FOURTEENTH EDITION

# The Kovels' Antiques Price List

A guide to the 1981–1982 market for
professionals, dealers, and collectors

## by Ralph and Terry Kovel

*Illustrated*

Crown Publishers, Inc.
New York

## BOOKS BY RALPH AND TERRY KOVEL

Dictionary of Marks—Pottery and Porcelain
A Directory of American Silver, Pewter and Silver Plate
American Country Furniture, 1780–1875
The Kovels' Antiques Price List
The Kovels' Bottle Price List
The Kovels' Collector's Guide to American Art Pottery
Kovels' Organizer for Collectors
The Kovels' Price Guide for Collector Plates, Figurines,
    Paperweights, and Other Limited Editions
The Kovels' Illustrated Price Guide to Royal Doulton
The Kovels' Illustrated Price Guide to Depression Glass and
    American Dinnerware
Kovels' Know Your Antiques
Kovels' Know Your Collectibles

Inquiries should be addressed to Crown Publishers, Inc., One Park
Avenue, New York, New York 10016

Printed in the United States of America

Published simultaneously in Canada by General Publishing Company
Limited

Library of Congress Catalog Card Number: 72-84290

ISBN: 0-517-544741

10 9 8 7 6 5 4 3 2 1

# Introduction

This has been another year with most prices rising steadily. For some types of antiques and collectibles, the prices have merely kept up with inflation, but in other areas the prices have skyrocketed. Antique silver has finally settled back to its old patterns. The value of antique silver is about five times the meltdown value. The only problem is that the meltdown value has been decreasing. Several major auction houses have had sales with many of the items "bought in." Many dealers claim that this has been caused by too many sales too close together. Because of the keen competition among the leading auction galleries, various dealers placed unrealistic reserve prices on their antiques. Many types of antiques and collectibles have shown a rise: Art Deco, Mission furniture by name makers, toys and dolls, to mention just a few. Oriental rugs are still feeling the insecurities of the Iranian market and top quality rugs seem to be selling at the same or at lower prices than last year. Art glass prices are at a plateau. Not a single record was set for glass of any type.

Pottery and porcelain records for the year included an earthenware teapot by George Ohr of Biloxi, Mississippi, for $6,000; a Lonhuda vase painted with monks for $3,000; a Wymyss tankard made in 1900 for $1,046; a Rookwood iris glaze vase for $2,750; a Meissen teacup and saucer decorated with swans made by Kaendler about 1740 for $44,100; and the amazing record for a Chinese chicken cup (1465–1487) of $941,176.

Eighteenth- and nineteenth-century American furniture sold well. A Goddard and Townsend Chippendale block-and-shell carved mahogany chest sold for $360,000; an American Federal clock by Sanford and Wheaton went for $75,000; a Federal grain painted bed sold for $23,000; a New York tea table for $170,000; and a Connecticut piece—a Chippendale bookcase—sold for $145,000. Other types of furniture of interest were Belter furniture (record for a single piece), $60,000 for a rococo rosewood center table, and a Gustav Stickley settle for $21,000. English furniture actually set the highest price with a George II mahogany fifteen-piece suite selling for $340,000.

A few records were set for objects made of metal. A pewter flat-top tankard made by William Bradford, Jr., sold for $15,000, while a gold Swiss hunting case watch with a perpetual calendar and moon phases, about 1890, brought $165,000.

Textiles and clothing have been interesting more collectors during the past 10 years. An American Indian textile record was set by a Navajo sarape made about 1850 that sold for $54,000; an eighteenth-century Boston school needlework picture brought $28,500; a Pennsylvania sampler dated 1830 set a record price of $38,000; a Paul Poiret evening dress, about 1914, sold for $5,000; a Fortuny hood, made about 1930, $5,000.

Toys have been rising in price and many new records were set. A pair of miniature lead figures by Sir Richard Courtenay brought $500; a still bank "Possum on Base" sold for $4,700; a 1931 Packard sports roadster pedal-car toy sold at $5,700; a cap shooter known as "Two Dogs on a Bench" brought $3,400; a celluloid Mickey Mouse windup toy from the 1930s went for $1,350; a glass candy container of a World War I soldier and a tent sold for $1,700; a Lenci doll polo player sold for $2,700; while a Bru oriental doll brought a record $16,500.

There were also many unusual records set. A Cox-Roosevelt jugate campaign button astounded everyone at a price of $30,000; a netsuke of a horse brought $78,000. This set a new record for a netsuke and regained its title because it had been the top priced netsuke in 1962. A Chinese 1898 bond sold for $14,000; a dowitcher decoy brought $13,000. There were even records set on postcards: $761 was paid for a Diamond Jubilee Queen Victoria card. A modern Kaziun paperweight of a yellow rose sold for $3,800, while a Paul Ysart paperweight went for $900. Once again, many photographs by twentieth-century photographers set record prices. The most interesting to antiques buffs was an Edward Curtis photograph, "Before the Storm—Apache," about 1910, which sold at $6,000, while a French daguerreotype of a postmortem by Le Blondel, about 1849, was purchased for $15,000.

Some of these prices are startling, but the everyday world of antiques has little to do with most of the record prices. However, the publicity for each record sale stirs more interest in the field of collecting. This is why all collectors should be acquainted with prices of many things that could be resting in an attic or even a basement.

The prices listed in the remainder of this book are reports of the more general antiques market. All of the record prices we have mentioned were set at auctions. The other prices that are listed in this book are retail prices when the items were offered in ships, sales, antiques shows, and flea markets, and they represent the actual price asked for an actual item. *None of these prices are estimates.* If a range of prices is given, it is because we have found the identical item offered during the year at two different times and at different prices. If you are selling your antiques and collectibles, do not expect to get the retail value unless you are a dealer. Wholesale prices for antiques can be from 20 to 50 percent less than retail. We must all remember that the antique dealer, like any other store owner, must make a profit or go out of business.

# Biltmore House and Gardens Color Pictures

The cover and color pictures in this book were taken at the Biltmore House and Gardens in Asheville, North Carolina, which was once the private home of George Washington Vanderbilt. The house was ready for occupancy in 1895 and was first opened to the public as a museum in 1930. Collectors and touring families will enjoy the acres of formal gardens and informally landscaped grounds that were originally designed by Frederick Law Olmsted, who was the creator of Central Park in New York City. At the center of the grounds is the house, built in the style of a sixteenth-century French château. Construction on the house began in 1890 and it took a thousand people five years to complete. It consists of one hundred and fifty rooms including thirty-two bedrooms, stables, an indoor pool, an outdoor pool, a greenhouse, and barns.

The family lived in the house for many years and the original furnishings and the additions are still on display. Some of the rooms are spectacular: the 72-foot by 42-foot banquet hall, the 75-foot-long entrance hall, and the twenty-thousand-book library. Some rooms show family life at the turn of the century with authentic bathrooms, kitchen, pantries, and servants' quarters. It is a unique opportunity to see how a wealthy family lived in 1900. The house is open every day of the year except New Year's, Thanksgiving, and Christmas. The full tour is $12 for adults, $9 for children 12 to 17, free for younger children. All tours are self-conducted. There is food available for the public on the grounds.

The library of the Biltmore house contains 20,000 volumes. The walnut paneling, black marble fireplace, painted ceiling, and brass railings add to the grandeur of this classical Baroque room. Carvings by Karl Bitter are over the mantel. The andirons represent Vulcan and Venus. *(Courtesy Biltmore House and Gardens)*

# How to Use This Book

There are just a few simple rules to follow in using this book. Each listing is arranged in the following manner: CATEGORY (such as pressed glass, silver, or furniture); OBJECT (such as vase, spoon, table); DESCRIPTION (which includes as much information as possible about size, age, color, and pattern). Pressed glass is the only exception to this rule, and it is listed CATEGORY, PATTERN, OBJECT, DESCRIPTION. All items are presumed to be in good condition, undamaged, unless otherwise noted.

Several special categories were formed to make a more sensible listing of items possible. "Kitchen" and "tool" include special equipment. Since it would be unreasonable to expect the casual collector to know the proper name for each variety of tool, such as an "adze" or a "trephine," we have lumped them together in the special categories. Other special categories are "commemorative," "store," "nautical," "fire," "weapon," and "railroad." The index can help you locate items in these sections.

This book has several idiosyncrasies of style that must be noted before it can be used properly. The final prices are compiled by a computer, and the machine has dictated several strange rules. Everything in the book is listed alphabetically according to the IBM alphabetic system. This means that words such as "mt." are alphabetized as "M-T," not as "M-O-U-N-T." Another peculiarity of the machine alphabetizing is that all numerals come after all letters, thus 2 comes after z. A quick glance at a listing will make this clear, as the alphabetizing is consistent throughout the book. We have not listed any pieces priced over $9,999.

We have made several editorial decisions that affect the use of the book. A bowl is a bowl and not a dish unless it is a special type of dish, such as a pickle dish. A butter dish is a "butter" and a celery dish is a "celery." A salt dish is called a "salt" to differentiate it from a saltshaker. A toothpick holder is called a "toothpick." It is always a "sugar and creamer," never a "creamer and sugar." Where one dimension is given, it is the height of the piece, or if the object is round, the dimension is the diameter. Height of a picture is listed before width. Glass is clear unless a color is indicated.

This book does not include price listings of fine art paintings, books, comic books, stamps, coins, and a few other categories that are covered in specialized books. Prices for collector's editions, bottles, Royal Doulton, depression glass, and American dinnerware are included although they are more completely reported in *The Kovels' Price Guide for Collector Plates, Figurines, Paperweights, and Other Limited Editions; The Kovels' Bottle Price List; The Kovels' Illustrated Price Guide to Royal Doulton;* and *The Kovels' Illustrated Price Guide to Depression Glass and American Dinnerware.*

Several categories such as "milk glass" and "bottles" include special reference numbers. These numbers refer the reader to the most widely known books about the category. When these numbers appear, the name of the special book is given in the paragraph heading. All of these numbers take the form "B-22," "McK-G-11," and so forth. The letter is the author's initial; the number refers to a picture in the author's book.

All black-and-white pictures in *The Kovels' Antiques Price List* are of antiques sold during the past year. The prices are as reported by the seller. Each piece pictured is listed with the word "Illus" as part of the description. Pictures are placed as close to the price listing as is possible. Color pictures are all from the collection of Biltmore House and Gardens and no prices are given for these antiques.

All prices included in this book are reports, not estimates. This means that at some sale in the United States between June 1980 and June 1981 the antiques described were offered for sale at the prices we have listed. A few prices are from auctions, but most are from shops and shows. The prices have been taken from sales in all parts of the country, and variations may be caused by geographic differences in pricing. Every price has been checked for accuracy, but we cannot be responsible for any errors that may have occurred. We welcome any suggestions for future editions of this book but cannot answer letters asking for advice or appraisals.

*Ralph M. Kovel, American Society of Appraisers, Senior Member*
*Terry H. Kovel, American Society of Appraisers, Senior Member*

# Update for Prices Available

Each year *The Kovels' Antiques Price List* is completely rewritten. Every entry is new because of the rapidly changing antiques market. The only way so complete a revision can be accomplished is by using a computer, making it possible to publish the bound book two months after the last price is received.

Yet many price changes occur between editions of *The Kovels' Antiques Price List.* Important sales produce new record prices each day. Inflation, the changing price of silver and gold, and the international demand for some types of antiques influence sales in the United States.

You can keep up with developments from month to month. *Kovels on Antiques and Collectibles* is a nationally distributed illustrated newsletter, published monthly. It covers prices, best buys, special interest antiques, refinishing and first aid for your possessions, marks, book reviews, and other pertinent antiques news.

Information about the newsletter is available from the authors at P.O. Box 22200, Beachwood, Ohio 44122.

# Picture Acknowledgments

ABCD Auction Gallery; Alt Print Haus; Al Anderson; Richard Bourne; E. J. Canton; Charles Chiarchiaro; Christie's; D. S. Clarke Auction Gallery; Douglas Galleries; William Doyle Galleries; Du Mouchelle Art Galleries; Roger Early; Garth's Auction; Francis Horgan; Carl Kukkonen; Litchfield Auction Gallery; Maritime Antique Auctions; New England Rare Coin Auctions; Allan Petretti; Lloyd Ralston; Schneider's Antiques; Robert Skinner; Soho East Auctions; Sotheby's; Biff Taylor; Auctions by Theriault; Richard Withington; Wolf's Shaker Galleries; John Woody.

Almaric Walter made pate-de-verre glass under contract at the Daum glassworks from 1908 to 1914. He started his own firm in Nancy, France, in 1919. Pieces made before 1914 are signed "Daum, Nancy" with a cross. After 1919 the signature is "A. Walter Nancy."

**A. WALTER,Paperweight,** Insects & Flowers, Pate-De-Verre ............................ 750.00
**Penholder,** Pate-De-Verre ...................................................................... 250.00

ABC plates, or children's alphabet plates, were popular from 1780 to 1860. The letters on the plate were meant as teaching aids for children learning to read. The plates were made of pottery, porcelain, metal, or glass.

**ABC, Ashtray,** Braille ............................................................................. 10.00
**Cup,** Letters & Animals .......................................................................... 16.00
**Cup,** Saucer, & Plate, Embossed Alphabet, Germany ................................. 45.00
**Mug,** Rust Lettering & Transfer, Cream Ground, 3 In. ................................ 55.00
**Mug,** Whole Alphabet, Country Scene Each Side, 2 3/4 In. .......................... 34.00
**Plate,** Alphabet In Gold On Rim, Baby's Plate, Germany ............................ 35.00
**Plate,** Alphabet, Tin, 6 In. ...................................................................... 32.00
**Plate,** Bear With Cubs, 7 1/2 In. ............................................................. 45.00
**Plate,** Bird With Frog, Frosted, 6 In.Diam. ............................................... 35.00
**Plate,** Black Alphabet, Girls Feeding Teddy Bear, 7 1/2 In. ....................... 28.00
**Plate,** Buster Brown ............................................................................... 20.00
**Plate,** Campbell Kids ............................................................................. 25.00
**Plate,** Child's Portrait, Bears, Snow Scenes On Border, Tin ....................... 30.00
**Plate,** Children Shipbuilding, Black Transfer, 6 In.Diam. ........................... 35.00
**Plate,** Clock Center, Alphabet Border, Glass, 6 In., Pair ........................... 38.00
**Plate,** Cock Robin, Raised Letter Border & Center, 8 In. ........................... 48.00
**Plate,** Cow Jumped Over The Moon, Tin, 8 3/4 In. .................................... 25.00
**Plate,** Crusoe Rescues Friday, 8 1/4 In. .................................................. 45.00
**Plate,** Dr.Franklin's Maxims, 6 1/2 In. ..................................................... 75.00
**Plate,** Droopy-Jowled Dog's Head Center, Clear Glass, 6 1/3 In. ............... 32.00
**Plate,** Elephant With Howdah, Signed R. & Co., 6 In.Diam. ...................... 135.00
**Plate,** Embossed Letters, Purple Transfer Print, 6 1/4 In. ......................... 45.00
**Plate,** Feeding, Children In Center .......................................................... 37.00
**Plate,** Feeding, Stork In Center, Marigold ............................................... 45.00
**Plate,** Hi Diddle Diddle, Tin, 8 1/2 In. .................................................... 45.00
**Plate,** Horses & Dogs, 6 1/4 In.Diam. ..................................................... 45.00
**Plate,** Independence Hall ....................................................................... 70.00
**Plate,** Jumbo, Raised Letter Border & Center, 5 1/2 In. ............................ 58.00
**Plate,** Lamb, Syracuse China ................................................................. 20.00
**Plate,** Little Bo-Peep & Numbers, Clear Glass ......................................... 40.00
**Plate,** Little Boys At Marbles, Play On The Summer Holiday, 6 In. .............. 68.00
**Plate,** Little Girl In Barn Feeding Animals, 6 1/2 In. .................................. 38.00
**Plate,** Little Miss Muffet, 6 1/4 In.Diam. .................................................. 33.00
**Plate,** Mary Had A Little Lamb, Tin, 8 In. ................................................ 55.00
**Plate,** McNichols, Two Kittens, Signed John Welch .................................. 37.00
**Plate,** Plough Theme, Meaken ................................................................ 28.00
**Plate,** Raised Letters On Rim, Girl & Rabbit Center, Staffordshire, 7 In. ...... 25.00
**Plate,** Roosters & Chickens, Germany, 7 In.Diam. .................................... 38.00
**Plate,** Stork Center, Carnival Glass, Marigold .......................................... 49.00
**Plate,** Thousand Eye Pattern, Sapphire Blue, 6 In.Diam. ........................... 46.00
**Plate,** Transfer, Center Fan, Horse With Birds, England, 8 In. .................... 30.00

Abingdon Pottery was established in 1934 by Raymond E. Bidwell as the Abingdon Sanitary Manufacturing Company. The company made art pottery. The factory ceased production in 1950.

**ABINGDON, Bowl,** Blue Flowers, Signed, 3 1/2 X 14 In.Long ..................... 19.50
**Bowl,** Console, Green, Oval, 14 1/2 In. Long ........................................... 9.50
**Cookie Jar,** Humpty Dumpty On Wall ..................................................... 35.00
**Cookie Jar,** Miss Muffet ....................................................................... 35.00
**Dish,** Pink, Large ................................................................................. 6.00
**Figurine,** Fish ...................................................................................... 8.00

**Jar,** Jam .................................................................................................. 4.00
**Salt & Pepper,** Humpty Dumpty ....................................................... 16.00
**Vase,** Cornucopia, White, Double ...................................................... 8.50
**Vase,** Cornucopia, White, Single ....................................................... 5.50
**Vase,** Green, 10 In. ........................................................................... 8.00
**Vase,** Handled, Pink, 10 In. ............................................................... 22.00
**Vase,** Trumpet Shape, Cream Ground, Handled, 9 In., Pair ............... 25.00

*Adams china was made by William Adams and Sons of Staffordshire,
England. The firm was founded in 1769 and is still working.*

**ADAMS, see also Flow Blue**
**ADAMS, Bowl,** Cries Of London, 6 1/2 In. ........................................ 18.00
**Creamer,** Square Handle ................................................................. 35.00
**Jar,** Biscuit, Jasperware, Blue & White, 6 1/2 In. ............................ 125.00
**Jar,** Powder, Covered, Fresh Gathered Peas .................................... 45.00
**Plate,** Clipper Ship Red Jacket, 10 1/4 In. ....................................... 28.00
**Plate,** Columbia, Blue, 7 In. ............................................................. 15.00
**Plate,** Rose, Scalloped, Red & Green, Marked, 9 1/4 In. .................. 105.00
**Plate,** The Star Of The Road, Lady, Horses, 10 1/2 In. ..................... 25.00
**ADVERTISING, see Store**

*Agata glass was made by Joseph Locke of the New England Glass
Company of Cambridge, Massachusetts, after 1885. A metallic stain was
applied to New England Peachblow and the mottled design characteristic of
agata appeared.*

**AGATA, Celery,** Pinched Quatrefoil Top, 4 Dimples, 6 In. ............... 1750.00
**Cruet,** Frosted Stopper ................................................................. 1250.00
**Cup,** Punch, Peachblow, New England Glass Co., C.1887 ........*Illus* 600.00
**Cup,** Punch, Rose To Pale Pink, Caramel Mottling, C.1887, 2 1/2 In. ... 600.00
**Cup,** Punch, 2 5/8 X 2 5/8 In.Diam. ................................................ 750.00
**Pitcher,** Water, 3 Tumblers, Squared Neck, C.1890, Pitcher, 7 In. .... 700.00
**Toothpick,** Square Mouth ............................................................... 375.00
**Vase,** Lily, Gold Mottling, Rose Shading To White At Foot, 9 In. .... 1250.00
**Vase,** Pinched Rose Top, Shades To White, Mottled, 4 1/2 In. ....... 1200.00

**AGATE, Box,** Brass Bands, 1 3/8 X 4 X 3/4 In. ................................ 95.00
**Box,** Cigarette, Chinese Green Jade Panel, Rose Diamonds, 4 3/8 In. ... 6000.00
**Easter Egg,** Chicken Size ............................................................... 9.00
**Figurine,** Horse, Gray & Blue With Brown, 2 1/4 X 4 1/2 In. ........... 110.00
**Knife,** Paper, Gray, French, Rose Diamond Tip, Gold Collet, 10 In. ... 1100.00
**Paperweight,** Faceted Urn Shape, 19th Century, Europe, 4 1/4 In.Diam. ... 150.00

Agata, Cup, Punch, Peachblow,
New England Glass Co., C.1887

*Akro agate glass was made in Clarksburg, West Virginia, from 1932 to 1951. Before that time the firm made children's glass marbles. Most of the glass is marked with a crow flying through the letter A.*

| | |
|---|---|
| **AKRO AGATE, Ashtray,** Leaf Shape, Blue & White Marbleized, 4 X 3 In. | 1.75 |
| **Ashtray,** Marbleized Green | 2.50 |
| **Ashtray,** Orange & White, 3 1/2 X 4 In. | 3.95 |
| **Ashtray,** Shell Shape, Green & White, 3 1/2 X 4 In. | 3.95 |
| **Basket,** Pumpkin & White | 12.50 |
| **Bowl,** Black Satin Enameled Trim, Low, 10 In.Diam. | 22.50 |
| **Bowl,** Cereal, Concentric Rings, Blue, Large | 12.00 |
| **Bowl,** Footed, Blue, 5 1/2 In.Diam. | 6.00 |
| **Bowl,** Footed, Pumpkin, 6 1/2 In.Diam. | 25.00 |
| **Box,** Powder, Colonial Lady, Blue | 35.00 |
| **Child's Set,** Interior Panel, 21 Piece | 210.00 |
| **Compote,** Jelly, Green, 6 In. | 4.95 |
| **Cup & Saucer,** Child's | 10.00 |
| **Cup,** Pumpkin | 11.00 |
| **Dish,** Powder, Scotty, Blue | 75.00 |
| **Dish,** Shell, Yellow | 10.00 |
| **Dish,** Soap, Blue & White | 10.00 |
| **Figurine,** Colonial Lady, Pink | 50.00 |
| **Figurine,** Colonial Lady, White | 50.00 |
| **Figurine,** Scotty, Pink | 55.00 |
| **Flowerpot,** Blue, Small | 6.00 |
| **Flowerpot,** Yellow | 2.00 To 6.50 |
| **Jar,** Powder, Colonial Lady, White | 35.00 |
| **Jar,** Powder, Mexicali, Pickwick Cosmetics | 35.00 |
| **Jar,** Powder, Pink Lady | 35.00 |
| **Pitcher,** Blue | 30.00 |
| **Planter,** Milk Glass, 5 1/2 X 3 In. | 11.00 |
| **Planter,** Red & Orange Marbleizing, Metal Stand, 6 X 3 1/4 In. | 10.95 |
| **Shell,** Clam, Green With Orange, 4 In., Set Of 3 | 12.00 |
| **Soup Plate,** Child's, Clear Green | 7.00 |
| **Sugar & Creamer,** Child's, Paneled, Blue, Open | 13.00 |
| **Sugar & Creamer,** Cobalt Blue | 22.00 |
| **Tea Set,** Child's, Green & Amber, 12 Piece | 75.00 |
| **Tea Set,** Child's, Teapot, 2 Cups & Saucers, Green | 32.50 |
| **Tea Set,** Jade Luster, Boxed, 21 Piece | 100.00 |
| **Teapot,** Light Blue | 35.00 |
| **Toothpick,** Hand-Shaped, Blue | 10.00 |
| **Urn,** Footed, 3 In. | 8.00 |
| **Vase,** Floral, Embossed, White, 4 1/4 In. | 8.00 |
| **Vase,** Lily Design, 4 1/2 In. | 20.00 |
| **Vase,** Opaque White, Green, White, & Brown Marbelizing, 4 1/2 In. | 5.50 |
| **Vase,** Raised Lily Design, Green & White Marbleized, 4 1/2 In. | 6.50 |
| **Water Set,** Blue, 7 Piece | 75.00 |
| **Water Set,** Green Transparent Stippled Band, 7 Piece | 45.00 |
| **Water Set,** Transfer Stacked Disc & Panel Green, 7 Piece | 45.00 |
| | |
| **ALABASTER, Figurine,** Greek Lady, White, C.1900, 10 In. | 500.00 |
| **Jar,** Powder, Pink, Gold Trim, Footed, Hinged Cover, 4 1/2 In. | 65.00 |
| 　　　　　**ALBUM, PHOTOGRAPH, Photography, Album** | |

*Alexandrite glass was first made by Thomas Webb & Sons at the beginning of the twentieth century. It is a transparent glass shading from pale yellow to rose to blue. Stevens & Williams later produced Alexandrite glassware by plating a transparent yellow body with rose and blue glass.*

| | |
|---|---|
| **ALEXANDRITE, Figurine,** Venus, Satin Finish, Polished Base, 8 In. | 85.00 |
| **Finger Bowl,** Honeycomb, Ruffled, 2 X 5 In.Diam. | 650.00 |
| **Goblet,** Amber Body, Violet Base & Top Rim, C.1890, Set Of 3 | 600.00 |
| **Vase,** Petal Top, 6 In. | 750.00 |

Alhambra

*Alhambra is a pattern of tableware made in Vienna, Austria, in the twentieth century. The geometric designs are applied in gold, red, and dark green.*

| | |
|---|---|
| **ALHAMBRA, Bowl,** Sugar | 85.00 |
| **Plate,** 9 In. | 65.00 |
| **Tea Set,** 6 Cups & Saucers, 17 Piece | 335.00 |
| | |
| **ALUMINUM, Box,** Advertising Flossie Handkerchiefs, C.1905, 5 3/4 In. | 12.00 |
| **Dish,** Candy, Divided Amber Glass, Farber Bros.Holder | 28.00 |
| **Pitcher,** Wire Bail, Wooden Grip | 25.00 |

*Amber glass is the name of any glassware with the proper yellow-brown shade. It was a popular color after the Civil War.*

| | |
|---|---|
| **AMBER GLASS, Bottle,** Barber, Frosted, Marked | 45.00 |
| **Bowl,** Dimpled Sides, Blown, French, 3 1/4 In.Square | 75.00 |
| **Bowl,** Fruit, Thumbprint Pattern, Enameled, James Tufts Frame | 300.00 |
| **Bowl,** Holly, Oval, 7 1/2 X 4 1/2 X 2 In. | 400.00 |
| **Bowl,** Signed, 3 3/4 X 10 In.Diam. | 40.00 |
| **Box,** Jewel, Grapevine Design, Velvet Lined Lid | 400.00 |
| **Cake Stand,** Dahlia, 10 1/2 In.Diam. | 75.00 |
| **Champagne,** Wildflower | 75.00 |
| **Condiment Set,** Daisy & Button, Original Tops, 4 Piece | 75.00 |
| **Creamer,** Hobnail With Thumbprint | 42.00 |
| **Creamer,** Inverted Thumbprint, Square Mouth, Applied Handle | 40.00 |
| **Creamer,** Pioneer | 43.00 |
| **Creamer,** Wheat & Barley | 20.00 |
| **Cruet,** Amber Applied Handle, White Flowers, Stopper, 6 In. | 80.00 |
| **Cruet,** Pedestal, Bubble Stopper, Enameled Flowers, 8 3/4 In. | 85.00 |
| **Goblet,** Basket Weave | 29.00 |
| **Jar,** Cigar, Dated 1894 | 45.00 |
| **Match Holder,** Cane Pattern | 50.00 |
| **Pitcher,** Water, Ruffled, Thumbprint | 75.00 |
| **Pitcher,** Water, White Flowers, Green Leaves, Reeded Handle, 7 In. | 135.00 |
| **Plate,** Daisy & Button, 7 In.Diam. | 17.50 |
| **Salt & Pepper,** Figural, Pig, Pewter Heads | 30.00 |
| **Sauce,** Daisy & Button, Square | 19.50 |
| **Shoe,** Striker On Sole, Daisy & Button, Patent 1886 | 35.00 |
| **Spooner,** Hobnail, Ruffled Edge | 25.00 |
| **Spooner,** Pioneer | 48.00 |
| **Spooner,** Thousand Eye, 3 Knob Base | 35.00 |
| **Syrup,** Basket Weave, Tin Top | 80.00 |
| **Syrup,** Inverted Thumbprint | 65.00 |
| **Syrup,** Rope & Thumbprint, Original Top, Patent June 1884 | 45.00 |
| **Tankard,** Glass Hinged Top, Encased In Pewter, 15 In. | 195.00 |
| **Toothpick,** Rabbit With Basket On Back | 40.00 |
| **Tumbler,** Daisy & Button, Round Bottom | 35.00 |
| **Water Set,** Madrid, 6 Flat Tumblers | 100.00 |
| **Wine,** Scroll Wtih Flowers, Pair | 23.00 |
| | |
| **AMBER, Cigar Holder,** 14K Gold Band, Boxed | 25.00 |
|     **AMBERETTE, see Pressed Glass, Klondike** | |

*Amberina is a two-toned glassware made from 1883 to about 1900. It was patented by Joseph Locke of the New England Glass Company. The glass shades from red to amber.*

    **AMBERINA, see also Baccarat, Bluerina, Plated Amberina**

| | |
|---|---|
| **AMBERINA, Basket,** Swirled Design, Applied Ruffle Top, Thorn Handle, 6 In. | 425.00 |
| **Bottle,** Water, Inverted Thumbprint | 175.00 |
| **Bottle,** Wine, Swirl, Amber Cut Stopper, 9 5/8 X 3 1/4 In.Diam. | 138.00 |

**Bowl & Saucer,** Finger, Fluted ............................................................................ 260.00
**Bowl,** Basket Weave, Lattice Edge, 6 1/2 In. .................................................... 70.00
**Bowl,** Basket Weave, Openwork Top, 6 In. ........................................................ 28.00
**Bowl,** Fan Shape, Wishbone Feet, Enameled Flowers, 12 3/8 In.Diam. ............. 350.00
**Bowl,** Fluted, Enameled Flowers, Coin Gold Stem, Red To Amber ..................... 395.00
**Bowl,** Fluted, Fuchsia, 5 In.Diam. ....................................................................... 155.00
**Bowl,** Fluted, Iridized, 8 X 3 In. ......................................................................... 275.00
**Bowl,** Fruit, Diamond-Quilted, Amber Rope Rim, 9 1/2 In.Diam. ....................... 295.00
**Bowl,** Fuchsia, Fluted, 5 In. ................................................................................ 165.00
**Bowl,** Inverted Diamond, Fuchsia Crown, 4 1/2 In. ........................................... 300.00
**Bowl,** Inverted Thumbprint, Amber To Cranberry ........................................... 295.00
**Bowl,** Lion Heads On Legs, Fluted, 8 1/2 X 9 3/4 In. ........................................ 375.00
**Bowl,** Tricorn Shape, White Flowers, Gold Leaves, 4 1/4 X 6 In.Diam. ............. 195.00
**Bride's Basket,** Applied Ribbon Edge, Cased Outside, Frame, 11 In. ................. 295.00
**Candleholder,** Basket Weave & Lattice Trim, Amber Foot, 2 In., Pair ................ 50.00
**Castor Set,** American, C.1890 ....................................................................*Illus* 350.00
**Castor Set,** Inverted Thumbprint, Acme Plated Frame, 3 Piece ......................... 300.00
**Castor Set,** Silver Plated Frame, C.1890, 4 Piece ............................................. 350.00
**Castor,** Pickle, Enameled Flowers & Fruit, Silver Plated Frame ........................ 400.00
**Castor,** Pickle, Fuchsia, Silver Plated Frame .................................................... 295.00
**Celery,** Daisy & Button, Boat Shape, C.1890, 13 3/4 In. ................................... 175.00
**Celery,** Diamond-Quilted, Square Scalloped Rim, Fuchsia, 6 1/2 In. ................. 245.00
**Celery,** Ruffled Top, Inverted Thumbprint, 6 1/4 In. .......................................... 325.00
**Compote,** Signed Libbey, 7 3/4 X 3 In. ............................................................. 625.00
**Condiment Set,** Thumbprint, Silver Plated Frame .............................................. 750.00
**Creamer,** Comical Body, Baby Thumbprint Pattern, C.1885, 2 3/4 In. ............... 200.00
**Creamer,** Inverted Thumbprint, Square Mouth, Red To Amber, 4 3/8 In. ............ 350.00
**Creamer,** Inverted Thumbprint, Square Mouth, 5 X 4 In.Diam. .......................... 135.00
**Creamer,** Reeded Handle, Quatrefoil Top, Amber, 4 1/2 In. .............................. 165.00
**Creamer,** Reverse, 5 In. ...................................................................................... 125.00
**Cruet,** Amber Stopper, Cranberry Top ............................................................. 395.00
**Cruet,** Diamond Thumbprint ............................................................................ 250.00
**Cruet,** Diamond-Quilted, Amber Stopper & Handle, 5 1/2 In. ............................ 225.00
**Cruet,** Inverted Thumbprint, Petal Top, Faceted Stopper, 5 5/8 In. ................... 295.00
**Cruet,** Melon Sectioned Herringbone, Amber Handle, 6 3/4 In. ........................ 225.00
**Cruet,** Swirl ........................................................................................................ 225.00
**Cruet,** Vinegar, Inverted Thumbprint, New England Glass Co., 6 In. ................ 295.00
**Cruet,** Wine, Amber Applied Handle, Bubble Stopper, 9 In. .............................. 195.00
**Dish,** Celery, Daisy & Button, Boat-Shaped, 13 3/4 In. ..................................... 175.00
**Dish,** Cheese .................................................................... 345.00 To 379.00
**Dish,** Jam, Silver Plate Frame .......................................................................... 135.00
**Dish,** Sauce, Daisy & Button, Scalloped, Flint, Square, 5 In. ............................ 88.00
**Finger Bowl,** Hobnail, Ruffled Edge, Polished Pontil ........................................ 105.00
**Finger Bowl,** Inverted Thumbprint .............................................. 40.00 To 110.00

Amberina, Castor Set, American, C.1890

Finger Bowl, Inverted Thumbprint, 10-Crimp Top, 2 1/4 X 4 1/2 In. ............................ 185.00
Finger Bowl, Saucer, Fluted ............................................................................................ 260.00
Finger Bowl, Swirl Pattern, 4 1/4 In.Diam. ................................................................. 130.00
Finger Bowl, 10-Panel ...................................................................................................... 95.00
Globe, Coin Spot Design, Attached Metal Bell, 19th Century ................................. 375.00
Jar, Cold Cream, Swirl Pattern, Silver Plate Top, 2 1/2 In.Diam. ........................... 35.00
Mustard Pot, Diamond-Quilted, Silver Plated Top, 3 In. ........................................ 150.00
Pitcher, Bulbous, Melon Ribbed, Applied Amber Reeded Handle, 6 In. ............... 50.00
Pitcher, Bulbous, Paneled, 8 In. .................................................................................. 225.00
Pitcher, Clear Applied Handle, 4 Glasses, Inverted Thumbprint ........................... 65.00
Pitcher, Cream, Inverted Thumbprint, Reed Handle, 5 In. ..................................... 170.00
Pitcher, Daisy & Button, 5 1/4 In. ............................................................................... 275.00
Pitcher, Deep Red Melon Ribbed, 8 In. ..................................................................... 175.00
Pitcher, Diamond-Quilted, Amber Handle, 6 3/4 X 4 In.Diam. .............................. 375.00
Pitcher, Fluted Top, Clear Handle, 6 1/2 In. .............................................................. 175.00
Pitcher, Honey Amber To Cranberry, Applied Handle, 4 3/4 In. ........................... 135.00
Pitcher, Inverted Daisy & Plume, Rope Rigaree & Handle, 8 1/2 In. .................. 395.00
Pitcher, Lemonade, Amber Reeded Handle, 6 1/8 In. ............................................. 225.00
Pitcher, Milk, Diamond-Quilted, Ruby To Golden Amber, 6 3/4 In. ..................... 375.00
Pitcher, Milk, Tankard Shape, Diamond Thumbprint, 6 3/4 In. .............................. 395.00
Pitcher, Rattail Collar, Braided To Form Handle, 6 1/2 In. ..................................... 400.00
Pitcher, Reversed Inverted Thumbprint, Square Mouth, 4 3/4 In. ......................... 135.00
Pitcher, Tapering Cylindrical Form, Vertical Ribbing, C.1890, 7 In. ..................... 375.00
Pitcher, Thumbprint Pattern, Clear Applied Handle, Small ................................... 375.00
Pitcher, Thumbprint Pattern, Enameled ....................................................................... 375.00
Pitcher, Water, Amber Ribbed Handle, Square Mouth ............................................. 195.00
Pitcher, Water, Crackle Glass, Amber Reeded Handle, 10 1/4 In. ........................ 225.00
Pitcher, Water, Diamond-Quilted, Square, 8 1/2 In. ............................ 185.00 To 200.00
Plate, Daisy & Button, Scalloped Edge, Flint, 7 In.Diam. ....................................... 145.00
Plate, Daisy & Button, 7 In. .......................................................................................... 110.00
Plate, Ruffled Edge, Quilted Pattern, C.1900, Blue, 5 5/8 In. ............................... 475.00
Plate, 7 1/2 In. .................................................................................................................... 35.00
Punch Cup, Amber Reeded Handle, C.1890, 2 3/4 In., Set Of 5 ......................... 375.00
Punch Cup, Amber Reeded Handle, Diamond-Quilted ............................................... 55.00
Punch Cup, Applied Amber Handle, C.1890, 2 3/4 In., Set Of 5 ......................... 375.00
Punch Cup, Applied Handle, Baby Thumbprint Pattern ............................................ 95.00
Punch Cup, Diamond Pattern ........................................................................................ 195.00
Punch Cup, Diamond-Quilted, Amber Reeded Handle, Set Of 6 .......................... 525.00
Punch Cup, Diamond-Quilted, Amber Reeded Handle, 5 1/2 In. .......................... 140.00
Punch Cup, Diamond-Quilted, Applied Reeded Handle, Set Of 8 ........................ 840.00
Punch Cup, Diamond-Quilted, Fuchsia, Amber Reeded Handle ............................ 125.00
Punch Cup, Inverted Thumbprint, Amber Reeded Handle, 2 5/8 In. .................... 118.00
Punch Cup, Ribbed Pattern, Fuchsia Into Amber, Reeded Handle ...................... 130.00
Rose Bowl, Daisy & Button ............................................................................................. 70.00
Salt & Pepper, Meridan Silver Holder, 6 1/2 In. ..................................................... 295.00
Saltshaker, Baby Thumbprint, Original Pewter Lid, Pair ......................................... 175.00
Saltshaker, Original Top ................................................................................................. 685.00
Sauce, Footed, Daisy & Button, Fuchsia To Amber, 4 1/4 In.Square ................... 75.00
Sherbet, Pair ........................................................................................................................ 90.00
Sugar Shaker, Inverted Thumbprint, Smoky .............................................................. 225.00
Sugar, Open, Amber Wishbone Feet, Berry Pontil, 4 1/4 X 3 In. ....................... 745.00
Syrup, Inverted Thumbprint, Silver Plated Fitting .................................................... 425.00
Tieback, Curtain, Sandwich Glass ................................................................................. 40.00
Tieback, Pewter Shank, Pair .......................................................................................... 28.50
Toothpick, Boot Shape .................................................................................................... 125.00
Toothpick, Figural, Boiling Pot With Handle, Honey ................................................ 33.50
Toothpick, Footed, Butter Chip & Dish, Daisy & Button, 7 In. .......................... 225.00
Toothpick, Footed, Hobnail ............................................................................................ 90.00
Toothpick, Goblet Shape ................................................................................................ 218.00
Toothpick, Inverted Baby Thumbprint, Flared & Ruffled ....................................... 140.00
Toothpick, Inverted Diamond, Fuchsia ....................................................................... 185.00
Toothpick, Venetian Diamond Pattern, 2 1/2 In. ..................................................... 95.00
Tumbler, Baby Inverted Thumbprint, 19th Century ................................................. 50.00

Tumbler, Deep Fuchsia, Diamond Pattern, New England .............. 140.00
Tumbler, Diamond Optic ................................................... 87.50
Tumbler, Diamond Thumbprint, Rolled Edge, 3 3/4 In. ............... 90.00
Tumbler, Expanded Diamond, Fuchsia Upper ......................... 85.00
Tumbler, Ground Pontil, 4 In. ........................................... 85.00
Tumbler, Multicolored Enameled Daisies & Foliage, 4 In. ........... 68.00
Tumbler, Paneled, 4 1/2 In. .............................................. 75.00
Tumbler, Reverse Diamond-Quilted, 3 7/8 In. ......................... 45.00
Tumbler, Swirl ............................................................ 80.00
Tumbler, Thumbprint ..................................................... 67.00
Tumbler, Thumbprint, Pale Rose To Pale Straw ...................... 45.00
Tumbler, Water, Swirl, Belltone, New England Glass Co., 4 In. ..... 95.00
Tumbler, Whiskey, Diamond-Quilted, 2 5/8 X 2 1/8 In.Diam. ....... 175.00
Tumbler, 10-Row Hobnail, Cramberry To Amber, 4 In. ..... 195.00 To 235.00
Vase, Applied Honey-Colored Rim, Optic Swirl, Turned Collar, 11 In. .... 225.00
Vase, Celery, Inverted Thumbprint, Crimped, Ruby To Amber, 6 1/4 In. .... 335.00
Vase, Cranberry To Amber, Bulbous Bottom, 5 3/4 In. ............... 125.00
Vase, Fluted Top, Pinched Sides, Enameled Flowers, 5 In. .......... 165.00
Vase, Footed, Fan Shape, Amber Wishbone Feet, 6 3/8 X 7 7/8 In. .... 185.00
Vase, Indented Corners, Stork & Grass Design, C.1884, 4 1/2 In. .... 300.00
Vase, Inverted Thumbprint, Amber, 12 1/2 In. ........................ 250.00
Vase, Lily, C.1890, 10 In, Pair .......................................... 200.00
Vase, Lily, Ribbed, 8 In. ................................................ 225.00
Vase, Lily, Signed Libbey Amberina, 12 In. ........................... 650.00
Vase, Lily, 11 3/4 In. ................................................... 335.00
Vase, Optic Swirl, Applied Honey-Colored Edge, 11 In. ............. 195.00
Vase, Reverse Thumbprint, Ruffled, Cranberry To Amber, 12 In. .... 150.00
Vase, Ruffled Rim, Ground Pontil, 12 In. ............................. 85.00
Vase, Ruffled Top, Ribbed, Blown, 9 1/2 In. .......................... 190.00
Vase, Swirl Footed, Amber Serpentine Trim, Gold Flowers, 12 1/4 In. .... 245.00
Vase, Swirl Footed, Colored Enamel Design, Amber Feet, 11 In. .... 265.00
Vase, Swirl Pattern, 10 1/2 In. ........................................ 245.00
Vase, Trumpet, Signed Libbey, 10 In. ................................. 325.00
Vase, Yellow To Fuschia, Bulbous, 8 1/4 In. .......................... 62.50
Water Set, Clear Handle, 6 Tumblers, Pitcher 7 In. .................. 400.00
Wine, Deep Fuchsia Top ................................................ 285.00

*American Encaustic Tiling Co. of Zanesville, Ohio, worked from 1879
to 1935. Decorative glazed, embossed, and faience tiles were made.*

AMERICAN ENCAUSTIC TILING CO., Tile, Man & Woman, 7 Lines Of Verse ........ 33.00
Tile, Roman Man & Woman, 6 X 6 In. .................................. 225.00
Tile, 2 Hunting Dogs, Foliage, 6 X 18 In. ............................. 250.00

*Amethyst glass is any of the many glasswares made in the proper dark purple
shade. It was a color popular after the Civil War.*

AMETHYST GLASS, Bottle, Cologne, Cut Panels, Matching Stopper, 7 3/4 In. ....... 118.00
Bottle, Cut Flowers & Leaves, Gold Trim, Stopper, 9 3/4 In. ....... 175.00
Bottle, Perfume, Double, Sterling Lids, 1 Hinged, 1 Screw-On ..... 235.00
Box, Hinged, Brass Side Rings, Sanded Grapes, 5 1/4 X 6 In. ..... 195.00
Claret, Nude Stem, 4 1/2 Oz. ........................................... 55.00
Compote, Silver Rim At Top & Foot .................................... 40.00
Cracker Jar, Silver Top & Handle, 9 In. ............................... 125.00
Cup, Punch, S-Repeat, Gold Trim ...................................... 21.00
Decanter, Bulbous Base, Sterling Silver Overlay, 7 In. .............. 185.00
Dish, Candy, Lion Cover, Marked K ................................... 65.00
Glass, Shot, Marked ..................................................... 165.00
Goblet, Nude Stem, 9 In. ................................................ 60.00
Holder, Placecard, Disc Form, Set Of 8 ............................... 15.00
Ivy Ball .................................................................... 80.00

**Jug,** Farber Holder, 48 Ounce ............................................................. 25.00
**Lamp,** Fairy, Herringbone Pattern, Ruffled Underplate, 7 In. ......... 149.00
**Lamp,** Whale Oil, Square Base, C.1840, 8 3/4 In. ............................ 250.00
**Mug,** Souvenir Of Eaton, Ohio ........................................................... 24.00
**Pitcher,** Fluted Top, Crystal Applied Handle ................................... 89.00
**Pitcher,** Inverted Thumbprint, Ruffled Top, Clear Handle ............ 125.00
**Pitcher,** Ribbon Swirl, Ruffled Lid, Handled, 6 Tumblers ............. 115.00
**Pitcher,** Silver Deposit & Festooning On Body, 7 3/4 X 8 In. ....... 225.00
**Pitcher,** Water, Applied Handle, 8 1/2 In. ....................................... 50.00
**Salt & Pepper,** Inverted Thumbprint, Original Tops ....................... 60.00
**Salt,** Hobnail Pattern, 4 In.Diam. ..................................................... 5.00
**Slipper,** Daisy & Button ................................................................... 13.00
**Spooner,** Jefferson Optic, Gold Band .............................................. 47.00
**Sugar & Creamer,** C.1840, 5 In. ...................................................... 38.00
**Sugar Shaker,** Paneled Sprig .......................................................... 125.00
**Tobacco Jar,** Copper Cover, Fluted Sided, 7 In. ............................ 35.00
**Toothpick,** Souvenir, Urichsville, Ohio, 1904 ................................ 45.00
**Toothpick,** Swag & Bracket, Gold Trim ........................................... 10.00
**Tumbler,** Inverted Thumbprint .......................................................... 8.50
**Tumbler,** Swag With Brackets .......................................................... 30.00
**Vase,** Fan Shape, Catalonian, 7 In. ................................................ 32.00

**AMOS & ANDY, Ashtray,** Chalkware ............................................... 65.00
    **Map,** Weber City .............................................................................. 25.00
       **AMPHORA, see Teplitz**
       **ANDIRON and related fireplace items, see Fireplace**

**ANIMAL TROPHY, Lion,** Head, Large ............................................. 150.00
       **APOTHECARY JAR, see Bottle, Apothecary**
       **APPLE PEELER, see Kitchen, Peeler, Apple**

**ARCHITECTURAL, Backbar,** Barber Shop, Holds 60 Mugs, C.1880, 116 X 96 In. ............... 6500.00
    **Backbar,** Barber, Double, Marble Top, Oak, 8 X 10 1/2 Ft. .......................... 2200.00
    **Backbar,** Barber, Marble Counter Top ....................................... 2500.00
    **Backbar,** Barber, 7 Beveled Mirrors, Marble Tops, Basins ......... 900.00
    **Backbar,** Built-In Beer Cooler, Mahogany, 18 Ft. ...................... 35.00
    **Backbar,** Drugstore, Marble Front, Oak, 10 X 9 1/2 Ft. ........... 1900.00
    **Backbar,** Flower Fixtures, C.1900, Oak, 9 1/2 Ft. X 22 In. ...... 5000.00
    **Backbar,** Marble Top & Doors, 12 X 8 Ft.High ........................ 1000.00
    **Backbar,** Marble Top, Coolers, 10 Syrup Pumps, 6 Stools ...... 4000.00
    **Backbar,** Saloon, Oak, 10 X 9 Ft. ............................................. 3000.00
    **Backbar,** Soda Fountain, Small .................................................. 895.00
    **Backbar,** Stained Glass, 8 Ft. ................................................... 2850.00
    **Backbar,** Tavern, 2 Liquor Cabinets .......................................... 8000.00
    **Backbar,** Tobacco & Candy, Black Trim, C.1920, 10 X 7 3/4 Ft. ......... 3500.00
    **Baker's Bin,** 8 Walnut Drawers, Lift-Lid Base, Cherry ............ 1450.00
    **Banister Railing,** 1 End Post, Pine, 6 1/4 Ft. ............................ 50.00
    **Bathtub,** Copper Lined, Wooden Frame .................................... 250.00
    **Bin,** Amana, Iowa, Spice Drawers, 4 Shelves, 3 Bins ............ 1450.00
    **Box,** Mail, Cast Iron, 6 X 12 In. ................................................ 12.50
    **Building Plate,** First National Bank, Chicago, 5 X 19 3/4 In. ... 27.50
    **Building Plate,** Fruit Growers Express Co., 5 X 19 3/4 In. ...... 27.50
    **Cabinet,** Apothecary, Sliding Glass Doors, 25 Drawers, Cherry ...... 800.00
    **Cabinet,** Country Store, Paneled All Sides, 11 Drawers, Oak .... 450.00
    **Cabinet,** Drugstore, Sliding Glass Doors, Cherry, 6 X 8 Ft. .... 800.00
    **Cabinet,** Feed Store, 23 Drawers, Oak, 12 Ft. X 33 In.High ... 750.00
    **Cage,** Bank Teller's, Ironwork Panels, 6 1/2 X 9 5/6 Ft. ....... 3250.00
    **Cage,** Teller's, Brass Gate, Frosted Glass, Victorian ................ 450.00
    **Carving,** Man's Head, From Barber Shop, C.1890, 5 X 5 In. ... 110.00
    **Case,** Butcher, 1/2 In.Thick Glass, Beveled, Brass Frame, Oak ... 475.00
    **Column,** Marble, Soda Fountain, Pair ........................................ 395.00
    **Column,** Oak Tongue & Groove, C.1909, 9 Ft. X 22 In., Set Of 3 ... 1000.00
    **Counter,** Marble Top, Fluted Pillars, Carved Flowers, Oak, 6 Ft. ... 650.00
    **Cupboard,** Shaving Mug, 56 Dividers, Walnut, 7 Ft. ............... 2400.00
    **Desk,** Bank Lobby, Inkwells Dated 1893 .................................. 425.00

Door, Beveled Leaded Glass, 4 Section, Oak, 16 X 77 In. ........................................................ 450.00
Door, Elevator, Grillwork & Cast Bronze, 1894, 3 1/2 X 7 Ft. .................................... 2500.00
Door, Etched Glass, Vase & Floral Design, Missouri ............................................... 500.00
Door, French, 12 Beveled Panes, Oak, Pair .................................................................... 600.00
Door, Front, Carved Oak, Oval Beveled Glass ................................................................... 800.00
Door, Postal, Copper & Glass .................................................................................................. 20.00
Door, Saloon, Beveled Glass, 5 Ft.Wide, Pair ............................................................. 1400.00
Door, Saloon, 19th Century, American, Oak, 26 X 55 In., Pair .......................... 395.00
Door, Vault, Lock & Key, Cast Iron, Framing, Pair ........................................................... 500.00
Entryway Door & Panels, Oak, 10 X 7 1/2 Ft. ................................................... Illus 8000.00
Fan, Federal, For House Doorway .......................................................................................... 95.00
Faucet, For Bathtub, Nickel Over Brass .............................................................................. 12.50
Faucet, Hot & Cold Handles, Nickel Plated Brass ........................................................ 27.00
Fence & Gate, Fleur-De-Lis, Medallions, Turnings, Iron, 60 In. .......................... 1150.00
Fence, Balustrades, & Gate, Victorian, Cast Iron, 40 Ft. ......................................... 800.00
Fence, 8 Posts, 2 Gates, Cast Iron, 110 X 3 Ft. ....................................................... 1000.00
Fountain, Front & Back Bar, Bishop, Babcock, & Becket, 1908 ......................... 7500.00
Fountain, Soda, Backbar, Stained Glass Panels, C.1920, 12 Ft. ....................... 8000.00
Fountain, Water, School, Iron Stand, Tin Tank, Porcelain Cup ............................. 149.50
Frontbar & Backbar, Mirror, 6 Stools, 9 Ft. ................................................................ 2350.00
Globe, Free Standing, Courthouse, 7 Light, Bronze, Pair ..................................... 5000.00
Hinge, Barn Door, Iron, 12 In., Pair .................................................................................... 75.00
Hinge, Etched Foliage, Wrought Iron, Pair ...................................................................... 185.00
Holder, Toilet Tissue, Peck Bros., Brass ........................................................................ 27.50
Ironwork From Widow's Walk, 100 Pieces ...................................................................... 100.00
Keyhole Lock, Sentry, Patent 1925 ...................................................................................... 16.00
Lamp, Street, Gas, Steel Base, Cast Iron Top, 23 In. ............................................... 300.00
Light, Porch, Gas, Electrified, Ceiling Mounted, Iron .................................................. 95.00
Newel Post, Green Opaline Pineapple, Brass Fitting, 7 1/2 In. ............................ 85.00
Panel, Carved, Beefeater Guard & Woman, 18th Century, Oak, Pair .................. 500.00
Shield, Paris Panel, Iron, Hector Guimard, C.1900, 29 X 24 In. ......................... 3000.00
Sink, Copper Lined, With Water Pump ................................................................................. 850.00
Sink, Corner, Embossed Bowl, Cast Iron .......................................................................... 50.00
Sink, Corner, Splashboard All Marble, Oak Cabinet .................................................... 100.00
Snow Birds, Used On Slate Roofs, Cast Iron, Set Of 10 ............................................ 40.00
Staircase, Paneling, Newel, Golden Oak, 1870s, 4 X 12 Ft. ............................... 1500.00
Tile, Roof, Bird On Curved Base, Chinese, 10 In., Pair .............................................. 95.00
Toilet Seat, 1918, Oak ................................................................................................................ 18.00
Valance Strip, Victorian, Brass, In Factory Wrapping ................................................. 10.00
Window Tops, Gingerbread, Side Trim, Set Of 20 ....................................................... 500.00
Window, Gothic Church, Amber Panels, 3 Part, Pair ................................................... 300.00
Window, Stained Glass, Multicolored, 24 X 24 In., Pair ............................................. 400.00

*Arequipa Pottery was produced from 1911 to 1918 by the patients of the Arequipa Sanitorium in Marin County Hills, California.*

AREQUIPA, Candleholder, Brown Matte, Floral Design, Square Form, 7 In. ............................. 150.00

Architectural, Entryway Door & Panels, Oak,
10 X 7 1/2 Ft.

**ARITA, Charger,** Blue & White, C.1800, 26 In.Diam. .................................... 1800.00
  **Plate,** Blue & White, 10 In. ........................................................................ 200.00

> *Art Deco, or Art Moderne, is a style started at the Paris Exposition*
> *of 1925, characterized by linear, geometric designs. All types of furniture*
> *and decorative arts, jewelry, bookbindings, and even games were designed*
> *in this style.*

**ART DECO, Box,** Powder, Alabaster, Inlaid Flower Top ............................... 35.00
  **Buckle,** White & Black Glass, Boxed, Pair ............................................... 20.00
  **Cocktail Shaker,** Hammered Silver Plate, Meriden ................................. 75.00
  **Compact,** 3 Flowers, Richard Hudnut ...................................................... 17.00
  **Figurine,** Dancer, Gilt Bronze, Carved Ivory, C.1935 ................... *Illus* 3250.00
  **Flower Frog,** 2 Nudes & Tulip Blossom ................................................... 35.00
  **Goblet,** Swirls, Blue Rooster In Stem Knob, Red & White ......................... 50.00
  **Lamp,** Labrador Retriever, Chasing Globe, White Frosted ........................ 65.00
  **Plate,** Three Water Lilies, Signed, 7 1/4 In. ............................................. 10.00
  **Rose Bowl,** Turquoise, Czech, 6 In. ........................................................ 48.00
  **Vase,** Geometrics, Signed, 1915, Austrian, 15 In. ................................... 35.00
  **Vase,** Graduated Steps, Turquoise, 16 In.Circumference, 7 In. ................. 45.00

Art Deco, Figurine, Dancer, Gilt Bronze, Carved Ivory, C.1935

> *Art glass means any of the many forms of glassware made during the late*
> *nineteenth or early twentieth century. These wares were expensive and*
> *made in limited production. Art glass is not the typical commercial glass*
> *that was made in large quantities, and most of the art glass was produced by*
> *hand methods.*

  **ART GLASS,** see also separate headings such as Burmese, Nash,
  Schneider, etc.
**ART GLASS, Basket,** Lemon Yellow, Clear Arched Handle, Ribbed Body .................. 110.00
  **Basket,** Thorn Handle, Crimped, Opalescent White Lining, 5 1/2 In. ..................... 275.00
  **Box,** Colored Enamel, Gold, Amber Crackle, Hinged, 3 1/2 In. .......................... 145.00
  **Box,** Semiprecious Stone Cover, Amber Base, 3 3/4 X 2 1/4 In. ........................ 165.00
  **Candlestick,** Opaline, Blue To White, C.1900, 8 In. ....................................... 95.00
  **Compote,** Blue Petal Bowl & Foot, Lemon Twist Stem, 6 In. ............................ 65.00
  **Darning Egg,** Spangled, 1800s ................................................................. 200.00
  **Dish,** Candy, Star & Button, Clear To Pumpkin, Footed, 5 In. ........................... 23.00
  **Lamp,** Table, Flowers, Green & Caramel Leaded Shade, Brass Base .................. 275.00
  **Pitcher,** Bacchante Face Spout, Nude Handle, A.Ledru, 14 In. ....................... 3000.00
  **Rose Bowl,** Striped Overshot, Purple, Dimpled, 5 X 5 In. .............................. 119.00
  **Shade,** Feather Pull-Up, Marked, 4 1/2 In. ................................................. 145.00
  **Shade,** Green & Gold Leaves, Vertical Vines, Gold Lined ................................ 145.00
  **Shade,** Pearl Iridescent Ground, Green Feathers, 6 1/2 In. ............................. 65.00
  **Spittoon,** Lady's, Polished Bottom, Green ................................................... 47.00
  **Tumbler,** Peach Opal Diamond .................................................................. 68.00

| | |
|---|---|
| **Vase,** Allover Raised & Beaded Enamel Flowers & Scrolls, 10 In. | 110.00 |
| **Vase,** Blue Heart, Vine & Red Star, 5 1/4 In. | 125.00 |
| **Vase,** Chrysanthemum, American, 19th Century, Green, 9 1/4 In. | 375.00 |
| **Vase,** Enameled Poppies, Topaz, 15 In. | 189.00 |
| **Vase,** Hand-Painted, Signed Leune, 20 In. | 850.00 |
| **Vase,** Opalescent To Clear Yellow, C.1900, American, 7 3/4 In. | 25.00 |
| **Vase,** Orchid, Silver Scroll, Green To White, Oval, 8 1/4 In. | 70.00 |
| **Vase,** Puffed-Out Beetle, Signed Montieres, 5 In. | 250.00 |
| **Vase,** Red, Yellow Stripes, White Interior, 10 1/2 In. | 35.00 |
| **Vase,** Trumpet, Pink Inside, Green Outside, Hand-Blown, 10 X 6 In. | 165.00 |
| **Vase,** Twisted & Dimpled, Peacock & Maroon Variegated, 6 In. | 110.00 |
| **Vase,** White Swirls, Clear Glass, Crimped Flared Top, 4 1/2 In. | 75.00 |
| **Vase,** 5 Layers Of Glass, Yellow, Orange, & Black, Firlentin, 9 In. | 385.00 |

*Art Nouveau, a style characterized by free-flowing organic design, reached its zenith between 1895 and 1905. The style encompassed all decorative and functional arts from architecture to furniture and posters.*

**ART NOUVEAU, see also Furniture, various glass categories, etc.**

| | |
|---|---|
| **ART NOUVEAU, Bust,** Woman, Bronze Clad, 9 In. | 75.00 |
| **Cover,** Fireplace, Lady With Blooming Flowers, Tin | 90.00 |
| **Figurine,** Bust Of Woman, Bronze Clad, 9 In. | 75.00 |
| **Inkwell,** Bust, Lady, Large Hat, France | 30.00 |
| **Lamp,** 6 Bent & 6 Straight Panels, Tree Scene, 3 Light, 21 In. | 1900.00 |
| **Mirror,** Shaving, Lady, Gown, Beveled, Brass & Copper, 17 In. | 75.00 |
| **Pin,** Collar, Lady With Flowing Hair | 35.00 |
| **Tray,** Bread, Reticulated Floral Rim, Maiden Heads, Silver Plate | 48.00 |
| **ART POTTERY, see under factory name** | |

# AURENE

*Aurene glass was made by Frederick Carder of New York about 1904. It is an iridescent gold glass, usually marked Aurene or Steuben.*

**AURENE, see also Steuben**

| | |
|---|---|
| **AURENE, Atomizer,** Perfume, Blue, 9 3/4 In. | 225.00 |
| **Bonbon,** Gold, Ruffled Edge, Blue, Signed, 3 3/4 X 1 1/4 In. | 125.00 |
| **Bonbon,** Ruffled Rim, Signed & Numbered, 1 3/4 X 4 3/4 In.Diam. | 135.00 |
| **Bonbon,** Ruffled, Iridescent Blue, 1 1/4 X 3 3/4 In.Diam. | 125.00 |
| **Bowl,** Calcite, Flared, Blue | 595.00 |
| **Bowl,** Purplish Highlights, Original Label, 2 1/4 X 10 In.Diam. | 700.00 |
| **Compote,** Champagne Glass Shape, Signed, 6 In. | 275.00 |
| **Creamer,** Clover Shape Handle, Blue & Violet, Signed, 4 In. | 450.00 |
| **Dish,** 3 Stretch Triangle, Blue & Gold, Signed, 4 X 2 1/4 In. | 190.00 |
| **Dish,** 4-Footed, Ruffled, Signed, 6 X 7 1/4 In.Diam. | 225.00 |
| **Pitcher,** Gold, Signed, No.3064, 6 In. | 365.00 |
| **Tumbler,** Gold, Signed | 350.00 |
| **Vase,** Dimpled & Pointed, Signed, 5 In. | 265.00 |
| **Vase,** Feather Design, Signed & Numbered, 7 3/4 In. | 595.00 |
| **Vase,** Iridescent, Urn Form, Blue, Inscribed Aurene, 2 1/2 In. | 275.00 |
| **Vase,** Rainbow Iridescent, 3-Prong Tree Stump, Signed, 6 In. | 450.00 |
| **Vase,** Ruffled Stretched Glass Top, C.1910, Marked, 12 1/4 In. | 1100.00 |
| **Vase,** Urn Form, Flared Rim, Iridescent Blue, C.1910, Marked, 2 1/2 In. | 275.00 |
| **Vase,** 3-Prong Tree Stump, Gold Iridescent, Signed, 10 In. | 525.00 |
| **AUSTRIA, see Royal Dux, Kauffmann, Porcelain** | |

*Auto parts and accessories are collectors' items today.*

| | |
|---|---|
| **AUTO, Can,** Oil, Autoline, C.1906, 1 Gallon | 15.00 |
| **Can,** Oil, Valvoline, C.1906, 1 Gallon | 15.00 |
| **Carrier,** Luggage, Fender, Metal | 11.00 |
| **Carrier,** Running Board, Expandable, Metal | 25.00 |
| **Clock,** Lux, With Case | 25.00 |
| **Cup,** Grease, Texaco Motor, Tin, 1 Pound | 7.00 |

**Emblem,** Monte Carlo Rally ................................................................................ 16.50
**Gas Pump & Globe,** Cloverleaf Shape, Cities Service, Brass Nozzle .................... 500.00
**Gas Pump Globe,** American Gas, 15 In.Diam. ...................................................... 175.00
**Gas Pump Globe,** Ashland ................................................................................... 40.00
**Gas Pump Globe,** Atlantic Hi-Arc, Unused, Boxed ............................................... 140.00
**Gas Pump Globe,** Atlantic White Flash, Unused, Boxed ..................... 130.00 To 250.00
**Gas Pump Globe,** Barnsdall, Capcolite Plastic Body ...................................*Illus* 95.00
**Gas Pump Globe,** Bell Oil Derrick ........................................................................ 165.00
**Gas Pump Globe,** Buffalo .................................................................................... 99.00
**Gas Pump Globe,** Calso Supreme, Unused, Boxed .............................................. 140.00
**Gas Pump Globe,** Cavalier .................................................................................. 85.00
**Gas Pump Globe,** Cities Service Ethyl, Cloverleaf Design ................................... 350.00
**Gas Pump Globe,** Crescent Gasoline, Metal Frame ............................................ 250.00
**Gas Pump Globe,** Crown, Frye ........................................................................... 700.00
**Gas Pump Globe,** Cushing Premium .................................................................... 90.00
**Gas Pump Globe,** Dixcel Pioneer ........................................................................ 140.00
**Gas Pump Globe,** Dixcel Trial Tells ..................................................................... 150.00
**Gas Pump Globe,** Dixie Oils, Gasoline, The Power To Pass, Jeweled .................. 275.00
**Gas Pump Globe,** Dorco, Pictured Wings ........................................................... 100.00
**Gas Pump Globe,** DX Lubricating Gas ................................................................. 75.00
**Gas Pump Globe,** Elreco Buy Miles ..................................................................... 175.00
**Gas Pump Globe,** Esta Motor Fuel, Gold Ripple Glass Frame ............................. 175.00
**Gas Pump Globe,** Figural, Shell, White Glass, Red Letters ................................. 90.00
**Gas Pump Globe,** Fleetwing, Pictured Flying Wing, Unused ............................... 95.00
**Gas Pump Globe,** Fry, Crown Globe ................................................................... 700.00
**Gas Pump Globe,** Fuel Oil, 1 Piece ..................................................................... 350.00
**Gas Pump Globe,** Gulf, Unused, Boxed, Small .................................................... 100.00
**Gas Pump Globe,** Hi Speed ................................................................................ 140.00
**Gas Pump Globe,** Imperial Refineries, 13 1/2 In.Diam. ........................................ 75.00
**Gas Pump Globe,** Indian, Metal Frame ................................................................ 300.00
**Gas Pump Globe,** Kanotex, Rippled Glass Body .........................................*Illus* 505.00
**Gas Pump Globe,** Kendall, 1 Piece, Etched, Round ............................................ 590.00
**Gas Pump Globe,** Keystone Ethyl, Design, Steel Screw-On Base ....................... 150.00
**Gas Pump Globe,** Marathon Super M, Pictured Running Athlete .......................... 150.00
**Gas Pump Globe,** Marathon, Best In Long Run, Running Athlete ......................... 100.00
**Gas Pump Globe,** Marathon, Milk Glass Body ...........................................*Illus* 210.00
**Gas Pump Globe,** Marie's ................................................................................... 110.00

Auto, Gas Pump Globe, Barnsdall, Capcolite Plastic Body

Auto, Gas Pump Globe, Kanotex, Rippled Glass Body

Auto, Gas Pump Globe, Marathon, Milk Glass Body

**Gas Pump Globe,** Marland, 15 In. .................................................................. *Illus* 440.00
**Gas Pump Globe,** Merit Hi-Test, Screw-On Base ........................................... 145.00
**Gas Pump Globe,** Mobil Gas Special, Metal Frame ...................................... 275.00
**Gas Pump Globe,** Mobil, Flying Red Horse Design, Unused, Boxed ............ 250.00
**Gas Pump Globe,** Musgo, Fired-On Painted Design, 6 In. ..................... *Illus* 645.00
**Gas Pump Globe,** Phillips 66 Ethyl ............................................................... 110.00
**Gas Pump Globe,** Phillips 66 Unique ............................................................ 250.00
**Gas Pump Globe,** Pierce, Etched Design ............................................... *Illus* 500.00
**Gas Pump Globe,** Premier ............................................................................... 60.00
**Gas Pump Globe,** Pure ................................................................................... 130.00
**Gas Pump Globe,** Red Crown, 1 Piece ......................................................... 150.00
**Gas Pump Globe,** Richfield Hi Octane, Shield & Eagle Emblem, Unused ..... 300.00
**Gas Pump Globe,** Richfield Hi Octane, 15 In.Diam., Pair ............................ 175.00
**Gas Pump Globe,** Shamrock .......................................................................... 60.00
**Gas Pump Globe,** Shell ................................................................ 125.00 To 175.00
**Gas Pump Globe,** Sinclair Dino Gasoline, Pictured Dinosaur, Unused ......... 65.00
**Gas Pump Globe,** Sinclair H-C, Green Ground ............................................. 150.00
**Gas Pump Globe,** Sinclair Power-X, The Super Fuel ................................... 100.00
**Gas Pump Globe,** Skelly Premium ................................................................ 100.00
**Gas Pump Globe,** Skelly S Regular, Unused ................................................. 75.00
**Gas Pump Globe,** Skelly S Supreme, Unused, Boxed .................................. 75.00
**Gas Pump Globe,** Skelly, Powermax ........................................................... 110.00
**Gas Pump Globe,** Solite Oil Co. ................................................................... 150.00
**Gas Pump Globe,** Sovereign, Two Shields Design, Jeweled, Unused ......... 250.00
**Gas Pump Globe,** Standard Flame ............................................................... 175.00
**Gas Pump Globe,** Standard Oil, Gold & White, 16 X 17 In. ....................... 135.00
**Gas Pump Globe,** Standard, Esso Extra ...................................................... 250.00
**Gas Pump Globe,** Standard, Green Crown Design, 1 Piece ........................ 250.00
**Gas Pump Globe,** Standard, Red Crown Design, Unused, Boxed ............... 150.00
**Gas Pump Globe,** Sun Oil, Blue Sunoco Legend, Unused, Boxed .............. 225.00
**Gas Pump Globe,** Texaco Diesel Chief, 13 1/2 In.Diam. .............................. 75.00
**Gas Pump Globe,** Texaco Sky Chief, Base, 6 In. ........................................ 165.00
**Gas Pump Globe,** That Good Gulf Gasoline, 1 Piece, Etched ..................... 500.00
**Gas Pump Globe,** Tydol, Unused, Boxed ..................................................... 275.00
**Gas Pump Globe,** Vance Ethyl ...................................................................... 150.00
**Gas Pump Globe,** Westland ............................................................................ 99.00
**Gas Pump Globe,** White Eagle, Molded Eagle Shape ................................. 550.00

Auto, Gas Pump Globe, Marland, 15 In.

Auto, Gas Pump Globe, Musgo, Fired On Painted Design, 6 In.

Auto, Gas Pump Globe, Muso, Fired-On Painted Design, 6 In.

Auto, Gas Pump Globe, Wirt Franklin, 15 In.

| | |
|---|---|
| **Gas Pump Globe,** Wirt Franklin, 15 In. .................................................*Illus* | 1000.00 |
| **Gasoline Measure Stick,** Ford, 1909 .................................................. | 15.00 |
| **Gasoline Pump. City Service,** Hand Crank, Complete, 9 Ft.4 In. .................... | 550.00 |
| **Gauge,** Balloon Tire, Schrader .......................................................... | 7.50 |
| **Gauge,** Tire, Buick, Patent 1923, Leather Case .................................... | 16.00 |
| **Gauge,** Tire, Pocket Watch Style, Brass .............................................. | 8.50 |
| **Gauge,** Tire, Schrader, Dated 1922, Leather Case .............................. | 4.00 |
| **Gearshift Knob,** American Legion Insignia, Screw-On .......................... | 35.00 |
| **Gearshift Knob,** Red & White Swirl .................................................... | 18.00 |
| **Globe,** Free Air & Water, Orange On Milk Glass, 15 In. ........................ | 300.00 |
| **Goggles,** Driving, Green Lens, Wilson ................................................ | 6.50 |
| **Grinder,** Valve, Ford, Model T .......................................................... | 8.00 |
| **Holder,** Crank, Ford Model T ............................................................ | 5.00 |
| **AUTO, HOOD ORNAMENT, see also Lalique** | |
| **Hood Ornament,** Airplane, Chrome, 14 In. .......................................... | 8.50 |
| **Hood Ornament,** Airplane, Display Flags, Tin ...................................... | 30.00 |
| **Hood Ornament,** Bulldog, Mack Truck ................................................ | 40.00 |
| **Hood Ornament,** Charging Ram ........................................................ | 20.00 |
| **Hood Ornament,** Chevrolet, 1950s .................................................... | 25.00 |
| **Hood Ornament,** Chrysler, Gold, Red, & Black .................................... | 12.00 |
| **Hood Ornament,** Dodge Brothers, 1924 ............................................ | 25.00 |
| **Hood Ornament,** Flying Lady, Chrome On Walnut Base ........................ | 30.00 |
| **Hood Ornament,** Horse With Jockey .................................................. | 23.00 |
| **Hood Ornament,** Kaiser .................................................................. | 6.50 |
| **Hood Ornament,** Lady's Head .......................................................... | 18.00 |
| **Hood Ornament,** Pontiac Super Chief, Illuminated, Boxed .................... | 25.00 |
| **Hood Ornament,** Pontiac, 1930s ...................................................... | 30.00 |
| **Hood Ornament,** Quail, Model A Ford ................................................ | 22.00 |
| **Hood Ornament,** Ram .................................................................... | 10.00 |
| **Horn,** Model T, Klaxon .................................................................... | 40.00 |
| **Horn,** 1909, Buick, Original Bulb, Brass ............................................ | 125.00 |
| **Hubcap,** Chevrolet, C.1920, Brass .................................................... | 5.00 |
| **Jack,** Ford, Model T ...................................................................... | 25.00 |
| **Lamp,** Carbide, Rubber Bumper Grip Ring, Brass, 4 In. ........................ | 17.50 |
| **Lamp,** Carbidge, 2-Way Pivoting Searchlight, New York ........................ | 450.00 |
| **Lamp,** Kerosene, Adlake, Red & Clear Lens, Oldsmobile, Pair .............. | 80.00 |
| **Lamp,** Model T, Front, 1914 ............................................................ | 65.00 |
| **Lamp,** Side, Kerosene, Model T ........................................................ | 50.00 |
| **Lamp,** Side, Pierce Arrow Truck, 1923, Engraved ................................ | 275.00 |
| **Lamp,** Studebaker Brothers, 23 1/2 In., Pair ...................................... | 485.00 |
| **License Plate,** Arkansas, 1932, Pair .................................................. | 15.00 |
| **License Plate,** Georgia, 1935, Pair .................................................... | 20.00 |
| **License Plate,** Illinois, Soybean, 1946 .............................................. | 30.00 |
| **License Plate,** Kansas City, 1923, Commercial Vehicle ........................ | 15.00 |
| **License Plate,** Maine, 1948, Brass .................................................... | 10.00 |
| **License Plate,** Massachusetts, 1932-35, Set Of 4 .............................. | 10.00 |
| **License Plate,** Massachusetts, 1964 .................................................. | 1.50 |

License Plate, Mississippi, 1932 ........................................................................................... 5.00
License Plate, New Hampshire, 1915 ................................................................................ 35.00
License Plate, New York, Farm, 1949 ................................................................................ 6.00
License Plate, Oregon, 1969 ............................................................................................. 1.50
License Plate, Pennsylvania, 1949 ................................................................................... 2.00
License Plate, Pennsylvania, 1955 ................................................................................... 2.00
License Plate, Rhode Island, 1913 ................................................................................. 40.00
License Plate, Rhode Island, 1955 ................................................................................... 2.00
License Plate, Texas, 1957 ............................................................................................... 2.00
License Plate, Vermont, 1953 ........................................................................................... 2.00
License Plate, Wyoming, 1936 ......................................................................................... 3.00
Light, Brass, Cadillac, 1902-08 ..................................................................................... 90.00
Lighter, Cigarette, Figural Blue Bird ............................................................................. 12.00
Nozzle, Gas Pump, Brass ............................................................................................... 11.00
Pump, Tire, Ford Script, Brass ...................................................................................... 20.00
Pump, Tire, Mounts On Running Board ......................................................................... 12.00
Radiator Cap, Durant, Dragon Embossed ..................................................................... 18.00
Radio, Packard Motor Car .............................................................................................. 35.00
Spotlight, Mirror On Back, Stewart, 1920s, 6 In. ......................................................... 20.00
Trunk, Contoured Back, Leatherette Cover, 1920s, 19 X 16 In.Diam. ......................... 95.00
Vase, Ruffled Edge, Clear, 7 1/2 In. ............................................................................... 6.00
Vase, Studebaker, Bracket, Etched Glass .................................................................. 100.00
Wrench, Model A Ford ....................................................................................................... 5.00

*Autumn Leaf pattern china was made for the Jewel Tea Company from 1933. Hall China Company of East Liverpool, Ohio, Crooksville China Company of Crooksville, Ohio, Harker Potteries of Chester, West Virginia, and Paden City Pottery, Paden City, West Virginia, made dishes with this design. Autumn Leaf dishes have been made in the 1970s.*

AUTUMN LEAF, Bowl, Jewel Tea, 5 1/2 In. ..................................................................... 4.00
Bowl, Jewel Tea, 6 In.Diam. ............................................................................................. 8.00
Bowl, Mixing, Jewel Tea, Set Of 3 ................................................................................. 24.00
Bowl, Salad, Jewel Tea, 9 In.Diam. ................................................................................. 9.00
Bread Box, Jewel Tea ..................................................................................................... 22.00
Butter, Cover, Jewel Tea .............................................................................................. 127.50
Butter, Covered, Jewel Tea .......................................................................................... 125.00
Cake Safe, Jewel Tea, Tin, 1935 ................................................................................... 35.00
Casserole, Covered, Jewel Tea, Round .................................................. 18.00 To 25.00
Coffee Grinder, Jewel Tea, Cream ................................................................................. 70.00
Coffeepot, Jewel Tea, Black & Orange Flowers, Silver On Edge ............................... 22.00
Coffeepot, Jewel Tea, Ivory ........................................................................................... 25.00
Creamer, Jewel Tea ........................................................................................................... 6.00
Cup & Saucer, Jewel Tea ..................................................................... 6.00 To 6.50
Cup, Custard, Jewel Tea ................................................................................................... 3.50
Gravy Boat, Jewel Tea ................................................................................................... 10.00
Marmalade, Jewel Tea, Underplate, Spoon .................................................................. 42.00
Mug, Jewel Tea ............................................................................................................... 12.00
Mustard, Jewel Tea ............................................................................. 35.00 To 40.00
Percolator, Jewel Tea, Electric .................................................................................... 125.00
Pitcher, Milk, Jewel Tea ................................................................................................. 18.00
Pitcher, Water, Jewel Tea ............................................................................................... 18.00
Plate, Jewel Tea, 9 In.Diam. ............................................................................................ 5.00
Plate, Luncheon, Jewel Tea, Gold Trim ......................................................................... 4.00
Plate, 6 In.Diam. ............................................................................................................... 2.50
Plate, 9 1/4 In.Diam. ......................................................................................................... 5.50

Autumn Leaf, Plate, 10 In.Diam.

| | |
|---|---|
| **Plate**, 10 In.Diam. ......................................................................................... *Illus* | 7.00 |
| **Platter**, Jewel Tea, 11 In. ............................................................................... | 9.50 |
| **Platter**, Jewel Tea, 13 1/2 In. ........................................................................ | 7.50 |
| **Platter**, Jewel Tea, 14 In. ............................................................................... | 35.00 |
| **Range Set**, Jewel Tea ................................................................................... | 20.00 |
| **Salt & Pepper**, Jewel Tea ............................................................................ | 8.00 |
| **Salt & Pepper**, Jewel Tea, Long-Handled .................................................... | 12.00 |
| **Soup**, Cream, Jewel Tea ............................................................................... | 14.00 |
| **Sugar & Creamer**, Jewel Tea ........................................................................ | 12.00 |
| **Sugar**, Covered ........................................................................................... | 7.50 |
| **Teapot**, Jewel Tea, Aladdin ......................................................................... | 25.00 |
| **Teapot**, Jewel Tea, Long-Spouted ............................................................... | 55.00 |
| **Tray**, Handled, Jewel Tea, Wooden .............................................................. | 57.50 |
| **Tray**, Tidbit, Jewel Tea, 3-Tiered .................................................................. | 30.00 |
| **Tumbler**, Jewel Tea, Frosted, 10 Ounce ....................................................... | 12.00 |
| **Tumbler**, Jewel Tea, Frosted, 14 Ounce ....................................................... | 12.00 |
| **Warmer Base**, Jewel Tea, Oval ..................................................................... | 75.00 |
| **Warmer**, Candle, Jewel Tea, Round .............................................................. | 75.00 |
|     **AVON, see Bottle, Avon** | |
| **AVON POTTERY, Vase**, Beige Ground, Red Cherries, C.1902, 6 1/2 X 6 In. ............ | 52.00 |
|     **AYNSLEY, see also Chelsea Grape** | |
| **AYNSLEY, Coffee Set**, Floral, Cobalt Blue, Gold, C.1900, 3 Piece ............................ | 145.00 |

*Baccarat glass was made in France by La Compagnie des Cristalleries de Baccarat, located 150 miles from Paris. The factory was started in 1765. The firm went bankrupt and began operating again about 1822. Cane and millefiori paperweights were made during the 1860 to 1880 period. The firm is still working near Paris making paperweights and glasswares.*

| | |
|---|---|
| **BACCARAT, Ashtray**, Automobile, Semielliptical Cut Glass, Pair ............................. | 30.00 |
| **Bird**, Frosted, 2 1/2 In. .................................................................................. | 30.00 |
| **Bobeche**, Signed, Pair ................................................................................... | 40.00 |
| **Bottle Perfume**, Yellow Stripes, Purse Size, 3 In. ......................................... | 22.00 |
| **Bottle**, Atomizer, Blue Panels, Pyramidal Stars, Signed, 8 In. ....................... | 105.00 |
| **Bottle**, Cologne, Cranberry Swirl, Stopper, 5 1/2 In. ..................................... | 65.00 |
| **Bottle**, Perfume, Carved Deco Nude, Black, Clear Stopper, Signed ................ | 95.00 |
| **Bowl**, Rose Teinte, Swirl Pattern, Ormolu Mounting, 6 1/2 X 12 In. ................ | 250.00 |
| **Candleholder**, Spiraled Glass, Prisms, Emerald Green, 14 1/2 In., Pr. ........... | 90.00 |
| **Compote**, Aqua Swirled To Scalloped Rim, Signed, 2 X 5 1/2 In.Diam. ........... | 40.00 |
| **Compote**, Swirl Pattern, Clear, 6 1/2 X 8 In. ................................................ | 65.00 |
| **Decanter**, Teardrop Cut Design, Signed, 10 In. ............................................. | 25.00 |
| **Dish**, Relish, Rose Teinte, Signed, 9 1/2 X 3 1/2 In. ...................................... | 70.00 |
| **Dolphin**, Clear, 4 3/4 In. ............................................................................... | 30.00 |
| **Dresser Set**, 3 Bottles, Powder Jar, English Sterling Fittings ........................ | 350.00 |

**Figurine,** Duck, Signed, 4 1/2 In. ....................................................................................... 22.00 To 30.00
**Goblet,** Electric Blue, Pinwheel, Marked ............................................................................. 58.00
**Holder,** Toothbrush, Amberina ............................................................................................. 75.00
**Inkwell,** Hinged Brass-Domed Top, Swirled Crystal, 3 X 4 In.Square ............................. 195.00
**Inkwell,** Swirl, Hinged Brass-Domed Top, Ray Star Bottom, 5 3/4 In. ........................... 195.00
**Knife Rest,** Clear ................................................................................................................ 15.00
**Lamp,** Fairy, Amberina, Signed .......................................................................................... 345.00
**Liquor Set,** Green, Clear Handles & Stopper, Gold Trim .................................................. 435.00
**Paperweight,** Candy Cane, Signed ...................................................................................... 300.00
**Paperweight,** Faceted, Concentric ...................................................................................... 255.00
**Paperweight,** Kennedy, John F., Box & Certificate, Waffle Cut Base ............................... 185.00
**Paperweight,** Kennedy, John F., Overlay ............................................................................ 675.00
**Paperweight,** Lafayette, Presentation Box .......................................................................... 300.00
**Paperweight,** Lincoln, Pink To White, Clear Overlay, 1954, Signed .................................. 650.00
**Paperweight,** Monroe, James, Sulfide, Box & Certificate ................................................... 125.00
**Paperweight,** Paine, Thomas ............................................................................................... 75.00
**Paperweight,** Paine, Thomas, Sulfide ................................................................................. 75.00
**Paperweight,** Roosevelt, Eleanor, Sulfide, 1971 ............................................................... 75.00
**Paperweight,** Wilson, Woodrow, Sulfide ............................................................................ 60.00
**Paperweight,** 3 Different Colored Millefiori Rings, Signed, 2 In. ...................................... 90.00
**Pitcher,** Lemonade, 9 Glasses, Diamond Panel Cut ........................................................ 240.00
**Tray,** Rubina Swirl, Signed, Rectangular, 13 In. .............................................................. 75.00
**Vase,** Bulbous, Swirl, Amberina, 7 In. .............................................................................. 85.00
**Vase,** Double Gourd Shape, Gilding, 12 In. ...................................................................... 115.00
**Vase,** Etched, Floral, 8 In. ................................................................................................. 40.00
**Vase,** Snake Winding Around Body, White, Clear, Signed, 8 1/2 In. ............................... 110.00
**Vase,** Trumpet, Gold Enamel Design, Signed, 12 In. ...................................................... 155.00

**BADGE, Agent,** New York Military Census, 1917, Shield ................................................. 35.00
**Cap,** Stage Driver's, A.Briggs, Pomeroy, Iowa, C.1850 .................................................... 85.00
**Chauffeur's,** New York, 1919 ............................................................................................. 8.00
**Deputy Constable,** Blue Township, Missouri Seal, Hallmarked ....................................... 75.00
**Deputy Sheriff,** C.1932, Monroe City, Michigan, Aluminum Clad ................................... 20.00
**Deputy Sheriff,** Hamilton County, Ohio, State Seal, Shield Shape ................................... 70.00
**Deputy Sheriff,** Posse, Wyandotte County, Kansas .......................................................... 47.50
**Deputy Sheriff,** St.Clair County, Illinois, Hallmarked ..................................................... 45.00
**Deputy Sheriff,** St.Clair County, Michigan ....................................................................... 20.00
**Detective Police,** Pacific Electric, 7 Point Star, Silver, Logo Center ............................... 27.50
**Fireman's,** C.1900 .............................................................................................................. 24.00
**Patrolman,** Shield Shape, Chevrolet Motor Co., St.Louis .............................................. 65.00
**Police Detective,** Pacific Electric, 7 Point Star, Silver .................................................... 27.50
**Police Village Of Cahokie,** Illinois, Eagle Top, Hallmarked ........................................... 45.00
**Police,** Cap, Michigan ....................................................................................................... 18.00
**Police,** Captain, Iowa ........................................................................................................ 25.00
**Police,** Chief, Foster Township, Michigan ......................................................................... 20.00
**Police,** Investigator, Hawaii Five-O, Gold Shield ............................................................. 22.50
**Police,** Special, Kansas City, Missouri, 1925, Hallmarked .............................................. 37.50
**Police,** Wallet, Foster Township, Michigan ....................................................................... 10.00
**Prohibition Officer's,** Padlock & Key, For Locking Speakeasies .................................... 240.00
**Public Hack Driver,** New York, 1933 ................................................................................. 25.00
**Sheriff,** Cap, Gold, Ogenaw County, Michigan ................................................................ 20.00
**Sheriff,** Deputy, 5 Point, Full Brass Ends, Cook County ................................................. 80.00
**Shooting,** Russian .............................................................................................................. 18.00
**Watchman,** Kerr S.S.Line, Eagle, Silvered Finish Brass .................................................. 45.00
     BAG, BEADED, see Beaded Bag

*Metal banks have been made since 1868. There are still banks, mechanical banks, and registering banks (those which total money deposited on the face of the bank). Many old banks have been reproduced since the 1950s in iron or plastic.*

**BANK, Ada Cottage,** Converted Toy, Painted Tin, 8 In. ........................................*Illus* 170.00
     **Advertising,** Pittsburgh Corning, Glass Block, 3 1/4 X 3 1/4 In. ............................... 15.00

**Alligator,** Climbing On Rocks, Gold Paint, Die Cast, 5 1/2 X 5 X 3 In. ..................................... 40.00
**Amish Boy,** Sitting On Hay Bale, Holding Pig, 1930s ......................................................... 65.00
**Animal Scenes,** Oval, Tin ................................................................................................. 35.00
**Arabian Safe,** Cast Iron ................................................................................................... 50.00
**Army Tank,** Turret For Coins, Tin Lithograph, 6 In. ......................................................... 32.00
**Aunt Jemima,** Cast Iron, 9 In. .......................................................................................... 50.00
**Aunt Jemima,** Original Paint, Cast Iron, 5 1/2 In. ........................................................... 60.00
**Bank Building,** Cupola, Blue Paint, Red Roof, Tin, 4 1/4 In. ........................................... 45.00
**Barney Google,** Candy Container, Tin & Glass, 3 In. ..................................... *Illus* 375.00
**Barrel,** Girl At Side, Pot Metal, 2 In. ............................................................... *Illus* 210.00
**Baseball Player & Bat,** Candy Container, 3 1/4 In. ........................................ *Illus* 350.00
**Baseball,** Lou Gehrig, Glass ............................................................................................ 50.00
**Baseball,** Official League, Tin, Key ................................................................................. 10.00
**Basket With 5 Scotty Dogs,** Ivory Paint, Die Cast, 4 1/4 In. ........................................ 35.00
**Bear With Honey Pot,** Cast Iron, 6 1/2 In. ..................................................................... 150.00
**Bear With Honey Pot,** Cast Iron, 6 3/4 In. ..................................................................... 135.00
**Bear,** Snowcrest, Glass, Label, 16 Oz. ............................................................................. 9.00
**Bed,** Standing, Cast Iron, 5 In. ......................................................................................... 12.00
**Ben Franklin,** Bust, Pot Metal ........................................................................................... 38.00
**Ben Franklin,** Bust, Suffolk Franklin Bank, Coppertone .................................................. 15.00
**Billiken,** Cast Iron ............................................................................. 38.50 To 48.00
**Bird On Log,** 1930, Bisque, 3 1/2 X 5 In. ........................................................................ 125.00
**Black Beauty,** Signed, Cast Iron ...................................................................................... 65.00
**Black Boy,** Plaster ........................................................................................................... 15.00
**Blackpool Tower,** England, Cast Iron ................................................................................ 95.00
**Book,** Banthrico, Leather Bound, Month & Day, 3 1/2 X 4 1/2 In. ................................. 25.00
**Book,** Brass Bound, Springfield, Mass., 5 Cent Savings Bank ........................................ 10.00
**Book,** Brass Bound, 4 1/2 In. ........................................................................................... 10.00
**Book,** Brass Edge, Investors Syndicate ............................................................................ 7.50
**Book,** Union Trust, New Haven, Conn., Key, 3 1/2 X 5 In. ............................................. 16.00
**Bottle,** Lincoln, Glass ....................................................................................................... 15.00
**Boy Scout,** Cast Iron, 5 3/4 In. ........................................................................................ 75.00
**Boy Scout,** Staff, In Uniform, Traces Of Gilt Paint, Cast Iron, 5 3/4 In. ....................... 50.00
**Buddy L,** Savings ............................................................................................................. 40.00
**Buffalo,** Gilded Metal ........................................................................................................ 75.00
**Buffalo,** Gold Paint, Cast Iron, 3 X 4 1/4 In. ................................................................... 70.00
**Buffalo,** Iron ..................................................................................................................... 50.00
**Building,** Cast Iron ............................................................................. 35.00 To 85.00
**Building,** Clyde Savings, Metal ......................................................................................... 12.50
**Building,** Dome, 7 Stories, 76 Windows, Gilt Paint, Cast Iron, 3 5/8 In. ....................... 35.00
**Building,** Dome, 8 Stories, 134 Windows, Some Gold Paint, Cast Iron, 5 In. ................ 25.00
**Building,** Triangular, Cast Iron ......................................................................................... 45.00
**Building,** 6-Sided, Cast Iron .............................................................................................. 125.00
**Bulldog,** Brown, Cast Iron ................................................................................................ 40.00
**Bulldog,** Cast Iron ............................................................................. 32.00 To 100.00
**Bulldog,** No Paint, Cast Iron, 6 X 8 In. ............................................................................ 35.00
**Bulldog,** Seated, Gold Paint, Wax Finish, Cast Iron, 4 1/2 X 4 In. ................................ 45.00
**Bulldog,** Sitting, Original Gilding, Cast Iron, 4 1/2 In. .................................................... 35.00
**Bunny,** Royal Doulton, 1967 ............................................................................................. 65.00
**Bunnykins** ........................................................................................................................ 45.00
**Bust,** Indian Head National Bank, Cast Iron .................................................................... 50.00
**Bust,** Lindy 1928 .............................................................................................................. 65.00
**Buster Brown & Tige,** Cast Iron ....................................................... 70.00 To 150.00
**Calumet Baking Powder** ................................................................................................. 90.00
**Camel,** Cast Iron, Small .................................................................... 85.00 To 160.00
**Cannon Shell,** Cast Iron .................................................................................................... 65.00
**Cannon Shell,** World War I, Embossed Eagle Seal, Cast Iron, 8 In. ............................... 50.00
**Captain Kidd,** Repainted Red, Cast Iron, 5 1/2 In. ......................................................... 130.00
**Car,** City Bank Of Lorain, Ohio, Cast Iron ........................................................................ 20.00
**Car,** North Carolina National Bank, Cast Iron ................................................................... 20.00
**Cash Register,** Cast Iron, 3 1/2 X 4 1/4 In.Wide ............................................................. 42.50
**Cash Register,** Thrift, Benjamin Franklin, Marx, Tin, 4 X 2 In. ...................................... 20.00

Bank, Ada Cottage, Converted Toy, Painted Tin, 8 In. (See Page 17)

Bank, Church, Clock Steeple, Painted, Stenciled, Tin, 12 1/2 In.

Banks, Candy Containers, from left to right, Barney Google, Dog & Barrel (See Page 21), Happifats (See Page 22), and Baseball Player & Bat

| | |
|---|---|
| **Cat,** Standing, Bronze Finish, Cast Iron, 6 3/4 In. ...............................................*Illus* | 1200.00 |
| **Century Of Progress,** Chicago, 1934, Tin ............................................................. | 13.50 |
| **Charlie McCarthy,** Coin Through Mouth Or Bottom, Composition, 11 In. ............................ | 100.00 |
| **Chipmunk,** Tin ........................................................................................... | 45.00 |
| **Church,** Clock Steeple, Painted, Stenciled, Tin, 12 1/2 In. ..............................*Illus* | 1800.00 |
| **Church,** J.Chein & Co. ............................................................................ | 10.00 To 22.50 |
| **Circus Elephant,** Howdah, Gray Paint Over Gilt, Cast Iron, 3 X 4 In. ...................... | 35.00 |
| **Circus Merry-Go-Round,** Dated 1875, Cast Iron, 5 In. ..................................... | 65.00 |

Banks, from left to right, Barrel With Girl At Side (See Page 18); Elephant With Drum (See Page 22); Rabbit, Heart Lock (See Page 27); and Sailor Boy (See Page 27)

Banks, Cast Iron, from left to right, Standing Cat (See Page 19), Clock With Pendulum

**Clock With Pendulum,** Cast Iron, 5 1/2 In. ........................................................................ *Illus* 400.00
**Clock,** Kinsbury, Art Deco, Chrome, 7 In. ........................................................................... 22.00
**Clock,** Tin & Cast Iron ........................................................................................................ 90.00
**Clown On Globe,** Cast Iron ................................................................................................ 700.00
**Clown,** Riding Pit, Chalkware, Dated 1949, 11 1/2 X 8 1/2 In. ........................................... 30.00
**Cocker Spaniel,** Rear End Up, Brown, 7 X 5 1/2 In. ........................................................... 22.50

Combination Safe, Dual, Kenton, Cast Iron ............................................................ 75.00
Combination Safe, National Safe Co., Cast Iron, 3 1/2 X 3 1/2 X 5 In. ........................ 32.00
Commonwealth, Registering, 1905 ......................................................................... 20.00
Covered Wagon, Bank Of Stockton ....................................................................... 10.00
Covered Wagon, Banthrico, Metal .......................................................................... 20.00
Cow, Cast Iron ................................................................................. 75.00 To 90.00
Cube, 1939 World's Fair, Glass, 5 1/2 In.Square .................................................... 35.00
Daisy Safe, Cast Iron ........................................................................................... 50.00
Deer, Cast Iron, 6 In. ........................................................................................... 45.00
DeSoto, 1952, Banthrico ...................................................................................... 50.00
Dime Register, Astronaut ..................................................................................... 12.00
Dime Register, Cash Register Shape, Number Column, 2 X 2 1/2 In. ....................... 18.00
Dime Register, Clown & Monkey, Tin ..................................................................... 18.00
Dime Register, Davy Crockett, Metal ..................................................................... 35.00
Dime Register, Embossed Capitol Building, Metal .................................................. 10.00
Dime Register, F. & R.Mfg.Co., Steel, 3/4 X 2 5/8 In. ............................................ 4.00
Dime Register, Gem, Embossed Eagle ................................................................... 18.00
Dime Register, Little Cowboy ................................................................................ 12.00
Dime Register, Popeye ...................................................................... 24.00 To 25.00
Dime Register, Popeye, 1929, Decal, Deer Park, Illinois ......................................... 46.00
Dime Register, Popeye, 1956 ............................................................................... 16.00
Dime Register, Prince Valiant ............................................................................... 45.00
Dime Register, Shape Of Cash Register, J.Chein ................................... 9.00 To 14.00
Dime Register, Snow White & Seven Dwarfs, 1938 ............................................... 25.00
Dime Register, 1964 World's Fair ......................................................................... 12.00
Dime, Raised Indian Chief, Round, Flat, Tin ........................................................... 9.50
Dime, Superman ................................................................................................. 125.00
Dirigible, Cast Iron ............................................................................................. 50.00
Dog & Barrel, Candy Container, Painted, 3 1/4 In. ............................... *Illus* 210.00
Dog With Pack On Back, Black Paint, Cast Iron, 5 1/2 X 8 In. ............................... 65.00
Dog, Fido, Black & White, Cast Iron ...................................................................... 130.00
Dog, Standing, Bundle On Back, Cast Iron ............................................................ 55.00
Donald Duck, Chalkware ...................................................................................... 20.00
Donald Duck, Glazed Bisque, 6 1/2 In. ................................................................. 20.00
Donkey, Cast Iron ............................................................................................... 60.00
Donkey, Saddled & Bridled, Gold Paint, Red Trim, Cast Iron, 4 1/2 In. .................. 75.00
Duck On Tub, Top Hat & Umbrella, Red Tub, Cast Iron, 5 1/2 In. ......................... 100.00
Duck, Yellow, Standing, Green Ground, Cast Iron, 5 1/2 In. ................................... 18.00
Duckling, Orange Bill & Feet, Spread Wings, Cast Iron, 5 X 6 1/4 In. .................... 100.00
Dutch Colonial House, Cast Iron .......................................................................... 85.00
Eagle On Hemisphere, Cast Iron .......................................................................... 50.00
Eagle, Cast Iron ................................................................................................. 15.00
Ear Of Corn, Art Nouveau, Pottery ...................................................................... 150.00
Eight O'clock Coffee ........................................................................................... 5.00
Eisenhower, Bronze, 5 In. .................................................................................... 10.00
Electric Railroad Trolley, Cast Iron, 4 1/2 X 8 3/4 In. ............................ *Illus* 1400.00

Bank, Electric Railroad Trolley, Cast Iron, 4 1/2 X 8 3/4 In.

Elephant On Tub ................................................................................................................ 70.00
Elephant With Drum, Pot Metal, 4 1/2 X 4 In. ................................................ *Illus* 45.00
Elephant, Cast Iron ............................................................................ 25.00 To 45.00
Elephant, China, German ................................................................................. 12.00
Elephant, Curled Trunk, Some Old Gilt Paint, Cast Iron, 4 1/2 In. ......................... 25.00
Elephant, Grapette, Glass, 16 Oz. ..................................................................... 15.00
Elephant, Movable Trunk, Mascon Toy Co., Plastic, 7 In. ................................... 15.00
Elephant, Penny Bank, Plaster, Pink ................................................................... 2.00
Elephant, Raised Trunk, Ceramic ..................................................................... 15.00
Elsie The Cow, Cast Iron ................................................................................ 25.00
Figural, Barrel, Chein, Tin ............................................................................... 10.00
G.E.Refrigerator, 3 3/4 In. ............................................................................. 45.00
Garage, Iron ................................................................................................. 30.00
George Washington, Bust, Iron ..................................................................... 275.00
George Washington, Cast Iron, 6 1/2 In. ............................................ 38.00 To 45.00
Globe On Arc, Cast Iron ............................................................................... 125.00
Golliwog, Cast Iron, 6 1/4 In. ........................................................... *Illus* 290.00
Golliwog, Metal Alloy ..................................................................................... 70.00
Grapette, Bottle Shape, Clear Glass, Tin Lid ..................................................... 10.00
Grasshopper, Pottery ..................................................................................... 35.00
Hansel & Gretel House, Lithographed Tin, 2 1/4 In. ........................... *Illus* 95.00
Happifats, Candy Container, 4 1/2 In. ............................................... *Illus* 185.00
Hen On Nest, Redware, 6 X 6 In. ..................................................................... 55.00
Hopalong Cassidy ......................................................................................... 24.00
Horse, Black Beauty, Arcade, C.1932, Cast Iron, 4 X 5 X 1 In. ............................ 60.00
Horse, Cast Iron, 2 3/4 In. .............................................................................. 65.00
Horse, Encircled With Horseshoe, Bust Of Columbus At Top, Cast Iron ............... 150.00
Horse, Prancing, Original Gilding, Cast Iron, 7 In. ............................................. 45.00
Horse, Red, Small, Cast Iron ........................................................................... 75.00
Horse, Standing ............................................................................................ 30.00
House With Porch, Cast Iron, Small ................................................................. 40.00
House, Cast Iron, Small ..................................................................... 25.00 To 30.00
House, Shoe Shape, Pot Metal ........................................................................ 15.00
Humpty Dumpty, Shepard Hardware, Buffalo, 7 1/2 In. .................................... 150.00
Hungry Hippo, Windup, Tin .............................................................................. 5.00
Independence Hall, Cast Iron, 10 X 9 1/4 In. ..................................... *Illus* 500.00
Indian Baby, Slot In Head, C.D.Kenny Co., Cast Iron, 4 In. ................................ 50.00

Banks, Lithographed Tin, from left to right, Punch & Judy Puppet Show (See Page 27), Jockey Head, Poor Weary Willie (See Page 27), Hansel & Gretel House

Bank, Independence Hall, Cast Iron, 10 X 9 1/4 In.

| | |
|---|---|
| **Indian Head,** Penny, 1 5/8 In. | 8.00 |
| **Indian Papoose,** Navajo, Chalkware, 11 1/2 In. | 20.00 |
| **Indian,** Full-Bodied, Cast Iron | 65.00 |
| **Indian,** Standing, Cast Iron | 50.00 |
| **Iron Horse,** Arcade, Label | 65.00 |
| **Jockey Head,** German, Lithographed Tin, 2 1/4 In. *Illus* | 150.00 |
| **John Kennedy,** Bronze, 5 In. | 10.00 |
| **Kitten,** Cast Iron | 20.00 To 45.00 |
| **Liberty Bell,** Copper, Patented 1919, 4 1/2 In. | 10.00 |
| **Liberty Bell,** Glass | 15.00 To 45.00 |
| **Liberty Bell,** Proclaim Liberty Throughout The Land, Arcade, Cast Iron | 50.00 |
| **Liberty Bell,** 1926, Cast Iron | 50.00 |
| **Lincoln,** Bottle | 7.00 |
| **Lion On Tub,** Cast Iron | 47.00 |
| **Lion,** Cast Iron, Large | 45.00 To 75.00 |
| **Lion,** Cast Iron, Medium | 27.00 |
| **Lion,** Gold Paint, Red Mouth, Cast Iron, 5 1/4 X 6 1/2 In. | 55.00 |
| **Lion,** Standing, Cast Iron, 3 1/2 In. | 12.00 |
| **Little Red Schoolhouse,** Tin | 10.00 |
| **Log Cabin Syrup,** Tin | 20.00 |
| **Log Cabin,** Cast Iron | 10.00 |
| **Log Cabin,** Glass | 20.00 |
| **Mailbox,** All-American, Green | 9.00 |
| **Mailbox,** Green, Tin, Large | 20.00 |
| **Mailbox,** Hanging, U.S.Mail Bank, Embossed Eagle, Cast Iron, 5 1/4 In. | 65.00 |
| **Mailbox,** Lift-Up Slot, Green Paint, Gold Trim, Cast Iron, 3 3/4 In. | 30.00 |
| **Majestic Radio,** Cast Iron | 100.00 |
| **Mammy With Spoon,** Cast Iron | 40.00 |
| **Mammy,** Cast Iron | 60.00 To 70.00 |
| **Man Squatting,** Pants Down, Papier-Mache, Hand-Painted, 1890s, 11 In. | 75.00 |
| **Man's Head,** Pottery, 2 In. | 45.00 |
| **Mantel Clock,** Camel Back, Movable Hands, Time To Save, Metal | 15.00 |
| **Mary & Lamb,** Cast Iron, 4 1/2 In. *Illus* | 525.00 |
| **Mary & Lamb,** Pot Metal | 35.00 |
| **Mason Jar,** Atlas Strong Shoulder, 3 1/4 In. | 20.00 |

Banks, Cast Iron, from left to right, Minute Man Soldier (See Page 28), Mary & Lamb (See Page 23), Gollywog (See Page 22)

*Mechanical banks were first made about 1870. Any bank with moving parts is considered mechanical, although those most collected are the metal banks made before World War I. Reproductions are being made.*

**Mechanical,** Adams Family, Thing, Box, Battery ............................................................ 25.00
**Mechanical,** Birdhouse, Tin, Lithograph .......................................................................... 18.50
**Mechanical,** Black Man In Cabin ..................................................................................... 225.00
**Mechanical,** Black Minstrel, Original Paint, Tin .......................................................... 185.00
**Mechanical,** Book Of Knowledge, Black Man Riding Mule, 1950s ............................ 70.00
**Mechanical,** Bowling Alley, Battery, Boxed .................................................................... 40.00
**Mechanical,** Breadwinners, Cast Iron ........................................................................ 4500.00
**Mechanical,** Bulldog ...................................................................................................... 275.00
**Mechanical,** Bulldog, Base, Cast Iron ............................................................................ 79.00
**Mechanical,** Bulldog, Seated, Glass Eyes, Iron, Dated 1880, 7 1/2 In. ................... 350.00
**Mechanical,** Cabin .......................................................................................................... 250.00
**Mechanical,** Chief Big Moon, Indian, Tepee, Frog, Fish, Iron ................... 450.00 To 700.00
**Mechanical,** Clown On Globe, Cast Iron .............................................................*Illus* 375.00
**Mechanical,** Clown's Head, Chein, Tin ........................................................................... 35.00
**Mechanical,** Coffin, Tin, Boxed ...................................................................................... 25.00
**Mechanical,** Creedmore Bank Of 1877 ........................................................................ 275.00
**Mechanical,** Darktown, 3 Black Boys, Baseball, Battery, Iron, 9 3/4 In. ................... 450.00
**Mechanical,** Dog In Kennel, Tin .................................................................................... 40.00
**Mechanical,** Dog On Turntable, Cast Iron .................................................................. 150.00
**Mechanical,** Dog With Tray, Cast Iron ......................................................................... 275.00
**Mechanical,** Dog, Speaking, Girl & Dog, Shephard Hdwr.Co. ................... 225.00 To 500.00
**Mechanical,** Down The Drain, 1967 ................................................................................ 50.00
**Mechanical,** Eagle & Eaglets ....................................................................... 325.00 To 525.00
**Mechanical,** Elephant, Cast Iron ................................................................................... 87.50
**Mechanical,** Elephant, Chein ........................................................................................ 22.00
**Mechanical,** Elephant, Howdah, Swings Trunk ........................................................... 165.00
**Mechanical,** Elephant, Pink .......................................................................................... 100.00
**Mechanical,** Elephant, Windup, Tin .............................................................................. 20.00
**Mechanical,** Feed The Kitty, Book Of Knowledge, Cast Iron ..................................... 135.00
**Mechanical,** Frog On Rock ............................................................................ 250.00 To 350.00
**Mechanical,** Frog On Round Base ............................................................................... 275.00
**Mechanical,** Frog On Stump ......................................................................... 345.00 To 395.00

**Mechanical,** Hall's Excelsior ........................................................................................ 175.00
**Mechanical,** Haunted House, Battery, Boxed ................................................................. 50.00
**Mechanical,** Hershey Chocolate, Tin & Plastic, 1950s, Boxed .................................... 25.00
**Mechanical,** High Hat, Black Man .................................................................................. 600.00
**Mechanical,** Hippo, Coin In Slot Opens Mouth To Eat It, Metal ............................... 8.50
**Mechanical,** Humpty Dumpty, Shephard Hdwr., Buffalo, 7 1/2 In. .......................... 150.00
**Mechanical,** I Always Did Spise A Mule, Black Man, 10 In. .................. 130.00 To 275.00
**Mechanical,** Initiating First Degree, Cast Iron ...........................................................3500.00
**Mechanical,** Jolly Black Man With Top Hat .................................................................. 375.00
**Mechanical,** Jolly Black Man, C.1955, Tin ................................................................... 25.00
**Mechanical,** Jolly Nigger, Cast Iron ............................................................................. 150.00
**Mechanical,** Lilliput, Hall, Cast Iron ............................................................................. 235.00
**Mechanical,** Lion & Monkey, Gilt Paint, Iron, 19th Century .................................... 110.00
**Mechanical,** Lion & Monkeys, Cast Iron ...................................................................... 375.00
**Mechanical,** Magic Bank ............................................................................................... 425.00
**Mechanical,** Magician, Cast Iron ................................................................................. 550.00
**Mechanical,** Merry-Go-Round ....................................................................................... 38.00
**Mechanical,** Minstrel .................................................................................................... 80.00
**Mechanical,** Monkey, Coin Is Dropped, Tips Hat, Tin, Chein ................... 32.50 To 35.00
**Mechanical,** Monkey, Organ Grinder, Iron, 8 3/4 In. ................................................ 75.00
**Mechanical,** Owl, Turns Head .................................................................. 175.00 To 225.00
**Mechanical,** Punch & Judy ........................................................................ 300.00 To 450.00
**Mechanical,** Recording, 1891 ...................................................................................... 125.00
**Mechanical,** Rooster .................................................................................. 150.00 To 275.00
**Mechanical,** Rooster Crowing ...................................................................................... 160.00
**Mechanical,** Santa At The Chimney ............................................................ 600.00 To 650.00
**Mechanical,** Santa Claus .............................................................................................. 500.00
**Mechanical,** Santa Claus At Chimney, Iron, 6 1/4 In. ................................................ 300.00
**Mechanical,** Satellite Loan Association, Cast Iron, 10 In. .......................................... 40.00
**Mechanical,** Sewing Machine, Cast Iron ...................................................................2100.00
**Mechanical,** Soldier Shooting Penny From Cannon ...................................... 325.00 To 575.00
**Mechanical,** Southern Comfort ..................................................................................... 30.00
**Mechanical,** Stump Speaker, Black Man Drops Coin Into Suitcase ...........................1250.00
**Mechanical,** Tammany .................................................................................. 135.00 To 180.00
**Mechanical,** Teddy Roosevelt & Bear, Original Paint ................................. 250.00 To 600.00
**Mechanical,** Tennis Player, King-Riggs, Boxed, Cast Iron .......................................... 165.00
**Mechanical,** Toad On Stump ......................................................................................... 350.00
**Mechanical,** Trick Dog, Clown Holding Hoop, Dog Jumps Through .......................... 350.00
**Mechanical,** Turntable .................................................................................................. 285.00

Bank, Mechanical, Clown On Globe, Cast Iron

Bank, Model T Touring Car,
Repaired Roof, Cast Iron

| | |
|---|---|
| **Mechanical,** Uncle Sam, Drops Coin Into Suitcase, New | 25.00 |
| **Mechanical,** Uncle Sam, Iron | 425.00 To 475.00 |
| **Mechanical,** Wall Telephone, Coin Rings Bell, 1920s, 12 In. | 95.00 |
| **Mechanical,** William Tell | 150.00 To 375.00 |
| **Mechanical,** Windmill, Tin | 110.00 |
| **Mechanical,** World's Fair, Iron, Patented Feb.2, 1875 | 275.00 To 395.00 |
| **Mechanical,** 1892 Columbian Exposition | 225.00 |
| **Merry-Go-Round** | 350.00 |
| **Model T Touring Car,** Repaired Roof, Cast Iron | *Illus* 450.00 |
| **Monkey,** Chein, Tin | 45.00 |
| **Moon,** Papier-Mache | 22.50 |
| **Mosque,** Embossed Bank, Over Door, Cast Iron, 4 1/4 X 4 1/4 X 2 1/2 In. | 40.00 |
| **Mosque,** Old Silver Paint, Cast Iron, 3 X 2 1/2 X 5/8 In. | 30.00 |
| **Mr.Peanut,** Composition | 10.00 |
| **Mr.Peanut,** Iron | 25.00 |
| **Mr.Peanut,** Tin | 10.00 |
| **Mulligan The Cop,** Cast Iron | 85.00 To 100.00 |
| **Mutt & Jeff,** Iron | 68.00 |
| **Nipper,** R.C.A. Victor, Ceramic, 12 In. | 75.00 |
| **Oil Can,** Tin, Miniature | 15.00 |
| **Old Dutch Cleanser Can,** 3 In. | 30.00 |
| **Organ Grinder** | 65.00 |
| **Owl,** Carnival Glass, 7 In. | 10.00 |
| **Owl,** Cast Iron | 125.00 |
| **Owl,** Raimond Silver Mfg.Co., Italy, 6 In. | 22.00 |
| **Penny Register,** Pail, Cast Iron | 160.00 |
| **Penny,** Foxy Grandpa, Figural, Ceramic | 38.00 |
| **Penny,** Man's Face, Staffordshire, 2 In. | 60.00 |
| **Pepsi-Cola,** Tin | 45.00 |
| **Pershing,** Cast Iron | 85.00 |
| **Phillips 66 Tire,** Tin | 6.00 |
| **Phillips 66,** Tin | 10.00 |
| **Pig,** Brown Spots, Standing, Metal | 35.00 |
| **Pig,** Carnival Glass, Marigold | 7.00 To 25.00 |
| **Pig,** Cast Iron, 1 3/4 X 3 In. | *Illus* 2600.00 |

Bank, Pig, Cast Iron, 1 3/4 X 3 In.

Pig, Cast Iron, 4 In. ............................................................................................. 10.00
Pig, Cobalt Blue, Glass ...................................................................................... 20.00
Pig, Glass, 4 In. ................................................................................................... 8.00
Pig, Glazed, White With Pink & Blue, Hull Pottery, 7 In.Long ....................... 24.50
Pig, People's Savings, Worcester, Mass., Cast Iron, 5 In. ............................ 15.00
Pig, Pink China, Applied Flowers ..................................................................... 10.00
Pig, Poem On Front, Cast Iron ......................................................................... 55.00
Pig, Red Overalls, Green Bib, Red Clay, 4 In. ................................................. 50.00
Pig, Seated, Cast Iron ....................................................................................... 23.00
Pig, Seated, Gold Paint, Red Mouth, Cast Iron, 4 1/2 X 3 In. ........................ 20.00
Pig, Spongeware ................................................................................................. 35.00
Pig, Standing, Bennington, Unglazed Gray ..................................................... 25.00
Pig, Windup, J.Chein, Tin .................................................................................. 20.00
Piggy, Daily Dime, Kalan Mfg., Tin ................................................................... 10.00
Piggy, Glass, 4 X 3 In. ....................................................................................... 3.50
Pinocchio Doll, Movable Arms, Head, Wooden, 11 1/2 In. ............................. 25.00
Pinocchio, Crown Mfg. Co., Composition ......................................................... 75.00
Pirate Sitting On Chest ..................................................................................... 375.00
Pirate's Chest, Metal ......................................................................................... 15.00
Poll Parrot, On Wire Perch, Chalkware, 18 1/2 In. .......................................... 65.00
Poor Weary Willie, Tin, 5 In. ..................................................................*Illus* 160.00
Porky Pig, Ceramic, Cork Nose, Marked .......................................................... 10.00
Porky Pig, Iron ................................................................................................... 100.00
Possum, Seated On Haunches, Tail Wraps Body, Pottery, 5 3/4 In. .............. 36.00
Post Box, Cast Iron ........................................................................................... 60.00
Pot-O-Gold, Buy War Bonds, World War II, Tin ................................. 7.00 To 10.00
Prancing Horse, Cast Iron, 7 1/2 X 7 In. .......................................................... 85.00
Prancing Pony, Cast Iron, Original Gold Paint, 4 1/4 In. ................................ 40.00
Presto, Round, Side Wings, Cast Iron .............................................................. 26.50
Punch & Judy ......................................................................... 425.00 To 450.00
Punch & Judy Puppet Show, Lithographed Tin, 3 In. ...........................*Illus* 225.00
Puppy With Bee, Cast Iron ............................................................................... 45.00
Puppy, Cast Iron ................................................................................................ 30.00
Rabbit, Heart Lock, Cast Iron, 2 3/4 In. ................................................*Illus* 475.00
Rabbits, Security, Tin ........................................................................................ 40.00
Radio, Cast Iron ................................................................................. 60.00 To 90.00
Radio, Clear Glass ............................................................................ 10.00 To 22.00
Radio, Kenton, Cast Iron ................................................................................... 125.00
Raggedy Ann, Composition ............................................................................... 10.00
Rearing Horse, Silver Paint, Cast Iron ............................................ 35.00 To 75.00
Red Circle Coffee, Yellow, Tin ......................................................................... 9.00
Red Goose Shoes ............................................................................................... 135.00
Republic Pig Iron, Cast Iron ............................................................................. 65.00
Rocket, Mechanical ........................................................................................... 25.00
Roller Safe, Roller Skating Scene, Iron ........................................................... 95.00
Rooster, Bronze, 4 3/4 In. ................................................................................. 65.00
Rooster, Cast Iron ............................................................................................. 65.00
Rooster, Mean Looking, Cast Iron, 4 3/4 X 3 1/4 In. ....................................... 60.00
Rooster, Red Comb, Sculptured Feathers, Cast Iron, 5 In. ........................... 85.00
Sad & Happy Face, Pottery .............................................................. 50.00 To 55.00
Safe Deposit, Combination, Cast Iron ............................................................. 50.00
Safe Deposit, Ideal, Cast Iron .......................................................................... 45.00
Safe Deposit, Painted Girl On Side, Boy On Other, Cast Iron, 5 1/4 In. ....... 225.00
Safe Style, Combination, Dated February 22, 1916, Steel, 3 1/2 X 3 In. ....... 25.00
Safe, Daisy, Cast Iron ........................................................................................ 50.00
Safe, Handle, Kenton, Cast Iron ....................................................................... 30.00
Safe, Key Lock, Cast Iron, Small ..................................................................... 35.00
Safe, White City Puzzle, Cast Iron ................................................................... 80.00
Safe, 3 1/4 In. ..................................................................................................... 35.00
Sailor Boy, Pot Metal, 4 1/4 In. ..............................................................*Illus* 320.00
Santa, On Chimney, Cast Iron, Boxed ............................................................. 150.00
Santa, Sleeping In Chair, Banthrico ................................................ 35.00 To 75.00
Santa, Sleeping In Chair, Plaster ..................................................................... 12.50

| | |
|---|---|
| Santa, Trim A Tree, Battery Operated | 200.00 |
| Santa, Trim A Tree, Cast Iron | 200.00 |
| Santa, With Tree, Cast Iron, 6 In. | 85.00 |
| Savings Deposit, Kenton, 4 In. | 30.00 |
| Scotty Dog, Black With Red Collar, Cast Iron, 5 In. | 22.00 |
| Scotty, Seated, Metal, 4 1/2 In. | 25.00 |
| Scrooge In Bed, Ceramic, 1961 | 18.00 |
| Seated Chinaman, Enamel Over Chinese Silver | 125.00 |
| Sharecropper, Cast Iron | 60.00 To 85.00 |
| Sheep, Cast Iron | 25.00 |
| Sheep, White, Black Face, Cast Iron | 38.00 |
| Shoe House, Pot Metal | 10.00 To 15.00 |
| Skyscraper, Cast Iron, 6 In. | 55.00 |
| Snowman, Chalkware, 12 In. | 7.00 |
| Soldier, Minute Man, Cast Iron, 6 In. .......................*Illus* | 425.00 |
| Spaniel Head, Black & White, Gold Lock, Staffordshire | 85.00 |
| Spaniel, Golden Brown, Porcelain, Head Locks With Key, 7 X 5 In. | 20.00 |
| Squirrel, Acorn In His Paw, Metal | 18.00 |
| St. Louis Fair | 38.00 |
| St.Bernard, Iron, 8 In. | 85.00 |
| State Bank, Iron | 115.00 |
| Stove, Acorn, Pottery | 25.00 |
| Suitcase, Marx, Tin, 2 1/4 X 4 In. | 25.00 |
| Sunflower Blossom, Art Nouveau, Pottery | 150.00 |
| Superman, China | 65.00 |
| Table, Drop Leaf, Penny, Wooden | 29.50 |
| Talk-O-Phone, Mechanical, Tin | 35.00 |
| Tank, Cast Iron | 45.00 |
| Tank, World War I Type, Tin | 45.00 |
| Teddy Bear, Blue Overalls, Neckerchief, Flower Cart, 7 X 6 1/2 In. | 25.00 |
| Telephone Booth, Tin, Marx | 35.00 |
| Tennis Players, Cast Iron mechanical, John Wright | 165.00 |
| The Globe, Claw & Ball Tripod, Cast Iron, 5 1/4 In. | 175.00 |
| Three-Dial Radio, Cast Iron | 60.00 To 65.00 |
| Time Around The World, Iron | 200.00 |
| Tom Thumb, Cast Iron | 35.00 |
| Transformer, Cast Iron | 65.00 |
| Traveling Teller, Oval, Nickel Plated | 10.00 |
| Treasure Bank, Children Playing, Tin | 15.00 |
| Treasure Chest, Captain Flint, Tin, Key | 10.00 |
| Treasure Chest, 1930s, Glass, 4 In. | 10.00 |
| Truck, Bankamerica, Smith & Miller | 115.00 |
| Two-Story Bank, Cast Iron | 60.00 |
| U.S.Mail Box, Cast Iron | 20.00 To 35.00 |
| U.S.Mail Box, Cast Iron, 2 1/4 X 1 3/4 X 3 1/4 In. | 40.00 |
| U.S.Mail Box, Original Green Paint, Cast Iron, 5 3/4 In. | 40.00 |
| Uncle Sam Register Bank, Red, Gold, & Silver, Tin | 25.00 |
| Uncle Sam, High Hat, Chein, Tin | 14.00 |
| Uncle Sam, High Hat, Presidential Campaign, 1890, Milk Glass | 55.00 |
| Uncle Sam, 25 Cent Register, Orange, Tin | 15.00 |
| Union Bank Safe, Kenton Brand, Cast Iron | 30.00 To 45.00 |
| Wall Telephone, Embossed Public Telephone, C.1920, Black, Tin, 7 In. | 62.00 |
| Woolworth Building, Cast Iron | 45.00 To 85.00 |
| World Globe, Arc-Shaped Stand, Cast Iron, 5 X 3 1/2 X 3 In. | 125.00 |
| World Globe, Glass | 10.00 |
| World War I Soldier, C.1918, Cast Iron | 45.00 |
| World War I Tank, Cast Iron | 60.00 |
| World War II Savings Bond | 15.00 |
| World, Tin, Ohio Art | 5.00 |

*Banko is a Japanese pottery first produced at Kuwana, Ise province, in the seventeenth century. Many potters produced this ware and marked it with the Banko seal. It is still being produced.*

**BANKO, Creamer,** Tapestry Design, 4 In. ............................................................................. 75.00
    **Flask,** 3 Figures, Teahouse In Handle, 11 In. .................................................................. 285.00
    **Sugar,** Tapestry Design, Openwork, Oversized, 6 In. ..................................................... 75.00
    **Tea Set,** 2-Cup Size, Souvenir Of Watertown, S.D., 1905, 3 Piece ............................... 65.00
    **Teapot,** Five Masks ....................................................................................................... 150.00
    **Teapot,** Stick Handle, Geometric Design ...................................................................... 30.00
    **Vase,** Teahouse In Handle, Applied Porcelain Figures, 11 In. ....................................... 275.00

**BARBER, Cabinet,** Brylcream Advertising, 18 X 11 X 21 1/2 In. .................................... 30.00
    **Cabinet,** Marble & Glass Shelves, 18 X 12 X 82 In. ...................................................... 100.00
    **Chair,** Berninghaus, Oak & Brass ................................................................................. 800.00
    **Chair,** Koch, Oak & Porcelain ....................................................................................... 395.00
    **Chair,** Koch's Hydraulic Model, Wooden ...................................................................... 750.00
    **Chair,** Koch's Hydraulic, Brass Claw Feet, Dated 1898 ................................................ 250.00
    **Chair,** Koken, Chrome, Porcelain Base ......................................................................... 500.00
    **Chair,** Koken, Oak ......................................................................................................... 750.00
    **Chair,** Koken, Red Upholstery, Porcelain ...................................................................... 750.00
    **Chair,** Leather Back & Headrest, Adjustable, Walnut & Oak ........................................ 625.00
    **Chair,** Oak & Brass ........................................................................... 800.00 To 850.00
    **Chair,** Recliner With Swan's Heads .............................................................................. 650.00
    **Chair,** Swan Carved Handholds, Archer's Patent, Walnut, 44 In. .................................. 450.00
    **Mirror,** 3 Beveled Diamonds At Top, Canopy, 1890s, 28 X 58 In. ................................ 350.00
    **Pole,** Koken, Red & White Art Glass, Wall Mount, 34 In. ............................................. 600.00
    **Pole,** Revolving, Porcelain & Glass .............................................................................. 350.00
    **Pole,** Square Shape, Chamfered Corners, Painted, 19th Century, 49 In. ...................... 100.00
    **Pole,** Wooden, 7 Ft. ....................................................................................................... 275.00
    **Sign,** Red, White, & Blue, Double Face, Porcelain, 24 X 12 In. .................................... 68.00
    **Sterlizer,** Comb, Milk Glass ......................................................................................... 18.00

**BAROMETER, Copper,** 10 In.Diam. ............................................................................... 75.00
    **Foliate Case,** Silvered Dials, Cairns, Liverpool, Mahogany, 26 In. ........................... 1900.00
    **Pocket,** English, 19th Century, Case ............................................................................ 45.00
    **Pocket,** James Lucking, Birmingham, England, C.1870, Leather Case ....................... 65.00
    **Thermometer,** Mahogany, Pediment Top, Brass Dial, 19th C., 40 In. ........................ 3800.00
    **BASKET, see also Indian, Basket**

**BASKET, Alternating Colors & Widths Of Splint,** 1800s, 10 X 12 In. .......................... 165.00
    **Apple Gathering,** 16 In.Diam. ...................................................................................... 110.00
    **Apple,** Side Handled, Double Wrap Top, Shaker Star Bottom, 14 3/4 In. ...................... 48.00
    **Apple,** Splint, 2 Looped Handles, Hand-Woven, 18 X 15 1/2 In. ................................... 95.00
    **Bentwood Rim & Handle,** Modified Buttocks Shape, C.1870, 6 X 7 In. ........................ 110.00
    **Berry,** Oak Splint, Bentwood Handle, 1900s, 7 X 9 X 9 In. .......................................... 80.00
    **Berry,** Splint, Woven Border, Hand-Carved Handle, 1800s, 6 X 10 In. ......................... 85.00
    **Bread Rising,** Rye Straw, Hickory Splint Wrapped, 1850s, 19 X 2 In. .......................... 110.00
    **Bread,** Wide Splints, 8 X 7 In. ....................................................................................... 65.00
    **Buttocks,** Curved Sides, Oak, Bent Oak Handle, C.1830, 16 X 17 X 18 In. ................... 250.00
    **Buttocks,** Oak Splint & Rib, St.Genevieve, Mo., C.1880, 18 X 11 In. ............................ 110.00
    **Buttocks,** Twined Handle, Splint, 8 X 4 1/2 X 5 1/4 In. ................................................ 110.00
    **Canteen Covered With Woven Willow,** 9 1/2 In.Diam. .............................................. 135.00
    **Carrier,** Bread, Maple, Hickory, Wooden Bottom, C.1800, 22 1/2 X 9 In. ..................... 145.00
    **Carrier,** Peeled Willow, Wooden Divider, 21 X 14 In. .................................................... 55.00
    **Cheese,** Handled, Hexagonal, 5 1/2 In.Diam. .............................................................. 60.00
    **Cheese,** 20 In.Diam. ...................................................................................................... 500.00
    **Coiled Rye Straw,** 12 X 6 1/2 In. .................................................................................. 38.00
    **Cone Shape,** 2 Side Handles, Darkened Color, 15 In. ................................................. 125.00
    **Corn Husks,** Small Splint Handle, 4 1/2 In.Diam. ....................................................... 30.00
    **Cradle,** Red & Blue Splint, Woven Hood, Curlicues, C.1890, 8 X 18 In. ........................ 75.00
    **Double Handle,** Reed Openwork, 6 X 9 In.Diam. ......................................................... 75.00
    **Double Handled Swing,** Bentwood Rim, 1850s, 15 X 13 X 15 In. ................................ 125.00
    **Eel Trap,** Splint, 21 In.Long ........................................................................................ 185.00
    **Egg,** Bentwood Handle, Ash Splint, C.1880, 12 X 12 In. .............................................. 75.00
    **Egg,** Gathering, Oak, Ash, 14 In.Diam. ......................................................................... 85.00
    **Egg,** Melon Shape, Pennsylvania, C.1880, 11 X 12 X 11 In. ......................................... 125.00
    **Egg,** Oak Splint, Exaggerated Corners, 1870s, 10 1/2 X 12 1/2 In. ............................. 110.00

**Feather,** Laced On Peeled Sapling, Handle ......................................................... 135.00
**Footed,** Oak Splint, 13 In.Diam. ......................................................................... 55.00
**Gathering,** Carolina, C.1900, Splint, Swinging Handles ...................................... 75.00
**Gathering,** Oak Splint, Handle, Side Carrying Holes, C.1880, 17 In. .................... 125.00
**Gathering,** Splint Swing Handle, Colored, C.1890, 13 1/2 X 16 In. ...................... 75.00
**Gathering,** Splint, Yellow Color, 19 In.Diam. ..................................................... 135.00
**Gizzard,** Oak Ribs, Splint, Bentwood Handle & Rim, C.1870, 8 X 8 In. ............... 110.00
**Gizzard,** Oak Splint, Bentwood Handle, C.1860, 13 1/2 X 12 1/2 In. .................. 110.00
**Gizzard,** Splint Handle, Blue & Tan Weave, Signed, 11 1/2 X 6 3/4 In. ............... 125.00
**Green Rib,** 11 X 15 In. ....................................................................................... 100.00
**Half Melon,** One Above The Other, Attached By Splint, 2-Color, 25 In. ................ 425.00
**Half Round Shape,** Carved Handle, Pennsylvania, C.1850, 11 X 10 In. ................ 100.00
**Hand-Woven,** 19th Century, Mingei ................................................................... 250.00
**Hat,** Covered, Ash Splint, C.1850s, 44 X 7 1/2 In. ............................................. 85.00
**Havesting,** Splint, Square Bottom, Round Top, 2 1/2 X 4 In.Diam. ...................... 50.00
**Hearth,** Painted, 14 X 21 In. .............................................................................. 52.00
**Herb Drying,** Handle, Brick Red, Laced Edge, 26 1/2 X 15 X 2 1/2 In. ............... 145.00
**Herb,** Bentwood Handles, 1800s, 13 X 19 X 9 1/4 In. ......................................... 45.00
**Hickory Splint,** Raised Bottom, Back-In Top, C.1860, 12 X 11 In. ....................... 95.00
**Horizontal & Vertical Ash Splint,** Wrapped Rim, C.1860, 10 X 6 In. .................. 65.00
**Lidded Storage,** Horizontal Splints, 11 1/2 In.Diam. ........................................... 58.00
**Maine Berry,** Hand-Carved Swing Handle, 15 In.Diam. ....................................... 75.00
**Market Herringbone Weave,** Handle, Tulipwood, C.1880, 15 X 11 X 11 In. ......... 60.00
**Market,** Black Ash, Bentwood Handle, C.1880, 6 X 12 X 10 In. ........................... 85.00
**Market,** Vegetable Dyed Red, Notched Handle, C.1880, 10 X 1, X 13 In. ............ 80.00
**Market,** Wide Splint, 9 1/4 In. ............................................................................ 38.00
**Market,** Wood Base, Peeled Willow, Bentwood Handle, 18 X 14 In. .................... 85.00
**Melon,** Dated 1862 On Handle, 12 In.Long ......................................................... 95.00
**Melon,** Double, Splint Attached, 5 In.Apart, Hale Circle, 26 In. ........................... 450.00
**Melon,** Gray Brown, 9 1/2 In.Diam. ................................................................... 75.00
**Melon,** Handle, 12-Rib Construction, Woven Oak Spliht, 3 X 9 In.Diam. ............. 85.00
**Miniature Tin,** 3 X 3 1/2 In. ............................................................................... 65.00
**Oak Staves,** Peeled Willow Sides, Wooden Bottom, Bushel, 21 X 10 In. .............. 125.00
**Onion,** New England, Multicolors ...................................................................... 65.00
**Piecrust,** Decorated Splint, 14 X 12 In. ............................................................. 145.00
**Potato,** Ash Splint, 19th Century, Aroostook County, Maine, 1/2 Bushel ............ 85.00
**Rectangular Rib,** 14 1/2 X 13 In. ....................................................................... 65.00
**Rectangular Splint,** Oval Top, Bentwood Handle, 15 X 9 In. .............................. 48.00
**Round Splint,** Honey Color, 11 In.Diam. ............................................................ 75.00
**Round,** Splint, Patinized Brown, Smooth Bentwood Handle, 14 1/2 In.Dia .......... 95.00
**Sewing,** Nantucket, Hinged Wooden Handle, 19th Century, 8 In.Diam. ............... 375.00
**Side Handles,** Old Gray Green, 17 In.Diam. ....................................................... 110.00
**Splint Ash,** Swing Handle ................................................................................. 145.00
**Splint,** Wooden Handles, 5 X 7 In. ..................................................................... 30.00
**Storage,** Black Ash Splint, Vegetable Dye Decorated, C.1860, 9 X 6 In. .............. 85.00
**Swing Handle,** Pinky Red Early Paint, 14 In. ...................................................... 185.00
**Symmetrical Design,** Dyed Colors, Signed VA, 11 1/2 X 11 In.Diam. ................. 100.00
**Table,** Woven Willow, 4 1/2 X 13 In.Diam. ......................................................... 15.00
**Top Handle,** Openwork Bottom, Silver-Brown Color, 7 1/2 In. ............................ 48.00
**Top Handle,** Varied Width Splint, 15 1/2 X 9 1/4 In. .......................................... 45.00
**Urn Shape,** Reed & Splint, 8 X 8 In.Diam. ......................................................... 65.00
**Vertical & Horizontal Splint,** Handle, Green Paint, C.1880, 18 X 8 In. ............... 95.00
**Woven Herringbone Design,** Lidded, Handled, C.1790, 12 X 21 X 15 In. ............. 225.00
**Wrapped Handles,** Bentwood Rim, Splint Bands, C.1800, 12 X 18 X 10 In. ......... 135.00


**BATMAN, Buckle,** Utility Belt Radio, 1941 ........................................................ 65.00
**Coloring Book,** 1966, Uncolored ....................................................................... 12.00
**Game,** 1966, Milton Bradley .............................................................................. 25.00
**Puppet** ............................................................................................................ 7.50
**Shooting Gallery** ............................................................................................. 12.00


*Battersea enamels are enamels painted on copper and made in the Battersea*

*District of London from about 1750 to 1756. Many similar enamels are mistakenly called Battersea.*

| | |
|---|---:|
| **BATTERSEA, Box,** Heart Shape, Flowers, A Token Of Love | 50.00 |
| **Box,** Transfer, In Memory Of A Friend, Pink, 1 3/8 X 1 1/8 X 1 In. | 185.00 |
| **Box,** When This You See Remember Me | 48.00 |
| **Box,** With Love On This Special Day, Couple In Garden | 48.00 |
| **Knob,** Eagle Banner | 250.00 |
| **Mirror Rest,** Black & White Transfer, Country Scene, Pair | 140.00 |
| **Tieback,** Hope Leaning On Anchor, 19th Century, Pair | 110.00 |

*Bavaria was a district where many types of pottery and porcelain were made for centuries. The words "Bavaria, Germany, " appeared after 1871.*

**BAVARIA, see also Rosenthal**

| | |
|---|---:|
| **BAVARIA, Bowl,** Drop Rose Pattern, 9 1/2 In.Diam. | 36.00 |
| **Chocolate Pot,** Versailles | 38.00 |
| **Cookie Jar,** Embossed, Yellow & Orange Daisies, Gold Trim | 32.00 |
| **Cracker Jar,** Hand-Painted Pink Roses, Signed Ragouse | 52.00 |
| **Hatpin Holder,** Pink Roses, Signed | 22.50 |
| **Plate,** Cake, Open End, Pink Morning Glories, Green, 9 1/2 In. | 18.00 |
| **Plate,** Chop, Drop Rose Pattern, 12 In. | 36.00 |
| **Plate,** Fruit, Apples, Leaves, Gold Trim, Crown H. & Co., 9 3/4 In. | 17.00 |
| **Plate,** Game, Punch, Brown, Green, & Ivory, Grouse, Gold Border | 35.00 |
| **Plate,** Game, Snipes, 12 In. | 35.00 |
| **Plate,** Hand-Painted Grape Design, A.Koch, 8 1/2 In. | 100.00 |
| **Plate,** Portrait, A.Lincoln, Flow Blue | 40.00 |
| **Plate,** Portrait, Cobalt & Gold, Girl With Red Hair, 12 In. | 75.00 |
| **Plate,** Portrait, Queen Louise | 45.00 |
| **Plate,** Punch, Cottage & Farmyard Scene, Brown, Green, & Ivory | 25.00 |
| **Plate,** Roses, Green, Gold Edge, Marked, J & C, 8 In. | 20.00 |
| **Plate,** Roses, 6 In. | 6.00 |
| **Plate,** Service, Scalloped Rim, Gold Trim, 11 In., Set Of 12 | 285.00 |
| **Plate,** Strawberries, Scalloped Edge, J & C Bavaria, 8 1/2 In. | 27.00 |
| **Relish,** Wild Roses, 11 1/2 In. | 20.00 |
| **Sugar & Creamer,** Violets, Satin Finish | 40.00 |
| **Sugar Shaker,** Yellow & Salmon Flowers, Gold Top, Signed | 40.00 |
| **Vase,** Pink & Yellow Roses, Pastel Ground, Marked, 10 1/2 In. | 85.00 |
| **Vase,** Pink Roses On Green, 11 In. | 60.00 |
| **Vase,** Roses, Pin, , 8 1/2 In. | 25.00 |
| **BAYONET, see Weapon, Bayonet** | |

| | |
|---|---:|
| **BEADED BAG, Child's,** Drawstring, White & Gold Beads, 5 In. | 12.50 |
| **Figural Clasp,** Pushing A Cat That Catches Mouse, Dated 1909 | 27.00 |
| **Red Floral,** Fringe, Victorian | 90.00 |
| **Roses,** Blue, Tortoiseshell Frame & Handle, Lined | 45.00 |
| **Silver Plate Mirrored Frame,** Blue | 95.00 |

| | |
|---|---:|
| **BEATLES, Bandana** | 15.00 |
| **Card,** Gum, Set Of 28 | 25.00 |
| **Doll,** 4 3/4 In., Set Of 4 | 32.00 |
| **Locket,** Holds 4 Beatle Pictures | 22.00 |
| **Lunch Box** | 24.50 |
| **Nodder,** Blue Suit, 4 In. | 50.00 |
| **Nodder,** Blue Suit, 8 In. | 200.00 |
| **Note Pad,** Yellow Submarine | 6.00 |
| **Pillow,** 4 Pictures On Front, Official | 30.00 |

**BECK, see also Buffalo Pottery**

| | |
|---|---:|
| **BECK, Plate,** Antlered Deer & Doe, Forest Setting, Signed, 12 3/4 In. | 40.00 |
| **Plate,** Spaniel With Rabbit, Spaniel With Bird, Signed, 9 1/4 In., Pair | 85.00 |
| **Platter,** Three Grazing Cows, Signed, 13 In. | 45.00 |

| | |
|---|---:|
| **BEDWARMER, Bail Handle,** Soapstone | 10.00 |
| **New England,** Brass | 285.00 |

*Beehive, Austria, or Beehive, Vienna, china includes all the many types of decorated porcelain marked with the famous beehive mark. The mark has been used since the eighteenth century.*

**BEEHIVE, see also Royal Vienna**

| | |
|---|---|
| **BEEHIVE, Charger,** Gleaners, 12 1/2 In. | 125.00 |
| **Cup & Saucer,** Alpine Village Scene On Interior Of Cup, Logo, Signed | 245.00 |
| **Cup & Saucer,** Demitasse, Pink Roses, Portrait Children | 35.00 |
| **Dish,** Bone, Medallion & Gold Design, Yellow, Marked | 12.00 |
| **Jar,** Powder, Design On Interior & Cover, Marked, 5 In.Diam. | 90.00 |
| **Plate,** Cupid With Lyre, Dancing Maidens, Marked, 8 3/4 In.Diam. | 35.00 |
| **Plate,** Hand-Painted Castle, Signed, Marked, 9 3/4 In. | 95.00 |
| **Plate,** Odysseus & Telemachus, Blue, Gold Border, J.Reiff, 10 1/2 In. | 180.00 |
| **Plate,** Pierced Handles, Hand-Painted Lady, Marked, 10 In. | 95.00 |
| **Plate,** Roses In Gold, Center Portrait Of 3 Maidens, Marked, 10 In. | 225.00 |
| **Plate,** Thrushes, Baroque Gold Border, Signed W.Hein, 13 In.Diam. | 235.00 |
| **Sugar,** Covered, Black & White, Marked | 39.50 |

*Beer cans have been made since the 1930s. Collectors search for old or new cans.*

| | |
|---|---|
| **BEER CAN, Bavarian Select,** Flat | 20.00 |
| **Beverwyck,** Cone Top | 35.00 |
| **Billy** | 2.00 |
| **Burgemeister Premium,** Flat | 15.00 |
| **Cone Top,** Bruck's Jubilee | 45.00 |
| **Cone Top,** Butte | 25.00 |
| **Cone Top,** Country Club | 40.00 |
| **Cone Top,** Duke | 25.00 |
| **Cone Top,** Eastlake | 25.00 |
| **Cone Top,** Falstaff, With Cap | 22.00 |
| **Cone Top,** German | 1.50 |
| **Cone Top,** Gluek | 50.00 |
| **Cone Top,** Gold Colored Metal, 1930, Quart | 150.00 |
| **Cone Top,** Iron City | 25.00 |
| **Cone Top,** Keeley Half & Half | 60.00 |
| **Cone Top,** Kingsbury Pale | 50.00 |
| **Cone Top,** Northern | 10.00 |
| **Cone Top,** Reisch | 35.00 |
| **Cone Top,** Royal Bohemian | 40.00 |
| **Cone Top,** Schlitz, With Cap | 22.00 |
| **Cone Top,** Schmidt's, Quart | 18.00 |
| **Cone Top,** Stag | 24.00 |
| **Cone Top,** Stoneys | 25.00 |
| **Dorf Bohemian,** Flat | 10.50 |
| **Eastern Brewery,** Hammonton, N. J., Arabian Script | 6.00 |
| **Eastlake,** Punch | 16.50 |
| **Fauerbach,** Flat | 20.00 |
| **Goebel Gold Label,** Flat | 50.00 |
| **Gold Coast,** Flat | 32.00 |
| **Goldeater,** Flat Top, 12 Ounce | 30.00 |
| **Highlander,** Cone Top | 18.50 |
| **Hull's Cream Ale,** Flat | 40.00 |
| **Iron City Beer,** Buck Player | 6.50 |
| **Iron City Beer,** 1979 Steeler Team | 6.50 |
| **Land Of Lakes,** Flat | 10.00 |
| **Mile Hi,** Flat | 20.00 |
| **Monarch,** Flat | 20.00 |
| **Schaeffer,** Handled, 16 Ounce | 5.00 |
| **Southern Select,** Faint Markings | 25.00 |
| **Tennents,** Angela | 4.00 |
| **Tennents,** Penny | 4.00 |
| **Tennents,** Vicky & Susan | 4.00 |

*Bells have been made of china, glass, or metal. All types are collected.*

| | |
|---|---|
| **BELL, African,** Entwined Snakes, Applied Frogs, Brass, 11 X 6 In. | 375.00 |
| **Apostle,** Bronze, 2 1/2 X 3 1/2 In. | 22.00 |
| **Apostle,** Bronze, 8 In. | 395.00 |
| **Assyrian Raised Figures Around Sides,** Brass, 6 1/2 X 5 In.Diam. | 110.00 |
| **Bicycle,** Cast Iron, Bevin | 10.00 |
| **Black Mammy** | 20.00 |
| **Brass,** Dated March 14, 1878 | 80.00 |
| **Brass,** Door Type | 40.00 |
| **Brass,** Dutch Girl, Figural, C.1890, 3 1/4 In. | 30.00 |
| **Brass,** Farm, Original Clapper, 6 In. | 44.00 |
| **Brass,** Filigree, Oak Base, Latin Phrases, Pierced Scroll, 1890, 10 In. | 225.00 |
| **Bronze,** C.1870, 3 1/2 In. | 22.00 |
| **Bronze,** 5 1/2 X 6 In. | 75.00 |
| **Camel,** Brass, 3 1/2 In. | 20.00 |
| **Champleve,** Enameled Symbols, Floral Medallions, 19th Century, Chinese | 95.00 |
| **Courting,** Tingle If You're Single, Pennsylvania Dutch, Brass | 195.00 |
| **Cow,** Gilt Paint, Cast Iron | 15.00 |
| **Cow,** Original Clapper, Cast Iron, 6 X 4 1/2 In. | 8.00 |
| **Cow,** Partial Lithograph, Sargents & Co., New Haven, Conn., 5 1/2 In. | 10.00 |
| **Cow,** 5 In. | 8.50 |
| **Cow,** 6 1/4 In. | 12.00 |
| **Dragon Handle,** Korean, Brass, 4 1/2 In. | 10.00 |
| **Dredge No. 2,** Nome, Alaska, Brass | 195.00 |
| **Embossed Animals,** Latin Wording, Brass, 6 3/4 X 4 1/2 In.Diam. | 110.00 |
| **Figural,** Lady In Ruffled Dress, Brass, 4 1/2 In. | 20.00 |
| **Figural,** Lady, Carrying Basket, Brass, 5 1/4 X 4 1/8 In.Diam. | 75.00 |
| **Figural,** Lady, Green, Lavender, & White, China Clapper, China, 4 3/4 In. | 48.00 |
| **Figural,** Lady, Purple, Blue, Yellow, & Green Dress, China, 4 1/4 In. | 48.00 |
| **Figural,** Servant Man Holding Bell On Head, Brass, 7 In. | 165.00 |
| **Figural,** Southern Lady Carrying Flowers, Brass, 4 1/2 X 3 In.Diam. | 60.00 |
| **Firewagon,** Iron Bracket, Brass & Silver | 800.00 |
| **Gong,** Hexagon Shape, Chinese, Brass, 5 In. | 22.50 |
| **Goose,** Double Clapper, Brass | 15.00 |
| **Hotel,** Ornate, Brass, Tap | 8.20 |
| **King's Highway Mission,** El Camino Real, 1914, 9 In. | 75.00 |
| **Lion's International** | 32.00 |
| **Marriage,** White Applied Threading, Inside Looping, Victorian, 12 In. | 175.00 |
| **Monastery,** Figural Bronze Backplate, Pull Chain, Bronze, 12 In. | 245.00 |
| **Ring For Jersey's,** Drink Bottled Sunlight | 12.50 |
| **School,** Hand, Brass, Wooden Handle, 2 7/8 In.Diam. | 13.00 |
| **School,** Hand, Brass, Wooden Handle, 3 In.Diam. | 15.00 |
| **School,** Hand, Brass, Wooden Handle, 3 3/4 In.Diam. | 29.00 |
| **School,** Hand, Brass, Wooden Handle, 4 3/4 In.Diam. | 34.00 |
| **School,** Hand, Brass, Wooden Handle, 5 1/2 In. | 25.00 |
| **School,** Hand, Brass, Wooden Handle, 5 3/4 In. | 30.00 |
| **School,** Hand, Brass, Wooden Handle, 6 1/4 In. | 35.00 |
| **School,** Hand, Brass, Wooden Handle, 6 1/2 In.Diam. | 53.00 |
| **School,** Hand, Brass, Wooden Handle, 7 1/2 In. | 40.00 |
| **School,** Hand, Brass, Wooden Handle, 8 In. | 45.00 |
| **School,** Hand, Brass, 6 In. | 30.00 |
| **School,** Hand, Brass, 8 In. | 30.00 |
| **School,** Turned Handle, Brass | 45.00 |
| **Sheep,** Brass, 1 7/8 In. | 13.00 |
| **Sheep,** Brass, 3 1/2 In. | 16.00 |
| **Sheep,** Leather Strap | 8.50 |
| **Siren,** Fire Wagon, Hand-Operated, Brass | 250.00 |
| **Sleigh,** Acorn Shaped, Red Leather Strap, Buckled End, 32 In., Set Of 12 | 70.00 |
| **Sleigh,** Brass, Acorn, 25 Bells, Leather Strap, 1 1/4 In. | 75.00 |
| **Sleigh,** Graduated In Size, String Of 19 | 165.00 |
| **Sleigh,** Graduated Size, Brass, Set Of 23 | 275.00 |
| **Sleigh,** No.6 To No.14, Brass, String Of 23 | 250.00 |

Sleigh, Rump, Original Strap, Brass, Set Of 4 ............................................................... 80.00
Sleigh, Strung On Leather, 1 In.Diam., Set Of 35 .......................................................... 275.00
Smoke, Hobnail, Opalescent, 8 X 6 1/2 In. ...................................................................... 45.00
Solid Brass, Clapper, 2 1/4 In. ............................................................................................ 10.00
Steam Locomotive, Cast Iron ........................................................................................... 400.00
Street Car, Brass ................................................................................................................. 110.00
Temple, Geometric Design & Hobnails, Japan, Bronze, 19th Century, 11 In. ........................ 150.00

> *Belle Ware was made in 1903 by Carl V. Helmschmied. In 1904 he*
> *started a corporation known as the Helmschmied Manufacturing Company.*
> *His factory closed in 1908 and he worked on his own until his death in 1934.*

BELLE WARE, Box, Jewel, Roses, Pink, Brass Collar, Signed, 7 In. ................................. 350.00
Box, Lid, Pink Rose, Buds, Pebbled Finish, Marked, 2 3/4 In.Diam. ......................... 375.00

*Belleek china is made in Ireland, other European countries, and the*
*United States. The glaze is creamy yellow and appears wet. The first*
*Belleek was made in 1857. All pieces listed are Irish Belleek.*
*The mark changed through the years: First mark, black, dates 1863 to 1890.*
*Second mark, black, dates 1891 to 1926 and includes the words "Co.*
*Fermanagh, Ireland". Third mark, black, dates 1926 to 1946 and has the*
*words "Deanta in Eirinn". Fourth mark, same as third mark but green,*
*dates 1946 to 1955. Fifth mark, green, dates 1955 to 1965 and has the R in*
*a circle added in the upper right. Sixth mark, green, dates after 1965 and*
*the words "Co. Fermanagh" have been omitted.*

**BELLEEK, see also Ceramic Art Co., Haviland, Lenox, Matt**
**Morgan, Ott & Brewer, Willets**

BELLEEK, Basket, Lily, 3-Strand, Woven, 9 3/4 In.Diam. ............................................. 1000.00
Basket, Shamrock Shape, 3 Applied Roses, 1890, 6 1/2 In.Diam. ................................. 395.00
Basket, 4 Strand, Pearl .................................................................................................... 1400.00
Bottle, Scent, Hawthorne Purple Luster, 1st Black Mark, 5 1/2 In. ............................... 400.00
Bowl, Covered, Figural, Bacchus Mask, Black Mark, 6 1/2 In. ...................................... 155.00
Bowl, Covered, Shell, Twig Handle, 2nd Black Mark, 4 1/2 In.Diam. ............................ 275.00
Bowl, Gold Border, Flowers, Artist Signed, 4 1/2 X 2 1/2 In. ......................................... 30.00
Bowl, Green Hound Mark, 4 In. ....................................................................................... 35.00
Bowl, Rose, Ribbed Melon, Pink Top, 4 In. .................................................................... 100.00
Bowl, Woven Double Strand, 7 In.Diam. ......................................................................... 375.00
Box, Trinket, Mask, 3rd Black Mark, 3 3/4 X 6 1/2 In. ................................................... 350.00
Bread Plate, Twig Handles, 2nd Black Mark, 10 In. ....................................................... 65.00
Bust, Clytie, 3rd Black Mark ............................................................................................ 950.00
Cake Plate, Pretzel Handles, Octagonal, Ribbon Mark, 9 1/2 In.Diam. ......................... 275.00
Candleholder, Boy On A Dolphin, 1st Black Mark, 7 1/2 In. ......................................... 1150.00
Cauldron, 2nd Black Mark, 2 1/8 In. ................................................................................ 85.00
Cauldron, 2nd Black Mark, 4 In. ...................................................................................... 95.00
Celery, Purple Luster, 1st Black Mark, 7 In. ................................................................... 625.00
Cheese House, 4th Green Mark ....................................................................................... 90.00
Christmas Plate, 1970 ...................................................................................................... 95.00
Cookie Jar, 1st Black Mark, 5 In. .................................................................................... 275.00
Creamer, Echinus, Coral Handled, Trim, 1st Black Mark ................................ 235.00 To 250.00
Creamer, Grasses, Gilt Rim, Lavender Trim, 1st Black Mark ......................................... 144.00
Creamer, Lotus, 2nd Black Mark ..................................................................................... 80.00
Creamer, Mask, Pink Handle, 2nd Black Mark, 4 3/4 In. .............................................. 190.00
Creamer, Mask, 3rd Black Mark ...................................................................................... 90.00
Creamer, Nautilus, Pearl, 1st Black Mark, 2 7/8 In. ...................................................... 190.00
Creamer, Shamrock, 2nd Black Mark .............................................................................. 40.00
Creamer, Shell, Child's, 3rd Black Mark ......................................................................... 50.00
Cup & Saucer, Artichoke, Registery Mark, 1868, 1st Black Mark .................................. 225.00
Cup & Saucer, Demitasse, Limpet Pattern, 2nd Green Mark ......................................... 37.50
Cup & Saucer, Demitasse, Limpet, 3rd Black Mark ........................................................ 58.00
Cup & Saucer, Demitasse, Pearl & Pink Trim, 2nd Black Mark ..................................... 135.00
Cup & Saucer, Demitasse, Shamrock, 3rd Black Mark ............................... 58.00 To 68.50
Cup & Saucer, Echinus Pattern, 1st Black Mark ............................................................ 125.00

Cup & Saucer, Harp & Shamrock, 2nd Black Mark ......................................... 55.00
Cup & Saucer, Harp & Shamrock, 3rd Black Mark ......................................... 70.00
Cup & Saucer, Hawthorne, 1st Black Mark ................................................. 75.00
Cup & Saucer, Mask, 3rd Black Mark ........................................................ 75.00
Cup & Saucer, Neptune, Green Trim, 2nd Black Mark ................................. 85.00
Cup & Saucer, Neptune, Luster Trim, 3rd Black Mark ................................ 50.00
Cup & Saucer, Neptune, Pink Trim, 2nd Black Mark ................. 35.00 To 75.00
Cup & Saucer, New Shell Pattern ............................................................. 28.00
Cup & Saucer, Ring-Handled Cup, Hand-Painted, Blue Border ................. 125.00
Cup & Saucer, Shamrock, 3rd Black Mark ................................................ 68.00
Cup & Saucer, Shell, 1st Green Mark ....................................................... 28.00
Cup & Saucer, Shell, 2nd Black Mark ..................................................... 125.00
Cup & Saucer, Thistle, Gilded & Pearl, 2nd Black Mark .......................... 125.00
Cup & Saucer, Tridacna, 2nd Black Mark ................................................ 65.00
Cup, Inlaid Sterling, Fluted Top ............................................................... 25.00
Dessert Set, Tridacna, Pink, 1st Black Mark, 7 Piece ............................ 450.00
Dish, Heart Shape, Green Mark ................................................................ 15.00
Dish, Heart Shape, 2nd Black Mark .......................................................... 23.00
Dish, Muffin, Covered, 1st Black Mark .................................................. 225.00
Dish, Muffin, Shamrock Pattern, 2nd Black Mark, 8 5/8 In.Diam. ......... 295.00
Dish, Shell, Seaweed Tab Handle, 1st Black Mark, 5 1/4 X 4 1/4 In. ...... 35.00
Eggcup, Tridacna, 2nd Black Mark ........................................................... 50.00
Ewer, Nile, 1st Green Mark ..................................................................... 25.00
Fernery, Green & Lilac, 1st Black Mark, 9 1/2 In. .................................. 750.00
Figurine, Leprechaun On A Toadstool, Pot O' Gold, Green Mark, 5 In. ..... 35.00
Figurine, Leprechaun, No Color, 3rd Black Mark ................................... 240.00
Figurine, Owl, Green Mark, 7 In. .............................................................. 75.00
Figurine, Swan, 1st Black Mark ............................................................... 50.00
Figurine, Swan, 2nd Black Mark, 4 In. .................................................. 112.00
Flask, Wine, Ceremonial, Star Of David Design, 1st Black Mark ........... 890.00
Flower Pot, Swirl, Applied Flowers, 2nd Black Mark, 3 1/2 In. ............... 70.00
Font, Sacred Heart, 2nd Black Mark, 6 1/2 In. ......................................... 80.00
Frame, 2nd Black Mark, Oval, 6 1/2 In. .................................................. 550.00
Honey Pot, Shamrock, Bees, 3rd Black Mark, 6 In. ................................. 295.00
Honey Pot, Shamrock, 2nd Black Mark ........................... 240.00 To 360.00
Honey Pot, Stand, 3 Legs, Yellow Luster Ground, 3rd Black Mark ......... 325.00
Jam Pot, Pink Ribbon, 1st Black Mark ...................................................... 35.00
Jug, Aberdeen, 2nd Black Mark, 6 In. ..................................................... 325.00
Jug, Harp Handle, 1st Black Mark, 6 In. .................................................. 220.00
Jug, Milk, Mask, 2nd Green Mark ........................................................... 120.00
Jug, Milk, Shamrock, 3rd Black Mark ...................................................... 55.00
Jug, Milk, Tridacna, 2nd Black Mark, 5 1/2 In. ...................................... 195.00
Kettle, Echinus, Handle, Undecorated, 2nd Black Mark ......................... 325.00
Lily Basket, 3 Strand, Round, Large ...................................................... 1100.00
Mug, Fermanagh, Shamrock Basket Weave, Black Mark ......................... 35.00
Mug, Shamrock, 2nd Black Mark, Name .................................................. 95.00
Mustache Cup, Tridacna, lst Black Mark, Oversized ............................. 300.00
Night-Light, Figural, Lighthouse, 1st Black Mark, 7 3/4 In. ................... 400.00
Pitcher, Aberdeen, Applied Floral Design, 2nd Black Mark ................... 295.00
Pitcher, Applied Roses & Shamrocks, Green Mark, 6 In. ......................... 95.00
Pitcher, Berries & Ivy Leaf Raised Design, Green Mark, 6 In. ................ 35.00
Pitcher, Green Mark, 3 1/2 In. ................................................................. 40.00
Pitcher, Leaf & Vine Design, Green Mark, 6 In. ....................................... 35.00
Plate, Basket Weave, Gilded Edge, 1st Black Mark, 9 1/4 In. ............... 135.00
Plate, Butter, Primrose, 3rd Black Mark ................................................ 30.00
Plate, Cake, Pretzel Handles, Ribbon Mark, Octagonal, 9 1/2 In. ......... 275.00
Plate, Echinus, Green Trim, lst Black Mark, 9 1/4 In. ............................ 65.00
Plate, Hawthorne, 1st Black Mark, 9 In.Diam. ...................................... 275.00
Plate, Leaf, Gold Trim, Green, 2nd Black Mark, 9 In. ............................ 130.00
Plate, Limpet, 3rd Black Mark, 8 In.Diam. .............................................. 42.00
Plate, Mask, 3rd Black Mark, Lease No.560 ............................................ 46.50
Plate, Mask, 3rd Black Mark, 4 3/4 In. .................................................... 46.50

| | |
|---|---|
| Plate, Neptune Pattern, 2nd Black Mark, 6 In.Diam | 20.00 |
| Plate, Neptune, Pink Trim, 3rd Black Mark | 46.50 |
| Plate, Oriental Bird, Floral, Pomegranate, 7 1/4 In., Pair | 45.00 |
| Plate, Primrose, 3rd Black Mark | 30.00 |
| Plate, Rose & Poppy Design, 8 In. | 12.00 |
| Plate, Shamrock & Basket Weave, 2nd Black Mark, 8 In.Diam. | 35.00 |
| Plate, Shamrock, 2nd Black Mark, Set Of 6 | 120.00 |
| Plate, Shell, 3rd Black Mark, 9 In.Diam. | 80.00 |
| Plate, Sydney, Green Trim, 3rd Black Mark, 6 In.Diam. | 69.50 |
| Platter, Flowers & Birds, White, 1st Green Mark, 13 In. | 195.00 |
| Platter, 3rd Black Mark, 13 1/2 X 10 1/2 In. | 75.00 |
| Salt, Boat Shape, Embossed Design, Green Mark | 25.00 |
| Salt, Shell, 3rd Black Mark | 30.00 |
| Salt, 6 Scallops, Green Mark, 3 In. | 25.00 |
| Saltshaker, Harp Shamrock, Oval, 2nd Black Mark | 22.50 |
| Saucer, Neptune Pattern, Green Border, 2nd Black Mark | 15.00 |
| Shell, Conch, Pink Coral Trim, 1st Black Mark, 6 1/2 In. | 450.00 |
| Spill, Polychrome Fowers, 2nd Black Mark, Signed, 6 In. | 145.00 |
| Sugar & Creamer, Basket Weave & Shamrock, 3rd Green Mark | 65.00 |
| Sugar & Creamer, Basket Weave, Shamrock, 3rd Black Mark | 95.00 |
| Sugar & Creamer, Bowtie & Swirl, Green Mark | 37.50 |
| Sugar & Creamer, Cleary Pattern, 3rd Black Mark | 95.00 |
| Sugar & Creamer, Cone Pattern, Green Shading, 2nd Black Mark | 185.00 |
| Sugar & Creamer, Covered, Shamrock, 3rd Black Mark | 95.00 |
| Sugar & Creamer, Erne, 2nd Black Mark | 85.00 |
| Sugar & Creamer, Harp & Shamrock, 3rd Black Mark | 65.00 To 85.00 |
| Sugar & Creamer, Ivy, 2nd Black Mark | 140.00 |
| Sugar & Creamer, Ivy, 3rd Black Mark | 95.00 |
| Sugar & Creamer, Lily Pattern, 3rd Black Mark | 105.00 |
| Sugar & Creamer, Lotus Pattern, 3rd Black Mark | 65.00 To 95.00 |
| Sugar & Creamer, Ribbon & Bow, Mark Swirled | 99.00 |
| Sugar & Creamer, Ribbon, 3rd Black Mark | 75.00 To 85.00 |
| Sugar & Creamer, Shamrock Basket Weave, Green Mark | 35.00 |
| Sugar & Creamer, Shamrock, 1st Green Mark | 45.00 |
| Sugar & Creamer, Shamrock, 2nd Black Mark | 75.00 |
| Sugar & Creamer, Shamrock, 3rd Black Mark | 90.00 |
| Sugar & Creamer, Thistle Pattern, 2nd Black Mark, 3 1/2 In. | 175.00 |
| Sugar, Child's, Celtic, 1st Green Mark | 25.00 |
| Sugar, Covered, Tridacna, Pearl, 1st Black Mark | 190.00 |
| Sugar, Echinus Pattern, 1st Black Mark, 3 3/4 In. | 250.00 |
| Sugar, Ivy, White, 3rd Black Mark | 22.00 |
| Sugar, Lily Pattern, 3rd Black Mark | 40.00 |
| Sugar, Lotus Pattern, 3rd Black Mark | 40.00 |
| Sugar, Shamrock, 3rd Black Mark | 40.00 |
| Swan, 2nd Black Mark, 4 1/2 X 3 1/4 X 5 1/2 In. | 145.00 |
| Tankard, Roses, Jewels, Iridescent Base, 14 In. | 329.00 |
| Tea Kettle, Neptune, 1st Black Mark | 430.00 |
| Tea Set, Harp Handle, Shamrock, 2nd Black Mark, 9 Piece | 985.00 |
| Tea Set, Hexagon Pattern, Pink Trim, 2nd Black Mark, 3 Piece | 375.00 |
| Tea Set, Limpet, 3rd Black Mark, 21 Piece | 525.00 |
| Tea Set, Shamrock & Basket Weave, 2 Cups & Saucers, 8 Piece | 1425.00 |
| Tea Set, Tridacna, Pink Trim, 1st Black Mark, 4 Piece | 635.00 |
| Tea Set, Tridacna, 2 Cups & Saucers, 2 Cake Plates, 1st Black Mark | 750.00 |
| Teakettle, Grass, Overhead Handle, 1st Black Mark | 450.00 |
| Teakettle, Grasses, 1st Black Mark, Lavender Trim | 440.00 |
| Teapot, Bamboo, White, Gold Trim, 1st Black Mark | 450.00 |
| Teapot, Covered, Shamrock, 3rd Green Mark | 95.00 |
| Teapot, Hexagon Pattern, Green Trim, 2nd Black Mark | 235.00 |
| Teapot, Limpet Design, Yellow Tinted Trim, Black Mark, 10 In. | 245.00 |
| Teapot, Neptune Pattern, Yellow Trim, 2nd Black Mark, 4 5/8 In. | 195.00 |
| Teapot, Neptune, Green Trim, 2nd Black Mark | 75.00 To 290.00 |
| Teapot, Neptune, Pearl Luster, Pink Trim, 2nd Black Mark | 250.00 |

Teapot, Pink, Gilt Edge, 1st Black Mark, 4 X 7 1/2 In. ......... 390.00
Teapot, Shamrock Pattern, 3rd Black Mark ......................... 150.00 To 195.00
Teapot, Shamrock, 1st Green Mark ........................................ 125.00
Teapot, Sugar & Creamer, Mask, Green Mark ...................... 125.00
Teapot, Tinted Yellow Trim, Black Mark ............................ 260.00 To 275.00
Teapot, Tridacna Pattern, Gold Trim, 1st Mark .................... 325.00
Teapot, Tridacna, Pearl, Pink Handle & Trim, 1st Black Mark, 8 In. ....... 390.00
Teapot, Tridacna, 2nd Black Mark, 7 In. ............................ 250.00
Tray, Dragon, 1st Mark, 15 In. ........................................... 800.00
Tray, Oval, Hawthorne Pattern, 1st Mark, 15 1/2 X 12 In. ........ 350.00
Tray, Spider, 1st Black Mark, 14 1/2 In.Square ................... 1150.00
Tumbler, Pink Lining, 1st Black Mark, 4 In. ....................... 110.00
Vase, Aberdeen, Pearl Luster, 3rd Black Mark, 6 In. ............ 265.00
Vase, Aberdeen, 2nd Black Mark, 7 1/2 In., Pair ................. 550.00
Vase, Applied Flowers & Leaves, Ruffled, Green Mark, 8 In., Pair ..... 165.00
Vase, Applied Flowers, Pearl Luster, 2nd Black Mark, 8 In. .... 125.00
Vase, Black & Gold On Pearl, 3rd Black Mark, 7 3/4 In. ........ 315.00
Vase, Bud, Lilac & Pearl, 1st Black Mark .......................... 390.00
Vase, Dolphin Handles, C.1940, Black Mark, 6 1/2 In. .......... 150.00
Vase, Double Fish, 1st Black Mark, 12 In. .......................... 950.00
Vase, Handled, Yellow Luster Panels, 4th Mark, 6 In. ........... 45.00
Vase, Lily Spill, 3rd Black Mark, Lease No.460 ................... 109.00
Vase, Nautilus, 1st Black Mark, 8 1/2 In. ........................... 350.00
Vase, Nile, Pearl Luster, Yellow Leaves, 3rd Black Mark, 13 In. ..... 385.00
Vase, Pastel Florals, Cylindrical, 16 In. ............................ 175.00
Vase, Phoenix Bird Design, Octagonal, 8 In. ...................... 300.00
Vase, Pink & White, Footed, 1st Mark, 7 In. ...................... 375.00
Vase, Prince Of Wales, 8 1/2 In. ...................................... 1550.00
Vase, Sea Horse, 1st Black Mark, 5 In. .............................. 360.00
Vase, Shamrock, Pierced, 3rd Black Mark, 9 In. ................. 135.00
Vase, Spill, Figural Fish, , 1st Black Mark, 7 3/4 In. ............ 390.00
Vase, Spill, Onion, 1st Black Mark, 9 7/8 In. ..................... 300.00
Vase, Spill, Pearl, 2nd Black Mark, 6 1/2 In. ...................... 160.00
Vase, Sunflower, 2nd Black Mark ..................................... 130.00
Vase, Thistle, 2nd Black Mark, Miniature .......................... 95.00
Vase, Tree Stump, Purple Luster, Gilding On Pear, 1st Black Mark ..... 290.00
Vase, Trunk Stump, Ivy Trim, 1st Black Mark ..................... 92.50
Vase, Trunk Stump, Shamrock, 3rd Black Mark, 6 In. ........... 85.00
Vase, Tulip, Green Trim, 2nd Black Mark, 6 In. .................. 290.00
Vase, Tulip, Yellow Trim, 2nd Black Mark, 6 In. ................. 300.00

*Bennington ware was the product of two factories working in Bennington, Vermont. Both firms were out of business by 1896. The wares include brown and yellow mottled pottery, Parian, scroddled ware, stoneware, graniteware, yellowware, and Staffordshire-like vases.*

BENNINGTON TYPE, Teapot, Miniature ............................. 100.00
     BENNINGTON, see also Rockingham
BENNINGTON, Bedpan ..................................................... 95.00
Bowl, Dough, Egg & Dart Design, 12 1/2 In.Diam. ............. 120.00
Chamberstick, Leaf Shape .............................................. 65.00
Crock, Blue Floral Bouquet, Stylized Ribbon, 6 Gallon ....... 150.00
Cuspidor, Swimming Ducks ............................................. 62.00
Cuspidor, 10 In.Diam. .................................................... 35.00
Flask, Book, Flint, Ned Butline's Own, Marked .................. 550.00
Flask, Book, Ladies' Companion, Enamel Glaze, 5 3/4 In. ..... 125.00
Flask, Boot, Dark Glaze, 8 X 6 1/2 In. ............................. 155.00
Flask, Cream Body, Brown & Yellow Glaze, 5 1/2 In. .......... 225.00
Flask, Figural, Woman's Bust ......................................... 225.00
Inkwell, Phrenology Head ............................................... 400.00
Jar, Batter, Bale Handle, Brown Slip, Dark Glaze, Tin Lid ..... 250.00

Jug, Batter, Ale, Signed E. Norton, 1 Gallon ............................................. 345.00
Mug, Frog In Bottom, Mottled Brown Glaze, 3 3/4 In. ........................... 135.00
Mug, Parrots In Relief ..................................................................................... 75.00
Pan, Milk, Mottled, 9 1/2 X 2 3/4 In. ........................................................... 85.00
Pan, Milk, 9 X 2 1/2 In. ................................................................................. 75.00
Pitcher, Lemonade, Brown Glaze, 8 In. ....................................................... 65.00
Pitcher, Paneled Sided, White Interior, 8 In. .............................................. 65.00
Pitcher, Parian, Corn, Large ........................................................................ 550.00
Plate, Pie, 7 3/4 In. ...................................................................................... 105.00
Plate, Pie, 10 In.Diam. ................................................................................. 95.00
Plate, Pie, 11 1/2 In. .................................................................................... 145.00
Spittoon, Lion Head ....................................................................................... 55.00
Spittoon, Shell Design ................................................................................... 95.00
Teapot, Miniature ........................................................................................... 40.00
Toby, Ben Franklin, Grape Handle .............................................................. 275.00
Vase, Blackberry, 4 In. .................................................................................. 75.00
Vase, Parian, Grapes & Tendrils, Blue & White .......................................... 30.00
Vase, Parian, Poppy Design, Blue & White, 11 1/4 In. ............................. 250.00

*Berlin, a German porcelain factory, was started in 1751 by Wilhelm Kaspar Wegely. In 1763 the factory was taken over by Frederick the Great and became the Royal Berlin Porcelain Manufactory. It is still in operation today.*

BERLIN, Figurine, Dancing Girl, Jeweled Headdress, Puce Bodice, Marked, 6 In. ................... 1300.00
Figurine, Retriever, Brown Fur, Red Collar, Marked, 4 1/2 In. ...................... 500.00
Plaque, Eve, Nude Maiden, Standing, Coiling Serpent, Marked, 9 1/4 In. ............................ 2250.00
Plaque, Praying Girl, Olive & Amber Tones, Impressed Mark, 9 1/2 In. .................... 3250.00
Plate, Flowers, Pierced, C.1880, K.P.M. Mark, Set Of 12 ...................... *Illus* 5000.00
Urn, Cover, Striated Lappets, C.1913, Marked, 30 1/4 In. ...................... *Illus* 3000.00

BERNARD LEACH, Jug, Molded Oak Leaf, St.Ives Mark, 7 1/2 In. ....................... 1000.00

BESWICK, Bank, Bunnykins, 9 1/4 In. ........................................................... 47.50
Figurine, Barracuda ....................................................................................... 38.00
Figurine, Blue Tit, No.992 ............................................................................ 15.00
Figurine, Great Dane ..................................................................................... 45.00
Figurine, Labrador Retriever ......................................................................... 45.00
Figurine, Mare & Colt, 7 1/2 X 9 1/4 In. ..................................................... 65.00
Slipper, Old Woman Who Lived In A Shoe .................................................. 15.00
Teapot, Peggotty ............................................................................................ 45.00

BETTY BOOP, Playing Cards ........................................................................ 45.00
Soap, Boxed ................................................................................................... 65.00
Vase, Holding Cat, Beige, Yellow, Black, 4 In. ............................................ 45.00
Vase, Wall, Betty Twisting Bimbo's Ear, 3 X 5 1/4 In. ............................... 150.00

BICYCLE, High Wheel, Leather Seat, Cast Iron, Wheel 53 In. ..................... *Illus* 1200.00
Lamp, Colored Set, English .......................................................................... 25.00
Touring, Man's, Ace Mfg., Varnished Wood Rims, 27 In. ........................... 285.00
Tricycle, All Wood ...................................................................... *Illus* 250.00
Tricycle, 1920, Iron ....................................................................................... 52.00
Velocipede, 3 Wheel, Railroad ..................................................................... 750.00

*Bing & Grondahl is a famous Danish factory making fine porcelains from 1853 to the present. Their Christmas plates are especially well known.*

BING & GRONDAHL, Chocolate Pot, Geisha Girl, Orange ........................... 48.00
Dish, Mint, Flower, Blue, 4 In.Diam. ............................................................. 6.00
Figurine, Ballerina ......................................................................................... 65.00
Figurine, Blacksmith, No.2225, Signed Axel Locher, 11 In. ...................... 395.00

Berlin, Plate, Flowers, Pierced, C.1880, K.P.M. Mark, Set Of 12

Berlin, Urn, Cover, Striated Lappets, C.1913, Marked, 30 1/4 In.

Bicycle, High-Wheel, Leather Seat, Cast Iron, Wheel, 53 In.

Bicycle, Tricycle, All Wood

Figurine, Boy & Girl On Bench, Drinking Milk, No.2175 ............................................. 150.00
Figurine, Boy Kissing Girl, 8 In. ................................................................................. 115.00
Figurine, Boy With Horse, No. 2195, Signed ........................................................... 295.00
Figurine, Bulldog, Standing, Porcelain, 3 1/4 X 4 In. ................................................ 75.00
Figurine, Girl Holding Kitten, Porcelain, 7 In. ........................................................... 115.00
Figurine, Girl Kneeling By Basket, Kitten, 4 X 4 In. .................................................. 110.00
Figurine, Girl Playing With Puppy ............................................................................. 70.00
Figurine, Girl With Cat, 8 In. ..................................................................................... 125.00
Figurine, Lioness, Seated, Tan, 6 In. ........................................................................ 165.00
Figurine, Monkeys, 4 Huddled, Tan .......................................................................... 165.00
Figurine, Mouse, Tail In Mouth, Artist Initialed, 2 In. ............................................... 35.00
Figurine, Old Man Feeding Hens & Ducks, 7 In. ...................................................... 150.00
Figurine, Parakeet ..................................................................................................... 50.00
Figurine, Pig, Sow Sitting On Haunches, 2 1/2 X 5 In. ............................................. 60.00
Figurine, Playing In The Waves, R.Gauguin, Artist, 19 In. ....................................... 3500.00
Figurine, Polar Bear, Seated, No.1954, Signed, 17 X 16 In. .................................... 1400.00
Figurine, Sea Sprite, Holding Starfish, White ........................................................... 78.00
Figurine, Seagull, Holding A Fish In Beak, 1 3/4 X 5 In. .......................................... 45.00
Figurine, Siamese Cat, Seated, 5 1/2 In. ................................................................. 28.00
Figurine, Sitting Cat ................................................................................................... 75.00
Figurine, Springer Spaniel, Brown, Tan, & White, 4 3/4 In. ...................................... 58.00
Figurine, St. Bernard Puppy, Seated, 4 1/2 In. ......................................................... 90.00
Figurine, Waltzing Couple, 8 In. ................................................................................ 225.00
Figurine, White Clown, Art Deco ............................................................................... 125.00
Figurine, Youthful Boldness, No. 2162 ...................................................................... 140.00
Jar, Jam, Covered, Hand-Painted, Signed ................................................................ 22.00
Plate, Annual, 1977, Madonna ................................................................................... 35.00
Plate, Christmas, 1910 .............................................................................................. 75.00
Plate, Christmas, 1957 .............................................................................................. 90.00
Plate, Christmas, 1958 ........................................................................... 70.00 To 80.00
Plate, Christmas, 1961 ......................................................................... 63.00 To 110.00
Plate, Christmas, 1963 .............................................................................................. 110.00
Plate, Christmas, 1966, Boxed .................................................................................. 35.00
Plate, Christmas, 1971 .............................................................................................. 15.00
Plate, Christmas, 1977 .............................................................................................. 29.00
Plate, Christmas, 1978 .............................................................................................. 32.00
Plate, Christmas, 1980 .............................................................................................. 35.00
Plate, Mother's Day, 1969 ..................................................................... 350.00 To 400.00
Plate, Mother's Day, 1979, Jubilee ........................................................................... 45.00
Plate, Mother's Day, 1980 ......................................................................................... 26.50

BINOCULARS, English, 3 Different Eye Lenses, Carrying Case, 30 Mm. ................. 35.00
Marked Merchand F.Pairs, Leather Case, 5 X 6 In. ............................................... 25.00
Seaver & Williams, Case, 10X .............................................................................. 25.00

BIRDCAGE, Brass Pedestal Base, Hendry, New Haven, Conn., Brass, 14 In. ........... 75.00
Cloth Bird, Miniature ............................................................................................... 110.00
Cone Shape, Made In New Haven, Conn., Brass, 28 In. ........................................ 550.00
Dowels Form Caging, Handmade, Wooden, 6 1/2 X 6 1/4 X 5 In. .......................... 35.00
Fencing Around Cage, High Pedestal, Folk Art, Wooden, 5 1/2 Ft. ........................ 1000.00
Hendryx, Brass, 13 X 10 In. .................................................................................... 55.00
3 Cast Iron Oriental Figures, Milk Glass, Feeder, Hendryx .................................... 35.00

*Bisque is an unglazed baked porcelain. Finished bisque has a slightly sandy
texture with a dull finish. Some of it may be decorated with various colors.
Bisque gained favor during the late Victorian era when thousands of bisque
figurines were made.*

#### BISQUE, see also named porcelain factories

BISQUE, Bust, Girl, Hair Tied With Ribbon, Signed A.Carrier, 1800s ........................ 950.00
Figurine, Daddy Warbucks, Germany, 3 1/2 In. ....................................................... 40.00
Figurine, French, Ram, Ormolu Base, 6 X 7 In. ....................................................... 450.00
Figurine, Girl With Kitty, Boy With Dog, Floral, French, 16 In., Pair ......................... 750.00
Figurine, Koko The Clown, 4 In. ................................................................................ 20.00

**Figurine,** Lady, Applied Rose At Neck & In Hair, French, 7 1/2 In. ............................................. 265.00
**Figurine,** Organ Grinder, Monkey On Top Tipping Hat, French, 11 In. ............................. 115.00
**Figurine,** Swimmer, Full Length Of Woman Diving, German, 18 In. ............................... 75.00
**Figurine,** Victorian Woman, Gown, Letter, Rosebuds, Brass Base, 15 In. ............... 295.00
**Figurine,** Young Boy & Girl, Children On Shoulders, 8 In., Pair ................................ 250.00
**Night-Light,** Figural, Castle, Green & Blue Steeples, White, 6 1/2 In. ....................... 195.00
**Night-Light,** Figural, Dog Head, Glass Eyes, 3 5/8 X 3 In.Diam. ................................ 145.00
**Toothpick,** Boy Kneeling By Laundry Barrel, Pastel ................................................ 34.00
**Vase,** Laughing Mask, Winged Imp On Side, 3 1/2 In. ............................................... 125.00

*Black amethyst glass appears black until it is held to the light, then a dark*
*purple can be seen. It was made in many factories from 1860 to the present.*

**BLACK AMETHYST, Ashtray,** Coal Hod Shape, Wire Handle ................................. 8.00
**Ashtray,** Figural, Top Hat, Dobbs ......................................................................... 15.00
**Ashtray,** Harold's Club, Reno, Set Of 3 ................................................................ 20.00
**Basket,** Bushel ...................................................................................................... 29.00
**Bowl,** Console, Fostoria, 9 3/4 In.Diam. ................................................................ 25.00
**Bowl,** Covered ....................................................................................................... 60.00
**Bowl,** Handled, Beaded Edge, Enameled Flowers, 8 In.Diam. ............................... 22.50
**Bowl,** Held By Metal Female, Outstretched Arms, 7 1/2 In. .................................. 25.00
**Bowl,** Sterling Design, 8 1/2 In. ........................................................................... 25.00
**Box,** Hinged, Pedestal, Heron & Flowers, 4 7/8 X 5 1/4 In. ................................ 110.00
**Candleholder,** Classical Design, Gold Feet, 6 In. ................................................... 40.00
**Candleholder,** Gold Band, Polished Top ................................................................ 20.00
**Candleholder,** 3 In. ............................................................................................... 15.00
**Candleholder,** 3 Light, 4 1/4 In., Pair .................................................................. 32.00
**Candlestick,** Beads, 7 In. ...................................................................................... 15.00
**Candlestick,** Gold Trim, Pair ................................................................................. 38.00
**Candlestick,** Imperial Mold, 8 1/2 In., Pair .......................................................... 35.00
**Compote,** Geometric Pattern, 6 1/2 X 7 In. .......................................................... 45.00
**Compote,** Gold Trim, 7 1/2 In. .............................................................................. 25.00
**Cookie Jar** ................................................................................. 25.00 To 55.00
**Cruet** ................................................................................................................... 195.00
**Cup Plate,** Set Of 4 .............................................................................................. 12.00
**Dish,** Powder, Covered, Footed, Enameled ........................................................... 25.00
**Figurine,** Cat, 1 1/2 In. ......................................................................................... 15.00
**Figurine,** Cat, 2 In. ............................................................................................... 10.00
**Figurine,** Swan, Some Gold, 9 In. ........................................................................ 95.00
**Flower Frog,** Rectangular, 7 X 3 In. ...................................................................... 4.95
**Holder,** Plant, Frog Insert, 4 X 7 In. ...................................................................... 50.00
**Ivy Ball,** Crystal Ribbed Optic .............................................................................. 35.00
**Planter,** Dancing Ladies, Signed L.E.Smith ........................................................... 60.00
**Plate,** Cake, Pedestal, Low, 11 In. ......................................................................... 17.50
**Plate,** Fairfax Pattern, 6 In., Set Of 4 ................................................................... 15.00
**Salt & Pepper Set,** 4 1/2 In. ................................................................................. 25.00
**Sugar,** Diamond-Quilted ........................................................................................ 6.00
**Toothpick Holder** ................................................................................................ 30.00
**Tray,** Handled, 14 X 10 In. ................................................................................... 15.00
**Tray,** Pin, Heart Shape .......................................................................................... 10.00
**Tumbler,** Ribbed, Barrel Shape ............................................................................. 30.00
**Vase,** Applied Clear Handle, 10 In. ....................................................................... 55.00
**Vase,** Bud, 7 3/4 In. .............................................................................................. 16.00
**Vase,** Classic Shape, 9 In. ..................................................................................... 15.00
**Vase,** Confetti & Spears, 8 1/2 In. ......................................................................... 17.00
**Vase,** Dancing Girls, 2-Handled, 7 1/4 In. ............................................................. 30.00
**Vase,** Handled, Nude Dancing Girls, 7 In. .............................................................. 25.00
**Vase,** Handled, 8 In. .............................................................................................. 35.00
**Vase,** Mother, World's Fair, 1934 .......................................................................... 40.00
**Vase,** Nudes, 10 In. ............................................................................................... 22.50
**Vase,** Ruffled Top, 6 1/4 In. ................................................................................... 10.00
**Vase,** Silver Deposit On Back, 10 X 5 1/2 In. ........................................................ 65.00
**Vase,** 2-Handled, 7 In. ........................................................................................... 20.00

**BLACK, Aunt Jemima,** Salt & Pepper, Plastic .................................................................... 14.00
    **Aunt Jemima,** Shaker, Paprika, 4 In. ........................................................................ 10.00
    **Cookie Jar,** Mammy ...................................................................................................... 25.00
    **Doorstop,** Aunt Jemima ............................................................................................... 45.00
    **Figurine,** Aunt Jemima, Iron, Original Paint, 9 In. .................................................. 75.00
    **Figurine,** Bisque, Boy In Outhouse, C.1940 ............................................................. 7.00
    **Mammy,** Walking, Wooden, Cardboard Doll ............................................................. 20.00
    **Salt & Pepper,** Aunt Jemima & Uncle Mose, Celluloid, 3 1/2 In. .......................... 10.00
    **Salt & Pepper,** Aunt Jemima, Plastic ......................................................................... 5.50
    **Salt & Pepper,** Aunt Jemima, 1 Blue, 1 Yellow, Porcelain .................................... 18.00
    **Syrup,** Aunt Jemima, Red & White, Plastic, 5 1/4 In. ......................... 18.00 To 20.00
    **Trivet,** Aunt Jemima ...................................................................................................... 8.00

**BLANC DE CHINE, Figurine,** Kwan Yin, Hands Clasped Over Knee, 7 X 17 In. ......................... 395.00

*Blown glass was formed by forcing air through a rod into molten glass.
Early glass and some forms of art glass were hand-blown. Other types of
glass were molded or pressed.*

**BLOWN GLASS, Ball,** Target, Amber, 2 3/4 In.Diam. ................................................. 35.00
    **Bell,** Fraternal Eagle Between Layers Of Glass, 9 In. .............................................. 110.00
    **Bottle,** Case, Tulip Design, American, 18th Century, 10 1/2 In. ............................ 185.00
    **Bottle,** Ink, Tapered, Octagonal, 2 X 2 In. ............................................................... 20.00
    **Bottle,** Perfume, Flask Shape, Silver Hinged Lid, Green, 3 1/2 In. ........................ 65.00
    **Bottle,** Port, Applied Strap Handle, Amber, Pint ..................................................... 70.00
    **Bottle,** 2 Panels With Indian Maidens, C.1830, French, 9 1/2 In. ......................... 500.00
    **Creamer,** 3 Mold, 5 In. ................................................................................................. 266.00
    **Decanter,** Applied Triple Neck Rings, Double Rigaree, 1 Quart, Pr. ...................... 385.00
    **Flip Glass,** Copper Wheel Engraving, C.1700, Engraved, 7 In. .............................. 150.00
    **Fly Catcher,** Hangs From Ceiling ............................................................................... 45.00
    **Jug,** Handled, Blue, 1/2 Gallon .................................................................................... 25.00
    **Pitcher,** Applied Rings On Body, C.1815, T.Caines, 6 3/4 In. ................................ 350.00
    **Pitcher,** Hollow Handle, Early American ................................................................... 75.00
    **Pitcher,** 2 Applied Rings On Body, Boston Glass Co., C.1815 ............................... 350.00
    **Sugar,** Covered, Zanesville, Ohio, 1820s, Blue, 8 In. ............................................. 325.00
    **Sugar,** Galleried Rim, New Hampshire, Green, 1830 .............................................. 150.00
        **BLUE AMBERINA, see Bluerina**
        **BLUE GLASS, see Cobalt Blue**
        **BLUE ONION, see Onion**

*Blue Willow pattern has been made in England since 1780. The pattern
has been copied by factories in many countries, including Germany, Japan, and
the United States. It is still being made. Willow was named for a
pattern that pictures a bridge, birds, willow trees, and a Chinese landscape.*

**BLUE WILLOW, Butter,** Covered, Burslem .................................................................. 35.00
    **Canister,** Coffee ............................................................................................................ 14.00
    **Canister,** Sugar ............................................................................................................. 18.00
    **Cup & Saucer,** Allerton .............................................................................................. 20.00
    **Cup & Saucer,** England, Large .................................................................................. 10.00
    **Dish,** Vegetable, Covered, Serpentine Shape, 11 X 8 1/2 In.Diam. ....................... 45.00
    **Dish,** Vegtable, Straus & Sons, 10 In. ...................................................................... 35.00
    **Eggcup,** Double ............................................................................................................ 6.00
    **Funnel** ............................................................................................................................ 15.00
    **Jar,** Covered, Lady's Head On Sides, Maddock & Sons, 4 1/2 In. ......................... 28.00
    **Pitcher,** Allerton, 4 In. ................................................................................................ 20.00
    **Pitcher,** Bulbous, Marked, 5 1/4 In. ......................................................................... 28.00
    **Pitcher,** Roses, Green, 8 In. ........................................................................................ 24.00
    **Planter,** 1909, 14 X 11 In. .......................................................................................... 50.00
    **Plate,** Allerton, 9 In.Diam. .......................................................................................... 20.00
    **Plate,** Soup, 2 People, Arched Bridge, Scalloped Rim, 7 1/2 In. ........................... 25.00
    **Plate,** 3 People, 3-Arched Bridge, 6 In.Diam. ......................................................... 18.00
    **Plate,** 9 1/2 In. .............................................................................................................. 12.00

Platter, Allerton, 13 1/2 In. ............................................................................... 45.00
Platter, Allerton, 15 1/2 In. ............................................................................... 65.00
Platter, Booth, England, 18 1/2 In. ................................................................... 50.00
Platter, Boston Statehouse, Spreadeagle Border, Blue & White ..................... 300.00
Soup Dish, Wide Edge, Royal China, 8 1/4 In.Diam. ........................................ 5.00
Sugar & Creamer .............................................................................................. 20.00
Tea Set, Doll's, Sugar, Creamer, Teapot, 2 Cups & Saucers ........................... 65.00
Teapot, Advertising Ringston's Tea .................................................................. 24.00
Tray, Gilded Rim, Two People On Arched Bridge, 6 X 7 1/4 In. ........................ 30.00

*Bluerina is a type of art glass which shades from light blue to ruby. It is often called blue amberina.*

BLUERINA, Vase, Jack-In-The-Pulpit, Red To Blue ........................................... 265.00

*Boch Freres Factory was founded in 1841 in La Louviere in eastern Belgium. The wares resemble the work of Villeroy & Boch. The factory is still in business.*

BOCH FRERES, Vase, Art Deco, Marked Gres Keramis, 9 3/4 In. ...................... 650.00
Vase, Stylized Blossoms, Marked, C.1925, 10 1/2 In. .........................*Illus* 200.00

BOEHM, Bird, Fledgling, Red Poll, No.495w, 3 In. ........................................... 215.00
Bookend, Owls, White, Pair ............................................................................. 650.00
Figurine, Baby Chickadee ................................................................................ 250.00
Figurine, Basset Hound, Glazed, 1950 ............................................................ 650.00
Figurine, Blackheaded Grosbeak ................................................................... 1275.00
Figurine, Blue Grosbeak ................................................................................ 1050.00
Figurine, Cactus Wren .................................................................................... 1560.00
Figurine, Canada Geese, Pair ........................................... 700.00 To 715.00
Figurine, Chrysanthemum With Butterfly ....................................................... 1275.00
Figurine, Crested Flycatcher, Gray Pot .......................................................... 450.00
Figurine, Falcon Head, King Tut Collection, 10 1/2 In. ................................... 300.00
Figurine, Fledgling, White-Throated Sparrow ................................................ 250.00
Figurine, Goldfinch ......................................................................................... 175.00
Figurine, Kestrels, Pair .................................................................................. 2350.00

Boch Freres, Vase, Stylized Blossoms,
Marked, C.1925, 10 1/2 In.

**Figurine,** Orchard Orioles .................................................................. 1575.00
**Figurine,** Robin ................................................................................... 150.00
**Figurine,** Sitting Bunny, Pink Eyes & Ears, White, 2 1/2 X 3 In. ........ 200.00
**Figurine,** Sleeping Signet ..................................................................... 150.00
**Figurine,** St.Maria Goretti, Kneeling Girl, 6 In. ................................... 495.00
**Figurine,** Verdins ................................................................................ 1085.00
**Figurine,** Western Bluebirds ................................................................. 250.00
**Figurine,** Western Meadowlark ............................................................ 1250.00

*Bohemian glass is an ornate, overlay, or flashed glass made during the Victorian era. It has been reproduced in Bohemia, which is now a part of Czechoslovakia. Glass made from 1875 to 1900 is preferred by collectors.*

**BOHEMIAN GLASS, Beaker,** White & Blue Overlay, Gilt Rim, Marked, 5 1/2 In. ......... 320.00
  **Bell,** Overlay Cut, White Over Green, 5 In. ....................................... 35.00
  **Biscuit Jar,** Cut, Blue ...................................................................... 100.00
  **Bowl & Underplate,** Ruby .................................................................. 70.00
  **Candlestick,** Light Blue, Etched Deer & Tree, 10 1/2 In., Pair ............ 120.00
  **Cordial,** Deer, Ruby Cut To Clear, Stemmed ...................................... 10.00
  **Creamer,** Yellow & Red Flowers ........................................................ 35.00
  **Cruet,** Red To Clear, Frosted Bird On Branch ................... 60.00 To 65.00
  **Decanter,** Amber Bird Design ............................................................ 95.00
  **Decanter,** Amber, Deer Scene, 8 In. .................................................. 165.00
  **Decanter,** Bird & Nest Design, Original Stopper ................................ 80.00
  **Decanter,** Castles, Birds, Fernery, Amber, 16 1/2 In., Pair ................. 145.00
  **Decanter,** Deer & Castle, Ruby Cut To Clear, 9 1/4 In. ....................... 95.00
  **Decanter,** Ruby Cut To Clear, Stopper, 15 1/2 In. .............................. 85.00
  **Decanter,** Ruby Cut To Clear, Tumbler On Top .................................. 110.00
  **Decanter,** Whiskey, Crystal Bubble Stopper, 14 1/2 In. ...................... 135.00
  **Goblet,** Cover, Blue, Castle & Flower, Flaring Stem, 9 1/2 In. ............. 425.00
  **Goblet,** Red, Stemmed, 7 1/2 X 3 1/2 In. ........................................... 185.00
  **Lampshade,** Deer, Trees, & Birds, Ruby Ground, 18 In.Diam. ........... 95.00
  **Plate,** Etched Animals & Castle, Rabbit Center, 8 1/2 In. .................... 85.00
  **Stein,** Etched Landscape Scene, Pewter Fittings, C.1900, 6 In. .......... 275.00
  **Stein,** Etched Landscape With Deer, Pewter Fittings, 6 In. ................. 275.00
  **Tumble-Up,** Flower Design, Ruby ...................................................... 90.00
  **Tumbler,** White Overlay, Barrel Shape, 3 In. ...................................... 48.00
  **Vase,** Acid Cut Cherubs, Blue To Clear, C.1900, 7 1/4 In., Pr. ........... 450.00
  **Vase,** Bud, Frosted Floral Decoration, Ruby, 7 In. ............................. 60.00
  **Vase,** Cut Cherubs, Blue To Clear, C.1900, 7 1/4 In., Pair ................. 450.00
  **Vase,** Deer & Castle, Footed, Amber, 8 In. ........................................ 65.00
  **Vase,** Floral Designed, Enameled Panels .......................................... 45.00
  **Vase,** 3 Deer, Oak Trees, Ruby To Clear, C.1840, 15 In. .................. 1050.00
    **BOOK, see Paper, Book and others**
    **BOSTON & SANDWICH CO., see Fireglow, Lutz ; Sandwich Glass**
**BOTTLE OPENER, Alligator Biting Black Man,** Cast Iron ........................ 30.00
  **Alligator,** Cast Iron, 5 1/2 In. ............................................................. 12.50
  **Alligator,** Old Paint, Cast Iron, 6 1/4 In. ............................................. 45.00
  **Billy Goat,** Horn Removes Cap, Partial Paint, 4 In. ............................ 17.50
  **Bulldog Face,** Wall, Cast Iron ............................................................ 45.00
  **Chapman Dairy** ................................................................................. 10.00
  **Chicken,** Cast Iron ............................................................................. 12.00
  **Elephant,** Opener In Trunk, Cast Iron ................................................ 35.00
  **Four-Eyed Man With Mustache,** Wall, Cast Iron ................................ 45.00
  **Heilman's Old Style Lager** ................................................................. 5.00
  **Horn Shape,** Sterling Silver Cap, Opener, Cast Iron, 7 In. ................. 4.50
  **Horse's Derriere,** Iron ........................................................................ 15.00
  **Indian,** Iroquois, Buffalo, N.Y., Advertising ........................................ 16.00
  **Man,** Cast Iron ................................................................................... 10.00
  **Negro,** Wall ....................................................................................... 30.00
  **Nude,** Art Deco, Holds Ring Over Head, Bronze, 8 In. ....................... 38.00
  **Nude,** Brass ...................................................................................... 15.00
  **Nude,** Utica Club ............................................................................... 8.00

| | |
|---|---|
| Oliver Hardy | 20.00 |
| Oliver Hardy, Wooden | 25.00 |
| Parrot, Cast Iron, 4 In. | 5.00 |
| Parrot, Stands Up, 3 1/2 In. | 25.00 |
| Pelican, Open Beak Is Opener, Traces Of Paint, 3 In. | 16.50 |
| Pepsi-Cola Bottle, Red, White, & Blue, 4 In. | 10.00 |
| Pepsi-Cola, Tin | 8.00 |
| Rearing Horse, Cast Iron | 20.00 |
| Rooster, Cast Iron | 20.00 |
| Semi-Side Ear Donkey, Cast Iron, 3 In. | 10.00 |
| Setter Dog, Cast Iron, 4 X 4 1/2 In. | 28.00 |
| Ship, Brass, 5 In. | 15.00 |
| Squirrel On Log, Iron, 3 In. | 18.00 |
| Standing Parrot | 22.00 |
| U Bang | 3.00 |
| Ugly Man In Top Hat, Iron | 15.00 |
| Woman's Hand, Art Nouveau, Bronze | 12.50 |

*Bottle collecting has become a major American hobby. There are several general categories of bottles such as historic flasks, bitters, household, figural, and others. The McK numbers refer to the book "American Glass" by George and Helen McKearin and "American Bottles and Flasks and Their Ancestry" by Helen McKearin and Kenneth Wilson. For modern bottle prices and more old bottle prices see the book "The Kovels' Bottle Price List" by Ralph and Terry Kovel.*

| | |
|---|---|
| **BOTTLE, Apothecary,** Acorn Shape, Blown, Crystal Stopper, 13 1/2 In. | 25.00 |
| **Apothecary,** Clear, C.1930s, 31 In. | 325.00 |

*Avon started in 1886 as the California Perfume Company. It was not until 1929 that the name Avon was used. In 1939 it became Avon Products Inc. Each year Avon sells figural bottles filled with cosmetic products. Ceramic, plastic, and glass bottles are made in limited editions.*

| | |
|---|---|
| **Avon,** Angel | 3.00 |
| **Avon,** Bicentennical, Betsy Ross | 10.00 |
| **Avon,** Boot, Pincushion Lid, Milk Blue Pastel, Purple Cushion | 5.00 |
| **Avon,** Butterfly, Iridescent, Gold Cap | 5.00 |
| **Avon,** Christmas Tree | 3.00 |
| **Avon,** Coffee Grinder, Gold Handles, Milk Glass | 3.00 |
| **Avon,** Courting Carriage, Crystal, Gold Cap | 2.00 |
| **Avon,** Leisure Hours Clock, Large, Milk Glass | 3.00 |
| **Avon,** Mug, Train On Front, White Ground | 25.00 |
| **Avon,** Sea Maiden, Crystal, Gold Crown | 3.00 |
| **Avon,** World's Greatest Dad Trophy | 5.00 |
| **Bar,** Bride Of York Whiskey, Enameled | 80.00 |
| **Barber,** Bird & Cartoon, Osiris Dandruff Cure, Opaque White | 175.00 |
| **Barber,** Blossoms & Sea Foam, Opaque White Ground, Blue Neck | 145.00 |
| **Barber,** Clambroth | 35.00 |
| **Barber,** Dresser Set, Milk Glass Design, Pair | 23.00 |
| **Barber,** Embossed Leaves, Gold Trim, White | 35.00 |
| **Barber,** Enamel Decorations, Open Pontil, Light Blue Green | 75.00 |
| **Barber,** Enameled Amethyst Design | 47.50 |
| **Barber,** Enameled Flowers, Amethyst, Original Top | 98.00 |
| **Barber,** Pear-Shaped Body, Freeblown, Metal Spout, England, 8 3/4 In. | 50.00 |
| **Barber,** Witch Hazel, Original Stopper | 22.50 |

*Beam bottles are made to hold Kentucky Straight Bourbon made by the James B.Beam Distilling Company. The Beam series of ceramic bottles began in 1953.*

| | |
|---|---|
| **Beam,** Antique Globe | 17.95 |
| **Beam,** Captain & Mate | 17.95 |
| **Beam,** Civil War, North | 27.50 |

| | |
|---|---|
| Beam, Coffee Mill | 11.50 |
| Beam, Edison Light Bulb | 9.95 |
| Beam, Executive, 1966 | 34.95 |
| Beam, French Cradle Telephone | 12.95 |
| Beam, Humidor, Red Fox, 1972 | 250.00 |
| Beam, Jewel Tea | 89.00 |
| Beam, Model A Ford, Red | 25.00 |
| Beam, Model T, Black | 45.00 |
| Beam, Panda Bear | 12.00 |
| Beam, Short Timer | 24.00 |
| Beam, Shriner, Western Association | 34.95 |
| Beam, Volkswagen, Red | 23.00 |
| Beam, Woodpecker | 7.95 |
| Beer, Eagle Brewery, Snap Top, Embossed Brewery Scene | 20.00 |
| Beer, L.Simond's, Stoneware, 1/2 Size | 50.00 |
| Beer, Pilsner 1884, Brown, 9 1/2 In. *Illus* | 2.00 |
| Beer, Ruby Red, Quart | 8.00 |
| Beer, Schlitz, Ruby, 7 Ounce | 35.00 |
| Beer, Signed M.O.Fuller, Stoneware | 50.00 |
| Bitters, Atwood's Jaundice, Georgetown, Mass., 12-Sided | 75.00 |
| Bitters, Atwood's Jaundice, 12-Sided, Aqua, Embossed, 6 In. | 4.50 |
| Bitters, Brown's Indian Queen, Light Amber | 240.00 |
| Bitters, Caldwell's Herb, Iron Pontil, Amber | 190.00 |
| Bitters, Doctor Fish's, Figural Fish, C.1845, 11 1/2 In. | 100.00 |
| Bitters, Doyle's Hop Bitters, Red Amber | 22.50 |
| Bitters, Dr.Fenner's Capitol, Clear | 15.00 |
| Bitters, Dr.Harter's Wild Cherry Bitters, Dayton, O., Amber | 35.00 |
| Bitters, Dr.Harter's, Miniature | 12.00 |
| Bitters, Dr.Petzold's German, Amber | 90.00 |
| Bitters, Eagle Angostura, Amber | 38.00 |
| Bitters, Greeley's Bourbon, Barrel, Dark Puce, 9 1/4 In. | 275.00 |
| Bitters, Hostetter's, Cork, Amber | 12.50 |
| Bitters, Kaiser Wilhelm | 125.00 |
| Bitters, Lash, Clear, 12 In. | 5.00 |
| Bitters, Log Cabin, 1860s, Amber | 75.00 |
| Bitters, N.K.Brown, Iron & Quinine | 85.00 |
| Bitters, Oxygenated, For Dyspepsia, Asthma, & General Debility | 75.00 |
| Bitters, Royal Pepsin Stomach, Amber, 9 In. | 85.00 |
| Bitters, Sanborn's Kidney & Liver Vegetable Laxative, Amber | 68.00 |
| Bitters, Yerba Buena, San Francisco, Amber, 1 Pint | 90.00 |
| Chemist, Laboratory, Civil War Merchant, Lockport, N.Y., Green | 65.00 |
| Chestnut, Free-Blown, 18th Century, American, Green, 7 3/4 In., Pair | 125.00 |
| BOTTLE, COCA-COLA, see Coca-Cola, Bottle | |
| Cologne, Cross-Hatched Diamond-Point, 7 1/2 X 5 In. | 125.00 |
| Cologne, Paperweight Bottom, Enameled, French, Pair | 125.00 |
| Cologne, Scarlet, Gone With The Wind, Pinaud | 35.00 |
| Decanter, Blown-Molded, Stopper, Swirled Rib, Quart | 195.00 |
| Demijohn, Green, German, 24 In. | 20.00 |
| Double Springs, Dusenberg S.J., 1931 | 17.00 |
| Dr.Thompson's Eye Water, Stopper Type, Embossed, 4 In. | 10.00 |
| Dresser, Bristol, Stopper, 11 In. | 28.00 |
| Ezra Brooks, American Legion, Hawaii | 9.00 |
| Ezra Brooks, Big Red, No.1 | 20.00 |
| Ezra Brooks, Brahma | 15.00 |
| Ezra Brooks, Iowa Statehouse | 37.00 |
| Ezra Brooks, Moose | 25.00 |
| Ezra Brooks, North Carolina | 10.00 |
| Ezra Brooks, Owl No.1 | 50.00 |
| Ezra Brooks, Phoenix Bird | 27.00 |
| Ezra Brooks, Phonograph | 15.00 |
| Ezra Brooks, Saddle, Silver | 19.95 |
| Ezra Brooks, Salmon | 20.00 |
| Figural, A Little Scotch, Maid With Tray & Dog, Japan | 35.00 |

Bottle, Beer, Pilsner 1884, Brown, 9 1/2 In.

| | |
|---|---:|
| **Figural,** Baseball Mitt, Ceramic | 7.50 |
| **Figural,** Baseball Player, Caricature, German, 9 1/2 In. | 88.00 |
| **Figural,** Bather-On-The-Rocks, Clear, 12 In. | 100.00 |
| **Figural,** Clam With Closure, Amber | 200.00 |
| **Figural,** George Washington, Bust, Green, 9 3/4 In. | 65.00 |
| **Figural,** Just A Little Nip, Flapper Girl, Dog, Japan | 25.00 |
| **Figural,** Liberty Bell, Tin Closure On Base, Green, 3 1/2 In. | 22.00 |
| **Figural,** Parrot, Cloisonne On Silver, 3 1/2 In., Pair | 100.00 |
| **Figural,** Pig, Fireman, Pink, 5 In. | 150.00 |
| **Figural,** Pretzel, Ceramic | 22.50 |
| **Figural,** Skeleton, Marked Poison, Germany, Tan & White | 65.00 |
| **Figural,** Turtle, Iridescence, Good Luck | 15.00 |
| **Figural,** Washington, Standing, Clear, 9 1/2 In. | 20.00 |
| **Flask,** B.P.O.E. | 85.00 |
| **Flask,** Chestnut, Zanesville, Ohio, Amber To Ruby, 1880-1900, 5 1/4 In. | 125.00 |
| **Flask,** Embossed Chestnuts, Monkey On Front, Lady's Corset On Back | 65.00 |
| **Flask,** For Pike's Peak, Eagle On Reverse Side | 50.00 |
| **Flask,** George Washington, Albany Works, Green | 150.00 |
| **Flask,** Green Swirled, 4 3/4 In. | 335.00 |
| **Flask,** Hip, Dated 1890s | 12.00 |
| **Flask,** Leather Covered, 18th Century, England | 52.00 |
| **Flask,** Masonic, 1/2 Pt. | 1250.00 |
| **Flask,** Pittsburgh Pattern, Double Eagle, Green | 100.00 |
| **Flask,** Police, Revolver Shape, 1900s | 75.00 |
| **Flask,** Saddle, Persian, Dark Green, Blown, 14 In. | 20.00 |
| **Flask,** Tin Lined, Hammered, Cowhide Case, 8 1/4 X 4 1/4 In. | 22.00 |
| **Flask,** U.S.Warship Maine, Glass | 165.00 |
| **Food,** Lea & Perrin Worcestershire, Glass Stopper, Green, Pair | 8.00 |
| **Fruit Jar,** Atlas E-Z Seal, Olive Green, 2 Quart | 10.00 |
| **Fruit Jar,** Atlas E-Z Seal, 1/2 Pint | 2.00 |
| **Fruit Jar,** Atlas Improved Mason, Quart | 3.50 |
| **Fruit Jar,** Atlas, Mason's Patent Nov.30th, 1858, Aqua, 1/2 Gallon | 5.50 |
| **Fruit Jar,** Ball Ideal, 1/2 Pint | 3.00 |
| **Fruit Jar,** Ball Perfect Mason, Aqua, 1/2 Pint | 18.00 |
| **Fruit Jar,** Ball Perfect Mason, 1/2 Pint | 3.00 |
| **Fruit Jar,** Battleship Maine, Eagle Insert, Milk Glass, Pint | 250.00 |
| **Fruit Jar,** Boyd Perfect Mason, Aqua, Pint | 3.00 |
| **Fruit Jar,** Crown Mason, 1/2 Gallon | 1.00 |
| **Fruit Jar,** Crown, Imperial, 1/2 Pint | 8.50 |
| **Fruit Jar,** Drey Mason, Sloping Shoulder, 1/2 Gallon | 15.00 |

Fruit Jar, Economy, Original Lid & Clamp, Quart .................................................................. 5.50
Fruit Jar, Gem, The, Aqua, Quart ....................................................................................... 4.50
Fruit Jar, Griffin's, Patent 1862 ......................................................................................... 90.00
Fruit Jar, Kerr Self-Sealing Mason, Amber, Quart ............................................................. 9.50
Fruit Jar, Lightning, Aqua, Quart ........................................................................................ 10.00
Fruit Jar, Lorillard, Patent 1872, Bail & Cover, Amber ...................................................... 20.00
Fruit Jar, Mason Star, Embossed ........................................................................................ 4.25
Fruit Jar, Mason, Aqua, Pint .......................................................................................*Illus* 4.00
Fruit Jar, Mason, Loop Underline, Light Vaseline, Pint ...................................................... 6.50
Fruit Jar, Mason, Swayzee Improved, Aqua, 1 Quart ......................................................... 7.50
Fruit Jar, Mason's, C.F.J.Co., Patent Nov.30th, 1858, Quart ............................................ 3.50
Fruit Jar, Mason's, Patent November 30, 1858, Aqua, 1 Quart ......................................... 3.00
Fruit Jar, Putnam Lightning Fruit Jar, Wire Closure, Blue, Pint ......................................... 15.00
Fruit Jar, Schram ................................................................................................................. 15.00
Fruit Jar, Stoneware, Weir, 1 Quart ................................................................................... 15.00
Fruit Jar, Sure Seal, Script, Aqua, Quart ........................................................................... 3.50
Fruit Jar, Swayzee's Improved Mason, Aqua, Pint ............................................................ 4.50
Fruit Jar, Winslow Canning Jar, Patent 1870 .................................................................... 80.00
Fruit, Weir, Stoneware, 1 Quart ......................................................................................... 15.00
Gourd, Stopper ..................................................................................................................... 12.00
Hot Water, Chromed Steel, 1912, 8 In.Diam. .................................................................... 25.00
Ink, Carter's Cathedral, Blue ............................................................................................... 45.00
Ink, Carter's, Cathedral, Quart ........................................................................................... 28.00
Ink, Carter's, Figural, Seated Man, Head Stopper, Porcelain, 3 1/2 In. ............................ 55.00
Ink, Carter's, Porcelain, Ma Carter, 3 3/4 In. .................................................................... 37.50
Ink, Stoddard, Cylinder, Open Pontil, Olive Amber, 2 1/2 In. ........................................... 45.00
Ink, Umbrella, Open Pontil, Aqua ....................................................................................... 15.00
Ink, Underwood, Cobalt Blue, Large ................................................................................... 45.00
Ink, Waterman, Sterling Silver Hinged Top, Red Stone ..................................................... 60.00
Jar, Battery, Edison, Glass, Ceramic Lid ............................................................................. 22.00
Lord Calvert, Wood Duck ..................................................................................................... 35.00
McCormick, Elvis, No.1 ........................................................................................................ 30.00
McCormick, Mail Car ............................................................................................................ 69.95
McCormick, Pony Express ..................................................................................................... 20.00
McCormick, Train Locomotive .............................................................................................. 37.50
Medicine, Cod Liver Oil, Fish Shape, Amber, 9 3/4 In. ..................................................... 18.00

Bottle, Fruit Jar, Mason, Aqua, Pint

**Medicine,** Dr.Fenner's Cure, Embossed Shoulder ............................................................ 22.00
**Medicine,** Dr.Kilmer's Female Remedy .............................................................................. 18.00
**Medicine,** Dr.M.M.Fenner's Kidney & Backache Cure, Amber, 1872-1898 .................... 15.00
**Medicine,** Dr.Ranney's Botanic Blood & Liver Cure ......................................................... 10.00
**Medicine,** Dr.Richmond, Samaritan Nervine, 1880s ......................................................... 4.00
**Medicine,** Dr.Taft's Asmalene, New York ........................................................................... 5.00
**Medicine,** Kickapoo Indians' Tapeworm Secret, Green ................................................... 5.00
**Medicine,** Owl, Amber, One Wing, 3 1/2 In. ..................................................................... 40.00
**Medicine,** Radam's Microbe Killer ................................................................................... 50.00
**Medicine,** Rohrer's Expectoral, Lancaster, Pa., Amber ................................................... 95.00
**Medicine,** Schenck's Pulmonic Syrup ............................................................................. 35.00
**Medicine,** Veno's Cough Cure ........................................................................................... 8.50
**Medicine,** Warner's Safe Diabetes Cure, Amber, Pint ..................................................... 25.00
**Medicine,** Warner's Safe Rheumatic Cure ....................................................................... 45.00
**Medicine,** Wishart's Pine Tree Cordial, Green ................................................................. 50.00
**Middletown Mineral Springs,** Nature's Remedy ............................................................. 48.00
**Milk,** Akron Pure Milk Co., Embossed, 12 Ounce ........................................................... 5.00
**Milk,** Alderney Green Meadow Dairy, Cow's Head, Embossed, Quart ........................... 6.50
**Milk,** Amber, Picture Of Elk, Challenge Milk Co. ........................................................... 17.50
**Milk,** Annapolis Dairy, Embossed, Round, 1/2 Pint ......................................................... 3.00
**Milk,** Campbell's Creamery Inc., Blake-Hart Square, Embossed, Pint ........................... 7.50
**Milk,** Capitol Dairy Co., Chicago, Embossed, Round, 1/2 Pint ....................................... 2.50
**Milk,** Clover Brand Dairy Products, 3-Leaf Clover, Embossed, Pint ............................... 5.00
**Milk,** Cloverdale Dairy, Wheeling, With Clover ............................................................... 9.00
**Milk,** Cobel Dairy, Amber ................................................................................................. 5.00
**Milk,** Fayette B.Weiss Dairy, Embossed, Round, Pint ..................................................... 3.50
**Milk,** Hill Bros., Canton, N.Y., Embossed, Round, 1/4 Pint ............................................ 5.50
**Milk,** Hill's Dairy, Jersey Milk, Barstow, Embossed, Round, Quart ................................. 7.50
**Milk,** Humboldt Dairy Chicago Products Co., Embossed, Pint ....................................... 4.50
**Milk,** Humboldt Dairy Chicago Products Co., Embossed, 8 Ounce ................................ 4.00
**Milk,** Independent Creamery, Chicago, Ill., Pint .............................................................. 5.00
**Milk,** Jarosz Milk Co., Chicago, Ill., Embossed, Round, Pint ......................................... 3.50
**Milk,** L.A.Creamery Co., Embossed, Round, Pint ........................................................... 4.00
**Milk,** Mitchells's, Screw Top, Red Pyro, Round, Quart .................................................... 20.00
**Milk,** Modern Dairy Co., La Crosse, Wis., Orange Pyro, Round, 1/2 Pint ...................... 2.50
**Milk,** Mt.Fern Dairy, Dover, N.J., Embossed, Pint ........................................................... 5.00
**Milk,** Producer's Dairy Co., Double Neck, Embossed, Round, Quart ............................. 5.00
**Milk,** Shaw's Dairy, Thatcher, Embossed, Round, 1/4 Pint ............................................ 3.50
**Milk,** Shawsheen Dairy, Indian Head, Embossed, Round, Quart .................................... 9.00
**Milk,** Tumbling Run, J.H.Brokhoff Park Dairy, Embossed, Pint ...................................... 5.00
**Milk,** Twin City Dairy, Hurley, 1 Pint ............................................................................... 1.50
**Milk,** Vallotton's Milk, Picture Of Dentist, Maroon Pyro, Round, Quart ......................... 8.50
**Milk,** Wild Oak Dairy, Green Tint, Embossed, Round, Quart .......................................... 12.00
**Miniature,** Ski Country, Bob Cratchit ............................................................................. 20.00
**Miniature,** Ski Country, Bull Rider ................................................................................... 18.00
**Nurser,** , Embossed Rabbit, Scenery On Front, Tiny Rabbits All Around ...................... 23.00
**Nurser,** Hazel Atlas, Embossed Rabbits ........................................................................ 10.00
**Nursing,** Betsy Brown Safety ......................................................................................... 20.00
**Nursing,** Crying Baby ...................................................................................................... 65.00
**Nursing,** Embossed Baby On Front, 8 Ounce ................................................................ 12.00
**Nursing,** Embossed Cat & Kittens .................................................................................. 13.50
**Nursing,** Embossed Elephant, Wide Mouth .................................................................... 12.00
**Nursing,** Graduated Nursing ........................................................................................... 12.00
**Nursing,** Happy Baby, Embossed, 8 Ounce ................................................................... 10.00
**Nursing,** Temp-Guard, Thermometer In Molded Cutout, 1920s .................................... 38.00
**OBR,** Pierce Arrow Car .................................................................................................... 24.95
**Oil,** Battery, Edison ......................................................................................................... 10.00
**Opium,** Porcelain & Brass .............................................................................................. 43.00
**Pepsi-Cola,** Amber ......................................................................................................... 195.00
**Perfume,** Betty Boop, Topped, 2 1/2 In. ......................................................................... 35.00
**Perfume,** Enameled Yellow Garland & Bow, Emerald Green, 3 1/8 In. .......................... 55.00
**Perfume,** Figural Bird Stopper ........................................................................................ 23.00
**Perfume,** Figural, Black Baby, Germany, 1930s, Glass, Miniature .................................. 22.50

| | |
|---|---|
| **Pickle,** Green Glass, Cathedral Type, 11 1/2 In. | 20.00 |
| **Poison,** Cobalt Blue, Lattice & Points, 3 3/8 In. | 10.00 |
| **Poison,** Kilner Bros., Makers, Ribbed, Marked, 3 1/2 In. | 26.00 |
| **Poison,** Star Hobbed, Embossed, Not To Be Taken | 19.00 |
| **Scent,** Etched Nudes Suspended From Branches, Tiara Stopper, D'orsey | 2300.00 |
| **Scent,** Facet Cut, Metal Lid, 4 X 3/4 In. | 30.00 |
| **Schnapps,** Aromatic, Olive, Graphite Pontil | 85.00 |
| **Seltzer,** Cheyenne, Wyoming, Green | 25.00 |
| **Seltzer,** Pink, Pewter Top | 65.00 |
| **Ski Country,** Bassett Hound | 53.00 |
| **Ski Country,** Hawk Eagle | 118.00 |
| **Ski Country,** Snake River Stampede | 75.00 |
| **Snuff,** Carved Brown Puddingstone Agate, Agate Stopper | 175.00 |
| **Snuff,** Lady's, Laque Burgate, Matching Stopper | 170.00 |
| **Snuff,** Lapis Lazuli, White Jade Stopper, 3 In. | 65.00 |
| **Snuff,** Moonstone Stopper, Brown Agate | 140.00 |
| **Snuff,** Pyramidal Shape, Carved Phoenix Bird & Dragon, 3 3/4 In. | 265.00 |
| **Snuff,** Reverse Painting, Chinese, Signed | 400.00 |
| **Snuff,** Symbolic Horses On Sides, Agate Stopper, C.1920, Chinese | 150.00 |
| **Soda,** Electric Blue, Sands Baltimore | 25.00 |
| **Soda,** Erie Ginger Beer, Original Top | 30.00 |
| **Soda,** Hutchinson, Jim Riddle, Ironwood, Michigan, Quart | 15.00 |
| **Soda,** Seltzer, Cobalt Blue | 15.00 |
| **Soda,** Seltzer, Emerald Green | 15.00 |
| **Sunburst,** Blown-In-Mold, Deep Green, C.1825, 6 1/4 In. _Illus_ | 900.00 |
| **Whiskey,** Bushwick Glass Works, Golden Amber, 3/4 Quart | 65.00 |
| **Whiskey,** Hayner Whiskey, Troy, Ohio, Clear, 14 In. | 1.50 |
| **Whiskey,** Jesse Moore, Blob Top, Golden Amber | 40.00 |
| **Whiskey,** Jones Garvin & Co., Yellow Amber, Square, Pint | 30.00 |
| **Whiskey,** Mount Vernon Pure Rye, Sample, Amber | 35.00 |
| **Whiskey,** New Hampshire Statehouse, Ezra Brooks | 5.00 |
| **Whiskey,** Old Quaker, In Relief | 10.00 |
| **Whiskey,** Pre-Civil War, Light Blue, 5 3/4 In. | 110.00 |
| **Whiskey,** Union Forever, A Bumper To The Flag, Flint, 1863 | 75.00 |
| **Wild Turkey,** No.2 | 250.00 |

*Boxes of all kinds are collected. They were made of thin strips of inlaid
wood, metal, tortoiseshell, embroidery, or other material.*
**BOX, see also Ivory, Box; Porcelain, Box; Shaker, Box; Store,
Box; Tin, Box; and various porcelain categories
BOX, BATTERSEA, see Battersea, Box**

Bottle, Sunburst, Blown-In-Mold,
Deep Green, C.1825, 6 1/4 In.

Box, Knife, Divided By Carved Running Horses, Pine, 6 1/4 In.

**BOX, Bible,** Cover, Wrought Iron Harp & Lock, 17th Century, Chestnut, 7 3/4 In. .................. 100.00
  **Brass Corners,** Nails & Fastener, Teak, Camphorwood Lined, 7 1/2 X 17 In. ............. 160.00
  **Bride's,** Norwegian, Rose Nailing, Pegged & Laced, 18th Century ......................... 275.00
  **Brides,** Lid, Straw Laced, Oval ................................................. 135.00
  **Caddy,** Tea, Inlaid Satinwood & Mahogany, George III, 5 1/2 In. ...................... 50.00
  **Candle,** Carved, New England, Dated 1698, Marked GCB ......................... 585.00
  **Candle,** Chipped Carved Lid, Moravian, Walnut, 3 X 4 X 8 In. ...................... 95.00
  **Candle,** Dovetailed, Chamfered Slide Top, Buttermilk Red, Pine, 14 3/4 In. .......... 165.00
  **Candle,** Dovetailed, Original Paint, Set-On Lid .............................. 65.00
  **Candle,** Lid, Walnut ........................................................ 175.00
  **Candle,** Original Red Paint ................................................. 98.00
  **Candle,** Sliding Lid, Dovetailed, Oak, 8 X 9 X 12 In. ........................ 90.00
  **Candle,** Wall, 2-Drawer, 18th Century, Buttermilk Red, 5 1/2 X 17 1/2 In. ........ 375.00
  **Candle,** 2-Drawer, Hand-Forged Nails, Buttermilk Red, Pine, 5 1/2 X 17 In. ....... 385.00
  **Candy,** Heart, Victorian ................................................... 20.00
  **Candy,** Lady In Sedan Chair, Schrafft's, Brass .............................. 19.00
  **Candy,** Snowman, Victorian ................................................. 35.00
  **Carrier,** Butter, Stenciled, Blanchard, Nashua, N.H., 16 X 12 X 10 In. .......... 125.00
  **Cartridge,** Ammunition, 12 Gauge ........................................... 12.00
  **Chalk,** 24 Partitions, Slide Top, Rainbow-Hued Chalk, 26 X 10 In. ............. 20.00
  **Cheese,** Ratchet Lid, Pennsylvania Dutch, 7 1/2 X 5 1/2 X 4 1/2 In. ........... 75.00
  **Chip Carved Compass Slide Cover,** Maple & Birch, 6 X 2 1/8 X 3 1/8 In. ......... 775.00
  **Cigar,** Burnt Wood Lady On Lid, La Forma Perfecto, Lithograph Inside ............. 7.50
  **Cigar,** Clasp, Garcia Club House Cigars, 5 Cents, Wooden .................... 15.00
  **Cigar,** Jose Lovera Co., Wooden, 4 1/2 X 5 In. ............................. 10.00
  **Cigar,** Lillian Russell On Top, Music Sheet Liner .......................... 50.00
  **Coffee,** Dwinnel Wright, Paper Labels, Wooden, 15 X 21 X 16 In. ............. 65.00
  **Collar & Cuff,** Brass Medallion Of Old Collars, Leatherette, 8 X 7 In. ........ 10.00
  **Deed,** Dome Top, Tin, Asphaltum Ground, Stenciled Flowers & Vines, 8 In. ....... 65.00
  **Deed,** Dome Top, Tin, Stenciled, Brushwork In Alizarin & Blue ............... 65.00
  **Deed,** Leather Over Pine, Brass Nail Design, 18th Century ................... 175.00
  **Deed,** Stenciled Pattern On Top, Maine, 3 1/4 X 5 X 3 In. .................. 34.00
  **Deed,** Stenciled, Rectangular .............................................. 55.00
  **Deed,** Tin, Floral Spray On Lid, White Ground, Maine, 4 1/4 X 2 3/4 In. ....... 65.00
  **Deed,** Wooden, Initials B.B.N. ............................................. 60.00
  **Display,** Remington Ammunition, 1950s ...................................... 10.00
  **Document,** Salmon Colored, 14 X 10 X 6 In. ................................. 49.00
  **Dovetailed,** Striped, Brown Ground, Wooden, 18 1/4 X 9 3/4 X 8 In. ........... 75.00
  **Dresser,** Gilded Art Deco, Reverse Painted Glass Top, 5 1/2 X 3 1/2 In. ....... 40.00
  **Eggshell,** Green & Brown, 3 1/2 In. ........................................ 205.00
  **French,** Enamel, Scalloped, Hinged Lid, Farm Scenes, Signed, 3 1/2 X 4 In. ..... 175.00
  **Frisian,** Carved Slide Lid, Allover Pattern, 18th Century, 1/ 3/4 X 2 In. ...... 145.00
  **Gold & Iron Red On Lid,** 3 Ladies, Garden, Lacquer, Japan, 4 3/8 In. ......... 70.00
  **Grain Painted,** Marked Dr.Cary, Warwick, N.Y. .............................. 110.00
  **Handkerchief,** 7 Drawer, Oak ............................................... 125.00
  **Hat,** Cover Paper Scene Of Port Buffalo, Lake Erie, Silk Bonnet ............. 325.00
  **Hat,** Oval, Cardboard, Covered In Blue Wallpaper, Large .................... 225.00
  **Hat,** Wallpaper Covered, Gray Ground, Flowers, Leaves, 10 1/2 X 14 In. ........ 138.00
  **Hat,** Wallpaper Covered, Label, Tarbell, Albany, N.Y., 11 1/4 X 2 3/4 In. ...... 165.00
  **Jeweler's,** 15 Different Shaped Drawers, Ivory Pulls ........................ 190.00
  **Knife,** Divided By Carved Running Horses, Pine, 6 1/4 In. .............. *Illus* 525.00
  **Knife,** Mahogany, George III, Serpentine Front, 10 1/4 In. ................. 700.00
  **Knife,** 2 Finger Holes, Yellow, Green Edges, New England, C.1830, 6 1/8 In. ...... 400.00
  **Leather Covered,** Brass Ring Handle & Knobs, Wooden, 6 X 10 In. ............. 35.00
  **Match,** Art Nouveau Design On Hinged Lid, Enameled, Bronze & Brass .......... 50.00
  **Oriental,** Women On Cover, Fruit On Side, Leather, C.1900, 10 In. ........... 85.00
  **Pantry,** Dark Brown, Wooden, 6 3/4 In.Diam. ................................ 38.00
  **Pantry,** Straight Lap, Early Green Paint, Oval, Wooden, 7 1/2 In. ........... 95.00
  **Pantry,** Straight Lap, Marked Sprague, Wooden, 4 1/4 In. ................... 42.00
  **Pantry,** Unpainted, 4 In.Diam. ............................................. 42.00
  **Pantry,** V Lap Top, Unpainted, Wooden, 4 1/2 In.Diam. ...................... 38.00
  **Paper Covered,** Rust, Black, White, & Green, Oval, 5 1/4 In. ............... 48.00
  **Patch,** Hinged, Enameled Lid, Green Glass, 1 3/4 In.Diam. .................. 95.00

**Pipe,** Circular Holder, 1 Drawer, Enamel Paint, Walnut & Pine, 18 In. ....................................... 1300.00
**Pipe,** 1 Drawer, Brass Knob, Red Paint, New England, Pine, 10 7/8 In. ............................... 550.00
**Salt,** Hanging, Walnut, Lid ............................................................................................................... 175.00
**Scouring,** Knife, C.1870, Pine, 12 X 6 1/2 X 3 1/4 In. ................................................................... 68.00
**Scouring,** Knife, 3 Compartment, Raised Block & Tool ................................................................ 45.00
**Seed,** Dovetailed, Tiger Oak .......................................................................................................... 38.00
**Shaving,** Brass Bound, Pewter & Ivory Appurtenances ........................................................... 165.00
**Slate Pencils,** Covered, One Piece Of Wood, Blue Paint, 8 X 3 X 1 3/4 In. ........................... 65.00
**Slide Cover,** Cut Nails, Wooden, 6 1/2 In. ................................................................................. 28.00
**Slide Cover,** Dovetailed, Morse Twist Drill & Machine, 4 1/2 X 2 3/8 In. ................................ 3.75
**Slide Cover,** Hand-Forged Nails, Walnut, 6 3/4 X 6 3/4 X 1 1/2 In. ..................................... 75.00
**Slide Cover,** One Piece Of Wood, Greenish Blue Paint, 8 X 6 X 1 3/4 In. ........................... 65.00
**Slide Cover,** One Piece Of Wood, Greenish Blue, 7 3/4 X 3 X 1 3/4 In. .............................. 65.00
**Snuff,** Silver Rivets, Wooden ....................................................................................................... 25.00
       **BOX, TEA CADDY, see Furniture, Tea Caddy**
**Tinder,** Snuffer Cover, Striker, Candleholder, & Cover, Wooden ............................................ 225.00
**Tool,** Arched Handle, 19th Century, American, Dark Gray Paint, 2 Ft. 4 In. ......................... 75.00
**Tool,** Carpenter's, Tray Inside, Slot For Saws In Lid, Pine ....................................................... 75.00
**Tool,** Dovetailed Drawers, Homemade ....................................................................................... 195.00
**Trinket,** Art Nouveau, Gold Gilded, Lined, 2 1/2 In. ................................................................... 8.00
**Trinket,** Mustard Yellow, Striping, Drop Tray, 10 X 6 1/4 X 5 In. ............................................ 69.00
**Wooden,** Covered With Early Wallpaper, Small Pattern, 14 X 7 X 6 In. .................................. 88.00
**Writing,** 6-Drawer, Mother-Of-Pearl Birds, Lacquer, 9 X 12 1/2 X 10 In. ........................... 335.00
**Zebra Design,** Red & Mustard, Small ........................................................................................ 95.00

**BOY SCOUT, Ashtray,** 1969 National Jamboree, 1969, Round ............................................... 6.00
**Badge,** Eagle Scout, Miniature Eagle, Sterling Silver ............................................................... 55.00
**Badge,** Merit, On Sash, 1933, Set Of 15 ...................................................................................... 18.00
**Badge,** Valley Forge Council ........................................................................................................ 20.00
**Binoculars,** Boxed .......................................................................................................................... 12.00
**Book,** Billy, 1916 ............................................................................................................................. 18.00
**Book,** Indoor Hobby Trails, Hardbound, 1939 ............................................................................ 5.00
**Card,** Membership, 1931 ................................................................................................................ 4.00
**Compass,** Official, Taylor Instruments, C.1940, Boxed .......................................................... 12.50
**Compass,** 1930s, 2 In. ................................................................................................................... 10.00
**Compass,** 1948, Original Box ....................................................................................................... 8.50
**Diary,** 1931, Not Used .................................................................................................................... 7.00
**Drum,** Toy.Metal, Pat.1908 ........................................................................................................... 38.00
**Handbook,** Master's, 1956 ............................................................................................................ 3.00
**Hat Band,** Leather .......................................................................................................................... 12.00
**Key Ring & Tag,** National Staff Emblem .................................................................................... 8.00
**Kit,** Fire Making, 1930s ................................................................................................................. 12.00
**Kit,** First Aid, Tin Box, Contents ................................................................................................. 10.00
**Knife,** Brass Slide, Buckle, & Whistle ........................................................................................ 25.00
**Knife,** With Chain, Germany ......................................................................................................... 12.00
**Merit Badge,** Swimming, Tan Square .......................................................................................... 3.50
**Mug,** Seal, Milk Glass ................................................................................................................... 2.00
**Neckerchief,** Slide, Bicentennial ................................................................................................ 1.00
**Patch,** Patrol Leader, 1960s ......................................................................................................... 1.00
**Patch,** 50th Anniversary Jubilee Camporee, 1960 .................................................................... 2.00
**Pin,** Lapel, Hand Sign .................................................................................................................... 1.00
**Sash,** Merit Badge, 25 Crimped Edge Badges ......................................................................... 60.00
**Scarf,** National Jamboree, Irvine Ranch, California, 1953 ....................................................... 6.00
**Seal,** Iceland, 1960 ........................................................................................................................ .75
**Sun Watch,** Compass & Sundial, 1921 ...................................................................................... 16.00
**Yearbook,** 1915, 243 Pages ............................................................................. 25.00 To 30.00

*Bradley & Hubbard Manufacturing Company made lamps and other metal
objects in Meriden, Connecticut, around the turn of the century.*

**BRADLEY & HUBBARD, Bookends,** Dante & Homer, Signed ............................................. 45.00
**Bookends,** Lion Design, Brass Finish ............................................................ 25.00
**Bookends,** Profile Of Roosevelt, Bronze, 4 1/2 X 6 1/4 In. ............................... 100.00
**Bookends,** Ships In Relief, Brass, Signed .................................................. 45.00
**Chandelier,** 3-Light, Kerosene, Brass, 1896 .......................................... 1000.00
**Desk Set,** Green Enameled Design On Brass, Signed, 5 Piece ........................ 150.00
**Desk Set,** Letter Knife, Pen Tray, Rocking Blotter, Brass ............................. 50.00
**Figurine,** The Beginner, Boy Smoking Cigarette .................................... 450.00
**Inkwell,** Art Deco, Signed, 4 In.Square ............................................. 37.50
**Inkwell,** 2 Hole, Lid ........................................................................ 55.00
**Lamp,** Country Store, Brass ........................................................... 150.00
**Lamp,** Dome Shade, Victorian Style Base, Signed ................................ 650.00
**Lamp,** Floor, Mica Shade, Dated April, 1924, 62 In. ............................. 590.00
**Lamp,** Gone With The Wind, No.23353 ............................................. 300.00
**Lamp,** Gone With The Wind, Red Satin Glass Globe ............................ 450.00
**Lamp,** Green Marbled Panels, Brass Acanthus Leaves, 19 In. ............... 595.00
**Lamp,** Kerosene, Embossed Flowers, 7 1/4 In., Pair ........................... 250.00
**Lamp,** Oil, Cranberry Shade .......................................................... 225.00
**Lamp,** Student, Single ................................................................. 565.00
**Lamp,** Studio, Seminudes Over Slag Panels, 42 In. ........................... 250.00
**Lamp,** Table, Caramel Slag Panels, Spelter Frame, Signed ................. 365.00
**Lamp,** Table, Carmel Slag Paneled Shade, Signed ............................. 385.00
**Lamp,** Table, Orange & White Slag Glass, Signed ............................. 445.00
**Lamp,** Table, Ribbed Paneled Shade, Signed .................................... 600.00
**Lamp,** Table, 8 Caramel Slag Panels, Signed, 19 In. ......................... 350.00
**Lamp,** 3 Shade, Chipped Jewels, Lead Around, Signed ...................... 700.00
**Smoking Stand,** Petal Design Base, Match Holder, Signed ................... 35.00
**Tray,** Girls In Tub, Iron, Signed, 7 1/2 In.Long ................................. 35.00

*Brass has been used for decorative pieces and useful tablewares since ancient times. It is an alloy of copper, zinc, and other metals.*

**BRASS, see also Bell, Tool, Trivet, etc.**
**BRASS, Andirons,** C.1800, 23 X 18 1/2 In. ...................................... 200.00
**Ashtray,** Face Of The Devil, 4 1/2 X 6 In. ....................................... 47.50
**Ashtray,** Figural, Frog, Hinged, Marked China ............................... 14.00
**Ashtray,** Pettit's Eye Salve, 1807-1907 ......................................... 6.00
**Ashtray,** Shell With Anchor, 4 3/4 In.Tall ...................................... 16.00
**Ashtray,** Trench Art, 1918, German .............................................. 10.00
**Bed Warmer,** Engraved Floral Hinged Lid, Maple Handle, C.1800, 46 In. ........... 225.00
**Bed Warmer,** Tulip Design, Handle Painted Black, 41 1/2 In. .............. 200.00
**Bed,** Doll, Tall Headboard, Vertical Rounds, 29 1/2 X 19 1/2 In. ......... 495.00
**Beverage Pot,** Handmade, Signed, Russian .................................... 49.00
**Bleeder,** 2 Blades, Signed Borwick, 3 In. ...................................... 75.00
**Bookends,** Clipper Ship, Marked, 1928 ......................................... 20.00
**Bookends,** German Shepherd Dog, 9 In. ........................................ 172.00
**Boot Jack,** Beetle, 10 In. ............................................................ 72.50
**Bowl,** Dragon, Engraved, Chinese, Marked, 7 1/2 X 4 In. ................. 47.50
**Bowl,** Oriental, Enameled Flowers, Marked China, 4 1/2 X 9 1/2 In.Diam. ....... 100.00
**Box,** Cigar, 3 Stars On Top, Belonged To General George Patton ....... 75.00
**Box,** Enameled Birds, Insects, Trees, Marked, 3 X 4 In. ................... 45.00
**Box,** Snuff, Artillery Officer's, Book Shape, C.1865, 3 X 2 1/8 In. ...... 95.00
**Box,** Stamp, Engraved, China ...................................................... 15.00
**Bucket,** Handwrought, Marked, B.C., 17 1/2 In.Diam. ...................... 200.00
**Bucket,** Spun, Iron Bail Handle, 1866, 9 X 12 1/2 In. ...................... 85.00
**Burner,** Bunsen, 8 In. ................................................................ 15.00
**Candleholder,** Church, Claw Feet, 16 In., Pair ............................... 150.00
**Candleholder,** Cobra Shape, 8 In. ................................................ 45.00
**Candlestick,** Barrel Shape Sockets, Twisted Stems, C.1875, 12 In., Pair ....... 95.00
**Candlestick,** Beehive, C.1840, English, Pair .................................. 85.00
**Candlestick,** Brass, Chinese, Small, Pair ...................................... 45.00
**Candlestick,** Dore, Marble Base, Figure Of Man & Woman, 14 In., Pair ..... 160.00
**Candlestick,** Double, Art Nouveau, Maiden With Flowing Hair, 13 In. ... 75.00

| | |
|---|---|
| **Candlestick,** English, Square Base, C.1800, 6 In. | 225.00 |
| **Candlestick,** French, Embossed Lily-Of-The-Valley, 7 1/4 In., Pair | 195.00 |
| **Candlestick,** French, Figural, Griffin, 7 1/2 X 8 In.Long, Pair | 140.00 |
| **Candlestick,** Leaf, 7 3/8 In. | 20.00 |
| **Candlestick,** Lift & Thumbrest Handle, 4 3/4 X 5 1/2 In.Diam. | 62.00 |
| **Candlestick,** Peacock, 6 1/4 In. | 20.00 |
| **Candlestick,** Push-Up, The Diamond Prince Pattern, 12 In., Pair | 250.00 |
| **Candlestick,** Queen Anne, Matching Vertical Snuffer Stand, Brass, Pair | 2200.00 |
| **Candlestick,** Queen Anne, Petal Base, 18th Century, 6 In. | 250.00 |
| **Candlestick,** Russian, Square Base, 4 Triangular Feet, 10 1/2 In., Pair | 165.00 |
| **Candlestick,** Shaped Foot, 1735-50, 6 1/2 In. | 225.00 |
| **Candlestick,** Soldiers Holding Candleholder, Pair | 110.00 |
| **Candlestick,** Traveler's, Brass, Pair | 35.00 |
| **Candlestick,** Wall Mounted, Signed E.Muller, Paris | 45.00 |
| **Chandelier,** C.1912, 48 Prisms | 175.00 |
| **Clamp,** C, Copper Screw, 12 In. | 20.00 |
| **Coffeepot,** Russian, Long Spout, Covered, 9 In. | 35.00 |
| **Cross,** Opens To Hold Relic, European, 6 3/4 In. | 185.00 |
| **Dispenser,** Stamp, Round | 4.00 |
| **Door Knocker,** Figural, Robert Burns, Small | 16.00 |
| **Door Knocker,** Lady's Hand Holding Mirror | 25.00 |
| **Door Knocker,** Woodpecker | 10.00 |
| **Doorbell,** Twist Model | 55.00 |
| **Doorknob,** Embossed | 5.00 |
| **Doorstop,** Alligator, 12 In. | 8.00 |
| **Doorstop,** German Shepherd, Marble Base | 85.00 |
| **Doorstop,** Stork, 13 1/2 In. | 135.00 |
| **Ewer,** Hand-Hammered, Copper Trim, Double Eagle Mark, 6 In. | 40.00 |
| **Fender,** Fireplace, Centennial, 40 X 12 X 8 1/4 In. | 150.00 |
| **Figurine,** Bird, Pedestal, Oxidized, Signed, 6 In. | 145.00 |
| **Fireplace Tools,** 18th Century, Shovel 23 1/2 In., Tongs 24 1/2 In. | 95.00 |
| **Flask,** Pocket, Embossed, Mirox Glass Cleaner | 7.00 |
| **Footrest,** Shoeshine | 28.00 |
| **Frame,** Picture, Easel Back, Signed L. & T., 3 1/2 X 6 1/2 In. | 55.00 |
| **Frame,** Raised Top, Easel Back & Hanger, 2 1/4 X 1 5/8 In. | 45.00 |
| **Glove Warmer,** Wooden Handle, 6 In. | 35.00 |
| **Hook,** Jamb, 18th Century, Pair | 75.00 |
| **Horn,** Fox Hunting, Copper, English | 35.00 |
| **Horseshoe,** Simmons Liver Regulator, Take In Time, 5 1/2 X 6 1/2 In. | 50.00 |
| **Humidor,** Lined, La Palinas Senators | 20.00 |
| **Incense Burner,** Oriental ............................................................. *Illus* | 700.00 |
| **Inkwell,** Glass Bottle, Covered, 4 1/2 In.Square | 45.00 |
| **Inkwell,** Lion Head, Double, 11 In. | 40.00 |
| **Inkwell,** Traveling | 15.00 |
| **Jardiniere,** Onion Shape, Lion & Ring Handles, 19th Century, 12 In. | 160.00 |
| **Jardiniere,** Russian, Elephant Head Handles, Czar Mark, 11 X 9 1/2 In. | 140.00 |
| **Jardiniere,** Sphinx On 3 Sides, Footed | 35.00 |
| **Kettle,** American, C.1860 | 85.00 |
| **Kettle,** Jelly, Iron Handle, Copper Rivets, Rolled Rim, 13 In. | 110.00 |
| **Kettle,** Tea, Amber Handle, Button Feet | 69.00 |
| **Lantern,** Bobby, Dietz, Bull's-Eye | 75.00 |
| **Letter Opener,** Dragon, 9 In. | 40.00 |
| **Lock,** Figural, Dog Key | 65.00 |
| **Match Holder & Ashtray,** Black Porter Carrying Bags | 45.00 |
| **Match Safe,** McKinley, Figural | 100.00 |
| **Measure,** Powder & Shot, Wood Handle, James Dixon & Sons | 65.00 |
| **Mold,** Bullet | 8.50 |
| **Mold,** Candle, 5 X 12 X 4 1/2 In. | 35.00 |
| **Mortar & Pestle,** Relief Faces, Stamped Spain, 3 X 4 3/4 In., 2 Pounds | 60.00 |
| **Mortar & Pestle,** 3 In. | 80.00 |
| **Padlock,** Embossed International Harvester Co. | 50.00 |
| **Pail,** Spun, American Brass Kettle Co., 10 In. | 25.00 |
| **Pin Tray,** Art Nouveau, Female Head With Flowing Hair | 65.00 |

Pin Tray, Enameled, Signed A.Farre, Egyptian Design ........................................................ 150.00
Planter, 19th Century, Russian, Signed, 12 1/2 In.Diam. ...................................................... 110.00
Plate, Collection ................................................................................................................ 20.00
Pocket, Match, Lady's Button Shoe, Nickel Plated, 5 1/4 In. .............................................. 45.00
Pot, Russian, Handmade, Czarist Period, Double Eagle Mark, 7 X 8 In. .............................. 85.00
Probe, Grain, Seedburo Equipment Co., Chicago, 50 In.Long .............................................. 95.00
Rack, Book, Expandable, Medallion Design, 12 In. .............................................................. 26.00
Rack, Letter, Plated, Art Nouveau, Owl Design, 7 X 5 In. .................................................... 28.00
Samovar, Dated 1857, Marked, 18 In. ................................................................................ 310.00
Samovar, Russian, Crown Mark, Miniature ........................................................................ 65.00
Samovar, 14 Medals Imprinted On Front, Russian, Electrified ............................................ 275.00
Saucepan, Iron Handle, 10 1/4 Diam., 5 1/4 Deep, 10 In. Long .......................................... 165.00
Screen, Fire, Folding, Oriental Woman In Center, 48 In. .................................................... 118.00
Shoehorn, 9 1/2 In. .......................................................................................................... 28.00
Slipper Chest, Slant Top, 8 People In Pub, English, 16 X 11 X 8 In. ..................................... 139.00
Spittoon, Marked Property Of Pullmam Silver Palace Co. .................................................. 145.00
Spittoon, Pony Express Chewing Tobacco Cut Plug, 11 In. ................................................ 85.00
Spool Rack, 3 Tiers, 19th Century, English, 12 1/2 In. ................................................*Illus* 230.00
Spoon, Cow Terminal, 6 3/4 In. ........................................................................................ 55.00
Stand, Plate, Collar Base & Top, C Shape Legs, 6 1/4 X 5 In.Diam. ..................................... 35.00
Sugar & Creamer, Cranberry Lining, Russian ................................................................... 125.00
Tamper, Tobacco, Figural, Shoe ........................................................................................ 20.00
Teapot, Amber Handle & 4 Feet, 11 X 10 In. ..................................................................... 120.00
Teapot, Raised Design, Two Jewels, Signed, Chinese ........................................................ 35.00
Teapot, Swing Handle, Domed, Marked E.Lewis, Lexington, Ky., C.1860 ............................ 375.00
Teapot, Swing Handle, Gooseneck, J.Ebert, 7 In. ............................................................. 385.00
Toothpick, Footed, Hunter, Dogs, Rabbit, Tree, In Releif .................................................. 15.00
Trivet, Figural Lyre, Footed, C.1800 ................................................................................. 65.00
Trumpet, Parabolic Ear, Painted ...................................................................................... 110.00
Watch Stand, C.1840, Ivory .............................................................................................. 185.00
Whistle, Steam, Tri-Tone, Buckeye Brass Works, Dayton, Ohio, 12 In. ............................... 295.00
Whistle, Steamboat, Mounted On Walnut Base, 19 1/2 X 4 1/2 In. .................................... 1975.00
      BREAD PLATE, see various Pressed Glass patterns

BRETBY, Figurine, Lady, Brown Tones, Derbyshire, 1891, Henry Toth, 30 In. ....................... 595.00
Vase, Carved Bamboo Pattern, C.1895, Japanese Scenes, 10 In., Pair ............................... 175.00

*Brides' baskets of glass were usually one-of-a-kind novelties made in
American and European glass factories. They were especially popular about
1880 when the decorated basket was often given as a wedding gift. Cut glass
baskets were popular after 1890. All brides' baskets lost favor about 1905.*

BRIDE'S BASKET, Cased Apricot Shaded To Clear Green, Enameled, Holder ....................... 325.00
Fern & Daisy Insert, Opalescent, Silver Plate Frame, Signed ............................................. 195.00

Brass, Incense Burner, Oriental

Brass, Spool Rack, 3 Tiers,
19th Century, English, 12 1/2 In.

Hand-Painted Flowers, White Beading, Silver Plate Frame ............................................ 225.00
Pink To Custard, Silver Plate Holder, Canada, 10 3/4 In. ............................................ 160.00
Pleated Edge, Enameled Flowers, White Outside, Holder, 11 In. .................................. 325.00
Ruffled Bowl, Enameled Flowers, Silver Plate Base .................................................... 225.00
Ruffled Cranberry Bowl, Silver Plate Holder .............................................................. 135.00
Ruffled Edge, Quilted, Opalescent Blue, 7 In.Square .................................................. 75.00
Ruffled Edge, White Exterior, Shaded Pink, 11 In.Diam. ............................................ 100.00
Ruffled Insert, Seaweed Pattern, Silver Plate Holder .................................................. 110.00
Ruffled Optic, Silver Plate Holder, Blue Opalescent .................................................. 145.00
Ruffled, Emerald To White, Silver Plate Holder, 10 In. .............................................. 145.00
Ruffled, Pink Overlay & Inside, 4 1/2 X 4 1/2 In.Diam. ............................................ 65.00
Spatter, Rose Overlay, Mica Flakes, Silver Plate Holder .............................................. 385.00
White Overlay, Gold Trim, Blue Enamels, 8 3/4 In. .................................................... 79.00

BRIDE'S BOWL, Crimped, Blue, Clear Overlay ............................................................ 55.00
Hand-Painted Pansies, Butterscotch Satin Glass ........................................................ 250.00
Ruffled & Fluted, Cased White Shading To Pink, 11 In. .............................................. 70.00
White To Pink, Enameled Daisies, Rockford Silver Frame ............................................ 150.00

> Bristol glass was made in Bristol, England, after the 1700s. The
> Bristol glass most often seen today is a Victorian lightweight opaque glass
> that is often blue. Some of the glass was decorated with enamels.

BRISTOL, Bottle, Perfume, Petticoat Stopper, Enameled Storks, Tan, Pair ...................... 95.00
Bottle, Scent, Children On Branch, Bird's Nest With Eggs, 9 1/4 In. .............................. 40.00
Cookie Jar, Silver Plate Top, Enameled, Translucent Blue, 6 1/4 In. ............................ 110.00
Cookie Jar, Silver Plate Trim, Enameled Flowers, Lavender, 6 3/4 In. .......................... 135.00
Cracker Jar, Red Poppies, Blue, Green, Silver Lid ...................................................... 85.00
Epergne, Pedestal Base, 2 Section Ruffled Rim, Blue, 7 X 13 In. ................................ 52.00
Jar, Sweetmeat, Enameled Design, Silver Plate Rim, Gray, 5 1/4 In. ............................ 75.00
Vase, Apricot Ground, Hand-Painted Flowers, 12 1/2 In. ............................................ 35.00
Vase, Blue, Gray Flowers, Baluster, 12 X 4 In. .......................................................... 45.00
Vase, Cherub, 12 In. ............................................................................................ 60.00
Vase, Floral, White Enamel, Gray, Gold, 7 1/2 In., Pair .............................................. 45.00
Vase, Fluted Top, Pink Lining, Enameled Flowers, 5 In., Pair ...................................... 65.00
Vase, Gold Design, 13 1/2 In., Pair ........................................................................ 195.00
Vase, Hand-Painted Daisies, 9 1/2 In. ...................................................................... 42.50
Vase, Hand-Painted Design, Tan Ground, 9 3/4 In. .................................................... 50.00
Vase, Pink, Enamel Butterflies & Flowers, 22 In., Pair ................................................ 225.00
Vase, White Flowers, Fawn Ground, 12 1/2 In., Pair .................................................. 125.00
    BRITANNIA, see Pewter

BRONZE, Ashtray, Hayes Equipment Mfg.Co., Wichita, Ks., Compressor In Relief .................. 10.00
Bookends, Anchor, Pair ........................................................................ 25.00 To 30.00
Bookends, Dante & Beatrice, Figural, Bust Style, 5 1/2 In. .......................................... 65.00
Bookends, Elephant Heads, Japanese, Signed ............................................................ 195.00
Bookends, Figural, Bengal Tiger, Rearing, China, 8 X 6 1/2 In. .................................... 425.00
Bookends, French, Rodin, Thinker, 7 In. .................................................................. 295.00
Bookends, German Shepherd, 9 In. .......................................................................... 172.00
Bookends, Indian, Full Feather Headdress .................................................................. 30.00
Bookends, Lincoln, Signed Cox ................................................................................ 65.00
Bookends, Scotty, Signed Edith Parsons .................................................................... 185.00
Bookends, Scotty, Signed J.B., 6 1/2 In. .................................................................. 125.00
Bookends, Sitting Bull .......................................................................................... 89.00
Bookends, T.Roosevelt, Profile, Ionic Columns, B & H, 6 1/4 In. .................................. 100.00
Bookends, Young Wisdom, Marked & Signed K.R.W., Nude Child Seated .......................... 75.00
Box, Covered, Figural, Standing Pig, 3 X 4 1/4 In. .................................................... 95.00
Box, Hinged Green Onyx Lid, Mermaid On Lid, Marked, 6 1/4 X 4 In. ............................ 225.00
Box, Lidded, Shape Of Standing Pig, 3 X 4 1/4 In. ........................................ 75.00 To 100.00
Bracelets, Slave, African ...................................................................................... 100.00
Brazier, 18th Century, Oriental .............................................................................. 195.00
Burner, Incense, Mythical Animal On Lid, 3 3/4 X 4 1/2 In. ........................................ 60.00
Bust, Baldwin, Indian Warrior, Signed, 8 1/4 In. ...................................................... 750.00
Bust, Cristophe Gabriel Allegrain, Woman Bather, 19 In. ............................................ 550.00

**Bust,** D.D.Franoz, Napoleon In Relief, Signed, 4 1/4 In. ............................................ 75.00
**Bust,** G.E.Bissell, Abraham Lincoln, Life Size, C.1895 .............................................. 3200.00
**Bust,** Henri A.Nelson, Young Woman, With Topknot Hair, C.1889 ................................ 1050.00
**Bust,** Iffland, Man, Marble Base, Signed, 9 In. ...................................................... 225.00
**Bust,** M.Geflowski, Queen Victoria, With Crown, Signed, 1901, 7 In. ............................ 195.00
**Bust,** M.Jose, Lady, Art Deco, Marble & Bronze, Signed, 15 In. ................................... 1350.00
**Bust,** Man, Bronze Base, Signed F.Barbedienne Fondeur, 11 In. ................................. 250.00
**Bust,** Raoul Larchet, Joan Of Arc, C.1895, Numbered, 14 X 16 In. ............................... 1150.00
**Bust,** Shakespeare, Signed Tiffany, 9 1/2 Pounds ................................................. 540.00
**Candelabra,** French, C.1800, 16 In., Pair ............................................................. 350.00
**Candlestick,** 5 Candle, Single Cherub Figure, 24 In., Pair .......................................... 950.00
**Cross,** Priest's, Russian Orthodox, 20th Century .................................................... 40.00
**Cuspidor,** Removable Top, 3 1/2 X 7 1/2 In.Diam. ................................................. 45.00
**Desk Set,** Figural, Pheasants In Various Positions, F.Gornik, 4 Piece ............................ 800.00
**Doorknob,** Art Nouveau Scrolled ...................................................................... 17.00
**Figurine,** A.Alexandre, Swallows In Brush, C.1870, 7 1/2 In. ...................................... 500.00
**Figurine,** Adrien-Etienne Gaudez, Woman, Pastoral, Marble Base, 28 In. ....................... 1600.00
**Figurine,** Albert Patrisse, Seated Nude, Butterfly On Finger, 22 In. .............................. 1350.00
**Figurine,** Aug.Moreau, Girl With Stick, Chasing Rooster, C.1880, 11 In. ........................ 2250.00
**Figurine,** Austria, Eagle, 4 3/4 X 3 1/4 In. ........................................................... 150.00
**Figurine,** Austria, Macaw, Perched On Stump, 19th Century, 12 In., Pair ...................... 1700.00
**Figurine,** Barye, Bear Playing On Its Back, Signed, 4 1/2 In. ..................................... 275.00
**Figurine,** Barye, Crocodile, 7 1/2 In. .................................................................. 600.00
**Figurine,** Barye, Horse Attacked By A Lion, Brown Patina, 15 1/2 In. ............................ 4750.00
**Figurine,** Barye, Hound Dog, Collar, 7 In. ............................................................ 265.00
**Figurine,** Barye, Joan Of Arc, 19th Century, 36 1/2 In. ............................................ 2250.00
**Figurine,** Barye, Peacock On Tree, Hollow, Signed, 3 1/2 In. ..................................... 375.00
**Figurine,** Barye, Tiger Devouring A Gavial, Marble Base, 10 3/4 In. .............................. 900.00
**Figurine,** Barye, Startled Hare, Greenish Brown Patina, 2 3/16 In. ............................... 300.00
**Figurine,** Bear Walking, Growling, Signed, Russian, 6 1/2 X 8 1/2 In. ........................... 465.00
**Figurine,** Besserdich, Boy With Pitcher & Ewer, Base, 6 1/4 In. .................................. 245.00
**Figurine,** Besserdich, Vienna, La Lecture Gaie, Signed, 7 In.Long ............................... 160.00
**Figurine,** Bonheur, Bear, Bronze Plinth, Signed, Large .............................................. 450.00
**Figurine,** Bonheur, Bull, Greenish Brown Patina, 20 In. ............................................ 2200.00
**Figurine,** Bonheur, Fox, Peers Into Ledge For Food, 21 X 10 In. ................................. 2950.00
**Figurine,** Buffalo, Marble Base, 13 In. ................................................................ 695.00
**Figurine,** C.Anfrie, Young Woman Knitting, 3 Pieces, 25 In. ...................................... 950.00
**Figurine,** C.DeBlezer, Lady In Klismos Chair, 12 1/2 X 11 In. .................................... 250.00
**Figurine,** C.Humphriss, Indian On Horse, Dated 1904, 17 X 15 In.Long ........................ 2450.00
**Figurine,** C.Masson & Susse Fes Edes, Pheasant, 27 In. ......................................... 550.00
**Figurine,** C.Perron, Illuminated, Lavender Shade, C.1900, 26 1/2 In. ........................... 875.00
**Figurine,** Cain, Donkey, Marble Base, 6 1/2 X 5 3/4 In. ........................................... 575.00
**Figurine,** Cana, Elk, Head Lifted, Marble Base, France, 7 1/2 In. ................................. 550.00
**Figurine,** Cat, Seated On Rug With Ball Of Yarn, 4 1/2 X 6 1/2 In. ............................... 265.00
**Figurine,** Chemin, Boar Sitting On Haunches, Signed, 7 1/4 In. ................................. 235.00
**Figurine,** Chemin, Boar, Sitting On Haunches, Signed, 7 X 7 In. ................................. 285.00
**Figurine,** Claude Michel, Wood Sprite, Marble Base, 24 In. ....................................... 700.00
**Figurine,** Conille, Napoleon, Seated On Horse, France, 14 1/2 In. ............................... 425.00
**Figurine,** Cossack On Horseback, 19th Century, Russian, 10 3/8 In. ............................. 750.00
**Figurine,** Coustou, Man In Loincloth, Rearing Stallion, 19 1/2 In. ................................ 450.00
**Figurine,** De La Brierre, Horse, C.1870, 16 X 16 In. ................................................ 2200.00
**Figurine,** Diane, 22 In. .................................................................................. 400.00
**Figurine,** E.Butti, Knight, Medieval Tunic, Carrying Shield, 38 1/2 In. ........................... 900.00
**Figurine,** E.Drouot, Art Nouveau Woman, Marble Base, C.1900, 20 1/2 In. .................... 1150.00
**Figurine,** E.Gruet, Eve, Nude, Head In Hands, Foundry Mark, 7 In. .............................. 750.00
**Figurine,** E.Villanis, Sappho, A Muse, Paris Seal, 20th Century .................................. 2000.00
**Figurine,** Elephant, Roman Bronze Works, N.Y., Brown Patina, 9 1/4 In. ....................... 350.00
**Figurine,** Elephant, Trunk Raised, Ivory Tusks, Man, 4 1/4 X 3 In. ............................... 190.00
**Figurine,** Elephant, 8 X 5 In. .......................................................................... 225.00
**Figurine,** Eli Harvey, Stag, On Rocky Base, 15 1/2 In. ............................................ 700.00
**Figurine,** Emile Bouvier, Dante, Full Figure, 26 In. ................................................. 1175.00
**Figurine,** Emile Louis Picault, A Harvester, C.1900, 25 1/2 In. ................................... 1100.00
**Figurine,** Emile Louis Picault, Blacksmith, 19th Century, 29 In. .................................. 2250.00

**Figurine,** F.Pautrot, Parrot, Poised To Catch Butterfly, Signed, 10 In. ........................................ 650.00
**Figurine,** F.Pautrot, Sandpiper Holding Sea Worm In Beak, 6 1/2 In. ................................... 400.00
**Figurine,** Fontana, Indian, Brown & Green Patina, 17 3/4 In. ............................................ 1700.00
**Figurine,** France, Bird In Flight, Brown Patina, C.1930, 13 In. ......................................... 3250.00
**Figurine,** France, Cupid, Forging An Arrow, 19th Century, 10 In. ..................................... 400.00
**Figurine,** Fratin, Goat, Reclining, Signed, Small ............................................................ 128.00
**Figurine,** French, Sans Famille, Orphaned Itinerant Musician, 19 In. ............................. 1300.00
**Figurine,** G.Tionet, Clown, Ivory Head, Playing Instrument, 4 3/4 In. ........................... 265.00
**Figurine,** Georgio Sommer, Nude Baby, Crawling, 6 In. ................................................ 185.00
**Figurine,** Gibson Girl, Mounted On White Marble Base, 5 In. ......................................... 150.00
**Figurine,** Girl, Dore & Ivory, Signed, 7 3/4 In. ............................................................... 725.00
**Figurine,** Grace Helen Talbot, Nude Woman, Arms Extended, 1922, 17 In. ..................... 950.00
**Figurine,** H.Darsow, Young Buck Grazing, Green Patina, 11 1/4 In. .............................. 400.00
**Figurine,** Hagenauer, Rowboat, Movable Oarlocks, 2 Oars, Vienna, 4 In. ...................... 150.00
**Figurine,** Hans Muller, Woman Carrying A Basket, 20th Century, 17 In. ........................ 600.00
**Figurine,** Harriet W.Frishmuth, The Star, Nude Female, 20 In. ....................................... 2500.00
**Figurine,** Humphries, Dance Leader, Indian Beating Tom-Tom ...................................... 1200.00
**Figurine,** Indian On Horseback, Greenish Black Patina, 19 In. ....................................... 2250.00
**Figurine,** Ivory, Art Deco, Preiss, 8 1/2 In. ..................................................................... 2800.00
**Figurine,** J.Cauffe, Semidraped Nude Woman Holding A Letter, 28 In. ........................... 200.00
**Figurine,** J.E.Masson, Retriever With Bird, 19th Century, 18 1/2 In. .............................. 1900.00
**Figurine,** J.Germanin, Allegorical, Young Man, C.1900, 39 1/2 In. ............................... 3000.00
**Figurine,** Jean-Leon Gerome, La Joyeuse De Boules, Gilt, 32 In. ................................... 2500.00
**Figurine,** Johan Axel Wetterlund, Tiger, C.1900, 15 1/4 In. ........................................... 350.00
**Figurine,** Kauba, Arab On Camel, Hand-Painted, Signed, 5 1/2 In. ................................ 695.00
**Figurine,** Kauba, Little Finger, Multicolor Indian, Signed, 7 1/2 In. ............................... 495.00
**Figurine,** Knight In Suit Of Armor & An Angel, 14 3/4 X 14 X 7 In. .............................. 1475.00
**Figurine,** L.Pilet, Indian Maid, Holding Weapons, Signed, 19th Century ........................ 200.00
**Figurine,** LeVasseur, Loincloth Clad Man With Sword, 15 In. ....................................... 600.00
**Figurine,** Longhorn Steer, Splayed Legs, Signed CMR, 7 1/4 In.Long .......................... 400.00
**Figurine,** M.Moreau, La Source, Allegorical Female, 26 3/8 In. ..................................... 2500.00
**Figurine,** Max Kruse, Nenikhkamen, Nude Male Runner, 23 X 19 In. ........................... 1200.00
**Figurine,** Moigniez, Bird ................................................................................................ 650.00
**Figurine,** Moigniez, Egret, Wading, Black Base, 19 In. .................................................. 1500.00
**Figurine,** Moigniez, Pointing Hound, Collared, 16 1/2 In. .............................................. 850.00
**Figurine,** Moigniez, Sandpiper, Hunting Fish In Pond, Signed, 11 In. ............................ 525.00
**Figurine,** Moigniez, Standing Bull, 3 1/2 X 2 3/4 In. ..................................................... 275.00
**Figurine,** Moigniez, Terrier Dogs Ratting, 4 1/2 X 3 1/2 In. .......................................... 495.00
**Figurine,** Moigniez, Wading Egret, Black Base, 19 1/2 In. ............................................. 1700.00
**Figurine,** Nude Youth Running, Carrying Olive Branch, 23 X 19 In. ............................... 1450.00
**Figurine,** Nude, Art Nouveau, Artist Signed, 10 In. ....................................................... 375.00
**Figurine,** P.E.Hebert, Le Champion, Sculling Champion, 32 In. ...................................... 1950.00
**Figurine,** P.J.Mene, Bull, Signed, 6 X 3 1/2 In. ........................................................... 550.00
**Figurine,** P.J.Mene, Huntsman & Hound, 18 1/2 In. ..................................................... 2500.00
**Figurine,** P.J.Mene, Huntsman, Signed, 26 In. .............................................................. 2500.00
**Figurine,** P.J.Mene, Irish Setter, Thistle Of Debris, 11 In. ............................................ 750.00
**Figurine,** P.J.Mene, Mare & Foal, Dark Brown Patina, 6 3/4 In. .................................... 2600.00
**Figurine,** P.J.Mene, Mare & Stallion, 5 X 3 In. ............................................................. 750.00
**Figurine,** P.J.Mene, Pointer & Setter, 5 X 1 1/2 In. ...................................................... 450.00
**Figurine,** P.J.Mene, Whippet, Shaped Base, 3 1/4 In. ................................................... 150.00
**Figurine,** P.L.Kowalczewski, Danae, Gilt Bronze, 8 7/8 In. ........................................... 3000.00
**Figurine,** P.Lecourtier, Horse & Jockey, 19th Century, 16 1/2 In. .................................. 1600.00
**Figurine,** Panther, Marble Base, Gorham Foundries, 15 1/2 X 4 3/4 In. ......................... 450.00
**Figurine,** Paul Dubois, Florentine Singer, C.1865, 44 In. .............................................. 4000.00
**Figurine,** Peacock, Chinese, 23 In. ............................................................................... 940.00
**Figurine,** Pierre Julien, Girl With A Goat, Marble Base, C.1900, 46 In. ........................... 2750.00
**Figurine,** Pitkanen, Eagle, Signed, 14 In. ..................................................................... 550.00
**Figurine,** Pitkanen, Eagle, 16 1/2 In.Wingspan, Signed, 14 1/2 In. .............................. 450.00
**Figurine,** R.E.Laglad, African Gazelle, Signed, Stand, 15 X 13 In. ............................... 1000.00
**Figurine,** R.Edeglud, Elan, Wooden Base, Signed, 15 X 13 In. ..................................... 1000.00
**Figurine,** Remington, Bronco Buster ............................................................................. 3200.00
**Figurine,** Remington, The Mountainman, Signed, 2. 1/4 In. .......................................... 3200.00
**Figurine,** Rousseau, Bare-Bosomed Dancer, Tambourine, Signed, 26 In. ...................... 3000.00

**Figurine,** Running Elephant, 4 X 3 In. ...................................................................................................... 400.00
**Figurine,** Russell, Bear & Cubs ...................................................................................................... 975.00
**Figurine,** S.Vander-Sharter, Dore, Signed, 8 3/4 In. .................................................................. 275.00
**Figurine,** Samurai On Horse, Battle Dress, C.1900, 17 1/2 In. ................................................ 3300.00
**Figurine,** Schmidt-Felling, Boy Lighting Cigarette, , Signed, 7 3/4 In. .................................. 395.00
**Figurine,** Scotty, Wirehaired, 2 1/2 X 4 In. .................................................................................. 37.50
**Figurine,** V.Szczeblewski, Mousse Siffleur, Signed, 17 In. ...................................................... 500.00
**Figurine,** Victor Seifert, Nude Woman, Broken Sword, Signed, 32 In.Long ........................... 2350.00
**Figurine,** Vienna, Black & White Bulldog, 5 Piece Band, 1 1/2 In. ........................................ 485.00
**Figurine,** Vienna, Black Boy With 10 Piece Band, 1 In. ............................................................ 225.00
**Figurine,** Vienna, Cat In Chair, Reading Paper .......................................................................... 85.00
**Figurine,** Vienna, Cat On Basket Of Flowers, 1 1/2 In. ............................................................ 85.00
**Figurine,** Vienna, Cat On Pot .......................................................................................................... 85.00
**Figurine,** Vienna, Frog On Chair, 1 3/4 In. .................................................................................. 85.00
**Figurine,** Vienna, Owl On A Book, 4 1/4 In. ................................................................................ 75.00
**Figurine,** Vienna, Rug Merchant, Offering Rug, Marble Base, 5 In. ...................................... 450.00
**Figurine,** Vienna, Standing Lion, Green Onyx Base, 6 X 8 In. ................................................ 295.00
**Figurine,** Vienna, Waltzing Cats, Small ...................................................................................... 125.00
**Figurine,** Vienna, 3 Mice On Carrot .............................................................................................. 85.00
**Figurine,** Wolf Caught In A Trap, Marble Base, 5 1/2 X 4 1/2 In. .......................................... 1050.00
**Figurine,** Woman, Victorian, 18 X 9 In. ...................................................................................... 975.00
**Figurine,** Zelezny, Young Man With Cigar In Mouth, Vienna, Signed .................................... 89.00
**Figurine,** 19th Century, 29 1/2 X 29 In. ...................................................................... *Illus* 1400.00
**Group,** Barye, Lion & Serpent, Reddish Patina, 7 In. ................................................ *Illus* 1100.00
**Group,** Barye, Panther Devouring Muntjac Deer, 9 In. ............................................ *Illus* 400.00

Bronze, Figurine, 19th Century, 29 1/2 X 29 In.

Bronze, Groups, Bayre, from left to right, Panther Devouring Muntjac Deer, Lion & Serpent

Bronze, Vase, French, Shell Mounted On Gilt Base, 16 In.

Group, E.Napoli, Alexander The Great, Equestrian, 19 1/2 In. .................................................. 520.00
Group, Guillaume Coustou, Horses & Trainers, 19th Century, 23 In. ........................................ 950.00
Group, J.Hatfield, Allegorical, U.S.Leading Americans, 31 In. ........................................ 2250.00
Group, P.J.Mene, Stallion & Dog, Saddled, Shrub & Rock Base, 27 In. ...................... 4250.00
Group, P.Lenordez, Three Horses, Galloping, Leaping, 30 In. .................................... 2500.00
Humidor, Sterling Overlay, Silhouette Of Golfer, Signed, 6 In. .................................. 150.00
Humidor, 6-Sided, Scrolls Of Danish History, Wooden Interior, C.1920 ...................... 75.00
Incense Burner, Japanese, 18th Century, 6 1/4 In. ............................................................ 225.00
Jardiniere, French, Bombe Shape, Enameled & Gilded, 12 1/2 In. ............................ 1300.00
Knife Rest, Vienna, Two Mice ............................................................................................ 265.00
Lamp, Cloisonne Overlay, Marked Japan, 22 In. .............................................................. 195.00
Lantern, Hall, American Gothic, Traces Of Gilding, C.1830, 2 X 22 In. .................... 225.00
Match Striker, Monk, English ............................................................................................ 25.00
Paperweight, Prudential, 1925 .......................................................................................... 55.00
Penholder, Pointer Dog On Marble, American, 6 1/4 In. ................................................ 90.00
Plaque, Alsatian Woman, Scene, Signed ........................................................................ 65.00
Plaquette, Barye, Pointer, Black Patina, 5 3/4 In. .......................................................... 375.00
Plate, Signed Tiffany, 9 In. ................................................................................................ 98.00
Porringer, Handled, Reticulated, Signed, Oscar B.Bach, 13 X 8 1/2 In. ...................... 129.00
S.Vander-Sharter, Figurine, Dore, Signed, 8 3/4 In. ...................................................... 275.00
Seal, Woman With Old-Fashioned Riding Costume, 4 1/4 In. ........................................ 75.00
Sundial, B.Pike & Sons, N.Y.C., C.1840, 7 1/2 In.Diam. ................................................ 425.00
Tieback, Flower Shape, Set Of 12 .................................................................................... 100.00
Tray, Art Nouveau, Full Figure Girl, 6 1/4 In.Long ........................................................ 85.00
Urn, Japanese, Dragons & Birds, C.1870, 4 Feet, Pair .................................................. 4500.00
Vase, French, Shell Mounted On Gilt Base, 16 In. ................................................ *Illus* 2000.00
Vase, Japanese, Raised Water Plants, Swimming Carp, Signed, 11 1/2 In. ................ 325.00
Vase, Raised Foot, Applied Dragon, Bird, & Florals, Oriental, 30 In. .......................... 600.00
Vase, Sculptured Child Reaching For Lizard, Signed Moreau, 6 1/2 In. ...................... 495.00

*Brownies were first drawn in 1883 by Palmer Cox. They are
characterized by large round eyes, down-turned mouths, and skinny legs.*

BROWNIE, Bowling Pins, Palmer Cox, Complete Set .................................................... 385.00
Box, Cigar, Palmer Cox, Tin ................................................................................................ 20.00
Clip, Letter, Palmer Cox, Brownie Head, Pop Eyes, Mustache, 2 1/8 In. .................... 25.00
Cup & Saucer, Palmer Cox ................................................................................................ 19.50
Cup, Six Around Sides, Floral Engraving, 1866-99 ........................................................ 140.00
Figurine, Chinaman, Palmer Cox, C.1892 ...................................................................... 25.00
Lithograph, Palmer Cox, Musician, Wood, 8 In. .............................................................. 22.00
Marionette, Palmer Cox, Commercial .............................................................................. 75.00
Pin Tray, Palmer Cox .......................................................................................................... 11.00
Spoon, Palmer Cox, Sterling Silver, Set Of 4 ................................................................ 50.00
Stickpin, Palmer Cox .................................................................................. 12.00 To 15.00
Toothpick, Palmer Cox ........................................................................................................ 475.00

| | |
|---|---:|
| **Trade Card,** Palmer Cox, Set Of 6 | 10.00 |
| **Tray,** Palmer Cox, Ice Cream Advertising | 45.00 |

| | |
|---|---:|
| **BUCK ROGERS, Badge,** Solar Scout | 40.00 |
| **Book,** Pop-Up, 1935 | 150.00 |
| **Doom Comet** | 24.00 |
| **Game,** Card, All Fair, Boxed | 55.00 |
| **Pistol,** Atomic, Daisy | 200.00 |
| **Pistol,** Sonic Ray, Boxed | 50.00 |
| **Punch-Out,** Rubber Band Gun, 1940 | 35.00 |
| **Puzzle,** Inlay, 1952 | 35.00 |
| **Ray Gun,** Daisy, 1930s, Gun Metal Finish | 75.00 To 95.00 |
| **Ship,** Attack | 85.00 |
| **Space Gun,** 25th Century Disintegrator, Daisy Mfg. | 82.50 To 100.00 |
| **Spaceship,** Flash Blast, 1937, Tootsietoy | 35.00 |
| **Strato Kite,** Origial Envelope, 1946, 18 1/2 X 18 1/2 In. | 45.00 |
| **Supersonic Space Glasses,** 3 X 4 In., 1953 | 15.00 |
| **Watch,** Pocket, Ingraham | 200.00 |

*Buffalo pottery was made in Buffalo, New York, after 1902. The company was established by the Larkin Company, famous manufacturers of soap. The wares are marked with a picture of a buffalo and the date of manufacture. Deldare ware is the most famous pottery made at the factory. It is a khaki-colored transfer-decorated ware.*

| | |
|---|---:|
| **BUFFALO POTTERY DELDARE, Bowl,** Berry, Village Tavern, 4 1/2 X 9 1/4 In.Diam. | 425.00 |
| **Bowl,** Fallowfield Hunt, The Death, A.Stiller, 9 In. | 318.00 |
| **Bowl,** Nut, Ye Lion Inn | 365.00 |
| **Bowl,** Ye Olden Days, 9 In. | 350.00 |
| **Bowl,** Ye Village Tavern, Signed, 9 1/4 In.Diam. | 385.00 |
| **Candlestick,** Untitled, 1909, Signed, 9 In., Pair | 500.00 |
| **Candlestick,** 1909, Signed, 6 1/2 In., Pair | 650.00 |
| **Charge,** An Evening At Ye Lion Inn, Signed, 13 In. | 475.00 |
| **Creamer,** Breaking Cover, 2 3/4 In. | 85.00 |
| **Creamer,** Emerald, Dr.Syntax, Dairymaid, Signed | 300.00 |
| **Cup & Saucer,** Ye Olden Days | 165.00 To 220.00 |
| **Hair Receiver,** Ye Village Street | 275.00 To 295.00 |
| **Humidor,** Lid, Ye Lion Inn, Octagon | 545.00 To 745.00 |
| **Humidor,** There Was An Old Sailor, Signed, 8 In. | 950.00 |
| **Mug,** At The Three Pigeons, 4 1/2 In. | 175.00 |
| **Mug,** Fallowfield Hunt, 1909, Signed | 240.00 To 290.00 |
| **Mug,** Ye Lion Inn, 3 1/2 In. | 125.00 To 225.00 |
| **Mug,** Ye Lion Inn, 4 1/4 In. | 250.00 |
| **Pitcher,** Fallowfield Hunt, Octagonal, 9 1/2 In. | 495.00 |
| **Pitcher,** Manner Of Telling Stories, Signed, 6 In. | 339.00 |
| **Pitcher,** Tankard, The Controversy, 1909, Signed | 825.00 |
| **Plaque,** An Evening At Ye Lion Inn | 125.00 |
| **Plaque,** The Fallowfield Hunt, Signed, 12 In.Diam. | 400.00 |
| **Plate,** At Ye Lion Inn, 6 1/2 In.Diam. | 95.00 To 145.00 |
| **Plate,** Dr.Syntax Soliloquizing, Emerald, 7 1/2 In. | 310.00 |
| **Plate,** Fallowfield Hunt, Breaking Cover, 7 In. | 160.00 |
| **Plate,** Fallowfield Hunt, 6 1/4 In. | 130.00 |
| **Plate,** Fallowfield Hunt, 9 1/2 In. | 295.00 To 495.00 |
| **Plate,** Lion Inn, Gerhardt, 13 1/2 In. | 450.00 |
| **Plate,** The Death, 8 1/2 In.Diam. | 195.00 |
| **Plate,** Village Street, Signed, 7 1/4 In. | 85.00 |
| **Plate,** Ye Olden Days, 6 1/2 In. | 90.00 |
| **Plate,** Ye Olden Days, 9 1/2 In. | 140.00 |
| **Plate,** Ye Olden Times, Artist Signed, 9 In. | 265.00 |
| **Plate,** Ye Olden Times, 1908, 9 1/2 In. | 169.00 To 170.00 |
| **Plate,** Ye Town Crier, 8 In. | 115.00 |
| **Plate,** Ye Town Crier, 8 1/2 In. Diam. | 165.00 To 195.00 |

**Plate,** Ye Village Street, 1908, 7 In. ............................................................ 85.00 To 140.00
**Saucer,** Ye Olden Days ...................................................................................... 55.00
**Sugar & Creamer,** Scenes Of Village Life ...................................................... 295.00
**Sugar & Creamer,** Ye Olden Days ................................................................... 295.00
**Teapot,** Breaking Ground, Artist Signed ......................................................... 345.00
**Teapot,** Village Life In Ye Olden Days, 1909, Signed ................................... 300.00
**Tile,** Dr.Syntax, C.1911, 6 1/4 In. ................................................................... 300.00
**Tile,** Traveling In Ye Olden Days ..................................................... 145.00 To 175.00
**Tray,** Calling Card, Dr.Syntax Robbed Of Property ........................................ 300.00
**Tray,** Calling Card, Fallowfield Hunt ................................................................ 270.00
**Tray,** Calling Card, Ye Lion Inn ....................................................................... 225.00
**Tray,** Dr.Syntax, Sports, 12 X 9 In. ................................................ 725.00 To 850.00
**Tray,** Minuet, Signed Simpson, 9 X 12 In. ....................................................... 425.00
**Vase,** Village Schoolmaster, Parson, 8 1/4 In., Pair ..................................... 850.00
**Ye Village Gossips,** 10 In.Diam. ...................................................... 180.00 To 200.00

**BUFFALO POTTERY, Bowl,** Blue & White, C.1900, 9 X 5 X 3 In. ................... 50.00
**Bowl,** Yellow Roses, Green Ground, Gold Trim, 10 In. .................................... 85.00
**Butter Pat,** Blue Willow, 1911, Set Of 9 ......................................................... 55.00
**Cup & Saucer,** Child's, Teddy Bears ............................................................... 125.00
**Cup,** Bread & Milk, Blue Willow ....................................................................... 28.00
**Dish,** Feeding, Campbell Kids, Boy, Girl, & Doll ............................. 35.00 To 55.00
**Dish,** Feeding, Picture Of Cat, Brown Mark ..................................................... 35.00
**Game Set,** Platter & 4 Plates, Signed Beck .................................................... 195.00
**Match Holder & Ashtray,** Blue Trim, Transfer Of Woman .............................. 25.00
**Mug,** Celebration & Renunciation ..................................................................... 135.00
**Pitcher,** Blue, Gloriana, 1907 ........................................................................... 340.00
**Pitcher,** Bluebirds, 7 In. ................................................................................... 125.00
**Pitcher,** Cinderella .............................................................................................. 260.00
**Pitcher,** Cinderella, 1906, 6 In. ....................................................................... 245.00
**Pitcher,** Flow Blue, Oriental Scene ................................................................... 65.00
**Pitcher,** Gaudy Willow, 1907, 5 1/2 In. ........................................................... 285.00
**Pitcher,** George Washington, 7 1/2 In. ............................................ 250.00 To 400.00
**Pitcher,** Landing Of Roger Williams ................................................................. 285.00
**Pitcher,** Robin Hood, 8 1/2 In. ........................................................ 225.00 To 295.00
**Pitcher,** Roosevelt Bears, No.1436v, 1907, Pair ...........................................1250.00
**Pitcher,** Sailor ..................................................................................................... 300.00
**Pitcher,** The Gunner, Dated 1907, Green ........................................................ 150.00
**Plate,** Blue, Dr.Syntax Disputing His Bill, 1909, 9 1/4 In. ............................. 165.00
**Plate,** Broadwater Natatorium, Helena, 7 In. .................................................. 75.00
**Plate,** Calendar, 1911, Antique Touring Car, Signed, 7 In. ............................ 165.00
**Plate,** Child's, Teddy Bears, 7 1/4 In. .............................................................. 95.00
**Plate,** Christmas, 1950 ...................................................................................... 45.00
**Plate,** Christmas, 1955 ...................................................................................... 45.00
**Plate,** Christmas, 1957 ...................................................................................... 45.00
**Plate,** Christmas, 1960 ...................................................................................... 45.00
**Plate,** Dinner, Black Border, Gold Trim, Set Of 4 ........................................... 35.00
**Plate,** Federal Building, Helena, 7 1/2 In. ....................................................... 75.00
**Plate,** Gaudy Willow, 7 1/4 In.Diam. ................................................................ 45.00
**Plate,** Mt.Vernon, Blue & White, 10 1/2 In.Diam. ........................................... 35.00
**Plate,** Mt.Vernon, Dark Green, 7 1/2 In. .......................................................... 35.00
**Plate,** Niagara Falls, Green, 7 1/2 In. ............................................... 30.00 To 38.00
**Plate,** State Capitol, Helena, Montana, 7 In. ................................................... 75.00
**Plate,** The Gunner, Beaver Falls, Pa., 7 In. ..................................................... 60.00
**Plate,** Trinity Church, N.Y. City, 7 In. ............................................................... 65.00
**Plate,** White House .............................................................................................. 40.00
**Plate,** White House & Faneuil Hall, Green, 10 1/4 In. ...................................... 50.00
**Plate,** Wild Ducks, 9 In. ...................................................................................... 39.00
**Platter & 4 Plates,** Green Rimmed, Deer Game Set, Signed ......................... 225.00
**Platter,** Blue Willow, 14 In.Diam. ...................................................................... 45.00
**Platter,** Blue Willow, 1900-10, 16 In. ................................................................ 40.00
**Platter,** Buffalo Hunt, Scalloped Gold Edge, 11 3/8 X 14 In. .......................... 55.00
**Platter,** Fish, R.Beck, 15 X 11 In. ..................................................................... 60.00

| | |
|---|---|
| **Platter,** Multifloral, Oval, Small | 20.00 |
| **Teapot,** Blue Flowers | 18.00 |
| **Vase,** Spray Of Clematis, Signed, Apple Green, 1905-07, 10 In. | 75.00 |
| | |
| **BUGGY, Baby,** Fold-Back Canopy, Large Rear Wheels, Smaller Front | 340.00 |
| **Baby,** Large Wire Wheels, Wicker | 275.00 |
| **Baby,** Original Parasol, Victorian | 450.00 |
| **Baby,** With Parasol, Wicker, 1880s | 200.00 |
| **Doll,** Heywood Wakefield, Wicker, 29 X 10 X 16 In. | 145.00 |
| **Doll,** 19th Century, 26 X 9 X 24 In. | 165.00 |
| | |
| **BURGUN & SCHVERER, Bowl,** Raspberry Swirls, Citron, 7 X 4 In. | 1000.00 |
| **Bowl,** Swirls Of Raspberry, Grapes, Signed, 7 1/2 In. | 1000.00 |

*Burmese glass was developed by Frederick Shirley at the Mt.Washington Glass Works in New Bedford, Massachusetts, in 1885. It is a two-toned glass, shading from peach to yellow. Some have a pattern mold design. A few Burmese pieces were decorated with pictures or applied glass flowers of colored Burmese glass.*

**BURMESE, see also Gunderson**

| | |
|---|---|
| **BURMESE, Basket,** Satin Finish, Wild Rose & Bowknot, 7 In. | 33.00 |
| **Bottle,** Perfume, Enameled Blue Flowers, Silver Hallmarked, 2 In. | 265.00 |
| **Bottle,** Perfume, Painted Bamboo, Dragonfly, 4 7/8 In. | 275.00 |
| **Bride's Bowl,** Pink Fluting, Enameled Flowers, C.1890 | 425.00 |
| **Condiment Set,** Kate Greenaway Silver Plate Holder, Mt.Washington | 450.00 |
| **Creamer,** Folded Top, Pigtail Handle | 115.00 |
| **Creamer,** Small | 385.00 |
| **Cup & Saucer,** Gold, Saucer 6 In. | 800.00 |
| **Cup & Saucer,** Mt.Washington, 3 Applied Feet On Cup | 650.00 |
| **Dish,** Condiment, English Silver Plate Frame, 2 3/4 X 5 In.Diam. | 485.00 |
| **Dish,** Jam, Butterflies & Flowers, Silver Plate Holder | 895.00 |
| **Finger Bowl,** Ruffled Edge, Mt.Washington, 5 5/8 X 2 1/2 In. | 235.00 |
| **Finger Bowl,** Undertray, Pinched On 2 Sides, C.1890, Bowl, 2 3/4 In. | 350.00 |
| **Flower Frog,** Mt.Washington, Raised Enameled Flowers | 175.00 |
| **Lamp,** Fairy, Base, Signed Clarke, 11 In. | 595.00 |
| **Lamp,** Fairy, Pink & Lemon, C.1890, Signed, 4 In. | 277.00 |
| **Lamp,** Fairy, Pyramid Shade & Base, Marked Clarke, 4 In. | 420.00 |
| **Lamp,** Fairy, Signed T.Webb, Queen's Burmese, Clarke Insert | 975.00 |
| **Lamp,** Fairy, 6 In. | 375.00 |
| **Mug,** Lemonade, Lemon Yellow | 290.00 |
| **Mustard,** Ribbed Body, Salmon Pink, Mt.Washington | 250.00 |
| **Mustard,** Ribbed Body, Silver Plate Fittings, C.1900, 4 5/16 In. | 150.00 |
| **Pitcher,** Diamond Pattern, Blue & White Forget-Me-Nots, 4 In. | 395.00 |
| **Pitcher,** Lemonade, Tapering Cylindrical Form, C.1890, 8 3/4 In. | 275.00 |
| **Plate,** Mt.Washington, 1880s, Acid Finish, 7 In. | 265.00 |
| **Rose Bowl,** Apple Blossom Design, Small | 375.00 |
| **Rose Bowl,** Rose To Pink | 450.00 |
| **Rose Jar,** Raised Enamel Flowers, Mt.Washington, 4 X 5 1/4 In.Diam. | 575.00 |
| **Salt & Pepper,** Enameled Holly Design, Mt.Washington, Plated Holder | 450.00 |
| **Salt & Pepper,** Mt.Washington, Tuft Holder, Ribbed | 475.00 |
| **Saltshaker,** Ribbed, Mt.Washington, 4 In. | 125.00 |
| **Saltshaker,** Ribbed, Pansy Design, Mt.Washington | 200.00 |
| **Saltshaker,** Ribbed, 4 In. | 245.00 |
| **Saltshaker,** Tomato, Mt.Washington | 110.00 |
| **Sugar & Creamer,** Footed, 3 In. | 400.00 |
| **Sugar & Creamer,** Silver Plate Holder | 1275.00 |
| **Sugar Shaker,** Maidenhair Fern Design, Mt.Washington | 250.00 |
| **Toothpick,** Bulbous Bottom, Square Top | 245.00 |
| **Toothpick,** Diamond-Quilted, Enameled | 275.00 |
| **Toothpick,** Lobe & Scroll | 350.00 |
| **Toothpick,** Prunus Blossoms, Hand-Painted, Square Mouth | 250.00 |
| **Toothpick,** Square Top, Honeycomb | 178.00 |
| **Tumbler,** Mt.Washington, Reheated Yellow Top Edge, 3 3/4 In. | 185.00 |

Tumbler, Satin Glass, 5 In. ........................................................................................ 100.00
Tumbler, 4 In. ....................................................................................................... 175.00
Vase, Acid Finish, Stick, 8 In. ................................................................................. 235.00
Vase, Acorn Feet & Applied Leaves, Signed, 5 1/2 In. ............................................ 325.00
Vase, Blue Forget-Me-Nots, Black-Edged Band, 3 1/2 X 3 1/2 In. ........................... 275.00
Vase, Crimped Top, Flower & Leaf Design, Salmon To Yellow, 3 In., Pr. ................... 700.00
Vase, Enameled & Gilt, Daisy & Vine, C.1890, 11 3/4 In. ...................................... 1150.00
Vase, Enameled Design, Yellow To Salmon, Bees, 6 1/2 In. .................................... 425.00
Vase, Enameled Flowers & Leaves, Hexagonal Top, 3 In. ....................................... 305.00
Vase, Five-Petal Rose Design, 2 1/4 In. ................................................................. 330.00
Vase, Hobnail, 5-Sided Top, Bulbous Base, 7 1/2 X 4 1/4 In.Diam. ........................ 375.00
Vase, Jack-In-The-Pulpit, Mt.Washington, 9 1/2 In. ............................................... 850.00
Vase, Labeled Mt.W.G.Co., C.1890, 11 3/4 In. ................................................. *Illus* 1150.00
Vase, Leaf & Fig Design, 4 In. ............................................................................... 375.00
Vase, Lily Form, Pinched To Form 3 Lobes, C.1890, 8 1/8 In. ................................ 200.00
Vase, Mirrored Wall Sconce, Beveled Oval, Vase 3 3/8 In. ..................................... 350.99
Vase, Mount Washington, Gourd Shape, 12 In. ....................................................... 360.00
Vase, Peach To Yellow, Bulbous Bottom, Ruffled Top, 3 1/2 In. .............................. 275.00
Vase, Pink To Raspberry, 12 X 5 In. ..................................................................... 225.00
Vase, Raised Gold Design, 9 1/2 In. ...................................................................... 850.00
Vase, Ruffled Top, Polychrome Enamel, 3 1/4 In. ................................................... 350.00
Vase, Stick, Enameled, 6 In. ................................................................................. 450.00
Vase, Trefoil, Glossy Finish, 7 1/2 In. ..................................................................... 85.00
Vase, Yellow To Pink, 4-Point Ruffled Top, C.1885, 13 1/2 In. ............................... 460.00
Vase, Yellow To Salmon, Enameled Design, Bee Mark, 6 1/2 In. ............................ 425.00
    BURMESE, WEBB, see Webb Burmese

BUSTER BROWN, Bank, Tige, Chalk ....................................................................... 12.00
  Bill Hook .......................................................................................................... 8.00
  Box Camera ..................................................................................................... 20.00
  Calendar, Tread Straight Shoes .......................................................................... 10.00
  Cards, Playing, Original Box, 1906 ..................................................................... 15.00
  Cigar Band, 1910 .............................................................................................. 7.00
  Cup & Saucer ................................................................................................... 32.00
  Cup, Saucer, & Creamer .................................................................................... 55.00
  Display, Celluloid Shoe ...................................................................................... 38.00
  Doll, Cloth, 14 In. ............................................................................................. 55.00
  Game, Pin The Tie On Buster, Tige, Oilcloth, 1930s ............................................ 175.00
  Knife, Spoon, & Fork, Illustrated Box, Dated 1904 .............................................. 39.50
  Knife, Table ...................................................................................................... 12.50
  Mannikin, One Year Old, Four Years Old, Pair ..................................................... 75.00
  Mug, Tige .......................................................................................................... 45.00
  Periscope .......................................................................................................... 6.00
  Plate, 6 In. ........................................................................................................ 40.00
  Postcard, Calendar, 1912 .................................................................................. 20.00
  Postcard, 1909 ................................................................................................. 10.00
  Runner, Carpet, Buster & Tige Woven 3 Times, 8 1/2 X 2 1/4 Ft. ........................ 300.00
  Stickpin, Buster & Tige Playing .......................................................................... 22.00
  Stickpin, Figural, 1930s, Buster Standing ........................................................... 18.00
  Teapot, Stand, Tige Balancing Pot On Nose, 6 1/4 In. ......................................... 25.00
  Tobacco Jar, Tam Lifts Off As Lid ...................................................................... 150.00
  Watch, Pocket ................................................................................................... 125.00
  Whistle, Tin ......................................................................................... 15.00 To 22.00
  Wristwatch ....................................................................................................... 85.00
    BUTTER MOLD, see Kitchen, Mold, Butter
    BUTTERMILK GLASS, see Custard Glass

*Buttons have been known throughout the centuries, and there are millions of styles. Only a few of the most common types are listed for comparison.*

BUTTON, Bicycle, Sterling Silver ............................................................................ 14.00
  Clothing, Shape Of Pepsi Bottle Cap .................................................................. 5.00
  Confederate, South Carolina, Silver, Marked, 1 1/16 In. ............................. *Illus* 450.00

Burmese, Vase, Labeled Mt.W.G.Co., C.1890, 11 3/4 In.

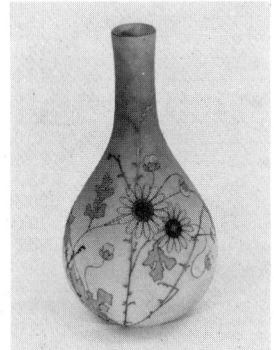

Button, Confederate, South
Carolina, Silver, Marked, 1 1/16 In.

Button, Washington Inaugural,
Sheffield Silver, 1 1/2 In.

| | | |
|---|---|---|
| **Elsie The Cow,** 4 Different Cards Of 4 Each | | 8.00 |
| **Gods Of Good Luck,** Satsuma, 3/4 In. | | 55.00 |
| **Gods Of Good Luck,** Satsuma, 1 In. | | 75.00 |
| **Indian Head Nickel,** 1937, Pair | | 9.00 |
| **James Whitcomb Riley,** Greenfield, Indiana | | 12.50 |
| **Raised Bust Of Jenny Lind,** Gutta-Percha, Civil War Period, 5/8 In. | | 9.00 |
| **Rope Edge,** Round Bead Center, Sterling Silver, 1 1/8 In., Set Of 8 | | 125.00 |
| **Shoe,** Celluloid Handle, Amber & Pink, 5 In. | | 4.95 |
| **Uniform,** Police & Fire Department, Set Of 35 | | 15.00 |
| **Uniform,** Police, Hartford, Brass, Set Of 12 | | 8.00 |
| **Uniform,** Texas, Raised Star, Bronzed Metal | | 5.00 |
| **Washington Inaugural,** Sheffield Silver, 1 1/2 In. | *Illus* | 2200.00 |
| | | |
| **BUTTONHOOK, Art Nouveau,** Maiden In Flowing Gown, Marked Sterling, 8 1/2 In. | | 40.00 |
| **Art Nouveau,** Sterling Silver, 7 In. | | 25.00 |
| **Glove,** Flattened Steel Handle, Wire Loop, White Shirt | | 7.50 |
| **Wire,** Flattened Handle, My Store Shoe Department, 5 In. | | 4.50 |
| **Wire,** Flattened Handle, Will Hall The Shoe Man, 5 In. | | 4.95 |
| **Woman's Shapely Leg,** Engraved Boot, Steel, Figural | | 45.00 |
| | | |
| **BYBEE, Vase,** 3 Handled, 1927, Virginia, 5 1/2 In. | | 110.00 |

**CALENDAR PAPER, 1881,** John J.Tower, N.Y. Police Goods ......................... 12.00
**1882,** Boston & Maine Railroad ......................................... 12.00
**1882,** Eastern Railroad ......................................... 16.00
**1888,** Scotts Emulsion, Little Girl, Kitten & Puppy ......................... 10.00
**1888,** Sunnyside Whiskey, Sun, Comical Face, 11 X 11 In. ................. 55.00
**1890,** Sulphur Bitters ......................................... 55.00
**1892,** Hood's Sarsaparilla, First Issue ......................... 35.00
**1892,** Walter Wood, Little Girls ......................................... 20.00
**1895,** Golden Treasure, Original Box ......................... 45.00
**1895,** Maude Humphrey, Color Plates, 13 1/2 X 11 In. ................. 300.00
**1895,** N.Y.Life Insurance Co., Prang ......................... 20.00
**1897,** Larkin, Embossed ......................................... 85.00
**1898,** Continental Insurance ......................................... 10.00
**1900,** DuPont Powder, U.S.Battleship, Spanish-American War ........... 275.00
**1900,** DuPont Powder, U.S.Battleship, 28 X 14 In. ................. 225.00
**1900,** Every Dog Has His Day, 7-Color Illustration ................. 32.00
**1900,** Hosmer's Ben-Zo-Ine, Pretty Woman ......................... 25.00
**1900,** McCormick Harvester, Soldier, Horse, 14 X 28 In. ........... 165.00
**1900,** Santa Fe Aztec ......................................... 50.00
**1900,** Sarsaparilla ......................................... 20.00
**1901,** Hill's Quinine ......................................... 12.00
**1902,** Hood's ......................................... 38.00
**1903,** Antikamnia ......................................... 12.00
**1904,** Dr.Mile's ......................................... 21.00
**1904,** Lord's Prayer, Tuck ......................................... 13.00
**1905,** Hill's Cascara Quinine ......................................... 18.00
**1905,** Hood's Sarsaparilla ................................ 28.00 To 38.00
**1907,** Hood's Sarsaparilla ......................................... 16.00
**1909,** Pacific Mutual Life Ins., Pictures Employees ................. 12.50
**1910,** Comfort, Mother, Child, & Kitten, Complete ................. 30.00
**1912,** Buster Brown Shoes, White House Queen, 13 X 32 In. ......... 130.00
**1912,** Deering International Harvester, 23 X 14 In. ................. 95.00
**1912,** Mother Holding Baby, 17 X 8 In. ......................... 65.00
**1913,** Dr.King's New Discovery Medicine ......................... 40.00
**1913,** Hood's Sarsaparilla ......................................... 22.00
**1913,** Kent & Burroughs Blacksmiths, Alstead, N.H., Girl, Pony ..... 20.00
**1913,** Swift's, Eleanor Colburn Picture ......................... 40.00
**1914,** Hood's Sarsaparilla, Original Envelope ..................... 20.00
**1915,** Continental Fire Ins., Signed Patriotic Print At Top ......... 10.00
**1915,** Hood's School Days ......................................... 35.00
**1920,** Munsingwear ......................................... 25.00
**1920,** Remington, Bear Destroying Camp, 30 X 15 In. ............. 175.00
**1923,** Peters, Hunter & Dog, Porcupine, 30 X 15 In. ............. 295.00
**1924,** Bromo-Quinine ......................................... 10.00
**1924,** Clare City Savings Bank ......................................... 3.00
**1927,** Goodrich Silvertowns, Flapper ......................... 15.00
**1927,** Hercules Powder, Hunter, Dog, 29 X 13 In. ................. 125.00
**1927,** Hercules Powder, Old Hunter, Dogs, Pals, 29 X 13 In. ....... 150.00
**1929,** Golden Hours, Mazda Edison ......................... 135.00
**1929,** U.S.Cartridge, Hunter Pulling Beagle, 35 X 16 In. ......... 250.00
**1930,** Ecstasy, Mazda Edison ......................................... 135.00
**1930,** Jewel Tea Co. ......................................... 15.00
**1934,** Natures Remedy, With Thermometer ......................... 8.00
**1935,** Old Judge, Cardinals Baseball Team ..................... 175.00
**1936,** Deco Nude ......................................... 75.00
**1936,** Quintuplets ......................................... 10.00
**1937,** De Laval ......................................... 8.00
**1937,** John Deere Centennial ......................................... 300.00
**1937,** Kinter Milling Co., Hunter, Chair, Petting Dog ............. 125.00
**1937,** Kinter Milling Co., Hunter, Shotgun, Dog, 36 X 18 In. ..... 125.00
**1937,** Liberty Magazine ......................................... 4.00
**1939,** Jamestown Mutual Ins., Pictures 1939 Packard ............. 12.00
**1941,** Allis Chalmer, 12 Page ......................................... 7.00

**1941,** Anaconda Brewing Co. ................................................................................ 25.00
**1942,** Morrell Meats, Disney Cartoon Scenes ................................................. 100.00
**1942,** Vargas ........................................................................................................ 18.00
**1942,** Walt Disney ............................................................................................... 45.00
**1944,** Great Northern Railway, Blackfoot Indian Chief ................................. 60.00
**1948,** Esquire ....................................................................................................... 14.00
**1956,** Marilyn Monroe ......................................................................................... 75.00

*Calendar plates were very popular in the United States from 1906 to 1929.
Since then plates have been made every year. A calendar, the name of a
store, a picture of flowers, a girl, or a scene was featured on the plate.*

**CALENDAR PLATE, 1877,** Liverpool Almanac, Advertising, Blue & White, 7 3/4 In. ........... 195.00
**1904,** World's Fair, Gold Painted Center ......................................................... 20.00
**1908,** Pittsburgh Mercantile Co., Roses, Pink ................................................. 20.00
**1909,** Dog Center, Krebs Coffee, Bloomington, Illinois ................................. 35.00
**1909,** Dog's Head, Mrs.Mark Cohen & Sons, Sharon, Pa. ............................ 35.00
**1909,** Flowers ...................................................................................................... 16.00
**1909,** Gibson Girl, Glen Elder, Kansas ............................................................ 30.00
**1909,** Lady's Head, Mrs.Mark Cohen & Sons, Sharon, Pa. ........................... 35.00
**1909,** Peace Bird .................................................................................................. 14.00
**1909,** Souvenir, Boone, Iowa .............................................................................. 28.00
**1909,** Two Flags, 7 1/4 In. .................................................................................. 24.00
**1910,** Cherubs & Bell .......................................................................................... 15.00
**1910,** Cherubs, Ruffled Edge, Ribbons, Blue Flowers, 8 1/4 In. .................. 39.00
**1910,** Cupids Ringing Bell .................................................................................. 42.50
**1910,** Four Seasons, Woman In Bonnet, Steubenville, Ohio ....................... 26.00
**1910,** Lighthouse, Ship, 8 In. ............................................................................ 34.00
**1910,** Mt.Vernon, 9 1/2 In. ................................................................................ 22.00
**1910,** Niagara Falls, 8 In. ................................................................................... 22.50
**1910,** Orange & Yellow Flowers ........................................................................ 22.00
**1910,** Swimming Hole .......................................................................................... 35.00
**1910,** Watertown, Wis., 9 1/2 In. ...................................................................... 22.00
**1911-12,** Farm Scene ........................................................................................... 17.00
**1911-12,** Sunrise ................................................................................................... 16.00
**1911,** Clocks Around World, Violets, Advertising, 8 1/2 In. ......................... 22.00
**1911,** Floral Center, E.F.Wilcox, Depew, N.Y., 9 In. ...................................... 22.00
**1911,** Helfrich & Raab, Ohio .............................................................................. 28.00
**1911,** Rural Scene, Joe Darches, Credit Jewelers .......................................... 20.00
**1912,** Cherries & Cherubs, 8 In. ....................................................................... 24.00
**1912,** Cherries, E.F.Lahey, Middleport, N.Y., 7 3/4 In. .................................. 22.00
**1912,** Indian Squaw Husking Corn, Tepee Scene ........................................... 28.50
**1912,** Lady Picking Flowers, Sports Equipment ............................................. 22.50
**1912,** O.C.Smith, Canal Street, Winchester, Ohio .......................................... 27.50
**1913,** Black Swans ............................................................................................... 20.00
**1913,** Clocks, Time Around The World, American Flag .................................. 30.00
**1914,** Hunt Scene, Red-Coated Riders, 7 1/2 In. ........................................... 27.50
**1915,** Flags & Panama Canal, 7 1/2 In. ............................................................ 28.00
**1915,** Panama Map, 7 3/4 In. ............................................................................ 15.00
**1916,** Flower, Compliments Of Harper General Store .................................... 20.00
**1917,** Cat Head, Tom's Cleaning Service, Janitor Service ............................. 20.00
**1919,** Ship, Thank You From Lawrence & Edith Lerch .................................. 20.00
**1920,** Shorebird Scene, Signed R.K.Beck ........................................................ 20.00
**1923,** Flowers, Hoover Jewelers ....................................................................... 20.00
**1928,** Flowers, Vest Home Center, Vest Surplus Center ............................... 20.00
**1932,** Flowers, Meshoppen Lumber & Building Supplies .............................. 20.00

**CALENDAR, Pocket,** 1898, Acorn Stove ............................................................. 5.00
**Ruler,** 1918, Bates Street, Maine, Celluloid ...................................................... 7.00
**Tile,** 1903, Elmwood, Cambridge, Home Of James Russell Lowell ............... 65.00
**Tile,** 1910, Mayflower Arriving, Provincetown Harbor, 1620 ......................... 50.00
**Tile,** 1922, Cathedral Church Of St.Paul, Erected 1820 .................................. 45.00

| | |
|---|---|
| **CAMARK, Candleholder,** Yellow, Double | 15.00 |
| **Console Set,** Double Candleholder, Paper Label, Bowl, 12 In.Diam. | 12.50 |
| **Creamer,** Parrot Handle, Yellow, High-Glaze Body, Marked | 25.00 |
| **Planter,** Rooster, Green | 9.00 |
| **Planter,** Swan, White, Double, Marked | 12.00 |
| **Vase,** Cylindrical, Black Pebbled Ground, Metallic Glaze, 12 In. | 135.00 |
| **Vase,** Mottled Blue & Gray, 6 X 4 1/2 In.Diam. | 8.00 |
| **Vase,** Raised Plumes, Light Blue, Label, 6 1/2 X 8 In.Diam. | 28.00 |
| **Vase,** Tulip, Green, 6 In. | 12.50 |
| **Vase,** Yellow, Wide Flared Top, 13 X 10 In. | 9.50 |

*Cambridge art pottery was made in Cambridge, Ohio, from about 1895 until World War I. The factory made brown-glazed decorated wares marked with a variety of marks including an acorn, the name Cambridge, the name Oakwood, or the name Terrhea.*

| | |
|---|---|
| **CAMBRIDGE POTTERY, Vase,** Brown Glaze, Marked Oakwood, 5 In. | 100.00 |
| **Vase,** Floral, Artist, M.W., 6 In. | 135.00 |

*Cambridge Glass Company was founded in 1901 in Cambridge, Ohio. The company closed in 1954, reopened briefly, and closed again in 1954. The firm made all types of glass. Their early wares included heavy pressed glass with the mark "Near Cut." Later wares included etched stemware, crystal, colored, and Crown Tuscan. The firm used a C in a triangle mark after 1920.*

| | |
|---|---|
| **CAMBRIDGE, Ashtray,** Crown Tuscan, Seashell, 4 In. | 23.00 |
| **Ashtray,** Crown Tuscan, 7 In.Diam. | 25.00 |
| **Ashtray,** Crystal Stem, Gold Krystol, 3 1/2 In. | 24.00 |
| **Ashtray,** Footed, Shell Shape, Name Card Slot, 2 In., Set Of 4 | 20.00 |
| **Ashtray,** Nude Stem, Forest Green, Pair | 75.00 |
| **Ashtray,** Nude Stem, Royal Blue, Pair | 80.00 |
| **Ashtray,** Seashell, Yellow | 4.00 |
| **Ashtray,** Shell, Clear | 6.00 |
| **Ashtray,** 3-Footed, Caprice, Crystal, 2 3/4 In. | 5.00 |
| **Atomizer,** Gold Stippled, Opaque Jade, Silk Lined Box, 6 1/4 In. | 125.00 |
| **Banana Boat,** Candlelight | 75.00 |
| **Basket,** Decagon, Pink, 7 In. | 7.00 |
| **Basket,** Footed, Red, 6 In. | 24.75 |
| **Berry Set,** Marjorie, Near Cut, 7 Piece | 55.00 |
| **Blotter,** Elephant, Black | 35.00 |
| **Bonbon,** Caprice, Blue, 6 In.Square | 16.00 |
| **Bonbon,** Cleo, Blue, 5 1/2 In. | 14.00 |
| **Bonbon,** Decagon, Pink, Etched, 5 1/2 In.Diam. | 6.50 |
| **Bonbon,** Rose Point, 5 1/4 In. | 16.50 |
| **Bookends,** Eagle | 110.00 To 165.00 |
| **Bookends,** Lion | 225.00 |
| **Bookends,** Pouter Pigeon, Original Label | 85.00 |
| **Bookends,** Scotty | 75.00 To 125.00 |
| **Bowl & Flower Frog,** Bashful Maiden, Pink, 13 In. | 175.00 |
| **Bowl,** Bulb, Footed, Green | 22.00 |
| **Bowl,** Caprice, Crystal, 3-Toed, 13 In.Diam. | 18.00 |
| **Bowl,** Caprice, Gold Floral Overlay, 4-Footed, 10 In. | 65.00 |
| **Bowl,** Centerpiece, Azurite, Flat Rim, 11 1/2 In.Diam | 57.00 |
| **Bowl,** Console, Crown Tuscan, Flying Lady | 160.00 |
| **Bowl,** Console, Jade, 10 In.Diam. | 25.00 |
| **Bowl,** Crown Tuscan, Flowers & Gold Trim, 3-Toed, 13 In. | 115.00 |
| **Bowl,** Crown Tuscan, Shell, Footed, 8 1/2 In. | 25.00 |
| **Bowl,** Daffodil Floral Design, Signed, 3 X 5 In. | 95.00 |
| **Bowl,** Diane, Gadroon, 7 1/2 In.Diam. | 18.50 |
| **Bowl,** Divided, Caprice, 6 In.Diam. | 12.50 |
| **Bowl,** Everglades Amber, Dolphin, Footed, 12 In. | 40.00 |

**Bowl,** Everglades Pattern, Blue, 15 In.Diam. ........................................ 125.00
**Bowl,** Figural, Swan, Green, 6 1/2 In. ..................................................... 50.00
**Bowl,** Footed, Cascade, Gold Trim, 5 In.Diam. ...................................... 15.00
**Bowl,** Footed, Crown Tuscan, 11 1/2 In.Square ..................................... 90.00
**Bowl,** Footed, Shell Shape, Crown Tuscan, Pink, Footed, 8 1/2 In. ........ 48.00
**Bowl,** Gold Daisies, 12 X 1 3/4 In. ....................................................... 50.00
**Bowl,** Ivory, Gold Encrusted Band, 8 X 3 1/2 In. ................................... 50.00
**Bowl,** Jade, 10 X 3 In. ......................................................................... 40.00
**Bowl,** Lorna, Crystal, 12 In.Diam. ....................................................... 14.00
**Bowl,** Martha Washington Heatherbloom, 12 In. .................................. 12.50
**Bowl,** Ram's Head, Crystal, Etched Elaine, 9 1/2 In. ............................. 95.00
**Bowl,** Ram's Head, Jade, 10 In. ........................................................... 150.00
**Bowl,** Rose Point, Oval, 12 In. ............................................................. 60.00
**Bowl,** Rose Point, 4-Footed, 12 In.Diam. ............................ 48.00 To 65.00
**Bowl,** Rubina Honeycomb, Signed, 10 In.Diam. ................................... 130.00
**Bowl,** Salad, Rose Point, 3-Footed, Scalloped Edge ............................. 55.00
**Bowl,** Seashell Design, 3-Toed, Crown Tuscan, 9 In. ........................... 100.00
**Bowl,** Shell, Crown Tuscan, 8 1/2 In.Diam. ........................ 35.00 To 38.00
**Bowl,** Shell, Crown Tuscan, 9 In. ......................................................... 55.00
**Bowl,** Shell, Flying Nude, Hand-Painted Flowers, Gold, 11 In. ............... 175.00
**Bowl,** Swan, Green, 6 1/2 In. ............................................................... 50.00
**Bowl,** Thistle Pattern, Emerald Green, Gold Trim, 9 1/4 In.Diam. .......... 90.00
**Box,** Candy, Crown Tuscan, 3 Sections, Covered ................................. 90.00
**Box,** Cigarette, Cover, Crown Tuscan ................................................. 30.00
**Box,** Cigarette, Covered, Nude Stem, Mandarin Gold ........................... 150.00
**Box,** Cigarette, Crown Tuscan, Dolphin Feet ....................... 25.00 To 65.00
**Box,** Cigarette, Footed, Diane, Pair .................................................... 75.00
**Box,** Crown Tuscan, Scroll Handle, Paneled Lid, 4 X 6 In. .................... 35.00
**Brandy,** Amethyst ............................................................................... 60.00
**Brandy,** Green ................................................................................... 60.00
**Brandy,** Nude Stem, Yellow Top, Optic Bowl ...................................... 65.00
**Butter,** Portia, Covered ...................................................................... 55.00
**Cake Plate,** Chantilly, Handled, 11 In.Diam. ....................................... 25.00
**Cake Plate,** Etched Flowers, Silver Overlay, Octagonal ....................... 50.00
**Cake Plate,** 25th Anniversary, Sterling Flowers & Bells, 13 In. ............ 32.00
**Cake Stand,** Crown Tuscan ................................................................ 40.00
**Candelabra,** Elaine, 2-Light, Pair ........................................................ 50.00
**Candelabra,** Rose Point, 2-Light, Pair ................................................. 50.00
**Candleholder,** Alpine, Prisms, Caprice ................................................ 45.00
**Candleholder,** Crown Tuscan, Dolphin Stem, Seashell Bowl, 4 In. ........ 95.00
**Candleholder,** Diane, 5 In., Pair ......................................................... 35.00
**Candleholder,** Double, Caprice, Blue ................................................... 75.00
**Candleholder,** Double, Crown Tuscan, Pair ......................................... 85.00
**Candleholder,** Jack-In-The-Pulpit ....................................................... 20.00
**Candleholder,** Rose Point, Double Keyhole ........................ 55.00 To 65.00
**Candleholder,** Rose Point, 3-Light ...................................................... 95.00
**Candlestick,** Azurite, Hexagon, Pair ................................................... 45.00
**Candlestick,** Caprice, Clear, 2 1/2 In., Pair ......................................... 14.00
**Candlestick,** Caprice, 1 Prism, Crystal, Pair ........................................ 25.00
**Candlestick,** Cleo, Pink, 4 In., Pair ..................................................... 25.00
**Candlestick,** Crown Tuscan, Nude, Pair .............................................. 175.00
**Candlestick,** Cut Pattern, Pair ............................................................ 48.00
**Candlestick,** Dolphin, Green, Pair ..................................... 75.00 To 140.00
**Candlestick,** Glass Ball, Signed, Pair .................................................. 15.00
**Candlestick,** Helio, Hexagonal, 7 In., Pair ........................................... 65.00
**Candlestick,** Keyhole Pattern, 2-Light, Silver Trim On Base ................. 17.50
**Candlestick,** Mandarin, Gold .............................................................. 26.00
**Candlestick,** Near Cut, Amber, 6 1/4 In., Pair ..................................... 25.00
**Candlestick,** Nude, Crown Tuscan, Pair .............................................. 250.00
**Candlestick,** Rose Point, 3-Light, 6 In., Pair ....................................... 72.50
**Candlestick,** Rose Point, 7 In., Pair .................................................... 32.00
**Candlestick,** Silver Embossed Flowers, Pair ....................................... 50.00
**Candlestick,** Twist, Satin, Green, Pair ................................................ 48.00

| | |
|---|---|
| Celery, Daffodil | 14.50 |
| Celery, Rose Point, Footed, 9 1/4 In. | 16.00 |
| Center Bowl, Navarre, Cut Panels, Oval | 47.50 |
| Champagne, Portia | 17.00 |
| Champagne, Rose Point | 18.00 |
| Champagne, Wildflower, Plumed Stem | 20.00 |
| Coaster, Caprice, Set Of 6 | 15.00 |
| Cocktail, Blue Satin Stem | 87.50 |
| Cocktail, Carmen, Satin Stem | 92.50 |
| Cocktail, Crown Tuscan Base, Nude Mandarin, Gold Top | 65.00 |
| Cocktail, Crown Tuscan, Nude Stem, Amber Bowl, 3 Ounce | 110.00 |
| Cocktail, Nude Stem, Amethyst | 40.00 |
| Cocktail, Nude Stem, Green Top | 70.00 |
| Cocktail, Nude Stem, Mocha | 110.00 |
| Cocktail, Rose Point, 3 Ounce | 25.00 |
| Cocktail, Satin Stem, Carmen | 92.50 |
| Cocktail, Satin Stem, Frosted, Amber | 115.00 |
| Cocktail, Satin Stem, Royal Blue | 105.00 |
| Cocktail, Seafood, Crown Tuscan, 4 1/2 Ounce | 50.00 |
| Compote, Amethyst, Farber Ware Chrome Holder | 21.00 To 28.00 |
| Compote, Covered, Queen Anne | 25.00 |
| Compote, Crown Tuscan, Emerald | 75.00 |
| Compote, Crown Tuscan, Shell, 4 In. | 40.00 |
| Compote, Crown Tuscan, Shell, 6 1/2 In.Diam. | 25.00 To 30.00 |
| Compote, Crystal Stem, Amethyst Top, 5 1/2 In. | 25.00 |
| Compote, Cupped, Nude, Red, 7 In. | 75.00 |
| Compote, Elaine, Gold Trim, Handled, 7 3/4 In. | 25.00 |
| Compote, Footed, Caprice, Crystal, 7 In.Diam. | 16.75 |
| Compote, Footed, Primrose | 45.00 |
| Compote, Jelly, Diamond-Quilted | 17.50 |
| Compote, Nude Stem, Amethyst, Farber Ware | 40.00 |
| Compote, Open, Primrose, Helio | 20.00 |
| Compote, Radiance, Ruby, 5 X 9 1/4 In. | 34.00 |
| Compote, Rose Point, Nude Stem, Cobalt Blue, 8 1/2 In. | 80.00 |
| Compote, Rose Point, 6 In. | 35.00 |
| Compote, Shell, Crown Tuscan, Pink, 6 1/2 In. | 28.00 |
| Compote, Silver Berries & Leaves, Marked, Footed | 35.00 |
| Compote, Topaz, Farber Ware Holder, 8 In., Pair | 40.00 |
| Console Bowl, Caprice, Yellow, 13 In.Diam. | 32.50 |
| Console Set, Calla Lily, Candlesticks & Bowl, Green, 3 Piece | 35.00 |
| Console Set, Crown Tuscan, Flying Lady, Nude Lady Candlesticks | 595.00 |
| Console Set, Ebony, Chrome Openwork Cover & Base, Bowl, 7 1/2 In. | 48.00 |
| Console Set, Rose Point, Candlesticks, Bowl, 12 In.Diam. | 85.00 |
| Console Set, Rose Point, Double Candleholders | 95.00 |
| Cordial Set, Amber, 7 Piece | 28.00 |
| Cordial, Amethyst | 55.00 |
| Cordial, Crystal Stem, Carmen Top, 1 Ounce, Set Of 4 | 34.00 |
| Cordial, Diane | 16.00 |
| Cordial, Rose Point | 45.00 |
| Cracker Jar, Wheat Sheaf, C.1920 | 45.00 |
| Creamer, Moonlight Blue | 6.00 |
| Creamer, Rose Point, Miniature | 35.00 |
| Cruet Set, Crystal Tray, Keyhole Stoppers, Cobalt | 40.00 |
| Cruet, Chantilly, Sterling Foot & Stopper | 85.00 |
| Cruet, Late Thistle, Signed | 40.00 |
| Cruet, Oil & Vinegar, Diane Pattern, Farber Ware Holders | 18.00 |
| Cruet, Portia, Footed, Green | 125.00 |
| Cruet, Urn Shape, Diane, Stopper | 70.00 |
| Cup & Saucer, Apple Blossom | 10.00 |
| Cup & Saucer, Ashburton, Red | 10.00 |
| Cup & Saucer, Caprice, Blue | 25.00 |
| Cup & Saucer, Caprice, Crystal | 10.00 |
| Cup & Saucer, Chantilly | 25.00 |

Cup & Saucer, Decagon, Crystal ............................................................................... 4.50
Cup & Saucer, Decagon, Green ................................................................. 6.50 To 7.00
Cup & Saucer, Decagon, Pink ................................................................... 6.00 To 7.00
Cup & Saucer, Mt.Vernon, Crystal ............................................................................ 7.50
Cup & Saucer, Rose Point ...................................................................... 25.00 To 30.00
Cup & Saucer, Tally-Ho, Cobalt ............................................................................. 22.50
Cup, Apple Blossom, Crystal ................................................................................... 4.50
Cup, Cascade ......................................................................................................... 2.50
Cup, Punch, Rose Point, Crystal ............................................................................ 24.00
Cup, Punch, Swan ................................................................................................ 42.00
Cup, Saucer & Plate, Mt.Vernon, Plate, 8 In., Set Of 12 ......................................... 118.00
Decanter, Crown Tuscan, Farber Holder, Apple Green ............................................. 55.00
Decanter, Opaque Black, Clear Stopper, Ball-Shaped, 8 Tumblers ........................... 80.00
Decanter, Pinch, Black .......................................................................................... 50.00
Decanter, Tally-Ho, Amber .................................................................................... 45.00
Decanter, Wine, Amethyst, 7 Pieces ...................................................................... 40.00
Decanter, 8 Tumblers, Opaque Black, Farber Holders ............................................. 80.00
Dish, Butter, Green, Chrome Lid, Signed ............................................................... 25.00
Dish, Candy, Caprice, Rolled Edge, Blue ............................................................... 24.00
Dish, Candy, Cover, 3-Part, Crown Tuscan, Cobalt Blue .......................................... 55.00
Dish, Candy, Covered, Caprice, Blue, 6 In. ............................................................ 47.50
Dish, Candy, Covered, Caprice, Clear .................................................................... 15.00
Dish, Candy, Covered, Crown Tuscan, Label .......................................................... 40.00
Dish, Candy, Covered, Weatherford, Green ............................................................ 30.00
Dish, Candy, Crown Tuscan, Shell Cover, Finial, Gold Design, 7 In. ........................ 135.00
Dish, Candy, Crown Tuscan, 3-Section, 7 In.Diam. ................................................. 40.00
Dish, Candy, Divided, Amber, No.704 .................................................................... 25.00
Dish, Candy, First Love, 3-Section, Sterling Silver Base .......................................... 50.00
Dish, Candy, Nude Stem, Amethyst Insert, Farber Holder ........................................ 27.00
Dish, Candy, Shell, Crown Tuscan, Cover & Shell Finial, 7 1/4 In. .......................... 135.00
Dish, Covered, Crown Tuscan, Footed Brass Holder, 3 Sections .............................. 45.00
Dish, Covered, Gadroon, 3-Section, Signed ........................................................... 20.00
Dish, Diane, Divided, Sterling Silver Base, Large .................................................... 47.50
Dish, Mayonnaise, Rose Point ............................................................................... 50.00
Dish, Pickle, Rose Point, 9 1/2 In. ......................................................................... 35.00
Dish, Relish, Caprice, 3-Section, Blue ................................................................... 15.00
Dish, Relish, Caprice, 4-Section ............................................................................ 65.00
Dish, Relish, Chantilly .......................................................................................... 22.50
Dish, Relish, Crown Tuscan, Handled, Divided ....................................................... 38.00
Dish, Relish, Rose Point, Footed, 2-Section, 7 In. .................................................. 19.00
Dish, Relish, Rose Point, Footed, 3-Section, 12 In. ................................................ 38.00
Dish, Relish, Roselyn, Crystal, 12 In. .................................................................... 17.00
Dish, Shell Shape, Pedestal, Crown Tuscan, Hand-Painted, 8 In. ............................ 75.00
Dish, Shell, Crown Tuscan, Signed, 10 In. ............................................................ 75.00
Figurine, Child Seated On Book, Crown Tuscan, 3 In. ............................................. 75.00
Figurine, Draped Lady, Crystal, 12 3/4 In. ............................................................ 135.00
Figurine, Draped Lady, Crystal, 16 In. .................................................................. 115.00
Figurine, Draped Lady, Dianthus, 13 In. ............................................................... 185.00
Figurine, Draped Lady, Green, 8 In. ...................................................................... 65.00
Figurine, Ladies, Draped, Pink, 8 1/2 In. .............................................................. 100.00
Figurine, Lady, Draped, Green, Glass, 8 In. ........................................................... 65.00
Figurine, Sea Gull, Clear, 10 In. ............................................................................ 35.00
Figurine, Swan, Clear, Sterling Overlay, 3 1/2 In. .................................................. 95.00
Figurine, Swan, Crown Tuscan, Signed, 10 In. ....................................................... 85.00
Figurine, Swan, Crown Tuscan, 4 1/2 In. .............................................................. 150.00
Figurine, Swan, Crystal, 4 1/2 In. .......................................................................... 20.00
Figurine, Swan, Crystal, 9 In. ............................................................................... 75.00
Figurine, Swan, Pink, 8 In. ................................................................................... 62.00
Figurine, Swan, Yellow, 3 In. ................................................................................ 35.00
Flower Frog, Bashful Charlotte, Nude, Clear, 8 In. ................................... 60.00 To 75.00
Flower Frog, Bashful Charlotte, Pomona, 8 1/2 In. ................................................. 90.00
Flower Frog, Bashful Maiden, Pink, 13 In. ............................................................ 175.00
Flower Frog, Blue Frosted Seminude, 7 In. ............................................................ 45.00

**Flower Frog,** Draped Lady, Amber, 13 In. ............................................................. 235.00
**Flower Frog,** Draped Lady, Clear, 5 1/2 In. ........................................................... 42.50
**Flower Frog,** Draped Lady, Green, 8 1/2 In. .......................................................... 85.00
**Flower Frog,** Draped Lady, Pink, 5 1/2 In. ............................................................ 66.50
**Flower Frog,** Globe, Rose Point, 5 In.Diam. ......................................................... 39.50
**Flower Frog,** Heron, 9 In. ....................................................................................... 65.00
**Flower Frog,** Sea Gull, 8 1/2 In. .......................................................................... 38.50
**Flower Frog,** Sea Gull, 10 In. ..................................................... 35.00 To 40.00
**Goblet,** Apple Blossom, Pale Yellow, 8 Ounce ................................................... 15.00
**Goblet,** Caprice, Blue, 7 3/4 In. ......................................................... 19.50 To 21.50
**Goblet,** Caprice, Crystal, 7 3/4 In. ......................................................................... 6.50
**Goblet,** Carmen .......................................................................................................... 12.00
**Goblet,** Diane, 9 Ounce .............................................................. 16.75 To 18.50
**Goblet,** Elaine, Footed, 10 Ounce ........................................................................... 20.00
**Goblet,** Ice Tea, Blossom Time ............................................................................... 12.50
**Goblet,** Ice Tea, Stem, Rose Point, 7 1/2 In. ...................................................... 22.00
**Goblet,** Ice Tea, Wildflower ...................................................................................... 22.50
**Goblet,** Lynbrook, Rock Crystal .............................................................................. 10.00
**Goblet,** Martha Washington Heatherbloom, 6 1/2 In. ......................................... 17.90
**Goblet,** Moongleam, Blue, 7 3/4 In., Set Of 6 ..................................................... 55.00
**Goblet,** Mt.Vernon, Crystal, 5 3/4 In. .................................................................... 7.95
**Goblet,** Mt.Vernon, Crystal, 9 Ounce ..................................................................... 7.50
**Goblet,** Portia, 10 Ounce .......................................................................................... 19.00
**Goblet,** Rose Point, Crystal, 10 Ounce ............................................ 20.00 To 30.00
**Goblet,** Versailles, 3 Ounce ..................................................................................... 22.00
**Goblet,** Wildflower, Plumed Stem ........................................................................... 20.00
**Gravy Boat & Platter,** Cleo ..................................................................................... 55.00
**Holder & Ashtray,** Cigarette, Mt.Vernon ............................................................... 18.00
**Holder,** Cigarette, Ashtray Base, Cobalt Blue ...................................................... 23.00
**Ice Bucket,** Etched, Blue ......................................................................................... 48.00
**Ice Bucket,** Forest Green, Marked ......................................................................... 20.00
**Ice Bucket,** Tally-Ho, Cobalt Blue, Handled ......................................................... 40.00
**Ice Bucket,** Tongs, Caprice Alpine, Crystal .......................................................... 30.00
**Ice Tea,** Wildflower, Footed, Set Of 6 ................................................................... 90.00
**Ice Tub,** Rose Point ................................................................................................. 55.00
**Ivy Ball,** Cobalt Blue ................................................................................................ 35.00
**Ivy Ball,** Crown Tuscan, Nudes ............................................................................... 100.00
**Ivy Ball,** Crown Tuscan, Rose Design, Gold Trim, 8 1/2 In. .............................. 78.00
**Ivy Ball,** Nude Figure Stem, Crystal, 9 1/2 In. ..................................................... 55.00
**Ivy Ball,** Red ............................................................................................................. 40.00
**Jar,** Candy, Covered, Bird Etching, Pink, 8 In. ..................................................... 45.00
**Jar,** Candy, Covered, Cut Flower Design, Amber, 6 In. ...................................... 20.00
**Jar,** Candy, Footed, Caprice, Blue, 6 In. ............................................................... 47.50
**Jar,** Candy, Green, Pink Flower Design, Signed, 8 In. ........................................ 60.00
**Jar,** Candy, Helio ....................................................................................................... 35.00
**Jar,** Marmalade, Chantilly, Sterling Silver Base & Cover ................................... 35.00
**Jar,** Marmalade, Diane, Sterling Silver Base & Lid ............................................. 28.50
**Jug,** Ball, Fuchsia, 80 Ounce .................................................................................. 75.00
**Jug,** Ice Lip, Green, 80 Ounce ............................................................................... 24.50
**Liquor Set,** Forest Green, 6-Ounce Tumblers, Farber Ware Tray ..................... 75.00
**Marmalade,** Diane, Open .......................................................................................... 24.75
**Mayonnaise Set,** Caprice, Blue, 3 Piece ............................................................... 30.00
**Mayonnaise Set,** Chantilly, Gold Encrusted, 3 Piece .......................................... 45.00
**Mustard,** Cover, Farber Ware Holder, Cobalt Blue ............................................. 40.00
**Pitcher,** Applied Reeded Handle ............................................................................ 65.00
**Pitcher,** Cream Color, Pewter Lid, Thumb Lift ..................................................... 290.00
**Pitcher,** Crystal Handle, Emerald, 76 Ounce ........................................................ 24.00
**Pitcher,** Diane ............................................................................................................ 125.00
**Pitcher,** Moonlight, Blue, 80 Ounce ....................................................................... 40.00
**Pitcher,** Mt.Vernon, 6 In. .......................................................................................... 10.00
**Pitcher,** Rose Point, 80 Ounce ......................................................... 125.00 To 195.00
**Pitcher,** Water, Pinched Sides, Silver Plated Handle, Amethyst ...................... 80.00
**Plate,** Apple Blossom, 4 1/2 In. ............................................................................. 4.50

**Plate,** Caprice, Blue, 8 1/2 In.Diam. .................................................................. 12.00 To 12.50
**Plate,** Caprice, Blue, 9 In.Diam. ...................................................................... 35.00
**Plate,** Caprice, Crystal, 8 1/2 In.Diam. ..................................................... 4.00 To 5.50
**Plate,** Caprice, Pistachio Green, 8 1/2 In. ........................................................ 12.00
**Plate,** Chantilly, Cobalt, 8 1/2 In. ................................................................... 10.00
**Plate,** Cheese & Cracker, Rose, 12 In.Diam. .................................................... 30.00
**Plate,** Cleo, Amber, 8 In.Diam. ...................................................................... 6.50
**Plate,** Crown Tuscan, Design, 5 In. ................................................................ 35.00
**Plate,** Decagon, Blue, 8 In.Diam. .................................................................. 6.00
**Plate,** Decagon, Green, 8 3/8 In.Diam. ........................................................... 5.00
**Plate,** Decagon, Green, 9 1/2 In.Diam. ........................................................... 7.00
**Plate,** Decagon, Pink, 7 In.Diam. ................................................................... 3.75
**Plate,** Decagon, Pink, 8 3/8 In.Diam. .............................................................. 5.00
**Plate,** Decagon, 6 In.Diam. ........................................................................... 3.50
**Plate,** Diane, Footed, 8 In. ........................................................................... 18.50
**Plate,** Diane, 12 1/2 In.Diam. ....................................................................... 28.00
**Plate,** Everglades, Clear, 16 In.Diam. ............................................................ 25.00
**Plate,** Martha Washington Heatherbloom, 12 In. ............................................... 12.50
**Plate,** Mt.Vernon, Crystal, 6 3/8 In.Diam. ....................................................... 2.75
**Plate,** Mt.Vernon, Crystal, 8 1/2 In.Diam. ....................................................... 4.75
**Plate,** Parrot, Green, 7 1/2 In. ...................................................................... 12.00
**Plate,** Peach Blow, 8 In. .............................................................................. 12.00
**Plate,** Rose Point, 6 1/2 In. ................................................................. 8.00 To 10.00
**Plate,** Rose Point, 7 1/2 In. ............................................................... 10.00 To 14.00
**Plate,** Rose Point, 8 In. .................................................................... 12.50 To 14.00
**Plate,** Rose Point, Handled, 8 In. ................................................................. 19.00
**Plate,** Rose Point, 10 In. ............................................................................. 45.00
**Plate,** Rose Point, Handled, 12 1/2 In.Diam. ................................................... 65.00
**Plate,** Rose Point, 14 In. ............................................................................. 30.00
**Plate,** Salad, Lynbrook, Rock Crystal ............................................................ 8.00
**Plate,** Tally-Ho, Amber, 8 In. ....................................................................... 7.00
**Plate,** Tally-Ho, Carmen, 10 1/2 In. .............................................................. 24.00
**Plate,** Torte, Crown Tuscan, Gold Floral, 13 1/2 In. ........................................ 150.00
**Plate,** Wildflower, 8 In., Set Of 12 ............................................................... 125.00
**Rose Bowl,** Caprice, Blue, 8 In. .................................................................... 38.00
**Salt & Pepper,** Rose Point, Egg Shape .......................................................... 65.00
**Salt,** Master, Swan, Figural ......................................................................... 15.00
**Salt,** Mt.Vernon, Signed, Paper Label ............................................................ 10.00
**Salt,** Swan, Apple Green, Signed, 4 1/2 In. ..................................................... 50.00
**Salt,** Swan, Clear, Signed ............................................................................ 20.00
**Saltshaker,** Diane, Flat ............................................................................... 14.50
**Saltshaker,** Handled, Farber Trim, Mulberry, Pair ........................................... 15.00
**Sauce Set,** Daffodil, 3 Piece ....................................................................... 30.00
**Shell,** Dolphin Base, Crown Tuscan, Pink Frosted, 14 In. ................................... 65.00
**Sherbet,** Apple Blossom, Pale Yellow, 6 Ounce .............................................. 10.00
**Sherbet,** Diane, Tall ................................................................................... 15.00
**Sherbet,** Lynbrook, Low, Crystal ........................................................ 4.00 To 10.00
**Sherbet,** Martha Washington Heatherbloom ................................................... 6.90
**Sherbet,** Mt.Vernon, Crystal, 4 1/4 In. .......................................................... 5.50
**Sherbet,** Rose Point, Short .......................................................................... 16.00
**Sherbet,** Rose Point, Tall ............................................................................ 18.00
**Sherbet,** Wildflower, Footed, Set Of 6 .......................................................... 60.00
**Sherry,** Diane, Amethyst, 2 Ounce ............................................................... 7.00
**Spooner,** Colonial, Green ............................................................................ 30.00
**Stein,** Amber, 14 Ounce .............................................................................. 35.00
**Sugar & Creamer,** Amber, Farber Holder, Metal Tray ...................................... 20.00
**Sugar & Creamer,** Apple Blossom, Crystal ................................................... 20.00
**Sugar & Creamer,** Caprice, Blue, 3 In. ........................................................ 24.00
**Sugar & Creamer,** Caprice, Footed, Clear, Individual, 3 In. ............................. 18.00
**Sugar & Creamer,** Cascade, Crystal ............................................................ 16.00
**Sugar & Creamer,** Cone-Shaped, Footed, Etched Flowers, Pink, 5 In. .............. 26.50
**Sugar & Creamer,** Decagon, Green .............................................................. 10.00
**Sugar & Creamer,** Decagon, Pink ................................................................ 15.00

**Sugar & Creamer,** Diane, Farber Ware Holders ........................................... 18.00
**Sugar & Creamer,** Emerald, 4 Feet, Sticker, Individual ................................ 20.00
**Sugar & Creamer,** Gadroon, Rose Point, Individual .................................... 27.00
**Sugar & Creamer,** Lightning ........................................................................ 18.00
**Sugar & Creamer,** Lynbrook ........................................................................ 25.00
**Sugar & Creamer,** Moonlight Blue, Tray ...................................................... 19.75
**Sugar & Creamer,** Mt.Vernon, Crystal ......................................................... 11.00
**Sugar & Creamer,** Rose Point, Gadroon, Individual .................... 20.00 To 30.00
**Sugar & Creamer,** Rose Point, Gold Encrusted ............................ 38.00 To 45.00
**Sugar,** Chantilly, Sterling Silver Base ......................................................... 42.50
**Sugar,** Colonial, Cobalt Blue, Covered ........................................................ 30.00
**Sugar,** Covered, Wildflower, Blue ............................................................... 42.00
**Sugar,** Decagon, Blue .................................................................................. 8.50
**Sugar,** Gadroon, Amber, Individual .............................................................. 9.00
**Sugar,** Mt.Vernon, Crystal ........................................................................... 5.00
**Syrup,** Rose Point ...................................................................................... 250.00
**Table Set,** Child's, Colonial ......................................................................... 95.00
**Toothpick,** Amberina, Ebony Feet, Inverted Strawberry, Signed ............... 100.00
**Tray,** Caprice, Crystal, 13 3/4 In. ................................................................. 15.00
**Tray,** Sandwich, Apple Blossom, Green ....................................................... 19.00
**Tray,** Sandwich, Decagon, Center Handle, Green ........................................ 12.50
**Tray,** Sandwich, Floral, Sterling Outlining, Marked, 11 1/4 In. ..................... 38.00
**Tumbler,** Amethyst, Georgian, 5 In., Set Of 8 ............................................. 80.00
**Tumbler,** Caprice, Green, Footed, Set Of 4 ................................................. 10.00
**Tumbler,** Cobalt Blue, 12 Ounce .................................................................. 9.50
**Tumbler,** Decagon, Footed, Green, 9 Ounce ................................................ 5.00
**Tumbler,** Diane, Flat, 14 Ounce ................................................................... 20.00
**Tumbler,** Elaine, Footed, 10 Ounce ............................................................. 15.50
**Tumbler,** Georgian, 4 Ounce ........................................................................ 6.00
**Tumbler,** Heatherbloom, 5 Ounce ................................................................ 15.00
**Tumbler,** Hunt Scene, Amber, 4 1/4 In. ....................................................... 15.50
**Tumbler,** Mt.Vernon, 10 Ounce .................................................................... 4.00
**Tumbler,** Rose Point, 5 Ounce ...................................... 24.00 To 26.00
**Tumbler,** Rose Point, 10 Ounce .................................................................... 23.00
**Tumbler,** Royal Lace, 4 1/8 In. ..................................................................... 22.00
**Tumbler,** Tally-Ho, Amber Bottom, Clear, 4 3/4 In., Set Of 4 ....................... 32.50
**Tumbler,** Wildflower, Footed, 5 Ounce ......................................................... 16.50
**Tumbler,** Wildflower, 10 Ounce .................................................................... 12.50
**Urn,** Covered, Crown Tuscan, Chintz Pattern, Gold, Marked, 10 In. ........... 195.00
**Vase,** Bud, Rose Point, 10 1/4 In. ................................................................ 35.00
**Vase,** Caprice, Amber, 8 3/4 In. ................................................................... 55.00
**Vase,** Cornucopia, Crown Tuscan, Shell Base, 5 In., Pair ............................ 50.00
**Vase,** Cornucopia, Ruffled, Weighted Sterling Silver Base, 11 In. .............. 125.00
**Vase,** Crown Tuscan, Trumpet, 10 In. .......................................................... 38.00
**Vase,** Diane, 11 In. ...................................................................................... 55.00
**Vase,** Enameled, Gold Rim, Green, 11 In. .................................................... 95.00
**Vase,** Feather Cut, 10 In. ............................................................................. 27.50
**Vase,** Flared Lip, Cobalt Blue, 8 1/4 In. ....................................................... 14.00
**Vase,** Keyhole, Rosepoint, 12 In. ................................................................. 49.00
**Vase,** Mandarin Gold, Cornucopia ............................................................... 33.00
**Vase,** Portia, Bulbous, 8 Crimp, 9 3/4 In. .................................................... 72.50
**Vase,** Portia, Gold Trim, 10 In. ..................................................................... 18.00
**Vase,** Purple, Keyhole Stem, 12 In. .............................................................. 30.00
**Vase,** Rose Point, Crystal, 11 In. .................................................................. 80.00
**Vase,** Rose Point, Crystal, 12 In. .................................................................. 50.00
**Vase,** Rose Point, Gold Encrusted, Squat, 5 In. ........................................... 55.00
**Vase,** Rust To Brown, Green Leaves, 2-Handled, Gourd Shape, 8 In. ......... 325.00
**Vase,** Shell, Amethyst .................................................................................. 55.00
**Vase,** Shell, Crystal, 9 3/4 In. ...................................................................... 75.00
**Vase,** Stick, Primrose, 10 In. ........................................................................ 42.50
**Vase,** Sweet Pea, Azurite, 7 1/2 In. .............................................................. 50.00
**Vase,** Wildflower, Gold Border, 12 In. ........................................................... 40.00
**Water Set,** Royal Lace, 4 Tumblers, Cobalt, Pitcher, 8 1/2 In. ................... 285.00

**Wine Set,** Amethyst Decanter, 6 Wines, Farber Ware Casing & Tray ........................ 155.00
**Wine,** Diane, Farber Ware Holder, 3 Ounce ................................................. 7.00
**Wine,** Near Cut, Gold Trim .................................................................... 8.00
**Wine,** Nude Stem, Amethyst ................................................................ 70.00
**Wine,** Nude Stem, Blue ...................................................................... 75.00
**Wine,** Nude Stem, Clear Foot & Bowl, Ebony ............................................ 50.00
**Wine,** Nude Stem, Green ........................................................ 65.00 To 70.00
**Wine,** Wildflower, Plumed Stem ........................................................... 20.00
**Wine,** Wildflower, Set Of 6 .............................................................. 120.00

*Cameo glass was made in much the same manner as a cameo in jewelry. Parts
of the top layer of glass were cut away to reveal a different colored glass
beneath. The most famous cameo glass was made during the nineteenth
century.*
**CAMEO GLASS, see also under factory names**
**CAMEO, see also Bakowitz, D'Arcy, Daum & Majorelle, Daum Nancy,**
**D'Aurys, De Vez, E. Rigor, G. De Feure, G. Raspillier,**
**Galle, L. Cie St. Denis, Le Verre Francais, Meado, Richard,**
**Vessiere, Nancy, Webb, Weis, Woodall**
**CAMEO, Bottle,** Perfume, English, Allover Cut Flowers, Stand-Up, Blue, 2 1/2 In. ................... 595.00
**Bowl,** French, Clipper Ship, Frosted, Enameled, Signed V.S., 8 In. ........................... 350.00
**Bowl,** French, Pedestal, Orange Stain, Signed Barz, 6 1/8 In. ................................ 495.00
**Box,** Amethyst Flowers, Gold Gilt, Signed St.Louis, 5 1/4 In.Diam. ........................... 400.00
**Bulb Bowl,** French, Cut Tortoiseshell Flowers, C.1900, 10 1/4 In.Diam. ..................... 150.00
**Carafe,** English, Two Butterflies, White Relief, Silver Top, 9 In. ........................... 1575.00
**Compote,** 3-Color, Pinecones In Cameo Relief, Charder, 11 In.Diam. ...................... 450.00
**Jar,** Tobacco, Acid Finish Blue Glass, Boar Finial, 8 1/2 In. ................................... 97.00
**Lamp,** Mottled Ice, Green & Brown Trees, Signed Lorainne, 19 1/4 In. ................. 2495.00
**Nappy,** English, Heart Shape, White Flowers, Citron Ground, 5 1/4 In. ................... 595.00
**Pitcher,** English, Pedestal Foot, Tangerine, 10 In. .......................................... 495.00
**Tumbler,** French, Orange Opaque Gloss Ground, Signed Lamiral, 3 3/4 In. ............ 195.00
**Vase,** Cranberry & White, C.1900, 9 3/4 In. ........................................... *Illus* 2800.00
**Vase,** Enameled Violets, St.Dennis, 6 In. .................................................. 195.00
**Vase,** English, Bulbous Base, Stick Shape Top, Red & White, 9 In. ...................... 2250.00
**Vase,** English, Citron, Cut All Around, 15 In. ........................................... 2250.00
**Vase,** English, Cut Swirling, White Leaves & Berries, 9 1/2 In. ....................... 1000.00
**Vase,** English, Passion Flower, Red Ground, 5 In. ...................................... 2500.00
**Vase,** English, Pink, White Floral, Numbered, Signed, 7 3/4 In., Pair .............. 1250.00
**Vase,** English, White Flowers, Pink Ground, Crimped, Bands At Top, 8 In. ........... 475.00
**Vase,** English, White Lining, Opaque Carved Flowers, Green, 2 3/8 In. ............... 595.00
**Vase,** French, Blue Roses, Gold Trim, Clear, Signed E.Bourgeois, 11 In. ............ 295.00
**Vase,** French, Clear Floral & Leaves, Gold Outline, St.Dennis, 12 In. ................. 695.00
**Vase,** French, Iris, Silvery Yellow Iridescence, C.De Pantin, 9 In. .................... 1500.00
**Vase,** French, Mottled Pink & Cream, Water Scene, Gauthier, 10 3/4 In. ............. 350.00
**Vase,** French, Oval, River Landscape, Gold Ground, Signed Weis, 5 7/8 In. .......... 550.00

Cameo, Vase, Cranberry & White, C.1900, 9 3/4 In.

Vase, French, Palm Tree, Arab & Camel, Signed De Veau, 11 1/2 In. .................................... 950.00
Vase, French, Swans On Water, Green, Yellow, & Black, Chouvenin, 5 In. ............................ 495.00
Vase, French, Three Cutting Jonquils, Red On White, 12 In. .................................................. 1250.00
Vase, French, Tree & Leaves, Intaglio Path, Signed Lemartine, 6 1/2 In. ........................... 1250.00
Vase, Pink & Burgundy, Signed Raspillier, 4 1/4 In. ........................................................... 395.00
Vase, Pink Flowers, 11 French Cameo Words, Signed C.Vessiere, 12 In. ........................... 785.00
Vase, Shasta Daisy Design, Purple Cut To Amber, Europe, Signed, 6 In. ........................... 80.00
Vase, Stylized Mauve Flowers, Mottled Orange, Charder, 14 In. ........................................ 490.00
Vase, Trees Lake, Men In Boat, Fishing, Signed C.Vessiere, 8 In. ..................................... 885.00
 CAMPAIGN, see Political Campaign

CAMPBELL KID, Doll, Boy, All Original, 12 1/2 In. ............................................................. 235.00
 Doll, Girl, All Original, 12 1/2 In. ................................................................................ 235.00
 Doll, Red & White Dress ............................................................................................. 15.00
 Doll, Rubber, 10 In. .................................................................................................... 15.00
 Pen & Pencil ............................................................................................................. 15.00
 Plate, Kid Painting A Sign, Give-Away ....................................................................... 25.00
 Pla-Vac Cleaner, Miro, Battery Operated, 1956 ........................................................ 24.00
 Potholder, Pair .......................................................................................................... 12.50
 Spoon, Soup, Boy ...................................................................................................... 7.00
 Spoon, Soup, Girl ...................................................................................................... 7.00

*Camphor glass is a cloudy white glass that has been blown or pressed. It was made by many factories in the Midwest during the mid-nineteenth century.*

CAMPHOR GLASS, Bottle, Perfume, Rose Shape, Butterfly Stopper .................................. 20.00
 Creamer, Bohemian Pattern ........................................................................................ 28.00
 Dish, Powder, Colonial Lady ....................................................................................... 25.00
 Dish, Powder, Covered, Bathing Beauty Seated On Lid Top ......................................... 32.00
 Dish, Swan Cover, 7 In. .............................................................................................. 13.00
 Plate, Kitten, Souvenir, Jamestown, N.Y. ..................................................................... 25.00
 Toothpick, Oaken Bucket ........................................................................................... 15.00
 Vase, Souvenir, 1876 Centennial, 7 In. ........................................................................ 28.00
 CANARY GLASS, see Vaseline Glass

CANDELABRA, Art Nouveau, Polychromed Metal Figure, Electric, 22 In. ........................... 325.00
 Enamel Inlay , Brass, 5-Branch, 20 In., Pair ............................................................... 795.00
 Gilt Bronze, Paw Feet, Fluted Column, 5-Light, 23 1/2 In., Pair ................................... 750.00
 CANDLEHOLDER, see also Brass; and various porcelain categories

CANDLEHOLDER Jeweled Vermont, Red & Green Design ................................................. 55.00
 Pricket, Fitted To Hand Or Carry, Wrought Iron, 7 In. .................................................. 150.00
 Ratchet Post, Adjustable Socket, Red Stain, Wooden, 46 In. ....................................... 600.00
 Rush, Wooden Base, 18th Century .............................................................................. 185.00
 CANDLESTICK, see also Brass, Candlestick; Pewter, Candlestick;
 Sandwich Glass, Candlestick; Silver, Sterling, Candlestick;
 and various porcelain categories

CANDLESTICK, Full-Figure Devil Creatures, Medieval, Brass, Pair ................................... 200.00
 Hog Scraper, Finger Hook, Push-Up, Tin, 4 1/2 In. ..................................................... 35.00
 Hog Scraper, Finger Hook, Push-Up, Tin, 6 1/4 In. ..................................................... 33.00
 Hog Scraper, Wedding Band Pattern, Hanging Hook, Signed ....................................... 265.00
 Hog Scraper, Wedding Band, Brass, 8 In. ................................................................... 240.00
 Knopped Stem, Bell Based, 17th Century, Germany ..................................................... 875.00
 Push-Up, Brass, Federal .............................................................................................. 42.00
 Push-Up, The Diamond Prince, English, Brass, 12 In., Pair .......................................... 250.00
 Queen Anne, Bell Metal, 4 In.Square Base, 5 1/2 In. ................................................... 90.00
 Queen Anne, Matching Vertical Snuffer Stand, Brass, Pair ........................................... 2200.00
 Spiral, Brass, 8 1/2 In. ................................................................................................ 165.00
 Spiral, Ejector, Wooden Base, 18th Century, 7 In., Pair ............................................... 175.00
 Tulip Socket, Pewter Inserts, C.1880, Boston, 9 5/8 In., Pair ..................................... 250.00

*Candy containers, especially those made of glass, have been popular since the late Victorian era. The S-XX numbers refer to the book "A Century of Glass Toys" by Mary Louise Stanky.*

| | |
|---|---:|
| **CANDY CONTAINER, Airplane,** Original Paint, Marked Victory | 68.50 |
| **Armored Tank,** Driver | 15.00 |
| **Army Bomber** | 15.00 |
| **Army Hat,** Large | 20.00 |
| **Army Hat,** Small | 10.00 |
| **Auto,** Coupe, Long Hood | 78.00 |
| **Auto,** Ford, Corrugated Hood | 60.00 |
| **Auto,** Streamlined | 15.00 To 20.00 |
| **Auto,** Streamlined, Yellow | 20.00 To 25.00 |
| **Baby Parrot,** Red & Blue | 9.00 |
| **Bank,** Liberty Bell, Amber, Tin Closure | 50.00 |
| **Barn Lantern,** Ruby | 35.00 |
| **Baseball Bank,** S-52, Flying Red Horse | 25.00 |
| **Battleship** | 12.50 To 14.50 |
| **Battleship,** S-221 | 15.00 |
| **Battleship,** Tin, Germany, 3 3/4 X 1 1/4 X 1 In. | 35.00 |
| **Bearded Musician,** Horn Down Front | 22.00 |
| **Beau Brummel** | 40.00 |
| **Bell,** Amber, Closure | 40.00 |
| **Bell,** Blue, 1926 Stamp | 45.00 |
| **Bellows Camera** | 150.00 |
| **Binoculars,** Red-Flashed, Bottom Closures | 60.00 |
| **Boot** | 4.00 |
| **Boot,** Candy & Closure, Merry Christmas Sticker | 12.00 |
| **Bottle,** Clamshell, 3 5/8 In. | 22.00 |
| **Bugle** | 15.00 |
| **Bulldog** | 6.00 To 25.00 |
| **Bulldog,** Round Tin Screw Base, 4 In. | 40.00 |
| **Bulldog,** Sitting On Small Ball | 16.00 |
| **Bureau** | 110.00 |
| **Bus** | 80.00 To 100.00 |
| **Butterfly,** Dresden | 150.00 |
| **Camera** | 95.00 |
| **Candlestick Telephone,** Whistle At Top, Contents & Label | 14.00 |
| **Car,** Cork Closure, 3 In. | 18.00 |
| **Car,** Cork Closure, 4 In. | 18.00 |
| **Cash Register** | 300.00 |
| **Chamberstick,** Clear | 9.00 |
| **Chamberstick,** Milk Glass | 12.00 |
| **Chamberstick,** Opal | 12.00 |
| **Charlie Chaplin** | 40.00 To 85.00 |
| **Charlie Chaplin,** Borgfeldt | 100.00 |
| **Charlie McCarthy** | 42.00 |
| **Chicken On Nest,** Closure & Candy | 18.00 |
| **Chicken On Nest,** Original Closure | 18.00 To 35.00 |
| **Chicken,** Rope Basket | 30.00 |
| **Chicken,** S-183 | 35.00 |
| **Chicken,** S-189 | 27.50 |
| **Clock,** Closure | 55.00 |
| **Clock,** Mantel, With Scrolls | 105.00 |
| **Clock,** Octagonal | 125.00 |
| **Colt Revolver** | 55.00 |
| **Cowboy Boot** | 12.00 |
| **Crowing Rooster** | 75.00 |
| **Cruiser,** S-226 | 7.50 |
| **Derringer,** 5 In. | 25.00 |
| **Dirigible** | 30.00 To 65.00 |
| **Dirigible,** Los Angeles | 55.00 |

| | |
|---|---|
| **Dog,** Pluto Type | 15.00 |
| **Dog,** Scotty | 6.00 To 18.00 |
| **Dog,** Seated Hound, T.H.Stough Co., Jeannette | 6.50 To 12.00 |
| **Dog,** Tige | 40.00 |
| **Doll Head,** Face Both Sides, Yellow Hair | 22.00 |
| **Doll,** Papier-Mache | 30.00 |
| **Dolly's Carpet Sweeper** | 175.00 |
| **Don't Park Here** | 125.00 |
| **Duck,** On Rope Basket | 35.00 |
| **E & A Plane,** Glass | 45.00 |
| **Electric Car** | 35.00 To 55.00 |
| **Farm Lantern** | 20.00 |
| **Fedora,** Milk Glass | 37.00 To 40.00 |
| **Fighter Ship** | 15.00 |
| **Fire Engine** | 12.00 To 30.00 |
| **Fire Engine,** S-427 | 15.00 |
| **Fire Engine,** With Man | 15.00 |
| **Fire Truck** | 20.00 |
| **Fish,** Pink To Pale Yellow | 12.00 |
| **French Telephone** | 10.00 |
| **G.O.P.Elephant** | 80.00 To 95.00 |
| **Gay Head Lighthouse** | 50.00 |
| **Gobbler** | 50.00 |
| **Grand Piano** | 65.00 |
| **Gun** | 7.00 |
| **Gun,** Amber | 45.00 |
| **Gun,** S-416 | 25.00 |
| **Gun,** S-1228 | 20.00 |
| **Gun,** S-1232 | 26.00 |
| **Gun,** Silvered Glass, 8 In. | 8.50 |
| **Happifats On Drum,** Light Purple | 50.00 |
| **Hay Wagon** | 32.00 |
| **Hearse,** 4 1/4 In. | 95.00 |
| **Hen On Nest,** Glass | 15.00 To 25.00 |
| **Hen On Sagging Basket** | 50.00 |
| **Horse-Pulled Wagon,** 3 In. | 3.00 |
| **Horse's Head,** 6 In., Pair | 25.00 |
| **Hound Pup** | 4.00 |
| **Idaho Potato** | 50.00 |
| **Independence Hall** | 20.00 |
| **Jack-O-Lantern** | 110.00 |
| **Jack-O-Lantern,** Cornflower Blue | 125.00 |
| **Jeep** | 12.50 To 15.00 |
| **Kettle** | 7.00 |
| **Kewpie,** By Barrel | 40.00 To 55.00 |
| **Kewpie,** Signed | 69.00 |
| **Kiddie Clock** | 5.00 |
| **Lamp,** Crepe Shade | 45.00 |
| **Lantern** | 7.00 To 10.00 |
| **Lantern,** Bail Handle, Paper Label Closure | 14.00 |
| **Lantern,** Bail, Jeanette, Pa. | 13.00 |
| **Lantern,** Light Blue | 18.00 |
| **Lantern,** Metal Top & Base, Dated 1904 | 32.00 |
| **Lantern,** Original Contents, Small | 11.00 |
| **Lantern,** Pewter Top, Green | 18.00 |
| **Lantern,** S-630 | 17.50 |
| **Lantern,** S-660 | 25.00 |
| **Lantern,** S-666 | 15.00 |
| **Lantern,** T.H.Stough Co. | 20.00 |
| **Learned Fox** | 70.00 |
| **Lemon,** Large | 8.00 |
| **Liberty Bell,** Amber | 25.00 To 27.50 |

| | |
|---|---|
| **Liberty Bell,** Clear | 34.00 To 40.00 |
| **Liberty Bell,** Milk Glass | 50.00 |
| **Limousine** | 75.00 |
| **Locomotive,** Glass | 15.00 |
| **Locomotive,** Original Tin Closure, 4 In. | 20.00 |
| **Locomotive,** S-706 | 7.50 |
| **Locomotive,** S-719 | 25.00 |
| **Locomotive,** S-748 | 10.00 |
| **Locomotive,** Tin Lithograph Closure | 35.00 To 40.00 |
| **Megaphone** | 25.00 |
| **Midget Washer,** Scrub Board | 20.00 |
| **Military Hat,** Original Closure & Candy | 20.00 |
| **Monkey,** Sitting Up, Holds Stick, Pink | 30.00 |
| **Moon Mullins,** S-293, Pair | 20.00 To 25.00 |
| **Mother Goose,** Holds Goose At Waist | 30.00 |
| **Motorboat** | 6.00 |
| **Mule Pulling Barrel** | 47.50 |
| **Newlywed,** Pictures Of Newlywed Comic Strip | 138.00 |
| **Nurser,** Full | 7.00 |
| **Nursing Bottle** | 7.00 |
| **Opera Glasses,** Milk Glass | 95.00 |
| **Peep-Peep Baby Chick** | 50.00 To 60.00 |
| **Peter Rabbit** | 10.00 To 20.00 |
| **Peter Rabbit,** Original Closing, Candy | 25.00 |
| **Phonograph,** Brass Horn | 150.00 |
| **Pipe,** Dresden | 150.00 |
| **Pipe,** Wicker Bowl | 50.00 |
| **Pistol,** Glass | 7.00 To 25.00 |
| **Pocket Watch,** Poor Paint | 15.00 |
| **Powder Horn,** Paneled | 25.00 |
| **Rabbit,** Carrying Basket | 15.00 |
| **Rabbit,** Eating Carrot | 25.00 To 35.00 |
| **Rabbit,** Emerging From Cracked Egg | 55.00 |
| **Rabbit,** German, Papier-Mache, 6 1/2 In. | 15.00 To 25.00 |
| **Rabbit,** Laid-Back Ears, Paint, Glass | 100.00 |
| **Rabbit,** Paws Next To Body | 30.00 |
| **Rabbit,** Running | 45.00 |
| **Rabbit,** S-858 | 15.00 |
| **Rabbit,** Seated | 12.00 |
| **Rabbit,** Sitting, Cracked Egg | 60.00 |
| **Rabbit,** Standing, Papier-Mache | 30.00 |
| **Racer,** Glass, 5 1/2 In. | 25.00 |
| **Radio** | 36.00 To 85.00 |
| **Radio,** Speaker | 75.00 |
| **Reindeer,** Papier-Mache, 1900s, Pair | 160.00 |
| **Republican Elephant** | 70.00 |
| **Revolver,** Aqua | 25.00 |
| **Revolver,** Clear | 15.00 To 30.00 |
| **Rocking Horse,** Clown Rider | 75.00 |
| **Rowboat,** Metal Sail | 15.00 |
| **Sailboat** | 10.00 |
| **Santa,** Descending Chimney, Original Paint, Tin Cap | 95.00 |
| **Santa,** Full-Bodied, Celluloid Head, 6 In. | 48.00 |
| **Santa,** In A Balloon, Red Woven Basket, Papier-Mache Hands | 55.00 |
| **Santa,** Long Coat, 4 X 2 In. | 45.00 |
| **Santa,** S-884 | 65.00 |
| **Santa,** Screw Bottom | 65.00 |
| **Santa,** With Pointed Cap | 50.00 |
| **Santa's Boot** | 10.00 |
| **Santa's Boot,** Red Plastic, Label | 5.00 |
| **Sedan,** Closure | 55.00 To 70.00 |
| **Ship On Waves** | 42.00 |

Snowman, 7 1/2 In. ............................................................................... 5.00
Spark Plug ...................................................... 30.00 To 75.00
Spirit Of Good Will ...................................... 25.00 To 100.00
Spirit Of Good Will, Paint .............................................. 125.00
Spirit Of St.Louis .......................................................... 150.00
Station Wagon ................................................................. 25.00
Station Wagon, Woody .................................................... 15.00
Station Wagon, Woody, S-73 ......................................... 15.00
Straw Hat ......................................................................... 30.00
Suitcase, Large ................................................................ 34.50
Suitcase, Small ................................................................ 20.00
Suitcase, Small, Tin Closure .......................................... 12.00
Suitcase, Wire Handle, Tin Closure ............................... 25.00
Swimming Duck Family ................................................... 60.00
Tank With Driver ............................................................ 15.00
Tank, Miniature ............................................................... 25.00
Tank, S-1138 ................................................................... 15.00
Tank, Screw Cap, 3 In. ................................................... 10.00
Tank, World War I, Paint ................................................. 65.00
Tank, World War II, Paint ................................................ 20.00
Telephone ........................................................ 7.00 To 12.00
Telephone, Closure & Candy .......................................... 25.00
Telephone, Dial, Wooden Receiver, Original Closing & Candy ......... 22.00
Telephone, Stick ............................................................. 25.00
Telephone, Upright, Ribbed ............................................ 27.50
Toonerville Trolley, Some Paint ................................... 500.00
Top Hat, Milk Glass ........................................................ 35.00
Tot Telephone ................................................................. 10.00
Train ................................................................. 18.00 To 30.00
Train, S-1028 ................................................................... 12.00
Train, 3 1/2 In. ................................................................ 20.00
Turkey, German ............................................................... 30.00
Turkey, On Stump, Nodding, Papier-Mache, Germany ............. 8.00
Turkey, Papier-Mache ................................... 30.00 To 35.00
U.S.Army Bomber ........................................................... 10.00
Uncle Sam Hat, Clear ..................................................... 35.00
Uncle Sam Hat, Milk Glass ............................................ 20.00
Uncle Sam, Fanny Farmer ............................................. 17.50
Victory Bus ...................................................................... 22.00
Wales Goodyear .............................................................. 55.00
Water Wagon .................................................................... 20.00
Wheelbarrow ................................................... 22.00 To 50.00
Willy's Jeep .................................................... 12.50 To 24.50
Windmill, S-1150 ............................................................. 30.00
Yellow Cab, Paint ........................................................... 75.00

CANE, Bamboo .................................................................. 25.00
Carved Bone, Plated Bronze Eagle Head Top, 19th Century, American ....... 575.00
Carved Coiled Snake Head, Brass Tip, 18th Century, 35 1/2 In. ..... 200.00
Cast Iron & Mother-Of-Pearl Handle ............................. 12.00
Century Of Progress, Bentwood, 35 1/2 In. .................. 17.00
Chicago World's Fair, 1934, 12 Buildings Pictured, Aluminum ......... 60.00
Figural, Thomas Jefferson ........................................... 125.00
Friendship Hand, Hand-Carved ..................................... 125.00
G.A.R. Encampment, 1897 ............................................. 35.00
Glass, Twisted Pattern, Knurled Crooked Handle, Honey Amber, 31 In. ....... 95.00
Handle, Alligator, Hand-Carved, 9 In. ......................... 125.00
Handle, Jockey Riding Race Horse ................................ 30.00
Percussion Gun, Day's Patent, C.1850 ......................... 575.00
Tiger Stripe ..................................................................... 75.00
Twisted Tree Vines Over Branch, 1890s, Irish ............. 25.00
Walking Stick, Black Inlay, Ivory ................................ 350.00
Walking Stick, Carved Ebony ........................................ 75.00

**Walking Stick,** Chicago World's Fair, 1933 ................................................................ 10.00
**Walking Stick,** Ivory Head, 34 In. ........................................................................ 30.00
**1934 Century Of Progress,** Chicago, Building Exhibits, Aluminum ................. 75.00

*Canton china is a blue-and-white ware made near Canton, China, from about
1785 to 1895. It is hand-decorated with Chinese scenes.*

**CANTON, Bowl,** Serving, 9 1/2 In. ........................................................................ 400.00
**Ginger Jar,** Covered, Landscape, 7 In., Set Of 3 ............................................... 275.00
**Ginger Jar,** Temple Building & Garden Scenes, 8 3/4 In. ................................. 200.00
**Plate,** Chop, Scenic Center, Blue Brocade, 14 In. ............................................. 200.00
**Platter,** Cut Corners, Rectangular, 18 1/4 In. .................................................. 350.00
**Platter,** Rectangular, 6 1/4 X 10 3/4 In. ........................................................... 99.50
**Platter,** 20 In. ........................................................................................................ 495.00
**Tureen,** Sauce, Underplate, Boar's Head Handles, Spur Finial, 5 In. ............... 175.00
**Tureen,** Soup ........................................................................................................ 225.00
**Tureen,** Vegetable, Oval, Acorn Design, 10 1/2 In. .......................................... 325.00
**Umbrella Stand,** 19th Century, 24 1/4 In. ...................................................*Illus* 1300.00

*Capo-Di-Monte porcelain was first made in Naples, Italy, from 1743 to
1759. The factory moved near Madrid, Spain, and reopened in 1771 and
worked to 1834. Since that time the Doccia factory of Italy acquired the molds
and is using the N and crown mark.*

**CAPO-DI-MONTE, Bottle,** Flask, Wine, 18th Century, Signed, Pair ................. 950.00
**Box,** Trinket, Mitered Corners, 4 X 3 In. ............................................................ 175.00
**Bust,** Cavalier, Signed, 6 In. ............................................................................... 135.00
**Casket,** Jewel, Gloria On Cover, Crown N Mark ............................................... 375.00
**Cup & Saucer,** Raised Horses, Chariot, Driver, 22K Gold ............................... 150.00
**Dish,** Candy, Covered, Lion On Cover, Figures, Signed .................................... 135.00
**Plaque,** Figures, Colorful Enamels, C.1900, 16 X 23 In. ................................. 2000.00
**Plaque,** 5 Children Romping In Garden, 4 1/4 X 3 In. ..................................... 110.00
**Plate,** Armorial Coat Of Arms Center, 18th Century ........................................ 375.00
**Stein,** Adults & Children In Garden, Lion On Lid, Signed ................................. 125.00
**Stein,** Elephants & Warriors ............................................................................... 1500.00
**Tea Set,** Creamer, Sugar, Dragon Spout, Gold & Red ...................................... 395.00
**Tea Set,** Dragon Spout, 4 Cups & Saucers, Red & Gold, 11 Piece ................. 425.00
**Urn,** Cherubs In Garden, 2-Handled, Covered, 8 X 25 In. ............................... 280.00
**Urn,** Seminudes Back & Front, Cherub Finial, C.1880, 18 In. ......................... 325.00
**Vase,** Allegorical Scene, 4 Cupids On Base, Holder, 2 In., Pair ...................... 350.00

Canton, Umbrella Stand, 19th Century, 24 1/4 In.

**CAPTAIN MARVEL, Racing Car, Lightning** ............................................. 300.00
    **Tatoos,** In Envelope, 1940s .................................................................. 20.00
    **Tooter,** 1946 ......................................................................................... 8.00


**CAPTAIN MIDNIGHT, Decoder & Pitcher** ...................................... 40.00
    **Decoder,** 1940 ....................................................................................... 65.00
    **Decoder,** 1949 ....................................................................................... 20.00
    **Mug,** Ovaltine ......................................................................................... 14.00
    **Ring,** Initial ............................................................................................ 40.00
    **Ring,** Secret Compartment ................................................................... 55.00
    **Shaker,** Ovaltine ................................................................................... 25.00
    **Skelly Badge,** Insert ............................................................................. 22.00
        **CARAMEL SLAG, see Chocolate Glass**


        **CARD, see also Postcard**
**CARD, Baseball,** Sweet Caporal, Set Of 60 ....................................... 135.00
    **Christmas,** Andy Gump, 1920s ............................................................ 2.50
    **Christmas,** Folding, Fringe, C.1890, Set Of 4 .................................. 500.00
    **Fortune,** Owl Drug, Movie Star, Set Of 100 ..................................... 15.00
    **Fortune,** Owl Drug, Movie Star, Set Of 200 ..................................... 20.00
    **Gum,** Mickey Mouse Bread, Set Of 20 Different .............................. 80.00
    **Playing,** American Airlines ................................................................... 2.00
    **Playing,** American President Lines ....................................................... 5.00
    **Playing,** Arbuckle Coffee ....................................................................... 65.00
    **Playing,** Burlington Northern, Sealed Double Deck .......................... 13.00
    **Playing,** Burlington Route, 1925 .......................................................... 20.00
    **Playing,** Burlington Zephyr, Dated 1935 ............................................ 6.50
    **Playing,** C.M.& St.Paul Railway .......................................................... 45.00
    **Playing,** Catapres Tablets ...................................................................... 2.00
    **Playing,** Century Of Progress ............................................................... 9.50
    **Playing,** Chessie The Cat ....................................................................... 8.50
    **Playing,** Chlor-Trimeton Tablets ........................................................... 2.00
    **Playing,** Contentment, Maxfield Parrish, Box ................................... 40.00
    **Playing,** Continental Airlines ................................................................ 2.00
    **Playing,** Cunard ...................................................................................... 5.00
    **Playing,** Erie Railroad, 100th Anniversary, Gold Edge, Double Deck ........ 24.00
    **Playing,** Greyhound ................................................................................ 2.00
    **Playing,** Hard-A-Port Cut Plug ............................................................ 225.00
    **Playing,** Harley Davidson, Unopened ................................................. 4.00
    **Playing,** Harrah's Reno Casino ............................................................ 2.00
    **Playing,** Little Duke, 1 1/2 X 1 1/2 In. .............................................. 12.50
    **Playing,** Man From Uncle ..................................................................... 5.00
    **Playing,** Movie Star, 1916 .................................................................... 85.00
    **Playing,** Norman Rockwell, Unopened .............................................. 3.00
    **Playing,** Peerless Pump ......................................................................... 2.00
    **Playing,** Political Personalities, Nixon Era ......................................... 5.00
    **Playing,** Popeye, 1937 .......................................................................... 16.00
    **Playing,** Portina Cigars, Pinochle ....................................................... 5.00
    **Playing,** Redwood Trees, Double ........................................................ 3.50
    **Playing,** San Francisco, Different Scenes, Double ............................ 5.00
    **Playing,** Santa Fe R.R. .......................................................................... 6.00
    **Playing,** Silent Movie Stars, 1916 ...................................................... 32.50
    **Playing,** Southern Pacific ..................................................................... 15.00
    **Playing,** Tulare, Double ......................................................................... 3.50
    **Trading,** Dwight's Soda, Arm & Hammer Birds, Set Of 100 .......... 75.00
    **Valentine,** Boy Dressed Like George Washington ............................ 7.00
    **Valentine,** Boy Holding Hearts, Movable Arms, Eyes, Germany, 9 In. .... 16.00
    **Valentine,** Dirigible ............................................................................... 25.00
    **Valentine,** Fold-Over, Silk Fringe, Tassle, Prang, 1884, 4 X 3 1/2 In. .... 7.00
    **Valentine,** Fold-Over, Whitneys, 6 X 4 1/2 In. ................................ 2.00
    **Valentine,** Heart-Shaped Fold-Over, Whitneys, C.1920, Marked, Set Of 5 .... 8.00
    **Valentine,** Henry & Maggie, Moving Parts, 1920s ......................... 15.00
    **Valentine,** Inscribed Elizabeth, Dated 1772, 3 3/4 X 6 1/4 In. ...... 125.00

| | |
|---|---|
| **Valentine,** Lacy, Signed W.J.Meek & Son, 7 1/2 X 9 1/2 In. | 40.00 |
| **Valentine,** Snow White, Disney, 1938 | 15.00 |
| **Valentine,** Standing, Pull-Out, Dimensional, German | 4.00 |
| **CARDER, see Aurene; Steuben** | |

*Carlsbad, Germany, is a mark found on china made by several factories in
Germany. Most of the pieces available today were made after 1891.*

| | |
|---|---|
| **CARLSBAD, Biscuit Jar,** Victoria, Cherubs, Blue | 68.00 |
| **Bowl,** Scalloped Edge, Flowers, Gold Rim, Oval, 16 X 9 In. | 45.00 |
| **Ewer,** Orange & Green Leaves, Cream Ground, 12 In. | 52.00 |
| **Fish Set,** 8 Plates, Crayfish, Platter, 21 X 9 3/4 In. | 350.00 |
| **Plate,** 3 Ladies In Grecian Dress, Emerald Border, 8 1/4 In. | 35.00 |
| **Tray,** Bread, Old Glory | 60.00 |
| **Vase,** Floral Design, Gold Enamel, Ivory Ground, 8 In. | 55.00 |
| **Vase,** Gold Outline, Enameled Poppies, Ivory Ground, 9 1/2 In. | 40.00 |
| **Vase,** Hand-Painted, Poppies, Gold Outline, 9 1/4 In. | 45.00 |
| **Vase,** Ivory Satin Finish, Floral, Gold Enamel, Signed, 8 In. | 35.00 |
| **Vase,** Portrait, Seminude Lady, Cherubs, 9 In. | 50.00 |
| **Vase,** Twig Handles, Rose & Gold, Ivory Ground, 7 In. | 32.00 |
| **Vase,** White Ground, Lilac Flowers, Purple Crown Mark, 9 In. | 35.00 |

*Carlton ware was made at the Carlton Works of Stoke-on-Trent,
England, about 1890. The firm traded as Wiltshaw & Robinson until
1957. It was renamed Carlton Ware Ltd. in 1958.*

| | |
|---|---|
| **CARLTON WARE, Biscuit Box,** White Figures, Blue Ground, Silver Bail & Cover | 110.00 |
| **Bowl,** Enameled, Gold Oriental Scene, Ivory Luster, 13 1/4 In. | 250.00 |
| **Candleholder,** Rouge Royale | 35.00 |
| **Dish,** Feeding, Hand-Tinted Scene, Seesaw, 7 3/4 In. | 48.00 |
| **Dish,** Feeding, Jack & Jill, Deep | 21.00 |
| **Napkin Ring,** Crinoline Lady, Different Color Each, Set Of 4 | 130.00 |
| **Vase,** Gold Edge, Lady & Horse, Signed, 2 1/2 X 9 In.Diam. | 15.00 |

*Carnival, or taffeta, glass was an inexpensive, pressed, iridescent glass made
from about 1900 to 1920. Over 200 different patterns are known.
Carnival glass is currently being reproduced. If the letter N for
Northwood is included in the description, it appears on the piece of glass.*

**CARNIVAL GLASS, see also Northwood**

| | |
|---|---|
| **CARNIVAL GLASS, Ashtray,** Dutch Boy & Girl, Marigold | 25.00 |
| **Ashtray,** Figural, Stetson Hat, Marigold | 17.50 |
| **Banana Boat,** Grape & Cable, Ice Green, 12 In. | 400.00 |
| **Banana Boat,** Grape & Cable, Marigold | 125.00 |
| **Banana Boat,** Grape & Cable, Purple | 150.00 |
| **Banana Boat,** Kittens, Marigold | 50.00 To 85.00 |
| **Banana Boat,** Thistle, Water Lily, & Cat, Blue | 185.00 |
| **Banana Boat,** Wreathed Cherry, White, 6 In. | 65.00 |
| **Basket,** Basket Weave, Bushel, 2-Handled, Marigold, 5 1/2 In. | 45.00 |
| **Basket,** Basket Weave, Fenton, Purple | 40.00 |
| **Basket,** Fenton, Ice Green, 5 1/2 In. | 70.00 |
| **Basket,** Handled, Basket Weave, Marigold, Miniature | 25.00 |
| **Bell,** Daisy Cut, Marigold | 450.00 |
| **Berry Bowl,** Blackberry Wreath, Marigold, Millersburg, 6 In. | 20.00 |
| **Berry Bowl,** Butterfly & Berry, Fantail Interior, Cobalt | 70.00 |
| **Berry Bowl,** Butterfly & Berry, Marigold | 49.00 To 60.00 |
| **Berry Bowl,** Floragold, Marigold, 4 1/2 In. | 2.95 |
| **Berry Bowl,** Grape & Gothic Arches, Blue | 17.50 |
| **Berry Bowl,** Northwood, Peach | 85.00 |
| **Berry Bowl,** Palm Beach & Gooseberry, White | 26.00 |
| **Berry Bowl,** Panther, Claw-Footed, Marigold | 22.00 To 39.00 |
| **Berry Bowl,** Peacock At Fountain, Marigold | 69.00 |

| | |
|---|---|
| Berry Bowl, Rose & Daisy, Marigold, Set Of 3 | 40.00 |
| Berry Bowl, Ski Star, Purple | 25.00 |
| Berry Set, Atlas, Northwood, Purple, 6 Piece | 55.00 |
| Berry Set, Butterfly & Berry, Blue, Footed, 7 Piece | 295.00 |
| Berry Set, Diamond Point Columns, Marigold, 7 Piece | 58.00 |
| Berry Set, Maple Leaf, Marigold, 7 Piece | 55.00 |
| Berry Set, Open Rose, Purple, 7 Piece | 255.00 |
| Berry Set, Peach, White, 7 Piece | 550.00 |
| Berry Set, Peacock At Fountain, Marigold, 7 Piece | 115.00 |
| Berry Set, Peacock At Fountain, White, 7 Piece | 525.00 |
| Berry Set, Petal & Fern, Opalescent Peach, 7 Piece | 275.00 |
| Berry, Bowl, Acorn Burrs, Green | 22.00 |
| Berry, Bowl, Singing Birds, Green, N | 22.00 |
| Boat, Daisy & Block, Marigold, 12 In. | 250.00 |
| Bonbon, Birds & Cherries, Blue | 80.00 |
| Bonbon, Brocaded Palms, Pink, 6 In. | 70.00 |
| Bonbon, Butterfly, Northwood, Green | 45.00 |
| Bonbon, Fine Cut & Roses, Northwood, Purple | 40.00 |
| Bonbon, Floral & Wheat, Stemmed, Opalescent Peach | 70.00 |
| Bonbon, Fruits & Flowers, Blue, Stemmed | 50.00 |
| Bonbon, Fruits & Flowers, Footed, Aqua Opalescent | 200.00 |
| Bonbon, Fruits & Flowers, Lavender, Stemmed, 2-Handled | 75.00 |
| Bonbon, Fruits & Flowers, Purple, Stemmed | 50.00 |
| Bonbon, Fruits & Flowers, White, Stemmed | 150.00 |
| Bonbon, Grape & Cable, Blue | 40.00 |
| Bonbon, Grape & Cable, Marigold | 29.00 |
| Bonbon, Grape & Cable, Purple | 40.00 |
| Bonbon, Netted Roses, Green, Northwood, 9 In. | 35.00 |
| Bonbon, Northern Star, Marigold | 15.00 |
| Bonbon, Panel Holly, Green | 45.00 |
| Bonbon, Persian Medallion, Aqua | 45.00 To 150.00 |
| Bonbon, Persian Medallion, Red | 500.00 |
| Bonbon, Theee Fruits, Blue, Handled, Pedestal, Basket Weave | 40.00 |
| Bonbon, Three Fruits, 2-Handled, Northwood, Amethyst | 45.00 |
| Bottle, Cologne, Grape & Cable, Stopper, Purple | 175.00 To 235.00 |
| Bottle, Cologne, Grape & Cable, Stopper, White | 90.00 |
| Bottle, Corn, Marigold | 300.00 |
| Bottle, Water, Imperial Grape.Green | 150.00 |
| Bottle, Water, Imperial Grape, Marigold | 135.00 |
| Bottle, Water, Imperial Grape, Purple | 95.00 To 164.00 |
| Bowl, Amethyst, Ruffled, 9 In. | 30.00 |
| Bowl, Apple Blossom Twigs, White, 8 3/4 In. | 125.00 |
| Bowl, Apple Twigs, Peach Opalescent, 9 In. | 49.00 |
| Bowl, Autumn Acorns, Candy Ribbon Edge, Green, 8 In. | 40.00 |
| Bowl, Banana, Cherry & Wreath, Purple, Oval, Footed | 135.00 |
| Bowl, Basket Weave, Ice Green, 5 In. | 45.00 |
| Bowl, Bells & Beads, Peach Opalescent, 7 In. | 40.00 |
| Bowl, Berries, Purple, Scalloped, 9 In. | 79.00 |
| Bowl, Blackberry Wreath, Green, Millersburg, 10 In. | 95.00 |
| Bowl, Blackberry Wreath, Millersburg, Green, 8 1/4 In.Diam. | 65.00 |
| Bowl, Blue, Sunray, Northwood, 5 In. | 25.00 |
| Bowl, Bowl, Iris & Herringbone, Scalloped, Marigold, 12 In. | 10.00 |
| Bowl, Brocaded Summer Garden, Ice Green, 11 In. | 125.00 |
| Bowl, Brooklyn Bridge, Marigold, 8 1/2 In. | 150.00 To 350.00 |
| Bowl, Bull's-Eye & Leaves, Marigold, Northwood, 8 1/2 In. | 35.00 |
| Bowl, Butterflies, Amethyst, Handled, 7 In. | 50.00 |
| Bowl, Butterfly & Tulip, Flared, Marigold, 11 In. | 300.00 |
| Bowl, Cable, Marigold, 8 In. | 50.00 |
| Bowl, Carnival Holly, Red, 9 In. | 450.00 |
| Bowl, Caroline, Fluted, Peach Opalescent, 8 1/2 In. | 55.00 |
| Bowl, Center, Brocaded Palms, Pink, 12 In. | 125.00 |
| Bowl, Centerpiece, Double Scroll, Red, 10 1/2 In. | 200.00 |
| Bowl, Cherries & Leaves, Marigold, Handled, 6 1/2 In. | 35.00 |

**Bowl,** Cherry Circles, Flared, 10 1/2 In. ..................................................................... 125.00
**Bowl,** Cherry Wreath, Marigold, Oval, 13 X 9 In. ............................................... 60.00
**Bowl,** Cherry Wreath, Purple, Oblong, 9 X 12 In. ............................................. 105.00
**Bowl,** Chrysanthemum, Blue, 10 1/2 In. ............................................................. 150.00
**Bowl,** Chrysanthemum, Marigold, 9 In. ............................................................... 43.00
**Bowl,** Chrysanthemum, Red, 8 In. ....................................................................... 1250.00
**Bowl,** Coin Dot, Amethyst, 9 In. ......................................................................... 22.00
**Bowl,** Coin Dot, Marigold, 9 In. ......................................................................... 16.00
**Bowl,** Coin Dot, Purple, 9 In. ............................................................................. 40.00
**Bowl,** Cosmos & Cane, Headdress Interior, Green, 6 In. ................................ 58.00
**Bowl,** Cosmos & Cane, White, 10 1/2 In. ......................................................... 25.00
**Bowl,** Cosmos Variant, Marigold, 10 In. ........................................................... 39.00
**Bowl,** Cut Arcs, Marigold, 9 In. ......................................................................... 20.00
**Bowl,** Daisy & Plume, Marigold, 3-Footed, 5 In. ............................................. 40.00
**Bowl,** Daisy Wreath, Blue Opalescent, 9 In. .................................................... 175.00
**Bowl,** Dogwood Spray, White, 8 1/2 In. ............................................................ 55.00
**Bowl,** Dogwood, Orange & White Overlay, Fluted, 7 In. ................................ 50.00
**Bowl,** Dragon & Lotus, Amethyst, 9 In. ............................................................. 32.00
**Bowl,** Dragon & Lotus, Green Opalescent, Footed, 8 In. ................................ 125.00
**Bowl,** Dragon & Lotus, Marigold, Flat, 9 In. .................................................... 32.00
**Bowl,** Dragon & Lotus, Orange, 8 1/2 In. ......................................................... 65.00
**Bowl,** Dragon & Lotus, Peach Opalescent, Footed, 8 In. ............................... 150.00
**Bowl,** Dragon & Lotus, Peach Opalescent, 8 3/4 In. ....................................... 125.00
**Bowl,** Dragon & Lotus, Red, 9 In. ............................................. 350.00 To 500.00
**Bowl,** Dragon & Strawberry, Blue, 9 In. ........................................................... 600.00
**Bowl,** Embroidered Mums, Ice Blue, 9 In. ....................................................... 179.00
**Bowl,** Embroidered Mums, Ice Green, 8 3/4 In. ............................................... 145.00
**Bowl,** Embroidered Mums, Purple, 9 In. ........................................................... 85.00
**Bowl,** Farmyard, Purple ............................................................ 1800.00 To 2100.00
**Bowl,** Fashion, Smoky, Imperial, Ruffled, 9 In. ............................................... 50.00
**Bowl,** Floral & Optic, Footed, Red, 9 In. .......................................................... 300.00
**Bowl,** Fluted, Red, 9 3/4 In. ............................................................................... 200.00
**Bowl,** Garden Path, White, 9 1/2 In. ................................................................. 85.00
**Bowl,** Golden Grape, Marigold, 7 1/2 In.Diam. ............................................... 29.00
**Bowl,** Golden Honeycomb, Opalescent Peach, 7 1/4 In. ................................ 50.00
**Bowl,** Good Luck, Amethyst, 9 In. ..................................................................... 125.00
**Bowl,** Good Luck, Aqua Opalescent, 9 In. ................................. 500.00 To 525.00
**Bowl,** Good Luck, Blue Stippled, 9 In. ............................................................. 110.00
**Bowl,** Good Luck, Blue, Ruffled, 9 In. ............................................................. 110.00
**Bowl,** Good Luck, Green Iridescent, 9 In. ........................................................ 150.00
**Bowl,** Good Luck, Marigold, Ruffled, 9 In. ..................................................... 67.00
**Bowl,** Good Luck, Marigold, 9 In. ..................................................................... 79.00
**Bowl,** Good Luck, Purple, 9 In. ......................................................................... 135.00
**Bowl,** Grape & Cable, Aqua, Fenton, 7 1/2 In. ............................................... 90.00
**Bowl,** Grape & Cable, Blue, 3-Footed, 8 In. .................................................... 45.00
**Bowl,** Grape & Cable, Electric Blue, 9 In. ....................................................... 75.00
**Bowl,** Grape & Cable, Green, Spatula-Footed, 9 In. ...................................... 32.50
**Bowl,** Grape & Cable, Purple, Ruffled, 8 In. ................................................... 66.00
**Bowl,** Grape & Cable, Purple, 8 In. ................................................................. 65.00
**Bowl,** Grape & Leaf, Blue, Fluted, 7 1/2 In. .................................................... 85.00
**Bowl,** Grape Arbor, Double Pattern, 9 1/2 X 5 1/2 In. .................................... 135.00
**Bowl,** Grape Leaves, Northwood, Marigold, 8 3/4 In. ..................................... 34.00
**Bowl,** Grape Wreath, Amethyst, 6 1/2 In. ........................................................ 65.00
**Bowl,** Grape, Clambroth, 6 In. ........................................................................... 30.00
**Bowl,** Grapes & Leaves, Marigold, Northwood, 8 3/4 In. ............................... 38.00
**Bowl,** Hearts & Flowers, Ice Blue, 8 3/4 In. .................................................... 125.00
**Bowl,** Hearts & Flowers, Ice Green, 8 1/2 In. .................................................. 185.00
**Bowl,** Hobstar & Arches, Marigold, 9 In. ......................................................... 20.00
**Bowl,** Holly & Berry, Marigold, 9 In. ......................................... 30.00 To 36.00
**Bowl,** Holly Carnival, Amber, 9 In. ................................................................. 75.00
**Bowl,** Holly Carnival, Aqua, 8 3/4 In. ............................................................. 75.00
**Bowl,** Holly Carnival, Blue, 8 1/2 In. ............................................................. 45.00
**Bowl,** Holly Carnival, Red, 9 In. ....................................................................... 450.00

**Bowl,** Holly Carnival, Ruffled, Blue, 9 In. ........................................................................ 65.00
**Bowl,** Holly Pattern, White, Scalloped Edge, 9 In. ............................................................ 70.00
**Bowl,** Holly Spring, Ribbon Edge, Opalescent Peach, 7 In. .............................................. 65.00
**Bowl,** Holly, Flat, Marigold, 9 In. ..................................................................................... 35.00
**Bowl,** Horse Medallion, Footed, Blue .............................................................................. 100.00
**Bowl,** Horse's Head, Amethyst, 8 1/2 In. ........................................................................ 145.00
**Bowl,** Horse's Head, Marigold, 6 In. ................................................................................ 60.00
**Bowl,** Ice Cream, Grape & Cable, White, 11 In. .............................................................. 195.00
**Bowl,** Ice Cream, Peacock & Urn, Electric Blue, 11 In. ................................................... 189.00
**Bowl,** Ice Cream, Peacock & Urn, Green, 11 In. .............................................................. 400.00
**Bowl,** Ice Cream, Peacock & Urn, White, 11 In. .............................................................. 250.00
**Bowl,** Ice Cream, Persian Garden, White, 11 1/2 In. ...................................................... 150.00
**Bowl,** Imperial Grape, Purple, 11 In. ................................................................................ 40.00
**Bowl,** Indian Tree, Marigold, 7 In. .................................................................................... 35.00
**Bowl,** Iris & Herringbone, Scalloped, Marigold, 11 In. ..................................................... 15.00
**Bowl,** Kingfisher, Marigold, 9 1/2 In. ............................................................................... 89.00
**Bowl,** Leaf Chain, Red, 7 1/4 In. ...................................................................................... 400.00
**Bowl,** Leaf Chain, 8 1/2 In. ............................................................................................... 125.00
**Bowl,** Little Fishes, Blue, 9 1/4 In. ................................................................................... 200.00
**Bowl,** Little Flowers, Amethyst, 10 In. .............................................................................. 75.00
**Bowl,** Lotus & Dragon, Blue, 9 In. ................................................... 40.00 To 95.00
**Bowl,** Lustre Rose, Clambroth, 3-Footed, 11 In. ............................................................. 50.00
**Bowl,** Lustre Rose, Marigold, 3-Footed, 7 1/2 In. ........................................................... 30.00
**Bowl,** Lustre Rose, Purple, 3-Footed, 11 In. .................................................................... 89.00
**Bowl,** Nesting Swan, Purple, Millersburg, 9 1/2 In. ......................................................... 160.00
**Bowl,** Nesting Swan, Purple, 10 In. .................................................................................. 300.00
**Bowl,** Nippon, Ice Blue, 8 1/2 In. ..................................................................................... 125.00
**Bowl,** Open Rose, Clambroth, 8 In. .................................................................................. 20.00
**Bowl,** Open Rose, Marigold, Footed, 10 In. ..................................................................... 29.00
**Bowl,** Orange Tree, Cobalt Blue, 9 In. .............................................................................. 48.00
**Bowl,** Orange Tree, Red, Footed, 8 In. ............................................................................. 600.00
**Bowl,** Panther, Blue, Footed, 9 1/2 In. ............................................................................. 200.00
**Bowl,** Panther, Blue, 5 In. ................................................................................................. 65.00
**Bowl,** Panther, Butterflies Outside, Purple, 9 In. ............................................................. 130.00
**Bowl,** Peacock & Grape, Amethyst, 8 1/2 In. ................................................................... 42.00
**Bowl,** Peacock & Grape, Blue, 9 In. .................................................................................. 45.00
**Bowl,** Peacock & Grape, Green, 9 In. ................................................................................ 65.00
**Bowl,** Peacock & Grape, Red, 8 1/2 In. .................................................. 275.00 To 375.00
**Bowl,** Peacock & Grape, Red, 9 In. ................................................................................... 325.00
**Bowl,** Peacock & Urn, Purple, 2 1/2 In. ........................................................................... 60.00
**Bowl,** Peacock & Urn, White, 8 3/4 In. ............................................................................. 125.00
**Bowl,** Peacock At Well, Marigold, 9 In. ............................................................................ 85.00
**Bowl,** Peacock On Fence, Aqua Opalescent, 8 3/4 In. .................................................... 400.00
**Bowl,** Peacock On Fence, Green, 8 3/4 In. ...................................................................... 200.00
**Bowl,** Peacock On Fence, Pearl, 9 In. ............................................................................... 350.00
**Bowl,** Persian Garden, White, 6 In. ..................................................... 30.00 To 70.00
**Bowl,** Persian Medallion, Light Green, 5 In. ..................................................................... 18.00
**Bowl,** Persian Medallion, Marigold, 8 3/4 In. ................................................................... 30.00
**Bowl,** Petal & Fan, Purple, 5 1/2 In. ................................................................................. 30.00
**Bowl,** Peter Rabbit, Marigold, 9 In. ................................................................................... 1300.00
**Bowl,** Plaid, Green, 9 In. ................................................................................................... 75.00
**Bowl,** Pony, Greek Key, Marigold, Ruffled, 9 In. .............................................................. 65.00
**Bowl,** Poppy Show, Ice Green, 8 3/4 In. ........................................................................... 500.00
**Bowl,** Poppy Show, Marigold, Flared, 9 In. ...................................................................... 250.00
**Bowl,** Posey & Pod, Gold Exterior, Marigold, 9 In.Diam. ................................................. 40.00
**Bowl,** Primrose, Purple, Millersburg, 10 In. ..................................................................... 79.00
**Bowl,** Raindrops, Ribbon Edge, Footed, Peach, 9 In. ...................................................... 60.00
**Bowl,** Ray, Orange, 10 In. ................................................................................................. 35.00
**Bowl,** Reindeer & Holly, Marigold, Footed, 11 In. ............................................................ 98.00
**Bowl,** Rose Show, Aqua Opalescent, 8 3/4 In. ................................................................ 300.00
**Bowl,** Rose Show, Green, Flared, 9 In. ............................................................................. 250.00
**Bowl,** Rose Show, Ice Green, 8 3/4 In. ............................................................................ 500.00
**Bowl,** Rosette, Purple, 9 In. .............................................................................................. 45.00

Bowl, Scroll, Purple, 7 In. ............................................................................................ 30.00
Bowl, Single Flower, Opalescent Peach, 7 3/4 In. .................................................. 50.00
Bowl, Ski Star, Peach Opalescent, 10 1/2 In. .......................................................... 47.00
Bowl, Stag & Holly, Footed, Green, 10 In.Diam. ...................................................... 220.00
Bowl, Stag & Holly, Marigold, Footed, 8 In. ............................................................. 55.00
Bowl, Stag & Holly, Marigold, 10 1/2 In. .................................................................. 79.00
Bowl, Stag & Holly, Marigold, 11 In. .......................................................................... 79.00
Bowl, Stag & Holly, Purple, Spatula-Footed, 3 3/8 In. ............................................ 75.00
Bowl, Star & Holly, Marigold, Ruffled, Footed, 7 In. ................................................ 145.00
Bowl, Star Medallion, Clambroth, 7 1/2 In. ............................................................... 30.00
Bowl, Star Of David, Amethyst, 9 In. .......................................................................... 40.00
Bowl, Star Of David, Green, 9 In. ............................................................................... 50.00
Bowl, Star Of David, Purple, 9 In. .............................................................................. 60.00
Bowl, Stemmed Rays, Green, 6 In. ............................................................................. 27.50
Bowl, Stippled Rays, Green, 8 In. ............................................................................... 30.00
Bowl, Stippled Rays, Purple, 9 In. .............................................................................. 35.00
Bowl, Strawberry, Ice Green, 8 1/2 In. ....................................................................... 250.00
Bowl, Strawberry, Purple, 8 1/2 In. ............................................................................ 65.00
Bowl, Strawberry, White, Flared, 10 In. ..................................................................... 150.00
Bowl, Sunflower, Meander Exterior, Green, 8 1/2 In. .............................................. 50.00
Bowl, Ten Mums, Fluted & Ruffled, Marigold, Footed, 9 1/4 In. ............................ 95.00
Bowl, Ten Mums, Green, Footed, 10 In. ..................................................................... 79.00
Bowl, Thistle, Amethyst, 8 1/2 In. ............................................................................... 45.00
Bowl, Three Fruits Inside, Basket Weave Outside, Green, 8 In. ............................ 48.00
Bowl, Three Fruits, Aqua Opalescent, 9 In. .............................................................. 250.00
Bowl, Three Fruits, Green, Footed, N, 5 In. ............................................................... 75.00
Bowl, Three Fruits, Green, N, 9 1/2 In. ...................................................................... 48.00
Bowl, Three Fruits, Purple To Red, N, 9 In. .............................................................. 85.00
Bowl, Three Fruits, White, Flared, 8 1/2 In. ............................................................... 175.00
Bowl, Trout & Fly, Marigold, 9 1/2 In. ........................................................................ 165.00
Bowl, Twist, Marigold, 3 1/4 X 8 In. ........................................................................... 30.00
Bowl, Two Flowers, Footed, Cobalt, 6 1/2 In. ........................................................... 65.00
Bowl, Two Flowers, Green, 10 In. ............................................................................... 42.00
Bowl, Vintage, Amethyst, 9 In. .................................................................................... 54.50
Bowl, Vintage, Marigold, Ruffled & Fluted, 8 1/2 In. ............................................... 32.00
Bowl, Waffle, Marigold, Square, 7 3/4 In. .................................................................. 35.00
Bowl, Whirling Leaves, Green, Millersburg, 9 1/2 In. .............................................. 85.00
Bowl, White, Poppy Show, 8 3/4 In. ........................................................................... 200.00
Bowl, Windmill, Marigold, 7 In. .................................................................................. 23.00
Bowl, Windmill, White, 7 1/2 In. ................................................................................. 50.00
Bowl, Wishbone, Green, Footed, 3 1/4 In. ................................................................ 68.00
Bowl, Wishbone, Green, Scallop Edge, Footed, 8 In. ............................................. 65.00
Bowl, Wishbone, Purple, Footed, Northwood, 8 1/2 In. .......................................... 75.00
Bowl, Wishbone, White, Flared, Footed, 8 1/2 In. ................................................... 125.00
Bucket, Brocaded Acorn, Lavender, 4 3/4 X 2 1/2 In. ............................................. 90.00
Butter, Butterfly & Berry, Marigold, Covered ........................................................... 70.00
Butter, Grape & Cable, Purple, Covered ........................................... 160.00 To 220.00
Butter, Grape & Gothic Arches, Marigold, Covered ................................................ 95.00
Butter, Iris & Herringbone, Marigold, Covered ........................................................ 18.00
Butter, Little Lamb, Marigold, Covered, Miniature ................................................... 125.00
Butter, Lustre Rose, Marigold, Covered .................................................................... 50.00
Butter, Palm Beach, White, Cover .............................................................................. 450.00
Butter, Peacock At Fountain, Purple, Covered ......................................................... 89.00
Butter, Singing Birds, Marigold, Covered ................................................................. 125.00
Button, Shell Shape With Beetle, Red, Pair .............................................................. 20.00
Candleholder, Grape & Cable, Amethyst .................................................................. 95.00
Candlestick, Double Scroll, White, Pair ..................................................................... 125.00
Candlestick, Grape & Cable, Domed Base, Purple ................................................. 110.00
Candlestick, Grape & Cable, Green, Northwood .......................................... 85.00 To 185.00
Candlestick, Grape & Cable, Marigold ....................................................................... 75.00
Candlestick, Grape & Cable, Northwood, Purple ..................................................... 330.00
Candlestick, Grape & Cable, Purple ........................................................................... 120.00
Chalice, Double Loop, Blue .......................................................................................... 30.00

Compote, Basket Weave, Marigold, Dated 1874, 4 In. ....................................................... 25.00
Compote, Birds & Cherry, Blue ........................ 55.00
Compote, Blackberry, Green, 5 X 6 In. ........................ 35.00
Compote, Brocaded Palms, Pink, Covered, 7 X 9 1/2 In. ........................ 85.00
Compote, Cherry, Amethyst, Millersburg ........................ 725.00
Compote, Embossed Scroll, Purple ........................ 27.50
Compote, File & Fan, Milk Glass, Marigold ........................ 85.00
Compote, Folded Fan, Opalescent Peach, Stemmed ........................ 65.00
Compote, Fruit & Flowers, Aqua Opalescent ........................ 200.00
Compote, Grape & Cable, Purple, Covered, Large ........................ 425.00
Compote, Grape, Marigold, Imperial ........................ 22.00
Compote, Grape, Purple, Northwood ........................ 125.00
Compote, Hearts & Flowers, Aqua Opalescent, 6 X 6 In. ........................ 200.00
Compote, Hearts & Flowers, Ice Blue, 6 X 7 In. ........................ 125.00
Compote, Hearts & Flowers, White ........................ 95.00
Compote, Iris, Amethyst ........................ 45.00
Compote, Iris, Green, 5 1/2 In. ........................ 45.00
Compote, Paneled Forget-Me-Not, Marigold, 6 In. ........................ 39.50
Compote, Peacock & Urn, Marigold ........................ 45.00
Compote, Persian Garden, Purple, 6 X 7 In. ........................ 85.00
Compote, Persian Medallion, Marigold, Footed ........................ 35.00
Compote, Question Mark, Opalescent Peach, 3 X 6 1/2 In. ........................ 50.00
Compote, Rib & Holly Sprig, Blue, Fenton, 3 In. ........................ 125.00
Compote, Scalloped Rim, Marigold, 8 1/2 In. ........................ 21.50
Compote, Tulip, Marigold, 6-Lip Ruffle, Pedestal, 5 3/4 In. ........................ 25.00
Console Set, Brocaded Acorns, Ice Blue ........................ 250.00
Cookie Jar, Grape & Cable, Purple ........................ 85.00 To 135.00
Cracker Jar, Grape & Cable, Purple, Northwood ........................ 350.00
Cracker Jar, Inverted Feather, Green ........................ 150.00
Creamer, Acorn Burrs, Marigold ........................ 79.00
Creamer, Acorn Burrs, Purple ........................ 125.00
Creamer, Beaded Shell, Marigold ........................ 52.00
Creamer, Butterfly & Berry, Marigold ........................ 40.00
Creamer, Grape & Cable, Marigold, Northwood ........................ 42.00
Creamer, Grape & Cable, Purple ........................ 75.00
Creamer, Grape & Gothic Arches, Blue ........................ 37.00
Creamer, Grape & Gothic Arches, Pearl ........................ 350.00
Creamer, Orange Tree, Cobalt Blue, Footed ........................ 75.00
Creamer, Peacock At Fountain, White ........................ 150.00
Cruet, Buzz Saw, Green ........................ 175.00 To 495.00
Cruet, Buzz Saw, Marigold ........................ 350.00
Cup & Saucer, Grape & Cable, Amethyst, Northwood ........................ 85.00
Cup, Punch, Acorn Burrs, Green ........................ 22.00 To 50.00
Cup, Punch, Acorn Burrs, Ice Green ........................ 50.00
Cup, Punch, Acorn Burrs, White ........................ 50.00
Cup, Punch, Grape & Cable, Amethyst ........................ 20.00
Cup, Punch, Grape & Cable, Blue, Northwood ........................ 18.00
Cup, Punch, Grape & Cable, Purple, Northwood ........................ 20.00
Cup, Punch, Grape & Cable, White, Northwood ........................ 65.00
Cup, Punch, Hobstar & Feather, Marigold ........................ 25.00
Cup, Punch, Kitten, Marigold ........................ 75.00
Cup, Punch, Memphis, Purple, Northwood ........................ 35.00
Cup, Punch, Orange Tree, Marigold ........................ 10.00 To 12.00
Cup, Punch, Wreath Of Roses, Grape Interior, Green ........................ 26.00
Cuspidor, Crackle, Marigold ........................ 38.00
Cuspidor, Peacock & Urn, Marigold, Millersburg ........................ Illus 3400.00
Decanter, Golden Harvest, Marigold, 6 Wines ........................ 195.00
Decanter, Grape & Cable, Marigold, Northwood ........................ 420.00
Decanter, Imperial Grape, Marigold, Stopper ........................ 50.00
Decanter, Imperial Grape, Purple ........................ 150.00
Decanter, Octagon, Marigold, 6 Wines ........................ 189.00
Dish, Acorn, Blue, 7 1/2 In. ........................ 30.00
Dish, Acorn, Red, 6 3/4 In. ........................ 300.00

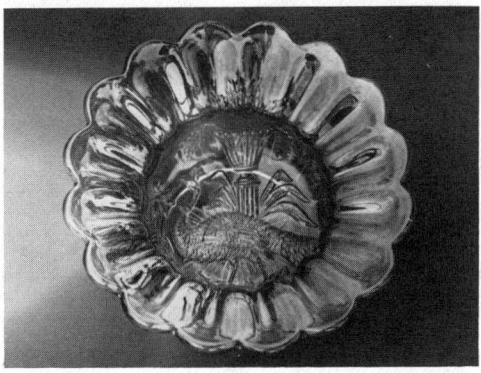

Carnival Glass, Cuspidor, Peacock & Urn, Marigold, Millersburg

**Dish,** Amethyst, Good Luck, 9 In. ..................................................................... 125.00
**Dish,** Candy, Drapery, Triangular, Ice Blue, N, 7 1/2 In. ............................... 97.00
**Dish,** Candy, Fine Cut & Roses, Ice Blue .......................................................... 150.00
**Dish,** Candy, Fine Cut & Roses, White ............................................................. 84.00
**Dish,** Candy, Grape Design, Marigold, Ruffled Sides, 6 In. ....................... 19.00
**Dish,** Candy, Robin, Red, Covered, 7 In. ........................................................ 20.00
**Dish,** Candy, Stippled Leaf, Marigold, 5 In. ................................................... 18.00
**Dish,** Candy, Wild Rose, Green ......................................................................... 40.00
**Dish,** Diamond Pattern, Peach Opalescent, Pedestal, Fluted ................... 35.00
**Dish,** Holly, Purple, Fluted, 9 In. ...................................................................... 60.00
**Dish,** Ice Cream, Grape & Cable, Purple, Stemmed ................................... 50.00
**Dish,** Little Fishes, Aqua, 6 In. ......................................................................... 100.00
**Dish,** Peacock Tail, Green, 5 In. ....................................................................... 25.00
**Dish,** Pin, Grape & Cable, Amethyst ............................................................... 95.00
**Dish,** Starspray, Smoke, 7 1/2 In. ................................................................... 40.00
**Dish,** Stippled Ray, Red, 6 1/4 In. .................................................................. 250.00
**Dish,** Three Fruits, Purple, Signed, Pedestal, 8 1/2 In. .............................. 115.00
**Dish,** Water Lily, Red, Footed, 6 In. ................................................................ 450.00
**Epergne,** Lily, Diamond Jewel, Peach Opalescent ...................................... 250.00
**Fernery,** Butterfly & Berries, Marigold, Ball & Claw Feet ......................... 40.00
**Fernery,** Grape & Cable, Amethyst .................................................. 595.00 To 895.00
**Fernery,** Grape & Cable, Marigold, Insert ..................................................... 1250.00
**Fernery,** Panel Of Roses, Marigold ................................................................. 60.00
**Fernery,** Vintage, Brick Red, 6 In. ................................................................... 500.00
**Figurine,** Swan, Ice Green, 5 In. ...................................................................... 30.00
**Goblet,** Imperial Grape, Marigold ....................................................... 35.00 To 40.00
**Goblet,** Octagon, Marigold, Stemmed ........................................................... 35.00
**Goblet,** Orange Tree, Marigold, Clear Stem, 5 1/2 In. ................................ 25.00
**Goblet,** Star Medallion, Marigold, Stemmed ................................................ 35.00
**Hat,** Basketweave, Marigold .............................................................................. 12.50
**Hat,** Holly, Marigold, 3 1/2 In. .......................................................................... 22.00
**Hat,** Lattice Edge, Red, Fenton ......................................................................... 149.00
**Hatpin Holder,** Cock O' The Walk, Purple ..................................................... 25.00
**Hatpin Holder,** Grape & Cable, Green, N ........................................... 140.00 To 148.00
**Hatpin Holder,** Grape & Cable, Marigold ...................................................... 110.00
**Hatpin Holder,** Grape & Cable, Purple, Northwood ......................... 145.00 To 195.00
**Hatpin Holder,** Peacock, Purple ..................................................................... 30.00
**Humidor,** Grape & Cable, Purple, Northwood ................................... 350.00 To 375.00
**Humidor,** Grape, Marigold, Northwood ......................................................... 225.00
**Ice Cream Set,** Peacock & Urn, Blue, 5 Piece ............................................. 265.00

Jar, Powder, Bambi, Marigold ........................................................... 12.00
Jar, Powder, Bambi, Orange, Jeanette ........................................... 9.50
Jar, Powder, Bambi, White ............................................................ 7.00
Jar, Powder, Classic Arts, Marigold, 4 1/2 In. ............................... 250.00
Jar, Powder, Grape, Green, N ....................................................... 65.00
Jar, Powder, Orange Tree, Blue, Covered ..................................... 40.00
Jar, Powder, Orange Tree, Marigold, Covered ............................... 65.00
Jar, Powder, Poodle, Covered ...................................................... 26.00
Lamp, Peacock Base, Front & Back Views, White ......................... 300.00
Lampshade, Brass Chandelier, Northwood ................................... 25.00
Lemonade Set, Open Rose, Marigold, 6 Tumblers ........................ 195.00
Loving Cup, Orange Tree, Amethyst .............................................. 95.00
Loving Cup, Orange Tree, Blue ...................................................... 100.00
Loving Cup, Orange Tree, Purple ................................................... 155.00
Mug, Beaded Shell, Blue ............................................................... 75.00
Mug, Dandelion, Aqua Opalescent ..................................... 275.00 To 400.00
Mug, Fisherman's, Purple ......................................................... 69.00 To 90.00
Mug, Orange Tree, Blue ........................................................... 45.00 To 55.00
Mug, Orange Tree, Marigold .................................................... 12.50 To 25.00
Mug, Robin, Marigold ................................................................... 29.00
Mug, Singing Birds, Blue ......................................................... 72.00 To 150.00
Mug, Singing Birds, Marigold, Northwood .............................. 40.00 To 65.00
Mug, Singing Birds, Marigold, Stippled, N .................................... 65.00
Mug, Singing Birds, Purple ...................................................... 50.00 To 70.00
Mug, Stork & Rushes, Marigold .................................................... 25.00
Mug, Vintage Band, Marigold ....................................................... 15.00
Nappy, Fine Rib, Flowers On Underside, Peach ........................... 65.00
Nappy, Holly Sprig, Purple ........................................................... 45.00
Nappy, Leaf Rays, Marigold .......................................................... 22.50
Nappy, Leaf Rays, White ........................................................ 32.00 To 40.00
Nappy, Strawberry, Amethyst, 2-Handled ..................................... 30.00
Pitcher, Apple Tree, White, Ruffled Top ........................................ 450.00
Pitcher, Blackberry, Green, N ....................................................... 125.00
Pitcher, Butterfly & Fern, Purple & Green, Ruffled, 9 1/2 In. ......... 175.00
Pitcher, Cherry, Cobalt Blue, Painted .......................................... 125.00
Pitcher, Child's, Acorn & Burrs, Purple, 6 Tumblers, N ................. 900.00
Pitcher, Concave Diamond, Vaseline, 2 Tumblers ........................ 1000.00
Pitcher, Diamond Lace, Purple, 6 Tumblers .................................. 475.00
Pitcher, Double Star, Green, 2 Tumblers ...................................... 445.00
Pitcher, Floral & Grape, Cobalt Blue ............................................ 145.00
Pitcher, Grape Arbor, Marigold, 2 Tumblers ................................. 195.00
Pitcher, Iris, Marigold .................................................................. 32.00
Pitcher, Iris, White ....................................................................... 32.00
Pitcher, Maple Leaf, Blue ............................................................. 150.00
Pitcher, Milk, Poinsettia, Marigold ........................................ 49.00 To 79.00
Pitcher, Milk, Raspberry, Marigold, Northwood ............................ 80.00
Pitcher, Milk, Raspberry, Purple, Northwood ............................... 165.00
Pitcher, Milk, Star Medallion, Clambroth ..................................... 20.00
Pitcher, Milk, Star Medallion, Marigold ........................................ 22.00
Pitcher, Octagon, Marigold .......................................................... 60.00
Pitcher, Oriental Poppy, White ..................................................... 500.00
Pitcher, Tiger Lily, Marigold .......................................................... 125.00
Pitcher, Town Pump, Purple, Northwood ...................................... 500.00
Pitcher, Vineyard, Purple, 6 Glasses ........................................... 425.00
Pitcher, Water, Butterfly & Fern, Blue .......................................... 435.00
Pitcher, Water, Butterfly & Fern, Purple ....................................... 250.00
Pitcher, Water, Crocus, Enameled, Ice Green ............................... 200.00
Pitcher, Water, Diamond Lace, Purple .......................................... 175.00
Pitcher, Water, Diamond, Marigold ............................................... 75.00
Pitcher, Water, Double Star, Green ............................................... 200.00
Pitcher, Water, Fashion, Marigold ................................................ 145.00
Pitcher, Water, Floral & Grape, White .......................................... 275.00
Pitcher, Water, Flute & Cane, Marigold ........................................ 125.00

Pitcher, Water, Grape & Cable, Purple .................................................................. 200.00
Pitcher, Water, Grape & Cable, Thumbprints, Purple .................................... 185.00
Pitcher, Water, Grape, Marigold, Imperial ....................................................... 70.00
Pitcher, Water, Grapevine Lattice, Purple ........................................................ 350.00
Pitcher, Water, Magnolia Drape, Marigold ....................................................... 125.00
Pitcher, Water, Orange Tree, Footed, Marigold ............................................... 165.00
Pitcher, Water, Palm Beach, White .................................................................... 650.00
Pitcher, Water, Peacock At Fountain, Marigold ............................................... 195.00
Pitcher, Water, Twins, Orange ............................................................................ 70.00
Pitcher, Water, Wreathed Cherry, Purple .................................... 200.00 To 275.00
Planter, Nude Dancing Girls, Orange, Square, 3 1/4 X 8 In. .......................... 15.00
Plate, Acanthus, Clambroth, 10 1/2 In. .............................................................. 200.00
Plate, Brocaded Palms, Pink, 7 In. .................................................................... 85.00
Plate, Captive Rose, Blue, 9 In. ....................................................... 75.00 To 85.00
Plate, Captive Rose, Marigold, 9 In. ................................................................. 79.00
Plate, Carnival Shell, Smoky, 9 1/2 In. ............................................................. 90.00
Plate, Chop, Chain Leaf Pattern, Green, 9 In. ................................................. 69.00
Plate, Chop, Cosmos, Marigold, 10 1/2 In. ...................................................... 75.00
Plate, Chop, Garden Path, Purple ....................................................*Illus* 2000.00
Plate, Chop, Hattie, Green .................................................................................. 250.00
Plate, Chop, Imperial Jewels, Red, 11 In. ........................................................ 95.00
Plate, Chop, Peacock & Urn, Purple, Northwood ........................................... 400.00
Plate, Chop, Persian Medallion, Blue ............................................................... 180.00
Plate, Chop, Stag & Holly, Footed, Marigold ................................................... 350.00
Plate, Clambroth, Ice Green, 9 1/2 In. ............................................................... 100.00
Plate, Double Peacock, Purple, 9 In. ................................................................. 190.00
Plate, Fishscale & Beads, Marigold, 7 In. ......................................................... 20.00
Plate, Four Flowers, Peach Opalescent, 6 In. ................................................. 40.00
Plate, Good Luck, Green, Northwood, 9 In. .................................. 125.00 To 175.00
Plate, Good Luck, Purple, 9 In. .......................................................................... 195.00
Plate, Grape, Purple, 8 In. .................................................................................. 55.00
Plate, Holly, Marigold, 9 1/2 In. ......................................................................... 45.00
Plate, Horse Medallion, Marigold, 7 1/2 In. ..................................................... 135.00
Plate, Iris & Herringbone, Marigold, 11 3/4 In. ............................................... 9.00
Plate, Kittens, Marigold, 3 3/4 In. ..................................................................... 125.00
Plate, Leaf Chain, Blue, 9 In. ............................................................................. 115.00
Plate, Orange Tree, Marigold, 9 1/4 In.Diam. .................................................. 55.00
Plate, Peacock & Urn, Blue, 9 In. ...................................................................... 130.00
Plate, Peacock & Urn, Blue, 9 1/4 In. ............................................................... 225.00
Plate, Peacock On Fence, Green, 8 3/4 In. ....................................................... 185.00
Plate, Peacock On Fence, Ice Green, 9 In. ....................................................... 250.00
Plate, Peacock On Fence, Purple, 9 In. ............................................................ 145.00

Carnival Glass, Plate, Chop, Garden Path, Purple

**Plate,** Peacock On Fence, White, Northwood, 9 In. ........................................................ 145.00
**Plate,** Peacock, Basket Of Fruit & Bee, Purple, 9 1/2 In. ............................................ 100.00
**Plate,** Peacock, White, Ruffled Edge, Northwood, 9 In. ................................................ 185.00
**Plate,** Persian Medallion, Blue, 9 In. ............................................................................ 125.00
**Plate,** Persian Medallion, Marigold, 6 In. ...................................................................... 27.50
**Plate,** Pinecone, Amethyst, 6 1/2 In. .............................................................................. 40.00
**Plate,** Pinecone, Blue, 7 3/4 In. ...................................................................................... 85.00
**Plate,** Pinecone, Green, 6 In. ........................................................................................... 45.00
**Plate,** Pinecone, Marigold, 6 In. ...................................................................................... 28.00
**Plate,** Pods & Posies, Green, Scalloped Edge, 9 1/4 In. .............................................. 95.00
**Plate,** Pony, Marigold .......................................................................................................... 275.00
**Plate,** Poppy Show, Ice Blue, 9 1/2 In. ........................................................................... 500.00
**Plate,** Ribbon Tie, Ruffled, 9 In. ...................................................................................... 110.00
**Plate,** Rose Show, Blue ....................................................................................................... 500.00
**Plate,** Roundup, Opalescent Peach, 9 In. ...................................................................... 450.00
**Plate,** Sailboat & Windmill, Marigold, 6 1/2 In. ............................................................ 50.00
**Plate,** Scroll Embossed, Purple, 9 In. .............................................................................. 75.00
**Plate,** Stippled Rays, Marigold, 6 In. ............................................................................... 15.00
**Plate,** Strawberry, Basket Weave Back, Marigold, 9 In. .............................................. 47.50
**Plate,** Three Fruits, Amethyst, 9 In. ................................................................................. 87.50
**Plate,** Three Fruits, Blue, Millersburg, 9 1/2 In. ........................................................... 175.00
**Plate,** Three Fruits, Green, 9 In. ..................................................... 65.00 To 95.00
**Plate,** Three Fruits, Marigold, 12-Sided, 9 In. .............................................................. 45.00
**Plate,** Three Fruits, Purple ................................................................................................ 79.00
**Plate,** Vintage, Blue, 7 In. .................................................................................................. 65.00
**Plate,** Vintage, Green, 7 3/4 In. ........................................................................................ 55.00
**Plate,** Windmill & Checkerboard, Marigold, 8 In. ......................................................... 8.00
**Powder Jar,** Grape & Cable, Northwood, Green ........................................................... 50.00
**Punch Bowl,** Grape & Cable, 11 Cups, N ......................................................... *Illus* 400.00
**Punch Bowl,** Orange Tree, Cobalt Blue, 11 Cups ........................................................ 285.00
**Punch Bowl,** Wreath Of Roses & Grape, 6 Cups, Green ............................................ 375.00
**Punch Bowl,** Wreath Of Roses, Amethyst, 12 In. ......................................................... 100.00
**Punch Set,** Acorn Burrs, Ice Green, 8 Piece ................................................................. 2300.00
**Punch Set,** Acorn Burrs, Purple ....................................................................................... 550.00
**Punch Set,** Grape & Cable, Marigold, 6 Cups, 10 1/2 X 10 In. ................................ 375.00
**Punch Set,** Peacock, Quail, & Grapes, Marigold, 7 Cups ........................................... 365.00
**Rose Bowl,** Beaded Cable, Marigold ............................................................................... 45.00
**Rose Bowl,** Beaded Cable, Purple ..................................................... 60.00 To 65.00
**Rose Bowl,** Beaded Chain, Cobalt .................................................................................... 60.00
**Rose Bowl,** Bow & Wreath, Marigold, Footed .............................................................. 35.00
**Rose Bowl,** Crackle, White, 7 In. ..................................................................................... 50.00
**Rose Bowl,** Daisy & Plume, Purple, 3-Footed .............................................................. 45.00
**Rose Bowl,** Drapery, Opalescent Aqua ........................................... 140.00 To 180.00
**Rose Bowl,** Drapery, Orange & Amber ........................................................................... 100.00
**Rose Bowl,** Fenton's Basket, Ice Blue ............................................................................ 250.00
**Rose Bowl,** Fine Cut & Roses, Amber ............................................................................ 35.00
**Rose Bowl,** Fine Cut & Roses, Purple ............................................................................ 65.00
**Rose Bowl,** Golden Grapes, Marigold ............................................................................. 20.00
**Rose Bowl,** Grape Delight, Purple, 6-Footed ................................. 65.00 To 75.00
**Rose Bowl,** Grape Delight, White .................................................................................... 60.00
**Rose Bowl,** Hobnail Swirl, Marigold ............................................................................... 250.00
**Rose Bowl,** Honeycomb, Opalescent Peach, Millersburg ........................................... 190.00
**Rose Bowl,** Leaf & Beads, Aqua Opalescent ................................. 149.00 To 175.00
**Rose Bowl,** Leaf & Beads, Blue ....................................................................................... 110.00
**Rose Bowl,** Leaf & Beads, Green ..................................................................................... 50.00
**Rose Bowl,** Leaf & Dots, Marigold, Pair ......................................................................... 95.00
**Rose Bowl,** Persian Medallion, Blue ............................................................................... 120.00
**Rose Bowl,** Swirl Hobnail, Purple .................................................................................... 225.00
**Rose Bowl,** Vintage, White, 6-Footed .............................................. 65.00 To 125.00
**Salt,** Swan, Pink, Master ..................................................................................................... 30.00
**Saucer,** Vintage, Marigold ................................................................................................. 10.00
**Sherbet,** Grape & Cable With Thumbprint, Purple, Footed ....................................... 25.00
**Sherbet,** Grape & Cable, Purple, Stemmed ..................................... 35.00 To 39.00

Carnival Glass, Punch Bowl, Grape & Cable,
11 Cups, N

| | |
|---|---|
| **Sherbet,** Holly, Red, Stemmed | 300.00 |
| **Spooner,** Acorn Burrs, Purple | 110.00 |
| **Spooner,** Butterfly & Berry, Marigold | 40.00 |
| **Spooner,** Butterfly & Berry, Purple, Ball Feet, 4 In. | 70.00 |
| **Spooner,** Cord & Tassel, Marigold | 65.00 |
| **Spooner,** Grape & Cable, Purple | 60.00 To 129.00 |
| **Spooner,** Grape & Gothic Arches, Pearl | 95.00 |
| **Spooner,** Grape, Marigold, Northwood | 75.00 |
| **Spooner,** Hobstar, Marigold | 15.00 To 20.00 |
| **Spooner,** Kittens, Blue | 250.00 |
| **Spooner,** Lustre Rose, Marigold | 25.00 To 30.00 |
| **Spooner,** Nautilus, Peach Opalescent | 300.00 |
| **Spooner,** Palm Beach, White | 190.00 |
| **Spooner,** Peacock At Fountain, White | 90.00 To 150.00 |
| **Spooner,** Shell & Tassel, Green | 75.00 |
| **Sugar & Creamer,** Estates, Peach Opalescent | 150.00 |
| **Sugar & Creamer,** Grape & Cable, Purple, Northwood | 145.00 |
| **Sugar & Creamer,** Melon Ribbed, Marigold | 15.00 |
| **Sugar & Creamer,** Peacock, Red, 5 In. | 20.00 |
| **Sugar,** Apple Panels, Marigold | 14.00 |
| **Sugar,** Basket Weave & Cable, Marigold, Covered | 30.00 |
| **Sugar,** Butterfly & Berry, Marigold | 70.00 |
| **Sugar,** Grape & Cable, Green | 45.00 |
| **Sugar,** Grape & Cable, Marigold | 25.00 |
| **Sugar,** Grape & Gothic Arches, Pearl, Covered | 375.00 |
| **Sugar,** Palm Beach, White, Covered | 350.00 |
| **Table Set,** Grape & Gothic Arches, Blue | 400.00 |
| **Table Set,** Peach, White, 4 Pieces | 650.00 |
| **Toothpick,** Button & Daisy, White, Hat Shape | 8.00 |
| **Toothpick,** Flute, Purple | 22.50 To 69.00 |
| **Toothpick,** Kittens & Mice, Marigold | 75.00 |
| **Toothpick,** Owl, Red | 6.00 |
| **Toothpick,** Ribbed & Beaded, Vaseline | 30.00 |
| **Toothpick,** Water Lilies & Cattails, Marigold | 335.00 |
| **Tray,** Brocaded Acorns, Ice Blue, Handled | 95.00 |
| **Tray,** Dresser, Grape & Cable, Northwood, Marigold | 115.00 |
| **Tray,** Dresser, Grape & Cable, Purple | 175.00 To 185.00 |
| **Tumbler,** Acorn Burrs, Marigold, Northwood | 35.00 To 38.00 |
| **Tumbler,** Acorn Burrs, Purple | 45.00 To 75.00 |
| **Tumbler,** Apple Tree, Marigold | 26.00 |
| **Tumbler,** Arbor, Marigold | 26.00 |
| **Tumbler,** Arched Panels, Marigold | 26.00 |

**Tumbler,** Beaded Shell, Blue ............................................................. 49.00 To 50.00
**Tumbler,** Beaded Shell, Purple ............................................................. 45.00
**Tumbler,** Blackberry Block, Blue ......................................................... 59.00
**Tumbler,** Blackberry Block, Purple ...................................................... 59.00
**Tumbler,** Blueberry, Marigold ............................................................. 26.00
**Tumbler,** Butterfly & Berry, Black ........................................................ 25.00
**Tumbler,** Butterfly & Berry, Blue ................................................. 20.00 To 35.00
**Tumbler,** Butterfly & Fern, Marigold ............................................ 24.00 To 26.00
**Tumbler,** Concave Diamond, Ice Blue ........................................... 45.00 To 50.00
**Tumbler,** Crab Claw, Marigold ............................................................. 70.00
**Tumbler,** Crocus, Enameled, Ice Green ................................................. 50.00
**Tumbler,** Daisy & Lattice, Cobalt Blue .................................................. 75.00
**Tumbler,** Dandelion, Marigold, Northwood ................................... 30.00 To 40.00
**Tumbler,** Diamond Lace, Purple ........................................................... 25.00
**Tumbler,** Egyptain Art, Marigold .......................................................... 800.00
**Tumbler,** Fashion, Marigold ......................................................... 24.00 To 26.00
**Tumbler,** Feather & Heart, Marigold ..................................................... 75.00
**Tumbler,** Fentonia, Blue ....................................................................... 75.00
**Tumbler,** Fentonia, Marigold ............................................................... 26.00
**Tumbler,** Field Flower, Marigold .................................................. 22.00 To 26.00
**Tumbler,** Floral & Grape, Amethyst .............................................. 15.00 To 30.00
**Tumbler,** Floral & Grape, Cobalt Blue .................................................. 35.00
**Tumbler,** Floral & Grape, Marigold ...................................................... 26.00
**Tumbler,** Floral & Grape, White ........................................................... 55.00
**Tumbler,** God & Home, Blue ................................................................ 115.00
**Tumbler,** Grape & Cable With Thumbprint, Marigold .............................. 15.00
**Tumbler,** Grape & Cable With Thumbprint, Purple ................................. 25.00
**Tumbler,** Grape & Cable, Amethyst, Northwood ........................... 25.00 To 35.00
**Tumbler,** Grape & Cable, Blue, N, Set Of 6 ........................................... 350.00
**Tumbler,** Grape & Cable, Green ........................................................... 35.00
**Tumbler,** Grape & Cable, Purple .......................................................... 28.00
**Tumbler,** Grape & Gothic Arches, Blue ................................................. 25.00
**Tumbler,** Grape & Lattice, Marigold ............................................. 22.50 To 26.00
**Tumbler,** Grape Arbor, Purple ...................................................... 45.00 To 50.00
**Tumbler,** Grape Arbor, White .............................................................. 75.00
**Tumbler,** Grape, Blue, Flat .................................................................. 10.00
**Tumbler,** Grape, Marigold, Northwood .......................................... 26.00 To 30.00
**Tumbler,** Grapevine Lattice, Marigold .................................................. 12.00
**Tumbler,** Harvest Flower, Marigold ...................................................... 69.00
**Tumbler,** Heavy Iris, Purple ................................................................ 35.00
**Tumbler,** Hobstar Band Varient, Marigold ............................................. 35.00
**Tumbler,** Imperial Grape, Marigold ...................................................... 13.00
**Tumbler,** Imperial Grape, Purple ......................................................... 49.00
**Tumbler,** Laurel Band, Marigold .......................................................... 26.00
**Tumbler,** Lustre Rose, Marigold ........................................................... 17.00
**Tumbler,** Maple Leaf, Blue .................................................................. 49.00
**Tumbler,** Maple Leaf, Purple ............................................................... 40.00
**Tumbler,** Milady, Amethyst ................................................................. 65.00
**Tumbler,** Milady, Blue ......................................................................... 75.00
**Tumbler,** Milady, Marigold .................................................................. 24.00
**Tumbler,** Octagon, Marigold ........................................................ 17.00 To 26.00
**Tumbler,** Orange Tree, Blue ................................................................ 50.00
**Tumbler,** Oriental Poppy, Blue ............................................................ 50.00
**Tumbler,** Oriental Poppy, Dark Marigold ............................................... 35.00
**Tumbler,** Oriental Poppy, Green .................................................. 35.00 To 65.00
**Tumbler,** Oriental Poppy, Marigold ...................................................... 26.00
**Tumbler,** Oriental Poppy, White .......................................................... 150.00
**Tumbler,** Palm Beach, White ............................................................... 75.00
**Tumbler,** Paneled Dandelion, Blue ............................................... 40.00 To 65.00
**Tumbler,** Peach, Blue, Northwood ................................................ 45.00 To 65.00
**Tumbler,** Peacock At Fountain, Blue ............................................. 25.00 To 40.00
**Tumbler,** Peacock At Fountain, Cobalt Blue .......................................... 35.00
**Tumbler,** Peacock At Fountain, Marigold ...................................... 29.00 To 35.00

| | | |
|---|---|---|
| **Tumbler,** Rambler Rose, Marigold | | 10.00 |
| **Tumbler,** Raspberry, Amethyst | | 40.00 |
| **Tumbler,** Raspberry, Green | | 35.00 |
| **Tumbler,** Scroll, Blue | | 26.00 |
| **Tumbler,** Singing Birds, Green | 35.00 To | 40.00 |
| **Tumbler,** Singing Birds, Purple | | 50.00 |
| **Tumbler,** Springtime, Purple | | 65.00 |
| **Tumbler,** Star Medallion, Marigold | | 26.00 |
| **Tumbler,** Stork & Rushes, Blue | | 28.00 |
| **Tumbler,** Stork & Rushes, Marigold | | 18.00 |
| **Tumbler,** Three Fruits, Marigold | | 20.00 |
| **Tumbler,** Tiger Lily, Green | | 36.00 |
| **Tumbler,** Tiger Lily, Marigold | | 11.00 |
| **Tumbler,** Tiger Lily, Purple | | 55.00 |
| **Tumbler,** Tree Bark, Marigold | | 26.00 |
| **Tumbler,** Windmill, Marigold | | 26.00 |
| **Tumbler,** Wishbone, Green | | 130.00 |
| **Vase,** Acorn Burrs, Green, Northwood | | 38.00 |
| **Vase,** Butterfly & Berry, Red, 8 1/2 In. | | 250.00 |
| **Vase,** Corn, Green | | 400.00 |
| **Vase,** Corn, Ice Green | | 200.00 |
| **Vase,** Corn, White | | 170.00 |
| **Vase,** Daisy & Drape, Blue | | 300.00 |
| **Vase,** Daisy & Drape, Ice Blue, 6 1/4 In. | | 475.00 |
| **Vase,** Daisy & Drape, White, 6 1/4 In. | | 200.00 |
| **Vase,** Diamond Point, Purple, 10 In. | | 14.00 |
| **Vase,** Diamond, Amethyst, 8 In. | | 35.00 |
| **Vase,** Double Dolphin, Ice Blue, Fan-Shaped | | 125.00 |
| **Vase,** Fine Rib, Aqua, 9 1/2 In. | | 35.00 |
| **Vase,** Fine Rib, Red, 8 3/4 In. | | 200.00 |
| **Vase,** Fine Rib, Red, 9 1/2 In. | | 179.00 |
| **Vase,** Fine Rib, Red, 13 In. | | 225.00 |
| **Vase,** Fluted, Marigold, 10 In. | | 25.00 |
| **Vase,** Lined Lattice, Blue, 9 In. | 30.00 To | 65.00 |
| **Vase,** Mary Ann, Marigold, 2-Handled | | 40.00 |
| **Vase,** Panel, Marigold, Northwood, 11 In. | | 30.00 |
| **Vase,** Peacock At Fountain, Footed, Signed, 9 1/2 In. | | 175.00 |
| **Vase,** Rib & Panel, Purple, 7 In. | | 25.00 |
| **Vase,** Ripple, Green, 10 In. | | 25.00 |
| **Vase,** Rustic, Ice Blue, 11 1/2 In. | | 95.00 |
| **Vase,** Rustic, White, 16 In. | | 89.00 |
| **Vase,** Thorn, Blue, 16 In. | | 75.00 |
| **Vase,** Tornado, Amethyst, 6 In. | | 60.00 |
| **Vase,** Tree Trunk, Green, 9 In. | | 30.00 |
| **Vase,** Tree Trunk, Marigold, Northwood, 9 3/4 In. | | 30.00 |
| **Vase,** Tree Trunk, Marigold, 16 In. | | 45.00 |
| **Wall Pocket,** Fishscale, Marigold, Pair | | 28.00 |
| **Water Set,** Acorn Burrs, Marigold, 7 Piece | | 550.00 |
| **Water Set,** Ball & Swirl, Red, Westmoreland, 7 Piece | | 140.00 |
| **Water Set,** Bark, Marigold, 5 Piece | | 55.00 |
| **Water Set,** Butterfly & Berry, Marigold, 7 Piece | | 335.00 |
| **Water Set,** Butterfly & Fern, Green, 6 Piece | | 495.00 |
| **Water Set,** Butterfly & Fern, Marigold, 7 Piece | | 395.00 |
| **Water Set,** Concave Diamond, Ice Blue, 8 Piece | | 675.00 |
| **Water Set,** Concave Diamond, Peacock Blue, 7 Piece | | 300.00 |
| **Water Set,** Crab Claw, Marigold, 7 Piece | | 400.00 |
| **Water Set,** Crocus, Enameled, Ice Green, 5 Piece | | 400.00 |
| **Water Set,** Diamond & Lace, Purple, 7 Piece | 425.00 To | 475.00 |
| **Water Set,** Grape & Cable, Marigold, 6 Piece | | 295.00 |
| **Water Set,** Grape & Cable, Purple, 7 Piece | 390.00 To | 575.00 |
| **Water Set,** Grape & Gothic Arches, Pearl, 7 Piece | | 1200.00 |
| **Water Set,** Grape Arbor, Ice Blue, 7 Piece | | 1500.00 |
| **Water Set,** Hand-Painted, Marigold, 7 Piece | 225.00 To | 350.00 |

Water Set, Hobstar & Crosshatch, Marigold, 5 Piece ................................................ 90.00
Water Set, Lattice & Grape, Blue, 7 Piece ................................................ 800.00
Water Set, Lattice & Grape, Marigold, 7 Piece ................................................ 145.00
Water Set, Maple Leaf, Oxblood, 7 Piece ................................................ 350.00
Water Set, Maple Leaf, Purple, 7 Piece ................................................ 449.00
Water Set, Orange Tree Orchard, Blue, 7 Piece ................................................ 495.00
Water Set, Oriental Poppy, Ice Blue, Northwood, 7 Piece ................................................ 600.00
Water Set, Paneled Dandelion, Amethyst, 5 Piece ................................................ 500.00
Water Set, Paneled Dandelion, Green, 7 Piece ................................................ 850.00
Water Set, Peacock At Fountain, Blue, 7 Piece ................................ 400.00 To 595.00
Water Set, Peacock At Fountain, Marigold, 7 Piece ................................................ 350.00
Water Set, Peacock At Fountain, Purple, 7 Piece ................................................ 685.00
Water Set, Peacock At Fountain, White, 5 Piece ................................................ 1100.00
Water Set, Rambling Rose, Blue, 7 Piece ................................................ 700.00
Water Set, Raspberry, Green, 7 Piece ................................................ 495.00
Water Set, Raspberry, Marigold, 5 Piece ................................................ 235.00
Water Set, Singing Birds, Green, 7 Piece ................................ 565.00 To 650.00
Water Set, Singing Birds, Purple, 7 Piece ................................ 400.00 To 575.00
Water Set, Spider Web, Marigold, Footed, 7 Piece ................................................ 125.00
Water Set, Strutting Peacock, Ice Blue, Child's, 7 Piece ................................................ 55.00
Water Set, Swirl, Marigold, Northwood, 7 Piece ................................................ 175.00
Water Set, Vineyard, Purple, 7 Piece ................................................ 425.00
Water Set, Wishbone, Green, 7 Piece ................................ 1850.00 To 995.00
Wine Set, Diamond & Sunburst, Purple, 6 Piece ................................................ 295.00
Wine Set, Imperial Grape, Green, 6 Piece ................................................ 175.00
Wine Set, Imperial Grape, Marigold, 6 Piece ................................................ 160.00
Wine Set, Imperial Grape, Purple, 7 Piece ................................................ 250.00
Wine, Orange Tree, Marigold ................................ 25.00 To 26.00
Wine, Rib & Holly Sprig, Marigold ................................................ 8.00
Wine, Sailboats, Marigold ................................ 27.50 To 90.00
Wine, Sailboats, Stemmed, Blue ................................................ 75.00
Wine, Wine & Roses, Marigold ................................................ 35.00
Wine, Wreath Of Roses, Marigold ................................................ 22.00

CAROUSEL, Horse, C.W.Parker, Signed ................................ 1500.00 To 2500.00
Horse, C.1900, Stein & Goldstein, N.Y. ................................................ 6500.00
Horse, Cast Aluminum ................................................ 275.00
Horse, Hand-Carved, Parker, Original Paint ................................................ 2200.00
Horse, Pine, Carved, American, 19th Century ................................................ 1600.00
2-Horse, 2 Wonder Horses, Mechanized, Canopy, 5 Ft.High ................................................ 450.00

CARRIAGE, Seat, Buggy, Tufted Velvet, Handmade Tressle Base ................................................ 350.00
Surrey, Tongue, Complete ................................................ 175.00
Surrey, 2 Seater, Canopy ................................................ 2500.00
Wagon, Farm, Wooden Wheel ................................................ 900.00

CASH REGISTER, Cash Till, Sliding Drawer, Lock System, Bell, Wooden ................................................ 65.00
English, Walnut ................................................ 200.00
Hough, Oak ................................................ 125.00
Lock Box, National, Nickel Plated & Glass, 6 X 6 3/4 In. ................................................ 150.00
McCaskey, Account ................................ 95.00 To 125.00
McCaskey, Brass Trim, Stenciling ................................................ 150.00
Monitor, No. la, Decal, Patent 1900, Oak, Small ................................................ 275.00
National, Amount Purchased Sign, No.349, Brass ................................................ 325.00
National, Box, Supplies, 9 X 6 X 3 In. ................................................ 22.50
National, Brass Inkwell, Nameplate & Trim, Oak ................................................ 400.00
National, Floor Model, Multidrawer, Oak ................................................ 1450.00
National, Floor Model, 8 Drawer, G.C.Horsman, 32 X 60 In. ................................................ 1750.00
National, Floor Model, 9 Drawer, Oak Base ................................................ 600.00
National, Lock Box, Nickel Plated & Glass, 6 X 6 3/4 In. ................................................ 150.00
National, Model 35, English Denominations, Brass ................................................ 350.00
National, Model 92, C.1898, Crank, Rings To 99.99, Brass ................................................ 675.00
National, Model 313, Brass, 21 1/2 In. ................................................ *Illus* 900.00

Cash Register, National, Model 313, Brass, 21 1/2 In.

**National,** Model 332, C.1910, Rings To 3.99, Brass ............................................................. 375.00
**National,** Model 333 ........................................................................................................ 475.00
**National,** Model 356, Brass ............................................................................................. 295.00
**National,** Model 441, Crank Operated, Bronze ................................................................ 750.00
**National,** Model 442, C.1912, Crank, Rings To 9.99, Brass ........................................... 575.00
**National,** Model 544 ......................................................................................................... 350.00
**National,** Model 711, 1920 .............................................................................................. 75.00
**National,** Model 1064, Brass ............................................................... 250.00 To 350.00
**National,** Model 6064g, Brass .......................................................................................... 350.00
**Simplex,** Showcase Ends, Drop Marbles To Ring Sales, 1880s ...................................... 750.00
**St. Louis,** Rings To 4.99 .................................................................................................... 175.00

*Castor sets have been known as early as 1705. Most of those found today
date from Victorian times. A castor set usually consists of a silver-plated
frame that holds three to seven condiment bottles. The pickle castor is a
single glass jar about six inches high, held in a silver frame. A cover and
tongs were kept with the jar. They were popular from 1890 to 1900.*

**CASTOR SET, see also various porcelain and glass categories**
**CASTOR SET, Horseshoe Frame,** Boot Mustard & Pepper, Silver Plate, 6 In. ........................... 260.00
**3 Bottle,** Gothic Pattern Inserts, Woven Wire Holder, C.1860 ....................................... 100.00
**4 Bottle,** Cut Glass, American, Papier-Mache & Mother-Of-Pearl ................................... 150.00
**4 Bottle,** English Silver Plate, Crystal Inserts, 6 3/4 In. ................................................. 135.00
**4 Bottle,** English Silver Plate, Square Frame, 5 1/2 X 8 In. ............................................ 125.00
**4 Bottle,** Gothic Pattern Inserts, Plated Holder, C.1890 ................................................. 200.00
**4 Bottle,** Pewter, I.Trask, Beverly, Massachusetts, C.1830, 8 In. .................................. 175.00
**4 Bottle,** Sandwich Glass, Pewter Frame, Trask ............................................................ 225.00
**4 Bottle,** Scalloped Swirl, Flint, Ripley & Co. ................................................................ 78.00
**4 Bottle,** 3-Mold Bottles, Pewter Frame, R.Gleason, 7 1/2 In. ....................................... 95.00
**5 Bottle,** Grape Pattern Bottles, Silver Plate Frame ..................................................... 60.00
**5 Bottle,** Ribbed Palm, Silver Plate Frame ................................................................... 120.00
**5 Bottle,** Silver Plate Stand, Medallion Head Handle, 6 In. .......................................... 110.00
**6 Bottle,** Gothic Bottles, Matching Stoppers, Pewter ................................................... 65.00
**6 Bottle,** Revolving, Sterling Silver Frame, Derby ........................................................ 195.00
**7 Bottle,** Cut Crystal, Silver Plate Holder, English ....................................................... 400.00

**CASTOR, Pickle, see also various glass categories**
**CASTOR, Pickle,** Bird & Cupid On Top Gallery, Block Pattern, Meriden Co. ........................... 125.00
**Pickle,** Blue Glass Insert, Silver Plate Frame, Matching Fork ........................................ 165.00
**Pickle,** Carved Leaves On Insert, Tongs ....................................................................... 85.00
**Pickle,** Claw Feet, Banded Clear Container .................................................................. 75.00
**Pickle,** Cranberry Glass Insert, Webster & Son Silver Plate ......................................... 125.00
**Pickle,** Cranberry Opalescent Windows ........................................................................ 235.00
**Pickle,** Crystal Prism Jar, Acid Etched, Silver Plate Frame, Tongs ............................... 85.00
**Pickle,** Cupid & Venus Insert, Quadruple Plate, Talon Tongs ....................................... 80.00
**Pickle,** Cut Jar, Cutout Silver Plate Frame ................................................................... 70.00
**Pickle,** Daisy & Button Bottle, Quadruple Plate, Tongs, Amber .................................... 100.00

Pickle, Daisy & Button Insert, Vaseline ....................................................................... 175.00
Pickle, Diamond Pattern, Cabriole Legs, Tongs, Poole Silver Co. .................................. 95.00
Pickle, Diamond-Quilted Turquoise Glass, Silver Plated ............................................... 120.00
Pickle, Diamonds & Squares, Vaseline Jar, Silver Plate, 8 1/2 In. ................................ 155.00
Pickle, Double, Claw Tongs, Block & Star Inserts, Meriden Silver ................................. 125.00
Pickle, Double, Frosted Set, Intaglio Cut ..................................................................... 150.00
Pickle, Double, Tongs, Floral Design On Bail, Daisy & Button Inserts ......................... 225.00
Pickle, Embossed Floral & Bird Silver Plate Frame, Tongs ........................................... 75.00
Pickle, Embossed Frame, Diamond Pattern Jars, Signed, Tongs .................................. 97.00
Pickle, Fork, Clear Paneled Insert, Reed & Barton Frame, C.1870 .............................. 135.00
Pickle, Green Enameled, Footed Shape, Tongs ............................................................. 200.00
Pickle, Inverted Thumbprint Insert, Enameled, Ruby ................................................... 225.00
Pickle, Inverted Thumbprint, Amberina ....................................................................... 325.00
Pickle, Maidenhair Fern Insert, Silver Plated Holder & Lid .......................................... 225.00
Pickle, Ruby Thumbprint Bottle, Silver Plate Cover, Frame, & Tongs ......................... 245.00
Pickle, Thumbprint Insert, Enameled Flowers, Blue .................................................... 180.00
Pickle, York Herringbone, Ruby Glass Insert, Silver Plate Frame ................................ 135.00
      CATALOG, see Paper, Catalog

*The firm Cauldon Limited worked in Staffordshire, Great Britain,
and went through many name changes. John Ridgway made porcelain at
Cauldon Place, Hanley, until 1855. The firm of John Ridgway,
Bates and Co. of Cauldon Place worked from 1856 to 1859. It became
Bates, Brown-Westhead, Moore and Co. from 1859 to 1862. Brown-
Westhead, Moore and Co. worked from 1862 to 1904. About 1890 this firm
started using the word Cauldon or Cauldon ware as part of the mark.
Cauldon Ltd. worked from 1905 to 1920, Cauldon Potteries from 1920 to 1962.*

      CAULDON, see also Indian Tree
CAULDON, Pitcher, Festoon Of Roses, 2 3/4 In. ............................................................ 40.00
    Plate, Blue Transfer ................................................................................................. 45.00
    Plate, Views Of Phillips Exeter Academy, Pink & White, 10 In. ................................... 70.00

*Celadon is a Chinese porcelain having a velvet-textured green-gray glaze.
Japanese and Korean factories also made a celadon-colored glaze.*

CELADON, Ashtray, 4 1/2 In. ........................................................................................ 18.00
    Basket, Fluted Handle & Rim, Japanese Legend, 10 1/2 In.Diam. ............................. 230.00
    Bowl, Enameled, Crackle Finish, 19th Century, 3 1/2 X 8 1/2 In. ............................. 175.00
    Bowl, 3 Knobbed Feet, Enamel Beads, Blue Stalks, 3 5/8 In.Diam. ........................... 35.00
    Bowl, 6 X 2 1/2 In. .................................................................................................. 30.00
    Creamer, Flowers & Butterfly, Triangular, 4 X 4 In. .................................................. 45.00
    Planter, Footed, White & Blue Trees, Bird, Hexagonal, 6 1/4 X 7 In. ........................ 99.50
    Plate, Enamel Butterflies, Birds & Flowers, 18th Century, 7 1/4 In. .......................... 135.00
    Plate, 8 1/2 In. ........................................................................................................ 30.00
    Teapot, Reeded Handle ............................................................................................. 58.00
    Vase, Drum Shape, 8 X 10 In. .................................................................................. 75.00
    Vase, Embossed Lotus Leaf, 19th Century, Signed, 15 In. ........................................ 265.00
    Vase, Ovoid Body, Painted Geometric Designs, Korea, 11 1/2 In. ............................. 125.00
    Vase, Temple, Blue Ceremonial Figures, 17 In. ......................................................... 290.00
    Wall Pocket, Floral Trim, Green ................................................................................. 32.50

CELLULOID, Box, Collar, Bust Portrait ......................................................................... 28.00
    Box, Collar, Sculptured Sides, Lady On Cover ........................................................... 45.00
    Box, Elk, Tree Bark, 11 X 8 X 4 In. .......................................................................... 55.00
    Box, Glove, Allover Embossed Violets ....................................................................... 22.00
    Box, Lady On Cover, Shaving Mug Inside ................................................................. 75.00
    Box, Pin, Painted Portrait Of Woman, C.1910, 2 1/2 In.Diam. .................................. 20.00
    Box, Tree Bark Look, 11 X 8 X 4 In. ......................................................................... 55.00
    Bulldog, University Of Georgia ................................................................................. 10.00
    Button, Indian Motorcycle ........................................................................................ 30.00
    Case, Cigarette, Tortoiseshell, C.1910, 3 X 3 1/2 In. ................................................ 40.00
    Dresser Set, Amber & Gold, 9 Piece .......................................................................... 80.00

**Dresser Set,** Black & Green, Stainless Steel, 3 Piece ........................................... 18.00
**Dresser Set,** Ivory & Blue, 10 Piece ................................................................. 95.00
**Dresser Set,** Pink, 17 Piece ............................................................................ 75.00
**Dresser Set,** 10 Piece ................................................................................... 28.50
**Holder,** Cigarette, Raised Twist Center, Ruby, Lined Case ............................... 14.00
**Holder,** Stamp, 1902 .................................................................................... 300.00
**Letter Opener,** Alligator, Black Boy's Head In Mouth, Germany ...................... 25.00
**Match Holder,** Ad For Buckwalter Stoves ...................................................... 18.00
**Mirror,** Hand, Art Deco .................................................................................. 9.50
**Santa Claus,** Reindeer On Cardboard Base ................................................... 75.00
**Shoe Horn,** Embossed Lady's Face On Handle, 18 In. .................................... 12.50
**Swan,** Colored, Pair ..................................................................................... 25.00
**Tobacco Jar,** Roly Poly, Brownie Type ........................................................... 12.00
**Whistle,** Crowing Rooster ............................................................................. 8.50

*The Ceramic Art Company of Trenton, New Jersey, was established
in 1889 by J. Coxon and W. Lenox, and was an early producer of
American Belleek porcelain.*

**CERAMIC ART CO., Bottle,** Pilgrims, Roses, Belleek, Dated 1934, Signed ............................. 225.00
**Bottle,** Pilgrims, Yellow & Peach Roses, Signed, Dated 1904 ......................... 225.00
**Figurine,** Shelf Sitters, Boy & Girl Kissing ................................................... 34.00
**Jelly,** Scenic, Green, Sterling Overlay, Palette Mark ...................................... 48.00
**Mug,** Colorful Fruits, Palette Mark, 5 1/2 In. ................................ 72.00 To 75.00
**Mug,** Gold Dragon Handle, Stag Portrait, Palette Mark ................................. 110.00
**Mug,** Madame Butterfly, Gold, Marked ......................................................... 95.00
**Mug,** Minstrel Playing Banjo, Dated 1902, 7 In. ........................................... 75.00
**Pitcher,** Lemonade, Palette Mark ................................................................. 60.00
**Salt & Pepper,** Mother Cat & Kitten, Black .................................................. 25.00
**Tankard,** Jewels At Neck, Flowers, Palette Mark, 14 1/2 In. ........................... 350.00
**Tankard,** Red Roses, Jewels, Palette Mark, 14 1/4 In. .................................. 330.00
**Tea Set,** Hand-Painted, Gold Palette Mark, 3 Piece ...................................... 295.00
**Vase,** Green Prisms, Deco, Green Palette Mark, 10 1/2 In. ............................ 110.00
**Vase,** Silver Overlay, Palette Mark ............................................................... 125.00

*Chalkware is really plaster of Paris decorated with watercolors. The
pieces were molded from known Staffordshire and other porcelain models and
painted and sold as inexpensive decorations.*

**CHALKWARE, Figurine, see also Kewpie**
**CHALKWARE, Bookends,** Lincoln In Chair, Painted Gold ............................... 18.00
**Figurine,** Boy Scout, Signed McKenzie, 1915, 17 1/2 In. ............................... 155.00
**Figurine,** Clothed Woman, Painted Gold, Marked Moreau ............................. 45.00
**Figurine,** Donald Duck, Carnival Doll ........................................................... 25.00
**Figurine,** Ewe & Lamb, 8 3/4 In. ................................................................. 100.00
**Figurine,** Girl Standing, Hands Holding Skirt In Curtsy, 16 In. ...................... 90.00
**Figurine,** Lighthouse, 11 X 9 In. ................................................................... 15.00
**Figurine,** Old Woman In Chair With Cat, 7 In. ............................................. 35.00
**Figurine,** Thinker, Rose O'Neill .................................................................... 50.00
**Figurine,** Usher, Universal Theaters, Chicago, 5 In. ...................................... 12.50
**Lamp,** Art Deco, Clothed Women Standing, 20 In. ........................................ 85.00
**Mutt,** 6 In., Jeff, 9 In., 1909, Fisher ............................................................ 75.00
**Salt & Pepper,** Figural, R.C.A.Victor Dog .................................................... 15.00

**CHARLIE CHAPLIN, Box.Glove,** Picture & Sign, Wooden .............................. 40.00
**Box,** Pencil ................................................................................................. 22.00
**Doll,** Walking, Composition Head, Cloth Suit, Windup .............................. 1250.00
**Figurine,** Musical, 7 In. ................................................................................ 18.00
**Playing Cards,** 1916 .................................................................................... 45.00
**Poster,** Chaplin Review, World War II Release, 30 X 40 In. ........................... 150.00
**Poster,** Gold Rush, 60 X 24 In. .................................................................... 550.00
**Poster,** Great Dictator, 30 X 40 In. ............................................................. 175.00

| | |
|---|---|
| **Poster,** Limelight, 30 X 40 In. | 150.00 |
| **Poster,** Modern Times, 30 X 40 In. | 175.00 |
| **Toy,** Walking Figure, Cast Iron Feet, 1920s, Windup | 650.00 |

| | |
|---|---|
| **CHARLIE MC CARTHY, Car,** Windup, Tin | 160.00 |
| **Car,** Windup, 1938 | 275.00 |
| **Dummy,** Cardboard | 20.00 |
| **Game,** Bingo | 18.00 |
| **Game,** Flying Hats | 25.00 |
| **Radio** | 175.00 |
| **Radio Party,** Chase & Sanborn, 21 Figures | 30.00 |
| **Spoon,** Silver Plate | 6.00 To 12.50 |

*Chelsea grape pattern was made before 1840. A small bunch of grapes in a raised design, colored with purple or blue luster, is on the border of the white plate. Most of the pieces are unmarked. The pattern is sometimes called Aynsley or Grandmother. Chelsea sprig is similar but has a sprig of flowers instead of the bunch of grapes.*

| | |
|---|---|
| **CHELSEA GRAPE, Coffeepot,** Covered | 195.00 |
| **Cup & Saucer,** Handleless | 28.00 To 32.00 |
| **Cup & Saucer,** Wishbone Handle | 25.00 |
| **Cup & Saucer,** 4 Sets | 135.00 |
| **Teapot,** 11 In. | 120.00 |
|     **CHELSEA KERAMIC ART WORKS, see Dedham** | |
| **CHELSEA SPRIG, Coffeepot,** Floral, Luster, Covered, 10 In. | 185.00 |
| **Cup & Saucer,** Tea, Blue | 20.00 |

*Chelsea porcelain was made in the Chelsea area of London from about 1745 to 1784. Recent copies of this work have been made from the original molds.*

| | |
|---|---|
| **CHELSEA, Bottle,** Applied Flowers, Cobalt Blue & Gold, 18 1/2 In., Pair | 5750.00 |
| **Bowl,** Cover, Cabbage, Red Anchor Mark, 4 1/2 In. | 1800.00 |
| **Bowl,** Pierced Cover, Loop Finial, C.1760, Red Anchor Mark, 6 1/2 In. | 900.00 |
| **Bowl,** Sunflower, Cover, Red Anchor Mark, 5 1/8 2n. | 2000.00 |
| **Dish,** Sunflower, Red Anchor Mark, 8 1/2 In. | 2500.00 |
| **Figurine,** Seal Seated On Barrel, Gilt Metal Ring, C.1755, 1 1/4 In. | 350.00 |
| **Platter,** Bouquet, Flowers, Trellis Design, Butterflies, 12 In. | 700.00 |
| **Tureen,** Cover, Asparagus, Red Anchor Mark, 7 In. | 4000.00 |
| **Tureen,** Cover, Cauliflower, Red Anchor Mark, 4 1/2 In. | 1600.00 |
| **Vase,** Figural, 2 Draped Boys Holding A Fish, C.1755, 8 5/8 In. | 1700.00 |

*Chinese export porcelain is all the many kinds of porcelain made in China for export to America and Europe in the eighteenth and nineteenth centuries.*

| | |
|---|---|
|     **CHINESE EXPORT, see also Canton, Celadon, Nanking** | |
| **CHINESE EXPORT, Bowl,** Chinese Family Scene, 9 In.Diam. | 80.00 |
| **Bowl,** Famille Rose, 9 1/2 In.Diam., Pair | 585.00 |
| **Bowl,** Pedestal, Chinese Family Scene, 9 3/4 In.Diam. | 200.00 |
| **Bowl,** Pedestal, Chinese Family, 10 1/2 X 7 3/4 In.Diam. | 200.00 |
| **Brush Pot,** American Eagle Holding Branch Of Peace, 5 In. | 155.00 |
| **Chamberstick,** Gold Star Rim, 18th Century, 5 1/2 In. | 50.00 |
| **Cup,** Pedestal, Gilded, Scalloped Edge, Coat Of Arms, 2 In. | 55.00 |
| **Pitcher & Bowl,** Blue & White Flowers, Bowl, 16 1/4 In.Diam. | 500.00 |
| **Pitcher,** Helmet, Brown Leaf & Berry Design, 5 In. | 165.00 |
| **Pitcher,** Helmet, Gold Banding, Monogram AN, C.1770, 5 In. | 90.00 |
| **Plate,** Chinese Family Scene, 10 1/2 In.Diam. | 100.00 |

Plate, Chop, Blue & Gray Calligraphic Signature, 15 3/4 In. ........................................... 265.00
Plate, Cut Corner, Lake Scene, 18th Century, 11 1/4 In. ............................................ 275.00
Plate, Fitzhugh Border, Pair ..................................................................................... 900.00
Plate, Floral Swags & Bands, 18th Century, 8 5/8 In.Diam. ...................................... 140.00
Platter, Blue & White, 12 1/8 X 15 1/8 In. ............................................................. 245.00
Platter, Chinese Family Scene, 14 In. ...................................................................... 400.00
Platter, Chinese Family Scene, 16 In. ...................................................................... 500.00
Platter, Lake Scene, Fruit Border, 18th Century, 11 1/4 In. ...................................... 275.00
Tea Bowl & Saucer, Polychrome, C.1790 .................................................................. 85.00
Tea Caddy, Flower Center, Purple Trim, White Ground ............................................. 150.00
Teapot & Undertray, Strap Handle, Fruit Finial, 19th Century ................................... 100.00
Tureen & Undertray, Covered, Strap Handles, 14 In. ..............................................2350.00
Umbrella Stand, Battle Scene Band, Floral Band, 24 1/2 In. .................................... 500.00
Vase, Baluster Form, Elephant Head Handles, 17 In., Pair .....................................2700.00

*Chocolate glass, sometimes mistakenly called caramel slag, was made by the Indiana Tumbler and Goblet Company of Greentown, Indiana, from 1900 to 1903.*

CHOCOLATE GLASS, Berry Set, Leaf Bracket Pattern, 7 Piece ................................... 175.00
Bride's Bowl, 10 In.Square .................................................................................... 115.00
Butter, Covered, Dewey ........................................................................................... 90.00
Butter, Covered, Leaf Bracket ................................................... 105.00 To 175.00
Compote, Cactus, Small ......................................................................................... 140.00
Compote, Cactus, 5 3/4 X 5 3/8 In.Diam. ............................................................. 145.00
Compote, Geneva, 3 1/2 X 4 1/2 In. ....................................................................... 80.00
Creamer, Austrian ................................................................................................... 120.00
Cruet, Cactus ......................................................................................................... 175.00
Cruet, Cactus, Dewey Stopper ................................................................................ 145.00
Cruet, Leaf Bracket ................................................................................................ 145.00
Cup, Punch, Shuttle ................................................................................................. 75.00
Dish, Berry, Geneva, 4 1/2 In.Diam. ........................................................................ 40.00
Dish, Dolphin Cover ............................................................................................... 265.00
Dish, Rabbit On Nest Cover, 5 1/2 X 4 In. ............................................................. 210.00
Dish, Relish, Leaf Bracket, Oval ............................................................................... 55.00
Dish, Sauce, Footed, Leaf Bracket ........................................................................... 35.00
Lamp, Dome Shade, 8 Panels, White Metal Base, 22 In. ......................................... 185.00
Mug, Cactus Design ................................................................................................. 38.75
Mug, Castle Scene, 4 1/2 In. .................................................................................... 80.00
Mug, Shuttle ............................................................................................................. 95.00
Nappy, Cactus .......................................................................................................... 65.00
Nappy, Leaf Bracket, Ruffled Edge ............................................... 30.00 To 49.00
Nappy, Masonic ........................................................................................................ 25.00
Nappy, 3-Cornered .................................................................................................... 50.00
Pitcher & Tray, Paneled, Tray 10 1/2 In. ................................................................ 330.00
Pitcher, Syrup, Shuttle ............................................................................................. 75.00
Pitcher, Water, Cactus ............................................................................................ 175.00
Pitcher, Water, Squirrel Pattern .............................................................................. 150.00
Plate, Serenade, 8 In. ............................................................................................... 75.00
Saltshaker, Cactus Pattern ......................................................... 32.50 To 50.00
Sauce, Leaf Bracket .................................................................................................. 30.00
Saucer, Shell Pattern ................................................................................................ 40.00
Spooner, Cactus ....................................................................................................... 85.00
Spooner, Dewey ........................................................................................................ 53.00
Spooner, Wild Rose & Bowknot ............................................................................... 95.00
Stein, Drinking Scene, 5 Matching Small Steins ...................................................... 900.00
Sugar & Creamer, Leaf Bracket ................................................................................ 84.00
Syrup, Cord Drapery ............................................................................................... 145.00
Syrup, Shuttle ......................................................................................................... 115.00
Toothpick, Figural, Witch's Head .............................................................................. 98.00
Tray, Chrysanthemum, 10 X 8 In. ........................................................................... 160.00
Tumbler, Cactus .......................................................................... 40.00 To 65.00
Tumbler, Leaf Bracket ............................................................................................... 40.00

**Tumbler,** Lemonade, Cactus Pattern .................................................................. 35.00
**Tumbler,** Shuttle .......................................................................................... 135.00
**Tumbler,** Uneeda Milk Biscuit, 5 1/2 In. ............................... 80.00 To 150.00
**Vase,** Paneled, 6 In. ...................................................................................... 65.00
**Water Set,** Cactus, 8 Piece ......................................................................... 350.00
      **CHRISTMAS PLATE, see Collector Plate**
**CHRISTMAS TREE, Light Bulb,** Andy Gump, Milk Glass ...................... 40.00 To 50.00
  **Light Bulb,** Angel ..................................................................................... 27.00
  **Light Bulb,** Angel, Celluloid ...................................................................... 8.00
  **Light Bulb,** Angel, Red Sash, Blue Robe, Clear Glass .............................. 35.00
  **Light Bulb,** Apple ..................................................................................... 15.00
  **Light Bulb,** Babe In Boot, Red, Milk Glass ............................................... 22.00
  **Light Bulb,** Bell ........................................................................................ 10.00
  **Light Bulb,** Betty Boop, Figural, 1930 ...................................................... 45.00
  **Light Bulb,** Bird ....................................................................................... 5.00
  **Light Bulb,** Bird, Milk Glass ..................................................................... 4.00
  **Light Bulb,** Bluebird ................................................................................. 5.00
  **Light Bulb,** Bunch Of Grapes, Green Leaves, Purple, 3 1/2 In. ................... 35.00
  **Light Bulb,** Comic Characters, Milk Glass, Set Of 7 ................................. 245.00
  **Light Bulb,** Diamond-Quilted, Milk Glass, Blue ........................................ 14.50
  **Light Bulb,** Dick Tracy, Milk Glass ........................................................... 50.00
  **Light Bulb,** Dirigible, Blue Gondola & Fin, Japan ...................................... 37.00
  **Light Bulb,** Dirigible, Electric, Orange, Blue, Flags, Stripes ...................... 37.00
  **Light Bulb,** Doll Head ............................................................................... 22.00
  **Light Bulb,** Figural, Milk Glass, Box Of 25 .............................................. 250.00
  **Light Bulb,** Flower, 9-Pointed, Amber Glass ............................................ 10.00
  **Light Bulb,** House .................................................................................... 10.00
  **Light Bulb,** Japanese Lantern, Set Of 3 ................................................... 16.00
  **Light Bulb,** Lantern ................................................................... 3.00 To 4.00
  **Light Bulb,** Mickey & Minnie Mouse, Diamond Brite, Pair ......................... 85.00
  **Light Bulb,** Mickey Mouse ....................................................................... 20.00
  **Light Bulb,** Monkey ................................................................................. 35.00
  **Light Bulb,** Old Woman In Shoe .............................................................. 35.00
  **Light Bulb,** Orphan Annie & Sandy, Figural, 1930, Pair ............................. 85.00
  **Light Bulb,** Parakeet ................................................................................ 10.00
  **Light Bulb,** Popeye, Action ....................................................................... 18.00
  **Light Bulb,** Popeye, Noma, 1930, Set Of 7 .............................................. 125.00
  **Light Bulb,** Red Riding Hood .................................................................... 22.00
  **Light Bulb,** Santa ...................................................................... 10.00 To 15.00
  **Light Bulb,** Santa Head, Flame Cone, White Milk Glass, Pair .................... 10.00
  **Light Bulb,** Santa Head, 3 Faces ............................................................. 18.00
  **Light Bulb,** Santa, Celluloid ..................................................................... 8.00
  **Light Bulb,** Santa, Straight Beard, Body Tapers To Base ........................... 12.00
  **Light Bulb,** Snail On Mushroom House, 3 In. ............................................ 55.00
  **Light Bulb,** Snowman ................................................................ 10.00 To 12.00
  **Light Bulb,** Star ....................................................................................... 3.00
  **Light Bulb,** Teapot, Applied Spout & Handle, Blown Glass ........................ 18.00
  **Light Bulb,** Yellow Rose, Green Leaves, Round, 3 In. ............................... 35.00
  **Light Bulb,** Zeppelin, Pink Gondola, Blue Flags ....................................... 18.00
  **Light,** Diamond Pattern, Amber, Blue, & Green, 3 1/2 In. ......................... 8.00
  **Light,** Milk Glass, Blue ............................................................................. 15.00
  **Light,** Quilted, Milk Glass ......................................................................... 15.00
  **Light,** Thousand-Eye, Cobalt Blue ............................................................ 12.00
  **Ornament,** Airplane, Gold Beads, Czechoslovakia, 5 In. ............................ 25.00
  **Ornament,** Airplane, Silver Beaded, Czechoslovakia, 5 In. ........................ 25.00
  **Ornament,** Angel Hair Angel, 7 1/2 In.Diam. ............................................ 10.00
  **Ornament,** Angel Head, 3 Dimensional, Center Of Star, Dresden ............... 28.50
  **Ornament,** Angel, Lithograph, Double ....................................................... 14.00
  **Ornament,** Angel, Lithograph, Single ........................................................ 10.00
  **Ornament,** Angel, Tinsel, Green Cellophane Trim, 4 1/2 In. ....................... 20.00
  **Ornament,** Ball With Star, Blown Glass .................................................... 4.00
  **Ornament,** Beetle, Glass, 2 1/2 In. .......................................................... 45.00

| | |
|---|---|
| Ornament, Bell, Cotton | 5.00 |
| Ornament, Bird, Brush Tail, Blown Glass, Tin Clip | 15.00 |
| Ornament, Bird, Clip-On | 14.00 |
| Ornament, Birdcage, 3 X 1 1/2 In. | 30.00 |
| Ornament, Boat, Tinsel Wrapped, Hanger, C.1900, 3 1/4 In. | 25.00 |
| Ornament, Boy, Hands In Pocket, German, 3 1/2 X 2 In. | 45.00 |
| Ornament, Boy, On Skis, Bisque Head, Cotton Batting Snowsuit | 95.00 |
| Ornament, Boy, Red Cap, Scarf, Black Eyes, C.1910, 2 3/4 In. | 40.00 |
| Ornament, Butterfly, 2-Sided, Gold, Flat, Dresden | 8.50 |
| Ornament, Camel, Dresden | 6.50 To 15.00 |
| Ornament, Candle Clip, Set Of 5 | 3.00 |
| Ornament, Candy Cane, Glass, 6 3/4 X 1/2 In. | 15.00 |
| Ornament, Candy Container, Bell, Red Silk & Paper | 25.00 |
| Ornament, Candy Container, Boot, Angel In Coat, 3 3/4 In. | 25.00 |
| Ornament, Candy Container, Santa In Balloon, 2 1/4 In. | 55.00 |
| Ornament, Candy Container, Santa With Child, 3 3/4 In. | 3.50 |
| Ornament, Candy Container, Walnut, 2 In., 2 Piece | 25.00 |
| Ornament, Carousel, 4 Figures On Horses, C.1930, 2 1/4 In. | 35.00 |
| Ornament, Circle Of Spun Glass, 2 Spun Glass Angels, 5 In. | 30.00 |
| Ornament, Clamshell With Pearl, 3 X 2 1/2 In. | 30.00 |
| Ornament, Clown With Accordion, C.1930, 3 1/4 In. | 45.00 |
| Ornament, Clown, 4 1/2 X 2 In. | 35.00 |
| Ornament, Crescent, 2-Sided, Silver, Dresden | 7.50 |
| Ornament, Cross, 2-Sided, Gold, Dresden | 6.00 |
| Ornament, Crown, Gold, 2 X 2 1/2 In. | 50.00 |
| Ornament, Devil's Head, Glass | 85.00 |
| Ornament, Doll's Head, Glass Eyes, Glass | 85.00 |
| Ornament, Drum, Silver & Blue Triangles, C.1950, 2 1/2 In. | 4.00 |
| Ornament, Elephant, Glass | 85.00 |
| Ornament, Elephant, 3 Dimensional, Dresden, 2 In. | 45.00 |
| Ornament, Father Christmas Head, On Tinsel, C.1920 | 25.00 |
| Ornament, Father Christmas, Papier-Mache | 250.00 |
| Ornament, Father Christmas, Spun Glass Skirt, Diecut, 9 In. | 50.00 |
| Ornament, Father Christmas, Spun Glass Skirt, 9 1/2 In. | 50.00 |
| Ornament, Father Christmas, 3 Dolls & Lamb, Tinsel, 13 In. | 35.00 |
| Ornament, Fish | 9.00 |
| Ornament, Fish, Tinsel Wrapped, C.1920, 3 3/4 In. | 20.00 |
| Ornament, Fruit Basket, Glass | 15.00 |
| Ornament, Girl, Diecut Face, Dressed, Cotton Batting, 7 In. | 60.00 |
| Ornament, Grapes, Wire Wrapped, Glass | 6.00 |
| Ornament, Head With Glass Eyes | 85.00 |
| Ornament, Heart, Glass | 15.00 |
| Ornament, Horn, Glass | 8.00 |
| Ornament, Horse, Gold, Black Eyes, Red Ears, Germany, 2 3/4 In. | 20.00 |
| Ornament, Horseshoe, Tinsel Outline, Angel Heads, 7 1/2 In. | 35.00 |
| Ornament, House, Silver, Green Roof, Red Window, 2 In. | 10.00 |
| Ornament, Icicle, Blown Glass | 5.00 |
| Ornament, Icicle, Twisted, Tin, 22 Piece | 20.00 |
| Ornament, Icicle, Wire Garland Inside, 7 1/2 X 3/4 In. | 28.00 |
| Ornament, Jack Frost Face, Pinecone | 60.00 |
| Ornament, Lyre, Silver, 2-Sided, Dresden | 9.50 |
| Ornament, Man On The Moon | 34.00 |
| Ornament, Man, Fat, Playing Accordion, 4 X 2 1/4 In. | 35.00 |
| Ornament, Man's Face, 2-Sided, 3 X 2 1/4 In. | 45.00 |
| Ornament, Mushroom, 2 1/2 X 1 1/4 In. | 25.00 |
| Ornament, Owl, Glass | 28.00 |
| Ornament, Peacock, Crown On Head, Gold Bill, 4 1/4 X 3 In. | 10.00 |
| Ornament, Pinecone, Blown Glass, Red | 6.00 |
| Ornament, Rabbit Eating Carrot, 3 1/2 X 1 3/4 In. | 60.00 |
| Ornament, Santa Face, In Pinecone, C.1920, 2 3/4 In. | 60.00 |
| Ornament, Santa Head, 3 Dimensional, Center Of Star, Dresden | 37.50 |
| Ornament, Santa, Blown Glass | 8.00 To 12.00 |
| Ornament, Santa, Coming Out Of Ball | 57.00 |

| | |
|---|---:|
| Ornament, Santa, Cotton With Paper Printed Face | 45.00 |
| Ornament, Santa, Papier-Mache Face, Cotton Beard, Red Suit | 22.50 |
| Ornament, Santa, Red Jacket, Blue Pants, Papier-Mache | 6.50 |
| Ornament, Silver Bird In Nest, Wire Wrapping, C.1930, 3 In. | 55.00 |
| Ornament, Silver Bird With Brush Tail | 15.00 |
| Ornament, Snake, Detailed Head, White, C.1920, 5 3/4 In. | 40.00 |
| Ornament, Snow White & 7 Dwarfs, Disney Enterprises, Boxed | 500.00 |
| Ornament, Snow White, Dwarfs, Candy Holder, Papier-Mache, 1934 | 240.00 |
| Ornament, Snowman, Glass | 27.50 |
| Ornament, Spun Glass Circle, Lithograph Santa Both Sides | 12.50 |
| Ornament, Spun Glass Semicircle, Angel Lithograph | 27.50 |
| Ornament, Squirrel With Nut, Frosted, C.1890, 3 1/4 In. | 70.00 |
| Ornament, Stag, Silver, Gold Ears, 2 3/4 In. | 20.00 |
| Ornament, Star, Sterling Silver, Gorham | 30.00 |
| Ornament, Swan, Free Blown, Tinsel Tail, C.1890, 7 X 11 In. | 25.00 |
| Ornament, Swan, Glass, Bent Neck, 2 3/4 X 3 1/2 In. | 30.00 |
| Ornament, Teapot, Hand-Painted, Blown Glass | 7.50 |
| Ornament, Teddy Bear, Glass, 4 1/2 In. | 65.00 |
| Ornament, Tree, Base Clip | 65.00 |
| Ornament, Tulip, Candleholder On Top, 3 1/4 X 2 3/4 In. | 45.00 |
| Ornament, Umbrella, 1890, Wire On Top | 40.00 |
| Ornament, Vase, Tinsel Wrapped, Bowl Shape, C.1890, 2 1/4 In. | 50.00 |
| Ornament, Wing Shape, Pink Cotton, Angel Center, 3 1/4 In. | 15.00 |
| Ornament, Wire Wrapped, Victorian, Thin Glass | 12.00 |
| Stand, Lador, Tree Cup, Musical | 100.00 |
| Stand, Santa & Reindeer, Noma, 8 X 14 In. | 55.00 |
| Wreath, Brass Ornaments, Hand-Soldered On Wreath, 15 In. | 60.00 |

*Art Deco chrome items became popular in the 1930s. Collectors are most interested in pieces made by the Chase Brass and Copper Company of Waterbury, Connecticut.*

| | |
|---|---:|
| CHROME, Cocktail Set, Shaker, 6 Beakers, Red Knobs, Farber Ware | 60.00 |
| Coffeepot, Black Handle, Chase, 10 1/2 In. | 25.00 To 45.00 |
| Percolator, Fluted Black Bakelite Handle, 10 1/2 In. | 14.00 |
| Punch Bowl, Red Plastic Coil Knob, 10 In. | 24.00 |
| Teakettle, Over Copper | 8.00 |
| Tray, Octagonal, Chase | 37.00 |
| Warming Oven, Electric, Chase | 95.00 To 125.00 |
| CIGAR CUTTER see Brass, Cutter, Cigar; Store, Cutter, Cigar | |
| CIGAR STORE FIGURE, Black Figure With Pipe, 19th Century, 22 In. | 9000.00 |
| Chinese Tea Shop Merchant, 44 In. | 6750.00 |
| Indian Princess, On Pedestal, C.1880, 6 Ft. 2 In. | 4500.00 |
| Indian, Cast Metal, Demuth, 6 Ft. 10 In. | 5000.00 |
| Indian, Scouting Chief, 1860–1890 | 3000.00 |
| Scotsman, Snuff Shop Figure, 31 1/4 In. | 1900.00 |

*Cinnabar is a vermilion or red lacquer. Some pieces are made with hundreds of thicknesses of the lacquer that is later carved.*

| | |
|---|---:|
| CINNABAR, Bookends, 2 Set-In Carved Jade Medallions | 235.00 |
| Bottle, Snuff, Inlaid Stones | 75.00 |
| Box, Card, Red, 6 X 4 X 2 In. | 85.00 |
| Box, Cigarette, Black & Red | 125.00 |
| Box, Red, Yamanaka & Co., N.Y., 6 X 4 X 2 1/2 In. | 75.00 |
| Box, Sitting Hen Cover, Blue Enamel Inside, 12 X 9 X 9 In. | 850.00 |
| Jar, Ginger, Covered, Deep Relief All Around, 6 In., Pair | 125.00 |
| Lamp, 29 In. | 350.00 |
| Vase, Baluster Shape, Carved Pagodas, Trees, & Mountains, 7 In. | 80.00 |

*Civil War mementos are important collectors' items. Most of the pieces are military items used from 1861 to 1865.*

| | |
|---|---:|
| CIVIL WAR, Amputation Kit, Charles Lentz & Sons, Philadelphia, Pa. | 695.00 |

Boots & Spurs, Colonel's, Cavalry ........................................................ 350.00
Boots, Officer's, Small, 25 In.High ........................................................ 165.00
Box, Musket, 1858 Model, Leather ........................................................ 45.00
Canteen, Officer's, Earthenware, Applied Handle, Brown, 12 1/2 In. ........... 65.00
Carbine, Spencer ................................................................................ 500.00
Desk, Field Dispatch, Brigadier General's, Name In Gold ......................... 360.00
Epaulets, Fishscale, Metal ................................................................... 125.00
Flag, Confederate, 60 X 36 In. ............................................................ 15.00
Hat, Gold Cord, Crossed Swords, Wide Brim ........................................ 165.00
Match Safe, Knapsack Matches ............................................................ 28.00
Photograph, 17th New York Volunteers, Framed ..................................... 185.00
Powder Horn, Indian On Horse, Spearing Buffalo, Copper & Brass ............. 125.00
Shaving Cup, Marked On Handle, 26 M.E., Inf., Tin ................................. 67.50
Sword, Scabbard, Dated 1864 .............................................................. 45.00
      CKAW, see Dedham

*Clambroth glass, popular in the Victorian era, is a grayish color and is*
*semiopaque like clambroth.*

CLAMBROTH, Basket, Souvenir, Friendship, Wisconsin, 5 In. ..................... 28.00
Bowl, Basket Weave Body, Fluted Opalescent Rim, 5 1/2 In.Diam. ............. 85.00
Candlestick, Petal & Column, Pair ......................................................... 250.00
Canoe, Pink Flowers, Souvenir New York ............................................... 9.00
Creamer, Swimming Swans ................................................................... 45.00
Goblet, Button Arches ......................................................................... 45.00
Goblet, Souvenir, Glenfield, North Dakota ............................................. 17.00
Jar, Barber, Lettered Antiseptic Cotton, Nickel Lid .................................. 40.00
Lamp, Log Cabin, Dated On Brass, Blue, Miniature .................................. 465.00
Lamp, Oil, Blown, Russian Blue ............................................................ 125.00
Lamp, Whale Oil, Paneled Font ............................................................. 175.00
Nappy, Prayer Rug Pattern ................................................................... 16.00
Toothpick, Button & Arches, Souvenir, Youngstown, Ohio ......................... 30.00
Toothpick, Pipe, Souvenir, Mt.Pleasant, Michigan, 5 1/2 In. ..................... 14.50

CLARICE CLIFF, Plate, Basket Of Flowers, 8 In. ..................................... 45.00

*Clewell ware was made in limited quantities by Charles Walter Clewell*
*of Canton, Ohio, from 1902 to 1955. Pottery was covered with a thin coat-*
*ing of bronze, then treated to make the bronze turn different colors. Pieces*
*covered with copper, brass, or silver were also made. Mr. Clewell's secret*
*formula for blue patina bronze was burned when he died in 1965.*

CLEWELL, Vase, Mottled Turquoise, Green, Copperclad, Signed, Marked, 7 3/4 In. ...... 195.00
Vase, Tarnish Technique, 4 1/2 In. ........................................................ 100.00
Vase, 7 In. ......................................................................................... 165.00

*Clews pottery was made by George Clews & Co. of Brownhill Pottery,*
*Tunstall, England, from 1806 to 1861.*
      CLEWS, see also Flow Blue
CLEWS, Cup & Saucer, Handleless, Castle Scene, C.1820 ......................... 80.00
Plate, Black Solar Rays, 10 1/2 In. ....................................................... 29.50
Plate, Dr.Syntax, The Garden Trio, Blue, 8 In.Diam. ................................ 20.00
Plate, Landing Of Lafayette, 7 3/4 In. .................................................... 285.00
Plate, Landing Of Lafayette, 9 In.Diam. ................................................. 360.00
Plate, Landing Of Lafayette, 10 In.Diam. ............................................... 350.00
Plate, Marine Hospital, Dark Blue ......................................................... 285.00
Plate, States, 7 3/4 In. ........................................................................ 285.00

Clock, Acorn, Mahogany, Forestville
Mfg. Co., C.1850, 28 1/2 In.

The Clifton Pottery was founded by William Long in Clifton,
New Jersey, in 1905. He worked there until 1908 making a line
called Crystal Patina. The Clifton Pottery made art pottery.
Another firm, the Chesapeake Pottery, sold majolica marked Clifton
Ware.

**CLIFTON, Humidor,** Covered, Indian Design ................................................................................ 65.00
   **Pitcher,** Spout, Indian Type, Signed ................................................................................ 125.00
   **Vase,** Indian Design, Signed ................................................................................ 75.00

**CLOCK, Aaron Crane,** Year Clock, Torsion Pendulum, C.1845, Glass Dial ................................ 3500.00
   **Acorn,** Mahogany, Forestville Mfg. Co., C.1850, 28 1/2 In. ................................ *Illus* 1300.00
   **Ada,** Mantine Sonora Bell, Time & Strike ................................................................ 325.00
   **Advertising,** AC Spark Plugs, Electric ................................................ 75.00 To 100.00
   **Advertising,** Blatz Beer, 4 In. ................................................................................ 9.00
   **Advertising,** Budweiser, Girl, Revolving, Light ................................................ 50.00
   **Advertising,** Budweiser, Hanging, Swag Chain, Revolving, Illuminated ................ 335.00
   **Advertising,** Calvert Whiskey, Electric, Picture Of Owl ................................ 65.00
   **Advertising,** Carstairs White Seal, Seal Balancing Ball ................................ 135.00
   **Advertising,** Cow, Clock Insert, St.Charles Evaporated Milk, Cast Iron ................ 95.00
   **Advertising,** Croft Ale, Large ................................................................................ 50.00
   **Advertising,** Dr.Pepper, Good For Life, Neon Light ................................ 70.00
   **Advertising,** Dr.Pepper, 1940s ................................................................ 75.00
   **Advertising,** Drink Coca-Cola, Please Pay Cashier, Aluminum Base ................ 135.00
   **Advertising,** Four Roses ................................................................................ 20.00
   **Advertising,** General Electric Refrigerator ................................................ 65.00
   **Advertising,** Keebler, 8-Day, Cuckoo Clock, Lux ................................ 35.00 To 55.00
   **Advertising,** Lucky Strike Tobacco, Regulator ................................ 150.00
   **Advertising,** Miller Beer, Electric ................................................ 20.00
   **Advertising,** Mr. Peanut, Alarm ................................................ 35.00
   **Advertising,** Nash's Coffee, Electric, 15 In.Diam. ................................ 15.00
   **Advertising,** Old Shay Beer, Marked Sunshine, Round ................ 20.00
   **Advertising,** Olympia Beer ................................................ 60.00
   **Advertising,** Pabst Blue Ribbon, Picture Beer Glass, Wood, 11 X 19 In. ................ 50.00
   **Advertising,** Pearl Beer, Bottle Cap ................................ 32.00
   **Advertising,** Peko Coffee, Short Drop, Walnut, 1881, Lewis ................ 485.00
   **Advertising,** Pepsi, The Light Refreshment, Wrought Iron ................ 35.00
   **Advertising,** Polk's Dairy, Carriage Type, Stem Wind, Small ................ 45.00
   **Advertising,** Prince George Cigars, With Clipper, Cast Iron ................ 650.00
   **Advertising,** Repeal Of Prohibition, Metal ................................ 85.00
   **Advertising,** Royal Crown, 1963 ................................ 20.00
   **Advertising,** Schlitz, 7 X 11 In. ................................ 14.00
   **Advertising,** Seven Up, Square With Wood Frame ................ 50.00
   **Advertising,** St.Joseph Aspirin, Wall, 15 In.Diam. ................ 45.00

**Advertising,** Star Brand Shoes Are Better, Alarm, Ansonia .................................. 75.00
**Advertising,** Star Brand Shoes, Shape Of Horseshoe, 3 In. ................................. 25.00
**Advertising,** Sun-Crest Soda, Electric ................................................................ 25.00
**Advertising,** Sun-Crest, Bottle Shape, 15 In. ..................................................... 45.00
**Advertising,** Sun-Crest, Wall, Bottle Of Orange On Glass Front, 5 In. .................. 45.00
**Advertising,** Talking, Says Pepsi-Cola On The Hour & Half Hour, Signed ............... 265.00
**Advertising,** Tetley Tea, Tin, Square ................................................................. 75.00
**Advertising,** Tootsie Pop, Alarm ...................................................................... 15.00
**Advertising,** Upright Sweepers, Electric ............................................................ 42.50
**Advertising,** Vantage Cigarettes, Battery Operated ............................................ 30.00
**Advertising,** Vernors Ale ................................................................................ 22.00
**Advertising,** Wells Fargo Depot, Double Face, Walnut ...................................... 1500.00
**Animated,** F.D.Roosevelt, Celebrate End Of Prohibition .................................... 115.00
**Ansonia,** Alarm, Metal Case, 4 X 3 1/2 In. ...................................................... 22.00
**Ansonia,** Art Nouveau, Metal .......................................................................... 85.00
**Ansonia,** Beveled Glass, Brass Frame, 6 X 7 X 10 1/4 In. ................................. 295.00
**Ansonia,** Black Marble, Statue ........................................................................ 625.00
**Ansonia,** Cherub, Porcelain Face, Beveled Glass, 8 1/2 In. ............................... 125.00
**Ansonia,** Gingerbread, 24 In. .................................................... 135.00 To 180.00
**Ansonia,** Gingerbread, 8-Day, Time & Strike, Walnut ...................................... 175.00
**Ansonia,** Long Drop, Time & Strike, Walnut .................................................... 375.00
**Ansonia,** Mantel, Black Iron, Brass Dial ......................................................... 75.00
**Ansonia,** Mantel, Dated 1882, Lion Trim, Brass Face ...................................... 145.00
**Ansonia,** Mantel, Marble, Exposed Escapement .............................................. 290.00
**Ansonia,** Mantel, 8-Day, Alarm, Chimes, 14 X 22 In. ...................................... 200.00
**Ansonia,** Mantel, 8-Day, Time & Strike, Brass Plated, 13 1/2 In. ...................... 350.00
**Ansonia,** Mercury Pendulum, Visible Works, Brass .......................................... 275.00
**Ansonia,** Rococo Revival Ceramic, German Case, 19th Century, 15 In. .............. 225.00
**Ansonia,** School, 8-Day, Original Label .......................................................... 295.00
**Ansonia,** Shelf, Royal Bonn Case, Time, Strike, 8 X 10 In. .................. 200.00 To 295.00
**Ansonia,** Wall, Time & Strike, Queen Elizabeth, Walnut ................................... 600.00
**Ansonia,** 8-Day, Time & Strike, C.1883, 32 In. ............................................... 550.00
**Austrian,** Figural, F.Goldscheider, 1900, 16 1/2 In. ............................... *Illus* 1000.00
**Austrian,** Fusee Movement, Silver & Enamel, Gothic Case, 5 1/4 In. ................. 1500.00
**Banjo,** Horace Tifft, Black & Gold Glass, C.1830, Mahogany, 33 1/2 In. ............. 1300.00
**Barnes & Bartholomew,** Ives Movement, 3 Tier .............................................. 800.00
**Big Bad Wolf,** Alarm, Animated, Ingersoll, 1933 ............................................ 150.00
**Blakeborough,** Calendar, 8-Day, Painted Dial, C.1800, 7 Ft. 8 In. ..................... 2900.00
**Bradley & Hubbard,** Topsy Blinking Eye ........................................................ 1175.00
**Bugs Bunny,** Germany ........................................................... 25.00 To 40.00
**Bundy Co.,** Time, Oak ................................................................................ 650.00
**Calendar,** Ingraham, Rooster Head, 8-Day, Oak .............................................. 150.00
**Calendar,** Lovell Mfg, Co, , Erie Pa.Meridian, Pine, 24 In. ................................ 450.00
**Calendar,** 8-Day, Remember To Die, Skull, Crossbones, C.1760, Oak, 7 Ft. ......... 3300.00
**Carriage,** Porcelain Face, Visible Escapement, 2 3/4 X 4 1/2 In. ....................... 75.00
**Cartier,** Travel, Malachite Easel Frame, Enameled ........................................... 8500.00

Clock, Austrian, Figural, F.Goldscheider,
1900, 16 1/2 In.

**Chelsea,** Carriage, Beveled Glass, Embossed Birds, Foliage, 8-Day .......................... 675.00
**Chelsea,** Ship, Time, 6-In. Dial, Solid Glass ...................... 230.00
**Chelsea,** Wall Bracket, U.S.Navy Ship, Deck, Nickel Plated Brass ...................... 150.00
**Cut Glass,** Harvard & Daisy, 5 1/2 X 4 In. ...................... 165.00
**Dutch,** Cottage, Bobbing Bird, 8-Day, Red, White, & Blue ...................... 125.00
**E.Howard,** Time, For Diebold Safe & Lock, 72-Hour ...................... 85.00
**English,** Cows, Porcelain, 11 X 14 In. ...................... 215.00
**Figural,** Art Nouveau, Pendulum, Bronze, Marked, 16 In. ...................... 110.00
**French,** Carriage, Time, Large ...................... 295.00
**French,** Floor, Ebony Ground, Ormolu, C.1740, 7 Ft. ...................... 3500.00
**French,** L'Iroux, Walnut & Brass, C.1850, 24 In. ...................... 1050.00
**French,** Mantel, Black Marble, Colored Inlay, 8-Day ...................... 125.00
**French,** Mantel, Ivory Painted Panel Under Dial, Bronze, C.1900, 14 In. ...................... 700.00
**French,** Mantel, White Marble, 8-Day, Time & Strike ...................... 175.00
**French,** Marble, Front Escapement, Mercury Pendulum, C.1855 ...................... 925.00
**French,** Mechanical Ferris Wheel Runs On Top, 1900, 11 In. ...................... 595.00
**French,** Pendulum, Marquetry, 19th Century ...................... *Illus* 850.00
**French,** Ship, Octagonal, 30-Hour, Wooden Case ...................... 100.00
**George Marsh,** Hartford, Conn., 1-Day, Wooden Works ...................... 475.00
**Gilbert,** China Case, Green With Flowers, Gold Trim ...................... 400.00
**Gilbert,** Gingerbread, 8-Day, Time & Strike, Oak ...................... 195.00
**Gilbert,** Kitchen, Painted Metal ...................... 32.00
**Gilbert,** Mantel, Bell On Top, 8-Day, 16 X 17 1/2 In. ...................... 500.00
**Gilbert,** Mantel, Black, 4 Free Standing Columns ...................... 125.00
**Gilbert,** Mantel, Hour & Half Hour Strike, 18 In. ...................... 80.00
**Gilbert,** Mantel, Mahogany Case, 18 In. ...................... 30.00
**Gilbert,** Regulator, Rosewood ...................... 1100.00
**Gilbert,** Regulator, Stepped Base, Quarter Oak Case, 45 X 18 1/2 In. ...................... 475.00
**Gold Wash Case,** Wedgwood Paneled, C.1866, 17 In. ...................... *Illus* 2650.00
**Hanson,** Grandfather, 8-Day, Westminster Chimes, Mahogany, 17 X 72 In. ...................... 450.00
**Heco,** Cuckoo, 8-Day ...................... 20.00
**Hersheide,** Grandfather, 5-Tube, C.1919, Double Columns, 7 Ft. ...................... 1500.00
**Howard,** Seconds Pendulum, Oak Case, 59 In. ...................... 1450.00
**Howard,** Wall, Double Faced, 12 In.Dials, Dark Oak Case ...................... 450.00
**Howard,** Wall, Weight Driven, Square Dial ...................... 950.00
**Illinois Watch Co.,** Time, 120-Hour ...................... 85.00
**Ingersoll,** Alarm, Mickey Mouse, 1940s ...................... 50.00
**Ingraham,** Banjo, Nyanze, 8-Day, Time & Strike, Reverse Glasses ...................... 325.00
**Ingraham,** Banjo, 38 In. ...................... 275.00
**Ingraham,** Banjo, 8-Day, Time & Strike, Yankee Clipper, 34 In. ...................... 240.00
**Ingraham,** Mantel, Hour Strike, 20 X 24 In. ...................... 70.00

Clock, French, Pendulum, Marquetry, 19th Century

Clock, Gold Wash Case, Wedgwood
Paneled, C.1866, 17 In.

Clock, Mantel, Bronze-Mounted,
Art Deco, 16 X 19 In.

| | |
|---|---:|
| **Ingraham,** Mantel, Scroll In Wood, Hour & Half Hour Strike | 85.00 |
| **Ingraham,** Regulator, Wall, Time, Walnut | 225.00 |
| **Ingraham,** Shelf, 8-Day, Pine | 95.00 |
| **Ingraham,** Shell Encased, Time & Strike, Key Wind | 9500.00 |
| **Ingraham,** 3 Pillars Each Side, 8-Day, Roof Atop Face, 16 X 11 1/2 In. | 200.00 |
| **Ithaca,** Calendar, Farmer's Model, C.1880, 25 In. | 975.00 To 1250.00 |
| **J.Trenaman,** Tall Case, Charlottetown, Prince Edward Island | 3200.00 |
| **Jerome & Darrow,** Split Column, Paper Inside, C.1825, 32 In. | 400.00 |
| **Jerome & Darrow,** Wooden Works, Mirror Door, C.1820, 32 In. | 290.00 |
| **John Birge,** Rosewood Veneer, Hand-Painted, C.1832, 8-Day | 395.00 |
| **Junghans,** Open Swinger, Westminster Chime, Walnut Case | 695.00 |
| **Kitchen,** Calendar | 215.00 |
| **Kneeling Nude,** Art Deco | 90.00 |
| **Lux,** Animated, Alarm, Spinning Wheel | 45.00 To 80.00 |
| **Lux,** Cuckoo | 35.00 |
| **Lux,** Happy Days, Animated, Beer Drinker | 125.00 |
| **Mantel,** Bronze Mounted, Art Deco, 16 X 19 In. | *Illus* 750.00 |
| **McCoy,** Tabletop, Mottled Blue & White, Marked, 4 1/4 In. | 95.00 |
| **Mechanical,** Stagecoach & Horse, Whip Goes Up & Down, Lighted | 150.00 |
| **Mickey Mouse,** Alarm, Ingersoll, 1933 | 265.00 |
| **Mickey Mouse,** Alarm, Ingersoll, 1947, Boxed | 250.00 |
| **New England,** Case, Victorian Carving, Brass, 8-Day, C.1810 | 1550.00 |
| **New England,** Tall Case, 30-Hour, Wooden Works, Cherry | 1600.00 |
| **New Haven,** Banjo, Time & Strike, Medium Size | 295.00 |
| **New Haven,** Banjo, 8-Day, Time & Strike, Pendulum | 325.00 |
| **New Haven,** Banjo, 8-Day, Time & Strike, Reverse Glasses, Whitney Label | 225.00 |
| **New Haven,** Royal Bonn China, Scalloped Design, 6 X 5 In. | 125.00 |
| **New Haven,** School, Satinwood Inlaid With Oak, 27 In. | 190.00 |
| **New Haven,** Statue, Small | 40.00 |
| **Newberry,** Calendar, Walnut | 375.00 |
| **R.Henderson,** Calendar, 8-Day, Brass Dial, Oak, C.1720, 6 Ft. 6 In. | 3300.00 |
| **Riley Whiting,** Shelf, Wooden Works | 600.00 |
| **Schoolhouse,** Mickey Mouse, Electric, 14 In. | 40.00 |
| **Sessions,** Arcadia, Mantel | 135.00 |
| **Sessions,** Banjo, Pendulum, 8-Day, Picture Of Ship | 145.00 |
| **Sessions,** Humpback, Mahogany | 40.00 |
| **Sessions,** Mantel, Black, Cast Iron | 10.00 |
| **Sessions,** Mantel, Lion's Head & Column, Black | 75.00 |
| **Sessions,** School, 8-Day, Octagon, Oak | 185.00 |
| **Sessions,** Shelf, Time & Strike, Walnut, 8-Day, 11 In. | 55.00 |
| **Sessions,** 8-Day, Alarm, Dated 1912 | 35.00 |
| **Sessions,** 8-Day, Open Face, Chimes, 10 X 18 In. | 200.00 |
| **Seth Thomas,** Banjo, 8-Day, Time & Strike, Reverse Glass, Plymouth Dial | 225.00 |

Seth Thomas, Calendar, Double Dial, 3 Feet ......................................................... 1200.00
Seth Thomas, Camel Back, 8-Day, Miniature, 8 In. ................................................. 32.00
Seth Thomas, Chime, 30-Hour, Papers, 25 In. ....................................................... 165.00
Seth Thomas, Crystal Regulator, Glass With Brass Trim ........................................ 425.00
Seth Thomas, Gingerbread Style, Glass Door, Gold Scroll Bottom ...................... 95.00
Seth Thomas, Half Column, Weight, Time & Strike, Brass ..................................... 200.00
Seth Thomas, Mantel, Chimes, Pillars, Lion Heads On Sides, 11 In. ................... 200.00
Seth Thomas, Mantel, Flat Top, 8-Day ..................................................................... 125.00
Seth Thomas, Mantel, Hour & Half Hour Strike ..................................................... 55.00
Seth Thomas, Mantel, Walnut, Art Deco, 8-Day, Westminster ................... 65.00 To 95.00
Seth Thomas, Mantel, Westminster Chimes, Electric ............................................ 45.00
Seth Thomas, Mantel, 2 Columns, Strikes On Hour, 16 X 10 1/2 In. ................... 195.00
Seth Thomas, Mantel, 8-Day, Pillars & Lion Heads Each Side, 11 In. ................. 200.00
Seth Thomas, Perpetual Calendar, Rosewood, C.1885 ........................................ 1200.00
Seth Thomas, Regulator, All Original, Oak ............................................................. 1350.00
Seth Thomas, School, Office No.3, Walnut ............................................................. 325.00
Seth Thomas, Shelf, Victorian Head On Side ......................................................... 225.00
Seth Thomas, Ship's, Outside Bell ........................................................................... 425.00
Seth Thomas, Time, For Diebold Safe & Lock, 120-Hour, Brass Case ............... 175.00
Ship, U.S.Navy, C.1941 ............................................................................................. 150.00
Tall Case, Connecticut, C.1800, Butternut ............................................................. 2000.00
Tall Case, Satinwood Inlay, Barraclough Of England, C.1820, 94 In. ................. 4200.00
Terry, Beehive, Shelf, Alarm, Patent 1868 ............................................................ 200.00
**CLOCK, TIFFANY, see Tiffany, Clock**
Travel, Brass & Red Leatherette, 2 1/4 X 3 1/2 In. ............................................... 32.00
Turler, Zurich, 8-Day Repeater, Silver Dial, C.1900, 2 3/8 In. ............................. 1300.00
Viennese, Ball Held By Man, Domed Base, Silver Gilt, 7 1/2 In. ......................... 3000.00
Viennese, Boudoir, Figural, Bronze & Enamel, 19th Century, 7 1/2 In. ............... 2500.00
Viennese, Gnomes In Jeweled Arbor, Enameled, Pearls In Nest, 8 In. ............... 4250.00
Viennese, Ludwig Pollizer, Oval Case, Diana Knop, 19th Century, 8 In. ............ 3000.00
Viennese, Scene Of Lovers On Dome, Silver Gilt & Enamel, 10 3/4 In. .............. 8500.00
Wall, Mickey Mouse, Animated, Wooden, 11 In. ................................................... 185.00
Waterbury, Gingerbread, 8-Day ................................................................................ 235.00
Waterbury, Kitchen, 8-Day, Time & Strike, Walnut ............................................... 145.00
Waterbury, Mantel, 8-Day, Brass Plated Chimes, 9 3/4 X 12 1/2 In. ................. 250.00
Waterbury, Perpetual Calendar, Double Dials, Dated 1898 ................................. 850.00
Waterbury, Shelf, Walnut, Time & Strike ................................................................ 150.00
Waterbury, 24-Hour, Alarm, Chimes, 11 3/4 X 19 1/2 In. ..................................... 200.00
Waterbury, 30-Hour, Weight Driven, Rosewood Veneer, C.1864 ......................... 250.00
Welch, Mantel, Black Case, Lion's Head ................................................................. 125.00
Welch, School, 8-Day, Rosewood & Veneer .......................................................... 575.00
Welch, School, 8-Day, Time & Strike, Oak ............................................................. 235.00
Westclox, Alarm, Bluebird, Nickel Case, Bell On Top, 1924 ................................ 20.00
Westclox, Baby Ben, Alarm, Chrome Case, Ring Handle, Black Face ................. 24.00
Westclox, Big Ben, Alarm .......................................................................... 15.00 To 24.00
Westclox, Travel, Pickwick, Original Box & Instructions ....................................... 38.00
Winterhalter & Hofmeir, Bracket, Bim Bam Chimes ............................................. 525.00
Yale & Town, Time, 72-Hour ..................................................................................... 75.00

*Cloisonne enamel was developed during the tenth century. A glass enamel was applied between small ribbonlike pieces of metal on a metal base. Most Cloisonne is Chinese or Japanese.*

**CLOISONNE, Ashtray,** Square, 4 In. .................................................................... 45.00
Bottle, Snuff, Blue, Floral Design, Phoenix Bird, 1 1/2 X 3 In. ........................... 180.00
Bottle, Snuff, Panels Of Dragons, 2 3/4 In. ............................................. 365.00 To 395.00
Bowl, Flowers, Blue Ground, 4 In.Diam. .................................................................. 65.00
Bowl, Monteith, Multicolored Blossoms, Butterflies, C.1850, 6 In. ..................... 1250.00
Bowl, Multicolor Flowers, Apple Green Ground, 4 In. ........................................... 20.00
Bowl, Multicolored, Blue & Green, 4 1/4 In. ......................................................... 110.00
Bowl, Plique-A-Jour, Multicolor Flowers, Green Ground, 4 3/4 In. ..................... 1200.00
Bowl, Rice, Cream & Black Design, 4 1/2 In. ......................................................... 25.00
Box, Allover Blue Design, 3 1/4 In.Diam. ................................................................ 52.00

| | |
|---|---|
| **Box,** Arched Lid, Overall Scrolling, 4 1/2 X 3 In. | 165.00 |
| **Box,** Dark Green, Multicolored, Egg Shape, 5 In. | 495.00 |
| **Box,** Drum Shape, Enameled Interior, Floral Edge Lid, 4 X 4 In. | 185.00 |
| **Box,** Foo Dog Brass Finial, Floral, Blue Ground, Round, 7 In. | 175.00 |
| **Box,** Foo Dog Design, Yellow, Pink & Blue Flowers, Round, 7 In. | 250.00 |
| **Box,** Garden Seat Shape, Covered, Butterflies, Red Trim, 2 1/2 In. | 245.00 |
| **Box,** Hinged, 4 Compartments, Butterflies, 6 X 4 1/2 In. | 350.00 |
| **Box,** Lid, Phoenix Bird, Brown Ground, Gold Flecks, 2 X 1 3/4 In. | 140.00 |
| **Box,** Red, Butterflies, Flowers, Hinged, 3 3/4 X 3 X 1 1/2 In. | 55.00 |
| **Box,** Stamp, Multicolored Wheels On Green, 2 1/2 X 3 1/2 In. | 195.00 |
| **Box,** Stamp, 3 Compartments, Flowers On Green Ground | 58.00 |
| **Box,** Thousand Flower Design, 4 1/2 X 2 1/2 X 3 1/2 In. | 175.00 |
| **Candlestick,** Dragon Chasing, Flaming Pearl, 5 7/8 In., Pair | 225.00 |
| **Candlestick,** Dragon, Floral, Black, 5 3/4 In., Pair | 195.00 |
| **Candlestick,** Prunus, Rust Ground, 9 1/4 In., Pair | 130.00 |
| **Case,** Cigarette, Phoenix Bird, Green & Pink, 3 1/8 X 3 3/8 In. | 300.00 |
| **Chalice,** Brass Filigree, White & Blue Peonies, Lidded, 8 1/2 In. | 285.00 |
| **Charger,** Bird & Floral Design, 14 In. ............................................*Illus* | 325.00 |
| **Charger,** Bird & Flowers, Turquoise, 12 In. | 450.00 |
| **Charger,** Butterflies & Chrysanthemums, 12 In.Diam. | 600.00 |
| **Charger,** Deep Blue Ground, Multicolor Bird & Foliage, 12 In. | 325.00 |
| **Charger,** Diaper Design, Seated Priest Center, 19th Century, 12 In. | 600.00 |
| **Charger,** Fans, Flowers, 3 Birds, 19th Century, 15 1/2 In. | 675.00 |
| **Charger,** Geese & Hibiscus, Blue Ground, Diaper Border, 12 In.Diam. | 450.00 |
| **Charger,** Gold Center With Dragon, Multicolor, 14 In. | 700.00 |
| **Charger,** Goldstone, Shields, Flowers, 19th Century, 18 In. | 1500.00 |
| **Charger,** Japanese Scene, 12 In., Pair | 500.00 |
| **Charger,** White Flowers, 12 In. | 250.00 |
| **Charger,** Yellow Ground, Eagle, Crane, & Sparrow, C.1900, 18 In. | 2250.00 |
| **Charger,** 4 Birds In Tree, Wooden Holder, C.1915, 15 In.Diam. | 975.00 |
| **Cup,** Sake, Turquoise Ground | 75.00 |
| **Decanter,** Figural, Lidded Duck, Swinging Handles, 8 1/2 In., Pair | 1400.00 |
| **Dish,** Nut, Orchid Blossom, Sea Green | 40.00 |
| **Egg,** In Silk Box, Wooden Stand | 55.00 |
| **Figurine,** Lions, Temple, 5 X 4 In. | 1450.00 |
| **Figurine,** Peacock, Turquoise & Coral Beadwork, 5 1/2 In., Pair | 375.00 |
| **Figurine,** Rhinoceros, Scrolls, Multicolored, 8 In., Pair | 1600.00 |
| **Figurine,** Unicorn, Brass Filigree, Enameled, 10 3/4 X 6 In., Pair | 1500.00 |
| **Hand Mirror & Hairbrush,** Butterflies & Flowers, Brass Handles | 200.00 |
| **Inkwell,** Foo Dog Finial | 175.00 |
| **Jar,** Cigarette, Black & Gold | 30.00 |
| **Jar,** Covered, Footed, Butterfly & Floral Design, 3 1/2 X 4 In. | 250.00 |
| **Jar,** Covered, Paneled Multidesign, 3-Footed, 4 In. | 225.00 |
| **Jar,** Covered, Paneled, Flowers & Butterflies, Goldstone, 4 X 4 In. | 295.00 |
| **Jar,** Covered, Panels With Ducks & Flowers, Aqua & Brick, 3 7/8 In. | 275.00 |
| **Jar,** Ginger, Blue Ground, Lotus Scrolls, 7 In. | 275.00 |
| **Jar,** Ginger, Cover, Blue & Black Goldstone, Butterfly, 4 1/2 In. | 125.00 |
| **Jar,** Ginger, Famille Verte, 4 In., Pair | 165.00 |
| **Jar,** Ginger, 3 Cartouches, Centered Dragon, Cover, 10 In., Pair | 595.00 |
| **Jar,** Potpourri, Butterfly & Flower Design, Mica Flecks, 3 1/2 In. | 215.00 |
| **Jar,** Tea, Prunus Blossoms, C.1850, Teakwood Stand, 8 X 7 In.Diam. | 575.00 |
| **Jar,** Temple, Covered, Flowers & Scrolls, Brick Red, 9 1/2 In. | 235.00 |
| **Lamp,** Base, Dark Bronze, Marked On Base Plate, 22 In. | 195.00 |
| **Lamp,** Floral Design, Silver Base, Scrolled Feet, Paper Shade, 9 In. | 450.00 |
| **Lamp,** Raised Birds, Foliage, & Designs, Brass Ground, 10 1/2 In. | 150.00 |
| **Matchbox,** Flowers, Rust Ground | 20.00 |
| **Matchbox,** Wire Scrolls, Yellow Ground | 15.00 |
| **Napkin Ring,** Black Fishscale, Blue Enamel, Turquoise Interior | 55.00 |
| **Napkin Ring,** Multicolored Flowers, Black Ground, 19th Century | 32.50 |
| **Napkin Ring,** Pink & White Flowers, Yellow Ground | 42.00 |
| **Pipe,** Opium Or Water | 225.00 |
| **Planter,** Multicolored Flowers & Scrolls, Turquoise Ground, 4 In. | 295.00 |
| **Plaque,** Marble, Ivory, Enameled, Brass Mounted, 6 X 8 In. | 135.00 |

Cloisonne, from left to right, Plate, Scalloped With Birds In Flight; Charger With Bird & Floral Design (See Page 111); Plate, Scalloped With Oriental Design

| | | |
|---|---|---|
| **Plate,** Birds & Flowers, 12 In.Diam. | | 175.00 |
| **Plate,** Blue Floral & Birds, Japanese, 8 1/2 In. | | 185.00 |
| **Plate,** Dragon, 8 In. | | 150.00 |
| **Plate,** Flowers On Red Ground, Marked, 3 3/4 In. | | 35.00 |
| **Plate,** Prunus Blossoms, 8 1/8 In. | | 150.00 |
| **Plate,** Scalloped, Birds In Flight, 12 In. | *Illus* | 300.00 |
| **Plate,** Scalloped, Oriental Design, 12 In. | *Illus* | 300.00 |
| **Plate,** Stork, Flowering Tree, 12 In. | | 400.00 |
| **Plate,** Stylized Flowers, 19th Century, 7 1/8 In.Diam. | | 140.00 |
| **Plate,** Swallow, Flower, & Cloud, 19th Century, 10 7/8 In., Pair | | 425.00 |
| **Pot,** Brush, 100 Antiques Design, 12 Color, 5 In. | | 270.00 |
| **Pot,** White Jade Blooms, Coral Center, Green Jade Leaves, 14 In. | | 450.00 |
| **Purse,** Lady's, 4 1/2 In.Wide | | 420.00 |
| **Purse,** Multicolored Peacock On Both Sides, 3 X 4 In. | | 175.00 |
| **Purse,** Worn Around Neck Or On Belt, 3 X 4 In. | | 175.00 |
| **Salt,** Ball Footed Underplate, Spoon | | 75.00 |
| **Salt,** Flowers & Leaves, Turquoise, Footed | | 24.00 |
| **Saltshaker & Dip,** Enameled Flowers, 1 1/2 In. | | 70.00 |
| **Teapot,** Dark Blue, White Design, Colored Circles, Miniature | | 185.00 |
| **Teapot,** Pink Lotus Blossoms, Lime Green, 5 X 4 1/2 In. | | 325.00 |
| **Teapot,** Red & Green, 3 In. | | 325.00 |
| **Teapot,** Swirled Floral Design, Miniature, Covered, 3 3/4 In. | | 165.00 |
| **Tray,** Birds, Flowers, & Butterflies, 8 1/4 X 9 3/4 In. | | 245.00 |
| **Tray,** Bronze Rail, Aqua & Yellow Fishscale, 9 3/4 X 5 1/2 In. | | 125.00 |
| **Tray,** Gallery, Thousand Flower Pattern, Bronze Feet, 15 In.Diam. | | 895.00 |
| **Urn,** Brass, Elephant Head Handles, 12 In. | | 125.00 |
| **Urn,** Covered, Multicolored Flowers, Turquoise Ground, 8 1/2 In. | | 160.00 |
| **Urn,** Dragons, Yellow & Lavender On Black, Pedestal, 11 In. | | 355.00 |
| **Urn,** Panels Of Phoenix & Mythical Cow, 8 In.Diam. | | 350.00 |
| **Urn,** White & Green Jade Inlay, Blue, 30 In. | | 2550.00 |
| **Vase,** Allover White Flowers, Blue Collar, Black Ground, 2 1/2 In. | | 55.00 |
| **Vase,** Aqua Foil Body, Flowers, Teak Stand, 4 In. | | 65.00 |
| **Vase,** Bird & Foliage, Bark Pottery, Japanese, 7 In. | | 200.00 |
| **Vase,** Bird On Floral Branch, Green, 7 1/2 In. | | 60.00 |
| **Vase,** Birds & Flowers, Turquoise Ground, 3 3/4 In. | | 80.00 |
| **Vase,** Birds, Flowers, Handles, Dark Blue Ground, 12 In., Pair | | 695.00 |
| **Vase,** Blue Fishscale, Tree Of Life, Marked, 8 1/2 In. | | 250.00 |
| **Vase,** Blue Floral, Silver Wire, Japanese, 8 1/2 In. | | 700.00 |
| **Vase,** Blue Flowers, Rust & Yellow, Blue Ground, 10 In. | | 145.00 |

Vase, Blue, Green, Silver, 7 1/2 In. .................................................................. 240.00
Vase, Blues, Red, Yellow, & Green, Black Ground, 10 1/2 In. .................. 175.00
Vase, Buds & Blossoms, 7 In. ............................................................................ 165.00
Vase, Bulbous, Cloud Scrolls, Blue Ground, Flying Birds, 9 1/2 In. ........ 250.00
Vase, Chrysanthemums, Dark Ground, 4 Ft., Pair ...................................... 9500.00
Vase, Chrysanthemums, White Ground, 6 In. ................................................ 58.00
Vase, Dragon, Black Ground, Goldstone Stars, 7 1/2 In., Pair ................ 550.00
Vase, Dragons, Flaming Pearl, 7 1/2 In. .......................................................... 90.00
Vase, Enamel On Green, Prunus Tree, Sterling Rim, 9 3/4 In. ................ 298.00
Vase, Enamel On Green, Silver Ground, Flowers, Sterling Rim, 9 In. ...... 298.00
Vase, Enameled, Blossoms, Sterling Silver Base & Rim, 9 3/4 In. .......... 300.00
Vase, Famille Noir, 5 In. ...................................................................................... 125.00
Vase, Fan Design, Garlic Shape Neck, 7 1/2 In. .......................................... 420.00
Vase, Fishscale, Electric Cobalt Blue, Floral Sprays, 5 In. ...................... 195.00
Vase, Fishscale, Green Dragon On Foil, 5 In. .................................................. 95.00
Vase, Fishscale, Melon Shape, Flowers, Silver Foil, 2 1/2 In. ...................... 40.00
Vase, Flared Mouth, Bulbous, Flared Foot, Signed Kinkozan, 19 In. ...... 1500.00
Vase, Floral & Butterfly Design, Goldstone, 7 1/4 In. ................................ 195.00
Vase, Floral & Curls, White, Blue, Silver Base, Marked, 5 1/2 In. ............ 78.00
Vase, Floral Design, Brown Ground, Stand, 5 1/4 In. .................................... 75.00
Vase, Floral Spray, Maroon Ground, Teak Base, 5 X 9 In., Pair .............. 270.00
Vase, Floral, Famille Noir, 5 In., Pair ................................................................ 140.00
Vase, Flower & Leaf Design, 2 3/4 X 5 1/2 In. .............................................. 285.00
Vase, Flowers, Dark Green Ground, Incised China, 6 1/2 In. ...................... 95.00
Vase, Gold & Black, Flowers, 10 In. .................................................................. 150.00
Vase, Gold Foil Panels, One Bird, One Butterfly, 8 1/4 In. ........................ 235.00
Vase, Green Floral, Japanese, 9 1/2 In. .......................................................... 450.00
Vase, Green Foil, Florals, Blue & Black Ground, 5 1/8 In. .......................... 135.00
Vase, Houses & Boats, C.1850, 10 In. ............................................................ 850.00
Vase, Key Cloisons, Petals, Flowers, Cobalt Blue Ground, 9 In. ............ 215.00
Vase, Melon, Divided, Bulbous Feet, Red, 6 In. ............................................ 475.00
Vase, Multicolored Dragon, Kyoto, 9 3/4 In. .................................................. 450.00
Vase, Multicolored, Blue Ground, 12 In. .......................................................... 695.00
Vase, Multicolored, Signed, 18 X 14 In.Diam. .............................................. 1790.00
Vase, On Stand, Green, Blue, Red Floral, 4 In., Pair .................................. 125.00
Vase, Phoenix Bird, Dragon, Shield Panels, Goldstone, 12 1/4 In. ........ 550.00
Vase, Pink & White Flowers, Black Ground, 4 In. .......................................... 65.00
Vase, Pink Flowers, 19th Century, Turquoise Ground, 6 1/2 In. .............. 165.00
Vase, Red Dot Design, Butterflies & Flowers, 3 1/2 In. ................................ 45.00
Vase, Red, Silver Rim Neck & Foot, 4 X 4 In. ................................................ 65.00
Vase, Silver Wires, Dragon, Factory Mark, C.1900, 18 In. ........................ 800.00
Vase, Swirl Panels With Florals, Goldstone, 6 In. ........................................ 150.00
Vase, White, Blue Ground, Purple Iris, Orange, 7 1/2 In. .......................... 295.00
Vase, Wisteria & Goldfish, Blue Ground, 10 In. ............................................ 410.00
Vase, Yellow Dragons, 10 In., Pair .................................................................... 130.00
Vase, Yellow, Blue, Green, Pink, Bird, Flower, 9 1/2 In., Pair .................. 550.00
Vase, 6 Sided, Birds & Trees, Signed, 7 1/4 In. .............................................. 65.00
   **CLOTHING, see Textile**

> *Cluthra glass is a two-layered glass with small air pockets that form white
> spots. The Steuben Glass Works of Corning, New York, made it after
> 1903. Kimball Glass Company of Vineland, New Jersey, made Cluthra
> from about 1925.*

   **CLUTHRA, see also Steuben**
**CLUTHRA, Vase,** Orange Mottled, Signed, 10 In. .......................................... 300.00
Vase, Strawberry, Steuben Signature, 9 X 11 In. ........................................ 1250.00
Vase, Wide Gourd Form, Signed Kimball, 7 3/4 In. ...................................... 160.00

> *Coalport ware has been made by the Coalport Porcelain Works of
> England from 1795 to the present time.*

   **COALPORT, see also Indian Tree**
**COALPORT, Creamer,** Panels Of Applied Grapes, Silver Trim, Pink, C.1798 ............................ 120.00

Cup & Saucer, Athens Shape, Pedestal, Cobalt Blue & Gold, C.1914 .................... 50.00
Cup & Saucer, Blue Rim, Lines On Upswept Handle, C.1891 ...................... 50.00
Cup & Saucer, Blue Transfer, Gold Rim, C.1831 ...................... 30.00
Cup & Saucer, Brick Red Outside, Turquoise Inside, Gold Rim, C.1881 .................... 60.00
Cup & Saucer, Cairo Pattern, Gold Rim, Bluebirds, C.1850 ...................... 30.00
Cup & Saucer, Demitasse, Pink, Gold Tracery, Enamel Dots, C.1900 .................... 185.00
Cup & Saucer, Double Handled, Panels Of Gold Scrolls, Roses, C.1911 .................... 30.00
Cup & Saucer, Gold Rim & Handle, Gold Leaf Garland, C.1900 .................... 25.00
Cup & Saucer, Handleless, Canton Pattern ...................... 19.00
Cup & Saucer, Harebell Pattern, Gold Rims, C.1964 ...................... 34.00
Cup & Saucer, Pink Roses, Yellow Daisies, C.1909, Marked ...................... 45.00
Cup & Saucer, Scalloped Gold Rim, Gold Band Around Well, C.1891 .................... 40.00
Cup, Scalloped Rim, Gold Band Inside, Pedestal, Scalloped, C.1910 .................... 14.00
Dish, Oystershell, Footed, Pearlized Interior, 1891 Mark, Set Of 10 .................... 60.00
Figurine, Lady On Hassock, 1920s ...................... 30.00
Inkwell, Spider & Web In Gilt, Signed, Dark Blue ...................... 48.00
Plate, Cake, Imari Colors, Large ...................... 45.00
Plate, Gold Embossed Border, Tiffany & Co., 5 1/2 In.Diam. ...................... 60.00
Plate, Imari Pattern ...................... 75.00
Platter, Serving, Imari Pattern, Large ...................... 350.00
Urn, Portrait, 7 In. ...................... 150.00
Vase, Cylindrical, Flower Design, 2 3/8 X 1 3/4 In.Diam. ...................... 35.00
Vase, White, Signed, 6 3/4 In., Pair ...................... 60.00

*Cobalt blue glass was made using oxide of cobalt. The characteristic bright dark blue identifies it for the collector. Most cobalt glass found today was made after the Civil War.*

### COBALT BLUE, see also Shirley Temple

COBALT BLUE, Bell, Marriage, Applied White Threading, Ornate Handle, 12 In. .................... 235.00
Bottle, Perfume, Cut To Clear Crystal, Bronze Collar, 4 3/4 In. ...................... 165.00
Bottle, Perfume, Gold Bands, Enameled Flowers, 5 3/8 In. ...................... 88.00
Bowl, Berry, Footed, Leaf Medallion, 9 In.Diam. ...................... 65.00
Bowl, Portrait, Oblong, 7 X 3 In. ...................... 22.00
Bowl, Punch, 6 Cups, Ladle ...................... 225.00
Box, Hinged, Footed, Gold Bands, Pink Roses, 4 7/8 X 6 In. ...................... 175.00
Box, Jewelry, Silver Mounted ...................... 125.00
Bride's Basket, White Ruffled Edge, Hallmarked Frame, 10 In. ...................... 250.00
Champagne, Ribbed Optic ...................... 10.00
Compote, Covered, Cut To Clear, 10 X 8 In.Diam. ...................... 225.00
Compote, Footed, Cut In Vintage Pattern, 7 X 8 1/2 In.Diam. ...................... 150.00
Creamer, 4 In. ...................... 16.00
Decanter, Clear Handle, Enameled Flowers, 10 1/2 In. ...................... 135.00
Decanter, Clear Panels, Stars, Thumbprint, 14 In. ...................... 125.00
Dresser Set, Oval Tray, Gold Flowers & Foliage, 6 Piece ...................... 245.00
Lamp, Clear Font, Ribbed Bottom, Burner & Chimney ...................... 85.00
Lustres, White Enamel Flowers, 10 In. ...................... 315.00
Mug, Darts & Balls, Miniature ...................... 15.00
Mustard, Gold Design, Red Roses ...................... 22.00
Mustard, Sterling Silver Holder & Cover ...................... 52.50
Pipe, Souvenir, Hot Springs, Arkansas ...................... 22.00
Pitcher, Lemonade, 4 Tumblers ...................... 47.50
Saltshaker, Beaded Bird Base ...................... 19.00
Toothpick, Footed, Colorado ...................... 25.00
Toothpick, Hat Shape ...................... 10.00
Tumbler, Teardrop & Thumbprint ...................... 33.00
Vase, Bulbous, Ruffled Rim, 10 1/2 In. ...................... 30.00
Vase, 2 Panels, Ladies In Garden, 8 1/2 In. ...................... 250.00
Water Set, Clear Handle, 4 Tumblers ...................... 35.00

*Coca-Cola advertising items have become a special field for collectors.*

COCA-COLA, Bag, Money, Canvas, Charleston, South Carolina ...................... 10.00
Billboard, 1939, Soda Fountain, Girl With Sailor Cap, Framed ...................... 175.00

Billfold, Gold Bottle & Motto, Original Box ............................................................... 20.00
Billfold, Inside Calendar & Stamp Holder, Leather, 1918 ....................................... 55.00
Blackboard, Girl Drinking Coke, Tin, 19 X 27 In. ................................................. 50.00
Blotter, Dated 1941, 3 X 7 In., Set Of 3 ............................................................ 10.00
Blotter, Skiing Scene, 1947 ................................................................................. 3.00
Blotter, 50th Anniversary .................................................................................... 25.00
Bottle Opener, Knife, Pearl Handled ................................................................... 75.00
Bottle, Cigarette Lighter ...................................................................................... 22.00
Bottle, Display, 1923, 2 Ft. ............................................................................... 100.00
Bottle, Huntington, West Virginia, Amber .......................................................... 95.00
Bottle, Korean .................................................................................................... 2.50
Bottle, Marked Nashville, Amber ........................................................................ 45.00
Bottle, Perfume, Lid, Glass ................................................................................. 25.00
Bottle, Seltzer, Bradford, Pennsylvania, Blue .................................................... 55.00
Bottle, Syrup, Backbar, White Enamel Script Letters, Wreath ........................... 165.00
Bottle, 1910, Amber ........................................................................................... 20.00
Bottle, 75th Anniversary, Full ............................................................................. 10.00
Bowl, Pretzel, 1935 .......................................................................... 40.00 To 55.00
Box, Pencil, Original Contents, C.1937 ............................................................... 25.00
Calendar, 1924 ................................................................................................. 115.00
Calendar, 1930, Top, Boy Seated On Well, Signed Norman Rockwell ................... 95.00
Calendar, 1935, Gone Fishing Print, Rockwell ................................................... 150.00
Calendar, 1937, Complete, Cover Sheet ............................................................. 85.00
Calendar, 1938, Calendar Girl, Oval, Canadian ................................................... 5.00
Card, Nature Study, Wrapper, 1930s, Set Of 12 ............................... 75.00 To 100.00
Card, Playing, Party Girl With Rose In Hair, Box ............................................... 30.00
Card, Playing, Woman Holding Coke Bottle & Scorecard, 1960 ......................... 25.00
Card, Playing, 1943 ............................................................................................ 22.50
Carrier, For 6-Ounce Bottles, Wooden ............................................................... 35.00
Case, Train, 1910 ............................................................................................. 225.00
Chair, Metal, Folding, Set Of 4 .......................................................................... 50.00
Checkers Set, Drink Coca-Cola On Each Checker, Original Box ........................... 20.00
Clock, Octagon, Aluminum ................................................................................ 100.00
Clock, Wall, Glass Front, Fish Logo, Electric, 15 X 15 In. ................................... 45.00
Cooler, Drink Coca-Cola, 1937, Bottle Opener End ............................................ 35.00
Cutout, 1931, Rockwell, Cardboard ................................................................... 575.00
Dispenser, Bottle, Cooler .................................................................................. 125.00
Dispenser, Bottle, Upright, 5 Cent ..................................................................... 150.00
Door Push, 1901, Brass, 10 X 3 3/4 In. ............................................ 45.00 To 75.00
Glass, Fountain, 1935 ......................................................................................... 35.00
Ice Pick ............................................................................................. 3.00 To 15.00
Jar, Chewing Gum ............................................................................................. 350.00
Menu, 1902, Hilda Clark .................................................................................... 575.00
Menu, 1942, Enameled, Embossed, 19 1/4 X 27 1/4 In. ................................... 68.00
Paddle, Ping-Pong, 1940, Pair ............................................................................ 40.00
Paperweight, Glass, Red & Blue Drink Coca-Cola, 1950, 3 In. ............................ 12.50
Paperweight, Mirror Bottom, World War II, W.A.F. ............................................. 20.00
Pencil Set, School, 1937 .................................................................................... 25.00
Pencil Sharpener, Bottle Shape, C.1930 ............................................................. 20.00
Pencil, Mechanical, Red ..................................................................................... 30.00
Policeman, Advertising, Traffic Sign Other Side, Porcelain, 6 Ft. ...................... 175.00
Poster, Lifeguard, Female, 33 X 20 In. ............................................................... 75.00
Radio, Cooler Shape, 1949 ............................................................................... 365.00
Ruler .................................................................................................................. 5.00
Santa, 1956, Cardboard ..................................................................................... 9.00
Scorekeeper, Baseball ....................................................................................... 75.00
Sign & Blackboard, Specials Today, C.1930s, Tin, 19 X 27 In. ........................... 75.00
Sign, Berry, 1914, Cardboard, 27 X 38 In. ........................................................ 400.00
Sign, Bottle Shape, Tin, 17 In. ........................................................................... 15.00
Sign, Drink Coca-Cola, Christmas Bottle, Tin, 12 X 33 In. .................................. 95.00
Sign, Drink Coca-Cola, Refresh, Porcelain, 1939, 30 In.Diam. ............................ 40.00
Sign, Figural, Bottle, 14 In. ................................................................................ 25.00
Sign, Fountain Service, Red, Yellow, Green, & White, 12 X 27 In. ...................... 65.00

**Sign,** Ice Cold Coca-Cola Sold Here, Dated 1931, Tin, 20 In. ................................................ 100.00
**Sign,** Please Pay When Served, Fluorescent ........................................................................ 175.00
**Sign,** Refresh With Our Special Coke, 1930s, Cardboard, 16 X 20 In. ....................... 18.00
**Sign,** Shaped Like U.S. Map, 1930, 15 X 15 In. ............................................................... 180.00
**Sign,** 1923 Christmas Coca-Cola Bottle, 27 X 20 In. ..................................................... 85.00
**Thermometer,** Bottle Shape, Dated 1936, 16 In. ............................................................. 40.00
**Thermometer,** Bottle Shape, Full-Color Bottle, Tin, 5 X 16 1/2 In. ............................ 22.00
**Thermometer,** Bottle Shape, Signed Robertson, 17 1/2 In. .......................................... 30.00
**Thermometer,** Bottles On Each Side, C.1941, Tin .......................................................... 50.00
**Thermometer,** Drink Coca-Cola, Tin, 11 1/2 In. ............................................................... 6.00
**Thermometer,** Sign Of Good Taste, 8 X 27 In. ................................................................ 45.00
**Thermometer,** Silhouette, Girl Drinking, C.1940 ............................................................. 75.00
**Thermometer,** Trade Mark, Patent Dec.25, 1923, 5 X 16 In. ....................................... 95.00
**Tin,** Pepsin Gum, 1909 .......................................................................................................... 750.00
**Tray,** Duster Girl, Canadian ............................................................................... 5.00 To 8.00
**Tray,** Elaine, Oval, Canadian ............................................................................. 5.00 To 7.50
**Tray,** Game, Commonwealth, Canadian ............................................................................ 15.00
**Tray,** Lillian Nordica, Red, Canadian ................................................................................. 18.00
**Tray,** Lillian Russell, Green, Canadian ............................................................................... 24.00
**Tray,** Tip, 1904, St.Louis Fair ......................................................................... 160.00 To 185.00
**Tray,** Tip, 1909, Coca-Cola Girl ......................................................................................... 135.00
**Tray,** Tip, 1912, Girl With Rose In Hat ............................................................................. 125.00
**Tray,** Tip, 1914, Betty ........................................................................................ 85.00 To 125.00
**Tray,** Tip, 1917, Elaine ...................................................................................... 65.00 To 135.00
**Tray,** Tip, 1920, Girl In Yellow Dress ................................................................................ 175.00
**Tray,** Tip, 1923, Flapper ..................................................................................................... 55.00
**Tray,** 1912, Girl With Rose In Hat ...................................................................................... 200.00
**Tray,** 1914, Betty ................................................................................................ 110.00 To 175.00
**Tray,** 1917, Elaine ............................................................................................... 50.00 To 135.00
**Tray,** 1921, Summer Girl ..................................................................................................... 150.00
**Tray,** 1923, Flapper ............................................................................................ 85.00 To 150.00
**Tray,** 1925, Girl At Party ..................................................................................130.00 To 135.00
**Tray,** 1926, Golfers ............................................................................................................. 120.00
**Tray,** 1927, Curb Service .................................................................................................... 225.00
**Tray,** 1928, Lady In Fur Scarf, 7 3/4 X 13 3/4 In. ........................................................... 175.00
**Tray,** 1929, Girl In Swimsuit Holding Bottle ................................................ 150.00 To 200.00
**Tray,** 1930, Bathing Beauty ................................................................................................. 97.00
**Tray,** 1931, Boy With Dog, Fishing, Norman Rockwell .......................... 205.00 To 225.00
**Tray,** 1932, Girl In Yellow Bathing Suit .............................................................................. 100.00
**Tray,** 1934, Johnny Weissmuller & Maureen O'Sullivan ................................................ 250.00
**Tray,** 1935, Madge Evans .................................................................................. 85.00 To 125.00
**Tray,** 1937, Running Girl ...................................................................................................... 30.00
**Tray,** 1940, Girl Fishing ....................................................................................................... 35.00
**Tray,** 1941, Skater ............................................................................................... 40.00 To 55.00
**Tray,** 1942, Two Girls At Car .............................................................................................. 35.00
**Tray,** 1950, Girl With Menu ................................................................................. 25.00 To 30.00
**Truck,** 3 Bottles, 1930 ........................................................................................................ 150.00
**Watch Fob,** Bulldogs, Bronze ............................................................................................. 85.00

*Coffee grinders, home size, were first made about 1894. They lost favor by*
*the 1930s.*

**COFFEE GRINDER, Arcade,** Crystal Glass Top ............................................................... 35.00
  **Arcade,** Wall ...................................................................................................... 65.00 To 70.00
  **Blue & White Celluloid Tiles,** 1800s ............................................................................ 200.00
  **Brass & Mahogany,** Dovetailed, English ........................................................................ 80.00
  **C.Parker & Co.,** Red Metal, Marked ............................................................................... 55.00
  **Elgin National,** Two 12 In.Wheels, 20 In. ....................................................................... 225.00
  **Enterprise,** Original Stencils & Eagle, 28 In. ................................................................ 695.00
  **Enterprise,** Wall Mount, Cast Iron .................................................................................... 50.00
  **Enterprise,** 2 Wheels, Iron Drawer, 12 1/2 In. ............................................................. 450.00
  **Enterprise,** 2 Wheels, 19 1/2 In. ..................................................................................... 275.00
  **Golden Rule,** Columbus, Ohio, Lacy Iron, Glass Front ................................................. 65.00

| | |
|---|---|
| Hoffmans | 245.00 |
| L.F. & Co., New Britain, Connecticut, Old Red Paint, 11 In. | 85.00 |
| Lap Type, Dovetailed Corners, Wooden | 65.00 |
| Parker Bros., Wall, Original | 85.00 |
| Parker, No.50, Embossed Eagle, Black Tin & Cast Iron | 60.00 |
| Swift Mill, Man, Woman, Child, Covered Wagon, C.1875, 40 In. | 2300.00 |
| Wall Mount, Crank Handle, Tin & Cast Iron | 35.00 |
| Wood & Iron, Miniature | 50.00 |

| | |
|---|---|
| COFFEE MILL, Daisy, Wood & Cast Iron, Miniature | 55.00 |

| | |
|---|---|
| COFFIN, Original Brown Paint, Green & Yellow Trim, Pine, 10 X 7 X 4 In. | 90.00 |

| | |
|---|---|
| COIN SPOT, Basket, Opalescent Vaseline | 24.00 |
| Bottle, Perfume, Opalescent, Original Stopper | 20.00 |
| Bowl, Blue Opalescent, Ruffled Rim | 43.00 |
| Castor, Pickle, Pink Satin Glass, Silver Plate Holder, 11 3/4 In. | 395.00 |
| Compote, Canary Opalescent, Pressed | 24.00 |
| Creamer, Cranberry | 85.00 |
| Cruet, Cranberry | 85.00 |
| Hat, White Opalescent | 90.00 |
| Lamp, White Milk Glass Base, Blue Opalescent | 148.00 |
| Muffineer, Cranberry | 85.00 |
| Pitcher, Blue Opalescent | 95.00 |
| Pitcher, Blue Opalescent, 20 Ounce | 39.50 |
| Pitcher, Cranberry & White, Clear Handle, 9 In. | 125.00 |
| Pitcher, Cranberry, C.1919, 4 In. | 35.00 |
| Pitcher, Green Opalescent | 110.00 |
| Pitcher, Pink, Small | 35.00 |
| Pitcher, Ruffled Rim, White | 125.00 |
| Pitcher, Ruffled Top, Blue Opalescent, 8 1/2 In. | 95.00 To 125.00 |
| Pitcher, Tricolor Top, Applied Handle, Opalescent | 155.00 |
| Pitcher, Water, Green | 110.00 |
| Pitcher, Water, Square Top, Blue | 95.00 |
| Sugar Shaker, Ring Neck, Blue Opalescent | 85.00 |
| Sugar Shaker, 9 Panel, Blue | 35.00 To 95.00 |
| Syrup, Blue Opalescent | 100.00 |
| Syrup, Cranberry Opalescent | 95.00 |
| Syrup, Ring Neck, Blue Opalescent | 95.00 |
| Syrup, Swirl, Blue | 65.00 To 110.00 |
| Syrup, Swirl, Blue Opalescent | 110.00 |
| Syrup, White Opalescent | 60.00 |
| Toothpick, Opalescent | 85.00 |
| Tumble-Up Set, Cranberry, Carafe, 7 1/2 In. | 45.00 |
| Tumbler, Blue Opalescent | 24.00 |
| Tumbler, Clear | 15.00 |
| Tumbler, Golden Amber | 20.00 |
| Tumbler, Green | 12.00 |
| Tumbler, Juice, Amber | 9.00 |
| Tumbler, Sapphire Blue | 20.00 |
| Vase, Blue Opalescent, 5 1/2 In. | 18.00 |
| Vase, Celery, Rainbow Coloring, 6 3/4 X 4 3/4 In.Diam. | 300.00 |
| Vase, Ruffled & Crimped Top, Blue Opalescent, 9 In. | 65.00 |
| Vase, Ruffled Top, Blue Opalescent, 8 1/2 In. | 55.00 |
| Water Set, Green Opalescent, 7 Piece | 210.00 |

| | |
|---|---|
| COIN-OPERATED MACHINE, A.B.T.Pistol Game, 2 Cent, Your Score | 165.00 |
| Bowling, 10 Cent, Complete With Puck, 1949 | 450.00 |
| Boxing, Hand-Painted Scenery, Ring, English, Oak | 1995.00 |
| Coin Vendor, 25 Cent | 75.00 |
| Dice Game, Match Dispenser, & Cigar Lighter | 450.00 |
| Dice, Midget, Fey | 1300.00 |
| Digger, Arcade | 1200.00 |

**Digger,** Magic Finger .................................................................................... 1100.00
**Dispenser,** Match, 1959, 25 Match Books ................................................ 35.00
**Dispenser,** Perfume, Bull's Head ............................................................ 1500.00
**Foot Vibrator,** 1 Cent ............................................................................ 325.00
**Game & Gum,** Hunter, Duck .................................................................. 135.00
**Grandma,** Hands, Eyes, Head Move, Fortune Cards, 1940s ...................... 1395.00
**Grip Test,** Push Or Pull, Peter Beetz ...................................................... 3250.00
**Gum Ball,** Baseball Card, Premiere ......................................................... 140.00
**Gum Ball,** Baseball, 1 Cent ..................................................................... 75.00
**Gum Ball,** Basketball, 1 Cent ................................................................. 75.00
**Gum Ball,** Bluebird, Penny Drop ............................................................. 350.00
**Gum Ball,** Columbus, Round Globe ............................................ 65.00 To 95.00
**Gum Ball,** E-Z ....................................................................................... 315.00
**Gum Ball,** Football ................................................................................ 100.00
**Gum Ball,** Jennings, 5 Cent ................................................................... 450.00
**Gum Ball,** Perfection Supreme ............................................................... 275.00
**Gum Ball,** Silver King, 1 Cent ................................................................ 55.00
**Gum Ball,** Two Domes, Each Dispenses Balls .......................................... 250.00
**Gum,** Adam, 1 Cent .............................................................................. 35.00
**Gum,** Adam's Pepsin Tutti-Frutti ........................................................... 550.00
**Gum,** Beechies, 1 Cent, Metal ............................................................... 25.00
**Gum,** Chiclets, Bakers Chocolate, Wall Hung, Porcelain .......................... 375.00
**Gum,** Penny King, Bar Top Model .......................................................... 125.00
**Gum,** Pulver, Policeman ......................................................................... 275.00
**Gum,** Wrigley, Pictures Blonde With Brimmed Hat ................................... 75.00
**Gum,** Wrigley, 5 Column, Rotating, Glass & Tin ....................................... 65.00
**Gum,** Zeno, White Porcelain .................................................................. 495.00
**Gum,** Zeno, Wood ................................................................................. 500.00
**Gun Game,** A.B.T.Challenger, 5 Cent ..................................................... 175.00
**Gypsy Reads Fortune Through Viewer** .................................................. 895.00
**Henrietta Hen,** Chicken On Stand, Iron, Automatic ................................. 2650.00
**Jukebox,** Wurlitzer Mill, Troubadour ..................................................... 6000.00
**Jukebox,** Wurlitzer, Model 1015 ........................................................... 2750.00
**Jukebox,** Wurlitzer, Model 750s ............................................................ 795.00
**Jukebox,** Wurlitzer, Sonata, New In Crate ............................................. 3895.00
**Kicker-Catcher,** 5 Cent ......................................................................... 140.00
**Lung Test-Grip Test,** 1 Cent, Caille Brothers ......................................... 2300.00
**Match Vendor,** Cast Iron ....................................................................... 85.00
**Mints & Chewing Gum,** National, 5 Cent .......................................... *Illus* 50.00
**Monkey Climb,** Crank Monkey Up Tree, Skill Race .................................. 225.00
**Mutoscope,** Clamshell, Cast Iron ............................... 1150.00 To 1500.00
**Mutoscope,** Indian ................................................................................ 1800.00
**Mutoscope,** Old Mill .............................................................................. 650.00

Coin-Operated Machine, Mints & Chewing Gum, National, 5 Cent

**Mutoscope,** World's Fair, Wooden Postcard Vendor ........................................................ 450.00
**Nickelodeon,** Western Electric ........................................................................................ 5750.00
**Peanut,** Advance, 1912 .................................................................................................... 65.00
**Peanut,** Columbus, Cast Iron Gooseneck, Round Globe ................................................. 100.00
**Peanut,** Master ................................................................................................................ 125.00
**Peanut,** 1 Cent, Nickel On Brass, Football Globe .............................................................. 87.50
**Photoscope,** 1 Cent, Peep Show ..................................................................................... 550.00
**Pinball,** Bally Derby, Payout ............................................................................................ 975.00
**Pinball,** Hy-Skor, Bally, Marble ....................................................................................... 225.00
**Pinball,** Mills, Pace Poinsettia ...................................................................................... 2100.00
**Pinball,** Rockola World Series ......................................................................................... 400.00
**Pinball,** Shoot The Bull's-Eye, Exhibits .......................................................................... 500.00
**Pinch Hitter,** Williams Baseball Game, Wooden Rails .................................................... 250.00
**Poker,** 1 Cent, Floor Model, Cast Iron ........................................................................... 1650.00
**Poor Box,** English Penny, Blind Man Fortune-Teller ....................................................... 265.00
**Popcorn Vendor,** 10 Cent, 40 In. ................................................................................... 695.00
**Safety Matches,** 3 Column, Cast Iron, 1904 .................................................................. 385.00
**Selectum,** Dice, 25 Cent ................................................................................................. 225.00
**Shoot To Chew,** Shoots Penny At Target, 1 Cent ........................................................... 135.00
**Slot,** Bantam, Pace, 1 Cent ........................................................................................... 1295.00
**Slot,** Bones, Buckley, 5 Cent, C.1935, 13 In. ................................................................. 4250.00
**Slot,** Buckley, Point Maker, Nonpayout, Control Box ..................................................... 395.00
**Slot,** Caille, Commander, 5 Cent .................................................................................... 850.00
**Slot,** Caille, Dictator, 5 Cent ......................................................................................... 1750.00
**Slot,** Caille, Doughboy, 1 Cent ...................................................................................... 1150.00
**Slot,** Caille, Jumbo Success, Counter Top, Cast Iron ..................................................... 1000.00
**Slot,** Caille, Silent Sphinx, 10 Cent ............................................................................... 1375.00
**Slot,** Chicago, Gabel's, Upright ..................................................................................... 9500.00
**Slot,** Fey, Jumping Jack, 1 Cent .................................................................................... 275.00
**Slot,** Golf Ball .................................................................................................................. 295.00
**Slot,** Groetchin, Columbia Deluxe, 5 Cent, C.1936 ........................................................ 1200.00
**Slot,** Jennings, Bronze Chief, 5 Cent ............................................................................. 950.00
**Slot,** Jennings, Century Vender, 5 Cent ......................................................................... 1400.00
**Slot,** Jennings, Duchess, 1 Cent .................................................................................... 895.00
**Slot,** Jennings, Dutch Boy, 5 Cent ................................................................................. 1250.00
**Slot,** Jennings, Four Star Chief, 5 Cent .......................................................................... 1200.00
**Slot,** Jennings, Gooseneck ............................................................................................. 795.00
**Slot,** Jennings, One Star Chief, 5 Cent .......................................................................... 1175.00
**Slot,** Jennings, Standard Chief, 5 Cent .......................................................................... 700.00
**Slot,** Jennings, Vest Pocket, 5 Cent ............................................................................... 450.00
**Slot,** Jennings, Victory Chief, 5 Cent ............................................................................. 800.00
**Slot,** Mills, Black Beauty, 5 Cent .................................................................................... 950.00
**Slot,** Mills, Black Cherry ................................................................................................ 1250.00
**Slot,** Mills, Bursting Cherry ............................................................................................ 1350.00
**Slot,** Mills, Castle Front .................................................................................................. 1395.00
**Slot,** Mills, Chrome 21, Hightop, Front Loaded ............................................................... 900.00
**Slot,** Mills, Dewey, 5 Cent, C.1900, 66 In. ............................................................ *Illus* 9000.00

Coin-Operated Machine, Slot, Mills, Dewey, 5 Cent, C.1900, 66 In.

**Slot,** Mills, Diamond Front, 5 Cent .................................................. 950.00 To 1250.00
**Slot,** Mills, Golden Falls .................................................. 1275.00
**Slot,** Mills, Gooseneck, Takes English Pennies, 1928 .................................................. 725.00
**Slot,** Mills, Jewel Bell, 5 Cent .................................................. 950.00
**Slot,** Mills, Jockey .................................................. 1800.00
**Slot,** Mills, Operator's Bell, 5 Cent, C.1911, 25 In. .................................................. 6500.00
**Slot,** Mills, Owl, Jockey Mechanical Wheel, 5 Cent .................................................. 7500.00
**Slot,** Mills, Poinsettia, Gooseneck, 5 Cent .................................................. 1100.00
**Slot,** Mills, Roman Head .................................................. 1500.00 To 1975.00
**Slot,** Mills, Side Vendor & Future Pay .................................................. 1775.00
**Slot,** Mills, Silent F.O.K., 5 Cent .................................................. 1500.00
**Slot,** Mills, War Eagle, C.1931, 25 In. .................................................. *Illus* 3000.00
**Slot,** Pace, Bantam, 5 Cent .................................................. *Illus* 1000.00
**Slot,** Pace, Five Star Bell, 50 Cent .................................................. 1300.00
**Slot,** Pace, Royal Comet, Console, 5 Cent .................................................. 1295.00
**Slot,** Rol-A-Top, Gold Plated .................................................. 3650.00
**Slot,** Watling, Blue Seal, 5 Cent .................................................. 1095.00
**Slot,** Watling, Jack Pot Brownie .................................................. 3250.00
**Slot,** Watling, Operator Bell, Cast Iron .................................................. 4200.00
**Slot,** Watling, Rol-A-Top .................................................. 3100.00 To 3295.00
**Slot,** Watling, 5 Cent, Three Reel, C.1936, Award Card .................................................. 5250.00
**Spear The Dragon,** Arcade .................................................. 4500.00
**Stamp,** Caille Bros., 1904, Drop Coin, Copper Plated .................................................. 1650.00
**Stamp,** Glass Front & Back, Cast Iron .................................................. 75.00
**Stamp,** Mills, C.1915, Shield Front, Drop Coin Here .................................................. 2000.00
**Stamp,** Postage, Crank Type .................................................. 25.00
**Stamp,** Roovers Stamper, Quartered Oak, 1901 .................................................. 1000.00
**Strength Tester** .................................................. 1500.00
**Target Pistol,** Bunny Shoot, Skill Game .................................................. 300.00
**The Great Hugo,** Life-Size Magician, Sound Effects .................................................. 1750.00
**Trade Card,** Stittman Pitt, C.1890 .................................................. 2500.00
**Vending,** Comic Card, With Cards .................................................. 175.00
**Wheel Of Fortune,** Griswold, Trade Stimulator .................................................. 475.00

Coin-Operated Machine, Slot, Pace, Bantam, 5 Cent

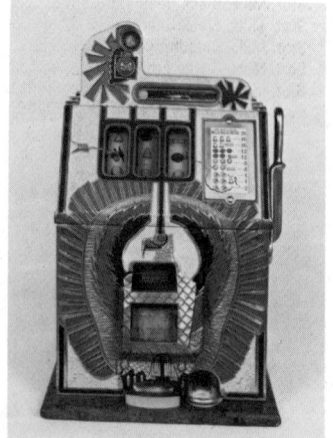

Coin-Operated Machine, Slot, Mills,
War Eagle, C.1931, 25 In.

Satsuma vases, 17½ in. high, Japan, c. 1890

Sugar, part of tea service, Sèvres, France, 1888

"Thetis Consoling Achilles on the Death of Patroele," Berlin charger, 16¾ in. diameter, mid-19th century

Celadon vase, Chien Lung style,
14 in. high

Blue and white dragon vase,
Oriental

Apostle James and candlestick,
part of complete altar set,
Meissen, sculpted by Kandler,
18th century, c. 1750

Bird pattern, dessert service plate, Minton, c. 1880–1890

Japanese influence, dessert service, Royal Worcester, c. 1880–1890

Rococo-style marquetry chair, fruitwood

Moonlight lustre tureen, Wedgwood, c. 1820

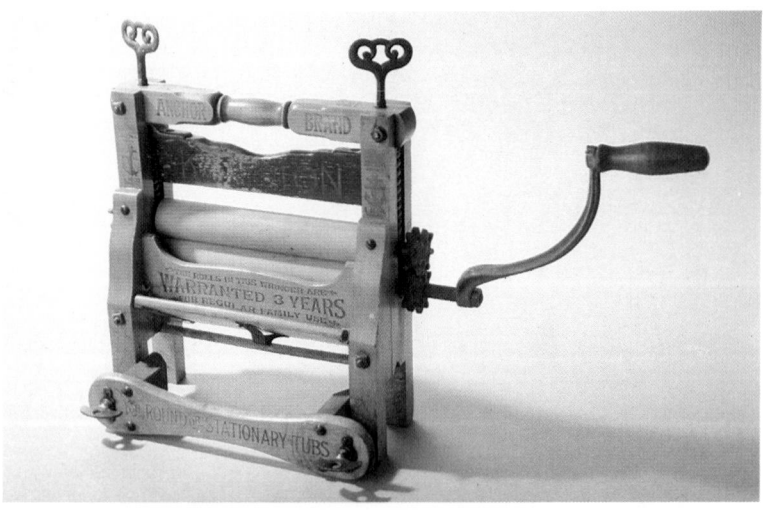

Clothes wringer, Anchor Brand, Erie, Pennsylvania

Crimping iron, Crown, Pat. November 2, 1875

Mrs. Potts Sadiron, patented 1871

Assorted food packaging from the turn of the century

American meat chopper, patented 1865

Copper pan, Bramhall Deane Co., New York, c. 1890

Adam and Eve brass alms dish, 18¼ in. diameter

Louis XV style brass andirons, 24 in. high

Baroque-style six-light candelabrum, 21½ in. high, brass

Chinese sacrificial vessel, Chou Dynasty,
14 in. high

Brass-covered wine cistern, 22
in. high

Japanese figurine in wood,
gesso, and lacquer, 22 in.
high, 19th century

*Collector plates are modern plates produced in limited editions. Some will be found listed under the company. Pictures and more price information can be found in "Kovels' Price Guide for Collector Plates, Figurines, Paperweights and other Limited Editions."*

| | |
|---|---:|
| **COLLECTOR PLATE, Anri,** Christmas, 1971 | 95.00 |
| **Anri,** Christmas, 1978 | 65.00 |
| **Anri,** Christmas, 1979 | 95.00 |
| **Berlin,** Christmas, 1979 | 40.00 |
| **COLLECTOR PLATE, BING AND GRONDAHL, see Bing & Grondahl** | |
| **D'Arceau,** Spring Girl, Limoges | 92.00 |
| **Disney,** Mother's Day, 1980 | 17.50 |
| **Ferrandiz,** Christmas, 1977 | 95.00 |
| **Ferrandiz,** Christmas, 1980 | 110.00 |
| **Ferrandiz,** Mother's Day, 1977, Orchard, First Edition | 105.00 |
| **Ferrandiz,** Mother's Day, 1978, Pastoral | 75.00 |
| **Ferrandiz,** Mother's Day, 1979 | 95.00 |
| **Goebel,** Annual, 1979 | 20.00 |
| **Haviland,** Christmas, 1971 | 55.00 |
| **Hutschenreuther,** Christmas, 1978 | 190.00 |
| **Hutschenreuther,** Christmas, 1979 | 250.00 |
| **Jansen,** Mother's Day, 1978 | 39.00 |
| **Lenox,** Raccoons, 1973 | 70.00 |
| **Pickard,** Christmas, 1979 | 70.00 |
| **Poole,** Christmas, 1978, First Edition | 25.00 |
| **Poole,** Christmas, 1979 | 25.00 |
| **Poole,** Mother's Day, 1979 | 25.00 |
| **Rockwell,** Christmas, 1980, Scotty Plays Santa | 24.00 |
| **Rockwell,** Letter To Santa, 1980 | 24.50 |
| **Royal Bayreuth,** Mother's Day, 1980 | 45.00 |
| **COLLECTOR PLATE, ROYAL COPENHAGEN, see Royal Copenhagen** | |
| **Veneto Flair,** Annual, 1979, Hansel | 50.00 |
| **Veneto Flair,** Annual, 1980, Gretel | 60.00 |
| **Wedgwood,** Christmas, 1969 | 200.00 |
| **Wedgwood,** Christmas, 1970 | 20.00 |
| **Wedgwood,** Christmas, 1971 | 25.00 |
| **Wedgwood,** Christmas, 1972 | 30.00 |
| **Wedgwood,** Christmas, 1973 | 30.00 |
| **Wedgwood,** Christmas, 1979 | 50.00 |
| **Wedgwood,** Christmas, 1980 | 50.00 |
| **Wedgwood,** Mother's Day, 1981 | 42.00 |
| **COMIC ART, CELLULOID see also, Disneyana, Celluloid** | |
| **COMIC ART, Action Comics No.1,** June 1938, First Superman   *Illus* | 6000.00 |

Comic Art, Action Comics No.l, June, 1938, First Superman

| | |
|---|---:|
| **Book,** Barney Google, 1924 | 25.00 |
| **Film,** Popeye Express, Flap Door Missing | 195.00 |
| **Flash Gordon,** Sunday Comics, 1938 | 15.00 |
| **Maggie & Jiggs,** Back Of Menu, Signed George A McManus, 1929 | 145.00 |
| **Tom Mix,** Sunday Comics, 1938 | 15.00 |

*Commemorative items have been made to honor members of royalty and those of great national fame. World's fairs and important historical events are also remembered with commemorative pieces.*

**COMMEMORATIVE, see also Coronation, World's Fair**

| | |
|---|---:|
| **COMMEMORATIVE, Cup & Saucer,** King George & Queen Mary, Portraits | 35.00 |
| **Cup,** Silver Jubilee, Queen Elizabeth II, 3 1/4 X 3 In. | 7.00 |
| **Cup,** Silver Jubilee, 1935, King George V & Queen Mary, 6 In. | 20.00 |
| **Dish,** Sir W.Churchill, Finest Hour On Reverse, 5 1/2 In. | 35.00 |
| **Dish,** Sweetmeat, Queen Elizabeth II, Portrait, Tuscan, 4 In. | 15.00 |
| **Dish,** Sweetmeat, Sir Winston Churchill, Wedgwood, 4 1/4 In. | 17.00 |
| **Figurine,** Edward VII, Prince Of Wales, C.1860, 17 In. | 245.00 |
| **Jar,** Bust Of Queen Victoria Cover, Royal Seal, 8 X 4 In.Diam. | 135.00 |
| **Mug,** George V, Mary, 1911 | 35.00 |
| **Mug,** George VI & Queen Elizabeth | 32.00 |
| **Mug,** Victoria, 1897 Jubilee | 70.00 |
| **Picture With Calendar,** 1937, King George VI & Elizabeth | 45.00 |
| **Pitcher & Beaker,** Queen Victoria, 1897 | 300.00 |
| **Plate,** King George VI, Queen Elizabeth, Canada, 9 In. | 18.00 |
| **Plate,** Queen Elizabeth II Silver Jubilee, 9 3/4 In. | 13.00 |
| **Plate,** Queen Elizabeth Silver Jubilee, 5 In. | 22.00 |
| **Shot Glass,** Queen Elizabeth II, Silver Jubilee | 2.40 |
| **Spoon,** Sterling Silver, Edward VII, 1932 | 27.50 |
| **Teapot,** Sugar, & Creamer, Jasperware, George VI & Elizabeth | 350.00 |
| **Tin Biscuit,** Queen Elizabeth II & Prince Phillip, 4 In. | 22.00 |

*Coors ware was made by a pottery in Golden, Colorado, owned by the Coors Beverage Company. It was produced from the turn of the century until the pottery was destroyed by fire in the 1930s. The name Coors is marked on the back of the pottery.*

| | |
|---|---:|
| **COORS, Creamer,** Dark Green, 2 In. | 6.00 |
| **Mug,** Green, 4 1/2 In. | 10.00 |
| **Mug,** Yellow, 4 1/2 In. | 10.00 |
| **Pitcher,** Green, 64 Ounce | 18.00 |
| **Pitcher,** Mellotone, Pink, 2 Quart | 35.00 |
| **Salt & Pepper,** Bottle Shape, Yellow | 15.00 |
| **Vase,** Aqua Interior, Peach, 8 In. | 10.00 |
| **Vase,** Beige & Turquoise, 10 In. | 15.00 |
| **Vase,** Footed, Handled, White Inside, Pink Outside, 6 In. | 18.00 |
| **Vase,** Golden, Colorado, Cream, Satin Finish, Signed, 8 1/2 In. | 22.00 |
| **Vase,** Handled, Green, 6 In. | 9.00 |
| **Vase,** White & Turquoise, 5 1/2 In. | 12.00 |
| **Vase,** Yellow, 6 In. | 18.00 |
| **Vase,** 2 Ring Handles, Tan & Turquoise Inside, Matte Finish, 6 In. | 21.50 |

*W.T.Copeland & Sons, Ltd., ran the Spode Works in Staffordshire, England, from 1847 to the present. Copeland & Garrett was the firm name from 1833 to 1847.*

**COPELAND SPODE, see also Flow Blue, Spode**

| | |
|---|---:|
| **COPELAND SPODE, Bowl & Pitcher Set,** Italian Pattern, Blue & White | 260.00 |
| **Bowl,** Italian, 2 3/4 X 9 1/2 In.Diam. | 22.50 |
| **Cup & Saucer,** Bouillon, Red & Blue Floral, Gold Rim, C.1888 | 15.00 |
| **Cup & Saucer,** Florence, 3 Sets | 25.00 |

**Cup & Saucer,** Gold & White Pattern, C.1840 ............................................................ 50.00
**Cup & Saucer,** Tower, Pink ............................................................................................ 15.00
**Cup,** Bouillon, Cover, 2-Handled, Italian Blue & White .......................................... 10.00
**Decanter,** Coronation Of George V & Queen Mary, 10 1/2 In. .............................. 175.00
**Figurine,** Turnips & Carrots, Marked, No.778048, 8 In. .......................................... 385.00
**Game Platter,** Peacock Center, Raised Flowers, 14 1/2 In. ...................................... 99.50
**Pitcher,** Blue Tower, Quart ............................................................................................ 115.00
**Pitcher,** Water, Raised Drinking Scene, Blue Ground, 7 3/4 In. ............................ 125.00
**Plate,** King Pattern, 9 In.Diam. .................................................................................... 10.00
**Plate,** Tower, 6 1/2 In. .................................................................................................... 20.00
**Platter,** Basket Of Fruit Center, Marked, 22 1/4 X 17 1/2 In. .............................. 75.00
**Saucer,** Cobalt & Gold Trim, White, Davis Collamore & Co., Pr. ............................ 15.00
**Sugar & Creamer,** Sorrento .......................................................................................... 20.00
**Teapot,** Dog Finial, 6-Sided, Blue, White, 1868-83, Inscribed .............................. 135.00
**Toby,** Winston Churchill, Ivory Glazed, 8 1/2 In. ...................................................... 115.00

### COPELAND, see also Copeland Spode, Spode

**COPELAND, Bowl,** Footed, Flowers & Birds Inside, Blue, Green, Pink ...................... 118.00
**Cheese Keeper,** Foliate Borders & Figures, C.1847, 10 1/4 In. .............................. 450.00
**Coffee Set,** Ship Design, 3 Piece .................................................................................. 100.00
**Cup & Saucer,** Demitasse, Blue Willow, 1847 ............................................................ 22.00
**Cup,** Demitasse, Primrose, Dated 1881 ...................................................................... 20.00
**Pitcher,** Figures, White On Blue .................................................................................. 45.00
**Pitcher,** Jasperware, Hunt Scene, White On Tan, Signed, 4 3/4 In. ...................... 95.00
**Pitcher,** Raised Hunt Scene, Tan Ground, 4 1/8 In. ................................................ 69.00
**Pitcher,** White Relief, Hunters, Blue & White, 5 1/4 In. ........................................ 58.00
**Plate,** Blue & White, White Edged .............................................................................. 85.00
**Plate,** Peacocks In Blue & Red, Green & Gold Rim, 9 In., Set Of 6 ........................ 130.00
**Platter,** Castle Ruins, Acorn Trim, Brown, Oval, 10 1/2 X 13 1/2 In. .................... 40.00
**Platter,** Floral Design, Imari Colors, 1847 Mark, 20 X 10 1/2 In. .......................... 125.00
**Sugar,** Covered, Figural, Pineapple, White Salt Glazed, 6 In. ................................ 65.00
**Tumbler,** Blue Ground, White Relief, Classical Figures, 4 In., Pair ........................ 30.00
**Vase,** Jasperware, White Cherubs, Brown Ground, 4 1/2 In. .................................. 50.00
### COPPER LUSTER, see Luster, Copper

**COPPER, Bed Warmer,** Stylized Floral Design, American, 40 In. .............................. 125.00
**Bed Warmer,** Sun Symbol, 11 In.Diam. ...................................................................... 65.00
**Bed Warmer,** Turned Wooden Handle ........................................................................ 175.00
**Bedpan,** Handmade ........................................................................................................ 70.00
**Bookends,** Woman, Flowing Hair, Pair ........................................................................ 148.00
**Bucket,** Fire ...................................................................................................................... 65.00
**Canister,** Tea, 18th Century, Small Round Cap, 10 In. ............................................ 65.00
**Coffeepot,** Curved Spout, 4 Copper Cups ................................................................ 80.00
**Coffeepot,** Espresso, C.1830, Copper, 3 Part ............................................................ 97.00
**Compote,** Handmade, 1920s, Polished, 6 X 12 In.Diam. ........................................ 45.00
**Dipper,** Bowl, Hand-Shaped, Wrought Iron Handle, Doughnut .............................. 70.00
**Fernery,** Russian, 3 Ft., 8 In. ........................................................................................ 110.00
**Frame,** Picture, Oval, Hammered, C.1910, 4 In. ...................................................... 40.00
**Kettle,** Fish, Oval ............................................................................................................ 150.00
**Letter Holder,** Indian Head, Quill Pens, Victorian .................................................... 65.00
**Mask,** Mirth & Sorrow, Signed Orvelo, Pair .............................................................. 125.00
**Matchbox,** Century Of Progress .................................................................................. 10.00
**Pan,** Dovetailed, Marked Baker, Philadelphia, 30 In. ................................................ 200.00
**Pan,** Sauce, Dovetailed, Wrought Iron Handle, 7 1/2 X 5 In. ................................ 89.00
**Pitcher,** Measure, Handled, Graduated, C.1820, D.M.Smith, Set Of 6 .................... 500.00
**Pitcher,** Measuring, Strap Handle, Tin Lined, 1 Gallon, 10 In. .............................. 65.00
**Sconces,** Wall, Mission Hammered, C.1910, Marked, 8 3/4 In., Pair ...................... 125.00
**Sign,** Molded Fish, Gold Leafed, Tackle Painted Both Sides, 36 In. ........................ 1350.00
**Skillet,** Iron Handle, 11 In. ............................................................................................ 95.00
**Still,** Moonshine .............................................................................................................. 75.00
**Teakettle,** English, Dovetailed Back & Bottom, Signed, J.C. & W.Lord .................... 245.00
**Tray,** Pen, & Letter Opener, Dirk Van Erp, C.1915 .................................................. 200.00
**Tray,** Sailing Ships, Handled, 16 X 11 In. .................................................................. 40.00

*Coralene glass was made by firing many small colored beads on the outside of glassware. It was made in many patterns in the United States and Europe in the 1880s. Reproductions are made today.*

**CORALENE, Basket**, Cobalt & Gold, Footed, Signed & Dated ...................................... 225.00
**Bowl**, Blue Mother-Of-Pearl, 2 1/4 X 4 1/4 In. .................................................... 450.00
**Bowl**, Sheafs Of Wheat, Yellow Mother-Of-Pearl, Satin Glass, Footed ................... 145.00
    **CORALENE, JAPANESE POTTERY, see Japanese Coralene**
**Jar**, Bulbous Stopper, Orange On Satin Frost, 5 3/4 In. ........................................ 130.00
**Tumbler**, White Lining, Yellow Beading Outside, Blue, 3 5/8 In. ........................... 395.00
**Vase**, Allover Beading, Blue Body, 6 In. ............................................................... 432.00
**Vase**, Basket, Beaded Chrysanthemums, Green Ground, Signed, 8 1/2 In. .............. 265.00
**Vase**, Bleeding Hearts, Green, Yellow Ground, 13 In. .......................................... 275.00
**Vase**, Blue & Yellow Flowers On Amber Ground, 5 In. ........................................... 50.00
**Vase**, Bottle Shaped, Blues, 1909, 9 In. ............................................................. 270.00
**Vase**, Bulbous, Green Coralene Flowers, Brown Body, 1909, 6 In. ........................ 165.00
**Vase**, Double Handled, Peonies, Gold Enamel, Purple Mark, 9 1/2 In. ................... 165.00
**Vase**, Floral & Bluebird Design, 2 Handles, Stick Neck, Signed, 7 In. .................... 195.00
**Vase**, Gold Beaded Bands, Allover Coralene, 7 In. .............................................. 345.00
**Vase**, Gold Handles, Beading, Patent Mark, 6 1/2 In. .......................................... 249.00
**Vase**, Green Ground, Floral Pink Beading, 1909, 9 1/4 In. .................................. 225.00
**Vase**, Handled, Allover Pastel Floral, Orange Ground, Signed, 13 In. ..................... 225.00
**Vase**, Handled, Bamboo Beading, Green Matte, 6 In. ........................................... 45.00
**Vase**, Handled, Stylized Coralene Flowers, Painted 1909, 15 1/2 In. ..................... 395.00
**Vase**, Orange, Pastel Floral, Handled, Signed, 13 In. ........................................... 225.00
**Vase**, Pink Beaded Flowers, Beaded Gold Lip, 7 3/4 In. ....................................... 225.00
**Vase**, Pink Flowers, Orange, Yellow, 2 Handles, Signed, 13 In. ............................. 250.00
**Vase**, Pink, Green, Gold, 9 1/2 In. ..................................................................... 195.00
**Vase**, Pink, 6 X 4 In.Diam. ................................................................................ 100.00
**Vase**, Poppy Handled, Footed, Cobalt Blue Trim, 5 1/2 In. ................................... 150.00
**Vase**, Raised Gold Beading & Trim, Shaded Green Ground, 9 1/4 In. ..................... 225.00
**Vase**, Ruffled Top, White Lining, Beaded Coral Pattern, 7 3/4 In. .......................... 525.00
**Vase**, Sprays Of Flowers, Powder Blue Ground, 5 1/2 In. .................................... 95.00
**Vase**, Yellow Stemmed Puff Flowers, Allover Design, 1909, 9 1/2 In. .................... 165.00
**Vase**, Yellow, Blue Satin Ground, Seaweed Design, 8 1/2 In. ............................... 325.00
**Vase**, Yellow, Marigolds, 7 In. .......................................................................... 165.00
**Vase**, 3-Handled, Flowers, Green Bisque Ground, 1909 Mark, 9 1/2 In. ................. 265.00

*Cordey China Company was founded in 1942 by Boleslaw Cybis in Trenton, New Jersey. The firm produced gift shop items. Production stopped in 1950 and Cybis Porcelains was founded.*

**CORDEY, Box**, Covered, 4 Legs, Applied Rosebud, Gold Outlined, Signed, 5 X 5 In. ......... 85.00
**Box**, 4-Footed, Blossoms On Lid, Gold Outlined Flowers, 3 1/2 X 5 In. .................... 75.00
**Box**, 4-Footed, Pink Rosebuds & Leaves, Oval, Numbered, 6 X 5 X 4 In. ................. 75.00
**Box**, 4-Footed, Red Rose In Green Leaves On Lid, No.6018, Square ....................... 55.00
**Bust**, Ladies, Blue Hat, Long Ringlets, Ruffled Bodice, 5 1/2 In. ........................... 30.00
**Bust**, Lady With Napoleon-Type Hat, Blue Coat, No.5038, 7 1/2 In. ...................... 90.00
**Bust**, Lady, Lavender Flowers, Paper Label, 6 In. ............................................... 50.00
**Bust**, Lady, No.5010 ........................................................................................ 45.00
**Bust**, Man & Lady, Elizabethan Dress, Pair ........................................................ 125.00
**Dish**, Leaf Shape, Pierced Design, Roses & Leaves, 5 X 5 1/2 In., Pair .................. 60.00
**Figurine**, Bird, Outstretched Wings, On Tree Trunk, No.6004r, 10 In. ..................... 95.00
**Figurine**, Bust Of Young Lady, Floral Blouse, No.5064, 6 1/4 In. ........................... 75.00
**Figurine**, Court Gentleman, Signed & Numbered, 11 In. ....................................... 85.00
**Figurine**, Female, No.5014, 6 1/2 In. ................................................................. 30.00
**Figurine**, French Lady, No. 5084a, 11 1/2 In. ..................................................... 95.00
**Figurine**, Lady With Bonnet, 7 1/2 In. ................................................................ 45.00
**Figurine**, Lady, No.5087a, 11 In. ....................................................................... 125.00
**Figurine**, Lady, No.5089 .................................................................................. 85.00
**Figurine**, Man In Waistcoat, Knee-High Pants, No. 5043, 10 3/4 In. ....................... 145.00
**Figurine**, Oriental Woman, Kimono, Lace & Flowers, 24 In. ................................... 495.00
**Lamp**, Flower Trim ........................................................................................... 50.00

**Tray,** Rosebud & Green Leaves, Cream Ground ......................................................... 25.00
**Vase,** Blown-Out Oriental Man & Woman, 9 X 8 1/2 In.Wide ............................... 55.00
**Wall Pocket,** Swirled Cone Shape, Nude Draped Lady, 8 1/2 In. ........................... 115.00

**CORKSCREW, Anheuser Busch,** Patent 1897, White Metal & Brass ...................... 20.00
**Figural,** Bottle, Busch ................................................................................................... 35.00
**Figural,** Bullet Shape, Drink Lemp, St.Louis ............................................................ 25.00
**Figural,** Lady's Legs, Green Striped Stockings ......................................................... 27.50
**Figural,** Old Curiosity Shop, Brass .......................................................................... 12.50
**Figural,** Perky Porky, Hind End, Chrome, Marked ................................................. 16.00
**Horse's Head,** Bronzed, Metal, 5 In. ...................................................................... 20.00
**Iron,** Turned Ivory Handle, Bottle Brush, Victorian, 6 In. .................................... 100.00
**Listerine** ...................................................................................................................... 6.50
**Turned Wooden Handle,** Nickeled Iron ................................................................... 9.00

*Coronation cups have been made since the 1800s. Pottery or glass with a
picture of the monarch and date have been souvenirs for many coronations.*
**CORONATION, see also Commemorative**
**CORONATION, Ashtray,** Queen Elizabeth II, Wedgwood, 5 1/2 In. ...................... 20.00
**Beaker,** King Edward VIII, Portrait, 4 1/4 In. ......................................................... 45.00
**Button,** King George V & Queen Mary, Metal, 4 In. ............................................. 18.00
**Creamer,** Edward VIII ................................................................................................. 18.00
**Cup,** King George VI & Queen Elizabeth, 3 In. ...................................................... 15.00
**Cup,** Queen Elizabeth II, Portrait & Flags, 4 In. .................................................... 12.00
**Mug,** Edward VIII, 1937 .......................................................................... 30.00 To 52.00
**Mug,** George VI .......................................................................................................... 18.00
**Pitcher,** Elizabeth II, Blue, White Relief Profile ...................................................... 37.00
**Plate,** Edward VIII, Laura Knight, 6 In. .................................................................... 65.00
**Plate,** King Edward VIII, Wedgwood, 8 1/2 In. ....................................................... 90.00

*Cosmos pattern glass is a pressed milk glass pattern with colored flowers.*

**COSMOS, Butter,** Covered, Pink Band ................................................. 90.00 To 150.00
**Butter,** Covered, Pink Band, 10 Colors .................................................................. 195.00
**Lamp Base,** Miniature, Yellow Band ....................................................................... 75.00
**Lamp,** Burner & Original Chimney, Miniature ......................................................... 78.00
**Lamp,** Kerosene, Swirl & Lattice, Polychrome Flowers, 15 1/2 In. ...................... 175.00
**Lamp,** Matching Shade, Original Paint .................................................................... 155.00
**Lamp,** Miniature, Original Shade ............................................................................. 150.00
**Lamp,** Spider Chimney, Clear .................................................................................. 58.00
**Lamp,** Yellow Band, Original, 15 In. ....................................................................... 295.00
**Pitcher,** Brown & Green ........................................................................................... 65.00
**Salt & Pepper,** Original Tops ................................................................................. 100.00
**Salt,** Blue .................................................................................................................... 60.00
**Sugar & Creamer,** Pink Band, Flowers, Pastels, Covered ...................... 275.00 To 298.00
**Sugar,** Covered .......................................................................................................... 150.00
**Syrup,** Pewter Top, Patented 1882 ......................................................................... 150.00
**Wall Pocket,** White .................................................................................................... 15.00
**COUNTRY STORE, see Store**

*Cowan pottery was made in Cleveland, Ohio, from 1913 to 1931. Most pieces
of the art pottery were marked with the name of the firm in various ways.*

**COWAN, Bowl,** Blue Iridescent, 7 1/2 In. ................................................................ 15.00
**Bowl,** Blue Luster, 11 X 4 In. .................................................................................... 20.00
**Bowl,** Centerpiece, Green Inside, Cream, Gargoyle Handles, 15 In. ..................... 12.00
**Bowl,** Iridescent Lavender, Signed, 9 In. ................................................................. 17.50
**Bowl,** Punch, Signed V.Schrechengost, C.1931, 16 1/2 In. .......................... *Illus* 5500.00
**Candleholder,** Seahorse, Blue, Pair ........................................................................ 47.00
**Candleholder,** Textured Orange Matte, Deco, Pair ................................................ 50.00
**Candlestick,** Blue Luster, 2 3/4 In. .......................................................................... 8.00
**Compote,** Seahorse Base, Pink Interior, 15 In. ....................................................... 13.00

Cowan, Bowl, Punch, Signed V.Schrechengost, C.1931, 16 1/2 In. (See Page 125)

| | |
|---|---|
| **Figurine,** Nude, 6 In. | 88.00 |
| **Holder,** Cigarette, Seahorses | 20.00 |
| **Lamp,** Green Crystalline, 11 In. | 125.00 |
| **Pitcher,** Water, Rust, 9 In. | 50.00 |
| **Vase,** Blue Iridescent, 4 In. | 12.00 |
| **Vase,** Blue Luster, 7 In. | 15.00 To 20.00 |
| **Vase,** Bud, Green, Seahorse, 7 In. | 18.00 |
| **Vase,** Bulbous, Incised Squirrel, Peacock, & Star, Blue On White, 9 In. | 85.00 |
| **Vase,** Fan Shape, Seahorse Base, Metallic Blue, 8 In. | 30.00 |
| **Vase,** Fan Shape, Seahorse Base, Mottled Rose, Signed, 6 In. | 19.00 |
| **Vase,** Orange Luster, 10 In. | 10.00 To 20.00 |
| | |
| **COXON, Plate,** Belleek, 10 In. | 18.00 |
| | |
| **CRACKER JACK, Bookmark,** Dog Head | 3.00 |
| **Caboose,** Plastic | 5.00 |
| **Cart,** 2 Wheel | 5.00 |
| **Delivery Truck,** Signed | 15.00 |
| **Plate** | 19.00 |
| **Token,** President, Metal | 5.00 |
| **Van** | 5.00 |
| **Wheelbarrow,** Wheels Turn, Tin | 15.00 To 18.00 |
| **Whistle,** Signed | 15.00 |
| **Whistle,** Single | 5.00 |
| **Whistle,** Tin, 6 Pieces | 12.00 |

> *Crackle glass was originally made by the Venetians, but most of the ware found today dates from the 1800s. The glass was heated, cooled, and refired so that many small lines appeared inside the glass. It was made in many factories in the United States and Europe.*

**CRACKLE GLASS, see also Fry**

| | |
|---|---|
| **CRACKLE GLASS, Pitcher,** Amber Reeded Handle, 7 1/2 In. | 140.00 |
| **Pitcher,** Bulbous, Clear Applied Handle, Cranberry, 6 1/4 In. | 85.00 |
| **Pitcher,** Pontil, Amber, 5 X 6 1/2 In. | 40.00 |
| **Pitcher,** Water, Lid, 8 1/2 In. | 40.00 |
| **Vase,** Green, 9 In. | 28.00 |
| **Vase,** Spill, Green, 5 In. | 10.00 |
| **Water Set,** Pitcher, Lidded, 5 Glasses, Light Blue | 145.00 |

> *Cranberry glass is an almost transparent yellow-red glass. It resembles the color of cranberry juice.*

**CRANBERRY GLASS, see also Northwood, Rubena Verde, etc.**

| | |
|---|---|
| **CRANBERRY GLASS, Atomizer,** 10 Panel, 3 1/2 In. | 65.00 |

| | |
|---|---|
| **Banana Boat,** Gold Trim, 11 1/4 In. | 155.00 |
| **Basket,** Clear Handle, Berry Prunts, Clear Foot, 3 In.Diam. | 65.00 |
| **Basket,** Thumbprint Ruffled Top, Clear Reeded Handle, 7 In. | 125.00 |
| **Bell,** Opaque White Handle, Glass Clapper, 2 1/8 X 4 5/8 In. | 125.00 |
| **Bell,** Wedding, Clear Handle, 10 In. | 185.00 |
| **Bell,** Wedding, Opaque White Edge, Handle, Blue Finial, 13 In. | 175.00 |
| **Bottle,** Cologne, Gold Embossed Tulips | 50.00 |
| **Bottle,** Cologne, Gold Outlined Flowers, Gold Ground, 7 In. | 245.00 |
| **Bottle,** Cologne, Gold Scales, Colored Foliage, 6 1/2 In. | 225.00 |
| **Bottle,** Cologne, Stopper, Enamel Overlay, 4 1/2 In. | 90.00 |
| **Bottle,** Perfume, Gold Flowers, Clear Faceted Stopper, 5 In. | 115.00 |
| **Bottle,** Perfume, Gold Intaglio Cut Deer, 6 In. | 118.00 |
| **Bottle,** Perfume, Green Foliage, Gold Trim, Stopper, 8 1/2 In. | 125.00 |
| **Bottle,** Perfume, Mushroom Stopper, Gold Design | 95.00 |
| **Bottle,** Water, Inverted Fern, Blown Clear Stopper, 1 1/4 Qt. | 135.00 |
| **Bottle,** Wine, White & Gold Flowers, Sanded Gold Bands, 9 In. | 145.00 |
| **Bowl,** Finger, Ground Bottom, Underplate | 40.00 |
| **Bowl,** Hobnail, Applied White Ribbon Rim, 7 3/4 In.Diam. | 195.00 |
| **Bowl,** Jam, Clear Rigaree, Silver Plate Holder | 95.00 |
| **Bowl,** Mat-Su-Noke Design, Branches & Flowers, 6 In.Diam. | 550.00 |
| **Bowl,** Punch, 12 Cups, Inverted Panel, Bowl, 10 In.Diam. | 375.00 |
| **Bowl,** Rose, Cystal Applique Top, 4 1/4 In. | 110.00 |
| **Bowl,** Swirl Pattern, White Rim, 9 3/4 X 4 In. | 185.00 |
| **Box,** Blue Enamel Flowers, Hinged | 135.00 |
| **Box,** Covered, White Enameled Fan Design, 2 7/8 X 2 3/4 In. | 95.00 |
| **Box,** Dresser, Footed, White, Gold Enameling | 110.00 |
| **Box,** Hinged, Gold Design, White Flowers, 3 X 4 1/4 In. | 165.00 |
| **Box,** Hinged, Gold Enamel, Flower Shape Bottom, 2 3/4 X 2 In. | 175.00 |
| **Box,** Hinged, Gold Scrolls, White Dots, 3 3/4 X 3 1/8 In. | 195.00 |
| **Box,** Patch, Gold Enamel, Hinged, 3 X 2 3/4 In.Diam. | 195.00 |
| **Bride's Basket,** Poinsettia Pattern, Ruffled, No Holder | 125.00 |
| **Bride's Bowl,** Ruffled, Silver Plate Holder, 10 X 4 In. | 175.00 |
| **Butter,** Covered, 4 1/2 X 5 3/4 In. | 95.00 |
| **Castor,** Pickle, Enameled | 485.00 |
| **Castor,** Pickle, Hobnail, Figural Tulips, Forbes | 185.00 |
| **Castor,** Pickle, Inverted Thumbprint, Lantern Shape, Tongs | 195.00 |
| **Celery,** Scalloped Top, Overshot Glass, 5 7/8 In. | 85.00 |
| **Celery,** Scalloped Top, 6 X 3 1/4 In.Diam. | 85.00 |
| **Chandelier,** Electrified | 495.00 |
| **Compote,** Gold Band, Pink Flowers, 3 X 8 1/4 In.Diam. | 165.00 |
| **Cookie Jar,** Round Crystal Handle On Cranberry Lid | 119.00 |
| **Cracker Jar,** Clear Leaf On Lid, Ribbed, 7 1/2 In. | 165.00 |
| **Creamer,** Applied Clear Crystal Handle | 60.00 |
| **Creamer,** Crystal Foot & Rim, 4 1/2 In. | 95.00 |
| **Creamer,** Opaque Threading, Clear Handle & Feet, 3 7/8 In. | 70.00 |
| **Creamer,** Paneled Sprig, Applied Handle | 125.00 |
| **Cruet,** Boy On Bicycle In White, Clear Stopper, Handle, 6 In. | 40.00 |
| **Cruet,** Bubble Stopper, Clear Applied Handle, Enameled, 7 In. | 175.00 |
| **Cruet,** Bubble Stopper, Clear Handle, Yellow Pansies, 7 In. | 175.00 |
| **Cruet,** Clear Applied Handle, Clear Bubble Stopper, 8 In. | 195.00 |
| **Cruet,** Clear Handle, Allover White Enamel Design, 8 3/8 In. | 145.00 |
| **Cruet,** Clear Handle, Enameled Flowers, Gold Trim, 5 In. | 118.00 |
| **Cruet,** Clear Handle, 3 Petal Top, Enamel Dots, 7 1/8 In. | 145.00 |
| **Cruet,** Clear Reed Handle, Enamel Scroll & Dot, 7 3/8 In. | 145.00 |
| **Cruet,** Flattened Bulbous Shape, Gold Leaves, 8 X 3 X 5 In. | 175.00 |
| **Cruet,** Hobnail, Stopper | 15.00 |
| **Cruet,** Inverted Thumbprint, Cut Glass Stopper | 75.00 |
| **Cruet,** Inverted Thumbprint, Floral, Faceted Stopper | 195.00 |
| **Cruet,** Vinegar, Pansies Design, Bubble Stopper, 7 In. | 165.00 |
| **Cruet,** Wine, Clear Handle, Jeweled, 14 1/2 X 5 In.Diam. | 325.00 |
| **Cruet,** Wine, Clear Reeded Handle, Bubble Stopper, 11 3/4 In. | 165.00 |
| **Cruet,** Wine, Three Petal Top, Clear Handle, 10 In. | 115.00 |
| **Cruet,** Wine, 9 In. | 115.00 |

Cup, Custard, Clear Handle, Pair ............................................................................................. 40.00
Decanter, Clear Applied Handle & Stopper, Enameled, 10 In. ..................................... 165.00
Decanter, Teardrop Stopper, Star Bottom, 8 X 17 1/4 In. ........................................... 95.00
Decanter, Wine, 9 In. ................................................................................................................ 115.00
Dish, Jam, Ruffled, Silver Plated Holder, 8 1/2 In. ......................................................... 165.00
Dish, Jam, Silver Plated Holder, Rigaree, 5 1/2 In.Diam. ............................................. 110.00
Dish, Sweetmeat, Double, Silver Plate Holder, 7 X 10 1/2 In. ................................... 175.00
Epergne, Clear Rigaree, Opalescent Vaseline, 11 In. ..................................................... 395.00
Epergne, Opaque Threading, Serpentine Trim, 15 1/2 X 11 In. ................................... 295.00
Epergne, 3 Lily, Clear Rigaree, 20 1/2 In. .......................................................................... 175.00
Epergne, 3 Lily, Ruffled Base, 22 1/2 X 10 1/8 In.Diam. .............................................. 345.00
Epergne, 4 Lily, Clear Rigaree, Mirror Plateau, 18 In. .................................................. 295.00
Epergne, 4 Lily, Crystal Rigaree, 19th Century, 24 In. .................................................. 345.00
Finger Bowl, Inverted Thumbprint ....................................................................................... 110.00
Flask, Laydown, White Loopings, 7 1/4 X 5 3/4 In. ....................................................... 55.00
Goblet, Shield Design, Large .................................................................................................. 20.00
Hat, Coin Dot, 3 In. ................................................................................................................... 30.00
Jar, Candy, Lid, Cone Shape, Footed ................................................................................. 28.00
Jar, Covered, Applied Berry Prunts, Clear Knob, 5 3/8 In. .......................................... 110.00
Jar, Covered, Bubble Finial, Orchid & Green Leaves, 5 In. ......................................... 125.00
Jar, Covered, Crystal Feet & Knob, 5 1/4 In. .................................................................. 115.00
Jar, Covered, Cut To Crystal, 5 In. ..................................................................................... 98.00
Jar, Sweetmeat, Berries, Leaves & Bird Decoration ...................................................... 165.00
Lamp, Fairy, Clear Marked Clarke Base, 3 1/2 In. ......................................................... 100.00
Lamp, Fairy, Ivory Flowers ..................................................................................................... 125.00
Lamp, Fairy, Pedestal, Signed Clarke Cup, Red Dome, 14 In. .................................. 295.00
Lamp, Fairy, Verre Moire, Marked Clarke Base, 4 1/2 In. ........................................... 165.00
Lamp, Hanging, Inverted Thumbprint, Brass Mountings, 29 In. ................................. 295.00
Lamp, Snowflake, Clear Stem, Opalescent, 8 In. ............................................................ 235.00
Lamp, Verre Moire Metal Base, Ruffled Shade, 8 7/8 In. ............................................ 295.00
Liqueur, Crystal Stem .............................................................................................................. 48.00
Muffineer, 12-Sided, Domed Top .......................................................................................... 80.00
Mug, Gold Flowers, Applied Handle, 3 X 2 In. ................................................................ 50.00
Mustard, Pewter Lid & Handle, 3 1/4 In. .......................................................................... 65.00
Nappy, Clear, Open Handle, 5 X 4 In.Diam. ........................................... 55.00 To 65.00
Pickle Castor, Lantern Shape, Inverted Thumbprint, 9 In. ........................................... 195.00
Pitcher, Applied Clear Handle, 7 In. ................................................................................... 125.00
Pitcher, Applied Clear Handle, 8 In. ................................................................................... 85.00
Pitcher, Buttons & Braids, Green ......................................................................................... 95.00
Pitcher, Gray Enameled Swallow, Gold Thistle, 11 3/4 In. .......................................... 175.00
Pitcher, Ice Pocket Above Clear Handle, 11 1/2 In. ...................................................... 195.00
Pitcher, Intaglio Cut Dragonfly, Applied Gold ................................................................. 150.00
Pitcher, Inverted Thumbprint, Clear Handle, 6 3/4 In. .................................................. 85.00
Pitcher, Inverted Thumbprint, Enameled Flowers, 7 1/2 In. ........................................ 165.00
Pitcher, Mary Gregory Boy In White, 3 1/2 In. ............................................................... 135.00
Pitcher, Nailsea White Loopings, Clear Handle, 7 3/8 In. ........................................... 175.00
Pitcher, Ribbed, Reeded Applied Clear Handle, 8 In. ................................................... 165.00
Pitcher, Silver Plate Pierced Holder, 4 In. ....................................................................... 115.00
Pitcher, Tankard Shape, Clear Applied Handle, 10 1/2 In. .......................................... 195.00
Pitcher, Tankard Shape, Clear Handle, 5 In. .................................................................... 115.00
Pitcher, Thumbprint, Ruffled Top, Clear Ribbed, 6 Glasses ....................................... 295.00
Pitcher, Water, Leaf Umbrella .......................................................... 250.00 To 325.00
Pitcher, Water, Nailsea White Looping, Bulbous, 5 3/8 In. ......................................... 175.00
Pitcher, Water, Optic Rib, Applied Reeded Handle, 7 1/4 In. ..................................... 135.00
Pitcher, Water, Optic Swirl, Controlled Bubbles ............................................................. 125.00
Pitcher, Water, Seaweed, Opalescent ................................................................................. 285.00
Pitcher, White Enameled Flowers, Gold Leaves, 7 1/4 In. ........................................... 115.00
Pitcher, White Enameled Lilies Of The Valley, 5 3/4 In. .............................................. 125.00
Rose Bowl, Diamond-Quilted, Crystal Applique Top, 4 1/4 In. .................................. 115.00
Rose Bowl, Optic Rib, 8 Crimp Top, Enamel Design, 3 In.Diam. ............................. 175.00
Rose Bowl, Swirl, Crimped Edges, 5 In. ............................................................................ 28.00
Rose Bowl, Threaded, 2 1/4 In. ............................................................................................ 95.00

| | |
|---|---|
| **Rose Bowl,** Threaded, 12 Crimp Top, Oval, 2 1/4 X 3 In.Diam. | 75.00 |
| **Rose Bowl,** 8 Crimp, Blue & White Forget-Me-Nots, 3 1/2 In. | 125.00 |
| **Salt & Pepper,** Bulbous Base | 40.00 |
| **Salt & Pepper,** Eire Twist Pattern | 37.50 |
| **Salt & Pepper,** Flower Band | 125.00 |
| **Salt & Pepper,** Inverted Thumbprint, 1 Enamel Flower | 55.00 |
| **Salt,** Crystal Shell Trim, Silver Plated Holder, 3 In.Diam. | 68.00 |
| **Salt,** Enameled White Flowers, Gold Trim, 3 In.Diam. | 42.00 |
| **Salt,** Pinched Crystal Feet & Top | 70.00 |
| **Salt,** Shaped Like Petals Of Flower | 58.00 |
| **Salt,** Silver Rim, Cut Glass | 45.00 |
| **Saltshaker,** Enameled Flower | 18.00 |
| **Spooner,** Floradora, Gold Trim, Footed | 100.00 |
| **Sugar Shaker,** Corset Shape, Silver Plate Rim, Top, 5 1/2 In. | 58.00 |
| **Sugar Shaker,** Cut & Flashed, 5 3/4 In. | 350.00 |
| **Sugar Shaker,** Cut Panels, Silver Plate Top, 5 7/8 In. | 58.00 |
| **Sugar Shaker,** Cut To Clear, Emerald Green, 5 In. | 195.00 |
| **Sugar Shaker,** Daisy & Fern | 70.00 |
| **Sugar Shaker,** Hobnail, 7 In. | 175.00 |
| **Sugar Shaker,** Leaf Umbrella | 110.00 |
| **Syrup,** Broken Column Design | 95.00 |
| **Toothpick,** Inverted Thumbprint | 32.00 |
| **Tumbler,** Baby Inverted Thumbprint | 50.00 |
| **Tumbler,** Baby Thumbprint | 24.00 |
| **Tumbler,** Bubble Lattice | 35.00 |
| **Tumbler,** Daisy & Fern | 35.00 |
| **Tumbler,** Inverted Thumbprint, Enameled Sprays, 3 3/4 In. | 45.00 |
| **Tumbler,** Mother-Of-Pearl, White Casing | 80.00 |
| **Vase,** Acid Cut Back To Geometric Design, Leaded, 7 1/4 In. | 75.00 |
| **Vase,** Applied Medallions, Gold Over Leaves, 10 1/4 In., Pair | 3250.00 |
| **Vase,** Blown, Enameled, Ruffled Top, 8 In., Pair | 125.00 |
| **Vase,** Blue Enameled Forget-Me-Nots, Clear Trim, 9 3/4 In. | 118.00 |
| **Vase,** Celery, Handled, 8 In. | 30.00 |
| **Vase,** Clear Applied Handles, Gold Foliage, 11 1/2 In. | 295.00 |
| **Vase,** Clear Wafer Foot, Clear Drape At Top, 12 1/4 In. | 225.00 |
| **Vase,** Covered With Hand-Painted Flowers, 3 1/2 In. | 22.00 |
| **Vase,** Crimped, Clear Applied Rigaree At Middle, 9 1/2 In. | 95.00 |
| **Vase,** Curled Feet, Metal Holder, Black, Green Accent, 13 In. | 225.00 |
| **Vase,** Daisy Enamel Design, 10 In. | 95.00 |
| **Vase,** Enameled Coralene Flowers, Scroll Feet, 10 In. | 375.00 |
| **Vase,** Enameled Gold Florals & Scrolls, Footed, 14 In. | 80.00 |
| **Vase,** Ewer Shape, Flowers, 14 3/4 In., Pair | 555.00 |
| **Vase,** Flowers & Butterflies, Gold, 11 In., Pair | 325.00 |
| **Vase,** Footed, Crystal Leaves, Ruffle Rim, 4 3/4 In. | 235.00 |
| **Vase,** Gold Bands, Enameled Forget-Me-Nots, 3 1/4 In., Pair | 175.00 |
| **Vase,** Gold Leaf & Enamel Design, 9 In. | 85.00 |
| **Vase,** Goldstone Foot, Cream Spatter, 10 3/8 In., Pair | 375.00 |
| **Vase,** Green Rigaree Trim, Bulbous Bottom, 8 In., Pair | 125.00 |
| **Vase,** Jack-In-The-Pulpit, Ruffled Top, 2 7/8 In. | 55.00 |
| **Vase,** Man & Boy Fishing, Enameled Colors, 6 1/4 In., Pair | 245.00 |
| **Vase,** Ormolu Feet, Ruffled, Enameled Flowers, 7 1/2 In. | 195.00 |
| **Vase,** Ormolu Feet, Ruffled, Enameled Flowers, 8 In. | 195.00 |
| **Vase,** Paneled Effect, Gold Enameled Leaves, 9 In. | 115.00 |
| **Vase,** Paneled, Enameling, 5 In., Pair | 150.00 |
| **Vase,** Sterling Silver Overlay, 1909 Date, Alvin, 6 1/4 In. | 550.00 |
| **Vase,** Thorned Ribs, Clear Petal Feet, Hexagonal, 12 In. | 75.00 |
| **Vase,** Trumpet Shape, Ruffled Rim, Clear Foot, 11 1/2 In. | 85.00 |
| **Vase,** White Enameled Tree Scene, Sanded Gold Flowers, 9 In. | 175.00 |
| **Vase,** 3 Applied Feet, Enameled Flowers, 12 3/4 In., Pair | 595.00 |
| **Vial,** Perfume, Double, Cut To Clear, Brass Caps, 5 1/4 In. | 295.00 |
| **Water Set,** Thumbprint, C.1900, 4 Piece | 295.00 |
| **Wine,** Champagne Shape, Cut To Clear | 50.00 |

*Creamware, or queensware, was developed by Josiah Wedgwood about 1765. It is a cream-colored earthenware that has been copied by many factories.*

**CREAMWARE, see also Wedgwood**

| | |
|---|---|
| **CREAMWARE,** Figurine, Seated Woman, Man In Greek Costume, 9 1/4 In., Pair | 225.00 |
| **Mug,** Stick Spatter Design, Peacocks, Leaf-End Handle, 4 In. | 185.00 |
| **Plate,** Pierced Border, 18th Century, Feather Edge, 8 In. | 165.00 |
| **Plate,** Toddy, Pink Luster Trim, Spiral Ribbon Border, 19th Century | 45.00 |

*The Creil Factory at Oise, France, made earthenware from 1794 to 1895. It joined the firm of Montereau in the early nineteenth century.*

| | |
|---|---|
| **CREIL,** Plate, Montereau, Captivity Of Napoleon, Sepia & Black, 8 In. | 35.00 |

**CROESUS, see Pressed Glass, Croesus**

*Crown Derby is the nickname given to the works of the Royal Crown Derby Factory which began working in England in 1859. An earlier and more famous English Derby factory existed from 1750 to 1848. The two factories were not related. Most of the porcelain found today with the Derby mark is the work of the later Derby factory.*

**CROWN DERBY, see also Royal Crown Derby**

| | |
|---|---|
| **CROWN DERBY,** Bowl, Fruit Center, Gilding & Filigree Work, Cobalt, 9 1/4 In. | 485.00 |
| **Cup & Saucer,** Phoenix Bird Pattern, Orange | 20.00 |
| **Dish,** Botanical, C.1820, Dot & D Mark, 11 1/4 In.Diam., Pair | 400.00 |
| **Plate,** Triumphant Stag, Standing Over Wolf, Signed, 9 1/4 In. | 135.00 |
| **Urn,** Covered, Imari Pattern, Red Mark, 1887-1890, 5 1/2 In. | 225.00 |
| **Vase Pistol Handles,** Allover Enameled Gold Flowers, 1884, 6 In. | 165.00 |

*Crown Milano glass was made by Frederick Shirley about 1890. It is a plain biscuit color with a satin finish. It is decorated with flowers, and often had large gold scrolls.*

| | |
|---|---|
| **CROWN MILANO,** Biscuit Jar, Burmese Coloring, Cactus Flower, Marked | 700.00 |
| **Bowl,** Swirl Ribbing, Scalloped 4-Pointed Top, Enameled, 3 In. | 545.00 |
| **Box,** Covered, Applied Gold Irises & Sprays, Signed, 8 X 3 In. | 650.00 |
| **Carafe,** Wine, Footed, Steeple Stopper, Gold Design, , 17 1/2 In. | 850.00 |
| **Cookie Jar,** Ribbed, Gilded, Enamel Opalescent, Marked, 4 1/2 In. | 895.00 |
| **Cracker Jar,** Albertine, Burmese Shading, Mt.Washington Lid | 695.00 |
| **Cracker Jar,** Apricot Shading To Yellow, Gold Acorns, Signed | 425.00 |
| **Cracker Jar,** Apricot To Yellow, Gold Acorns, Signed | 125.00 |
| **Cracker Jar,** C.1885, Marked, 7 1/4 In. *Illus* | 500.00 |
| **Cracker Jar,** Gilded, Enameled, Raised Berries, Marked, 7 1/2 In. | 1250.00 |
| **Cracker Jar,** Melon Shape, Gold Beaded Foliage, Green, Signed | 500.00 |
| **Cracker Jar,** Orange To Cream, Flowering Prunus, Marked, 7 In. | 500.00 |
| **Cracker Jar,** Round, Signed *Illus* | 650.00 |
| **Cracker Jar,** Silver, Top, Rim & Bale, White Lining, Gold Trim | 695.00 |
| **Creamer,** Tan & Blue, Gold Flowers | 95.00 |
| **Cup & Saucer,** Chrysanthemum | 1250.00 |
| **Cup & Saucer,** Demitasse, Scroll Banded Over Enamel, C.1890 | 375.00 |
| **Dish,** Sweetmeat, Signed CM Base, Mt.Washington Signed Lid | 1250.00 |
| **Ewer,** Gold Feet, Rope Handle, Gold Stopper, Signed, 17 In. | 650.00 |
| **Ewer,** Mottled Ground, 10 In. | 1500.00 |
| **Mustard Jar,** Silver Plated Cover *Illus* | 600.00 |
| **Rose Bowl,** Raised Enamel Oak Leaf & Acorn, C.1895, 5 In. | 225.00 |
| **Salt,** Figural, Enamel Flowers, Bark Texture | 110.00 |
| **Sugar & Creamer,** Blue & Beige, Gold Trim | 250.00 |
| **Syrup,** Melon Ribbed, Cream Colored, Silver Plated Top, 6 In. | 1100.00 |
| **Toothpick** | 335.00 To 345.00 |
| **Vase,** Brown, Tan, & Gold Design, Beige Ground, 14 In. | 1600.00 |
| **Vase,** Gold Flowers On Cream Mottled Ground, Label, 6 In. | 1500.00 |
| **Vase,** Gold Handles, Enameled, Gold Trim, Matte, Dated 1892, 3 In. | 375.00 |

Crown Milano, Cracker Jar, C.1885, Marked, 7 1/4 In.

Crown Milano, from left to right, Cracker Jar, Round; Mustard Jar With Silver-Plated Cover

**Vase,** Melon Ribbed, Fold-Over Neck, Pastels, Signed, 13 In. ................................................. 1645.00
**Vase,** Ribbed Body, Begonia Leaf Design, 5 In. ........................................................................ 225.00
**Vase,** Swirled & Designed Flowers, 7 1/2 In. .......................................................................... 3200.00
**CROWN TUSCAN, see Cambridge**

*Cruets of glass or porcelain were made to hold vinegar or oil. They were especially popular during Victorian times.*
**CRUET, see also various glass sections**
**CRUET, Amberina** ......................................................................................................................... 150.00
**Baby Coin Spot,** Vaseline, Opalescent ........................................................................................ 35.00
**Checkerboard,** Cerise ................................................................................................................... 30.00
**Checkerboard,** Mother-Of-Pearl, Crimson ................................................................................... 35.00
**Croesus,** Green ............................................................................................................................. 70.00
**Cut Crystal,** 8 X 3 In. .................................................................................................................. 95.00
**Cut Log,** 4 In. ............................................................................................................................... 30.00
**Gold Design,** Amethyst To Clear ................................................................................................. 45.00
**Hobnail,** Cranberry Opalescent .................................................................................................... 75.00
**Jeweled Heart,** Green .................................................................................................................. 85.00
**Sunk Honeycomb** ......................................................................................................................... 20.00

**C.T.** *CT Germany porcelain was made by C. Tielsch & Company of Altwasser, Silesia, in 1845. It is a hard-paste porcelain.*

**CT GERMANY, Bowl,** Boat, Reticulated, Footed ......................................................................... 225.00
**Sugar,** Holly ................................................................................................................................. 15.00

*Cup plates are small glass or china plates that held the cup while a lady or gentleman of the mid-nineteenth century drank coffee or tea from the saucer. The most famous cup plates were made of glass at the Boston and Sandwich Factory in Sandwich, Massachusetts.*

**CUP PLATE, Beauties Of China,** C.1845, Venables, Flow Blue ............................................... 48.00
**Black Transfer Of Man & Woman On Donkey** .......................................................................... 27.00
**Double Heart With Arrows,** Flint ................................................................................................ 30.00

Eagle, Dated 1831, Sandwich Glass ......................................................................................... 25.00
Eagle, Smooth Rim, Sandwich Glass ...................................................................................... 28.00
Elongated Dots, Clear, 3 7/16 In. ........................................................................................... 30.00
Henry Clay, Sandwich Glass ........................................................................... 65.00 To 85.00
Henry Clay, Stars & Alternate Serrations, Sandwich Glass ............................................ 65.00
Lacy Pattern, Sandwich, Mass., C.1835, 3 1/4 In. .......................................................... 35.00
Log Cabin ............................................................................................................................ 55.00
Morea, C.1878, Goodwin, Flow Blue ..................................................................................... 48.00
Oregon, C.1845, Mayer, Flow Blue ........................................................................................ 48.00
Penn's Treaty, 3 3/4 In. ........................................................................................................ 95.00
Rose Lee, White Opalescent ................................................................................................. 50.00
Rust Girl With Bird On Finger, Cream Ground, Wood ...................................................... 50.00
Ship, Octagonal ................................................................................................................... 55.00
Thistle & Beehive, Apple Green, Octagon, 5 1/2 In., Set Of 6 ..................................... 600.00
Troy, C.1840, Meigh, Flow Blue ........................................................................................... 48.00
White Slag In Body, Clear .................................................................................................... 25.00
13 Heart Border, Opalescent ............................................................................................... 60.00
13 Hearts, Sandwich Glass .................................................................................................. 85.00

*Currier & Ives made the famous American lithographs marked with their
name from 1857 to 1907.*

CURRIER & IVES, A Home In The Wilderness, Winter Scene ........................................ 325.00
A Mansion Of The Olden Time, Dog, Home, River ........................................................ 150.00
American Country Life, Pleasures Of Winter ............................................................... 1200.00
American Feathered Game, Wood Duck & Golden Eye, C.1854 ................................... 395.00
American Field Sports, Colored, Framed, 6 1/2 X 4 In. ................................................. 125.00
American Homestead Spring, 1869 .................................................................................. 200.00
Battle Of Buena Vista, 1847, Mexican War Battle ......................................................... 125.00
Birthplace Of Washington, Westmoreland County, Virginia ......................................... 250.00
Bride, Margin Mends ........................................................................................................... 45.00
Burning Of The Ocean Monarch Of Boston .................................................................... 150.00
Cornelia ................................................................................................................................ 45.00
Daughter Of Erin, Girl Playing Harp ................................................................................. 35.00
Drawing Fust Blood, Darky Series, Dated 1882 ............................................................. 160.00
Falls Of Niagara .................................................................................................................. 140.00
First Step, Come To Mamma .............................................................................................. 100.00
Franklin At The Court Of France, 1778, Black & White ................................................. 450.00
Fruits Of The Seasons, Grapes, Apple, & Others ............................................................ 90.00
Fruits Of The Tropics, Colored ........................................................................................... 55.00
General Israel Putnam, The Iron Son Of '76 .................................................................. 150.00
Good Night, Little Playfellow, Baby & Dog ....................................................................... 40.00
Great Eastern ...................................................................................................................... 125.00
James K.Polk, Green Curtain .............................................................................................. 75.00
Landscape & Cattle, Woodlands ....................................................................................... 145.00
Little Cherubs, 2 Winged Infants, Black & White .............................................................. 28.00
Niagara Falls, From Goat Island ....................................................................................... 125.00
Noah's Ark, Mounted ........................................................................................................... 35.00
Noontide, A Shady Spot, Cattle & Sheep ........................................................................... 85.00
Partridge Shooting, 2 Dogs & 2 Birds ............................................................................. 250.00
Skating Pond, Central Park Winter, Lithograph, Framed ................................................ 200.00
Stanch Pointer, C.1871, Wide Margins ............................................................................ 325.00
Sunset Tree, 3 Ladies Resting Under Tree ......................................................................... 85.00
Tree Of Life .......................................................................................................................... 50.00
Two Pets ............................................................................................................................... 40.00
View Down The Ravine, At Trenton Falls, New York ....................................................... 250.00
Washington Family, Seated At Table .................................................................................. 95.00
Woodcock Shooting, 2 Dogs & Hunter At Left, 1873 ..................................................... 345.00

CURRIER, Burial Of The Bird, Black & White .................................................................... 42.00
High Bridge At Harlem, 1849 ............................................................................................ 475.00
The Dove, Two Women, One Holding Dove ........................................................................ 28.00

*Custard glass is an opaque glass sometimes known as buttermilk glass. It was first made in America after 1886 at the La Belle Glass Works, Bridgeport, Ohio.*

**CUSTARD GLASS, see also Maize**

| | |
|---|---:|
| **CUSTARD GLASS, Banana Boat,** Grape & Cable, Pearlized | 215.00 |
| **Banana Boat,** Louis XV, Gold Trim, 8 X 11 In. | 98.00 To 140.00 |
| **Bell,** Rose Design, Souvenir | 100.00 |
| **Berry Bowl,** Argonaut Shell, Large | 255.00 |
| **Berry Bowl,** Chrysanthemum Sprig, Blue, Northwood | 350.00 |
| **Berry Bowl,** Diamond Peg, 6 Sauces | 600.00 |
| **Berry Bowl,** Grape & Gothic Arches, Gold Trim, Master | 125.00 |
| **Berry Bowl,** Inverted Fan & Feather | 185.00 To 200.00 |
| **Berry Set,** Argonaut Shell | 425.00 |
| **Berry Set,** Cherry & Scale, Nutmeg, 7 Piece | 385.00 |
| **Berry Set,** Chrysanthemum Sprig, Blue, 6 Piece | 1250.00 |
| **Berry Set,** Geneva, 5 Piece | 325.00 |
| **Berry Set,** Louis XV, 5 Piece | 360.00 |
| **Bottle,** Cologne, Grape, Northwood | 250.00 |
| **Bowl,** Fruit, Louis XV | 150.00 |
| **Bowl,** Grape & Cable, Ruffled, 7 1/2 In. | 32.00 |
| **Bowl,** Lattice, Northwood, 6 In.Diam. | 25.00 |
| **Bowl,** Tom & Jerry, 6 Mugs, McKee | 80.00 |
| **Bowl,** Waste, Vermont | 65.00 |
| **Butter,** Chrysanthemum Sprig, Signed, Covered | 195.00 To 275.00 |
| **Butter,** Geneva, Green, Red Trim | 150.00 |
| **Butter,** Georgia Gem, Flared Design, Covered | 165.00 |
| **Butter,** Indiana, Covered | 55.00 |
| **Butter,** Intaglio, Green, Covered | 165.00 |
| **Butter,** Inverted Fan & Feather, Covered | 235.00 To 250.00 |
| **Butter,** Jefferson Optic, Covered | 145.00 |
| **Butter,** Louis XV, Covered | 140.00 |
| **Butter,** Victoria, Green, Covered | 190.00 |
| **Candleholder,** Cornucopia | 17.50 |
| **Candleholder,** Jeweled, Vermont, Red & Green Design | 55.00 |
| **Celery,** Ring Band, Red Roses | 400.00 |
| **Compote,** Argonaut Pattern, Signed N, 5 In. | 100.00 |
| **Compote,** Horn Of Plenty, Signed Northwood, 9 In. | 100.00 |
| **Compote,** Jelly, Chrysanthemum | 70.00 |
| **Compote,** Jelly, Chrysanthemum Sprig | 50.00 To 95.00 |
| **Compote,** Jelly, Chrysanthemum Sprig, Blue | 485.00 |
| **Compote,** Jelly, Geneva | 90.00 |
| **Compote,** Jelly, Intaglio, Blue | 125.00 |
| **Compote,** Jelly, Intaglio, Green Design | 120.00 |
| **Creamer,** Argonaut Shell | 115.00 To 150.00 |
| **Creamer,** Beaded Circle | 85.00 |
| **Creamer,** Chrysanthemum Sprig | 80.00 To 110.00 |
| **Creamer,** Geneva | 75.00 |
| **Creamer,** Geneva, Red & Green Design | 65.00 |
| **Creamer,** Georgia Gem, Hand-Painted Rosebud | 70.00 |
| **Creamer,** Georgia Gem, Souvenir Of Colorado Springs | 40.00 |
| **Creamer,** Inverted Fan & Feather | 145.00 |
| **Creamer,** Louis XV | 65.00 To 80.00 |
| **Creamer,** Ring & Beads | 40.00 |
| **Creamer,** Ring & Beads, Carthage, New York, Individual | 20.00 |
| **Creamer,** Souvenir, Diamond Point | 40.00 |
| **Creamer,** Souvenir, Iowa Falls | 17.00 |
| **Creamer,** Souvenir, Pulaski, New York, Individual | 18.00 |
| **Creamer,** Souvenir, Salem, Massachusetts, Green | 20.00 |
| **Creamer,** Thumbprint | 25.00 |
| **Creamer,** Trailing Vine | 55.00 |
| **Creamer,** Wild Bouquet | 145.00 |
| **Cruet,** Argonaut Shell | 225.00 |
| **Cruet,** Chrysanthemum Sprig, Faceted Amber Stopper | 275.00 |

**Cruet,** Geneva, Original Stopper ................................................ 245.00
**Cruet,** Inverted Fan & Feather, Original Stopper ............. 495.00 To 595.00
**Cruet,** Inverted Fan & Feather, Original Stopper, Green ............... 495.00
**Cruet,** Iris, Stopper ....................................................... 600.00
**Cruet,** Louis XV, Clear Faceted Stopper ............................... 185.00
**Cruet,** Rib Draped, Glass Stopper ..................................... 375.00
**Cruet,** Ring Band, Gold Band ............................................ 255.00
**Cruet,** Ring Band, Rose Design ......................................... 235.00
**Cruet,** Wild Bouquet, Northwood, Plastic Stopper ................. 475.00
**Cup,** Punch, Daisy & Button With Narcissus, Set Of 3 .............. 12.00
**Cup,** Tea, Souvenir, Scranton, Pennsylvania ......................... 48.00
**Dish,** Ice Cream, Peacock At Urn, Master ............................ 265.00
**Dish,** Pickle, Winged Scroll, Gold Trim, 6 In. ......................... 80.00
**Fernery,** Grape & Cable, Nutmeg Stain, Signed, 2 Piece ........... 500.00
**Flour Shaker,** Metal Top, Square, Pair ................................ 15.75
**Goblet,** Beaded Loop, Fond Du Lac, Wisconsin ...................... 60.00
**Goblet,** Beaded Swag With Roses ...................................... 75.00
**Goblet,** Beaded Swag, Souvenir, New Holstein, Heisey ............. 25.00
**Goblet,** Beaded Swag, Souvenir, Revere Beach ...................... 60.00
**Goblet,** Egg In Sand, Set Of 6 .......................................... 125.00
**Goblet,** Grape & Gothic Arches ................................ 50.00 To 65.00
**Jar,** Powder, Flower Scroll .............................................. 65.00
**Jar,** Powder, Winged Scroll, Hand-Painted, Covered ................. 95.00
**Lamp,** Kerosene, Hearts & Painted Pansies ......................... 400.00
**Mug,** Bucksport, Maine ................................................... 29.00
**Mug,** Diamond & Peg ...................................................... 45.00
**Mug,** Gilmanton Iron Works, New Hampshire ......................... 38.00
**Mug,** Lewiston, Maine ..................................................... 35.00
**Mug,** Ribbed Thumbprint ................................................. 30.00
**Mug,** Ribbed Thumbprint, Souvenir .................................... 35.00
**Mug,** Souvenir, Locust Street Market, Dover, New Hampshire ...... 22.00
**Mug,** Thumbprint .......................................................... 30.00
**Mug,** Tiny Thumbprint ..................................................... 30.00
**Nappy,** Peacock & Dahlia, 7 In. ......................................... 55.00
**Nappy,** Prayer Rug ......................................................... 50.00
**Nappy,** Three Fruits, 2-Handled ........................................ 50.00
**Pitcher,** Jackson Pattern, 5 1/4 In. .................................... 65.00
**Pitcher,** Monessen, 2 1/2 In. ............................................ 32.00
**Pitcher,** Water, Argonaut Shell, Gold Trim & Design ................ 295.00
**Pitcher,** Water, Cannonball, 4 Tumblers, Clear, Enameled Flowers ... 87.00
**Pitcher,** Water, Louis XV, Gold Trim ......................... 165.00 To 225.00
**Pitcher,** Water, Maple Leaf With Tree Of Life, Gold & Colors ....... 350.00
**Plate,** Spiraea, Blue, Pierced Handles, 12 In. ....................... 130.00
**Plate,** Three Fruits, Basket Weave, Marked, 7 3/4 In. ............... 45.00
**Punch Bowl,** Inverted Fan & Feather, 8 Cups ...................... 3000.00
**Rose Bowl,** Persian Medallion .......................................... 60.00
**Salt & Pepper,** Bulging Teardrop ....................................... 65.00
**Salt & Pepper,** Geneva, Gold Trim, Emerald Green .................. 95.00
**Salt & Pepper,** Jackson, Gold Design ................................. 95.00
**Salt & Pepper,** Jefferson Optic, Opera House, Logan, Kansas ...... 75.00
**Salt & Pepper,** Louis XV .................................................. 175.00
**Salt & Pepper,** Maple Leaf .............................................. 675.00
**Salt & Pepper,** Overlapping Leaf Pattern, Green ..................... 55.00
**Salt & Pepper,** Pineapple Pattern, Green ............................ 50.00
**Saltshaker,** Beaded Border, Beechers Falls, Vermont .............. 25.00
**Saltshaker,** Beaded Circle .............................................. 125.00
**Saltshaker,** Chrysanthemum Sprig ......................... 55.00 To 70.00
**Saltshaker,** Diamond Peg ................................................ 45.00
**Sauce Boat,** Louis XV, Gold Trim, Footed ............................. 55.00
**Sauce,** Argonaut Shell ........................................ 45.00 To 50.00
**Sauce,** Chrysanthemum Sprig, Blue .................................... 80.00
**Sauce,** Chrysanthemum Sprig, Oval, Northwood, Footed ............ 55.00
**Sauce,** Intaglio, Blue ...................................................... 55.00

| | |
|---|---|
| **Sauce,** Inverted Fan & Feather | 55.00 |
| **Sauce,** Louis XV | 65.00 |
| **Sauce,** Souvenir, Diamond Peg, Coney Island | 25.00 |
| **Saucer,** Geneva, Oval | 35.00 |
| **Saucer,** Indiana | 3.50 |
| **Shot Glass,** Souvenir, Ponca City, Oklahoma | 25.00 |
| **Shot Glass,** Thumbprint & Rose | 20.00 |
| **Shot Glass,** 14 Panels, Apple Transfer, Motto | 32.00 |
| **Spooner,** Argonaut Shell | 120.00 To 125.00 |
| **Spooner,** Beaded Circle | 80.00 |
| **Spooner,** Chrysanthemum Sprig | 70.00 To 95.00 |
| **Spooner,** Chrysanthemum Sprig, Blue | 250.00 To 310.00 |
| **Spooner,** Diamond Peg, Red Rose, 4 1/4 X 4 In. | 75.00 |
| **Spooner,** Fan | 55.00 |
| **Spooner,** Geneva, Red & Green | 65.00 |
| **Spooner,** Georgia Gem | 65.00 |
| **Spooner,** Inverted Fan & Feather, Gold Trim | 115.00 |
| **Spooner,** Iris | 165.00 |
| **Spooner,** Louis XV | 65.00 To 90.00 |
| **Spooner,** Trailing Vine | 50.00 |
| **Spooner,** Verde, Ivorina, Gold | 80.00 |
| **Spooner,** Winged Scroll | 55.00 |
| **Sugar & Creamer,** Argonaut Shell, Marked | 420.00 |
| **Sugar & Creamer,** Louis XV | 150.00 |
| **Sugar,** Argonaut Shell, Covered | 95.00 To 160.00 |
| **Sugar,** Chrysanthemum Sprig, Covered | 145.00 To 195.00 |
| **Sugar,** Chrysanthemum Sprig, Open | 70.00 |
| **Sugar,** Georgia Gem, Covered | 95.00 |
| **Sugar,** Horn Of Plenty, Flint, Signed Northwood, Covered | 60.00 |
| **Sugar,** Inverted Fan & Feather, Covered | 150.00 To 170.00 |
| **Sugar,** Little Gem, Enameled Flowers, Open | 30.00 |
| **Sugar,** Little Gem, Souvenir, Warner, New Hampshire, Green | 23.00 |
| **Sugar,** Louis XV, Covered | 110.00 |
| **Sugar,** Northwood, Grape | 75.00 |
| **Sugar,** Ring Band, Roses Trim, Covered | 150.00 |
| **Sugar,** Trailing Vine, Blue, Covered | 185.00 |
| **Syrup,** Geneva | 230.00 |
| **Table Set,** Chrysanthemum Sprig, Blue, 4 Piece | 1075.00 To 1450.00 |
| **Table Set,** Chrysanthemum Sprig, Gold Trim, 4 Piece | 575.00 |
| **Table Set,** Feather & Fan, Pink & Gold, 4 Piece | 750.00 |
| **Table Set,** Intaglio, Gold & Green Design, 4 Piece | 550.00 |
| **Table Set,** Louis XV, 4 Piece | 325.00 To 375.00 |
| **Tankard,** Pineapple & Fan, Newport, N.H., Marked, 1/2 Pint | 65.00 |
| **Toothpick,** Beaded Ring, Brunswick, Massachusetts | 50.00 |
| **Toothpick,** Button Arches, Revere Beach | 22.00 |
| **Toothpick,** Chrysanthemum Sprig | 185.00 |
| **Toothpick,** Geneva, Green & Gold Design | 110.00 |
| **Toothpick,** Georgia Gem | 55.00 |
| **Toothpick,** Georgia Gem, Green | 30.00 |
| **Toothpick,** Harvard | 30.00 |
| **Toothpick,** Inverted Fan & Feather, Gold Trim | 585.00 To 595.00 |
| **Toothpick,** Jefferson Optic, Conneaut Lake, Expo Park Shows | 55.00 |
| **Toothpick,** Lacy Medallion, Branch Mills, Maine | 16.00 |
| **Toothpick,** Ring & Beads | 20.00 |
| **Toothpick,** Roses, Wheaton, Minnesota | 75.00 |
| **Toothpick,** Souvenir, Fairbury, Nebraska | 35.00 |
| **Toothpick,** Souvenir, Manawa, Wisconsin | 45.00 |
| **Toothpick,** Souvenir, Old Orchard, Maine | 35.00 |
| **Toothpick,** Thumbprint | 40.00 |
| **Toothpick,** Tiny Thumbprint, Souvenir | 40.00 |
| **Toothpick,** Vermont, Blue Design | 75.00 |
| **Toothpick,** Wing Scroll | 325.00 |
| **Tray,** Dresser, Wing Scroll, Flowers | 230.00 |

Tumbler, Ale, Hotel Conneaut, Inscribed & Pictured ............................................................ 28.00
Tumbler, Chrysanthemum Sprig ............................................................ 50.00 To 60.00
Tumbler, Chrysanthemum Sprig, Gold Trim, Blue ............................................................ 240.00
Tumbler, Chrysanthemum Swirl ............................................................ 60.00
Tumbler, Fan Pattern, Northwood ............................................................ 75.00
Tumbler, Flute, Northwood ............................................................ 35.00
Tumbler, Geneva ............................................................ 50.00
Tumbler, Grape & Gothic Arches, Set Of 6 ............................................................ 295.00
Tumbler, Grape & Leaf, Purple, Northwood ............................................................ 40.00
Tumbler, Intaglio, Blue Design ............................................................ 48.00 To 65.00
Tumbler, Intaglio, Green, Gold Trim ............................................................ 58.00
Tumbler, Inverted Fan & Feather ............................................................ 55.00 To 65.00
Tumbler, Jackson ............................................................ 39.00 To 50.00
Tumbler, Louis XV ............................................................ 40.00 To 60.00
Tumbler, Maple Leaf, Northwood ............................................................ 65.00
Tumbler, Ring Band ............................................................ 50.00
Tumbler, Rose & Diamond Peg, Souvenir, Madison, Maine ............................................................ 55.00
Tumbler, Scroll With Flower, Fluted ............................................................ 40.00
Tumbler, Souvenir, High School, Brodhead, Wisconsin ............................................................ 55.00
Tumbler, Souvenir, Newaygo, Michigan ............................................................ 35.00
Tumbler, Souvenir, Norfolk, Virginia ............................................................ 35.00
Tumbler, Souvenir, Phoenix, Arizona ............................................................ 40.00
Vase, Crystal Edge, 8 In. ............................................................ 20.00
Vase, Howard, South Dakota ............................................................ 34.00
Vase, Pogo, Green, 7 1/2 In. ............................................................ 30.00
Vase, Prison Stripe, Signed, 4 1/2 In. ............................................................ 30.00
Water Set, Chrysanthemum Sprig, 7 Piece ............................................................ 625.00 To 750.00
Water Set, Diamond Peg, Rose Design ............................................................ 785.00
Water Set, Grape & Cable, Nutmeg, 7 Piece ............................................................ 1100.00
Water Set, Louis XV, Gold Trim, 7 Piece ............................................................ 450.00
Water Set, Maple Leaf, 7 Piece ............................................................ 645.00
Water Set, Vermont, 7 Piece ............................................................ 775.00
Whiskey, Diamond Peg, Souvenir, Jamaica, Vermont ............................................................ 38.00

*Cut glass has been made since ancient times, but the large majority of the pieces now for sale date from the brilliant period of glass design, 1880 to 1905. These pieces had elaborate geometric designs with a deep miter cut.*

### CUT GLASS, see also listings under factory names

CUT GLASS, Banana Boat, Fan Shaped, Pedestal, 8 1/2 X 9 X 4 1/4 In. ............................... 250.00
Banana Boat, Harvard Hobstars, Flowers, Scalloped, 7 1/2 X 11 In. ............................... 155.00
Banana Boat, Harvard, 14 In. ............................................................ 375.00
Basket, Allover Cut, Rope Handle, 5 X 8 1/2 In. ............................................................ 325.00
Basket, Diamond Field, Chain Of Bull's-Eyes, Oval, 6 X 5 1/2 In. ............................... 85.00
Basket, Floral, Cane & Crosshatch, Notched Handle, 7 1/2 In. ............................... 95.00
Basket, Fluted Top, Signed J.Hoare & Co., 1853, 9 1/2 X 14 In. ............................... 1500.00
Basket, Hobstars, Fan, Buzz Stars, Twisted Handle, 6 In. ............................................ 195.00
Bell, Dinner, Allover Cut Hobstars, 5 1/2 In. ............................................................ 285.00
Berry Set, Russian Pattern, 6 Sauces, 9 In.Diam.7 Piece ............................................ 100.00
Bonbon, Heavy Blank, Deep Cut, Signed Hoare, 7 X 6 1/2 In. ............................... 85.00
Bottle Cologne, Laydown, Cane Pattern, Silver Screw Top, 7 In. ............................... 165.00
Bottle, Barber, Sterling Stopper ............................................................ 255.00
Bottle, Cologne, Diamond Cut, Sterling Silver Top, 4 X 3 In.Diam. ............................... 95.00
Bottle, Cologne, 8-Star Cut, Stopper ............................................................ 90.00
Bottle, Perfume, Brilliant Cut, Allover Cut Stopper ............................................................ 75.00
Bottle, Perfume, Footed, Signed, Libbey, 8 In. ............................................................ 175.00
Bottle, Perfume, Hinged Lid, Allover Cut Circles, Royal Blue, 5 In. ............................... 350.00
Bottle, Perfume, Intaglio Flower & Design, Sterling Top, 4 3/4 In. ............................... 135.00
Bottle, Perfume, Squares & Stars, 6 X 8 In.Diam. ............................................................ 25.00
Bottle, Smelling Salts, Middlesex Pattern ............................................................ 75.00
Bottle, Water, Hobstar ............................................................ 65.00
Bowl, Adonis, Signed Clarke, 8 In.Diam. ............................................................ 225.00
Bowl, Allover Cut, Round, 22 In. ............................................................ 43.00

**Bowl,** American Brilliant, Hobstar Base, 9 In. ............................................................ 175.00
**Bowl,** American Brilliant, 4 Oval Russian Panels, 9 In.Diam. .............................. 265.00
**Bowl,** Beveled Prisms & Hobstars, 8 In.Diam. ........................................................ 125.00
**Bowl,** Brilliant Cut, Hobstar Rows, Intaglio Panels, 9 1/2 In.Diam. ................. 225.00
**Bowl,** Cluster Pattern, Allover Hobstars, 3 1/2 X 8 In.Diam .............................. 270.00
**Bowl,** Combination Of Cuttings, Signed Hoare, 12 X 8 1/2 In.Diam. ................ 765.00
**Bowl,** Cornucopia Variation, 8 1/2 In.Diam. ............................................................ 250.00
**Bowl,** Creswick, Signed Egginton, 2 X 8 In.Diam. ......................... 165.00 To 195.00
**Bowl,** Crossbars In Strawberry Diamond, Signed Hoare, 8 In.Diam. ................... 90.00
**Bowl,** Diamond Vesicas & Chain Vesicas, 5 1/2 X 11 3/4 In.Diam. ................... 225.00
**Bowl,** Eggnog, Double X Split Vesicas, Feathered, 10 1/2 X 8 In. ................... 750.00
**Bowl,** Expanding Harvard Pattern, 7 3/4 In.Diam. .................................................. 235.00
**Bowl,** Expanding Star, 9 In.Square ............................................................................ 425.00
**Bowl,** Fan & Pinwheels, 24-Point Bottom, 4 X 6 1/2 In.Diam. ............................. 48.00
**Bowl,** Fern, Hobstars & Feathered Fans, 3 Feet, 4 X 8 In.Diam. ..................... 125.00
**Bowl,** Finger, Russian Cut, Heavy Blank, Star Cut Buttom, 5 In. ....................... 160.00
**Bowl,** Footed, Harvard & Flowers, 7 3/4 X 5 1/2 In.Diam. ............................... 150.00
**Bowl,** Footed, Harvard Bands, Intaglio Flowers, 7 X 2 1/2 In. ............................ 85.00
**Bowl,** Fruit, Scalloped Rim, Hobstar & Crosshatch, 9 In.Diam. .......................... 50.00
**Bowl,** Hindoo Pattern, Curved-In Rim, Signed Hoare, 8 In. ............................... 295.00
**Bowl,** Hobstar & Fan Cut, 2 X 8 In.Diam. ................................................................ 80.00
**Bowl,** Hobstar, Hobnail, & Strawberry Diamonds, Signed Clarke, 7 In. ........... 150.00
**Bowl,** Hobstar, Ornate Sterling Rim, 3 X 3 In. ........................................................ 110.00
**Bowl,** Hobstars Rim, Strawberry Diamonds, Signed Hoare, 9 In.Diam. ............ 235.00
**Bowl,** Hobstars, Cane, Beading, Dorflinger, 8 In.Diam. ...................................... 165.00
**Bowl,** Hobstars, Signed Straus, 3 1/2 X 8 In.Diam. ............................................ 150.00
**Bowl,** Hobstars, Vesicas & Prism Cut, 10 1/4 In. .................................................. 185.00
**Bowl,** Lotus Design, Flat Bottom, Cut Hobstar, Signed, 8 In. ............................ 225.00
**Bowl,** Orange, Blackmere's Columbia Pattern .......................................................... 265.00
**Bowl,** Parisian Pattern, Scalloped Edge, Dorflinger, 10 X 5 In. ......................... 650.00
**Bowl,** Pinwheel, 8 In. ........................................................................................................ 140.00
**Bowl,** Pinwheels, Canes, & Hobstars, Scalloped Rim, 8 In.Diam. ........................ 85.00
**Bowl,** Pinwheels, Strawberries, Scalloped Edge, 8 X 3 1/2 In. ......................... 175.00
**Bowl,** Propellor Pattern, 8 In.Diam ............................................................................ 195.00
**Bowl,** Punch, Astoria Pattern, 10 In.Diam. ................................................................ 350.00
**Bowl,** Punch, Cross Star & Hatch, 11 Cups, 11 1/4 X 12 In. ............................... 475.00
**Bowl,** Sawtooth Rim, Hobstar & Cane, American, 10 In.Diam. .......................... 175.00
**Bowl,** Sawtooth Rim, Hobstar, Pinwheel, & Crosshatch, 9 In.Diam. .................... 70.00
**Bowl,** Star Rosette Pattern, W.C.Anderson Design, 9 In.Diam. ......................... 185.00
**Bowl,** Stratford Pattern, Turned-In Sides, 8 In.Diam. ............................................ 165.00
**Bowl,** Strawberry & Diamond, Feather Fan, Clarke, 9 In. ................................... 325.00
**Bowl,** Strawberry Diamonds, Gothic Points, 5 Panels, 5 X 9 1/2 In. ............... 325.00
**Bowl,** Strawberry Hobnail & Fan Cutting, C.1880, 10 1/2 In.Diam. .................. 175.00
**Bowl,** Thistles, Scalloped Sawtooth Rim, Signed Clarke, 6 In.Diam. ................... 90.00
**Bowl,** Vintage Pattern, Blue To Amber To Clear, 2 1/2 X 5 In.Diam. ............... 225.00
**Bowl,** Vintage, Flared, 3-Footed, Signed Tuthill, 6 X 3 1/2 In. ......................... 360.00
**Box,** Blown-Out Scalloped Sides, Diamond Field, 5 X 3 1/2 In. ........................... 85.00
**Box,** Collar, Cosmos Pattern, 4 X 7 1/2 In. .............................................................. 225.00
**Box,** Covered, Cane Pattern, Intaglio Cut, 4 3/4 X 3 In. ........................................ 85.00
**Box,** Jelly, Cover, Hobstar, Lapidary Knob Stem, 5 X 5 In.Diam. ....................... 150.00
**Box,** Powder, Daisies, Frosted, Leaves & Stems, Rayed Base, 5 In. ..................... 95.00
**Box,** Powder, Sterling Silver Hinged Lid, 3 X 5 In. ................................................ 225.00
**Box,** Star Cut Cover, Amber, Cranberry, & Clear, 4 In.Square ........................... 325.00
**Butter Pat,** Diamond & Fan, 3 In.Diam., Set Of 12 ............................................... 275.00
**Butter,** Allover Hobstars, Covered ............................................................................ 375.00
**Butter,** Harvard & Floral, Dome Top ......................................................................... 145.00
**Butter,** Hobstars & Fans, Covered ............................................................................. 200.00
**Butter,** Hobstars, Crosshatching, Covered, Signed Dorflinger .......................... 650.00
**Butter,** Hobstars, Zipper & Smooth Panels, Albany Design, 8 In. ..................... 325.00
**Butter,** Pinwheels, Cane, & Strawberries, Covered ............................................... 250.00
**Cake Stand,** Russian Pattern, Starred Buttons, 4 X 14 In., Pair ..................... 1500.00
**Cake Tray,** 3 Feet, Fluted Rim, Harvard & Cane, 9 In.Diam. ............................. 490.00
**Candleholder,** Hobstar Base, Teardrop Stem, 7 1/2 In., Pair ............................. 250.00

Candlestick, Diamond, Stars, & Fans, Teardrop, 8 In., Pair ................................ 395.00
Candlestick, Prism Pattern, Silver Plated Top & Bottom, Pair ........................... 125.00
Candlestick, St.Louis Diamond, Teardrop Stem, 8 1/2 In., Pair ......................... 940.00
Candlestick, Teardrop, Flute Cut, Rayed Base, Signed, 6 1/2 In. ....................... 145.00
Candlestick, Vintage Grape, Signed Tuthill, 10 In., Pair ..................................... 1300.00
Candlestick, Wild Rose Pattern, Signed, Roden Bros., 10 In., Pair ................... 350.00
Carafe, Bull's-Eye, Crosshatching, Diamond Fields, Fans ................................... 70.00
Carafe, Chrysanthemum Variation .......................................................................... 100.00
Carafe, Hobstars, Diamond & Fan, Rayed Base ................................................... 85.00
Carafe, Notched Panel Neck, Hobstars, Fans ....................................................... 85.00
Carafe, Pineapples, Stars, 8 In. ............................................................................... 75.00
Carafe, Russian Cut, Plain Bottom, 6 1/4 In. ....................................................... 145.00
Carafe, Water, Pinwheel & Hobstars ...................................................................... 65.00
Castor Set, 6 Bottles, Silver Plated Holder, Center Handle ............................... 325.00
Celery, Allover Cut, Serrated Edge, Heavy Blank ................................................ 85.00
Celery, Boat Shape, Strawberry & Cut Hobs, 11 1/2 X 4 3/4 In. ...................... 85.00
Celery, Cane Pattern, Signed Fry, 12 In. ............................................................... 85.00
Celery, Diamond Point, Flint ................................................................................... 20.00
Celery, Hobstar Center, Pinwheel End, Allover Cut, 10 1/2 In. ......................... 95.00
Celery, Hobstars & Thatching, 5 X 12 In. ............................................................. 250.00
Celery, Hunt's Royal, 11 1/2 In. .............................................................................. 165.00
Celery, Princeton, Pairpoint ................................................................................... 185.00
Chamberstick, Handle, Hobstars ........................................................................... 60.00
Champagne Cooler, Arcadia Pattern, 8 1/2 X 9 In.Diam. ................................... 625.00
Chandelier, 20 Light, George III Style, Ball Central, 43 In. ............................... 2200.00
Cheese Dish, Dome Cover, Hobstars, Plate, 9 3/4 In. ........................................ 450.00
Cheese Dish, Hobstars, Feathered Fans, 7 1/2 X 9 1/2 In.Wide ...................... 725.00
Clock, Harvard & Daisy, 5 1/2 X 4 In.Diam. ......................................................... 165.00
Clock, Harvard Pattern Sides, Allover Cut ........................................................... 375.00
Coaster, Wine Bottle, Hobstars & Notched Prisms, 9 1/2 In. ............................ 85.00
Cocktail, Notched Stem, Double Lozenge .............................................................. 60.00
Coffeepot, Baluster Body, Star Design, Banded Borders, 8 In. ......................... 1200.00
Compote, Comet Pattern, 5 1/2 In.Square ............................................................ 225.00
Compote, Crossed Ellipticals, Pinwheel, Step-Cut Base, 6 X 6 In. .................. 120.00
Compote, Double Teardrop Stem, Signed Hoare, 9 X 10 In.Diam. ................... 575.00
Compote, Fan & Hobstar, 8 In. ............................................................................... 165.00
Compote, Folded Rim, All Hobstars, 6 X 9 In. ...................................................... 135.00
Compote, Handled, Cut Hobs, Strawberry Diamond, 9 1/4 X 9 1/2 In. ........... 395.00
Compote, Harvard & Hobstars, Allover Cut, 11 1/2 X 8 In. ............................... 345.00
Compote, Hobstar, Fan & Diamond, Rayed Base, 7 1/2 X 6 In.Diam. ............. 125.00
Compote, Hobstars & Pinwheels, 7 X 7 In.Diam. ................................................ 410.00
Compote, Hobstars, Hobstar Base, 8 1/2 In. ....................................................... 325.00
Compote, Jelly, Hobstar Base, Notched Stem, 5 X 6 3/4 In. ............................. 110.00
Compote, Jelly, Lotus Pattern, Signed Egginton, 12 In. .................................... 565.00
Compote, Pluto Pattern, Signed Hoare, 8 1/2 In. ................................................ 275.00
Compote, Small Harvard & Hobstars, 11 1/2 X 8 In.Diam. ............................... 345.00
Compote, Strawberry Diamond Band, Hollow Stem, C.1865, 8 X 8 In. ........... 235.00
Compote, Swirl Pattern, Strauss, 8 1/2 X 6 In.Diam. ......................................... 235.00
Compote, Teardrop In Knob Stem, 6 3/4 X 7 In.Diam. ....................................... 365.00
Compote, Teardrop Stem, Turned-In Rim, Signed Hunt, 8 X 10 In. ................. 285.00
Compote, Vintage Design, Rolled Rim, Signed Tuthill, 10 In. ........................... 375.00
Compote, Vintage Pattern, Signed Sinclaire, 8 X 10 In.Diam. ......................... 525.00
Compote, 4-Sided, Starling Pattern, Square Top, 9 1/2 X 6 1/4 In. ................ 365.00
Cookie Jar, Allover Pinwheel & Beading, Brass Rim, 8 1/2 In. ......................... 295.00
Cordial Set, Clear & Cranberry, 10 Glass, Decanter 10 In. ............................... 350.00
Cracker Jar, Double X Split Vesicas, Feathered, Cut Base & Lid ..................... 595.00
Cracker Jar, Greek Key Pattern, Sterling Silver Cover, 8 1/2 In. ..................... 300.00
Creamer & Sugar, Royal Design .............................................................................. 255.00
Creamer & Sugar, Taylor, Pinwheel, Signed ........................................................ 125.00
Creamer, Hobstars .................................................................................................... 20.00
Cruet, Daisy & Fern, Blue Opalescent .................................................................... 70.00
Cruet, Diamond Cut Buttons, Pedestaled, Russian, Pair .................................... 225.00
Cruet, Diamond Point, Fan, & Star, 24-Point Bottom Star ................................ 35.00

Cruet, Double Lozenge Pattern, Cone Shape .................................................... 95.00
Cruet, Hobstars, Fans, Beaded Shoulders, Teardrop Stopper, 7 In. ................... 85.00
Cruet, Hobstars, Fans, Cut Handles, Pair ......................................................... 185.00
Cruet, Pineapple Cut, Zipper Neck, Original Stopper, 6 1/4 In., Pr. ................ 140.00
Cruet, Pinwheels, Allover Cut ........................................................................... 72.50
Cruet, Russian Pattern, 3 Corner, Step Cut Neck ............................................. 90.00
Cruet, Strawberry, Diamond, & Fan, Triple Cut Handle, 7 1/4 In. .................... 190.00
Cruet, Triple Spout, Lotus Variant, Faceted Stopper ........................................ 70.00
Cruet, Whirling Star With Hobstar, Stopper ...................................................... 48.00
Cup, Footed, Mortenson's Butterfly, 3 1/2 In., Set Of 4 .................................. 180.00
Cup, Punch, Brilliant Hobstars, Set Of 5 .......................................................... 120.00
Cup, Punch, Cranberry Cut To Clear, Brilliant ................................................. 200.00
Cup, Punch, Hobstar, Crosshatch, & Fan, 19th Century, Set Of 10 ................. 275.00
Cup, Punch, Hobstars, Fan, 8 Cups ................................................................. 200.00
Cup, Punch, Monarch, Set Of 6 ........................................................................ 175.00
Decanter, Allover Hobnail Pattern, Faceted Stopper, 8 1/2 In. ........................ 145.00
Decanter, Allover Hobstars, 11 In. ................................................................... 395.00
Decanter, Celtic Pattern, Ship Type, Dorflinger, 5 1/2 X 9 In. ........................ 530.00
Decanter, Crosscut Diamond, 12 In. ................................................................ 195.00
Decanter, Diamond Field, Star Cut, Cut Flower Blossom, 10 1/2 In. ............... 155.00
Decanter, Facet Stopper, Hobstars, Pinwheels, 13 1/2 In. .............................. 225.00
Decanter, Medallions, Blossom Shape Stopper, 10 1/2 In., Pair ..................... 155.00
Decanter, St.Louis Diamond Pattern, Teardrop Stopper, 10 1/2 In. ................ 275.00
Decanter, Star & Flower Design, Stopper, Signed Egginton, 11 In. ................. 175.00
Decanter, Teardrop Within, Honeycomb Neck, Dorflinger, 11 In. .................... 190.00
Decanter, Wine, Dorflinger, Cranberry To Clear, Stopper ............................... 900.00
Decanter, Yellow & Green Cut To Clear, 15 In. ............................................... 285.00
Dish, Allover Harvard Pattern, Triangular, 5 1/2 X 5 1/4 In., Pr. ..................... 225.00
Dish, American Shield Pattern, 5 X 3 X 12 In. ............................ 195.00 To 225.00
Dish, Candy, Allover Hobstars & Diamond, 6 In. .............................................. 45.00
Dish, Candy, Handle, Prism Pattern, 7 1/2 In.Diam. ....................................... 169.00
Dish, Candy, Handled, Pedestal, 4 1/2 X 7 In.Diam. ...................................... 90.00
Dish, Chip & Dip, Floral & Leaf Cutting, 10 1/4 In. ........................................ 90.00
Dish, Divided, Intaglio, Sterling Rim, 4 Compartment, 10 In. ......................... 250.00
Dish, Expanding Star, 2-Handled, 5 Section, 12 In.Diam. .............................. 325.00
Dish, Hobstars, Folded-Up Handles, 3 X 6 3/4 In. ......................................... 85.00
Dish, Hobstars, Strawberry Diamond, & Fans, Signed Hoare, 7 In. ................. 95.00
Dish, Stick, Hobnail Vesicas, 6 1/2 X 9 In.Diam ............................................ 335.00
Dish, Tricornered, Paris Pattern, Auerback ..................................................... 85.00
Ewer, Triple Overlay, Blue & White To Clear, 10 In. ....................................... 475.00
Feeder, Invalid, Harvard & Cosmos Pattern ..................................................... 85.00
Fernery, Allover Hobstars, Footed .................................................................... 135.00
Fernery, Footed, Hobstars & Fans, 4 1/2 X 8 In.Diam. ................................... 75.00
Fernery, Footed, Hobstars, Strawberry Diamonds, 4 X 6 3/4 In.Diam. ........... 75.00
Fernery, Footed, Pinwheels & Hobstars, 8 In.Long ......................................... 60.00
Fernery, Footed, Pinwheels, Hobstars, 7 1/2 In. ............................................. 55.00
Fernery, 3 Feet, Hobstars & Feathered Fans, 8 X 4 In. ................................... 95.00
Finger Bowl, Hobstars & Notched Prisms, Dorflinger, Set Of 6 ...................... 270.00
Finger Bowl, Russian Pattern, Set Of 6 ........................................................... 325.00
Flask, Harvard Design, Sterling Cap ................................................................ 85.00
Flask, Unger, Sterling Top ................................................................................ 150.00
Glue Pot, Brush, Silver Plated Lid .................................................................... 29.00
Goblet, Red Cherry Inside, Dorflinger, 5 1/4 In. ............................................. 135.00
Goblet, Strawberry Diamond, Zipper Stem, Rayed Base, 6 1/4 In. .................. 50.00
Goblet, Teardrop Stem, Diamond & Fan, 7 In., Set Of 12 ............................... 995.00
Goblet, Water, Double Lozenge Pattern ........................................................... 65.00
Goblet, Water, Kalana Hawthorne, Dorflinger .................................................. 85.00
Holder, Cigarette, Rock Crystal Design, Signed Hawkes ................................. 125.00
Humidor, Diamond & Fans, Cut Dome Dover, Ball Finial, 8 In. ...................... 145.00
Humidor, Diamond Field & Fans, Dome Cover, Ball Finial, 4 1/2 In. .............. 145.00
Humidor, Repousse Top, Inside Gold Wash, 6 1/2 X 5 1/2 In.Diam. ............. 375.00
Humidor, Ruby Stone Centered, Zipper Design, 5 1/2 In. ............................... 70.00
Humidor, Stopper & Base Cut In Pillar & Diamond, Oval ............................... 475.00

**Humidor,** Tobacco, Sterling Silver Cover .......................................................... 110.00
**Ice Bucket,** Allover Harvard Cut, 6 In. ............................................................... 295.00
**Ice Cream Set,** Russian Pattern, Tray, 15 X 8 In., 11 Piece .......................... 1100.00
**Inkwell,** Blue Prism, 2 1/2 In. ............................................................................. 135.00
**Inkwell,** Multifaceted Ball Stopper, Electric Blue, 3 1/2 In. ............................. 160.00
**Inkwell,** Sterling Top ........................................................................................... 165.00
**Jar,** Pill, Feathered Pinwheels, Hollow Stopper, 4 1/2 In. ................................. 110.00
**Jar,** Powder, Notched Prisms, Sterling Silver Top, 1 3/4 X 2 In. ....................... 28.00
**Jar,** Powder, Sterling Monogrammed Lid, Puff Top, 5 X 3 In. ........................... 100.00
**Jar,** Tobacco, Buzz Pattern, 9 In. ...................................................................... 125.00
**Jug,** Bull's-Eye Handles, Pinwheels On Sides, 6 1/2 X 5 1/4 In. ....................... 210.00
**Jug,** Cider, Allover Cut, 24 Ray Base .................................................................. 120.00
**Jug,** Syrup, Silver Top, 4 In. ................................................................................ 95.00
**Knife Rest,** Faceted Ball Ends, 5 1/2 In. ............................................................. 45.00
**Knife Rest,** Geometric Design, Ball Ends, 7 Panel Cut Bar .............................. 35.00
**Knife Rest,** Horizontal V Cuts, 6-Sided Center Bar ........................................... 45.00
**Knife Rest,** Notched Prism Cut Ball Ends & Bar, 5 1/2 In. ................................ 105.00
**Knife Rest,** Russian Pattern, Extra Large .......................................................... 150.00
**Knife Rest,** Square On Each End ........................................................................ 25.00
**Lamp,** Harvard Pattern, Long Prisms, 21 1/2 In. ................................................ 985.00
**Lamp,** Near Cut, Dome Shade, Silver Ring, Crystal Prisms, 18 In., Pr. ........... 750.00
**Lamp,** Pointed Dome, Harvard, Cornflowers & Leaves, Prisms, 18 In. ............ 395.00
**Lamp,** Vesicas Of Cane Shade, Harvard Cut Base, Prisms, 13 In. .................. 625.00
**Lamp,** Whale Oil, Blue, White, Clear, Brass Stem, 11 In. ................................. 295.00
**Liquor,** New Jersey Glass Co., 1915, Set Of 6, 5 In. ........................................ 100.00
**Loving Cup,** 3-Handled, Middlesex Pattern, Dorflinger, Large ....................... 1800.00
**Mayonnaise Set,** Hobstars & Cane, 5 1/2 In.Diam. .......................................... 185.00
**Mayonnaise Set,** Hobstars, Strawberries, 2 Piece .......................................... 95.00
**Muffineer,** Cane Pattern, 8-Sided, Pierced Dome Cover, 6 1/2 In. ................... 50.00
**Muffineer,** Pear Shape, Pedestal, Bull's-Eyes, Pierced Dome, 6 In. ............... 35.00
**Mustard,** Covered, Notched Prism, 4 In. ............................................................ 50.00
**Mustard,** Pewter Lid & Handle, 3 1/4 In. ............................................................ 65.00
**Napkin Ring,** 6-Sided, Harvard Pattern, 2 In. .................................................... 75.00
**Nappy,** Allover Cut, Handled, Divided Center, 10 In.Diam. ............................... 187.00
**Nappy,** Honeycomb Handles, 4 Section, Expanding Star, 12 In.Diam. ............. 395.00
**Nappy,** 3 Curled Legs, Handled, Fans & Hatching, 4 1/8 In.Diam. .................... 50.00
**Paperweight,** Russian Pattern, Border Flowers, 3 1/4 X 2 3/4 In. ..................... 240.00
**Pitcher,** Barrel Shape, Russian Pattern, 6 1/2 In. ................................. *Illus* 700.00
**Pitcher,** Cane Panels, Notched Handle, 19th Century, 10 3/4 In. ..................... 225.00
**Pitcher,** Champagne, Diamond & Intaglio, 9 In. ................................................ 495.00

Cut Glass, Pitcher, Barrel Shape, Russian Pattern, 6 1/2 In.

**Pitcher,** Cider, Avon Pattern, Bergen ........................................................................ 195.00
**Pitcher,** Cider, Parisian Pattern, Dorflinger ............................................................. 325.00
**Pitcher,** Diamond Fan Pattern, Bulbous Base, 5 In. ............................................... 125.00
**Pitcher,** Double Notch Cut Handle, Single Star Bands, 10 1/2 In. ....................... 135.00
**Pitcher,** Harvard Hobstars & Cane, 11 In. ................................................................ 345.00
**Pitcher,** Hindoo Pattern, Signed Hoare, 9 In. .......................................................... 325.00
**Pitcher,** Hobs, Pinwheel, Cane, Diamond, Scalloped Top, 12 1/2 In. .................... 300.00
**Pitcher,** Hobstars, Cane, Fan, Pedestaled, 15 In. .................................................. 1600.00
**Pitcher,** Hobstars, Diamond & Fan, Notched Handle, 8 1/2 In. .............................. 175.00
**Pitcher,** Hobstars, Diamond, Notched Handles, 4 1/4 In. ....................................... 110.00
**Pitcher,** Hobstars, Notched Handle, Rayed Base, 11 1/2 In. .................................. 185.00
**Pitcher,** Honeycomb Neck, Thumbprint Handle, Bulbous, 7 In. ............................. 225.00
**Pitcher,** Lotus Pattern, 11 In. ..................................................................................... 295.00
**Pitcher,** Milk, Barrel Shape, Strawberry Diamond & Fan, 5 1/2 In. ........................ 250.00
**Pitcher,** Milk, Colonial Pattern, Dorflinger, Diamond Handle, 6 In. ...................... 195.00
**Pitcher,** Milk, Russian Pattern, Scalloped Top, Dorflinger, 7 In. .......................... 850.00
**Pitcher,** Pinwheel Fans, Strawberry Diamond, Crosscut, 6 1/2 In. ....................... 145.00
**Pitcher,** Water, Brilliant Period, Crosscut Fan, Hobstar Base .............................. 325.00
**Pitcher,** Water, Crosscut Diamonds, Daisy Floral, 10 In. ...................................... 130.00
**Pitcher,** Water, Daisy & Foliage, 10 1/2 In. ............................................................... 65.00
**Pitcher,** Water, Deep Cut, Handle Triple Cut, 9 1/2 In. ........................................... 310.00
**Pitcher,** Water, Pinwheels, Long Spout, 13 In. ......................................................... 425.00
**Plate,** Floral & Harvard Design, 10 In. ...................................................................... 135.00
**Plate,** Hobstars, Fans & Miter Cuts, Scalloped Rim, 7 In. ....................................... 65.00
**Plate,** Parisian Pattern, Dorflinger, 8 1/2 In. ............................................................ 225.00
**Plate,** Prism Pattern, Bergen, 7 In. ........................................................................... 175.00
**Plate,** Russian Pattern, Pinched Sides, Square, 7 In. ............................................. 185.00
**Plate,** Stars, Fans, Miters, Scalloped In 8 Sections, 7 In. ....................................... 65.00
**Plate,** Swirl, Signed Hoare, 7 In. ............................................................................... 165.00
**Plate,** Wedding Ring, Sterling Border, 6 In. ............................................................... 35.00
**Rose Bowl,** Russian Pattern, American, 7 X 5 In.Diam. .......................................... 250.00
**Salt & Pepper,** Mother-Of-Pearl Centers, 3 1/4 In., Pair ......................................... 35.00
**Salt & Pepper,** Pinwheel, Sterling Silver Tops, 3 In. ................................................ 13.50
**Salt,** Diamond & Fans, Open, 1 3/4 In. ...................................................................... 22.00
**Salt,** Pedestal, Vintage Pattern, Set Of 3 ................................................................. 75.00
**Salt,** Sawtooth Edge, Pedestal .................................................................................. 20.00
**Salt,** Zipper Pattern, Set Of 6 .................................................................................... 50.00
**Shade,** Strawberry, Diamonds, & Fans, 4 3/4 X 4 1/4 In.Diam. ............................... 30.00
**Shaving Mug,** Notched Prism, Embossed Sterling Silver Rim ................................ 135.00
**Shot Glass,** Sunburst & Fan, 2 1/4 In. ....................................................................... 30.00
**Spooner,** Allover Crosscut Diamond, Scalloped, 5 1/4 In. ...................................... 105.00
**Spooner,** Child's, Allover Diamond & Fan, 3 1/4 In. ................................................. 90.00
**Spooner,** Child's, Diamond Field, Serrated Top, 3 1/2 In. ....................................... 250.00
**Spooner,** Radiant Pattern, Scalloped Rim ................................................................ 95.00
**Spooner,** Triple Notched Handles, Flared Top ......................................................... 140.00
**Sugar & Creamer,** Allover Cane Cut ......................................................................... 175.00
**Sugar & Creamer,** Baker & Gothic Pattern, T.B.Clark ........................................... 1000.00
**Sugar & Creamer,** Beverly Design ............................................................................ 115.00
**Sugar & Creamer,** Cambria Pattern, Egginton ........................................................ 245.00
**Sugar & Creamer,** Harvard Design ........................................................................... 165.00
**Sugar & Creamer,** Hobstar, Allover Cut, Triple Notched Handles ........................ 150.00
**Sugar & Creamer,** Hobstars, Allover Cut ................................................................. 110.00
**Sugar & Creamer,** Pear Shape, Floral, Crosshatch, & Cane, 5 In. ....................... 100.00
**Sugar & Creamer,** Pinwheel Design, Signed Taylor ............................................... 125.00
**Sugar & Creamer,** Roses With Cane ........................................................................ 60.00
**Sugar & Creamer,** Thumbprint Rims, Beverly Pattern, 7 In.Wide ......................... 115.00
**Sugar Shaker,** Allover Crosscut, Ornate Top, Sterling ........................................... 175.00
**Sugar Shaker,** Sterling Cover, Puffed-Out Flowers ................................................ 65.00
**Syrup,** Cranberry To Clear, Sterling Frame & Lid .................................................... 785.00
**Syrup,** Diamond & Fan, Rayed Base, Sterling Mountings & Lid ............................. 135.00
**Syrup,** Glenwood Pattern, Bergen, Silver Plated Top ............................................. 125.00
**Syrup,** Hinged Sterling Lid, Dorflinger's Renaissance ........................................... 100.00
**Syrup,** Hobstars & Fans, Silver Hinged Top, Collar, & Handle ............................... 135.00

Syrup, Intaglio Cut Grasshopper, Sterling Silver Hinged Cover .......................... 75.00
Syrup, Intaglio Cut, Silver Collar & Handle, Rayed Bottom, 9 In. ....................... 125.00
Syrup, Notched Prisms, Silver Plate Hinged Top & Handle ............................... 80.00
Syrup, Pineapple Design & Hobstar, Bulbous .............................................. 110.00
Syrup, Renaissance, Hinged Sterling Lid, Dorflinger ..................................... 100.00
Syrup, Vertical Notch Cut Prisms, Silver Hinged Top, Lid, & Handle ................... 125.00
Tankard, Cornflowers, Notched Top & Handle, 9 1/4 In. ................................. 75.00
Tankard, Hobstars, Crosshatching, & Prism, Single Star, 8 In. .......................... 150.00
Tankard, Pinwheels & Hobstars, Prism Spout, 9 1/2 In. ................................. 105.00
Tankard, Pitcher, Flower Design ............................................................. 95.00
Tankard, Step Cut Spout, Hunt's Royal ..................................................... 485.00
Tobacco Jar, Hexagonal Shape, Star Bottom, Sterling Lid ............................... 125.00
Toothpick, Strawberry Diamond & Fan, Canary Glass ................................... 35.00
Toothpick, Trough Shape, Side Tabs, Cane Pattern, 4 In. ............................... 25.00
Tray, Celery, Flashed Pinwheels ............................................................. 58.00
Tray, Cornucopia Pattern, 13 1/2 X 8 1/2 In. .......................................... 1500.00
Tray, Dresser, Allover Cut Flowers & Vines, 6 1/4 X 10 In. ............................ 145.00
Tray, Fans, Hobstars & Miter Cuts, Heavy Blank, 12 In. ................................ 285.00
Tray, Floral & Harvard, Oval, 10 1/2 X 17 In. ........................................... 275.00
Tray, Hobstars, Fans, Vesicas, 12 In.Diam. ............................................... 135.00
Tray, Hobstars, Nailhead Diamond, 12 In. ................................................. 395.00
Tray, Ice Cream, Empire Glass, Nelson ..................................................... 195.00
Tray, Ice Cream, Hobstar, Crosshatch, American, C.1900, 15 X 10 In. ............... 575.00
Tray, Ice Cream, Hobstar, Diamond Nailhead, 14 X 7 1/2 In. .......................... 300.00
Tray, Ice Cream, Russian Ambassador Pattern, 14 X 7 1/2 In. ......................... 250.00
Tray, Ice Cream, Vesicas, Fans, & Zippers, 16 In. ....................................... 900.00
Tray, Ice Cream, 41 Hobstars In Vesicas, Oval, 14 X 8 In. ............................. 395.00
Tray, Imperial, By Strauss, 7 1/2 X 14 In. ................................................ 125.00
Tray, Leaf Shape, Allover Hobs, Fans, & Beading, 12 X 5 1/2 In. ..................... 215.00
Tray, Monarch Pattern, Signed Hoare, 12 In.Diam. ...................................... 450.00
Tray, Pie, Allover Hobstars, Crossed Bars, 8 3/4 In.Diam. .............................. 355.00
Tray, Russian & Intaglio Pattern, Signed Tuthill, Oval, 1i 1/2 In. ..................... 425.00
Tray, Shagbark, Signed Libbey, 7 3/4 X 11 3/4 In. ...................................... 190.00
Tub, Ice, Dahlia Pattern, 22-Point Star Bottom, 7 X 5 1/2 In. ........................ 350.00
Tumble-Up, Harvard Pattern, Lip On Pitcher ............................................. 275.00
Tumble-Up, Pinwheel, Vesicas Of Strawberry Diamond, 5 X 7 In. .................... 675.00
Tumbler, Ginger Ale, 8 Gold Bands, Dorflinger, 6 Oz. ................................... 80.00
Tumbler, Hobstar & Drape Fan, Set Of 4 .................................................. 220.00
Tumbler, Hobstar & Fan, Crosshatching, 24-Star Base, 4 In. .......................... 25.00
Tumbler, Lemonade, Pinwheel Pattern, 5 In., Set Of 5 .................................. 60.00
Tumbler, Parisian Pattern ..................................................................... 65.00
Tumbler, Pineapple & Fan Pattern .......................................................... 13.75
Tumbler, Pinwheel ............................................................................. 22.00
Tumbler, Pinwheel, Fan, & Stars ............................................................ 15.00
Tumbler, Rose Pattern, Signed Tuthill, Pair ............................................... 100.00
Tumbler, Sand & Diamond Pattern, Set Of 6 ............................................. 75.00
Tumbler, Shagbark Pattern, Hoare ........................................................... 65.00
Vase, Aster Engraving, Signed Sinclaire, 10 In. .......................................... 100.00
Vase, Bergen's Comet, 24-Point Hobstar Base, 14 In. ................................... 300.00
Vase, Bucket Shape, Various Cuttings, 8 X 5 In. ......................................... 175.00
Vase, Chain Of Hobstars, Strawberry, & Prisms, 14 In. ................................. 195.00
Vase, Corset Shape, Daisy & Leaf, Sawtooth Edge, 14 In. .............................. 250.00
Vase, Corset Shape, Harvard Cut, Rayed Base, 8 In. .................................... 80.00
Vase, Corset Shape, Hobstars, Strawberries, 12 In. ..................................... 40.00
Vase, Cut Through Blue & White To Clear, Triple Overlay, 9 In. ...................... 400.00
Vase, Cylinder, Hobstars, Strawberries, & Diamonds, 14 In. ........................... 550.00
Vase, Daisies, 10 1/4 In. ..................................................................... 65.00
Vase, Dorflinger, Prism Cut, Emerald To Clear, 10 1/2 In. ............................. 250.00
Vase, Flower Shape, Bull's-Eyes, Hobstar Chains, Hoare, 12 In. ...................... 350.00
Vase, Fluted, Sprays Of Flowers & Leaves, 18 In. ....................................... 850.00
Vase, Henry VIII Pattern, Emerald Green, 8 In. .......................................... 365.00
Vase, Hobstars, Fans, Diamond, Signed, Taylor Boggess, 13 In. ...................... 175.00
Vase, Holly Pattern, 6 1/4 In. ............................................................... 200.00

Vase, Kalana Pansy, Stained, Dorflinger, Purple To Gold, 6 1/2 In. ........................................ 165.00
Vase, Maple Leaf Pattern, Maple City Glass, 11 7/8 In. .................................................... 395.00
Vase, Miniature, Strawberry Diamond & Fan, 3 3/4 In. ....................................................... 50.00
Vase, Paperweight Base, Lapidary Knob, 8 In. ............................................................... 115.00
Vase, Pedestal, Hobstar Paperweight Base, Intaglio Cut, 18 In. .......................................... 2000.00
Vase, Pinwheel, Fan, Hobstars, Notched Stem, 10 1/2 In. .................................................. 125.00
Vase, Russian Cutting On Rim, Floral & Leaves, 12 In. ...................................................... 90.00
Vase, Strawberry, Diamond, & Fan, Scalloped Rim, 3 3/4 In. ................................................ 50.00
Vase, Trumpet, Prism Columns, Unger Bros., Rims, 7 1/2 In., Pair ........................................ 145.00
Vase, Trumpet, Venetian, Notched Hobstar Base, 12 In. ..................................................... 550.00
Vase, Trumpet, Zipper Panels Alternating With Rayed Stars, 14 In. ....................................... 325.00
Vase, Tulip Shape, Hobstars, Diamond, & Fan, 17 In. ....................................................... 295.00
Vase, Violet, Pedestal, Faceted Knob Stem, Hobstars & Fans, 5 In. ...................................... 145.00
Vase, Zipper Stem, Bulbous Body, 9 1/2 In. ................................................................. 120.00
Vial, Perfume, Flute, Silver Caps, 1 Hinged, 1 Screw, 5 In. ............................................... 145.00
Vial, Perfume, Howard, Double, Brass Hinged Cap Each End, 6 In. ....................................... 175.00
Violet Bowl, Pedestal, Hobstars, Elongated Sunburst, 7 1/4 In. .......................................... 245.00
Wine Cooler, Sterling Silver Handle & Collar, 11 X 7 In.Diam. ............................................ 750.00
Wine, Faceted Stem, Green Bowl, Enameled, Dorflinger, 7 In., Pair ..................................... 100.00
Wine, Frosted Grape Design, Rayed Base, Set Of 6 ........................................................ 150.00
Wines, Rhine, Rayed Footing, Notched 6 Panel, Set Of 6 .................................................. 230.00

*Cut velvet is a special type of art glass made with two layers of blown glass, which shows a raised pattern. It usually had an acid finish or velvetlike texture. It was made by many glass factories during the late Victorian years.*

CUT VELVET, Vase, Diamond-Quilted, Pink, 10 In. ........................................................... 145.00
Vase, Pink & White, Ruffled, 9 In. ............................................................................. 180.00

*D'Argental is a mark used by the St. Louis, France, glassworks. The firm made multilayered, acid-cut cameo glass in the late nineteenth and twentieth centuries. D'Argental is the French name for the city of Munzthal, home of the glassworks. Later they made enameled etched glass. Compagnie des Cristalleries de St. Louis is still working.*

D'ARGENTAL, Atomizer, Bleeding Heart Pattern, 3 3/4 X 5 In. ........................................... 325.00
Bottle, Perfume, Scenic, Flying Birds, Yellow Ground, 4 In. ............................................... 795.00
Bowl, Autumnal Colors, 3 Cuttings, 3 1/2 X 6 In.Diam. ................................................... 795.00
Bowl, Brown Floral On Lighter Brown Ground, 5 1/2 X 10 In.Diam. ..................................... 985.00
Vase, Amber To Maroon, Leaves & Flowers, 12 1/2 In. ................................................... 1200.00
Vase, Autumnal Colors, 3 Cuttings, 6 In. ................................................................... 750.00
Vase, Blooming Flowers, Frosted Yellow Ground, 4 1/2 In. ............................................... 390.00
Vase, Blue Cut To Yellow, Frosted Landscape, Signed, 3 1/8 In. ........................................ 335.00
Vase, Boat Scene, Frosted Purple To White, Signed, 5 3/4 In. ........................................... 650.00
Vase, Boats On Water, Purple To White Ground, Signed, 5 3/4 In. ...................................... 650.00
Vase, Cobalt Blue & Pale Blue, 13 1/2 In. ................................................................. 875.00
Vase, Dark Blue To Hot Pink Flowers, Signed, 6 In. ...................................................... 795.00
Vase, Frosted Gold Ground, Landscape Scene, Signed, 4 X 3 1/2 In. ................................... 550.00
Vase, Frosted Pink Ground, Tree Landscape, Signed, 12 1/2 In. ......................................... 995.00
Vase, Gray Trumpet Flowers & Berries, Frosted Yellow, 4 1/2 In. ....................................... 310.00
Vase, Houses, Flying Birds, Apricot & Brown, Signed, 10 In. ........................................... 1350.00
Vase, Magenta Poppies, Umber Ground, 10 1/2 In. ....................................................... 725.00
Vase, Maroon Landscape, Frosted Gold Ground, Signed, 6 1/2 In. ...................................... 550.00
Vase, Pear Shape, Orange, Brown Floral Ground, Signed, 4 In. .......................................... 325.00
Vase, Pinecones & Needles, Pumpkin Ground, Signed, 9 1/4 In. ......................................... 875.00
Vase, Pink Gold Ground, Landscape, Acid Cut, Signed, 12 1/2 In. ...................................... 995.00
Vase, Rose Landscape Scene, Gold Ground, Signed, 3 1/2 In. ........................................... 550.00
Vase, Scenic Town, Stork & Little Ones In Nest, Signed, 9 3/4 In. ..................................... 2275.00
Vase, Translucent White Ground, Landscape, Signed, 2 3/8 In. .......................................... 275.00

Vase, Wine Colored Clematis, Blue Ground, 14 In. ............................................... 950.00
Vase, 2 Shades Of Blue, 7 1/4 In. ............................................... 800.00

*D'Aurys is a mark found on French cameo glass wares of the nineteenth century.*

D'AURYS, Vase, Mottled Green & Red, 7 1/2 In. ............................................... 350.00
    Vase, Mottled Green To Chartreuse, Roses, 5 1/2 In. ............................................... 235.00
      DAGUERREOTYPE, see Photography, Daguerreotype
      DANISH CHRISTMAS PLATE, see Bing & Grondahl, Collector Plate,
      Royal Copenhagen

*Daum Nancy is the mark used by Auguste and Antonin Daum on pieces of French cameo glass made after 1875.*

DAUM NANCY, Bottle, Perfume, Trumpet Flowers, Yellow Ground, Signed, 6 1/2 In. ......... 550.00
    Bowl, Autumn Forest Scene, Enameled Petal Top, Signed, 4 3/4 In. ............................. 850.00
    Bowl, Enameled Oranges & Foliage, Signed, 2 3/4 X 7 In. ............................. 435.00
    Bowl, Green Floral, Multicolor Frosted Ground, Signed, 8 In.Diam. ............................. 950.00
    Bowl, Green Flowers, Multicolored Ground, Signed, 3 1/2 In. ............................. 950.00
    Bowl, Rose, Gold Enameled Flowers, Gold Flakes, Signed, 6 1/2 In. ............................. 395.00
    Bowl, Stained Glass Cameo, Green Stylized Design, 9 X 3 3/4 In. ............................. 475.00
    Bowl, Winter Scene, Gold Ground, Enameled, Signed, 5 X 2 1/2 In. ............................. 750.00
    Bowl, Winter Snow & Tree Scene, Signed, 3 1/2 X 8 In.Diam. ............................. 1200.00
    Bowl, Yellow, Green, Persimmon Flowers, Signed, 2 1/2 X 5 In. ............................. 525.00
    Box, Cover, Winter Scene, Yellow Orange Ground, 3 In.Wide ............................. 750.00
    Box, Covered, Autumn Leaves & Cones, Frost Ground, 4 In.Wide ............................. 675.00
    Box, Covered, Winter Scene, Snow On Trees, Orange Ground, 3 In. ............................. 750.00
    Box, Nutlike Cones, Brown & Yellow, Frosted Ground, 4 In.Wide ............................. 550.00
    Cachepot, Forest Scene, Brown, Blue, Gray, Signed, 5 X 4 In. ............................. 985.00
    Chandelier, Aqua Bells, Berries, White Ground, Signed, 14 In.Diam. ............................. 1500.00
    Chandelier, Brass Chains & Frame, Blue & Green, Signed, 18 In. ............................. 1800.00
    Cordial Set, Gold Rim & Design, C.1920, Signed, Set Of 6 ............................. 350.00
    Dish, Mottled Orange, Purple, Gold Frog Center, Signed, 6 In. ............................. 695.00
    Glass, Shot, Lily Of The Valley, Gold Enameled, 1 1/2 In. ............................. 135.00
    Inkwell, Knob Top, Gold Foil Inside, Red-Orange & Gold, 5 In. ............................. 950.00
    Jardiniere, Blown Into Brass & Iron Frame, Signed, 12 X 12 In. ............................. 2000.00
    Lamp Base, Cameo & Enamel, Winter Scene, 8 In. ............................. 675.00
    Lamp, 6 Boats On Globe, City In Ground, Signed, 12 In. ............................. 3000.00
    Rose Bowl, Enameled Flowers, Mottled, Lobed, Signed, 5 1/2 In. ............................. 475.00
    Rose Bowl, Multicolored, Yellow Ground, Signed, 3 1/4 X 3 In. ............................. 325.00
    Rose Bowl, Squared Top, Purple & Gold, 2 3/4 In.Diam. ............................. 435.00
    Salt, Summer Scene, Oval ............................. 350.00
    Shade, Mottled Glass, Ruffled 5 In.Bottom, Signed, 5 In. ............................. 250.00
    Toothpick, Cut To Frosty White, Gold Enameled Flowers, Signed ............................. 225.00
    Toothpick, Enameled Palm Trees, House, & Water, Marked, 2 In. ............................. 700.00
    Toothpick, Enameled Scene, C.1900, Signed, 1 3/4 In. ............................. 700.00
    Toothpick, Enameled Trees & Houses, Marked, C.1900, 1 3/4 In. ............................. 700.00
    Tumbler, Barrel Shape, Frosted Ground, Mottled, Signed, 5 In. ............................. 335.00
    Tumbler, Emerald Green, Cased In Lime Green Foil, Signed ............................. 269.00
    Tumbler, Gold Leaf, Cranberry, Enameled & Cut, Signed, 5 In. ............................. 325.00
    Tumbler, White Enamel Dots, Gold Limbs, Green ............................. 225.00
    Vase, Allover Green Bottom, Pink & Purple, Mottled, 10 In. ............................. 495.00
    Vase, Apple Green, Black Layer Cut In Cameo, 1 1/2 X 1 3/4 In. ............................. 395.00
    Vase, Autumn Leaves, Gold Ground, Signed, 13 1/2 In. ............................. 650.00
    Vase, Banjo Shape, Scenic, Frosted Ground, Signed, 10 1/4 X 12 In. ............................. 2395.00
    Vase, Beige, Pink & Purple, Green Leaves, Applied Acorns, 5 In. ............................. 995.00
    Vase, Black & White, Blackbirds, Snowtrees, Signed, 4 In. ............................. 950.00

**Vase,** Blown-Out Landscape, Pebbled Ground, 11 1/4 In. ....................................... 4750.00
**Vase,** Blue Ground, Blue & Green Overlay, Signed, 7 5/8 In. ............................... 725.00
**Vase,** Boats On Lake, Autumn Colors, 14 In. ........................................................ 1350.00
**Vase,** Butterflies, Dragonfly, Embedded Carved Flowers, 22 In. ...................... 2400.00
**Vase,** Cameo & Enamel, Thistle Pattern, Amber, Signed, 9 In. ......................... 695.00
**Vase,** Chinese Red Poppies, Yellow Ground, Signed, 4 3/4 In. ......................... 650.00
**Vase,** Cone Shape, Yellow, 6 1/4 In. .................................................................... 310.00
**Vase,** Cut & Enameled, Frosted Ground, Signed, 6 7/8 X 4 1/4 In. ................... 450.00
**Vase,** Cut-Back & Gilt Fleur-De-Lis, Signed, 6 In. ............................................. 175.00
**Vase,** Dark Green & Peach Frosted, Signed, 6 In. .............................................. 595.00
**Vase,** Diamond-Shaped, Summer Scene, Enameled, Signed, 4 3/8 In. ............. 595.00
**Vase,** Emerald Green, Pink, White, & Blue Flowers, Signed, 12 In. ................... 495.00
**Vase,** Enameled Flowers, Buds, Gold Outlined, Signed, 12 In. .......................... 295.00
**Vase,** Flattened Oval, Barren Forest Landscape, Signed, 4 In. .......................... 795.00
**Vase,** Floral Design, Gold Outlined, Gold Rim, Square, 4 3/4 In. ...................... 455.00
**Vase,** Frosted Design, Etched, Signed, 11 1/2 In. .............................................. 350.00
**Vase,** Gilt Floral, Green To Clear Ground, Ovoid, Signed, 3 1/2 In. .................. 350.00
**Vase,** Grapevine Design, 2 Cuttings, 5 3/4 In. ................................................... 585.00
**Vase,** Green & Red, Cut Thistle, Gold Enameling, 4 In. ..................................... 675.00
**Vase,** Green Fern & Yellow Berries, Orange Ground, 18 In. ............................... 550.00
**Vase,** Green, Misletoe Design, Enamel Berries, 5 1/4 In. .................................. 225.00
**Vase,** Hen, Rooster, 2 Chicks, Enamel, Signed, 3 1/2 In. .................................. 875.00
**Vase,** Lake Scene, Frosted, Pinecones, Enameled, Signed, 5 1/4 In. ................ 395.00
**Vase,** Mottled Cream, Pink, & Purple, Enameled Cameo, 7 1/2 In. ................... 795.00
**Vase,** Mottled Gold, Trees, Enameled, Signed, 3 7/8 X 4 3/8 In. ...................... 850.00
**Vase,** Mottled Green & Amber, Gray Overlay, C.1900, Signed, 11 In. ................ 900.00
**Vase,** Nautical Scene, 5 Colors, Signed, 16 1/2 In. ........................................... 1850.00
**Vase,** Orange, Amber Frosted Ground, Berries, Blue, 8 1/2 In. .......................... 1650.00
**Vase,** Pink, Blue, Lavender Flowers, Bumblebee, Signed, 4 1/2 In. ................... 975.00
**Vase,** Pink, Frosted Pink Ground, Blossoms, Leaves, Signed, 11 In. ................. 400.00
**Vase,** Poppies & Bachelor Buttons, Yellow, Rust, Signed, 3 3/4 In. .................. 425.00
**Vase,** Purple Leaves & Ground, Gold Tracery, Signed, 4 1/4 In. ....................... 350.00
**Vase,** Rain Scene, Signed, 2 In. ......................................................................... 595.00
**Vase,** Red Berries, Chartreuse Leaves, Mottled, Signed, 15 In. ........................ 1250.00
**Vase,** Rising Sun, 7 Swallows, Signed, 9 3/4 In. ............................................... 1500.00
**Vase,** Rustic Fruit Design, Gold Frosted, Signed, 2 X 4 3/4 In. ......................... 195.00
**Vase,** Scenes In 3 Shades Of Red, Yellow Ground, Signed, 8 In. ...................... 995.00
**Vase,** Scenic, Boats, Lake, Autumn Colors, 14 In. ............................................. 1750.00
**Vase,** Scenic, Purples, Signed, 3 1/2 X 4 1/2 In. ............................................... 225.00
**Vase,** Scenic, 2 Spider Webs, 4 Colors, Signed, 4 X 4 In. ................................. 595.00
**Vase,** Smoky Glass, Concentric Bands, Barrel Shape, Signed, 8 In. .................. 300.00
**Vase,** Stick, Rose Color, Homogeneous, 17 1/4 In. ............................................. 140.00
**Vase,** Summer Scene, Urn, Pedestal Base, Signed, 12 1/2 In. ........................... 595.00
**Vase,** Sunset Scene, Sailboats On Red, Signed, 9 1/2 In. .................................. 985.00
**Vase,** Sunset Scene, Yellow & Pink Ground, Signed, 7 1/2 In. ........................... 750.00
**Vase,** Sweet Pea & Leaf Design, Yellow Ground, Signed, 6 1/2 In. .................... 325.00
**Vase,** Thistle, 5 In. ............................................................................................. 340.00
**Vase,** Trapped Air Bubbles, Crystal, Signed, 7 In. .............................................. 95.00
**Vase,** Trees, Water, Orange & Rust, Oval, Signed, 4 In. ...................................... 425.00
**Vase,** Trumpet Shape, Overlay Of Berries, Red, Signed, 7 1/2 In. ...................... 995.00
**Vase,** White, Pink, Lavender, Frosted, Signed, 3 1/4 In. ...................................... 385.00
**Vase,** Winter Scene, Flattened Cylinder, Signed, 6 1/2 In. .................................. 875.00
**Vase,** Winter Scene, Snow-Covered Ground, 18 Crows, Signed, 5 In. ................ 1750.00
**Vase,** Winter Scene, 20 1/2 In. ........................................................................... 2400.00
**Vase,** Yellow Mimosas, Gold Stem, Leaves, 5 5/8 In. ........................................ 350.00
**Vase,** 3-Color Ground, Blue & Green Overlay, C.1905, 7 5/8 In. ........................ 725.00
**Water Set,** Applied Amethyst Handle, Blue Cluthra, 5 Glasses ......................... 250.00

*Davenport pottery and porcelain were made at the Davenport Factory in Longport, Staffordshire, England, from 1793 to 1887. Earthenwares, creamwares, porcelains, ironstone wares, and other products were made. Most of the pieces are marked with a form of the word Davenport.*

DAVENPORT
LONGPORT
STAFFORDSHRE

**DAVENPORT, Bowl,** Vegetable, Covered, Flower Band, Gold Rim, C.1932 ................................ 18.00
    **Cup & Saucer,** Gold Rim, Scrolled Panels In Gold, C.1850 ...................................... 72.00
    **Cup & Saucer,** Gold Rims, Gold Band On Pedestal, C.1873 ................................ 40.00
    **Cup & Saucer,** Handleless, Floral Border, Rose In Bottom, C.1820 ..................... 70.00
    **Cup & Saucer,** 16 Scroll Panels, Gold Medallion In Well, C.1850 ..................... 72.00
    **Cup,** Handleless, Floral Border Inside Cup, C.1820 ......................................... 70.00
    **Dish,** Covered, Oriental Pattern, Blue & White, Oblong, 7 In. ......................... 45.00
    **Mug,** The Little Plunderer, Boy Robbing Bird Nest, 1805-20 ......................... 40.00
    **Plate,** Amoy, C.1844, Flow Blue, 9 In.Diam. .................................................. 68.00
    **Plate,** Blue, Ironstone, Impressed Anchor, 9 1/4 In. ...................................... 25.00
    **Plate,** Mulberry Print, View From Scott's Novels, C.1850, 10 In. .................... 40.00
    **Plate,** Orange Flowers, Cobalt, Gold Rim, 9 3/4 In.Square ......................... 60.00
    **Platter,** Impressed Anchor, Flowers & Birds ............................................... 100.00
    **Teapot,** Amoy, C.1844, Bulbous, Flow Blue ............................................... 340.00
    **Vase,** Gold Lion's Head Either Side, Gold Feet, C.1860, 6 In. ..................... 265.00

**DAVY CROCKETT, Bedspread** ............................................................................... 10.00
    **Bowl,** Cereal ................................................................................................ 5.00
    **Brush** ......................................................................................................... 95.00
    **Game,** Adventure ....................................................................................... 20.00
    **Jigsaw Puzzle** ........................................................................................... 6.00
    **Lunchbox** ................................................................................................... 10.00
    **Mug** ................................................................................ 4.00 To 10.00
    **Pistol,** Official, Flint Action .......................................................................... 18.00
    **Planter,** Canoe Shape, Ceramic ................................................................ 10.00
    **Puzzle,** Tray, Framed ................................................................................... 5.00
    **Rifle,** Original Package, 34 In. ..................................................................... 22.00
    **Ring,** Brass ................................................................................................. 15.00
    **Scarf,** With Slide ........................................................................................ 20.00
    **Suitcase** .................................................................................................... 12.50
    **Tray** ........................................................................................................... 15.00

**DE MORGAN, Tile,** Tan Flowers, Green Leaves, Blue Stripes, Signed, 6 In.Square ................ 125.00

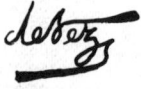

*De Vez is a name found on special pieces of French cameo glass made by
the Cristallerie de Pantin about 1890. Monsieur de Varreux was the art
director of the glassworks and he signed pieces "de Vez."*

**DE VEZ, Bowl,** Tricorn, Scenic, Gold Ground, Signed, 3 3/4 X 4 7/8 In.Diam. ......................... 895.00
    **Lamp,** Flowers, Fernery, Greens, Frosted Ground, Signed, 14 X 11 In. .................... 2750.00
    **Vase,** Blue Satin Ground, Brown Flowers, 2 Cuttings, Signed, 6 1/4 In. .................... 245.00
    **Vase,** Boat Scene, Maroon To Pink, Aqua Ground, Signed, 4 1/4 In. ...................... 495.00
    **Vase,** Bottle Shape, Sailboats, Pink Frosted Ground, Signed, 8 In. ...................... 695.00
    **Vase,** Cameo Scenic, Vines Hang Over Boats, 10 In. ...................................... 1250.00
    **Vase,** Navy Blue, Yellow On Pink, 3 Cuttings, Signed, 16 3/4 In. ...................... 2250.00
    **Vase,** Palm Trees, Mosque, 3 Cuttings, Gold Ground, Signed, 5 In. ...................... 695.00
    **Vase,** Sailboat, Fishermen, 16 In. ............................................................... 3500.00
    **Vase,** Sailboats, Salmon & Blue, Pink Ground, Signed, 6 1/2 In. ...................... 975.00
    **Vase,** Scalloped Top, Island & Houses, Yellow & Blue, Signed, 8 In. .................... 375.00
    **Vase,** Scenic, Blue, Yellow On Pink, 3 Acid Cuttings, Signed, 16 1/4 In. .................... 2250.00
    **Vase,** Signed, French, C.1905, 7 3/4 In. .................................................... *Illus* 550.00
    **Vase,** Translucent Pink Scene, Blue Cut To Yellow, 6 1/4 In. ...................... 550.00
    **Vase,** Venice Scene, Pink Lining, Yellow Ground, Signed, 8 7/8 In. .................... 995.00
    **Vase,** Water & Trees, Island, Frosted Gold Ground, Signed, 5 7/8 In. .................... 650.00
    **Vase,** Water Scene, Islands, Pink Frosted Ground, Signed, 6 1/4 In. .................... 650.00
    **Vase,** Winter Scene, Blue To Green, Signed, 5 3/4 In. .................................. 520.00
    **Vase,** Winter Scene, 2 People Walking, Blue Ground, Signed, 5 3/4 In. .................... 525.00

*Decoys are carved or turned wooden copies of birds. The decoy was placed in
the water to lure flying birds to the pond for hunters.*

**DECOY, Blue Bill Drake,** Crowell, Low Head, C.1910, Original Paint ......................... 975.00

De Vez, Vase, Signed, French, C.1905, 7 3/4 In.

Decoy, Canada Goose, Tin, Removable
Head, 21 1/2 In.

| | |
|---|---|
| **Blue Bill Hen,** Slope-Breasted, Mason, Original Paint | 450.00 |
| **Blue Wing Teal** | 55.00 |
| **Canada Goose,** Canvas Covered | 125.00 |
| **Canada Goose,** Metal Eyes, Gray & Black, 19th Century, 17 3/4 In. | 500.00 |
| **Canada Goose,** Tack Eyes, One Piece | 250.00 |
| **Canada Goose,** Tin, Removable Head, 21 1/2 In. ...........*Illus* | 200.00 |
| **Canvasback Drake,** Delaware River ...........*Illus* | 1300.00 |
| **Challenge Goldeneyes,** Mason, Original Paint, Pair | 475.00 |
| **Curlew,** Metal Beak & Feet, Carved, Wooden | 325.00 |
| **Dorwitcher,** Spring Plumage, William Bowman ...........*Illus* | 4600.00 |
| **Duck,** Arched Neck, Black Body, White On Head & Rear, 26 In. | 125.00 |
| **Duck,** Hand-Painted, Papier-Mache, Lacquered, Red & Gold, 24 In. | 100.00 |
| **Duck,** Papier-Mache, Victor Verilite Label | 43.00 |
| **Goose Shadow,** Neck Folds Down, Large | 65.00 |
| **Goose,** Balsa Wood, Herter | 80.00 |
| **Goose,** Preening Position, Head Buried In Feathers | 225.00 |
| **Goose,** Straight Neck, Gray & White Body, Feather Effect Back, 23 In. | 125.00 |
| **Mallard Drake,** Dodge, Hollow, All Original | 500.00 |
| **Mallard Drake,** Hollowed Body, Original Paint, C.1935 | 475.00 |
| **Mallard Drake,** Mason Factory ...........*Illus* | 900.00 |
| **Mallard Hen,** Mason Factory ...........*Illus* | 850.00 |
| **Mallard Hen,** Snaky Head, Hollow Body, Mason Challenge, Original Paint | 375.00 |
| **Mallard,** Glass Eye, Mason, Original Condition, Pair | 450.00 |
| **Mallard,** Patented 1887, Tin | 145.00 |
| **Mallard,** Swimming, Down East Decoy Co. | 475.00 |
| **Merganser Drake,** W.Cleaves, Chebeague Island, Original Paint | 600.00 |
| **Owl,** Glass Eyes, Large | 46.50 |
| **Owl,** Glass Eyes, Papier-Mache, 16 1/2 In. | 65.00 |
| **Premier Mallard Hen,** Mason, Original Paint | 550.00 |
| **Redhead Hen,** Glass Eye, Mason | 165.00 |
| **Redhead,** Mason, Original Paint | 325.00 |
| **Root-Headed Feeder,** Old Paint, Tack Eyes, 28 In. | 225.00 |
| **Shorebird,** Flat Type, Original Paint | 110.00 |
| **Shorebird,** New York | 175.00 |
| **Shorebird,** Stilt | 85.00 |
| **Shorebird,** Turnstone | 65.00 |
| **Shorebird,** Yellowlegs | 75.00 |
| **Snipe,** Folding, Painted, Metal | 24.50 |
| **Wood Duck Hen,** Dodge, Original Paint | 500.00 |

Decoy, Mallard Hen, Mason Factory

Decoy, Mallard Drake, Mason Factory

Decoy, Dorwitcher, Spring Plumage,
William Bowman

Decoy, Canvasback Drake, Delaware River

*(See Page 147)*

*Chelsea Keramic Art Works was established in 1872 in Chelsea,
Massachusetts, by members of the Robertson family. The factory closed
in 1889, and was reorganized as the Chelsea Pottery U.S. in 1891. It
became the Dedham Pottery of Dedham, Massachusetts, in 1895. The
factory closed in 1943. It was famous for its crackleware dishes, which
picture blue outlines of animals, flowers, and other natural motifs.*

| | |
|---|---:|
| **DEDHAM, Bowl,** Azalea, 5 1/4 In.Diam. | 185.00 |
| **Bowl,** Duck, 5 1/4 In.Diam. | 185.00 |
| **Bowl,** Grape, 7 X 3 In. | 150.00 |
| **Bowl,** Horsechestnut, 5 1/4 In.Diam. | 185.00 |
| **Bowl,** Iris, 5 1/4 In.Diam. | 185.00 |
| **Bowl,** Rabbits, 4 X 8 1/2 In.Diam. | 250.00 |
| **Bowl,** Snowtree, 5 1/4 In.Diam. | 195.00 |
| **Bowl,** Swan, 5 1/4 In.Diam. | 225.00 |
| **Bowl,** Turkey, 5 1/4 In.Diam. | 225.00 |
| **Cup & Saucer,** Azalea | 155.00 |
| **Cup & Saucer,** Duck | 165.00 |
| **Cup & Saucer,** Horsechestnut | 165.00 |
| **Cup & Saucer,** Magnolia | 145.00 |
| **Cup & Saucer,** Polar Bear | 250.00 |
| **Cup & Saucer,** Rabbit | 95.00 |
| **Cup & Saucer,** Snowtree | 155.00 |
| **Mug,** Rabbit Border Pattern, 2 Ear, Gray Ground, Marked, 5 1/2 In., Pr. | 550.00 |
| **Pitcher & Bowl,** Rabbit Design, Bowl With Swan, C.1920, 7 1/2 In. | 275.00 |
| **Pitcher,** Blue & White, Night & Day, 5 In. | 350.00 |
| **Pitcher,** Cock, Sunrise, Sunset, 4 1/2 In. | 400.00 |
| **Pitcher,** Rabbit Design, 5 In. | 210.00 |

Plate, Azalea, 8 In. .................................................................................................. 95.00
Plate, Azalea, 10 In. ................................................................................................ 145.00
Plate, Butterfly, White On Blue, Signed, 8 1/2 In. .................................................. 95.00
Plate, Butterfly, 6 In. ............................................................................................... 225.00
Plate, Duck, 6 In. .................................................................................................... 125.00
Plate, Duck, 8 In. .................................................................................................... 110.00
Plate, Duck, 8 1/2 In. ............................................................................................. 30.00
Plate, Duck, 10 In. .................................................................................................. 125.00
Plate, Elephant, 6 In. .............................................................................................. 235.00
Plate, Elephants, 9 3/4 In. ...................................................................................... 80.00
Plate, Grape, Blue On Gray, Signed, 9 3/4 In. ...................................................... 80.00
Plate, Horsechestnut, 8 In. ..................................................................................... 95.00
Plate, Horsechestnut, 10 In. ................................................................................... 155.00
Plate, Iris, 6 In. ....................................................................................................... 115.00
Plate, Iris, 8 In. ....................................................................................................... 95.00
Plate, Iris, 10 In. ..................................................................................................... 110.00
Plate, Lobster Center, 8 1/2 In. .............................................................................. 150.00
Plate, Magnolia, 6 In. .............................................................................................. 115.00
Plate, Magnolia, 8 In. .............................................................................................. 95.00
Plate, Polar Bear, 6 In. ........................................................................................... 245.00
Plate, Polar Bear, 8 In. ........................................................................................... 245.00
Plate, Polar Bear, 10 In. ......................................................................................... 285.00
Plate, Pond Lily Pattern, Impressed & Stamped Marks, 6 In. ............................... 55.00
Plate, Rabbit, 6 In. .................................................................................................. 95.00
Plate, Rabbit, 8 In. .................................................................................................. 85.00
Plate, Rabbit, 8 1/2 In. ..................................................................... 85.00 To 100.00
Plate, Rabbit, 10 In. ................................................................................................ 95.00
Plate, Snowtree, 6 In. ............................................................................................. 125.00
Plate, Snowtree, 8 In. ............................................................................................. 100.00
Plate, Snowtree, 10 In. ........................................................................................... 125.00
Plate, Swan, 6 In. .................................................................................................... 200.00
Plate, Swan, 8 In. .................................................................................................... 245.00
Plate, Turkey, 6 In. .................................................................................................. 225.00
Plate, Turkey, 8 In. .................................................................................................. 225.00
Plate, Turkey, 8 1/2 In. ........................................................................................... 195.00
Plate, Turkey, 10 In. ................................................................................................ 250.00
Salt & Pepper, Rabbits ........................................................................................... 275.00
Sugar, Open, Azalea, 3 1/2 X 2 In. ........................................................................ 100.00
Vase, Oxblood, Impressed, C.1895, 11 In. ...........................................*Illus* 4700.00
Vase, Oxblood, Volcanic Glaze, Chelsea Keramic, C.1895, 11 In. ...................... 4700.00

DEGUE, Vase, Art Deco, Deep Blue, Acid Signature, 7 1/4 In. ............................ 150.00
    Vase, Bulbous Base, Scenic, 2 Houses, Trailing Leaves, Signed, 6 In. ................ 645.00

Dedham, Vase, Oxblood, Impressed, C.1895, 11 In.

*Delatte glass is a French cameo glass made by Andre Delatte. It was first made in Nancy, France, in 1921. Lighting fixtures and opaque glassware in imitation of Bohemian opaline were made.*

**DELATTE, Box,** Lidded, Lavender & Purple, Signed, 3 1/4 X 4 1/2 In. ....... 600.00
**Jar,** Sweetmeat, Frosted Gold, Brown Mushroom, Signed, 3 5/8 In. ....... 650.00
**Vase,** Girl At Lake, Boat, Castles, Blue Ground, Signed, 10 1/2 In. ....... 975.00
**Vase,** Mauve Scene, 2 Acid Cuttings, Pink Ground, Signed, 7 In. ....... 695.00
**Vase,** Mottled Blues & Greens, White Flowers, Signed, 9 3/4 In. ....... 895.00
**Vase,** Translucent Ground, 2 Cuttings, 7 1/2 In. ....... 395.00
    **DELAWARE, see Custard Glass, Pressed Glass**
    **DELDARE, see Buffalo Pottery, Deldare**

*Delft is a tin-glazed pottery that has been made since the seventeenth century. It is decorated with blue on white or with colored decorations. Most of the pieces sold today were made after 1891, and the name Holland appears with the Delft factory marks.*

**DELFT, Bottle,** Liquor, House Shape, Dutch Airlines ....... 12.00
**Butter Pat,** Blue Scalloped Edge, Windmill & Building, 3 1/2 In., Pr. ....... 30.00
**Canister Set,** Blue & White, 12 Piece ....... 195.00
**Canister,** Sugar, Blue, White, & Gold ....... 28.00
**Charger,** Flowering Plants, Liverpool, C.1760, 13 1/4 In. ....... 500.00
**Coffee Grinder** ....... 125.00
**Creamer,** Cow, Blue ....... 5.00
**Decanter,** Wine, Musical, 4 Cups, Windmill Scene, Blue ....... 125.00
**Dish,** Quatrefoil, Flower Center, C.1765, 9 3/4 In.Diam. ....... 400.00
**Dish,** 2 Dancing Dwarfs, Jester Costumes, C.1731, 11 1/4 In.Diam. ....... 500.00
**Inkstand,** Trefoil, Polychrome, Silver Inkwells, C.1733, 7 3/4 In. ....... 2800.00
**Jar,** Apothecary, Farm Landscape In Scrolls, Blue, 9 1/4 In. ....... 150.00
**Plaque,** Blue & White, Allegorical, 16 In. ....... 225.00
**Plaque,** Couple On One-Horse Sleigh, Marked, 15 1/2 In.Diam. ....... 55.00
**Plate,** Cake, Cottage Scene ....... 47.50
**Plate,** Floral Medallions, Windmills, Sailboats, Marked, 8 1/2 In. ....... 36.00
**Plate,** Flower Border, Marked, 8 In. ....... 18.00
**Plate,** Peacock Center, Regina Crown Mark, 9 In. ....... 95.00
**Plate,** Polychrome Peacock, Iron Red, C.1765, 8 3/4 In., Pair ....... 550.00
**Plate,** Polychrome Vases Of Flowers, C.1765, 9 1/4 In. ....... 420.00
**Salt & Pepper,** Windmill, Blades Turn, Marked Holland ....... 15.00
**Sugar & Creamer,** Windmill ....... 20.00
**Tay,** Pin, Reticulated Rim, Marked, 5 In. ....... 23.00
**Tea Set,** Portrait On Pot, Sugar & Creamer, Blue & White ....... 65.00
**Tile,** Dutch Scene, Blue, 6 X 6 In. ....... 28.00
**Tobacco Jar,** Blue, Stylized Flowers, Rolled Rim, 18th Century, 7 In. ....... 325.00
**Tray,** Pin, 5 In. ....... 22.00
**Tumbler,** Hand-Painted, Signed, Groningen, Holland ....... 40.00
**Tureen,** Windmills & Sailboats, Handled, Covered ....... 95.00
**Vase,** Blue On White Blossoms & Sprigs, C.1830, 7 In., Pair ....... 650.00
**Vase,** Scenic, Blue & White, 6 1/2 In. ....... 67.50
    **DENTIST, see Medical**

*Depression glass was an inexpensive glass manufactured in large quantities during the 1920s and early 1930s. It was made in many colors and patterns by dozens of factories in the United States. The name "Depression glass " is a modern one.*

**DEPRESSION GLASS, Ashtray,** Pineapple & Floral, Crystal ....... 10.00
**Berry Bowl,** Bubble, Blue, 8 3/8 In. ....... 9.00
**Berry Bowl,** Cherry Berry, Green, 7 1/2 In. ....... 8.00
**Berry Bowl,** Fortune, Pink, 4 In. ....... 2.00
**Berry Bowl,** Lorain, Green, 8 In. ....... 50.00
**Berry Bowl,** Lorain, Yellow, 8 In. ....... 75.00

Berry Bowl, Lydia Ray, Green, 8 In. .................................................................... 6.00
Berry Bowl, Normandie, Iridescent, 5 In. ............................................................ 4.00
Berry Set, Cherry Blossom, Pink  ........................................................................ 55.00
Berry Set, Diana, Pink, 7 Piece  .......................................................................... 25.00
Bonbon, Strawberry, Green, Open Handles, 6 In.Diam. ..................................... 16.50
Bottle, Cologne, Moonstone .................................................................................. 10.00
Bowl Set, Waterford, Graduated, Large Bowl, 8 In.Diam. ................................. 35.00
Bowl, Block, Green, 4 1/4 In. ............................................................................... 2.50
Bowl, Bubble, Blue, 4 1/2 In. ............................................................................... 3.00
Bowl, Cameo, Green, 8 1/2 In. ............................................................................. 15.00
Bowl, Cereal, American Sweetheart, Cremax  ...................................................... 10.00
Bowl, Cereal, American Sweetheart, Monax  ........................................................ 10.00
Bowl, Cereal, American Sweetheart, Pink  ........................................... 5.00 To 6.50
Bowl, Cereal, Dogwood, Green ............................................................................. 7.50
Bowl, Cereal, Georgian, Green  ............................................................................. 7.00
Bowl, Cereal, Petal Ware, Off-White  .................................................................... 2.50
Bowl, Cereal, Ring, Crystal  .................................................................................. 1.50
Bowl, Cherry Blossom, Delphite, 4 3/4 In. .......................................................... 8.50
Bowl, Cherry Blossom, Green, 9 In. ..................................................................... 18.50
Bowl, Cherry Blossom, Pink, 1-Handled, 10 In.  .................................................. 10.00
Bowl, Colonial, Green, 9 In. .................................................................................. 13.00
Bowl, Console, American Sweetheart, Red  ....................................................... 1095.00
Bowl, Console, Madrid, Amber  ............................................................................. 10.00
Bowl, Coronation, Pink, 6 1/2 In. .......................................................................... 2.50
Bowl, Cubist, Green, 4 1/2 In. ............................................................................... 3.50
Bowl, Diamond-Quilted, Blue, 7 In. ....................................................................... 9.50
Bowl, Doric, Green, 4 1/2 In. ................................................................................ 6.00
Bowl, Doric, Pink, Handled, 9 In. .......................................................................... 20.00
Bowl, Floragold, Iridescent, Ruffled, 5 1/2 In. ..................................................... 3.00
Bowl, Floral, Green, 7 1/2 In. ................................................................................ 2.00
Bowl, Fruit, Iris, Crystal, 11 In. ............................................................................. 8.50
Bowl, Fruit, Lace Edge, Pink, 3-Footed, 10 1/2 In.  ............................................ 65.00
Bowl, Fruit, Sharon, Pink, 10 1/2 In. ..................................................................... 13.00
Bowl, Georgian Lovebirds, Green, 4 1/2 In. ......................................................... 4.00
Bowl, Lace Edge, Pink, 9 1/2 In. ........................................................................... 7.50
Bowl, Laurel Band, Jadite, 9 In. ............................................................................ 12.00
Bowl, Lorain, Green, 7 1/4 In. ............................................................................... 28.00
Bowl, Lotus & Dragon, Pink, 8 1/2 In. .................................................................. 15.00
Bowl, Madrid, Amber, 5 In. .................................................................................... 3.00
Bowl, Mayfair, Blue, Scalloped, 12 In. .................................................................. 32.00
Bowl, Mayfair, Frosted, Hand-Painted, Pink, 9 1/2 In. ......................................... 8.00
Bowl, Mayfair, Pink, Flared, 12 In. ........................................................................ 25.00
Bowl, New Century, Green, 8 In. ........................................................................... 6.50
Bowl, Oyster & Pearl, Ruby, 10 1/2 In. ................................................................. 20.00
Bowl, Radiance, Ruby, Crimped, Flat, 10 In. ........................................................ 35.00
Bowl, Radiance, Ruby, Flat, 13 In. ........................................................................ 35.00
Bowl, Royal Lace, Blue, 10 In. ................................................................ 18.00 To 26.00
Bowl, Royal Lace, Cobalt Blue, Rolled Edge, 10 1/2 In. ...................................... 37.50
Bowl, Royal Lace, Cobalt Blue, 3-Footed, 10 In. .................................................. 40.00
Bowl, Salad, Royal Ruby, 11 In. ........................................................................... 20.00
Bowl, Salad, Swirl, Ultramarine, 9 In. ................................................................... 10.00
Bowl, Sharon, Amber, 8 1/2 In. ............................................................................. 3.50
Bowl, Sharon, Pink, 10 1/2 In. .............................................................................. 12.50
Bowl, Sierra, Pink, 8 In. ........................................................................................ 6.00
Bowl, Sierra, Pinwheel, Pink, 5 In. ....................................................................... 6.00
Bowl, Swirl Petal, Ultramarine, 9 In. ..................................................................... 8.50
Bowl, Vegetable, Moderntone, Cobalt Blue, 8 3/4 In. .......................................... 20.00
Bowl, Wedding Band, Blue, 4 3/4 In. ..................................................................... 6.00
Bowl, Windsor, Pink, 4 3/4 In. ............................................................................... 4.50
Box, Cigarette, Moonstone, Opalescent, Covered  ............................................... 6.00
Butter, Adam, Green  .......................................................................................... 295.00
Butter, Adam, Pink ................................................................................. 25.00 To 50.00
Butter, Cherry Blossom, Pink ............................................................................... 60.00

**Butter,** Cherry, Green ............................................................................... 35.00
**Butter,** Cherry, Green, Covered ............................................................ 65.00
**Butter,** Cherry, Pink, Covered .............................................................. 35.00
**Butter,** Chinex, Ivory, Covered ............................................................ 75.00
**Butter,** Colonial, Green, Covered ......................................................... 30.00
**Butter,** Columbia, Crystal ..................................................................... 12.00
**Butter,** Floral & Diamond, Green ......................................................... 80.00
**Butter,** Floral, Green, Covered ............................................. 48.00 To 50.00
**Butter,** Florentine, Pink ...................................................................... 240.00
**Butter,** Holiday, Pink, Covered ............................................................ 30.00
**Butter,** Iris & Herringbone, Clear, Covered ......................... 25.00 To 28.00
**Butter,** Lace Edge, Pink, Covered ...................................................... 45.00
**Butter,** Madrid, Amber ......................................................................... 45.00
**Butter,** Madrid, Amber, Covered ......................................................... 22.00
**Butter,** Madrid, Green, Covered .......................................................... 17.00
**Butter,** Mayfair, Blue ......................................................................... 225.00
**Butter,** Mayfair, Pink ........................................................... 12.50 To 35.00
**Butter,** Miss America, Crystal ........................................................... 185.00
**Butter,** Miss America, Green .............................................................. 450.00
**Butter,** Miss America, Pink ................................................................ 350.00
**Butter,** Patrician, Amber ...................................................................... 58.00
**Butter,** Patrician, Amber, Covered ...................................................... 45.00
**Butter,** Pinwheel, Green, Covered ....................................................... 37.50
**Butter,** Princess, Pink .......................................................................... 20.00
**Butter,** Princess, Pink, Covered .......................................................... 50.00
**Butter,** Royal Lace, Clear, Covered ..................................... 35.00 To 75.00
**Butter,** Royal Lace, Green .................................................................. 280.00
**Butter,** Sharon, Amber, Covered ......................................................... 25.00
**Butter,** Sharon, Pink ............................................................................ 27.50
**Butter,** Sharon, Pink, Covered ............................................................ 30.00
**Butter,** Swirl, Ultramarine, Covered .................................................. 175.00
**Butter,** Windsor, Crystal ...................................................................... 16.00
**Butter,** Windsor, Crystal, Covered, Tall Knob ..................................... 19.75
**Candleholder,** Dolphin, Green, Hexagon Base ..................................... 30.00
**Candleholder,** Dolphin, Green, 4 In. ..................................................... 15.00
**Candleholder,** Moonstone, Opalescent, Pair ......................................... 8.75
**Candlestick,** Dolphin, Pink, 3 1/4 In., Pair .......................................... 25.00
**Celery,** Miss America, Pink .................................................................. 12.50
**Celery,** Tearoom, Green ......................................................................... 2.00
**Child's Set,** Cherry Blossom, Delphite Blue, 14 Piece ....................... 225.00
**Coaster,** Adam, Green ........................................................................... 15.00
**Coaster,** Cherry Blossom, Pink ............................................................ 50.00
**Cocktail,** Boopie, Forest Green .............................................................. 3.00
**Compote,** Cameo, Green, 4 In. ............................................................. 14.00
**Compote,** Moondrops, Amethyst, 4 In. ................................................. 20.00
**Compote,** Pineapple & Floral, Crystal, 6 1/2 In. ................................... 3.00
**Compote,** Rock Crystal, Pink, Footed, 7 In. ......................................... 23.00
**Console Bowl,** Cameo, Green .............................................................. 38.00
**Console Bowl,** Rock Crystal, Green, Footed, 12 In. ............................. 39.75
**Console,** Cameo, Green ........................................................................ 38.00
**Cookie Jar,** Cameo, Green .................................................... 25.00 To 35.00
**Cookie Jar,** Cobalt Blue, Royal Lace, Metal Top ................................. 45.00
**Cookie Jar,** Madrid, Amber .................................................................... 8.00
**Cookie Jar,** Mayfair, Pink ..................................................... 12.00 To 25.00
**Cookie Jar,** Open Lace, Pink ................................................................ 10.00
**Cookie Jar,** Patrician, Amber ................................................ 42.00 To 50.00
**Cookie Jar,** Princess, Green .................................................. 12.00 To 27.50
**Cookie Jar,** Royal Lace, Blue .............................................................. 225.00
**Cookie Jar,** Royal Lace, Green ............................................................ 16.00
**Cookie Jar,** Royal Lace, Pink ............................................................... 18.00
**Cracker Jar,** Mayfair, Pink ................................................................... 20.00
**Creamer,** Adam, Pink ............................................................................. 7.00
**Creamer,** Cherry Blossom, Delphite ................................................... 15.50

Creamer, Cherry Blossom, Pink .................................................................... 9.00
Creamer, Cherry, Pink, Child's ................................................................... 25.00
Creamer, Cubist, Green ............................................................................. 6.50
Creamer, Floragold, Iridescent ................................................................. 3.00
Creamer, Georgian, Green, 4 In. ............................................................... 6.00
Creamer, Laurel Band, Ivory ...................................................................... 8.00
Creamer, Laurel Band, Ivory, Child's ...................................................... 15.00
Creamer, Laurel Band, Jadite .................................................................... 8.00
Creamer, Madrid, Amber ........................................................................... 5.00
Creamer, Miss America, Pink .................................................... 9.50 To 12.00
Creamer, Moderntone, Blue .......................................................... 4.50 To 5.00
Creamer, Patrician, Green .......................................................................... 6.00
Creamer, Princess Feather, Amber ............................................................ 7.50
Creamer, Royal Lace, Blue ...................................................... 15.00 To 21.00
Creamer, Sharon, Amber ........................................................................... 6.00
Creamer, Starlight, Clear ........................................................................... 5.00
Creamer, Victory, Green ............................................................................ 5.00
Cup & Saucer, Adam, Green ..................................................................... 18.00
Cup & Saucer, American Sweetheart, Monax ............................... 8.00 To 9.00
Cup & Saucer, Bubble, Blue ...................................................................... 4.00
Cup & Saucer, Bubble, Ruby ..................................................................... 7.00
Cup & Saucer, Cameo, Green .................................................................. 13.00
Cup & Saucer, Candlewick, Crystal .......................................................... 7.50
Cup & Saucer, Cherry Blossom, Pink ...................................... 13.00 To 14.00
Cup & Saucer, Cloverleaf, Black .............................................................. 12.50
Cup & Saucer, Coronation, Pink ............................................................... 3.50
Cup & Saucer, Cremax, White, Child's ..................................................... 3.00
Cup & Saucer, Daisy, Amber ........................................................ 4.50 To 5.00
Cup & Saucer, Dogwood, Pink .................................................................. 8.50
Cup & Saucer, Floral, Green .................................................................... 11.00
Cup & Saucer, Georgian, Green ................................................................ 6.50
Cup & Saucer, Golden Wedding, Marigold ............................................... 6.50
Cup & Saucer, Horseshoe, Green ............................................................. 8.00
Cup & Saucer, Iris, Iridescent ................................................................... 8.00
Cup & Saucer, Iris, Marigold ..................................................................... 7.00
Cup & Saucer, Jubilee, Yellow ................................................................... 8.50
Cup & Saucer, Laurel Band, Jadite ........................................................... 7.00
Cup & Saucer, Lydia Ray, Green ............................................................... 8.00
Cup & Saucer, Madrid, Amber ................................................................... 7.50
Cup & Saucer, Miss America, Pink ........................................ 15.00 To 17.50
Cup & Saucer, Moderntone, Blue ............................................................. 6.00
Cup & Saucer, Moderntone, Pink .............................................................. 1.50
Cup & Saucer, Molly, Cobalt Blue Opalescent ........................................ 19.75
Cup & Saucer, Moondrops, Amber ............................................................ 9.50
Cup & Saucer, Moondrops, Amethyst ...................................................... 14.75
Cup & Saucer, Newport, Blue .................................................................... 5.50
Cup & Saucer, Normandie, Amber ............................................................ 6.00
Cup & Saucer, Parrot, Green ................................................................... 29.50
Cup & Saucer, Patrican, Amber, Set Of 12 ............................................. 15.00
Cup & Saucer, Petalware, Cremax ............................................................ 6.00
Cup & Saucer, Petalware, Cremax, Pastel Bands ..................................... 6.50
Cup & Saucer, Pinwheel, Pink ................................................................... 7.50
Cup & Saucer, Pretzel, Crystal .................................................................. 3.50
Cup & Saucer, Princess, Green ................................................................. 9.00
Cup & Saucer, Princess, Yellow ................................................................ 7.00
Cup & Saucer, Queen Mary, Pink .............................................................. 6.50
Cup & Saucer, Rosemary, Amber .............................................................. 3.75
Cup & Saucer, Round Robin, Green .......................................................... 4.25
Cup & Saucer, Sharon, Amber ...................................................... 5.00 To 7.00
Cup & Saucer, Victory, Green .................................................................... 6.00
Cup & Saucer, Victory, Pink .......................................................... 4.00 To 6.00
Cup, Block, Green ..................................................................................... 3.50
Cup, Diana, Clear, Child's ......................................................................... 3.00

| | |
|---|---:|
| **Cup,** Laurel Band, Ivory | 4.50 |
| **Cup,** Madrid, Amber | 5.00 |
| **Cup,** Mayfair, Amber | 7.00 |
| **Cup,** Miss America, Green | 16.00 |
| **Cup,** Moderntone, Amethyst | 5.00 |
| **Cup,** Moondrops, Cobalt Blue | 8.00 |
| **Cup,** Normandie, Pink | 4.00 |
| **Cup,** Patrician, Green | 4.00 |
| **Cup,** Primo, Green | 3.50 |
| **Cup,** Queen Mary, Pink | 4.00 |
| **Cup,** Raindrops, Green | 3.50 |
| **Cup,** Roulette, Green | 3.00 |
| **Cup,** Royal Lace, Blue | 13.00 |
| **Cup,** Sierra, Pink | 5.25 |
| **Decanter,** Mayfair, Pink, Stopper | 65.00 To 75.00 |
| **Decanter,** Radiance, Ruby, Stopper | 75.00 |
| **Dish,** Candy, Adam, Pink, Covered | 40.00 |
| **Dish,** Candy, Cameo, Green, Covered | 40.00 To 44.95 |
| **Dish,** Candy, Cloverleaf, Green, Covered | 30.00 |
| **Dish,** Candy, Cubist, Pink, Covered, Footed | 20.00 |
| **Dish,** Candy, Doric, Pink, Covered | 14.00 |
| **Dish,** Candy, Forest, Green, Aluminum Handles & Base | 3.00 |
| **Dish,** Candy, Iris, Crystal | 75.00 |
| **Dish,** Candy, Mayfair, Blue | 125.00 |
| **Dish,** Candy, Mayfair, Yellow, Covered | 500.00 |
| **Dish,** Candy, Miss America, Crystal, Covered | 40.00 |
| **Dish,** Candy, Ribbon, Green, Covered | 12.00 To 15.00 |
| **Dish,** Candy, Sharon, Pink, Covered | 30.00 |
| **Dish,** Miss America, Pink, 4-Sectioned | 15.00 |
| **Flower Frog,** Figural, Owl, Green, 5 In. | 22.00 |
| **Goblet,** Cape Cod, Crystal, 8 Ounce | 3.50 |
| **Goblet,** Herringbone & Iris, Clear, 4 1/4 In. | 8.50 |
| **Goblet,** Iris, Crystal, Water | 12.50 |
| **Goblet,** Moondrop, Red, 4 Ounce | 9.75 |
| **Ice Bucket,** Cameo, Green | 85.00 |
| **Ice Bucket,** Frosted Ribbon, Ruby Red | 20.00 |
| **Jar,** Candy, Princess, Green, Covered | 26.00 |
| **Ladle,** Candlewick, Crystal, 5 In. | 2.00 |
| **Lamp,** Dolphin, Electrified, Pink, Figural, 12 In., Pair | 80.00 |
| **Lamp,** English Hobnail, Pink, 9 1/4 In. | 75.00 |
| **Measuring Cup,** Hazel Atlas, Green | 6.00 |
| **Measuring Cup,** Kellog's, Pink | 9.00 |
| **Mug,** Bubble, Blue, Fire King, Hocking, 8 Ounce | 14.00 |
| **Mug,** Cherry Blossom, Pink, Pair | 125.00 |
| **Mustard,** Swirl, Green | 5.00 |
| **Nappy,** Block, Green, 4 1/2 In. | 3.00 |
| **Nappy,** Candlewick, Crystal, Heart Shape, 6 In. | 8.50 |
| **Pitcher,** American Sweetheart, Pink, 7 1/2 In. | 310.00 |
| **Pitcher,** Cherry Blossom, Pink, 8 In. | 22.00 |
| **Pitcher,** Floral, Pink, 7 1/2 In. | 20.00 |
| **Pitcher,** Juice, Cameo, Green | 45.00 |
| **Pitcher,** Juice, Madrid, Amber | 20.00 |
| **Pitcher,** Juice, Manhattan, Crystal | 10.00 |
| **Pitcher,** Juice, Mayfair, Blue | 60.00 |
| **Pitcher,** Lydia Ray, Green, 8 In. | 17.50 |
| **Pitcher,** Lydia Ray, Pink, 7 3/4 In. | 15.00 |
| **Pitcher,** Mayfair, Blue, 8 1/2 In. | 105.00 |
| **Pitcher,** Mayfair, Blue, 80 Ounce | 60.00 |
| **Pitcher,** Mayfair, Pink, 6 In. | 12.00 |
| **Pitcher,** Mayfair, Pink, 8 In. | 22.00 |
| **Pitcher,** Milk, Windsor, Clear, 16 Ounce | 7.50 |

Pitcher, New Century, Pink, 60 Ounce ................................................................................. 16.00
Pitcher, Old English, Amber, Covered, 6 Footed Tumblers ............................. 100.00
Pitcher, Princess, Green, 8 In. ........................................................................................... 30.00
Pitcher, Royal Ruby, 42 Ounce ......................................................................................... 15.00
Pitcher, Water, Cherry Blossom, Green ...................................................................... 20.00
Pitcher, Water, Floragold, Marigold ............................................................................... 45.00
Pitcher, Water, Iris, Crystal ......................................................................... 12.00 To 19.50
Pitcher, Water, Iris, Pink, Footed, 9 In. .................................................................... 18.00
Pitcher, Water, Mayfair, Pink .......................................................................................... 25.00
Pitcher, Water, Royal Lace, Cobalt Blue .......................................... 70.00 To 85.00
Pitcher, Water, Sailboat, Cobalt Blue ................................................. 25.00 To 33.00
Pitcher, Windsor, Crystal, 16 Ounce ........................................................................... 12.00
Pitcher, Windsor, Crystal, 52 Ounce ............................................................................. 8.00
Pitcher, Windsor, Pink, 52 Ounce ................................................................................. 24.00
Plate, Adam, Green, 7 3/4 In. ............................................................. 5.00 To 6.00
Plate, Adam, Pink, 6 In. ....................................................................................................... 4.00
Plate, Adam, Pink, 7 3/4 In. .............................................................................................. 6.00
Plate, Adam, Pink, 8 In. ....................................................................................................... 8.00
Plate, Adam, Pink, 10 In. .................................................................................................... 10.00
Plate, American Sweetheart, Monax, 8 In. ..................................... 4.00 To 6.00
Plate, American Sweetheart, Monax, 10 In. ........................................................... 11.00
Plate, American Sweetheart, Pink, 6 In. .................................................................... 2.50
Plate, American Sweetheart, Pink, 12 In. ...................................... 8.00 To 12.00
Plate, American Sweetheart, Red, 8 In., Three ...................................................... 80.00
Plate, Block Optic, Yellow, 8 In., Set Of 6 ............................................................ 15.00
Plate, Bubble, Blue, 6 3/4 In. .......................................................................................... 1.25
Plate, Bubble, Blue, 9 1/2 In. ........................................................................................... 3.00
Plate, Cake, Holiday, Pink ................................................................................................. 25.00
Plate, Cake, Mayfair, Blue, Open Handles, 14 In. ............................................. 45.00
Plate, Cake, Miss America, Pink ........................................................ 18.00 To 25.00
Plate, Cake, Petalware, Monax, Gold Trim .............................................................. 6.00
Plate, Cake, Sharon, Pink ..................................................................................Illus 16.00
Plate, Cake, Sunflower, Pink ............................................................................................ 12.00
Plate, Cameo, Green, 6 In. ................................................................................................ 2.50
Plate, Cameo, Green 10 In. ................................................................... 10.00 To 11.50
Plate, Cameo, Yellow, 6 In. ................................................................................................ 1.50
Plate, Candlewick, Crystal, 8 1/2 In. ........................................................................... 7.00
Plate, Cherry Blossom, Delphite, Child's ................................................................. 6.50
Plate, Cherry Blossom, Pink, 7 In. ................................................................................. 9.95
Plate, Cherry Blossom, Pink, 7 In., Set Of 6 ........................................................ 50.00
Plate, Cherry Blossom, Pink, 10 In. ...........................................................Illus 9.00
Plate, Coronation, Pink, 8 1/2 In. ................................................................................. 3.00
Plate, Cubist, Pink, 6 In. .....................................................................................Illus 1.50
Plate, Daisy, Amber, 6 In. ...................................................................... 1.50 To 1.95
Plate, Delphite, Green, 6 In. ............................................................................................. 10.00
Plate, Diamond-Quilted, Pink, 8 In. ............................................................................. 3.25
Plate, Dogwood, Green, 8 In. ........................................................................................... 4.00
Plate, Dogwood, Pink, 6 In. .............................................................................Illus 3.50
Plate, Dogwood, Pink, 9 1/2 In. ..................................................................................... 12.50
Plate, Dogwood, Pink, 10 In. ............................................................................................ 12.00
Plate, Doric, Pink, 10 In. ..................................................................................................... 5.00
Plate, Floral, Pink, 6 In. .......................................................................................Illus 3.00
Plate, Florentine No.I, Green, 6 In. ...........................................................Illus 1.50
Plate, Florentine No.2, Topaz, 9 1/2 In. ...............................................Illus 10.00
Plate, Fruits, Green, 8 In. ................................................................................................... 3.25
Plate, Georgian, Green, 8 1/2 In. .................................................................................. 8.00
Plate, Grill, Cameo, Green ................................................................................................. 6.50
Plate, Grill, Cameo, Yellow .................................................................... 5.00 To 6.50
Plate, Grill, Cloverleaf, Green .......................................................................................... 2.00
Plate, Grill, Daisy, Crystal, 10 3/8 In. ........................................................................ 2.00
Plate, Grill, Dogwood, Pink ............................................................................................... 7.50

*(See Page 155)*

Depression Glass, Plate, Cherry Blossom, Pink, 10 In.

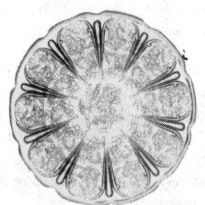

Depression Glass, Plate, Cake, Sharon, Pink

Depression Glass, Plate, Cubist, Pink, 6 In.

Depression Glass, Plate, Dogwood, Pink, 6 In.

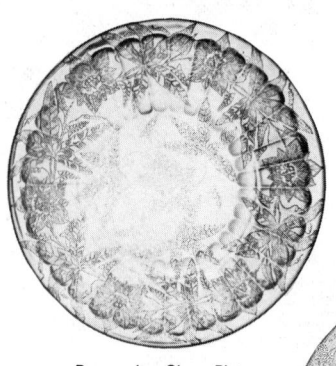

Depression Glass, Plate,
Floral, Pink, 6 In.

Depression Glass, Plate,
Florentine No.I,
Green, 6 In.

Depression Glass, Plate, Florentine No.2, Topaz, 9 1/2 In.

Depression Glass, Plate, Grill, Patrician, Crystal

Depression Glass, Plate, Grill,
Normandie, Iridescent

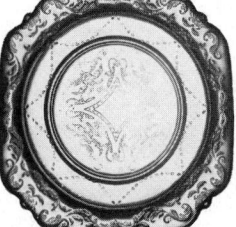

Depression Glass, Plate, Madrid,
Amber, 10 1/2 In.

Depression Glass, Plate,
Mayfair, Pink, 6 1/2 In.

Depression Glass, Plate, Miss
America, Pink, 8 In.

| | | |
|---|---|---|
| **Plate,** Grill, Mayfair, Blue | | 16.00 |
| **Plate,** Grill, Miss America, Pink | | 10.00 |
| **Plate,** Grill, Normandie, Iridescent | *Illus* | 4.00 |
| **Plate,** Grill, Patrician, Amber | | 5.00 |
| **Plate,** Grill, Patrician, Crystal | *Illus* | 6.50 |
| **Plate,** Grill, Princess, Amber | | 7.50 |
| **Plate,** Grill, Princess, Green, Tab-Handled | | 5.50 |
| **Plate,** Grill, Princess, Yellow | | 5.50 |
| **Plate,** Grill, Rosemary, Amber | | 3.25 |
| **Plate,** Grill, Royal Lace, Blue | | 14.00 |
| **Plate,** Iris, Marigold, 10 In. | | 11.00 |
| **Plate,** Jubilee, Yellow, 8 3/4 In. | | 4.50 |
| **Plate,** Knife & Fork, Pink, 6 In. | | 2.00 |
| **Plate,** Laurel, Green, 6 In. | | 2.50 |
| **Plate,** Laurel, Jade, 8 3/4 In. | | 4.00 |
| **Plate,** Lorain, Topaz, 10 In. | | 30.00 |
| **Plate,** Lorain, Yellow, 7 In. | | 6.00 |
| **Plate,** Madrid, Amber, 10 1/2 In. | *Illus* | 5.00 |
| **Plate,** Mayfair, Pink, 6 1/2 In. | *Illus* | 6.50 |
| **Plate,** Miss America, Pink, 8 In. | *Illus* | 7.00 |
| **Plate,** Miss America, Pink, 8 1/2 In. | | 8.75 |
| **Plate,** Miss America, Pink, 10 In. | | 14.00 To 15.00 |
| **Plate,** Moderntone, Cobalt Blue, 8 In. | *Illus* | 4.00 |
| **Plate,** Molly, Green Opalescent, 8 In. | | 5.00 |

Depression Glass, Plate, Moderntone,
Cobalt Blue, 8 In.
(See Page 157)

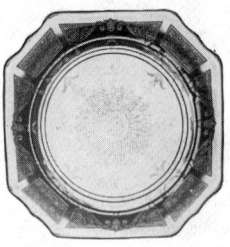

Depression Glass, Plate,
Princess, Green, 7 In.

| | |
|---|---:|
| **Plate**, Moondrop, Amber, 6 In. | 2.50 |
| **Plate**, Moonstone, Opalescent, Ruffled, 10 1/2 In. | 12.50 |
| **Plate**, Moonstone, Opalescent, 8 In. | 6.25 |
| **Plate**, Moroccan, Amethyst, 8 In. | 4.00 |
| **Plate**, Newport, Blue, 8 In. | 2.00 |
| **Plate**, Newport, Blue, 8 1/2 In. | 6.00 |
| **Plate**, Oyster & Pearl, Ruby, 13 1/2 In. | 17.00 |
| **Plate**, Parrot, Green, 9 In. | 19.75 |
| **Plate**, Patrician, Amber, 7 1/2 In. | 5.50 |
| **Plate**, Patrician, Amber, 9 In. | 5.00 |
| **Plate**, Patrician, Amber, 11 In. | 8.00 |
| **Plate**, Patrician, Crystal, 9 In. | 6.50 |
| **Plate**, Patrician, Green, 7 In. | 7.50 |
| **Plate**, Petal Swirl, Ultramarine, 6 1/2 In. | 2.25 |
| **Plate**, Petalware, Cremax, Pastel Bands, 8 In. | 5.00 |
| **Plate**, Petalware, Cremax, 9 In. | 5.00 |
| **Plate**, Petalware, Cremax, 10 1/2 In. | 10.00 |
| **Plate**, Pineapple & Floral, Amber, 8 3/8 In. | 10.00 |
| **Plate**, Pink Cherry, 10 In., Set Of 5 | 45.00 |
| **Plate**, Princess, Green, 7 In. *Illus* | 5.00 |
| **Plate**, Ring, Crystal, 6 In. | .50 |
| **Plate**, Rock Crystal, Crystal, 12 In. | 14.00 |
| **Plate**, Rock Crystal, Green, 8 In. | 6.00 |
| **Plate**, Rock Crystal, Red, 8 In. | 14.00 To 20.00 |
| **Plate**, Rope, Green, 9 1/2 In. | 14.50 |
| **Plate**, Rosemary, Amber, 6 3/4 In. | 2.50 |
| **Plate**, Roulette, Green, 6 In. | 1.00 |
| **Plate**, Royal Lace, Blue, 6 In. | 3.50 |
| **Plate**, Royal Lace, Blue, 10 In. | 16.00 |
| **Plate**, Royal Lace, Pink, 9 1/2 In. | 7.00 |
| **Plate**, Sherbet, Aunt Polly, Blue | 3.00 |
| **Plate**, Sherbet, Florentine II, Yellow | 2.25 |
| **Plate**, Sierra, Green, 10 In. | 5.00 |
| **Plate**, Starlight, Clear, 8 In. | 3.50 |
| **Plate**, Twisted Optic, Green, 8 In. | 1.25 |
| **Plate**, Waterford, Pink, Handled, 10 1/2 In. | 6.00 To 6.50 |
| **Platter**, Cherry Blossom, Green, 11 In. | 15.00 To 16.00 |
| **Platter**, Cherry Blossom, Pink, 13 In. | 27.50 |
| **Platter**, Doric, Green, 12 In. | 14.00 |
| **Platter**, Petalware, Cremax, 13 In. | 12.00 |
| **Reamer**, Jenny, Ultramarine, Footed | 75.00 |
| **Relish**, Cameo, Green | 5.00 |
| **Relish**, Cameo, Green, 3-Section | 11.00 |
| **Relish**, Florentine No.2, Pink, Divided | 10.50 |
| **Relish**, Horseshoe, Yellow | 4.50 |

| | |
|---|---|
| **Relish,** Lorain, Green, 4-Section | 12.50 |
| **Relish,** Miss America, Pink | 12.50 |
| **Relish,** Moondrops, Dark Green, 3-Section, 8 1/4 In. | 22.50 |
| **Relish,** Moonstone, Opalescent, Cloverleaf Shape | 5.75 |
| **Salt & Pepper,** American Sweetheart, Monax | 185.00 |
| **Salt & Pepper,** Cameo, Green | 50.00 |
| **Salt & Pepper,** Cloverleaf, Green | 15.00 To 20.00 |
| **Salt & Pepper,** Colonial, Green | 80.00 |
| **Salt & Pepper,** Dogwood, Green | 27.00 |
| **Salt & Pepper,** Floral Pattern, Pink | 21.00 |
| **Salt & Pepper,** Florentine No.2, Green | 28.00 |
| **Salt & Pepper,** Florentine, Pink | 43.00 |
| **Salt & Pepper,** Lydia Ray, Green | 20.00 |
| **Salt & Pepper,** Madrid, Amber | 30.00 To 32.50 |
| **Salt & Pepper,** Mayfair, Frosted Pink, Pair | 40.00 |
| **Salt & Pepper,** Mayfair, Pink, Pair | 45.00 |
| **Salt & Pepper,** Miss America, Green, Square-Footed, Pair | 375.00 |
| **Salt & Pepper,** Moderntone, Blue | 5.00 |
| **Salt & Pepper,** Moderntone, Cobalt Blue | 20.00 |
| **Salt & Pepper,** Moderntone, Pink | 5.00 |
| **Salt & Pepper,** Moderntone, White | 5.00 |
| **Salt & Pepper,** Patrician, Amber | 20.00 To 40.00 |
| **Salt & Pepper,** Shamrock, Black | 70.00 |
| **Salt & Pepper,** Sharon, Amber | 20.00 |
| **Salt & Pepper,** Sharon, Pink | 25.00 To 30.00 |
| **Salt & Pepper,** Sharon, Pink, Pair | 38.00 |
| **Salt & Pepper,** Swirl, Ultramarine | 20.00 To 21.00 |
| **Salt & Pepper,** Tearoom, Green | 39.75 |
| **Saltshaker,** Cloverleaf, Green | 7.50 To 9.00 |
| **Saltshaker,** Doric, Pink | 8.00 |
| **Saltshaker,** Florentine No.2, Topaz | 12.50 |
| **Saltshaker,** Normandie, Amber | 12.00 |
| **Saltshaker,** Royal Lace, Blue | 55.00 |
| **Saucer,** Adam, Green | 3.50 |
| **Saucer,** Block, Green, 6 1/8 In. | 2.00 |
| **Saucer,** Florentine No.2, Yellow | 20.00 |
| **Saucer,** No.612, Horseshoe, Green | 2.00 |
| **Saucer,** Royal Lace, Green | 3.50 |
| **Saucer,** Royal Lace, Pink | 2.50 |
| **Server,** Mayfair, Blue, Center-Handled | 40.00 |
| **Server,** Victory, Amber, Handled | 15.00 |
| **Sherbet,** American Sweetheart, Crystal, Metal Holder | 5.00 |
| **Sherbet,** American Sweetheart, Monax | 8.50 |
| **Sherbet,** American Sweetheart, Pink, Footed | 6.75 |
| **Sherbet,** Block, Green, Footed | 3.50 |
| **Sherbet,** Block, Pink, 4 3/4 In. | 6.00 |
| **Sherbet,** Boopie, Forest Green | 3.00 |
| **Sherbet,** Cameo, Green, Footed, 3 1/8 In. | 8.50 |
| **Sherbet,** Candlewick, Crystal, Stemmed, 5 In. | 8.00 |
| **Sherbet,** Cape Cod, Crystal, 3 3/4 In. | 2.50 |
| **Sherbet,** Clover, Green | 4.50 |
| **Sherbet,** Cloverleaf, Pink | 4.00 |
| **Sherbet,** Cloverleaf, Yellow | 8.00 |
| **Sherbet,** Coronation, Pink, Footed | 2.75 |
| **Sherbet,** Doric, Delphite | 6.50 |
| **Sherbet,** Florentine, Green | 4.50 |
| **Sherbet,** Florentine, Pink | 6.50 |
| **Sherbet,** Iris, Marigold | 6.00 |
| **Sherbet,** Mayfair, Pink, Stem, 5 In. | 32.00 |
| **Sherbet,** Mayfair, Pink, 3 In. | 6.50 To 9.00 |
| **Sherbet,** Moderntone, Blue | 4.00 |
| **Sherbet,** Patrician, Amber | 5.00 |
| **Sherbet,** Patrician, Spoke, Crystal | 6.75 |

**Sherbet,** Petalware, Cremax .................................................................... 5.00
**Sherbet,** Roxana, Yellow ........................................................ 3.50 To 5.00
**Sherbet,** Royal Ruby, Red, Footed ............................................ 4.50
**Shot Glass,** Colonial, Green, Set Of 7 .................................... 6.00
**Shot Glass,** Moondrops, Amber ................................................ 5.75
**Shot Glass,** Moondrops, Pink .................................................... 2.75
**Soup Dish,** American Sweetheart, Monax, Flat ...................... 32.00
**Soup Dish,** American Sweetheart, Pink ................................ 17.50
**Soup Dish,** Bubble, Blue, 7 3/4 In. ........................................ 3.50
**Soup,** Cream, Daisy, Amber .................................................... 5.50
**Soup,** Cream, Newport, Blue .................................................. 6.50
**Soup,** Cream, Royal Lace, Blue ............................................ 20.00
**Soup,** Cream, Sweetheart, Pink .............................................. 18.00
**Spooner,** Colonial, Pink .......................................................... 48.00
**Sugar & Creamer,** Adam, Pink .............................................. 12.00
**Sugar & Creamer,** American Sweetheart, Pink ...................... 15.00
**Sugar & Creamer,** Block, Green ............................................ 20.00
**Sugar & Creamer,** Cameo, Green, 3 1/4 In. .......................... 18.00
**Sugar & Creamer,** Cherry Blossom, Pink .............................. 20.00
**Sugar & Creamer,** Cherry, Pink .............................................. 18.00
**Sugar & Creamer,** Chinex, Ivory ............................................ 16.00
**Sugar & Creamer,** Cloverleaf, Yellow .................................... 16.50
**Sugar & Creamer,** Cube, Pink, 2 In. ............................ 4.00 To 6.00
**Sugar & Creamer,** Diana, Amber ............................................ 12.00
**Sugar & Creamer,** Floragold, Marigold .................................. 35.00
**Sugar & Creamer,** Floral, Pink, Covered .............................. 12.00
**Sugar & Creamer,** Florentine, Green ...................................... 25.00
**Sugar & Creamer,** Homespun, Pink ........................................ 8.00
**Sugar & Creamer,** Horseshoe, Green .................................... 20.00
**Sugar & Creamer,** Iris, Crystal, Covered .............................. 12.50
**Sugar & Creamer,** Lace Edge, Pink ...................................... 25.00
**Sugar & Creamer,** Lorain, Yellow .......................................... 20.00
**Sugar & Creamer,** Lovebirds, Green ...................................... 15.00
**Sugar & Creamer,** Madrid, Amber .............................. 6.00 To 25.00
**Sugar & Creamer,** Mayfair, Frosted Pink .............................. 25.00
**Sugar & Creamer,** Moderntone, Amethyst .............................. 12.00
**Sugar & Creamer,** Moderntone, Blue ...................................... 6.00
**Sugar & Creamer,** Moderntone, Cobalt Blue .......................... 9.00
**Sugar & Creamer,** Molly, Green Opalescent ................ 25.75 To 28.00
**Sugar & Creamer,** Moondrops, Amethyst .................... 26.50 To 28.00
**Sugar & Creamer,** Moondrops, Ruby, Miniature ...................... 32.50
**Sugar & Creamer,** Newport, Cobalt & Amethyst ...................... 10.00
**Sugar & Creamer,** Normandie, Iridescent .............................. 10.00
**Sugar & Creamer,** Parrot, Green .................................. 20.00 To 35.00
**Sugar & Creamer,** Poinsettia, Green ...................................... 18.00
**Sugar & Creamer,** Poppy, Green ............................................ 12.00
**Sugar & Creamer,** Princess, Pink .......................................... 15.00
**Sugar & Creamer,** Pyramid, Green ........................................ 15.00
**Sugar & Creamer,** Ribbon, Green, Miniature .......................... 19.00
**Sugar & Creamer,** Rosemary, Amber .................................... 11.00
**Sugar & Creamer,** Round Robin, Green, Footed ...................... 11.00
**Sugar & Creamer,** Royal Lace, Blue, Covered ...................... 95.00
**Sugar & Creamer,** Royal Lace, Pink ...................................... 25.00
**Sugar & Creamer,** Royal Ruby, Red, Flat .............................. 7.00
**Sugar & Creamer,** Sandwich, Crystal, Covered ...................... 10.00
**Sugar & Creamer,** Sharon, Amber .......................................... 6.00
**Sugar & Creamer,** Tearoom, Pink .............................. 16.00 To 18.00
**Sugar & Creamer,** Windsor, Clear .............................. 4.50 To 6.75
**Sugar & Creamer,** Windsor, Pink, Covered ............................ 15.00
**Sugar Shaker,** Colonial, Pink .................................................. 45.00
**Sugar,** Adam, Pink, Covered .................................................. 20.00
**Sugar,** American Pioneer, Green, 3 1/2 In. ............................ 6.00
**Sugar,** American Sweetheart, Pink ........................................ 5.50

| | |
|---|---|
| **Sugar,** Cameo, Yellow, Label | 10.00 |
| **Sugar,** Cherry Blossom, Green, Covered | 15.00 |
| **Sugar,** Holiday, Pink, Covered | 20.00 |
| **Sugar,** Iridescent Iris, Covered | 7.50 |
| **Sugar,** Madrid, Amber, Covered | 22.50 |
| **Sugar,** Madrid, Green, Covered | 25.00 |
| **Sugar,** Parrot, Green | 15.00 |
| **Sugar,** Patrician, Amber, Covered | 35.00 |
| **Sugar,** Princess, Green, Covered | 13.00 |
| **Sugar,** Royal Ruby, Red, Footed | 4.50 |
| **Sugar,** Sharon, Pink, Covered | 25.00 |
| **Sugar,** Sierra, Green | 3.50 |
| **Sugar,** Tearoom, Green, Footed, Small | 8.50 |
| **Tray,** Louisa, Floragold, Oval, 11 1/2 In. | 13.00 |
| **Tray,** Sandwich, Cherry Blossom, Delphite | 12.00 |
| **Tray,** Sandwich, Cherry Blossom, Pink | 9.00 |
| **Tray,** Sandwich, Holiday, Pink | 6.00 |
| **Tray,** Sandwich, Moderntone, Cobalt Blue | 12.00 |
| **Tray,** Sandwich, Princess, Green, 12 In. | 9.00 |
| **Tray,** Waterford, Pink, 13 3/4 In. | 8.00 |
| **Tumbler,** Block, Pink, Flat, 5 In. | 5.00 |
| **Tumbler,** Cameo, Green, Flat, 5 In. | 16.50 |
| **Tumbler,** Cameo, Yellow, Cone Shape, Footed, 9 Ounce | 10.00 |
| **Tumbler,** Cherry Blossom, Pink, 4 Ounce | 15.00 |
| **Tumbler,** Cherry Blossom, Pink, 9 Ounce | 14.00 |
| **Tumbler,** Cloverleaf, Green, 9 Ounce, Pair | 10.00 |
| **Tumbler,** Fine Rib, Cobalt Blue, 5 In. | 7.50 |
| **Tumbler,** Florentine, Topaz, 9 Ounce | 12.50 |
| **Tumbler,** Fortune, Pink, 5 Ounce | 2.50 |
| **Tumbler,** Georgian, Cobalt Blue, 4 In. | 8.00 |
| **Tumbler,** Iris, Crystal, Footed, 7 In. | 12.50 |
| **Tumbler,** Iris, Iridescent, Footed, 6 In. | 7.50 To 9.00 |
| **Tumbler,** Juice, Candlewick, Crystal, Footed, 4 1/2 In. | 8.00 |
| **Tumbler,** Juice, Florentine No.l, Footed, 5 Ounce | 5.75 |
| **Tumbler,** Lydia Ray, Amethyst, 9 Ounce | 6.00 |
| **Tumbler,** Lydia Ray, Cobalt Blue, Flat, 5 Ounce | 6.50 |
| **Tumbler,** Lydia Ray, Green, 9 Ounce | 5.00 |
| **Tumbler,** Madrid, Amber, 12 Ounce | 12.00 |
| **Tumbler,** Moondrops, Ruby, Footed, 5 Ounce | 9.00 |
| **Tumbler,** Patrician, Amber, Flat, 5 1/2 In. | 26.00 |
| **Tumbler,** Patrician, Amber, Footed, 5 In., Set Of 6 | 25.00 |
| **Tumbler,** Queen Mary, Pink, 5 In., Pair | 10.00 |
| **Tumbler,** Ring, Crystal, 12 Ounce | 2.50 |
| **Tumbler,** Sailboat, Sportsman Series, Cobalt Blue, 10 Ounce | 5.00 |
| **Tumbler,** Windsor Diamond, Green, 3 1/4 In., Set Of 6 | 35.00 |
| **Tumbler,** Windsor Diamond, Pink, 9 Ounce | 7.00 |
| **Tumbler,** Windsor, Clear, Footed, 7 1/4 In. | 8.00 |
| **Vase,** Bud, Scalloped, Emerald Green, 8 In. | 8.00 |
| **Vase,** Cameo, Green, 5 3/4 In. | 95.00 |
| **Vase,** Cameo, Green, 8 In. | 20.00 |
| **Vase,** Genie, Opalescent Blue, Footed, 5 In. | 14.00 |
| **Vase,** Iris, Iridescent, 9 In. | 8.00 |
| **Vase,** Iris, White, 9 In. | 9.50 |
| **Vase,** Princess, Pink, 8 In. | 10.00 |
| **Vase,** Radiance, Ruby, 11 In. | 35.00 |
| **Vase,** Rock Crystal, Crystal, 6 In. | 24.50 |
| **Vase,** Tearoom, Crystal, 12 In. | 7.00 |
| **Vegetable,** Cherry Blossom, Pink | 15.00 |
| **Vegetable,** Cameo, Green, Oval | 13.00 |
| **Vegtable,** Patrician, Amber | 18.00 |
| **Water Set,** Dogwood, Pink, Pitcher & 4 Tumblers | 45.00 |
| **Water Set,** New Century, Amethyst, 12 Tumblers | 125.00 |
| **Water Set,** Thistle, Pink, 6 Tumblers | 50.00 |

| | |
|---|---|
| **Whiskey,** Mayfair, Pink, Pair | 60.00 |
| **Whiskey,** Rings, Crystal, Design | 5.00 |
| **Wine,** Iris, Crystal, 4 In., Set Of 4 | 28.00 |
| **Wine,** Moondrops, Ruby, Footed, 4 In. | 14.00 |
| **Wine,** Rock Crystal, Pink | 15.50 |

 *Derby porcelain was made in Derby, England, from 1756 to the present. The factory changed names and marks several times. Chelsea Derby (1770 to 1784), Crown Derby (1784 to 1811), and the modern Royal Crown Derby are some of the most famous periods of the factory.*

**DERBY, see also Chelsea, Crown Derby, Royal Crown Derby**

| | | |
|---|---|---|
| **DERBY, Coffee Can,** Puce Crown, Bird & Fruit, C.1790, Marked | *Illus* | 3500.00 |
| **Plate,** Imari Design, Red Mark, 8 In. | | 25.00 |
| **Teapot,** Oriental Design | | 50.00 |

| | |
|---|---|
| **DE VILBISS, Atomizer,** Allover Gold Design, Tapered Top, Amber Stone In Cap | 225.00 |
| **Atomizer,** Round Tray, Lidded Box, Gold Overlay, Iridescent | 235.00 |
| **Bottle,** Perfume, Black, Chrome | 65.00 |

| | |
|---|---|
| **DICK TRACY, Badge,** Secret Service Patrol Member | 10.00 |
| **Badge,** Sergeant | 30.00 |
| **BO Plenty,** Pocket Knife, Camco, Crime Whistle, Clue Detector | 100.00 |
| **Book,** Coloring, Unused, 1946 | 10.00 |
| **Book,** Meets The Night Crawler, 1945 | 22.50 |
| **Camera** | 32.00 |
| **Detective Set,** Original Box, 1933 | 85.00 |
| **Detective Set,** Suspenders & Badge, C.1940, Original Box | 17.50 |
| **Foto Reel & Film** | 20.00 |
| **Game,** Target, Gun, 2 Darts, Tin Lithograph, Marx | 65.00 |
| **Handcuffs,** Suspenders, & Brass Emblem, Box | 40.00 |
| **Lunch Box** | 5.00 |
| **Pin,** Girl's Division | 55.00 |
| **Pin,** Lapel | 55.00 |
| **Printing Set,** 1935, Boxed | 80.00 |
| **Radio** | 20.00 |
| **Ring** | 85.00 |
| **Wristwatch,** Ingersoll, Boxed | 150.00 |

**DICKENS WARE, see Weller, Royal Doulton**

| | |
|---|---|
| **DIONNE QUINTUPLETS, Book,** Going On Three | 20.00 |
| **Bowl,** Metal | 15.00 |
| **Calendar,** 1936, Colored Picture | 20.00 |
| **Calendar,** 1937 | 10.00 |
| **Calendar,** 1945, Harvest Days | 10.00 |

Derby, Coffee Can, Puce Crown, Bird & Fruit, C.1790, Marked

**Fan** ......................................................................................................................... 10.00 To 12.00
**Fan,** St.Paul Milk Co., Seated At Desks ....................................................... 25.00
**Game,** Domino ........................................................................................................ 25.00
**Handkerchief,** Picture Of 5 Girls, Dates, Names ...................................... 15.00
**Paperdolls,** All Aboard Shut Eye Town, Uncut ........................................ 35.00
**Spoon,** Figural, Silver Plated, Set Of 5 ...................................................... 75.00

**DISNEYANA, Album,** Bubble Gum, Mickey Mouse, 14 Cards ................. 45.00
**Ball,** Picture Mickey Mouse, Sun Rubber Co. ............................................ 35.00
**Bank,** Donald Duck, Ceramic ......................................................................... 20.00
**Bank,** Gum, Mickey Mouse ............................................................................ 7.00
**Bank,** Mickey Mouse, Glass ............................................................................ 15.00
**Bank,** Mickey Mouse, Plastic, 11 In. ............................................................. 25.00
**Bank,** Mickey, Book, Red, Tin, Mickey's First Step, 1935 ....................... 225.00
**Bank,** Pinocchio Book ....................................................................................... 60.00
**Bank,** Snow White, Ceramic .......................................................................... 15.00
**Book,** Mickey Never Fails, 1939 .................................................................... 10.00
**Book,** Pop-Up, Mickey Mouse, 1933 ............................................................ 85.00
**Book,** Pop-Up, Minnie Mouse ........................................................................ 85.00
**Bottle,** Donald Duck, Cola ............................................................................... 4.00
**Camera,** Mickey Mouse ................................................................................... 18.00
**Can,** Sprinkling, Donald Duck, 1938, 3 In. .................................................. 60.00
**Can,** Sprinkling, Mickey Mouse, 1933, 3 In. ............................................... 110.00
**Card Game,** Donald Duck, 1949 ..................................................................... 10.00
**Card,** Birthday, Mickey, C.1936, 19 X 23 In. ................................................ 25.00
**Card,** Mickey Mouse, No.95 ............................................................................ 3.00
**Celluloid,** Chip & Dale, Full Figures, Dancing, 1960 ................................. 66.00
**Celluloid,** Chip The Squirrel, Full Figure Standing, 1950 ........................ 55.00
**Celluloid,** Cinderella, Dress For Wedding .................................................... 140.00
**Celluloid,** Dale The Squirrel, Full Figure, Walnut On Head ................... 55.00
**Celluloid,** Dodo Bird, Alice In Wonderland, Large Figure ...................... 120.00
**Celluloid,** Donald Duck, In Santa Claus Suit, Full Figure ....................... 85.00
**Celluloid,** Donald Duck, Red Coat & Hat, Camera On Neck .................. 80.00
**Celluloid,** Fairy Godmother, Waist Up, Full Face ...................................... 80.00
**Celluloid,** Goofy, Hawaiian Shirt, Holding Window, Knees Up ............. 85.00
**Celluloid,** Goofy, Standing Next To Camera, 1940, Full Figure ............. 85.00
**Celluloid,** Goofy, Wearing Blue Suit & Glasses, 1940, Full Figure ....... 85.00
**Celluloid,** Lady, Lady And The Tramp, Full Face ...................................... 100.00
**Celluloid,** March Hare, Full Figure, Holding Cup In Hand ...................... 120.00
**Celluloid,** Mickey Mouse, As Bandleader, Full Figure ............................ 140.00
**Celluloid,** Mickey Mouse, Holding A Match, Waist Up, 1950 ................. 150.00
**Celluloid,** Stepmother, Knees Up, Full Face .............................................. 140.00
**Celluloid,** Tramp, From Lady And The Tramp, Walking, Full Figure ..... 90.00
**Chair,** Beach, Mickey Mouse ......................................................................... 100.00
**Charm,** Mickey Mouse, Celluloid ................................................................. 14.99
**Choo Choo,** Pull-Bell Ringer, Donald Duck, 1940 ................................... 29.00
**Christmas Seals,** Mickey Mouse, Different Scenes, Unopened .............. 95.00
**Clock,** Alarm, Animated, Mickey Mouse ..................................................... 55.00
**Cookie Jar,** Alice In Wonderland ................................................... 25.00 To 30.00
**Cookie Jar,** Donald Duck ................................................................................. 35.00
**Cookie Jar,** Mickey & Minnie, Turnabout .................................................... 25.00
**Crayon Box,** Mickey & Donald, Tin, Transogram, 1946 .......................... 13.00
**Creamer,** Mickey, Oriental Character .......................................................... 25.00
**Cup,** Baby's, Mickey Mouse, Silver Plated, 1 3/4 In. ............................... 35.00
**Dish,** Donald Duck, Pink, Plastic, Stamped Walt Disney ....................... 4.50
**Dish,** Soap, Donald Duck, Rubber ................................................................ 18.00
**Doll,** Alice In Wonderland, Jointed, Vinyl, 12 In. ....................................... 13.50
**Doll,** Grumpy, Gund .......................................................................................... 75.00
**Doll,** Mickey Mouse, Knickerbocker, 11 In. .............................. 185.00 To 225.00
**Doll,** Mickey Mouse, Plastic, 12 In. .............................................................. 30.00
**Doll,** Mickey Mouse, Rubber, 4 In. ............................................................... 5.00
**Doll,** Mickey Mouse, Steiff, Tagged Ear, Large ........................................ 850.00
**Doll,** Minnie Mouse, Cloth .............................................................................. 35.00

| | |
|---|---|
| **Doll,** Minnie Mouse, Rubber, 7 In. | 15.00 |
| **Doll,** Pinocchio, Cloth | 50.00 |
| **Donald Duck,** Carnival Chalk, 14 In. | 35.00 |
| **Donald Duck,** Full Figure, Holding An Elephant's Trunk, 1950 | 75.00 |
| **Ears,** Mickey Mouse Club, C.1950, Packaged | 5.00 |
| **Explorer Outfit,** Mickey Mouse Club, C.1950, Original Box | 25.00 |
| **Figure,** Mickey, Minnie, & Pluto, Wood Jointed, Labeled, 4 In. | 250.00 |
| **Figurine,** Bashful, Bisque, White, 4 In. | 18.00 To 25.00 |
| **Figurine,** Donald Duck, Strutting, Bisque, Closed Bill, 3 1/4 In. | 20.00 |
| **Figurine,** Dopey, Bisque, 3 In. | 15.00 To 18.00 |
| **Figurine,** Ferdinand, Bisque, 3 In. | 20.00 To 42.00 |
| **Figurine,** Mickey Mouse, Porcelain, Watch Display, 5 1/2 In. | 50.00 |
| **Figurine,** Minnie Mouse, Bisque, 4 1/2 In. | 30.00 |
| **Fork,** Donald Duck | 10.00 |
| **Fork,** Minnie Mouse | 10.00 |
| **Game,** Board, Pinocchio, 1939 | 30.00 |
| **Game,** Mickey Mouse Club, 1955 | 9.00 |
| **Game,** Target, Mickey Mouse, 18 In. | 15.00 |
| **Game,** Tomorrowland, Rocket To The Moon, 1956 | 35.00 |
| **Hairbrush,** Donald Duck, 1938 | 24.00 |
| **Holder,** Toothbrush, Donald Duck, Bisque, Signed Walt Disney | 65.00 |
| **Holder,** Toothbrush, Mickey & Minnie, Bisque | 95.00 |
| **Holder,** Toothbrush, Three Little Pigs, Bisque | 30.00 |
| **Holder,** Toothpick, Sneezy, China, 1937 | 42.00 |
| **Knife,** Davy Crockett, Barlow | 7.00 |
| **Lunch Box,** Disney World | 14.00 |
| **Mask,** Pinocchio & Jiminny Cricket, 1939, Boxed | 26.00 |
| **Megaphone,** Mickey Mouse Club, C.1950 | 5.00 |
| **Moviejector,** Mickey Mouse | 100.00 |
| **Napkin Ring,** Figural, Mickey, Celluloid, 1938 | 22.00 |
| **Napkin Ring,** Figural, Pluto, Plastic | 12.50 |
| **Pail,** Donald Duck, 1938 | 22.00 |
| **Paint Set,** Alice In Wonderland | 28.00 |
| **Phonograph,** Mickey Mouse | 45.00 |
| **Pitcher,** Figural, Dumbo, Walt Disney, 5 1/2 In. | 5.00 To 10.00 |
| **Planter,** Figural, Bambi, Label, 6 1/4 In. | 6.50 |
| **Planter,** Figural, Pluto & Cart, 6 1/2 In. | 8.00 |
| **Planter,** Snow White | 18.00 To 20.00 |
| **Plate,** Mickey Mouse, Silver Plated, 8 1/4 In. | 120.00 |
| **Plate,** Pinocchio, Tin | 7.00 |
| **Playing Cards,** Three Little Pigs, 1934 | 15.00 |
| **Puppet,** Dumbo, Original Box | 10.00 |
| **Roadster,** Parade, Windup, Boxed | 100.00 To 165.00 |
| **Rug,** Disney Characters, 20 X 36 In. | 20.00 |
| **Salt & Pepper,** Donald Duck | 6.00 To 18.00 |
| **Salt & Pepper,** Dumbo, 1947 | 9.00 |
| **Salt & Pepper,** Little Red Riding Hood | 12.00 |
| **Salt & Pepper,** Mickey & Minnie | 12.00 |
| **Salt & Pepper,** Pluto | 16.00 |
| **Shade,** Lamp, Mickey Mouse, Glass | 35.00 |
| **Sharpener,** Pencil, Mechanical, Mickey Mouse Chews Pencil | 35.00 |
| **Sheet Music,** Who's Afraid Of The Big Bad Wolf, 1933 | 10.00 |
| **Soap,** Dopey, Castile, Boxed | 42.00 |
| **Stamp Pad,** Mickey Mouse, C.1930 | 18.00 To 20.00 |
| **Swimsuit,** Child's, Pictures Mickey, 1930s | 95.00 |
| **Tea Set,** Mickey Mouse, China, 17 Pieces | 75.00 |
| **Teapot,** Snow White, Musical, China | 35.00 |
| **Toy,** Dancing Cinderella & Prince, Battery Operated | 45.00 |
| **Toy,** Disneyland Express, Engine, 3 Cars, Windup, 1950 | 55.00 |
| **Toy,** Donald & Pluto In Roadster, Hard Rubber, Wood Wheels | 35.00 |
| **Toy,** Donald Duck On Motorcycle, Tin | 15.00 |
| **Toy,** Donald Duck, Cart Pulled By Pluto, Celluloid, Windup, 1939 | 750.00 |
| **Toy,** Donald Duck, Fisher Price, Pull | 140.00 |

Toy, Donald Duck, Wood Pull Toy, 1930s ................................................................. 45.00
Toy, Dumbo, Stuffed ............................................................................................... 65.00
Toy, Ferris Wheel, Mickey Mouse, Windup, 17 In. ................................................. 150.00
Toy, Fire Truck, Mickey Mouse, Rubber ................................................................ 20.00
Toy, Handcar, Donald & Pluto, Lionel, Boxed ....................................................... 1650.00
Toy, Handcar, Mickey & Minnie .............................................................................. 500.00
Toy, Mickey & Minnie Play Piano, Mechanical, Salco Series, 1940 ........................ 295.00
Toy, Mickey Mouse Playing Xylophone, Linemar Toys, Windup ............................... 175.00
Toy, Minnie Mouse In Rocker, Windup .................................................................... 225.00
Toy, Porky Pig Twirls Umbrella, 1938, Windup, Boxed ........................................... 155.00
Toy, Truck, Fire, Mickey Mouse, Rubber ................................................................ 20.00
Toy, Xylophone, Mickey Mouse, Tin, Windup, Japan, 5 1/2 X 7 In. ........................ 250.00
Umbrella, Mickey Mouse, Costume Top .................................................................. 10.00
Umbrella, Pluto, 1947 ............................................................................................ 45.00
Watch Fob, Mickey Mouse ..................................................................................... 45.00
Watch, Pocket, Mickey Mouse, 1939 ..................................................................... 250.00
Western Outfit, Mickey Mouse Club, Gun & Holster, Boxed ................................... 25.00
Wristwatch, Daisy Duck .......................................................................................... 35.00
Wristwatch, Donald Duck ........................................................................................ 60.00
Wristwatch, Mickey Mouse, Ingersoll, Boxed, 1947 ............................ 110.00 To 150.00
Wristwatch, Mickey Mouse, Ingersoll, C.1940 ....................................................... 55.00
Wristwatch, Mickey Mouse, 1935, Round Dial, Second Hand, Metal Band ............. 225.00
Wristwatch, Mickey Mouse, 1938 ........................................................................... 85.00
Wristwatch, Snow White, Original Strap .................................................................. 25.00
Yo-Yo, Mickey Mouse .............................................................................................. 5.00
	DOCTOR, see Medical


*Doll entries are listed by marks printed or incised on the doll, if possible.*
*If there are no marks, the doll is listed by name of subject or country.*

DOLL, A.B.G. 1361, Character Baby, Wobbly Tongue, Open Nostrils, 17 In. ............ 475.00
A.M., Baby Betty, Ball-Jointed Body, Marked, 14 In. .............................................. 275.00
A.M., Baby, Set Blue Eyes, Bent Limb Body, Blue Dress, 11 In. ............................ 85.00
A.M., Ball-Jointed, Fixed Brown Eyes, 33 In. ......................................................... 450.00
A.M., Bisque Socket Head, Jointed, Human Hair, White Dress, 11 1/2 In. .............. 225.00
A.M., Boy, Blue Velvet Suit, Jointed, Bisque, 21 In. .............................................. 250.00
A.M., Dream Baby, Bent Limb Body, Stationary Eyes, 10 In. ................................. 210.00
A.M., Dream Baby, Bisque, Cloth Body, 16 In. ....................................................... 275.00
A.M., Dream Baby, Sleep Eyes, White Dress, Pink Ribbon Insets, 12 In. ............... 300.00
A.M., Floradora, Sleep Eyes, Lashes, Human Hair, Ball-Jointed, 23 In. .................. 350.00
A.M., Floradora, Turned Head, Fur Eyebrows, Kid Body, 23 In. .............................. 225.00
A.M., Girl, Original Nun's Outfit, 17 In. ................................................................... 220.00
A.M., Indian, Bisque, 10 In. .................................................................................... 150.00
A.M., Indian, Bisque, 12 In. .................................................................................... 225.00
A.M., Leather Body, Gray Paperweight Eyes, 20 In. ............................................... 400.00
A.M., Mabel, Long Blonde Hair, 12 In. .................................................................... 98.00
A.M., Rosebud, Kid Body, Gibson Girl Dress, 17 In. ............................................... 175.00
A.M., Scowling Indian, Bisque Head, Original Clothes, 9 In. ................................... 195.00
A.M., Sleep Eyes, Dress, Bonnet To Match, Jointed, Bisque, 16 1/2 In. ................. 250.00
A.M., Toddler, Chubby Wide Face, Chemise, Organdy Dress, Bisque, 20 In. ........... 250.00
A.M., Toddler, Set Eyes, Chunky Pink Body, Dressed, Bisque, 14 In. ..................... 250.00
A.M., 17, Blue Eyes, Ball-Jointed, 39 In. ................................................................ 795.00
A.M., 165, Googly, Watermelon Mouth, Chubby Toddler, 13 In. ............................. 3600.00
A.M., 323, Googly, Lace Dress, Hat, 10 In. ............................................................ 695.00
A.M., 323, Googly, 7 1/2 In. ................................................................................... 525.00
A.M., 341/14, Dream Baby, Jointed Cloth Body, Signed, 14 1/2 In. ....................... 495.00
A.M., 351/9k, Toddler, Molded Curls, Bisque Head, Sleep Eyes, 25 In. ................. 1800.00
A.M., 353, Googly, Sleep Eyes, Molded Wig, 5-Part Body, 11 3/4 In. ..................... 895.00
A.M., 370, Bisque Head, Original Wig, Kid Body, Dressed, 20 In. ........................... 150.00
A.M., 370, Kid Body, 18 In. ..................................................................................... 175.00
A.M., 390, Bisque Head, Nun's Outfit, Open Mouth, 24 In. ..................................... 265.00
A.M., 390, Bisque, Ball-Jointed Body, Dressed, 24 In. ........................................... 185.00

A.M., 390, Bisque, Human Hair, Dressed, 25 In. ........................................ 850.00
A.M., 390, Bisque, Socket Head, Blonde Wig, Tin Stand, 9 In. ...................... 400.00
A.M., 390, Blue Sleep Eyes, Jointed Body, Stockings, 19 In. ......................... 155.00
A.M., 390, Fully Jointed, Original Crepe Paper Dress, 10 In. ......................... 130.00
A.M., 390, Red Velvet, Red Straw Hat, Ball-Jointed, Bisque Head, 25 In. ........ 265.00
A.M., 971, Character Baby, Head Circumference, 11 In. ................................ 250.00
A.M., 985, Character Baby, Blonde, Composition, Baby Dress, 14 In. .............. 200.00
A.M., 992, Toddler, Blonde Wig, Sleep Eyes, Dressed, 13 In. ....................... 375.00
A.M., 1894, Bisque Head, Jointed Composition Body, Open Mouth, 10 In. ......... 95.00
A.M., 1894, Composition Body, Mohair Wig, Middy Dress, 16 In. ................... 145.00
A.M., 1894, Dimple In Chin, Old Dress, Boots, Kid Body & Arms, 14 In. ......... 150.00
A.M., 3200, Kid Fashion Body, Gibson Girl Dress, 14 In. ............................ 150.00
Agness, Turned Head, Molded Hair, China Arms & Legs, 19 In. .................... 135.00
    DOLL, ALEXANDER, see Doll, Madame Alexander
Alice In Wonderland, Wax, Leather Arms, Dressed, 26 In. ........................... 225.00
Amelia Bloomer, Parian Shoulder Head, Kid Hands, Cloth Feet, 15 In. ........... 395.00
American Character, Annie Oakley, 18 In. ................................................ 125.00
    DOLL, ARMAND MARSEILLE, see also Doll, A.M.
Aunt Jemima, Oilcloth ........................................................................ 50.00
Baby Crissy, Black, Boxed ................................................................... 75.00
Baby Dumps, Bisque Head, Cloth Body, Black, 8 In. .................................. 225.00
Barbie, Winter Holiday Outfit, Plaid Bag, Accessories, 1958 ....................... 140.00
Bear, Jointed, Hump, Straw Stuffed, 7 In. .............................................. 110.00
Bebe Jumeau, Bisque Head, Paperweight Eyes, Jointed Body, 21 In. .......... 4000.00
Bebe Jumeau, Paperweight Eyes, Eiffel Tower Mark, 21 In. ..................... 2600.00
Bebe, Open Mouth, Set Paperweight Eyes, Brown Curls, 22 In. ................. 1100.00
Belton, Blue Paperweight Eyes, Closed Mouth, Ball-Jointed, 18 1/2 In. ....... 1295.00
Belton, Closed Mouth, Paperweight Eyes, Mohair Wig, 15 In. ..................... 950.00
Ben Casey, Doctor, Original Box, 28 In. ................................................... 25.00
    DOLL, BERGMANN, see also Doll, S & H; Doll, Simon & Halbig
Bergmann, Ball-Jointed Body, Blue Stationary Eyes, Dressed, 36 In. ............ 650.00
Bergmann, Floradora Kid, 28 In. ........................................................... 300.00
Bergmann, Lashed Sleep Blue Eyes, Jointed, 17 In. .................................. 225.00
Bergmann, Simon & Halbig, Blue Moire Dress, Blonde Human Hair, 22 In. ...... 300.00
Bergmann, Sleep Eyes, Brown Hair, Ball-Jointed, 26 In. ............................. 350.00
Bestor, Composition, Ball-Jointed, 22 In. ................................................ 125.00
Bisque, Baldy, Stiff Legs, Movable Arms, 1 1/2 In. .................................... 15.00
Bisque, Bathing Beauty, Marked Germany, 3 In. ........................................ 50.00
Bisque, Boy, Inset Eyes, Jointed, Composition, Knickers, Tam, 11 1/2 In. ...... 375.00
Bisque, German, No.2015-2, 24 In. ....................................................... 300.00
Black Toddler, Painted Side Eyes, Original Fur Hair, 12 1/2 In. .................... 125.00
Black, Poured Wax, Mohair Wig, Painted Eyes, Cloth Body, 14 In. ............... 225.00
Borgfeldt, Compostion Body, Brown Wig, Blue Eyes, 24 In. ........................ 300.00
Boudoir, Composition, Cloth Body, 28 In. ................................................. 25.00
Bride & Groom, Short Gown, Bisque, Dated 1920's, 4 In. ............................ 45.00
Bru, Mechanical, Walks, Talks, & Throws Kisses, 22 In. ........................... 3250.00
Buddy Lee, Composition, Original Jeans Outfit ......................................... 95.00
Buschow & Beck, Metal Head, Kid Body, Velvet Suit, 19 In. ....................... 150.00
Bye-Lo, Baby, Painted Eyes & Blue Shoes, Bisque, 4 In. ........................... 265.00
Bye-Lo, Baby, 1923, All Original, 12 In. .................................................. 450.00
Bye-Lo, Bisque Head, Celluloid Hands, Cloth Body, Dressed, 18 In. ............. 895.00
Bye-Lo, Bisque Head, Stamped Cloth Body, Celluloid Hands, 12 In. .............. 425.00
Bye-Lo, Molded Hair, Jointed At Shoulders & Hips, Label, 4 1/2 In. .............. 210.00
Bye-Lo, Putnam, Head Circumference 13 In. ............................................ 225.00
Bye-Lo, Sleep Eyes, Celluloid Hands, Shirt, Slip, Diaper, Dress, 12 In. .......... 650.00
Bye-Lo, Socket Head, Original Body, 12 In. ............................................. 600.00
Campbell Kid, Horsman, Composition Head & Hands, C.1910, 11 In. ............... 90.00
Campbell Kid, Original Playsuit, Grace Drayton ........................................ 45.00
Carmen Miranda, Composition .............................................................. 145.00
Chad Valley, Girl, Red Velvet Coat & Hat, Glass-Eyed, 14 In. ..................... 200.00
Charlie Chaplin, Composition, Original Clothes ......................................... 250.00
Chase, Baby, Christening Dress, 13 1/2 In. .............................................. 395.00
Chatty Baby Brother, Black, 15 In. ........................................................ 65.00

| | |
|---|---|
| **Chatty Cathy,** Black | 115.00 |
| **Chin Chin Baby,** Original Label, 4 1/2 In. | 120.00 |
| **Chubby Toddler,** Cloth Body, Tin Sleep Eyes, Original Hair, 27 In. | 135.00 |
| **Cloth,** Pug, Puppy, 1892 | 25.00 |
| **Cloth,** Tatters, Dog, 1892 | 65.00 |
| **Cream Of Wheat Man,** Cloth | 45.00 |
| **Cuno & Otto Dressel,** Girl, Composition Body, Flirty Eyes, 2, In. | 485.00 |
| **Cuno & Otto Dressel,** Kid Body, Bisque Arms, Sleep Brown Eyes, 14 In. | 175.00 |
| **Dale Evans,** Hat & Boots, 21 In. | 40.00 |
| **DeLux Lame Co.,** Little Dressmaker, Cardboard Suitcase, Clothes | 12.00 |
| **Dianna Durbin,** 24 In. | 250.00 |
| **Dionne Quintuplets,** Dressed, Bonnets, Playpen | 685.00 |
| **Dionne Quintuplets,** In Wicker Basket, Bent-Limb, Organdy Dresses | 325.00 |
| **Dream Baby Toddler,** Sleep Eyes, Molded Hair, 5-Part Body, 14 1/2 In. | 425.00 |
| **Dream Baby,** Dressed, 9 In. | 300.00 |
| **Dream Baby,** 11 In.Circumference, Celluloid Handle, 9 In. | 225.00 |
| **Dressel,** Composition Body, Brown Wig & Eyes, 24 In. | 300.00 |
| **Dressel,** Leather Body, Open Mouth, Turned Head, Dressed, 23 In. | 225.00 |
| **Dutch Girl,** Stuffed Body, Ball-Jointed, Wooden Shoes, Bisque, 12 In. | 150.00 |
| **Edison,** Reproduction Mechanism | 1250.00 |
| **Effanbee,** Ann Shirley, Compostion, 20 In. | 225.00 |
| **Effanbee,** Ann Shirley, Little Lady, Composition, 27 In. | 255.00 |
| **Effanbee,** Anne Shirley, Composition, Redressed, 16 In. | 100.00 |
| **Effanbee,** Baby, Cloth Body, Blue Sleep Eyes, 18 In. | 345.00 |
| **Effanbee,** Baby, Composition, Flirty Eyes, Lamb's Wool Curls, 24 In. | 85.00 |
| **Effanbee,** Bride, Composition, 18 In. | 250.00 |
| **Effanbee,** Brownie, 1966, 12 In. | 30.00 |
| **Effanbee,** Bubbles, Composition, 1924, 24 In. | 125.00 To 175.00 |
| **Effanbee,** Bubbles, Original Clothes, 29 In. | 450.00 |
| **Effanbee,** Champagne Lady, Lawrence Welk Show, 20 In. | 45.00 |
| **Effanbee,** Chuckles, 23 In. | 75.00 |
| **Effanbee,** Coquette, Lady Grey, 15 In. | 35.00 |
| **Effanbee,** Crowning Glory | 85.00 |
| **Effanbee,** Dream Baby, Cloth Body, Sleep Eyes, Voile Dress, 17 In. | 65.00 |
| **Effanbee,** Dy-Dee Baby, Caracul Wig, 12 In. | 20.00 |
| **Effanbee,** Fluffy, Negro, Official Girl Scout Uniform, 1965, 8 In. | 13.50 |
| **Effanbee,** Half-Pint, White Dress, Straw Hat, Flirty Eyes, 1966, 11 In. | 25.00 |
| **Effanbee,** Honeybun, Hard Plastic, 14 In. | 32.00 To 35.00 |
| **Effanbee,** Little Lady, Yarn Hair, Composition, 17 In. | 90.00 |
| **Effanbee,** Little Lady, 28 In. | 300.00 |
| **Effanbee,** Little Tubber, Black, Boxed, 10 In. | 15.00 |
| **Effanbee,** Lucifer, Puppet, Black, C.1937 | 85.00 |
| **Effanbee,** My Precious, Boxed | 200.00 |
| **Effanbee,** Patsy Babyette, Original Clothes | 45.00 |
| **Effanbee,** Patsy Lou, 22 In. | 175.00 |
| **Effanbee,** Patsy, Jr., Mohair Braids, Wrist Bracelet | 85.00 |
| **Effanbee,** Patsy, 1946, 14 In. | 75.00 |
| **Effanbee,** Rosemary, 18 In. | 42.00 |
| **Effanbee,** Tommy Tucker, Curly Wig, Flirty Eyes, 22 In. | 95.00 |
| **Effanbee,** W.C.Fields, Centennial, Vinyl, Jointed, Top Hat, Spats, 15 In. | 44.95 |
| **Einco,** Baby, Bisque Head, Painted Hair & Features, Bent-Limb | 1200.00 |
| **Ella Cinders,** Labeled Dress, 18 In. | 275.00 |
| **Emma Clear,** Barbary Coast Gent, Dressed 18 In. | 195.00 |
| **Emma Clear,** Parian Head, Glass Eyes, Hairdo With Comb, Flowers, 21 In. | 285.00 |
| **Emperor & Empress,** Crowns, Sword, Dressed, Pre-World War II, Pair | 245.00 |
| **English,** Peddler, Costumed, Carrying Baskets, Pair | 550.00 |
| **English,** Peddler, Jointed Wood Body, C.1830, Original Clothes, 12 In. | 1600.00 |
| **English,** Shepherd, Smock & Staff, 10 In. | 65.00 |
| **F.G.,** Girl, Fashion, Kid Body, Dress & Coat, 18 In. | 825.00 |
| **F.S. & Co.,** Baby, Pierced Nostrils, Blue Sleep Eyes, 26 In. | 850.00 |
| **Fanny Brice,** Original Clothes | 100.00 |
| **Flapper,** Bed, Blonde Wig, Original, 26 In. | 75.00 |
| **Floradora,** Ball-Jointed, Stationary Eyes, 24 In. | 225.00 |

**Floradora,** Composition Body, Original Clothes, 19 In. ................................................. 160.00
**Floradora,** Jointed, Bisque Head, 12 1/2 In. ............................................................. 125.00
**Floradora,** Kid Body, 15 In. ..................................................................................... 150.00
**Floradora,** Sleep Eyes, Bent-Limb Body, Flowered Pajamas, 10 In. ........................... 150.00
**Floradora,** Sleep Eyes, Brown Mohair Wig, Kid Body, Wool Dress, 18 In. .................... 150.00
**Freddie,** Red Skelton ............................................................................................... 15.00
**French,** Bisque, Swivel Head, Glass Eyes, Anchor Mark, 8 1/2 In. .............................. 425.00
**French,** Boudoir, With Cigarette, Original Clothes ...................................................... 135.00
**French,** Cherie, Paperweight Eyes, Dressed, F.Francaise, 16 In. ................................. 475.00
**French,** Fashion, Kid Body, Jewel Eyes, 14 In. ........................................................... 800.00
**French,** Fashion, Leather Body & Arms, Original Dress, 16 In. .................................... 900.00
**French,** Fashion, Paperweight Eyes, Kid Body, Bisque Shoulder, 16 1/2 In. ............... 1475.00
**French,** Fish Peddler Woman With Basket Of Fish, Terra-Cotta, 8 In. ........................... 75.00
**French,** Open Mouth, 5-Piece Body, Labeled Au Bas De Soie, 8 1/2 In. ...................... 195.00
**French,** Pierced Ears, Blue Silk & Lace Dress, Bonnet, Schmitt, 20 In. ..................... 4600.00
**French,** Swivel Neck, Bisque, Original Costume, Heeled Shoes, 5 3/4 In. ..................... 600.00
**Frozen Charlie,** Marked 12/0, 2 1/2 In. ..................................................................... 45.00
**Frozen Charlie,** Red, White, & Blue Knitted & Crocheted Suit, 16 In. .......................... 650.00
**Frozen Charlie,** 15 In. ............................................................................................. 400.00
**Frozen Charlotte,** Black, Red Mouth, White Eyes, 2 In. .............................................. 25.00
**Frozen Charlotte,** Black, 5 In. .................................................................................. 48.00
**Frozen Charlotte,** Glazed, Original Clothes, 3 1/2 In. ................................................ 75.00
**Frozen Charlotte,** White, Chunky, Marked 500 On Back, 2 In. ..................................... 25.00
    **DOLL, FULPER, see also Doll, Horsman**
**Fulper,** American, Girl, Kid & Cloth Body, Bisque Hands, 20 In. .................................. 400.00
**Fulper,** Girl, Pink Linen Dress, Marked, 19 In. ........................................................... 500.00
**Fulper,** Toddler, Green Sleep Eyes, 18 In. ................................................................. 425.00
**Georgene Averill,** Baby Dimples, Bisque Head, Blue Glass Eyes, 19 In. ................... 1250.00
**Georgene Averill,** Blue Sleep Eyes, Pink Dress, Sweater, Bonnet, 16 In. ..................... 795.00
**Gerber,** Baby, Rubber, 12 In. .................................................................................... 15.00
**Gerbruder Krauss,** No.165, Bisque Head, Ball-Jointed Body, C.1907, 24 In. ............... 450.00
**German,** Bisque, Glass Eyes, Mohair Wig, Bare Feet, 3 1/2 In. ................................... 95.00
**German,** Boy, Bald Head, Intaglio Eyes, Ball-Jointed, Bisque, 10 In. ......................... 500.00
**German,** Celluloid Chunky Body, Flirty Eyes, Open Mouth, 21 In. ................................ 130.00
**German,** Character Baby, Brown Glass Eyes, All Bisque, 5 1/2 In. ............................... 130.00
**German,** Floradora, Kid Body, Bisque Hands, 15 In. ................................................... 175.00
**German,** Girl, H109, Socket Head, Bisque, White Dress, 27 In. .......................... *Illus*  325.00
**German,** Little Imp, All Bisque, 7 In. .......................................................................... 200.00
**German,** No.1316, Character Toddler, Bisque Head, 4-Piece Body, 13 In. ................... 295.00
**German,** Sleep Eyes, Lashes, Open Mouth, Ball-Jointed, Bisque, 21 In. ..................... 350.00
**German,** Turned Shoulder Head, Sleep Eyes, Taffeta Dress, Cap, 22 In. ..................... 285.00
**Gladdy Boy,** Original Shirt & Velvet Pants, 15 In. ....................................................... 465.00
**Greiner,** Blonde, 1872, Labeled, Old Arms, Replaced Body, 28 In. ............................. 325.00
**Greiner,** Girl, Glass-Eyed, Brush Marks, 23 In. ......................................................... 875.00
**Greiner,** Molded Hair, Bisque Face, Original Paint, C.1858, 23 In. ............................. 550.00
**Handwerck & Halbig,** Pierced Ears, Human Hair Wig, Jointed Body, 27 In. ................. 230.00
**Handwerck,** Ball-Jointed Body, Dressed, 27 In. ......................................................... 425.00
**Handwerck,** Girl, Kid Body, Black Velvet Dress, Mink Cape & Hat, 27 In. .................... 600.00
**Handwerck,** Girl, Sleep Eyes, Mohair Wig, Ball-Jointed, Dressed, 24 In. ..................... 300.00
**Handwerck,** Simon & Halbig, Paperweight Eyes, 31 In. ...................................... *Illus*  375.00
**Handwerck,** Slant Blue Eyes, Ball-Jointed Body, 24 In. .............................................. 395.00
**HEbee,** Composition, Head, Arms, & Hips Move, Blue Shoes, 11 1/2 In. ...................... 195.00
**Heinrich Halbig,** Girl, Bisque Head, Blue Set Eyes, White Dress, 29 In. ..................... 650.00
**Herm Steiner,** Character Baby, Toddler Body, 14 In. ................................................... 450.00
**Heubach Koppelsdorf 250,** Girl, Composition Body, 23 In. ......................................... 245.00
**Heubach Koppelsdorf 267,** Character Baby, 19 In. ..................................................... 382.00
**Heubach Koppelsdorf 430-5/0,** Character Baby, Breather, 13 In. ................................ 265.00
**Heubach Koppelsdorf 458,** Polynesian, All Original, 10 In. ........................................ 275.00
**Heubach Koppelsdorf 7602,** Character Baby, Closed Mouth ...................................... 350.00
**Heubach Koppelsdorf,** Baby Stewart, Molded Hat, 12 In. ......................................... 1150.00
**Heubach Koppelsdorf,** Baby, Jointed Body, White Clothes, 24 In. ............................... 325.00
**Heubach Koppelsdorf,** Character Baby, Bent-Limb, Dressed, 27 In. ............................ 700.00
**Heubach Koppelsdorf,** Character Girl, Kid Body, Bisque Arms, 14 In. .......................... 775.00

Dolls, from left to right; Simon & Halbig 512H, Girl Ball-Jointed, Bisque (See Page 176); German, Girl, H109, Socket Head, Bisque, White Dress; Handwerck, Simon & Halbig, Paperweight Eyes

| | |
|---|---:|
| **Heubach Koppelsdorf,** Character Toddler, Dimpled, 14 In. | 195.00 |
| **Heubach Koppelsdorf,** Coquette, 14 In. | 500.00 |
| **Heubach Koppelsdorf,** Girl, Blonde Hair, All Original, 13 In. | 175.00 |
| **Heubach Koppelsdorf,** Girl, Original, 8 In. | 87.50 |
| **Heubach Koppelsdorf,** Laughing Boy, Molded Hair, Kid Body, Bisque, 9 In. | 375.00 |
| **Heubach Koppelsdorf,** Sleep Eyes, Closed Mouth, Molded Teeth, 14 In. | 1800.00 |
| **Heubach Koppelsdorf,** Toddler, Chubby, Sleep Eyes, Open Mouth, 9 In. | 350.00 |
| **Heubach Koppelsdorf,** Whistling Boy, Original Body, 13 In. | 875.00 |
| **Horsman,** Baby Jeanne, Composition, Topknot, 15 In. | 55.00 |
| **Horsman,** Little Sister, Blonde Hair, Sleep Eyes, Bow In Hair, 16 In. | 45.00 |
| **Horsman,** Mary Poppins, All Original, Vinyl, 26 In. | 225.00 |
| **Horsman,** Mary Poppins, Dressed All Original, Missing Umbrella, 12 In. | 18.00 |
| **Horsman,** Mary Poppins, Original Outfit, With Umbrella, 36 In. | 155.00 |
| **Horsman,** Poor Pitiful Pearl, Dress-Up Outfit, Boxed, 11 In. | 42.00 |
| **Hummel,** Christy Girl, Scarf & Basket, Rubber, 11 In. | 95.00 |
| **Hummel,** Holding Accordion, 1960 | 95.00 |
| **Hummel,** Rubber, 1956 | 195.00 |
| **Hummel,** Wanderbub, Rubber, Full Bee | 90.00 |
| **Ideal,** Baby Coo, Hand-Painted Head, 20 In. | 40.00 |
| **Ideal,** Baby Peggy, Flirty Eyes, Composition, 22 In. | 125.00 |
| **Ideal,** Baby, Composition, Blonde Ringlets, Organdy Outfit, 20 In. | 125.00 |
| **Ideal,** Betsy Wetsy, With Layette, 1950, Boxed, 16 In. | 45.00 |
| **Ideal,** Black Baby, 1971, 14 In. | 20.00 |
| **Ideal,** Campbell Kid, 16 In. | 85.00 |
| **Ideal,** Cinnamon | 15.00 |
| **Ideal,** Cricket | 25.00 |
| **Ideal,** Fanny Brice, Baby Snooks | 150.00 |
| **Ideal,** Fanny Brice, Composition | 175.00 |
| **Ideal,** Ferdinand The Bull | 75.00 |
| **Ideal,** Grow Hair Crissy, Black | 35.00 |
| **Ideal,** Harriet Hubbard Ayers, Vinyl & Hard Plastic, 1956, 15 In. | 60.00 |

**Ideal,** Judy Garland, Dressed, 21 In. ............................................................................. 275.00
**Ideal,** Kerry, Crissy, & Velvet, Growing Hair, Set Of 6 ............................................... 18.00
**Ideal,** Kissy, Makes Tweaking Sound When Kissing, Jointed Wrists, 22 In. ............... 35.00
**Ideal,** Liberty Boy, Movable Head, Legs, & Arms, 12 In. .............................................. 85.00
**Ideal,** Liberty Boy, World War I, Composition, 12 In. .................................................. 165.00
**Ideal,** Miss Goody Two Shoes .......................................................................................... 45.00
**Ideal,** Shirley, Tagged Velvet Hat & Coat, 20 In. ........................................................ 300.00
**Ideal,** Snow White, Red & White Dress, 15 In. ........................................................... 200.00
**Ideal,** Suzy Walker, 1950, 19 In. ...................................................................................... 25.00
**Ideal,** Tiny Tears, Black, Dressed In Panties Only, 13 In. ............................................ 10.00
    **DOLL, INDIAN, see Indian, Doll**
**J.D.F.,** Character Baby, Solid Dome Head, Baby Body, 19 In. ...................................... 695.00
    **DOLL, J.D.K., see also Doll, Kestner**
**J.D.K.,** Kid Body, Streamer Marked, 16 In. .................................................................... 225.00
**J.D.K.152,** Baby, Sleep Eyes, 12 In. ................................................................................ 250.00
**J.D.K.211,** Blue Sleep Eyes, Composition Body, Original Wig, 11 In. ........................ 225.00
**J.D.K.211,** Blue Sleep Eyes, Original Body, 18 In. ....................................................... 695.00
**J.D.K.221,** Googly, Toddler Body, Blue Eyes, 12 In. ................................................... 1950.00
**J.D.K.257,** Baby, Blue Sleep Eyes, 14 In. ...................................................................... 275.00
**J.D.K.260,** Character, On Toddler Body, Original Blue Dress, 9 In. ............................ 350.00
**Jackie Coogan,** 13 In. ...................................................................................................... 400.00
**Jackie,** Pillbox Hat, Blue Suit, 21 In. ............................................................................ 550.00
**Jane Withers,** Original, 20 In. ................................................................. 650.00 To 695.00
**Japanese Lady,** Fabric Face, Painted Features, Wire Armature, 16 In. ...................... 40.00
**Japanese,** Mohair Pigtails, Painted Bisque, 4 In. ......................................................... 35.00
**Joe Palooka,** Wood, Jointed ............................................................................................ 35.00
**Joey Stivic,** Baby Boy, First Sexed Doll, Vinyl ............................................................. 10.75
**Judy Garland,** Teenage, All Original, 20 1/2 In. ........................................................... 375.00
**Jules Steiner,** Baby, Set Eyes, Mohair Wig, C.1884, 12 3/4 In. ............................... 675.00
**Jumeau,** Bisque Head, Glass Eyes, Ball-Jointed, Dressed, Marked, 14 In. .............. 1100.00
**Jumeau,** Brown Eyes, Original Wig, Incised E.J., 12 1/2 In. ..................................... 2995.00
**Jumeau,** Brown Paperweight Eyes, Closed Mouth, Marked, 14 In. ........................... 1850.00
**Jumeau,** Closed Mouth, Bisque Face, Jointed, Original Wig, C.1885, 30 In. ........... 1200.00
**Jumeau,** Composition Body, Velvet Coatdress, 1907, 19 In. ..................................... 1500.00
**Jumeau,** Fashion, Swivel Neck, Cloth Body, Leather Arms, 19 In. ............................ 1400.00
**Jumeau,** Open Mouth, All Original, 20 In. ................................................................... 1350.00
**Jumeau,** Open Mouth, Composition, Jointed Body & Wrists, Marked, 23 In. ............ 950.00
**Jutta,** Little Girl, Ball-Jointed, 22 In. ............................................................................ 650.00
**K • R 36,** Baby, Wavy Molded Hair, Velvet Suit, Ball-Jointed, 19 In. ....................... 850.00
**K • R 101,** Marie, Painted Eyes, Human Hair, Braids, Jointed, 12 In. ..................... 1075.00
**K • R 101,** Marie, 12 In. ................................................................................................ 1150.00
**K • R 114,** Hans, Composition Body, Wig, 7 In. .......................................................... 725.00
**K • R 114,** Pouty Boy, Painted Blue Eyes, Ball-Jointed Body, 22 In. ...................... 1350.00
**K • R 116/a,** Brown Open & Close Eyes, New Costume & Wig, 16 1/2 In. ............ 1850.00
**K • R 116/a,** Character Baby, Composition Body, Bisque, 19 1/2 In. ...................... 1975.00
**K • R 126,** Baby, Blue Sleep Eyes, 20 In. .................................................................... 475.00
**K • R 126,** Character Baby, Blonde, White Baby Dress, 15 In. .................................. 295.00
**K • R 126,** Flirty Eye, Wobble Tongue, Bisque Head, Bent-Limb, 19 In. .................. 595.00
**K • R 126,** Toddler, Flirt, Ball-Jointed, 26 In. .............................................................. 250.00
**K • R 402,** Girl, Flirty Eye, Bisque Head, Jointed Body, Dressed, 19 In. ................. 500.00
**K • R,** Boy, Sleep Eyes, Ball-Jointed, Bisque, 11 In. ................................................... 250.00
**K • R,** Character, Painted Eyes, Composition Baby Body, 22 In. ............................... 750.00
**K • R,** S & H 126, Character Baby, Bent-Limb Body, Baby Clothes, 21 In. ............. 550.00
**K • R,** Toddler, Bisque Head, Sleep Eyes, Ball-Jointed, Dressed, 18 In. .................. 295.00
**K • R,** Toddler, Character Face, Ball-Jointed, 22 In. .................................................... 550.00
**Kabuki,** Rotating Faces, Ivory, 6 In. .............................................................................. 350.00
**Kaiser,** Baby, Brown Eyes, Original Body, 19 In. ......................................................... 750.00
**Kallas,** Baby Bo Kaye, Bisque Head, 24 In. ............................................................... 2700.00
**Kallas,** Baby Bo Kaye, Sleep Eyes, All Bisque, 4 3/4 In. ......................................... 1000.00
**Kathe Kruse Girl,** Original Wig, 20 In. .......................................................................... 295.00
**Ken,** 1961, Mattel, Original Box ...................................................................................... 12.50
    **DOLL, KESTNER, see also Doll, J.D.K.**
**Kestner 148,** Kid Body, Sleep Eyes, Dressed, 20 In. ................................................... 250.00

**Kestner 152,** Sleep Eyes, Open Mouth, Bent-Limb Body, 15 In. .................................................. 200.00
**Kestner 154,** Bertha Collar On Dress, Bisque Head, Kid Body, 16 In. ..................................... 250.00
**Kestner 154,** Kid Body, Bisque Arms, Velvet Graduation Gown, Hat, 16 In. ........................... 165.00
**Kestner 154,** Kid Body, Brown Eyes, Brown Wig, 17 In. ............................................................. 285.00
**Kestner 156,** Brown Sleep Eyes, Ball-Jointed Body, 23 In. ....................................................... 495.00
**Kestner 164,** Ball-Jointed Body, 28 In. ....................................................................................... 485.00
**Kestner 164,** Ball-Jointed, Pale Bisque, 32 In. .......................................................................... 585.00
**Kestner 171,** Ball-Jointed Body, 24 In. ....................................................................................... 300.00
**Kestner 171,** Girl, Brown Sleep Eyes, Lashes, Long Hair Wig, 28 In. ...................................... 375.00
**Kestner 183,** Closed Mouth, Painted Blue Eyes, Smiling Face, 17 In. .................................... 1200.00
**Kestner 192,** Ball-Jointed, 32 In. ................................................................................................ 300.00
**Kestner 307/9,** Bisque, Jointed Arms & Legs, Original Clothing, 4 In. ...................................... 175.00
**Kestner,** Baby, Bald Head, Victorian Christening Dress, Life Size ............................................ 800.00
**Kestner,** Baby, Open & Close Mouth, 8 In. .................................................................................. 240.00
**Kestner,** Bisque, Sleep Eyes, Open Mouth, 6 In. ........................................................................ 225.00
**Kestner,** Character Baby, Kid Body, Bisque Arms & Face, 15 In. ............................................... 795.00
**Kestner,** Composition Body, Blonde Wig, Brown Eyes, Marked, 15 In. ..................................... 425.00
**Kestner,** Girl, Sleep Brown Eyes, 24 1/2 In. ................................................................................ 350.00
**Kestner,** Innocent Face, Sleep Eyes, Long Curls, Marked C, 18 In. ......................................... 300.00
**Kestner,** Open Mouth, Ball-Jointed, Bisque, Dressed, 23 In. .................................................... 235.00
**Kestner,** Velvet Outfit, Kid Torso, Brown Eyes, 12 In. ............................................................... 500.00
    **DOLL, KEWPIE, see Kewpie, Doll**
**Kley & Hahn,** Boy, Velvet 2-Piece Suit, Bisque, Jointed, 20 1/2 In. .......................................... 300.00
**Kley & Hahn,** Character Baby, Molded Tongue, Jointed Body, 13 1/2 In. ............................... 350.00
**Knickerbocker,** Dopey, Original Clothes, 9 In. ............................................................................. 200.00
**Lenci,** Alice In Wonderland, Felt Over Celluloid, Boxed, 12 In. ................................................... 300.00
**Lenci,** Amelia Earhart, Felt Swivel Head, C.1930, 16 In. ...................................................*Illus* 1550.00
**Lenci,** Boudoir, Painted Face, Muslin Body, C.1930, 22 In. ...................................................*Illus* 500.00
**Lenci,** Brazilian Lady ........................................................................................................................ 175.00
**Lenci,** Dutch Girl, Original, 8 In. ..................................................................................................... 110.00
**Lenci,** Girl, Glass Flirty Eyes, Felt Body, Peasant Costume, 20 1/2 In. .................................... 850.00
**Lenci,** Girl, Holding Hoop, Sticker Tag, 8 In. ................................................................................ 110.00
**Lenci,** Girl, Long-Legged, 21 In. ..................................................................................................... 215.00
**Lenci,** Girl, Pink Jacket & Cap, Marked, C.1930, 13 In. .........................................................*Illus* 275.00
**Lenci,** Girl, Red Felt Costume, Marked, 19 In. .........................................................................*Illus* 600.00
**Lenci,** Girl, Sundress & Bonnet, C.1930, 17 In. .......................................................................*Illus* 350.00

Doll, Lenci, Girl, Red Felt Costume, Marked, 19 In.

Dolls, Lenci, from left to right, Boudoir With Painted Face & Muslin Body (See Page 171); Girl With Swivel Head & Pajamas, Jointed; Girl With Swivel Head & Dress, Jointed; Russian Boy With Swivel Head, Felt; Amelia Earhart With Swivel Head, Felt (See Page 171)

| | |
|---|---|
| **Lenci,** Girl, Swivel Head, Jointed, Dress, C.1925, 21 In. ........................................ *Illus* | 900.00 |
| **Lenci,** Girl, Swivel Head, Jointed, Pajamas, C.1925, 14 In. ................................... *Illus* | 350.00 |
| **Lenci,** Lucia, Blue Eyes, Unusual Hairdo ......................................................... | 550.00 |
| **Lenci,** Russian Boy, Felt Swivel Head, C.1930, 17 In. ........................................ *Illus* | 1250.00 |
| **Lenci,** Swiss Boy, Embroidered Vest, C.1930, Marked, 17 In. ............................. *Illus* | 600.00 |
| **Lenci,** Teddy Bear, No.524, Signed On Leg, 18 In. .......................................... | 165.00 |
| **Leuzzi,** Paperweight Eyes, Mohair Wig, Molded Hair, 10 1/2 In. ........................... | 500.00 |
| **Liberty Belle,** Cloth, 1926 .............................................................................. | 65.00 |
| **Lily,** The Maid, 1890 Hairdo, Original Clothes, 7 In. .......................................... | 195.00 |
| **Lucy Peck,** Poured Wax Head, Glass Eyes, Signed, 20 In. ................................. | 950.00 |
| **Madame Alexander,** Africa, 8 In. ................................................................... | 275.00 |
| **Madame Alexander,** Agatha ......................................................... 165.00 To | 300.00 |
| **Madame Alexander,** Alice In Wonderland, Vinyl & Cloth, 29 In. ........................... | 250.00 |
| **Madame Alexander,** Alice In Wonderland, 18 In. .............................................. | 195.00 |
| **Madame Alexander,** American Girl, 8 In. ......................................................... | 450.00 |
| **Madame Alexander,** Amish Boy, Boxed ........................................................... | 275.00 |
| **Madame Alexander,** Amy, Walker, Boxed ........................................................ | 95.00 |
| **Madame Alexander,** April Birthday Girl, Composition, 7 1/4 In. ........................... | 100.00 |
| **Madame Alexander,** Argentine Boy, Knee Bender, Walker, 8 In. ......................... | 295.00 |
| **Madame Alexander,** Baby Jane, Child Movie Star, Composition, 17 In. ................. | 500.00 |
| **Madame Alexander,** Baby Victoria, White Wooden High Chair ............................ | 75.00 |
| **Madame Alexander,** Baby, Lovey Dovey, Hard Plastic, 11 1/2 In. ....................... | 90.00 |

Dolls, Lenci, from left to right, Swiss Boy With Embroidered Vest; Little Girl In Pink Jacket; Girl, Sundress & Bonnet, C. 1930 (See Page 171)

**Madame Alexander,** Ballerina, Walker, Hand-Painted, 17 1/2 In. ............................................ 100.00
**Madame Alexander,** Binnie, Walker, Hand-Painted, Original ...................................................... 185.00
**Madame Alexander,** Bride, Blue Sleep Eyes, Blonde Hair, Alex Tag, 15 In. ........................... 115.00
**Madame Alexander,** Bride, Red Hair, Brown Eyes, 1930s, Tag, 18 In. ................................... 215.00
**Madame Alexander,** Brigetta, 14 In. ......................................................................................... 150.00
**Madame Alexander,** Caroline, Pink Corduroy Outfit, 15 In. ....................................................... 350.00
**Madame Alexander,** Cinderella, Pink & Silver Ballgown, 14 1/2 In. .......................................... 95.00
**Madame Alexander,** Cinderella, 21 In. ...................................................................................... 650.00
**Madame Alexander,** Cissette, Brunette, Tagged Dress, Boxed, 10 In. ...................................... 175.00
**Madame Alexander,** Cissette, Southern Belle, No.1170 ............................................................ 250.00
**Madame Alexander,** Cynthia, Walker, Black ............................................................................. 450.00
**Madame Alexander,** Dionne Quintuplet, Lavender Sun Suit, 7 1/2 In. ...................................... 100.00
**Madame Alexander,** Dionne Quintuplets, Sunday Suits, Bonnets, 7 1/2 In. ............................. 695.00
**Madame Alexander,** Easter, Boxed, 8 In. ...............................................................................1295.00
**Madame Alexander,** Elise Ballerina, White Tutu, Toe Shoes, 15 1/2 In. ............................... 130.00
**Madame Alexander,** Elise Bride, Necklace, 17 In. .................................................................... 85.00
**Madame Alexander,** Enchanted Doll, Boxed, 8 In. ................................................................... 350.00
**Madame Alexander,** First Ladies, Abigail Adams .................................................................... 150.00
**Madame Alexander,** First Ladies, Dolley Madison ................................................................... 150.00
**Madame Alexander,** First Ladies, First Set, Boxed ................................................ 825.00 To 900.00
**Madame Alexander,** Flora McFlimsey, All Original, 19 1/2 In. ................................................. 195.00
**Madame Alexander,** Girl, French, Black, 8 In. ......................................................................... 40.00
**Madame Alexander,** Girl, Tagged Sunday School, 1955, 8 In. ................................................ 155.00
**Madame Alexander,** Grande Dame, Boxed, 20 In. ................................................................... 35.00
**Madame Alexander,** Greek Boy & Girl, Pair, 8 In. ................................................................... 500.00
**Madame Alexander,** Gretel, Wrist Tag, 8 In. ........................................................................... 85.00
**Madame Alexander,** Groom, Jointed-Knee Walker, Original Outfit, 8 In. ............................... 125.00
**Madame Alexander,** Jacqueline Kennedy, Formal Dress, 10 In. .............................................. 500.00
**Madame Alexander,** Janie, Original, 36 In. .............................................................................. 225.00
**Madame Alexander,** Jeannie, Walker, Dressed, Composition, 19 In. ....................................... 175.00

Madame Alexander, Kate Greenaway, Original, 15 In. ......................................................... 125.00
Madame Alexander, Kathy Cry, Pink & White Checked Dress, 14 In. ................................... 45.00
Madame Alexander, Lissy, 1956, 11 1/2 In. ........................................................................ 90.00
Madame Alexander, Little Genius, Caracul Wig, 7 In. .......................................................... 50.00
Madame Alexander, Little Genius, Composition, All Original, 12 In. .................................... 125.00
Madame Alexander, Little Genius, Composition, Sleep Eyes, 11 In. ................................... 295.00
Madame Alexander, Little Lady, All Original, 28 In. ............................................................. 300.00
Madame Alexander, Little Shaver, 12 In. ............................................................................. 27.50
Madame Alexander, Little Women & Marmee, Boxed, 8 In. ................................................. 300.00
Madame Alexander, Madame, 14 In. .................................................................................... 225.00
Madame Alexander, Madelaine, All Original, 18 In. ............................................................. 265.00
Madame Alexander, Maggie, Walker, Tagged Dress, 17 In. ................................................. 90.00
Madame Alexander, Magnolia, 1977 ................................................................................... 350.00
Madame Alexander, Margaret O'Brien, 14 In. ...................................................................... 400.00
Madame Alexander, Marta, Wrist Tag, 8 In. ......................................................................... 85.00
Madame Alexander, Mary Ellen, Hard Plastic, Only In 1955, 31 In. ..................................... 165.00
Madame Alexander, Mary Martin, 18 In. .............................................................................. 450.00
Madame Alexander, MaryBel-Get-Well, In Suitcase, Original, 16 In. .................................... 175.00
Madame Alexander, MaryBel-Get-Well, Uniform, 14 In. ....................................................... 95.00
Madame Alexander, McGuffey Anna, Composition, 9 In. ............................. 200.00 To 265.00
Madame Alexander, McGuffey Anna, Composition, 13 In. .................................................... 140.00
Madame Alexander, McGuffey Anna, Taffeta Dress, Original, 19 1/2 In. ............................. 295.00
Madame Alexander, Melanie, 1974, 21 In. ......................................................................... 340.00
Madame Alexander, Patty Playpal, 26 In. ........................................................................... 65.00
Madame Alexander, Peru, Knee Bender, Walker, Boy, Boxed, 8 In. .................................... 295.00
Madame Alexander, Pig Face, Composition, 11 In. ............................................................. 135.00
Madame Alexander, Princess Elizabeth, Closed Mouth, 13 In. ........................................... 125.00
Madame Alexander, Princess Elizabeth, Little Colonel Outfit, 13 In. ................................... 195.00
Madame Alexander, Princess Elizabeth, Nurse, Tagged ..................................................... 160.00
Madame Alexander, Princess Elizabeth, Original, In Trunk .................................................. 250.00
Madame Alexander, Puppets & Stage, Tony Sarg, Pair ...................................................... 450.00
Madame Alexander, Riley's Little Annie, 1965 Only ............................................................ 300.00
Madame Alexander, Rosy, Boxed, 12 In. ............................................................................ 325.00
Madame Alexander, Scarlett O'Hara, Original Clothing, 1939, 18 In. ................................. 275.00
Madame Alexander, Scarlett, 1978, 21 In. .......................................................................... 245.00
Madame Alexander, Snow White, Composition, 1937, Original Box, 13 In. ......................... 140.00
Madame Alexander, Snow White, Hard Plastic, Tagged Dress, 17 In. ................................ 175.00
Madame Alexander, Snow White, Original Clothes, Label, 16 In. ....................................... 225.00
Madame Alexander, Sonja Henie, 1939, 15 In. ................................................................... 125.00
Madame Alexander, Sonja Henie, 1951, 18 In. ................................................................... 260.00
Madame Alexander, Sound Of Music, Set Of 7 ................................................................... 950.00
Madame Alexander, Spanish Boy & Girl, 8 In., Pair ........................................................... 750.00
Madame Alexander, Tyrolean, Boy & Girl, Boxed, Pair ....................................................... 125.00
Madame Alexander, Wendy Ann, Original Clothes, 8 In. ..................................................... 150.00
Madame Chapeaux, Voodoo Queen ................................................................................... 50.00
Madame Hendren, Indian, 14 In. ........................................................................................ 85.00
Majestic, Sleep Eyes, Kid Body, Composition Lower Arms, 16 In. ..................................... 140.00
Man Friday, Black, Composition, Handmade, Fur Skirt, 8 1/2 In. ....................................... 75.00
Marx, General Eisenhower, Boxed, 12 In. ........................................................................... 45.00
Mason Taylor, Jointed, Metal Feet, C.1879, Wooden, 12 In. ............................................. 500.00
Mattel, Hush Little Baby, Black .......................................................................................... 14.00
Mattel, Saucy, Makes Faces, Boxed .................................................................................. 30.00
Mechanical, Bisque, Plays Mandolin, Taps Foot, Head Turns, 16 1/2 In. .......................... 725.00
Mechanical, Boy, Musical, Sylvaine, Bisque ...................................................................... 250.00
Melitta Baby, 16 In. ........................................................................................................... 670.00
Milliner's Model, Original Clothing, 1850s, 18 In. ............................................................ 1650.00
Minerva, Tin Head, 16 In. ................................................................................................... 55.00
Miss Charming, Original, With Button, Composition, 20 In. ................................................ 165.00
Miss Sunbeam, Advertising, Composition & Rubber, Marked Clothes ................................ 45.00
Morimura, Baby, Bisque Head, Composition Body, Brown Hair, 13 In. ............................... 180.00
Morimura, Bisque Head, Kid Body, Auburn Wig, Dressed, Marked, 18 In. ......................... 150.00
Morimura, Character Baby, Blue Sleep Eyes, Brown Wig, 10 In. ....................................... 65.00
Motschmann, Alice, Silk Dress, Velvet Yoke, Face On Swivel, 10 1/2 In. .......................... 250.00

| | |
|---|---|
| **Mr.Peanut,** Rag, 14 In. | 6.50 |
| **Mr.Peanut,** Wooden, Ball-Jointed Body, 9 In. | 100.00 |
| **Mussolini,** Character Saroff, 12 In. | 195.00 |
| **My Girlie,** Ball-Jointed Body, Red Hair, 25 In. | 300.00 |
| **My Sweetheart,** Sleep Eyes, Ball-Jointed, White Lace Dress, 28 In. | 375.00 |
| **Nippon,** Character Baby, Bisque Head, Composition Body, 14 In. | 185.00 |
| **Nippon,** Happy Fats, Miniature | 125.00 |
| **Norah Wellings,** Sailor, Original Clothes, 10 1/2 In. | 35.00 |
| **P.M.914,** Baby, Blue Sleep Eyes, 19 In. | 300.00 |
| **P.M.914,** Toddler, 20 1/2 In. | 422.00 |
| **DOLL, PAPER, see Paper Doll** | |
| **Papier-Mache,** Ball-Jointed, Dressed, Signed, Belgium, 27 In. | 175.00 |
| **Papier-Mache,** Blonde Molded Hair, Label Marked C.B., 15 In. | 150.00 |
| **Papier-Mache,** Booted Feet, Cotton Body, 2-Piece Dress, Beadwork, 41 In. | 950.00 |
| **Papier-Mache,** Flirty Eyes, 33 In. | 950.00 |
| **Papier-Mache,** Toddler, 12 In. | 250.00 |
| **Parian,** Boy, Blond, 19 In. | 425.00 |
| **Parsons Jackson,** Baby, Biskoline, 11 In. | 125.00 |
| **Patty Play Pal,** Original Clothes & Box, 36 In. | 85.00 |
| **Phonograph,** Mae Star | 400.00 |
| **DOLL, PINCUSHION, see Pincushion Doll** | |
| **Policeman,** Palmer Cox Brownie, Papier-Mache Head, Wooden Arms, 10 In. | 55.00 |
| **Popeye,** Rubber Head, Seasick Motion, Musical, Japan, 1940s, 16 In. | 185.00 |
| **Queen Louise,** Brown Sleep Eyes, Ball-Jointed, 30 In. | 395.00 To 425.00 |
| **R & B,** Nancy Lee, Composition, 14 In. | 75.00 |
| **Rag,** Black, Girl & Boy, C.1890, All Original, 11 In., Pair | 250.00 |
| **Rag,** Black, Knitted Fabric Face, Embroidered Features, Dressed, 23 In. | 150.00 |
| **Rag,** Embroidered Face, Auburn Hair, Handmade Dress, Linen Head, 17 In. | 85.00 |
| **Rag,** Painted Hair, Eyes, & Mouth, Checked Dress, Slip, 14 In. | 65.00 |
| **Regal,** Charles Lindbergh, Composition Head, Cloth Body & Limbs, 27 In. | 200.00 |
| **Revalo,** Coquette, Molded Hair, Bows, Intaglio Eyes, Toddler Body, 10 In. | 450.00 |
| **Rheinische Gummi,** Boy, Celluloid, 14 In. | 55.00 |
| **Rock-A-Bye Baby,** Black, Cloth Body, Sleep Eyes, 7 1/2 In. | 245.00 |
| **Rock-A-Bye Baby,** Black, 26 In. | 650.00 |
| **S & H 939,** Paperweight Blue Eyes, Closed Mouth, 20 In. | 1500.00 |
| **S & H 1078,** Lashed Sleep Eyes, French Torso, 18 In. | 295.00 |
| **S & H 1159,** Lady, Brown Sleep Eyes, Brown Hair, 20 In. | 895.00 |
| **S & H 1912-4,** Ball-Jointed Body, Brown Wig, Undressed, 22 In. | 95.00 |
| **S & H,** Ball-Jointed Body, Dressed, 24 In. | 495.00 |
| **S & H,** Bonnie Babe, Brown Sleep Eyes, 16 In. | 765.00 |
| **S & H,** Brown Sleep Eyes, 36 In. | 550.00 |
| **S.F.B.J.,** French Child, Composition Body, Bisque Face & Hands, 24 In. | 575.00 |
| **S.F.B.J.,** Girl, Lashed Sleep Eyes, Fully Jointed, 15 In. | 475.00 |
| **S.F.B.J.60,** Girl, Blue Eyes, Blonde Wig, Jointed, Dressed, 14 In. | 425.00 |
| **S.F.B.J.236,** French, Laughing Child, Bisque, Marked, 27 In. | 1775.00 |
| **S.F.B.J.247,** French Toddler, Molded Teeth, Silk Dress, Marked, 28 In. | 3700.00 |
| **S.F.B.J.247,** Twirp, Molded Teeth, Sleep Eyes, Ball-Jointed, 18 In. | 1850.00 |
| **S.F.B.J.301,** Rudy, Original, 18 In. | 425.00 |
| **DOLL, S & H, see also Doll, Bergmann; Doll, Simon & Halbig** | |
| **Sandy McCall,** Original, 36 In. | 190.00 |
| **Santa Claus,** Straw Stuffed, Silk Suit, Electrified Eyes, 18 In. | 275.00 |
| **Saucy Walker,** Black, 22 In. | 90.00 |
| **Scarecrow,** Wizard Of Oz, 1940s, 28 In. | 65.00 |
| **Schoenau & Hoffmeister,** Composition Body, Corduroy Coat & Hat, 22 In. | 225.00 |
| **Schoenau & Hoffmeister,** Fashion, Cloth Body, Bisque Hands, 13 1/2 In. | 650.00 |
| **Schoenhut,** Baby, Mohair Wig, Dressed, 17 In. | 450.00 |
| **Schoenhut,** Baby, Wigged, Original Clothes, 14 1/2 In. | 350.00 |
| **Schoenhut,** Boy, Brown Intaglio Eyes, Nude, Incised Mark, 15 In. | 360.00 |
| **Schoenhut,** Boy, Nude, Molded Hair, 19 In. | 575.00 |
| **Schoenhut,** Female, Long Hair, Dressed, Marked, 15 In. | 335.00 |
| **Schoenhut,** Girl, Smiling, Two Teeth, Original, 21 In. | 895.00 |
| **Schoenhut,** Pouty Boy, 16 In. | 310.00 |
| **Schoenhut,** Pouty Girl, Blue Eyes, 16 In. | 395.00 To 450.00 |

Schoenhut, Pouty Girl, Brown Eyes, 22 In. ............................................................. 500.00
Schoenhut, Pouty Girl, Intaglio Eyes, 18 In. ......................................................... 485.00
Schoenhut, Pouty Girl, 14 In. ................................................................................. 275.00
Schoenhut, Suzy Smart, 24 In. ................................................................................. 25.00
Schoenhut, Toddler, Original Rompers, 12 In. ...................................................... 395.00
Schwellies, Clown, China ......................................................................................... 40.00
SHEbee, Japanese, Jointed, 4 1/2 In. .................................................................... 175.00
    DOLL, SHIRLEY TEMPLE, see Shirley Temple
    DOLL, SIMON & HALBIG, see also Doll, Bergmann; Doll, S & H
Simon & Halbig 550, Blue Sleep Eyes, 24 In. ...................................................... 350.00
Simon & Halbig, Bisque Head, Fur Eyebrows, Pierced Ears, 29 In. ................... 950.00
Simon & Halbig, Coral Taffeta & Lace Costume, 26 In. ...................................... 395.00
Simon & Halbig, Feathered Brows, Blue Sleep Eyes, Dressed, 22 In. ............... 400.00
Simon & Halbig, Lady, Sleep Eyes, Pierced Ears, Jointed, 27 In. .................... 1450.00
Simon & Halbig 512h, Girl, Ball-Jointed, Bisque, 24 In. .................*Illus* 350.00
Simon & Halbig 939, Blue Paperweight Eyes, 14 In. ........................................ 1200.00
Simon & Halbig 1039, Bisque Head, Open & Close Eyes, Jointed, 16 In. ........... 495.00
Simon & Halbig 1079, Sleep Eyes, Pierced Ears, Ball-Jointed, 20 In. ............... 250.00
Simon & Halbig 1329, Oriental, Olive Bisque, 16 In. ...................................... 1100.00
Simon Halbig, Set Eyes, Open Mouth, Sailor Dress, Jointed, Bisque, 14 In. ....... 300.00
Simone, Fashion, Completely Original, Signed, 17 In. ..................................... 2595.00
Skookum Squaw, Boxed, 16 In. ................................................................................ 60.00
Skookum, Papier-Mache, Funny Paper Character, 11 1/2 In. ................................. 98.00
Sonja Henie, Composition, Original & Mint, 15 In. ............................................. 125.00
Sonja Henie, 18 In. ................................................................................................ 200.00
Steiner, Googly, Glass Eyes, Bisque Head, 7 In. .................................................. 325.00
Steiner, Paperweight Eyes, Closed Mouth, Pierced Ears, 9 In. ......................... 1550.00
Sunbaby Babee, Rubber Body, Composition Head, Sleep Eyes, 12 1/2 In. .......... 55.00
Sweet Sue, Blonde, Red & White Dress, Rooted Cap, Bent-Knee, 24 In. ............. 60.00
Terri Lee, Baby, Linda, Christening Outfit ............................................................. 60.00
Terri Lee, Benji, Painted Flirty Eyes, Blue Shorts, Print Shirt, 16 In. ............... 250.00
Terri Lee, Girl Scout, Several Outfits, 16 In. ...................................................... 150.00
Terri Lee, Strawberry Blonde, Confirmation Dress, 16 In. .................................. 125.00
Tete Jumeau, Paperweight Eyes, Human Hair, Ball-Jointed, Marked, 25 In. ...... 2000.00
Tin Head, Metal Sleep Eyes, 2 Teeth, Voice Box, 22 In. ...................................... 215.00
Tinker Bell, Vinyl, Molded Hair, 13 In. ................................................................... 45.00
Tony Sarge, Marionette, Alice ................................................................................. 75.00
Tony Sarge, Marionette, Prince Charming .............................................................. 65.00
Topsy Turvy, Black Figure On One Side ................................................................. 28.00
Twins, Dream Babies, Socket Heads, Sleep Eyes, White Dresses, 8 1/2 In. ....... 300.00
Uneeda, Freckles, Red Hair, Green Eyes, 32 In. .................................................... 38.00
Uneeda, Littlest So-Soft, Pink Sleeper, Bonnet, Unopened ................................... 10.00
Unis, 301, French Girl, Open Mouth, Composition Body, 25 In. .......................... 575.00
Vogue, Dearest One, 1967 ....................................................................................... 35.00
Walker, Sleep Eyes, Blonde Curly Wig, Pierced Ears, White Dress, 28 In. ......... 395.00
Walking, Autoperipatetikos, Dressed, Key & Box, 9 1/2 In. ...................*Illus* 800.00
Wax Over Composition, Open & Close Eyes, Original Clothes, 11 1/2 In. ......... 165.00
Wax Over Papier-Mache, Girl, Glass Eyes, C.1850, 24 In. ................................. 300.00
Wax Over Papier-Mache, Molded Hair, Curls, Wood Hands & Feet, 30 In. ........ 595.00
Wax Over Papier-Mache, Wooden Arms, Molded Boots, Wig, 20 1/2 In. ........... 160.00
Wax, Baby Emerging From Papier-Mache Egg, Dome, French ............................. 325.00
    DONALD DUCK, see Disneyana
    DOORSTOP, see Iron, Doorstop

        *Doulton pottery and porcelain were made by Doulton and Co. of Burslem,*
        *England, after 1882. The name Royal Doulton appeared on their wares*
        *after 1902.*
    DOULTON, see also Royal Doulton
DOULTON, Biscuit Barrel, Lambeth, Sheep, Sterling Cover & Trim, Marked ............. 425.00
Bowl, Lambeth, Blues & Grays, 2 X 3 In.Diam. ..................................................... 25.00
Candlestick, Lambeth, Silicone, 6 1/4 In., Pair ..................................................... 110.00
Candlestick, Stoneware, Butterflies, Mottled Ground, 3 1/2 In., Pair .................... 135.00
Coffeepot, Covered, Stoneware, Assyrian Scene, 7 1/4 In. ................................... 165.00

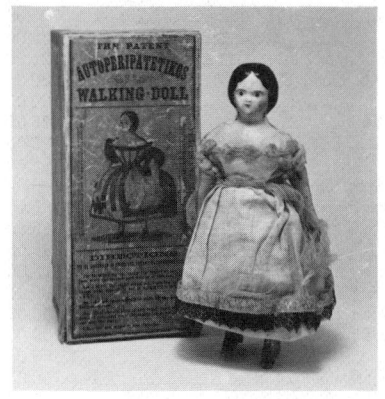

Doll, Walking, Autoperipatetikos,
Dressed, Key & Box, 9 1/2 In.

Cookie Jar, Burslem, Flowers, Marked, 6 3/4 X 5 3/8 In.Diam. ............................................ 115.00
Cookie Jar, Lambeth Silicon, Signed C.Rymer ............................................................ 245.00
Cracker Jar, Fish, C.1882, Signed & Numbered, Handled, Covered ............................... 175.00
Creamer, Lambeth, Dogwood On Green Ground, Marked ................................................ 40.00
Cup & Saucer, Burslem, Floral Design ........................................................................ 25.00
Cup & Saucer, Demitasse, Burslem, Fluted, Hand-Painted Flowers ............................... 65.00
Dish, Strainer, Burslem, Cobalt, Red, Gold, Oval ........................................................ 50.00
Ewer, Burslem, Blow Blue, Gold Trim, Beaded Neck, C.1882, 9 1/2 In. ......................... 150.00
Ewer, Burslem, Gold Dragon Handle, Burgundy Flowers, 11 1/2 In. .............................. 350.00
Ewer, Cobalt Handle & Neck, Gilded Tapestry, Flowers, 5 1/2 In. ................................... 95.00
Ewer, Lambeth, Art Nouveau, Artist Signed, 6 1/2 In. .................................................. 50.00
Ewer, Lambeth, Sterling Silver Rim, Signed E.P. ........................................................ 200.00
Ewer, Morrisian Ware, Pedestal, Dancing Girl, Gold, Brown, 7 1/2 In. .......................... 225.00
Flask, Reform, Figural, Watts, C.1832 ...................................................................... 425.00
Humidor, Lambeth, Brownware, Applied Floral & Medallion, Signed ............................... 50.00
Jug, Brown & Cream Stoneware, Raised Figures, 6 1/2 In. ........................................... 75.00
Jug, Brownware, Monk Scenes, 6 1/2 In. ................................................................... 80.00
Jug, Lambeth, Green Flowers, Blue, Brown Upper, 8 In. ............................................. 110.00
Jug, Lambeth, Incised Flowers, Leaves, Hallmarked Silver Rim, 8 In. ............................ 95.00
Jug, Lambeth, Incised Swirling, Brown Ground, Dated 1874, 7 1/2 In. ........................... 125.00
Jug, Lambeth, Queen Victoria, 1897 Diamond Jubilee, 7 1/2 In. ................................... 165.00
Jug, Leatherware, Raised Wording, Silver Plated Band, 8 1/4 In. .................................. 125.00
Lamp, The Huntsman Fox ........................................................................................ 200.00
Mug, Stoneware, Raised Figures Of Man With Dogs, White, 3 3/4 In. ............................. 55.00
Pitcher, Burslem, Allover Blue & White Pinwheel Shapes ........................................... 160.00
Pitcher, Burslem, Alphabet, Tan, 7 1/2 In. .................................................................. 85.00
Pitcher, Burslem, Bands Of Sailing Ships & Fish, 7 1/2 In. ............................................ 50.00
Pitcher, Burslem, Horseshoe Design, Hand-Painted Flowers, 8 In. ................................ 98.00
Pitcher, Burslem, Pinwheel-Type Flowers, Dark Blue On White, 9 In. ........................... 175.00
Pitcher, Hot Water, Lambeth, Brownware, Embossed Stag Hunt Scene ......................... 150.00
Pitcher, Lambeth, Brownware, Applied Hunting Scene, 6 1/2 In. .................................. 115.00
Pitcher, Lambeth, Leatherware, Sterling Band, C.1890, 6 1/2 In. .................................. 150.00
Pitcher, Lambeth, Raised Hunt Scene ........................................................................ 82.00
Pitcher, Lambeth, Silicone, Signed, 7 3/4 In. .............................................................. 98.00
Pitcher, Leathercraft, Sterling Rim, 8 In. .................................................................. 145.00
Planter, Lambeth, Indian Design, Brown Ground, 6 1/2 X 6 1/2 In. ............................... 85.00
Planter, Lambeth, Marbleized Colors, Raised Scrolls, 10 X 11 In. ................................. 190.00
Plate, Cake, Scalloped, Flowers, Silver Plated Handle .................................................. 60.00
Plate, Pompeii, Black & White Design, Dated 1871, 8 In. ............................................. 25.00
Platter, Asiatic Pheasant, 17 1/2 14 1/2 In. ................................................................. 42.50
Platter, Burslem, Flow Blue, Turkey Center, 22 1/2 X 18 1/2 In. ................................... 200.00

Platter, Burslem, Melrose Pattern, 18 In. ............................................................................................ 150.00
Platter, Retriever, 13 1/2 X 9 3/4 In. ................................................................................................. 125.00
Puzzle Jug, Lambeth, Green Design, White Letter Saying, 7 In. ......................................................... 125.00
Salt, Blue, Brown, & White, Hallmarked Silver Rim & Spoon, 2 1/4 In. ................................................. 80.00
Saltshaker, Lambeth, Supported By Openwork ................................................................................ 100.00
Soap Dish, Raised Dragonfly, Stoneware, 4 1/2 X 6 In. ...................................................................... 85.00
Soup Plate, Melrose, 10 1/2 In.Diam. .................................................................................................. 25.00
Sweetmeat Jar, Silver Top, Rim, & Handle, Dated 1881, 4 1/2 In. .................................................... 195.00
Syrup, Lambeth, Brownware, Silver Plated Float, Stag, Hunt Scene .................................................... 145.00
Syrup, Lambeth, Embossed Stag Hunt Scene, Silver Plated Lid .......................................................... 145.00
Tea Set, Lambeth, 3 Piece ................................................................................................................ 395.00
Teapot, Burslem, Jacobean Pattern, Flow Blue ................................................................................. 135.00
Teapot, Coronet Pattern ..................................................................................................................... 25.00
Teapot, Covered, Moorish Gate, 2 Arabs In Color, 5 1/2 X 5 3/4 In. .................................................... 95.00
Teapot, Lambeth, Terra-Cotta, Reds, Browns, & White, 5 In. ............................................................. 150.00
Tray, Burslem, 3 Curves Forming Triangle, Swags, Blossoms, 7 In. .................................................. 100.00
Tumbler, Brass Rim, Tinsworth, 5 1/2 In. .......................................................................................... 150.00
Umbrella Stand, Lambeth, Flared, Sgraffito Design, Marked, 24 In. .................................................. 200.00
Vase, Burslem, Blue & Gold Daffodils, 11 1/2 In., Pair ....................................................................... 195.00
Vase, Burslem, Cows Grazing, Artist Signed, 22 In. ........................................................................ 1900.00
Vase, Burslem, Iris, Blue & White, Gilt Trim, 6 In. .............................................................................. 75.00
Vase, Fish Handles, Dutch Scene, 4 In. ............................................................................................. 65.00
Vase, Green, Tan, Gold, Brown, Blue Floral.9 In., Pair ...................................................................... 275.00
Vase, Lambeth, Green & Tan Ground, Branches & Leaves, 10 In. ...................................................... 95.00
Vase, Pedestal, Collared Top, Cobalt & Brown Flowers, 9 1/2 In. ...................................................... 75.00
Vase, Ship Scenic, Hand-Painted, Gold Handles, Marked M, 5 3/4 In. ............................................. 150.00
Vase, Silicon, 8 1/2 In., Pair ............................................................................................................. 180.00
Washbowl & Pitcher, Burslem, Gold Edge, Oblong, Bowl, 14 X 17 In. .............................................. 345.00
    DR.SYNTAX, see Adams, Staffordshire

    *Dresden china is any china made in the town of Dresden, Germany. The*
    *most famous factory in Dresden is the Meissen factory.*
    DRESDEN, see also Meissen
DRESDEN, Bowl, Floral Design, Reticulated, Applied Handles, Blue Mark, 6 In. ...................... 100.00
Bowl, Hand-Painted, Reticulated, 7 1/2 In. ...................................................................................... 225.00
Cake Plate, Portrait, Love Scene, Gold Border ................................................................................ 125.00
Cake Set & Compote, 4 Plates, Flowers, Cutout Borders, 1895 ....................................................... 255.00
Cake Stand, Openwork Border, Floral Design, 5 X 10 In.Diam. .......................................................... 50.00
Candelabra, Cherubs, 4 Candle, 19 1/2 In., Pair ............................................................................. 2900.00
Candlestick, Angels & Flowers, Pair ................................................................................................ 125.00
Cup & Saucer, Hand-Painted Flowers, Gold Trim, Signed .................................................................. 30.00
Cup & Saucer, Melon Shape, Alternating Panels Of People & Flowers ................................................ 85.00
Cup, Chocolate, Cover & Stand, Sporting Figures, Marked ............................................................... 250.00
Cup, Portrait, Lady & Man, Gold Leaf, Tall ....................................................................................... 100.00
Figurine, Ballerina, Blue & Lace Dress, Gold Trim, 6 In. .................................................................... 30.00
Figurine, Ballerina, Porcelain, Lace Skirt, Pink, 4 1/4 In. ................................................................... 55.00
Figurine, Girl Wearing Bonnet, Flower Cluster, Purple Feather, 3 In. ............................................... 125.00
Figurine, Girl, Applied Lace & Varicolored Flowers, 8 1/4 In. ........................................................... 250.00
Figurine, King Charles Spaniel, Gray & White, 8 1/2 X 14 In. ........................................................... 395.00
Figurine, Ladies, Pink Dressed, Lace Flowers, 4 1/2 In. ..................................................................... 95.00
Figurine, Lady In Lavender Dress, Man In Green Jacket, 6 In., Pair .................................................. 234.00
Figurine, Lady, Pink Dress, Lace, Flowers, 4 1/2 In. .......................................................................... 95.00
Figurine, Madonna, 8 In. .................................................................................................................... 85.00
Figurine, Man Walking With Basket Of Eggs & Dead Bird, 6 In. ......................................................... 95.00
Figurine, Mary Stuart, C.Thieme, 1870s, 8 In. ................................................................................. 275.00
Figurine, Nude, Signed Schaubach, 9 1/2 In. ................................................................................... 125.00
Figurine, Seated Lady, Playing Mandolin, Lace Skirt, Blue Mark, 4 In. .............................................. 125.00
Figurine, Young Man & Woman On Floral Settee, 9 1/4 X 10 In. ....................................................... 585.00
Jardiniere, Handled, Enameled, 6 In. ................................................................................................. 50.00
Lemonade Set, Green, White, Red Poppies, 7 Pieces ....................................................................... 125.00
Nut Cup, Basket Weave, Flower Center, Gold Trim, Lamb Mark .......................................................... 35.00
Oyster Plate, Blue Seashells, White Ground, 8 1/4 In.Diam. ............................................................ 125.00
Plaque, Boy, Rustic Clothing, Medallion, Gold Ring In Ear, 6 In. ....................................................... 600.00

Plaque, Maiden Carrying Sheaf Of Corn, C.1900, 8 1/2 X 5 1/2 In. ........................ 475.00
Plaque, Princess Louise, White Gown, Pink Bow, Marked, 9 X 5 In. ..................... 1100.00
Plaque, Psyche, Woodland Ground, Goddess, Water, 7 1/2 X 5 In. ........................ 400.00
Plaque, The Zither Player, Muted Tones, Marked, 7 In. ........................................ 325.00
Plaque, Wall, Rape Of Daughters Of Leucippus, Blue-Green, 19 3/4 In. .............. 3500.00
Plate, Maiden, White Gown, Green Robe, Red Ground, C.1900, 9 In. .................... 450.00
Rose Jar, Floral Wreaths, Gold Stripes, Rose Finial, Signed, 8 In. ....................... 169.00
Tankard, Portrait Of Monk Pouring Wine, 11 In. .............................................. 500.00
Tea Caddy, Hand-Painted ...................................................................................... 50.00
Tea Set, Dragon Spout, 8 Demitasse Cups & Saucers, Crossed Swords ................ 495.00
Teapot, Sugar, & Creamer, Hand-Painted, Blue Mark ........................................ 250.00
Vase, Painted Marie Antoinette, Butterflies, Encrusted Gold, 19 In. .................. 1950.00

*Duncan & Miller glass was made at the George A. Duncan and Sons*
*Company in Washington, Pennsylvania. The company was started in 1894,*
*with James E. Duncan, president, and Edwin C. Miller, secretary.*

DUNCAN & MILLER, Ashtray, Figural, Duck, Crystal, 4 In. ................................. 15.00
Ashtray, Fish Shape, Blue Opalescent .............................................................. 45.00
Ashtray, Teardrop, Individual, Set Of 6 ............................................................ 15.00
Ashtray, Terrace, Square, Small ...................................................................... 12.00
Basket, Handled, Canterbury, Crimped, Pink, 4 1/2 In. ...................................... 65.00
Basket, Tavern, Floral Cutting, 12 In. ............................................................ 55.00
Berry Bowl, Tepee .......................................................................................... 26.00
Bonbon, Handled, Sylvan Crystal, 5 1/2 In. ...................................................... 5.00
Bottle, Toilet Water, Block Pattern .................................................................. 7.50
Bottle, Water, Tepee ...................................................................................... 28.00
Bowl, Canterbury, Crimped, Opalescent Blue, 9 In.Diam. .................................. 50.00
Bowl, Canterbury, Pink, Opalescent, Flared, 10 In.Diam. .................................. 35.00
Bowl, Crimped, Multicolored Enamel Flowers, 10 X 5 In. .................................. 58.00
Bowl, Gardenia, 6 1/2 In.Diam. ...................................................................... 22.00
Bowl, Grapefruit, Sandwich, Crystal, 7 In.Diam. .............................................. 7.00
Bowl, Hobnail, Crystal, Crimped, 10 In.Diam. .................................................. 18.00
Bowl, Lace Edge, Opalescent, Blue, 10 1/2 In.Diam. ........................................ 45.00
Bowl, Oval, 10 In.Diam. .................................................................................. 39.00
Bowl, Punch, Diamond & Sunbrust .................................................................. 26.50
Bowl, Punch, Diamond With Fans, 13 In.Diam. ................................................ 30.00
Bowl, Salad, Sanibel, Pink, 10 1/2 In.Diam. .................................................... 80.00
Bowl, Terrace, 10 In.Square ............................................................................ 38.00
Bowl, Underplate, Canterbury, Silver Overlay, 5 1/2 In.Diam. ............................ 32.50
Box, Cigarette, Duck Covered ........................................................................ 35.00
Butter, Covered, Mardi Gras Pattern, Gold Trim .............................................. 85.00
Cake Salver, Footed, Sandwich, Crystal, 13 In.Diam. ........................................ 40.00
Candelabra, Early American Pattern, Prisms, Pair .......................................... 150.00
Candelabra, Prisms & Flowers, 3 Arms, Center Ring, Pair ................................ 95.00
Candleholder, American Way, Pink, 2 In., Pair .................................................. 35.00
Candleholder, Canterbury ................................................................................ 6.50
Candlestick, First Love, 2-Light, 6 In. .............................................................. 18.00
Candlestick, Lacy Sandwich, Pair .................................................................... 20.00
Candlestick, Teardrop, Crystal, 4 In. ................................................................ 6.00
Candlestick, 4 In., Pair .................................................................................... 20.00
Castor, Mustard & Relish, Caribbean .............................................................. 65.50
Celery, Craquelle, Scalloped Rim, Amber, C.1880, 7 In. .................................... 50.00
Champagne, First Love, Etched, 5 Ounce .......................................................... 18.50
Champagne, Hobnail, Crystal ............................................................................ 9.00
Cocktail, Kimberly, Set Of 6 ............................................................................ 30.00
Cocktail, Sandwich, Crystal, 3 Ounce .............................................................. 5.00
Cocktail, Seafood, Spiral Flutes, Green ............................................................ 6.50
Compote, Flowered Scroll, Ruffled Top, 7 In. .................................................... 25.00
Compote, Swirl, Green, 6 In. ............................................................................ 10.00
Console Set, Crystal Caribbean, Prisms ............................................................ 55.00
Cornucopia, Blue Opalescent, 8 1/2 In. ............................................................ 32.00
Cracker Jar, Lid, Ladder With Diamonds .......................................................... 60.00
Creamer, Arlington Pattern, Opalescent ............................................................ 22.50

| | |
|---|---|
| **Creamer,** Individual, Diamond Ridge | 12.50 |
| **Creamer,** Late Block, Applied Handle, Small | 10.00 |
| **Creamer,** Tree Of Life, Silver Plated Holder | 35.00 |
| **Creamer,** Zipper Slash | 40.00 To 45.00 |
| **Cruet,** Button Panels, Patterned Stopper | 25.00 |
| **Cruet,** Latticed Block | 15.00 |
| **Cup & Saucer,** Canterbury, Crystal | 10.00 |
| **Cup & Saucer,** Spiral Flutes, Pink | 9.50 |
| **Cup,** Punch, Diamond Ridge | 6.00 |
| **Cup,** Punch, Mardi Gras, Crystal | 8.00 |
| **Cup,** Punch, Tepee | 8.00 |
| **Cup,** Spiral Fluted, Green | 7.00 |
| **Dish,** Candy, Canterbury, 3-Handled, Covered | 45.50 |
| **Dish,** Candy, Covered, Canterbury, Chartreuse, 8 In. | 42.50 |
| **Dish,** Candy, Covered, Canterbury, Pink, 8 In. | 45.00 |
| **Dish,** Candy, Crimped, Murano, 7 In. | 12.50 |
| **Dish,** Candy, Harp & Thistle, 7 In. | 20.00 |
| **Dish,** Divided, Canterbury, Blue Opalescent | 27.00 |
| **Dish,** Nut, Handled, Divided, Teardrop, Crystal | 5.00 |
| **Dish,** Relish, Heart Shape, Teardrop, Crystal | 7.00 |
| **Dish,** Relish, 3 Compartment, Sanibel, 8 1/2 In. | 24.00 |
| **Dish,** Sanibel Shell, Blue Opalescent, 12 X 12 In. | 65.00 |
| **Dish,** Sauce, Shell, Flat, Set Of 6 | 40.00 |
| **Dish,** Swan, 10 1/2 In. | 30.00 |
| **Dish,** Teardrop, Amber, 10 In.Diam. | 15.00 |
| **Figurine Duck,** Standing, Open Back | 20.00 |
| **Flower Bowl,** First Love, Oval, 12 In. | 35.00 |
| **Goblet,** Diamond Band, Etched Fern | 20.00 |
| **Goblet,** Late Block, Etched Leaves, Tendrils | 20.00 |
| **Goblet,** Sandwich, Crystal, 9 Ounce | 10.00 |
| **Goblet,** Spiral Flute, Footed, Green, 4 1/2 In. | 5.00 |
| **Holder & Tray,** Card, Pink Opalescent | 45.00 |
| **Ivy Ball,** Pink | 24.00 |
| **Lamp,** Kerosene, 3-Faced | 275.00 |
| **Martini Mixer,** Chanticleer, Ruby, 16 Ounce | 135.00 |
| **Nappy,** Spiral Fluted, Green, 4 In. | 5.00 |
| **Pitcher,** Sandwich, Ice Lip, Clear | 45.00 |
| **Pitcher,** Water, Adoration | 92.00 |
| **Pitcher,** Water, Beaded Swirl, Emerald Green, 1/2 Gallon | 85.00 |
| **Plate,** Caribbean, Sapphire Blue, 10 1/2 In. | 12.00 |
| **Plate,** Harp & Thistle, Octagonal, 6 In. | 50.00 |
| **Plate,** Sandwich, Crystal, 13 3/4 In. | 20.00 |
| **Plate,** Sandwich Pattern, Amber, 7 In. | 4.50 |
| **Plate,** Sandwich, Crystal, 6 In. | 5.50 |
| **Plate,** Sandwich, Crystal, 7 In. | 6.50 |
| **Plate,** Sandwich, First Love, 11 In. | 20.00 |
| **Plate,** Spiral Flutes, Pink, 8 1/2 In. | 4.50 |
| **Plate,** Teardrop, Crystal, 8 3/4 In. | 8.00 |
| **Relish,** Sylvan, Red Stem, Divided | 17.50 |
| **Salt & Pepper,** Teardrop | 10.00 |
| **Sherbet,** Sandwich Design, Paneled Stem, Set Of 6, 4 In. | 40.00 |
| **Sugar & Creamer,** Canterbury, Individual | 15.00 |
| **Sugar & Creamer,** Tray, Language Of Flowers, Individual | 35.00 |
| **Sugar,** Covered, Footed, Duncan Ribbon | 85.00 |
| **Sugar,** Covered, Indian Feather | 22.50 |
| **Sugar,** Creamer, & Tray, Canterbury, Individual | 75.00 |
| **Sugar,** Creamer, & Tray, Hobnail, Crystal | 20.00 |
| **Sugar,** Diamond Ridge, Gold, Covered | 25.00 |
| **Swan,** Crystal Neck, Blue, 7 In. | 65.00 |
| **Swan,** Crystal, Cut Stars, 8 In. | 22.00 |
| **Swan,** Crystal, 5 In. | 20.00 |
| **Swan,** Crystal, 8 In. | 16.00 |
| **Swan,** Crystal, 14 In. | 28.00 To 35.00 |

| | |
|---|---:|
| **Swan,** Crystal, 15 In. | 38.00 |
| **Swan,** Green Body, Crystal Neck, 10 1/2 In. | 48.00 |
| **Swan,** Green, 11 In. | 48.00 |
| **Swan,** Pall Mall, Chartreuse, 8 In. | 38.00 |
| **Swan,** Pall Mall, Crystal Neck, Chartreuse, 10 In. | 65.00 |
| **Swan,** Pall Mall, Crystal Neck, Medium Green, 10 In. | 40.00 |
| **Swan,** Pall Mall, Ruby, 7 In. | 35.00 |
| **Swan,** Pall Mall, Solid, 3 In. | 20.00 To 30.00 |
| **Swan,** Pall Mall, 3 In. | 18.00 |
| **Swan,** Ruby Bowl, Clear Head & Neck, 10 1/2 In. | 65.00 |
| **Swan,** Short Body, Spread Wing, Pink Opalescent, 12 In. | 125.00 |
| **Swan,** Silver Overlay | 65.00 |
| **Swan,** Solid, 3 In. | 18.00 |
| **Swan,** Solid, 4 1/2 In. | 20.00 |
| **Swan,** Solid, 5 In. | 20.00 |
| **Swan,** Solid, 7 In. | 45.00 |
| **Swan,** Sylvan, Elongated Head, Round Eyes & Mouth, 11 In. | 40.00 |
| **Swan,** Sylvan, Pink Opalescent, Pink Neck, 6 In. | 65.00 |
| **Swan,** Sylvan, Pink Opalescent, 7 In. | 75.00 |
| **Swan,** Vaseline, 11 1/2 In. | 85.00 |
| **Swan,** Vaseline, 11 3/4 X 8 1/2 In. | 135.00 |
| **Swordfish** | 75.00 |
| **Syrup,** Squat, Tepee | 35.00 |
| **Toothpick,** Diamond Ridge | 25.00 |
| **Toothpick,** States | 25.00 |
| **Toothpick,** Tepee | 28.00 |
| **Tumbler,** Chanticleer, Crystal, Frosted, 3 In. | 25.00 |
| **Tumbler,** Hobnail, Crystal, 13 Ounce | 4.00 |
| **Tumbler,** Sandwich, Crystal, 13 Ounce | 10.00 |
| **Vase,** Bud, Caribbean, Blue | 24.50 |
| **Vase,** Canterbury, Blue Opalescent, 8 1/2 X 7 1/2 In. | 40.00 |
| **Vase,** Canterbury, Clover, 3 1/2 In. | 19.00 |
| **Vase,** Canterbury, Pink Opalescent, 4 1/2 In. | 20.00 |
| **Vase,** Horn Of Plenty, 4 1/2 In. | 7.00 |
| **Vase,** Violet, 3 In. | 19.00 |
| **Wine,** Mardi Gras, 3 Ounce, Stemmed, 4 In. | 20.00 |

*Durand glass was made by Victor Durand from 1879 to 1935 at several factories. Most of the iridescent Durand glass was made by Victor Durand, Jr., from 1912 to 1924 at the Durand Art Glass Works in Vineland, New Jersey.*

| | |
|---|---:|
| **DURAND, Base,** Lamp, Iridescent Green Shaft, Calcite Body, King Tut, 11 In. | 300.00 |
| **Bottle,** Perfume, Bulbous, Raised Gold Design, Sterling Cap, 2 1/2 In. | 285.00 |
| **Box,** Cover, King Tut Pattern, Green Luster & Gold, 3 1/2 X 2 3/4 In. | 950.00 |
| **Champagne,** Green Base, Hollow Amber Stem | 250.00 |
| **Champagne,** Rose Base, Hollow Amber Stem, Rose Bowl | 250.00 |
| **Champagne,** Ruby & Amber, Tall | 225.00 |
| **Cracker Jar,** Iridescent Green, Black Webs, Silver Top | 350.00 |
| **Ginger Jar,** Lid, King Tut Pattern, Gold & Green, Signed, 10 1/2 In. | 1850.00 |
| **Goblet,** White Feather On Ruby, Pedestal, 6 1/2 In. | 300.00 |
| **Inkwell,** Peacock Feathers Of Green & Blue, Art Nouveau, Numbered | 275.00 |
| **Lamp,** Egyptan, Crackle, Green & Silver Design, Bronze Base, 10 In. | 595.00 |
| **Lamp,** King Tut Pattern | 285.00 To 345.00 |
| **Paperweight,** Satin Swirl, Blue Flower On Top | 95.00 |
| **Plate,** Gold, Yellow Scalloped, Green Glass Trim, 14 In. | 210.00 |
| **Plate,** Peacock, Engraving On Underside, Bridgeton Rose, 7 1/4 In. | 275.00 |
| **Shade,** Opal Feather Edge, Green On Gold, 7 In., Set Of 4 | 550.00 |
| **Sherbet,** Peacock Pulled Feather, Allover Luster, 3 1/2 In. | 365.00 |
| **Sherbet,** White & Pink Peacock Feather, Red Ground, 3 1/2 In. | 265.00 |
| **Tazza,** Spider Webbing, Gold Iridescence, Signed, 6 3/4 X 7 3/4 In. | 695.00 |
| **Vase,** Allover King Tut Swirls, Gold Ground, 11 In. | 450.00 |
| **Vase,** Beehive, Iridescent Blue, Gold, Signed, 5 3/4 X 6 In.Diam. | 775.00 |

Vase, Blue & Crystal Egyptian Crackle Glass, 12 1/2 In. ........................................ 485.00
Vase, Blue Iridescent Transparent, Applied Gold Threading, 8 In. ........................... 375.00
Vase, Blue Luster Outside, Silver Luster Inside, Signed, 11 1/2 In. ......................... 750.00
Vase, Feather Design, Cranberry Collar & Foot, White, 9 3/4 In. .............................. 895.00
Vase, Feather Design, Spun Glass, Gold & Green, 9 In. ........................................... 850.00
Vase, Gold & Orange Iridescence, Green Lily Pads, Signed, 12 In. ......................... 850.00
Vase, Gold Iridescent, Blue-Green Swirls, 11 In. ...................................................... 550.00
Vase, Gold Threading, Blue & Cream Feathering, Signed, 9 In. .............................. 950.00
Vase, Gray & Orange Hearts, Opal Body, Signed, 10 1/2 In. ................................... 575.00
Vase, Heart Shaped Leaves, Gold Threading, Orange Lining, 12 In. ........................ 750.00
Vase, King Tut, Gold Over White, 9 In. ..................................................................... 650.00
Vase, Oiled Luster, Opal Leaf & Vines, Signed, 7 In. ............................................... 350.00
Vase, Orange & Gray Heart Shaped Leaves, White Ground, Signed, 10 In. ............ 475.00
Vase, Pink Gold, Signed, 7 1/2 In. ............................................................................ 675.00
Vase, Silver Feathering, Maroon Cased, Pewter Frame, Marked, 10 In. .................. 750.00
Vase, Tapering Form, White Flowers, Blue Ground, C.1910, Signed, 5 In. .............. 150.00
Vase, Trumpet, Footed, Aurene, 15 In. ..................................................................... 1350.00
Vase, Urn Shape, Iridescent Blue Threaded, Signed, 6 1/2 In. ............................... 1050.00
Vase, Urn Shaped, King Tut, Green To Gold To Apricot, Signed, 8 In. ..................... 750.00
Vase, Vine & Leaf, Luster Blue Ground, Gold Interior, Signed, 7 In. ........................ 685.00
Vase, White Flowers & Stems, Blue Ground, C.1910, Signed, 5 In. ........................ 150.00
Vase, White, Orange & Gray Heart Shaped Leaves, Signed, 10 In. ......................... 475.00

ECANADA, Ashtray, Blue & White ............................................................................. 18.00

ELVIS PRESLEY, Card, Arcade, 8 Different, Set Of 100 ........................................... 8.00
Hat, 1956 .................................................................................................................. 35.00
Pillow Case ............................................................................................................... 12.50
Scarf, Neck, Hilton Hotel, Signed ............................................................................. 10.00
        ENAMEL WARE, see Graniteware

ENAMEL, Chinese, Box, Flowers, Butterflies, Blue Ground, 3 X 4 In. ..................... 145.00
French, Box, Enameled Top, Lovers On Bench, Metallic Clothes, 3/4 In. ................ 295.00
French, Vase, Cone Shape, Sunset Landscape, 19th Century, 6 1/8 In. .................. 775.00
        ENAMEL, RUSSIAN, see also Faberge
Russian, Beaker, Tin, Nicholas II, 1896 ................................................................... 115.00
Russian, Box, Colored Flowers, On Silver, Signed K.T., 4 1/2 X 2 In. ..................... 1700.00
Russian, Plate, Ball-Footed, Spoon, Cut Glass Salt, 3 Piece .................................. 150.00
Russian, Saltshaker, Bowl Shape, Gold Wash, Signed, 7/8 X 1 In.Wide ................. 800.00
Russian, Spoon, Demitasse, Floral Designed Bowl, Marked 950, 3 1/2 In. .............. 30.00
Russian, Spoon, Salt, Footed, Silver Band, Hallmarked, Initialed ........................... 475.00
Russian, Spoon, Salt, On Silver & Copper, C.1930, Royal Blue ............................... 75.00
Russian, Spoon, St.Petersburg In Bowl, Marked 84, 4 1/4 In. ................................. 165.00
Russian, Teaspoon, Multicolored, Hallmarked, 4 1/4 In., Set Of 6 .......................... 750.00
Russian, Tongs, Sugar, Initial .................................................................................. 287.00
Russian, Tumbler, Tsar Nicholas, On Tin ................................................................. 150.00
Viennese, Tray, Lobate Body, 8 Crystal Plaques, Collet Foot, 10 In. ....................... 5500.00
        END OF DAY GLASS, see Spatter Glass

ERIKSON, Vase, Bubble Base, Banana Shape Top, Green, 9 X 10 1/4 In. ............... 95.00

 ES Germany porcelain was made at the factory of Erdmann Schlegelmilch from 1861 to 1925 in Suhl, Germany. The porcelain was sold decorated or undecorated.

ES GERMANY, Ashtray, Pinecone Design, Triangular Shape ................................. 40.00
Bowl, Open Handles, Portrait Of 5 Women, 13 1/2 X 9 1/2 In. ................................ 75.00
Bowl, Portrait, Hortense, Napoleon, 5 1/2 In., Pair ................................................. 50.00
Chocolate Set, Roses, Yellow, 11 Piece .................................................................. 295.00
Dish, Bun, Autumn Leaves, Ornate Gold Rim ........................................................ 26.50
Dish, Leaf Shape, Tapestry, Windmill By Stream, 7 In., Pair ................................. 110.00
Dish, Lobster, White, Gold Trim ............................................................................. 45.00

**Dish,** Relish, White Chrysanthemums, Gold Edge, 8 In. ................................................ 25.00
**Figurine,** Bird, Porcelain, 14 In. ................................................ 350.00
**Hatpin Holder,** Rose Swag, Gold Trim ................................................ 35.00
**Hatpin Holder,** Yellow, White & Fuchsia Flowers, 4 3/4 In. ................................................ 45.00
**Plate,** Cottage & Lake Scene, Green, Purple, Pink, Marked, 9 1/2 In. ................................ 135.00
**Plate,** Pink & Salmon Flowers, Gold Leaves, 8 1/2 In. ................................................ 30.00
**Plate,** Portrait, Open Handled, 11 1/2 In. ................................................ 95.00
**Tankard,** Vase, Portrait Of Chinese Lady ................................................ 175.00
**Tray,** Serving, 7 In.Square ................................................ 85.00
**Vase,** Cabinet, Pink & Yellow, Lady, Roses, Enameled, Gold ................................................ 65.00
**Vase,** Portrait, 2-Handled, 9 1/4 In. ................................................ 175.00
**Vase,** Purple Iridescent Ground, Enameled Flowers, 8 1/2 In. ................................................ 125.00
**Vase,** Woman With Peacock, Raised Beading, 11 1/2 In. ................................................ 275.00
**Vase,** Woman With Seashell, 10 1/2 In. ................................................ 200.00

**ES PRUSSIA, Cake Set,** Open Handle, 5 Servers, Yellow Roses, 10 In. ................................ 75.00
**Dresser Set,** Tray, Pin Tray, Powder Jar, Ring Tree, Violets ................................................ 160.00
**Hair Receiver,** Footed, Pink Flowers, Blue, Gold Trim ................................................ 47.50
**Strainer,** Tea, Handled Undercup, Floral ................................................ 50.00
**Strainer,** Tea, Handled Undercup, Mother-Of-Pearl Finish ................................................ 50.00

**ESKIMO, Box,** Walrus Ivory, Engraved Drum Scene, 19 Figures, 10 In.Diam. ........................ 450.00
**Comb,** Walrus Ivory, Engraved, Thule Culture, 2 1/2 X 3 1/2 In. ................................................ 50.00
**Container,** Harpoon Blades, Walrus Ivory, Fluke Effigy, 4 1/4 In. ................................................ 200.00
**Doll,** Walrus Ivory, St.Lawrence Island, Prehistoric, 7 1/2 In. ................................................ 1600.00
**Figurine,** Duck, Walrus Ivory, Used In Gambling Game, 1 1/2 In. ................................................ 75.00
**Figurine,** Fox, Walrus Ivory, 4 1/2 In. ................................................ 375.00
**Figurine,** Okuik Female Torso, Walrus Ivory, St.Lawrence Islands ................................................ 200.00
**Figurine,** Thule, Headdress, On Pedestal, 1 1/8 In. ................................................ 60.00
**Fish Lure,** Walrus Ivory, Shishmaref, Alaska, 4 In. ................................................ 35.00
**Game Piece,** Duck, Walrus Ivory, Used In Gambling Games, 1 1/2 In. ................................................ 75.00
**Handle,** Box, Walrus Ivory, Engraved Drum Scene, 19 Figures, 10 In. ................................................ 450.00
**Handle,** Engraving Tool, Walrus Ivory, Western Thule, 7 3/4 In. ................................................ 75.00
**Harpoon Head,** Walrus Ivory, Prehistoric, 2 X 4 In. ................................................ 12.00
**Knife,** Snow, Child's, Ivory, 20th Century, 3 1/4 In. ................................................ 12.00
**Lure,** Fish, Walrus Ivory, 3 In. ................................................ 25.00
**Net Sinker,** 1 Ivory, 1 Stone, Pair ................................................ 10.00
**Snow Knife,** Walrus Tusk, Scrimshaw Eagle, Whale, & Scenes, 18 In. ................................................ 975.00
**Spearhead,** Polished Bone, 8 3/8 In. ................................................ 25.00
**Thumb Guard,** Archer's, Bone, Engraved, Seward Peninsula, 2 In. ................................................ 25.00
    **ETRUSCAN MAJOLICA, see Majolica**

*Faberge was a firm of jewelers and goldsmiths founded in St.
Petersburg, Russia, in 1842, by Gustav Faberge. Peter Carl
Faberge, his son, was jeweler to the Russian Imperial Court from
about 1870 to 1914.*

**FABERGE, Buckle,** Belt, Loose Dagger Forms Closure ................................................ 395.00
**Flower,** Gold, Stem Set Into Rock Crystal, Jade Leaves, 7 1/2 In. ................................................ 900.00
**Pitcher,** Crystal & Silver, Workmaster, Rappaport, 14 In., Pair ................................................ 7500.00
**Spoon,** Shell Design, Signed ................................................ 125.00

**FAIENCE, Compote,** Le Nove, Birds & Flower Sprays, 8 3/4 In., Pair ................................ 220.00
**Dish,** Nevers, Shepherd & Dog Center, C.1750, 13 1/4 In.Diam. ................................................ 300.00
**Inkstand,** Gargoyle Handles, Blue & White Flowers, 13 X 8 In. ................................................ 145.00
**Jar,** Covered, Handled, Bands Of Gilt, Ivory Ground, 19 1/8 In. ................................................ 650.00
**Jug,** Montpellier, Loop Handle, Flower Spray, C.1760, 9 1/2 In. ................................................ 200.00
**Plate,** Central Flower Vase, Enameled, Foliage Rim, 8 1/2 In., Pair ................................................ 120.00
**Plate,** Chinoiserie Figure In Landscape, C.1800, 9 In.Diam. ................................................ 120.00

*Fairings are small souvenir china boxes sold at country fairs during the nineteenth century.*

| | |
|---|---:|
| **FAIRING, Box,** Last One Into Bed Put Out The Light | 68.50 |
| **Box,** Trinket, Boy & Dog | 35.00 |
| **Box,** Trinket, Boy Looking In Mirror On Fireplate | 35.00 |
| **Box,** Trinket, Lid Has Picture Of Child, Oval, Pastel Colors | 95.00 |
| **Box,** Trinket, Old-Fashioned Couple Before Mirror | 48.00 |
| **Box,** Trinket, Oval Basket, 2 Cats On Lid | 75.00 |
| **Box,** Trinket, Parents & Child, White | 52.00 |
| **Figurine,** Last Into Bed Put Out The Light | 68.50 |
| **Figurine,** Man & Wife Bedroom Scene, First To Bed, 4 In. | 85.00 |
|     **FAMILLE ROSE, see Chinese Export** | |
| | |
| **FAN, Abie's Irish Rose,** 3 Movable Panels | 25.00 |
| **Advertising,** Bakers Chocolate, Folding, Hand | 35.00 |
| **Advertising,** Columbus, Indiana, Paper | 10.00 |
| **Advertising,** Moxie Soda, 2-Sided, Frank Archer & Girl | 7.00 |
| **Advertising,** Moxie, Celluloid | 40.00 To 50.00 |
| **Advertising,** Moxie, Man & Boy On Horses, Pointing Finger, 7 In. | 16.00 |
| **Advertising,** Moxie, 2-Sided, Frank Archer & Girl | 7.00 |
| **Advertising,** Putman Dye, Cardboard | 5.00 |
| **All Lace,** Mother-Of-Pearl Stays, Presentation Silk Box, 28 In. | 175.00 |
| **Ballroom,** French Ivory On Lace | 45.00 |
| **Black Lacquer Stick,** Chinese Painting On Paper | 150.00 |
| **Brass & Mother-Of-Pearl Stick,** Painting On Paper | 45.00 |
| **Brass Blade,** Robbins, Meyers | 20.00 |
| **Ceiling,** Fan-O-Plane, Electric, Airplane Shaped | 350.00 |
| **Ceiling,** 4-Bladed, C. 1915 | 250.00 |
| **Ceiling,** 6-Bladed, C.1915 | 300.00 |
| **Celluloid Ivorine,** Applied Mother-Of-Pearl, Hand-Painted Flowers, 6 In. | 85.00 |
| **Celluloid Stick,** French, Black Chantilly Lace | 30.00 |
| **Child's,** Spanish Scene, Folding | 18.00 |
| **Cisco Kid** | 8.00 |
| **Electric,** Winchester | 150.00 |
| **Embroidered,** Ivory | 15.00 |
| **Embroidered,** Silk | 15.00 |
| **English,** Ostrich, Black Plumes, 16 In. | 220.00 |
| **Feather,** Velvet Handle | 15.00 |
| **Fly,** Clockwork | 475.00 |
| **French,** Mother-Of-Pearl Stick, White Ostrich Plumes, 16 In. | 125.00 |
| **French,** Ostrich Plume, Scarlet Plume, Tortoiseshell Frame, 22 In. | 70.00 |
| **French,** Tortoiseshell Stick & Tip, Scene On Black Silk, 13 1/2 In. | 300.00 |
| **General Electric Whiz,** Brass Blades | 35.00 |
| **GGG Drugs,** Goddess Diana & Hunting Dog, 7 X 11 In. | 7.50 |
| **Gilt Tortoise & Carved Stick,** Figures In French Garden, Sequin Border | 175.00 |
| **Ivory Frame,** Silk With Sequins, 7 1/2 In. | 35.00 |
| **Ivory Stick,** Butterflies & Flowers, Applied Sequins, 9 1/2 In. | 150.00 |
| **Ivory Stick,** Hand-Carving, Hand-Painted Paper, Classical Scene | 35.00 |
| **Ivory Stick,** Hand-Painted Roses On Silk, 11 1/2 In. | 55.00 |
| **Ivory,** Filigree Carved | 65.00 |
| **Ivory,** Folding, Ribbon Guider, Cutwork | 10.00 |
| **Ivory,** Hand-Painted Silk, Gold Leaf Case | 450.00 |
| **Ivory,** White Satin, Embroidered, Gold Leaf Case | 400.00 |
| **Lacquer Butterfly** | 60.00 |
| **Lisbon,** Ohio, September 1933, Cardboard | 6.00 |
| **Metal & Enamel Sticks,** Chinese Painting | 250.00 |
| **Mother-Of-Pearl Sticks,** Brown & White Plumes, Gilt Monogram, 13 In. | 150.00 |
| **Mother-Of-Pearl Sticks,** French, Black Lace Over Silk, 10 In. | 300.00 |
| **Mother-Of-Pearl Sticks,** Gold, Silver, English Scene, Silk Tassel, Signed | 45.00 |
| **Mother-Of-Pearl Sticks,** Painted Gold & Silver Kid | 70.00 |
| **Mother-Of-Pearl Sticks,** Scene, Tiffany & Co., Signed, 1880s *Illus* | 550.00 |
| **Mother-Of-Pearl Sticks,** White Plumes, Tipped In Black, 12 In. | 125.00 |
| **Moxie,** Celluloid | 75.00 |

Fan, Mother-Of-Pearl Sticks, Scene, Tiffany
& Co., Signed, 1880s

| | |
|---|---|
| **Ostrich Feather,** Ivory | 15.00 |
| **Pierced & Carved Sandlewood,** Embroidered Silk, Oriental Design, 6 In. | 25.00 |
| **Pierced & Carved Sandlewood,** 7 1/2 In. | 25.00 |
| **Pressed Ivory Sticks,** Chinese People With Brocade Clothing | 90.00 |
| **Putnam Dye,** Wooden Handle, Paper | 5.00 |
| **Railroad,** Northern Pacific, 24 In. | 30.00 |
| **Red Cloth Cockade,** Open, 13 In. | 20.00 |
| **Red,** White, & Blue, Wooden | 45.00 |
| **Sandalwood,** Long Handle, Pleated Brown Silk, 10 In. | 100.00 |
| **Silk,** Wood Ribs, Hand-Painted Roses, 14 In. | 45.00 |
| **Westinghouse,** Electric, 60 Cycle, 1936 | 50.00 |
| **20 Section,** Decoratively Pierced, 9 1/4 In. | 95.00 |

*Fenton Art Glass Company, founded in Martins Ferry, Ohio, by
Frank L.Fenton, is now located in Williamstown, West Virginia. It
is noted for early carnival glass produced between 1907 and 1920.
Many other types of glass were also made.*

| | |
|---|---|
| **FENTON, Basket,** Carnival, Cobalt, 6 In. | 18.00 |
| **Basket,** Cased, Ruffled Edge, Green, Cane Handle, 11 1/2 In. | 65.00 |
| **Basket,** Daisy & Button, Amber, 6 In. | 20.00 |
| **Basket,** Green Cane Handle, Green & White, 11 1/2 In. | 68.00 |
| **Basket,** Ruby Cased White, Large | 17.50 |
| **Basket,** Thumbprint, Cranberry, 7 In. | 35.00 |
| **Basket,** White Cased Glass, Blown Caramel, Amber Handle, 6 In. | 65.00 |
| **Basket,** White Cased Glass, 7 1/2 In. | 40.00 |
| **Bell,** Rosealene | 35.00 |
| **Bonbon,** Blackberries, Ruffled | 20.00 |
| **Bonbon,** Celeste Blue, Covered, Footed | 38.00 |
| **Bottle,** Cologne, French Opalescent, Wooden Stopper | 40.00 |
| **Bowl,** Console, San Toy, Crystal, 12 In.Diam. | 22.50 |
| **Bowl,** Cupped, Blue Stretch, 10 In.Diam. | 32.50 |
| **Bowl,** Dolphin Handles, Amethyst, 6 1/4 In.Diam. | 15.00 |
| **Bowl,** Dolphin Handles, Footed, Floral & Leaf Cutting, Jade, 10 1/2 In. | 45.00 |
| **Bowl,** Dolphin, Diamond Optic, Pink, 8 1/2 In.Diam. | 40.00 |
| **Bowl,** Dolphin, Floral & Leaf Cutting, Aquamarine, 6 In. | 25.00 |
| **Bowl,** Dolphin, Handled, Oval, Footed, 10 1/2 In. | 45.00 |
| **Bowl,** Dolphin, Jade, 6 In.Diam. | 20.00 |
| **Bowl,** Dolphin, Ruffled, Jade, Flat, 9 In.Diam. | 45.00 |
| **Bowl,** Jade, 9 1/2 In. | 20.00 |
| **Bowl,** Ming, Green, 8 In.Diam. | 27.50 |
| **Bowl,** Red Slag, Pedestal Bowl & Base, 3 1/4 X 7 1/4 In. | 75.00 |
| **Candleholder,** Dolphin, Frosted Flower Underneath, 3 1/2 In., Pair | 17.00 |
| **Candlestick,** Pink, 4 In., Pair | 25.00 |
| **Centerpiece,** Green Opaque, Flowers On Side, 7 1/2 X 4 1/2 In. | 30.00 |
| **Compote,** Mikado, Mandarin Red | 150.00 |
| **Cookie Jar,** Covered, Jade, Bamboo Handles | 75.00 |
| **Cup & Saucer,** Lincoln Inn, Red | 10.00 |
| **Hat,** 3-Sided, Child's, Opalescent Swirl, White | 35.00 |
| **Jug,** Squat, Opalescent, Hobnail | 18.00 |
| **Paperweight,** Blue Carnival Fish, 6 In. | 25.00 |

| | |
|---|---|
| **Pitcher**, Hanging Heart, 7 In. | 105.00 |
| **Pitcher**, Hobnail, Opalescent, Blue, 7 In. | 30.00 |
| **Plate**, Lincoln Inn, Jade, 8 In. | 15.00 |
| **Shaker**, Hobnail, Opalescent, Pair | 20.00 |
| **Toothpick**, Blue Opalescent | 30.00 |
| **Tumbler**, Grape & Cable | 12.00 |
| **Tumbler**, Grape & Lattice | 40.00 |
| **Vase**, Burmese, Signed, 6 1/2 In. | 30.00 |
| **Vase**, Butterfly & Berry, Amethyst Base, 9 In. | 22.50 |
| **Vase**, Empress, White Milk Glass, 8 In. | 75.00 |
| **Vase**, Fan, Aqua Crest, 6 1/4 In. | 20.00 |
| **Vase**, Fan, Jade, Dolphin Handled, 8 In. | 30.00 |
| **Vase**, Peach Crest, Crimped, C.1940, 6 In. | 38.00 |
| **Vase**, Peach Crest, Crimped, Square Top, 5 1/2 In. | 40.00 |
| **Vase**, Pulled Feather, Blue, 8 1/2 In. | 125.00 |
| **Vase**, Pulled Feather, 10 In. | 125.00 |
| **Vase**, Silvercrest, 4 1/2 X 3 3/4 In.Diam. | 15.00 |
| **Water Set**, Buttons & Braids, Green, Opalescent, 7 Piece | 215.00 |

*Fiesta dinnerware was introduced in 1936 by the Homer Laughlin China Co., redesigned in 1969, and withdrawn in 1973. The simple design was characterized by a band of concentric circles, beginning at the rim. Cups had full-circle handles until 1969, when partial-circle handles were made. Harlequin and Riviera were related wares.*

| | |
|---|---|
| **FIESTA WARE**, Ashtray, Red | 25.00 |
| **Bowl**, Fruit, Yellow, 5 1/2 In. | 5.50 |
| **Bowl**, Medium Green, 8 1/2 In.Diam. | 19.50 |
| **Bowl**, Onion Soup, Covered, Cobalt Blue | 60.00 |
| **Bowl**, Onion Soup, Covered, Green | 60.00 |
| **Bowl**, Yellow, 11 In.Diam. | 45.00 |
| **Butter**, Covered, Red | 39.00 |
| **Candleholder**, Green, Square Base, Footed | 28.00 |
| **Carafe**, Green | 35.00 |
| **Carafe**, Red | 35.00 |
| **Casserole**, Covered, Handled, Light Green | 26.00 |
| **Casserole**, Covered, Medium Green | 15.00 |
| **Coffeepot**, Ivory | 32.50 |
| **Coffeepot**, Light Green | 22.50 |
| **Coffeepot**, Medium Green | 28.00 |
| **Coffeepot**, Red | 75.00 To 95.00 |
| **Coffeepot**, Turquoise | 32.50 |
| **Cookie Jar**, Blue, Large | 50.00 |
| **Cream Soup**, Red | 20.00 |
| **Cream Soup**, Yellow | 15.00 |
| **Cup & Saucer**, Blue | 12.00 |
| **Cup & Saucer**, Green | 12.00 |
| **Cup & Saucer**, Yellow | 12.00 |
| **Cup**, Cobalt | 8.50 To 12.00 |
| **Cup**, Yellow | 8.50 |
| **Dish**, Relish, Red, Green, & Cobalt Inserts, Turquoise | 35.00 |
| **Eggcup**, Ivory | 15.00 |
| **Grill Plate**, Italian Green, 11 3/4 In.Diam. | 19.00 |
| **Jug**, Yellow, 2 Pint | 15.00 |
| **Mug**, Red | 25.00 |
| **Mustard**, Cover, Red | 40.00 |
| **Mustard**, Cover, Turquoise | 32.00 |
| **Mustard**, Green | 35.00 |
| **Pitcher**, Blue, 3 Pint | 37.00 |
| **Pitcher**, Ice Lip, Yellow | 65.00 |
| **Pitcher**, Juice, Yellow | 10.00 To 11.50 |
| **Pitcher**, Syrup, Cobalt | 55.00 |

Fiesta Ware, Plate, Amberstone, 10 1/4 In.Diam.

Fiesta Ware, Plate, Hawaiian 12-Point Daisy, Turquoise, White

| | | |
|---|---|---|
| **Plate,** Amberstone, 10 1/4 In.Diam. | *Illus* | 4.50 |
| **Plate,** Chop, Green, 13 In. | 9.00 To | 15.00 |
| **Plate,** Chop, Yellow, 15 In. | | 15.00 |
| **Plate,** Dessert, Yellow, 6 1/2 In. | | 2.25 |
| **Plate,** Divided, Red | | 20.00 |
| **Plate,** Hawaiian 12-Point Daisy, Turquoise, White | *Illus* | 5.00 |
| **Plate,** Red, 10 In.Diam. | | 11.00 |
| **Plate,** Turquoise, 15 In. | | 10.00 |
| **Plate,** Yellow, 10 In.Diam. | | 7.00 |
| **Salt & Pepper,** Red | | 12.00 |
| **Salt & Pepper,** Turquoise | | 3.50 |
| **Salt & Pepper,** Yellow | | 3.50 |
| **Saltshaker,** Red | | 7.00 |
| **Saltshaker,** Yellow | | 3.50 |
| **Saucer,** Red, Set Of 6 | | 20.00 |
| **Soup,** Onion, Green, Covered | | 95.00 |
| **Sugar,** Yellow, Covered | | 7.00 |
| **Syrup,** Turquoise | | 85.00 |
| **Syrup,** Yellow | | 90.00 |
| **Tumbler,** Juice, Blue | | 10.00 |
| **Tumbler,** Juice, Rose | | 10.00 |
| **Tumbler,** Water, Green | | 18.00 |

*Findlay, or onyx, glass was made using three layers of glass. It was manufactured by the Dalzell Gilmore Leighton Company about 1889 in Findlay, Ohio. The silver, ruby, or black pattern was molded into the glass. The glass came in several colors, but was usually white or ruby.*

| | | |
|---|---|---|
| **FINDLAY ONYX, Berry Bowl** | | 450.00 |
| **Bowl,** Sugar, Opalescent, Covered, 5 3/4 In. | *Illus* | 175.00 |
| **Celery** | 275.00 To | 350.00 |
| **Muffineer,** Original Cover, Cream | | 275.00 |
| **Spooner,** Cream | | 315.00 |
| **Spooner,** 4 In. | | 260.00 |
| **Syrup,** Original Top | | 500.00 |
| **Tumbler,** Barrel Shape, Platinum | | 280.00 |

| | |
|---|---|
| **FIREFIGHTING, Alarm Box,** Gamewell | 40.00 |
| **Alarm Gong,** Floor Mounted In Steam Fire Engine, Rotary | 350.00 |
| **Alarm Register,** Brass | 125.00 |
| **Badge,** San Antonio, Hose, Hat, & Nozzle On Side | 35.00 |
| **Belt,** Assistant Foreman, Leather | 50.00 |
| **Belt,** Parade, Gravesend, N.Y., Leather | 45.00 |

Belt, Parade, New Utrecht, N.Y., Leather ................................................................. 45.00
Belt, Volunteer .................................................................................................... 50.00
Bucket, Green Body, Leather, Massachusetts, C.1809, 21 1/2 In. ........................ 200.00
Bucket, Labeled Boston Fire Club, 19th Century, 13 In. ...................................... 150.00
Bucket, Leather, Markings .................................................................................. 185.00
Bucket, Leather, 1814 ........................................................................................ 335.00
Bucket, Tin .......................................................................................................... 29.00
Decal, Reflective, Word Fire ................................................................................ 2.00
Extinguisher, American LaFrance, 2 Man, Brass Nozzle ...................................... 175.00
Extinguisher, Blue Glass, Grenade Type ............................................................. 28.00
Extinguisher, Bulb Shape, Holder ....................................................................... 10.00
Extinguisher, Embossed C.& N.W.Ry., Glass, 18 In. ........................................... 50.00
Extinguisher, Fyr-Fyter, Wall Mounted, Brass ..................................................... 15.00
Extinguisher, Grenade, Fireen ............................................................................ 15.00
Extinguisher, Grenade, Flamite .......................................................................... 12.00
Extinguisher, Grenade, Fryicide ......................................................................... 15.00
Extinguisher, Grenade, Hazelton ........................................................................ 125.00
Extinguisher, Grenade, Phoenix ......................................................................... 20.00
Extinguisher, Hardens Star, Glass, Blue ............................................................. 50.00
Extinguisher, Light Bulb Shape, Sealed Shur-Stop, Bracket ............................... 10.00
Extinguisher, Phoenix, Tin, 16 In. ....................................................................... 14.00
Extinguisher, Throw On Fire, Tin Lithograph, 1904 ............................................. 15.00
Hat, Eagle On Front, Leather, R.B.X.Jr., Large .................................................. 100.00
Helmet, High Eagle, Aluminum ........................................................................... 55.00
Lantern, Bull's-Eye Globe, Brass, August 27, 1907 ............................................ 145.00
Nozzle, Brass, 21 In. ........................................................................................... 90.00
Nozzle, Hose, Brass, 15 In.High .......................................................................... 55.00
Nozzle, LaFrance, 29 1/2 In. ............................................................................... 43.00
Nozzle, Leather Handled ..................................................................................... 135.00
Openers, Door, Detroit ........................................................................................ 50.00
Wagon, Pipe, Handwheels, Mounts, & Cradle, Akron, Brass .............................. 750.00

> *Fireglow glass resembles English Bristol glass, but a reddish-brown*
> *color can be seen when the piece is held to the light. It is a form of art*
> *glass made by the Boston and Sandwich Glass Co. of Massachusetts,*
> *and other companies.*

FIREGLOW, Plaque, Enameled Heron, Flowers, & Lake Scene, 1880s, 7 3/4 In. ..................... 135.00

FIREPLACE, Andirons, Albany, N.Y., C.1800, Brass ............................................. 950.00
Andirons, Anchor Shape, Cast Iron ..................................................................... 135.00
Andirons, Ball Top, Decagonal Belt At Center, Brass, 12 X 21 In. ....................... 350.00
Andirons, Ball Top, Spur & Snake Feet, C.1800, Brass, 14 1/2 In. ...................... 275.00
Andirons, Baluster Shape Stems, E.Smylie, N.Y., Brass, 20 In. ........................... 650.00
Andirons, Blades Ending In Rings, Wrought-Iron, 18 1/2 In. ............................... 90.00
Andirons, Blades Narrow To Gooseneck Top, 18th Century, 16 In. ...................... 120.00
Andirons, Double Lemon Finials, Cabriole Legs, Brass, 18 3/4 In. ...................... 450.00
Andirons, Empire Period, New York State, Brass ................................................ 225.00
Andirons, Gooseneck, Diamond Head, Penny Feet, 13 X 11 In. .......................... 275.00
Andirons, Gooseneck, Round Ball Top, 18th Century, 10 X 18 In. ....................... 225.00
Andirons, Hessian Heads, Facing Left, Cast Iron, 9 1/2 In. ................................ 150.00
Andirons, Knife Blade Fronts, Rounded Neck, 15 1/2 In. .................................... 125.00
Andirons, Knife Blade, Wrought-Iron, 18th Century, 18 In. ................................. 195.00
Andirons, Louis XV, Bronze, Pair ........................................................................ 145.00
Andirons, Multirigged Column, 20th Century, Brass, 22 1/2 In. .......................... 200.00
Andirons, Queen Anne, Engraved Eagles, Brass ................................................ 1100.00
Andirons, Spurred Legs, Shovel & Tongs, Brass, C.1810, 17 1/2 In. ................... 350.00
Andirons, Stuart Brass & Iron, Scroll Feet, 17th Century, 23 In. ........................ 650.00
Andirons, Wide Blade To Gooseneck Top, Faceted Balls, 16 In. ......................... 120.00
Bellows, Brass Tip, Wood & Leather, 7 In. .......................................................... 38.00
Bellows, Brown, Black, & Gold Leaf, Grape Design ............................................ 30.00
Bellows, Fruit & Leaves Design, Yellow Ground, Brass Tip, C.1820 ................... 120.00
Bellows, Hand-Carved Mahogany, Brass Nails & Tip, 18 In. .............................. 95.00

| | |
|---|---|
| Bellows, Original Grained Wood, Turtleback, 15 1/2 In. | 35.00 |
| Bellows, Stenciled Fruit & Brushwork, Wood & Leather | 65.00 |
| Bellows, Stenciled Tomatoes, Gold Leaves, Red Striping | 65.00 |
| Box, Coal, Brass & Copper, Original Tin Liner, C.1870 | 250.00 |
| Box, Tinder, Pocket, Domed Cover, Striker, C.1780, Steel, 3 1/2 In. | 220.00 |
| Broiler, Wrought-Iron, Flat Bars, 4-Footed, Handles, 10 X 11 In. | 85.00 |
| Broom, Bamboo Handle | 6.50 |
| Broom, Hearth, Birch, 41 1/2 In. | 85.00 |
| Broom, Peeled Birch, Round Bottom, 56 In. | 110.00 |
| Brush, Sheraton, Original Gold Stenciling, Black Ground, Iron | 85.00 |
| Cover, Man Riding Camel, Tin, Copper Wash, 27 X 21 1/2 In. | 130.00 |
| Crane Plate, Wrought-Iron Handle, Swivel Ring, Footed | 165.00 |
| Fireback, 19th Century, Cast Iron | 90.00 |
| Fireboard, Leather, Painted Floral Design | 180.00 |
| Fireboard, Urn With Flowering Plant, Wood | 3100.00 |
| Grate, Multicolored Jewels, Brass & Glass, 22 X 15 3/4 In. | 375.00 |
| Heater, Kerosene, Dietz, Patent 1873, Cast Iron | 295.00 |
| Mantel, Carved, Winged Griffins, Oak, 7 Ft.5 In. X 10 Ft. | 5000.00 |
| Mantel, Cast Iron, Masonic Emblems, Brass Fender & Tools | 95.00 |
| Mantel, Cherubs, Coat Of Arms, Walnut, 6 Ft.8 In. X 10 Ft. | 7500.00 |
| Mantel, Molded & Beaded Cornice, Cameo Urn, C.1790, 52 In. | 1300.00 |
| Mantel, 3 Beveled Mirrors In Top, Spindled Galleries, Oak | 475.00 |
| Mantel, 3 Mirrors, Display Shelves, Oak, 3 Piece | 450.00 |
| Pan, Hand-Hammered Iron, Wood Handle, 3-Footed | 30.00 |
| Pan, Spouted, Hanging Ring, Iron, 10 In.Diam. | 45.00 |
| Roaster, Bird, Tin, 8 Hanging Hooks | 120.00 |
| Screen, Beaded Embroidery, Walnut, 45 1/4 In. | 425.00 To 450.00 |
| Screen, English Cottage, Copper | 65.00 |
| Screen, Framed Needlepoint Picture, C.1860, Walnut, 53 1/2 In. | 225.00 |
| Screen, Gilt & Ebonized, C.1870, 42 1/2 X 28 1/4 In. | *Illus* 500.00 |
| Screen, Portable, Silk & Brass, In Fitted Box | 200.00 |
| Screen, Stained Glass, Brass Frame, 38 1/2 X 24 In. | *Illus* 425.00 |
| Screen, Victorian, Rosewood, 45 X 26 In. | 250.00 |

Findlay Onyx, Bowl, Sugar, Opalescent, Covered,
5 3/4 In. (See Page 187)

Fireplace, Screen, Gilt & Ebonized,
C.1870, 42 1/2 X 28 1/4 In.

Fireplace, Screen, Stained Glass, Brass Frame, 38 1/2 X 24 In.

Shovel, Ash, Doughnut Handle, Wrought-Iron, 29 In. ............................................ 35.00
Shovel, Wrought-Iron, 33 In.Long ...................................................................... 45.00
Spit Holder, Wrought-Iron Goose, Pessuh, 18th Century ...................................... 110.00
      FIREPLACE, STOVE, see Stove
Surround, Marble & Terra-Cotta, Inlaid Bronze, 4 X 4 Ft. ................................... 1900.00
Tilter, Kettle, Faceted Ball End, Wrought-Iron ................................................... 285.00
Tinderbox, Snuffer Cover, Striker, Handled ....................................................... 235.00
Toaster, Flip-Style, Wqod Handle, Straight Bars, 12 X 28 In. ............................... 89.00
Toaster, Hinged Handle, Wrought Iron, 18 In. ..................................................... 90.00
Toaster, On Swivel, Shaped Handle & Feet, New England, 14 In. .......................... 100.00
Tongs, Brass, 8 In. ......................................................................................... 18.00
Tongs, Coal, Brass, 8 In. ................................................................................ 18.00
Tongs, Empire Period, New York State, Brass .................................................... 45.00
Tongs, Snake Handle, Bog Iron, Pair ................................................................ 95.00
Tool Set, Ball Finials, 2 Hearth Ornaments, C.1900, Signed ................................ 195.00
Trammel, 2 Hooks, Iron ................................................................................... 65.00
Waffle Iron, Wrought-Iron, Waffle Pattern, 23 In. ............................................... 45.00

*Fischer porcelain was made in Herend, Hungary. The factory was founded
in 1839, and has continued working into the twentieth century. The wares are
sometimes referred to as Herend porcelain.*

FISCHER, Ewer, Openwork Flowers, Multicolored, Square Handle, Signed, 8 In. .......... 175.00
Ewer, Pink, Blue, Bold Yellow & Black, Raised Design, 18 In. ............................... 575.00
Pitcher, Handle, Allover Design, 12 1/4 In. ....................................................... 295.00
Plaque, Covered With Gold & Flowers, 13 1/2 In. .............................................. 340.00
Plate, Flowers, Colorful, 13 In. ....................................................................... 340.00
Vase, Blue & Gold Leaves, Double Gold Handles, Shield Mark .............................. 220.00
Vase, Draped Handles, Reticulated Body, Pink Flowers, 8 In. ............................... 210.00
Vase, Gold Flowers, Green Enamel Beads, Signed, 12 1/2 In. ............................... 295.00
Vase, 2 Gold Handles, Reticulated Blue Flowers, Shield Mark, 8 In. ....................... 220.00

FISHING, Box, Lure, Al Foss, Tin ...................................................................... 9.00
Catalog, Heddon's Dowagiac, 1911, 36 Page .................................................... 25.00
Creel, Hand-Hewn Pine Lid, Splint ................................................................... 95.00
Creel, Trout, Wicker, Leather Binding ............................................................... 25.00
Lure, Creek Club, Jointed Pike, 6 In. ............................................................... 6.00
Lure, Heddon, Flap-Tail, 5 In. ......................................................................... 12.00
Lure, Meadow Mouse, 4 In. ............................................................................. 9.00
Lure, Tease-O-Reno, 4 In. .............................................................................. 9.00
Reel, Casting, Pflueger .................................................................................. 11.00
Reel, Hendryx, 1888, Brass, Small .................................................................. 27.50
Reel, J.A.Coxe Coronet, Leather Case, 25 In. .................................................... 35.00
Reel, Landley, 1950s, Original Box, Unused ...................................................... 22.00
Reel, Level-Winding Musky, Kalamazoo Tackle Co. ............................................ 22.00
Reel, Ocean, Fortescue Free Spool, Ocean City, German Silver ........................... 18.50
Reel, Shakespeare, Level Wind, 1920 .............................................................. 18.00
Reel, Victory, Brass, Patented 1894 ................................................................. 12.00
Rod & Nonlevel Wind, Sunnybrook, Union Hardware .......................................... 32.00
Rod & Reel, Winchester ................................................................................. 150.00
Rod, Casting, Heddon Pal .............................................................................. 20.00
Rod, Union Hardware Co., 4 Sections, Steel, 4 1/2 Ft. ........................................ 12.00
Rod, Winchester, Bamboo ............................................................................... 20.00
Spool, Winchester .......................................................................................... 8.00
Tackle, Salmon & Trout, William Mills & Son, 1932 ............................................ 12.00
      FLAG, see Textile, Flag

FLASH GORDON, Compass, Wrist ..................................................................... 38.00
Gun, Dated 1935, Boxed, Blue ........................................................................ 350.00
Pencil Box, Magic Slate, Picture, 1951, 4 1/2 X 10 3/8 In. ................................... 48.00
Pistol, Radio Repeater Click, Boxed ................................................................. 135.00
Pistol, Water, Space Design, Yellow Plastic, 7 X 4 1/2 In. .................................... 75.00

**Ring,** 1949, Tin ............................................................................................................ 15.00
**Solar Commando,** 3 Plastic Spacemen & Ship, 3 X 4 In. ...................................... 10.00

*Flow blue, or flo blue, was made in England about 1830 to 1900. The plates*
*were printed with designs using a cobalt blue coloring. The color flowed from*
*the design to the white plate so the finished plate had a smeared blue design.*
*The plates were usually made of ironstone china.*

**FLOW BLUE, Bone Dish,** Albany, Grindley ........................................................ 23.00
**Bone Dish,** Arcadia, Wilkinson, Set Of 8 ........................................................ 150.00
**Bone Dish,** Fairy Villas, Adams, 1891 ................................................................ 38.00
**Bone Dish,** Gironde, Grindley, 1891 .................................................................. 24.00
**Bone Dish,** Lorne, Grindley, C.1900 ................................................................. 28.00
**Bone Dish,** Messina, Cauldon, C.1905 .............................................................. 24.00
**Bone Dish,** Romeo, Wedgwood, C.1908 ............................................................ 25.00
**Bowl,** Cereal, Gironde, W.H.Grindley, 1891 ..................................................... 26.00
**Bowl,** Cereal, Portman, 6 3/4 In. ...................................................................... 24.00
**Bowl,** Conway, New Wharf Pottery, Round, 9 In. ....................................... 30.00 To 40.00
**Bowl,** Fairy Villas, W.Adams, 6 1/2 In. ............................................................. 27.00
**Bowl,** Fruit, La Belle, Wheeling Potteries, Ruffled Edge ................................. 125.00
**Bowl,** Handled, Touraine, 9 1/2 In.Diam. ........................................................... 50.00
**Bowl,** Meissen, 1891, 9 3/4 In. ......................................................................... 70.00
**Bowl,** Nonpareil, Burgess & Leigh, 1891, 9 1/2 X 7 3/4 In. .............................. 45.00
**Bowl,** Persian Moss, Utzschneider & Co., 1891, 6 In. ....................................... 18.00
**Bowl,** Salad, Pekin, Royal Staffordshire, C.1909, 9 3/4 In. ............................... 55.00
**Bowl,** Serving, Victoria, Wood & Sons, C.1890, 10 1/4 In. ................................ 45.00
**Bowl,** Soup, Touraine, Stanley, 7 1/2 In., Pair .................................................. 32.50
**Bowl,** Touraine, Handled, 9 1/2 In. ................................................................... 50.00
**Bowl,** Touraine, 6 1/4 In. .................................................................................. 20.00
**Bowl,** Trilby, 9 1/2 In. ............................................................................. 47.50 To 65.00
**Bowl,** Vegetable, Acantha, Meakin, Open, 9 1/2 X 7 1/4 In. .............................. 25.00
**Bowl,** Vegetable, Amoy, Davenport, Open, 1844, 8 3/4 X 6 1/2 In. .................. 145.00
**Bowl,** Vegetable, Argyle, Oval ......................................................................... 30.00
**Bowl,** Vegetable, Baltic, Grindley, Open, 1891, 10 In. ...................................... 65.00
**Bowl,** Vegetable, Beaufort, Grindley, Covered, C.1902, 10 1/4 In. ................... 110.00
**Bowl,** Vegetable, Bristol, Covered, 5 3/4 X 12 1/4 In. ....................................... 110.00
**Bowl,** Vegetable, Chapoo, Wedgwood, Open, C.1850, 7 1/2 X 5 1/2 In. .......... 145.00
**Bowl,** Vegetable, Chen-Si, Open, 8 1/2 X 6 In. ................................................. 95.00
**Bowl,** Vegetable, Chiswick, Covered ............................................................... 65.00
**Bowl,** Vegetable, Chusan, Oblong, 8 1/2 In. ................................................... 155.00
**Bowl,** Vegetable, Covered, Pansy, Rectangular, 12 In. .................................... 110.00
**Bowl,** Vegetable, Delaware, Open ................................................................... 35.00
**Bowl,** Vegetable, Formosa ............................................................................... 63.50
**Bowl,** Vegetable, Gironde, Grindley, Open, 1891, 8 1/4 In. ............................... 38.00
**Bowl,** Vegetable, Gironde, Grindley, Open, 1891, 9 X 6 3/4 In. ......................... 65.00
**Bowl,** Vegetable, Lahore, Phillips, Covered, 10 1/2 In. ..................................... 275.00
**Bowl,** Vegetable, Martha, Bridgett & Bates, Open, C.1896, 9 In. ....................... 40.00
**Bowl,** Vegetable, Melbourne, Grindley, Open, C.1900, 9 In. .............................. 45.00
**Bowl,** Vegetable, Nanking, 8-Sided, Covered, 9 In. ........................................ 175.00
**Bowl,** Vegetable, Nonpareil, Burgess & Leigh, Open ....................................... 45.00
**Bowl,** Vegetable, Oriental, Ridgway, Rectangle, 1891, 9 1/2 X 7 In. .................. 95.00
**Bowl,** Vegetable, Pansy, Covered, Rectangular, 12 In. ................................... 110.00
**Bowl,** Vegetable, Pansy, Floral Design, 1880 .................................................. 110.00
**Bowl,** Vegetable, Scinde, Alcock, Rosebud Finial, C.1840, 12 X 9 In. ............... 410.00
**Bowl,** Vegetable, Scinde, Covered, Rose Finial ............................................... 120.00
**Bowl,** Vegetable, Temple, Covered ................................................................. 175.00
**Bowl,** Vegetable, Waldorf, Open, 9 In. ............................................................. 40.00
**Bowl,** Vegetable, Watteau, Round, Covered ................................................... 145.00
**Bowl,** Vegetable, White, Blue Trim, Covered, 1912, 13 X 7 1/2 In. ................... 11.00
**Bowl,** Victoria, 10 In. ...................................................................................... 65.00
**Bowl,** Waldorf, 8 3/4 In. ................................................................................... 65.00
**Bowl,** Waste, Oriental, Ridgway, 1891 ............................................................. 65.00

Bowl, Waste, Sobraon, Furnival, C.1850, 7 In. ........................................................... 195.00
Bowl, Watteau, New Wharf Pottery, 1891, 2 X 9 In. ................................................ 45.00
Box, Indian, 3 Ball Feet, Braiding, Covered, 6 In. .................................................. 25.00
Butter Pat, Grace, Grindley, 1897 ......................................................................... 20.00
Butter Pat, Holland, Johnson Bros., 1891 ............................................................ 22.00
Butter Pat, La Francais, French China Co., 1890 ................................................. 9.50
Butter Pat, Messina, Cauldon, 1905 ..................................................................... 15.00
Butter Pat, Muriel, Upper Hanley, New Wharf Pottery, 1895 ............................... 15.00
Butter Pat, Oriental, Ridgway, 1891 ...................................................................... 22.00
Butter Pat, Osborne, Ridgway, 1905 ..................................................................... 15.00
Butter Pat, Ovando, Meakin, 1891 ......................................................................... 18.00
Butter Pat, Princeton, Johnson Bros., 1900 ......................................................... 15.00
Butter Pat, Verona, Wood & Sons, 1891 ............................................................... 18.00
Butter, Florida, Covered ......................................................................................... 85.00
Butter, Kyber, Covered ........................................................................................... 145.00
Butter, Manhattan, Alcock, Covered ...................................................................... 20.00
Butter, Milan, Wood & Son, Insert, Covered, 1893 ............................................... 70.00
Butter, Normandy, Covered .................................................................................... 110.00
Butter, Scinde, Alcock, Covered, 1840 .................................................................. 415.00
Cake Plate, Bombay, Japan, C.1835, 9 In. ............................................................ 25.00
Cake Plate, Lancaster, New Wharf Pottery, 1891, 10 X 9 1/8 In. ......................... 40.00
Chamber Pot, Ning Po, Hall, Covered, 1845 ......................................................... 375.00
Chamber Pot, Sharon ............................................................................................. 210.00
Chamber Pot, Willow, Doulton & Co. ..................................................................... 175.00
Chamber Set, Rose, Gold Trim, C.1900, 16 1/2 In. .............................................. 225.00
Charger, La Belle, 14 In. ......................................................................................... 90.00
Chocolate Pot, Florence, Bennett, 1890 ................................................................ 115.00
Chop Plate, Fairy Villas, Adams, 12 1/2 In. ........................................................... 75.00
Coffeepot, Scinde, 7 1/2 In. .................................................................................... 350.00
Coffeepot, Temple ................................................................................................... 265.00
Coffeepot, Tulip & Sprig .......................................................................................... 450.00
Cracker Jar, Anemone ............................................................................................. 125.00
Creamer, La Belle ................................................................................................... 50.00
Creamer, Lorne, Grindley, 1900 ............................................................................. 65.00
Creamer, Meissen, Ridgway, 1910 ......................................................................... 38.00
Creamer, Nonpareil, Burgess & Leigh, 1891 ........................................................ 95.00
Creamer, Oregon, Mayer, Straight Sided, Paneled, 1845 .................................... 210.00
Creamer, Paisley, Mercer, 1890 ............................................................................. 60.00
Creamer, Scinde, Alcock ......................................................................................... 195.00
Creamer, Singa, Cork, Edge, & Malkin, 1865 ....................................................... 160.00
Creamer, Temple ................................................................... 185.00 To 200.00
Creamer, Tonquin, 8-Paneled ................................................................................ 65.00
Creamer, Touraine ................................................................................................... 175.00
Creamer, Waldorf ..................................................................................................... 75.00
Cup & Saucer, Acantha, Meakin ............................................................................ 25.00
Cup & Saucer, Athens, Handleless, Slate Blue, C.1849 ...................................... 75.00
Cup & Saucer, Chapoo, Wedgwood, Handleless, 1850 ....................................... 85.00
Cup & Saucer, Chen-Si, Meir, Handleless, 1835 ................................................. 85.00
Cup & Saucer, Corean, Garden, Scroll Borders, Handleless, C.1884 ................. 100.00
Cup & Saucer, Harlington, Grindley ....................................................................... 20.00
Cup & Saucer, Holland, Johnson Bros., 1891 ...................................................... 45.00
Cup & Saucer, Idris, Grindley, Demitasse ............................................................. 25.00
Cup & Saucer, Indian Jar, Handleless ................................................................... 70.00
Cup & Saucer, Japan Pattern, Handleless ............................................................ 40.00
Cup & Saucer, Kyber, Adams, 1891 ....................................................................... 60.00
Cup & Saucer, Kyber, J.Meir, Handleless, 1844 ................................................... 86.50
Cup & Saucer, Leaves & Bar, Handleless ............................................................. 60.00
Cup & Saucer, Lorne, Demitasse ........................................................................... 30.00
Cup & Saucer, Martha, Bridgett & Bates, 1896 .................................................... 35.00
Cup & Saucer, Meissen, Demitasse ....................................................................... 32.00
Cup & Saucer, Messina, Cauldon, 1905 ................................................................ 42.00
Cup & Saucer, Mikado, Wilkinson .......................................................................... 30.00
Cup & Saucer, Nonpareil, Burgess & Leigh, 1891, 4 In. ...................................... 48.00

Cup & Saucer, Oriental, Ridgway, 1891 ............................................................ 48.00
Cup & Saucer, Pelew, Challinor, Paneled, 1843 ................................................ 85.00
Cup & Saucer, Scinde, Alcock, Handleless, 1840 ........................ 72.00 To 90.00
Cup & Saucer, Shapoo, Boote, Handleless, 1860 ............................................. 85.00
Cup & Saucer, Shell, Challinor, Handleless, 1860 ............................................ 62.00
Cup & Saucer, Sobraon, Furnival, Handleless, 1850 ........................................ 85.00
Cup & Saucer, Spinach ...................................................................................... 30.00
Cup & Saucer, Touraine .......................................................... 35.00 To 60.00
Cup & Saucer, Touraine, Coffee ........................................................................ 55.00
Cup & Saucer, Valencia, S.Hancock & Sons, 1910 ......................................... 10.00
Cup & Saucer, Vermont, Burgess & Leigh, Demitasse ..................................... 35.00
Cup Plate, Amoy ................................................................................................ 30.00
Cup Plate, Berlin Groups, C.1860 ..................................................................... 55.00
Cup Plate, Corean, C.1850 ................................................................................ 35.00
Cup Plate, Gothic, Furnival, 1850 ..................................................................... 48.00
Cup Plate, Kaolin, Podmore & Walker, 1850 ................................................... 48.00
Cup Plate, Montilla, Davenport, Slate Blue, 1844 ........................................... 50.00
Cup Plate, Tonquin ............................................................................................ 50.00
Cup, Marie ......................................................................................................... 30.00
Cup, Shell, Wood & Challinor, Handleless, 1860 ............................................. 40.00
Dish, Candy, Blossom, Square, Covered ........................................................... 45.00
Dish, Ferrara, Heart Shape, Wedgwood, 8 X 9 3/4 In. ................................... 60.00
Dish, Soap, California, Podmore Walker & Co., Drainer & Lid ......................... 95.00
Dish, Soap, Indian Jar, Furnival, Covered, Liner, 1843 ................................. 125.00
Eggcup, Raleigh, Burgess & Leigh, 1906 ......................................................... 35.00
Flowerpot, Peony, 6 3/4 X 6 In. ..................................................................... 145.00
Gravy Boat & Tray, Coburg, Edwards, 1860 .................................................. 235.00
Gravy Boat & Tray, Marie, Grindley, 1891 ...................................................... 85.00
Gravy Boat & Tray, Oriental, Ridgway, 1891 ................................................. 155.00
Gravy Boat & Tray, Spodes Tower, Copeland .................................................. 95.00
Gravy Boat, Athol, Doulton, 1900 .................................................................... 45.00
Gravy Boat, Baltic, Grindley, 1891 ................................................................... 65.00
Gravy Boat, Gironde, Grindley .......................................................................... 45.00
Gravy Boat, Kyber, Adams ................................................................................ 75.00
Gravy Boat, La Belle .......................................................................................... 65.00
Gravy Boat, Larch, S.Hancock & Son, 1906 ..................................................... 35.00
Gravy Boat, Lorne, Grindley ............................................................................. 38.50
Gravy Boat, Luzerne, Mercer, 1890 .................................................................. 45.00
Gravy Boat, Nonpareil, Burgess & Leigh, 1891 ............................................... 70.00
Gravy Boat, Portman, Grindley ......................................................................... 35.00
Gravy Boat, Tivoli, T.Furnival, 1875 .............................................................. 100.00
Gravy Boat, Underplate, Arcadia, Wilkinson .................................................... 58.00
Gravy Boat, Underplate, Gironde, W.H.Grindley, 1891 .................................... 85.00
Gravy Boat, Undertray, Mentone, Johnson Bros. ............................................. 55.00
Holder, Toothbrush, Gothic .............................................................................. 145.00
Hot Plate, Persian Moss, Utzschneider & Co. ................................................... 80.00
Jar, Spice, Oriental, 3 3/4 X 2 3/8 In.Square .................................................. 45.00
Jardiniere, La Belle .......................................................................................... 150.00
Jardiniere, Peony, Gold Trim, 6 In. ................................................................. 145.00
Jardiniere, Poppy ............................................................................................... 85.00
Ladle, Curved Molded Handle, 10 In. ............................................................... 65.00
Ladle, Sauce, Montana ...................................................................................... 65.00
Pitcher & Bowl, Blue & White ......................................................................... 235.00
Pitcher & Bowl, E.Challinor, Marked, Bowl 12 1/2 In. .................................. 1000.00
Pitcher & Bowl, Pelew Ironstone, Marked, Bowl 12 1/2 In. .......................... 1000.00
Pitcher & Bowl, Scinde, Alcock, Paneled Bowl, 1840, 13 In. ......................... 875.00
Pitcher & Bowl, Scinde, Alcock, Scalloped Bowl, 1840, 14 In. ....................... 875.00
Pitcher, Allover Florals, Royal Doulton, 5 1/4 In. ............................................ 88.00
Pitcher, Hofburg, C.1891, 6 In. ........................................................................ 80.00
Pitcher, Ivy, Gold Trim, 8 1/2 In. ..................................................................... 65.00
Pitcher, La Belle .............................................................................................. 125.00
Pitcher, Lemonade, Floral Design, Bamboo Handle, Covered .......................... 50.00
Pitcher, Marked Wood & Son, England, 12 In. ............................................... 250.00

Pitcher, Milk, Beauties Of China, C.1845, Venables, 5 1/2 In. ................................. 165.00
Pitcher, Milk, California, C.1849, 8 In. ................................. 95.00
Pitcher, Milk, Canton, Maddock, 1850, 9 In. ................................. 325.00
Pitcher, Milk, Chapoo, 5 1/2 In. ................................. 135.00
Pitcher, Milk, Formosa, Ridgway, 1834, Large ................................. 325.00
Pitcher, Milk, Idris, Grindley, 6 In. ................................. 60.00
Pitcher, Milk, Jeddo, 1 Quart ................................. 145.00
Pitcher, Milk, La Belle ................................. 150.00
Pitcher, Milk, Margot, Embossed, 6 In. ................................. 110.00
Pitcher, Milk, Touraine ................................. 125.00
Pitcher, Paneled, Raised Flowers, Blue Ground, Gold Trim, 6 In. ................................. 68.00
Pitcher, Spodes Tower, Copeland, 9 1/2 In. ................................. 155.00
Pitcher, Water, Lotus, Grindley, 2 1/2 Quart ................................. 110.00
Pitcher, Water, Lynton, 10 In. ................................. 265.00
Pitcher, Waverly, J.Maddock & Son, 1 1/2 Quart ................................. 125.00
Plaque, Wall, Lake Lucerne, Gold Trim, Raised Scroll, 16 3/4 In. ................................. 275.00
Plate Soup, Arcadia, W.Adams, 9 1/4 In.Diam., Set Of 5 ................................. 85.00
Plate, Abbey, 10 1/2 In. ................................. 45.00
Plate, Acantha, Meakin, 9 In. ................................. 18.00 To 20.00
Plate, Acantha, Meakin, 10 In. ................................. 19.00 To 25.00
Plate, Acantha, 8 In. ................................. 15.00 To 16.00
Plate, Alaska, Grindley, 1891, 9 In. ................................. 28.00
Plate, Amoy, Davenport, 1844, 10 1/2 In. ................................. 75.00
Plate, Amoy, Davenport, 8 In. ................................. 45.00
Plate, Ancient Ruins, 9 In. ................................. 17.50
Plate, Arabesque, Mayer, 14-Sided, 1845, 10 1/2 In. ................................. 75.00
Plate, Arabesque, 9 1/2 In. ................................. 25.00
Plate, Arabesque, 9 3/4 In. ................................. 85.00
Plate, Arcadia, Wilkinson, 1907, 7 3/4 In. ................................. 20.00
Plate, Argyle, 7 In. ................................. 27.50
Plate, Argyle, 8 1/2 In. ................................. 32.50
Plate, Asiatic Pheasants, 9 3/4 In. ................................. 30.00
Plate, Astoria, 10 In. ................................. 35.00
Plate, Baltic, Grindley, 1891, 10 In. ................................. 38.00
Plate, Beaufort, Grindley, 1902, 10 In. ................................. 30.00
Plate, Beaufort, 1903, 9 In. ................................. 30.00
Plate, Blue Danube, Johnson Bros., 1900, 10 In. ................................. 30.00
Plate, Brunswick, New Wharf Pottery, 1891, 8 3/4 In. ................................. 25.00
Plate, Cabul, Challinor, 1847, 10 1/2 In. ................................. 85.00
Plate, Cake, Royal Blue, Tab Handle, 10 In. ................................. 85.00
Plate, Carlton, Alcock, 1840, 9 In., Pair ................................. 52.00
Plate, Cashmere, Morley, 1850, 9 1/2 In. ................................. 70.00
Plate, Chapoo, J.Wedgwood, 8 In. ................................. 50.00
Plate, Chapoo, Wedgwood, 1850, 10 1/2 In. ................................. 70.00
Plate, Chapoo, 1850, 8 1/2 In. ................................. 64.00
Plate, Chen-Si, J.Meir, 1835, 7 1/2 In. ................................. 39.50
Plate, Chen-Si, J.Meir, 1835, 8 1/2 In. ................................. 60.00
Plate, Chop, La Belle, 12 In. ................................. 75.00
Plate, Chrysanthemum, Pratt, 1870, 6 In. ................................. 28.00
Plate, Chusan, 7 1/2 In. ................................. 45.00
Plate, Coburg, Edwards, 1860, 8 1/2 In. ................................. 60.00
Plate, Colonial, Meakin, 1891, 10 In. ................................. 30.00
Plate, Conway, 9 In. ................................. 30.00
Plate, Conway, 10 1/2 In. ................................. 36.00
Plate, Corean, Clementson, 1860, 9 1/4 In. ................................. 38.00
Plate, Corean, Mulberry Brown, Paneled Sides, C.1884, 9 3/4 In. ................................. 70.00
Plate, Corean, Walker, 1850, 6 3/4 In. ................................. 28.00
Plate, Corean, Walker, 1850, 9 3/4 In. ................................. 45.00
Plate, Corey Hill, C.1845, 8 1/2 In. ................................. 20.00
Plate, Delamere, Alcock, 1900, 7 In. ................................. 18.00
Plate, Delamere, Alcock, 1900, 8 3/4 In. ................................. 28.00
Plate, Dinner, Conway, 10 In. ................................. 40.00
Plate, Dinner, Lancaster ................................. 22.00

**Plate,** Excelsior, 8 In. .......................................................................................... 15.00
**Plate,** Excelsior, 9 In. .......................................................................................... 75.00
**Plate,** Fairy Villas, Adams, 1891, 9 In. ................................................ 38.00 To 45.00
**Plate,** Formosa, 8 In. ........................................................................................... 45.00
**Plate,** Gainsborough, Ridgway, 1905, 10 In. ...................................................... 35.00
**Plate,** Gem, R.Hammersley, 8 3/4 In. ................................................................. 75.00
**Plate,** Gironde, Grindley, 10 In. ......................................................................... 30.00
**Plate,** Gironde, W.H.Grindley, 1891, 7 In. ....................................... 16.00 To 18.00
**Plate,** Gironde, W.H.Grindley, 1891, 8 3/4 In. .................................................. 26.00
**Plate,** Haddon, 8 In. ............................................................................................ 18.00
**Plate,** Hanley, 10 In. ........................................................................................... 35.00
**Plate,** Hizen, 9 1/2 In. ........................................................................................ 45.00
**Plate,** Holland, 9 In. ........................................................................................... 12.00
**Plate,** Holland, 10 In. .......................................................................................... 32.00
**Plate,** Hong Kong, Meigh, 1845, 9 1/4 In. ........................................................ 68.00
**Plate,** Hong Kong, Meigh, 1845, 10 1/2 In. ....................................................... 75.00
**Plate,** Idris, Grindley, 1910, 8 3/4 In. ................................................................ 15.00
**Plate,** Indian Bridge, Alcock, 8 In. ..................................................................... 35.00
**Plate,** Indian Bridge, Alcock, 10 1/4 In. ............................................................. 75.00
**Plate,** Indian, Pratt, 1843, 8 1/4 In. .................................................................... 38.00
**Plate,** Iris, Royal Staffordshire, 1907, 10 1/2 In. ............................................... 25.00
**Plate,** Ivanhoe, Wedgwood, 1901, 10 In. ........................................................... 75.00
**Plate,** Jenny Lind, 9 In. ....................................................................................... 55.00
**Plate,** Jewel, 7 In. ............................................................................................... 16.00
**Plate,** Kelvin, Meaking, 1891, 9 3/4 In. .............................................................. 30.00
**Plate,** Kin Shan, 10 1/2 In. .................................................................................. 85.00
**Plate,** Kyber, Adams, 1891, 9 In. ......................................................... 38.00 To 45.00
**Plate,** Kyber, Adams, 1891, 10 In. ...................................................................... 48.00
**Plate,** La Belle, Wheeling Pottery, 1900, 9 In. ................................................... 30.00
**Plate,** La Belle, 7 1/2 In. ..................................................................................... 25.00
**Plate,** La Belle, 8 1/2 In. ...................................................................... 25.00 To 30.00
**Plate,** La Belle, 9 1/2 In. ..................................................................................... 35.00
**Plate,** Lancaster, Handled, 10 In. ....................................................................... 35.00
**Plate,** Lancaster, 9 In. .......................................................................... 18.00 To 25.00
**Plate,** Lancaster, 9 1/4 In. .................................................................... 25.00 To 35.00
**Plate,** Le Pavot, 10 1/2 In. .................................................................................. 36.00
**Plate,** Libertas, Prussia, 1890, 9 In. ................................................................... 24.00
**Plate,** Lorne, Grindley, 1900, 5 3/4 In. ............................................................... 20.00
**Plate,** Lorne, 6 3/4 In. ......................................................................................... 15.00
**Plate,** Lucania, Clarke, 1885, 9 In. ..................................................................... 22.00
**Plate,** Madras, Davenport, Some Gold, 9 In. ...................................... 32.00 To 35.00
**Plate,** Madras, Davenport, 1844, 8 3/4 In. ......................................................... 35.00
**Plate,** Madras, Doulton, 10 1/2 In. ...................................................................... 38.00
**Plate,** Madras, Doulton, 1900, 6 1/2 In. .............................................................. 28.00
**Plate,** Manilla, Walker, 1845, 12-Paneled, 7 3/4 In. .......................................... 60.00
**Plate,** Manilla, Walker, 1845, 12-Paneled, 8 3/4 In. .......................................... 65.00
**Plate,** Manilla, Walker, 1845, 12-Paneled, 9 3/4 In. .......................................... 75.00
**Plate,** Marechal Niel, W.H.Grindley, 1895, 8 In. ............................................... 25.00
**Plate,** Marechal Niel, 10 1/2 In. .......................................................................... 36.00
**Plate,** Marguerite, W.H.Grindley, 1891, 10 In. .................................... 35.00 To 40.00
**Plate,** Marie, Grindley, 1891, 10 In. .................................................................... 35.00
**Plate,** Martha Washington, Daniel Law & Co., 1900, 9 In. ................................. 35.00
**Plate,** Medina, 12-Sided, Furnival, 1840, 10 In. ................................................ 25.00
**Plate,** Melbourne, Grindley, 1900, 8 3/4 In. ....................................................... 32.00
**Plate,** Nonpareil, Burgess & Leigh, 1891, 8 1/2 In. ........................................... 38.00
**Plate,** Nonpareil, 8 In. ......................................................................................... 28.00
**Plate,** Nonpareil, 9 In. ......................................................................................... 35.00
**Plate,** Normandy, 7 In. ......................................................................................... 25.00
**Plate,** Oregon, T.J. & J.Mayer, 1845, 7 1/2 In. .................................................. 40.00
**Plate,** Oregon, T.J. & J.Mayer, 1845, 8 1/2 In. .................................................. 46.50
**Plate,** Oregon, T.J. & J.Mayer, 1845, 9 3/4 In. .................................................. 70.00
**Plate,** Oregon, 9 1/2 In. ....................................................................................... 22.00
**Plate,** Oregon, 10 In. ........................................................................................... 85.00

Plate, Oriental, New Wharf Pottery Co., 1891, 8 3/4 In. ........................................ 38.00
Plate, Oriental, Ridgway, 1891, 8 In. ........................................ 32.00
Plate, Oriental, Ridgway, 1891, 9 In. ........................................ 36.00
Plate, Oriental, 9 In. ........................................ 22.00
Plate, Osborne, Grindley, 1900, 8 3/4 In. ........................................ 30.00
Plate, Osborne, Ridgway, 1905, 5 3/4 In. ........................................ 16.00
Plate, Osborne, Ridgway, 1905, 9 3/4 In. ........................................ 28.00
Plate, Ovando, A.Meakin, 1891, 7 In. ........................................ 25.00
Plate, Paris, New Wharf Pottery, 1894, 9 In. ........................................ 20.00
Plate, Pekin, Albert Jones, 12 In.Diam. ........................................ 55.00
Plate, Pelew, Challinor, 14-Paneled, 1840, 10 In. ........................................ 75.00
Plate, Penang, W.Ridgway, 1840, 10 1/2 In. ........................................ 55.00
Plate, Poppy, 8 3/4 In. ........................................ 25.00
Plate, Portsmouth, New Wharf, 8 In. ........................................ 22.00
Plate, Princeton, 10 In. ........................................ 35.00
Plate, Progress, 8 3/4 In. ........................................ 12.00
Plate, Rebecca, 10 In. ........................................ 58.00
Plate, Rhone, Furnival, 12-Paneled, 1845, 10 1/2 In. ........................................ 68.00
Plate, Rhone, 7 1/4 In. ........................................ 35.00
Plate, Rhone, 10 In. ........................................ 50.00 To 55.00
Plate, Richmond, Johnson Brothers, 10 1/4 In. ........................................ 32.00
Plate, Roslyn, Alfred Culley, 1900, 10 In. ........................................ 35.00
Plate, Scinde, Alcock, 10 1/2 In. ........................................ 80.00
Plate, Scinde, Alcock, 1830, 10 1/2 In. ........................................ 90.00
Plate, Scinde, Alcock, 1840, 10 1/2 In. ........................................ 85.00
Plate, Scinde, Alcock, 8 In. ........................................ 52.00
Plate, Scinde, Alcock, 9 1/4 In. ........................................ 60.00
Plate, Scinde, Alcock, 1840, 9 1/4 In. ........................................ 68.00
Plate, Scinde, 8 1/4 In. ........................................ 65.00
Plate, Scinde, 9 1/2 In. ........................................ 65.00
Plate, Scinde, 10 1/2 In. ........................................ 75.00 To 95.00
Plate, Shanghai, Adams, 1870, 10 1/2 In. ........................................ 75.00
Plate, Shanghai, Furnival, 12-Sided, 1860, 8 1/4 In. ........................................ 45.00
Plate, Shanghai, 10 In. ........................................ 75.00
Plate, Sobraon, Floral Border, 10 1/2 In. ........................................ 40.00
Plate, Temple, Walker, Paneled, 1850, 9 In. ........................................ 70.00
Plate, Temple, Walker, 1850, 8 3/4 In. ........................................ 55.00
Plate, Temple, Walker, 8 In. ........................................ 58.00
Plate, Timor, Luneville, France, 1875, 7 1/4 In. ........................................ 25.00
Plate, Tonquin, Adams, 10 1/4 In. ........................................ 75.00
Plate, Tonquin, Adams, 12-Paneled, 1845, 7 1/2 In. ........................................ 58.00
Plate, Tonquin, Adams, 12-Paneled, 1845, 10 1/2 In. ........................................ 75.00
Plate, Touraine, Alcock, 8 3/4 In. ........................................ 28.00 To 35.00
Plate, Touraine, Stanley, 1891, 6 1/2 In. ........................................ 10.00 To 18.00
Plate, Touraine, Stanley, 8 13/16 In. ........................................ 30.00
Plate, Touraine, 8 In. ........................................ 22.50
Plate, Touraine, 9 In. ........................................ 14.00 To 35.00
Plate, Troy, 9 In. ........................................ 30.00
Plate, Verona, 9 In. ........................................ 25.00
Plate, Vignette, J.Maddock & Son, 1891, 9 In. ........................................ 30.00
Plate, Virginia, 8 In. ........................................ 27.00
Plate, Waldorf, New Wharf Pottery, 10 In. ........................................ 30.00
Plate, Waldorf, New Wharf Pottery, 1892, 8 3/4 In. ........................................ 38.00
Plate, Waldorf, New Wharf Pottery, 1892, 10 In. ........................................ 35.00 To 38.00
Plate, Waldorf, 9 In. ........................................ 15.00 To 25.00
Plate, Waldorf, 9 3/4 In. ........................................ 32.00
Plate, Washington Vase, 1850, 9 3/4 In. ........................................ 48.00
Plate, Watteau, Doulton, 1896, 10 In. ........................................ 35.00 To 48.00
Plate, Watteau, 9 In. ........................................ 25.00
Plate, Yedo, Ashworth & Bros., 1870, 7 In. ........................................ 30.00
Platter, Abbey, Adams, 13 1/2 X 10 1/4 In. ........................................ 90.00
Platter, Acantha, Meakin, 12 X 15 1/2 In. ........................................ 60.00
Platter, Acantha, 9 X 12 In. ........................................ 25.00

**Platter,** Amoy, Davenport, 12 1/4 X 9 1/4 In. ........ 125.00
**Platter,** Amoy, Davenport, 1844, 8 X 6 In. ........ 120.00
**Platter,** Arabesque, Mayer, 1845, 15 3/4 X 12 In. ........ 195.00
**Platter,** Argyle, Grindley, 1896, 10 In. ........ 65.00
**Platter,** Argyle, Grindley, 1896, 15 In. ........ 115.00
**Platter,** Argyle, 17 X 12 In. ........ 10.00
**Platter,** Baltic, Grindley, 1891, 14 In. ........ 115.00
**Platter,** Baltic, Grindley, 1891, 18 In. ........ 155.00
**Platter,** Beaufort, Grindley, 1902, 14 In. ........ 60.00
**Platter,** Beaufort, Grindley, 1902, 18 In. ........ 110.00
**Platter,** Carlton, Alcock, 13 1/2 In. ........ 135.00
**Platter,** Catherine, Grindley, 14 X 10 In. ........ 65.00
**Platter,** Cecil, 14 In. ........ 50.00
**Platter,** Celtic, 17 1/2 X 11 1/2 In. ........ 50.00
**Platter,** Clarissa, C.1900, 16 X 12 In. ........ 85.00
**Platter,** Clayton, 10 1/2 In. ........ 65.00
**Platter,** Coburg, Edwards, 1860, 12 1/2 X 9 1/4 In. ........ 175.00
**Platter,** Corean, Walker, 1850, 16 X 11 In. ........ 135.00
**Platter,** Countess, 12 In. ........ 30.00
**Platter,** Crumlin, 11 In. ........ 65.00
**Platter,** Cyprus, Davenport, 1850, 8 X 11 In. ........ 95.00
**Platter,** Delmar, 12 1/2 In. ........ 65.00
**Platter,** Fairy Villas, Adams, 12 1/2 In. ........ 75.00
**Platter,** Fairy Villas, 18 In. ........ 145.00
**Platter,** Fisherman, Walker, 1850, 10 1/2 X 10 3/4 In. ........ 155.00
**Platter,** Formosa, Ridgway, 1834, 15 1/2 X 12 In. ........ 290.00
**Platter,** Gironde, Grindley, 1891, 15 1/4 X 10 3/4 In. ........ 85.00
**Platter,** Gironde, Grindley, 1891, 20 X 13 In. ........ 100.00
**Platter,** Glenmore, C.1892, 16 1/4 X 12 1/2 In. ........ 80.00
**Platter,** Glenwood, Johnson, 7 1/2 X 10 1/2 In. ........ 38.00
**Platter,** Holland, Johnson Bros., 1891, 14 1/4 X 10 1/2 In. ........ 68.00
**Platter,** Idris, Grindley, 1910, 10 X 7 3/4 In. ........ 22.00
**Platter,** Indian Jar, Furnival, 1843, 16 1/2 X 12 1/2 In. ........ 190.00
**Platter,** Indian, Pratt, 1840, 12 1/4 X 9 1/2 In. ........ 155.00
**Platter,** Indian, Pratt, 1840, 15 1/2 X 11 1/2 In. ........ 220.00
**Platter,** Indian, 13 1/2 X 17 1/4 In. ........ 255.00
**Platter,** Indian, 17 In. ........ 275.00
**Platter,** Japan Pattern, Octagonal Shape ........ 195.00
**Platter,** Japan, Bennett & Co., 1890, 16 1/2 X 11 3/4 In. ........ 75.00
**Platter,** Kyber, Adams, 1891, 10 X 7 1/4 In. ........ 95.00
**Platter,** Lancaster, 12 1/2 In. ........ 45.00
**Platter,** Le Pavot, W.H.Grindley, 14 In. ........ 55.00
**Platter,** Linda, J.Maddock, 15 X 11 In. ........ 65.00
**Platter,** Lois, New Wharf Pottery, 1891, 10 3/4 X 9 In. ........ 48.00
**Platter,** Lois, 11 In. ........ 65.00
**Platter,** Lonsdale, 15 In. ........ 110.00
**Platter,** Lorne, Grindley, 14 X 10 In. ........ 45.00
**Platter,** Manhattan, Alcock, 1900, 15 X 10 1/4 In. ........ 60.00
**Platter,** Manilla, Walker, 1845, 10 3/4 X 8 1/4 In. ........ 185.00
**Platter,** Manilla, Walker, 1845, 13 1/2 X 10 1/2 In. ........ 245.00
**Platter,** Manilla, Walker, 1845, 15 1/2 X 12 In. ........ 325.00
**Platter,** Marguerite, Grindley, 1891, 16 1/2 X 11 1/4 In. ........ 68.00
**Platter,** Marlborough, Grindley, England, Oval, 10 X 14 In. ........ 59.50
**Platter,** Melbourne, Grindley, 1900, 14 X 10 In. ........ 80.00
**Platter,** Melbourne, Oval, 10 In. ........ 20.00
**Platter,** Napier, Wedgwood, 19 X 16 In. ........ 85.00
**Platter,** Ning Po, 12 1/2 In. ........ 210.00
**Platter,** Nonpareil, Burgess & Leigh, 1891, 13 1/2 X 11 1/2 In. ........ 120.00
**Platter,** Nonpareil, 10 X 8 In. ........ 50.00
**Platter,** Orchid, Well & Tree, Covered, 12 In. ........ 75.00
**Platter,** Oriental, 15 1/2 In. ........ 150.00
**Platter,** Oriental, 17 X 14 1/2 In. ........ 125.00
**Platter,** Peach Royal, 16 In. ........ 120.00

**Platter,** Portman, 16 X 11 3/4 In. ............................................................ 40.00
**Platter,** Portsmouth, 16 In. ...................................................................... 90.00
**Platter,** Royal Blue, Burgess & Campbell, 18 1/2 In. ............................... 75.00
**Platter,** Saxon, Daisies & Pansies In Center, 8 1/2 X 11 1/2 In. .............. 22.00
**Platter,** Scinde, Alcock, Scalloped, 1840, 13 1/2 X 10 1/2 In. .............. 245.00
**Platter,** Scinde, Alcock, 1840, 20 1/2 X 16 In. .................................... 625.00
**Platter,** Scinde, 12 1/4 In. ..................................................................... 235.00
**Platter,** Scinde, 13 1/2 In. ..................................................................... 265.00
**Platter,** Scinde, 16 In. ............................................................................ 345.00
**Platter,** Scinde, 16 X 13 In. .................................................................. 225.00
**Platter,** Shanghai, Grindley, 14 X 10 In. ................................................ 75.00
**Platter,** Shell, Challinor, 1860, 10 X 7 1/4 In. ...................................... 115.00
**Platter,** Shell, 16 In. .............................................................................. 150.00
**Platter,** Strawberry, C.1856, 16 X 12 1/2 In. ........................................ 125.00
**Platter,** Tonquin, Heath, 1850, 15 1/2 X 11 3/4 In. .............................. 275.00
**Platter,** Tonquin, 10 1/2 In. ................................................................... 195.00
**Platter,** Tonquin, 17 In. .......................................................................... 300.00
**Platter,** Touraine, Stanley, 10 1/4 X 6 7/8 In. ........................................ 58.00
**Platter,** Touraine, 8 1/2 X 12 1/2 In. ........................................ 20.00 To 50.00
**Platter,** Touraine, 10 X 15 In. ................................................................. 75.00
**Platter,** Turin, 12 X 16 In. ..................................................................... 40.00
**Platter,** Turkey Pictured, Cauldon, 1890, 20 1/2 In. .............................. 185.00
**Platter,** Verona, 12 1/2 In. ..................................................................... 65.00
**Platter,** Victor, 10 1/2 In. ...................................................................... 45.00
**Platter,** Waldorf, New Wharf Pottery, 1892, 10 3/8 X 8 In. .................... 42.00
**Platter,** Waldorf, New Wharf Pottery, 1892, 11 X 9 In. .......................... 58.00
**Platter,** Waldorf, 10 3/4 In. ................................................................... 40.00
**Platter,** Warwick, Podmore & Walker, 1850, 18 X 10 1/2 In. ................ 125.00
**Platter,** Watteau, Doulton, 1896, 17 X 13 1/2 In. ................................. 225.00
**Platter,** Watteau, New Wharf Pottery, Oval, 1891, 11 X 9 In. ................. 45.00
**Platter,** Waverly, J.Maddock & Son, 11 X 8 1/4 In. ................................ 35.00
**Platter,** Westbourne, 14 In. ................................................................... 110.00
**Platter,** Whampoa, 13 In. ....................................................................... 275.00
**Platter,** White, Blue Trim, Marked Globe & Crown, 16 X 11 In. ............... 45.00
**Platter,** Yedo, Ashworth & Bros., Oval, 1870, 11 X 8 1/4 In. .................. 75.00
**Platter,** 17 1/2 X 15 In. ........................................................................ 175.00
**Posset Cup,** Indian Jar, Furnival, 1843 ................................................... 55.00
**Relish,** Beaufort, Grindley ....................................................................... 16.00
**Relish,** Beauties Of China, Mellor, Venables & Co., 1845, 8 X 5 In. ...... 135.00
**Relish,** Fairy Villas, Adams, 1891 .......................................................... 95.00
**Relish,** Hartwell, 8 1/2 In. ..................................................................... 33.50
**Relish,** La Belle, Wheeling Pottery, 1890, 13 1/2 X 4 In. ...................... 115.00
**Relish,** Lakewood, Wood & Son, 1900 ................................................... 48.00
**Relish,** Nonpareil .................................................................................... 66.00
**Relish,** Sweet Pea, 9 In. ......................................................................... 28.00
**Relish,** Tillenberg, Clementson ............................................................... 75.00
**Relish,** Wild Rose, Warwick, C.1900, 12 1/4 X 5 1/2 In. ....................... 40.00
**Sauce Tureen,** Carlton, Alcock, Covered, 1850 ..................................... 120.00
**Sauce,** Arcadia, Wilkinson, 1907 ........................................................... 12.00
**Sauce,** Fairy Villas, Adams, 1891 .......................................................... 24.00
**Sauce,** Indian Stone, Walley, 1850 ........................................................ 40.00
**Sauce,** Indian, 5 In. ................................................................................ 50.00
**Sauce,** Iris ............................................................................................. 10.00
**Sauce,** Lancaster ................................................................................... 15.00
**Sauce,** Melbourne, Grindley, 1900, 5 1/4 In. ......................................... 20.00
**Sauce,** Nonpareil, Burgess & Leigh, 1891, 5 In. .................................... 24.00
**Sauce,** Oregon, Mayer, 12-Paneled, 1845 ............................................. 48.00
**Sauce,** Pelew, Challinor, 14-Paneled, 1840 ........................................... 48.00
**Sauce,** Pelew, 5 In. ................................................................................ 55.00
**Sauce,** Scinde, Alcock, 1840 ................................................................. 48.00
**Sauce,** Shanghai, Furnival, 1860 ........................................................... 42.00
**Sauce,** Tonquin, Heath, 12-Paneled, 1850 ............................................ 48.00
**Sauce,** Touraine, Stanley Pottery ............................................. 15.00 To 20.00

Saucer, Arcadia, Wilkinson, 1907 ..................................................... 15.00
Saucer, Gironde, Grindley ........................................................... 7.00
Saucer, Holland, Johnson Bros., 1893 .............................................. 16.00
Saucer, Marechal Niel, W.H.Grindley, 1895 ........................................ 10.00
Saucer, Martha Washington, Daniel Low & Co., 1900 ................................ 15.00
Saucer, Martha, Bridgett & Bates, 1896 ........................................... 15.00
Saucer, Milan, 6 In. .............................................................. 6.50
Saucer, Oregon .................................................................... 29.00
Saucer, Persian Spray, Doulton & Co., 1885 ....................................... 14.00
Saucer, Regina, Societe Ceramique, 1891 .......................................... 12.00
Saucer, Shanghai, W.& E.Corn, 1900 ............................................... 12.00
Saucer, Touraine, 5 3/4 In. ...................................................... 16.00
Soup, Dish, Alexandria ............................................................ 25.00
Soup, Dish, Baltic, Grindley, 1891, 7 3/4 In. .................................... 28.00
Soup, Dish, Carlton ............................................................... 23.00
Soup, Dish, Cashmere, Moreley, Rim, 1850, 10 1/2 In. ............................. 90.00
Soup, Dish, Cashmere, 10 1/2 In. ................................................. 50.00
Soup, Dish, Ceylon, Furnival, Rim, 1876, 10 1/2 In. .............................. 45.00
Soup, Dish, Chapoo, Wedgwood, Rim, 1850, 9 1/4 In. ............................... 68.00
Soup, Dish, Chrysanthemum, 9 1/4 In. ............................................. 25.00
Soup, Dish, Denton, Grindley, 1891, 7 3/4 In. .................................... 22.00
Soup, Dish, Fairy Villas, 7 1/2 In. .............................................. 32.00
Soup, Dish, Geneva, Royal Doulton, 10 1/2 In. .................................... 22.50
Soup, Dish, Gironde, 8 1/2 In. ................................................... 27.00
Soup, Dish, Madras ................................................................ 30.00
Soup, Dish, Montana, Johnson Bros., Rim, 1900, 9 In. ............................. 30.00
Soup, Dish, Nonpareil ............................................................. 39.00
Soup, Dish, Nonpareil, Burgess & Leigh, 8 3/4 In. ............................... 32.00
Soup, Dish, Oregon, Mayer, Paneled, 1845, 9 3/4 In. ............................. 72.00
Soup, Dish, Oriental, Scenic, Scalloped Rim, 9 In. .............................. 30.00
Soup, Dish, Osborne, Ridgway, 1905 ............................................... 30.00
Soup, Dish, Scinde, Alcock, 1840, Rim, 9 In. ..................................... 75.00
Soup, Dish, Scinde, Alcock, 1840, 10 1/4 In. ..................................... 85.00
Soup, Dish, Spinach, Libertas, 1900, 7 1/4 In. ................................... 28.00
Soup, Dish, Touraine .............................................................. 35.00
Soup, Dish, Touraine, Stanley, 7 1/2 In. ......................................... 25.00
Soup, Dish, Troy, Meigh, Rim, 1840, 10 1/4 In. ................................... 68.00
Soup, Dish, Verona, Wood & Son, 9 In. ............................................ 36.00
Spittoon, La Belle ................................................................ 250.00
Sugar & Creamer, Gironde, Grindley, 1891 ......................................... 185.00
Sugar & Creamer, Holland .......................................................... 165.00
Sugar & Creamer, Oriental, Ridgway, 1891 ......................................... 195.00
Sugar & Creamer, Scinde, Walker .................................................. 225.00
Sugar, Amor, Davenport, Covered, Bulbous, 1844 ................................... 185.00
Sugar, Coburg ..................................................................... 175.00
Sugar, Coburg, Edwards, 1860 ..................................................... 195.00
Sugar, Gironde, Grindley, Covered ................................................ 65.00
Sugar, Indian ..................................................................... 38.00
Sugar, Linda, Covered ............................................................. 45.00
Sugar, Manilla, Walker, Straight-Sided, Open, 1845 ............................... 125.00
Sugar, Marie, Grindley, 1891 ..................................................... 45.00
Sugar, Milan, Grindley, 1893 ..................................................... 75.00
Sugar, Moyune, Coverd ............................................................. 75.00
Sugar, Pelew, Covered ............................................................. 195.00
Sugar, Tonquin, Adams, 1845 ...................................................... 115.00
Tea Set, Amoy, Davenport, Straight-Sided, 3 Piece, 1844 .......................... 725.00
Tea Set, Lahore, Phillips, Teapot, Creamer, & Sugar, 1840 ........................ 825.00
Teapot, Amoy, Davenport, Bulbous, 1844 ........................................... 385.00
Teapot, Coburg .................................................................... 125.00
Teapot, Corean, Walker, 1850 ..................................................... 225.00
Teapot, Lobelia, English Registry Mark 1845 ...................................... 245.00
Teapot, Manilla, Walker, 1845 ......................................... 365.00 To 415.00
Teapot, Oregon, Mayer, Bulbous, 1845 ............................................. 410.00

| | |
|---|---|
| **Teapot,** Pelew, Challinor, 1840 | 300.00 |
| **Teapot,** Scinde, Alcock, Bulbous, 1840 | 300.00 To 385.00 |
| **Teapot,** Shanghai, C.1860, Furnival, Bulbous | 390.00 |
| **Teapot,** Shell, Challinor | 165.00 |
| **Teapot,** Touraine, Alcock | 180.00 |
| **Toothbrush Holder,** Harvest, Sampson Hancock & Son, 1906 | 70.00 |
| **Toothpick,** Barrel-Shaped, Scalloped Bottom & Top, Steeple Mark | 150.00 |
| **Touraine,** 8 3/4 In. | 28.00 |
| **Tray,** Dresser, Maling, 6 X 11 In. | 55.00 |
| **Tray,** Hindostan, 1860, 14 1/2 In. | 175.00 |
| **Tray,** Sauce Tureen, Scinde, Alcock, 1840, 7 1/2 X 5 3/4 In. | 185.00 |
| **Tray,** Soup Tureen, Formosa, Ridgway, Scrolled Handles, 1834 | 385.00 |
| **Tureen,** Holland | 15.00 |
| **Tureen,** Princess, Covered | 75.00 |
| **Tureen,** Sauce, Benjapore, Ladle, 3 Piece | 150.00 |
| **Tureen,** Sauce, Covered, Manila | 150.00 |
| **Tureen,** Soup, Baltic, Grindley | 225.00 |
| **Tureen,** Soup, Canton, Maddocks, Ladle, 1850 | 695.00 |
| **Tureen,** Soup, Geneva, Doulton, Ladle & Tray, 1906 | 595.00 |
| **Tureen,** Soup, Grace | 275.00 |
| **Tureen,** Soup, Marguerite, Tab-Handled, Covered, 11 In. | 135.00 |
| **Tureen,** Soup, Osborne, Grindley, 1900 | 165.00 |
| **Tureen,** Soup, Togo | 30.00 |
| **Tureen,** Soup, Versailles, Furnival, 1894, 12 1/2 X 7 1/2 In. | 115.00 |
| **Tureen,** Soup, Victor, John Maddox, Covered, 14 In. | 55.00 |
| **Tureen,** Touraine, Oval, Covered, 9 In. | 175.00 |
| **Tureen,** Vegetable, Covered, Acantha, Footed, Handled, Scalloped | 60.00 |
| **Tureen,** Vegetable, Covered, Acantha, Meakin, Pointed Ends | 60.00 |
| **Tureen,** Vegetable, Covered, Bristol, Ford & Sons, 12 X 5 1/2 In. | 110.00 |
| **Tureen,** Vegetable, Covered, Messina, Cauldon Ltd., 1905 | 150.00 |
| **Tureen,** Vegetable, Covered, Verona, Fore & Sons, 5 1/4 X 11 1/4 In. | 110.00 |
| **Urn,** Gold Open Handles, Gold Flowers At Top, Marked, 7 In. | 155.00 |
| **Vase,** Bud, Flowers, Gold Accent, Impressed England, 9 3/4 In. | 125.00 |
| **Vase,** Lily, W.A.Adderley & Co., Ovoid, 1885, 5 In. | 50.00 |
| **Vase,** Portrait, Scrolled Handles, Scalloped Foot, Marked, 12 In. | 135.00 |
| **Vase,** Warwick Castle Scene, Marked, 8 1/2 In. | 125.00 |
| **Wash Pitcher,** Cyprus, Davenport, 1850 | 215.00 |
| **Wash Pitcher,** Floral Pattern, Knowles, Taylor, & Knowles | 210.00 |
| **Wash Pitcher,** Mikado, Wilcox & Till Ltd., 1890 | 155.00 |
| **Wash Pitcher,** Pagoda, Ridgway, 1834, 12 In. | 210.00 |
| **Wash Pitcher,** Temple, Walker, Straight-Sided, 1850 | 225.00 |
| **Washbasin,** Chinese, T.Dimmock, 13 In. | 150.00 |
| **Washbasin,** Scinde, Alcock, Scalloped, 1840, 13 In. | 410.00 |
| **Washbowl & Pitcher,** Ning Po, Hall, 1850 | 385.00 |
| **Waste Bowl,** La Belle | 25.00 |
| **Waste Bowl,** Malta, F.A.Mehlem, 1891, 4 1/4 In. | 35.00 |
| **Waste Bowl,** Manhattan, H.Alcock.1891 | 50.00 |
| **Waste Bowl,** Regina, Societe Ceramique, 1891 | 45.00 |
| **Waste Bowl,** Scinde, 3 1/2 X 6 In. | 35.00 |
| **Waste Bowl,** Spinach, Societe Ceramique, 1891, 4 1/2 In. | 50.00 |

**FOLK ART is listed in many sections of the book under the actual name of the object.
See categories such as Box, Weather Vane, Wooden Cigar Store Figure, etc.**

| | |
|---|---|
| **FOLK ART, Church,** Stamped WPA Project, Wooden | 12.00 |
| **Dollhouse** | 75.00 |
| **Fish,** Gilt Copper, 3-Dimensional, Signed Tackle, 36 In. Long | 1350.00 |
| **Horses & Royal Carriage,** Hand-Carved, C.1890, 24 In. | 550.00 |
| **Monkey,** Hand-Carved, Jointed With Wire, Climbs Pole, Black Paint | 75.00 |
| **Ornament,** Lawn, Rabbit, Wooden, 18 In. | 18.00 |
| **Puppet,** Man, Carved Wooden Head, Cloth Arms, Cardboard Body | 1950.00 |
| **Sheep,** On Wheels, Hand-Carved, Wooden | 140.00 |

Whirligig, Carved Bone Man, Articulated Arms & Legs, 15 1/2 In. ......................................... 475.00
Whirligig, Indian With Headdress, In Canoe, Paddle In Hand, 16 In. ................................... 450.00
Whirligig, Santa Claus, Sleigh, Reindeer, & Trees ............................................................. 220.00
Whirligig, Standing Soldier, Articulated Shoulders, 18 1/4 In. ........................................ 1050.00
Whirligig, Windmill With Small Elephant, 21 X 11 In. ......................................................... 65.00

FOOT WARMER, Carpeted ........................................................................................................... 12.00
Figural, Pig, Stoneware ........................................................................................................... 40.00
Gray Stoneware, 10 1/2 X 5 In.Diam. ..................................................................................... 25.00
Marked Do Not Put On Hot Stove, Glass ............................................................................ 65.00
Punched Circles & Heart Design ........................................................................................ 110.00
Tan Stoneware ......................................................................................................................... 22.00
Wood & Pierced Tin, Hearts ................................................................................................ 175.00

# FOSTORIA

*Fostoria glass was made in Fostoria, Ohio, from 1887 to 1891. The factory was moved to Moundsville, West Virginia, and most of the glass seen in shops today is a twentieth-century product.*

FOSTORIA, see also Milk Glass

FOSTORIA, Bonbon, Victoria, Frosted, Triangular, Handled ............................................. 15.00
Bonbon, 3-Footed, Baroque, Crystal .................................................................................... 7.00
Bookends, Rearing Horse ........................................................................................................ 19.75
Bottle, Water, Edgewood ........................................................................................................ 25.00
Bowl, American, Shallow, 13 In.Diam. ................................................................................... 15.00
Bowl, American, Straight Sides, Oval, 9 In. .......................................................................... 9.00
Bowl, Beverly, Amber, 10 In.Diam. ........................................................................................ 12.00
Bowl, Handled, Century, 6 In.Diam. ....................................................................................... 20.00
Bowl, Heirloom, Clear, Opalescent, Oval, 14 In. .................................................................. 25.00
Bowl, Heirloom, Opalescent Blue & Green, 7 In.Square ..................................................... 15.00
Bowl, Swirl, Ultramarine, 9 In.Diam. ..................................................................................... 6.25
Bowl, Trojan, Yellow, Flared, 3-Footed, 12 In. ..................................................................... 28.00
Bowl, Versailles, 12 Panel, Green, 11 1/2 In.Diam. .............................................................. 16.00
Bowl, Whipped Cream, Versailles, Yellow ............................................................................. 12.50
Butter, American, Round, Covered ........................................................................................ 20.00
Butter, Fairfax, Pink ............................................................................................................... 45.00
Butter, Holiday, Pink, Covered ............................................................................................... 27.00
Candleholder, American, Crystal, 6 In., Pair ........................................................................ 22.00
Candleholder, American, 7 In.Square, Pair .......................................................................... 20.00
Candleholder, Double, Navarre, Crystal, Pair ...................................................................... 25.00
Candleholder, Etched, Sapphire Blue, 2 In., Pair ................................................................ 14.00
Candleholder, Pink, Footed, Pair .......................................................................................... 18.00
Candleholder, Seascape, Pink Opalescent, Pair ................................................................. 45.00
Candleholder, Versailles, Yellow ........................................................................................... 12.00
Candlestick, American, Octagonal Base, 6 1/4 In., Pair ...................................................... 25.00
Candlestick, Colony, 3 In., Pair .............................................................................................. 12.00
Candlestick, Colony, 7 In. ....................................................................................................... 14.00
Candlestick, Double, Navarre Pattern, Clear, Pair .............................................................. 35.00
Candlestick, Lyre, Pair ............................................................................................................ 35.00
Candlestick, Navarre, Double, 4 1/2 In., Pair ....................................................................... 35.00
Candlestick, Triple, Romance, Pair ....................................................................................... 35.00
Candlestick, Trojan, Yellow, 3 In. .......................................................................................... 22.50
Candlestick, 2-Light, Baroque, Etched, Pair ........................................................................ 25.00
Champagne, Corsage Pattern, 5 1/2 Ounce ......................................................................... 15.00
Champagne, June, Yellow ....................................................................................................... 20.00
Claret, Navarre ........................................................................................................................ 14.00
Coaster, Sunray ....................................................................................................................... 3.00
Cocktail, Oyster, Versailles .................................................................................................... 13.95
Compote, Dolphin, Ribbon, Green ........................................................................................ 65.00
Console Set, Bowl, Candlesticks, June, Azure, 5 In. ........................................................... 95.00
Console Set, Meadow Rose, 2-Light Candelabra, Bowl, 12 In.Diam. ................................. 125.00
Console Set, Royal Blue, Bowl & Candlesticks .................................................................... 65.00
Creamer & Sugar, Trojan, Yellow .......................................................................................... 35.00

| | |
|---|---|
| **Creamer,** Century | 5.00 |
| **Creamer,** Colony, Footed | 3.00 |
| **Creamer,** Holiday, Pink | 4.25 |
| **Creamer,** Swirl, Ultramarine | 4.20 |
| **Cruet,** Colony | 22.50 |
| **Cup & Saucer,** Fairfax, Blue | 12.00 |
| **Cup & Saucer,** Footed, Fairfax, Amber | 5.00 |
| **Cup & Saucer,** Footed, Fairfax, Green | 5.00 |
| **Cup & Saucer,** Footed, June, Topaz | 25.00 |
| **Cup & Saucer,** June | 16.00 |
| **Cup & Saucer,** Petalware, Pink | 6.50 |
| **Cup & Saucer,** Sharon, Amber | 1.70 |
| **Cup & Saucer,** Versailles | 25.00 |
| **Cup & Saucer,** Vesper, Amber | 12.50 |
| **Cup,** Bouillon, Seville, Amber | 5.00 |
| **Cup,** Colony | 4.98 |
| **Cup,** Fairfax, Topaz, Footed | 4.00 |
| **Cup,** Royal Lace, Blue | 15.00 |
| **Cup,** Versailles, Azure | 10.00 |
| **Cup,** Windsor, Clear | 2.00 |
| **Decanter,** Wine, 4 Stemmed Wineglasses, Clear, Etched | 30.00 |
| **Dish,** Candy, Stemmed, Covered | 28.00 |
| **Dish,** Celery, Chintz | 25.00 |
| **Dish,** Ice Cream, Manor, Crystal | 10.00 |
| **Dish,** Lemon, Handle, Trojan, Topaz | 7.00 |
| **Dish,** Lemon, June, Pink | 15.00 |
| **Dish,** Lemon, Navarre | 6.00 |
| **Dish,** Relish, American, 3 Section | 35.00 |
| **Dish,** Relish, Chintz, 3 Section | 25.00 |
| **Dish,** Relish, Divided, American, 12 In. | 7.00 |
| **Dish,** Relish, Divided, June, Pink, Oval, 9 In. | 20.00 |
| **Dish,** Relish, Romance, 3 Section | 35.00 |
| **Dish,** Relish, Vogue, Flat | 7.00 |
| **Dish,** Sweetmeat, Handled, Lafayette, Cobalt Blue, 4 1/4 In. | 10.00 |
| **Eggcup,** American | 6.00 |
| **Figurine,** Avocado, Running, Blue | 35.00 |
| **Figurine,** Chanticleer | 250.00 |
| **Figurine,** Colt, Crystal | 25.00 |
| **Figurine,** Deer, Crystal | 25.00 |
| **Figurine,** Deer, Standing | 32.00 To 34.75 |
| **Figurine,** Horse, Rearing, Blue, Pair | 62.00 |
| **Figurine,** Madonna, Clear | 38.00 |
| **Figurine,** Madonna, Frosted, 9 3/4 In. | 38.00 |
| **Figurine,** Seahorse | 85.00 |
| **Figurine,** Seal, Lilac | 75.00 |
| **Figurine,** Squirrel, Seated, Amber | 30.00 |
| **Goblet,** American Lady, 6 In. | 5.00 |
| **Goblet,** American, Crystal, 6 1/2 In. | 6.00 |
| **Goblet,** Baroque | 12.00 |
| **Goblet,** Cobalt, Royal Blue, Set Of 6 | 100.00 |
| **Goblet,** Colony | 8.00 |
| **Goblet,** Corsage | 7.00 |
| **Goblet,** Ice Tea, June, Pink | 22.50 |
| **Goblet,** June, Topaz, 10 Ounce | 25.00 |
| **Goblet,** Mayflower | 10.00 |
| **Goblet,** Navarre, 9 Ounce | 15.00 |
| **Goblet,** Rogene | 10.00 |
| **Goblet,** Trojan, Pink, Set Of 6 | 125.00 |
| **Goblet,** Vernon, Green, Stemmed | 18.00 |
| **Goblet,** Versailles, Blue, 8 1/4 In. | 28.00 |
| **Goblet,** Versailles, Green | 21.75 |
| **Goblet,** Washington, Footed, 8 Ounce | 15.00 |
| **Goblet,** Water, Baroque, Clear, 6 1/2 In. | 10.00 |

| | |
|---|---|
| Ice Tea, June, Yellow, Footed | 20.00 |
| Jar, Candy, Covered, Navarre | 28.00 |
| Jug, Footed, Navarre | 55.00 |
| Lemonade Set, Green, 9 Piece | 90.00 |
| Mayonnaise & Underplate, Footed, Fairfax, Green | 8.00 |
| Mayonnaise Set, Lafayette, Crystal, 6 1/2 In., 2 Piece | 9.00 |
| Mayonnaise Set, Swirl, Clear, 3 Piece | 16.50 |
| Pioneer Plate, Seville, Amber, 6 In.Diam. | 1.50 |
| Pitcher, American, Leaded Crystal | 125.00 |
| Pitcher, Century, 3 Pint | 25.00 |
| Pitcher, Royal Lace, Blue, 8 1/2 In. | 40.00 |
| Pitcher, Water, American, 1 Gallon | 22.00 |
| Plate, Baroque, 6 In. | 2.00 |
| Plate, Beverly, Amber, 6 In.Diam. | 2.50 |
| Plate, Colony, 7 1/4 In. | 4.00 |
| Plate, Fairfax, Blue, 6 In.Diam. | 3.50 |
| Plate, Fairfax, Blue, 8 3/4 Ind.Aim. | 4.00 |
| Plate, Fairfax, Blue, 9 1/4 In.Diam. | 8.00 |
| Plate, Fairfax, Green, 8 3/4 In.Diam. | 3.00 |
| Plate, Fairfax, Topaz, 7 1/2 In.Diam. | 3.00 |
| Plate, Grill, Mayfair Open Rose, Pink | 15.00 |
| Plate, Holiday, Pink, 9 1/2 In. | 6.50 |
| Plate, June, Blue, 7 1/2 In. | 8.50 |
| Plate, June, Topaz, 8 3/4 In.Diam. | 9.00 |
| Plate, June, Yellow, 6 In. | 7.00 |
| Plate, Mayfair Open Rose, Pink, 6 1/2 In. | 5.00 |
| Plate, Mayfair, Pink, 8 1/4 In.Diam. | 4.00 |
| Plate, Meadow Rose, Blue, 7 1/2 In. | 8.75 |
| Plate, Meadow Rose, Crystal, 7 In. | 6.00 |
| Plate, Petalware, Pink, 8 In. | 3.00 |
| Plate, Royal, Amber, 7 1/2 In.Diam. | 4.00 |
| Plate, Salad, Seville, Green, Set Of 12 | 42.00 |
| Plate, Serving, Trojan, Yellow, Handled, 12 In. | 25.00 |
| Plate, Swirl, Ultramarine, 6 1/2 In. | 2.50 |
| Plate, Torte, American, 10 1/2 In.Diam. | 26.00 |
| Plate, Torte, Colony, 15 In.Diam. | 18.00 |
| Plate, Versailles, Blue, 8 3/4 In. | 9.00 |
| Plate, Versailles, Green, 8 1/2 In. | 5.50 |
| Plate, Versailles, Green, 10 1/4 In.Diam | 18.50 |
| Plate, Versailles, Yellow, 7 1/2 In. | 7.25 |
| Plate, Versailles, 6 In. | 5.00 |
| Plate, Vesper, Green, 10 1/2 In. | 20.00 |
| Plate, Willowmere, 8 1/4 In. | 6.00 |
| Platter, Vesper, Green, 12 In. | 20.00 |
| Punch Bowl, American, 18 In.Diam. | 65.00 |
| Punch Bowl, Ladle, American, Clear, 14 In.Diam. | 50.00 |
| Punch Set, American, Bowl, Base, & 24 Cups | 185.00 |
| Relish, Boat, Victoria, Frosted | 24.00 |
| Sherbet, Baroque, Clear, 4 In. | 6.50 |
| Sherbet, Chintz, 6 Ounce | 10.00 |
| Sherbet, Colony | 6.00 |
| Sherbet, Fruits, Pink | 7.90 |
| Sherbet, Mayflower | 10.00 |
| Sherbet, Rose On Trellis, Pink | 4.25 |
| Sherbet, Royal, Amber, Low | 5.00 |
| Sherbet, Thistle, Azurite Engraved, Clear Stem | 12.00 |
| Sherbet, Versailles, Low | 14.50 |
| Sherbet, Windsor, Clear | 5.20 |
| Soup, Cream, Patrician, Pink | 12.00 |
| Soup, Cream, Vesper, Green | 12.50 |
| Spooner, Hat-Shaped, America Pattern | 15.00 |
| Spooner, Paneled Grape | 14.00 |
| Sugar & Creamer, American, Crystal | 5.00 |

Sugar & Creamer, American, 2 1/2 In. ................................................................ 6.50
Sugar & Creamer, Chintz ................................................................................ 35.00
Sugar & Creamer, Fairfax, Black, Individual ................................................... 5.50
Sugar & Creamer, Fuchsia, Footed .................................................................. 15.00
Sugar & Creamer, Hermitage, Footed .............................................................. 8.00
Sugar & Creamer, June, Topaz ........................................................................ 34.50
Sugar & Creamer, Monax ................................................................................ 7.25
Sugar, Footed, Baroque, Azure ....................................................................... 10.00
Sugar, Footed, Fairfax, Amber ........................................................................ 5.00
Sugar, Footed, Fairfax, Blue ........................................................................... 5.00
Sugar, Krystol, Dated 1907 ............................................................................. 5.00
Sugar, Petalware, Pink ................................................................................... 320.00
Sugar, Sharon, Amber ..................................................................................... 5.50
Sugar, Sunray, Open .......................................................................... 3.00 To 5.00
Syrup, American, Chrome Cover ...................................................................... 18.00
Syrup, 2-Handled Tray, Cut Flower Design, Pink ........................................... 18.50
Table Set, Priscilla, Gold Trim, Green, 4 Piece ............................................... 250.00
Toothpick, Edgewood ...................................................................................... 16.00
Tray, American, Closed Handles, Clear, 7 1/4 In.Diam. .................................. 6.50
Tray, Handled, Sunray, Oval, 9 In. .................................................................. 7.00
Tray, Sandwich, Center Handle, Meadow Rose ............................................... 15.00
Tumbler, American, Flat, 5 1/4 In. ................................................................... 5.00
Tumbler, Baroque, 9 Ounce ............................................................................. 8.00
Tumbler, Brazilian, Green ................................................................................ 14.00
Tumbler, Edgewood Pattern, Clear, Set Of 6 .................................................. 55.00
Tumbler, Ginger Ale, Regent, 6 Ounce ........................................................... 10.00
Tumbler, June, Footed ..................................................................................... 7.00
Tumbler, Navarre, Footed, 5 7/8 In. ................................................................ 13.00
Tumbler, Oakwood, Azure Iridescent, Footed, 5 Ounce ................................. 12.00
Tumbler, Royal, Amber, Footed, 5 Ounce ....................................................... 9.00
Tumbler, Versailles, Footed ............................................................................. 14.95
Tumbler, Versailles, Pink, Footed, 5 1/4 In. .................................................... 17.00
Tumbler, Versailles, Topaz, 9 Ounce, Set Of 6 .............................................. 85.00
Tumbler, Vesper, Green, Footed, 5 Ounce ...................................................... 12.00
Tumbler, Windsor, Footed, 5 1/4 In. ............................................................... 3.20
Vase, American, 8 In. ....................................................................................... 17.50
Vase, Heirloom, Pink, 20 In. ........................................................................... 25.00
Vase, Orchid, Ribbed, 7 X 6 1/2 In. ................................................................ 30.00
Vase, Pink, Heirloom, 19 In. ........................................................................... 25.00
Vase, Shirley, Flame, Etched, Pair .................................................................. 30.00
Vase, Swirl, Ultramarine, 8 1/2 In. .................................................................. 11.25
Wine, Christiana .............................................................................................. 21.00
Wine, Crystal Ball Stem, Cobalt Bowl ............................................................. 25.00
Wine, Versailles ............................................................................................... 25.00
  FOVAL, see Fry Foval
  FRAME, see Furniture, Frame


*Francisware is an amber hobnail glassware made by Hobbs Brockunier and Company, Wheeling, West Virginia, in the 1880s.*

FRANCISWARE, Bowl, Frosted Hobnail Amber Rim, 4 1/2 In.Diam. ............... 25.00
Bowl, Waste, Hobnail, Amber Band, Frosted, 4 1/2 X 3 3/4 In. ..................... 55.00
Celery, Swirl Frosted, Amber Rim ................................................................... 20.00
Dish, Sauce ...................................................................................................... 15.00
Pitcher, Water, Hobnail ...................................................................... 65.00 To 85.00
Plate, Parrot Center, Reticulated Rim, Signed, Pair ....................................... 30.00
Saltshaker, Hobnail, Frosted ........................................................................... 95.00
Sugar, Amber Fluted Rim, Covered ................................................................. 50.00
Sugar, Yellow Stain, Covered .......................................................................... 65.00
Toothpick, Frosted With Amber ....................................................................... 75.00
Toothpick, Hobnail, Clear With Amber ............................................................ 60.00
Vase, Celery, Frosted Hobnail, Amber Trim .................................................... 50.00

*Frankart, Inc., New York, New York, mass-produced nude "dancing-lady" lamps, ashtrays, and other decorative Art Deco items in the 1920s and 1930s. They were made of white lead composition and spray painted. Frankart Inc. and the patent number and year were stamped on the base.*

| | |
|---|---|
| **FRANKART, Ashtray,** Nude On Brass Ball Holding Up Brass Tray | 495.00 |
| **Creamer,** Figural, Ram's Head | 10.00 |
| **Figurine,** Art Deco, Nude, 24 In. | 525.00 |
| **Figurine,** Dog, Bronzed | 35.00 |
| **Figurine,** Little Sailor, Boy Carrying Sailboat, Signed, 7 1/2 In. | 75.00 |
| **Figurine,** Nude, Arms Upstretched, Signed, 1922, 9 1/4 In. | 60.00 |
| **Figurine,** Nude, 7 1/2 In. | 85.00 |
| **Lamp,** Full Figure Nude, Arms Over Head, Holds Globe, 17 In. | 195.00 |
| **Light,** Night, Masonic, Man's Head, Pot Metal, Dated 1927 | 40.00 |

*Frankoma Pottery was originally known as The Frank Potteries when John F. Frank opened shop in 1933. The factory is now working in Sapulpa, Oklahoma.*

| | |
|---|---|
| **FRANKOMA, Bowl,** Console, Brown & Green, 17 In.Long | 17.50 |
| **Candlestick,** Double Candle, Swirled Pattern, Glossy, Pair | 20.00 |
| **Dish,** Green Shading To Brown | 10.00 |
| **Flask,** Lavender, Thong Holder | 28.00 |
| **Pitcher,** Water, Green, Brown, 4 Mugs | 45.00 |
| **Sugar & Creamer,** Brown | 22.50 |
| **Vase,** Aqua, 7 1/2 In. | 8.00 |
| **Vase,** Handled, Green & Brown Swirl, 6 In. | 15.00 |
| **Vase,** Mauve, Leaf Handles, 11 In. | 25.00 |
| **FRUIT JAR, see Bottle, Fruit Jar** | |

*Fry glass was made by the H.C.Fry Glass Company of Rochester, Pennsylvania. It includes cut glass, but the famous Fry glass today is the foval, or pearl, art glass. This is an opal ware decorated with colored trim. It was made from 1922 to 1933.*

| | |
|---|---|
| **FRY FOVAL, Ashtray,** Pink & Blue, Pedestal Foot, 3 In. | 80.00 |
| **Bottle,** Perfume, Jade Green Foot, Engraved Flowers, 7 3/4 In. | 110.00 |
| **Bowl,** Console, Green, Blue Base, Applied Blue | 60.00 |
| **Bowl,** Fruit, Delft Blue Pedestal, 12 X 7 1/2 In. | 450.00 To 525.00 |
| **Candlestick,** Blue & Opalescent, Wafer Stem, 10 1/2 In., Pair | 225.00 |
| **Candlestick,** Blue Spiral Threading On Shaft, 10 3/4 In., Pair | 250.00 |
| **Candlestick,** Wafer Stem, Blue & Opal, 10 1/2 In. | 175.00 |
| **Compote,** Jade Stem, Signed & Numbered | 325.00 |
| **Cup & Saucer,** Demitasse, Applied Blue Handle | 60.00 |
| **Pitcher,** Lemonade, 2 Tumblers, Cobalt Blue Handles, Stripes | 225.00 |
| **Pitcher,** Water, Cobalt Blue Handle & Base, 10 In. | 125.00 |
| **Sugar,** Delft Blue Handles & Base, Sterling Overlay Leaf Pattern | 130.00 |
| **Teapot,** Green Handle, Lid | 55.00 |
| **Vase,** Applied Delft Blue Rim, Opalescent Green, 4 1/2 In. | 145.00 |
| **Vase,** Blue Rim & Foot, 6 X 5 3/4 In. | 175.00 |
| **Wine,** Conical, Jade Foot | 75.00 |
| **FRY, see also Cut Glass** | |
| **FRY, Bowl,** Basket Pattern, Signed, 8 X 2 1/2 In. | 175.00 |
| **Casserole,** Holder, Covered | 30.00 |
| **Dish,** Olive, Unusual Shape, 8 X 4 In.Diam. | 120.00 |
| **Epergne,** 3-Trumpet, Light & Dark Blue | 250.00 |
| **Lemonade Set,** Yellow Iridescent, Cobalt Handles, 4 Glasses | 180.00 |
| **Pitcher,** Lemonade, Applied Emerald Green Handle, Clear Crackle, 8 In. | 110.00 |
| **Reamer,** Juice, Fluted, Opalescent | 16.00 To 20.00 |
| **Sauce,** Beaded Swirl, Green | 12.00 |
| **Shade,** Trumpet Flair, Matched, 4 1/2 In., Pair | 100.00 |
| **Toothpick,** Light & Dark Blue | 35.00 |

| | |
|---|---|
| **Tray,** Duquesne, Geometric Design, 14 In.Diam. | 850.00 |
| **Tumbler,** Lemonade, Signed, Set Of 6 | 395.00 |
| **Vase,** Center Baskets Of Flowers, Vertical Ribbing, Signed, 9 1/4 In. | 250.00 |
| **Vase,** Crackle, 3 Blue Rosettes, 8 1/2 In. | 55.00 |
| **Vase,** Hobstars & Fans, Signed, 9 In. | 175.00 |

> F
> U
> L
> P
> E
> R
>
> *Fulper is the mark used by the American Pottery Company of*
> *Flemington, New Jersey. The art pottery was made from 1910 to 1929.*
> *The firm had been making bottles, jugs, and housewares from 1805. Doll heads*
> *were made about 1928. The firm became Stangl Pottery in 1929.*

**FULPER, see also Doll**

| | |
|---|---|
| **FULPER, Basket,** Rope Handle, White, 15 1/2 In. | 75.00 To 110.00 |
| **Bell,** Figural, Morning Glory Shape | 75.00 |
| **Bell,** Hollyhock, Blue | 65.00 |
| **Bookends,** Egyptian Design, Dark Green Matte | 100.00 |
| **Bowl,** Blue & Ivory, Flambe Glaze, Ink Stamp, 10 1/2 In. | 75.00 |
| **Bowl,** Blues, Browns, White, Flange Rim, 10 In. | 165.00 |
| **Bowl,** Chinese, 4-Footed, Flambe Glaze, Marked, 4 X 12 In.Diam. | 85.00 |
| **Bowl,** Console, Matte Rose, 13 In.Diam. | 85.00 |
| **Bowl,** Five Embossed Fish Inside, Old Mark, Green, 11 In. | 125.00 |
| **Bowl,** Footed, Black & Green, 8 In. | 65.00 |
| **Bowl,** Footed, Green Flambe Inside, Outer Copper Glaze, Marked, 10 In. | 165.00 |
| **Bowl,** Green & Tan, Metallic, Matte, 3 3/8 X 10 1/2 In.Diam. | 50.00 |
| **Bowl,** Handled, Greek Kylix, Yellow, Dusting Of Crystals, 5 In. | 100.00 |
| **Bowl,** High Handles, Rose & Purple, 4 1/2 X 4 1/2 In.Diam. | 75.00 |
| **Bowl,** Mirror Black, Ribbed, Scalloped Rim, 7 1/2 X 3 1/4 In. | 85.00 |
| **Bowl,** Mottled Green & Black, Crystals, 3-Footed, 2 1/4 X 8 In.Diam. | 75.00 |
| **Bowl,** Periwinkle Flambe Over Olive & Blue Ground, 8 In.Diam. | 50.00 |
| **Bowl,** Rolled Edge, Mottled Green & Blue Glaze, 2 1/4 X 9 In.Diam. | 100.00 |
| **Bowl,** Rose Matte, Turquoise To Olive Green, 2-Handled, 6 1/2 In. | 135.00 |
| **Box,** Powder, Egyptian Lady On Top, Orange, Marked, 8 X 5 In. | 210.00 |
| **Candlestick,** Blue, Green, & Ivory, 10 In., Pair | 125.00 |
| **Candlestick,** Blue, Mustard, Vasekraft Label, 8 3/4 In., Pair | 250.00 |
| **Candlestick,** Blue, Saucer Type | 45.00 |
| **Candlestick,** Green Crystal, 3 Deco Handles, 6 In., Pair | 75.00 |
| **Candlestick,** Green, Blue & Cream Flambe Glaze, Rusty Orange, 10 In. | 50.00 |
| **Candlestick,** Rose, Beige, 3 In. | 39.00 |
| **Candlestick,** Turquoise, Crystalline Glaze, 3 In., Pair | 15.00 |
| **Chamberstick,** Scalloped Rim, Scroll-Shaped Handle, Marked, 7 X 4 In. | 45.00 |
| **Coffee Set,** Pot, 6 Cups & Saucers, Trivet | 150.00 |
| **Crock,** Ice Water, Blue Bands | 120.00 |
| **Crock,** 2 Mourning Doves, Blue Glaze | 1000.00 |
| **Ewer,** Purple, 5 In. | 35.00 |
| **Figurine,** Frog, Seated On Brown Round Base, Green, Marked, 4 X 4 In. | 55.00 |
| **Flower Frog,** Blue Flambe Glaze, 2 X 4 In. | 15.00 |
| **Flower Frog,** Holes In Back, Green & Brown, 4 X 4 1/2 In. | 48.00 |
| **Flower Frog,** Ivory Nude, Green Base, Yellow Flowers, Signed | 55.00 |
| **Flower Frog,** Lily Pad, Blue | 35.00 |
| **Flower Frog,** Lily Pad, 1 1/2 X 4 In.Wide | 12.00 |
| **Flower,** Frog, Pierced Lid, Geometric Relief, Marked, C.1915, 5 In. | 125.00 |
| **Jar,** Coiled, Gunmetal Mottled Glaze, Mustard Ground, 9 In. | 55.00 |
| **Lamp,** Perfume, Art Deco Lady, Pink & Purple Gown | 175.00 |
| **Lamp,** Perfume, Ballerina In Lavender, Signed | 175.00 |
| **Lamp,** Perfume, Ballerina, Green Skirt, Orange Base | 140.00 |
| **Lamp,** Perfume, Ballerina, Rose Skirt, Signed M.Stangl | 175.00 |
| **Lamp,** Perfume, Ballerina, Turquoise Dress, Signed | 200.00 |
| **Lamp,** Perfume, Blue Ballerina | 200.00 |
| **Lamp,** Perfume, Cerise | 125.00 |
| **Lamp,** Perfume, Dutch Girl | 60.00 |
| **Lamp,** Perfume, Lavender Dancer | 120.00 |
| **Light,** Night, Perfume, Colonial Lady With Fan, 8 1/2 In. | 165.00 |
| **Mug,** Brown Mirror Glaze | 58.00 |

**Pitcher,** Lemonade, Green Glaze, Detachable Juicer, 13 In. ............................ 325.00
**Pot,** Handled, Blue & Brown, 3 In. ...................................................... 45.00
**Rose Bowl,** Grayish Green, Rust, Label, 6 X 7 In. ....................................... 145.00
**Tumbler,** Green Metallic Glaze, 3 1/2 In. ................................................ 45.00
**Vase,** All Black Luster, Paper Label, 3 1/2 In. ............................................ 40.00
**Vase,** Art Deco, Crystalline, 9 1/2 X 7 In.Diam. .......................................... 80.00
**Vase,** Art Deco, Mirror Glaze, 8 In., Pair ................................................. 140.00
**Vase,** Black Mirror Finish, 2-Handled, Signed, 10 X 9 1/2 In. ........................... 300.00
**Vase,** Blue Crystaline, Double Handle, Bulbous, Signed, 8 In. .......................... 150.00
**Vase,** Blue Drip Over Rose, 4 In. ........................................................ 60.00
**Vase,** Blue Flambe Drip, Yellow-Blue Matte, Bottle Shape, 8 1/2 In. .................. 225.00
**Vase,** Blue Flambe Over Mustard, 3 1/2 In. .............................................. 42.00
**Vase,** Blue Luster Glaze, 2 Angular Handles, Marked, 8 In. ............................. 120.00
**Vase,** Bottle Shape, Blue Flambe Over Yellow, Marked, 8 1/2 In. ...................... 50.00
**Vase,** Bracket Handles, Blue Dripped Over Citron, Marked, 14 1/2 In. ............... 1000.00
**Vase,** Bud, Flared, Green Glaze, Marked, 7 In. .......................................... 55.00
**Vase,** Bud, Matte Glaze, 8 In. ........................................................... 28.00
**Vase,** Bulbous, Green & Rose, 7 1/2 In. ................................................. 75.00
**Vase,** Charcoal Glaze, Gray Flecks, Ring Handles, 13 In. ............................... 550.00
**Vase,** Cornucopia, Green Drip, Crystalline Over Blue Ground, 9 X 8 In. ............... 135.00
**Vase,** Crystalline Glaze, 9 In. ........................................................... 115.00
**Vase,** Crystalline Leopard Skin, 10 In. ................................................... 95.00
**Vase,** Crystalline, Art Deco, 9 1/2 X 7 In.Diam. ......................................... 80.00
**Vase,** Crystalline, Design At Top Rim, 7 1/2 In. ......................................... 85.00
**Vase,** Drip Glaze Over Brown, 4 In. ...................................................... 30.00
**Vase,** Famille Rose, Matte, 8 1/2 In. ..................................................... 70.00
**Vase,** Fan Shaped, Handled, Tree Top & Interior, 8 1/2 In. ............................. 75.00
**Vase,** Fan Shaped, Handles, Green Rose, 8 In. .......................................... 60.00
**Vase,** Fan Shaped, Roses, Green Ground, 8 In. .......................................... 75.00
**Vase,** Handled, Black Mirror Finish, 10 In. .............................................. 350.00
**Vase,** Lavender Matte, 8 1/2 In. ......................................................... 95.00
**Vase,** Leopard Skin, Vasekraft, Octagon, 7 1/2 In. ...................................... 125.00
**Vase,** Light Green, Vertical Stamp, 4 1/2 In. ............................................ 54.00
**Vase,** Oatmeal Glaze, 4 In. .............................................................. 34.00
**Vase,** Oval, Blue-Green, 2 Handled, 8 1/2 In. ........................................... 75.00
**Vase,** Rose With Purple Drip, 4 In. ...................................................... 30.00
**Vase,** Sea-Green, Olive Green Splash, 6 In. ............................................. 68.00
**Vase,** Shoulder Handles, Green Runs Over Rose, 7 1/2 In. .............................. 85.00
**Vase,** Stick, Plum Matte, 8 1/2 In. ...................................................... 25.00
**Vase,** Streaked Olive Green Glaze, C-Scroll Handles, Marked, 6 In. .................... 160.00
**Vase,** Urn Shape, Olive Flambe Over Ivory ............................................... 68.00
**Vase,** Volcanic Blue, 6 1/2 In. ........................................................... 75.00
**Wall Pocket,** Entwined Horn Design, Paper Label, 12 In. ................................ 85.00

**FURNITURE, Armchair,** Banister Back ....................................................... 450.00
**Armchair,** Belter, Rosewood, Book-Match Graining ..................................... 3750.00
**Armchair,** Brass Inlaid, Teakwood, Chinese, C.1850 ..................................... 650.00
**Armchair,** Carved Shell & Feather Back, Walnut, 54 3/4 In. ............................. 375.00
**Armchair,** Charles Stickley, Oak, C.1915, Spring Seat, Decal Mark ..................... 400.00
**Armchair,** Child's, Ladder Back, Rush Seat, American, 21 1/2 In. ...................... 150.00
**Armchair,** Cupid's-Bow Rail, Red Seat, Walnut, Chippendale ............................ 975.00
**Armchair,** Dutch, Rococo, Fruitwood, Open, 18th C., Drop-In Seat ..................... 480.00
**Armchair,** Ebonized, Savonarola, Ivory Inlaid, Italian .................................. 500.00
**Armchair,** Founders' Names Of Odd Fellows, Wisconsin, Bentwood ..................... 185.00
**Armchair,** George II, Upholstered, Mahogany ...................................... *Illus* 1700.00
**Armchair,** Jacobean Style, Inset Caned Seat & Back .................................... 100.00
**Armchair,** L. & J.G.Stickley, Original Label ............................................. 95.00
**Armchair,** Ladder Back, Shawl Back, Shaker ............................................ 650.00
**Armchair,** Lady's, American Rococo, Pierce-Carved, Rosewood, C.1850 ................ 950.00
**Armchair,** Mahogany, Regency, Open, Reeded Arms, Caned Seat, Pair ............... 2300.00
**Armchair,** New England, Mid-18th Century, 35 3/4 In. .......................... *Illus* 2700.00
**Armchair,** Oak & Mahogany, George III, Drop-In Seat, Open .......................... 320.00
**Armchair,** Open, Hunzinger, C.1875, Inlaid Walnut ............................... *Illus* 350.00

Furniture, Armchair, George II, Upholstered, Mahogany (See Page 207)

Furniture, Armchair, New England, Mid-18th Century, 35 3/4 In. (See Page 207)

Furniture, Armchair, Open, Hunzinger, C.1875, Inlaid Walnut (See Page 207)

Furniture, Bed, American Rococo, Walnut, C.1845, 65 1/2 In.

| | | |
|---|---|---|
| **Armchair,** Portuguese Baroque, Caned Seat, Beechwood, Pair | | 350.00 |
| **Armchair,** Reclining, Eastlake, C.1890, J.McKenley, Philadelphia | | 400.00 |
| **Armchair,** Rush Seat, Hickory & Maple, Shaker | | 600.00 |
| **Armchair,** Vented Splat, Taffeta Drop Seat, C.1790, Mahogany | | 895.00 |
| **Armchair,** Vertical Slat Back, Charles Stickley, Decal, C.1915, Oak | | 400.00 |
| **Armchair,** William & Mary, Shaped Arms, 18th Century, 42 1/2 In. | | 600.00 |
| **Armchair,** Windsor, Green Paint, Utilitarian Box Under Seat | | 695.00 |
| **Armchair,** With Magazine Holder, Wicker | | 325.00 |
| **Armchair,** 19th Century, American, Painted Cast Iron, Pair | | 1600.00 |
| **Bassinet,** Canoe Shape, Wicker, Wooden Wheels, C.1870 | | 995.00 |
| **Bassinet,** Handle For Pushing, Wicker, On Wheels | | 225.00 |

**Bed,** Acanthus Carved Posts, Pineapple Finials, Mahogany, 58 In. .......................... 275.00
**Bed,** Acanthus Carving, Cherry, Set Of 4 ................................................. 795.00
**Bed,** American Rococo, Walnut, C.1845, 65 1/2 In. ...................................*Illus* 1600.00
**Bed,** Bow End, Brass, Single ........................................................... 675.00
**Bed,** C.1851, New York, Painted Iron, 3 2/3 Ft. X 4 Ft. 8 1/2 In. ....................... 1400.00
**Bed,** Cannonball, Turned Posts & Feet, American, C.1820, Painted ........................ 275.00
**Bed,** Carved & Applied Crest, Panels, C.1880, Walnut, 81 1/2 In. ........................ 675.00
**Bed,** Carved Pineapple Posts & Head, C.1820, Tiger Maple, 50 In. ........................ 450.00
**Bed,** Carved, Victorian, Burled Maple, 7 Ft. ........................................... 4500.00
**Bed,** Child's, Drop Side, C.1873, Oak .................................................. 250.00
**Bed,** Curved Foot, Solid Brass, Ornate ................................................. 2200.00
**Bed,** Enfield, Conn., Hickory, Maple, Pine, & Ash, Shaker ............................... 550.00
**Bed,** Farmhouse, Ohio, Maple, Double ................................................... 700.00
**Bed,** High Back, Spoon-Cut, Walnut .......................................................... 5.00
**Bed,** Italian Baroque, Painted, 41 In.Wide, Pair ....................................... 200.00
**Bed,** Lacquered Brass, Iron Painted White, Full Size .................................... 675.00
**Bed,** Murphy, Beveled Mirror, Golden Oak ................................................ 1550.00
**Bed,** Murphy, Oak ...................................................................... 525.00
**Bed,** Pineapple, American, C.1840, Cherry, 53 In. ...................................... 500.00
**Bed,** Post, Cannonball, Old Red, 54 In. .................................................. 360.00
**Bed,** Rolled Headboard, Brass Screws, C.1820, Maple, 51 X 47 In. ........................ 800.00
**Bed,** Rope, Child's, Jack-Planed, Single ................................................. 335.00
**Bed,** Rope, Pegs Intact, Turned Posts, Walnut, 40 In.Wide ................................ 300.00
**Bed,** Sleigh, Carved, Mahogany, Double ................................................... 550.00
**Bed,** Sleigh, Fan-Shaped Head, Polychrome Cast Iron, 4 1/2 X 7 Ft. ....................... 950.00
**Bed,** Tester, Carved Posts, American, C.1820, Cherry & Pine, 68 In. ..................... 1050.00
**Bed,** Tester, Maple & Tiger Maple, Red Finish, C.1830 .................................... 2550.00
**Bed,** Tester, Sheraton, Reeded & Carved Footposts ........................................ 1650.00
**Bed,** Trundle, On Casters, Maple, 13 In.Posts, 36 X 60 In. ............................... 100.00
**Bed,** Under-The-Eaves, Rope, C.1840, Old Red Paint, Twin Size ............................ 595.00
**Bed,** Victorian, Poplar, Double Size ...................................................... 265.00
**Bed,** Victorian, Walnut, 3/4 Size .......................................................... 250.00
**Bed,** Youth, Carved Headboard & Footboard, C.1840, Burled Panels ......................... 450.00
**Bed,** 4-Poster, C.1825, Old Blue, 3/4 Size ............................................... 595.00
**Bed,** 5 Vertical Slats On Headboard & Foot, C.1910, G.Stickley ........................... 3250.00
**Bedroom Set,** Eastlake, Bed, Dresser & Mirror, Cherry .................................... 1000.00
**Bedroom Set,** Loving Cup Pattern, Marble, C.1850, Walnut, 4 Piece ........................ 8000.00
**Bench Bed,** Top Raised At Night, Drawer Pulled Out, Texas, Pine ........................... 750.00
**Bench,** Carpenter's, Tiger Maple Top ...................................................... 350.00
**Bench,** Cobbler's, Pink, 4 Feet ........................................................... 300.00
**Bench,** Country, Spindle Back, Blue, 12 Ft. ............................................... 225.00
**Bench,** Deacon's, Carved Back Inserts, Golden Oak ......................................... 850.00
**Bench,** Desk Form, 3 Drawers Right Of Knee, Green Paint .................................... 395.00
**Bench,** Garden, 19th Century, American, Cast Iron, 3 Ft. 7 1/2 In. ........................ 400.00
**Bench,** Hand-Carved, Hand-Woven Fabric Cover, 21 X 97 In. ................................. 1500.00
**Bench,** Kneeling, C.1860, Original Brown Paint ............................................. 95.00
**Bench,** Organ, Lift-Top Seat, Oak .......................................................... 85.00
**Bench,** Red Star Shoes, Oak, 5 Ft.Long ..................................................... 325.00
**Bench,** Settle, Pennsylvania, Pine .......................................................... 425.00
**Bench,** Water Bucket, Bootjack Ends, Pine, 48 X 38 X 9 In. ................................. 200.00
**Bench,** Work, Cabinet With 3 Drawers, Wood Screws, Maple ................................... 535.00
**Bookcase,** Bronze-Mounted Mahogany, Glazed Doors, 5 3/4 X 5 Ft. ........................... 1300.00
**Bookcase,** Bureau, Oak, George II, 5 Drawers, Bracket Feet, 79 In. ......................... 1200.00
**Bookcase,** Glass Door, Beveled Mirror At Top, Dark Oak ..................................... 350.00
**Bookcase,** Mullioned Doors, G.Stickley, C.1904, 35 1/2 X 55 1/2 In. ........................ 2000.00
**Bookcase,** Student's, 3 Sections, 6 Shelves, Pine, 48 X 56 In. ............................. 800.00
**Bookcase,** 2 Door, 12 Glass Panes, C.1910, Oak, G.Stickley ................................ 3250.00
**Bookcase,** 2 Drawers On Bottom, 2 Door, Oak ................................................ 350.00
**Bookcase,** 3 Door, Claw Feet, Oak, 63 X 58 In. ............................................. 700.00
**Bookshelf,** A.Roux, New York, C.1850, Rosewood, 3 Ft. 10 In. X 3 Ft. ...................... 2250.00
**Box,** Blanket, Child's, Lift Top, Pennsylvania, Pine, 25 X 18 In. ......................... 375.00
**Box,** Blanket, Lift Top, Shaker, Dated 1830, Pine, 42 X 22 In. ............................ 400.00

| | |
|---|---|
| **Box,** Comb, Hanging, Decorated, Pine | 75.00 |
| **Box,** Dough, Cover, Original Buttermilk Paint | 145.00 |
| **Box,** Dough, Sliding Lid, Pennsylvania, Hand-Pegged, Splay Legs, Pine | 375.00 |
| **Box,** Dough, Sliding Top, Made Of 1 Piece Of Walnut | 365.00 |
| **Box,** Storage, Dovetailed, Old Black Over Red Graining, Poplar | 400.00 |
| **Box,** Storage, Truro, Nova Scotia | 725.00 |
| **Box,** Wall, 2 Shelf, Old Gray Over Green, 11 X 10 In. | 210.00 |
| **Bracket,** Shelf Above Female Mask, C.1860, Gilt Wood, Pair | 225.00 |
| **Breakfront,** Triple Beveled Doors, Carved, Oak, 6 X 8 1/2 Ft. | 2500.00 |
| **Breakfront,** 4 Glass Doors, 4 Drawers, Mahogany, 72 X 82 In. | 1050.00 |
| **Buffet,** Jacobean Style, Carved Frieze, New York, 33 X 60 In. | 450.00 |
| **Buffet,** Queen Anne Feet, Piecrust Molding On Front, Oak, 1920s | 315.00 |
| **Bureau,** Oval Mirror, Glove Drawers, Mahogany, 36 X 58 1/2 In. | 125.00 |
| **Bureau,** Rope-Turned Quarter Columns, C.1790, Tiger Maple | 1200.00 |
| **Cabinet,** Barber Shop, Splashboard, Oak, 15 X 20 In., Pair | 225.00 |
| **Cabinet,** China, Bow Front, Mirrored Backs, Paine, C.1900, 62 In. | 450.00 |
| **Cabinet,** China, Curved Glass Front, Claw Feet, C.1890 | 485.00 |
| **Cabinet,** China, Curved Glass, Beveled Mirror, Pillared Hood, Oak | 1050.00 |
| **Cabinet,** China, Curved Glass, Mirror Back, C.1915, Oak, 5 Ft., 7 In. | 695.00 |
| **Cabinet,** China, Curved Glass, Oak | 500.00 To 590.00 |
| **Cabinet,** China, Leaded, Beveled Glass Top, Oak, 53 X 75 1/2 In. | 2500.00 |
| **Cabinet,** China, Queen Anne Style, Baroque | 250.00 |
| **Cabinet,** Corner, Victorian Copy Of Chinese Style, Mahogany | 515.00 |
| **Cabinet,** Display, Ivory Inlaid, Walnut, 7 1/4 X 3 Ft. 10 In. | 1600.00 |
| **Cabinet,** File, 12 Various Sized Drawers, Bookcase Top, Oak | 650.00 |
| **Cabinet,** File, 32 Drawer, Civil War | 800.00 |
| **Cabinet,** Hanging, Asymetrically Arranged Shelves, 21 X 25 In. | 40.00 |
| **Cabinet,** Hardware, Octagonal, 72 Triangular Drawers | 1350.00 |
| **Cabinet,** Hoosier, Copper Bins, Oak | 395.00 |
| **Cabinet,** Jelly, 2 Drawer, C.1850 | 255.00 |
| **Cabinet,** Kitchen, Dated 1919, Golden Oak | 390.00 |
| **Cabinet,** Kitchen, Hoosier Style, Porcelain Top, Roll Front, Sifter | 375.00 |
| **Cabinet,** Kitchen, Seller's, Dated 1919 | 390.00 |
| **Cabinet,** Kitchen, Zinc Top, 2 Bin Drawers, Chestnut | 575.00 |
| **Cabinet,** Marble Top, Bowed Door, France, Walnut Veneer, 54 3/4 In. | 550.00 |
| **Cabinet,** Medicine, Mirror, Oak | 85.00 |
| **Cabinet,** Medicine, Mirror, Wooden, 14 1/2 X 19 1/2 In. | 20.00 |
| **Cabinet,** Napoleon III, Marble Top, Walnut Marquetry, 3 1/2 In. | 650.00 |
| **Cabinet,** Open Shelves, 4 Drawers, Eastlake, Walnut, 78 1/2 In. | 300.00 |
| **Cabinet,** Renaissance Revival, Baroque, German, 69 In. ........ *Illus* | 625.00 |

Furniture, Cabinet, Renaissance Revival,
Baroque, German, 69 In.

Furniture, Canterbury, Rosewood, C.1840,
21 1/4 X 21 In.

Cabinet, School, Glass Doors, Art Drawers, Oak, 70 X 31 X 91 In. ........................................ 750.00
Cabinet, Sewing, Mirror On Lid, C.1850, Rosewood, 28 X 20 1/2 In. ............................... 250.00
Cabinet, Shelf Top, Glazed Doors, Grain-Painted Pine, 29 X 32 In. ............................... 275.00
Cabinet, Spice, Inlaid Eagle, Chester County, 18th Century, 3 Ft. ............................... 9000.00
Cabinet, Spice, Original Stenciling, Oak  ............................................................... 125.00
Cabinet, Spice, Porcelain Knobs, 6 Drawer, Drop Top  ............................................... 650.00
Candle Holder, Adjustable Ratchet, Tin Sockets, American, 28 In. ............................... 575.00
Candlestand, Chippendale, New England, C.1770, Maple, 28 In. ............................... 750.00
Candlestand, Chippendale, Tilt Top, Snake Feet, Cherry & Maple ............................... 750.00
Candlestand, Edge Pattern, Center Pedestal, Walnut, 19 1/2 In. ............................... 25.00
Candlestand, Marble Top, Victorian, Walnut ........................................ 135.00 To 215.00
Candlestand, Queen Anne, Scalloped, New England, Cherry, 25 1/2 In. ............................... 600.00
Candlestand, Queen Anne, Urn & Shaft Shape, C.1800 ............................................... 950.00
Candlestand, Rectangular, American, C.1780, Cherry & Birch, 27 In. ............................... 475.00
Candlestand, Spider Leg, Maple .......................................................................... 245.00
Candlestand, Tilt Top, C.1920, Massachusetts, Tiger Maple, 24 In. ............................... 525.00
Candlestand, Tilt Top, Federal, T.Chase, C.1795, Birch, 15 1/2 In. ............................... 300.00
Candlestand, Tilt Top, Oval, Spider Legs, C.1800, Mahogany, 22 In. ............................... 650.00
Candlestand, Tilt Top, Snake Feet, C.1755, Mahogany, 19 1/2 In. ............................... 1300.00
Candlestand, Vase-Turned Post, New England, Walnut, 18 In. ............................... 125.00
Candlestand, 2-Light, Tin, Weighted, C.1810, 20 1/2 In. ....................................... 1850.00
Candlestand, 3 Legs Set Into Pedestal, Maple, 29 In. ............................................. 25.00
Canterbury, Rosewood, C.1840, 21 1/4 X 21 In. .............................................. *Illus* 600.00
Case, Type, 18 Drawer, Standing, Iron Pulls, Oak, 20 X 17 X 43 In. ............................... 250.00
Chair-Table, Maple Arms, Legs, & Supports, Pine ............................................... 1350.00
Chair, American Rococo, Laminated Rosewood, C.1855  ............................................... 800.00
Chair, American Rococo, Pierce-Carved, C.1850, Cabriole Legs, Pair ............................... 400.00
Chair, Arm, C.1910, Gustav Stickley, Oak, 39 In. .................................................... 150.00
Chair, Arm, Open Wing, Elm, Bentwood, 29 1/2 In.  ............................................... 900.00
Chair, Arm, Vented Splat, Green Drop Seat, Chippendale  ............................................... 895.00
Chair, Arrow Back, Rabbit Ears, Plank Bottom  ............................................... 150.00
Chair, Arrow Back, Stylized Fruit Design, New England, C.1825, Pair ............................... 700.00
Chair, Art Deco, Composition, Joseph Urban, Pair ............................................... 1900.00
Chair, Banister Back, Original Seat & Paint, New York ............................................... 325.00
Chair, Banister Back, Splint Seat, Black Paint, C.1750, 45 In.  ............................................... 475.00
Chair, Banister Back, 3 Stretchers, Pair ............................................................ 1500.00
Chair, Bentwood, Cane Seat, Signed, Set Of 4  ............................................... 275.00
Chair, Billiard Parlor, Oak  ........................................................................... 125.00
Chair, Birdcage Windsor, Shaped Seat, American, C.1800, Set Of 6 ............................... 1600.00
Chair, Birthing, Pegged, C.1800s, Detachable Legs, German, Walnut ............................... 120.00
Chair, Boston, Black Lacquer, Gold Stenciling, Set Of 8 ............................................... 1950.00
Chair, Bow Back, Signed Wallace Nutting, C.1910, Set Of 6 ............................................... 5800.00
Chair, Bow Back, 9 Spindle, Bamboo-Turned, White, Family History  ............................... 450.00
Chair, Brass Inlay On Rails & Slats, Caned Seat, C.1810, Pair ............................................... 1200.00
Chair, Carved Back, Jacob & Josef Kohn, Bentwood, 37 1/2 In., Pair ............................... 175.00

Furniture, Chair, Carved, Oak

Chair, Carved, Oak ........................................................................... *Illus* 350.00
Chair, Child's, Hitchcock, Straight ................................................. 125.00
Chair, Child's, Shaker, North Union ............................................... 200.00
Chair, Child's, Wicker Arms & Back, Cane Seat ........................... 175.00
Chair, Child's, Wooden, Bentwood Arms ...................................... 135.00
Chair, Chippendale, Cupid's-Bow Rail, Taffeta Seat, C.1775, Walnut ........ 975.00
Chair, Corner, Cloven Feet, German, Mahogany, 3/ 1/2 In. ......... 200.00
Chair, Corner, Queen Anne, New England, C.1730, 31 In. ........... 6750.00
Chair, Corner, Slip Seat, Chippendale Legs, Mahogany ............... 450.00
Chair, Cross Cut Cigarettes, Pack Of Cigarettes, Lady ............... 275.00
Chair, Desk, Windsor, Hoop Back, Bamboo Turnings ................. 795.00
Chair, Dining, High Back, Original Hair Seat, Walnut, Set Of 4 ..... 275.00
Chair, Dining, Regency, Striped Velvet Seat Cover, English ......... 100.00
Chair, Fanback, Crest Rail, Saddle Seat, Ash & Maple, 36 3/4 In. ...... 400.00
Chair, Finger-Carved Back, Medallions, American, 39 In., Pair ...... 875.00
Chair, Fly Whisk, Pink, Maple ........................................................ 1750.00
Chair, Folding, Holmes' Patent Label, C.1871, Walnut & Burl Walnut ..... 175.00
Chair, Folding, Original Red Upholstery, Patent 1868 .................. 85.00
Chair, Half-Arrow Back, Painted, Set Of 6 .................................. 675.00
Chair, Hall, Victorian, Carved Crest, Arms, & Legs, 51 In. ........... 300.00
Chair, Hitchcock Style, Rush Seat, Gold Stenciling ..................... 85.00
Chair, Hitchcock, Rush Seat, Original Black Paint, Gold Stenciling ..... 85.00
Chair, Hoop Back, Windsor Style, Child's, Oak, Set Of 4 ............. 140.00
Chair, Horn, Texas, C.1820, 6 Sets Of Longhorn Steer Horns ...... 1000.00
Chair, Horn, 14 Longhorn Steer Horns ......................................... 350.00
Chair, John Henry Belter, Molded Back, Needlepoint Seat, Rosewood ..... 2500.00
Chair, Kitchen, Plank Seat, Set Of 6 ............................................. 450.00
Chair, Ladder Back, Child's, Old Red Paint, 29 1/2 In. ................ 100.00
Chair, Ladder Back, New England, C.1880 .................................. 350.00
Chair, Ladder Back, Pennsylvania, 19th Century, Set Of 4 .......... 1400.00
Chair, Ladder Back, 3 Slat, Harvard Colony, Shaker, Green, 31 In. ..... 40.00
Chair, Ladder Back, 6 Slats, Original Green Paint, Set Of 6 ......... 595.00
Chair, Lady's, Queen Anne Legs, 1800s, Mahogany ................... 225.00
Chair, Lady's, Upholstered In Machine Tapestry, Walnut ............. 250.00
Chair, Lady's, Victorian, Upholstered, Walnut .............................. 187.50
Chair, Louis XVI, Gris Trianon, Painted, Pair ............................... 550.00
Chair, Louis XVI, Original Needlepoint Cover, Walnut .................. 300.00
Chair, Lyre Back, Needlepoint Seat Cover ................................... 90.00
Chair, Matching Stool, Windsor, Child's, Thumb Back, Painted ..... 475.00

Chair, Morris, L. & J.G.Stickley, C.1915, Oak ............................................... 200.00 To 350.00
Chair, Morris, Lion's-Paw Feet, Oak ............................................................. 245.00
Chair, Morris, Mahogany, Reclining Back, C.1910 ...................................... 60.00
Chair, Morris, 5 Vertical Slats, C.1910, Oak, G, Stickley, Marked .............. 4250.00
Chair, Napoleon III, Caned, C.1900, Leaf-Carved, Gilt Wood, Pair ............ 650.00
Chair, Oak & Ash Turned, Elizabeth I, 3 Legs, Diamond-Shaped Seat ....... 300.00
Chair, Office, Swivel, Casters, Oak ............................................................. 50.00
Chair, Pennsylvania, Salmon Ground, Grape Design, Set Of 6 .................. 1075.00
Chair, Pillow Back, Hitchcock, Green & Gold, C.1820, Set Of 6 ................ 950.00
Chair, Porch, Wicker, Set Of 3 .................................................................... 180.00
Chair, Potty, Pine, 18 X 13 In. Wide ......................................................... 75.00
Chair, Pressed Back, Cane Seat, Oak, Set Of 4 ......................................... 395.00
Chair, Pressed Back, Spindles, Set Of 4 ..................................................... 350.00
Chair, Queen Anne, Carved Crest Rail, New England, C.1760, 42 In. ....... 1250.00
Chair, Queen Anne, Rush Seat, Black Paint, Gold Striping, Pair ............... 1400.00
Chair, Queen Anne, Yoke Crest, Rush Seat, 18th Century, 41 In., Pair ..... 400.00
Chair, Recliner, Child's, Mission Style, Oak ............................................... 105.00
Chair, Red Paint, C.1850, Maple & Ash, 4-Slat, 43 In., Pair ..................... 550.00
Chair, Revolving, Shaker, Enfield, N.H. ...................................................... 2500.00
Chair, Sheraton, Original Black Finish & Yellow Seats, Set Of 6 ............... 450.00
Chair, Side, Bow Back, Saddle Seat, C.1780, Maple & Ash, 37 In., Pr. ..... 600.00
Chair, Side, Caned Seat, Rosewood Finish, English, C.1810, Set Of 6 ....... 2500.00
Chair, Side, Eastlake, Brass & Mother-Of-Pearl Inlay, C.1885 ................. 1600.00
Chair, Side, Elm, Bentwood, Ebonized Spheres, 29 1/2 In., Pair .............. 2200.00
Chair, Side, Floral Carved Crests, Victorian, Mahogany, Set Of 4 ............. 640.00
Chair, Side, George III, Mahogany, Pair ................................................ Illus 1400.00
Chair, Side, Laminated Rosewood, J.Belter, C.1855 .............................. Illus 4750.00
Chair, Side, Mahogany, Regency, 19th Century, Caned Seat, Pair ............. 800.00
Chair, Side, Pierce-Carved, C.1860, John & Joseph Meeks, Rosewood ....... 700.00
Chair, Side, Queen Anne, Hudson River Valley, C.1710 ............................ 925.00
Chair, Side, Rococo, Laminated Rosewood, C.1855 .............................. Illus 800.00
Chair, Side, Rococo, Laminated Rosewood, Meeks, C.1855 .................. Illus 650.00

Furniture, Chair, Side, George III, Mahogany, Pair

Furniture, Chairs, Side, Rococo, Laminated Rosewood, C. 1855 (See Page 213)

**Chair**, Side, Victorian, Walnut, Pair ............................................................................................. 285.00
**Chair**, Side, Walnut, American Gothic, C.1845, Pair ................................................. *Illus* 550.00
**Chair**, Side, Walnut, Needlepoint Cover, C.1845 ..................................................... *Illus* 150.00
**Chair**, Smoke Paint & Stenciled, Plank Seat, C.1860, Pair ........................................ 135.00
**Chair**, Square Slip Seat, Cabriole Legs, C.1760, Mahogany, 38 In. .................... 1400.00
**Chair**, Tavern, Schlitz, Set Of 5 ........................................................................................... 600.00
**Chair**, Tilter, Ladder Back, Shaker, 40 1/2 In., Set Of 6 ...................................... 2000.00
**Chair**, Tilter, Mixed Seats, Shaker, Set Of 4 .................................................................. 3200.00
**Chair**, V Back, 5 Vertical Slats, C.1910, G.Stickley, Oak, Pair ............................... 225.00
**Chair**, Weaver's, Pittsford, Vt., 1850-60 ............................................................................ 195.00
**Chair**, Weaver's, Shaker, Ohio ............................................................................................... 375.00
**Chair**, William & Mary, Banister Back, Rush Seat, C.1700, 43 In., Pr. ................ 650.00
**Chair**, Windsor, Bow Back, C.1765, E.Tracy, 36 In., Pair ..................................... 6000.00
**Chair**, Windsor, Box Stretcher, Bow Back ...................................................................... 200.00
**Chair**, Windsor, Comb Back, C.1830, Old Finish, 18 1/2 X 36 In. ....................... 625.00
**Chair**, Windsor, Continous Arm, Bamboo Turnings ..................................................... 590.00
**Chair**, Windsor, Fanback, 7 Spindle, Old Red Paint ................................................... 450.00
**Chair**, Windsor, Revolving, Original Paint & Design ................................................ 1050.00
**Chair**, Windsor, Step-Down, Bamboo Turnings, Set Of 4 ........................................ 775.00
**Chair**, Windsor, 9 Spindle, Original Finish .................................................................... 575.00
**Chair**, Wing, Chippendale, Cabriole Legs, Mahogany, 45 In. ................................... 400.00
**Chair**, Wing, Chippendale, Scrolled Arms, Claw Feet, 46 In. ................................... 500.00
**Chair**, 6-Plank Bottom, Hand-Painted Design, Pine, Set Of 6 ................................. 750.00
**Chaise Lounge,** Adjustable Knee-Bend & Headrest, Brass Castors ............................ 5.00
**Chest-On-Chest,** Chamfered, Satinwood Inlay, 18th Century, Mahogany ............... 4500.00
**Chest-On-Chest,** Chippendale, Flame Finials, Mahogany, 21 In. ............................ 1400.00
**Chest-On-Chest,** Queen Anne, 18th Century, Blind Fretwork ................................... 8500.00
**Chest-On-Chest,** William & Mary, English, C.1850, 38 X 60 In. ............................. 2600.00
**Chest-On-Chest,** 5 Drawers, New England, C.1770, Tiger Maple, 71 In. ................ 8500.00
**Chest,** American Hepplewhite, 3-Over-3 Drawer, Beading, C.1800 ........................... 890.00
**Chest,** Apothecary, 12 Drawer, C.1873, Brass Pulls, Poplar ..................................... 550.00
**Chest,** Apothecary, 55 Drawer .............................................................................................. 750.00
**Chest,** Bachelor's, Fold-Over Dusting Top, C.1750, English, Mahogany ............... 1450.00
**Chest,** Blanket, Bootjack End, Red ...................................................................................... 225.00
**Chest,** Blanket, Bracket Base, Lock, Escutcheon & Red Paint, 36 In. ................... 255.00
**Chest,** Blanket, Bun Feet, C.1840, Pennsylvania Dutch, Painted ............................. 425.00

Furniture, Chair, Side, Walnut, American Gothic, C.1845, Pair

Furniture, Chair, Side, Walnut, Needlepoint Cover, C.1845

**Chest,** Blanket, Chippendale, 6 Drawer, 3 Secret, Dated 1821, Penna. ................................. 2600.00
**Chest,** Blanket, Grained Poplar ........................................................................................ 225.00
**Chest,** Blanket, Green Base & Top, Initialed H.W.M. ................................................... 515.00
**Chest,** Blanket, Hudson Valley, 18th Century, Strap Hinges ........................................ 850.00
**Chest,** Blanket, Mustard Ground, C.H.Young, Littleton, N.H., C.1830 ...................... 1065.00
**Chest,** Blanket, Pennsylvania, C.1780, Secret Till, 3 Drawers ................................... 595.00

Furniture, Chest, Burled Elm & Walnut, G.Rohde, C.1937

**Chest,** Blanket, Pine, 2 Drawer, Signed & Dated, C.1836 .......................................................... 1200.00
**Chest,** Blanket, Slant-Top, Grain Painted .................................................................................. 950.00
**Chest,** Blanket, Southern Illinois, Walnut, Tall .......................................................................... 695.00
**Chest,** Blanket, Sponge Design, 35 1/2 X 18 1/2 X 15 In. ....................................................... 200.00
**Chest,** Blanket, Tulip Design, Pennsylvania, C.1830, 52 X 22 1/2 In. ..................................... 150.00
**Chest,** Blanket, 1 Drawer, High Bootjack, Original Red ........................................................... 395.00
**Chest,** Blanket, 2 Drawer, Grain Painted, Bun Feet ................................................................. 450.00
**Chest,** Blanket, 2 Drawer, New England, Signed & Dated, 1836, 38 In. ................................ 1200.00
**Chest,** Blanket, 2 Drawer, Ochre Paint, C.1800, 41 X 19 1/2 In. ........................................... 300.00
**Chest,** Blanket, 2 Drawer, 18th Century, Blue Over Red, 1760, 43 In. ................................. 1400.00
**Chest,** Blanket, 5 Drawer, Lift Top, American, Pine, 48 X 36 In. ............................................ 800.00
**Chest,** Bow Front, Demilune Stringing, Bracket Feet, Mahogany ......................................... 4500.00
**Chest,** Burled Elm & Walnut, G.Rohde, C.1937 ...............................................*Illus* 1500.00
**Chest,** Campaign, English, C.1800 ......................................................................................... 3000.00
**Chest,** Campaign, English, Documented History, C.1800 ...................................................... 3000.00
**Chest,** Campaign, Mahogany, Victorian, Brass Corners, 41 In. ............................................ 1000.00
**Chest,** Captain's Sea, Signed T. Hunter, C.1778 ...................................................................... 375.00
**Chest,** Carved, Camphorwood Lines, Brass Fittings, 7 X 17 X 8 In. ...................................... 160.00
**Chest,** Cedar, Queen Anne Feet, Walnut .................................................................................. 185.00
**Chest,** Chamfered 1/4 Columns, C.1790, Signed J.W.Blair ................................................... 2000.00
**Chest,** Chamfered, Bracket Feet, 4 Drawer, Walnut & Maple, Miniature .............................. 650.00
**Chest,** Chippendale, New England, C.1760, Pine, Walnut Finish, 38 In. .............................. 1495.00
**Chest,** Chippendale, Ogee Feet, Pennsylvania, Curly Maple ................................................. 6250.00
**Chest,** Chippendale, Serpentine Front, Walnut & Mahogany ................................................. 850.00
**Chest,** Chippendale, Split Drawers, C.1760, Maple, 43 X 35 In. ........................................... 600.00
**Chest,** Chippendale, 4 Drawer, Philadelphia, Mahogany ...................................................... 2400.00
**Chest,** Chippendale, 5 Graduated Drawers, 18th Century, Cherry ........................................ 2850.00
**Chest,** Cupboard Top, 6 Drawer, Shaker, Mt.Lebanon, N.Y. ................................................ 6500.00
**Chest,** Dated 1829, Painted, Mahantango Valley, Pennsylvania ........................................... 1700.00
**Chest,** Dower, Pennsylvania, C.1813, Painted By J.Seltzer ................................................... 8500.00
**Chest,** Dressing, 2 Split Drawers, 2 Long Drawers, Mirror, Oak ........................................... 220.00
**Chest,** Empire, Curly Maple Drawer Fronts, Cherry ............................................................... 235.00
**Chest,** Empire, 3 Drawer, New York State, Miniature ........................................................... 3800.00
**Chest,** Empire, 8 Drawer, Split Column On Sides, Cherry ..................................................... 1500.00
**Chest,** English, 4 Drawer, 19th Century, Mahogany, 38 X 35 1/2 In. .................................... 1550.00
**Chest,** Federal, 4 Drawer, New England, Maple, 39 1/2 In. .................................................. 1700.00
**Chest,** Forged Hardware, Wooden Pegs, Scandinavian, Chestnut, C.1780 .......................... 525.00
**Chest,** Globe-Wernicke Co., 22 Drawer, Oak, Marked, 33 X 42 In. ...................................... 125.00

**Chest,** Graduated Drawers, Brass Hardware, C.1770, Birch, 17 1/2 In. ................................ 1100.00
**Chest,** Hand-Forged Nails, New Hampshire, Pine & Chestnut ...................................... 3400.00
**Chest,** Hepplewhite, Cherry & Mahogany, 8 Drawer ................................................... 2160.00
**Chest,** Hepplewhite, Cherry, 4 Drawer, Inlaid Escutcheons, C.1795 ......................... 1150.00
**Chest,** Hepplewhite, Mahogany, Swell Front, French Bracket Feet ............................ 975.00
**Chest,** Hepplewhite, String Inlay, 5 Drawer ............................................................... 775.00
**Chest,** Hepplewhite, Swell Front, 4 Drawer, Signed Brasses, Cherry ........................ 1275.00
**Chest,** Hepplewhite, 19th Century, Mahogany Inlay, Cherry ...................................... 900.00
**Chest,** Hepplewhite, 2 Drawers Over 5, C.1790, 62 1/2 In. ..................................... 2850.00
**Chest,** Hoof Feet, Carved Skirt, Quebec County ....................................................... 1750.00
**Chest,** Lift Top, 2 Drawer, C.1710, 37 X 51 In. ........................................................ 4800.00
**Chest,** Lift Top, 2 Drawer, Grain Painting ................................................................. 1450.00
**Chest,** Liquor, Step-Back Top, American, Pine & Chestnut ........................................ 650.00
**Chest,** Lockside, Victorian, 47 X 41 X 22 In. ............................................................. 450.00
**Chest,** Mahogany, George III, 2 Short & 3 Long Drawers, 17 In. ............................. 800.00
**Chest,** Mule, Tilt Box, Amherst, N.H., Original Red, Pine .......................................... 650.00
**Chest,** Oak Joined, Stuart, Lozenges & Rosettes, 49 In. ........................................... 1600.00
**Chest,** Old Red, Pine, 39 X 19 X 43 1/2 In. ............................................................. 1800.00
**Chest,** Pennyslvania, Single Board Construction, C.1870 .......................................... 225.00
**Chest,** Peterson, 1830-40, Painted, Yellow Pine ..................................................... *Illus* 200.00
**Chest,** Sheraton, Ivory Shield Shaped Escutcheons, Curly Maple .............................. 650.00
**Chest,** Sheraton, Reeded Front, Paneled Sides, Mahogany ...................................... 600.00
**Chest,** Sheraton, 4 Graduated Drawers, Pennsylvania, C.1800, Walnut ..................... 950.00
**Chest,** Spice, Porcelain Knobs, 8 Drawer ................................................................. 125.00
**Chest,** Storage, Korean, White Brass, C.1780, 40 X 17 X 36 In. .............................. 3500.00
**Chest,** Sugar, Sheraton Feet, Reeded Posts, Cherry ................................................. 1000.00
**Chest,** Walnut, C.1860, 42 1/2 X 24 1/2 X 21 In. .................................................. *Illus* 1000.00
**Chest,** 2 Drawers Inside, Dovetailed, C.1870 ............................................................ 265.00
**Chest,** 4 Drawer, Brass Pulls, Mahogany, 43 1/2 X 20 X 41 In. ............................... 420.00
**Chest,** 4 Drawer, Brown Paint, Pin Striping, Pine, 17 X 6 X 21 In. ........................... 265.00
**Chest,** 4 Drawer, Cherry, Hepplewhite, Inlaid Escutcheons, C.1795 ......................... 1150.00
**Chest,** 4 Drawer, Pennsylvania, C.1830, Walnut ....................................................... 385.00
**Chest,** 4 Drawer, Solid Tiger Maple & Cherry, 49 X 42 X 22 1/2 In. ......................... 850.00
**Chest,** 5 Drawer, Figured Maple, 39 1/2 X 18 X 48 In. ............................................ 2750.00
**Chest,** 6 Drawer, C.1830, Cherry & Tiger Maple ....................................................... 525.00

Furniture, Chest, Peterson, 1830-40,
Painted, Yellow Pine

Furniture, Chest, Walnut, C.1860,
42 1/2 X 24 1/2 X 21 In.

Furniture, Chest, 6 Drawer, Stand,
Olivewood, Marquetry, 41 In.

| | |
|---|---|
| **Chest,** 6 Drawer, Stand, Olivewood, Marquetry, 41 In. .............................. *Illus* | 7500.00 |
| **Chest,** 7 Drawer, Eastern Maryland, C.1790, Cherry ............................................. | 4500.00 |
| **Chest,** 8 Drawer, Cock Bead Molding, C.1810, Cherry ......................................... | 4250.00 |
| **China Cabinet,** Carved, Louis XV Style ................................................................. | 2500.00 |
| **China Cabinet,** Curved Glass Front, Claw Feet .................................................... | 485.00 |
| **China Cabinet,** Curved Glass, Leaded Bottom Door, Carved Legs ..................... | 2200.00 |
| **China Cabinet,** Jester Head Crest On Cabinet, 74 X 51 X 21 In. ...................... | 125.00 |
| **China Closet,** Curved Sides, Bowed Door, Columns, Oak, 64 X 46 In. ............... | 600.00 |
| **Church Pew,** Golden Oak, 45 In. ........................................................................... | 245.00 |
| **Coatrack,** Brass Ends, 3 Wooden Rings For Hanger, Wooden ............................ | 30.00 |
| **Coatrack,** Oval Mirror, Umbrella Holder Base, Wrought Iron, 89 In. .................. | 175.00 |
| **Coatrack,** Wall, 6 Cast Iron Hooks ...................................................................... | 12.00 |
| **Coattree,** Bentwood, Czechoslovakia, Paper Label, 76 In. ................................. | 150.00 |
| **Commode,** Carved Seat, Carrying Handle, Burl Walnut, 20 X 21 In. ................... | 225.00 |
| **Commode,** Carved, Cherry, Miniature ................................................................... | 325.00 |
| **Commode,** Eastlake, Dated 1888, Oak ................................................................. | 210.00 |
| **Commode,** Lift Top, Blue Interior, Original Graining, C.1840 ............................... | 400.00 |
| **Commode,** Lift Top, Hand-Painted Graining, Pine, 27 1/2 X 30 In. ..................... | 275.00 |
| **Commode,** Lift Top, Walnut ................................................................................... | 150.00 |
| **Commode,** Marble Top, 3 Drawer, American, 29 1/2 X 23 1/2 In. ....................... | 725.00 |
| **Commode,** Mirror & Towel Bar, Oak .................................................. 110.00 To | 265.00 |
| **Commode,** Pink Marble Top, 3 Drawers, 1 Door, Carved Front, Walnut ............. | 575.00 |
| **Commode,** Rosewood & Fruitwood Parquetry, 3 X 2 3/4 Ft. ............................... | 5500.00 |
| **Commode,** Satinwood, George III Style, Semicircular, 29 In., Pair ..................... | 1400.00 |
| **Console,** Nickel-Plated Metal, Marble, French, C.1925 ................................. *Illus* | 1500.00 |
| **Couch,** Carved, Leather Tuft & Button Upholstery, Mahogany, 8i In. ................ | 2800.00 |
| **Cradle,** Bentwood, Made By Thonet ..................................................................... | 1100.00 |
| **Cradle,** Foot Pedal, Walnut ................................................................................... | 695.00 |
| **Cradle,** Jenny Lind ................................................................................................ | 97.00 |
| **Cradle,** Quebec, 1840-50, Chestnut & Pine ....................................................... | 300.00 |
| **Cradle,** Stand, Shaped Slats, American, 18th Century, Walnut, 36 In. ............... | 200.00 |
| **Cradle,** Wooden Pegs, Square Nails, Handmade, Walnut, 39 In. ....................... | 195.00 |
| **Crib,** Child's, Victorian, Collapsible, American, 51 1/2 In. .................................. | 250.00 |
| **Crib,** Drop Sides, Brass & Cast Iron, 28 1/2 X 52 In. ......................................... | 375.00 |
| **Crib,** French, Original Casters, Iron ..................................................................... | 145.00 |
| **Crib,** Painted Head & Foot Panels, Metal, French, 56 X 19 1/2 In. .................... | 500.00 |
| **Cupboard-Over-Chest,** 7 Drawer, Grain Painting, Shaker, 26 In.Wide .............. | 4050.00 |
| **Cupboard,** Baking, Hutch Top, Maple .................................................................. | 475.00 |
| **Cupboard,** Cant Back, New England, Original Paint, 18th Century ..................... | 6500.00 |
| **Cupboard,** Chestnut, Cherry, Butternut, 4 Doors, 2 Drawers, 48 In. ................. | 600.00 |

Furniture, Console, Nickel-Plated
Metal, Marble, French, C.1925

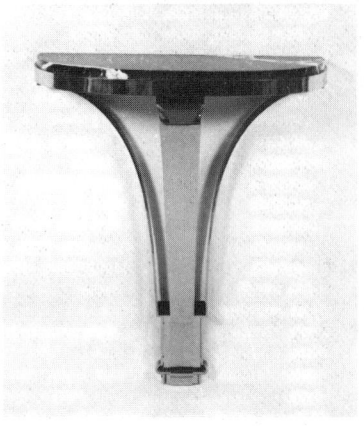

| | |
|---|---|
| **Cupboard,** Child's, Yellow Comb Graining | 475.00 |
| **Cupboard,** Corner, Blind Doors, Cherry | 1750.00 |
| **Cupboard,** Corner, C.1820, Dovetailed, 7 1/4 X 3 3/4 Ft. | 2200.00 |
| **Cupboard,** Corner, Center Drawers Tiger Maple, Old Red | 1950.00 |
| **Cupboard,** Corner, Cherry, Glass Top, 2 Piece | 750.00 |
| **Cupboard,** Corner, Cherry, Pennsylvania, C.1774, I Piece | 2200.00 |
| **Cupboard,** Corner, Chippendale, Raised Panels, Butternut, 29 In. | 3000.00 |
| **Cupboard,** Corner, George IV, C.1840, Arched Doors, Mahogany | 2500.00 |
| **Cupboard,** Corner, Georgian, 18th Century, Pine, 33 X 53 X 95 In. | 4200.00 |
| **Cupboard,** Corner, Hanging, Fitted Desk Interior, Pennsylvania | 750.00 |
| **Cupboard,** Corner, New England, 19th Century, Pine, 82 X 42 X 20 In. | 1200.00 |
| **Cupboard,** Corner, Pennsylvania, Original Blue Paint | 3600.00 |
| **Cupboard,** Corner, 1 Piece Blind Doors, C.1820, Cherry | 1300.00 |
| **Cupboard,** Corner, 2 Doors Over 2 Doors, New England, Pine, 51 In. | 1100.00 |
| **Cupboard,** Corner, 8-Light Doors, C.1800, Pennsylvania, 87 X 51 In. | 2800.00 |
| **Cupboard,** Dutch, Chamfered Doors, Walnut, 2 Piece | 1450.00 |
| **Cupboard,** Flat Back, 2 Piece, Oak | 895.00 |
| **Cupboard,** Flat, Painted Basket Of Tulips, Scandinavian, C.1848 | 3400.00 |
| **Cupboard,** Glass Doors Above, 2 Drawers | 850.00 |
| **Cupboard,** Glass Front, Dovetailed Top, Pine | 450.00 |
| **Cupboard,** Glazed Door Top, Pennsylvania Dutch, 110 X 73 In. | 695.00 |
| **Cupboard,** Hanging, Cherry Doors, Pine | 175.00 |
| **Cupboard,** Jelly, Butterfly Tin, Walnut | 385.00 |
| **Cupboard,** Jelly, C.1840, Painted & Grained Surface, Pennsylvania | 975.00 |
| **Cupboard,** Jelly, C.1850, Original Brown Paint, Cherry | 575.00 |
| **Cupboard,** Jelly, Legs, Pine, 5 Ft. X 32 In. | 295.00 |
| **Cupboard,** Jelly, Walnut With Tin | 190.00 |
| **Cupboard,** Jelly, 1 Drawer, 2 Doors, Walnut | 550.00 |
| **Cupboard,** Jelly, 2 Door, Old Red, Pine | 175.00 |
| **Cupboard,** Jelly, 2 Drawers Over 2 Doors, Chestnut | 250.00 |
| **Cupboard,** Kitchen, Flour Bin, Scalloped Top, Ash, 2 Piece | 325.00 |
| **Cupboard,** Kitchen, Hoosier | 350.00 |
| **Cupboard,** Kitchen, New England, 1880, Miniature | 225.00 |
| **Cupboard,** Kitchen, Original Finish, Tall | 100.00 |
| **Cupboard,** Mennonite, Thief River, Minn., C.1840, Walnut, 7 Feet | 1500.00 |
| **Cupboard,** Original Pulls, 1800s, Oak, 61 X 29 X 96 In. | 2100.00 |
| **Cupboard,** Pennsylvania, Spice Drawers, Walnut, 83 1/2 X 49 In. | 3000.00 |
| **Cupboard,** Pewter, Indiana, Gray-Green Paint, Pine & Poplar | 1050.00 |
| **Cupboard,** Pewter, Step Back, C.1820 | 595.00 |
| **Cupboard,** Shelf At Bottom, 2 Drawer, 2 Doors, Red & Gray | 495.00 |

**Cupboard,** Step Back, Piedmont, N.C., C.1890, 86 X 46 1/2 X 16 In. ................................. 4800.00
**Cupboard,** Step Back, Tulip Wood ................................................................ 695.00
**Cupboard,** Step Back, 1800s, Pine, 40 X 17 X 74 In. ........................................ 600.00
**Cupboard,** Tan Over Original Salmon ............................................................ 1075.00
**Cupboard,** Two 2-Panel Doors, Pegged, Cutout Base, Gallery, Red .................... 415.00
**Cupboard,** Wall, Blue Interior, 2 Door, 28 X 20 1/2 X 12 1/2 In. .......................... 125.00
**Cupboard,** Wall, Mahogany, Regency, Bonnet Top, Secret Door, 39 In. ................ 200.00
**Cupboard,** Walnut & Ash, 2 Piece ................................................................ 425.00
**Cupboard,** 12 Lights, Pennsylvania Dutch, Walnut .......................................... 2750.00
**Cupboard,** 17th Century, Oak ................................................................ *Illus* 1800.00
**Cupboard,** 2 Raised Panels On Door, Pine, 30 In. .......................................... 350.00
**Cupboard,** 3 Tiered Shelves, Drying Rack, England, Pine, 54 X 75 In. ................ 1300.00
**Cupboard,** 5 Drawer, 5 Paneled Doors, Short Turned Legs, Walnut .................... 295.00
**Curio Shelf,** C.1880, Solid Brass ................................................................ 1500.00
**Desk Secretary,** C.1780, Pine .................................................................. 1250.00
**Desk,** Campaign, 1810-12, Mahogany & Bird's-Eye Maple ................................ 1850.00
**Desk,** Chippendale, Slant Front, C.1740, Pine & Poplar .................................... 4200.00
**Desk,** Chippendale, Slant Front, Document Drawers, Walnut .............................. 4500.00
**Desk,** Chippendale, Slant Front, New England, C.1790, Cherry .......................... 5150.00
**Desk,** Columnettes On Sides, Drop Front, English, Oak, 35 X 39 In. .................... 900.00
**Desk,** Document Drawers, Inlaid Escutcheons, Ohio, C.1820, Cherry .................... 2150.00
**Desk,** Double, Pedestal, Oak, 60 In. ............................................................ 225.00
**Desk,** Drop Front, Applied Carvings, Walnut .................................................. 735.00
**Desk,** Kneehole, Japanned, Black, George I, 6 Drawers, 31 In. .......................... 1500.00
**Desk,** Kneehole, Tramp Art ........................................................................ 475.00
**Desk,** Lady's, Flat Top, 5 Drawers, C.1900, Oak, 29 1/2 In. ................................ 450.00
**Desk,** Lady's, Grain Painted ...................................................................... 310.00
**Desk,** Lady's, Mirror At Top, Drop Lid, Pigeonholes, Oak .................................. 325.00
**Desk,** Lady's, Side Cupboards Around Kneehole, Oak ...................................... 2000.00
**Desk,** Lap, Inlaid Walnut .......................................................................... 95.00
**Desk,** Lap, Oak, 18 X 14 In. ...................................................................... 40.00
**Desk,** Lap, Pewter Covered Wells, Rosewood, C.1850 ...................................... 125.00
**Desk,** Lap, Sand Bottle, Secret Drawer, Walnut .............................................. 65.00
**Desk,** Lap, Striped Border, Compartments, 19th Century, 8 3/4 In. ...................... 45.00
**Desk,** Lap, Velvet Lined, 2 Inkwells, Walnut, 13 1/2 X 8 3/4 In. .......................... 165.00
**Desk,** Lap, Velvet Writing Area, 3 Compartment, 8 3/4 X 12 1/4 In. .................... 45.00
**Desk,** Lap, Walnut, Ink Bottle, Compartments, 9 X 14 X 4 In. ............................ 95.00
**Desk,** Lap, Walnut, 13 X 9 In. .................................................................... 35.00
**Desk,** Larkin, Miror, Key, Oak .................................................................... 375.00
**Desk,** Lift Top, Mirror, Lyre Base, C.1870, Rosewood & Walnut, 31 In. ................ 450.00
**Desk,** On Frame, 18th Century, Tiger Maple Box, Stretcher Base ........................ 725.00
**Desk,** Partner's, Leather Top, Kittinger & Co., 72 X 36 X 30 In. .......................... 675.00

Furniture, Cupboard, 17th Century, Oak

**Desk,** Partner's, Walnut, Pair .................................................................................. 820.00
**Desk,** Pennsylvania, 2 Drawer, Original Mustard Paint ........................................ 475.00
**Desk,** Post Office, 32 Holes For Letters ............................................................... 395.00
**Desk,** Queen Anne Style, Slant Front, American, C.1900, 39 In. .......................... 750.00
**Desk,** Queen Anne, Slant Front & Galleried, American, Walnut .......................... 1200.00
**Desk,** Queen Anne, Slant Top, 2 Drawers, C.1720, Mahogany ............................ 750.00
**Desk,** Railroad, Wainscoting Back, Stool, Maple, 1800s, 36 X 84 In. .................. 900.00
**Desk,** Reeded 1/4 Columns, Curly Cherry & Bird's-Eye Maple ............................ 3200.00
**Desk,** Rolltop, C Curve, Matching Swivel Chair, Mahogany ................................. 700.00
**Desk,** Rolltop, Carved Gallery, Custom Interior, 66 In. ......................................... 3900.00
**Desk,** Rolltop, Carved Pulls, Mail File Center, Oak, 66 In. .................................. 4500.00
**Desk,** Rolltop, Jeweler's, Walnut, 43 1/2 X 25 1/2 X 39 In. ................................. 585.00
**Desk,** Rolltop, Raised Panels, Carved Pulls, Oak, 60 In. ..................................... 3400.00
**Desk,** Rolltop, S Curve, Child's, Oak .................................................................... 135.00
**Desk,** Rolltop, S Curve, Clamshell Pulls, 13 Drawer, Oak, Chair ....................... 3350.00
**Desk,** Rolltop, S Curve, Golden Oak, 54 X 50 In. ................... 1400.00 To 1810.00
**Desk,** Rolltop, S Curve, Oak Writing Surface, C.1893, Steel, 50 In. ................... 7600.00
**Desk,** Rolltop, S Curve, Raised Panel, Oak, 48 X 36 In. ..................................... 1600.00
**Desk,** Rolltop, S Curve, Upper Letter Boxes, 60 In. ............................................. 3500.00
**Desk,** Rolltop, S Curve, 2 Internal Drawers, Oak, 48 In. ..................................... 1095.00
**Desk,** Rolltop, S Curve, 25 Drawers In Center Section, Oak, 48 In. ................... 1200.00
**Desk,** Schoolmaster's, New Hampshire, C.1835 ................................................. 175.00
**Desk,** Schoolmaster's, Tapered Legs, Bowed Drawer, Cherry ............................ 500.00
**Desk,** Serpentine Slant Front, Claw & Ball Feet, C.1773, 45 In. ........................ 1900.00
**Desk,** Sewing, Shaker, Alfred, Maine .................................................................. 6800.00
**Desk,** Sheraton, Walnut Veneer Front, 20 Drawers, Walnut ................................ 2450.00
**Desk,** Ship, Gallery, 19th Century, English, Mahogany ....................................... 1100.00
**Desk,** Slant Front, Chippendale, Mahogany, 36 In.Wide ...................................... 2250.00
**Desk,** Slant Front, Compartments, 3 Drawer, New England, 41 In. ..................... 2000.00
**Desk,** Slant Front, Cubbyholes, Maple, Cherry Legs, 24 X 29 In. ....................... 375.00
**Desk,** Slant Front, Flame Birch, Nova Scotia, John Wade .................................. 9500.00
**Desk,** Slant Front, New England, Brass Pulls, C.1780, Maple .............................. 2800.00
**Desk,** Slant Front, Original Brasses, Black Walnut .............................................. 325.00
**Desk,** Slant Front, 2 Short, 3 Long Drawers, G.Stickley, 45 In. ........................... 3000.00
**Desk,** Slant Front, 4 Drawer, French Feet, American, C.1795, 43 In. .................. 1900.00
**Desk,** Slant Front, 4 Drawer, 18th Century, Red Cherry ..................................... 3250.00
**Desk,** Spinet, Empire, C.1840 ............................................................................ 265.00
**Desk,** Spinet, Lady's, Mahogany ......................................................................... 265.00
**Desk,** Storekeeper's, Countertop, Slant Top, 29 1/2 X 20 In. .............................. 500.00
**Desk,** Tambour, 3 Bottom Drawers, 8 Cubbyholes, Mahogany ........................... 3675.00
**Desk,** Traveling, Teakwood, Brass Bound, 3 Drawers, 12 1/4 In. ........................ 400.00
**Desk,** Wooton ....................................................................................... *Illus* 7900.00

Furniture, Desk, Wooton

**Desk,** Wooton, No.101 .................................................................................................. 4750.00
**Dining Set,** Art Deco, 1923, 10 Pieces ..................................................................... 3500.00
**Dining Set,** Duncan Phyfe Style, Dropped Apron, 6 Chairs ................................. 1200.00
**Dining Set,** Scroll Feet, Solid Oak, Table 60 In., 10 Piece ................................... 2500.00
**Dining Set,** Stickley, Cross Cut Oak, 4 Chairs, 54 In.Wide ..................................... 900.00
**Dining Set,** Tudor Style, 7 Piece ............................................................................... 4000.00
**Dining Set,** 6 Caned Seat Chairs, Sideboard, Table 54 In.Oval ........................... 4200.00
**Dresser Desk,** Slant Front, 4 Drawers, Carved, C.1890, Mahogany ....................... 475.00
**Dresser,** Carved Fruit Pulls, Glove Boxes, Wishbone Frame Mirror ...................... 595.00
**Dresser,** Marble Top, Mirror, Walnut ......................................................................... 310.00
**Dresser,** Mirror, Marble Top, Jewelry Drawer, Walnut ............................................ 695.00
**Dresser,** Mirror, 2 Short Drawers, 3 Long, Oak, G.Stickley, 33 In. ...................... 2500.00
**Dresser,** Welsh, Oak, George II, 3 Shelves, 3 Drawers, 73 In. ............................ 1000.00
**Dresser,** Wishbone Mirror, Fruit Pulls, Walnut ........................................................ 400.00
**Dresser,** 2 Drawer, Rectangular Mirror, Carved Wood Frame ............................... 295.00
**Dresser,** 4 Drawer, G. Stickley, Oak, C.1910, 33 In. .............................. *Illus* 2500.00
**Dresser,** 4 Drawer, Handkerchief Boxes, Brass Hardware, Cherry ....................... 395.00
**Dressing Glass,** On Stand, Queen Anne, 1760-70, Mahogany, English ............... 1450.00
**Dressing Table,** Kneehole, Block Front, Massachusetts, Mahogany ...................... 5500.00
**Dry Sink,** Boxed Drain, Red Paint, Pennsylvania, Pine, 20 X 56 In. .................... 2500.00
**Dry Sink,** Child's, Salmon Center Panels, Original Blue Paint ............................... 725.00
**Dry Sink,** Hutch Top, Pennsylvania, 1 Drawer ....................................................... 850.00
**Dry Sink,** Pennsylvania, Pine & Poplar .................................................................. 900.00
**Dry Sink,** Pine, 33 X 33 X 13 In. ............................................................................. 180.00
**Dry Sink,** Small Drawer, Original Hardware, Lehigh Valley, Chestnut ................. 500.00
**Dry Sink,** Unusual Door & Drawer Arrangement, Pine & Poplar .......................... 900.00
**Dry Sink,** 2 Door, 1 Small Drawer, Original Green Paint ....................................... 750.00
**Easel & Panel,** Neoclassically Draped Female, Carved Birch .............................. 600.00
**Easel,** Victorian, Bamboo ........................................................................................... 40.00
**Etagere,** Napoleon III, Gilt, Bronze-Mounted Onyx, 4 X 2 1/2 Ft. ..................... 2500.00
**Fern Stand,** Acanthus Carved, Louis XIV, 5 1/2 Ft., Set Of 4 .............................. 2000.00
**Fern Stand,** Oak ................................................................................ 60.00 To 125.00
**Fernery,** Serpentine Pilaster Supports, C.1880, Teak, 37 In. ................................ 400.00
**Field Bed,** Duncan Phyfe, 4 Carved Posts, Mahogany, 8 Ft.High ....................... 8000.00
**Flower Box,** Wicker ...................................................................................................... 60.00
**Foot Warmer,** Walnut & Tin ....................................................................................... 98.00
**Footstool,** Black Graining, Shaker, 25 1/2 X 9 1/2 X 9 1/2 In. .......................... 122.00
**Footstool,** Iron Legs, Velvet Top ............................................................................... 55.00
**Footstool,** Maroon Needlepoint, Iron Legs, Small, Round ..................................... 37.50
**Footstool,** Victorian, Patchwork Cover, Walnut, 18 In. ........................................... 85.00
**Footstool,** Wicker ........................................................................................................ 65.00
**Frame,** Carved Rosewood, Easel, 4 1/4 X 8 X 10 In. ............................................. 35.00
**Frame,** Floral Embossed, Scalloped, Cast Iron, 10 X 7 In. ................................... 25.00
**Frame,** Gold Leaf Inside, Walnut, Oval ..................................................................... 75.00
**Frame,** Gold Liner, Carved, Walnut, 14 X 18 In. ..................................................... 45.00
**Frame,** Painted & Grained, 23 1/2 X 20 In. ............................................................. 65.00
**Frame,** Shadowbox, Double Gilt Liner, Walnut, 15 X 17 In. .................................. 75.00
**Hall Rack & Mirror,** Victorian .............................................................. *Illus* 875.00
**Hall Seat,** Beveled Mirror, Leather Medallion, C.1890, Oak, 81 In. ...................... 375.00
**Hall Stand,** English, Oak, Barley Twist .................................................................... 345.00
**Hall Tree,** Pink Marble Base, Cherry ........................................................................ 425.00
**High Chair & Stroller,** Adjustable, Oak .................................................................. 270.00
**High Chair,** Arrow Back, Oak ..................................................................................... 85.00
**High Chair,** Child's, C.1900, G.Stickley, Oak, 38 In. ............................... *Illus* 800.00
**High Chair,** Folds Into Play Table, 1930s, Maple & Birch ...................................... 95.00
**High Chair,** Kilgore ...................................................................................................... 10.00
**High Chair,** Original Wood-Tone Finish, Maple & Wicker ..................................... 165.00
**High Chair,** Wicker Seat ............................................................................................ 175.00
**High Stool,** 4 Legs, Shaker, Enfield, Connecticut .................................................. 185.00
**Highboy,** Chippendale, Triple Fan Carving, Scrolled Apron, Maple ..................... 6750.00
**Highboy,** Duck Feet, 4 Upper Drawers, 5 Lower, Connecticut, Cherry ................ 8000.00
**Highboy,** Flat Top, Beaded Apron, Walnut & Burl Veneer, 39 3/4 In. ................... 800.00
**Highboy,** Queen Anne, Tiger Maple ......................................................................... 3200.00

Furniture, Dresser, 4 Drawer, G.Stickley,
Oak, C.1910, 33 In.

Furniture, Hall Rack & Mirror, Victorian

Furniture, High Chair, Child's, C.1900,
G.Stickley, Oak, 38 In.

| | |
|---|---|
| **Highboy,** String Inlay, 1700-30, Walnut, 20 X 36 X 69 In. | 1500.00 |
| **Highboy,** 18th Century, Grained Pine | 1400.00 |
| **Holder,** Magazine, Wall, Victorian, Walnut | 48.00 |
| **Huntboard,** English Hepplewhite, C.1800, Mahogany | 2200.00 |
| **Huntboard,** Moravian, Painted, Davidson County | 3200.00 |

**Huntboard,** 2 Dovetailed Drawers, Pine, 43 X 49 In. ............................................................... *Illus* 1500.00
**Hutch,** French, Carved, C.1780 .............. 2500.00
**Hutch,** Handmade Square Nails, C.1875, Cherry & Poplar, 2 Piece .............. 425.00
**Hutch,** Wide Overhang, Pennsylvania, Pine & Poplar ........................ 1600.00
**Kas,** Double Panel Doors, Ball Feet, New York, Cherry, 73 X 63 In. .................... 225.00
**Knife Urn,** Regency, C.1840, English, Hardwood, 25 In., Pair ................ 1000.00
**Library Steps,** Pine, 1 Side Rail, 19 1/2 In. .............................. 245.00
**Linen Press,** Pine, 36 X 18 X 84 In. ............................ 475.00
**Linen Press,** 1 Drawer, Cupboard Base, Cherry ........................ 2600.00
**Linen Press,** 3 Graduated Drawers, C.1760, Walnut, 43 3/4 X 71 In. ................ 2200.00
**Love Seat,** Finger-Carved, Gold Velvet Upholstery, Victorian ................. 650.00
**Love Seat,** Finger-Carved, Mirror Back, Velvet Covered, Walnut ..................... 1400.00
**Love Seat,** Queen Anne Legs, Green Velvet, 1900s, Pair ................. 400.00
**Love Seat,** Tufted Back, Wine Velvet Cover, Victorian, 60 X 32 In. ................ 650.00
**Lowboy,** Chippendale, Shaped Apron, Claw Feet, Mahogany, 35 X 31 In. ............ 200.00
**Lowboy,** Queen Anne Style, C.1900, Walnut ........................ 500.00
**Magazine Rack,** Hanging, Oak ............................ 185.00
**Map Case,** 10 Drawer, Oak ............................ 400.00
**Mirror,** Baroque, Gilt, Metal Crest, Beveled, 66 X 44 In. ................. 500.00
**Mirror,** Cheval, Beveled, Reeded Columns, American, Mahogany, 73 In. .............. 275.00
**Mirror,** Chippendale, C.1820, Wayne & Biddle, Mahogany, 38 X 20 In. ............... 1100.00
**Mirror,** Chippendale, Line Inlay, Walnut & Pine, 11 1/2 X 7 3/4 In. ............... 255.00
**Mirror,** Chippendale, Scrolled, American, Mahogany, 19 1/2 X 12 In. ............... 175.00
**Mirror,** Convex, Carved Eagle Crest, Gilt, Europe, 20th Century ................. 35.00
**Mirror,** Crest, Gilt Phoenix Bird, Mahogany, 39 1/4 X 19 3/4 In. ................. 225.00
**Mirror,** Dressing, Carved, Footed, Walnut, 25 In. ........................ 140.00
**Mirror,** Dressing, Federal, Inlaid Drawer, Sandwich Pulls ................. 275.00
**Mirror,** Dressing, Mahogany, Poplar, Inlay, 14 X 6 7/8 X 18 5/8 In. ............... 235.00
**Mirror,** Dressing, Mahogany, Poplar, Line Inlay, 13 X 6 X 18 In. ................. 235.00
**Mirror,** Eastlake, Marble Shelf, C.1880, Walnut, C.1883, 15 X 95 In. ............... 450.00
**Mirror,** Federal, Pilaster Trim, C.1830, 2 Part ........................ 75.00
**Mirror,** Gilt Girandole, Eagle & Acanthus Crest, C.1800, 21 In. ................. 350.00
**Mirror,** Gilt Spherules, Columns, W.Gould & Son, C.1840, 54 X 33 In. ............... 350.00
**Mirror,** Gilt Wood, George III, Knots & Husk Festoons, 47 In. ................ 2000.00
**Mirror,** Gilt Wood, Regency, Scrolled Foliate Cresting, 44 In. ................. 650.00
**Mirror,** Gold Leaf Design, Painted Fruit Above Glass, C.1880, Frame ................. 125.00
**Mirror,** Gold Leaf, Carved Crest, 19th Century, 25 X 74 In. ................. 250.00
**Mirror,** Gothic, Hand-Carved Walnut Frame, 42 In. ........................ 400.00
**Mirror,** Hall, Matching Marble Top Bench, 10 Ft. ........................ 500.00
**Mirror,** House In Upper Part, American, Walnut, 33 1/2 X 15 1/2 In. ................. 600.00
**Mirror,** Italian Baroque, Gilt Wood, Center Mask, 5 X 3 1/2 Ft. ................. 800.00

Furniture, Hunt Board, 2 Dovetailed Drawers, Pine, 43 X 49 In.

Furniture, Mirror, Louis XV, Gilt Wood, Carved, 65 In.

**Mirror,** Louis XV, Gilt Wood, Carved, 65 In. ............................................................ *Illus* 7500.00
**Mirror,** Pier, Eastlake, Marble Shelf, C.1880, 95 1/2 In. ............................................... 450.00
**Mirror,** Pier, Gilt Incised, C.1865, Rosewood, 5 Ft. .................................................... 1400.00
**Mirror,** Pier, Renaissance Revival, Columns, C.1870, 21 X 30 In. ................................. 200.00
**Mirror,** Pier, Rococo Gilt Wood, 19th Century, 5 Ft. X 2 Ft.9 In. ................................. 275.00
**Mirror,** Pier, Wall, Marble Shelf, Walnut Frame ....................................................... 325.00
**Mirror,** Plateau, Beveled Edge, Silver Border, 12 In. .................................................. 30.00
**Mirror,** Plateau, Fleur-De-Lis Forms Border Over Bevel, 14 In. ..................................... 60.00
**Mirror,** Plateau, Lion Heads & Claws, Beveled, Hexagonal, 12 In. ............................... 110.00
**Mirror,** Plateau, Scroll Feet, 14 In.Diam. ................................................................ 35.00
**Mirror,** Plateau, Scrolled & Fruit Embossed Silver Border, 15 In. ................................. 145.00
**Mirror,** Plateau, Silver Plated Feet, Beaded Sides, Beveled, 12 In. ............................... 75.00
**Mirror,** Reverse Painting On Glass, Sea Battle Scene Of 1812 .................................... 1250.00
**Mirror,** Rococo Fruit & Flowers, Germany, Walnut, Oval, 41 1/2 In. ............................. 200.00
**Mirror,** Shaving, , Bevel Rim, Oak Frame, Humphrey's Witch Hazel ............................. 90.00
**Mirror,** Shaving, Art Nouveau, Beveled Glass, 16 In. ................................................ 32.50
**Mirror,** Shaving, Art Nouveau, Beveled, Cupids Holding Mirror ................................... 50.00
**Mirror,** Shaving, Art Nouveau, 18 In. ..................................................................... 65.00
**Mirror,** Shaving, Beveled, Nickel Plated Brass Base, 8 X 6 In. .................................... 75.00
**Mirror,** Shaving, Federal, 2 Drawer, Maine, Mahogany, 17 In. .................................... 225.00
**Mirror,** Sheraton, Gilt, Reverse Painting Of Eagle, C.1800 ........................................ 1950.00
**Mirror,** Split Column, Acorn Drops, Beveled Mirror, 25 X 43 1/2 In. ............................. 75.00
**Mirror,** Swinging, Beveled, Lady Figurine, Art Deco ................................................. 95.00
**Mirror,** Venetian Style, Etched Floral Design, 25 X 38 In. .......................................... 150.00
**Mule Chest,** 2 Drawer, Grain Painted, C.1820 ......................................................... 1175.00
**Music Stand,** Oak ............................................................................................. 75.00
**Nightstand,** Curly Maple Veneer On Drawer & Legs, C.1830, Cherry ........................... 325.00
**Nightstand,** Drop Leaf, Walnut & Curly Maple ......................................................... 190.00
**Nightstand,** Sheraton, 2 Drawer, Cherry ................................................................ 300.00
**Parlor Set,** Carved Cherubs On Arms, Paw Feet, Mahogany, 3 Piece ........................... 850.00
**Parlor Set,** Grape Carved Crests, American, Walnut, 3 Piece ...................................... 800.00
**Parlor Set,** Hunzinger, Ebonized Walnut, 4 Piece ........................................... *Illus* 8000.00
**Parlor Set,** Victorian, Carved Crests, American, Walnut, 4 Piece ................................. 600.00
**Pew,** Church, Oak, 8 Ft. ..................................................................................... 50.00
**Pie Safe,** Checkerboard Pattern, North Carolina, Mustard, Tin .................................... 350.00
**Pie Safe,** Hand-Punched Tin, Original Red Paint ..................................................... 1495.00

Furniture, Parlor Set, Hunzinger, Ebonized Walnut, 4 Piece (See Page 225)

**Pie Safe,** Hanging, Punched Flags, Hearts, Birds, 1881, Hex Signs ..................... 1950.00
**Pie Safe,** Pierced Tin Front, Top Drawer ................................................ 785.00
**Pie Safe,** Pierced Tin, Walnut ........................................................ 170.00
**Pie Safe,** Screened, Adjustable Shelves, Original Grain Paint ......................... 160.00
**Pool Table,** Balls & Rack, Eastlake, Walnut, Mahogany, 52 X 100 In. .................. 800.00
**Pool Table,** Brunswick, Balke Collender, C.1895, 4 1/2 X 9 Ft. ...................... 3000.00
**Pool Table,** Brunswick, C.1880, Leather Pockets, 9 X 4 1/2 Ft. ..................... 7000.00
**Pool Table,** Brunswick, 1920s, Solid Mahogany ..................................... 5500.00
**Pool Table,** Brunswick, 6-Legged, Pre-1910, Walnut ................................ 6500.00
**Porch Set,** Sofa, Rocker, & Chair, Rush, Painted White .............................. 790.00
**Rack,** Cue, Brunswick, With Mirror & Coat Hooks ................................... 195.00
**Rack,** Folio, 3 Parquetry Dividers, Inlaid Fruitwood, C.1870, 38 In. ................ 700.00
**Rack,** Print, Adjustable, Saber Legs, C.1840, Mahogany, 7 X 29 In. ................. 450.00
**Rack,** Tie, Victorian, Mirror, 9 X 10 In. .......................................... 27.50
**Rack,** Wall, Comb & Brush, Lattice, Pine, 15 X 10 1/2 In. .......................... 15.00
**Rocker Swing,** Cane Back & Seat ................................................... 135.00
**Rocker,** Armless, Tape Back, Shaker ............................................... 400.00
**Rocker,** Arms, Tape Back, Shaker .................................................. 550.00
**Rocker,** Bamboo Turned Birdcage Back, C.1800, American, 39 In. ..................... 300.00
**Rocker,** Barrel, Miniature, Primitive ............................................. 250.00
**Rocker,** Boston, Child's, Fruit Stenciling ......................................... 35.00
**Rocker,** Cane Bottom, 1850s, Walnut ............................................... 350.00
**Rocker,** Carvings, Oak ............................................................. 70.00
**Rocker,** Child's, Bentwood, Hand-Caned Seat, Thonet ............................... 375.00
**Rocker,** Child's, C.1900, Small .................................................... 70.00
**Rocker,** Child's, Cane Seat, Stenciled, New England ............................... 135.00
**Rocker,** Child's, Old Green ....................................................... 110.00
**Rocker,** Child's, Thonet, Bentwood, Hand-Caned Seat & Back, Label ................. 375.00
**Rocker,** Child's, Victorian, Cane Back & Seat ..................................... 175.00
**Rocker,** Child's, Wicker .................................................. 48.00 To 60.00
**Rocker,** Continous Arm, Comb Back, Gold Design, C.1800, 41 In. ..................... 500.00

Furniture, Rocker, Ladderback,
Hickory Split Seat, Walnut

Furniture, Rocker, Platform, Hunzinger,
C.1880, Turned Walnut

Furniture, Rocker, Platform, Hunzinger,
C.1885, Turned Walnut

**Rocker,** Eastlake, Platform, Victorian ........................................................................................ 300.00
**Rocker,** Heart Shape, Wicker ...................................................................................................... 500.00
**Rocker,** Hunzinger, C.1870, Mesh Seat, Cherry ........................................................................ 175.00
**Rocker,** Ladder Back, Hickory Split Seat, Walnut .............................................................. *Illus* 100.00
**Rocker,** Lady's, Hunzinger, Turned Walnut, C.1870 .................................................................. 300.00
**Rocker,** Low Arms, Cane Seat, Walnut Burl Trim .................................................................... 165.00
**Rocker,** Mission Oak, C.1910 ......................................................................................................  90.00
**Rocker,** Original Tape Seat, Mt.Lebanon, Shaker .................................................................... 475.00
**Rocker,** Pennsylvania, Red Striping, Colored Design, C.1835 ............................................... 375.00
**Rocker,** Peter Cooper, Trenton, N.J., C.1845, Wrought Iron ................................................. 3250.00
**Rocker,** Pierce Carved, C.1855, Carved Headrest, Laminated Oak ........................................ 650.00
**Rocker,** Pillow Bar, Shaker No.7 Stamped On Back ............................................................... 525.00
**Rocker,** Platform, Hunzinger, C.1880, Turned Walnut ...................................................... *Illus* 160.00
**Rocker,** Platform, Hunzinger, C.1885, Turned Walnut ...................................................... *Illus* 400.00

**Rocker,** Platform, Victorian ........................................................................... 250.00
**Rocker,** Pressed Back, Cane Seat ..................................................................... 130.00
**Rocker,** Rolled Hoop Back, 19th Century, Wicker, 39 In. ........................................ 125.00
**Rocker,** Sewing, Victorian, Wicker ..................................................................... 75.00
**Rocker,** Shawl Bar, Tape Seat, Marked Shaker No. 7, Mt.Lebanon ........................... 425.00
**Rocker,** Slat Back, Rush Seat, Original Design On Back ......................................... 285.00
**Rocker,** Spindle Back, Side Arms, Victorian ......................................................... 150.00
**Rocker,** Splint Seat, Shaker, Watervliet Finial, Groveland, N.Y. ............................... 375.00
**Rocker,** Vase Turned Posts, Painted, Shaker, 19th Century, 33 In. ........................... 100.00
**Rocker,** Watervliet, N.Y., Splint Seat, C.1820, Shaker .......................................... 350.00
**Rocker,** Webbed Seat, Shaker ........................................................................... 325.00
**Rocker,** Wicker, Upholstered Back & Seat ........................................................... 110.00
**Rocker,** Windsor, Continuous Arm, 7 Spindles, New England, 37 In. ......................... 275.00
**Rocker,** 4 Back Slats, Mushroom Knobs, Rush Seat, Shaker, C.1790 ......................... 600.00
**Salon Set,** Louis XIV, Carved, Silk Upholstery, Walnut ......................................... 1500.00
**Screen,** Chinese, Terra-Cotta, 4 Panel Scene, C.1880 .......................................... 1050.00
**Screen,** Dragon Inlay, Teakwood & Lacquer, C.1830, 75 X 35 In. ............................. 1750.00
**Screen,** Eastlake, Cherry ................................................................................... 165.00
**Screen,** Folding, Art Deco, Eve Picking Apple ....................................................... 315.00
**Sea Chest,** Hinged, Original Black-Green Paint, 6 1/8 X 7 1/8 In. ............................. 300.00
**Seat,** Airplane, Wicker, Leather Back .................................................................. 50.00
**Secretary Bookcase,** Drop Front, Walnut, 7 Ft. .................................................... 1250.00
**Secretary,** Barrel-Roll, Burl Trim, Spoon-Carved, Walnut ...................................... 2050.00
**Secretary,** Burl On Walnut, 45 X 93 In. ............................................................... 2500.00
**Secretary,** Cylinder Top, Original Glass ............................................................... 1550.00
**Secretary,** Glass Door Top, Rolltop Desk, Grand Rapids Desk Co. ............................ 2950.00
**Secretary,** Kneehole, Slant Lid, Carved Pulls, C.1860, Walnut, 88 In. ........................ 950.00
**Secretary,** Leaded Glass Upper Doors, English, Oak .............................................. 600.00
**Secretary,** Original Glass & Casters, Drop Front Desk, Walnut ................................ 1250.00
**Secretary,** Rolltop, Mahogany Veneer, 7 Ft.High ..................................... *Illus* 1400.00
**Secretary,** Stop Fluting, Rhode Island Cabinetry, Mahogany .................................. 7800.00
**Secretary,** Walnut & Burl Veneer, C.1865, 111 In.Tall .............................. *Illus* 3000.00
**Secretary,** Wisconsin Butternut ......................................................................... 1850.00
**Server,** Corner, Hand Decorated & Carved, 2 Piece ............................................... 1650.00

Furniture, Secretary, Rolltop,
Mahogany Veneer, 7 Ft.High

Furniture, Secretary, Walnut & Burl Veneer,
C.1865, 111 In.Tall

Furniture, Shaving Stand, Marble Top, Walnut

Furniture, Sideboard, Georgia, C.1830, Tiger Maple

Server, Drop Leaf, Open Shelf, 2 Drawers, Mahogany, 58 X 19 In. ............................... 225.00
Server, Marble Top, Beveled Glass Mirrors, American, Walnut, 8 Ft. ........................ 1595.00
Server, Pennsylvania Dutch, Buttermilk Paint, C.1790 ............................... 500.00
Settee, Chippendale, Carved Knees, Scrolled Feet, Mahogany, 59 In. ....................... 350.00
Settee, Federal, 20 Slat Back, Rush Seat, New England, 17 1/2 In. ....................... 300.00
Settee, Greco-Roman, Acanthus Carved Crest, C.1830, 83 In. ....................... 500.00
Settee, Hepplewhite, Caned ............................... 1200.00
Settle, Black, Red Stripes, Pennsylvania ............................... 1500.00
Settle, Carved Angels, Faces, 19th Century, Walnut, 54 X 48 In. ....................... 1250.00
Settle, 5 Vertical Slats, 1910, Oak, Signed G.Stickley, 56 In. ....................... 5000.00
Shaving Stand, Marble Top, Walnut ............................... *Illus* 725.00
Shaving Stand, Victorian, Walnut ............................... 450.00
Shelf, Book, Collapsible, Leaf & Acorn Ends, Oak, 5 1/2 X 15 In. ....................... 27.00
Shelf, Plate & Spoon, Bird Design, 18th Century, American Pine ....................... 750.00
Showcase, Floor, Claw Feet, Jewelry Store, Oak ............................... 600.00
Showcase, Gun Cabinet & Bookcase, 3 Drawers, 8 X 9 1/2 Ft. ....................... 1500.00
Sideboard & Backbar, Beveled, Bowed Glass, Mahogany, 10 X 7 Ft. ....................... 7500.00
Sideboard, Bow Front Drawer, 2 Doors, Carved, Oak Barley Twist ....................... 325.00
Sideboard, Carved Fretwork, Frank L.Wright, Mahogany, 86 In.Wide ....................... 2500.00
Sideboard, Carved Lions, Oak, Large ............................... 1900.00
Sideboard, Country French, C.1840, 13 Large Drawers, Pine ....................... 625.00
Sideboard, Curved Glass Cabinet, Claw Feet ............................... 485.00
Sideboard, Gargoyles, Curved Beveled Leaded Glass Doors ....................... 2700.00
Sideboard, Georgia, C.1830, Tiger Maple ............................... *Illus* 1050.00
Sideboard, Hunter, Marble Top, Curved Side Glass, 8 X 6 1/2 Ft. ....................... 5000.00
Sideboard, Inlay Stringing, 19th Century, New England, Mahogany ....................... 3250.00
Sideboard, Mahogany, George III, 2 Short Drawers, 47 In. ....................... 750.00
Sideboard, Mirror, Bowed Center Door, Claw Feet, Oak ............................... 195.00
Sideboard, Regency, Bowed Front, Mahogany ............................... 3900.00
Sideboard, Scalloped Edge, 3 Drawer, 4 Door, C.1850, Pine, 6 X 4 Ft. ....................... 1950.00
Sideboard, Sheraton Empire, Transitional, Bow Front, Tiger Maple ....................... 975.00
Sideboard, Spindle Work, Mirror, English Burled Walnut, Small ....................... 750.00
Sideboard, With Mirror, Pressed Design, Oak, Small ............................... 145.00
Sideboard, 3 Beveled Mirrors, 4 Drawers & Doors, Oak, 77 X 90 In. ....................... 1200.00
Smoking Cabinet, C.1910, G.Stickley, Oak ............................... *Illus* 1200.00
Sofa & Armchair, Gilt Incising, J.Jeliffe, Walnut, 1870 ............................... 2500.00
Sofa & Chair, Mohair, Art Deco, Channel Back ............................... 750.00
Sofa, Beechwood, George III, Cream, Blue & Black Design, 78 In. ....................... 650.00
Sofa, Camelback, Carved Cabriole Legs, Mahogany, 37 X 89 In. ....................... 850.00

Furniture, Smoking Cabinet, C.1910, G.Stickley, Oak (See Page 229)

Furniture, Sofa, Mahogany, American, C.1795, 77 In.Wide

| | |
|---|---|
| **Sofa,** Chippendale, Camelback, Ball & Claw Feet | 500.00 |
| **Sofa,** Country Sheraton, Birch | 1425.00 |
| **Sofa,** Federal, Serpentine Back, C.1700, Massachusetts, 78 In. | 1500.00 |
| **Sofa,** J. & J.W.Meeks, New York, Rosewood, 6 Ft. 6 3/4 In. | 3500.00 |
| **Sofa,** Laminated Rosewood, C.1855, J.H.Belter, Serpentine Seat | 1300.00 |
| **Sofa,** Mahogany, American, C.1795, 77 In.Wide | *Illus* 3600.00 |
| **Sofa,** Mahogany, George III, Bowed Seat, Green Brocade, 80 In. | 600.00 |
| **Sofa,** Mahogany, George III, Carved Upholstered Back, 79 In. | 1200.00 |
| **Sofa,** Victorian, Serpentine Back, Carved Crest, C.1890, Walnut | 400.00 |
| **Spoonholder,** Hanging, 18 Slots, Jigged Apron, Brown Paint, Pine | 135.00 |
| **Stand,** Federal, 2 Drawer, Gold Leaf, Bamboo Spools, 42 X20 In. | 650.00 |
| **Stand,** Plant, Adjustable, C.1875, Iron, 4 Ft. 5 In. | *Illus* 750.00 |
| **Stand,** Plant, Marble Top, Teakwood, Chinese, 16 X 30 In. | 300.00 |
| **Stand,** Plant, Pedestal, Oak | 49.00 |
| **Stand,** Plant, 3 Twisted Legs, 2 Shelves, Victorian, Walnut, 44 In. | 100.00 |
| **Stand,** Shaving, Fitted Door For Mug & Brush, Mahogany | 325.00 |
| **Stand,** Shoe Shining, Like Ice Cream Chair, 1904 | 450.00 |
| **Stand,** 1 Drawer, C.1840, Cherry | 275.00 |
| **Stand,** 1 Drawer, Tapered Round Legs, C.1830, 16 X 15 3/4 X 29 In. | 95.00 |
| **Stand,** 1 Drawer, Tiger Cherry | 325.00 |
| **Stand,** 1 Drawer, Walnut, Miniature | 400.00 |
| **Stand,** 2 Drawer, Inlaid, All Original, Shaker | 1500.00 |
| **Step Chest,** C.1850, Cherry | 850.00 |
| **Stool,** Covered, Victorian, Walnut | 22.00 |
| **Stool,** Ice Cream | 37.50 |
| **Stool,** Mahogany, George II, Drop-In Seat, Cabriole Legs, 23 In. | 1500.00 |
| **Stool,** Milk, 3-Legged, Gray Paint | 24.00 |

Furniture, Stand, Plant, Adjustable,
C.1875, Iron, 4 Ft. 5 In.

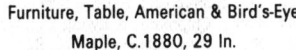

Furniture, Table, American & Bird's-Eye
Maple, C.1880, 29 In.

| | | |
|---|---|---:|
| **Stool,** Milking, 9 1/2 X 18 1/2 In.Long | | 8.50 |
| **Stool,** Oak Joined, Charles I, Plant Top, Baluster Legs, 20 In. | | 380.00 |
| **Stool,** Organ, Black Horsehair Cover, C.1870 | | 39.00 |
| **Stool,** Organ, Glass Ball Feet | | 45.00 |
| **Stool,** Piano, Adjustable, Swivel Type, Glass Ball Feet | | 85.00 |
| **Stool,** Piano, Oak, Iron, Glass Claw Feet | | 265.00 |
| **Stool,** Primitive, Stamped J.S.Noyes, Red & Black Paint, 11 X 6 In. | | 55.00 |
| **Stool,** Shoeshine, Bent Wire | | 37.00 |
| **Stool,** Wicker, White, 1o X 13 In.Diam. | | 35.00 |
| **Stool,** 4-Legged, Enfield, Conn., Shaker | | 185.00 |
| **Sugar Chest,** Dovetailed Pine, Flat Top, 6 X 2 X 3 1/2 Ft. | | 275.00 |
| **Swing,** Child's, Porch, Victorian | | 95.00 |
| **Swing,** Porch, Wicker, Natural | | 400.00 |
| **Table & Chair,** Child's, C.1880, Red Paint, 13 7/8 X 13 7/8 In. | | 65.00 |
| **Table,** Adirondack Twig, 12 X 12 X 24 In. | | 65.00 |
| **Table,** American & Bird's-Eye Maple, C.1880, 29 In. | *Illus* | 350.00 |
| **Table,** Baking, 1 Drawer, Pine Top, Oak Legs | | 95.00 |
| **Table,** Bread Making, Homemade | | 145.00 |
| **Table,** Breakfast, Piecrust Tilt Top, American, C.1700, 27 3/4 In. | | 1200.00 |
| **Table,** Butcher Block, 18 X 31 In. | | 100.00 |
| **Table,** Card, Duncan Phyfe Style | | 185.00 |
| **Table,** Card, Flip Top, Inlaid Ebony, C.1865, Rosewood, 2 1/2 X 3 Ft. | | 550.00 |
| **Table,** Card, George III, Serpentine Folding Top, Mahogany, 40 In. | | 3500.00 |
| **Table,** Card, Greco-Roman Revival, C.1815, Mahogany, 37 X 30 In. | | 800.00 |
| **Table,** Card, Hepplewhite, Swing Legs, Tiger & Regular Maple, C.1810 | | 750.00 |
| **Table,** Card, Inlaid, Serpentine Ends, C.1790, Massachusetts, 29 In. | | 4500.00 |
| **Table,** Card, New Hampshire, String Inlay, Bird's-Eye Maple | | 950.00 |

**Table,** Card, Oval Center Panel, C.1790, Massachusetts, 36 X 29 In. ........................................ 2100.00
**Table,** Card, Serpentine Shape, Inlay On Skirt, 18 X 36 X 30 In. ........................................... 325.00
**Table,** Card, 1 Swing Leg, Ball Feet, C.1800, Mahogany, 29 1/2 In. ................................. 550.00
**Table,** Card, 1 Swing Reeded Leg, Lunette Inlay, Boston ............................................... 3100.00
**Table,** Carved Teak, Chinese, 19th Century ............................................................. 500.00
**Table,** Child's, 2 Chairs, Oak ......................................................................... 125.00
**Table,** Chippendale, Birch, New England, C.1770, 35 In. ........................................... *Illus* 850.00
**Table,** Claw Feet, Round, Oak ......................................................................... 1500.00
**Table,** Console, Empire, Claw Feet, Mahogany, C.1840, Marble Top ............................ 650.00
**Table,** Console, Italian Rococo, Gilt Wood, 3 X 3 1/4 Ft., Pair ................................ 6250.00
**Table,** Console, 5-Legged Support, Tiger Maple & Cherry .................................... 650.00
**Table,** Country Chippendale, 1-Board Top, C.1770, Original Paint ............................. 1350.00
**Table,** Crop Leaf, Federal, Acanthus Legs, C.1830, 48 X 70 In. ........................... 525.00
**Table,** Dice, Built-In Chip Rack, B.C.Wills Co., C.1950, 4 X 8 Ft. ...................... 975.00
**Table,** Dining, Chippendale, Swing Leg, New England, Birch ................................ 445.00
**Table,** Dining, Drop Leaves, C.1770, Boston, Walnut, 49 X 29 In. ...................... 550.00
**Table,** Dining, Federal, American, C.1795, Birch ............................................... 425.00
**Table,** Dining, Gateleg, George II, Cloven Feet, Mahogany, 59 In. .................... 800.00
**Table,** Dining, Queen Anne, Drop Leaf, American, C.1760, 27 3/4 In. ............... 1700.00
**Table,** Dining, Round Pedestal, Claw Feet, 5 Leaves, Square, Oak .................... 525.00
**Table,** Dining, Thumb-Molded, C.1845, Mahogany, 2 Ft. 5 In. X 9 Ft. .............. 900.00
**Table,** Dining, 5 Legs, 2 Leaves, C.1910, G.Stickley, 48 In. ............................. 450.00
**Table,** Dining, 6 Leaves, Pedestal Base, Oak, G.Stickley, 54 In. ...................... 3250.00
**Table,** Dining, 6 Square Legs, C.1770, 40 1/2 X 51 X 28 1/2 In. ...................... 500.00
**Table,** Dough, Shaker, Alfred, Maine ........................................................... 365.00
**Table,** Dressing, Inlaid Mahogany, George III, 32 In. ....................................... 650.00
**Table,** Dressing, Sheraton, Original Varnish, Pine .......................................... 175.00
**Table,** Dressing, Yellow, Stenciled, Original Hardware, C.1810 ........................ 1250.00
**Table,** Drop Leaf, Acanthus Legs, Mahogany, C.1850, 28 X 52 In. .................. 225.00
**Table,** Drop Leaf, American, C.1795, Tiger Maple, 46 In.Square ...................... 1150.00
**Table,** Drop Leaf, Breadboard Ends, Pine, 7 Ft. ........................................... 1100.00
**Table,** Drop Leaf, C.1790, Tiger Stripe Maple, 42 X 21 1/2 X 29 In. ............... 1150.00
**Table,** Drop Leaf, C.1820, Birch .............................................................. 245.00
**Table,** Drop Leaf, Cabriole Legs, C.1730, Mahogany, 42 X 40 In. ................... 5200.00
**Table,** Drop Leaf, Cherry & Burl Maple ....................................................... 285.00
**Table,** Drop Leaf, Dovetailed Drawer ........................................................... 250.00
**Table,** Drop Leaf, Ireland, C.1750, Mahogany, 63 X 46 In. ............................ 700.00
**Table,** Drop Leaf, Marlboro Legs, New England, C.1780, 27 3/4 In. ................ 1100.00
**Table,** Drop Leaf, Pine, 72 In. ................................................................. 500.00
**Table,** Drop Leaf, Red Paint, Pine ............................................................. 225.00
**Table,** Drop Leaf, Scalloped Top Edge, Queen Anne Legs, C.1890 ................. 350.00
**Table,** Drop Leaf, Shaker, For Hancock Community Use, Cherry ..................... 1200.00
**Table,** Drop Leaf, Trestle Ends, L. & J.G.Stickley, 41 3/4 In.Diam. ............... 1200.00
**Table,** Drop Leaf, 1 Drawer, Walnut ......................................................... 375.00
**Table,** Drop Leaf, 18th Century, Mahogany, Open, 38 In.Diam. .................... 1850.00

Furniture, Table, Chippendale, Birch,
New England, C.1770, 35 In.

**Table,** Drum Top, Biedermeier, Walnut, Hexagonal Pedestal, 24 In. ........................... 1300.00
**Table,** Drum, Chippendale, Leather Top, American, 34 X 28 1/2 In. ........................... 200.00
**Table,** Empire, Marble Top, Ebonized, 3 Ft. 7 In. X 2 1/2 Ft. ........................... 4250.00
**Table,** End, Federal, Scalloped Apron, Medial Shelf & Drawer ........................... 200.00
**Table,** English Pub, Pullout Leaves, C.1910 ........................... 285.00
**Table,** Faro, Brunswick, Balke & Collender, Walnut ........................... 1200.00
**Table,** Faro, Gambling, Claw Feet, Covered, Tonapa Nevada ........................... 975.00
**Table,** French, Marquetry, C.1860 ........................... 395.00
**Table,** Galle, Inlaid Wood, Shield Shape Top, 3 Legs, Poem On Top ........................... 875.00
**Table,** Galle, Nest, Oak, Sycamore, & Fruitwoods, Signed ........................... 4000.00
**Table,** Game, Double Lift Top, Backgammon & Other Board, C.1730 ........................... 4750.00
**Table,** Game, Stenciled, C.A.Baudouine, 2 Ft. 2 In. X 1 Ft. 10 In. ........................... 300.00
**Table,** Game, Tilt Top, Carved, Artist Signed, Hardwood ........................... 750.00
**Table,** Gateleg, William & Mary, 1 Drawer, Walnut, 29 X 31 In. ........................... 1100.00
**Table,** George III, 2 Tier, Revolving, Mahogany, 24 X 36 In. ........................... 850.00
**Table,** Gilt Bronze, Mahogany & Rosewood, Paris, 2 1/3 X 2 3/4 Ft. ........................... 4000.00
**Table,** Glass, Radiating Wheat Sheaths Molding, Pyramid Base, Ovoid ........................... 7500.00
**Table,** Handcrafted, 1820s, English Mahogany, 30 X 33 X 19 In. ........................... 400.00
**Table,** Hutch, Red Finish, Maine, C.1800, 42 X 42 X 27 1/2 In. ........................... 1500.00
**Table,** Hutch, 2-Board Top, Shoe Feet, 19th Century, American ........................... 1100.00
**Table,** Inset Leather Drum Top, 12 Drawers, 52 In. ........................... *Illus* 2500.00
**Table,** Kitchen, 1 Drawer, C.1875, Pine ........................... 185.00
**Table,** Leather Topped, 6 Legs, G.Stickley, C.1905, Oak, 48 X 29 In. ........................... 4500.00
**Table,** Library, Brass & Glass Claw Feet, Golden Oak ........................... 350.00
**Table,** Library, C.1875, Rosewood & Maple, 28 1/2 X 44 In. ........................... 2000.00
**Table,** Library, Marble Top, Victorian ........................... 575.00
**Table,** Library, Ornately Carved, Solid Walnut ........................... 800.00
**Table,** Library, 2 Drawer, C.1900, Oak, G.Stickley, 29 In. ........................... 750.00
**Table,** Lift Top, 1 Drawer, Zoar ........................... 650.00
**Table,** Mahogany, American, C.1840, 31 X 35 In. ........................... *Illus* 500.00
**Table,** Marble Top, Bronze Center, C.1894, Tiffany, 2 Ft. 5 In. ........................... 4750.00
**Table,** Napoleonic, Painted Porcelain Corners, 21 X 29 In. ........................... 3500.00
**Table,** Nightstand, Sheraton, 2 Drawer, Glass Pulls, Mahogany ........................... 375.00
**Table,** Oak, Square, 48 In. ........................... 225.00
**Table,** Occasional, 8 Turned Legs, Spider Shaped, Mahogany ........................... 150.00
**Table,** Paw Feet, Porcelain Painted Scene Insert, Oriental, 23 In. ........................... 895.00
**Table,** Pedestal, Golden Oak, Round, Scroll Legs, 5 Leaves, 58 In. ........................... 2000.00

Furniture, Table, Inset Leather Drum Top,
12 Drawers, 52 In.

Furniture, Table, Mahogany, American,
C.1840, 31 X 35 In.

**Table,** Pembroke, Inlay, C.1895, Mahogany ............................................................ 435.00
**Table,** Pembroke, Mahogany, George III, Satinwood, 39 1/2 In. ........................... 1300.00
**Table,** Pembroke, New England, C.1795, Cherry, 32 1/2 In.Square ...................... 750.00
**Table,** Pier, Satinwood, Semicircular, George III, 50 1/2 In. ................................. 2000.00
**Table,** Plank Top, Pine, 36 X 52 In. ...................................................................... 195.00
**Table,** Pub, Draw Leaves, 4-Legged, English ........................................................ 265.00
**Table,** Pub, Trestle, Pullout Leaves, English Oak, C.1910 ..................................... 285.00
**Table,** Sewing, Mother-Of-Pearl Inlaid Papier-Mache, Octagonal .......................... 850.00
**Table,** Sewing, Victorian, 2 Drawer, Curly Maple .................................................. 185.00
**Table,** Sheraton, Drop Leaf, Reeded Legs, 1 Drawer, Cherry ................................ 375.00
**Table,** Side, Marble Top, Gilt Bronze, Durand & Cie, Paris, 2 Ft., Pr. ................... 4000.00
**Table,** Side, Oak, George II, Queen Anne Style, Pad Feet, 43 In. ......................... 850.00
**Table,** Snooker, Brunswick, Balke, Collender, C.1890 ........................................... 2800.00
**Table,** Snooker, Brunswick, Balke, Collender, 5 X 10 Ft. ...................................... 2800.00
**Table,** Splay Leg, Dated 1750-1850, New England, Maple ..................................... 5800.00
**Table,** Tap, 1 Board, Turned Legs, Shaker, Small ................................................. 275.00
**Table,** Tavern, Breadboard Top, Overlapping Drawer, Pegged, C.1800 .................. 1250.00
**Table,** Tavern, William & Mary, New England, Pine & Maple, 26 In. ...................... 2000.00
**Table,** Tavern, 1 Drawer, New England, Birch & Pine, 27 1/2 X 32 In. .................. 950.00
**Table,** Tea, Beaded Legs, Beige Paint, C.1770, Maple, 25 3/4 X 28 In. ................. 1200.00
**Table,** Tea, Dish Top, Chippendale, Mahogany, 29 In.Diam. ................................. 1275.00
**Table,** Tea, Oriental, Round ................................................................................... 90.00
**Table,** Tea, Pad Feet, Virginia, C.1740, English Walnut ....................................... 3500.00
**Table,** Tea, Pennsylvania, 1760-1810, Chestnut & Pine ........................................ 2150.00
**Table,** Tea, Porringer Top, C.1730, Walnut, 22 1/2 X 33 1/2 In. .......................... 4000.00
**Table,** Tea, Tilt Top Birdcage, Cherry, 1800s, 33 In.Diam. ................................... 950.00
**Table,** Tea, Tip-Top, 18th Century, Mahogany, 31 X 31 X 27 1/2 In. .................... 550.00
**Table,** Tea, 2 Candle Slides, 2 Drawer, Brass Gallery, French .............................. 350.00
**Table,** Tilt Top, Birdcage Base, Square ................................................................. 195.00
**Table,** Tilt Top, C.1840, Cherry ............................................................................. 275.00
**Table,** Tilt Top, New Hampshire, Oval, Spider Legs ............................................... 525.00
**Table,** Tilt Top, 18th Century, Mahogany, 28 In. ................................................... 900.00
**Table,** Tip-Top, Dish Edge, American, Cherry ........................................................ 1250.00
**Table,** Wicker, 20 X 16 X 24 In. ............................................................................ 35.00
**Table,** Work, Federal, Square Tray Top, C.1820, 18 X 19 1/2 In. .......................... 275.00
**Table,** Work, Inlaid Walnut, C.1860, 5 Ft.5 1/2 In. X 2 1/2 Ft. ............................. 950.00
**Table,** Work, Serpentine Outline, Canted Corners, C.1800, Mahogany .................. 1450.00
**Table,** Writing, Mahogany, George III, Sham Drawers, 48 In. ................................ 3000.00
**Table,** Writing, Pedestal, Walnut, Victorian, 6 Drawers, 63 In. .............................. 900.00
**Table,** 2 Drawer, Stretcher Base, 18th Century, Pine ........................................... 1750.00
**Table,** 2 Small Drawers, English Mahogany, 33 X 19 X 30 In. ............................... 400.00
**Table,** 3 Plank, Breadboard Ends, Pine, 72 X 39 In. ............................................. 695.00
**Table,** 3-Tiered, Wicker ......................................................................................... 89.00
**Table,** 5 Leg, Quartered Oak Top, Oak, Square ..................................................... 200.00
**Table,** 5 Original Leaves, Oak, Square ................................................................... 565.00
**Table,** 6 Leg, Claw Feet, Oak, Square ................................................................... 275.00
**Table,** 6 Leg, Walnut, 48 X 69 In. ......................................................................... 850.00
**Tabouret,** L. & J.G.Stickley, C.1910, Oak ........................................... 40.00 To 60.00
**Tea Caddy,** Filigree Paper, Shell, Mahogany, 6 1/2 In. ......................................... 1800.00
**Tea Caddy,** Partridgewood, Marquetry, George III, 12 1/2 In. .............................. 300.00
**Tea Cart,** Child's, 2 Shelves, Wicker ..................................................................... 150.00
**Tea Cart,** Glass Tray, Large Wheels, 1920s, Cherry ............................................. 175.00
**Tea Cart,** Wicker, Wood Wheels, Glass Tray ........................................................ 250.00
**Tray,** Art Deco, Wicker Frame, H.H.Morson, 10 X 15 In. ...................................... 150.00
**Tray,** Butler's, Folding Stand, Oval, George IV, 39 In. .......................................... 500.00
**Tray,** Knife, Federal, 2 Compartments, Dovetailed, C.1790, 16 1/2 In. .................. 175.00
**Umbrella Stand,** Mirror, Hat Hooks, Walnut ......................................................... 500.00
**Urn Stand,** Egyptian Design, American, C.1873, 3 Ft. 3 In., Pair .......................... 1000.00
**Urn,** Knife, Regency, Hardwood, C.1840, 25 In., Pair ........................................... 1000.00
**Wall Shelf,** Carved, 1 Drawer, Walnut .................................................................. 200.00
**Wardrobe,** C.1810, Fruitwood ............................................................................... 550.00
**Wardrobe,** Corner, Chestnut, C.1860 .................................................................... 450.00
**Wardrobe,** Crest, Walnut, Large ............................................................................ 650.00

Wardrobe, Crown Molding, 2 Dovetailed Drawers, C.1865, Walnut .......................................... 900.00
Wardrobe, Mirrored Door & Drawer In Bottom, Oak ......................................................... 345.00
Wardrobe, Walnut, 7 Ft. ...................................................................................................... 350.00
Wardrobe, 1700s, Pine, 50 X 20 X 69 In. ...................................................................... 1600.00
Washstand, American Empire, 2 Drawer, Milk Glass Knobs, 29 In. ...................................... 175.00
Washstand, Bow Drawer, Lyre Towel Rack, Oak ............................................................... 165.00
Washstand, Corner, C.1840, Mahogany ............................................................................ 475.00
Washstand, Corner, Federal, C.1790, New England, 39 1/2 X 22 In. .................................. 350.00
Washstand, Drawer In Bottom, Poplar ............................................................................... 175.00
Washstand, Marble Top, Brass Hardware, Tile Back, Mahogany ........................................... 185.00
Washstand, Marble Top, 4 Drawers, 2 Cupboards, Tile Back, 54 In. .................................... 495.00
Washstand, Mirror & Towel Bar, Oak ................................................................................ 195.00
Washstand, Side Towel Bars, C.1898, Oak ........................................................................ 110.00
Washstand, Splash Back, Medial Drawer, C.1810, Mahogany, 20 In. .................................. 500.00
Washstand, Splash Bar, 3 Drawer, Oak ............................................................................. 175.00
Washstand, Tile Back-Splash, Walnut & Maple .................................................................. 325.00
Washstand, Towel Bar, Ash ............................................................................................... 125.00
Washstand, Towel Bar, Oak ............................................................................................... 175.00
Washstand, Victorian, Grained Design ............................................................................... 105.00
Whatnot Shelf, Design, Black Lacquer, 9 In.Wide ............................................................... 25.00
Wheelchair, Cane Back, Seat & Foot Rests, Label ............................................................. 125.00
Wine Cooler, Walnut, George I, Octangular Top, Drawer, 18 In. ........................................ 3500.00

FURSTENBERG, Tray, Handled, Bouquets, Butterflies, C.1765, Marked, 15 1/2 In. ............... 350.00
Vase, Rose Finial On Cover, C.1770, Marked, 15 1/2 In. .................................................... 950.00

 Galle glass was made by the Galle factory founded in 1874 by Emile
Galle of France. The firm made cameo glass, furniture, and other
Art Nouveau items, including some pottery. After Galle's
death in 1904, the firm continued in production until 1935.

GALLE POTTERY, Figurine, Cat, Medallion, Signed, 13 In. ................................................ Illus 1000.00
Pitcher, Art Nouveau Shape, Earth Tones, Signed, 7 1/4 In. ............................................... 950.00
Vase, Old Town Scene, Bird, Flowers, Signed Galle, Nancy, 6 In. ....................................... 475.00

GALLE, Bonbon, Lid, Enameled, Ribbons, Blossoms, & Bees, Signed, 5 X 7 1/4 In. ............... 1085.00
Bowl, Ball Form, Pink Overlay, Cut Fuchsia, C.1905, Signed, 5 3/4 In. ............................... 725.00
Bowl, Brown, Berry Branches, Butterflies, Canoe Shape, Signed, 26 In. ............................... 1500.00
Bowl, Flower Form Top, Flowers, Yellow Frosted Ground, 7 X 4 1/2 In. ............................... 1500.00
Bowl, Oval Basket, Inverted Rim, Floral Decoration, Gilt Rim, 10 In. .................................. 315.00
Box, Covered, 2 Color, Lid & Base Signed, 6 X 3 In. ......................................................... 775.00

Galle Pottery, Figurine, Cat, Medallion, Signed, 13 In.

Centerpiece, Blue Body, Pink, Blue & White Thistles, Signed, 12 In. ..................... 1800.00
Cordial, Little Boy Blowing Bubbles, Crystal & Enamel, Signed, 5 In. ..................... 275.00
Cordial, Six Frogs Jumping, Crystal & Enamel, Signed, 5 In. ............................... 350.00
Cup & Saucer, Enameled, Signed .......................................................... 345.00
Cup & Saucer, Topaz, Enameled Insects, Signed, Set Of 6 .............................. 2000.00
Decanter, Enameled, Green Ribbed, Applied Rope Handle, Signed, 13 In. ............ 1295.00
Ewer, Ribbed Form, Handle, Etched Leaf Design, Signed, 19th Century ............... 250.00
Glass, Frosted Ground, Orange Flowers & Leaves, Signed, 1 1/2 In. ................... 295.00
Glass, Shot, Amber Crystal, Multicolor Enamel, Signed, 2 In. ........................... 185.00
Jardiniere, Green & Brown Etched, Forest, Lake, Cameo Signed, 11 In. .............. 1100.00
Lamp, Birds In Flight, Scenic Base, Yellow Ground, 15 In. ............................... 7500.00
Lamp, Flowers, Mushroom Shade, Signed, 24 In. ......................................... 9500.00
Light, Night, Red, Gold Ground ............................................................ 1750.00
Rose Bowl, Floral, Frost & Gold, Purple-Brown Flowers, 3 1/2 In. ...................... 450.00
Rose Bowl, Thistle Pattern, Rose & White, Chartreuse, 2 1/2 In. ....................... 395.00
Vase, Amber & Pink Wildflowers, Signed, 5 In. ........................................... 550.00
Vase, Amber, Yellow, Grape Leaves & Grapes, Signed, C.1910, 18 In. ................ 1100.00
Vase, Amethyst Leaves, 4 In. ............................................................... 295.00
Vase, Banjo Shape, Peach, Mauve Floral Design, 6 1/2 In. .............................. 825.00
Vase, Banjo Shape, Scenic, 4 Colors, Trees Reflected In Water, 6 In. .................. 625.00
Vase, Bird & Flowers, 2 Ladies Marketing, Old Town Scene, 6 In. ...................... 475.00
Vase, Blooming Flowers & Foliage, Lemon Frosted Ground, 7 3/4 In. .................. 695.00
Vase, Blown-Out Clematis, Signed, 9 1/2 In. ............................................. 6400.00
Vase, Blue, Green, Purple, Mountain & Trees, Pear Shaped, 8 In. ...................... 975.00
Vase, Brown Flowers In 2 Layers, Pink To Frosted Ground, 6 1/2 In. ................... 695.00
Vase, Brown Grapevine, Pink & Yellow Ground, Signed, 3 1/2 In. ...................... 425.00
Vase, Brown, Bud, Flowers, Yellow Ground, Signed, 5 In. ............................... 495.00
Vase, Brown, Tan, Yellow, White, Landscapes, 6 In. ..................................... 1220.00
Vase, Bud, Cylindrical, Yellow & Pink, C.1910, Signed, 6 5/8 In. ...................... 450.00
Vase, Bud, Flat Sided, Cut With Phlox & Leaf, C.1910, Signed, 8 In. .................. 600.00
Vase, Bud, Multicolor Greens, Yellows, & Apricot, Foliage, 3 1/2 In. .................. 475.00
Vase, Bud, Pink & Green Sides, Green Berries, Signed, 4 In. ........................... 300.00
Vase, Bullet Shape Of Landscape, Mountains & Lakes, 7 1/4 In. ....................... 950.00
Vase, Bullet Shape, Delphiniums, Frosted Yellow Ground, 14 1/2 In. .................. 1375.00
Vase, Cascading Wisteria, Lavender Blossoms, Pink Ground, 12 3/8 In. ............... 3850.00
Vase, Chrysanthemums, Double Spout Lip, 6 X 14 In. ................................... 1950.00
Vase, Cobalt Beetle Flying Over Leaves, Blue Ground, Signed, 5 1/4 In. .............. 2850.00
Vase, Crescent Shaped Top, Orange Flowers, Frosted, Signed, 5 1/2 In. .............. 595.00
Vase, Cut & Polished Floral Design, Multicolored, Signed, 6 In. ........................ 450.00
Vase, Deep Cut Orange Floral On Frosted, Signed, 2 1/2 In. ............................ 385.00
Vase, Enameled Blossoms, Acid Icicles At Rim, Clear, Signed, 6 In. ................... 750.00
Vase, Enameled Thistles, Lug Handles, C.1889, 12 X 15 In. ............................ 1250.00
Vase, Flared Base & Top, Amber & Yellow, Signed, C.1910, 18 In. ..................... 1100.00
Vase, Flared Rim, Flattened Body, Cut Floral, C.1910, Signed, 6 5/8 In. .............. 450.00
Vase, Flared, Brown Base, Cone Shape, Frosted Ground, 16 1/2 In. ................... 1200.00
Vase, Flat Sided Body, Cut Phlox Design, Signed, C.1910, 8 In. ....................... 600.00
Vase, Flower Design, Caramel, Pink Frosted Ground, Signed, 6 1/2 In. ............... 995.00
Vase, Flowers & Leaves, White, Purple, & Yellow, 9 1/2 In. ............................. 875.00
Vase, Flowers Cut In 2 Layers, Frosted, Signed, 6 1/4 In. .............................. 575.00
Vase, Frosted Body, Rose Floral & Butterfly, 3 Cut Layers, 11 In. ...................... 975.00
Vase, Frosted Green To Orange, Signed, 3 3/4 In. ....................................... 450.00
Vase, Frosted Lemon Ground, Flowers, Rust, Lavender, Bulbous, 3 In. ............... 385.00
Vase, Frosted Lime-Green, Blue & Brown Overlaid, Orchids, Signed .................. 1200.00
Vase, Fruiting Grapevine, Rust-Red, Yellow Ground, Signed, 11 In. ................... 4500.00
Vase, Ginkgo Trees, Lake & Mountains, Pedestal, Signed, 6 1/2 In. ................... 985.00
Vase, Gray & Green Water Lilies, 3 Color, C.1910, Signed, 6 1/8 In. .................. 400.00
Vase, Green & Brown Trees, Orange Ground, Signed, 4 In. ............................. 875.00
Vase, Green Ground, Brown Etched Plants, Signed, 6 In. ............................... 750.00
Vase, Green Leaves, Pink & White Frosted Ground, 5 X 3 In. ........................... 595.00
Vase, Green Leaves, Stems, Acorns, Pink & White Frosted, Signed, 5 In. ............ 595.00
Vase, Lavender, Purple & Green Floral On Clear, Pink Body, Signed ................... 385.00
Vase, Leaves, Flowers, Vines, Clear To Yellow, Signed, 17 1/2 In. .................... 1295.00
Vase, Lemon-Yellow Sides, Brown Blossoms, Ovoid, Signed, 4 In. .................... 400.00

Vase, Maroon Berries & Leaves On Yellow, 4 1/4 In. .................................................. 395.00
Vase, Maroon On Green Ground, 3 Layers, Signed, 13 In. ....................................... 900.00
Vase, Mauve Flowers, Frosted Peach, Globular Base, 6 In. ...................................... 775.00
Vase, Orange & Amber Frosted, Leaves, Berries, 3 1/2 In. ...................................... 425.00
Vase, Orange & Red Flowers, 5 In. ......................................................................... 465.00
Vase, Orange Floral, Frosted Ground, Signed, 3 3/4 In. ........................................... 375.00
Vase, Orange Leaves, Frosted Ground, Signed, 4 In. .............................................. 415.00
Vase, Paneled Neck, Pink To Clear, Frosted Matte, Signed, 4 In. ............................. 895.00
Vase, Peach Body, 2 Layer Pine Boughs, Amber & Green, 6 1/2 In. ......................... 675.00
Vase, Pedestal, Ivy Design, Green, Signed, 9 In. ................................................... 750.00
Vase, Pilgrim, Amethyst Flowers, 7 In. .................................................................. 700.00
Vase, Pink, Frosted Ground, Gray Bamboo, Signed, 6 1/2 In. .................................. 345.00
Vase, Plum Colored Acorns & Foliage, Yellow Ground, Signed, 15 In. ..................... 3600.00
Vase, Polished Berries & Leaves Allover, Gold & Orange, 6 X 13 In. ........................ 1250.00
Vase, Purple Berries & Leaves, Frosted Ground, 4 In. ............................................ 325.00
Vase, Purple Floral On Yellowish Ground, Signed, 5 In. .......................................... 375.00
Vase, Purple Flowers, Frost & Gold Ground, 5 3/4 In. ............................................. 565.00
Vase, Purple Flowers, Frosted Glass, Narrow Neck, Flared Top, 6 1/4 In. ................. 575.00
Vase, Purple Leaves, Yellow Ground, Signed, 4 In. ................................................ 475.00
Vase, Red Amber On Camphor, Flowers & Buds, 10 In. ......................................... 750.00
Vase, Red Berries, Stems On Front, Leaf On Back, Signed, 6 1/2 In. ....................... 475.00
Vase, Red, Gold, Burgundy, Pedestaled, 6 In. ....................................................... 850.00
Vase, Reddish-Brown, Opaque, Orange Ground, 5 1/4 In. ...................................... 550.00
Vase, Scenic Wheel Cut, Ginkgo Trees, Mountains, Signed, 6 1/2 In. ...................... 985.00
Vase, Seven Boats Around Vase, Blue Sea & Sky, Signed, 5 1/4 In. ........................ 2450.00
Vase, Shocking Pink, Orange & Amber Flowers, 5 1/8 In. ...................................... 550.00
Vase, Shrimp, Greens, 18 In. ............................................................................... 1700.00
Vase, Stick, Banjo Shape, Green, Rose, & White, Deep Cutting, 7 In. ...................... 525.00
Vase, Stick, Banjo Shape, Pink Ground, Gray Bamboo, Signed, 6 In. ....................... 345.00
Vase, Stick, Lavender Flowers On White, Silver Collar, Green, 3 1/2 In. ................... 445.00
Vase, Stick, Red To Orange, Signed, 3 3/4 In. ....................................................... 575.00
Vase, Stick, Vine & Leaf, 3 Shades Of Green & White, 23 1/2 In. ............................ 1450.00
Vase, Stick, 3 Color, Pink Base, Flared Top, 12 1/2 In. ........................................... 1200.00
Vase, Water Lilies, Pink & Purple, 9 1/2 In. ........................................................... 1100.00
Vase, White, Purple, & Yellow, Flowers, 9 1/2 In. .................................................. 875.00
Vase, Windowpane See-Through Flower, Gold, Purple, Blue, & Brown, 10 In. ........... 1450.00
Vase, Yellow, Gray, Green, Water Lilies, Signed, C.1910, 6 1/8 In. ......................... 400.00
Vase, 3-Color Woodland Scene, 4 Cuttings, Green To Yellow, 7 3/4 In. ................... 1200.00
Wine, Amber, Crystal, Boy & Girl, Signed, 4 3/4 In. ............................................... 250.00

*Game plates are any type of plate decorated with pictures of birds, animals, or fish. The game plates usually came in sets consisting of twelve dishes and a serving platter. These game plates were most popular during the 1880s.*

GAME PLATE, Gold Rococo Border, Gold Encrusted Jewels Each Side, Signed ........ 85.00
Grouse, Bavaria, Signed, 9 In. ............................................................................ 25.00
Hunting Dogs, Limoges, Signed ......................................................................... 75.00

GAME SET, Scalloped, Hand-Painted Birds, 12 Plates, Platter 16 In. ....................... 175.00
GAME, see also Disneyana, Game; Lone Ranger, Game; Popeye,
    Game
GAME, Ally Oop, 1937, Complete With Directions ................................................. 12.00
Alphabet, Campbell Kids ................................................................................... 16.00
American Jack Straws, C.1910, Milton Bradley, Original Box ................................ 18.00
Anagrams, Picture Of Mother & Daughter Playing, 1800s, Bradley ...................... 7.00
Answer, Robot, Battery Operated, Amico, Box ................................................... 90.00
Bagatelle, Mickey Mouse, 23 1/2 In. .................................................................. 185.00
Barney Google ................................................................................................. 25.00
Bet Your Life, Groucho Marx, 1955, Boxed ........................................................ 20.00
Bingo, Charlie McCarthy .................................................................................... 18.00
Board, Chess, Brown & Blonde Wood Attached To Fabric, Roll-Up, 10 In. ........... 50.00
Board, Uncle Wiggly ......................................................................................... 12.00
Bonanza, Picture Of Original Cast ...................................................................... 10.00
Bringing Up Father, Book, 1919, 2nd Series ...................................................... 19.00

| | |
|---|---|
| **Calling All Cars,** Original Metal Autos | 10.00 |
| **Captain Video,** Space Game | 25.00 |
| **Card,** Playing, Movie Star, 1916 | 85.00 |
| **Challenger,** Shooting | 125.00 |
| **Charlie McCarthy Radio Party,** 1938 | 30.00 |
| **Checkerboard,** Blue, Red, & Yellow, Primitive | 190.00 |
| **Checkerboard,** Reverse Painted Tinsel | 110.00 |
| **Checkers,** Standard Oil | 8.50 |
| **Chess Set,** Boxwood Pieces, Inside Divider, Mahogany Box | 52.00 |
| **Chess Set,** Boxwood, Original Mahogany Box, English | 50.00 |
| **Chess Set,** Florentine, Gold & Silver Plated | 125.00 |
| **Chessboard,** Brown & Blonde Wood, Roll-Up, Fabric, 13 In. | 18.00 |
| **Chinese Checker,** Board, Akro Agate Marbles, Boxed | 25.00 |
| **Chiromagica,** Magnetic Question-Answer, 1870s, McLoughlin Bros. | 145.00 |
| **Cinderella,** Cloth, 1896, Selchon & Righter's | 50.00 |
| **Circus Shooting Gallery,** Ohio Art | 25.00 |
| **Coming Home,** Mickey Mouse, C.1930 | 25.00 |
| **Cowboy,** C.1889, Chaffee & Selchow | 18.00 |
| **Cowboy,** Chaffee & Selchow, 1898 | 18.00 |
| **Cows In The Corn,** Parker Brothers, C.1930 | 30.00 |
| **Cribbage Board,** Cast Iron | 65.00 |
| **Cribbage Board,** Permanent Brass Pegs, Cast Iron, 10 1/2 X 3 3/4 In. | 100.00 |
| **Cribbage Board,** Veneer Inlay In Light, Medium, & Dark Pieces, 2 X 9 In. | 18.00 |
| **Cribbage,** Original Wooden Box, Dated 1879 | 45.00 |
| **Derby Classic,** Horse Racing, Board | 13.00 |
| **Dominoes,** Brass Pegged Bone & Ebony, Wooden Box, C.1900, 28 Piece | 38.00 |
| **Dominoes,** Ivory & Ebony, 27 Pieces | 36.00 |
| **Dominoes,** Ivory, Miniature, Boxed, Set Of 28 | 30.00 |
| **Dominoes,** To Double 6, Ebony, Ivory, Brass Pegged, Wooden Box | 25.00 |
| **Drew Pearson's Predict A Word** | 6.00 |
| **Fan-Tel Fortune Telling,** 1937, Schoenhut | 10.00 |
| **Faro,** Dealing Box, Will & Finck, San Francisco | 750.00 |
| **Fibber McGee,** 1940, Boxed | 10.00 |
| **Fish Pond,** McLaughlin, Original Box | 65.00 |
| **Fishing Party,** Cloth, 1916, Saalfield | 45.00 |
| **Football,** Bernie Bierman's | 20.00 |
| **Foxy Grandpa,** Wood Carrying Box | 25.00 To 32.00 |
| **Gard,** Shakespeare, Instructions, 1901 | 12.50 |
| **Gee-Whiz Horse Race,** Operates On Flywheel, Bouncing Balls, Boxed | 95.00 |
| **Gilbert Problem Puzzles,** Atomic Bomb Game, Boxed | 60.00 |
| **Graf Zeppelin,** Freiderichshafen To Lakehurst | 25.00 |
| **Happy Landing,** Airplane, 1938, Transogram | 5.00 |
| **Hearts,** 1916, Parker Brothers | 7.00 |
| **Hickety Pickety,** 1924, Parker Bros. | 5.00 |
| **Hoko,** Catch Ring On Nose Of Santa | 12.00 |
| **Honeymooners,** Gleason | 20.00 |
| **Horseshoe,** Brownie, Palmer Cox | 20.00 |
| **Jack & Jill Jungle Jinks** | 60.00 |
| **Jack Pot,** Buffalo Toy Co., Oak & Tin | 95.00 |
| **Jigsaw,** Victor Talking Machine, C.1910 | 60.00 |
| **Kings & Quoits,** McLoughlan Bros., 1891 | 10.00 |
| **Library Of Games,** Snow White, Old Maid, Authors, Etc. | 35.00 |
| **Little Black Sambo** | 20.00 |
| **Lotto,** Milton Bradley | 7.50 |
| **Mah Jong,** Ivory Sticks, Wooden Tiles, Tin Box | 40.00 |
| **Mah Jong,** 5 Drawers, Wooden Tiles, Celluloid Strips, Dice, Boxed | 35.00 |
| **Major Bowes' Amateur Hour,** 1930s, Boxed | 15.00 |
| **Parcheesi,** 1935 | 8.00 |
| **Penny Challenger** | 200.00 |
| **Picture Lotto,** Early | 30.00 |
| **Pitch-Em-Winks** | 13.00 |
| **Popeye Jump-Up,** Wooden | 17.50 |
| **Puzzle Blocks,** Lithograph On Wood, 6 Children, Dated 12-25-1865 | 40.00 |

**Puzzle,** Blocks 6 Different, Wooden Box, C.1915, 6 X 5 In. ........................................ 25.00
**Puzzle,** Captain Marvel, 1941 ........................................ 10.00
**Puzzle,** Child's, Maid Milking Cow, C.1900, 4 Piece ........................................ 6.00
**Puzzle,** Cow, Blocks In Box ........................................ 45.00
**Puzzle,** Dunlop Tires, Hexagon, 1920s ........................................ 17.00
**Puzzle,** Firestone Tire World Map ........................................ 9.00
**Puzzle,** Greyhound Line ........................................ 10.00
**Puzzle,** Home Sweet Home, Maggie & Jiggs, C.1932, 7 3/4 X 9 3/4 In. ........................ 20.00
**Puzzle,** Jigsaw, Lux ........................................ 8.00
**Puzzle,** Jigsaw, Peanuts Cartoon Character, Milton Bradley, Dated 1952 ........................ 5.00
**Puzzle,** Our Gang, Marked McKesson & Robbins & Hal Roach, Framed ........................ 30.00
**Puzzle,** The Bug House, Complete In Box ........................................ 4.50
**Puzzle,** Uncle Wiggly ........................................ 6.00
**Puzzle,** Wheatena Advertising ........................................ 9.00
**Puzzle,** 20 Mule Team Borax, 1930 ........................................ 28.00
**Racquets,** Spalding, Bentwood, C.1900 ........................................ 30.00
**Rich Uncle** ........................................ 15.00
**Ring Toss,** Aunt Sally ........................................ 65.00
**Rolling Ball,** Barney Google ........................................ 35.00
**Roulette Wheel,** French, 36 In.Diam. ........................................ 750.00
**Sinking Of The Titanic,** Ideal, Box ........................................ 12.00
**Sleeping Beauty,** Walt Disney, 1958 ........................................ 15.00
**Table,** Roulette, Wheel, H.C.Evans, Claw Feet ........................................ 2600.00
**The Jolly Darkie Target,** 1890s, Lithographed Toss Game, 11 3/4 In. ........................ 150.00
**Today,** Dave Garroway ........................................ 12.00
**Toss,** Black Chuck, Standup, 1890 ........................................ 50.00
**Uncle Wiggly Hat,** Original Envelope ........................................ 30.00
**Uncle Wiggly,** Box & Game Board, 1920s ........................................ 12.00 To 20.00
**Uncle Wiggly,** Boxed ........................................ 14.00
**Wells Fargo** ........................................ 8.00
**Wheel Of Fortune,** Floor Model, Original Paint, 31 In.Diam. ........................ 275.00
**Who Am I,** Pinky Lee ........................................ 18.00

*Gaudy Dutch pottery was made in England for America from about 1810 to*
*1820. It is a white earthenware with Imari style decorations of red, blue,*
*green, yellow, and black. Only sixteen patterns of Gaudy Dutch were made:*
*Butterfly, Carnation, Dahlia, Double Rose, Dove, Grape, Leaf,*
*Oyster, Primrose, Single Rose, Strawflower, Sunflower, Urn,*
*War Bonnet, Zinnia, and No Name. Other similar wares are called*
*Soft Paste, Gaudy Ironstone, or Gaudy Welsh.*

**GAUDY DUTCH, Cup & Saucer,** Grape ........................................ 200.00 To 275.00
**Cup & Saucer,** War Bonnet ........................................ 295.00 To 350.00
**Plate,** Double Rose, 7 1/4 In. ........................................ 300.00
**Plate,** Grape, 7 In. ........................................ 275.00
**Plate,** Grape, 8 1/4 In. ........................................ 300.00
**Plate,** Oyster, 5 3/4 In. ........................................ 350.00
**Plate,** War Bonnet, 9 3/4 In. ........................................ 350.00

**GAUDY IRONSTONE, Bowl,** Eggnog, Transfer Of Birds, C.1870, 6 X 10 In.Diam. ................ 135.00
**Orange,** Purple, & Pink, Gold Trim, 10 In.Diam. ........................................ 65.00
**Pitcher,** Graduated, Set Of 4 ........................................ 425.00
**Pitcher,** Peonies & Green Vegetation, Ribbed Handle, 7 In. ........................ 65.00
**Pitcher,** Tiger Handle, Orange, Blue, Green, Marked, 5 1/2 In. ........................ 125.00
**Plate,** Blinking Eye, Niagara Shape, 1856 Mark, Set Of 6 ........................ 450.00
**Plate,** C.1820, New Stone, 8 In.Diam. ........................................ 45.00
**Plate,** Pink & Orange Flowers, Gold Veining, 10 1/4 In. ........................ 65.00
**Plate,** Pink Chrysanthemum, Blue Leaves, Ridgway, 1814, 10 In. ........................ 70.00
**Platter,** Blue Leaves, Orange Flowers, Marked, 8 X 11 In. ........................ 110.00
**Platter,** Blue, Green & Rose Red, Marked, 15 In.Diam. ........................ 275.00
**Platter,** Oriental Floral Design, C.1850, Marked, 13 In.Diam. ........................ 75.00
**Platter,** Oriental Pond Foliage, Mason's, 17 In.Diam. ........................ 275.00

*Gaudy Welsh is an Imari decorated earthenware with red, blue, green, and gold decorations. It was made after 1820.*

**GAUDY WELSH, Bowl,** Oriental Design, Copper Luster Trim, 6 3/4 In.Diam. ........................... 75.00
**Bowl,** Wagon Wheel, 7 1/2 In.Diam. ................................................................................ 38.00
**Cup & Saucer,** Cobalt Blue, Red, & Green, Copper Luster Trim ........................................ 60.00
**Cup & Saucer,** Columbine ............................................................................................ 35.00
**Cup & Saucer,** Copper Luster, Pink Luster Trim, Set ..................................................... 22.00
**Cup & Saucer,** Demitasse, Oyster Pattern ................................................................... 40.00
**Cup & Saucer,** Feather Design, Set Of 6 ....................................................................... 135.00
**Cup & Saucer,** Rhoda Design, Set Of 6 ........................................................................ 135.00
**Cup & Saucer,** Tulip Pattern, Colored Enamels ............................................................ 55.00
**Cup & Saucer,** Wagon Wheel Pattern ........................................................ 45.00 To 70.00
**Cup & Saucer,** Wildflowers, 19th Century, Cobalt Blue ................................................. 30.00
**Ginger Jar,** Single Jewel, 4 1/2 X 7 In. ....................................................................... 110.00
**Jug,** Soft Paste, Pink Luster Trim, Fruits, C.1800, 5 In. ................................................ 95.00
**Plate,** Columbine Pattern ........................................................................................... 30.00
**Plate,** Nebula Pattern, Blue Border .............................................................................. 38.00
**Plate,** Oyster Pattern, 5 1/2 In. ................................................................................... 35.00
**Plate,** Oyster Pattern, 6 In. ......................................................................................... 35.00
**Plate,** Tulip Pattern .................................................................................................... 20.00
**Plate,** Tulip Pattern, C.1860, 6 In. ............................................................................... 17.50
**Plate,** Wagon Wheel Pattern, 5 1/2 In. ......................................................................... 32.00
**Tea Set,** Child's, Oyster Pattern, Copper Luster Trim, 3 Piece ...................................... 125.00
**Tea Set,** Child's, Oyster Pattern, Purple Luster Rims, 14 Piece ..................................... 450.00
**Tea Set,** Tulip Pattern, 4 Cups & Saucers, C.1850, 11 Piece .......................................... 385.00
**Tea Set,** 4 Cups & Saucers, 4 5 1/2 In.Plates, 15 Piece ................................................. 300.00
**Teapot,** Cobalt & Red ................................................................................................. 55.00
**Tureen,** Footed, Urn Pattern, Cover, 9 1/2 In.Wide ...................................................... 150.00

**GENE AUTRY, Billfold** ................................................................................................ 12.00
**Cap Pistol,** Boxed ...................................................................................................... 28.00
**Cap Pistol,** Red Grips, Kenton, Cast Iron, 6 1/2 In. ...................................................... 35.00
**Charm,** With Champion, Sterling Silver, Original Card, 1946 ......................................... 45.00
**Guitar,** Adult Size ...................................................................................................... 25.00
**Gun,** Revolver, Cast Iron ............................................................................................ 45.00
**Mirror,** Photo, Black & White, Pocket .......................................................................... 6.00
**Pencil,** Mechanical, Light-Up, Trigger .......................................................................... 8.50
**Pistol,** Cap, Repeater, Cast Iron ................................................................................. 15.00
**Ranch Outfit,** Unused, Boxed ...................................................................................... 45.00
**Slippers,** Child's, Boxed .............................................................................................. 35.00

*Black and blue decorated Gibson girl plates were made in the early 1900s. Twenty-four different 10 1/2 inch plates were made by the Royal Doulton Pottery at Lambeth, England. These pictured scenes from the book "A Widow and Her Friends" by Charles Dana Gibson. Another set of twelve 9 inch plates featuring pictures of the heads of Gibson girls had all blue decoration.*

**GIBSON GIRL, Plate,** A Message From The Outside World ............................................. 70.00
**Plate,** A Quiet Dinner With Dr.Bottles, 10 1/4 In. ...................................... 64.00 To 85.00
**Plate,** Day After Arriving At Her Journey's End .......................................... 38.00 To 85.00
**Plate,** Decides To Die In Spite Of Dr.Bottles, 10 1/2 In. ............................................... 65.00
**Plate,** Failing To Find Rest & Quiet ............................................................................. 85.00
**Plate,** Miss Babbles The Authoress Calls And Reads Aloud .......................................... 65.00
**Plate,** Mr.Waddles Arrives Late ............................................................... 55.00 To 65.00
**Plate,** Mrs.Babbles Brings A Copy .............................................................................. 75.00
**Plate,** Mrs.Diggs Is Alarmed .................................................................... 50.00 To 85.00
**Plate,** Quiet Dinner With Dr.Bottles ............................................................................ 65.00
**Plate,** She Becomes A Trained Nurse ........................................................ 65.00 To 85.00
**Plate,** She Contemplates The Cloister ......................................................................... 95.00
**Plate,** She Decides To Die .......................................................................................... 95.00

| | |
|---|---|
| **Plate,** She Finds Some Consolation | 85.00 |
| **Plate,** She Goes Into Colors | 75.00 |
| **Plate,** She Longs For Seclusion | 75.00 |
| **Plate,** She Looks For Relief From Among The Old Ones | 70.00 |
| **Plate,** They Go Fishing | 50.00 To 55.00 |
| **Plate,** They Take A Morning Run | 65.00 |

## GILLINDER

*Gillinder pressed glass was first made by William T. Gillinder of Philadelphia in 1863. Many glass items were made for the Centennial.*

| | |
|---|---|
| **GILLINDER, Figurine,** Buddha, Orange, Signed, 5 3/4 In. | 75.00 |
| **Paperweight,** Frosted Lion, Marked Centennial | 80.00 |
| **Paperweight,** Ruth The Gleaner | 100.00 |
| **Shoe,** Patent 1886, Signed, Clear | 30.00 |
| **Toothpick,** Bird, Frosted, Signed | 55.00 |

| | |
|---|---|
| **GIRL SCOUT, Book,** The Adventures Of A Brownie | 4.00 |
| **Patch,** National Girl Guides, Britain | 3.00 |
| **Seal,** Sweden, 1955 | .60 |
| **Whistle** | 5.00 |

| | |
|---|---|
| **GLASSES, Lorgnette,** Black Silk Ribbon, 3 Spacers, 14K Gold | 75.00 |

| | |
|---|---|
| **GOLDSCHEIDER, Figurine,** Bust Of Old-Fashioned Girl | 35.00 |
| **Figurine,** Elephant, Gray, 9 X 9 1/2 In. | 125.00 |
| **Figurine,** Female Head, Blue Glazed Corkscrew Curls, 13 In. | 300.00 |
| **Figurine,** Flying Ducks, 9 X 15 In. | 175.00 |
| **Figurine,** Lady In Full Ruffled Pink Dress, 10 In. | 85.00 |

| | |
|---|---|
| **GONDER, Vase,** Cornucopia, Gray, Pink Interior, 8 In. | 9.00 |
| **Vase,** Cornucopia, Pink & Gray Exterior, Pink Interior, 8 In. | 9.50 |
| **Vase,** Marbleized Turquoise & Brown, Pink Interior, 9 In. | 10.00 |
| **Vase,** Urn Shape, Handled, Mottled Brown, 9 In. | 17.50 |

*Goofus glass was made from about 1900 to 1920 by many American factories. It was originally painted gold, red, green, bronze, pink, purple, and other bright colors.*

| | |
|---|---|
| **GOOFUS GLASS, Bottle,** Apothecary, Statue Of Liberty | 60.00 |
| **Bowl,** Gold With Red Flowers | 7.50 |
| **Candleholder & Bowl,** 3 Piece | 30.00 |
| **Dish,** Gold, Black, & Red, Oval, 6 1/2 X 3 1/2 X 1 x 1/2 In. | 13.00 |
| **Dish,** Jeweled Heart Shape, Northwood, 9 X 9 In. | 18.00 |
| **Plate,** Apples, Red, Gold, 8 1/2 In. | 12.50 |
| **Plate,** Red Roses, Gold, 11 In. | 15.00 |
| **Platter** | 30.00 |
| **Powder Jar,** Red | 18.00 |
| **Tray,** Molded Stars & Red Flower Underside, Gold Ground, 5 In. | 18.00 |
| **Vase,** Peacock, Black, Gold, & Red Enamel Design | 75.00 |

*Goss china has been made since 1858. English potter William Henry Goss first made it at the Falcon Pottery in Stoke-on-Trent. In 1934 the factory name was changed to Goss China Company when it was taken over by Cauldon Potteries. Goss china resembles Irish Belleek in both body and glaze. The company also made popular souvenir china.*

W.H.COSS

| | |
|---|---|
| **GOSS, Bust,** Shakespeare, 4 In. | 40.00 |
| **Figurine,** Swiss Lion, 4 1/4 In.Long | 70.00 |
| **Hair Receiver,** Floral, 2 Butterflies, Hair-Tidy, W.H.Goss, 3 3/8 In. | 45.00 |
| **Pitcher,** Coat Of Arms, Salisbury Leather Gill, 3 In. | 28.00 |

*Pottery has been made in Gouda, Holland, since the seventeenth century. Two firms, The Zenith pottery, established in the eighteenth century, and the Zuid-Hollandsche pottery, made the brightly colored Art Nouveau wares marked Gouda from 1880 to about 1940.*

| | |
|---|---|
| GOUDA, Ashtray, Black Ground, House Mark, 4 1/4 In. | 30.00 |
| Bowl, Handled, Cobalt Blue Geometric Design, Green Rim, 2 X 4 In.Diam. | 32.00 |
| Bowl, Interior Design, Signed, 2 3/4 X 8 1/2 In.Diam. | 80.00 |
| Candlestick, Matapan, Blue & Green, 12 In. | 125.00 |
| Candlestick, NGRA Mark, 12 In. | 35.00 |
| Carafe, Covered, House Mark, 11 In. | 105.00 |
| Chamberstick, Art Nouveau Geometric Styling, House Mark, 3 X 7 In. | 115.00 |
| Chamberstick, Handled, Dripcatch, Forum Pattern, House Mark, 5 In. | 60.00 |
| Chamberstick, Shield Back, Corona Pattern, Olive Ground, 7 In. | 130.00 |
| Creamer, Cow | 65.00 |
| Ewer, Canteen Shape, Multicolored Flowers, Black Ground, 4 1/4 In. | 58.00 |
| Ewer, Strap Handled, C.1940, 7 In. | 42.50 |
| Inkwell, Triangular Shape, Crown Mark, Regina | 50.00 |
| Lamp, Base, 2-Light, Brass, Isa House Mark, 15 In. | 165.00 |
| Pitcher, Art Nouveau, High Glaze, House Mark, 6 3/4 In. | 145.00 |
| Pitcher, Flowers On Mottled Yellow, Cream Ground, 2 3/4 In. | 30.00 |
| Pitcher, Flowers On White, 2 1/2 In. | 20.00 |
| Pitcher, Handle, Multicolored Flowers, Black Top & Bottom, 3 1/4 In. | 45.00 |
| Plaque, Wall, Birches In Country, Zuid-Holland, Scenic, 9 In. | 150.00 |
| Rose Bowl, Scenic Ground, Windmill, 3 In. | 18.00 |
| Smoke Set, Cigarette Holder, Match Holder, Ashtray | 75.00 |
| Teapot, Aladdin Lamp Shape, Matte Finish, House Mark, 9 1/2 In. | 185.00 |
| Vase, Art Nouveau, Double Gourd Shape, House Mark, 6 1/2 In. | 70.00 |
| Vase, Art Nouveau, Handled, High Glaze, 9 In. | 225.00 |
| Vase, Art Nouveau, High Glaze, 5 1/2 In. | 125.00 |
| Vase, Black Ground, Green & Rust, Flowers & Foliage, 9 In., Pair | 175.00 |
| Vase, Black Handles, Cobalt Blue Flowers, 2 3/8 In. | 28.00 |
| Vase, Blue, Yellow, & Orange Flowers, Yellow Ground, 5 1/4 In. | 65.00 |
| Vase, Bulbous, Flowers & Branches, Mottled White Ground, 2 3/4 In. | 35.00 |
| Vase, Bulbous, Long Neck, Art Nouveau, High Glaze, Signed, 6 1/2 In. | 110.00 |
| Vase, Flower Design, Marked Royal, 10 1/2 In. | 95.00 |
| Vase, Frog, Black, Multicolor Design | 70.00 |
| Vase, High Glaze, Art Nouveau, 5 1/2 In. | 125.00 |
| Vase, Olive Green Top & Handles, Multicolored, Black Base, 4 In. | 38.00 |
| Vase, Schoonoven Corel, 7 1/2 In. | 95.00 |
| Vase, Signed House Gluck, 7 In. | 75.00 |
| Vase, Stylized Design, Handled, Signed, 10 In. | 155.00 |
| Vase, Teardrop Form, Flowers, Black Ground, Marked, 9 3/4 In., Pair | 280.00 |
| Vase, Trumpet Shape, Phoenix Bird, Black Ground, Marked, 10 In. | 110.00 |

*Graniteware is an enameled tinware that has been used in the kitchen from the late nineteenth century to the present. Earlier graniteware was green or turquoise blue, with white spatters. The later ware was gray with white spatters. Reproductions are being made in all colors.*

| | |
|---|---|
| GRANITEWARE, Bathtub, Baby's, Cover, White, Blue Trim, 23 In. | 18.00 |
| Bedpan, Gray | 22.00 |
| Bedpan, Urinal | 14.00 |
| Bowl, Mixing, Blue, 11 1/4 In. | 9.00 |
| Can, Cream, Brown, Wire & Wood Bail, 2 Quart | 40.00 |
| Can, Cream, Gray, Tin Lid, Bail Handle | 25.00 |
| Can, Cream, Green Wire & Wood Bail Handle | 38.00 |
| Can, Green & White, Lid & Handle, 1/2 Gallon | 30.00 |
| Can, Milk, Tin Cover, 1/2 Gallon | 28.00 |
| Candlestick, Blue | 20.00 |
| Coaster, White | 2.00 |
| Coffee Boiler, Blue & White | 50.00 |

Coffeepot, Blue & White ........................................................................ 17.50 To 28.00
Coffeepot, Copper Bottom, Pewter Handle, Spout, & Top, 12 In. ......................... 95.00
Coffeepot, Dark Blue, White Speckled, Lid, 6 In.Tall ..................................... 20.00
Coffeepot, Floral Design, Copper Bottom, Handle, Spout, & Top ......................... 95.00
Coffeepot, Gray ............................................................................................ 12.50
Coffeepot, Green, Large ............................................................................... 28.00
Coffeepot, Lid, Dark Blue & White Speckled .......................................... 18.00 To 20.00
Coffeepot, Red & White ................................................................................ 55.00
Coffeepot, Sky Blue Top & Bottom, Off-White Center, Flowers ......................... 25.00
Coffeepot, White & Black, 8 1/2 In. ............................................................... 18.00
Colander, Blue & White Speckled ................................................................. 14.00
Colander, Brown, Wire Handle ...................................................................... 35.00
Colander, Gray, Handled, 10 In.Diam. ........................................................... 12.00
Colander, Gray, 1 Long Handle ..................................................................... 12.00
Colander, Pedestal Base, Dark Blue & White ................................................. 10.00
Cup, Blue & White Speckled ......................................................................... 14.50
Cup, Child's ................................................................................................... 9.50
Cup, Measure, Gray ..................................................................................... 19.50
Cuspidor, Gray ............................................................................................. 10.00
Dipper, Blue, C.1900 .................................................................................... 14.00
Dish, Feeding, Humpty Dumpty, Rhyme Center, Blue, 6 1/2 In. ....................... 30.00
Dish, Pan, Cobalt Marbled ........................................................................... 38.00
Dish, Soap, Blue & White Swirled ................................................................. 24.50
Dish, Soap, Wall Hanging, Back Splash, Gray, 2 Piece ..................................... 18.00
Dish, Soap, Wall Hung, 6 1/2 In. ..................................................................... 8.00
Dishpan, Handles, 16 In.Diam. ....................................................................... 8.50
Double Boiler, Shaded Blues ......................................................................... 15.00
Funnel, Gray, 4 3/4 In. ................................................................................... 8.00
Funnel, Handle, White, Blue Edge, 2 In. ......................................................... 7.00
Funnel, White ................................................................................................ 7.50
Grinder, Food, Green Porcelain On Cast Iron, Harper ...................................... 45.00
Kettle, Covered, Wooden Swing Handle, Gray ................................................ 12.00
Kettle, Lid, Blue, 10 1/4 In. ............................................................................ 9.50
Ladle, Gray, Pierced ...................................................................................... 6.00
Lunch Box, Gray ........................................................................................... 28.50
Mold, Pudding, Gray, 9 In.Diam. .................................................................... 30.00
Muffin Tin, Gray ........................................................................................... 12.50
Mug, Blue ...................................................................................................... 5.00
Pail, Blueberry, Bail Handle, Gray ................................................................. 10.00
Pail, Milk, Gray, 6 In. .................................................................................... 35.00
Pan, Angel Food Cake, Gray ......................................................................... 15.00
Pan, Angel Food, Aqua & White .................................................................... 25.00
Pan, Loaf, Gray ............................................................................................ 14.50
Pan, Milk, Blue & White, 11 In. ..................................................................... 15.00
Pan, Muffin, 6 Cup, Gray .............................................................................. 17.00
Pie Tin, Gray, 9 3/4 In.Diam. ........................................................................... 4.00
Pitcher, Cream & Green Trim, 9 1/2 In. ............................................................ 8.50
Pitcher, Gray, 6 In. ......................................................................................... 7.50
Pitcher, Water, Green & White ....................................................................... 30.00
Pitcher, Water, 5 Tumblers, Shaded Blue ...................................................... 35.00
Plate & Cup, Child's, Nursery Rhyme, Blue .................................................... 25.00
Pot, Slop, Blue .............................................................................................. 42.00
Roaster, Embossed Savory, White & Black ..................................................... 20.00
Roaster, Inner White Granite Tray, Cobalt Blue & White Mottled ..................... 65.00
Saucepan, Pouring Lip, Gray, 5 In.Diam. .......................................................... 7.00
Stein, Transfer, Spirit Of Liberty, Columbia Brewing, 9 In. .............................. 150.00
Syrup, Gray, 3 1/2 In. .................................................................................... 15.00
Tea Set, Child's, Gray, 11 Piece .................................................................... 135.00
Tea Steeper, White, Blue Trim ...................................................................... 20.00
Teakettle, Gray, 2 Quart ............................................................................... 40.00
Teapot, Blue & White .................................................................................... 27.50
Teapot, Gooseneck, Blue & White ................................................................. 20.00
Teapot, Gray .................................................................................... 22.00 To 27.00

**Teapot,** Squatty, White ......................................................................................... 18.00

*Greentown glass was made by the Indiana Tumbler and Goblet Company of Greentown, Indiana, from 1894 to 1903. In 1899, the factory name was changed to National Glass Company. A variety of pressed, milk, and chocolate glass was made.*

**GREENTOWN, see also Chocolate Glass; Custard Glass; Holly Amber; Milk Glass; Pressed Glass**

**GREENTOWN, Berry,** Dewey, Vaseline ................................................................. 40.00
**Bowl,** Daisy & Button .............................................................................................. 35.00
**Bowl,** Dewey, Amber .............................................................................................. 26.00
**Butter,** Covered, Teardrop & Tassel, Clear ......................................................... 55.00
**Butter,** Dewey, Vaseline ......................................................................................... 85.00
**Compote,** Teardrop & Tassel, Clear, 6 In. ............................................................ 40.00
**Cracker Jar,** Herringbone, Clear ........................................................................... 40.00
**Creamer,** Austrian, Clear, Miniature ..................................................................... 35.00
**Creamer,** Cord Drapery ........................................................................................... 25.00
**Creamer,** Dewey, Vaseline ..................................................................................... 55.00
**Creamer,** Herringbone Buttress ............................................................................. 50.00
**Creamer,** Honeycomb With Flower Rim, Amber .................................................. 31.50
**Creamer,** Pleat Band ................................................................................................ 25.00
**Cruet,** Ruby Crossbars ............................................................................................ 65.00
**Dish,** Olive, Michigan, Handled .............................................................................. 18.00
**Dish,** Relish, Teardrop & Tassel, Clear, Oval ....................................................... 40.00
**Dolphin,** Red Agate .................................................................................................. 450.00
**Dustpan,** Vaseline ............................................................... 100.00 To 135.00
**Lamp,** Wild Rose With Bowknot, Chocolate Glass Base, 9 1/4 In. .................... 500.00
**Mug,** Elf, Opaque Blue, Label ................................................................................ 28.00
**Mug,** Elves Scenes, Milky Blue, Large .................................................................. 45.00
**Mug,** Green Serenade .............................................................................................. 35.00
**Mug,** Shuttle, Clear .................................................................................................. 12.00
**Pitcher,** Grape With Thumbprint, 8 In. .................................................................. 48.00
**Pitcher,** Squirrel On Branch .................................................................................... 150.00
**Pitcher,** Syrup, Chocolate, Cactus ........................................................................ 80.00
**Pitcher,** Water, Cord Drapery ................................................................................. 58.00
**Pitcher,** Water, Dewey, Yellow .............................................................................. 75.00
**Pitcher,** Water, Ruffled Eye, Amber ....................................................................... 110.00
**Pitcher,** Water, Squirrel, Clear ............................................................................... 125.00
**Pitcher,** Water, Teardrop & Tassel, Clear ............................................................. 30.00
**Pitcher,** Water, Teardrop & Tassel, Green ............................................................ 180.00
**Pitcher,** Water, Wild Rose With Bowknot, Frosted .............................................. 35.00
**Relish,** Dewey, Serpentine, Vaseline .................................................................... 38.00
**Salt & Pepper,** Amethyst Sprig Medallion, Original Tops ................................... 60.00
**Sauce,** Cord Drapery ............................................................................................... 12.50
**Smoke Set,** Wild Rose & Bowknot, Tray, Cigarette, & Match Holder ................ 85.00
**Spooner,** Austrian, Clear ......................................................................................... 30.00
**Spooner,** Dewey, Amber .......................................................................................... 55.00
**Spooner,** Herringbone Buttress, Green ................................................................. 55.00
**Spooner,** Paneled Holly, Clear Beaded Top ......................................................... 225.00
**Stein,** Castle, Chocolate .......................................................................................... 85.00
**Stein,** Indoor Drinking Scene, Chocolate .............................................................. 85.00
**Stein,** Troubadour, Transparent Green, 4 3/4 In. ................................................. 65.00
**Sugar & Creamer,** Cord & Drapery, Clear ............................................................ 65.00
**Sugar & Creamer,** Teardrop & Tassel, Covered, Green ...................................... 100.00
**Sugar,** Dewey, Open, Yellow .................................................................................. 30.00
**Sugar,** Herringbone Buttress, Gold Gilt, Cover ................................................... 65.00
**Syrup,** Chocolate ...................................................................................................... 68.00
**Table Set,** Dewey, Amber, 4 Piece ......................................................................... 210.00
**Tray,** Dewey, Serpentine, Amber, 10 In. ............................................................... 42.50
**Tumbler,** Wild Rose With Bowknot, Frosted ......................................................... 17.00
**Vase,** Herringbone Buttress, Emerald Green, 5 1/2 In. ....................................... 130.00
**Wine,** Beehive ........................................................................................................... 35.00

*Grueby Faience Company of Boston, Massachusetts, was incorporated in 1897 by William H. Grueby. Garden statuary, art pottery, and architectural tiles were made until 1920.*

| | |
|---|---|
| GRUEBY, Bowl, Flared, Matte Green, 7 In.Diam. | 125.00 |
| Bowl, Dark Green, Yellow Buds, Flat Leaves, Impressed Mark, 6 In. | 800.00 |
| Tile, Footed Brass Frame, Green & White, Blue Ground, 6 1/2 In.Square | 450.00 |
| Tile, Impressed & Sgraffito Galleon, Bird Overhead, 6 In.Square | 350.00 |
| Tile, Impressed & Sgraffito Turtle, Artist Signed, 6 In.Square | 550.00 |
| Tile, Sgraffito Tulip, Yellow & Green, Signed, 6 In.Square | 150.00 |
| Tile, Trojan Horses, Blue & Green Ground, Initialed, 6 X 6 In. | 500.00 |
| Vase, Bud & Leaf Design, Green, 7 In. | 425.00 |
| Vase, Cucumber & Avocado Matte, Broad Leaves, Bottle Form, 6 In. | 425.00 |
| Vase, Cucumber Glaze, Leaves & Buds, Spherical, Marked, 7 3/4 In. | 700.00 |
| Vase, Flat Leaves & Buds, Impressed Mark, 10 3/4 In. | 2500.00 |
| Vase, Green, Kendrick, 12 3/4 X 9 In.Diam. | 1650.00 |
| Vase, Green, 9 X 12 3/4 In. | 1650.00 |
| Vase, Leaves & Flowers, Green Matte, Yellow Flowers, Marked, 8 In. | 2500.00 |
| Vase, Light Green, Flat Leaves, Impressed Mark, 10 In. | 450.00 |
| Vase, Monumental, Cucumber Matte, 7 Elongated Leaves, 23 In. | 1800.00 |
| GUM BALL MACHINE, see Store, Machine | |

*Gunderson glass was made at the Gunderson Pairpoint Works of New Bedford, Massachusetts, from 1952 to 1957. Gunderson Peachblow is especially famous.*

| | |
|---|---|
| GUNDERSON, Compote, Blue Bowl, Clear Stem & Foot, 6 1/2 X 7 1/2 In. | 45.00 |
| Creamer, Peachblow, Knob Handle, 5 1/2 X 2 1/2 In. | 170.00 |
| Cup & Saucer, Peachblow | 250.00 |
| Goblet, Peachblow, 5 1/2 In. | 125.00 |
| Paperweight, Butterfly Suspended On Bubble, Paper Label | 58.00 |
| Pitcher, Peachblow, Ruffled, Applied Handle, 6 In. | 100.00 |
| Sugar & Creamer, Peachblow, Applied Shell Handles, Pink To White | 235.00 |
| Toothpick, Burmese, Lemon To Light Rose, Flared & Ruffled Rim | 120.00 |
| Toothpick, Peachblow, Tricornered, Rose To White | 170.00 |
| Tumbler, Peachblow, 4 1/2 In. | 90.00 |
| Vase, Burmese, 5-Sided Opening, Overall Hobnails, 7 1/2 In. | 115.00 |

| | |
|---|---|
| GUTTA-PERCHA, see also Photography, Daguerreotype Case | |
| GUTTA-PERCHA, Mirror, Hand, Winged Dragon In Center Medallion, Dated 1865 | 28.00 |
| Mirror, Pocket, Patent 1867 | 55.00 |

| | |
|---|---|
| HALCYON, Vase, 13 X 8 X 2 1/2 In. | 125.00 |

*Hall China Company started in East Liverpool, Ohio, in 1903. The firm made all types of wares, including Autumn Leaf pattern dishes. It is still working.*

HALL'S
SUPERIOR
QUALITY
KITCHENWARE

| | |
|---|---|
| HALL, see also Autumn Leaf | |
| HALL, Bean Pot, Rose Parade, Blue | 20.00 |
| Bowl Set, Mixing, Poppy, 4 Piece | 22.50 |
| Bowl, Poppy, 9 In.Diam. | 6.00 |
| Canister Set, Red Poppy, 4 Piece | 24.00 |
| Casserole, Cover, Orange Poppy, 8 1/2 In. | 22.50 |
| Casserole, Covered, Handled, Golden Glow | 42.00 |
| Coffee Dispenser, Crocus, Metal | 16.00 |
| Coffee Dispenser, Wall, Original Instructions, Crocus | 25.00 |
| Cookie Jar, Puss 'n Boots | 20.00 |
| Cookie Jar, Taverne, Pretzel Handles | 30.00 |
| Cookie Jar, Zeisel, Gold Dots | 20.00 |
| Cream & Sugar, Orange Poppy | 20.00 |
| Dish, Leftover, Orange Poopy | 20.00 |
| Dish, Scalloped Shell, Green, 5 In.Diam. | 4.00 |
| Dish, Tavern Scene, Covered | 22.00 |

| | |
|---|---|
| **Jug,** Cadet Doughnut | 15.00 |
| **Jug,** Red Poppy | 8.00 |
| **Match Holder,** Red Poppy | 12.00 |
| **Mug,** Irish Coffee, Footed, Set Of 5 | 35.00 |
| **Pitcher,** Straight Sided, Orange Poppy | 10.00 |
| **Pitcher,** Water, Covered, Westinghouse, Blue | 18.00 |
| **Pitcher,** Water, Hotpoint, Refrigerator | 12.00 |
| **Plate,** Pie, Orange, 10 In. | 12.00 |
| **Pot,** Bean, Lid, Orange Poppy | 27.50 |
| **Salt & Pepper,** Handled, Red Poppy, Large | 11.00 |
| **Salt & Pepper,** Handled, Rose Parade, Ivory | 8.50 |
| **Sugar & Creamer,** Sanigrid, Chinese Red | 10.00 |
| **Sugar,** Covered, Rose Parade, Ivory | 10.00 |
| **Teapot,** Aladdin's Lamp Shape, Cobalt, Strainer | 30.00 |
| **Teapot,** Blue, Boston | 12.00 |
| **Teapot,** Brown, Small | 4.00 |
| **Teapot,** Chartreuse, Large | 15.00 |
| **Teapot,** Covered, Hook, Blue Flowers | 12.00 |
| **Teapot,** Drip-O-Later, Daffodil Design | 18.00 |
| **Teapot,** Maroon, Gold, Floral Design | 15.00 |
| **Teapot,** Sunshine, Bud Ray Lid | 60.00 |
| **Teapot,** Surfside, Canary, Gold Design | 22.00 |
| **Teapot,** Turquoise Star | 16.00 |
| **Teapot,** White & Gold | 12.00 |
| **Teapot,** Windshield, Ivory, Gold Dot | 12.00 |
| **Teapot,** Yellow Basket | 22.00 |
| **Tom & Jerry Set,** 10 Cups, Bowl, Cover, Black, Gold Writing | 45.00 |

*Hampshire pottery was made in Keene, New Hampshire, between 1871 and 1923. Hampshire developed a line of colored glazed wares as early as 1883, including a Royal Worcester-type pink, olive green, blue, and mahogany.*

| | |
|---|---|
| **HAMPSHIRE, Creamer,** Twisted Side Handle, Bulbous, Barklike Texture | 38.00 |
| **Ewer,** Matte Green, 7 In. | 47.00 |
| **Jardiniere,** Matte Green, Signed, 3 In. | 25.00 |
| **Mug,** Dark Green & Brown High Glaze, Signed J.S.Taft & Co. | 49.00 |
| **Mug,** Handled, Matte Green, White Interior | 60.00 |
| **Plate,** Old Witch House, 6 1/2 In. | 32.00 |
| **Plate,** Souvenir, Windham Town Hall, Red Mark | 23.00 |
| **Rose Bowl,** Green Matte, Impressed Mark, 5 In. | 35.00 |
| **Sugar & Creamer,** Green, Large | 60.00 |
| **Teapot,** Sweeping Deco Handle, Matte Finish, Butterfly Finial | 55.00 |
| **Vase,** Bud, Serpent Handle, Green, Marked, 6 In. | 85.00 |
| **Vase,** Bulbous, Matte Green, 7 1/2 In. | 60.00 |
| **Vase,** Green, Bulbous, Marked, 4 X 5 In. | 55.00 |
| **Vase,** Matte Green, Geometric Pattern, Signed M In D, 8 In. | 105.00 |
| **Vase,** Melon Rib, Green Speckle, Marked, 2 3/4 X 4 3/4 In. | 24.00 |
| **Vase,** Molded Leaves, Brown, 7 In. | 85.00 |
| **Vase,** Mottled Blue, Shape No.40, 4 In. | 35.00 |
| **Vase,** Yellow, Green Leaves, 9 In. | 135.00 |

*Philip Handel worked in Meriden, Connecticut, about 1885 and in New York City from about 1900 to the 1930s. His firm made art glass and other types of lamps.*

| | |
|---|---|
| **HANDEL, Humidor,** Moose Design, Metal Top, Signed | 275.00 |
| **Humidor,** Opalescent Russet & Green, Owl On Branch, Signed, 5 1/4 In. | 250.00 |
| **Humidor,** Owl Sitting On Branch, Cover Is Match Holder, Signed, 5 In. | 275.00 |
| **Jar,** Cigar, Indian On Horse, Spearing Buffalo, Green Ground, Signed | 595.00 |

**Lamp,** Boudoir, Reverse Painted 16 Rib Shade, Signed, 7 In. ........................................ 650.00
**Lamp,** Boudoir, Reverse Painted, Art Deco Style, Signed, 12 In. ................................... 850.00
**Lamp,** Cabbage Base, Leaded Shade, 20 In.Diam. ................................................... 1800.00
**Lamp,** Dark Bronze, Silk Label, 22 In. ............................................................... 275.00
**Lamp,** Desk, Green & White Shade, Bronze Base, Signed ........................................ 650.00
**Lamp,** Desk, Leaded, Signed, 16 In. ................................................................. 850.00
**Lamp,** Desk, Long Brown Shade, Bronze Base, Signed ........................................... 600.00
**Lamp,** Desk, Pine Needle Design, Chocolate Glass Liner, C.1915, 14 In. ................... 450.00
**Lamp,** Floor, Leaded Shade, Signed ................................................................ 1800.00
**Lamp,** Four Lilies & Two Buds, Lily Bud Base, Signed, 16 In. ................................. 2450.00
**Lamp,** Gooseneck, Bronze ............................................................................. 150.00
**Lamp,** Leaded Shade, Birds In Flight, Caramel & Orange, Signed, 24 In. ................... 2750.00
**Lamp,** Leaded Shade, Flowers, Signed, 23 In. .................................................... 2800.00
**Lamp,** Piano, Obverse & Reverse Painted, Bronze Foot, Label, 6 1/2 In. ................... 1900.00
**Lamp,** Reverse Painted Chipped Ice Shade, Bronze Base, Signed, 14 In. .................. 1150.00
**Lamp,** Reverse Painted Shade, C.1922, Fabric Label, 23 In. .................................. 2100.00
**Lamp,** Reverse Painted Shade, Teakwood Stand, Bronze Stem, 23 1/4 In. ................ 8100.00
**Lamp,** Wall, Globe, Cobalt Bluebird, Floral Ground, Signed, 18 In.Diam. ................... 395.00
**Lamp,** 4 Lilies, 2 Buds, Lily Pad Bronze Base, Signed, 16 X 22 In.Wide ................... 2450.00
**Lamp,** 96 Leaded Pieces, Signed, 23 In. ......................................................... 2400.00
**Shade,** Hanging, Bronze Plated Hardware, Signed, 25 In. ......................... *Illus* 5800.00
**Shade,** Reverse Painted Scene Of Ship & Moon, Signed ..................................... 1000.00
**Vase,** Cameo, Amber, Signed, Amber, 11 In. .................................................... 450.00
**Vase,** Ledham, Scenic, Artist Signed, 8 In. ..................................................... 1100.00

Handel, Shade, Hanging, Bronze Plated Hardware, Signed, 25 In.

*Harlequin dinnerware was produced by the Homer Laughlin Company
from 1938 to 1964, and sold without trademark by the F.W. Woolworth Co.
It has a concentric ring design like Fiesta, but the rings are separated
from the rim by a plain margin and cup handles were angular in shape.*

**HARLEQUIN WARE, Creamer,** Novelty, Gray ..................................................... 4.50
**Figurine,** Donkey, Maroon ........................................................................... 23.00
**Figurine,** Donkey, Yellow ............................................................................ 23.00
**Figurine,** Duck, Green ................................................................................ 40.00
**Figurine,** Fish, Mauve ................................................................................ 40.00
**Figurine,** Lamb, Yellow & Gold ..................................................................... 20.00
**Figurine,** Penguin, White With Gold ............................................................... 23.00
**Jug,** Water, Red, Large ................................................................................ 15.00
**Platter,** Turquoise, 11 1/2 In. ....................................................................... 4.75
**Platter,** Yellow, 13 In. ................................................................................ 6.00

**HATPIN HOLDER, see also Porcelain and various porcelain categories**
**HATPIN HOLDER, Filigree Mounting,** Elongated Pointed Shape, Cobalt, Pair ........................ 48.00

**HATPIN, Etruscan Work,** Gold Filled, 6 1/4 In. ................................................. 25.00
    **Figural,** Indian Maid, Sterling Silver, 10 1/2 In. ....................................... 85.00

# HAVILAND & CO.

*Haviland china has been made in Limoges, France, since 1842. The factory*
*was started by the Haviland Brothers of New York City. Other*
*factories worked in the town of Limoges making a similar chinaware.*

**HAVILAND, Basket,** Pink Rose Design, Artist Signed ........................... 50.00 To 60.00
  **Berry Set,** 12 Bowls, Pink Chrysanthemums, Gold Trim ........................ 175.00
  **Bonbon,** Ranson, Cloverleaf Shape, Marked, 6 1/2 In. ........................... 16.50
  **Bowl,** Apple Blossom, Covered, Gold Handles, 10 1/2 In. ...................... 65.00
  **Bowl,** Poppies, Gold Band, Baroque, 10 X 4 In. ................................. 195.00
  **Bowl,** Punch, Hand-Painted Grapes, Covered, Signed, 9 1/2 X 10 In. ....................... 250.00
  **Bowl,** Vegetable, Ranson, Covered, Oval, 11 In. ................................ 50.00
  **Bowl,** Vegetable, Ranson, Marked, Oval, 10 In. ................................. 45.00
  **Bowl,** Vegetable, Ranson, Marked, 9 1/4 In. ..................................... 24.50
  **Box,** Roses, Covered, 3 In. ....................................................... 32.00
  **Butter Pat,** Moss Rose ............................................................ 9.00
  **Butter Pat,** Ranson, Marked ...................................................... 6.50
  **Butter,** Pink Roses, Covered, Liner, Green Mark ............................. 48.50
  **Candlestick,** Molded Designs, Enameled Flowers, 7 1/2 In., Pair ........... 65.00
  **Chamberstick,** White & Pink Floral ............................................ 65.00
  **Charger,** Hand-Painted Grapes, Gold Scalloped Border, 13 In. ............. 95.00
  **Chocolate Pot,** Ribbon Handle & Lid, Hand-Painted Flowers ................ 185.00
  **Chocolate Set,** Bouquets Allover, Gold Handle, Signed, 8 In. .............. 295.00
  **Chocolate Set,** Orange Flowers, Pear Luster, 4 Cups & Saucer ............ 185.00
  **Chocolate Set,** The Princess, 4 Cups & Saucers ............................. 250.00
  **Coffeepot,** Blue Flowers, Gold Handle, Spout, & Finial, 7 1/2 In. .......... 55.00
  **Coffeepot,** Moss Rose, Incised Mark .......................................... 65.00
  **Coffeepot,** Petal Foot, Gold Trim, Green & Red Mark, 7 1/2 In. ............ 65.00
  **Coffeepot,** Pink Floral ........................................................... 85.00
  **Cracker Jar,** Underplate, Floral ............................................... 103.00
  **Creamer,** Moss Rose, Marked ................................................... 20.00
  **Cup & Saucer,** Chocolate, White, Gold Trim .................................. 20.00
  **Cup & Saucer,** Cloverleaf ....................................................... 20.00
  **Cup & Saucer,** Demitasse, Ranson ............................................. 15.00
  **Cup & Saucer,** Emerald Pattern, 2-Handled ................................... 35.00
  **Cup & Saucer,** Gold Handles, Flowers, Set Of 5 .............................. 65.00
  **Cup & Saucer,** No.599-B3 ....................................................... 20.00
  **Cup & Saucer,** Pink Flowers, Blue & Green Foliage, Green Mark ........... 12.00
  **Cup & Saucer,** Ranson, White ................................................... 30.00
  **Cup & Saucer,** Rosalinde ......................................................... 15.00
  **Dish,** Cloverleaf Shape, 6 1/2 In. ............................................... 40.00
  **Dish,** Soap, Pansies, Gold Trim ................................................. 23.50
  **Dish,** Vegetable, Open, Pink Flowers, Gold Trim, Oval, 10 In. ............. 39.50
  **Fish Set,** Platter, 12 Plates, Irregular Edge, Design In Gold ............... 425.00
  **Gravy Boat,** American Rose, Underplate, 2 Piece ............................ 30.00
  **Gravy Boat,** Attached Plate, Marie ............................................. 30.00
  **Ice Cream Set,** Raised Floral Enameling, Tray, 12 Plates, Marked ......... 250.00
  **Oyster Plate,** Flower Center, 5 Indentations .................................. 55.00
  **Oyster Plate,** Violets, Sponged Gold Edge, Set Of 6 ......................... 145.00
  **Pitcher,** Acanthus Leaf, Leaf Lip, Gold Handle, 10 X 6 In. ................. 95.00
  **Pitcher,** Lemonade, Sprigs Of Yellow Flowers, 9 In. ......................... 30.00
  **Plate,** Autumn Leaf Design, 9 1/2 In. .......................................... 10.00
  **Plate,** Cake, Multicolor Flowers, Handkerchief Corners, 10 1/2 In. ....... 49.50
  **Plate,** Cloverleaf, 8 1/2 In. ..................................................... 15.00
  **Plate,** Cloverleaf, 9 1/2 In. ..................................................... 20.00
  **Plate,** Coupe, Art Deco, Celadon Green, Signed, 12 In. .................... 55.00
  **Plate,** Court Lady Decal, 9 1/2 In. ............................................. 10.00

Plate, Hand-Painted Roses, Dated, 8 In. .......................................................... 22.50
Plate, Lady, Gold Headpiece, Gold Border, Signed, 8 3/4 In. ................................ 60.00
Plate, Marie, 10 In. .......................................................................................... 10.00
Plate, Marie, 8 In. ............................................................................................ 7.00
Plate, Monk, Hand-Painted, Brown Ground, 12 1/2 In. ....................................... 285.00
Plate, Moss Rose, 9 1/2 In., Set Of 8 ................................................................. 85.00
Plate, No.158, Gold Trim, 7 3/8 In. .................................................................... 10.00
Plate, Pink Spray, 7 1/2 In. ............................................................................... 2.00
Plate, Portrait, Redhaired Young Woman, Copper Rim, Signed, 9 In. .................... 125.00
Plate, Ranson, White, 6 In. ................................................................................ 10.00
Plate, Ranson, 7 1/2 In. ..................................................................................... 13.50
Plate, Ranson, 9 3/4 In. ....................................................... 22.50 To 25.00
Plate, Rosalinde, 7 1/2 In. ................................................................................. 8.00
Plate, Roses, Dated 1902, Artist Signed, 12 1/2 In. ............................................ 40.00
Plate, Scrolled Border, Colored Violets, Red Mark, 9 In. ..................................... 19.50
Plate, The Ardennes, 6 In. ................................................................................. 5.00
Plate, The Ardennes, 8 1/2 In. ........................................................................... 8.00
Plate, The Ardennes, 9 1/2 In. ........................................................................... 10.00
Plate, Touraine, 10 In. ...................................................................................... 10.00
Platter, Apple Blossom, Oval, 16 In. ...................................... 50.00 To 65.00
Platter, Apple Blossom, 14 In. ........................................................................... 45.00
Platter, Marie, Oval, 16 In. ............................................................................... 50.00
Platter, Pink Flowers, Gold Trim, 16 In. .............................................................. 59.50
Platter, Ranson, Oval, 14 In. ............................................................................. 28.00
Platter, Ranson, 11 1/2 In. ................................................................................. 48.50
Platter, Red & Green, Gold Edge, Chain Pattern, 14 X 10 In. .............................. 75.00
Pot De Creme, Blue, Yellow Floral, Gold Leaves, Finial, Set Of 12 ...................... 295.00
Relish, Ranson, Cloverleaf Shape, White, 6 1/2 In. ............................................ 16.50
Soup, Cream, Gold Twisted Ribbon Handles ...................................................... 25.00
Soup, Cream, Ranson, Gold Border, Set Of 6 .................................................... 90.00
Soup, Dish, Montreux, Rim ............................................................................... 10.00
Soup, Dish, Ranson, Marked, 7 1/2 In. ............................................................. 15.00
Sugar & Creamer, Hand-Painted Orange Poppies, Gold Trim, Marked ................ 50.00
Sugar & Creamer, Melon Ribbed, Scalloped Rim, Green Mark, 5 1/4 In. ............. 65.00
Sugar & Creamer, St.Lazare Pattern ................................................................. 175.00
Sugar & Creamer, Tankard Type, Marked, Covered ........................................... 50.00
Sugar, Moss Rose ............................................................................................ 45.00
Tea Set, Green Trim, Pink Flowers, Dated Jan.1917, Service For 6 ...................... 225.00
Tray, Dresser, Easel Shaped, Gold Edge, 12 1/2 X 8 3/4 In. ............................... 35.00
Tray, Gold Rim, Clusters Of Pink Flowers, Oval, 8 1/2 X 10 1/2 In. ..................... 20.00
Tray, Green Rim, Painted Cottage Scene, Green Mark, 7 X 13 1/2 In. ................. 35.00
Tureen, Soup, Saint Cloud, 13 1/2 In. ............................................................... 75.00
Tureen, Soup, Tray, 11 Soup Dishes, Salmon Asters, Tureen 3 Quart .................. 400.00
Vase, Footed, Bulbous Body, Marked, 19th Century, Pottery, 5 In. ...................... 50.00
Waste Bowl, Ranson, Marked, 5 3/4 In. ............................................................ 17.50

*T.G.Hawkes & Company of Corning, New York, was founded in 1880.*
*The firm cut glass made at other firms until 1962. Many pieces are marked*
*with the trademark, a trefoil ring enclosing a fleur-de-lis and two hawks.*
HAWKES, see also Cut Glass
HAWKES, Atomizer Bottle, Blue, Footed, Signed, 6 In. ...................................... 95.00
Bottle, Cologne, Centauri, Signed, 7 1/2 X 5 In. ................................................ 375.00
Bowl, Carnation, Rock Crystal Finish, 8 In. ....................................................... 235.00
Bowl, Expanding Star, 8 In. .............................................................................. 395.00
Bowl, Floral Garland, Engraved, Signed, 8 In. ................................................... 145.00
Bowl, Fruit, Iris, Sterling Pedestal, Signed, 12 In. .............................................. 850.00
Bowl, Gladys, Signed, 10 In. ............................................................................ 225.00
Bowl, Gravic, Intaglio Walnut & Leaf, Scalloped Rim, 8 1/2 In. .......................... 350.00
Bowl, Hobstar & Crosshatch, Serrated Rim, C.1900, 12 In. .................... *Illus* 450.00
Bowl, Iris, Signed, 8 In. .................................................................................... 235.00
Bowl, Iris, Sterling Silver Pedestal, Signed, 12 In. ............................................. 850.00
Bowl, Panel, Hobstars In Diamonds, Signed, 3 X 6 In. ...................................... 110.00

Hawkes, Bowl, Hobstar & Crosshatch, Serrated Rim,
C.1900, 12 In. (See Page 249)

| | |
|---|---|
| **Bowl,** Venetian, 4 X 10 1/2 In. | 400.00 |
| **Candlestick,** Wreath & Flower Design, 12 In. | 200.00 |
| **Cigarette Holder,** Rock Crystal, Footed, Silver Base, Signed | 125.00 |
| **Cocktail Shaker,** Forest Scene, Signed, 5 X 9 1/2 In. | 110.00 |
| **Compote,** Gravic, Iris, Elongated Teardrop Stem, Signed, 7 1/2 In. | 375.00 |
| **Compote,** Waffle Pattern, Sterling Silver Base, Signed, 5 X 5 In. | 95.00 |
| **Cruet,** Chain Hobstars & Crosshatched Fans, Petticoat Shape, Signed | 90.00 |
| **Cruet,** Floral Engraving, Blown Stopper, 7 1/2 In. | 50.00 |
| **Cup,** Punch, Corinthian Pattern, Pedestal, Signed | 55.00 |
| **Cuspidor,** Lady's, Floral, Signed | 135.00 |
| **Decanter,** Chrysanthemum, Cut Base, 12 In. | 495.00 |
| **Decanter,** Engraved Polished Floral Design, Pedestal, Stopper, 13 In. | 225.00 |
| **Dish,** Candy, Rock Crystal, 2 Tier, Sterling Silver Handle, 7 X 9 In. | 225.00 |
| **Finger Bowl,** Aquila, Set Of 6 | 80.00 |
| **Goblet,** Intaglio Cut Leaf Design, Amber Foot, Signed, Pair | 35.00 |
| **Ice Bucket,** Aberdeen, Silver Plated Rim & Handle, 4 X 6 1/2 In. | 650.00 |
| **Jar,** Dresser, Floral, Sterling Cover, Both Signed | 48.00 |
| **Pitcher,** Brunswick, Signed, 8 3/4 In. | 240.00 |
| **Pitcher,** Water, Phoenix Bird, Copper Wheel On Front, Signed, 12 In. | 200.00 |
| **Pitcher,** Water, Pinwheel & Feathered Fan, Signed, 12 In. | 160.00 |
| **Plate,** Brunswick, Signed, 7 In. | 275.00 |
| **Plate,** Bull's-Eye Alternating With Hobstars, Signed, 6 In. | 175.00 |
| **Rose Bowl,** Engraved Flowers, Gold Trim, Signed, Green | 55.00 |
| **Spittoon,** Lady's, Allover Cut, Signed, 3 1/4 X 9 In. | 1500.00 |
| **Sugar & Creamer,** Floral Engraving, Signed | 195.00 |
| **Sugar & Creamer,** Strawberry Pattern, Hobstar Base, Signed | 285.00 |
| **Syrup,** Venetian Pattern, Silver Plated Handle & Top | 350.00 |
| **Tray,** Fishtail Shaped, Signed, 6 1/2 X 9 1/2 In. | 325.00 |
| **Tray,** Hobstars & Fans, Rayed Center, Signed, 10 In. | 200.00 |
| **Tumbler,** Chrysanthemum, Pair | 100.00 |
| **Tumbler,** Hobstars, Signed | 40.00 |
| **Tumbler,** Jubilee, Signed, Set Of 5 | 125.00 |
| **Vase,** Baluster Shape, Frosted Top Band, Copper Wheel Floral, 8 In. | 38.00 |
| **Vase,** Bud, Hobstar, Crosshatch, & Thumbprint, 10 1/4 In. | 200.00 |
| **Vase,** Cornucopia, Intaglio Leaf & Berry, Bronze Holder, Signed, 7 In. | 125.00 |
| **Vase,** Cranberry, 6 1/2 In. | 165.00 |
| **Vase,** Easter Pattern, Hob Base, Signed, 14 In. | 365.00 |
| **Vase,** Engraved Grapes & Leaves, Signed, Green, 8 In. | 85.00 |
| **Vase,** Flared, Venetian, 8 In. | 190.00 |
| **Vase,** Flowers & Columns, Tube Shape, 9 1/4 In. | 75.00 |
| **Vase,** Gravic, Chrysanthemum Design, Signed, 10 1/2 In. | 550.00 |
| **Vase,** Green, Horn Shaped, Etched Berry & Leaf Design, 7 1/2 In. | 115.00 |
| **Vase,** Hobstars & Fan, Trumpet, Ruffled Top, Signed, 11 In. | 155.00 |
| **Vase,** Navarre Design, Hobstars & Bull's Eyes, Signed, 12 In. | 215.00 |
| **Vase,** Notched Rim, Flowers & Punties, Signed, 11 X 5 1/2 In. | 285.00 |
| **Vase,** Queen's Design, Signed, 11 1/2 In. | 285.00 |
| **Vase,** Queen's, Trumpet, Faceted Knob At Base, 16 In. | 1095.00 |
| **Vase,** Sheraton, Signed, 10 In. | 450.00 |
| **Vase,** Tiger Lily, Flowers & Ferns, 8 In. | 140.00 |

Vase, Trumpet, Brunswick, 12 In. .................................................................... 225.00 To 295.00
Vase, Trumpet, Easter Pattern, Scalloped Base, Signed, 13 1/2 In. ........................ 425.00
Vase, Trumpet, Swirl & Comet, Signed, 12 In. ...................................................... 335.00
Vase, Trumpet, Venetian Pattern, Notched Base, 12 In. .......................................... 550.00
Vase, Venetian, Flared, 8 In. ............................................................................... 190.00
Water Set, Grapes, Leaves, 6 Glasses, C.1925, Signed, Green, 10 In. ....................... 375.00
Water Set, Vintage, Pitcher, 4 Goblets, Teardrop Handle ........................................ 550.00
Whiskey Jug, Brazilian, Strap-Handled, Signed .................................................... 575.00
Wine, Russian, Knobbed Teardrop Stem, Signed .................................................. 135.00
Wine, Russian, Knobbed Teardrop Stem, Signed, Set Of 6 ................................... 1600.00

*Heintz Art Metal shop made jewelry, copper, silver, and brass in Buffalo, New York, from 1915 to about 1935. It became Heintz Brothers Manufacturers about 1935.*

HEINTZ ART, Match Holder, Sterling On Bronze .................................................... 35.00
Vase, 2-Handled, Sterling On Copper, 8 In. .......................................................... 75.00

*Heisey glass was made from 1895 to 1958 in Newark, Ohio, by A.H. Heisey and Co., Inc.*

HEISEY, see also Custard Glass

HEISEY, Ashtray, Crystolite ................................................................................. 4.00
Ashtray, Diamond Point, Individual ...................................................................... 6.00
Ashtray, Duck, Moongleam ................................................................................. 225.00
Ashtray, Empress, Cobalt Blue ............................................................................ 110.00
Base, Punch Bowl, Greek Key, 8 1/4 X 9 1/2 In. ................................................... 55.00
Basket, Double Rib & Panel, Flamingo, 6 In. ......................................................... 60.00
Basket, Paneled, Dated 8-17-15, 10 1/2 In. .......................................................... 100.00
Basket, Raised Panel, Etched Border, 12 In. .......................................................... 125.00
Basket, Raised Panel, 9 In. ................................................................................. 95.00
Basket, Raised Panel, 10 In. ............................................................................... 105.00
Basket, Rope Handle, Ruffled, Marked, 12 In. ....................................................... 30.00
Berry Bowl, Beaded Swag, Gold Trim, Crystal, 4 1/2 In. ........................................ 10.00
Berry Bowl, Empress, 8 In. ................................................................................. 32.50
Berry Bowl, Pinwheel & Fan, Signed, Set Of 6 ...................................................... 65.00
Berry Set, Beaded Swag, Clear, Gold Trim, 7 Piece ............................................... 250.00
Berry Set, Etched Rose, 5 Piece .......................................................................... 85.00
Berry Set, Prince Of Wales, Gold Trim, 7 Piece ..................................................... 175.00
Berry Set, Rose Pattern, Etched, 5 Piece .............................................................. 85.00
Berry Set, Winged Scroll Pattern, 7 Piece ............................................................ 535.00
Berry Set, Winged Scroll, Custard, 6 Piece ........................................................... 450.00
Berry Set, 4 Sauces, Scalloped Gold Top, Gold Beads, Marked ............................... 450.00
Bonbon, Hawthorne, 6 In. .................................................................................. 25.00
Bookends, Fish, 6 5/8 In. ................................................................ 85.00 To 150.00
Bookends, Horsehead, Marked ............................................................................ 85.00
Bottle, Apothecary, Stopper, 5 1/2 In. .................................................................. 25.00
Bottle, Oil & Vinegar, Original Label, Recipes ....................................................... 57.50
Bottle, Water, Fancy Loop, Bulbous, 9 1/2 In. ....................................................... 50.00
Bottle, Water, Punty & Diamond .......................................................................... 40.00
Bowl & Underplate, Zodiac Limelight, 8 In. ........................................................... 50.00
Bowl, Beaded Swag, Green, 8 In. ........................................................................ 75.00
Bowl, Colonial, 7 In. ......................................................................................... 16.00
Bowl, Console, Dolphin Footed, Flower Frog, Pink, 12 In. ....................................... 35.00
Bowl, Console, Orchid, 13 In.Diam. ..................................................................... 35.00
Bowl, Console, Pink, 11 In. ................................................................................ 80.00
Bowl, Console, Sahara, Queen Anne .................................................................... 30.00
Bowl, Console, Seahorse, Footed, Crystal, 11 In. .................................................. 30.00
Bowl, Crystolite, Etched Flowers, Oval, Marked, 13 In. ........................................... 35.00
Bowl, Divided, Orchid Etch, Oval, 5 X 8 In. ........................................................... 30.00

Bowl, Flamingo, Twist Handle, 5 In. .......................................................................... 10.00
Bowl, Fluted, Diamond Loop, Signed, 10 1/4 X 3 3/4 In. ...................................... 35.00
Bowl, Fruit, Waverly, 12 In. ......................................................................................... 20.00
Bowl, Gold Border, Oblong, 8 X 10 In. .................................................................... 20.00
Bowl, Greek Key, 3 1/2 X 8 1/2 In. ..................................................... 30.00 To 55.00
Bowl, Horn Of Plenty, Floral, Crystal, 10 In. .......................................................... 60.00
Bowl, Lariat, Collared Base, Sterling Silver Overlay, 7 1/2 In. ............................. 25.00
Bowl, Lariat, Crystal, 9 In. .......................................................................................... 12.00
Bowl, Minuet, Symphony Stem, 5 In. ........................................................................ 20.00
Bowl, Narrow, Fluted, Dated & Signed, 9 In. .......................................................... 35.00
Bowl, Old Sandwich, Oval, Footed, Marked, 12 In. ................................................ 43.50
Bowl, Orchid Etch, Low, 9 In. ................................................................................... 30.00
Bowl, Orchid Etch, 10 In. .................................................................... 30.00 To 32.00
Bowl, Peerless, Oval, 9 In. .......................................................................................... 35.00
Bowl, Pineapple & Hobstars, Marked, 4 X 8 1/4 In. ............................................. 65.00
Bowl, Pinwheel & Fan, Clear, 8 1/2 In. .................................................................... 65.00
Bowl, Pinwheel & Fan, 8 In. ....................................................................................... 30.00
Bowl, Punch, Beaded Panel & Sunburst, Base, Signed ........................................ 22.00
Bowl, Punch, Greek Key, Pedestal, 12 Cups, Bowl, 15 In. .................................... 295.00
Bowl, Punch, Greek Key, Separate Base, Signed, 15 X 15 In. ............................. 195.00
Bowl, Punch, Pineapple Design, 12 Cups, Signed, 13 1/2 X 8 1/2 In. ................ 395.00
Bowl, Raided Panel, Copper Wheel Etched, 8 1/2 In. ............................................ 25.00
Bowl, Ridgeleigh, Silver Overlay, 3 X 12 In. ............................................................ 30.00
Bowl, Rose Pattern, Silver Overlay, Ribbed Back, Signed, 13 In. ........................ 70.00
Bowl, Seahorse Feet, Swirl, 11 1/2 In. ..................................................................... 45.00
Bowl, Sunburst, 8 In. .................................................................................................. 15.00
Bowl, Waste, Fandango, 2 1/4 X 4 3/4 In. ............................................................... 15.00
Bowl, Waverly, 12 In. ................................................................................................... 20.00
Box, Cigarette, Carcassone ....................................................................................... 65.00
Box, Cigarette, Colonial, Footed .............................................................................. 18.00
Box, Cigarette, Crystolite, 2 Ashtrays, Cover ....................................................... 22.00
Box, Cigarette, Horsehead, Covered .................................................... 50.00 To 60.00
Box, Cigarette, Ridgeleigh, 4 Ashtrays ................................................................... 75.00
Box, Cigarette, Whirlpool, Cover ............................................................................. 35.00
Bust, M.J.Owens, Frosted .......................................................................................... 95.00
Butter Pat, Diamond Pattern, Marked, 3 1/2 In. ................................................... 8.00
Butter, Colonial, Covered, Marked ........................................................................... 75.00
Butter, Narcissus, Covered ........................................................................................ 37.50
Butter, Orchid Etch, Covered .................................................................................... 85.00
Butter, Orchid, Square, Covered ............................................................................... 65.00
Butter, Plantation, Covered ....................................................................................... 50.00
Butter, Winged Scroll, Gold Trim, Covered ............................................................ 235.00
Candlestick, Cherub, Frosted, Large ....................................................................... 300.00
Candlestick, Crystolite, 3-Light, Pair ...................................................................... 30.00
Candlestick, Crystolite, 5 1/4 In., Pair .................................................................... 25.00
Candlestick, Flamingo, Frosted Cherub, Pair ......................................................... 395.00
Candlestick, Gardenia, Etched ................................................................................. 15.00
Candlestick, Gascony, 6 1/4 In., Pair ...................................................................... 50.00
Candlestick, Lariat, 2-Light ....................................................................................... 20.00
Candlestick, Lariat, 2-Light, Pair ..................................................... 28.00 To 45.00
Candlestick, Moongleam, Cut, Silver, Pair .............................................................. 55.00
Candlestick, Orchid Etch, 2-Light, Pair ................................................................... 40.00
Candlestick, Orchid, 1-Light ...................................................................................... 15.00
Candlestick, Orchid, 3-Light, Pair ............................................................................ 60.00
Candlestick, Prisms, Pair ........................................................................................... 90.00
Candlestick, Regency, 2-Light ................................................................................... 25.00
Candlestick, Ridgeleigh, Bobeche & Prisms, Pair .......................... 120.00 To 150.00
Candlestick, Swan, Flamingo, 6 1/2 In. ................................................................... 125.00
Celery, Colonial, Marked, 9 In. ................................................................................. 18.00
Celery, Empress, Flamingo, Marked, 12 In. ............................................................ 25.00
Celery, Fandango ......................................................................................................... 80.00
Celery, Yeoman, 12 In. ................................................................................................ 22.50
Champagne, Ipswich, 5 In. ........................................................................................ 18.50

| | |
|---|---|
| **Champagne,** Le Rose Etching | 15.00 |
| **Champagne,** Minuet, Symphony Stem | 22.00 |
| **Champagne,** Orchid, Tyrolean Stem | 20.00 |
| **Champagne,** Oxford, Saucer | 16.00 |
| **Champagne,** Trojan | 20.00 |
| **Claret,** Tally-Ho | 35.00 |
| **Coaster,** Colonial, Pink, Set Of 6 | 30.00 |
| **Coaster,** Crystolite, Marked, 3 In. | 7.00 |
| **Coaster,** Lariat | 5.00 |
| **Cocktail Shaker,** Coaching Scene & Inn, Deep Etched, 22 In. | 225.00 |
| **Cocktail Shaker,** Horsehead, Small | 90.00 |
| **Cocktail Shaker,** Limelight, Frosted Madonna | 1200.00 |
| **Cocktail Shaker,** Ram's Head | 250.00 |
| **Cocktail Shaker,** Rooster Head Stopper, Crystolite, 3 Piece | 90.00 |
| **Cocktail Shaker,** Rooster Head, Etched | 150.00 |
| **Cocktail Shaker,** Rooster Head, Raffia Handles, 3 Piece | 165.00 |
| **Cocktail Shaker,** Rooster Head, 4 Chanticleer Cocktails | 275.00 |
| **Cocktail Shaker,** Rooster, Strainer | 85.00 |
| **Cocktail Shaker,** Seahorse | 115.00 |
| **Cocktail Shaker,** Tally-Ho, Etched | 175.00 |
| **Cocktail Shaker,** 8 Cocktails, Rooster, Etched | 500.00 |
| **Cocktail,** Alexandrite, Creole Stem | 50.00 |
| **Cocktail,** Alexandrite, 4 Ounce | 85.00 |
| **Cocktail,** Alexandrite, 11 Ounce | 100.00 |
| **Cocktail,** Carcassone, Sahara | 12.00 |
| **Cocktail,** Chintz Etching, Footed | 15.00 |
| **Cocktail,** Fisherman, 4 Ounce | 50.00 |
| **Cocktail,** New Era | 15.00 |
| **Cocktail,** Plantation | 18.50 |
| **Cocktail,** Puritan, 3 Ounce | 6.00 |
| **Cocktail,** Rooster Stem | 50.00 To 59.75 |
| **Cocktail,** Seahorse, Crystal | 200.00 |
| **Cocktail,** Skier Silhouette, Etched, 4 Ounce | 50.00 |
| **Compote,** Candy, Etched | 25.00 |
| **Compote,** Candy, Ipswich | 40.00 |
| **Compote,** Colonial, 5 X 4 In. | 12.50 To 17.50 |
| **Compote,** Cut Flowers, Sterling Silver Cover, Footed, 5 1/2 X 3 In. | 65.00 |
| **Compote,** Dual Tone, Caramel, Petal & Loop, Scalloped Rim, 10 In. | 75.00 |
| **Compote,** Empress, Sahara, Dolphin Footed, 6 In. | 110.00 |
| **Compote,** Fancy Loop, High Stand, 8 3/4 In. | 55.00 |
| **Compote,** Flamingo, Dolphin, Sterling Overlay | 175.00 |
| **Compote,** Green, 7 In. | 12.50 |
| **Compote,** Hamilton, Flint, Covered, 6 1/4 X 6 In. | 100.00 |
| **Compote,** Jelly, Footed, Colonial, 4 1/2 In. | 16.50 |
| **Compote,** Plantation, Covered, 8 In. | 65.00 |
| **Compote,** Plantation, 6 1/2 In. | 28.00 |
| **Compote,** Rib & Panel, Marked, 5 In. | 14.00 |
| **Conosle,** Set, Center Fish Bowl, Candlesticks, Marked, Bowl 8 1/2 In. | 675.00 |
| **Console Bowl,** Footed, 8-Sided, Marked, Pink, 11 In.Diam. | 38.00 |
| **Console Set,** Twist Flamingo, 3 Piece | 65.00 |
| **Console Set,** Waverly, Orchid Etch | 59.50 |
| **Cordial,** Block Optic | 20.00 |
| **Cordial,** Minuet | 45.00 |
| **Cordial,** Old Colonial | 30.00 |
| **Cordial,** Old Dominion | 20.00 |
| **Cordial,** Orchid, Clear, Marked, 4 3/4 In. | 95.00 |
| **Cordial,** Peerless, 3 3/8 In. | 25.00 |
| **Cordial,** Plantation | 45.00 |
| **Cordial,** Yorktown | 30.00 |
| **Cornucopia,** Clear, Signed, 6 In., Pair | 225.00 |
| **Cornucopia,** Clear, Signed, 9 In., Pair | 225.00 |
| **Creamer,** Cane Pattern, Custard Paneled, Marked | 60.00 |
| **Creamer,** Colonial, Child's | 30.00 To 32.00 |

Creamer, Fancy Loop .......................................................................... 35.00
Creamer, Greek Key, Clear, Oval .................................................. 35.00
Creamer, Pinwheel & Fan .................................................................. 23.00
Creamer, Provincial ............................................................................ 12.00
Creamer, Punty Band, St.Joseph, Michigan, Individual ............ 45.00
Creamer, Swingtime ........................................................................... 18.75
Cruet, Banded Flute ...................................................... 24.00 To 40.00
Cruet, Colonial, Marked ................................................ 25.00 To 32.00
Cruet, Cut Log ...................................................................................... 18.00
Cruet, Fandango, 6 Ounce .............................................................. 35.00
Cruet, Flowers & Leaves, Cut, Marked ...................................... 22.00
Cruet, Grape, Etched ......................................................................... 16.00
Cruet, Marigold, Twist ....................................................................... 45.00
Cruet, Pineapple & Fan, Gold Trim, Emerald Green ............... 245.00
Cruet, Plantation Ivy .......................................................................... 65.00
Cruet, Pleat & Panel, Pink .............................................................. 25.00
Cruet, Queen Anne .............................................................................. 50.00
Cruet, Rose, Stopper .......................................................................... 75.00
Cruet, Victorian .................................................................................... 25.00
Cruet, Waldorf Astoria ....................................................................... 25.00
Cruet, Waverly, Gold Trim ............................................................... 45.00
Cruet, Whirlpool, Original Stopper ............................................... 30.00
Cup & Saucer, Colonial ..................................................................... 14.00
Cup & Saucer, Empress, Alexandrite ........................................... 59.75
Cup & Saucer, Empress, Sahara, Marked .................................. 25.00
Cup & Saucer, Etched Save America, Elect Landon ............... 200.00
Cup & Saucer, Heritage, Crystal ................................................... 4.00
Cup & Saucer, Queen Anne, Pink ................................................. 20.00
Cup & Saucer, Shelley ....................................................................... 24.50
Cup, Crinoline ....................................................................................... 16.75
Cup, Custard, Colonial, Marked ..................................................... 9.00
Cup, Custard, Punty & Diamond, Marked .................................. 15.00
Cup, Fancy Loop ................................................................................... 18.00
Cup, Punch, Beaded Panel & Sunburst ...................................... 10.00
Cup, Punch, Colonial Pattern, Signed, Set Of 9 ..................... 45.00
Cup, Punch, Optic, 4 Ounce ............................................................ 5.00
Cup, Punch, Pinwheel & Fan, Set Of 6 ...................................... 45.00
Cup, Punch, Plantation ...................................................................... 10.00
Cup, Punch, Sunburst, Crystal ....................................................... 18.00
Cup, Punch, Victorian ......................................................................... 6.00
Decanter, Etched, Rooster ............................................................... 60.00
Decanter, Orchid, Sterling Silver Stopper ................................. 175.00
Decanter, Peerless .............................................................................. 55.00
Decanter, Penguin, Stopper ..................................... 225.00 To 250.00
Decanter, Rooster Design, Etched ................................................ 60.00
Dish, Berry, Pinwheel & Fan, Signed, Set Of 6 ...................... 65.00
Dish, Butter, Plantation ..................................................................... 50.00
Dish, Candy, Bird Finial, Covered ................................................. 65.00
Dish, Candy, Brass Lid, Fruit Attached ...................................... 50.00
Dish, Candy, Crystolite, Sectional ............................. 12.00 To 20.00
Dish, Candy, Ridgeleigh, Grapes At End Of Handles, 4 X 10 In. .......... 40.00
Dish, Candy, Waverly, Seahorse Handle, Yellow, Covered ... 25.00
Dish, Candy, Woman In Medallion, Sterling Overlay, 6 1/2 In. ...... 30.00
Dish, Chip & Dip, Colonial, Gold Etched .................................... 30.00
Dish, Greek Key, 28-Point Star Center, Oval, Signed, 4 X 9 In. ........ 38.00
Dish, Ice Cream, Silver Plated Holders ...................................... 20.00
Dish, Lemon, Empress, Sahara, Oval, Covered, 6 1/2 In. ..... 36.50
Dish, Mayonnaise, Waverly Rose, Liner ..................................... 39.50
Dish, Mint, Queen Anne, 5 In. ........................................................ 20.00
Dish, Nut, Empress, Sahara, Footed, Individual ...................... 20.00
Dish, Nut, Greek Key, Footed .......................................................... 15.00
Dish, Nut, Puritan, Footed ................................................................ 16.00
Dish, Nut, Swan, Crystal, 5 Piece ............................... 50.00 To 65.00

| | |
|---|---|
| **Dish,** Nut, Swan, Crystolite, Master | 30.00 To 35.00 |
| **Dish,** Nut, Swan, Crystolite, Small | 10.00 To 15.75 |
| **Dish,** Nut, Twist Design, Marigold | 35.00 |
| **Dish,** Pickle, Beaded Edge, Marked, Oblong, 6 1/2 X 4 In. | 22.00 |
| **Dish,** Pickle, Orchid, Oval | 34.75 |
| **Figurine,** Asiatic Pheasant | 150.00 To 265.00 |
| **Figurine,** Bull | 1800.00 |
| **Figurine,** Clydesdale | 375.00 To 425.00 |
| **Figurine,** Colt, Kicking | 160.00 |
| **Figurine,** Colt, Standing | 60.00 |
| **Figurine,** Elephant, Amber | 1200.00 |
| **Figurine,** Fighting Rooster | 70.00 To 185.00 |
| **Figurine,** Filly Horse, Head Back | 2495.00 |
| **Figurine,** Fish, Clear, Pair | 110.00 |
| **Figurine,** Flamingo Kingfisher | 285.00 |
| **Figurine,** Gazelle, 11 In. | 1500.00 |
| **Figurine,** Geese, Set | 500.00 |
| **Figurine,** Giraffe | 135.00 To 185.00 |
| **Figurine,** Goose, Wings Down | 325.00 |
| **Figurine,** Goose, Wings Half Up | 65.00 To 125.00 |
| **Figurine,** Mallard, Wings Half Up | 90.00 |
| **Figurine,** Mallard, Wings Up | 90.00 |
| **Figurine,** Pheasant | 85.00 To 125.00 |
| **Figurine,** Piglet | 80.00 |
| **Figurine,** Plug Horse | 85.00 To 90.00 |
| **Figurine,** Pony, Rearing | 20.00 To 150.00 |
| **Figurine,** Pony, Standing | 60.00 To 75.00 |
| **Figurine,** Pouter Pigeon, Pair | 35.00 |
| **Figurine,** Ringneck Pheasant | 100.00 To 125.00 |
| **Figurine,** Scotty | 85.00 To 95.00 |
| **Figurine,** Sparrow | 65.00 |
| **Figurine,** Swan, Crystolite, Large | 28.00 |
| **Finger Bowl,** Greek Key | 12.50 |
| **Flower Frog,** Sahara | 25.00 |
| **Fork,** Salad, Signed | 25.00 |
| **Glass,** Colonial, Molded Mark, 4 In., Set Of 5 | 100.00 |
| **Glass,** Shot, Fox Chase | 45.00 |
| **Glass,** Shot, Old Sand | 20.00 |
| **Glass,** Shot, Tally-Ho | 35.00 |
| **Glass,** Soda, Chateau, Cut Stemware | 30.00 |
| **Glass,** Soda, Jamestown, Cobalt Blue, Footed | 45.00 |
| **Glass,** Soda, Lancaster, 12 Ounce | 35.00 |
| **Glass,** Soda, Sailboat, Carving, 8 Ounce | 35.00 |
| **Glass,** Soda, Tally-Ho, 8 Ounce | 35.00 |
| **Goblet,** Americana | 15.00 |
| **Goblet,** Barley | 22.50 |
| **Goblet,** Carcassone Stem, 11 Ounce | 20.00 |
| **Goblet,** Carcassonne, Alexandrite | 55.00 |
| **Goblet,** Champagne, Orchid | 20.00 |
| **Goblet,** Charter Oak | 18.00 |
| **Goblet,** Colonial, Marked, 6 1/4 In. | 12.00 |
| **Goblet,** Colonial, 7 Ounce | 15.00 |
| **Goblet,** Crystolite, Set Of 4 | 73.00 |
| **Goblet,** Empress | 15.00 |
| **Goblet,** Fancy Loop, Green | 50.00 |
| **Goblet,** Frontenac, Etched | 15.00 |
| **Goblet,** Greek Key, 6 In. | 65.00 |
| **Goblet,** Honeycomb, Signed | 27.50 |
| **Goblet,** Ipswich, 5 1/2 In. | 18.50 |
| **Goblet,** Mayflower, Etched, 10 Ounce, Pair | 25.00 |
| **Goblet,** Minuet, Symphony Stem | 28.00 |
| **Goblet,** New Era | 10.00 To 65.00 |
| **Goblet,** Orchid Etch | 18.00 To 25.00 |

| | |
|---|---:|
| **Goblet,** Pied Piper | 15.00 |
| **Goblet,** Plantation, Etched Ivy | 24.00 |
| **Goblet,** Portsmouth, Flamingo Red, 9 Ounce | 42.50 |
| **Goblet,** Renaissance, Etched | 15.00 |
| **Goblet,** Rose | 35.00 |
| **Goblet,** Seahorse Stem | 350.00 |
| **Goblet,** Shawl Dancer, Etched, Set Of 12 | 145.00 |
| **Goblet,** Spanish Stem, Crystal, Killarney Cutting | 30.00 |
| **Goblet,** Victorian | 16.00 |
| **Goblet,** Victorian, 2-Knob Stem | 10.00 |
| **Goblet,** Water, Frontenac, Crystal | 14.00 |
| **Goblet,** Water, New Era, 6 1/2 In. | 20.00 |
| **Goblet,** Water, Olympiade | 24.00 |
| **Goblet,** Waverly, 9 Ounce | 27.00 |
| **Goblet,** Whirlpool, Signed | 12.00 |
| **Hair Receiver & Powder Box,** Pinwheel & Fan, Silver Plated Tops | 65.00 |
| **Hair Receiver & Powder Jar,** Dancing Ladies, Signed, 4 X 4 In., Pair | 80.00 |
| **Hair Receiver,** Colonial, Celluloid Lid | 24.00 |
| **Hair Receiver,** Pinwheel & Fan, Silver Plated Top, Signed | 32.00 |
| **Heisey,** Creamer, Cabochon, Crystal | 10.00 |
| **Honey Pot & Tray,** Amethyst, Dated & Signed, 8 In. | 60.00 |
| **Ice Bucket,** Greek Key, Small | 55.00 |
| **Ice Bucket,** Green Swirl, Aluminum Bail | 65.00 |
| **Ice Bucket,** Marigold Swirl, Intaglio Cutting, Handle, Oval | 90.00 |
| **Ice Bucket,** Moongleam, Tongs, In Stand, Marked | 75.00 |
| **Ice Bucket,** Old Colony, Dolphin Footed, Etched, Metal Handle | 50.00 |
| **Ice Bucket,** Queen Anne, Footed, Silver Overlay | 55.00 |
| **Ice Tea,** Ipswich, Footed, 6 1/4 In. | 18.50 |
| **Jar,** Candy, Flower Design, Cut, Sterling Cover, C.1915, 10 In. | 195.00 |
| **Jar,** Candy, Ipswich, Amethyst, Covered | 35.00 |
| **Jar,** Candy, Pleat & Panel, Cover, Marked | 50.00 |
| **Jar,** Marmalade, Apple Pattern, Cover | 45.00 |
| **Jar,** Pickle, Colonial, Covered | 22.50 |
| **Jug,** Moongleam, Footed, 54 Ounce | 130.00 |
| **Lemonade Set,** Hand-Painted Roses, Gold Trim, Custard Band, 7 Piece | 750.00 |
| **Mayonnaise & Ladle,** Empress, Alexandrite | 75.00 |
| **Mayonnaise & Ladle,** Empress, Sahara | 15.00 |
| **Mayonnaise Set,** Crystolite, Marked | 22.00 To 25.00 |
| **Mayonnaise Set,** Grape, Plate, 7 1/2 In. | 22.00 |
| **Mayonnaise Set,** Moongleam, Footed | 24.50 |
| **Mayonnaise Set,** Pheasant Border, Ornate Gold, Ladle, Footed | 44.00 |
| **Mayonnaise Set,** Twist Design, Flamingo, Footed, Signed | 25.00 |
| **Mug,** Beer, Fox Chase, Deep Plate | 95.00 |
| **Mug,** Child's, Custard Glass, Colorado Springs | 35.00 |
| **Mug,** Orange Tree, Marigold | 25.00 |
| **Mug,** Pineapple Fan | 25.00 |
| **Mug,** Punty Band, Custard | 35.00 |
| **Mug,** Ring Band, Custard | 50.00 |
| **Mustard,** Broad Flute Pattern, Covered, Finial Lid, Marked | 24.50 |
| **Mustard,** Crystolite, Covered | 15.00 |
| **Mustard,** Oceanic, Pink | 42.00 |
| **Nappy,** Greek Key, 4 1/2 In., Set Of 4 | 45.00 |
| **Nappy,** Touraine, Signed, 8 In. | 14.00 |
| **Parfait,** Moonglo, Cut | 23.00 |
| **Pitcher,** Cider, Pink, Swirl Design | 98.00 |
| **Pitcher,** Colonial, Squat, 3 Quart | 100.00 |
| **Pitcher,** Flamingo, 54 Ounce | 75.00 |
| **Pitcher,** Gravy, Colonial, Footed, Pink, Matching Ladle | 25.00 |
| **Pitcher,** Paneled, 4 Quart | 45.00 |
| **Pitcher,** Rib & Panel, 4 Tumblers, Clear | 80.00 |
| **Pitcher,** Water, Crystolite | 55.00 |
| **Pitcher,** Water, Fancy Loop | 75.00 |
| **Pitcher,** Water, Greek Key | 120.00 To 125.00 |

| | |
|---|---|
| Pitcher, Water, Loop | 100.00 |
| Pitcher, Water, Pinwheel & Fan | 100.00 |
| Plaque, Display | 165.00 |
| Plate, Amber, 5 In., Set Of 6 | 65.00 |
| Plate, Beehive, Flamingo, 5 In. | 15.00 |
| Plate, Cake, Colonial, Marked | 150.00 |
| Plate, Cake, Maple Leaf, Gold Center Flower, White Ground, 9 In. | 45.00 |
| Plate, Cake, Orchid, Center-Handled | 30.00 |
| Plate, Colonial, Marked, 7 1/2 In. | 16.00 |
| Plate, Colonial, Marked, 10 1/2 In. | 25.00 |
| Plate, Colonial, 30-Point Cut Rayed Bottom, Signed, 7 1/4 In. | 20.00 |
| Plate, Crystolite, 10 1/2 In. | 40.00 |
| Plate, Dessert, Crystolite, Marked | 22.50 |
| Plate, Dessert, Diana, 6 In. | 5.00 |
| Plate, Diana, 8 In. | 7.00 |
| Plate, Diana, 8 In., Set Of 12 | 120.00 |
| Plate, Eagle, 8 In. | 65.00 |
| Plate, Empress, Etched, Pink | 8.00 |
| Plate, Empress, Moongleam, 7 In. | 6.00 |
| Plate, Empress, Moongleam, 10 1/2 In. | 25.00 |
| Plate, Empress, Moonglo, Marked, 8 In.Square | 15.00 |
| Plate, Empress, Sahara, 7 1/2 In., Set Of 6 | 125.00 |
| Plate, Frontenac, 7 1/2 In. | 7.00 |
| Plate, Heritage, Crystal, 9 1/4 In. | 4.00 |
| Plate, Moongleam, Marked, 7 In. | 5.00 To 6.00 |
| Plate, Moongleam, Marked, 8 In. | 10.00 To 35.00 |
| Plate, Moongleam, 6 In. | 5.00 |
| Plate, Moongleam, 9 In. | 20.00 |
| Plate, Muffin, Hawthorne | 16.00 |
| Plate, Oceanic, Green, 8 In. | 10.00 |
| Plate, Orchid Etch, 7 In., Pair | 11.50 |
| Plate, Orchid Etch, 8 In. | 10.00 To 15.00 |
| Plate, Orchid Etch, 10 1/2 In. | 22.00 |
| Plate, Pied Piper, 7 In. | 6.00 |
| Plate, Pleat & Panel, Marked, 7 1/2 In., Pair | 10.00 |
| Plate, Pleat & Panel, Marked, 8 In. | 8.00 |
| Plate, Prince Of Wales, Gold, 7 In. | 45.00 |
| Plate, Rib & Panel, 8 In. | 8.00 |
| Plate, Ridgeleigh, 6 1/2 In. | 10.00 |
| Plate, Sandwich, Empress, 12 In. | 35.00 |
| Plate, Sunflower, Crystal, 14 In. | 25.00 |
| Plate, Torte, Fern, 13 In. | 20.00 |
| Plate, Twist Design, Green, Signed | 15.00 |
| Plate, Waverly, 8 In. | 10.00 |
| Platter, Colonial, 19 In. | 50.00 |
| Platter, Lariat, 14 In. | 25.00 To 30.00 |
| Punch Bowl, Beaded Panel & Sunburst, 14 1/2 In. | 110.00 |
| Punch Set, Colonial, 12 Cups | 195.00 |
| Punch Set, Pineapple, 12 Cups, Marked, Bowl 8 1/2 X 13 1/2 In. | 395.00 |
| Punch Set, Whirling Star, 12 Cups, Marked, Bowl 15 X 14 1/2 In. | 395.00 |
| Relish, Crystolite, 4 Compartments | 15.00 |
| Relish, Diana, 3-Section, Pink, 8 In. | 15.00 |
| Relish, Lariat, 3 Section, 11 In.Diam. | 24.00 To 30.00 |
| Relish, Ridgeleigh, 5 Compartments, Marked, 10 In. | 33.00 |
| Relish, Sahara, 3-Section, 10 In. | 26.50 |
| Relish, Waverly, 3 Section | 28.00 To 32.00 |
| Relish, Whirlpool, Divided | 20.00 |
| Rose Bowl, Alexandrite, 12 In. | 675.00 |
| Rose Bowl, Barcelona, Metal Stand | 75.00 |
| Rose Bowl, Optic, 6 In. | 55.00 |
| Rose Bowl, Serrated Top, Etched, 3-Footed, Yellow, 5 In.Diam. | 15.00 |
| Salt & Pepper, Crystolite | 36.00 |
| Salt & Pepper, Greek Key | 75.00 |

| | |
|---|---|
| Salt & Pepper, Orchid Etch | 55.00 |
| Salt & Pepper, Waverly | 38.00 |
| Saltshaker, Colonial, Stem | 20.00 |
| Saltshaker, Pineapple & Fan | 15.00 |
| Saltshaker, Waverly Rose | 27.50 |
| Sauce, Button & Arches | 35.00 |
| Sauce, Continental, Signed, Set Of 2 | 11.00 |
| Sauceboat & Tray, Enameled Floral Border, Signed | 45.00 |
| Saucer, Button & Arches | 35.00 |
| Saucer, Empress, Alexandrite, Square | 12.50 |
| Saucer, Empress, Sahara, Marked, 4 In. | 4.00 To 10.00 |
| Sherbet, Americana | 12.00 |
| Sherbet, Colonial, Flared, Marked | 8.00 To 10.00 |
| Sherbet, Colonial, Footed, Signed, 4 Ounce, Set Of 12 | 90.00 |
| Sherbet, Greek Key, Low, Flared, Marked, 6 Ounce | 10.00 |
| Sherbet, Heisey Rose | 30.00 |
| Sherbet, Ipswich | 12.50 |
| Sherbet, Minuet, Etched Stem, Set Of 4 | 70.00 |
| Sherbet, Narrow Flute, 5 Ounce | 6.00 To 12.50 |
| Sherbet, New Era | 18.00 |
| Sherbet, Olympiade | 22.00 |
| Sherbet, Rose | 30.00 |
| Sherbet, Victorian | 9.00 |
| Sherbet, Waverly | 7.00 |
| Sherry, Orchid, Tyrolean Stem, 2 Ounce | 48.00 |
| Soup, Cream, Empress, Flamingo, 2-Handled, Marked | 20.00 |
| Spooner, Colonial | 12.00 |
| Spooner, Crystalite | 25.00 |
| Spooner, Narcissus | 22.50 |
| Spooner, Victorian | 30.00 |
| Sugar & Creamer, Colonial | 35.00 |
| Sugar & Creamer, Crystolite | 20.00 |
| Sugar & Creamer, Custard, Marked | 235.00 |
| Sugar & Creamer, Equator, Flamingo | 40.00 |
| Sugar & Creamer, Etched Design, Ring Handle, Footed | 95.00 |
| Sugar & Creamer, Greek Key, Hotel | 24.00 |
| Sugar & Creamer, Lariat, Marked | 14.00 |
| Sugar & Creamer, Moongleam | 36.50 |
| Sugar & Creamer, Moonglo | 38.00 To 40.00 |
| Sugar & Creamer, Narrow Flute, Cube, Gold Trim, 8 In. | 35.00 |
| Sugar & Creamer, Octagonal, Pink | 27.50 |
| Sugar & Creamer, Pink Panel | 25.00 |
| Sugar & Creamer, Ridgeleigh | 25.00 To 35.00 |
| Sugar & Creamer, Rose Pattern, Footed, Signed | 57.00 |
| Sugar & Creamer, Sahara | 30.00 |
| Sugar & Creamer, Waverly | 30.00 To 48.00 |
| Sugar & Creamer, Whirlpool, Imperial, Amethyst | 30.00 |
| Sugar & Creamer, Zodiac, Crystal | 55.00 |
| Sugar Shaker, Flamingo | 25.00 |
| Sugar, Colonial, Covered, Marked | 35.00 |
| Sugar, Creamer, & Tray, Crystolite, Oval, Individual | 22.00 |
| Sugar, Fancy Loop | 35.00 |
| Sugar, Flamingo, Covered, Marked | 15.00 |
| Sugar, Plantation, Crystal, Open | 15.00 |
| Sugar, Ribbed Octagon, Moongleam, 2-Handled | 15.00 |
| Syrup, Colonial, Cut, Marked | 35.00 |
| Syrup, Cut Pattern, 6-Sided, Marked | 49.00 |
| Syrup, Fandango, Metal Lid | 80.00 |
| Tankard, Banded Flute, 1 Quart | 48.00 |
| Toddy, Sahara | 22.00 |
| Toothpick, Beaded Swag, Ruby Flashed | 65.00 |
| Toothpick, Empress, Flamingo | 20.00 |
| Toothpick, Fancy Loop | 30.00 To 49.00 |

| | |
|---|---|
| Toothpick, Locket On Chain, Ruby Stained, Gold | 500.00 |
| Toothpick, Loop Pattern | 28.00 |
| Toothpick, Pineapple & Fan, Emerald Green | 125.00 |
| Toothpick, Pineapple & Fan, Gold Trim, Emerald Green | 195.00 |
| Toothpick, Pink Pattern Glass | 35.00 |
| Toothpick, Priscilla | 25.00 |
| Toothpick, Ring Band | 85.00 |
| Toothpick, Star Design, Cobalt Blue, Signed | 18.00 |
| Toothpick, Swag Bead | 25.00 |
| Toothpick, Winged Scroll, Gold Trim, Custard | 125.00 |
| Toothpick, Zion City In Red, Gold Trim | 45.00 |
| Tray, Celery, Flamingo, Marked | 30.00 |
| Tray, Sandwich, Empress Design, 12 1/2 In. | 20.00 To 35.00 |
| Tray, Sandwich, Waverly, Seahorse Center Handle, 14 In.Diam. | 45.00 |
| Tray, Torte, Orchid, 14 In. | 52.00 |
| Tumbler, Bar, Coleport, 13 Ounce | 10.00 |
| Tumbler, Bar, Tally-Ho, Etched, 3 1/2 In. | 45.00 |
| Tumbler, Brazilian, Emerald | 18.00 |
| Tumbler, Carcassone, 11 Ounce | 20.00 |
| Tumbler, Colonial, 7 Ounce | 12.00 |
| Tumbler, Cross-Lined, Flute | 20.00 |
| Tumbler, Dawn | 25.00 |
| Tumbler, Greek Key, Signed, 8 Ounce | 35.00 |
| Tumbler, Iced Tea, Ipswich, Footed, 6 1/4 In. | 18.50 |
| Tumbler, Iced Tea, Victorian, Footed | 16.00 |
| Tumbler, Ipswich, Footed, Crystal, 12 Ounce | 12.00 |
| Tumbler, Juice, Whirlpool | 12.50 |
| Tumbler, Loop Variant, Gold Trim | 26.00 |
| Tumbler, Old Sandwich, 5 Ounce | 12.50 |
| Tumbler, Optic | 12.00 |
| Tumbler, Orchid, 6 1/2 In. | 20.00 |
| Tumbler, Pineapple & Fan, Gold Trim, Emerald | 55.00 |
| Tumbler, Prince Of Wales | 20.00 |
| Tumbler, Punty Band, Marked, Blandburg, Pa. | 40.00 |
| Tumbler, Ring Band | 50.00 |
| Tumbler, Rose, Footed, 12 Ounce | 25.00 |
| Tumbler, Victorian | 10.00 |
| Vase, Bristol, Floral, 7 1/2 In. | 35.00 |
| Vase, Cornucopia, Marked, Clear, 9 In. | 145.00 |
| Vase, Cornucopia, Marked, 5 In., Pair | 35.00 |
| Vase, Cornucopia, 7 In., Pair | 40.00 |
| Vase, Fancy Loop, 8 In. | 30.00 |
| Vase, Lariat, Crimped, 7 1/2 In. | 10.00 |
| Vase, Optic Tooth, Flamingo, 10 In. | 50.00 |
| Vase, Ridgeleigh, 8 3/4 In. | 24.00 |
| Vase, Trumpet Shape, Clear, 12 X 5 In. | 32.00 |
| Vase, Violet, Panel Ribs, Marked, 3 In. | 23.00 |
| Vase, Whirlpool, Crimped, Amethyst, 5 In. | 35.00 |
| Water Set, Tiger Lily, Azure, 7 Piece | 275.00 |
| Wine Set, Grape, Azure, 9 Piece | 225.00 |
| Wine, Alexandrite, 2 1/2 Ounce | 95.00 |
| Wine, Colonial, Molded Mark, Set Of 5 | 100.00 |
| Wine, Fancy Loop, Emerald | 110.00 |
| Wine, Minuet, Symphony Stem, 3 1/2 Ounce | 32.00 |
| Wine, New Era, Venus Cut | 35.00 |

### HEREND, see also Fischer

| | |
|---|---|
| HEREND, Figurine, Boy, Chasing Goose, 7 1/2 X 1 1/2 In. | 85.00 |
| Figurine, Shepherd Boy & Girl, 7 1/2 X 5 1/2 In. | 175.00 |

*Gebruder Heubach, a German firm working from 1820 to 1925, is best known for bisque dolls and doll heads, their principal products. They also manufactured bisque figurines, including piano babies, beginning in the 1880s, and glazed figurines in the 1900s.*

**HEUBACH, Ashtray,** 2 Horses, Match Holder, 5 X 5 1/2 In. ............................................. 265.00
    **Dish,** Jasperware, Indian With Bow & Arrow, Signed, 4 1/4 In. ......................... 50.00
    **Ewer,** Scenic, Green, 4 In., Pair .............................................................. 135.00
    **Ewer,** Scenic, House & Trees, 4 1/2 In., Pair ........................................... 135.00
    **Figurine,** Bear, Gray & White, Seated, Marked, 3 1/2 X 3 In. ...................... 135.00
    **Figurine,** Boy, Pouring Milk Into Seashell, 9 In. ...................................... 165.00
    **Figurine,** Chick, Yellow & Tan, White Oval Base, Marked, 3 1/8 In. ............. 50.00
    **Figurine,** Children, Dutch Dress, Seated, Marked, 7 X 9 In. ....................... 950.00
    **Figurine,** Colonial Gentleman, Dressed In Blue, Gilding, Marked, 8 In. ........ 145.00
    **Figurine,** Colonial Man Holding Hat, Gilded Gold, White, 8 3/4 In. ............. 175.00
    **Figurine,** Colonial Man, Blue With Gold Gilding, Marked, 8 In. ................... 195.00
    **Figurine,** Dog, Long-Haired White Dog, Red Collar, Marked, 7 1/2 In. ......... 265.00
    **Figurine,** Dove, Tinted Eyes, Beak, & Feet, White, Marked ......................... 250.00
    **Figurine,** Dutch Boy & Girl, Signed, 7 3/4 In. ......................................... 895.00
    **Figurine,** Dutch Boy, Book In Hands Behind Him, Marked, 10 1/2 In. .......... 295.00
    **Figurine,** Dutch Boy, Gray & White, Marked, 10 1/8 In. ............................ 135.00
    **Figurine,** Dutch Girl, Blue & White, Marked, 4 1/4 X 2 1/4 In. ................... 88.00
    **Figurine,** Dutch Girl, Green & Red, Signed, 5 In. .................................... 125.00
    **Figurine,** Dutch Girl, Shades Of Blue & White, Marked, 4 1/4 In. ............... 88.00
    **Figurine,** Girl & Holder, Pastel Colors, Signed, 6 In. ............................... 95.00
    **Figurine,** Herring Gull, 5 In.Long ....................................................... 55.00
    **Figurine,** Kittens, Two, 4 X 3 X 2 In. ................................................... 65.00
    **Figurine,** Lad On Flower-Laden Ladder, Open Basket, Bisque, 7 In. ............ 53.00
    **Figurine,** Laughing Dutch Boy, Marked, 7 1/2 In. .................................... 150.00
    **Figurine,** Peasant Girl, Hands Above Head ......................................... 295.00
    **Figurine,** Polar Bear, White ............................................................... 125.00
    **Figurine,** Sailor Boy, Lavender & Green Outfit, Marked, 9 3/8 In. .............. 110.00
    **Figurine,** Young Boy, Cream Trousers, Jacket & Hat, Marked, 9 3/4 In. ........ 85.00
    **Figurine,** Young Girl In Nightgown, Praying, Marked, 10 In. ..................... 110.00
    **Vase,** Dutch Mother & Child, Blown-Out, Sunburst Mark, 5 In. ................... 95.00
    **Vase,** Roses, Sunburst Mark, 4 In., Pair ............................................... 110.00
    **Vase,** Woman, Flowers, Swan, Bisque, 8 In. ......................................... 50.00

**H I G**

    *Higbee glass was made by the J.B.Higbee Company of Bridgeville,*
    *Pennsylvania, about 1900.*
    **HIGBEE, see also Pressed Glass**
**HIGBEE, Vase,** Sling, Marked, 12 In. .................................................... 22.50
    **HISTORIC BLUE, see Adams; Clews; Ridgway; Staffordshire**

    *Hobnail glass is a pattern of glass with bumps in an allover pattern.*
    *Dozens of hobnail patterns and variants have been made. Reproductions of*
    *many types of hobnail glass can be found.*
    **HOBNAIL, see also Francisware**
**HOBNAIL, Bottle,** Cologne, Stopper, Lavender, 1920s .............................. 20.00
    **Bowl,** Applied White Opaque Ribbon Edge, Cranberry, 7 3/4 In.Diam. ........ 250.00
    **Mug,** Blue, 9 Rows ......................................................................... 40.00
    **Pitcher,** Pink, 8 In. ......................................................................... 55.00

    *Holly amber, or golden agate, glass was made by the Indiana Tumbler and*
    *Goblet Company from January 1, 1903 to June 13, 1903. It is a pressed*
    *glass pattern featuring holly leaves in the amber-shaded glass.*

**HOLLY AMBER, Butter,** Covered ......................................................... 1250.00
    **Sauce** ...................................................................... 200.00 To 325.00
    **Sugar,** Open, 4 In. ......................................................................... 495.00
    **Vase,** Parfait, 6 In. ......................................................................... 600.00

**HONESDALE, Cocktail,** Colored Fighting Roosters, Enameled ..................... 22.50
    **Vase,** Gold Enameled, Flowers, Emerald Green Ground, 14 In., Pair ........... 200.00
    **Vase,** Leaded, Stained Green, Gold Outlines, Etched, Signed, 12 In. .......... 225.00

**HOPALONG CASSIDY, Bar 20 Ranch Badge,** Star Shape, 1950, On Card ............................ 15.00
  **Bedspread,** Single Size ......................................................................................... 175.00
  **Belt & Spurs** ........................................................................................................ 25.00
  **Belt,** Extra Buckle, Original Card ........................................................................... 25.00
  **Book,** Pop-Up, 1950 ............................................................................................ 19.00
  **Bowl,** Cup, & Plate ............................................................................................... 30.00
  **Button,** Pan-O-Gold, Bread .................................................................................. 6.00
  **Cookie Jar,** Original Label, 1950 ......................................................................... 55.00
  **Cowgirl Outfit,** Boxed ......................................................................................... 38.00
  **Dental Kit,** Boxed .................................................................................................. 20.00
  **Drum,** 1952 .......................................................................................................... 34.00
  **Field Glasses,** Boxed ........................................................................................... 35.00
  **Flashlight** .............................................................................................................. 12.50
  **Flatware,** Knife, Fork, Spoon, Original Box ........................................................... 45.00
  **Game,** Dominoes, Boxed ...................................................................................... 35.00
  **Game,** Ring Toss .................................................................................................. 7.25
  **Gun & Holster,** Boxed, Pair .................................................................................. 50.00
  **Gun & Spurs Set,** Boxed ...................................................................................... 65.00
  **Horse,** Topper, Inflatable, Original Box ................................................................. 50.00
  **Knife,** Pen ............................................................................................................. 25.00
  **Lamp,** Bullet Shape, Aladdin Alacite, Original Shade ........................................... 125.00
  **Lunch Box,** With Thermos, 1954 .......................................................................... 35.00
  **Mug,** Milk Glass ........................................................................... 8.50 To 15.00
  **Night-Light,** Gun In Holster, Alacite ........................................... 60.00 To 75.00
  **Plate & Glass,** Milk Glass ..................................................................................... 25.00
  **Pocketwatch,** 1950 .............................................................................................. 225.00
  **Puzzle,** Boxed, Set Of 3 ....................................................................................... 30.00
  **Radio,** Arvin ................................................................................. 30.00 To 90.00
  **Ring** ...................................................................................................................... 15.00
  **Roller Skates** ....................................................................................................... 85.00
  **Spurs,** 1950s ....................................................................................................... 22.50
  **Tin,** Potato Chips ................................................................................................. 10.00
  **Tumbler,** 5 In. ...................................................................................................... 12.00
  **Watch,** 1950, Smaller Size ................................................................................... 65.00
  **Wristwatch,** Good Luck Hoppy On Back .............................................................. 30.00

**HOWDY DOODY, Camera,** Sun Ray ...................................................................... 25.00
  **Glasses,** Juice, 6 Character, 1953, Set Of 6 ....................................................... 20.00
  **Handkerchief** ........................................................................................................ 10.00
  **Lamp,** Electric ...................................................................................................... 45.00
  **Marionette** ................................................................................... 30.00 To 95.00
  **Night Light,** Boxed ............................................................................................... 15.00
  **Rag Doll,** Flub A Dub ........................................................................................... 35.00
  **Sketch Set,** Boxed ............................................................................................... 22.00
  **Spoon,** Silver Plate .............................................................................................. 12.00
  **Straw Holder,** Boxed ............................................................................................ 8.00
  **Tube,** Swimming, Inflatable ................................................................................. 12.50
  **Tumbler,** Kraft, 1953, Orange .............................................................................. 2.00

*Hull pottery is made in Crooksville, Ohio. The factory started in 1903*
*as the Acme Pottery Company. Art pottery was first made in 1917.*

**HULL, Ashtray,** Serenade, Yellow, 13 X 10 1/2 In. ............................................... 12.00
  **Banana Bowl,** Scalloped, Shaded Green, Marked, 7 X 10 3/4 X 2 In. .................... 15.00
  **Basket,** Bowknot, Pink & Blue, 10 1/2 In. ............................................................ 60.00
  **Basket,** Dogwood, Beige & Pink, 7 1/2 In. ........................................................... 32.00
  **Basket,** Overhandle, Wheat Design, Green Ground, 16 1/2 In. .............................. 32.00
  **Basket,** Parchment & Pine, Green, 8 X 5 In. ........................................................ 35.00
  **Basket,** Pink & White Spatter, Glazed, 11 X 11 In. .............................................. 32.00
  **Basket,** Wildflower, 10 1/2 In. .............................................................................. 50.00
  **Basket,** Woodland, 10 1/2 In. ............................................................................... 25.00
  **Bowl,** Console, Water Lily, 14 X 5 In. ................................................................... 17.00
  **Bowl,** Flowers & Pink Birds, Ruffled Cover, 9 1/2 In. ........................................... 28.00

**Bowl,** Fruit, Pink To Green, 9 In. .............................................................................. 18.00
**Butter,** Red Riding Hood, Covered ........................................................ 40.00 To 45.00
**Candleholder,** Magnolia, Pair .............................................................................. 25.00
**Candleholder,** Parchment & Pine, Green, Pair ...................................................... 20.00
**Candleholder,** Single, Wildflower, Pink & Blue, 2 1/2 In. ....................................... 14.00
**Candleholder,** Wildflower, Pair ............................................................................ 25.00
**Candleholder,** Woodland, Matte, 5 In. .................................................................. 10.00
**Console Set,** Serenade, Candlestick 6 3/8 In., Bowl 7 X 11 1/2 In. ........................ 75.00
**Cookie Jar,** Baby Duck .......................................................................... 28.00 To 32.00
**Cookie Jar,** Bear ................................................................................................. 12.00
**Cookie Jar,** Brown Glaze ..................................................................................... 12.50
**Cookie Jar,** Drum ................................................................................................ 15.00
**Cookie Jar,** Duck, Glazed, 12 In. ......................................................................... 14.00
**Cookie Jar,** Red Riding Hood ............................................................... 25.00 To 44.00
**Cornucopia,** Camelia, 8 1/2 In. ............................................................................ 32.00
**Cornucopia,** Dark Green At Opening, Shell Shape, 10 1/4 X 5 X 4 1/4 In. .............. 10.75
**Cornucopia,** Dogwood, 11 1/2 In. ........................................................................ 44.00
**Cornucopia,** Double, Bowknot ............................................................................. 35.00
**Cornucopia,** Magnolia, 8 1/2 In. .......................................................................... 16.00
**Cornucopia,** Parchment & Pine, Green, 7 1/2 In. .................................................. 18.00
**Cornucopia,** 11 X 10 In.Wide .............................................................................. 25.00
**Creamer,** Magnolia .............................................................................................. 10.00
**Creamer,** Red Riding Hood .................................................................................. 22.50
**Ewer,** Jack-In-The-Pulpit, 11 In. ........................................................................... 45.00
**Ewer,** Magnolia, Pink & Blue, 13 1/2 In. ............................................................... 45.00
**Ewer,** Orchid, 13 In. ............................................................................................. 45.00
**Ewer,** Parchment & Pine, Gold Design, Green, 15 In. ............................................ 65.00
**Ewer,** Tokay, White & Green, 13 In. ...................................................................... 22.00
**Ewer,** White Blossoms, Pink, 7 1/4 In. .................................................................. 20.00
**Ewer,** Wildflower, 13 In. ....................................................................................... 50.00
**Jar,** Candy, Red Riding Hood ............................................................................... 65.00
**Jardiniere,** Orchid, No.310, 9 1/2 In. .................................................................... 25.00
**Jardiniere,** Tulip, 6 X 8 In.Diam. ........................................................................... 38.00
**Lamp,** Vase Shape, Bulbous Bottom, Yellow & Orange Flowers, 11 1/2 In. ............. 89.50
**Lavabo Set,** White, Butterflies, Flowers ................................................................ 30.00
**Pepper Shaker,** Pink Flower, Green Leaves, Yellow Ground ...................................... 4.95
**Pitcher,** Blue, Crisscross Design, 5 In. ................................................................... 9.00
**Pitcher,** Butterfly, 13 1/2 In. ................................................................................ 25.00
**Pitcher,** Magnolia, Yellow Flower, Pink Bud, Open Handle, 7 In. ............................ 26.50
**Pitcher,** Red Riding Hood, 8 In. ........................................................................... 77.50
**Pitcher,** Rosella, White Flowers, Handle, Label, 7 1/4 In. ...................................... 15.95
**Pitcher,** Yellow Matte, 10 1/2 In. ......................................................................... 25.00
**Planter,** Baby Swan, Glossy Green With Darker Green, Marked, 4 X 3 In. ................ 6.95
**Planter,** Butterfly Design, Ivory & Aqua ................................................................ 10.00
**Planter,** Butterfly, Lavabo ..................................................................................... 25.00
**Planter,** Cat ......................................................................................................... 18.00
**Planter,** Duck ...................................................................................................... 15.00
**Planter,** Fighting Cocks, Pair ............................................................................... 22.00
**Planter,** Flying Goose, Pair ................................................................................... 60.00
**Planter,** Green Leafy Base, Ribbed & Scalloped Top, 10 1/4 X 4 X 5 In. ................ 17.50
**Planter,** Kitten ..................................................................................................... 14.00
**Planter,** Mother Cat & Kitten, Siamese, 12 In. ...................................................... 25.00
**Planter,** Pig, Blue, Yellow, Matte Finish .................................................................. 9.50
**Planter,** Poodle ..................................................................................................... 8.00
**Planter,** Seminude Woman ................................................................................... 18.00
**Planter,** St. Francis, Cream, 12 In. ....................................................................... 15.00
**Planter,** Swan, Green, 7 1/2 In. ........................................................................... 15.00
**Salt & Pepper,** Red Riding Hood, 5 1/2 In. ............................................ 15.00 To 25.00
**Saltshaker,** Pink Flower, Green Leaves, Yellow Ground ........................................... 4.95
**Stein,** Frothy White Around Top, Brown, Marked, 16 Ounce ................................... 6.50
**Sugar & Creamer,** Open, Magnolia, Matte Brown To Tan, 3 1/4 In. ....................... 21.50
**Sugar Shaker,** Red Riding Hood ........................................................................... 12.50
**Tea Set,** Parchment & Pine, 3 Piece ..................................................................... 45.00

| | |
|---|---|
| **Tea Set,** Woodland, 3 Piece | 55.00 |
| **Teapot,** Butterfly Design | 30.00 |
| **Teapot,** Red Riding Hood | 45.00 |
| **Teapot,** Sugar, & Creamer, Cover, Water Lily Pattern | 55.00 |
| **Teapot,** Sugar, & Creamer, High Gloss | 55.00 |
| **Vase,** Bowknot, Green & Blue, 6 1/2 In. | 18.00 |
| **Vase,** Bowknot, Pink & Blue, 8 1/2 In. | 22.00 |
| **Vase,** Bowknot, 8 1/2 In. | 32.00 |
| **Vase,** Bud, Double, Woodland, Pink To Green, 8 1/2 In. | 30.00 |
| **Vase,** Butterflies, Triangular | 21.00 |
| **Vase,** Camelia, 8 1/2 In. | 20.00 |
| **Vase,** Fan Shape, Wildflower, Beige & Brown, 10 1/2 In. | 24.00 |
| **Vase,** Flamingo, Pink & Yellow Bird, Glossy, 8 3/4 In. | 19.50 |
| **Vase,** Hat Shape, Serenade, Pink | 18.00 |
| **Vase,** Jack-In-The-Pulpit, Blue & Pink, 8 In. | 32.00 |
| **Vase,** Magnolia Pattern, Pink & Blue Matte, 8 1/2 In. | 20.00 |
| **Vase,** Magnolia, Brown To Yellow, 8 1/2 In. | 28.00 To 30.00 |
| **Vase,** Magnolia, 13 In. | 35.00 |
| **Vase,** Narcissus, Original Seal, 8 1/2 In. | 25.00 |
| **Vase,** Orange-Gold, Green Base, 9 In. | 32.00 |
| **Vase,** Parchment & Pine, Scrolled Base, Pine Design, 6 3/4 In. | 17.50 |
| **Vase,** Pastel Brushstroke, H In Circle, 8 In. | 18.00 |
| **Vase,** Pink Floral, 6 1/2 In. | 15.00 |
| **Vase,** Pink To Blue Matte, Marked, 8 3/4 In. | 25.00 |
| **Vase,** Shell & Fish, 7 In., Pair | 20.00 |
| **Vase,** Thistle, Blue, 6 1/2 In. | 16.00 To 22.00 |
| **Vase,** Tokay, Handled, Pink & Green, 5 1/2 In. | 12.00 |
| **Vase,** Tulip, 6 In. | 12.00 |
| **Vase,** Water Lily, 6 1/2 In. | 12.00 To 15.00 |
| **Vase,** Water Lily, 8 1/2 In. | 22.00 |
| **Vase,** Wildflower, Blue To Pink, 9 In. | 30.00 |
| **Vase,** Wildflower, Yellow, Pink, 13 In. | 35.00 |
| **Vase,** Wildflower, Yellow, 7 1/2 In. | 18.00 |
| **Wall Pocket,** Blue Speckled, 7 1/2 In. | 14.00 |
| **Wall Pocket,** Bowknot, Blue | 20.00 |
| **Wall Pocket,** Butterfly | 8.50 |
| **Wall Pocket,** Open Rose, 8 In. | 12.00 |
| **Wall Pocket,** Pink Heart With Flowers, 6 1/4 In. | 12.00 |
| **Wall Pocket,** Red Riding Hood | 40.00 |
| **Wall Pocket,** Rose & White, 7 1/2 In. | 15.00 |
| **Wall Pocket,** Teapot Shape, Pink Flower & Butterfly | 15.00 |
| **Wall Pocket,** Whiskbroom, Paper Sticker | 18.00 |
| **Wall Pocket,** Woodland | 15.00 |

*Hummel figurines, based on the drawings of Berta Hummel, are made by the W. Goebel Porzellanfabrik of Oeslau, Germany. They were first made in 1934. The mark has changed slightly through the years. The "crown" mark dates 1935 to 1949. "U.S. Zone, Germany" dates 1946 to 1948, "West Germany" dates after 1949, "incised bee" dates 1950 to 1955, "full bee" dates 1950 to 1959, "stylized bee" dates 1960 to 1972, "three line mark" dates after 1968.*

| | |
|---|---|
| **HUMMEL, Bookends,** Bookworm, No.141/a & b, Stylized Bee, 5 1/2 In. ............ *Illus* | 225.00 |
| **Creamer,** Friar Tuck, 2 1/2 In. | 15.00 |
| **Figurine,** Accordion Boy, No.185, Stylized Bee | 80.00 |
| **Figurine,** Adoration, No.23/0, Stylized Bee | 185.00 |
| **Figurine,** Angel Serenade, No.83, Crown & Full Bee | 500.00 To 550.00 |
| **Figurine,** Angel With Yellow Bird, No.167, Full Bee Mark | 275.00 |
| **Figurine,** Apple Tree Boy, No.142/I, Incised Crown Mark, 6 In. | 275.00 |
| **Figurine,** Apple Tree Boy, No.142/I, Stylized Bee | 120.00 To 140.00 |
| **Figurine,** Apple Tree Boy, No.142/3/0, Brown Base, Full Bee | 135.00 |
| **Figurine,** Apple Tree Girl, No.141/I, Incised Crown Mark | 275.00 |
| **Figurine,** Apple Tree Girl, No.141/I, Stylized Bee | 120.00 |

Hummel, Bookends, Bookworm, No. 141/a & b,
Stylized Bee, 5 1/2 In. (See Page 263)

**Figurine,** Apple Tree Girl, No.141/3/0, Stylized Bee ........................................................................ 75.00
**Figurine,** Apple Tree Girl, No.141/3/0, Tree Trunk Base, Full Bee .......................................... 125.00
**Figurine,** Bandleader, No.129, Full Bee ............................................................... 135.00 To 160.00
**Figurine,** Barnyard Hero, No.195/I, Stylized Bee, 5 1/2 In. ...................................................... 145.00
**Figurine,** Barnyard Hero, No.195/2/0, Full Bee ........................................................................ 150.00
**Figurine,** Begging His Share, No.9, Full Bee, 5 3/4 In. ............................................................. 325.00
**Figurine,** Birthday Serenade, No.218/0, Reverse Mold, Full Bee ............................................. 725.00
**Figurine,** Birthday Serenade, No.218/2/0, Reverse Mold, Three Line .................................... 170.00
**Figurine,** Blessed Event, No.333, Full Bee ............................................................................... 215.00
**Figurine,** Bookworm Bookend, No.14/a, Incised Bee .............................................................. 200.00
**Figurine,** Boots, No.143/0, Stylized Bee ........................................................... 70.00 To 75.00
**Figurine,** Boy With Toothache, No.217, Full Bee ..................................................................... 130.00
**Figurine,** Brother, No.95, Stylized Bee .................................................................................... 65.00
**Figurine,** Carnival, No.328, No Holes In Pompoms, Three Line .............................................. 140.00
**Figurine,** Chick Girl, No.57/0, Stylized Bee ............................................................................ 110.00
**Figurine,** Christ Child, No.18, Full Bee .................................................................................... 75.00
**Figurine,** Christ Child, No.18, Stylized Bee ............................................................................ 100.00
**Figurine,** Culprits, No.56/a, Eyes Open, Full Bee ................................................................... 225.00
**Figurine,** Doctor, No.127, Stylized Bee ................................................................................... 100.00
**Figurine,** Doll Mother, No.67, Stylized Bee ............................................................................ 150.00
**Figurine,** Drummer, No.240, Three Line .................................................................................. 90.00
**Figurine,** Duet, No.130, Stylized Bee ...................................................................................... 105.00
**Figurine,** Farewell, No.65, Stylized Bee ........................................................... 150.00 To 160.00
**Figurine,** Farm Boy, No.66, Full Bee ....................................................................................... 170.00
**Figurine,** Feeding Time, No.199/0, Full Bee ........................................................................... 150.00
**Figurine,** Feeding Time, No.199/0, Stylized Bee ...................................................................... 90.00
**Figurine,** Festival Harmony With Flute, No.173/II, Stylized Bee ............................................ 210.00
**Figurine,** Festival Harmony With Flute, No.173/II, Three Line ............................................... 140.00
**Figurine,** Forest Shrine, No.183, Full Bee, 9 In. .................................................................... 750.00
**Figurine,** Friends, No.136/I, 3 Line ......................................................................................... 115.00
**Figurine,** Globetrotter, No.79, Stylized Bee ............................................................................ 100.00
**Figurine,** Goodnight, No.214/c, Three Line ............................................................................ 55.00
**Figurine,** Goose Girl, No.47/II, Stylized Bee ........................................................................... 240.00
**Figurine,** Goose Girl, No.47/0, Stylized Bee ..................................................... 100.00 To 120.00
**Figurine,** Goose Girl, No.47/3/0, Stylized Bee ......................................................................... 70.00
**Figurine,** Happiness, No.86, Full Bee Mark, 4 3/4 In. ............................................................ 155.00
**Figurine,** Happy Pastime, No.69, Stylized Bee ................................................ 95.00 To 100.00
**Figurine,** Hear Ye, Hear Ye, No.15/I, Stylized Bee ................................................................. 120.00
**Figurine,** Heavenly Angel, No.21/0, Full Bee .......................................................................... 125.00
**Figurine,** Herald Angels, No.37, Full Bee ................................................................................ 155.00
**Figurine,** Home From Market, No.198/2/0, Three Line Mark .................................................. 60.00
**Figurine,** Joyful, No.53, 1/4 In. Oversized, Stylized Bee ....................................................... 85.00

**Figurine,** Joyous News, No.27/III, Stylized Bee .................................................................. 600.00
**Figurine,** Just Resting, No.112/3/0, Full Bee .................................................................. 90.00
**Figurine,** Kiss Me, No.311, Three Line .................................................................. 115.00
**Figurine,** Knitting Lesson, No.256, No Eyelashes, Three Line .................................. 275.00
**Figurine,** Let's Sing, No.110/0, Full Bee .................................................................. 160.00
**Figurine,** Little Cellist, No.89/I, Stylized Bee .................................................................. 90.00
**Figurine,** Little Fiddler, No.4, Stylized Bee .................................................. 70.00 To 80.00
**Figurine,** Little Gardener, No.74, Raised Flower, Stylized Bee .................................. 90.00
**Figurine,** Little Helper, No.73, Stylized Bee .................................................. 105.00 To 115.00
**Figurine,** Little Hiker, No.16/I, Stylized Bee .................................................................. 75.00
**Figurine,** Little Scholar, No.80, Full Bee .................................................................. 175.00
**Figurine,** Little Sweeper, No.171, Full Bee .................................................. 125.00 To 215.00
**Figurine,** Little Tooter, 214/h, 3 Line Mark .................................................. 40.00 To 65.00
**Figurine,** Lost Sheep, No.68/0, Stylized Bee .................................................................. 75.00
**Figurine,** Lost Sheep, No.68, Gray Pants, Full Bee .................................................... 300.00
**Figurine,** Mail Is Here, No.226, Stylized Bee .................................................................. 210.00
**Figurine,** March Winds, No.43, Full Bee .................................................................. 145.00
**Figurine,** Max & Moritz, No.123, Three Line .................................................................. 100.00
**Figurine,** Mother's Darling, No.175, 2-Color Handkerchiefs, Full Bee ......................... 290.00
**Figurine,** Playmates, No.58/0, Full Bee .................................................................. 175.00
**Figurine,** Postman, No.119, 5 Letters, Shoelaces, Stylized Bee .................................. 160.00
**Figurine,** Schoolboy, No.82/0, Crown Mark .................................................................. 170.00
**Figurine,** Schoolboy, No.82/0, Stylized Bee .................................................................. 135.00
**Figurine,** Schoolgirl, No.81/0, Pink Blouse, Stylized Bee .......................................... 140.00
**Figurine,** Schoolgirl, No.81/2/0, Pink Blouse, Stylized Bee ....................................... 130.00
**Figurine,** Sensitive Hunter, No.6/II, Stylized Bee .................................................... 170.00
**Figurine,** Sensitive Hunter, No.6/0, Bee Mark, 4 3/4 In. .......................................... 175.00
**Figurine,** Signs Of Spring, No.203/2/0, Three Line Mark .......................................... 70.00
**Figurine,** Singing Lesson, No.63, Crown Mark .................................................................. 225.00
**Figurine,** Singing Lesson, No.63, Stylized Bee .................................................................. 120.00
**Figurine,** Soloist, No.135, Full Bee .................................................. 100.00 To 160.00
**Figurine,** Spring Cheer, No.72, Full Bee & Crown Mark .......................................... 295.00
**Figurine,** Stormy Weather, No.71, Full Bee, 6 1/4 In. .................................... *Illus* 330.00
**Figurine,** Stormy Weather, No.71, Stylized Bee .................................................... 250.00
**Figurine,** Surprise, No.94/I, Octagon Base, Full Bee .......................................... 180.00
**Figurine,** Surprise, No.94/2/0, Square Base, Full Bee .......................................... 180.00
**Figurine,** Surprise, No.94/3/0, Full Bee .................................................. 95.00 To 125.00

Hummel, Figurine, Stormy Weather, No.71, Full Bee, 6 1/4 In.

| | |
|---|---|
| **Figurine**, Sweet Music, No.186, Full Bee | 130.00 |
| **Figurine**, Trumpet Boy, No.97, Open Doughnut Base, Full Bee, 5 In. | 115.00 |
| **Figurine**, Umbrella Boy, No.152/a/II, Full Bee, 8 In. | 785.00 |
| **Figurine**, Umbrella Girl, No.152/b/O, Three Line | 325.00 |
| **Figurine**, Umbrella Girl, No.152/b/O, Three Line, 4 3/4 In. | 225.00 |
| **Figurine**, Waiter, No.154/O, Stylized Bee | 100.00 |
| **Figurine**, Wayside Devotion, No.28/II, Stylized Bee | 190.00 |
| **Figurine**, Wayside Harmony, No.111/I, Full Bee, 5 1/2 In. | 210.00 |
| **Figurine**, Wayside Harmony, No.111/3/0, Full Bee | 90.00 |
| **Figurine**, Weary Wanderer, No.204, Stylized Bee | 90.00 |
| **Figurine**, Which Hand, No.258, Three Line | 70.00 |
| **Figurine**, Worship, No.84/O, Stylized Bee, 8 In. | 90.00 |
| **Lamp**, Apple Tree Girl, No.M/229, Stylized Bee | 210.00 |
| **Lamp**, Culprits, No.44/a, Switch On Base, Full Bee | 350.00 |
| **Lamp**, Out Of Danger, No.M44b, Culprits, No.44/a, Full Bee, Pair | 500.00 |
| **Lamp**, Volunteers, No.102 | 5000.00 |
| **Pitcher**, Fat Monk, Miniature, Full Bee | 65.00 |
| **Plaque**, Flitting Butterfly, No.139, 2 1/2 In.Square | 30.00 |
| **Plaque**, Madonna, No.48/II, 4 3/4 X 6 In. | 75.00 |
| **Salt & Pepper**, Friar Tuck | 16.00 |

LORENZ
HUTSCHEN REUTER

GERMANY

*Hutschenreuther Porcelain Company of Selb, Germany, was established
in 1814 and is still working.*

| | |
|---|---|
| **HUTSCHENREUTHER, Bust**, Gentleman, Parian, Signed, 7 In. | 95.00 |
| **Cup & Saucer**, Demitasse, U.S.Zone | 15.00 |
| **Demitasse Set**, Cream Colored, Gold Trim, 15 Piece | 125.00 |
| **Dinnerware**, The Ferndale, 5 Piece | 45.00 |
| **Figurine**, Butterfly, Flying Over Flowers, 2 X 2 3/4 In. | 50.00 |
| **Figurine**, Chihuahua, Standing, 4 X 4 In. | 85.00 |
| **Figurine**, Dachshund, Standing, Brown Hair, 3 1/2 X 5 1/2 In. | 78.00 |
| **Figurine**, Dachshund, Standing, Smooth Hair, 5 X 8 3/4 In. | 165.00 |
| **Figurine**, Elephant | 70.00 |
| **Figurine**, Fish Over Seaweed, 2 1/2 X 4 1/2 In. | 95.00 |
| **Figurine**, Flying Butterfly, 2 X 2 1/2 In. | 50.00 |
| **Figurine**, Hummingbird, Perched Over Lily, 4 1/2 In. | 100.00 |
| **Figurine**, Kittens Playing, Ball, Signed, 4 In. | 55.00 |
| **Figurine**, Mermaid Holding Fish, 6 In. | 110.00 |
| **Figurine**, Mother & Child Walking, Pastel Colors | 225.00 |
| **Figurine**, Mother & Child, 10 In. | 110.00 |
| **Figurine**, Redhead Finch, Holding Berry, 9 1/2 In. | 100.00 |
| **Figurine**, Sailfish, Signed, 4 X 5 1/2 In. | 100.00 |
| **Figurine**, Seated Cat, Matte Glaze, 5 X 4 In. | 130.00 |
| **Figurine**, Skater, Leg Extended, White Porcelain, 5 1/2 In. | 170.00 |
| **Figurine**, Squirrel, 3 1/4 In. | 45.00 |
| **Figurine**, Two Cats, Seated Side By Side, Signed, 7 X 7 In. | 265.00 |
| **Figurine**, Wirehaired Terrier, Standing, 8 In. | 125.00 |
| **Plaque**, Napoleon, Murat Family, C.1900, 5 X 7 1/4 In. | 600.00 |
| **Plaque**, Odalisque, Maiden, Profile, C.1900, 4 X 6 In. | 950.00 |
| **Plate**, Cake, Gold & Floral, Handled, 12 In. | 62.00 |
| **Plate**, Cobalt, Gold Border | 35.00 |
| **Plate**, Gold, Rococo Edge, 8 1/2 In. | 54.00 |
| **Plate**, Portrait, Duchess Of Devonshire, Marked, 10 1/4 In. | 325.00 |
| **Ramekin**, Gold Design, Signed | 9.00 |
|     **ICEBOX, see Kitchen, Icebox** | |

| | |
|---|---|
| **ICON, Archangels**, Gilt Frame & Background, 18th Century, Pair | 750.00 |
| **Russian Silver**, Madonna & Child, Hallmarked, 1 3/4 X 1 1/2 In. | 125.00 |
| **Russian**, Christ Pantocrator, Enameled Halo, Wooden Case, 10 X 12 In. | 2500.00 |
| **Russian**, Holy Man & Angel, On Porcelain, Ivory Frame, 3 3/4 X 2 3/4 In. | 200.00 |

*Imari patterns are named for the Japanese ware decorated with orange and blue stylized flowers. The design on the Japanese ware became so characteristic that the name Imari has come to mean any pattern of this type. It was copied by the European factories of the eighteenth and early nineteenth centuries.*

| | |
|---|---|
| **IMARI, Bottle,** Sake, Blue & White, Scenic, 5 1/4 In. | 28.00 |
| **Bowl,** Allover Blue Inside & Out, 8 In. | 65.00 |
| **Bowl,** Basket Of Flowers Center, Cobalt & Red Design, 5 In.Diam. | 55.00 |
| **Bowl,** Cartouche Design, Surrounded By Tiger, Coins, 12 1/4 X 8 3/4 In. | 1700.00 |
| **Bowl,** Fish Design, Flowerpot Center, 9 1/2 X 4 In. | 235.00 |
| **Bowl,** Footed, Gold Rim, Genre Scene, 19th Century, 19 In.Diam. | 800.00 |
| **Bowl,** Footed, 9 1/2 In.Diam. | 245.00 |
| **Bowl,** Panel Design Inside & Out, Blue & Gold, Octagonal, 11 In.Diam. | 275.00 |
| **Bowl,** Pine, Bamboo, Plum, Turtle Design, Covered, C.1830, 11 1/2 In. | 2000.00 |
| **Bowl,** Red, Blue, Green, Paneled, 8 In. | 85.00 |
| **Bowl,** Reds & Gold, Oriental Bird, 6 In. | 45.00 |
| **Bowl,** Shaped Cartouches, Tiger, Coins, & Clouds, 12 1/4 In.Diam. | 1700.00 |
| **Bowl,** Tiger, Coins, & Clouds, Cartouches, 19th Century, 8 3/4 X 12 In. | 1700.00 |
| **Charger,** Birds, Blue, 12 In. | 85.00 |
| **Charger,** Blue & White Rim, Crysanthemum Cherry Blossom, Signed, 16 In. | 160.00 |
| **Charger,** Blue, White, Red, & Gold, 14 In.Diam. | 125.00 |
| **Charger,** Brown Border, Blue & White, 12 In.Diam. | 95.00 |
| **Charger,** Chrysanthemum Design, Tokugawa Period, C.1850, Stand, 18 In. | 3500.00 |
| **Charger,** Cobalt Blue & White Scene, 9 Fire Points, C.1830, 14 In. | 195.00 |
| **Charger,** Exotic Bird Center, Paneled Rim, 19th Century, 14 3/4 In. | 375.00 |
| **Charger,** Full Colored Oriental Pheasants, Signed, 24 1/4 In.Diam. | 1350.00 |
| **Charger,** Pheasants & Flowers, Blue Vines & Flowers, Signed, 24 In. | 1350.00 |
| **Charger,** Scenic Center, Gold Tracery, Fluted Rim, C.1860, Signed, 16 In. | 295.00 |
| **Chop Plate,** Scalloped, Fan Shaped Panels, Shields, 14 3/4 In.Diam. | 250.00 |
| **Dish,** Blue & White, Dragon, Peacock, Feathers, Oval, 6 X 4 In. | 30.00 |
| **Dish,** Japan, 19th Century, 11 3/4 In. ..................................*Illus* | 175.00 |
| **Figurine,** Devil Dog, Gold & Silver Pearls Allover, 5 X 8 In. | 145.00 |
| **Figurine,** Japanese Woman Holding & Reading Scroll, C.1850, 14 In. | 555.00 |
| **Hibachi,** Kikko Shape, Tortoiseshell, Tokugawa Period, C.1730, 10 In. | 3500.00 |
| **Jars,** Temple, Meji Period, C.1880, 17 In., Pair | 5000.00 |
| **Plate,** Brocade Border, Flower Center, C.1875, 8 1/4 In., Set Of 4 | 550.00 |
| **Plate,** Brown Reds & Underglaze, Blue & Green Design, 7 X 9 In. | 36.00 |
| **Plate,** C.1850s, 8 In. | 100.00 |
| **Plate,** Dragon, Fruit & Flower Basket Border, C.1865, 8 1/2 In. | 325.00 |
| **Plate,** Fan, 13 In. | 120.00 |
| **Plate,** Notched Brown Edge, 10 In.Diam. | 95.00 |
| **Plate,** Peacocks & Flowers, Oriental Signs On Underbase, 7 In. | 75.00 |
| **Plate,** Pierced Circle Border, Iron Red & Gold, 10 In. | 85.00 |

Imari, Dish, Japan, 19th Century, 11 3/4 In.

| | |
|---|---|
| **Plate,** Scalloped Edge, 6 1/2 In. | 55.00 |
| **Plate,** Scalloped, Birds, & Fans In Reds, Greens, & Oranges, 12 In.Square | 195.00 |
| **Plate,** 6 Panel, Blue Dragon Center, 8 1/2 In. | 75.00 |
| **Platter,** Scalloped, Floral & Bird Design, Oval, 11 1/4 X 9 In. | 175.00 |
| **Tea Bowl,** Flowers, Brocade, 5 Colors, C.1860, 3 1/4 In. | 32.00 |
| **Temple Jar,** Domed Cover, Foo Dog Finial, Coblat Blue, 21 In. | 175.00 |
| **Umbrella Stand,** Blue & White Floral & Bird Design, 24 1/2 In. | 400.00 |
| **Umbrella Stand,** Cylindrical, Floral Panels, Tans & Reds, 24 1/2 In. | 525.00 |
| **Umbrella Stand,** Floral & Bird Design, 19th Century, 24 1/2 In. | 400.00 |
| **Umbrella Stand,** Hand-Painted, Transfer Floral Design, 8 1/4 In. | 375.00 |
| **Vase,** Blown-Out Dragon Entwining Piece, Blue & White, 12 In. | 340.00 |

*Imperial Glass Corporation was founded in Bellaire, Ohio, in 1902.
Stretch glass and art glass are two of the many kinds of glass made.*

| | |
|---|---|
| **IMPERIAL, Bottle,** Perfume, Candlewick Pattern, Marked, 4 1/2 In. | 18.00 |
| **Bowl,** 3 Aurene Loop Feet, Orange Luster Interior, 7 X 5 In. | 195.00 |
| **Candleholder,** Candlewick, Single Teardrop, Pair | 6.00 |
| **Candlestick,** Eagle Insert, 3 Section | 75.00 |
| **Cup,** Sake, Gold Chrysanthemums & Peacocks, C.1880 | 125.00 |
| **Plate,** Jewels, Green, 7 3/4 In. | 30.00 |
| **Salt Dip,** Red Slag, Marked IG, Set Of 4 | 20.00 |
| **Sign,** Dealer, Elephants | 20.00 |
| **Tumbler,** Spun, Amber, Footed, Set Of 6 | 12.00 |
| **Vase,** Amethyst Base | 55.00 |
| **Vase,** Ball Bottom, Trumpet Flare To Rim, Blue Iridescent, 9 1/2 In. | 180.00 |
| **Vase,** Blue, Gold, Cream, Pulled Design, Paper Label, 11 1/2 In. | 285.00 |
| **Vase,** Blue, Orange & Red Hearts & Vines, 6 1/2 In. | 275.00 |
| **Vase,** Bud, White Leaf & Vine Design, Cobalt Blue Ground, 8 1/2 In. | 155.00 |
| **Vase,** Candlewick, Yellow, 8 1/4 In. | 16.00 |
| **Vase,** Cobalt Blue, Opal Hearts & Vines, Orange Luster, 10 1/2 In. | 275.00 |
| **Vase,** Freehand, Leaf & Vine, Luster Ground, Orange Lining, 9 In. | 295.00 |
| **Vase,** Ground Top, Iridescent, 7 In. | 30.00 |
| **Vase,** Jewel, Green Iridescent, Old Mark, 5 X 5 1/4 In. | 80.00 |
| **Vase,** Marbleized Blue, Orange Iridescent Inside Of Neck, 8 In. | 125.00 |
| **Vase,** Orange & Black, Mirror, Pedestaled, Art Deco, 11 In. | 150.00 |
| **Vase,** Orange & Cobalt Looped, 10 1/4 In. | 75.00 |
| **Vase,** Stick, Green Ribbed, 6 In. | 83.00 |
| **Vase,** Tangerine, Opal Panels, Signed, 8 X 8 1/2 In. | 75.00 |
| **Vase,** White Drape, Yellow Ground, Orange Interior, 11 In. | 375.00 |
| **Water Set,** Grape Pattern, Iridescent, Smoke | 595.00 |

*Indian Tree is a china pattern that was popular during the last half of
the nineteenth century. It was copied from earlier patterns of English
china that were very similar. The pattern includes the crooked branch of a
tree and a partial landscape with exotic flowers and leaves. It is colored
green, blue, pink, and orange.*

| | |
|---|---|
| **INDIAN TREE, Cup & Saucer,** Gold Key Border, Octagon, Coalport, C.1891 | 33.00 |
| **Cup & Saucer,** Scalloped, Coalport | 30.00 |
| **Dish,** Vegetable, Covered, Johnson Bros., 10 In. | 36.50 |
| **Pitcher,** Coalport, 5 In. | 29.50 |
| **Plate,** Blue, Pink, & Green, Gold Trim, Spode, 10 In.Diam. | 22.50 |
| **Plate,** Coalport, 7 In.Diam. | 8.50 |
| **Plate,** Fluted, Coalport, 8 In.Diam. | 12.50 |
| **Plate,** Soup, Maddock, 8 In.Diam. | 12.00 |
| **Platter,** C.1780, Spode, 18 1/2 In. | 100.00 |
| **Platter,** Drainer, 18 In. | 135.00 |
| **Platter,** Meakin, 9 1/2 X 12 In. | 34.50 |
| **Sugar,** Covered, Coalport | 35.00 |
| **Teapot,** Maddock | 42.00 |

**Teapot,** Sadler, Signed, Large .................................................................... 30.00

*Indian art from North America has attracted the collector for many years.*
*Each tribe has its own distinctive designs and techniques. Baskets, jewelry,*
*and leatherwork are of greatest collector interest.*

**INDIAN, Ashtray,** Pueblo Of Santa Clara, Bird Effigy, Paper Label .............. 35.00
  **Bag,** Apache, Beaded Amulet, Star & Moon Design, C.1870 ................. 65.00
  **Bag,** Bandolier, Chippewa, 1880s ........................................................ 600.00
  **Bag,** Beaded, Deerskin ......................................................................... 150.00
  **Bag,** Crow, Beaded, 1890 .................................................................... 125.00
  **Bag,** Iroquois, Beadwork On Velvet, Front & Back, 7 X 7 1/2 In. ......... 125.00
  **Basket,** Algonquin, Vegetable-Dyed Red, C.1870, 10 X 11 X 5 In. ...... 65.00
  **Basket,** Apache, Olla, Figures Of Dogs & Men, C.1900 ...................... 1850.00
  **Basket,** Covered, Potato Stamp Stencil, Square ................................. 125.00
  **Basket,** Covered, Wide Splint, Yellow & Red, 11 X 14 1/2 In. ............ 165.00
  **Basket,** Hopi, Natural, Red, & Green Design ...................................... 150.00
  **Basket,** Makah, Covered, Allover Design, 4 1/2 In.Diam. .................... 75.00
  **Basket,** Micmac, Eastern Maine .......................................................... 295.00
  **Basket,** Navajo, Rattlesnake Design, 11 1/4 In.Diam. ........................ 200.00
  **Basket,** Papago, Golden With Dark Brown Designs, 10 In. .................. 65.00
  **Basket,** Papago, Willow, 13 1/2 In.Diam. ........................................... 140.00
  **Basket,** Papago, Yucca Fiber, Black Devil's Claw ............................... 100.00
  **Basket,** Penobscot, Bentwood Handles, Blue, C.1800, 12 X 15 X 7 1/2 In. ..... 110.00
  **Basket,** Penobscot, Black Ash Painted, Round, C.1870, 10 X 5 In. ..... 185.00
  **Basket,** Pima, Coiled, Interwoven Horse Design .................................. 85.00
  **Basket,** Pima, 13 In.Diam. ................................................................... 150.00
  **Basket,** Root, Cedar, Klickitat, 11 1/2 In. ........................................... 675.00
  **Basket,** Seminole, Everglade Scene In Bottom, 8 1/2 X 5 1/2 X 3 In. ..... 75.00
  **Basket,** Southwest, Cactus & Human Figure Design, C.1940, 6 In. ...... 150.00
  **Beads,** Trade, Northwest Coast, Polished Bugles, C.1873, 6 Ft. ......... 36.00
  **Bell,** Hohocom, Arizona, Cast Copper .................................................. 4.00
  **Belt,** Cheyenne, Turtle Design, C.1900, 2 1/2 X 39 In. ....................... 50.00
  **Blanket,** Navajo Chief's, C.1890, Wool, Vegetable Dyes, 5 X 6 Ft. ..... 600.00
  **Blanket,** Shoulder, Chief's, C.1880, 18 X 33 In. ................................. 580.00
  **Blanket,** Shoulder, Chief's, C.1880, 48 X 33 In. ................................. 5800.00
  **Bottle,** Water, Caddo, Body Nodes, Rim Restoration ........................... 85.00
  **Bowl,** Hopi, Small ................................................................................ 25.00
  **Box,** Pantry, Micmac, Fruit Dye Design, Oval, 19th Century, 7 In. ....... 75.00
  **Bracelet,** Navajo, Man's, Silver Leaves, Blue Turquoise, Signed Cactus ..... 245.00
  **Bracelet,** Navajo, Pawn, Turquoise & Coral, Silver, Signed A.B. .......... 125.00
  **Bracelet,** Pawn, Oval Turquoise Stone, Silver Mounting, C.1940 ......... 485.00
  **Bracelet,** Shell, Hohocom, Arizona ..................................................... 10.00
  **Carpet,** Navajo, Center Red Cross, Brown Ground, 9 X 12 Ft. ............. 5500.00
  **Case,** Awl, Plains, Beaded, Horsehair Design ..................................... 65.00
  **Case,** Knife, Iroquois, Hide, Beadwork, C.1870 ................................... 40.00
  **Coverlet,** Seminole, 40 X 68 In. .......................................................... 250.00
  **Doll,** Clay Bisque, Children, Leather Clothes, 5 To 8 In., Set Of 8 ....... 110.00
  **Doll,** Family, Blankets, Hair, Mom, Pop, Papoose, 7 1/2 To 3 In. ......... 30.00
  **Doll,** Frowning, Open Mouth, Ball-Jointed, Bisque, 12 1/2 In. .............. 125.00
  **Doll,** Miniature, Buckskin, Painted Face, Bead Eyes, Fringe On Legs .... 200.00
  **Doll,** Navajo, Painted Features, Hair In Bun, 16 In. ............................ 30.00
  **Doll,** Peruvian, Composition Head, 11 In. ........................................... 75.00
  **Dough Bowl,** Cochiti, 11 X 17 In.Diam. ............................................. 3000.00
  **Dough Bowl,** Santa Clara, 12 X 21 In.Diam. ..................................... 1200.00
  **Dough Bowl,** Santa Domingo, 9 X 18 In.Diam. .................................. 3000.00
  **Dress,** Wedding, Plains, Leather, Beadwork & Silver .......................... 800.00
  **Drum,** Double Headed & Painted, C.1900, Acoma Pueblo .................... 175.00
  **Earrings,** Crowfoot, 1884 ................................................................... 150.00
  **Fetish,** Umbilical, Sioux, Beaded ........................................................ 125.00
  **Gourd Dipper,** Furnace Creek Ruins ................................................... 25.00
  **Indian,** Hammer, Maul, Santa Fe, Double Headed .............................. 20.00
  **Jug,** Water, Black On Black, Carved Dragon, Signed Isaac Pena, 6 In. ..... 165.00
  **Knife,** Tlingit, Carved Bone Handle ..................................................... 1800.00

Lariat, Sioux, Horsehair, 5 Strand, 22 Ft. ........................................................................ 47.00
Legging, Red Trade Cloth, Men's, Beaded, Strip, Pawnee, C.1900 ........................ 155.00
Mace, Sioux, Sandstone, 21 In. .......................................................................................... 500.00
Moccasins, Beaded, Multicolor, Geometric Design, Sky Blue, C.1920 .................. 120.00
Moccasins, Crow Tribe, Full Beaded .............................................................................. 165.00
Moccasins, Eastern Woodland, Beaded, Lined, Child's ........................... 65.00 To 75.00
Neckalce, Zuni, Squash Blossom, Arizona Blue Stones ......................................... 800.00
Necklace, Burial, Hohocom, Arizona, Disc Shells ..................................................... 75.00
Necklace, Colorado, Elkhorn .............................................................................................. 175.00
Necklace, Zuni, Squash Blossom, Several Shades Of Turquoise .......................... 800.00
Pipe, Effigy, Warrior's Head, Lightning & Tears, Stone ........................................... 215.00
Pipe, Greenstone, Hatchet Shape ..................................................................................... 200.00
Pipe, Squaw, Carved ............................................................................................................ 45.00
Pitcher, Cochiti, Hand-Painted Wheat Frond, C.1900, Large ............................... 3500.00
Pitcher, Pueblo, 2nd Period, Black On White, 6 X 8 In. ........................................... 210.00
Plate, Doe-Wah-Jack, 9 In.Diam. ...................................................................................... 45.00
Pot, Carved Lightning Serpent, Black Matte, Signed, 29 1/2 In.Diam. ............... 1000.00
Pot, Cooking, Navajo, Rim Design, 6 X 6 In. ............................................................... 35.00
Pot, Pueblo, Black With Feather Design, San Ildefonso, 2 1/2 In. ....................... 110.00
Pot, San Ildefonso Pueblo, Blue Corn, 3 1/4 X 5 1/4 In. ......................................... 150.00
Purse, Change, Beaded, 2 1/2 In.Diam. ......................................................................... 20.00
Quilt, Axis Design, Blue On White .................................................................................. 250.00
Quilt, Seminole, Flower Sack Backing ............................................................................ 65.00
Quilt, Seminole, Patchwork & Applique, C.1920, 41 X 65 In. ................................ 150.00
Quiver, Hide, Cutout Design, C.1890 .............................................................................. 125.00
Rug, Navajo, Brown Ground, Central Red Cross, 9 X 12 Ft. ................................ 5500.00
Rug, Navajo, Brown, White, Gray, & Pink, 31 X 5. In. ............................................. 135.00
Rug, Navajo, C.1880, 10 Ft. X 5 Ft.11 In. ..................................................................... 350.00
Rug, Navajo, Germantown, 1910, 4 X 6 Ft. ............................................................... 6500.00
Rug, Navajo, Hand-Loomed, Browns, Tans, Black, & White, 60 X 30 In. .......... 40.00
Rug, Navajo, Multicolored, Hand-Woven, 1920s, 52 X 72 In. .............................. 500.00
Rug, Navajo, Red, White, & Gray Diamonds, Black Border, 60 X 33 In. ......... 1200.00
Rug, Navajo, Shades Of Brown, Red, & Tan, 18 X 40 In. ....................................... 85.00
Rug, Navajo, Single Saddle, Storm Pattern, Klagetoh ........................................... 40.00
Rug, Red, Green, Blue, & Yellow Tassels, 7 X 3 Ft. ................................................. 150.00
Sash, Woodland, Finger-Woven, Geometric Design, 2 1/2 X 60 In. ................... 32.00
Snowshoes, Maine, 19th Century, 20 1/2 X 6 In.Wide ............................................. 55.00
Snowshoes, Ojibwa, Hide Laces, 37 In. ....................................................................... 175.00
Stick, Sioux, Used In Kettle Dance, Beads, Feathers, Tin Cones, Pair .............. 85.00
Totem Pole, Coast Salish, Thunderbird, Grizzly Bear, & Crest, 12 Ft. ........... 3500.00
Vase, Wedding, Acoma Pueblo, C.1890, Pottery, 8 X 9 In. ................................... 120.00
Vest, Plains, Fully Beaded ............................................................................................... 4200.00
Water Storage Olla, Papago, 17 X 14 In. .................................................................... 135.00
Whip Stick, Sioux, Brass Tacks ....................................................................................... 55.00

INKSTAND, Double, Lids Are Mask Of Bacchus, Signed Geschutz ..................... 110.00
Raised Pastoral Scenes, Footed, 2 Clear Glass Inserts ......................................... 45.00
Regency Style, Oval, Brass, 15 In.Wide ........................................................................ 295.00
Round, Original Well, Hallmarked Sterling Silver, Large ........................................ 300.00
Terrier One Side, Square Holds Well, Gilt Cover ..................................................... 95.00
2 Glass Wells, Iron Covers, Raised Brass Pen Rest, Iron ..................................... 47.00
3-Pen Holder, Glass Insert, C.1879, Cast Iron, 3 1/2 X 7 1/2 In. ......................... 44.50
      INKWELL, see also Brass, Inkwell; Pewter, Inkwell; and various
      Porcelain Categories
INKWELL, Art Deco, Bronze, Hinged Lid, Glass Inserts ........................................ 75.00
Art Deco, Glass Insert, Brass, 3 1/2 In. ........................................................................ 37.50
Art Nouveau Face, Peacock Feathers, Metal Cap ..................................................... 275.00
Attached Underplate, Hinged Top, Fan Corners, Porcelain, 4 5/8 In. ............... 65.00
Bearded King, Crown Lid, Maltese Cross Top, Brass, 7 1/2 X 6 1/2 In. ........... 75.00
Blown Molded, Dark Olive Amber ................................................................................. 75.00
Blown Three Mold, Dark Amethyst, 2 1/2 X 2 5/8 In. .............................. *Illus* 700.00
Blue Pillow, Gold Trim, Dog Lying On Lid, Porcelain, 5 3/4 X 3 In. ................. 445.00
Brass Griffins On Sides, Covered, C.1900, Brass & Glass, 8 X 5 In. .................. 125.00

Inkwell, Blown Three Mold, Dark Amethyst,
2 1/2 X 2 5/8 In.

Inkwell, Covered, Free-Blown, Greenish
Aqua, 5 5/8 X 3 3/4 In.

**Brass Hinged Top,** Blue Glass, 2 1/2 In.Square ........................................ 170.00
**Brass Top,** Crystal, Salamander Holder, Glass Eyes, 3 3/4 X 2 3/8 In. ..................... 195.00
**Brass Top,** Royalty Crest, Pair ........................................ 165.00
**Buffalo,** N.Y., Decorated, Wooden ........................................ 110.00
**Carved Sheaf Of Wheat,** Wooden, French, Walnut, Large ........................ 115.00
**Chester,** Conn., Grain Painted, Wooden ........................................ 55.00
**Copper Base & Floral Design,** Marked M & Cn. & Co., Hoboken, N.J. ................. 42.00
**Covered,** Free-Blown, Greenish Aqua, 5 5/8 X 3 3/4 In. ....................... *Illus* 300.00
**Diamond Point,** 3-Mold, Green, Connecticut, C.1825, 1 7/8 In., Pair .............. 170.00
**Double Glass Inserts,** Brass Covers, Victorian, Brass ............................ 65.00
**Double,** Enameled Design, Gold Trim, Brass Fittings, Glass, 3 X 4 In. .............. 65.00
**Double,** Indian Arrowhead Mounts, Signed, Copper & Silver, 10 In. ............... 275.00
**Double,** Pen Holder, 3 Fully Formed Dutch Children, Bronze ...................... 465.00
**Figural,** Bears At Table, Eating Berries, Porcelain, 3 1/2 X 5 In. ................. 225.00
**Figural,** Camel Lying Down, Lid On Back Opens, Metal, 9 1/2 X 6 In. .............. 115.00
**Figural,** Camel, Brown, Red & Black Trim, C.1810, White Metal, 8 In. ............. 185.00
**Figural,** Camel, Well In Saddle, Brass ........................................ 45.00
**Figural,** Comical Clown Dog, Head Is Cover, Porcelain, 4 1/2 In. .................. 42.00
**Figural,** Dragonfly, Pen Holder, Art Nouveau, Metal, 5 1/2 X 6 1/2 In. ............ 75.00
**Figural,** Flowerpot, Potted Pansies, Natural Colors, Bronze ..................... 125.00
**Figural,** Hessian Helmet, Crossed Swords, Brass .............................. 175.00
**Figural,** King, Crown Lid, Maltese Cross Top, Brass, 7 1/2 X 6 1/2 In. ............. 75.00
**Figural,** Lady's Head Cover, Art Nouveau, Brass Wash .......................... 95.00
**Figural,** Laughing Evil Man, Pen Over Ear, 3 Piece ............................. 75.00
**Figural,** Oriental Seated Man, 3 3/4 In. ...................................... 48.00
**Figural,** Reclining Lady, Well Beside Her, Bronze, 6 3/4 In. ..................... 80.00
**Figural,** Spike Helmet ..................................................... 25.00
**Figural,** Stag Head, Antlers Beside Well, Hinged, Brass, 6 1/2 In. ............... 75.00
**Figural,** Stag, Gilding On Iron, Crystal Well, Rack Of Horns ..................... 65.00
**Figural,** Striped Tabby Head, 19th Century, English, Cast Iron, 4 In. ............. 250.00
**Figural,** Taj Mahal, Glass Base ............................................. 30.00
**Figural,** Viking Ship, Liner, Bronze, Art Nouveau .............................. 135.00
**Figural,** Walnut, Green & Brown Patina, Glass Insert, 9 In. ..................... 65.00
**Figural,** 4-Leaf Clover, Lady Swivels To Side, Art Nouveau ...................... 70.00
**Floral Design,** Emerald Green, 2 1/2 X 2 3/4 In.Diam. ...................... *Illus* 300.00
**Free-Blown Funnel Type,** Pedestal, Amber, 2 7/8 In. ....................... *Illus* 225.00
**Glass,** Geometric Cuts, Hinged Crystal Lid, Brass Connector .................... 100.00
**Glass,** Sterling Overlay, Clear, 2 1/2 X 2 3/4 In. .............................. 98.50

Inkwell, Free-Blown Funnel Type,
Pedestal, Amber, 2 7/8 In.
(See Page 271)

Inkwell, Floral Design, Emerald Green,
2 1/2 X 2 3/4 In. Diam.
(See Page 271)

Inkwell, Red & White Stripes, Pewter
Cap, Sandwich, 3 1/4 In.

| | |
|---|---:|
| **Glass,** Sterling Overlay, Round, 3 1/2 In. | 98.00 |
| **Glass,** Umbrella Form, New England, 19th Century, Blue, 2 1/2 In. | 225.00 |
| **Grain Painted,** Wooden, Chester, Conn. | 55.00 |
| **Half Moon Shape,** Winged Griffin, Paw On Shield, Ceramic, 5 X 4 In. | 65.00 |
| **Lion Overlooking Stand,** Delft Blue & White, 7 1/2 X 9 In. | 175.00 |
| **Porcelain,** Hinged Lid, Cobalt Blue | 69.00 |
| **Porcelain,** Hinged Lid, Pastel Ground, Flowers, Square, 3 1/8 X 5 In. | 95.00 |
| **Pottery,** Hinged Lid, Flowers, 3 1/2 In. | 32.00 |
| **Pressed Glass,** Swirl Design, Hinged Lid | 25.00 |
| **Red & White Stripes,** Pewter Cap, Sandwich, 3 1/4 In. *Illus* | 1050.00 |
| **Saucer,** Pedestal, Hinged Lid, Glass Insert, Medallions, 7 1/2 X 4 In. | 95.00 |
| **Snail Form,** Iron Frame, White | 45.00 |
| **Soapstone,** Concentric Circle On Top, 2 1/4 In.Square | 30.00 |
| **INKWELL, TIFFANY, see Tiffany, Inkwell** | |
| **Traveling,** Glass Well Inside Wooden Case | 25.00 |
| **Traveling,** Leather, Brass | 65.00 |
| **Traveling,** Lignum Vitae | 15.00 |
| **Traveling,** Silver & Red Leather, Vesta Vase, C.1860 | 250.00 |
| **Traveling,** Winged Screw Lock Top | 45.00 |
| **4-Sided Brass Cutout Base,** Iridescent Pink Glass, 4 3/4 X 3 In. | 115.00 |

*Insulators of glass or pottery have been made for use on telegraph or telephone poles since 1844.*

| | |
|---|---:|
| **INSULATOR, A.G.M.,** Red Amber | 3.00 |
| **American,** Embossed, Repair Spot On Dome | 50.00 |
| **Brookfield,** Lime Green | 10.00 |
| **C.G.I.Co.** | 1.00 |
| **California,** Aqua | 5.00 |
| **Canadian Pacific,** Vertical & Horizontal Ridges | 22.00 |
| **Carnival Glass,** Rainbow Colored, 10 In. | 20.00 |
| **Chicago,** Embossed | 200.00 |
| **Columbia,** Patent May 12, 1891, Threads Inside Skirt | 35.00 |
| **D512,** Dark Green | 8.00 |
| **E.R.W.,** Ice Blue | 200.00 |
| **Gayner,** No. 90, Aqua | 7.00 |
| **H.G.Co.,** Patent May 2, 1893, Petticoat, Open Bubbles, Royal Purple | 100.00 |
| **Hemingray,** No.12, Light Purple | 12.00 |
| **Hemingray,** No.19, Clear | 20.00 |
| **Hemingray,** No.660, Carnival Glass | 10.00 |
| **Hemingray,** No.95, Aqua | 42.00 |
| **Homer Brookes,** Blue | 22.00 |
| **Jumbo,** Porcelain | 160.00 |
| **K.C.G.W.,** Fairmount, Green | 10.00 |
| **Knowles Cable,** Patent June 17, 1890, Blue | 38.00 |
| **L.A.C.,** Patent Date, Aqua Green | 60.00 |
| **Lynchburg,** No. 10, Drips, Straw | 1.50 |
| **Lynchburg,** No. 43, Aqua | 8.00 |
| **Maydwell,** No. 10, Pale Green | 5.00 |
| **Maydwell,** No. 42, Straw | 1.00 |
| **McLaughlin,** No.9, Light Blue | 1.00 |
| **Montreal Telegraph Co.,** Blue | 11.00 |
| **National** | 80.00 |
| **P.R.R.,** Aqua | 60.00 |
| **Postal Telegraph Co.,** Aqua | 5.00 |
| **Pyrex No. 661,** Purple Carnival Glass | 30.00 |
| **Pyrex,** Carnival Glass, Rainbow Colored, 10 In. | 20.00 |
| **Pyrex,** No. 61, Clear | 1.50 |
| **Rainbow Colored Carnival Glass,** Pyrex | 20.00 |
| **S.B.T. & T.Co.,** Aqua, Embossed Center | 25.00 |
| **S.McKee & Co.,** Blue | 100.00 |
| **S.N.E.T.Co.,** Commemorative, Cobalt Hat | 12.00 |
| **Telegrafos Nacionales,** Amber | 20.00 |
| **Telephonos Ericsson,** Aqua | 30.00 |
| **W.Brookfield,** Emerald Green | 12.00 |
| **W.Brookfield,** New York, S.C.A.Flat Base | 8.00 |
| **W.G.M.Co.,** Purple, Flat Base | 10.00 |
| **Western Union Co.,** Soft Black Rubber, 3 X 1 1/2 In. | 10.00 |
| **Western Union Telegraph Co.,** Rubber, Inside Thread, 4 X 2 3/8 In. | 15.00 |
|     **IRISH BELLEEK, see Belleek** | |
| | |
|     **IRON, see also Kitchen; Tool; Store** | |
| **IRON, Andirons,** Boston Terrier | 75.00 |
| **Andirons,** Daisy Collar, Penny Feet, Pair | 725.00 |
| **Andirons,** Drawn Loop Finial, Knife-Blade Style, 18th Century, 18 In. | 195.00 |
| **Aquarium,** Building Shape, Original Paint, 10 3/4 X 20 1/4 In. | 325.00 |
| **Ashtray,** Bullet Cigar Cutter | 85.00 |
| **Ashtray,** Floor Model, Scotty Dog On Hind Legs, Removable Tray | 25.00 |
| **Bed,** Baby, Toy, Iron Wheels, Original Paint, 2 3/4 In. | 23.00 |
| **Bookends,** Art Deco, Dancing Girl | 20.00 |
| **Bookends,** Clipper Ship | 12.00 |
| **Bookends,** Colonial Ladies, Bronze Finish | 24.00 |
| **Bookends,** Elephant | 17.50 |
| **Bookends,** Flower Basket, Green, Eureka Still Range Co., Pair | 25.00 |
| **Bookends,** Full Face Indian Chief In Relief, 4 1/4 X 3 3/4 In. | 15.00 |

| | |
|---|---:|
| **Bookends,** Full Headdress Indian Bust | 25.00 |
| **Bookends,** Indian Head, Full Headdress | 25.00 |
| **Bookends,** Kitten | 23.00 |
| **Bookends,** Log Cabin, Tall Pines, Moon | 30.00 |
| **Bookends,** Old Ironsides | 14.50 |
| **Bookends,** Prancing Black Horse, Red Bridle, C.1880, 11 In., Pair | 98.00 |
| **Bookends,** Shakespeare, Bronze Finish | 15.00 |
| **Bookends,** The Thinker | 9.50 To 12.50 |
| **Boot Scraper,** Curled Top Ends | 25.00 |
| **Boot Scraper,** Design, Victorian | 28.00 |
| **Boot Scraper,** Ends Fasten To Wall, Curved, 14 X 19 In.Tall | 58.00 |
| **Boot Scraper,** Witch | 195.00 |
| **Bootjack,** Beetle, 10 1/2 In. | 30.00 |
| **Bootjack,** Devil | 90.00 |
| **Bootjack,** Jockey | 32.00 |
| **Bootjack,** Naughty Nellie | 23.00 |
| **Bowl,** Embossed Rearing Horse, Bronzed, 5 1/2 In. | 14.00 |
| **Bowl,** Rimmed Bottom, 19th Century, 8 1/2 In.Diam. | 38.00 |
| **Bracket,** Shelf, Lacy, 8 3/4 X 10 3/4 In. | 18.00 |
| **Bracket,** Shelf, Lacy, 10 In., Pair | 20.00 |
| **Burner,** Incense, Camel, Signed Vamlinez | 65.00 |
| **Candle Snuffer,** Cone Shape, Handled, 3 1/4 In. | 38.00 |
| **Candlestick,** Figural, Victorian Squire, Pair | 50.00 |
| **Candlestick,** Saucer Base, Turned Pedestal, 18th Century, 4 1/2 In. | 95.00 |
| **Chandelier,** Brackets Hold Kerosene Lamps | 150.00 |
| **Clamp,** Buggy Rein, Horse Shape, 1875, Set Of 3 | 27.50 |
| **Clipper,** Yankee Cigar | 150.00 |
| **IRON, COFFEE GRINDER, see Coffee Grinder** | |
| **Door Knocker,** Basket Of Flowers Shape, 4 X 3 In. | 22.50 |
| **Door Knocker,** Parrot | 22.00 |
| **Door Knocker,** Victorian, Knights Of Pythias | 28.00 |
| **Door Latch,** Lebanon County, Pa. | 130.00 |
| **Doorknob,** Embossed, Pair | 6.50 |

*Iron doorstops have been made in all types of designs. The vast majority of the doorstops sold today are cast iron and were made from about 1890 to 1930. Most of them are shaped like people, animals, flowers, or ships.*

| | |
|---|---:|
| **Doorstop,** Basket Of Flowers, 8 1/2 In. | 16.00 To 25.00 |
| **Doorstop,** Basket Of Flowers, 10 1/2 In. | 25.00 To 38.00 |
| **Doorstop,** Bearded Dwarf, 11 In. | 28.00 |
| **Doorstop,** Black Boy, Hitching Post, Ring In Hand, 11 1/2 In. | 45.00 |
| **Doorstop,** Boston Terrier, Green & Brown Paint, 9 In. | 45.00 |
| **Doorstop,** Bulldog | 50.00 To 65.00 |
| **Doorstop,** Bullfrog | 50.00 |
| **Doorstop,** Campbell Kid | 125.00 |
| **Doorstop,** Cat, Black, Red Bow | 32.00 |
| **Doorstop,** Cat, Tabby, Red Bow, 11 X 5 1/2 In. | 40.00 |
| **Doorstop,** Cockatoo, 7 In. | 25.00 |
| **Doorstop,** Cottage With Flowers Growing Around It | 27.50 To 34.00 |
| **Doorstop,** Court Jester | 13.00 |
| **Doorstop,** Dog, Pug, Black & White, 9 1/2 X 10 In. | 40.00 |
| **Doorstop,** Dog, Scotty, Sitting | 23.00 |
| **Doorstop,** Dog, Scotty, Standing | 30.00 |
| **Doorstop,** Dog, Terrier, Birmingham, Alabama Foundry | 55.00 |
| **Doorstop,** Dutch Girl With Ball, Red Dress, Green Apron | 34.00 |
| **Doorstop,** English Stagecoach & Driver | 65.00 |
| **Doorstop,** Fisherman At Wheel | 27.00 |
| **Doorstop,** Frog | 25.00 |
| **Doorstop,** Girl In Canoe, Lake, Trees | 38.00 |
| **Doorstop,** High Button Shoes, 19th Century | 35.00 |
| **Doorstop,** Horse, Parade Saddle, Black, 7 1/2 X 7 1/2 In. | 60.00 |
| **Doorstop,** Horse, 12 X 12 In. | 75.00 |

Doorstop, Judy & Baby .................................................................................. 135.00
Doorstop, Kitten, Female, 7 1/2 In. ............................................................. 45.00
Doorstop, Kitten, Male, 7 1/2 In. ................................................................ 45.00
Doorstop, Kittens, Twin, Standing Side By Side, 7 1/2 In. ......................... 45.00
Doorstop, Monkey Holding Cigar, 13 In. ..................................................... 95.00
Doorstop, Parrot, On Tree Stump, 7 1/2 In. ............................................... 20.00
Doorstop, Pelican ....................................................................................... 17.50
Doorstop, Penguin, Kool Cigarette Ad ........................................................ 70.00
Doorstop, Raggedy Ann With Doll, 9 1/2 In. ............................................... 47.50
Doorstop, Shepherd Dog ............................................................................ 40.00
Doorstop, Ship ............................................................... 18.00 To 25.00
Doorstop, Squirrel ...................................................................................... 17.50
Doorstop, Sunbonnet Girl ........................................................................... 45.00
Doorstop, Teddy Rough Rider, Dated 1899 ................................................ 70.00
Doorstop, Windmill ...................................................................................... 30.00
Doorstop, Windmill & House With Flowers ................................................. 35.00
Eggbeater, Glass ........................................................................................ 85.00
Footscraper, Ram's Horn Ends, 17 X 10 1/2 In. ........................................ 65.00
Footscraper, Scroll Top, Hand-Wrought, Pair ............................................ 85.00
Fork, Meat, Hand-Forged, 2-Tine, 11 In. .................................................... 150.00
Frame, Easel, Eagle, Drums, & Flags In Relief, 9 X 6 3/4 In. ..................... 30.00
Frog, Compliments Of Michigan Stove Co., Opens To Hold Matches .......... 45.00
Gophering Iron, Wood Handle, On Brass Trivet .......................................... 140.00
Hames, Brass Balls, Pair ............................................................................ 10.00
Handcuffs, H. & R.Arms Co. ....................................................................... 75.00
Hat, Derby, White Enamel Interior, 5 X 7 X 3 In. ....................................... 12.00
Hinge, Strap, Half H, 11 1/2 In., Pair ......................................................... 45.00
Holder, Buggy Whip .................................................................................... 50.00
Holder, String, Beehive Shape, C.1855 ...................................................... 35.00
Holder, String, Beehive Shape, 6 In. .......................................................... 25.00
Holder, String, Figural, Apple ..................................................................... 10.00
Holder, String, Figural, Chef ....................................................................... 8.00
Holder, String, Figural, Sailor ..................................................................... 10.00
Holder, String, Turtle Shape ....................................................................... 10.00
Holder, Watch, Victorian, Green, Gilt Leaf & Flower Design ....................... 65.00
Hook, Meat, 3 Hooks, Forged ..................................................................... 50.00
Hook, Pot, Fireplace ................................................................................... 15.00
Horse, Tan & White, Saddle Cast, Chain Lead, 4 X 3 In. ............................ 15.00
Ice Pick, Capital Ice Co., Washington, D.C. ................................................ 4.00
Ice Tongs ................................................................................................... 18.00
Kettle, Gooseneck Spout, Flat Bottom, B Mark, 12 X 7 3/4 In. .................. 150.00
Kettle, Gooseneck Spout, 3 Feet, 2-Part Mold, 11 1/2 X 7 In. ................... 175.00
Kettle, Wrought-Iron Bail, Black Paint, 10 In.Diam. ................................... 48.00
Ladle, Hand-Wrought, Brass Bowl, 14 1/2 In. ............................................ 95.00
Leg Irons, Harvard Lock Co. ....................................................................... 80.00
Leg Irons, Tower, Dated 1882 .................................................................... 150.00
Lighting Device, Tripod Feet, Wrought Iron, 24 1/2 In. .............................. 215.00
Loggerhead, Hand-Wrought, 24 In. ............................................................ 110.00
Mailbox, 6 X 11 1/2 In. .............................................................................. 10.00
     **IRON, MATCH HOLDER, see also Match Holder**
Match Holder, Art Nouveau, Bronze Patina, 4 In. ...................................... 60.00
Match Holder, Devil .................................................................................... 40.00
Match Picker, Figural, Black Bird Picks Up Match, 4 1/2 In. ...................... 125.00
Match Scratch & Dispenser, Figural, Donkey, Cast Iron, 6 In. ................... 75.00
Match Scratch, Figural, Donkey, C.1900.9 3/4 In. ..................................... 45.00
Matchbox, Figural, Turtle, Compliments Of Michigan Stove, 5 In. .............. 65.00
Mold, Cake, Lamb ....................................................................................... 50.00
Mold, Candy, Cross Of Flowers, 4 In Mold, 4 1/2 X 10 1/2 X 1 1/4 In. ...... 14.00
Mold, Candy, Rabbit On Hind Legs, 2 Rows, 7 In Row, 7 X 13 1/4 In., 2 Pc. ... 22.00
Mold, Candy, Running Rabbit, 4 Row, 3 In Row, 10 1/2 X 13 1/2 In., 2 Pc. ... 25.00
Mold, Candy, Seashell, 7 Rows, 8 1/4 X 14 1/4 In., 2 Piece ...................... 18.00
Mold, Candy, Squirrel, C.Weygandt Co., 4 X 9 1/2 2n., 2 Piece ................ 21.00
Mold, Rabbit, Basket On Back, 2 In Row, 7 X 5 1/4 X 1 In., 2 Piece .......... 19.00

| | |
|---|---:|
| **Mortar & Pestle,** 7 X 8 In. | 65.00 |
| **Nutcracker,** Alligator | 45.00 |
| **Nutcracker,** Elephant | 10.00 |
| **Nutcracker,** Squirrel, Dated 1913 | 15.00 |
| **Oven Peel,** Knob Top, 6 X 6 In. Blade, 42 In.Overall | 55.00 |
| **Padlock,** Keen Kutter, Emblem Shape, 1906 | 65.00 |
| **Pan,** Wrought Legs & Handle, Revolutionary War, 8 In.Diam. | 160.00 |
| **Paperweight,** High-Top Shoe | 25.00 |
| **Paperweight,** Scotty Dog | 20.00 |
| **Peel,** Button Terminus, 45 In. | 75.00 |
| **Plant Stand,** Incised Floral Design, Marked Musterschutz | 60.00 |
| **Plate,** Savery & Sons, New York, 19th Century, 9 1/2 In. | 165.00 |
| **Porringer,** Kendrick, Smallest Size, 4 1/4 In. | 65.00 |
| **Porringer,** Kendrick, 1 Pint | 135.00 |
| **Pot,** Glue, Handled, 2 Piece | 15.00 |
| **Rack,** Magazine | 65.00 |
| **Sadiron,** Charcoal, Marked E.Cummings, Patent 1852 | 32.00 |
| **Sadiron,** Child's | 13.75 |
| **Seat,** Implement, Walter A.Wood | 32.50 |
| **Seat,** Mower, Nixon & Co., Alliance, Ohio | 35.00 |
| **Seat,** Tractor, Whitely, Cast Iron | 30.00 |
| **Shears,** Tailor's, Brass At Joining, Large, 1859, R.Heinisch, Newark, N.J. | 60.00 |
| **Snuffer,** Candle, Footed | 30.00 |
| **Spindle,** Bill | 3.00 |
| **Spittoon,** Gray & White Porcelain Clad | 20.00 |
| **Spittoon,** Mechanical, Figural, Turtle, Dated November, 1891 | 150.00 |
| **Stamp,** Millinery, Maple Leaf, Brass Base, Wood Handle, 1 1/2 In. | 39.00 |
| **Stand,** Bible, Adjustable Book Boards, C.1897 | 135.00 |
| **Taoster,** Twisted Rods, Small Trees, Doughnut Top, 19 X 11 1/2 In. | 310.00 |
| **Teakettle,** Brass Handle, Brass Knob, Tin Lid | 110.00 |
| **Teakettle,** Domed Cover, Line Design, Gooseneck Spout, England, C.1830 | 300.00 |
| **Teakettle,** Domed Cover, Spherical Body, Gooseneck, 3 Legs, 8 1/4 In. | 125.00 |
| **Teakettle,** Domed Cover, Strap Handle, S.A. In Casting, 8 In.Diam. | 175.00 |
| **Teakettle,** Tilting, Footed, Wrought Bail | 320.00 |
| **Toaster,** Rectangular Frame, Arched Feet, Swing Handle, 13 X 5 In. | 50.00 |
| **Toaster,** Swivels, 11 1/2 X 19 In.Long | 310.00 |
| **Tobacco Jar,** Grotesque Face | 90.00 |
| **Tongs,** Blacksmith's, 22 In. | 10.00 |
| **Trivet,** Child's, Lacy Heart, Handled & Footed, 6 In. | 20.00 |
| **Trivet,** Horseshoe, Wooden Handle, 3-Footed, 1884 | 45.00 |
| **Trivet,** Man In Center | 25.00 |
| **Wall Hanging,** Musical Figural Lyre, C.1900, 6 1/2 X 8 In. | 30.00 |
| **Wall Pocket,** Coal Co. | 25.00 |
| **Weight,** Buggy | 15.50 |
| **Weight,** Windmill, Bologna Bull | 325.00 |
| **Weight,** Windmill, Horse | 48.00 |
| **Weight,** Windmill, Hummer Rooster | 75.00 |
| **Weight,** Windmill, Long-Tailed Horse | 295.00 |
| **Weight,** Windmill, Rooster, White, Red Comb, 19 1/2 In.   *Illus* | 1000.00 |

*Ironstone china was first made in 1813. It gained its greatest popularity during the mid-nineteenth century. The heavy, durable, off-white pottery was made in white or was decorated with any of hundreds of patterns. Much flow blue pottery was made of ironstone. Some of the decorations were raised.*

**IRONSTONE, see also Chelsea Grape; Gaudy Ironstone; Moss Rose; Staffordshire, Wedgwood**

| | |
|---|---:|
| **IRONSTONE, Bowl,** Oriental Pattern, Mason, 3 X 7 In.Diam. | 55.00 |
| **Bowl,** 12-Sided, Imperial Alcock, 10 In. | 13.50 |
| **Cachepot,** Cattle Scenery, Adams, C.1890, 6 1/2 In. | 125.00 |
| **Chamber Pot,** Oriental Scenes, Snake Handle, Mason, C.1845 | 125.00 |
| **Coffeepot,** Floral Finial On Lid, Marked Elsmore & Forster | 70.00 |
| **Creamer,** Ning-Po, C.1845 | 100.00 |
| **Cup & Saucer,** Coffee, Moss Rose, Meakin | 68.50 |

Iron, Weight, Windmill, Rooster,
White, Red Comb, 19 1/2 In.

Cup & Saucer, D Handle, Rose At Top, 8-Paneled Sides, Meakin ........................................ 20.00
Cuspidor, Lady's, Side Handle, Masked Spout ........................................ 48.00
Dish, Pickle, Tab Handles, Hand-Painted Flowers, Meakin, 8 1/4 In. ........................................ 6.50
Dish, Serving, Triangular Shape, Raised Dragon Head Each Corner ........................................ 27.50
Ginger Jar, Covered, Oriental Shape, 7 In. ........................................ 95.00
Holder, Toothbrush, Oriental Pattern, 5 1/2 In. ........................................ 50.00
Mold, Grapes ........................................ 26.00
Mold, Sheaf Of Wheat, Impressed Minton, Oval, 2 1/4 In. ........................................ 24.00
Mug, Flowers, Brown & White, 2 In. ........................................ 5.00
Mug, 2-Handled, Swansea Pattern, Mason's, 5 1/4 In. ........................................ 68.00
Pitcher, Bulbous, Scrolled Handle & Spout ........................................ 20.00
Pitcher, English, C.1864, 11 1/2 In. ........................................ 29.50
Pitcher, Flowers, Obverse, American Flag, T. & R.Boote, 10 In. ........................................ 100.00
Pitcher, Milk, Applied Handle, White, 7 1/2 In. ........................................ 13.50
Pitcher, Milk, Oriental Pattern, 5 1/2 In. ........................................ 55.00
Pitcher, Milk, Snake Handle, Birds & Flowers, 5 1/2 In. ........................................ 65.00
Pitcher, Relief Mythology Figures, Mason, 9 In. ........................................ 140.00
Pitcher, Shaded Pink Top Half, Gold Rim, Hand-Painted, 7 1/4 In. ........................................ 29.50
Pitcher, T. & R.Boote, 1853, 8 In. ........................................ 45.00
Plate, Baronial, Minarets, People, Boats, Lavender, W.England, 10 In. ........................................ 22.00
Plate, Cleopatra, Purple, 8 In.Diam. ........................................ 20.00
Plate, Heirloom, Straight Fluting, Scalloped, C.1962 ........................................ 3.00
Plate, Impressed Adams Rose, 7 1/2 In.Diam. ........................................ 125.00
Plate, Pearl Pattern, 9 In.Diam. ........................................ 14.00
Plate, Pearl Pattern, 10 In. ........................................ 18.00
Plate, Soup, Lily-Of-The-Valley, Wood & Son ........................................ 10.00
Plate, Soup, Pearl Pattern, 9 In.Diam ........................................ 23.00
Plate, Soup, Wheat Pattern, Set Of 3 ........................................ 35.00
Plate, Sousa, C.M.S. & P., Mulberry, 10 1/2 In. ........................................ 40.00
Platter, Black, Parrot Incised Center, Signed & Numbered, 10 In. ........................................ 79.00
Platter, Cobalt & Orange Floral Design, 6 1/2 X 10 In. ........................................ 75.00
Platter, Give Us This Day Our Daily Bread ........................................ 75.00
Platter, Mason's, Gold Trim, Marked, 19 1/2 X 15 3/4 In. ........................................ 175.00
Platter, Neva Pattern, Mulberry, 12 X 15 1/2 In. ........................................ 85.00 To 95.00
Platter, Oriental Scene, C.1850, Flow Blue, 11 3/4 X 15 1/4 In. ........................................ 60.00
Platter, Rose Pattern, Mulberry, E.Challinor, 14 X 18 In. ........................................ 110.00
Platter, Scalloped, Asiatic Pheasants, Marked, 15 X 18 In. ........................................ 60.00
Platter, Stylized Oriental Garden Foliage, Mason, 17 In.Diam. ........................................ 275.00
Platter, Thorn Pattern, C.1872, Registry Mark, 20 X 16 In. ........................................ 25.00
Potty, Oriental Scenes, Snake Handle, C.1845, Mason ........................................ 125.00
Soup, Wheat ........................................ 13.00
Spittoon, Lady's, White ........................................ 22.00
Stand, Umbrella, Victorian, Gold Flowers, Green, 21 In. ........................................ 115.00

Sugar & Creamer, Covered, Canton Pattern, Mason's, Blue, 1820s ........................ 125.00
Sugar, Cover, Moss Rose, J.M. & Co. ................................................................... 30.00
Tankard, Flowers, Dragon Handle, C.1860, Mason's, 3 1/2 In. ............................... 95.00
Tea Caddy, Cover, Hexagon Shaped, Blue & Gold Foliage, 6 1/2 In. ...................... 75.00
Tea Caddy, Mason ............................................................................................. 38.00
    IRONSTONE, TEA LEAF, see Tea Leaf Ironstone
Teapot, Lid, Bow & Tassel, 1878 Mark, Burgess & Goddard ................................. 28.00
Teapot, Ning-Po, C.1845 ................................................................................... 250.00
Tureen, Covered, Child's, Attached Underplate .................................................. 19.50
Tureen, Grape Cluster Handle, Red Cliff ............................................................ 58.00
Tureen, Gravy, Underplate & Ladle, Beachberry Pattern ..................................... 90.00
Tureen, Octagonal Urn Shape, Ladle, Log & Leaf Handles, Marked ...................... 90.00
Tureen, Soup, Pear Finial, White ....................................................................... 60.00
Tureen, Vegetable, Marked Clementson Brothers ............................................... 60.00
Washbowl & Pitcher, Sydenham, White .............................................................. 185.00
Washbowl, Corella Pattern, Mulberry, 12 In.Diam. ............................................. 125.00
Waste Bowl, Ning-Po, C.1845 ............................................................................ 125.00
Waste Pot, Polychrome Transfer, Hunter, Dogs, 18th Century, 14 In. ................... 130.00

    IVORY, see also Napkin Ring; Netsuke
IVORY, Ball, Mystery, Dragon Stand, 10 Carved Layers, Movable, 7 In. ............... 250.00
Ball, Opening With Interior Judaic Scene ........................................................... 225.00
Bone, Totem Pole, Hand-Carved & Painted, Alaska, 1900s, 4 In. ......................... 25.00
Bottle, Scent, Hand-Painted Scenes, Multicolors & Calligraphy, 4 In. .................. 295.00
Box, Jewel, Carved Allover, Elephants, Trees, 5 X 4 In. ...................................... 200.00
Brush Holder, Hand-Carved, Oriental Stand, 8 In. .............................................. 575.00
Buckle, Carved Flowers, 2 Piece ....................................................................... 25.00
Calculator, Chinese, Monkeys, Butterflies, Beetles, 2 1/4 X 3 1/2 In. .................. 150.00
Case, Calling Card, Carved Allover, 4 1/2 X 2 1/2 In. ......................................... 225.00
Case, Card Carrying, Egyptian, Carved, Dated 1889 .......................................... 160.00
Chess Set, Oriental, King, 3 1/2 In. .................................................................... 325.00
Chess Set, Wooden Case, Doubles As Board, King, 4 In. ..................................... 410.00
Chips, Poker, In Original Rack Case, Set Of 510 ................................................ 3000.00
Cricket Cage, Carved Dragons, Pierced Background, 4 1/4 In. ............................. 275.00
Crochet Hook .................................................................................................... 10.00
Doctor's Lady, Full Figure, Movable Bracelet, 4 In. ........................................... 70.00
Doctor's Lady, Full Figure, Movable Bracelet, 6 In. ........................................... 135.00
Doctor's Lady, Full Figure, Movable Bracelet, 8 In. ........................................... 195.00
Doctor's Lady, Reclining, Full Nude, 12 In. ........................................................ 295.00
Doll, Kabuki, 2 Faces Rotate, 6 In. .................................................................... 300.00
Elephant Tusk, Primitive, African, 34 In. ........................................................... 750.00
Figure, Foo Lion, 2 In. ....................................................................................... 85.00
Figurine, Andromeda, English, C.1925, Signed Andrew, 11 1/4 In. ...................... 800.00
Figurine, Black Man In Pain, Colored ................................................................. 500.00
Figurine, Chinese Peasant Eating Noodles, Signed, 1 In. ................................... 65.00
Figurine, Chubby Child, Recumbent Position, Hardwood Base, 6 In. .................... 500.00
Figurine, Cupid Hammering Arrow On Anvil, 3 3/4 In. ........................................ 250.00
Figurine, Diana, Hunting Horn At Her Shoulder, 13 3/4 In. ................................. 3500.00
Figurine, Elephant Being Attacked By Two Tigers, 4 X 6 1/2 In. .......................... 445.00
Figurine, Emperor & Empress, Teak Base, 4 1/2 In. & 5 3/4 In., Pair ................... 395.00
Figurine, Emperor & Empress, Wooden Base, 4 1/4 In., Pair ............................... 795.00
Figurine, Five Elephants & Shark's Head, Tusk, 21 In. ....................................... 225.00
Figurine, Horse, 19th Century, Japanese, Wood Base, 2 1/2 X 3 In. .................... 50.00
Figurine, Hotei, Seated, 3 1/2 In. ....................................................................... 70.00
Figurine, Hound Dog, 3 1/2 X 4 1/2 In. .............................................................. 150.00
Figurine, Kwan Yin, Buddha On Headdress, Lotus Pad, Marked, 6 1/2 In. ........... 450.00
Figurine, Kwan Yin, Teak Base, 36 In. ............................................................... 4800.00
Figurine, Lady, Hand-Carved, Base, 12 1/4 In. ................................................... 1950.00
Figurine, Lion, Growling, 8 1/2 In. ..................................................................... 350.00
Figurine, Moses, Studded Stones On Robe, Opens To Scene Of Life, 9 In. ........... 3500.00
Figurine, Organ Grinder, Silver Base, C.1900, 10 1/4 In. .................................... 1000.00
Figurine, Six Monkeys Climbing, Pomegranate, Cricket, Signed, 6 1/2 In. ........... 185.00
Figurine, Tigers Fighting Elephant, 13 In.Long ................................................... 950.00

**Figurine,** Warrior In Chain Armor, With Arrows & Spear, 6 3/4 In. ............................ 800.00
**Foo Lion Jar,** Removable Head, Stones, 5 In. ............................................................ 250.00
**Holder,** Cigar, Carved .............................................................................................. 25.00
**Holder,** Cigarette, Hand-Carved, Twisted Design, 4 In. .......................................... 30.00
**Horse,** Walking, Full Figure, Pair, 2 1/2 X 2 In. ....................................................... 35.00
**Horses,** Hand-Carved, Teak Stands, Set Of 6 .......................................................... 359.00
**Letter Opener,** English Silver Mountings, Hallmarked, 1891, E.Barnard ................ 135.00
**Napkin Ring,** Oriental, Carved Scrimshaw, Stalking Lion ....................................... 45.00
**Plaque,** Four Cavorting Putti & Dog, Black Wood Frame, Oval, 5 1/2 In. ............... 1300.00
**Plaque,** Soldier Home From Battle, Italy, 6 1/2 X 5 1/4 In. ..................................... 375.00
**Plate,** Carved, 3 In. ................................................................................................... 95.00
**Prayer Wheel,** Wooden Handle, 24 Prayers Inside .................................................. 85.00
**Stretcher,** Glove ...................................................................................... 15.00 To 18.00
**Teething Stick,** Scissors Shape ............................................................................... 22.00
**Tooth,** Whale's, Engraved Whale Ship, U.S.Flag, 5 1/2 In. ..................................... 275.00
**Triptych,** Dissolution Of Parliament, Trophy Center, 11 X 9 5/8 In. ....................... 2250.00
**Triptych,** Monk Preaching To Crowd, C.1900, 10 1/2 In. ......................................... 1100.00
**Triptych,** Virgin, Saint Anne, Christ Child, Pierced Canopy, 4 X 6 In. .................... 700.00
**Tusk Tips,** Maiden, Carved, 17 In. ............................................................................ 58.00
**Tusk,** Walrus, Portrait Of Young Bearded Man, Indian On Rise, 24 In. ................... 300.00
**Tusks,** Elephant, 3 Pounds, 14 In. ........................................................................... 160.00
**Urn,** Hunt Scene, Covered, C.1900, 17 In. ............................................................... 3250.00
**Urn,** Ring Handles, Foo Lions Top Ogre Mask, Ching Dynasty, 10 X 9 In. ............. 1600.00
**Walking Stick,** Black Inlay Design .......................................................................... 350.00
**Wall Pocket,** 12 In. Long .......................................................................................... 150.00

**JACK ARMSTRONG, Flashlight** ............................................................................. 12.00
**Hike-O-Meter** ........................................................................................ 9.00 To 18.00
**Pedometer** ................................................................................................................ 15.00
**Ring,** Siren ............................................................................................................... 50.00
**Ring,** With Code ....................................................................................................... 75.00
**Telescope,** Explorer ................................................................................................. 15.00
**Telescope,** 1930s ..................................................................................................... 19.00

*Jack-In-The-Pulpit vases were named for their odd trumpetlike shape
that resembles the wild plant called jack-in-the-pulpit. The design
originated in the late Victorian years.*

**JACK-IN-THE-PULPIT, Vase,** Amber Applied Clear Handle, Small ......................... 22.00
**Vase,** Amber Applied Top Edging, Swirl, 12 3/4 In. .................................................. 195.00
**Vase,** Enameled Gold, Opalescent Vaseline, 5 1/2 In. ............................................ 70.00
**Vase,** Enameled Pink Flowers, Sapphire Blue, 5 3/8 In. ......................................... 85.00
**Vase,** Fluted Top, Cranberry, 11 In., Pair ................................................................ 120.00
**Vase,** Footed, Cranberry & Vaseline Opalescent, 5 1/2 In. ..................................... 150.00
**Vase,** Footed, Flower Shape Top, Pink Overlay, 6 1/2 In. ....................................... 78.00
**Vase,** Hobnail Edge, Multicolored Spatter, 6 1/2 In. ................................................ 95.00
**Vase,** Hollow Hob, Deep Red To Baby Blue ............................................................. 265.00
**Vase,** Inverted Thumbprint, Amberina, 13 In. .......................................................... 200.00
**Vase,** Melon Ribbed, Green Outside, White Inside, 9 In. ......................................... 50.00
**Vase,** Olive Green, Diamond-Quilted, End-Of-Day Top, 5 In. .................................. 95.00
**Vase,** Opalescent Stripes, Petal Feet, 5 1/2 In. ...................................................... 110.00
**Vase,** Orchid, 5 1/4 In. .............................................................................................. 65.00
**Vase,** Pale Yellow, 4 3/4 In. ..................................................................................... 60.00
**Vase,** Petal Top, White Outside, Pink Overlay, 6 1/2 In. .......................................... 80.00
**Vase,** Pleated & Dimpled, White Outside, 11 In. ...................................................... 485.00
**Vase,** Purple Shading Inside, White Outside, 7 In. ................................................... 110.00
**Vase,** Quilted, Blue Cased, Pewter Base, 11 3/4 In., Pair ....................................... 75.00
**Vase,** Ruby Throat, Blue Filigree, 6 1/2 In. .............................................................. 80.00
**Vase,** Ruffled Edge, Pink Overlay, 7 1/4 In. ............................................................. 85.00
**Vase,** Spatter, Pink, 7 In. ......................................................................................... 59.00
**Vase,** Vaseline To Blue Opalescent, 8 In. ............................................................... 78.00
**Vase,** Vaseline To Blue, 7 In. ................................................................................... 69.00
**Vase,** White Bristol Body, Applied Leaf Feet, 6 1/4 In. ............................................ 52.00

Vase, White Opalescent, Pink, Yellow Stripe, 5 In. .................................................................... 95.00
Vase, White Outside, Pink Inside, Melon Ribbed, 7 In. ............................................................ 60.00
Vase, Yellow & White Enameld Flowers, Aqua ......................................................................... 85.00

*Jackfield ware was originally a black glazed pottery made in Jackfield,
England, from 1750 to 1775. A yellow glazed ware has also been called
Jackfield ware. Most of the pieces referred to as Jackfield are black
pieces made during the Victorian era.*

JACKFIELD, Creamer, Cow ........................................................................................................ 75.00
Dish, Cheese, Hand-Enameled Design, 12 1/2 X 11 1/4 In. ............................................... 250.00
Teapot, RN. 176424, Enameled On Gold Design ................................................................... 75.00

JADE, Bowl, Mottled Green, Made From One Piece Of Jade, 3 7/8 In., Pair .......................... 495.00
Box, Muttonfat, Carved Wading Bird & Lotus, 1 1/2 X 3 In.Diam. ..................................... 225.00
Bracelet, Bangle, Pale Green ..................................................................................................... 395.00
Elephant, 3 1/2 In. ..................................................................................................................... 85.00
Figurine, Goldfish, Swimming, Fantail, Apple Green, 3 1/4 X 5 1/4 In. .............................. 200.00
Figurine, Horned Beast, Spinach Green, Inlaid Base, Nephrite, 3 X 8 In. ............................ 240.00
Figurine, Mouse, 3 In. ................................................................................................................ 25.00
Figurine, Swan, Muttonfat, Head Back Over Body, Stand, 2 X 1 1/3 In. .............................. 95.00
Figurine, Turtle, 3 In. ................................................................................................................. 25.00
Incense Burner, Serpentine, Elephant Heads, Hanging Rings, 6 In. ....................................... 185.00
Ring, Lavender, 14K Gold ........................................................................................................... 300.00
Urn, Covered, Serpentine, 4 Rings, 9 1/2 X 5 1/4 In. ........................................................... 650.00

*Japanese Coralene is a pottery decorated with small raised beads and dots.
It was first made in the nineteenth century. Later wares made to imitate
coralene had dots of enamel.*

JAPANESE CORALENE, Vase, Bleeding Hearts, Lime To Green, Gold Trim, 13 In. .............. 425.00
Vase, Gold, Pink Flowers, Cobalt Blue Ground, 4 1/4 In. ....................................................... 135.00

JAR OPENER, Speedo, Cast Iron, 6 In. .................................................................................... 14.50

*Jasperware is a fine-grained pottery developed by Josiah Wedgwood in
1755. The jasper was made in many colors including the most famous, a light
blue. It is still being made.*
JASPERWARE, see also various art potteries; Wedgwood
JASPERWARE, Plaque, Green, White, Gentleman, Dog, Hanging, 5 1/4 In. ......................... 55.00
Stein, Tan, 12 Seminude Maidens Dancing, 7 In. .................................................................. 85.00
Syrup, Olive Green, Hunt Scene, Pewter Rim & Lid, Signed, 5 In. ...................................... 69.00
JEWEL TEA, see Autumn Leaf

JEWELRY, Bar Pin, Center Diamond, Filigree, Platinum On 14K Gold ................................ 75.00
Bar Pin, Pearl & Diamond, 15K Fold, C.1900, American ..................................................... 575.00
Baroque Pearl & Amethyst, Suspended On Gold Chain, C.1880, American ......................... 450.00
Beads, Amber, Faceted, Graduated From 1/4 To 1 In., 19 In. .............................................. 75.00
Beads, Amethyst, Vermeil Clasp, 24 In. .................................................................................. 175.00
Beads, Cloisonne On Wire, Leaf Design, Birdcage Shape, C.1920 ....................................... 200.00
Beads, Coral, Graduated, Gold Clasp, 36 In. .......................................................................... 75.00
Belt, Jet Beads, Tassels, 1870s, Whitby, England, 71 In. ..................................................... 87.50
Bracelet, Bangle, American, C.1880, Gold, Set Of 5 ......................................................... 1225.00
Bracelet, Bangle, Seed Pearls, Opens, Chain, 14K Yellow Gold .......................................... 285.00
Bracelet, Bangle, 3 Opals, Opens, Chain, 14K Yellow Gold, 1/8 In. ................................... 275.00
Bracelet, Black Enamel & Sterling Silver, Paste, 7 In. .......................................................... 28.00
Bracelet, Carved Agate, Freshwater Baroque Pearl, C.1820, European ............................... 150.00
Bracelet, Carved, Cinnabar, Marked China ............................................................................. 35.00
Bracelet, Engraved Design, Arrow Shape Ends, C.1890, American ...................................... 400.00
Bracelet, Gold & Amethyst, Flat Engraved Band, C.1880, American ................................... 150.00
Bracelet, Graduated Black & White Cabochons, Gold Bezels, C.1880 ................................. 250.00
Bracelet, Hair, Silver Trim ......................................................................................................... 20.00
Bracelet, Ivory & Silver, 8 Ivory Carvings, Chinese .............................................................. 125.00
Bracelet, Platinum & Diamond, Approximately 3 Carats ..................................................... 2250.00
Bracelet, Topaz Quartz Stone, 14K Gold Filigree ................................................................. 550.00

Jewelry, Brooch, Platinum, Gold, Diamond, & Pearl, Edwardian

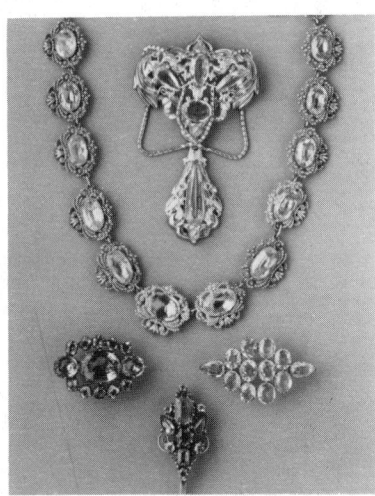

Top center, Brooch, Gold & Pink Topaz, and Necklace, Georgian Gold, Pink Topaz (See Page 283); bottom center left, Brooch, Gold & Foil-backed Quartz; bottom center right, Brooch, Gold & Yellow Topaz; below, Brooch, Silver & Pink Tourmaline

| | |
|---|---:|
| **Brooch & Earrings,** Cameos, White Cut To Black, Gold & Agate, C.1875 | 400.00 |
| **Brooch & Earrings,** Textured Leaves & Rosebuds, Yellow Gold, C.1880 | 225.00 |
| **Brooch,** Almandine Garnet, Octagonal, 14K Gold, 3/8 X 3/8 In. | 135.00 |
| **Brooch,** Butterfly, Ivory, With Mother-Of-Pearl, 2 In. | 125.00 |
| **Brooch,** Butterfly, Sterling Silver, 3 In. | 55.00 |
| **Brooch,** Cameo, Chain Loop, 14K Gold, 2 1/2 X 1 7/8 In. | 300.00 |
| **Brooch,** Cameo, Cream Against Brown, 10K Gold | 65.00 |
| **Brooch,** Cameo, Diamond, 14K Gold, Large | 225.00 |
| **Brooch,** Carved Lava Cameo, Head Of Young Woman, 2 In. | 55.00 |
| **Brooch,** Four-Leaf Clover, Black Enamel On Leaves, 14K Gold | 45.00 |
| **Brooch,** Gold & Foil-Backed Quartz, C.1830 .......................... *Illus* | 325.00 |
| **Brooch,** Gold & Pink Topaz, C.1860 ............................................ *Illus* | 900.00 |
| **Brooch,** Gold & Yellow Topaz, C.1830 ...................................... *Illus* | 650.00 |
| **Brooch,** Gold, Carved Onyx Cameo, Pearl & Diamond ............ *Illus* | 800.00 |
| **Brooch,** Gold, Hardstone Cameo & Pearl, C.1870 ................... *Illus* | 800.00 |
| **Brooch,** Gold, Platinum, & Diamond Bar .................................. *Illus* | 750.00 |
| **Brooch,** Platinum, Gold, Diamond, & Pearl, Edwardian ......... *Illus* | 3500.00 |
| **Brooch,** Shono, Sterling Silver, Queen's Hallmark, 2 X 3 In. | 175.00 |
| **Brooch,** Silver & Pink Tourmaline .............................................. *Illus* | 200.00 |
| **Brooch,** Silver, Pearl, Diamond, & Porcelain, C.1880 ........... *Illus* | 500.00 |
| **Buckle,** French Cut Steel, Pair | 25.00 |
| **Buckle,** Shoe, Stamped Design, Silver Overlay On Brass, 1760-70, 3 In. | 56.00 |
| **Buckle,** Shoe, Steel Cut, 1920s, 2 X 3 In., Pair | 5.00 |
| **Buckle,** Shoe, 18th Century, Pewter On Steel, Pair | 35.00 |
| **Button,** Collar, Hand-Carved Pearl, C.1875, Set Of 5 | 23.50 |
| **Chain,** Gold, Double Hollow Link, Applied Flower On Each, C.1880 | 450.00 |
| **Chain,** Lady's, Antique, 14K Rose Gold | 99.00 |
| **Chain,** Pendant, Diamond Shaped Links, Yellow Gold, 20th Century | 200.00 |
| **Chain,** Watch, Blue Enamel Bars, Yellow Gold Inlay, 14K Gold, 14 In. | 125.00 |
| **Chain,** Watch, Gold Filled Mesh, Fob | 15.00 |
| **Chain,** Watch, Hair, Gold Trim | 23.00 |
| **Chain,** Watch, 12K Gold, 13 In. | 58.00 |

Jewelry, Necklace, Gold & Carved Coral, C.1870

Jewelry, Brooch, Gold,
Carved Onyx Cameo,
Pearl & Diamond
(See Page 281)

Jewelry, Brooch, Gold, Hardstone
Cameo & Pearl, C.1870 (See Page 281)

Jewelry, Necklace, Cross Pendant
& Ear Clips, Gold Paste

Jewelry, Brooch, Silver, Pearl, Diamond,
& Porcelain, C.1880 (See Page 281)

| | |
|---|---:|
| **Charm,** Cash Register, Scroll Covered, Drawer Opens, 14K Gold | 65.00 |
| **Charm,** Horseshoe, Good Luck Across Front, Rose Gold, 14K | 19.00 |
| **Compact,** Gold Mesh | 7.00 |
| **Cross,** Engraved, Victorian, 14K Yellow Gold | 70.00 |
| **Cuff Links,** Engraved, 14K Green Gold | 125.00 |
| **Cuff Links,** Sterling Silver, Oval | 14.00 |
| **Ear Studs,** Peridot Stone, Green | 15.00 |
| **Earrings,** Carved Angel's Breath Coral, Center Seed Pearl, C.1880 | 250.00 |
| **Earrings,** Carved Ivory Flowers, Openwork, 14K Gold Wires | 40.00 |
| **Earrings,** Diamond In Stud & On Black Enameled Oval, 14K Gold | 170.00 |
| **Earrings,** Elongated Teardrop Agate, Banded In White, C.1880 | 100.00 |
| **Earrings,** Garnet, Set In Gold, 14K Wires | 160.00 |
| **Earrings,** Gold & Floral Carved Jade, C.1900, American | 125.00 |
| **Earrings,** Shell Cameo, Male Busts, C.1880, American | 50.00 |
| **Earrings,** With Pearls, Front Closure, 14K Yellow Gold | 70.00 |
| **Earrings,** 6 Small Diamonds, 14K White Gold, C.1900, American | 425.00 |
| **Flask,** Gold, Gadrooned & Embossed, 3 Small Diamonds, 19th Century | 325.00 |
| **Hairpin,** 3 Seed Pearls, Art Nouveau, 15K Gold, Pair | 45.00 |
| **Hatpin,** Figural, Snake, Amethyst | 55.00 |
| **Hatpin,** Gold Filigree, Signet S | 65.00 |
| **JEWELRY, INDIAN, see Indian** | |
| **Lavaliere,** Freshwater & Natural Pearls, 14K Gold | 105.00 |
| **Lavaliere,** Geometric Shaped Diamond, Gold Chain, C.1910, American | 450.00 |
| **Lavaliere,** Gold, Tourmaline & Diamond, Reticulated Chain, C.1900 | 575.00 |
| **Lavaliere,** Several Pearls, Yellow Gold, 14K Gold Chain | 90.00 |
| **Lavaliere,** 2 Amethysts & 2 Pearls, 2 Color 10K Gold | 65.00 |
| **Locket,** Twisted Wire & Ball Design, Cameo Center, C.1880, American | 300.00 |
| **Locket,** 12 Sepia Pictures Of General Tom Thumb, Wedding & Guests | 200.00 |

**Necklace,** Amber Glass Beads, 62 In. .......................................................................... 17.50
**Necklace,** Amber, 33 Beads, 16 1/2 In. ....................................................................... 55.00
**Necklace,** Angel Breath Coral, Graduated, C.1880, Far East ...................................... 75.00
**Necklace,** Carved Angel Skin Coral Beads, Gold Clasp .............................................. 225.00
**Necklace,** Carved Coral, Double Strand, Heads Of Goats, C.1880 ............................. 375.00
**Necklace,** Cinnabar, 29 In. ........................................................................................... 100.00
**Necklace,** Cloisonne, Blue On Silver, 33 In. ............................................................... 150.00
**Necklace,** Cross Pendant & Ear Clips, Gold Paste ...........................................*Illus* 1800.00
**Necklace,** Earrings & Pin, Hairwork, Mounted In Gold .............................................. 250.00
**Necklace,** Georgian Gold, Pink Topaz, 1810 ...................................................*Illus* 3250.00
**Necklace,** Gold & Carved Coral, C.1870 .........................................................*Illus* 1000.00
**Necklace,** Graduated Garnets & Faceted Crystal, C.1890, American .......................... 100.00
**Necklace,** Mesh, Beaded Scrolled Wire Frame, Tassel Drop, C.1870 ........................ 600.00
**Necklace,** Mourning, Gold & Jets, Plated Chain, C.1880, American .......................... 50.00
**Necklace,** Mourning, Jet Beads, Gold Findings, Set In Pendant, C.1880 ................... 150.00
**Necklace,** Silver & Jeweled Cross, C.1840, Hungarian .............................................. 850.00
**Necklace,** Silver Butterflies, Heishi, Turquoise, Signed ............................................. 165.00
**Nuggets,** Gold, C.1880, American, Set Of 3 ............................................................... 525.00
**Pearls,** 8mm., 42 In. ................................................................................................... 950.00
**Pendant & Ear Pendants,** Gold & Mosaic, C.1870 .........................................*Illus* 3000.00
**Pendant,** Cranes On Colored Blooming Flowers, Cloisonne, 1 3/4 In. ....................... 35.00
**Pendant,** Double Cameo, Man & Woman, Black & White Onyx, 14K Gold .................. 95.00
**Pendant,** Flowers In Field, Satsuma, 19th Century, Silk Cord, 2 In. ......................... 200.00
**Pendant,** Gold, Freshwater Pearl, Sapphire, & Diamond, C.1900, American .............. 450.00
**Pendant,** Iris, Satsuma, 19th Century, Silk Cord, 2 In. ............................................. 200.00
**Pendant,** Kambara, Sterling Silver, Queen's Hallmark, 2 1/2 In. ............................... 135.00
**Pendant,** Marcasite, Sterling Silver Chain ................................................................... 45.00
**Pendant,** Mt.Fuji, Hand-Enameled, Queen's Hallmark, 2 1/2 In. ............................... 125.00
**Pendant,** Opal With 6 Rose-Cut Diamonds, 14K Yellow Gold ................................... 138.00
**Pendant,** Persian Turquoise & Elongated Pearls, 18K Gold, Chain ............................. 62.00
**Pendant,** Rose Quartz, Carved Rose, Tear Shaped, 1 1/3 In. ..................................... 22.00
**Pendant,** Ryogoku Bridge, Hand Enameled, Queen's Hallmark, 2 In. ........................ 125.00
**Pendant,** Shell Cameo, Lady, Flowers In Hair, 10K Gold Setting ............................... 80.00

Jewelry, Pendant & Ear Pendants, Gold & Mosaic, C.1870

Jewelry, Ring, Carved Garnet Sphinx & Rose
Diamond, 18K Gold (See Page 284)

**Pendant,** Victorian, Yellow Gold Perfume Bottle ............................................................ 42.00
**Pin & Earrings,** Gold & Shell Cameo, Victorian ............................................................. 525.00
**Pin,** Art Deco Chatelaine, Seed Pearls, Sapphire, 10K Gold ......................................... 85.00
**Pin,** Art Nouveau, Grapes, Sterling Silver .................................................................... 45.00
**Pin,** Bar, Silver, Georg Jensen, 2 3/4 In. ...................................................................... 70.00
**Pin,** Blonde Hair Under Glass, Surrounded By Pearls ................................................... 80.00
**Pin,** Butterfly, Yellow Enamel, Sterling Silver, 2 1/2 X 1 1/4 In. ................................... 32.00
**Pin,** Cameo, Framed In 10K Gold, 1 In. ........................................................................ 65.00
**Pin,** Cameo, Gold Frame, Roman Soldier, C.1880, European ....................................... 125.00
**Pin,** Marcasite, Oval Ribbonlike Frame, Open Enter, 1 3/4 X 1 In. ............................... 29.00
**Pin,** Queen Victoria, 2 Hearts, V.R.Entwined, Crown, 1 1/2 X 3/4 In. .......................... 55.00
**Pin,** Seed Pearls, White Enamel On 14K Yellow Gold .................................................. 30.00
**Pin,** Silver, Butterflies, Flower, & Leaves, Georg Jensen, 2 1/4 In. ............................... 155.00
**Pin,** Silver, Double Leaf, Georg Jensen ......................................................................... 50.00
**Pin,** Two & One Half Dollar, Gold Coin, Dated 1878 ..................................................... 210.00
**Ring,** Baby, Persian Turquoise, 10K Yellow Gold ........................................................... 22.00
**Ring,** Baby, Topaz Stone, 10K Yellow Gold ................................................................... 22.00
**Ring,** Black Onyx, Diamond In Corner, 20K White Gold, Size 6 1/2 ............................... 90.00
**Ring,** Cameo, Gray, 14K Gold, Black Ground, Wedgwood, Size 6 1/2 ......................... 130.00
**Ring,** Carved Garnet Sphinx & Rose Diamond, 18K Gold .....................................*Illus* 4000.00
**Ring,** Center Amethyst, 6 Persian Turquoises, Seed Pearls, 14K Gold ......................... 110.00
**Ring,** Gold, Cabochon Cat's-Eye, 1 Carat, Victorian, Anchor Mark ............................... 125.00
**Ring,** Gold, Large Cabochon Cut Emerald, Surrounded By 16 Rubies .......................... 200.00
**Ring,** Onyx & Center Diamond, 10K Yellow Gold ........................................................... 62.00
**Ring,** Snake, Rubies Eyes, Winds Around Finger, 14K ................................................... 75.00
**Ring,** Star Ruby, .9 Carats, Flanked By 5 Diamonds, 14K Gold ................................... 1400.00
**Ring,** Victorian Persian Turquoise & Pearl Ring ............................................................. 95.00
**Ring,** Victorian, 6 Carat Amethyst, 14K Yellow Gold ..................................................... 65.00
**Ring,** Wedding, Embossed 14K & 18K Pink Gold, 1/4 In.Wide .................................... 62.00
**Ring,** Wedding, Man's, 14K Yellow Gold, Size 10, 1/2 In.Wide .................................... 185.00
**Ring,** Wedding, 6 Full-Cut 3 Point Diamonds, 14K Gold, Size 6 1/2 ............................. 105.00
**Ring,** Woman's Head On Right, Sapphire On Left, 14K Yellow Gold ............................. 135.00
**Ring,** 2 Amethysts, White Gold Filigree ........................................................................ 225.00
**Ring,** 2 Hands Holding Diamond, Victorian, 14K Pink Gold ........................................... 150.00
**Ring,** 2 Rubies, 4 Rose-Cut Diamonds, 14K Yellow Gold, Size 6 1/2 ........................... 155.00
**Ring,** 3 Garnets, Set Across, 14K Yellow Gold, Size 7 .................................................. 85.00
**Slide,** Opal, 14K Yellow Gold, Set With Opal ................................................................ 30.00
**Stickpin,** Baroque Pearl Dangles, 14K Yellow Gold With Diamond ............................... 65.00
**Stickpin,** Black Opals, Carved Woman's Head, Gold ..................................................... 750.00
**Stickpin,** Blue Enamel Leaf, Pearl, 10K Gold ................................................................ 25.00
**Stickpin,** Cameo, White On Brown, 14K Yellow Gold ..................................................... 52.00
**Stickpin,** Gold Nugget, On Gold Pin .............................................................................. 75.00
**Stickpin,** International Harvester, Brass .......................................................................... 16.00
**Stickpin,** John Deere, Brass .......................................................................................... 25.00
**Stickpin,** Lilac Amethyst & Seed Pearl, 14K Yellow Gold .............................................. 40.00
**Stickpin,** Lover's Knot, Center Pearl, 14K Yellow Gold ................................................. 26.00
**Stickpin,** Masonic, Set With Pearls, 14K Gold .............................................................. 32.00
**Stickpin,** Polished Green Tourmaline, 15K Gold, 5/8 In. ............................................... 30.00
**Stickpin,** Question Mark Shape, 14K Gold, Sapphire Center ........................................ 40.00
**Stickpin,** Shmoo, Al Capp Comic Character .................................................................. 10.00
**Stickpin,** Stirrups, 14K Gold ......................................................................................... 22.00
**Stickpin,** The Staver Carriage Co., Brass ..................................................................... 12.00
**Stickpin,** 10 Full Cut Diamonds, 14K White Gold ......................................................... 68.00
**Stickpin,** 6 Diamonds, 14K Yellow Gold ....................................................................... 60.00
**Tie Tack,** Gold, .985 Carat Diamond, C.1900, American .............................................. 500.00
    **JEWELRY, WATCH, see Watch**
**Watch Chain,** Interlocking Scrolled & Oval Links, Gold, 19th Century .......................... 450.00
**Watch Chain,** Rose Gold, 19th Century, 14 In. ............................................................. 650.00
**Watch Chain,** 13 Gold Nuggets, Miniature Gold Miner's Tools, 21 Cts. ....................... 300.00
**Watch Pin,** Fleur-De-Lis, Gold ..................................................................................... 195.00

*John Rogers statues were made from 1859 to 1892. The originals were*
*bronze, but the thousands of copies made by the Rogers Factory were of*
*painted plaster. Eighty different figures were made.*

**JOHN ROGERS, Group,** Council Of War ................................................................. 800.00
  **Group,** Courtship In Sleepy Hollow .............................................................. 750.00
  **Group,** Favorite Scholar ............................................................................... 550.00
  **Group,** Hide & Seek, 1874, 42 In. ........................................................... 4900.00
  **Group,** Is It So Nominated In The Bond .................................................... 300.00
  **Group,** The First Meeting ......................................... 375.00 To 400.00
  **Stereo Cards,** Set Of 10 ............................................................................. 100.00

Judaica, Lamp, Sabbath, Dutch, C.1700, Brass

Judaica, Lamp, Sabbath, Italian Brass,
18th Century

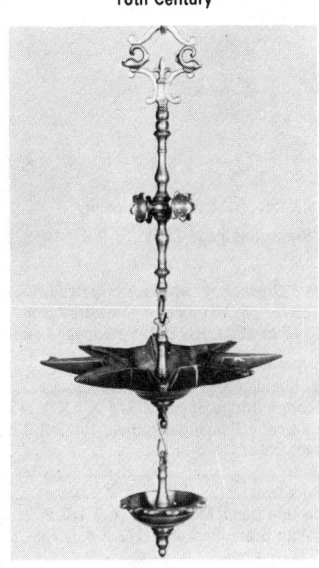

**JUDAICA, Lamp,** Sabbath, Dutch, C.1700, Brass ................................ *Illus* 1700.00
  **Lamp,** Sabbath, Italian Brass, 18th Century ................................ *Illus* 1900.00
  **Lamp,** Sabbath, 18th Century, Brass ............................................ *Illus* 600.00
  **Lamp,** Sabbath, 18th Century, Polish, Brass ............................... *Illus* 3400.00
  **Spice Holder,** Pyramid Shape, Banner On Top, Sterling Silver, 7 In. ......... 265.00
  **Spice Holder,** Sterling Silver, Tower Shape, Flying Flags, 6 1/2 In. ........... 325.00
  **Triptych,** Ivory Ball, Interior Scenes ......................................................... 225.00

> *Jugtown pottery refers to pottery made in North Carolina as far back as*
> *the 1750s. In 1915 Juliana and Jacques Busbee set up a training and*
> *sales organization for what they named Jugtown Pottery. In 1921 they*
> *built a shop at Jugtown, North Carolina, and hired Ben Owen as a*
> *potter in 1923. The Busbees moved the Village Store where the pottery*
> *was sold and promoted to 37 East Sixtieth Street in New York City.*
> *Juliana Busbee sold the New York store in 1926 and moved into a log*
> *cabin near the Jugtown Pottery. The pottery ended production in 1958.*

**JUGTOWN, Candleholder,** Orange ..................................................................... 30.00
  **Candleholder,** Yellow .................................................................................... 25.00
  **Pitcher,** Incised Design, Gray, 6 1/2 In. ........................................................ 45.00
  **Vase,** Reddish Purple Splotches, Turquoise Ground, 7 1/2 In. ...................... 75.00

Judaica, Lamp, Sabbath, 18th Century, Brass
(See Page 285)

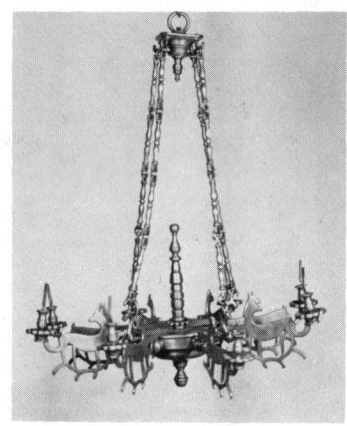

Judaica, Lamp, Sabbath, 18th Century,
Polish, Brass (See Page 285)

*Kate Greenaway, who was a famous illustrator of children's books, drew pictures of children in high-waisted Empire dresses. She lived from about 1846 to 1901. Her designs appear on china, glass, and other pieces.*

| | |
|---|---|
| KATE GREENAWAY, Almanac, Illustrated, 1885 | 70.00 |
| Book, Birthday, The Language Of Flowers, 1887 | 40.00 |
| Bowl, Blue Glass, London Bridge Scene, 1 1/4 X 4 X 1 1/2 In. | 85.00 |
| Bowl, London Bridge Scene, Rectangular, Blue, 1 1/2 X 8 In. | 85.00 |
| Box, Seesaw Children, Unus, 1 X 6 In. | 70.00 |
| Button | 20.00 |
| Cup & Saucer, Child's | 22.00 |
| Figurine, Girl, Doll In One Hand, Muff In Other, 6 1/2 In. | 65.00 |
| Match Holder, Girl With Green Basket, 5 1/2 X 4 1/2 In. | 40.00 |
| Mug, Gardening | 55.00 |
| Napkin Ring, Brass | 55.00 |
| Napkin Ring, Frog After Fly, Silver Plate | 200.00 |
| Napkin Ring, Rolling Hoop, Silver Plate | 250.00 |
| Plate, Card, Girl, Silver Plate | 145.00 |
| Salt & Pepper, Boy & Girl, Rope Borders | 15.00 |
| Saltshaker, Blue Coat, Brown Fur Trim Hat, 4 1/2 In. | 75.00 |
| Saltshaker, Girl In Coat, Hat, & Muff | 37.50 |
| Tea Set, Child's, 16 Pieces | 300.00 |
| Tiles, Four Seasons, Set Of 4 | 350.00 |
| Toothpick, Seated Girl, Embossed Holder | 135.00 |

*Kauffmann refers to the type of work done by Angelica Kauffmann, a painter and decorative artist for Adam Brothers in England between 1766 and 1781. She designed small-scale pictorial subjects in the neoclassical manner. Most porcelains signed Kauffmann were made in the 1800s.*

| | |
|---|---|
| KAUFFMANN, Bottle, Flask, Pilgrim, Luster, 3 Muses, Signed, 8 In. | 195.00 |
| Bowl, Classical Figures, Blue Ground, Signed, 9 1/2 X 9 1/2 In. | 100.00 |
| Bowl, Handled, Picture In Bottom, Cobalt, Signed, 8 1/2 In. | 45.00 |
| Box, Hinged Cover, Classical Scene, Ladies In Garden, Marked, 3 In. | 65.00 |
| Box, Hinged, Signed, 2 1/2 X 2 3/4 In. | 48.00 |
| Box, Jewelry, Heart Shaped, Signed, 4 X 3 In. | 55.00 |
| Box, Ladies & Shepherd On Lid, Brass Mounts, Signed, 3 X 3 In. | 55.00 |

Compote, Low, Beehive Mark, Signed, 8 In.Diam. ............................................................. 70.00
Creamer, Classical Figures, Blue Ground, Signed .............................................................. 85.00
Cup & Saucer, Demitasse, Gold Trim, Orange Luster Edge, Signed ............................... 20.00
Dish, Classical Figures, Blue Ground, Signed, Oblong, 16 X 15 In. ............................... 100.00
Inkwell, Hinged Top, Mother-Of-Pearl Luster, Square, 3 1/4 In. ................................... 75.00
Jar, Jam, Classical Figures, Blue Ground, 3 Piece, Signed ............................................. 85.00
Loving Cup, Gold Handles, Claw Legs, Cobalt Blue, Signed, 8 1/2 In. ......................... 225.00
Match Holder, Pink, Signed, 3 In. ..................................................................................... 30.00
Plate, Beehive, Gold Edge & Border, Lady & Child, Signed, 9 In. ................................. 75.00
Plate, Classical Figures, Blue Ground, Signed, 8 1/4 In.Diam. ...................................... 50.00
Plate, Gold Scalloped Rim, Dancing Maidens, Signed, 8 3/8 In.Diam. .......................... 50.00
Plate, 3 Maidens With Cupids, Green Border, Signed, 10 In. ........................................ 40.00
Tray, Pearlized, Maiden, Irregular Shape, Signed, 5 X 7 1/2 In. .................................... 50.00
Tray, Portrait Of Maidens, Cupid, Gold Beading, Beehive, 8 5/8 In. ............................. 50.00
Urn, Classical Scene, Gold, Yellow Trim, 16 X 9 In. ..................................................... 575.00
Urn, Covered, Scenes On Top & Bottom, Beehive Mark, 18 In. ................................... 325.00
Vase, Portait Of 4 Women, Flowing Robes, Gold Scrollwork, 7 In. ............................... 45.00
    KAYSERZINN, see Pewter
    KAZIUN, see Paperweight, Kaziun

# KELVA

*Kelva glassware was made by the C.F.Monroe Company of Meriden, Connecticut, about 1904. It is a pale pastel painted glass decorated with flowers, designs, or scenes.*

KELVA, Box, Avocado Green, Pink Wild Roses, 3 3/4 X 3 3/4 X 3 In. ............................ 345.00
Box, Clover, Pink Blossoms, 7 In. ..................................................................................... 395.00
Box, Covered, Lined, Scalloped Design, Pink & White, 5 1/2 X 4 X 3 In. ....................... 295.00
Box, Gray & White, Flowers On Cover, Footed, Hinged, Signed, 4 1/2 In. ..................... 325.00
Box, Hinged Lid, Enameled Flowers, Lined, Signed, 4 X 2 1/4 In. ................................. 240.00
Box, Jewelry, Mottled Green Ground, Mauve Roses, Signed ......................................... 350.00
Box, Mottled Blue, Pink Blossoms Allover, Signed, 8 In. ............................................... 495.00
Box, 6-Sided, Blown-Out Rose On Cover, Signed, 3 3/4 X 3 In. ................................... 375.00
Cracker Jar, Green, Blown-Out Pink Flowers, Brass Lid & Rim, Signed ........................ 475.00
Cracker Jar, Mottled Green Ground, Azaleas, Brass Rim & Lid, Signed ....................... 450.00
Dish, Open, Chickens, Signed, 4 In. ................................................................................. 125.00
Humidor, Cigar, Cigars Written In Gold, Pink Flowers, Gray, Signed ........................... 400.00
Planter, Azaleas, Green Ground, Signed, 8 In.Diam. ..................................................... 400.00
Vase, Ormolu Feet & Handles, Flowers, Gray Ground, 14 X 6 In.Diam. ....................... 650.00

*Kemple glass was made by John Kemple of East Palestine, Ohio, and Kenova, West Virginia, from 1945 to 1970. The glass was made from old molds. Many designs and colors were made. Kemple pieces are usually marked with a K on the bottom.*

KEMPLE, Goblet, Lace & Dewdrop, Amber ...................................................................... 15.00
Plate, Milk Glass, 8 In. ....................................................................................................... 9.00

*Kenton Hills Pottery was founded in 1937 in Erlanger, Kentucky. In 1945 all molds were destroyed and the factory was closed.*

KENTON HILLS, Figurine, Lady, 10 In. ............................................................................. 60.00

*Kew Blas is the name used by the Union Glass Company of Somerville, Massachusetts. The name refers to an iridescent golden glass made from the 1890s to 1924.*

KEW BLAS, Candlestick, Swirled Stem, Iridescent Gold, Signed, 8 In., Pair ................. 450.00
Creamer, Gold Iridescent, Signed, 3 1/4 In. ............................................... 250.00 To 400.00
Cuspidor, Lady's, Fluted Top, Pulled Green Feathers, Signed ................................... 1250.00
Vase, Hourglass Form, Gold Feather Design, C.1910, Signed, 8 In. ............................. 450.00

*Kewpies were first pictured in the "Ladies' Home Journal" by Rose*
*O'Neill. The pixielike figures were a success, and Kewpie dolls started*
*appearing in 1911. Kewpie pictures and other items soon followed.*

| | |
|---|---:|
| **KEWPIE, Book,** The Kewpies, Illustrated, Rose O'Neill, 18 Pages, 4 1/2 X 6 In. | 35.00 |
| **Bowl,** Feeding, Signed Rose O'Neill | 100.00 |
| **Cookbook,** Jell-O | 25.00 |
| **Creamer,** Pink Luster, Gold Trim, Rose O'Neill Copyright | 65.00 |
| **Cup & Saucer,** 2 Kewpies On Front Of Cup, Signed | 35.00 |
| **Doll,** Bisque, Signed, Original Sticker, 5 1/2 In. | 90.00 |
| **Doll,** Blue Wings, Movable Arms, Signed O'Neill, 5 In. | 95.00 |
| **Doll,** Jointed At Shoulders, In Glass Cradle, Marked, 4 In. | 100.00 |
| **Doll,** Jointed, Original Sunsuit, Composition, 13 In. | 40.00 |
| **Doll,** Lying On Side, Leg Raised, Signed, 4 1/2 In. | 210.00 To 235.00 |
| **Doll,** Movable Arms, Blue Wings, Signed Rose O'Neill, Bisque, 5 In. | 85.00 |
| **Doll,** Movable Arms, Signed Rose O'Neill, 4 1/4 In. | 97.50 |
| **Doll,** Paper Label On Back, Signed Rose O'Neill, 7 In. | 115.00 |
| **Doll,** Red Heart On Chest, Marked, Bisque, 5 In. | 125.00 |
| **Doll,** Seated On Leaf Of Rose, Bisque, Rose O'Neill, 2 1/2 In. | 125.00 |
| **Doll,** Seated, Chin In Hands, Chalk, 7 In. | 22.00 |
| **Doll,** Signed Rose O'Neill, 11 In. | 65.00 |
| **Doll,** Thinker, Bisque, Signed, 4 1/2 In. | 225.00 |
| **Doll,** Traveler, Signed O'Neill, 3 1/2 In. | 275.00 |
| **Holder,** Talcum Powder, Heart Front, 1913, Signed Rose O'Neill | 125.00 |
| **Planter,** Blue Ceramic | 28.00 |
| **Planter,** Jasperware, Pink Action Kewpies, Green, 2 X 3 1/2 In.Diam. | 175.00 |
| **Planter,** Pottery, Pink, Marked | 12.00 |
| **Plate,** Feeding, Signed O'Neill, Dated, 9 In.Diam. | 78.00 |
| **Salt & Pepper,** Japan | 25.00 |
| **Sign,** Santa, Royal Kewpie Society, 3-24-13, Cardboard, 11 1/2 In. | 19.00 |
|     **KIMBALL, see Cluthra** | |
|     **KING'S ROSE, see Soft Paste** | |
|     **KITCHEN, see also Iron; Store; Tool; Wooden** | |
|     **KITCHEN, APPLE, PEELER, see Kitchen, Peeler, Apple** | |
| **KITCHEN, Basket,** Egg, Wire | 25.00 |
| **Basket,** Potato, Wire | 90.00 |
| **Beater,** Cream & Egg, The Wonder Whip, Tinware | 15.50 |
| **Beater,** Egg & Cream, Lantz | 30.00 |
| **Board,** Bread, Beveled Edge, Octagonal, Pine, 9 In. | 9.00 |
| **Board,** Bread, Grooved Border, Maple, 11 In.Diam. | 18.00 |
| **Board,** Bread, Ivy Trim, Scalloped, Walnut, Button Feet, 12 X 14 In. | 75.00 |
| **Board,** Cookie, 4 Pattern, Birch, 4 X 5 In. | 50.00 |
| **Board,** Cutting, Kraut | 19.00 |
| **Board,** Noodle, Pennsylvania, 17 3/4 In.Diam. | 72.00 To 85.00 |
| **Board,** Noodle, Poplar Wood, 17 In.Diam. | 62.00 To 65.00 |
| **Board,** Pie, Arched Top, Hanging Hole, Breadboard Ends, 20 In. | 95.00 |
| **Boiler,** Potato, Folding Wire | 15.00 |
| **Bowl,** Cast Iron, 11 1/2 In. | 45.00 |
| **Bowl,** Chopping, Curly Maple | 75.00 |
| **Bowl,** Chopping, Handmade, Rectangular, Wooden, 20 5/8 X 9 In. | 65.00 |
| **Bowl,** Dough, North Carolina, Wooden | 65.00 |
| **Bowl,** Dough, Original Dough Paddle, Oval | 69.00 |
| **Bowl,** Dough, Walnut, Oval | 52.00 |
| **Bowl,** Pouring Spout, For Crushing Apples, Rectangular, 21 In. | 78.00 |
| **Box,** Pantry, Blue, 9 In.Diam. | 68.00 |
| **Box,** Pantry, Cover, Amish, 8 In.Diam. | 72.00 |
| **Box,** Pantry, Covered, Quaker, 8 1/2 In.Diam. | 84.00 |
| **Box,** Pantry, Lapped, Yellowish Putty Color, Oval, 8 In. | 76.00 |
| **Box,** Pantry, Old Red Paint, Oak, 11 3/4 In.Diam. | 46.00 |
| **Box,** Pantry, Red Stippled Paint, Compass Design On Cover, 4 7/8 In. | 115.00 |
| **Box,** Pantry, Stippled Old Paint, Salmon & Gray, 15 1/2 In.Diam. | 65.00 |
| **Box,** Pantry, Straight Lap, Old Red, 11 7/8 X 4 1/2 In. | 45.00 |
| **Box,** Pantry, Straight Seam, 4 1/2 X 7 1/4 In.Diam. | 25.00 |

**Box,** Pantry, V-Lap Top, Aqua Blue Paint, 7 1/4 In. .................................................... 38.00
**Box,** Pantry, V-Lap Top, Straight Bottom, 18th Century, 6 3/4 In. ...................... 68.00
**Box,** Pantry, 18th Century, Red Stain, 3 3/8 In.Diam. .......................................... 58.00
**Box,** Salt, Grain Painted .............................................................................................. 60.00
**Box,** Spice, 6 Boxes, Grater Inside Lid, Tin, 11 X 8 X 4 1/2 In. ........................... 55.00
**Breadboard,** Bread Carved On Edge, 10 In.Diam. .................................................. 30.00
**Broiler,** Footed, Square, Handle Ends In Heart ...................................................... 68.00
**Broiler,** Grease Trap, 19th Century, Cast Iron, 11 In. ............................................ 145.00
**Broom,** Oven, Peeled Splint, Turned Handle, 10 In. ............................................... 85.00
**Broom,** Splintered Birch, 48 In. .................................................................................. 95.00
**Bucket,** Bail, J.P.Schaum, Pennsylvania, Copper & Iron, 25 1/2 In. ................. 300.00
**Bucket,** Jelly, Brass ........................................................................................................ 75.00
**Bucket,** Milk, Pour Spout, Tip Handle, Copper, 3 Gallon ...................................... 125.00
  **KITCHEN, BUTTER, MOLD, see Kitchen, Mold, Butter**
**Can Opener,** Bull's Head, With Tail, Cast Iron ...................................................... 20.00
**Can Opener,** Hoppers, C.1896, Cast Iron ................................................................. 40.00
**Canister Set,** Red & Gold, Tin, 6 Piece Set .......................................................... 250.00
**Canister Set,** Winner Tobacco, Floral, Stoneware, 8 Piece ................................. 450.00
**Canister,** Brushwork In Green & Red, Asphaltum Ground, Tin, 4 1/2 In. ............ 125.00
**Canister,** Tea, Striped, Red & White, Sears ........................................................... 65.00
**Cheese Press,** Red Paint ............................................................................................. 175.00
  **KITCHEN, CHERRY, PITTER, see Kitchen, Pitter, Cherry**
**Chest,** Ice, Country Store, Pine, 58 X 29 X 19 In. .................................................. 350.00
**Chopper,** Food, Enterprise, Cast Iron ...................................................................... 7.00
**Chopper,** Food, Keen Kutter, Large ........................................................................... 10.00
**Chopper,** Food, Rocker Style, Wood Handles, Amish ............................................. 40.00
**Chopper,** Marked J.Stevens, Iron, 7 In. ..................................................................... 38.00
**Chopper,** Meat, Enterprise 1888, Cast Iron ............................................................ 27.50
**Churn,** Bentwood Oak .................................................................................................. 165.00
**Churn,** Bentwood, Wapokeneta Stenciling .............................................................. 105.00
**Churn,** Butter, Greenish-Blue Paint, Crank At Side, 15 X 17 In. .......................... 85.00
**Churn,** Butter, Handmade Nuts & Bolts, Original Blue Paint ................................. 245.00
**Churn,** Butter, Table Model, Barrel Shape, Wooden ............................................... 85.00
**Churn,** Butter, U-Shape, Cover, 3 Legs, Green Milk Paint ..................................... 225.00
**Churn,** Dazey, Glass, 2 Quart ...................................................................................... 49.50
**Churn,** Dazey, Glass, 4 Quart ...................................................................................... 39.50
**Churn,** Dazey, Glass, 6 Quart ...................................................................................... 59.50
**Cleaver,** Meat, Steer Stamp, Wm.Beatty & Sons, Chester, Penn., 6 In. ............. 9.00
  **KITCHEN, COFFEE GRINDER, see Coffee Grinder**
**Colander,** Tin ................................................................................................................. 6.00
**Container,** Bakery Flour, Sifter, Wall Hung, Tin, 24 In. ........................................ 65.00
**Cookie Peel,** Square Paddle, Hickory, Tin, 18th C., 11 1/2 lb. ............................ 75.00
**Corer,** Apple, Tin ................................................................................................ 7.00 To 8.00
**Corkscrew,** Monogram Whiskey ............................................................................... 6.00
**Corkscrew,** The Davis Corkscrew, Patented 1891, Folding ................................. 12.50
**Crimper,** Pie, Brass ....................................................................................................... 18.00
**Crimper,** Pie, Forged Iron, 1812 Coin Wheel, Wood Handle ............................... 95.00
**Crimper,** Pie, Wood, Bone Wheel, 5 In. ................................................................... 28.00
**Crimper,** Pie, Wrought Iron, Wooden Handle ......................................................... 15.00
**Crock,** Butter, Bail Handle, Word Butter, Blue & Gray ......................................... 125.00
**Cutter,** Biscuit, Marked Rumford, Tin, 3 3/4 X 2 In.Diam. ................................... 13.00
**Cutter,** Cabbage, Arched Top, Walnut, 8 X 22 In. ................................................ 42.00
**Cutter,** Cabbage, Cherry, 20 X 7 1/4 In. ................................................................. 39.00
**Cutter,** Cabbage, Lacy Cast Iron Side ..................................................................... 35.00
**Cutter,** Cabbage, Wooden Turning Handle & Press Bar, Patent 1900 ................ 50.00
**Cutter,** Cookie, Bird, Tin ............................................................................................. 12.00
**Cutter,** Cookie, Bobtailed Horse, C.1800, 4 1/2 X 7 In. ...................................... 60.00
**Cutter,** Cookie, Chick Shape, Handle, Tin ..................................................... 10.00 To 15.00
**Cutter,** Cookie, Christmas Tree, Tin, 4 2 1/4 In. .................................................... 12.00
**Cutter,** Cookie, Duck, Tin ........................................................................................... 10.00
**Cutter,** Cookie, Eagle, Tin, 4 1/4 X 3 1/4 In. ......................................................... 29.00
**Cutter,** Cookie, Eagle, Wings Spread, 6 X 3 1/2 In. ............................................. 35.00
**Cutter,** Cookie, Eagle, 5 3/4 X 2 1/2 X 3 1/2 In. ................................................... 35.00

**Cutter,** Cookie, Fish, Tin, 5 1/4 X 2 In. ..................................................... 20.00
**Cutter,** Cookie, Fish, Tin, 6 X 2 1/4 In. ......................................................... 20.00
**Cutter,** Cookie, Fish, Whale, Tin, Handled, 4 X 1 1/2 In. ........................... 12.00
**Cutter,** Cookie, Flower, Tulip, Crimped Edges, Tin ...................................... 20.00
**Cutter,** Cookie, Flying Bird, Handle, Rectangular, 3 X 4 In. ....................... 10.00
**Cutter,** Cookie, Goat, 7 X 5 1/2 In. ............................................................. 35.00
**Cutter,** Cookie, Goose, Tin ........................................................................... 30.00
**Cutter,** Cookie, Heart, Tin ............................................................................ 15.00
**Cutter,** Cookie, Horse, Handled, Tin, 4 X 3 In. .......................................... 15.00
**Cutter,** Cookie, Horse, Tin, Handmade ...................................................... 85.00
**Cutter,** Cookie, Horse, 10 X 6 In. ............................................................... 25.00
**Cutter,** Cookie, Horse, 8 X 1/2 In. ............................................................. 35.00
**Cutter,** Cookie, Lamb, Tin ............................................................................ 10.00
**Cutter,** Cookie, Lion, 6-Sided, Handle, Tin ................................................. 10.00
**Cutter,** Cookie, Rocking Horse, Handled, Tin, 4 X 3 In. ............................ 15.00
**Cutter,** Cookie, Rocking Horse, Tin ............................................................ 37.50
**Cutter,** Cookie, Sitting Bear, Tin ................................................................. 12.50
**Cutter,** Cookie, Smoking Pipe, Arched Stem, 5 In. .................................... 40.00
**Cutter,** Cookie, Sunbonnet Baby ................................................................ 25.00
**Cutter,** Cookie, Whale, Tin, Handled, 4 X 1 1/2 In. ................................... 12.00
**Cutter,** Doughnut, Rumford, Long Handle .................................................. 8.00
**Cutter,** Noodle, Acme Mincer ...................................................................... 5.00
**Cutter,** Pastry, Calumet, Aluminum ............................................................ 2.00
**Cutter,** Slaw, 1904, Sliding Box, Curly Maple, 25 X 9 In. ......................... 60.00
**Dish,** Butter, Covered, Blue Trim, Word Butter In Blue, Enamel ............... 45.00
**Drainer,** Cheese, Maple, 8 1/2 X 29 In. ..................................................... 67.00
**Dutch Oven,** Bail Handle, Griswold, Cast Iron, 1920, 10 1/4 In. .............. 35.00
**Egg Poacher,** Single, Wire Handle, Tinware ............................................... 15.50
**Eggbeater,** Double Looped, Wheel, Cast Iron ........................................... 23.00
**Eggbeater,** Dover, Dated 1891, Cast Iron ................................................. 12.00
**Eggbeater,** Turbine, Tin ............................................................................... 15.00
**Flue Cover,** Pictorial Design ....................................................................... 20.00
**Fork,** 2-Tine, Doughnut Top, Wrought-Iron, 18th Century ......................... 38.00
**Fork,** 2-Tine, Elongated Diamond Handle, 18th Century, 19 1/2 In. .......... 32.00
**Fork,** 3-Tine, Hook On Back, 42 In. ............................................................ 45.00
**Fork,** 3-Tine, Twisted Wire, 12 In. .............................................................. 7.50
**Freezer,** Ice Cream, Acme Can Co., Philadelphia, July 10, 1912, Tin ...... 30.00
**Freezer,** Ice Cream, White Mountain, Cedar Tub, 2 Quart ....................... 18.50
**Fryer,** Egg, 7 Eye, Griswold, Iron ............................................................... 10.00
**Frying Pan,** Griswold, Iron, 11 3/8 In. ........................................................ 20.00
**Funnel,** White Porcelain, 7 1/2 In.Diam. ..................................................... 60.00
**Grater,** Clamp-On, Schroeter, Cast Iron ..................................................... 27.50
**Grater,** Hand-Pierced, Top Grip, Forged Rose Head Nails, Tin, 12 In. ..... 155.00
**Grater,** Nutmeg, Patent June 7, 1870, Cast Iron ....................................... 125.00
**Grater,** Nutmeg, Patent 1891, Edgar Mfg., Tin & Wood ............................ 42.00
**Grater,** Nutmeg, Stand & Tray, Italy .......................................................... 10.00
**Grater,** Rind, Patent 1901, Tin ................................................................... 12.00
**Grater,** Sweet Corn, Brass Screws, Cherry, 10 In. .................................... 22.50
**Griddle,** Hanging Handle, Pre-1760 Mark, Case Iron, 9 In.Diam. ............. 35.00
**Grinder,** Chain Driven, Cast Iron, Table Mount ......................................... 14.00
**Grinder,** Coffee, Pewter Hopper, Hand-Dovetailed Box ........................... 120.00
**Grinder,** Food, Keen Kutter, Patent 1906 .................................................. 10.00
**Grinder,** Meat, Winchester, Marked ........................................................... 55.00
**Grinder,** Sausage, Cylinder Type, Cast Iron ............................................. 35.00
**Grinder,** Sausage, Keen Kutter ................................................................. 4.00
**Grindstone** ................................................................................................. 15.00
**Holder,** Skewer, Twisted Shank, 18th Century, 2 Skewers, 3 1/2 In. ........ 95.00
**Huller,** Strawberry, Dated 1894, Brass ...................................................... 10.00
**Icebox,** Carved, Beveled Mirror, Oak ....................................................... 1300.00
**Icebox,** Golden Oak, 4 X 4 X 2 Ft. ............................................................. 550.00
**Icebox,** Lift Top, Legs, Pine, 3 Ft. Wide ..................................................... 185.00
**Icebox,** Oak, 30 X 60 In. ............................................................................. 250.00
**Icebox,** 3 Door, Oak ................................................................................... 535.00

Iron, Charcoal, Cast Iron ............................................................................................................. 18.00
Iron, Miniature, Star Laundry, Fall River ................................................................................. 12.00
Iron, Waffle, Cast Iron ................................................................................................................. 12.00
Iron, Waffle, Keen Kutter ............................................................................................................ 55.00
Iron, Waffle, Marked Chatham, Connecticut, 19th Century, Iron, 27 In. ............................... 35.00
Iron, Waffle, Stand, Hearts & Diamond, Abbott & Lawrence, 8 1/2 In. ................................. 28.00
Kettle, Apple Butter, Copper ........................................................................ 145.00 To 175.00
Kettle, Candy, Copper, Brass Footed ........................................................................................ 85.00
Kettle, Cover, Cast Iron, Carlisle ............................................................................................... 10.00
Kettle, Griswold, Iron .................................................................................................................. 22.00
Kettle, Jelly, C.1890, Brass ........................................................................................................ 100.00
Kettle, Swinging, Burner Stand, Manning Bowman, Connecticut, Copper ............................. 85.00
Kettle, Wrought Iron Handle, Hangs On Crane, 19th Century, 10 In. ..................................... 68.00
Kitchen, Dutch Oven, Lid Rim Holds Coals, Iron, 13 In. ......................................... 325.00 To 375.00
Ladle & Strainer, Brass, Hook, Hand-Wrought, 5 In.Bowl ..................................................... 150.00
Lifter, Kettle, Hinged Bail, Hand-Forged Iron, 18th Century .................................................. 50.00
Lifter, Pie, Wooden Handle, 2 Metal Prongs, 14 1/2 In. .......................................................... 19.00
Lifter, Pie, 7 Wire Circles Inside, Wooden Handle, Elliptical, Wire ........................................ 30.00
Lifter, Pot, Hook Ends, Swivel Hanging Hook ......................................................................... 32.00
**KITCHEN, MATCH SAFE, see Match Safe**
Measures, Graduated Sizes, Tin, 2 In. To 3 5/8 In. .................................................................. 65.00
**KITCHEN, MOLD, see also Pewter, Mold; Tin, Mold**
Mold, Brown Bread, Covered, Tin .............................................................................................. 25.00
Mold, Butter, Acorn, Chip-Carved Edge, Pennsylvania Dutch, 1 Pound ............................... 75.00
Mold, Butter, Acorn, Double, Round .......................................................................................... 42.00
Mold, Butter, Beaver, Plunger, 2 1/2 X 3 In.Diam. .................................................................. 22.00
Mold, Butter, Carved Flowers & Leaves, Plunger, Round ....................................................... 35.00
Mold, Butter, Carved Hops, Wooden, 4 1/2 In.Diam. .............................................................. 58.00
Mold, Butter, Cherry Design ....................................................................................................... 18.00
Mold, Butter, Cow, Glass, Wooden Handle ............................................................................... 40.00
Mold, Butter, Daisy & Fern, Maple, Round ............................................................................... 39.50
Mold, Butter, Double B, Rectangular ......................................................................................... 45.00
Mold, Butter, Double Pineapple, Rectangular ........................................................................... 45.00
Mold, Butter, Double Sheaf Of Wheat, Dated 1866, Brass Plunger ........................................ 95.00
Mold, Butter, Double 5-Point Star .............................................................................................. 25.00
Mold, Butter, Fleur-De-Lis, Glass & Wood ............................................................................... 36.00
Mold, Butter, Flower Leaf, Double Print, Brass Hinges & Rod ............................................... 45.00
Mold, Butter, Geometric Design, Miniature ............................................................................... 85.00
Mold, Butter, Hinged Sides, Rectangular, 2 Piece ................................................................... 65.00
Mold, Butter, Maple Leaf ........................................................................................ 25.00 To 36.00
Mold, Butter, Oak With Leaf, Dated 1866, Plunger, Round ..................................................... 95.00
Mold, Butter, Pine Twig ............................................................................................................... 29.00
Mold, Butter, Pineapple ........................................................................................... 35.00 To 47.50
Mold, Butter, Pineapple, Dated 1866, Plunger ......................................................................... 95.00
Mold, Butter, Pineapple, Ring Border, 3 In. .............................................................................. 17.00
Mold, Butter, Rose & Leaf Design, Plunger Type, Round ....................................................... 35.00
Mold, Butter, Rosette Design, 4 In.Square ................................................................................ 80.00
Mold, Butter, Sheaf Of Wheat, Dated 1866, Plunger ............................................................... 95.00
Mold, Butter, Strawberry & Leaves, Rectangular, 7 X 4 In. ................................................... 60.00
Mold, Butter, Sunburst ................................................................................................................ 90.00
Mold, Butter, Swan, Dated 1866, Plunger, Round .................................................................... 125.00
Mold, Butter, Swan, Pound ......................................................................................................... 50.00
Mold, Butter, Thistle, Plunger, Walnut, Pewter, 3 Piece .......................................................... 85.00
Mold, Butter, Wheat & Berries, Square Box Type .................................................................... 28.00
Mold, Butter, Wheat Design ........................................................................................................ 45.00
Mold, Butter, 4 Wheat Sheaves, Brass Handle, Dated 1866, Square ..................................... 135.00
Mold, Butter, 5-Point Star, Round .............................................................................................. 37.00
Mold, Butter, 8-Point Star ........................................................................................................... 27.50
Mold, Cake, Lamb, Aluminum, With Screws, 2 Piece .............................................................. 14.00
Mold, Cake, Lamb, Baker's Coconut ......................................................................................... 25.00
Mold, Cake, Rabbit, Full-Bodied, Griswold, Cast Iron, 11 In, 2 Piece .................................... 39.00
**KITCHEN, MOLD, CANDLE, see also Tin, Mold, Candle**
Mold, Candle, Crimped Edge, Handled, 10 1/4 In. ................................................................... 195.00

| | |
|---|---|
| **Mold,** Candle, 16 Tube, Stands Either End, Handle, Square | 125.00 |
| **Mold,** Candle, 18 Hole, 10 Tube, Double Handle, 10 In. | 120.00 |
| **Mold,** Candle, 24 Tube, 3 X 8 In. | 150.00 |
| **Mold,** Candle, 48 Tube, Stand, 11 3/4 X 11 1/2 X 7 3/4 In. | 290.00 |
| **Mold,** Candy, Butterflies, White Metal, 12 Sections, 4 1/2 X 8 In. | 20.00 |
| **Mold,** Candy, Clover, White Metal, 48 Sections, 10 X 13 In. | 20.00 |
| **Mold,** Candy, Hand, 3 In Mold, Metal, 3 X 4 1/2 X 1 In. | 19.00 |
| **Mold,** Candy, Horse, Double | 35.00 |
| **Mold,** Candy, Leaves, Pressed Tin, 21 Sections, 10 X 13 In. | 20.00 |
| **Mold,** Candy, Leaves, White Metal, 7 Sections, 4 X 8 In. | 20.00 |
| **Mold,** Candy, Seashells, White Metal, 15 Sections, 4 X 7 In. | 20.00 |
| **Mold,** Candy, Shamrocks, White Metal, 12 Sections, 4 X 6 In. | 20.00 |
| **Mold,** Candy, Spearmint Leaves, White Metal, 5 Sections, 4 X 6 In. | 20.00 |
| **Mold,** Cheese, Cottage, 2 Handles, 5 X 5 In. | 60.00 |
| **Mold,** Cheese, Heart, Pierced, Tin, Handle, 3 Legs, 6 X 7 1/2 In. | 35.00 |
| **Mold,** Cheese, Pierced, Round, 5 X 5 In. | 60.00 |
| **Mold,** Chocolate, Chicken Little, 5 1/4 X 3 3/4 In. | 35.00 |
| **Mold,** Chocolate, Chicken On Basket, Tin | 25.00 |
| **Mold,** Chocolate, Hen On Basket, Double, 4 X 9 In. | 20.00 |
| **Mold,** Chocolate, Holly Bell, 3 1/4 In. | 35.00 |
| **Mold,** Chocolate, Huckleberry Hound, 2 Rows, 10 1/2 X 9 X 2 In. | 22.50 |
| **Mold,** Chocolate, Lamb | 25.00 |
| **Mold,** Chocolate, Little Girl With Cat | 40.00 |
| **Mold,** Chocolate, Rabbit Cowboy On Back Of Larger Rabbit, 8 X 6 In. | 35.00 |
| **Mold,** Chocolate, Rabbit In Shoe, Double, 8 1/4 X 7 X 1 1/2 In. | 18.00 |
| **Mold,** Chocolate, Rabbit, Basket On Back, Double, 6 3/4 X 6 In. | 17.00 |
| **Mold,** Chocolate, Rabbit, Basket On Back, Double, 9 1/2 X 8 In. | 19.00 |
| **Mold,** Chocolate, Rabbit, Laughing, Tin, 2 X 3 1/2 In. | 10.00 |
| **Mold,** Chocolate, Rabbit, Lop-Eared, Slip-On Clamp | 25.00 |
| **Mold,** Chocolate, Rabbit, Sitting, 3 3/4 In. | 35.00 |
| **Mold,** Chocolate, Rabbit, Standing Up | 25.00 |
| **Mold,** Chocolate, Rabbit, 2 Rows, 3 Each Row, 5 X 2 X 2 In. | 20.00 |
| **Mold,** Chocolate, Rooster, 2 Rows, 4 In Row, 7 1/2 X 8 1/2 X 1 1/4 In. | 20.00 |
| **Mold,** Chocolate, Santa & Sleigh | 25.00 |
| **Mold,** Chocolate, Santa, German | 55.00 |
| **Mold,** Chocolate, St.Nick, Long Coat, Switch & Bag In Hand, 7 1/2 In. | 65.00 |
| **Mold,** Chocolate, Standing Turkey, Hinged & Clamped | 35.00 |
| **Mold,** Chocolate, Two Chickens On Nest | 25.00 |
| **Mold,** Chocolate, Two Hearts | 25.00 |
| **Mold,** Chocolate, 3 Crouching Rabbits, 10 X 6 1/2 In. | 30.00 |
| **Mold,** Chocolate, 4 Upright Rabbits, 9 X 5 In. | 30.00 |
| **Mold,** Cookie, Happy New Year In Script, 1800s, Cast Iron, 5 3/4 In. | 95.00 |
| **Mold,** Cookie, Santa Claus With Pack, Standing, Tin, 5 1/4 In. | 95.00 |
| **Mold,** Fish, Shows Eyes, Scales, Tail, C.1840, Cast Iron, 5 1/2 X 3 In. | 65.00 |
| **Mold,** Fish, Tin, Large | 22.00 |
| **Mold,** Food, Fluted Sides, Pineapple, Tin Over Copper | 48.00 |
| **Mold,** Food, Fluted Sides, Rose, Tin Over Copper | 48.00 |
| **Mold,** Food, Fluted Sides, Wheat, Tin Over Copper | 48.00 |
| **Mold,** Food, Melon Ribbed, Wire Loop Handle, Tin, 7 X 5 1/4 In. | 12.50 |
| **Mold,** Gelatin, Sheaf Of Wheat, Tin & Copper, 4 3/4 X 6 5/8 In. | 45.00 |
| **KITCHEN, MOLD, ICE CREAM, see Pewter, Mold, Ice Cream** | |
| **Mold,** Jell-O, Green Glass | 4.00 |
| **Mold,** Jell-O, Heart, Aluminum | 5.00 |
| **Mold,** Maple Sugar, Beaver, Wide Tail, 11 X 5 1/2 X 1 1/4 In. | 11.75 |
| **Mold,** Maple Sugar, Cookie Boy, 6 X 1 1/8 X 4 1/2 In. | 7.00 |
| **Mold,** Maple Sugar, Cookie Girl, 6 X 4 3/4 X 1 1/8 In. | 8.00 |
| **Mold,** Maple Sugar, Cow, 6 1/4 X 4 1/2 X 1 1/8 In. | 8.00 |
| **Mold,** Maple Sugar, Double Heart, 4 1/2 X 15 In. | 55.00 |
| **Mold,** Maple Sugar, Duck, 7 X 5 X 1 1/8 In. | 7.50 |
| **Mold,** Maple Sugar, Elephant With Long Trunk, 7 X 5 X 1 1/4 In. | 8.00 |
| **Mold,** Maple Sugar, Fish, 10 X 4 X 1 1/8 In. | 8.00 |
| **Mold,** Maple Sugar, Heart Shape, Hand-Carved, Pine, 3 X 5 X 7 1/2 In. | 95.00 |
| **Mold,** Maple Sugar, Horse, 5 3/4 X 4 3/4 X 1 1/8 In. | 8.00 |

| | |
|---|---:|
| **Mold,** Maple Sugar, Lion, 7 X 5 X 1 1/4 In. | 8.00 |
| **Mold,** Maple Sugar, Rooster With Flowing Tail, 6 3/4 X 4 1/2 In. | 8.00 |
| **Mold,** Maple Sugar, Sheep, 6 X 5 X 1 1/8 In. | 7.50 |
| **Mold,** Maple Sugar, Turkey, Tail Feathers Ruffled, 6 X 5 X 1 1/8 In. | 8.00 |
| **Mold,** Meat, Wooden, Funnel Shaped, Pine, 4 3/4 In. | 50.00 |
| **Mold,** Plum Pudding, Tin | 24.00 |
| **Mold,** Pudding, Cabbage Rose, Tin | 40.00 |
| **Mold,** Pudding, Fluted, Tin | 8.00 |
| **Mold,** Pudding, Santa Claus, Griswold, Cast Iron, 12 In. | 75.00 |
| **Mold,** Pudding, Wheat Center, Tin | 22.00 |
| **Mold,** Pudding, 3 Fruit Patterns, Oval, Copper, Tin, 3 X 4 In. | 65.00 |
| **Mold,** Rice Cake, Oriental | 60.00 |
| **Mold,** Turtle, Copper Over Tin | 95.00 |
| **Oven,** Biscuit, Used In Fireplace, Tin | 125.00 |
| **Paddle,** Butter Worker, Short Handle, 12 1/4 In. | 27.00 |
| **Paddle,** Butter, Chip Carved On Knob End, Wooden, 19 1/4 In. | 24.00 |
| **Paddle,** Butter, Flat, Corrugated Surface, Wooden, 3 In.Wide | 3.50 |
| **Paddle,** Butter, Wooden, 1868 | 25.00 |
| **Pan,** Bread, Baker's, 3 Compartment, Tin | 18.00 |
| **Pan,** Bread, Baker's, 4 Compartment | 27.50 |
| **Pan,** Cake, Angel Food, Swan's Down, Tin | 10.00 |
| **Pan,** Cake, Heart Shape, Rolled Tin | 25.00 |
| **Pan,** Corn Stick, Cast Iron, 6 X 13 In. | 18.00 |
| **Pan,** Corn Stick, 7 Ear, Iron | 8.00 |
| **Pan,** Crane, Pouring Spout, Swivel Ring, Iron, 13 In. | 165.00 |
| **Pan,** Dough Rising, Footed, Tin | 25.00 |
| **Pan,** Footed, Long Handled, Cast Iron, 26 1/4 In. | 155.00 |
| **Pan,** Frying, Chamfered Handle, 38 In. | 125.00 |
| **Pan,** Frying, Footed, Handled, Wrought Iron, 13 1/4 X 8 In. | 165.00 |
| **Pan,** Frying, Footed, Wrought Iron, 36 1/2 In. | 165.00 |
| **Pan,** Frying, Long Handle, Wrought Iron, 42 In. | 155.00 |
| **Pan,** Hammered, Dovetailed, 19th Century, Copper, Iron Handle, 10 In. | 150.00 |
| **Pan,** Muffin, Rosettes, 12 Sections, Iron, 9 X 12 In. | 49.00 |
| **Pan,** Muffin, 11 Hole, Cast Iron | 17.50 |
| **Pan,** Muffin, 6 Cup, Fluted & Bulbous Ribbed, Cast Iron | 12.00 |
| **Pasta Maker,** Rippled Carved Center, Maple, 2-Part, Hinged | 65.00 |
| **Pastry Jigger & Pie Crimper,** Double Ended, Wooden, Smooth Patina | 60.00 |
| **Pastry Wheel,** Ball End, 18th Century, Hand-Forged Iron, 5 1/2 In. | 50.00 |
| **Pastry Wheel,** Brass, Wooden Handle | 18.00 |
| **Peeler,** Apple, Belt Driven, 2 Gear, Chip Carved Board, Wooden | 195.00 |
| **Peeler,** Apple, Clamp, Cast Iron, 10 X 6 In. | 34.00 |
| **Peeler,** Apple, Hudson, Cast Iron | 30.00 To 55.00 |
| **Peeler,** Apple, Keen Kutter, Cast Iron | 48.00 |
| **Peeler,** Apple, Lockey & Howland, Patent 1856, Cast Iron | 35.00 To 42.00 |
| **Peeler,** Apple, Reading Hardware, Patent 1868, Cast Iron | 40.00 |
| **Peeler,** Apple, Signed Maxam, Dated 1855, Cast Iron | 95.00 |
| **Peeler,** Apple, White Mountain, Cast Iron | 27.00 |
| **Peeler,** Apple, Wooden, Belt Driven, 2 Gear, Mounted On Board | 195.00 |
| **Peeler,** Ram's Horn Top, Wrought Iron, 48 In. | 90.00 |
| **Pie Juicer,** Black Mammy | 17.00 |
| **Pie Peel,** Ring Hook, Forged Iron, 20 In. | 32.00 |
| **Pitter,** Cherry, Clamps To Table, Enterprise, 1877 | 26.50 |
| **Pitter,** Cherry, Enterprise, Cast Iron | 12.50 |
| **Pitter,** Cherry, Enterprise, Double | 25.00 |
| **Pitter,** Cherry, 2 Prong, Table Clamp, Goodell Co., Antrim, N.H. | 45.00 |
| **Plate,** Rounded Over Edge, 18th Century, Wooden, 10 7/8 In. | 125.00 |
| **Pot,** Cooking, Footed, 18th Century, Wrought Iron Handle, 7 1/2 In. | 45.00 |
| **Pot,** Side Ears, Footed, Cover, Wrought Iron Handle, 18th Century | 110.00 |
| **Pot,** Stew, 3-Legged, English, 18th Century, Cast Iron, 7 X 6 7/8 In. | 150.00 |
| **Potato Masher,** Wooden, 9 1/2 In. | 10.00 |
| **Potato Masher,** Wooden, 16 1/2 In. | 12.00 |
| **Press,** Lard | 27.00 |
| **Rack,** Pie, Twisted Wire, Holds 4 Pies | 25.00 |

| | |
|---|---|
| **Reamer,** Clown, 7 In., 2 Piece | 10.00 |
| **Reamer,** Lemon, Cast Iron, Wooden Cup, Marked Pearl | 35.00 |
| **Reamer,** Lemon, Wooden | 22.50 To 30.00 |
| **Reamer,** Lemon, Wooden Cup Marked Pearl, Cast Iron | 35.00 |
| **Reamer,** Milk Glass, Sunkist | 5.00 |
| **Reamer,** Sunkist, Blue Opaline | 35.00 |
| **Reamer,** Sunkist, Green | 12.00 |
| **Reamer,** Sunkist, Milk Glass | 8.00 |
| **Reamer,** Sunkist, Opalescent | 26.00 |
| **Ricer,** Potato, Dated 1881 | 22.50 |
| **Roaster,** Bird, For Fireplace, Tin | 175.00 |
| **Roller,** Butter, Wooden, 3 Design Bands, Birch Yoke | 150.00 |
| **Rolling Pin,** Blown Glass, Forget-Me-Nots, Cobalt Blue, 15 In. | 75.00 |
| **Rolling Pin,** Blown Glass, Robin's Egg Blue, 29 In.Long | 110.00 |
| **Rolling Pin,** China, White With Flowers | 40.00 |
| **Rolling Pin,** Cigar Shape, Turned Knobs, 16 In. | 34.00 |
| **Rolling Pin,** Cookie, Grooved, 10 In.Long | 29.00 |
| **Rolling Pin,** Flattened Knob Handles, Cigar Shape, 18th Century, Ash | 32.00 |
| **Rolling Pin,** Glass, Cork Ends | 15.00 |
| **Rolling Pin,** Grooved Handle, Maple | 7.00 |
| **Rolling Pin,** Maple, 1 Piece | 9.00 |
| **Rolling Pin,** Milk Glass, Wooden Handles | 30.00 |
| **Rolling Pin,** Noodle, Grooved, 17 In.Long | 30.00 |
| **Rolling Pin,** Noodle, Wooden | 32.50 |
| **Rolling Pin,** Oak | 10.00 |
| **Rolling Pin,** Shaker, 3 1/2 In.Long | 165.00 |
| **Rolling Pin,** Springerle, Simple Carved Pattern, 4 3/4 In. | 65.00 |
| **Rolling Pin,** Springerle, Wooden | 26.00 |
| **Rolling Pin,** Springerle, 20 Patterns | 145.00 |
| **Rolling Pin,** Springerle, 5 In. | 65.00 |
| **Rolling Pin,** Tiger Stripe Maple, One Piece, C.1880, 20 In. | 95.00 |
| **Rundlet,** Maple With Pine Ends, 3 1/2 In. | 85.00 |
| **Sadiron,** Everready, Coal Burning, Patent 1917 | 30.00 |
| **Sadiron,** Hammer Look, Loop Handle, 7 In. | 14.00 |
| **Sadiron,** Marked B. & Co., No.7, 6 In. | 10.00 |
| **Scoop,** Ice Cream, Gilchrist 31, Brass | 48.00 |
| **Scoop,** Ice Cream, Tin, Cone-Shaped, Wallace Co. | 20.00 |
| **Scoop,** Spice, Wooden, 5 1/2 In.Handle | 60.00 |
| **Scoop,** Tin, Quart Measure | 12.00 |
| **Scrubber & Peeler,** Vegetable, Hamlinite, 1920, Fluted Tin, Handle | 20.00 |
| **Scrubber,** Metal Link, Handle | 17.00 |
| **Seeder,** Raisin, Table Clamp, Crown, Landers, Frary & Clark | 40.00 |
| **Seeder,** Raisin, The Everett, Patent 1888, Wood & Wire | 28.00 To 30.00 |
| **Separator,** Cream, Hand Crank, Floor Model, 4 Ft. Tall | 125.00 |
| **Separator,** Cream, Marvel | 35.00 |
| **Separator,** Egg, Tin | 2.75 |
| **Sheller,** Corn, Patent 1859, 39 In. | 200.00 |
| **Sheller,** Corn, Tabletop, Fulton, Cast Iron | 75.00 |
| **Sieve,** Flour, Oak, 13 1/2 In. | 18.00 |
| **Sifter,** Flour, Bromwell, Tin | 14.00 |
| **Sifter,** Flour, Wooden, Wire Mesh, 12 In. | 135.00 |
| **Sifter,** Green, Wood Handle, Lidded, Duplex | 35.00 |
| **Skimmer,** Arched Handle, Mustard Paint, 18th Century, Ash, 6 1/8 In. | 95.00 |
| **Skimmer,** Brass | 45.00 |
| **Skimmer,** Classic Form, Wooden, 5 1/2 In. | 55.00 |
| **Skimmer,** Riveted On Bowl, Wrought Iron, 24 In. | 65.00 |
| **Skimmer,** Shell, Wooden, Nut Brown, 5 1/2 In. | 65.00 |
| **Slicer,** Bread, Wood & Iron | 39.50 |
| **Slicer,** Green Bean, Clamps, Tin Panels, French, Wooden, 9 1/2 In. | 145.00 |
| **Slicer,** Vegetable, Sliding Block, Maple, 20 In. | 21.50 |
| **Spice Box,** Lid, 6 Containers & Shaker, Round, Tin | 75.00 |
| **Spice Box,** 8 Inner Boxes, C.1870 | 125.00 |
| **Spice Rack,** 8 Drawer | 75.00 |

### KITCHEN, SPINNING WHEEL, see Tool, Spinning Wheel

| | |
|---|---|
| **Spit,** Bird, Hood Style, 6 Hooks, Tin | 135.00 |
| **Squeezer,** Lemon, Wooden | 35.00 To 38.50 |
| **Stamp,** Butter, Acorn With 2 Oak Leaves, 3 1/2 In. | 85.00 |
| **Stamp,** Butter, Cow, Hand-Carved, 4 In. | 135.00 |
| **Stamp,** Butter, Flower Pattern, Hand-Cut, 5 In.Diam. | 75.00 |
| **Stamp,** Butter, Leaves, Four Circles, Wooden, 3 3/4 In. | 37.00 |
| **Stamp,** Butter, Lollipop, Floral Design, 3 X 6 In. | 170.00 |
| **Stamp,** Butter, Lollipop, Shaped Handle, Maine | 175.00 |
| **Stamp,** Butter, Pineapple, Hand-Hewn Pine Handle, 1 X 1 1/2 In. | 95.00 |
| **Stamp,** Butter, Pineapple, 3 1/2 In. | 55.00 |
| **Stamp,** Butter, Rose & Thistle | 125.00 |
| **Stamp,** Butter, Sheaf Of Wheat, Circles, Geometric, Wooden, 4 In. | 48.00 |
| **Stamp,** Butter, Sheaf Of Wheat, 3 3/4 In. | 59.00 |
| **Stamp,** Butter, Stylized Leaf Design, Words Try Me, 7 1/4 In. | 350.00 |
| **Stamp,** Butter, Sunflower, Leaves, 3 Circles, Wooden, 3 3/4 In. | 49.00 |
| **Stamp,** Butter, Tulip, Hand-Carved, 3 In.Diam. | 85.00 |
| **Stamp,** Butter, Wild Flower & Pointed Branches, 3 3/4 In. | 60.00 |

### KITCHEN, STOVE, see Stove

| | |
|---|---|
| **Strainer,** Brass Bowl, Iron Handle | 68.00 |
| **Strainer,** Tea, Puffed Handle, Brass | 23.00 |
| **Stuffer,** Sausage, Maple Plunger, Tin | 85.00 |
| **Stuffer,** Sausage, Tin & Wood | 17.50 |
| **Teakettle,** Dated 1867, Cast Iron | 62.50 |
| **Teakettle,** Dovetailed Seams, C.1840, Signed D.Stoehr | 195.00 |
| **Teakettle,** Footed, Sweep Tilter, Wrought Iron Bail, Cast Iron | 320.00 |
| **Teakettle,** Gooseneck, Footed, Wrought-Iron Handle | 125.00 To 145.00 |
| **Teakettle,** Gooseneck, Marked S.C., 18th Century, Cast Iron | 185.00 |
| **Teakettle,** Porcelain Knob, Copper | 45.00 |
| **Teakettle,** Tilting, Footed, Wrought Iron Handle, Iron | 250.00 |
| **Timer,** Egg, Blown Glass | 8.00 |
| **Timer,** Egg, Humpty Dumpty, Colored, Cast Iron | 15.00 |
| **Toaster,** Double Shaped Handle With File Design, 7 1/2 In. | 240.00 |
| **Toaster,** Fancy Universal, Electric, 1913-1920 | 18.00 |
| **Toaster,** Single, 18th Century, Wrought Iron, 12 X 8 In.Wide | 235.00 |
| **Tongs,** Ice, Chain Handled | 10.00 |
| **Tray,** Apple, Blue Asphaltum Ground, Allover Pattern, 11 1/2 In. | 68.00 |
| **Tray,** Coffin, Original Red & Green Design, Tin, 9 X 6 In. | 95.00 |
| **Tray,** Utensil, Enameled, 4 Piece Set | 125.00 |
| **Washboard,** Wood Frame, Tin Soap Saver, Brass Scrubber Insert | 45.00 |
| **KNIFE, A.W.Wadsworth,** Knife, Fork, & Spoon Combination, Horn Handle | 55.00 |
| **Beekeeper's,** Cuts Wax Foundation, C.1910, 14 In. | 7.50 |
| **Bowie,** Ka-Bar, Pearl Handle, Scabbard, Union Cutlery, 7 3/8 In. | 95.00 |
| **Bowie,** Prostitute's, J.Allen & Son, Pearl Handle, 6 3/4 In. | 110.00 |
| **Case Bros.,** Little Valley, N.Y., 2 Blades, Stag Handle, 3 1/2 In. | 45.00 |
| **Case,** Muskrat Design, Brown Bone | 125.00 |
| **Challenge Cut Co.,** Bridgeport, Conn., Bone Stock | 60.00 |
| **Champion,** Tobacco Plug, Cutter | 37.50 |
| **Clasp,** Bone Handled, Single Blade, Loop, Sheffield, England, 6 In. | 18.00 |
| **Corn,** IXL, C.1880, Ivory Handle | 35.00 |
| **Golden Rule Cutlery Co.,** Partial Nude On Handle, 4 1/4 In. | 45.00 |
| **Hook,** IXL Washington Works, Both Edges Honed, 12 In. | 45.00 |
| **Hunting,** Bleeder Blade, Leather Handle | 35.00 |
| **Hunting,** Remington, Rh-50 | 30.00 |
| **Hunting,** Scabbard, Marked, Ka-Bar | 40.00 |
| **Hunting,** Schmidt, Ziegler Solingen, Stag Handle, 1920, 13 1/2 In. | 35.00 |
| **Hunting,** Union Cutlery Co., Stag Handle, Brass Bound | 45.00 |
| **J.S.Cantello,** Draw, Folding, 15 In. | 23.00 |
| **Jack,** Coin Silver, 1 Blade, Toothpick, Floral Embossed | 35.00 |
| **Jack,** Hibbard Spencer Bartlett Co., Bone Handle | 45.00 |
| **Jack,** J.Rodgers & Sons, Sheffield, C.1850, 6 1/8 In. | 190.00 |
| **Jack,** Lady's Leg & High-Heeled Steel Shoe, 2 Blades, 3 1/4 In. | 24.00 |

Jack, N.Y.Knife Co., 4 1/4 In. ..................................................................... 45.00
Jack, Old Crow Whiskey ............................................................................. 30.00
Jack, Remington, No.R575 ......................................................................... 35.00
Jack, Valley Forge, 2 Blade, Celluloid Handle ........................................ 15.00
Ka-Bar, Stag Doghead ............................................................................... 185.00
Leather, Wooden Handle, Brass Ferule, Wooden .................................. 9.50
Letter Opener, Remington, Brass ............................................................ 40.00
Miller Bros., Conn., 2 Blade, Mother-Of-Pearl Handle, 3 1/2 In. ......... 65.00
Paring, Hoof, Marked T.U.Pope, September, 1899 ................................ 6.00
Pen, Blade Hallmarked & Dated 1868 ..................................................... 25.00
Pennsylvania Knife Co., Peep Picture, Inset Of Fannie Davenport ....... 115.00
Pocket, A.W.Wadsworth, With Fork & Spoon, Horn Handle .................. 55.00
Pocket, Anheuser Busch, Peephole, A.Busch, 1900, Sterling Silver ...... 225.00
Pocket, Case XX ........................................................................................ 15.00
Pocket, Case XXX, 5220, Stag Handle ..................................................... 27.50
Pocket, Challenge Cut Co., Bridgeport, Conn., Bone Stock .................. 60.00
Pocket, Dockash Stoves ............................................................................ 24.00
Pocket, E.C.Simmon's Keen Kutter, Pearl, 3 In. ................................... 37.00
Pocket, Engraved Flowers, 2 Blades, Pouch, Sterling Silver, 3 In. ....... 30.00
Pocket, Golden Rule Cutlery Co., Chicago, Partial Nude On Handle ..... 45.00
Pocket, H.Boker Improved Cutlery, Silver & Mother-Of-Pearl Handle .... 35.00
Pocket, Henry Ears & Son, 1865, Stag Handle, 2 Blade ........................ 35.00
Pocket, Imperial Cutlery, 2 Blade, Germany, Steel, 3 1/2 In. ............... 22.50
Pocket, Ka-Bar, Stag, Doghead ................................................................ 185.00
Pocket, Keen Kutter Emblem, 2 Blade .................................................... 17.50
Pocket, Lock Blade, Celluloid Handle, Game Scenes, Open, 10 In. ...... 75.00
Pocket, Mascot Tobacco ............................................................................ 22.00
Pocket, Mechanical, Quaker State Oil Co., 1 Blade .............................. 42.50
Pocket, Mother-Of-Pearl On 3 Sides, 2 Blades, Germany, 3 In. .......... 35.00
Pocket, Muller Bros., 2 Blades, Mother-Of-Pearl Handle, 3 1/2 In. ...... 65.00
Pocket, Old Fitzgerald ............................................................................... 5.00
Pocket, Remington Bullet No.1306, Etched Blade ................................. 390.00
Pocket, Remington Bullet, Stag Handles ................................................ 200.00
Pocket, Remington Bullet, V.M.C., 7 1/2 In. .......................................... 200.00
Pocket, Remington, Scout Emblem .......................................................... 100.00
Pocket, Russell Barlow, Bone Handle, Arrow Through R Markings ........ 95.00
Pocket, Shapleigh, 2 Blade, Diamond Edge, 3 1/2 In. .......................... 15.00
Pocket, Simmon's Hardware Co. .............................................................. 125.00
Pocket, Ulster USA, 3 Blades ................................................................... 3.50
Pocket, Wade & Butcher, Bone, With Corkscrew, C.1873 ..................... 45.00
Pocket, White House Coffee ..................................................................... 23.00
Pocket, William Penn Rye Whiskey, 1 Blade With Corkscrew ............... 15.00
Pocket, Winchester, Black Handle, Large ............................................... 26.00
Pocket, Winchester, 2 Blade, Scissors, Pearl ........................................ 65.00
Pruning, Hooked Blade, Wood Bolster On Side, J.Rodgers & Sons, 10 In. .......... 17.50
Russel & Co., Green River Works, 2 Blade, Bone Handles, 4 In. .......... 165.00
Scutching, Maple, Brass Hanging Ring, 25 In. ....................................... 50.00
Sharpener, Crescent Hill Milk Co. ........................................................... 7.00
Skinning, Wilson, Indian Trade, Boxed, Set Of 6 .................................. 145.00
Survival, Cattaraugus, Sheath .................................................................. 10.00
Walden Knife Co., 2 Blade, Wood Handle, 3 In. .................................... 20.00
Winchester, 4 Blade, No.4942 ................................................................. 100.00
       KNOWLES, TAYLOR & KNOWLES, see KTK; Lotus Ware

KOCH, Bowl, Grape Design, 7 In.Diam. ................................................... 37.50
Bowl, Shaded, Apple Design, Signed, 10 In.Diam. ................................. 40.00
Cup & Saucer, Grape Design ................................................................... 37.50

> *Korean ware is a heavy-glazed pottery usually featuring three-dimensional
> figures of people and animals as decorations. Dull orange and gray-blue are
> favored colors. Korean ware is still being made.*

KOREAN WARE, Teapot, Celadon Type, 19th Century ......................... 55.00

KOSTA, Vase, Intaglio Cut, Pulled Black Spiral, 12 1/2 In. .................. 200.00

*K.P.M*  Most dealers and collectors use the term "KPM" to refer to Berlin porcelain but the same initials were used alone and in combination with other symbols by several German porcelain makers. They include the Konigliche Porzellan Manufaktur of Berlin, initials used in mark 1823-1847; Meissen, 1723-1724 only; Krister Porzellan Manufaktur in Waldenburg, after 1831; Kranichfelder Porzellan Manufaktur in Kranichfeld, after 1903; and the Kister Porzellan Manufaktur in Scheibe, after 1838.

| | |
|---|---|
| KPM, Basket, Two Children Each Side, Woven Canelike Handle | 215.00 |
| Bottle, Figural, Court Jester, Hat Stopper, C.1830, Marked, 4 1/2 In. | 225.00 |
| Bowl, Covered, Gold Trim, Blue, Large | 145.00 |
| Bowl, Scepter, Flowers, Gold Trim, Open Handles, 12 3/4 In. | 120.00 |
| Celery, Handles, Roses, Gold Trim, Marked | 18.50 |
| Clock Case, American Works, 10 1/2 In. | 290.00 |
| Clock, American Brass Works, Porcelain, Signed, 10 1/2 In. | 250.00 |
| Coffeepot, Scattered Flowers On White, 10 1/2 In. | 40.00 |
| Cup & Saucer, Demitasse, Hand-Painted Flowers, Green Crown Mark | 18.00 |
| Cup & Saucer, Demitasse, Lozenge Shaped, 1830 Globe & Cross Mark | 35.00 |
| Cup & Saucer, Floral Design | 85.00 |
| Dish, Hand-Painted Apple Blossom, Signed, Oblong | 25.00 |
| Figurine, Girl With Two Baskets, 9 In. | 130.00 |
| Figurine, Merchant, Green Hat & Coat, C.1880, Scepter Mark, 11 1/2 In. | 350.00 |
| Jar, Tobacco, Black Girl, Bisque, 4 1/2 In. | 75.00 |
| Lamp, Fairy, Three-Faced Owl | 250.00 |
| Panel, Girl Tasting Wine, Girl & Book, Lithophane, C.1850, 8 3/4 In., Pr. | 400.00 |
| Plaque, Boys In Ragged Clothes, C.1860, Scepter Mark, 8 3/4 X 6 1/4 In. | 2000.00 |
| Plaque, Cherubs Embracing, 18th Century, 9 1/4 X 6 1/4 In. | 1050.00 |
| Plaque, Chocolate Girl, Impressed Mark, 9 1/4 X 6 1/2 In. | 1750.00 |
| Plaque, Dutch Boy, 5 X 4 In. | 750.00 |
| Plaque, Fairy With Butterfly On Finger, Signed, 12 1/4 X 10 In. | 1200.00 |
| Plaque, Lassitude, Young Lady In Pensive Mood, Signed, 8 X 10 1/2 In. | 2200.00 |
| Plaque, Painted Bust Of Man, Scepter Mark, 5 X 7 In. | 750.00 |
| Plaque, Portrait, Young Woman With Hat, Marked, 9 1/2 X 6 1/2 In. | 1700.00 |
| Plaque, Psyche, C.1870, Impressed Scepter Mark, 6 X 4 1/2 In. | 1095.00 |
| Plaque, Woman With Hat, 3/4 View, Marked & Signed, 9 1/2 X 6 1/2 In. | 1800.00 |
| Plaque, Young Woman With Hat & Cross, Signed Bayerlein, 9 X 6 In. | 1800.00 |
| Plaque, Young Woman With Hat, Profile View, Marked, 9 1/2 X 6 1/2 In. | 1700.00 |
| Plate, Band Of Pink Roses, Gilt Rim, C.1835, Blue Scepter Mark, Set Of 6 | 1100.00 |
| Plate, Hand-Painted Peaches, 8 In.Diam. | 25.00 |
| Plate, Openwork, 11 In.Diam. | 45.00 |
| Plate, Scrolled Band, Gilt Rim, C.1835, Scepter Mark, 9 1/2 In., Set Of 12 | 1200.00 |
| Sugar & Creamer, Covered, Roses, 2-Toned Ground, Gold Trim | 45.00 |
| Vase, Temple, Lidded, Bouquets Of Flowers, Gold Filigree, 16 1/2 In. | 145.00 |

**K.T.&K.**
**CHINA**  KTK are the initials of the Knowles, Taylor and Knowles Company of East Liverpool, Ohio, founded by Isaac W.Knowles in 1853. They made Lotus Ware.

**KTK LOTUS WARE, see Lotus Ware**

| | |
|---|---|
| KTK, Cuspidor, Lady's, 7 X 8 In.Diam. | 75.00 |
| Dish, Shell Shape, Knight Templar, Marked | 85.00 |
| Jar, Openwork Lid & Sides, Turquoise-Tipped White Balls, 6 In. | 800.00 |
| Jug, China, Old Maryland Whiskey | 90.00 |
| Jug, Old Maryland Whiskey, G.Riesmeyer, St.Louis, Mo. | 90.00 |
| Pitcher, Milk, Blue & White | 45.00 |
| Platter, Fighting Bucks, 13 1/2 In. | 40.00 |
| Syrup, Pansy Design | 135.00 |
| Vase, Ruffled, Hand-Painted Flowers, Beading | 295.00 |

| | |
|---|---|
| KU KLUX KLAN, Cap, Beanie Type, Tassel | 14.00 |
| Records, By American & Rhinehart Bros., Lot Of 12 | 275.00 |
| Sash, Felt | 14.00 |

| | |
|---|---|
| **Token,** Convention, 1907 | 7.00 |
| **Uniform,** Hood Attached, Black | 46.00 |

*Kutani ware is a Japanese porcelain made after the mid-seventeenth century. Most of the pieces found today are nineteenth century.*

| | |
|---|---|
| **KUTANI, Bowl,** Waste, 6 In.Diam. | 25.00 |
| **Chocolate Set,** Gold Leaf & Rust, 5 Cups & Saucers | 375.00 |
| **Cracker Jar,** Scenic Medallions, Pink & Gold | 135.00 |
| **Cup & Saucer,** Demitasse, Geisha Girl, Red Handled & Rimmed, Set Of 5 | 130.00 |
| **Ewer,** Floral & Bird Design, 18th Century, Signed, 9 5/8 In., Pair | 275.00 |
| **Jar,** Ginger, Gold Design, Birds In Black, Orange, 5 X 2 1/2 In.Diam. | 65.00 |
| **Luncheon Set,** Japanese Country Scene, Gray Ground, 21 Piece | 185.00 |
| **Pitcher,** Burgundy Top, Medallions & Roses, Fat Belly | 115.00 |
| **Pitcher,** Flowers & Bird Design, 4 In. | 30.00 |
| **Plate,** Flowers, Birds, Orange & Cream, C.1850, 8 1/2 In.Diam. | 99.50 |
| **Plate,** Gold Brocade, C.1850 | 50.00 To 75.00 |
| **Plate,** Hot Water, Orange & Blue, 11 In.Diam. | 390.00 |
| **Plate,** 8 1/4 In. | 85.00 |
| **Sugar & Creamer,** Blue Skies, White Birds, Yellow Beaks, Flower Finial | 50.00 |
| **Sugar & Creamer,** Geishas, White, Orange, & Gold | 45.00 |
| **Tea Set,** Demi, Gold Dragons, White Ground, 13 Pieces | 125.00 |
| **Tea Set,** 12 Cups & Saucers, 12 Tea Plates, Scenes, 40 Piece | 525.00 |
| **Vase,** Imperial Palace, Flying Birds On Reverse, Prunus Trees, 24 In. | 2400.00 |
| **Vase,** Raised Dragon Base, Melon Ribs, Quail, Gold, 19th Century, Pair | 2000.00 |

| | |
|---|---|
| **LACQUER, Box,** Gold Apricot Blossom, Black Ground, Japanese, 2 1/2 In.Square | 175.00 |
| **Box,** Oriental, Deer, Birds, Tree, Inlaid In Pearl, 3 1/2 X 5 1/2 In. | 18.00 |
| **Tray,** Gilt & Polychrome Bird & Floral Design, C.1900, 16 In.Square | 50.00 |

R. LALIQUE

LALIQUE

*Lalique glass was made by Rene Lalique in Paris, France, between the 1890s and his death in 1945. The glass was molded, pressed, and engraved in Art Nouveau and Art Deco styles. Pieces were marked with the signature "R. Lalique." Lalique glass is still being made. Pieces made after 1945 bear the mark "Lalique."*

| | |
|---|---|
| **LALIQUE, Ashtray,** Bird With Fish In Mouth | 275.00 |
| **Ashtray,** Boat With Mast In Center, Signed, 3 3/4 In. | 40.00 |
| **Ashtray,** Fish, Frosted, 6 In. | 95.00 |
| **Ashtray,** Molded Fish In Bubbles, Signed, 6 In. | 40.00 |
| **Ashtray,** Naiade, Clear & Frosted, Signed, 5 In. | 250.00 |
| **Ashtray,** Swan | 45.00 |
| **Atomizer,** Perfume, Female Figures | 225.00 |
| **Atomizer,** Purse, Brown Wash Daisy, Block Embossed, 3 1/2 In. | 225.00 |
| **Bell,** Frosted & Clear, Sparrow Handle, Signed, 5 1/2 In. | 125.00 |
| **Bonbon,** Hanging Leaf Design On Cover, Signed, 4 1/2 X 6 In.Diam. | 495.00 |
| **Bonbon,** Molded Fish Each Side, Signed, 9 X 3 In. | 235.00 |
| **Bookends,** Swallow | 225.00 |
| **Bottle,** Air Du Temps, Double Doves, Signed, 32 Ounce | 1200.00 |
| **Bottle,** Cologne, Dahlia, 7 In. | 100.00 |
| **Bottle,** Cologne, Nude Children In Relief, Signed, Pair | 675.00 |
| **Bottle,** Nudes, Silver Plated Stopper, 4 1/2 In. | 425.00 |
| **Bottle,** Perfume, Apple Shape, Signed | 70.00 |
| **Bottle,** Perfume, Blooming Flower, Concave Center, Black Enamel | 140.00 |
| **Bottle,** Perfume, Blooming Flower, Relief, Black Enamel, 5 1/4 In. | 165.00 |
| **Bottle,** Perfume, Bouchon Fleurs De Pommier, Stopper Inscribed, 5 In. | 650.00 |
| **Bottle,** Perfume, Capricorn, Lacquered Beetles, Signed, 3 In. | 295.00 |
| **Bottle,** Perfume, Dahlia Pattern, Raised Petals, Signed, 5 In. | 350.00 |
| **Bottle,** Perfume, Emilione Pattern, Flower Stopper, Signed, 7 In. | 350.00 |
| **Bottle,** Perfume, Enameled, Basket Weave Design, Signed, 6 1/4 In. | 200.00 |
| **Bottle,** Perfume, Entwined Thorn, Brown Toning, Signed, 6 1/4 In. | 375.00 |
| **Bottle,** Perfume, Frosted Dove Stopper, Signed, 3 1/2 In. | 125.00 |
| **Bottle,** Perfume, Frosted, Shape Of 2 Flowers, Signed, 3 3/4 In. | 275.00 |

**Bottle,** Perfume, Green, Bullet Shaped Stopper, Signed, 2 1/2 In. ............................................ 175.00
**Bottle,** Perfume, Impressed Flowers, Stopper, Label, 3 1/4 In. ............................................ 85.00
**Bottle,** Perfume, Lily-Of-The-Valley Stopper ............................................ 79.00
**Bottle,** Perfume, Scalloped Heart Shape, Garlands, Signed, 5 3/4 In. ............................................ 275.00
**Bottle,** Perfume, Sea Urchin, Enameled Bosses, Signed, 4 1/2 In. ............................................ 350.00
**Bottle,** Perfume, Seashell, Stopper, Signed R.Lalique, 3 1/2 In. ............................................ 160.00
**Bottle,** Perfume, Worth, Blue, Sapphire Body, Pale Blue Stopper, 2 In. ............................................ 125.00
**Bottle,** Scent, Cased Green Glass, Bird Of Paradise In Flight ............................................ 2000.00
**Bowl & Charger,** Swirling Leaves, Frosted Opalescent, Signed, 8 In. ............................................ 875.00
**Bowl & Underplate,** Coquilles ............................................ 325.00
**Bowl,** Dandelion Leaf, Brown Wash, Signed, 9 1/2 In. ............................ 350.00 To 450.00
**Bowl,** Frosted Amber, Bands Of Serrated Arcs, Signed, 9 1/2 In. ............................................ 600.00
**Bowl,** Frosted Blown-Out Wild Horses, 6 X 8 In.Diam. ............................................ 135.00
**Bowl,** Fruit Trees, Signed In Script, France, 8 1/4 In. ............................................ 450.00
**Bowl,** Fruit, Wheat Pattern, Signed, 9 1/4 In. ............................................ 210.00
**Bowl,** Martigues, Yellow Glass, Signed, 14 1/2 In. ............................................ 900.00
**Bowl,** Mistletoe, Opalescent & Clear, Block Signature, 8 1/4 In.Diam. ............................................ 395.00
**Bowl,** Opalescent Frosted Stem, Berries & Vines, Signed, 4 1/2 In. ............................................ 120.00
**Bowl,** Patterned Leaves From Center Outward, Signed, 5 In.Diam. ............................................ 80.00
**Bowl,** Punch, Leaf Pattern, Underplate, Marked, 13 X 5 1/4 In. ............................................ 1150.00
**Bowl,** Shell, Opalescent, Signed, 5 1/4 In.Diam. ............................................ 225.00
**Bowl,** Starfish, Opalescent, Signed, 9 1/2 X 3 In. ............................................ 350.00
**Bowl,** Striated Luster, Frosted Berries On Stem, Signed, 4 In.Diam. ............................................ 110.00
**Bowl,** Two Birds Perched On Rim, Signed, 12 In.Diam. ............................................ 545.00
**Bowl,** Underplate, Coquilles, Signed ............................................ 335.00
**Bowl,** Veronique, 8 1/2 In. ............................................ 275.00
**Bowl,** Water Lily Design, Opaque, Signed, 4 X 11 In.Diam. ............................................ 210.00
**Bowl,** Wheat Pattern, 3-Footed, Signed ............................................ 250.00
**Bowl,** 7 Stylized Fruit Trees, Signed, 8 1/8 In. ............................................ 395.00
**Box,** Cigarette, Beads On Undercover, Scale Design, Signed, 5 X 4 In. ............................................ 450.00
**Box,** Cover, Dahlia Blossoms, Blue Satin Glass, Signed, 8 1/4 In.Diam. ............................................ 425.00
**Box,** Covered, 8 Triangular Panels, Signed, 1 1/2 X 2 1/4 In.Diam. ............................................ 350.00
**Box,** Powder, Cactus Design, Original Label ............................................ 135.00
**Box,** Powder, Cactus Pattern ............................................ 125.00
**Box,** Powder, Dancing Girls ............................................ 165.00
**Box,** Powder, Dancing Nudes, Signed ............................................ 135.00
**Box,** Powder, Flowering Rambling Roses, Black Glass, 3 1/2 In. ............................................ 250.00
**Box,** Powder, Libellules, Opalescent Glass, Signed, 6 1/2 In. ............................................ 550.00
**Box,** Powder, 3 Dancing Nudes, Frosted Brown Stain, Signed ............................................ 275.00
**Box,** Powder, 3 Nudes Cover, Leaf Design, Signed, 3 3/4 In.Diam. ............................................ 225.00
**Box,** Rows Of Swimming Swans, Covered, Signed, 2 1/2 X 4 1/4 In. ............................................ 170.00
**Candlestick,** Cherubs, Signed, Pair, 3 1/2 In. ............................................ 350.00
**Car Mascot,** Longchamps, Chrome Mount, Signed, 5 1/4 In. ......................... *Illus* 3800.00
**Car Mascot,** Pintade, Chrome Mount, Black Glass Base, Signed, 5 In. ............................................ 2500.00
**Chalice,** Striated Threaded, Iridescent Bowl, Frosted, 4 X 2 In. ............................................ 120.00

Lalique, Car Mascot, Longchamps, Chrome Mount, Signed, 5 1/4 In.

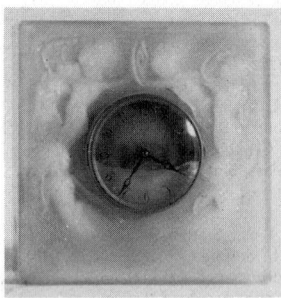

Lalique, Clock, Sirenes, Engraved R.Lalique, France, 11 In.

Chandelier, Peony Blossoms, Leaves, Domical Shape, Signed, 12 In. .................................... 800.00
Christmas Plate Set, 1965-1973 ............................................................................. 1800.00
Clock, Deux Figurines, C.1930, Marked, 15 1/2 In. .......................................................... 4500.00
Clock, Sirenes, Engraved R.Lalique, France, 11 In. ............................................... Illus 2500.00
Decanter, Frosted, Frog's Heads, Nymphs, Signed, 12 1/2 In. ............................................ 1300.00
Dish, Bonbon, Hanging Leaves, Opalescent, Signed, 6 X 4 1/2 In. ......................................... 495.00
Dish, Candy, Frosted Roses, 3 Cherubs, 5 In. ............................................................... 45.00
Dish, Green, Molded Birds, 4 In. ............................................................................ 45.00
Dish, Peacock Feather, Opalescent Eyes, Signed, 11 In.Wide ............................................... 395.00
Dish, Perles Pattern, Signed .................................................................................. 155.00
Figure, Tete Penchee, Woman, Hands Clasped, Long Robe, Signed, 14 In. .......................... 2200.00
Figurine, Angelfish, Blue-Green, Signed, 2 1/2 In. ......................................................... 85.00
Figurine, Bird, Camphor Finished, 2 1/2 In. ............................................................... 175.00
Figurine, Bird, Signed, 3 1/2 In. ........................................................................... 275.00
Figurine, Fish, Green, 2 In. ................................................................................... 50.00
Figurine, Madonna & Child, Halos, Black Amethyst Base, 14 In. ......................................... 250.00
Figurine, Sirene, Opalescent & Brown Stained, Signed, 4 1/4 In. ....................................... 700.00
Figurine, Source De La Fontaine, C.1925, Marked, 28 In. ............................................... 1800.00
Figurine, Suzanne, Bronze Base, Incised Peacocks, Signed, 6 1/2 In. ................................. 3300.00
Figurine, Suzanne, Opalescent Glass, Tinged Yellow, Marked, 9 In. .................................... 1100.00
Figurine, Suzanne, Opalescent, Signed, 9 In. ............................................................. 2500.00
Goblet, Duncan Pattern, Nude Figure Stem, 6 1/4 In. ..................................................... 115.00
Goblet, Five Nude Figures On Stem, Signed, 6 1/4 In. .................................................... 115.00
Holder, Menu, Semicircular Form, Cherries Design, Signed, 2 In. ....................................... 110.00
Holder, Menu, Semicircular Shape, Cherries, Signed, 1 3/4 X 2 In. ..................................... 100.00
Holder, Placecard, Filigree Metal Base, Set Of 12 ........................................................ 450.00
Hood Ornament, Archer, Frosted & Clear, Signed, 5 In. ................................................... 950.00
Hood Ornament, Chevaux, 5 Horses ........................................................................ 2600.00
Hood Ornament, Comet ....................................................................................... 2500.00
Hood Ornament, Female Head, Flowing Hair ................................................................ 125.00
Hood Ornament, Grande Libellule, Dragonfly .............................................................. 2300.00
Hood Ornament, Pullman Express, Cote D'Azur, Nude ..................................................... 3200.00
Hood Ornament, Tete De Belier, Ram's Head ............................................................... 3200.00
Hood Ornament, Victoire ...................................................................................... 4500.00
Jar, Powder, D'orsay, Frosted Top .......................................................................... 150.00
Mirror, Hand, Gray, Clear & Frosted, Ladies On Handle, 12 In. ......................................... 1650.00
Paperweight, Baby Impressed In Frosted Glass, Oval, 4 X 3 In. .......................................... 65.00
Paperweight, Bison, Clear & Frosted, Signed, 4 In. ....................................................... 750.00
Paperweight, Faucon, Clear & Frosted, Signed, 6 In. ..................................................... 1650.00
Paperweight, Sanglier, Smoky Green Frosted, Signed, 3 In. .............................................. 1950.00
Plaque, Siren Of The Sea, Glass Base, 4 1/2 In. ........................................................... 85.00
Plate, Annual 1966, Signed, Boxed, 8 1/2 In. .............................................................. 295.00
Plate, Annual, 1967, Fish ........................................................................ 100.00 To 175.00

Plate, Annual, 1968, Gazelle .............................................................. 80.00
Plate, Annual, 1969, Papillion .............................................................. 80.00
Plate, Annual, 1970, Peacock ................................................ 65.00 To 100.00
Plate, Annual, 1972, Coquillage ............................................ 50.00 To 60.00
Plate, Annual, 1973, Haying .............................................................. 50.00
Plate, Annual, 1976 ...................................................................... 125.00
Plate, Brown Stained Floral Border, 8 X 8 In. ...................................... 200.00
Plate, Coquille Pattern, Signed, 8 In.Diam. ......................................... 495.00
Plate, Flame Design, Black, Block Signature, 8 In., Pair .......................... 275.00
Plate, Flowers & Leaves, 7 3/4 In. ..................................................... 40.00
Plate, Scallop Shells Design, 20th Century, Signed, 6 3/8 In.Diam. ............. 75.00
Plate, Scrolling Scalloped Bands, C.1930, Acid Stained, 9 1/2 In. ............. 175.00
Plate, Shell Design, Signed ............................................................. 595.00
Plate, Wheat Pattern, Frosted, Molded Signature, 9 3/8 In.Diam. .............. 170.00
Salt, Master, Flower Base, Footed, 2 In. ............................................... 45.00
Tray, Bull's-Eye Handles, Signed, 5 X 7 In. ......................................... 175.00
Tray, Entwined Thorn Design At Bottom, Signed, 4 1/2 X 3 In. ................. 150.00
Tray, Frosted Oak Leaves & Acorns, 13 X 17 In. ................................... 985.00
Tray, Pin, Shepherd Dog In Center, Signed, 3 1/2 In. .............................. 95.00
Tray, Pin, Shield Shape, Center Handle, Intaglio Carved Siren ................... 95.00
Tray, Pink, Madonna, 4 1/2 In. .......................................................... 85.00
Tray, Scalloped Frosted Fish Border, Oval, Signed, 11 X 9 In. .................. 145.00
Tumbler, Blown-Out Berries, Signed, 4 1/2 In. ..................................... 150.00
Tumbler, Pedestal, Overall Pattern, Signed, 6 1/4 In. ............................. 150.00
Tumbler, Vertical Ribbed, Molded Raspberries Around Base, 4 1/4 In. .......... 70.00
Vase, Allover Leaf Design, Blue Wash, Signed & Numbered, 6 3/4 In. ........ 1000.00
Vase, Amber Glass, Epines, C.1925, Marked, 9 1/2 In. ........................... 800.00
Vase, Amber, Palm Leaves, 5 In. ....................................................... 395.00
Vase, Beliers, Opalescent Glass, Signed, 6 1/2 In. ................................. 800.00
Vase, Black Glass, Lizards Et Bluets, Signed, 13 1/2 In. ........................ 6000.00
Vase, Blue Glass, Perruches, C.1925, Impressed, 10 1/4 In. ................... 2000.00
Vase, Blue Staining, Frolicking Nude Ladies, Signed, 9 3/4 In. ................ 3000.00
Vase, Blue Tinted, Plumes, Signed, 8 1/4 In. ....................................... 650.00
Vase, Blue-Green Glass, Poissons, Marked, 9 1/2 In. ............................. 2250.00
Vase, Bouchardon, Gray Glass, Frosted, Signed, 4 1/2 In. ............. Illus 1200.00
Vase, Brambles, Opalescent, Block Letters, 9 1/4 In. ............................. 1100.00
Vase, Cire Perdu Glass, Eucalyptus Leaves, Signed, 6 1/4 In. ................. 3500.00
Vase, Deer In Woodland, Brown Patination, Signed, 7 In. ......................... 295.00
Vase, Farandole, Clear & Frosted Blue, Signed, 7 1/4 In. ....................... 4500.00
Vase, Fern Leaves All Around, Blue Cast, Frosted, Signed, 7 1/2 In. .......... 450.00
Vase, Fish Heads, Frosted Rippled, 3-Footed, Signed, 7 In. ..................... 200.00
Vase, Frosted Body, 24 Molded Fish Around, Signed, 3 1/2 X 3 3/4 In. ...... 380.00
Vase, Frosted Crystal, Leaf & Berry Design, Signed, 6 In. ....................... 120.00
Vase, Frosted Leaves, Signed, 5 In. .................................................... 100.00
Vase, Frosted Luster Birds, Fernery, 7 X 6 1/2 In. ................................ 700.00

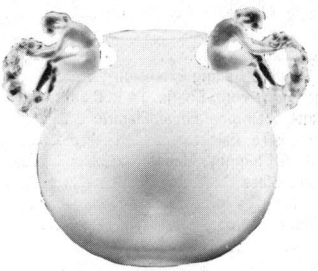

Lalique, Vase, Bouchardon, Gray Glass, Frosted, Signed, 4 1/2 In.

Vase, Frosted Nudes, Paneled, Clear, Signed, 8 1/4 In. ................................................ 685.00
Vase, Frosted Oak Leaves, 4 3/4 In. ........................................................................ 55.00
Vase, Gold Filigree Trim, Frosted, Bulbous ................................................................ 375.00
Vase, Gros Scarabees, Allover Beetles, Picked In Enamel, C.1922 .......................... 6600.00
Vase, Herd Of Deer Feeding On Fruit Trees, Signed, 6 1/2 In. .............................. 550.00
Vase, Herd Of Deer Feeding, Tree & Foliage, Frosted, Signed, 7 In. ...................... 485.00
Vase, Leaf & Berry Design, Signed, 6 In. ................................................................ 120.00
Vase, Leafing & Fruiting Mistletoe, Frosted & Clear, Marked, 7 In. ........................ 275.00
Vase, Lotus Blossom Form, Stand-Out Ribs, Clear, Signed, 5 3/4 In. .................... 395.00
Vase, Lovebirds, Opalescent, Signed, 9 1/2 In. ...................................................... 595.00
Vase, Molded Swimming Fish All Around, Signed, 3 1/2 X 4 In.Diam. .................... 425.00
Vase, Monnaie De Pape, Frosted, 9 1/2 In. ............................................................ 850.00
Vase, Monnaie Du Pape, Blue, Opalescent, Signed, 8 In. ........................................ 750.00
Vase, Nude Sirens All Around, Blue Wash, Signed, 5 X 3 1/2 In.Diam. .................... 550.00
Vase, Opalescent Birds Protruding All Around, Signed, 7 In. .............................. 1050.00
Vase, Oranges, Black Enameled, Frosted, Signed, 12 In. ...................................... 4500.00
Vase, Poissons, Cased Opaque Green, Signed, 10 In. ............................................ 4000.00
Vase, Poivre, Signed, 9 1/2 In. ............................................................................ 1200.00
Vase, Rows Of Sea Gulls, Frosted Ground, Signed, 5 1/2 In. ................................ 250.00
Vase, Sophora, Frosted Amber & Clear, Signed, 10 1/4 In. .................................. 4500.00
Vase, Spheroid Shape, Sparrows On Limbs, Luster Ground, Signed, 7 In. .............. 750.00
Vase, Stylized Opalescent Flowers, Oval, Signed, 8 X 6 3/4 In. ............................ 950.00
Vase, Thistle, Translucent Blue White, 9 In. .......................................................... 695.00
Vase, 4 Female Nudes Supporting Geometric Festoons, C.1925 .......................... 4200.00
Vase, 7 Frosted Bands, 3 Birds, Cone Shaped, Block Signed, 6 1/2 In. .................. 575.00
Wine, Raised Grapevines, Square Deco Stem, Signed, 6 In. .................................... 75.00
Wine, Stem, 18 Block, Black Enameled Top, Signed ................................................ 86.00
Wine, 2 Nude Figures On Stem, Signed, 5 1/2 In. .................................................. 115.00
       LAMP, see also Bradley & Hubbard, Lamp; Burmese, Lamp; Handel,
       Lamp; Pairpoint, Lamp; Tiffany, Lamp
LAMP, Advertising, Richard Hudnut Perfume, Reverse Painting, 19 1/4 In. .............. 2500.00
Aladdin, Alacite, No.G16 ...................................................................................... 300.00
Aladdin, Alacite, No.G24 ...................................................................................... 135.00
Aladdin, Alacite, No.G375 .................................................................................... 475.00
Aladdin, Beehive, Red .......................................................................................... 225.00
Aladdin, Clear Beta Crystal Font, Black Base, B-104 .............................................. 65.00
Aladdin, Corinthian, Green .................................................................................... 65.00
Aladdin, Corinthian, No.B-76-A ............................................................................ 115.00
Aladdin, Corinthian, No.B-101 .............................................................................. 60.00
Aladdin, Corinthian, No.B-105 .............................................................................. 60.00
Aladdin, Corinthian, No.B-114 .............................................................................. 80.00
Aladdin, Corinthian, No.B-115 .............................................................................. 80.00
Aladdin, Cupid, Alacite, Pair ................................................................................ 225.00
Aladdin, Desk, Reverse Painted Tree Scene Shade, 13 1/2 In. .............................. 175.00
Aladdin, Drape Design, C Burner .......................................................................... 87.00
Aladdin, Dresser, Scroll Design, Natural Color, Alacite, 20 In., Pair ........................ 65.00
Aladdin, Figurine, No.G-16 .................................................................................. 150.00
Aladdin, Hanging, Double Angle, Alacite, Nickel Plated .......................................... 245.00
Aladdin, Hanging, No.5 ........................................................................................ 260.00
Aladdin, Hanging, No.6 ........................................................................................ 150.00
Aladdin, Hanging, No.616s, Shade & Ceiling Extension .......................................... 500.00
Aladdin, Hanging, White Moonstone Font, Shade, 14 In.Diam. .............................. 250.00
Aladdin, Lily-Of-The-Valley Pattern, Original Finial, Electric .................................... 25.00
Aladdin, Lincoln Drape, Alacite, B-75, Pair .......................................... 67.00 To 75.00
Aladdin, Lincoln Drape, Burner & Chimney, Alacite ................................................ 90.00
Aladdin, Lincoln Drape, Custard Glass .................................................................. 65.00
Aladdin, Lincoln Drape, Flint, Clear, 24 In. .......................................................... 165.00
Aladdin, Lincoln Drape, Miniature .......................................................................... 85.00
Aladdin, No.B-76a ................................................................................................ 95.00
Aladdin, No.B-87 ................................................................................................ 115.00
Aladdin, No.B-153, Alacite Font ............................................................................ 50.00
Aladdin, No.8, Brass ............................................................................................ 75.00
Aladdin, No.11, Nickel, Shade .............................................................................. 175.00

Aladdin, No.26 ............................................................................................................... 210.00
Aladdin, No.100 ............................................................................................................. 60.00
Aladdin, No.104, Hobnail Shade ................................................................................ 165.00
Aladdin, No.107, Crystal Cathedral ........................................................................... 55.00
Aladdin, Red Lincoln Drape, Tall ............................................................................... 375.00
Aladdin, Short Lincoln Drape, Alacite, No.8-60 ....................................................... 300.00
Aladdin, Wall, Bracket, White Moonstone Font ....................................................... 70.00
Aladdin, Washington Drape, Amber ............................................... 48.00 To 135.00
Aladdin, Washington Drape, Clear .............................................................................. 42.00
Angel, Wall Mount, Etched Birds & Leaves, Brass .................................................. 225.00
Astral, Cut Glass Shade, Marble Base, Dated 1842, Signed, 20 In. ....................... 595.00
Astral, Double Step Marble Base, Prisms, Shade, 19 In. ........................................ 145.00
Atterbury Cottage, C.1870 .......................................................................................... 85.00
Banquet, Applied Brass Flowers On Globe, Dated 1888, Signed, 28 1/2 In. ......... 295.00
Banquet, Kerosene, Marble Stem, Green & Gold Mums On Globe, 30 1/2 In. ...... 395.00
Banquet, Kerosene, Owl Head Sides ......................................................................... 200.00
Banquet, Painted Floral Ball Shade, Brass Base, Enameled, 28 In. ....................... 48.00
Banquet, Pink Flowers On White Glass, Patent 1895 ........................................... 1250.00
Banquet, Polychrome Globe, Cast Metal Foot, American, 31 In. ............................. 150.00
Banquet, Swirled Brass Shaft, Frosted Shade, American, Brass, 9 In. .................. 75.00
Banquet, The New Juno No.1, Yellow Shade ............................................................ 225.00
Barber's Singe, Emerald, Tin Stand, Patent .............................................................. 150.00
Beaded Swirl, Cranberry, Miniature ........................................................................... 395.00
Berry, Double, Cast Iron ............................................................................................... 38.00
Berry, Tinned Sheet Iron, Hinged Cover, 19th Century, 5 1/4 In. ............................ 175.00
Betty, Iron, Covered, 18th Century, Complete .......................................................... 200.00
Betty, Oxydized Red Paint, Tin, 7 1/2 In. ................................................................... 225.00
Betty, Spouted, Tin ........................................................................................................ 62.00
Betty, Whale Oil .............................................................................................................. 75.00
Bicycle, Carbide, Badger Brass Co., 1899 ................................................................ 40.00
Bicycle, Colored Sets, English ..................................................................................... 25.00
Billiard Table, 3 Green Slag Glass, Lined In Opal Panel .......................................... 450.00
Boutique, Mini, Imperial, Blue With Blue Chimney, Pair ......................................... 95.00
     **LAMP, BRADLEY & HUBBARD, see Bradley & Hubbard, Lamp**
Brass, Ford Victor, Carbide Head ............................................................................... 37.50
Bronze, Floor, Chinese, Birds On Front, Gold Wash, 68 In. ......................... *Illus* 850.00
Camphene, Newell Patent, 1853, Cast Handle, 2 3/4 In.Diam. .............................. 225.00
Camphene, Standing, Conical Weighted Base, American, Tin, 34 In. ..................... 275.00
Canadian Bull's-Eye, Green, 10 In. ............................................................................ 125.00

Lamp, Bronze, Floor, Chinese, Birds On Front, Gold Wash, 68 In.

Lamp, Chandelier, Sabino Metal Mounted, C.1925, 18 X 24 In.

| | |
|---|---|
| **Carriage,** Beveled Glass, Brass, Burner | 50.00 |
| **Chandelier,** Center Bowl, 4 Lower Egg-Shaped Bowls, 17 In.Diam. | 1800.00 |
| **Chandelier,** Gas, Eastlake, 3-Light, Brass | 215.00 |
| **Chandelier,** Gas, 3-Light, Satin Glass Shades, Brass, C.1890 | 295.00 |
| **Chandelier,** Grape & Leaf Design, Crystal & Glass, 2 Tier, 45 In. | 2000.00 |
| **Chandelier,** Leaded Paneled Glass Inserts, Chained, Bronze, 36 In. | 1250.00 |
| **Chandelier,** Matching Wall Sconces, Steuben Shades, 6-Light, Brass | 2500.00 |
| **Chandelier,** Sabino Metal Mounted, C.1925, 18 X 24 In. | *Illus* 1400.00 |
| **Chandelier,** 20-Light, C.1865, Gilt Bronze, 3 X 3 1/3 Ft., Pair | 2750.00 |
| **Clear Heart With Thumbprint,** 8 In. | 45.00 |
| **Cleveland Safety Library,** Patented Nov.18, 1871 | 425.00 |
| **Coach,** Cunningham Co., New York City, Glass Panels, Brass, Pair | 1450.00 |
| **Coach,** Tin, Beveled Glass, Pair | 160.00 |
| **Columbian Coin Base,** Large Gold Coins | 185.00 |
| **Coolidge Drape** | 75.00 |
| **Coreopsis,** All Original, Miniature | 200.00 |
| **LAMP, COSMOS, see Cosmos, Lamp** | |
| **Cut Glass Stand,** 3 Blue Nailsea Fairy Lamps, Clarke Base, 17 1/2 In. | 625.00 |
| **Cut Glass,** Butterfly, Tulips, Daisies, 19 In. | 2500.00 |
| **Desk,** Slag Shade, Scenic Metal Overlay, Bronzed Spelter | 285.00 |
| **Eiffel Tower Shape,** Wicker, 6 Ft. | 450.00 |
| **Elephant Head & Trunk Tripod Legs,** Font, Globe, 50 In. | 950.00 |
| **Fairy,** Apricot, White, Satinized, 2 Piece, Ruffled Saucer | 150.00 |
| **Fairy,** Blue Moire, 2-Tiered, 11 In. | 845.00 |
| **Fairy,** Castle Tower, Opalescent | 125.00 |
| **Fairy,** Castle, Bisque, Light Shines Through Window, 7 In. | 345.00 |
| **Fairy,** Castle, Porcelain, German, 5 X 3 1/2 In. | 175.00 |
| **Fairy,** Clear Bottom, Green Diamond Point Top, Signed | 100.00 |
| **Fairy,** Coralene Pink, Deep Rose Tulip, Clear Clarke Base, Wheat | 125.00 |
| **Fairy,** Cranberry, Coralene Beading, Pears & Leaves, Clear Base | 325.00 |
| **Fairy,** Figural Owl Head, Frosted Green, Orange Eyes, 4 1/2 In. | 175.00 |
| **Fairy,** Frosted Blue, White, 3 Piece, Clarke Cup, Stars On Top | 400.00 |
| **Fairy,** Frosted Cranberry, Bowl Base, Clear Clarke Cup, 4 7/8 In. | 495.00 |
| **Fairy,** Frosted Cranberry, 3 Piece, Clarke Cup, Ruffled Base | 450.00 |
| **Fairy,** Frosted Etched Cranberry, Clear Clarke Base | 125.00 |
| **Fairy,** Golden Amber Overshot Embossed Swirl, Clear Clarke Base, 3 In. | 110.00 |
| **Fairy,** Green, Pyramid Lighthouse, Clarke Cup | 150.00 |
| **Fairy,** Green, White, Satinized, 2 Piece, 4 Jeweled Inserts | 165.00 |
| **Fairy,** Green, 2-Faced Owl, Painted Eyes, Pyramid Clarke Cup | 175.00 |
| **Fairy,** Hobnail Shade, Clarke Base, Ruby Red | 85.00 |
| **Fairy,** Intaglio Butterscotch, 2 Piece, Pyramid, Deep Cutting | 450.00 |
| **Fairy,** Jeweled, Lacy, Ruffled Brass Plate, Dome Shade, 6 In. | 225.00 |
| **Fairy,** Jeweled, Ruffled Brass Plate, Signed Clarke, 4 In. | 225.00 |

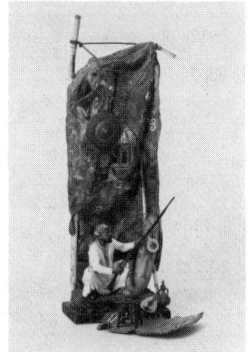

Lamp, Figural, Austrian, Cold-Painted,
C.1900, Marked, 17 In.

Lamp, Gone With The Wind, American,
P & G Co., 23 1/2 In.

Fairy, Lemon Yellow, Clarke Bottom, Verre Moire Glass Top, Signed, 4 In. ............................ 245.00
Fairy, Nailsea, Red, Clarke Cricklite Base ................................................................................. 100.00
Fairy, Opalescent Swirl Pyramid, Amber, 3 7/8 In. .................................................................. 100.00
Fairy, Pyramid, Quilted, Yellow, Satin, 4 In. .............................................................................. 165.00
Fairy, Red Hobnail Shade, Clarke Base ....................................................................................... 90.00
Fairy, Red Nailsea, 3 Piece, Deep Ruffled Base, Applied Feet ................................................. 475.00
Fairy, Ruby Diamond-Quilted Glass, Clear Clarke Base, 3 1/2 In. .............................................. 75.00
Fairy, Ruby Red, Hobnail Shade, Clark Base ............................................................................... 85.00
Fairy, Ruby, Enamel Hand-Painted Flowers ................................................................................ 85.00
Fairy, Verre Moire, Clear Marked Clarke Base, Blue, 4 1/2 In. .................................................. 165.00
Fairy, Verre Moire, Clear Marked Clarke Base, Chartreuse, 4 1/2 In. ....................................... 165.00
Figural, Austrian, Cold-Painted, C.1900, Marked, 17 In. .................................................*Illus* 1700.00
Figural, Boar's Head, Cut Glass Shade, Bronze, C.1830, Argand, 9 In., Pair ...................... 1250.00
Figural, Mercury, Marble Base, Gian De Gologna, Bronze, 3 Ft. ............................................. 800.00
Finger, Heart Pedestal ................................................................................................................. 75.00
Finger, Oil, Erin Fan, Green, 5 1/2 In. ....................................................................................... 145.00
Finger, Peacock Feather, Blue, Pedestal .................................................................................... 195.00
Finger, Pressed Glass, Leaf & Dart, Handled ............................................................................. 40.00
Finger, Riverside Fern, Dated, Clear ........................................................................................... 60.00
Finger, Thuro 304-A, Peanut ...................................................................................................... 85.00
Floor, Champleve, Bronze Shaft, Brown Patina, Oriental, 60 In., Pair ..................................... 450.00
Floor, Champleve, Palace, 72 In. ................................................................................................ 900.00
Floor, Pierced Shade, Brass, 6 Feet ........................................................................................... 895.00
Fluted Base, Dragon Wrapped Around Body, Japan, Bronze, 34 In. ......................................... 750.00
French, Opaline Pillar, Ormolu Mounted, Royal Blue, 20 In. ..................................................... 450.00
Gas, Coleman, Quick Lite, Nickel Over Brass, 18 In. .................................................................. 40.00
Gas, Table, Multicolored Shade, No.1045, Signed E.M. & Co., 17 In. ....................................... 650.00
Glow, Opalescent Top, Clear Base .............................................................................................. 24.00
Gone With The Wind, Allover Azalea, Yellow Ground, Dated 1890, Signed ........................ 295.00
Gone With The Wind, American, P & G Co., 23 1/2 In. ........................................................*Illus* 300.00

Gone With The Wind, Baby Face Top, Red Satin Glass ............................................ 495.00
Gone With The Wind, Brass Slip-In Font, Tea Roses, Blue Ground ........................... 550.00
Gone With The Wind, Brown, Tan, Purple, 26 In. .................................................... 595.00
Gone With The Wind, Daffodil & Roses, C.1890, Electrified, 26 In. ......................... 295.00
Gone With The Wind, Dated 1895, Red Satin Glass .............................................. 600.00
Gone With The Wind, Gold Satin .......................................................................... 1000.00
Gone With The Wind, Lavender & Maroon Tulips, Original, 1936 ........................... 175.00
Gone With The Wind, Miniature, Camphor Glass, Kerosene .................................. 125.00
Gone With The Wind, Poppies, Blue Ground, Dated 1888, Signed, 24 In. ............... 550.00
Gone With The Wind, Poppyseed Pattern, Red Satin Glass, 28 In. ........................ 875.00
Gone With The Wind, Puffed Rose Garlands, Green Satin, 14 In. ............................ 365.00
Gone With The Wind, Regal Ties Pattern, Ball Top, Wired ..................................... 450.00
Gone With The Wind, Sunflower Design Top & Bottom, 22 1/2 In. ........................ 725.00
Gone With The Wind, White, Blown Baby Faces, 24 1/2 In. ................................... 450.00
Hand, Footed, Green Bull's-Eye, Safety Handle ................................................... 150.00
Hand, Footed, Lowell Loop, Milk Glass ............................................................... 120.00
LAMP, HANDEL, see Handel, Lamp
Hanging Pan, Candleholder Over Pan, Wrought Iron, 20 3/4 In. ............................. 375.00
Hanging, Amber Bull's-Eye, Teardrop Shape ....................................................... 350.00
Hanging, Diamond-Quilted, Brass Frame, Prisms, Ruby, 14 In.Diam. .................... 485.00
Hanging, Teardrop Shape, Amber Bull's-Eye ....................................................... 350.00
Hearse, Silver Plate, Pair ................................................................................... 1950.00
Hobnail, Amber, Miniature .................................................................................. 80.00
Horn Of Plenty Pattern, Sandwich Glass ............................................................. 195.00
Horn Of Plenty, Purple Glass, Brass, Marble Base ............................................... 185.00
Hurricane, White & Burgundy, 5 In.Prisms, Pair .................................................. 85.00
Inverted Bull's Eye, Enameled Flowers, Amberina ............................................... 1650.00
Jefferson, Sunset & House Scene, 21 In. ............................................................. 790.00
Kerosene, Cast Iron Base, Greek Key Font, Milk Glass Shade, 21 1/2 In. .............. 95.00
Kerosene, Climax, C.1906, Brass, 10 In. .............................................................. 37.50
Kerosene, Colonial, Matching Hobnail Shade, No.701b ........................................ 150.00
Kerosene, Coolidge Drape, Clear ........................................................................ 70.00
Kerosene, Cut & Etched Shade, Brass Base, Eldorado, HB & H, 28 IN. ................. 225.00
Kerosene, Etched Birds & Leaves, 5 In. ............................................................... 40.00
Kerosene, Feathered Design, White Milk Glass .................................................... 150.00
Kerosene, Florentine, White Moonstone, No.1221 ............................................... 425.00
Kerosene, Fuel Gauge, Air Pump, Parlor Picture, Brass ........................................ 50.00
Kerosene, Jeweled Heart Pattern, Clear ............................................................. 85.00
Kerosene, Kitchen, Brass Font & Fittings, Milk Glass Shade, 14 In.Diam. .............. 395.00
Kerosene, Owls In Flight, 4 Panels, Double Wicks, Brass, 13 In. ........................... 185.00
Kerosene, Petal Pattern, 7 In. ............................................................................. 40.00
Kerosene, Pressed Glass, 101, Clear ................................................................... 65.00
Kerosene, Princess Feather Pattern, Cranberry Glass, 20 In. ............................... 265.00
Kerosene, Princess Feather, Cobalt Blue ............................................................. 200.00
Kerosene, Ruffled Bull's-Eye, Quarter Block ....................................................... 55.00
Kerosene, Shield & Star, Brass Connector, Clambroth Base ................................. 85.00
Kerosene, Warren Patent, Glass .......................................................................... 95.00
Kerosene, Wreath & Torch .................................................................................. 55.00
Kerosene, 4 Glass Sides, Brass, 13 In., Pair ........................................................ 185.00
Kettle, Wrought Iron Base, Shank, & Arms, Copper Oil Holder, 7 5/8 In. ............... 390.00
Lard Oil, Canting, Reflector, Chamberlain Patent, Tin ........................................... 375.00
Lard, C.1854, Smith & Stonesifer, Tin .................................................................. 325.00
Lard, Pump Type, Matby, Neal, Tin ...................................................................... 225.00
Lard, Saucer Base, Pedestal, Original Tin Shade, Tin, 10 In. ................................. 165.00
Leaded Glass Shade, Marble Base ................................................................ Illus 3900.00
Library, Cleveland Safety Lamp Co., 1871 ........................................................... 425.00
Library, Kerosene, Pull-Down, Hand-Painted Shade, Signed Juno ........................ 425.00
Library, Pull-Down, Brass Font & Frame, Signed, Dated 1885, Shade 14 In. .......... 550.00
Library, Pull-Down, Kerosene, Enameled Lilies, Gold Trim, Signed Miller .............. 595.00
Little Banner, Miniature ...................................................................................... 75.00
Locomotive, German, Pair .................................................................................. 400.00
Lomax, Plinth, Stem, & Handle Marked Oil Guard, Dated 1873 ............................. 45.00
Loom, With Candle & Splint Holder, Wrought Iron, Sliding Staple, 37 In. ............... 460.00

Lamp, Leaded Glass Shade, Marble Base

| | |
|---|---|
| Milk Glass, Alba, Blue, Melon Shaped | 95.00 |
| Miner's, Carbide, 1920, Brass | 20.00 |
| Miner's, Fold-Up | 45.00 |
| Miner's, Hinged Top & Spout, Donlaps, Pittsburgh, 2 1/2 In. | 25.00 |
| Miner's, Reflector, Brass | 25.00 |
| Miniature, Kerosene, Basket Weave, Blue, Match Holder Handle | 250.00 |
| Miniature, Little Beauty Night Lamp, Cobalt Shade, Nickel Plated | 75.00 |
| Miniature, Red Dimpled Satin Glass | 100.00 |
| Nellie Bly, Pink Rose Design | 125.00 |
| Night, Climax Reflector, Brass, Miniature, 7 In., Pair | 120.00 |
| Night, Lithophane Of Girl & Kittens, Germany, Porcelain, 5 3/4 In. | 300.00 |
| Nurse's, Asphaltum Ground, Original Burner, Tin | 60.00 |
| Nursery, Merry-Go-Round Shade, Clown Base, Camphor Glass | 35.00 |
| Oil, Acanthus Leaf, Sandwich Glass | 200.00 |
| Oil, Brass Stem, Marble Base, Flint Font, Punty, & Sawtooth | 85.00 |
| Oil, Brass, Double Wick, Etched Globe, Crystal Chimney, 25 In. | 125.00 |
| Oil, Bull's-Eye, Clear Font, Green Base, 12 In. | 195.00 |
| Oil, Coolidge Drape, Cobalt Blue | 125.00 |
| Oil, Dazelle Oval Window, Green, 6 1/2 In. | 145.00 |
| Oil, Diamond Band & Shield, Flat Finger, Amethyst | 210.00 |
| Oil, Egret Standing On Tortoise, Balancing Lamps, 19th Century | 160.00 |
| Oil, Erin Fan Pattern, Pedestaled, Green, 5 1/2 In. | 145.00 |
| Oil, Erin Fan, Green, 9 In. | 135.00 |
| Oil, Frosted Font, Iron Base | 19.00 |
| Oil, Hand, Poppy Band, Clear | 65.00 |
| Oil, Hanging, Hand-Painted Shade, Wrought Iron Bracket, Victorian | 495.00 |
| Oil, Lard, Tin, Saucer Base, Kinnear | 135.00 |
| Oil, Miniature, Hand-Blown, Applied Handle, 1 1/4 X 2 1/4 In. | 150.00 |
| Oil, Owl Bottom, Miniature | 78.00 |
| Oil, Pear Shaped Font, White Marble Base, C.1850, 10 3/4 In. | 275.00 |
| Oil, Pressed Glass, Cable With Fan Top & Front | 225.00 |
| Oil, Riverside Fern, Emerald Green | 145.00 |
| Oil, Shrine Pattern, 10 In. | 115.00 |
| Oil, Square Porcelain Body, Windows With Children, American, 17 In. | 320.00 |
| Oil, Success Brand, Ruby Glass Shade, C.1890 | 250.00 |
| Oil, Swirled Rosettes, Clear | 40.00 |
| Oil, Trigger Handle, Cobalt Blue | 125.00 |
| Oil, Turkey Legs Pattern | 38.50 |
| Oil, Wavecrest, Floral Decoration, Blue Base, 12 In. | 300.00 |
| Onion Fluid, Stemmed | 105.00 |
| Opalescent Reverse Swirl, Iron Base | 55.00 |
| Opium, Enamel Over Brass, Miniature | 85.00 |
| LAMP, PAIRPOINT, see Pairpoint, Lamp | |
| Pan, Adjustable, 16 3/4 In. | 300.00 |
| Pan, Pear Shape, Spike & Hook, 18th Century, Wrought Iron, 3 1/4 In. | 125.00 |
| Parlor, Gasoline, Coleman, Nickel Over Brass, C.1929, 18 In. | 45.00 |
| Pearl Thistles, C.1910, Persimmon, Phoenix, 18 In. | 450.00 |
| Piano, Adjustable, Victorian, Brass | 595.00 |
| Piano, Gilt Brass & Marble | 275.00 |
| Piano, Globe Shade, Polychrome Floral Design, Brass, 60 In. | 125.00 |
| Piano, Kerosene, Original Ball Shade | 350.00 |
| Pig, 3 Spouts, Whale Oil Wicks, Handled, Asphaltum Coated, 7 In. | 265.00 |

Lamp, Shade, Leaded, 3-Colored Slag, Tulip Design,
26 1/4 In.

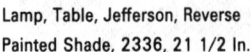

Lamp, Table, Jefferson, Reverse
Painted Shade, 2336, 21 1/2 In.

| | |
|---|---|
| Pool Table, Custom Designed, 3-Light, Brass | 1500.00 |
| Puffy Grape, Dated 1910 | 800.00 |
| Rayo, Applied Handle, Pink Ribbed Shade, Marked, 11 1/2 In. | 125.00 |
| Reverse Painted Scenic Shade, Tropical Landscape, 19 In. | 425.00 |
| Reverse Painted Shade, Bronze Adjustable Base, Pittsburgh, 1i In.Diam. | 875.00 |
| Reverse Painting On Glass Dome, Polychromed Design, 17 In. | 250.00 |
| Ruffled Bull's-Eye, Pink Eyes & Base | 65.00 |
| Saloon, Hanging, Brass Rope, Harp & Filigree, Star Etched, C.1870 | 195.00 |
| Sandwich Glass, Blue & White Acanthus Leaf, Blue Base, Pair | 1250.00 |
| Sandwich Glass, Jade Green & White Acanthus Leaf, Pair | 3500.00 |
| Sandwich Glass, Sweetheart, Burners, 9 3/4 In., Pair | 300.00 |
| Sandwich Glass, Whale Oil, Clear, Blown Front, 6 1/4 In. | 65.00 |
| LAMP, SATIN GLASS, see Satin Glass, Lamp | |
| Sconce, 4-Light, C.1880, Philadelphia, Gilt Bronze, 15 In., Pair | 250.00 |
| Sewing, Riverside, Large | 80.00 |
| Shade, Leaded Slag, Umbrella Shape, Green Petal Design, 22 1/2 In. | 800.00 |
| Shade, Leaded, 3-Colored Slag, Tulip Design, 26 1/4 In. .............................. Illus | 750.00 |
| Shade, Threaded, Signed Quezal, Set Of 2 | 180.00 |
| Shadow, Polychromed Figure, Ivory Head, Alabaster Base, C.1925, E.Movier | 600.00 |
| Soda Shop, White Cased, Opal Shades, Geometric Shape, C.1910 | 90.00 |
| Stained Glass, Patinated Metal, Handel Type, 22 1/4 In. | 500.00 |
| Student, Adjustable, Single, American, 19th Century, Brass, 21 N. | 300.00 |
| Student, Sand-Weighted Base, Adjustable Shade, Candle Arm, Tin | 1400.00 |
| Student, Single Arm, Opaque White Shade, American, 20 1/4 In. | 190.00 |
| Table, Coinspot Mother-Of-Pearl Shade, Brass, 24 1/4 In. | 695.00 |
| Table, Jefferson, Reverse Painted Shade, 2336, 21 1/2 In. ........................ Illus | 550.00 |
| Table, Princess Feather, Squat, Milk Glass | 295.00 |
| Table, Reverse Painted Shade, Spelter Base, Forest Scene | 195.00 |
| Table, Stained Glass, 6 Panels, H.Z.Best Lamp Co., Chicago, 21 In. | 200.00 |
| Teardrop-Eyewinker, Plume Frosted Font | 150.00 |
| Thuro 250 Degree, Teardrop Thumbprint | 65.00 |
| LAMP, TIFFANY, see Tiffany, Lamp | |
| Tulip, Alabaster Shades, Bronze, A.Cheuret, 15 In., Pair .......................... Illus | 5000.00 |
| Vienna Polychromed, Arab Figure | 300.00 |
| Whale Oil, Amethyst Cut To Clear, Marble Base | 175.00 |
| Whale Oil, Ball Font, Wafer Connector, 3-Step Scalloped Base, 3 1/4 In. | 145.00 |
| Whale Oil, Bird Holds Shell Between Feet, Wick Out Of Mouth, Bronze | 300.00 |

Lamp, Tulip, Alabaster Shades, Bronze, A.Cheuret, 15 In., Pair

| | |
|---|---:|
| Whale Oil, Brass Collar, Blown & Pressed, Paneled Font, 8 1/2 In. | 125.00 |
| Whale Oil, Brass, 2-Wick Burner, Inverted Acorn Font, 3 3/4 In. | 310.00 |
| Whale Oil, Bull's Eye, Flint, Pewter Burner | 85.00 |
| Whale Oil, Cast Handle Chamber, 2 Wick, 6 In. | 175.00 |
| Whale Oil, Cylindrical Font, Single Wick, Pewter, 4 In. | 175.00 |
| Whale Oil, Diamond Point Font, Sandwich Glass, C.1850, 10 1/4 In., Pair | 250.00 |
| Whale Oil, Double Wick Holder, Ring Burner, Flint Glass, 6 1/2 In. | 90.00 |
| Whale Oil, Ellipse, Coach Lamp Burner, 10 In. | 115.00 |
| Whale Oil, Hand, Moon & Star Pattern | 95.00 |
| Whale Oil, Haystack Shape, Tin, 7 1/4 In. | 45.00 |
| Whale Oil, Pear Shape, Opaque White, Sandwich Glass, C.1825, 10 In. | 300.00 |
| Whale Oil, Peg, Single Burner, Tin | 55.00 |
| Whale Oil, Petticoat, Handled, 3-Wick Burner, Tin, 5 1/2 In. | 125.00 |
| Whale Oil, Ring Stem, Trefoil Base, Paw Feet, American, 12 1/2 In., Pair | 150.00 |
| Whale Oil, Sandwich Glass Clambroth Base, Double Wick, 12 1/2 In. | 100.00 |
| Whale Oil, Sandwich Glass, Pewter Collar, Twin Tube Burner, 7 In. | 130.00 |
| Whale Oil, Sandwich, Horn Of Plenty, Pair | 450.00 |
| Whale Oil, Sparking, Miniature | 75.00 |
| Whale Oil, Thumbprint & Waffle, Hexagonal Base, American, 12 In., Pair | 125.00 |
| Whale Oil, Tin, Cone Shaped, Pewter Handle, Double Wick, 5 In. | 110.00 |
| Whale Oil, Triple Flute Pattern, Brass Column, Marble Base | 155.00 |
| Whale Oil, Twin Tube, Pewter Fittings, Pedestal Glass, 6 3/4 In. | 195.00 |
| Whale Oil, Umbilicated Sawtooth, 2 Thumbprints | 135.00 |
| Wheat In Shield, Pressed Glass, 7 In. | 60.00 |
| Windmill & Boat Scene, Bass Base, Handle, 16 1/2 In. | 1000.00 |
| LANTERN, Buggy, Dietz, Dated 1904, Red Glass | 35.00 |
| Buggy, Dietz, Eureka | 35.00 |
| Buggy, Rayco, Stamped C. & O. | 85.00 |
| Candle, Cage Form, Tin | 225.00 |
| Candle, Folding, Triangular, C.1810, Tin | 68.00 |
| Clear Globe, Brass Burner, Glass Font, New England Glass Co., Tin | 175.00 |
| Coach, Oval Beveled Fronts, Silver Plated Inside, 14 1/2 In., Pair | 300.00 |
| Dietz, Kerosene, High Low | 10.00 |
| Dietz, Navy, Deck, Brass, C.1910 | 110.00 |
| Dietz, Policeman's, Bull's-Eye Lens, Brown | 30.00 |
| Dietz, Scout, Skater's, C.1904 | 39.00 |
| Dietz, Traffic Guard, No.40, Red With Red Globe, 8 In. | 21.00 |
| Embossed The Stonebridge, Folding, Dated 1908, Tin | 38.00 |
| Fireman's, Dietz, Steel, Clear Globe | 15.00 |
| Hanging, Half Round, Glass Face, Pierced Tin Door, Iron & Tin, 14 In. | 165.00 |
| Horn, Original Horn, Tin, 15 In. | 225.00 |
| Horn, 17 In. | 225.00 |
| Kerosene, Hanging, Stove, Copper Frame, Milk Glass Chimney, 16 In. | 95.00 |

Mercury Metal Reflector, Wall Mounted, Cast Iron Trivet, 16 In. ............................................. 140.00
Miner's, Permissible Flame Safety Lamp ................................................................................. 50.00
Parade, Marked Abraham The Faithful, C.1860, Tin, 10 In. .................................................... 400.00
Pierced, Top Loop, Brass, Miniature .................................................................................... 625.00
    LANTERN, RAILROAD, see, Railroad, Lantern
Skater's, Globe, Tin ............................................................................................................... 45.00
Skater's, Tubular Shaped, Hurricane Lantern Co., Brass ........................................................ 68.00
Whale Oil, Tin Top & Base, Original Glass Globe ................................................................. 200.00

*Le Verre Francais*

Le Verre Francais cameo glass was made in France between 1920 and 1933
by the C. Schneider Factory. It is mottled and usually
decorated with floral designs, and bears the incised signature
Le Verre Francais.

LE VERRE FRANCAIS, Bowl, Green Base, Shaded To Purple, Rectangular, 7 1/2 In. ........... 350.00
Charger, Cameo, Art Deco Design, Mottled, Marked, 12 In. ................................................. 300.00
Pitcher, Orange & White, Purple Handles, Signed, 11 In. ..................................................... 325.00
Planter, Green, Deep Red, & Clear ...................................................................................... 275.00
Vase, Brown & Blue Sides, Cut Design, Mottled, 14 In. ....................................................... 750.00
Vase, Brown, Blue, Green, Gold, France-Ovington, 9 In. ...................................................... 550.00
Vase, Burgundy Drapes Against Mottled Ground, 15 In. ...................................................... 295.00
Vase, Mottled Design, Orange Ground, Signed, 5 1/2 In. ..................................................... 650.00
Vase, Orange & Green Canes, Orange Base, Signed, 10 In. ................................................. 367.00
Vase, Orange Leaves, Frosted Ground, Signed, 3 3/4 In. ..................................................... 150.00
Vase, Pedestal, Flower Down Full Length, Purple, 19 1/2 In ................................................ 845.00
Vase, Pedestal, Stylized Landscape, 4 1/2 In. ..................................................................... 375.00
Vase, Pedestal, Yellow & Green Berries, Signed, 10 X 6 In. ................................................ 750.00
Vase, Red Dotted Flowers, Mottled Ground, 17 In. .............................................................. 390.00
Vase, Tortoiseshell Outside, Orange, Green, Signed, 19 In. ................................................. 875.00
Vase, Vertical Canes, Orange Pedestal Base, Signed, 10 In. ............................................... 367.00

LEATHER, Album, Photograph, 11 X 8 In. ............................................................................. 27.50
Bag, Marble ........................................................................................................................... 10.00
Bookends, Hinged, Italian, 4 X 5 In. .................................................................................... 10.00
Case, 3 Cigar, Spanish ......................................................................................................... 10.00
Collar, Horse, Steel Hame, Brass Knobs ............................................................................... 29.50
Hat, Fireman's ....................................................................................................................... 85.00
Muffler, Horse Hoof, Funereal, Handmade, Set Of 4 ........................................................... 360.00
Pack Saddle, Miner's, Blanket .............................................................................................. 99.00
Pocketbook, Embossed White House On Metal Lid, Brown Shoe Co. .................................. 22.50
Saddle Bags, Hexagonal Medallion, Anatolian, 2 1/2 X 4 Ft. 11 In. ................................... 700.00
Saddle, Bonnie Allen, Dated 1873 ..................................................................................... 1000.00
Saddle, Side, Hand-Tooled ................................................................................................... 425.00
Valise, Tooled, Dover, N.H. Label ......................................................................................... 48.00

# LEEDS POTTERY.

Leeds pottery was made at Leeds, Yorkshire, England, from 1774 to 1878.
Most Leeds ware was not marked. Early Leeds pieces had distinctive
twisted handles with a greenish glaze on part of the creamy ware. Later ware
often had blue borders on the creamy pottery.

LEEDS, Jug, Yellow Glazed, Black Transfer Printed, Dated 1812 ..........................*Illus* 1100.00
Plate, Blue Embossed Border, Feather Edge, C.1790, 10 In., Set Of 6 .................................. 330.00
Plate, C.1790, Blue Embossed, 10 In., Set Of 6 .................................................................... 325.00
Plate, Creamware, Blue Embossed Border Design, C.1790, 10 In., Set Of 6 ........................ 330.00
Platter, Green Feather Edge, 18 1/2 X 14 1/2 In. .................................................................. 150.00
Teapot, Pagodas & Plants, Flower Finial, C.1780, 7 In. ........................................................ 200.00

Leeds, Jug, Yellow Glazed, Black Transfer Printed, Dated 1812

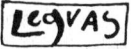 *Legras was founded in 1864 by Auguste Legras at St. Denis, France.
It is best known for Art Nouveau and cameo glass wares. Legras merged
with Pantin in 1920 and became the Verreries et Cristalleries de St.
Denis et de Pantin Reunies.*

| | |
|---|---|
| **LEGRAS, Bowl,** Green Ivy & Red Cherries, Enameled, Signed, 8 1/2 In. | 300.00 |
| **Cookie Jar,** Open Flower Cut To Peach Ground, Brass Fittings, Signed | 600.00 |
| **Lamp,** Birds In Flight, White & Pink Ground, Signed, 12 1/2 In. | 995.00 |
| **Rose Bowl,** Pink Tint, Cameo Leaves & Berries, Signed, 3 1/2 X 4 In. | 325.00 |
| **Vase,** Acid Cut, Gold Design, Etched Marking, 8 In. | 500.00 |
| **Vase,** Cameo & Enamel, Scenic, Trees, Lake, Mountains, 5 3/4 In. | 324.00 |
| **Vase,** Cameo, Berry, 9 In. | 550.00 |
| **Vase,** Cameo, Butterfly & Leaves, Pink To Apricot, 6 1/2 In. | 795.00 |
| **Vase,** Cameo, Pink Ground, Purple Flowers, Signed, 8 1/2 In. | 250.00 |
| **Vase,** Clear Base, Blue, Yellow, & Green Enameling, 13 In., Pair | 1000.00 |
| **Vase,** Deep Cut Floral, 2-Handled, 12 In. | 800.00 |
| **Vase,** Enameled Trees, Lake, Hexagonal Top, 11 In. | 275.00 |
| **Vase,** Enameled Winter Scene, 4-Sided, Signed, 11 1/2 In. | 235.00 |
| **Vase,** Floral Maroon Squares, Rose Pink, Bulbous, 10 X 29 In.Diam. | 185.00 |
| **Vase,** Frosted Blue & Green Ground, Autumn Scene, Signed, 5 1/2 In. | 475.00 |
| **Vase,** Frosted Cherries & Leaves, Signed, 4 1/2 In. | 150.00 |
| **Vase,** Orange, Cameo Bridge, Stream, Bushes, Trees, Signed, 4 In. | 675.00 |
| **Vase,** Pink & White Blossoms, Green Ground, Signed, 19 1/2 In. | 1250.00 |
| **Vase,** Purple Foliage, Wine Frosted Ground, Bullet Shape, 11 In. | 325.00 |
| **Vase,** Purple Geometric Design, Pink & White, Signed, 12 3/4 In. | 995.00 |
| **Vase,** Purple Grapes & Leaves, 8 1/4 In. | 425.00 |
| **Vase,** Scenic Mountains, Trees, Pink Frosted Ground, Signed, 6 In. | 350.00 |
| **Vase,** Seaweed & Butterfly, Green & Brown, Beige Ground, 15 1/2 In. | 750.00 |
| **Vase,** Topaz, Peach, Blossoms, Leafage, Burgundy, Ovoid, Signed, 10 In. | 275.00 |
| **Vase,** Trees & Bushes In Shaded Brown, Colored Ground, Signed, 24 In. | 1875.00 |
| **Vase,** Two Swirled Bands, Geometric Carved Design, 6 1/2 In. | 550.00 |
| **Vase,** Two White Swans On Water, Enameled, 11 1/2 In. | 550.00 |
| **Vase,** White Flowers, Enameled, Burnt Orange Neck, 6 In. | 150.00 |
| **Vase,** Winter Scene, Woman Walking On Snow-Clad Terrain, 14 1/4 In. | 310.00 |
| **Vase,** Yellow, Gold, Brown, & Green Ground, 2 Swirled Bands, 6 1/2 In. | 550.00 |

 *Lenox china was made in Trenton, New Jersey, after 1906. The firm also
makes a porcelain similar to Belleek.*

**LENOX, see also Ceramic Art Co.**

| | |
|---|---|
| **LENOX, Atomizer,** Penguin, Figural, Felt Wings, Marked De Vilbiss | 90.00 To 125.00 |
| **Bottle,** Hattie Carnegie Bath Oil, Figural Head Stopper | 85.00 |

| | |
|---|---|
| **Bowl,** Baby Chicks, Gold Trim, Marked, Green Wreath, 5 X 2 1/4 In. | 55.00 |
| **Bowl,** Blossom Shape, Underplate, Silver Overlay Radials, 6 In.Diam. | 55.00 |
| **Bowl,** Blue, Pink, Yellow, Floral, Palette Mark, Signed, 9 X 5 1/4 In. | 225.00 |
| **Bowl,** Centerpiece, Gold Handle & Rim, Footed, 12 In. | 38.00 |
| **Bowl,** Centerpiece, Priscilla, Blue Cornflowers, Fluted, 12 In. | 45.00 |
| **Bowl,** Covered, Ming Pattern, Black Wreath Mark, 4 X 5 1/2 In.Diam. | 95.00 |
| **Bowl,** Enameled Flower Border | 55.00 |
| **Bowl,** Flanged, Gilt Rim, Oval, 9 3/8 In.Long, Pair | 110.00 |
| **Bowl,** Fruit, Ming | 75.00 |
| **Bowl,** Nautilus Shape, Ivory, Green Mark, 9 In.Diam. | 17.00 |
| **Bowl,** Priscilla Pattern, Blue Cornflowers, Fluted Top, 12 X 4 In. | 50.00 |
| **Bowl,** Priscilla, Blue Cornflowers, Fluted, 12 X 4 In. | 50.00 |
| **Bowl,** Slanted Top, Embossed Rim, Green Wreath, 4 1/4 In.Diam. | 20.00 |
| **Box,** Cigarette, Hand-Painted Pheasants, Gold Mark, 5 X 3 1/2 In. | 50.00 |
| **Box,** Powder, Covered, Woman's Head Finial, Green Wreath Mark, 4 1/2 In. | 135.00 |
| **Box,** Powder, Hattie Carnegie, Figural Head Finial | 75.00 |
| **Candlestick,** Roses On Vine, Palette Mark, 8 1/4 In., Pair | 145.00 |
| **Character Jug,** William Penn, 3/4 Figure, Cream Glaze, 6 3/4 In. | 225.00 |
| **Coffeepot,** Fairmount | 75.00 |
| **Coffeepot,** Medallions, Turquoise Enamel Beading, Gold Trim | 75.00 |
| **Compote,** Blue Bands, Fruit On Border, Green Wreath, 5 1/4 X 2 1/2 In. | 55.00 |
| **Compote,** Pedestal, Silver Overlay, Green Wreath Mark, 5 1/2 In.Diam. | 195.00 |
| **Creamer,** Weatherly | 20.75 |
| **Cup & Saucer,** Coral, Demitasse | 25.00 |
| **Cup & Saucer,** Fluted & Scalloped, Flower Inside Cup, Green Wreath | 40.00 |
| **Cup & Saucer,** Gold Handle & Rim, Stylized Flowers | 20.00 |
| **Cup & Saucer,** Ming | 15.00 |
| **Cup & Saucer,** Ming, Demitasse | 25.00 |
| **Cup & Saucer,** Mt.Vernon, Pair | 95.00 |
| **Cup & Saucer,** Peachtree, Large | 10.00 |
| **Cup & Saucer,** Red Rose & Coin Gold Leaves | 23.00 |
| **Cup & Saucer,** Saratoga Springs, N.Y., 1831, 1933 Historical China | 45.00 |
| **Cup & Saucer,** Shell, Demitasse, Green Wreath Mark | 25.00 |
| **Cup & Saucer,** Wishbone Handle, White Ribbed, Demitasse | 25.00 |
| **Cup,** Bouillon, Saucer, Pink Roses, Tiffany Silver Holder | 195.00 |
| **Cup,** Boullion, Wedding Band Design, Sterling Silver Holder | 38.00 |
| **Cup,** Cherubs, Pedestal, Square Base | 85.00 |
| **Cup,** Gold Trim, Copper Holder, Handled | 35.00 |
| **Dish,** Candy, Blossom Shape, Silver Plate Holder, 6 In.Diam. | 65.00 |
| **Dish,** Candy, Low Pedestal, Silver Overlay, Marked, R.S.Co., 5 3/4 In. | 55.00 |
| **Dish,** Candy, Shell Shape, Blue, 6 In. | 29.50 |
| **Dish,** Candy, Shell Shape, White, 6 In. | 29.50 |
| **Dish,** Fruit, Cretan, 12 In. | 120.00 |
| **Dish,** Leaf Shape, Gold Rim, 8 1/2 In. | 22.00 |
| **Dish,** Shell Shape, Coral, Gilded, Green Wreath Mark, 2 X 6 In. | 38.00 |
| **Dish,** Shell Shape, Scroll-Type Handle, Oval, 3 1/2 X 6 X 2 1/2 In. | 28.00 |
| **Dish,** Soup, Coral Around, Gold Rim, Green Mark, 9 1/2 In., Set Of 8 | 65.00 |
| **Feeding Set,** Child's, Black & Red Roosters, Green Wreath Mark, 2 Piece | 95.00 |
| **Figurine,** Bird, Tail Up, Tail Down, Green Mark, Pair | 30.00 To 32.00 |
| **Figurine,** Bird, Wings Down, White, Green Wreath Mark | 25.00 |
| **Figurine,** Bird, Wings Over Back, White, Green Wreath Mark | 25.00 |
| **Figurine,** Swan, Coral & Gilding, Green Wreath Mark, 3 X 4 1/4 In. | 38.00 |
| **Honey Pot,** Cover, Applied Gold Bees Top & Sides, Green Mark, 5 In. | 79.50 |
| **Jar,** Jam, Grape, Blue, 3 1/2 In., Underplate | 30.00 |
| **Jug,** Brandy, Silver Stopper, Handle, Green To Brown, Green Mark, 7 In. | 145.00 |
| **Lamp,** Nude Lady, 1929 | 500.00 |
| **Letter Holder & Blotter,** Rolling, Ivory, Pink Ribbon Design | 250.00 |
| **Mayonnaise Set,** Blue Bands, Fruit Border, Green Wreath, 3 1/2 In. | 60.00 |
| **Mug,** Acorn Design, Brown & Rust, Hand-Painted | 85.00 |
| **Mug,** Gilt Handled, Landscape In Berry Border, Signed, 1912 | 95.00 |
| **Mug,** Hand-Painted, Gold Rim, 5 In. | 75.00 |
| **Mug,** Masonic Temple, Atlantic City Convention, Green Wreath | 75.00 |
| **Mug,** River Scene, Blackberries On Edge, Gold Trim & Handle | 65.00 |

**Mug,** W.Penn Treaty, 3/4 Figure, Indian Head Handle, Green Mark, 7 In. ............... 195.00
**Pitcher,** Cider, Allover Grapes & Leaves ............................................................. 125.00
**Pitcher,** Cream, Pedestal, Gold Handle, Marked, 6 1/2 In. ..................................... 33.00
**Pitcher,** Dimpled Surface, Mask Spout, Cream Glaze, 3 X 5 X 8 In. ......................... 95.00
**Pitcher,** Gold Leaf Handle, Enamel & Gold Florals, Scepter Mark, 8 In. ................... 185.00
**Pitcher,** Milk, Stylized Bird Design, 7 In. ............................................................. 45.00
**Plate,** Art Deco Design In Silver, Green, & Black, Green Wreath, 9 In. ..................... 55.00
**Plate,** Dinner, Blue Tree ..................................................................................... 14.50
**Plate,** Dinner, Harvest ........................................................................................ 15.00
**Plate,** Sheraton, Black, Set Of 12 ....................................................................... 240.00
**Plate,** Sheraton, 10 1/2 In.Diam. ......................................................................... 40.00
**Plate,** Swimming Fish, Coral & Seaweed, Signed, Green Wreath, 9 In. ..................... 95.00
**Plate,** Trent Pattern, 5 3/4 In.Diam. ..................................................................... 35.00
**Plate,** Washington, Wakefield, 12 1/2 In.Diam. ..................................................... 40.00
**Ramekin,** Underplate, Embossed Gold Band, Ovington Bros. .................................. 35.00
**Salt & Pepper,** His Master's Voice, Pair ........................................... 25.00 To 30.00
**Salt & Pepper,** World's Fair, Yellow ..................................................................... 50.00
**Salt & Pepper,** 1934 World's Fair, White ............................................................. 30.00
**Salt,** Figural, Swan, Green Mark .......................................................................... 20.00
**Sugar & Creamer,** Brown, Silver Overlay, L In Green Wreath, Unicorn ..................... 60.00
**Sugar & Creamer,** Fairmount .............................................................................. 40.00
**Sugar & Creamer,** Floral Silver Overlay, Cobalt Blue ............................................ 95.00
**Sugar & Creamer,** Footed, Gold Handles, Palette Mark ......................................... 95.00
**Sugar & Creamer,** Footed, Gold Incrustations On Cream Body ............................... 95.00
**Sugar,** Weatherly .............................................................................................. 22.75
**Swan,** Open, Ivory Glaze, Gilded Top Edge, 4 1/2 In. ............................................. 32.00
**Swan,** Open, Pink Glaze, Green Mark, 6 1/2 In. ..................................................... 55.00
**Syrup,** Silver Overlay, 5 3/4 In. ........................................................................... 90.00
**Tankard,** Copper & Silver Top, Friar Emptying Keg Into Bottle, 16 In. ..................... 395.00
**Tankard,** Seated Friar, Dated 1896, Purple Wreath Mark, 16 In. ............................. 350.00
**Tea Caddy,** Covered, White, Palette Mark ........................................................... 25.00
**Tea Set,** Art Nouveau, Sterling Silver Overlay Trim, 3 Piece ................................... 175.00
**Tea Set,** Hawthorne Pattern, Black Mark, 3 Piece ................................................ 165.00
**Teapot,** Ming, 6 In. ........................................................................................... 90.00
**Teapot,** Sterling Overlay On Brown, Green Wreath ............................................... 110.00
**Teapot,** Swan Shape, Neck & Head Form Spout, Swan Finial, Green Wreath ............ 325.00
**Toby Mug,** George Washington, C.1896, Signed, 5 In. ............................................ 575.00
**Toby Mug,** William Penn, Green Mark, 6 3/4 In. ............................. 115.00 To 165.00
**Tray,** Hand-Painted Flower Chain, Open Handles, Palette Mark, 14 In. ..................... 125.00
**Tray,** Handled, 2 Gold Bands On Edge, Cream Ground, 9 In.Square .......................... 45.00
**Tray,** Plume Shape, Marked ................................................................................ 40.00
**Tray,** Sterling Overlay, White, Palette Mark, 19 X 11 In. ....................................... 185.00
**Urn,** Reticulated Wing Shape, Footed, Covered, Green Mark, 9 In. ........................... 225.00
**Urn,** Swan Handles, Square Pedestal Base, Green Mark, 11 In., Pair ........................ 140.00
**Urn,** 3-Handled, Silver Medallion, Green Wreath Mark, 5 1/4 In. ............................. 145.00
**Vase,** Art Nouveau, Turquoise Ground, Gold Trim, Marked, 11 1/2 In. ...................... 120.00
**Vase,** Beige, White Flower Design, 8 1/2 In. ......................................................... 45.00
**Vase,** Bud, Bulbous, Ribbed Neck, Flared Top, Green Wreath Mark, 7 In. ................... 35.00
**Vase,** Bulbous Bottom, Rose Design, White Ground, Green Mark, 7 1/2 In. ................ 25.00
**Vase,** Coral Ribbed, Relief Flowers, Green Wreath Mark, 6 In. ................................ 52.00
**Vase,** Double, Curved Tube Shape, Pink Handle, 7 In. ............................................. 55.00
**Vase,** Drape Design, Cobalt Ground, Green Mark, 12 In. ......................................... 40.00
**Vase,** Fluted, Green Wreath, 10 In. ...................................................................... 45.00
**Vase,** Footed, Lenox Rose, Pink, Green Wreath Mark, 7 In. ..................................... 42.00
**Vase,** Gold Handles, Hand-Painted Yellow & Red Roses, 18 In. ............................... 140.00
**Vase,** Gold Leaves & Blossoms, White Ground, Green Wreath Mark, 10 In. ............... 265.00
**Vase,** Hand-Painted Urns Of Fruit, Cockatoos, Palette Mark, 11 1/2 In. .................... 95.00
**Vase,** Hexagonal, Artist Signed, 8 In. ................................................................... 120.00
**Vase,** Horn Of Plenty Shape, Rose Pattern, Signed, 8 In. ........................................ 55.00
**Vase,** Horn Of Plenty, Handled, Gold Rim, Green Mark, 6 1/4 In. .............................. 35.00
**Vase,** Lenox Rose Design, Reticulated Handles, Green Mark ................................... 125.00
**Vase,** Melon Ribbed Bottom, Claw Feet, Green Wreath Mark, 5 In. ........................... 40.00
**Vase,** Purple Iridescent, Palette Mark, 8 In. ......................................................... 30.00

Vase, Rose Bouquets, Green Mark, 4 1/2 X 10 1/4 In. ...................................................... 38.00

LETTER OPENER, Athey Truss Wheel Co., Chicago, Caterpillar Tracks, Brass ...................... 22.50
  Bone, Carved Design, 8 1/2 In. ...................................................................................... 12.00
  Brass Turkey Claw, Embossed Inglovin .......................................................................... 12.00
  Child's Head, Marked Vienna, Bronze, 7 3/4 In. ........................................................... 60.00
  Cloisonne Handle, Brass ................................................................................................ 25.00
  Cowboy Boot Shape, Copper ......................................................................................... 8.00
  Dagger Shape, Ivory, 8 1/2 In. ...................................................................................... 15.00
  Dagger Shape, Sterling Silver Handle, 6 1/4 In. ............................................................ 12.00
  El Belmont Cigars, New York Cigar Co. On Reverse, Celluloid ....................................... 22.00
  Embossed Royal Typewriter, Cast Iron, 9 1/2 In. .......................................................... 22.00
  Figural, Gold Club ........................................................................................................ 13.50
  Figural, Hand-Carved, Elijah Pierce ............................................................................... 225.00
  Figural, Mother-Of-Pearl Indian Chief, Head, 3 1/2 In. .................................................. 12.50
  Figural, Saumari Sword, Bamboo Handle, Advertising, 7 1/2 In. ..................................... 13.00
  Figural, Uneeda Boy ..................................................................................................... 52.00
  Fuller Brush ................................................................................................................. 2.50
  Gold, Dore Zodiac, Tiffany ........................................................................................... 85.00
  Indian On Handle, Lake Geneva, Wisc., Celluloid .......................................................... 10.00
  Kansas City Barrel Co., Bronze ..................................................................................... 15.00
  Lincoln, Full Figure ...................................................................................................... 28.00
  Marked Verdun, 1918, Handmade, Copper ..................................................................... 18.00
  Mother-Of-Pearl Handle, Sterling Silver Blade ............................................................... 45.00
  New Process Stoves ...................................................................................................... 8.00
  Ohio Valley Casket Co., Cincinnati, Metal ..................................................................... 9.00
  Ornate Ivory Handle ..................................................................................................... 9.00
  Pictures Bird Dog's Head, Bird In Mouth, Kansas City Roofing ...................................... 25.00
  Piece Of World War I Shrapnel ..................................................................................... 21.00
  Prisoner Of War, France, 1917, Crown & Cross On Top ................................................. 32.00
  Samurai Sword Shape, Eardley's Dixie Oil & Gas, 7 1/2 In. ........................................... 13.00
  Shape Of Wrench, Advertising, Celluloid ....................................................................... 18.00
  Souvenir, Blakesley, Tuttle Stove Co., Kansas, Bakelite ................................................. 15.00
  St.Louis World's Fair, Figural, 1904, Brass ................................................................... 45.00
  Vermont Mutual Fire Ins., Brass ................................................................................... 11.00
  Victor Chemical Works, Embossed Barrel ...................................................................... 25.00
  Vienna, Signed, Bronze, 6 X 9 In. ................................................................................ 135.00
  1921 Triennial Convocation R.A.M.Of Iowa .................................................................. 26.00

LIBBEY, Banana Boat, Brilliant Cut, 5 In.Wide ................................................................ 250.00
  Basket, Lovebirds Pattern, Signed, 12 In. ..................................................................... 90.00
  Biscuit Jar, Delft Design, Oval Punties, Covered, Signed, 6 In. ...................................... 175.00
  Bottle, Water, 2-Way Beveled Bulbous Body, Signed ..................................................... 145.00
  Bowl, American Brilliant Cut, Signed, Saber Mark, 9 X 4 1/2 In. .................................... 295.00
  Bowl, Bishop's Hat Type, Tab Handles, Signed, 11 1/4 In.Diam. ..................................... 535.00
  Bowl, Brilliant Cut, Signed, 9 X 4 1/2 In. ..................................................................... 289.00
  Bowl, Colonna Pattern, Signed, 9 In.Diam. .................................................................... 325.00
  Bowl, Flower, Venetia Pattern, Signed, 6 X 8 In.Diam. .................................................. 250.00
  Bowl, Harvard Pattern, Straight Sides, 10 X 4 In. .......................................................... 395.00
  Bowl, Rib Cut & Blocks On Rim, Signed, 9 X 1 1/4 In. ................................................. 35.00
  Bowl, Sawtooth Edge, Ornate Design, Signed ................................................................ 95.00
  Butter, Covered, Underplate, Diamond & Hobstar, Floria Pattern, 8 In. ........................... 325.00
  Celery, Laurent Pattern, Signed .................................................................................... 200.00
  Cocktail, Black Kangaroo Stem, Signed ......................................................................... 110.00
  Compote, Amberina, Signed, 5 In.Diam. ....................................................................... 495.00
  Compote, Flute, Signed, Pair ........................................................................................ 495.00
  Compote, Fuchsia, Amberina, Signed, 5 X 4 3/4 In. ...................................................... 235.00
  Compote, Hobstars, Strawberries, Pyramidal Stars, Signed, 8 X 7 In. .............................. 275.00
  Cordial, Hobstar, Diamond, Fan, Signed, 3 1/8 In. ........................................................ 75.00
  Cordial, Morning Mist, Opalescent, 3 1/2 In. ................................................................ 125.00
  Cup, Punch, Marcella, Cut Handle ................................................................................ 135.00
  Decanter, Harvard Pattern, 11 3/4 In. ........................................................................... 350.00
  Decanter, Princess Pattern, Signed, 12 1/2 In. .............................................................. 435.00

| | |
|---|---|
| **Dish,** Acorn Shape, Kimberly Pattern, 9 1/2 X 8 3/4 In. | 425.00 |
| **Dish,** Ice Cream, Diamonds & Fans, Signed, 6 In., Set Of 6 | 125.00 |
| **Dish,** Jewel Pattern, Signed, 10 In. | 150.00 |
| **Dish,** Pickle, Scalloped, Hobstar & Crosshatch, 4 X 8 In.Diam. | 50.00 |
| **Dish,** Polished Oval Cutting Underneath, 7 In. | 25.00 |
| **Glass,** Juice, Corinthian, Signed, Pair | 75.00 |
| **Glass,** Juice, Harvard, Pair | 70.00 |
| **Goblet,** Champagne Shape, Intaglio Cut Floral & Leaf, Pair | 75.00 |
| **Goblet,** Eagle Stem, Crystal | 17.50 |
| **Goblet,** Intaglio Cut Flowers & Leaf, Panel Cut Stem, Signed, Pair | 75.00 |
| **Mayonnaise,** Underplate, Flute Cut, Signed | 105.00 |
| **Mayonnaise,** Underplate, Gem Pattern, Signed | 195.00 |
| **Paperweight,** Frosted Lady's Head, Columbian Exposition, 1893, Signed | 225.00 |
| **Paperweight,** Lady's Profile, World's Fair, Libbey Glass Co., Toledo | 285.00 |
| **Pitcher,** Champagne, Hobstars, Cane, 11 In. | 295.00 |
| **Plate,** Colonna Pattern, Signed, 7 In.Diam. | 225.00 |
| **Plate,** Gloria Pattern, 8 In.Diam. | 150.00 |
| **Rose Bowl,** Crosshatching, Diamond & Fan, Signed, 6 X 3 1/2 In. | 165.00 |
| **Rose Bowl,** Hobstar, Crosshatch, & Fan, 6 1/2 X 5 1/4 In.Diam. | 250.00 |
| **Salt & Pepper,** Egg On Side, 1893 Exposition, Blue, Signed | 150.00 |
| **Stemware,** Animal Silhouette, Opalescent Cat, Signed | 125.00 |
| **Sugar & Creamer,** Gem Pattern, Signed | 145.00 |
| **Sugar & Creamer,** Matching Lid, Pedestal, Signed | 2000.00 |
| **Tumbler,** Allover Cut, 24-Point Star On Base, Signed | 60.00 |
| **Tumbler,** Butterflies, Cattails, & Dragonflies, Signed | 35.00 |
| **Tumbler,** Flat Flute Cuts, Signed, 3 In., Set Of 4 | 35.00 |
| **Tumbler,** Square Footed, Signed, Set Of 6 | 180.00 |
| **Vase,** Cobalt Blue, Cut To Clear, Overlay, 12 In. | 685.00 |
| **Vase,** Crimped, Engraved Floral Design, C.1816, 8 In. | 95.00 |
| **Vase,** Flowers & Ferns, Crystal, Footed, Signed | 195.00 |
| **Vase,** Harvard Pattern, Green Cut To Clear, 12 In. | 600.00 |
| **Vase,** Leaves & Flowers, Swirling Around, Signed, 14 In. | 400.00 |
| **Vase,** Radiant Pattern, Paper Label Over Signature, Signed, 1i In. | 385.00 |
| **Vase,** Sweet Pea, Lily-Of-The-Valley, Signed, 4 1/4 X 6 In.Diam. | 245.00 |
| **Whiskey Set,** Jug & 6 Shots, Star In Circle Mark, 7 Piece | 925.00 |
| **Wine,** Hobstar Cutting, 4 1/2 In. | 70.00 |

**LIGHTING DEVICES, see Candleholder; Candlestick; Lamp; etc.**

*Lightning rod balls are collected for their variety of shape and color. These glass balls were at the center of the rod that was attached to the roof of a house or barn to avoid lightning damage.*

| | |
|---|---|
| **LIGHTNING ROD, Ball,** Blue, Large | 21.00 |
| **Ball,** D. & S., 10-Sided, Blue | 10.00 |
| **Ball,** D. & S., 10-Sided, Clear | 18.00 |
| **Ball,** D. & S., 10-Sided, Opaque Turquoise | 18.00 |
| **Ball,** Moon & Star, Milk Glass, White | 10.00 |
| **Ball,** Ribbed Grapes, Opaque, Turquoise | 18.00 |
| **Ball,** 10-Sided, Blue Milk Glass, Marked D. & S. | 15.00 |

*Limoges porcelain has been made in Limoges, France, since the mid-nineteenth century. Fine porcelains were made by many factories, including Haviland, Ahrenfeldt, Guerin, Pouyat, Elite, and others.*

**LIMOGES, see also Haviland**

| | |
|---|---|
| **LIMOGES, Basket,** Bowtie Shape, Gold Handle, 1911, Marked, 10 X 7 X 3 1/2 In. | 47.50 |
| **Basket,** Handled, Gold Trim, Hand-Painted Inside & Out, Dated 1915 | 75.00 |
| **Basket,** Waste, Handled, Oval Top, Cupids With Globe, Gold Trim, 5 In. | 55.00 |

Bird Plate, Coronet, Signed, 11 In. ............................................................................. 95.00
Biscuit Jar, Handled, Roses, Blue Forget-Me-Nots, Gold Trim ............................... 85.00
Bone Dish, Leaf Shape, Set Of 8 ................................................................................ 50.00
Bottle, Cologne, Forget-Me-Nots, Gold Finial & Trim, 6 1/2 In. ............................. 45.00
Bottle, Cologne, Rose Design, Gold Stopper, Signed, 6 1/2 In. .............................. 35.00
Bottle, Perfume, Enameled, Gold Mark, 5 1/2 In., Pair ........................................... 52.50
Bowl, Coronet, Pink & Green Floral, Gold Trim, 6 In. .............................................. 38.00
Bowl, Covered, Berries & Vines, Rococo Border, Signed, 6 1/2 In. ........................ 140.00
Bowl, Cupids With Bows & Arrows, Clouds, Gold Swirls, 9 1/2 In. ......................... 95.00
Bowl, Footed, Gold Over White Florals, Signed, 10 In. ........................................... 125.00
Bowl, Fruit, Hand-Painted Peaches, Signed, Square, 10 In. ................................... 85.00
Bowl, Fruit, Irises, Gold Trim, Fluted Gold Border, Signed .................................... 45.00
Bowl, Gold Twig Handle, 11 X 9 In. ............................................................................ 195.00
Bowl, Irises, Artist Signed, 10 3/8 In. ....................................................................... 40.00
Bowl, Orange Poppies, Mint Green Ground, Gold Trim, 5 1/2 X 23 In. .................. 105.00
Bowl, Pastel Coloring, Swan On Lily Pad, 6 1/2 In.Diam. ....................................... 45.00
Bowl, Punch, Chrysanthemums, Scalloped, Raised Rim, 13 In. ............................. 225.00
Bowl, Punch, Grape Design, Gold Tracery, Verses At Base, 6 Mugs ...................... 1800.00
Bowl, Punch, Hand-Painted Flowers Inside & Out, 13 In. ...................................... 125.00
Bowl, Red Poppies On Cream, Elite, Gold Swag Border, 9 In. ............................... 55.00
Bowl, Soup, Pink Flowers, White, Open Rim, Ahrenfelt ......................................... 30.00
Bowl, Vegetable, Divided, Signed Ahrenfeldt .......................................................... 42.50
Box, Collar Button, Hand-Painted, Red Roses On Blue .......................................... 23.00
Box, Covered, Handkerchief, Hand-Painted Violets, Green, Square ...................... 95.00
Box, Match, Covered, Striker Base, Gold Design, Signed & Dated ........................ 25.00
Box, Powder, Covered, Pink Flowers, Green Leaves ............................................... 25.00
Box, Powder, Hand-Painted Roses, Covered ........................................................... 45.00
Box, Powder, Hinged Lid, Ivory Ground, Gold Trim, Marked, 7 X 3 In. ................. 75.00
Box, Powder, Portrait On Lid, Raised Turquoise & Gold Beads, 5 In. ................... 45.00
Box, Sardine, Hand-Painted Fish On Lid, Marked, 5 1/4 X 4 In. ............................ 32.00
Box, Stamp, 3 Sections, Gold Lines, Marked, 4 1/4 X 2 1/2 In. ............................ 45.00
Box, Trinket, Egg Shape, Floral Design, Brass Hinge & Clasp ............................... 25.00
Butter, Covered, Gold Trim, Blue ............................................................................... 35.00
Cake Plate, Gold Handles, Scalloped, Rose Design, Signed .................................. 60.00
Cake Plate, Pedestal, Silver Design .......................................................................... 25.00
Candlestick, Pink Flowers In Gold Baskets, Cream Ground ................................... 23.00
Celery, Hand-Painted, Floral Design, 11 1/2 X 5 1/2 In. ....................................... 25.00
Celery, Yellow Roses, Green Leaves, Yellow Ground, Signed, 14 In. ..................... 60.00
Chalice, Man Painted In Cartouche, Dated 1906, Signed, 10 In. ........................... 225.00
Charger, Forest Scene, Gold Rim & Leaves, Open Handled, 13 1/2 In. ................. 135.00
Charger, Hand-Painted, Peaches & Leaves, Artist Signed, 13 In. ......................... 55.00
Chocolate Pot, Cluster Of Forget-Me-Nots, White Ground, 9 1/2 In. .................... 45.00
Chocolate Pot, Floral Design, Ribbon Handle .......................................................... 139.00
Chocolate Pot, Gold & Roses ..................................................................................... 78.00
Chocolate Pot, Pink, Gold Trim .................................................................................. 85.00
Chocolate Pot, Violet, Gold Border, Marked ............................................................ 50.00
Chocolate Set, Cups With Lids, Gold Edged Tray, Birds & Flowers ....................... 125.00
Chocolate Set, Pink, Green, & White, Marked, Dated 1906 ...................... Illus 750.00
Chocolate Set, White Porcelain, Tooled Gold, Square Pedestal Base ................... 200.00
Chop Plate, Flowers, Coronet Pattern, 12 In. .......................................................... 35.00
Cider Set, Bulbous Pitcher, 4 Mugs, Hanging Apples, Marked .............................. 195.00
Cider Set, Geometric Rose, 3 Tumblers, Underplate, 5 Piece ............................... 125.00
Cup & Saucer, Demitasse, Elite, Roses .................................................................... 8.00
Cup & Saucer, Europa In Chariot, Diana & Cupid, Black Ground .......................... 450.00
Cup, Mustache, Underplate, Hand-Painted Roses .................................................. 40.00
Dish, Candy, Pink & Yellow Roses, Gold Handle, 10 X 7 In. ................................... 40.00
Dresser Set, Floral, Tray, Hair Receiver, Powder Jar, Bottles, Pin Box ................ 225.00
Dresser Set, Hand-Painted, Gray Ground, Gold Finials, 3 Piece .......................... 110.00
Egg Plate, 6 Wells, Chick, Hens, & Rooster Border, 5 1/2 X 9 1/2 In. ................. 65.00
Egg, Hand-Painted Design, Embellished With Gold, Hinged ................................. 35.00
Ewer, Beige, Hand-Painted Flowers, Gold Tracery, 7 1/4 In. ................................ 135.00
Ewer, Green Clover, Orange Ground, Gold Interior, Dated 1903, 12 In. ............... 175.00
Ewer, Wine, Lid, Gilded Scroll Finial, Hanging Grapes, Marked, 12 In. ............... 175.00

Limoges, Chocolate Set, Pink, Green,
& White, Marked, Dated 1906

| | |
|---|---:|
| **Fernery,** Hand-Painted Autumn Leaves | 75.00 |
| **Fernery,** Pastel Shaded, Enamel Flowers & Leaves, 7 1/2 X 5 In. | 85.00 |
| **Fish Set,** Artist Signed, 7 Piece | 275.00 |
| **Fish Set,** Coronet, Gravy Boat, Underplatter, 12 Plates | 1000.00 |
| **Fish Set,** Gold Trim, 10 Plates, Signed Dubois, Platter, 24 In. | 495.00 |
| **Fish Set,** Green, Gold Trim, Platter, 6 Plates, 6 Dishes | 375.00 |
| **Fish Set,** Marine Life Design, Green, C.1890, 6 Plates, Platter, 24 In. | 275.00 |
| **Fish Set,** Scalloped, Pink, 7 Piece | 750.00 |
| **Fish Set,** Sunset Ground, Marsh Scene With Trout, Signed, 7 Piece | 250.00 |
| **Fish Set,** 6 Plates, Gold Trim, Fish & Water Lilies, Platter 16 In. | 225.00 |
| **Fish Set,** 6 Plates, Hand-Painted, Signed, Platter, 16 X 11 In. | 275.00 |
| **Furniture,** Dollhouse, Miniature, Porcelain, Signed, 22 Pieces | 250.00 |
| **Game Plate,** Bird On Tree Limb, Rococo Gold, Signed, 11 1/2 In. | 150.00 |
| **Game Plate,** Gold Rococo Border, Marked, 9 In., Pair | 110.00 |
| **Game Plate,** Gold Twisted Rope Rim, Signed, 9 In.Diam., Pair | 90.00 |
| **Game Plate,** Hand-Painted Pheasants, Gold Border, Marked, 13 1/4 In. | 145.00 |
| **Game Plate,** Hunting Dogs, Signed | 75.00 |
| **Game Plate,** Pheasant, Marked B. & H. | 65.00 |
| **Game Plate,** Rococo Gold, Scalloped, Hand-Painted, Signed, 11 1/2 In. | 250.00 |
| **Game Plate,** Speckled Breast Bird, Rococo Gold Border, Signed, 10 In. | 110.00 |
| **Game Set,** Grouse Design, Dated 1909, 11 Plates, Platter | 252.00 |
| **Game Set,** Hand-Painted Birds, 12 Plates, Platter | 1650.00 |
| **Gravy Boat,** Attached Underplate, Autumn Leaf | 38.00 |
| **Hair Receiver,** Flowers, Artist Signed | 45.00 |
| **Hair Receiver,** Rose Design, Gold Stopper, Signed, 5 X 3 In. | 35.00 |
| **Hatpin Holder,** Flowers, Gold Leaves & Trim, 5 1/4 In. | 68.00 |
| **Hatpin Holder,** Pink Flowers, Outlined In Gold, Marked, 4 In. | 47.50 |
| **Hatpin Holder,** Silver Overlay Of Tulips & Leaves, Pink, 4 In. | 38.50 |
| **Humidor,** Brown, Peach, Blue Ground, Acorns & Leaves, 1908 | 60.00 |
| **Humidor,** Pine Design Allover, Pipe On Top, 5 In.Diam. | 50.00 |
| **Ice Bucket,** Open Handles, Artist Signed | 65.00 |
| **Jar,** Potpourri, Floral Design, Embossed Gold Scroll On White | 35.00 |
| **Jardiniere,** Purple & Gold, Footed | 245.00 |
| **Lemonade Set,** Mother-Of-Pearl Glaze, 6 Tumblers | 50.00 |
| **Lemonade Set,** Tray, Pitcher, 4 Tumblers, Grape Pattern, Signed | 270.00 |
| **Mug,** Apples & Leaves, Multicolor, 5 1/2 In. | 45.00 |
| **Mug,** Easter 1905, Grapes & Leaves, Black, Purple Border, Signed, 6 In. | 60.00 |
| **Mug,** Forget-Me-Not, Pearlized, Signed, 3 3/4 In. | 40.00 |
| **Mug,** Grapes, Signed Lynch, 5 In. | 45.00 |
| **Mug,** Green, Blue, Yellow, Pink Design, Yellow Violets, 3 1/2 In. | 22.00 |
| **Mug,** Pearlized, Forget-Me-Nots, Dated 1911, Signed | 40.00 |
| **Mug,** Purple Raspberries, Foliage & Blooms, Signed | 65.00 |
| **Mustard,** White To Pink, Tiny Pink Roses, Gold Trim | 35.00 |
| **Oyster Plate,** Gold Flowers, White Ground, Marked | 35.00 |
| **Oyster Plate,** Rococo Border, Hand-Painted, Signed, 21 X 8 1/2 In. | 150.00 |

| | |
|---|---:|
| **Oyster Plate,** Roses | 45.00 |
| **Oyster Set,** Scalloped Platter, C.1900, 6 Plates | 275.00 |
| **Pitcher,** Bulbous, Water Lily Pattern, 6 In. | 95.00 |
| **Pitcher,** Cherries On Brown & Peach Ground, Signed Wagner, 12 In. | 75.00 |
| **Pitcher,** Cider, Black Berries, Cream, Gold Handle, Squatty, Marked | 58.00 |
| **Pitcher,** Cider, Grapes, Hand-Painted, Gold Handle, 5 1/2 In. | 110.00 |
| **Pitcher,** Cider, Hand-Painted Apples, Dated 1902, 7 In.Diam. | 85.00 |
| **Pitcher,** Cider, Hand-Painted Raspberries & Flowers, 5 3/4 In. | 95.00 |
| **Pitcher,** Cider, Hand-Painted, Berries, Gold Handle & Trim, 6 In. | 95.00 |
| **Pitcher,** Gold Band & Handle, Cream, 8 In. | 55.00 |
| **Pitcher,** Gold Grape Handle, Pink Roses, Signed, Cornet, 13 1/2 In. | 110.00 |
| **Pitcher,** Gold Handle, Purple Plum & Leaves, 8 In. | 65.00 |
| **Pitcher,** Hand-Painted Grape Clusters, Gold Trim, Signed, 12 3/4 In. | 195.00 |
| **Pitcher,** Hand-Painted Green Apples & Blossoms, Gold Trim | 95.00 |
| **Pitcher,** Lemonade, Grapes, Gold Trim | 60.00 |
| **Pitcher,** Lemonade, Purple Plum, Green Leaves, Yellow Ground | 110.00 |
| **Pitcher,** Pink Roses, Green Ground, Signed, 10 3/4 In. | 135.00 |
| **Planter,** Rose & Lilac Design, Gold Trim, 6 1/2 In. | 40.00 |
| **Plaque,** Hand-Painted Red & Pink Roses, Green Ground, 12 In. | 85.00 |
| **Plaque,** Hand-Painted, Signed A.Broussilon, 10 1/4 In. | 150.00 |
| **Plaque,** Indian Chief, Gold Border, Artist Signed, 11 In. | 300.00 |
| **Plaque,** Irises & Gold, Pierced, Signed, 12 1/2 In. | 175.00 |
| **Plaque,** Young Man Drinking, With Bottle, Framed, 8 3/4 X 6 1/2 In. | 600.00 |
| **Plate,** Asparagus, White & Pink Rim, Gold Trim, Anchor Mark | 22.00 |
| **Plate,** Cake, Hand-Painted Bird, 10 In. | 35.00 |
| **Plate,** Cake, Silver Design, Pedestal | 25.00 |
| **Plate,** Chop, Elite, Orchids, Gold Edge, 12 In. | 35.00 |
| **Plate,** Chop, Flowers, Rococo Gold Border, Signed | 99.00 |
| **Plate,** Chop, Purple & Gold Grapes, Signed | 120.00 |
| **Plate,** Cobalt Blue & Gold, Marked, 7 In., Set Of 12 | 150.00 |
| **Plate,** Coronet, Gold Design, Ecru Ground, 10 1/2 In., Set Of 16 | 240.00 |
| **Plate,** Coronet, Signed Coudert, Pair | 150.00 |
| **Plate,** Coronet, 2 Foxes, Artist Signed, 9 1/2 In. | 60.00 |
| **Plate,** Demure Maria The Cat, Hand-Painted, Gold Outline | 95.00 |
| **Plate,** Fish, Hand-Painted & Signed, 10 In. | 39.00 |
| **Plate,** Fish, Scalloped Edge, Gilded, Artist Signed, 9 1/2 In. | 35.00 |
| **Plate,** Game Bird, Gold Scalloped Border, 10 In. | 90.00 |
| **Plate,** Game, Duck & Partridge, Signed | 120.00 |
| **Plate,** Game, 2 Birds, Green Gound, Scalloped Border, Signed, 11 In. | 110.00 |
| **Plate,** Gold On Green Edge, Marked, 8 1/2 In. | 45.00 |
| **Plate,** Gooseberries, Signed, 6 3/4 In. | 25.00 |
| **Plate,** Green & Gold Banded, Garlands, Pink Blossoms.7 1/4 In. | 42.00 |
| **Plate,** Hand-Painted Border Of Roses, Signed, 9 1/2 In. | 20.00 |
| **Plate,** Handled, Blue & Gold Border, 4 Baskets Of Fruit, 10 1/2 In. | 35.00 |
| **Plate,** Hanging, Peach Design, Gold Border, Signed Baumy, 14 In. | 100.00 |
| **Plate,** Jumping Fish In Lake, Gold Rococo Border | 55.00 |
| **Plate,** Miniature, Rose, 2 In. | 7.50 |
| **Plate,** Oyster, Coronet, Signed, Set Of 6 | 250.00 |
| **Plate,** Oyster, Fish & Floral Design, White & Gold Ground, 8 In. | 45.00 |
| **Plate,** Oyster, Flowers, Gold Leaves & Stems, Blue & Pink | 39.50 |
| **Plate,** Oyster, White & Gilt Ground, Pink Floral, 8 3/4 In. | 45.00 |
| **Plate,** Pink Blossoms, Blue Garlands, Green & Bold Banded, 7 1/4 In. | 9.00 |
| **Plate,** Portrait, Cobalt Blue & Gold Border | 75.00 |
| **Plate,** Portrait, Ladies, Lambs, Castle, Gold Tracery, 9 1/2 In. | 57.00 |
| **Plate,** Queen Louise, 6 In. | 35.00 |
| **Plate,** Red Currants, Green Leaves, Signed Roby, 8 In. | 38.00 |
| **Plate,** Roses, Green & Gold Border, C.1890, 9 In. | 65.00 |
| **Plate,** Scalloped Gold Rim, Different Birds, 9 1/2 In., Set Of 12 | 1500.00 |
| **Plate,** Scalloped Gold Rim, Pink & Blue Flowers, Marked, 10 In.Diam. | 25.00 |
| **Plate,** Scalloped, Pastel Flowers, Gold Trim, 8 In.Diam., Set Of 6 | 85.00 |
| **Plate,** Sly Sir Thomas Cat, Hand-Painted, Scalloped, Marked | 95.00 |
| **Plate,** Soup, Turtle Medallions On Rim, Turtle Center, 7 3/8 In.Diam. | 85.00 |
| **Plate,** Three Large Orange Poppies, Marked, 8 3/4 In. | 30.00 |

Limoges, Punch Bowl, 19th Century, Signed, 14 1/8 In.

| | |
|---|---|
| **Plate,** Three Rabbits, Wooded Ground, Scalloped, Edge Beaded In Gold | 155.00 |
| **Platter,** Hand-Painted, 20 1/2 In. | 435.00 |
| **Platter,** Pink Flowers, Gold Trim, 11 1/2 In. | 39.50 |
| **Powder Box,** Footed, Gold Bow On Lid, Gold Handles, 5 1/2 In. | 45.00 |
| **Punch Bowl,** Purple Grapes, Green & Blue Leaves, Rust Ground, 9 In. .......... *Illus* | 475.00 |
| **Punch Bowl,** 19th Century, Signed, 14 1/8 In. ........................................ *Illus* | 900.00 |
| **Ramekin,** Elite, Pink Flowers, Green, Gold Trim | 16.00 |
| **Ramekin,** Sterling Silver Holder, Set Of 4 | 110.00 |
| **Ramekin,** Underplate, Elite, Pink & White Roses Inside & Out | 12.00 |
| **Ramekin,** Underplate, Pink & White Flowers | 14.00 |
| **Ramekin,** Underplate, Roses On Border, Turquoise Edge, Set Of 6 | 95.00 |
| **Snuffer,** Ivy Design, Shell Shape | 45.00 |
| **Sugar & Creamer,** Elite, Pink & White Flowers, Ruffled Edge | 65.00 |
| **Sugar & Creamer,** Green Luster Bottoms, Hand-Painted Gold Deco | 65.00 |
| **Sugar & Creamer,** Lake & Trees, Gold Trim, Hand-Painted | 35.00 |
| **Sugar & Creamer,** Lilac Sprays, Gold Handles, Tiffany Color, Signed | 85.00 |
| **Sugar & Creamer,** Silver Overlay | 65.00 |
| **Tankard,** Berries, Hand-Painted, 11 In. | 190.00 |
| **Tankard,** Cherry Design | 135.00 |
| **Tankard,** Grape Design, Signed, 11 In. | 105.00 |
| **Tankard,** Hand-Painted Purple Berries, Marked, 11 In. | 190.00 |
| **Tankard,** Purple Grapes, 11 In. | 195.00 |
| **Tankard,** Raspberries & Blossoms, Gold Bands, Signed | 65.00 |
| **Tazza,** Pink, Flowers, Double, 10 X 10 In. | 125.00 |
| **Tea Caddy,** Hand-Painted, Magenta Flowers, Green Leaves, 4 In. | 38.00 |
| **Tea Caddy,** Magenta & Green, Flowers & Ivy | 30.00 |
| **Tea Set,** Coin Gold On Green Bands, 3 Piece | 49.00 |
| **Tea Set,** 4 Cups & Saucers, Geometric Pattern, 11 Piece | 175.00 |
| **Teapot,** Figural Spout | 65.00 |
| **Tile,** Hand-Painted Roses, 11 1/2 X 8 1/2 In. | 45.00 |
| **Tray,** Bread, Pansies, Gold Trim, 14 X 6 1/2 In. | 55.00 |
| **Tray,** Chrysanthemums, Scalloped Edge, Gold, 11 1/2 X 8 In. | 35.00 |
| **Tray,** Dresser, Blue, Gold Trim | 70.00 |
| **Tray,** Dresser, Flowers, Scalloped Gold Edges, 14 In. | 50.00 |
| **Tray,** Dresser, Gold Rococo Edge, Pink Flowers & Buds, 11 X 8 1/2 In. | 40.00 |
| **Tray,** Dresser, Hand-Painted Red Roses, Gold Trim, 8 1/4 X 12 1/8 In. | 70.00 |
| **Tray,** Dresser, Powder Jar, Perfume Bottle, Forget-Me-Nots, Signed | 135.00 |
| **Tray,** Hand-Painted Poppies, Gold Trim, Dated 1911, 11 X 7 In. | 60.00 |
| **Tray,** Hand-Painted, Kidney Shape, Center Medallion, 12 X 9 In. | 100.00 |
| **Tray,** Hand-Painted, Wavy Edge, 12 1/2 X 9 In. | 45.00 |
| **Tray,** Narcissus Design, Gold Trim, Signed, 14 In. | 175.00 |
| **Tray,** Scalloped In Gold, Hand-Painted, 11 1/2 X 8 In. | 35.00 |
| **Tray,** Violets On White Ground, 6 1/2 X 9 1/4 In. | 25.00 |

Tray, Yellow Roses, Wavy Edge, Hand-Painted, 12 1/2 X 9 In. ............................................ 45.00
Tray, 2-Handled, Bale Handle, Gold Trim, 7 1/2 In.Long ................................................ 25.00
Tree, Ring, Blue Flowers, 1902, Artist Signed ............................................................ 22.00
Tree, Ring, Gold & Violets Design ........................................................................ 30.00
Tumbler, Gold Flower Border, Leaves, Light Green, 3 3/4 In. ............................................ 22.00
Tumbler, Handled, Hand-Painted Dutch Boy .............................................................. 35.00
Tureen, Covered, Poppies, Leaves, Gold Trim, Sterling Silver Ladle .................................... 165.00
Tureen, Soup, Pink Flowers, Covered, L.Bernardaud Co. ................................................. 75.00
Urn, Dark Blue, Gold Trim, C.1840, 12 In., Pair ........................................................ 475.00
Vase, Art Deco, Red, White, & Green, Signed, 5 In. .................................................... 15.00
Vase, Asters, Artist Signed, 10 In. ..................................................................... 145.00
Vase, Blue Ground, Dark Blue Stems, White Flowers, Signed, 8 In. ...................................... 100.00
Vase, Bluejays, Acorns & Oak Leaves, Green To Blue, 12 1/2 In. ........................................ 125.00
Vase, Bud, Enameled, Signed, 4 3/4 In., Pair ........................................................... 900.00
Vase, Cylindrical, Polychrome Design Of Pyramid, C.1900, 13 3/4 In. ................................... 250.00
Vase, Enamel & Jeweled, Signed, 4 1/2 In. .............................................................. 650.00
Vase, Five White Geese, Brown Ground, 7 X 11 1/4 In. .................................................. 210.00
Vase, Handled, Bluebirds In Flight, Gold Trim, White Matte, 6 1/2 In. ................................. 150.00
Vase, Irises, Lilies, Yellow & White, Gold Trim, 12 In. ............................................... 110.00
Vase, Pink Flowers, Classical Scene, Footed, 17 1/2 X 11 In. .......................................... 85.00
Vase, Portrait, 10 Figures, 2 Handles, Black Mark, 14 In. ............................................. 225.00
Vase, Red & Pink Roses, 13 1/2 In. ..................................................................... 150.00
Vase, Red & White Roses, Blue, 9 1/2 X 4 In. .......................................................... 45.00
Vase, Red Flowers On Green & White Ground, Marked, 12 In. ............................................. 200.00
Vase, Red Poppies, Green Ground, Gold Rim, Signed, 8 In. .............................................. 35.00
Vase, Roses, Pink, White, Green, Gold Trim, Coronet, Signed, 15 In. ................................... 225.00
Vase, Storks, Ruby Red, Medallions, Spherical Body, 7 1/2 In. ......................................... 325.00
Vase, Tricolored, Soaring Birds, Enameled, Signed, 10 In. ............................................. 110.00
Vase, Two Geishas In Flowing Robes, Gold Base, 11 In. ................................................. 120.00
Vase, Wisteria, Ornate Handles, Gold Design, Signed, 12 X 14 In. ...................................... 300.00
Wine Set, Tankard Pitcher, 15 1/4 In., Tray, Footed Cups, 6 Piece ..................................... 475.00

LINDBERGH, Banner, Portrait, Welcome, Red, White, & Blue, 56 1/2 X 33 1/2 In. ........................ 225.00
Banner, Welcome Captain Lindbergh, New York, Paris, 1927 ............................................. 85.00
Bookends, Signed Verona ................................................................................. 65.00
Bottle, Perfume, Lucky Lindy ........................................................................... 20.00
Box, Pencil, Spirit Of St.Louis, Metal ................................................................ 22.00
Box, Photograph On Lid, Under Glass, Wood Lined, Metal, 7 1/2 In. ..................................... 45.00
Mirror, Flight, Plane, Statue, Tower, 2 3/8 X 3 1/2 In. ............................................... 25.00
Tapestry, Fliers, Planes, France, 50 X 20 In. ......................................................... 100.00
Tapestry, French & N.Y.Scenes, Byrd, Chamberlain, 19 X 56 In. ......................................... 65.00
Watch, Pocket, Chrome Plated Brass .................................................................... 75.00

*Lithophanes are porcelain pictures made by casting clay in layers of various thicknesses. When a piece is held to the light, a picture of light and shadow is seen through it. Most lithophanes date from the 1825 to 1875 period. A few are still being made.*

LITHOPHANE, Candle Shield, Boy Holding Yarn, Opaque Font, 5 X 4 1/4 In. .............................. 445.00
Candle Shield, Soldier, Child, Cast Iron, 7 3/4 X 6 1/2 X 23 In. ...................................... 695.00
Child In Cradle Praying In German, Pewter, 5 7/8 X 4 3/4 In. .......................................... 75.00
Cup & Saucer, Purple Luster, Souvenir, San Francisco .................................................. 25.00
Cup, Can You See Through It, Gold Letters, Porcelain, 1 3/4 In. ....................................... 47.50
Dream Series, Author Under Tree, Dreaming Of Lady, 3 5/8 X 3 In. ...................................... 65.00
Half Shade, Single Cast, 5 Scenes, 5 5/8 X 9 3/4 In.Diam. .............................................1100.00
Lamp, Candle Heater, Castle Scene, 5 X 4 X 4 3/4 In.Diam. ............................................. 250.00
Lamp, Fairy, Children & Animals, 5 1/2 X 6 In.Diam. ................................................... 425.00
Lamp, Fairy, Panels Depict Mothers & Children Sewing, Cooking ......................................... 800.00
Lamp, Fairy, Pedestal, 1 Piece Top, 4 Panels .......................................................... 375.00
Lamp, Fairy, 3 Scenes On Shade, C.1900, France, 8 1/2 In. ............................................. 225.00
Lamp, 3-Panel Shade, Fisherman, Lighthouse, & Rescue At Sea ..........................................1175.00
Lamp, 5 Trapezoid Panels, Scenes Of Mother & Children ................................................. 900.00
Lamp, 5 Trapezoid Panels, Scenes Of Women, Sandwich Base .............................................. 850.00

Lamp, 6-Sided Shade, Victorian Base, Brass Top & Base ............................................ 990.00
Matchbox, Girl Sitting On Shore Watching Boats, 3 X 2 In. ...................................... 90.00
Mug, Monk, Marked, 4 X 6 In. ................................................................................... 95.00
Panel, Boat Paddled By Man, Passengers, 6 1/4 X 4 3/4 In. .................................... 175.00
Panel, Colored Hunt Scene, Impressed 44, 5 3/4 X 6 In. ......................................... 125.00
Panel, Lady Smelling Flower, Marked Francaise, Paris, 5 X 4 In. .............................. 95.00
Panel, 4 Angels Leading Child With Halo, 9 1/4 X 8 1/8 In. .................................... 295.00
Panel, 6 People In Rowboat, One With Flag, Hills, 6 X 4 1/8 In. ............................. 125.00
Plaque, Cows Crossing Bridge, Thatched Barn, 4 3/8 X 5 1/4 In. ............................ 90.00
Plaque, Magdalen Kneeling At Christ's Feet, 10 X 12 1/4 In. ................................... 450.00
Plaque, Rheinstein, Black Border, Hanger, 6 1/8 X 4 1/2 In. ................................... 250.00
Plaque, Turreted Castle, Horseman In Archway, 4 X 4 5/8 In. .................................. 90.00
Plaque, View From West Point .................................................................................. 125.00
Plaque, 3 Children Kneeling Before Priest, 4 X 5 1/8 In. ......................................... 85.00
Plaque, 4 Children Having Picnic, Waving Boy, 4 X 4 11/16 In. ............................... 85.00
Shade, Candle, The Tempest, Curved, Stamped P.R.Ormolu .................................... 200.00
Shade, Hand-Painted Festoons, 5-Sided Trapezoid Shade ...................................... 690.00
Shade, 5 Panel, All Scenic, Signed, PPPM ............................................................... 700.00
Stein, Regimental, Porcelain, 1906 .......................................................................... 185.00
Stein, Snow Scene, German Soldier ......................................................................... 195.00

LITHYALIN, Bottle, Cologne, 4-Sided Body, Pedestal, Mottled Lavender, 6 In. ......................... 300.00

> Liverpool, England, has been the site of several pottery and porcelain
> factories from 1716 to 1785. Some earthenware was made with transfer
> decorations. Sadler and Green made print-decorated wares from 1756. Many
> of the pieces were made for the American market and featured patriotic
> emblems such as eagles, flags, and other special-interest motifs.

LIVERPOOL, Jug, Creamware, Enameled, Poem, C.1800, 8 1/8 In. ..................................... *Illus* 325.00

LOBMEYR, Bowl & Stand, Enameled Court Figures, Gilt Rim, C.1880, 14 In. ......................... 1500.00
Flask, Gold Filigree, Enameled Jewels, Clear, 6 1/2 In. ........................................... 165.00
Tumbler, Engraved Birds & Hearts, Flowering Foliage, Set Of 28 ............................ 350.00
Vase, Rotating Stand, Porcelain & Glass, Beehive Mark ............................... *Illus* 4200.00
Wine, Faceted Green Tinted, Cut Stem, C.1900, 5 1/2 In., Set Of 24 ...................... 600.00

LOCKE ART, Cordial, Stem, Poppy Pattern, Signed, 3 1/4 In. ........................................... 65.00
Cordial, Vintage Pattern, Signed, 4 1/2 In. .............................................................. 75.00
Dish, Candy, Grape & Vine Design, Pedestal, 3 X 4 In. ............................................ 150.00
Goblet, Ivy Pattern, Intaglio Cut & Etched, Signed, 6 1/2 In. .................................. 65.00
Goblet, Poppy, Matching Underplate, Signed, 6 In. .................................................. 125.00

Liverpool, Jug, Creamware, Enameled, Poem,
C.1800, 8 1/8 In.

Lobmeyr, Vase, Rotating Stand,
Porcelain & Glass, Beehive Mark

| | |
|---|---|
| **Goblet,** Water, Ivy Leaf Pattern, 6 1/2 In. | 78.00 |
| **Sherbet,** Ivy Pattern, Engraved & Etched, 3 1/4 X 3 1/2 In. | 80.00 |
| **Tumbler,** Intaglio Cut & Etched Daisies, 3 5/8 In., Pair | 85.00 |
| **Vase,** Blown-Out Base, Engraved & Etched Orchids, 11 In. | 148.00 |
| **Vase,** Flared Top, Etched Design Of Roses, Signed, 6 In. | 350.00 |
| **Vase,** Flared Top, Etched Rose Design, Signed, 6 1/4 In. | 325.00 |
| **Vase,** Frosted Roses, Thorny Stems, Signed, 11 1/4 In. | 325.00 |

*Johann Loetz-Witwe bought a glassworks in Austria in 1840. He died in 1848
and his widow ran the company, then in 1879 his grandson took over. Loetz
glass was varied. Most collectors recognize the iridescent gold glass similar to
Tiffany but many other types were made. The firm was closed in World War II.*

| | |
|---|---|
| **LOETZ, Basket,** Iridescent Green, Threaded In Silver, Coin Spots, 10 X 6 In. | 475.00 |
| **Bowl,** Green, Purple, Iridescent, Fluted Inverted Rim, 2 3/4 X 8 In. | 195.00 |
| **Bowl,** Iridescent Mottled Spots, Dimples, Cobalt Blue, 4 X 10 In.Diam. | 495.00 |
| **Bowl,** Mottled Gold Iridescence, Signed, 5 X 4 In. | 300.00 |
| **Bowl,** Random Threading Outside, Iridescent, 8 In.Diam. | 225.00 |
| **Bowl,** Ruffled, Iridescent Purple, 6 1/2 In. | 155.00 |
| **Bowl,** Silver Coin Spots, Green Luster, Crimped, 4 1/2 X 7 In. | 345.00 |
| **Bowl,** Silver Coin Spots, Green Threading, Iridescent Green, 7 3/4 In. | 295.00 |
| **Compote,** Purple Exterior, Oil Interior, Bronze Mounted | 200.00 |
| **Cuspidor,** Melon Ribbed, Dimples, Iridescent Green, 4 1/2 X 5 In.Diam. | 95.00 |
| **Dish,** Red Threading, Art Nouveau Brass Stand, 7 In. | 175.00 |
| **Elephant,** Metallic Luster, Gold, Blue, & Pink, 7 X 9 1/2 In. | 285.00 |
| **Ewer,** Applied Art Nouveau Sterling Silver Overlay, 8 In. | 125.00 |
| **Ewer,** Bronze Mounted Handles & Leaves, Green Ground, 10 1/4 In. | 425.00 |
| **Humidor,** Blown-Out, Teardrops, Gilt Lid, Green Iridescent | 250.00 |
| **Inkwell,** Art Nouveau Lid, Iridescent Purples & Blues | 269.00 |
| **Inkwell,** Blue Iridescent, Brass Rim, Signed, 2 X 2 1/2 In. | 75.00 |
| **Inkwell,** Cobalt Blue, Purple, Glass Insert, Featherlike Design | 269.00 |
| **Inkwell,** Feather Design, Iridescent Cobalt Blue, Glass Insert | 270.00 |
| **Inkwell,** Hinged Brass Petal Shaped Lid, Iridescent Green, 5 1/4 In. | 170.00 |
| **Inkwell,** Iridescent Blue, Green, Purple, Brass Cover, Squatty, 2 In. | 575.00 |
| **Jar,** Biscuit, Green Crackle, Metal Top & Bail | 185.00 |
| **Jar,** Sweetmeat, Enameled Apples & Leaves, Brass Bail & Cover | 65.00 |
| **Jar,** Sweetmeat, Red Threaded, Silver Plate Handle, Signed, 5 In.Diam. | 475.00 |
| **Pitcher,** Blue-Green, Applied Clear Handle, 6 1/4 In. | 135.00 |
| **Rose Bowl,** Folded-In Rim, Iridescent Green, 5 X 6 In.Diam. | 65.00 |
| **Shade,** Corset Shape, Gold Oil Spots, Green, 5 1/2 In., Set Of 4 | 240.00 |
| **Toothpick,** Blue, Signed | 60.00 |
| **Vase,** Alligator Surface, Iridescent Blues, Greens, Purples, 8 In. | 380.00 |
| **Vase,** Amethyst Inside, Mottled Exterior, 8 In. | 425.00 |
| **Vase,** Applied Rust Flower, Iridescent Gold, Signed, 3 3/4 In. | 395.00 |
| **Vase,** Austria, Gold Iridescent, Raindrops, Signed, 10 In. | 335.00 |
| **Vase,** Bands Of Gold Waves, Applied Gold Lily Pads, 7 In. *Illus* | 2200.00 |
| **Vase,** Blue & Gold, Feathered Design, 3 1/2 X 4 In. | 225.00 |
| **Vase,** Blue Iridescent Drapery, Pinched-In Neck, Gold, 4 3/4 In. | 150.00 |
| **Vase,** Cameo, Pink Etched Ground, 2-Layer Green Floral, Signed, 6 In. | 675.00 |
| **Vase,** Carved Thistles & Branches, Emerald Green, 11 1/2 In. | 500.00 |
| **Vase,** Cobalt Papillon, 8 X 6 3/4 In.Wide | 270.00 |
| **Vase,** Colored Bands, Gold Ribs Form Feet, 7 In. *Illus* | 3400.00 |
| **Vase,** Deep Purple, Melon Ribbed, Blown-Out, 3 3/4 In. | 150.00 |
| **Vase,** Double Gourd Shape, Blue Iridescent, Crossed Arrows, 7 In. | 500.00 |
| **Vase,** Enameled Painting Designs, Pastel Aqua, Signed, 8 1/4 In. | 185.00 |
| **Vase,** Fan Shape, Signed, 7 In. | 350.00 |
| **Vase,** Flared, Iridescent Green & Blue Swirled Design, 12 1/4 In. | 55.00 |
| **Vase,** Flower Form, Gold Dust, 14 In. | 375.00 |
| **Vase,** Flower Opening, Apple Green & Gold, 13 In. | 375.00 |
| **Vase,** Formosa Pattern, Blue Threads Over Green Ground, 3 1/2 In. | 195.00 |
| **Vase,** Gold & Blue Iridescent, 4 In. | 225.00 |
| **Vase,** Gold Dust, Green, 15 X 5 In.Diam. | 375.00 |
| **Vase,** Gold Iridescent, Corset Shaped, 12 In. | 275.00 |

| | |
|---|---|
| **Vase,** Green With Gold Dust, 15 X 5 In. | 375.00 |
| **Vase,** Green, Iridescent Raised Design, Acid Cut Back, 8 In. | 200.00 |
| **Vase,** Iridescent Brown & Yellow, Peacock Eye, Fan Shape, 5 In. | 290.00 |
| **Vase,** Iridescent Gold & Blue, Dimpled, 2-Handled, 2 X 3 In. | 195.00 |
| **Vase,** Iridescent Raised Loops, Oil Spot Base, Green, 4 1/4 In. | 80.00 |
| **Vase,** Luster Crackled Purple, Gold Ground, Metallic Luster, 7 3/4 In. | 395.00 |
| **Vase,** Mahogany Spider Web, Green, Silver Overlay, 3-Handled, 7 In. | 650.00 |
| **Vase,** Melon Ribbed Base, Cylindrical Top, Green & Gold, 10 In. | 225.00 |
| **Vase,** Pear Shape, Brown Flat Threading, Clear Base, Signed, 10 1/8 In. | 285.00 |
| **Vase,** Pinched Bulbous Base, Amber Oil Spots, Pink, 5 1/4 In. | 75.00 |
| **Vase,** Pinched Gourd Shape, Treebark Texture, Green, 5 1/2 In. | 50.00 |
| **Vase,** Pinched, Multicolored Pulls, Ruffled, Midnight Blue, 9 In. | 165.00 |
| **Vase,** Pinched, Treebark Texture With Knots, Green, 7 In. | 75.00 |
| **Vase,** Pulled Feather Design, Purple, Green, & Amber Iridescent, 12 In. | 195.00 |
| **Vase,** Purple, Yellow, & Pink, Sterling Silver Overlay, Marked, 7 3/8 In. | 695.00 |
| **Vase,** Quilted Pattern, Applied Flower & Stem, Signed, 3 3/4 In. | 395.00 |
| **Vase,** Random Swirl, Set Into Bronze Tree, Blossoms At Top, 6 1/4 In. | 450.00 |
| **Vase,** Red & Brown Design, 3-Layer Cameo, Pink Ground, Marked, 10 In. | 450.00 |
| **Vase,** Rows Of Gold Dots & Waves, Pink, Signed, 16 1/4 In. *Illus* | 3200.00 |
| **Vase,** Ruffled Top, Silver Overlay, 4 1/2 X 4 1/2 In. | 145.00 |
| **Vase,** Silver Overlay, Blue Iridescent, 6 X 6 In.Diam. | 595.00 |
| **Vase,** Six Rigaree Bands, Blue-Green Iridescent, 11 3/4 In. | 195.00 |
| **Vase,** Swirled Iridescent Green, Applied Bronze Grapes, 10 In. | 250.00 |
| **Vase,** Swirled Purple & Blue Iridescent, Green Ground, 8 3/4 In. | 325.00 |
| **Vase,** Threaded, 5 X 3 1/2 In. | 20.00 |
| **Vase,** Thumbprint, 5 In. | 65.00 |
| **Vase,** Tri-Pinched, Blue-Black Oil Spots, Clear Green Ground, 6 1/2 In. | 165.00 |
| **Vase,** Twisted, Rectangular, Iridescent Blue, 12 In. | 185.00 |
| **Vase,** 3-Handled, Mahogany Spider Web On Green, Silver Overlay, 7 In. | 650.00 |
| **Vase,** 3-Handled, Pinched Base, Iridescent Amber, Signed, 7 In. | 295.00 |
| **Vase,** 3-Layer Cameo, Pink Satin Ground, Marked, 10 In. | 395.00 |

Loetz, Vase, Rows Of Gold Dots & Waves, Pink, Signed, 16 1/4 In.

Loetz, Vase, Colored Bands
Gold Ribs Form Feet, 7 In.

Loetz, Vase, Bands Of Gold Waves,
Applied Gold Lily Pads, 7 In.

| | |
|---|---|
| **LONE RANGER, Badge,** Deputy, Numbered | 6.00 To 15.00 |
| **Badge,** Deputy, Store Display, 12 On Card | 80.00 |
| **Bank,** Silver Reared, Cast Iron, 11 X 15 In. | 95.00 |
| **Box,** First Aid, Tin | 25.00 |
| **Bullet,** Red | 30.00 |
| **Bullet,** Silver | 15.00 |
| **Bullet,** Silver, 1941 | 10.00 |
| **Doll,** Chaps, Hat, Boxed | 125.00 |

| | |
|---|---|
| **Doll,** Composition Head, Latex Body, 1950s, 9 1/2 In. | 10.00 |
| **Field Glasses** | 5.00 |
| **Flashlight,** Signal Siren, Silver Bullet Code, Boxed | 45.00 |
| **Game,** Parker Bros. | 15.00 To 28.00 |
| **Game,** Pop-Up, Boxed | 14.00 |
| **Guitar** | 8.00 |
| **Gun,** Target, Boxed, Large | 70.00 |
| **Gun,** Target, Boxed, Small | 55.00 |
| **Hairbrush,** Men's, Wood, Tonto, Dated 1939 | 18.00 |
| **Knife,** Pocket, 2 Blades, Ring, Ranger Pictured, 3 In. | 40.00 |
| **Necktie** | 6.50 |
| **Paperweight,** Roundup, Snow Globe | 30.00 |
| **Pedometer,** Boxed | 15.00 To 50.00 |
| **Pen Knife,** With Silver Bullet | 19.00 |
| **Pen,** Danger Signal, 1940s, Pair | 15.00 |
| **Pin,** Star Shape | 12.00 |
| **Pistol,** Click, Boxed | 45.00 |
| **Pistol,** Silver, Ivorylike Handle, 1939, Boxed | 65.00 |
| **Projector,** Movie, 3 Films, 1944, Boxed | 25.00 |
| **Ring,** Atomic Bomb | 9.00 |
| **Ring,** Film Strip | 25.00 |
| **Ring,** | 45.00 |
| **Ring,** View, Original Box | 45.00 |
| **Watch,** Pocket, Ranger & Silver Illustrated, 1939 | 250.00 |
| **Wristwatch,** Boxed, 1939 | 275.00 |

*Longwy Workshop of Longwy, France, first produced wares in 1798. It is best known for enamels. The workshop is still in business.*

| | |
|---|---|
| **LONGWY, Box,** Bird In Flight, Crackle Blue Ground, Marked, 4 1/2 In.Diam. | 100.00 |
| **Box,** Multicolored Bird, Flower, Cobalt Trim, Signed, 2 1/2 X 4 1/2 In. | 125.00 |
| **Box,** Yellow Wavy Lines, Design On Green Lid, Marked, 5 1/2 In.Diam. | 90.00 |
| **Salt & Pepper,** Chinese Enamel Design, Pewter Tops | 50.00 |
| **Tray,** Footed, Faience, Enameled, Floral Design, 4 3/4 X 3 In. | 75.00 |
| **Vase,** Bulbous, Overall Floral, Blue Ground, 8-Sided Top, Marked, 6 In. | 125.00 |
| **Vase,** Cobalt Ground, Singed, 10 In. | 190.00 |
| **Vase,** 4 Leaf-Shaped Panels, Flowers, Beige Ground, Marked, 4 1/4 In. | 45.00 |
| **Vase,** 8-Sided, Flowers, Blue Ground, Marked, 6 X 5 1/2 In.Diam. | 90.00 |

*Lotus ware was made by the Knowles, Taylor & Knowles Company of East Liverpool, Ohio, from 1890 to 1900.*

| | |
|---|---|
| **LOTUS WARE, Bowl,** Floral, Gold Beads, Bulbous, Signed, 5 1/4 X 5 In. | 575.00 |
| **Bowl,** Rose | 350.00 |
| **Creamer,** Fishnet Design, Marked, Small | 210.00 |
| **Pitcher,** Covered, Flowers & Leaves, Gold Rim, Signed, 11 In. | 350.00 |
| **Pitcher,** Uptilted Spout, Gold & Turquoise Handle, 6 1/2 In. | 225.00 |
| **Sugar & Creamer,** White Raised Design, Ribbed Flat Handles | 200.00 |
| **Teapot,** Hand-Painted Flowers, Blue, White, & Gold | 125.00 |
| **Vase,** Lavender Florals, Gilded Handles, Signed A.H.P., 7 1/2 In. | 350.00 |

**J.&J.G.LOW**    *Low art tiles were made by the J. and J.G. Low Art Tile Works of Chelsea, Massachusetts, from 1877 to 1902. A variety of art and other tiles were made.*

| | |
|---|---|
| **LOW, Box,** Tile Insert, Brass, Signed | 145.00 |
| **Tile,** Child Kneeling At Vase, 1880s | 30.00 |

Tile, Grecian Head Of Man, 1880s ....................................................................................... 30.00
Tile, High-Glaze Green, Swirls & Geometrics, 6 In.Square ............................................. 42.00
Tile, Profile Of Girl, Flowing Hair, Shades Of Brown, 1880s ......................................... 30.00
Tile, Seated Oriental With Instrument, Fishscale Pattern, Signed, 6 In. ..................... 150.00

> *The Lowestoft factory in Suffolk, England, worked from 1757 to 1802.*
> *They made many commemorative gift pieces and small dated, inscribed pieces*
> *of soft paste porcelain.*

**LOWESTOFT, see also Chinese Export**
**LOWESTOFT, Bowl,** Blue & White, Oriental Scene, 5 In. ............................................ 200.00
    **LOY-NEL-ART, see McCoy**

**LUDWIGSBURG, Figurine,** Dancer, Tree Stump Base, C.1765, Crown Mark, 5 1/2 In. ......... 1400.00
    **Group,** Skaters, Boy & Girl, C.1765, Crown Mark, 5 3/4 In. ....................................... 4500.00

> *Luneville, a French faience factory, was established in 1731 by Jacques*
> *Chambrette. It is best known for its fine biscuit figures and groups and*
> *for large faience dogs and lions. The early pieces were unmarked. The*
> *Terre de Lorraine or T.D.L. impression was used after 1766.*

**LUNEVILLE, Bowl,** Fruit, Roses, 9 In. ........................................................................... 35.00
    **Pitcher,** Marine Ground, Red Roses, Quart ................................................................. 30.00
    **Pitcher,** Nasturtiums On Green Ground, 8 X 7 1/2 In. ............................................... 75.00
    **Plaque,** Red Roses, Foliage, Blue Ground, 12 1/4 In. ................................................ 45.00
    **Plate,** Deep Red Border, Spongeware, Gold Trim, Set Of 3 ....................................... 25.00
    **Plate,** Oriental Ladies, Pagoda, Marked, 8 In. ............................................................ 60.00
    **Plate,** Oriental Scene, Mother Scolding Son, 8 In. ..................................................... 50.00

> *Lusterware was meant to resemble copper, silver, or gold. It has been used*
> *since the sixteenth century. Most of the luster found today was made during*
> *the nineteenth century.*

**LUSTER, Canary,** Mug, Child's, Bucolic Scene Transfer, Pink Luster Band ...................... 95.00
    **Copper,** Bowl, Fish & Seaweed, Center Medallion, English, 8 In. .............................. 250.00
    **Copper,** Chocolate Set, 6 Cups & Saucers, Long-Spout Pot, England ....................... 385.00
    **Copper,** Creamer, Blue Design, Wide Band ................................................................ 35.00
    **Copper,** Creamer, Blue Plaid Pattern, 4 1/4 In. ......................................................... 39.00
    **Copper,** Creamer, Diamond Pattern, 5 1/2 In. ........................................................... 70.00
    **Copper,** Creamer, Orange Ring At Top, 4 3/4 In. ....................................................... 78.00
    **Copper,** Cup & Saucer, Handleless, Scroll & Swastika Design .................................. 35.00
    **Copper,** Cup & Saucer, Orange Band & Flowers Outline ............................................ 40.00
    **Copper,** Cup, Demitasse, 2 1/2 In. ............................................................................. 12.50
    **Copper,** Cup, Green ...................................................................................................... 40.00
    **Copper,** Goblet, Dark Green Band ................................................................................ 35.00
    **Copper,** Goblet, Hand-Brushed Enamel Floral, C.1835, 4 1/8 X 3 1/2 In. ................ 95.00
    **Copper,** Jug, White, Yellow, Pink Luster, C.1820, 7 1/2 In. ...................................... 300.00
    **Copper,** Mug, Band At Top & Base, Yellow Midband, 2 3/4 In. ................................. 45.00
    **Copper,** Mug, Clovers On Mustard Ground, Pink Luster Band Inside ......................... 75.00
    **Copper,** Pitcher, Blue Band, 5 1/2 In. ........................................................................ 65.00
    **Copper,** Pitcher, Cream Band, 7 In. ............................................................................ 18.00
    **Copper,** Pitcher, Dancers, Scroll Design, English Mark, 7 In. ................................... 85.00
    **Copper,** Pitcher, Diamond Band, Painted Flowers, 7 1/2 In. ..................................... 10.00
    **Copper,** Pitcher, Flowers In Relief, Painted, 6 In. ..................................................... 57.00
    **Copper,** Pitcher, Girl & Boy On Sides, Face On Spout, 8 In. .................................... 65.00
    **Copper,** Pitcher, Girl On Fence, Blue Band, 3 1/2 In. ............................................... 45.00
    **Copper,** Pitcher, Hand-Painted Flowers, Diamond Base, 8 In. .................................. 85.00
    **Copper,** Pitcher, Lady With Umbrella In Relief, 8 In. ................................................ 85.00
    **Copper,** Pitcher, Mask Spout, Children On Sides, Green Trim, 6 1/2 In. ................... 65.00
    **Copper,** Pitcher, Orange Band At Top, 6 In. ............................................. 32.00 To 45.00
    **Copper,** Pitcher, Painted Flowers, Blue Trim, 6 1/2 In. ............................................ 65.00
    **Copper,** Pitcher, Pink Band, 6 In. ............................................................................... 50.00
    **Copper,** Pitcher, Pink Design, Signed Cumbow, 4 1/2 In. ........................................ 35.00
    **Copper,** Pitcher, Pink Floral Band, Miniature ............................................................ 35.00

| | |
|---|---|
| Copper, Pitcher, Raised Dancers On Sides, Blue Trim, 6 1/2 In. | 65.00 |
| Copper, Pitcher, Sand Band, 4 1/2 In. | 55.00 |
| Copper, Pitcher, Two Blue Bands, 6 In. | 58.00 |
| Copper, Pitcher, Two Tan Bands, Flowers, 5 In. | 65.00 |
| Copper, Pitcher, White Band With Daisies, 4 1/2 In. | 32.00 |
| Copper, Plate, Blue Flower Border, 1850-60, 8 5/8 In. | 35.00 |
| Copper, Plate, Elsmore & Forster, 8 3/4 In. | 18.00 |
| Copper, Plate, Sand Colored Band, C.1830, 7 1/2 In.Diam. | 40.00 |
| Copper, Royal Blue & Copper Stripes At Top & Base, 2 3/4 In. | 60.00 |
| Copper, Salt, Master, Pedestal Base, Blue Band | 38.00 |
| Copper, Salt, Pedestal, Blue Band, 2 1/2 In. | 42.00 |

**LUSTER, COPPER, TEA LEAF, see Tea Leaf, Ironstone**

| | |
|---|---|
| Tea Set, 6 Cups & Saucers, England, 20 Piece | 500.00 |

**LUSTER, FAIRYLAND, see Wedgwood, Fairyland Luster**

| | |
|---|---|
| Pink, Boot, Red & Gold Trim, German, 4 1/4 X 1 3/4 X 3 3/4 In. | 40.00 |
| Pink, Bowl, House Design, 6 1/2 In.Diam. | 40.00 |
| Pink, Bowl, Pink Rim, Center Scene Of Hill, Trees, & Country, 7 1/4 In. | 50.00 |
| Pink, Creamer, White Flowers, Gold, 4 In. | 15.00 |
| Pink, Cup & Saucer | 25.00 To 49.00 |
| Pink, Cup & Saucer, Faith, Hope, & Charity, Three Children, C.1835 | 100.00 |
| Pink, Cup & Saucer, Fish Hook Handle, Rosebuds, C.1815 | 54.00 |
| Pink, Cup & Saucer, Hand-Painted Flowers In White Reserves | 40.00 |
| Pink, Cup & Saucer, Handleless, Trees & Fence | 36.00 |
| Pink, Cup & Saucer, Pink Band | 27.00 |
| Pink, Cup & Saucer, Ship Transfer | 22.50 |
| Pink, Cup & Saucer, 2 Bands In Well, Loop Panels, C.1820 | 42.00 |
| Pink, Cup Plate | 15.00 |
| Pink, Cup, Mustache | 25.00 |
| Pink, Mug, Cloud Pattern | 65.00 |
| Pink, Mug, Cobalt Trim, German, 3 In. | 20.00 |
| Pink, Pitcher, Copper Top & Bottom, 6 X 7 In.Diam. | 85.00 |
| Pink, Plate, Copper Rim, This Is A Good World To Live In, 8 3/4 In. | 75.00 |
| Pink, Plate, General Jackson, Hero Of New Orleans, 9 In. | 135.00 |
| Pink, Plate, Luster Borders, Enamel Flowers, 7 In. | 20.00 |
| Pink, Plate, Square, Scalloped, 9 1/2 In. | 35.00 |
| Pink, Plate, Yellow Flowers, Silver Resist Reserve, 7 In. | 45.00 |
| Pink, Sugar Shaker, Sanded Midband | 40.00 |
| Pink, Sugar, Creamer, & Spooner, White Flowers | 35.00 |
| Pink, Tea Service, Stylized Floral Drapery, England, 22 Piece | 125.00 |
| Pink, Teapot, Pink Band, Red Roses, Ornate Handle | 85.00 |
| Pitcher, Andrew Jackson, Hero Of New Orleans | 600.00 |
| Plate, Pink Band, 5 3/4 In. | 11.00 |
| Silver, Creamer, Sugar, Teapot | 575.00 |
| Silver, Pitcher, Foliage & Fruit Design, 6 In. | 100.00 |
| Silver, Pitcher, Grape & Leaf Pattern, Marked Ridgeway, 4 1/2 In. | 50.00 |
| Silver, Pitcher, Grape & Leaf Pattern, 5 1/4 In. | 50.00 |
| Silver, Pitcher, Hexagon Pattern, Foliage, 5 1/2 In. | 60.00 To 75.00 |
| Silver, Sugar & Creamer | 150.00 |
| Silver, Tea Set, Hot Plate, Stoke-On-Trent, Burslem | 40.00 |
| Silver, Tea Set, 6 Cups & Saucers, Daisies, Bavaria, 15 Piece | 145.00 |

**LUSTER, SUNDERLAND, see Sunderland**

*Lustre Art Glass Company was founded in Long Island, New York, in
1920 by Conrad Vahlsing and Paul Frank. The company made lampshades
and globes that are almost indistinguishable from those made by Quezal.*

| | |
|---|---|
| LUSTRE ART, Candlestick, White Pulled Feathers, Gold, Signed, 9 1/2 In. | 350.00 |
| Shade, Gold Webbing Over Green & Gold Leaves, Signed, 6 In. | 110.00 |
| Shade, White Feathers, Gold Ribbing, Signed, 5 1/4 In., Pair | 250.00 |

*Lustres are mantel decorations, or pedestal vases, with many hanging glass prisms. The name really refers to the prisms, and it is proper to refer to a single glass prism as a lustre. Either spelling, luster or lustre, is correct.*

LUSTRE, Figure, Colonial Couple, Brass, Prisms, Set Of 3 ............................................. 250.00

*Lutz glass was made in the 1870s by Nicholas Lutz at the Boston and Sandwich Company. He made a delicate and intricate threaded glass of several colors. Other similar wares are referred to as Lutz.*

LUTZ, Bowl, Opalescent Pink, Threaded, Ruffled Edge, 2 1/2 X 4 3/4 In. ................................ 95.00
Bowl, Underplate, Ruffled, Gold Luster, Threaded, 7 In.Diam. ........................................ 125.00

*Petrus Regout established the De Sphinx pottery in Maastricht, Holland, in 1836. The firm was noted for its transfer-printed earthenware. Many factories in Maastricht are still making ceramics.*

MAASTRICHT Bowl, Hong Kong Pattern, 7 3/4 In.Diam. .............................................. 23.00
Cup & Saucer, Oriental, C.1900, Flow Blue .......................................................... 30.00
Cup & Saucer, Timor, C.1875, Flow Blue ............................................................. 40.00
Plate, Black Transfer, Napoleon On Horseback, 7 In. ............................................... 55.00
Plate, Oriental Design, Cobalt Blue, 8 1/2 In.Diam., Set Of 4 ..................................... 225.00
Plate, Oriental Scene, Blue, Black, & Pink, 8 1/2 In.Diam. ........................................ 55.00
Plate, Ruth & Boaz, Red Transfer, 10 In.Diam. ..................................................... 55.00
Plate, Windmill Scene, Flower Border, Flow Blue .................................................... 25.00
Waste Bowl, Pompeia, C.1875, Flow Blue ............................................................. 50.00

MAC INTYRE, Vase, Marbleized Brown, Signed, 2 3/4 In. ............................................. 85.00

*Maize glass, sold by the W.L.Libbey & Son Company of Toledo, Ohio, was made by Joseph Locke in 1889. It is pressed glass formed like an ear of corn. Most pieces were made for household use.*

MAIZE, Bowl, Suppressed Bulbous Form, Blue Husk Design, 3 3/4 X 9 In.Diam. ...................... 100.00
Bowl, Suppressed Bulbous Form, Opaque White Design, Green Husks, 9 In. ............................ 85.00
Carafe, Water, Opaque Yellow, Blue Husks, 19th Century, 8 In. .................................... 100.00
Celery, Gold Color Leaves, Cream Opaque Glass, 6 1/2 In. ......................................... 145.00
Celery, Green On White, Libbey ................................................................... 110.00
Celery, Ovoid, Amber Husks, Gilt, 6 1/2 In., Pair ................................................. 75.00
Celery, White & Green ............................................................................ 77.50
Cruet, Blue Husks, Original Stopper .............................................................. 375.00
Sugar Shaker, Blue Leaves ........................................................................ 145.00
Sugar Shaker, Green Leaves Tipped With Brown, Libbey .............................................. 175.00
Sugar Shaker, Yellow Leaves ...................................................................... 155.00
Tumbler, Barrel Shape, Raised Kernels, Gold Edging, Libbey, 4 In. ................................. 695.00
Tumbler, Ovoid Form, Green & Brown Husks, 4 In., Set Of 5 ......................................... 150.00
Tumbler, Yellow Leaves ................................................... 65.00 To 125.00
Vase, Celery, Iridescent Gold, Blue Leaves, 6 1/4 In. ............................................. 95.00

*Majolica is any pottery glazed with a tin enamel. Most of the majolica found today is decorated with leaves, shells, branches, and other natural shapes and in natural colors. It was a popular nineteenth-century product.*

MAJOLICA, see also Wedgwood
MAJOLICA, Bank, Pig ............................................................................. 30.00
Basket, Yellow, Lavender Lining, 2 Handles, 10 X 7 In. ............................................ 30.00
Bowl, Applied Grapes, 4 X 1i 1/2 In.Diam. ........................................................ 85.00
Bowl, Etruscan Shell & Seaweed, 8 1/2 In. ........................................................ 35.00
Bowl, Raised Daffodils, Purple Lining, Unglazed Outside, 6 3/4 In. ................................ 25.00
Bowl, Salad, Green Leaves, Blue Ground, 11 In.Diam. .............................................. 48.00

| | |
|---|---|
| **Bread Tray,** Oak, Signed | 65.00 |
| **Butter Pat,** Etruscan, Geranium Leaf | 18.00 |
| **Butter Pat,** Etruscan, Lily Pad | 15.00 |
| **Butter Pat,** Etruscan, Shell & Seaweed | 8.00 |
| **Cake Plate,** Cobalt Blue Center, Wild Roses, 11 In. | 50.00 |
| **Cake Plate,** Geranium Pattern, Impressed Mark, 12 In. | 70.00 |
| **Cake Plate,** Handled, Geranium Design, Impressed G.H.S., 12 In. | 70.00 |
| **Cake Stand,** Leaf Design | 55.00 |
| **Candlestick,** The Policeman, Figural, 8 In. | 165.00 |
| **Charger,** Raised Butterflies, Flowers, & Leaves, 11 1/2 In. | 50.00 |
| **Compote,** Etruscan, Maple Leaves, Signed | 80.00 |
| **Compote,** Pedestal, Mottled Underside, Dated 1875, 4 X 11 In.Diam. | 195.00 |
| **Compote,** Salad, Daisy, Signed | 135.00 |
| **Compote,** Scalloped, Pink Interior, Daisies & Leaves, Marked, 10 In. | 155.00 |
| **Compote,** Shell Shape, Lavender Lining, Blue, 6 1/2 X 9 1/2 In.Diam. | 50.00 |
| **Compote,** Stemmed, Vines & Leaves Border, Cupid Center, 10 In. | 40.00 |
| **Console Set,** Flowers & Leaves, Signed, Bowl, 11 In.Diam. | 90.00 |
| **Creamer,** Bamboo, Signed | 75.00 |
| **Creamer,** Bird, Butterfly, 3 1/2 X 3 1/4 In. | 38.00 |
| **Creamer,** Crane & Water Lilies, Stemmed Heart Mark, 6 In. | 40.00 |
| **Creamer,** Spout, Butterfly, 4 1/2 In. | 35.00 |
| **Cup & Saucer,** Bamboo Design | 65.00 |
| **Cup & Saucer,** Shell & Seaweed | 85.00 |
| **Cuspidor,** Pineapple | 90.00 |
| **Cuspidor,** Shell & Seaweed Pattern | 55.00 |
| **Dish,** Calla Leaf Shape, Green & Buff, Signed, 9 1/2 In. | 16.00 |
| **Dish,** Leaf Shape, Bird On Nest, Strawberries, 11 X 9 In. | 48.00 |
| **Dish,** Leaf, Brown Handle, Green, Acorns & Leaf, 11 1/2 X 8 1/2 In. | 27.00 |
| **Dish,** Serving, Leaf Shape, Etruscan, Seal Sign, 8 1/2 In.Diam. | 45.00 |
| **Dresser Set,** Bird, Butterfly, & Fan, Tray, 12 1/2 X 6 1/2 In., 4 Pc. | 120.00 |
| **Ewer,** Acorn, 9 In., Pair | 35.00 |
| **Ewer,** Basket Weave, Gold Leaves, Yellow, Pink, Gold, On Cobalt Blue | 125.00 |
| **Ewer,** Journey Of The Magi Design, Copper Red, 27 1/2 In. | 950.00 |
| **Ewer,** Portrait Center, Yellow & Green Trim, Cobalt, 7 In. | 32.50 |
| **Figurine,** Dolphin Boy, Holding Shell, 1869, Minton | 160.00 |
| **Figurine,** Man Pushing Wheelbarrow, Signed, 12 1/2 X 12 1/2 In. | 540.00 |
| **Figurine,** Pig, With Mandolin, Place For Cigars & Matches | 125.00 |
| **Figurine,** Reclining Black Boy & Girl, Pair | 130.00 |
| **Flower Pot,** Fern & Flowers | 90.00 |
| **Humidor,** Head Of Arab Wearing Turban, 9 In. | 115.00 |
| **Humidor,** Tree Stump, Serpent | 110.00 |
| **Jar,** Cigar, Shell & Seaweed | 177.00 |
| **Jar,** Tobacco, Frog | 80.00 |
| **Jar,** Tobacco, Indian, 6 In. | 75.00 |
| **Jar,** Tobacco, Mushroom Shape, Dwarf Seated, Drinking From Mug | 35.00 |
| **Jar,** Tobacco, Old Man With Beany Hat, Pipe In Mouth, 5 7/8 In. | 55.00 |
| **Jardiniere,** Emerald Green, Snarling Dragons, 34 In. | 350.00 |
| **Jardiniere,** Forest Mold, 8 3/8 X 10 In. | 85.00 |
| **Jug,** Syrup, Sunflower, Blue | 135.00 |
| **Jug,** Whiskey, Uncle Sam | 45.00 |
| **Lamp,** Oil, Urn Shape, Wine & Gold Color | 52.00 |
| **Match Holder,** Boy With Basket, Striker | 65.00 |
| **Match Holder,** Boy, 2 Spaniels, Fresh Chestnuts Sir, Marked | 95.00 |
| **Match Holder,** Happy Hooligan, Striker, 5 In. | 65.00 |
| **Match Holder,** Mandolin Player, Tray, Colored, 5 In. | 26.50 |
| **Mug,** Barrel Shaped, Applied Flowers, Turquoise Interior | 21.50 |
| **Mug,** Pebble Surface, Strawberry Blossom Sprays, Marked | 28.00 |
| **Pitcher,** Bamboo Pattern, English Red, Dated 1876, 9 In. | 55.00 |
| **Pitcher,** Bark, Roses, 6 In. | 35.00 |
| **Pitcher,** Bird On Leaves, 8 1/2 In. | 40.00 |
| **Pitcher,** Bluebirds, Aqua Lining, Pebbled Ground, 6 In. | 35.00 |
| **Pitcher,** Butterfly Spout, Etruscan, Signed | 45.00 |
| **Pitcher,** Commemorative, Our Army & Navy Brave Volunteers, 1860 | 285.00 |

Pitcher, Corn, Green, Gold, Impressed, 5 1/4 X 3 1/4 In. ........................................................... 35.00
Pitcher, Corn, 6 In. ........................................................................................................................ 20.00
Pitcher, Corn, 8 In. ........................................................................................................................ 70.00
Pitcher, Corn, 8 1/2 In. .................................................................................................................. 35.00
Pitcher, Fan With Dragonfly & Dogwood, Mauve Interior, 7 In. ................................................. 40.00
Pitcher, Figural, Bulldog, Brown, Green, & Red ....................................................................... 65.00
Pitcher, Fish, 9 In. ..................................................................................................................... 110.00
Pitcher, Fish, 9 3/4 In. .................................................................................................................. 45.00
Pitcher, Fish, 11 In. ....................................................................................................................... 75.00
Pitcher, Flowers, Cobalt Blue & Yellow, 7 1/2 In. ....................................................................... 35.00
Pitcher, Goat, Children, 9 In. ........................................................................................................ 48.00
Pitcher, Hummingbird Design, 6 1/2 In. ....................................................................................... 45.00
Pitcher, Iris, 8 1/2 In. .................................................................................................................... 60.00
Pitcher, Milk, Brown & Turquoise ................................................................................................ 22.50
Pitcher, Milk, Cows Grazing Under Trees, C.1820, 7 In. ............................................................. 75.00
Pitcher, Olive Green, Vertical Fish, 6 In. ...................................................................................... 75.00
Pitcher, Pear Shape, Burgundy Interior, Green Exterior, 7 3/4 In. .............................................. 45.00
Pitcher, Pear Shape, Ice Lip, Geometric Apples & Pears, 10 1/2 In. .......................................... 50.00
Pitcher, Pear Shape, Poppies, Cobalt Blue, Numbered, 13 1/2 In. ............................................. 60.00
Pitcher, People Drinking, Dancing Around, 9 X 4 1/2 In. ............................................................. 70.00
Pitcher, Pineapple, 7 In. ............................................................................................................... 50.00
Pitcher, Pink Inside, Cobalt Flowers, 6 1/4 X 3 1/2 In. ................................................................ 42.00
Pitcher, Pistol & Snake Handle, Frog Mouth Pouring Spout ..................................................... 165.00
Pitcher, Ram's Head On Front Legs For Handle, 8 1/2 In. .......................................................... 75.00
Pitcher, Ram's Head, Yellow & Green, Lavender, 8 1/2 In. ......................................................... 75.00
Pitcher, Roses, Green Ground, 7 1/2 In. ...................................................................................... 50.00
Pitcher, Sanded On Burgundy Red, Applied Rose, 10 1/2 In. ..................................................... 48.00
Pitcher, Seaweed & Shell, 6 In. .................................................................................................. 125.00
Pitcher, Tree Trunk & Leaf, 8 1/4 In. ............................................................................................ 60.00
Pitcher, Water Lilies, 8 In. ............................................................................................................ 75.00
Pitcher, Water, Shell & Seaweed, 6 In. ........................................................ 90.00 To 135.00
Pitcher, White, Leaves & Buds, Moss Green Coral, Marked, 2 Quart ...................................... 150.00
Pitcher, Yellow Flowers On Bottom, Light Blue Ground, 6 1/2 In. ............................................... 40.00
Planter, Handled, Footed, Blue, Green Leaves, Brown Tree Trunk, Pair .................................. 155.00
Plaque, Fruit In Relief, Cream & Brown Ground, 10 1/8 In.Diam., Pr. ..................................... 175.00
Plate, Bamboo & Seaweed, 6 Corner, 8 In. ................................................................................ 95.00
Plate, Bamboo, 8 In. ..................................................................................................................... 35.00
Plate, Begonia Leaf On Pink Basket Weave, Signed, 8 3/4 In. .................................................. 35.00
Plate, Brown Basket Weave, Raspberries, Flowers, 8 1/4 In. .................................................... 25.00
Plate, Cauliflower, Signed, 9 In. ................................................................................................... 35.00
Plate, Choisy-Le-Roi ..................................................................................................................... 16.00
Plate, Cobalt Blue, Basket Weave, Fruit, 10 In. .......................................................................... 50.00
Plate, Cream, Applied Strawberries, White, 8 1/4 In.Diam. ........................................................ 50.00
Plate, Cupid Animal, Etruscan ...................................................................................................... 50.00
Plate, Cupid On Tiger, Etruscan, 9 1/4 In. ................................................................................... 42.00
Plate, Flower Petals, Cabbage Leaf Design, Signed .................................................................. 12.00
Plate, Flower, Green, 9 In. ............................................................................................................ 15.00
Plate, Flying Crane Center, Turquoise Pebble Ground, Marked, 8 In. ........................................ 35.00
Plate, Fruit Leaves, Incised, Yellow, 8 1/2 In.Diam., Set Of 6 .................................................... 60.00
Plate, Gold, Green, & Rust, 7 1/2 In.Diam. .................................................................................. 28.00
Plate, Grape Leaf Center, Strawberries On Rim, 9 In., Set Of 12 ............................................ 550.00
Plate, Green & Gold Begonia Leaf, 9 1/4 In. ............................................................................... 30.00
Plate, Green Raised Design, C.1880, 8 1/4 In.Diam. ................................................................... 65.00
Plate, Green, Daisies, 7 1/4 In. ..................................................................................................... 12.00
Plate, Green, Griffin, Smith & Hill Co., 8 3/4 In., Pair ................................................................. 90.00
Plate, Hand-Painted Cottage Scene, 12 In. ................................................................................. 45.00
Plate, Leaf Shape, Large Veins, 8 1/2 In. ....................................................... 20.00 To 28.00
Plate, Maple Leaf ......................................................................................................................... 22.00
Plate, Orchid & Pink Geraniums, Open Handles .......................................................................... 62.00
Plate, Pink Wild Roses, 9 In. ........................................................................................................ 20.00
Plate, Pink, Green Center Grape Leaves ..................................................................................... 35.00
Plate, Raised Green & Brown Leaves, Marked, 8 1/2 In.Diam. ................................................... 60.00
Plate, Shell & Seaweed, 9 1/4 In.Diam. ..................................................................................... 135.00

Plate, Starfish, Etruscan, 6 In. ............................................................................. 14.00
Plate, Yellow & Green Flowers, 8 3/4 In. .......................................................... 14.00
Plate, 6 Shells, One In Center, 1880 Date, Artist's Mark, 7 In. ..................... 55.00
Platter, Albino, Shell & Seaweed ....................................................................... 125.00
Platter, Avalon, Blackberry, 13 X 9 1/2 In. ...................................................... 45.00
Platter, Bamboo, Marked ..................................................................................... 40.00
Platter, Dog, Green & Brown ............................................................................... 45.00
Platter, Floral, Etruscan, 9 X 10 In. ................................................................... 50.00
Platter, Leaf, Begonia, 12 X 8 In. ...................................................................... 45.00
Platter, Turquoise Ground, Irregularly Shaped, Marked, 9 X 12 In. ............... 70.00
Shaving Mug, Soap Rest, Pansies, Green & Blue ............................................ 48.00
Smoking Set, Boy Sitting Against Wall, Covered, 9 X 7 In. ........................... 35.00
Spittoon, Lined In Orchid, Raised Flowers, Flared, 6 X 7 In.Diam. ............... 40.00
Spooner, Barrel, Blackberry Blue Inside, 4 1/2 X 3 In. ................................... 42.00
Spooner, Bird, Signed .......................................................................................... 65.00
Spooner, Shell & Seaweed ................................................................................. 50.00
Sugar & Creamer, Albino, Gold Trim, Signed ................................................. 200.00
Sugar & Creamer, Pansies, Impressed ............................................................. 35.00
Sugar, Cauliflower ................................................................................................ 95.00
Sugar, Pineapple ................................................................................................... 115.00
Sugar, Raised Clusters Of Oak Leaves, Twig Handles, Acorn Knob ............. 12.00
Syrup, Shell & Seaweed, Pewter Lid, 6 3/4 In. ............................................... 75.00
Syrup, Sunflowers, Pewter Lid, 8 1/2 In. ........................................ 85.00 To 95.00
Teapot, Albino, Shell & Seaweed ....................................................................... 165.00
Teapot, Bamboo ................................................................................................... 95.00
Teapot, Brown Geometric Design, Bamboo Handle & Finial, 6 In. ............... 55.00
Teapot, Pineapple ................................................................................................ 115.00
Teapot, Shell & Seaweed .................................................................................... 185.00
Teaset, Shell & Seaweed, Etruscan, 3 Piece ................................................... 350.00
Tray, Begonia, Leaf Shape, 5 X 9 In. ................................................................ 25.00
Tray, Begonia, Ruffled Edge, Leaf, 9 X 7 In. .................................................. 20.00
Tray, Etruscan Leaf, Open Stem Handle, 9 X 11 In. ....................................... 75.00
Umbrella Stand, Pink Inside, Yellow, Pink Tulips, 20 In. ................................ 150.00
Urn, Purple Splashed With White, Turquoise Handles, C.1877, Signed ....... 240.00
Vase, Applied Figure Of Dutch Girl, Vine, Flowers, 13 In. ............................. 165.00
Vase, Art Nouveau, Iris, 4 1/2 In. ...................................................................... 20.00
Vase, Little Boy Goat Herder, 4 1/2 In. ............................................................ 25.00
Vase, Shield & Cock On 4 Panels, C.1900, 7 1/4 In., Pair ........................... 100.00

**MALACHITE, Ashtray** ......................................................................................... 60.00
Basket, Glass, Figures Of Woman & Children, 5 1/4 X 5 1/4 In. .................. 350.00
Bowl, Held By Kneeling Girl, 3 In. ..................................................................... 50.00
Box, Nude On Lid Holding Hourglass, Zodiac Signed, 4 X 5 1/4 In. ............ 145.00
Egg, Larger Than Hen's, Colored, Marked ....................................................... 125.00

**MAP, Africa,** Color, 1873, Collins & Sons, Glasgow, 9 X 11 3/4 In. ............ 10.00
Boston, Cram's Atlas, 1891, 9 X 12 In. ............................................................ 8.00
Chicago & Century Of Progress, Shell Oil Co. ................................................. 9.00
Chicago, Boston Journal, Pictorial Atlas, 1891, Color, 9 X 12 In. ................ 8.00
City Of San Francisco, 20 X 36 In. .................................................................... 35.00
Cleveland, Boston Journal, Pictorial Atlas, 1891, Color, 9 X 12 In. .............. 8.00
Delaware, World Wide Encyclopedia, Color, 1896, 7 1/2 X 10 1/2 In. ......... 4.00
Flight, World War II, Silk ...................................................................................... 15.00
Florida, Halifax To Cape Canaveral, Black & White, 1881, 12 X 13 In. ....... 7.00
German Empire, Collins & Sons, Glasgow, 1873, Color, 9 X 11 3/4 In. ....... 10.00
Kansas, Union Pacific Prominent, Color, 1887, 9 X 12 In. ............................. 14.00
Kentucky & Tennessee, Johson, Color, 1872, 16 X 24 In. ............................. 25.00
Naples, The Two Sicilies, Cowperthwait & Co., Color, 1850, 14 X 12 In. .... 8.00
New Jersey, 1812, Carey ..................................................................................... 85.00
Ohio, Johnson, Color, 1872, 16 X 24 In. .......................................................... 22.00
Pennsylvania, Mitchell, Color, 1867, 12 X 14 In. ............................................ 18.00
South Dakota, Old Farm, Post Offices, C.1920, 48 X 50 In. ......................... 22.50
State Of New York, J.H.French & R.P.Smith, 1860, City Scenes, 6 X 5 Ft. .. 50.00

| | |
|---|---|
| **United States,** School, 1860, 3 X 3 In. | 100.00 |
| **Wall,** School, Roll-Up, Europe, 1931, 48 In.Wide | 35.00 |

| | |
|---|---|
| **MARBLE CARVING, Bust,** Girl In Lace Bonnet, C.1878, F.G.Villa, C.1878, 58 In. | 575.00 |
| **Fruit,** Apple | 38.00 |
| **Fruit,** Ripe Fig | 35.00 |
| **Statue,** Woman Wearing Toga, Left Foot Raised, 24 1/4 In. | 325.00 |
| **Vase,** Gilt Bronze, Ovoid, Handles, Gray, Rust, 21 3/4 In., Pair | 650.00 |

*Marbles of glass were made during the nineteenth century. Venetian swirl, clear glass, sulfides, and marbles with frosted white animal figures embedded in the glass were popular. Handmade clay marbles were made in many places, but most of them came from the pottery factories of Ohio and Pennsylvania. Occasionally, real stone marbles of onyx, carnelian, or jasper can be found.*

| | |
|---|---|
| **MARBLE, Agate,** 3/4 In. | 8.00 |
| **Sulfide,** Angel | 50.00 |
| **Sulfide,** Baby Chick, 5 In. | 68.00 |
| **Sulfide,** Bimbo, Comic | 35.00 |
| **Sulfide,** Bird, 1 1/2 In. | 60.00 |
| **Sulfide,** Camel | 50.00 |
| **Sulfide,** Chicken | 50.00 |
| **Sulfide,** Dog, Large | 68.00 |
| **Sulfide,** Fish, 1 3/4 In. | 135.00 |
| **Sulfide,** Frog | 50.00 |
| **Sulfide,** Herbie | 35.00 |
| **Sulfide,** Lamb, 1 1/4 In.Diam. | 50.00 |
| **Sulfide,** Lamb, 1 3/4 In. | 40.00 |
| **Sulfide,** Monkey, Standing, 2 In. | 155.00 |
| **Sulfide,** Rooster, 6 In.Diam. | 85.00 |
| **Sulfide,** Salmon, Large | 73.00 |
| **Sulfide,** Setter Dog, 1 1/2 In. | 55.00 |
| **Sulfide,** Sheep, 1 In. | 75.00 |
| **Sulfide,** Sheep, 1 3/4 In. | 135.00 |
| **Sulfide,** Smitty, Comic | 35.00 |
| **Sulfide,** Swan | 75.00 |
| **Sulfide,** Swirl | 10.00 |
| **Sulfide,** Wild Pigeon, Large | 85.00 |
| **Swirl,** Onionskin | 8.00 |
| **Swirl,** Tricolored, Large | 40.00 |
| **Swirl,** Twin Pontil, 1/2 In. | 4.00 |
| **Swirl,** Twin Pontil, 3/4 In. | 6.00 |

*The Marblehead Pottery was founded in 1905 as a rehabilitative program for the patients of a Marblehead, Massachusetts, sanitarium by Dr. J. Hall. Two years later it was separated from the sanitarium, and it continued operations until 1936. Many of the pieces were decorated with marine motifs.*

| | |
|---|---|
| **MARBLEHEAD, Ale Set,** 6 Mugs, Gray & Blue, Pitcher, 8 In. | 250.00 |
| **Plate,** Hand-Decorated, 10 In. | 55.00 |
| **Tile,** Floral Design, Yellow-Brown Glaze, 6 1/2 X 6 1/2 In. | 125.00 |
| **Tile,** Ocean Liner In Slate & Brown, Gray Ground, Label, 6 1/4 In. | 100.00 |
| **Tile,** Rear View Of Galleon Ship On Water, 4 1/2 In.Square | 135.00 |
| **Tile,** Sailing Ship, Impressed Mark, 6 1/2 In.Square | 250.00 |
| **Tile,** Stylized Bird, Flowers, Ivory Border, Marked, 6 1/4 In. | 90.00 |
| **Vase,** Olive Green, Marked, 5 In. | 40.00 |
| **Vase,** Stylized Leaf Design, Blue, Signed, 3 3/4 In. | 275.00 |
| **Vase,** White Inside, Mauve, 2 1/2 In. | 40.00 |
| **Wall Pocket,** Blue, 4 X 5 In. | 60.00 |
| **Wall Pocket,** Brown, 4 X 5 In. | 60.00 |

    **MARINE, see Nautical**

*Martinware is a salt-glazed stoneware made by the Martin Brothers of Middlesex, England, between 1873 and 1915. Many figural jugs and vases were made.*

**MARTIN BROTHERS, Bottle,** Brown, 8 In. .................................................................................. 235.00
  **Box,** Cover, Celtic Dragons, 8 1/2 In.Square ........................................................... 1200.00
  **Figurine,** Owl, Caricature, Dated 1900, 9 In. ......................................................... 3500.00
  **Pitcher,** Cherry Blossoms, 7 In. .................................................................................... 300.00
  **Pitcher,** Coat Of Arms, Brown, 9 In. ............................................................................. 375.00
  **Pitcher,** Leaves, 10 In. ....................................................................................................... 275.00
  **Pitcher,** 2 Spouts, Loop Handle, 7 In. ......................................................................... 150.00
  **Pitcher,** 2-Faced Caricature, Dated 1897, 7 1/4 In. ........................................... 1200.00
  **Vase,** Bird Head Handles, Blue Leaves, 13 In. ....................................................... 1000.00
  **Vase,** Blue Matte, 3 1/2 In. .............................................................................................. 110.00
  **Vase,** Flowers & Leaves, 11 In. ....................................................................................... 1000.00
  **Vase,** Flying Cranes, 14 In. .............................................................................................. 1200.00
  **Vase,** Geometric Design, 2 1/2 In. ................................................................................. 175.00
  **Vase,** Grape Leaves In Relief, 8 1/2 In. ........................................................................ 700.00
  **Vase,** Incised & Painted, London, 10 1/4 In. ............................................................. 250.00
  **Vase,** Incised Fish, Stoneware, 7 In. .............................................................................. 250.00
  **Vase,** Incised Flowers, Stoneware, 7 In. ....................................................................... 200.00
  **Vase,** Leaves, 8 1/2 In. ........................................................................................................ 600.00
  **Vase,** Morning Glories, 9 In. ............................................................................................. 375.00
  **Vase,** Stoneware, 1887, 10 1/4 In. ............................................................................... 1000.00
  **Vase,** Stylized Leaves & Flowers, 9 In. ......................................................................... 700.00
  **Vase,** Sunflowers, 9 In. ....................................................................................................... 350.00
  **Vase,** 2-Handled, Butterfly, 10 In. ................................................................................ 800.00
  **Vase,** 4-Handled, White Leaves, 8 In. ........................................................................... 850.00

*Mary Gregory glass is identified by a characteristic white figure painted on dark glass. It was made from 1870 to 1910. The name refers to any glass decorated with a white silhouette figure and not just the Sandwich glass originally painted by Miss Mary Gregory.*

**MARY GREGORY, Beaker,** White Enamel Boy Figure, Cranberry ................................... 75.00
  **Bell,** Blue ..................................................................................................................................... 12.00
  **Bottle,** Barber, Bubbles & Pontil Mark, Amethyst .................................................... 165.00
  **Bottle,** Barber, Girl With Flowers, Amethyst ............................................................... 115.00
  **Bottle,** Cologne, Amethyst, Stopper, 5 In. ..................................................................... 85.00
  **Bottle,** Cologne, Deep Amethyst, Original Stopper, 5 In. ....................................... 85.00
  **Bottle,** Perfume Atomizer, Inverted Thumbprint, Cranberry, 3 In. .................... 135.00
  **Bottle,** Perfume, Champagne Color, Boy, White Enamel, 4 In. ........................... 118.00
  **Bottle,** Perfume, Clear, 6 In. ............................................................................................. 58.00
  **Bottle,** Perfume, Cranberry, 4 1/2 In. ............................................................................ 60.00
  **Bottle,** Perfume, Figure Of Girl, 4 1/2 In. .................................................................... 95.00
  **Bottle,** Perfume, Olive Green, White Girl, Chain, Cap & Stopper ..................... 185.00
  **Bottle,** Perfume, White Enamel Girl, Stopper, Green, 3 1/8 In. ......................... 145.00
  **Bottle,** Wine, White Boy Blowing Bubbles, Cranberry, 9 In. ............................... 195.00
  **Bottle,** Wine, White Boy With Bubble Pipe, Cranberry, 8 3/4 In. ..................... 195.00
  **Bottle,** Wine, White Enamel Girl, Emerald Green, 9 In. ........................................ 125.00
  **Bottle,** Wine, White Enamel Girl, Stopper, Blue, 10 3/4 In. ................................ 125.00
  **Bowl,** Finger, Goldstone, Applied Baby Face, 7 In. ................................................ 400.00
  **Box,** Covered, Knob Finial, Young Boy, Chartreuse, 4 1/2 X 2 In. ..................... 135.00
  **Box,** Green, White, Shepherd Boy, Hinged, 3 1/2 X 4 1/2 In. ............................. 225.00
  **Box,** Hinged Cover, Ormolu Feet, Enamel Girl, Ruby, 6 In.Diam. ....................... 195.00
  **Box,** Hinged, Girl & Foliage, White Enamel, Blue, 4 In.Diam. ............................. 345.00
  **Box,** Knob Finial, All-White Boy, Chartreuse, 4 1/4 X 2 1/2 In. .......................... 125.00
  **Box,** Patch, Hinged, White Girl, Chartreuse, 4 X 1 7/8 In. .................................. 145.00
  **Box,** Trinket, White Enamel Design, Aqua Blue, 3 In. ............................................ 80.00
  **Carafe,** Water, Matching Tumbler, White Enamel Figure, Green .......................... 195.00
  **Compote,** Sapphire Blue, Ruffled, Girl Feeding Birds, 4 3/4 In. .......................... 125.00
  **Creamer,** Blue, Clear Applied Handled, White Girl Figure ...................................... 110.00
  **Cruet,** Enameled Girl & Dove, Reeded Handle, Green, 11 In. ............................. 325.00
  **Cruet,** Green Applied Handle, White Enamel Boy, Green, 7 In. ......................... 195.00

**Cruet,** Green Handle & Stopper, Girl With Basket, Green, 7 In. ............................................ 175.00
**Cruet,** Teardrop Stopper, White Girl, Chartreuse, 7 1/4 In. ................................................. 165.00
**Decanter,** Blue, White Enamel Boy, Girl, Trees, Birds, 12 In. ............................................. 125.00
**Decanter,** Inverted Panel, Handled, Stopper, Blue, 10 In. .................................................. 295.00
**Decanter,** White Enamel Boy Blowing Bubbles, Gold Trim, 9 In. ......................................... 235.00
**Glass,** Juice, Amber, White Girl In Field .............................................................................. 38.00
**Glass,** Liquor, Boy Holding Branch, 3 1/4 In. ....................................................................... 35.00
**Glass,** White Girl Figures, Green, 4 In. ................................................................................ 50.00
**Goblet,** Blue And White, Figures Of Elves, 7 In., Pair .......................................................... 55.00
**Holder,** Hatpin, Boy & Girl, Lime Green, 1 1/2 X 2 1/4 In., Pair .......................................... 300.00
**Inkwell,** Black Glass, Beveled, Square, 2 1/2 In. .................................................................. 95.00
**Jar,** Biscuit, Blue, White Enamel, Girl, Gold Florals, 6 In. .................................................... 75.00
**Jar,** Cracker, Cranberry, Bronze Handled Lid, 7 X 5 In. ....................................................... 250.00
**Jar,** Pomade, Girl In White On Lid, Cranberry, 3 X 1/2 In.Diam. .......................................... 175.00
**Jar,** Powder, Covered, Cranberry, Small ............................................................................... 125.00
**Lamp,** Base, Cranberry, Miniature ....................................................................................... 175.00
**Lamp,** Oil, Black Amethyst, Child Chasing Butterfly, 24 In., Pair ...................................... 1500.00
**Lemonade Set,** 6 Tumblers, Gold Design, Cranberry, 19th Century ................................... 425.00
**Liqueur Set,** Tray, White Boy, Sapphire Blue, Bottle, 9 1/8 In. ........................................... 395.00
**Mug,** Amber, Girl Holding Flag, 3 1/2 In. ............................................................................. 75.00
**Mug,** Clear Handle, Girl In All-White Enamel, 3 3/8 In. ........................................................ 68.00
**Mug,** Cranberry, 1 3/4 In. .................................................................................................... 85.00
**Pitcher,** Applied Clear Handle, Cranberry Color Boy .......................................................... 225.00
**Pitcher,** Blue Coin Spot, Applied Ribbed Handle, 6 In. ........................................................ 75.00
**Pitcher,** Canberry, Flared Top, 10 In. .................................................................................. 195.00
**Pitcher,** Clear Handle, White Boy With Hat, Cranberry, 9 1/4 In. ........................................ 168.00
**Pitcher,** Green, Applied Handle, Girl With Lily Of Valley, 6 In. ............................................ 125.00
**Plate,** Lattice Rim, White Figures, Black Milk Glass, 8 1/2 In. ............................................ 175.00
**Salt,** Boy & Girl At Well, Sterling Silver Overlay, Bell Shape .............................................. 135.00
**Syrup,** Inverted Iris, Embossed .......................................................................................... 55.00
**Tankard,** Boy Figure, Green ................................................................................................ 200.00
**Toothpick,** White Enameled, Boy Blowing Horn .................................................................. 125.00
**Tray,** Boy & Girl In White, Champagne Color, 6 1/2 X 9 1/4 In. .......................................... 195.00
**Tumble-Up,** Girl With Bird, Sapphire Blue ........................................................................... 165.00
**Tumbler,** Boy & Girl, Flowers In Hand, Pair ........................................................................ 125.00
**Tumbler,** Boy Holding Hat & Flower, White Enamel, 4 7/8 In. ............................................. 65.00
**Tumbler,** Lemonade, Tinted Boy & Girl, Green .................................................................... 79.00
**Tumbler,** White Enamel Boy, Clear Flint, 3 1/2 In. .............................................................. 38.00
**Tumbler,** White Enamel Girl, Cranberry, 3 5/8 In. ............................................................... 60.00
**Tumbler,** White Figure, Trees, Birds, Samuel 1904 ............................................................. 28.00
**Vase,** Amber, Boy, White Enameled, Gold Snail Handles, 9 In. .......................................... 235.00
**Vase,** Amber, Footed, Girl Feeding Birds, 6 1/4 In. .............................................................. 60.00
**Vase,** Amber, Frosted, Girl Waving Hat, 5 1/8 X 3 3/4 In. ................................................... 110.00
**Vase,** Applied Crystal Sides, White Boy, Emerald Green, 10 In. ......................................... 135.00
**Vase,** Applied Shells On Sides, Boy With Oar, Cranberry, 9 In. .......................................... 195.00
**Vase,** Blue & White Enameling, 6 In. .................................................................................. 275.00
**Vase,** Bowl, Lime Green, Girl, Boy With Hoop, White Enamel, 5 In ..................................... 250.00
**Vase,** Boy & Girl At Pump, Opaque Green, 13 3/4 In. .......................................................... 295.00
**Vase,** Boy & Girl Picking Flowers, Cranberry, 8 1/4 In. ....................................................... 295.00
**Vase,** Bud, White Enamel Girl, Sapphire Blue, 6 1/4 In. ...................................................... 95.00
**Vase,** Cherub Head Feet, Enameled, Atlantic City, 6 In., Pair ............................................. 385.00
**Vase,** Children & Dogs, White Design, Lime Green, 13 1/4 In., Pr. ...................................... 750.00
**Vase,** Cobalt Blue, Bottle Shape, Girl Climbing Tree, 6 1/4 In. ............................................ 85.00
**Vase,** Cranberry, Brass Base, Cherub's Head Feet, 6 In., Pair ........................................... 385.00
**Vase,** Cranberry, Girl Carrying Basket, 4 1/2 X 2 3/4 In. ..................................................... 95.00
**Vase,** Cranberry, Girl With Balloon, 5 1/8 X 2 5/8 In. .......................................................... 95.00
**Vase,** Cranberry, Young Boy, 5 1/8 X 2 1/4 In. .................................................................... 95.00
**Vase,** Crystal Applique On Sides, Boy With Paddle, 9 In. .................................................... 195.00
**Vase,** Crystal Handles, White Enamel Girl, Blue, 6 1/4 In. ................................................... 115.00
**Vase,** Cylinder, Iridized Green, 7 In. ................................................................................... 145.00
**Vase,** Emerald Green, Girl Facing Boy, Ruffled Top, 10 In., Pair ........................................ 450.00
**Vase,** Emerald Green, White Head Of Girl, 6 1/2 In. ............................................................ 90.00
**Vase,** Facing Boy & Girl, White Enamel, Cranberry, 9 In., Pair ........................................... 365.00

| | |
|---|---|
| **Vase,** Girl Carrying Flowers, Frosted Emerald Green, 9 In. | 150.00 |
| **Vase,** Girl In Garden, 3-Footed Brass Holder, Green, 6 1/2 In. | 85.00 |
| **Vase,** Girl With Basket, Boy With Tray, White, 4 3/8 In., Pair | 450.00 |
| **Vase,** Girl With Bird In White, 10 1/4 In. | 195.00 |
| **Vase,** Girl With Butterfly Net, Blue, 8 3/4 In. | 165.00 |
| **Vase,** Girl With Hat In White Enamel, Lime Green, 6 In. | 88.00 |
| **Vase,** Girls With Birds, White Enamel, Cranberry, 12 In., Pair | 575.00 |
| **Vase,** Girls, Birds, Facing, White Enamel, 12 3/8 In., Pair | 695.00 |
| **Vase,** Green Trim, White Ground, C.1890, 7 In., Pair | 95.00 |
| **Vase,** Green, Figures, Blossoms, Enameled Angel & Child, 12 In. | 145.00 |
| **Vase,** Green, White Boy, 9 1/4 In. | 170.00 |
| **Vase,** Green, White Enameled Boy, Rigaree On Side, 11 In. | 485.00 |
| **Vase,** Inverted Thumbprint, White Boy, Cranberry, 2 1/2 In. | 98.00 |
| **Vase,** Lime Green, Boy In All White, 11 In. | 110.00 |
| **Vase,** Ormolu Foot, White Enamel Girl With Hat, Amber, 7 1/2 In. | 110.00 |
| **Vase,** Ruffled, Inverted Thumbprint, White Enamel, 5 In. | 100.00 |
| **Vase,** Ruffled, White Enamel Girl & Trees, Green, 10 3/4 In. | 150.00 |
| **Vase,** Ruffled, White Enamel Girl, Cobalt Blue, 12 In. | 195.00 |
| **Vase,** White Enamel Boy With Hat & Cane, Blue, 9 1/4 In. | 125.00 |
| **Vase,** White Enamel Boy With Hoop, Pink, White Lining, 9 In. | 195.00 |
| **Vase,** White Enamel Boy, Cranberry, 7 X 3 1/4 In.Diam. | 110.00 |
| **Vase,** White Enamel Girl, Gold Trim, Chartreuse, 3 7/8 In. | 88.00 |
| **Vase,** White Enamel Girl, Ruby, 7 1/4 X 3 3/4 In.Diam. | 135.00 |
| **Vase,** White Girl Seated On Branch, Pink Opaque, 11 7/8 In. | 225.00 |
| **Vase,** White Girl With Bird On Finger, Pink, 10 1/4 In. | 195.00 |
| **Vase,** Young Girl Carrying Basket, White Enamel, 4 1/2 In. | 95.00 |
| **Wine,** Stemmed, Boy & Girl, Sapphire Blue, 3 7/8 In., Pair | 120.00 |
| **Wine,** Stemmed, White Enameled Boy, Dots At Base, 4 5/8 In. | 85.00 |

*Masonic Shrine glassware was made from 1893 to 1917. It is occasionally called Syrian Temple Shrine glassware. Most pieces are dated.*

| | |
|---|---|
| **MASONIC, Banner,** Shriner, 1912, Set Of 17 | 8.00 |
| **Bottle,** Ear Of Corn, Green & Yellow Paint, Milk Glass, Shrine, 3 In. | 50.00 |
| **Can,** Ballot, Trace Of Painted Masonic Emblems | 225.00 |
| **Chalice,** Pittsburgh 1899, Lion | 55.00 |
| **Chalice,** St.Paul, 1908 | 65.00 |
| **Champagne,** 1911 | 65.00 |
| **Cocktail,** Syria Shrine, Pittsburgh, Pa., 1909, Louisville, Ky. | 65.00 |
| **Cup & Saucer,** Chocolate, Eastern Star Emblem | 7.50 |
| **Door Knocker,** Brass, 6 1/2 In. | 50.00 |
| **Ewer,** Melita Lodge, No.295, White China, 11 In. | 85.00 |
| **Glass,** Syria-Pittsburgh, New Orleans, 1910, Shrine | 35.00 |
| **Goblet,** Pittsburgh, 1909, Iridescent | 35.00 |
| **Hatpin,** Gold Filigree, Masonic Emblem | 35.00 |
| **Hatpin,** 1 1/4 In.Top | 60.00 |
| **Lap Robe,** Shriners Emblem | 125.00 |
| **Mug,** Fish Handle, Pittsburgh, Atlantic City, 1904, 3 1/2 In. | 65.00 |
| **Mug,** Saratoga, Shriner, Indian Head, 1903 | 45.00 |
| **Mug,** Shrine, Pittsburgh, 1903, Sword Handle, Indian In Relief | 50.00 |
| **Paperweight,** Boston, Patent 1892, Glass, Oblong | 4.50 |
| **Paperweight,** Masonic Home, Utica | 7.00 |
| **Pin,** Lady's Slipper, Compass & Square, Emblem, Blue Enamel On Gold | 20.00 |
| **Planter,** Eastern Star, 3 1/4 In. | 6.00 |
| **Plate,** Dated 1903, 9 1/2 In.Diam. | 25.00 |
| **Plate,** Lodge No. 605, Blue & Gold, 1905 | 40.00 |
| **Plate,** Shriner, Los Angeles, 1906, 6 In. | 37.50 |
| **Platter,** B.P.O.E., Purple Border, Emblem, 12 1/2 In. | 25.00 |
| **Ring,** Emblem In Ruby Square, Diamond On Each Side, 10K Gold | 300.00 |
| **Ring,** Rebecca Lodge, 14K Gold, Onyx | 45.00 |
| **Spoon,** Sterling Silver, Masonic Silver Conclave, Colo., 1892 | 25.00 |
| **Stein,** Utica, N.Y., San Francisco, 1902, 1 In. | 65.00 |
| **Tankard,** Blue, 1912, 12 1/2 In. | 75.00 |

| | |
|---|---|
| **Teaspoon,** Enamel Design, 32nd Degree, Sterling Silver | 45.00 |
| **Teaspoon,** Souvenir, Chicago Temple, Sterling Silver | 26.00 |
| **Tie Bar,** 10K Gold | 22.00 |
| **Uniform,** Knights Templar, Frock Coat, Hats, Belts, Cape, In Trunk | 65.00 |
| **Watch Fob,** Grand Lodge Of The State Of Iowa | 45.00 |
| **Watch Fob,** Missouri, 1915, Quit Kickin' My Dawg Around | 30.00 |
| **Watch Fob,** Rochester International, Tortoiseshell, Rhinestones | 30.00 |
| **Watch Fob,** Terre Haute, Ind., Temple Dedication, July 1917, Strap | 15.00 |

**C.M**

**Golfe-Juan.**    *Massier pottery is iridescent French art pottery made by Clement Massier in Golfe-Juane, France, in the late nineteenth and early twentieth centuries. It is characterized by a metallic luster glaze.*

| | |
|---|---|
| **MASSIER, Vase,** Floral Design, Iridescent, 6 In. | 200.00 |
| **MATCH HOLDER, see also Iron, Match Holder; Staffordshire, Match Holder; Store, Match Holder** | |
| **MATCH HOLDER, Adriance Buckeye,** Mowers & Reapers, Poughkeepsie, N.Y. | 24.00 |
| **Barrel Shape,** 2 X 9 1/2 In. | 9.50 |
| **Bowl Of Pipe Shape,** 2 3/4 X 7 In. | 9.00 |
| **Boy Standing By Hollow Tree,** Dated 1882, Gutta-Percha | 155.00 |
| **Boy Wearing Nightshirt,** Sitting On Potty, 3 1/4 X 3 1/4 In. | 95.00 |
| **Bucket On Base,** Pot Metal | 15.00 |
| **Bullock Ward,** Chicago, Tin | 16.00 |
| **Cat,** Bisque | 75.00 |
| **Cigarettes,** Dog In Center, Pot Metal | 25.00 |
| **Cloisonne,** China, 3/4 X 1 1/2 X 2 1/4 In. | 25.00 |
| **Cresota,** Little Boy With Loaf Of Bread | 45.00 |
| **Cylinder Shape,** Stamped Flowers, Brass, 2 1/2 In. | 17.50 |
| **DeLaval Cream Separator,** Tin, Boxed      45.00 To | 80.00 |
| **Dockash Stove Factory,** Picture Of Factory, Scranton, Pa. | 22.00 |
| **Dog Sitting Up Holding Hat,** China, German, 6 X 2 1/4 In.Diam. | 45.00 |
| **Double,** Deerhead Top, Rabbit Sides, Gun, Bugle | 45.00 |
| **Dr.Shoop's,** Tin | 60.00 |
| **Dutch Boy,** Tin | 125.00 |
| **Dwarf Lighting Cigar On Candle,** Bisque, 6 In. | 60.00 |
| **Figural,** Child Sitting On Potty, China | 25.00 |
| **Figural,** Lizard, China | 23.00 |
| **Figural,** Scotty, Blue, Brass | 27.50 |
| **Figural,** Skull, Striker, Porcelain | 50.00 |
| **Hinged Lid,** Bottom Striker, Red Design, Tin, 2 X 4 1/2 X 2 In. | 18.00 |
| **Jenny Lind,** Clear | 52.00 |
| **Lion Brewing,** Girl & Umbrella, Cardboard | 50.00 |
| **Michigan Stove Co.,** Cast Iron | 45.00 |
| **Milk Glass,** Gold Trim | 15.00 |
| **Milwaukee Binders & Mowers,** Tin | 30.00 |
| **Mother's Worm Syrup** | 150.00 |
| **Old Sunnybrook Whiskey,** Wall, Tin | 30.00 |
| **Open Purse,** Blue Glass | 29.00 |
| **Pocket,** Double, Embossed Star, Tin | 16.00 |
| **Pocket,** San Felice Quality Cigars | 20.00 |
| **Rush Club,** Crimped & Flared Top, Tin | 45.00 |
| **Sharples Separator Co.,** Woman With Separator      49.00 To | 59.00 |
| **The Hunt,** Double Pouch, Rabbit, Bird, Horn, Cast Iron | 75.00 |
| **Usher's Whiskey,** Kipling Poem, Stoneware | 90.00 |
| **Wall,** Figural, Shovel & Pail, Bail For Matches, Brass, 9 1/2 In. | 50.00 |
| **Wall,** Old Judson Whiskey, Man, Woman, Little Girl | 35.00 |
| **White Rock,** China | 12.50 |
| | |
| **MATCH SAFE, see also Silver-Sterling, Match Safe** | |
| **MATCH SAFE, Anheuser Busch,** Embossed Brass | 50.00 |
| **Art Nouveau Flowers,** German Silver | 32.50 |
| **Art Nouveau,** Rococo, Gem, Sterling Silver | 100.00 |

| | |
|---|---|
| **Birds,** Matches | 63.50 |
| **Bridgeport,** Conn., Shield On Cover, Brass | 22.50 |
| **Cherubs,** Flowers, Vines, Sterling, 925 Fine, Hinged Top | 95.00 |
| **Crimped Top,** Brushwork Around Hinging Hole, Painted, 7 1/2 In. | 130.00 |
| **Diamond Matches,** Tin | 9.00 |
| **Dog On Sugar Crate,** Hinged Lid, Brass, Brench | 70.00 |
| **Drake's Palmetto Wine,** Colored, Tin | 55.00 |
| **Dutch Boy,** Tin | 65.00 |
| **Embossed Flowers Allover,** Ribbons, Sterling Silver | 85.00 |
| **Embossed Flowers,** Scrolls, Sterling Silver, English, Hallmark | 35.00 |
| **Embossed Scene Of Deer,** Silver Plate, Dated 1904 | 15.00 |
| **Figural,** Cigar Box, El Telegrafo, Key West | 45.00 |
| **Figural,** Pig, Head Opens, Brass | 28.00 |
| **Figural,** Stern-Faced Old Man's Head, Dated 1888, Brass, 2 1/2 In. | 35.00 |
| **Fisherman's,** Sterling Silver | 50.00 |
| **Fishing Rod & Net Engraving,** Nickel Over Brass | 16.00 |
| **Grape Design On Front,** Tin | 10.00 |
| **Ideal Pharmacy,** Taloga, Okla. | 11.00 |
| **Imperial Council,** California, 1907, Saladin Temple | 32.00 |
| **Lady,** Flowing Hair, In Garden, Etched, Marked, 2 5/8 X 1 1/4 In. | 75.00 |
| **Louisiana Purchase,** Thomas Jefferson, Nickel Plated Brass | 37.50 |
| **Profile Of Woman,** Floral, Silver, Sterling | 50.00 |
| **Saddles & Riding Equipment,** Sterling Silver | 80.00 |
| **Silver State Cigar,** Denver, Embossed Stag | 45.00 |
| **Souvenir,** Jamestown, 1904 | 22.50 |
| **Spanish American War,** Enameled Brass Emblem & Shield | 25.00 |
| **St.Louis Exposition,** Palace Of Arts, U.S.Government Building | 22.00 |
| **St.Louis Exposition,** 1904, Palace Of Arts | 30.00 |
| **St.Louis World's Fair,** 1904, Jefferson & Napoleon Obverse | 34.00 |
| **Topeka Linseed Oil Works,** Topeka, Kansas | 40.00 |
| **Trousers,** Patent 1886 | 65.00 |
| **U.S.Injector,** Aluminum | 35.00 |
| **Woman Among Flowers,** Silver, Sterling | 59.00 |

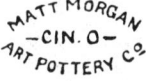

*Matt Morgan opened an art pottery company in Cincinnati, Ohio, in 1883.
It lasted in business for only a year, closing because of money problems.*

**MATT MORGAN, Vase,** White & Green Flowers, Impressed Mark, C.1883, 5 In., Pair .......... 200.00

*McCoy pottery is made in Roseville, Ohio. The J.W. McCoy
Pottery was founded in 1899. It became the Brush McCoy Pottery
Company in 1911. The name changed to the Brush Pottery in 1925. The
Nelson McCoy Sanitary and Stoneware Company was founded in
Roseville, Ohio, in 1910. This firm made art pottery after 1926. In 1933
it became the Nelson McCoy Pottery. Pieces marked McCoy were
made by the Nelson McCoy Company.*

| | |
|---|---|
| **MC COY, Bank,** Pig, Marbleized, Brown, Yellow Glaze, Pieced Eyes | 46.00 |
| **Basket,** Oak Leaf & Acorn, Dark Green | 15.00 |
| **Bowl,** Flower Frog, Zuniart, 7 X 2 In. | 55.00 |
| **Bowl,** Loy-Nel-Art, Yellow Blossoms, Brown Glaze, 6 1/4 In.Diam. | 125.00 |
| **Bowl,** Nested Shoulder, Green, C.1926, 9 1/2 In. | 20.00 |
| **Candlestick,** Bird, Blue, 7 In. | 12.00 |
| **Candlestick,** Jetwood, 10 1/2 In. | 175.00 |
| **Casserole,** Rooster | 16.00 |
| **Clock,** Mottled Blue, Brush McCoy Period | 88.00 |
| **Clock,** Table Top, Mottled Blue & White, Marked, 4 1/4 X 4 In. | 95.00 |
| **Cookie Jar,** ABC, Churn Boy | 22.00 |
| **Cookie Jar,** Apple | 13.00 |
| **Cookie Jar,** Banana | 20.00 To 28.00 |

Cookie Jar, Barnum's Animal Crackers ......................................................................... 38.00
Cookie Jar, Barrel ........................................................................................................ 12.00
Cookie Jar, Basket ....................................................................................................... 18.00
Cookie Jar, Bear ............................................................................................ 15.00 To 28.00
Cookie Jar, Bear On Stump ............................................................................ 20.00 To 25.00
Cookie Jar, Black Chef .................................................................................................. 22.50
Cookie Jar, Black Lantern ............................................................................................. 21.00
Cookie Jar, Bushel Basket With Fruit Top .................................................................... 32.00
Cookie Jar, Cabin ......................................................................................... 20.00 To 26.00
Cookie Jar, Chef Head ................................................................................................. 25.00
Cookie Jar, Chinese Lantern ........................................................................................ 22.00
Cookie Jar, Chipmunk ................................................................................... 18.00 To 45.00
Cookie Jar, Circus Horse .............................................................................................. 45.00
Cookie Jar, Circus Horse, Monkey Lid, Black ............................................................... 35.00
Cookie Jar, Clown Out Of Basket ................................................................................. 32.00
Cookie Jar, Clown, Bust ................................................................................ 10.00 To 25.00
Cookie Jar, Clown, Full Body ........................................................................................ 25.00
Cookie Jar, Coffee Grinder ............................................................................ 10.00 To 18.00
Cookie Jar, Coffeepot ................................................................................................... 15.00
Cookie Jar, Cookie Boy ................................................................................................. 42.00
Cookie Jar, Cookie Cabin .............................................................................................. 28.00
Cookie Jar, Cookie House .............................................................................. 35.00 To 40.00
Cookie Jar, Cookie Jug ................................................................................................. 15.00
Cookie Jar, Cookstove, Black ....................................................................................... 12.00
Cookie Jar, Cookstove, White ........................................................................ 12.00 To 17.00
Cookie Jar, Corn ........................................................................................................... 50.00
Cookie Jar, Covered Wagon ........................................................................... 15.00 To 36.00
Cookie Jar, Dalmatians ................................................................................................ 60.00
Cookie Jar, Davy Crockett ............................................................................................ 45.00
Cookie Jar, Doughboy ................................................................................................... 19.50
Cookie Jar, Dresser ...................................................................................................... 20.00
Cookie Jar, Dutchman ................................................................................................... 16.00
Cookie Jar, Elephant ..................................................................................................... 60.00
Cookie Jar, Fireplace .................................................................................................... 46.00
Cookie Jar, Fortune Cookie ........................................................................................... 15.00
Cookie Jar, Frontier Family ............................................................................ 12.00 To 18.00
Cookie Jar, Globe .......................................................................................................... 40.00
Cookie Jar, Green Pepper ............................................................................................. 25.00
Cookie Jar, Have A Happy Day ..................................................................................... 11.00
Cookie Jar, Honey Bear ................................................................................................ 23.00
Cookie Jar, Horse Pulling Milk Wagon .......................................................................... 15.00
Cookie Jar, House ......................................................................................................... 35.00
Cookie Jar, Humpty Dumpty ......................................................................................... 35.50
Cookie Jar, Indian Head ................................................................................. 82.00 To 95.00
Cookie Jar, Kettle, Immovable Bale .............................................................................. 12.00
Cookie Jar, Kettle, Movable Bale, Large ....................................................................... 15.00
Cookie Jar, Kissing Penguins ....................................................................................... 30.00
Cookie Jar, Kitten In Pink Basket, Signed ...................................................... 22.00 To 24.00
Cookie Jar, Kittens On Ball Of Twine, Signed .............................................................. 25.00
Cookie Jar, Kookie Kettle ............................................................................................. 12.00
Cookie Jar, Lamb On Basket ........................................................................................ 24.00
Cookie Jar, Lantern ...................................................................................................... 20.00
Cookie Jar, Locomotive ................................................................................................ 36.00
Cookie Jar, Lovebirds ................................................................................................... 15.00
Cookie Jar, Mammy ....................................................................................... 16.50 To 40.00
Cookie Jar, Modern Cookie ........................................................................................... 16.00
Cookie Jar, Mr.& Mrs.Owl .............................................................................. 28.00 To 30.00
Cookie Jar, Oak'n Bucket .............................................................................................. 12.00
Cookie Jar, Old Hen ...................................................................................................... 15.00
Cookie Jar, Owl .............................................................................................. 10.00 To 30.00
Cookie Jar, Peach ......................................................................................................... 30.00
Cookie Jar, Pears On Basket ........................................................................................ 22.00
Cookie Jar, Pepper ....................................................................................................... 30.00

**Cookie Jar,** Picnic Basket ........................................ 25.00 To 30.00
**Cookie Jar,** Pineapple ............................................ 16.00 To 19.00
**Cookie Jar,** Potbelly Stove ..................................... 12.00 To 20.00
**Cookie Jar,** Pumpkin ............................................................. 40.50
**Cookie Jar,** Puppy ................................................. 18.00 To 32.00
**Cookie Jar,** Puss 'n Boots ................................................... 30.00
**Cookie Jar,** Raggedy Ann ...................................................... 22.00
**Cookie Jar,** Rocking Horse ..................................... 28.00 To 40.00
**Cookie Jar,** Rooster ............................................... 30.00 To 38.00
**Cookie Jar,** Sad Clown ......................................................... 24.00
**Cookie Jar,** Sad Puppy ......................................................... 28.00
**Cookie Jar,** Schoolhouse ....................................................... 20.00
**Cookie Jar,** Scotty Dog ......................................................... 20.00
**Cookie Jar,** Snoopy On House, Signed ...................................... 16.00
**Cookie Jar,** Snow Bear .......................................................... 20.00
**Cookie Jar,** Squirrel On Log ................................................... 30.00
**Cookie Jar,** Strawberry .......................................... 18.00 To 24.00
**Cookie Jar,** Teakettle ........................................................... 20.00
**Cookie Jar,** Teapot, Dutch Design ........................................... 15.00
**Cookie Jar,** Tepee ................................................. 75.00 To 95.00
**Cookie Jar,** Touring Car ......................................... 22.50 To 35.00
**Cookie Jar,** Train ................................................................. 30.00
**Cookie Jar,** Tudor House ........................................................ 32.00
**Cookie Jar,** Turkey ............................................................... 50.00
**Cookie Jar,** W.C.Fields .......................................... 35.00 To 50.00
**Cookie Jar,** Wedding Jar ........................................................ 22.00
**Cookie Jar,** Windmill ............................................................. 28.00
**Cookie Jar,** Wishing Well ....................................... 15.00 To 18.00
**Creamer,** Pinecone, Green & Brown ............................................ 4.75
**Dish,** Dog Feeder, Embossed Dog On Side, Green, 6 1/2 X 3 1/4 In. ...... 12.95
**Dish,** Shell Shape, Burnished Gold Inside, Ivory Underside, 7 1/4 In. ...... 17.95
**Figurine,** Frog, Bird Bath ...................................................... 22.50
**Figurine,** Negro, Playing Guitar, Seated By Barrel ......................... 30.00
**Figurine,** Pelican ............................................................... 45.00
**Jardiniere,** Basket Weave, Cherry, 10 In. ................................... 28.00
**Jardiniere,** Cameo, Green & Ivory, 10 In. ................................... 50.00
**Jardiniere,** White Dogwood, Pink, Signed .................................... 35.00
**Lamp,** Cowboy Boot, Shade ..................................................... 12.00
**Pitcher,** Angelfish ............................................................. 10.00
**Pitcher,** Buttermilk, Shield Mark ............................................. 25.00
**Pitcher,** Chicken, White ....................................................... 13.50
**Pitcher,** Grape Design, Blue, 9 In. .......................................... 20.00
**Pitcher,** Grape Design, Yellow, 9 In. ........................................ 14.00
**Pitcher,** Olympia, Floral Design, 3-Footed, Signed, 5 X 4 In. .............. 100.00
**Pitcher,** Raised Butterfly On Sides, 10 In. .................................. 25.00
**Pitcher,** Tavern, Green ........................................................ 75.00
**Planter,** Basket Weave ......................................................... 4.00
**Planter,** Bird Dog .............................................................. 40.00
**Planter,** Blacksmith ............................................................ 10.00
**Planter,** Dutch Shoe ............................................................ 5.00
**Planter,** Frog ................................................... 8.00 To 15.00
**Planter,** Frog With Umbrella ................................................... 24.00
**Planter,** Gondola ............................................... 8.00 To 15.00
**Planter,** Lamb, Large ........................................................... 7.00
**Planter,** Log, Gnomes .......................................................... 10.00
**Planter,** Mill Stream ........................................................... 6.00
**Planter,** Old Mill .............................................................. 8.00
**Planter,** Parrot, Green ......................................................... 8.00
**Planter,** Peacock, 13 In. ...................................................... 14.00
**Planter,** Pelican, Marked NM ................................................... 5.00
**Planter,** Pelican, Matte, White, Marked, 7 X 5 1/4 In. ...................... 7.50
**Planter,** Pig & Clown .......................................................... 12.00
**Planter,** Plow Boy .............................................................. 18.00

| | |
|---|---|
| **Planter,** Pulled By Duck, Aqua | 3.00 |
| **Planter,** Quail | 9.00 To 20.00 |
| **Planter,** Rabbit | 10.00 |
| **Planter,** Rocking Chair | 14.00 |
| **Planter,** Rooster | 14.00 |
| **Planter,** Spinning Wheel | 8.00 To 15.00 |
| **Planter,** Squirrel | 15.00 |
| **Planter,** Tree Stump | 4.50 To 5.00 |
| **Planter,** Turtle | 15.00 |
| **Planter,** Wishing Well | 6.00 To 7.50 |
| **Sprinkler,** Turtle | 15.00 |
| **Sugar & Creamer,** Pinecone | 6.00 To 15.00 |
| **Sugar,** Covered, Decal Of Elmer The Bull | 6.50 |
| **Tea Set,** Floral, 3 Piece | 25.00 |
| **Tea Set,** Gold Brocade | 12.50 |
| **Tea Set,** Pinecone, 3 Piece | 25.00 To 35.00 |
| **Teapot,** Daisy | 12.00 |
| **Teapot,** Green | 12.00 |
| **Teapot,** Yellow | 8.50 |
| **Urn,** Grecian, 24K Gold Trim, 10 In. | 50.00 |
| **Vase,** Bird In Middle, 9 In. | 8.00 |
| **Vase,** Blooming Jonquils, Brown High-Glaze, Loy-Nel-Art, 9 In. | 140.00 |
| **Vase,** Blossomtime, Applied Flower, Embossed Leaves, 6 1/4 In. | 7.50 |
| **Vase,** Bud, King Tut, 8 In. | 175.00 |
| **Vase,** Butterfly, Matte Ivory, Marked, 6 X 3 In. | 7.50 |
| **Vase,** Loy-Nel-Art, Embossed Berries & Leaves, Green Matte, 8 In. | 19.50 |
| **Vase,** Marbleized, 7 1/2 In. | 10.00 |
| **Vase,** Molded Pinecones, Green Accents, Mottled Brown, Redware, 10 In. | 55.00 |
| **Vase,** Onyx, Blue, 6 In. | 8.00 |
| **Vase,** Peacock, 8 In. | 13.00 |
| **Vase,** Swan, Tall Curling Grass, Green, 9 1/2 In. | 8.00 |
| **Vase,** Swan, 9 In. | 7.00 To 15.00 |
| **Vase,** Wheat Pattern, 8 In. | 12.00 |
| **Vase,** Wine Trimmed, Fluted, Green, 7 In. | 9.00 |
| **Vase,** World's Fair, 1933, Onyx | 35.00 |
| **Wall Pocket,** Dogwood | 8.00 |
| **Wall Pocket,** Leaf, Yellow & Green | 17.50 |
| **Wall Pocket,** Rustic | 6.00 |
| **Wall Pocket,** Single Lily, Original Label, 7 1/2 In. | 11.50 |

**PRESCUT**

*The McKee name has been associated with various glass enterprises in the United States since 1836, including J. & F. McKee (1850), Bryce, McKee & Co. (1850-1854), McKee and Brothers (1865), and National Glass Co. (1899). In 1903 the McKee Glass Company was formed in Jeanette, Pennsylvania. It became McKee Division of the Thatcher Glass Co. in 1951, and was bought out by the Jeanette Corporation in 1961. Pressed glass, kitchenware, and tableware were produced.*

| | |
|---|---|
| **MC KEE, Banana Boat,** Autumn Pattern, Green Custard, 10 1/2 In. | 35.00 |
| **Bowl,** Jadite, Scalloped, Signed, 8 1/2 In. | 8.00 |
| **Bowl,** Mixing, Jade, 8 In.Diam. | 7.00 |
| **Bowl,** Tom & Jerry, 6 Mugs, Beaded Edge, Red Scroll | 35.00 |
| **Bowl,** Tom & Jerry, 6 Mugs, Custard | 55.00 |
| **Butter,** Covered, Yellow | 15.00 |
| **Clock,** Tambour, Daisy & Button, Amber | 360.00 |
| **Cup,** Custard, Jade | 5.00 |
| **Dish,** Refrigerator, Yellow, 4 X 8 In. | 11.00 |
| **Dish,** Relish, Prescut, Clear, 7 1/2 In. | 16.00 |
| **Figurine,** Chow Dog, Milk Glass | 150.00 |
| **Jug,** Batter, French Ivory | 15.00 |
| **Mug,** Tom & Jerry, Milk Glass | 4.00 |

| | |
|---|---|
| **Plate,** Cake, Rock Crystal | 5.00 |
| **Reamer,** Jadite | 12.50 |
| **Refrigerator Set,** Jade, 3 Piece | 25.00 |
| **Saltshaker,** French Ivory | 6.00 |
| **Shot Glass,** Red Rock Crystal, 2 7/8 In. | 37.00 |
| **Tumbler,** Bottoms Up, Jade | 15.00 |
| **Wine,** Champion | 9.50 |

**MECHANICAL BANK, see Bank, Mechanical**

| | |
|---|---|
| **MEDICAL, Bag,** Instruments, C.1875, 36 Pieces | 185.00 |
| **Bleeder,** 16 Blade, Spring Loaded, Brass | 125.00 |
| **Bottle,** Ether, Fits Over Mouth, 1890s, Blown | 15.00 |
| **Bottle,** Hot Water, Child's, Picture & Nursery Rhyme | 20.00 |
| **Bowl,** Bleeding, Brass, Curve Cut Back, Fits Body Areas, 7 In. | 365.00 |
| **Cabinet,** Dental, Glass Knobs, C.1870 | 450.00 |
| **Cabinet,** Dental, Sterilizer, Mission Style, Mahogany | 800.00 |
| **Cabinet,** Dental, 6 Drawer, Brass Knobs, C.1920, 12 1/2 X 13 In. | 125.00 |
| **Case,** Delivery, Pharmacist's, Red Paint, Gold Letters, Tin | 195.00 |
| **Chair,** Dental, With Unit, Green Enamel, 1920 | 2500.00 |
| **Chest,** Apothecary, Dovetailed, Original Paint, 7 X 7 X 31 In. | 295.00 |
| **Dilators,** Rectal, Dr.Young's, Set | 8.00 |
| **Ear Trumpet,** Tin, Black Japanning & Gold Trim, 19 In. Long | 60.00 |
| **Electro Poise,** Quack, Dated 1891 | 8.00 |
| **Eye Patch,** Pleated Silk, Lead Weighted | 3.00 |
| **Eyecup,** Milk Glass | 6.00 |
| **Eyeglasses,** 5 Graduated Pince-Nez, Set Of 5 | 30.00 |
| **Feeder,** Invalid, Porcelain, German | 18.00 |
| **Feeder,** Invalid, Tin | 300.00 |
| **Feeder,** Invalid, White China | 22.00 |
| **Frost's Artificial Eye,** Curry & Paxton, C.1890, Fitted Box | 500.00 |
| **Hearing Aid,** Black | 25.00 |
| **Hearing Aid,** Horn | 60.00 |
| **Instrument,** Optical Testing, 1928 | 8.00 |
| **Kit,** 6 Bottles, Name & Design On Front, Tin | 115.00 |
| **Lamp,** Alcohol, Laboratory, Screw-Off Cap, Brass, 2 X 8 In. | 14.00 |
| **Lens,** Eye Testing, 1890s, Set Of 36 | 22.00 |
| **Liniment,** Wrang Tang, Original Box | 1.50 |
| **Microscope,** Bausch & Lomb, Brass & Iron, Mahogany Box | 85.00 |
| **Microscope,** Brass, Mahogany Box, 5 1/2 X 11 In. | 340.00 |
| **Microscope,** Emil Busch, Brass & Iron, 12 1/2 In. | 275.00 |
| **Microscope,** Leitz, Brass & Iron, Boxed, 13 1/4 In. | 36.00 |
| **Mirror,** Pocket, Frank Mollema, Chiropractor | 20.00 |
| **Mold,** Dental, Brass Alloy, 8 1/2 In. | 30.00 |
| **Mold,** Suppository, C.1870, Brass | 120.00 |
| **Opener,** Urethra, 16 Sizes, Sterling Silver, Case, 6 X 2 1/2 In., 8 Pc. | 45.00 |
| **Pestle,** Druggist's, Double Ended Mushroom, Brass, 8 1/2 In. | 40.00 |
| **Pill Box & Medicine Cup,** Silver Gilt, Hallmarked, C.1899 | 200.00 |
| **Pump,** Breast | 7.00 |
| **Scalpel,** Marked Rosers, Sheffield, Case, Pair | 10.00 |
| **Scissors,** Surgeon's | 8.50 |
| **Spoon,** Carleton & Havey, Established 1827, Lowell, Mass., Glass | 12.00 |
| **Spoon,** Castor Oil, C.1837, Gibson, Pewter | 350.00 |
| **Stretcher,** Jar, Dentist's | 9.00 |
| **Surgical Kit,** Leather Case | 8.00 |
| **Syringe,** Pewter, 4 5/8 In. | 45.00 |
| **Tools,** Dental, 1880-1910 | 195.00 |

*Meerschaum pipes and other carved pieces of meerschaum date from the nineteenth century to the present time.*

| | |
|---|---|
| **MEERSCHAUM, Candleholder,** Elf & Tree Trunk, Fluted Base, Signed, 7 1/2 In. | 125.00 |
| **Holder,** Cigar, Amber, Case | 30.00 |
| **Holder,** Cigar, Carved, Dog Chasing Horse, 5 1/2 In. | 65.00 |
| **Holder,** Cigarette, Pipe Shape, Horse On Top, Case, 3 In. | 38.00 |

Pipe, Amber Stem, Original Case, 4 1/2 In. ......................................................................... 175.00
Pipe, Bacchus Head, Covered With Grapes & Vines, 20 In. ................................................ 250.00
Pipe, Carved Man With Jeweled Turban, Amber Stem, 12 In. ............................................ 115.00
Pipe, Carved Hound At Tree Trunk Bowl, C.1890, 3 1/2 In. .............................................. 100.00
Pipe, Carved Turk's Head .................................................................................................... 15.00
Pipe, Cigarette, Cupid Riding Dog, Case .............................................................................. 90.00
Pipe, Cupid & Garlands Of Flowers, 4 In. ............................................................................ 150.00
Pipe, Cupid Riding Behind Dog's Head, 3 3/4 In. ............................................................... 75.00
Pipe, Cupid Riding Crab, 3 3/4 In. ....................................................................................... 75.00
Pipe, Deer Across Front, Original Case ................................................................................ 40.00
Pipe, Eagle Claw Clutching Bowl, Leather Case, Marked ..................................................... 75.00
Pipe, Eagle Talons, Amber Stem, Fitted Case, Label .......................................................... 105.00
Pipe, Five Bulldogs On Bowl, Original Holder, 5 1/2 In. ...................................................... 75.00
Pipe, Full Figure Seated Lady, Holding Basket, Stem, 5 1/4 In. ......................................... 85.00
Pipe, Full-Busted Mermaid, 8 1/2 In. ................................................................................... 150.00
Pipe, Horse's Head With Mane & Reins, 7 1/2 In. .............................................................. 250.00
Pipe, Horses Around Flower, Amber Stem, Case, 19th Century, 7 In. ................................ 125.00
Pipe, Indian Fighting Spanish Soldier With Tomahawk, 8 1/4 In. ....................................... 850.00
Pipe, Nude On Top, 5 In. ...................................................................................................... 95.00
Pipe, Three Pug Dogs On Top, 3 3/4 In. .............................................................................. 60.00
Pipe, Two Cupids Playing Cymbals & Mandolin, 8 In. ........................................................ 350.00

Meissen is a town in Germany where porcelain has been made since 1710.
Any china made in that town can be called Meissen, although the famous
Meissen factory made the finest porcelains of the area.

**MEISSEN, see also Dresden; Onion**

MEISSEN, Bottle, Scent, In Fitted Shagreen Case ............................................................. 1600.00
Bowl, Basket Weave, Applied Flowers, 2 1/2 X 3/4 In. ................................ 35.00 To 45.00
Bowl, Berry, Libertas, 10 In. ................................................................................................ 45.00
Bowl, Gold Flowers, Molded Relief Rim, Crossed Swords, 11 In.Diam. .......................... 195.00
Bowl, Raised Gold & White Leaves, Blue, Crossed Swords, 12 In.Diam. ........................ 295.00
Bowl, Raised Gold Flowers, Paneled, Crossed Swords Mark, 12 In.Diam. ...................... 370.00
Bowl, Raised Gold Flowers, 12 In. ...................................................................................... 250.00
Bowl, Square Design, Garden Scene, Crossed Swords, 10 In. ......................................... 495.00
Box, Gold Trim & Design, Hand-Painted Lid, Crossed Swords, 2 X 4 In. ........................ 25.00
Cachepot, Applied Flowers, Pastoral Scene ...................................................................... 165.00
Charger, Floral Medallion, White Ground, Gold Trim, Crossed Swords ........................... 250.00
Charger, Roses, Floral Center, Baroque Border, Blue Swords, 12 In. ............................. 275.00
Compote, Floral Design, Gold Trim, Reticulated Top & Base, 7 In. ................................. 215.00
Compote, Reticulated Edge, Crossed Swords Mark, Pair .................................................. 250.00
Compote, Top & Bottom Floral Reticulation, Signed, 7 X 9 In.Diam. .............................. 225.00
Compote, White & Gold, Blue Crossed Swords Mark ....................................................... 215.00
Compote, 1 Geese & Gosling, 1 Chicken Center, C.1840, 8 In.Diam., Pr. ....................... 750.00
Cup & Saucer, Blue, Floral, Wishbone Handle ................................................................... 75.00
Cup & Saucer, Demitasse, Cobalt & Gilded, Crossed Swords ......................................... 115.00
Cup & Saucer, Demitasse, Small Bouquet Allover, Set Of 6 ............................................ 150.00
Cup & Saucer, Gold Roses, C.1724 ..................................................................................... 60.00
Cup & Saucer, Green Leaf Border, Gold Trim, Crossed Swords ...................................... 35.00
Cup & Saucer, Marcolini, C.1780, Crossed Swords & Star ............................................... 180.00
Cup & Saucer, Signed Augustus Rex, 1725 Mark .............................................................. 340.00
Cup & Saucer, Swan Neck Handles ..................................................................................... 55.00
Cup, Gold Rim, Twisted Handle, Leaf Sprig Inside, C.1800 ............................................... 7.50
Dish, Dancing Court Figures, Pierced Rim, Crossed Swords, 9 3/4 In. ........................... 500.00
Dish, Lovers, Leaf Shaped, Floral Garlands ....................................................................... 65.00
Dish, Nut, Shell Shape, Gold Edge, Butterfly, Crossed Swords ....................................... 79.50
Figurine, Boston Bull Terrier, 6 X 5 In.Long ...................................................................... 295.00
Figurine, Boy Holding Garland Of Flowers, 6 1/2 In. ......................................................... 595.00
Figurine, Bull Terrier, Red, Gold Collar, Crossed Swords ................................................. 375.00
Figurine, Child Vintners, Blue Crossed Swords, C.1885, 3 3/4 In., Pr. ............................ 350.00
Figurine, Colonial Man, Red Coat, Cane, Pocket Watch, 6 In. .......................................... 525.00
Figurine, Boy, Loincloth, Basket Of Flowers, Crossed Swords, 5 In. ............................... 395.00

**Figurine,** Cupid, Dressed As Actor, C.1755, Crossed Swords, 4 1/4 In. ................................. 600.00
**Figurine,** Double, Lady & Gentleman ................................................ 375.00
**Figurine,** Europa & The Bull, 19th Century, 8 1/2 X 8 In.Wide ................................. 650.00
**Figurine,** Gardener, Rustic Clothes, Spade, Gilt Edge, Marked, 5 In. ................................. 375.00
**Figurine,** Girl Holding Flowers Away From Goat, 7 In. ................................................ 650.00
**Figurine,** Girl With Basket Of Flowers, 6 1/2 In. ................................................ 550.00
**Figurine,** Grandmother's Birthday, No.M184 ................................................ 2500.00
**Figurine,** Lady With Apron, Dot Period, 5 In. ................................................ 375.00
**Figurine,** Lady, 18th-Century Clothes, Feather Muff, Marked, 7 In. ................................. 650.00
**Figurine,** Lover Group, Crossed Swords, 10 X 8 1/2 In. ................................. 1950.00
**Figurine,** Man On White Horse, Crossed Swords, 6 X 11 1/2 In., Pair ................................. 2500.00
**Figurine,** Musketeer, 2 1/2 In. ................................................ 85.00
**Figurine,** Nymph, Blue Dress, Pink Cloak, Book, Marked, 6 1/2 In. ................................. 275.00
**Figurine,** Nymph, C.1840, Blue Crossed Swords, 6 1/2 In. ................................. 320.00
**Figurine,** Peasant, C.1860, Pair ................................................ 750.00
**Figurine,** Pug Dog, Black & Beige, C.1740, Crossed Swords, 2 In. ................................. 820.00
**Figurine,** Sleeping Baby Over Dog, Crossed Swords, 6 1/2 X 6 In. ................................. 375.00
**Figurine,** Street Vendor, C.1745, Crossed Swords, 6 1/4 In. ................................. 1600.00
**Figurine,** Street Vendor, C.1880, Blue Crossed Swords, 6 1/2 In. ................................. 700.00
**Figurine,** Three Soldiers At Well, Crossed Swords, 8 X 11 1/2 In. ................................. 1500.00
**Figurine,** Turkish Lady, Gilt Edged Coat, C.1745, 6 3/4 In. ................................. 900.00
**Figurine,** Woman & Child, Crossed Swords, 8 In. ................................................ 295.00
**Figurine,** Woman Seated, Man At Side, 7 In. ................................................ 985.00
**Group,** Ballet Dancers, Harlequin Costume, C.1925, Marked, 10 3/4 In. ................................. 2000.00
**Group,** Young Satyr & Nude Girl, C.1900, Crossed Swords, 2 3/4 In. ................................. 480.00
**Inkwell Set,** Tray, Sand Holder, Well, Crossed Swords, 6 X 8 1/2 In. ................................. 495.00
**Plate,** Blue, Floral, Blue Crossed Swords, 11 1/2 In. ................................................ 175.00
**Plate,** Bouquets & Flower Sprays, Gilt Rim, Marked, 9 In. ................................................ 300.00
**Plate,** Burgundy Border, Flower Spray Center, Crossed Swords, 12 In. ................................. 110.00
**Plate,** Costumed Lovers In Garden, Gold Scrolls, 18th Century ................................. 195.00
**Plate,** Embossed Fans, Busts Of Children, Crossed Swords, 8 1/2 In. ................................. 85.00
**Plate,** Family Scene, Raised Gold Rim, 1774-1814, Crossed Swords ................................. 295.00
**Plate,** Gold & White On Waffle Ground, Crossed Swords, 9 1/4 In. ................................. 75.00
**Plate,** Gold & White, 9 In. ................................................ 165.00
**Plate,** Gold Vines & Grapes, Crossed Swords, 10 In. ................................................ 90.00
**Plate,** Leaf Shape, 10 1/2 In.Diam. ................................................ 75.00
**Plate,** Lovers In Garden Scene, 1774-1814, Crossed Swords ................................. 295.00
**Plate,** Poinsettia Form, Gold On White, Crossed Swords, 8 In. ................................. 95.00
**Plate,** Reticulated Rim, White Ground, C.1860, Crossed Swords, 8 In. ................................. 55.00
**Plate,** Scalloped, Gold Encrusted & Raised Red Design, Marked, 11 In. ................................. 175.00
**Plate,** Scenic, Gold Border, Crossed Swords, 6 In.Square ................................. 185.00
**Plate,** Sweet Peas, 8 1/2 In., Set Of 4 ................................................ 100.00
**Plate,** Sweetmeat, 18th Century, Set Of 6 ................................................ 215.00
**Plate,** Topless Victorian Girl Entering Pond, Crossed Swords ................................. 10.00
**Platter,** Gold Medallion, Floral, Yellow Border, 9 In. ................................................ 210.00
**Platter,** Pierced Insert, Crossed Swords, 10 X 22 In. ................................................ 300.00
**Syrup,** Bulbous, Silver Plated Top, Blue Flowers, Opaque, 7 In. ................................. 55.00
**Tea Bowl & Saucer,** Puce & Gilt, Plants, C.1745, Crossed Swords, Pair ................................. 800.00
**Tea Bowl,** Blue, Iron Red, Green, & Yellow, Flowers, Marked ................................. 125.00
**Tea Caddy,** Cover, Baluster Shape, 8-Paneled, C.1720, 4 3/4 In. ................................. 8000.00
**Tea Caddy,** Cover, White, Baluster Shape, Plants & Birds, 4 1/2 In. ................................. 2500.00
**Tea Set,** 6 Cups & Saucers, Gold Dragon Pattern, Signed, 18 Piece ................................. 270.00
**Teapot,** Ball Shaped, Blue Flowers, Bird On Branch, Brass Stand ................................. 110.00
**Teapot,** Globular, River Landscape, C.1730, Crossed Swords, 7 In. ................................. 2200.00
**Tureen,** Cover, Stand, Cauliflower Finial, C.1820, Marked, 22 3/4 In. ................................. 3500.00
**Urn,** Snake Handles, Cobalt Blue & Gold, 16 In. ................................................ 2500.00
**Vase,** Bouquets Of Flowers, Gilded Design, Crossed Sword, 6 1/4 In. ................................. 155.00
**Vase,** Grape Leaf Pattern, Green, Crossed Swords, 5 1/2 In. ................................. 45.00
**Vase,** Orange Dragon, White Ground, 6 In. ................................................ 75.00
**Vase,** Pink Roses, Summer Flowers, Fluted Foot, Marked, 11 In., Pair ................................. 600.00
**Vase,** Yellow Tiger Design, Pear Shaped, Brown Rim, 2 In. ................................. 900.00

*Mercury, or silvered, glass was first made in the 1850s. It lost favor for a*
*while but became popular again about 1910. It looks like a piece of silver.*

| | |
|---|---|
| **MERCURY GLASS, Candleholder,** Ball Shape, Ribbed, Light Blue, 3 In., Pair | 16.00 |
| **Compote,** Acid Etched, Floral Design, Open, 8 1/4 In. | 75.00 |
| **Compote,** 7 X 10 In.Diam. | 75.00 |
| **Pitcher,** Water, Handle, Cut Panels, C.1860, 9 1/2 In. | 245.00 |
| **Plate,** Cake, Pedestaled, 8 In. | 55.00 |
| **Salt,** Eggcup Shaped, Floral Design, Footed, 3 In. | 32.50 |
| **Salt,** Master | 40.00 |
| **Tieback,** C.1860, Pair | 16.00 |
| **Vase,** Floral Design, Swirled, 6 In., Pair | 30.00 |
| **Vase,** Grapes & Leaves, 3 1/2 X 4 1/2 In. | 35.00 |
| **Wig Stand** | 65.00 |

*Mettlach, Germany, is a city where the Villeroy and Boch factories*
*worked. Steins from the firm are known as Mettlach steins. They date from*
*about 1842. PUG means painted under glaze.*

| | |
|---|---|
| **METTLACH, Beaker,** No.2327/1302, Eagle On U.S.Flag, Capitol Building | 50.00 |
| **Beaker,** No.2327/6146, Man's Portrait, Brown Ground | 70.00 |
| **Beaker,** No.2368/1032, Elves, Cream Ground | 65.00 |
| **Beaker,** No.2842/1170, Dwarf | 60.00 |
| **Bowl,** Punch, No.3037, Handled, 6 Portraits, Castle Mark, 15 X 15 In. | 649.00 |
| **Candlestick,** No.3339, Geometric Design, Marked, 8 In., Pair | 110.00 |
| **Cup,** No.5029, Faience | 200.00 |
| **Jar,** Sweetmeat, 6 Cows, Silver Plate Rim, Handle, & Lid, Marked, 5 In. | 325.00 |
| **Loving Cup,** No.2260, Serpent Handles, Musician Medallion, 7 In. | 225.00 |
| **Mug,** Artist Signed Portrait, Castle Mark, 1/2 Liter | 125.00 |
| **Mug,** Hires, Pictures Boy With Bib, 1906 | 115.00 |
| **Mug,** No.1023, Boy Playing Violin | 60.00 |
| **Mug,** No.3095, Hires Root Beer | 70.00 To 90.00 |
| **Pitcher,** No.1169, Portrait Busts, Silver Lid, Marked, 14 In. | 250.00 |
| **Pitcher,** No.1632, Pedestal, Round Flat Body, Signed, 21 In. | 1700.00 |
| **Pitcher,** Twig Handle, Applied Leaves, Branches, C.1890, 8 1/2 In. | 255.00 |
| **Pitcher,** Yellow, Silver, Floral, Medallions, Relief, 10 1/4 In. | 269.00 |
| **Plaque,** No.1044, Men & Woman On Terrace, Polychrome, 17 1/2 In. | 200.00 |
| **Plaque,** No.1044, Pastoral Scene, Village Background, PUG, 12 In. | 145.00 |
| **Plaque,** No.2113, Gnome, 16 In. | 1650.00 |
| **Plaque,** No.2442, Cameo, Mythological Figures On Ship | 1450.00 |
| **Plaque,** No.2443, Cameo, Mythological Figures, 18 In. | 1450.00 |
| **Plaque,** No.2874, Cameo, Two Women And Man | 950.00 |
| **Plaque,** No.2875, Cameo, Two Women And Man | 600.00 |
| **Plaque,** No.3130, Country Scene, Signed, 12 In. | 135.00 |
| **Plaque,** No.5041, Man With Lute, Signed, 12 In. | 165.00 |
| **Plaque,** No.7051, Baby, Altar, Children Dancing, 10 X 23 1/2 In. | 1000.00 |
| **Plaque,** No.7060, 3 Children Playing Cards, Castle Mark, 14 3/4 In. | 400.00 |
| **Plate,** Blue & Brown, Hexagonal, 7 In. | 70.00 |
| **Plate,** No. 2712, Head & Shoulders Of Girl, C.1900, 9 1/4 In. | 275.00 |
| **Plate,** Old Tower, Mercury Mark, 11 In. | 70.00 |
| **Stein,** No.6, 3 Liter, 3 Panels, Scales Of Justice, Noah, Harp | 650.00 |
| **Stein,** No. 62, 1/2 Liter, Relief Student Crest | 220.00 |
| **Stein,** No.100, 1/4 Liter, Raised Coat Of Arms, Italian Gray | 135.00 |
| **Stein,** No.171, 1/2 Liter, 5 Figures, White Relief, Blue Ground | 275.00 |
| **Stein,** No.280, 1/2 Liter, Street Scene, 14 People | 275.00 |
| **Stein,** No.485, 1/2 Liter, Ten People, Bold Relief | 275.00 |
| **Stein,** No.485, 1 Liter, Ten People, Bold Relief | 350.00 |
| **Stein,** No.675, 1/2 Liter, Keg Shape | 200.00 |
| **Stein,** No.812, 1/2 Liter, 3 Panels, Hunting Scenes | 335.00 |
| **Stein,** No.1028, 1/2 Liter, Couple With Grapes & Hops *Illus* | 250.00 |
| **Stein,** No.1180, 1/2 Liter, Cream Relief, Poem | 200.00 |

Mettlach, Steins, from left to right, No. 1645, Man With Stein & Mandolin; No. 1467, Four Seasons, Mercury Mark; No. 1028, Couple With Grapes & Hops (See Page 343); No. 1526, Man & Innkeeper, V & B Mark

Mettlach, Steins, from left to right, No. 2382, Knights, Heinrich Schlitt (See Page 347); No. 2190, Cyclists; No. 2373, Spanish Coat Of Arms (See Page 347); No. 1508, Drinking Scene

Metlach, Steins, from left to right, No. 2097, Bands Of Music; No. 2778, Castle Interior (See Page 347); No. 1675, Heidelberg; No. 1577, Man On Bicycle

Stein, No.1266, 1/4 Liter, Three Panels, Drinking Scenes ............................................ 175.00
Stein, No.1403, 1/2 Liter, Seven People And Tavern Keeper ...................................... 500.00
Stein, No.1467, 1/2 Liter, Four Seasons, Mercury Mark ............................*Illus* 375.00
Stein, No.1476, 1/2 Liter, Dwarfs ....................................................................*Illus* 600.00
Stein, No.1508, 1/2 Liter, Drinking Scene ........................................................*Illus* 575.00
Stein, No.1526, 1/2 Liter, Man & Innkeeper, V & B Mark ....................................*Illus* 425.00
Stein, No.1577, 1/2 Liter, Man On Bicycle, C.1910 ..........................................*Illus* 700.00
Stein, No.1577, 5 Liter, Panoramic Dinner Scene ............................ 1300.00 To 2000.00
Stein, No.1645, 1/2 Liter, Man With Stein & Mandolin ......................................*Illus* 275.00
Stein, No.1675, 1/2 Liter, Heidelberg, C.1910 ................................................*Illus* 675.00
Stein, No.1725, 1/2 Liter, Shield With Man & Woman .....................................*Illus* 375.00
Stein, No.1733, 1/2 Liter, Horses & Jockeys .....................................................*Illus* 575.00
Stein, No.1734, 2 Liter, Polychrome Of Man & Woman ......................................... 725.00
Stein, No.1742, 1/2 Liter, Gottingen, 1737-1887, Signed .................................*Illus* 475.00
Stein, No.1745, 1/4 Liter, German Verse, Yellow Relief ................. 160.00 To 200.00
Stein, No.1786, 1 Liter, St.Florian Pouring Beer On Fire ..................................... 700.00
Stein, No.1796, 1/2 Liter, Swashbuckler ............................................................. 450.00
Stein, No.1797, 1/2 Liter, Jesters & Musicians, C.1910 ..................................*Illus* 475.00
Stein, No.1837, 1/2 Liter, Floral Buds ..............................................................*Illus* 275.00
Stein, No.1909, 1/2 Liter, Pilsner Export Beer, N.Y. ........................ 150.00 To 185.00
Stein, No.1914, 1/2 Liter, Man Holding Banner ...............................................*Illus* 525.00
Stein, No.1939, 1/2 Liter, Diagonal Inlay With Cream Border .............................. 150.00
Stein, No.1946, 1/2 Liter, Love Scene .................................................................. 460.00
Stein, No.1968, 1/2 Liter, Lovers, Stork .............................................................. 450.00
Stein, No.1972, 1/2 Liter, Four Seasons ...........................................................*Illus* 375.00
Stein, No.1997, 1/2 Liter, George Ehret ........................................ 235.00 To 390.00
Stein, No.2001, 1/2 Liter, Banker ................................................. 450.00 To 600.00
Stein, No.2002, 1/2 Liter, Housetops Of Munich ............................ 400.00 To 425.00
Stein, No.2002, 1 Liter, Housetops Of Munich ............................... 525.00 To 625.00
Stein, No.2003, 1/2 Liter, 3 Panel, Medieval Men, Eagle .................................... 450.00
Stein, No.2005, 1/2 Liter, Banqueting Scene, C.1910 ......................................*Illus* 425.00
Stein, No.2007, 1/2 Liter, Opera-Black Cat ......................................................... 600.00
Stein, No.2024, 1/2 Liter, Berlin Scene .............................................................*Illus* 600.00
Stein, No.2025, 3/10 Liter, Nude Cherubs At Play ............................................... 200.00
Stein, No.2028, 1 Liter, Drinking Scene, German Verse ....................................... 575.00
Stein, No.2033, 1/2 Liter, Deer & Oak Tree .....................................................*Illus* 650.00
Stein, No.2035, 3/10 Liter, Nude Satyrs & Revelers ....................... 325.00 To 375.00
Stein, No.2035, 1/2 Liter, Nude Satyrs & Revelers .............................................. 400.00
Stein, No.2036, 1/2 Liter, Owl, Figural ............................................................. 1050.00
Stein, No.2038, 4 Liter, Black Forest, Roofs Of Gersprenze ............................... 2000.00
Stein, No.2051, 1/2 Liter, University Students In Tavern ...................................... 650.00
Stein, No.2057, 1/2 Liter, Dancing Figures ......................................................... 500.00
Stein, No.2065, 3 Liter, H.Schlitt, Girl With Keg ............................................... 1400.00
Stein, No.2076, 2 Liter, Four Panels, German Eagle & Owls ................................ 500.00
Stein, No.2076, 3 Liter, Four Panels, German Eagle & Owls ................................ 600.00
Stein, No.2077, 1/2 Liter, Bulbous Body, Low Pedestal Base ............................. 275.00
Stein, No.2089, 1/2 Liter, Angel, White Wings, Old Fellow .................................. 625.00
Stein, No.2090,, 3/10 Liter, Man At Club, Wife At Home ..................................... 350.00
Stein, No.2090, 1/2 Liter, Man At Club, Wife At Home .....................................*Illus* 450.00
Stein, No.2092, 1/2 Liter, Man On Ladder, Winding Clock ................. 600.00 To 650.00
Stein, No.2093, 1/2 Liter, Small Card ................................................................. 700.00
Stein, No.2097, 1/2 Liter, Bands Of Music, C.1910 .........................................*Illus* 650.00
Stein, No.2100, 3/10 Liter, Drunken Roman Soldier ............................................ 385.00
Stein, No.2140/952, 1/2 Liter, Bicycler ............................................................. 325.00
Stein, No.2140, 1/2 Liter, Old Lady Selling Fruit ................................................ 200.00
Stein, No.2179/961, 3/10 Liter, Gnome .............................................................. 200.00
Stein, No.2184, 1/2 Liter, Dwarfs In Foliage ...................................................*Illus* 400.00
Stein, No.2190, 1/2 Liter, Cyclists ..................................................................*Illus* 650.00
Stein, No.2206, 3 Liter, Cavaliers Drinking, Pewter Cover, Marked .......................... 950.00
Stein, No.2211, 3/10 Liter, Bowlers, Terra-Cotta Body ....................................... 275.00
Stein, No.2246, 3/10 Liter, Dancing Figures ....................................................... 225.00
Stein, No.2247, 3/10 Liter, Figures In Relief ....................................................... 135.00
Stein, No.2277, 3/10 Liter, Burg Nurnburg, Panoramic Scene ............................... 325.00

Mettlach, Steins, from left to right, No. 1742, Gottingen, 1737–1887, Signed (See Page 345); No. 2886, Men Discussing Politics; No. 2716, Men Drinking; No. 1725, Shield With Man & Woman (See Page 345)

Mettlach, Steins, from left to right, No. 1914, Man Holding Banner (See Page 345); No. 1733, Horses & Jockeys (See Page 345); No. 2585, Munich; No. 2033, Deer & Oak Tree

Mettlach, Steins, from left to right, No. 2005, Banqueting Scene; No. 2880, Tavern; No. 1797, Jesters & Musicians (See Page 345); No. 5006, Man's Portrait, V & B Mark

**Stein,** No.2281, 1/2 Liter, National Guard, Flags & Military Items ............................................ 425.00
**Stein,** No.2282, 1/2 Liter, Scene In Wine Cellar ................................................................................ 575.00
**Stein,** No.2285, 1/2 Liter, Lovers In Panel, Floral ................................................. 400.00 To 475.00
**Stein,** No.2286, 3 Liter, Cavaliers ......................................................................................................... 1450.00
**Stein,** No.2373, 1/2 Liter, Spanish Coat Of Arms ......................................................*Illus* 700.00
**Stein,** No.2382, 1/2 Liter, Knights, Heinrich Schlitt ..................................................*Illus* 650.00
**Stein,** No.2382, 1/2 Liter, 3 Scenes, The Thirsty Rider ........................................................ 600.00
**Stein,** No.2391, 1/2 Liter, Wedding March Of Swan Knight ................................................. 1000.00
**Stein,** No.2441, 1/2 Liter, Etched Dice & Cards ................................................ 475.00 To 495.00
**Stein,** No.2557, 1/2 Liter, 3 Panels, Playing Cards ........................................... 300.00 To 425.00
**Stein,** No.2580, 1/2 Liter, DeKannenburg, Parapet ........................................ 1000.00 To 1050.00
**Stein,** No.2581, 1/2 Liter, Lady Playing Harp .......................................................................... 425.00
**Stein,** No.2583, 1 Liter, 3 Comic Egyptian Panels, 8 1/2 In. ............................................ 600.00
**Stein,** No.2585, 1 Liter, Munich ......................................................................................*Illus* 850.00
**Stein,** No.2632, 1/2 Liter, Bowling ................................................................................................ 550.00
**Stein,** No.2640, 1/2 Liter, Cavalier Drinking At Table ............................................................. 600.00
**Stein,** No.2716, Men Drinking, Signed FQ, 10 1/8 In. ................................................*Illus* 775.00
**Stein,** No.2755, 1/2 Liter, Etched Ground, White Tavern Figures .................................... 475.00
**Stein,** No.2778, 1 Liter, Castle Interior, C.1910 .............................................................*Illus* 900.00
**Stein,** No.2780, 1/2 Liter, Two Men Drinking In Wine Cellar ........................................... 450.00
**Stein,** No.2832, 1/2 Liter, Thirsty Knight ..................................................................................... 1050.00
**Stein,** No.2836, 1/2 Liter, Cameo, Five Men Discussing Politics .................................... 875.00
**Stein,** No.2872, 1/2 Liter, Cornell University ................................................................................ 925.00
**Stein,** No.2880, 1/2 Liter, Tavern, C.1910 .........................................................................*Illus* 525.00
**Stein,** No.2880, 1 Liter, Tavern ........................................................................................................ 750.00
**Stein,** No.2886, 1/2 Liter, Men Discussing Politics ...............................................*Illus* 600.00
**Stein,** No.2888, 1 Liter, 3 Men, Arm In Arm ................................................................................ 700.00
**Stein,** No.2935, 1/4 Liter, Etched Art Deco Flowers ............................................................. 325.00
**Stein,** No.2956, 1 Liter, Bowler, Inlaid Lid ...................................................................................... 750.00
**Stein,** No.2957, 1/2 Liter, Etched, Old-Time Bowling Alley .............................................. 450.00
**Stein,** No.3090, 1/2 Liter, Man Playing Guitar, Earthenware ........................................... 500.00
**Stein,** No.3092, 1/2 Liter, Man Drinking Beer, Signed ...................................................... 475.00
**Stein,** No.5006, 1/2 Liter, Man's Portrait, V & B Mark ...........................................*Illus* 525.00
**Tea Set,** White, Blue, & Mustard, Teapot, Creamer, Open Sugar ................................... 800.00
**Tile,** Brass Frame, Footed ........................................................................................................ 60.00
**Tile,** Pastoral Scene ...................................................................................................................... 65.00
**Tumbler,** Stadt Nurnberg, 5 In. ............................................................................................... 38.00
**Tumbler,** 1/4 Liter, Elves Drinking & Playing .......................................................................... 40.00
**Tumbler,** 1/4 Liter, Girl Holds Peacock & Pitcher On Tray .................................................. 50.00
**Tureen,** 6 Portraits, Covered, 2 Handles, 15 X 15 In. ........................................................ 495.00
**Urn,** Brown, Twisted Asps Handle, Footed, 12 In. ................................................................. 395.00

Mettlach, Steins, No. 1972, Four Seasons (See Page 345); No. 2090, Men At Club, Wife At Home (See
Page 345); No. 2184, Dwarfs In Foliage (See Page 345); No. 1837, Floral Buds (See Page 345); No. 2024,
Berlin Scene (See Page 345)

Vase, Blue Medallions, Dancing Figures, Signed, 9 In. ............................................... 215.00
Vase, Colored Flowers, Elephant Head Handles, 11 3/4 In., Pair ........................... 300.00
Vase, No.1256, Etched & Relief, 14 3/8 In. ............................................................. 350.00
Vase, No.1829, Beading, Enameled, Etched, Castle Mark, 9 In. ............................. 295.00
    **MICKEY MOUSE, see Disneyana**

> *Milk glass was named for its milky white color. It was first made in*
> *England during the 1700s. The height of its popularity in the United*
> *States was from 1870 to 1880. It is now correct to refer to some colored*
> *glass as blue milk glass, black milk glass, etc.*

    **MILK GLASS, see also Cambridge; Cosmos**
MILK GLASS, Banana Boat, Footed, Wicket Edge ........................................... 27.50
Bank, Log Cabin ...................................................................................................... 45.00
Basket, Basket Weave, Signed Sowerby, 2 X 3 In. ................................................ 20.00
Basket, Hobnail, Ruffled, Applied Handle, Blue & Silver, 7 X 7 In. ....................... 35.00
Basket, Raised Fruit All Around, 12 In.Diam. ........................................................ 45.00
Biscuit Jar, Metal Lid & Handle, Flowers, Portrait Of Lady ................................. 75.00
Bonbon, Grape Pattern, White ............................................................................... 35.00
Bottle, Barber, Cover, Hand-Painted Roses, Shaped Top, White ........................... 18.00
Bottle, Barber, Lily-Of-The-Valley Perfume ......................................................... 65.00
Bottle, Grotesque Lion & Scroll, Stopper, 9 In., Pair .......................................... 90.00
Bottle, Perfume, Lilacs & Violets, Hand-Painted, White ....................................... 30.00
Bottle, Pomade, Figural, Standing Bear, White, 3 1/2 In. ..................................... 65.00
Bottle, Statue Of Liberty, No Stopper ................................................................... 125.00
Bowl, Atterbury, Knobby Edge, Oval, 10 In. .......................................................... 75.00
Bowl, Blue, Latice Edge, 8 In. ............................................................................... 45.00
Bowl, Daisy & Tree Of Life, 6 Panel, Scalloped Rim .......................... 55.00 To 58.00
Bowl, Daisy, Scalloped Rim, 8 In. ......................................................................... 60.00
Bowl, Footed, Picture Of Disraeli, July, 1878, English ........................................ 125.00
Bowl, Hobnail, Blue, Flint, Ruffled, 10 In. ............................................................ 50.00
Bowl, Waste, Pointed Hobnail, Blue ...................................................................... 25.00
Bowl, 3 Birds, Widespread Wings, Pink, 9 In. ...................................................... 55.00
Box, Patch, Brass Trim, Hand-Painted Capitol, Washington, D.C. ......................... 30.00
Box, Trinket, Blue Enameled, C.1898 .................................................................... 325.00
Box, Trinket, Cover, Swirl Design On Outside, 3 In. ............................................. 18.00
Butter, Apple Blossom, Covered ........................................................................... 50.00
Cake Stand, Scroll Pattern, Blue, Large ................................................................ 50.00
Candleholder, Dish Shape, Grape Pattern, Marked W.C., White, Pair .................... 37.50
Candleholder, Footed, Ring Handle, Blue, 4 1/2 In. .............................................. 32.00
Candlestick, Crucifix, 6-Sided, INRI Across Front, 13 In., Pair ........................... 50.00
Candlestick, Dolphin, Pair ..................................................................................... 35.00
Candlestick, Patterned, Blue, 8 In., Pair .............................................................. 58.00
Compote, Atlas, White, 9 X 8 In.Diam. .................................................................. 75.00
Compote, Blue, Banana Lattice Edge, 11 1/2 In. ................................................... 75.00
Compote, Child's, Little Red Riding Hood .............................................................. 20.00
Compote, Covered, Sawtooth, 6 1/2 X 9 In. ......................................................... 105.00
Compote, Lattice Edge, Basket Weave Pedestal .................................................... 45.00
Compote, Opaque Scrolls, Hexagonal, 8 X 8 In. ................................................... 70.00
Compote, Open, Grape Pattern, Pink ..................................................................... 7.50
Compote, Open, Sawtooth Edge, 8 X 8 In. ........................................................... 55.00
Compote, Open, Sawtooth, Flint Wafer Connector, 8 X 8 In. ................................ 65.00
Compote, Scroll, Hexagonal Bowl, 8 X 8 In. ......................................................... 45.00
Compote, Scroll, 8 X 8 In. ..................................................................................... 45.00
Condiment Set, Cosmos Scroll, 3 Piece ................................................................ 75.00
Cracker Jar, Raised Apple Blossoms, Silver Plate Bail ........................................ 55.00
Creamer & Sugar, Blue, Stippled Peacock Design, Covered .................................. 125.00
Creamer, Atterbury, Ribbed, Looped Edge, 4 X 5 In.Diam. ................................... 50.00
Creamer, Ball & Claw Foot, Crossed Fern ............................................................. 25.00
Creamer, Ceres ...................................................................................................... 25.00
Creamer, Child's, Blocks & Bars, Blue, 3 In. ........................................................ 20.00
Creamer, Diamond Sunburst, Flattened ................................................................ 15.00
Creamer, Feather, Blue .......................................................................................... 27.00
Creamer, Figural, Owl, Blue .................................................................................. 42.50

| | |
|---|---|
| Creamer, Flickering Flame, Covered | 23.00 |
| Creamer, Luster Rose, Satin Finish | 28.00 |
| Creamer, Melon With Leaf & Net, Marked 1878 | 40.00 |
| Creamer, Metal Handle & Rim, Waterfall Scene | 25.00 |
| Creamer, Sawtooth | 18.00 |
| Creamer, Swan | 55.00 |
| Crucifix, White Opaque, 11 1/2 In. | 14.00 |
| Cup & Saucer, Banded Raindrop | 12.50 |
| Cuspidor, Opalescent Edge, 6 In. | 49.00 |
| Decanter, Actress Pattern | 45.00 |
| Decanter, Jenny Lind, Stopper, 11 In. | 38.00 |
| Dish, Admiral Dewey Cover, Ship Base | 22.50 |
| Dish, Admiral Dewey Cover, Tile Base | 65.00 |
| Dish, American Hen Cover | 80.00 |
| Dish, Battleship Cover | 47.00 |
| Dish, Battleship Oregon Cover | 55.00 |
| Dish, British Lion Cover | 60.00 |
| Dish, Candy, Covered, Grape Pattern, Pink | 15.00 |
| Dish, Cat Cover, Blue Eyes, Lacy Edge | 100.00 |
| Dish, Cat Cover, Lacy Base, Westmoreland, Blue | 26.00 |
| Dish, Cat Cover, Split Rib Base, 5 1/2 In. | 25.00 To 35.00 |
| Dish, Cat Cover, Wide Rib Base, White, 5 In. | 25.00 |
| Dish, Cherries On Round, Basket | 45.00 |
| Dish, Chick Hatching From Egg On Nest Cover | 35.00 |
| Dish, Chick On Sleigh Cover | 25.00 |
| Dish, Chicken & Eggs Cover, Glass Eyes | 130.00 |
| Dish, Chicken On Nest Cover | 35.00 |
| Dish, Chicks In Basket Cover, Square | 195.00 |
| Dish, Chicks On Round, Cover | 55.00 |
| Dish, Cow Cover, Basket Base, White, 7 In. | 65.00 |
| Dish, Dog Cover, White | 45.00 |
| Dish, Dog Cover, White, 5 In. | 25.00 |
| Dish, Dove, Cover Signed McKee | 145.00 |
| Dish, Enamel Design In Bottom, French, C.1860, 9 3/4 X 6 3/4 In. | 35.00 |
| Dish, Fish Cover, Amber Eyes, 1880s, Supported On Fins, 8 3/4 In. | 55.00 |
| Dish, Fish Cover, Dated | 125.00 |
| Dish, Fox Cover, Glass Eyes, Lacy Base | 100.00 |
| Dish, Hen Cover, Basket Weave Base, Deep Blue, 5 In. | 30.00 |
| Dish, Hen Cover, Black, 5 In. | 110.00 |
| Dish, Hen On Nest Cover, Head Turned, Red Comb, V Tail, 8 In. | 50.00 |
| Dish, Hen On Nest, White Head, Blue, 6 In. | 40.00 |
| Dish, Horse Cover, Split Rib Base, White | 40.00 |
| Dish, Lion Cover, Basket Base, 7 In. | 40.00 |
| Dish, Lion Cover, Picket Fence Base, 5 1/2 X 6 6/4 X 4 In. | 85.00 |
| Dish, Lion Cover, Ribbed, Lacy Base | 85.00 |
| Dish, Pintail Duck Cover, Basket Base, Blue | 65.00 |
| Dish, Quail Cover | 55.00 |
| Dish, Rabbit Cover, Domed, Split Rib Base, 5 1/2 In. | 50.00 |
| Dish, Rabbit Cover, Glass Eyes, 9 1/2 In. | 100.00 |
| Dish, Reclining Horse Cover | 65.00 |
| Dish, Relish, Fish Shape, Dated 1872 | 24.00 |
| Dish, Rooster Cover, Wide Rib Base, White, 5 In. | 20.00 |
| Dish, Santa On Sleigh Cover | 65.00 |
| Dish, Swan Cover, Square | 95.00 |
| Dish, Turkey Cover, Split Rib Base, White, 5 1/2 In. | 25.00 |
| Duck, Amethyst Head, Eyes | 250.00 |
| Egg, Easter, Chick Coming Out, Yellow, Gold Design, 4 In. | 25.00 |
| Egg, Easter, Embossed Greetings, 6 X 3 In. | 20.00 |
| Egg, Easter, Pink Flowers, 3 1/4 In. | 22.00 |
| Egg, Embossed Horseshoe, 6 X 4 In. | 25.00 |
| Eggcup, Painted Chicken Base | 15.00 |
| Epergne, 4 Lilies, Blue Rigaree, Pre-Civil War, White, 17 1/2 In. | 195.00 |
| Figurine, Rabbit, Mule-Eared | 38.00 |

| | |
|---|---|
| **Figurine,** Standing Deer | 36.00 |
| **Figurine,** Swan, Allover Gold, 5 X 4 In. | 30.00 |
| **Goblet,** Blackberry | 45.00 |
| **Goblet,** Fruit In Oval Panel | 35.00 |
| **Goblet,** Honeycomb, Footed, Flint | 75.00 |
| **Goblet,** Sawtooth | 22.00 |
| **Goblet,** Strawberry Pattern, Flint | 30.00 |
| **Goblet,** Two Panel, Blue | 32.50 |
| **Hat,** Signed McKee, Shape Of Captain's Cap | 20.00 |
| **Inkwell,** Figural, Wheelbarrow With Snail | 225.00 |
| **Jar,** Eagle, C.1876 | 110.00 |
| **Jar,** Owl, Screw Closure | 65.00 |
| **Jar,** Queen Victoria, Covered | 75.00 |
| **Ladle,** Punch, Polished Bottom, 13 In. | 25.00 |
| **Lamp Base,** Paneled Dogwood On Pedestal & Font | 105.00 |
| **Lamp,** Boudoir, Pink, 1920s, Peachy Pink Silk Shade, 24 In., Pair | 125.00 |
| **Lamp,** Centennial, Base, Original Paint | 55.00 |
| **Lamp,** Finger, Brass Band & Finger Ring, Miniature | 60.00 |
| **Lamp,** Gilt Corner Design, Miniature | 50.00 |
| **Lamp,** Kerosene, Hand-Painted | 60.00 |
| **Lamp,** Paneled Base, Egg Shape Shade, Embossed, 6 1/2 In. | 90.00 |
| **Match Holder,** Embossed For Burnt Matches, Flint | 21.00 |
| **Match Holder,** Indian Chief | 30.00 To 43.00 |
| **Match Holder,** Triple Swans, 2 1/4 In. | 25.00 |
| **Mug,** Mephistopheles, Blue | 30.00 |
| **Mug,** Washington & Lafayette | 35.00 |
| **Mustard,** Beehive | 20.00 |
| **Mustard,** Bull's Head, Blue | 215.00 |
| **Mustard,** Ladle, Bull's Head | 85.00 |
| **Napkin Ring,** Dotted Edge, Scrolls | 25.00 |
| **Paperweight,** Figural, Rabbit | 12.00 |
| **Pitcher,** Boudoir, Dutch, Miniature | 35.00 |
| **Pitcher,** Cream, Swan | 48.00 To 50.00 |
| **Pitcher,** Figural, Owl, Original Eyes, Blue, 3 1/4 In. | 95.00 |
| **Pitcher,** Juice, Grape Pattern, White, 9 1/2 In. | 35.00 |
| **Pitcher,** Water, Blackberry, White | 175.00 |
| **Pitcher,** Water, Dart Bar, Blue | 110.00 |
| **Plate,** Angel Head, 9 In. | 15.00 |
| **Plate,** Angel With Lute, Gold Trim, 7 1/2 In.Diam. | 39.50 |
| **Plate,** Apple Blossom, Lattice Edge, 10 1/4 In. | 30.00 |
| **Plate,** Battleship Maine | 35.00 |
| **Plate,** Blue, Lattice Edge, 8 In. | 30.00 |
| **Plate,** Bo-Peep | 35.00 |
| **Plate,** Cake, Diamond, Sawtooth Border, 6 Pounds | 65.00 |
| **Plate,** Cake, Openwork Edge & Foot, Triple Stem | 29.00 |
| **Plate,** Cake, Pedestal, Hand-Painted Wild Roses, White | 35.00 |
| **Plate,** Columbus | 35.00 |
| **Plate,** Cupid & Psyche, 7 In. | 18.00 To 25.00 |
| **Plate,** Diamond & Shell | 15.00 |
| **Plate,** Easter Ducks | 30.00 |
| **Plate,** Fleur-De-Lis & Sheaf Wheat, Open Edge, Pair | 19.00 |
| **Plate,** Floral Center, Crisscross Edge, 10 In.Diam. | 28.00 |
| **Plate,** Forget-Me-Not, Single | 15.00 |
| **Plate,** Forget-Me-Not, Triple, Plain Yoke, Set Of 6 | 25.00 |
| **Plate,** Gothic, 9 In. | 12.00 |
| **Plate,** Half Pinwheel, 7 1/2 In. | 50.00 |
| **Plate,** Lattice Edge, Hand-Painted Iris Center, 11 In. | 40.00 |
| **Plate,** Open Border, A.Lincoln Bust, Bearded, White, 9 1/4 In. | 35.00 |
| **Plate,** Open Border, U.S.Maine, Colored Transfer, White, 7 1/4 In. | 12.00 |
| **Plate,** Open Diamond Border, 10 1/2 In.Diam. | 10.00 |
| **Plate,** Quarter Circle, 11 In. | 30.00 |
| **Plate,** Remember The Maine, 7 In. | 20.00 |
| **Plate,** S Border, Black, 8 1/2 In. | 22.00 |

| | |
|---|---|
| Plate, Scroll & Waffle, 7 In. | 25.00 |
| Plate, Sheaf Wheat, Open Edge | 19.00 |
| Plate, Spring Meets Winter | 45.00 |
| Plate, The Little Red Hen | 40.00 |
| Plate, Three Kittens, 8 In. | 15.00 To 21.00 |
| Plate, Winged Cupids, Openwork Edge, Blue | 35.00 |
| Plate, Woof Woof, 5 3/4 In. | 18.00 To 25.00 |
| Plate, 3 Owls, Figural, Patent 1901 | 20.00 |
| Platter, Retriever, 9 5/8 X 13 5/8 In. | 138.00 |
| Platter, Vine Handles, End Flowers, 1870s, 9 1/2 X 14 3/4 In. | 85.00 |
| Reamer, White, Sunkist | 12.00 |
| Rolling Pin | 25.00 |
| Rolling Pin, Wooden Handle, Embossed Imperial Jf. Co., Cambridge | 40.00 |
| Salt & Pepper, Basket Weave Pattern | 22.50 |
| Salt & Pepper, Cosmos, Blue, Metal Tops, 3 1/2 In. | 75.00 |
| Salt & Pepper, Diamond Point & Leaf, Blue | 45.00 |
| Salt & Pepper, Forget-Me-Nots, Original Tops | 55.00 |
| Salt & Pepper, G.E.Refrigerator, Coil On Top | 20.00 |
| Salt & Pepper, Moonstone | 30.00 |
| Salt & Pepper, Roman Key Base, Original Celluloid Tops | 37.50 |
| Salt & Pepper, Thistles, 2 In. | 8.00 |
| Salt & Pepper, 3 Large Flowers, Pink, Yellow, 3 1/2 In. | 45.00 |
| Salt, Birch, Flint | 20.00 |
| Salt, Covered, Sawtooth, Flint | 38.00 |
| Salt, Diamond Point & Leaf, Blue | 35.00 |
| Salt, Kettle, Master, 3 Feet, Bail Molded In Pattern | 20.00 |
| Salt, Master, Blackberry, Footed | 45.00 To 55.00 |
| Salt, Rib & Swirl | 10.00 |
| Saltshaker, Apple Blossom, Pair | 45.00 |
| Saltshaker, Basket Weave | 12.00 |
| Saltshaker, Creased Scroll, C.1870 | 10.00 |
| Saltshaker, Creased Waist, Yellow | 30.00 |
| Saltshaker, Daisy & Button, Original Top, Blue | 25.00 |
| Shade, Umbrella Shape, 10 Ribs In Relief, Tin Foot | 135.00 |
| Shoe, Tramp | 20.00 |
| Sign, Guests, 8 X 24 In. | 60.00 |
| Spooner, Blackberry | 32.00 To 55.00 |
| Spooner, Coreopsis | 65.00 |
| Spooner, Sawtooth | 45.00 |
| Spooner, Strawberry, Flint | 45.00 |
| Spooner, Wheat | 25.00 |
| Spooner, Wild Rose | 75.00 |
| Spooner, Wild Rose, Child's | 40.00 |
| Sugar & Creamer, Baltimore Pear, Pink | 35.00 |
| Sugar & Creamer, Cubist, Open | 5.95 |
| Sugar Shaker, Allover Small Yellow Flowers, Enameled, 4 1/2 In. | 25.00 |
| Sugar Shaker, Enameled Flowers, Original Top | 45.00 |
| Sugar Shaker, Forget-Me-Not | 20.00 |
| Sugar Shaker, Guttate | 75.00 |
| Sugar Shaker, Melon Ribbed, Flint, Blue, 6 1/2 X 3 In. | 50.00 |
| Sugar Shaker, Nettled Oak | 60.00 |
| Sugar Shaker, Sawtooth Band Around Base, Flint | 22.00 |
| Sugar, Covered, Blackberry | 35.00 To 38.00 |
| Sugar, Strawberry, Covered, Strawberry Finial | 65.00 |
| Sugar, Swan Pattern, Open | 10.00 |
| Syrup, Alba, Floral Design | 45.00 To 60.00 |
| Syrup, Applied Handle, Tin Top, Dated | 28.00 |
| Syrup, Catherine Ann, Metal Top | 40.00 To 45.00 |
| Syrup, Chain & Fan | 25.00 |
| Syrup, Embossed Corn Ears On Tin Top | 65.00 |
| Syrup, Loop Pattern, Applied Handle | 45.00 |
| Syrup, Palmette Pattern, Pewter Cover, Dated 1871, Bird Finial | 60.00 |
| Syrup, Scroll & Net | 45.00 To 55.00 |

| | |
|---|---|
| **Table Set,** Child's, Flattened Diamond | 18.00 |
| **Table Set,** Diamond Square, Westmoreland | 15.00 |
| **Table Set,** Swan, Butter, Covered, Sugar, & Creamer, 1930-40 | 85.00 |
| **Tobacco Jar,** Hand-Painted, Brass Lid | 65.00 |
| **Toothpick,** Blue, Square | 7.00 |
| **Toothpick,** Daisy & Button, Top Hat Shape, 2 1/4 In. | 12.50 |
| **Toothpick,** Rose Urn | 22.00 |
| **Toothpick,** Shell & Seaweed, Blue Trim | 35.00 |
| **Toothpick,** Thousand Eye, Blue | 32.00 |
| **Toothpick,** Vermont Pattern, Blue | 90.00 |
| **Tray,** Dresser, Lion's Head At Each End, 11 X 7 1/2 In. | 20.00 |
| **Tray,** Dresser, Raised Bloom Center, Gold Ruffled Edge, 7 X 10 In. | 25.00 |
| **Tray,** Pin, Raised Roses, Blue, 6 X 4 In. | 24.00 |
| **Tumbler,** Hand-Painted Flower, Green Leaves, White | 20.00 |
| **Tumbler,** Hobnail, Blue, Rayed Bottom | 18.00 |
| **Tumbler,** Hobnail, White | 16.00 |
| **Tumbler,** Ivy In Snow | 15.00 |
| **Tumbler,** Louisiana Purchase, 1904 | 15.00 |
| **Tumbler,** Netted Oak | 35.00 |
| **Tumbler,** Scenic Birds & Butterfly | 50.00 |
| **Tumbler,** Scroll Pattern, Blue | 25.00 |
| **Tumbler,** Shell & Jewel, Blue | 35.00 |
| **Tumbler,** St.Louis World's Fair, 1904 | 14.00 To 22.00 |
| **Vase,** Blown-Out Swans, Fluted Top, 8 In. | 65.00 To 95.00 |
| **Vase,** Dutch Lady & Child | 7.00 |
| **Vase,** Footed, Maltese Cross Design, Blue, 5 1/4 In. | 30.00 |
| **Vase,** Grape With Vine, Green, 10 In. | 65.00 |
| **Vase,** Grape With Vine, White, 10 In. | 85.00 |
| **Vase,** Hand-Painted Flowers, Basket Weave Sides, C.1870, 9 X 3 In. | 55.00 |
| **Vase,** Lacy Edge, Flares To Flat Top, Pink, 5 In. | 15.00 |
| **Vase,** Lily Of The Valley, 8 In. | 22.00 |
| **Vase,** Ringed Handle, Ruffled, Blue, 8 1/2 In. | 37.50 |
| **Vase,** Tumbler Shape, Crimped, Geometric Design, 5 1/2 In. | 9.95 |
| **Vase,** 3 Swans, 6 1/2 In. | 14.00 |
| **Water Set,** Beaded Swag, 7 Piece | 395.00 |

*Millefiori means many flowers. It is a type of glasswork popular in paperweights. Many small flowerlike pieces of glass are grouped together to form a design.*

**MILLEFIORI, see also Paperweight**

| | |
|---|---|
| **MILLEFIORI, Basket,** Paperweight, Red, Cased Whte Liner, Jade Inserts | 275.00 |
| **Paperweight,** Marked China, 2 1/2 In. | 40.00 |
| **Rose Bowl,** 3 1/2 In. | 125.00 |
| **Vase,** 2 1/2 In. | 75.00 |

*Minton china has been made in the Staffordshire region of England from 1793 to the present. Many marks have been used; the one shown dates from c. 1873 to 1911.*

| | |
|---|---|
| **MINTON, Beaker,** Jester Lid, Medieval Figures, Vine Handle, C.1868, 13 1/4 In. | 400.00 |
| **Bowl,** Multicolored Rooster, Wine Border, Mottled, Luster, 10 In. | 135.00 |
| **Charger,** Exotic Bird Design, Pink Flowers, 15 In. | 65.00 |
| **Cup & Saucer,** Demitasse, Yellow Ground, Lacy Gold Edge, Set Of 6 | 80.00 |
| **Cup & Saucer,** Enameled Design, 2 Sets | 25.00 |
| **Cup & Saucer,** Multicolored, Oversized, Artist Signed | 95.00 |
| **Cup,** Chocolate, Embossed Gilt Bands & Handle | 55.00 |
| **Egg & Stand,** Floral, Birds, Limited Edition | 45.00 |
| **Figurine,** Fisherman, Signed, April, 1864 Mark, 15 1/4 In. | 365.00 |
| **Figurine,** La Lace, Maiden Holding One Knee, Incised Date, 16 In. | 90.00 |
| **Figurine,** Parrot, Blue-Green, Brass Rim, Marked Minton, 8 1/2 In. | 95.00 |

| | |
|---|---|
| Group, Gamekeeper, No.112 | 795.00 |
| Pitcher & Bowl, Wine & Yellow Floral Medallions, Lavender | 129.00 |
| Pitcher, Cream, Bird & Flower Design, Pink & Green | 20.00 |
| Plate, Floral Centers, Flowers, Hand-Painted | 20.00 |
| Plate, Raised Black & Gold Leaves, Peach Ground, 10 In.Diam. | 35.00 |
| Tile, Birthplace Of Oliver Wendell Holmes, Dated 1888, 6 In.Square | 35.00 |
| Tile, Embossed Sea Life, Ground Of Greens, Stoke-On-Trent, 6 X 6 In. | 95.00 |
| Tile, Green, Gold Trim | 12.50 |
| Tile, Stoke-On-Trent, Beauty & The Beast, Sepia, 6 In.Square | 25.00 |
| Tureen, Soup, Multicolored Flowers, C.1910 | 85.00 |
| Vase, Cherub, Pate-Sur-Pate, Double Handles, C.1900, Signed, 11 In. | 650.00 |
| Vase, Turquoise Ground, Black, Oriental Birds, Marked, 11 In., Pair | 600.00 |
|     MIRROR, see Furniture, Mirror | |

*Mocha ware is an English-made product that was sold in America during the early 1800s. It is a heavy pottery with pale coffee and cream coloring. Designs of blue, brown, green, orange, black, and white were added to the pottery.*

| | |
|---|---|
| MOCHA, Bowl, Blue Seaweed Design, 8 In. | 80.00 |
| Bowl, Green Seaweed Design, 12 1/2 In.Diam. | 95.00 |
| Bowl, Mixing | 48.50 |
| Butter Tub, Blue Seaweed Design, 5 1/2 X 6 3/4 In.Diam. | 90.00 |
| Creamer, Allover Marbled Brown, Oranges, & Tans, 3 In. | 245.00 |
| Mug, Striped, Embossed Imperial Measure, Blue & Green On Cream | 175.00 |
| Mustard, White & Blue Design | 335.00 |
| Pitcher, Earthworm Design, Orange Band, Strap Handle, 7 3/4 In. | 285.00 |
| Salt, Pedestal, Seaweed Design | 33.00 |
|     MOLD, BULLET, see Weapon, Mold, Bullet | |
|     MOLD, ICE CREAM, see Pewter, Mold, Ice Cream | |
| MOLD, Maple Sugar, Scroll Carved Base, Butternut, 2-Part, 6 X 9 In. | 130.00 |

| | |
|---|---|
| MONART, Bowl, Blue, Mottled Brown, Aventurine, Goldstone, Pebbled, 9 In. | 125.00 |
| Vase, Bud, Fluted Top, Pinched-In Center, Blue Matte, 5 7/8 In. | 5.95 |
| Vase, Mottled Blues With Goldstone, Paper Label, 5 7/8 X 5 5/8 In. | 145.00 |
| Vase, Shaded Blue, Gold Flecks, Signed, Partial Label, 8 In. | 48.00 |
| Vase, Swirl Design, Multicolored, Paper Label, 7 X 7 In. | 125.00 |

| | |
|---|---|
| MONMOUTH, Bowl, Green Glazed Inside, Unglazed Outside, Green, 2 X 5 1/2 In. | 9.50 |
| Console Set, Bowl & Cornucopias, Powder Blue, Bowl, 6 In.Diam. | 19.50 |
| Vase, Impressed Stem & Leaf, Handled, Ivory, Label, 7 1/2 In. | 9.95 |
|     MONT JOYE, see Mt.Joye | |

*William Moorcroft managed the art pottery department for James Mac Intyre & Company of England from 1898 to 1913. In 1913 he started his own company, Moorcroft Pottery, in Burslem, England. The earlier wares are similar to those made today, but color and marking will help indicate the age.*

| | |
|---|---|
| MOORCROFT, Ashtray, Pink Poppy, Green Ground, Signed | 32.00 |
| Base, Iridescent Green Over Pink, 1913, 10 3/8 In. | 100.00 |
| Bowl, Pomegranate, 3 In.Diam. | 105.00 |
| Bowl, Raised Flowers Inside, Marked, 1 1/4 X 3 In.Diam. | 20.00 |
| Box, Lid, Blooming Flowers, Script Signature, 6 In.Diam. | 160.00 |
| Cachepot, Pomegranate Pattern, Signed, 7 1/4 In. | *Illus* 280.00 |
| Candlestick, Flowers, Dark Blue, Script Signed, 3 1/2 X 4 In.Diam. | 70.00 |
| Candlestick, Pomegranate, Silver Plate Rim, 8 In. | 165.00 |
| Compote, Silver Foot, Pomegranate | 125.00 |
| Compote, Tudric, Deep Blue, 5 1/4 In. | 195.00 |
| Cup & Saucer, Demitasse, Multicolor Fruits, Label | 75.00 |
| Cup & Saucer, Green, Signed | 50.00 |
| Cup & Saucer, Leaves & Berries, Flambe Glaze, Demitasse | 65.00 |
| Cup & Saucer, Orchid Spray On Side & In Well, C.1914 | 54.00 |

Moorcroft, Vase, Crimson Flowers,
Citron, Signed, 7 1/2 In.

Moorcroft, Cachepot, Pomegranate Pattern,
Signed, 7 1/4 In. (See Page 353)

| | |
|---|---|
| **Dish,** Spade Shape, Cobalt, Pink Hibiscus, Signed, 4 1/2 X 5 1/2 In. | 37.50 |
| **Dish,** Sweetmeat, Red Pomegranates, Silver Mounts, 5 In., Diam. | 150.00 |
| **Ewer,** Florian Ware, 2 Shades Of Blue, White Outline | 595.00 |
| **Jar,** Covered, Multicolored Flowers, High Glaze, 5 In. | 150.00 |
| **Jar,** Jam, Covered, Medallion On Lid, Green Mark | 95.00 |
| **Jardiniere,** Frieze Of Yellow Poppies, Label, Signed, 12 In. | 450.00 |
| **Jardiniere,** Mac Intyre, Blue-Green, 7 In. | 875.00 |
| **Lamp,** Flower Design, Dark To Light Blue, Signed, 12 In. | 495.00 |
| **Mug,** Commemorative, Edward VII, 4 1/2 In. | 325.00 |
| **Mug,** Commemorative, George V | 350.00 |
| **Plate,** Fruit, Cobalt Rim, Blue Label, 8 1/2 In. | 42.00 |
| **Plate,** Reds & Greens, Yellow Ground, 9 1/2 In. | 150.00 |
| **Tazza,** Fruits, Pewter Stand, Paper Label, 6 X 8 1/2 In.Diam. | 160.00 |
| **Teapot,** Mushroom, 6 Cup Size | 275.00 |
| **Tobacco Jar,** Commemorative, George VI | 325.00 |
| **Tobacco Jar,** Pomegranate | 235.00 |
| **Vase,** Berries, Blue To Green, 4 In. | 45.00 |
| **Vase,** Blue Poppies, Green Stems & Leaves, White Ground, 8 1/2 In. | 600.00 |
| **Vase,** Bottle, Florian, Blue-Green On White, 5 In. | 475.00 |
| **Vase,** Burslem, Iridescent Green Over Pink, 1913, 10 3/8 In. | 95.00 |
| **Vase,** Cobalt Blue, Rose & Green Design, 3 1/4 In. | 65.00 |
| **Vase,** Cobalt Ground, Embossed Pansies, Leaves, Signed, 8 In., Pair | 485.00 |
| **Vase,** Crimson Flowers, Citron, Signed, 7 1/2 In. .................................*Illus* | 380.00 |
| **Vase,** Fish, Green, 7 In. | 325.00 |
| **Vase,** Flambe Leaf Design, 3 1/2 In. | 95.00 |
| **Vase,** Flamminian, Silver Plated Rim, 3 In. | 100.00 |
| **Vase,** Flared, Tudric Base, Pomegranates, Cobalt, Signed, 5 1/2 In. | 130.00 |
| **Vase,** Florian Ware, Blue, 9 In. | 375.00 |
| **Vase,** Florian Ware, Peacock Feathers, 6 3/4 In. | 395.00 |
| **Vase,** Florian Ware, Yellow Flowers, Leaves | 600.00 |
| **Vase,** Grape, 5 1/2 In. | 200.00 |
| **Vase,** Green, Pink Flowers, Bulbous Bottom, 6 1/2 In. | 88.00 |
| **Vase,** Green, Pomegranates & Grapes, Signed, 4 1/2 In. | 80.00 |
| **Vase,** Handled, Mac Intyre, Flowers, Cream Ground, Gold Rim, 8 In. | 750.00 |
| **Vase,** Handled, Wisteria, 5 In. | 190.00 |
| **Vase,** Orange Luster, 1912-22, Signed, 12 1/2 X 23 In.Diam. | 245.00 |
| **Vase,** Pansy, 3 In. | 75.00 |
| **Vase,** Pansy, 4 1/2 In. | 110.00 |
| **Vase,** Polychrome Fruit Design, Mustard Ground, 17 In. | 275.00 |
| **Vase,** Pomegranate, Cobalt Blue Ground, Purple Grapes, 8 In. | 325.00 |
| **Vase,** Pomegranate, Green Mark, 8 1/4 X 4 5/8 In.Diam. | 165.00 |
| **Vase,** Pomegranate, 4 In. | 125.00 |

| | |
|---|---|
| **Vase,** Pomegranate, 7 In. | 195.00 |
| **Vase,** Poppy, Pewter Base, 6 1/2 In. | 400.00 |
| **Vase,** Poppy, 4 1/2 In. | 115.00 |
| **Vase,** Raised Pansies, Cobalt, 7 1/2 In. | 65.00 |
| **Vase,** Rose & Green Design, Cobalt Blue, 3 1/4 In. | 65.00 |
| **Vase,** Wisteria, 3 1/2 In. | 95.00 |
| **Vase,** Wisteria, 5 In. | 500.00 |

*Moriage is used to identify Japanese pottery to which a raised overglaze decoration has been added. This relief ornamentation may be elaborate. The term applies to the style or technique.*

| | |
|---|---|
| **MORIAGE, Ashtray,** Green Flowers, Rust, White Beads, Footed, 5 In. | 30.00 |
| **Ashtray,** Red Roses | 85.00 |
| **Bell,** Flowers, Hand-Painted | 45.00 |
| **Berry Bowl,** Underplate, Burgundy & White Flowers, Green Ground | 175.00 |
| **Bowl,** Blue, Coralene, 5 X 5 1/2 In. | 55.00 |
| **Bowl,** Cucumber, Underplate, Scalloped Edges, Roses, Gold Trim | 75.00 |
| **Bowl,** Floral Design, Footed, 6 In. | 85.00 |
| **Box,** Heart Shape, Scene On Top, 3 1/2 In. | 48.00 |
| **Candlestick,** Flowers, Lavender Ground, Blue Maple Leaf, 9 1/2 In. | 69.00 |
| **Charger,** Flowers, Green Ground, 12 1/2 In.Diam. | 150.00 |
| **Chocolate Pot,** Dragon, Orange On White, 3 Cups & Saucers | 45.00 |
| **Chocolate Pot,** Gold Ground, Allover Lacy Slip | 295.00 |
| **Chocolate Pot,** Red Roses, Allover Beading, Pink Ground | 245.00 |
| **Chocolate Set,** Floral Medallion, Handles, Pot & 2 Cups & Saucers | 250.00 |
| **Chocolate Set,** Raised Enamel Design, 2 Cups & Saucers, Pot, 11 In. | 250.00 |
| **Coffee Set,** Dragon Slipware, Gray, Gold Luster, 19 Piece | 55.00 |
| **Cracker Jar,** Off-White, Green & Pink Roses, Melon Shaped | 125.00 |
| **Creamer,** Six Floral Medallions, Jewels, Turquoise Ground | 30.00 |
| **Creamer,** Six Floral Medallions, Turquoise | 35.00 |
| **Cup & Saucer,** Bamboo Design | 22.00 |
| **Demitasse Set,** Erotic Lithophane Cups, Dragon, Gray | 175.00 |
| **Dish,** Fluted, Slipware & Flowers, Green, 5 1/2 In.Diam. | 47.50 |
| **Ewer,** Gold Grapes, Geometric Swags | 170.00 |
| **Ewer,** Green, Medallions, 4 In. | 175.00 |
| **Ewer,** Green, Medallions, Squatty, 4 1/2 In. | 165.00 |
| **Fernery,** Dragon, Blue Mark, 7 1/2 In.Diam. | 125.00 |
| **Hatpin Holder,** Pierced Top, Green Beading, Red Flowers | 57.50 |
| **Humidor,** Blue Dragon, Glass Bead Eyes, Beige & Brown Ground | 295.00 |
| **Humidor,** Flower Medallion | 130.00 |
| **Jar,** Cookie, Green, Lacy Design | 225.00 |
| **Jardiniere,** Footed, Handled, Cartouche, Hand-Painted Flowers, 11 In. | 395.00 |
| **Lamp,** Handled, Stylized Japanese Scene, 24 In. | 250.00 |
| **Lamp,** Raised Gray Dragons, Pink, Pair | 95.00 |
| **Mayonnaise Set,** Red & Pink Roses, 3 Piece | 45.00 |
| **Mustard Pot,** Floral Medallion | 125.00 |
| **Plate,** Allover Design, 6 In. | 28.00 |
| **Rose Bowl,** Blue, Green, Pink, & Crimson, Off-White Ground, 7 1/2 In. | 115.00 |
| **Sake Set,** Barrel, Elephant Finial, Scenic, 7 Piece | 85.00 |
| **Salt & Pepper,** Slipware On Upper Part | 17.50 |
| **Stein,** Red Roses, 5 1/2 In. | 250.00 |
| **Sugar & Creamer,** Dragon, Gray Ground | 75.00 |
| **Sugar & Creamer,** Garnet, Gold Beading, Scenic | 47.50 |
| **Sugar & Creamer,** Green Ground, Medallions On Side, Covered | 75.00 |
| **Sugar & Creamer,** Lid, Blue-Green Shaded Ground, 4 Medallions | 95.00 |
| **Sugar & Creamer,** Pedestal Base, Green, Wine, & Gold | 175.00 |
| **Tankard,** Pale Green Ground, 11 In. | 140.00 |
| **Tea Set,** Dragons, 4 Cups & Saucers | 175.00 |
| **Teapot,** Floral Design, Green Ground, 7 In. | 175.00 |
| **Teapot,** Reeded Handle, 6 X 6 In. | 25.00 |
| **Tobacco Jar,** Green Slipware On Shaded Ground, 6 1/2 X 7 In.Diam. | 285.00 |
| **Vase,** Beaded Handles, Pastel Flowers, Fluted Top, 12 In., Pair | 800.00 |

Vase, Birds & Flowers, Enameled, Closed Handles, 11 In. ............................................. 95.00
Vase, Blue Birds, Shaded Yellow, Blue & Green Ground, 18 In. .................................... 125.00
Vase, Bouquet Of Flowers In Center, Handled, Pastel Green, 9 In. ............................... 225.00
Vase, Brown, Yellow, Green, Rust, 6 In. ......................................................................... 115.00
Vase, Bulbous, Handles, Floral Design, 8 In. ................................................................. 100.00
Vase, Foo Dog Handles, Flowers & Dragons, Beading, Green, 22 In. ........................... 130.00
Vase, Footed, Egret, Gold Trim, Signed, 6 1/2 In. ....................................................... 125.00
Vase, Footed, 3 Handles Swirling Around Lower Half, Pink, 6 1/4 In. .......................... 160.00
Vase, Handled, White Beading Allover, Flowers, 9 In. ................................................... 195.00
Vase, Lacy Slipware Top & Bottom, Cobalt Blue, Signed, 9 In. .................................... 275.00
Vase, Marbleized Ground, Red Roses, 4 1/2 In. ........................................................... 189.00
Vase, Pagoda Scene On Both Sides, Cream Ground, 18 In. .......................................... 400.00
Vase, Peonies, Jewels, 7 In. ........................................................................................... 225.00
Vase, Scenic, 6-Sided, Artist Signed, 10 In. ................................................................... 95.00
Vase, Spider Web & Flowers, 11 1/2 In. ........................................................................ 185.00
Vase, Three People Each Side, Bulbous, Handled, 7 In. ............................................... 150.00
Vase, Violet & Pink Flowers, Fluted, 3 Handles, 12 In., Pair ........................................ 800.00
Vase, Yellow & Red Roses, Green Slip, Red & Gold Ground, 15 In. ............................. 235.00

 *Mosaic Tile Company of Zanesville, Ohio, was started by Karl Langenbeck and Herman Mueller in 1894. Many types of plain and ornamental tiles were made until 1959. The company closed in 1967.*

MOSAIC TILE CO., Tile, Lincoln, Blue, White, Hexagonal, 3 1/2 In. ............................ 30.00 To 50.00
Tile, Woodrow Wilson, Blue, White ............................................................................. 45.00

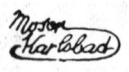 *Moser glass was made by Ludwig Moser and Sohne, a Bohemian glass house founded in 1857. Art Nouveau type glassware and iridescent glassware were made. The firm is still working.*

MOSER, Bottle, Perfume, Amber, Gold, Floral Design, Signed, 4 1/2 In. ..................... 395.00
Bowl, Amethyst, Gold Engraved Border, Footed, 4 In. ................................................ 195.00
Bowl, Band Of Amazons, Fluted Bottom, Incised Karlsbad, 4 1/2 In. .......................... 195.00
Bowl, Centerpiece, Intaglio, Green To Clear, Signed, 11 In.Long ................................ 295.00
Bowl, Enameled Oak Leaves, Applied Acorns, Signed, 10 1/4 X 2 1/2 In. ................... 1100.00
Bowl, Finger, Applied Glass Grapes, Enameled, Signed, 4 3/4 In. ............................... 325.00
Bowl, Flaring, Gold Band, Clear Amber, Karlsbad, 12 X 3 In. ...................................... 200.00
Bowl, Fruit, Pedestal, Diamond Sawtooth Pattern, 5 1/2 X 8 In.Diam. ....................... 150.00
Bowl, Ruby To Clear, 14-Paneled, Signed, 6 X 3 1/4 In. .............................................. 175.00
Box, Covered, Etched Border On Lid, Amber, Signed, 3 1/2 X 3 1/4 In. ....................... 125.00
Box, Dresser, Hinged, Multicolor Enameling, Amber, Signed, 5 In. ............................. 225.00
Box, Patch, Enamel Design, Frosted Ground, Signed .................................................. 155.00
Butter, Covered, White Enameling, Honey Amber ...................................................... 150.00
Candlestick, Emerald Green, Gold Trim, Signed, 8 1/4 In., Pair ................................. 195.00
Candlestick, Gold Frieze Of Figures, Signed, 1o 1/2 In., Pair ..................................... 495.00
Candlestick, Hollow Columnar Body, Warrior Band, 13 3/4 In. ................................... 65.00
Cruet, Wine, Gold Bands & Yellow Dots, Green Stopper, Signed, 7 3/8 In. ................ 135.00
Cup & Saucer, Demitasse, Cranberry, Enameled Flowers .......................................... 90.00
Cup, Apothecary, Numbers In Gold, Blue, Signed, 4 3/4 In. ....................................... 395.00
Decanter, Amber Faceted, Signed, 8 In. ...................................................................... 65.00
Decanter, Deep Green & Gold Floral Overlay ............................................................. 150.00
Decanter, Stopper, Ruby Cut To Frosted, Signed, 14 In. ............................................ 295.00
Dish, Amber, Enamel Oak Leaves & Bee, Signed, 3 1/4 In. ........................................ 180.00
Dish, Sweetmeat, Enameled, Signed ........................................................................... 375.00
Glass, Juice, Gold Floral, Green, Metal Holder, Hallmark, 4 In. ................................. 230.00
Goblet, Gold Top Band, Red Jewels, Enameled Florals, Signed, 5 1/2 In. .................. 175.00
Goblet, Nature Scenes, Color Cut To Clear, Signed, Set Of 6 ..................................... 2000.00
Humidor, Covered, Gold & White Enamel, Green, Signed, 6 1/4 In. ........................... 295.00
Pitcher, Clear Handle, Gold Enameled Foliage, Cranberry, Signed, 3 In. ................... 295.00
Pitcher, Raised Acorns, Colored Enameling, Dragonfly, 5 In. ..................................... 650.00

Ring Tree, Signed ...................................................................................................... 125.00
Tumbler, Enameled Leaves, Applied Glass Acorns, Signed, 3 7/8 In. ...................... 225.00
Tumbler, Juice, Art Deco Enameling, Blue & White, Gold Trim, 4 In. ...................... 30.00
Tumbler, Juice, Cranberry, Blue, & White, Geometric Design, 4 In. ...................... 30.00
Tumbler, Juice, Enameled Grape Leaves, Gold Foliage, Signed, 3 7/8 In. .............. 225.00
Tumbler, Juice, Jeweled, Enameled Bands, Signed, Royal Blue, 3 1/2 In. ............... 225.00
Urn, Multicolored Coralene Design, Signed, 13 1/2 In. ...................................... 1295.00
Vase, Allover Enamel Design, Cranberry Glass, Gold Trim, 6 In. .......................... 275.00
Vase, Amber Wishbone Feet, Applied Acorns, Signed, 6 1/4 In. .......................... 550.00
Vase, Amber, Waisted Fluted Paneled Form, Impressed, 6 In. ............................. 800.00
Vase, Amethyst To Clear, Chrysanthemums, White & Yellow Enamel, 11 In. .......... 143.00
Vase, Art Deco Shape, Amethyst To Blue, Signed, 13 In. ................................... 225.00
Vase, Bud, 8 Side Panels, Intaglio Poppies, 6 In. ............................................. 150.00
Vase, Clear Shading To Blue At Top Half, Pansies, Signed, 9 1/2 In. ................... 250.00
Vase, Cobalt To Clear, Peacock Design, Signed, 7 X 10 In. ............................... 240.00
Vase, Cranberry Pedestal, Enameled Gold Butterfly, Foliage, 6 3/4 In. ............... 265.00
Vase, Cranberry, Gold, Blue & White Daises, Scrolling, 15 In. ........................... 175.00
Vase, Diamond Pattern, Frosted Angelfish, Footed, Signed, 8 1/4 In. ................. 290.00
Vase, Emerald Green, Gold, Hexagonal, Signed, 13 In. ..................................... 295.00
Vase, Enameled Spider Mums, Gold Tracery, 14 In. .......................................... 125.00
Vase, Enameled White & Yellow Flowers, Amethyst, 12 In. ............................... 125.00
Vase, Frieze At Bottom, Impressed In Gold, Signed, 20 In. ............................... 750.00
Vase, Intaglio Cut, Gourd Shape, Gold Trim, Opaque, Signed, 10 In.Pair ............ 175.00
Vase, Karlsbad, Allover Cut, 5 X 10 In. ......................................................... 395.00
Vase, Leaf At Base, Gold Rim, Gold Outlined Acorns, Bug, 6 In. ........................ 395.00
Vase, Molded & Colored Parrot, Acorns, Diamond Shape, 14 In. ........................ 750.00
Vase, Pedestal, Enameled Gold Acorns & Butterfly, 6 3/4 In. ........................... 265.00
Vase, Pink Swirled Ribs, Gold Design, 13 In. .................................................. 175.00
Vase, Sculptured, Amethyst, 14 In. ................................................................ 155.00
Vase, Wishbone Feet, Enameled Oak Leaves, Butterfly, Signed, 6 3/4 In. ........... 495.00
Vase, 2 Layer Red Over Amber, Cameo Frieze, Enameled, Signed, 13 In. ........... 2000.00
Wine, Cased Overlay, Gold Bands, Signed, Label, 8 In. ..................................... 195.00
Wine, Etched Bird Scene, Stem, Signed .......................................................... 125.00


*Moss rose china was made by many firms from 1808 to 1900. It refers to any china decorated with the moss rose flower.*

MOSS ROSE, Bowl, Irregular Edge, Ironstone, 6 1/2 X 9 In., Nest Of 4 ................ 115.00
Butter Pat, Ironstone, Meakin ....................................................................... 7.50
Spittoon ..................................................................................................... 125.00


*Mother-of-pearl glass, or pearl satin glass, was first made in the 1850s in England and in Massachusetts. It was a special type of mold-blown satin glass with air bubbles in the glass, giving it a pearlized color.*
MOTHER-OF-PEARL, see also Pearl
MOTHER-OF-PEARL, Basket, Camphor Rim, Thorn Handle, White Lining, 8 In. ....... 395.00
Basket, Diamond-Quilted, 7 1/4 In. ................................................................ 450.00
Bottle, Perfume, Diamond-Quilted, White Inside, Rose, 5 In. ............................. 195.00
Bottle, Scent, Diamond-Quilted, Blue, 3 3/4 X 1 3/4 In.Diam. ........................... 165.00
Bride's Basket, Yellow, 10 In. ....................................................................... 135.00
Bride's Bowl, Diamond-Quilted, On Silver Ring ............................................... 500.00
Bride's Bowl, Scalloped, Piecrust Rim, 4 X 8 1/4 In.Diam. ................................ 535.00
Creamer, Grape, Signed Deponiet & Germany .................................................. 125.00
Jug, Diamond-Quilted, Pink, 4 1/4 In. ............................................................ 370.00
Lamp, Fluted Shade, , Quilted, Pink .............................................................. 450.00
Lamp, Frosted Petal Feet, Square Ruffled Shade, 10 In. ................................... 695.00
Lamp, Peg, Blue Swirl, Silver Plate & Copper, 17 1/2 In. ................................. 550.00
Mustard Pot, Diamond-Quilted, Pewter Top, Coral, 3 1/2 In. ............................ 325.00
Rose Bowl, American Beauty Rose, 3 3/4 In.Diam. .......................................... 295.00
Rose Bowl, Dark Gold, Shiny Gold Stripes, Wafer Base, 3 In. ........................... 135.00
Rose Bowl, Diamond-Quilted, Egg Shape, 2 3/4 In.Diam. ................................. 295.00

Rose Bowl, Swirl Pattern, White, 2 1/4 In. ................................................ 148.00
**MOTHER-OF-PEARL, SATIN GLASS, see also Satin Glass; Smith**
**Brothers; Tiffany Glass; etc.**
Shade, Gas, Ruffled Top, Blue Quilted, 8 In. ........................................... 135.00
Sugar & Creamer, Acorn & Flower, Camphor Handle, 3 In. .................... 350.00
Tumbler, Diamond-Quilted Pattern, Rainbow Colors ............................... 395.00
Tumbler, Diamond-Quilted, Deep Rose ..................................................... 175.00
Vase, Blue Diamond Design, White Inside, Long Neck, 13 In. ................. 145.00
Vase, Blue Iridescent, Floral Design, Pink Ground, C.1880 .................... 700.00
Vase, Bud, Pink, 7 1/4 In. .......................................................................... 175.00
Vase, Bulbous, Ruffled, White Lining, 5 1/4 In. ....................................... 135.00
Vase, Diamond Design, Ruffled, Yellow To Ivory, 5 1/2 In. .................... 110.00
Vase, Diamond Pattern, Blue Satin Glass, 10 3/8 In. .............................. 150.00
Vase, Diamond Pattern, Cased White, 4 3/4 In. ........................................ 75.00
Vase, Drape Pattern, Pink, 5 3/4 In. .......................................................... 275.00
Vase, Flower & Acorn Pattern, Chartreuse, 3 7/8 X 4 3/4 In. ................. 425.00
Vase, Frosted Amber Rigaree At Neck, Cream, 5 1/8 In. ....................... 235.00
Vase, Frosted Handle, Blue Swirl, 9 1/2 In. .............................................. 265.00
Vase, Herringbone, Ruffled Top, Apricot, 6 1/2 In. ................................. 135.00
Vase, Pink Satin, Quilted, 7 1/2 In. ........................................................... 175.00
Vase, Purple, Swirl, 13 In. .......................................................................... 850.00
Vase, Rainbow Satin Glass, Blue, 6 3/4 In. ............................................... 175.00
Vase, Raindrop Pattern, Flared, White Lining, 9 In. ................................ 275.00
Vase, Raindrop, Butterscotch, 8 1/2 In. ..................................................... 150.00
Vase, Ruffled, Butterscotch, 5 In. .............................................................. 118.00
Vase, Rust, Swirl, 5 In. ............................................................................... 450.00
Vase, Snowflake Pattern, Peach, 5 1/2 X 4 1/2 In.Diam. ........................ 450.00
**MOUSTACHE CUP, see Mustache Cup**

*Mt. Joye is an enameled cameo glass made in the late nineteenth and the
twentieth centuries by Saint-Hilaire Touvoir de Varraux and Co. of
Pantin, France. This same company produced De Vez glass.*

**MT.JOYE, Bowl,** Enameled Blossoms, Gilt Rim, Frosted, Signed, 2 1/2 X 8 In. ........ 225.00
Bowl, Enameled Flowers, Acid Frosted, Sawtooth Border, 2 1/4 X 8 In. ................... 155.00
Bowl, Gold Leaf & Cameo Leaves, Frosted Green Ground, Signed, 9 In. ................... 275.00
Bowl, Iris Blossom, Acid Frosted, Sawtooth Border, Signed, 8 In. ........................... 155.00
Bowl, Iris, Signed, 9 In.Diam. .................................................................................... 115.00
Ewer, Handled, Gold Flowers, Brown Accents, Green Ground, 9 1/2 In. .................... 265.00
Rose Bowl, Iris Pattern, Signed, 4 X 3 In. ................................................................ 145.00
Vase, Acid Etched, Applied Silver & Gold Acorns, Green, 18 In. ............................... 650.00
Vase, Amber, Green Tint, 7 In. ................................................................................... 325.00
Vase, Amethyst, Gold Flowers & Leaves, Marked, 13 1/2 In. .................................... 395.00
Vase, Applied Opals, Signed, 6 1/4 In. ...................................................................... 300.00
Vase, Blossoms, Acid Textured Frosted Surface, Signed, 6 1/2 In. ........................... 285.00
Vase, Bronze Ground, Acid Cut, Gold Larkspurs, Gold Border, 10 In. ....................... 450.00
Vase, Brown & Gold, Signed, 12 In. ........................................................................... 185.00
Vase, Cameo & Enamel, Amethyst, Violet Flowers, Signed, 6 In. .............................. 495.00
Vase, Cameo, Floral, Brown, Black, Gold, Green Glass, Signed, 10 In. ..................... 265.00
Vase, Cameo, Ice Green, Roman Gold, Floral, Signed, 13 X 6 In. ............................. 575.00
Vase, Cameo, Red, Green, Gold Enameled, Green Ground, Signed, 10 In. ................ 395.00
Vase, Cut Art Deco Design, Golden Yellow, 7 X 4 1/4 In.Diam. ............................... 275.00
Vase, Egg Shape, Internally Ribbed, Enameled Flowers, Gilt, 3 1/2 In. ..................... 95.00
Vase, Embossed Flowers, Brass Rim & Holder, Signed, 8 In. .................................... 395.00
Vase, Enameled Leaves & Red Poppies, Signed, 8 1/2 In. ........................................ 500.00
Vase, Enameled Leaves, Red Poppies, Icy Ground, Signed, 8 In. .............................. 425.00
Vase, Enameled Pansies, Cranberry To Clear, 13 In., Pair ........................................ 350.00
Vase, Frosted Chipped Ice Ground, Enameled Flower, Signed ................................... 445.00
Vase, Gold & Brown Cameo Cut Flowers, Green, Signed, 9 1/2 In. ........................... 265.00
Vase, Gold & Orchid Enamel, Frosted, Signed, 16 In. ............................................... 675.00

| | |
|---|---|
| Vase, Gold Band At Top, Enameled Flowers, Clear Frosted, 11 In. | 185.00 |
| Vase, Green Acid Cutback, Gold Chrysanthemums, Signed, 7 1/2 In. | 185.00 |
| Vase, Green Stippled Ground, Enameled, Gold Band, Signed, 9 3/4 In. | 295.00 |
| Vase, Purple Iris, Foliage, Gold, Frosted, Signed, 10 In. | 185.00 |
| Vase, Purple Pansies, Green Leaves & Vines, Gilt Etched, 8 In. | 295.00 |
| Vase, Ripple Surface, Brass Holder Embossed, Signed, 8 In. | 345.00 |
| Vase, Roman Gold Enameled Leaves, Ice Green Ground, Signed, 13 In. | 415.00 |
| Vase, Rose Flowers, Gold Rim, Vine, Stem, Leaves, Signed, 10 In. | 550.00 |
| Vase, Triple Cut, Frosted, Clear Cabbage Roses, Olive Green, 12 In. | 285.00 |
| Vase, Trumpet, Gilt Etched, Raised Chrysanthemums, Marked, 13 1/2 In. | 240.00 |
| Vase, Yellow & Lavender Iris, Ruby, 11 3/4 In., Pair | 400.00 |
| Vase, Yellow, Lavender Iris, 11 3/4 In., Pair | 400.00 |

*Mt.Washington Glass was made at the Mt.Washington Glass Co. located in New Bedford, Massachusetts. Many types of art glass were made there from 1850 to the 1890s.*

**MT.WASHINGTON, see also Burmese; Crown Milano**

| | |
|---|---|
| MT.WASHINGTON, Bottle, Cologne, Blown-Out Fronds, Enameled, 10 In., Pair | 250.00 |
| Bowl, Amber, Seaweed & Fish Design, Crackled Glass, 4 1/2 In. | 75.00 |
| Bowl, Burmese, Acid Finish, 2 3/4 X 5 1/2 In.Diam. | 395.00 |
| Bowl, Floral Design Around Exterior, 18 In. | 130.00 |
| Bowl, Melon Shape, Lusterless, Leaves & Berries, 3 1/2 X 5 In. | 260.00 |
| Bowl, Peachblow, Gold Rim, Enameled Flowers, 2 3/4 In. | 110.00 |
| Bowl, Tricorner, Burmese, Yellow Top Edge, 2 X 5 In.Diam. | 195.00 |
| Box, Powder, Pale Pink To Yellow, Pansy Design, Hinged | 110.00 |
| Bride's Bowl, Pleated, White Outside, Pairpoint Frame | 165.00 |
| Castor Set, 2 Salts, Berry & Leaves, Pairpoint Frame | 150.00 |
| Celery, Amberina, Diamond-Quilted, 6 1/2 In. | 320.00 |
| Cracker Jar, Blown-Out Scrolls, Silver Plated Lid, 8 1/2 In. | 100.00 |
| Cracker Jar, Flowers, Pairpoint, Ornate Embossing | 185.00 |
| Cracker Jar, Melon Ribbed, White Enameled Flowers | 195.00 |
| Cracker Jar, Raised Dot Enamel Flowers, Uranium Glass, 7 In. | 525.00 |
| Cracker Jar, Translucent, Plated Silver Cover, Bail, 9 In. | 150.00 |
| Cruet Set, Enameled | 155.00 |
| Egg, Easter, White Satin, Lily-Of-The-Valley, Hand-Painted, 6 In. | 35.00 |
| Ewer, Apple Green, Enameled Flowers, 6 In. | 85.00 |
| Flower Frog, Mushroom Shape, 3 X 5 1/2 In.Wide | 185.00 |
| Holder, Flower, Mushroom Shape, Allover Dogwood Blossoms | 165.00 |
| Holder, Hatpin, Mushroom Shape, Pink Blossoms | 145.00 |
| Muffineer, Enameled Design | 335.00 |
| Muffineer, Ribbed, Apple Blossom, Blue Beaded Top, Pewter Lid | 195.00 |
| Mustard, Bail, Pink & Blue Flowers, White | 90.00 |
| Mustard, Barrel Shape, Ribbed, Satin Yellow, Dotted Flower | 55.00 |
| Pitcher, Water, Painted Flowers, Lusterless White, 9 3/4 In. | 210.00 |
| Plaque, Ruffled Edge, Carnations, Lusterless, 11 X 13 In. | 85.00 |
| Plate, Girl Portrait, Lusterless, 11 1/2 In. | 65.00 |
| Salt & Pepper, Acorn | 95.00 |
| Salt & Pepper, Satin Ribbed, Leaf & Berry, Pairpoint Frame | 160.00 |
| Salt, Cockleshell, Pink & Blue | 195.00 |
| Salt, Enameled Flowers, Tomato Shape, Original Top | 50.00 |
| Salt, Fig Shape, Enameled Design | 75.00 |
| Salt, Melon Rib, Beige & Orange Design, Gold Trim | 50.00 |
| Salt, Tomato, Pair | 40.00 To 100.00 |
| Saltshaker, Apple Blossom | 48.00 |
| Saltshaker, Egg Shape, Original Tops | 85.00 |
| Saltshaker, Egg, Columbian 1893 Exhibition, Orange & Blue | 90.00 |
| Saltshaker, Fig, Green & Purple Flowers, Original Top | 135.00 |
| Saltshaker, Flat Egg, Pewter Top | 50.00 |
| Saltshaker, Holly Design | 48.00 |
| Saltshaker, Leaf & Berry | 75.00 |
| Saltshaker, Melon Ribbed, Yellow Enameled Flowers | 70.00 |
| Saltshaker, Melon Shape, Original Top, Enameled Flowers | 45.00 |
| Saltshaker, Melon, Enameled | 40.00 |

| | |
|---|---:|
| Saltshaker, Tomato Shape, Flowers, Original Top | 85.00 |
| Saltshaker, Tomato, Original Top, Green Enamel Flowers, 2 In. | 55.00 |
| Shaker, Blue, Enamel Floral Design, Melon Shape | 45.00 |
| Sugar & Creamer, Seaweed & Shell, Enameled, Silver Tops | 250.00 |
| Sugar Shaker, Blue Stain, Pink Roses | 115.00 |
| Sugar Shaker, Egg Shape, Flowers On Yellow Ground | 130.00 |
| Sugar Shaker, Egg Shape, Opaque Yellow, 4 1/4 In. | 225.00 |
| Sugar Shaker, Egg Shape, Pastel Apple Blossoms | 150.00 |
| Sugar Shaker, Egg, Blue Satin, Pink Rose | 185.00 |
| Sugar Shaker, Egg, Daisy Design, White | 120.00 |
| Sugar Shaker, Egg, Purple Violets | 175.00 |
| Sugar Shaker, Fig, Decorated | 385.00 |
| Sugar Shaker, Fig, Gold Flowers, Cranberry Glass | 305.00 |
| Sugar Shaker, Melon Ribbed, Original Top, Floral Design | 185.00 |
| Sugar Shaker, Melon Ribbed, Pink Blossoms, Original Top | 195.00 |
| Sugar Shaker, Melon Ribbed, Tomato | 160.00 |
| Sugar, Tomato, Pierced Cover, Enameled, 2 3/4 In.Diam | 90.00 |
| Syrup, Cherry Blossom Sprays, Lusterless, Cover, 7 1/2 In. | 175.00 |
| Syrup, Loop & Daisy, Hand-Painted Flowers, 3 1/2 In. | 235.00 |
| Table Set, Mustard & Salts, White Ribbed, Pairpoint Frame | 220.00 |
| Tazza, Amethyst With Floral Design, 3 1/2 In. | 245.00 |
| Toothpick, Burmese, Enamel Forget-Me-Nots, 2 3/4 In. | 250.00 |
| Toothpick, Burmese, Tricorner, Diamond-Quilted, Flowers | 325.00 |
| Toothpick, Melon Ribbed Bottom, Satin, Dotted Top | 80.00 |
| Toothpick, Melon Ribbed, Chimney Neck, Beaded Top, 2 1/4 In. | 85.00 |
| Tumbler, Whiskey, Diamond-Quilted, 2 3/4 In. | 185.00 |
| Vase, Birds & Other Figures, Slim, 6 1/2 In. | 43.00 |
| Vase, Celery, Pairpoint Holder, Rose Amber | 750.00 |
| Vase, Clear Daffodils & Leaves, Gold Highlights, 12 In. | 985.00 |
| Vase, Coralene, Flemish Windowpanes, Pink To Blue, 7 In. | 1250.00 |
| Vase, Enameled Mums, Crimped Top, Amethyst Shading, 12 In., Pr. | 235.00 |
| Vase, Jack-In-The-Pulpit, Crimped Yellow Edge, 9 3/4 In. | 650.00 |
| Vase, Jack, Apple Blossoms On Stem & Foot, Crimped Rim, 9 In. | 295.00 |
| Vase, Lemon Yellow, Cased In White | 200.00 |
| Vase, Peachblow, Lily, 6 1/8 In. | 1200.00 |
| Vase, Peachblow, Ribbed, 4 1/2 In. | 1195.00 |
| Vase, Peachblow, 12 In. | 1050.00 |
| Vase, Scalloped, Banded Rigaree, Streamers, C.1890, 4 1/4 In. | 2500.00 |

*Mud figures are small Chinese pottery figures made in the twentieth century. The figures usually represent workers, scholars, farmers, or merchants. Other pieces are trees, houses, and similar parts of the landscape. The figures have unglazed faces and hands but glazed clothing. The figures were originally made for fish tanks or planters.*

| | |
|---|---:|
| MUD FIGURE, Fisherman, Chinese, 1930, 4 1/2 In. | 15.00 |
| Lady, Blue Dress, 1930s, 5 In. | 20.00 |
| Man Seated, Yellow, Blue, & Green, 3 3/4 In. | 49.50 |
| Man Standing, Yellow, Blue, & Green, 6 1/2 In. | 69.50 |

| | |
|---|---:|
| MULBERRY, Creamer, Pelew, Challinor, 5 In. | 75.00 |
| Cup & Saucer, Carrara, Handleless | 48.00 |
| Cup & Saucer, Cyprus, Davenport, Handleless | 65.00 |
| Cup & Saucer, Handleless, Pelew | 38.00 |
| Cup, Dresden | 35.00 |
| Pitcher, Corean Pattern, 8-Sided, 9 1/2 In. | 75.00 |
| Pitcher, Milk, Corean | 85.00 |
| Pitcher, Schenectady On The Mohawk, 8 In. | 155.00 |
| Plate Warmer, Cork & Porcelain Plug, 10 In. | 185.00 |
| Plate, Alleghany, T.Goodfellow, 10 1/2 In. | 25.00 |
| Plate, Corean, 9 In. | 100.00 |
| Plate, Corean, 10 In. | 32.00 |

| | |
|---|---|
| **Plate,** Cyprus, 7 1/2 In., Set Of 4 | 85.00 |
| **Plate,** Hunting Scene, 9 1/4 In. | 35.00 |
| **Plate,** Mogul Scenery, Stoke, 10 1/2 In. | 32.00 |
| **Plate,** Palestine, 9 1/4 In. | 22.00 |
| **Plate,** Panama, 9 3/4 In. | 30.00 |
| **Plate,** Peruvian, Scenic, Marked, 9 1/2 In. | 30.00 |
| **Plate,** Schuylkill Water Works, 9 3/8 In. | 195.00 |
| **Plate,** Temple, 10 In. | 29.00 |
| **Platter,** Fountain Scenery, 13 X 10 In. | 45.00 |
| **Relish,** Shell Shaped, The Temple | 40.00 |
| **Soup Dish,** Peru, 10 3/4 In. | 35.00 |
| **Sugar,** Unina, Covered, Clementson | 75.00 |
| **Teapot,** Jeddo, C.1850, Adams | 150.00 |
| **Tile,** Spider Head Corners, 5 In.Square, Pair | 50.00 |
| **Vase,** Washington, 9 In. | 34.00 |

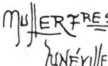

*Muller Freres, French for Muller Brothers, made cameo and other art glass from the early 1900s to the late 1930s. Their factory was first located in Luneville and later moved to Croismaire, France.*

| | |
|---|---|
| **MULLER FRERES, Bowl,** Orange, Blue-Green, Orchid, Signed, 4 3/4 In.Diam. | 125.00 |
| **Light,** Ceiling, Luneville, 3 Shades, Mottled, Fixture, Signed | 895.00 |
| **Vase,** Burgundy Leaves, Thorny Stems, Mottled Ground, 7 1/2 In. | 1500.00 |
| **Vase,** Cameo, Antarctic Scenic, Signed, 15 In. | 3300.00 |
| **Vase,** Cameo, Battle Scene, Medal Of Honor, Signed, 7 X 7 In. | 950.00 |
| **Vase,** Cameo, Brown Scenic, Orange Ground, Signed, 4 X 4 In. | 495.00 |
| **Vase,** Cameo, Cone Laden, Flying Beetles, Signed, 4 1/2 In. | 485.00 |
| **Vase,** Fern Design, Maroon, Gray, Grasshopper, Pedestal, 12 In. | 675.00 |
| **Vase,** Forest Scene, Orange, 4 Crimps, Signed, 4 3/4 In.Diam. | 955.00 |
| **Vase,** Leaves & Flowers, Grasshopper, Green, Signed, 1i 1/4 In. | 985.00 |
| **Vase,** Red Leaves & Flowers, 3-Color Ground, Signed, 12 1/4 In. | 985.00 |
| **Vase,** Water Scene, Clear Gound, Signed, 9 1/4 In. | 775.00 |

| | |
|---|---|
| **MUSIC, Accordion,** Amplifier, Extra Plug-Ins, Italian | 3600.00 |
| **Accordion,** Deer Design, Red Stones In Eyes, Italian, Case, 16 X 17 In. | 500.00 |
| **Album,** Photo, Plays Irish Eyes, Celluloid & Velvet | 145.00 |
| **Album,** Photo, 2 Tunes, Leather Cover, Pictures | 220.00 To 330.00 |
| **Album,** Photo, 2-Tune Cylinder Box Inside, Velvet Covered | 150.00 |
| **Banjo-Mandolin,** Trapdoor, C.1925 | 150.00 |
| **Banjo,** Maxitone, 4 String, Canvas Case | 140.00 |
| **Banjo,** Tenor, Bacon & Day, Silver Bell, C.1923 | 1500.00 |
| **Banjo,** Tenor, Liberty, 1920s, Inlaid Resonator | 325.00 |
| **Barrel Orchestrion,** Vossen, Art Glass, Oak Case, 10-Tune, 7 Ft.10 In. | 3700.00 |
| **Barrel Organ,** Gavioli, 40 Key, 8 Tunes, 19 X 28 X 24 In. | 4400.00 |
| **Baton,** Conductor's, Ivory & Ebony | 40.00 |
| **Baton,** Conductor's, Ivory Grip, Sterling Silver Tip, Ebony, Boxed | 55.00 |
| **Bird In Cage,** Mechanical, French | 275.00 |
| **Box,** Baker, Troll Co., Swiss, 20 X 9 X 5 1/2 In. | 450.00 |
| **Box,** Calliope, Christmas Tree Attachment, 4 Discs | 1200.00 |
| **Box,** Calliope, 10 Discs, 17 3/4 In. | 1250.00 |
| **Box,** Criterion, Double Comb, 15 3/4 In. | 2500.00 |
| **Box,** Cylinder, 4 Striking Bells, 6-Tune | 1800.00 |
| **Box,** Cylinder, 5 Bells, Drum, Castanets, 12-Tune, Inlaid Top, 13 In. | 2650.00 |
| **Box,** Cylinder, 5 Bells, 8-Tune | 1400.00 |
| **Box,** Empress, 23 Discs, 12 In. | 1200.00 |
| **Box,** Ideal, Drawer In Base, Zither Attachment, Mahogany, 12 X 28 In. | 5500.00 |
| **Box,** Imperial Symphonion, Duplex Combs, Mahogany Case, 11 Ft. | 2500.00 |
| **Box,** Junghans, 3 Bells, Music, Album, Victorian, 4 1/2 In.Metal Disc | 550.00 |
| **Box,** Mandolin Basso Piccolo, Interchangeable Cylinder, 38 X 20 In. | 5900.00 |
| **Box,** Mermod Freres, Cylinder, 19th Century, 13 3/4 In. ... *Illus* | 300.00 |
| **Box,** Mermod Freres, 6-Tune, Inlaid Lid, 20 X 8 1/2 X 6 1/2 In. | 1450.00 |

Music, Box, Mermod Freres, Cylinder, 19th Century, 13 3/4 In. (See Page 361)

Music, Box, Regina Corona, Automatic Changer, 31 Discs, 67 In.

Music, Box, Symphonion, Inlaid Floral Lid, 14 Discs, 13 1/2 In.

**Box,** Mermod Freres, 10-Tune, Coin-Operated, Carved Oak .................................................. 1900.00
**Box,** Mermod Ideal Piccolo, 8 Cylinders, 40 X 24 X 50 In. .................................................. 7750.00
**Box,** Mira, 36 Discs, Matching Base Cabinet, 18 1/2 In. .................................................. 4200.00
**Box,** Miraphone, Horn, 20 Discs, Slow-Fast Lever, 30 X 25 X 30 In. .................................. 6000.00
**Box,** Olympia, Double Comb, Carved Golden Oak, 12 Discs ..............................................  800.00
**Box,** Olympia, Table Model, Single Comb, Storage Drawer .............................................. 2300.00
**Box,** Otto, Pianette Disc Piano, Coin-Operated, 33 1/4 X 17 X 66 In. .................................. 6000.00
**Box,** Paillard, Interchangeable 4-Tune Cylinders, Inlay All Sides .................................... 8400.00
**Box,** Penny Coin-Operated, 12-Tune .................................................................... 2500.00
**Box,** Polyphon, Double Comb, Oak Case, 12 1/2 In.Disc .................................................. 1200.00
**Box,** Polyphon, Picture On Inside Lid, Walnut, 25 X 2o X 13 In. ........................................ 2800.00
**Box,** Powder, Celluloid Legs, Metal ....................................................................   12.50
**Box,** Regina Corona, Automatic Changer, 31 Discs, 67 In. .................................... *Illus* 7500.00
**Box,** Regina Hexaphone, Style 104, Case With Sign .................................................... 4500.00
**Box,** Regina, Carved Rococo Case, 11 In.Double Comb .................................................. 2750.00
**Box,** Regina, Double Comb, 8 Discs, Oak, 15 1/2 In.Disc .................................................. 2200.00
**Box,** Regina, Double Comb, 10 Discs, Oak .............................................................. 1250.00
**Box,** Regina, Double Comb, 20 Discs, Storage Stand, 15 1/2 In.Disc .................................. 4200.00

**Box,** Regina, Double Comb, 20 3/4 In.Disc, Library Table, Mahogany ....................................... 8500.00
**Box,** Regina, Set In Desk, Double Comb, Quartered Oak ............................................................ 7900.00
**Box,** Regina, Stand With Compartment, 22 Discs, 15 1/2 In. ..................................................... 3500.00
**Box,** Regina, Style 22, Twenty 8 In.Discs ................................................................................. 900.00
**Box,** Regina, Style 113, Serpentine Cabinet ............................................................................. 1800.00
**Box,** Regina, Table Model, Accordion Format, 50 Records, 27 In. .............................................. 4800.00
**Box,** Reginaphone, Lion Head Corners, 36 Discs, 22 X 20 X 50 In. ........................................... 5500.00
**Box,** Reginaphone, 15 1/2 In.Double Comb, Rookwood Finish ................................................... 5750.00
**Box,** Signet, Side Wind, Flowers On Lid, Card Inside, Metal Discs ............................................. 495.00
**Box,** Stella, Crank, Eight 15 1/2 In.Discs .................................................................................. 1800.00
**Box,** Swiss, Bells, Butterflies, Others, Pearl Inlay, 17 X 14 In. ................................................. 8500.00
**Box,** Swiss, Cylinder, On 2-Drawer Marquetry Inlaid Stand, 19th Century ............................... 4700.00
**Box,** Symphonion, Inlaid Floral Lid, 14 Discs, 13 1/2 In. .................................................. *Illus* 850.00
**Box,** Symphonion, Monster Automation, Coin-Operated, 25 1/4 In. ........................................... 7200.00
**Box,** Symphonion, Original Picture On Inside Lid, Disc, 7 5/8 In. ............................................. 475.00
**Bugle,** Regulation, Army, Brass ................................................................... 32.50 To 50.00
**Castanets,** Silk Cord, Elton, Pair ............................................................................................ 5.00
**Clarinet,** Albert, Bflat, A. & C., Rosewood, English, Signed ....................................................... 490.00
**Clarinet,** Bundy, Blue Velvet Lined Case ................................................................................. 75.00
**Clarinet,** Selmer, Contra Bass, Rosewood ............................................................................... 1500.00
**Cornet,** E.K.Blessing, Elkhart, Brass ...................................................................................... 110.00
**Drum,** Snare, Military, Polychrome Eagle, V.J.Lunt, Newburyport, 11 In. .................................. 675.00
**Grammaphone,** Columbia, 2-Minute Cylinder .......................................................................... 325.00
**Graphophone,** Columbia, Floor Model, Coin-Operated ............................................................. 4500.00
**Graphophone,** Columbia, Model AH, Brass Horn, Oak Case ..................................................... 700.00
**Graphophone,** Key Wind, Carrying Case .................................................................................. 265.00
**Graphophone,** Type BS, Coin-Operated, 5 Cent ....................................................................... 2350.00
**Guitar Zither,** Henzenhauer, Dated May 29, 1897, Original Case ............................................. 135.00
**Guitar,** Gibson, Model L-5c.1932 ............................................................................................ 1100.00
**Guitar,** Lady's, Abalone Inlay, 19th Century ........................................................................... 600.00
**Guitar,** Martin, 1871, Original Wooden Case ........................................................................... 3000.00
**Harmonica,** Hohner, Counter Display, Revolves, Wood & Metal ............................................... 195.00
**Harmonica,** Hohner, Echo Model ............................................................................................. 8.00
**Harmonica,** Hohner, Echo Model, 1937, German ..................................................................... 35.00
**Harmonica,** Koch, International Pitch, 3 1/4 2(9 ...................................................................... 10.00
**Harmonica,** Nor-Cos, Uses Play-A-Sax Rolls, 3 Rolls Included ................................................. 85.00
**Harmonica,** Pohl, Germany, Boxed .......................................................................................... 18.00
**Harmonica,** Rolmonica, Roll Operated .......................................................... 75.00 To 100.00
**Harmonica,** Zeppelin, Brass .................................................................................................. 299.00
**Hurdy Gurdy,** All Wooden Pipes, 8 Tunes, German ................................................................. 2000.00
**Jukebox,** Bimbo Baby, 6 Monkeys Playing Instruments, Miniature .......................................... 1600.00
**Jukebox,** Bing Crosby, Table Model, Lights Flash, 78 RPM ...................................................... 125.00
**Jukebox,** Manhattan, Packard Pla-Mor, Capehart, No.37 ......................................................... 1600.00
**Jukebox,** Mills, Ferris Wheel .................................................................................................. 450.00
**Jukebox,** Packard, Manhattan ................................................................................................ 1500.00
**Jukebox,** Rock Ola, Model 1426 .............................................................................................. 1195.00
**Jukebox,** Rock Ola, Model 16283, Series B-2, 1936 ................................................................ 675.00
**Jukebox,** Rock Ola, Monarch Model, Walnut ........................................................................... 600.00
**Jukebox,** Scopitone, With Movies, 36 Films, Free Play & 25 Cent Slot ..................................... 1450.00
**Jukebox,** Seeburg, Coin-Operated, 1928, 46 X 35 X 25 In. ...................................................... 6000.00
**Jukebox,** Seeburg, Model 100a, 33 1/3 R.P.M.Records ............................................................ 1000.00
**Jukebox,** Seeburg, Symphonola, Model 147ma ....................................................................... 800.00
**Jukebox,** Wurlitzer IX, Art Glass, Marshall Wendell, 5 Ft. ........................................................ 4250.00
**Jukebox,** Wurlitzer, Model 41, Countertop ............................................................................. 1500.00
**Jukebox,** Wurlitzer, Model 71, Countertop ............................................................................. 2000.00
**Jukebox,** Wurlitzer, Model 800 ............................................................................................... 750.00
**Jukebox,** Wurlitzer, Model 1015 ............................................................ 1800.00 To 2800.00
**Jukebox,** Wurlitzer, Model 1080, 45 R.P.M.Records ................................................................ 3495.00
**Jukebox,** Wurlitzer, Model 1315, 45 R.P.M. ........................................................................... 1900.00
**Mandolin,** Bowl Back, Stella, 1920s ....................................................................................... 75.00
**Mandolin,** Calacci, Tortoiseshell, Inlaid Mother-Of-Pearl ........................................................ 600.00
**Mandolin,** Kay, 1930s ........................................................................................................... 85.00
**Mandolin,** Lignatone, Czechoslovakian .................................................................................. 85.00

**Mandolin,** Venetian, 16 Rib, Signed Carrying Case ........................................ 95.00
**Mandolin,** Victoria, C.1898 ........................................................................ 135.00
**Melo-Harp,** Lap, Tuning Key, Patent 1895 ................................................. 125.00
**Melodeon,** O.Follett, Ivory & Teak Keys, Signed, Dated 1873, Rosewood ......... 650.00
**Melodeon,** Street, C.1895, 2 Sets Of Reeds, No Stops, 24 X 54 X 52 In. ..... 1120.00
**Nickelodeon,** Cremona, Roll, Art Glass Front, Coin-Operated ......................... 4500.00
**Nickelodeon,** Engelhardt, With Xylophone, Art Glass, Oak ............................. 8700.00
**Nickelodeon,** Hupfeldt, 1915, Burled Rosewood Case ................................... 6000.00
**Nickelodeon,** Kohler Chase, Berry Wood, 1901, Quarter-Sawn Oak ................ 9750.00
**Nickelodeon,** Nelson Wiggens, Casino X, Xylophone & Banjo Attachment ........ 7800.00
**Nickelodeon,** Watling, Coin Front, Walnut Stand ......................................... 5000.00
**Nickelodeon,** Western Electric, Cabinet Piano ............................................. 4600.00
**Nickelodeon,** Wurlitzer, Art Glass, Satin Lacquer Finish Oak, 5 Rolls ............ 6900.00
**Nickelodeon,** Wurlitzer, Model SA, Flute Pipes ........................................... 8000.00
**Nickelodeon,** Wurlitzer, Roman Style Case, Roll Changer .............................. 4500.00
**Nickleodeon,** Western Electric Piano Co., Cabinet Style ............................... 4600.00
**Organ,** Artizan, Military Band, Plays Wurlitzer 125 Rolls ............................... 7600.00
**Organ,** Band, Book Style, W.B.Sohn, Germany, C.1895, 12 X 7 Ft. .............. 8200.00
**Organ,** Band, 45 Pipes, 7-Tune, C.1860, Small .......................................... 3500.00
**Organ,** Barrel, Pistor, 58 Pipes, 10-Tune, 1801, Crank Wound, 5 1/2 Ft. ....... 3000.00
**Organ,** Chicago Cottage, Pump, Stool With Ball & Claw Feet ......................... 3500.00
**Organ,** Crank, 15 Wood Spools, 12 X 14 In. ................................................ 400.00
**Organ,** Davis Piano Player Co., Pulaski, Tenn., Mahogany ............................... 600.00
**Organ,** Estey, Folding Field Model, 4 Octave, 2 Levers & Foot Pumps ............. 450.00
**Organ,** Estey, Pump, Child's, C.1900, 3 Octave, Ivory Keys, Bench, Maple ...... 150.00
**Organ,** Estey, Reed, 2 Manual Pedal Boards ................................................. 600.00
**Organ,** Estey, 2 Keyboards, Hand Crank, Full Foot Pedals, 6 X 5 Ft. ............ 1800.00
**Organ,** Gavioli, Fairground, Keyless, Set For Continuous Playing .................... 8000.00
**Organ,** Gem, Roller, 2 Combs, Original Box, Walnut ....................................... 425.00
**Organ,** Hammond, B3, Leslie Cabinet ........................................................ 4500.00
**Organ,** Mason & Hamlin, Foot Pedal, C.1875, Walnut Case ............................. 465.00
**Organ,** Pipe, Aeolian, Residential, 16 Rank, Harp & Chimes ......................... 7500.00
**Organ,** Pipe, Wurlitzer, Theater, Toy Counter ............................................. 7500.00
**Organ,** Player, Aeolian-Hammond, 28 Rolls, Bench, 49 X 49 1/2 X 47 In. ...... 5200.00
**Organ,** Seeburg, Pipe, Mortuary, MSR Rolls ................................................ 3500.00
**Organ,** Street, Dutch, 60 Key, Music Book ................................................. 7500.00
**Organ,** Wurlitzer, Pipe, Theater, Toy Counter .............................................. 7500.00
**Organette,** Ariston, 12 Cardboard Discs ..................................................... 425.00
**Organette,** Clariona, 3 Rolls ..................................................................... 375.00

*The phonograph, invented by Thomas Edison in the 1880s, has been made by
many firms.*

**Phonograph & Lamp,** Electric Phonograph Corp., N.Y., 32 In. ....................... 650.00
**Phonograph,** Amberola 30, Edison Cylinder ................................................. 325.00
**Phonograph,** Busy Bee, Cylinder, Key Wind .................................................. 350.00
**Phonograph,** Busy Bee, Morning Glory Horn ................................................. 475.00
**Phonograph,** Cirola, Portable, Mahogany Case .............................................. 185.00
**Phonograph,** Clark, Johnson, Hand-Driven .................................................. 600.00
**Phonograph,** Coin-Operated, 1 To 10 Cents, Mazda Bulb, 42 X 22 X 18 In. ..... 1200.00
**Phonograph,** Columbia B.K.T., Cylinder, Mounted Green Petaled Horn ............. 600.00
**Phonograph,** Columbia, Graphonola, Regent, Desk Type ................................ 475.00
**Phonograph,** Columbia, Q Cylinder, Tin Horn, C.1900, Key Wind, Lid ............. 420.00
**Phonograph,** Edison Amberola VI, Mahogany Case ........................................ 450.00
**Phonograph,** Edison Amberola, Model DX, Oak .............................................. 235.00
**Phonograph,** Edison Amberola, Model No.75, Floor Model, Cylinder ................ 375.00
**Phonograph,** Edison Fireside, Cylinder, 2-Piece Horn .................................... 550.00
**Phonograph,** Edison Home Model, Brass Horn, 1 Cylinder .............................. 560.00
**Phonograph,** Edison Standard, Horn, C.1906, 85 Records, 16 In. .................... 425.00
**Phonograph,** Edison, Banner Triumph, 2 Minute ........................................... 575.00
**Phonograph,** Edison, Concert Banner, Maroon Gem ....................................... 650.00
**Phonograph,** Edison, Gem, Baby Morning Glory Horn ..................................... 500.00
**Phonograph,** Edison, Gem, Cylinder, Key Wind ............................................. 295.00

Phonograph, Edison, Gem, Type I, 10 In.Gem Horn ........................................................... 425.00
Phonograph, Edison, Home, Large Brass Horn, Birdcage Stand ............................... 650.00
Phonograph, Edison, Opera, Oak, Music Master Horn ............................................ 1850.00
Phonograph, Edison, Standard, Suitcase, Oak ............................................................ 145.00
Phonograph, Edison, Triumph, Banner, 2 Minute ..................................................... 575.00
Phonograph, Lyre, Cast Iron, String Drive Cylinder .................................................. 145.00
Phonograph, Paillard, Cylinder, Reproducer, Swiss ................................................... 375.00
Phonograph, Polly Portable, Key Wind, Wooden Case .............................................. 75.00
Phonograph, Silvertone, Open Top, Inside Horn, Oak ............................................... 75.00
Phonograph, Sonora, C.1920, Filing System For 160 Records Beneath .................. 250.00
Phonograph, Thoren, Disassembles For Folding, Case, 10 3/4 X 4 3/4 In. ............. 250.00
Phonograph, Victor III, Oak Horn ................................................................................. 975.00
Phonograph, Victor V, Floating Turntable, Brass Horn, 24 In. ............................... 1500.00
Phonograph, Victor, Orthophonic, Credenza .............................................................. 450.00
Phonograph, Victor, Orthophonic, French Provincial Console ................................... 450.00
Phonograph, Victor, Upright, Carving, Circassian Walnut Case ................................ 500.00
Piano, Ampico B, Baby Grand, William & Mary Art Case, 1931 ............................ 7500.00
Piano, Ampico, C.1924, Walnut, Ampico Rolls ........................................................ 1200.00
Piano, Ampico, Chickering, 5 Ft.8 In. ...................................................................... 9500.00
Piano, Ampico, Grand, Marshall & Wendall, 5 Ft. ................................................... 5500.00
Piano, Ampico, Knabe, Upright, Walnut ................................................................... 1300.00
Piano, Baby Grand, Lester, Cabriole Legs, 5 Ft. 6 In. ............................................. 2000.00
Piano, Barrel, Favorite, With Cart ............................................................................. 900.00
Piano, Chickering & Sons, Circassian Walnut, Upright Grand, Carved ................... 5500.00
Piano, Chickering, Grand, Eastlake Bench, Ebony, 7 Ft. ......................................... 1200.00
Piano, Child's, Thoren's Disc Movement, 18 X 9 X 13 In. ........................................ 75.00
Piano, Cremona, Roll, Coin, 3 Beveled Glass Panels ............................................. 3500.00
Piano, George Steck, Grand, Original Ivories, Walnut, 5 1/2 Ft. ............................. 2100.00
Piano, Haines Bros., Grand, Ivory Keys, C.1860, Square, Rosewood .................... 5000.00
Piano, Hallet & Allen, Square, C.1850, Rosewood .................................................. 1150.00
Piano, Henry G.Johnson, Art Glass Front, C.1928, Coin-Operated, 3 Rolls ............ 6500.00
Piano, Horace Waters, Made In 1927, Alligatored Mahogany, 5 Ft.4 In. ................ 2000.00
Piano, J.Broadwood & Sons, Grand, C.1860 ........................................................... 1000.00
Piano, J.W.Brackett, Grand, C.1880, Rosewood Case, Square, 5 Ft.7 In. ............... 850.00
Piano, Kimball, Console, Pianocorder Mechanism & Tapes .................................... 3000.00
Piano, Lighte & Bradbury, Grand, C.1850, Square ................................................. 3500.00
Piano, Marshall & Wendell, Grand, Reproducing, Spanish Art Case, Bench ........... 9500.00
Piano, National Electric Co., Art Glass, Mandolin & 24 Flute Pipes ...................... 8500.00
Piano, Player & Crank, Kohler & Campbell .............................................................. 1500.00
Piano, Player, Aeolian, George Steck, Grand, C.1923, 6 Legs, Rolls ..................... 3500.00
Piano, Player, Angelus Orchestral ............................................................................. 300.00
Piano, Player, Baldwin, Pump Or Electric, 1905, Mahogany Finish ....................... 1200.00
Piano, Player, Brinkerhoff, Electric ........................................................................... 1400.00
Piano, Player, Kimball, 20 Rolls, Mahogany ........................................................... 1000.00
Piano, Player, Kohler & Campbell, Crank, Victorola ................................................ 1500.00
Piano, Player, Mandolin Attachment, Art Glass, Coin-Operated ............................ 4000.00
Piano, Player, Upright, Oak ....................................................................................... 2400.00
Piano, R.Gors & K.Berlin, Upright, Black Lacquer, Rolls ......................................... 1200.00
Piano, Regina, Mandolin Orchestra .......................................................................... 4300.00
Piano, Reproducing, Welte, Baby Grand, Mahogany .............................................. 2500.00
Piano, Southwell Of Dublin, C.1825, Square .......................................................... 1500.00
Piano, Southwell, Dublin, Ireland, C.1725, Square ................................................. 1500.00
Piano, Steinway, Grand, Duo Art, Matching Bench, Mahogany .............................. 6200.00
Piano, Steinway, Square Grand, Cabriole Legs, Built In 1877 ................................ 4800.00
Piano, Street, Spanish ............................................................................................... 1750.00
Piano, Weber Duo-Art, Reproducing Grand, Walnut, 68 In. .................................... 5000.00
Pianoforte, C.1810, Thomas Western & Son, New York ........................................ 2200.00
Pianolodeon, Chein ..................................................................................................... 150.00
Record, Amos & Andy, 1929 Episode, Electra Label, Set Of 12 ............................ 475.00
Record, Cylinder, Edison, Original Box, Set Of 10 .................................................... 15.00
Record, Fats Domino, Counting Boy & If You Need Me ............................................. 2.00
Record, Jimmy Durante, One Of These Days .............................................................. 2.00
Record, Ku Klux Klan, Set Of 78 .............................................................................. 165.00

**Record,** Superman, 1975, LP ............................................................. 25.00
**Recordo,** Baldwin, Made In 1931, Walnut Case, 4 Ft.8 In. ........................... 2100.00
**Recordo,** Mehlin, Made In 1933, Light Walnut Case, Matching Bench ............. 1600.00
**Roll,** Nickelodeon, 10 Tunes, Gray Paper, 11 1/4 In.Wide ......................... 20.00
**Rolmonica,** Blow & Crank, Plays Music, 3 Rolls .................................... 135.00
**Saxophone,** Mother-Of-Pearl Buttons, Dated 1914, Elkhart, Indiana ............... 90.00
**Saxophone,** Saxello, Byassee Keyboard ............................................. 800.00
**Sheet,** After The War Is Over, 1917 ................................................. 3.00
**Sheet,** Al Jolson, 1915-23, 3 Piece ................................................. 20.00
**Sheet,** At An Ole Virginia Wedding, 1900, Lithograph ............................... 10.00
**Sheet,** Au Revoir, But Not Good-Bye, Doughboy & French Girl, 1917 ............... 5.00
**Sheet,** Babes In Toyland ............................................................ 18.00
**Sheet,** Barney Google & Spark Plug ................................................ 15.00
**Sheet,** Barney Google, 1923 ........................................................ 25.00
**Sheet,** Boy Scouts Parade, 1912 .................................................... 15.00
**Sheet,** But Beautiful, Road To Rio, Bob Hope, Dorothy Lamour, 1947 ............. 3.00
**Sheet,** Cheek To Cheek, Astaire, Rogers, 1935 ..................................... 15.00
**Sheet,** Darktown Strutters Ball, 1917 ............................................... 15.00
**Sheet,** Deanna Durbin, 36-Page Folio, 1938 ........................................ 15.00
**Sheet,** Don't Be Like That, Helen Kane ............................................. 8.50
**Sheet,** Franklin D.Roosevelt March, 1933, Cover Photo ............................. 10.00
**Sheet,** Go Way Back & Sit Down, 1901 .............................................. 20.00
**Sheet,** Golden Earrings, Marlene Dietrich .......................................... 1.50
**Sheet,** Good Ship Lollipop, Shirley Temple ......................... 10.00 To 18.50
**Sheet,** Good-Bye Betty Brown, Harrison Fisher Cover, 1912 ........................ 16.00
**Sheet,** Goody Goody, Johnny Mercer, Featuring Jackie Heller, 1936 ............... 1.00
**Sheet,** Heartbreak Hotel, Elvis Presley ............................................ 10.00
**Sheet,** Hello Central, Harris, 1901 ................................................. 8.00
**Sheet,** Heroes Of Peace, Rose O'Neill Illustration ................................. 20.00
**Sheet,** High & Mighty, John Wayne, 1954 ........................................... 12.50
**Sheet,** How Could You, Ann Sheridan & Humphrey Bogart Cover ................... 5.00
**Sheet,** Huggable, Kissable You, Rudy Vallee ........................................ 10.00
**Sheet,** I Can't Begin To Tell You, Betty Grable .................................... 10.00
**Sheet,** I Can't Do Without You, Iving Berlin, 1928 ................................ 1.00
**Sheet,** I Got Stung, Elvis Presley .................................................. 12.00
**Sheet,** I'm Forever Blowing Bubbles, Picture Of June Caprice, 1919 ............... 4.00
**Sheet,** I've Got The Time, I've Got The Place, Hetty King, 1910 .................. 3.00
**Sheet,** It's A Long, Long Way To Tipperary, 1912 .................................. 5.00
**Sheet,** Jersey Bounce, 1941 ......................................................... 1.00
**Sheet,** June In January, Bing Crosby, 1934 ........................................ 15.00
**Sheet,** Laughing On The Outside, 1946, Dinah Shore, Sammy Kaye ............... 1.00
**Sheet,** Little Annie Rooney, Mary Pickford, Signed, 1925 ......................... 15.00
**Sheet,** Little Orphan Annie Song ................................................... 35.00
**Sheet,** Long Ago And Far Away, Rita Hayworth .................................... 10.00
**Sheet,** Love Me Tender, Elvis Presley .............................................. 15.00
**Sheet,** March To The White House, 1924, Photo Of John Davis .................... 5.00
**Sheet,** Maybe, 1901, Rosa Olitzka On Cover ....................................... 1.00
**Sheet,** Missouri Waltz, Bing Crosby ................................................ 10.00
**Sheet,** Moonlight Becomes You, Bing Crosby ...................................... 8.50
**Sheet,** Moxie, Advertising, 1921 ................................................... 25.00
**Sheet,** My Buddy, Introduced By Al Jolson, 1922 .................................. 2.00
**Sheet,** My Sunny Tennessee, Eddie Cantor, 1921 .................................. 2.00
**Sheet,** Nevada, Tommy Dorsey, 1945, Barbelle Cover ............................. 1.00
**Sheet,** Oh Mister Gallagher, Yes Mister Shean, Ziegfelds, 1922 ................. 5.00
**Sheet,** Oh, How I Hate To Get Up In The Morning, Irving Berlin .................. 5.00
**Sheet,** Oh, How She Could Yacki Hacki Wicki Wacki Woo, 1916 ................. 1.00
**Sheet,** Orphan Annie Song, Ovaltine, 1931 ........................................ 35.00
**Sheet,** Over There, Rockwell ....................................................... 25.00
**Sheet,** Paper Doll, Frank Sinatra .................................................. 10.00
**Sheet,** Peerless March, 1918, Peerless Motor Car ................................. 17.00
**Sheet,** Pepsodent Theme Song, Amos 'n Andy, 1929 ............................. 12.00
**Sheet,** Pronounced You Man & Wife, 1898, Child Bride & Groom ............... 2.00
**Sheet,** Roses In The Rain, Frank Sinatra .......................................... 10.00

Sheet, Rudolph Valentino, 1926, Photograph On Cover ................................................ 9.75
Sheet, Salvation Lassie Of Mine, 1919, Salvation Army ............................................. 10.00
Sheet, San Fernando Valley, Bing Crosby ................................................................ 10.00
Sheet, Sleep Soldier Boy, Soldier Playing Bugle Over Coffin, 1926 ......................... 3.00
Sheet, Song Of The South, 1946 ............................................................................ 9.00
Sheet, Sonny Boy, Al Jolson ................................................................................... 6.00
Sheet, Stars & Stripes, Sousa, 1897 ...................................................................... 30.00
Sheet, Sweet Rosie O'Grady, Betty Grable ............................................................ 10.00
Sheet, The Old Oaken Bucket, 1882 ....................................................................... 9.00
Sheet, The Right Somebody To Love, Shirley Temple, 1937 ................................... 15.00
Sheet, The Sheik Of Araby, Illustrated Cover, 1921 ................................................ 1.00
Sheet, The Trolley Song, Judy Garland .......................................................... 8.00 To 8.50
Sheet, The Whole World Is Singing My Song, Mary Small, 1946 ............................ 1.00
Sheet, There's No You, 1944, Frank Sinatra .......................................................... 1.00
Sheet, They Called It Dixieland, Whiting, 1916 ...................................................... 6.00
Sheet, Toot Toot Tootsie, Al Jolson, 1922 ............................................................. 10.00
Sheet, Trail Of The Lonesome Pine, 1913, Illustrated ............................................ 5.00
Sheet, Trolley Song, Judy Garland ........................................................................ 7.50
Sheet, Under The Anheuser-Busch ........................................................................ 15.00
Sheet, When I'm With You, Shirley Temple ............................................................ 15.00
Sheet, When The Moon Comes Over The Mountain, Kate Smith, 1931 ................... 7.00
Sheet, When You Come Back, George M.Cohan, 1918 ............................................ 7.50
Sheet, When You Wish Upon A Star, 1939 ............................................................. 7.50
Sheet, When You Wore A Tulip, 1914 ..................................................................... 12.00
Sheet, Whistle While You Work, 1937 ........................................................... 7.00 To 7.50
Sheet, White Christmas, Irving Berlin, 1942 .......................................................... 30.00
Sheet, Wizard Of Oz ............................................................................................. 12.00
Sheet, Yes We Have No Bananas, 1923 ................................................................. 1.00
Sheet, Yours & Mine, Guy Lombardo, 1930 ........................................................... 1.00
Sheet, Zip-A-Dee-Doo-Dah, 1946 .......................................................................... 7.50
Songbook, Bill Haley & The Comets ...................................................................... 12.00
Songbook, Blue Wallpaper Cover, Dated 1808, 9 X 5 1/4 In. ................................ 95.00
Trombone, Campo, New Orleans, Nickel Over Brass, Case ................................... 100.00
Trombone, Slide, Compo Bros., New Orleans, Nickel Over Brass, Case ................ 65.00
Trumpet, Fireman's, Presentation Broadside, 1857 .............................................. 50.00
Ukulele, Martin, C.1919 ........................................................................................ 75.00
Violin, William B.Knox, 1909, Case, 2 Bows ......................................................... 600.00
Xylophone, Guatemalan, Rosewood Notes & Keys, Front Parquetry ................... 1000.00
Zither, Queen ........................................................................................................ 85.00

*Mustache cups were popular from 1850 to 1900. A ledge of china or silver held the hair out of the liquid in the cup.*

MUSTACHE CUP & SAUCER, Applied Flowers, Lavender, Manchester, N.H. ......... 13.00
Lilac Design ......................................................................................................... 45.00
Portrait ................................................................................................................ 38.00
Portrait Of Mother & Child, Gold Trim, Tetau Mark .............................................. 65.00
Raised White Design, Gold Rims ........................................................................... 38.00
Roses, Germany ................................................................................................... 18.00
Roses, Pink & White, Gold Ribbons ....................................................................... 25.00
Scenic, Beaded Trim, Nippon, Rising Sun Mark .................................................... 145.00
White Ground, Gold Trim, Royal Crown Derby ...................................................... 55.00

MUSTACHE CUP, Forget-Me-Nots, Germany ......................................................... 30.00
Pink Flowers & Gold Lines ..................................................................................... 22.00
Remember Me, Floral Design, Germany ................................................................ 35.00
Think Of Me .......................................................................................................... 20.00

*MZ Austria is a mark used by Moritz Zdekauer from about 1900. The firm worked in the town of Alt-Rohlau, Austria.*

**MZ AUSTRIA, Bowl,** Morning Glory Gold Rim Inside, Blue Tint Ground, 2 X 8 In. ................. 45.00
    **Cookie Jar,** Floral Design, Satin Finish, Gold Trim, 8 1/2 In. ............................................. 85.00
    **Dish,** Vegetable, Covered, Pink Flower ....................................................................... 20.00
    **Plate,** Blown-Out Floral Edge, Satin Finish ................................................................ 34.00
    **Plate,** Portrait, Constance, Scalloped Edge, Gold Trim, 9 3/8 In. ..................................... 95.00
    **Tray,** Pin, Red Roses, Green & Gold Trim, 3 X 4 In. ..................................................... 28.00
    **Vase,** Hand-Painted Roses, Gold Trim, 11 In. ............................................................. 50.00

*Nailsea glass was made in the Bristol district in England from 1788 to
1873. Many pieces were made with loopings of colored glass as decorations.*

**NAILSEA, Bell,** Wedding.Clear Handle & Clapper, Loopings, Cranberry, 12 In. ...................... 195.00
    **Bottle,** White Swirls, Clear, 12 In. ............................................................................ 95.00
    **Cruet,** Spatter White, Applied Handle, 4 1/4 In. ........................................................... 45.00
    **Lamp,** Fairy, Pegged Clarke Base In Brass Candlestick, Cranberry .................................. 198.00
    **Rolling Pin,** Dark & Light Blue ................................................................................ 95.00
    **Shade,** Lily Pad Design, Small, Set Of 4 .................................................................... 235.00
    **Shade,** Ruffled, Blue, Small ................................................................................... 100.00

# NAKARA

*Nakara is a trade name for a white glassware made around 1900 that was
decorated in pastel colors. It was made by the C.F. Monroe Company
of Meriden, Connecticut.*

**NAKARA, Bonbon Basket,** Cream Panels, Enameled Flowers, Signed, 6 In.Diam. ................... 195.00
    **Bonbon,** Basket, Bail, Orchids, White Beading, Crown Mold, 8 In. ................................... 298.00
    **Box,** Allover Roses, Green Ground, Crown Mold, Signed, Large ....................................... 900.00
    **Box,** Blue, Marked C.F.Monroe Co., Large .................................................................. 750.00
    **Box,** Covered, 6-Sided, Pansies, White Beading, 3 X 3 In. ............................................. 345.00
    **Box,** Crown Mold, Olive Green To Pink, Ormolu Rims, Signed, 5 X 8 In. ........................... 950.00
    **Box,** Floral, Pink & Turquoise, Marked, 3 In.Diameter .................................................. 290.00
    **Box,** Hinged Cover, Pink & White Flowers, Signed, 4 In.Diam. ....................................... 175.00
    **Box,** Hinged, Pink Flowers, Gray Ground, Octagon, 6 1/2 In. .......................................... 495.00
    **Box,** Jewel, Gold Ormolu, Footed, Enameled, Beading, 4 In.Diam. ................................... 345.00
    **Box,** Peachblow, Pansy Design, Hinged, Signed, 4 1/2 X 2 1/2 In. ................................... 375.00
    **Box,** Pink Flowers, Beaded, Beige & White, Signed, 5 In.Wide ........................................ 295.00
    **Box,** Trinket, Beaded Medallions On Lid, Signed, 2 X 2 1/2 In. ....................................... 225.00
    **Box,** Trinket, Open, Brass Rim, Ormolu Handles, Flowers, Signed .................................... 150.00
    **Casket,** Ring, Blue & Beaded, Lined, Signed .............................................................. 275.00
    **Dish,** Pin, Floral, Blue, Apricot, Ormolu Rim & Handles ................................................ 145.00
    **Holder,** Letter, Pink Blossoms, Brass Trim, Signed, 2 1/2 X 5 1/4 In. ............................... 225.00
    **Humidor,** Cigar, Indian Chief Portrait, Red Banner Mark, 6 In. ....................................... 390.00
    **Humidor,** Pink Flowers, Cigars Written In Gold, 6 In. .................................................... 450.00
    **Letter Holder,** Puffy, Enameled, Brass Trim, Signed, 5 1/4 X 4 1/8 In. .............................. 225.00
    **Vase,** Blue Design, 8 In. ....................................................................................... 225.00

*Nanking china is a blue-and-white porcelain made in China for export during
the eighteenth century.*

**NANKING, Ginger Jar,** Wooden Base, Covered, 7 In. ...................................................... 195.00
    **Jug,** Covered, Foo Dog Finial, Gold Leafed, 9 1/2 In., Pair ............................................ 625.00

*Napkin rings were popular from 1869 to about 1900.*

**NAPKIN RING, ABC,** Embossed Alphabet Around, Sterling, 3/4 In. ..................................... 80.00
    **Beaded Edge,** Sam, Sterling Silver .......................................................................... 22.00
    **Beaded Edges,** Initial E.F.T., Sterling, 1 In.Wide ........................................................ 20.00
    **Cloisonne** ......................................................................................................... 25.00
    **Embossed Bird On Sled,** Wilcox, Silver Plate ............................................................ 80.00
    **Figural,** A Frame, 2 Tall Ornaments On Sides, Silver Plate ............................................ 70.00
    **Figural,** Alligator At Ring, Miami, Florida Emblem, Silver Plate ........................................ 30.00
    **Figural,** Animal, Celluloid ...................................................................................... 5.00
    **Figural,** Barrel Shape, Branches & Leaves, Silver Plate ................................................ 35.00

**Figural,** Bashful Cherub, J.W.Tufts, Silver Plate, 4 In.Figure ................... 129.00
**Figural,** Begging Dog, Silver Plate ................... 65.00
**Figural,** Best Wishes, Kneeling Cupid, Heart Shaped, Silver Plate ................... 60.00
**Figural,** Betty Boop, China ................... 18.00
**Figural,** Bird Beside Ring, Supported On Cart, Silver Plate ................... 125.00
**Figural,** Bird On Flower, Derby Co. ................... 19.50
**Figural,** Bird On Wishbone, Rogers Brothers ................... 35.00
**Figural,** Bird Peering Into Nest, Webster ................... 150.00
**Figural,** Bird Perched On Stem, Leaf Base, Silver Plate, Meriden ................... 85.00
**Figural,** Boy & Girl Kissing Over Ring Top, China ................... 10.00
**Figural,** Boy Taking Off Shoes & Socks, Silver Plate ................... 125.00
**Figural,** Bulldog Chained To Dog House, Silver Plate ................... 225.00
**Figural,** Butterflies Base, Flared & Embossed, Silver Plate ................... 70.00
**Figural,** Carved Bird Effigy, Eastern Sioux Catlinite, 4 In. ................... 35.00
**Figural,** Cherub Girl Holds Ring, Dated May 5, 1905, Derby ................... 135.00
**Figural,** Cherub In Soldier Hat, Sitting On Turtle, Silver Plate ................... 235.00
**Figural,** Cherub On Rectangular Base, Silver Plate ................... 80.00
**Figural,** Cherub Playing Trumpet, Silver Plate ................... 125.00
**Figural,** Cherub Pulls Sled With Ring, Silver Plate ................... 135.00
**Figural,** Cherub Sits On Pedestal, Reed & Barton ................... 135.00
**Figural,** Cherubs, Applied Floral Design, Silver Plate ................... 29.00
**Figural,** Chick On Leafy Branch, Silver Plate ................... 85.00
**Figural,** Chick On Twigs, Engraved, Silver Plate ................... 48.00
**Figural,** Chick On Wishbone, Broken Egg, Derby, Silver Plate ................... 75.00
**Figural,** Chinese Mandarin & Performing Dog, Silver Plate ................... 189.00
**Figural,** Crawling Infant, Ring On Back, Silver Plate ................... 110.00
**Figural,** Diamond & Fan, Silver Plate ................... 49.00
**Figural,** Dog Next To Barrel Shaped Ring, Tufts, Triple Plate ................... 65.00
**Figural,** Dog Peers Out On Both Sides Of Doghouse, Silver Plate ................... 95.00
**Figural,** Dog Pulling Ring, Angel Riding ................... 125.00
**Figural,** Dog Pulling Ring, Movable Wheels, Racine, Silver Plate ................... 225.00
**Figural,** Dove On Each Side, Silver Plate ................... 60.00
**Figural,** Eagle On Each Side, Silver Plate, Meriden ................... 40.00 To 55.00
**Figural,** Elephant Standing Next To Holder, Tufts ................... 55.00
**Figural,** Elves, One On One, Pushing Ring, Simpson Hall ................... 125.00
**Figural,** Fans Holding Ring Over Butterfly, Silver Plate ................... 96.00
**Figural,** Floral Engraved, Silver Plate, 1 X 1 1/2 In. ................... 8.00
**Figural,** Frog With Glass Eyes, Seashell, Victorian, Silver Plate ................... 165.00
**Figural,** Girl, Center Ring, Salt & Pepper, 8 1/2 X 5 In.Wide ................... 145.00
**Figural,** Goat Before Ring, Oblong Platform, Silver Plate ................... 105.00
**Figural,** Goat Pulls Wheeled Flower Cart, Silver Plate ................... 250.00
**Figural,** Horse Pulling Ring On Movable Wheels ................... 175.00 To 250.00
**Figural,** Horse Pulling Wheeled Sulky, Silver Plate ................... 250.00
**Figural,** Horseshoe Leans Against Ring, Silver Plate ................... 63.00
**Figural,** Horseshoe, Oval, Footed Base, Silver Plate, Tufts ................... 80.00
**Figural,** Kate Greenaway Children, Double Figure, New Haven ................... 125.00
**Figural,** Kate Greenaway Girl Pushes Ring, Silver Plate ................... 145.00
**Figural,** Kewpie, Silver Plate ................... 85.00
**Figural,** Lily Pad, Bridgeport, Silver Plate ................... 35.00
**Figural,** Lily Pad, Flower & Ring At Center, Silver Plate ................... 65.00
**Figural,** Long-Tailed Bird Perched On Branch, Silver Plate ................... 115.00
**Figural,** Nude Leaning Against Ring, Leaf Base, Silver Plate ................... 95.00
**Figural,** Ostrich Standing Beside Ring, Silver Plate ................... 65.00
**Figural,** Owl On Wishbone, Silver Plate ................... 59.00
**Figural,** Peacock, Silver Plate, Meriden ................... 65.00
**Figural,** Pug Dog With Glass Eyes On Pie Plate, Van Berg Co. ................... 165.00
**Figural,** Rabbits Against Ring, On Good Earth, Silver Plate ................... 250.00
**Figural,** Reindeer, Rectangular Base, Meriden Co. ................... 125.00
**Figural,** Sailor Boy Pushes Ring, Silver Plate ................... 160.00
**Figural,** Squirrel, Acorns On Leaf Base, Scrolled, Silver Plate ................... 95.00
**Figural,** Squirrel, Glass Eyes, Holding Songbook, Silver Plate ................... 250.00
**Figural,** Standing Lion Beside Ring, Silver Plate ................... 118.00
**Figural,** Stork With Ring On Back, Silver Plate ................... 172.00

| | |
|---|---|
| **Figural,** Turtle, Signed Pairpoint, Silver Plate | 65.00 |
| **Figural,** Turtles On Round Base, Ring On Backs, Meriden | 100.00 |
| **Figural,** 2 Cox Brownies On Ring, Marked S.H.M., Silver Plate | 225.00 |
| **Flower Borders,** Monogrammed ADA, Sterling Silver, 2 X 1 3/4 In. | 100.00 |
| **Flowers & Leaves On Oval Base,** Hallmarked, Sterling | 50.00 |
| **Flowers On Sides Of Ring,** Oval Base, Sterling Silver | 50.00 |
| **Frog,** Mouth Open For Place Card, Ring On Back, Sterling Silver | 125.00 |
| **Horseshoe On Footed Base,** Tufts, Silver Plate | 80.00 |
| **Ivory Colored,** Celluloid, Opening, 1 1/2 In., Pair | 3.50 |
| **Souvenir Of Niagara Falls,** Silver Plate, 2 X 1 1/4 In.Diam. | 5.00 |

*Nash glass was made in Corona, New York, by Arthur Nash and his sons
after 1919. He worked at the Webb factory in England and for the
Tiffany Glassworks in the United States.*

| | |
|---|---|
| **NASH, Bottle,** Perfume, Stopper, Signed, 7 3/4 In. | 475.00 |
| **Bowl & Underplate,** Platinum & Gold, Iridescent, Signed, Numbered | 325.00 |
| **Compote,** Green Chintz, Signed, 4 1/2 X 7 1/4 In.Diam. | 235.00 |
| **Goblet,** Chintz, Lime Green, Clear & Lavender, Signed, 6 1/2 In. | 115.00 |
| **Goblet,** Green Stem, Pulled Feather Design On Bottom Of Bowl, Signed | 550.00 |
| **Salt,** Bronze, Blue, & Purple Iridescence, Signed, 4 In.Diam. | 175.00 |
| **Salt,** Iridescent Bronze, Blue, & Purple, Signed, 4 In.Diam. | 175.00 |
| **Vase,** Chintz, Orange & White Stripe, 9 1/2 In. | 375.00 |
| **Vase,** Chrome Green, Enameled Flowers, 2 Butterflies, 1930, 4 In. | 295.00 |
| **Vase,** Gold Iridescent, Pedestal, Optic Rib, 4 1/2 In. | 135.00 |
| **Vase,** Pedestal, Molded Rib Lower Half, Scalloped, Blue, Signed, 4 1/2 In. | 225.00 |

| | |
|---|---|
| **NAUTICAL, see also Scrimshaw** | |
| **NAUTICAL, Bed,** Captain's, On Rockers, Collapsible, Double | 450.00 |
| **Bell,** Ship's, Brass, 2 Ft. | 1100.00 |
| **Binocular,** Le Maire, Paris, Lenses | 70.00 |
| **Chest,** Carved Oak, Scene Of Mermaids, 2 Ft. X 9 In. | 250.00 |
| **Chest,** Handmade Hinges, Inscribed Pearl, Walnut, 5 X 2 1/2 In. | 110.00 |
| **Chest,** Hinged Lid, Fitted Inside, Camphor Wood, C.1840, 42 X 17 In. | 650.00 |
| **Clock,** Ashcroft, Brass | 150.00 |
| **Compass,** Binnacle In Box | 85.00 |
| **Compass,** Binnacle, Brass-Mounted, 4 Ft.10 In. | 500.00 |
| **Compass,** Boxed, Inside Swivel, S.Thaxter & Son, Boston, 5 1/8 In. | 100.00 |
| **Compass,** Brass Ring For Chain, 1 1/4 In.Diam. | 28.00 |
| **Compass,** Mahogany Box, Brass, Star, Boston, U.S.A., 5 In. | 300.00 |
| **Harpooning Gun,** Whaler's, Ocean Stead, Iron, 3 Ft.11 In. | 450.00 |
| **Helmet,** Diving, Brass | 850.00 |
| **Horn,** Fog, Iron Base, Foot Operated, C.1860, Brass | 385.00 |
| **Lantern,** Brass, 12 In. | 85.00 |
| **Lantern,** Harbor, 3-Sided Glass, Tin Frame, C.1840, 8 1/2 X 6 1/2 In. | 48.00 |
| **Lantern,** Masthead, Brass | 200.00 |
| **Lantern,** Masthead, Galvanized, Brass Top | 250.00 |
| **Lantern,** Port & Starboard, Brass, Copper Hinges, 9 In., Pair | 200.00 |
| **Lantern,** Red Ball Globe, 2 Bails, Steel, 12 X 5 In.Diam. | 65.00 |
| **Light,** Masthead, C.1915, 2 Ft. | 225.00 |
| **Light,** Ship's, Spot, Brass, Wall Mounted, American, 19th Century | 70.00 |
| **Mallet,** Sail Maker's, Raw Hide | 7.00 |
| **Octant,** English, Cased | 400.00 |
| **Pipe,** Boatswain's, Lanyard, Sterling Silver | 20.00 |
| **Port Hole,** Brass, 10 In. | 160.00 |
| **Propeller,** Brass, 11 1/2 In. | 25.00 |
| **Sextant,** Rosewood & Brass, Ivory Inlays, English, 13 X 14 1/2 In. | 500.00 |
| **Sextant,** 19th Century, Original Mahogany Case, Signed Wm. Cardiff | 350.00 |
| **Ship's Log,** U.S.Steam Frigate, Merrimac, Captain Pendergast, 1856 | 700.00 |
| **Stamp,** Whale, Used For Journal Logbook, Wooden | 1000.00 |
| **Telegraph,** Engine, 2 Controls & Speaking Tube, Brass | 495.00 |
| **Telescope,** Ancient Mariner's, Brass, Leather Case, 20 In. | 95.00 |
| **Telescope,** Brass & Mahogany, Adjustable Lenses, American, 43 In. | 575.00 |
| **Telescope,** Dust Covers, C.1860, 3 Drawer, Brass | 275.00 |

Telescope, 4-Section, American, Signed, Brass ......................................................... 235.00
Trumpet, Speaking, Captain's, Brass, Carrying Rings, American ............................. 160.00
Wheel, Brass Trim ...................................................................................................... 450.00
Wheel, Pilot, 3 Ft.Diam. ............................................................................................. 175.00
Wheel, Satinwood Inlay, Compass Points, Brass Hub, Teak, 31 In. ......................... 550.00
Wheel, 10 Spoke, Mississippi River Boat, C.1880, 5 Ft., Diam. ............................. 2100.00
Whistle, Steam, Brass ................................................................................................ 125.00
     NEEDLEWORK, see Textile, Picture; Textile, Sampler

*Netsuke are small ivory, wood, metal, or porcelain pieces used as the button on the end of a cord holding a Japanese money pouch. The earliest date from the sixteenth century.*

NETSUKE, Bowl, Gold-Eyed Dragon On Shibuishi Lid, Kagamibuta, Wooden ........................... 350.00
Buaku The Angry Warrior, Bronze Mask ................................................................. 135.00
Chinese Man Holding A Sword ................................................................................. 38.00
Crouching Woman, Wood ........................................................................................... 150.00
Figure Sitting Next To Rock, C.1890, 1 1/2 X 1 1/4 In. ........................................ 45.00
Fisherman With Basket, 19th Century, Signed Roichi ........................................... 1200.00
Foo Dog, Signed ......................................................................................................... 125.00
Ivory, Dog .................................................................................................................. 36.00
Ivory, Fox 18th Century ............................................................................................ 2500.00
Ivory, Horse ............................................................................................................... 36.00
Ivory, Hotei Seated, Child On Lap, Holding Fan .................................................... 125.00
Ivory, Man On Water Buffalo, 1 3/4 In. ................................................................ 125.00
Ivory, Man Pouring Water From Net Into Barrel, 2 In. ........................................ 65.00
Ivory, Man Sitting, Holding Monkey On Rope, Monkey With Fruit, 2 In. ............. 65.00
Ivory, Mouse ............................................................................................................. 36.00
Ivory, Revolving Face, Angry To Happy, 2 In. ....................................................... 60.00
Ivory, Standing Wrestler, 2 In. ............................................................................... 60.00
Ivory, Turtles ............................................................................................................ 50.00
Ivory, Two Men Holding Pedestal On Steps, 2 In. ................................................ 65.00
Ivory, Woman Standing, In Kimono, Holding Skull, 2 In. ..................................... 58.00
Monkey Clinging To Back Of Water Buffalo, Signed, 1 5/8 In. ............................. 175.00
Old Woman With Child On Back, 2 In. .................................................................... 125.00
Owl, Pelican & Turtle, Signed ................................................................................. 500.00
Samuri Warrior, Sword In Hand & Head Of Adversary By Hair, 2 In. ................. 48.00
Sleeping Dog, Wood, 18th Century .......................................................................... 1000.00
Snake Coiled Around Frog, Signed .......................................................................... 98.00
Staghorn, 19th Century, Okame .............................................................................. 200.00
Wise Man, White Beard, Green Robe, Gnarled Staff & Apple, 2 In. ..................... 42.00
Wood Wolf, 19th Century, Signed Masakiuo ......................................................... 1200.00

*New Martinsville Glass Manufacturing Company was established in 1901 in New Martinsville, West Virginia. It was bought and renamed the Viking Glass Company in 1944 and is still producing fine glasswares.*
     NEW MARTINSVILLE, see also Peachblow
NEW MARTINSVILLE, Ashtray, Swan ....................................................................... 12.00
Bookends, Eagle ........................................................................................................ 55.00
Bookends, Elephant .................................................................................................. 125.00
Bookends, Seal .......................................................................................................... 62.50
Bookends, Ship, Pair ................................................................................................ 45.00
Bookends, Squirrel .................................................................................................... 42.50
Bookends, Squirrels ....................................................................................... 42.50 To 65.00
Bookends, Starfish, Crystal ..................................................................................... 45.00
Bowl, Peachblow, Pink To Butterscotch, 8 1/2 X 3 In. ........................................ 180.00
Bride's Basket, Peachblow, Holder, 8 1/2 In. ........................................................ 350.00
Bride's Bowl, Peachblow, Ribbed, Fluted Edge, 10 In. ......................................... 135.00
Bride's Bowl, Yellows, Pink Underside, 4-Cornered, 9 In. .................................... 175.00
Candelabra, Rectangular Base, 3-Hole Branch, Pair ............................................ 95.00
Candleholder, Swan, Dark Green, Pair ................................................................... 19.75
Cup & Saucer, Jade ................................................................................................... 11.00
Decanter, Moondrop, Red, Small ............................................................................ 40.00

**Decanter,** Ruby Radiance With Overlay ............................................................ 75.00
**Dish,** Swan, Blue Neck & Head, Clear, 10 In. ....................................................... 22.50
**Figurine,** Baby Bear ............................................................................ 35.00 To 47.50
**Figurine,** Baby Chick ............................................................................................ 45.00
**Figurine,** Bird, Small ............................................................................................ 65.00
**Figurine,** Dog, Frosted, Seated, Rhinestone Eyes, 3 In. ...................................... 15.00
**Figurine,** Elephant ............................................................................. 35.00 To 50.00
**Figurine,** Gazelle ............................................................................... 30.00 To 85.00
**Figurine,** Hen, Glass ............................................................................................ 32.00
**Figurine,** Mama Bear ......................................................................................... 145.00
**Figurine,** Panther, Seated .................................................................................... 60.00
**Figurine,** Seal With Ball, Large ........................................................... 42.75 To 60.00
**Figurine,** Squirrel .............................................................................. 30.00 To 45.00
**Figurine,** Squirrel, On Base ............................................................... 32.50 To 50.00
**Figurine,** Swan, Cobalt Neck ............................................................. 19.75 To 35.00
**Figurine,** Swan, Emerald, 7 1/2 In. ................................................................... 20.00
**Figurine,** Swan, Ruby ......................................................................................... 20.00
**Figurine,** Wolfhound ........................................................................... 65.00 To 87.75
**Plate,** Center Handle, Jade, 10 In. .................................................................... 17.00
**Shell,** Nautilus, Snail ........................................................................................... 21.50
**Sugar & Creamer,** Jade ..................................................................................... 15.00
**Tumbler,** Lorraine ............................................................................................... 14.00
**Wine Set,** Decanter & 5 Glasses, Red ............................................................... 80.00
**Wine,** Footed, Blue ................................................................................................ 7.50

*Newcomb Pottery was founded by Ellsworth and William Woodward at Sophie Newcomb College, New Orleans, Louisiana, in 1896. The work continued through the 1940s. Pieces of this art pottery are marked with the letter N inside the letter C.*

**NEWCOMB, Bowl,** Blue Flowers, Cream Ground, High Glass, 2 3/4 X 5 In. ............ 725.00
**Bowl,** Pink Flowers, Matte, 1 3/4 X 3 3/4 In. ....................................................... 375.00
**Bowl,** Pink Morning Glories, 2 1/2 X 8 In. ............................................................ 400.00
**Candlestick,** Blue Matte, Pink Floral Border, 7 1/2 In. ........................................ 375.00
**Case,** Purple, Shiny Glaze, 4 X 4 3/4 In. ............................................................. 275.00
**Plaque,** Wall, Incised Crowns, Blue, Green, Yellow, Round, 7 1/4 In. ................... 575.00
**Rose Bowl,** Allover Flowers, Applied Roses, Incised Mark ...................................... 225.00
**Rose Bowl,** Flowers, Applied Roses & Leaves, Incised Mark .................................. 100.00
**Trivet,** Flowers, S.Irvine, 3 In.Diam. ................................................................... 195.00
**Vase,** Grapevine Rim, Blue Ground, Initialed & Numbered, 6 3/4 In. ................... 400.00
**Vase,** Moss Draped Trees, Coral Sky, Marked, 6 1/2 In. ...................................... 700.00
**Vase,** Oleander Design, Signed, Paper Label, 5 In. .............................................. 425.00
**Vase,** Oviform, Band Of Roses, Semigloss Glaze, Marked, 8 1/4 In. ..................... 380.00
**Vase,** Pink, Cream, Green Foliage, Blue Ground, Signed, 6 In. ............................. 450.00
**Vase,** Purple, Shiny Glaze, 4 X 4 3/4 In. .............................................................. 275.00
**Vase,** Signed Sadie Irvine, 3 3/4 In. ................................................................... 460.00
**Vase,** Signed Sadie Irvine, 6 3/4 X 8 1/4 In.Diam. ............................................ 1300.00
**Vase,** Swirling Jonquil Design, Matte, 5 3/4 In. .................................................. 600.00
**Vase,** Yellow Flowers, Incised Design, Signed S Irvine ......................................... 495.00

*Newhall Porcelain Manufactory was started at Newhall, Shelton, Staffordshire, England, in 1782. Simple decorated wares were made. Between 1810 and 1825, the factory made a glassy bone porcelain marked with the factory name.*

**NEWHALL, Cup & Saucer,** Handleless, Mother & Child, Luster Rims.C.1820 ........... 120.00
**Cup & Saucer,** Mill At Ombersley, Blue Rims, Cottage Scene, C.1830 ................... 40.00
**Cup & Saucer,** Seashell Design, Orange Rims, Green & Orange, C.1820 ............... 46.00
**Teapot,** C.1790, Hand-Painted Sprays, Pineapple Finial ...................................... 250.00
**Teapot,** Polychrome Design ................................................................................. 140.00

*Niloak Pottery (Kaolin spelled backwards) was made at the Hyten Brothers Pottery in Benton, Arkansas, between 1909 and 1946. Although the factory did make cast and molded wares, collectors are most interested in the marbleized art pottery line.*

| | |
|---|---:|
| **NILOAK, Ashtray,** Pink & Blue | 12.00 |
| **Ashtray,** Swirl, 3 3/4 In. | 7.00 |
| **Bowl,** Swirl, 5 In. | 25.00 |
| **Candleholder,** Swirl, 6 In. | 60.00 |
| **Candlestick,** Marbleized Swirl, 8 1/2 In. | 50.00 |
| **Candlestick,** Swirl, 10 In., Pair | 140.00 |
| **Dutch Shoe,** Blue | 9.00 |
| **Dutch Shoe,** Green | 9.00 |
| **Ewer,** Blue, 6 1/4 In. | 30.00 |
| **Ewer,** Handled, Flying Eagle, Dark Gray Matte, 10 In. | 35.00 |
| **Ewer,** Marbleized, Pair | 30.00 |
| **Figurine,** Circus Elephant, Pink | 10.00 |
| **Figurine,** Lady, Matte Pink, 8 In. | 44.00 |
| **Figurine,** Southern Belle Lady, 11 In. | 95.00 |
| **Figurine,** Squirrel | 15.00 |
| **Figurine,** Swan, Blue, 6 In., Pair | 16.00 |
| **Figurine,** Turtle | 15.00 |
| **Humidor,** Swirled | 65.00 |
| **Pitcher,** Pink, 7 In. | 8.50 |
| **Planter,** Beige Parrot Perched On Edge | 10.00 |
| **Planter,** Bird, Glossy Yellow, Marked, 5 In.Long | 2.95 |
| **Planter,** Cradle, Burgundy, Signed | 12.00 |
| **Planter,** Elephant, Mauve To Blue, Matte Finish, Impressed Mark | 23.00 |
| **Planter,** Figural, Camel | 40.00 |
| **Planter,** Seal | 15.00 |
| **Planter,** White, Bear | 12.00 |
| **Rose Bowl,** Multicolored Swirl, Incised Mark, Paper Label, 3 X 4 In. | 45.00 |
| **Vase,** Blue, Brown Swirl | 25.00 |
| **Vase,** Blue, 7 1/2 In. | 8.00 |
| **Vase,** Brown & Cream, Blue Swirled, Signed, 3 1/2 X 4 In. | 35.00 |
| **Vase,** Brown, Aqua & Cream, Marbleized Swirl, 3 1/2 In., Pair | 30.00 |
| **Vase,** Bulbous, Marbleized Swirl, 3 1/4 In. | 35.00 |
| **Vase,** Cornucopia, Glossy Pink, 7 In. | 17.00 |
| **Vase,** Green, Yellow, 6 1/2 In. | 25.00 |
| **Vase,** Lavender Fading To Aqua, Matte Finish, Paper Label, 6 X 3 In. | 12.00 |
| **Vase,** Pink Matte, Signed, 7 X 6 In. | 10.00 |
| **Vase,** Swirl, Brown & Blues, 5 1/2 In. | 45.00 |
| **Vase,** Swirl, Brown, 5 In. | 30.00 |
| **Vase,** Swirl, 3 1/2 In. | 25.00 |
| **Vase,** Swirl, 4 In. | 30.00 |
| **Vase,** Swirl, 4 1/2 In. | 33.00 To 40.00 |
| **Vase,** Swirl, 6 In. | 40.00 |
| **Vase,** Swirl, 6 1/2 In. | 34.00 |
| **Vase,** Swirl, 8 1/2 In. | 75.00 |
| **Vase,** Wing Handle, 6 In. | 5.00 |
| **Wall Pocket,** Swirl, 6 In. | 55.00 |

*Nippon-marked porcelain was made in Japan from 1891 to 1921. "Nippon" is the Japanese word for "Japan."*

| | |
|---|---:|
| **NIPPON, Ashtray & Match Holder,** Blossoms, Gold & Green Trim, Blue Leaf Mark | 55.00 |
| **Ashtray,** Blown-Out Cartoon Characters, Set Of 4 | 450.00 |
| **Ashtray,** Blown-Out Horse Heads, Green M In Wreath, 5 1/2 In. | 260.00 |
| **Ashtray,** Hunting Dog, Relief, Black & White, 5 1/4 X 4 1/4 In. | 95.00 |
| **Ashtray,** Jiggs, Comic Face, Eyes, Mouth, Cigar, Green Tie, Bisque | 155.00 |

Ashtray, Scenic, Green Wreath Mark, 4 X 3 In. ........ 35.00
Ashtray, Skull ........ 130.00
Ashtray, Windmill Scene, Matte, Pastels, 3 In.Deep ........ 85.00
Basket, Acorns, Brown, Bisque, Blown-Out, Handles ........ 210.00
Basket, Gold Handled, Scenic, Rising Sun Mark, 6 1/2 X 10 In. ........ 55.00
Basket, Pink & Yellow Roses, Gold Rim, 8 X 4 1/2 In. ........ 38.00
Basket, Purple & Yellow Grapes, Green Ground, Beaded, Oak Leaf, 5 In. ........ 150.00
Basket, Rosebuds On Loop Handle, Green Maple Leaf, 5 In. ........ 80.00
Basket, Sailboat Shape, Blue Leaf Mark, 8 In. ........ 145.00
Basket, Sailboat, Enameled Handle, Green M, 7 3/4 X 5 In. ........ 145.00
Basket, Woodland Scene, Enameled Beading On Handle, Green Mark, 8 In. ........ 32.00
Berry Bowl, Cobalt Blue, Roses, Beading, Gold ........ 20.00
Berry Bowl, Pink Flowers, Gold Border, Green M, Footed, 7 1/2 In. ........ 75.00
Berry Dish, Floral & Gold, M In Wreath, 5 In., Set Of 6 ........ 40.00
Berry Set, Floral, White, Gold Handles, Signed, M In Wreath, 5 Piece ........ 60.00
Berry Set, Pierced Handle & Rims, 6 Sauces, Crown Mark ........ 150.00
Biscuit Jar, Blue Floral ........ 78.00
Biscuit Jar, Dragons, Signed ........ 165.00
Biscuit Jar, Footed, Red, Green, & Gold Geometrics ........ 135.00
Biscuit Jar, Gold Feet & Finial, Gold Design, Green Wreath, 8 1/2 In. ........ 75.00
Blotter, Rocking, Flowers, Gold Beading, Jeweled, Magenta Wreath ........ 75.00
Bonbon, Hand-Painted, Green Border, Roses, Crimped Sides, 7 In. ........ 50.00
Bottle, Cologne, Blue Flowers, White Ground ........ 27.00
Bowl, Acorn Shape, M In Wreath, 6 X 8 In. ........ 70.00
Bowl, Acorns & Leaves, 3 Ball Feet, 8 In. ........ 40.00
Bowl, Beaded Handles, Pond Scene, M In Green Wreath, 7 In. ........ 30.00
Bowl, Blown-Out Acorns, Enamel Trim, Bisque Finish, 7 1/4 X 6 In. ........ 70.00
Bowl, Cherries, Shaded, Gold Handles, Matte Finish, 7 1/4 In. ........ 35.00
Bowl, Cobalt, Floral, Gold, 10 In. ........ 65.00
Bowl, Coup, Covered, Handled, Pedestal Feet, Underplate, 9 3/8 In., Pair ........ 330.00
Bowl, Egyptian Scene, 3 Handled, Marked, 5 1/2 X 2 In. ........ 35.00
Bowl, Elk, Green Mark, 8 In. ........ 70.00
Bowl, Enameled Egyptian Figures Inside, Bouquets Outside, 8 In. ........ 245.00
Bowl, Floral Design, Footed, 8 1/2 In. ........ 25.00
Bowl, Footed, Grapes & Leaves, Gold Trim, M In Wreath, 7 In. ........ 85.00
Bowl, Footed, Kidney Shaped, Butterflies, Blue, M In Wreath, 7 In. ........ 65.00
Bowl, Footed, Molded Acorns, 7 1/2 In. ........ 55.00
Bowl, Footed, Molded Squirrel, Enameled Acorns, Green Mark, 8 1/2 In. ........ 375.00
Bowl, Footed, Raised Gold Rim, Bisque Scene Inside, Blue Mark, 10 In. ........ 135.00
Bowl, Gaudy, Roses, Gold & Cobalt Blue Design, Maple Leaf Mark, 10 In. ........ 35.00
Bowl, Gold Eagles In Cobalt Border, Marked, 7 3/4 In. ........ 95.00
Bowl, Gold Handles, Shaggy Pink Flowers, 9 In. ........ 28.00
Bowl, Gold Handles, Stylized Flowers, Green M In Wreath, 10 X 9 In. ........ 75.00
Bowl, Gold Scalloped, Pink & Red Roses, 8 In. ........ 35.00
Bowl, Hand-Painted Flowers Inside, M In Wreath, 6 In. ........ 25.00
Bowl, Hand-Painted Gold Roses, Gold Beading, M In Wreath, 7 1/2 In. ........ 45.00
Bowl, Hand-Painted Nut Design, Green M Mark, 8 1/2 In. ........ 75.00
Bowl, Hand-Painted, Gold Rim & Handles, Shore Scene, 9 X 2 In. ........ 57.00
Bowl, Handled, Rural Scene, Beaded Edge, Green M Wreath, 6 3/4 In. ........ 35.00
Bowl, Handled, Swans, Gold Beading, Green Wreath, 7 1/2 In. ........ 140.00
Bowl, Lake Scene, Beading On Rim, Handles, M In Wreath, 7 1/4 In. ........ 95.00
Bowl, Lavender Beet Design, Gold Trim, Green Wreath, 8 In. ........ 75.00
Bowl, Lovebirds, Colored Flowers, Black Enameled, 8 1/2 In. ........ 125.00
Bowl, Lovebirds, Flowers, 8 In. ........ 43.00
Bowl, Mayonnaise, Pink Flowers, Ladle & Underplate ........ 25.00
Bowl, Mayonnaise, Underplate & Ladle, Azalea ........ 45.00
Bowl, Molded Acorn Shape, M In Wreath, 6 X 8 In. ........ 70.00
Bowl, Nut, Ball Beet, Moriaga Nuts, Maple Leaf Mark, 7 1/2 In.Diam. ........ 35.00
Bowl, Nut, Blown-Out Nuts, 2 Handled, Green Mark, Signed, 9 1/2 In. ........ 75.00
Bowl, Nut, Blown-Out, Crimped Top, 7 In. ........ 45.00
Bowl, Nut, Enameled Walnuts, Green Wreath, Pair ........ 32.50
Bowl, Nut, Footed, Royal Kaga, 6 In. ........ 25.00
Bowl, Nut, Painted Nuts, Signed, 6 In. ........ 32.00

Bowl, Nut, Windmill & Lake Design, Blue Crown, 4 1/2 In. .......................... 8.00
Bowl, Nut, 2-Handled, Matte Finish, Acorns & Leaves, Green Wreath ................. 65.00
Bowl, Nut, 5-Sided, Beaded, Textured Nuts, 9 1/2 In. ............................. 165.00
Bowl, Opalescent Handles, Gold & Green Rim, Pedestal, 7 In. ...................... 35.00
Bowl, Peanut Design, Blown-Out, Footed .......................................... 75.00
Bowl, Pedestal, Handles, Flowers, Gold Beaded Edge, 4 In. ........................ 18.00
Bowl, Pierced Handles, Scenic, Gold Wreath Mark, 6 1/4 In.Diam. .................. 18.00
Bowl, Pink & Red Zinnias, Gold Beading, 8 In. ................................... 89.00
Bowl, Pink Flowers, Gold Handles, 9 1/2 In. ..................................... 25.00
Bowl, Pink Orchids, Open Handled, 8 X 8 In. ..................................... 45.00
Bowl, Pink Roses, Dripping Gold, Deep Scallops, 12 In. .......................... 165.00
Bowl, Poppies, 7 In. ............................................................ 40.00
Bowl, Portrait, Victorian Lady, Hat, Yellow & Black, Signed, 6 In. .............. 150.00
Bowl, Punch, Hand-Painted Roses, Gold Trim, 10 In.Diam. ......................... 350.00
Bowl, Red & Pink Roses, Gold Overlay, Octagon, 10 1/2 In. ....................... 85.00
Bowl, Relish, White Ground, Gold Wreaths, Black Mark, 11 1/2 In. ................ 38.00
Bowl, Roses, Jeweled, Gold Design, Footed, Blue Mark, 6 In. ..................... 45.00
Bowl, Strawberry, Pierced, Underplate, Roses, Gold Trim, 7 1/4 In.Diam. ......... 145.00
Bowl, Sunset Scene, Handled, Green Mark, 6 In. .................................. 12.00
Bowl, Violets, 7 In. ............................................................ 21.00
Bowl, White, Black & Gold, Scenic, Handled, 7 1/2 In. ........................... 30.00
Bowl, Wild Roses, 10 In. ........................................................ 35.00
Bowl, Windmill Scene, 3 Jeweled Handles, Gold Trim, 6 1/2 X 9 In. ............... 125.00
Bowl, 3-Handled, Lavender Beets & Leafage, Blue Maple Lead, 7 In. ............... 45.00
Bowl, 6 Panels, Divided With Gold, Beaded, Jeweled, Marked ...................... 55.00
Box, Bulldog Design, Green M, Cover, 5 1/2 X 3 In. .............................. 175.00
Box, Cut Corners, Beaded Trim, Swans, M In Wreath, Cover, 3 1/2 In. ............. 125.00
Box, Gold, Footed, Pastoral Scene, Cover, Green Mark, 6 X 3 In. ................. 69.00
Box, House On Lid, Mountain Scene, Beading, Maple Leaf, 5 1/2 X 3 In. ........... 225.00
Box, Jewel, Violets, Gold Beading, 3 1/2 X 1 3/4 In. ............................ 15.00
Box, Landscape On Lid, Round, Cover ............................................. 45.00
Box, Pink & Green Flowers, Gold Trim, Marked, Footed, 4 X 2 3/4 In. ............. 90.00
Box, Pink, Gold, & Turquoise Jewels, Cover, 5 In. ............................... 50.00
Box, Powder, Covered, White Moriage Slip, 4 5/8 In.Diam. ........................ 75.00
Box, Powder, Pink & Gold Intertwined, Footed, MW Mark, 4 In. .................... 110.00
Box, Ring, Gold Beading, Green Mark ............................................. 28.00
Box, Scenic, Pastel Color, Footed, Covered, Round, 6 X 4 In. .................... 95.00
Box, Stamp, Divided, Blue & Pink Flowers, White Ground, Gold Border ............. 65.00
Bread Tray, Hand-Painted Roses, Butterfly, Hoo Birds Mark, 11 1/2 In. ........... 45.00
Butter Tub, Violets, Purple, White, Liner ...................................... 15.00
Butter, Beaded Gold Trim, Green Jewels, Pink Florals, Green M ................... 50.00
Butter, Blossom Pattern, Gold Beading, Covered, Royal Crown Mark ................ 42.50
Butter, Child's, Florals & Gold, EE Mark, Covered .............................. 22.00
Cake Plate, Gold Beaded Rim, Roses, Hand-Painted, 12 In. ........................ 75.00
Cake Plate, Gold Scrolling Over Red Border, Medallions, 11 In. .................. 110.00
Cake Plate, Hand-Painted Roses, Gold Bead Rim, 12 In. ........................... 75.00
Cake Plate, Open Ends, Scenic & Floral, Beaded, Gold Trim, 11 In. ............... 45.00
Cake Plate, Orange & White Flowers, Gold Beading ............................... 40.00
Cake Plate, Red Border, Bold Overlay, Center Medallion, 11 In.Diam. ............. 110.00
Cake Plate, Tree In The Meadow, Green Mark, 10 In. .............................. 40.00
Cake Set, Art Deco, Yellow & Blue Stripes, 7 Piece ............................. 22.00
Cake Set, Autumn Leaves On White, 5 Piece ...................................... 25.00
Cake Set, Camel & Rider ......................................................... 98.00
Cake Set, Camel & Sailboat Scene, 4 Plate, TN Mark ............................. 115.00
Cake Set, Floral, Gold Ground, 7 Piece .......................................... 125.00
Cake Set, Pierced Handles, Scenic Center, Gold Rims, Jewels, 7 Piece ........... 150.00
Cake Set, Violets, Crown Mark, 7 Piece .......................................... 50.00
Candleholder, Orange Blossoms, Outlined In Gold, M In Wreath, Pair .............. 175.00
Candlestick, Birds & Apple Blossom, 5 1/2 In. .................................. 30.00
Candlestick, Black, Pink Flowers, Green Vine, 6 In. ............................. 48.00
Candlestick, Dogwood, Gold, Maple Leaf Mark, 8 1/2 In. .......................... 45.00
Candlestick, Floral With Moriage Trim, 6 In. ................................... 29.00
Candlestick, Floral, Hexagonal, Pair ........................................... 65.00

| | |
|---|---|
| **Candlestick,** Pansies, Yellow Stripe Ground, Green Mark, 8 In., Pair | 115.00 |
| **Candlestick,** Peonies, Sprays, Hexagon, Green Wreath, 8 In., Pair | 225.00 |
| **Candlestick,** White, Black & Gold, Scenic, 6 1/4 In. | 40.00 |
| **Candlestick,** Yellow Ground, Ornate Design, Signed, Pair | 162.00 |
| **Canoe,** Snow Scene With Flying Geese, 7 1/2 In. | 53.00 |
| **Celery,** Bluebirds | 38.00 |
| **Celery,** Gold & Bead Work, Maple Leaf Mark, 12 In. | 35.00 |
| **Celery,** Red Robin | 45.00 |
| **Cereal Set,** Bowl, Underplate, Creamer, Black & Gold, Green M | 37.00 |
| **Chamberstick,** Gold Bead Design, Green M In Wreath | 65.00 |
| **Charger,** Chrysanthemums, Jeweled, Gold Tracery, Pagoda Mark, 12 In. | 125.00 |
| **Cheese Dish,** Slant Top, Pink Flowers, Gold Trim | 55.00 |
| **Chocolate Pot,** Geishas, Blue, 9 In. | 35.00 |
| **Chocolate Pot,** Pink Roses, Gold Trim, Maple Leaf Mark | 70.00 |
| **Chocolate Pot,** Pleated Base, Gold & Beading, Blue Mark, 10 1/2 In. | 185.00 |
| **Chocolate Pot,** Raised Gold, Lavender, & Pink Flowers, Turquoise | 65.00 |
| **Chocolate Pot,** Scenic With Swans, Trees, & House, 5 Cups & Saucers | 185.00 |
| **Chocolate Pot,** Stylized Design, Gold | 85.00 |
| **Chocolate Pot,** Swimming Swans, 4 Cup & Saucers | 85.00 |
| **Chocolate Pot,** Windmill Scene, Scroll Handle, Grrem Mark, 9 1/2 In. | 95.00 |
| **Chocolate Set,** Cobalt Floral, Gold, Pot, 5 Cups & Saucer | 395.00 To 475.00 |
| **Chocolate Set,** Floral Medallion, Blue Ground, 5 Cups | 500.00 |
| **Chocolate Set,** Floral, Parrot | 145.00 |
| **Chocolate Set,** Floral, Pink, Blue, White, Gold, Crown Mark, 9 Piece | 82.00 |
| **Chocolate Set,** Gold On Handles & Saucers, White Ground, 13 Piece | 75.00 |
| **Chocolate Set,** Green, Orange Poppies, Green Mark, 4 Cups & Saucers | 250.00 |
| **Chocolate Set,** Purple Violets, Gold Trim, 5 Cups & Saucers, Signed | 295.00 |
| **Chocolate Set,** Rose, White, 7 Piece | 95.00 |
| **Chocolate Set,** Square Shape, Black Border, Rose Medallion, Marked | 120.00 |
| **Chocolate Set,** Violets, Gold & Raised Beading, 4 Cups & Saucers | 199.00 |
| **Cider Set,** Grapes, Brown, Tan, Pitcher & 2 Mugs | 65.00 |
| **Coaster,** Boat Scene, Set Of 6 | 40.00 |
| **Cocoa Pot,** Cobalt, Geishas, Gold Trim | 105.00 |
| **Coffeepot,** Cobalt Flowers, Gold Trim | 65.00 |
| **Coffeepot,** Purple Flowers, 6-Sided, 12 In. | 125.00 |
| **Compote,** Bands Of Gold Beading, Green Wreath, 8 3/4 X 6 X 4 In. | 125.00 |
| **Compote,** Fruit, Gold, Green, Lavender, Bunch Of Grapes, 10 In. | 135.00 |
| **Compote,** Gold Outlined Fruit & Leaves, Signed, 6 3/4 In. | 175.00 |
| **Compote,** Rose Floral Center Pedestal, 2-Handled, 7 In. | 185.00 |
| **Condiment Set,** China Holder, Gold Trim, Hand-Painted, Marked, 3 Piece | 68.00 |
| **Cookie Jar,** Floral Design, Blue, White, & Cream, Covered, 7 In. | 95.00 |
| **Cookie Jar,** Footed, Autumn Scene, House, Lake | 115.00 |
| **Cookie Jar,** Knob Handles, Violets, Leaves & Gold | 75.00 |
| **Cookie Jar,** Oriental Scene, Gold Trim | 295.00 |
| **Cookie Jar,** Purple Flowers, Yellow Building | 145.00 |
| **Cracker Jar,** Boat & Desert Scene, Gold Palm Trees, Footed, 6 1/2 In. | 225.00 |
| **Cracker Jar,** Butterfly Design, Wreath Mark | 80.00 |
| **Cracker Jar,** Flowers In Panels, Gold Trim, Rising Sun Mark, 4 X 7 In. | 30.00 |
| **Cracker Jar,** Gold Handles & Medallions, Blue Jewels, Beading | 145.00 |
| **Cracker Jar,** Gold Raised Beading, Double Handles, 6 Legs | 190.00 |
| **Cracker Jar,** Hand-Painted, Gold Trim, Marked | 225.00 |
| **Cracker Jar,** Handled, Bottom Design, Green Wreath, 9 In. | 95.00 |
| **Cracker Jar,** Raised Dragon, Bisque Ground, Ribbed, Footed, Covered | 75.00 |
| **Creamer & Sugar,** Canal Scene, Mustache | 60.00 |
| **Creamer & Sugar,** Pink & Burgundy, Gold Trim, Squatty, Footed | 155.00 |
| **Creamer,** Beading, Gold Trim, Green Ground, 3 In. | 28.00 |
| **Creamer,** Blown-Out Child's Face | 50.00 |
| **Creamer,** Fiji, Behind Islands, Gold Trim | 16.00 |
| **Creamer,** Floral Coralene & Gold, Maple Leaf | 13.00 |
| **Creamer,** Gray Moriage Dragon, Signed | 25.00 |
| **Creamer,** Violets, Enamel Dots, Gold Beading, Green Wreath Mark | 47.50 |
| **Creamer,** 4-Colored Band, Gold Rim, Beading, Blue Leaf Mark | 15.00 |
| **Cup & Saucer,** Boat On Lake | 10.00 |

Louis XV-style gilt mirror, 30½ in. high

Blue overlay cut glass jar with lid, 16½ in. high

Blown glass bowl with applied decoration, 6 in. diameter, c. 1880

Scent bottles in glass carriage or railway car, 13 in. long x 8 in. high, 19th century

Renaissance-style clock, wood and metal, 31 in. high, 19th century

Elephant chinoiserie clock, ormolu and bronze, 16¾ in. high

Ebonized William and Mary bracket clock by Edmund Card, 14 in. high, c. 1680

Bagpipe player, Meissen monkey band

Figurine, Samson Golden Anchor mark, 25 in. high, France, c. 1890

Candelabra, Samson, France, Meissen mark, c. 1890

Vanderbilt bathroom china, Copeland, England, c. 1890

Goddess of Mercy, porcelain figurine, 15 in. high, 19th century

Leather "Knole"-style armchair, Morant and Company, London, 1895

Baroque gilt and painted cassone and mirror, Italian, 85 in. high

Oak Louis XV-style cabinet bookcase

Renaissance-style ornate cabinet, walnut

Bronze figure of Roger and Angelique on the Hippogriff by Antoine
Louis Bayre, 25 in. high, c. 1850

Bronze figure, metalworker by
C. Meunier, 19¼ in. high, c. 1890

Bronze figure, bear fighting dogs,
A. L. Bayre, 11½ in. high, c. 1850

Rocker, made by L. J. Colony,
Keene, N.H., c. 1890

Sheraton-style painted satinwood bed

Ebony cabinet, Antwerp, 17th century

Renaissance-style walnut table, 70 in. long

Louis XV ormolu and marquetry desk, French, c. 1740

George II marbletop commode, English, c. 1740

| | |
|---|---|
| Cup & Saucer, House, Trees, & Water, Green Mark | 95.00 |
| Cup & Saucer, Pink Roses, Hand-Painted | 17.00 |
| Cup & Saucer, Purple, Black & Gold, Mauve & Pink Roses Inside | 65.00 |
| Cup & Saucer, Rising Sun, Boat On Lake | 9.50 |
| Cup, Nut, 3-Footed, 8-Sided, Chestnut Design, Green Wreath, Set Of 6 | 58.00 |
| Demitasse Set, Swans On Lake, Green Wreath Mark, 12 Piece | 195.00 |
| Dish & Underplate, Red, Gold, Blue, Covered, 2 Handled, 6 1/2 In. | 90.00 |
| Dish, Cheese & Cracker, Flowers, Rising Sun Mark | 18.00 |
| Dish, Cheese, Pink & Yellow Flowers, 9 In. | 46.00 |
| Dish, Cheese, Red Rose Design Center, Green Wreath, 9 In. | 45.00 |
| Dish, Cheese, Roses, Gold Trim, Slant Top, Signed, 7 1/2 In. | 60.00 |
| Dish, Child's, Design Of Mother, Boy, & Dog | 75.00 |
| Dish, Child's, Girl, Boy, Dog Design | 68.00 |
| Dish, Collar Button, Shape Of Collar, Rising Sun Mark | 25.00 |
| Dish, Mayonnaise, Attached Plate, Blue Bird & Gold Center, Rising Sun | 40.00 |
| Dish, Mayonnaise, Green Wreath Mark, 2 Piece | 35.00 |
| Dish, Mayonnaise, Pink Roses, Gold Beading | 25.00 |
| Dish, Mayonnaise, Underplate, Floral Trim | 25.00 |
| Dish, Pancake, Cover, Cobalt Trim & Butterflies, Flowers | 45.00 |
| Dish, Pancake, Cover, Gold Band, Scrolls, Gray Flowers, R.C.Mark | 85.00 |
| Dish, Pancake, Gold, Flower Design | 75.00 |
| Dish, Pancake, Pierced Dome, Cobalt & Gold Bands | 69.50 |
| Dish, Relish, Pinched Sides, Gold & Black Tree, M In Wreath, 9 In. | 45.00 |
| Dish, Relish, Scenic, Open Handles, Mauve Ground, Blue Leaf Mark | 20.00 |
| Dish, Rose Design, Wedgwood Border, 4 X 9 1/4 In. | 125.00 |
| Dish, Sauce, Floral Design, Gold Trim | 55.00 |
| Dresser Set, Hand-Painted, Gold | 65.00 |
| Dutch Shoe, Scenic Boat & Enamel Design | 65.00 |
| Dutch Shoe, Violets, Gold, Green Mark | 20.00 |
| Ewer, Allover Moriage Design, Green Ground, Blue Maple Leaf Mark | 275.00 |
| Ewer, Cranes, 8 In. | 60.00 |
| Ewer, Green Ground, 2 Gold Jeweled Butterflies, 11 In. | 200.00 |
| Ewer, Pinched Top, Gold & Purple Grapes, Blue Maple Leaf, 5 1/2 In. | 95.00 |
| Fernery, Blue, White Moriage Design, Signed Green Mark, 5 In. | 175.00 |
| Fernery, Deer In Forest, Enameled Design | 115.00 |
| Fernery, Egyptian Head, 8 In. | 125.00 |
| Fernery, Gold Flowers On Yellow | 40.00 |
| Fernery, Pink Flowers, Jeweled | 65.00 |
| Fish Set, Underwater Scene, 4 Plates, Sauce Boat, Platter, 22 1/2 In. | 450.00 |
| Flask, Talcum Powder, Pink Roses, Green Ivy, White Ground | 80.00 |
| Hair Receiver, Band On Cover, Enamel Flowers, Green Wreath Mark | 35.00 |
| Hair Receiver, Bluebirds, Footed | 40.00 |
| Hair Receiver, Border Of Roses, Rising Sun Mark | 22.00 |
| Hair Receiver, Gold & Pink Flowers, Footed | 57.00 |
| Hair Receiver, Gold Bamboo Design, Hand-Painted, TS Mark | 50.00 |
| Hair Receiver, Medallions, Roses, Jewels, Gold, 5 1/2 In.Diam. | 98.00 |
| Hair Receiver, Oriental Figures, Royal Kaga | 25.00 |
| Hair Receiver, Pedestaled, Pastel Floral | 35.00 |
| Hair Receiver, Pink Roses, Gold Beading | 40.00 |
| Hair Receiver, Ruby & Gold Bead Trim, Cobalt, Scenic Center | 85.00 |
| Hatpin Holder, Beaded Pink Roses, 4 1/2 In. | 32.00 |
| Hatpin Holder, Floral, 4 1/2 In. | 22.00 |
| Hatpin Holder, Violets, 4 3/4 In. | 23.00 |
| Hatpin Holder, Woodland Design, Blue Maple Leaf, 4 3/4 In. | 125.00 |
| Holder, Condensed Milk, Raised Gold, White Ground | 40.00 |
| Holder, Milk, Condensed, Plate & Cover | 65.00 |
| Holder, Stickpin, Twist Shape, Coral & Black, Gold Trim | 95.33 |
| Hostess Set, Scenic, Black Design, Swan On Lake, 5 Compartments | 96.00 |
| Humidor, All-Around Scenic Design, 5 1/2 In. | 145.00 |
| Humidor, Art Nouveau Forest Scene, Beading, Green Wreath Mark, 7 In. | 245.00 |
| Humidor, Art Nouveau Pattern, Blue Maple Leaf | 225.00 |
| Humidor, Farmhouse, Yellow & Earth Tones, Bisque, 5 1/4 In. | 110.00 |
| Humidor, Floral Diapers, Beaded, Gold Trim, Signed, 6 In. | 180.00 |

**Humidor,** Flying Cranes, Jewels, 3 Gold Feet, Green Wreath, 8 In. ............................ 145.00
**Humidor,** Forest Scene, Colored Beading, Green Wreath Mark ........................... 245.00
**Humidor,** Gold Chrysanthemum, Beading, Blue Maple Leaf, 6 1/2 In. ..................... 135.00
**Humidor,** Green, Floral Medallions, Blue Maple Leaf Mark, 6 1/2 In. ...................... 285.00
**Humidor,** Hand-Painted Tropical Scene, IOH Mark, 5 1/4 X 4 1/4 In. ...................... 75.00
**Humidor,** Indian On Horseback, Blown-Out ............................................. 550.00
**Humidor,** Island Scene, Palm Trees, Boats, Signed, 5 3/4 In. ............................. 130.00
**Humidor,** Painted Horse's Head On Front, Beaded, Bisque Finish ......................... 225.00
**Humidor,** Pastoral Scene, Yellow, Green Mark, 6 X 6 In. ................................. 225.00
**Humidor,** Raised Palm Trees, Signed .................................................... 175.00
**Humidor,** Scenic Medallions ............................................................ 195.00
**Humidor,** Windmill Scene, Enamel Design On Lid, Green Wreath ......................... 85.00
**Humidor,** Woodland Scene, Cameo-Type Painting, Green M Mark, 5 1/2 In. ............... 185.00
**Humidor,** 6-Sided, Flowers, Gold Trim ................................................... 90.00
**Inkwell,** Brown Cartouches, Enameled, Gray Ground, Green M In Wreath ................. 165.00
**Inkwell,** Camel & Rider ................................................................. 95.00
**Inkwell,** Covered, Jewels, Matte Finish, Green Wreath ................................... 175.00
**Jar,** Covered, Roses On Matte Finish, 12 In. ............................................ 80.00
**Jar,** Cricket, Scenic ................................................................... 95.00
**Jar,** Dresser, Hand-Painted, Green Wreath, Signed, 5 In. ..................... 17.00 To 20.00
**Jar,** Jam, Gold Grapes, White Ground, 3 Piece ......................................... 40.00
**Jar,** Jam, Lid, Plate, Pink Flowers, Gold Trim, Green Mark ............................. 80.00
**Jar,** Jam, Underplate, Flowers, Gold Beading, Green Ground ............................ 55.00
**Jar,** Mustard, Roses, Gold, Green Wreath, Attached Underplate .......................... 20.00
**Jar,** Powder, Covered, Pink Roses, Footed .............................................. 46.00
**Jar,** Raised Moriage Design, Hunting Scene, Blue Maple Leaf, 9 In. ..................... 300.00
**Jar,** Rose Petal, Pastel Ground, Floral, Holes In Lid, 5 In. ............................ 65.00
**Jug,** Wine, Fox Hunt Scene ............................................................. 450.00
**Jug,** Wine, Scenic Medallion, Overall Beading, Signed ................................. 285.00
**Jug,** Wine, Turquoise Jeweling, Scenic Medallion, Blue Maple Leaf .................... 365.00
**Jug,** Wine, Wisteria, Raised Gold Leaves, Green Bisque Ground, 11 In. ................ 325.00
**Lamp,** Lake Scene, Jeweling, Teakwood Base, Green Wreath Mark, 23 In. ............... 295.00
**Lemonade Set,** Pink & Green Floral, Pitcher & 5 Mugs ................................. 110.00
**Lemonade Set,** Roses, Pink, Green, Gold Outline & Beaded Rims, 6 Piece .............. 155.00
**Lemonade Set,** 5 Mugs, Red Flowers & Buds Cover Sides, E-Oh Mark ................... 225.00
**Mantel Set,** Bolted Bases, Jeweled, Gold Beading, Marked, Urn, 11 In. ................ 300.00
**Match Holder & Striker,** Dome Shaped, 2 Piece ........................................ 155.00
**Match Holder,** Geometric Design ....................................................... 40.00
**Match Holder,** Hanging, Horse Head ................................................... 75.00
**Match Holder,** Open Side Striker, Fatima Cigarettes Advertisement .................... 60.00
**Matchbox Holder,** Small Pink Roses, White ............................................. 18.00
**Muffineer,** Greek Key, Cobalt & Gold Band, Hexagonal, Green M Wreath ............... 65.00
**Muffineer,** Pink Flowers, Gold Trim, Green Wreath, 4 3/4 In. .......................... 75.00
**Mug,** Shaving, Scenic, Windmill, Jeweled Handle ..................................... 100.00
**Mustache Cup & Saucer,** Scenic, Beaded Trim, Rising Sun Mark ...................... 145.00
**Mustache Cup,** Flowers, Allover Gold ................................................. 150.00
**Mustard & Underplate,** Cobalt Bands, Drippy Gold .................................... 25.00
**Mustard Pot,** Cobalt Blue Trim, Gold Design, Roses & Leaves ......................... 18.50
**Mustard Pot,** Desert Scent, Bisque .................................................... 30.00
**Mustard,** Attached Plate, Spoon, Poppy Design, Green Mark ........................... 20.00
**Mustard,** Attached Underplate, Flowers, Gold, Signed ................................. 35.00
**Mustard,** Lid, Underplate & Ladle, Desert Scene, Marked .............................. 75.00
**Mustard,** Underplate, Egyptian Scenery, Cobalt Trim .................................. 20.00
**Mustard,** Windmill, Trees, Signed ..................................................... 12.00
**Nappy,** Handle, Cobalt Blue Trim, Roses, Maple Leaf ................................. 32.00
**Nappy,** Pierced Handle, Black & White Scenic, Green Wreath Mark, 6 In. ............. 20.00
**Nut Set,** Cobalt, Gold Trim, Maple Leaf Mark, 5 Piece ................................ 85.00
**Nut Set,** Floral, Beige, 3 Ball Feet, Set Of 4 ......................................... 35.00
**Nut Set,** Gold, Flowers & Jewels, Green M Mark ...................................... 95.00
**Nut Set,** Jewels, Double Handle, 5 Pedestal Cups ..................................... 89.00
**Nut Set,** Rose, 3-Legged, Maple Leaf Mark, 5 Piece .................................. 55.00
**Nut Set,** 3 Ball Feet, 6-Sided, 4 Dishes, Green Wreath Mark, 7 Piece ................. 90.00
**Nut Set,** 3 Small Bowls, Twigs & Leaves, M In Wreath, 7 1/4 In. ..................... 80.00

| | |
|---|---|
| **Pitcher,** Allover Country Lane Scene, 7 In. | 110.00 |
| **Pitcher,** Dark Green, Hand-Painted Violets, Some Gold | 40.00 |
| **Pitcher,** Hand-Painted, Jeweled, Signed, 4 1/2 X 6 In.Diam. | 75.00 |
| **Pitcher,** Pink & Orange Flowers, Gold Rim & Handle, Maple Leaf, 11 In. | 225.00 |
| **Pitcher,** Syrup, Floral, Gold Trim, Wreath Mark | 40.00 |
| **Pitcher,** Syrup, Pink & Blue Flowers, Green Leaves, Gold Scroll, 5 In. | 50.00 |
| **Planter,** Desert Scene, Moriage Trim, 11 In. | 165.00 |
| **Plaque,** Antlered Moose, Trees & Acorns, Green Mark, 10 In. | 225.00 |
| **Plaque,** Blown-Out Indian On Horseback, M In Green Wreath, 10 1/2 In. | 495.00 |
| **Plaque,** Blown-Out Indian, Headdress, Rifle, On Horseback, 10 1/2 In. | 550.00 |
| **Plaque,** Castle Scene, 10 In. | 150.00 |
| **Plaque,** Cow, Mauve To Tan, Green Wreath, 10 1/4 In. | 90.00 |
| **Plaque,** Desert Scene With Arab | 59.00 |
| **Plaque,** Dutch Children In Field, Animal Border, Blue Wreath, 10 In. | 195.00 |
| **Plaque,** Dutch Woman & Children, Moriage Border | 195.00 |
| **Plaque,** English Hunt Scene, 8 In. | 165.00 |
| **Plaque,** Farmer Hand-Plowing, Horses, 10 In. | 250.00 |
| **Plaque,** Female & Drake Duck On Shore, Pond, Green Mark, 8 In. | 65.00 |
| **Plaque,** Fishing Scene, Greek Key Border, Maple Leaf, 10 In. | 85.00 |
| **Plaque,** Flying Owl, Full Moon, Green M In Wreath, 9 In. | 245.00 |
| **Plaque,** Foaming Stein, Cards, Pipe, Bisque, 11 In. | 250.00 |
| **Plaque,** Four Sheep Grazing In Meadow, Bisque, Green Mark, 10 In. | 135.00 |
| **Plaque,** Fox Hunters On Horseback, Dog, Green M In Wreath, 9 In. | 245.00 |
| **Plaque,** Garden Scene, Trees, Flowers, Home, Green Mark, 11 In. | 139.00 |
| **Plaque,** Geometric Border, 6-Pointed Star, Elks, Marked | 193.00 |
| **Plaque,** Gold Branches & Leaves, Scenic, Pierced, 9 3/4 In. | 120.00 |
| **Plaque,** Gold Leaves, Floral Purple & White, Maple Leaf Mark | 165.00 |
| **Plaque,** House & Lake Scene, Enameled Border, Blue Maple Leaf, 9 In. | 185.00 |
| **Plaque,** Lion & Lioness, Blown Out | 495.00 |
| **Plaque,** Moonlight Scene Of Swans On Water, M In Wreath, 7 1/2 In. | 60.00 |
| **Plaque,** Nile Scene, Egyptian Design Border, Bisque, 8 In. | 68.00 |
| **Plaque,** Palm Trees, Looking At Lake, Mountains, Gold Border, 9 1/2 In. | 125.00 |
| **Plaque,** Sheep Grazing In Meadow, 10 In.Diam. | 135.00 |
| **Plaque,** Star Center, Elks In Woods, Green M In Wreath, 8 1/2 In. | 190.00 |
| **Plaque,** Thatched Cottage Pastoral, Green M, 9 In. | 60.00 |
| **Plaque,** Two Ducks By Pond, Signed, 8 In. | 45.00 |
| **Plaque,** Water Scene, Moriage On Palms & Ferns, Beaded Edge, 10 In. | 115.00 |
| **Plate,** Azalea, Rising Sun Mark, 7 1/2 In.Diam. | 7.00 |
| **Plate,** Bisque, Sailing Ship, Palms, 8 1/2 In. | 45.00 |
| **Plate,** Blown-Out Collie & Bird Dog, Signed, 10 5/8 In. | 495.00 |
| **Plate,** Child's Face, Blown Out, 8 In. | 55.00 |
| **Plate,** Deep Purple Violets, Pierced Handles, Oval, 7 In. | 23.00 |
| **Plate,** Dessert, Roses, Enameled, Pawlonia Mark, 6 In., Set Of 4 | 20.00 |
| **Plate,** Double Handles, Gold On Figures, Royal Kaga, 11 In. | 65.00 |
| **Plate,** Egyptian Boat Scene, Green M Mark, 8 1/2 In. | 47.50 |
| **Plate,** Floral Edge, White, Gold Trim, 7 1/2 In. | 6.00 |
| **Plate,** Flower Design, Blue Maple Leaf, 10 In. | 225.00 |
| **Plate,** Flowers, Rising Sun Mark, 8 1/2 In. | 7.00 |
| **Plate,** Gold Design, 7 3/4 In. | 20.00 |
| **Plate,** Lavender, Green, Gold, 10 In. | 45.00 |
| **Plate,** Leaves, Pink & White Blossoms, Green Wreath Mark, 7 3/4 In. | 18.00 |
| **Plate,** Pink Flowers, Gold Cones, Cherry Blossom Mark, 10 In. | 20.00 |
| **Plate,** Rose Medallions, Gold Trim, Dark Green, Signed, 10 In. | 70.00 |
| **Plate,** Roses, Red, Gold Beading, 8 1/2 In. | 45.00 |
| **Plate,** Ruby Jewels & Gold Trim, Scenic Center, 9 In. | 165.00 |
| **Plate,** Scalloped, Gaudy, 9 1/2 In. | 25.00 |
| **Plate,** Scenic, Animals, Raised Gold, Green Border, Green Mark, 8 In. | 49.00 |
| **Plate,** Tree Design, Pink Rose Band, Marked, 9 In. | 55.00 |
| **Plate,** Windmill, Lake, 8 1/2 In. | 27.00 |
| **Plate,** 2 Sailor Boys, Rifles & Bayonets, Rising Sun Mark, 6 1/2 In. | 75.00 |
| **Plate,** 3 Swans, Lilies, Beaded Edge, M In Wreath Mark, 10 In. | 95.00 |
| **Ramekin & Underplate,** Blue & Pink Roses | 20.00 |
| **Relish,** Roses, Gold Trailings | 15.00 |

Rose Jar, Yellow Ground, Blue Hieroglyphic Animals, Signed ........................ 85.00
Salt & Pepper, Hand-Painted Flowers, Gold Trim ........................ 14.00
Salt & Pepper, Quilted Phlox, Crystal ........................ 55.00
Sauce Boat, Underplate, Blue Band, Gold Edge, Roses, Green M Wreath ........................ 35.00
Sauce, Pink Flowers, Set Of 6 ........................ 25.00
Server, Pancake, Covered, Pink Roses On Rim, Green Leaves ........................ 40.00
Server, Pancake, Gold Grapes, Leaves, Geometric Swags, White ........................ 57.00
Server, Pancake, Pink & Blue Floral, 8 3/4 In. ........................ 65.00
Server, Sauce, Gaudy Colors, Pointed ........................ 95.00
Shaker, Sugar, Florals, Gold, Green Wreath Mark ........................ 45.00
Shoe, Dutch, Scenic, Raised Design, Green Wreath Mark, 3 1/2 In. ........................ 65.00
Smoke Set, Tray, 3 Jars, Horsehead In Triangular Medallion, 4 Piece ........................ 500.00
Spoon, Mayonnaise, Rising Sun, Marked ........................ 8.00
Spooner, Barberry ........................ 20.00
Stein, Horse & Two Dogs, Relief, Handle, Green M In Wreath, 5 1/2 In. ........................ 350.00
Stein, Red Floral, Green Ground, Tankard Shaped, 5 1/2 In. ........................ 185.00
Strainer, Tea, Cobalt & Gold Design, 6 In. ........................ 125.00
Sugar & Creamer, Azalea, Covered, Marked ........................ 38.00
Sugar & Creamer, Bands Of Gold Beading, Green Mark ........................ 65.00
Sugar & Creamer, Flowers, Leaves, Covered, Rising Sun Mark ........................ 19.50
Sugar & Creamer, Footed, Gold Scrolling & Beading, Blue Wreath Mark ........................ 65.00
Sugar & Creamer, Gold With Blue, Square Bases ........................ 95.00
Sugar & Creamer, Gold, Blue, Pink Flowers, Green Mark, Square ........................ 55.00
Sugar & Creamer, Green & Pink Flowers, Ivorene With Gold ........................ 50.00
Sugar & Creamer, Melon Ribbed, Gold Beading, Rose Design ........................ 45.00
Sugar & Creamer, Pink Roses, Green Leaves, Blue Band ........................ 35.00
Sugar & Creamer, Poppies, Gold Trim ........................ 12.00
Sugar & Creamer, Trees, Water, Swan ........................ 125.00
Sugar Shaker, Pink Roses, Gold Scrolling, Beading Allover ........................ 60.00
Sugar Shaker, Red Roses, Gold Trim, Maple Leaf Mark, 4 In. ........................ 37.50
Sugar Shaker, Roses, Gold Trim, Cobalt ........................ 65.00
Sugar, Handled, Woodland Scene, Covered ........................ 75.00
Sugar, Roses, Gold Trim, Covered ........................ 25.00
Syrup & Underplate, Green Floral Band, Gold, 4 In. ........................ 32.50
Syrup, Black & Gold, Lake Scene Silhouette, Covered ........................ 48.00
Syrup, Hand-Painted Flowers, Crown Mark ........................ 10.00
Syrup, Underplate, Woodland Scene, Beading, Imperial Nippon Mark ........................ 95.00
Tankard, Blossoms, Raised Gold Enamel Centers, Green Mark, 11 1/2 In. ........................ 145.00
Tankard, Floral, Gaudy, 12 3/4 In. ........................ 250.00
Tankard, Maroon & Gold, 12 In. ........................ 150.00
Tea & Toast Set, Gold Design, Red Mark, M In Wreath ........................ 35.00
Tea & Toast Set, Royal Sametuke, Signed, 8 In. ........................ 50.00
Tea Set, Brown Beading, Jewels, Arabian Scene, Matte, 3 Piece ........................ 275.00
Tea Set, Child's Face, Blown Out, 3 Cups & Saucers, 9 Piece ........................ 165.00
Tea Set, Geisha Girl, Cobalt Trim, 3 Piece ........................ 95.00
Tea Set, Gold Gilding, 6 Cups & Saucers, Purple Mark, 15 Piece ........................ 145.00
Tea Set, Gold Leaves, Berries, White Ground, Spoke Mark, 15 Piece ........................ 59.00
Tea Set, Gold, Swans, Nagoya Mark ........................ 125.00
Tea Set, Green Ground, Gold Flowers, 3 Swans, 3 Piece ........................ 175.00
Tea Set, Hand-Painted White Birds, Gold Trim, Green Mark, 13 Piece ........................ 125.00
Tea Set, Moriage Medallion, Rust & White, Green Ground, 3 Piece ........................ 95.00
Tea Set, Rose & Gold, 3 Piece ........................ 90.00
Tea Set, Roses On Black, Gold Trim, 4 Cups & Saucers, Signed, 11 Piece ........................ 145.00
Tea Set, Yellow, Brown Beading, Jewels, Arabian Scene ........................ 275.00
Tea Strainer, Underplate, M In Wreath ........................ 55.00
Teacup, Strainer, & Underplate, Gold & Flowers ........................ 47.00
Teapot, Red, Beaded Gold, Floral ........................ 125.00
Teapot, Sugar & Creamer, Panels Of Flowers ........................ 65.00
Teapot, Wicker Handle, Oriental Rider On Blanket ........................ 25.00
Teapot, 5 Cups & Saucers, Gold Outlined Flowers, Imperial Mark ........................ 140.00
Tile, Enameled Horse Heads, Medallion, Green Wreath Mark, 6 In.Diam. ........................ 60.00
Tile, Scenic, 5 In.Square ........................ 25.00
Toast Rack, Scattered Flowers, Gold Ring Handle, White, Rising Sun ........................ 135.00

**Tobacco Jar,** 3 Blown-Out Horses' Heads, Horseshoe On Back .......... 500.00
**Toothpick,** Cobalt Band, Gold Beading, Gold Feet, M In Wreath .......... 55.00
**Toothpick,** Floral Border, Gold Trim, Rising Sun Mark .......... 20.00
**Toothpick,** Gold & Stylized Flower Design, 3-Handled .......... 45.00
**Toothpick,** Gold Over White Ground .......... 18.00
**Toothpick,** Rosebuds, Blue, Gold, Green Mark .......... 20.00
**Toothpick,** Scenic, 3 Handled .......... 55.00
**Toothpick,** Woman Feeding Geese, 3 Ball Feet, Green M In Wreath .......... 70.00
**Tray,** Celery, Gold Grapes & Flowers, Green M In Wreath .......... 30.00
**Tray,** Celery, Lakeside Landscape In Black & White, Gold Trim .......... 25.00
**Tray,** Dresser, Egyptian Pattern, Green Wreath Mark .......... 45.00
**Tray,** Dresser, Green M In Wreath, Roses .......... 25.00
**Tray,** Dresser, Scenic, House, Birds, 11 1/2 In. .......... 58.00
**Tray,** Handled, English Hunting Scene, 10 1/2 In. .......... 225.00
**Tray,** Moriage Grape Border, Castles, Grazing Sheep, 10 1/2 In. .......... 195.00
**Tray,** Pin, Blue Leaf Mark, 5 In. .......... 22.50 To 23.00
**Tray,** Sailing Scene, Matte, Gold Design, Cobalt Blue Edge, 12 1/2 In. .......... 150.00
**Trivet,** Green Wreath Mark .......... 35.00
**Trivet,** Windmill Scene .......... 23.00
**Urn,** Cobalt Blue Floral, Moriage Cover, 11 In. .......... 225.00
**Urn,** Cobalt, Gold Beading, Covered, 11 3/4 In. .......... 259.00
**Vase,** Allover Design, Maple Leaf Mark, 10 1/2 In. .......... 150.00
**Vase,** Applied Conquistador On Horseback, Marked, 12 In. .......... 240.00
**Vase,** Basket Shape, Footed, Flowers, Gold Trim, 9 In. .......... 125.00
**Vase,** Beige Ground, Dark Brown Handles, Yellow & Pink Roses, 9 In. .......... 95.00
**Vase,** Bird On Flowering Limb, Tan Ground, 8 In. .......... 85.00
**Vase,** Bisque, Scene Front & Back, Beading On Blue, 11 3/4 In. .......... 150.00
**Vase,** Black Panels, Silver & Green Filigree, Green Mark, 18 In. .......... 295.00
**Vase,** Black, Purple, Gold, Marked, 11 In. .......... 210.00
**Vase,** Blossoms, Pink, Green M In Wreath, 6 1/2 In. .......... 35.00
**Vase,** Blown-Out Leaves, Grapes, Marbleized Bottom, Green M, 10 1/2 In. .......... 285.00
**Vase,** Blue Ocean, Red Sunset, White Moriage Birds, 7 In. .......... 195.00
**Vase,** Bluebird, Gilt Handled, Green Mark, 10 In. .......... 165.00
**Vase,** Brown Ground, Floral, 2-Handled, 6 In. .......... 50.00
**Vase,** Brown Handles & Beading, Beige Ground, Marked, 9 In. .......... 95.00
**Vase,** Bud, Jeweled Floral Design, 5 1/2 In., Pair .......... 125.00
**Vase,** Bulbous, Ear-Shaped Handles, Flowers, Gold Trim, 12 X 9 In.Diam. .......... 225.00
**Vase,** Calla Lily Design, Open Handle, Royal Nishiki Mark, 13 In. .......... 100.00
**Vase,** Camels, Green, 5 In. .......... 16.00
**Vase,** Cameo Of Sailboat, Green M In Wreath, 4 1/2 In. .......... 25.00
**Vase,** Castle On Cliff, Two Gold Shell Handles, 9 In. .......... 95.00
**Vase,** Cobalt Trim, Pink Flowers, Bulbous Top, Small Base, 12 In. .......... 100.00
**Vase,** Coralene Handled, Lavender Flowers, Patent 1908 Mark, 4 1/2 In. .......... 195.00
**Vase,** Coralene, 10 In. .......... 250.00
**Vase,** Deer & Trees, Geometric Design, Blue Wreath Mark, 2 3/4 In. .......... 30.00
**Vase,** Dutch Scene, Handles, 6 In. .......... 55.00
**Vase,** Egyptian Scene, Gold Tracery, Hand-Painted, 11 1/2 In. .......... 200.00
**Vase,** Egyptian Scene, Gold, 2-Handled, Green M In Wreath, 8 In. .......... 175.00
**Vase,** Embossed Butterflies, Gold Handles, Green Mark, 12 X 9 In. .......... 165.00
**Vase,** Falcon Chained, Black Over Gold, 12 1/4 In. .......... 95.00
**Vase,** Fishing Scene, Double Handled, 14 In. .......... 295.00
**Vase,** Five Medallions, Seascape, Gold Handles, Green Mark, 9 1/2 In. .......... 125.00
**Vase,** Floral Design, Blue, Square With Ring Handles, 8 In. .......... 475.00
**Vase,** Floral Design, Gold Top, Green M Mark, 10 1/2 In. .......... 110.00
**Vase,** Floral Design, Gold Trim, 2 Ear-Shaped Handles, 12 In. .......... 225.00
**Vase,** Floral, Gold, Green Wreath Mark, 7 1/2 In. .......... 40.00
**Vase,** Flowered, Gold Trim, M Wreath Mark, 14 1/2 In. .......... 250.00
**Vase,** Flowers, Browns, Yellows, & Gold, Green Mark, 9 In. .......... 125.00
**Vase,** Flowers, Cobalt Blue & Gold, Maple Leaf, 9 In. .......... 110.00
**Vase,** Flowers, Leaves, Geometric Design, 6-Footed, Green Mark, 9 In. .......... 125.00
**Vase,** Geometric Design, Green, Gold Base & Handles, 10 In., Pair .......... 135.00
**Vase,** Geometric Pattern, 7 1/2 In. .......... 85.00
**Vase,** Gold & Jeweled Trim, Scenic, 12 In. .......... 225.00

| | |
|---|---|
| **Vase,** Gold Design, Scenic, Floral Base, 2-Handled, 11 1/2 In. | 135.00 |
| **Vase,** Gold Roses, Stems, & Leaves, Black & Green, 2-Handled, 5 In. | 50.00 |
| **Vase,** Gold, Roses, Beading, Cobalt, 15 In. | 195.00 |
| **Vase,** Island Scene, Gold Handled, Gold Outline, 6 1/2 In. | 45.00 |
| **Vase,** Jewels & Beading, Gold Handles, Green Mark, 13 3/4 In. | 275.00 |
| **Vase,** Leaves, Roses, 12 1/2 In. | 245.00 |
| **Vase,** Man On Camel, 9 1/2 In. | 225.00 |
| **Vase,** Middle East Scene, Bisque, Pyramids, Camels, 9 In. | 125.00 |
| **Vase,** Moriage Bird, Blue Maple Leaf Mark, 9 In. | 210.00 |
| **Vase,** Moriage, Dragon Slipwork Design, Maple Leaf, 7 1/2 In. | 160.00 |
| **Vase,** Mountain & Lake Scene, Imperial Mark, 11 1/2 In. | 150.00 |
| **Vase,** Orchids & Leaves, Gold Tracery, Cobalt Blue Trim, 9 1/2 In. | 195.00 |
| **Vase,** Petals Beaded In Gold, Yellow Ground, Marked, 12 In. | 125.00 |
| **Vase,** Pink Roses, Beige Ground, Gold, 9 1/2 In. | 200.00 |
| **Vase,** Pink Roses, 2-Handled, 4 1/2 In. | 16.00 |
| **Vase,** Pink, Green Floral, Lake Ground, Bulbous, 5 In., Pair | 80.00 |
| **Vase,** Pleated Angles, Octagonal, 12 X 6 In.Diam. | 175.00 |
| **Vase,** Portrait Of Madame Potocka, Gold, 13 In. | 295.00 |
| **Vase,** Portrait, Cobalt Blue, Gold, Jewels, 2-Handled, Signed, 9 In. | 375.00 |
| **Vase,** Purple Flowers, White Ground, 10 1/2 In. | 95.00 |
| **Vase,** Raised Dogwood, Jeweled Border, Aqua Ground, 9 In. | 180.00 |
| **Vase,** Ram's Head Ring Handles, Blooming Roses, Enameled, 6 1/2 In. | 135.00 |
| **Vase,** Red Roses, Gold Beading, 5 1/2 In. | 68.00 |
| **Vase,** Red Roses, Green Ground, Gold Trim, Marked, 8 In. | 88.00 |
| **Vase,** River Scene, Gold Tracery, Green Wreath, 5 3/4 In. | 200.00 |
| **Vase,** Rose Bouquet, Gold Trim, 10 X 8 In. | 155.00 |
| **Vase,** Roses & Geometric Panels, Gold Beading, 7 1/2 In. | 30.00 |
| **Vase,** Roses, Hand-Painted, Hexagonal, 6 In. | 40.00 |
| **Vase,** Roses, Maple Leaf Mark, 7 In., Pair | 120.00 |
| **Vase,** Roses, Red, Pink, Blue, Gold Trim, Maple Leaf Mark, 7 In. | 65.00 |
| **Vase,** Roses, Sky, & Trees, Green Mark, 8 In. | 40.00 |
| **Vase,** Sailboat, Blue & Gray, Yellow Green & Blue Border, 10 In. | 45.00 |
| **Vase,** Scenic & Floral, Handled, 6 In. | 38.00 |
| **Vase,** Scenic, Black, Rust, Green, Turquoise, Jewels, 4 3/4 In. | 48.00 |
| **Vase,** Scenic, Gold Beaded, 2-Handled, 14 In. | 85.00 |
| **Vase,** Scenic, Gold Trim & Handled, EE Mark, 8 1/2 In. | 95.00 |
| **Vase,** Scenic, Windmill, Green Wreath Mark, 7 In. | 55.00 |
| **Vase,** Stylized Flowers, Beaded At Top, Gold Trim, Green Wreath, 10 In. | 165.00 |
| **Vase,** Tapestry Bands Top & Bottom, Royal Nishiki Mark, 12 In. | 350.00 |
| **Vase,** Tapestry, Grapes, Corset Shape, 8 In. | 395.00 |
| **Vase,** Tapestry, Plum Design, Signed, 8 In. | 450.00 |
| **Vase,** Victorian Lady, Cylindrical Foot, Marked Dowsie Nippon, 10 In. | 118.00 |
| **Vase,** Wall, Hanging, Cone Shape | 30.00 |
| **Vase,** White Azaleas, Brown, Green M In Wreath, 10 In. | 125.00 |
| **Vase,** White Cranes In Flight, Enameled Trees, Bisque, 10 In. | 185.00 |
| **Vase,** White Ground, Green, Gold Trim, Roses, 9 1/2 In. | 235.00 |
| **Vase,** White Narcissus, Mocha Ground, Gold Collar & Handles, 10 In. | 125.00 |
| **Vase,** Windmill, House, Flowers, Footed, 5 1/2 In. | 25.00 |
| **Vase,** Woodland, Footed, Blue Maple Leaf, 6 1/2 In. | 250.00 |
| **Vase,** Yellow Ground, Orange Poppies, Petals In Gold, 12 In. | 125.00 |
| **Wall Pocket,** Butterfly Design, Blue | 35.00 |

*Nodders or nodding figures, or pagods, are porcelain figures with heads and hands that are attached to wires. Any slight movement causes the parts to move up and down. They were made in many countries during the eighteenth and nineteenth centuries.*

| | |
|---|---|
| **NODDER, Black Boy,** Papier-Mache | 6.50 |
| **Black Child,** Blue Dress, Bank At Side, Chalkware, 13 1/2 In. | 352.00 |
| **Black Girl Wearing Blue Dress,** Chalkware, Bank, 13 1/2 In. | 335.00 |
| **Candlestick,** Boys On Teeter-Totter, Double, Bisque, German, 8 1/4 In. | 175.00 |
| **Chinese Man,** Green Dress, Tongue Comes Out As Head Moves, 1 3/4 In. | 65.00 |
| **Choir Boy,** Papier-Mache, 6 1/2 In. | 17.00 |

Choir Girl, Papier-Mache, 6 1/2 In. ........................................................................ 17.00
Chubby Chauncy, Germany ........................................................................ 100.00
Colonial Man, Woman, Birds On Shoulder, Bisque, 8 1/2 In., Pair ........................ 450.00
Daddy Warbucks, Germany ........................................................................ 100.00
DeLong Jones, Germany ........................................................................ 100.00
Dog, Bisque, German, 5 X 2 1/2 In. ........................................................................ 45.00
Donkey, Head Bobs, Celluloid, 3 1/2 X 4 1/4 In. ................................................ 17.00
Double, Pug & Husky Seated Side By Side, Bisque, 5 In. ................................ 110.00
Double, Pug Seated Beside Husky, Bisque ........................................................ 120.00
German Bisque, Boy, Black Gown, Sitting, Vessel Between Knees, 4 In. ............ 72.50
Girl In Coat & Bonnet, Staffordshire ........................................................ 50.00
Hawaiian Girl, Bisque, 6 In. ........................................................................ 15.00
Huntsman, Holds Hatchet, 2 Movable Parts, Germany, Bisque, 8 1/2 In. ............ 185.00
Irish Boy & Girl, German, Pair ........................................................................ 65.00
Jackie Copper, Germany ........................................................................ 100.00
Lady, Seated At Piano, Hands & Head Move, Bisque, 8 1/2 In. ........................ 300.00
Little Fat Boy, German ........................................................................ 35.00
Monk, Holding Water Jug, Marked Portugal ........................................................ 27.00
Mouse, Felt Head, Clay Body, 4 In. ........................................................................ 13.50
Mr.Wicker, Germany ........................................................................ 100.00
Oriental Boy & Girl, German, Pair ........................................................................ 85.00
Oriental Lady, Side To Side, Hand-Painted, 7 1/2 In. ........................................ 195.00
Oriental Man & Woman Jugglers, Bisque, Large, Pair ........................................ 165.00
Oriental Man In Kimono, Holding Fan Behind Head, Germany, 7 X 7 In. ............ 295.00
Oriental Man, Seated, Fan In Hand, Matte Green, Bisque, 7 X 6 1/2 In. ............ 295.00
Oriental Queen, Fanning Herself, Tree Trunk Vase, Bisque, 8 3/4 In. ................ 145.00
Oriental, Blue Clothes, Comical Face, 3 X 6 1/8 In. ........................................ 95.00
Orphan Annie, Germany ........................................................................ 75.00
Poodle, Plastic, Germany ........................................................................ 22.50
Pug & Large Dog Sitting Side By Side, Heubach, 5 In. ........................................ 145.00
Rabbit, Brown & White, Papier-Mache, Germany, 4 1/2 In. ................................ 20.00
Santa, Papier-Mache, 6 1/2 In. ........................................................................ 20.00
Sitting Man, Head Large As Body, Cigar In Mouth, Clay, 2 1/2 In. ........................ 14.00
The Happy Monk, German, 7 1/4 In. ........................................................................ 195.00
Wheezer, Germany ........................................................................ 100.00
Woman Seated Cross-Legged, Kimono, Bisque, Marked, 5 X 3 3/8 In. ................ 125.00

*Noritake-marked porcelain was made in Japan after 1904 by Nippon Toki Kaisha.*

NORITAKE, Ashtray, Blown-Out Fox, Puffed-Out Floral & Trees, 5 In.Diam. ............ 195.00
Ashtray, Hand-Painted, Trees, Lake, & Sky, Green Mark ........................................ 10.00
Basket, Azalea, 2 1/2 X 4 1/2 In. ........................................................................ 85.00
Basket, Hand-Painted Plums Inside ........................................................................ 24.00
Basket, House Scene, Bisque Finish, M Mark, 6 In. ........................................ 40.00
Berry Set, Green & Gold Border, Flowers, 13 Piece ........................................ 68.00
Bowl, Azalea, Divided ........................................................................ 185.00
Bowl, Azalea, 10 In.Diam. ........................................................................ 30.00
Bowl, Azalea, 2-Handled, 10 In. ........................................................................ 22.00
Bowl, Blown-Out Brazil Nuts, 6 X 6 In. ........................................................................ 72.00
Bowl, Center Handle, Birds & Flowers, Gold Trim, 9 In.Diam. ........................ 40.00
Bowl, Floral, Gold Center & Border, Open Handles, 7 1/2 In. ........................ 20.00
Bowl, Footed, Tree In The Meadow, Ladle, 4 1/2 In.Diam. ................................ 20.00
Bowl, Gold Rim & Handles, Snow Farm Scene, 8 X 10 In. ................................ 65.00
Bowl, Hand-Painted Bridge Scene, 5 In.Square ........................................ 10.00
Bowl, Nut, Florals & Gold, Fluted Shell, Footed ........................................ 55.00
Bowl, Raised Enamel Flowers, Silver Overlay, Pedestaled ................................ 38.00
Bowl, Scenic, Open Handles, Oval, 7 1/2 In. ........................................ 22.00
Bowl, Soup, Azalea ........................................................................ 15.00
Bowl, Sugar, Tree In Meadow, Covered ........................................................ 10.00

**Bowl,** Swan On Lake, 8 In. ..................................................................................... 16.00
**Bowl,** Twig Handles, Blown-Out Chestnuts, Owls On Rim, 6 1/2 In. .......... 60.00
**Bowl,** Vegetable, Azalea, Oval, 10 1/2 In. ........................................................ 32.00
**Bowl,** Vegetable, Azalea, 10 1/2 In. ................................................................. 18.00
**Box,** Lid, Figural, Clown, Signed, 6 In. ............................................................ 35.00
**Box,** Trinket, Gold Finial, Yellow Flowers, Green Ground, 2 3/4 In. ............ 25.00
**Butter Tub,** Drainer, Azalea ............................................................................... 30.00
**Butter,** Desert Scene, Gold Trim ...................................................................... 85.00
**Cake Plate,** Azalea ...................................................................... 20.00 To 30.00
**Cake Plate,** Tree In The Meadow .................................................................... 15.00
**Cake Set,** Gold Flowers, Peacock, Spider, C. 1912, 7 Piece ........................ 55.00
**Cake Set,** Orchid Pattern, Hand-Painted, 7 Piece .......................................... 45.00
**Candlestick,** Masted Sailing Ship, Gold, 7 1/4 In., Pair ................................ 75.00
**Celery,** Azalea, 12 1/2 In. ......................................................... 24.00 To 35.00
**Celery,** Minaret Pattern, 8 1/2 In. ................................................................... 12.00
**Cheese,** Blue Flying Turkey, Round ................................................................ 32.50
**Cheese,** Covered, Azalea ........................................................... 50.00 To 85.00
**Cheese,** Parrot Finial, Luster, Red M In Wreath ............................................ 15.00
**Child's Set,** Azalea, 15 Piece ..................................................................... 1350.00
**Chocolate Pot,** White, Gold Trim .................................................................... 45.00
**Chocolate Set,** Cobalt & Gold, Cream Band, 6 Cups & Saucers .................. 115.00
**Chocolate Set,** Maroon Wreaths, Pink Roses, Green Leaves, 5 Piece ........ 135.00
**Coffeepot,** Azalea ............................................................................................. 450.00
**Compote,** Pink & Yellow Roses On Interior, Gold Border, 8 1/2 In. ............ 75.00
**Creamer,** Child's, Nursery Rhyme .................................................................. 16.00
**Creamer,** Minaret Pattern ................................................................................ 10.00
**Creamer,** Valiere .............................................................................................. 10.00
**Cruet,** Azalea, Original Stopper ...................................................................... 185.00
**Cup & Saucer,** Azalea ............................................................... 8.00 To 12.00
**Cup & Saucer,** Azalea, Demitasse, Set Of 6 ................................................ 425.00
**Cup & Saucer,** Peach Luster, Ship, Demitasse, M In Red Wreath .............. 12.00
**Cup & Saucer,** Rosalie, Gold Trim, Demitasse .............................................. 35.00
**Cup & Saucer,** The Venice, Plates, Set Of 8 Each ........................................ 30.00
**Cup & Saucer,** Tree In Meadow, Red Wreath Mark ...................................... 15.00
**Cup & Saucer,** Valiere ..................................................................................... 10.00
**Dish,** Candy, Handled, Flowers, Green Wreath Mark, 6 3/4 In.Diam. .......... 37.00
**Dish,** Lemon, Handle, Tree In Meadow, 5 1/2 In.Diam. ................................ 24.00
**Dish,** Mayonnaise, Ladle, Azalea Pattern ...................................................... 15.00
**Dish,** Relish, Azalea, Oval, 8 1/4 In. .............................................................. 12.00
**Dish,** Relish, Divided, Edgewood Pattern, 7 X 10 In. ................................... 14.00
**Dish,** Vegetable, Greek Key, Large ................................................................ 12.00
**Gravy Boat,** Attached Underplate, Azalea ..................................................... 25.00
**Gravy Boat,** Valiere, Stand ............................................................................. 15.00
**Grill Plate,** Azalea, Gold Trim ......................................................................... 75.00
**Holder,** Spoon, Oblong .................................................................................... 16.00
**Humidor,** Elk, Wreath & M .............................................................................. 185.00
**Humidor,** Pipe On Cover, M In Wreath, Green .............................................. 55.00
**Mayonnaise Bowl & Spoon,** Pink Flowers, Gold Trim ................................. 25.00
**Mayonnaise Set,** Azalea, 3 Piece ............................................ 22.50 To 25.00
**Mayonnaise Set,** Birds, Flowers, 4 Piece ...................................................... 38.00
**Mayonnaise Set,** Blue, Cream With Flowers, Marked, 3 Piece .................... 45.00
**Mayonnaise Set,** Leaf Shape, Gold Trim, 3 Piece ........................................ 24.00
**Mayonnaise Set,** Luster, 3 Piece ................................................................... 22.00
**Mustard,** Covered, Spoon, Azalea .................................................................. 30.00
**Mustard,** Figural Cherries, Green Mark .......................................................... 15.00
**Mustard,** Underplate & Spoon, House & Trees, Orange ............................... 35.00
**Mustard,** Vermillion With Grape Lid ............................................................... 14.00
**Napkin Ring,** Porcelain, Pink, Black Medallion With Flowers ....................... 20.00
**Nappy,** Blue Border, Bird & Flower Center, M In Wreath ............................. 25.00
**Nappy,** Scenic ................................................................................................. 20.00
**Pitcher,** Milk, Azalea, 6 In. ..................................................... 125.00 To 135.00
**Plate,** Art Deco, White With Blues, Black & Yellow, Red Wreath, 6 In. ...... 12.50
**Plate,** Azalea, 6 1/2 In. ............................................................. 3.00 To 7.50

Plate, Azalea, 7 1/2 In. ............................................................................................ 4.00 To 6.50
Plate, Azalea, 8 1/4 In. ............................................................................................ 12.00
Plate, Azalea, 10 In. ................................................................................................ 11.00
Plate, Edgewood Pattern, 10 1/2 In.Diam. ................................................................ 8.00
Plate, Hand-Painted Floral Sprays & Gold, Green Wreath, 9 In. ............................... 32.00
Plate, Howo Bird, 10 In. ............................................................................................ 25.00
Plate, Laureate Pattern, 7 1/2 In. ............................................................................. 3.25
Plate, Scenic, 6 1/2 In. ............................................................................................. 7.50
Plate, Scenic, 8 1/2 In. ............................................................................................. 14.50
Plate, Tree By Lake, Ring Handle, Green M, 7 In. ..................................................... 25.00
Plate, Tree In Meadow, Gold Scrolls & Roses On Rim, 8 In. ..................................... 15.00
Plate, Valiere, 7 5/8 In. ............................................................................................. 5.00
Plate, Valiere, 8 In. ................................................................................................... 6.00
Plate, Valiere, 10 In. ................................................................................................. 8.00
Platter, Azalea, 10 1/4 In. .......................................................................... 105.00 To 110.00
Platter, Azalea, 12 In. ............................................................................................... 32.00
Platter, Azalea, 14 In. ............................................................................................... 38.00
Platter, Azalea, 16 In. ............................................................................................... 295.00
Platter, Cavalier, 13 1/2 In. ...................................................................................... 12.50
Platter, Edgewood Pattern, M In Wreath, 10 X 13 1/2 In. ......................................... 21.00
Platter, Edgewood Pattern, M In Wreath, 12 X 16 In. ............................................... 65.00
Platter, Minaret Pattern, 16 In. ................................................................................ 20.00
Platter, Westminster Pattern, Red Wreath Mark, 14 X 10 1/2 In. ............................. 10.00
Relish, Hand-Painted Flowers, Gold Rim, 12 1/2 X 6 In. ........................................... 22.50
Relish, Twin Loop, Azalea ......................................................................................... 260.00
Salt & Pepper, Tray, Azalea ...................................................................................... 45.00
Sauce, Azalea, 5 1/4 In. ........................................................................................... 7.50
Shaker, Azalea, Bulbous, 3 In. ................................................................................. 9.00
Snack Set, Tree In Meadow ....................................................................................... 35.00
Soup Dish, Azalea ..................................................................................................... 15.00
Spoon Holder, Azalea .............................................................................. 45.00 To 55.00
Spoon Holder, Pastel Flowers, Gold Trim, Green M .................................................. 30.00
Spooner, Lay Down, Urns Of Fruit, Gold Trim .......................................................... 32.50
Sugar & Creamer, Azalea ......................................................................... 21.50 To 30.00
Sugar & Creamer, Azalea, Gold Finial ...................................................... 75.00 To 105.00
Sugar & Creamer, Azalea, Ruffled Edge .................................................................. 250.00
Sugar & Creamer, Blue & Gold ................................................................................ 14.50
Sugar & Creamer, Flowers & Gold Trim, M In Wreath ............................................. 20.00
Sugar & Creamer, Montclair Design ......................................................... 12.50 To 15.00
Sugar & Creamer, Orange, Black Band & Flowers, Green Wreath ............................. 35.00
Sugar & Creamer, Tremont, Covered ....................................................................... 30.00
Sugar Shaker & Creamer, Scene, Lake, House ......................................................... 30.00
Sugar, Valiere .......................................................................................................... 10.00
Syrup Set, Azalea, 3 Piece ....................................................................................... 55.00
Syrup Set, Gold Trim, 3 Piece .................................................................................. 19.50
Tea Set, Child's, Gold Band, White, 21 Piece ........................................................... 95.00
Tea Set, Orchids, Green Leaves, Gold Trim, 7 Piece ................................................ 75.00
Teapot, Azalea .......................................................................................... 50.00 To 55.00
Teapot, Azalea, Gold Finial ...................................................................... 350.00 To 375.00
Teapot, Minaret Pattern ........................................................................................... 20.00
Teapot, Sugar, & Creamer, Enchantress, Nitto Ware ................................................ 45.00
Teapot, Valiere ......................................................................................................... 25.00
Teapot, 4 Flower Medallions, Gold Trim ................................................................... 45.00
Tile, Azalea ............................................................................................... 28.00 To 35.00
Toast Tray, Blue Luster, Flowers, Green M, 2 Slices ................................................ 20.00
Toast Tray, Blue Luster, Orange Bird, Green M, 4 Slices .......................................... 28.50
Toothpick, Azalea ..................................................................................... 70.00 To 85.00
Tray, Handled, Hand-Painted Flowers, Cream Ground, 7 X 18 In. ............................. 30.00
Tray, Sandwich, Gold Trim, 16 X 6 In. ...................................................................... 27.00
Trivet, Blue Willow, Green M In Wreath, 6 In.Diam. ................................................. 12.00
Vase, Handled, Bunches Of Gold Grapes, Black Ground, 10 In. ................................ 95.00
Vase, Handled, Flowers On Top, Gold Trim, M In Wreath, 7 3/4 In. .......................... 35.00
Vase, Handled, Lake Scene, Gold Beading At Top, 5 1/2 In. ..................................... 35.00

| Vase, Pastoral Scene, Signed, 9 In. | 75.00 |
|---|---|
| Vase, Pink & White Mums, Magenta, Green, & Gold Trim, 8 1/2 In. | 45.00 |
| Vase, Pink Flowers, Gold Handles, Gold Top & Bottom, 8 In. | 45.00 |
| Vase, Scenic, Green M In Wreath, 10 In. | 50.00 |
| Vase, Tree In The Meadow, 8 3/4 In. | 35.00 |
| Vase, Tree, Cottage At Lake, Peach With Gold Handles, 5 1/2 In. | 35.00 |
| Wall Pocket, Country Scene, Signed, 8 In. | 15.00 |

| NORSE, Vase, Black Over Gold, Geometric Design, 3 1/2 X 4 In. | 40.00 |
|---|---|

*The North Dakota School of Mines was established in 1892 at the University of North Dakota.*

| NORTH DAKOTA SCHOOL OF MINES, Bowl, Green & Aqua, Signed, 1 1/4 X 3 1/4 In. | 40.00 |
|---|---|
| Candleholder, Terra-Cotta, Signed | 95.00 |
| Pot, Rose Over Gray, Marked, 6 1/2 In. | 40.00 |
| Vase, Blue, Black, Glossy, 7 3/4 In. | 60.00 |
| Vase, Buff, Green, 3 5/8 X 4 In. | 120.00 |
| Vase, Cobalt Blue, Signed, 7 In. | 35.00 |
| Vase, Green, Tan, Squatty, Signed, 7 X 4 In. | 45.00 |
| Vase, Indian, Black & Red, Signed, 5 In. | 125.00 |

**N**

*Northwood Glass Company worked in Martins Ferry, Ohio, in the 1880s to c. 1923. They marked some pieces with the underlined letter N. Many pieces of carnival glass were made by this company.*

NORTHWOOD, see also Carnival Glass; Custard Glass; Goofus Glass; Pressed Glass

| NORTHWOOD, Basket, Bushel, Black, Signed N In Circle | 85.00 |
|---|---|
| Basket, Bushel, Vaseline Opalescent, Signed N | 165.00 |
| Berry Set, Atlas, 5 Piece | 50.00 |
| Berry Set, Jeweled Heart, Opalescent, 3 Piece | 35.00 |
| Berry Set, Strawberry Pattern, 7 Piece | 95.00 |
| Berry Set, 6 Sauces, Leaf Medallion, Green | 500.00 |
| Bowl, Center, Emerald Green, Footed, Signed, 11 In. | 65.00 |
| Bowl, Winged Scroll, Gold Trim, Footed, Green, 5 In.Diam. | 11.00 |
| Butter, Gold Rose, Signed | 175.00 |
| Butter, Intaglio, Emerald Green, Gold Trim | 165.00 |
| Compote, Strawberry, Covered | 42.00 |
| Creamer, Jackson, White Opalescent | 35.00 |
| Dish, Sauce, Footed, Intaglio Pattern, Blue Opalescent | 26.00 |
| Pitcher, Water, Cornflower, Gold Trim, Green | 125.00 |
| Pitcher, Water, Geneva, Green & Gold | 95.00 |
| Pitcher, Water, Leaf Umbrella, Cranberry | 225.00 |
| Rose Bowl, Beaded Cable, Blue To Opalescent | 42.00 |
| Sugar & Creamer, Covered, Grape & Gothic Arches, Green | 65.00 |
| Sugar, Belladonna, Covered, Gold & Enamel Trim, Blue | 35.00 |
| Sugar, Everglades, Blue, Opalescent, Gold Cover | 95.00 |
| Sugar, Fluted Scrolls, Blue Opalescent, Covered | 85.00 |
| Sugar, Intaglio, Covered, Emerald Green, Gold Trim | 110.00 To 165.00 |
| Syrup, Grape & Leaf, Turquoise | 145.00 |
| Tankard, 6 Tumblers, Enameled Lilies Of The Valley, Green | 225.00 |
| Tumbler, Enameled Cherries, Cobalt | 15.00 |
| Tumbler, Green With Gold, N Mark | 33.00 |
| Tumbler, Holly, Green | 30.00 |
| Tumbler, Oriental Poppy, Emerald Green & Gold, Set Of 6 | 150.00 |
| Tumbler, Regal, Opalescent White | 35.00 |
| Vase, Lily, Clear To Pumpkin, 10 In. | 30.00 |
| Vase, Panels With Bark Design, Amethyst To Red, 7 In. | 85.00 |

**Vase,** Rust Pull-Up, Pink Liner, Tan Ground, Signed, 10 In. ........................................ 950.00
**Vase,** Tree Bark, Purple, 13 X 6 In.Diam. ................................................................... 115.00
**Water Set,** Cornflower, Emerald Green, 5 Piece ........................................................ 135.00
**Water Set,** Drapery Design, Opalescent, 6 Tumblers, Marked ................................... 335.00
**Water Set,** Gold Rose, Green, Gold Trim, 7 Piece ..................................................... 385.00
**Water Set,** Grape & Lattice, Green, Gold Trim, Blown, 6 Piece ................................. 95.00
**Water Set,** Green Grape & Gothic Arches, Pitcher & 6 Tumblers .............................. 250.00
**Water Set,** Inverted Fan & Feather, 7 Piece .............................................................. 695.00
**Water Set,** Lattice & Grape, 6 Tumblers, Green, Gold Trim, 7 Piece ........................ 150.00
**Water Set,** Strawberry & Cable, Gold Trim, 6 Piece ................................................. 375.00
**Water Set,** 6 Glasses, Enameled Flowers, Fired Enamel On Pitcher ........................ 185.00

*Nuart was a trademark registered by the Imperial Glass Co. of
Bellaire, Ohio, about 1920.*

**NUART, Shade,** Lamp, Gold Iridescent Pattern Around Bottom, Bell Shape, 6 In. ................... 25.00

**NUTCRACKER, Alligator,** Brass ..................................................................................... 25.00
**Crocodile,** 1900, Brass .................................................................................................. 45.00
**Double,** Silver ................................................................................................................ 27.50
**Figural,** Cat, Cracker Face & Mouth, Paw Handles, Brass, 4 1/2 In. ............................ 35.00
**Figural,** Cat, Face & Mouth Cracker, Paw Handles, Brass, 4 3/4 In. ........................... 35.00
**Figural,** Dog, Cast Iron ................................................................................................. 65.00
**Figural, Snail,** Hand-Carved, C.1820 ........................................................................... 85.00
**Figural,** Soldier, Painted, All Wood, 14 In. ................................................................... 18.00
**Figural, Squirrel,** C.1820 ........................................................................................... 100.00
**Hand-Carved Man,** Fruitwood, German ........................................................................ 35.00
**Rooster,** Brass ....................................................................................... 6.50 To 22.00
**Screw Type,** Table Clamps, Cast Iron ........................................................................... 10.00
**Takes 3 Sizes Of Pecans,** Table Clamp, Cast Iron, Patent, 1911 ................................ 12.00

*Nymphenburg, a German porcelain factory, was established at
Neudeck-ob-der-Au in 1753 and moved to Nymphenburg in 1761. The company
is still in existence. Modern marks include a shield superseded by a star or
crown, and a crowned CT with a checkered shield.*

**NYMPHENBURG, Candleholder,** Swirled, Cream Colored, Pair ................................ 300.00
**Figurine,** Clio, Holding Book, C.1765, Shield Mark, 4 In. .......................................... 320.00
**Figurine,** Old Man, Naked, Bearded, Yellow Clothes, 8 1/4 In. ................................. 150.00
**Figurine,** Putto, Dour Seasons Series, C.1760, Marked, 4 In. .................................. 2500.00
**Figurine,** Seated, Clio, White, Holding Book, Marked, 3 1/2 In. ................................ 500.00
**Group Of Lovers,** Dog, Goat, Ruins, Marked, 10 1/2 In. .......................................... 8000.00

*Occupied Japan is the mark used on pieces of pottery and porcelain made
during the American occupation of Japan after World War II, from 1945
to 1952. Collectors are now buying these pieces. The items were made for
export to the United States.*

**OCCUPIED JAPAN, Bell,** Fat Lady, 3 In. ....................................................................... 18.00
**Bootie,** Bisque ............................................................................................................... 13.00
**Bowl,** Maruni, Red, Gold, Lacquer, Metal, 10 X 4 In. ................................................... 25.00
**Box,** Powder, Cobalt Blue, Silver Plated Frame ........................................................... 47.50
**Candleholder,** Double, Figural Woman ......................................................................... 11.00
**Celluloid Elephants On Wooden Bridge,** Original Box ............................................... 12.00
**Clock,** Figural, Scotty, China, Marked .......................................................................... 8.00
**Coaster,** Lacquered Box, Set Of 6 ............................................................................... 20.00
**Coaster,** Lacquered, Original Box, Set Of 5 ................................................................ 18.00
**Coffee Set,** Gold Dragon, White, 11 Piece .................................................................. 65.00
**Condiment Set,** Dog Mustard, Attached Salt & Pepper, Spoons ................................. 20.00
**Cornucopia,** Drawn By Cherubs, Marked In Gold, 7 In., Pair .................................... 110.00
**Creamer,** Figural, Cow .......................................................................... 15.00 To 18.00
**Cup & Saucer,** Blue Phoenix ....................................................................................... 12.00
**Cup & Saucer,** Demitasse, Floral & Gold, Marked ...................................................... 5.50

| | |
|---|---|
| **Cup & Saucer,** Demitasse, Flower, Plant Design, Set Of 6 | 30.00 |
| **Cup & Saucer,** Demitasse, Moriage Dragons | 10.00 |
| **Demitasse Set,** Lacquerware, 6 Cups & Saucers, Gold Inside | 45.00 |
| **Dish,** Leaf Shape, Multicolor Green & Gold, 5 X 5 1/2 In. | 15.00 |
| **Doll,** Sitting, 3 1/2 In. | 15.00 |
| **Egg Timer,** Black Mammy Holding Glass | 15.00 |
| **Eggcup,** Blue Willow | 10.00 |
| **Elephant,** 3, Glass Ball In Trunk, Celluloid, Marked | 6.00 |
| **Elephant,** 3, Wooden Bridge, Celluloid, Boxed, Marked | 8.00 |
| **Elf On Shoe,** Pink Elf, Gray Shoe, 3 1/2 X 3 1/2 In. | 14.00 |
| **Figurine,** Boy, 9 In. | 20.00 |
| **Figurine,** Cat & Kittens In Shoe, Porcelain, 4 In. | 12.50 |
| **Figurine,** Cinderella & Chariot, 6 In. | 25.00 |
| **Figurine,** Colonial Couple, 6 In. | 8.00 |
| **Figurine,** Courting Couple, Bisque, 6 In. | 45.00 |
| **Figurine,** Flamingo, Standing, 6 In., Pair | 20.00 |
| **Figurine,** Girl Seated On Vase, Bisque, 7 In. | 32.50 |
| **Figurine,** Girl, On Stump, Bird On Hat, 6 In. ........ 13.00 To 18.00 | |
| **Figurine,** Girl, 9 In. | 25.00 |
| **Figurine,** Kewpie Type, Bisque, Dressed, 2 3/4 In. | 20.00 |
| **Figurine,** Lady Seated, 7 In. | 11.00 |
| **Figurine,** Man By Stump, 6 In. | 11.00 |
| **Figurine,** Nude Boy, Seated On Blue Fountain, 6 1/4 In. | 35.00 |
| **Figurine,** Reindeer, Celluloid | 8.00 |
| **Lamp,** Colonial Man & Woman | 15.00 |
| **Lighter,** Camera On Tripod, Marked | 27.50 |
| **Lighter,** Cowboy Hat, Crown Lighter, Brim Ashtray, C.1945 | 16.00 |
| **Lighter,** Pocket | 12.00 |
| **Mug,** Cowboy, Handle | 25.00 |
| **Mustard,** Beehive | 9.00 |
| **Planter,** Figural, Swan, 5 In., Pair | 23.00 |
| **Plaque,** Butterfly, Gold Outline, 6 X 5 In. | 20.00 |
| **Plaque,** Colonial Couple, Frame Border, 5 1/4 X 6 1/4 In. | 30.00 |
| **Plaque,** Colonial Figure, Bisque, 7 1/4 In. | 25.00 |
| **Plate,** Flying Phoenix Bird, Blue, 9 1/2 In. | 18.00 |
| **Plate,** Spring Violets, Rosetti, 10 In. | 12.00 |
| **Powder Jar,** Figural, Woman, Bare Shoulders, Colonial Dress | 65.00 |
| **Salt & Pepper,** Beehive Shape, Molded Bee On Side, 3 In. | 18.00 |
| **Salt & Pepper,** Blue Phoenix ........ 10.00 To 16.00 | |
| **Salt & Pepper,** Bunny, Marked | 10.50 |
| **Salt & Pepper,** Dragon, Moriage Type, Marked | 14.00 |
| **Salt & Pepper,** Pelican ........ 8.00 To 10.00 | |
| **Salt & Pepper,** Tomato Shape, Leaf Base, 4 In. | 18.00 |
| **Santa,** Papier-Mache | 12.00 |
| **Shoe,** Elf Sitting On Front, Pink & Gray, 3 1/2 X 3 1/2 In. | 14.00 |
| **Sugar & Creamer,** Dragon, Raised, Blue, Marked | 12.50 |
| **Sugar & Creamer,** Figural, Birds, Yellow Bills | 8.50 |
| **Sugar & Creamer,** Teapot, Tomato | 35.00 |
| **Sugar,** Bird On Tree, 2-Handled | 12.00 |
| **Tea Set,** Art Deco, 15 Piece | 42.00 |
| **Tea Set,** Cottage Shape, 3 Piece | 95.00 |
| **Tea Set,** Dragons, Gray, White, Green, Coral, 15 Piece | 155.00 |
| **Tea Set,** Lacquerware, 6 Cups & Saucers, Black, Gold Inside | 55.00 |
| **Tea Set,** Miniature, 3 Piece | 17.50 |
| **Teapot,** Brown, 3 In. | 12.00 |
| **Teapot,** Dark Brown, Glazed, Lid | 18.50 |
| **Teapot,** Figural, Red Tomato, Green Spout & Handle | 20.00 |
| **Teapot,** Floral, Relief, Brown, Hadson | 17.00 |
| **Teapot,** Winking, Cigar Smoking Man, Hat Cover | 16.50 |
| **Toby Mug,** Man With Black Top Hat & Bowtie, 5 In. | 16.00 |
| **Toby,** MacArthur, 4 1/2 In. | 75.00 |
| **Toothpick,** Black Bear Climbing Tree Trunk | 12.00 |

**Toothpick,** Lady Bug With Accordion .......................................................................... 5.00
**Toothpick,** Seated Boy, Bluebird On Hand ................................................................. 12.00
**Toothpick,** Spotted Dog, Marked ................................................................................. 8.00
**Toothpick,** 3 Figures ...................................................................................................... 15.00
**Toy,** Cat With Ball, Windup ........................................................................................... 25.00
**Toy,** Cheery Cook, Movable Arms, Celluloid & Tin, Windup ...................................... 25.00
**Toy,** Crawling Baby, Cotton Romper, Tin & Celluloid, Windup .................................. 95.00
**Toy,** Dog With Shoe, Windup ........................................................................................ 25.00
**Toy,** Kangaroo, Windup, Tin .......................................................................................... 35.00
**Toy,** Ostrich, Windup, Tin .............................................................................................. 35.00
**Toy,** Playful Poodle, Windup, Tin ........................................................ 28.50 To 35.00
**Toy,** Pocket Watch, With Chain, Stamped ................................................................... 15.00
**Toy,** Santa, Sleigh, Reindeer, Bell Ringer, Keywind ................................................... 28.00
**Toy,** Singing Bird, Windup ............................................................................................. 25.00
**Umbrella,** Child's, Silk, Hand-Painted ......................................................................... 12.50
**Vase,** Children In Garden, Blue, Green, Urn Shape, 7 1/4 In. .................................. 60.00

**G. E. OHR,** *Ohr pottery was made by George E.Ohr in Biloxi, Mississippi, between*
**BILOXI.** *1883 and 1918. The pieces were made of very thin clay and were twisted, folded, and dented into odd, graceful shapes.*

**OHR, Bank,** Pear Shaped, Nonglazed, 4 In. .............................................................. 235.00
**Bowl,** Folded Rim, Mottled Green, 2 In.High ............................................................. 210.00
**Bowl,** Folded Rim, Mottled Green, 5 In. ..................................................................... 210.00
**Bowl,** Globular Body, Elliptical Rim, High Glaze, Marked, 3 1/4 In. ......................... 450.00
**Bowl,** Gun-Metal Glaze, Footed, Crimped Rim, 4 3/4 In. .......................................... 225.00
**Bowl,** Gun-Metal Glaze, Metallic, Crimped Rim, Footed, Marked, 4 3/4 In. ............ 220.00
**Bowl,** Thumbprint Band, 3 Lizards Over Collar & Sides, Marked, 2 3/4 In. .............. 850.00
**Bowl,** Yellow & Green Glaze, Globular Body, Pinched End, Marked, 3 In. ............... 450.00
**Mug,** Puzzle, Bracket Handle, Pierced Rim, Burnt Sienna, Marked, 3 1/2 In. .......... 320.00
**Mug,** Puzzle, Iridescent Brown, 3 1/2 In. .................................................................. 200.00
**Mug,** Puzzle, Rabbit Head Handle, Mottled Brown & Black, Signed, 3 1/2 In. ........ 225.00
**Mug,** Puzzle, Sienna Glaze, Leaves & Vines, Metallic Flecks, 3 1/2 In. .................. 215.00
**Pitcher,** Applied Handle, Gun-Metal Glaze, 3 1/2 In. ............................................... 235.00
**Pitcher,** Diagonal Fluting, Trilobed Rim, Mottled Brick Red, Marked, 6 In. ............ 2500.00
**Pitcher,** Green Glaze, Bracket Handle, Marked, 3 3/4 In. ......................................... 550.00
**Pitcher,** Green Mottled Glaze, Dented Side, Applied Handle, 3 3/4 In. ................... 650.00
**Pitcher,** Gun-Metal Glaze, 3 1/2 In. .......................................................................... 235.00
**Pitcher,** Red Speckled Glaze, Folded Neck, 6 1/2 In. ............................................... 550.00
**Teapot,** Arched Handle, Serpentine Spout, Marked, 5 1/2 In. ................................ 1300.00
**Teapot,** Midnight Blue Glaze, Serpentine Spout & Handle, 5 1/2 In. ....................... 650.00
**Teapot,** Midnight Blue, Serpentine Spout, Arched Handle, Marked, 5 In. .............. 1300.00
**Teapot,** Serpentine Spout, Red & Gray Volcanic Glaze, Marked, 7 In. .................. 6000.00
**Vase,** Applied Snake, Mottled Green, Brown, Tan, 6 1/2 In. .................................... 325.00
**Vase,** Arrowhead Design, Rose Glaze, Pear Shape, Footed, Marked, 5 In. ............ 380.00
**Vase,** Black Speckled Olive Green, Oviform Body, Footed, Marked, 6 In. .............. 450.00
**Vase,** Burnt Sienna, Ocher Glaze, Turquoise Dripping, Bell Form, 7 In. ................. 850.00
**Vase,** Death's Head, Sunken Eyes, Olive Green, Signed, 4 1/4 In. .......................... 650.00
**Vase,** Green & Brown, Applied Snake, 6 X 5 In. ....................................................... 325.00
**Vase,** Gun-Metal Glaze, Metallic, Flecked, Oviform, Marked, 7 1/2 In. .................. 380.00
**Vase,** Inverted Bell Form, Handle, Turquoise Dripping, Marked, 7 In. ..................... 850.00
**Vase,** Olive Green Glaze, Heart Shaped Rim, Speckled, Marked, 5 In. .................. 1100.00
**Vase,** Oviform, Covered In Metallic Gun-Metal Glaze, Marked, 7 1/2 In. ............... 380.00
**Vase,** Punched-In Top, Greenish Tan, Signed, 5 1/4 X 4 1/2 In. ............................. 495.00
**Vase,** Sienna & Ocher Glaze, Turquoise Drippings, Signed, 7 In. ............................ 325.00
**Vase,** Speckled Green, Brown, Twisted, 2 3/4 In. ..................................................... 210.00
**Vase,** Spherical Form, Speckled Green Glaze, Marked, 5 In. .................................. 1100.00
**Vase,** Swirl Design, Tan, 2 1/2 In. ............................................................................. 210.00
**Vase,** Wide Thin Lip, Green Mottling, Signed, 4 1/4 In. ........................................... 145.00
**Vase,** Yellow & Green, 4 1/2 In. ................................................................................. 240.00
**Vase,** Yellow, Green, Script Signature, 4 1/2 In. ....................................................... 240.00

OLD IVORY    Old ivory china was made in Silesia, Germany, at the end of the nine-
**84**         teenth century. It is often marked with a crown and the word Silesia.
              The pattern numbers appear on the base of each piece.

| | |
|---|---|
| OLD IVORY, **Berry Bowl,** Trianon, 5 Saucers, Bowl, 10 In. | 185.00 |
| **Berry Bowl,** Trianon, 5 Saucers, Bowl, 9 1/2 In. | 185.00 |
| **Berry Set,** Silesia, Bowl, 10 In., 7 Piece | 260.00 |
| **Berry Set,** 6 Saucers, Silesia, Bowl, 9 1/2 In. | 225.00 |
| **Berry Set,** 7 Piece | 175.00 To 195.00 |
| **Bonbon,** Top Handle, 6 1/2 In. | 40.00 |
| **Bowl,** Sugar, Silesia | 24.00 |
| **Bowl,** Waste, 5 1/2 In. | 45.00 |
| **Bowl,** 9 1/2 In. | 55.00 To 75.00 |
| **Cake Set,** 6 Dessert Plates, Signed, 10 In. | 175.00 |
| **Celery,** Silesia, 8 1/2 X 5 In. | 80.00 |
| **Celery,** Thistle, Oval, 12 X 5 1/2 In. | 50.00 |
| **Chocolate Set,** 7 Piece | 435.00 |
| **Coffee Set,** Pot, Creamer, & Covered Sugar, Silesia | 425.00 |
| **Cracker Jar** | 195.00 |
| **Creamer,** Silesia | 50.00 |
| **Cup & Saucer** | 24.00 |
| **Cup & Saucer,** Demitasse, Silesia, Set Of 6 | 200.00 |
| **Cup & Saucer,** Silesia | 30.00 To 36.50 |
| **Dish,** Celery, 11 In. | 45.00 |
| **Dish,** Pickle, Silesia, 6 1/2 X 4 1/2 In. | 65.00 |
| **Dish,** Sauce, Silesia, Set Of 6 | 100.00 |
| **Hair Receiver,** Brown Rose Design | 40.00 |
| **Mustache Cup,** Saucer | 290.00 |
| **Plate,** Cake, Closed Handles, Silesia, 10 In. | 45.00 |
| **Plate,** Cake, Double Handled | 75.00 |
| **Plate,** Cake, Open Handles, 10 In. | 95.00 |
| **Plate,** Cake, 10 1/4 In. | 55.00 |
| **Plate,** Chop, Silesia, 13 In. | 125.00 |
| **Plate,** Multicolored Flowers, Silesia, 8 3/8 In. | 30.00 |
| **Plate,** Silesia, 6 In., Set Of 6 | 125.00 |
| **Plate,** Silesia, 8 In., Set Of 6 | 225.00 |
| **Plate,** 6 In. | 21.00 To 22.50 |
| **Plate,** 7 In. | 35.00 |
| **Plate,** 7 3/4 In. | 25.00 |
| **Plate,** 8 1/2 In. | 30.00 To 38.00 |
| **Platter,** Silesia, 11 X 6 In. | 90.00 |
| **Relish,** Thistle, Oval, 9 X 4 1/2 In. | 38.00 |
| **Salt & Pepper** | 125.00 |
| **Salt & Pepper,** Silesia | 105.00 |
| **Sugar & Creamer** | 95.00 To 185.00 |
| **Sugar & Creamer,** Silesia | 90.00 To 100.00 |
| **Sugar & Creamer,** Thistle Design | 65.00 |
| **Tray,** Dresser, Thistle, 8 3/4 X 6 1/2 In. | 50.00 |
| **Tray,** 6 X 11 1/4 In. | 85.00 |
| **Vase,** , Sticker, 9 1/4 In. | 300.00 |

    **OLD PARIS, see Paris**

Onion, originally named "bulb pattern," is a white ware decorated with
cobalt blue. Although it is commonly associated with Meissen, other
companies made the pattern in the latter part of the nineteenth century.

| | |
|---|---|
| ONION, **Bowl,** Soup, Rimmed, Blue, Meissen, 9 In. | 35.00 |
| **Cup & Saucer,** Blue & White, Signed Sachsen | 12.00 |
| **Cup & Saucer,** Blue, Crossed Swords | 48.00 |
| **Dish,** Handled, 2 Spouts, Meissen, Marked | 68.00 |
| **Dish,** Soap, Wall Type, Blue, Meissen | 35.00 |
| **Jar,** Vinegar, Blue & White, Stopper, Meissen | 225.00 |

| | |
|---|---|
| Plate, Meissen, Crossed Swords, 9 1/4 In. | 45.00 |
| Plate, Meissen, 10 In. | 22.00 |
| Platter, Crossed Swords, Meissen, 15 In. | 75.00 |
| Platter, Meissen, Crossed Swords, 17 X 12 In. | 250.00 |
| Platter, Meissen, 15 X 10 In. | 65.00 |
| Platter, Meissen, 20 X 16 In. | 175.00 |
| Platter, Pewter Hot Water Jacket, Meissen | 118.00 |
| Rolling Pin, Blue, Miniature, Meissen | 125.00 |
| Salt & Pepper, Meissen, Signed | 35.00 |
| Saucer, Blue & White, Meissen, 5 1/2 In. | 22.00 |
| Tea Strainer, Meissen | 25.00 |

*Opalescent glass is translucent glass that has the bluish-white tones of the opal gemstone. It is often found in pressed glassware made in Victorian times. Some dealers use the terms opaline and opalescent for any of the bluish-white translucent wares.*

| | |
|---|---|
| OPALESCENT, Banana Boat, Alaska, Vaseline | 425.00 |
| Basket, Cactus, Aqua, 7 In. | 25.00 |
| Basket, Hobnail, Cranberry, 8 In. | 30.00 |
| Basket, May Basket, Over Handle, Green, 5 3/4 In. | 38.00 |
| Basket, Ring Handled, Blue | 85.00 |
| Berry Bowl, Honeycomb & Clover, Blue | 55.00 |
| Berry Bowl, Master, Argonaut Shell, Boat Shape, Northwood, Blue | 195.00 |
| Berry Bowl, Master, Intaglio, Northwood, Blue | 135.00 |
| Berry Bowl, Reverse Swirl, Clear, Large | 60.00 |
| Berry Bowl, Tokyo, Master, Green | 55.00 |
| Berry Bowl, Wreath & Shell, Master, Blue | 85.00 |
| Berry Set, Beaded Heart, Emerald Green To Custard, 7 Piece | 95.00 |
| Berry Set, Beatty Rib, Blue, 7 Piece | 145.00 |
| Berry Set, Dolly Madison, Green, 5 Piece | 225.00 |
| Berry Set, Fluted Scrolls, Vaseline, 7 Piece | 285.00 |
| Berry Set, Iris With Meander, Vaseline, 6 Piece | 125.00 |
| Berry Set, Jeweled Heart, Blue, 7 Piece | 125.00 To 135.00 |
| Berry Set, Jeweled Heart, 7 Piece | 50.00 To 85.00 |
| Berry Set, Leaf Medallion, Amethyst, 7 Piece | 320.00 |
| Berry Set, Regal, Master & 4 Sauces, Green | 145.00 |
| Bonbon, Jefferson, Clear Barbells, 8 1/2 In. | 25.00 |
| Bonbon, Many Loops, Blue, 8 In. | 30.00 |
| Bonbon, Strawberry, Handle, White | 15.00 |
| Bottle, Barber, Fern Pattern, Blue | 95.00 |
| Bottle, Barber, Hobnail, Original Pewter Top, Cranberry | 135.00 |
| Bowl, Alaska, Scalloped Rim, Vaseline, 4 X 4 In. | 42.00 |
| Bowl, Argonaut Shell, Blue, Footed, 8 X 6 3/4 In. | 42.00 |
| Bowl, Argonaut Shell, Footed, Fluted, Ice Green, 9 In. | 32.50 |
| Bowl, Berry, Cactus, Aqua, 10 In. | 20.00 |
| Bowl, Berry, Honeycomb & Clover, Blue | 35.00 |
| Bowl, Berry, Honeycomb & Clover, Green | 45.00 |
| Bowl, Berry, Jeweled Heart, Blue, Small | 22.00 |
| Bowl, Blossoms, Gilt Collar, White, 8 1/2 In. | 28.50 |
| Bowl, Cactus, Crimped, Aqua, 7 In. | 16.50 |
| Bowl, Clarissa, Green, Flat, 8 In. | 35.00 |
| Bowl, Grapes & Cherries, Blue | 85.00 |
| Bowl, Greek Key, Ruffled, Northwood, Blue, 8 In. | 47.00 |
| Bowl, Green, Meander, Leaves, 3 Legs, Ruffled, 9 1/2 In. | 45.00 |
| Bowl, Hobnail, Ruffled, Square Top, Clear Bottom, White | 35.00 |
| Bowl, Honeycomb & Clover, Fenton, Green, 9 In. | 37.00 |
| Bowl, Inverted Fan & Feather, Pointed Rim, White, 3 X 6 1/2 In. | 14.00 |
| Bowl, Jackson, White | 28.00 |
| Bowl, Jefferson Wheel, Green, 9 In. | 38.00 |
| Bowl, Jeweled Heart, Clear To Blue, 4 X 10 In. | 85.00 |
| Bowl, Loop, Footed, Blue, 9 In. | 135.00 |
| Bowl, Netted Rose, Green | 30.00 |
| Bowl, Peacocks On A Fence, Ruffled, Northwood, Blue | 80.00 |

| | |
|---|---|
| Bowl, Reflecting Diamonds, Green, Flared, 9 In. | 35.00 |
| Bowl, Ribbed Spiral, Fluted, Blue, 8 1/4 In. | 44.00 |
| Bowl, Ruffled Rim, Green, 6-Footed, 8 In. | 25.00 |
| Bowl, Ruffles & Rings, Clear To White, 6 1/2 In. | 28.00 |
| Bowl, Ruffles & Rings, Green | 55.00 |
| Bowl, Ruffles & Rings, Green, Crimped Edge, 9 In. | 28.00 |
| Bowl, Shell & Dots, Ruffled, White, 8 In. | 32.00 |
| Bowl, Standing Bear In Base, White, 8 1/2 In. | 145.00 |
| Bowl, Swirl, Ruffled, Pink, 6 1/2 X 4 1/2 In. | 40.00 |
| Bowl, Tokyo, Ruffled, Blue, 7 3/4 In. | 22.00 |
| Bowl, White, Greek Key, Ribbed, Ruffled, Footed, Signed, 8 1/4 In. | 30.00 |
| Bowl, Wishbone & Drape, White, 2 2/3 X 6 1/4 In. | 12.00 |
| Bowl, Wreath & Shell, 6 1/2 In. | 25.00 |
| Box, Jewel, Fluted Scroll, Vaseline | 45.00 |
| Bride's Basket, Hobnail, Crimped, Silver Plate Frame, 10 1/2 In. | 105.00 |
| Bride's Basket, Hobnail, Frame, Cranberry | 175.00 |
| Bride's Basket, Ruffled Optic, Clear, Swirled | 70.00 |
| Bride's Basket, Ruffled Optic, Silver Plate Holder, Blue | 145.00 |
| Bride's Basket, Spanish Lace, Silver Plate Holder, Blue | 150.00 |
| Butter & Creamer, Covered, Jewel & Flower, Gold Trim, Blue | 325.00 |
| Butter, Circled Scroll, Covered, White | 95.00 |
| Butter, Dewey, Covered, Vaseline | 130.00 |
| Butter, Drapery, Covered, Blue & Gold | 175.00 |
| Butter, Everglades, Covered, Blue | 175.00 |
| Butter, Herringbone, Covered, Green | 60.00 |
| Butter, Hobnail, Covered, Blue | 145.00 |
| Butter, Hobnail, Covered, Vaseline | 150.00 |
| Butter, Idyll, Covered, Green | 85.00 |
| Butter, Inverted Fan & Feather, Covered, Northwood, Green | 200.00 |
| Butter, Jewel & Flower, Covered, White | 135.00 |
| Butter, Nail, Covered, Ruby | 175.00 |
| Butter, Paneled Holly, Covered, Blue | 200.00 |
| Butter, Regal, Covered, Green | 150.00 |
| Butter, Regal, Covered, Northwood, Gold Signed, White | 80.00 |
| Butter, Regal, Covered, Northwood, Green | 175.00 |
| Butter, Seaweed, Covered, Blue | 195.00 To 225.00 |
| Butter, Swag & Bracket, Covered, Clear | 30.00 |
| Butter, Swag With Brackets, Covered, White | 125.00 |
| Butter, Teardrop & Thumbprint, Covered, Cobalt Blue | 80.00 |
| Butter, Tokyo, Covered, Green | 55.00 To 145.00 |
| Butter, Wreath & Shell, Covered, Blue | 175.00 |
| Butter, Wreath & Shell, Covered, White | 85.00 |
| Candleholder, Florentine, Blue, 8 1/2 In., Pair | 54.00 |
| Candleholder, Florentine, Vaseline, 8 In. | 19.00 |
| Castor, Pickle, Reverse Swirl, Tongs, Blue | 150.00 |
| Celery, Beaded Swirl, Gold Trim, Green | 55.00 |
| Celery, Beatty Honeycomb, Northwood, Blue | 63.00 |
| Celery, Beatty Rib, White | 25.00 |
| Celery, Beatty Swirl, Blue | 45.00 |
| Celery, Beatty Swirl, White | 40.00 |
| Celery, Blown Twist, Cranberry Edge, Clear | 70.00 |
| Celery, Honeycomb, Scalloped Top, Amber | 75.00 |
| Celery, Jewel & Fan, Green | 28.00 |
| Celery, Seaweed, Blue | 75.00 |
| Celery, Windows, Cranberry | 75.00 |
| Celery, Wreath & Shell, Blue | 150.00 |
| Celery, Wreath & Shell, Clear | 65.00 |
| Compote, Dolphin, Stem, Blue, 5 1/2 In. | 35.00 |
| Compote, Hearts & Flowers, Blue | 45.00 |
| Compote, Hobnail, Blue, Stemmed, 6 In. | 12.00 |
| Compote, Jelly, Argonaut Shell, Pedestal, Vaseline | 55.00 |
| Compote, Jelly, Intaglio, Blue | 20.00 To 90.00 |
| Compote, Jelly, Maple Leaf, Northwood, Blue | 58.00 |

Compote, Jelly, Scroll & Acanthus ........................................................................ 32.00
Compote, Jelly, Swag With Bracket, Blue ............................................................ 55.00
Compote, Jelly, Swag With Bracket, Green ......................................................... 25.00
Compote, Swag With Brackets, Blue ..................................................................... 20.00
Creamer & Spooner, Alaska, Vaseline .................................................................. 95.00
Creamer, Alaska, Blue ............................................................................................ 45.00
Creamer, Alaska, Clear ............................................................................ 24.00 To 30.00
Creamer, Alaska, Vaseline ....................................................................... 50.00 To 95.00
Creamer, Argonaut Shell, Northwood, Blue ....................................... 75.00 To 110.00
Creamer, Beatty Rib, Blue ..................................................................................... 42.00
Creamer, Beatty Rib, White ................................................................................... 30.00
Creamer, Chrysanthemum Swirl, White ............................................................. 50.00
Creamer, Chrysanthemum, Blue ........................................................................ 325.00
Creamer, Circle Scroll, Blue ................................................................................. 65.00
Creamer, Flora, Blue ............................................................................................... 65.00
Creamer, Fluted Scroll, Blue ................................................................................. 50.00
Creamer, Fluted Scroll, Vaseline .......................................................................... 55.00
Creamer, Intaglio, Blue ............................................................................ 30.00 To 70.00
Creamer, Intaglio, White ........................................................................................ 24.00
Creamer, Iris, Green ................................................................................................ 70.00
Creamer, Jeweled Heart, Blue .............................................................................. 45.00
Creamer, Palm Beach, Blue ................................................................................... 95.00
Creamer, Raindrop, Sapphire Blue ...................................................................... 35.00
Creamer, Ribbed Spiral, Blue .................................................................. 65.00 To 75.00
Creamer, Shell, Blue ............................................................................................... 55.00
Creamer, Swag With Brackets, Blue ................................................................... 65.00
Creamer, Swag With Brackets, Canary ............................................................... 20.00
Creamer, Waterlily With Cattails .......................................................................... 19.00
Creamer, Waterlily With Cattails, Blue ............................................................... 45.00
Creamer, Wreath & Shell, Blue ............................................................. 65.00 To 135.00
Cruet, Alaska, Blue ............................................................................................... 225.00
Cruet, Cross-Cross, Pink ..................................................................................... 100.00
Cruet, Daisy & Fern, Clear ..................................................................................... 65.00
Cruet, Hobnail, Blue ............................................................................................... 25.00
Cruet, Reverse Swirl, Chrysanthemum Base, Blue ......................................... 145.00
Cruet, Reverse Swirl, Clear Hand & Stopper, 6 1/2 In. ................................... 75.00
Cruet, Seaweed, Original Stopper, Blue ........................................................... 165.00
Cruet, Tokyo, Green .............................................................................................. 150.00
Cup, Punch, Souvenir, Merrill, Michigan, Green ............................................... 15.00
Dish, Candy, Jackson, Blue ................................................................................... 20.00
Dish, Candy, Jackson, White ................................................................................. 25.00
Dish, Candy, 4-Footed, Beaded Cable, Green .................................................... 35.00
Dish, Daisy & Panel, Vaseline, Round, Futed, 7 3/8 In. ................................... 45.00
Dish, Green, Fluted, 8 1/2 In. ................................................................................ 35.00
Dish, Hobnail, Ruffled, Cranberry .......................................................... 30.00 To 50.00
Dish, Meander, Footed, Green, 9 In. .................................................................... 26.50
Doughnut Stand, Tokyo, Clear ............................................................................. 30.00
Epergne, 3-Lily, Blue ............................................................................................. 165.00
Epergne, 3-Lily, Hobnail, Vaseline ....................................................................... 75.00
Goblet, Hobnail, Clear ............................................................................................ 35.00
Hat, Hobnail, Blue, 2 1/2 In. .................................................................................. 22.50
Ice Cream Set, Hobnail, Vaseline, 7 Piece ....................................................... 220.00
Inkwell, Cover, Hobnail, 2 In.Square .................................................................... 68.00
Jar, Pomade, Diamond Band, Beading, Pewter Top, 2 1/2 X 1 1/8 In. .......... 165.00
Jelly, Scroll & Acanthus, Green ............................................................................ 35.00
Jug, Hobnail, Plum, 5 1/2 In. .................................................................................. 58.50
Lamp, Finger, Snowflake, Blue ............................................................................ 275.00
Lamp, Oil, Swirl, Turquoise Blue ......................................................................... 195.00
Lamp, Snowflake, Clear Base, Cranberry, 8 In. ............................................... 400.00
Mug, Beatty Waffle, White ..................................................................................... 24.00
Mustard, Reverse Swirl, Blue ............................................................................... 55.00
Nappy, S Repeat, Green ......................................................................................... 28.00
Pitcher, Buttons & Braids, Green ....................................................................... 295.00

Pitcher, Daisy & Fern, Clear .......................................................................... 125.00 To 175.00
Pitcher, Daisy & Fern, Clear Applied Handle, Ruffled, 9 In. ............................. 75.00
Pitcher, Drapery, Northwood, White ............................................................... 75.00
Pitcher, Eyelet & Flowers, Blue ...................................................................... 435.00
Pitcher, Hobnail, Vaseline, Miniature ............................................................ 175.00
Pitcher, Stripe, Canary .................................................................................... 295.00
Pitcher, Swirl, Green ....................................................................................... 275.00
Pitcher, Water, Buttons & Braids, Green ........................................ 75.00 To 110.00
Pitcher, Water, Chrysanthemum & Swirl ......................................................... 65.00
Pitcher, Water, Daffodil, Blue ......................................................................... 155.00
Pitcher, Water, Daisy & Fern, Clear ............................................................... 150.00
Pitcher, Water, Daisy & Fern, Vaseline .......................................................... 100.00
Pitcher, Water, Drapery, Northwood, Blue ..................................... 165.00 To 200.00
Pitcher, Water, Fluted Scrolls, Blue ............................................................... 285.00
Pitcher, Water, Fluted Scrolls, Vaseline ......................................................... 135.00
Pitcher, Water, Hobbs, Cranberry .................................................................. 245.00
Pitcher, Water, Hobnail, Clear, 4 1/2 In. ........................................................ 80.00
Pitcher, Water, Hobnail, Reeded Handle, Cranberry ..................................... 265.00
Pitcher, Water, Hobnail, Square Top, Blue .................................................... 110.00
Pitcher, Water, Hobnail, Vaseline .................................................. 225.00 To 275.00
Pitcher, Water, Honeycomb, Scalloped Edge, Amber .................................... 75.00
Pitcher, Water, Jefferson Drape, 4 Tumblers, Green ..................................... 295.00
Pitcher, Water, Jefferson, Cranberry ............................................................... 85.00
Pitcher, Water, Jefferson, Green ...................................................................... 69.00
Pitcher, Water, Reverse Swirl, Chrysanthemum Base, Cranberry ................ 325.00
Pitcher, Water, Reverse Swirl, White .............................................................. 100.00
Pitcher, Water, Seaweed, Cranberry ............................................................... 225.00
Pitcher, Water, Swirl, Applied Handle, Square Top, White ............................ 50.00
Pitcher, Water, Swirl, Bulbous, 4 Tumblers, Blue ......................................... 275.00
Pitcher, Water, Swirl, Cranberry ...................................................................... 125.00
Pitcher, Water, Wild Bouquet, White .............................................................. 95.00
Pitcher, Water, Wreath & Shell, Blue .............................................................. 75.00
Pitcher, Water, Wreath & Shell, Vaseline ....................................................... 150.00
Pitcher, Wild Bouquet, White .......................................................................... 75.00
Pitcher, Windows, 6 Tumblers, Dated 1880-90, Cranberry ........................... 500.00
Pitcher, Zipper, Vaseline ................................................................................. 65.00
Plate, Bead & Scroll, Green, 10 In. ................................................................. 65.00
Plate, Tokyo, Green .......................................................................................... 25.00
Platter, Hobnail, Pink, Round .......................................................................... 52.00
Rose Bowl, Beaded Cable, Blue ...................................................................... 30.00
Rose Bowl, Beaded Drape, Green ................................................................... 42.00
Rose Bowl, Beaded Drape, Vaseline ............................................................... 30.00
Rose Bowl, Button Panels, Crystal ................................................................. 28.00
Rose Bowl, Crimped Edge, Hand-Painted, Polished Pontil, Green ............... 60.00
Rose Bowl, Daisy & Button, Vaseline ............................................................. 48.00
Rose Bowl, Hobnail, Vaseline ......................................................................... 55.00
Rose Bowl, Peacock Feather, Scroll Legs, 8 Crimp, Clear ........................... 65.00
Rose Bowl, Polka Dot, Windows, Ruffled, Cranberry .................................... 45.00
Rose Bowl, Sanibel, Crimped, Blue, 14 In. ..................................................... 50.00
Rose Bowl, Swirl, Blue, 4 1/2 In.Diam. ........................................................... 30.00
Rose Bowl, Wreath & Shell, Blue .................................................................... 65.00
Salt & Pepper, Beaded Oval In Sand, Blue .................................................... 90.00
Salt & Pepper, Cotton Bale, Blue ................................................................... 36.00
Salt & Pepper, Fluted Scrolls, Blue ............................................................... 80.00
Salt & Pepper, Lattice, Original Tops, Clear .................................................. 20.00
Salt & Pepper, Nestor, Blue ............................................................................ 40.00
Salt & Pepper, Scrolls, Footed, Green ............................................................ 55.00
Salt & Pepper, Sunset, Blue ............................................................................ 55.00
Salt, Hobnail, Blue ........................................................................................... 10.00
Salt, Wreath & Shell, Vaseline ........................................................................ 55.00
Salt, Wreath & Shell, White ............................................................................. 40.00
Saltshaker, Alaska, Blue .................................................................................. 85.00
Saltshaker, Circled Scroll, Clear ..................................................................... 18.50

**Saltshaker,** Fluted Scroll, Blue .................................................................................... 85.00
**Saltshaker,** Princess Swirl, Blue Flowers, Pair ........................................................ 20.00
**Saltshaker,** Reverse Swirl, Blue ................................................................................. 20.00
**Sauce,** Beatty Rib, Blue .............................................................................................. 15.00
**Sauce,** Everglades, Vaseline ...................................................................................... 32.50
**Sauce,** Fluted Scrolls, Enameled Flowers, Blue ....................................................... 35.00
**Sauce,** Honeycomb & Clover, Green .......................................................................... 20.00
**Sauce,** Sunburst On Shield, Vaseline ........................................................................ 25.00
**Sauce,** Tokyo, Green ................................................................................................... 18.00
**Saucer,** Ribbed Spiral, Yellow .................................................................................... 20.00
**Shade,** Vertical Stripes, Ruffled, Vaseline, 2 In.Fitter ............................................. 25.00
**Shoe,** Pump, Medium Heel, Diaper Pattern, France, Pair ........................................ 35.00
**Slipper,** Hobnail, Fenton, Blue ................................................................................... 12.50
**Slipper,** Hobnail, Fenton, Green ................................................................................. 25.00
**Spittoon,** Lady's, Winged Scroll, Blue ....................................................................... 110.00
**Spittoon,** Lady's, Wreath & Shell, Vaseline .............................................................. 60.00
**Spooner,** Alaska, Northwood, Green .......................................................................... 25.00
**Spooner,** Alaska, Vaseline .......................................................................................... 75.00
**Spooner,** Alaska, White ............................................................................................... 45.00
**Spooner,** Beveled Star, Green .................................................................................... 30.00
**Spooner,** Dolly Madison, Green .................................................................................. 65.00
**Spooner,** Everglades, Gold Trim, Blue ....................................................................... 70.00
**Spooner,** Fine Cut & Roses, Clear ............................................................................. 40.00
**Spooner,** Flora, Blue ................................................................................................... 65.00
**Spooner,** Fluted Scrolls, Blue .......................................................... 45.00 To 55.00
**Spooner,** Hobnail & Pan, Blue ................................................................................... 55.00
**Spooner,** Hobnail, Vaseline ....................................................................................... 60.00
**Spooner,** Intaglio, Blue ..................................................................... 70.00 To 80.00
**Spooner,** Iris & Meander, Clear ................................................................................. 50.00
**Spooner,** Jackson, Blue .............................................................................................. 45.00
**Spooner,** Jewel & Flower, Blue .................................................................................. 85.00
**Spooner,** Paneled Holly, Northwood, Blue ................................................................ 95.00
**Spooner,** Princess Feather, C.1875, White .............................................................. 300.00
**Spooner,** Swag & Bracket, Blue ..................................................... 38.00 To 60.00
**Spooner,** Swag & Bracket, Green .............................................................................. 49.00
**Spooner,** Tokyo, Blue & Gold .................................................................................... 45.00
**Spooner,** Wild Bouquet, Blue, Northwood ................................................................ 78.00
**Spooner,** Wreath & Shell, Blue ...................................................... 60.00 To 110.00
**Spooner,** Wreath & Shell, Vaseline ........................................................................... 95.00
**Spooner,** Wreath & Shell, White ................................................................................ 75.00
**Sugar & Creamer,** Alaska, Northwood, Blue ............................................................ 135.00
**Sugar & Creamer,** Alaska, Vaseline .......................................................................... 135.00
**Sugar & Creamer,** Child's, Hobnail, Blue ................................................................. 25.00
**Sugar & Creamer,** Fluted Scrolls, Vaseline .............................................................. 150.00
**Sugar & Creamer,** Hobnail, Blue ............................................................................... 25.00
**Sugar & Creamer,** Hobnail, Cranberry ...................................................................... 55.00
**Sugar & Creamer,** Louis XV, Northwood, Green & Gold .......................................... 150.00
**Sugar Shaker,** Bubble Lattice, Tapered, Blue .......................................................... 120.00
**Sugar Shaker,** Chrysanthemum Base Swirl, White .................................................. 85.00
**Sugar Shaker,** Diamond-Quilted, Ribbed, Blue ........................................................ 90.00
**Sugar Shaker,** Diamond-Quilted, Ribbed, Cranberry ............................................... 90.00
**Sugar Shaker,** Leaf Mold, Northwood, Mica Flecks, Pink & White ......................... 165.00
**Sugar Shaker,** Reverse Swirl, Blue ........................................................................... 90.00
**Sugar Shaker,** Reverse Swirl, Canary ....................................................................... 95.00
**Sugar Shaker,** Ribbed Lattice, Cranberry ...................................... 85.00 To 135.00
**Sugar Shaker,** Swirl, Silver Plated Top, Cranberry, 5 3/4 In. ................................. 65.00
**Sugar Shaker,** Swirl, 9 Panel, Original Top, Cranberry ........................................... 65.00
**Sugar,** Creamer, & Butter, Covered, Bird & Strawberry .......................................... 175.00
**Sugar,** Everglades, Covered, Blue ............................................................................ 175.00
**Sugar,** Everglades, Covered, Vaseline ...................................................................... 150.00
**Sugar,** Fine Cut & Roses, Open, Green ..................................................................... 55.00
**Sugar,** Fluted Scroll, Covered, Blue .......................................................................... 95.00
**Sugar,** Intaglio, Covered, Northwood, White ............................................................ 65.00

**Sugar**, Iris & Meander, Clear .................................................................................................. 65.00
**Sugar**, Sunburst On Shield, Open, Blue ............................................................. 40.00 To 45.00
**Sugar**, Wreath & Shell, Covered, White ...................................................................... 95.00
**Sugar**, Wreath & Shell, Open, Blue ............................................................................. 60.00
**Syrup**, Daisy In Criss-Cross, Blue ............................................................................. 325.00
**Syrup**, Polka Dot, Blue ............................................................................................... 185.00
**Syrup**, Reverse Swirl, Blue .......................................................................... 135.00 To 145.00
**Syrup**, Reverse Swirl, Clear Handle, Cranberry ....................................................... 195.00
**Syrup**, Ring Neck, Blue .............................................................................................. 155.00
**Syrup**, Swastika, White ............................................................................................... 145.00
**Table Set**, Beaded Swag, 4 Piece ............................................................................... 295.00
**Table Set**, Drapery, Gold Trim, Northwood, Blue ...................................................... 425.00
**Table Set**, Hobnail With Paneled Thumbprint, Vaseline ............................................ 395.00
**Table Set**, Intaglio, Blue, 4 Piece ............................................................................... 675.00
**Table Set**, Paneled Holly, Northwood, White, 3 Piece ............................................... 250.00
**Table Set**, Wreath & Shell, Blue, 4 Piece .................................................................. 550.00
**Table Set**, Wreath & Shell, Vaseline, 4 Piece ................................................ 400.00 To 695.00
**Table Set**, Wreath & Shell, White .............................................................................. 550.00
**Tankard**, Reverse Swirl, White ................................................................................... 110.00
**Toothpick**, Beatty Honeycomb.Blue ............................................................................ 40.00
**Toothpick**, Beatty Honeycomb, White ......................................................................... 40.00
**Toothpick**, Beatty Rib ................................................................................................... 33.00
**Toothpick**, Beatty Rib, Blue ............................................................................ 25.00 To 30.00
**Toothpick**, Chrysanthemum Swirl, Cranberry ............................................................ 135.00
**Toothpick**, Daisy & Button, Cat Holding Holder, Vaseline .......................................... 36.00
**Toothpick**, Diamond Spearhead, Green ...................................................................... 345.00
**Toothpick**, Fleur-De-Lis, Blue ...................................................................................... 19.00
**Toothpick**, Flora, White ............................................................................................... 150.00
**Toothpick**, Florette, Yellow .......................................................................................... 37.50
**Toothpick**, Hobnail, Blue .............................................................................................. 25.00
**Toothpick**, Hobnail, Vaseline ...................................................................................... 165.00
**Toothpick**, Hobnail, White ............................................................................................ 55.00
**Toothpick**, Iris With Meander, Vaseline ....................................................................... 85.00
**Toothpick**, Petticoat, Vaseline, Gold Trim .................................................................. 325.00
**Toothpick**, Ribbed Lattice, Blue ................................................................................... 65.00
**Toothpick**, Ribbed Lattice, Cranberry ............................................................ 110.00 To 325.00
**Toothpick**, Ribbed Spiral, Vaseline .............................................................................. 75.00
**Toothpick**, Vermont Custard, Blue & Floral ................................................................. 75.00
**Toothpick**, Wild Bouquet, Blue ................................................................................... 225.00
**Toothpick**, Wild Bouquet, White ................................................................................. 125.00
**Toothpick**, Wreath & Shell, Blue .................................................................... 150.00 To 165.00
**Tray**, Card, Argonaut Shell, Northwood, Vaseline ........................................................ 42.00
**Tumbler**, Beaded Swag ................................................................................................ 58.00
**Tumbler**, Beatty Rib, Blue ............................................................................................ 48.00
**Tumbler**, Beatty Rib, Clear .......................................................................................... 37.00
**Tumbler**, Beatty Rib, White .......................................................................................... 24.00
**Tumbler**, Beaumont Columbia, Gold Trim, Vaseline ................................................... 45.00
**Tumbler**, Bubble Lattice, Cranberry ............................................................................ 35.00
**Tumbler**, Cherry & Lattice, Green ................................................................................ 18.00
**Tumbler**, Chrysanthemum ............................................................................................ 28.00
**Tumbler**, Chrysanthemum Sprig, Blue ....................................................................... 225.00
**Tumbler**, Chrysanthemum, Cranberry ......................................................................... 45.00
**Tumbler**, Daffodil, Blue ................................................................................................ 45.00
**Tumbler**, Daffodil, Green .............................................................................................. 35.00
**Tumbler**, Daisy & Fern, Blue ........................................................................................ 15.00
**Tumbler**, Diamond Spearhead, Vaseline ..................................................................... 47.50
**Tumbler**, Drapery, Northwood, Blue ............................................................................ 33.00
**Tumbler**, Everglades, N, Blue ...................................................................................... 65.00
**Tumbler**, Fluted Scrolls, Blue .......................................................................... 10.00 To 40.00
**Tumbler**, Hobnail, Pink, Juice, Set Of 6 ..................................................................... 115.00
**Tumbler**, Hobnail, 10-Row, Cranberry, 3 7/8 In. ........................................................ 95.00
**Tumbler**, Hobnail, 12 Rows Of Hobs On Each, Clear, Set Of 5 ................................. 160.00
**Tumbler**, Iris & Meander, Blue ..................................................................................... 45.00

Tumbler, Jackson, White ............................................................................................ 25.00
Tumbler, Jeweled Heart, Green ................................................................................ 42.00
Tumbler, Jeweled Heart, White ................................................................................ 28.00
Tumbler, Maiden Blush, Michigan, Gold Trim ...................................................... 45.00
Tumbler, Paneled Holly, Gold Trim, White ........................................................... 25.00
Tumbler, Poinsettia, Blue .......................................................................... 30.00 To 38.00
Tumbler, Poinsettia, Green, Signed N ..................................................................... 22.00
Tumbler, Regal, N, Blue .............................................................................................. 65.00
Tumbler, Reverse Swirl, Clear, With White ........................................................... 25.00
Tumbler, Swag With Brackets, Vaseline ................................................................ 35.00
Tumbler, Swirl Pattern, Blue & White Beading, Cranberry, 4 In. ..................... 110.00
Tumbler, Thumbprint, Blue, 5 1/4 In. ..................................................................... 35.00
Tumbler, Water Lily With Cattails, Blue ................................................................ 40.00
Tumbler, Wild Bouquet, Green, Northwood ......................................................... 25.00
Vase, Cafe Au Lait, Scenic, Raised Enameling, 11 1/2 In. ............................... 65.00
Vase, Corn, Vaseline, 8 In. ........................................................................................ 85.00
Vase, Dahlia Twist, White, 7 In. ............................................................................... 22.00
Vase, Diamond Point, Blue, Northwood, 11 In. .................................................... 30.00
Vase, Diamond Point, Clear, Northwood, 13 In. .................................................. 20.00
Vase, Fan Shape, Hobnail, Blue, 7 1/2 In. ............................................................ 47.50
Vase, Fan Shape, Hobnail, Vaseline, 6 In. ........................................................... 27.50
Vase, Footed, Basketweave, Green, 5 In. ............................................................. 20.00
Vase, Hobnail, Footed, Pink, 7 1/2 In. ................................................................... 25.00
Vase, Hobnail, Footed, Plum, 11 In. ....................................................................... 35.00
Vase, Hobnail, Ruffled Rim, White, 8 In. ............................................................... 23.00
Vase, Hobnail, Vaseline, 2 1/2 X 3 1/2 In. ............................................................ 24.00
Vase, Ocean Shell, Blue ............................................................................................ 40.00
Vase, Piasa Bird, Footed, White, 10 In. ................................................................. 30.00
Vase, Ribbed Spiral, Canary, 10 In. ........................................................................ 24.50
Vase, Ribbed, White, 7 1/2 In. .................................................................................. 16.00
Vase, Ribs & Diamonds, Clear, 12 3/4 In. ............................................................. 24.00
Vase, Spool, Green ...................................................................................................... 26.00
Vase, Swirl, Clear To White, 7 In. ........................................................................... 40.00
Vase, Swirl, Hat Shape, Ruffled Square Rim, Cranberry, 6 1/2 In. .................. 75.00
Vase, Tokyo, Green, 10 In. ......................................................................................... 25.00
Vase, Twig, Blue, 5 In. ................................................................................................ 45.00
Water Set, Cherry & Lattice, Gold Trim, Green, 7 Piece .................................... 187.00
Water Set, Drapery, Blue, 7 Piece ........................................................... 325.00 To 375.00
Water Set, Fenton, Vaseline ..................................................................................... 130.00
Water Set, Jeweled Heart, White, 7 Piece ........................................................... 325.00
Water Set, Memphis, N, Green, 7 Piece ................................................................ 350.00
Water Set, Paneled Holly, Northwood, White, Pitcher, 4 Tumblers ................. 250.00
Water Set, Swirl, Cranberry ...................................................................................... 135.00

*Opaline, or opal glass, was made in white, green, and other colors. The glass had a matte surface and a lack of transparency. It was often gilded or painted. It was a popular mid-nineteenth-century European glassware.*

OPALINE, Bottle, Perfume, Luster Pearl Opalescent Design, Nudes, 6 1/2 In. ........................ 100.00
Lamp, Enameled Children, Pink Ground, White, 22 In. ...................................... 245.00
Pitcher, Water, Spatter Glass, Clear, 10 In. .......................................................... 110.00
Vase, Campagna Form, Ormolu Mounts, 5 In. ..................................................... 110.00
Vase, Full Figure Girl, Hand-Painted, Signed, 8 In. ........................................... 285.00
Vase, Gilt Handled, Enameled Flowers, Jewels, Gray, 8 1/2 In., Pair ........... 295.00

OPERA GLASSES, Flowers, Mother-Of-Pearl, Enameled, French ................... 125.00
French, Bouquets Of Flowers, Enameled, Blue Ground ................................... 110.00
French, Brass & Pearl .................................................................................................. 35.00
Lemaire, Paris, Mother-Of-Pearl, Case ................................................................. 40.00
Lorgnette, Rococo Case, Victorian, Gold, C.1880, American ........................... 675.00
Mermode & Jaccards, France, Mother-Of-Pearl Handle ..................................... 35.00
Metal, Occupied Japan ............................................................................................... 20.00
Mother-Of-Pearl Covered, E.G.Wood, Boston ..................................................... 32.00
Mother-Of-Pearl, Brass Trim, Leping, Paris, 3 3/4 X 2 1/4 In. ....................... 14.00

Mother-Of-Pearl, Brass, Lemaire, Paris ........................................................ 40.00
Mother-Of-Pearl, Gold Trim, Case, Marked Latour, Paris ........................... 60.00
Mother-Of-Pearl, Paris, 1882, Telescopic Handle .................................... 57.00
Pearl, Handled, Marked Paris ...................................................................... 75.00
Red & Silver Brocade, Snap-Up Case, Vesta, Japan ............................... 25.00
Tortoise Handle, Gold Design On Handle, Signed Tiffany ........................ 140.00
    ORGAN, see Music, Organ

ORPHAN ANNIE, Ad, Ovaltine, 10 In. ........................................................ 5.00
Bandana ....................................................................................................... 45.00
Big Little Book ............................................................................................ 15.00
Book, Pop-Up, 1935 .................................................................................. 75.00
Book, Secret Society, Radio, 1936 ........................................................... 25.00
Code Manual, 1936 .................................................................................... 25.00
Coin, Good Luck ........................................................................................ 15.00
Cup, Ceramic ............................................................................................. 25.00
Cup, Shaker, Top ....................................................................................... 25.00
Decoder, 1935 ..................................................................... 22.00 To 25.00
Decoder, 1937 ........................................................................................... 18.00
Decoder, 1938 ........................................................................................... 12.00
Decoder, 1940 ........................................................................................... 20.00
Doll, Bisque, Jointed, German ................................................................... 32.00
Doll, Cloth Face & Body, Mohair Hair, Dressed, 18 In. ....................... 110.00
Doll, Sandy, Wooden, Jointed .................................................................. 80.00
Figural, Standing By Basket, Bisque, 3 1/2 In. ..................................... 15.00
Game, Treasure Hunt, 1933 .............................................. 40.00 To 45.00
Game, 1935 ................................................................................................ 45.00
Holder, Toothbrush .................................................................................... 50.00
Mug, Beetleware ........................................................................................ 25.00
Mug, Ovaltine ............................................................................................. 13.50
Mug, Signed Harold Gray .......................................................................... 30.00
Music, Sheet, Ovaltine, 1931 ................................................................... 10.00
Pastry Set ................................................................................................... 25.00
Pin, Secret Society ............................................................... 5.00 To 15.00
Purse, Carried By Sandy, 1920s ............................................................. 200.00
Shaker, Ovaltine, Bettleware ............................................ 12.00 To 35.00
Skipping Rope, Windup, Tin ..................................................................... 225.00
Stove, Electric, 1930s ............................................................................... 65.00
Stove, Tin .................................................................................................... 20.00
Wristwatch, Ingersoll, Boxed ................................................................... 150.00

Orrefors Glassworks, located in the Swedish province of Smaaland, was established in 1916.

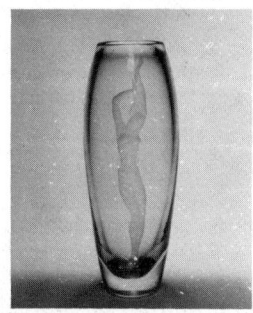

Orrefors, Vase, Designed By Karl Lindstrand, C.1930, 13 5/8 In.

ORREFORS, Ashtray, Internal Fish & Seaweed, Signed, 6 In. ................................................ 185.00
    Bowl, Etched, Inscribed, 8 3/4 In. ...................................................................................... 800.00
    Cathedral Set, Decanter, 2 Glasses .................................................................................. 90.00
    Cruet, Crystal, Clear .......................................................................................................... 80.00
    Toothpick, Ice Blue ............................................................................................................ 25.00
    Toothpick, Signed & Dated 1959 ...................................................................................... 45.00
    Vase, Acid Etched Fish, Dated 1916, Signed, 9 1/2 In. ................................................ 850.00
    Vase, Designed By Karl Lindstrand, C.1930, 13 5/8 In. .................................. *Illus* 700.00
    Vase, Full Figure Dancing Nude, 6-Sided, Signed, 9 1/2 In. ........................................ 225.00
    Vase, Nude Dancer, Smoky, 8 In. ...................................................................................... 150.00
    Vase, Swan, Signed, 6 1/2 In. .......................................................................................... 125.00

*Ott & Brewer Company operated the Etruria Pottery at Trenton,*
*New Jersey, from 1863 to 1893. It was under the direction of*
*William Bromley, Sr., from the Belleek factory at Belleek, Ireland,*
*from 1883.*

OTT & BREWER, Creamer, Pansies, 3 1/4 In. .................................................................. 165.00
    Cup & Saucer, Demitasse, Cactus, Gold Wishbone Handle, Marked ......................... 150.00
    Pitcher, Gold Paste, Sponge Gold, Cream Ground, Crown & Sword ......................... 385.00

OVERBECK, Figurine, Squirrel, Hand-Modeled, Signed, 1 X 1 In. .............................. 165.00

*Owens Pottery was made in Zanesville, Ohio, from 1891 to 1928. The*
**OWENS**   *first art pottery was made after 1896. Utopian Ware, Cyrano, Navarre,*
**UTOPIAN**  *Feroza, and Henri Deux were made. Pieces were usually marked with a form*
*of the name Owens. About 1907 the firm began to make tile and gave up the*
*art pottery wares.*

OWENS, Ewer, Utopian, Signed Steele, 6 In. .................................................................. 175.00
    Feeder, Invalid, Lotus, White Dogwood Blossoms, Gray Ground, 7 1/2 In. ............... 175.00
    Feeder, Invalid,White Dogwood Blossoms, Lotus, Gray Ground, 7 In. ..................... 175.00
    Jardiniere & Pedestal, Utopian, Matte ............................................................................ 350.00
    Jug, Ear Of Corn On Standard Glaze, Marked Utopian, 8 In. ...................................... 175.00
    Jug, Left Handed, Currants & Green Leaves, Signed, 5 1/2 In. .................................. 175.00
    Mug, Utopian, Berries, Artist Signed .............................................................................. 145.00
    Mug, Utopian, Cherry Clusters & Leaves ........................................................................ 155.00
    Mug, Utopian, Tulips & Leaves On Front, Dated April 21, 1908, 5 1/4 In. ............... 125.00
    Pitcher, Lotus, Stork On One Leg, Gray To Blue ............................................................ 275.00
    Pitcher, Utopian, Berry Design, Ice Lip, Signed F, 9 In. .............................................. 225.00
    Tile, Butterfly, Geometric, Carved, Marked, 5 3/4 In.Square .................................... 105.00
    Tile, Landscape, Rust, Green, & Blue, Outlined In White, 12 X 9 In. ......................... 350.00
    Vase, Bottle Shape, Utopian, Brown Matte, Signed, 10 In. ........................................ 265.00
    Vase, Brown, Orange, & Green Leaves, Marked, Artist Signed, 7 1/2 In. ................. 155.00
    Vase, Bulbous, Orange & Yellow Flowers, 12 In. .......................................................... 135.00
    Vase, Cylindrical, Green To Brown High-Gloss Ground, 11 In. .................................. 120.00
    Vase, Cyrano, Footed Pillow .............................................................................................. 95.00
    Vase, Green To Brown, High-Gloss, Florals, Cylindrical, 11 In. ................................ 120.00
    Vase, Handled, Nude Figure, Marked, 8 X 2 X 6 In. ...................................................... 98.50
    Vase, Leaf Design, High-Blending Glaze, Marked, 10 3/4 In. .................................... 150.00
    Vase, Mission, 11 1/2 In. .................................................................................................. 250.00
    Vase, Portrait, Indian, Silver Overlay, Brown, Green, C.1900, 7 1/4 In. ................. 3000.00
    Vase, Red Cherries, Utopian Matte, 3-Handled, Henry Fuchs, 7 In. ......................... 125.00
    Vase, Utopian, Cylindrical Neck, Brown & Green Leaves, 11 1/2 In. ....................... 133.00
    Vase, Utopian, Inverted Cone Shape, Tulips, Incised Mark, 11 1/4 In. ................... 130.00
    Vase, Utopian, Rose Tree, Signed, 12 In. ...................................................................... 85.00
    Vase, Utopian, Swirled, Nasturtium & Open Rose, 14 In., Pair .................................. 350.00

OYSTER PLATE, Bright Colors, Marked Austria, 8 X 9 In.Diam. .............................. 38.00
    Elite, Limoges .................................................................................................................... 39.50
    Fish Scene ............................................................................................................................ 32.00
    Horseshoe Shape ................................................................................................................ 45.00

| | |
|---|---|
| **Pink Blush,** Black Divisions, White | 85.00 |
| **Pink Luster Rim Inside,** White | 30.00 |
| **Purple Luster Trim,** 8 1/2 In. | 18.00 |
| **Turquoise,** Pink & Yellow, 10 In. | 80.00 |
| **4 Shells,** Scallop & Clamshell Center, Gold Border | 18.00 |

*Paden City Glass Manufacturing Company was established in 1916 at Paden City, West Virginia. It is best known for glasswares but also produced a pottery line. The firm closed in 1951.*

| | |
|---|---|
| **PADEN CITY, Bowl,** Fruit, Peacock & Rose, 10 In. | 18.00 |
| **Figurine,** Chinese Pheasant | 49.75 |
| **Figurine,** Fighting Cocks, Clear, Pair | 145.00 |
| **Figurine,** Horse, Solid, Clear, 11 In. | 65.00 |
| **Figurine,** Pheasant, Blue | 75.00 |
| **Figurine,** Pony, Light Blue, 11 1/2 In., Pair | 300.00 |
| **Figurine,** Pouter Pigeon | 42.25 |
| **Figurine,** Rooster, Head Down | 29.75 |
| **Figurine,** Standing Pony | 69.75 |
| **Lamp Base,** Dolphin, Amber | 55.00 |
| **Plate,** Ivory, Blue Stripe, Woman At Spinning Wheel, 13 In. | 9.50 |
| **Platter,** Ivory, Gold Design, Lavender Tulip, Salmon Rose, 14 In. | 8.50 |
| **Platter,** Reverse Willow, Oval, 12 In. | 20.00 |
| **Reamer,** Amber | 19.50 |
| **Server,** Green, Center Handle, Gypsy Etching, 11 In. | 35.00 |
| **Vase,** Peacock, Pink, Oval, 8 1/2 In. | 55.00 |

| | |
|---|---|
| **PAINTING, Ink & Watercolor On Silk,** Johann Strauss Home, Signed, 10 X 7 In. | 35.00 |
| **On Ivory,** Dutchman, Rembrandt Style, Framed, Limoges, 9 1/2 X 7 In. | 300.00 |
| **On Ivory,** Dutchmen At Inn, Gilt & Enamel Frame, 5 1/2 X 4 1/4 In. | 2000.00 |
| **On Ivory,** Gentleman, Ivory Frame, 5 5/8 X 4 7/8 In. | 195.00 |
| **On Ivory,** German, 1800-38, Ferdinand Berthold, 2 1/4 In. | 250.00 |
| **On Ivory,** Lady Hamilton, Signed JoulRy | 200.00 |
| **On Ivory,** Lady, Feathers In Hair, Ivory & Tortoise Frame, Signed | 425.00 |
| **On Ivory,** Lady, Ivory Frame, 5 5/8 X 4 7/8 In. | 195.00 |
| **On Ivory,** Lady's Portrait, Gilt Frame, Oval, 3 1/8 X 4 In. | 175.00 |
| **On Ivory,** Lady's Portrait, Oval Enamel & Gilt Frame, 3 1/4 X 4 In. | 175.00 |
| **On Ivory,** Lord Hamilton, Signed JoulRy | 200.00 |
| **On Ivory,** Lovely Lady, Framed, Oval, 1 5/8 X 2 In. | 125.00 |
| **On Ivory,** Marie Antoinette, Signed JoulRy | 200.00 |
| **On Ivory,** Two Rabbis Playing Chess, 5 X 7 In. | 135.00 |
| **On Ivory,** W.Cross, Black Coat, Gold Plated, Case, C.1804, American | 225.00 |
| **On Ivory,** Woman In Court Dress, Bronze Frame, Signed C.Fremont | 180.00 |
| **On Porcelain,** Boy In Turban, Gilt Bronze Frame, 3 3/4 X 2 3/4 In. | 165.00 |
| **On Porcelain,** Chateau Des Tuileries, Gilded Border, Sevres, 10 In. | 225.00 |
| **On Porcelain,** Couple, Baby Dressed For Christening, 6 1/2 X 4 In. | 300.00 |
| **On Porcelain,** Lady Holding Baby Jesus, Signed, 6 In. | 125.00 |
| **On Porcelain,** Lisette, Signed George Hom, Framed, 5 1/4 In. | 500.00 |
| **On Porcelain,** Madonna & Child, Gilt Rococo Frame, Gilt, 3 1/2 In. | 250.00 |
| **On Porcelain,** Madonna Della Sedia, Gilt Frame, Germany, 9 3/4 In. | 1900.00 |
| **On Porcelain,** Stately Gentleman, Gold Leaf Frame, Oval, 2 1/2 In. | 225.00 |
| **On Wood,** Mother Breast-Feeding Baby, 18th Century, 9 1/2 X 13 In. | 550.00 |
| **Reverse On Glass,** Billiard Room, Oak Frame, Gold Leaf, 9 X 5 In. | 750.00 |
| **Reverse On Glass,** George Washington, C.1800, Oval, 9 X 11 In. | 450.00 |
| **Reverse On Glass,** Panel, Perched Birds, Teak Frame, 13 X 19 In. | 350.00 |
| **Reverse On Glass,** Roses On Black Glass, Framed, 20 X 14 In. | 65.00 |
| **Reverse On Glass,** Shade, Flowers, Pink, Blue, & Black, Large | 375.00 |
| **Reverse On Glass,** Silhouette, Woman Spinning, Frame, 12 X 15 In. | 35.00 |
| **Reverse On Glass,** Spring, German, Oval Frame, 4 X 5 1/2 In. | 18.00 |
| **Reverse On Glass,** Titanic Sinking, Framed, 31 X 17 In. | 45.00 |
| **Reverse On Glass,** U.S.Capitol, Gold Oval Frame, 22 X 16 In. | 45.00 |
| **Watercolor,** Theorem, Shut The Cat, Velvet, 13 X 9 In. *Illus* | 600.00 |

Painting, Watercolor, Theorem, Shut
The Cat, Velvet, 13 X 9 In.

*Pairpoint Corporation was a silver and glass firm founded in New Bedford, Massachusetts, in 1880.*

| | |
|---|---|
| **PAIRPOINT, Atomizer,** Canary Color, Engraved Design, Bubble Ball Stem, 14 In. | 225.00 |
| **Basket,** Cake, Footed, Floral Repousse, Silver Plate, Square | 75.00 |
| **Basket,** Cherries, Silver Frosted, Handled, 10 In. | 75.00 |
| **Basket,** Cranberry Glass Liner, Ring Handled, C.1885, 7 X 4 In. | 95.00 |
| **Basket,** Fruit, Handled, Footed, Etched Lily Design | 68.00 |
| **Basket,** Handled, Silver Frosted Cherries, 10 In. | 75.00 |
| **Basket,** Little Bird Sits On Rim, Small | 28.00 |
| **Basket,** Sweetmeat, Footed, Pierced & Fluted, Beaded Edging | 35.00 |
| **Bonbon,** Basket, Openwork, Handle | 45.00 |
| **Bottle,** Perfume, Footed, Stopper, 11 In. | 89.00 |
| **Bowl,** Burmese, Basket Weave, Painted Pansies, 2 1/2 X 3 3/4 In. | 285.00 |
| **Bowl,** Cabbage Leaf Design, Footed, Silver Plate, 9 In. | 25.00 |
| **Bowl,** Fruit, Cabbage Leaf Pattern, Apple Twig Feet, 9 In.Diam. | 40.00 |
| **Bowl,** Nut, Double, Figural Squirrel | 275.00 |
| **Box,** Covered, Wing Collar Shape, Silk Lined, 2 1/2 In. | 45.00 |
| **Box,** Hairpin, Woman's Friend, Ornate | 20.00 |
| **Breakfast Set,** Scrolled Handled & Design, Signed, 6 Piece | 125.00 |
| **Bucket,** Ice, Intaglio Cut, Silver Plate Swing Handle, 6 In. | 75.00 |
| **Butter,** Nevada, Covered | 350.00 |
| **Butter,** Pressed Glass Cow Insert, Covered | 58.00 |
| **Candelabra,** 3-Branch, Applied Orchids, Signed | 60.00 |
| **Candletstick,** Diamond Cut, Gold Ormolu & Marble Base, 15 In., Pair | 1500.00 |
| **Castor,** Pickle, Silver Plated Inset, Lid, & Tongs | 95.00 |
| **Castor,** Pickle, Tongs, Ruby Enameled Flower Insert, Signed | 250.00 |
| **Chalice,** Controlled Bubble Stem, 12 In. | 185.00 |
| **Compote,** Amber Foot & Rim, Berries, Intaglio Cut, 4 1/2 In. | 70.00 |
| **Compote,** Bubble Ball, Amethyst, 8 X 8 In. | 50.00 |
| **Compote,** Design Of Raspberries & Leaves, Amber, 7 X 8 1/2 In. | 85.00 |
| **Compote,** Etched Grapes & Leaves, Amber, 7 X 9 In.Diam. | 165.00 |
| **Compote,** Marble Base, Silver Plate Cupids Support Bowl, 8 In. | 220.00 |
| **Compote,** Ruby Flashed, Covered, Ball Stem | 48.00 |
| **Compote,** Stemmed, Painted Grapes & Leaves Inside, Signed, 7 In. | 275.00 |
| **Compote,** Victoria, 7 1/4 X 8 1/4 In. | 100.00 |
| **Console Set,** Amber With Clear Controlled Bubble Stem, 8 X 15 In. | 500.00 |
| **Cracker Jar,** Burmese Design, Signed, 7 In. | 445.00 |
| **Cracker Jar,** Hand-Painted | 95.00 |
| **Cup,** Reticulated, Milk Glass Insert, Silver Plate | 25.00 |
| **Decanter,** Flambeau, Signed | 125.00 |
| **Decanter,** Intaglio Fruit, Flute Cut Neck, Teardrop, Stopper, 11 In. | 110.00 |
| **Dish,** Sweetmeat, Reticulated, Oval, 8 In. | 65.00 |
| **Dish,** Sweetmeat, Rose Design, Opaline | 95.00 |

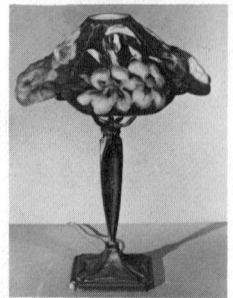

Pairpoint, Lamp, Puffy, 16 In.

| | |
|---|---|
| **Figurine,** Swan, Ruby, 12 In. | 142.00 |
| **Goblet,** Flambeau | 79.00 |
| **Hat,** Contemporary High-Crowned, Blue & Pink, Label, 4 In. | 55.00 |
| **Humidor,** Wine Bottle Shape, Bottom Stores Cigars, 10 1/2 In. | 165.00 |
| **Inkwell,** Controlled Bubbles, Sterling Silver Lid, 4 In. | 135.00 |
| **Ladle,** Hobstar Handle With Teardrop | 390.00 |
| **Lamp Base,** Quadruple Plate, Silver, 10 In. | 85.00 |
| **Lamp,** Blown Out, Poppy, Red, Signed Base, 12 X 18 In. | 2500.00 |
| **Lamp,** Dolphin Astral, Engraved Blue Glass Font, Cut Shade | 1150.00 |
| **Lamp,** Fleur-De-Lis Pattern, Coralene-Type Finish, Signed, 22 In. | 750.00 |
| **Lamp,** Kerosene, Oriental Design, Mice Feet | 325.00 |
| **Lamp,** Puffy Pansy, Yellow, White, Green, & Purple, Signed | 950.00 |
| **Lamp,** Puffy Piano, Poppies Design | 850.00 |
| **Lamp,** Puffy, 16 In. | *Illus* 2300.00 |
| **Lamp,** Reverse Floral Painted, 22 In. | 1450.00 |
| **Lamp,** Reverse Painted Shade, Mahogany Urn Shaped Base, 13 In. | 475.00 |
| **Lamp,** Reverse Painted Shade, Scenic, Signed, Shade, 16 In.Diam. | 2300.00 |
| **Lamp,** Reverse Painted, Carlisle, Signed, 4 In. | 1150.00 |
| **Lamp,** Rose Bouquet, Floral Base, Signed, 12 In. | 3975.00 |
| **Mustache Cup & Saucer,** Floral Embossing, Marked | 125.00 |
| **Mustache Cup,** Band Of Flowers On Top, Silver Plate Rim | 85.00 |
| **Penholder,** Chinaman Seated On Base Holds Receptacle, 3 In. | 65.00 |
| **Pitcher,** Golden-Amber, Vintage Pattern, Sterling Band At Top | 150.00 |
| **Pitcher,** Sugar, & Creamer, 10 In. | 35.00 |
| **Pitcher,** Water, Vintage Pattern, Sterling Silver Top Band | 125.00 |
| **Planter,** Brass Case, Glass Liner | 30.00 |
| **Salt,** Lay Down Egg, Blue Delft Decorated | 65.00 |
| **Shaker,** Cocktail, Intaglio Cut Flowers, Silver Plate Cover, 9 In. | 75.00 |
| **Shaving Mug,** Milk Glass Insert, Silver Plate | 50.00 |
| **Spooner,** Handles, Hunting Scene, Gold Washed Bowl | 65.00 |
| **Sugar & Creamer,** Tankard Shape, Art Nouveau, Signed | 58.00 |
| **Sugar & Creamer,** Twig Handles, Raised Fruit, Gold Washed | 75.00 |
| **Syrup,** Flower Etching, Silver Feet & Lid, 6 1/2 In. | 25.00 |
| **Tea Set,** Footed, Art Nouveau, Floral Engraving, 4 Piece | 225.00 |
| **Toothpick,** Blue, House, Glossy | 32.00 |
| **Tureen,** Trimmed Handles, Knob Finial, 60 Ounce | 75.00 |
| **Vase,** Clear Crystal, Engraved Flowers, Signed, 6 In. | 95.00 |
| **Vase,** Cornucopia, Paperweight Base, Red To Clear, 8 In. | 75.00 |
| **Vase,** Crystal, Flared Top, Paperweight Stem, 12 3/4 In. | 75.00 |
| **Vase,** End-Of-Day, Jack-In-The-Pulpit, Varicolored, Label, 9 In. | 65.00 |
| **Vase,** Flared, Paperweight Stem, Cut, 12 3/4 X 6 1/2 In.Diam. | 75.00 |
| **Vase,** Grape Leaf Pattern, Amber, 9 1/2 In. | 150.00 |
| **Vase,** Ruby, Air Bubble Ball Stem, 12 In. | 150.00 |
| **Vase,** Trumpet, Ruffled, Ruby Red Over Crystal, , 13 1/4 In. | 210.00 |
| **Wine Cooler,** Bubble Connector Ball, 9 1/2 X 10 In.Diam. | 95.00 |

| | |
|---|---|
| **PAPER DOLL, Amy Carter** | 4.50 |
| **Annie Laurie,** Uncut | 20.00 |
| **Baby Peggy Doll,** F.Tipton Hunter, Uncut, 1925 | 15.00 |
| **Baby,** 6 Dolls, Babies To Toddlers, Betty Sisson, 1949 | 14.00 |
| **Barbour's Irish Flax Threads,** Grape Costume, 2 Girls | 10.00 |
| **Betsy McCall & Linda,** Fold-Out Sheet Of Clothes, 1968 | 4.00 |
| **Betsy McCall,** 1951 Magazine, 60 Sheets | 60.00 |
| **Blondie,** Uncut, 1968 | 9.00 |
| **Captain Marvel,** Mary Marvel, & Captain Marvel, Jr., Punchout, 1945 | 15.00 |
| **Captain Marvel,** 1944 | 16.00 |
| **Clark's Dolls Of All Nations,** Turkish Boy | 5.00 |
| **Claudette Colbert,** 3 Dolls, 8 Pages, Uncut, 1945 | 68.00 |
| **College Cousins,** Graduation Gowns, Betty Bonnet, Uncut, 1917 | 10.00 |
| **College Sister,** Lady & Clothes, Betty Bonnet | 15.00 |
| **Cuba,** 3 Men, 2 Ladies, Chicago's Record Herald, Uncut, 1900s | 6.00 |
| **Debbie Reynolds,** Original Folder, Cut | 26.00 |
| **Deerfield Set,** Colonial Home, 6 Sheets Of Children, Uncut, 1919 | 50.00 |
| **Dennison's Dolls & Dresses** | 75.00 |
| **Dionne Quintuplets,** Sleepytown, Uncut | 40.00 |
| **Dolly Dingle,** Patriotic Party, Uncut, 1918 | 18.00 |
| **Donna Reed,** 2 Dolls, Bathing Suits & Clothes, Uncut, 1959-64 | 17.00 |
| **Doris Day,** Cut | 8.00 |
| **Dr.Kildaire & Nurse Susan,** Uncut | 10.00 |
| **Elizabeth Taylor,** Cut | 7.00 |
| **Eve Arden,** Cut | 12.00 |
| **Fairy Tale,** Puss 'n Boots, G.Drayton, Uncut | 25.00 |
| **Father & Mother,** Clothes, Betty Bonnet, 1916 | 15.00 |
| **Gale Storm,** Cut | 7.00 |
| **Gentleman,** Edwardian Type, Evening Dress, Moustache, 5 In. | 12.00 |
| **Gigi Perreau,** Uncut, 1951 | 12.00 |
| **Good Housekeeping,** 11 Sheets, 1925 | 75.00 |
| **Grace Kelly,** Cut | 8.00 |
| **Gulliver's Travels,** Clothes & Costumes, 1939 | 35.00 |
| **Haley Mills,** Cut | 7.00 |
| **Historical Deerfield,** Children, Indians, Wigwam, 1909 | 40.00 |
| **Housekeeping With Kuddle Kiddies,** 2 Children, Furniture, 1936 | 15.00 |
| **Italian Soldier,** Delineator, 1918 | 8.00 |
| **Italian Twins** | 7.00 |
| **Jack & Jill,** Uncut, 18 Cutouts, 1950s | 24.00 |
| **Jane Russell,** 3 Dolls, Clothes, Jeanne Voelz, Uncut, 1955 | 15.00 |
| **Japanese Twins** | 7.00 |
| **Julie Andrews,** Glamorous Clothes, 1958 | 20.00 |
| **Kewpie,** Coloring, Uncut | 18.00 |
| **Ladies Of The White House,** Uncut | 25.00 |
| **Lady,** Lithographed, Bustle Dress, Red Outfit | 15.00 |
| **Lennon Sisters,** Cut | 7.00 |
| **Lettie Lane,** 2 Sets | 38.00 |
| **Lettie's Party Of Little People,** Fancy Dress Costumes, 1909 | 15.00 |
| **Li'l Abner,** Half Cut, 1941 | 18.00 |
| **Little Flora Fair,** McLaughlin | 18.00 |
| **Little Miss Muffet,** 1 Doll, Clothes, Uncut, 1969 | 3.00 |
| **Lucky Strike Flat 50 With Lilyan Tashman Dolls** | 8.00 |
| **Margaret O'Brien,** Cut | 22.00 |
| **Marlo Thomas,** That Girl, Uncut | 8.00 |
| **Mary Pickford,** Cut, 1916 | 7.00 |
| **Mickey & Minnie Mouse,** Heavy Cardboard, 5 Outfits, 1932 | 45.00 |
| **Mother Goose,** Cutout Picture Book | 18.00 |
| **My Fair Lady,** 5 Dolls, Uncut, 1965 | 10.00 |
| **Nancy & Her Skates,** 1923 | 6.00 |
| **Natalie Wood,** Cut | 7.00 |
| **Nursery Rhyme,** Lion Coffee, Set Of 6 | 14.00 |
| **Old-Fashioned 1890s Lady,** Folding Skirt, Hat, & Blouse | 15.00 |

| | |
|---|---|
| **Pat Boone,** Cut | 7.00 |
| **Pat Nixon** | 15.00 |
| **Patty Duke,** Cut | 7.00 |
| **Peggy Pride & Her Playmates,** Uncut, 1926 | 10.00 |
| **Pepe,** Senoritas, Cantinflas Star | 12.00 |
| **Peter Pan,** Uncut, 1917 | 12.00 |
| **Peter Pan's Movie Contest,** Who Are They, Uncut, 1917 | 25.00 |
| **Polly & Her Playmates,** 4 Girls, Wrap-Around Dresses, Uncut, 1951 | 9.00 |
| **Polly Pratt Goes To Vacation Camp,** 2 Sheets, 1919 | 15.00 |
| **Polly's Paper Playmates,** Boston Post, Uncut, 1911 | 15.00 |
| **Polly's Sister Has A June Wedding,** Good Housekeeping, 1921 | 12.00 |
| **Queen Elizabeth II,** Coronation Gown, Uncut, 1953 | 15.00 |
| **Rose O'Neill,** Kewpieville | 50.00 |
| **Santa Claus & Judy,** Nursery Rhyme Figures, G.Kay, Uncut, 1923 | 6.00 |
| **Shirley Temple,** Uncut | 4.00 |
| **Shirley Temple,** 4 Dolls & Clothing, 1934 | 80.00 |
| **Sleeping Beauty,** Characters From Movie, Folder Book, Uncut | 21.00 |
| **Three Little Girls Who Grew & Grew,** Uncut, 1945 | 13.00 |
| **Tom Corbett,** Space Cadet, Uncut, 1952 | 20.00 |
| **Tricia Nixon,** Uncut | 8.00 |
| **Tuck Anne,** Cut, 1894 | 55.00 |
| **Tuesday Weld,** Cut | 7.00 |
| **Twiggy** | 12.50 |
| **Victorian Mother & Daughter,** Orangeine | 5.00 |
| **Wedding Of Paper Dolls,** 10 Figures, 41 Outfits, 1932 | 30.00 |
| **When The Snowman Sat By The Fire,** Uncut, 1923 | 16.00 |
| **Wide World Costume Dolls,** 4 Ladies, Costumes, Uncut | 60.00 |
| | |
| **PAPER, Almanac,** Farmer's, 1872 | 15.00 |
| **Book,** Abraham Lincoln Prairie Years, Sandburg, 1926 | 20.00 |
| **Book,** Almanac, Ayer's, 1900 | 6.50 |
| **Book,** Bennie & Jennie, Overall Boys & Sunbonnet Girls, 1907 | 65.00 |
| **Book,** Big Golden Book, Roy Rogers, 9 X 11 In. | 9.00 |
| **Book,** Big Little Book, Big Chief Wahoo | 15.00 |
| **Book,** Big Little Book, Billy The Kid | 15.00 |
| **Book,** Big Little Book, Billy The Kid, 1935 | 15.00 |
| **Book,** Big Little Book, Brad Turner In Transatlantic Flight, Whitman | 12.60 |
| **Book,** Big Little Book, Bringing Up Father, Whitman, 1936 | 9.40 To 10.00 |
| **Book,** Big Little Book, Buck Jones & The Rock Creek Cattlemen | 15.00 |
| **Book,** Big Little Book, Charlie McCarthy, 1938 | 13.00 |
| **Book,** Big Little Book, Chester Gump Finds Hidden Treasure, 1934 | 13.40 |
| **Book,** Big Little Book, Coach Bernie Bierman's Brick Barton | 14.00 |
| **Book,** Big Little Book, Dick Tracy, 1933 | 10.00 |
| **Book,** Big Little Book, Donald Duck Sees Stars | 9.00 |
| **Book,** Big Little Book, Ella Cinders | 15.00 |
| **Book,** Big Little Book, Ellery Queen's Adventure, Murdered Millionaire | 9.00 |
| **Book,** Big Little Book, Eric Nash & The Forty-Niners | 20.00 |
| **Book,** Big Little Book, Flash Gordon In The Water World Of Mongo | 25.00 |
| **Book,** Big Little Book, Foreign Legion | 12.00 |
| **Book,** Big Little Book, Frank Merriwell At Yale, 1936 | 15.00 |
| **Book,** Big Little Book, G-Men On The Crime Trail | 10.00 |
| **Book,** Big Little Book, Gene Autry Special Ranger | 8.00 |
| **Book,** Big Little Book, Iric Noble & The Forty-Niners, 1934 | 20.00 |
| **Book,** Big Little Book, Just Kids, 1937 | 9.40 |
| **Book,** Big Little Book, Little Orphan Annie | 20.00 |
| **Book,** Big Little Book, Lone Ranger & Great Western Span | 14.00 |
| **Book,** Big Little Book, Lone Ranger Vanishing Hero, 1936 | 16.00 |
| **Book,** Big Little Book, Mandrake & The Midnight Monster, 1939 | 12.60 |
| **Book,** Big Little Book, Men Of The Mounted, 1934 | 10.00 |
| **Book,** Big Little Book, Mickey & Pluto The Racer | 12.00 |
| **Book,** Big Little Book, Mickey Mouse & The Sacred Jewel | 12.00 |
| **Book,** Big Little Book, Mickey Mouse Sails For Treasure Island | 18.00 |
| **Book,** Big Little Book, Mickey Rooney Himself | 16.00 |

**Book,** Big Little Book, Moon Mullins & Kayo, 1939 ............................................ 11.20
**Book,** Big Little Book, Pete The Tramp ............................................................ 20.00
**Book,** Big Little Book, Pinocchio, 1940 ........................................................... 13.00
**Book,** Big Little Book, Popeye Sees The Sea ..................................................... 8.00
**Book,** Big Little Book, Railroad Detective ......................................................... 10.00
**Book,** Big Little Book, Roy Rogers, Robinhood Of The Range, 1942 ...................... 11.40
**Book,** Big Little Book, Shirley Temple ............................................................. 10.00
**Book,** Big Little Book, Skippy, 1929 ............................................................... 25.00
**Book,** Big Little Book, Smitty, 1934 ............................................................... 23.00
**Book,** Big Little Book, Tarzan's Revenge, 1938 ................................................. 15.00
**Book,** Big Little Book, Texas Ranger .............................................................. 10.00
**Book,** Big Little Book, The Adventure Of The Last Man Club, 1940 ....................... 16.50
**Book,** Big Little Book, The G-Man & The Gun Runners, 1940 .............................. 15.00
**Book,** Big Little Book, Tim McCoy On The Tomahawk Trail, 1937 ......................... 10.00
**Book,** Big Little Book, Tom Beaty Ace Service ................................................... 7.00
**Book,** Big Little Book, Tom Mix .................................................................... 15.00
**Book,** Big Little Book, Tracked By G-Man ........................................................ 12.00
**Book,** Big Little Book, Wash Tubbs & Captain Andy, Hunting For Whales ............... 35.00
**Book,** Big Little Book, Will Rogers ................................................................. 20.00
**Book,** Big Little Book, Zane Grey .................................................................. 13.00
**Book,** Boys & Girls Of Bookland, 11 Color Plates, Jessie Wilcox Smith .................. 30.00
**Book,** Children Of The Revolution, 12 Color Plates, M.Humphrey .......................... 75.00
**Book,** Coloring, Esther Williams ................................................................... 11.00
**Book,** From Southern Shores, R.Tuck, Diecut, 1895 .......................................... 18.00
**Book,** Grimm's Fairy Tales, 4 Color Plates ...................................................... 10.00
**Book,** Heritage Of The Desert, Zane Grey, Dust Cover, 1910 ............................... 5.00
**Book,** Hiawatha, Harrison Fisher Illustrations .................................................. 80.00
**Book,** Life Of McKinley ............................................................................. 5.00
**Book,** McGuffey's 4th Electric Speller ............................................................ 15.00
**Book,** Mother Goose, Kate Greenaway Illustrations, 4 1/2 X 6 1/2 In. ..................... 25.00
**Book,** Peeps Into Fairyland, Pop-Up, Colored, C.1896 ....................................... 30.00
**Book,** Rinkytink In Oz, Baum, 1916 .............................................................. 15.00
**Book,** Sander's School Reader, 1800s ............................................................ 9.00
**Book,** Sermons, Billy Sunday, Omaha, September, 1915 ..................................... 6.00
**Book,** Teddy Roosevelt, Miniature, 1 1/2 In. .................................................... 19.00
**Book,** The Brownies, Their Book, Palmer Cox, 1887 .......................................... 65.00
**Book,** The Doctors, Elbert Hubbard, Suede Cover, Ribbon Tie, 1909 ..................... 150.00
**Book,** The Patchwork Girl Of Oz, Baum, 1913 ................................................. 15.00
**Book,** Tom Corbett, Space Cadet, Push-Outs, 1952, 10 1/2 X 14 In. ...................... 40.00
**Bookmark,** Easter, 1904 ............................................................................ 3.00
    **PAPER, CALENDAR, see Calendar Paper**
**Catalog,** American Brewers Supply, C.1915 ..................................................... 35.00
**Catalog,** Larkin, Spring-Summer, 1915 .......................................................... 20.00
**Deed,** Transfer Of Property, Hampton, N.H., 1815, 13 X 9 1/2 In. ......................... 35.00
**Label,** La Rendicion Cigar, Pair ................................................................... 3.00
**Magazine,** Buffalo Bill Wild West, Souvenir, 1909 ............................................ 18.50
**Nursery Rhymes,** Fairbank's Soap, Signed Maud Humphrey, Set Of 4 .................. 245.00
**Program,** Ringling Bros. & Barnum & Bailey, 1949 ........................................... 15.00
**Punchboard,** Damon Runyon Cancer Fund, Baseball ......................................... 18.00
**Workbook,** Calligraphy Headings, Signed & Dated, 1839, 7 1/2 X 10 In. ................. 165.00

    **PAPERWEIGHT, see also Baccarat, Paperweight**
**PAPERWEIGHT, Abraham Lincoln,** Bust, Frosted, Gillinder & Sons, 6 1/4 In. ......... 195.00
  **Abraham Lincoln,** Sulfide, Signed St.Clair .................................................. 28.00
  **Advertising,** Maryland Casualty Insurance Co., 2898 ...................................... 15.00
  **Advertising,** National Lead Co., Dutch Boy Embossed .................................... 35.00
  **Agate In The Rough,** 2 Polished Sides, 2 X 3 X 5 In. ...................................... 10.00
  **Albert Schweitzer,** By D'Albert, Sulfide ..................................................... 100.00
  **Amherst Stoves,** Buffalo Cooperative Stove Co. ........................................... 16.00
  **Apple Shape,** Clear, Joe Zimmerman, Signed .............................................. 30.00
  **Art Glass,** Iridescent, Signed Vandermark ................................................... 28.00
  **Bell System,** Bell Shaped, Blue ................................................................ 25.00
  **Brass Brunswick,** Lady, Lyre, Ornate ........................................................ 30.00

| | |
|---|---:|
| **Burt's Seed Co.,** With Seeds | 15.00 |
| **Camel Reclining,** Court Jester Playing Violin, Iron | 30.00 |
| **Centennial,** 1776-1876, Memorial Hall | 250.00 |
| **Chameleon,** Sherwin Williams Paint, 4 X 5 3/4 In. | 75.00 |
| **Circles Of Blue,** Green & Clear, Signed Kosta, 1 X 2 In. | 20.00 |
| **Cluster Of Canes On Turquoise,** White Stripes, Clichy, 1 3/4 In. | 265.00 |
| **Daniel Webster Flour,** Glass | 15.00 |
| **Double Overlay,** Mushroom Of Latticinio, Signed Perthshire | 950.00 |
| **Figural,** Bulldog, Solid Brass, 5 In. | 38.00 |
| **Figural,** Dog, Bryant Heating, Cast Iron, 6 1/2 X 3 In. | 45.00 |
| **Figural,** Frog, Cast Iron | 25.00 |
| **Figural,** Frog, Dempster, Manufacturers Of Windmills, Buggies | 30.00 |
| **Figural,** Scotty, Cast Iron | 18.00 |
| **Francis The Talking Mule,** 1948, Metal | 20.00 |
| **Head Of Girl,** Glass | 5.00 |
| **Home Insurance Co.,** 1850-1915, Brass | 15.00 |
| **Indian On Rock,** Water Globe With Snow | 8.00 |
| **Johnson Hat Co.,** Black Face, Glass | 15.00 |
| **Kalak Water,** N.Y. | 6.00 |
| **Kaziun,** Pedestal, Water Lily, 4 Green Leaves | 325.00 |
| **Kaziun,** Ruby & White Stylized Lily, Goldstone Ground, 2 In. | 325.00 |
| **MacArthur,** General, Star Cut Base, D'Albert, Crystal | 170.00 |
| **Machinery Hall,** Columbian Exposition | 9.50 |
| **Memorial Hall,** Centennial 1776-1876, Pressed Glass | 325.00 |
| **Mutt & Jeff,** Boston American Newspaper, Mirror, Cruver, 3 In. | 25.00 |
| **New Idea Implements,** Pictures Manure Spreader, Brass | 14.00 |
| **Old Crow,** James Clay Delivering Whiskey Barrel To Henry Clay | 30.00 |
| **Pan American,** Machinery Building, Buffalo, N.Y., Oblong | 17.00 |
| **Pear,** Blown Glass, 7 In. | 15.00 |
| **Plymouth Rock** | 40.00 |
| **Prudential Insurance Co.,** Scene Of Home Office, Dated | 20.00 |
| **Quilted Mother-Of-Pearl,** Half Round Shape, Satin Glass, 4 In. | 275.00 |
| **R.C.A.Victor,** His Master's Voice, Mirror Back | 36.00 |
| **Remember The Maine** | 25.00 |
| **Sailor Teaching Lady To Swim,** Bronze, Europe, 6 1/2 X 3 7/8 In. | 475.00 |
| **Santa Maria Ship,** Marble Base, Metal, 3 1/2 In. | 65.00 |
| **Scrambled Candy,** New England, 2 3/4 In. | 125.00 |
| **Smith Brothers,** Model Of Cough Drop, Cast Iron, 2 In.Diameter | 30.00 |
| **Snow,** Penguin | 25.00 |
| **Souvenir,** Belleville, Kansas, Red, Oval | 20.00 |
| **Souvenir,** French Lick Springs, Ind. | 45.00 |
| **St.Louis Crown Weight,** Ribbons, Central Cane, White Lace Ground | 650.00 |
| **St.Louis,** Bouquet, Faceted, Upright | 1050.00 |
| **Sulfide,** Four Seasons, Summer, Bayel, France | 85.00 |
| **Sulfide,** Standing Lamb, Flattened Dome, 2 1/2 In.Diam. | 110.00 |
| **Thatcher Your Warm Friend,** Boilers, Man, Iron, 3 3/4 In. | 29.00 |
| **Three White Horses,** 1901 | 30.00 |
| **Truman,** Harry, Overlay, Signed, Baccarat | 175.00 |
| **Wells Fargo,** Dated 1852 | 20.00 |
| **World War II,** Stars, V, Red, White, & Blue | 25.00 |
| **Wright Aeronautical Co.,** Lindbergh's Flight, Pot Metal, 5 In. | 50.00 |
| **Ysart,** Fish Swimming Over Sandy Base, Rocks, Signed, 2 3/4 In. | 900.00 |

*Papier-mache is a decorative form made from paper mixed with glue, chalk, and other ingredients, then molded and baked. It becomes very hard and can be decorated. Boxes, trays, and furniture were made of papier-mache. Some of the early nineteenth-century pieces were decorated with mother-of-pearl.*

| | |
|---|---:|
| **PAPIER-MACHE, Box,** Jewelry, Hand-Painted Soccer Scene | 35.00 |
| **Box,** Snuff, Pewter Trim, Black | 25.00 |
| **Bulldog,** Clayton's Dog Remedies, C.1900, Life Size | 450.00 To 500.00 |
| **Case,** Glasses, Metal Inlay Design, C.1900 | 20.00 |
| **Coaster,** Wine, Georgian, C.1880, Gold, Black, & Green, Pair | 450.00 |

Egg, Easter, Germany, 6 In. ............................................................................. 20.00
Figures, Nativity, 3 Kings & Shepherds, Germany, 8 In. ..................................... 75.00
Figurine, Boy On A Tricycle ............................................................................ 250.00
Figurine, Shepherd, Bearded, Carrying Staff ................................................. 20.00
Marionette, Cloth, 22 In. ................................................................................ 50.00
Mask, Santa Claus .......................................................................................... 65.00
Nodder, Cat, Also A Bank ............................................................................... 25.00
Pitcher, Measuring, Set Of 3 .......................................................................... 75.00
Plate, Hand-Painted Flowers, C.1880, 10 In., Pair ........................................... 50.00
Rabbit, White, 8 1/2 In. ................................................................................... 20.00
Santa, Rabbit Fur Hair, Beard, 14 In. .............................................................. 45.00
    **PARASOL, see Umbrella**

*Parian is a fine-grained, hard-paste porcelain named for the marble it
resembles. It was first made in England in 1846 and gained in favor in the
United States about 1860. Figures, tea sets, vases, and other items were
made of Parian at many English and American factories.*

**PARIAN, Bust,** Burns, C.1885, 6 1/4 In. ............................................................. 48.00
Bust, Charles Dickens, 8 1/2 In. ...................................................................... 75.00
Bust, Clytie, Impressed Copeland, Art Union Of London, 1863, 10 In. .................... 400.00
Bust, Franz Liszt, 6 1/2 X 4 1/2 In.Wide ........................................................ 35.00
Bust, Gentleman, Hutschenreuther, Signed, 7 In. .......................................... 95.00
Bust, Grecian Woman, Laurel Leaf Crown On Head, 8 3/4 In. ............................ 65.00
Bust, Homer, 8 X 13 In. ................................................................................... 90.00
Bust, Juliet Type Woman, 9 1/2 In. .................................................................. 60.00
Bust, Mendelssohn, C.1885, 7 3/4 In. .............................................................. 65.00
Bust, Mozart, C.1885, 7 3/4 In. ....................................................................... 65.00
Bust, Queen Victoria, Incised Turner & Wood-Stoke, 7 In. ................................. 155.00
Bust, Scott, C.1885, 7 1/2 In. .......................................................................... 48.00
Bust, Shakespeare, Signed J. & T.B., 14 In. .................................................... 350.00
Bust, Shakespeare, 9 In. .................................................................................. 75.00
Bust, Young Girl Reading, Signed .................................................................... 550.00
Candlestick, Swans, Stretched Necks, 4 1/4 & 6 1/4 In., Pair ........................... 295.00
Creamer, Vintner, Embossed Scene, C.1840, 3 1/2 In. ..................................... 58.00
Cup & Saucer, Relief Pattern .......................................................................... 45.00
Figurine, Apollo, 15 In. .................................................................................... 269.00
Figurine, Basket Held By Lady's Hand, September 1873 Mark, 8 In. .................... 195.00
Figurine, Girl, Pearl Trimmed Dress, Holding Nest Of Eggs, 7 In. ...................... 65.00
Figurine, Little Girl, 2 In. ................................................................................ 8.00
Figurine, Mary & Lamb, 11 In. ........................................... 90.00 To 125.00
Figurine, Roman Soldier In Chariot, Horses, 8 X 6 In. ..................................... 85.00
Figurine, Three Graces, 7 1/4 In. .................................................................... 140.00
Figurine, Victorian Lady Talking To Gentleman, Signed, 9 1/4 In. ..................... 195.00
Figurine, Woman With Basket On Head, 8 In. ................................................. 30.00
Jug, Albion Corridor Base, Symbols Of Great Britain, 1863, 6 In. ....................... 70.00
Jug, Boy & Bird's Nest, 1850 Registry Mark, 7 1/2 In. ..................................... 195.00
Jug, Pewter Hinged Top & Thumb Rest, C.1847, Blue ..................................... 135.00
Owl, For A Candle, Glass Eyes, 3 In. ............................................................... 145.00
Pitcher, Cain & Abel Scenes, Marked, 7 1/2 In. .............................................. 150.00
Pitcher, Hound Handle .................................................................................... 150.00
Syrup, Floral Relief, White Ground, Tin Top, 5 In. ........................................... 75.50
Vase, Covered, Bird Finial, Raised Figures, 19th Century, 15 In. ....................... 110.00

*Vieux Paris, or Old Paris, is porcelain ware that is known to have been
made in Paris in the eighteenth or early nineteenth century but has no
identifying manufacturer's mark.*

**PARIS, Biscuit Jar,** Molded Handles, Enameled Flowers ................................. 125.00
Case, Clock, White & Gilt, French Movement, C.1840, 13 1/2 In. ....................... 120.00
Figurine, Winged Cupid With Dog, Signed, Parian, C.1770 ............................... 145.00
Jardiniere, Bouquets, Gilt Acorn & Leaves, C.1800, 9 3/4 In., Pair ..................... 480.00
Tobacco Jar, Napoleon Reaching Snuffbox, 10 Colors, 1800s, 10 In. .................. 235.00

Paris, Vase, Ovoid, Riverscape, Gilt
Rim, C.1815, 12 3/4 In., Pair

**Vase,** Baluster Shape, Ormolu Mounted, Blue Ground, C.1820, 9 3/4 In. ............................... 700.00
**Vase,** Floral Design, Flowing Leaf, 11 In., Pair ......................................................................... 300.00
**Vase,** Oval Centerpiece, Painted Landscape, Pink, 15 1/2 In., Pair ......................................... 1250.00
**Vase,** Ovoid, Riverscape, Gilt Rim, C.1815, 12 3/4 In., Pair .............................................*Illus*1000.00

> *Pate-de-verre is an ancient technique in which glass is made by blending and refining powdered glass of different colors into molds. The process was revived by French glassmakers, especially Galle, around the end of the nineteenth century.*

**PATE-DE-VERRE, Ashtray,** Open Rose Shape, Jade Green, A.Walter, 4 1/2 In. ....................... 500.00
**Base,** Lamp, 8 Colors, 48 Red Poppies, Brass Base, Signed, 9 In. ........................................... 1995.00
**Bowl,** Purple, Green & Orange Protruding Grapes ................................................................. 1450.00
**Bowl,** Translucent Light Tan, G.Argy Rousseau, 4 1/2 In.Diam. ............................................. 645.00
**Dish,** Embossed Pheasants, Signed Walter Nancy, 5 X 7 3/4 In. ............................................ 695.00
**Dish,** Yellow To Green, Applied Grasshopper, Signed, 4 3/4 In. ............................................. 1750.00
**Figurine,** Bird, C.1900, Turquoise Blue, Signed, 3 3/4 In., Pair ............................................. 1000.00
**Inkwell,** Covered, Signed A.Walter Nancy .............................................................................. 350.00
**Lamp Base,** 48 Poppies In Windows, Brass Base, Signed, 9 In. .............................................. 2500.00
**Pendant,** Pinecones & Needles, Green & Brown, 2 1/4 In. ...................................................... 325.00
**Vase,** Multicolored, Signed A.Walter Nancy, 5 3/4 In. ............................................................ 1575.00

> *Pate-sur-pate means paste on paste. The design was made by painting layers of slip on the ceramic piece until a relief decoration was formed. The method was developed at the Sevres factory in France about 1850. It became even more famous at the English Minton factory about 1870.*

**PATE-SUR-PATE, Box,** Full Figure Nude On Cover, Triangular, Signed, 6 In.Diam. ................. 395.00
**Chocolate Pot,** Scalloped Base, Pearlized, Gold Star Design ................................................... 125.00
**Cracker Jar,** Dandelions, Gold Insects, Green Ground, 6 3/4 In. ............................................. 50.00
**Lamp,** Flowers & Bird, Etched Shade, Brass Base, 20 1/2 In. .................................................. 650.00
**Plate,** Gold Dragonflies, Butterflies, Green, 8 1/2 In. ............................................................ 59.00
**Vase,** Celadon Green, Raised Poppies, Gold Trim, Signed, 10 In. ........................................... 195.00
**Vase,** Clusters Of Enamel Flowers, Dancing Muse, Blue, 6 In. .............................................. 375.00
**Vase,** Fan Shape, Angelfish & Seaweed, Beige Ground, 6 1/2 In. ........................................... 135.00
**Vase,** Lavender Medallion, Dancing Girl, Peacock Blue, 8 In. ................................................. 165.00

> *Paul Revere pottery was made at several locations in and around Boston between 1906 and 1942. The pottery was operated as a settlement-house type of program for teen-aged girls. Many pieces were signed S.E.G. for Saturday Evening Girls. The firm concentrated on children's dishes and tiles. Decorations were outlined in black and filled in with color.*

**PAUL REVERE, Bowl,** Tricolor Stylized Water Lilies, S.E.G., 11 In.Diam. ..................... 250.00
  **Charger,** Hen With Chick, Blue Band, S.E.G., Signed, 11 1/2 In. ............................ 130.00
  **Inkwell,** Four-Color Landscape, Covered ...................................................... 245.00
  **Pitcher,** Semigloss Speckled Blue, Frothy White Drip, 5 In. ............................. 78.00
  **Tile,** Riding Horse, Dated 1926, Round ....................................................... 67.50
  **Vase,** Dark Blue Matte, Light Blue Matte, Bulbous, 5 X 5 In. ............................ 65.00
  **Vase,** Landscape Band, Green Cylindrical Form, S.E.G., 9 In. ........................... 225.00

**PAULINE POTTERY, Jar,** Tobacco, Barrel Shaped, Gnome On Top, 1888 .................. 75.00

> *Peachblow glass originated about 1883 at Hobbs, Brockunier and Company*
> *of Wheeling, West Virginia. It is a glass that shades from yellow to*
> *peach. It was lined in white. New England peachblow is a one-layer*
> *glass shading from red to white. Mt. Washington peachblow shades from pink*
> *to blue. Reproductions of peachblow have been made, but they are of poor*
> *quality and can be detected.*

**PEACHBLOW, Bell,** New England, 6 1/2 In. ......................................................... 495.00
  **Bride's Bowl,** Wheeling, Rose To Yellow Cased, Silver Holder ......................... 750.00
  **Celery,** New England, Square Ruffled Top, C.1890, 6 1/2 In. ........................... 250.00
  **Creamer,** New England Ribbed, 4 In. ........................................................... 485.00
  **Creamer,** Ribbed, Satin, 2 1/2 In. ............................................................... 375.00
  **Creamer,** Wheeling, Drape Pattern ............................................................ 1100.00
  **Cup,** New England, 1893 World's Fair, Alabaster Handle, 2 3/4 In. .................... 475.00
  **Cup,** Punch, New England, Ribbed Handle, C.1890, 2 1/2 In. ........................... 250.00
  **Cup,** Punch, New England, World's Fair, 1893, Alabaster Handle ...................... 385.00
  **Cup,** Punch, Wheeling, Handled, Amber Handle, 1880 .................................... 390.00
  **Finger Bowl,** New England, Raspberry, 4 3/8 In.Diam. ................................... 395.00
  **Finger Bowl,** New England, Ruffled Rim, C.1890, 5 1/2 In.Diam. ...................... 300.00
  **Finger Bowl,** New England, 5 1/4 X 2 1/4 In. ............................................... 350.00
  **Finger Bowl,** Wheeling, 4 In.Diam. ........................................................... 450.00
    **PEACHBLOW, see Gunderson**
  **Lamp Base,** Wine Color To Yellow, 9 In. ..................................................... 750.00
  **Pear,** New England, Open End Stem ............................................................ 205.00
  **Pear,** Wheeling, C.1904, 4 1/2 In. ............................................................... 250.00
  **Pitcher,** Deep Rose To Yellow, Ruffled Rim, C.1890, 7 1/2 In. ......................... 650.00
  **Pitcher,** Milk, Wheeling, 7 1/2 In. ............................................................... 955.00
  **Pitcher,** 4 1/4 In. .................................................................................... 895.00
  **Punch Cup,** New England, Applied Ribbed Handle, C.1890, 2 1/2 In. ................. 250.00
  **Rose Bowl,** Acid Finish, 3 1/2 In. ............................................................... 350.00
  **Rose Bowl,** New England, 7 Crimp, 3 3/4 X 3 3/8 In. ..................................... 325.00
  **Rose Bowl,** Wheeling ............................................................................... 350.00
  **Salt & Pepper,** Acorn ............................................................................... 55.00
  **Saltshaker** ........................................................................................... 215.00
  **Sugar Bowl** ........................................................................................... 750.00
  **Sugar,** Inscribed World's Fair 1893 ............................................................ 500.00
  **Toothpick,** New England, Tricornered ........................................................ 269.00
  **Toothpick,** Pink Cased, Signed .................................................................. 325.00
  **Toothpick,** Pink Enamel Flowers ............................................................... 295.00
  **Tumbler,** Acid, Wheeling .......................................................................... 325.00
  **Tumbler,** Wheeling, White Lining, 2 1/8 X 3 3/4 In. ....................................... 350.00
  **Vase,** Enameled Cherry Leaf, Flowers, & Fruit, 11 In., Pair ............................. 850.00
  **Vase,** Lily, New England, Wild Rose Glassworks Label, 8 In. ........................... 895.00
  **Vase,** New England, Lily Form, C.1890, 9 In. ................................................ 325.00
  **Vase,** New England, Pink & White, Ruffled Rim, 3 1/2 X 7 In.Diam. .................. 175.00
  **Vase,** New England, Swollen Cylindrical Neck, C.1890, 6 1/8 In. ...................... 250.00
  **Vase,** New England, Wild Rose Pattern, 9 In. ............................................... 885.00
  **Vase,** New England, Wild Rose, White To Raspberry Red, 8 7/8 In. .................. 1000.00
  **Vase,** New England, 7 1/2 In. .................................................................... 750.00
  **Vase,** Pink To Yellow, Crimped Rim, Footed, 5 1/2 X 3 In. ............................... 225.00
  **Vase,** Ruffled, Applied Flowers, Stems, & Leaves, 9 1/2 In., Pair ...................... 500.00
  **Vase,** Seaweed Design, Coralene Cased, C.1890, 5 1/2 In. .............................. 350.00
  **Vase,** Stick, Wheeling, Glossy Finish, 8 In. .................................................. 525.00

**Vase,** Wheeling, Bulbous, C.1890, 2 3/8 In. ............................................................ 175.00
**Vase,** Wheeling, Double Gourd, 7 1/2 In. ................................................................ 850.00
**Vase,** Wheeling, Round Bulbous Form, C.1890, 2 3/8 In. ....................................... 175.00
    **PEACHBLOW, WEBB, see Webb, Peachblow**

**Pearl,** Letter Opener, Napoleon ............................................................................ 25.00
    **PEARL, OPERA GLASSES, see Opera Glasses**

      *Peking glass is a Chinese cameo glass of the eighteenth and nineteenth*
      *centuries.*

**PEKING GLASS, Bookends,** Foo Dogs, Light Green, Wood Plinth, 4 X 5 In. ............ 120.00
**Bottle,** Snuff, Blue To Clear, Inside Painted Scene, 2 1/2 In. ................................. 80.00
**Bottle,** Snuff, Reverse Painting ............................................................................. 40.00
**Bottle,** Snuff, Reverse Painting On Both Sides ...................................................... 50.00
**Bottle,** Snuff, Scenic Reverse Painting .................................................................. 35.00
**Bowl,** Birds & Flower, Wood Stand, Cobalt Blue, 6 1/2 In. ..................................... 300.00
**Bowl,** Blue Carved, White Hibiscus & Butterflies, 7 In. .......................................... 240.00
**Bowl,** Blue, 7 1/2 In. Diam. .................................................................................. 85.00
**Bowl,** Cameo, Flowers, Birds, Branches, Red, White, 3 1/2 In. ............................... 297.00
**Bowl,** Ibexes, Flamingos, Green Cut To White, 5 1/4 X 6 1/2 In. ............................ 300.00
**Bowl,** Water Lily & Duck, Carnelian To Opaque, 4 In.Diam., Pair ............................ 175.00
**Bowl,** White Design, Yellow Flowers & Foliage ....................................................... 285.00
**Box,** Trinket, Brass Bezel, White, 2 1/2 X 2 1/2 X 1 3/4 In. ................................... 55.00
**Cup & Saucer,** Demitasse, Filigree Silver Handled Framework .............................. 110.00
**Flower Tree,** Set In Jade ...................................................................................... 22.00
**Snuff Bottle,** Painted Inside, 3 3/8 In. ................................................................. 45.00
**Vase,** Bird & Floral Design, 19th Century, 4 3/8 In., Pair ..................................... 325.00
**Vase,** Blue Cameo Design, Dragonflies, White Ground, 6 In., Pair ......................... 300.00
**Vase,** Cameo, Red & White, Flowers, Butterflies, 6 1/4 In. Pair ............................ 595.00
**Vase,** Cut Back, Green On White, 6 In. ................................................................ 125.00
**Vase,** Flowers, Carved Bats On Border, 18th Century, 6 In. ................................... 950.00
**Vase,** Flying Birds, Turquoise On White, Signed, 10 In. ........................................ 250.00
**Vase,** Overlay, Cut Back To White Honeycomb Pattern, 6 In. ................................ 135.00
**Vase,** Red Base & Collar, Peony Flower Design, 5 X 10 In. .................................... 320.00
**Vase,** Red Flowers, Butterfly, White Ground, 6 1/8 In. ......................................... 395.00
**Vase,** Sculpted Red Floral On White, 6 In., Pair ................................................... 225.00
**Vase,** Silver Overlay, Red, 5 In. ........................................................................... 100.00

      *Peloton glass is European glass with small threads of colored glass rolled*
      *onto the surface of clear or colored glass. It is sometimes called spaghetti,*
      *or shredded coconut glass.*

**PELOTON, Basket,** Folded-Over Top, Applied Feet, Colored Strings, 8 In.Diam. ...... 300.00
**Epergne,** 3-Handled, Ruffled Trumpet, Fluted Base ............................................. 1250.00
**Sugar,** Covered, Underplate, Ribbed, Acid Finished Threads, 6 In. ....................... 135.00
**Vase,** Bud, Paperweight Style, Applied Strips Of Glass, 7 In., Pair ......................... 450.00
**Vase,** Multicolored Threading, Rim Turned Inward, 3 X 4 In. ................................ 485.00

**PEN & PENCIL SET, Waterman,** Lady's, Sterling Silver Overlay, Boxed .................. 95.00

**PEN, All Glass,** Including Point ............................................................................ 30.00
**Cobalt,** Glass ..................................................................................................... 10.00
**Conklin,** Gold Band, Blue ................................................................................... 10.00
**Dip,** Cloisonne, Black Enamel Ground ................................................................ 35.00
**Esterbrook,** Dripless Fountain Well .................................................................... 14.00
**Fountain,** Conklin, Lady's, Crescent Filler, Gold Plated, 14K Gold Nib .................. 30.00
**Fountain,** Esterbrook, Green ............................................................................. 10.00
**Fountain,** Esterbrook, Red ................................................................................ 10.00
**Fountain,** Lady Webster, Miniature .................................................................... 20.00
**Fountain,** Moore's Improved Nonleakable, Patent 1869, Box .............................. 7.00
**Fountain,** Schaeffer, In Marble Base, Brown ...................................................... 85.00
**Fountain,** Swan, Black, Dated 1915 .................................................................. 20.00

**Gold Point,** Mother-Of-Pearl, 6 In. ........................................................ 15.00
**Gold Tip,** Mother-Of-Pearl ................................................................ 27.50
**Mother-Of-Pearl Handle** ................................................................ 32.50
**Mother-Of-Pearl,** Brass ................................................................. 12.50
**Mother-Of-Pearl,** 14K Gold, Onyx Holder ........................................ 35.00
**New York World's Fair,** Gold Point & Handle, 1939 ......................... 45.00
**Parker,** Big Red, Duofold Point, 1923 ......................... 75.00 To 95.00
**Retractable Point,** Mother-Of-Pearl, 6 In. ...................................... 15.00
**Ribbon Striped,** Glass ..................................................................... 15.00
**Waterman,** Gold Band ...................................................................... 9.00
**Waterman,** Sterling ........................................................................ 50.00
**Waterman's Ideal,** 14K Gold ........................................................ 110.00
**Wearever,** Gold Plate Tip & Point, Two-Tone ................................... 30.00
**Winchester,** Fountain, 14K Point ................................................... 20.00

**PENCIL, Bold Swirled,** Ruby Set In Top, Mechanical ......................... 50.00
**Eversharp,** Gold & Brass Trim, Retractable, 1879, Fairchild .......... 29.50
**Eversharp,** Gold Filled, Fob .......................................................... 42.00
**Eversharp,** Ideal Motors, Gold, 6 In. ............................................... 8.00
**Eversharp,** Mr. Peanut .................................................................. 12.00
**Eversharp,** Silver, 1915 ............................................................... 12.00
**Eversharp,** Sterling Silver ............................................................. 15.00
**Figural,** Alligator, Black Man In Mouth, Celluloid .......................... 25.00
**Lady's,** Gold Filled, Hang On Chain, Set Of 3 ................................. 22.00
**Mechanical,** Budweiser, 1930s ....................................................... 6.50
**Mechanical,** Eversharp, Sterling Silver ......................................... 22.00
**Mechanical,** Rolled Gold ................................................................. 8.00
**Mechanical,** Silver Fish, Dated 1881 ............................................. 35.00
**Mechanical,** Swirled Ruby Set In Top, Gold ................................... 12.00
**Mr.Peanut Ritepoint,** Original Package .......................................... 5.00
**Parker,** Big Red, Patented September 5, 1916 ................................ 45.00
**Rolled Silver,** Willys, Overland ...................................................... 20.00
**Telescope,** Textured Design, Chain, Sterling Silver, 3 1/2 In. .......... 22.00
**Wahl,** Eversharp, Sterling .............................................................. 18.00
**Wahl,** Eversharp, Worn On Necklace, Gold Plated, C.1920 ............. 35.00

**PENNSBURY, Bowl,** Man & Woman, Oval, 8 1/2 In. ........................ 22.00
**Pitcher,** Rooster, 5 In. ................................................................... 15.00

*Peters and Reed Pottery Company of Zanesville, Ohio, was founded by
John D. Peters and Adam Reed in 1897. Chromal, Landsun, Montene,
Pereco, and Persian are some of the art lines that were made until the
company closed in 1920.*

   **PETERS & REED,** see also Zane
**PETERS & REED, Bowl,** Dragonfly, Moss Aztec ............................... 18.00
**Jardiniere,** Aztec, Floral Moss, 6 In. .............................................. 40.00
**Jardiniere,** Moss Aztec, Signed, 7 1/2 X 8 3/4 In.Diam. ................ 60.00
**Jug,** Brown Glazed ......................................................................... 88.00
**Pitcher,** Water, Brown Glaze, 7 X 5 In. ........................................... 88.00
**Umbrella Stand,** Signed Ferrel, 22 1/2 X 11 In.Diam. ................... 245.00
**Urn,** Irises, Green Ground, 5 In. ..................................................... 85.00
**Vase,** Aztec Pinecone, 8 In. ........................................................... 38.00
**Vase,** Candlestick Shaped, Applied Floral, 5 1/2 In. ....................... 34.00
**Vase,** Handled, Green Sprigs & Leaves, Brown Ground, 6 In. ........... 45.00
**Vase,** Moss Aztec, 8 In. ................................................................. 20.00
**Vase,** Red Sewer Pipe, Raised Berry & Leaf Design, 7 1/2 In. .......... 35.00
**Vase,** Terra-Cotta, Green Highlights, 6 In. ....................................... 35.00
   **PETRUS REGOUT,** see Maastricht

*Pewabic Pottery was founded by Mary Chase Perry Stratton in 1903 in Detroit, Michigan. Pewabic type pottery is still being made.*

| | |
|---|---|
| **PEWABIC, Ashtray,** Iridescent Green, Gold Trim, Marked, 4 1/4 In.Diam. | 65.00 |
| **Ashtray,** Mottled Glaze, 3 1/2 X 4 In. | 50.00 |
| **Box,** Cigarette, Art Deco Bird, Metallic Glaze, Signed, 3 1/2 X 5 In. | 275.00 |
| **Candleholder,** Hooded, Green | 86.00 |
| **Pitcher,** 1903-06, Metallic Glaze, 5 In. | 225.00 |
| **Tile,** 1930s, Marked & Numbered, Sample, 1 In.Square | 25.00 |
| **Vase,** Gold Drip Over Turquoise, 3 1/2 In. | 185.00 |
| **Vase,** Gray Luster Over Turquoise, 2 3/4 In. | 195.00 |

*Pewter is a metal alloy of tin and lead. Some of the pewter made after 1840 has a slightly different composition and is called Britannia metal.*

| | |
|---|---|
| **PEWTER, Bell,** Liberty, Weighted, Miniature | 6.00 |
| **Box,** Patch, Steel Mirror, 19th Century, French | 50.00 |
| **Box,** Soap, American | 135.00 |
| **Candlestick,** Lattice Design At Base, Marked J.B., 5 1/4 In., Pair | 45.00 |
| **Candlestick,** 7 In. | 45.00 |
| **Castor Set,** 4 Bottle, Revolving | 65.00 |
| **Chalice,** Pedestal, Kayserzinn, 6 1/2 In. | 110.00 |
| **Chalice,** Providence, R.I., Marked Calder | 525.00 |
| **Charger,** Marked Thomas D.Boardman, 13 1/2 In. | 485.00 |
| **Charger,** Touchmarks, Cotterell, C.1960, 16 1/2 In.Diam. | 245.00 |
| **Charger,** Wide Flat Rim, English, 18th Century, 19 In. | 130.00 |
| **Coaster,** Kayserzinn, Embossed Fish, 5 1/4 In., Set Of 4 | 65.00 |
| **Coffeepot,** Acorn Finial, A.Porter, Maine, C.1830, 12 In. ...........................*Illus* | 400.00 |
| **Coffeepot,** C.Cartwright & Sons, English, Acorn Finial, 8 In. | 95.00 |
| **Coffeepot,** Marked Donhaw, C.1830, American, 11 1/4 In. | 445.00 |
| **Coffeepot,** R.Dunham, American, 12 In. | 445.00 |
| **Coffeepot,** Ribbed Panel, Ivory Ring Handle, Flower Finial, 9 1/2 In. | 145.00 |
| **Coffeepot,** Wooden Wafer Finial, A.Porter, 11 1/2 In. ....................*Illus* | 275.00 |
| **Ewer,** Foo Dog Finial & Dragon, Chinese, Signed | 135.00 |
| **Inkstand,** Standish, 1760-70 | 900.00 |
| **Inkwell,** English, Quill Holder, Porcelain Insert, 7 1/2 X 2 In. | 68.00 |

Pewter, Coffeepot, Acorn Finial,
A.Porter, Maine, C.1830, 12 In.

Pewter, Coffeepot, Wooden Wafer
Finial, A.Porter, 11 1/2 In.

Pewter, Lamp, Dated June 3, 1856, Marked, 8 3/4 In.

| | |
|---|---|
| **Inkwell,** Turned Band, Covered, Ceramic Liner, American, 2 7/8 In. | 60.00 |
| **Inkwell,** Whitcome, C.1845, Signed | 70.00 |
| **Jardiniere,** Floral Design In Inlaid Brass, China, 7 In. | 175.00 |
| **Lamp,** Bell, American, 2 3/4 In. | 85.00 |
| **Lamp,** Dated June 3, 1856, Marked, 8 3/4 In. .......*Illus* | 600.00 |
| **Lamp,** Whale Oil, Turned Stem & Saucer, American, 3 1/2 In., Pair | 125.00 |
| **Letter Opener,** Gargoyle Of Notre Dame Forms Handle, 9 1/4 In. | 22.00 |
| **Measure,** Graduated Sizes, Hallmarked, 1 3/4 To 4 1/4 In., Set Of 5 | 175.00 |
| **Measure,** Pear Shape, Queen Victorian Mark, 1/4 Gill | 35.00 |
| **Measure,** Samuel Mason, Dublin, Handled, C.1796 | 250.00 |
| **Mold,** Chocolate, Lamb | 50.00 |
| **Mold,** Chocolate, Rabbit | 50.00 |
| **Mold,** Chocolate, Santa Claus With Sleigh | 65.00 |
| **Mold,** Ice Cream, American Flag, Hinged | 110.00 |
| **Mold,** Ice Cream, American Legion Emblem | 24.00 |
| **Mold,** Ice Cream, American Shield | 35.00 |
| **Mold,** Ice Cream, Apple Medallion | 47.00 |
| **Mold,** Ice Cream, Automobile, No.562 | 45.00 |
| **Mold,** Ice Cream, Baby, Dressed, No.286 | 38.00 |
| **Mold,** Ice Cream, Battleship | 35.00 |
| **Mold,** Ice Cream, Bear, No.222 | 38.00 |
| **Mold,** Ice Cream, Bird, No.172 | 25.00 |
| **Mold,** Ice Cream, Bird's Nest, With 4 Eggs | 75.00 |
| **Mold,** Ice Cream, Black Boy, Hands Around Neck Of Turkey | 40.00 |
| **Mold,** Ice Cream, Bride & Groom On Round Box, No.468 | 45.00 |
| **Mold,** Ice Cream, Bride With Veil | 40.00 |
| **Mold,** Ice Cream, Brownie | 33.00 |
| **Mold,** Ice Cream, Brownie, No.389 | 33.00 |
| **Mold,** Ice Cream, Buffalo On Round Box | 33.00 |
| **Mold,** Ice Cream, Bull | 38.00 |
| **Mold,** Ice Cream, Bunch Of Grapes | 50.00 |
| **Mold,** Ice Cream, Bust Of Admiral Byrd | 65.00 |
| **Mold,** Ice Cream, Calla Lily | 50.00 |
| **Mold,** Ice Cream, Canary | 55.00 |
| **Mold,** Ice Cream, Cat, No.170 | 33.00 |
| **Mold,** Ice Cream, Chick In Egg, No.292 | 25.00 |
| **Mold,** Ice Cream, Chicken Hatching From Egg, 2 3/4 X 4 In., 2 Parts | 45.00 |
| **Mold,** Ice Cream, Chrysanthemum | 45.00 |
| **Mold,** Ice Cream, Cooing Doves | 62.50 |
| **Mold,** Ice Cream, Cradle | 47.50 |
| **Mold,** Ice Cream, Deer | 33.00 |
| **Mold,** Ice Cream, Dolphin | 70.00 |

| | |
|---|---|
| **Mold,** Ice Cream, Donkey | 33.00 |
| **Mold,** Ice Cream, Dove Of Peace | 38.00 |
| **Mold,** Ice Cream, Duck | 33.00 |
| **Mold,** Ice Cream, Duck, Banquet Size | 550.00 |
| **Mold,** Ice Cream, Ear Of Corn | 50.00 |
| **Mold,** Ice Cream, Eastern Star, Masonic | 60.00 |
| **Mold,** Ice Cream, Elk's Head | 35.00 |
| **Mold,** Ice Cream, Eskimo | 38.00 |
| **Mold,** Ice Cream, Father Knickerbocker | 50.00 |
| **Mold,** Ice Cream, Firecaller, No.574 | 38.00 |
| **Mold,** Ice Cream, Floral Hammock | 60.00 |
| **Mold,** Ice Cream, Flowered Wedding Ring | 35.00 |
| **Mold,** Ice Cream, Football Player | 38.00 |
| **Mold,** Ice Cream, Fox | 38.00 |
| **Mold,** Ice Cream, Foxy Grandpa, No.594 | 38.00 |
| **Mold,** Ice Cream, Gables Club, Los Angeles | 90.00 |
| **Mold,** Ice Cream, Grapes, Round | 20.00 |
| **Mold,** Ice Cream, Guitar | 50.00 |
| **Mold,** Ice Cream, Halloween Cat | 33.00 |
| **Mold,** Ice Cream, Hen On Nest | 45.00 To 65.00 |
| **Mold,** Ice Cream, Hickory Nut In Bark | 50.00 |
| **Mold,** Ice Cream, Irishman | 34.00 |
| **Mold,** Ice Cream, Irishman, No.387 | 33.00 |
| **Mold,** Ice Cream, Jack Of Clubs | 30.00 |
| **Mold,** Ice Cream, Jack Of Diamonds | 30.00 |
| **Mold,** Ice Cream, Jack Of Hearts | 30.00 |
| **Mold,** Ice Cream, K. Of C.Maltese Cross | 30.00 |
| **Mold,** Ice Cream, Kiwanis Medallion | 20.00 |
| **Mold,** Ice Cream, Lamb | 29.00 |
| **Mold,** Ice Cream, Liberty Bell | 29.00 |
| **Mold,** Ice Cream, Liberty, No.559 | 49.00 |
| **Mold,** Ice Cream, Lily-Of-The-Valley Leaf | 40.00 |
| **Mold,** Ice Cream, Locomotive | 38.00 |
| **Mold,** Ice Cream, Man In Moon | 45.00 |
| **Mold,** Ice Cream, Mandolin | 62.50 |
| **Mold,** Ice Cream, Mikado, Standing | 34.00 |
| **Mold,** Ice Cream, National Guardsman | 80.00 |
| **Mold,** Ice Cream, Oak Leaf With Acorns | 24.00 |
| **Mold,** Ice Cream, Palmer Cox, Brownie Dude | 62.50 |
| **Mold,** Ice Cream, Palmer Cox, Brownie Irishman | 62.50 |
| **Mold,** Ice Cream, Peach | 22.50 |
| **Mold,** Ice Cream, Pumpkin | 45.00 |
| **Mold,** Ice Cream, Rabbit, England | 15.00 To 25.00 |
| **Mold,** Ice Cream, Rabbit, No.189 | 33.00 |
| **Mold,** Ice Cream, Rabbit, No.297 | 29.00 |
| **Mold,** Ice Cream, Ram | 33.00 |
| **Mold,** Ice Cream, Red Riding Hood | 45.00 |
| **Mold,** Ice Cream, Roast Turkey | 18.50 |
| **Mold,** Ice Cream, Roman Helmet | 75.00 |
| **Mold,** Ice Cream, Rooster | 33.00 |
| **Mold,** Ice Cream, Sailor | 33.00 |
| **Mold,** Ice Cream, Santa Claus, Banquet Size | 450.00 |
| **Mold,** Ice Cream, Santa, C.1890 | 33.00 |
| **Mold,** Ice Cream, Santa, No.991 | 33.00 |
| **Mold,** Ice Cream, Snowman | 33.00 |
| **Mold,** Ice Cream, Squirrel | 33.00 To 35.00 |
| **Mold,** Ice Cream, St.Bernard Dog | 70.00 |
| **Mold,** Ice Cream, Stork With Baby | 60.00 |
| **Mold,** Ice Cream, Streamliner, Engine & Coach, Pair | 100.00 |
| **Mold,** Ice Cream, Tomato Medallion | 45.00 |
| **Mold,** Ice Cream, Tulip Bud | 52.50 |
| **Mold,** Ice Cream, U.S.Flag | 33.00 |

| | |
|---|---:|
| Mold, Ice Cream, U.S.Shield | 33.00 |
| Mold, Ice Cream, Uncle Sam With Rifle | 45.00 |
| Mold, Ice Cream, Washington As Boy | 33.00 |
| Mold, Ice Cream, Washington On Shield | 38.00 |
| Mold, Ice Cream, Watermelon, With Slice Out | 23.00 |
| Mold, Spoon | 295.00 |
| Mug, Curved Lip, C Handle, Marked W.R., English, 4 3/8 In. | 90.00 |
| Mug, Mid Band, Marked George IV & 1826, Pint, 4 3/4 In. | 80.00 |
| Pan, Warming, Handled, 18th Century, Cotterell Mark, English, 9 1/2 In. | 90.00 |
| Pitcher, Ovoid Body, Wishbone Handle, Boardman & Hart Mark, 6 1/2 In. | 350.00 |
| Pitcher, Water, Covered, Marked Roswell Gleason, Mass. | 650.00 |
| Pitcher, Water, Ovoid Body, Wishbone Handle, Marked R. Dunham, 6 In. | 350.00 |
| Pitcher, Wishbone Handle, R.Dunham, C.1845, 4 3/4 In. *Illus* | 350.00 |
| Pitcher, With Agate, Copper Ring At Bottom, 11 In. | 80.00 |
| Plate, Curved Rim, Incised Line, Marked David Melvill, 8 In., Pair | 800.00 |
| Plate, Dated 1847-48, Sheldon & Feltman, Albany, 10 1/2 In.Diam. | 165.00 |
| Plate, Eagle & Badger, Boston, Marked, 1737-1815, 8 1/2 In.Diam. | 250.00 |
| Plate, English, Hallmarked, Freeman, London, 9 1/2 In.Diam. | 125.00 |
| Plate, Flange, Simon Edgell, Philadelphia, 1713-42, 13 In. | 350.00 |
| Plate, Hot Water, English, Hallmarked | 180.00 |
| Plate, Marked Freeman, London, 9 1/2 In. | 125.00 |
| Plate, Rolled Rim, Boardman & Hart Mark, C.1835, 9 3/8 In. | 325.00 |
| Plate, Rolled Rim, J.Danforth, Connecticut, 1780-88, 8 In.Diam. | 175.00 |
| Plate, Rolled Rim, Leonard, Reed, & Barton, Massachusetts, 1835, 12 In. | 55.00 |
| Plate, Serving, Touchmarks, C.1810, English, 10 In.Diam., Pair | 600.00 |
| Plate, 18th Century, R.Bush, England, 8 In.Diam. | 75.00 |
| Platter, Kayserzinn, Pond Fish Design, Water Swirls, 24 1/2 X 11 In. | 165.00 |
| Platter, Kayserzinn, Turkey, 14 In. | 195.00 |
| Platter, Steak, Tree Of Life | 35.00 |
| Porringer, Crown Handle, 5 1/2 In. | 15.00 |
| Porringer, Pierced Handle, Signed Stede, Touchmark, 6 In. | 60.00 |
| Porringer, Straight Rim, Cast Crown Handle, Marked I.C., 4 1/4 In. | 175.00 |
| Pounce Pot, C.1800, English | 85.00 |
| Scoop, Candy, Miniature | 1.00 |
| Spoon, Marked Wm.Mix, 7 1/2 In. | 20.00 |
| Spoon, Wedding, Bridal Couple On Top, 7 In. | 60.00 |
| Syrup, Marked William Savage, Conn. | 135.00 |
| Tankard, Art Nouveau, Lilies, Kayserzinn, 15 In. | 125.00 |
| Taster, Wine, French, Porringer Shape, 18th Century, 2 1/2 In.Diam. | 35.00 |
| Tea Set, Ribbed Body, Footed, Marked Dixon & Son, England, 4 Piece | 175.00 |
| Tea Set, Scroll Handles, Nekrasoff, 4 Piece | 140.00 |
| Teapot, American, 8 In. | 125.00 |
| Teapot, Boat Shape, Ball Feet, Wreath On Sides, Dixon & Smith, England | 95.00 |

Pewter, Pitcher, Wishbone Handle, R.Dunham, C.1845, 4 3/4 In.

| | |
|---|---|
| **Teapot,** Cluster Of Grapes, Signed Morey & Smith, 9 In. | 175.00 |
| **Teapot,** Handmade, Sheffield, England, Signed, 10 In. | 22.00 |
| **Teapot,** James Dixon & Sons, Sheffield, England, 7 In. | 95.00 |
| **Teapot,** Signed E.Porter, Westbrook, Me. | 395.00 |
| **Teapot,** Wooden Finial, Spherical, I.C.Lewis, 1939, Meriden, 8 1/2 In. | 225.00 |
| **Teaspoon,** Pseudo Shell On Back, Marked William Mix | 18.00 |
| **Toothpick,** Like Your Pick | 25.00 |
| **Tray** Kayserzinn, Art Nouveau, Shellfish In Relief, Signed, 13 In. | 225.00 |
| **Tray,** Pin, A Woman's Friend | 5.75 |
| **Tureen,** 3-Legged, Animal & Flower Design, Chinese, 7 X 7 1/2 In. | 195.00 |
| **Vase,** Flared Scallop Top, Fluted, Signed, 9 In. | 145.00 |
| **Vase,** Kayserzinn, Beetles, Lilies, 15 In. | 90.00 |
| **Warmer,** Foot, Signed I.T.Schroeder | 200.00 |

| | |
|---|---|
| **PEYNAUD, Vase,** Cameo & Enamel Florals, Frost Ground, 10 In. | 375.00 |

*Phoenix Bird, or flying Phoenix, is the name given to a blue and white chinaware made between 1900 and World War II. A variant is known as Flying Turkey.*

| | |
|---|---|
| **PHOENIX BIRD, Chocolate Pot,** Flying Turkey, Marked | 250.00 |
| **Creamer** | 6.00 |
| **Cup & Saucer** | 12.50 |
| **Eggcup,** Set Of 4 | 18.00 |
| **Gravy Boat,** 2 Piece | 35.00 |
| **Plate,** Dinner | 25.00 |
| **Plate,** 10 In. | 18.00 |
| **Strainer,** Tea, Twin Bird | 38.00 |
| **Tea Set,** Teapot, Sugar, Creamer, Covered | 79.00 |
| **Vase,** Dragonfly, Green, Brown On Frosted White | 40.00 |

*Phoenix Glass Company was founded in 1880 in Pennsylvania. The firm made commercial products such as lampshades, bottles, and glassware. Collectors today are interested in the sculptured glassware made by the company from the 1930s until the mid-1950s.*

| | |
|---|---|
| **PHOENIX, Bowl,** Boat Shape, Lemons & Foliage, White Ground, 8 In. | 85.00 |
| **Bowl,** Gold, Daffodlis & Birds, Footed, 3 In. | 45.00 |
| **Bowl,** Starflower Design, Ormolu Frame, 15 1/2 X 7 In. | 195.00 |
| **Bowl,** White Ground, Lemons & Foliage, Boat Shape, 8 In. | 85.00 |
| **Compote,** Frosted Green, Orchid Design, Footed, Open | 55.00 |
| **Glass,** Vase, White Thistle, Pale Blue Ground, 9 X 17 1/2 In. | 480.00 |
| **Lamp,** Floral, Blue Bells In Relief, Pink | 85.00 |
| **Lamp,** Orange Berries, Green Leaves, 22 In. | 88.00 |
| **Plate,** Art Nouveau, Dancing Nudes, Frosted, 8 1/2 In.Diam. | 50.00 |
| **Vase,** Acorns, Leaves, Cinnamon Color, White Ground, 6 1/2 In. | 99.00 |
| **Vase,** Amethyst Fish Extended Allover, Oblong Top, 6 1/2 In. | 125.00 |
| **Vase,** Ball, Salmon, Floral Design, 8 In. | 55.00 |
| **Vase,** Baluster Shape, 3-Color Peony, 12 1/2 In. | 350.00 |
| **Vase,** Bird Of Paradise, Fan Shape, Green, 6 3/4 X 6 3/4 In. | 58.00 |
| **Vase,** Bird, Green, 6 1/2 In. | 35.00 |
| **Vase,** Birds & Flowers, Purple, 6 1/2 In. | 70.00 |
| **Vase,** Birds In Flight, Wings Up, 10 X 10 In. | 145.00 |
| **Vase,** Birds On Branches, Gold Leaves, Aqua Birds, 11 In. | 225.00 |
| **Vase,** Birds, Butterscotch, 6 1/2 In. | 65.00 |
| **Vase,** Bittersweet Berries, Custard Ground, 9 1/2 In. | 69.00 |
| **Vase,** Bittersweet Berries, Green Leaves, White Ground, 10 In. | 95.00 |
| **Vase,** Bittersweet Berries, Red & White Opaque, 10 In. | 35.00 |
| **Vase,** Bittersweet Colored Flowers, Label, 9 1/2 In. | 65.00 |
| **Vase,** Bittersweet, Custard, 9 1/2 In. | 65.00 |
| **Vase,** Blue Berries, Vines, Cream Ground, 9 1/2 In. | 80.00 To 95.00 |
| **Vase,** Blue Peonies, Custard Ground, Green Leaves, Brown Stem, 10 In. | 65.00 |
| **Vase,** Blue, Moon, White Geese In Flight | 130.00 |

| | |
|---|---|
| **Vase,** Bluebell, Blue Overlay, White Bells, C.1915, 7 In. | 75.00 |
| **Vase,** Branches & Berries On Green, 9 1/2 In. | 62.00 |
| **Vase,** Cocoa Band, Floral Carvings Over Frost, 6 1/2 In. | 50.00 |
| **Vase,** Curved Fronds, Brown Tinged Leaves, 7 1/4 In. | 70.00 |
| **Vase,** Custard, Tan, Turquoise, Persimmon Birds | 289.00 |
| **Vase,** Dance Of Veils, Salmon Ground, 12 In. | 250.00 |
| **Vase,** Dancing Nudes, Coral & White, 12 In. | 120.00 |
| **Vase,** Dogwood Flowers, Blue, 11 X 6 In., 3 In.Opening | 70.00 |
| **Vase,** Dogwood, Blue & White, 10 In. | 135.00 |
| **Vase,** Dogwood, Salmon, 10 1/2 In. | 240.00 |
| **Vase,** Fern, Iridescent White, Gray Ground, 6 X 7 In. | 95.00 |
| **Vase,** Fish, Pillow Shape, Frosted, 9 X 8 In. | 85.00 |
| **Vase,** Flying Fish, White Frosted & Clear, 8 1/2 In. | 85.00 |
| **Vase,** Flying Geese, Aqua, Paper Label, 9 X 12 In. | 170.00 To 190.00 |
| **Vase,** Freesia, Fan, Aqua, 8 In. | 75.00 |
| **Vase,** Geese, White Frosted Ground, Label, 9 1/4 In. | 165.00 |
| **Vase,** Grasshopper, Fan Shape, Frosted & Clear, Pair | 60.00 |
| **Vase,** Grasshoppers, Brown, Green Leaves, Cream Ground, 7 X 8 1/2 In. | 95.00 |
| **Vase,** Gray Owls, 6 In. | 45.00 |
| **Vase,** Green Floral On White, 6 In. | 55.00 |
| **Vase,** Green Leaves, Blue Peonies, White Frosted Ground, 9 1/2 In. | 125.00 |
| **Vase,** Green Leaves, Lavender Peonies, Frosted Ground, 11 1/2 In. | 165.00 |
| **Vase,** Hummingbird, Lavender, 6-Sided, 6 In. | 55.00 |
| **Vase,** Ivory With Brown, 10 In. | 135.00 |
| **Vase,** Leaves & Flowers, Camphor, Paper Label, 7 In. | 50.00 |
| **Vase,** Little Flowers Pattern, Cream & Nutmeg Shading, 7 In. | 125.00 |
| **Vase,** Lovebirds, Bulbous, Green, Cherry Clusters | 180.00 |
| **Vase,** Lovebirds, Flowers, Amethyst, 6 1/2 In. | 69.00 |
| **Vase,** Lovebirds, Flowers, Purple, 6 1/2 In. | 69.00 To 72.00 |
| **Vase,** Lovebirds, Green, Pink Flowered Branches, 10 X 10 In. | 110.00 |
| **Vase,** Lovebirds, Yellow Frosted, 18 In. | 135.00 |
| **Vase,** Pearl Flowers, Pink Ground, 7 In. | 38.00 |
| **Vase,** Peonies, Yellow On White, 9 1/4 In. | 40.00 |
| **Vase,** Peony, Gold & White, 6 1/2 In. | 25.00 |
| **Vase,** Pinecone, 6 1/2 In. | 85.00 |
| **Vase,** Pink Blossoms, White Opaque, 3 Panels, Spherical, 6 1/2 In. | 80.00 |
| **Vase,** Pink Blossoms, 3 Panels, White Opaque Ground, 6 1/2 In. | 80.00 |
| **Vase,** Praying Mantis, Blue, White Ground, 8 X 7 1/2 In. | 80.00 |
| **Vase,** Rose Snapdragons, White Ground, 10 1/4 In., Pair | 135.00 |
| **Vase,** Siamese Fish | 80.00 |
| **Vase,** Stork In Cattails, Craquelle, Clear, 9 In. | 20.00 |
| **Vase,** Tropical Birds, Globular, White Ground, 9 X 32 In. | 245.00 |
| **Vase,** White Flowers, Beige Ground, 8 X 5 1/2 In. | 90.00 |
| **Vase,** White Flowers, Blue Ground, 7 1/2 In. | 60.00 |
| **Vase,** White Gulls, Gray Ground, Label, 9 1/2 In. | 145.00 |

**PHONOGRAPH, see Music, Phonograph**

*Albums were popular in Victorian times to hold the myriad pictures and cutouts favored by the collectors. All sorts of scrapbooks and albums can still be found.*

| | |
|---|---|
| **PHOTOGRAPHY, Album,** Class Of 1857, Williams College, 54 Portraits, Signed | 500.00 |
| **Album,** Hand-Painted Winter Scene, Cut Velvet Back | 20.00 |
| **Album,** 2-Tune Music Box, Leather Cover, Original Pictures | 220.00 |
| **Ambrotype,** Black Child With White Doll, Case, 6th Plate | 300.00 |
| **Ambrotype,** H.M.The Queen, 1887 | 10.00 |
| **Ambrotype,** Horse, Linus, Long Mane & Tail | 10.00 |
| **Ambrotype,** Salvation Army Lass With Tambourine | 20.00 |
| **Ambrotype,** Soldier Holding Pistol & Saber | 150.00 |
| **Ambrotype,** Swedish Girl In Costume | 5.00 |
| **Ambrotype,** Young Lady Wearing Ruffled Bonnet | 18.00 |
| **Cabinet Card,** Buffalo Bill | 45.00 |
| **Cabinet Card,** Postmortem Of Man | 12.50 |

**Cabinet Card,** Sarah Bernhardt ............................................................ 35.00
**Camera,** Argus C-3, Telephoto Lens, 35 MM ....................................... 45.00
**Camera,** Boston Camera Co., Bull's-Eye, Boston, Wooden Box .......... 150.00
**Camera,** Box, Brownie .......................................................................... 12.00
**Camera,** Brownie Target 6-20, Box ...................................................... 10.00
**Camera,** Brownie, Model A, Folding ..................................................... 32.00
**Camera,** Busch Pressman Reflex, Flashgun, 2 1/4 X 3 1/4 In. ......... 125.00
**Camera,** Cadet B-2 .............................................................................. 8.00
**Camera,** Dorelle, Single Lens Reflex ................................................... 40.00
**Camera,** Eastman No.3-A, Folding ....................................................... 35.00
**Camera,** Folding, Brownie, Brass Lens Mount, Red Bellows ............... 24.50
**Camera,** Folding, Kodak, Leather Bellows, Brass Lens, Pocket Size ... 46.50
**Camera,** Jiffy Kodak Twindar Lens ....................................................... 15.00
**Camera,** Kewpie No.3, Box ................................................................... 18.00
**Camera,** Kodak Co., Hawkeye Model B, Folding ................................. 10.00
**Camera,** Kodak Hawkeye No.2-A, Folding ........................................... 10.00
**Camera,** Kodak K, 1910 ....................................................................... 35.00
**Camera,** Kodak No.2, Hawkeye, Folding, 1910 ................................... 15.00
**Camera,** Kodak Signet 35, Case .......................................................... 35.00
**Camera,** Kodak, Model A, Original Leather Case ................................. 10.00
**Camera,** Kodak, Model B, Vest Pocket, Folding .................................. 12.00
**Camera,** Kodak, 1930, 30th Anniversary, Box ..................................... 7.00
**Camera,** Movie, Debrie, 35 MM, Leather Case .................................... 600.00
**Camera,** Movie, Keystone, Case .......................................................... 10.00
**Camera,** Pacemaker Speed Graphic, Range Finder, Case ................... 180.00
**Camera,** Pony Premo No.6, Plate Holder ............................................ 110.00
**Camera,** Speed Graphic, Range Finder, Wallensak Shutter, 2 Films ... 135.00
**Camera,** Studio, Empire State ............................................................. 110.00
**Camera,** Tasopey Deluxe, Attachments Included ................................. 425.00
**Camera,** Zeiss, Ikonta, 35 MM ............................................................ 15.00
**Candle Lamp,** Kodak, Darkroom, Folding ............................................ 12.00
**Carte De Visite,** Album, Civil War Soldiers, Band, Set Of 85 ............. 125.00
**Carte De Visite,** Andrew Johnson ........................................................ 15.00
**Carte De Visite,** Bringham Young, Beardless ....................................... 75.00
**Carte De Visite,** Charles Sumner ......................................................... 10.00
**Carte De Visite,** Civil War Soldier, Double Amputee ........................... 25.00
**Carte De Visite,** Colt Factory Fire, 1860s .......................................... 30.00
**Carte De Visite,** Daniel Webster, Brady .............................................. 30.00
**Carte De Visite,** Franklin Pierce, Brady .............................................. 35.00
**Carte De Visite,** General Grant ........................................................... 20.00
**Carte De Visite,** General Grant & Family ............................................ 20.00
**Carte De Visite,** General Lee .............................................................. 15.00
**Carte De Visite,** General Longstreet ................................................... 15.00
**Carte De Visite,** General McClellian ................................................... 20.00
**Carte De Visite,** General Thomas, Autographed ................................. 20.00
**Carte De Visite,** Henry Clay, Brady ..................................................... 35.00
**Carte De Visite,** Jean Petri, Chess Master ......................................... 25.00
**Carte De Visite,** Lincoln & Todd ......................................................... 15.00
**Carte De Visite,** Mark Twain, Young, 1870 ........................................ 100.00
**Carte De Visite,** Stonewall Jackson .................................................... 18.00
**Carte De Visite,** Tom Thumb & Wife In Wedding Dress, Brady ......... 225.00
**Carte De Visite,** Tom Thumb & Wife, Brady ....................................... 15.00
**Carte De Visite,** Washington & Family ................................................ 4.00
**Carte De Visite,** Woman, Indian, Modoc ............................................. 18.00
**Carte De Viste,** Abraham Lincoln ........................................................ 20.00
**Daguerreotype Case,** Brown Leather, Raised Thistles, Children ......... 19.00
**Daguerreotype Case,** Gutta-Percha, Beehive, Fruit, 2 1/2 X 3 In. ..... 75.00
**Daguerreotype Case,** Gutta-Percha, Double, Roses, 3 X 4 1/4 In. ..... 95.00
**Daguerreotype Case,** Gutta-Percha, Fortune-Teller, 4 X 5 In. ........... 115.00
**Daguerreotype Case,** Gutta-Percha, Lady On Milk Glass, C.1860 ...... 350.00
**Daguerreotype Case,** Gutta-Percha, Man Serenading Woman, Oval ... 47.50
**Daguerreotype Case,** Gutta-Percha, Rebecca At Well, 3 1/4 In. ........ 125.00
**Daguerreotype Case,** Gutta-Percha, Secret Meeting, 4 X 5 In. .......... 110.00

**Daguerreotype Case,** Gutta-Percha, Snowflake Medallion, 3 In. .................................................. 25.00
**Daguerreotype Case,** Leaf Design, Man, 3 1/4 X 3 3/4 In. .......................................................... 35.00
**Daguerreotype Case,** Mary & Lamb, 3 X 2 1/2 In. ...................................................................... 58.00
**Daguerreotype Case,** Mother & Child ............................................................................................ 110.00
**Daguerreotype Case,** Musicians ............................................................................. 100.00 To 125.00
**Daguerreotype,** Civil War Soldier, Maine, Soft Case ............................................................... 65.00
**Daguerreotype,** Civil War Soldier, Pistol, 3 Stripes On Arm ............................................... 95.00
**Daguerreotype,** Daniel Webster, Half Plate, Original ...................................................... 3750.00
**Ferrotype,** General Grant ............................................................................................................... 65.00
**Lantern,** Darkroom, Kerosene, Tin ............................................................................................. 15.00
**Lantern,** Darkroom, Red Glass, Tin, Vindex, 8 In. ............................................................... 24.00
**Magic Lantern,** Brass Stovepipe, Lens, 10 Glass Slides, Tin ............................................ 155.00
**Magic Lantern,** Delineascope, Model 0, 26 In.Long ............................................................ 350.00
**Magic Lantern,** Kerosene Burner, 23 Slides, Assorted Scenes ....................................... 145.00
**Magic Lantern,** Keystone View Co., Slide, Western, Set Of 80 ...................................... 75.00
**Magic Lantern,** 10 Hand-Colored Slides, Criterion, 17 1/2 In. ...................................... 150.00
**Mirroscope,** Postcard Projector .................................................................................................. 20.00
**Photograph,** Babe Ruth, Batting, Glossy Press Photo ......................................................... 27.00
**Photograph,** Buffalo Bill Cody, 1892, Autographed ............................................................ 300.00
**Photograph,** Vanishing Race, Signed Ed Curtis .................................................................... 400.00
**Projector,** Keystone, Crank ........................................................................................................... 45.00
      **PHOTOGRAPHY, STEREO, see Stereo**
**Tintype,** Carnival Booth Scene, Men Selling Dolls, Blankets ............................................ 40.00
**Tintype,** Civil War General ........................................................................................................... 20.00
**Tintype,** Civil War Sergeant Portrait ......................................................................................... 30.00
**Tintype,** Civil War Soldier ............................................................................................ 15.00 To 23.00
**Tintype,** Civil War Soldier In Union Case ................................................................................ 50.00
**Tintype,** Farm Scene, Barn, People, Team & Wagon, 4 X 7 In. ...................................... 35.00
**Tintype,** Gay 90s Dandy, Cased ................................................................................................. 15.00
**Tintype,** Girl Holding China Head Doll .................................................................................... 9.00
**Tintype,** Indian, White Girls, Beaded Frame .......................................................................... 65.00
**Tintype,** Little Girl, Tinted, 8 3/4 X 6 1/2 In. ......................................................................... 19.00
**Tintype,** Man Making Cigars ....................................................................................................... 24.00
**Tintype,** Young Man, Bridge Scene, Half Pearls Border, 1 3/4 In. ................................. 52.00
**Tintype,** Young Woman, Full Plate ............................................................................................ 18.00
**Tintype,** 2 Boys, Painted, 10 X 7 1/2 In. ................................................................................ 25.00
**Tintype,** 2 Men Playing Poker .................................................................................................... 17.00
**Tintype,** 3 Men, Gold Frame On Easel, 6 In. ......................................................................... 20.00
      **PIANO, see Music, Piano**

*About 1880 the well-decorated home had a shawl on the piano. The bisque*
*piano baby was designed to help hold the shawl in place. They range in size*
*from 6 to 18 inches. Most of the figures were made in Germany.*

**PIANO BABY, Baby Boy & Girl,** Lying On Back, Crossed Swords, 6 1/2 In., Pair ................. 120.00
  **Baby Sitting Beside Coal Bucket,** 4 In. .................................................................................. 75.00
  **Baby Tucked In Horn Of Plenty,** 3 1/2 In. ............................................................. 75.00 To 80.00
  **Blonde Hair,** Blue Eyes, Pink Trim, 4 1/2 In. ......................................................................... 75.00
  **Boy In Socks,** Shorts, Holds Gray Dog, 8 1/2 X 5 In. .......................................................... 125.00
  **Crawling Baby,** Nightie Trimmed In Blue, Marked, 7 X 4 1/2 In. ..................................... 215.00
  **Crawling,** One Foot In Air, Ruffled Dress, Marked, 5 1/2 In. ............................................. 135.00
  **Girl In Nightie Wearing Bonnet,** 4 X 3 1/2 In. ...................................................................... 55.00
  **Girl On Back,** Kicking Legs, Arms Raised, Dimpled, Bisque, Germany .......................... 160.00
  **Kate Greenaway,** Bisque, 7 In. .................................................................................................. 90.00
  **Kate Greenaway,** Bisque, 10 In. ................................................................................................ 125.00
  **Lying Down,** Holding Brown Vessel ......................................................................................... 22.00
  **Lying On Back,** Blue Trim, Heubach, 5 1/2 In. ...................................................................... 97.50
  **Lying On Back,** Blue Trim, Heubach, 8 In. ............................................................................. 175.00
  **Lying On Back,** Playing With Toes, Bonnet, 2 1/2 X 4 1/2 In. .......................................... 110.00
  **Lying On Back,** Playing With Toes, Nightie, Marked, 5 3/4 In. ........................................ 195.00
  **Lying On Side,** Bonnet Of Blooming Daisies, 3 X 4 In. ..................................................... 60.00
  **Lying On Stomach,** Bunny In Arms, Kitten On Back, 7 In. ................................................ 175.00
  **Lying On Stomach,** Holding Dog, Bisque, 10 In. ................................................................. 110.00

Lying On Stomach, Thumb Up To Mouth, Pink & White Gown, 5 In. .................... 45.00
On Back, Holding Toe, Blue Gown, 7 1/2 X 4 1/2 In. .................................... 300.00
On Back, Nightie & Hobnail Bonnet, Heubach, 12 In. ................................... 495.00
One Foot Raised, Impressed Mark, 8 X 4 1/2 In. ........................................ 299.00
Only Toes & Fingers Touch Floor, Real Brown Hair, 5 In. ............................ 150.00
Pink Trim, Blonde Hair, Blue Eyes, Bisque, German, 4 1/2 In. ..................... 75.00
Seated, Both Hands Raised, White Nightie, Bisque, Heubach ....................... 180.00
Seated, Holding Feet, White Nightie, Blue Trim, Marked, 10 1/2 In. ............. 425.00
Seated, Holding Feet, White Nightie, Marked, Heubach, 10 1/2 In. .............. 425.00
Seated, Intaglio Eyes, White Shirt, Green Rim, Heubach, 8 In. ................... 175.00
Seated, Legs Crossed, Arms Upraised, White Gown, Marked, 5 3/4 In. ........ 195.00
Seated, Pink Trim, Blonde, Blue Eyes, 4 1/2 In. ....................................... 75.00
Sitting, No.1467, 5 In. .......................................................................... 35.00
Sitting, Playing With Toes, Blue Ribbon Trim, Marked, 3 1/2 In. ................. 95.00
Twins, Boy & Girl, Sitting Up, Crossed Swords, 5 In., Pair ......................... 100.00

*Pickard china was started in 1898 by Wilder Pickard. Hand-painted china was a featured product. The firm is still working in Antioch, Illinois.*

PICKARD, Berry Set, Yellow, Blue Flowers, Signed Goose ......................... 195.00
Bonbon, Italian Garden, Signed Yesheck, 7 In.Diam. ................................ 65.00
Bowl, Berries & Leaves, Raised Gold Rococo, 1898, 10 1/2 In.Diam. ........... 150.00
Bowl, Bird Center, Gold Edge, Autumnal Colored Ground, 9 1/2 In. ............ 195.00
Bowl, Blue Berries, White Blossoms, Gilt, 1898-1904 Mark, 7 1/2 In. ......... 55.00
Bowl, Deserted Garden Pattern, Bold Trim, 1912 Mark, 11 1/2 In.Diam. ...... 225.00
Bowl, Folded Rim, Gold Etched, 6 1/2 In. ................................................ 50.00
Bowl, Gold Scalloped Rim, Feet, Painted Peaches, 1898 Mark, 11 In. ......... 300.00
Bowl, Hand-Painted, Water Lilies & Gold Pads, Signed, 10 In.Diam. ........... 175.00
Candlestick, Art Nouveau, Silver Luster & Gold Design, 8 In. ................... 60.00
Candlestick, Dutch Girl, Leaf Mark, Bisque Finish, 6 1/2 In., Pair ............. 165.00
Celery, Pheasant Game Scene, Signed, 13 In.Long .................................. 185.00
Charger, Crimson & Burgundy, Iridescent Gold, Signed, 12 1/2 In. ........... 185.00
Charger, Italian Garden Scene, Marble Columns, 1912, 12 1/4 In.Diam. ...... 325.00
Chocolate Set, Geometric Blue Design, Gold Band, Marked, 11 Piece ........ 225.00
Coffee Service, Tray, Pot, Sugar & Creamer ............................................ 90.00
Cup & Saucer, Dark Green, Gold Grapes ................................................. 25.00
Cup & Saucer, Floral, Gold, Signed ........................................................ 45.00
Dish, Candy, Chain Loop Border, All Gold, 7 1/2 In.Square ....................... 55.00
Dish, Candy, Gold Floral Etching, 1925-38 Mark, 1 1/2 X 6 1/2 In. ........... 65.00
Dish, Nut, Signed Vokral ...................................................................... 25.00
Dish, Pedestal, Hand-Painted Strawberries, Signed, 2 X 6 In. ................... 95.00
Hair Receiver, Hand-Painted, Flowers, Gold Trim, 4 1/4 X 2 1/2 In. ............ 75.00
Hatpin Holder, Gold Border, Pansy Design .............................................. 50.00
Hatpin Holder, Iris Design ..................................................................... 75.00
Jar, Jam, 1912 Mark, Art Deco .............................................................. 75.00
Mayonnaise Set, Leaf Shape Dish, Tray, Gold Trim, 1912-19 Mark ............ 98.00
Mustard, Spoon, Gold Etched, 1920 Mark ............................................... 32.00
Nappy, Handled, Castle Scene, Leaf Mark, 7 1/2 In.Diam. ......................... 85.00
Nappy, Violet & Green Leaves, Gold Trim, Signed, 1905 Mark ................... 60.00
Nappy, Violets, Green Leaves, Gold Design, Signed, Marked, 1889-1904 ..... 65.00
Pitcher, , Hand-Painted, Oak Leaves, 1905, Signed, 8 In. ......................... 125.00
Pitcher, Bulbous Base, Gold Handle, 3-Leaf Clovers Allover, 9 In. ............. 195.00
Pitcher, Bulbous, Pear Design, Signed Efdon, Circle Mark, 8 In. ................ 225.00
Pitcher, Cider, Clover, Gold Trim, Signed Lind ........................................ 160.00
Pitcher, Cider, Gold & Blue, Signed Beuttich ........................................... 200.00
Pitcher, Cider, Pink & Red Roses, Gold Trim, Signed, 9 X 7 In. ................ 300.00
Pitcher, Gold Base, Coral & Gold Leaves, Signed, 10 1/2 In. ................... 325.00
Pitcher, Red Poppy Design, Black Outlines, Gold, 7 In. ............. 165.00 To 200.00
Plate, Cake, Antique Enamel Pattern, Gold Center, Signed, 10 In. ............. 115.00
Plate, Cake, Gold Etched, Open Handles, 11 In. ...................................... 50.00
Plate, Currant Design, Gold, Signed, 8 1/2 In. ........................................ 55.00
Plate, Floral, Pink, Gold, C.1912, 8 1/2 In.Diam. ..................................... 30.00

Plate, Gardenias, Gold Trim, Green Ground, 1898 Mark, Signed, 9 In. .................................... 75.00
Plate, Gilded Scalloped Rim, Pastels, 1905-10, Signed, 7 1/2 In. ........................................ 58.00
Plate, Gilt Border, Acorns, Leaves, Circular Mark, Signed, 7 1/2 In. .................................... 85.00
Plate, Gold Band Edge, 10 1/4 In., Set Of 8 ........................................................... 195.00
Plate, Gold, Plum Design, Maple Leaf Marked, 8 1/2 In. ................................................. 75.00
Plate, Misty Forest Scene, Gold Border, Octagon, 11 1/2 In. ........................................... 375.00
Plate, Orange Poppies, Green Ground, Gold Leaf Mark, 7 1/2 In. ........................................ 35.00
Plate, Pink Floral, Signed Edward, 8 1/2 In. .......................................................... 65.00
Plate, Poppy Pattern, Artist Signed, 6 In.Diam., Set Of 6 .............................................. 70.00
Plate, Service, Floral Medallion Center, Bohemia China ................................................ 60.00
Plate, Stylized Stems & Leaves, Gold Rim, 1910 Mark, 8 1/2 In. ........................................ 65.00
Plate, Violets, Gold Border, Signed, 8 1/2 In. ........................................................ 95.00
Punch Set, Footed Bowl, 6 Pedestal Cups, Enameled Petals, 14 1/2 In. ................................ 525.00
Salt & Pepper, Allover Gold ................................................................ 25.00 To 35.00
Salt & Pepper, Gold Etched Flowers, 4 In. ............................................................. 35.00
Salt & Pepper, Gold Etched, 3 1/4 In. ................................................................. 50.00
Salt & Pepper, Gold Etched, 3 3/4 In. ................................................................. 40.00
Sugar & Creamer, Allover Gold, Black Mark ............................................................ 85.00
Sugar & Creamer, Floral Design, Signed .............................................................. 115.00
Sugar & Creamer, Flowers, Gold Trim, Art Deco ....................................................... 105.00
Sugar & Creamer, Fluted, Scalloped, 1925-38 Mark, 2 3/4 In. .......................................... 65.00
Sugar & Creamer, Gold Etched, 2 1/2 In. .................................................... 50.00 To 65.00
Sugar & Creamer, Lake Scene, Blue, Green, Gold, Signed, 1912-19 ..................................... 225.00
Sugar & Creamer, Raised Design, Large ............................................................... 145.00
Sugar Shaker, Tulips, Gold Decoration, C.1905, Signed J.Fisher ....................................... 145.00
Tankard, Gold & Purple Grapes, Gold Trim ............................................................ 195.00
Teapot, Sugar, & Creamer, Gold Etched, 1920 Mark .................................................... 135.00
Tray, Handled, Enamel Bowls Of Fruit, 1912-19 Leaf Mark, Signed ...................................... 75.00
Tray, Handled, Landscape Of Roman Portico, Signed, 7 In.Diam. ....................................... 125.00
Urn, Gold Iris Design, Artist Signed, 1910-20, 10 1/4 In. ............................................ 225.00
Vase, American Beauty Roses, Coin Gold, Green, C.1910, 13 1/2 In. ................................... 195.00
Vase, Art Nouveau, Signed Schoner, 9 1/2 In. .............................................. 225.00 To 249.00
Vase, Art Nouveau, 2-Handled, Coin Gold In Design, Signed, 9 1/2 In. ................................ 225.00
Vase, Birds, Florals & Insects, 2 Handles, Signed, 9 In. ............................................ 180.00
Vase, Fan, Gold, Marked, 5 1/2 In. .................................................................... 85.00
Vase, Farm Scene, Gold Trim, Artist Signed, 7 1/2 In. ............................................... 269.00
Vase, Flared Gold Top, Daisy Design, Signed, 7 3/4 In. .............................................. 155.00
Vase, Floral, Pink Roses, Ribboned Basket, Double Handles .......................................... 125.00
Vase, Green & Gold, Art Nouveau, Flowers & Gold Handles, 9 In. ..................................... 175.00
Vase, Lake Hill, Tropical Scene, Footed, Marked, 1905, 6 In. ........................................ 265.00
Vase, Lilies On Purple & Stippled Gold, Signed Yeschek, 8 1/2 In. ................................... 245.00
Vase, Moon Over Lake & Palm Trees, Signed, 9 In. ................................................... 325.00
Vase, Moonlight Scene, Matte Finish, Signed, 7 In. ................................................. 275.00
Vase, Moonlight Scene, Signed, 8 1/2 In. ............................................................ 165.00
Vase, Poppies, Beading, Silver Trim, White Ground, C.1912, 9 In. .................................... 135.00
Vase, Poppies, 2-Handled, C.1910, 9 1/4 In. ......................................................... 295.00
Vase, Red, Gold, Flowers, Signed, 7 In. .............................................................. 55.00
Vase, Scene Around One Third, Cascading Roses, Ovoid, Signed, 13 In. ............................... 325.00
Vase, Scenic, Moon Over Lake & Palm Trees, Signed, 9 In. ........................................... 325.00
Vase, Trees Covered With Colored Florals, 7 1/2 In. ................................................. 75.00
Vase, White Enamel On Flower Petals, 15 In. ........................................................ 225.00
Vase, Woodland Scene, Pastel Colors, C.1910, Signed, 6 1/2 In. ..................................... 365.00
Vase, Yellow Poppies, Scene On Back, Red, Signed ................................................... 275.00
Vase, Yellow Weeping Trees, River Scene, Handle, Signed, 6 1/4 In. ................................. 365.00

      PICTURE, see also Painting; Print
      PICTURE FRAME, see Furniture, Frame
PICTURE, Embroidered, Girl Seated In Garden, Silk Thread, 18th Century .............................. 145.00
Needlepoint, Biblical, 19th Century, Gilded Frame ................................................... 250.00
Silhouette, Boy Driving Geese ......................................................................... 9.00
Silhouette, Class Of 1823, Bowdoin College, Framed ................................................ 1100.00
Silhouette, Hollow Cut, Williams, 19th Century, Pair ............................................... 225.00
Silhouette, Victorian Girl, Made Of Ribbon & Lace, Taffeta Ground ................................... 15.00

Picture, Tinsel, Black Reverse Glass, 21 1/4 X 17 3/4 In.

Pilkington, Vase, Oviform, Swimming Angelfish, 6 3/4 In.

| | |
|---|---|
| **Silhouette,** Young Child, Signed & Dated 1832 ............................................................ | 65.00 |
| **Tinsel,** Black Reverse Glass, 21 1/4 X 17 3/4 In. .................................................*Illus* | 250.00 |
| **Woven Hair,** Memorial, Signed & Dated 1806, 6 1/2 X 7 1/2 In. ................................... | 125.00 |
|     **PIGEON BLOOD, see Cranberry Glass, Ruby Glass** | |
| | |
| **PIGEON FORGE, Vase,** 4 Legs, Spackled Black & White, 8 1/2 In.Diam. ..................... | 19.95 |
| | |
| **PILKINGTON, Vase,** Oviform, Swimming Angelfish, 6 3/4 In. ...............................*Illus* | 420.00 |
| | |
| **PINCUSHION DOLL, Arms & Hands Away,** Red Beads In Hairdo, Marked, 4 3/4 In. .......... | 165.00 |
| **Arms Away,** Spanish Queen, Beaded Gown, Feather Fan, 6 In. ..................................... | 300.00 |
| **Arms Out,** Wig, 6 In. ....................................................................................................... | 195.00 |
| **Black Bodice,** Hands On Hips, Yellow Bonnet, Germany, 4 In. .................................... | 18.00 |
| **Blue Bodice,** Yellow Hat, Pink Trim, 2 1/2 In. ............................................................. | 55.00 |
| **Colonial Lady,** Green Dress, German, 3 In. .................................................................. | 45.00 |
| **Flapper,** Red Hair, Blue Dress, German, 4 In. .............................................................. | 70.00 |
| **Gray Hair,** Arms On Breast, 11 In. ............................................................................... | 32.00 |
| **Green & Pink Plumes,** Gray Hair, 4 1/2 In. ................................................................. | 58.00 |
| **Green Bodice,** Cerise Fan & Flowers, 4 In. ................................................................. | 55.00 |
| **Hands On Waist,** Black Dress, German, 4 1/2 In. ......................................................... | 55.00 |
| **Nude,** Rose In Black Hair, German, 3 In. ...................................................................... | 40.00 |
| **Open Arm Raised To Head,** Germany, 3 1/4 In. ........................................................... | 15.00 |
| **Ringlets,** Bow, Roses In Hair, Silk Dress, Boots, 6 In. ................................................ | 250.00 |
| **Spanish Dancer,** Blue Comb In Black Hair, Germany, 3 3/4 In. ................................... | 28.50 |
| **Yellow Hat,** Orange Bow, 2 1/4 In. .............................................................................. | 35.00 |
|     **PINK SLAG, see Slag, Pink** | |
|     **PINOCCHIO, see Disneyana, Doll** | |
| | |
| **PIPE, Art Nouveau Lady's Head,** Bisque ....................................................................... | 145.00 |
| **China Bowl,** Carved Foxes & Rabbits ........................................................................... | 28.00 |
| **Cone Shaped Bowl,** C.1820, Tin, 6 In. ......................................................................... | 30.00 |
| **Corncob,** Bent Reed Stem .............................................................................................. | 12.00 |
| **Elephant Head With Tusks** ........................................................................................... | 25.00 |
| **German,** Porcelain Scenic Bowl, Stag Designs .............................................................. | 75.00 |
|     **PIPE, MEERSCHAUM, see Meerschaum, Pipe** | |
| **Mennonite,** Russian, C.1840 ......................................................................................... | 35.00 |
| **Miniature Hand Holding Bowl,** 2 5/8 In. ..................................................................... | 19.00 |
| **Opium,** Applied Flowers & Foo Dog, Hinged Cover, Bronze, 15 X 4 In.Diam. .......... | 135.00 |
| **Opium,** Cobra Head, Lacquered Bamboo, Silver Mounts, Copper Bats ..................... | 195.00 |
| **Opium,** Foo Dog & Foliage Applied To Stem, Bronze, 15 X 4 In. ............................... | 179.00 |
| **Opium,** Lacquered Bamboo, Silver Mounts, Inlaid With Copper Bats ....................... | 195.00 |
| **Porcelain,** Deer Scene, Transfer, German ................................................................... | 37.50 |

**Porcelain,** Painted Gibson Girl ............................................................................... 47.50
**Trade,** Indian, Ax Head, Bell Shaped, Heart Cut Out, 18th Century, 8 In. ............................ 400.00

*Pirkenhammer is a porcelain manufactory started in 1802 by Friedrich Holke and J.G. List.*

**PIRKENHAMMER, Cup & Saucer,** Demitasse, Set Of 6 ...................................... 220.00
    **Snack Tray & Cup,** Ivory Ground, Bird, Flower, & Butterfly ............................... 39.00

*Pisgah pottery pieces that are marked Pisgah Forest Pottery were made in North Carolina from 1926 until the present. Vases, teapots, jugs, candlesticks, and many other items were made.*

**PISGAH FOREST, Casserole,** Covered, Trivet With Warmer .......................................... 20.00
    **Creamer,** Blue & Aubergine, 3 1/2 X 3 1/4 In. .................................................. 10.00
    **Creamer,** Cameo, Dated 1942, 5 X 4 1/2 In.Diam. ........................................... 325.00
    **Mug,** Cameo, Signed Stephen, 3 1/2 In. ........................................................ 175.00
    **Pitcher,** Mottled Turquoise Outside, Pink Inside, 3 3/4 In. ................................. 34.50
    **Sugar & Creamer,** Lid, Handled, Aqua, Pink Inside, Dated 1934 ......................... 125.00
    **Sugar & Creamer,** Turquoise, Small ............................................................. 15.00
    **Vase,** Blue Crackle, 1940, 4 In. .................................................................. 25.00
    **Vase,** Burgundy High Gloss, 1941, 4 In. ....................................................... 45.00
    **Vase,** Flared, 1950, 6 In. ........................................................................... 28.50
    **Vase,** 1937, 4 In. ...................................................................................... 35.00
    **Vase,** 1950, Blue Crystalline, 7 In. .............................................................. 28.00
    **PLATE, see under special types such as ABC; Calendar**

*Plated amberina was patented June 15, 1886, by Edward D. Libbey and made by the New England Glass Works. It is similar to amberina, but is characterized by a cream-colored or chartreuse lining (never white) and small ridges or ribs on the outside.*

**PLATED AMBERINA, Tumbler** .................................................................................... 1900.00
    **Vase,** C.1890, 3 1/4 In. ...................................................................... *Illus* 1250.00
    **PLATED SILVER, see Silver Plate**

Plated Amberina, Vase, C.1890, 3 1/4 In.

*Plique a jour is an enameling process. The enamel is laid between thin raised metal lines and heated. The finished piece has transparent enamel held between the thin metal wires.*

| | |
|---|---|
| **PLIQUE A JOUR, Bowl,** Blooming Flowers, Green Ground, 4 1/4 In. | 765.00 |
| **Spoon,** Demitasse, Original Box, Set Of 6 | 400.00 |
| **Spoon,** Twisted Stem, Enamel Flowers, Marked, Set Of 12 | 795.00 |
| | |
| **POLITICAL CAMPAIGN, Banner,** Al Smith, Photograph On Cloth, U.S.Shield | 55.00 |
| **Banner,** F.D.R., Silk | 12.00 |
| **Box,** Ballot, McNulty, Key, Carrier, 45 X 21 In. | 495.00 |
| **Box,** Choice, Willkie Or Roosevelt | 15.00 To 25.00 |
| **Bust,** Woodrow Wilson, Plaster, Life Size, C.1916 | 46.50 |
| **Button,** Clean House With Dewey | 5.00 |
| **Button,** Dick, Ike | 5.00 |
| **Button,** Eisenhower & Nixon | 5.00 |
| **Button,** Figural, Donkey Head, Hee Haw Victory, 1932 | 15.20 |
| **Button,** For President, W.J.Bryan, Copper Frame, 1 In. | 20.00 |
| **Button,** Friends Of Franklin Roosevelt, Picture | 10.00 |
| **Button,** George Wallace, 1968, 1 3/4 In. | 1.75 |
| **Button,** Goldwater For President, Portrait | 5.00 |
| **Button,** Grant, Colfax, Jugate | 135.00 |
| **Button,** Harrison, 1888, Red, White, & Blue, Brass | 75.00 |
| **Button,** Henry Ford For Senator | 5.00 |
| **Button,** Hoover & Curtis, Blue & White | 4.00 |
| **Button,** Humphrey For Senate, Picture | 20.00 |
| **Button,** Kennedy & Johnson For Experience, Pictured | 20.00 |
| **Button,** La Follette Wheeler, Bronze | 6.00 |
| **Button,** Landon, Knox, Felt Back | 3.50 |
| **Button,** Landon, Knox, G.O.P.Elephant, 2 1/2 In.Diam. | 3.50 |
| **Button,** Lapel, Grover Cleveland, Mother-Of-Pearl | 45.00 |
| **Button,** McGovern In '72, Used Only In Oregon | 3.00 |
| **Button,** McKinley, Gold Bug | 9.00 |
| **Button,** Mechanical, Uncle Sam Hanging Hitler | 32.50 |
| **Button,** Oregonians For Nixon, Agnew | 2.00 |
| **Button,** President Nixon | 2.00 |
| **Button,** Sunflower, Landon, Knox | 2.00 |
| **Button,** Thomas Dewey For President, Pictured, 2 1/2 In. | 4.00 |
| **Button,** Uncle Sam, C.1870, Tin, 3 In. | 50.00 |
| **Button,** Warren Harding, Picture | 4.00 |
| **Button,** Willkie & McNary | 3.50 |
| **Button,** Win With Wilson, Colored, 1 1/2 In. | 15.00 |
| **Cane,** Golf Club Shape, W.Wilson Inauguration, 1917 | 95.00 |
| **Cigar,** Truman For President | 30.00 |
| **Cutter,** Cigar, Theodore Roosevelt, 1904-05, Bone, 9 In. | 45.00 |
| **Figurine,** Fighting Elephant & Donkey, Chalkware, 9 In. | 15.00 |
| **Flag,** Garfield, Arthur | 185.00 |
| **Flag,** Window, Wendell Willkie, Silk | 9.00 |
| **Handkerchief,** Picture Of Al Smith, Blue & White | 30.00 |
| **Hat,** Cowboy, Lyndon Johnson, Ceramic | 12.50 |
| **Hat,** Goldwater, Cloth | 12.00 |
| **Hot Plate,** Roosevelt Bear, China | 48.00 |
| **Invitation,** Inaugural, Autographed, F.D.Roosevelt | 40.00 |
| **Jackknife,** McKinley | 55.00 |
| **Jugate,** McKinley-Hobart | 95.00 |
| **Jugate,** Roosevelt & Wallace | 7.00 |
| **Mug,** Bobby For President | 8.00 |
| **Mug,** Covered, McKinley | 32.00 |
| **Mug,** Elephant, Signed Nixon & Agnew, 1969, Frankoma | 50.00 |
| **Mug,** G.O.P. Elephant, 1968, Frankoma | 60.00 |
| **Mug,** Nixon & Agnew, Cobalt Blue | 15.00 |
| **Music,** Sheet, Our Hats Off To You, Mr. Wilson | 15.00 |
| **Nodder,** Eisenhower | 15.00 |

| | |
|---|---|
| **Nodder,** Elephant, Nixon For President, Original Box | 12.50 |
| **Paperweight,** Eisenhower Inauguration | 25.00 |
| **Paperweight,** F.D.Roosevelt, 1932, Pewter | 25.00 |
| **Parade Shield,** George Washington, C.1870 | 625.00 |
| **Parade Torch,** Handle, 40 In. | 30.00 |
| **Picture,** McKinley In Carriage, Phoenix, 1901, 6 X 9 In. | 150.00 |
| **Pin,** Coolidge, Dawes Club, Albany County, N.Y., Jugate | 200.00 |
| **Pitcher,** Al Smith Pictured, White China | 60.00 |
| **Plate,** President Nixon | 11.00 |
| **Plate,** Taft, Turquoise Glass, 8 In.Diam. | 10.00 |
| **Plate,** Teddy Roosevelt, Animals, Pierced Edge, 7 1/2 In. | 65.00 |
| **Plate,** Ulysses Grant, Patriot & Soldier | 45.00 |
| **Plate,** Van Buren, Turquoise Glass, 8 In.Diam. | 10.00 |
| **Platter,** McKinley, It Is God's Way | 15.00 |
| **Postcard,** Nebraska For Taft, Tuck | 15.00 |
| **Poster,** Roosevelt & Truman | 30.00 |
| **Poster,** Stevenson For Governor, Pictured Waist Up | 15.00 |
| **Poster,** Vote Democratic, Truman, Roosevelt, 11 X 14 In. | 45.00 |
| **Program,** Teamsters Support Roosevelt | 4.00 |
| **Ribbon,** Abraham Lincoln, 1 3/4 In.Wide | 15.00 |
| **Ribbon,** Harrison | 35.00 |
| **Ribbon,** Landon, Knox, 1 In. | 12.00 |
| **Ribbon,** Late Lamented President Lincoln, Silk, 2 X 8 In. | 120.00 |
| **Ribbon,** Republican Rally, 1888 | 8.00 |
| **Ribbon,** Taft & Henricks, Jugate | 55.00 |
| **Ring,** Al Smith | 22.00 |
| **Ring,** Nixon, 1972, Metal | 3.75 |
| **Sign,** Bumper, Landon, Knox, Sunflower, Metal | 10.00 To 12.00 |
| **Sunflower,** With Wire, Alf Landon, Papier-Mache | 6.00 |
| **Thermometer & Mirror,** Pocket, Advertising | 5.00 |
| **Tin,** Pocket, Presidential Candidates Of 1880 Election | 252.00 |
| **Toby Jug,** Eisenhower | 45.00 |
| **Toby Jug,** Hoover, Al Smith, Pair | 95.00 |
| **Tray,** McKinley, Roosevelt, Jugate, Aluminum | 16.00 |
| **Tumbler,** G.O.P.Elephant, Raised Letters, Frosted | 18.00 |
| **Tumbler,** McKinley, Our President, 1896 To 1900 | 37.50 |
| **Tumbler,** McKinley, Protection & Plenty | 45.00 |
| **Wall Box,** John Buchanan | 40.00 |
| **Watch Fob,** A.Lincoln, Republican Nat'l.Convention, 1920 | 37.50 |
| **Watch Fob,** Busts Of Cox & Roosevelt | 50.00 To 80.00 |
| **Watch Fob,** For President Theodore Roosevelt, Shield | 30.00 |
| **Watch Fob,** Harding, Coolidge | 35.00 |
| **Watch Fob,** Inaugural, President W.H.Taft, March 4, 1900 | 60.00 |
| **Watch Fob,** Our Choice, Taft & Sherman | 40.00 To 60.00 |
| **Watch Fob,** Republican Convention, 1920, Hallmarked | 45.00 |
| **Watch Fob,** Roosevelt, Fairbanks, 1904, Brass | 12.50 |

*Pomona glass is clear with a soft amber border decorated with pale blue or rose-colored flowers and leaves. The colors are very, very pale. The background of the glass is covered with a network of fine lines. It was made from 1885 to 1888 by the New England Glass Company.*

| | |
|---|---|
| **POMONA, Bowl,** Cornflower Design, 2nd Grind, 8 X 3 1/2 In. | 315.00 |
| **Creamer,** Footed, Blue Cornflower Front, Butterfly On Back, 3 1/4 In. | 125.00 |
| **Cup,** Punch, Cornflower & Butterfly Design, 2nd Grind | 85.00 |
| **Finger Bowl,** Scalloped Rim, Amber Upper 1/3rd, Clear Lower 2/3rd | 130.00 |
| **Pitcher,** Frosted Bottom, Blue Flowers, Yellow Leaves, 4 3/4 In. | 250.00 |
| **Pitcher,** Frosted Bottom, Yellow Border Top, 5 X 3 In. | 85.00 |
| **Pitcher,** Lemonade, Diamond-Quilted, 2nd Grind, 13 In. | 140.00 |
| **Pitcher,** Water, Inverted Thumbprint, Amber Handle, Square Mouth | 275.00 |
| **Rose Bowl,** Crimped, Amber Stain, 2nd Grind, 2 1/2 X 4 1/4 In.Diam. | 140.00 |
| **Saltshaker,** Violets & Fuchsia, Pewter Collar & Lid, 4 In. | 45.00 |
| **Sugar & Creamer,** Cornflower Design, Ruffled Edges, C.1900, 5 In. | 200.00 |

Toothpick, Diamond-Quilted, Amber Stain, 2nd Grind, Tricornered ................................ 140.00
Toothpick, Inverted Thumbprint, Tricornered ................................ 140.00
Toothpick, Midwestern, Tricornered, Amber Top ................................ 125.00
Tumbler, Acanthus Amber Design, First Grind ................................ 125.00
Tumbler, Diamond Optic, Scalloped Top, 2nd Grind, 3 In. ................................ 78.00
Tumbler, Diamond-Quilted, Amber, Scalloped Border, 3 3/4 In. ................................ 115.00
Tumbler, 1st Grind ................................ 160.00
Vase, Amber Ruffled Top, Scalloped Base, 2nd Grind, 5 In. ................................ 350.00
Vase, Handles, 1st Grind, Signed, 2 1/2 In. ................................ 75.00
Vase, Pedestal, Optic Ribbed, Green, 12 In. ................................ 145.00
Vase, Ruffled, Applied Base, Palm Leaf Design, 2nd Grind, 6 In. ................................ 190.00
Vase, Ruffled, Blue & Amber Cornflower, C.1900, 6 1/2 In. ................................ 125.00
    PONTYPOOL, see Tole
    POO WARE, see Banko

POPE-GOSSER, Jam Set, Yellow Flowers, 2 Piece ................................ 12.00

POPEYE, Bandwagon, Paper Lithograph On Wood, Fisher Price ................................ 45.00
Bank, Dime Register, Pocket Type, C.1929 ................................ 60.00
Bank, Dime Register, 1956 ................................ 20.00
Beachball, C.1950, Packaged ................................ 12.50
Book, Animated, Popeye & The Pirates, 1945 ................................ 35.00
Book, Colored Illustrations, Hard Cover, 1937, 9 1/2 X 10 In. ................................ 28.00
Box, Pencil, 1929, Large ................................ 24.00
Box, Pencil, 1950s ................................ 20.00
Bubble Set, Transogram, 1937 ................................ 45.00
Cycle, Spinach, Hubley, 5 1/2 In. ................................ 350.00
Doorstop, Wooden ................................ 26.00
Fountain Pen ................................ 15.00
Game, Ball In Hole, C.1929, 4 X 5 In. ................................ 15.00
Game, Juggler, 1929 ................................ 32.00
Game, Jump-Up, Wood ................................ 17.50
Game, Pipe Toss, Original Box, 1935 ................................ 40.00
Game, Popeye The Juggler Game, 1929 ................................ 35.00
Game, Ring Toss, King Features ................................ 20.00
Game, The Juggler ................................ 50.00
Harmonica, 1929 ................................ 58.00
Lantern, Figural Man, Battery Operated, Linemar, Boxed ................................ 100.00
Marble Set, Boxed, 1929 ................................ 12.00
Notebook, 1929 ................................ 10.00
Olive, Figures, Soft Rubber, 1930s, 8 In. ................................ 145.00
Paddle Ball, Bifbat, 1929 ................................ 15.00
Paint Set, Popeye & Family, 5 X 4 X 1 1/2 In. ................................ 25.00
Pen & Pencil Set ................................ 45.00
Pencil Box, 1929 ................................ 24.00
Pencil, Extra Large ................................ 20.00
Photo-Fun Print Set, 1958 ................................ 12.00
Pipe, Kazoo ................................ 10.00
Pistol, Pirate, Boxed ................................ 135.00
Puppet, Olive Oyl ................................ 7.50
Toy, Express, Windup, Tin ................................ 250.00
Toy, In Barrel, C.1930, Chein ................................ 180.00
Toy, Olive On Cabin, Marx, Boxed ................................ 750.00
Toy, On Roof, Windup, Marx ................................ 425.00
Toy, Parrot Cage, Windup, Lehmann, Tin ................................ 175.00
Toy, Pilot ................................ 400.00
Toy, Pull, Fisher Price ................................ 65.00
Toy, Punching Bag, Floor Type, Marx ................................ 425.00
Toy, Pushing Wheelbarrow, Windup, Stationary Parrot ................................ 250.00
Toy, The Pilot, 1930s, Windup, Marx ................................ 375.00
Walker, Celluloid ................................ 35.00
Wallet, 1950 ................................ 18.00
Wristwatch, Ingersoll ................................ 80.00

PORCELAIN, see also Copeland; Nippon; RS Prussia; etc.

PORCELAIN, Bottle, Drug, Lambeth, Delft Blue & White, C.1680, 7 3/4 In., Pair ................. 2800.00
Bottle, Sake, Calligraphy On Side, 5 In. ............................................................................... 35.00
Bottle, Snuff, Men On Horses, Elephant & Dog, Ch'ien Lung Mark ................................... 185.00
Box, Blue Enamel, Draped Nude On Lid, C.1925, Viennese, 4 5/8 In. ......................... 1000.00
Box, Bureau Shape, Bronze & Enamel, 3 Drawers, Pull-Down, 8 3/4 In. ....................... 1600.00
Box, Covered, Double Happiness Design, Blue & White, Round ...................................... 52.00
Bust, Marie Antoinette, White, Gold Initials M A, 15 In. ................................................. 375.00
Charger, Blue & White, C.1580, Ming Dynasty, 18 In.Diam. ........................................... 795.00
Chocolate Set, Gilt Bronze & Enamel, 19th Century, Vienna, 8 Piece ......................... 3250.00
Chocolate Set, Tray, 6 Cups & Saucers, Alhambra Pattern ........................................... 800.00
Condiment Set, White, Magenta Bird & Floral, German, 4 Piece .................................... 55.00
Cup, Sake, Naughtie, Set Of 6 ........................................................................................ 70.00
Dish, Lobed, Chinoiserie Center Figure, C.1720, 13 3/4 In.Diam. ................................. 520.00
Dresser Set, Beige To Dark Brown, Gold Trim, Tray, 11 In., 6 Piece ............................ 245.00
Egg, Russian, Hand-Painted Flowers, Blue Ground, Silk Ribbon .................................... 600.00
Figurine, Boy With Lotus Seated On Carp, Chinese, 5 In. ............................................. 115.00
Figurine, Hoeti, Seated Beside Green Frog, C'hing, 10 1/2 X 8 In. ............................... 365.00
Figurine, Napoleon, Standing, Uniform, German, 9 1/2 In. ............................................. 175.00
Figurine, Sitting Hoeti, Enamel Flowers, Ch'ien Lung, 10 In. ........................................ 340.00
Figurine, Smiling Deity, Huge Frog, Chinese, 10 1/2 X 8 In. .......................................... 395.00
Frame, Gold Border, Signed Wagner, 4 X 5 1/4 In. ....................................................... 925.00
French, Plate, Footed, Musical, 2 Tunes, Marked, 2 1/4 X 9 In. .................................... 350.00
Humidor, Figural, Fox With Hat, Smoking Pipe, Multicolor, 5 1/2 In. ............................. 79.50
Jar, Tobacco, Figural, Man With Cigar, Green Hat With Feather ..................................... 65.00
Lamp, Incense Burner, Colonial Lady ............................................................................ 25.00
Mortar & Pestle, Coors, 6 1/2 In. .................................................................................. 47.00
Mustard, Figural, Pineapple, Yellow Finial, Twig Handle ................................................ 26.00
PORCELAIN, NAPKIN RING, see Napkin Ring
Seat, Garden, Barrel Shape, Chrysanthemum Design, 18 1/4 In. ................................... 850.00
Shoe, High Heel, 2 Cupids On Toe, Orange Heel On Pillow, Marked ............................. 195.00
Stein, Painted Frieze, Soldier Knop, Viennese, 4 1/2 In., Pair ...................................... 2500.00
Tea Set, 6 Cups & Saucers, Ch'ien Lung Dynasty, 15 Piece ........................................ 175.00
Teapot, Scenery Front & Back, Square, Helene Wolfsohn, 5 In. .................................... 135.00
Tray, Enamel & Gilt Bronze, 18th Century, Scene On Reverse, 16 In. .......................... 2500.00
Urn, Painted Vignettes, Mask Border, Scroll Handles, 5 3/4 In.Pr. ............................... 4000.00
Vase, Bird's Head Handles, Inlaid Enamel Design, China, 14 1/2 In. ............................ 225.00
Vase, Floral Panels, Marble Ground, Blue Border, 13 In., Pair ...................................... 175.00
Vase, Gilt Handle, Polychrome Floral & Heron, Japan, C.1900, 9 In. ............................ 475.00
Vase, 3 People In Relief, Red & Black, Sumida, Japan, 8 In. ........................................ 115.00
Wall Pocket, Egg Yolk & Spinach Glaze, C.1850, Chinese, 11 In. ................................ 185.00
Wig Stand, Royal Court Scene, Calligraphy, 11 1/2 In. ................................................. 65.00

*Postcards were first legally permitted in Austria on October 1, 1869.*
*The United States passed postal regulations allowing the card in 1873.*
*Most of the picture postcards collected today date from 1910.*

POSTCARD, A Christmas Wish, A New Year Wish, Cloth, Fringed .................................. 2.00
Album, Africa, Set Of 280 .............................................................................................. 35.00
American Red Cross, Washington, D.C. ......................................................................... .50
Atlantic City, Old Hotels, Set Of 16 ............................................................................... 15.00
Bangor & Aroostock Rail Road Hunting Scene, Maine ................................................... 20.00
Bathing Beauties, 1920s, Color, Unused, Set Of 6 ....................................................... 4.50
Children Looking In Window At Santa ............................................................................ 6.00
Chromo Vase Of Mums, Signed Loewenberg .................................................................. 7.00
City Hall, Philadelphia, Pennsylvania ............................................................................ .25
Congregational Church, Keosauque, Iowa ...................................................................... 3.50
Council House, Birmingham, England ............................................................................. .50
Doll, Madame Alexander, Set Of 12 ............................................................................... 1.50
Easter, 1907, P.Sanders, N.Y., Embossed ................................................................... 6.00
Elks Fraternal, Black Baby Riding Goat ......................................................................... 12.00
Fire Engine, Close-Up, Set Of 12 .................................................................................. 12.00
Girl, Real Hair ............................................................................................................... 15.00
H.J.Heinz Auditorium, 1900 .......................................................................................... 12.00

Heidi, English .......................................................................................... 15.00
Indian Pueblo Village .......................................................................... 7.00
Interior Of St.John's Church, Richmond, Virginia ............................ .25
Just Before The Start, Indianapolis Motor Speedway ...................... 12.00
Kewpie, Signed O'Neill ......................................................................... 20.00
Lighthouse, Waukegan, Illinois ............................................................ 4.50
May Christmas Morn Be Bright For You, Cloth, Fringed ................. 2.00
Nude Baby Holding Candlestick Telephone ...................................... 7.00
Out To Old Aunt Mary's, Riley ............................................................ 7.00
President McKinley, Dated 1886 ........................................................ 3.00
President Taft Speaking To Crowd, Set Of 5 ..................................... 25.00
Prince Charles Colored Investiture, 1969 ........................................ 3.00
Railroad, Set Of 4 .................................................................................. 4.00
Ralph Tuck & Sons, Pair ....................................................................... 5.00
Roosevelt Bears ...................................................................................... 14.00
Santa Carrying Balloons, C.1905 ....................................................... 5.00
Small Towns In Illinois, Pre-1910, Set Of 6 ..................................... 5.00
S. S. Marion, Woven On Silk ................................................................ 25.00
State Flower & State Bird ...................................................................... .25
Teddy Roosevelt & Family, Color, Marked 1906 ............................. 5.00
Thanksgiving Turkey, Ellen Clapsaddle, Set Of 10 ......................... 24.00
The Palace Hotel, Heliopolis, Egypt .................................................. .50
U.S.Arbuckle, Coffee ............................................................................. 2.00
Union Depot, Cheyenne, Wyoming ..................................................... 5.00
Union Pacific Railroad, Scenics, Set Of 8 ......................................... 6.00
West Main Street, Urbana, Illinois ...................................................... 6.00
Wishing You A Peaceful Easter, Cloth, Fringed ............................... 2.00
World War I, Embroidered, Set Of 3 ................................................... 10.00
1962 Seattle World's Fair, Set Of 12 ................................................. 7.00


POSTER, Alaska Refrigerators, Couple Beside 5-Door Ice Box, 22 X 28 In. ............ 150.00
Antislavery, The Negro Woman's Lamentation, 1775 ...................... 225.00
Arm & Hammer, Bird, Set Of 6 ............................................................ 27.00
Baldwin's Nervous Pills, 1905, 26 X 20 In. ...................................... 30.00
Barnum & Bailey, Chromolithograph Of Wallendas, 3 1/2 X 2 1/3 Ft. .......... 110.00
Circus, Donaldson Lithographing Co., Date Bills, 9 Sheet ........... 300.00
City Of Chattanooga, S.D., Steamship Co., 24 X 36 In. ................. 100.00
DuPont, Hunters With Dog & Guns, 20 X 31 In. .............................. 325.00
DuPpont, Pictures Powder Kegs, 14 X 21 In. ................................... 125.00
Enlist, World War I, Speer ..................................................................... 400.00
Hart, Schaffner, & Marx, Well-Dressed Man, C.1909, 27 X 19 1/4 In. .......... 35.00
Hercules Powder, Hunter With Gun, 14 X 21 In. ............................. 175.00
Hopkins & Allen, Picture Of Annie Oakley, Framed, 10 X 26 In. ........... 325.00
I Want You, World War I, Flagg ........................................................... 500.00
McLaughlin's Coffee, C.1910, 23 X 24 In. ........................................ 65.00
Movie, Red Skelton, Excuse My Dust, 1951 .................................... 75.00
Movie, To Hell & Back, Audie Murphy, 30 X 39 1/2 In. .................. 10.00
Myrtle Navy Tobacco, 1901, 23 X 16 In. ......................................... 135.00
Red Man Tobacco, 1930s, Pictures Indian Chief, 20 X 22 In. ...... 65.00
Remington, Big Game, Game & Target Cartridges, 20 X 36 In. ..... 225.00
Ringling Circus, Storbridge Lithograph, Ohio, 1911, 24 X 16 3/4 In. ........ 35.00
Rube Perkin's Novelty Act, 22 X 16 In. ............................................. 15.00
Santa Claus, Large Pack, 1930s, 9 In. ............................................. 28.00
Savage Washers & Dryers, Old Washing Machine, 21 X 26 In. ..... 45.00
Tom Mix, Buck Jones, & William Cody, 1931, 22 X 2 In., Set Of 3 ........ 175.00
U.S.Cartridge, Pictures Moose, 11 X 14 In. ..................................... 165.00
World War I, Over The Top For You, 3rd Liberty Loan, 20 X 30 In. ........ 40.00


POTLID, see also Pratt
POTLID, Cliff House, San Francisco, 2 1/2 In. ................................ 125.00
Cries Of London, Sweet Oranges .............................. 20.00 To 35.00
Room Shakespeare Was Born, 1564, Stratford On Avon .............. 75.00
Village Wedding, Framed ...................................................................... 65.00

**POTTERY,** see also Buffalo Pottery; Staffordshire; Wedgwood; etc.

| | |
|---|---|
| **POTTERY, Bowl,** Turquoise, Yellow, Ivory Ground, Wiener Werkstatte, 4 In. | 175.00 |
| **Candlestick,** 2 Branch, Blue, Yellow, Orange, Werkstatte, 8 In. | 250.00 |
| **Coffeepot,** Tin Covered, Ohio | 165.00 |
| **English,** Teapot, Caneware, Oriental Figures, 6 1/4 In. ............................*Illus* | 500.00 |
| **Figurine,** Group, Yellow, Green, Rose, Wiener Werkstatte, 6 In. | 350.00 |
| **Figurine,** Water Buffalo, Chinese, 10 X 3 1/2 In. | 200.00 |
| **Foot Warmer,** England, Lovatt Langley | 45.00 |
| **Jardiniere,** Molded Water Lily, Rose Ground, England, C.1900, 32 In. | 225.00 |
| **Jug,** Orange With Greens, Peoria Pottery, 1o 1/2 In. | 65.00 |
| **Pitcher,** Grape Pattern, Brown Glaze | 26.00 |
| **Plaque,** Tulle Panel, Geometric Banding, Werkstatte, 33 In. | 400.00 |
| **Salt,** Hanging, Blue & Gray Eagle | 250.00 |
| **Spittoon,** Grape Pattern, Earth Brown | 35.00 |
| **Vase,** Flow Blue, Embossed Gold Flowers, G.Jones, 12 In. | 225.00 |
| **Vase,** French, Earthenware, Marked, Signed, 21 In., Pair ...................*Illus* | 1000.00 |
| **Vase,** Wannapee, 9 3/4 X 8 X 8 1/2 In. | 95.00 |
| **Vase,** 4-Sided, 5 Petal Flowers, Oyster Bay, 5 X 3 1/2 In. | 385.00 |
| | |
| **POWDER FLASK, Brass** | 50.00 |
| **Copper,** Deer Heads, Oak Leaves & Acorns | 175.00 |
| **Fleur-De-Lis,** 4 Measures, Brass, 9 In. | 45.00 |
| **Zinc** | 32.50 |
| | |
| **POWDER HORN, Carved,** Alexander Corles, 1778 | 700.00 |
| **Engraved,** Gideon Webb's Horn, 1762, 12 In. | 4600.00 |
| **Made & Signed By T.M.Ross,** Texas, Dated 1860, 16 In. | 125.00 |

Pottery, Vase, French, Earthenware, Marked, Signed, 21 In., Pair

PRATT
FENTON

*Pratt ware means two different things. It was an early Staffordshire pottery, cream colored with colored decorations, made by Felix Pratt during the late eighteenth century. There was also Pratt ware made with transfer designs during the mid-nineteenth century in Fenton, England.*

| | |
|---|---|
| **PRATT, Jar,** Boar Hunt, Blue, 4 In. | 45.00 |
| **Jar,** Pomade, Blue Glaze, Hunt Scene, 4 1/8 In. | 22.00 |

| | |
|---|---|
| Jar, Snuff, Constantinople | 50.00 |
| Pitcher, Embossed Figures Making Wine, C.1820, 5 In. | 230.00 |
| Plate, End Of Hunt, Green Border, 8 1/2 In. | 55.00 |
| Plate, Shakespeare's House, White Ground, Green Border | 45.00 |
| Plate, The Battle Of The Nile, White Ground, Green Border | 45.00 |
| Plate, The Cavalier, Lavender Border, 7 In. | 42.00 |
| Plate, 7 1/4 In.Diam. | 100.00 |
| Plate, 8 1/2 In.Diam. | 100.00 |
| Potlid, The Sportsman | 110.00 |
| Potlid, Yellow Primroses | 47.50 |
| Sugar & Creamer, Covered, Signed | 90.00 |
| Sugar & Creamer, Waterfront, Ships, Grecian Ruins, Turquoise, Signed | 110.00 |
| Syrup, Medallions With Children, Pewter Lid | 155.00 |
| Tankard, Waterfront, Ships, Grecian Ruins, Turquoise, Signed, 7 In. | 110.00 |
| Tea Caddy, Woman On One Side, Man On Other, 18th Century Dress | 250.00 |
| Tea Tile, Waterfront, Ships, Grecian Ruins, Turquoise, Signed, 7 In. | 65.00 |

*Pressed glass was first made in the United States in the 1820s after the invention of pressed glass machines. Hundreds of patterns of pressed glass were made in complete table settings. Although the Boston and Sandwich Works was the most famous of the pressed glass factories, there were about sixteen other factories making pressed glass from 1830 to 1850, and still more from 1850 to 1900, when pressed glass reached its greatest popularity. It is now being widely reproduced.*

| | |
|---|---|
| **PRESSED GLASS, Aberdeen,** Goblet | 18.75 |
| **Aberdeen,** Spooner | 15.00 |
| **Aberdeen,** Tumbler, Footed | 19.00 |
| **ACANTHUS, see Ribbed Palm** | |
| **ACME, see Butterfly With Spray** | |
| **ACORN MEDALLION, BEADED, see Beaded Acorn Medallion** | |
| **Acorn,** Goblet | 20.00 To 28.00 |
| **Acorn,** Saltshaker, Pink To White | 42.00 |
| **Actress,** Cake Stand | 125.00 |
| **Actress,** Compote, 3 X 6 In. | 35.00 |
| **Actress,** Goblet | 75.00 |
| **Actress,** Goblet, Frosted | 85.00 |
| **Actress,** Marmalade, Frosted | 65.00 |
| **Actress,** Pitcher, Water | 275.00 |
| **Actress,** Sauce, Footed, Frosted | 15.00 |
| **Actress,** Sauce, Footed, 4 1/2 In. | 15.00 |
| **Actress,** Spooner | 62.00 |
| **Actress,** Spooner, Clear | 50.00 |
| **Admiral Dewey,** Tumbler, Etched | 20.00 |
| **Admiral Dewey,** Tumbler, Portrait Impressed In Base, 3 3/4 In. | 36.00 |
| **Admiral Dewey,** Water Set, 6 Molded Tumblers, Pitcher | 325.00 |
| **Adonis,** Celery | 28.00 |
| **Adonis,** Creamer, Green | 35.00 |
| **Aida,** Pitcher, Water | 85.00 |
| **Alabama,** Creamer | 18.50 To 35.00 |
| **Alabama,** Creamer, Large | 39.50 |
| **Alabama,** Dish, Relish | 18.00 |
| **Alabama,** Spooner | 30.00 |
| **Alaska,** Butter, Covered, Gold Trim, Emerald Green | 125.00 |
| **Alaska,** Creamer, Blue | 45.00 To 95.00 |
| **Alaska,** Creamer, Blue Opalescent | 65.00 |
| **Alaska,** Creamer, Vaseline, Opalescent | 95.00 |
| **Alaska,** Cruet, Enamel Flowers, Blue Opalescent | 185.00 |
| **Alaska,** Cruet, Vaseline | 225.00 |
| **Alaska,** Pitcher, Water, Vaseline | 325.00 |
| **Alaska,** Sauce | 18.00 |
| **Alaska,** Spooner, Blue | 95.00 |
| **Alaska,** Spooner, Blue Opalescent | 50.00 |

| | |
|---|---|
| **Alaska,** Spooner, Clear | 50.00 |
| **Alaska,** Spooner, Opalescent Vaseline | 50.00 |
| **Alaska,** Spooner, Vaseline | 65.00 |
| **Alaska,** Spooner, White Opalescent | 50.00 |
| **Alaska,** Sugar, Covered, Blue Opalescent | 110.00 |
| **Alligator Scales With Spearpoint,** Celery | 12.00 |
| **Almond Thumbprint,** Compote | 18.00 |
| **Almond Thumbprint,** Compote, Sweetmeat, Covered, 4 X 6 1/2 In. | 43.00 |
| **Almond Thumbprint,** Cruet, Flint | 45.00 |
| **Almond Thumbprint,** Salt | 25.00 |
| **Amazon,** Creamer | 28.00 |
| **Amazon,** Creamer, Child's | 30.00 |
| **Amazon,** Epergne | 40.00 |
| **Amazon,** Salt, Master | 25.00 |
| **Amazon,** Spooner | 35.00 |
| **Amazon,** Sugar, Covered | 40.00 |
| **Amazon,** Tumbler | 22.50 |
| **Amazon,** Wine | 5.00 |
| **Amber Block,** Creamer | 36.50 |
| **Amber Block,** Goblet | 36.50 |
| **AMBERETTE, see Klondike** | |
| **Angelus,** Wine | 15.00 |
| **Anthemion,** Sugar, Covered | 25.00 |
| **Apollo,** Goblet, Etched Tulip | 35.00 |
| **Apollo,** Tray, Water, Square, Large | 38.00 |
| **Arabesque,** Butter, Covered | 40.00 |
| **Arabesque,** Goblet | 100.00 |
| **Arabesque,** Saucer | 5.00 |
| **Arabesque,** Sugar, Covered | 48.00 |
| **Arch & Forget-Me-Not Bands,** Creamer | 18.00 |
| **Arch & Forget-Me-Not,** Pitcher, Advertising | 42.00 |
| **Arched Fleur-De-Lis,** Banana Boat | 48.00 |
| **Arched Fleur-De-Lis,** Plate, Square, 7 In. | 16.00 |
| **Arched Grape,** Goblet .................... *Illus* | 26.00 |
| **Arched Leaf,** Spooner, Flint | 65.00 |
| **Argus,** Champagne, Flint | 65.00 |
| **Argus,** Eggcup, Flint | 20.00 To 25.00 |
| **Argus,** Goblet | 28.00 |
| **Argus,** Goblet, Flint | 30.00 To 45.00 |
| **Argus,** Goblet, Flint, Flared Rim | 37.00 To 37.50 |
| **Argus,** Spooner, Flint | 48.00 |
| **Argus,** Sugar, Covered, Flint | 75.00 |
| **Argus,** Wine, Flint | 45.00 |
| **Arrow Sheaf,** Pitcher, Water | 38.00 |

Pressed Glass, Arched Fleur-De-Lis

Pressed Glass, Arched Grape, Goblet

**Art,** Banana Stand .................................................................................................. 60.00
**Artichoke,** Cake Stand, Frosted ........................................................................... 32.00
**Artichoke,** Spooner, Frosted ................................................................................. 22.00
**Ashburton,** Celery, Scalloped Top, Flint ............................................................ 125.00
**Ashburton,** Champagne, Flint ............................................................................... 55.00
**Ashburton,** Claret ................................................................................................... 35.00
**Ashburton,** Cordial ................................................................................................. 45.00
**Ashburton,** Creamer, Flint .................................................................................... 245.00
**Ashburton,** Decanter, Flint .................................................................................... 75.00
**Ashburton,** Decanter, Pewter Pouring Stopper, Flint, Quart ......................... 75.00
**Ashburton,** Eggcup, Flint ........................................................... 15.00 To 28.00
**Ashburton,** Goblet, Flint .............................................................. 25.00 To 30.00
**Ashburton,** Goblet, Gilded Etching, Flint ........................................................ 125.00
**Ashburton,** Long Tom Ale, Flint ........................................................................... 87.50
**Ashburton,** Sugar & Creamer, Covered, Flint .................................................. 245.00
**Ashburton,** Sugar, Covered ................................................................................... 60.00
**Ashburton,** Tumbler, Bar ....................................................................................... 38.00
**Ashburton,** Wine ...................................................................................................... 32.00
**Ashburton,** Wine, Flint ........................................................................................... 40.00
**Ashman,** Bread Plate, Motto ................................................................................. 30.00
**Ashman,** Cake Basket, Footed, Wire Handle .................................................... 75.00
**Ashman,** Cake Stand, 10 In. ................................................................................. 55.00
**Ashman,** Creamer ................................................................................................... 18.50
**Ashman,** Platter, Motto ........................................................................................... 45.00
**Ashman,** Wine, Etched ........................................................................................... 12.00
**Astro,** Bowl, Opalescent Blue .............................................................................. 26.00
**Atlanta,** Creamer ..................................................................................................... 45.00
**Atlanta,** Cruet, Stopper .......................................................................................... 16.00
**Atlanta,** Jar, Jam, Etched Flowers ....................................................................... 65.00
**Atlas,** Cake Stand, 8 In. ......................................................................................... 18.00
**Atlas,** Celery ............................................................................................................. 28.00
**Atlas,** Creamer .......................................................................................................... 18.50
**Atlas,** Spooner ........................................................................... 17.50 To 18.00
**Atlas,** Sugar, Covered ............................................................................................ 20.00
**Atlas,** Toothpick ......................................................................... 15.00 To 24.00
**Aurora,** Tray, Wine .................................................................................................. 26.50
**Aurora,** Tray, Wine, Ruby Stained ....................................................................... 28.00
**Aurora,** Wine ............................................................................................................. 25.00
**Austrian,** Berry Set, Clear, 5 Piece ..................................................................... 75.00
**Austrian,** Cup, Footed ............................................................................................ 16.00
**Austrian,** Pitcher & Bowl, Dolphin Handle, Green .......................................... 175.00
**Austrian,** Tumbler .................................................................................................... 24.00
**Baby Face,** Compote, Covered, Large Stem, Frosted ..................................... 275.00
    **BABY THUMBPRINT, see Dakota**
**Bakewell Block,** Goblet, Flint ............................................................................... 65.00
**Bakewell Block,** Tumbler, Flint ............................................................................ 95.00
    **BALDER, see also Pennsylvania**
**Balder,** Celery ........................................................................................................... 32.00
**Balder,** Cup, Punch ................................................................................................. 15.00
**Balder,** Goblet ............................................................................ 18.00 To 18.50
**Balder,** Syrup, Original Top ................................................................................... 38.00
**Balder,** Wine ............................................................................................................. 14.00
    **BALKY MULE, see Currier & Ives**
**Ball & Bar,** Creamer, Tankard, 5 In. .................................................................... 13.50
**Ball & Bar,** Tumbler ................................................................................................. 8.50
**Ball & Swirl,** Butter, Covered ............................................................................... 25.00
**Ball & Swirl,** Cake Stand, 9 In. ............................................................................. 21.00
**Ball & Swirl,** Creamer .............................................................. 18.00 To 21.00
**Ball & Swirl,** Eggcup, Handled .............................................................................. 16.00
**Ball & Swirl,** Pitcher, Footed ................................................................................. 35.00
**Ball & Swirl,** Pitcher, Milk ...................................................................................... 27.00
**Ball & Swirl,** Pitcher, Water .................................................................................... 27.00
**Ball & Swirl,** Spooner .............................................................................................. 20.00

Ball & Swirl, Wine ............................................................................................................ 17.50
Balloon, Goblet ................................................................................................................ 12.00
Balloon, Sugar, Covered, Flint ...................................................................................... 50.00
Baltimore Pear, Goblet ...................................................................... 20.00 To 34.00
Baltimore Pear, Plate, Scalloped Edge, Star Center, 9 In. ...................................... 24.00
Baltimore Pear, Sugar, Covered ................................................................................... 45.00
    BAMBOO, see Broken Column
Banded Buckle, Spooner ........................................................... 17.50 To 18.50
Banded Flute, Goblet, Flint .......................................................................................... 16.00
Banded Knife & Fork, Cordial, Green ........................................................................ 20.00
    BANDED PORTLAND, when flashed with pink, is sometimes called Maiden
    Blush
Banded Portland, Compote, Open, 8 In.Diam. ........................................................... 42.50
Banded Portland, Cup, Punch, Set Of 4 .................................................................... 45.00
Banded Portland, Dish, Pickle, Cranberry & Clear, 6 1/2 In. .................................. 28.00
Banded Portland, Dish, Relish, Pink, 8 1/2 In.Diam. ............................................... 15.00
Banded Portland, Goblet, Gold Trim .......................................................................... 23.00
Banded Portland, Pitcher, Water .................................................................................. 52.00
Banded Portland, Saltshaker, Pewter Lid .................................................................. 45.00
Banded Portland, Sugar & Creamer, Yellow, Individual .......................................... 90.00
Banded Portland, Syrup ................................................................................................. 35.00
Banded Portland, Toothpick .......................................................................................... 12.00
Banded Portland, Toothpick, Clear ............................................................................. 18.00
Banded Portland, Toothpick, Pink & Gold Rim ......................................................... 60.00
Banded Portland, Tumbler ............................................................................................. 35.00
Banded Portland, Tumbler, Gold Trim ........................................................................ 29.00
Banded Portland, Vase, 6 In. ....................................................................................... 14.00
Banded Portland, Vase, 9 In. ....................................................................................... 28.00
Banded Portland, Wine ................................................................................................. 32.50
    BANDED RAINDROP, see Candlewick
Banded Star, Celery ........................................................................................................ 35.00
Banded Star, Creamer ................................................................................................... 30.00
    OTHER BANDED PATTERNS, see under name of basic pattern: e.g., Banded
    Honeycomb, see Honeycomb, Banded
    BAR & DIAMOND, see Kokomo
Barberry, Cake Stand, 9 1/2 In. ................................................................................. 23.00
Barberry, Celery ............................................................................ 24.50 To 28.00
Barberry, Compote, 8 In.Diam. ................................................................................... 32.50
Barberry, Dish, Relish, 8 In. ........................................................................................ 16.00
Barberry, Eggcup ............................................................................................................ 22.50
Barberry, Goblet ........................................................................... 12.00 To 25.00
Barberry, Goblet, Oval ................................................................................................... 22.50
Barberry, Pitcher, Water, Applied Handle ................................. 49.00 To 75.00
    BARLEY & OATS, see Wheat & Barley
    BARLEY & WHEAT, see Wheat & Barley
Barley, Bread Plate ...................................................................... 22.50 To 24.00
Barley, Compote, 7 X 8 In. .......................................................................................... 25.00
Barley, Goblet ............................................................................... 16.00 To 22.00
Barley, Pitcher, Water ................................................................... 35.00 To 36.00
Barley, Sauce, 4 1/2 In. ................................................................................................. 6.50
Barred Forget-Me-Not, Cake Stand, 10 1/2 In. ....................................................... 21.00
Barred Forget-Me-Not, Creamer ................................................................................ 24.50
Barred Forget-Me-Not, Sauce, Flat .............................................................................. 6.00
    BARRED OVALS, see Banded Portland
Barred Star, Goblet ........................................................................................................ 15.50
Barred Star, Toothpick, Clear ...................................................................................... 13.50
Barrel Argus, Goblet ...................................................................................................... 25.00
Barrel Thumbprint, Goblet ........................................................................................... 16.00
    BARRELED BLOCK, see Red Block
Basket Of Flowers, Salt, Flint ..................................................................................... 50.00
Basket Weave, Pitcher, 2 Quart .................................................................................. 25.00
Basket Weave, Tray, Blue ............................................................................................. 65.00
Bead & Scroll, Water Set, 5 Piece ........................................................................... 110.00

Beaded Acorn Medallion, Goblet ................................................................ 18.50
Beaded Band, Butter, Covered ................................................................. 28.50
Beaded Band, Goblet .............................................................................. 24.00
Beaded Band, Spooner ........................................................................... 22.00
Beaded Band, Sugar, Covered ................................................................ 25.00
Beaded Band, Wine ............................................................................... 20.00
**BEADED BULL'S-EYE & DRAPE, see also Alabama**
Beaded Circle, Bottle, Perfume ............................................................... 40.00
Beaded Dart Band, Castor, Pickle, Amber ............................................. 145.00
Beaded Dewdrop, Butter, Covered .......................................................... 65.00
Beaded Dewdrop, Celery, Tray ............................................................... 37.50
Beaded Dewdrop, Cup ............................................................................ 19.00
Beaded Dewdrop, Dish, 6 1/4 X 4 1/4 In. .............................................. 32.50
Beaded Dewdrop, Pitcher ....................................................................... 65.00
Beaded Dewdrop, Pitcher, Water ............................................................ 52.50
Beaded Dewdrop, Sugar Shaker .............................................................. 48.50
Beaded Dewdrop, Wine, Gold Flashed ..................................................... 30.00
Beaded Fine Cut, Sugar, Creamer, & Spooner ......................................... 36.00
Beaded Grape Medallion, Eggcup ............................................................ 18.50
Beaded Grape Medallion, Goblet ................................................ 16.00 To 40.00
Beaded Grape Medallion, Honey, Flint, 3 3/4 In. ...................................... 20.00
Beaded Grape Medallion, Spooner ........................................................... 25.00
Beaded Grape Medallion, Spooner, Pedestal Base ..................................... 25.00
Beaded Grape Medallion, Sugar, Covered ................................................ 45.00
Beaded Grape Medallion, Tumbler, Buttermilk ......................................... 37.50
Beaded Grape, Butter, Covered, Green ..................................................... 65.00
Beaded Grape, Butter, Covered, 7 1/2 X 4 5/8 In.Diam. ........................... 28.00
Beaded Grape, Compote, Jelly, Green, Covered ........................................ 12.00
Beaded Grape, Compote, Jelly, Purple, Covered ....................................... 12.00
Beaded Grape, Cruet, Original Stopper ................................................... 100.00
Beaded Grape, Goblet .............................................................. 18.00 To 20.00
Beaded Grape, Spooner ........................................................................... 30.00
Beaded Grape, Spooner, Green ................................................................ 45.00
Beaded Grape, Toothpick, Green ............................................... 55.00 To 60.00
Beaded Grape, Tumbler ........................................................................... 28.00
Beaded Loop, Cruet ................................................................................ 30.00
Beaded Loop, Goblet ................................................................ 20.00 To 28.00
Beaded Loop, Pitcher, Milk ..................................................................... 25.00
Beaded Loop, Spooner ............................................................................ 18.00
Beaded Loop, Toothpick .......................................................................... 16.00
Beaded Loop, Wine ................................................................................... 9.00
**BEADED MEDALLION, see Beaded Mirror**
Beaded Mirror, Celery ............................................................... 37.50 To 38.50
Beaded Oval & Scroll, Goblet ................................................................. 20.00
Beaded Panel, Goblet ............................................................................. 19.00
Beaded Rosette, Goblet .......................................................................... 22.50
Beaded Swirl, Butter, Green, Gold ......................................................... 120.00
Beaded Swirl, Cup, Punch, Green, Gold Trim ........................................... 22.00
Beaded Swirl, Mug, Gold Trim .................................................................. 7.00
Beaded Swirl, Pitcher, Water, Green & Gold ............................................ 85.00
Beaded Tulip, Goblet .............................................................................. 35.00
Beaded Tulip, Pitcher, Milk ..................................................................... 55.00
Beaded Tulip, Pitcher, Water ................................................................... 45.00
Bear Climber, Goblet, Etched ................................................................. 55.00
**BEARDED MAN, see Viking**
Beatty Honeycomb, Celery, Opalescent ................................................... 65.00
Beatty Honeycomb, Toothpick, Mauve ..................................................... 50.00
Beautiful Lady, Celery ............................................................................ 22.00
Beehive, Bread Tray, Be Industrious, Deer & Stag, Frosted ....................... 80.00
Beehive, Plate, Octagonal, 9 1/4 In. ...................................................... 115.00
Beehive, Platter, Be Industrious, Frosted Center ..................................... 41.50
Bellflower With Loops, Goblet ............................................................... 185.00

**Bellflower,** Bowl, Scalloped, 8 1/2 X 4 1/2 In. ............................................................ 42.00
**Bellflower,** Butter, Covered ............................................................ 95.00
**Bellflower,** Celery ............................................................ 125.00
**Bellflower,** Celery, Scalloped, Rayed Base, 8 In. ............................................................ 175.00
**Bellflower,** Champagne ............................................................ 60.00
**Bellflower,** Compote, Covered, High ............................................................ 375.00
**Bellflower,** Compote, Scalloped, Flint, 8 X 8 In.Diam. ............................................................ 75.00
**Bellflower,** Decanter, Faceted, 1/2 Quart ............................................................ 125.00
**Bellflower,** Decanter, 1 Quart ............................................................ 125.00
**Bellflower,** Eggcup ............................................................ 23.00 To 25.00
**Bellflower,** Eggcup, Flint ............................................................ 25.00 To 28.00
**Bellflower,** Eggcup, Single Vine ............................................................ 20.00
**Bellflower,** Goblet ............................................................ 22.00 To 24.00
**Bellflower,** Goblet, Barrel Shape, Knop Stem, Rayed Base ............................................................ 45.00
**Bellflower,** Goblet, Flint ............................................................ 30.00
**Bellflower,** Goblet, Flint, Barrel Shape ............................................................ 27.50
**Bellflower,** Goblet, Flint, Straight Side ............................................................ 22.50
**Bellflower,** Goblet, Single Vine, Flint ............................................................ 25.00 To 35.00
**Bellflower,** Honey ............................................................ 8.50 18.50
**Bellflower,** Pitcher, Water, Flint ............................................................ 185.00
**Bellflower,** Salt, Scalloped ............................................................ 22.00
**Bellflower,** Sauce, Flint ............................................................ 10.00 To 12.00
**Bellflower,** Spooner ............................................................ 25.00 To 32.50
**Bellflower,** Spooner, Flint ............................................................ 25.00
**Bellflower,** Spooner, Single Vine ............................................................ 54.00
**Bellflower,** Sugar, Covered, Flint ............................................................ 75.00
**Bellflower,** Sugar, Open, Double Vine ............................................................ 60.00
**Bellflower,** Tumbler, Footed ............................................................ 195.00
**Bellflower,** Tumbler, Water ............................................................ 65.00
**Bellflower,** Tumbler, 3 1/2 In. ............................................................ 75.00
**Bellflower,** Whiskey ............................................................ 165.00
**Bellflower,** Whiskey, 3 1/2 In. ............................................................ 95.00
**Bellflower,** Wine, Knob Stem ............................................................ 58.00
    **BELTED WORCESTER, see Worcester, Belted**
    **BENT BUCKLE, see New Hampshire**
    **BERKELEY, see Blocked Arches**
**Bethlehem Star,** Pitcher, Water ............................................................ 35.00
**Bethlehem Star,** Sugar, Open ............................................................ 22.00
**Beveled Diamond & Star,** Creamer ............................................................ 18.00
**Beveled Diamond & Star,** Plate, 10 In. ............................................................ 10.00
**Beveled Diamond & Star,** Sugar Shaker ............................................................ 28.00
**Beveled Diamond & Star,** Toothpick, Green ............................................................ 150.00
**Beveled Star,** Spooner, Green ............................................................ 35.00
    **BIG BLOCK, see Henrietta**
**Bigler,** Goblet, Grooved ............................................................ 30.00
**Bird & Strawberry,** Cake Stand, 9 In. ............................................................ 40.00
**Bird & Strawberry,** Cake Stand, 9 1/2 In. ............................................................ 55.00
**Bird & Strawberry,** Compote, Open, 7 3/4 In. ............................................................ 58.00
**Bird & Strawberry,** Compote, Ruffled Top, Clear, 8 In. ............................................................ 75.00
**Bird & Strawberry,** Creamer ............................................................ 42.00 To 45.00
**Bird & Strawberry,** Dish, Candy, Heart Shaped ............................................................ 45.00
**Bird & Strawberry,** Pitcher, Water ............................................................ 195.00
**Bird & Strawberry,** Tumbler ............................................................ 35.00 To 40.00
**Bird At Fountain,** Goblet ............................................................ 45.00
    **BIRD IN RING, see Butterfly & Fan**
**Birds & Roses,** Goblet, Etched ............................................................ 30.00
**Birds At Fountain,** Compote, Covered, 8 In. ............................................................ 55.00
**Bismarc Star,** Goblet ............................................................ 12.50
**Bismarc Star,** Wine ............................................................ 22.00
**Blackberry,** Compote, Covered, Pedestal, 4 In.Diam. ............................................................ 82.00
**Blaze,** Goblet ............................................................ 47.50
**Bleeding Heart,** Bowl, Green, 6 In.Diam. ............................................................ 22.50
**Bleeding Heart,** Butter, Covered ............................................................ 55.00

Pressed Glass, Bleeding Heart, Goblet

Pressed Glass, Bellflower, Compote

| | | |
|---|---|---|
| Bleeding Heart, Goblet | *Illus* | 50.00 |
| Bleeding Heart, Goblet, Knob Stem | | 27.00 |
| Bleeding Heart, Spooner | 23.00 To | 32.00 |
| Block & Circle, Goblet | | 10.00 |
| Block & Circle, Goblet, 8 Ounces | | 10.00 |
| Block & Circle, Wine | | 15.00 |
| Block & Fan, Cake Stand | | 32.50 |
| Block & Fan, Carafe, Rayed, 8 In. | | 50.00 |
| Block & Fan, Cruet, Large | | 27.00 |
| Block & Fan, Ice Bucket | | 22.00 |
| Block & Fan, Plate, 6 In.Diam. | | 25.00 |
| Block & Fan, Plate, 10 In.Diam. | | 25.00 |
| Block & Fan, Rose Bowl, 4 In.Diam. | | 26.00 |
| Block & Fan, Saucer, 3 3/4 In. | | 5.50 |
| Block & Fan, Wine | | 35.00 |
| BLOCK & FINECUT, see Finecut & Block | | |
| BLOCK & STAR, see Valencia Waffle | | |
| BLOCK WITH STARS, see Hanover | | |
| Block, Creamer, 3 In. | | 6.00 |
| Block, Toothpick, 4-Mold Medallion Bottom, Blue | | 10.00 |
| BLOCKADE, see Diamond Block With Fan | | |
| Blocked Arches, Dish, Berry, Frosted, 5 In. | | 8.00 |
| Blocked Arches, Plate, Frosted | | 15.00 |
| BLOCKHOUSE, see Hanover | | |
| BLUEBIRD, see Bird & Strawberry | | |
| Bow Tie, Bowl, Orange, 9 1/4 In. | | 65.00 |
| Bow Tie, Compote, Open, 8 In. | 47.50 To | 52.00 |
| Bow Tie, Compote, Open, 8 1/2 In. | | 55.00 |
| Bow Tie, Goblet | | 28.00 |
| Bow Tie, Saltshaker, Clear | | 15.00 |
| Boxed Star, Tumbler | | 7.50 |
| BRADFORD BLACKBERRY, see Bradford Grape | | |
| Bradford Grape, Goblet, Flint | | 45.00 |
| Bradford Grape, Honey, Flint | | 8.50 |
| Branches, Pitcher, Water | | 65.00 |
| Brazilian, Syrup, Original Top | | 48.00 |
| Bridle Rosettes, Wine | 10.00 To | 12.00 |
| British Cane, Creamer | | 18.50 |
| Broken Column, Bowl, 9 In.Diam. | | 28.00 |
| Broken Column, Celery | 20.00 To | 35.00 |
| Broken Column, Compote, Flared, 6 In.Diam. | | 55.00 |
| Broken Column, Compote, Open, 6 In.Diam. | | 45.00 |
| Broken Column, Compote, 6 1/2 In. | | 42.50 |
| Broken Column, Cracker Jar | | 55.00 |
| Broken Column, Creamer | 25.00 To | 55.00 |
| Broken Column, Cruet | | 40.00 |
| Broken Column, Pitcher, Water | 65.00 To | 95.00 |
| Broken Column, Red Dots, Compote, 8 X 6 In. | | 195.00 |

Pressed Glass, Buckle, Goblet

Pressed Glass, Bull's Eye & Daisy, Goblet

Pressed Glass, Bull's Eye & Diamond Point, Goblet

| | |
|---|---|
| Broken Column, Spooner | 18.50 To 35.00 |
| Brooklyn, Celery, Flint, 8 3/4 In. | 100.00 |
| Brooklyn, Goblet, Flint | 35.00 To 85.00 |
| BRYCE, see Ribbon Candy | |
| Buck & Doe, Goblet, Etched | 55.00 |
| Buckingham, Butter, Covered, Design | 100.00 |
| Buckingham, Mug, Pink & Green | 24.00 |
| Buckle & Star, Wine | 24.00 To 25.00 |
| Buckle, Bowl, Rolled Rim, Flint, 10 In.Diam. | 55.00 |
| Buckle, Eggcup | 12.00 |
| Buckle, Goblet | *Illus* 65.00 |
| Buckle, Goblet, Flint | 30.00 |
| Buckle, Sugar, Acorn Finial, Covered, Flint | 55.00 |
| Budded Ivy, Goblet | 42.50 |
| Budded Ivy, Spooner, Footed | 28.00 |
| Bull's-Eye & Broken Column, Goblet, Flint | 95.00 |
| Bull's-Eye & Cube, Goblet, Flint | 95.00 |
| Bull's-Eye & Daisy, Berry Set, Gold Rim, 5 Piece | 85.00 |
| Bull's-Eye & Daisy, Spooner, Red Eyes | 30.00 |
| Bull's-Eye & Daisy, Table Set, Green Eyes, Gold Trim, 4 Piece | 175.00 |
| Bull's-Eye & Daisy, Water Set, Gold Eyes & Border, 7 Piece | 135.00 |
| Bull's-Eye & Daisy, Wine, Gold Trim, Green | 15.00 |
| Bull's-Eye & Diamond Panels, Goblet | 15.00 |
| Bull's-Eye & Diamond Point, Goblet | *Illus* 30.00 To 95.00 |
| Bull's-Eye & Diamond Point, Goblet, Flint | 85.00 To 110.00 |
| Bull's-Eye & Diamond Point, Pitcher, Water, Amber | 160.00 |
| Bull's-Eye & Diamond Point, Pitcher, Water, Transparent Blue | 185.00 |
| Bull's-Eye & Diamond Point, Spooner | 65.00 |
| Bull's-Eye & Diamond Point, Whiskey | 125.00 |
| Bull's-Eye & Drape, Creamer, Flint | 32.00 |
| BULL'S-EYE & FAN, see Daisies In Oval Panels | |
| Bull's-Eye & Gothic Arches, Decanter | 65.00 |
| Bull's-Eye & Spearhead, Wine, Clear | 24.00 |
| Bull's-Eye & Star, Compote, Open, 9 In. | 42.50 |
| Bull's-Eye & Thumbprint, Cracker Jar, Cobalt Blue, Cover | 65.00 |
| BULL'S-EYE BAND, see Reverse Torpedo | |
| BULL'S-EYE VARIANT, see Texas Bull's-Eye | |
| Bull's-Eye With Fleur-De-Lis, Goblet, Flint | 65.00 To 80.00 |

Bull's-Eye, Bottle, Water, Flint ............................................................................... 60.00
Bull's-Eye, Cordial, Flint ......................................................................................... 35.00
Bull's-Eye, Goblet, Flint .......................................................................................... 65.00
Bull's-Eye, Salt ......................................................................................................... 40.00
Bull's-Eye, Salt, Collared ........................................................................................ 22.00
Bull's-Eye, Spooner .................................................................................. 17.50 To 18.00
Bull's-Eye, Sugar, Covered ...................................................................................... 145.00
Bull's-Eye, Wine ....................................................................................................... 23.50
Bullet Emblem, Butter, Covered ................................................... 235.00 To 350.00
Bullet Emblem, Sugar, Covered ............................................................................. 225.00
Bumblebee Honeycomb, Goblet, Flint ................................................................... 40.00
Bunker Hill, Bread Plate ................................................................... 40.00 To 58.00
Butterfly & Fan, Celery ........................................................................................... 25.00
Butterfly & Fan, Dish, Fan Shape .......................................................................... 26.00
Butterfly With Spray, Butter, Covered .................................................................. 65.00
Butterfly With Spray, Mug, 3 1/2 In. .............................................. 31.50 To 32.00
Butterfly, Celery, Handles ....................................................................................... 32.00
Butterfly, Cup, Punch .............................................................................................. 6.00
Butterfly, Pitcher, Water ......................................................................................... 48.50
Button & Daisy, Bowl, Berry, Amber ...................................................................... 25.00
Button Arches, Butter, Covered, Gold Band ......................................................... 45.00
Button Arches, Cake Stand, Gold Band ................................................................. 45.00
Button Arches, Salt & Pepper, Ruby ...................................................................... 28.00
Button Arches, Tankard ........................................................................................... 65.00
Button Arches, Toothpick, Weyerhauser, Wisconsin ........................................... 22.50
Button Arches, Tumbler ........................................................................................... 20.00
Button Arches, Tumbler, Ruby Top ......................................................................... 30.00
Button Band, Pitcher, Milk ..................................................................................... 20.00
Button Panel, Butter, Covered, Miniature ............................................................. 65.00
Button Panel, Compote ............................................................................................ 27.00
Buttons & Bows, Sugar & Creamer, Pink .............................................................. 15.00
Buttressed Arch, Table Set, Amber, 4 Pieces ...................................................... 95.00
Buzz Star, Goblet ..................................................................................................... 26.00
Cabbage Rose, Butter, Pink .................................................................................... 45.00
Cabbage Rose, Celery .............................................................................................. 38.00
Cabbage Rose, Cup & Saucer, Pink ....................................................................... 12.50
Cabbage Rose, Goblet, Buttermilk ......................................................................... 40.00
Cabbage Rose, Pitcher, Water, Pink ...................................................................... 70.00
Cabbage Rose, Tumbler ........................................................................................... 45.00
Cabbage Rose, Wine ................................................................................................ 60.00
Cable With Ring, Sugar .......................................................................... 65.00 To 75.00
Cable With Ring, Sugar, Covered, Flint ................................................................. 65.00
Cable, Berry Bowl, Scalloped Top, 7 1/2 In.Diam. .............................................. 25.00
Cable, Butter, Covered ............................................................................................. 85.00
Cable, Compote, Low ............................................................................................... 30.00
Cable, Compote, Low Standard, Flint ..................................................................... 50.00
Cable, Compote, Open, Flint, 7 X 4 In. ................................................................. 34.00
Cable, Compote, Open, Flint, 8 X 5 In. ........................................... 39.00 To 40.00
Cable, Compote, Open, 9 In. ................................................................................... 55.00
Cable, Decanter, Quart ............................................................................................ 95.00
Cable, Eggcup ........................................................................................................... 40.00
Cable, Goblet ............................................................................................ 45.00 To 75.00
Cable, Goblet, Flint ................................................................................. 48.00 To 80.00
Cable, Honey ............................................................................................................. 9.50
Cable, Spooner ............................................................................................... *Illus*  31.50
Cable, Wine ............................................................................................................... 15.00
Cadmus, Toothpick ................................................................................................... 22.00
    CALIFORNIA, see Beaded Grape
    CANADIAN DRAPE, see Garfield Drape
Canadian Shield, Plate, Maple Leaf Border, 10 1/2 In. ....................................... 65.00
Canadian, Pitcher, Milk ........................................................................................... 85.00
Canadian, Pitcher, Water ........................................................................ 58.00 To 65.00

Pressed Glass, Cable, Spooner

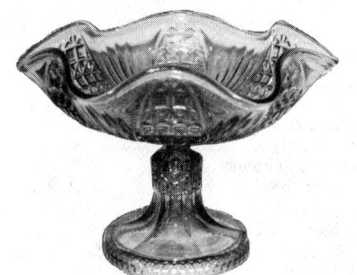

Pressed Glass, Cathedral

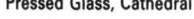

Pressed Glass, Chain & Shield, Creamer

| | |
|---|---|
| **Canadian,** Wine | 45.00 |
| **Candlewick,** Celery | 30.00 |
| **Candlewick,** Creamer | 14.00 |
| **CANDY RIBBON, see Ribbon Candy** | |
| **Cane Column,** Goblet | 10.00 |
| **Cane,** Creamer | 25.00 |
| **Cane,** Goblet | 14.00 |
| **Cane,** Goblet, Clear | 16.00 |
| **Cannonball,** Bowl, 9 1/4 In. | 14.00 |
| **Cape Cod,** Goblet | 40.00 |
| **Capitol Building,** Champagne | 15.00 To 25.00 |
| **Capitol Building,** Goblet | 19.00 |
| **Cardinal Bird,** Creamer | 30.00 To 45.00 |
| **Cardinal Bird,** Goblet | 35.00 To 45.00 |
| **Cardinal,** Creamer | 35.00 |
| **Cardinal,** Goblet | 26.00 To 45.00 |
| **Cardinal,** Spooner | 23.00 |
| **Cardinal,** Sugar, Open | 23.50 |
| **Cathedral,** Bowl, Vaseline, 6 In. | 38.50 |
| **Cathedral,** Relish, Amber, Fish Shaped | 22.00 |
| **Cathedral,** Sauce, Footed | 30.00 |
| **Cathedral,** Spooner, Clear | 24.00 |
| **Cathedral,** Wine, Blue | 32.50 |
| **Cattails & Fern,** Goblet | 22.00 |
| **Cavitt,** Celery | 20.00 |
| **CENTENNIAL, see also Liberty Bell; Washington Centennial** | |
| **Centennial,** Compote, Blue, Covered | 45.00 |
| **Chadwick,** Goblet, Amber | 23.00 |
| **Chain & Shield,** Creamer | *Illus* 18.50 |
| **Chain & Shield,** Goblet | 14.00 To 25.00 |
| **CHAIN WITH DIAMONDS, see Washington Centennial** | |
| **Chain With Star,** Creamer | 20.00 |
| **Chain With Star,** Goblet | 17.00 To 35.00 |
| **Chain With Star,** Spooner | 15.00 |
| **Chain,** Goblet | 20.00 |
| **Chain,** Spooner | 17.50 |
| **Chain,** Wine | 14.50 |
| **Champion,** Spooner | 27.00 |
| **Champion,** Toothpick, Green, Gold Trim | 32.00 |
| **Chandelier,** Creamer, Etched | 24.00 |

Checkerboard, Bowl, Flat, 9 In. .................................................................................. 18.50
Checkerboard, Celery ........................................................................ 15.00 To 18.00
Checkerboard, Goblet ............................................................................................ 42.50
Checkerboard, Spooner ......................................................................................... 20.00
Checkerboard, Wine ............................................................................................... 15.50
Cherry & Fig, Pitcher, Milk, 7 1/2 In. ..................................... 35.00 To 45.00
Cherry & Fig, Wine ................................................................................................. 9.00
Cherry, Goblet .......................................................................................................... 25.00
Chrysanthemum Leaf, Tumbler, Gold Trim .................................................... 24.00
Chrysanthemum Sprig, Compote, Jelly ......................................................... 250.00
          CHURCH WINDOWS, see Tulip Petals
Circled Scroll, Sauce, Blue, Footed ................................................................. 22.00
Clark, Cup .................................................................................................................. 9.00
Classic Medallion, Compote, Open, 7 1/2 X 4 In. ...................................... 15.00
Classic Medallion, Creamer ................................................... 14.00 To 16.50
Classic Medallion, Spooner ................................................................................ 14.00
Classic Medallion, Sugar, Open ........................................................................ 14.50
Classic, Bowl, Covered, 7 1/4 In. ................................................................... 125.00
Classic, Butter, Covered ..................................................................................... 55.00
Classic, Butter, Covered, Collared Base ........................................................ 85.00
Classic, Celery ...................................................................................................... 150.00
Classic, Celery, Collared Base ...................................................... 160.00 To 175.00
Classic, Compote, Covered, Log Feet ..................................................... Illus 150.00
Classic, Creamer, Collared Base ..................................................................... 110.00
Classic, Goblet ........................................................................... 180.00 To 185.00
Classic, Pitcher, Milk, Open Log Feet ........................................................... 550.00
Classic, Pitcher, Water, Collared Base .......................................................... 275.00
Classic, Pitcher, Water, Open Feet .................................................................. 295.00
Classic, Spooner, Paneled ................................................................................... 60.00
Classic, Spooner, 6 Legs ..................................................................................... 78.00
Clear Circle, Spooner ............................................................................................ 19.00
Clear Diagonal Band, Creamer ................................................................ Illus 18.50
Clear Panels With Cord Band, Plate, 7 In. .................................................... 14.00
Clear Panels With Cord Band, Wine ........................................... 16.00 To 18.00
Clear Ribbon, Compote, Covered, 14 In. ......................................................... 89.00
Clear Ribbon, Goblet ............................................................................................ 30.00
Clear Stork, Goblet ................................................................................................ 40.00
Cleat, Pitcher, Water, Flint ............................................................................... 150.00
Clematis, Cup, Punch ............................................................................................. 8.00
Clematis, Goblet, Stipple & Ruby Flashed .................................................... 35.00
Clematis, Sugar, Covered .................................................................................... 25.00
Clematis, Wine ........................................................................................................ 10.00
Cleopatra, Bread Plate ................................................................... 40.00 To 75.00
Climbing Ivy, Spill, Clear ..................................................................................... 45.00
Coachman's Cape, Goblet .................................................................................... 20.00
Coachman's Cape, Wine ............................................................... 15.00 To 23.50
Coarse Cut & Block, Cruet, Original Stopper ............................................... 26.00
          COIN SPOT, see Coin Spot category
Collared Bull's-Eye, Salt, Flint .......................................................................... 16.00
Colonial, Goblet, Knob Stem .............................................................................. 30.00
Colonial, Spooner, Flint ........................................................................................ 34.00
Colonial, Sugar & Creamer, Individual ........................................................... 20.00
Colorado, Bowl, Blue Violet ................................................................................ 55.00
Colorado, Bowl, Blue Violet, Gold Feet .......................................................... 25.00
Colorado, Bowl, Blue Violet, Miniature .......................................................... 40.00
Colorado, Bowl, Fluted Rim, Green, 10 In. .................................................... 30.00
Colorado, Butter, Green & Gold ...................................................................... 100.00
Colorado, Celery, Etched ...................................................................................... 35.00
Colorado, Compote, Clear Bowl, Crimped, Footed, 6 In. ........................... 19.00
Colorado, Creamer, Green .................................................................................... 38.00
Colorado, Creamer, Large .................................................................................... 32.00
Colorado, Cup & Saucer, Green ......................................................................... 30.00
Colorado, Mug, Green, 2 1/2 In. ....................................................................... 20.00

Pressed Glass, Classic, Compote, Covered, Log Feet

Pressed Glass, Clear Diagonal Band, Creamer

Pressed Glass, Colonial

| | |
|---|---|
| **Colorado,** Mug, Souvenir, Green | 20.00 |
| **Colorado,** Plate, Footed, 7 In. | 15.00 |
| **Colorado,** Sauce, Clear | 6.00 |
| **Colorado,** Sherbet, Blue | 18.00 To 35.00 |
| **Colorado,** Sherbet, Footed, Green | 35.00 |
| **Colorado,** Sherbet, Green | 20.00 |
| **Colorado,** Sherbet, Green, Souvenir | 14.00 |
| **Colorado,** Sugar & Creamer, Miniature | 22.50 |
| **Colorado,** Sugar & Creamer, Rye, N.Y., Individual | 49.00 |
| **Colorado,** Sugar, Covered | 35.00 |
| **Colorado,** Sugar, Open, Ruby & Clear, Souvenir | 45.00 |
| **Colorado,** Toothpick, Blue | 38.00 |
| **Colorado,** Toothpick, Clear, Gold Trim | 22.00 To 55.00 |
| **Colorado,** Toothpick, Green | 28.00 To 30.00 |
| **Colorado,** Toothpick, Green, Gold Trim | 38.00 |
| **Colorado,** Toothpick, Spittoon Shape, Souvenir | 35.00 |
| **Colorado,** Tray, 7 In. | 29.00 |
| **Colorado,** Tumbler, Green | 30.00 |
| **Colorado,** Tumbler, Ruby Top | 30.00 |
| **Colorado,** Wine | 18.00 |
| **Colossus,** Goblet | 15.00 To 42.50 |
| **Columbia,** Salt Dip | 10.00 |
| **Columbia,** Spooner | 15.00 |
| **Columbian Coin,** Bread Plate, Liberty Head | 45.00 |
| **Columbian Coin,** Compote, Open | 125.00 |
| **Columbian Coin,** Creamer | 85.00 |
| **Columbian Coin,** Syrup | 175.00 |
| **Columbian Coin,** Wine, Gilded | 70.00 |
| **Column Block,** Toothpick, Blue | 80.00 |
| **Comet,** Compote, Low | 135.00 |
| **Comet,** Goblet | 70.00 |
| **Comet,** Goblet, Flint | 65.00 To 85.00 |
| **COMPACT, see Snail** | |
| **Connecticut Flute,** Goblet, Flint | 16.00 |
| **Cord & Tassel,** Goblet | 20.00 To 30.00 |
| **Cord & Tassel,** Spooner | 21.50 To 25.00 |
| **Cord & Tassel,** Spooner, Scalloped Top, Pedestal | 22.00 |
| **Cord & Tassel,** Syrup, Applied Handle | 69.50 |
| **Cord Drapery,** Butter, Covered | 65.00 |

Cord Drapery, Creamer ............................................................ 18.00 To 45.00
Cord Drapery, Custard Cup, Clear, Footed ......................................... 15.00
Cord Drapery, Dish, Sauce, Flat, 4 1/2 In. ......................................... 12.50
Cord Drapery, Pitcher, Water ......................................................... 75.00
Cord Drapery, Spooner ................................................................. 40.00
Cord Drapery, Sugar, Covered ....................................................... 55.00
Cordova, Cup, Punch .................................................................... 8.00
Cordova, Toothpick ..................................................................... 15.00
Coreopsis, Cracker Jar, Raised Flower Sprays, Silver Band .................. 150.00
Cornell, Plate, 10 In. .................................................................... 8.00
Cornell, Punch Bowl, Stand, 10 Cups ............................................. 85.00
Corner Medallion, Creamer ........................................................... 15.00
Cornucopia, Cordial ..................................................................... 24.50
Cornucopia, Pitcher, Water ........................................................... 45.00
Cornucopia, Wine ................................................................. 12.00 To 22.00
    COSMOS, see Cosmos
Cottage, Cake Stand, 9 In. ............................................................ 24.50
Cottage, Compote, Jelly, Green ..................................................... 18.00
Cottage, Creamer ................................................................ 20.00 To 22.00
Cottage, Cup & Saucer ......................................................... 27.00 To 32.00
Cottage, Spooner ........................................................................ 16.00
Cottage, Wine ............................................................................ 19.50
Cradled Diamonds, Goblet ............................................................ 25.00
    CRANE, see Stork
    CRISSCROSS, see Rexford
Croesus, Berry Set, 6 Sauces, Green ......................................... *Illus* 230.00
Croesus, Butter, Covered, Amethyst ............................................. 163.00
Croesus, Butter, Covered, Gold Trim, Green ................................... 130.00
Croesus, Butter, Covered, Green ........................................ 145.00 To 175.00
Croesus, Butter, Sugar & Creamer, Covered, Gold Trim, Green ........... 350.00
Croesus, Creamer, Individual, Green .............................................. 85.00
Croesus, Cruet, Green ................................................................ 125.00
Croesus, Cruet, Green, Gold Trim ................................................ 195.00
Croesus, Cruet, Stopper ............................................................. 175.00
Croesus, Salt & Pepper, Footed, Amethyst ..................................... 55.00
Croesus, Sauce, Amethyst, Gold Trim, Set Of 4 .............................. 200.00
Croesus, Spooner, Green ............................................................. 75.00
Croesus, Sugar, Covered, Green ................................................... 135.00
Croesus, Sugar, Covered, Green With Gold ..................................... 165.00
Croesus, Table Set, Butter, Sugar, Creamer, & Celery, Purple ............ 595.00
Croesus, Table Set, Sugar, Creamer, & Spooner, Green ..................... 470.00
Croesus, Toothpick, Emerald ........................................................ 75.00
Croesus, Toothpick, Milk Glass ..................................................... 25.00
Croesus, Toothpick, Purple .......................................................... 70.00
Croesus, Tray, Scalloped ............................................................. 85.00
Croesus, Tumbler, Amethyst, Gold Trim .......................................... 85.00
Croesus, Tumbler, Green, Gold Trim ...................................... 35.00 To 40.00
Croesus, Tumbler, Purple, Gold Trim .............................................. 65.00
    CROSSBAR & FINECUT, see Ashman
Crossed Discs, Eggcup, 2 Handles ................................................ 15.00
Crowfoot, Creamer .............................................................. 18.00 To 24.00
Crowfoot, Dish, 5 1/2 In. ............................................................. 12.00
Crowfoot, Goblet ........................................................................ 36.50

Pressed Glass, Columbian Coin, Salt & Pepper

| | |
|---|---:|
| **Crowfoot,** Pitcher, Water | 45.00 |
| **Crowfoot,** Spooner | 20.00 |
| **Crowfoot,** Sugar, Covered | 35.00 |
| **Crowfoot,** Wine | 7.00 |
| **CROWN JEWELS, see also Chandelier; Queen's Necklace** | |
| **Crystal Wedding,** Compote, Covered, 7 In. | 78.00 |
| **Crystal Wedding,** Tumbler | 12.50 |
| **Crystal,** Eggcup, Flint | 12.00 |
| **CUBE & DIAMOND, see Milton** | |
| **CUBE & FAN, see Pineapple & Fan** | |
| **CUPID & PSYCHE, see Psyche & Cupid** | |
| **Cupid & Venus,** Berry Set, 9 Piece | 95.00 |
| **Cupid & Venus,** Bowl, Footed, 9 1/2 In. | 33.00 |
| **Cupid & Venus,** Bread Plate ................................................... *Illus* | 42.00 |
| **Cupid & Venus,** Cake Stand | 31.50 |
| **Cupid & Venus,** Celery | 24.00 To 47.50 |
| **Cupid & Venus,** Compote | 30.00 |
| **Cupid & Venus,** Compote Set, Clear, 6 Footed Sauces | 120.00 |
| **Cupid & Venus,** Cordial, 3 1/4 In. | 50.00 |
| **Cupid & Venus,** Creamer | 28.00 |
| **Cupid & Venus,** Cup, Child's, 2 1/2 In. | 32.00 |
| **Cupid & Venus,** Goblet | 42.00 To 65.00 |
| **Cupid & Venus,** Mug, 2 1/2 In. | 22.00 |
| **Cupid & Venus,** Mug, 3 1/2 In. | 25.00 |
| **Cupid & Venus,** Pitcher, Milk | 65.00 |
| **Cupid & Venus,** Pitcher, Water | 45.00 To 68.00 |
| **Cupid & Venus,** Plate, Amber, 10 1/2 In. | 65.00 |
| **Cupid & Venus,** Plate, 10 1/2 In. | 35.00 |
| **Cupid & Venus,** Spooner | 26.50 |
| **Cupid's Hunt,** Dish, Relish | 22.00 |
| **Curled Leaf,** Spooner | 18.50 |
| **Currant,** Spooner | 22.00 |
| **Currant,** Tumbler, Buttermilk | 20.00 |
| **Currier & Ives,** Compote, Open, 7 1/4 In. | 45.00 |
| **Currier & Ives,** Creamer | 35.00 |
| **Currier & Ives,** Cup & Saucer | 20.00 |
| **Currier & Ives,** Goblet | 16.00 To 23.00 |
| **Currier & Ives,** Pitcher, Milk | 30.00 To 45.00 |
| **Currier & Ives,** Pitcher, Water | 45.00 To 65.00 |
| **Currier & Ives,** Tray, Mule On Railroad Track, 12 In. | 75.00 |
| **Currier & Ives,** Tray, Water | 45.00 |
| **Currier & Ives,** Tray, Water, Dog Rabbit Series | 45.00 |
| **Currier & Ives,** Wine | 15.00 To 30.00 |
| **Curtain Tieback,** Goblet | 15.00 |
| **Curtain Tieback,** Pitcher, Water | 40.00 |
| **Curtain Tieback,** Sauce, Footed | 3.50 To 7.50 |
| **Cut Log,** Cake Stand, 10 In. | 75.00 |
| **Cut Log,** Celery | 55.00 |

Pressed Glass, Croesus, Berry Set, 6 Sauces, Green

Pressed Glass, Cupid & Venus, Bread Plate

| | |
|---|---|
| **Cut Log,** Compote, Covered, 5 1/2 In. | 45.00 |
| **Cut Log,** Compote, Jelly | 35.00 To 45.00 |
| **Cut Log,** Compote, Open, Low, 9 In. | 17.50 |
| **Cut Log,** Compote, Open, 7 1/2 In. | 47.00 |
| **Cut Log,** Creamer | 12.00 To 35.00 |
| **Cut Log,** Creamer, Large | 42.50 |
| **Cut Log,** Cruet, Cut Log Stopper | 37.50 To 45.00 |
| **Cut Log,** Cruet, Stopper | 32.00 |
| **Cut Log,** Goblet | 45.00 |
| **Cut Log,** Mug, 6 1/4 In. | 12.00 To 16.50 |
| **Cut Log,** Pitcher, Tankard, 12 1/2 In. | 79.00 To 95.00 |
| **Cut Log,** Pitcher, Water, 9 In. | 75.00 |
| **Cut Log,** Sugar & Creamer | 35.00 |
| **Cut Log,** Wine | 20.00 To 50.00 |
| **Cyclone,** Wine | 15.00 |
| **Dahlia,** Creamer | 25.00 |
| **Dahlia,** Eggcup, Double, Stippled | 44.00 |
| **Dahlia,** Goblet | 44.00 |
| **Dahlia,** Goblet, Etched | 15.00 |
| **Dahlia,** Mug, Amber, Large | 40.00 |
| **Dahlia,** Pitcher, Water | 35.00 To 48.00 |
| **Dahlia,** Plate, Handled, 9 In. | 22.00 To 30.00 |
| **Dahlia,** Wine | 37.50 |
| **Daisies In Oval Panels,** Creamer | 7.00 To 15.00 |
| **Daisies In Oval Panels,** Goblet | 12.00 |
| **Daisies In Oval Panels,** Toothpick | 17.50 |
| **Daisies In Oval Panels,** Tumbler | 13.50 |
| **Daisies In Oval Panels,** Tumbler, Gold | 12.00 |
| **Daisies In Oval Panels,** Tumbler, Green Eyes | 15.00 |
|    **DAISY & BUTTON, see also Paneled Daisy & Button** | |
| **Daisy & Button With Crossbar,** Butter, Covered, Amber | 35.00 |
| **Daisy & Button With Crossbar,** Cruet, Amber | 65.00 |
| **Daisy & Button With Crossbar,** Dish, Pickle | 14.00 |
| **Daisy & Button With Crossbar,** Pitcher, Milk, Amber | 34.00 |
| **Daisy & Button With Crossbar,** Pitcher, Water, Amber | 65.00 |
| **Daisy & Button With Narcissus,** Wine | 12.50 |
|    **DAISY & BUTTON WITH OVAL PANELS, see Hartley** | |
| **Daisy & Button With Thumbprint,** Goblet, Sapphire Blue | 45.00 |
| **Daisy & Button With V-Ornament,** Pitcher, Blue, 5 In. | 47.50 |
| **Daisy & Button With V-Ornament,** Tumbler, V Bar | 15.00 |
| **Daisy & Button,** Boot, 5 In. | 25.00 |
| **Daisy & Button,** Candleholder, Double | 20.00 |
| **Daisy & Button,** Celery, Amber | 33.00 |
| **Daisy & Button,** Celery, Crimped Flared Top | 36.00 |
| **Daisy & Button,** Compote, Scalloped Rim, Blue, 8 X 7 1/4 In. | 45.00 |
| **Daisy & Button,** Compote, Scalloped, Petticoat Base, 9 In.Diam. | 50.00 |
| **Daisy & Button,** Compote, 8 X 8 In. | 25.00 |
| **Daisy & Button,** Cup, Punch, Teal Blue Handle, Amber | 14.00 |
| **Daisy & Button,** Dish, Canoe Shaped, Olive Green, 6 1/4 In. | 18.50 |
| **Daisy & Button,** Pickle Castor, Amber, Silver Plated Holder | 125.00 |
| **Daisy & Button,** Pitcher, 2 3/4 In. | 45.00 |
| **Daisy & Button,** Sauce, Amber, 5 1/2 In.Square | 18.00 |
| **Daisy & Button,** Sauce, Honey Amber, 4 1/2 In.Square | 6.00 |
| **Daisy & Button,** Shoe, Dated 1895 | 28.00 |
| **Daisy & Button,** Shoe, Original Perfume Bottle Insert, Blue | 45.00 |
| **Daisy & Button,** Slipper, Green, 2 1/8 X 1 1/2 X 5 1/2 In. | 30.00 |
| **Daisy & Button,** Spooner, Blue | 35.00 |
| **Daisy & Button,** Spooner, Cylindrical Shape, Scalloped, Amber | 35.00 |
| **Daisy & Button,** Toothpick, Clear, Gold Trim | 25.00 |
| **Daisy & Button,** Toothpick, Hat Shaped, Amber | 22.00 |
| **Daisy & Button,** Tumbler, Ground Bottom, Amber | 22.00 |
| **Dakota,** Butter, Covered | 40.00 |
| **Dakota,** Butter, Covered, Etched, Pie Crust Edge | 65.00 |

| | |
|---|---|
| **Dakota,** Butter, Covered, Pie Crust Rim, Hotel | 44.00 |
| **Dakota,** Cake Stand, 10 In. | 45.00 |
| **Dakota,** Celery, Etched | 42.00 |
| **Dakota,** Celery, Hotel Style | 34.00 |
| **Dakota,** Compote, Covered, Etched | 55.00 |
| **Dakota,** Compote, Jelly, Etched, 8 1/2 In. | 32.50 To 35.00 |
| **Dakota,** Compote, Jelly, 6 In. | 34.00 |
| **Dakota,** Compote, 12 Footed Desserts, 9 In. | 170.00 |
| **Dakota,** Compote, 6 1/4 X 4 1/4 In. | 42.00 |
| **Dakota,** Compote, 7 In. | 24.50 |
| **Dakota,** Creamer, Etched | 52.00 |
| **Dakota,** Cruet | 110.00 |
| **Dakota,** Goblet | 18.50 To 35.00 |
| **Dakota,** Goblet, Etched | 27.50 To 37.50 |
| **Dakota,** Pitcher, Water | 65.00 |
| **Dakota,** Spooner | 25.00 |
| **Dakota,** Spooner, Etched | 35.00 |
| **Dakota,** Sugar, Covered | 38.50 |
| **Dakota,** Sugar, Covered, Etched | 50.00 |
| **Dakota,** Tray, Wine | 60.00 |
| **Dakota,** Tumbler | 32.50 |
| **Dakota,** Tumbler, Engraved Band | 24.00 |
| **Dakota,** Wine, Clear | 27.00 |
| **Dakota,** Wine, Ruby Flashing | 52.50 |
| **Dart,** Creamer | 18.75 |
| **Deer & Doe,** Goblet | 50.00 |
| **Deer & Dog,** Goblet | 68.50 |
| **Deer & Dog,** Goblet, Etched | 40.00 |
| **Deer & Dog,** Pitcher, Water, Etched Hunter | 125.00 |
| **Deer & Pine Tree,** Berry Dish, 3 1/2 X 4 1/2 In. | 26.00 |
| **Deer & Pine Tree,** Bread Plate | 30.00 |
| **Deer & Pine Tree,** Goblet | 37.50 |
| **Deer & Pine Tree,** Mug, Miniature | 25.00 |
| **Deer & Pine Tree,** Pitcher | 35.00 |
| **Deer & Pine Tree,** Platter | 48.00 |
| **Deer & Pine Tree,** Sugar, Covered | 47.50 |
| **Delaware,** Banana Boat, Clear To Cranberry | 75.00 |
| **Delaware,** Banana Boat, Green, Gold Trim, 11 1/2 X 7 1/4 In. | 68.00 |
| **Delaware,** Banana Boat, Metal Basket, Green, Gold Trim | 125.00 |
| **Delaware,** Banana Boat, Pink, Gold Trim | 40.00 |
| **Delaware,** Banana Boat, 4 Sauces, Rose & Gold | 225.00 |
| **Delaware,** Berry Dish, Rose | 22.50 |
| **Delaware,** Berry Set, Gold Trim, Green, 4 Sauces | 70.00 |
| **Delaware,** Bowl, Fluted, Green, 10 In.Diam. | 40.00 |
| **Delaware,** Bowl, Green, Gold Trim, 7 1/2 In.Diam. | 45.00 |
| **Delaware,** Bowl, Octagon, 9 In. | 32.00 |
| **Delaware,** Bowl, Silver Plate Holder, 6 1/2 In. | 25.00 |
| **Delaware,** Box, Powder, Covered, Cranberry | 180.00 |
| **Delaware,** Butter, Covered, Green | 145.00 To 175.00 |
| **Delaware,** Butter, Covered, Rose | 165.00 |
| **Delaware,** Creamer, Gold Trim, Green | 45.00 To 75.00 |
| **Delaware,** Cup, Punch, Green | 25.00 |
| **Delaware,** Fruit Boat, Green, Gold Edge | 40.00 |
| **Delaware,** Jar, Pomade, Jeweled Lid, Gold Trim | 195.00 |
| **Delaware,** Pitcher, Claret, 6 Tumblers, Rose | 325.00 |
| **Delaware,** Pitcher, Rose, 2 Rose & 2 Amethyst Tumblers | 175.00 |
| **Delaware,** Pitcher, Water, Clear, 6 Tumblers | 155.00 |
| **Delaware,** Rose Bowl, Metal Basket, Gold Trim | 95.00 |
| **Delaware,** Sauce, Oval | 26.00 |
| **Delaware,** Spooner, Green, Gold | 32.00 To 50.00 |
| **Delaware,** Spooner, Pink Flashed | 65.00 |
| **Delaware,** Table Set, Emerald Green, Gold Trim, 4 Piece | 265.00 |
| **Delaware,** Tankard, Green, Gold Trim, 9 1/2 In. | 85.00 |

Delaware, Toothpick ..................................................................................................... 18.00
Delaware, Toothpick, Clear, Gold Trim ..................................................................... 48.00
Delaware, Toothpick, Green, Gold Trim ..................................................................... 95.00
Delaware, Toothpick, Pink Stain ................................................................................ 85.00
Delaware, Tray, Pin ................................................................................................... 40.00
Delaware, Tumbler, Cranberry .................................................................................. 40.00
Delaware, Tumbler, Gold Trim, Green ...................................................................... 20.00
Delaware, Tumbler, Green ......................................................................................... 45.00
Delos, Spooner ........................................................................................................... 16.00
Dew & Raindrop, Spooner ......................................................................................... 35.00
Dew & Raindrop, Wine ................................................................................................ 7.00
Dewberry, Sugar, Covered ......................................................................................... 15.00
Dewdrop Bands, Goblet ................................................................................. 6.50 To 10.00
Dewdrop In Points, Bread Plate, Vine Border ......................................................... 11.00
Dewdrop With Sheaf Of Wheat, Bread Plate, Motto ........................... 22.00 To 30.00
Dewdrop With Star, Butter, Covered ....................................................................... 30.00
Dewdrop With Star, Cake Stand, 9 1/2 In. .............................................................. 20.50
Dewdrop With Star, Plate, 5 1/4 In. ......................................................................... 16.00
Dewdrop With Star, Plate, 7 1/4 In. ......................................................................... 20.00
Dewdrop With Star, Sugar, Covered ........................................................................ 45.00
Dewdrop, Goblet, Banded ........................................................................................... 6.50
    DEWEY, see also Admiral Dewey
Dewey, Butter, Amber, Covered ............................................................................... 45.00
Dewey, Cruet, Clear Stopper, Amber ....................................................................... 65.00
Dewey, Cruet, Green, Original Stopper ................................................................... 125.00
Dewey, Mug, Green ..................................................................................................... 45.00
Dewey, Pitcher, Water .................................................................................. 45.00 To 68.50
Dewey, Relish, Amber, Serpentine Shape .............................................................. 42.50
Dewey, Tumbler, Vaseline .......................................................................................... 32.00
Dewey, Water Set, 6 Molded Tumblers, 7 Piece .................................................. 325.00
Diagonal Band & Fan, Dish, Relish, Oval, 7 In. ....................................................... 9.00
Diagonal Band & Fan, Goblet ................................................................................... 17.00
Diagonal Band & Fan, Pitcher ................................................................................... 50.00
Diagonal Band & Fan, Plate, 7 In. ........................................................................... 15.00
Diagonal Band, Compote, Covered, 7 In. ................................................................ 55.00
Diagonal Band, Creamer ............................................................................................ 25.00
Diagonal Band, Dish, Sauce, Footed, 4 In. ............................................................. 12.50
Diagonal Band, Goblet .................................................................................. 11.00 To 35.00
Diagonal Band, Pitcher, Water, Clear ...................................................................... 20.00
Diagonal Sawtooth Band, Wine ................................................................................ 32.00
Diagonal Sawtooth Band, Wine, Flint ...................................................................... 29.00
    DIAMOND, see Umbilicated Sawtooth
    DIAMOND & SUNBURST, see Flattened Diamond & Sunburst
Diamond & Teadrop, Cruet ....................................................................................... 30.00
Diamond Band, Goblet, Amber ................................................................................. 45.00
Diamond Bar, Tray, Scalloped Sides, Oblong, 11 In. ............................................. 30.00
Diamond Block With Fan, Goblet ............................................................................. 20.00
Diamond Cut With Leaf, Creamer, Blue .................................................................. 45.00
Diamond Hobnail, Cruet, Stopper, C.1885 .............................................................. 50.00
    DIAMOND HORSESHOE, see Aurora
Diamond In Diamond, Goblet .................................................................................... 10.00
Diamond Medallion, Cake Stand, 8 1/4 In. .............................................................. 15.00
Diamond Medallion, Cake Stand, 9 1/2 In. .............................................................. 15.00
Diamond Medallion, Goblet ....................................................................................... 22.50
Diamond Medallion, Plate, 10 In.Diam. ................................................................... 15.00
Diamond Point Band, Wine, Amber .......................................................................... 35.00
    DIAMOND POINT DISCS, see Eyewinker
Diamond Point Loop, Bowl, 8 In. .............................................................................. 14.00
Diamond Point, Butter, Covered .............................................................................. 25.00
Diamond Point, Champagne, Flint ............................................................................ 75.00
Diamond Point, Claret, Flint ........................................................................... Illus 87.50
Diamond Point, Cordial, Knob Stem, Flint ............................................................... 75.00
Diamond Point, Goblet ............................................................................................... 40.00

Pressed Glass, Diamond Point, Claret, Flint

| | |
|---|---:|
| **Diamond Point**, Goblet, Flint | 35.00 To 36.00 |
| **Diamond Point**, Honey, Sunburst Center, 3 1/2 In. | 10.00 |
| **Diamond Point**, Pitcher, Milk, Flint | 125.00 |
| **Diamond Point**, Pitcher, Water, American, C.1850, Flint | 100.00 |
| **Diamond Point**, Plate, Flint | 16.00 |
| **Diamond Point**, Salt, Covered, Footed, Flint | 65.00 |
| **Diamond Point**, Spooner | 55.00 |
| **Diamond Point**, Spooner, Flint | 55.00 |
| **Diamond Point**, Toothpick, Flint, Teal | 125.00 |
| **Diamond Point**, Toothpick, Scalloped Rim, Blue | 75.00 |
| **Diamond Point**, Tumbler, Flint | 45.00 |
| **Diamond Ridge**, Toothpick | 25.00 |
| **Diamond Rosettes**, Goblet | 18.00 |
| **Diamond Splendor**, Spooner | 18.00 |
| **Diamond Sunburst**, Goblet | 12.00 |
| **Diamond Sunburst**, Pitcher, Water, 7 In. | 38.00 |
| **Diamond Sunburst**, Punch Set, Child's, Flattened, 7 Piece | 52.00 |
| **Diamond Swirl**, Syrup | 33.50 |
| **Diamond Thumbprint**, Carafe, Open, Flint | 115.00 |
| **Diamond Thumbprint**, Celery, Scalloped Rim, 9 1/2 In. | 200.00 |
| **Diamond Thumbprint**, Compote, Flint, 8 1/4 X 11 In.Diam. | 265.00 |
| **Diamond Thumbprint**, Compote, Low, Flint | 80.00 |
| **Diamond Thumbprint**, Compote, Open, Flint | 95.00 |
| **Diamond Thumbprint**, Creamer | 145.00 |
| **Diamond Thumbprint**, Creamer, Flint | 275.00 |
| **Diamond Thumbprint**, Glass, Whiskey, Flint | 100.00 |
| **Diamond Thumbprint**, Goblet, Flint | 325.00 To 350.00 |
| **Diamond Thumbprint**, Honey, Flint | 15.00 |
| **Diamond Thumbprint**, Pitcher, Water, Flint | 275.00 |
| **Diamond Thumbprint**, Pitcher, Water, Flint, 10 In. | 300.00 |
| **Diamond Thumbprint**, Sauce, Flint | 20.00 |
| **Diamond Thumbprint**, Sugar, Covered | 185.00 |
| **Diamond Thumbprint**, Tumbler | 95.00 |
| **Diamond Thumbprint**, Tumbler, Flint | 85.00 |
| **Diamond Thumbprint**, Tumbler, Water, Flint | 95.00 |
| **Diamond-Quilted**, Butter, Covered, Vaseline | 85.00 |
| **Diamond-Quilted**, Spooner, Amethyst | 38.00 |
| **Diamond**, Cake Stand, Blue, 5 X 10 1/2 In. | 55.00 |
| **Diamonds With Double Fans**, Wine | 12.00 |
| **Dickinson**, Goblet, Flint | 40.00 To 58.00 |
| **Dickinson**, Spooner | 30.00 To 55.00 |
| **Diedre**, Goblet | 12.00 |
| **Divided Hearts**, Eggcup, Flint | 40.00 |
| **Divided Hearts**, Goblet, Sandwich | 50.00 |
| **Dolly Madison**, Sugar, Green, Gold, Covered | 40.00 |

Pressed Glass, Dolphin, Pitcher, Water, Frosted

Pressed Glass, Egg In Sand, Goblet

Pressed Glass, Egyptian, Goblet

| | | |
|---|---|---|
| **Dolphin,** Compote, 6 1/2 In. | | 85.00 |
| **Dolphin,** Goblet, Clear | | 70.00 |
| **Dolphin,** Pitcher, Water, Frosted | *Illus* | 110.00 |
| **Dolphin,** Spooner | | 48.00 |
| **Dolphin,** Spooner, Etched | | 60.00 |
| **Dolphin,** Sugar, Covered | | 135.00 |
| **Dominion,** Goblet | | 40.00 |
| **DORIC, see Feather** | | |
| **Doric & Pansy,** Pitcher, Child's, Pink | | 28.00 |
| **Dot & Dash,** Creamer | | 15.00 |
| **Double Beetle Band,** Creamer | | 25.00 |
| **Double Beetle Band,** Creamer, Blue | | 32.00 |
| **Double Beetle Band,** Spooner, Blue | | 38.00 |
| **Double Doughnut,** Creamer | | 15.00 |
| **Double Doughnut,** Creamer, Pewter Top | | 36.00 |
| **Double Fan,** Celery, 7 In. | | 14.00 To 17.00 |
| **Double Fan,** Spooner, 6 In. | | 25.00 |
| **Double Leaf & Dart,** Goblet | | 16.00 To 28.00 |
| **DOUBLE LOOP, see Double Loop & Dart** | | |
| **Double Loop & Dart,** Goblet | | 12.00 To 22.50 |
| **Double Ribbon,** Frosted, Spooner | | 20.00 |
| **Double Snail,** Rose Bowl, 5 In. | | 30.00 |
| **Double Wedding Ring,** Goblet | | 18.50 |
| **Double Wedding Ring,** Goblet, Flint | | 40.00 |
| **Dragon,** Goblet | | 185.00 |
| **Draped Fan,** Pitcher, Water | | 23.00 |
| **Draped Window,** Goblet | | 135.00 |
| **Drapery,** Creamer | | 55.00 |
| **Drapery,** Goblet | | 15.00 To 21.00 |
| **Drapery,** Spooner | | 43.50 |
| **Drum,** Creamer, Miniature | | 60.00 |
| **Duchess Loop,** Eggcup, Flint | | 16.00 |
| **Duncan Block,** Celery | | 20.00 |
| **Duncan Block,** Wine, Souvenir, Etched, Ruby | | 25.00 |
| **Duncan,** Plate, 7 In. | | 16.00 |
| **Duquesne,** Goblet | | 33.50 |
| **E Pluribus Unum,** Mug | | 60.00 |
| **Eagle,** Salt, Flint | | 175.00 |
| **EARL, see Spirea Band** | | |
| **Egg & Dart,** Creamer, Individual | | 12.00 To 14.00 |
| **Egg & Sand,** Plate, Bread | | 18.00 |
| **Egg In Sand,** Bread Plate, 12 1/2 In. | | 15.00 To 26.00 |
| **Egg In Sand,** Goblet | *Illus* | 24.50 |

Pressed Glass, Excelsior, Bottle, Bitters

Pressed Glass, Fern Burst, Goblet,

5 1/2 In. (See Page 450)

| | |
|---|---:|
| **Egg In Sand,** Pitcher, Milk | 35.00 |
| **Egg In Sand,** Platter, Handled, 8 X 10 In. | 31.00 |
| **Egyptian,** Bread Plate, Cleopatra | 48.00 |
| **Egyptian,** Butter, Covered | 38.00 To 55.00 |
| **Egyptian,** Compote, 8 In.Diam. | 80.00 |
| **Egyptian,** Creamer | 29.50 To 34.00 |
| **Egyptian,** Creamer, Embossed Ruins Of Parthenon | 38.00 |
| **Egyptian,** Goblet | *Illus* 40.00 |
| **Egyptian,** Plate, Cleopatra | 42.00 |
| **Egyptian,** Plate, Pyramids, Large | 45.00 |
| **Egyptian,** Saucer, 4 1/2 In.Diam. | 15.00 |
| **Egyptian,** Spooner | 26.50 To 38.50 |
| **Elaine,** Bread Plate | 60.00 To 95.00 |
| **Elephant,** Berry Set, 6 Sauces, Gold Trim, Green Stain | 85.00 |
| **Elephant,** Creamer | 20.00 |
| **Elk & Doe,** Goblet | 120.00 |
| **Elk Medallion,** Compote, Open, 8 1/4 In. | 55.00 |
| **Empire Colonial,** Goblet | 95.00 |
| **Empress,** Berry Set, 5 Sauces, Gold Trim | 115.00 |
| **Empress,** Butter, Covered, Green | 175.00 |
| **Empress,** Butter, Covered, Green, Gold Trim | 125.00 |
| **Empress,** Creamer, Clear, Gold Trim | 18.00 |
| **Empress,** Pitcher, Water, Emerald, Gold Trim | 165.00 To 195.00 |
| **Empress,** Pitcher, Water, Green | 135.00 |
| **Empress,** Spooner, Green | 65.00 |
| **Empress,** Spooner, Green, Gold Trim | 40.00 |
| **Empress,** Sugar, Covered, Green | 95.00 |
| **Empress,** Table Set, Green, Gold Trim | 395.00 |
| **Empress,** Toothpick, Green, Gold Trim | 85.00 |
|     **ENGLISH HOBNAIL CROSS, see Klondike** | |
| **PRESSED GLASS, Esther,** Bowl, Green, 11 In. | 75.00 |
| **Esther,** Butter, Covered | 50.00 |
| **Esther,** Celery | 45.00 |
| **Esther,** Sugar, Covered, Amber Etched | 95.00 |
| **Esther,** Table Set, Gold Trim, Green, 4 Piece | 495.00 |
| **Esther,** Toothpick, Clear | 55.00 |
|     **ETCHED BAND, see Dakota** | |
|     **ETCHED FERN, see Ashman** | |
|     **ETCHED PATTERNS, see under main pattern: e.g., Etched Dakota, see** | |
|     **Dakota** | |
| **Eugenie,** Goblet | 32.00 |
| **Eugenie,** Goblet, Flint | 45.00 |
| **Eureka,** Bread Plate | 35.00 |

| | |
|---|---|
| **Eureka,** Goblet | 15.00 |
| **Eureka,** Goblet, Flint | 35.00 |
| **Excelsior,** Candlestick, 9 1/2 In. | 85.00 |
| **Excelsior,** Champagne | 32.00 |
| **Excelsior,** Creamer, Flint | 70.00 |
| **Excelsior,** Eggcup | 14.00 |
| **Excelsior,** Goblet | 45.00 |
| **Excelsior,** Goblet, Flint | 40.00 To 55.00 |
| **Excelsior,** Hat | 145.00 |
| **Excelsior,** Pitcher | 150.00 |
| **Excelsior,** Sugar, Covered | 60.00 |
| **Excelsior,** Wine, Flint | 28.00 To 35.00 |
| **Eyewinker,** Butter, Covered | 65.00 |
| **Eyewinker,** Compote, Open, 9 In. | 70.00 |
| **Eyewinker,** Creamer | 42.50 |
| **Eyewinker,** Fruit Stand | 42.00 |
| **Eyewinker,** Spooner | 35.00 |
| **Eyewinker,** Sugar, Covered | 50.00 |
| **FAGOT, see Vera** | |
| **Faith,** Hope, & Charity, Creamer | 32.00 |
| **Faith,** Hope, Charity, Plate, Cake | 55.00 |
| **Famous,** Spooner, Green | 55.00 |
| **FAN, see also Butterfly & Fan** | |
| **Fan Band** | 18.00 |
| **Fan With Diamond,** Spooner | 19.00 |
| **Fan With Diamond,** Sugar, Covered | 25.00 |
| **Fan With Diamond,** Wine | 35.00 |
| **Fancy Loop,** Creamer | 20.00 |
| **Fancy Loop,** Salt & Pepper, Clear | 25.00 |
| **Fancy Loop,** Wine, Clear | 35.00 |
| **Fashion,** Pitcher, Water, Clear, Gold Trim | 30.00 |
| **Feather Duster,** Goblet | 15.00 |
| **Feather Swirl,** Syrup | 34.50 |
| **Feather,** Bowl, Amber, 7 1/2 In. | 95.00 |
| **Feather,** Butter, Covered | 34.50 To 45.00 |
| **Feather,** Cake Stand, Green | 125.00 |
| **Feather,** Cake Stand, 10 In. | 21.00 To 28.00 |
| **Feather,** Cake Stand, 8 1/2 In. | 30.00 |
| **Feather,** Cake Stand, 9 1/2 In. | 33.00 |
| **Feather,** Celery | 25.00 |
| **Feather,** Compote, Jelly | 17.50 |
| **Feather,** Cordial | 65.00 |
| **Feather,** Creamer | 18.00 |
| **Feather,** Creamer, Green | 10.00 |
| **Feather,** Cruet, Feather Stopper | 50.00 |
| **Feather,** Goblet | 37.50 |
| **Feather,** Goblet, Amber Flashing | 210.00 |
| **Feather,** Green, 10 In. | 15.00 |
| **Feather,** Honey | 15.00 |
| **Feather,** Pitcher, Milk | 37.50 |
| **Feather,** Pitcher, Water | 30.00 To 50.00 |
| **Feather,** Plate, 7 3/4 In.Diam. | 18.00 |
| **Feather,** Sauce, 4 In.Square | 17.50 |
| **Feather,** Spooner | 12.00 To 13.50 |
| **Feather,** Spooner, Green | 55.00 |
| **Feather,** Sugar | 25.00 |
| **Feather,** Sugar, Covered | 38.00 To 40.00 |
| **Feather,** Tumbler | 45.00 |
| **Feather,** Wine | 8.00 To 32.50 |
| **Feathered Arches,** Bowl, Punch, Child's | 22.00 |
| **Fern Burst,** Goblet, 5 1/2 In. _Illus_ | 13.50 |
| **Fern Garland,** Syrup | 34.50 |
| **Fern,** Goblet | 10.00 |

| | |
|---|---|
| **Ferris Wheel,** Wine, Clear & Gold | 15.00 |
| **FESTOON & GRAPE, see Grape & Festoon** | |
| **Festoon,** Berry Bowl, 9 In. | 18.50 |
| **Festoon,** Bowl, 9 In.Diam. | 18.50 To 30.00 |
| **Festoon,** Butter | 55.00 |
| **Festoon,** Creamer | 15.00 |
| **Festoon,** Pitcher, Water | 55.00 To 65.00 |
| **Festoon,** Spooner | 15.00 |
| **Festoon,** Tray, Water, 10 In.Diam. | 18.00 |
| **Festoon,** Tumbler | 17.00 |
| **Festoon,** Water Set, 6 Piece | 160.00 |
| **Fickle Block,** Pitcher, Milk, 7 1/2 In. | 110.00 |
| **Fickle Block,** Spooner | 18.00 |
| **File,** Plate, 6 1/2 In.Diam. | 14.00 |
| **Fine Prism,** Goblet, Straight Edge, Flint | 14.00 |
| **Fine Rib With Cut Ovals,** Goblet, Flint | 185.00 |
| **Fine Rib,** Celery, Flint | 65.00 |
| **Fine Rib,** Goblet, Flint | 35.00 To 55.00 |
| **Fine Rib,** Wine, Flint | 38.00 |
| **Finecut & Block,** Celery | 32.00 To 32.50 |
| **Finecut & Block,** Cordial | 28.00 |
| **Finecut & Block,** Creamer, Amber | 45.00 |
| **Finecut & Block,** Eggcup | 19.50 |
| **Finecut & Block,** Eggcup, Pink Blocks | 20.00 |
| **Finecut & Block,** Spooner, Clear & Blue | 65.00 |
| **Finecut & Block,** Wine, Clear | 18.00 |
| **Finecut & Panel,** Bread Plate | 15.00 |
| **Finecut & Panel,** Creamer, Amber | 32.00 |
| **Finecut & Panel,** Goblet | 25.00 |
| **Finecut & Panel,** Wine | 35.00 |
| **Finecut & Panel,** Wine, Amber | 35.00 |
| **Finecut & Panel,** Wine, Blue | 25.00 To 32.50 |
| **Finecut & Panel,** Wine, Dark Amber | 30.00 |
| **FINECUT MEDALLION, see Austrian** | |
| **Finecut,** Butter, Amber, Shape Of Stove | 49.00 |
| **Finecut,** Goblet | 22.50 |
| **Finecut,** Pitcher, Water, Blue | 95.00 |
| **Finecut,** Plate, Sapphire Blue, 5 1/2 In.Diam. | 20.00 |
| **Finecut,** Spooner, Amber | 30.00 |
| **Finecut,** Toothpick, Top Hat | 30.00 |
| **Finecut,** Tray, Water, Vaseline, 9 1/2 X 12 In. | 34.00 |
| **Finecut,** Wine, Green | 25.00 |
| **Fishscale,** Butter, Covered | 35.00 |
| **Fishscale,** Cake Stand, 10 1/4 In.Diam. | 25.00 |
| **Fishscale,** Compote, Jelly | 12.50 To 25.00 |
| **Fishscale,** Compote, Open, 8 In.Diam. | 25.00 |
| **Fishscale,** Creamer | 25.00 |
| **Fishscale,** Goblet | 18.00 To 25.00 |
| **Fishscale,** Pitcher, Clear, 8 In. | 35.00 |
| **Fishscale,** Pitcher, Milk | 22.00 To 32.50 |
| **Fishscale,** Pitcher, Water | 21.00 |
| **Fishscale,** Pitcher, Water, Blue & White | 75.00 |
| **Fishscale,** Plate, 7 In. | 12.00 To 20.00 |
| **Fishscale,** Plate, 9 In. | 27.00 |
| **Fishscale,** Sauce | 4.50 |
| **Fishscale,** Sauce, Flat | 4.50 |
| **Fishscale,** Spooner | 20.00 |
| **Fishscale,** Sugar, Covered | 35.00 |
| **Flamingo Habitat,** Compote, Covered, 6 1/4 X 7 1/2 In. | 34.00 |
| **Flamingo Habitat,** Compote, Covered, 9 X 12 In. | 56.00 |
| **Flamingo Habitat,** Goblet | 45.00 |
| **Flamingo Habitat,** Goblet, Etched | 20.00 |
| **Flamingo,** Goblet | 39.00 |

Pressed Glass, Frosted Stork

Pressed Glass, Fruit Panels, Goblet

| | |
|---|---|
| Flamingo, Sugar, Covered | 60.00 |
| **FLAT DIAMOND & PANEL, see Lattice & Oval Panels** | |
| Flat Diamond, Celery | 15.00 |
| Flat Diamond, Eggcup | 15.00 |
| Flattened Diamond & Sunburst, Creamer, Oval, Clear, 5 In. | 6.95 |
| Flattened Finecut, Platter | 19.00 |
| Fleur-De-Lis & Drape, Plate, Emerald, 8 1/2 In. | 13.00 |
| Fleur-De-Lis & Drape, Sugar, Covered | 25.00 |
| Fleur-De-Lis & Tassel, Pitcher, Milk | 25.00 |
| Fleur-De-Lis & Tassel, Tumbler, Green | 28.00 |
| Fleur-De-Lis, Compote, Open, 8 In. | 24.00 |
| Fleur-De-Lis, Pitcher, Frosted | 47.50 |
| Fleur-De-Lis, Wine, Clear | 15.00 |
| Floral Oval, Creamer, Covered | 19.00 |
| Florette, Condiment Set, Pink Cased | 185.00 |
| **FLORIDA, see Herringbone** | |
| Flower & Pleat, Sugar, Frosted | 40.00 |
| Flower & Quill, Spooner | 16.00 |
| Flower & Quill, Sugar | 25.00 |
| Flower Band, Frosted, Celery | 65.00 |
| Flower Band, Frosted, Goblet | 55.00 |
| **FLOWER FLANGE, see Dewey** | |
| Flower Pot, Cake Stand, 10 1/2 In.Diam. | 45.00 |
| Flower Pot, Pitcher, 8 1/2 In. | 68.00 |
| Flower Pot, Platter, Motto | 39.00 |
| Flower With Cane, Water Set, Pitcher, 6 Tumblers | 155.00 |
| Flute, Decanter | 45.00 |
| Flute, Eggcup | 22.50 |
| Flute, Eggcup, Flint | 26.50 |
| Flute, Goblet, Sandwich | 22.00 |
| Flute, Goblet, Square Base | 22.00 |
| Flute, Taster, Whiskey, Cobalt, Flint | 70.00 |
| Flute, Wine | 14.00 |
| Fluted Scrolls, Creamer | 30.00 |
| Flying Birds, Goblet | 32.00 |
| **FLYING ROBIN, see Hummingbird** | |
| Flying Stork, Goblet | 40.00 |
| Forget-Me-Not In Scroll, Spooner | 17.00 To 22.00 |
| **FORGET-ME-NOT IN SNOW, see Stippled Forget-Me-Not** | |
| Forget-Me-Not, Butter, Paneled | 40.00 |
| Forget-Me-Not, Compote, Open | 30.00 |
| Forget-Me-Not, Goblet, Paneled | 32.00 |
| Forget-Me-Not, Spooner | 18.50 To 20.00 |
| Forget-Me-Not, Sugar Shaker, Pink | 90.00 |
| Forget-Me-Not, Wine | 18.00 |
| Four Petal, Sugar, Covered | 62.00 |
| Frazier, Toothpick, Maiden Blush & Flowers | 65.00 |
| Fringed Drape, Cruet, Clear | 20.00 |
| Frost Crystal, Plate, 6 In. | 12.00 |
| **FROSTED PATTERNS, see also under name of main pattern** | |

| | |
|---|---|
| **Frosted Artichoke,** Butter, Covered | 85.00 |
| **Frosted Artichoke,** Sauce, 5 In. | 8.50 |
| **Frosted Circle,** Compote, Open, Clear, 7 X 6 In. | 14.00 |
| **Frosted Circle,** Goblet | 35.00 |
| **Frosted Circle,** Pitcher, 1876, Bryce Bros., 12 1/2 In. | 58.00 |
| **Frosted Circle,** Plate, 8 In.Diam. | 35.00 |
| **Frosted Circle,** Spooner, Clear | 22.00 |
| **Frosted Circle,** Spooner, Frosted | 36.00 |
| **FROSTED CRANE, see Frosted Stork** | |
| **Frosted Dog,** Compote, Covered, Footed, Low, Dog Finial | 135.00 |
| **Frosted Dolphin,** Compote, 8 In. | 55.00 |
| **Frosted Double Ribbon,** Creamer | 27.50 |
| **Frosted Eagle,** Creamer, Etched | 75.00 |
| **FROSTED FLOWER BAND, see Flower Band, Frosted** | |
| **Frosted Fruits,** Pitcher, Water, Squirrel In Branches | 145.00 |
| **Frosted Leaf,** Celery | 145.00 |
| **Frosted Leaf,** Champagne | 165.00 |
| **Frosted Leaf,** Champagne, Flint | 165.00 |
| **Frosted Leaf,** Eggcup | 65.00 To 95.00 |
| **Frosted Leaf,** Goblet | 60.00 To 75.00 |
| **Frosted Leaf,** Goblet, Flint | 34.00 To 95.00 |
| **Frosted Leaf,** Sugar, Covered, Portland Glass Co., Flint | 95.00 |
| **Frosted Leaf,** Tumbler, Bar | 95.00 |
| **Frosted Leaf,** Wine, Flint | 135.00 |
| **Frosted Lion,** Bread Plate | 36.00 |
| **Frosted Lion,** Celery | 45.00 To 75.00 |
| **Frosted Lion,** Compote, Full Lion On Lid, Oval, 9 X 9 In. | 95.00 |
| **Frosted Lion,** Compote, Full Lion On Lid, 7 X 7 1/2 In. | 65.00 |
| **Frosted Lion,** Compote, Round, 12 X 8 In.Diam. | 110.00 |
| **Frosted Lion,** Creamer | 35.00 To 65.00 |
| **Frosted Lion,** Dish, Relish, Cable Edge | 35.00 |
| **Frosted Lion,** Eggcup | 50.00 To 75.00 |
| **Frosted Lion,** Goblet | 45.00 To 60.00 |
| **Frosted Lion,** Marmalade | 60.00 |
| **Frosted Lion,** Salt, Oval | 165.00 |
| **Frosted Lion,** Sauce | 12.50 To 25.00 |
| **Frosted Lion,** Sauce, Footed | 22.00 |
| **Frosted Lion,** Spooner | 25.00 To 54.00 |
| **Frosted Lion,** Spooner, 3 Reclining Lions | 35.00 |
| **Frosted Lion,** Sugar & Creamer, Covered | 185.00 |
| **Frosted Lion,** Sugar, Covered | 70.00 |
| **Frosted Lion,** Sugar, Covered, Crouched Lion Finial | 75.00 |
| **Frosted Lion,** Sugar, Open, Lion Collared Base | 25.00 |
| **Frosted Pheasant,** Butter, Covered, C.1860 | 145.00 |
| **Frosted Ribbon,** Compote, Flint, 6 1/2 In. | 46.00 |
| **Frosted Ribbon,** Pitcher, Water | 60.00 |
| **Frosted Roman Key,** Goblet, Flint | 35.00 |
| **Frosted Stork,** Bread Plate | 40.00 |
| **Frosted Stork,** Castor, Pickle | 90.00 |
| **Frosted Stork,** Creamer | 50.00 |
| **FROSTED WAFFLE, see Hidalgo** | |
| **Fruit Panels,** Goblet ................................................ *Illus* | 21.00 |
| **Gaelic,** Compote, 5 1/4 X 5 1/4 In. | 28.00 |
| **Gaelic,** Dish, Heart Shaped, 5 1/2 In. | 14.00 |
| **Gaelic,** Goblet, 7 In. | 16.00 |
| **Gaelic,** Pitcher, Milk | 17.00 To 45.00 |
| **Gaelic,** Pitcher, 5 1/2 In. | 18.00 |
| **Gaelic,** Toothpick | 22.00 |
| **Galloway,** Butter, Covered | 60.00 |
| **Galloway,** Cake Stand | 52.00 |
| **Galloway,** Creamer | 22.00 |
| **Galloway,** Cup, Punch | 8.00 |
| **Galloway,** Goblet, Gilt | 22.50 |

Pressed Glass, Garfield Drape, Pitcher, Water

Pressed Glass, Grape & Festoon, Cup

Pressed Glass, Hairpin,
Goblet, Flint

| | |
|---|---|
| Galloway, Spooner | 21.50 |
| Galloway, Toothpick | 21.00 |
| Galloway, Tumbler | 25.00 |
| Galloway, Vase, 11 1/2 In. | 14.00 To 20.00 |
| Garden Fruits, Goblet, Etched | 15.00 |
| **GARDEN OF EDEN, see Lotus & Serpent** | |
| Garfield Drape, Bread Plate | 38.00 |
| Garfield Drape, Creamer | 26.50 To 45.00 |
| Garfield Drape, Dish, Relish, Oval | 16.00 |
| Garfield Drape, Goblet | 29.50 To 35.00 |
| Garfield Drape, Pitcher | 49.50 |
| Garfield Drape, Pitcher, Milk, Applied Handle | 75.00 |
| Garfield Drape, Pitcher, Water | *Illus* 65.00 |
| Garfield Drape, Spooner | 22.00 |
| Garfield, Bread Plate | 35.00 |
| Garfield, Bread Plate, Egg & Dart Border, Iowa City | 45.00 |
| Garfield, Plate, Star Rim, 6 In. | 28.00 |
| Garfield, Tumbler | 15.00 |
| Geneva, Banana Boat, Emerald & Gold | 72.00 |
| Geneva, Pitcher, Water, Gold Trim, Green | 125.00 |
| Georgia Gem, Berry Bowl, Master, Gold Trim | 75.00 |
| Georgia Gem, Creamer, Custard | 48.00 |
| Giant Baby Thumbprint, Wine, Flint | 60.00 |
| Giant Prism With Thumbprint Band, Ale | 45.00 |
| Giant Prism, Goblet | 65.00 |
| Giant Sawtooth, Goblet, Flint | 85.00 |
| Giant Sawtooth, Spill | 40.00 |
| Giraffe, Goblet, Etched | 55.00 |
| Girl With Fan, Goblet | 35.00 To 65.00 |
| Goat's Head, Compote, High Standard | 45.00 |
| Goat's Head, Sauce, Figural | 32.50 |
| Goat's Head, Spooner, Frosted | 58.00 |
| Gonterman, Celery | 92.00 |
| Gonterman, Compote, Open, 7 1/2 X 8 In.Diam. | 155.00 |
| **GOOD LUCK, see Horseshoe** | |
| Gooseberry, Creamer | 30.00 To 35.00 |
| Gooseberry, Goblet | 21.00 |
| Gooseberry, Mug | 22.50 To 25.00 |
| Gothic Arch, Celery | 58.00 |
| Gothic, Eggcup, Flint | 25.00 To 45.00 |
| Gothic, Goblet, Flint | 35.00 To 80.00 |
| Gothic, Sauce, Flint | 15.00 |
| Gothic, Spooner, Flint | 28.00 |

Gothic, Sugar, Covered .......................................................................................... 98.00
Gothic, Sugar, Open, Flint ..................................................................................... 40.00
Gothic, Tumbler ...................................................................................................... 15.00
    GRACE, see Butterfly & Fan
    GRAND, see Diamond Medallion
Grant, Bread Plate, Peace, Amber ......................................................................... 42.00
    GRAPE, see also Beaded Grape, Beaded Grape Medallion, Magnet &
      Grape, Magnet & Grape with Frosted Leaf, Paneled Grape, Paneled
      Grape Band
Grape & Festoon, Butter, Covered, Acorn Finial ................................................... 35.00
Grape & Festoon, Dish, Pickle, Oval, 8 1/2 In. ................................................... 14.00
Grape & Festoon, Spooner ..................................................................................... 18.00
Grape Band, Spooner .............................................................................................. 19.00
Grape With Gothic Arches, Goblet ........................................................................ 45.00
Grape With Gothic Arches, Green & Gold, Table Set, 4 Piece ......................... 300.00
Grape With Gothic Arches, Sugar, Green ............................................................. 35.00
Grape With Gothic Arches, Sugar, Open, Green .................................................. 15.00
Grape, Eggcup ........................................................................................................ 12.00
Grape, Goblet .......................................................................................................... 10.00
Grasshopper With Insect, Goblet .......................................................................... 65.00
Grasshopper With Insect, Spooner ........................................................................ 28.00
Grasshopper With Insect, Sugar, Covered ............................................................ 75.00
Grasshopper, Bowl, Footed, 7 In. .......................................................................... 25.50
Grasshopper, Bowl, Footed, 8 In. .......................................................................... 25.50
Grasshopper, Butter, Covered, Vaseline ............................................................... 95.00
Grasshopper, Goblet, Amber .................................................................................. 40.00
Grasshopper, Goblet, Clear .................................................................................... 42.00
Grasshopper, Pitcher, Water, 9 In. ......................................................................... 42.50
Grasshopper, Sauce, Footed, 4 In. ........................................................................ 16.50
Grasshopper, Spooner ........................................................... 20.00 To 40.00
Grasshopper, Spooner, Vaseline ........................................................................... 65.00
Greek Key, Champagne, Flint ................................................................................ 65.00
Grogan, Goblet ........................................................................................................ 12.50
Grooved Bigler, Champagne ................................................................................... 85.00
Hairpin With Thumbprint, Goblet ........................................................................... 30.00
Hairpin, Celery, Flint ............................................................................................... 50.00
Hairpin, Compote, Opalescent, Flint, 9 In.Diam. ................................................. 175.00
Hairpin, Goblet, Flint ................................................................................ *Illus* 35.00
Hairpin, Tumbler, Blue, 2 1/4 In. ........................................................................... 15.00
Hairpin, Whiskey, Amber, 2 3/4 In. ....................................................................... 10.00
Halley's Comet, Bowl, 8 In.Diam. ......................................................................... 21.00
Halley's Comet, Tumbler ........................................................................................ 22.00
Halley's Comet, Wine .............................................................................................. 15.00
    HAMILTON WITH CLEAR LEAF, see Hamilton With Leaf
Hamilton With Leaf, Compote, Scalloped, Flint, 8 X 6 1/2 In. ............................ 50.00
Hamilton, Compote, High Standard, Flint ............................................... *Illus* 85.00
Hamilton, Eggcup, Flint ........................................................... 25.00 To 28.00
Hamilton, Goblet, Flint ............................................................. 35.00 To 37.50
Hamilton, Pitcher, Buttermilk, Footed ................................................................... 45.00
Hamilton, Spooner, Flint ........................................................... 22.50 To 45.00
Hamilton, Tumbler, Water, Flint ............................................................................. 75.00
    HAND, see Pennsylvania Hand
Hand & Bar, Sugar Covered ................................................................................... 55.00
Hanover, Sauce, Footed, 4 In. ............................................................................... 11.50
Harp, Pitcher, Water, Flint ........................................................................ *Illus* 125.00
Hartley, Bread Plate ................................................................................................ 18.00
Hartley, Creamer ..................................................................................................... 24.00
Hartley, Spooner, Green & Gold ............................................................................ 35.00
Harvard, Creamer .................................................................................................... 13.00
Hawaiian Lei, Sauce, Footed, Higbee, Signed ..................................................... 6.00
Hawaiian Lei, Sugar, Covered ................................................................................ 32.00
Heart & Thumbprint, Plate, Green, Gold, 6 In. ................................................... 34.00
Heart Band, Ruby, Creamer ................................................................................... 25.00

Pressed Glass, Hamilton, Compote, High Standard, Flint
*(See Page 455)*

Pressed Glass, Hobnail, Pitcher, Ruffled, Frosted Amber

Pressed Glass, Harp, Pitcher, Water, Flint (See Page 455)

| | |
|---|---:|
| **Heart Stem,** Creamer | 38.50 To 40.00 |
| **Heart With Thumbprint,** Bowl, Gold Trim, 8 In.Diam. | 26.00 |
| **Heart With Thumbprint,** Bowl, Waste | 40.00 |
| **Heart With Thumbprint,** Bowl, 4 1/2 In.Diam. | 10.00 |
| **Heart With Thumbprint,** Bowl, 9 In.Diam. | 14.00 To 24.00 |
| **Heart With Thumbprint,** Butter | 40.00 |
| **Heart With Thumbprint,** Creamer | 15.00 To 17.50 |
| **Heart With Thumbprint,** Cup, Punch | 12.00 |
| **Heart With Thumbprint,** Goblet | 55.00 |
| **Heart With Thumbprint,** Plate, Green, 6 1/4 In. | 65.00 |
| **Heart With Thumbprint,** Plate, 6 1/4 In. | 16.00 |
| **Heart With Thumbprint,** Sauce, 5 In. | 9.00 |
| **Heart With Thumbprint,** Sugar, Gold Rim, Individual | 20.00 |
| **Heart With Thumbprint,** Tray, Gold Trim, 8 1/4 X 2 1/2 In. | 20.00 |
| **Heart With Thumbprint,** Tumbler | 20.00 To 35.00 |
| **Heart With Thumbprint,** Wine | 35.00 |
|     **HEARTS OF LOCH LAVEN, see Shuttle** | |
| **Heavy Gothic,** Goblet | 32.00 |
| **Hen On Nest,** 4 1/2 In. | 22.00 |
| **Henrietta,** Cup, Punch | 11.00 |
| **Henrietta,** Sugar Shaker | 18.00 |
| **Hercules Pillar,** Goblet | 24.00 |
| **Hercules Pillar,** Syrup, Blue | 50.00 |
| **Heron,** Celery, Stemmed, Scalloped Edge | 45.00 |
| **Heron,** Goblet, Etched | 37.50 |
| **Heron,** Spooner, 3 Scenes, Wading, Feeding, Flying | 48.00 |
| **Herringbone,** Berry Set, 7 Sauces, Emerald Green, 8 In. | 70.00 |
| **Herringbone,** Bowl, Emerald Green, 8 3/4 In.Square | 15.00 |
| **Herringbone,** Creamer, Emerald | 20.00 |
| **Herringbone,** Goblet | 10.50 |
| **Herringbone,** Goblet, Buttermilk | 20.00 |
| **Herringbone,** Spooner | 14.00 |
| **Herringbone,** Sugar, Covered | 27.00 |

Pressed Glass, Holly Band

| | |
|---|---:|
| **Herringbone,** Water Set, Emerald Green, 7 Piece | 165.00 |
| **Hexagon Block,** Butter, Covered, Yellow Blocks | 55.00 |
| **Hey Diddle Diddle,** Plate, 6 In. | 22.50 |
| **Hickman,** Bottle, Cologne | 35.00 |
| **Hickman,** Bucket, Ice, Green | 45.00 |
| **Hickman,** Cruet, Faceted Stopper | 30.00 |
| **Hickman,** Mug, Lemonade, Green | 45.00 |
| **Hickman,** Pitcher, Water | 32.00 |
| **Hickman,** Spooner | 27.50 |
| **Hickman,** Vase, 12 In. | 22.50 |
| **Hidalgo,** Celery, Frosted | 20.00 |
| **Hidalgo,** Cruet, Original Stopper | 28.00 |
| **Hildago,** Goblet, Frosted Top | 16.00 |
| **Hobnail With Line Band,** Pitcher, Water | 29.00 |
| **Hobnail With Thumbprint Base,** Creamer, Amber | 22.00 |
| **Hobnail With Thumbprint Base,** Spooner | 20.00 |
| **Hobnail,** Hat, Clear, 6 X 10 In. | 65.00 |
| **Hobnail,** Pitcher, Ruffled, Frosted Amber *Illus* | 65.00 |
| **Hobnail,** Toothpick, Blue Frosted | 35.00 |
|     **HOLBROOK, see Pineapple & Fan** | |
| **Holland,** Pitcher | 32.00 |
| **Holly Band,** Pitcher, Water | 90.00 |
| **Honeycomb & Loop,** Goblet | 15.00 |
| **Honeycomb With Diamond,** Goblet, Flint | 18.00 |
| **Honeycomb With Flower Rim,** Creamer, Green | 35.00 |
| **Honeycomb With Pillar,** Wine | 22.50 |
|     **HONEY, see also Vernon Honeycomb** | |
| **Honeycomb With Star,** Salt & Pepper, Clear, 3 1/2 In. | 10.95 |
| **Honeycomb,** Bowl, Punch, 4 Cups, Miniature | 50.00 |
| **Honeycomb,** Celery, Flint | 32.00 |
| **Honeycomb,** Celery, 8 1/2 In. | 14.00 |
| **Honeycomb,** Compote, Clear, Flint, 5 X 6 In.Diam. | 75.00 |
| **Honeycomb,** Compote, Flint, 8 In. | 135.00 |
| **Honeycomb,** Eggcup, Flint | 12.00 |
| **Honeycomb,** Goblet | 15.00 To 27.00 |
| **Honeycomb,** Goblet, Barrel, Flint | 19.50 |
| **Honeycomb,** Goblet, Bumblebee | 22.00 |
| **Honeycomb,** Goblet, Engraved | 50.00 |
| **Honeycomb,** Goblet, Etched, Flint | 22.50 |
| **Honeycomb,** Spooner | 12.50 To 14.00 |
| **Honeycomb,** Spooner, Allover Cut, Star Cut Foot, 4 In. | 20.00 |
| **Honeycomb,** Sugar, Covered, Flint | 55.00 |
| **Honeycomb,** Wine, Clear | 14.00 To 15.00 |
| **Hooks & Eyes,** Goblet | 13.50 |
| **Hops Band,** Goblet | 18.75 |
| **Horn Of Plenty,** Celery, Flint | 135.00 |

| | |
|---|---|
| **Horn Of Plenty**, Creamer | 125.00 |
| **Horn Of Plenty**, Eggcup | 30.00 |
| **Horn Of Plenty**, Eggcup, Flint | 25.00 To 45.00 |
| **Horn Of Plenty**, Eggcup, Set Of 4 | 140.00 |
| **Horn Of Plenty**, Goblet | 46.00 To 65.00 |
| **Horn Of Plenty**, Goblet, Flint | 60.00 To 65.00 |
| **Horn Of Plenty**, Mug, Whiskey, Handled | 160.00 |
| **Horn Of Plenty**, Plate, Flint, 6 In. | 85.00 |
| **Horn Of Plenty**, Plate, 6 In., Set Of 4 | 165.00 |
| **Horn Of Plenty**, Sauce, Flint | 17.50 To 28.00 |
| **Horn Of Plenty**, Spooner, Flint | 18.00 To 45.00 |
| **Horn Of Plenty**, Sugar, Flint | 125.00 |
| **Horn Of Plenty**, Whiskey, Flint | 115.00 |
| **Horn Of Plenty**, Wine | 125.00 |
| **Horseheads Medallion**, Sugar, Open | 35.00 |
| **Horseheads Medallion**, Tumbler | 39.50 |
| **Horseshoe**, Bowl, Footed, 8 In.Diam. | 30.00 |
| **Horseshoe**, Bowl, Waste | 65.00 |
| **Horseshoe**, Bread Plate | 40.00 To 45.00 |
| **Horseshoe**, Cake Stand, 9 In. | 36.00 |
| **Horseshoe**, Cake Stand, 10 In.Diam. | 48.50 To 65.00 |
| **Horseshoe**, Celery | 45.00 |
| **Horseshoe**, Compote, Marmalade, 3 3/4 X 4 1/8 In.Diam. | 15.00 |
| **Horseshoe**, Creamer | 20.00 To 42.50 |
| **Horseshoe**, Creamer, Pedestal Base | 23.00 |
| **Horseshoe**, Dish, Relish | 16.00 |
| **Horseshoe**, Dish, 9 In. | 16.00 |
| **Horseshoe**, Goblet | 20.00 To 38.00 |
| **Horseshoe**, Goblet, Knob Stem | 14.00 |
| **Horseshoe**, Goblet, Plain Stem | 25.00 |
| **Horseshoe**, Pitcher, Water | 75.00 |
| **Horseshoe**, Plate, 7 1/4 In. | 45.00 |
| **Horseshoe**, Salt, Master | 50.00 |
| **Horseshoe**, Sauce, Footed | 13.50 |
| **Horseshoe**, Spooner | 16.00 To 27.00 |
| **Horseshoe**, Wine | 9.00 |
| **Hotel Argus**, Goblet, Flint | 32.50 |
| **Huber**, Eggcup, Flint | 14.00 |
| **Huber**, Whiskey, Handled | 47.50 |
| **Huber**, Wine, Flint | 25.00 |
|     **HUCKLE, see Feather Duster** | |
| **Hummingbird**, Celery | 49.50 |
| **Hummingbird**, Goblet | 35.00 |
| **Hummingbird**, Pitcher, Amber | 65.00 |
| **Hummingbird**, Pitcher, Footed, 5 3/4 In. | 37.50 |
| **Hummingbird**, Pitcher, Water | 55.00 To 95.00 |
| **Hummingbird**, Pitcher, Water, Blue | 95.00 |
| **Hundred Eye**, Wine | 15.00 |
| **Hundred Leaved Rose**, Butter, Covered | 25.00 |
| **Icicle With Chain Band**, Goblet | 30.00 |
| **Icicle**, Goblet, Fluted | 17.00 |
|     **IDA, see Sheraton** | |
|     **IDANO, see Snail** | |
| **Illinois**, Basket, Applied Reeded Handle | 58.00 |
| **Illinois**, Tray, Celery, Flat | 27.00 |
| **Illinois**, Vase, Spill | 40.00 |
|     **INDIAN TREE, see Sprig** | |
| **Indian**, Dish, Relish, Gold Trim, 7 X 4 1/2 In.Diam. | 10.00 |
|     **INDIANA SWIRL, see Feather** | |
| **Intaglio**, Spooner, Vaseline Opalescent | 75.00 |
| **Interlocked Hearts**, Creamer | 16.00 |
| **Inverted Fan & Feather**, Pitcher, Water, Green | 175.00 |
| **Inverted Fan & Feather**, Tumbler, Gold Trim, Green | 49.00 |

**Inverted Fan & Feather,** Water Set, Green, Gold Trim, 7 Piece ............................................ 475.00
**Inverted Fern,** Eggcup, Flint ................................................................. 22.00 To 28.50
**Inverted Fern,** Goblet ........................................................................... 18.00 To 35.00
**Inverted Fern,** Goblet, Flint .................................................................. 25.00 To 32.00
**Inverted Fern,** Goblet, Ribbed ........................................................................ 37.50
**Inverted Fern,** Honey, Flint ............................................................................. 8.00
**Inverted Fern,** Wine ..................................................................................... 125.00
**Inverted Fern,** Wine, Flint ............................................................................. 35.00
**Inverted Prism With Diamond Band,** Creamer, Flint ......................................... 30.00
    **INVERTED THISTLE, see Late Thistle**
**Inverted Thumbprint,** Compote, Designed Dome, Vaseline, 7 In. ........................ 36.00
**Inverted Thumbprint,** Goblet ............................................................................ 55.00
**Inverted Thumbprint,** Goblet, Blue ................................................................... 20.00
**Ionia,** Goblet ................................................................................................... 12.00
**Iowa,** Cup, Punch ............................................................................................. 5.00
**Iowa,** Plate, Be Affectionate, Frosted Bird Handles, 8 In.Diam. ......................... 45.00
**Iowa,** Sugar & Creamer .................................................................................... 14.00
**Iowa,** Toothpick ............................................................................................... 25.00
**Iris & Herringbone,** Butter, Covered ................................................................. 18.50
**Iris & Herringbone,** Pitcher ............................................................................. 15.00
**Iris & Herringbone,** Sugar & Creamer ................................................................ 7.00
**Iris With Meander,** Toothpick, Clear To Opalescent ........................................... 25.00
**Iris With Meander,** Toothpick, Green ................................................................. 45.00
**Isis,** Butter, Covered ........................................................................................ 15.00
**Ivy In Snow,** Celery .......................................................................................... 20.00
**Ivy In Snow,** Cup, Blue ..................................................................................... 45.00
**Ivy In Snow,** Plate, Blue Ivy, 10 In. .................................................................. 32.00
**Jacob's Ladder,** Bowl, 7 3/4 X 5 1/2 In. ............................................................ 14.00
**Jacob's Ladder,** Celery .................................................................... 22.00 To 40.00
**Jacob's Ladder,** Compote, Flint, 7 1/2 X 7 1/2 In. ............................................. 35.00
**Jacob's Ladder,** Compote, Open, 7 1/2 X 4 1/2 In. ............................................ 19.00
**Jacob's Ladder,** Compote, Open, 9 In. .............................................................. 40.00
**Jacob's Ladder,** Creamer .................................................................................. 36.50
**Jacob's Ladder,** Dish, Relish ............................................................................ 29.00
**Jacob's Ladder,** Eggcup ................................................................................... 15.00
**Jacob's Ladder,** Goblet ................................................................... 47.50 To 79.50
**Jacob's Ladder,** Pitcher, Milk .......................................................... 18.00 To 20.00
**Jacob's Ladder,** Pitcher, Water ........................................................................ 75.00
**Jacob's Ladder,** Plate, 6 In. ............................................................................. 20.00
**Jacob's Ladder,** Wine ...................................................................... 22.00 To 48.50
    **JASPER, see Late Buckle**
**Jenny Lind,** Match Holder, Clear ....................................................................... 58.00
**Jersey Swirl,** Celery ......................................................................... 22.00 To 25.00
**Jersey Swirl,** Compote, Open, Large .................................................................. 45.00
**Jersey Swirl,** Jar, Jam, Original Lid ................................................................... 45.00
**Jersey Swirl,** Plate, Amber, 8 In. ..................................................................... 28.00
**Jersey Swirl,** Plate, 6 In. .................................................................................. 14.00
**Jersey Swirl,** Salt ............................................................................................... 6.50
**Jewel & Crescent,** Dish, Pickle ......................................................................... 24.00
**Jewel & Dewdrop,** Berry Bowl, Cranberry Jewels, Master ................................... 22.00
**Jewel & Dewdrop,** Bread Plate, Our Daily Bread, Clear ...................................... 55.00
**Jewel & Dewdrop,** Dish, Relish, 8 1/4 In. .......................................................... 24.00
**Jewel & Dewdrop,** Goblet ................................................................................. 35.00
**Jewel & Dewdrop,** Pitcher, Water ..................................................................... 45.00
**Jewel & Dewdrop,** Platter, Motto ...................................................................... 35.00
**Jewel & Dewdrop,** Wine ................................................................................... 45.00
    **JEWEL & FESTOON, see Loop & Jewel**
    **JEWEL BAND, see Scalloped Tape**
**Jeweled Heart,** Butter, Covered ....................................................................... 170.00
**Jeweled Heart,** Butter, Gold Cover .................................................................... 45.00
**Jeweled Heart,** Creamer ................................................................... 17.50 To 25.00
**Jeweled Heart,** Pitcher, Water ................................................................*Illus* 75.00
**Jeweled Heart,** Sugar, Covered ........................................................................ 18.00

Pressed Glass, Jeweled Heart,
Pitcher, Water (See Page 459)

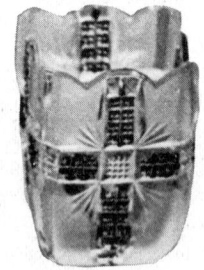

Pressed Glass, Klondike,
Bowl, Square, 7 In.

| | |
|---|---|
| **Jeweled Moon & Star,** Compote, 6 3/4 X 8 In.Diam. | 55.00 |
| **JOB'S TEARS, see Art** | |
| **JUBILEE, see Hickman** | |
| **Jumbo,** Butter, Covered | 360.00 |
| **Jumbo,** Creamer | 85.00 |
| **Jumbo,** Creamer, Man Under Handle | 215.00 |
| **KAMONI, see Balder** | |
| **KANSAS, see Jewel & Dewdrop** | |
| **Kentucky,** Cup, Punch, Green | 12.00 |
| **King's Crown,** Celery | 55.00 |
| **King's Crown,** Compote, Open, 8 1/2 In. | 39.50 |
| **King's Crown,** Creamer | 55.00 |
| **King's Crown,** Goblet | 14.00 To 32.00 |
| **King's Crown,** Sauce Boat, Ruby | 24.00 |
| **King's Crown,** Sauce, Oval | 25.00 |
| **King's Crown,** Spooner | 40.00 |
| **King's Crown,** Tankard, Etched | 165.00 |
| **King's Crown,** Toothpick | 21.50 To 30.00 |
| **King's Crown,** Wine | 16.00 |
| **King's Crown,** Wine, Clear | 9.00 |
| **King's 500,** Compote, Open, 10 X 8 1/2 In. | 19.00 |
| **King's 500,** Nappy, Handle, Gold Trim, Cobalt, 5 1/2 In. | 22.00 |
| **Kitten On Pillow,** Toothpick | 50.00 |
| **Klondike,** Bowl, Square, 7 In. *Illus* | 175.00 |
| **Klondike,** Butter, Covered | 450.00 |
| **Klondike,** Champagne | 645.00 |
| **Klondike,** Compote, Vertical Amber Panels, 11 In.Diam. | 125.00 |
| **Klondike,** Creamer | 275.00 |
| **Klondike,** Cruet | 475.00 |
| **Klondike,** Dish, Butter, Clear | 85.00 |
| **Klondike,** Dish, Pickle, Boat Shape, 9 X 4 In. | 85.00 To 95.00 |
| **Klondike,** Dish, Sauce | 12.00 |
| **Klondike,** Salt & Pepper, Original Tops | 175.00 |
| **Klondike,** Saltshaker, Clear | 30.00 |
| **Klondike,** Saucer, Vertical Amber Panels, 4 3/4 In. | 27.00 |
| **Klondike,** Sugar, Covered | 325.00 |
| **Klondike,** Sugar, Covered, Frosted & Gold | 290.00 |
| **Klondike,** Syrup | 675.00 |
| **Klondike,** Tumbler, Frosted, Amber Flashing, 4 In. | 145.00 |
| **Klondike,** Vase, Trumpet, Frosted, Amber | 125.00 |
| **Klondike,** Vase, Trumpet, 8 1/2 In. | 24.00 |
| **Knives & Forks,** Goblet | 16.00 |
| **Knobby Bull's-Eye,** Wine, Amethyst Eyes | 16.50 |
| **Kokomo,** Compote, Covered, 11 1/2 In. | 65.00 |
| **LACE, see Drapery** | |

Pressed Glass, Liberty Bell, Plate

Pressed Glass, Lily Of The
Valley (See Page 462)

| | |
|---|---|
| Lacy Daisy, Berry Set, Child's | 60.00 |
| Lacy Daisy, Spooner | 16.00 |
| Lacy Medallion, Mug, Handled, Etched Merry Christmas, 1906 | 35.00 |
| Lacy Medallion, Pitcher, Gold Trim, Green, 2 1/2 In. | 18.00 |
| Lacy Medallion, Toothpick, Gold Trim, Green | 35.00 |
| LACY SPIRAL, see Colossus | |
| LAMP, see Lamp | |
| Last Supper, Bread Plate | 12.00 |
| Late Buckle, Cake Stand, 10 In. | 17.00 |
| Late Thistle, Bowl, Footed, 5 1/2 In. | 19.50 |
| Lattice & Oval Panels, Claret | 75.00 |
| Lattice & Oval Panels, Creamer | 275.00 |
| Lattice & Oval Panels, Sugar, Covered | 275.00 |
| Lattice & Oval Panels, Wine, Flint | 40.00 |
| Lattice, Tumbler, Blue Opalescent | 35.00 |
| Leaf & Dart, Butter, Covered, Footed | 65.00 |
| Leaf & Dart, Creamer, Applied Handle | 29.00 |
| Leaf & Dart, Creamer, Applied Handle, Footed | 45.00 |
| Leaf & Dart, Cruet, Applied Handle, Original Stopper | 75.00 |
| Leaf & Dart, Eggcup | 20.00 To 30.00 |
| Leaf & Dart, Goblet | 16.00 To 25.00 |
| Leaf & Dart, Pitcher, Water, Applied Handle | 75.00 |
| Leaf & Dart, Salt, Covered | 75.00 |
| Leaf & Dart, Sugar, Covered, Footed | 55.00 |
| Leaf & Dart, Sugar, Open | 22.50 |
| Leaf & Dart, Tumbler, Footed, 5 3/4 In. | 28.00 |
| Leaf & Dart, Wine | 20.00 To 35.00 |
| Leaf & Star, Celery | 18.00 |
| Leaf Medallion, Berry Set, Amethyst, 7 Piece | 320.00 |
| Leaflets, Creamer | 15.00 |
| Lee, Celery | 125.00 |
| Lens & Block, Goblet | 18.50 |
| LENS & STAR, see Star & Oval | |
| LEVERNE, see Star In Honeycomb | |
| Liberty Bell, Bread Plate, Centennial, Signers | 75.00 |
| Liberty Bell, Butter | 85.00 |
| Liberty Bell, Compote, 8 In. | 65.00 To 85.00 |
| Liberty Bell, Mug, Snake Handled | 285.00 |
| Liberty Bell, Plate | Illus 55.00 |
| Liberty Bell, Platter, Signers' Names, 9 1/4 X 13 In. | 200.00 |
| Liberty Bell, Saltshaker, Original Top | 50.00 |
| Liberty Bell, Sauce | 22.00 |
| Liberty Bell, Sauce, Footed | 11.00 To 15.00 |

Pressed Glass, Lincoln Drape

Pressed Glass, Lion

| | |
|---|---|
| **Liberty Bell,** Spooner | 40.00 To 69.50 |
| **Lily Of The Valley,** Goblet | 12.50 To 18.00 |
| **Lily Of The Valley,** Goblet, Buttermilk | 22.50 |
| **Lily Of The Valley,** Goblet, Etched | *Illus* 12.50 |
| **Lincoln Drape With Tassel,** Goblet | 95.00 |
| **Lincoln Drape,** Cable Edge, Flint, 7 1/2 In. | 65.00 |
| **Lincoln Drape,** Dish, Sweetmeat, Covered | 65.00 |
| **Lincoln Drape,** Eggcup, Flint | 30.00 To 40.00 |
| **Lincoln Drape,** Goblet | 65.00 |
| **Lincoln Drape,** Goblet, Flint | 45.00 |
| **Lincoln Drape,** Master Salt | 125.00 |
| **Lincoln Drape,** Paperweight, Frosted Face, Oval | 145.00 |
| **Lincoln Drape,** Sauce | 15.00 |
| **Lincoln Drape,** Sugar, Covered | 75.00 |
| **Lincoln Drape,** Syrup | 40.00 |
| **Lincoln Drape,** Syrup, Applied & Crimped Handle, Tin Top | 110.00 |
| **Lined Smocking,** Goblet | 65.00 |
| **LION, see also Frosted Lion** | |
| **Lion & Baboon,** Butter, Covered | 90.00 |
| **Lion & Baboon,** Sauce | 22.50 |
| **Lion With Cable,** Creamer | 35.00 |
| **Lion,** Butter, 2 Face Lion Finial, 6 5/8 In.Square | 80.00 |
| **Lion,** Cup & Saucer, Child's, Clear | 50.00 To 70.00 |
| **Lion,** Goblet, Square | 75.00 |
| **Lion,** Sugar & Creamer | 175.00 |
| **Lion's Head,** Goblet | 12.00 |
| **LION'S LEG, see Alaska** | |
| **LIPPMAN, see Flat Diamond** | |
| **Little Gem,** Butter, Green | 65.00 |
| **Log & Star,** Cruet, Original Stopper, Amber | 40.00 |
| **Log & Star,** Mug, Amber | 16.00 |
| **Log Cabin,** Creamer | 50.00 |
| **Log Cabin,** Relish | 55.00 |
| **Log Cabin,** Salt, Master | 130.00 |
| **Log Cabin,** Spooner | 110.00 |
| **Loganberry & Grape,** Goblet | 20.00 |
| **Long Buttress,** Pitcher | 22.75 |
| **LOOP, see also Seneca Loop, Yuma Loop** | |
| **Loop & Block,** Celery | 39.50 |
| **Loop & Block,** Pitcher, Water | 84.00 |
| **Loop & Dart With Diamond Ornaments,** Creamer | 21.00 |
| **Loop & Dart With Diamond Ornaments,** Goblet | 18.00 To 28.00 |
| **Loop & Dart With Round Ornament,** Bowl, Flint, Oval, 8 1/4 In. | 46.00 |
| **Loop & Dart With Round Ornament,** Goblet, Flint | 25.00 To 30.00 |
| **Loop & Dart,** Buttermilk | 32.50 |

Loop & Dart, Celery ........................................................................................ 45.00
Loop & Dart, Creamer, Applied Handle ....................................................... 35.00
Loop & Dart, Creamer, Flint ........................................................................ 45.00
Loop & Dart, Eggcup ..................................................................................... 21.50
Loop & Dart, Goblet ......................................................... 17.50 To 25.00
Loop & Dart, Goblet, Flint ............................................... 25.00 To 30.00
Loop & Dart, Salt .......................................................................................... 17.50
Loop & Dart, Spooner ................................................................................... 13.50
Loop & Dart, Tumbler ................................................................................... 16.50
Loop & Dart, Tumbler, Footed .................................................................... 15.00
Loop & Dart, Wine ......................................................................................... 29.50
Loop & Honeycomb, Goblet ........................................... 19.00 To 20.00
Loop & Jewel, Dish, Pickle .......................................................................... 12.00
Loop & Jewel, Eggcup ................................................................................... 34.00
Loop & Jewel, Pitcher, Water, Footed ....................................................... 50.00
Loop & Jewel, Tray, Celery ......................................................................... 14.00
Loop & Moose Eye, Goblet, Flint ............................................................... 80.00
Loop & Pyramid, Goblet ............................................................................... 33.50
Loop & Pyramid, Plate, 5 1/2 In. ............................................................... 9.50
Loop & Pyramid, Toothpick ......................................................................... 25.00
Loop & Pyramid, Wine, Gold ...................................................................... 16.50
Loop With Dewdrop, Creamer .................................................................... 15.50
Loop With Dewdrop, Wine ........................................................................... 14.50
  **LOOP WITH STIPPLED PANELS, see Texas**
Loop, Celery ..................................................................... 20.00 To 26.00
Loop, Celery, 10 1/4 In. ............................................................................... 55.00
Loop, Compote, 10 In.Tall ........................................................................... 45.00
Loop, Compote, 7 X 9 1/2 In.Diam. ........................................................... 33.00
Loop, Goblet, Flint ........................................................................................ 40.00
Loop, Spooner ................................................................................................ 15.00
Loop, Syrup, Bulging, Pink Cased ............................................................. 225.00
  **LOOPS & DROPS, see New Jersey**
Loops & Diamonds, Goblet .......................................................................... 27.00
Loops & Fans, Plate, 7 In. ............................................................................ 12.00
Loops & Fans, Sauce, 3 1/2 In. ................................................................... 5.00
Loops & Ovals, Goblet .................................................................................. 17.00
Lotus & Serpent, Bread Plate ..................................................................... 36.50
Lotus & Serpent, Bread Plate, Give Us This Day, 9 X 12 1/2 In. .......... 24.00
Lotus & Serpent, Butter, Covered ............................................................. 35.00
Lotus & Serpent, Creamer ............................................. 27.50 To 45.00
Lotus & Serpent, Pitcher, Water ................................................................ 75.00
Lotus, Dish, Oval, 6 In. ................................................................................ 15.00
Louisiana, Celery, Footed ........................................................................... 32.00
Louisiana, Tumbler ....................................................................................... 10.00
Madison, Spooner, Flint ............................................................................... 28.50
Magnet & Grape With Frosted Leaf, Goblet, Flint ................................. 55.00
Magnet & Grape With Frosted Leaf, Tumbler, Flint .............................. 95.00
Magnet & Grape, Spooner, Pedestal Base ............................................... 22.00
Magnet & Grape, Wine, Clear & Stippled ................................................ 25.00
Magnolia, Cake Stand, Clear ...................................................................... 38.00
Magnolia, Sugar, Covered, Frosted ........................................................... 36.00
  **MAIDEN BLUSH, see Banded Portland**
Maine, Bowl, Berry, 8 1/2 In. ........................................................ *Illus* 30.00
Maine, Bowl, Oval, Large ............................................................................. 16.50
Maine, Cake Stand, 9 In. .............................................................................. 49.50
Maine, Sugar, Covered, Emerald Green ................................................... 23.00
Majestic, Toothpick ...................................................................................... 27.50
Majestic, Tumbler ......................................................................................... 5.00
Majestic, Wine ............................................................................................... 15.00
Man's Head, Spooner .................................................................................... 35.00
Manhattan, Berry Bowl, Gold Rim, 8 In. .................................................. 14.50
Manhattan, Butter, Covered ....................................................................... 55.00
Manhattan, Goblet ........................................................... 10.00 To 15.00

Manhattan, Plate, Handle, 5 1/2 In.Diam. ......................................... 8.00
Manhattan, Plate, 6 In.Diam. ......................................................... 6.00
Manhattan, Salt & Pepper ............................................................ 35.00
Manhattan, Sauce ....................................................................... 8.80
Manhattan, Sugar, Covered, Rose ................................................. 45.00
Manhattan, Toothpick ................................................. 17.50 To 28.50
Manhattan, Tumbler, Gold, 4 In. ................................................... 12.50
Manhattan, Vase, Green, Gold Rim, 6 1/2 In. ................................. 26.00
Maple Leaf Band, Goblet ............................................................. 28.00
Maple Leaf, Goblet ...................................................... 25.00 To 35.00
Maple Leaf, Goblet, Blue .............................................................. 55.00
Maple Leaf, Goblet, Tree Trunk Stem, Frosted ............................... 68.00
Maple Leaf, Plate, Blue, 9 In. ....................................................... 24.00
Maple Leaf, Sugar, Vaseline ........................................................ 30.00
Marquisette, Celery ..................................................................... 42.50
Marquisette, Celery Vase ............................................................. 42.50
Marquisette, Goblet .................................................... 20.00 To 27.50
Marquisette, Spooner .................................................................. 22.00
Marsh Pink, Cake Stand, Footed, Square ...................................... 45.00
Maryland, Bread Plate .................................................................. 16.00
Maryland, Compote, Jelly, 4 X 5 In. ............................... 12.00 To 15.00
Maryland, Creamer ...................................................................... 12.50
Maryland, Goblet ........................................................ 18.00 To 26.00
Maryland, Pitcher, Milk ................................................................ 25.00
Mascotte, Celery, Etched ............................................................. 45.00
Mascotte, Creamer, Etched .......................................... 27.00 To 45.00
Mascotte, Spooner ...................................................................... 35.00
Mascotte, Sugar, Covered ........................................................... 45.00
Mascotte, Wine ........................................................................... 32.50
Massachusetts, Butter, Covered ................................................... 85.00
Massachusetts, Cruet, Miniature .................................................. 37.00
Massachusetts, Dish, Candy ........................................................ 16.00
Massachusetts, Jug, Rum ............................................ 75.00 To 85.00
Massachusetts, Mug, Gold Trim .................................... 14.00 To 18.00
Massachusetts, Plate, 8 1/4 In. .................................................... 20.00
Massachusetts, Vase, Trumpet, Green, 9 3/4 In. ............ 20.00 To 32.00
Master Argus, Champagne ........................................................... 37.00
Master Argus, Goblet .................................................................. 36.00
McKinley, Bread Plate .................................................. 31.50 To 45.00
McKinley, Cup, Covered ............................................................... 45.00
McKinley, Plate, It's God's Way .................................... 20.00 To 30.00
McKinley, Tumbler ....................................................................... 15.00
Medallion Sprig, Pitcher, Water, Green Shaded .............................. 165.00
Medallion Sunburst, Pitcher, Water ............................................... 26.00
Medallion, Pitcher ....................................................................... 25.00
Medallion, Pitcher, Water, Blue .................................................... 35.00
Meloton, Creamer ....................................................................... 65.00
Melrose, Compote ....................................................................... 25.00
Melrose, Plate, 8 In. .................................................................... 12.00
Memphis, Cup, Punch .................................................... 6.00 To 6.50
Memphis, Saucer, Gold Trim, Green .............................................. 10.00
Memphis, Tumbler, Green ............................................ 15.00 To 28.00
Memphis, Tumbler, Green, Gold Trim ............................ 10.00 To 25.00
Memphis, Water Set, Emerald Green, Gold Trim, 7 Piece ................ 250.00
Mephistopheles, Glass, Ale, Frosted ............................................. 45.00
Mephistopheles, Goblet ............................................... 25.00 To 38.00
Mephistopheles, Goblet, Gold Band .............................................. 30.00
Michigan, Creamer, Pink Flowers, Individual .................................. 23.00
Michigan, Creamer, Small ............................................................ 20.00
Michigan, Mug, Lemonade, Handled .............................................. 9.00
Michigan, Sugar & Creamer, Covered, Pink .................................... 95.00
Michigan, Table Set, 4 Piece ........................................................ 185.00
Michigan, Toothpick ..................................................... 20.00 To 25.00

**Michigan,** Toothpick, Yellow Flashing, Pink Enameled Carnation ............................................. 75.00
**Michigan,** Tumbler, Green Stain ................................................................................................. 25.00
**Michigan,** Vase, 8 1/2 In. ........................................................................................ 20.00 To 25.00
**Michigan,** Water Set, Maiden's Blush With Gold, 7 Piece ................................................. 300.00
**Mikado Fan,** Goblet ...................................................................................................................... 10.00
**Milton,** Goblet .................................................................................................... 12.00 To 18.50
**Minerva,** Bread Plate ........................................................................................ 42.00 To 65.00
**Minerva,** Creamer ............................................................................................... 38.00 To 45.00
**Minerva,** Dish, Pickle, Inscribed ............................................................................................... 40.00
**Minerva,** Goblet ................................................................................................. 70.00 To 95.00
**Minerva,** Sauce .................................................................................................... 9.00 To 10.50
**Minerva,** Sauce, Flat, 5 In. ........................................................................................................ 15.00
**Minerva,** Sauce, Footed, 4 In. ...................................................................... 12.50 To 15.00
**Minnesota,** Berry Bowl .............................................................................................................. 30.00
**Minnesota,** Creamer, Individual .............................................................................................. 14.00
**Minnesota,** Mug ............................................................................................................................ 16.00
**Minnesota,** Pitcher, Water ........................................................................................................ 48.00
**Minnesota,** Spooner .................................................................................................................... 22.50
**Minnesota,** Toothpick, Clear, Gold Trim ................................................... 15.00 To 22.00
**Minnesota,** Toothpick, Emerald Green, Gold Trim ........................................................ 110.00
**Minnesota,** Tray, Celery, Flat .................................................................................................. 25.00
**Mirror,** Sugar, Covered, Flint .................................................................................................. 50.00
**Mirror,** Wine, Bulb Stem ............................................................................................................ 35.00
**Missouri,** Creamer ........................................................................................................................ 18.00
**Missouri,** Water Set, Green, 7 Piece ................................................................................... 250.00
**Mitered Bars,** Goblet .................................................................................................................. 15.00
**Mitered Bars,** Wine ...................................................................................................................... 13.00
    **MITERED DIAMOND POINT, see Mitered Bars**
**Mitered Prisms,** Compote, Open, 7 In. ............................................................................... 14.00
**Mitered Prisms,** Compote, Open, 8 In. ............................................................................... 16.00
**Mitered Prisms,** Goblet .............................................................................................................. 22.50
**Monkey Climber,** Goblet, Etched ........................................................... 75.00 To 120.00
**Monkey,** Creamer ...................................................................................................................... 130.00
**Monkey,** Mug ................................................................................................................................. 75.00
**Moon & Star,** Celery .................................................................................................................. 35.00
**Moon & Star,** Compote, Open, Flared Bowl, 9 X 6 1/2 In. .......................................... 38.00
**Moon & Star,** Compote, Open, 7 X 7 1/2 In. .................................................................... 27.00
**Moon & Star,** Compote, Scalloped, 6 1/2 X 9 In.Diam. ............................................... 32.50
**Moon & Star,** Compote, 8 1/4 In.Diam. ............................................................... *Illus* 45.00
**Moon & Star,** Goblet ........................................................................................ 30.00 To 33.00
**Moon & Star,** Spooner ................................................................................................................ 22.00
**Moon & Star,** Tumbler ................................................................................................................ 55.00
**Moon & Star,** Wine ...................................................................................................................... 30.00
    **MOON & STORK, see Ostrich Looking At The Moon**

Pressed Glass, Moon & Star,
Compote, 8 1/4 In.Diam.

Pressed Glass, Maine, Bowl, Berry,
8 1/2 In. (See Page 463)

Morning Glory, Eggcup ........................................................................................ 125.00
Morning Glory, Goblet, Buttermilk, Flint ......................................................... 200.00
Morning Glory, Goblet, Flint ............................................................................. 175.00
Morning Glory, Sauce ........................................................................................ 35.00
Morning Glory, Wine .......................................................................................... 175.00
Nail, Celery ......................................................................................................... 40.00
Nail, Creamer ...................................................................................................... 25.00
Nail, Pitcher, Water, Etched ............................................................................... 55.00
Nail, Sugar, Engraved, Covered ......................................................................... 40.00
Nailhead, Cake Stand, 9 In.Diam. ...................................................................... 26.50
Nailhead, Goblet .................................................................................................. 18.75
Nailhead, Pitcher, Water ..................................................................................... 35.00
Nailhead, Plate, Round, 8 In. .............................................................................. 18.00
Nailhead, Wine .................................................................................................... 17.00
    NEBRASKA, see Bismarc Star
Near Cut, Bowl, Punch, Miniature ...................................................................... 30.00
Needles & Pins, Goblet ....................................................................................... 19.00
Needles & Pins, Sugar, Open, Hamilton ............................................................ 34.00
Nellie Bly, Platter, 6 1/2 X 13 In. ....................................................................... 150.00
Nestor, Compote, Jelly, Footed, Blue ................................................................ 20.00
Nestor, Compote, Jelly, Footed, Purple ............................................................. 25.00
Nestor, Creamer, Enameled, Apple Green ......................................................... 45.00
New England Flute, Champagne, Flint ............................................................... 21.00
New England Flute, Goblet, Flint ..........................................................*Illus*  18.50
New England Pineapple, Compote, 5 X 5 In. ..................................................... 80.00
New England Pineapple, Decanter, Bar Lip, 1 Quart ........................................ 95.00
New England Pineapple, Dish, Sweetmeat, Covered ........................................ 250.00
New England Pineapple, Eggcup ................................................... 35.00 To 39.50
New England Pineapple, Eggcup, Set Of 4 ....................................................... 140.00
New England Pineapple, Goblet, Flint ......................................... 47.50 To 62.50
New England Pineapple, Sauce, Flint ................................................................ 15.00
New England Pineapple, Spooner, Flint ............................................................. 27.00
New England Pineapple, Sugar, Open, Scalloped Rim, Flint ............................ 45.00
New England Pineapple, Tumbler, Water ................................... 95.00 To 125.00
New Hampshire, Berry Bowl, 9 1/2 In. ............................................................... 30.00
New Hampshire, Creamer, Breakfast, Pink Rim ............................................... 15.00
New Hampshire, Cup, Gold Trim ....................................................................... 10.00
New Hampshire, Cup, Punch .............................................................................. 6.50
New Hampshire, Dish, Relish ............................................................................. 12.00
New Hampshire, Mug ......................................................................................... 12.00
New Hampshire, Sauce ...................................................................................... 6.00
New Hampshire, Sugar, Breakfast, Gold Rim ................................................... 10.00
New Hampshire, Toothpick ................................................................................ 19.50

Pressed Glass, New England
Pineapple, Pitcher

Pressed Glass, New England Flute, Goblet, Flint

New Hampshire, Wine ........................................................................................................... 17.00 To 18.00
New Hampshire, Wine, Flared ........................................................................................................... 14.00
New Jersey, Bowl, Footed, Scalloped, 9 1/2 In. ........................................................................ 31.00
New Jersey, Butter, Covered ........................................................................................................... 45.00
New Jersey, Dish, Relish, 7 1/2 In. ............................................................................................... 10.00
New Jersey, Goblet, Gold Loops & Trim ........................................................................ 35.00 To 36.00
New Jersey, Pitcher, Water, Gold Flashed Edge ........................................................................ 45.00
New Jersey, Plate, Cake, Deep Well, 10 1/2 In. ........................................................................ 28.00
New Jersey, Plate, 7 1/2 In. ........................................................................................................... 10.00
New Jersey, Plate, 10 1/2 In. ........................................................................................................... 10.00
New Jersey, Sauce ........................................................................................................................... 8.00
New Jersey, Stand, Doughnut, Scalloped Petticoat, 9 X 5 In. ............................................ 45.00
New York Honeycomb, Wine, Flint ........................................................................... 6.00 To 11.00
Nicotiana, Goblet, Etched ........................................................................................................... 15.00
O'hara Diamond, Banana Stand ................................................................................................... 28.00
O'hara Diamond, Bread Plate, 10 In. ............................................................................................ 15.00
Oak Leaf Band, Goblet ................................................................................................................... 20.00
Oak Wreath, Pitcher ........................................................................................................................... 53.00
Oaken Bucket, Pitcher, Water, Purple ........................................................................................ 65.00
Oaken Bucket, Spooner ................................................................................................................... 25.00
Oaken Bucket, Spooner, Amber ................................................................................................... 42.00
Oaken Bucket, Sugar, Covered ................................................................................................... 32.00
Oaken Bucket, Toothpick, Vaseline, 2 1/2 In. ........................................................................ 35.00
Oasis, Celery ...................................................................................................................................... 45.00
    ONE HUNDRED ONE, see One-O-One
One-O-One, Butter, Covered ........................................................................................................... 50.00
One-O-One, Celery ........................................................................................................................... 40.00
One-O-One, Champagne ................................................................................................................... 12.50
One-O-One, Creamer ........................................................................................................................... 12.00
One-O-One, Creamer, Footed ........................................................................................................ 28.00
One-O-One, Toothpick, Green ........................................................................................................ 40.00
One-O-One, Toothpick, Opaque Green ....................................................................................... 75.00
    ONE-THOUSAND EYE, see Thousand Eye
Open Plaid, Goblet ........................................................................................................................... 20.00
Open Rose, Eggcup, Raised Pattern ............................................................................................ 20.00
Open Rose, Goblet ........................................................................................................................... 16.50
Open Rose, Spooner ........................................................................................................................... 18.50
Open Rose, Tumbler ........................................................................................................................... 30.00
Opposing Pyramids, Goblet ........................................................................................................... 16.00
Opposing Pyramids, Wine ........................................................................................... 12.00 To 14.50
Optic, Toothpick, Paneled, Amethyst ......................................................................................... 21.00
Orange Peel, Goblet ................................................................................................................ *Illus* 10.00
    OREGON, see also Beaded Loop
Oregon, Carafe, Whiskey ................................................................................................................. 38.00
Oregon, Creamer ............................................................................................................................... 25.00

Pressed Glass, Orange Peel, Goblet

**Oregon,** Cruet, Stopper .................................................................................... 42.00
**Oregon,** Dish, Relish, 7 1/2 In. ...................................................................... 10.00
**Oregon,** Goblet ................................................................................................ 38.50
**Oregon,** Pitcher, Water, Footed .................................................................... 55.00
**Oregon,** Syrup .................................................................................................. 27.00
**Oriental Poppy,** Tumbler, Blue, Gold .......................................................... 20.00
**Oriental Poppy,** Tumbler, Green .................................................................. 20.00
**Oriental,** Butter, Covered ................................................................................ 48.00
     **ORION, see Cathedral**
**Ostrich Looking At The Moon,** Goblet ......................................... 55.00 To 70.00
**Oval Barberry,** Sauce .......................................................................................... 6.00
**Oval Panels,** Goblet ........................................................................................ 18.50
**Oval Star,** Creamer .......................................................................................... 16.00
**Oval With Long Bars,** Goblet ........................................................................ 30.00
**Overall Hob,** Sugar .......................................................................................... 12.00
     **OWL, see Bull's-Eye & Diamond Point**
     **OWL & FAN, see Parrot & Fan**
**Owl & Possum,** Goblet .................................................................... 50.00 To 60.00
**Owl & Pussycat,** Cheese Dish ..................................................................... 235.00
**Owl In Horseshoe,** Goblet .............................................................. 40.00 To 75.00
**Paisley,** Toothpick, 2 Handles ...................................................................... 25.00
**Paling,** Creamer ............................................................................................... 17.00
**Palm & Scroll,** Celery, Green ........................................................................ 29.00
**Palm & Scroll,** Compote, Scalloped, Green, 9 X 7 1/2 In. ........................ 40.00
**Palm & Scroll,** Pitcher, Green ...................................................................... 40.00
**Palm & Scroll,** Pitcher, Water, Green .......................................................... 80.00
**Palm Beach,** Butter, Covered, Red, Green, & Gold Design ...................... 225.00
**Palm Leaf Fan,** Compote, Jelly .................................................................... 12.00
**Palm Leaf Fan,** Plate, 7 In. ........................................................................... 10.00
**Palmette Variant,** Bread Plate, Amber ........................................................ 39.50
**Palmette,** Goblet ............................................................................................. 22.50
**Palmette,** Relish Scoop ................................................................................. 14.00
**Palmette,** Wine ............................................................................................... 26.50
**Pampas Flower,** Creamer ............................................................................... 30.00
**Panama,** Banana Boat .................................................................................... 15.00
**Panama,** Cake Stand ...................................................................................... 19.00
**Paneled Cane,** Pitcher, Gold Edge ............................................................... 45.00
**Paneled Cherry,** Berry Bowl ......................................................................... 10.00
     **PANELED DAISY & BUTTON, see also Daisy & Button With Amber**
     **Panels**
**Paneled Daisy & Button,** Sauce, Collared Base, Amber ............................ 32.50
**Paneled Daisy,** Plate, Square, 9 In. ............................................................. 18.00
**Paneled Dewdrop,** Bread Plate .................................................................... 24.00
**Paneled Dewdrop,** Pitcher, 6 1/2 In. ........................................................... 42.00
**Paneled Dewdrop,** Plate, 7 In. ..................................................................... 20.00
**Paneled Dewdrop,** Plate, 9 In. ..................................................................... 24.00
**Paneled Dewdrop,** Platter, Motto ............................................................... 30.00
**Paneled Dewdrop,** Wine .................................................................. 12.00 To 15.50
**Paneled Diamond Point,** Compote ............................................................. 35.00
**Paneled Diamond Point,** Goblet .................................................................. 35.00
**Paneled Diamond Point,** Goblet, Blue ........................................................ 30.00
**Paneled English Hobnail,** Tumbler ............................................................. 32.00
     **PANELED FAN TOP, see Shepherd's Plaid**
**Paneled Flowers,** Goblet ............................................................................... 20.00
**Paneled Forget-Me-Not,** Goblet .................................................................. 32.00
**Paneled Forget-Me-Not,** Pitcher, Milk ....................................................... 30.00
**Paneled Forget-Me-Not,** Pitcher, Water ....................................... 35.00 To 40.00
**Paneled Grape Band,** Goblet, Flint ............................................................. 35.00
**Paneled Grape,** Bowl, 8 In. ........................................................................... 27.50
**Paneled Grape,** Creamer ............................................................................... 19.00
**Paneled Grape,** Goblet, Flint ....................................................................... 35.00
**Paneled Grape,** Sugar .................................................................................... 25.00
**Paneled Grape,** Tumbler, Gold & Purple, 4 In. .......................................... 15.50

Pressed Glass, Paneled Nightshade, Goblet

Pressed Glass, Paneled Wheat

| | |
|---|---|
| **Paneled Heather,** Cake Stand, 10 3/8 In.Diam. | 26.00 |
| **Paneled Heather,** Wine | 12.00 |
| **Paneled Iris,** Goblet | 12.00 To 18.00 |
| **Paneled Jewel,** Goblet | 10.00 To 20.00 |
| **Paneled Jewel,** Goblet, Blue | 35.00 To 50.00 |
| **Paneled Julep,** Goblet | 10.00 |
| **Paneled Nightshade,** Goblet | *Illus* 22.50 |
| **Paneled Ovals,** Goblet, Flint | 35.00 |
| **Paneled Ovals,** Sugar, Covered, Flint | 50.00 To 55.00 |
| **Paneled Potted Flower,** Goblet | 40.00 |
| **Paneled Sagebrush,** Goblet | 45.00 |
| **Paneled Sprig,** Sugar Shaker | 29.00 |
| **PANELED STIPPLED BOWL, see Stippled Band** | |
| **Paneled Stippled Scroll,** Creamer | 8.50 To 17.00 |
| **Paneled Strawberry,** Berry Set, Key Band, 6 Piece | 160.00 |
| **Paneled Strawberry,** Butter, Covered, Key Band | 55.00 |
| **Paneled Sunflower,** Creamer | 15.00 |
| **Paneled Sunflower,** Goblet | 13.00 |
| **Paneled Sunflower,** Water Pitcher | 50.00 |
| **Paneled Thistle,** Bowl, Flared Rim, 9 In.Diam. | 28.00 |
| **Paneled Thistle,** Bowl, 6 In.Diam. | 18.00 |
| **Paneled Thistle,** Bowl, 8 In.Diam. | 20.00 |
| **Paneled Thistle,** Compote, Open, 8 In. | 28.00 |
| **Paneled Thistle,** Cruet | 30.00 |
| **Paneled Thistle,** Cup, Punch, Flared Handle | 23.00 |
| **Paneled Thistle,** Goblet, Bee Mark | 35.00 |
| **Paneled Thistle,** Pitcher, 7 1/4 In. | 28.50 |
| **Paneled Thistle,** Plate, 8 In.Diam. | 20.00 |
| **Paneled Thistle,** Plate, 9 In.Diam. | 32.00 |
| **Paneled Thistle,** Plate, 10 In.Diam. | 28.00 |
| **Paneled Thistle,** Rose Bowl, Footed | 28.00 |
| **Paneled Thistle,** Spooner | 18.00 |
| **Paneled Thistle,** Wine, With Bee | 18.00 |
| **Paneled Thumbprint,** Spooner, Beaded, Scalloped Edge | 25.00 |
| **Paneled Waffle,** Sugar, Covered, Footed, Flint, C.1860, 9 In., Pair | 75.00 |
| **Paneled Wheat,** Creamer | 27.50 |
| **Paneled Wheat,** Spooner | 22.00 |
| **Paneled Wild Daisy,** Goblet | 18.00 |
| **Paneled Zipper,** Compote, Open, 8 1/2 In. | 45.00 |
| **Paneled Zipper,** Cup, Set Of 3 | 12.00 |
| **Paris,** Celery | 20.00 |
| **Paris,** Plate, 8 In. | 12.00 |
| **Parrot & Fan,** Goblet | *Illus* 40.00 |
| **Parrot & Fan,** Wine | 30.00 |

Pressed Glass, Parrot & Fan, Goblet (See Page 469)

Pressed Glass, Pleat & Panel, Bowl

| | |
|---|---|
| Parthenon, Creamer | 30.00 |
| Pavonia, Pitcher | 35.00 |
| Pavonia, Wine, Etched | 28.00 To 35.00 |
| Peacock Feather, Berry Set | 46.00 |
| Peacock Feather, Butter, Covered | 44.50 |
| Peacock Feather, Compote, Jelly | 35.00 |
| Peacock Feather, Creamer, 4 In. | 27.50 To 35.00 |
| Peacock Feather, Cruet | 18.50 To 24.00 |
| Peacock Feather, Pitcher, Water | 50.00 |
| Peacock Feather, Salt & Pepper, Matching Glass Holder | 65.00 |
| Peacock Feather, Spooner | 35.00 |
| Peacock Feather, Sugar, Covered | 45.00 |
|     PEACOCK'S EYE, see Peacock Feather | |
| Peerless, Wine | 15.00 |
|     PENNSYLVANIA, see also Balder, Pennsylvania Hand | |
| Pennsylvania Hand, Celery | 45.00 |
| Pennsylvania, Butter | 55.00 |
| Pennsylvania, Spooner | 35.00 |
| Pennsylvania, Toothpick, Gold Trim | 40.00 |
| Pennsylvania, Wine | 18.00 |
| Pequot, Celery, Footed | 45.00 |
| Pequot, Goblet | 32.00 |
| Persian Spear, Goblet | 125.00 |
| Petal & Loop, Compote, Open, Flint | 10.00 |
| Pheasant, Compote, Covered, Footed, Frosted, 6 X 8 1/2 In. | 65.00 |
| Philadelphia Centennial, Goblet | 35.00 To 45.00 |
| Picket, Spooner | 20.00 |
| Pigs In Corn, Goblet | 175.00 To 200.00 |
|     PILLAR & BULL'S-EYE, see Thistle | |
| Pillar, Pitcher, Milk, 8 Ribs, Tooled Rim, Applied Handle | 290.00 |
| Pillow Encircled, Pitcher, Water | 35.00 |
|     PINAFORE, see Actress | |
| Pineapple & Fan, Bottle, Water | 35.00 |
| Pineapple & Fan, Cruet, Original Stopper | 28.00 |
| Pineapple & Fan, Cup, Punch | 6.00 |
| Pineapple & Fan, Pitcher, Bulbous | 37.00 |
| Pineapple & Fan, Saltshaker, Brass Plated Lid, 3 1/4 In. | 22.50 |
| Pineapple & Fan, Sugar, Covered | 35.00 |
| Pineapple & Fan, Sugar, Creamer, & Spooner | 65.00 |
| Pineapple & Fan, Syrup | 25.00 |
| Pineapple & Fan, Tumbler | 10.00 |
| Pineapple & Fan, Wine, Clear | 19.00 |
| Pinwheel, Compote, Bright Blue, Open, 7 In. | 85.00 |
| Pinwheel, Sugar, Covered, W.S.Co., Embossed On Finial | 20.00 |
| Pittsburgh Daisy, Wine | 23.00 |
| Pittsburgh Tree Of Life, Tumbler | 20.00 |

**PLAIN SMOCKING, see Smocking**

| | |
|---|---|
| **Pleat & Panel,** Bread Plate | 24.00 |
| **Pleat & Panel,** Creamer | 26.00 To 27.00 |
| **Pleat & Panel,** Goblet | 15.00 To 20.00 |
| **Pleat & Panel,** Plate, Square, 7 In. | 20.00 |
| **Pleat & Panel,** Plate, 7 In. | 17.50 |
| **Pleat & Panel,** Spooner | 22.50 |
| **Plume,** Berry Bowl, Square, Master | 25.00 |
| **Plume,** Berry Bowl, 5 In.Square | 8.00 |
| **Plume,** Cake Stand, 9 1/4 In. | 52.50 |
| **Plume,** Celery | 18.00 To 22.00 |
| **Plume,** Compote, Open, 6 1/2 X 7 1/2 In. | 19.00 To 22.50 |
| **Plume,** Compote, Open, 8 1/4 In. | 30.00 |
| **Plume,** Creamer | 27.50 To 29.50 |
| **Plume,** Dish, Relish | 12.00 |
| **Plume,** Goblet | 25.00 To 40.00 |
| **Plume,** Wine | 9.00 |
| **Plutec,** Bowl, Pink, 8 1/4 In. | 24.00 |
| **Plutec,** Celery | 17.00 |
| **Plutec,** Wine | 6.00 |
| **Pogo Stick,** Cruet, Fitted Stopper | 18.00 |
| **Pointed Hobnail,** Creamer, Child's, Amber | 15.00 |
| **Pointed Jewel,** Creamer | 25.00 |
| **Pointed Jewel,** Spooner | 20.00 |
| **Pointed Jewel,** Sugar & Creamer | 35.00 |
| **Pointed Jewel,** Tumbler | 15.00 |

**POINTED PANELED DAISY & BUTTON, see Queen**

**POINTED THUMBPRINT, see Almond Thumbprint**

| | |
|---|---|
| **Polar Bear,** Bowl, Waste | 85.00 |
| **Polar Bear,** Goblet | 92.00 |
| **Popcorn,** Goblet | 22.00 |
| **Popcorn,** Goblet, Line Ears | 35.00 |
| **Popcorn,** Spooner, Corn Ears | 39.00 |
| **Portland Log,** Salt | 16.00 |

**PORTLAND WITH DIAMOND POINT BAND, see Galloway; Virginia**

| | |
|---|---|
| **Portland,** Butter | 45.00 |
| **Portland,** Butter, Gold Trim | 45.00 |
| **Portland,** Carafe | 30.00 |
| **Portland,** Creamer | 20.00 |
| **Portland,** Toothpick | 14.00 To 22.00 |
| **Portland,** Tumbler | 14.00 |
| **Post,** Bowl, Covered, Footed, 6 3/4 In. | 30.00 |
| **Post,** Pitcher, Water, Etched | 30.00 |

**POTTED PLANT, see Flower Pot**

| | |
|---|---|
| **Powder & Shot,** Goblet | 60.00 |
| **Powder & Shot,** Goblet, Flint | 48.50 To 55.00 |
| **Powder & Shot,** Spooner | 30.00 |
| **Powder & Shot,** Sugar, Open | 35.00 |

**PRAYER RUG, see Horseshoe**

| | |
|---|---|
| **Pressed Diamond,** Bowl, Amber, 8 In.Diam. | 21.00 |
| **Pressed Diamond,** Spooner, Blue | 50.00 |
| **Pressed Leaf With Chain,** Goblet | 15.00 |
| **Pressed Leaf,** Compote, Covered, High Standard, Acorn Finial | 60.00 |
| **Pressed Leaf,** Creamer | 50.00 |
| **Pressed Leaf,** Eggcup, Flint | 15.00 |
| **Pressed Leaf,** Goblet | 15.00 To 32.00 |
| **Pressed Leaf,** Goblet, Buttermilk | 16.00 |
| **Pressed Leaf,** Honey, Flint | 6.00 |
| **Pressed Leaf,** Pitcher, Water | 90.00 |
| **Pressed Leaf,** Pitcher, Water, Applied Handle | 80.00 |
| **Pressed Leaf,** Wine | 40.00 |
| **Pretty Maid,** Toothpick, Figural | 45.00 |
| **Primrose,** Pitcher, Milk, Amber | 39.50 |

Primrose, Plate, Amber, 6 In. ....................................................................................... 14.00
Primrose, Plate, Amber, 7 In. ....................................................................................... 30.00
Primrose, Spooner ....................................................................................................... 18.00
Primrose, Wine ............................................................................................................. 28.00
Prince Albert, Goblet ................................................................................................... 22.50
     PRINCESS FEATHER, see also Lacy Medallion
Princess Feather, Celery .................................................................. 30.00 To 45.00
Princess Feather, Eggcup ............................................................................................ 16.00
Princess Feather, Goblet ............................................................................................. 27.50
Princess Feather, Spooner ............................................................. 20.00 To 22.00
Printed Hobnail, Mug, Covered, Blue ......................................................................... 28.00
Priscilla Tumbler, Emerald Green ............................................................................... 25.00
Priscilla, Bowl, 10 In.Diam. ........................................................................................ 14.00
Priscilla, Compote, Jelly, Covered ............................................................................. 55.00
Priscilla, Compote, Open, 9 In.Diam. ........................................................................ 38.00
Priscilla, Jelly, Footed ................................................................................................. 32.00
Priscilla, Rose Bowl, Ovoid, 3 X 1 3/4 In.Diam. ...................................................... 45.00
Priscilla, Wine ............................................................................................................. 26.00
Prism & Block Band, Tray, Water ............................................................................... 38.00
Prism & Broken Column, Compote, Open, 7 X 7 In. ................................................ 13.00
Prism & Bull's-Eye, Goblet ......................................................................................... 10.00
Prism & Crescent, Goblet ........................................................................................... 30.00
Prism & Daisy Bar, Wine, Blue ................................................................................... 32.00
Prism & Flattened Sawtooth, Spooner, Flint ............................................................. 28.00
Prism & Flute, Goblet .................................................................................................. 12.50
Prism Arc, Goblet ........................................................................................................ 18.00
Prism Arc, Wine, Amber .............................................................................................. 18.50
Prism With Diamond Points, Spooner ....................................................................... 15.00
Prism With Double Block Band, Wine ........................................................................ 15.00
Prism, Compote, Flint, 8 In. ........................................................................................ 27.50
Prism, Eggcup, Flint .................................................................................................... 30.00
Prism, Goblet ............................................................................................................... 35.00
Prism, Goblet, Flint ..................................................................................................... 27.50
Prism, Spooner, Flint ................................................................................................... 22.00
Prize, Spooner, 5 1/2 In. ............................................................................................. 18.00
Psyche & Cupid, Bread Plate ..................................................................................... 25.00
Psyche & Cupid, Celery .................................................................. 40.00 To 46.00
Psyche & Cupid, Creamer ........................................................................................... 35.00
Psyche & Cupid, Goblet .................................................................. 35.00 To 40.00
Psyche & Cupid, Spooner ........................................................................................... 30.00
Quartered Block, Toothpick ........................................................................................ 22.50
     QUEEN ANNE, see Viking
Queen, Creamer ........................................................................................................... 37.50
Queen, Pitcher, Water, Amber ..................................................................................... 95.00
Queen's Necklace, Wine .............................................................................................. 25.00
Quilted Phlox, Sugar Shaker, Green ........................................................................... 90.00
Rabbit In Tree, Toothpick ............................................................................................ 21.00
Rabbit Tracks, Goblet .................................................................................................. 22.50
Raindrop, Compote, Open, Amber, 8 X 4 In. ................................ 22.00 To 25.00
Rayed Flower, Wine ..................................................................................................... 18.00
Red Block, Butter, Covered ........................................................................................ 78.00
Red Block, Goblet ........................................................................................................ 20.00
Red Block, Sugar, Covered ......................................................................................... 57.00
Red Block, Sugar, Open .............................................................................................. 32.50
Red Block, Tumbler ...................................................................................................... 30.00
Red Block, Wine ............................................................................... 31.50 To 35.00
     REGAL, see Paneled Forget-Me-Not
Reticulated Cord, Pitcher, Water ................................................................................ 45.00
Retort, Plate, Turned-Up Edge, 6 7/8 In.Square ....................................................... 30.00
Reverse Torpedo, Banana Boat ................................................................................... 95.00
Reverse Torpedo, Goblet ............................................................................................ 75.00
Reverse Torpedo, Sugar, Covered, Etched ................................................................ 50.00
Reverse 44, Creamer, Silver Design ........................................................................... 15.00

Reverse 44, Pitcher, Water ........................................................................................ 35.00
Reverse 44, Sugar & Creamer, Covered ........................................................... 60.00
Reverse 44, Water Set, Pink & Gold, Marked, 7 Piece ............................... 225.00
Rexford, Cruet ................................................................................ 14.50 To 15.00
Rib & Bead, Creamer ............................................................................................ 12.00
Ribbed Acorn, Honey, Flint ................................................................................ 10.00
Ribbed Bellflower, Goblet ................................................................................... 70.00
Ribbed Forget-Me-Not, Creamer ....................................................................... 20.00
Ribbed Grape, Creamer, Applied Handle, Flint ................................................ 95.00
Ribbed Grape, Goblet, Buttermilk ..................................................................... 35.00
Ribbed Grape, Goblet, Flint ......................................................... 24.00 To 45.00
Ribbed Grape, Sauce, Flint .................................................................................. 12.50
Ribbed Ivy, Butter, Covered, Flint ............................................... 80.00 To 95.00
Ribbed Ivy, Compote, Cover, Footed, 8 X 5 In. .............................................. 45.00
Ribbed Ivy, Compote, Rope Rim, Flint, 7 X 6 In. ..................... 25.00 To 35.00
Ribbed Ivy, Creamer, Footed, Applied Handle, Flint .................................... 125.00
Ribbed Ivy, Eggcup, Flint .............................................................. 18.00 To 28.50
Ribbed Ivy, Goblet, Flint ............................................................... 30.00 To 65.00
Ribbed Ivy, Salt, Footed, Covered ................................................................... 135.00
Ribbed Ivy, Salt, Master, Covered, Footed, Flint .......................................... 150.00
Ribbed Ivy, Spooner, Flint .................................................................................. 15.00
Ribbed Ivy, Tumbler, Whiskey, Flint ................................................................ 40.00
Ribbed Ivy, Wine, Flint ................................................................. 95.00 To 125.00
Ribbed Lattice, Saltshaker, White, Opalescent .............................................. 22.00
Ribbed Lattice, Sugar Shaker, White, Opalescent ......................................... 55.00
    RIBBED LEAF, see Bellflower
Ribbed Palm, Celery, Scalloped, Flint, 8 3/4 In. ..................... 50.00 To 65.00
Ribbed Palm, Champagne ................................................................................... 95.00
Ribbed Palm, Eggcup, Flint ......................................................... 24.00 To 28.00
Ribbed Palm, Goblet, Flint ........................................................... 19.00 To 38.50
Ribbed Palm, Plate, 6 In. .................................................................................... 48.50
Ribbed Palm, Wine .......................................................................... 40.00 To 65.00
    RIBBED PINEAPPLE, see Prism & Flattened Sawtooth
Ribbon Candy, Compote, Covered, High Standard .......................................... 32.50
Ribbon Candy, Compote, Open, 8 1/4 In.Diam. .............................................. 22.50
Ribbon Candy, Cup ............................................................................................... 22.50
Ribbon Candy, Spooner .................................................................. 16.00 To 18.00
Ribbon, Celery ....................................................................................................... 25.00
Ribbon, Compote, Open, 8 1/4 In. .................................................................... 30.00
Ribbon, Platter, Motto ......................................................................................... 35.00
Ribbon, Sauce, Flint ............................................................................................. 10.00
Ribbon, Spooner, Flint ......................................................................................... 22.00
Ribbon, Sugar, Covered, Flint ............................................................................ 40.00
Rising Sun, Compote, Jelly ................................................................................ 12.00
Rising Sun, Goblet, Red Sun .............................................................................. 25.50
Rising Sun, Toothpick, Handled, Rose Stained Eyes ..................................... 30.00
Rising Sun, Tumbler, Gold Trim ........................................................................ 72.00
Rising Sun, Wine, Clear ....................................................................................... 12.00
    ROCHELLE, see Princess Feather
Rock Of Ages, Bread Plate, Dated ............................................... 55.00 To 60.00
Roman Key, Bowl, Flint, 2 X 9 1/4 In.Diam. .................................................. 40.00
Roman Key, Butter, Covered, Stippled Bottom, Flange ................................ 65.00
Roman Key, Champagne ...................................................................................... 28.00
Roman Key, Champagne, Frosted, Pair ............................................................ 65.00
Roman Key, Compote, Dated, 1858, 7 X 8 1/2 In. ....................................... 45.00
Roman Key, Creamer, Footed, Applied Handle .............................................. 30.00
Roman Key, Goblet, Flint .............................................................. 25.00 To 45.00
Roman Key, Spooner, Frosted ........................................................................... 22.00
Roman Key, Sugar, Open, Hexagonal Stem, Frosted, Flint .......................... 64.00
Roman Key, Tumbler, Bar, Frosted, Pair ......................................................... 95.00
Roman Rosette, Bread Plate, Oval .................................................................... 28.00
Roman Rosette, Cake Stand ............................................................................... 65.00
Roman Rosette, Creamer .................................................................... *Illus* 23.50

Pressed Glass, Roman Rosette, Creamer
*(See Page 473)*

Pressed Glass, Rose In Snow, Goblet

Pressed Glass, Rose Sprig, Goblet

| | | |
|---|---|---:|
| **Roman Rosette,** Goblet | | 25.00 |
| **Roman Rosette,** Spooner | | 23.00 |
| **Romeo,** Goblet | | 24.00 |
| **Roosevelt Teddy Bears,** Bread Tray | | 125.00 |
| **Rope & Thumbprint,** Spooner, Amber | | 30.00 |
| **Rope & Thumbprint,** Syrup, Amber | | 60.00 |
|     **ROPE BANDS, see Clear Panels With Cord Band** | | |
| **Rose In Snow,** Bowl, Footed, 4 Sauces, 8 1/4 In. | | 70.00 |
| **Rose In Snow,** Cake Stand, 9 1/4 In.Diam. | | 85.00 |
| **Rose In Snow,** Compote, Covered, 8 In. | | 55.00 |
| **Rose In Snow,** Compote, Open, Blue, 5 X 6 In.Diam. | | 45.00 |
| **Rose In Snow,** Compote, Open, 7 In.Diam. | | 45.00 |
| **Rose In Snow,** Creamer | | 30.00 |
| **Rose In Snow,** Creamer, Blue | | 55.00 |
| **Rose In Snow,** Creamer, Square | | 42.50 |
| **Rose In Snow,** Goblet | *Illus* | 32.00 |
| **Rose In Snow,** Goblet, Blue | | 8.00 |
| **Rose In Snow,** Goblet, Vaseline | | 10.00 |
| **Rose In Snow,** Pitcher, Water | | 60.00 |
| **Rose In Snow,** Plate, Amber, Handled, 10 In. | | 35.00 |
| **Rose In Snow,** Plate, 5 In. | | 36.00 |
| **Rose In Snow,** Plate, 7 In. | 15.00 To | 20.00 |
| **Rose In Snow,** Plate, 8 In. | | 22.00 |
| **Rose In Snow,** Sauce, 4 In. | | 8.00 |
| **Rose In Snow,** Spooner, Scalloped, Clear, Square, 4 1/2 In. | | 28.00 |
| **Rose Leaves,** Goblet | | 23.00 |
| **Rose Point Band,** Compote, 4 1/4 In. | | 14.00 |
| **Rose Point Band,** Compote, 6 1/2 In. | | 35.00 |
| **Rose Point Band,** Wine, Footed | | 12.00 |
| **Rose Sprig,** Cake Stand, Square | | 25.00 |
| **Rose Sprig,** Goblet | *Illus* | 35.00 |

| | |
|---|---|
| Rose Sprig, Pitcher, Water | 45.00 |
| Rose Sprig, Plate, Blue, Square, 6 1/2 In. | 14.00 |
| Rose Sprig, Plate, Square, 6 1/2 In. | 20.00 |
| Rose Sprig, Sauce, Amber | 12.00 |
| Rose Sprig, Sauce, Footed | 10.00 |
| Rose Windows, Pitcher | 49.00 |
| ROSETTE MEDALLION, see Feather Duster | |
| Rosette With Palms, Bowl, Waste, 4 1/2 In. | 14.00 |
| Rosette With Palms, Plate, 9 In. | 14.00 |
| Rosette, Cake Stand, 8 1/2 In. | 18.00 |
| Rosette, Compote, Jelly | 10.00 |
| Rosette, Creamer | 13.00 |
| Rosette, Goblet | 26.00 |
| Rosette, Pitcher, Water, Quart | 22.00 |
| Rosette, Spooner | 13.00 |
| Royal Crystal, Butter | 28.00 |
| Royal Crystal, Syrup | 39.00 |
| Royal Ivy, Bowl, Fruit, Frosted, Ruby Glass | 125.00 |
| Royal Ivy, Creamer, Frosted | 75.00 |
| Royal Ivy, Creamer, Frosted & Clear | 50.00 |
| Royal Ivy, Jar, Dresser, Frosted & Clear, Covered | 85.00 |
| Royal Ivy, Pitcher, Frosted & Clear, 4 1/2 In. | 60.00 |
| Royal Ivy, Pitcher, Water, Clear To Pink | 165.00 |
| Royal Ivy, Pitcher, Water, Rainbow Craquelle | 350.00 |
| Royal Ivy, Rose Bowl, Clear To Pink, Frosted | 125.00 |
| Royal Ivy, Salt & Pepper, Clear To Cranberry | 85.00 To 100.00 |
| Royal Ivy, Sauce, Frosted | 45.00 |
| Royal Ivy, Spooner, Cranberry & Frosted | 68.00 To 80.00 |
| Royal Ivy, Spooner, Frosted, Northwood | 125.00 |
| Royal Ivy, Sugar Shaker, Frosted, Covered | 50.00 |
| Royal Ivy, Sugar, Covered, Pink Cased Spatter | 175.00 |
| Royal Ivy, Toothpick, Frosted | 345.00 |
| Royal Ivy, Toothpick, Red To Clear | 50.00 |
| Royal Ivy, Tumbler, Frosted To Clear | 27.00 |
| Royal Lady, Bread Plate, Crying Baby Center | 35.00 |
| Royal Oak, Butter, Covered, Frosted | 175.00 |
| Royal Oak, Salt & Pepper | 125.00 |
| Royal Oak, Sugar Shaker, Frosted, Original Top | 195.00 |
| Royal Oak, Sugar, Covered, Clear To Pink | 155.00 |
| Royal Oak, Sugar, Covered, Clear To Pink, Frosted | 98.00 |
| Royal Oak, Sugar, Silver Lid | 72.00 |
| Royal Oak, Toothpick, Clear To Pink, Frosted | 150.00 |
| Royal Oak, Tumbler, Frosted | 95.00 |
| RUBY ROSETTE, see Pillow Encircled | |
| RUBY THUMBPRINT, see King's Crown | |
| S Repeat, Carafe, Amethyst, Gold Trim | 60.00 |
| S Repeat, Condiment Set, Apple Green, 5 Piece | 145.00 |
| S Repeat, Cruet, Green, Stopper | 70.00 |
| S Repeat, Toothpick, Dark Blue | 10.95 |
| S Repeat, Toothpick, Rayed Pattern Bottom, Flint | 29.50 |
| S Repeat, Tray, Condiment, Green | 30.00 |
| SANDWICH LOOP, see Hairpin | |
| Sandwich Star, Spooner | 30.00 |
| Sandwich Waffle & Thumbprint, Decanter | 65.00 |
| SAWTOOTH BAND, see Amazon | |
| Sawtooth Circle, Salt, Footed, Flint | 22.00 |
| Sawtooth, Cake Stand, Pedestal | 50.00 |
| Sawtooth, Celery | 17.00 |
| Sawtooth, Champagne, Flint | 30.00 |
| Sawtooth, Champagne, Knob Stem, Flint | 50.00 |
| Sawtooth, Compote, Flint, 10 X 9 In.Diam., Pair | 95.00 |
| Sawtooth, Compote, Flint, 7 3/4 X 6 1/4, In. | 65.00 |
| Sawtooth, Creamer, Straight Top | 14.00 |

| | |
|---|---:|
| **Sawtooth,** Dish, Butter, Covered, Flint | 85.00 |
| **Sawtooth,** Dish, Covered, Lion Handle & Finial, 8 1/2 In.Diam. | 40.00 |
| **Sawtooth,** Goblet | 36.00 |
| **Sawtooth,** Pitcher, Applied Handle | 90.00 |
| **Sawtooth,** Pitcher, Water | 25.00 |
| **Sawtooth,** Salt, Covered, Acorn Finial | 95.00 |
| **Sawtooth,** Salt, Covered, Flint | 48.00 To 55.00 |
| **Sawtooth,** Spill | 40.00 |
| **Sawtooth,** Spooner, Gold Rim & Base, Sandwich | 125.00 |
| **Sawtooth,** Tumbler, Flint | 25.00 |
| **Sawtooth,** Wine | 20.00 |
| **Sawtooth,** Wine, Flint | 26.00 |
| **Sawtooth,** Wine, Knob Stem | 35.00 |
| **Sawtoothed Honeycomb,** Goblet | 16.00 |
| **Saxon,** Wine | 15.00 |
| **Scalloped Swirl,** Toothpick, Green | 25.00 |
| **Scalloped Tape,** Bread Plate, Motto | 20.00 |
| **Scalloped Tape,** Creamer | 15.00 |
| **Scalloped Tape,** Eggcup | 14.00 To 16.00 |
| **Scalloped Tape,** Platter, Motto | 25.00 |
| **Scarab,** Goblet, Flint | 80.00 To 85.00 |
| **Scroll With Cane Band,** Plate, Amber Flash, 7 In. | 34.00 |
| **Scroll With Flowers,** Cake Plate, Handled, 10 In. | 35.00 |
| **Scroll With Flowers,** Celery | 17.50 To 28.50 |
| **Scroll With Flowers,** Compote, Opaque, Nile Green, 8 In. | 85.00 |
| **Scroll With Flowers,** Goblet | 24.00 |
| **Scroll With Flowers,** Pitcher, Water | 35.00 |
| **Scroll With Flowers,** Plate, 10 In. | 22.00 |
| **Scroll With Flowers,** Wine, Amber | 40.00 |
| **Scroll,** Eggcup | 12.00 To 18.00 |
| **Scroll,** Goblet | 12.50 To 14.00 |
| **Scroll,** Spooner | 14.00 To 18.00 |
| **Scroll,** Toothpick, Cane Band, Red | 40.00 |
| **Scroll,** Tumbler, Blue Opaque | 40.00 |
| **Seed Pod,** Spooner, Blue | 40.00 |
| **Seneca Loop,** Celery, Flint | 53.00 |
| **Seneca Loop,** Celery, Footed | 16.00 |
| **Seneca Loop,** Goblet | 15.00 |
| **Seneca Loop,** Goblet, Flint, Set Of 6 | 130.00 |
| **Sequoia,** Tray, Handled, Cut Corners, 8 X 12 In. | 15.00 |
| **Sexton Flute,** Goblet | 14.00 |
| **Sheaf & Block,** Celery | 30.00 |
|    **SHEAF & DIAMOND, see Fickle Block** | |
| **Sheaf Of Wheat,** Bread Plate | 60.00 |
| **Shell & Jewel,** Butter, Covered | 35.00 |
| **Shell & Jewel,** Cake Stand, 9 1/2 In. | 34.00 |
| **Shell & Jewel,** Creamer | 22.00 |
| **Shell & Jewel,** Pitcher | 35.00 To 42.00 |
| **Shell & Jewel,** Pitcher, Amber | 75.00 |
| **Shell & Jewel,** Pitcher, Water | 22.50 To 35.00 |
| **Shell & Jewel,** Spooner | 18.00 |
| **Shell & Jewel,** Sugar | 25.00 |
| **Shell & Jewel,** Tumbler | 14.50 To 25.00 |
| **Shell & Jewel,** Tumbler, Water | 14.50 |
| **Shell & Jewel,** Water Set, Clear, 5 Tumblers | 42.00 |
| **Shell & Jewel,** Water Set, 9 Piece | 87.00 |
| **Shell & Tassel,** Bowl, Oval, 10 In. | 30.00 |
| **Shell & Tassel,** Bowl, 12 X 6 1/2 In. | 45.00 |
| **Shell & Tassel,** Celery, Footed | 65.00 |
| **Shell & Tassel,** Celery, Round | 75.00 |
| **Shell & Tassel,** Compote, Covered, 7 In. | 45.00 |
| **Shell & Tassel,** Creamer, Square | 55.00 |
| **Shell & Tassel,** Platter, Oval, 9 X 13 In. | 65.00 |

Shell & Tassel, Platter, 8 X 12 In. ............................................................................ 52.00
Shell & Tassel, Saltshaker, Clear .............................................................................. 50.00
Shell & Tassel, Sauce, Flat, 4 1/2 In.Diam. ............................................................. 7.50
Shell & Tassel, Sauce, Footed, 4 1/2 In.Square ...................................................... 15.00
Shell & Tassel, Spooner ........................................................................ 18.00 To 37.00
Shell & Tassel, Sugar, Covered .................................................................................. 75.00
Shell, Sugar, Covered, Green ...................................................................................... 75.00
Shepherd's Plaid, Plate, 7 1/2 In. .............................................................................. 10.00
Sheraton, Celery ........................................................................................................... 25.00
Sheraton, Spooner ....................................................................................................... 12.50
Shield & Anchor, Goblet ............................................................................................. 45.00
Shimmering Star, Tumbler .......................................................................................... 16.00
Short Loops, Spooner ................................................................................................... 12.00
Shoshone, Banana Boat, Scalloped Sides ................................................................. 30.00
Shoshone, Cake Stand, Green .................................................................................... 45.00
Shoshone, Compote, Emerald Green, 5 3/8 In. ....................................................... 35.00
Shoshone, Compote, Open, 6 In. ............................................................................... 16.00
Shoshone, Cruet, Green, Original Stopper ................................................................ 75.00
Shoshone, Cruet, Original Stopper ............................................................................ 55.00
Shoshone, Nappy, Handled, Cobalt Blue .............................................. 15.00 To 22.00
Shoshone, Sugar, Covered, Green .............................................................................. 30.00
Shoshone, Toothpick .................................................................................................... 15.00
Shrine, Pitcher, Water .................................................................................................. 48.50
Shrine, Tumbler ............................................................................................................. 20.00
Shuttle, Celery ............................................................................................................... 45.00
Shuttle, Wine ................................................................................................................. 13.50
Singing Birds, Butter, Covered ................................................................................. 150.00
Six Panel Finecut, Celery ............................................................................................ 12.00
Six Panel Finecut, Goblet, Amber Stripe .................................................................. 45.00
Six Panel Finecut, Spooner, Clear With Amber ....................................................... 55.00
Slewed Horseshoe, Goblet .......................................................................................... 26.00
Smocking, Bowl, Footed, 7 In. .................................................................................... 50.00
Smocking, Creamer ...................................................................................................... 98.00
Smocking, Goblet, Flint ............................................................................................... 75.00
Smocking, Spooner, Flint ............................................................................................ 18.00
Snail, Celery .................................................................................................................. 28.00
Snail, Compote, Covered, 8 X 13 In. .......................................................................... 85.00
Snail, Creamer .............................................................................................................. 65.00
Snail, Goblet ........................................................................................... 40.00 To 85.00
Snail, Goblet, Etched ................................................................................................... 55.00
Snail, Spooner ......................................................................................... 24.00 To 28.00
Snakeskin & Dot, Goblet .............................................................................................. 12.00
Snakeskin & Dot, Plate, Blue, 6 In. ............................................................................ 24.00
Snakeskin & Dot, Plate, Blue, 7 In. ............................................................................ 14.00
    SPANISH AMERICAN, see Admiral Dewey
    SPANISH COIN, see Columbian Coin
Spearpoint Band, Compote, Jelly .............................................................................. 14.00
Spearpoint, Compote, Jelly, Ruby Band, 4 X 5 1/8 In.Diam. ................................... 65.00
Spearpoint, Goblet ....................................................................................................... 22.50
Spiked Argus, Tumbler, Bar ........................................................................................ 65.00
Spiked Argus, Wine ...................................................................................................... 65.00
Spiral & Maltese Cross, Creamer, Light Amber ...................................................... 22.00
Spiraled Ivy, Creamer .................................................................................................. 30.00
Spiraled Ivy, Spooner ................................................................................................... 12.00
Spirea Band, Cordial, Amber ...................................................................................... 30.00
Spirea Band, Goblet, Amber ....................................................................................... 20.00
Spirea Band, Pitcher, Amber ...................................................................................... 40.00
Spirea Band, Wine ........................................................................................................ 16.00
Spirea Band, Wine, Amber .......................................................................................... 23.00
Sprig, Cake Stand, 8 1/2 In. ........................................................................................ 30.00
Sprig, Celery ........................................................................................... 35.00 To 45.00
Sprig, Compote, Covered, Footed, 6 In. ..................................................................... 30.00
Sprig, Compote, Open, 7 In. ........................................................................................ 20.00

Pressed Glass, Squirrel

Pressed Glass, Strawberry

| | |
|---|---|
| **Sprig,** Creamer | 25.00 |
| **Sprig,** Goblet | 30.00 To 32.00 |
| **Sprig,** Sugar, Covered | 30.00 |
| **Sprig,** Sugar, Open | 10.00 |
| **Squirrel In Bower,** Goblet | 285.00 |
| **Squirrel In Bower,** Pitcher, Water | 195.00 |
| **Squirrel,** Butter, Covered, Squirrel Finial | 150.00 |
| **Squirrel,** Pitcher, Water | 125.00 |
| **Squirrel,** Pitcher, Water, Squirrels On Limbs & 2 On Ground | 105.00 |
| **Squirrel,** Sauce | 15.00 |
| **Star & Feather,** Plate, Blue, 7 In.Diam. | 28.00 |
| **Star & Oval,** Butter, Covered, Frosted & Clear | 35.00 |
| **Star & Oval,** Celery, Footed | 20.00 |
| **Star & Oval,** Tumbler | 10.00 |
| **Star & Pillar,** Creamer | 18.50 |
| **Star & Pillar,** Pitcher, Water, 1876 Pattern | 45.00 |
| **STAR & PUNTY, see Moon & Star** | |
| **Star Band,** Compote, Jelly | 10.00 |
| **Star In Bull's-Eye,** Creamer, Pink Flashing | 24.00 |
| **Star In Bull's-Eye,** Goblet, Gold | 19.50 |
| **Star In Bull's-Eye,** Pitcher, Water, Cranberry Flashed Top | 55.00 |
| **Star In Bull's-Eye,** Toothpick | 22.50 |
| **Star In Bull's-Eye,** Water Set, Gold Pitcher, 6 Tumblers | 120.00 |
| **Star In Honeycomb,** Celery | 20.00 |
| **Star Of David,** Bowl, Scroll, Embossed Underside | 65.00 |
| **Star Rosetted,** Compote, Covered, 8 1/2 In. | 46.50 To 48.00 |
| **Starred Scroll,** Wine | 7.00 |
| **Stars & Bars,** Celery | 11.00 |
| **Stars & Bars,** Cruet, Stopper | 35.00 |
| **Stars & Bars,** Goblet, Etched Moose Scene | 65.00 |
| **Stars & Stripes,** Wine | 8.00 |
| **States,** Bowl, Shallow, 9 1/2 In. | 16.00 |
| **States,** Compote, 5 1/2 In. | 45.00 |
| **States,** Cup, Gold Trim, 2 1/4 In. | 17.50 |
| **States,** Goblet | 23.00 |
| **States,** Plate, Gold Trim, 5 1/2 In. | 12.00 |
| **States,** Plate, 5 1/2 In.Diam. | 10.00 |
| **States,** Punch Bowl, 11 In.Diam., 2 Piece | 70.00 |
| **STAYMAN, see Tidy** | |
| **Stippled Band,** Spooner, Scalloped Top, Clear | 20.00 |
| **Stippled Chain,** Spooner | 15.00 To 25.00 |
| **Stippled Cherry,** Bowl, 8 In. | 25.00 |
| **STIPPLED DAHLIA, see Dahlia** | |
| **Stippled Daisy,** Compote, Open, 8 In. | 32.00 |
| **Stippled Double Loop,** Creamer | 22.50 |
| **Stippled Forget-Me-Not,** Cake Stand, 9 In. | 55.00 |
| **Stippled Fuchsia,** Goblet | 20.00 To 22.50 |
| **Stippled Grape & Festoon,** Butter, Covered | 35.00 |
| **Stippled Grape & Festoon,** Celery | 25.00 To 50.00 |

Stippled Grape & Festoon, Compote, Covered, 8 In. ............................................... 30.00
Stippled Grape & Festoon, Creamer, Applied Handle ........................................... 36.00
Stippled Grape & Festoon, Creamer, Clear Leaf ................................................... 41.50
Stippled Grape & Festoon, Goblet, Buttermilk ...................................................... 15.00
Stippled Grape & Festoon, Goblet, Clear Leaf ...................................................... 18.00
Stippled Grape & Festoon, Mug, Cobalt Blue ....................................................... 30.00
Stippled Grape & Festoon, Pitcher, Milk ............................................................... 60.00
Stippled Grape & Festoon, Pitcher, Water, Applied Handle ................................... 45.00
Stippled Grape & Festoon, Spooner .............................................. 11.00 To 22.00
Stippled Grape & Festoon, Sugar, Covered .......................................................... 35.00
Stippled Ivy, Buttermilk ......................................................................................... 33.50
Stippled Ivy, Sauce, Flat ......................................................................................... 5.50
Stippled Ivy, Spooner ............................................................................................ 22.50
Stippled Medallion, Eggcup, Flint ................................................ 22.50 To 29.00
Stippled Medallion, Sauce, Flint ........................................................................... 12.00
### STIPPLED PANELED FLOWER, see Maine
Stippled Roman Key, Goblet ................................................................................. 20.00
Stippled Sandburr, Sugar, Open ........................................................................... 15.00
### STIPPLED SCROLL, see Scroll
Stippled Star Flower, Wine .................................................................................... 12.00
### STIPPLED STAR VARIANT, see Stippled Sandburr
Stippled Star, Celery ................................................................. 29.00 To 30.00
Stippled Star, Goblet ............................................................................................. 27.00
Stippled Star, Spooner ............................................................... 22.00 To 27.00
### STORK LOOKING AT THE MOON, see Ostrich Looking At The Moon
Stork, Dish, Relish, One Hundred & One Border, Clear ........................................ 20.00
Stork, Tray, Water, 11 1/2 In. ................................................................................ 32.50
Strawberry & Currant, Goblet ............................................................................... 25.00
Strawberry & Fan, Champagne, Flint .................................................................. 125.00
Strawberry, Spooner .............................................................................................. 30.00
Strawberry, Spooner, Roman Key Band, Gold Trim .............................................. 18.00
Strawberry, Sugar, Covered, Roman Key Band, Gold Trim ................................... 28.00
Strawberry, Tumbler ............................................................................................... 30.00
Strigil, Celery ......................................................................................................... 18.50
Strigil, Cup & Saucer ............................................................................................. 25.00
Strigil, Spooner ...................................................................................................... 15.00
Sunburst & Diamond, Compote, Open .................................................................. 40.00
Sunburst, Cruet, Top ............................................................................................. 28.50
Sunburst, Eggcup ........................................................................ 12.00 To 15.00
Sunburst, Plate, 8 In. ............................................................................................ 10.00
Sunk Daisy, Compote ............................................................................................ 25.00
Sunk Daisy, Saltshaker .......................................................................................... 16.00
Sunk Honeycomb, Cruet, Original Stopper ........................................................... 28.00
Sunken Primrose, Spooner, Amber & Ruby ......................................................... 115.00
### SUNRISE, see Rising Sun
Swag Block, Eggcup .............................................................................................. 15.00
Swag With Brackets, Cruet, Gold Swags, Clear Stopper, Blue ............................. 85.00
Swan With Tree, Pitcher, Water ........................................................................... 110.00
Swan, Compote, Open, 10 X 7 1/2 In. .................................................................. 32.00
Swan, Creamer ...................................................................................................... 40.00
Swan, Spooner ....................................................................................................... 40.00
Swirl, Goblet ........................................................................................................... 11.00
Tacoma, Tumbler, Amber Stain ............................................................................. 40.00
Tandem Bicycle, Celery ......................................................................................... 48.00
Teardrop & Tassel, Berry Set, Blue, 7 Piece ........................................................ 95.00
Teardrop & Tassel, Dish, Relish ............................................................................ 20.00
Teardrop & Tassel, Pitcher, Water ........................................................................ 75.00
Teardrop & Tassel, Pitcher, Water, Blue .............................................................. 175.00
Teardrop & Tassel, Tumbler .................................................................................. 25.00
### TEARDROP & THUMBPRINT, see Teardrop
Teardrop, Wine ...................................................................................................... 18.50
Tennessee, Compote, Covered .............................................................................. 85.00
Tennessee, Dish, Pickle ......................................................................................... 24.00

Pressed Glass, Thistle

| | |
|---|---|
| **Tepee,** Spooner, Amber | 20.00 |
| **Tepee,** Toothpick, Clear | 19.00 |
| **Texas Bull's-Eye,** Goblet | 18.00 To 40.00 |
| **Texas Star,** Spooner | 34.00 |
| **Texas Star,** Sugar | 36.00 |
| **Texas Star,** Toothpick | 32.00 To 38.00 |
| **Texas Star,** Tumbler | 20.00 |
| **Texas,** Bowl, 7 In.Diam. | 18.00 |
| **Texas,** Butter, Covered | 165.00 |
| **Texas,** Creamer | 18.00 |
| **Texas,** Creamer, Individual | 15.00 |
| **Texas,** Sugar, Small | 8.00 |
| **Texas,** Vase, 9 1/4 In. | 28.00 |
| **The States,** Pitcher, Water | 50.00 To 110.00 |
| **The States,** Plate, 5 1/4 In.Diam. | 10.00 |
| **The States,** Tray, Celery, Flat | 29.00 |
| **The States,** Tumbler | 35.00 |
| **Thistle,** Champagne | 30.00 |
| **Thistle,** Pitcher, Water | 95.00 |
| **Thistle,** Spooner | 22.00 To 25.00 |
| **Thistle,** Syrup, Applied Handle | 95.00 |
| **Thistle,** Wine | 30.00 |
| **Thompson,** Goblet, Ruby Top | 22.00 |
| **Thousand Eye,** Celery, Knob Stem, Amber | 30.00 |
| **Thousand Eye,** Celery, 3 Knob | 48.00 |
| **Thousand Eye,** Compote, Apple Green, 6 In. | 25.00 |
| **Thousand Eye,** Compote, Square, 8 1/2 In. | 65.00 |
| **Thousand Eye,** Creamer | 20.00 |
| **Thousand Eye,** Dish, Pickle, Amber | 27.00 |
| **Thousand Eye,** Eggcup | 17.00 |
| **Thousand Eye,** Goblet, Amber | 25.00 |
| **Thousand Eye,** Goblet, Knob Stem | 35.00 |
| **Thousand Eye,** Holder | 45.00 |
| **Thousand Eye,** Pitcher, Milk, Knob Stem, Blue | 80.00 |
| **Thousand Eye,** Pitcher, Water, Flat, Blue | 125.00 |
| **Thousand Eye,** Pitcher, Water, Knob Stem | 95.00 |
| **Thousand Eye,** Plate, Blue, 6 In. | 25.00 |
| **Thousand Eye,** Plate, Blue, 8 In. | 30.00 |
| **Thousand Eye,** Plate, Blue, 10 In. | 35.00 |
| **Thousand Eye,** Spooner | 10.00 |
| **Thousand Eye,** Spooner, Knob Stem | 35.00 |
| **Thousand Eye,** Sugar, Covered | 30.00 |
| **Thousand Eye,** Tray, Water, Amber | 95.00 |
| **Three Bar Waffle,** Goblet | 12.00 |

Pressed Glass, Three Face, Compote, Frosted, 8 1/2 In.

Three Face, Cake Stand, 11 In.Diam. ..................................................................................... 140.00
Three Face, Celery, Allover Floral Etching ............................................................................. 75.00
Three Face, Claret ................................................................................................................ 125.00
Three Face, Compote, Cover, 6 In. ....................................................................................... 75.00
Three Face, Compote, Frosted, 6 1/2 In. .............................................................................. 175.00
Three Face, Compote, Frosted, 8 1/2 In. .............................................................. *Illus* 250.00
Three Face, Compote, Frosted, 13 In. ................................................................................... 350.00
Three Face, Creamer ............................................................................................................. 25.00
Three Face, Goblet, C.1883 .................................................................................................. 50.00
Three Face, Goblet, Etched Band ........................................................... 75.00 To 95.00
Three Face, Pitcher, Water .................................................................................................... 295.00
Three Face, Salt, Frosted, Set Of 5 ...................................................................................... 87.00
Three Face, Spooner .............................................................................. 30.00 To 85.00
Three Face, Spooner, Etched ................................................................................................ 95.00
    THREE GRACES, see Three Face
Three Panel, Bowl, Footed, Blue ........................................................................................... 35.00
Three Panel, Creamer, Amber ............................................................................................... 35.00
Three Panel, Salt, Sapphire Blue .......................................................................................... 16.00
Three Panel, Sauce, Footed, Amber ...................................................................................... 14.00
Three Panel, Spooner ............................................................................................................ 36.50
Three Panel, Tumbler, Amber ................................................................................................ 33.50
Three Presidents, Bread Plate, In Remembrance ............................................... 42.00 To 52.50
    THREE SISTERS, see Three Face
Thumbprint Block, Rose Bowl ............................................................................................... 10.00
Thumbprint, Berry Bowl, Master ........................................................................................... 22.50
Thumbprint, Bottle, Bitters, Flint .......................................................................................... 95.00
Thumbprint, Bowl, Flint, Shallow, 10 In.Diam. ..................................................................... 60.00
Thumbprint, Butter, Covered, Cherry .................................................................................... 90.00
Thumbprint, Celery ................................................................................................................ 55.00
Thumbprint, Compote, Covered, Flint, 6 1/2 X 7 1/2 In. ..................................................... 50.00
Thumbprint, Compote, Hexagonal Stem, Amber, 7 X 6 In. .................................................. 41.00
Thumbprint, Creamer, Ruby, Individual ................................................................................. 32.50
Thumbprint, Frosted, Sugar, Open, Large ............................................................................. 145.00
Thumbprint, Goblet, Flint ...................................................................... 42.00 To 65.00
Thumbprint, Goblet, Flint, Baluster ....................................................................................... 65.00
Thumbprint, Goblet, Knob Stem ........................................................................................... 48.00
Thumbprint, Sauce, Flint ....................................................................................................... 15.00
Thumbprint, Spooner ............................................................................................................. 27.00
Thumbprint, Spooner, Cherry ................................................................................................ 45.00
Thumbprint, Spooner, Scalloped Beaded Edge ..................................................................... 22.00
Thumbprint, Sugar & Creamer, Ruby, Individual .................................................................. 55.00
Thumbprint, Tumble-Up ......................................................................................................... 385.00
Thumbprint, Tumbler, Flint .................................................................................................... 28.00
Thumbprint, Wine, Clear ........................................................................................................ 34.00
Thumbprint, Wine, Flint, Baluster Stem ................................................................................. 60.00
Thumbprint, Wine, Reeded Stem ........................................................................................... 30.00
Tidy, Goblet ............................................................................................................................ 12.00

| | |
|---|---:|
| Tidy, Spooner | 18.50 |
| Tiny Finecut, Goblet | 13.00 |
| Tiny Lion, Celery, Engraved | 25.00 |
| Tiny Lion, Pitcher, Water, Cable Base | 55.00 |
|     TOBIN, see Leaf & Star | |
| Toltec, Syrup | 37.50 |
| Topedo, Spooner | 25.00 |
| Torpedo, Bowl, 9 In.Diam. | 14.00 To 20.00 |
| Torpedo, Bowl, 10 In.Diam. | 35.00 |
| Torpedo, Cake Stand | 40.00 |
| Torpedo, Celery, Scalloped Top | 20.00 To 25.00 |
| Torpedo, Compote, Open, Ruffled Rim, 8 X 7 1/4 In. | 65.00 |
| Torpedo, Cup | 22.50 |
| Torpedo, Goblet | 45.00 |
| Torpedo, Pitcher, 12 In. | 140.00 |
| Torpedo, Waste Bowl | 40.00 |
| Transcontinental Railroad, Platter | 42.00 |
| Tree Bark, Pitcher, Water | 22.00 |
| Tree Of Life, Bowl, Berry, 8 In.Diam. | 18.00 |
| Tree Of Life, Bowl, Berry, 10 In.Diam. | 25.00 |
| Tree Of Life, Butter Pat, Shell Shape | 13.00 |
| Tree Of Life, Cake Stand, 10 In.Diam. | 95.00 |
| Tree Of Life, Compote, Frosted Band, 8 1/4 X 8 In.Diam. | 60.00 |
| Tree Of Life, Compote, 8 In. | 60.00 |
| Tree Of Life, Creamer, Frosted Ball & Hand Stem | 50.00 |
| Tree Of Life, Dish, Shell Shape, Footed, 8 1/2 X 7 1/2 In. | 45.00 |
| Tree Of Life, Finger Bowl, Blue | 58.00 |
| Tree Of Life, Goblet, Portland | 35.00 |
| Tree Of Life, Mug, Gold Rim, 3 In. | 27.00 |
| Tree Of Life, Pitcher, Water | 55.00 |
| Tree Of Life, Portland, Tray, Ice Cream, Rectangular | 35.00 |
| Tree Of Life, Spooner | 35.00 |
| Tree Of Life, Sugar & Creamer | 80.00 |
| Tree Of Life, Syrup | 30.00 |
| Tree Of Life, Tumbler | 25.00 |
| Tree Of Life, Tumbler, 6 Paneled, Blue, Flint, 3 1/2 In. | 54.00 |
| Tree Of Life, Wine | 30.00 |
| Tremont, Creamer | 12.00 To 18.50 |
| Triangular Prism, Goblet, Flint | 29.50 |
| Triangular Prism, Pitcher, Water, Applied Handle, Flint | 135.00 |
| Triangular Prism, Spooner | 18.50 |
| Triangular Prism, Whiskey | 18.00 |
| Triple Band Miotin, Spooner | 12.00 |
| Triple Triangle, Mug | 65.00 |
| Triple Triangle, Wine | 40.00 |
| Tulip & Honeycomb, Butter, Creamer & Spooner, Child's | 65.00 |
| Tulip & Honeycomb, Punch Bowl, 5 Cups, Child's | 65.00 |
| Tulip Petals, Goblet | 26.00 |
| Tulip With Sawtooth, Cruet | 22.00 |
| Tulip With Sawtooth, Goblet, Flint | 40.00 |
| Tulip With Sawtooth, Tumbler, Flint | 28.00 |
| Tulip With Sawtooth, Wine | 15.00 |
| Tulip With Sawtooth, Wine, Knob Stem | 18.00 |
| Tulip, Celery, 10 1/4 In. | 62.00 |
| Tulip, Champagne | 45.00 |
| Tulip, Goblet, Pontil, Flint | 38.00 |
| Twin Snowshoes, Creamer | 12.50 |
| Twin Teardrops, Cake Stand, 9 1/4 In. | 18.00 |
| Twin Teardrops, Compote, Open, 8 In. | 16.00 |
|     TWINKLE STAR, see also Utah | |
| Twinkle Star, Pitcher, Water | 38.00 To 45.00 |
| Twinkle Star, Syrup | 38.00 |
| Two Band, Goblet | 33.00 |

Pressed Glass, U.S.Coin, Bread Plate, Frosted, 10 X 8 In.

| | |
|---|---:|
| **Two Camels,** Goblet, Etched | 55.00 |
| **Two Panel,** Bowl, Amber, 3 X 5 X 4 In.Diam. | 30.00 |
| **Two Panel,** Bowl, Amber, 6 3/4 X 5 1/2 In.Diam. | 25.00 |
| **Two Panel,** Bowl, Amber, 8 X 6 1/2 In.Diam. | 35.00 |
| **Two Panel,** Butter, Covered, Amber | 50.00 |
| **Two Panel,** Celery | 24.00 To 26.50 |
| **Two Panel,** Creamer, Amber | 35.00 |
| **Two Panel,** Pitcher, Water, Apple Green | 75.00 |
| **Two Panel,** Pitcher, Water, Clear | 45.00 |
| **Two Panel,** Spooner, Amber, Flared Top | 40.00 |
| **Two Panel,** Sugar, Covered, Amber | 40.00 |
| **Two Panel,** Tray, Water, Clover Leaf Shape, 12 X 12 In. | 45.00 |
| **Two Panel,** Tumbler, Amber | 30.00 |
| **Two Panel,** Tumbler, Apple Green | 30.00 |
| **U.S.Coin,** Bread Plate, Frosted, 10 X 8 In. *Illus* | 295.00 |
| **U.S.Coin,** Butter, Covered, 1892 Dollars | 400.00 |
| **U.S.Coin,** Cake Stand, Footed, Frosted Dollars | 350.00 To 375.00 |
| **U.S.Coin,** Cruet, Original Stopper | 525.00 |
| **U.S.Coin,** Goblet, Dimes | 175.00 |
| **U.S.Coin,** Pitcher, Water, U.S.Dollar, Clear | 495.00 |
| **U.S.Coin,** Sauce, Footed, Quarters, Scalloped | 105.00 |
| **U.S.Coin,** Saucer, Flat | 100.00 |
| **U.S.Coin,** Spooner | 150.00 |
| **U.S.Coin,** Sugar, 25 & 50 Cent Coins | 300.00 |
| **U.S.Coin,** Syrup | 475.00 |
| **U.S.Coin,** Syrup, Quarters, 1892 | 475.00 |
| **U.S.Coin,** Table Set, Sugar, Creamer, Spooner, Butter, Covered | 250.00 |
| **U.S.Coin,** Toothpick | 65.00 To 100.00 |
| **U.S.Coin,** Toothpick, Dollar | 140.00 |
| **U.S.Coin,** Tray, Halves & Dollars, Frosted, 10 X 8 In. | 380.00 |
| **U.S.Grant,** Plate, Clear, Square | 45.00 |
| **U.S.Rib,** Butter, Covered, Green | 75.00 |
| **U.S.Rib,** Sugar & Creamer, Open, Clear & Gold | 16.50 |
| **U.S.Rib,** Toothpick | 18.00 |
| **Umbilicated Sawtooth,** Eggcup | 35.00 |
| **Umbilicated Sawtooth,** Wine, Flint | 30.00 |
| **Utah,** Dish, Relish, Clear, 7 X 5 In.Diam. | 20.00 |
| **Utah,** Salt & Pepper, New Tops | 30.00 |
| **Valencia Waffle,** Bread Plate | 16.00 |
| **Valencia Waffle,** Pitcher, Milk, Amber, 7 1/2 In. | 75.00 |
| **Valencia Waffle,** Salt & Pepper, Apple Green, Original Tops | 40.00 |
| **Valencia Waffle,** Salt, Amber, Master | 24.00 |
| **Valencia Waffle,** Syrup, Apple Green | 85.00 |
| **Vera,** Compote, Covered, 7 1/2 In. | 90.00 |
| **Vermont,** Bonbon Basket, Emerald Green | 85.00 |

Pressed Glass, Viking, Compote,
Covered, 9 1/2 In.

Pressed Glass, Waffle &
Thumbprint

| | |
|---|---:|
| **Vernon Honeycomb,** Celery | 65.00 |
| **Vernon Honeycomb,** Champagne | 14.00 |
| **Vernon Honeycomb,** Goblet, Flint | 22.00 |
| **Vesta,** Tumbler, Opalescent | 35.00 |
| **Victoria,** Celery | 45.00 |
| **Victoria,** Creamer | 45.00 |
| **Victoria,** Goblet | 16.00 |
| **Victoria,** Spooner | 25.00 |
| **Viking,** Butter, Covered | 25.00 To 55.00 |
| **Viking,** Cake Stand, 10 In.Diam., Pair | 70.00 |
| **Viking,** Celery | 35.00 To 42.50 |
| **Viking,** Compote, Covered, 9 1/2 In. | *Illus* 85.00 |
| **Viking,** Creamer | 25.00 To 30.00 |
| **Viking,** Pitcher, Water | 65.00 To 125.00 |
| **Viking,** Sauce, Footed | 8.50 |
| **Viking,** Spooner | 22.50 To 45.00 |
| **Viking,** Sugar, Covered | 35.00 To 50.00 |
| **Viking,** Sugar, Open | 50.00 |
| **Viking,** Wine, Footed | 19.00 |
| **VIRGINIA, see also Galloway** | |
| **Virginia Dare,** Bread Plate | 22.00 To 30.00 |
| **Virginia,** Butter, Covered, Clear | 35.00 |
| **Virginia,** Creamer, Gold Trim | 24.00 |
| **Virginia,** Creamer, Rose Stained | 35.00 |
| **Virginia,** Sugar, Gold Trim, Covered | 30.00 |
| **Waffle & Spearhead,** Water Set, 7 Piece | 80.00 |
| **Waffle & Thumbprint,** Champagne, Flint | 60.00 |
| **Waffle & Thumbprint,** Claret | 85.00 |
| **Waffle & Thumbprint,** Compote, 6 5/8 In. | 35.00 |
| **Waffle & Thumbprint,** Sugar, Covered | 165.00 |
| **Waffle & Thumbprint,** Wine, Polished Pontil | 55.00 |
| **Waffle With Spearpoint,** Water Set, 7 Piece | 80.00 |
| **Waffle,** Celery, Sandwich, Flint | 40.00 |
| **Waffle,** Champagne, Flint | 135.00 |
| **Waffle,** Goblet | 65.00 |
| **Waffle,** Plate, Flint, 6 In.Diam. | 18.00 |
| **Waffle,** Spooner | 15.00 |
| **WASHBOARD, see Adonis** | |
| **Washington & Lafayette,** Mug, Blue | 30.00 |
| **Washington Centenial,** Pitcher, Water | 85.00 |
| **Washington Centennial,** Bread Plate, Dated | 50.00 |
| **Washington Centennial,** Celery | 42.00 |
| **Washington Centennial,** Compote, 10 1/4 In. | 95.00 |
| **Washington Centennial,** Creamer | 65.00 |
| **Washington Centennial,** Dish, Relish, Bear Handled, Dated | 45.00 |

Pressed Glass, Washington Centennial, Relish, Bear Handles

| | |
|---|---:|
| **Washington Centennial,** Eggcup | 52.50 |
| **Washington Centennial,** Pitcher, Water | 85.00 |
| **Washington Centennial,** Relish, Bear Handles .......... *Illus* | 45.00 |
| **Washington Hatchet,** 1893 World's Fair, Blue | 45.00 |
| **Washington,** Celery, Flint | 70.00 |
| **Washington,** Eggcup .................... 65.00 To | 75.00 |
| **Washington,** Eggcup, Flint | 30.00 |
| **Washington,** Goblet | 80.00 |
| **Washington,** Goblet, Lady's | 75.00 |
| **Washington,** Goblet, Large | 85.00 |
| **Washington,** Spooner | 55.00 |
| **WATER LILY, see Rose Point Band** | |
| **Way Colonial,** Champagne | 65.00 |
| **Wedding Ring,** Bowl, 9 In.Diam. | 75.00 |
| **Westmoreland,** Bottle, Water | 28.00 |
| **Westward Ho,** Berry Bowl, Footed, 3 1/2 In. | 45.00 |
| **Westward Ho,** Compote, 11 1/2 In.Diam. .......... *Illus* | 75.00 |
| **Westward Ho,** Goblet ........................ 35.00 To | 50.00 |
| **Westward Ho,** Sauce ........................ 17.00 To | 37.50 |
| **Westward Ho,** Sauce, Footed, 4 In. ............ 37.50 To | 40.00 |
| **Wheat & Barley,** Butter, Covered, Amber | 50.00 |
| **Wheat & Barley,** Compote, Jelly | 32.50 |
| **Wheat & Barley,** Creamer | 15.00 |
| **Wheat & Barley,** Creamer, Amber | 32.00 |
| **Wheat & Barley,** Goblet | 20.00 |
| **Wheat & Barley,** Pitcher, Water | 45.00 |

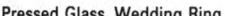

Pressed Glass, Wedding Ring

Pressed Glass, Westward Ho, Compote, 11 1/2 In.Diam.

**Wheat & Barley,** Pitcher, Water, Blue ............................................................................ 65.00
**Wheat & Barley,** Plate, Amber, 7 In. ............................................................................. 28.00
**Wheat & Barley,** Spooner ............................................................................................ 14.00
**Wheat & Barley,** Spooner, Amber ................................................................................ 25.00
**Wheat & Barley,** Sugar, Covered ................................................................... 23.00 To 25.00
**Wheat & Barley,** Sugar, Covered, Footed ..................................................................... 35.00
**Wheat & Barley,** Tumbler ............................................................................................ 22.50
**Wheat & Barley,** Tumbler, Amber ................................................................................ 18.50
**Wheat Sheaf,** Goblet .................................................................................................. 22.00
**Wheat Sheaf,** Punch Bowl & 6 Mugs, Miniature, 3 In. ................................................. 140.00
**Whirligig,** Punch Set, Child's ...................................................................................... 80.00
**Wild Bouquet,** Creamer .............................................................................................. 45.00
**Wild Fruits,** Goblet ..................................................................................................... 13.50
**Wild Rose With Bow Knot,** Sugar, Covered, Frosted ................................................... 35.00
**Wildflower,** Bowl, Square, Cut Corners ....................................................................... 15.00
**Wildflower,** Celery, Amber .......................................................................................... 39.50
**Wildflower,** Creamer ................................................................................................... 20.00
**Wildflower,** Creamer, Amber ....................................................................................... 38.50
**Wildflower,** Goblet ....................................................................................................... 7.00
**Wildflower,** Goblet, Amber ................................................................................ 16.00 To 18.00
**Wildflower,** Goblet, Blue .............................................................................................. 9.00
**Wildflower,** Pitcher, Water ................................................................................ 31.00 To 35.00
**Wildflower,** Platter, Blue, Green, Oval ......................................................................... 43.00
**Wildflower,** Spooner ................................................................................................... 10.00
**Wildflower,** Syrup, Dated July 15, 1884, Amber ......................................................... 185.00
**Wildflower,** Tumbler, Amber ....................................................................................... 45.00
**Wildflower,** Tumbler, Apple Green .............................................................................. 29.00
**Wildflower,** Water Set, Apple Green, 7 Piece ............................................................. 215.00
**Wildflower,** Wine, Amber ............................................................................................ 46.00
**Willow Oak,** Bowl, 7 1/4 In. .............................................................................. 16.00 To 35.00
**Willow Oak,** Butter, Covered, Amber ........................................................................... 42.50
**Willow Oak,** Cake Stand, 5 X 11 In.Diam. ................................................................... 40.00
**Willow Oak,** Compote, High Standard, Blue ................................................................ 60.00
**Willow Oak,** Creamer ....................................................................................... 24.00 To 29.00
**Willow Oak,** Creamer, Blue .............................................................................. 37.50 To 42.00
**Willow Oak,** Goblet ......................................................................................... 33.00 To 35.00
**Willow Oak,** Mug ............................................................................................ 32.50 To 35.00
**Willow Oak,** Pitcher, Milk ........................................................................................... 45.00
**Willow Oak,** Plate, Blue, 9 In. ..................................................................................... 24.50
**Willow Oak,** Spooner, Amber ...................................................................................... 40.00
**Willow Oak,** Tray, Water ............................................................................................. 25.00
**Willow Oak,** Tray, Water, Round, Clear ....................................................................... 22.00
**Willow Oak,** Tumbler .................................................................................................. 25.00
**Willow Oak,** Waste Bowl ................................................................................. 32.00 To 32.50
**Windflower,** Spooner ........................................................................................ 18.00 To 25.00
**Winged Scrolls,** Pitcher, Water, Clear, Gold Trim ...................................................... 195.00
**Wishbone,** Wine ......................................................................................................... 17.50
**Wooden Pail,** Pitcher, Water, Amber ........................................................................... 75.00
**Worcester,** Belted, Goblet, Flare Top .......................................................................... 32.00
**Worcester,** Belted, Tumbler, Water, Footed, Flint ........................................................ 25.00
**Worcester,** Belted, Whiskey, Flint ............................................................................... 18.00
**Worcester,** Goblet, Straight Banded ............................................................................ 35.00
**Wreath & Bars,** Goblet ............................................................................................... 12.00
**Wreath & Shell,** Celery, Vaseline .............................................................................. 125.00
**Wreath & Shell,** Center Set, Vaseline, 4 Piece .......................................................... 375.00
**Wreath & Shell,** Center Set, White Opalescent, 4 Piece ............................................ 300.00
**Wreath & Shell,** Creamer, Blue .................................................................................. 85.00
**Wreath & Shell,** Spooner, Blue .................................................................................. 75.00
**Wreath & Shell,** Spooner, Vaseline ............................................................................ 65.00
**Wreath & Shell,** Spooner, White Opalescent .............................................................. 50.00
**Wyoming,** Cake Stand, 8 1/2 In. ................................................................................. 25.00
**Wyoming,** Pitcher, Water ............................................................................................ 35.00
**X-Ray,** Bowl, Emerald Green, Gold Trim, 8 1/8 In. ..................................................... 45.00

**X-Ray,** Cruet, Green ............................................................................................ 165.00
**X-Ray,** Sugar, Covered, Green ........................................................ 25.00 To 50.00
**X-Ray,** Sugar, Covered, Green, Gold Trim ............................................................ 55.00
**X-Ray,** Sugar, Gold Trim, Covered ....................................................................... 32.50
**X-Ray,** Table Set, Green & Gold, 4 Piece ........................................................... 225.00
**X-Ray,** Toothpick, Gold Trim, Green ..................................................................... 50.00
**X-Ray,** Toothpick, Green ........................................................................................ 65.00
**X-Ray,** Tumbler, Amethyst, Gold Trim ................................................................... 28.00
**X-Ray,** Water Set, Green & Gold, 7 Piece ........................................................... 185.00
    **YALE, see Crowfoot**
**Yoked Loop,** Compote, Open, Flint, 7 X 3 1/2 In. ................................................ 20.00
**Yoked Loop,** Goblet, Flint ..................................................................................... 18.00
**York Colonial,** Champagne .................................................................................... 65.00
**Yuma Loop,** Tumbler, Footed, Flint ....................................................................... 18.00
**Zephyr,** Spooner, Amber ........................................................................................ 24.00
**Zipper Slash,** Butter, Covered, Yellow .................................................................. 85.00
**Zipper Slash,** Creamer, Applied Handle ............................................................... 45.00
**Zipper Slash,** Toothpick ......................................................................................... 17.00
**Zipper,** Compote, Open .......................................................................................... 25.00
**Zipper,** Jar, Jam, Covered, 6 In. ............................................................................ 35.00
**Zipper,** Syrup ......................................................................................................... 17.50
**Zipper,** Toothpick ................................................................................................... 18.50
      **100-EYE, see Hundred Eye**
      **100-LEAVED ROSE, see Hundred Leaved Rose**
      **101, see One-O-One**
      **1,000-EYE, see Thousand Eye**

*The size of the print is given, not the overall size with frame.*
    **PRINT, see also Store, Sign**
**PRINT, Audubon,** Killdeer Plover ........................................................................ 1250.00
**Audubon,** Snow Owl .............................................................................................. 750.00
**Audubon,** Starling, Havell Edition ....................................................................... 1250.00
**Baby,** Little Bit Of Heaven, Bessie Gutmann, Gold Frame, 14 X 17 In. .................. 20.00
**Bartlett,** Valley Of The Connecticut, Dated 1828 .................................................. 18.00
**Bartlett,** View From Ruggle's House, Dated 1838 ................................................. 18.00
**Becker,** Here We Are, 14 X 18 In. ........................................................................... 8.00
**Becker,** Morning Sunshine, 14 X 18 In. ................................................................... 8.00
**Becker,** Playmates, 14 X 18 In. ............................................................................... 8.00
**Becker,** Smiling Through, 14 X 18 In. ...................................................................... 8.00
    **PRINT, CURRIER, see Currier**
    **PRINT, CURRIER & IVES, see Currier & Ives**
**Frost,** Hunting Scene, 1904 .................................................................................... 37.50
**Gutmann,** A Call To Arms, 14 X 21 In. ................................................................... 30.00
**Gutmann,** Butterflies & Daisies, 14 X 21 In. .......................................................... 35.00
**Gutmann,** Goldilocks, 11 X 14 In. .......................................................................... 35.00
**Gutmann,** Little Bo Peep, 17 X 14 In. ..................................................................... 35.00
**Gutmann,** Little Boy Blue, 17 X 14 In. .................................................................... 35.00
**Gutmann,** Little Miss Muffet, 14 X 21 In. ............................................................... 35.00
**Gutmann,** Little Miss Muffet, 17 X 14 In. ............................................................... 35.00
**Gutmann,** Miss Flirt, 14 X 21 In. ............................................................................ 25.00
**Gutmann,** On The Up & Up, 14 X 21 In. ................................................................. 20.00
**Gutmann,** Symphony, 14 X 21 In. .......................................................................... 65.00
**Gutmann,** Two Sleepy Heads, 14 X 21 In. ............................................................. 45.00
**Gutmann,** Winged Aureole, 14 X 21 In. ................................................................. 95.00
**Gutmann,** Wood Magic, 14 X 21 In. ....................................................................... 75.00
**Haskell & Allen,** Washington Family, Seated At Table, Black & White ................... 45.00
**Icart,** Angry Steed ............................................................................................... 2100.00
**Icart,** Conchita, Dry Mounted ............................................................................. 1000.00
**Icart,** Etching, Mealtime, 1927, Signed, Windmill Mark, Oval, Framed .................. 775.00
**Icart,** Four Seasons ............................................................................................. 5000.00
**Icart,** German Shepherd With Girl, Artist's Work Copy With Notes ....................... 925.00
**Icart,** Golden Vail ............................................................................................... 3200.00
**Icart,** In The Trenches ........................................................................................ 2500.00

**Icart,** Joy Of Life ............................................................................................................. 2800.00
**Icart,** Morning Cup ............................................................................................................ 750.00
**Icart,** Peacock ................................................................................................................... 2000.00
**Icart,** Pink Slip .................................................................................................................. 1900.00
**Icart,** Retour De Promenade, Windmill Mark, Signed, 18 X 14 1/2 In. ........................... 595.00
**Icart,** Sleeping Beauty, Framed ........................................................................................ 1600.00
**Icart,** Speed ...................................................................................................................... 950.00
**Icart,** Tosca ....................................................................................................................... 975.00
**Icart,** Trenches .................................................................................................................. 1550.00
**Icart,** Voice Of The Cannon .............................................................................................. 2400.00
**Icart,** White Underwear ..................................................................................................... 975.00
**Icart,** Youth ........................................................................................................................ 2900.00
**Icart,** Zest .......................................................................................................................... 2000.00

*Japanese prints are listed as follows: Print, Japanese, name of artist,*
*title or description, type, size. The following terms are used to denote type:*
*Tate-e is a vertical composition. Yoko-e is a horizontal composition.*
*The words Aiban, Chuban, Hosoban, Oban, and Koban denote size.*
*The sizes are 13 x 9 inches, 10 x 7 1/2 inches, 12 x 6 inches,*
*15 x 10 inches, and 7 x 4 1/2 inches respectively.*

**Japanese,** Chikanobu, Woman Walking In Blue Kimono, Orange Floral ........................... 40.00
**Japanese,** Chikuto, Landscapes & Riverscapes, Ink On Paper, Signed ......................... 125.00
**Japanese,** Deities, Ink & Color On Paper, 18th Century, 61 X 19 3/4 In. ....................... 650.00
**Japanese,** Eisan, Rain On Hiratsuka Moor, Seal ................................................................ 700.00
**Japanese,** Female Figure, Ink & Color On Silk, Framed, Seal ..................................... 550.00
**Japanese,** Fifty-Three Stations Of Tokaido, C.1850, Toyokun III, Oban ...................... 300.00
**Japanese,** Harunobu, Woman & Child Walking Beside Sea ...................................... 200.00
**Japanese,** Hasui, A Great Image Of Buddha At Kamakura, Signed ......................... 250.00
**Japanese,** Hiroshige, Oji Waterfall .................................................................................. 300.00
**Japanese,** Hokusai, Man Pulling Oxen By Rope, Woodblock ................................... 175.00
**Japanese,** Hunsida, Courtesan & Lover, Erotic Embrace, On Silk ......................... 225.00
**Japanese,** Jacoulet, Bergers Des Hautes Montagnes, Signed, Seal ...................... 700.00
**Japanese,** Jacoulet, Homme De Menado Et Mangoustane, Signed ....................... 425.00
**Japanese,** Jacoulet, Jeune Fille De Saipan Et Fleurs, Mica Ground ...................... 550.00
**Japanese,** Jacoulet, Le Mairte Potier, And Nuit De Neige, Signed, Pair ............... 750.00
**Japanese,** Jacoulet, Souvenirs D'autrefois, Signed, Sparrow Seal ....................... 700.00
**Japanese,** Jacoulet, Vendeur De Masques, Signed, Butterfly Seal ...................... 375.00
**Japanese,** Koson, Album, Birds, Carp, & Landscape, Set Of 12 ........................... 950.00
**Japanese,** Kunisada, Two Courtesans, One Child Promenading, Framed ........... 200.00
**Japanese,** Kuniyoshi, Fully Armed Samurai, Holding Banner, Woodcut .............. 150.00
**Japanese,** Thirty-Six Beautiful Women, C.1880, Kunichika, Oban ........................ 125.00
**Japanese,** Tochiro, Bridge Of Five Wooden Arches Spanning Canal ................... 50.00
**Japanese,** Toyojuni, Scenes & Figures, Lavish Kimono, Framed ......................... 150.00
**Japanese,** Utamaro, Promenading Courtesan, Two Children ............................... 1300.00
**Japanese,** Utamaro, Three Women Arranging Their Hair, Seal ........................... 1100.00
**Japanese,** Yoshitora, Twelve Scenes, Depicting Fighting Samurai ..................... 350.00
**Japanese,** Yoshitoshi, One Hundred Views Of The Moon, Set ............... 1500.00 To 1600.00
**Kellogg,** Martha Washington, Bust ............................................................................. 30.00
**Kroger,** Wake Up Time, 14 X 18 In. ............................................................................. 8.00
**Lithograph,** A La Fontaine, Colored, Adolph Schreyer, 18 X 24 In. .......................... 100.00
**Lithograph,** A.Elsley, Grandpa, Children Riding Horse, 18 X 22 In. ........................... 58.00
**Lithograph,** Custer's Last Fight, Anheuser-Busch, Framed, 36 X 47 In. .................. 365.00
**Lithograph,** Flood, Thomas Hart Benton ...................................................................... 500.00
**Lithograph,** Johnstown Flood, 1890 ............................................................................. 75.00
**Lithograph,** Kissing Couple Playing Pool, Grant, 15 X 19 In. .................................. 45.00
**Lithograph,** Procession, Jean Charlot .......................................................................... 200.00
**Lithograph,** Sporting Scenes, Framed, Signed Henry Alken, Pair ....................... 500.00
**Lithograph,** Tree-Planting Group, Grant Wood, 1937 ............................................... 450.00
**Muller,** And Now Awake, 14 X 18 In. ........................................................................... 8.00
**Muller,** Devotion, 14 X 18 In. ...................................................................................... 8.00
**Nutting,** A Peep At The Hills, Framed, 11 X 17 In. ...................................................... 35.00
**Nutting,** A Portsmouth Door, Oak Frame, 15 X 19 In. ................................................ 40.00
**Nutting,** Announcing The Engagement, Framed, 16 1/2 X 16 1/2 In. ........................ 70.00

| | |
|---|---:|
| **Nutting,** Bean Porridge Hot, 1907, Framed, 14 1/4 In.Square | 65.00 |
| **Nutting,** Bonny Dale, Orange Flowers & Trees, 15 1/2 X 18 1/2 In. | 35.00 |
| **Nutting,** Brookside Blooms, Framed, 17 1/2 X 20 1/2 In. | 32.00 |
| **Nutting,** Honeymoon Blossoms, Framed, 10 1/2 X 13 In. | 30.00 |
| **Nutting,** Interior, Confidences, Ladies At Tea, Framed, 17 X 11 In. | 65.00 |
| **Nutting,** New Hampshire Birches, Framed, 12 X 15 In. | 35.00 |
| **Nutting,** Primrose Cottage, 5 X 6 In. | 30.00 |
| **Nutting,** The Coming Out Of Rosa, Framed, 12 X 10 In. | 65.00 |
| **Nutting,** The Swimming Pool, Glazed Frame, Signed, 17 1/2 In. | 33.00 |
| **Nutting,** The Treasure Bag, Framed, Signed, 14 1/4 In. | 55.00 |
| **Nutting,** Water Gambols, Framed, 15 X 18 In. | 32.00 |
| **Nutting,** Wilburton Slopes, Framed, 11 X 13 In. | 35.00 |
| **On Silk,** Canal At Gouda, Signed Louis K.Harlow | 65.00 |
| **Parkinson,** Cupid's Awake, Black & White, 8 1/2 In.Diam. | 56.00 |
| **Parrish,** Cadmus Sowing Dragon Teeth, Framed, 1908, 12 X 16 In. | 50.00 |
| **Parrish,** Daybreak, Framed, 18 X 30 In. | 125.00 |
| **Parrish,** Daybreak, Original Frame, 18 X 30 In. | 175.00 To 195.00 |
| **Parrish,** Entrance Of King Pompdebile, 10 X 13 In. | 55.00 |
| **Parrish,** Frog & Prince, 4 X 9 In. | 45.00 |
| **Parrish,** Garden Of Allah, Lithograph, Framed, 18 X 30 In. | 145.00 |
| **Parrish,** Garden Of Allah, Original Frame, 15 X 30 In. | 185.00 |
| **Parrish,** Lady Ursula Kneeling Before The King, 10 X 13 In. | 30.00 |
| **Parrish,** Lute Players, Label, Lithograph, 6 1/2 X 11 In. | 35.00 |
| **Parrish,** Lute Players, 16 X 20 In. | 215.00 |
| **Parrish,** Reveries, Original Frame, 6 X 10 In. | 50.00 |
| **Parrish,** Twilight, 1937, Framed, 14 X 16 In. | 60.00 |
| **Prang,** Apple Blossoms & Bees, Dated 1885, 7 1/2 X 10 3/4 In. | 14.00 |
| **Prang,** Battle Of Gettysburg, Chromolithograph, 26 X 20 In. | 95.00 |
| **Prang,** Cowslips, Dated 1886, 7 1/2 X 10 1/2 In. | 12.00 |
| **Prang,** Poultry Life, Framed, 13 X 11 1/2 In. | 80.00 |
| **Prang,** Quails, Male & Female Quail & 10 Chicks | 60.00 |
| **Prang,** Sheridan's Final Charge At Winchester, Chromolithograph | 95.00 |
| **Prang,** Trillium, Purple & White, Dated 1886, 7 1/2 X 10 1/2 In. | 12.00 |
| **Raphael Tuck,** Mr.Pecksniff Leaves For London, 18 X 25 1/4 In. | 35.00 |
| **Rockwell,** The Inventor, Signed & Numbered | 1400.00 |
| **The Kill,** English Hunting Scene, C.1880, Framed, 37 X 26 In. | 175.00 |
| **The Meet,** English Hunting Scene, C.1880, Framed, 37 X 26 In. | 175.00 |
|     **PURPLE SLAG, see Slag, Purple** | |

| | |
|---|---:|
| **PURSE, Art Deco Silver Mesh,** Enameled Ground, Geometric Design, 10 X 5 In. | 35.00 |
| **Art Nouveau,** Unger Bros., Sterling Silver | 125.00 |
| **Beaded,** White, Square, Gold Trim Pearl, 6 In. | 12.00 |
| **Card,** Art Nouveau Shape, Chain Handle, Silver Plate | 55.00 |
| **Carpet Bag,** Child's | 15.00 |
| **Chinese Brocade,** Coral Thumbpiece, Marked Cartier, Paris | 950.00 |
| **Coin,** Art Nouveau Metal Top, Embossed Lad1s Head, Leather | 22.50 |
| **Drawstring,** Beaded Edges, Black Suede | 40.00 |
| **Drawstring,** Black Silk, Appliqued Circles, Pink Lining, 6 1/2 In. | 32.00 |
| **Drawstring,** Quilted, Black Velvet | 8.00 |
| **Drawstring,** Silk, Appliqued Colored Circles, Black, Victorian | 24.00 |
| **Drawstring,** Silk, Velvet Applique Circles, Tassels, 6 1/2 In. | 32.00 |
| **Drawstring,** Solid Carnival Glass Beads | 20.00 |
| **Enameled Mesh** | 35.00 |
| **Envelope,** Beaded, White & Silver Bugle Beads, Czechoslovakia, 1920s | 15.00 |
| **Gold Mesh,** Pierced Floral Top, Mesh Change Bag, 14K | 1550.00 |
| **Leather,** Art Nouveau | 12.50 |
| **Mesh,** Art Deco, Enameled, Chain Handle, Whiting & Davis Co., 6 1/4 In. | 35.00 |
| **Mesh,** Dated 1909, German Silver, 7 X 5 In. | 22.00 |
| **Mesh,** Enameled, Full Colored, 6 In. | 30.00 |
| **Mesh,** Fringed Bottom, Sterling Silver, 1910s | 175.00 |
| **Mesh,** Gold Enamel, Art Deco Clasp | 18.00 |
| **Mesh,** Light & Dark Blue Design, Blue Enameled Frame | 34.00 |
| **Mesh,** Twisted Clasp, Whiting & Davis Co., 4 X 8 In. | 30.00 |

| | |
|---|---|
| Mesh, Whiting & David, Sterling Silver, 4 X 4 1/2 In. | 75.00 |
| Mesh, Whiting & Davis, Silver | 22.00 |
| Miser's, Glass Beads | 18.00 |
| Money & Cosmetic, Art Deco, Ribbon Scroll Bands, Sterling Silver | 225.00 |
| Silver Mesh, 1908, German | 25.00 |
| Silver-German, 2 Angels Holding God's Beard | 85.00 |
| Sovereign, Victorian, Wine Colored Leather, 2 Compartments | 42.00 |
| Tapestry, Beaded, 1890s | 25.00 |
| Turquoise & Rose Mesh | 20.00 |

| | |
|---|---|
| QUARTZ, Figurine, Goddess Of Mercy, Standing Kuan Yin, Rose, 6 3/4 In. | 185.00 |

# Quezal

*Quezal glass was made from 1901 to 1920 by Martin Bach, Sr. He made iridescent glass of the same type as Tiffany.*

| | |
|---|---|
| QUEZAL, Bottle, Cologne, Iridescent Gold, Art Deco, Signed, 7 1/2 In. | 295.00 |
| Bowl, Flared Rim, Iridescent Gold, Signed, 5 3/4 In.Diam. | 265.00 |
| Bowl, King Tut Pattern, 3 1/2 X 7 1/2 In.Diam. | 750.00 |
| Candlestick, Blue Iridescent, Signed, 8 In., Pair | 575.00 |
| Candlestick, Cobalt Blue Iridescent, Signed, 10 In. | 575.00 |
| Candlestick, Green, Bronze, & Purple, Cobalt Iridescent, Signed, 10 In. | 575.00 |
| Compote, Gold Inside, Gold Design On Foot & Stem, Signed, 6 In. | 1750.00 |
| Finger Bowl, Gold Iridescence, 4 In.Diam. | 175.00 |
| Salt, Ribbed, Gold Iridescence, Signed | 165.00 |
| Shade, Allover Gold Zipper On Opal, Set Of 5 | 750.00 |
| Shade, Aurene, Green Pulled Feather | 145.00 |
| Shade, Blue Double Hooked Feather, Gold Edge, Ruffled, Signed | 200.00 |
| Shade, Blue, Hooked, Signed, Pair | 350.00 |
| Shade, Calcite, Gold Interior | 72.00 |
| Shade, Enamel Design Outside, Gold Iridescent Inside, 5 1/2 In. | 245.00 |
| Shade, Gold Feather On Calcite, Gold Lined, Signed, 7 In., Set Of 4 | 860.00 |
| Shade, Gold Heart Shaped Leaves, Gold Lined, Webbing, Signed | 125.00 |
| Shade, Gold Iridescent, Signed, 2 1/4 X 5 1/4 In., Pair | 350.00 |
| Shade, Gold, Etched Leaves, Signed, 6 1/4 In. | 145.00 |
| Shade, Green Feather On Calcite, Gold Interior, Ribbed, Signed | 125.00 |
| Shade, Green Feather, Signed, 5 1/2 X 3 5/8 In. | 175.00 |
| Shade, Green Feathered, Gold Outlined, Signed, 6 1/4 X 4 3/4 In.Diam. | 110.00 |
| Shade, Hooked Feather, Signed, Blue | 200.00 |
| Shade, Ivory, Gold & Green, Set Of 4 | 500.00 |
| Shade, Marigold To Blue, Signed, 4 X 5 In.Diam. | 135.00 |
| Shade, Pulled Green Feathers, Gold Border, Signed, 6 3/4 In. | 145.00 |
| Shade, Pumpkin With Opalescent Lining, Scalloped, Signed, 4 In., Pair | 200.00 |
| Shade, Ruffled Bottom, White Swirl Design, Gold Lining, 6 X 8 1/2 In. | 125.00 |
| Shade, Threaded, Scalloped Rim, Signed, Pair | 300.00 |
| Shade, Translucent Gold, 4 Green Panels, 6 In.Diam., Pair | 1000.00 |
| Shade, 16 Swirling Stripes, Gold Interior, 3 1/2 X 3 1/4 In. | 675.00 |
| Shade, 3 Graduated Spheres, Gold, Signed, 4 3/4 In. | 85.00 |
| Vase, Engraved Silver Overlay, Flowing Flower Design, Signed, 15 In. | 4495.00 |
| Vase, Fernlike Design, Opalescent Outside, Gold Inside, Signed, 5 In. | 1150.00 |
| Vase, Frilled, Gold Interior, Green & Gold Feather, Signed, 4 In. | 785.00 |
| Vase, Gold & Blue, Signed, 8 In. | 495.00 |
| Vase, Gold & Purple Highlights, Signed, 4 1/2 X 3 1/2 In. | 377.00 |
| Vase, Gold With Purple Highlights, Signed, 4 1/2 X 3 1/2 In. | 375.00 |
| Vase, Green Feathers, Gold Outline, Crimped Top, Signed, 4 3/4 In. | 675.00 |
| Vase, Green Pulled Feather, Gold Rib Interior, Signed, 6 In. | 1500.00 |
| Vase, Jack-In-The-Pulpit, Iridescent Gold, Signed, 9 1/2 In. | 390.00 |
| Vase, King Tut Pattern, 8 1/2 In. | 850.00 |
| Vase, Lattice Design, Iridescent Gold Inside, Signed, 6 In. | 1350.00 |
| Vase, Moire Pattern Inside, Blue Iridescent, Signed, 7 In. | 465.00 |
| Vase, Pedestal Footed, Marigold Iridescence, Signed, 12 In. | 425.00 |

Vase, Pulled Feather Design, Gray-Green Base, 6 In. ......................................................... 60.00
Vase, Silver Overlay, Dated 1903, Gorham, Signed, 8 X 9 In.Diam. ......................... 1800.00
Vase, Silver Overlay, Gold Feathers, Green Outline, 6 1/4 In. ......................................... 800.00
Vase, Stick, Bulbous Base, Gold Iridescence, Signed, 5 In. .............................................. 300.00
Vase, White & Gold Coiling, Platform Foot, Turquoise Ground, 12 In. ..................... 1400.00

QUILT, see also Textile, Quilt

QUILT, Appliqued Daffodil, Yellow & Orange, White Ground, Amish, Full Size ......................... 150.00
Appliqued Sunbonnets, Hand Stitching, White Ground, 70 X 83 In. ........................... 295.00
Baby, Hand Stitching, Embroidered Animals In Squares ..................................... 40.00
Blue & White Star, Amish, Full Size ........................................................................ 135.00
Bride's, Trapunto, C.1830 ...................................................................................... 800.00
Crazy Pattern, Silk, Crib ........................................................................................ 40.00
Double Wedding Ring Pattern, Scalloped, 78 X 67 In. ........................................ 110.00
Eastern Star, 1932, Detroit, Twin Size .................................................................. 55.00
Flower Garden, Hand-Stitched, Octagonal Pieces, 1920s, 36 X 48 In. ................. 135.00
Grandma's Flower Garden, Amish, Full Size ........................................................ 175.00
Green, Yellow, Red, & Gray Squares, Pennsylvania Mennonite, Double ................. 475.00
Inverted Nine-Patch, Reds & Blues, Signed, Double Size ..................................... 85.00
Log Cabin, Red, Green, & Deep Rose, 62 X 72 In. ............................................... 225.00
Lone Star Pattern, Double Size .............................................................................. 315.00
Multicolored Pinwheel Design, Applique, 7 Ft. 7 In. X 7 Ft. 3 In. ....................... 600.00
Names In Ink On Stripes, C.1880, 7 Ft. 6 In. .........................................Illus 1200.00
Patch, Blue, White, Brown, 68 X 78 In. ................................................................. 135.00
Patch, Pink, Yellow, Blue, Green, 72 X 72 In. ....................................................... 135.00
Patchwork, American, Mid-19th Century, 72 X 90 In. ...................................Illus 325.00
Patchwork, Feather Stitching, Velvet, 66 X 48 In. ................................................. 55.00
Patchwork, Friendship, Signed Blocks, Dated 1862-65, 7 X 7 Ft. 5 In. ............... 2600.00
Red, White, & Blue, Signed & Dated 1931, Double ............................................ 500.00
Signature, Appliqued Stylized Flowers, Dated 1843, 100 In.Square .................... 725.00
Silk Square Within, Multicolor, 54 X 64 In. ........................................................... 45.00
Star Of Texas Pattern, Pastel Colors, 3/4 Size .................................................... 375.00
Star Pattern, Cotton String, Double Size ............................................................... 60.00
Star Pattern, Yellows, Red, & Blues, Green Ground, 90 X 92 In. ........................ 500.00
Top, Sunbonnet Sue, Hand Work, 65 X 90 In. ...................................................... 35.00
Trapunto, Bride's, C.1830, Double Size ................................................................. 800.00

Quilt, Patchwork, American, Mid 19th Century, 72 X 90 In.

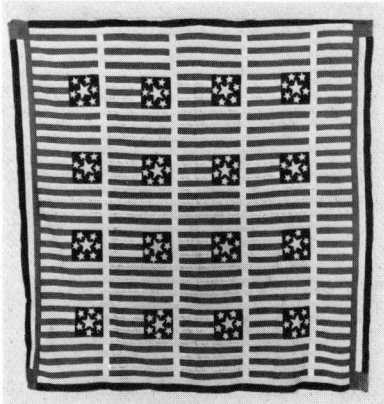

Quilt, Names In Ink On Stripes, C.1880, 7 Ft. 6 In.

Wedding Ring Pattern, C.1920, Twin Size ........................................ 125.00
Wedding Ring Pattern, Calicos, Prints, Double Size ........................ 65.00
White Hearts & Tulip Buds, Yellow, Green, & Orange, C.1900, 84 X 87 In. ........ 275.00
Yo-Yo Pattern, Red Scalloped Border, Orange Lining, Double Size ........ 110.00

HR.
Quimper

*Quimper pottery was made in Quimper, France. Most of the pieces found today were made during the nineteenth and twentieth centuries. A Quimper factory has worked in France since the eighteenth century.*

QUIMPER, Bank, Peasant, Allover Yellow, Signed ................................ 150.00
Bell, Figural, Woman Handle, Signed ................................................ 135.00
Bottle, Figural, Breton Lady, 12 In. ................................................ 130.00
Bowl, Covered, Handled, Inside Design Of Foliage, Gold Rim, 4 3/4 In. ........ 75.00
Bowl, Handled, Yellow & Blue Border, White Ground, Signed ................ 70.00
Cup & Saucer, Colonial Lady & Flowers ........................................ 20.00
Cup & Saucer, Signed P. Formillion, Large ...................................... 95.00
Cup, Coffee, Woman's Figure On Pink Ground, Flowers ...................... 50.00
Cup, Punch, Set Of 4 ................................................................ 100.00
Dish, Diamond Shape, Signed H.B., Yellow ...................................... 16.00
Eggcup & Napkin Ring, Combined, Signed ...................................... 45.00
Eggcup, Figural Man & Woman Holding Cup, Signed, Pair .................. 125.00
Eggcup, On Stand, Signed .......................................................... 110.00
Figurine, Woman Holding Urn On Table, Signed, 11 1/2 In. ................ 350.00
Inkwell, Double ...................................................................... 250.00
Jug, Man, Red Streamers On Hat, Pale Green Glaze, Winged, 6 In. ........ 85.00
Knife Rest ................................................................ 30.00 To 55.00
Oyster Plate .......................................................................... 60.00
Panel, Door, Peasant, White Design, 6 X 2 In. ................................ 70.00
Pitcher, Cream, Signed H.B. ...................................................... 20.00
Pitcher, Green, 7 In. ................................................................ 130.00
Pitcher, Milk, 8 1/2 In. ............................................................ 85.00
Pitcher, Peasant Girl, Flowers, Yellow Ground, Marked, 7 1/2 In. ........ 35.00
Pitcher, Signed, 5 1/2 In. .......................................................... 65.00
Pitcher, Treton Boys Dancing, Red Clay, Signed, 9 1/2 In. ................ 100.00
Planter, Green, Underplate, Man On Front, 5 1/2 In. ........................ 125.00
Planter, Swan Shape ................................................................ 230.00
Plate, Male & Female Figures, White Ground, Salad, Pair .................. 30.00
Plate, Man, Woman, Colored Border, 7 In.Diam., Pair ...................... 55.00
Plate, Orange Bird, Floral Sprays, 5-Dot Flowers, C.1930, 8 In. .......... 35.00
Plate, Peasant At A Task, Flowered Border, Octagon, 9 In., Set Of 4 ...... 400.00
Plate, Rooster & Foliage Center, Multicolored Border, Marked, 10 In. ...... 115.00
Plate, Sailboat Design, 9 1/2 In. .................................................. 75.00
Plate, Scalloped, Women & Men, Blue Ground, Signed, 8 In.Diam. ........ 45.00
Plate, 4 In.Diam. .................................................................... 22.00
Porringer, Rooster Design, 7 1/2 In. ............................................ 75.00
Pot, Espresso, Beige, Brown, Bluebirds, Flowers, Signed, 2 Cup .......... 130.00
Sugar & Creamer, Woman & Flowers, Spatter Handle, Pink, Signed ...... 80.00
Sugar, White, Signed .............................................................. 75.00
Tea Set, Art Deco, Apple Blossom Pattern, 3 Piece .......................... 150.00
Tea Tile .............................................................................. 48.00
Teapot, Man & Woman, Floral Sprays, 19th Century, Marked, Octagonal ...... 450.00
Teapot, Pink Daisies, Pink Band Trim, Large .................................. 80.00
Teapot, Tulips & Dutch Girl, 6 1/2 X 9 In. .................................... 170.00
Teapot, 6 1/2 X 9 In. .............................................................. 185.00
Tray & Box, Covered, Marked .................................................... 55.00
Tray & Cigarette Holder, Peasant Design ...................................... 150.00
Tray, Odetta, Black & Browns, 12 In. .......................................... 110.00
Tray, Pin, Fish, 4 1/2 In. .......................................................... 20.00
Tray, Relish, 11 In.Diam. .......................................................... 65.00
Vase, Bud, Pierced Handled, Portrait Of Lady, 7 In. ........................ 80.00
Vase, Busts Of Breton Man & Woman, Black & Orange, Signed, 9 In. ...... 110.00

**Vase,** Portrait, Man & Woman, Ivory & Brown, 3 3/4 In. .............................................. 85.00
**Wall Pocket,** Peasant Man, Yellow .......................................................................... 95.00

**RADIO, Atwater Kent,** Battery, Horn Speaker, 1924 .................. 675.00
  **Atwater Kent,** Beehive, 1931 ............................................................................. 575.00
  **Atwater Kent,** Cathedral .................................................................................... 250.00
  **Atwater Kent,** Floor Model 1920, A.C. ................................................................ 275.00
  **Atwater Kent,** Model M-55 ................................................................................. 190.00
  **Atwater Kent,** Model 20, 5 Tube, 6 Knobs ......................................................... 150.00
  **Atwater Kent,** Model 40 ....................................................................................... 25.00
  **Atwater Kent,** Model 52 ..................................................................................... 110.00
  **Atwater Kent,** Model 60 ..................................................................................... 180.00
  **Atwater Kent,** Speaker Model F2 ......................................................................... 65.00
  **Belmont,** Table ................................................................................................... 35.00
  **Bottle,** Pepsi Cola ............................................................................................. 375.00
  **Carlson,** 6 Volt, Battery ....................................................................................... 60.00
  **Claratone,** 5 Tube, Battery, 5 Tuning Knobs ........................................................ 67.50
  **Crebe Synchophase Receiver,** Wood Speaker ..................................................... 325.00
  **Crosley,** Table, Cathedral .................................................................................... 62.50
  **Crystal,** Philmore, Boxed ..................................................................................... 45.00
  **David Grimes,** Baby Grand, Duplex, 5 Tube ....................................................... 160.00
  **Dayfan,** 4 Tube, 5 Knobs ................................................................................... 135.00
  **Fada Neutrodyne,** 6 Tuning Dials, Battery, 5 Tube ................................................ 67.50
  **General Electric,** Clock, Potmetal, C.1932 ......................................................... 250.00
  **General Electric,** Model Rc-3 ............................................................................. 130.00
  **Goldentone,** Standard & Short Wave, Battery, C.1937 ........................................... 55.00
  **Hallicrafters,** Military, Sky Ranger, Model S-39a ................................................... 27.50
  **Jakson Bell,** Dome ............................................................................................. 85.00
  **Majestic,** Cathedral .......................................................................................... 240.00
  **Majestic,** Model 90 ........................................................................................... 125.00
  **Majestic,** Model 130-A ...................................................................................... 125.00
  **Marshall Cathedral,** Large ................................................................................ 160.00
  **Overseas,** Hallicrafter ......................................................................................... 75.00
  **Parmak,** 6 Volt, Battery ....................................................................................... 60.00
  **Philco,** Battery, Bakelite ...................................................................................... 60.00
  **Philco,** Battery, Bakelite, Model 40-90 ................................................................. 60.00
  **Philco,** Cathedral ............................................................................................... 85.00
  **Philco,** Model 87 .............................................................................................. 215.00
  **Philmore,** Crystal Set, Earphone, Boxed ............................................................ 110.00
  **R.C.A.,** Beehive ............................................................................................... 120.00
  **R.C.A.,** Gold Plastic Table Model, Label, 12 1/2 X 9 3/4 X 8 1/4 In. ..................... 59.00
  **R.C.A.,** 110 Volt, 11 X 26 X 11 In. ..................................................................... 35.00
  **Radiola III,** R.C.A., Instruction Book .................................. 140.00 To 275.00
  **Radiola,** Model 33 ........................................................................................... 150.00
  **Radiola,** R.C.A., Model 80 ................................................................................ 175.00
  **Radiola,** Speaker Model 100a, Service Book, 1927 .............................................. 80.00
  **Silvertone,** Push Button, Table Model, Regular & Shortwave, 1940s ....................... 37.00
  **Westinghouse,** Jukebox Type, C.1940 ................................................................. 35.00

**RAILROAD, Ashtray,** Floor, Weighted, Southern Pacific Lines, Medallion On Base ................ 185.00
  **Ashtray,** Union Pacific, Sun Valley, Idaho .............................................................. 6.00
  **Badge,** Cap, Flagman ........................................................................................ 12.50
  **Badge,** Conductor's, Upton R.R. ......................................................................... 45.00
  **Badge,** Hat, Brakeman's, C.& O. R.R. .................................................................. 20.00
  **Badge,** Police, Erie R.R., Shield, Logo Center, Hallmarked ..................................... 65.00
  **Bell,** Bronze, Steam Locomotive, 9 X 18 In. ....................................................... 375.00
  **Bell,** Locomotive, Mounting Bracket, 12 In.Diam. ................................................ 400.00
  **Bell,** Locomotive, Yoke & Clapper, Brass, 10 X 13 In. .......................................... 700.00
  **Bell,** Marked 312, Brass, 16 1/2 In. ..................................................................... 60.00
  **Blotter,** Dixie Flyer, N.C. & St.Louis, 1920s .......................................................... 9.00
  **Bowl,** Footed, Pacific Overland ........................................................................... 30.00
  **Bowl,** Union Pacific, Harriman Blue, 6 In. ............................................................ 25.00
  **Bowl,** Vegetable, Union Pacific Streamline, Small .................................................. 5.95

| | |
|---|---|
| **Box,** Held Matches, Wax & Official Seal, Tin | 40.00 |
| **Bucket,** Fire, Santa Fe R.R., Cone Shape | 38.00 |
| **Cabinet,** Map, 20th Century, Michigan & Pennsylvania, Oak Pullouts | 195.00 |
| **Calendar,** 1930, Great Northern R.R., Famous Indians, 8 X 10 In. | 15.00 |
| **Can,** Kerosene, C.N.W. R.R. | 11.00 |
| **Can,** Watering, For Steam Engine, P.R.R. Within Keystone, Tin, 12 In. | 25.00 |
| **Cap,** Flagman | 15.00 |
| **Cap,** Officer, Baltimore, Badge No.1911 | 19.00 |
| **Case,** Ticket, S Roll, Oak, 23 X 2, In. | 150.00 |
| **Catcher,** Mail Bag | 200.00 |
| **Celery,** Atlantic Coastline & Carolina, 10 In. | 16.50 |
| **Celery,** Bleeding Blue, Santa Fe, 5 3/4 X 12 1/2 In. | 175.00 |
| **Chocolate Pot,** Santa Fe, California Poppy, 6 In. | 65.00 |
| **Coffee Cup,** Pedestal, Union Pacific, Overland Shield, Pair | 25.00 |
| **Coffeepot,** Individual, Mimbreno Indian, Santa Fe, Syracuse | 100.00 |
| **Coverlet,** Canadian Natl. R.R., Maple Leaf Pattern, 45 X 80 In. | 125.00 |
| **Cup & Saucer,** C & O Lines, Martha Washington, Demitasse | 325.00 |
| **Cup & Saucer,** Central Pacific Logo, Demitasse | 12.00 |
| **Cup & Saucer,** N.Y.C., 9 In. | 35.00 |
| **Cup,** Marked, P.R.R., Tin | 5.00 |
| **Cuspidor,** Pullman, Brass Nickel Plated | 90.00 |
| **Dial,** Train On Line, Line Clear, Line Closed, Brass Bell On Bottom | 300.00 |
| **Eagle,** Locomotive, Cast Iron | 300.00 |
| **Glass,** The Chief, Reverse Picture, 25 In. | 275.00 |
| **Glass,** Whiskey, B & O | 18.00 |
| **Hat,** Ticket Agent, M.K.T. | 45.00 |
| **Heater,** Boxcar, Preco, Model GB2, Alcohol, Rock Island Lines | 45.00 |
| **Holder,** Globe & Smoke Bell, Wall Bracket, Wabash R.R. | 35.00 |
| **Holder,** Menu, Burlington Zephyr Logo, International Silver | 45.00 |
| **Key,** Coach, Adlake, Brass | 7.50 |
| **Key,** Switch, Santa Fe, A. & W., Brass | 20.00 |
| **Key,** Switch, Set Of 31 | 650.00 |
| **Knife,** Albany, Santa Fe | 15.00 |
| **Knife,** Pocket, P.R.R. | 3.25 |
| **Knife,** 2 Blade, B. & O.R.R. | 4.00 |
| **Ladder,** Berth, C. & O., Aluminum | 57.00 |
| **Lamp,** A. & W. Co., Candle, Brass, 1907 | 45.00 |
| **Lamp,** Caboose, Bracket, Aladdin, Model C., Brass | 50.00 |
| **Lamp,** Caboose, Kerosene, Pair | 65.00 |
| **Lamp,** Caboose, Red & Amber Lens, P.R.R. | 85.00 |
| **Lamp,** Caboose, Shade & Bracket, Kerosene, Brass | 37.50 |
| **Lamp,** Caboose, Wabash R.R. | 85.00 |
| **Lamp,** Candle, Parlor Car, Brass | 32.50 |
| **Lamp,** Kerosene, Adlake, Clear Globe, N.Y.C., 3 1/4 In. | 22.00 |
| **Lamp,** Kerosene, Switch, Bell Bottom | 95.00 |
| **Lamp,** Rayo, Green Cased Shade, Nickel Plated | 65.00 |
| **Lamp,** Switch Stand, Adlake, 2 Red & 2 Blue Lenses | 125.00 |
| **Lantern,** Black Over Tin, British | 34.00 |
| **Lantern,** Brakeman's, Casey, P.R.R. Globe, Keystone Monogram | 40.00 |
| **Lantern,** Carbide | 80.00 |
| **Lantern,** Chesapeake & Ohio, Red Globe | 38.00 |
| **Lantern,** Cobalt Globe, Signed, Penn R.R. | 125.00 |
| **Lantern,** Dietz, D.L. & W.R.R. | 60.00 |
| **Lantern,** Dietz, N.Y. Central, Clear Globe | 19.00 |
| **Lantern,** Dietz, N.Y.C. Lines, Cast Globe | 43.00 |
| **Lantern,** Dietz, N.Y.C., Cast Globe | 42.00 |
| **Lantern,** Dressel, Arlington, Va., Lens & Burner | 88.00 |
| **Lantern,** Embury, No. 40, Red Glass Globe, Marked | 25.00 |
| **Lantern,** Fire Station, Engraved Hibernia, Brass | 70.00 |
| **Lantern,** Frame & Globe, S.T.Co., 4 5/8 In. | 50.00 |
| **Lantern,** Hand, Dietz Vesta, New York Central R.R. | 26.00 |
| **Lantern,** Hand, Long Island, Short Blue Globe | 35.00 |
| **Lantern,** Illinois Central, Red Globe, Brass Plated | 75.00 |

| | |
|---|---:|
| **Lantern,** Inspector, D.L. & W.R.R. | 75.00 |
| **Lantern,** N.Y. & N.H.R.R., Ruby Globe | 40.00 |
| **Lantern,** Penn, Signed Cobalt Globe | 125.00 |
| **Lantern,** Red Globe, Burlington Route | 38.00 |
| **Lantern,** Red Paint, Clear Globe, Marked Syracuse, N.Y., Dietz | 15.00 |
| **Lantern,** Southern Railway, Red Globe | 38.00 |
| **Lantern,** Switch, Short Globe | 39.50 |
| **Light,** Coach, Patented 1907 | 45.00 |
| **Lighter,** Cigarette, Desk, Kansas City Southern Lines | 25.00 |
| **Lights,** Steam Engine, Marker, Green & White, Dated 1924 | 200.00 |
| **Lock,** Adlake, P.C.R.R., Brass | 35.00 |
| **Lock,** I.C.G.R.R., Key, Cast Iron | 15.00 |
| **Lock,** Main Central | 40.00 |
| **Lock,** Signal, G.N.R.R., Brass | 55.00 |
| **Lock,** Signal, Lackawanna, Embossed, Yale, Brass | 30.00 |
| **Lock,** Signal, P. & R., Brass | 26.00 |
| **Lock,** South Pacific R.R., Pair | 35.00 |
| **Lock,** Switch, Heart Shaped, Script, P.R.R., Brass | 45.00 |
| **Lock,** Switch, Heart Shaped, Union Pacific, Bronze | 67.50 |
| **Lock,** Switch, Key, N.Y.N.H.& H.R.R., Brass | 55.00 |
| **Lock,** Switch, Santa Fe, Keen Kutter, E.C.Simmons Co.Brass | 100.00 |
| **Lock,** Switch, Southern Ohio, Banjo Shaped, Iron | 25.00 |
| **Map,** Cumberland R.R., 1900, Set Of 78 | 19.00 |
| **Map,** Wall, Southern Pacific Lines, 1969, 36 X 5 In. | 35.00 |
| **Mug,** Coffee, Amtrak, Logo, Set Of 4 | 14.00 |
| **Padlock,** K.C.T.R.R., Union Station, Corbin, Brass | 65.00 |
| **Padlock,** Key, Heart Shaped, C. & N.W.R., Brass | 65.00 |
| **Padlock,** Sante Fe, Keen Kutter, Brass | 135.00 |
| **Paperweight,** Keystone, P.R.R. Logo, Nickel Plated Brass | 60.00 |
| **Pencil,** Union Pacific, 1 Dozen | 2.75 |
| **Pitcher,** Water, Southern Pacific, International Silver, 64 Ounce | 175.00 |
| **Plate,** Dinner, Adobe Design, Santa Fe, 10 In. | 80.00 |
| **Plate,** Prairie Mountain Wildflower, South Pacific, 5 1/2 In. | 11.00 |
| **Plate,** Southern Pacific R.R., Backstamp, Dated 1931 | 30.00 |
| **Plate,** Syracuse China, Great Northern, 7 In. | 25.00 |
| **Plate,** Union Pacific Tea Co., 1907 | 28.00 |
| **Platter,** Desert Flower, Union Pacific, Large | 48.00 |
| **Platter,** Milwaukee R.R., Backstamped, Oval, 8 In. | 18.00 To 28.00 |
| **Platter,** Northern Pacific, Eagle | 45.00 |
| **Platter,** Peacock, Milwaukee, Small | 32.00 |
| **Platter,** Pennsylvania Keystone, 12 In. | 33.00 |
| **Poster,** Go Pullman Next Time, Porter & Passengers, 23 X 18 In. | 30.00 |
| **Ruler,** Norfolk & Western R.R., Metal, 6 In. | 3.00 |
| **Scale,** Sliding, Clamps On Rails, 2 Levels, Buff Mfg., Co. | 150.00 |
| **Side Lamp,** Coach, Kerosene, Marked V. & T., Brass | 195.00 |
| **Sign,** Lamp, Caboose, Wabash R.R. | 85.00 |
| **Sign,** Providence Line For New York, Wooden | 35.00 |
| **Sign,** Railroad Private Property, Porcelain, 1939, 16 X 24 In. | 65.00 |
| **Sign,** Stop Tank Car Connected, Blue & White, Porcelain, 15 X 12 In. | 40.00 |
| **Sign,** Warning Close Clearance, Porcelain, Red & White, 20 X 12 In. | 45.00 |
| **Spittoon,** C. & E.l. R.R., Brass | 150.00 |
| **Spittoon,** Pullman Parlor Works, Chicago, Nickel Plated | 90.00 |
| **Stand,** Smoking, Rock Island Lines | 79.00 |
| **Step Stool,** Pullman, 14 1/2 X 11 1/2 X 11 In. | 130.00 |
| **Step Stool,** Seaboard Railroad, 14 X 9 1/2 X 10 In. | 135.00 |
| **Stove,** Caboose, M.K. & T. R.R. | 225.00 |
| **Stove,** Depot, Sante Fe Station, Burlingame, Kansas | 375.00 |
| **Sugar,** Missouri Pacific, Sterling Silver | 26.00 |
| **Switch Lock,** Union Pacific, Heart Shaped, Key, Bronze | 67.50 |
| **Switch Stand,** C.C.C. & St.L., Harp Style | 100.00 |
| **Switch,** Single Position, 2 Stops, Brass, C.1900, 2 5/8 X 2 1/8 In. | 25.00 |
| **Syrup,** Nickel Plate Railroad, Silver Plate, Signed | 25.00 |
| **Teapot,** Curved Spout, Southern Pacific R.R., Reed & Barton | 20.00 |

Telegraph Receiver, On Stand, Hooded .................................................................. 150.00
Telegraph Sounder, Bunnell ................................................................................... 65.00
Ticket-Taker, Depot, Chicago, Oak ........................................................................ 275.00
Tie Clasp, Figural, Train, A.T. & S.F. R.R. ............................................................ 12.50
Tongs, Sugar, Northern Pacific ............................................................................. 25.00
Tongs, Sugar, Southern Pacific ............................................................ 21.00 To 45.00
Tool, Adjustable Monkey Wrench, A.T. & S.F. R.R. ............................................. 17.50
Tool, Wrench, Adjustable, B. & O. R.R. ................................................................ 18.50
Torch, Marked P.R.R., Cast Iron ........................................................................... 12.50
Towel, Santa Fe .................................................................................................... 6.50
Tray, Rockford High Grade Watches, Tin, 5 X 3 1/2 In.Diam. ............................. 75.00
Truck, Baggage, Rubber Tires .............................................................................. 150.00
Tumbler, Southern Railway, Logo, Boxed, Set Of 6 ............................................. 18.00
Uniform, Conductor, C.& N.W.R.R. ...................................................................... 110.00
Uniform, Conductor's, Vest, Tie, Hat, Ticket Punch, Rock Island Lines .............. 60.00
Watch Fob, Bucyrus, Erie ..................................................................................... 14.00
Whistle, Caboose, Backup, Sherburne Co., Boston, Mass., Bronze ..................... 65.00
Whistle, Caboose, Peanut-Shaped, C.& O. .......................................................... 30.00
Whistle, Locomotive, Brass, 8 In. ......................................................................... 60.00
Whistle, Peanut, Brass, Backup, Caboose ........................................................... 35.00
Whistle, Sherburne Co., Brass, Caboose ...................................................... 37.00 To 65.00
Whistle, Steam, Lunkenheimer, Single Chime, Brass, 1 X 12 In. ........................ 300.00
Wrench, A.T. & S.F. R.R., Cast Iron ...................................................................... 7.50
Wrench, Curved Double End, Union Pacific, 20 In. ............................................. 20.00
Wrench, Monkey, Adjustable, A.T. & S.F.R.R., 8 In. ............................................ 17.50
Wrench, S, Adjustable, B. & O. R.R. ..................................................................... 18.50
     **RAINBOW, see Mother-of-Pearl; Satin Glass**
RAZOR, Case Co., Amber Celluloid ...................................................................... 25.00
Durham Duplex, Box ............................................................................................. 7.00
Eagle, Hand-Painted Shaving Set, German ......................................................... 85.00
Gillet, Marked Use Ivory Soap, Metal Case ......................................................... 8.50
Griffin ..................................................................................................................... 5.00
Hone, Swastika ...................................................................................................... 30.00
Keen Kutter, Safety, Boxed ................................................................................... 5.00
Kriss Kross, Hand Crank, Reversing Mechanical Stropper, 1921 ........................ 20.00
Lake Side Cutlery, Army & Navy ........................................................................... 18.00
Mustache, 1889, DePew's ..................................................................................... 35.00
Pipe, George Wastenholm, Maple Handles ......................................................... 20.00
Safety Razor Co., Valet Autostrop, Brass, Carton ............................................... 5.00
Safety, Autostrop, Box, Directions, Baldes ......................................................... 5.00
Safety, Keen Kutter, Boxed .......................................................................... 5.00 To 9.50
Safety, Single Blade, Dated 1909, Homer Merchant ........................................... 15.00
Shumate, Ben Hur .................................................................................................. 5.00
Stahly, Live Blade Spring, Vibrating, Brass ......................................................... 22.50
Straight, Dixie, Mottled Green & White Handle ................................................... 12.00
Straight, Durham Duplex, Celluloid Handle, Case, Patent 1907 ......................... 15.00
Straight, Etched Ship, S.S.Imperator On Balde, Imperial Razor ......................... 13.00
Straight, Holly Mfg., Co. ....................................................................................... 20.00
Straight, Ivory Handled, Engraved Design, Germany, 6 In. ................................. 25.00
Straight, J.R.Torrey, Gray Woodgrain Celluloid ................................................... 8.00
Straight, McLaughlin's Coffee ............................................................................... 10.00
Straight, Our Chief, Indian Embossed Blade, Ivory Handle ................................ 36.00
Straight, Silver Beauty, Case ................................................................................ 6.00
Straight, Wade & Butcher, Sheffield ..................................................................... 15.00
Straight, West Point Model, Black Handle, Reppenhagen, Germany .................. 15.00
Strop, Koken, Inner Wood Frame .......................................................................... 10.00
Strop, Kriss Kross .................................................................................................. 6.00
Strop, Silver Plated Cylindrical Holder ................................................................. 65.00
Strop, Valet Automatic, Tin Box, Blades .............................................................. 10.00
Torrey, Case .......................................................................................................... 5.00
     **REAMER, see also Kitchen, Reamer**
REAMER, Amber Glass .......................................................................................... 10.00
Beige With Maroon, Yellow Flower, Walker, Pottery ........................................... 25.00

Clown, Orange, Yellow, & White, 5 In. ........................................................................ 40.00
Clown, Orange, 6 In. .................................................................................................. 28.00
Clown, Pink, 6 In. ...................................................................................................... 28.00
Clown, 7 In. ............................................................................................................... 48.00
Cone Shape, Lip & Handle, Signed Anchor Hocking ................................................ 20.00
Crisscross, Green, Large ........................................................................................... 15.00
Duck ......................................................................................................................... 30.00
Floral Border, Made In Germany, 3 In. ...................................................................... 30.00
Grapefruit, Holes In Perimeter Drop Juice Into Cup, 4 1/2 X 7 In. .............................. 8.00
Handled, Aluminum ................................................................................................... 4.00
High Cone, Signed Sunkist ........................................................................................ 25.00
Juice, Vaseline Glass ................................................................................................ 22.50
Lemon, Cast Iron .......................................................................... 10.00 To 18.00
Lemon, Crisscross, Spout At Bottom Of Head, Crystal ............................................... 6.00
Lemon, White Ironstone Insert, Cast Iron, Patent 1868 .............................................. 36.00
Lemon, William's, Cast Iron & Glass ......................................................................... 35.00
Lemon, Wooden, 11 In. ................................................................... 28.00 To 37.00
Milk Glass, White, Sunkist ......................................................................................... 10.00
Opaline Blue, Sunkist ............................................................................................... 35.00
Orange, Crisscross, 4 X 7 1/4 In. .............................................................................. 12.00
Orange, Easley's New Model, Patent 1909, Tab Handle, 5 1/4 In. ............................... 6.00
Orange, Jeanette Glass, Amber, 3 3/4 X 7 In. ............................................................. 5.00
Orange, Rib Type Pattern, Hocking Glass, 3 1/2 X 6 3/4 In. ........................................ 5.00
Orange, Top Sets Into Retainer, Signed, 1 3/4 X 5 In. ................................................. 10.00
Pink Glass, 2 Piece ................................................................................................... 28.00
Scalloped, Fry ........................................................................................................... 35.00
Sigma, Full Bodied Clown .......................................................................................... 17.00
Sunkist, Blue Milk Glass ................................................................. 50.00 To 100.00
Sunkist, Custard Glass .............................................................................................. 40.00
Sunkist, Green Milk Glass .......................................................................................... 35.00
Sunkist, Jadite .......................................................................................................... 18.00
Sunkist, Pink ............................................................................................................. 40.00
Sunkist, Thatcher ...................................................................................................... 12.00
Sunkist, White Milk Glass ............................................................... 12.00 To 20.00
Sunkist, Yellow ......................................................................................................... 37.00
Yellow, Redwing, Pitcher ........................................................................................... 60.00

RED GOOSE, Bus, Wooden ....................................................................................... 26.00
Clicker ...................................................................................................................... 4.50
Top, Spinner ............................................................................................................. 4.00
Whirlybird ................................................................................................................. 8.00
Whistle ..................................................................................................................... 6.00

*The Red Wing Pottery of Red Wing, Minnesota, was a firm started in
1878. It was not until the 1920s that art pottery was made. It closed in
1967. Rumrill pottery was made for George Rumrill by the Red Wing
Pottery Company and other firms. It was sold in the 1930s.*

RED WING, Ashtray, Figural Wing ............................................................................... 15.00
Ashtray, Figural, Baseball, Minnesota Twins ............................................................. 35.00
Ashtray, Red ............................................................................................................. 30.00
Bowl, Batter, Sponge Band ........................................................................................ 350.00
Bowl, Blue & Rust Sponge, 7 In. ............................................................................... 25.00
Bowl, Design On Outside & Inside Top, Signed, 3 1/2 X 7 1/4 In. ............................... 25.00
Bowl, Green Inside, Green Design Outside, Marked, 7 1/2 In. ..................................... 45.00
Bowl, Lampert Yards, Saffron, 1937 .......................................................................... 40.00
Bowl, Salad, Hand-Painted Fruit, Brown Glazed, 11 In. .............................................. 22.50
Butter, Bobwhite ...................................................................................................... 30.00
Candlestick, Beige With Floral Cut, Pair .................................................................... 15.00
Casserole, Bobwhite, Iron Stand, 4 Quart ................................................................. 35.00
Churn, Union Oval Over Birch Leaves, 2 Gallon ......................................................... 65.00
Compote, Green Matte, 6 1/4 X 8 In. ......................................................................... 12.00
Console Bowl, Deer, Cream, 12 In. ............................................................................ 25.00
Console Set, Bowl, Double Candleholders, Flowers & Frog ......................................... 35.00

Cookie Jar, Apple, Yellow ............................................................... 22.00
Cookie Jar, Baker, Blue ............................................... 25.00 To 35.00
Cookie Jar, Baker, Yellow ............................................................... 25.00
Cookie Jar, Bobwhite ...................................................................... 45.00
Cookie Jar, Bunny, Blue .................................................................. 20.00
Cookie Jar, Dutch Girl, Turquoise .................................................. 25.00
Cookie Jar, Dutch Girl, Yellow ................................... 18.00 To 28.00
Cookie Jar, Monk, Beige .................................................................. 25.00
Cookie Jar, Monk, Thou Shall Not Steal, Green ........................... 25.00
Cookie Jar, Sponge Band ............................................ 65.00 To 88.00
Cookie Jar, Sponge Band, Lid ....................................................... 285.00
Creamer, Bobwhite ....................................................... 12.00 To 15.00
Crock, Wire Handles, 5 Gallon ....................................................... 30.00
Cup & Saucer, Demitasse, Twig & Green Berries, White ............. 12.00
Custard, Grayline ............................................................................ 90.00
Custard, Sponge Band ..................................................................... 85.00
Dish, Baking & Serving, Open, Dark Brown, 2 X 4 1/2 In., Pair ..... 8.50
Dish, Relish, Divided, Bobwhite ................................. 14.00 To 20.00
Dish, Relish, Oatmeal, 12 1/2 In. ................................................. 12.00
Feeder, Chick, Ko-Rec .................................................................... 45.00
Feeder, Poultry, Advertising ...................................... 65.00 To 78.00
Flowerpot, Frog Shaped .................................................................... 7.50
Jar, Beater, Blue Band ..................................................................... 28.00
Jar, Fruit, 1/2 Gallon ...................................................................... 87.00
Jar, Preserve, Brown, 6 1/2 In. ..................................................... 50.00
Jar, Raised Letters On Bottom, 1 Gallon ...................................... 30.00
Jar, Refrigerator, Small .................................................................. 85.00
Jardiniere, Brushstroke .................................................................. 60.00
Jardiniere, Green Glazed Interior, Profile Of Indian, 8 In. ............. 70.00
Jardiniere, Pedestal, Matte Pink Flowers, Grained Ground, 30 In. ...... 260.00
Jug, Beehive Shaped, Brown, 1/2 Gallon ...................................... 30.00
Jug, Souvenir Of Red Wing, Miniature ........................................... 95.00
Juicer, Yellow, Pedestal ................................................................ 125.00
Mug, Hamm's Beer ........................................................................... 65.00
Mug, Old Colony Brewing ................................................................ 18.00
Pitcher, Blue & Gray Spatter ....................................................... 135.00
Pitcher, Bobwhite, 12 In. .......................................... 18.00 To 25.00
Pitcher, Bulbous, Paper Label, 5 In. .............................................. 35.00
Pitcher, Cherries & Leaves, Blue-Gray, 6 In. ............................... 65.00
Pitcher, Figural, Girl, Yellow .......................................................... 30.00
Pitcher, Ice Lip, Orange, 8 In. ........................................................ 16.00
Pitcher, Sponge Band ............................................. 110.00 To 130.00
Pitcher, Water, Bobwhite ............................................................... 12.50
Pitcher, Water, Brown, Green Trim ................................................ 25.00
Pitcher, Water, Refrigerator, Kelvinator, White Pottery, Lid ........ 22.00
Planter, Aqua, 4 X 14 In. ................................................................ 15.00
Planter, Boat Shaped ........................................................................ 7.00
Planter, White Swan, 5 In. ............................................................... 6.00
Plate, Iris, 10 1/4 In. ........................................................................ 7.00
Plate, Sandwich, Iris, Hand-Painted, Signed .................................. 9.00
Salt & Pepper, Bobwhite ................................................................. 20.00
Salt & Pepper, Hamm's Brewery ................................................... 40.00
Salt, Hanging, Sponge Band ......................................................... 500.00
Shoe, High Button .......................................................................... 125.00
Sugar, Covered, Bobwhite ............................................................. 10.00
Teapot, Bobwhite, Warmer ............................................................ 35.00
Tile, Centennial, Yellow .................................................................. 30.00
Tray, Hors D'Oeuvre, Bobwhite ..................................................... 35.00
Vase, Brown, Leaf Cluster, 7 In. .................................................... 18.00
Vase, Brushware, 8 1/2 In. ........................................................... 270.00
Vase, Chartreuse, Dark Brown Interior, 7 1/4 In. ........................... 5.50
Vase, Cobalt Blue, Molded Flowers, Art Pottery, 13 In. ............... 50.00
Vase, Cornucopia, Pink, 6 In., Pair ............................................... 12.50

| | |
|---|---|
| **Vase,** Dark Green, 12 In. | 27.00 |
| **Vase,** Double Handled, Rust Interior, Gray, 7 1/2 In. | 14.00 |
| **Vase,** Embossed Flowers, 8 In. | 15.00 |
| **Vase,** Green & Yellow Lining, Handled, 8 1/4 In. | 12.00 |
| **Vase,** Handled, Gray, Rust Interior, Flossy Finish, 7 1/2 In. | 14.00 |
| **Vase,** Maroon, 2 Handles, 9 1/2 In. | 35.00 |
| **Vase,** Metallic Brown, Avocado Green Interior, 8 In. | 27.00 |
| **Vase,** Pink, 8 In. | 8.00 |
| **Vase,** Rose Basket, Pink, 10 In. | 18.00 |
| **Vase,** Rose In Relief, 10 In. | 20.00 |
| **Vase,** White, 7 1/2 In. | 10.00 |
| **Vase,** Woman's Face Each Side, Blown Out, Aqua, 12 In. | 45.00 |
| **Vase,** Yellow, Bow Design, 10 In. | 25.00 |
| **Wall Pocket,** Fiddle Shape, Pink | 8.00 |
| **Wall Pocket,** Violin Shape, Strings In Envelope, Pair | 32.00 |
| **Water Cooler,** 5 Gallon | 120.00 |
| **Waterer,** Chicken, Klondike Incubator Co., Marked | 37.50 |

*Redware is a hard red stoneware that originated in the late 1600s and continues to be made. The term is also used to describe any common clay pottery that is reddish in color.*

| | |
|---|---|
| **REDWARE, Ashtray,** Signed, Murray Quarry Tile | 6.00 |
| **Bank,** Hen On Nest, 6 X 6 In. | 55.00 |
| **Beanpot,** Glazed Inside, Incised Shoulder, B.W.Griffin, 7 & 5 In., Pr. | 265.00 |
| **Bottle,** Harvest, Ring, Orange, 8 1/2 In. | 195.00 |
| **Bottle,** Ring, Orangy Sienna Glaze, 7 1/2 In. | 165.00 |
| **Bowl,** Cover, Impressed John Bell, Waynesboro, Pa., 8 In.Diam. | 45.00 |
| **Bowl,** Inscribed, Present To Mrs.Robson, 1st, Jan.1886 | 550.00 |
| **Bowl,** Ridged, 10 1/2 In.Diam. | 70.00 |
| **Bowl,** Sussex Slipware, 19th Century, 14 1/2 X 11 1/4 X 3 In. | 300.00 |
| **Crock,** Narrow Neck, 8 1/2 In. | 68.00 |
| **Crock,** Storage, Ovoid Body, Line Design, Fitted Cover, 12 1/4 In. | 275.00 |
| **Cup,** Custard, Olive Green Glaze, 3 1/4 In. | 25.00 |
| **Dish,** Crimped, Combed & Trailed Slip, English, 13 3/4 X 17 1/2 In. | 825.00 |
| **Dish,** Loaf, Brown With Cream Slip Trailing, 13 X 14 1/2 In. | 825.00 |
| **Flask,** Dark Splotches, 8 3/4 In. | 195.00 |
| **Flower Frog,** Manganese Splotches Over Brown Glaze, 4 1/2 X 5 In. | 120.00 |
| **Flowerpot,** Attached Saucer, White Glaze, Marked S.Bell, 6 1/4 In. | 100.00 |
| **Jar,** Cover, Maine, Mustard Glaze, 6 1/2 In. | 130.00 To 155.00 |
| **Jar,** Dark Orangy Red Glaze, Small | 125.00 |
| **Jug,** Cider, Applied Handle & Pouring Spout, Mottled, Pennsylvania, 10 In. | 375.00 |
| **Jug,** Coggle Wheel Lines At Shoulder, Green Mustard, Speckled, 7 In. | 168.00 |
| **Jug,** Coggle Wheel Lines At Top, Rust To Brown, 4 1/2 In. | 85.00 |
| **Jug,** Orange-Red Glaze, 11 1/2 In. | 140.00 |
| **Jug,** Scarlet Rust, 7 In. | 60.00 |
| **Jug,** Yellow Slip Design | 150.00 |
| **Mold Cake,** Tube Type | 27.50 |
| **Mold,** Fish | 225.00 |
| **Mold,** Turk's Head, Glazed, 2 1/2 X 7 1/4 In.Diam. | 50.00 |
| **Pan,** Milk, Northeast, 13 1/2 In.Diam. | 70.00 |
| **Pie Plate,** Crackled Orange-Red Glaze, Flat Bottom, 8 In. | 40.00 |
| **Pitcher,** Dark Brown Glaze, 4 Gallon | 20.00 |
| **Pitcher,** Milk, Reddish Brown Glaze, Uneven Pale Spots, 4 3/4 In. | 65.00 |
| **Pitcher,** Signed Brown Pottery, Miniature | 85.00 |
| **Plate,** Brown Glaze, Touch Of Green, 2 1/2 X 13 1/4 In. | 75.00 |
| **Plate,** Orange Glaze, Swirls Of Green, 2 5/8 X 12 1/4 In. | 75.00 |
| **Plate,** Pie, Brown Glaze With Freckles & Streaks, 7 In.Diam. | 38.00 |
| **Porringer,** Handled, Manganese Glaze, 3 1/2 In. | 40.00 |
| **Pot,** Herb, Dark Brown Glaze, 5 3/4 X 4 3/4 In.Diam. | 25.00 |
| **Pot,** Rolled Edge, 4 1/4 In. | 35.00 |
| **Teapot,** Blue Enamel, Gold Tracing | 25.00 |
|     **REGOUT, see Maastricht** | |

**REVERSE PAINTING, see Painting, Reverse On Glass**

*Richard was the mark used on acid-etched cameo glass vases, bowls, night-lights, and lamps in Lorraine, France, during the 1920s.*

| | |
|---|---|
| **RICHARD, Bottle,** Perfume, Blue Flowers, Yellow Ground, Signed, 5 1/2 In. | 455.00 |
| **Bowl,** Footed, Orange Satin Bowl, Clover Leaves, Signed, 4 1/2 In. | 250.00 |
| **Bowl,** Village Scene, Light Brown On Chartreuse Body, Signed, 7 In. | 675.00 |
| **Box,** 3 Colored Flowers, Yellow Ground, Signed, 3 1/4 In.Diam. | 400.00 |
| **Lamp,** Cameo, Blue Mountains, Boat, Water, Trees, Yellow, 11 3/4 In. | 2450.00 |
| **Vase,** Blue Floral, Bright Red Ground, Label, Signed, 4 In. | 550.00 |
| **Vase,** Blue Flowers & Leaves, Orange Ground, Signed, 8 3/4 In. | 450.00 |
| **Vase,** Chateau Scenic, Red Satin Ground, Signed, 14 1/8 In. | 895.00 |
| **Vase,** Farm & Shore Scene, Gold Ground, Signed, 13 1/8 In. | 650.00 |
| **Vase,** Green, White, Rose Frosted, Signed, 12 1/4 In. | 695.00 |
| **Vase,** Hot Pink Cameo Flowers, Blue Ground, 8 1/2 In. | 595.00 |
| **Vase,** Lake, Mountains, Brown, Citron, Footed, Signed, 13 1/2 In. | 625.00 |
| **Vase,** Navy Blue On Opaque Orange Satin, 2 Cuttings, Signed, 10 In. | 950.00 |
| **Vase,** Navy Blue Scene, Trees, Water, & Chateau, Signed, 14 1/8 In. | 950.00 |
| **Vase,** Opaque Lime Green, Satin Ground, Flowers, Signed, 4 1/4 In. | 165.00 |
| **Vase,** Royal Blue Orchid, Rose Body, Signed, 8 In. | 425.00 |
| **Vase,** Scenic, Boats, Pink Ground, Brown Landscape, Signed, 3 5/8 In. | 275.00 |
| **Vase,** Shaded Blue Flowers, Red Ground, Sticker, Signed, 4 In. | 550.00 |
| **Vase,** Translucent Gold Ground, Blue Mountain Scene, 10 1/8 In. | 575.00 |
| **Wine,** Scene On Rose Ground, Clear Stem & Foot, Signed, 7 7/8 In. | 425.00 |

*Ridgway pottery has been made in the Staffordshire district in England since 1808 by a series of companies with the name Ridgway. The transfer-design dinner sets are the most widely known product. They are still being made.*

**RIDGWAY, see also Flow Blue**

| | |
|---|---|
| **RIDGWAY, Berry Bowl,** Budge Pattern, Scalloped, Set Of 6 | 50.00 |
| **Bowl,** Coaching Days, Scenic, Marked, 9 3/8 In. | 55.00 |
| **Bowl,** Coaching Days, 6 1/2 X 6 1/2 In.Diam. | 40.00 |
| **Coffee Set,** Coaching Days & Coaching Ways, 15 Piece | 185.00 |
| **Cup & Saucer,** Hilditch, Blue Willow, C.1825 | 30.00 |
| **Cup & Saucer,** Plate, Coaching Days, 7 In. | 60.00 |
| **Dish,** Cheese, Covered, Lahore Pattern, Gold Trim, 6 X 10 1/2 X 12 In. | 135.00 |
| **Dish,** Coaching Days, Oval, 4 1/2 X 9 1/2 In. | 35.00 |
| **Dish,** Vegetable, Covered, Oriental, Oval | 110.00 |
| **Dish,** Vegetable, Footed, Cover, Grecian Pattern | 55.00 |
| **Jug,** Celadon Green Bamboo Canes, 8 In. | 98.00 |
| **Jug,** Coaching Days, Black On Caramel, 4 3/4 In. | 45.00 |
| **Jug,** Coaching Days, Silver Luster Trim, 3 5/8 In. | 45.00 |
| **Jug,** Knights Jousting, Gray Ground, Dated 1849, Salt Glaze, 8 3/4 In. | 135.00 |
| **Jug,** Tam O'Shanter, Signed & Dated 1835, 9 1/2 In. | 160.00 To 245.00 |
| **Mug,** Coaching Days, Brown | 26.00 |
| **Mug,** John Peel, 4 In. | 28.00 |
| **Pitcher,** Harbor Scene, Copper Luster Handle & Trim, 4 In. | 40.00 |
| **Pitcher,** Mr.Pickwick, Silver Luster Trim, 2 3/8 In. | 45.00 |
| **Pitcher,** Oriental, Blue & White, 6 In., Pair | 75.00 |
| **Pitcher,** Pewter Rim, Hinged Lid, Jousting Knights, 1841-46, 7 1/2 In. | 190.00 |
| **Pitcher,** Pottery Lid, 19th Century, Blue, 7 In., Pair | 400.00 |
| **Pitcher,** Tom O'Shanter Design, Pewter Lid, Blue, 6 3/4 In. | 110.00 |
| **Pitcher,** Two Knights Jousting, Relief, Brown, Marked, 8 In. | 179.00 |
| **Plate,** Capitol, Washington, D.C., Brown | 32.00 |
| **Plate,** Coaching Days, Newburg Bridge, 9 In. | 35.00 |
| **Plate,** Coaching Days, Paying Toll, 9 In.Diam. | 20.00 |

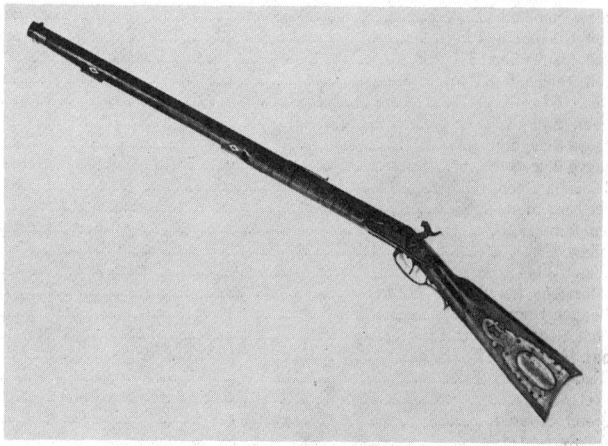

Rifle, Kentucky, Octagonal Barrel, Flintlock, Percussion

**Plate,** Medina, Blue & White, 10 5/8 In. ......................................................... 25.00
**Plate,** Moving Away, Fox Hunt Scene, Brown & Black, 9 3/4 In. ..................... 35.00
**Plate,** Royal Vistas, Gold Trim, Signed Dumbarton, 10 1/4 In. ....................... 35.00
**Platter,** Asiatic Palaces, C.1830, Blue, 13 In. ................................................. 75.00
**Platter,** Oriental, 15 In. ..................................................................................... 55.00
**Syrup,** Coaching Days, 2 Scenes ..................................................................... 55.00
**Tankard,** Coaching Days, 9 1/2 In. .................................................................. 48.50
**Tray,** Pin, Scene From Hamlet, Silver Luster Border, Diamond Shaped .......... 15.00
**Vase,** Coaching Days, Coaching Scene In Color, Marked, 4 3/8 In. .................. 48.00

**RIFLE, C.S.A. Bowie Company,** Marked, 15 3/4 In. ......................................... 165.00
    **Kentucky,** Octagonal Barrel, Flintlock, Percussion ........................... *Illus* 950.00
    **Kentucky,** Silver Mounted, Silver Inlays, Patch Box, Curly Maple Stock ......... 1975.00
    **Percussion,** Billinghurst, Tools, Bool Box, Bullets & Patches ..................... 1000.00
    **Remington,** 1871 ...................................................................................... 200.00
    **Remington,** 45 Caliber, Walnut Stock, American, 31 In. ........................... 550.00
    **Single Shot,** Bolt Action, 1874 Darm's Mfg., French Army ...................... 400.00
    **Target,** Billinghurst ................................................................................. 1000.00
    **Winchester,** Model 1906, 22 Caliber, Patented 2890 ................................ 50.00
    **Winchester,** Repeater, Model 1884, Octagon Barrel, 38 Caliber ............... 225.00

*Riviera Ware was made by the Homer Laughlin Co. from 1938 to 1950.
Plates were square and cup handles were squared.*

**RIVIERA, Bowl,** Mixing, Mexicana, 10 X 5 1/2 In. ......................................... 18.00
    **Creamer,** Green ........................................................................................ 6.00
    **Cup & Saucer,** Green ............................................................................... 6.50
    **Cup & Saucer,** Mauve Blue ..................................................................... 6.50
    **Cup,** Green ............................................................................................... 5.00
    **Cup,** Ivory ................................................................................................ 5.00
    **Mug,** Green, Handled ................................................................................ 32.50
    **Mug,** Mauve Blue, Handled ...................................................................... 32.50

| | |
|---|---|
| **Mug,** Yellow, Handled | 32.50 |
| **Plate,** Fruit, Green, 5 1/2 In. | 2.50 |
| **Plate,** Fruit, Mauve Blue, 5 1/2 In. | 2.50 |
| **Plate,** Fruit, Yellow, 5 1/2 In. | 2.50 |
| **Plate,** Green, 6 In. | 2.00 |
| **Plate,** Green, 9 In. | 4.00 |
| **Plate,** Mauve Blue, 6 In. | 2.00 |
| **Plate,** Mauve Blue, 9 In. | 4.00 |
| **Plate,** Mexicana, Deep | 8.00 |
| **Plate,** Mexicana, 6 In. | 4.00 |
| **Plate,** Red, 9 In. | 4.00 |
| **Plate,** Yellow, 6 In. | 2.00 |
| **Plate,** Yellow, 9 In. | 4.00 |
| **Platter,** Mexicana, Handled, 11 1/2 In. | 12.50 |
| **Salt & Pepper,** Ivory | 6.00 |
| **Sauce,** Fruit, Red, 5 1/2 In. | 2.50 |
| **Sauceboat,** Mauve Blue | 9.00 |
| **Saucer,** Red | 1.50 |
| **Saucer,** Yellow | 1.50 |
| **Sugar,** Green, Covered | 6.00 |
| **Sugar,** Yellow, No Lid | 3.00 |
| **Tumbler,** Juice, Mexicana, Blue | 10.00 |
| **Tumbler,** Juice, Mexicana, Green | 10.00 |
| **Tumbler,** Juice, Mexicana, Red | 10.00 |
| **Tumbler,** Juice, Mexicana, Yellow | 10.00 |
| **Tumbler,** Juice, Red | 24.00 |
| **Tumbler,** Juice, Yellow | 24.00 |
| **Tumbler,** Mexicana, Blue, 10 Ounce | 12.00 |
| **Tumbler,** Mexicana, Green, 10 Ounce | 12.00 |
| **Tumbler,** Mexicana, Red, 10 Ounce | 12.00 |
| **Tumbler,** Mexicana, Yellow, 10 Ounce | 12.00 |

**ROBERTSON, Bookends,** Reclining, Semiclad Woman, Blue, Maroon, 1910 ........... 375.00

**ROBJ, Bookends,** Chinese Guard, Crossed Arms, Yellow, Black, 7 In. ................. 280.00

R O B L I N

*Roblin Art Pottery was founded in 1898 by Alexander W. Robertson and Linna Irelan in San Francisco, California. The pottery closed in 1906.*

**ROBLIN, Mug,** Head Of Ram In Slip Relief, Iron-Oxide Ground, Signed ................. 850.00

*Rockingham in the United States is a brown glazed pottery with a tortoiseshell-like glaze. It was made from 1840 to 1900 by many American potteries. Mottled brown Rockingham wares were first made in England at the Rockingham factory. Other wares were also made by the English firm.*

| | |
|---|---|
| **ROCKINGHAM, Bottle,** Flask, Boot Warmer | 115.00 |
| **Bowl,** Spotted, 8 3/4 In. | 58.00 |
| **Bread Plate,** Appetite Obeys, Where Reason Rules, 13 X 10 1/2 In. | 155.00 |
| **Creamer,** Cow, Glazed, Brown & Yellow | 140.00 |
| **Cuspidor** | 42.00 |
| **Dish,** Soap, Foliage Pattern | 50.00 |
| **Jar,** Sweetmeat, Blue Flowers Outlined In Gold, 9 In.Pair | 175.00 |
| **Jug,** Fox On Handle, Marked | 12.50 |
| **Pan,** Milk, 10 1/4 In. | 85.00 |
| **Pie Plate,** Distinct Mottling, 8 1/4 In. | 65.00 |
| **Pie Plate,** Patterning, Beige Ground, 8 1/2 In.Diam. | 65.00 |
| **Pie Plate,** Speckling, 8 1/2 In. | 65.00 |
| **Pitcher,** Batter, Handled | 185.00 |
| **Pitcher,** Hound Handled, Stag, Boar, Rabbit, Eagle, Fox, 8 3/4 In. | 250.00 |
| **Pitcher,** Tavern Scene On One Side, Shepherd & Sheep On Other | 40.00 |

| | |
|---|---|
| Teapot, Double Spouted | 150.00 |
| Teapot, Rebecca At The Well, 8 In. | 75.00 |
| Teapot, 2 Spout | 150.00 |
| Toby, Man In Tricornered Hat | 75.00 |
| Toby, Snuff Taker, Brown, 8 In. | 50.00 |
| **ROGERS, see John Rogers** | |
| ROLL, Wallpaper Printing, Brass Trim, 24 In. | 25.00 |

*Rookwood pottery was made in Cincinnati, Ohio, from 1880 to 1960. All of this art pottery is marked, most with the famous flame mark. The R is reversed and placed back to back with the letter P. Flames surround the letters.*

| | |
|---|---|
| ROOKWOOD, Ashtray, Elk's Convention, 1904, Elk's Head In Relief, 4 In. | 95.00 |
| Ashtray, Semireclining Nude, White, 1929 | 67.50 |
| Ashtray, 50th Anniversary, Western Southern Ins., Yellow, 5 3/4 In. | 60.00 |
| Banana Boat, 1920, 6 X 4 In. | 40.00 |
| Bookends, Deco Girl, Blue | 120.00 |
| Bookends, Oak Tree Form, Yellow & Brown, Green Base, 1929 | 165.00 |
| Bookends, Oriental Figures, High Glaze Blue & Purple, 1922 | 285.00 |
| Bookends, Peacock, Blue, 1926, Pair | 80.00 |
| Bookends, Peafowl, 1925, Yellow | 70.00 To 87.50 |
| Bookends, Penguin Mates, Blue Matte, Pair | 65.00 |
| Bookends, Rook Eating Grapes, 1943, McD Mark | 120.00 |
| Bookends, Rook With Leaves & Berries, Signed & Numbered | 125.00 |
| Bookends, Rook, Green | 165.00 |
| Bookends, Seated Lady In Ruffled Dress, Matte Cream, 1936 | 110.00 |
| Bookends, Ship, 1825, Signed, Aqua | 105.00 |
| Bookends, Victorian Lady, Iridescent | 110.00 |
| Bookends, Water Lily, Gray Over Pink, 1934 | 85.00 |
| Bowl & Frog, Flower Interior, Black Exterior, 1927, 13 1/2 In. | 175.00 |
| Bowl, Band Of Pink Fowers, White Ground, 1918, Signed, 5 1/2 In. | 125.00 |
| Bowl, Black Glaze Outside, Wine Glaze Inside, 2 1/2 X 10 In. | 65.00 |
| Bowl, Flowers On Gray, Brown Rim, Signed W.E.H., 3 In. | 150.00 |
| Bowl, Geometrically Designed Flowers, C.1929, 3 X 8 In. | 375.00 |
| Bowl, Green Interior, Clay Exterior, Flairing, Shape No.2253, 3 In. | 48.00 |
| Bowl, Green Matte, 1920, 3 1/2 X 9 In. | 55.00 |
| Bowl, Matte Yellow, 1923, 4 1/2 In. | 25.00 |
| Bowl, Ram's Horn, Philodendron Leaves, No.618, 23 X 9 X 5 In. | 525.00 |
| Bowl, Red-Brown Blend, Matte Finish, 1909, 2 1/2 In. | 35.00 |
| Bowl, Teal Blue, Green, 3 Handled, 8 1/2 In. | 55.00 |
| Bowl, Three-Eared, Pink, Shape No.1222, 1916, Marked P, 9 In. | 65.00 |
| Bowl, Turquoise, 10 In. | 50.00 |
| Bowl, Yellow, Footed, 8 X 2 1/2 In. | 45.00 |
| Box, Dog, Tail & Back Lift Off | 125.00 |
| Candleholder, Blue, Round, Low, 1924 | 55.00 |
| Candleholder, Glendale | 55.00 |
| Candlestick, Blue, Dated 1920 | 55.00 |
| Candlestick, Cherubs, Brown With Ivory, 1921, 24 In., Pair | 1500.00 |
| Candlestick, Lily-Of-The-Valley, Iris Glaze, 1902, Signed, 7 1/2 In. | 385.00 |
| Candlestick, Rose, Tulips, 1922, 10 In., Pair | 75.00 |
| Candlestick, Yellow Blossoms, Enameled, Brown To Green, 5 1/2 In. | 185.00 |
| Candlestick, 3-Sided, Sea Horse Corners, 1927, S.Toohey, 4 In., Pr. | 78.00 |
| Chamberstick, Rose, Dated, 1920 | 85.00 |
| Chocolate Pot, Red Porcelain Glaze, Signed A.Van Briggle, 7 In. | 625.00 |
| Creamer, Daisy Design, Blue & Yellow Ground, 1890, Stamp, 3 In. | 225.00 |
| Creamer, Sara E.Coyne, 1894 | 225.00 |
| Cup & Saucer, Blue Sailing Pirate Ships, 1924 | 45.00 |
| Decanter, Cluster Of Grapes, Brown, C.1898, Stamp, 7 In. | 325.00 |
| Dish, Rook Perched On Side, Green Glaze, 6 1/2 In. | 220.00 |
| Ewer, Autumn Leaves, Orange To Brown Glaze, Dated 1894, 5 1/4 In. | 140.00 |
| Ewer, Brown Glaze, Yellow Flowers, 1907, Signed, 6 In. | 265.00 |

Rookwood, from left to right, Ewer, Silver Overlay; Vase, Tigereye, Gilt Flecks (See Page 506); Vase, Daffodils, Brown (See Page 506); Jug, Stopper, Ear of Corn; Mug, Painted Ear of Corn

| | |
|---|---|
| **Ewer,** Dogwood Design, Artist Initials, C.1894, 7 1/2 In. | 325.00 |
| **Ewer,** Floral Design, Bulbous, Narrow Neck, Signed, 1888, 9 In. | 250.00 |
| **Ewer,** Handled, Tricorner Lip, Brown Pansies, 6 In. | 365.00 |
| **Ewer,** Handled, Tricorner Lip, Sweet Peas, Dated 1898, Signed, 6 In. | 340.00 |
| **Ewer,** Lincoln, 7 In. | 325.00 |
| **Ewer,** Silver Overlay, A.M.Valentien, 1892, 5 1/2 In. _Illus_ | 600.00 |
| **Ewer,** Single Spout, Small Handle, Flowers, Japanese Signed, 1888 | 1500.00 |
| **Ewer,** Sweet Pea Design, Dated 1889, Artist Signed | 450.00 |
| **Ewer,** White & Gilded Prunus, Peach Body, Impressed Mark, 9 1/2 In. | 450.00 |
| **Ewer,** Wild Roses, Brown & Amber, 1899, Stamp, 8 In. | 425.00 |
| **Ewer,** Yellow Flowers, Leafed Twig, 1907, Signed, 6 In. | 265.00 |
| **Figurine,** Beatrice, Bronze Finish, 1912 | 350.00 |
| **Figurine,** Donkey, On Base, White | 185.00 |
| **Figurine,** Elephant, Signed | 100.00 |
| **Figurine,** Nude On Plinth, Turquoise, Signed Louise Abel, 1928 | 110.00 |
| **Figurine,** Rook, Dark Green, Matte Finish, 1909 Mark, 5 In. | 34.50 |
| **Flower Frog,** High Glaze, Aqua, 5 1/2 In. | 45.00 |
| **Humidor,** Light Green, Wax Matte, C.1921 | 265.00 |
| **Humidor,** Matte Green, Lid, Finial, Spider Design, 1901, 7 In. | 255.00 |
| **Jar,** Chartreuse, Shield On Top, Covered, 10 In. | 45.00 |
| **Jar,** Crest On Top, High Glaze, Covered, Dated 1950 | 65.00 |
| **Jug,** Corn, Stopper, Glazed, Artist Signed, 1900 | 950.00 |
| **Jug,** Floral, Shape No.767c, Signed Laura Lindeman, 5 3/4 In. | 260.00 |
| **Jug,** Flowers, Glazed, 5 1/4 In. | 260.00 |
| **Jug,** Grapevines, High Glaze, Stopper, 1900-04 | 350.00 |
| **Jug,** Stopper, Ear Of Corn, J.E.Zettel, Glaze, 7 In. _Illus_ | 450.00 |

Jug, Swallows Flying Over Marsh, Marked & Signed, C.1883, 6 1/2 In. ............................... 500.00
Jug, Water, Blue, 1946, 10 3/4 In. ........................ 165.00
Loving Cup, 3-Handled, Rose, 1907, 8 1/2 In. ........................ 105.00
Mask, Comedy, Green ........................ 125.00
Match Holder, Maroon, Green Feet, Square, 1922, 1 In. ........................ 45.00
Mug, Dutch Gentleman, 1895, Marked, 5 In. ........................ 250.00
Mug, Painted Ear Of Corn, L.Ashbury, 1902, 4 3/4 In. ........................ *Illus* 150.00
Mug, Portrait, Running Antelope, Onkpapa, 1898, Signed, 5 In. ........................ 750.00
Mug, Portrait, Two Strike, Sioux, 1897, Marked, 5 In. ........................ 2750.00
Mug, Puzzle, Portrait Of Black Boy, 1897, Marked, 5 In. ........................ 2750.00
Mug, Raised Snails, Matte Green, 1905, 5 3/4 In. ........................ 195.00
Mug, Stylized Flowers On Green Matte, Dated 1903, 5 1/2 In. ........................ 110.00
Mug, Yellow & Green Corn, Brown Ground, 1902, Marked, 5 In. ........................ 375.00
Paperweight, Donkey, Ivory, Figural ........................ 85.00
Paperweight, Figural, Donkey, White Vellum, Signed, 1935, 4 1/2 In. ........................ 98.00
Paperweight, Foo Dog, Green, 1924 ........................ 90.00
Paperweight, Rabbit, White, 1931 ........................ 45.00
Pitcher, Floral, Butterfly, Smear Glaze, Side Spout, 1884, 6 1/4 In. ........................ 495.00
Pitcher, Molded Putti Design, C.1886, 5 1/2 In. ........................ 275.00
Pitcher, Pansies, Stamped Name In Oval, 2 1/2 X 4 In. ........................ 220.00
Pitcher, Poppies, 1898, Signed, 4 1/2 In. ........................ 295.00
Pitcher, Tan-Mauve To Tan, High Glaze, 1953, 3 1/2 In. ........................ 35.00
Plaque, Landscape, Vellum, 1945, Signed, 12 1/2 X 14 1/2 In. ........................ 4750.00
Plaque, Riverbank Scene, Trees, Vellum, C.1912, Signed ........................ 950.00
Plaque, Scenic, E.Diers, 6 X 9 In. ........................ 995.00
Plaque, Stormy Lake Scene, Vellum, 1913, Marked, 8 1/2 X 10 3/4 In. ........................ 1600.00
Plaque, Winter Landscape, Blues & Pink, 1915, Stamp, 5 X 8 In. ........................ 1200.00
Plaque, Winter Sunrise, Vellum, 1917, Signed, 7 1/4 X 9 1/4 In. ........................ 4400.00
Plate, Blue Design On Creamy Ground, 1912, 7 1/2 In. ........................ 35.00
Plate, Floral, High Glaze Design, 1889 Ads, 10 In. ........................ 195.00
Rose Bowl, Clover On Swirled Body, Dated 1893, Marked, 5 1/2 In. ........................ 550.00
Saucer, Blue Floral, Signed Hew, 1886 ........................ 68.00
Spoon Holder, Blue & Green Peacock Feather, 1914 ........................ 55.00
Stein, Pewter Lid, Weidemann Co., 1948 Eagle Over W ........................ 210.00
Sugar & Creamer, Covered, Butterfly Handles, Floral Design ........................ 190.00
Sugar & Creamer, Matte Pink To Green, 1929 ........................ 37.00
Tea Caddy, Sweet Clover Design, Standard Glaze ........................ 475.00
Tea Set, Sailing Ships ........................ 185.00
Tea Set, White & Blue, High Gloss, Creamer & Sugar With Lid ........................ 60.00
Tile, Landscape, Mural, 25, C.1910, 40 X 38 In. ........................ 2750.00
Tile, Molded Duck Border, 1917 ........................ 40.00
Tile, Parrot, Blue, Pink, Beige, Green, 1936, 5 1/2 In. ........................ 125.00
Tile, Pigeon, Pastels, 1930 ........................ 85.00
Tile, Raven, Footed, 1922, 5 1/2 In.Square ........................ 75.00
Tile, Rook, Round, Blue, 1919 ........................ 145.00
Tile, Rook, Yellow, Dark Green, 1948, 5 3/4 In. ........................ 75.00
Tile, Water Lily, Dark Blue, 1916 ........................ 145.00
Tray, Card, Rook Perched On Rim, Green Glaze ........................ 135.00
Vase, Apple Blossoms, Vellum, 1906, 8 In. ........................ 365.00
Vase, Aqua Interior, White Matte Glaze, 11 In. ........................ 75.00
Vase, Beige, Indians, Donkey, Houses, 1946, 5 3/4 In. ........................ 135.00
Vase, Beige, White Tulips, 1907, 5 1/2 X 3 1/2 In. ........................ 40.00
Vase, Blue & Brown, Dated 1914, 7 1/2 In. ........................ 65.00
Vase, Blue & Green Design, Pink Ground, Dated 1924, 8 In. ........................ 295.00
Vase, Blue Matte, Drip Design, 16 Flames, 9 In. ........................ 55.00
Vase, Blue Matte, Finger Molds, 1928, 6 1/2 In. ........................ 70.00
Vase, Blue Matte, Handled, 1916, 6 In. ........................ 20.00
Vase, Blue, Molded Fish, 1931 ........................ 60.00
Vase, Blue, Signed H, 7 1/2 In. ........................ 135.00
Vase, Blue, Winter Landscape, Marked, 10 3/4 In. ........................ 800.00
Vase, Blues, Greens, White, Roses, Vellum, Marked, 6 In. ........................ 325.00
Vase, Brown & Blue Leaf Design, Aqua Matte, Signed, 4 In. ........................ 145.00
Vase, Brown & Yellow Ground, Applied Slip Lilies, Signed, 14 In. ........................ 1200.00

**Vase,** Bulbous, Flared, Light Green, 1918, Signed C.S.T., 6 In. ............................................. 120.00
**Vase,** Cabinet, Leaf & Flowers, Blue, Green, 1930, 4 1/2 In. ............................................. 135.00
**Vase,** Carp Swimming, Cresting Waves, Burnt Orange & Brown, 20 In. ........................ 1600.00
**Vase,** Crocuses, 1900, Carl Schmidt, 5 In. ............................................................... 275.00
**Vase,** Daffodils, Brown, A.B.Sprague, C.1902, 12 3/4 In. ............................... *Illus* 750.00
**Vase,** Deep Blue, Purple, 1914, 8 In. ...................................................................... 55.00
**Vase,** Drip Design, Blue Matte Glaze, Ovoid, 9 In. ................................................... 65.00
**Vase,** Dutch Gentleman, 1903, G.Young Monogram, Stamp, 10 In. ...................... 3700.00
**Vase,** Earth-Tone Flowers & Leaves, 1928, 4 In. ...................................................... 135.00
**Vase,** Flared Rim, Brown Glaze, 3 1/8 X 3 In. .......................................................... 25.00
**Vase,** Flared, Stylized Flowers, C.1887, Signed, 5 1/2 In. ...................................... 350.00
**Vase,** Floral Band, Gray & Blue, Patti Conant, 1918, 6 In. ...................................... 150.00
**Vase,** Floral, Cinnamon, 1920, 10 1/2 In. ................................................................ 40.00
**Vase,** Floral, Vellum, Poppy Design, 1907, 9 1/2 In. ............................................... 595.00
**Vase,** Flowers & Leaf Design, Dated 1898, Brown Glaze, Signed, 4 In. .................. 455.00
**Vase,** Flowers, Purple, Vellum, Artist Signed, 8 In. .................................................. 195.00
**Vase,** Flowers, Van Briggle, 1900, 2 Handles, 5 1/2 In. .......................................... 375.00
**Vase,** Flowers, Vellum, Edward Dyres, 1927, 9 In. .................................................. 675.00
**Vase,** Flowers, Vellum, Fred Rothenbush, 1909, 6 1/4 In. ...................................... 295.00
**Vase,** Geese & Stars, Omboroso, 5 1/2 In. ............................................................. 40.00
**Vase,** Gilt Collar & Foot, Geometric Design, 1886, Marked, 20 1/2 In. .................. 1800.00
**Vase,** Gray Porcelain, Floral Band, Signed Pc, 1918 ............................................... 200.00
**Vase,** Green Poppy Raised Design, 1930 Mark, 12 In. ............................................. 235.00
**Vase,** Greens & Yellows With Fish, 1901, Signed, 12 3/4 In. .............................. 4000.00
**Vase,** Greens With Fish, Vellum, C.1905, Marked, 6 1/4 In. .................................. 325.00
**Vase,** Handled, Grapes & Leaves Design, 1907, 6 1/2 In. ...................................... 450.00
**Vase,** Incised Design, Olive Ground, 1914, Signed C S Todd, 4 In. ........................ 250.00
**Vase,** Incised Floral Design, Wax Matte, 1912, 10 1/2 In. ...................................... 335.00
**Vase,** Indian Landscape, Vellum, 1910, Signed, 13 3/8 In. .................................. 4000.00
**Vase,** Iris Glaze, Crocus Painting, 8 In. .................................................................. 525.00
**Vase,** Iris Glaze, Snowberry Design, 4 In. ............................................................... 350.00
**Vase,** Landscape At Dusk, Vellum Glaze, 1910, Marked, 6 1/2 In. .......................... 500.00
**Vase,** Landscape, Dusk, Greens, Vellum Glaze, Marked, 6 In. ............................... 350.00
**Vase,** Leaves & Berries, Greens & Ambers, 1890, Signed, 6 1/2 In. ...................... 375.00
**Vase,** Lily-Of-The-Valley, Dated 1902, Signed ....................................................... 125.00
**Vase,** Matte Green, 1907, 12 1/2 In. ...................................................................... 95.00
**Vase,** Narcissus Blossoms, C.1907, Signed, 10 1/2 In. ...................................... 2750.00
**Vase,** Olive Green, 1930, 11 In. ............................................................................. 65.00
**Vase,** Peacock Blue, High Glaze, 1945, 6 1/2 In. .................................................... 55.00
**Vase,** Petaled Yellow Flowers, Dated, 1894, Signed, 7 1/4 In. ............................... 425.00
**Vase,** Pink Peonies, Blue, Green Foliage, Lilac & Cream, 9 In. ............................... 550.00
**Vase,** Pink Poppies, Vellum, E.F.McDonald, 1914, 7 In. ......................................... 250.00
**Vase,** Pink Shading To Green, 1921, 5 1/2 In. ........................................................ 26.50
**Vase,** Pink To Green, Flowers At Crown, E.N.Lincoln, 1911, 5 1/2 In. ..................... 200.00
**Vase,** Pink, Border Of Rooks, 6 In. ......................................................................... 58.00
**Vase,** Pink, C.1901, 6 In. ....................................................................................... 55.00
**Vase,** Pink, Shading To Gray-Green, 1950, 5 1/2 In. ............................................... 24.50
**Vase,** Plum Exterior, Turquoise Interior, 6 In. ......................................................... 45.00
**Vase,** Poppies, Brown & Amber, 1902, Marked, 12 1/2 In. .................................. 2100.00
**Vase,** Primroses, Brown Ground, Signed, 1903, 6 1/2 In. ...................................... 350.00
**Vase,** Red & Blue Floral On Pink Ground, Wax Matte, 1925, 9 1/2 In. .................. 185.00
**Vase,** Red Crab Apples, Wax Matte, 1905, OGR, 5 In. ........................................... 100.00
**Vase,** Red Nasturtiums, Brown Glaze, Ovoid, Dated 1898, 11 1/2 In. ..................... 495.00
**Vase,** Redware, Yellow Chrysanthemums, Handled, 1885 Mark, 5 3/4 In. ............... 75.00
**Vase,** Riverbank, Vellum, Greens & Cream, C.1907, Signed, 16 In. ..................... 1100.00
**Vase,** Robin On Branch, Blue-Gray Glaze, Artist Signed, 4 3/4 In. .......................... 325.00
**Vase,** Rose Color, Impressed Floral, C.1928, Art Deco ........................................... 40.00
**Vase,** Rose To Green, Amphora Shape, 1908, 8 In. ................................................ 25.00
**Vase,** Rust, Pinecones & Needles, 1906, Signed, 6 1/2 In. .................................... 165.00
**Vase,** Scenic, Vellum, Tapering Form, 1911, Blue & Pink, 7 In. .............................. 475.00
**Vase,** Sky-Blue, 1942, 13 In. ................................................................................. 190.00
**Vase,** Slip Lilies, Brown & Yellow Ground, 1901, Marked, 14 In. .......................... 1200.00
**Vase,** Tigereye, Gilt Flecks, Bailey, C.1890, 7 In. .............................. *Illus* 400.00

**Vase,** Trees, Rocks, Pentagonal, 4 3/4 In. ................................................................... 125.00
**Vase,** Tulip Pattern, Tan Overdrip, Matte Aqua, 10 In. ....................................... 45.00
**Vase,** White Flowers At Base, Mauve Matte, 1913, Signed, 8 1/2 In. ................. 110.00
**Vase,** White, Blue Interior, Bulbous, Marked 1939, 7 In. ..................................... 65.00
**Vase,** White, Turquoise, Geometic Molded, 5 3/4 In. ........................................ 95.00
**Vase,** Wild Daisies, Silver Overlay, Gorham, 1901, 10 1/2 In. ........................ 1600.00
**Vase,** Yellow Flowers, 1888, 2 In. ................................................................... 190.00
**Vase,** 5 Panels With Rooks, Lavender, 7 1/2 In. ............................................ 50.00
**Wall Pocket,** Geometric Design, Green To Rose, 1912 ................................... 75.00
**Wall Pocket,** Wisteria Vines On Plum Matte, 1911 ....................................... 90.00

> *Rose bowls were popular during the 1880s. Rose petals were kept in the open*
> *bowl to add fragrance to a room. The glass bowls were made with crimped tops,*
> *which kept the petals inside. Many types of Victorian art glass were made*
> *into rose bowls.*

**ROSE BOWL, Blown Satin Glass,** Pale Yellow ................................................ 95.00
**Blown Satin Glass,** Rose Color ....................................................................... 95.00
**Cerise,** Blue Ruffle & Feet, Signed S. & W. .................................................. 175.00
**Green Overlay Cut To Clear,** Intaglio Water Lilies, 5 1/2 In. ...................... 125.00
**Hobnail,** Pink Cased, 8 Crimp Top, 6 1/8 X 4 In.Diam. ................................. 65.00
**Pineapple Pattern,** Clear, Silver Plated Rim ................................................ 12.00
**Pink Applied Flower,** Opaque Cream, Vaseline, 4 1/4 In.Diam. ................... 85.00
**Translucent Blue Spangled,** Mica, 4 1/4 In. ................................................ 125.00
**Yellow Spangled,** Translucent, Mica, Egg Shape, 4 In. ................................ 115.00

> *Rose Canton china is similar to Rose Medallion except no people are*
> *pictured in the decoration. It was made during the nineteenth and twentieth*
> *centuries in greens, pinks, and other colors.*

**ROSE CANTON, Bowl,** Butterflies, Birds, & Roses, Marked, 5 In.Diam. .......... 75.00
**Bowl,** Butterflies, Birds, Roses, Inside & Out, 5 In. .................................... 155.00
**Bowl,** Marked, 2 X 4 1/2 In.Diam. ................................................................. 28.00
**Teapot,** 6 1/4 In. ......................................................................................... 110.00
**Vase,** Dragon, Raised Gilt, 10 In. ................................................................ 145.00
**Vase,** 4 Full-Figure Dragons & 2 Dogs, Paneled, 9 3/4 In. ......................... 275.00

> *Rose Medallion china was made in China during the nineteenth and*
> *twentieth centuries. It is a distinctive design picturing people, flowers,*
> *birds, and butterflies. They are colored in greens, pinks, and other colors.*

**ROSE MEDALLION, Bottle,** Snuff, Original Stopper & Ivory Spoon, C.1840 ........... 170.00
**Bowl,** Flower Sprigs On Outside, C.1830, 16 In.Diam. ................................ 1200.00
**Bowl,** Incurved Corners, Polychrome Design, 10 In.Diam. ......................... 400.00
**Bowl,** Marked, 10 3/4 In.Diam. ..................................................................... 675.00
**Bowl,** Oval, 9 In. ......................................................................................... 145.00
**Bowl,** Scalloped, C.1830, 10 1/2 X 2 1/2 In. .............................................. 445.00
**Bowl,** Teakwood Stand, 13 3/4 X 6 In. ....................................................... 895.00
**Bowl,** 8 1/4 In.Diam. ................................................................................... 145.00
**Box,** Barrel Shape, C.1885, 4 1/4 X 4 In. ................................................... 225.00
**Box,** Brush, Large ....................................................................................... 400.00
**Box,** Covered, Cylindrical, 4 1/2 In. ............................................................. 175.00
**Butter Pat,** 8-Sided, 2 3/4 In. ..................................................................... 35.00
**Cake Plate,** Pedestal, Oval, Marked, 5 X 10 In.Diam. ................................ 185.00
**Chop Plate,** Genre Scenes, Floral Panels, 12 In.Diam. .............................. 100.00
**Cup & Saucer** ................................................................. 75.00 To 85.00
**Cup & Saucer,** Fluted, Marked ..................................................................... 40.00
**Dish,** Footed, Floral & Domestic Scenes, 14 1/2 X 10 3/8 In. ..................... 375.00
**Dish,** Vegetable, Covered, Nut Finial, Genre Scenes, 9 1/2 In. .................. 250.00
**Dish,** Vegetable, Covered, 19th Century, Oval, 11 X 7 In. .......................... 350.00
**Dish,** Vegetable, Covered, 19th Century, Oval, 12 X 9 In. .......................... 400.00
**Jar,** Ginger ................................................................................................. 175.00
**Jardiniere,** Polychrome Bird, Butterfly, & Mandarin, 12 In. ........................ 675.00
**Mug,** Double Twisted Handle, 4 1/2 In. ....................................................... 295.00

| | |
|---|---|
| **Pitcher,** Ovoid Body, Genre & Floral Panels, 9 In. | 525.00 |
| **Pitcher,** Ovoid Body, Genre Scenes, Floral Panels, 6 1/8 In. | 125.00 |
| **Plate,** Alternating Scenes & Floral Panels, 10 In.Diam. | 75.00 |
| **Plate,** Cake, 6 In.Diam., Set Of 6 | 125.00 |
| **Plate,** Figures In Teahouse, Gold Hair, 8 1/2 In. | 90.00 |
| **Plate,** Flowers & Butterflies, 5 1/2 In. | 32.00 |
| **Plate,** Flowers & People, Bluebirds, 5 5/8 In.Diam. | 20.00 |
| **Plate,** Marked, 8 3/8 In.Diam. | 185.00 |
| **Plate,** 2 Medallions With People, Cutout Border, 7 1/4 In. | 70.00 |
| **Plate,** 3 Chinese Ladies Playing Game, 9 In.Diam. | 75.00 |
| **Plate,** 6 In. | 45.00 |
| **Plate,** 6 In., Set Of 6 | 120.00 |
| **Plate,** 7 1/2 In. | 24.00 To 65.00 |
| **Plate,** 8 In. | 55.00 To 85.00 |
| **Plate,** 8 1/2 In. | 65.00 |
| **Plate,** 9 In.Diam. | 75.00 |
| **Platter,** Marked, Octagonal, 8 1/4 In. | 115.00 |
| **Platter,** Oval, Marked, 13 X 10 1/2 In. | 285.00 |
| **Platter,** 13 In. | 95.00 |
| **Platter,** 14 1/2 In. | 185.00 |
| **Platter,** 19th Century, Oval, 14 In. | 195.00 To 250.00 |
| **Salt,** Pair | 28.00 |
| **Spittoon,** Bulbous, 2 Rectangular Cartouches, People, China | 525.00 |
| **Tazza,** C.1885, 3 1/2 X 7 1/2 In. | 285.00 |
| **Tea Set,** Curlicue Handles, Gold Trim, 1840-60 | 595.00 |
| **Tea Set,** 4 Octagonal Cups & Saucers, Marked, 11 Piece | 195.00 |
| **Teapot,** Domed Lid | 200.00 |
| **Teapot,** Footed, Domed Cover, Knob Finial, Urn Shape, 9 1/2 In. | 475.00 |
| **Teapot,** In Basket, Marked | 120.00 |
| **Teapot,** Miniature | 50.00 |
| **Teapot,** Pear Shape, C.1890 | 195.00 |
| **Teapot,** Wicker Case, Brass Hardware | 200.00 |
| **Teapot,** 2 Cups, Woven Basket Pattern, C.1840 | 395.00 |
| **Teapot,** 2-Handled Demitasse Cups, Raffia Basket | 175.00 |
| **Tray,** Cloverleaf Shape, 3 Court Scenes, Birds, 12 X 11 In. | 225.00 |
| **Urn,** Roses & Daisies On Sides, Gold Ground, 10 1/2 In., Pair | 145.00 |
| **Vase,** Cylinder, 8 In. | 80.00 |
| **Vase,** Raised Gold Dragon Circling Neck, 5 In. | 175.00 |
| **Vase,** Sacred Bird & Flower, Applied Foo Dogs, 11 In., Pair | 465.00 |
| **Vase,** Temple, Pastel Coloring, 15 1/2 In. | 775.00 |

     **ROSE O'NEILL, see Kewpie**

*Rose Tapestry porcelain was made by the Royal Bayreuth factory of Germany during the late nineteenth century. The surface of the ware feels like cloth.*

| | |
|---|---|
| **ROSE TAPESTRY, Ashtray,** Green Mark, Square | 100.00 |
| **Ashtray,** Square Rests, 6 In.Diam. | 120.00 |
| **Basket,** Handled, 4 In. | 285.00 |
| **Bell,** Castle Scene | 350.00 |
| **Bowl,** Radish, Leaf Underplate, Blue Mark, Bowl, 5 In.Diam. | 145.00 |
| **Box,** Covered, 3 Color, Gold Feet, Blue Mark, 2 1/2 X 4 In.Diam. | 325.00 |
| **Box,** Covered, 3 Gold Legs, 4 In. | 265.00 |
| **Box,** Hairpin, Covered, Blue Mark, 2 X 4 1/2 In.Diam. | 250.00 |
| **Box,** Pin, Pink Roses, 3 Gold Feet, Green Mark, 4 In.Diam. | 78.00 |
| **Box,** Pin, 3 Gold Feet, Pink Roses, Green Mark | 85.00 |
| **Box,** Pink & Yellow Roses, Blue Mark, 4 In.Diam., 2 Piece | 275.00 |
| **Box,** Powder, Flowers, 2 X 3 1/2 In.Diam. | 195.00 |
| **Box,** Powder, Pink Flowers, White Ground, 3 1/2 In.Diam. | 200.00 |
| **Can,** Watering, Swans, Miniature | 350.00 |
| **Chamberstick,** 3-Color Roses, 19th Century, 4 1/2 In. | 350.00 |
| **Chocolate Set,** 4 Cups & Saucers, Blue Mark | 1450.00 |
| **Creamer,** Corset Shape, 3 3/4 In. | 195.00 |

| | |
|---|---:|
| **Creamer,** Cow, Blue Mark, 3 1/4 In. | 175.00 |
| **Creamer,** Goose Girl, Blue Mark | 325.00 |
| **Creamer,** Pinched Spout, Tavern Scene, Blue Mark | 225.00 |
| **Creamer,** Pinched Spout, 3 1/2 In. | 210.00 |
| **Creamer,** Pinched Spout, 4 In. | 200.00 |
| **Creamer,** Royal Bayreuth, 3 3/4 In. | 200.00 |
| **Creamer,** 4-Color Roses, Pinched Spout, Blue Mark, 4 In. | 180.00 |
| **Dish,** Clover Shape, Floral Design, 1 1/2 X 5 In.Diam. | 75.00 |
| **Dish,** Relish, Handled, Tricolored, 8 1/8 X 4 1/8 In. | 115.00 |
| **Dish,** Relish, Tricolored, Blue Mark, 8 1/8 X 4 1/8 In. | 100.00 |
| **Hair Receiver,** Flowers, Gold Legs, Blue Mark | 175.00 |
| **Hair Receiver,** Pin Holder & Dish, Open, Gold Footed, Violets | 495.00 |
| **Hair Receiver,** Pink, White, & Yellow Roses | 185.00 |
| **Hatpin Holder,** Signed | 235.00 |
| **Hatpin Holder,** 3-Color, Filigree, Blue Mark, 4 1/2 In. | 425.00 |
| **Holder,** Hatpin, 3-Color, Rate Filigree, Blue Mark, 4 1/2 In. | 425.00 |
| **Pitcher,** Buildings Reflected In Lake, Blue Mark, 4 1/4 In. | 275.00 |
| **Pitcher,** Flow Blue Girl With Doll, Blue Mark, 5 1/4 In. | 175.00 |
| **Pitcher,** Milk, Goats & Trees, Blue Mark, 4 In. | 225.00 |
| **Pitcher,** Milk, Yellow & Pink Roses, Black Mark, 3 3/4 In. | 180.00 |
| **Pitcher,** Pinched Spout, Blue Mark, 4 1/2 In. | 205.00 |
| **Pitcher,** Pinched Spout, Goose Girl, 4 In. | 450.00 |
| **Planter,** Separate Insert, Miniature | 225.00 |
| **Plate,** Cake, Handles, Yellow, Pink, & White Roses, 10 1/2 In. | 355.00 |
| **Shoe,** Colonial Scene, Blue Mark | 340.00 |
| **Shoe,** Lady's & Gent's, Pair | 325.00 |
| **Shoe,** Lady's, High, Cuban Heel, Chrysanthemums, Blue Mark, 3 In. | 155.00 |
| **Shoe,** Lady's, 3-Color, Blue Mark | 450.00 |
| **Shoe,** Painted Colonial Couple | 350.00 |
| **Teapot,** White Mother-Of-Pearl | 125.00 |
| **Toothpick,** Footed, Double Handled, Signed | 325.00 |
| **Toothpick,** Handled, Lady With Horse | 175.00 |
| **Toothpick,** Lady With Horse, Blue Mark | 165.00 |
| **Toothpick,** 4 Feet, 2-Handled, Signed, 2 5/8 In. | 225.00 |
| **Tray,** Pin, Triangular, 3-Color Roses | 95.00 |
| **Tray,** Pink, White, & Yellow Roses, Blue Mark, Rectangular | 350.00 |
| **Tray,** Trinket, Blue Mark, 3 1/4 X 1 1/4 In. | 95.00 |
| **Vase,** Cavalier, Blue Mark, 6 1/2 In. | 125.00 |
| **Vase,** Classic Figures, Scenic Ground, 4 1/2 In. | 150.00 |
| **Vase,** Handled, Lady With Horse, Blue Mark, 8 1/2 In. | 395.00 |
| **Vase,** Pink Roses, Foliage, 8 1/2 In., Pair | 285.00 |
| **Vase,** Polar Bear, 5 In. | 300.00 |
| **Vase,** Royal Bayreuth, 5 In. | 250.00 |
| **Vase,** Scenic, Polar Bear, Blue Mark | 275.00 |
| **Vase,** White & Blue Flowers, Gold Ground, Doulton, 10 In., Pair | 135.00 |
| **Vase,** Woman On Horse, 7 In. | 350.00 |
| **Vase,** 3-Color Roses, Blue Mark, 3 X 5 1/2 In. | 250.00 |
| **Wall Pocket,** 3-Color Roses | 265.00 |
| **Watering Can,** Swans | 340.00 |

*Rosenthal porcelain was established in Selb, Bavaria, in 1880. The German factory still continues to make fine-quality tableware and figurines.*

| | |
|---|---:|
| **ROSENTHAL, Bonbon,** Handled, House & Tree, Blue & White, Marked | 35.00 |
| **Bowl,** Girl Playing Harp, Open Handles, Blue Border, 9 1/4 In. | 240.00 |
| **Bowl,** Moss Rose, Gold Trim, Openwork, 8 1/2 In. | 36.00 |
| **Bowl,** Open Handles, Girl Playing Harp Center, 9 1/4 In.Diam. | 240.00 |
| **Box,** Collar Button Shaped, Blue Forget-Me-Nots | 35.00 |
| **Box,** Collar Button, Covered, Collar Shaped, Pink Roses | 45.00 |
| **Condiment Set,** Sterling Silver Tops & Spoon, Blue On White, 4 Pc. | 55.00 |

**Cup & Saucer,** Garlands Of Roses ........................................................... 20.00
**Dish,** Chrysanthemum, Floral, White & Gold, 9 X 6 In. ................................ 65.00
**Dish,** Hand-Painted, Roses Inside Rim, Open Handles, Signed, 7 In. ............ 12.00
**Dish,** Pin, Covered, White, Gold Outline, Signed ..................................... 12.50
**Dish,** Vegetable, Boticelli, Oval, Covered, 13 In. ..................................... 18.00
**Figurine,** Black Amour, Arabian Nights Attire, Signed ........................... 185.00
**Figurine,** Boy And Rooster ..................................................................... 125.00
**Figurine,** Boy With Lamb, Green, White, & Beige, 6 In. ........................... 125.00
**Figurine,** Brown Bears, 8 In. .................................................................. 250.00
**Figurine,** Cat With 2 Kittens, No.739 ...................................................... 115.00
**Figurine,** Cat, Marked Face & Tail, 5 X 4 In. ............................................ 45.00
**Figurine,** Doe, Green Mark, 3 3/4 X 2 1/4 In. ........................................... 45.00
**Figurine,** Doe, Hand-Painted, Green Mark, Signed, 3 1/4 X 2 1/4 In. ......... 45.00
**Figurine,** Dragonfly, Flying, Porcelain, 1 1/4 X 3 In. ................................ 45.00
**Figurine,** Dragonfly, Insect Flying, Porcelain, 4 X 1 1/4 In. ..................... 45.00
**Figurine,** Fawn, Spotted, Brown, Black, White, 3 1/4 In. ........................... 85.00
**Figurine,** Girl With Geese, Signed, 2 1/2 X 3 X 5 In. ............................... 125.00
**Figurine,** Goat, Kid, 3 3/4 In. ................................................................... 25.00
**Figurine,** Hedgehog, White, Pair ............................................................. 35.00
**Figurine,** Horned Beetle ......................................................................... 45.00
**Figurine,** Horse, Dapple Gray, 17 In. .................................................... 1600.00
**Figurine,** Horse, Porcelain, 12 In. ........................................................... 350.00
**Figurine,** Kitten, Black & White, 5 1/4 In. ................................................ 65.00
**Figurine,** Kitty, Head Down, Paws Crossed, Gray & White, 2 1/2 In. .......... 15.00
**Figurine,** Lady Cynthia, Paragon No.67 ................................................. 200.00
**Figurine,** Mallard, U.S.Zone, 2 1/2 In. ..................................................... 40.00
**Figurine,** Naked Child Holding Baby Goat, 7 In. ..................................... 125.00
**Figurine,** Nude, Kneeling Female, White, Signed Ernst Wenck ............... 125.00
**Figurine,** Nude, White, Raised Arms, 7 1/2 In. ......................................... 95.00
**Figurine,** Poodle .................................................................................. 110.00
**Figurine,** Powder Pigeon, Swelled Chest, 6 1/4 In. ................................. 155.00
**Figurine,** Russian Wolfhound Lying, 11 In.Long ..................................... 225.00
**Figurine,** Squirrel, White, 2 1/2 In. .......................................................... 25.00
**Figurine,** Squirrel, 7 In. ......................................................................... 150.00
**Figurine,** Street Musician, Horn, Artist Signed, Himmerlstoss ............... 150.00
**Ice Cream Set,** Roses, Scalloped, Signed, Tray & 5 Plates ..................... 150.00
**Jar,** Ladies On Cover, Silhouette With Bird .............................................. 30.00
**Mug,** Blue, Green, & Red Grapes, Leaves, Gold Edge ............................... 40.00
**Mug,** Strawberries, Blossoms, Leaves, 5 1/2 In. ...................................... 55.00
**Plaque,** Fairies, Dead Robin, Forrest, Porcelain, Marked, 13 In. ............ 2500.00
**Plate,** Gilt Scalloped Border, Fruit Center, Marked, 8 1/2 In., Pair ............ 95.00
**Plate,** Oberammergau, 1922, Signed Anton Lang ................................... 175.00
**Plate,** Phoenix, 9 In.Diam. ...................................................................... 12.00
**Plate,** Portrait, Scalloped, Bare-Breasted Nymph, Marked, 9 In.Diam. ...... 65.00
**Plate,** The Dresden, Gold Edged, 10 3/4 In., Set Of 12 ............................ 250.00
**Platter,** Sterling Rim, R.Loewy Design, 11 1/2 In.Diam. ............................ 60.00
**Sugar & Creamer,** Art Nouveau, Gold Trim, Signed, Dated 1917, 4 In. ...... 60.00
**Tea Set,** Sugar & Creamer, 12 Cups & Saucers, Gold Lining .................... 175.00
**Tray,** Floral Spray, Beaded Center, Sterling Border, 3 1/2 In. .................... 20.00
**Tray,** Moubijon, Handled, 15 In. ............................................................... 55.00
**Vase,** Bud, Hand-Painted Jonquils, 7 3/4 In. ............................................ 35.00
**Vase,** Ivorine Ground, Fish Swimming, Seaweed, 5 X 6 1/2 In. ............... 150.00
**Vase,** Off-White, Oriental Vines, Signed, 7 1/2 In. .................................... 45.00

*Roseville*
*U.S.A.*

*Roseville Pottery Co. was organized in Roseville, Ohio, in 1890.*
*Another plant was opened in Zanesville, Ohio, in 1898. Many types of*
*pottery were made. The firm closed in 1954.*

**ROSEVILLE, Ashtray,** Bushberry, Green ................................................... 30.00
**Basket,** Bittersweet, Green, 6 In. ............................................................. 40.00
**Basket,** Bleeding Heart, Blue, 10 In. ......................................................... 55.00

| | |
|---|---|
| **Basket,** Bleeding Heart, Pink, 12 In. | 50.00 |
| **Basket,** Bushberry, Blue, 6 1/4 In. | 35.00 |
| **Basket,** Bushberry, Green, 12 In. | 70.00 |
| **Basket,** Bushberry, Orange To Green, Handled, Footing, 12 In. | 68.00 |
| **Basket,** Clematis, Brown, 7 1/4 In. | 28.00 |
| **Basket,** Columbine, Blue, 7 In. | 35.00 |
| **Basket,** Columbine, Blue, 8 In. | 26.00 |
| **Basket,** Columbine, Blue, 12 In. | 75.00 |
| **Basket,** Columbine, Orange To Green, Pedestal, 8 In. | 38.00 |
| **Basket,** Columbine, Pink, 7 In. | 32.00 |
| **Basket,** Cosmos, Blue, Ball Shaped, Pedestal, 10 In. | 68.00 |
| **Basket,** Freesia, Blue & Brown, 7 In. | 32.00 |
| **Basket,** Freesia, Green, 10 In. | 50.00 |
| **Basket,** Gardenia, Brown, 8 In. | 37.00 |
| **Basket,** Gardenia, Gray, 8 In. | 55.00 |
| **Basket,** Iris, Pink, 8 In. | 50.00 |
| **Basket,** Laurel, Ivory Glaze, 8 In. | 45.00 |
| **Basket,** Magnolia, Blue, 7 In. | 30.00 |
| **Basket,** Magnolia, Green, 8 In. | 32.50 |
| **Basket,** Peony, Gold, 7 In. | 35.00 |
| **Basket,** Peony, Green, Hanging | 60.00 |
| **Basket,** Peony, Yellow, 8 In. | 45.00 |
| **Basket,** Pinecone, Blue, 10 In. | 50.00 |
| **Basket,** Pinecone, Burnt Orange, Boat Shaped, 10 In. | 60.00 |
| **Basket,** Primrose, Blue, Hanging | 100.00 |
| **Basket,** Snowberry, Green, 10 In. | 48.00 |
| **Basket,** Snowberry, Hanging | 44.00 |
| **Basket,** White Rose, Green Handle, 8 In. | 40.00 |
| **Basket,** Wincraft, 8 In. | 35.00 To 50.00 |
| **Bookends,** Pinecone, Blue | 75.00 |
| **Bookends,** Zephyr Lily, Brown | 55.00 |
| **Bowl,** Apple Blossom, Green, 4 In. | 15.00 |
| **Bowl,** Bleeding Heart, Pink, 4 In. | 20.00 |
| **Bowl,** Bushberry, Blue, Handled, 6 1/2 X 9 3/4 In. | 45.00 |
| **Bowl,** Columbine, Pink, 8 In. | 25.00 |
| **Bowl,** Console, Foxglove, Green, 10 In. | 20.00 |
| **Bowl,** Console, Freesia, Blue, 12 In. | 25.00 |
| **Bowl,** Console, Freesia, Terra-Cotta, 8 In. | 22.50 |
| **Bowl,** Console, Magnolia, Brown, 11 In. | 25.00 |
| **Bowl,** Console, Poppy, Pink, 14 In. | 55.00 |
| **Bowl,** Console, Thorn Apple, Blue & Green, 13 In. | 45.00 |
| **Bowl,** Cosmos, Green, 14 In. | 38.00 |
| **Bowl,** Donatello, 8 1/2 In.Diam. | 28.00 |
| **Bowl,** Donatello, 9 In. | 25.00 |
| **Bowl,** Donatello, 9 1/2 In.Diam. | 50.00 |
| **Bowl,** Florentine, Brown, 2 1/4 X 5 1/2 In. | 18.00 |
| **Bowl,** Freesia, Green, 10 3/4 In. | 20.00 |
| **Bowl,** Fuchsia, Blue, Oblong | 65.00 |
| **Bowl,** Green Pinecone, 6 In. | 20.00 |
| **Bowl,** Iris, Pink & Green, 6 In. | 25.00 |
| **Bowl,** Magnolia, Blue, 10 In. | 30.00 |
| **Bowl,** Magnolia, Terra-Cotta With Green, Raised Flowers, 8 In. | 45.00 |
| **Bowl,** Mixing, Green Band, 5 1/2 In. | 50.00 |
| **Bowl,** Mostique, Stylized Roses, 7 In. | 20.00 |
| **Bowl,** Pinecone, Green, 6 In. | 20.00 |
| **Bowl,** Rosecraft, Black, 5 In. | 34.00 |
| **Bowl,** Rosecraft, Blue, 5 In. | 20.00 |
| **Bowl,** Russco, Blue, 12 In. | 75.00 |
| **Bowl,** Snowberry, Blue, Handled, 9 1/2 X 8 1/2 In. | 25.00 |
| **Bowl,** Snowberry, Pink, Magenta, Handled, Footing, 4 1/4 X 12 In. | 38.00 |
| **Bowl,** Tourmaline, Blue, 5 In. | 45.00 |
| **Bowl,** Water Lily, Pink, 3 In. | 27.00 |
| **Bowl,** With Frog, Ferrella, Brown, 9 1/2 In. | 295.00 |

| | |
|---|---|
| **Bowl,** With Frog, Tuscany, Pink, 9 In. | 50.00 |
| **Candleholder,** Burmese Girls, Green | 125.00 |
| **Candleholder,** Clematis, Pair | 25.00 |
| **Candleholder,** Gardenia, Green & Tan, 4 3/4 In., Pair | 30.00 |
| **Candleholder,** Water Lily, Pink To Green, 4 1/2 In., Pair | 30.00 |
| **Candleholder,** Wincraft, Brown, Pair | 10.00 |
| **Candleholder,** Zephyr Lily, Blue, 3 In. | 8.00 |
| **Candleholder,** Zephyr Lily, Brown, 2 In., Pair | 27.00 |
| **Candlestick,** Carnelian, Aqua, Pair | 18.00 |
| **Candlestick,** Carnelian, Blue Drip On Tan, 3 In., Pair | 25.00 |
| **Candlestick,** Freesia, Terra-Cotta, 4 1/2 In., Pair | 16.00 |
| **Compote,** Donatello, Children Frolicking, 4 1/4 X 5 1/2 In. | 45.00 |
| **Compote,** Donatello, 6 In. | 65.00 To 75.00 |
| **Compote,** Florentine, Brown, 1924-28, 5 In. | 35.00 |
| **Compote,** Velmoss II, Aqua, 5 In. | 30.00 |
| **Conch Shell,** Foxglove, Pink | 45.00 |
| **Console Set,** Ixia, Green, Bowl, 2 Candleholders, 12 In. | 55.00 |
| **Console Set,** Snowberry, Pink, Bowl, 2 Candleholders, 10 In. | 58.00 |
| **Cookie Jar,** Clematis, Green | 85.00 |
| **Cookie Jar,** Zephyr Lily, Brown | 125.00 |
| **Cornucopia,** Apple Blossom, Blue, 6 In. | 22.50 |
| **Cornucopia,** Clematis, Green, 6 In. | 20.00 To 38.00 |
| **Cornucopia,** Gardenia, Green, Double, 8 In. | 30.00 |
| **Cornucopia,** Peony, Pink, 6 In. | 22.50 |
| **Cornucopia,** Pinecone, Blue, 6 In. | 18.50 |
| **Cornucopia,** Pinecone, Green, 6 In. | 20.00 |
| **Cornucopia,** Snowberry, Blue, 6 In. | 24.00 |
| **Cornucopia,** Snowberry, Blue, 8 In. | 20.00 |
| **Cornucopia,** Water Lily, Brown, 6 In. | 21.00 |
| **Cornucopia,** Water Lily, Pink, 8 In. | 40.00 |
| **Cornucopia,** White Rose, Blue, 6 In. | 15.00 |
| **Cornucopia,** White Rose, Flower Frog, Blue, 5 In. | 26.00 |
| **Creamer,** Juvenile, Peter Rabbit | 20.00 |
| **Creamer,** White Rose, Pink, 3 X 5 In. | 20.00 |
| **Cuspidor,** Donatello, 8 In. | 85.00 |
| **Dish,** Child's, Bunnies | 45.00 |
| **Dish,** Child's, Ducks | 45.00 |
| **Dish,** Pinecone, Green, Matte, Signed, 9 X 3 1/2 In. | 10.00 |
| **Dish,** Pinecone, Green, 8 In. | 29.00 |
| **Ewer,** Apple Blossom, Blue, 8 In. | 40.00 |
| **Ewer,** Apple Blossom, Pink, 8 In. | 30.00 |
| **Ewer,** Clematis, Blue, 10 In. | 55.00 |
| **Ewer,** Columbine, Pink, 7 In. | 35.00 |
| **Ewer,** Foxglove, Pink, 10 In. | 55.00 |
| **Ewer,** Gardenia, Gray, 10 In. | 55.00 |
| **Ewer,** Gardenia, Green, 10 In. | 47.00 |
| **Ewer,** Peony, Pink, 10 In. | 42.00 |
| **Flower Frog,** Carnelian, Blue | 18.00 |
| **Flower Pot,** Zephyr Lily, Green, Under Dish | 55.00 |
| **Flowerpot,** Clematis, Brown | 20.00 |
| **Flowerpot,** Clematis, Brown, Under Dish | 60.00 |
| **Jardiniere,** Apple Blossom, Blue, 8 In. | 110.00 |
| **Jardiniere,** Bittersweet, Green, Pedestal, 24 1/2 In. | 325.00 |
| **Jardiniere,** Blackberry, 4 In. | 80.00 |
| **Jardiniere,** Blackberry, 4 1/2 In. | 110.00 |
| **Jardiniere,** Blackberry, 7 In. | 175.00 |
| **Jardiniere,** Bleeding Heart, Green, 7 In. | 60.00 |
| **Jardiniere,** Bushberry, Green, 4 In. | 20.00 |
| **Jardiniere,** Dahlrose, 6 X 8 1/2 In. | 32.00 |
| **Jardiniere,** Dahlrose, 7 1/2 In. | 55.00 |
| **Jardiniere,** Dogwood, Green, 9 In. | 75.00 |
| **Jardiniere,** Donatello, Children, Mandolin, 4 1/2 X 5 1/2 In. | 32.00 |
| **Jardiniere,** Donatello, 6 In. | 45.00 |

| | |
|---|---|
| **Jardiniere,** Florentine, Brown, 9 In. | 75.00 |
| **Jardiniere,** Freesia, Terra-Cotta, 5 In. | 20.00 |
| **Jardiniere,** Gardenia, Gray, Pedestal, 24 In. | 200.00 |
| **Jardiniere,** Mostique, Matte Green, 5 1/2 In. | 20.00 |
| **Jardiniere,** Pinecone, Brown, 14 1/2 In. | 98.00 |
| **Jardiniere,** Rosecraft, Green, Marked, 12 In. | 150.00 |
| **Lamp,** Baneda, Green Shade, 22 In. | 85.00 |
| **Mug,** Bushberry, Blue | 20.00 |
| **Mug,** Elk, Cream | 45.00 To 60.00 |
| **Mug,** Magnolia, Blue | 35.00 |
| **Pitcher,** Freesia, Blue & Green, 10 In. | 40.00 |
| **Pitcher,** Ice Tea, Bushberry, Green, Handled Jugs | 225.00 |
| **Planter,** Apple Blossom, Green, 12 In. | 30.00 |
| **Planter,** Freesia, Terra-Cotta, 8 In. | 18.50 |
| **Planter,** Lotus, Blue & Cream, 4 In.Square | 67.50 |
| **Planter,** Magnolia, Green, 6 In. | 25.00 |
| **Planter,** Pasadena, Blue & Green, Stand, 6 X 6 X 4 In. | 25.00 |
| **Planter,** Wincraft, Gray & Pink, 12 In. | 30.00 |
| **Planter,** Wincraft, Ming Tree Inside, Gray & Wine, 8 In. | 45.00 |
| **Plate,** Baby, Chicks | 10.00 |
| **Plate,** Child's, Creamware, Rolled Edge | 40.00 |
| **Plate,** Child's, Dog | 45.00 |
| **Plate,** Child's, Duck | 40.00 |
| **Plate,** Child's, Duck, Red Hat | 45.00 |
| **Plate,** Child's, Rabbits, 8 In. | 29.00 |
| **Rose Bowl,** Apple Blossom, Blue | 35.00 |
| **Rose Bowl,** Pinecone, Green, 4 In. | 30.00 |
| **Rose Bowl,** Primrose, Tan, 4 In. | 25.00 |
| **Rozane,** Yellow Iris, Pedestal, 15 1/2 In. | 165.00 |
| **Sugar,** White Rose, Pink | 18.00 |
| **Tankard Set,** Dutch, Pitcher & 4 Mugs | 375.00 |
| **Tankard,** Dutch Creamware | 45.00 To 75.00 |
| **Tea Set,** Apple Blossom, Green | 85.00 |
| **Tea Set,** Bushberry, Green | 75.00 |
| **Tea Set,** Wincraft, Blue, 3 Piece | 85.00 |
| **Teapot,** Clematis, Brown | 45.00 |
| **Umbrella Stand,** Bushberry, Brown | 400.00 |
| **Umbrella Stand,** Pinecone, Blue | 200.00 |
| **Urn,** Baneda, Pink, 7 In. | 40.00 |
| **Urn,** Bushberry, Terra-Cotta, Handled, 8 In. | 32.50 |
| **Urn,** Carnelian II, Green, 2-Handled, 8 In. | 45.00 |
| **Urn,** Florentine, Brown, Footed, 4 1/2 In. | 75.00 |
| **Vase,** Apple Blossom, Deep Pink, Twig Handles, 9 1/2 In. | 35.00 |
| **Vase,** Baldin, Blue, 12 In. | 145.00 |
| **Vase,** Baneda, Blue On Green, 2-Handled, 7 1/4 In. | 45.00 |
| **Vase,** Baneda, Green, 7 X 6 1/2 In. | 65.00 |
| **Vase,** Baneda, Green, 8 In. | 50.00 |
| **Vase,** Bittersweet, Yellow Terra-Cotta, 8 In. | 38.00 |
| **Vase,** Blackberry, 4 In. | 100.00 |
| **Vase,** Blackberry, 6 1/2 In. | 110.00 |
| **Vase,** Blackberry, 8 In. | 130.00 To 150.00 |
| **Vase,** Bleeding Heart, Blue, 4 In. | 20.00 |
| **Vase,** Bleeding Heart, Pink, 12 In. | 55.00 |
| **Vase,** Bud, Clematis, Brown, 7 In., Pair | 15.00 |
| **Vase,** Bud, Freesia, Green, 7 In. | 22.00 |
| **Vase,** Bud, Rosecraft, Black, Paper Sticker, 7 In. | 94.00 |
| **Vase,** Bud, Rosecraft, Black, 8 In. | 50.00 |
| **Vase,** Bushberry, Green, Terra-Cotta Reversed Handles, 7 In. | 95.00 |
| **Vase,** Bushberry, Green, 12 In. | 85.00 |
| **Vase,** Bushberry, Green, 14 In. | 95.00 |
| **Vase,** Bushberry, Green, 15 In. | 95.00 |
| **Vase,** Bushberry, Orange, 2-Handled, 6 In. | 25.00 |
| **Vase,** Bushberry, Terra-Cotta, 8 In. | 16.00 |

| | |
|---|---|
| **Vase,** Camark, Green, 5 In. | 12.50 |
| **Vase,** Cherry Blossom, Blue, 8 In. | 50.00 |
| **Vase,** Clematis, Blue, 7 In. | 20.00 |
| **Vase,** Clematis, Green, Rose Flower Handle, 6 In. | 38.00 |
| **Vase,** Clematis, Green, 15 In. | 80.00 |
| **Vase,** Columbine, Pink, 3 In. | 20.00 |
| **Vase,** Cornucopia, Green, 8 1/2 In. | 28.00 |
| **Vase,** Cremona, Green, 5 In. | 20.00 |
| **Vase,** Cremona, Green, 8 In. | 30.00 |
| **Vase,** Cremona, Pink, Flat, 6 In. | 25.00 |
| **Vase,** Dahlrose, Original Seal, 8 1/2 In. | 45.00 |
| **Vase,** Dahlrose, 2-Handled, 8 In. | 35.00 |
| **Vase,** Dahlrose, 10 X 6 In. | 70.00 |
| **Vase,** Dogwood II, 8 In. | 50.00 |
| **Vase,** Donatello, Cylinder, 8 In. | 40.00 |
| **Vase,** Donatello, Trumpet Shape, 12 In. | 110.00 |
| **Vase,** Ferrella, Brown, Handled, 9 1/4 In. | 325.00 |
| **Vase,** Florentine, Reverse Brown Handled, 8 In. | 95.00 |
| **Vase,** Foxglaze, Blue Ground, Pink & Yellow Flowers, 4 1/4 In. | 25.00 |
| **Vase,** Foxglove, Blue, 8 In. | 25.00 |
| **Vase,** Foxglove, Green, Handled, 7 In. | 22.00 |
| **Vase,** Freesia, Blue, 2-Handled, 7 In. | 20.00 |
| **Vase,** Fuchsia, Blue, Handled, 8 1/2 In. | 34.00 |
| **Vase,** Fuchsia, Brown, 6 In. | 40.00 |
| **Vase,** Fuchsia, Orange, 6 In. | 30.00 |
| **Vase,** Futura, Blue, 6 In. | 20.00 |
| **Vase,** Gardenia, Brown, 10 In. | 35.00 |
| **Vase,** Iris, Blue, 4 In. | 23.00 |
| **Vase,** Iris, Pink & Green, 8 In. | 40.00 |
| **Vase,** Jonquil, Brown To Green, 6 In. | 38.00 |
| **Vase,** Laurel, Green, 6 In. | 45.00 |
| **Vase,** Laurel, Yellow & Black, 4-Handled, Marked, 7 1/2 In. | 42.50 |
| **Vase,** Laurel, Yellow, 7 1/2 In. | 65.00 |
| **Vase,** Luffa, Tan, Gold Sticker, 6 In. | 48.00 |
| **Vase,** Magnolia, Blue, 2-Handled, 14 1/2 In. | 88.00 |
| **Vase,** Magnolia, Blue, 7 In. | 21.00 To 25.00 |
| **Vase,** Ming Tree, Aqua, Pink & Brown, 10 In., Pair | 50.00 |
| **Vase,** Ming Tree, Green, 8 In. | 40.00 |
| **Vase,** Ming Tree, White, 6 In. | 25.00 |
| **Vase,** Ming Tree, White, 8 In. | 65.00 |
| **Vase,** Montacello, Turquoise, 2-Handled, Bulbous, 7 3/4 In. | 65.00 |
| **Vase,** Morning Glory, Green, Fan Shape, 7 In. | 325.00 |
| **Vase,** Morning Glory, Green, 7 1/2 In. | 175.00 |
| **Vase,** Mostique, Gray, 8 In. | 28.00 |
| **Vase,** Peony, Green, 4 In. | 20.00 |
| **Vase,** Peony, Green, 8 In. | 22.00 |
| **Vase,** Peony, Yellow, 6 In. | 32.00 |
| **Vase,** Pinecone, Blue, 9 1/2 In. | 50.00 |
| **Vase,** Pinecone, Green, 7 In. | 45.00 |
| **Vase,** Pinecone, Green, 12 In. | 55.00 |
| **Vase,** Pinecone, Orange, 12 1/2 In. | 95.00 |
| **Vase,** Pinecone, Terra-Cotta, Twig Handles, 8 In. | 85.00 |
| **Vase,** Poppy, Pink, 6 In. | 25.00 |
| **Vase,** Primrose, Pink, 6 In. | 24.00 To 30.00 |
| **Vase,** Primrose, Pink, 7 In. | 20.00 |
| **Vase,** Royal Capri, Gold, 6 In. | 785.00 |
| **Vase,** Rozane, Della Robbia, Signed E.L., 9 1/2 In. | *Illus* 675.00 |
| **Vase,** Rozane, White, 7 In. | 25.00 |
| **Vase,** Russco, Blue, 6 1/2 In. | 20.00 |
| **Vase,** Russco, Salmon, Paper Label, 9 1/4 In. | 30.00 |
| **Vase,** Savona, Ivory, 10 In. | 65.00 |
| **Vase,** Silhouette, Burgundy, Leaf Design, 5 In. | 65.00 |
| **Vase,** Silhouette, Burgundy, 12 In. | 35.00 |

Roseville, Vase, Rozane, Della Robbia, Signed E.L., 9 1/2 In.

| | |
|---|---|
| **Vase,** Silhouette, Red, 8 In. | 125.00 |
| **Vase,** Silhouette, Rust, Fan Shape, 7 In. | 65.00 |
| **Vase,** Silhoutte, Aqua, 14 In. | 90.00 |
| **Vase,** Snowberry, Green, Slanted, 7 In. | 17.00 |
| **Vase,** Snowberry, Green, 9 In. | 30.00 |
| **Vase,** Snowberry, Pink, 6 In. | 24.00 |
| **Vase,** Thorn Apple, Green & White, Pink, 6 1/4 In. | 24.00 |
| **Vase,** Topeo, Blue, 7 In. | 75.00 |
| **Vase,** Topeo, Blue, 9 In. | 75.00 |
| **Vase,** Tourmaline, Blue & Italian Gold, 7 1/2 In. | 38.00 |
| **Vase,** Tourmaline, Blue-Green, 6 In. | 95.00 |
| **Vase,** Tourmaline, Blue, Bowl Shape, 5 In. | 28.00 |
| **Vase,** Tuscany, Gray, 8 In. | 35.00 |
| **Vase,** Water Lily, Blue & Aqua, 6 In. | 24.00 |
| **Vase,** Water Lily, Pink, 4 In. | 23.00 |
| **Vase,** White Rose, Rose To Green, 6 In. | 38.00 |
| **Vase,** Wincraft, Blue, 6 In. | 30.00 To 32.00 |
| **Vase,** Wincraft, Yellow & Green, 12 In. | 60.00 |
| **Vase,** Wisteria, Brown, 6 In. | 55.00 |
| **Vase,** Wisteria, Tan, 8 In. | 75.00 |
| **Vase,** Zephyr Lily, Blue, 7 In. | 22.50 |
| **Vase,** Zephyr Lily, Blue, 8 In. | 20.00 |
| **Vase,** Zephyr Lily, Blue, 15 In. | 125.00 |
| **Wall Pocket,** Apple Blossom, Pink, 8 In. | 35.00 |
| **Wall Pocket,** Blackberry | 165.00 To 250.00 |
| **Wall Pocket,** Corinthian, 8 In. | 45.00 |
| **Wall Pocket,** Corinthian, 9 1/2 In. | 60.00 |
| **Wall Pocket,** Dahlrose, Black Sticker, 8 In. | 45.00 |
| **Wall Pocket,** Dogwood II, 10 In. | 40.00 |
| **Wall Pocket,** Donatello, Impressed Mark, 12 In. | 95.00 |
| **Wall Pocket,** Donatello, 10 In. | 45.00 To 55.00 |
| **Wall Pocket,** Foxglove, Blue | 50.00 |
| **Wall Pocket,** Foxglove, Green Shades To Pink | 50.00 |
| **Wall Pocket,** Foxglove, Pink, 8 In. | 35.00 |
| **Wall Pocket,** Iris, Pink | 60.00 |
| **Wall Pocket,** Snowberry, Blue, 8 In. | 35.00 |
| **Wall Pocket,** Tuscany Pink & Green, 7 In. | 55.00 |
| **Wall Pocket,** Zephyr Lily, Brown | 45.00 |
| **Wall Pocket,** Zephyr Lily, Green, 8 In. | 45.00 |
| **Water Set,** Peony, Green, 7 Piece | 280.00 |

*Rowland & Marsellus Company is a mark which appears on historical
Staffordshire dating from the late nineteenth and early twentieth centuries.
Rowland & Marsellus is believed to be the British Anchor Pottery
Co. of Longton, England. Many American views were made.*

| | |
|---|---|
| **ROWLAND & MARSELLUS, Plate,** Albany, N.Y., Rolled Edge, 10 In. | 30.00 |
| **Plate,** Denver, C.1905, 9 3/4 In. | 35.00 |
| **Plate,** Historic, Detroit | 75.00 |
| **Plate,** Historic, Kalamazoo | 75.00 |
| **Plate,** Lakewood, N.Y., Rolled Edge, 10 In. | 30.00 |
| **Plate,** Norristown, Penn., 1912, Blue, 10 In. | 30.00 |
| **Plate,** Portland, Me., Rolled Edge, 10 In. | 30.00 |
| **Plate,** Scranton, Penn., Rolled Edge, Sepia | 95.00 |
| **Plate,** Souvenir, Albany, N.Y., Blue, 7 1/2 In. | 22.00 |
| **Plate,** Theodore Roosevelt | 45.00 |
| **Plate,** Valley Forge, Penn., 1910, 10 In. | 30.00 |
| **Vase,** Handled, Bust Of Classic Maiden On Front, 12 In. | 85.00 |
| | |
| **ROY ROGERS, Badge,** Deputy | 10.00 |
| **Bandana,** Red, With Trigger | 7.50 |
| **Bank,** With Trigger | 18.00 |
| **Book,** Raiders Of Sawtooth Edge, 1946, Whitman | 7.00 |
| **Boot Tops,** Leatherette | 10.00 |
| **Cap Gun,** Cast Iron | 18.00 |
| **Cap Gun,** Tuckaway Miniature, Original Store Card | 5.00 |
| **Cart,** Pulled By Wooden Horse, Wooden, 19 1/2 In. | 35.00 |
| **Chaps,** Vinyl | 9.00 |
| **Chuckwagon,** Pull Toy | 25.00 |
| **Clock,** Alarm | 90.00 |
| **Clock,** Animated, Boxed | 65.00 |
| **Creamer,** Figural | 15.00 |
| **Cup,** Molded Face, Original Paint, Plastic | 9.00 |
| **Dog,** Bullet, Plastic, Hartland | 15.00 |
| **Gloves,** Leather | 10.00 |
| **Guitar,** Pictures On Case & Guitar, Wooden, 1956, 33 In. | 65.00 |
| **Gun & Spurs Set,** 1940, Original Box | 40.00 |
| **Harmonica,** On Original Card | 15.00 |
| **Holster,** Leather | 9.00 |
| **Kiddie-Car,** Figural, Horse, Paper On Wood, Marked Trigger | 85.00 |
| **Lamp,** Riding Trigger | 35.00 |
| **Lantern,** Ranch, Boxed | 32.00 |
| **Lunch Box** | 8.00 To 10.00 |
| **Mug,** Plastic | 8.00 |
| **Necktie,** 1940s | 7.00 |
| **Pencil Box** | 10.00 |
| **Ranchhouse,** Tin | 25.00 |
| **Ring,** Branding Iron | 20.00 To 35.00 |
| **Ring,** Photograph Of Hero, C.1950 | 35.00 |
| **Toy,** Wagon Train, Windup | 75.00 |
| **Watch,** Fastens To Blouse, 7-Jewel, Swiss Movement | 50.00 |
| **Western Town,** Lithographs, Tin Buildings, 100 Accessories, Marx | 50.00 |
| | |
| **ROYAL AUSTRIA, Berry Bowl,** White Pearl Interior, Yellow Roses, Signed, 7 In. | 75.00 |
| **Fish Set,** Platter, 8 Plates, 20 In. | 150.00 |
| **Salt & Pepper,** Pastel, Pink Apple Blossoms, Gold Trim | 25.00 |
| **Stickpin Holder,** Hand-Painted, Artist Signed, 1 1/2 In. | 125.00 |
| **Teapot,** Sugar & Creamer, Covered, 1916, Green Wreath Mark | 60.00 |
| **Tureen,** Soup, Green, Yellow Flowers | 45.00 |
| **Vase,** Seminude Goddess Of Love, 4 Cupids, Gold, 4 1/2 X 9 In. | 285.00 |

*The Royal Bayreuth factory was founded in Tettau, Bavaria, in 1794.
It has continued to modern times. The marks have changed through the years.*

*A stylized crest, the name "Royal Bayreuth," and the word "Bavaria"
appear in slightly different form from 1870 to about 1919. Later dishes may
include the words "U.S. Zone," the year of the issue, and do not have
the word "Bavaria."*

**ROYAL BAYREUTH, see also Rose Tapestry; Sand Babies; Snow
Babies; Sunbonnet Babies**

| | |
|---|---|
| **ROYAL BAYREUTH, Ashtray,** Cattle Scene | 45.00 |
| **Ashtray,** Club Shaped, Dutch Girl, Bird, House, Blue Mark | 45.00 |
| **Ashtray,** Coral Shell, Signed | 27.00 |
| **Ashtray,** Elk | 35.00 To 135.00 |
| **Ashtray,** Goats, Trees, 2 Rests, Marked | 42.00 |
| **Ashtray,** Hunter & Dog, Blue Mark | 58.00 |
| **Ashtray,** Spade Shape, Goose Girl, Blue Mark | 55.00 |
| **Ashtray,** Stork, Green, Blue Mark | 25.00 |
| **Babies Under Umbrella,** 4 1/2 In. | 160.00 |
| **Basket,** Miniature, Peach, Mother-Of-Pearl, 3 In. | 95.00 |
| **Basket,** Mother-Of-Pearl, Gold Trim, 4 1/2 X 5 X 2 1/2 In. | 60.00 |
| **Bell,** Little Boy Blue, Saying, Wood Clapper | 125.00 |
| **Bowl,** Berry, 6 Leaf Dishes, Green, Pink Splatches, Green Mark | 185.00 |
| **Bowl,** Egg Shaped, Footed, Scenic, Green Mark | 75.00 |
| **Bowl,** Girl, Hands In Fur Muff Center, Spider, 10 1/2 In. | 175.00 |
| **Bowl,** Grape, Mother-Of-Pearl, Blue Mark, 4 1/2 X 9 1/2 In. | 225.00 |
| **Bowl,** Portrait, Girl With Her Hands In Fur Muff, 10 In. | 175.00 |
| **Bowl,** Portrait, Tapestry, Victorian Lady, 6 In. | 125.00 |
| **Bowl,** Red Poppy, Blue Mark, 8 In.Diam. | 70.00 |
| **Bowl,** Roses, Gold Trim, Rolled Over Edge, 10 In. | 575.00 |
| **Bowl,** Sauce, Tray, Swan Design, Blue Mark | 150.00 |
| **Bowl,** Scalloped, 4 Blown-Out Areas, 10 1/2 In. | 117.00 |
| **Bowl,** Scenic, Blue Mark, 10 1/2 In.Diam. | 435.00 |
| **Bowl,** Tomato, Blown Out, Green Mark, 9 In. | 95.00 |
| **Bowl,** Woman & Chickens In Field, Blue Mark, 9 1/2 In. | 135.00 |
| **Bowl,** 3 Toed, Blue Mark, 9 In.Diam. | 95.00 |
| **Box,** Candy, 3 Compartment, Covered, Blue Mark | 50.00 |
| **Box,** Covered, Turtle, Blue Mark, 7 In.Square | 650.00 |
| **Box,** Figural, Turtle, Covered, 7 In. | 650.00 |
| **Box,** Powder, Cover, Elk Scene On Lid, Black Mark | 75.00 |
| **Box,** Powder, Gold Footed, Roses | 55.00 |
| **Box,** The Fox Hunt, Round, Footed, Covered, Blue Mark | 85.00 |
| **Box,** Turtle, Figural, 7 In. | 650.00 |
| **Butter,** Covered, Arabs On Horses Design, 6 X 4 1/4 In. | 170.00 |
| **Cake Plate,** Bo Peep, Handled | 145.00 |
| **Cake Plate,** Raised Gold Concentric Rings, Blue Mark, 10 In. | 75.00 |
| **Candleholder,** Beach Babies, Blue Mark | 100.00 To 125.00 |
| **Candleholder,** Cavalier Scene On Shield, 7 1/2 In. | 95.00 |
| **Candleholder,** Figural, Clown, Short | 150.00 |
| **Candleholder,** Little Miss Muffet | 150.00 |
| **Candlestick,** Bellringer | 210.00 |
| **Candlestick,** Brown Grazing Cows, Green Ground, 6 In., Pair | 85.00 |
| **Candlestick,** Devil & Cards, Low, Pair | 175.00 |
| **Candlestick,** Figural, Basset, Black Mark | 190.00 |
| **Candlestick,** Floral Design, Green Ground | 65.00 |
| **Candlestick,** Goose Girl | 135.00 |
| **Candlestick,** Jack & Jill, Blue Mark | 135.00 |
| **Candlestick,** Jester, Signed, Blue Mark, 4 3/4 In. | 70.00 |
| **Candlestick,** Little Bo Peep, Pair | 145.00 |
| **Candlestick,** Low, Penguin, Yellow, Blue Mark | 35.00 |
| **Candlestick,** Peasant Musicians, Blue Mark, 4 1/2 In. | 65.00 |
| **Candlestick,** Red Clown Sitting | 250.00 |
| **Card Holder,** Stork, Green, Covered, Blue Mark | 30.00 |
| **Celery,** Lobster, Figural | 145.00 |
| **Chamberstick,** Corinthian, Handled, Saucer, Blue Mark | 75.00 |
| **Chamberstick,** Sunbonnet Babies, Folding & Ironing | 225.00 |

**Chocolate Pot,** Hunter & Dog, 8 In. ........................................................................... 280.00
**Chocolate Pot,** Red Poppy, Blue Mark ....................................................................... 200.00
**Cracker Jar,** Corinthian, Red, Black Trim, Blue Mark ............................................ 150.00
**Cracker Jar,** Tomato, Covered ................................................................................... 125.00
**Creamer & Sugar,** Corinthian Grecian Design, Marked ........................................ 115.00
**Creamer & Tray,** Peacock & Scenic, Blue Mark ...................................................... 75.00
**Creamer,** Alligator, Blue Mark ................................................................ 75.00 To 145.00
**Creamer,** Apple, Blue Mark .................................................................... 55.00 To 60.00
**Creamer,** Art Nouveau Lady, Blue Mark ................................................................. 175.00
**Creamer,** Aukland Exposition, 1913 ......................................................................... 50.00
**Creamer,** Bird Of Paradise ....................................................................................... 140.00
**Creamer,** Black Bull, Red Horns, Tettau Mark ........................................................ 95.00
**Creamer,** Black Cat, Marked, 5 In. ......................................................... 105.00 To 145.00
**Creamer,** Black Crow, Blue Mark ............................................................................ 105.00
**Creamer,** Black Water Buffalo .................................................................. 115.00 To 155.00
**Creamer,** Bull, Red Mouth & Horns, Blue Mark ..................................... 90.00 To 140.00
**Creamer,** Calico Cat, Figural .................................................................................... 350.00
**Creamer,** Cat, Black, Figural .................................................................... 70.00 To 80.00
**Creamer,** Cat, Gray To Black, Blue Mark ............................................... 87.00 To 130.00
**Creamer,** Clown, Red ................................................................................................ 175.00
**Creamer,** Clown, Red, Blue Mark ........................................................... 125.00 To 130.00
**Creamer,** Coachman, Blue Mark .............................................................................. 120.00
**Creamer,** Cow, Scenic ............................................................................................... 55.00
**Creamer,** Crow, Black & Red, Marked .................................................... 75.00 To 125.00
**Creamer,** Dachshund, Figural, Blue Mark ............................................. 125.00 To 150.00
**Creamer,** Devil & Card, Blue Mark .......................................................... 85.00 To 125.00
**Creamer,** Duck ........................................................................................................... 35.00
**Creamer,** Dutch ......................................................................................................... 65.00
**Creamer,** Eagle .......................................................................................................... 135.00
**Creamer,** Elk, Blue Mark, 4 1/2 In. .......................................................................... 45.00
**Creamer,** Elk, Blue Mark, 5 In. ................................................................................. 70.00
**Creamer,** Floral .......................................................................................................... 45.00
**Creamer,** Frog, Blue & Orange, Blue Mark ............................................................. 49.00
**Creamer,** Frog, Green ................................................................................................ 55.00
**Creamer,** Girl Feeding Chickens ............................................................................. 95.00
**Creamer,** Girl With Handle, Scenic .......................................................................... 65.00
**Creamer,** Hand-Painted Rose, Her Majesty, Blue Mark, 6 1/2 In. ......................... 40.00
**Creamer,** Horsehead .................................................................................................. 145.00
**Creamer,** Hounds ....................................................................................................... 65.00
**Creamer,** Hunt Scene, Pinched Spout, 4 In. ........................................... 40.00 To 55.00
**Creamer,** Hunting Scene, Green, Blue Mark ........................................................... 45.00
**Creamer,** Lady, Art Nouveau, Blue Mark ................................................................. 175.00
**Creamer,** Lamplighter, Green Coat, Signed ........................................................... 185.00
**Creamer,** Lemon, Blue Mark .................................................................... 60.00 To 70.00
**Creamer,** Lemon, Figural, Blue Mark ..................................................... 85.00 To 105.00
**Creamer,** Lettuce, Lobster Handled, Blue Mark ..................................... 25.00 To 45.00
**Creamer,** Little Jack Horner, Blue Mark .................................................................. 55.00
**Creamer,** Lobster, Marked ....................................................................... 37.00 To 65.00
**Creamer,** Lobster, Matching Underplate ................................................................. 95.00
**Creamer,** Man In Mountain, Marked ........................................................................ 110.00
**Creamer,** Melon, Green Branch, Flowers, Signed .................................................. 145.00
**Creamer,** Mountain Goat, Blue Mark ...................................................... 95.00 To 105.00
**Creamer,** Musicians, Double Handled, Blue Mark .................................................. 75.00
**Creamer,** Oak Leaf, Pearlized, Blue Mark .............................................................. 95.00
**Creamer,** Oak Leaf, Satin ......................................................................................... 135.00
**Creamer,** Old Man Of The Mountain, Gray, Figural ................................................ 45.00
**Creamer,** Old Man Of The Mountain, Green Mark .................................................. 65.00
**Creamer,** Orange, Blue Mark ................................................................... 70.00 To 85.00
**Creamer,** Pansy, Blue Mark ...................................................................................... 125.00
**Creamer,** Pansy, Green Mark .................................................................................... 85.00
**Creamer,** Parakeet, 3 3/4 In. ..................................................................................... 165.00
**Creamer,** Peacock Design, Blue Mark, 4 1/4 In. ..................................................... 95.00
**Creamer,** Pink Rose, Blue Mark ............................................................................... 125.00

**Creamer,** Poodle, Gray, Blue Mark, 4 1/4 In. ............................................................ 140.00
**Creamer,** Poppy, Red, Black Mark ............................................................................... 85.00
**Creamer,** Poppy, Red, Blue Mark .................................................... 70.00 To 95.00
**Creamer,** Robin ............................................................ 110.00 To 140.00
**Creamer,** Rooster, Black Mark ................................................................................... 115.00
**Creamer,** Rose ......................................................................................................... 175.00
**Creamer,** Shell, Figural Sea Horse, Handled ............................................................ 35.00
**Creamer,** Shell, Murex, Blue Mark ............................................................................ 30.00
**Creamer,** Shell, Pink, Blue, Orange, & Tan, 4 In. ..................................................... 25.00
**Creamer,** Shell, Spiky, Pearl ...................................................................................... 70.00
**Creamer,** St.Bernard Dog Head, Black, Gray, & Brown, 3 1/2 In. ........................... 155.00
**Creamer,** St.Bernard Head, Gray, 4 In. ................................................................... 145.00
**Creamer,** Stirrup ........................................................................................................ 150.00
**Creamer,** Stork, Green, Blue Mark ............................................................................. 30.00
**Creamer,** Strawberry, Blue Mark ......................................................... 85.00 To 125.00
**Creamer,** Striped Cat Handle ..................................................................................... 95.00
**Creamer,** Sunflower, Blue Mark ............................................................................... 150.00
**Creamer,** Toby Coachman, Figural ........................................................................... 145.00
**Creamer,** Tomato .......................................................................... 35.00 To 45.00
**Creamer,** Tomato, Blue Mark ........................................................... 51.00 To 62.50
**Creamer,** Trout, Green, Black, Red On Beige, 4 In. ................................................. 145.00
**Creamer,** Turtle, Black Mark, Small ......................................................................... 175.00
**Creamer,** Twig Handle, Apple, 3 1/4 In. .................................................................... 90.00
**Creamer,** Washer Woman, Blue Mark ........................................................................ 75.00
**Creamer,** Water Buffalo, Yellow Horns, Blue Mark ......................... 95.00 To 120.00
**Cruet,** Cattle Scene, Blue Mark, 5 In. ...................................................................... 125.00
**Cup & Saucer,** Girl, Dog On Leash, Blue Mark ............................... 98.00 To 110.00
**Cup & Saucer,** Rose Design, Demitasse, Blue Mark .................................................. 65.00
**Cup & Saucer,** Rose, Demi, Blue Mark .................................................................... 175.00
**Cup,** Loving, Hunting Scene, Blue Mark, 3 3/4 In. .................................................... 95.00
**Dish,** Candy, Maple Leaf, Bopeep ........................................................................... 155.00
**Dish,** Celery, Shell, Blue Mark ................................................................................ 100.00
**Dish,** Child's, Little Jack Horner, 8 In. ...................................................................... 115.00
**Dish,** Conch Shell Shaped, Divided, 11 In. .............................................................. 165.00
**Dish,** Heart Shaped, Jack & Jill ................................................................................ 65.00
**Dish,** Heart Shaped, Little Bopeep, Blue Mark .......................................................... 55.00
**Dish,** Leaf Shaped, Handle, Blue Mark, 5 1/2 In.Diam. ............................................ 24.00
**Dish,** Lettuce .......................................................................... 14.50 To 15.00
**Dish,** Mayonnaise, Red Poppy Ladle, Blue Mark ...................................................... 50.00
**Dish,** Pickle, Hunting Scene ...................................................................................... 60.00
**Dish,** Pin, Devil & Cards, Blue Mark ....................................................................... 200.00
**Dish,** Pin, Heart Shaped, 2 Cows, Blue Mark .......................................................... 135.00
**Dish,** Relish, Lobster, Curved Tail Forms Handle, 6 In. ............................................ 30.00
**Dish,** Relish, Roses & Gold Panels, Blue Mark, 7 3/4 In. ......................................... 95.00
**Dish,** Shell, Pearlized, Green Mark, Small ................................................................ 25.00
**Dish,** Shell, 5 In. ....................................................................................................... 45.00
**Dish,** Soap, 3 Children At Beach .............................................................................. 75.00
**Dish,** Tomato, Covered, Blue Mark, 3 In. ........................................ 30.00 To 45.00
**Dish,** Twiglike Handled, Tomato Center, 6 In. ........................................................... 30.00
**Ewer,** Cockfight, Green Handles ................................................................................ 95.00
**Ewer,** Green, Couple In Hunting Scene, 5 1/2 In. ................................................... 125.00
**Figurine,** Oxford Shoe, Man's, Original Laces, Signed ............................................... 85.00
**Flower Holder,** Covered, Hunt Scene, Blue Mark, 3 5/8 In. ...................................... 85.00
**Hair Receiver,** Cover, Little Bopeep .......................................................................... 25.00
**Hair Receiver,** Venetian Scene, Blue Mark, 3 1/2 In. ............................................... 45.00
**Hair Receiver,** White Roses, Pink & Green, Blue Mark ............................................. 50.00
**Hatpin Holder,** Oyster & Pearl ................................................................................. 195.00
**Hatpin Holder,** Penguin ............................................................................................ 495.00
**Holder,** String, Rooster .............................................................................................. 95.00
**Holder,** String, Rooster, Blue Mark ................................................ 163.00 To 175.00
**Humidor,** Card & Devil, Green Mark, 8 1/4 In. ........................................................ 350.00
**Humidor,** Castle Scene, Black Mark ......................................................................... 135.00
**Inkwell,** Beach Baby ................................................................................................ 225.00

**Jam Jar & Ladle,** Tomato ............................................................................ 38.00
**Jar,** Lobster, Red, Covered, 4 In. ................................................................ 42.00
**Jar,** Powder, Venetian Scene, Blue Mark, 3 1/2 In. ...................................... 45.00
**Ladle,** Red Poppy, 7 In. .............................................................................. 25.00
**Lid,** Hair Receiver, Rose Tapestry, Pink, Yellow Roses ................................ 55.00
**Match & Cigarette Holder,** Corinthian, Striker On Base, Pair ...................... 65.00
**Match Holder,** Children At Beach, Wall, Blue Mark ...................................... 130.00
**Match Holder,** Clown, Wall ........................................... 175.00 To 295.00
**Match Holder,** Devil & Card, Wall ............................................................... 175.00
**Match Holder,** Devil & Cards, Marked ........................................................ 225.00
**Match Holder,** Devil & Cards, Wall ............................................................. 95.00
**Match Holder,** Elk, Green Mark ................................................................... 130.00
**Match Holder,** Musicians, Double Pocket .................................................... 145.00
**Match Holder,** Poppy, Blue Mark ................................................................ 40.00
**Match Holder,** Poppy, Red ........................................................................... 40.00
**Match Holder,** Poppy, Wall ......................................................................... 75.00
**Match Holder,** Shell Shape, Wall ................................................................ 110.00
**Match Holder,** Violets, Green Mark ............................................................. 18.00
**Mug,** Beer, Elk, Antler Handle, Blue Mark .................... 150.00 To 195.00
**Mug,** Devil & Cards, Marked ....................................................................... 195.00
**Mug,** Tankard, Green Cavalier Scene, Black Mark ...................................... 70.00
**Mug,** White Cat, Green, Handle, Blue Mark ................................................ 225.00
**Mug,** 3-Handled, Orange Top Band With Cows, Blue Mark ......................... 40.00
**Mustard,** Attached Plate, Boy With Reins Of Horses, Blue Mark ................. 65.00
**Mustard,** Lobster, Red, Covered, Blue Mark ............................................... 59.00
**Mustard,** Poppy, Red, Covered, Spoon ....................................................... 85.00
**Mustard,** Red Poppy, Covered, Blue Mark .................................................. 65.00
**Mustard,** Red Poppy, Green Mark ............................................................... 25.00
**Mustard,** Tomato ........................................................................................ 35.00
**Nappy,** Diamond Shaped, Roses, Blue Mark .............................................. 40.00
**Nappy,** Leaf Shape, 3 Blown-Out Grapes, Blue Mark, 5 1/2 In. .................. 70.00
**Nut Set,** Poppy, White Mother-Of-Pearl ...................................................... 250.00
**Pinbox,** Hunting Scene, Diamond Shaped, Covered, Blue Mark .................. 75.00
**Pipe Rest,** Basset, Marked .......................................................................... 145.00
**Pitcher,** Apple, Blue Mark, 6 In. ................................................................. 115.00
**Pitcher,** Butterfly, Blue Mark ...................................................................... 187.50
**Pitcher,** Cream, Man Fishing In Boat, Blue Mark, 2 1/2 In. ......................... 75.00
**Pitcher,** Fishing Scene, Blue Mark, 5 1/4 In. .............................................. 95.00
**Pitcher,** Goats, Lower Half Orange, Blue Mark, 5 1/4 In. ............................ 75.00
**Pitcher,** Hunter With Dogs & Geese, Blue Mark, 4 1/2 In. .......................... 90.00
**Pitcher,** Hunting Scene, 4 In. ..................................................................... 65.00
**Pitcher,** Ladies & Sheep, Square, Blue Mark, 3 In. ..................................... 50.00
**Pitcher,** Left Handed, Nude Ladies, Blue Mark, 5 3/4 In. ............................ 200.00
**Pitcher,** Little Miss Muffet, Verse ............................................................... 90.00
**Pitcher,** Milk, Band Of Figures On Horseback, Green ................................. 195.00
**Pitcher,** Milk, Butterfly ............................................................................... 325.00
**Pitcher,** Milk, Coachman, Blue Mark .......................................................... 195.00
**Pitcher,** Milk, Cockatoo ............................................................................. 195.00
**Pitcher,** Milk, Devil & Cards, 5 In. .............................................. 150.00 To 250.00
**Pitcher,** Milk, Fish Head, Marked ............................................................... 75.00
**Pitcher,** Milk, Fish, Figural ........................................... 125.00 To 145.00
**Pitcher,** Milk, Lamplighter, Figural ............................................................. 195.00
**Pitcher,** Milk, Lobster Form, 19th Century, 7 In. ........................................ 95.00
**Pitcher,** Milk, Melon, Blue Mark ................................................................. 150.00
**Pitcher,** Milk, Oak Leaf, Blue Mark ............................................................ 150.00
**Pitcher,** Milk, Pansy, Blue Mark ................................................................. 225.00
**Pitcher,** Milk, Parrot Handle ....................................................................... 380.00
**Pitcher,** Milk, Parrot, Figural ...................................................................... 195.00
**Pitcher,** Milk, Pinched Spout, Pastoral Scene, 6 1/8 In. ............................. 115.00
**Pitcher,** Milk, Rose ..................................................................................... 575.00
**Pitcher,** Milk, Seal, Blue Mark ................................................................... 225.00
**Pitcher,** Milk, Sunbonnet ........................................................................... 198.00
**Pitcher,** Milk, Tomato, Blue Mark ................................................. 75.00 To 90.00

| | |
|---|---|
| Pitcher, Mountain Goat Scene, 3 3/4 In. | 90.00 |
| Pitcher, Musicians, Blue Mark, 3 1/2 In. | 95.00 |
| Pitcher, Pastoral Scene, Blue Mark, 15 1/2 In.Diam. | 125.00 |
| Pitcher, Pinch-Nose, Scene Of Cows Grazing, 10 In. | 190.00 |
| Pitcher, Poodle, Black, Blue Mark, 5 In. ............. 125.00 To | 150.00 |
| Pitcher, Riders & Hounds, Lower 2/3 Yellow, Blue Mark, 6 In. | 140.00 |
| Pitcher, Ring-Around-The-Rosie, Blue Mark, 3 1/4 In. | 130.00 |
| Pitcher, Sheep In Pasture, Pinched Spout, Signed, 7 In. | 245.00 |
| Pitcher, Sheep In Pasture, Signed, 7 In. | 245.00 |
| Pitcher, Stork, Yellow, Blue Mark, 6 1/2 In. | 35.00 |
| Pitcher, Water, Buffalo Black, Red Horns | 125.00 |
| Pitcher, Water, Grapes, White, Mother-Of-Pearl | 375.00 |
| Pitcher, Water, Orange, Figural | 295.00 |
| Pitcher, Water, Sailing Scene, Blue Mark | 225.00 |
| Pitcher, Water, Shell & Coral | 150.00 |
| Pitcher, Water, Tomato ............. 150.00 To | 395.00 |
| Pitcher, 2 Musicians, Blue Mark, 7 In. | 48.00 |
| Planter, Elk, Wall | 28.50 |
| Planter, Handled, Turkey Boy, Insert, Blue Mark, 3 1/2 X 4 In. | 100.00 |
| Planter, Shell, Murex, 9 In. | 210.00 |
| Planter, Yellow & Pink Roses, Green Ground, 2 3/4 In. | 225.00 |
| Plate, Boat Scene, Blue Mark, 6 1/2 In. | 38.00 |
| Plate, Cake, Pink Roses, Green Leaves, Circled, 10 1/2 In. | 250.00 |
| Plate, Children Playing Ring-A-Rosie, Blue Mark, 8 In. | 85.00 |
| Plate, Devil & Cards, Blue Mark, 7 In. | 85.00 |
| Plate, Dutch Boat Scene, Blue Mark, 6 In. | 25.00 |
| Plate, Goose Girl, 8 In. | 85.00 |
| Plate, Hand-Painted Roses, Blue Mark, 9 In. | 150.00 |
| Plate, Jack & Jill, 7 1/2 In. | 130.00 |
| Plate, Leaf Shape, Handle, 5 1/2 In. | 38.00 |
| Plate, Lettuce, Handles, 4 1/4 In., Pair | 15.00 |
| Plate, Little Bopeep, Blue Mark, 6 1/2 In. | 78.00 |
| Plate, Little Boy Blue, 7 1/2 In. | 50.00 |
| Plate, Oak Leaf, 5 1/4 In. | 30.00 |
| Plate, Pheasants, Gold Edge, Scalloped, Blue Mark, 11 1/2 In. | 325.00 |
| Plate, Poppy, 8 In., Pair | 100.00 |
| Plate, Scene Of Musicians, Blue Mark, 6 In. | 95.50 |
| Plate, Tomato, 7 1/2 In. | 58.00 |
| Rose Bowl, Rose, Figural, White To Pink, Blue Mark | 235.00 |
| Salt & Pepper, Coachman | 100.00 |
| Salt & Pepper, Elk Head, Blue Mark | 115.00 |
| Salt & Pepper, Leaf Bases | 20.00 |
| Salt & Pepper, Strawberry | 18.00 |
| Salt & Pepper, Tomato | 10.00 |
| Salt, Devil & Card, Blue Mark | 65.00 |
| Saltshaker, Spiky Murex, Marked | 20.00 |
| Sauce, Little Bopeep, Blue Mark, 4 1/2 In. | 50.00 |
| Sauce, Little Bopeep, Holly & Berries, 4 In. | 40.00 |
| Shoe, Lady, Purple, White, Chrysanthemums, Marked, 3 1/2 In. | 155.00 |
| Shoe, Lady's, Medium Heel, Laced, Brown | 75.00 |
| Shoe, Man's Laced Oxford, Signed | 125.00 |
| Shoe, Man's Oxford, Tan | 80.00 |
| Shoe, Man's, High, Black With White Tab | 85.00 |
| Shoe, Man's, High, Blue Mark, Original Lace | 95.00 |
| Shoe, Man's, High, Laced, Cinnamon, Dotted, Tab Back | 75.00 |
| Spooner, Peacock Design, Blue Mark | 95.00 |
| String Holder, Rooster, Black Mark | 163.00 |
| Sugar & Creamer, Belmont, Green Mark | 25.00 |
| Sugar & Creamer, Black & White Penguins, Covered, Blue Mark | 100.00 |
| Sugar & Creamer, Donkey, Boy, Farm, Covered, 3 In. | 225.00 |
| Sugar & Creamer, Grape, Black Mark, Dated 1794, 3 Piece | 105.00 |
| Sugar & Creamer, Musicians In White, Black | 125.00 |
| Sugar & Creamer, Pearlized Painted Violets, Gold Handles | 70.00 |

Sugar & Creamer, Red Poppy, Blue Mark ........................................................ 150.00 To 195.00
Sugar & Creamer, Salt & Pepper, Grape ........................................................ 235.00
Sugar & Creamer, Shell ........................................................ 40.00
Sugar & Creamer, Strawberry ........................................................ 120.00
Sugar & Creamer, Tomato, Blue Mark ........................................................ 85.00
Sugar & Creamer, Tray, Grape Pattern, Dated 1794, Black Mark ........................................................ 105.00
Sugar, Elk, Covered, Blue Mark ........................................................ 125.00
Sugar, Grape ........................................................ 25.00
Sugar, Rose, Yellow, Open, Figural ........................................................ 165.00
Sugar, Tomato, Covered, 4 In. ........................................................ 40.00
Sugar, Tomato, 3 Piece, Blue Mark ........................................................ 45.00
Syrup, Covered, Elk Figural, Blue Mark ........................................................ 185.00
Syrup, 2 Musicians, Brown Ground, Blue Mark, 4 In. ........................................................ 45.00
Tankard, Polychrome Plants, Pewter Lid, C.1760, 7 3/4 In. ........................................................ 1200.00
Tea Set, Miniature Flowers, Blue Mark, 18 Piece ........................................................ 250.00
Tea Set, Tomato, Blue Mark ........................................................ 265.00
Tea Strainer, Poppy, Cream & Rust ........................................................ 50.00
Teapot, Scenic, Black Mark ........................................................ 125.00
Teapot, Sugar, & Mustard, Purple Leaves, Pearlized, Blue Mark ........................................................ 225.00
Teapot, Sugar, & Plate, Tomato, Blue Mark, Plate, 7 In. ........................................................ 300.00
Teapot, Tomato, Blue Mark ........................................................ 85.00
Thread Holder, Rooster, Blue Mark ........................................................ 125.00
Toothpick, Corner Handles, Musicians, Square Top, Blue Mark ........................................................ 75.00
Toothpick, Elk, Figural, Blue Mark ........................................................ 60.00 To 75.00
Toothpick, Hat Shape, Hand-Painted Goat Scene ........................................................ 35.00
Toothpick, Hunter With Dog & Geese, 3-Handled, Blue Mark ........................................................ 125.00
Toothpick, 2 Horses, Man With Gun, 3-Handled, Blue Mark ........................................................ 195.00
Tray, Card, Hunt Scene, Footed, Marked ........................................................ 125.00
Tray, Dresser, Flowers Design ........................................................ 95.00
Tray, Dresser, George & Martha Washington ........................................................ 72.00
Tray, Dresser, Goose Girl, Blue Mark, 8 X 11 1/2 In. ........................................................ 125.00
Tray, Dresser, Green Rim, Butterflies, Center Rose, 10 X 7 In. ........................................................ 35.00
Tray, Horse & Rider, Blue Mark, 7 In. ........................................................ 125.00
Tray, Lettuse Leaf Shape, Handled, Blue Mark, 3 In. ........................................................ 22.00
Tray, Pin, Dutch Girl, Scenic, White, Gray, 4 3/4 In.Square ........................................................ 46.00
Tureen, Blue Mark, 6 In.Diam. ........................................................ 325.00
Tureen, Covered, Underplate, Figural, Rose, Blue Mark ........................................................ 225.00
Tureen, Rose, Blue Mark, 6 In.Diam. ........................................................ 325.00
Vase, Arab, Horses Scene, Silver Rim, Handled, Blue Mark, 3 In. ........................................................ 48.00
Vase, Boat Scene, 5 1/2 In. ........................................................ 90.00
Vase, Boat Scene, 5 3/4 In. ........................................................ 85.00
Vase, Brittany Girl, Blue Mark, 8 In. ........................................................ 175.00
Vase, Bud, Urn Shape, Cattle In Stream, 3 1/2 In. ........................................................ 45.00
Vase, Cavalier Scene, Tans & Grays, Blue Mark, 3 1/2 In. ........................................................ 45.00
Vase, Cavaliers Drinking, Playing Mandolin, Blue Mark, 10 In. ........................................................ 225.00
Vase, Dutch Children Scene, Silver Top Rim, Green Mark, 3 In. ........................................................ 45.00
Vase, Dutch Girl, Boats, Hallmarked Rim, Blue Mark, 3 1/8 In. ........................................................ 48.00
Vase, Female Figure, Forest Ground, Green, 4 1/4 In., Pair ........................................................ 138.00
Vase, Floral Scene, Shades Of Brown, Blue Label, 5 In. ........................................................ 62.00
Vase, Hunting Scene, Blue Mark, 6 In. ........................................................ 30.00
Vase, Hunting Scene, Green, Blue Mark, 6 In. ........................................................ 40.00
Vase, Ladies & Sheep Scene, Handled, Blue Mark, 3 1/4 In. ........................................................ 50.00
Vase, Lady & Ship, 3-Handled, Blue Mark, 3 1/4 In. ........................................................ 70.00
Vase, Man, Hound Pack, All-Around Scenic, 7 In. ........................................................ 340.00
Vase, Men In Boat, Fishing Scene, Blue Mark, 5 In. ........................................................ 60.00
Vase, Portrait, Pink & Gold Trim, Black Mark, 8 In. ........................................................ 120.00
Vase, Red, Black, Corinthian Ware, Classic Figures, 6 In. ........................................................ 75.00
Vase, Red, Mountain Goats Scene, 7 1/2 In. ........................................................ 115.00
Vase, Roman Key Bands, Seated Figures, White, 5 1/2 In. ........................................................ 95.00
Vase, Sailing Ship, Silver Rim, 3 In. ........................................................ 50.00
Vase, Sheep With Moon, Blue Mark, 2 3/4 In. ........................................................ 70.00
Vase, Turkeys, Woman, Blue Mark ........................................................ 55.00
Vase, Wide Body, Thin Top, Goat Scene, Blue Mark, 6 1/4 In. ........................................................ 80.00

Vase, 3 Tab Handles, Sheep Scene, Blue Mark, 2 3/4 In. ......................................... 45.00
Vase, 4-Handled, 2 Men On Horses, Dogs, Blue Mark, 3 1/4 In. ............................. 50.00
Wall Pocket, Courting Scene, Pink Roses, 9 In. ....................................................... 650.00
Wall Pocket, Little Bopeep, Verse, Marked, 4 1/2 In. .............................................. 75.00
Wall Pocket, Pink, Green Leaves, Blue Mark ........................................................... 225.00
    **ROYAL BERLIN, see KPM**

*Royal Bonn is the nineteenth-century trade name for the Bonn China Manufactory established in 1755 at Bonn, Germany. A general line of porcelain dishes was made.*

**ROYAL BONN, see also Flow Blue**

ROYAL BONN, Clock, Blue, Pink, Yellow Flowers, New Haven Works, 6 X 5 In. ...................... 175.00
Dish, Cheese, Covered, Slant Top, Pink & Blue Flowers ......................................... 40.00
Dish, Cheese, Moss Rose, Impressed Mark ............................................................. 70.00
Dish, Cucumber, Underplate, Franz Art Meklam, Turquoise ................................... 70.00
Dish, Serving, Sardine ............................................................................................. 35.00
Ewer, Tapestry Design, Blue, Red, Gold, Gray Swirl, Signed, 12 In. ...................... 125.00
Plaque, Blue Onion, Blue & White, Oval, Signed, 12 In. ......................................... 89.00
Plaque, Delft, Windmill & Water Scene, Floral Design, Signed ............................... 79.00
Plate, Fish In Center, 9 In. ...................................................................................... 85.00
Plate, Scalloped, Embossed Rim, Roses & Violets, 9 In.Diam. ................................ 36.00
Urn, Pink, Blue, & Yellow Flowers, Gold Outlined, 15 1/2 In. .................................. 225.00
Urn, Satin Finish, Lion's Head Handles, 15 1/2 In. .................................................. 225.00
Vase, Autumn Coloring, Gold & Orange Flowers, Marked, 8 In. .............................. 88.00
Vase, Ball, Moss Green, Orchids, Signed, 13 X 13 In. ............................................ 275.00
Vase, Blue & White, Signed, 8 1/2 X 8 In. ............................................................... 120.00
Vase, Bud Opening, Hand-Painted, C.1900, Gold Design, Signed, 5 In. ................. 175.00
Vase, Cobalt Blue, Gold Trim, 11 In. ....................................................................... 75.00
Vase, Dark Glass Ground, Roses, Signed Sieber, 7 In. ........................................... 85.00
Vase, Delft, Blue & White, Signed, 8 1/2 X 8 In. ..................................................... 120.00
Vase, Double Gold Handles, Flower Design, 11 In., Pair .......................................... 325.00
Vase, Double Handled, Pansy, 14 In. ...................................................................... 45.00
Vase, Floral, Bulbous, 8 In. ..................................................................................... 35.00
Vase, Flower Design, Double Gold Handle, Pair ....................................................... 325.00
Vase, Green Bands, Pink & Yellow Roses, 5 1/2 X 6 1/2 In.Diam. ......................... 125.00
Vase, Hand-Painted Flowers, Raised Gold, 10 1/2 In. ............................................. 95.00
Vase, Hand-Painted Flowers, 5 1/2 In. .................................................................... 30.00
Vase, Hand-Painted, Gold Trim, C.1840, Ivory Ground, 20 In. ............................... 650.00
Vase, Handled, Hand-Painted Ships & Flowers, 20 In. ............................................ 50.00
Vase, Handled, Musical Designs, Signed, 7 In. ........................................................ 40.00
Vase, Lady Portrait, Pastoral Scene, Banded, Marked, 8 1/8 In. ............................. 175.00
Vase, Large Mums, Baluster Form, Signed, 9 1/2 In. .............................................. 50.00
Vase, Multicolored Flowers, Blue & Orange Ground, Marked, 10 In. ....................... 115.00
Vase, Mum Design, Baluster Form, Signed, 9 1/2 In. .............................................. 50.00
Vase, Old Dutch, 10 X 7 In.Diam. ........................................................................... 149.00
Vase, Pink Flowers, Turquoise Ground, 4 1/2 In. .................................................... 45.00
Vase, Poppies, Brown & Yellow Ground, Marked, 7 3/4 In. ..................................... 95.00
Vase, Portrait, Gold Trim, Artist Signed, 10 1/2 In. ................................................. 385.00
Vase, Portrait, Lady, Long Hair, Gown, Artist Signed, 9 In. ..................................... 150.00
Vase, Portrait, Lady, Mottled Green Ground, Gold Trim, 7 In. ................................. 165.00
Vase, Portrait, Woman, Green, Yellow Ground, 7 In. .............................................. 145.00
Vase, Urn Shape, Handled, Hand-Painted Ships & Flowers, 20 In. ......................... 50.00
Vase, 2 Lion Heads, Cream Ground, Yellow Flowers, 6 In. ..................................... 75.00

*Royal Copenhagen porcelain and pottery have been made in Denmark since 1772. They are still being made. One of their most famous wares is the Christmas Plate Series.*

**ROYAL COPENHAGEN, Bowl,** Blue Fluted, Full Lace, 8 In. ................................................. 71.00

| | |
|---|---|
| **Box,** Nude & Swan On Cover, Porcelain, 4 In.Square | 40.00 |
| **Cactus Flower Design,** 4 1/2 In. | 39.00 |
| **Chocolate Pot,** Blue Fluted, 1/2 Lace, 4 Cups & Saucers | 450.00 |
| **Compote,** Blue Fluted Pattern, 1/2 Lace, 1 In. | 158.00 |
| **Compote,** Pedestaled, Hand-Painted Flowers, Signed, 7 In. | 40.00 |
| **Compote,** Triangular, Blue & White, Marked, 8 1/4 In. | 135.00 |
| **Cruet,** Blue Fluted, 1800-1923 | 95.00 |
| **Cup & Saucer,** Demitasse, Blue Fluted, 1/2 Lace | 80.00 |
| **Dish,** Candy, Mouse On Edge, 6 In. | 75.00 |
| **Dish,** Nut, Blue Fluted Pattern, 1/2 Lace, 4 In. | 45.00 |
| **Dish,** Powder, Green, Gold Trim, Octagonal Lidded | 38.00 |
| **Dish,** Powder, Lid, Gray-Green Crackle, Octagon Shape | 30.00 |
| **Dish,** Salad, Flora Danica, 18k Gold Border, 9 In. | 550.00 |
| **Eggcup,** Blue Fluted | 24.00 |
| **Figurine,** Ape, Stoneware, Arms Around Self, Marked, 3 In. | 150.00 |
| **Figurine,** Boy With Ball, No.3542 | 145.00 |
| **Figurine,** Boy With Gourd, No.4539 | 142.00 |
| **Figurine,** Boy With Teddy Bear, No.3468 | 200.00 |
| **Figurine,** Boy, Wearing Overalls, Smoking Pipe, 6 1/4 In. | 115.00 |
| **Figurine,** Cat, Siamese, Head, Blue Eyes | 95.00 |
| **Figurine,** Cat, Siamese, No.2851/3281, 8 In. | 215.00 |
| **Figurine,** Chicken, 6 1/2 In. | 95.00 |
| **Figurine,** Chickens, Pair, 5 1/2 In. | 150.00 |
| **Figurine,** Child Crawling, No.1739 | 86.00 |
| **Figurine,** Child With Accordion, No.3667 | 125.00 |
| **Figurine,** Children With Dog, No.707 | 238.00 |
| **Figurine,** Chinoiserie Group, Eastern Dress, Marked, 13 In. | 1000.00 |
| **Figurine,** Crawling Child, No.1518 | 95.00 |
| **Figurine,** Drummer, No.3647 | 116.00 |
| **Figurine,** Elephant, No.2998 | 105.00 |
| **Figurine,** Farmer With Woman, No.1352, Signed, 17 1/2 In. | 1250.00 |
| **Figurine,** Girl Dressing Her Hair, No.4648 | 175.00 |
| **Figurine,** Girl In Gray Bonnet, Shawl, No.1251, 7 3/4 In. | 145.00 |
| **Figurine,** Girl With Doll, No.1938 | 175.00 |
| **Figurine,** Goose Girl, No.527 | 275.00 |
| **Figurine,** Goose Girl, No.528 | 180.00 |
| **Figurine,** Man Riding Ram, Bird In Hand, 8 1/2 In. | 175.00 |
| **Figurine,** Match Girl, No.4438, 4 1/2 In. | 67.50 |
| **Figurine,** Neptune Rising, Arm Around Maiden, 22 1/2 In. | 1600.00 |
| **Figurine,** Polar Bear Cub, No.729 | 80.00 |
| **Figurine,** Polar Bear Cubs, No.1107 | 145.00 |
| **Figurine,** Polar Bear, No.320 | 75.00 |
| **Figurine,** Pony, No.4653 | 225.00 |
| **Figurine,** Sandman | 85.00 |
| **Figurine,** Siamese Cat, Sitting, 8 In. | 125.00 |
| **Figurine,** Sitting Siamese Cat, No.2851, Signed, 8 In. | 125.00 |
| **Figurine,** Sjalland, Girl, Costume, Blue, Marked, 4 In. | 350.00 |
| **Figurine,** Terrier, Crown Mark, Pair | 85.00 |
| **Figurine,** Wirehair Terrier, Standing, 5 X 4 In. | 75.00 |
| **Figurine,** 2 Monkeys Nit Picking | 85.00 |
| **Gravy Boat,** Attached Underplate, Dated 1897 | 95.00 |
| **Group,** Elfin Maiden, Marked, 9 In. _Illus_ | 850.00 |
| **Group,** Lady With Fan, Girl, Marked, 9 3/4 In. _Illus_ | 700.00 |
| **Knife Rest,** Blue Fluted | 50.00 |
| **Pitcher,** Milk, Blue & White, Covered | 75.00 |
| **Pitcher,** Milk, Covered, 8 In. | 110.00 |
| **Plate,** Blue Fluted, 1/2 Lace, 1800-1923, 9 In. | 28.50 |
| **Plate,** Blue Fluted, 1/2 Lace, 6 In. | 21.50 |
| **Plate,** Blue Fluted, 1/2 Lace, 8 In. | 32.50 |
| **Plate,** Christmas 1916 | 85.00 |
| **Plate,** Christmas 1922 | 75.00 |
| **Plate,** Christmas, 1940 | 375.00 |
| **Plate,** Christmas, 1942 | 375.00 |

Royal Copenhagen, Group, from left to right, Lady With Fan, Girl, Marked; Elfin Maiden, Marked

| | |
|---|---|
| **Plate,** Christmas, 1949 | 150.00 |
| **Plate,** Christmas, 1951 | 295.00 |
| **Plate,** Christmas, 1959 | 100.00 |
| **Plate,** Christmas, 1961 | 127.00 |
| **Plate,** Christmas, 1965 | 45.00 |
| **Plate,** Christmas, 1974 | 20.00 |
| **Plate,** Mother's Day, 1974 | 14.00 |
| **Plate,** Mother's Day, 1978 | 21.50 |
| **Plate,** Mother's Day, 1979 | 25.00 |
| **Salt & Pepper,** Blue Fluted, Lace, 2 1/2 In. | 58.00 |
| **Salt,** Dip, Blue Fluted | 25.00 |
| **Sugar & Creamer,** Blue Fluted, Full Lace | 166.00 |
| **Vase,** Cactus Flower Design, 4 1/2 In. | 40.00 |
| **Vase,** Cactus Flower Design, 5 In. | 35.00 |
| **Vase,** Rose, Leaves, Blue Ground, Shaded To White, 1923 Mark | 95.00 |
| **Vase,** Variegated, 4 1/2 In.Square | 65.00 |
| **Vase,** White & Gray, Signed, 5 1/2 In. | 75.00 |

*Royal Copley was produced by the Spaulding China Company of Sebring, Ohio, from 1939 to 1960.*

| | |
|---|---|
| **ROYAL COPLEY, Planter,** Doe & Fawn, 9 In. | 10.00 |
| **Planter,** Elephant, White, Green Polka Dots, Smiling Face, 8 In. | 9.00 |
| **Planter,** Rooster, Matching Hen Figurine | 15.00 |
| **Planter,** Window Box, Ivy, 7 In. | 6.00 |
| **Vase,** Multicolored Flowers Transfer, White Glaze, 6 1/4 In. | 10.00 |
| **Vase,** Pink, Black Leaves, Paper Label, Set Of 3, 8-6-3 In. | 12.00 |

*Royal Crown Derby Company, Ltd., was established in England in 1876.*
**ROYAL CROWN DERBY, see also Derby**

| | |
|---|---|
| **ROYAL CROWN DERBY, Cup & Saucer,** Blue, Gold | 95.00 |
| **Cup & Saucer,** Brittany | 15.00 |
| **Cup & Saucer,** Derby Posies, Demitasse, Set Of 6 | 100.00 |
| **Cup & Saucer,** Orange & Blue | 60.00 |
| **Figurine,** Group Of Birds On Tree Stump, Signed Jacob | 50.00 |
| **Figurine,** Sealyham Dog | 75.00 |

| | |
|---|---|
| **Plate,** White, Blue Floral, Gold Rim, 7 In. | 12.00 |
| **Sugar & Creamer,** Blue & Gold | 125.00 |

*Royal Doulton was the name used on pottery made after 1902. The Doulton factory was founded in 1815. Their wares are still being made. For a more complete listing see "Kovels' Illustrated Price Guide to Royal Doulton."*

| | |
|---|---|
| **ROYAL DOULTON, Animals,** Chestnut Mare & Foal, HN 2533 | 295.00 |
| **Ashtray & Holder,** Tony Weller | 50.00 |
| **Ashtray,** Dickensware, Tony Weller | 28.00 |
| **Ashtray,** Roosevelt, Army Club | 35.00 |
| **Baby Set,** 3 Piece, Bunnykins | 27.00 |
| **Bank,** Bunny | 47.00 |
| **Beaker,** Brown Earthenware, 5 1/2 In. | 65.00 |
| **Bottle,** George The Guard, Dewars, Original Stopper, 9 In. | 145.00 |
| **Bottle,** Zorro, A Mark | 38.00 |
| **Bottle,** Zorro, Red Glass | 45.00 |
| **Bottle,** Zorro, Yellow Glass, 4 1/2 In. | 115.00 |
| **Bowl & Pitcher,** Blue On White, Cloverleaf Design | 300.00 |
| **Bowl,** Barnaby Rudge, Dickens Ware, 6 In. | 30.00 |
| **Bowl,** Bill Sykes, Dickens Ware, 6 In. | 30.00 |
| **Bowl,** Bunnykins, Bunnies Golfing, Signed B.Vernon, 5 In. | 36.50 |
| **Bowl,** Caramel, English Street Scene, Signed, 10 1/4 In. | 125.00 |
| **Bowl,** Desert Scenes Series, Arabs On Camels, 8 In.Diam. | 85.00 |
| **Bowl,** Design On Brass Around Middle, Cobalt Blue, 13 1/2 In. | 45.00 |
| **Bowl,** Dickens Ware, Scenes Inside & Out, 7 1/2 In. | 80.00 |
| **Bowl,** Dr.Johnson At Temple Bar, Signed, 9 1/4 In | 45.00 To 50.00 |
| **Bowl,** Dutch Women, 5 1/2 In. | 25.00 |
| **Bowl,** Flambe, Handled, Oriental Syle, 9 3/4 X 3 In. | 225.00 |
| **Bowl,** Jackdaw Of Rheims, 7 1/2 In. | 55.00 |
| **Bowl,** Jackdaw Of Rheims, 8 In. | 105.00 |
| **Bowl,** Mr.Squeers, 6 In. | 35.00 |
| **Bowl,** Mrs Bardell, 9 X 2 1/4 In. | 95.00 |
| **Bowl,** Pope, 8 1/2 In. | 150.00 |
| **Bowl,** Portia, Shakespeare Series, 9 In. | 95.00 |
| **Bowl,** Rosalind, 6 In. | 65.00 |
| **Bowl,** Sairey Gamp, 8 In. | 40.00 |
| **Box,** Covered, Multicolored Birds & Flowers, 5 1/2 X 4 In. | 47.50 |
| **Box,** Little Tommy Tucker, Cover, 9 In. | 100.00 |
| **Breakfast Set,** Bachelors Buttons, Pink, 8 Piece Set | 50.00 |
| **Bulldog,** British Flag On Back, 6 In. | 150.00 |
| **Bulldog,** HN 1043 | 155.00 |
| **Butterfly,** HN 1456, Potted | 700.00 |
| **Candlestick,** Welsh Ladies Series, Lady, Girl, Square, 6 1/2 In. | 75.00 |
| **Candlesticks & Pitcher,** Monk & Keg, D 2385, June 5, 1906 | 325.00 |
| **Cat,** Persian, 4 1/2 In. | 28.00 |

*Character jugs are modeled of the head and shoulders of the subject. They were made in four sizes: large - 5 1/4 to 7 inches, small - 3 1/4 to 4 inches, miniature - 2 1/4 to 2 1/2 inches, and tiny - 1 1/4 inches. Toby mugs depict a full seated figure.*

| | |
|---|---|
| **ROYAL DOULTON, Character Jug,** 'ard Of 'earing, Miniature | 1000.00 |
| **Character Jug,** 'Ard Of 'Earing, Small | 575.00 To 625.00 |
| **Character Jug,** 'Arry & 'Arriet, Miniature | 60.00 |
| **Character Jug,** 'Arry, A Mark, Miniature | 65.00 |
| **Character Jug,** Athos, Large | 79.50 |
| **Character Jug,** Auld Mac, A Mark, Small | 40.00 |
| **Character Jug,** Barleycorn, Miniature | 45.00 |
| **Character Jug,** Barlycorn, A Mark, Large | 105.00 |
| **Character Jug,** Beefeater, A Mark, Green, Miniature | 40.00 |
| **Character Jug,** Blood Money, 5 1/2 In. | 165.00 |

| | |
|---|---|
| Character Jug, Buz Fuz, Small | 95.00 |
| Character Jug, Cap'n Cuttle, A Mark, Small | 85.00 |
| Character Jug, Captain Hook, Small | 220.00 |
| Character Jug, Cardinal, A Mark, Large | 95.00 To 112.50 |
| Character Jug, Cardinal, Tiny | 175.00 |
| Character Jug, Cavalier, Small | 60.00 |
| Character Jug, Falconer, Large | 75.00 |
| Character Jug, Farmer John, A Mark, Large | 110.00 |
| Character Jug, Farmer John, A Mark, Small | 65.00 |
| Character Jug, Fortune Teller, Miniature | 250.00 |
| Character Jug, Fortune Teller, Small | 250.00 |
| Character Jug, Gladiator, Small | 295.00 |
| Character Jug, Gondolier, Miniature | 325.00 |
| Character Jug, Gondolier, Small | 250.00 To 295.00 |
| Character Jug, Granny, A Mark | 85.00 |
| Character Jug, Jarge, A Mark, Small | 140.00 |
| Character Jug, Jarge, Miniature | 135.00 |
| Character Jug, Jarge, Small | 125.00 To 150.00 |
| Character Jug, Jester, A Mark, Small | 80.00 |
| Character Jug, John Barleycorn, Large | 110.00 |
| Character Jug, John Peel, A Mark, Miniature | 40.00 |
| Character Jug, Lord Nelson, D 6336, Large | 165.00 |
| Character Jug, Mephistopheles, A Mark | 495.00 |
| Character Jug, Micawber, A Mark, Miniature | 45.00 |
| Character Jug, Micawber, Small | 45.00 |
| Character Jug, Mikado, Miniature | 195.00 To 250.00 |
| Character Jug, Mr.Pickwick, A Mark, Large | 88.00 |
| Character Jug, Mr.Pickwick, Miniature | 65.00 |
| Character Jug, Mr.Pickwick, Small | 110.00 |
| Character Jug, Old Charley, A Mark, Large | 65.00 |
| Character Jug, Old King Cole, A Mark, Small | 75.00 |
| Character Jug, Punch & Judy, Miniature | 325.00 |
| Character Jug, Regency Beau, Miniature | 325.00 |
| Character Jug, Regency Beau, Small | 325.00 |
| Character Jug, Robin Hood, A Mark, Miniature | 50.00 |
| Character Jug, Sairey Gamp, A Mark, Large | 60.00 |
| Character Jug, Sairey Gamp, Tiny | 85.00 |
| Character Jug, Sam Johnson, A Mark, Small | 160.00 |
| Character Jug, Sam Weller, Small | 50.00 |
| Character Jug, Sam Weller, Tiny | 85.00 |
| Character Jug, Scaramouche, Miniature | 325.00 |
| Character Jug, Scaramouche, Small | 325.00 |
| Character Jug, Sergeant Buz Fuz, A Mark, 4 1/4 In. | 150.00 |
| Character Jug, St.George, Large | 100.00 |
| Character Jug, St.George, Small | 55.00 To 75.00 |
| Character Jug, Tam O'Shanter, Large | 60.00 |
| Character Jug, Tony Weller, A Mark, Miniature | 45.00 |
| Character Jug, Town Crier, Miniature | 90.00 To 120.00 |
| Character Jug, Town Crier, Small | 85.00 To 125.00 |
| Character Jug, Turpin, Mask Off, Small | 45.00 |
| Character Jug, Ugly Duchess, Miniature | 200.00 |
| Character Jug, Ugly Duchess, Small | 160.00 |
| Character Jug, Vicar Of Bray, Large | 165.00 |
| Character Jug, Viking, Large | 60.00 |
| Character Jug, Viking, Miniature | 125.00 |
| Character Jug, Viking, Small | 125.00 |
| Character Jug, Walrus And The Carpenter, Large | 60.00 |
| Cocker Spaniel With Pheasant, HN 1029 | 85.00 |
| Cocker Spaniel, HN 1020 | 40.00 |
| Cocker Spaniel, HN 1021 | 90.00 |
| Cocker Spaniel, HN 1188 | 80.00 |
| Coffee Set, Demitasse, Rose, 1920 | 95.00 |
| Collie, HN 1059 | 85.00 |
| Cookie Jar, Tony Weller | 225.00 |

| | |
|---|---:|
| **Creamer,** Dickensware, Old Peggoty, Marked, 3 1/4 In. | 97.50 |
| **Cup & Saucer,** Coaching Days, Marked | 25.00 |
| **Cup & Saucer,** Dickensware | 50.00 |
| **Cup & Saucer,** Glamis Thistle | 35.00 |
| **Cup & Saucer,** Greek-Style Border, Flowers | 45.00 |
| **Cup & Saucer,** Tea, Bunnykins | 13.00 |
| **Cup & Saucer,** The Cardinal | 40.00 |
| **Cup & Saucer,** Witches Series, Brown Witches, Roman Key Design | 48.00 |
| **Cup,** Blue & White, Shield With Anchor | 8.00 |
| **Dessert Set,** Rochester, Set Of 4 | 130.00 |
| **Dish,** Baby, Three Blind Mice, Toys Around Rim, 8 In. | 42.50 |
| **Dish,** Celery, Beefeaters At Tower Of London | 65.00 |
| **Dog,** Sealyham, HN 2508 | 85.00 |
| **Dragon,** Flambe | 495.00 To 500.00 |
| **Ewer,** Babes In Wood, Miniature | 65.00 |
| **Figurine,** Abdulla, HN 2104 | 575.00 To 675.00 |
| **Figurine,** Annette, HN 1472 | 350.00 |
| **Figurine,** Anthea, HN 1669 | 485.00 |
| **Figurine,** Antoinette, HN 2326 | 115.00 |
| **Figurine,** Autumn Breeze, HN 2147 | 275.00 |
| **Figurine,** Autumn Breeze, Red, HN 1911 | 95.00 |
| **Figurine,** Ballerina, HN 2116 | 225.00 To 235.00 |
| **Figurine,** Balloon Man, HN 1954 | 350.00 |
| **Figurine,** Balloon Seller, HN 583 | 250.00 |
| **Figurine,** Basket Weaver, HN 2245 | 450.00 |
| **Figurine,** Beggar, HN 2175 | 410.00 |
| **Figurine,** Belle O' The Ball, HN 1997, 6 In. | 175.00 To 265.00 |
| **Figurine,** Bess, HN 2002 | 200.00 To 275.00 |
| **Figurine,** Betsy, HN 2111 | 265.00 |
| **Figurine,** Biddy-Penny-Farthing, HN 1843 | 95.00 |
| **Figurine,** Blithe Morning, HN 2065 | 175.00 |
| **Figurine,** Bonnie Lassie, HN 1626, Potted | 175.00 |
| **Figurine,** Bridesmaid, HN 2148 | 195.00 |
| **Figurine,** Bridesmaid, M 12 | 250.00 |
| **Figurine,** Bridesmaid, M 30 | 240.00 |
| **Figurine,** Bridget, HN 2070 | 265.00 |
| **Figurine,** Broken Lance, HN 2041 | 475.00 |
| **Figurine,** Bunny, HN 2214 | 125.00 |
| **Figurine,** Carmen, HN 2545 | 225.00 |
| **Figurine,** Carolyn, HN 2112 | 250.00 |
| **Figurine,** Celeste, HN 2237 | 250.00 |
| **Figurine,** Cerise, HN 1607, Potted | 225.00 |
| **Figurine,** Charley's Aunt, HN 35 | 625.00 To 695.00 |
| **Figurine,** Charmian, HN 1568, Potted | 360.00 |
| **Figurine,** Cleopatra & The Slave, HN 2868 | 1000.00 |
| **Figurine,** Clockmaker, HN 2279 | 250.00 |
| **Figurine,** Coachman, HN 2282 | 375.00 |
| **Figurine,** Corinthian, HN 1973 | 850.00 |
| **Figurine,** Cradle Song, HN 2246 | 345.00 |
| **Figurine,** Daffy Down Dilly, HN 1712 | 295.00 |
| **Figurine,** Dainty May, HN 1656 | 200.00 |
| **Figurine,** Daisy, HN 1575, Potted | 150.00 |
| **Figurine,** Damaris, HN 2079 | 875.00 |
| **Figurine,** Darling, HN1319 | 110.00 |
| **Figurine,** Debutante, HN 2210 | 265.00 |
| **Figurine,** Delight, HN 1772 | 125.00 To 215.00 |
| **Figurine,** Delphine, HN 2136 | 300.00 |
| **Figurine,** Denise, HN 2273 | 275.00 |
| **Figurine,** Dorcas, HN 1490 | 225.00 |
| **Figurine,** Dorcas, HN 1558, Potted | 230.00 |
| **Figurine,** Easter Day, HN 2039 | 295.00 |
| **Figurine,** Ellen Terry, HN 379 | 875.00 |
| **Figurine,** Ermine Coat, HN 1981 | 195.00 To 250.00 |

**Figurine,** Esmeralds, HN 2168, 5 3/4 In. ............................................................ 385.00
**Figurine,** Family Album, HN 2321 ................................................ 285.00 To 350.00
**Figurine,** Fat Boy, HN 555 ......................................................... 250.00 To 265.00
**Figurine,** Fiona, HN 1925 ............................................................................ 450.00
**Figurine,** Fiona, HN 2694 .............................................................................. 90.00
**Figurine,** First Waltz, HN 2862 ................................................................... 139.00
**Figurine,** Fleurette, HN 1587 ...................................................................... 425.00
**Figurine,** Fortune-Teller, HN 2159 ........................................... 375.00 To 425.00
**Figurine,** Forty Winks, HN 1974 .............................................. 185.00 To 225.00
**Figurine,** Fox In Red Frock Coat, HN 100 .................................................. 450.00
**Figurine,** Fragrance, HN 2334 ...................................................................... 90.00
**Figurine,** French Peasant, HN 2075 ........................................................... 450.00
**Figurine,** Friar Tuck, HN 2143 ................................................................... 375.00
**Figurine,** Gainsborough Hat, HN 705, 8 3/4 In. ....................................... 750.00
**Figurine,** Gay Morning, HN 2135 ............................................. 170.00 To 325.00
**Figurine,** Giselle, HN 2139 ........................................................................ 275.00
**Figurine,** Glory, HN 2484 .......................................................................... 125.00
**Figurine,** Golly Wog, HN 1979, 5 5/8 In. ................................................... 165.00
**Figurine,** Good King Wenceslas, HN 2118 ................................................. 225.00
**Figurine,** Good Morning, HN 2671 ............................................................. 125.00
**Figurine,** Gossips, HN 2025 ..................................................... 300.00 To 350.00
**Figurine,** Grand Manner, HN2723 .............................................................. 145.00
**Figurine,** Griselda, HN 1993 .................................................... 395.00 To 400.00
**Figurine,** Grossmith's Tsang Ihang Perfume, HN 582 ................................ 525.00
**Figurine,** Hazel, HN 1797 .......................................................................... 325.00
**Figurine,** He Loves Me, HN 2046 .............................................................. 160.00
**Figurine,** Heart To Heart, HN 2276 ......................................... 300.00 To 320.00
**Figurine,** Her Ladyship, HN 1977 ............................................ 270.00 To 350.00
**Figurine,** Herminia, Potted, HN 1646 ........................................................ 500.00
**Figurine,** Hilary, HN 2335 ......................................................................... 135.00
**Figurine,** Honey, HN 1909 ......................................................................... 250.00
**Figurine,** Hornpipe, HN 2161 .................................................................... 775.00
**Figurine,** Huntsman, HN 2492 ................................................................... 175.00
**Figurine,** Indian Temple Dancer, HN 2830 ................................................ 500.00
**Figurine,** Irene, HN 1621 .......................................................................... 225.00
**Figurine,** Janice, HN 2022 ......................................................................... 475.00
**Figurine,** Jasmine, HN 1862, Potted ......................................................... 700.00
**Figurine,** Jean, HN 2032 ........................................................................... 250.00
**Figurine,** Jersey Milkmaid, HN 2057 ......................................................... 300.00
**Figurine,** Karen, HN 1994, 8 In. ................................................................ 340.00
**Figurine,** Kate Hardcastle, HN 1719, 8 1/4 In. ......................................... 575.00
**Figurine,** Kate Hardcastle, HN 2028 .......................................................... 575.00
**Figurine,** Lady Betty, HN 1967 ................................................ 250.00 To 295.00
**Figurine,** Lady Charmian, HN 1949 ........................................................... 225.00
**Figurine,** Lady Ermine, HN 54, Potted ................................... 750.00 To 775.00
**Figurine,** Lady Fayre, HN 1265, Potted .................................. 475.00 To 525.00
**Figurine,** Lavinia, HN 1955 ......................................................... 60.00 To 95.00
**Figurine,** Leisure Hour, HN 2055 ............................................................... 325.00
**Figurine,** Linda, HN 2106 ............................................................ 98.00 To 130.00
**Figurine,** Lisa, HN 2310 .............................................................................. 90.00
**Figurine,** Little Boy Blue, HN 2062 .............................................................. 90.00
**Figurine,** Little Jack Horner, HN 2063 ...................................................... 295.00
**Figurine,** Little Land, HN 67, Potted, 7 1/2 In. ....................................... 1100.00
**Figurine,** Long John Silver, HN 2204, 9 In. ............................................... 465.00
**Figurine,** Lorna, HN 2311 ............................................................................ 85.00
**Figurine,** Margaret, HN 1989 .................................................................... 245.00
**Figurine,** Margot, HN 1628 ....................................................................... 525.00
**Figurine,** Marguerite, HN 1928 ................................................................. 300.00
**Figurine,** Marietta, HN 1341 ..................................................................... 695.00
**Figurine,** Masquerade, HN 599 ................................................................. 210.00
**Figurine,** Master Sweep, HN 2205 ............................................................ 675.00
**Figurine,** Matilda, HN 2011 ....................................................................... 675.00
**Figurine,** Mayor, HN 2280 ....................................................... 350.00 To 425.00

**Figurine,** Melody, HN 2202 ............................................ 265.00 To 275.00
**Figurine,** Memories, HN 2030 ........................................ 250.00 To 350.00
**Figurine,** Midinette, HN 2090 ........................................................... 260.00
**Figurine,** Midsummer Noon, HN 1899 .......................................... 420.00
**Figurine,** Miss Demure, HN 1402 .................................................... 320.00
**Figurine,** Miss Demure, HN 1402, Potted ..................................... 185.00
**Figurine,** Mr.Micawber, HN 557, 7 1/2 In. .................................... 250.00
**Figurine,** Mr.Micawber, HN 2097 .................................................... 265.00
**Figurine,** Mr.Pickwick, HN 556 ....................................................... 250.00
**Figurine,** Mr.Pickwick, HN 2099 ..................................................... 265.00
**Figurine,** My Pet, HN 2238 ............................................... 95.00 To 100.00
**Figurine,** Nana, HN 1766 ................................................................. 135.00
**Figurine,** New Bonnet, HN 1728 ................................... 525.00 To 575.00
**Figurine,** Noelle, HN 2179 .............................................................. 350.00
**Figurine,** Old Balloon Seller, HN 1315 .......................................... 350.00
**Figurine,** Olga, HN 2463 ................................................. 175.00 To 275.00
**Figurine,** Once Upon A Time, HN 2047 .......................................... 145.00
**Figurine,** One Of The Forty, HN 677 .............................................. 795.00
**Figurine,** One That Got Away, HN 2153 ......................................... 225.00
**Figurine,** Orange Lady, HN 1953 .................................................... 175.00
**Figurine,** Owd Willum, HN 2042 ..................................................... 175.00
**Figurine,** Paisley Shawl, HN 1987 ................................. 235.00 To 250.00
**Figurine,** Paisley Shawl, M 4 .......................................................... 250.00
**Figurine,** Paisley Shawl, M 26 ........................................................ 275.00
**Figurine,** Pantalettes, HN 1362 ...................................................... 375.00
**Figurine,** Patchwork Quilt, HN 1984 ............................. 250.0/ To 275.00
**Figurine,** Patricia, HN 1431 ............................................................ 500.00
**Figurine,** Peggy, HN 2038 ................................................................ 98.00
**Figurine,** Philippa Of Hainault, HN 2008 ...................................... 695.00
**Figurine,** Phyllis, HN 1420, Potted ................................................ 450.00
**Figurine,** Pirouette, HN 2216 ......................................................... 235.00
**Figurine,** Poke Bonnet, HN 612 ...................................................... 750.00
**Figurine,** Polka, HN 2156 ................................................................ 200.00
**Figurine,** Polly Peachum, HN 589 .................................................. 265.00
**Figurine,** Priscilla, HN 1337, Potted .............................................. 275.00
**Figurine,** Queen Elizabeth II, HN 5202 .......................................... 975.00
**Figurine,** Rag Doll, HN 2142 ............................................. 45.00 To 50.00
**Figurine,** Rendezvous, HN 2212 ..................................................... 375.00
**Figurine,** Rhoda, HN 1573 .............................................................. 475.00
**Figurine,** Rockinghorse, HN 2072 ................................................ 1450.00
**Figurine,** Schoolmarm, HN 2223 .................................................... 127.50
**Figurine,** Seashore, HN 2263 .......................................................... 235.00
**Figurine,** She Loves Me Not, HN 2045 ........................................... 160.00
**Figurine,** Silks & Ribbons, HN 2017 ............................................... 105.00
**Figurine,** Simone, HN 2378 ............................................................... 90.00
**Figurine,** St. George, HN 2067 ...................................................... 2650.00
**Figurine,** St. George, HN 2856 ...................................................... 3500.00
**Figurine,** Suitor, HN 2132 .............................................................. 325.00
**Figurine,** Summer, HN 2086 ........................................................... 400.00
**Figurine,** Suzette, HN 2026 ............................................ 300.00 To 375.00
**Figurine,** Sweet & Twenty, HN 1298 .............................. 195.00 To 200.00
**Figurine,** Sweet Anne, HN 1331, Potted ........................................ 180.00
**Figurine,** Sweet Anne, HN 1496 ..................................................... 168.00
**Figurine,** Sweet Anne, M 5 ............................................................. 250.00
**Figurine,** Sweet Sixteen, HN 2231 ................................................. 250.00
**Figurine,** This Little Pig, HN 1793 .................................................... 50.00
**Figurine,** Top Of The Hill, HN 1849 ............................................... 250.00
**Figurine,** Toymaker, HN 2250 ......................................................... 365.00
**Figurine,** Treasure Island, HN 2243 ............................................... 125.00
**Figurine,** Vanity, HN 2475 ................................................................ 60.00
**Figurine,** Veronica, HN 1517 .......................................... 250.00 To 295.00
**Figurine,** Victorian Lady, HN 728, Potted ...................................... 325.00
**Figurine,** Vivienne, HN 2073 .......................................... 260.00 To 275.00

| | |
|---|---|
| **Figurine,** Wood Nymph, HN 2192 | 180.00 |
| **Figurine,** Young Master, HN 2872 | 200.00 |
| **Fish,** Flambe, 12 1/2 In. | 750.00 |
| **Gude Grey Mare,** HN 2569 | 225.00 |
| **Humidor,** Barrel Shaped, 3 Panels Of Monks Smoking, 7 In. | 155.00 |
| **Humidor,** Cobalt & Beige Scene, Man Drinking, 6 In. | 150.00 |
| **Humidor,** Green, Game Birds | 75.00 |
| **Humidor,** Kingsware, Brown Glazed, Terrier On Lid, 2 1/2 In. | 225.00 |
| **Humidor,** Monks At Work, 3 Panels, Signed, 5 1/4 In. | 145.00 |
| **Humidor,** Tan & Brown, Applied Relief Figures, 6 In. | 105.00 |
| **Humidor,** Tan, Blue, & White Scrolls, Concentric Rings | 25.00 |
| **Jar,** Covered, Stoneware, 6 In. | 95.00 |
| **Jar,** Rose, Foliage Ware, Holes In Lid, 4 1/4 X 4 1/2 In.Diam. | 95.00 |
| **Jardiniere,** Glazed Reptile Finish, Enamel Designs | 125.00 |
| **Jardiniere,** Monk Scenes, 9 1/4 X 6 In. | 175.00 |
| **Jug,** Columbian Exposition, 1890 | 300.00 |
| **Jug,** Dickensware, Poor Jo, Square, 3 3/4 X 7 1/2 In. | 80.00 |
| **Jug,** Highland Whiskey | 48.00 |
| **Jug,** Isaac Walton, Timrous Trout, Devours My Bait, 8 1/2 In. | 110.00 |
| **Jug,** Leatherware, Don't Sware, Drinke Faire, Dated 1900, 5 In. | 165.00 |
| **Jug,** Monk Series, Blue Monks, Tan Ground, 3 X 3 In.Diam. | 75.00 |
| **Jug,** Monks Series, Blue Scene, Tan Ground, 7 X 3 5/8 In.Diam. | 110.00 |
| **Jug,** Welsh Ladies, 2 3/4 X 1 3/4 In. | 55.00 |
| **Jug,** Whiskey, Viking Ship | 85.00 |
| **Jug,** Ye Olde Cheshire Cheese 1667 | 55.00 |
| **Lamp,** Autumn Breeze, Red | 225.00 |
| **Lamp,** Figural, Fair Lady, Green | 150.00 |
| **Lamp,** Flambe, Marked, 23 In., Pair | 1200.00 |
| **Lighter,** Bacchus | 50.00 |
| **Loving Cup,** Mayflower, Basalt, Dated 1970, Boxed, 8 In. | 200.00 |
| **Match Holder,** Bayeux Tapestry, 2 7/8 In. | 40.00 |
| **Match Holder,** Mr.Pickwick, Dickensware, Square, 2 1/2 In. | 55.00 |
| **Monkeys,** Blue Flambe | 300.00 |
| **Mug,** Blood Money, Car, Driver, & Dead Goose, C.1922, 5 1/4 In. | 145.00 |
| **Mug,** Bowl, Plate, Bunnykins | 85.00 |
| **Mug,** Bunnykins, 1 Handle | 10.00 |
| **Mug,** Bunnykins, 2-Handled, Signed | 35.00 |
| **Mug,** Cottage Scenes, 5 1/2 In. | 35.00 |
| **Mug,** Lambeth, Sterling Silver Rim, 3-Handled, 4 X 3 In. | 85.00 |
| **Mug,** Nelson, 2-Handled | 240.00 To 250.00 |
| **Mug,** Nursery Rhyme, Handled, Peter Piper | 50.00 |
| **Mug,** Oliver Twist, Square | 150.00 |
| **Mug,** The Gleaners, 2-Handled, 4 In. | 65.00 |
| **Mustard Pot,** Mr.Squeers, Dickensware | 65.00 |
| **Owl,** Flambe, Sung | 262.50 To 390.00 |
| **Pepper Shaker,** Brown Earthenware | 28.00 |
| **Piper Minstrel,** Flambe, 16 In. | 1500.00 |
| **Pitcher & Bowl,** Adams Pattern | 295.00 |
| **Pitcher & Bowl,** Flow Blue | 450.00 |
| **Pitcher & Bowl,** Sailboat Scene, Green & Gold, Art Glaze | 290.00 |
| **Pitcher,** Admission Of Utah Into The Union In 1895 | 185.00 |
| **Pitcher,** Arabian Night Series, Ali Baba, Marked, 4 1/2 In. | 65.00 |
| **Pitcher,** Art Nouveau Design, Signed Morrisian, 6 3/4 In. | 85.00 |
| **Pitcher,** Battle Of Hastings, 4 3/4 In. | 65.00 |
| **Pitcher,** Brown & Tan, Deer, Hounds, Man On Horse, 8 1/4 In. | 125.00 |
| **Pitcher,** Burslem, Falconry, Hunting Scene, 8 In. | 60.00 |
| **Pitcher,** Coaching Days, 7 In. | 75.00 |
| **Pitcher,** Commemorative, Edward & Alexander, Cobalt, Pair | 140.00 |
| **Pitcher,** David Garrick, Green, Pinched, Signed, 6 3/4 In. | 90.00 |
| **Pitcher,** Dickensware, Dick Swiveller, 8 In. | 150.00 |
| **Pitcher,** Dickensware, Old Peggoty, Square, 5 1/8 In. | 65.00 |
| **Pitcher,** Dickensware, Old Pegotty, 8 In. | 235.00 |
| **Pitcher,** Dickensware, Sam Weller Scene, 2 X 2 1/2 In. | 68.00 |

| | |
|---|---|
| **Pitcher,** Dickensware, Ye Old Curiosity Shoppe | 75.00 |
| **Pitcher,** Don Quixote, Cobalt Blue, 8 1/4 In. | 159.50 |
| **Pitcher,** Gold Scrolls, Hand-Painted Roses, Signed, 9 1/4 In. | 175.00 |
| **Pitcher,** Golfing, Raised Figures, 9 1/2 In. | 135.00 |
| **Pitcher,** Head Of Horse Running, Silver Rim, Signed, 8 1/2 In. | 335.00 |
| **Pitcher,** Horseman, Brown, 7 3/4 In. | 79.00 |
| **Pitcher,** Jack's The Lad For Work, Signed Noke, 7 1/2 In. | 300.00 |
| **Pitcher,** John Barleycorn, A Mark, 3 In. | 60.00 |
| **Pitcher,** Longfellow, Black & White | 40.00 |
| **Pitcher,** Monk Scenes, Signed Noke, 7 In. | 225.00 |
| **Pitcher,** Monk Scenes, 6 1/2 In. | 125.00 |
| **Pitcher,** Morrisian, 7 1/2 In. | 125.00 |
| **Pitcher,** Oliver Twist, Square, 6 In. | 160.00 |
| **Pitcher,** Pewter Lid, Slaters, 7 1/2 In. | 150.00 |
| **Pitcher,** Pickwick Papers, Square | 125.00 |
| **Pitcher,** Pinched & Puckered, Leather Effect, 6 1/2 In. | 135.00 |
| **Pitcher,** Polar Bears, Blue, Green, 5 X 8 In.Diam. | 140.00 To 155.00 |
| **Pitcher,** Scene Of People At Wedding Celebration, 7 1/4 In. | 125.00 |
| **Pitcher,** Sketches From Teniers, 5 1/2 In. | 95.00 |
| **Pitcher,** Slater's, Pink Flowers, Pester Lid, 7 1/2 In. | 150.00 |
| **Pitcher,** Welsh Ladies, 6 X 3 In.Diam. | 65.00 |
| **Plaque,** Long John Silver, 14 In. | 100.00 |
| **Plate,** Anne Page, 9 In. | 110.00 |
| **Plate,** Autumn Breezes, Green | 150.00 |
| **Plate,** Battle Of The Nile, Blue & White, 10 1/2 In. | 65.00 |
| **Plate,** Battle Of Trafalgar, Blue Transfer | 25.00 |
| **Plate,** Bunnykins, 5 In. | 9.00 |
| **Plate,** Bunnykins, 8 In. | 11.00 |
| **Plate,** Cake, Handled, Garlands & Roses, 9 In. | 12.00 |
| **Plate,** Cap'n Cuttle, Dickensware, Signed, 10 1/2 In. | 45.00 |
| **Plate,** Churchill, 4 In. | 35.00 |
| **Plate,** Cobbler, D 6302, 10 1/2 In. | 25.00 |
| **Plate,** Countess, Blue & White, 1908 Mark, 10 1/4 In. | 20.00 |
| **Plate,** Desert Scene Series, Arab On Camel, Marked, 8 1/2 In. | 85.00 |
| **Plate,** Desert Scene, Gold Rim, Signed, 10 1/4 In., Set Of 6 | 600.00 |
| **Plate,** Dick Turpin At Bootham Bar, A Mark, 6 X 9 In. | 40.00 |
| **Plate,** Dickensware, Artful Dodger, Signed Noke, 10 1/2 In. | 75.00 |
| **Plate,** Dickensware, Fagin, 10 1/4 In. | 55.00 |
| **Plate,** Dickensware, Old Curiosity Shoppe, 12 In. | 35.00 |
| **Plate,** Dr.Johnson At The Cheshire Cheese, 10 1/4 In. | 45.00 |
| **Plate,** Egglington Tournament, Lion On Crown Mark, 10 In. | 50.00 |
| **Plate,** Falconer, 10 1/2 In. | 45.00 |
| **Plate,** Giraffes, African Series, 13 1/2 In. | 80.00 |
| **Plate,** Golfers In Colonial Garb, 9 1/2 In. | 55.00 |
| **Plate,** Green & Gold Border, Pink Roses In Center, 8 1/2 In. | 36.00 |
| **Plate,** Hamlet, 9 In. | 59.00 |
| **Plate,** Hunters With Gun & Hunting Dogs, 10 1/2 In. | 42.50 |
| **Plate,** Indian Head, Wigwam, Hiawatha Quote, 10 In | 75.00 To 120.00 |
| **Plate,** Isaac Walton, 10 1/2 In.Diam. | 75.00 |
| **Plate,** Jackdaw Of Rheims, 9 1/2 In.Diam. | 40.00 |
| **Plate,** Jackdaw Of Rheims, 10 In. | 65.00 |
| **Plate,** Jester, 10 1/2 In. | 47.50 To 58.00 |
| **Plate,** Mayor | 45.00 |
| **Plate,** Monks Toasting Cavalier, Beige & Brown | 40.00 |
| **Plate,** Mother Goose, 6 In.Diam. | 32.00 |
| **Plate,** Norfolk Pattern, 8 In. | 18.00 |
| **Plate,** Othello Scene, Cream Ground, Black Border, 12 5/8 In. | 75.00 |
| **Plate,** Portia, 8 In. | 38.00 |
| **Plate,** Portrait, Welsh Lady, Floral Border, Marked, 10 5/8 In. | 85.00 |
| **Plate,** Robert Burns, 10 1/2 In. | 40.00 To 45.00 |
| **Plate,** Sam Weller, 7 1/2 In. | 40.00 |
| **Plate,** Sam Weller, 10 1/2 In. | 50.00 |
| **Plate,** Shakespeare Portrait, 14 Names On Rim, 10 1/2 In. | 50.00 |

| | |
|---|---|
| Plate, Shakespeare Series, Juliet, 10 In. | 65.00 |
| Plate, Shakespeare Series, Orlando, 10 In. | 65.00 |
| Plate, Shakespeare Series, Rosalind, 10 In. | 65.00 |
| Plate, Shakespeare Series, Sir Andrew Aguecheek, 10 1/2 In. | 50.00 |
| Plate, Shakespeare Series, Wolsey, 10 In. | 65.00 |
| Plate, Sir Toby Belch | 40.00 |
| Plate, Spanish Armada, 10 1/2 In. | 55.00 |
| Plate, Temple Pattern, C.1905, Enameled Pinks, Greens, & Blues | 35.00 |
| Plate, The Justices Late Meeting, 10 1/4 In.Diam. | 35.00 |
| Plate, Timber Wagon, 10 1/2 In.Diam. | 25.00 |
| Plate, Wolsey, 10 In. | 85.00 |
| Plate, Ye Squire, Ye Passenger, Marked, 10 1/2 In. | 42.00 |
| Plate, 3-Horse Coach, Luggage Atop, 2 Gentlemen, 10 1/2 In. | 50.00 |
| Soup, Cream & Underplate, Fox Hunt | 35.00 |
| Soup, Dish, Geneva Pattern, 10 1/2 In.Diam. | 22.50 |
| Spittoon, 2 Roman Head Medallions, Greek Key Border, 8 In. | 145.00 |
| Sugar & Creamer, Argonaut Shell Custard | 220.00 |
| Sugar & Creamer, Glamis Thistle | 80.00 |
| Sugar, Jackdaw Of Rheims, Covered | 30.00 |
| Tea Set, Stoneware, Raised Figures, Off-White, 3 Piece | 145.00 |
| Teapot, Madras, Flow Blue | 195.00 |
| Teapot, Marqueterie | 200.00 |
| Teapot, Terra-Cotta With Reds, Brown, & White, 5 In. | 150.00 |
| Teapot, Tony Weller | 110.00 |
| Tile, Dickensware, Sam Weller, 6 1/2 In.Square | 110.00 |
| Tobacco Jar, Isaac Walton, Covered | 145.00 |
| Tobacco Jar, Kingsware, Mr.Pickwick Proposes, 7 In. | 195.00 |
| Tobacco Jar, Paddy | 350.00 |
| Toby Jug, Fat Boy | 45.00 |
| Toby Jug, Sam Weller | 75.00 |
| Toby Jug, The Huntsman, 7 1/4 In. | 40.00 |
| Toothpick, Paddy | 80.00 |
| Tray, Canterbury Pilgrims Series, Marked, 3 3/4 X 4 1/4 In. | 40.00 |
| Tray, Cardinal Wolsey, 11 X 5 In. | 45.00 |
| Tumbler, George VI, Elizabeth | 40.00 |
| Tumbler, Stag Hunt, Tan & Brown, White Figures, 5 In. | 90.00 |
| Tureen, Sauce, Leaf Handle & Finial, Italian Blue | 55.00 |
| Vase, Artful Dodger, 2 5/8 In. | 65.00 |
| Vase, Babes In Woods, Flow Blue, Girls Under Tree, 12 3/4 In. | 495.00 |
| Vase, Babes In Woods, Girl Picking Flowers, 7 1/2 In. | 295.00 |
| Vase, Babes In Woods, Hide & Seek, Marked, 4 In. | 175.00 To 210.00 |
| Vase, Babes In Woods, 2 Girls Sitting Under Tree, 8 1/2 In. | 345.00 |
| Vase, Babes In Woods, 2 Girls Under Tree, 4 X 12 In. | 265.00 |
| Vase, Chang, Green, 6 In. | 250.00 |
| Vase, Coaching Days, Marked, 4 3/8 In. | 48.00 |
| Vase, Dickensware, Dombey & Son, 8 In. | 425.00 |
| Vase, Dickensware, Little Nell, 2 3/4 X 6 1/4 In. | 68.00 |
| Vase, Dickensware, Mr.Micawber, 2-Handled, Porcelain, 2 In. | 55.00 |
| Vase, Dickensware, Old Pegotty, 4 1/2 In.Square | 48.00 |
| Vase, Dutch, Sea Horse Handles, 4 In. | 67.50 |
| Vase, Flambe, Bulbous, Veined Sung Design, 9 In. | 225.00 |
| Vase, Flambe, Ploughman & Horses Tilling Soil, 4 1/4 In. | 75.00 |
| Vase, Flambe, Veined, 6 In. | 55.00 |
| Vase, Flambe, Woodcut Scene, House, Trees, 9 1/2 In. | 140.00 |
| Vase, Flowers & Curlicues, 2-Color Design, Stoneware, 14 In. | 169.00 |
| Vase, Flowers & Leaves, Ivory Ground, C.1880, 7 In., Pair | 145.00 |
| Vase, Foliage, C.1925, Initialed A.L., 12 1/2 In. | 125.00 |
| Vase, Foliage, Tan & Blue, 9 1/2 In. | 100.00 |
| Vase, Gray Earthenware, Applied Flowers, 9 1/4 In., Pair | 230.00 |
| Vase, Impressed Leaf, Browns, 12 1/4 In. | 155.00 |
| Vase, Iris, 5 1/2 In. | 54.00 |
| Vase, Isaac Walton, Snake Handles, 4 In. | 85.00 |
| Vase, Isaac Walton, 4 3/4 In. | 75.00 |

**Vase,** Jackdaw Of Rheims, He Solemnly Cursed, 8 3/4 In. ........................................ 85.00
**Vase,** Pastoral Sheep Scene, Mottled Green Ground, 5 1/2 In. .............................. 175.00
**Vase,** Pink, Yellow, Green, Blue, Persian, Signed, 14 In., Pair ............................... 135.00
**Vase,** Red Poppies, Leaves, Signed, Burslem Marked, 8 3/4 In. ............................ 135.00
**Vase,** Sheep, 6 1/2 In. ........................................................................................... 350.00
**Vase,** Spill, Babes In Woods, 5 In. ...................................................................... 165.00
**Vase,** Spill, Brown Earthenware, 5 In. .................................................................. 60.00
**Vase,** Tapestry, Golden, 9 1/2 In. ......................................................................... 149.00
**Vase,** Tapestry, Tan & Cobalt, White Flowers, 12 In. ........................................... 160.00
**Vase,** Veined Flambe, 5 In. ................................................................................... 90.00
**Vase,** Welsh Ladies Series, 3 Ladies On Front, 5 1/2 In. ...................................... 85.00
**Vase,** Welsh Ladies, 6 1/4 X 1 3/4 In. ................................................................. 55.00
**Wall Mask,** Marlene Dietrich .................................................................................. 375.00

*Royal Dux is a porcelain made by Duxer Porzellanmanufaktur, a factory established in 1860 in Dux, Bohemia (now Czechoslovakia). Reproductions are being made.*

**ROYAL DUX, Bowl,** Figural, Girl, Parasol, Lily Pond, 13 X 12 In. ......................... 250.00
**Bust,** Elly Strobach, Pink Triangle, Pair .............................................................. 150.00
**Bust,** Woman, Pale Green & Mauve Matte Finish, Signed ................................... 750.00
**Candleholder,** Shepherdess, Shepherd, 10 In., Pair ........................................... 700.00
**Chess Set,** Genghis Khan, Entourage, Board, 32 Piece ....................................... 500.00
**Figurine,** Bavarian Hunter & Wife, Natural Colors, 22 In. .................................... 600.00
**Figurine,** Bohemian Water Carriers, Marked, 8 1/4 In., Pair ................................. 340.00
**Figurine,** Boy & Girl, Green, Beige, Rose, Signed, 10 In., Pair ............................. 485.00
**Figurine,** Boy Riding Donkey, Pink Triangle Mark, 11 X 15 1/2 In. ....................... 345.00
**Figurine,** Boy Water Carrier, Gold, Green, Triangle Mark, 9 3/8 In. ....................... 195.00
**Figurine,** Cherub Holds Shell, 6 1/2 X 8 In. ........................................................ 275.00
**Figurine,** Colonial, Double, Pink Triangle .............................................................. 175.00
**Figurine,** Dancing Woman, Swirling Dress, Foot Raised, Blue, 22 In. .................... 450.00
**Figurine,** Fisher Boy & Girl, Gold Trim, Marked, 10 3/8 In., Pair .......................... 350.00
**Figurine,** Girl Standing Beside Tree Trunk, 16 1/4 In. ...............................*Illus* 275.00
**Figurine,** Girl, Seashell On Back, Waves At Feet, Marked, 11 In. .......................... 375.00
**Figurine,** Harlequin With Lute, Kissing Columbine's Hand, 11 In. ......................... 350.00

Royal Dux, Figurine, Girl Standing Beside Tree Trunk, 16 1/4 In.

**Figurine,** Harvester, Cobalt, 11 1/2 In. .................................................................... 550.00
**Figurine,** Horse, Pink Triangle Mark, 9 X 8 1/2 In. ............................................. 110.00
**Figurine,** Indian Chief, 20 In. .......................................................................... 145.00
**Figurine,** Lions, 23 In. Long, 12 In. High, Pair ................................................ 975.00
**Figurine,** Nude Woman, Eyeing Male Dancer, Gold Brushed, 10 In. .................. 675.00
**Figurine,** Polar Bear, Seated, Paws Raised, White, Black, 14 In. ...................... 125.00
**Figurine,** Polar Bear, Seated, White, Black Eyes, Marked, 10 1/2 In. ................. 95.00
**Figurine,** Roman Girl, Pink Triangle Mark, 11 In. .............................................. 395.00
**Figurine,** Seated Princess, 13 In. ..................................................................... 200.00
**Figurine,** Setter With Duck, 14 In. ..................................................................... 100.00
**Figurine,** Shepherd, Earth Tones, Pink Triangle, 25 1/2 In. ............................... 1200.00
**Figurine,** Shepherdess, Pink Mark, 20 In. ........................................................ 485.00
**Figurine,** Spooked Mule ................................................................................... 95.00
**Figurine,** Water Carrier, Lavender & Gold Dress, Marked, 8 In., Pair ................. 340.00
**Figurine,** Water Carrier, Man & Lad, Marked, 8 1/4 In., Pair ............................. 360.00
**Figurine,** Water Carrier, Rose, Gold Burnishing, 7 1/2 In., Pair ......................... 300.00
**Figurine,** Woman Dressing, Art Deco, 8 In. ...................................................... 40.00
**Figurine,** Woman With Melons, Kneeling, Basket, 10 In. .................................... 495.00
**Lamp,** Two Women, 35 In., Pair ....................................................................... 995.00
**Light,** Night, Figure, Seminude, 13 In. .............................................................. 450.00
**Vase,** Flowers, Leaves, Yellow Ground, 11 1/2 In. ............................................ 32.00
**Vase,** Green, Applied Roses & Leaves, 6 1/2 In. ............................................... 75.00
**Vase,** Pink Flowers, Cream Ground, Marked, 10 In. .......................................... 50.00
**Vase,** Pink Luster, Petal Form, Woman's Face, White Flower ........................... 375.00
**Vase,** Pink Mark, 20 In., Pair ........................................................................... 500.00

*Royal Flemish glass was made during the late 1880s in New Bedford, Massachusetts, by the Mt.Washington Glass Works. It is a colored satin glass decorated in dark colors with gold designs.*

**ROYAL FLEMISH, Biscuit Jar,** Covered, Moss Roses, Signed MW 4413 ................. 1175.00
**Cookie Jar,** Moss Roses, Pink & Purple, Marked, 9 In. ...................................... 990.00
**Cracker Jar,** Stained Glass Flowers, Frosted Ground, Signed ........................... 1200.00
**Jar,** Sweetmeat, Mums, Gold Trim, Turtle On Edge, Sticker, 4 In. ...................... 1060.00
**Lamp,** Dragon Design, Russet & Green, No Shade, 20 In. .................................. 1400.00
**Vase,** Coat Of Arms In Panel, Gold Trim, 7 X 10 1/2 In. .................................... 2100.00
**Vase,** Gold Enameled Eagles's Head, 9 1/2 In. ................................................. 1400.00
**Vase,** Pastel Chrysanthemum Blossoms, 12 In. ................................................ 1450.00
**Vase,** Robins In Flight On Panels, 3 Feet, Marked, 6 7/8 In. .............................. 1450.00
**Vase,** Rose, Jewels & Flowers, Crown Shaped, 15 In. ....................................... 1500.00
**Vase,** Winged Dragon Design, Gold Trim, 8 In. ................................................. 2850.00
**Vase,** 2-Handled, Roman Coin Design, 8 In. ..................................................... 2800.00
**Vase,** 4 Medallions, Flower-Form Top, 7 In. ...................................................... 2700.00

**ROYAL HAEGER, Bowl,** Nude Astride Dolphin, Signed, 10 In. ............................. 50.00
**Cup & Saucer,** Old Willow ................................................................................ 25.00
    **ROYAL IVY, see Pressed Glass, Royal Ivy**
    **ROYAL OAK, see Pressed Glass, Royal Oak**

**ROYAL SAXE, Tray,** Dresser, Green & Pink, Gold Outline & Trim, Signed ........... 100.00
**Vase,** Portrait, Gray, Gold Scrolling ................................................................. 32.00

*Royal Vienna was established in Vienna by Claude Innocentius du Paquier in 1719. The factory closed in 1865. Since then, various German and Austrian factories have reproduced Royal Vienna wares, complete with the original beehive mark.*

**ROYAL VIENNA, see also Beehive**
**ROYAL VIENNA, Beaker & Saucer,** Flower Sprays, C.1765, Beehive Mark ........... 180.00
**Biscuit Jar,** Signed Kauffmann, Beehive Mark .................................................. 159.00
**Bowl,** Molded Rim, Beaded Ground, Gold Trim, Marked, 10 In.Diam. ................. 75.00
**Bowl,** Scalloped Edge, 10 X 3 In. ...................................................................... 75.00

**Box,** Cobalt Blue Top, Woman With Horse, 3 1/2 In. ................................................ 95.00
**Coffee Set,** Gold & Magenta, C.1900, Medallions, 7 Piece ................................ 425.00
**Dish,** Jupiter & Calisto, C.1880, Beehive Mark, 6 1/4 In.Diam. ........................ 700.00
**Ewer,** Portrait, Cupid Handle, Lion's Head Base, 16 In. .................................. 155.00
**Figurine,** Man & Girl, Flowers In Apron, 7 1/2 In. .......................................... 395.00
**Figurine,** Military Figure On Rearing Horse, Signed, 11 1/4 In. ...................... 175.00
**Figurine,** Porcelain, Seated Boy, Beehive Mark, 6 In. .................................... 250.00
**Figurine,** Porcelain, Seated Girl, Beehive Mark, 5 1/4 In. .............................. 250.00
**Group,** Couple In Colonial Dress, Dog In Back, 19th Century ........................ 500.00
**Jar,** Powder, Heart Shaped, Beehive Mark, 5 X 3 In. ...................................... 65.00
**Jug,** Owl Sitting On Handle, Stoneware, 6 In. ................................................ 125.00
**Mustache Cup,** Saucer, Man & Woman Seated On Ground, Marked .............. 110.00
**Plaque,** Mythological, Signed A.Kauffmann, 10 In., Pair ................................ 295.00
**Plaque,** The Guitar Player, White & Yellow Robe, 19 X 9 In. ........................ 1700.00
**Plate,** Bust Of Blonde, Maroon, Gold Etching, Beehive Mark ........................ 85.00
**Plate,** Cupids & Nymphs, Gold, Green, & Pink Border, Marked, 8 In. ............ 70.00
**Plate,** Diana Et Endymean, Gold Border, Beehive Mark ................................ 265.00
**Plate,** Diana With 3 Figures, Gold Border, Beehive Mark .............................. 195.00
**Plate,** Die Sehnsucht, Gold & Polychrome Border, Beehive, 9 In. .................. 285.00
**Plate,** Dutch People In Colorful Dress, Green Ground, 9 5/8 In. ...................... 50.00
**Plate,** Figure Of Woman, Flowers, 12 1/2 In. ................................................ 135.00
**Plate,** Figures, Horses, Floral Border, C.1900, 13 3/4 In. .............................. 450.00
**Plate,** Gold Trim, Cobalt, 9 1/2 In. ................................................................ 65.00
**Plate,** Hand-Painted Castle, Signed, Beehive Mark, 9 3/4 In. ........................ 95.00
**Plate,** Hand-Painted, Gold Birds & Animals, 9 1/2 In., Set Of 4 .................... 300.00
**Plate,** Pictured Lady With Fan, Blue Beehive Mark ...................................... 35.00
**Plate,** Pierced Handles, Lady At Pond, Beehive Mark, 10 In. ........................ 95.00
**Plate,** Portrait, Brunette, Beehive Mark, 9 1/2 In.Diam. ................................ 190.00
**Plate,** Portrait, Girl, Gold & Turquoise Border, Signed, 10 In. ...................... 450.00
**Plate,** Portrait, Louise, Cobalt & Floral Border, Signed, 10 In. ...................... 400.00
**Plate,** Psyche Showing Jewels To Sisters, Animal Border, 11 In. .................. 400.00
**Plate,** Psyche, Hand-Painted, Beehive Mark, 9 In. ........................................ 650.00
**Plate,** Theseus Et Kalvnso, Gold Border, Beehive Mark .............................. 265.00
**Sugar & Creamer,** Portrait Beaded In Gold, Beehive Mark ............................ 195.00
**Syrup,** Underplate, Classical Figures, Beehive Mark .................................... 140.00
**Tea Caddy,** Hand-Painted Picture Of 2 Young Ladies .................................. 250.00
**Tea Caddy,** Story Of Renaldo & Armida, Signed, 6 1/2 In. ............................ 250.00
**Tea Set,** Individual, Scenic Panels, Beehive Mark, 3 Piece .......................... 145.00
**Tray,** Cupids, 10 In. Long ............................................................................ 65.00
**Tray,** Dresser, Gold & Flowers On Lavender, Beehive Mark, 12 In. ................ 48.50
**Urn,** Man, Maiden, Warrior, Plum, Yellow, Blue, Covered, 17 1/2 In. ............ 600.00
**Urn,** Scene, Royal Blue & Gold, Beehive Mark, Pair .................................... 175.00
**Vase,** Cobalt Blue, Portrait Of Lady, 4 In. .................................................... 250.00
**Vase,** Floral Silhouette, White, 5 In., Pair .................................................... 30.00
**Vase,** Girl & Apple, Gold, Handled, Blue Beehive, 7 1/4 In., Pair .................. 125.00
**Vase,** Portrait, Gold On Iridescent Green, Signed, 6 3/4 In. .......................... 650.00
**Vase,** Wisteria, 9 1/2 In. ............................................................................ 58.00
**Vase,** 2-Handled, Medallions & Butterflies, Signed ...................................... 165.00

 *Royal Worcester porcelain was made in the later period of Worcester pottery, which was originally established in 1751. The Royal Worcester trade name has been used by Worcester Royal Porcelain Company, Ltd., since 1862.*

**ROYAL WORCESTER, Ashtray,** Fox Figure, C.1930, D.Lindner ...................... 100.00
**Ashtray,** Hound, D.Lindner, C.1930 ............................................................ 100.00
**Ashtray,** Sealyham Terrier, D.Lindner, 5 1/2 X 4 1/2 In. ................................ 350.00
**Basket,** Beige Satin, Floral, Dated 1903, 6 In. .............................................. 180.00
**Basket,** Celery, Bamboo, 9 In. .................................................................... 140.00
**Bowl,** Elephant Head Handles, Gold Trim, Blue, 6 X 14 In. .......................... 250.00
**Bowl,** Hand-Painted Pheasants, Signed, 8 1/2 In.Diam. ................................ 695.00
**Bowl,** Lusterware, Fruit In Bottom, Blue, Gold, C.1920, 10 In. ...................... 175.00

**Bowl,** Palm Fronds Form Handle, Gold To Eggshell, 9 In.Diam. ............................................ 345.00
**Bowl,** Pierced Loop Rim, C.1897, Purple Mark, 9 1/4 In. ...................................................... 550.00
**Bowl,** Scalloped, Hand-Painted, Gold Band, 5 3/4 In.Diam. ................................................. 115.00
**Bowl,** Waste, Green Enamel, Gilt Rim, C.1765, Marked, 6 1/2 In. ........................................ 260.00
**Box,** Covered, Flowers, 2 1/2 X 1 X 3 1/2 In. ..................................................................... 75.00
**Box,** Green & Gold, Purple Mark, 2 5/8 In.Diam. ................................................................ 35.00
**Bust,** Veiled Lady, Hope, C.1897, Ivory Porcelain, 11 In. ................................................ 1550.00
**Candlesnuffer,** Cook, Gold Trim, 1907 Mark, 2 1/2 In. ....................................................... 145.00
**Candlesnuffer,** Granny Snow, C.1950 .............................................................................. 110.00
**Candlesnuffer,** Japanese Lady, Purple Mark ..................................................................... 125.00
**Candlesnuffer,** Monk, Carries Bible, 1930 Mark, 4 3/4 In. .................................................. 88.00
**Candlesnuffer,** Nun, Purple Mark ..................................................................................... 85.00
**Candlesnuffer,** Plumed Hat, C.1901, Grainger Mark ......................................................... 110.00
**Candlestick,** Cherub Blowing Horn, Pink Drape, 7 3/4 In. ................................................. 365.00
**Candlestick,** Lily Pad, Frog, Dated 1888, 7 1/4 In., Pair ..................................................... 695.00
**Coffee Set,** Sterling Bands & Handles, Individual, 3 Piece ................................................ 120.00
**Compote,** Pedestal, Pheasants, 1907 Mark, Signed, 7 3/4 In. ........................................... 595.00
**Cracker Jar,** Melon Shape, Floral & Gilt, Marked, 7 In. ..................................................... 200.00
**Creamer,** Flat Back, Gold & Flower Design, 6 In. ............................................................. 125.00
**Cup & Saucer,** Blue Dragons, White Ground, Demitasse, 1903 .......................................... 55.00
**Cup & Saucer,** Flower Design ........................................................................................... 35.00
**Cup & Saucer,** Lavinia ..................................................................................................... 20.00
**Cup & Saucer,** Quadrefoil Top, C.1887, Gilded Rim, Demitasse ........................................ 45.00
**Cup,** Hand-Enameled Flowers, Beige, 2-Handled, 1 1/2 In. ................................................ 55.00
**Cup,** Left Handed, Yellow To Rose, Flowers, Gold Handle, 4 In. ........................................ 125.00
**Cup,** 2-Handled, Hand-Enameled Flowers, 1 1/2 X 1 5/8 In. ............................................... 52.00
**Ewer,** Dragon Handle, 11 In. ............................................................................................ 375.00
**Ewer,** Floral, Hand-Painted, Left Handed, 4 1/2 In. ........................................................... 185.00
**Ewer,** Gilt Lizard Handle, Polychrome, C.1889, 12 In. ...................................................... 425.00
**Ewer,** Gold Satyr Mask Under Handle, Dated 1888, 10 3/4 In. .......................................... 325.00
**Ewer,** Hand-Painted Flowers, Left Handed, 4 1/2 In. ......................................................... 185.00
**Ewer,** Handled, Flowers, Beige Ground, C.1903, 6 1/8 In. ................................................. 175.00
**Ewer,** Pierced Cover, Pink Flowers, Purple Mark, 15 1/2 In. ............................................ 1100.00
**Figurine,** Amaryllis, Numbered, 9 1/4 In. .......................................................................... 235.00
**Figurine,** Blutit, 2 1/2 In. ................................................................................................. 45.00
**Figurine,** Bullfinch, 2 1/2 In. ............................................................................................ 45.00
**Figurine,** Burmah, Porcelain, 5 1/4 In. .............................................................................. 80.00
**Figurine,** Canary, Yellow, White, Gold Flower Tree, 6 1/2 In. ............................................ 125.00
**Figurine,** Chinese Boy With Chopsticks ............................................................................ 75.00
**Figurine,** Duchess Dress, No.3106, C.1940, 6 In. ............................................................ 200.00
**Figurine,** Dutch Boy & Girl, Blue Mark, 5 1/2 In., Pair ...................................................... 160.00
**Figurine,** Dutch Boy, No. 2923 ........................................................................................ 120.00
**Figurine,** Eastern Water Carrier, 1897 Mark, 8 In. ............................................................ 295.00
**Figurine,** Egyptian Musician, Apricot Robe, 12 1/2 In. ...................................................... 475.00
**Figurine,** England ............................................................................................................ 135.00
**Figurine,** Fortune Teller ................................................................................................... 150.00
**Figurine,** Foxhound, Seated, 7 In. .................................................................................... 150.00
**Figurine,** Friday's Child ................................................................................................... 75.00
**Figurine,** Girl Holds Dead Bird, Draped Luster Gown, 10 In. ............................................. 450.00
**Figurine,** Girl With Apron Spread, Marked, 8 1/2 In. .......................................................... 375.00
**Figurine,** Goosie Goosie Gander, No.3304, 6 1/4 In. ........................................................ 155.00
**Figurine,** Grandmother's Dress, Blue ............................................................................... 75.00
**Figurine,** Grecian Lady Water Carrier, 1918 Mark, 9 1/4 In. .............................................. 295.00
**Figurine,** Irishman, Decorated, C.1896 ............................................................................ 350.00
**Figurine,** Kingfisher, Blue, Salmon, On Tree Stump, 6 1/2 In. ........................................... 200.00
**Figurine,** Lady With Tambourine, Dated 1916, 5 3/4 In. .................................................... 425.00
**Figurine,** Little Jack Horner ............................................................................................. 135.00
**Figurine,** Man & Woman Turk, Gilt & Green, C.1885, 8 1/2 In. ......................................... 1200.00
**Figurine,** Masquerade Girl, No.3360, Boy, No.3359, Pair .................................................. 250.00
**Figurine,** Mockingbirds, Peach Tree, C.1940, 10 3/8 In., Pair ........................................... 800.00
**Figurine,** Naked Cherub, 2 Goats .................................................................................... 125.00
**Figurine,** Near Eastern Figures, Hadley, Pair ..................................................... *Illus* 2800.00

Royal Worcester, Figurine, Near Eastern
Figures, Hadley, Pair (See Page 537)

| | |
|---|---|
| Figurine, Only Me | 125.00 |
| Figurine, Parakeet, Blue, On Stump, Lavender, Black, 5 1/2 In. | 190.00 |
| Figurine, Polly-Put-Kettle-On | 85.00 |
| Figurine, Robin, Signed & Numbered | 40.00 |
| Figurine, Saturday's Child, Blue, White, Red, 6 In. | 95.00 |
| Figurine, Sea Breeze, Girl, Signed, 8 In. | 195.00 |
| Figurine, Sea Urchin, Dated 1938, 6 1/2 In. | 145.00 |
| Figurine, Spain, No.3070, 5 In. | 75.00 |
| Figurine, Spring, Girl Holding Lamb, Signed, 9 In. | 389.00 |
| Figurine, Spring, 8 1/2 In. | 195.00 |
| Figurine, Sunday's Child, Blue, Yellow, 4 1/2 In. | 95.00 |
| Figurine, Sunshine, No.3083 | 200.00 |
| Figurine, Three Circus Horses Rearing, 1936 | 2900.00 |
| Figurine, Tommy, No.2913, C.1930s | 150.00 |
| Figurine, Two Babies, Doughty | 110.00 |
| Figurine, Veiled Lady, Ivory Porcelain, 1867 Mark, 11 In. | 1575.00 |
| Figurine, Wednesday's Child, Pink, Green, 6 1/2 In. | 90.00 |
| Figurine, Woman Holding Basket, Marked, 1918, 9 1/2 In. | 240.00 |
| Figurine, Wood Warbler, 2 3/4 In. | 47.50 |
| Figurine, Woodland Dance, No.3076 | 150.00 |
| Figurine, Wren, 2 3/4 In. | 47.50 |
| Figurine, Yankee, No.836, Gold & Color Trim, 7 In. | 475.00 |
| Finger Bowl, Gold & Brown, Leaf On White Porcelain | 40.00 |
| Honey Dish, Clear Yellow | 15.00 |
| Jar, Covered, Burgundy Flowers, Purple Mark, 4 1/2 In. | 150.00 |
| Jug, Ice, Tusk Pattern, Raised Enamel & Gold Florals, 10 In. | 255.00 |
| Jug, Left Handed, Blown-Out Handle, C.1890, Signed, 7 1/2 In. | 235.00 |
| Jug, Raised Gold Salamander, Branch Handle, 1917 Mark, 6 In. | 225.00 |
| Lamp Base, Roses, Lilac Ground, Blue & Lilac, 12 3/4 In. | 425.00 |
| Mug, Sabbath Child | 20.00 To 28.00 |
| Nappy, Water Lily Pad | 75.00 |
| Pie Bird | 11.00 |
| Pitcher, Bamboo Handle, Flowers, Signed | 98.00 To 115.00 |
| Pitcher, Cabbage Leaf, White & Rust, 1944, 3 1/2 In. | 40.00 |
| Pitcher, Colored Flowers, 1903 Mark, 7 1/8 X 4 1/2 In.Diam. | 175.00 |
| Pitcher, Dragon Handle, Gold & Silver, 1880 Mark, 11 1/4 In. | 495.00 |
| Pitcher, Flowers, Bamboo Handle, Purple Mark, 8 In. | 450.00 |
| Pitcher, Flowers, Roped Handles, 1899 Mark, 8 3/4 In. | 195.00 |
| Pitcher, Hand-Painted Bird, Artist Signed, 4 In. | 58.00 |
| Pitcher, Ivory Ground, Flowers, Gold Handle, Flat Back | 120.00 |
| Pitcher, Lion's Head Spout, Paw Handle, Victorian, 4 3/4 In. | 210.00 |
| Pitcher, Mask Spout, Marked, C.1884, 10 1/2 In. *Illus* | 450.00 |
| Pitcher, One Side Flat, Handled, Gold Trim, 1867 Mark, 6 In. | 100.00 |
| Pitcher, Pink Salamander, Branch Handle, 1917 Mark, 6 In. | 225.00 |
| Pitcher, Red Bird On Ivorine, Artist Signed, 1911, 3 1/4 In. | 115.00 |
| Pitcher, Roped Gold Handle, Beige, 1897 Mark, 8 3/8 In. | 185.00 |
| Pitcher, Sweet Peas & Yellow Leaves, Gold Outlined, 9 In. | 160.00 |

Royal Worcester, Pitcher, Mask Spout, Marked, C.1884, 10 1/2 In.

| | |
|---|---:|
| **Plaque,** Wall, Orchids, Gold & Beige, Pair | 500.00 |
| **Plate,** Bird, Flower, Butterflies, Dated 1879, 9 In. | 40.00 |
| **Plate,** Blue & Pink Flowers, Gold Outlined & Trim, 9 1/4 In. | 28.00 |
| **Plate,** Blue & White, Oriental Scene, C.1880, 10 1/2 In. | 60.00 |
| **Plate,** Bouquets & Flower Sprays, C.1765, 7 3/4 In., Pair | 360.00 |
| **Plate,** Commemorative, St. Augustine | 38.00 |
| **Plate,** Commemorative, Victoria 1887 Jubilee, Stowell | 55.00 |
| **Plate,** Commemorative, 1896, 10 1/2 In. | 60.00 |
| **Plate,** Dorchester, 8 In.Diam., Set Of 8 | 75.00 |
| **Plate,** Floral, Gold Detail, 9 1/4 In. | 35.00 |
| **Plate,** Hand-Painted Design, Crackle Glaze, 1880, 9 In., Pair | 80.00 |
| **Plate,** Leaf, Flower Design, Gold Border, 8 In., Set Of 10 | 650.00 |
| **Plate,** Rosemary, Dated 1929, 9 1/4 In. | 15.00 |
| **Plate,** St.Augustine, Florida, 9 1/2 In. | 22.50 |
| **Platter,** Elephant Head Handles, Gold Trim, 19 X 15 In. | 250.00 |
| **Rose Bowl,** Rust, Lavender, Gold Flowers, Signed, 3 In. | 95.00 |
| **Rose Jar,** Covered, Gold Outline, 1906 Mark, 4 3/8 In. | 175.00 |
| **Rose Jar,** Slip Design Panels, Green Ground, 1904, 4 In. | 145.00 |
| **Sauceboat,** Flowers On Beige, 1896, 2 3/4 X 6 In. | 110.00 |
| **Sauceboat,** Hand-Painted Flowers, 1896, 2 3/4 X 6 In. | 110.00 |
| **Shell,** Nautilus, Snail, Seaweed, On Pedestal, 8 1/2 In. | 275.00 |
| **Sugar & Creamer,** Blue Willow, Gold Trim, Dated 1882 | 65.00 |
| **Teapot,** Melon Shape, Scalloped Lid, Flower Finial, 5 1/2 In. | 385.00 |
| **Toby Jug,** Dated 1929, Marked, 1 3/4 In. | 98.00 |
| **Toothpick,** Applied Lizard, Hand-Painted Flowers, 2 X 2 In. | 175.00 |
| **Tray,** Green, Gold Trim, White Blossoms, Signed, 4 3/8 X 6 In. | 245.00 |
| **Tureen,** Gold Elephant Head Handles, 1880 Mark, 15 1/4 In. | 300.00 |
| **Urn,** Beaded Rim, Pistol Grip Handles, Marked, 17 1/4 In. | 850.00 |
| **Urn,** Covered, Reticulated, Gold Trim, 1889 Mark, 9 1/2 In. | 795.00 |
| **Urn,** Pedestal, Beige, Gold Border, C.1904 | 225.00 |
| **Vase,** Animal Handles, Mouth Open, Flowers, 10 In. | 265.00 |
| **Vase,** Bamboo Shoot & Butterfly Design, C.1880, 5 3/4 In. | 50.00 |
| **Vase,** Bands & Buckles, Hoof Feet, 1899 Mark, 5 1/4 In.Diam. | 225.00 |
| **Vase,** Beige Satin, Floral, Gold Handles, Dated 1902, 10 In. | 240.00 |
| **Vase,** Blackberries, Fruit, Flower, Signed K, 5 1/2 In. | 150.00 |
| **Vase,** Butterfly, Floral, Snake Handles, C.1890, 10 In. | 325.00 |
| **Vase,** Coiled Snakes On Shoulder, C.1880, 7 1/2 In. | 325.00 |
| **Vase,** Coral Ground, Gold Trim, Marked Locke, 3 3/8 In. | 50.00 |
| **Vase,** Covered, Flying Ducks Over Marshlands, 13 1/4 In. | 770.00 |
| **Vase,** Covered, Hand-Painted Florals, Gold Trim, C.1901, 8 In. | 225.00 |
| **Vase,** Covered, Pansies, Gilding, Apricot, 19 In. ................*Illus* | 550.00 |
| **Vase,** Double, Bamboo-Handled, Curved, Ivory, C.1885, 7 In. | 150.00 |
| **Vase,** Figural, Covered, Open Handle, Hand-Painted, 9 In. | 255.00 |
| **Vase,** Flowers Outlined In Gold, 1907 Mark, 7 3/4 In. | 210.00 |
| **Vase,** Flowers, Gold Greek Key Rim, 1901 Mark, 3 In., Pair | 145.00 |
| **Vase,** Gilt Mythological Handles, C.1878, Purple Mark, 13 In. | 650.00 |
| **Vase,** Gold Ball Feet, Handles, Hand-Painted, 1911, 3 1/2 In. | 105.00 |

Royal Worcester, Vase, Covered, Pansies,
Gilding, Apricot, 19 In. (See Page 539)

| | |
|---|---:|
| Vase, Gold Handles & Outlining, 1908 Mark, 6 5/8 In. | 175.00 |
| Vase, Gold Serpent Handles, Butterfly, Dated 1882, 8 3/4 In. | 550.00 |
| Vase, Hand-Painted Peacock, Signed, 2 5/8 X 4 1/8 In. | 265.00 |
| Vase, Hand-Painted, Gold Outlines, 1897, 8 3/4 In. | 5.00 |
| Vase, Handled, Hand-Painted Flowers, 1900, 2 7/8 In. | 85.00 |
| Vase, Handled, Multicolored, Dated 1886, 9 X 12 In. | 385.00 |
| Vase, Handles, Pedestal, Roman Gold Trim, 1907 Mark, 7 In. | 218.00 |
| Vase, Highland Cattle Scene, Signed J.Stinton, 16 In., Pair | 5850.00 |
| Vase, Multicolored Flowers, Gold Outlining, 1910 Mark, 8 In. | 235.00 |
| Vase, Nautilus Shell, Beige & Blush, Gold Trim, 6 X 8 In. | 235.00 |
| Vase, Peacock On Branch, Hand-Painted, Signed, 14 1/8 In. | 265.00 |
| Vase, Pedestal, Handled, Flowers, 1907 Mark, 7 1/2 In. | 225.00 |
| Vase, Polychrome Floral & Leaf Design, Marked, 10 In. | 175.00 |
| Vase, Shell On Coral Stand, Tan, Gold, & Ivory, Marked, 7 In. | 250.00 |
| Vase, Stick, Flowers, Cream Ground, Purple Mark, 7 In. | 90.00 |
| Vase, Trumpet, Flowers, Green Trim, Dated 1898, 8 7/8 In. | 245.00 |
| Vase, Yellow To Pink, Flowers, Gold Handles, 1900, 3 In. | 115.00 |
| Vase, Yellow To Rust, Hand-Painted Flowers, 1890, 6 In. | 225.00 |
| Wall Pocket, Orchid, Gold & Beige, Pair | 550.00 |
| Watering Can, Ivorine Ground, Dragon Handle, 5 X 10 1/2 In. | 585.00 |

*Roycroft products were made by the Roycrofter community of East Aurora, New York, in the late nineteenth and early twentieth centuries. The community was founded by Elbert Hubbard. The products included furniture, metalware, leatherwork, and jewelry.*

| | |
|---|---:|
| ROYCROFT, Bookends, Art Deco Design, Handmade Brass & Enamel | 22.50 |
| Bookends, Copper, Floral Relief Design | 65.00 |
| Bookends, Dome Shaped Center, Copper, 3 1/4 X 4 In., Pair | 30.00 |
| Bookends, Hammered Copper, Incised Design, 3 X 3 X 5 In., Pair | 52.00 |
| Bookends, Triangular Shape, Copper | 50.00 |
| Bowl, Hammered Copper, 8 In.Diam. | 42.50 |
| Box, Figural, Cigarette Holder, Marked, 3 1/4 X 2 1/2 In. | 20.00 |
| Candelabrum, Applied Scrolling, Spreading Base, C.1910, 20 In. | 275.00 |
| Candlestick, Bronze Finish, Impressed Mark, 8 In., Pair | 85.00 |
| Candlestick, Drip Pan On Twin Columns, Marked, 7 3/4 In., Pair | 85.00 |
| Candlestick, Twisted Stem, Copper, 12 In., Pair | 75.00 |
| Drawer Pull | 25.00 |
| Inkwell, Round | 45.00 |
| Jug, Brown, 6 In. | 22.00 |
| Lamp, Helmet Shape Shade, Standard Base, Marked, 14 In. | 425.00 |
| Nut Set, Flower Center, Hammered Border, C.1910, 7 Piece | 150.00 |
| Plate, Hammered Copper, 8 1/2 In. | 70.00 |
| Scrapbook, Hubbard, 1926 | 6.00 |
| Smoker's Stand, Matchbox Holder, Ashtray, Marked, 23 3/4 In. | 500.00 |
| Vase, American Beauty, 12 In. | 390.00 |
| Vase, Bud, Glass Insert, 4 In., Pair | 37.50 |

Rozenburg, Vase, Eggshell, Lilac,
& Yellow Flowers, Ivory, 7 In.

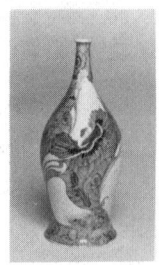

Vase, Flower In Relief, Marked, 7 1/8 In. ................................................................................... 75.00
Vase, Silver Finish Over Copper, 8 1/2 In. ................................................................................ 55.00
Vase, Spherical, Cylindrical Neck, Folded Rim, Marked, 18 1/2 In. ......................................... 400.00
Vase, Stylized Floral Design, Green Paint, Marked, C.1910, 7 In. ........................................... 125.00
  **ROZANE, see Roseville**

ROZENBURG, Vase, Eggshell, Lilac, & Yellow Flowers, Ivory, 7 In. ....................................*Illus* 2200.00

*RRP is the mark used by the firm of Robinson-Ransbottom. The firm was
founded by the Ransbottom brothers in 1900 in Ironspot, Ohio. In 1920
they merged with the Robinson Clay Product Company of Akron, Ohio,
to become Robinson-Ransbottom. Pieces are often confused with those
of the Roseville Pottery. The factory is still working.*

RRP CO., Cookie Jar, Sheriff Pig ................................................................................................ 32.00

*RS Germany porcelain was made at the factory of Rheinhold Schlegelmilch
after 1869 in Tillowitz, Germany. It was sold decorated or undecorated.*

RS GERMANY, Ashtray, Orange Poppies, 3 Rests, 4 1/2 In. ....................................................... 28.00
Ashtray, Pink Poppies, Large ................................................................................... 40.00 To 50.00
Ashtray, White, Pink Flowers ....................................................................................................... 34.00
Basket, Strawflowers, Open Handled, 3-Footed ........................................................................ 36.00
Berry Set, Pink Floral, Gold Trim, 7 Piece ................................................................................. 175.00
Berry Set, Scalloped Edges, Opened Pink Roses, 5 Piece ....................................................... 100.00
Berry Set, Scalloped Edges, 4 Small Bowls, Opened Pink Roses ............................................. 160.00
Berry Set, 6 Sauces, Underplates, Gold Edge, Set Of 6 ............................................................ 125.00
Biscuit Jar, Calla Lilies, Handled, 5 1/2 In. ................................................................................ 125.00
Bonbon, Cotton Design, Gold Trim, Open Handles, Blue Mark ................................................. 48.00
Bonbon, Orange & Black, Handled ............................................................................................. 58.00
Bonbon, 3-Footed, Scalloped, Peach Roses, White Ground, Marked ....................................... 60.00
Bone Dish, Gold Trim, White, Set Of 8 ....................................................................................... 58.00
Bottle, Cologne, Pink Roses, Green Ground, Stopper ............................................................... 10.00
Bottle, Perfume, Forget-Me-Nots ................................................................................................ 20.00
Bowl, Berry & Underplate, Green & Gold Trim, Violets, Embossed .......................................... 28.00
Bowl, Berry, Blue Mark, Flowers, Pink, White, 5 In., Set Of 4 ................................................. 40.00
Bowl, Berry, Poppies, Gold Beaded Edge, Blue Mark, Set Of 6 .............................................. 180.00
Bowl, Berry, Violets, Green, Gold Trim ...................................................................................... 12.00
Bowl, Blown Roses On Rim, Luster Finish, 11 X 3 In. .............................................................. 120.00
Bowl, Blue Flowers & Butterflies, Handled, Square, 4 1/2 In. ................................................... 38.00
Bowl, Candy, Farmhouse Amid Foliage, Signed, 6 In. .............................................................. 115.00
Bowl, Centerpiece & Candlestick, Orange Luster ..................................................................... 120.00
Bowl, Centerpiece, Lotus Leaf Shaped, Silver Overlay, 8 In. .................................................... 47.50
Bowl, Cottage Scene, Signed, 10 In.Diam. ................................................................................ 165.00
Bowl, Floral, Reticulated Border, Square, 6 1/2 In. ................................................................... 58.00

| | |
|---|---|
| **Bowl,** Fruit, White Rose, Gold Band, 10 In.Diam. | 45.00 |
| **Bowl,** Gold Iris, White, Castle Red Mark, 9 3/4 In. | 175.00 |
| **Bowl,** Gold Trim, White Roses, 9 X 2 1/2 In. | 35.00 |
| **Bowl,** Gold, Green, Blossom Shaped, 4 1/2 X 2 1/2 In. | 35.00 |
| **Bowl,** Green, Blue, White Tulip, Footed, Blue Mark, 9 X 7 In. | 60.00 |
| **Bowl,** Green, Lilies, Lilacs, Molded Rim, Green Mark, 9 1/4 In. | 32.00 |
| **Bowl,** Matte Green, Gold Rim Design, Green Star & Wreath, 10 In. | 40.00 |
| **Bowl,** Molded Cabbage Leaf, Crimped, Gold Trim, 10 In.Diam. | 135.00 |
| **Bowl,** Open Handles, Gold Trim Edge, Roses, Blue Mark, 10 In. | 55.00 |
| **Bowl,** Peach Lilies, Green, White Ground, 9 1/2 In. | 65.00 |
| **Bowl,** Poppy, Scalloped, 10 In. | 50.00 |
| **Bowl,** Sugar, Yellow Strawflowers, Gold, Rein.Schl. Signed | 28.00 |
| **Bowl,** White & Pink Roses, Gray To Green, Blue Mark, 9 1/4 In. | 42.00 |
| **Bowl,** White Oriental Flowers, Pale Green, 9 1/2 In. | 45.00 |
| **Bowl,** Yellow & Green Peonies, 8 In. | 55.00 |
| **Bowl,** Yellow Rose, Cream Ground, Blue Mark, 6 X 3 1/2 In. | 65.00 |
| **Bowl,** Yellow Roses, Poppies, Flower Edge, Oblong, 13 X 8 3/4 In. | 110.00 |
| **Bowl,** Yellow Roses, Salmon Border, 9 1/2 In. | 45.00 |
| **Bowl,** 4-Footed, Scalloped Edge, Pink Roses, 5 7/8 X 4 1/2 In. | 45.00 |
| **Bowl,** 5 Folded-In Sides, Silver, Blue Mark, 8 1/4 In.Diam. | 56.00 |
| **Box,** Butterfly Shape, Covered, Blue & White, Gold Trim, 3 X 4 In. | 65.00 |
| **Box,** Covered, Hand-Painted Roses, 2 5/8 In.Square | 21.00 |
| **Box,** Dresser, Covered, Daisies, Hand-Painted | 45.00 |
| **Box,** Jewelry, White & Pink Roses, Green Ground, Blue Mark, Round | 20.00 |
| **Bread Tray,** Bluebird, 15 1/2 In. | 55.00 |
| **Bread Tray,** Slit Handles, White Roses, Green Ground, 13 X 8 In. | 95.00 |
| **Bulb Bowl,** Yellow Rose, Cream Ground, Blue Mark, 3 1/2 X 6 In. | 65.00 |
| **Cake Plate,** Open Handled, Flowers, Green Mark, 9 3/4 In.Diam. | 40.00 |
| **Cake Plate,** Open Handled, Orange Nasturtiums, 9 1/4 In.Diam. | 37.00 |
| **Cake Plate,** Pink Roses, Open Handled, 9 1/2 In. | 65.00 |
| **Cake Plate,** Scalloped Gold Edge, Flowers, 6 1/2 In. | 18.00 |
| **Cake Plate,** Water Lily Scene, Open Handled, Green Mark, 9 1/4 In. | 75.00 |
| **Cake Plate,** White Floral Design, Cream Ground, Green Mark | 35.00 |
| **Cake Set,** Open Handled Tray, 6 Plates, Tray, 9 3/4 In. | 150.00 |
| **Candleholder,** Lily Of The Valley, 5 In. | 29.00 |
| **Celery Set,** Lily Design | 58.00 |
| **Celery,** Green, Roses Inside Daisies, Open Edge, Signed, 13 In. | 40.00 |
| **Celery,** Open Handled, Water Lilies | 42.00 |
| **Chocolate Pot,** Beige, Pastel Lilacs | 125.00 |
| **Chocolate Pot,** Hand-Painted Roses | 90.00 |
| **Chocolate Pot,** Pastel Flowers, Single Serving, 6 In. | 62.00 |
| **Chocolate Pot,** Roses, Red, Pink, & White, Marked | 95.00 |
| **Chocolate Pot,** Underplate, Orange & Green, Green Mark, 8 1/2 In. | 125.00 |
| **Chocolate Pot,** Underplate, Tiger Lily Design | 95.00 |
| **Chocolate Pot,** White Rose Design, Shaded Ground, 9 In. | 125.00 |
| **Chocolate Set,** Pink Orchids, Gold Rimmed, Blue Mark, 13 Piece | 350.00 |
| **Chocolate Set,** Roses, Pot, 6 Cups & Saucers | 375.00 |
| **Chocolate Set,** White Lilacs, Gold Trim, Green Ground, 13 Piece | 350.00 |
| **Chocolate Set,** White, Gold, Apple Blossoms, Marked | 350.00 |
| **Coffeepot,** White Rose Design, 9 In. | 115.00 |
| **Cracker Jar,** Floral Handled, Marked | 75.00 |
| **Cracker Jar,** Flowers, Green Ground | 95.00 |
| **Cracker Jar,** Green & Gold, Red & White Roses | 110.00 |
| **Cracker Jar,** Green Flowers & Leaves, Gold Trim | 110.00 |
| **Cracker Jar,** Orange Lilies, Green Mark | 100.00 |
| **Creamer,** Blue Flowers, White Ground, Gold Tracery, Marked, 4 In. | 28.00 |
| **Creamer,** Orange Poppy & 2 Daisies, Green Mark | 25.00 |
| **Creamer,** Pale Green, Pink Roses At Top, Gold Handle, 3 In. | 10.00 |
| **Creamer,** Pebble Blown-Out Rim, Easter Lily On Green | 26.00 |
| **Creamer,** Yellow, Green, Pink & White Flowers, 1916, 4 1/2 In. | 22.00 |
| **Cup & Saucer,** Lily Of The Valley | 18.00 |
| **Cup & Saucer,** Pedestal, Pink, Gold Handles, Demitasse, Set Of 6 | 85.00 |
| **Cup & Saucer,** Ribbed Sides, White, Gold Rim, Marked, Demitasse | 50.00 |

**Dish,** Cheese & Cracker, Pastel Design, Green Ground, Gold Trim ........................................... 60.00
**Dish,** Cupids Around Fire, Open Handled, 5 1/2 In. ................................................................... 75.00
**Dish,** Mint, Flowers, 2-Handled, Signed ..................................................................................... 22.50
**Dish,** Open Handled, Flowers, Signed, 3 3/4 In.Diam. ............................................................. 20.00
**Dish,** Parakeet, 6 1/4 In. ............................................................................................................. 110.00
**Dish,** Pickle, Floral, Green Mark, 3 X 7 In. ............................................................................... 25.00
**Dish,** Pink Flowers, Brown Tones, Bow Shaped, 4 X 7 1/2 In. .............................................. 38.00
**Dish,** Relish, Canoe Shaped, Handled, Mint Ground, 9 1/2 In. ............................................ 32.50
**Dish,** Relish, Flowers, Green Mark, 4 X 8 1/2 In.Diam. ........................................................... 27.00
**Dish,** Relish, Handled, White Flowers, Gold Trim, Blue Mark, 10 In. ................................... 40.00
**Dish,** Relish, Roses, Earth Tones, Gold Trim, Blue Mark ....................................................... 55.00
**Gravy Boat,** Underplate, Yellow Roses, Gray & Green Ground ........................................... 22.50
**Hair Receiver,** White Flowers, Green Shading, Gold Trim ..................................................... 95.00
**Hatpin Holder,** Brown Design, Gold Top, Blue Mark, 4 1/2 In. ........................................... 17.25
**Hatpin Holder,** Floral Design, Gold Top & Bottom, 4 1/2 In. .............................................. 40.00
**Hatpin Holder,** Flowers On Brown & White Ground, Marked .............................................. 55.00
**Hatpin Holder,** Lily .................................................................................................................... 32.50
**Hatpin Holder,** Peach Roses, 4 1/4 In. ..................................................................................... 32.00
**Hatpin Holder,** Pink Rose, 4 1/4 In. ......................................................................................... 32.00
**Hatpin Holder,** Pink Roses, Green Mark, 4 1/2 In. ................................................................. 50.00
**Hatpin Holder,** Purple Violets, Pierced Top, Marked ............................................................ 48.00
**Hatpin Holder,** Scalloped Bottom, Ring Handles .................................................................. 55.00
**Hatpin Holder,** Violets, Shaded, Large ................................................................................... 45.00
**Hatpin Holder,** Windflowers, Green Shading, 4 1/4 In. ......................................................... 32.00
**Inkwell,** Bridge Design Across Cover, Pink Rose Design ....................................................... 75.00
**Inkwell,** Gold Design, Green Luster, Signed, 2 Piece ............................................................ 20.00
**Inkwell,** Hand-Painted, Art Nouveau, Square ....................................................................... 75.00
**Inkwell,** Handled Cover, Pink Rose ......................................................................................... 85.00
**Inkwell,** Rosebuds Design, Covered ....................................................................................... 60.00
**Inkwell,** White & Green With Pink Roses, Marked ................................................................. 60.00
**Jam Set,** Toned White Roses .................................................................................................... 58.00
**Mayonnaise Set,** Peach & Ivory Poppies, Daisies, 3 Piece .................................................. 58.00
**Muffineer,** Iris Design ................................................................................................................ 45.00
**Mustache Cup,** Beveled Mirror, Floral, Steeple Mark, 3 In. ................................................. 140.00
**Mustache Cup,** Pink Blossoms, Blue Mark ............................................................................. 65.00
**Mustache Cup,** Pink Blossoms, Swirled Ribs, Red Mark ...................................................... 125.00
**Mustard Pot,** Roses, Covered .................................................................................................. 30.00
**Mustard,** Flowers, White Ground, Orange Mark ................................................................... 55.00
**Mustard,** Handled, Green Poppies .......................................................................................... 25.00
**Mustard,** Handled, Green Trim, White Flowers ..................................................................... 32.00
**Mustard,** Hydrangeas, Gold Trim ........................................................................................... 45.00
**Mustard,** Lid, Ladle, Flowers On Brown & White Shading, Marked .................................... 50.00
**Mustard,** Pink Roses, Yellow Ground, Gold Pierced Handled Top ...................................... 35.00
**Mustard,** Rose Design, Ornate Handle & Finial ..................................................................... 40.00
**Mustard,** Tureen Shaped, Attached Underplate .................................................................... 20.00
**Nut Set,** Pale Green & White Tulip, Satin Finish, 6 Bowls ..................................................... 150.00
**Nut Set,** 6 Small Bowls, Pedestal Base, Tulips, Green Ground ............................................ 150.00
**Pitcher,** Water, Shadow Design, Mauve, White Flowers, Signed, 8 In. ................................ 100.00
**Planter,** Rose Design, Original Insert, Marked, 7 In. ............................................................. 80.00
**Plate,** Beige, Green Poppies, Scalloped, 8 In. ....................................................................... 35.00
**Plate,** Bird, Hand-Painted Pheasants, Open Handled, 7 In. ................................................ 65.00
**Plate,** Chop, Carnation On Green Ground, Green Mark, 11 In.Diam. ................................. 55.00
**Plate,** Daffodils, 6 1/2 In. .......................................................................................................... 20.00
**Plate,** Dessert, Floral Design, Set Of Seven, 6 1/2 In. ........................................................... 40.00
**Plate,** Different Floral Designs, 6 1/2 In., Set Of 7 .................................................................. 40.00
**Plate,** Gold Scalloped Edge, Purple Violets, 7 In., Set Of 7 ................................................. 75.00
**Plate,** Hand-Painted Roses, Blue Mark, 8 In.Diam. ............................................................... 32.00
**Plate,** Orchids, Gold Trim, White Ground, Blue Mark, 9 1/4 In. ........................................... 45.00
**Plate,** Pansies On Green Ground, 8 1/2 In. ............................................................................ 15.00
**Plate,** Peach Roses, White, Blue Mark, 11 In. ......................................................................... 36.50
**Plate,** Peonies, Pink Ground, Gold Border, 8 1/2 In. ............................................................. 40.00
**Plate,** Poppies, 3-Handled, 7 3/4 In. ....................................................................................... 25.00
**Plate,** Red & White Tulips, 6 In. ................................................................................................ 17.50

| | |
|---|---:|
| **Plate,** Rose Design, 6 In. | 10.00 |
| **Plate,** Roses, 8 1/2 In. | 20.00 |
| **Plate,** Satin Finish Border, Gold, 9 In., Set Of 6 | 105.00 |
| **Plate,** Tulips, Gold Edge, Green, 8 In. | 30.00 |
| **Plate,** Violets, Gold, Hand-Painted, 6 1/2 In. | 10.00 |
| **Plate,** White & Yellow Flower, Blue Mark, 6 1/2 In. | 14.00 |
| **Plate,** White Flowers, Green, 6 1/4 In. | 10.00 |
| **Plate,** White, Gold, Flowers, 11 In. | 65.00 |
| **Plate,** Yellow Roses, Green & Peach Ground, 8 1/4 In. | 28.00 |
| **Plate,** Yellow Roses, Signed, 8 In. | 22.00 |
| **Plate,** 3-Handled, Cream Flowers, Green Mark, 8 In. | 32.00 |
| **Ramekin,** Pink Roses, Shadow Roses Outside | 27.00 |
| **Ramekin,** Underplate, Ivory Glaze, Set Of 4 | 40.00 |
| **Relish,** Pinecones, Open Handled, 4 X 5 In. | 15.00 |
| **Rose Bowl,** Blown-Out Handles, Scalloped, Green Luster, Marked | 49.00 |
| **Rose Bowl,** Frog Top, Marked Wreath | 50.00 |
| **Salt & Pepper,** Rose Design | 40.00 |
| **Salt,** Handled, Pink Rose, Gold Trim, 2 3/4 X 1 3/4 In., Set Of 6 | 50.00 |
| **Server,** Cheese & Cracker, Brown To Gold Earth Tones | 80.00 |
| **Spooner,** Flat, Flowers | 45.00 |
| **Sugar & Creamer,** Blue, Butterflies, Gray Ground, Gold Handled | 32.00 |
| **Sugar & Creamer,** Covered, Optic Melon Ribbed | 35.00 |
| **Sugar & Creamer,** Flowers, Shaded Green Ground | 50.00 |
| **Sugar & Creamer,** Luster, Black Design | 48.00 |
| **Sugar & Creamer,** Magnolias, Gold Trim, White & Green | 35.00 |
| **Sugar & Creamer,** Orange Nasturtiums, Peach Ground | 20.00 |
| **Sugar & Creamer,** Pansies, Black Mark | 40.00 |
| **Sugar & Creamer,** Peach Ground, Orange, Pink Nasturtiums | 50.00 |
| **Sugar & Creamer,** Peonies, Lavender Ground | 35.00 |
| **Sugar & Creamer,** White Flowers, Green, Covered | 25.00 |
| **Sugar & Creamer,** Yellow Roses | 50.00 |
| **Sugar Shaker,** Paneled Lavender, Forget-Me-Nots | 38.00 |
| **Sugar,** Covered, Band Of Roses, Gold Handle & Knob, Green, 3 In. | 10.00 |
| **Sugar,** Pink & Orange Floral, Covered | 15.00 |
| **Sugar,** Pink Roses, Gold Trim | 25.00 |
| **Sugar,** Roses, Pink, Marked, Covered | 18.00 |
| **Syrup,** Underplate, White Blossoms, Green Leaves, Blue Mark | 40.00 |
| **Tankard,** Gold, Daisies, Mums, Steeple Mark, 11 1/2 In. | 250.00 |
| **Tea & Toast Set,** Pink Roses On Brown & White Ground, Marked | 80.00 |
| **Tea Set,** Azalea Design, 4 Piece | 145.00 |
| **Teapot,** Figural, Lady | 65.00 |
| **Teapot,** Sugar & Creamer, Cream Pearlized Ground, Black Trim | 125.00 |
| **Teapot,** Tan, White, Gray, Black Trim, Deco Design | 60.00 |
| **Toothpick,** Floral, Trihandled | 52.00 |
| **Tray & Cup,** Snack, Parrot Design | 50.00 |
| **Tray,** Beige Gold Ground, White, Yellow Roses, Handles, 15 In. | 70.00 |
| **Tray,** Bread, Bellflowers, Open Handled, 14 In. | 38.00 |
| **Tray,** Celery, 3 Scallop Shape, Green Mark, 12 1/2 X 5 1/2 In. | 60.00 |
| **Tray,** Dresser, Gold & White Flowers | 75.00 |
| **Tray,** Open Handled, Pink Roses, Blue Mark, 6 1/4 X 7 1/2 In. | 17.00 |
| **Tray,** Pin, Flowers, Marked, 5 In.Diam. | 24.00 |
| **Tray,** Pin, White Flower On Gray Ground | 15.00 |
| **Tray,** Relish, Cotton Plant, Pierced Handles, Blue Mark | 35.00 |
| **Tray,** Serving, Blue Grapes, White Leaves | 65.00 |
| **Tray,** Tidbit, Tiered, Lily-Of-The-Valley Design, Gold Trim | 110.00 |
| **Vase,** Castle Scene, Green, 4 1/2 In. | 47.50 |
| **Vase,** Cupid & 3 Ladies, Beehive Mark, Double Handled, 4 1/2 In. | 50.00 |
| **Vase,** Flowers, Cream Ground, 2-Handled, Green Mark, 5 1/4 In. | 38.00 |
| **Vase,** Nightwatch Scene, Double Handled, Green Mark, 5 In. | 295.00 |
| **Vase,** Orange Poppies, 10 1/4 In. | 89.00 |
| **Vase,** Portrait, Indian Chief, Pistol Handles, 5 1/4 In. | 85.00 |
| **Vase,** Purple Iris Design, 4 1/2 In. | 45.00 |
| **Vase,** Violets, 5 1/4 In. | 55.00 |
| **Vase,** 2-Handled, Wide Top, Narrow Base, Green Ground, 6 1/4 In. | 62.00 |

**RS POLAND, Bowl,** Chinese Pheasants, 4 In. .................................................. 295.00
   **Bowl,** Shell Shape, Flowers, Signed, 9 1/2 In.Diam. ................................ 225.00
   **Hair Receiver,** Flowers ................................................................................ 105.00
   **Jar,** Covered, Leaves, Acorns, Cream Ground, Red Mark, 4 X 3 3/4 In. ........... 75.00
   **Vase,** Gold Link Handles, Flowers Form Trees, Red Mark, 9 In. ................ 125.00
   **Vase,** Scenic, 2 Swans In White, 7 3/4 In. .............................................. 225.00
   **Vase,** Yellow Rose, Gold Trim, Cobalt Blue Band, Red Mark, 7 1/8 In. ....... 125.00
   **Vase,** Yellow Roses, 4 1/2 In. ................................................................... 125.00

*RS Prussia porcelain was made at the factory of Reinhold Schlegelmilch after 1869 in Tillowitz, Germany. It was sold decorated or undecorated.*

**RS PRUSSIA, Basket,** Hanging, 6 Medallions, Red Mark ...................................... 200.00
   **Berry Bowl,** Footed, Underplate, Drain, Flowers, Red Mark ...................... 120.00
   **Berry Set,** Carnation, Red Mark ................................................................ 560.00
   **Berry Set,** Dogwood Pattern, Red Mark, 7 Piece ..................................... 525.00
   **Berry Set,** Green With White Flowers, Red Mark, 5 Piece ......................... 325.00
   **Berry Set,** Lilies, Blossoms, Gold Trim, Red Mark, 6 Piece ....................... 285.00
   **Berry Set,** Medallion Mold, 4 Sauces, Poppies & Daisies, Red Mark ......... 385.00
   **Berry Set,** Pink Roses, Master Bowl, 4 Sauces, 10 1/2 In. ........................ 245.00
   **Berry Set,** Roses & Shadow Flowers, Rose Center, Red Mark, 7 Piece ...... 375.00
   **Berry Set,** Starfish Design, 6 Desserts, Red Mark, 9 1/4 In.Diam. ............ 300.00
   **Biscuit Jar,** Pink Roses, Cream Ground, Red Mark ................................... 145.00
   **Bowl-In-Bowl,** Blown-Out Flowers, 10 1/2 In. ......................................... 450.00
   **Bowl-In-Bowl,** Fruit Design, Gold Tones, Pleated Mold ............................ 355.00
   **Bowl,** Apple Blossoms, Leaves, Ruffled, Red Mark, 10 In.Diam. ............... 130.00
   **Bowl,** Berry, Scalloped Gold Edge, White Roses, 5 In. ............................... 20.00
   **Bowl,** Blown Fan, Berry & Iris Rim, Red Star, 10 1/2 In. ........................... 275.00
   **Bowl,** Blown-Out Flower Edge, Roses, 10 In.Diam. .................................... 80.00
   **Bowl,** Blown-Out Flowers, Gold Handles, Red Mark, 10 X 3 1/2 In. .......... 175.00
   **Bowl,** Blown-Out Flowers, Yellow To Orange Roses, Red Mark, 11 In. ....... 185.00
   **Bowl,** Blown-Out Flowers, 10 1/4 X 3 In. ................................................ 185.00
   **Bowl,** Blown-Out Iris, Pink & Yellow Roses, 8 1/2 In. .............................. 100.00
   **Bowl,** Blown-Out Panels, 8 Panels, Red Mark, 10 1/2 In. ......................... 125.00
   **Bowl,** Blown-Out Poppies, Red Mark, 11 In. ............................................ 175.00
   **Bowl,** Blue & Gold Scalloped, Pink Roses, White Daisies, 10 In. ............... 360.00
   **Bowl,** Blue & Pink, Florals, Shaded Blue Edge, 8 1/2 In. .......................... 120.00
   **Bowl,** Blue Flowers, Red Crown Mark, 10 1/2 In. ..................................... 240.00
   **Bowl,** Blue With Flowers, 3 Feet, Round, 6 In. .......................................... 75.00
   **Bowl,** Brown To Bone, Brown Iris, Red Mark, 6 1/2 In. ............................. 40.00
   **Bowl,** Carnations, Matte Finish, 10 X 2 1/2 In. ....................................... 125.00
   **Bowl,** Castle Scene, Pastel Colors, 10 1/2 In.Diam. .................................. 495.00
   **Bowl,** Colored Roses On Yellow Ground, Red Mark, 11 In.Diam. ............... 185.00
   **Bowl,** Fall Season, Red Mark, 12 In.Diam. ............................................. 1650.00
   **Bowl,** Farm, Icicle Scene, Red Mark ..................................................... 1100.00
   **Bowl,** Floral Center, Gold Scalloped Edge, Green, 10 In.Diam. ................... 60.00
   **Bowl,** Floral Design, Scalloped, Red Mark, 11 In. .................................... 150.00
   **Bowl,** Floral, Blown Irises, 10 1/4 In. ..................................................... 195.00
   **Bowl,** Floral, Blue, Pink, Gold, Red Mark, 10 1/2 In. ............................... 177.00
   **Bowl,** Floral, Iridescent Edges, Scalloped, Red Mark, 11 In. .................... 125.00
   **Bowl,** Floral, Reflected In Water, Icicles, Pearlized, 5 1/2 In. .................... 45.00
   **Bowl,** Floral, White, Iridescent, Scalloped Edges, Red Mark, 11 In. ........... 150.00
   **Bowl,** Flowers, Puffed Rim, 10 1/2 In.Diam. ........................................... 175.00
   **Bowl,** Flowers, Red Mark, 10 In. ............................................................ 225.00
   **Bowl,** Fluted, Blown-Out Sides, Green & Red Mark, 10 1/2 In. ................. 195.00
   **Bowl,** Fluted, White Roses, Holly Berries, Red Mark, 10 3/4 In. ................ 220.00
   **Bowl,** Footed, Hand-Painted Roses, Gold Trim, Red Mark, 8 In. ............... 150.00
   **Bowl,** Footed, Red Roses Inside & Out, Red Mark, 8 1/2 In.Diam. ............ 110.00
   **Bowl,** Footed, Roses, Eggshell Ground, Red Mark, 7 1/2 In.Diam. ............ 145.00
   **Bowl,** Footed, Swan, Red Mark, 7 In.Diam. ............................................ 145.00
   **Bowl,** Four Seasons, Medallions, Floral Center, Red Mark, 11 In. ............ 2250.00

**Bowl,** Fruit Design, Luster, Scalloped, Red Mark, 11 In. .................................. 185.00
**Bowl,** Fruit, Blown-Out Grape Pods, 10 1/2 In. .................................. 185.00
**Bowl,** Fruit, Blown-Out Petaled Flowers, Red & Gold, 11 In.Diam. .................. 135.00
**Bowl,** Gold Edge, Green Ground, Raised Flowers, 10 1/2 In. .................. 150.00
**Bowl,** Gold Scalloped Edge, Roses, Red Mark, 10 1/2 In. .................. 150.00
**Bowl,** Green & White, Pink Roses, Footed, Red Mark, 6 1/2 In. .................. 65.00
**Bowl,** Green, Pink, & White Flowers, 11 In. .................. 225.00
**Bowl,** Green, White Flowers, Marked Red, 10 In. .................. 165.00
**Bowl,** Green, White Lily, Scalloped, Red Mark, 11 In. .................. 215.00
**Bowl,** Handled, Lotus On Water, Gold Garlands, Red Mark, 13 In. .................. 95.00
**Bowl,** Hanging Basket, Red Mark, 10 In.Diam. .................. 195.00
**Bowl,** Ice Cream, 6 Dessert Plates, Green Satin, Red Mark, 8 Piece .................. 650.00
**Bowl,** Icicle Mold, Snowbird, 15 In.Diam. ..................*Illus* 6400.00
**Bowl,** Jeweled Border, 10 1/2 In. .................. 225.00
**Bowl,** Jeweled Border, 2 Turkeys, Pine Trees, Red Mark, 10 3/4 In. .................. 850.00
**Bowl,** Lady With Dog, Red Mark, 10 In.Diam. .................. 275.00
**Bowl,** Lilies Floating In Water, Rose Panels, Red Mark, 10 3/4 In. .................. 200.00
**Bowl,** Madame LeBrun, Self-Portrait, 5 Panels, Gold, 10 In. .................. 950.00
**Bowl,** Mallard Duck In Forest, Icicle Mold, 5 1/2 In. .................. 125.00
**Bowl,** Melon Eaters, Green Tones, Red Mark, 10 1/2 In.Diam. .................. 1600.00
**Bowl,** Mill Scene, Gold Trim, Red Mark, 10 1/2 In.Diam. .................. 450.00
**Bowl,** Open Handled, Lotus On Water, Garland, Red Mark, 13 In. .................. 87.50
**Bowl,** Open Handled, Pearlized, Gold Trim, Fluted, Red Mark, 10 In. .................. 159.00
**Bowl,** Openwork Edge, Raised Iris On Rim, 2 3/4 X 10 In.Diam. .................. 165.00
**Bowl,** Orange, 8 Blown-Out Pockets, Green, Red Mark, 11 In.Diam. .................. 170.00
**Bowl,** Paneled, Flowers, Red Mark, 11 In. .................. 195.00
**Bowl,** Peace Bringing Plenty, Browns, Red Mark, 9 1/2 In.Diam. .................. 1200.00
**Bowl,** Pearlized Jeweled Rim, Cinder Marks, Red Mark, 10 1/2 In. .................. 115.00
**Bowl,** Pedestal, Roses Inside & Out, Red Mark, 5 X 10 1/4 In.Diam. .................. 95.00
**Bowl,** Pink & Yellow Bow, Roses, Gold Trim, Red Mark, 10 In.Diam. .................. 160.00
**Bowl,** Pink Roses & Snowball Center, Gold & Floral Rim, 11 In. .................. 125.00
**Bowl,** Pink, White, Apple Blossoms, Green Leaves, Gold, 10 In. .................. 130.00
**Bowl,** Poppies & Daisies Reflecting In Water, Red Mark, 11 In. .................. 185.00
**Bowl,** Portrait Of Lady, Blown-Out Center, 10 1/2 In. .................. 125.00
**Bowl,** Purple Violets, Green Leaves, Gold Trim, Signed, 9 1/2 In. .................. 85.00
**Bowl,** Queen Louise, Red Mark, 10 1/2 In.Diam. .................. 750.00
**Bowl,** Red & Pink Roses, Blue, Red Mark, 3 X 10 1/2 In.Diam. .................. 155.00
**Bowl,** Red Flowers, 10 1/4 In. .................. 190.00
**Bowl,** Red Leaf Border, Floral Center, Pink Shading, 10 1/2 In. .................. 88.00
**Bowl,** Rose Design, 9 1/2 In. .................. 38.00
**Bowl,** Roses In Center, 8 Dimpled Sides, Gold Trim, 10 3/4 In. .................. 250.00
**Bowl,** Roses On Raised Scroll Rim, Luster, Red Mark, 10 1/2 In. .................. 105.00
**Bowl,** Roses With Gold, Red Mark, 10 1/2 In.Diam. .................. 250.00
**Bowl,** Salmon, Pink & Yellow Roses, Red Mark, 8 In. .................. 150.00
**Bowl,** Satin White, Soft Green, Purple On Edge, Poppies, 11 In. .................. 110.00
**Bowl,** Scalloped Rim, White & Green Ground, Red Star, 10 1/2 In. .................. 145.00
**Bowl,** Scalloped, Embossed, Gold Trim, Red Mark, 11 In.Diam. .................. 185.00
**Bowl,** Scalloped, Gold Rim, 8 Side Scoops, Red Mark, 10 1/4 In. .................. 150.00
**Bowl,** Schooner Ship Scene, Tan, Yellow, & Brown, Signed, 9 1/2 In. .................. 600.00
**Bowl,** Shadow Flowers, Scrolled Rim, Pink, Red Mark, 8 1/2 In. .................. 100.00
**Bowl,** Shell Shape, Scalloped, Gold Accents, Red Mark, 10 In. .................. 200.00
**Bowl,** Snowbird, Icicle Mold, Red Mark .................. 990.00
**Bowl,** Spring Season, Iris, Red Mark, 9 1/4 In.Diam. .................. 995.00
**Bowl,** Sugar, Pink Roses, Green Ground, Red Mark .................. 60.00
**Bowl,** Summer Season, Red Mark, 10 1/2 In. .................. 1500.00
**Bowl,** Swan Pattern, Icicle Mold, 10 In.Diam. .................. 1000.00
**Bowl,** Swans, Pine Trees, 11 In. .................. 225.00
**Bowl,** Swirl Rim, Gold Trim, Wicker Basket Center, Red Mark, 11 In. .................. 185.00
**Bowl,** Violets, 11 In. .................. 185.00
**Bowl,** White Ground, Roses, Floral Border, 11 In. .................. 150.00
**Bowl,** White Roses, Scalloped Gold Trim Edge, 10 In. .................. 325.00
**Bowl,** Winter Season, Lebrun Medallion, Red Mark, 10 1/2 In. .................. 1550.00
**Bowl,** 3 Legs, 3 Shades Of Gold Rimmed Flowers, Red Mark, 7 In. .................. 165.00

RS Prussia, from left to right, Chocolate Pot, Icicle Mold;
Bowl, Icicle Mold, Snowbird

RS Prussia, Cake Plate, Gazelles, Red Mark

| | |
|---|---|
| **Bowl,** 3-Footed, Snowbird, Icicle Mold, Red Mark | 1190.00 |
| **Bowl,** 8 Dimpled Sides, Gilded Stars, Gold Trim, Marked, 10 3/4 In. | 260.00 |
| **Bowl,** 8 Wide & 8 Narrow Panels, Blossoms, Red Mark, 10 1/2 In. | 125.00 |
| **Bowl,** 12 Pointed, Pink Roses, Blown-Out Lilies, Ring Mark, 11 In. | 125.00 |
| **Box,** Dresser, Floral, Gold, Satin Finish, 5 1/4 X 2 1/2 In. | 110.00 |
| **Box,** Powder, Roses, Blue Ground, Red Mark, 5 In.Diam. | 75.00 |
| **Box,** Stud, Collar Shape, Gold & White, Green Mark | 28.00 |
| **Cake Plate,** Floral Design, Blue & Cream Ground, Red Mark, 11 In. | 185.00 |
| **Cake Plate,** Fruit Design, 11 In. | 240.00 |
| **Cake Plate,** Gazelles, Red Mark | *Illus* 3150.00 |
| **Cake Plate,** Handled, Pink Roses, Green Leaves, Red Mark, 11 In. | 175.00 |
| **Cake Plate,** Leaves & Berries Border, Floral Design, White Glaze | 100.00 |
| **Cake Plate,** Open Handled, Pink Roses, Red Mark, 11 In. | 175.00 |
| **Cake Plate,** Open Handled, Red Mark, 12 In.Diam. | 175.00 |
| **Cake Plate,** Pink Roses, Open Handled, 11 In. | 140.00 |
| **Cake Plate,** Puffed Out Molded Green Leaves, 11 1/2 In.Diam. | 115.00 |
| **Cake Plate,** 6 Jewels, Pink Rose Center, Red Mark, 10 1/2 In.Diam. | 190.00 |
| **Cake Set,** Rose Clusters, Molded Flowers On Rim, 7 Piece | 300.00 |
| **Celery,** Blown-Out Flowers, Raised Gold Flowers, Red Mark, 9 In. | 185.00 |
| **Celery,** Canterbury Bells, Satin Finish | 95.00 |
| **Celery,** Icicle, Swan | 300.00 |
| **Celery,** Pink & White Poppies, 12 1/4 X 6 1/8 In. | 50.00 |
| **Celery,** Satin Finish, Canterbury Bells | 95.00 |
| **Celery,** Shaded White & Pink Poppies, 12 1/4 X 6 1/8 In. | 60.00 |
| **Celery,** Shadow Flowers, Beaded Medallions, Red Mark, 12 1/4 In. | 125.00 |
| **Celery,** White Florals, Signed | 75.00 |
| **Celery,** White Lily | 100.00 |
| **Chocolate Pot,** Blown-Out Shoulder, Pink & Gold Flowers, Red Mark | 395.00 |
| **Chocolate Pot,** Calla Lilies, Raised Leaf Under Spout, Red Mark | 265.00 |
| **Chocolate Pot,** Cottage | 1300.00 |
| **Chocolate Pot,** Courting Scene | 425.00 |
| **Chocolate Pot,** Covered, Satinized, 6 Cups & Saucers, Red Mark | 950.00 |
| **Chocolate Pot,** Fall Season | 1150.00 |
| **Chocolate Pot,** Floral Sprays, Iridescent Petal Feet, Red Mark | 359.00 |
| **Chocolate Pot,** Gold Outlined Lily Of The Valley, Green & White | 85.00 |
| **Chocolate Pot,** Gold Scrolled, Blown-Out Top, Leaf Feet, Red Mark | 385.00 |
| **Chocolate Pot,** Icicle Mold | *Illus* 275.00 |

Chocolate Pot, Iridescent Petal Feet, Handled, Red Mark, 10 In. ......................... 359.00
Chocolate Pot, Lady With Fan, Red Mark ..................................................................... 395.00
Chocolate Pot, Lilies, 6 Cups & Saucers ..................................................................... 575.00
Chocolate Pot, Magnolias & Ferns, Steeple Finial, 8 In. ........................................ 265.00
Chocolate Pot, Olive Brown Ground, Pink & Cream Roses, 10 In. ......................... 195.00
Chocolate Pot, Pedestal, Satin Finish, Red Mark ....................................................... 45.00
Chocolate Pot, Pink & Yellow Roses, Salloped Base, Red Mark ........................... 295.00
Chocolate Pot, Pink Roses, Green Leaves .................................................................. 275.00
Chocolate Pot, Red Star, Green Wreath ...................................................................... 200.00
Chocolate Pot, Rococo Cover, Flower Forms, Red Mark ......................................... 195.00
Chocolate Pot, Roses, Leaves, Olive Brown Ground, Red Mark, 10 In. ............... 195.00
Chocolate Pot, Roses, Pearlized Gold, Red Mark ..................................................... 300.00
Chocolate Pot, Roses, 9 In. ........................................................................................... 185.00
Chocolate Pot, Swan & Bluebird, Roses, Red Mark ................................................. 425.00
Chocolate Pot, Turkey, Icicle Mold, Red Mark ........................................................1675.00
Chocolate Pot, Yellow, Green & Lavender, Pink & Yellow Roses .......................... 195.00
Chocolate Pot, 2 Cups & Saucers, Demitasse, Pink Roses, Signed ...................... 350.00
Chocolate Pot, 4 Cups & Saucers, Beige Ground, Red Mark .................................. 565.00
Chocolate Set, Blown-Out Swirl Shape, White Flowers, Red Mark ....................... 400.00
Chocolate Set, Florals, Green, Pink Roses, Luster, Red Mark ................................ 465.00
Chocolate Set, Leaves Pattern, Red Mark .................................................................. 850.00
Chocolate Set, Pink Roses, 6 Cups & Saucers, Red Mark ...................................... 300.00
Chocolate Set, Roses & Pearlized, 5 Cups & Saucers, Signed ............................. 450.00
Chocolate Set, Scalloped Tops, Gold Trim, Luster Finish, Red Mark ................... 465.00
Chocolate Set, White Puffed & Swirled Pot, Gold Design, 4 Cups ........................ 325.00
Coffeepot, Carnations, White To Beige, 6 Cups ........................................................ 295.00
Coffeepot, Demitasse, Scalloped Base, Wild Roses, Red Mark ............................. 185.00
Compote, Basket Of Flowers Center, Red Mark, 4 1/2 X 9 1/2 In. ....................... 265.00
Compote, Christmas Roses, Holly Leaves, Red Mark, 4 X 5 In.Diam. ................. 210.00
Compote, Hanging Basket Of Flowers, Red Mark, 4 1/2 X 9 In.Diam. ................. 280.00
Cookie Jar, Roses, Marked ............................................................................................ 295.00
Cracker Jar, Blown-Out Carnations, Blue & Pink Flowers ........................................ 65.00
Cracker Jar, Curlicue Handles, Gold Beaded, Pearlized, Red Mark ..................... 350.00
Cracker Jar, Footed, Poppies & Dogwood, Red Mark ............................................. 225.00
Cracker Jar, Handled, Footed, Roses, Ivory & White, Red Mark ........................... 150.00
Cracker Jar, Hanging Basket With Roses, 2-Handled, Red Mark ........................... 295.00
Cracker Jar, Melon Boys, Red Mark .........................................................................2175.00
Cracker Jar, Pearlized Finish, Pink & White Flowers, 8 1/2 In. ............................. 295.00
Cracker Jar, Pink & Cream Rose, Green Ground, Red Mark ................................... 265.00
Cracker Jar, Pink Poppies, Green Ground, Red Mark, 7 1/4 In. ............................ 220.00
Cracker Jar, Red & White Roses, Red Mark ............................................................. 225.00
Cracker Jar, Roses, Purple Ground, Red Mark ......................................................... 255.00
Cracker Jar, Swans & Castle, Red Mark, 7 X 3 1/2 In.Diam. ................................. 650.00
Cracker Jar, Water Lilies ................................................................................................ 250.00
Cracker Jar, 4 Feet, Hand-Painted Roses, White Ground, 7 In. ............................ 295.00
Creamer, Blown Flowers Base & Rim, Pink Floral Design, 4 In. ............................. 87.00
Creamer, Bluebirds, Pedestaled, 6-Footed ................................................................ 200.00
Creamer, Brown Flowers, Pink Floral Design, 4 In. .................................................... 87.00
Creamer, Cottage Scene, Yellow, Orange, Brown, Red Mark .................................. 75.00
Creamer, Lebrun .............................................................................................................. 145.00
Creamer, Pedestal, Mill Scene ....................................................................................... 95.00
Creamer, Pink, Blown-Out Flowers ............................................................................... 75.00
Creamer, Ruffled Rim, Pearlized Green With Pink, Red Mark ................................. 48.00
Creamer, Scallop On Foot .............................................................................................. 40.00
Creamer, Underplate, Red Rose, Green, Signed, 4 3/4 X 6 In. ............................. 250.00
Creamer, White Carnations, Green, Red Mark ............................................................ 45.00
Cup & Saucer, Beaded Scalloped Rim, Roses, Red Mark, Demitasse ................... 75.00
Cup & Saucer, Chocolate, Cabbage Roses, Red Mark ............................................. 48.00
Cup & Saucer, Floral, Red Mark .................................................................................... 65.00
Cup & Saucer, Flowers, Red Mark, Demitasse ........................................................... 45.00
Cup & Saucer, Footed, Child's ..................................................................................... 125.00
Cup & Saucer, Footed, Lavender Clematis .................................................................. 30.00
Cup & Saucer, Green Luster, Dogwood Blossoms ..................................................... 25.00

Cup & Saucer, Pearlized, Pink & Blue Flowers, Red Mark, Set Of 6 ........................................ 280.00
Cup & Saucer, Pink & Blue Floral, Red Mark, Set Of 6 ................................................... 280.00
Cup & Saucer, Pink Roses, Gold Tracery, Demitasse ...................................................... 135.00
Cup & Saucer, Purple Violets, Red Mark, Demitasse ....................................................... 22.50
Cup & Saucer, Satinized Pedestal, Red Mark ............................................................. 55.00
Cup & Saucer, Satinized Portrait, Footed ................................................................ 95.00
Cup & Saucer, 4-Footed, Blown & Molded Florals, Red Mark ................................................ 82.00
Cup, Swans, Castle, Red Mark ........................................................................... 110.00
Demitasse Set, Pink Floral Design, 4 Cups & Saucers .................................................... 400.00
Dish, Candy, Dice Player, Red, Jewels, Footed, Marked .................................................. 675.00
Dish, Candy, Fox Hunter Design, Diamond Shaped, Blue Mark ............................................... 45.00
Dish, Candy, Winter Portrait, Footed, Red Mark, 6 In. ................................................. 635.00
Dish, Celery, Floral, Scalloped Edge, Red Mark .......................................................... 75.00
Dish, Celery, Pink Roses, Green & Blue Ground, 12 1/2 X 6 In. ......................................... 135.00
Dish, Cheese, Covered, Hand-Painted Flowers ........................................................... 250.00
Dish, Handled, Poppies, Roses, Gold Rim, Oval, 10 1/2 X 8 1/2 In. ..................................... 195.00
Dish, Open Handled, Roses, Scalloped Edge, Beige Ground, 9 1/2 In. ..................................... 65.00
Dish, Relish, Flowers, Gold Stamens, Handled, Red Mark, 12 In. ....................................... 105.00
Dish, Relish, Green, Gold Flowers, Swags, 8 X 3 1/2 In. ................................................ 68.50
Dish, Relish, Pink & Gold Flowers, Red Mark ........................................................... 115.00
Dish, Relish, Raised Flowers On Rim, Steeple Mark ....................................................... 50.00
Dish, Relish, Roses, Gold Trim, Blue Ground, 3 X 12 1/4 In. ........................................... 67.50
Dish, Relish, Roses, Red Mark, 8 In. .................................................................. 85.00
Dish, Roses & Daisies, Blown Out, Pierced Handle, 11 In. ............................................... 75.00
Dish, Serving, Flowers, Beaded Medallions, Red Mark, 13 X 8 In. ...................................... 250.00
Dish, White Roses, Pink, Satinized, Footed, 6 1/2 In. .................................................. 85.00
Ewer, Allover Flowers & Gold Design, Green, Red Mark, 9 In. ............................................ 40.00
Fernery, Footed, Blown Base, Gold Rim, Red Mark, 9 In.Diam. ........................................... 595.00
Fernery, Green Maple Leaves, Shell Feet, 8 1/2 In. ..................................................... 95.00
Fernery, Lily Of The Valley, Gold, Shell Feet, 4 1/4 In. .............................................. 225.00
Fernery, Shell Feet, Maple Leaves, Flared, Red Mark, 4 1/2 X 8 In. ................................... 155.00
Fernery, 4-Footed, Red & White Roses, Gold Trim, Red Mark, 8 In. ..................................... 265.00
Hair Receiver, Cobalt With Gold, Red Mark .............................................................. 35.20
Hair Receiver, Flowers, Red Mark ....................................................................... 70.00
Hair Receiver, Gold Trim, Octagon, Red Mark ............................................................ 80.00
Hair Receiver, Pink & Yellow Roses, Pompoms, Red Mark .................................................. 70.00
Hair Receiver, Pink Roses, Red Mark .................................................................... 62.00
Hair Receiver, Scalloped Base, Extending Petals, Red Mark .............................................. 95.00
Hair Receiver, Tan, Bouquet Of Flowers On Lid, Red Mark ................................................ 95.00
Hair Receiver, 4-Footed, Green & White Design, 2 1/4 X 5 In. ........................................... 75.00
Hair Receiver, 6-Sided, Pink Roses .................................................................... 115.00
Hatpin Holder, Attached Box With Lid .................................................................. 225.00
Hatpin Holder, Deep Pink Poppies, Green Leaves, 3 1/4 In. .............................................. 75.00
Hatpin Holder, Floral, Attached Dish, Red Mark ........................................................ 195.00
Hatpin Holder, Hanging Basket ......................................................................... 195.00
Hatpin Holder, Pink Flowers, Flared Base, Red Mark ..................................................... 75.00
Hatpin Holder, Pink Roses, Reflected In Water, Red Mark ............................................... 140.00
Hatpin Holder, Roses On Shaded Green, 4 Scallop Base, Red Mark ........................................ 135.00
Hatpin Holder, Sheepherder Scene, Red Mark ............................................................ 325.00
Hatpin Holder, The Hanging Basket ..................................................................... 185.00
Holder, String, Signed, Blue Mark ..................................................................... 125.00
Jar, Jam, Underplate, Flowers, Green & White Ground, Red Mark ........................................ 160.00
Jar, Powder, Covered, Teal Blue Trim, Pink Flowers .................................................... 119.00
Mug, Red & Yellow Shading, Blown Out Florals, Red Mark ................................................ 145.00
Mug, Shaving, Floral .................................................................................. 135.00
Mug, Shaving, Icicle Mold, Rose & Pansies, Red Mark ................................................... 165.00
Mug, Shaving, Multicolored Poppies, Blue Shading, Footed, Marked ...................................... 135.00
Mustache Cup & Saucer, Calla Lily ..................................................................... 195.00
Mustache Cup, 3 Feet, Snow Blossoms, Scalloped & Lustered .............................................. 95.00
Mustard Pot, Ladle, Melon Blossom Shape, Pink, Gold Edging ............................................. 85.00
Mustard Pot, Roses, Satin Finish, Covered, Red Mark ................................................... 96.00
Mustard, Green Swirl .................................................................................. 35.00
Mustard, Lily Pad ..................................................................................... 55.00

**Mustard,** Pond Lilies, Green Ground, Footed, Red Mark ............................................. 75.00
**Mustard,** Roses, Red Mark ............................................................................................ 47.50
**Nut Dish,** Swallows, Triangular ..................................................................................... 85.00
**Nut Set,** Master & 6 Individual Bowls, Red Mark ...................................................... 450.00
**Nut Set,** Yellow Roses, Satin, 5 Piece ......................................................................... 355.00
**Pitcher,** Cider, 3 Swans, Tree, & Lake, 6-Sided, Pearlized, 6 1/2 In. ...................... 220.00
**Pitcher,** Lemonade, Blue, Pink Roses, Leaf Handle, Blown-Out Edge ..................... 150.00
**Pitcher,** Lemonade, Footed, Raised Gold Flower Stems, Red Mark ......................... 275.00
**Pitcher,** Orchids, Red Star, Green Wreath, 5 X 4 In.Diam. ......................................... 160.00
**Planter,** Footed, Poppies, Gold Fluted Edge, Red Mark, 9 In.Diam. .......................... 165.00
**Planter,** Lily Of The Valley, Shell Feet, Red Mark, 8 In. ............................................ 125.00
**Planter,** Poppies, Gold Fluted Edge, Red Mark, 9 In.Diam. ....................................... 195.00
**Planter,** Shell Feet, Lily Of The Valley, Red Mark, 4 X 8 In.Diam. ........................... 125.00
**Plate,** Autumn, Pink Design, Red Mark, 6 In. ............................................................. 495.00
**Plate,** Blossoms, Leaves On White, Handled, 10 In. .................................................. 95.00
**Plate,** Blown-Out Flower Center, Pink & Coral Poppies, 10 1/2 In. .......................... 160.00
**Plate,** Bread, Roses, Red Mark, 10 In. ......................................................................... 165.00
**Plate,** Cake, Embossed Rim, Flowers, Green Shading, Red Mark, 11 In. .................. 115.00
**Plate,** Cake, Floral, Blown Irises, Open Handled, 10 3/4 In. ...................................... 210.00
**Plate,** Cake, Floral, Pierced Handled, Scalloped, 11 In. ............................................. 65.00
**Plate,** Cake, Fruit Design, 11 In. .................................................................................. 240.00
**Plate,** Cake, Mill Scene, Open Handled, 10 In. ........................................................... 750.00
**Plate,** Cake, Old Man In The Mountain, Red Mark, 11 In.Diam. ................................ 395.00
**Plate,** Cake, Pink Flowers, Gold Trim, Red Mark, 11 In. ............................................ 200.00
**Plate,** Cake, Portrait, Dice Boys, Gold Trim, Red Mark ............................................. 950.00
**Plate,** Cake, Swan & Bluebird, Red Mark ................................................................... 295.00
**Plate,** Carnation, 8 In. ................................................................................................... 85.00
**Plate,** Cottage Scene, Red Mark, 8 1/2 In. .................................................................. 375.00
**Plate,** Dogwood, 8 In. ................................................................................................... 45.00
**Plate,** Drapery Embossing, Flowers, Red Mark, 10 5/8 In. ......................................... 165.00
**Plate,** Easter Lily, Double Open Handled .................................................................... 125.00
**Plate,** Embossed Ecru Starfish, Red Mark, 10 1/4 In. ................................................ 135.00
**Plate,** Fall Season, Red Mark ....................................................................... *Illus* 1500.00
**Plate,** Floral, Beading, Scalloped Edge, Open Handled, 10 In. ................................... 125.00
**Plate,** Floral, Pink & White, Red Star, Green Wreath ................................................. 75.00
**Plate,** Flossie, Sunflower, Gold Trim, Open Handled, 11 1/2 In. ................................ 350.00
**Plate,** Flowers, Scalloped, Red Mark, 7 3/4 In.Diam. .................................................. 75.00
**Plate,** Flowers, Turquoise, Yellow, & White, Red Mark, 7 1/2 In. ............................. 50.00
**Plate,** Fruit Design, Beaded Gold Rim, Red Mark, 7 1/2 In.Diam. ............................. 75.00
**Plate,** Gold & Tan Petal Scoops, Gold Trim, Red Mark, 7 7/8 In. .............................. 80.00
**Plate,** Handled, Scalloped, 8 Panels, Raspberries, 11 1/2 In. ..................................... 335.00
**Plate,** Hanging Basket, 8 In. ........................................................................................ 185.00
**Plate,** Lilacs, Greens, Golds, 6 Fluted Panels, 6 1/2 In. ............................................. 150.00
**Plate,** Lion, Red Mark .................................................................................... *Illus* 2700.00
**Plate,** Mill Scene, Blown-Out Iris, Pink, Red Mark, 9 1/2 In. .................................... 650.00
**Plate,** Old Man In Mountain, Blue & Yellow, Red Mark, 9 In. ................................... 375.00
**Plate,** Old Mill, Blown-Out Border, Red Mark, 8 1/2 In. ............................................ 350.00
**Plate,** Open Handled, Blown-Out Flowers, Red Mark ................................................ 195.00
**Plate,** Open Handled, Gold Beaded Border, Red Mark, 11 1/4 In. ............................. 170.00
**Plate,** Ostrich, Red Mark ............................................................................... *Illus* 1850.00
**Plate,** Peacock, Chicks, Swallows, Orange, 7 1/2 In. ................................................. 725.00
**Plate,** Pheasant In Forest, Open Handled, Red Mark, 10 1/4 In. ................................ 95.00
**Plate,** Portrait, Autumn, Red Mark, 11 In.Diam. ......................................................... 450.00
**Plate,** Portrait, Scenic, Flowers, Red Mark, 8 1/2 In. .................................................. 95.00
**Plate,** Purple Iridescent Border, Roses, Red Mark, 8 1/2 In.Diam. ............................ 110.00
**Plate,** Queen Louise & King, Medallions Around Rim, Red Mark .............................. 275.00
**Plate,** Raised Petal Forms, White Flowers, Red Mark, 8 1/2 In. ................................ 100.00
**Plate,** Rose, Purple Iridescent Border, 8 1/2 In, ......................................................... 125.00
**Plate,** Roses , Gold Edge, Red Mark, 6 1/2 In. ............................................................ 250.00
**Plate,** Roses, Green, Gold, Open Handle, 12 1/2 In. .................................................... 55.00
**Plate,** Roses, Purple Iridescent Border, 8 1/2 In. ....................................................... 125.00
**Plate,** Satinized Dogwood Blossoms, 7 1/2 In. ........................................................... 65.00
**Plate,** Satinized Floral, Puffed Irises, Open Handled, 10 In. ...................................... 210.00

RS Prussia, Plate, Fall Season, Red Mark

RS Prussia, Plate, Lion, Red Mark

RS Prussia, Plate, Ostrich, Red Mark

| | |
|---|---|
| **Plate,** Scalloped, Roses, Pearlized, 7 3/4 In. | 65.00 |
| **Plate,** Scenic, Masted Schooner, Signed, Red Mark, 6 In. | 225.00 |
| **Plate,** Spring, Iris Mold, Red Mark, 7 1/2 In. | 675.00 |
| **Plate,** Stag, Satin, Red Mark, 9 1/2 In. | 925.00 |
| **Plate,** Swan Design, Satin Finish, Handled, 9 1/2 In. | 150.00 |
| **Plate,** Swan Scenic, Satin, Pearlized, Blown-Out Berries, 8 1/2 In. | 200.00 |
| **Plate,** Tumbling Rose, Gold, Open Handled, 10 1/2 In. | 150.00 |
| **Plate,** Turkey, Icicle Mold, Wheelock Mark, 8 1/2 In. | 395.00 |
| **Plate,** Turkey, Red Mark, 8 In. | 350.00 |
| **Plate,** Turkeys, Icicle Mold, Red Mark, 11 In.Diam. | 950.00 |
| **Plate,** White Satin, Pink & White Roses, Gold Center, 8 In. | 155.00 |
| **Plate,** 5 Portrait Medallions, Cobalt Blue & Gold, 6 In.Diam. | 350.00 |
| **Relish,** Green, Gold Flowers, Swags, 8 X 3 1/2 In. | 68.50 |
| **Relish,** Pink & White Poppies, Lilies On Rim, Open Handled, 13 In. | 100.00 |
| **Shaving Mug,** Flowers On Light Blue Ground, Red Mark | 65.00 |
| **Shaving Mug,** Poppy Form, Oval Mirror Inset, C.1900, 4 In. | 375.00 |
| **Shaving Mug,** Puffed-Out Base, Multicolored Poppies, Red Mark | 115.00 |
| **Shaving Mug,** Swan & Pine Trees, Red Mark | 165.00 |
| **Sugar & Creamer,** Allover Floral, Large | 145.00 |
| **Sugar & Creamer,** Ball Shape, Upturned Feet, Castle, Red Mark | 850.00 |
| **Sugar & Creamer,** Bluebirds Flying, Pedestaled, Red Mark | 250.00 |
| **Sugar & Creamer,** Boy Courting Girl | 450.00 |
| **Sugar & Creamer,** Castle Scene, Green, Covered | 400.00 |
| **Sugar & Creamer,** Christmas Reef Pattern, Roses, Red Mark | 195.00 |
| **Sugar & Creamer,** Cottage & Castle Scene, Red Mark | 250.00 |
| **Sugar & Creamer,** Covered, Luster Pearl Ground, Roses | 235.00 |
| **Sugar & Creamer,** Covered, Old Man In Mountain, Red Mark | 350.00 |

**Sugar & Creamer,** Covered, Pink Roses, Green Ground, Red Mark ........................................... 165.00
**Sugar & Creamer,** Dogwood Design, Red Mark ................................................................. 150.00
**Sugar & Creamer,** Footed, Green Holly, White Ground, Red Mark ................................... 195.00
**Sugar & Creamer,** Footed, Holly On White Ground, Red Mark ......................................... 195.00
**Sugar & Creamer,** Footed, Rose Pattern, 14K Gold Trim ................................................. 175.00
**Sugar & Creamer,** Laurel Leaf ....................................................................................... 80.00
**Sugar & Creamer,** Lavender & Green, Red & Green Mark, 4 3/4 In. ................................ 145.00
**Sugar & Creamer,** Lilies Of The Valley, White Ground, Marked ....................................... 295.00
**Sugar & Creamer,** Melon Boy, Red Mark ......................................................................... 325.00
**Sugar & Creamer,** Off-White, Pink Rosebuds, Red Mark ................................................. 140.00
**Sugar & Creamer,** Pearl Ground, Pink Roses & Gold Trim .............................................. 250.00
**Sugar & Creamer,** Pedestal, Cupid Scenes, Gold Trim, Signed ....................................... 550.00
**Sugar & Creamer,** Pedestal, Flowers & Leaves, Signed .................................................. 165.00
**Sugar & Creamer,** Pheasant, Pedestal, Red Mark .......................................................... 875.00
**Sugar & Creamer,** Pink Flowers, Covered, Red Mark ...................................................... 190.00
**Sugar & Creamer,** Pink Roses, Green & White Ground, Red Star .................................... 90.00
**Sugar & Creamer,** Pond Lilies, Feather Mold, Covered, Red Mark .................................. 300.00
**Sugar & Creamer,** Roses & Fruit .................................................................................... 50.00
**Sugar & Creamer,** Roses On Body & Pedestal ............................................................... 225.00
**Sugar & Creamer,** Satin Finish, Gold Rims, Red Mark .................................................... 145.00
**Sugar & Creamer,** Swan ................................................................................................ 450.00
**Sugar & Creamer,** 6 Panels Of Roses, Gold Edges, Red Mark ....................................... 200.00
**Sugar Shaker,** Flowers, Red Mark .................................................................................. 85.00
**Sugar,** Covered, Footed, Floral, Satin Finish .................................................................. 50.00
**Sugar,** Lid, Floral, Satin Finish, Footed Handled ........................................................... 50.00
**Sugar,** Melon Boy, Jeweled Cover, 2-Handled, Red Mark ............................................... 250.00
**Sugar,** Mill Scene, Pedestal ........................................................................................... 295.00
**Sugar,** Pink Rose, Covered, Marked ............................................................................... 100.00
**Sugar,** 2-Finger Handles, Square Base, Covered, Flowers ............................................. 175.00
**Syrup,** Scenic, Red Mark ............................................................................................... 145.00
**Syrup,** Underplate, Solid Gold Drapery & Dots, Jeweled, Red Mark ............................... 225.00
**Tankard,** Blown-Out Carnations, Satin, Red Mark, 13 In. ................................................ 850.00
**Tankard,** Fall Season, Poppy Mold ............................................................... *Illus* 5600.00
**Tankard,** Floral Design, Red Mark, 14 In. ...................................................................... 580.00
**Tankard,** Flowers, Bulbous To Tip Of Spout, Red Mark, 13 In. ...................................... 600.00
**Tankard,** Flowers, Red Mark, 10 1/2 In. ....................................................................... 250.00
**Tankard,** Jeweled, 9 In. ................................................................................................. 475.00
**Tankard,** Molded Flowers, Red Mark, 10 3/4 In. ............................................................. 490.00
**Tankard,** Roses, Olive Green Ground, Red Mark, 10 3/4 In. ........................................... 650.00
**Tankard,** Summer Season, Poppy Mold ........................................................ *Illus* 4650.00
**Tea Set,** Child's, 17 Piece ............................................................................................. 175.00
**Tea Set,** Pedestal, Lilacs, Pot, 6 1/4 In., 9 Piece ........................................................... 395.00
**Tea Set,** Purple Ground, Roses, Footed, Red Mark, Covered Sugar ............................... 390.00
**Tea Set,** White Orchid Design, Green Ground, Pearlized ................................................ 425.00
**Teapot,** Blown-Out Top & Handle, White Flowers, Marked ............................................. 185.00
**Teapot,** Leaf Handle, Gold Flowers, Melon Ribbed, Flower Finial .................................. 175.00

RS Prussia, from left to right, Tankard, Summer Season, Poppy Mold; Tankard, Fall Season, Poppy Mold

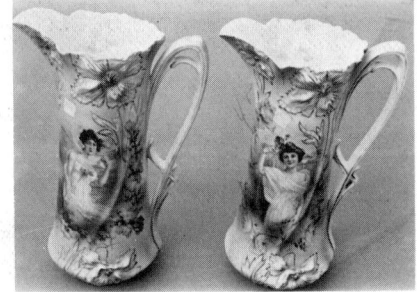

Teapot, Lilies, Red Mark ............................................................................................ 140.00
Teapot, Pedestal, Floral Design, Gold Trim, Red Mark, 5 3/4 In. ......................... 175.00
Teapot, Pink Roses, Melon-Ribbed Shape, Squatty, Luster Finish ......................... 125.00
Toothpick, Clown ...................................................................................................... 155.00
Toothpick, Handled, Basket Design, Red Mark ........................................................ 260.00
Toothpick, Handled, 6 Feet, Roses, Signed ............................................................. 75.00
Toothpick, Mill Scene, 3-Handled ............................................................................ 345.00
Toothpick, Pink Roses, Green Ground ...................................................................... 75.00
Toothpick, 3-Handled, Castle Scene ......................................................................... 285.00
Toothpick, 3-Handled, Flowers, Gold Trim, Red Mark ............................................. 100.00
Tray, Blown Irises, Floral, Open Handled, 13 X 6 1/2 In. ....................................... 110.00
Tray, Blown-Out Iris, Red Mark, 9 1/2 X 4 1/2 In. ................................................ 650.00
Tray, Bread, Blown-Out Handled, Blown-Out Iris ..................................................... 125.00
Tray, Bun, Pierced Ends, Baroque Design, Red Mark, 13 1/4 X 6 In. ................... 155.00
Tray, Bun, Pink Flowers, Green, Gray Shading, Red Mark ...................................... 95.00
Tray, Celery, Basket Of Roses, Red Mark ................................................................ 90.00
Tray, Celery, Branches & White Blossoms, Red Mark, 12 X 6 In. .......................... 100.00
Tray, Celery, Castle Scene, Handled, Red Mark ....................................................... 200.00
Tray, Cottage, 11 3/4 X 7 1/2 In. ........................................................................... 500.00
Tray, Dresser, Allover Roses, Blown-Out Iris, Red Mark ......................................... 150.00
Tray, Dresser, Pink Roses, Embossed Flowers, Green & Blue ................................ 75.00
Tray, Dresser, Portrait, Cherubs, Cream To Green, Steeple Mark .......................... 235.00
Tray, Dresser, Spring Season, Vertical Satin Mold, Red Mark ............................. 1650.00
Tray, Dresser, White Swans, Red Mark .................................................................... 325.00
Tray, Dresses, Cutout Handles, Poppies, Scalloped, Red Mark .............................. 185.00
Tray, Handled, Magnolias, Oval, Red Mark, 12 3/8 X 9 In. .................................... 125.00
Tray, Handled, Roses, Gold Trim, Red Mark, 9 1/2 In.Diam. .................................. 95.00
Tray, Lebrun Medallion, Red Mark, 14 In. ............................................................... 825.00
Tray, Molded Iris Corners, Green Ground, Red Mark, 11 1/4 X 7 In. ..................... 150.00
Tray, Pin, Basket Of Roses Center, Red Mark, 5 1/2 X 3 1/2 In. .......................... 30.00
Tray, Pink, Basket Of Roses, Red Mark, 5 1/2 X 3 1/2 In. ................................... 30.00
Tray, Pond Lilies, Signed, 12 1/2 X 5 3/4 In. ........................................................ 115.00
Tray, Relish, Carnation Mold ................................................................................... 115.00
Tray, Shaded Lavender, Yellow & White Flowers, 6 X 10 1/2 In. ........................... 70.00
Vase, Allover Roses, Satin Finish, Miniature .......................................................... 140.00
Vase, Bulbous, Hand-Painted Flowers, Yellow Ground, 4 In. .................................. 78.00
Vase, Bulbous, Roses On Green To Yellow Ground, 4 In. ....................................... 78.00
Vase, Church Steeple Scene, 4 In. ........................................................................... 90.00
Vase, Cottage Scene, Yellow & Green, Red Mark, 8 In. ......................................... 395.00
Vase, Cottage, Red Mark, Green, 9 In. .................................................................... 495.00
Vase, Dice Player Shape, 7 1/2 In. ......................................................................... 550.00
Vase, Double Handled, Portrait, Red Mark ............................................................ 1200.00
Vase, Flower Form Opening, Hand-Painted Roses, Red Mark, 8 In. ....................... 325.00
Vase, Golden Pheasant, Red Mark, 6 In. ................................................................. 375.00
Vase, Handled, Jeweled & Footed Base, Red Mark, 10 In. ..................................... 355.00
Vase, Handled, Melon Boys, Jeweled, Red Mark, 6 In. ......................................... 1100.00
Vase, Handled, Pedestal, Pheasant, Red Mark, 10 In. ............................................ 495.00
Vase, Melon Boy, Green Ground, 4 3/8 X 2 1/8 In.Diam. ....................................... 225.00
Vase, Melon Boys, Bulbous, 4 In. ............................................................................ 500.00
Vase, Melon Boys, Green Ground, 6 1/2 In. ............................................................ 495.00
Vase, Melon Boys, Jeweled, Red Mark, 13 1/2 In. ............................................... 2500.00
Vase, Melon Boys, Jeweled, 2-Handled, Red Mark, 6 In. ..................................... 1100.00
Vase, Melon Boys, Sister On Cover, 7 3/4 In. ......................................................... 695.00
Vase, Parrot, Handled, Red Mark, 6 In. ................................................................... 775.00
Vase, Portrait, Ball Shape, Spring Season, 6 1/2 In. ............................................. 800.00
Vase, Roses, Flower Form, Red Mark, 8 3/4 In. ...................................................... 325.00
Vase, Sheepherder, Red Mark, 9 In. ........................................................................ 495.00
Vase, Spring Season, Cobalt Blue, 9 In. ................................................................ 1150.00
Vase, White & Yellow Flowers, Yellow Ground, Red Mark, 6 In. ............................ 285.00
Vase, 4-Footed, Ring Handles, Swans, Castle, Red Mark, 6 1/4 In. ....................... 490.00

RS SUHL, Bowl, Portrait, Cobalt Blue & Gold, 2 1/2 X 1/ 1/2 In.Diam. ................. 1300.00
Plate, 8 Cavaliers, Green Mark, 7 1/2 In.Diam. ...................................................... 85.00

Tray, Pin, Nightwatch, Handled, Signed, 4 1/2 In.Diam. .................................................. 325.00
Vase, Handled, Blown-Out Top, Roses, 8 In. ................................................................. 195.00
Vase, Nightwatch Scene, 7 In. ...................................................................................... 350.00
Vase, Sheepherder With Man, 7 In. .............................................................................. 395.00

*R.S.Tillowitz porcelain factory was started at Tillowitz near Silesia in 1869 by Rheinhold Schlegelmilch. Table services and ornamental pieces were made.*

RS TILLOWITZ, Berry Bowl, White Flowers, Set Of 5 ................................................... 30.00
Bowl, Handled, Hand-Painted Flowers, Marked, 10 In.Diam. ....................................... 65.00
Bowl, Open Handled, Floral Clusters On Sides, Gold Trim, 10 In. .............................. 65.00
Butter Pat, Melon Eaters, Green, Brown Ground, EPOS Mark .................................... 45.00
Dish, Relish, Lily Of The Valley, 10 1/2 In.Diam. ........................................................ 32.00
Pitcher, Cider, White Flowers, Outlined In Black, Caramel ........................................ 125.00
Plate, Cake, Flower Design, 10 In. ................................................................................ 25.00
Plate, Snack, Cup, Parrot Design ................................................................................. 20.00
Tray, Pin, Flowers & Gold Trim, Oblong, 5 In. ............................................................ 24.00

*Rubena Verde is a Victorian glassware that was shaded from red to green. It was first made by Hobbs, Brockunier and Company of Wheeling, West Virginia, about 1890.*

RUBENA VERDE, Bowl, Hobnail, 4 1/2 In.Diam. ........................................................... 48.00
Bride's Basket, Hobnail, Opalescent ........................................................................... 385.00
Epergne, Center Trumpet & Bowl, Hanging Baskets, 22 In. ....................................... 325.00
Vase, Enamel Floral Design, Blue Bow, 10 1/2 In. ..................................................... 260.00
Vase, Opalescent Jack-In-The-Pulpit, Leaf Feet, 12 In. ............................................. 210.00
Vase, Pinched Sides, 10 1/4 In., Pair ........................................................................... 95.00
Vase, Ruffled Top, Threaded Body, 6 In. ..................................................................... 175.00
Vase, Stick, Applied Clear Rigaree, Cranberry, 10 In., Pair ...................................... 320.00
Vase, 3-Handled, Applied Gold Scroll & Flowers, 8 In. ............................................. 250.00

*Rubena is a glassware that shades from red to clear. It was first made by George Duncan and Sons of Pittsburgh, Pennsylvania, about 1885.*

RUBENA, see also Pressed Glass, Royal Ivy, Royal Oak
RUBENA, Bottle, Cologne, Red Running Into Clear Swirls, Original Stopper ............................ 40.00
Bottle, Perfume, Clear Cut Stopper, 6 In. .................................................................... 70.00
Bottle, Wine, Gold Medallions, Jewel Centers, Stopper, 11 1/2 In. .......................... 495.00
Bowl, Applied Feet, Ribbed, 9 In.Diam. ....................................................................... 85.00
Bowl, Honeycomb, 10 In.Diam. ..................................................................................... 135.00
Carafe, Swirled & Ribbed, Clear To Red At Top, 8 1/2 In. ......................................... 75.00
Celery, Reverse, Inverted Thumbprint, 6 In. ................................................................ 78.00
Cruet, Hobnail ................................................................................................................ 165.00
Cup, Punch ..................................................................................................................... 20.00
Dish, Jam, Ruffled, Silver Plated Holder, Petal Rigaree, 6 X 6 In. ........................... 95.00
Dish, Jam, Vaseline Applied Edge & Rigaree, Square, 5 1/2 In. ............................... 125.00
Jam, Swirl Pattern ......................................................................................................... 110.00
Jar, Jam, Swirl ............................................................................................................... 110.00
Pitcher, Applied Handle, Clear To Cranberry ............................................................. 175.00
Pitcher, Clear Handle, Overshot, 5 1/4 X 3 1/4 In.Diam. ........................................... 95.00
Pitcher, Melon Sectioned, Round Mouth, Clear Reeded Handle, 5 3/4 In. ............... 115.00
Pitcher, Overshot, Clear Applied Handle, 5 1/4 In. ................................................... 95.00
Pitcher, Overshot, Clear Applied Handle, 7 1/2 In. ................................................... 160.00
Pitcher, Overshot, Clear Reeded Handle, Crimped 3-Corner Top, 6 In. ................... 395.00
Pitcher, Overshot, Clear Reeded Handle, Melon-Ribbed, 5 3/4 In. ........................... 125.00
Pitcher, Overshot, 7 1/2 In. .......................................................................................... 150.00
Pitcher, Water, Clear Reeded Handle, 10 In. .............................................................. 175.00
Pitcher, Water, Opalescent Swirl, Inside Ribs, Square Pleated Mouth ..................... 225.00
Pitcher, Water, Square Top, Twisted Rope Handle Encircling Neck .......................... 350.00
Pitcher, Water, Tankard Shape, Clear Reeded Handle ............................................... 195.00

| | |
|---|---|
| Rose Bowl, Inverted Baby Thumbprint, Enamel Fan & Flowers | 110.00 |
| Salt & Pepper, Cut Glass, Original Lead Tops | 55.00 |
| Saltshaker, Paneled | 30.00 |
| Saltshaker, Threaded, Northwood | 35.00 |
| Sugar Shaker, Frosted, Crackle | 225.00 |
| Syrup, Threaded | 225.00 |
| Toothpick, Bulbous Base, Thumbprint Pattern | 58.00 |
| Tumbler, Enameled | 75.00 |
| Tumbler, Hobnail, 10 Rows, Frosted | 125.00 |
| Tumbler, Pioneer's Victoria | 28.00 |
| Tumbler, Ten-Row Hobnails, Frosted, 3 1/4 In. | 125.00 |
| Tumbler, Water, Embossed Swirl, Cranberry To Clear, 3 3/4 In. | 60.00 |
| Vase, Bud, Enameled Floral Design, 10 1/2 In. | 40.00 |
| Vase, Celery, Diamond-Quilted, 6 1/2 In. | 68.00 |
| Vase, Enameled Flowers, Gold Trim, 11 In. | 125.00 |
| Vase, Enameled, 12 In. | 36.00 |
| Vase, White Enameled Flowers, Raised Gold Lily Pads, 12 3/4 In. | 115.00 |
| Wine, Cathedral, Blue & Vaseline | 35.00 |

*Ruby glass is a dark red color. It was a Victorian and twentieth-century
ware. The name means many different types of red glass.*

**RUBY GLASS, see also Cranberry Glass; Pressed Glass; Souvenir**

| | |
|---|---|
| RUBY GLASS, Basket, Rim Upturned, Openwork, 6 In. | 75.00 |
| Bell, Elkhorn Fair, 1913, Clear Paneled Handle, 6 1/2 In. | 55.00 |
| Berry Bowl, Button Arches, 11 Sauces, Etched Flowers & Leaves | 190.00 |
| Berry Bowl, Loop & Block | 55.00 |
| Berry Bowl, Master, Boat Shape, Thumbprint, Etched | 125.00 |
| Berry Bowl, Pleating | 35.00 |
| Berry Bowl, Truncated Cube | 16.00 |
| Bowl, Silver Plated Rim, 8 1/2 In. | 85.00 |
| Butter, Button Arches, Frosted Band, Covered | 85.00 |
| Butter, Diamond Pattern, Covered | 115.00 |
| Butter, Etching, Thumbprint, Covered | 115.00 |
| Butter, Imperial, Clear Areas, Covered | 150.00 |
| Butter, Loop & Block, Covered | 105.00 |
| Butter, Red Block, Covered | 85.00 |
| Butter, Star In Square, Covered | 135.00 |
| Candleholder, Fish On Each Side Of Base, 4 In., Pair | 115.00 |
| Canoe, 11 3/4 X 4 In. | 65.00 |
| Celery, Ivy In Snow, Ruby Buds | 95.00 |
| Celery, Souvenir, Florida | 48.00 |
| Celery, Thumbprint | 45.00 To 48.50 |
| Celery, Truncated Cube | 48.00 |
| Chamber Pot, Souvenir Of Niagara Falls | 14.00 |
| Champagne, Thumbprint, Berry Etching | 28.00 |
| Claret, Block Band, St.Mary's, Pa. | 28.00 |
| Claret, Button Arches | 25.00 |
| Claret, Thumbprint | 50.00 |
| Claret, Truncated Cube | 35.00 |
| Compote, Broken Column, Open, 8 3/4 X 8 1/4 In. | 275.00 |
| Compote, Oregon, 7 X 6 In. | 55.00 |
| Cracker Jar, Enameled Open Heart | 325.00 |
| Creamer, Barreled Oval | 18.00 |
| Creamer, Box In Box, Miniature | 35.00 |
| Creamer, Co-Op Block | 40.00 |
| Creamer, Colorado, Individual | 45.00 |
| Creamer, Nail | 65.00 |
| Creamer, Plume, Large | 60.00 |
| Creamer, Red Block | 65.00 |
| Creamer, Ring & Beads, 2 3/4 In. | 15.00 |
| Creamer, Souvenir, Colorado, Compliments Of Roy Meek | 24.50 |
| Creamer, Souvenir, Niagara Falls, 4 In. | 12.00 |
| Creamer, Spearpoint, Frosted Band | 42.00 |

| | |
|---|---|
| **Creamer**, Triple Triangle | 45.00 |
| **Creamer**, Truncated Cube, 3 In. | 14.00 |
| **Cruet**, Beaded Swirl, Oval Lenses | 80.00 |
| **Cruet**, Block & Lattice, Original Stopper | 110.00 |
| **Cruet**, Button Arches, Clear Faceted Stopper | 185.00 |
| **Cruet**, Inverted Thumbprint | 50.00 |
| **Cruet**, Truncated Cube, Etched Berries | 125.00 |
| **Cup & Saucer**, Sea, Mermaids, Blown, Hand-Painted, Pedestal | 85.00 |
| **Decanter**, Red Block | 125.00 |
| **Decanter**, Wine, Diamond & Star, Original Stopper | 85.00 |
| **Goblet**, Colonial Flute | 22.00 |
| **Goblet**, Dakota | 30.00 |
| **Goblet**, Loop & Block | 38.00 |
| **Goblet**, Mioton | 25.00 |
| **Goblet**, Red Block | 30.00 To 35.00 |
| **Goblet**, Roanoke | 35.00 |
| **Goblet**, Thumbprint | 30.00 To 35.00 |
| **Goblet**, Truncated Cube | 35.00 |
| **Jar**, Powder, Gilt Trim, Souvenir, Coney Island | 18.00 |
| **Milk Glass**, Plate, Admiral Dewey, Club Border | 22.50 |
| **Mug**, Brookfield, Ill. | 19.00 |
| **Mug**, Button Arches, Souvenir, Elsie Friddle, 1910 | 30.00 |
| **Mug**, Clear Handled, Souvenir, David 1896 | 22.00 |
| **Mug**, Fleur-De-Lis, Gold Trim | 55.00 |
| **Mug**, Handled, Double Block, 3 1/8 In. | 32.50 |
| **Mug**, Lacy Medallion, Souvenir, Dottie Krug | 27.50 |
| **Mustard**, Lid, Button Arches, Souvenir | 85.00 |
| **Paperweight**, Souvenir, Atlantic City, Flat, 4 X 2 3/8 In. | 45.00 |
| **Pitcher**, Durand, Michigan, 4 In. | 24.00 |
| **Pitcher**, Melon Ribbed, Clear Applied Handle, 9 In. | 235.00 |
| **Pitcher**, Milk, Button Arches, Engraved | 65.00 |
| **Pitcher**, Milk, Washington, World's Fair 1893, Ruby & Clear | 125.00 |
| **Pitcher**, Mother, 1933 Fair, Button & Arches, 3 1/2 In. | 20.00 |
| **Pitcher**, Sheaf & Block, 7 1/2 In. | 95.00 |
| **Pitcher**, Swirl Pattern, 2 Qt. | 13.00 |
| **Pitcher**, Syrup, Clear Applied Handle | 110.00 |
| **Pitcher**, Thumbprint, 7 1/2 In. | 70.00 |
| **Pitcher**, Water, Button Arches | 175.00 |
| **Pitcher**, Water, Carnation | 150.00 |
| **Pitcher**, Water, Hexagonal Block | 125.00 |
| **Pitcher**, Water, Nail | 175.00 |
| **Plate**, Cake, York Herringbone, 7 X 10 In. | 110.00 |
| **Plate**, Sandwich, Oyster & Pearl, 13 1/2 In. | 20.00 |
| **Rose Bowl**, Leaves & Birds Under Glaze, Silver Rim, 3 1/2 In. | 85.00 |
| **Salt & Pepper**, Souvenir, Elsie & Mary Duncan, 1912 | 35.00 |
| **Saltshaker**, Broken Column | 75.00 |
| **Saltshaker**, Button & Arches, Peoria, Ill. | 12.00 |
| **Saltshaker**, Red Block, Pair | 85.00 |
| **Saltshaker**, Snail | 25.00 |
| **Saltshaker**, Souvenir, Center Lovell, Maine | 18.00 |
| **Shaker**, Cocktail, Chrome Top, 6 Footed Tumblers | 60.00 |
| **Spooner**, Button Arches, Etched Band | 45.00 |
| **Spooner**, Co-Op Block | 40.00 |
| **Spooner**, Nail | 60.00 |
| **Spooner**, Paneled Dogwood | 55.00 |
| **Spooner**, Red Block | 30.00 |
| **Spooner**, Royal Crystal | 30.00 |
| **Spooner**, Sunken Primrose | 115.00 |
| **Spooner**, Thumbprint | 38.00 To 45.00 |
| **Spooner**, Triple Triangle | 40.00 |
| **Spooner**, Truncated Cube | 45.00 |
| **Sugar & Creamer**, Royal | 110.00 |
| **Sugar**, Broken Columns | 50.00 |

Sugar, Button Arches, Etched, Covered ............................................................. 65.00
Sugar, Crystal Wedding, Covered ..................................................................... 75.00
Sugar, Loop & Block, Covered .......................................................................... 55.00
Sugar, Nail, Open .............................................................................................. 30.00
Syrup, Hexagonal Block ................................................................................... 150.00
Syrup, Torpedo ................................................................................................ 185.00
Table Set, Red Block, 4 Piece ......................................................................... 235.00
Table Set, Triple Triangle, 4 Piece ................................................................... 235.00
Tankard, Button & Arches, Clear Band ............................................................. 80.00
Tankard, Oregon .............................................................................................. 100.00
Tankard, Ribbed Thumbprint, Orange & Gold Band, 11 1/2 In. ........................ 65.00
Toothpick, Button Arches, Grantham, N.H. ...................................................... 15.00
Toothpick, Columbian Coin .............................................................................. 100.00
Toothpick, Heart Band, Souvenir, 1904 ........................................................... 24.00
Toothpick, Late Block ...................................................................................... 195.00
Toothpick, Shamrock ....................................................................................... 22.00
Toothpick, Souvenir, Elwood, Ind. ................................................................... 10.00
Toothpick, Souvenir, Mother 1902 ................................................................... 18.00
Toothpick, Souvenir, Omaha Exposition, 1898 ................................................ 35.00
Toothpick, Souvenir, Onaway, Michigan .......................................................... 17.00
Toothpick, Souvenir, Ontario Beach, New Hampshire ...................................... 50.00
Toothpick, Sunken Honeycomb ........................................................................ 28.00
Toothpick, Swirl, Scalloped .............................................................................. 48.00
Toothpick, Thumbprint ............................................................ 21.50 To 30.00
Toothpick, Truncated Cube ...................................................... 30.00 To 35.00
Toothpick, Zipper Slash, Souvenir, Mt.Vernon ................................................. 28.00
Tray, Pin, Banded Portland, Souvenir, Newburyport, Mass. .............................. 10.00
Tumbler, Ashbury Park, 1894, Mother ............................................................. 28.00
Tumbler, Block & Leaves, Frosted ................................................................... 15.00
Tumbler, Flat Diamond ..................................................................................... 22.00
Tumbler, Kokomo ............................................................................................. 28.50
Tumbler, Leta, Script ....................................................................................... 22.00
Tumbler, Paneled Dogwood ............................................................................. 25.00
Tumbler, Red Block .......................................................................................... 30.00
Tumbler, Shoshone, Set Of 6 .......................................................................... 225.00
Tumbler, Star Of Bethlehem ............................................................................ 28.50
Tumbler, Thumbprint, Flowers ......................................................................... 45.00
Tumbler, Triple Triangle .......................................................... 23.00 To 32.00
Vase, Bud, Metal Crane, C.1890, 13 3/4 In. .................................................... 350.00
Vial, Perfume, Central Divider, One Hinged, One Screw Top, 5 In. ................... 325.00
Vinaigrette, Polished Panels, Sterling Silver Caps, 4 In. .................................. 58.50
Water Set, Greek Key Pattern, Pitcher & 5 Tumblers ....................................... 225.00
Water Set, Late Block, Bulbous, 7 Piece .......................................................... 325.00
Water Set, Pavonia, Fern Etching, 5 Piece ....................................................... 200.00
Water Set, Pillow Encircled, 7 Piece ................................................................ 285.00
Water Set, Red Block, 7 Piece ......................................................................... 275.00
Water Set, Thumbprint, 7 Piece ....................................................................... 285.00
Water Set, Triple Triangle, 7 Piece .................................................................. 275.00
Wine, Aurora ................................................................................................... 30.00
Wine, Block Band, A.E.Schmeling, Milwaukee, 1902 ....................................... 35.00
Wine, Button Arches ....................................................................................... 40.00
Wine, Red Block .............................................................................................. 30.00
Wine, Souvenir, Hot Springs, 1892 ................................................................. 20.00
Wine, Souvenir, Madison, Wisconsin .............................................................. 26.00
Wine, Sunk Honeycomb ................................................................................... 42.50
Wine, Thumbprint ............................................................................................ 35.00
Wine, Triple Triangle, Set Of 8 ........................................................................ 175.00

*Rudolstadt was a faience factory in the Thuringia region of Germany
from 1720 to about 1791. In 1854, Ernst Bohne began working in the area
and in 1882, L Straus & Sons began production of luxury decorative
porcelain at Rudolstadt. Collectors often refer to late pieces as Royal*

*Rudolstadt. Late nineteenth- and early twentieth-century pieces are most commonly found today.*

**RUDOLSTADT, ROYAL RUDOLSTADT, see Kewpie**

| | |
|---|---:|
| **RUDOLSTADT, Bowl,** Cornflowers, Wheat Stalks, Gold Rim, Royal, 11 In. | 175.00 |
| **Bowl,** Flowers Inside, Gold Banding, Irregular Shape, Royal, 11 In. | 235.00 |
| **Cake Set,** 6 Cake Plates, White Roses, Gold Rim, Royal, 7 Piece | 135.00 |
| **Cup & Saucer,** Floral Design, Royal | 25.00 |
| **Dish,** Cheese, Covered, Pink & Blue Design, Royal | 50.00 |
| **Dish,** Child's, Happifats, Royal, 13 Piece | 150.00 |
| **Dish,** Handle, Leaf Shaped, Blue & White Birds, Royal | 15.00 |
| **Dish,** Pickle, Pink Roses, Gold Trim, Royal, 8 1/4 In. | 28.50 |
| **Dresser Set,** Poppies, Signed, Royal, 4 Piece | 210.00 |
| **Ewer,** Gilded Handle, Flowers, Cream Satin, Royal, 9 1/2 In. | 58.00 |
| **Ewer,** Raised Flower Sprays, Gold Branches, Signed | 95.00 |
| **Ewer,** Turquoise Beading, Sand Finish, 12 In. | 149.00 |
| **Figurine,** Elephant, Royal, 6 In. | 75.00 |
| **Figurine,** Lady, Bust, 8 In. | 195.00 |
| **Figurine,** Young Girl, Ivory & Brown, Royal, Signed, 14 In. | 90.00 |
| **Group,** Diana & Hind, Nymphs & Putto, Marked, 25 In. *Illus* | 800.00 |
| **Mayonnaise Set,** Footed, Ladle & Underplate, Royal | 40.00 |
| **Nappy,** Roses, Gold Rim, Open Handled, Royal | 18.00 |
| **Pitcher,** Gold Mermaid Handle, Royal, 13 1/4 In. | 245.00 |
| **Plate,** Blue Shading, Pink, Yellow Roses, Green Leaves, Royal | 30.00 |
| **Plate,** Daisies, Purple & Pink, Signed, Royal, 8 1/2 In. | 40.00 |
| **Plate,** Flowers, Gold Trim, Signed, Royal, 7 3/4 In. | 20.00 |
| **Plate,** Fruit, Gold Trim, Apple Clusters, Poppies, 8 1/2 In.Diam. | 33.00 |
| **Plate,** Lattice Rim, Gold Florals, Signed, Royal, 7 1/4 In.Diam. | 95.00 |
| **Plate,** Roses, Royal, 8 1/2 In.Diam. | 42.50 |
| **Plate,** Scalloped Gold Rim, Hand-Painted Grapes, Royal, 8 1/2 In. | 45.00 |
| **Plate,** Scenic, Royal, 7 In. | 75.00 |
| **Plate,** Tidbit, Yellow & Cream, Royal | 65.00 |
| **Saucer,** Hand-Painted Bachelor Buttons, Signed, Royal, Set Of 6 | 60.00 |
| **Shoe,** Lady's, Floral Design, Signed | 65.00 |
| **Sugar & Creamer,** Beige Ground, Green & Brown Ferns, Royal | 25.00 |
| **Sugar & Creamer,** Covered, Hand-Painted Roses, Gold Trim, Royal | 60.00 |
| **Syrup,** Ovoid Shape, Cream Ground, White Roses, Gold Handle, Royal | 68.00 |
| **Teapot,** Underliner Plate, White Roses, Gold Rim, Royal, 3 1/2 In. | 57.00 |
| **Tray,** Celery, Pink & White Roses, Royal, 12 3/4 X 5 1/2 In. | 40.00 |
| **Tray,** Dresser, White Roses, Royal, Signed | 75.00 |
| **Urn,** Spherical Body, Polychrome Floral Design, Royal, 12 1/2 In. | 125.00 |
| **Vase,** Applied Flowers, Royal, 22 In. | 350.00 |
| **Vase,** Baroque Base & Top, Flowers, 11 In. | 160.00 |
| **Vase,** Cream Ground, Pink & Blue Morning Glories, Royal, 5 In. | 35.00 |
| **Vase,** Figural, Elephant, Beige, Brown, Royal, 9 In. | 280.00 |

Rudolstadt, Group, Diana & Hind, Nymphs & Putto, Marked, 25 In.

Vase, Flowers & Vines, Royal, 10 In. .................................................................................... 85.00
Vase, Gold Handles, Pastel Flowers, Royal, Signed, 14 1/2 In. ....................................... 250.00
Vase, Gold Scrolled Handles, Cream Ground, Signed, 15 In. ........................................... 75.00
Vase, Morning Glories, Gold Side Handle, Royal, Signed, 5 1/2 In. ................................. 40.00
Vase, Yellow, Flowers, Royal, 8 1/2 In. .............................................................................. 95.00

RUG, Ada-Melas Prayer, Apricot, Rose & Green, 5 Ft. X 42 In. ....................................... 1000.00
Aubusson, Central Bouquet Medallion, Olive Green, 14 3/4 X 11 1/4 Ft. ...................... 2250.00
Autumn Leaf Pattern, Hand-Hooked, Virgin Wool, Oval, 45 X 22 In. .............................. 65.00
Bauluchistan, 4 X 7 Ft. ..................................................................................................... 700.00
Beshir, Red, Pistachio, Blue, Indigo, 6 Ft. X 13 1/2 Ft. .................................................... 2800.00
Bibikabad, Petal-Formed Medallion, Floral Field, 21 X 9 1/3 Ft. ..................................... 2000.00
Bokoma, 4 X 6 Ft. .............................................................................................................. 800.00
Chinese, Plum Red Flower, Saffron, Lavender, 9 X 12 Ft. ................................................ 1600.00
Chinese, Silk, 6 Cranes, Ivory, Black, & Olive, 4 X 3 Ft. ................................................... 650.00
Clamshell Pattern, Reddish Brown, Red, & Beige, 51 1/2 X 30 In. ................................... 155.00
Dagestan, Pistachio, Brown, Ivory, 12 Ft. X 39 In. ............................................................ 400.00
Eastern Caucasian, Polychrome Star Design, 3 1/4 X 5 Ft. 1 In. ...................................... 1700.00
French, Needlepoint, Allover Floral, Yellow Ground, 8 3/4 X 7 1/2 Ft. ............................ 2200.00
Hamadan, Ivory Field, Geometrical Flowers, 2 Ft. 10 In. X 9 Ft. 10 In. ........................... 200.00
Hamadan, Oriental, Pink, Blue Flowers, 9 X 12 Ft. ........................................................... 1600.00
Hamadan, Red Field, Blue Spandrels, 7 Ft. 3 In. X 3 Ft. 5 In. .......................................... 325.00
Hamadan, Star & Rosettes, Blue Ground, 24 X 148 In. ..................................................... 350.00
Hamadan, Stepped Medallions & Spandrels, Blue, 4 Ft. 2 In. X 5 3/4 Ft. ........................ 425.00
Heriz, Red Field, Square Stepped Medallion, 12 1/2 X 8 Ft. 2 In. ..................................... 1850.00
Heriz, 3 Medallions, Blue Ground, 4 Ft. 10 In. X 17 Ft. 4 In. ............................................ 1400.00
Hooked, Alternating Flowers & Geometric Squares, 27 X 42 In. ....................................... 40.00
Hooked, Bouquet, Wool, 1910-20, 37 X 23 In. ................................................................... 150.00
Hooked, Brick Pattern, Gray & Black, 55 X 35 In. ............................................................. 95.00
Hooked, Center Floral, Shades Of Greens, Brown Ground, 24 1/2 X 37 In. ...................... 65.00
Hooked, Center Medallion, Border Of Colored Leaves, 28 1/2 X 44 1/2 In. ..................... 68.00
Hooked, Center Medallion, Multicolored, 28 X 46 In. ........................................................ 90.00
Hooked, Colored Oak Leaves, Gray Ground, Black Border, Oval, 24 X 36 In. ................... 40.00
Hooked, Corner Cornucopia, Floral Clusters, 50 X 29 In. ................................................. 90.00
Hooked, Crazy Quilt Pattern, 19th Century, 35 X 72 In. ............................................ *Illus,* 425.00
Hooked, Crazy Quilt, Wool, 1910-20, 56 X 29 1/4 In. ....................................................... 350.00
Hooked, Crisscross Pattern, Multicolors, 37 X 51 In. ........................................................ 85.00
Hooked, Floral Design, C.1900, 3 X 5 Ft. ........................................................................... 40.00
Hooked, Floral, A.W.Phillips, 19th Century, 62 X 55 In. ............................................ *Illus* 1300.00
Hooked, Geometric Bricks, Diamond Shaped Pattern, 50 X 30 In. .................................. 110.00
Hooked, Geometric Edge, 1 Inch Squares, Groups Of 4, 31 X 60 In. ............................... 145.00

Rug, Hooked, Crazy Quilt Pattern, 19th Century, 35 X 72 In.

Rug, Hooked, Floral, A.W.Phillips, 19th Century, 62 X 55 In. (See Page 559)

Rug, Hooked, Ivory Ground, 1886, American, 60 X 42 In.

| | | |
|---|---|---|
| **Hooked,** Geometric Pattern, Multicolored, 31 1/2 X 48 In. | | 75.00 |
| **Hooked,** Geometric Squares, Flowers & Stripes, 27 X 42 In. | | 45.00 |
| **Hooked,** Geometric, Crisscross Pattern Of Squares, 35 1/2 X 65 1/2 In. | | 125.00 |
| **Hooked,** Geometric, Multicolored, 23 1/2 X 40 In. | | 75.00 |
| **Hooked,** Ivory Ground, 1886, American, 60 X 42 In. | *Illus* | 3600.00 |
| **Hooked,** Lions & Floral, 19th Century, American, 31 X 57 In. | *Illus* | 1200.00 |
| **Hooked,** Log Cabin Pattern, Multicolored, 23 X 41 In. | | 48.00 |
| **Hooked,** Log Cabin Pattern, Multicolored, 31 X 37 In. | | 75.00 |
| **Hooked,** Multicolored, 4 In.Border, 32 X 44 In. | | 75.00 |
| **Hooked,** Pictorial, American, 19th Century, 48 X 84 In. | *Illus.* | 400.00 |
| **Hooked,** Runner, Floral Rectangles, Navy Ground, 32 1/2 X 62 1/2 In. | | 115.00 |
| **Hooked,** Shaded Gray-Brown To Brown Ground, Diamond Pattern, 56 X 32 In. | | 110.00 |
| **Hooked,** Shirred, Gray With Red Spots Overall, 42 1/2 X 20 1/2 In. | | 45.00 |
| **Hooked,** Square, Zigzag Lines, Multicolored, 28 X 44 In. | | 75.00 |
| **Hooked,** Squares, Zigzag Line Divider, Dark Rose Ground, 52 X 30 In. | | 85.00 |
| **Hooked,** Three Bears, Wool, 1910-20, 39 X 24 In. | | 295.00 |
| **Hooked,** Tulip Pattern, 3 X 4 Ft. | | 125.00 |
| **Hooked,** W.Virginia, Dated 1931, Blue, Brown, & Orange, 38 X 27 In. | | 90.00 |
| **Hooked,** Waldoboro, Homespun Linen, C.1820, Gray Ground, 30 1/2 X 18 In. | | 185.00 |
| **Hooked,** Whale & Ship Pattern, American, C.1930 | *Illus* | 350.00 |
| **Hooked,** 19th Century, American | *Illus* | 950.00 |
| **Indian,** Chimayo, Dusty Rose & Blue, Pre-1920s, 86 X 54 In. | | 250.00 |
| **Kazak,** Cloud Band, Blue & Green Medallions, 4 X 9 Ft. 2 In. | | 3700.00 |

Rug, Hooked, 19th Century, American

Rug, Hooked, Pictorial, American, 19th Century, 48 X 84 In.

Rug, Hooked, Whale & Ship Pattern, American, C.1930

Rug, Hooked, Lions & Floral, 19th Century, American, 31 X 57 In.

Kazvin, Center Blue Medallion, Ivory Field, 12 Ft. 2 In. X 9 Ft. ...................................................3700.00
Kerman, Blue Rose Floral Sprays, Ivory Field, 6 Ft. 10 In. X 3 Ft. .......................................... 600.00
Kerman, Central Palmette Medallion, 13 Ft. 2 In. X 9 Ft. 8 In. ................................................3500.00
Kerman, Floral Center, Blue Border, Ivory Ground, 84 X 52 In. ................................................1100.00
Kerman, Runner, Central Rose Medallion, Ivory Field, 7 X 2 Ft. 5 In. ...................................... 400.00
Kuba, Indigo, 3 Geometric Borders, 6 Ft. X 43 In. .....................................................................1900.00
Makri Prayer, Ivory, Madder, Blue, Pistachio, 4 X 6 Ft. ............................................................ 750.00
Moghan, Ivory, Salmon, Brown, Blue, & Pink, 7 Ft. X 45 In. ...................................................1200.00
Needlepoint, English, 4 1/2 X 2 1/4 Ft. ...................................................................................... 125.00
Needlepoint, Polychrome Floral Cluster, 10 Ft. 7 In. X 18 1/2 Ft. ...........................................2100.00
Oriental, Agra, Turkey, 11 Ft.7 In. X 9 Ft.6 In. ........................................................................... 400.00
Oriental, Balulichstan, 4 X 7 Ft. ................................................................................................. 700.00
Oriental, Bokhara, Burnt Orange & Black Medallions, 51 X 70 In. ........................................... 500.00
Oriental, Bokoma, 4 X 6 Ft. ....................................................................................................... 800.00
Oriental, Chinese, Brown Ground, 9 Ft.10 In. X 12 Ft.5 In. ....................................................... 400.00
Oriental, Chinese, Central Phoenix, Floral, 4 Ft. 2 In. X 6 3/4 Ft. ............................................ 700.00
Oriental, Ivory, Indigo, Madder, Olive, Gold, 4 X 5 Ft. ............................................................. 950.00
Oriental, Kabistan, Geometrical Design, Fringed, 4 X 6 Ft. ...................................................... 450.00
Oriental, Kabistan, Predominately Red, 70 X 38 In. .................................................................. 145.00
Oriental, Tabriz, 8 X 11 Ft. .........................................................................................................2000.00
Oriental, 4 Borders, 3 Medallions, 4 1/4 X 6 1/4 Ft. .................................................................. 425.00
Persian, Royal Kerman, Cranberry Field, 9 X 12 Ft. ..................................................................3200.00
Pictorial, Kerman, Rose, Ivory, Blue, & Salmon, 5 X 9 Ft. ........................................................3500.00
Pink Field, Diamond Medallion, Flowered Edge, 6 1/2 X 3 3/4 Ft. ........................................... 550.00
Prayer, Eastern Caucasian, Trellis Design, 3 Ft. 8 In. X 5 Ft. 3 In. ........................................... 950.00
Prayer, Indo, Silk, 4 X 7 Ft. ........................................................................................................1500.00
Prayer, Ladik, Spandrels, Serrated Leaves, 3 3/4 X 9 1/2 Ft. ...................................................2700.00
Rag, Hooked, Flowers & Scrolls, 2 X 3 Ft. ................................................................................. 15.00
Sampler, Flowers In Rim Squares, Center Stripes, 37 X 34 In. ................................................. 185.00
Sarouk, Floral Sprays, Magenta Field, 4 Ft. 5 In. X 6 Ft. 8 In. .................................................1500.00
Sarouk, Floral Sprays, Red Border, Blue Field, 8 X 10 Ft. ........................................................1300.00
Sarouk, Wine Red, 11 Ft.5 In. X 13 Ft.5 In. ...............................................................................2500.00
Senneh Kelim, Madder, Green Medallion, 4 X 6 Ft. 7 In. ..........................................................1800.00
Serapi, Diamond-Shaped Medallion, Rust Ground, 11 X 15 Ft. .................................................3600.00
Shaker, Crocheted, Bands Of Color, 41 In.Diam. ...................................................................... 125.00
Shaker, Knitted Base, Strips Of Material Drawn Through, 48 X 23 In. ...................................... 75.00
Spanish, Flowering Urn Design, Ivory Field, 16 3/4 X 14 Ft. ....................................................1800.00
Sultanabad, Lobed & Pendanted Medallion, Red Field, 10 1/2 X 12 1/2 Ft. ............................1600.00
Sultanabad, Medallion & Spandrels, Blue Field, 6 Ft. 7 In. X 4 Ft. ........................................... 900.00
Sunburst Pattern, Earth Tones, Brick Red, Mustard, & Beige, 53 In.Diam. ............................. 125.00
Tabriz, Palmette & Floral Arabesques, Scrolled Vines, 9 1/2 X 12 Ft. .....................................7000.00
Tabriz, 8 X 11 Ft. .......................................................................................................................2000.00
Turkman Tekke Juval, Madder, Guls, 32 X 45 In. ..................................................................... 350.00
Waldeboro On Burlap, Raised Flowers, C.1860, White Ground, 46 X 22 In. ........................... 135.00

RumRill  *Rumrill Pottery was designed by George Rumrill of Little Rock,
Arkansas. From 1930 to 1933, it was produced by the Red Wing
Pottery of Red Wing, Minnesota. In 1938, production was transferred
to the Shawnee Pottery, Zanesville, Ohio.*

RUMRILL, Candleholder, Blue, 4 In., Pair ................................................................................. 15.00
Pitcher, Ball Shape, Tilt Top, Ice Lip, Orange & Red, Marked ............................................... 17.50
Vase, Drape Handles, Matt White, Marked, 4 X 12 In. ........................................................... 25.00
Vase, Fan Shape, 7 In. ............................................................................................................. 6.00
Vase, White & Blue, 7 1/2 In. ................................................................................................... 6.00

*Ruskin Pottery was established in 1898 at West Smethwick,
Birmingham, England. The factory worked until 1935.*

RUSKIN, Vase, Blue, Red Glaze, 8 In. ........................................................................................ 120.00

*Russel Wright*
*Wright*
*MFG. BY*
*STEUBENVILLE*

*Russel Wright designed dinnerwares in modern shapes for four companies. Iroquois China Company, Harker China Company, Steubenville Pottery, and Justin Therod and Sons made dishes marked Russel Wright. The Steubenville wares, first made in 1938, are the most common today.*

| | |
|---|---|
| **RUSSEL WRIGHT, Bowl,** Green Lid, Dark Brown, 2 X 10 In.Diam. | 15.00 |
| **Butter,** Covered, Iroquois Pattern, Pale Green | 28.50 |
| **Casserole,** Covered, Chartreuse | 16.00 |
| **Casserole,** Covered, Iroquois Pattern, Charcoal Gray | 17.00 |
| **Coffeepot,** Pink | 18.00 |
| **Creamer,** Blue, Signed | 6.00 |
| **Creamer,** Modern Pattern, Cedar Green | 7.50 |
| **Gravy Boat,** Underplate, Gray | 8.00 |
| **Nappy,** Iroquois Pattern, Dark Green, 5 1/2 In. | 2.50 |
| **Pitcher,** Water, Green | 25.00 |
| **Plate,** Iroquois Pattern, Brown, 9 1/4 In.Diam. | 2.75 |
| **Platter,** Iroquois Pattern, Light Blue, 14 1/2 In. | 10.00 |
| **Platter,** Rose | 40.00 |
| **Salt & Pepper,** Iroquois, Pale Green | 7.50 |
| **Teapot,** Bluish Gray, Signed | 15.00 |
| **Teapot,** Gray | 35.00 |
| **Teapot,** Iroquois Pattern, Light Blue | 17.50 |
| **RUSSIAN, Silver, see Silver-Russian** | |

*Sabino*
*France*

*Sabino glass was made in the 1920s and 1930s in Paris, France. Founded by Marius-Ernest Sabino, the firm was noted for Art Deco lamps, vases, nudes, figures, and animals in clear, colored, and opalescent glass. Production stopped during World War II, but resumed in the 1960s with manufacture of nudes and small opalescent glass animals. The new pieces are a slightly different color and can be recognized.*

**SABINO FRANCE**

| | |
|---|---|
| **SABINO, Bottle,** Perfume, Art Deco, Dancing Woman, Luster Pear, Ice Blue, 6 In. | 110.00 |
| **Bowl,** Sloping Opalescent Sides, High Relief, Clamshells, 6 In. | 150.00 |
| **Figurine,** Dragonfly, Signed, 6 In. | 72.50 |
| **Figurine,** Kneeling Nude Holding 3 Pouter Pigeons, Signed, 6 1/4 In. | 195.00 |
| **Figurine,** 3 Birds In Flight, Outstretched Wings, 5 1/2 In. | 200.00 |
| **Plaque,** Stork, 3 Huge Birds, 1920-30, Molded, Signed, 12 1/2 In. | 1400.00 |
| **Vase,** Beehive, Signed, 7 X 7 1/2 In. | 190.00 |
| **Vase,** Frosted With Sculpted Flowers & Leaves, Signed, 6 In. | 69.50 |
| **Vase,** La Danse, Ladies All Around, 14 In. | 870.00 |
| **Vase,** Smocked Pattern, Gray Glass, Signed, 5 1/8 X 5 In.Diam. | 375.00 |

*Salt glaze is a hard, shiny glaze that was developed for pottery during the eighteenth century. It is still being made.*

| | |
|---|---|
| **SALT GLAZE, Bowl,** Blue, Gray, Crown Mark, 9 In. | 65.00 |
| **Crock,** Apricot, Blue & White | 56.00 |
| **Dish,** Cheese, Covered, Raised White Figures, 10 1/2 X 9 In. | 250.00 |
| **Figurine,** Ewe & Lamb, 5 1/2 X 1/2 In. | 75.00 |
| **Jar,** Snuff, 8 In. | 40.00 |
| **Jug,** American, Brown & Tan, Small | 25.00 |
| **Jug,** Arabic, Pewter Hinged Lid, C.1840, Gray, 7 1/4 In. | 110.00 |
| **Jug,** C.Herman, Fitzgerald Finest Whiskey, Marked, 3 Gal. | 365.00 |
| **Jug,** Donatello, Silver Plate Lid, 1861 Mark, English | 48.00 |
| **Pitcher,** Apostle, 8 1/4 In. | 95.00 |
| **Pitcher,** Apostle, 11 In. | 195.00 |
| **Pitcher,** Face On Spout | 75.00 |
| **Pitcher,** Grape Pattern, Green | 75.00 |
| **Spooner,** Double Handled, Metal Rim, Hunting Scene | 50.00 |
| **Syrup,** Molded Pattern | 20.00 |
| **Teapot,** Figural, Squirrel, C.1760, White | 1050.00 |
| **Teapot,** Pewter Lid, Ivory Colored, English | 55.00 |
| **Vase,** Dragonfly, 7 1/2 In. | 75.00 |

**SAMPLER, see Textile, Sampler**

*Samson and Company, a French firm specializing in the reproduction of collectible wares of many countries and periods, was founded in Paris in the early nineteenth century. Chelsea, Meissen, Famille Verte, and Oriental Lowestoft are some of the wares that have been reproduced by the company. The company uses a variety of marks to distinguish its reproductions. It is still in operation.*

**SAMSON, Desk Set,** Ormolu Mounted, Pink Diapering, Flowers, 2 Quill Holes .................... 85.00
**Figurine,** Bolognese Hound, Blue Swastika Mark, 5 3/4 In., Pair ................................... 420.00
**Figurine,** Malabar, Oriental Hat, Yellow Cloak, Marked, 7 In. ....................................... 50.00
**Snuffbox,** Double Lidded, Barrel Shape, Gilt Metal, 2 1/2 In. ....................................... 200.00

**SAND BABIES, Pitcher,** Blue Mark, 4 In. ......................................................................... 85.00
**Pitcher,** 3 Children At Water Edge, Signed, 3 In. ........................................................ 80.00
**Sugar,** Open ..................................................................................................................... 25.00

*Sandwich glass is any one of the myriad types of glass made by the Boston and Sandwich Glass Works in Sandwich, Massachusetts, between 1825 and 1888. It is often very difficult to be sure whether a piece was really made at the Sandwich factory because so many types were made there and similar pieces were made at other glass factories.*

**SANDWICH GLASS, see also Pressed Glass, etc.**
**SANDWICH GLASS, Basket,** Looped Handle With Thorns, Overshot, Ruffles, Large ............ 230.00
**Bottle,** Bar, Flute Pattern, Applied Neck Ring, 11 3/8 In. ............................................. 365.00
**Bottle,** Cologne, Loop & Punty, Blown Out, Flint, Green, 5 In. ..................................... 95.00
**Bowl,** Industry, 6 1/4 In. ................................................................................................... 185.00
**Bowl,** Sapphire Blue Loop, 5 1/2 In.Diam. ..................................................................... 375.00
**Bowl,** Tulip & Acanthus Leaf, Lacy, Blue, 5 1/2 In. ...................................................... 575.00
**Bowl,** Wash, Miniature, Paneled, Flint ........................................................................... 15.00
**Candelabrum,** Prisms, 10 In., Pair ................................................................................. 90.00
**Candlestick,** Acanthus, Blue Over White, 11 In. ........................................................... 625.00
**Candlestick,** Clamwater Blue Petal & Loop .................................................................... 350.00
**Candlestick,** Dolphin, Blue Petticoat, 6 3/4 In., Pair ..................................................... 425.00
**Candlestick,** Dolphin, Clear ............................................................................................ 125.00
**Candlestick,** Hexagonal Form, C.1840, Clambroth, 4 In., Pair ..................................... 275.00
**Candlestick,** Hexagonal, 1835-45, Amethyst, 7 1/2 In., Pair ....................................... 725.00
**Candlestick,** Petal & Loop, Blue Socket On Clambroth Base ....................................... 575.00
**Candlestick,** Petal & Loop, 7 3/4 In., Pair ...................................................................... 200.00
**Candlestick,** Pointed Lobed 5-Step Base, 6 3/4 In. ...................................................... 175.00
**Candlestick,** Purple, Blue Acid Finish, Hexagonal, 7 In. ............................................... 375.00
**Candlestick,** Single-Step Dolphin, Electric Blue ........................................................... 975.00
**Candlestick,** Stippled Socket, Waterfall Base, Pair ....................................................... 350.00
**Celery,** Elongated Loop, Scalloped Rim, Marble Base, 11 In. ....................................... 450.00
**Celery,** Standing, Diamond Thumbprint, Pair .................................................................. 400.00
**Compote,** Footed, Melon Ribbed, Scalloped Rim, Flint .................................................. 159.00
**Compote,** Frosted White Overshot, 4 1/2 X 5 3/4 In.Diam. ............................................ 85.00
**Cracker Jar,** Covered, Indiana ........................................................................................ 26.00
**Creamer,** Star & Punty, Ribbed Handle, C.1840, 5 1/4 In. ............................................ 125.00
**Creamer,** Turned Up Handle, Course Rib, Double Vine .................................................. 135.00
**Cup & Saucer,** Miniature, Clear ..................................................................................... 350.00
**Decanter,** Original Tablet Stopper, Clear Blown, C.1825 ............................................... 150.00
**Decanter,** Shell & Rib, Rib Stopper, 1 Quart ................................................................. 195.00
**Goblet,** Star & Scroll, Green, Set Of 6 ........................................................................... 55.00
**Honey Dish,** Peacock Eye ............................................................................................... 10.00
**Ice Bucket,** Cut Handle, 6 X 5 In. ................................................................................... 25.00
**Inkwell,** Star Pattern, Brass Hinged Top ......................................................................... 135.00
**Jar,** Candy, Covered, 8 1/2 In. ........................................................................................ 35.00
**Jar,** Pomade, Figural, Muzzled Bear, C.1845, Amethyst, 3 3/4 In. ............................... 200.00
**SANDWICH GLASS, LAMP, see also Lamp**
**Lamp,** Blue & White Acanthus Leaf, Blue Bases, Pair ................................................... 1250.00

**Lamp,** Jade Green, White Acanthus Leaf, Pair ....................................... 3500.00
**Lamp,** Kerosene, Jade Green Base, Clear Font, 8 1/4 In. ....................... 125.00
**Lamp,** Oil, Acanthus Leaf ................................................................................ 200.00
**Lamp,** Peg, Original Burner & Chimney, Clear, 19 In., Pair ................... 400.00
**Lamp,** Sparking, Knop Stems, Single Wick, C.1820, 4 1/4 In. ............... 650.00
**Lamp,** Sweetheart, Burners, Clear, 9 3/4 In., Pair ................................ 300.00
**Lamp,** Whale Oil, Amethyst Tulip Font, Milk Glass Base, 12 In. ......... 450.00
**Lamp,** Whale Oil, Blown Font, Clear, 6 1/4 In. ..................................... 65.00
**Lamp,** Whale Oil, Blown Font, Pewter Collar, 7 1/4 In. ...................... 95.00
**Lamp,** Whale Oil, Double Drop Tin Burners, Canary, Pair ................... 800.00
**Overshot,** Frosted White, Form Of A Tazza, 4 1/2 In. .......................... 85.00
**Pitcher,** Applied Handle, Clear & Frosted Crackle, 5 1/2 In. ............... 70.00
**Pitcher,** Ice Pocket, Rope Handle, 11 In. ................................................ 120.00
**Pitcher,** Lemonade, Cranberry & Clear, Bulbous, 8 In. ......................... 225.00
**Pitcher,** Overshot, Reeded Handle, 10 1/2 In. ........................................ 175.00
**Pitcher,** Water, First Love ........................................................................... 125.00
**Pitcher,** Water, Ice Bladder, Twisted Handle, Flint, 11 In. ................... 200.00
**Plate,** Beehive, Octagonal .............................................................................. 90.00
**Plate,** Green, 6 In. ........................................................................................... 2.00
**Plate,** Lacy Pattern, 8 In., Set Of 5 ......................................................... 300.00
**Plate,** Molded Beehive Pattern, C.1840, Hexagonal ............................... 140.00
**Plate,** Plaid Pattern, 6 In.Diam. ................................................................. 10.00
**Plate,** Toddy, Lacy, Pale Green .................................................................. 97.50
**Plate,** Toddy, Profile Head Of Victoria & Albert ...................................... 82.00
**Rose Bowl,** Icicle Pattern, Green, 2 1/2 In. ............................................ 55.00
**Salt,** Agitator, Dated Top, Amber, Canary & Cobalt Blue ..................... 85.00
**Salt,** Agitator, Pewter Top, Dated Dec.25, 1877, Cobalt Blue ............. 95.00
**Salt,** Amethyst, Rectangular, Flint .............................................................. 175.00
**Salt,** Christmas, Original Top & Agitator, Dated 1877, Amber .............. 95.00
**Salt,** Christmas, Original Top & Agitator, 1877, Cobalt Blue ................ 95.00
**Salt,** Clear, Oval .............................................................................................. 95.00
**Salt,** Light Green, Pair .................................................................................. 350.00
**Salt,** Lion's Paw Footed ................................................................................ 130.00
**Sauce,** Peacock Feather & Scrolled Eye .................................................. 16.00
**Spooner,** Bellflower, Rayed Base, Double Vine ....................................... 58.00
**Spooner,** Roman Key, Flint, Silver Plated Holder, C.1870 ................... 38.00
**Sugar & Creamer,** Open, Diamond ............................................................ 7.50
**Taster,** Whiskey, Canary ............................................................................... 225.00
**Tieback,** Curtain, Pair .................................................................................... 12.50
**Tumbler,** Blue Footed, Opaque, Miniature ................................................ 425.00
**Tumbler,** Clear & Cranberry Overshot, Roman Key ............................... 100.00
**Tumbler,** Water, Forest Green ..................................................................... 3.00
**Vase,** Block & Printie, Amber, 11 In., Pair .............................................. 875.00
**Vase,** Block & Punty, 1835-45, Amethyst, 9 1/2 In., Pair ..................... 500.00
**Vase,** Circle & Ellipse, Gaffered Rim, Canary, 7 1/2 In. ....................... 275.00
**Vase,** Footed, Loop Pattern, C.1840, 5 3/4 In. ...................................... 425.00
**Vase,** Icicle, Crimped Rim, Honey Amber, 9 In. ...................................... 650.00

*Sarreguemines*

*Sarreguemines pottery was first made in Lorraine, France, about 1770. Most of the pieces found today date from the late nineteenth century.*

**SARREGUEMINES, see also Kate Greenaway**

**SARREGUEMINES, Box,** Kate Greenaway, Seesaw Children, 1 X 6 In. ....................... 70.00
**Character Jug,** Man's Head, Red Nose, Marked, 5 1/4 In. ...................... 55.00
**Character Jug,** Smiling Man, High Collar, Impressed Mark, 4 In. .......... 65.00
**Plate,** Fables De La Fontaine, Brown Sepia, Set Of 6 ......................... 45.00
**Plate,** Grape Leaves, Cream Ground, 8 1/2 In.Diam. ............................ 35.00
**Plate,** Incised Rust & Green Rose Hips, 8 1/4 In.Diam. ....................... 40.00
**Platter,** Oyster, Brown & Turquoise, Signed, 14 1/2 In.Diam. ............. 69.50
**Pocket,** Wall, Figural, Beetle, Iridescent, 9 1/2 In. ............................... 110.00
**Teapot,** 6 1/2 In. ............................................................................................. 22.00

| | |
|---|---|
| **Tray,** Calling Card, Encased In Wire Basket, 5 X 8 In. | 20.00 |
| **Vase,** Lilies, Snake, & Apple Design, Marked, 15 3/8 In., Pair | 325.00 |

*Satin glass is a late nineteenth-century art glass. It has a dull finish that is caused by a hydrofluoric acid vapor treatment. Satin glass was made in many colors and sometimes had applied decorations.*

| | |
|---|---|
| **SATIN GLASS, Basket,** Pink, White, Rope Handle | 90.00 |
| **Bottle,** Perfume, Green, Crystal Stopper | 24.00 |
| **Bottle,** Perfume, Umbrella Shape, Mother-Of-Pearl Drops, 6 In. | 120.00 |
| **Bowl,** Footed, Scalloped, Gilt Design, Rose Ground, C.1883, 7 In. | 300.00 |
| **Bowl,** Green, White Inside, Scalloped Ruffles, 6 In. | 95.00 |
| **Bowl,** Quilted, Lime Cased White Lining, 7 X 8 1/4 In. | 295.00 |
| **Bowl,** Rose Ground, 3 Clear Feet, Scalloped Top, 7 In. | 300.00 |
| **Bowl,** Rose, Lime Green Striped, Napkin Fold Underplate | 60.00 |
| **Bowl,** Rose, Pink, 5 1/2 In. | 65.00 |
| **Bowl,** Yellow, 4 1/4 X 4 3/4 In. | 100.00 |
| **Bride's Basket,** Drape Pattern, Silver Plate Holder, 15 1/2 In. | 475.00 |
| **Bride's Bowl,** White Flowers, Orange Branches, 10 1/2 In.Diam. | 245.00 |
| **Butter,** Six Panel, Amber, Covered | 47.00 |
| **Compote,** Blue Crackle, Marked, 7 In. | 40.00 |
| **Cracker Jar,** Beaded Drape, Apple Green | 165.00 |
| **Cracker Jar,** Floret Pattern, Applied Flowers, Twist Bail | 225.00 |
| **Cracker Jar,** Pink Fleurette Overlay, 6 1/2 In. | 210.00 |
| **Cracker Jar,** White To Yellow, Pink Blossoms, Silver Cover | 95.00 |
| **Cracker Jar,** White, Silver Plate Top, Hand-Painted Flowers | 85.00 |
| **Epergne,** Pink, Gold Plated Metal Mounting, 19 1/2 X 19 In. | 425.00 |
| **Epergne,** 4-Lily, Blue Quilted | 225.00 |
| **Ewer,** Applied Thorn Handle, Ruffled Top, Yellow & White, 13 In. | 265.00 |
| **Ewer,** Diamond-Quilted, Ribbed Handle, Light Blue, 9 In. | 325.00 |
| **Ewer,** Frosted Handles, Flowers, Coral Berries, Peach, 10 In., Pair | 195.00 |
| **Ewer,** Jack-In-The-Pulpit Shape, Frosted Thorn Handle, 6 In. | 90.00 |
| **Ewer,** Pink Herringbone, 8 In. | 485.00 |
| **Ewer,** Ruffled, Frosted Applied Handle, Yellow Garland, 10 In. | 95.00 |
| **Ewer,** Thorn Handle, Herringbone, Pink, 8 1/2 In. | 195.00 |
| **Ewer,** Tricorn, Ribbed Body, Coiled Handle, C.1880, 12 X 11 In. | 275.00 |
| **Ewer,** Twisted Handle, Pink Floral Front, 12 3/4 In. | 145.00 |
| **Jar,** Biscuit, Quilted, Pink, Silver Cover | 125.00 |
| **Jar,** Sweetmeat, Coralene, Opaque Ground, Beaded, Coral, 5 In. | 225.00 |
| **Lamp,** Basket Weave, Green, 2 1/4 In. | 65.00 |
| **Lamp,** Fairy, Brass Base, Pink, Maroon Lace Design, 8 In. | 295.00 |
| **Lamp,** Fairy, Diamond-Quilted, Cup Base, White Lining, 5 In. | 295.00 |
| **Lamp,** Fairy, Diamond-Quilted, 5 Feet, Frosted Raspberry | 265.00 |
| **Lamp,** Oil, Parlor, Brass Fittings, 21 In. | 400.00 |
| **Lamp,** Peg, Blue Swirl Mother-Of-Pearl, 20 1/4 In. | 600.00 |
| **Lamp,** 3 Owl Heads, Kerosene, Metal Base | 325.00 |
| **Pitcher & Bowl,** Red Tortoise Cased Interior, C.1880 | 175.00 |
| **Pitcher & Bowl,** Ruffled, Ribbed Bodies, Ruby Cased, C.1880 | 175.00 |
| **Pitcher,** Cut Velvet, Diamond-Quilted, Rose Pink, 3 1/4 In. | 245.00 |
| **Pitcher,** Diamond-Quilted, Apricot To White, 10 In. | 225.00 |
| **Pitcher,** Hobnail, Lemon Yellow, Pink Top, Amber Handle, 8 In. | 235.00 |
| **Pitcher,** Water, Blue, Pink, & Yellow Stripes, Lined | 195.00 |
| **Pitcher,** Water, Mother-Of-Pearl, Blue On White, 9 In. | 975.00 |
| **Pitcher,** 5 Tumblers, Apricot, Pitcher, 8 In. | 595.00 |
| **Rose Bowl,** Apricot, Cream & Blue Floral, Gold Foliage, 4 1/4 In. | 145.00 |
| **Rose Bowl,** Blue, Footed, 4 1/2 X 4 1/4 In. | 125.00 |
| **Rose Bowl,** Blue, Pansies Design, Footed, 5 1/4 In. | 145.00 |
| **Rose Bowl,** Blue, 4 1/2 In. | 125.00 |
| **Rose Bowl,** Blue, 5 1/2 In. | 68.00 |
| **Rose Bowl,** Cabbage Leaf Mold, Yellow Cased | 95.00 |
| **Rose Bowl,** Chartreuse Green, Ribbon Mother-Of-Pearl, 2 7/8 In. | 195.00 |
| **Rose Bowl,** Crimped, Blue, 3 1/2 In. | 45.00 |
| **Rose Bowl,** Crimped, Dimpled Sides, Pink, 4 In. | 45.00 |
| **Rose Bowl,** Egg Shape, 6 Clear Feet, Rose To Pink, 6 In. | 175.00 |

**Rose Bowl,** Enamel Design, 4 Young Girls, 10 3/4 In. .................................................................. 250.00
**Rose Bowl,** Enamel Mums, Blue ................................................................................................. 50.00
**Rose Bowl,** Frosted Feet, Pansies & Foliage, 4 Crimp, 5 1/4 In. ............................................. 145.00
**Rose Bowl,** Herringbone, Yellow, 6 In. .................................................................................... 30.00
**Rose Bowl,** Mother-Of-Pearl, Blue, 8 Crimp Top, 4 In. ........................................................... 100.00
**Rose Bowl,** Petal Feet, 8 Crimp, Apricot To Rose, 4 1/2 X 5 In. ............................................ 150.00
**Rose Bowl,** Shaded Apricot, Footed, 5 In. ............................................................................... 145.00
**Rose Bowl,** Shell & Seaweed, Green ............................................................. 125.00 To 155.00
**Rose Bowl,** Shell & Seaweed, Pink .......................................................................................... 158.00
**Rose Bowl,** Shell Pattern, Blue ................................................................................................ 130.00
**Rose Bowl,** Striped, Crimped, Underplate, 2 1/2 X 2 1/2 In. .................................................. 60.00
**Salt & Pepper,** Floral, Pink & White ........................................................................................ 25.00
**Salt & Pepper,** Original Lids, Red ............................................................................................ 125.00
**Salt & Pepper,** Wedding Bells ................................................................................................. 75.00
**Spooner,** Yellow, Quilted, Cased White Lining, Silver Top, 4 In. ............................................ 145.00
**Syrup,** Squatty, Cone, Pink ....................................................................................................... 150.00
**Tumbler,** Diamond-Quilted, Shading Pink To White, 4 In. ...................................................... 110.00
**Tumbler,** Mother-Of-Pearl, Pink To White, Diamond-Quilted ................................................ 112.00
**Tumbler,** White Enameled Flowers, Foliage, & Bird, Yellow ................................................... 95.00
**Vase,** Apricot, Pearl Diamonds, White Lining, 6 X 6 3/4 In. .................................................... 60.00
**Vase,** Black, Silver Deposit, 6 1/2 In. ....................................................................................... 165.00
**Vase,** Black, Trumpet Shape, 10 1/2 In. ................................................................................... 45.00
**Vase,** Blue, Raindrop Diamond Design, White Edge, 4 1/2 In. ............................................... 115.00
**Vase,** Blue, 9 1/4 X 7 In. .......................................................................................................... 325.00
**Vase,** Bulbous Base, Green Cut Velvet, 6 1/4 In. ..................................................................... 130.00
**Vase,** Bulbous, Pleated Top, Scroll, Green, Handled, 7 1/2 In. .............................................. 95.00
**Vase,** Bulge Body, Trumpet Top, Mushroom Base, Blue, 8 In. .............................................. 140.00
**Vase,** Butterscotch, Cased, Flat Bodies, 9 1/2 In. ................................................................... 165.00
**Vase,** Coralene Design, 9 1/4 In. .............................................................................................. 395.00
**Vase,** Diamond-Quilted, Frosted Wishbone Feet, 5 3/8 In. ................................................... 135.00
**Vase,** Diamond-Quilted, White Lining, Pink, 8 1/4 In. ............................................................ 195.00
**Vase,** Enameled Flowers & Leaves, 12 In. .............................................................................. 60.00
**Vase,** Enameled Woodland Scene, Purple & Gold Wreath, 7 1/2 In. ..................................... 50.00
**Vase,** Ewer Shape, Flowers, White Ground, Pair ................................................................... 75.00
**Vase,** Fluted, Melon Sectioned, Pink, Green Roses, 10 1/4 In., Pair ..................................... 195.00
**Vase,** Frosted Handles, Yellow Scrolls, 9 1/8 In., Pair ........................................................... 195.00
**Vase,** Green, Lavender Flowers, 11 In. .................................................................................... 75.00
**Vase,** Handled, Blue Quilted, Enameling, 4 In. ....................................................................... 375.00
**Vase,** Herringbone, Rose White, Cased, 6 1/2 In. .................................................................. 175.00
**Vase,** Herringbone, Ruffled, Frosted Edging, Enameled, 6 3/4 In. ....................................... 325.00
**Vase,** Hobnail, Yellow & Red, 19th Century, 2 1/2 In. ............................................................ 80.00
**Vase,** Melon Sectioned, Frosted Handle, White Lining, 12 1/2 In. ........................................ 265.00
**Vase,** Moire Pattern, Mother-Of-Pearl, Blue, 4 1/2 In. ........................................................... 175.00
**Vase,** Mother-Of-Pearl, American, C.1880, 7 In. ..................................................*Illus* 175.00
**Vase,** Mother-Of-Pearl, Bulbous Base, Apricot, 7 In. ............................................................. 155.00

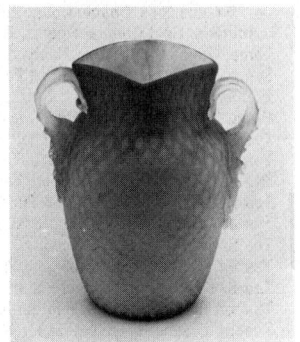

Satin Glass, Vase, Mother-Of-Pearl, American, C.1880, 7 In.

Vase, Mother-Of-Pearl, Diamond Pattern, C.1880, 10 3/8 In. ........................ 150.00
Vase, Mother-Of-Pearl, Ormolu Feet, White Lining, 6 7/8 In. ...................... 145.00
Vase, Mother-Of-Pearl, Pink, Ruffled, 6 1/2 In. ..................................... 225.00
Vase, Network Of Branches & Blossoms, Blue Cased, 11 In. ....................... 75.00
Vase, Peach Overlay, White Lining, Enameled Flowers, 9 In., Pair .............. 195.00
Vase, Picture Of Niagara Falls, Pink To Red, 8 In. .................................. 125.00
Vase, Pink, Flared & Ruffled Top, 10 In. ............................................. 30.00
Vase, Quilted, Blue, Fluted, White Lining, 4 In.Diam. ............................. 118.00
Vase, Rainbow Colors, Yellow Lining, 7 In. .......................................... 35.00
Vase, Ruffled Top, Pink Cut Velvet, 6 In. ............................................ 180.00
Vase, Ruffled, Shaded Blue Overlay, Frosted Handle, 14 1/2 In. ................ 195.00
Vase, White Enameled Flowers, Leaves, & Foliage, Blue, 7 In. .................. 125.00
Water Set, 2 Tumblers, Diamond-Quilted, Mother-Of-Pearl, Apricot ........... 450.00
    **SATIN GLASS, Webb, see Webb**

*Satsuma is a Japanese pottery with a distinctive creamy beige crackled glaze. Most of the pieces were decorated with blue, red, green, orange, or gold. Almost all the Satsuma found today was made after 1860. Japanese faces are often a part of the decorative scheme.*

**SATSUMA, Bottle,** Bulbous Top & Bottom, Oriental People, Gold Color, 6 In. ........... 375.00
Bottle, Elongated Neck, Gold Speckled Dragon, C.1830, 15 1/2 In. ................. 1790.00
Bottle, Feudal Lords, C.1890, 7 1/2 In. ................................................ 125.00
Bottle, Squat, 1885, 5 1/2 In. ........................................................... 110.00
Bowl, Bird On Bamboo Shoots, Covered, Handled, 5 1/2 In. ....................... 245.00
Bowl, Bird On Bamboo Shoots, Covered, 2-Handled, 4 1/2 X 3 1/2 In. ........... 190.00
Bowl, Cherry Blossoms, Thatched House, Bridge, People, 8 1/2 X 4 In. ......... 295.00
Box, Powder, Jeweling On Porcelain, Scene On Top .............................. 55.00
Button, 7 Gods Of Good Luck, Large, Set Of 3 ..................................... 75.00
Button, 7 Gods Of Good Luck, Medium, Set Of 3 ................................... 55.00
Chamberstick, Kinkozan, Florals, 1884 ............................................... 170.00
Charger, Oriental Florals, Bluebirds .................................................. 300.00
Chocolate Set, 6 Cups & Saucers, Gold Trim, 11 In. .............................. 175.00
Cup & Saucer, Allover Arhats, Dragon Wrapped Around Piece, Marked ....... 295.00
Cup & Saucer, 12 Seated Men On Cup, Dragon Face Handle, 1860-75 ......... 169.00
Dish, Medallion Of People, Footed, Covered, Handled, Marked, 5 In. .......... 595.00
Ewer, Moriage, People, Knotted Handle .............................................. 185.00
Goblet, Mother & Child, C.1925, 2 3/4 In. ............................................ 100.00
Hatpin, Flowers & Gold Trim, 1 1/2 In. ............................................... 75.00
Incense Burner, Ball Shaped, Mill Scene, 1920s, Signed, 6 In. .................. 370.00
Incense Burner, Blue, Bamboo Motif, 1930 .......................................... 120.00
Incense Burner, Enameled With Arhats, Lion-Dog Finial, Signed, 5 In. ....... 225.00
Incense Burner, Mother & Children, C.1910, 2 In. ................................. 125.00
Jar, Cracker, Chrysanthemum & Figural Design, C.1890, 6 1/2 In. ............. 195.00
Jar, Ginger, Oriental People, Cream & Gold, Signed, 4 In. ....................... 110.00
Jar, Medallions Of 50 Women & Warriors, 2 3/4 In. ............................... 275.00
Jar, 6 Medallions, Double Gourd Shape, Footed, Handled, 2 3/4 In. ........... 250.00
Jardiniere, Gold Oriental Figures, Teak Base, Covered, 16 X 12 In. .......... 1250.00
Lamp, Oriental Girl Riding Elephant, Gold Beading, 25 In. ...................... 150.00
Lamp, Pagoda Scene, Scalloped Panel, Clear, 6 3/4 In. .......................... 60.00
Pitcher, Warlords, Pedestal, 7 In. ..................................................... 179.00
Plate, Cherry Blossoms, Birds, Crackly, 9 3/4 In. ................................. 150.00
Tea Set, Blooming Flowers, Cobalt Blue, 15 Piece ................. 300.00 To 325.00
Tea Set, Dragon Head Spouts & Finials, White Beading, 15 Piece ............. 240.00
Tea Set, Gilded, Warrior Design, Teapot, Sugar, 2 Cups & Saucers ........... 185.00
Tea Set, Gold Dragon Spout & Finials, Beading, Enameled, 3 Piece .......... 185.00
Tea Set, Gold Dragon Spout, Crest, Oriental Figures, Marked, 3 Piece ....... 195.00
Tea Set, Gold Tree, 27 Piece ............................................................ 245.00
Tea Set, Kinkozan, 3 Piece ............................................................. 100.00
Tea Set, Thousand Flowers Pattern, Black Mark, 14 Piece ...................... 550.00
Teapot, Black Ground, Scenic Gardens, Gold Gilding, 4 1/2 In. ................ 60.00
Teapot, Dragon Handles & Spout, Miniature, 4 In. ................................ 600.00

Teapot, Gold Handles, House By Sea, Autumn Ivy, Mountains ............................................ 58.00
Teapot, Molded Dragon Spout, Oriental Figures, Circle Mark ........................................... 115.00
Teapot, Mums, Leaves, & Blossoms Outline In Gold, 7 3/4 In. ........................................ 85.00
Teapot, Mums, Red Leaves, Outlined In Gold, 4 1/4 In. ................................................... 85.00
Temple Burner, Bisque Peony Handles, Edo Period ..................................................... 3500.00
Tile, Flowers, C.1830, 3 X 3 In. ..................................................................................... 350.00
Toothpick, Owl On Log, 1900, 4 1/2 In. ......................................................................... 385.00
Tray, Peach Shape, Applied Leaves, Motif Of Elders, 13 1/2 In. ................................... 1575.00
Urn, Cobalt Blue, Gold Trim, Scene, Covered, 6 In. ......................................................... 75.00
Urn, Green Leaf Design, Overall Brown, 22 In. .............................................................. 450.00
Vase, Allover Design, Gold Trim, 18 In. .......................................................................... 135.00
Vase, Bamboo & Birds, 8 3/4 In. ..................................................................................... 350.00
Vase, Blue & Lavender Wisteria, 10 In. ........................................................................... 325.00
Vase, Blue & Pink Design, Sea Horse Handles, C.1900, 16 In. ....................................... 105.00
Vase, Children & Lady Panel, Chrysanthemums Back, 1860s, 24 1/2 In. ...................... 850.00
Vase, Children, C.1880, 3 3/4 In. ..................................................................................... 135.00
Vase, Crackle Glaze, Warrior With Mustache, Meiji Period, 10 In. ................................... 50.00
Vase, Cylindrical, Peonies & Cranes, Kinkozan, C.1840, 12 In. ................................... 1300.00
Vase, Double Gourd Shape, Deities & Dragon, 7 In. ....................................................... 225.00
Vase, Elongated Fingerhole Handles, Raised Figures, 18 In. .......................................... 225.00
Vase, Female Figure, Gold Dragon Handles, 10 In. ......................................................... 225.00
Vase, Foo Dog Handles, Flowers, Cream Ground, 9 1/2 In. .............................................. 65.00
Vase, Foo Dogs On Top Part, Dragon On Neck, Enameled, 15 1/2 In. ........................... 200.00
Vase, Geishas, Double Handled, C.1910, 12 In., Pair ..................................................... 195.00
Vase, Gold & White Flowers, 12 3/4 In. ........................................................................... 75.00
Vase, Hand-Painted Flowers, Raised Gold, Matte Ground, 15 1/2 In. ............................. 105.00
Vase, Holy Men & Elephant Molded In Relief, 13 1/2 In. ................................................. 300.00
Vase, Japanese Figures & Scenes In Panels, C.1860, Red Mark, Pair ........................... 365.00
Vase, Jesus, Moses, Dragons, Gold, 1860, 9 3/4 In. ....................................................... 620.00
Vase, Kinkozan, Peonies & Cranes, C.1840, 12 In. ..................................................... 1300.00
Vase, Ladies & Children, Cobalt Panels, C.1900, Signed, 4 3/4 In. ............................... 155.00
Vase, Lords & Ladies, Enameled, Rust, Cream, & Turquoise, 1800s, 18 In. .................. 300.00
Vase, Molded Figures In Panels, Scenic, C.1930, Signed, 12 1/2 In. ............................. 475.00
Vase, Moriage, Roses, 12 1/4 In. ..................................................................................... 130.00
Vase, Moriage, Scent On Front, Gold Trim, 15 1/4 In. .................................................... 150.00
Vase, Multicolor Designs, Blue Ground, 3 1/2 In. ........................................................... 195.00
Vase, Multicolor Flowers, 8-Sided, 6 In. ........................................................................... 95.00
Vase, Orange Design, Gold & Raised Enamels, 5 1/2 In., Pair ........................................ 65.00
Vase, Orange Flowers, Gold Outlined Green Leaves, Marked, 8 5/8 In. .......................... 325.00
Vase, Oriental Figures, Raised Gold & Enamel, 12 In. .................................................... 275.00
Vase, Painted Panels, Cobalt Blue Ground, 2 In. ............................................................. 25.00
Vase, Rust Design, Gold Overlay, C.1860, 22 In. ............................................................ 500.00
Vase, Scene On Both Sides, Blue Ground, 18 In. .............................................. 475.00 To 500.00
Vase, Scenes Overall, Tapestry, Gold Trim, 7 In., Pair .................................................... 550.00
Vase, Scenic Panels, Gold Design, 19th Century, 4 13/16 In., Pair ............................... 400.00
Vase, Sumari Warriors, Beading, 18 1/2 In. .................................................................... 195.00
Vase, Terra-Cotta & White, 19th Century, 10 X 12 In. .................................................... 145.00
Vase, Warlord Design, C.1900, 12 In., Pair ..................................................................... 185.00
Vase, Warriors In Battle, 25 In. ..................................................................................... 1800.00
Vase, Warriors Relaxing & Seated, Courtesans, 24 1/2 In. ............................................. 385.00
Vase, Wisteria & Birds, 7 1/2 In. ...................................................................................... 95.00
Vase, 19th-Century Warriors, 15 1/2 In., Pair ................................................................. 300.00
Vase, 4 Circular Panels, Each With Scene, 3 In., Pair ..................................................... 325.00
Vase, 6 Gold Halloed Men, Ornate, C.1920, 16 In. ......................................................... 140.00
Wall Pocket, Dragon Design, Raised Enamel Features, Brown, 8 1/2 In. ........................ 35.00

**SCALE, Apothecary,** American, All Weights ................................................................ 115.00
Apothecary, Henry Troemner ........................................................................................... 145.00
Apothecary, Marble Base, Copper Pans, 6 X 16 X 4 1/2 In. ............................................. 75.00
Army, Howe, Dated October 4, 1862 ............................................................................... 500.00
Baby, Wicker ..................................................................................................................... 48.00
Balance, Cupid Holding Arm With Hanging Trays, 6 1/2 In. ............................................. 35.00
Balance, Scrolled, Cast Iron ............................................................................................. 65.00

| | |
|---|---:|
| **Brass & Mahogany,** Weights, C.1825, 22 In. | 395.00 |
| **Butter,** Clothespin Top, Hangs From Beam, Handmade | 125.00 |
| **Butter,** Hangs From Beam, Wooden Arm & Platforms | 155.00 |
| **Candy,** Brass Tray, Cast Iron With Gilt Paint | 65.00 |
| **Candy,** Dayton, Brass Pan, 1906 | 115.00 |
| **Candy,** Toledo, Brass Scoop, 3 Pound | 65.00 |
| **Cockfight,** Weights | 65.00 |
| **Coin,** Balance, Weights, French, 1700s, Hinged Wooden Case | 175.00 |
| **Coin,** Fairbanks, Coin Slots, Brass Arm & Top, Patent 1879 | 65.00 |
| **Cotton,** Brass Face, Capacity 200 Pound | 45.00 |
| **Counter,** Railway Express Agency | 40.00 |
| **Counter,** Wolverine Corner Grocer | 125.00 |
| **Counting,** National, Brass | 275.00 |
| **Country Store,** Cast Iron & Brass | 40.00 |
| **Eastman Kodak,** 5 Weights | 85.00 |
| **Egg,** Sears, Roebuck | 15.00 |
| **Gold Dust,** 2 Pans, 5 Weights, Lined Box, Brass, 5 1/2 X 2 1/2 In. | 45.00 |
| **Gold,** Brass In Wood & Glass Box, Testing Kit | 250.00 |
| **Gold,** Brass Pans & Weights, C.1850, Oak Box | 75.00 |
| **Gold,** Tray Weights, C.1840, Brass, 11 X 13 In. | 340.00 |
| **Gold,** 2 Round Pans, Brass, Beam, 6 In. | 75.00 |
| **Grain,** Convert To Pounds Per Bushel, Corcoran Witt, London, 11 In. | 750.00 |
| **Guinea,** Signed Thos.Williams, London, Scale Maker, C.1800, 5 Weights | 750.00 |
| **Hanging,** Cylindrical, Weighs To 50 Pounds, Brass Face, Cast Iron | 17.00 |
| **Hanging,** Old Viding Jr., Model 890, 25 Pound | 9.50 |
| **Hanson Dairy,** 50 Pound | 22.00 |
| **Hardware,** Belmont, C.1900 | 7.00 |
| **Ice,** Springer Balancer, Brass Dial, Cast Iron | 8.50 |
| **Jeweler's,** Springer Balance Co., Dated 1882 | 48.00 |
| **Kitchen,** Old Kentucky Home, White Enamel | 17.50 |
| **Letter,** Clip, Ring & Weight, Brass | 22.00 |
| **Meat,** Spring Balance, 24 Pound, By Ounce, Enamel Pan | 35.00 |
| **Medical,** Wood, Ivory, & Brass, Chinese | 75.00 |
| **Milk,** Top & Bottom Hooks, Brass Face, Weighs To 60 Pounds, 13 In. | 79.00 |
| **Mills,** Cast Iron, 1908 | 1295.00 |
| **Money,** Cup Weights, Original Label, French | 240.00 |
| **Penny,** National, Cast Iron | 495.00 |
| **Pharmaceutical,** 2 Brass Pans, Oak Box, Cover, Troemner, 13 X 7 1/2 In. | 115.00 |
| **Platform,** Industrial, Brass & Wood On Wheels | 375.00 |
| **Platform,** 1 Cent, Which Way Are You Growing | 500.00 |
| **Postal,** Counterweighted With Brass, English, 12 In. | 550.00 |
| **Postal,** Standard, Brass Pan | 28.00 |
| **Postal,** Toledo, 1927, Brass Pan | 45.00 |
| **Questions & Answers,** Watling, Red & Yellow Porcelain | 295.00 |
| **Seed,** Trade Reporting Bureau, Chicago, Brass, 12 In.Long | 85.00 |
| **Silver,** 200 Troy Ounce, Brass, English, 12 1/2 In. | 50.00 |
| **Spring,** Excelsior, Brass Faced, Hanging | 12.00 |
| **Steelyard,** Complete Weights & Hooks, Iron | 22.00 |
| **Torsion Balance,** Glass Case, Oak Stand | 300.00 |
| **Watling,** Horoscope, Side Crank | 295.00 |
| **Weight,** Fortune-Telling Watling | 125.00 |
| **2 Suspended Trays,** Eagle On Top Ribbed Column, Silver Plate, 15 In. | 115.00 |

*Schafer & Vater, makers of small ceramic items, are best known for their amusing figurals. The factory was located in Volkstedt, Germany, from 1890 to 1917.*

| | |
|---|---:|
| **SCHAFER & VATER, Ashtray,** Figural, Lady In Bed, Humorous, Signed, 3 1/2 In. | 85.00 |
| **Bottle,** What A Night, Signed, 6 In. | 55.00 |
| **Box,** Lobster, Covered, Orange, Signed, 5 In.Long | 55.00 |

| | |
|---|---|
| **Creamer,** Dutch Boy's Head, Blue Glaze, 3 1/2 In. | 35.00 |
| **Creamer,** Figural, Impish Santa Clause, 4 In. | 95.00 |
| **Creamer,** Maid With Fan, Blue Glaze, Signed, 3 1/2 In. | 45.00 |
| **Creamer,** Oriental With Bird, Signed, 3 1/2 In. | 45.00 |
| **Figurine,** Children In Big Chair, Humorous, Signed, 3 In. | 85.00 |
| **Figurine,** Scotsman, Humorous, Multicolor, 5 1/2 In. | 65.00 |
| **Match Holder,** Figural, Dancing Couple, Signed, 4 1/4 In. | 115.00 |
| **Match Holder,** Figural, Fat Man In Chair, Signed, 3 In. | 85.00 |
| **Mug,** Advertising, Houtens Hot Chocolate, Signed, 3 In. | 55.00 |
| **Nodder,** Little Boy Holding Up Bathing Suit, Signed, 4 In. | 95.00 |
| **Planter,** Blown-Out Comical Cat, Duck's Head, 5 X 4 In. | 65.00 |

*Schneider*

*Schneider Glassworks was founded in 1903 at Epinay-sur-Seine, France, by Charles and Ernest Schneider. Art glass was made between 1903 and 1930. The company still produces clear crystal glass.*

| | |
|---|---|
| **SCHNEIDER, Bowl,** Blue, Ribbed, Red Flecks, Chalice, Signed, 9 X 6 In. | 125.00 |
| **Bowl,** Centerpiece, Iron Mounted, Red To Yellow, Signed, 10 In.Diam. | 295.00 |
| **Bowl,** Shallow, Signed, 6 In. | 150.00 |
| **Bowl,** Smoky Topaz, Wrought-Iron Frame, Signed, 5 1/2 X 3 1/4 In. | 225.00 |
| **Bulb Bowl,** Cherry Red & Yellow, Signed | 115.00 |
| **Compote,** Amethyst Stem, Mottled Orange Center, Signed, 8 In. | 165.00 |
| **Compote,** Footed, Red, Black, & Purple With Gold Trim, Signed | 185.00 |
| **Compote,** Purple, Blue, & Brown, Signed, 12 In.Diam. | 175.00 |
| **Ewer,** Multicolored Pink, White Flakings, Amethyst Handle, 6 In. | 355.00 |
| **Plate,** Cameo Ribs, Acid Panels, Purple To Clear, Signed, 18 In. | 375.00 |
| **Plate,** Orange, Yellow, Amethyst, Signed, Round, 16 In. | 175.00 |
| **Rose Bowl,** Yellow Satin Glass | 100.00 |
| **Tray,** Mottled Orange, Blue, & Yellow, Signed, 16 In.Diam. | 150.00 |
| **Vase,** Applied Clear Design, Amethyst Foot, Bubble, Signed, 15 In. | 275.00 |
| **Vase,** Bulb, Yellow & Cherry Red, Signed | 135.00 |
| **Vase,** Clear Over Blue, Red Cased, Signed, 8 3/4 In. | 150.00 |
| **Vase,** Lavender, Blue, Lemon, 11 In. | 385.00 |
| **Vase,** Mottled Frosted Pinks, Yellow, Orange, Signed, 17 In. | 345.00 |
| **Vase,** Mottled Pinks & Yellow, Signed, 7 1/4 In. | 285.00 |
| **Vase,** Pillow Shaped, Pink, Yellow, & Amethyst, Signed, 7 1/4 In. | 322.00 |
| **Vase,** Pink Ground, Yellow Mottling, Signed, 7 1/4 In. | 325.00 |
| **Vase,** Pink, Yellow, Amethyst, Pillow Shaped, Signed, 7 In. | 322.00 |

*Scrimshaw is bone or ivory or whale's teeth carved by sailors and others for entertainment during the sailing-ship days. Some scrimshaw was carved as early as 1800.*

**SCRIMSHAW, see also Nautical**

| | |
|---|---|
| **SCRIMSHAW, Club,** Arctic Scene, Polar Bears, Eskimos, Seals, Map, 20 1/2 In. | 350.00 |
| **Elephant Tusk,** Eagle Head, Abalone Inlay, Whaling Scenes, 33 In. | 1200.00 |
| **Holder,** Cigarette, Ivory | 65.00 |
| **Ivory,** Bracelet & Earrings, Gold Nuggets, Walrus Tusk Ring, Set | 37.50 |
| **Plaque,** Profile Of Whale, 2 Harpoons, Inscribed Cuttings, 10 In. | 300.00 |
| **Stick,** Walking, Whale Form Handle, Gold Inset Eyes, 2 Ft.10 In. | 600.00 |
| **Turtle Shell,** Flags, Eagle, Washington, Mottos, Signed, 24 X 18 In. | 3000.00 |
| **Tusk,** Elevation Map At St.George's Island | 150.00 |
| **Vase,** Flowers, Rigged Ship, Whales, Vine Border, 8 In., Pair | 550.00 |
| **Walrus Tusk,** Theatrical Figures, 5 Point Star, 2 Ft., Pair | 1400.00 |
| **Walrus Tusk,** Whaling Scene, Signed Nantucket 1838, 13 1/2 In. | 385.00 |
| **Whale's Tooth,** Boat, Ship, Freedom, C.1700, 5 In. | 675.00 |
| **Whale's Tooth,** Early Sailing Ship | 220.00 |
| **Whale's Tooth,** Erotic, Man Looking Through Telescope, 6 1/2 In. | 400.00 |
| **Whale's Tooth,** Philadelphia Harbor, Tricolor | 900.00 |
| **Whale's Tooth,** The Royal George, King George III | 395.00 |
| **1831 Between 2 Flags,** The Comet Under Whale At Top, 6 1/4 In. | 129.00 |

SCUTTLE MUG, see Shaving Mug, Scuttle
SEG, see Paul Revere Pottery

 Sevres porcelain has been made in Sevres, France, since 1769. Many copies of the famous ware have been made. The name originally referred to the works of the Royal factory. The name now includes any of the wares made in the town of Sevres, France.

SEVRES, Bowl, Gilded Bronze Mounting, Pedestal, Courting Scene, 10 1/2 In. ...................... 450.00
Box, Chateau De St.Cloud, Cherubs, Blue, Dated, Royal Cipher ................................ 275.00
Box, Clasp Of 2 Leaves, Scenic, Coin Gold Trim, Marked, 5 3/4 In.Diam. ................. 335.00
Box, Man & Woman On Top, Coin Gold Sides, Blue Mark, 5 3/4 In.Diam. .................. 335.00
Bust, Louis XVI, Enameled, C.1900, 11 1/2 In. ................................................ 175.00
Cake Stand, 2-Tier, Hand-Painted Gold & Flowers, Signed, 14 In. ......................... 695.00
Candelabra, Louis XIV, Soft Paste, Signed Leroy, 9 7/8 In. ............................... 215.00
Casket, Jewelry, Footed, Watteau Design, Signed, 6 1/2 X 4 1/4 X 4 In. ................ 475.00
Cup & Saucer, Cupid On Cloud Scrolls, C.1765, Green Ground .......................... 750.00
Cup & Saucer, Cylindrical, Cornflower & Rose Sprays, C.1787, Signed ................. 350.00
Cup & Saucer, Flowers, Portrait, Celeste Blue ............................................. 150.00
Cup & Saucer, Rose, Cupids .................................................................. 75.00
Cup, Cherubs, Gold Tracery, 1836 Royal Mark ............................................ 60.00
Dish, Blue Celeste, Shell Form, Maiden, Basket, Marked, 8 1/2 In. ..................... 500.00
Dish, Sweetmeat, Lovers Scene In Bowl, Insert, 6 X 6 In., Pair .......................... 160.00
Humidor, Covered, Arcaded Panels, Gilding, C.1765, L Mark, 6 1/4 In. ................. 2200.00
Jug, Cream, Pear Shape, Berried Foliage, Branch Handle, C.1770, L Mark ............ 350.00
Lamp, Base, Parian, Brass Mounted & Fitted, 19th Century, 19 In. ..................... 690.00
Plaque, Marie Antoinette, Gilt Border, Blue Ground, 9 In. ............................... 325.00
Plate, Center Fruit & Flower Spray, C.1770, L Mark, 9 3/4 In. ........................... 480.00
Plate, Chateau De St.Cloud, Signed, 9 1/2 In. ............................................ 150.00
Plate, Chateau De Versailles, Blue, Gold Rim, 1846, Signed, 8 1/4 In. ................. 150.00
Plate, Josephine, Scalloped Gold Rim, Medallions, Signed, 9 1/2 In. ................... 225.00
Plate, Napoleon, Laurel Wreath In Gold, Signed .......................................... 125.00
Plate, Pastoral Scene, Gold Border, Robin's Egg Blue, 11 X 7 1/2 In. .................. 300.00
Plate, Portrait, Duc De Bourgogne, Hand-Painted, Signed, 9 1/2 In. .................... 195.00
Plate, Portrait, Josephine, Gold Tracery, 9 1/2 In. ....................................... 150.00
Plate, Portrait, Madame De Lavalliere, Hand-Painted, Signed, 9 1/2 In. ............... 195.00
Plate, Portrait, Madame Du Barry, Gold Tracery, 9 1/2 In. .............................. 150.00
Plate, Portrait, Madame Elisabeth, Gold Tracery, 9 1/2 In. ............................. 150.00
Plate, Portrait, Marie Louise, Gold Border, Marked 1856 ................................ 125.00
Plate, Portrait, Signed Debrie, Chateau & 1848 Mark .................................... 160.00
Sauceboat, Gold Trim, C.1850, Napoleonic Monogram, 11 In., Pair ..................... 350.00
Saucer, Demitasse, Portrait, Silver Overlay, 1844, Signed .............................. 235.00
Urn, Bullet Shape, Domed Lids, Rosebud Medallions, 13 1/2 In., Pair .................. 750.00
Urn, Covered, Amphora Shaped, Gold Designs, Signed, 26 1/2 In. ...................... 425.00
Urn, Covered, Gilded Bronze Mountings, 16 In. ........................................... 250.00
Urn, Covered, Ormolu Frame, Artist Signed, 8 1/2 In. ................................... 290.00
Urn, Gilt Bronze, Amorous Couple, Covered, 18 In., Pair ............................... 1000.00
Urn, Romantic Scene Medallion, Cobalt Blue & Gold, 15 1/2 In., Pair .................. 625.00
Vase, Brown At Bottom, Shading To Yellow, Gold Trim, Dated 1887, 6 In. ............. 135.00
Vase, Brown Shading To Beige, 8 X 6 In.Diam. ........................................... 225.00
Vase, Drawstring Pouch, Floral Wreaths, Gold Trim, C.1890, 4 In. ..................... 155.00
Vase, Empress Josephine Bust Medallion, Gold Handles, 8 3/4 In. ..................... 125.00
Vase, Gilt, Bronze Mounted, Maiden Spinning Thread, Cupids, 15 In. .................. 450.00
Vase, Jeweled, Bronze, Trumpet Form, Nymphs, Dolphin, Blue, 10 In. ................. 450.00
Vase, Portrait & Champleve At Top & Base, 9 1/2 In., Pair ............................... 425.00
Vase, Woman Sitting In Field, Pedestal, Ormolu Trim, Signed, 6 In. .................... 145.00
Writing Set, 3 Inkwells, Birds & Flowers, Marked ..............................*Illus* 1100.00

Sewer tile figures were made by workers in the sewer tile factories in the Ohio area during the late nineteenth and early twentieth centuries.

SEWER TILE, Cowboy Boot, 2 3/4 X 3 1/2 In. ............................................ 35.00

Sevres, Writing Set, 3 Inkwells, Birds & Flowers, Marked

| | |
|---|---|
| **Figurine,** Duck | 55.00 |
| **Figurine,** Head | 45.00 |
| **Figurine,** Pig | 125.00 |
| **Jug** | 110.00 |
| **Planter,** Brown Glaze Sculptured Tree Trunk, Ohio, 4 X 6 In. | 60.00 |
| | |
| **SEWING, Basket,** Armadillo, Silk Crepe Lining | 50.00 |
| **Basket,** Fitted Round Top, Wicker, 12 In.Top, Tapers To 7 In.Bottom | 28.00 |
| **Basket,** Holds Pincushion, Needle Case, Crochet Hook | 28.00 |
| **Basket,** Standing, Wicker, 29 In. | 150.00 |
| **Basket,** Woven Reed, 11 1/2 In.Diam. | 20.00 |
| **Bird,** C.1740, English, Cast Iron | 140.00 |
| **Bird,** Carved Ivory, No Pincushion | 125.00 |
| **Bird,** Clamp-On, 1800s, Steel | 175.00 |
| **Bird,** Embossed Brass, Maroon Double Felt Cushion | 110.00 |
| **Bird,** Embossed Brass, Velvet Pincushion, Clamp | 95.00 |
| **Bird,** 2-Cushion, Brass, Large | 80.00 |
| **Bird,** 2-Cushion, Dated 1853, Embossed Brass | 60.00 |
| **Box,** Cradle Style, Wooden | 15.00 |
| **Box,** Needle, Carved Wooden Cover, Silk Lined, C.1870, 2 1/2 In. | 45.00 |
| **Box,** Thread, J. & P.Coats, Advertising Under Lid, 5 1/4 X 3 1/2 In. | 15.00 |
| **Box,** Wallpaper Covered, Wooden | 86.00 |
| **Box,** Wicker, 9 In.Diam. | 10.00 |
| **Case,** Japanned Scenes, Ivory Fittings, Lacquered, 14 X 6 1/2 In. | 400.00 |
| **Case,** Needle, Boyde, Slide Type, Metal | 5.00 |
| **Case,** Needle, Carved Man On Pedestal | 30.00 |
| **Case,** Needle, Chessman Shape, Pincushion Top, Wooden, 6 1/2 In. | 22.00 |
| **Case,** Needle, Ivory, C.1850, 2 1/2 In. | 22.00 |
| **Case,** Needle, Selector, Holder Stand, Germany, Wooden | 15.00 |
| **Case,** Needle, Worcester Iodized Salt, Cardboard | 6.00 |
| **Case,** Thimble, Egg Shape, Brass | 60.00 |
| **Darner,** Ebony With Sterling Handle | 28.00 |
| **Darner,** Foot Form, Patented | 12.50 |
| **Darner,** Glove, Marbleized | 9.50 |
| **Darner,** Green, Glass | 27.50 |
| **Darner,** Marbleized, Sterling Handle, 6 In. | 29.00 |
| **Darner,** Sock, Sterling Silver Handle | 35.00 |
| **Darner,** Toadstool Shape, Wooden | 4.50 |
| **Darner,** Umbrella | 14.50 |
| **Darner,** Wheel, Metal Band, Dated 1900 | 16.00 |
| **Dish,** Shell Shaped, Sterling Silver | 55.00 |
| **Doll,** Pincushion, Colonial Lady, Germany, 1 1/2 In. | 25.00 |

**Footstool,** Sewing Compartment, Queen Anne, C.1925 .................................................... 29.50
**Iron,** Fluting, Shepard Hardware, 1880, 3 Piece .......................................................... 38.00
**Kit,** Advertising, Lydia Pinkham ................................................................................ 25.00
**Lacer,** Ribbon, Sterling Silver ..................................................................................... 23.00
**Machine,** Black Paint Design, Claw Feet, 19th Century, 11 X 7 X 9 In. ................. 100.00
**Machine,** Child's, Gateway, Tin .................................................................................. 11.00
**Machine,** Child's, German, 7 In. ................................................................................ 15.00
**Machine,** 1875 Victor, Walnut ................................................................................... 150.00
**Needle,** Knitting, Basse-Taile On Sterling Top, Celluloid, Pair ................................. 8.00
**Pattern,** Dressmaker's, Adjustable, McKowell Co., Patent 1886, Brass ................. 150.00
    **SEWING, PINCUSHION, see also Pincushion Doll**
**Pincushion,** Beadwork, American Flag, Indian ......................................................... 28.00
**Pincushion,** Figural, Canoe Set In Waves, 6 1/2 In.Long ......................................... 16.00
**Pincushion,** Figural, Duck ........................................................................................... 4.50
**Pincushion,** Figural, Elephant & Camel, Pair ........................................................... 8.50
**Pincushion,** Figural, Sitting Pig, Silver Plate ........................................................... 45.00
**Pincushion,** Heart, Sterling ....................................................................................... 60.00
**Pincushion,** Lace ........................................................................................................ 20.00
**Pincushion,** Lady's Boot Shape, Beaded Bird Sitting On Branch ............................. 45.00
**Pincushion,** Pennsylvania Amish .............................................................................. 70.00
**Pincushion,** Pink, Pale Green, Beige, Amish, Handmade ......................................... 26.00
**Pincushion,** Shoe Shape, Red Celluloid, 3 1/2 X 2 3/4 In. ..................................... 6.95
**Pincushion,** Strawberry Shape, Sterling Silver Top, 3 In. ......................................... 23.50
**Pincushion,** Swan, Pewter, 3 1/2 In. ........................................................................ 25.00
**Pincushion,** 6-Pointed Star, Victorian Needlework, 7 1/4 In.Square ....................... 30.00
**Pinking Device,** Clamp-On ....................................................................................... 15.00
**Scissors,** American, 18th Century, Wrought-Iron ...................................................... 22.00
**Scissors,** Bird Shape, Blades Are Beak, Handle Is Body, 4 In. ................................. 20.00
**Scissors,** Embroidery, Floral Sterling Handles ......................................................... 15.00
**Scissors,** Figural Shoes In Handle, Star Brand Shoes Are Better .............................. 30.00
**Scissors,** Figural, Stork, Germany ............................................... 15.00 To 25.00
**Scissors,** Floral Design, Sterling Silver ..................................................................... 27.50
**Shuttle,** Tatting, Celluloid ......................................................................................... 10.00
**Shuttle,** Tatting, Metal, Scroll Design ....................................................................... 15.00
**Shuttle,** Wooden, Loom, 12 In., Set Of 6 ................................................................ 40.00
**Stand,** Wicker ............................................................................................................ 115.00
**Tape Measure,** Abbot's Ice Cream, Milkmaid & Pail, Celluloid .............................. 8.50
**Tape Measure,** Advertising, Whitehead Metal, Tin .................................................. 4.00
**Tape Measure,** Angelus Marshmallow ...................................................................... 27.50
**Tape Measure,** Cat On Each Side, Celluloid, 1 1/2 In. Diam. ................................. 23.50
**Tape Measure,** Celluloid Flower Basket, Germany, 1 3/4 X 1 1/2 In. ..................... 26.00
**Tape Measure,** Celluloid, Asbury Park, Sailboat Races ........................................... 21.00
**Tape Measure,** Dutch Children Scene, German Celluloid ........................................ 35.00
**Tape Measure,** Embossed Cat's Head, Glass Eyes, Brass, 1 1/2 In. ....................... 35.00
**Tape Measure,** Figural Salt Dip, Brass ..................................................................... 38.00
**Tape Measure,** Figural, Apple .................................................................................. 12.00
**Tape Measure,** Figural, Buffalo, Nickel Plated ........................................................ 26.00
**Tape Measure,** Figural, Clamshell ............................................................................ 55.00
**Tape Measure,** Figural, Fishing Reel, Wood & Brass ............................................... 55.00
**Tape Measure,** Figural, Hat ...................................................................................... 35.00
**Tape Measure,** Figural, High Shoe, Brass ................................................................ 38.50
**Tape Measure,** Figural, Hoover Vacuum Sweeper ......................... 15.00 To 20.00
**Tape Measure,** Figural, Indian, Celluloid Face, Blanket Warp ................................. 18.00
**Tape Measure,** Figural, Lady, German ............................................ 27.00 To 30.00
**Tape Measure,** Figural, Owl ..................................................................................... 25.00
**Tape Measure,** Figural, Pig, Celluloid ...................................................................... 20.00
**Tape Measure,** Figural, Pig, With Winding Tail, Metal ............................................ 55.00
**Tape Measure,** Figural, Poodle, Winding Tail, Brass ................................................ 65.00
**Tape Measure,** Figural, Shoe, Silver Plate, Three In One Shoe ............................... 18.00
**Tape Measure,** Figural, Spiked Helmet, Spike Rewinds Tap ............ 100.00 To 125.00
**Tape Measure,** Figural, Straw Hat, Embossed Words On Top .................................. 65.00
**Tape Measure,** Figural, Turtle, Pull My Head .......................................................... 35.00
**Tape Measure,** Flags, Liberty Bell, Celluloid, 1776-1926 ....................................... 45.00

| | |
|---|---|
| **Tape Measure,** Hawk Work Clothes, Picture Of Hawk | 15.00 |
| **Tape Measure,** Kansas City Life Insurance | 12.50 |
| **Tape Measure,** Lewis Lye | 20.00 |
| **Tape Measure,** Morrell Meat, Plastic, Round | 12.00 |
| **Tape Measure,** Pincushion Doll, Mammy, 1930s, Japan | 12.00 |
| **Tape Measure,** Pittsburgh Paint, Celluloid | 4.75 |
| **Tape Measure,** Pyramid Shape, Insert Of Girl, Gold Colored Metal | 24.00 |
| **Tape Measure,** Robin Hood Flour | 20.00 |
| **Tape Measure,** Souvenir, Spring Valley, Wisc., Celluloid | 7.00 |
| **Tape Measure,** Taylor Trousers, Newton, Iowa, Metal, Round | 9.00 |
| **Thimble Holder,** Acorn Shape, Floral & Foliage Design, Sterling | 75.00 |
| **Thimble,** Anne Hathaway, Original Cottage Box | 15.00 |
| **Thimble,** Buick, Aluminum | 3.00 |
| **Thimble,** Coin Silver, Band Of Houses | 35.00 |
| **Thimble,** Greek Key Border, 10K Gold | 75.00 To 85.00 |
| **Thimble,** Indiana Coffee Co., Milwaukee, Aluminum | 1.50 |
| **Thimble,** Old Gold, 14K | 60.00 |
| **Thimble,** Raised Design Of Berries & Leaves, Sterling Silver | 24.00 |
| **Thimble,** Raised Scroll Border, 14K Gold | 90.00 To 100.00 |
| **Thimble,** Scroll Border, Sterling Silver | 22.00 |
| **Thimble,** Sterling Silver & 14K Gold, Etched | 50.00 |
| **Thimble,** Sterling Silver, Border Fleur-De-Lis, 6 Stones, Mark 800 | 65.00 |
| **Thimble,** Sterling Silver, Diamond Band, Size 10 | 21.00 |
| **Thimble,** Sterling Silver, Engraved M.R. | 22.50 |
| **Thimble,** Sterling Silver, Engraved Wide Band, Beaded Rim, Size 9 | 25.00 |
| **Thimble,** Sterling Silver, Plain | 7.50 To 18.00 |
| **Thimble,** Sterling Silver, Sailor, Open End, Scroll Band, Size 8 | 15.00 |
| **Thimble,** Sterling Silver, Scalloped & Scroll Opening, Size 10 | 20.00 |
| **Thimble,** Sterling Silver, Scotch Thistle | 32.00 |
| **Thimble,** Sterling Silver, Scroll & Dotting Band, Beaded Edge, Size 12 | 18.00 |
| **Thimble,** Sterling Silver, Tudor Rose | 32.00 |
| **Thimble,** Sterling Silver, Westminster Abbey & Tudor Rose | 32.50 |
| **Thimble,** Sterling Silver, Wide Floral Band, Size 10 | 21.00 |
| **Thimble,** Sterling Silver, With Thread Cutter | 12.00 |
| **Thimble,** Tailor's, Open End | 4.50 |
| **Thimble,** Wide Band Scrollwork, 14K Gold | 45.00 |
| **Thimble,** 14K Gold Border | 110.00 |
| **Thread Holder,** Figural, Greenaway Type Figure With Bonnet, Brass | 28.00 |
| **Thread Holder,** Round Robin, Celluloid, Holds 6 | 8.00 |
| **Thread Holder,** 3 Tiers, 5-Spool Holder, 3 Scrolled Feet, Brass, 12 In. | 320.00 |

*Shaker-produced items are characterized by simplicity, functionalism, and orderliness. There were many Shaker communities in America from the eighteenth century to the present day.*

| | |
|---|---|
| **SHAKER, Basket,** Carrier Type, Rectangular, 12 X 18 In. | 265.00 |
| **Basket,** Cheese, Dark Greenish Blue Paint, 14 In.Diam. | 265.00 |
| **Basket,** Cheese, Hexagonal Weave, Dark Blue Paint, 14 In.Diam. | 245.00 |
| **Basket,** Cheese, Narrow Splint, Hexagonal Weave, 9 3/4 In.Diam. | 190.00 |
| **Basket,** Covered, Round, 2 1/2 X 3 In., Square, 2 1/4 X 3 In., Pair | 140.00 |
| **Basket,** Covered, Side Handles, Woven Blue Bands, 7 1/2 In. | 75.00 |
| **Basket,** Covered, Woven, 2 1/2 X 3 In.Diam. | 135.00 |
| **Basket,** Double Wrap Top, Laced Splint Bottom, Handle, 10 1/4 In. | 95.00 |
| **Basket,** Feather, Top Handle, Attached Lid, 7 In.Diam. | 75.00 |
| **Basket,** Grayish Brown Splint, Star Bottom, 5 X 8 1/2 In.Diam. | 26.00 |
| **Basket,** H Stiffeners On Bottom, Rectangular, 21 X 16 X 10 In. | 200.00 |
| **Basket,** Handle, Crisscross Lacing, Star Bottom, Maine, 10 In. | 95.00 |
| **Basket,** Handle, Double Wrap Top, Star Bottom, Enfield, N.H., 15 1/2 In. | 125.00 |
| **Basket,** Handle, Nut Brown, Star Bottom, Chas.Drummond, 11 1/2 In. | 95.00 |
| **Basket,** Handle, Single Wrap Round Top, Openwork Square Bottom, 9 In. | 74.00 |
| **Basket,** Narrow Splint Top Handle, Blue Band, 6 In. | 65.00 |
| **Basket,** Open, Palm Leaf, Pleasant Hill, Kentucky, 6-Sided, 6 3/4 In. | 45.00 |

**Basket,** Open, Side Handles, 13 1/2 In. .................................................................................... 45.00
**Basket,** Sewing, Splint, Blue Satin Liner, Needle Case, Beeswax ................................. 60.00
**Basket,** Side Handle, Star Bottom, Splint Sides, Red Stain, 8 1/2 In. ........................... 85.00
**Basket,** Similar To Goose Basket Shape, 5 1/4 In. ............................................................. 65.00
**Basket,** Storage, Narrow Splints & Ribs, Carved Handles, C.1800, 18 In. ................... 145.00
**Basket,** Storage, Pumpkin Shape, 3 Coats Of Paint, 12 1/2 X 10 3/4 In. .................... 125.00
**Basket,** Swing Handle, Dark Color, 12 X 12 In. ................................................................. 130.00
**Basket,** Swing Handle, 13 In.Diam. ....................................................................................... 138.00
**Basket,** Top Handle, Corners Woven To Make Feet, 7 1/2 In. ...................................... 65.00
**Basket,** Top Handle, Double Strap Top, Enfield, N.H., 15 1/2 In. .................................. 125.00
**Basket,** Top Handle, Enfield, N.H. ......................................................................................... 125.00
**Basket,** Top Handles, Crisscross Weave Edge, 12 In., Pair ........................................... 135.00
**Beater,** Rug, 41 1/4 In. ............................................................................................................ 65.00
**Bonnet Stand,** With 2 Bonnets ............................................................................................. 175.00
**Bonnet,** Woven Straw ............................................................................................................. 65.00
**Bottle,** Open Pontil, Marked Canterbury, N.H., Aqua Glass, 7 In. ................................ 67.00
**Box,** Carved, Initials A.I. McB ................................................................................................ 295.00
**Box,** Cheese, Buttonhole Lap, 14 1/2 In. ............................................................................. 110.00
**Box,** Cheese, Lap, Buttonhole, 12 In.Diam. ......................................................................... 155.00
**Box,** Cheese, Lap, Buttonhole, 14 3/4 In.Diam. .................................................................. 165.00
**Box,** Copper Nails, Oval ......................................................................................................... 120.00
**Box,** Copper Nails, Wood Pins, 2-Fingered Bottom, Lid, 10 In.Diam. .......................... 295.00
**Box,** Glove, Woven Poplar, Sabbathday Lake, Maine, 12 1/4 In. .................................. 105.00
**Box,** Harvard, V-Lap, Oval, Never Painted, 6 1/8 In. ......................................................... 68.00
**Box,** Harvard, V-Lap Top & Bottom, Brown, 2 In.Diam. ................................................... 35.00
**Box,** Harvard, V-Lap Top & Bottom, Brown, 4 1/2 In. ....................................................... 55.00
**Box,** Harvard, V-Lap Top & Bottom, Uneven Headed Nails, 7 7/8 In. .......................... 60.00
**Box,** Knife, Bentwood ............................................................................................................. 65.00
**Box,** Knife, Wooden ................................................................................................................. 65.00
**Box,** Knife, 13 X 8 1/4 In. ........................................................................................................ 65.00
**Box,** Natural Finish, Oval, 6 1/2 In. ...................................................................................... 85.00
**Box,** Original Gray Paint, Oval, 6 1/2 In. .............................................................................. 90.00
**Box,** Oval, 6 1/2 In. .................................................................................................................. 150.00
**Box,** Oval, 10 1/4 X 7 In. ......................................................................................................... 225.00
**Box,** Pantry, Covered In Early Wallpaper, Green & White, 5 7/8 In. ............................ 85.00
**Box,** Pantry, Cut Nails, Harvard, 4 1/2 In.Diam. ................................................................. 50.00
**Box,** Pantry, Dark Blue Paint, Oval, 6 1/8 In. ...................................................................... 85.00
**Box,** Pantry, Dark Green Paint, Round, 7 In. ...................................................................... 68.00
**Box,** Pantry, Double Hinged Bottom, Copper Tacks, Oval, 5 1/4 In. ............................ 98.00
**Box,** Pantry, Harvard, Orange Paint Over Gray, 6 1/2 In.Diam. ..................................... 70.00
**Box,** Pantry, V-Lap, 6 1/4 In.Diam. ...................................................................................... 58.00
**Box,** Pantry, V-Lap Top & Bottom, Harvard, Oval, 6 1/4 In. .......................................... 65.00
**Box,** Spice, 6 Drawer, Porcelain Knobs ............................................................................. 275.00
**Box,** Trinket, Sabbath Day Lake, Poplar ............................................................................. 50.00
**Box,** Utensil, Double Section, Center Handle, Hickory, 12 3/4 X 8 In. ......................... 115.00
**Box,** 3 Fingers, Oval, 10 In. .................................................................................................. 275.00
**Broadcaster,** Seed, Chest Type ........................................................................................... 40.00
**Brush,** Clothes ......................................................................................................................... 28.00
**Brush,** Shaving ........................................................................................................................ 22.50
**Bucket,** Bail Handle, Red Outside, White Inside, 4 1/2 In. .............................................. 75.00
**Bucket,** Cover, Original Gray, 10 In. ................................................................................... 48.00
**Bucket,** Sugar .......................................................................................................................... 40.00
**Chest,** Tabletop, Alligatored, Old Red, 18 X 8 X 12 1/2 In. ............................................ 250.00
**Dipper,** Painted Black, Tin ..................................................................................................... 26.00
**Dustpan,** Original Finish, Tin, 16 In. .................................................................................... 55.00
**Firkin,** Buttonhole Laps, Handle, Old Red, 9 1/2 In. ......................................................... 75.00
          **SHAKER, FURNITURE, see Furniture**
**Hoop,** Embroidery, Screws On Table, Maine ..................................................................... 68.00
**Label,** Family Pill, Cure Sick Headache, 3 X 5 In. ............................................................. 50.00
**Lamp,** Tin, 8 X 5 3/4 In.Diam. ............................................................................................... 115.00
**Pegboard,** 6 Shirt Pegs, 38 In. ............................................................................................. 100.00
**Pincushion,** White & Maroon Check, Sabbathday Lake ................................................. 35.00

| | |
|---|---|
| **Rolling Pin,** Clothespin-Type Knobs, 19 1/4 In. | 35.00 |
| **Shawl,** Dark Gray & Black | 65.00 |
| **Sieve,** Horsehair, Bound 2-Hoop, Copper Nails, 4 1/2 In.Diam. | 145.00 |
| **Sieve,** Horsehair, 11 1/2 In. | 60.00 |
| **Sifter,** Flour, Labeled & Dated 1861 | 125.00 |
| **Spice Box,** 5 Black Stenciled Wooden Containers, 9 1/4 In.Diam. | 60.00 |
| **Textile,** Cloak, Woven Ribbon | 100.00 |
| **Yarn Winder** | 225.00 |

*Shaving mugs were popular from 1860 to 1900. Many types were made, including occupational mugs featuring pictures of the man's job. There were scuttle mugs, silver plated mugs, glass-lined mugs, and others.*

| | |
|---|---|
| **SHAVING MUG, Chariot Scene,** Marked Germany | 45.00 |
| **Cobalt Blue Flowers,** Peach Background | 20.00 |
| **Elk,** Hand-Painted, B.P.O.E. | 48.50 |
| **Elk,** Raised, Bisque | 60.00 |
| **Flowers,** Gold Trim, A Present, German | 16.50 |
| **Flowers,** Hand-Painted, Dated 1873 | 35.00 |
| **G.A.R.,** Insignia, We Drank From The Same Canteen, 4 In. | 60.00 |
| **Gadroon Border,** Hexagonal Shape, Silver Plate, Signed | 48.00 |
| **Lady's,** Pink Luster, Pink Lined Box | 27.50 |
| **Mother-Of-Pearl,** Flowers, Gold Trim | 25.00 |
| **Occupational,** Artist, Brush & Palette | 125.00 To 130.00 |
| **Occupational,** Baseball, Batter, Umpire, France | 185.00 |
| **Occupational,** Boy On Bike | 125.00 |
| **Occupational,** Butcher, Steer's Head & Tools Of Trade | 130.00 |
| **Occupational,** Carpenter, Hunter, Pig, Mortar, & Pestle | 100.00 |
| **Occupational,** Cigar Store, Bar Scene | 145.00 |
| **Occupational,** Coal Wagon With Driver & Name | 125.00 |
| **Occupational,** Druggist, Mortar & Pestle & Name In Gold | 125.00 |
| **Occupational,** Fire Chemical Wagon, Horse Drawn | 325.00 |
| **Occupational,** Fisherman | 95.00 |
| **Occupational,** Florist Name, Man, Horse, & Wagon With Flowers | 155.00 |
| **Occupational,** Horse Heads In Stall Window, Name, O'Connell | 160.00 |
| **Occupational,** Horse Heads, J.C.Eldredge | 100.00 |
| **Occupational,** Horse Pulling Milk Wagon & Man | 195.00 |
| **Occupational,** Horses, Surrey, Koken & Boppert | 90.00 |
| **Occupational,** Lawyer, Justice, Holding Balance Scales & Sword | 105.00 |
| **Occupational,** Man Driving Horse & Wagon With Furniture | 110.00 |
| **Occupational,** Man Driving Racing Sulky | 200.00 |
| **Occupational,** Men Loading Lumber, Wagon, 2 Horses | 55.00 |
| **Occupational,** Oil Field Scene | 175.00 |
| **Occupational,** P.R.R., Wood Fired Engine & Tender | 100.00 |
| **Occupational,** Paper Mill Wagon & Rider | 135.00 |
| **Occupational,** Plasterer, D.M.Campbell, Ruby, Gold Trim | 165.00 |
| **Occupational,** Printer At Case | 100.00 |
| **Occupational,** 4 Men, Barbershop Quartet, Gold Trim | 125.00 |
| **Picture Of Paddle Boat,** Gold Banded | 25.00 |
| **Roses,** Gold, China | 35.00 |
| **Scenic,** Nippon | 95.00 |
| **Scuttle,** Mother-Of-Pearl Luster Strawberries, 3 Crown Mark | 45.00 |
| **Scuttle,** Spray Of Flowers Design | 30.00 |
| **Scuttle,** Turquoise Flowers, Gold Trim | 115.00 |
| **Silver Plated Pierced Holder,** Brush Rest, Milk Glass Liner | 62.00 |
| **Tin,** Handled, Side Compartment, 4 1/4 In. | 58.00 |
| **Violets,** Gold Script | 75.00 |
| **Winter Scene,** Left Handed | 35.00 |

Shawnee
USA

*Shawnee pottery was made in Zanesville, Ohio, from 1935 until 1961.*
*Shawnee also produced pottery for George Rumrill during the late 1930s.*

| | |
|---|---|
| **SHAWNEE, Bookends,** Grinning Buddhas, Pair | 25.00 |
| **Bowl,** Corn King, 7 3/4 In. | 9.50 |
| **Butter,** Corn King | 25.00 |
| **Butter,** Corn, Covered | 25.00 To 35.00 |
| **Butter,** Red Riding Hood, Covered | 95.00 |
| **Casserole,** Corn, Covered, 11 In. | 28.50 |
| **Cookie Jar & Bank,** Smiley Pig | 27.50 |
| **Cookie Jar & Bank,** Winnie Pig, Brown Coat | 38.00 |
| **Cookie Jar,** Basket Of Fruit | 12.00 |
| **Cookie Jar,** Bell, Real Bell In Top | 15.00 |
| **Cookie Jar,** Cat | 20.00 To 26.50 |
| **Cookie Jar,** Clown | 45.50 |
| **Cookie Jar,** Corn King, Signed | 40.00 |
| **Cookie Jar,** Corn Queen | 47.50 |
| **Cookie Jar,** Corn Stalk | 15.00 |
| **Cookie Jar,** Dutch Boy | 18.00 To 34.00 |
| **Cookie Jar,** Dutch Girl | 20.00 |
| **Cookie Jar,** Farmer Pig | 24.00 |
| **Cookie Jar,** French Chef | 28.00 |
| **Cookie Jar,** Log & Stone Cabin, No.2754 | 16.00 |
| **Cookie Jar,** Miss Muffet | 20.00 |
| **Cookie Jar,** Monkey, DeForest | 30.00 |
| **Cookie Jar,** Mugsey | 32.50 |
| **Cookie Jar,** Owl | 45.50 |
| **Cookie Jar,** Pig, Bandana Around Neck, 11 1/2 In. | 12.75 |
| **Cookie Jar,** Pumpkin Carriage | 22.50 |
| **Cookie Jar,** Puss 'n Boots | 22.00 To 32.00 |
| **Cookie Jar,** Red Riding Hood | 70.00 |
| **Cookie Jar,** Red Wing, Gold | 20.00 |
| **Cookie Jar,** Sailor Boy | 14.00 |
| **Cookie Jar,** Tweety Bird-Type | 22.00 |
| **Cookie Jar,** Winking Owl | 36.00 |
| **Cookie Jar,** Winnie The Poo | 32.50 |
| **Cornucopia,** Upright, Short Pedestal, Feather Design, 4 3/4 In., Pair | 9.95 |
| **Creamer,** Cat | 8.00 To 9.00 |
| **Creamer,** Corn | 8.00 To 10.00 |
| **Creamer,** Corn King | 10.00 To 15.00 |
| **Creamer,** Elephant | 7.00 To 10.00 |
| **Creamer,** Pig | 8.00 |
| **Creamer,** Puss 'n Boots | 6.00 To 10.00 |
| **Jug,** Chanticleer | 15.00 |
| **Mug,** Corn King | 8.50 To 22.50 |
| **Pitcher,** Beige, Dolphin Handles, 8 In. | 9.50 |
| **Pitcher,** Bopeep, 7 1/2 In. | 20.00 |
| **Pitcher,** Chanticleer | 14.00 To 20.00 |
| **Pitcher,** Corn King, Small | 10.00 |
| **Pitcher,** Corn, 5 In. | 10.50 |
| **Pitcher,** Corn, 8 In. | 12.00 To 30.00 |
| **Pitcher,** Cows, Blue & White | 80.00 |
| **Pitcher,** Elephant | 8.50 |
| **Pitcher,** Puss 'n Boots | 7.50 To 15.00 |
| **Pitcher,** Sailor Boy, 7 1/2 In. | 18.00 |
| **Pitcher,** Smiley Pig, Milk | 19.50 To 22.50 |
| **Planter,** Clock, Gold Hands & Numbers, 6 In. | 11.50 |
| **Planter,** Coolie Pulling Cart, Multicolored, 5 1/2 X 2 3/4 In. | 5.95 |
| **Planter,** Dark Green, 10 In. Long | 4.50 |
| **Planter,** Deer | 10.00 |
| **Planter,** Donkey & Cart | 5.00 |
| **Planter,** Elephant | 5.00 To 15.00 |

| | |
|---|---|
| Planter, Gristmill ................................................. | 7.00 |
| Planter, Man Pushing Cart ................................. | 6.00 |
| Planter, Pig ....................................................... | 4.00 |
| Planter, Shell, Blue .......................................... | 5.00 |
| Planter, Wishing Well .......................... 8.00 To 10.00 |
| Plate, Corn King, 10 In. .................................... | 10.00 |
| Salt & Pepper, Black Face, 7 1/2 In. ................. | 28.50 |
| Salt & Pepper, Bopeep & Sailor ....................... | 6.00 |
| Salt & Pepper, Corn ........................ 10.00 To 13.50 |
| Salt & Pepper, Flowerpot ................................. | 4.50 |
| Salt & Pepper, Milk Can ..................... 6.00 To 7.00 |
| Salt & Pepper, Mugsy ...................................... | 7.00 |
| Salt & Pepper, Owl .......................................... | 8.00 |
| Salt & Pepper, Pigs ........................... 5.00 To 18.50 |
| Salt & Pepper, Puss 'n Boots .............. 6.00 To 8.00 |
| Salt & Pepper, Sprinkling Can ......................... | 7.50 |
| Salt & Pepper, Winnie & Pig Boy ..................... | 7.00 |
| Saltshaker, Bopeep ............................ 4.00 To 5.00 |
| Saltshaker, Corn King, 5 1/2 In. ....................... | 8.00 |
| Saltshaker, Corn Queen .................................. | 5.00 |
| Saltshaker, Elephant, Figural, Blue Ears, 3 1/4 In. .. | 2.50 |
| Saltshaker, Mugsy, Large ................................ | 25.50 |
| Saltshaker, Sailor Boy ..................................... | 4.00 |
| Server, Nut ...................................................... | 12.00 |
| Spooner, Corn .................................................. | 12.00 |
| Sugar & Creamer, Corn King, Covered .............. | 24.00 |
| Sugar & Creamer, Red Riding Hood .................. | 70.00 |
| Sugar Shaker, Salt, & Pepper, Red Riding Hood .. | 18.00 |
| Sugar, Corn King .............................................. | 12.00 |
| Teapot, Corn King ............................ 38.00 To 45.00 |
| Teapot, Corn Queen ......................... 20.00 To 32.50 |
| Teapot, Corn, Individual ................... 25.00 To 45.00 |
| Teapot, Granny Ann .......................... 26.50 To 35.00 |
| Teapot, Red Riding Hood .................................. | 85.00 |
| Teapot, Tom The Piper's Son ............. 18.00 To 32.00 |
| Vase, Bowknot, Gold Accents, Cream Ground, 8 3/4 In. .. | 10.95 |

    **SHEFFIELD, see Silver**
    **SHIP, see Nautical**

*Shirley Temple dishes, blue glassware, and any other souvenir-type objects with her name and picture are now collected. Cobalt blue glassware decorated with Shirley Temple's picture was made by the Hazel Atlas Glass Company from 1934 to 1942.*

| | |
|---|---|
| **SHIRLEY TEMPLE, Book,** Heidi, 1st Edition ........ | 10.00 |
| Book, Little Star, Her Life In Pictures ............... | 35.00 |
| Bowl, Cobalt Blue ............................ 50.00 To 55.00 |
| Box, Puffed Wheat ........................................... | 50.00 |
| Cereal Set, Pitcher & Bowl ............................... | 50.00 |
| Creamer ........................................... 18.00 To 37.50 |
| Doll, Composition, Flirty Eyes, Original Wig, 28 In. .. | 425.00 |
| Doll, Composition, 13 In. .................................. | 225.00 |
| Doll, Composition, 18 In. .................. 250.00 To 395.00 |
| Doll, Composition, 27 In. .................. 350.00 To 595.00 |
| Doll, Cowgirl, Ranger Outfit, Original, 18 In. ...... | 425.00 |
| Doll, Flirty Eyes, Original Wig, Old Clothing, Marked, 25 In. .. | 550.00 |
| Doll, Flirty Eyes, Plaid Dress, Labeled, Composition, 27 In. .. | 495.00 |
| Doll, Glass Eyes, Open Mouth, Blonde, Bisque, 16 In. .. | 55.00 |
| Doll, Ideal, Original Dress, 16 In. ..................... | 225.00 |
| Doll, Jointed Wrist, Vinyl, 36 In. ...................... | 1250.00 |
| Doll, Music Dress, Original, Composition, 22 In. .. | 495.00 |
| Doll, Soap ....................................................... | 50.00 |
| Film, Little Miss Marker, 16MM, Sound .............. | 250.00 |
| Lobby Card, Little Princess, 1935 ..................... | 50.00 |

Mug ............................................................................................................................ 30.00 To 49.50
Mug, Bowl, Pitcher .................................................................................................... 115.00
Paper Doll, Uncut ...................................................................................................... 35.00
Pitcher & Bowl ........................................................................................................... 50.00
Pitcher, Cobalt Blue ........................................................................................ 26.00 To 29.00
Postcard, View Of Home, Inset As Child, Set Of 3 ................................................... 5.00
Postcard, 1949 ............................................................................................................ 8.50
Poster, Movie, Susannah Of The Mounties, 1939 ................................................. 100.00
School Bag ................................................................................................................. 49.00
Sheet Music, Good Ship Lollipop ................................................................ 10.00 To 18.00
Sheet Music, The Right Somebody To Love, 1937 .................................................. 15.00
Teapot, Pink .............................................................................................................. 12.00
Trunk, Doll ................................................................................................................. 40.00

SILESIA, Bowl, Beaded Edge, White Roses, 9 In. ..................................................... 30.00
Bowl, Gold Border, Flowers, 9 1/4 In. ..................................................................... 37.50
Butter, Pink Clover, Covered, 7 In. .......................................................................... 70.00
Celery, White, Pink Flowers, Gold Stem, Scalloped Rim, 11 X 6 In. ....................... 45.00
Creamer, Pink Clover, 3 1/2 X 4 1/2 In. .................................................................. 40.00
Cup & Saucer, Demitasse, Hand-Painted, Gold Rim ................................................. 9.00
Dish, Candy, Hibiscus, Square, 7 1/2 In. ................................................................. 22.50
Dish, Cheese & Cracker, Open Roses, Gold Florals, Green Mark ............................ 50.00
Gravy Boat, Underplate, Pink Clovers, 7 1/2 X 4 In. ................................................ 48.00
Hair Receiver & Pin Box, All White ........................................................................... 28.00
Mustard Jar, Pink Roses, Signed .............................................................................. 15.00
Plate, Beaded Edge, Flowers, 6 In., Set Of 6 .......................................................... 35.00
Plate, Cake, Blue Flowers, 9 1/2 In. ........................................................................ 60.00
Plate, Dessert, Geometric Border, Set Of 8 ............................................................. 15.00
Plate, Hand-Painted Floral Design, Signed, 15 In. ................................................... 95.00
Plate, Hand-Painted Lilies Of The Valley, Gold Rim, 7 1/2 In. ................................. 20.00
Plate, High Glaze, Marked, 12 In. ............................................................................ 75.00
Plate, Pink Clover, 9 1/2 In. ..................................................................................... 60.00
Plate, Roses, Gold Trim, 8 In. .................................................................................. 12.00
Plate, The Capitol, Light Green Ground, 7 1/2 In. ................................................... 45.00
Plate, Turquoise, White, & Pink Flowers, Serrated Rim, Beaded, 12 In. .................. 75.00
Plate, White House, Light Green Ground, 7 1/2 In.Diam. ......................................... 45.00
Soup Dish, Pink Clover, Covered, Handled, 9 In. ..................................................... 75.00
Sugar & Creamer, Gold Band At Top, Scalloped & Beaded ...................................... 25.00
Teapot, Pearl Luster ................................................................................................. 35.00
Tray, Dresser, Roses, Hand-Painted, Signed ........................................................... 29.00
Tumbler, Hand-Painted Water Lilies, Tent Mark, Set Of 4 ....................................... 60.00
    SILHOUETTE, see Picture, Silhouette

> Silver deposit glass was made during the late nineteenth and early twentieth
> centuries. Solid sterling silver was applied to the glass by a chemical
> method so that a cutout design of silver metal appeared against a clear or
> colored glass. It is sometimes called silver overlay.

SILVER DEPOSIT, Creamer, Blue Porcelain ............................................................. 75.00

> Silver plate is not solid silver. It is a ware made of a metal such as
> nickle or copper, then covered with a thin coating of silver. The letters
> EPNS are often found on American and English silver plated wares.

SILVER PLATE, Basket, Etched Birds, C.1880, Handle, Reed & Barton, 9 1/2 In. ..... 68.00
Bottle, Perfume, Screw-On Top, Raised Flowers, Wilcox .......................................... 28.00
Bowl, Fruit, Ram's Heads & Chains, Cranberry Liner, C.1865 ................................... 95.00
Bowl, Sugar, Victorian, Blue Thumbprint Insert, 12 Spoons ................................... 125.00
Box, Sardine, Floral Engraving, Fish Finial On Lid ................................................... 110.00
Box, Sardine, Footed Holder, Glass Insert, Wilcox ................................................... 57.00
Box, Sardine, Victorian Footed, 5 1/4 X 2 1/2 In. .................................................... 75.00
Bread Plate, Corn Design, P.A.Coon Silver Co., 12 X 7 In. ...................................... 45.00
Butter, Engraved Dome, Lily Pad Base, Knife Rest & Knife ...................................... 38.00
Candlestick, Cupid On Leaf, Brass Bobeche, J.W.Trefts, 5 In. ................................. 75.00

Coffee Urn, Brass Spigot, C.1886, Simpson, Hall, Miller & Co. ............................. 125.00
Coffee Urn, Ivory Spigot, Meriden, 15 In. ............................................................. 185.00
Compact, Art Deco, Winged Nymphs Kissing, Embossed Lid, 1917 ....................... 14.00
Compote, Winged Cherubs, Marble Base, Pairpoint, 7 In., Pair ........................... 195.00
Cooler, Wine, Pedestal, C.1833, Sheffield, 12 In., Pair ...................................... 3950.00
Cup & Saucer, Bright Cut, Gold Washed, Pairpoint, 12 Ounce ............................ 65.00
Cutter, Cigar, With Match Holder, Bird On Wishbone, 4 3/4 In. ........................... 85.00
Cutter, Cigar, 1880 ............................................................................................. 35.00
Dish, Dessert, Stemmed, Fred Harvey, Reed & Barton, Set Of 7 ......................... 140.00
Egg Server, Handled Cups, 4 Matching Spoons .................................................. 90.00
English, Salver, 3 Ball & Claw Feet, 8 In. ........................................................... 50.00
Epergne, Three Lilies, Vaseline Glass, 12 1/4 X 14 In. ....................................... 195.00
Feeder, Hot Water, Child's, Engraved Mother Goose Characters ......................... 75.00
Flask, Art Nouveau, Girl With Flowing Hair, Flowers ........................................... 65.00
Fork & Spoon, Child's, Little Red Riding Hood ................................................... 21.00
Fork, Cold Meat, Raphael, Roger, Simon ............................................................. 38.00
Fork, Seafood, Assyrian Head, 1847 Rogers Bros., Box, Set Of 6 ....................... 30.00
Goblet, Leaves In Relief, Wilcox & Co., 5 In. ..................................................... 35.00
Goblet, Wine, Repousse Dutch Scenes, Barbour Silver Plate Co. ......................... 39.00
Knife Rest, Cow On Each End, 4 1/2 In. .............................................................. 95.00
Knife Rest, Dachshund, Head Up ........................................................................ 35.00
Knife Rest, Running Dog ..................................................................................... 35.00
Knife Rest, Running Rabbit .................................................................................. 35.00
Knife Rest, Sphinx .............................................................................................. 27.50
Knife Rest, Squirrels At Each End With Nut, 2 In. ............................................... 59.00
    SILVER PLATE, MUSTACHE CUP, see Mustache Cup
Mustard, Handle, Glass Liner, Meriden ............................................................... 22.00
Penholder, Pairpoint, Quadruple, 3 In. ............................................................... 55.00
Pipe, Opium, Oriental Engraving Design ............................................................. 35.00
Pitcher, Syrup, Girl Head Finial, Rogers & Smith Co., 1865 ................................ 45.00
Pitcher, Water, Countess, International ................................................................ 45.00
Pitcher, 6 Panel, Baluster Form, Scrolled Handle, 6 In. ...................................... 100.00
Plate, Openwork, Raised Cherries Center, Tufts, 9 1/2 In. .................................. 32.00
Rattle, Cat & Dog Design, C.1880 ...................................................................... 35.00
Spoon Warmer, Victorian, Nautilus Shell, 6 3/4 X 5 1/4 In. ............................... 85.00
Spoon, Grapefruit, Sunkist, Rogers, Set Of 5 .................................................... 15.00
    SILVER PLATE, SPOON, SOUVENIR, see Souvenir, Spoon, Silver Plate
Sugar Shell, Scoop, Helmet Shape, Footed, Handled, Victorian .......................... 55.00
Syrup, Ladies' Heads On Handle & Finial, Pairpoint, 8 In. .................................. 85.00
Syrup, Lady's Head On Handle & Lid, C.1868 .................................................... 75.00
Syrup, Sheffield Lid, Butterfly Transfer, C.1874, 7 1/2 In. ................................. 60.00
Tea Caddy, Raised Swirls, Engraved Hinged Lid, C.1865, English ....................... 175.00
Tea Set, Barbour International, Flower Basket, Footed, 3 Piece ........................... 100.00
Tea Set, Hoof Feet, Ball Shape, Sphinx Finial, C.1877, 5 Piece .......................... 525.00
Teapot, Colonial Silver Co., Portland, Maine ...................................................... 65.00
Teapot, Swinging, Ceramic Lined, Tray, C.1850, Forbes, 21 In. .......................... 440.00
Teaspoon, Ramon Navarro ................................................................................. 15.00
    SILVER PLATE, TOOTHPICK, see Toothpick
Tray, Card, Figural, Cherubs Holding Plate, 6 1/2 X 3 In. ................................... 36.00
Tray, Crumb, Lily Pattern .................................................................................... 9.00
Watch Holder, Boy Running, Wreath Around Feet, Glass Dome ........................... 225.00


*American silver was usually marked with the name or initials of the silver-*
*smith or silver company. The word "Sterling" was not in general use until*
*about 1860.*
    SILVER-AMERICAN, see also Tiffany Silver; Silver-Sterling
SILVER-AMERICAN, Baby Cup, Inscribed In German, April, 1888, 2 5/8 In. ............ 95.00
Basket, Sugar, Beaded Rims, Ball, Black, & Co., N.Y.C., C.1855 .......................... 475.00
Basket, Sweetmeat, Lincoln & Foss, C.1850, Coin, 6 1/2 In. ............................... 350.00
Beaker, Churchill & Treadwell, 3 7/16 In., Pair .................................................. 575.00
Bowl, Applied Molded Base Ring, J.Targee, C.1815, 6 1/8 In. ............................. 750.00

**Bowl,** Berry, Art Nouveau Flower Design, Unger Bros. ............................................... 450.00
**Bowl,** Child's, J.Ewan, Dated 1846, 6 1/2 In. ............................................... 675.00
**Bowl,** Pierced Border, Unger Bros., 9 1/2 In.Diam ............................................... 130.00
**Bowl,** Pierced Grapevine, C.1894, New Orleans, 16 In.Diam. ............................................... 1500.00
**Bowl,** Repousse, C.1895, Bailey, Banks, & Biddle Co., 6 In. ............................................... 55.00
**Bracelet,** Baby, Initial A, Coin ............................................... 35.00
**Brooch,** Profile Of Diane, Unger Bros., 2 1/8 In. ............................................... 275.00
**Brushes & Shoehorn,** Love's Dream Lost, Unger Bros.3 Piece ............................................... 195.00
**Butter Knife,** Engraved Design, M.S.Smith, 7 5/8 In. ............................................... 48.00
**Butter,** 3 Cast Birds, C.1880, Brown & Spaulding, N.Y. ............................................... 450.00
**Candelabra,** Gorham, 15 1/2 In., Pair ............................................... *Illus* 2000.00
**Candlesnuffer,** C.1810, Coin, 7 In. ............................................... 750.00
**Case,** Card, B.P.O.E., Ocala, No.2861 1/2 X 2 In. ............................................... 65.00
**Case,** Card, Engine Turned Design, Gorham ............................................... 95.00
**Case,** Thimble, Openwork, Unger Bros. ............................................... 150.00
**Cheese Scoop,** Applied Mouse, N.Harding & Co., C.1860 ............................................... 150.00
**Cheese Scoop,** Olive Pattern, George Sharp, Philadelphia ............................................... 140.00
**Cheese Scoop,** Oval Thread, N.Harding & Co., C.1865, 8 In. ............................................... 75.00
**Child's Set,** Merriman Byrd & Co., C.1850, Coin, 3 Piece ............................................... 125.00
**Coffee Set,** Georgian Style, C.1900, Alvin, 3 Piece ............................................... 1100.00
**Creamer,** C.1815, Signed Edward Lownes, Philadelphia, 5 In. ............................................... 350.00
**Creamer,** Gadroon Border, 3 Shell Feet, Theodore B.Starr ............................................... 165.00
**Creamer,** Pedestal, H.Erwin, Philadelphia, C.1825, 6 3/4 In. ............................................... 250.00
**Cup,** Cartouche Over Half Of Cup, E.G.Ryans, 3 3/8 In. ............................................... 125.00
**Cup,** Handled, Floral & Scroll, C.1850, Boston, Coin, 4 In. ............................................... 140.00
**Cup,** Handled, 19th Century, Jones, Lows, & Ball, 3 1/4 In. ............................................... 90.00
**Cup,** Julep, Jaccard & Co., Marked St.Louis, Coin, 3 1/4 In. ............................................... 375.00
**Cup,** Julep, John B.Akin, Danville, Ky., 3 1/2 In. ............................................... 450.00
**Cup,** Julep, Peter L.Krider, Ky., 6 1/2 In. ............................................... 450.00
**Cup,** Julep, Watson & Hildeburn, 1833-49, 3 1/4 In. ............................................... 550.00
**Cup,** S-Scroll Handle, T. & W.Bird, Coin, 3 3/8 In. ............................................... 145.00
**Dish,** Footed, Embossed, Beaded Rim, Signed, Coin, 5 1/2 In. ............................................... 350.00
**Dresser Set,** Dated 1903, Signed Unger Bros., 5 Piece ............................................... 585.00
**File,** Nail, Love's Dream, Unger Bros. ............................................... 85.00
**Fish Server,** Fiddle, Engraved, John Ewan, Coin.11 1/2 In. ............................................... 650.00
**Fish Server,** Pierced, Baldwin Gardiner, Coin, 10 3/4 In. ............................................... 475.00
**Fish Slice,** King Pattern, Bailey & Co., Openwork Design ............................................... 185.00

Silver-American, Candelabra, Gorham, 15 1/2 In., Pair

**Fish Slice,** Thomas Evans & Co., 1855, Marked FHSE, 10 In. ..................................................... 275.00
**Flask,** Repousse Florals, C.1880, Gorham, 4 X 7 X 1 3/4 In. ........................................ 600.00
**Fork,** Beaded Edge, Crane & Co., C.1842, 7 7/8 In. .............................................................. 60.00
**Fork,** Beaded Edge, Mitchell & Tyler, Richmond, 7 7/8 In. ............................................. 45.00
**Fork,** David Rait, C.1833, Fiddle Thread, Hallmarked, Set Of 5 ................................... 325.00
**Fork,** Fiddle Thread, A.Knapp, Mobile, 8 In., Set Of 5 ................................................... 475.00
**Fork,** Fiddle Thread, Bailey & Co., C.1848, Set Of 6 ...................................................... 375.00
**Fork,** Fiddle Thread, Tenney, N.Y., Coin, Set Of 6 .......................................................... 350.00
**Fork,** Fiddle Thread, William I.Tenney, N.Y., Coin ...................................... 60.00 To 85.00
**Fork,** Jenny Lind, B.C.Hoff, 7 1/8 In., Set Of 6 ................................................................. 360.00
**Fork,** Luncheon, J.W.Tucker, C.1860, Pair .......................................................................... 150.00
**Fork,** Oval End, E.B.Horn, Boston, C.1847, Coin, Set Of 5 ........................................ 350.00
**Fork,** Oyster, Richard Smith, Newark, N.J., C.1850, 10 3/4 In. ................................. 110.00
**Fork,** Pierced Bowl, Tines, H.B.Stanwood, Coin, 9 1/4 In. .......................................... 95.00
**Fork,** Ribbon Design, Wood & Hughes, C.1843, 8 In. ..................................................... 50.00
**Fork,** Serving, Design On Tines, K.Kinsey, Cincinnati, C.1865 .................................. 125.00
**Fork,** Serving, J.J.Low, Boston, C.1828, 8 3/4 In. ............................................................ 27.00
**Fork,** Thread & Shell, R. & W.Wilson, C.1830, Set Of 10 .............................................. 500.00
**Fruit Bowl,** Gilt, W.B.Kerr .............................................................................*Illus* 1000.00
**Funnel,** Wine, Gorham ......................................................................................................... 50.00
**Goblet,** John Kitts, Shield Shaped Cartouche, 6 1/2 In., Pair ................................... 800.00
**Goblet,** Presentation, Elk Head Handles, 9 X 3 7/8 In.Diam. ..................................... 595.00
**Inkstand,** 2 Bottles, Footed Tray, Sheffield, 13 1/4 In. ............................................. 750.00
**Key,** Wine Taster's, C.1882, Chain, Reed & Barton, 5 In. ............................................ 60.00
**Knife & Fork,** Bull's Head At Handle Top, P.L.Krider, Penn. ...................................... 295.00
**Knife Rest,** Andiron Shape, Gold Wash Ball, Gorham, 3 In. ....................................... 100.00
**Knife Rest,** Andiron Shape, Gorham, Coin ...................................................................... 25.00
**Knife,** Butter, Jones, Ball & Poor, C.1846, Coin, 7 1/2 In. ......................................... 30.00
**Knife,** Cake, Engraved, George C.Vaughan, Buffalo, Coin ......................................... 190.00
**Knife,** Dessert, 9-Ribbon Design, Jones, Ball, & Poor, C.1846 .................................. 30.00
**Knife,** Spreader, Twist Handle, F.A.Brahe, Augusta, Georgia .................................... 75.00
**Ladle,** Gravy, Fiddle Thread, Thomas Fletcher, Coin, 8 In. ....................................... 175.00
**Ladle,** Gravy, Fiddle, Joseph Draper, C.1840, Coin ..................................................... 250.00
**Ladle,** Gravy, Fiddle, Thomas Whartenby, Coin, 7 In. ................................................ 125.00
**Ladle,** Gravy, Palmer & Bachelders, C.1850, 7 3/8 In. .............................................. 125.00
**Ladle,** Mustard, J. & I.Cox, C.1850, Arched Handle, 5 1/4 In. ................................... 45.00
**Ladle,** Mustard, Prince Albert, Stebbins & Co., C.1850 ............................................ 45.00
**Ladle,** Oyster, Richard Smith, C.1850, Marked Coin, 10 3/4 In. .............................. 110.00
**Ladle,** Punch, Bright Cut, P.L.Krider, C.1850, 12 1/4 In. ........................................... 395.00

Silver-American, Fruit Bowl, Gilt, W.B.Kerr

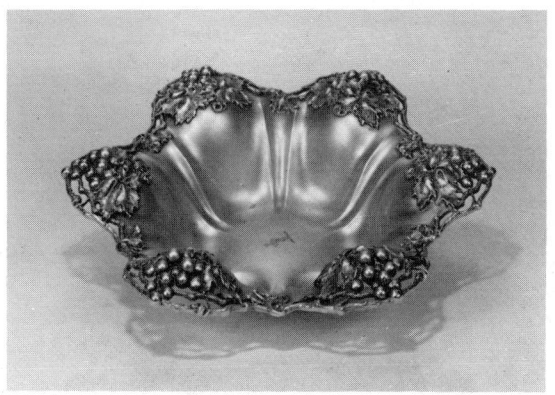

**Ladle,** Punch, Mazarin Pattern, Dominick & Haff, C.1892 ................................................ 170.00
**Ladle,** Punch, Ribbon Pattern, N.Harding & Co., 19th Century ................................................ 175.00
**Ladle,** Sauce, Fiddle, C.Butman, Coin, 6 1/4 In. ................................................ 45.00
**Ladle,** Sauce, Fiddle, D.D.R.Ormsby, C.1832, 6 1/4 In. ................................................ 75.00
**Ladle,** Sauce, Fiddle, Newell Watson, C.1845, Coin, 6 In. ................................................ 55.00
**Ladle,** Sauce, Oval Tip, W.H.Talbott, C.1855, Coin, 6 1/4 In. ................................................ 65.00
**Ladle,** Soup, Beaded Pattern, Bigelow Bros. & Kennard ................................................ 350.00
**Ladle,** Soup, Beaded, Crest & Oval, S.T.Crosby & Son, 13 In. ................................................ 245.00
**Ladle,** Soup, Benedict & Scudder, C.1827, Marked, 14 3/4 In. ................................................ 395.00
**Ladle,** Soup, C.A.Burnett, Georgetown, C.1815, 11 3/4 In ................................................ 1200.00
**Ladle,** Soup, Coffin End, M.Merriman, Conn., C.1810, 12 In. ................................................ 285.00
**Ladle,** Soup, Fiddleback, C.Bard & Co., Coin, 13 In. ................................................ 175.00
**Ladle,** Soup, J.W.Tucker, C.1860, Coin, 13 1/2 In. ................................................ 300.00
**Ladle,** Soup, Old English, George Sharp, Coin.14 In. ................................................ 450.00
**Ladle,** Soup, Samuel C.Brown, N.Y., 1824-30, 13 1/2 In. ................................................ 275.00
**Ladle,** Soup, Tipped Back, Shreve, Crump, & Low, Boston, 12 In. ................................................ 350.00
**Ladle,** Soup, 6 Forks, 6 Tablespoons, T.Fletcher, C.1825 ................................................ 2350.00
**Letter Opener & Ink Eraser,** He Loves Me, Unger Bros. ................................................ 75.00
**Marrow Scoop,** AR In Oval Cartouche, Coin ................................................ 585.00
**Match Safe,** Nude With Lyre, Unger Bros., 4 5/8 X 2 3/4 In. ................................................ 255.00
**Mirror,** Handled, Beveled Glass, Unger Bros., 9 3/4 X 5 In. ................................................ 150.00
**Mirror,** Love's Dream, Embossed Woman & Cherub, Unger Bros. ................................................ 250.00
**Monteith Bowl,** Baltimore Roses, S.Kirk, C.1840, 9 1/2 In. ................................................ 1700.00
**Mug,** Child's, Beaded Border, T.W.Radcliffe, C.1830, 3 5/8 In. ................................................ 325.00
**Mug,** Child's, Beaded Border, Wm.Carrington & Co., C.1850 ................................................ 450.00
**Mug,** Child's, Engraved Design, Gregg & Hayden, C.1849, 3 In. ................................................ 350.00
**Mug,** Child's, Victorian, Chased Design, Name & Date, 1878 ................................................ 95.00
**Mustard Spoon,** Coffin End, W.Roe, Kingston, N.Y., C.1800 ................................................ 125.00
**Mustard Spoon,** Fiddle Tipped, J.Owne, Phila., C.1804, Coin ................................................ 55.00
**Mustard Spoon,** Fiddle Tipped, R.& W.Wilson, Phila., C.1850 ................................................ 45.00
**Mustard Spoon,** Fiddleback, Cuthbert Warner, C.1840, Coin ................................................ 25.00
**Mustard Spoon,** Old Maryland Pattern, Canfield, C.1860 ................................................ 25.00
**Mustard Spoon,** Shell Pattern, Coin, Pair ................................................ 37.50
**Mustard Spoon,** William Brown, Fiddleback, C.1845, Coin ................................................ 25.00
**Mustard,** Blue Glass Liner, Pierced Sides, Sheffield ................................................ 200.00
**Nailfile,** Rococo, Unger Bros. ................................................ 55.00
**Olive Spoon,** Twist Stem, Pierced Shell Bowl, Coin, 9 1/2 In. ................................................ 75.00
**Platter,** Fish, Martele, 23 1/2 In. ................................................ *Illus* 4250.00
**Porringer,** Lion Crest On Handle, John Edwards, 1724 Mark ................................................ 3500.00
**Punch Bowl,** Baltimore Rose Pattern, S.Kirk & Son, 9 In. ................................................ 1600.00
**Punch Bowl,** Ladle, Chased, Stieff Co., 1914, 1/ 1/2 In.Diam. ................................................ 2600.00

Silver-American, Platter, Fish, Martele, 23 1/2 In.

**Punch Bowl,** Theodore B.Starr, 1882 ............................................. 8500.00
**Salt Spoon,** Bailey & Co., C.1845, Beaded Edge ............................ 25.00
**Salt Spoon,** Bigelow Bros.& Kennard, C.1845, Shell Bowl ............ 22.00
**Salt Spoon,** Edward Brown, Liberty & Lynchburg, Va., Coin ......... 85.00
**Salt Spoon,** Fiddle Shell Bowl, E.Lownes, Philadelphia, Coin ...... 45.00
**Salt Spoon,** Fiddle Thread, R. & W.Wilson, Coin, Pair ................. 65.00
**Salt Spoon,** Fiddle Tipped, Bard & Lamont, Phila., C.1841 .......... 45.00
**Salt Spoon,** Fiddle Tipped, E.Benjamin, New Haven, 1830 ......... 25.00
**Salt Spoon,** Fiddle Tipped, Ezra Whitton, Boston, Coin ............... 35.00
**Salt Spoon,** Fiddle Tipped, Watson & Hildeburn, C.1833 ............. 45.00
**Salt Spoon,** Fiddle, Drummond, Shell Bowl ................................. 35.00
**Salt Spoon,** Fiddle, Fletcher & Gardiner, Philadelphia, Coin ........ 45.00
**Salt Spoon,** Fiddle, Harvey Lewis, Philadelphia, Marked, Pair ..... 75.00
**Salt Spoon,** Flared, Palmer & Bachelders, C.1850, 6 5/8 In. ...... 20.00
**Salt Spoon,** Gilt Finish, Hyde & Goodrich, C.1860, Coin, Pair ..... 90.00
**Salt Spoon,** Greeg & Hayden, Charleston, S.C., C.1840, Pair ..... 75.00
**Salt Spoon,** Pointed End, J.Proctor Trott, New London, C.1795 ... 45.00
**Salt Spoon,** Shell Bowl, Littleton Holland, 4 1/2 In. .................... 75.00
**Salt Spoon,** Shell Bowl, 4 1/2 In. ............................................. 75.00
**Salt Spoon,** Steward, Stevens, & Dewey, Shell Bowl, Coin ........ 25.00
**Saucepan,** T.Underhill & J.Vernon, C.1785, Coin .................... 1900.00
**Server,** Pastry, Pierced, Fenno & Hale, C.1840, Engraved ......... 95.00
**Server,** Vegetable, J.Dolfinger & Co., Louisville, C.1845 ........... 85.00
**Shoehorn,** Love's Dream, Unger Bros. ...................................... 45.00
**Slat Spoon,** Fiddle, Marcus Merriman, C.1810, 4 1/4 In. ........... 35.00
**Spoon,** Berry, Trousseau, Scalloped Bowl, International, 9 In. .... 120.00
**Spoon,** Birdback, Pointed End, John Myers, 9 In., Pair ............. 350.00
**Spoon,** Condiment, S.Baker & Son, Coin .................................. 65.00
**Spoon,** Dessert, B.B.Hasting, Cleveland, Ohio, C.1830, Coin ..... 35.00
**Spoon,** Dessert, B.E.Cook, 1827-45, 7 1/2 In. .......................... 30.00
**Spoon,** Dessert, C.L.Boehme, Oval Tip, C.1780, Coin ............... 60.00
**Spoon,** Dessert, Canfield Bros. & Co., C.1840, Coin, Set Of 4 ... 100.00
**Spoon,** Dessert, Coffin End, S. & E., C.1800, 6 3/4 In. .............. 45.00
**Spoon,** Dessert, Fiddle Thread, R. & W.Wilson, Coin, Pair ......... 85.00
**Spoon,** Dessert, Fiddle, A.E.Warner, 1818 Marks, 7 1/4 In. ....... 75.00
**Spoon,** Dessert, Fiddle, B.E.Cook, 1827-45, Coin .................... 35.00
**Spoon,** Dessert, Fiddle, C.F.Beckel, C.1840, 7 1/8 In. .............. 28.00
**Spoon,** Dessert, Fiddle, R. & W.Wilson, C.1850, 6 7/8 In. ......... 85.00
**Spoon,** Dessert, Fiddle, Rudd & Scudder, V-Drop, 7 1/4 In. ...... 30.00
**Spoon,** Dessert, Flared Handle, W.B.Durgin, C.1803 ................. 25.00
**Spoon,** Dessert, J.W.Tucker, C.1860, Set Of 6 ........................ 600.00
**Spoon,** Dessert, Jehu W.Bear, 7 1/8 In. .................................. 75.00
**Spoon,** Dessert, Kings, William I.Tenney, N.Y., Coin ................. 45.00
**Spoon,** Dessert, Oval End, Scovil, Willey, & Co., 1836 .............. 30.00
**Spoon,** Dessert, Pinched Fiddle, D.Smiley, N.H., 7 In. .............. 28.00
**Spoon,** Dessert, Sheaf Wheat, J.Dyer, Star At End, Coin .......... 90.00
**Spoon,** Dessert, Twist Stem, F.A.Brahe, Augusta, Ga., Coin ..... 45.00
**Spoon,** Dessert, 2-Part Construction, C.Yates, Coin, Pair .......... 70.00
**Spoon,** Egg, Douglas & Heckman, Philadelphia, Coin ................ 45.00
**Spoon,** Feather Edge, V. & R., C.1760, 5 1/8 In., Set Of 5 ....... 500.00
**Spoon,** Lily Of The Valley, Whiting, Demitasse ......................... 18.00
**Spoon,** Medallion Handle, Duhme & Co., 1842, 8 1/8 In. .......... 75.00
**Spoon,** Medallion Pattern, C.1860, Vanderslice, Coin ............... 75.00
**Spoon,** Raised Design, C.1815, Garrett Eoff, Coin, 6 3/4 In. ..... 50.00
**Spoon,** Rattail, Marked I.P., C.1725, Mid-Rib, Coin, 7 1/4 In. ... 300.00
**Spoon,** Serving, Bright Cut, Wm.Homes, C.1795, Oval Drop ..... 175.00
**Spoon,** Serving, Coffin End, Andrew Dewilt, C.1805, Large Bowl ... 85.00
**Spoon,** Serving, Dog Nose, T.Edwards, C.1725, 7 3/8 In. ........ 475.00
**Spoon,** Serving, Embossed, Mulford, Wendell & Co., C.1855 ..... 195.00
**Spoon,** Serving, Farrington & Hunnewell, Coin, Pair .................. 55.00
**Spoon,** Serving, Fiddle Thread, Gale, Wood, & Hughes, C.1836 ... 95.00
**Spoon,** Serving, Fiddle Tip, D.Chapin, C.1850, 8 5/8 In. ........... 40.00
**Spoon,** Serving, Fiddle Tip, Isaac Spear, C.1850, 8 3/8 In. ....... 55.00

**Spoon,** Serving, Fiddle Tip, Richard Huntington, C.1823, 8 In. .......................... 50.00
**Spoon,** Serving, Fiddle, S.Kirk, 1824 Assay Mark, 8 3/4 In. .............................. 85.00
**Spoon,** Serving, Flared Handle, E.Ferren, Manchester, C.1840 ...................... 30.00
**Spoon,** Serving, Forward Tipped, J.Clarke, Newport, C.1730 ........................ 495.00
**Spoon,** Serving, J.E.Brinsmaid, C.1850, Coin, 8 1/2 In. .................................. 65.00
**Spoon,** Serving, M.S.Smith, Detroit, C.1850, 8 3/4 In .................................... 50.00
**Spoon,** Serving, Olive Pattern, S.W.Pepper, Coin, 8 1/2 In. .......................... 95.00
**Spoon,** Serving, Oval End Tipped, A.Underhill, C.1780, 8 In. ....................... 135.00
**Spoon,** Serving, Oval Tip, S.B.Walcott, C.1840, Coin, 8 1/2 In. ...................... 35.00
**Spoon,** Serving, Pointed End, J.Vernon, C.1795, 9 1/8 In. ............................ 175.00
**Spoon,** Serving, Pointed End, John Wood, C.1790, 9 1/2 In. .......................... 75.00
**Spoon,** Serving, Pointed End, Judah Hart, C.1805, 9 In. .............................. 185.00
**Spoon,** Serving, Pointed End, S.Merriman, New Haven, C.1795 ...................... 70.00
**Spoon,** Serving, Pointed, Marcus Merriman, C.1790, 8 3/4 In. ...................... 80.00
**Spoon,** Serving, R.Humphreys, Wilmington, Delaware, C.1770 ...................... 450.00
**Spoon,** Serving, Repousse, C.1880, Kirk ...................................................... 150.00
**Spoon,** Serving, Shell Back, Benjamin & Benjamin, C.1825 .......................... 40.00
**Spoon,** Serving, Twisted Handle, D.Kinsey, C.1860, 8 5/8 In. ........................ 65.00
**Spoon,** Soup, Fiddle, Welles Gelston & Porter, 13 1/4 In. ............................ 275.00
**Spoon,** Sugar, Embossed Handle, Elias Baker, N.J., C.1860, Coin .................... 45.00
**Spoon,** Sugar, Fiddle Tipped Handle, Shell Bowl, Pearson, Coin ...................... 50.00
**Spoon,** Tea Caddy, Joseph Bird, 1825-35, 4 In. ............................................ 400.00
**Sugar & Creamer,** C.1835, Signed Gale, Wood & Hughes, Coin ...................... 2500.00
**Sugar & Waste Bowl,** C.L.Boehme, C.1799, Ball Feet .................................... 3000.00
**Sugar Shell,** Fiddle Thread, Baile & Co., C.1850, 7 In. .................................. 85.00
**Sugar Shell,** Fiddle Tipped, J.B.Scott, N.Y.C., C.1840, 6 In. ............................ 25.00
**Sugar Shell,** Fiddle, G.L.Ames & Bros., C.1850, 6 1/2 In. .............................. 45.00
**Sugar Shell,** Fiddleback, P.Miller, Rhode Island, C.1820, Coin ...................... 35.00
**Sugar Shell,** Pinched Fiddle, Jaccard & Co., C.1840, 4 In. ............................ 55.00
**Sugar Shell,** R.Smith, New Jersey .............................................................. 45.00
**Sugar Shell,** Shovel, William H.Walker, Philadelphia, Coin .......................... 60.00
**Sugar Sifter,** Jenny Lind, Pierced, Albert Cole, 7 3/4 In. .............................. 145.00
**Sugar Tongs,** Basket Of Flowers, Welles & Gelston, C.1840 .......................... 225.00
**Sugar Tongs,** Fiddle Arms, Bolles & Childs, C.1840 ...................................... 45.00
**Sugar Tongs,** Flowers On Arms, Shell Nipper, G.Beatty, C.1830 .................... 375.00
**Sugar Tongs,** Sheaf Of Wheat, Shell Nipper, W.B.North, C.1818 .................... 250.00
**Tablespoon,** B.Willey, Cincinnati, C.1840, Coffin Corner, Coin ...................... 50.00
**Tablespoon,** Basket Of Flowers, Benedict, Coin .......................................... 150.00
**Tablespoon,** Bright Cut, Bernard Wenman, N.Y.C., Coin .............................. 100.00
**Tablespoon,** Bright Cut, John D.Germon, Philadelphia, Coin ........................ 125.00
**Tablespoon,** Bright Cut, Robert Evans, Boston, Coin .................................... 125.00
**Tablespoon,** Bright Cut, William Roe, Albany, N.Y., Coin .............................. 125.00
**Tablespoon,** E. & D.Kinsey, C.1840, Coin, Set Of 3 ...................................... 180.00
**Tablespoon,** E.Benjamin, New Haven, Conn., C.1825, Coin .......................... 58.00
**Tablespoon,** Edward Winslow, Boston, 1660-1753, Coin .............................. 1000.00
**Tablespoon,** Elias Davis, Boston, C.1820, Coin ............................................ 58.00
**Tablespoon,** Fiddle Shell, Bailey & Co., Philadelphia, Coin .......................... 75.00
**Tablespoon,** Fiddle Tipped, E.Thompson, C.1850 ........................................ 30.00
**Tablespoon,** Fiddle Tipped, J.Conning, Marked, 8 3/4 In. ............................ 145.00
**Tablespoon,** Fiddle Tipped, J.Stevenson, N.Y.C., C.1850 .............................. 28.00
**Tablespoon,** Fiddle Tipped, R.Huntington, Utica, C.1823, 8 In. ...................... 45.00
**Tablespoon,** Fiddle, Clark, Rackett & Co., C.1840, 8 1/4 In. .......................... 165.00
**Tablespoon,** Fiddle, Ivory Hall, Concord, N.H., Coin .................................... 40.00
**Tablespoon,** Fiddleback, C.1828, J.Stockman, Coin ...................................... 60.00
**Tablespoon,** Fiddleback, I.Black, Philadelphia, C.1811, Coin ........................ 65.00
**Tablespoon,** Fiddleback, N.LeHuray, Deleware, C.1830 ................................ 75.00
**Tablespoon,** Fiddleback, Theophilus Bradbury, C.1815, Coin ........................ 60.00
**Tablespoon,** Forward Rib, Edward Winslow, Boston, Coin ............................ 235.00
**Tablespoon,** Frederick Marquand, Savannah, Georgia, 1826, Coin .................. 190.00
**Tablespoon,** Gregg & Hayden, Charleston, S.C., 1847, Set Of 6 .................... 450.00
**Tablespoon,** Gregg, Hayden & Co., Dated 1849, 8 3/4 In. ............................ 48.00
**Tablespoon,** H.R.Hollman & Co., Kansas City, C.1850, Set Of 3 .................... 225.00
**Tablespoon,** J.Baldwin, Salem, Mass., C.1810, Coin .................................... 68.00

Tablespoon, J.G.Joseph, Cincinnati, C.1840, Coin ........................................................ 85.00
Tablespoon, King's Pattern, F.Marquand, N.Y., C.1830 .............................................. 75.00
Tablespoon, Marked Revere, 1735-1818, 8 5/8 In. .................................................. 1000.00
Tablespoon, Narrow Handle, Crooks & Phelps, 8 1/8 In. ............................................ 35.00
Tablespoon, Old English, John Myers, Philadelphia, Coin ......................................... 275.00
Tablespoon, Old English, Joseph Shoemaker, Philadelphia ......................................... 75.00
Tablespoon, Oval Tip, J.Warner, Wilmington, C.1780, Coin, Pair .............................. 400.00
Tablespoon, Pelletreau, Bennett, & Cooke, N.Y.C., Coin ......................................... 125.00
Tablespoon, Pinched Fiddle, E.& D.Kinsey, C.1840, 8 1/2 In. ................................... 30.00
Tablespoon, Pointed End, C.1790, John Proctor Trott, Coin ...................................... 125.00
Tablespoon, Pointed, Downturned End, C.1790, Terry Geer, Coin ............................. 150.00
Tablespoon, R.Mathews, Charlottesville, C.1836, 8 7/8 In. ....................................... 135.00
Tablespoon, Rattail, Daniel Russel, Newport, R.I., Coin ........................................... 400.00
Tablespoon, Rattail, Eliakim Hitchcock, Coin ........................................................ 325.00
Tablespoon, Rattail, Joseph Clark, Danbury, Conn. & N.Y.C. ................................... 375.00
Tablespoon, S.Brown, New York City, C.1825, Fiddleback ....................................... 20.00
Tablespoon, Thomas Edwards, Boston, Shell Back, Coin ......................................... 200.00
Tablespoon, Tipped Back, Mulford & Wendell, Albany, C.1843 ............................... 35.00
Tablespoon, Tipped, Oskamp & Bros., Cincinnati, Ohio, Coin .................................. 45.00
Tablespoon, V-Shaped Drop, J.Scheffer, C.1820, 9 1/2 In. ..................................... 58.00
Tea & Coffee Service, Bailey & Kitchen ................................................. *Illus* 4250.00
Tea & Coffee Set, Repousse Pattern, C.1898, 5 Piece ........................................ 1400.00
Tea Ball, Figural, Japanese Lantern, Chain & Ring ................................................. 125.00
Tea Ball, Figural, Pear, Ring & Chain, Gorham ...................................................... 135.00
Tea Ball, Figural, Saltshaker, Chain, B.S.C.S. Co. .................................................. 25.00
Tea Ball, Figural, Teapot, Artcraft, Battlesboro, Mass. ............................................ 55.00
Tea Ball, Hinged Cover, Looped Back Forms Grip, 5 1/8 In. .................................... 45.00
Tea Ball, Webster & Co. ...................................................................................... 48.00
Tea Service, Fluted Shoulders, N.J.Bogert, Coin, 3 Piece ..................................... 2350.00
Tea Set, Grape & Leaf, Wm.Gale & Son, Vine Finials, 4 Piece ............................... 5500.00
Teapot, Fletcher & Gardiner, Philadelphia, C.1820, 5 In. ...................................... 1500.00
Teapot, Peter Chitry, N.Y., C.1814, Signed, Coin ................................................. 3000.00
Teaspoon, Basket Of Flowers, Aaron Dikeman, N.Y.C., Coin .................................... 65.00
Teaspoon, Benjamin Judd, Burton, Ohio, C.1820, Coin, Set Of 6 ............................. 120.00
Teaspoon, Bird On Reverse Of Bowl, W.Walker, Set Of 6 ........................................... 7.50
Teaspoon, Birdback, Pointed End, Wm.Haverstick, Phila. .......................................... 95.00
Teaspoon, Bright Cut, Daniel Parker, Boston, Coin .................................................. 50.00
Teaspoon, Bright Cut, Ezekiel Burr, Providence, R.I., Coin ....................................... 50.00
Teaspoon, Bright Cut, George Armitage, Philadelphia, Dozen .................................. 325.00

Silver-American, Tea & Coffee Service, Bailey & Kitchen

**Teaspoon,** Bright Cut, Joel Sayre, 1802-18, 6 1/4 In. .............................. 40.00
**Teaspoon,** Brinsmaid & Hildreth, Vermont, 1854-1902, Coin ................. 28.50
**Teaspoon,** C.T.Gifford, Keokuk, Iowa, Coin, Set Of 7 ........................... 150.00
**Teaspoon,** Cartouche, J.Loring, Boston, 18th Century, Set Of 6 .............. 85.00
**Teaspoon,** Charleston, N.C., Javain, C, 1895 ...................................... 200.00
**Teaspoon,** Coffin End, A. & C.Brandt, 1800-14, 6 In. ........................... 50.00
**Teaspoon,** Coffin End, David Greenleaf, C.1800, 6 In .......................... 45.00
**Teaspoon,** Coffin End, E.Baker, Ashford, Conn., C.1810 ....................... 35.00
**Teaspoon,** Coffin End, Ebenezer Moulton, C.1810, 5 1/4 In. .................. 35.00
**Teaspoon,** Coffin End, George Carlton, N.Y., 1810, Set Of 3 .................. 65.00
**Teaspoon,** Coffin End, J.F.Vent, Boston, C.1805, Coin, Set Of 4 ............. 100.00
**Teaspoon,** Coffin End, S.Brown, 5 1/2 In., Set Of 6 ............................. 200.00
**Teaspoon,** Coffin End, Saunders Pitman, C.1810, 5 5/8 In. ................... 45.00
**Teaspoon,** Crested, Ebenezer Moulton, Boston, C.1790, Set Of 6 ........... 300.00
**Teaspoon,** D.N.Dole, Mass., C.1805, Coin, 5 1/4 In. ............................ 30.00
**Teaspoon,** Feather Edge, Thomas Arnold, Newport, R.I., Coin ............... 50.00
**Teaspoon,** Fiddle Shell, J.Stockman, Phila., 1828, 6 1/4 In. ................. 18.00
**Teaspoon,** Fiddle Thread, Canfield & Bro., Baltimore, Coin .................. 45.00
**Teaspoon,** Fiddle Thread, Samuel Kirk, Baltimore, Coin ....................... 55.00
**Teaspoon,** Fiddle Tipped, C.Spence, Newark, N.J., 1830-40 .................. 16.00
**Teaspoon,** Fiddle Tipped, W.Gennet, N.Y., C.1850, Set Of 6 ................. 120.00
**Teaspoon,** Fiddle, A.Hanford, 1820-30, 6 1/4 In. ............................... 20.00
**Teaspoon,** Fiddle, Chedell & Co., Auburn, N.Y., C.1827 ...................... 16.00
**Teaspoon,** Fiddle, D.Dupuy, Jr., C.1813, 5 5/8 In., Set Of 12 ............... 700.00
**Teaspoon,** Fiddle, E.Coit, Norwich, Conn., C.1825, 5 3/4 In. ................ 20.00
**Teaspoon,** Fiddle, E.Shaw, C.1850, 5 7/8 In. ..................................... 16.00
**Teaspoon,** Fiddle, F.H.Clark & Co., Memphis, C.1840 ......................... 55.00
**Teaspoon,** Fiddle, J.Gorham & Son, Providence, C.1842 ...................... 16.00
**Teaspoon,** Fiddle, J.S.Blackman & Son, Danbury, Conn., C.1830 .......... 18.00
**Teaspoon,** Fiddle, L.Badget, Painted Post, N.Y., C.1830 ...................... 20.00
**Teaspoon,** Fiddle, Moses Morse, Boston, Set Of 6 .............................. 210.00
**Teaspoon,** Fiddle, Sheaf Of Wheat, Taylor & Hinsdale, 1801 ................ 40.00
**Teaspoon,** Fiddle, T.Perry, Westerly, R.I., C.1828, 5 3/4 In. ................ 16.00
**Teaspoon,** Fiddle, Tipped Back, T.B.Herbert, N.Y.C., C.1806 ............... 18.00
**Teaspoon,** Fiddleback, E. & D.Kinsey, C.1840, Coin, Set Of 6 .............. 120.00
**Teaspoon,** Fiddleback, G.Sharp, Danville, Ky., C.1840, Set Of 7 ........... 350.00
**Teaspoon,** Fiddleback, G.Vaker, Rhode Island, C.1815, Coin ................ 25.00
**Teaspoon,** Fiddleback, John Hall, Louisville, Ky., C.1845, Coin ............ 30.00
**Teaspoon,** Fiddleback, Lynch, Baltimore, C.1820 ............................... 20.00
**Teaspoon,** Fiddleback, R.Clayton, C.1830, Coin, Pair ......................... 40.00
**Teaspoon,** Fiddleback, Turned Down Tip, N.Harding, Boston ................ 25.00
**Teaspoon,** Flared Handle, B.Ranger, Vermont, C.1840, Set Of 5 ........... 100.00
**Teaspoon,** Flat Stem, Saunders Pitman, Rhode Island, Coin ................. 60.00
**Teaspoon,** Forward Tipped, D.Dupuy, C.1760 .................................... 160.00
**Teaspoon,** Grand Colonial, Engraved Date, Wallace, Set Of 12 ............. 300.00
**Teaspoon,** H.L.Webster, Prov.R.I., C.1838, Coin, Set Of 4 ................... 75.00
**Teaspoon,** I.Pittman, Baltimore, C.1795, Oval Tip, Coin ...................... 30.00
**Teaspoon,** Lily Of The Valley, Whiting, Set Of 8 ................................ 150.00
**Teaspoon,** M.Noyes, Burlington, C.1840, Set Of 6 .............................. 120.00
**Teaspoon,** Matthias Haverstick, 5 3/4 In. ......................................... 95.00
**Teaspoon,** Mid-Rib, W.Thomson, N.Y.C., C.1810, 6 In. ....................... 45.00
**Teaspoon,** O.D.Griswald, Coin ....................................................... 22.50
**Teaspoon,** Old English, Andrew Clark, N.Y.C., Coin, 4 3/4 In. .............. 45.00
**Teaspoon,** Old English, Robert Brookhouse, Salem, Mass., Coin ........... 25.00
**Teaspoon,** Oval End, Birdback, Lewis & Smith, C.1805, 6 In. ............... 110.00
**Teaspoon,** Oval End, Joel Sayre, Dot Engraved, C.1810 ...................... 35.00
**Teaspoon,** Oval End, Joseph Richardson, Jr., 5 1/8 In. ....................... 125.00
**Teaspoon,** Oval End, Lewis & Smith, 6 In. ....................................... 110.00
**Teaspoon,** Oval Tipped, P.Ford, C.1850, 6 1/8 In. .............................. 16.00
**Teaspoon,** Pinched Fiddle, O.Gerrish, Portland, Maine, C.1840 ............ 18.00
**Teaspoon,** Pinchwaist, C.1830, Fall River, Mass., Coin ....................... 20.00
**Teaspoon,** Pointed End, Birdback, J.David, Jr., C.1785 ....................... 95.00
**Teaspoon,** Pointed End, W.Homes, Sr., Boston, C.1780, Set Of 4 .......... 225.00

Teaspoon, R. & W.Wilson, Philadelphia, C.1830, Set Of 8 ................................................ 400.00
Teaspoon, Semicoffin End, Jesse Churchill, C.1805, Coin ................................................ 40.00
Teaspoon, Serrated Rectangle, Double Drop, Coin ................................................ 50.00
Teaspoon, Shell Back, William Homes, C.1760, 4 7/8 In. ................................................ 175.00
Teaspoon, Twist Stem, F.A.Brahe, Augusta, Coin, Set Of 6 ................................................ 125.00
Thimble Holder, Reticulated, Unger Bros. ................................................ 105.00
Tongs, Acorn Grips, W.Moulton, Newburyport, C.1820 ................................................ 85.00
Tongs, Acorn Nippers, B.Cleveland, C.1806, 6 1/4 In. ................................................ 175.00
Tongs, Bird Feet Nippers, G.A.Hoyt, C.1830, 6 5/8 In. ................................................ 225.00
Tongs, Fiddle Arms, Eolles & Childs, C.1840 ................................................ 45.00
Tongs, Fiddle Shape, Joseph Draper, 6 In. ................................................ 275.00
Tongs, Leaf Engraving, Henry McKeen, Coin, 6 1/4 In. ................................................ 65.00
Tongs, Sheaf Of Wheat, W.B.North, C.1818, 6 5/8 In. ................................................ 250.00
Tongs, Shell Shaped Ends, E.Benjamin, Conn., C.1830, Coin ................................................ 75.00
Tongs, Spoon Ends, Maltby Pelletreau, Coin, 6 1/2 In. ................................................ 95.00
Tongs, Tapered, Maltby Pelletreau, N.Y., Coin, 6 1/2 In. ................................................ 95.00
Tongs, Thomas Rockwell, Connecticut, C.1775 ................................................ 135.00
Toothpick, Figural, Mouse, Derby ................................................ 48.00
Tray, Dresser, Art Glass Insert, Unger Bros. ................................................ 125.00
Trophy Cup, Acorns & Leaves, Dominick & Haff, 1899, 10 In. ................................................ 900.00
Vinaigrette, Book Form, 1840, Taylor & Perry, Birmingham ................................................ 275.00
Yo-Yo, Raised Acanthus Leaves, Gorham ................................................ 68.00

SILVER-AUSTRIAN, Dresser Set, Repousse In Rococo Design, 3 Piece ................................... 225.00
Sauceboat, Leaf Capped Handle, 19th Century, 10 1/4 In. ................................................ 550.00

SILVER-CANADIAN, Punch Bowl, C.1910, 14 1/4 In.Diam. ................................................*Illus*1400.00

SILVER-CHINESE, Case, Calling Card, Twining Serpents On Both Side, Filigree ..................... 110.00
Rattle, Repousse ................................................ 50.00
Tray, Floral & Dragon Design, 4 Ft., MIQ Mark, 6 In. ................................................ 145.00

SILVER-CONTINENTAL, Box, Bear, Garnet Eyes, 2 1/4 In. ................................................ 750.00

SILVER-DANISH, Bottle Opener, 3 In., Knife, 4 1/2 In., Signed Jensen ................................... 50.00
Compact, Scalloped Edge, Acorn Design, Georg Jensen ................................................ 110.00
Compote, Georg Jensen, 4 X 4 1/2 In.Diam. ................................................ 240.00
Dish, Entree, Covered, Art Deco, Georg Jensen, Pair ................................................*Illus*5500.00

Silver-Canadian, Punch Bowl, C.1910, 14 1/4 In.Diam.

Silver-Danish, Dish, Entree, Covered, Art Deco, Georg Jensen, Pair

Silver-Dutch, from left to right, top row, Figurine, Schoolmaster At Blackboard; Tea Set, Miniature, Tray; Coach and Horses, Miniature; bottom row, Teakettle On Pierced Stand; Gramophone With Horn, Miniature; Sewing Machine & Chair, Miniature

**Fork,** Lemon, Georg Jensen ................................................................................................................. 55.00
**Fork,** Meat, Acanthus, Georg Jensen ...................................................................................................... 75.00
**Fork,** Pickle, Georg Jensen ...................................................................................................................... 45.00
**Fork,** Serving, Scroll, Georg Jensen, 9 3/8 In. ...................................................................................... 250.00
**Jug,** Water, Pear Form, Ebony Handle, Jensen, 9 In. ............................................................................ 1200.00
**Knife,** Butter, Horn Blade, Georg Jensen ............................................................................................. 45.00
**Ladle,** Gravy, Cactus Pattern, Georg Jensen, 7 1/4 In. ........................................................................ 145.00
**Match Holder,** Figural, Standing Dog ................................................................................................... 25.00
**Salad Set,** Blossom Type, Georg Jensen .............................................................................................. 425.00
**Salt,** Open, Acanthus, Liner, Spoon, Georg Jensen, Set Of 4 .............................................................. 375.00
**Spoon,** Berry, Cactus Pattern, Georg Jensen, 6 In. .............................................................................. 250.00
**Tablespoon,** Etched Handle, Dated 1818 ............................................................................................ 38.00

**SILVER-DUTCH, Basket,** Flowers, Shellwork, 2-Handled, Footed, 16 1/2 In. ............................... 1000.00
**Coach & Horses,** Miniature, 5 In. ....................................................................................... *Illus* 500.00
**Figurine,** Schoolmaster At Blackboard, 5 In. ..................................................................... *Illus* 150.00
**Frame,** Desk, C.1900, Ollan & Touched Mark, 3 1/2 X 6 In. ............................................................ 35.00
**Gramophone With Horn,** Miniature, 1 1/4 In. ................................................................... *Illus* 100.00
**Plaque,** Crenellated Rim, Medieval Dressed Figures, 35 1/2 In. .................................................... 2100.00
**Scissors,** For Chatelaine, Dated 1816 ................................................................................................ 125.00
**Sewing Machine & Chair,** Miniature, 2 In. ..................................................................... *Illus* 125.00
**Snuffbox,** Clog Shape, 3 In. ............................................................................................................... 165.00
**Tea Caddy,** Teniers Scene, People Drinking, Oval, 3 7/8 In. ............................................................. 600.00
**Tea Set,** Miniature, Tray, 1 1/2 In. ................................................................................... *Illus* 100.00

*English silver is marked with a series of 4 or 5 small hallmarks. The standing lion is the most commonly seen sterling quality mark.*

**SILVER-ENGLISH, Beaker,** Henry Chawner, London, 1790-1801 ................................................ 700.00
**Bottle,** Perfume, Lying Down, Electric Blue, 4 In. ............................................................................ 145.00
**Bowl,** Engraved Presentation, Hemispherical, 5 1/2 In. .................................................................. 150.00
**Bowl,** Handled, Beaded Quatrefoils, John Harris, 1801, 10 In. ..................................................... 1400.00
**Bowl,** Putti & Panthers, Mask Ends, Hunt & Roskell, 24 In. ......................................................... 5750.00
**Cake Basket,** Pierced, E.Aldridge Jr. & Sr., 1760, 12 3/4 In. ...................................................... 1200.00
**Cake Basket,** Victorian ...................................................................................................................... 850.00

Silver-English, Cake Basket, Victorian

Silver-English, Centerpiece Bowl, Gilt, Victorian, M.Hall & Co.

| | |
|---|---:|
| **Candelabra,** 3 Light, Fluted Base, R.Hennell, 1859, 22 In., Pair | 5000.00 |
| **Candlestick,** Sheffield, C.1875 | 250.00 |
| **Castor,** 4 Bottle, Pierced Silver Frame, 10 In. | 135.00 |
| **Centerpiece Bowl,** Gilt, Victorian, M.Hall & Co. | *Illus* 5750.00 |
| **Chatelaine,** Nurse's | 375.00 |
| **Creamer,** C Scroll Handle, 1780, 4 In. | 75.00 |
| **Dessert Spoon,** T.Northcote, London, 1779-80, Set Of 5 | 350.00 |
| **Dish Cross,** S.Buttall, London, 1770, 12 1/2 In. | *Illus* 1400.00 |
| **Dish Ring,** Engraved Birds, Marked J.P., 1908, 8 1/4 In.Diam. | 400.00 |
| **Dish Ring,** Victorian | *Illus* 400.00 |
| **Fork & Spoon,** Salad, Hunting Scene, 1836 Mark, 9 In. | 300.00 |
| **Inkstand,** 4 Claw Feet, Cut Glass Bottles, 12 In. | 850.00 |
| **Jug,** Hot Milk, Cylindrical Form, Hinged Domed Cover, 6 In. | 300.00 |
| **Ladle,** Gravy, Shell Shape, William Eaton, 1806-07 | 200.00 |
| **Ladle,** Sauce, London, Samuel Hennell, 1807-08 | 75.00 |
| **Ladle,** Soup, Bright Cut Pattern, Bateman, C.1801 | 475.00 |
| **Ladle,** Soup, George III, William Sumner I, 1789 | 190.00 |
| **Marriage Cup,** Form Of Maiden, 19th Century, 9 Oz. | 425.00 |
| **Match Safe,** Figural, Rugby Ball | 110.00 |
| **Muffineer,** Engraving, Birmingham, 6 1/2 In. | 155.00 |
| **Mustard,** Hinged Lid, Embossed Bows, Hallmarked, 1911 | 68.00 |
| **Pepperette,** Owl Form, Brown Glass Eyes, Liner, 2 3/8 In. | 275.00 |
| **Pepperette,** Penguins, Inset Eyes, Pair, 2 1/2 In. | 150.00 |
| **Punch Bowl,** Rococo Foliate Scrolls, Garards, 1899, 21 1/2 In. | 4750.00 |
| **Salt Cellar,** Owl, Feathers, Hinged Head, Glass Liner, 4 In. | 650.00 |
| **Salt,** Shell Shape, Spoon, Birmingham, 1898, Hallmarked | 55.00 |
| **Salver,** Gilt, William Eaton, 1836, 22 1/2 In. | *Illus* 4500.00 |
| **Skewer,** Peter, Ann, & William Bateman, 1802, Crest, 13 3/4 In. | 300.00 |
| **Snuffbox,** Elongated Octagonal Form, T.Willmore, 1796 | 250.00 |
| **Snuffbox,** Engraved Rays & Dots, T.Phipps & E.Robinson, 1798 | 325.00 |

Silver-English, Dish Cross, S.Buttall, London, 1770, 12 1/2 In. (See Page 591)

Silver-English, Dish Ring, Victorian (See Page 591)

Silver-English, Salver, Gilt, William Eaton,
1836, 22 1/2 In. (See Page 591)

| | |
|---|---|
| **Spoon,** Basting, George III, Thomas Barker, 1813 | 90.00 |
| **Spoon,** Berry, Hallmarked, Elhengton, 1904, Pair | 85.00 |
| **Spoon,** Black & White Enameled Handles, Demitasse, Set Of 6 | 95.00 |
| **Spoon,** Sugar Sifter, Fiddleback, E.Eaton, 1849, Falcon Crest | 200.00 |
| **Spoon,** Tea Caddy, Chased Bowl, Jonathan Hayne, 1823 | 240.00 |
| **Strainer,** Lemon, Thomas Daniell, 1774, 10 In. | *Illus* 900.00 |
| **Strainer,** Tea, Peter & Ann Bateman, 3 1/2 In. | 235.00 |
| **Table Ornament,** Figural, Victorian, Pair | *Illus* 3750.00 |
| **Tablespoon,** Squirrel Engraved, W.Chawner, London, 1798 | 100.00 |
| **Tankard,** J.Langlanas, Newcastle, 1769, 7 3/4 In. | *Illus* 2000.00 |
| **Tankard,** Pickslay & Sons, Weighs 52 Ounces, 12 1/2 In. | 2800.00 |
| **Tea & Coffee Set,** R.Hennell, 1846-56, 6 1/4 In. | *Illus* 1800.00 |
| **Tea Caddy,** 1811-12, Alexander Hewat, London | 600.00 |
| **Tea Service,** William IV, Mappin & Webb, 1918, 6 Piece | 7000.00 |
| **Tea Set,** Half Fluted Body, George III, 1798, 3 Piece | 800.00 |
| **Teakettle,** Stand, J.S.Hunt, London, 1843, 16 In. | *Illus* 4500.00 |
| **Teakettle,** Tilt, Stand, Dated 1873 | 950.00 |
| **Teapot,** Wooden Handle & Finial, William Plummer, 1790, Oval | 700.00 |
| **Teaspoon,** Bright Cut Design, A. & P.Bateman, C.1797 | 55.00 |
| **Teaspoon,** Thistle & Cairngorm Stone On Top, Chester, 1901 | 32.00 |
| **Toast Rack,** C.1880, Signed J. Deakin | 45.00 |
| **Tongs,** Dated 1785, Bright Cut, Hester Bateman, C.1785 | 500.00 |
| **Tray,** Meat, Hot Water Base, P.Storr, 1827, 17 In. | *Illus* 6500.00 |
| **Tray,** Meat, J.Collins, London, 1826, 17 3/4 In. | *Illus* 1600.00 |
| **Vinaigrette,** Ledsam, Vale, & Wheeler, 1830, 1 1/4 In. | 260.00 |
| **Vinaigrette,** Satchel Shape, Gold Wash, 1820 | 275.00 |

Silver-English, Strainer, Lemon,
Thomas Daniell, 1774, 10 In.

Silver-English, Table Ornament,
Figural, Victorian, Pair

Silver-English, Tankard, J.Langlanas, Newcastle, 1769, 7 3/4 In. (See Page 593)

Silver-English, Tea & Coffee Set, R.Hennell, 1846-56, 6 1/4 In. (See Page 593)

Silver-English, Teakettle, Stand, J.S.Hunt, London, 1843, 16 In. (See Page 593)

Silver-English, Tray, Meat, Hot Water Base, P.Storr, 1827, 17 In. (See Page 593)

Silver-English, Tray, Meat, J.Collins, London, 1826, 17 3/4 In. (See Page 593)

Silver-French, Coffeepot, Odiot, Paris, C.1875, 9 1/2 In.

**SILVER-FRENCH, Coffeepot,** Odiot, Paris, C.1875, 9 1/2 In. ..................................................*Illus* 900.00
   **Spoon,** Demitasse, Crested & Engraved, 1809-19, 5 In. .................................................. 25.00
   **Tea & Coffee Set,** Pear Form Tray, C.1840, 6 Piece ................................................ 4000.00

**SILVER-GERMAN, Candelabra,** 4 Light, Lion Masks & Foliage, 18 1/2 In., Pair ..................... 1100.00
   **Case,** Coin, Vanity, Money Clip, Chain, 2 1/2 X 3 1/2 In. ................................................ 30.00
   **Case,** Lady's, On Chain, Engraved ................................................................. 45.00
   **Cocktail Set,** 2 Gas Cylinders, Wheeled Handcart, 16 In. ................................................ 1500.00
   **Cup,** Stirrup, Bell Form, Fox, Horse, Rabbit, Boat, Moose, 4 In. ................................................ 1000.00
   **Dessert Set,** 12 Demitasse Spoons, Berry Spoon, 19th Century ................................................ 150.00
   **Fork,** Pie, Blade On Side, Scroll Handle, Hallmarked, Set Of 4 ................................................ 60.00
   **Goblet,** Foliage Stem, C.1850, W.Zeitz, 5 5/8 In. ................................................ 325.00
   **Goblet,** Medieval Style, Grape Cluster Applied, C.1900, 13 In. ................................................ 475.00
   **Goblet,** Pineapple Shape, Lid, Man Knop, 19th Century, 14 In. ................................................ 1000.00
   **Ladle,** Punch, English King Pattern, Hallmarked, 1850, 14 In. ................................................ 800.00
   **Letter Opener,** Sword Shape, Engraved Handle, 7 1/2 In. ................................................ 25.00

Silver-Irish, Tea Urn, J.Locker, Dublin, C.1765, 21 1/4 In.

Silver-Japanese, Humidor, Camphorwood Lined, 9 3/4 In.

| | |
|---|---|
| **Ornament,** Figural, Fighting Cocks, 19th Century, 10 In., Pair | 800.00 |
| **Sauceboat,** Stand, Boat Form, Laurel Borders, 10 In. | 300.00 |
| **Ship,** 4 Masted, Dolphin & Wheel Supports, C.1900, 16 1/2 In. | 1900.00 |
| **Smoking Set,** Form Of Airship, C.1930, 9 1/2 In. | 1900.00 |
| **Spoons,** Ice Cream, Armorial, Foliate Mantle, Set Of 12 | 200.00 |
| **Teaspoon,** Reich Hallmark, 8 Troy Ounce, Set Of 12 | 185.00 |
| **Tray,** Coronet & Crest, Leaves, Foliate Rim, Marked, 26 1/2 In. | 1800.00 |
| **Tray,** Oval, Punched Rim, Stylized Leaf Tips, 13 1/4 In. | 1400.00 |
| | |
| **SILVER-IRISH, Chalice,** C.1850, 11 1/2 In. | 500.00 |
| **Ladle,** Punch, Ribbed Bowl, 1797 Dublin Mark, 14 In. | 375.00 |
| **Spoon,** Salt, Engraved Crest, C.1797, Hallmarked, Dublin, 4 In. | 45.00 |
| **Spoon,** Serving, John Sheilds, Dublin, 1803 | 85.00 |
| **Tea Urn,** J.Locker, Dublin, C.1765, 21 1/4 In. | *Illus* 3700.00 |
| | |
| **SILVER-JAPANESE, Humidor,** Camphorwood Lined, 9 3/4 In. | *Illus* 1000.00 |
| | |
| **SILVER-MEXICAN, Bottle,** Perfume, Purse, Cylindrical, Ball Screw Stopper, 3 In. | 14.00 |
| **Box,** Pill, Hinged Lid With Applied Flower, 1 3/8 X 3/4 In. | 14.50 |
| **Plate,** Juarez, Weight, 4 Ounce | 125.00 |
| **Plate,** Made In Juarez, Marked, 6 In., Set Of 3 | 450.00 |
| **Plate,** Molded Border, C.1780, Gonzales, 9 In. | 425.00 |
| **Shot Glass,** Inlaid Abalone Shell | 25.00 |
| | |
| **SILVER-PERSIAN, Vessel,** Peacock Form, Hinge Back Opening, Paste Eyes, 14 In. | 650.00 |
| | |
| **SILVER-PERUVIAN, Holder,** Placecard, Llama, Marked 900 | 22.50 |
| | |
| **SILVER-POLISH, Tea & Coffee Set,** Maler, C.1840, 9 Piece | *Illus* 2000.00 |
| | |
| **SILVER-PORTUGUESE, Salver,** Paw & Foliage Feet, C.1845, Oporto, Signed | 375.00 |
| **Tea & Coffee Set,** Art Deco, C.1930 | *Illus* 3500.00 |
| **Tureen,** Ovoid Bombe Form, Strawberry Knop, 14 In.Long | 1300.00 |

Silver-Polish, Tea & Coffee Set,
Maler, C.1840, 9 Piece

Silver-Portuguese, Tea & Coffee Set, Art Deco, C.1930

*Russian silver is marked with the cyrillic or Russian alphabet. The numbers 84, 88, or 91 indicate the content of solid silver pieces. Russian silver may be higher or lower than sterling standard. Other marks indicate maker, assayer, or city of manufacture.*

**SILVER-RUSSIAN, see also Faberge**
SILVER-RUSSIAN, **Basket,** Swing Handle, Dated 1884, Ovchinnikov, 4 1/2 In.Diam. ........... 825.00
  **Box,** Niello, 1876 Silver Marks For Moscow, Villiliky Ustiug ................................................ 500.00
  **Case,** Cigarette, Gold Script Name, Hallmarked, 8 Troy Ounce ........................................ 375.00
  **Case,** Semiprecious Stone Thumbpiece, Hallmarked, 4 X 3 In. ........................................ 225.00
  **Cup & Saucer,** White Ground, Multicolored Enamel, 4 1/2 In. ......................................... 750.00
  **Cup,** Vodka, Blue, Green, Mauve Enameled, White Trim, 1 1/2 In. .................................. 400.00
  **Holder,** Tea Glass, Art Nouveau Engravings ................................................................ 90.00
  **Salt Cellar,** Pink & Blue Enameled Flowers, 1 5/8 In. ................................................... 500.00
  **Salt,** Silver Bands, 3 Ball Feet, Hallmarked ................................................................ 650.00
  **Salt,** Sterling Silver Bands, Hallmarked, Pair ............................................................... 750.00
  **Snuffbox,** Engraved, Niello Allover, Marked, 3 X 2 In. .................................................. 195.00
  **Spice Box,** Dated 1867, Marked 84, Hinged Lid, 3 X 2 1/2 In. ...................................... 265.00
  **Spoons,** Serving, Moscow, 1894, 9 1/4 In. ................................................................ 95.00
  **Strainer,** Tea, Bucket, Rope Handle, Gold Wash, 1887 ................................................. 95.00
  **Teapot,** Bullet Form, Loop Handle, Swan Neck, Marked, 4 In. ...................................... 400.00

SILVER-SCOTCH, **Scoop,** Marrow, Castle Crest, Hallmarked, C.1780 ........................................ 195.00
  **Tongs,** Sugar, Hallmarked ..................................................................................... 30.00
  **Urn,** Tea, Leaf Form Handles, William Davie, 1779, 20 1/2 In. .................................... 200.00

*Sterling silver is made with 925 parts of silver out of 1, 000 parts of metal. The word sterling is a quality guarantee used in the United States after about 1860.*

**SILVER-STERLING, see also Silver-American; Silver-English; etc.**

| | |
|---|---:|
| **SILVER-STERLING, Belt Buckle,** Chrysler Corp., Award To Master Technician | 25.00 |
| **Biscuit Holder,** Shell Shaped Covers, Wallace, 10 X 12 In. | 275.00 |
| **Box,** Hinged Lid, Crystal, Foster & Bailey, 2 X 1 1/2 In. | 45.00 |
| **Brush,** Art Deco, 5 In. | 65.00 |
| **Butter,** Covered, Knife, Tufts, Boston | 85.00 |
| **Butter,** Pad Feet, Ball Trim, Bailes & Co., C.1850, 5 1/2 In. | 850.00 |
| **Buttonhook & Nailfile,** Beaded | 10.00 |
| **Buttonhook,** Nailfile, & Cuticle Pusher, Beaded Edge, Set | 25.00 |
| **Candlesnuffer,** Cone End, Twist Handle, Long | 39.00 |
| **Candlestick,** Chantilly, Gorham, 4 3/4 In., Pair | 155.00 |
| **Candlestick,** Gadroon & Shell Border, M.Boulton, C.1790 | 800.00 |
| **Case,** Calling Card, Chain, C.1880, Whiting, 3 1/2 X 2 1/2 In. | 95.00 |
| **Case,** Calling Card, Full Figure Woman, Hallmarked | 95.00 |
| **Case,** Card, Engine Turned Design, Gorham, Marked | 95.00 |
| **Case,** Coin, Dimes & Nickels, Hinged, Chain, Lined, 2 1/8 In. | 30.00 |
| **Case,** Needle, Hinged Top, Embossed Fish Forms | 50.00 |
| **Cigarette Case,** Enameled Setter, Game Bird | 400.00 |
| **Coffeepot,** Leaf At Spout, M.McMullin, C.1795, 14 In. | 4000.00 |
| **Compact,** Japanese Scene | 75.00 |
| **Creamer,** Cow, Bee Embossed On Lid, 4 X 6 1/2 In. | 425.00 |
| **Creamer,** Shell Feet, Gadroon Border, Beaded Line, T.B.Starr | 185.00 |
| **Cross,** Underglaze Design Enamel, Rope Twist Chain, 15 In. | 38.00 |
| **Dish,** Coronation, George VI, Queen Elizabeth, 5 In. | 98.00 |
| **Ewer,** S-Scroll Handle, Engraved, Forbes & Son, C.1838, 15 In. | 3200.00 |
| **Figurine,** Bulldog, Standing, 2 3/4 X 4 In. | 215.00 |
| **Figurine,** Rabbit, Crouching, 2 1/2 X 2 3/4 In. | 160.00 |
| **Flask,** Floral, Cherub, Repousse, Crown, 925 Fine | 225.00 |
| **Flask,** Horn Shaped, Moon & Star, Applied Frog, Crane | 225.00 |
| **Fork,** Asparagus, Ornate Cutout Bowl, 8 1/2 In. | 25.00 |
| **Fork,** Baby, Joan Of Arc | 19.50 |
| **Fork,** Serving, Lily, Whiting | 185.00 |
| **Frame,** Picture, 2 Ball Feet, Easel Back, Hanger, 3 In.Diam. | 35.00 |
| **Funnel,** Perfume, Applied Wirework Design, Handle, 1 1/4 In. | 15.00 |
| **Holder,** Corn, Figural Ears Of Corn, Pair | 10.00 |
| **Holder,** Matchbox, Inscribed Top Score | 28.00 |
| **Inkstand,** Double, Pen Rest Either Side, Sheffield | 195.00 |
| **Iron,** Curling | 36.50 |
| **Jar,** Dresser, Art Nouveau, Unger Bros. | 150.00 |
| **Label,** Rum Bottle, Chain, Cutout Lettering | 18.00 |
| **Ladle,** Cream, Gadroon, Feathered Handle, Towle, 6 1/2 In. | 35.00 |
| **Ladle,** Soup, Mayflower, Kirk, 1896-1903 Mark, 13 In. | 250.00 |
| **Ladle,** Soup, Swiss Pattern, Gorham, C.1873, 10 1/2 In. | 100.00 |
| **Match Safe,** Leaf Design, Hallmarked Birmingham, 1885, 2 In. | 45.00 |
| **Mirror,** Hand, Art Nouveau, 5 1/2 In. | 400.00 |
| **Mirror,** Hand, Initial D, Floral | 10.00 |
| **Muffineer,** Pedestal, Pierced Dome Cover, Marked, 5 1/2 In. | 90.00 |
| **Mug,** Child's, Dated 1909 | 55.00 |
| **Napkin Ring,** Tree Bark Pattern, Initialed, Marked | 110.00 |
| **Nut Picks,** Set Of 4 | 150.00 |
| **Nut Set,** Gilded, Scalloped Shell, 7 Small Shells, Card Clip | 275.00 |
| **Perfumer,** Cut Glass, Sterling Top, Unger Bros., 2 3/4 In. | 30.00 |
| **Rattle,** Bell Hooked Onto Celluloid Ring, 1 1/2 In. | 20.00 |
| **Salt,** Master, Cobalt Blue Liner, Ball Feet, Oval, 3 1/2 In. | 39.00 |
| **Server,** Cheese, Floral Design | 135.00 |
| **Shuttle,** Tatting, Greek Key Design Border, Engraved Name | 39.00 |
| **Soup,** Cream, Etruscan, Gorham | 50.00 |

**SILVER-STERLING, Spoon, Souvenir, see Souvenir, Spoon, Sterling Silver**

| | |
|---|---:|
| **Spoon & Fork,** Serving, Salad, Lily, Frank Whiting | 225.00 |
| **Spoon,** Baby, International, Applied Alphabet Blocks | 35.00 |

| | |
|---|---|
| Spoon, Demitasse, Head Of Indian On Handle | 25.00 |
| Spoon, Folding, Double | 25.00 |
| Spoon, Ice Cream, Mt.Vernon, Watson, Newell, Set Of 6 | 95.00 |
| Spoon, Lemonade Sipper, Tubular Handled, Gorham, Set Of 6 | 95.00 |
| Spoon, Serving, Honeysuckle, Shovel Shape, J.Polhemus, 9 In. | 75.00 |
| Sugar Tongs, Hindostanee, Gorham | 65.00 |
| Tamper, Pipe, Loop To Attach To Watch Chain | 22.50 |
| Tea Ball, Hinged Top, Double Chain With Ring | 45.00 |
| Tea Ball, Hinged, Gold Wash Interior, Chain & Loop | 22.00 |
| Tea Ball, Sterling Handle, 5 1/8 In. | 85.00 |
| Tea Ball, Teapot Shape, Cover, Chain, Battlesboro, Mass. | 55.00 |
| Tea Caddy, Fluted Body, Hinged Lid, Bone Finial, C.1870 | 195.00 |
| Teaspoon, English Gadroon | 30.00 |
| Teaspoon, Pointed End, Robert Brookhouse, C.1800, 5 7/8 In. | 55.00 |
| Teaspoon, Zodiac, August, Gorham | 35.00 |
| Teaspoon, Zodiac, September, Gorham | 35.00 |
| Tongs, Shell Grips, Chased Flowers, C.1870 | 75.00 |
| Tongs, Sugar, Spiral Prongs, 3 1/2 In. | 15.00 |
| Tongs, Wishbone Shaped, Spring Mechanism, 4 1/4 In. | 50.00 |
| Tray, Heart Shaped, Footed, Reticulated, Gorham, 3 3/4 In. | 35.00 |
| Trimmer, Cuticle | 22.00 |
| Vase, Bud, Marked, 6 1/4 In. | 40.00 |
| Vase, Ivy & Lizard, Hand Hammered, Hallmarked, 8 In. | 225.00 |
| Warmer, Biscuit, Sides Unfold To Open, 2 Inside Trays | 500.00 |
| SILVER-VIENNESE, Bottle, Pilgrim, Classical Dress, H.Boehm, 7 1/2 In. | 1400.00 |
| Box, Clown On Lid, Pearl Nose, Gems On Base, 5 3/4 In. | 1400.00 |
| Etui, Cylindrical, Figures, Polychrome Enamel, 4 3/4 In. | 1400.00 |
| Figurine, Heron, Enameled & Jeweled Plumage, C.1910, 4 In. | 650.00 |
| Wine, Barrel Shape, Figure Supported, C.1900, 7 In. | 3500.00 |

*Sinclaire cut glass was made by H.P.Sinclaire and Company of Corning, New York, between 1905 and 1929. Pieces were made of crystal as well as amber, blue, green, or ruby. Only a small percentage of Sinclaire glass is marked.*

| | |
|---|---|
| SINCLAIRE, Bottle, Cologne, Etched Flowers, Signed, 6 In. | 125.00 |
| Bowl, Adam Pattern, 6-Sided, Signed, 3 1/2 X 9 1/4 In. | 250.00 |
| Bowl, Amethyst, Signed, 3 1/4 X 10 In. | 45.00 |
| Bowl, Pale Green, Pedestal, Rolled Rim, Signed, 16 3/4 In. | 65.00 |
| Bowl, Poppy Pattern, Intaglio Poppies, Scalloped, 4 X 8 In. | 225.00 |
| Compote, Dorglinger, Flutes & Festoons, Signed, 9 1/2 X 8 In. | 475.00 |
| Dish, Card, Hobs & Engraved, Signed, 7 X 4 X 1 In. | 75.00 |
| Dish, Sweetmeat, Silver Plated Cover, Bail & Handle, Signed | 175.00 |
| Plate, Adam Pattern, 8-Sided, Signed, 10 In. | 250.00 |
| Plate, Green, Signed, 8 1/2 In. | 35.00 |
| Plate, Strawberry, Diamond, Fan, & Hobstar, Signed, 10 In. | 50.00 |
| Vase, Etched Tulips, Crystal, Signed, 13 1/2 In. | 250.00 |
| Vase, Fan, Light Green, Signed, 7 X 5 In. | 40.00 |
| Vase, Holly Pattern, 6 1/4 In. | 150.00 |
| Vase, Lily Pattern, Amethyst To Clear, 6 In. | 125.00 |
| Vase, Tulips, Etched, Crystal, Signed, 13 1/2 In. | 250.00 |
| Water Set, Blown Handle, Wafer Base Tumblers, Signed, 3 Piece | 345.00 |
| | |
| SITZENDORF, Figurine, Musical Group, 5 Figures On Podium, 20 X 10 In. | 1450.00 |
| Figurine, Putto Sitting Astride Pink Dolphin, 7 In. | 95.00 |
| | |
| SKY KING, Ring, Electronic Television | 50.00 |
| Ring, Navajo | 55.00 |

*Slag glass is streaked with several colors. There were many types made from about 1880. Pink slag was an American Victorian product of unknown origin. Purple and blue slag were made in American and English factories. Red slag is a very late Victorian product. Other colors are known, but are of less importance to the collector. The numbers B-XX refer to the book "Milk Glass" by E. Belknap.*

| | |
|---|---:|
| **SLAG, Blue,** Compote, Diamond Lattice | 60.00 |
| **Blue,** Match Holder, 4 Ashtrays | 15.00 |
| **Blue,** Toothpick, Barrel On Circular Base, C.1882 | 30.00 |
| **Blue,** Vase, Fused Peacock Design, English, 8 In. | 100.00 |
|     **SLAG, Caramel, see Chocolate Glass** | |
| **Green,** Jar, Perfume, Renaud, Label | 20.00 |
| **Green,** Lamp, Hanging, Black Metal, 18 In.Square | 180.00 |
| **Orange,** Vase, 15 In. | 25.00 |
| **Pink,** Cup, Punch, Footed | 295.00 |
| **Pink,** Sauce, Inverted Fan & Feather, Set Of 6 | 800.00 |
| **Pink,** Tumbler, Inverted Fan & Feather | 175.00 To 300.00 |
| **Pink,** Tumbler, Water, Fan & Feather, 4 X 2 3/4 In. | 395.00 |
| **Purple,** Bell | 21.50 |
| **Purple,** Bowl, Raindrop, 8 3/4 In. | 45.00 |
| **Purple,** Butter, Round | 20.00 |
| **Purple,** Compote, C.1910, 4 1/2 X 6 In. | 65.00 |
| **Purple,** Compote, Grapes, 4 In. | 20.00 |
| **Purple,** Compote, Jelly, Acanthus | 32.00 |
| **Purple,** Compote, Threaded & Ruffled | 45.00 |
| **Purple,** Compote, Vertical Pattern, Hexagonal Stem, Scalloped, 4 In. | 45.00 |
| **Purple,** Compote, 5 X 5 In. | 50.00 |
| **Purple,** Creamer, English | 70.00 |
| **Purple,** Creamer, Flower Panel, Milk Glass | 48.00 |
| **Purple,** Creamer, Sunflower | 75.00 |
| **Purple,** Cruet | 25.00 |
| **Purple,** Jar, Honey, Glossy | 20.00 |
| **Purple,** Jar, Honey, Satin Finish | 25.00 |
| **Purple,** Jar, Owl | 30.00 |
| **Purple,** Match Holder | 28.00 To 45.00 |
| **Purple,** Pitcher, Embossed Floral & Flutes, English, 3 1/4 In. | 37.00 |
| **Purple,** Pitcher, Milk, Figural, Fish | 95.00 |
| **Purple,** Pitcher, Water, Fan & Basket Weave Pattern | 225.00 |
| **Purple,** Plate, Basket Weave, Open Edge, 8 In. | 70.00 |
| **Purple,** Plate, Lattice Edge, 10 In. | 95.00 |
| **Purple,** Shot Glass, Thimble Shape, Just A Thimble Full, England | 80.00 |
| **Purple,** Spooner, Fluted | 75.00 |
| **Purple,** Sugar & Creamer, Holly | 60.00 |
| **Purple,** Sugar & Creamer, Owl | 30.00 |
| **Purple,** Swan, 4 In. | 20.00 |
| **Purple,** Toothpick Holder | 30.00 |
| **Purple,** Tray, 2-Handled, Round, 4 1/2 In. | 30.00 |
| **Purple,** Tumbler, 4 3/4 In. | 25.00 |
| **Purple,** Vase, 2 1/2 X 3 In. | 15.00 |
| **Purple,** Vase, 4 3/4 In. | 42.00 |
| **Red,** Bowl, Fenton, Pedestal, 4 X 3 1/4 In. | 75.00 |
| **Red,** Bowl, Fenton, Pedestal, 7 1/4 In. | 75.00 |

*Sleepy Eye pottery was made to be given away with the flour products of the Sleepy Eye Milling Co., Sleepy Eye, Minnesota, from about 1893 to 1952. It is a heavy stoneware with blue decorations, usually the famous profile of an Indian.*

| | |
|---|---:|
| **SLEEPY EYE, Bottle,** Blue & White, 1/2 Pint | 137.50 |
| **Butter,** Covered, Stenciled Butter, Blue & White | 80.00 |
| **Creamer,** Blue & White, Signed Western Pottery, 1930s | 85.00 |
| **Creamer,** Cobalt Blue, Monmouth | 192.50 |

Creamer, Yellow & Cobalt .................................................................................................. 400.00
Crock, Salt .......................................................................................... 325.00 To 355.00
Mug, Cobalt & White, 4 1/2 In. ....................................................................................... 245.00
Pitcher, Cobalt Blue & White, Pint ................................................................................ 175.00
Pitcher, Cobalt Blue & White, 1 Quart .......................................................... 178.00 To 220.00
Pitcher, Cobalt Blue & White, 1/2 Gallon .................................................................... 250.00
Pitcher, Cobalt Blue & White, 1/2 Pint ........................................................ 140.00 To 165.00
Pitcher, Standing Indian .......................................................................................... 1250.00
Pitcher, W.S. Co., Monmouth, Ill., 6 1/2 In. ................................................................. 95.00
Spoon, Picture Of Sleepy Eye ..................................................................................... 75.00
Stein, Blue & Gray, No Handle ................................................................................... 125.00
Stein, Brown Glaze, 8 In. .......................................................................................... 385.00
Stein, Cobalt Blue, Marked, 8 In. ............................................................................... 650.00
Stein, White & Blue, Light ......................................................................................... 500.00
Stein, Yellow & Brown ............................................................................................... 580.00
Sugar Bowl ................................................................................................................ 425.00
Vase, Cylinder, Cattails, Dragonfly, 8 1/2 In. ............................................................. 180.00
Vase, Gray & Blue, 9 In. ............................................................................................ 105.00
Vase, Indian, Cattails & Dragonfly, Cylindrical, 6 3/4 In. ........................................... 155.00
Vase, 8 1/2 In. .......................................................................................................... 350.00

> *Slip is a thin mixture of clay and water, about the consistency of sour cream, that is applied to the pottery for decoration.*

SLIPWARE, Plate, Pie, Potter John Bell, Waynesboro, Penn. ..................................... 125.00
Syrup, Wheel Etched, Slip Decorated, C.1900 ............................................................ 75.00
    SLOT MACHINE, see Store, Machine

## *Smith Bros. Co.*

> *Smith Brothers glass was made after 1878. The owners had worked for the Mt. Washington Glass Company in New Bedford, Massachusetts, for seven years before going into their own shop.*

SMITH BROTHERS, Bottle, Cologne, Rampant Lion, Signed, 10 3/4 X 5 3/4 In. ............ 265.00
Bowl, Rampant Lion, Melon Shaped, Brass Rim, Signed, 4 In. ................................... 389.00
Bowl, Rose, Beige Ground, Blue Overall Pansies, 5 In. .............................................. 185.00
Bowl, White To Pink, Beads Around Neck, Lion Sign, 4 In. ........................................ 175.00
Box, Powder, Beige, Pansies, Melon Ribbed, Covered, Signed .................................. 225.00
Cracker Barrel, Silver Plated Cover, Gold Outlined, Signed ...................................... 375.00
Dish, Hand-Painted Daises, Dated June, 1894, Signed, 5 1/2 In. ............................... 395.00
Finger Bowl, Floral Rim, Silver Plated Holder, Signed .............................................. 135.00
Jar, Mustard, Glazed Porcelain Base, Sterling Top, Signed ....................................... 140.00
Jar, Pedestal Base, Blue Flowers, 3 1/4 X 4 1/4 In. ................................................... 150.00
Jar, Sweatmeat, Covered, Signed ............................................................................... 300.00
Muffineer, Covered, Flowers, Beige Ground, Rampant Lion ....................................... 280.00
Muffineer, Melon Ribbed, Daisies, Cream, Yellow, 3 X 3 1/4 In. ................................ 278.50
Mustard Pot, Porcelain Base, Sterling Top, Signed, 3 X 2 In. ................................... 140.00
Plaque, Pansies, Marked, 10 In. Diam. ......................................................................... 60.00
Rose Bowl, Beige Ground, Blue Pansy, Beaded Top, 5 X 5 In. ................................... 185.00
Rose Bowl, Melon Ribbed, Signed, 2 1/2 In. ............................................................. 200.00
Rose Bowl, Melon Shape, Morning Glories, 5 1/2 X 3 1/2 In. .................................... 230.00
Rose Bowl, Queen's Design, Moire Ground, Beaded, Signed, 4 In. ............................ 350.00
Rose Jar, Pansy Design, Beige Ground, 4 X 4 1/4 In. Diam. ...................................... 160.00
Rose Jar, Shasta Daisy Design, White Dots On Top Edge, 4 In. ................................ 160.00
Salt, Melon Ribbed, Coin Gold Beaded Rim ................................................................ 65.00
Salt, Open, Melon Rib, Gold Floral Design, Beaded, 3 1/4 In. .................................... 35.00
Saltshaker, Melon Shape, Pewter Top ......................................................................... 60.00
Saltshaker, Squat Melon Shape, Pink, Pewter Top, 2 1/2 In. ...................................... 60.00
Sugar Shaker, Burmese, Maiden Hair Fern, 5 3/4 In. ............................................... 250.00
Sugar Shaker, 5-Ribbed, Pansies, Pink To White, 5 In. ............................................ 275.00
Sweetmeat, Daisies, Melon Ribbed, Bail & Lid, Signed, 5 In. .................................... 395.00
Sweetmeat, Melon Ribbed, Signed, Bail & Handle ..................................................... 375.00
Vase, Hand-Painted, Gold Trim, 11 1/2 In., Pair ....................................................... 325.00

| | |
|---|---:|
| Vase, Heron In Water Scene, Butterscotch Ground, 6 In. | 50.00 |
| Vase, Heron, White Ground, Silver Plated Holder, 5 3/4 In. | 95.00 |
| Vase, Melon Ribbed, Allover Daisy Design, Signed, 2 1/2 In. | 210.00 |
| Vase, Pinched-In Sides, Carnation Sprays, Signed, 4 1/2 In. | 315.00 |
| Vase, Ribbed, Season's Greetings In Gold, Signed, 2 1/2 In. | 210.00 |

*Snow Babies, made from bisque and spattered with glitter sand, were first manufactured in 1864 by Hertwig and Company in Thuringia. Other German and Japanese companies copied the Hertwig designs. Originally, Snow Babies were made of candy and used as Christmas decorations.*

| | |
|---|---:|
| SNOW BABIES, Bowl, Girl & Dog, 9 1/2 In.Diam. | 175.00 |
| Box, Club Shape, Signed | 120.00 |
| Creamer, Black Cat | 75.00 |
| Creamer, Blue Mark, Small | 68.00 |
| Figurine, Bell, On Sled, Blue Mark | 200.00 |
| Figurine, On Polar Bear, Germany, 2 1/2 In. | 75.00 |
| Figurine, On Skis, Bisque, 1 1/2 In. | 25.00 |
| Figurine, Seated On Log, 1 In. | 25.00 |
| Figurine, Seated, 1 1/4 In. | 30.00 |
| Figurine, Singer, Standing, Jointed, Bisque, Set Of 3 | 55.00 |
| Figurine, Standing, Bisque, 2 1/2 In. | 60.00 |
| Figurine, Two On Sled | 60.00 |
| Mustard, Red Poppy, Leaf Spoon | 60.00 |
| Pitcher, Babies Sliding Down Hill, Royal Bayreuth, 4 1/2 In. | 125.00 |
| Pitcher, Blue Mark, 1 Quart | 225.00 |
| Plate, 9 In.Diam. | 165.00 |
| Postcard, Christmas Greetings | 12.00 |
| Rose Bowl, Footed, Square Mouth, Shell Each Corner, Blue Mark | 85.00 |
| Saltshaker, Royal Bayreuth | 65.00 |

| | |
|---|---:|
| SNUFF BOTTLE, see Bottle, Snuff | |
| SNUFFBOX, Birch Bark, Punched Diamonds & Circles, Leather Tab, 2 In. | 65.00 |
| Black Lacquered Papier-Mache, Pewter Inlay, Hinged Lid, 3 1/2 In. | 28.00 |
| C.Parker, C.1860, Tin | 21.00 |
| Cornucopia Shape, Pressure Fit Lid, Old Black Paint, Wooden, 3 In. | 35.00 |
| Curly Maple, Tortoise Lined | 85.00 |
| Dated 1895, Sterling Silver, Gorham | 100.00 |
| Enamel On Wood | 30.00 |
| Engraved Angel On Cover, Copper, 2 In. | 10.00 |
| French, Raised General Foch On Lid, 1914 | 10.00 |
| Papier-Mache | 22.00 |
| Pewter Inlay, Rectangular | 20.00 |
| Pewter, Round, Stamped | 110.00 |
| Russian, Scenes Front & Back, 1840, M.Chermazov, 2 5/8 X 1 5/8 In. | 550.00 |

*Soapstone is a mineral that was used for foot warmers or griddles because of its heat-retaining properties. Soapstone was carved in many countries in the nineteenth and twentieth centuries.*

| | |
|---|---:|
| SOAPSTONE, Ashtray, Carved, Signed China | 9.00 |
| Ashtray, Leaf Shape, Small | 5.00 |
| Bookends, Openwork Flowers, Maroon | 45.00 |
| Bookends, Urns With Flowers, 4 1/2 X 3 3/4 In. | 35.00 |
| Bookends, Vase & Peony | 57.00 |
| Cup, Wine, Green Gray, 2 X 2 1/4 In., Set Of 4 | 45.00 |
| Dish, Pin, Carved Foliage, 3-Legged, Signed | 15.00 |
| Figurine, Bearded God, 2 3/4 In. | 28.00 |
| Figurine, Dragon, 4 In. | 16.00 |
| Figurine, Fisherman On Rocky Mound, Holding Carp, 12 In. | 145.00 |
| Figurine, Foo Dog, Chinese, 6 1/2 In., Pair | 120.00 |
| Figurine, Horse & Rider, Raspberry Patina, 1900s, 11 X 10 In. | 195.00 |
| Figurine, Horse, 4 In. | 12.00 |
| Figurine, Lady With Bottle & Branch | 300.00 |

**Figurine,** Man With Cane, 10 In. .................................................................................. 95.00
**Figurine,** Monkeys, Black, 4 In. ................................................................................... 22.00
**Figurine,** Peacock, Jade Green, Wood Base, 6 1/2 In., Pair ......................................... 96.00
**Figurine,** Peacock, 8 In. .............................................................................................. 32.00
**Figurine,** Seated Foo Lion, Tan, 4 X 6 X 9 In. ............................................................. 95.00
**Figurine,** Wolf & Crane ............................................................................................... 75.00
**Figurine,** 2 Men On Reclining Water Buffalo, Wood Base, 6 In. .................................... 75.00
**Figurine,** 3 Rearing Horses, 1900s, Wooden Base, 11 X 10 In. .................................. 195.00
**Foot Warmer,** Bail Handle .......................................................................................... 13.00
**Lamp,** Figural, Geisha Girl, Fringed Shade, Green, 22 In. ........................................... 285.00
**Lamp,** Oil, Head Of Bacchus, 19th Century, Europe, 2 1/2 In. .................................... 200.00
**Match Holder,** Footed, Carved Front, 6 In. ................................................................. 27.00
**Match Holder,** Vase On Side, Flowers ........................................................................ 30.00
**Mold,** Bullet, Single Cavity, Hardwood Handles ......................................................... 110.00
**Planter,** Pierced Foliage, 6 X 4 In. ............................................................................. 22.00
**Toothpick,** Three Monkeys ................................................................ 18.50 To 28.50
**Tray,** Handles, Metal Rim, Oval, 16 1/2 In. ................................................................. 18.00
**Tray,** Pin, Carved, Chinese, Signed .......................................................................... 12.50
**Vase,** Carved Filigree Flowers, Birds, 6 X 9 In. .......................................................... 48.00
**Vase,** Carved Peony, Leaves, Footed Red Brown Base, 12 In. .................................... 90.00
**Vase,** Carved With Foliage, C.1900, 7 In. ................................................................... 85.00
**Vase,** Carved, Green & Rust, 5 1/4 In. ....................................................................... 135.00
**Vase,** Cherry Blossom, 8 In. ....................................................................................... 32.00
**Vase,** Double, Rust Brown, Mottled Gray & Green, 5 1/2 X 3 1/2 In. .......................... 122.00
**Vase,** Flat Sides, Mottled Rust & Gray Green, Incised Design, 3 In. ............................ 19.00
**Vase,** Floral & Leaf Design, Green, Rust, Ornate, 4 1/2 In. ........................................ 125.00
**Vase,** Leaves & Flowers, 5 In. .................................................................................... 35.00
**Vase,** Mums, 8 In. ....................................................................................................... 32.00
**Vase,** Oriental, Carved, Green, Pair, 5 In. .................................................................. 135.00
**Vase,** Peony Bushes, Yellow, Gray, Tan Base, S Form, 10 1/2 In. ............................... 80.00
**Wall Pocket,** Carved, Brown & Beige, 3 Pocket ......................................................... 45.00

**SOFT PASTE, Creamer,** Salt Glazed, Small ............................................................. 485.00
**Cup & Saucer,** Raised Basket Weave Outside & Inside, C.1850 ................................. 20.00

**SOUVENIR, Ashtray,** Carlsbad Caverns, Vernon Kilns ............................................... 5.00
**Ashtray,** Coney Island, New York, Metal .................................................................... 8.00
**Brush,** Clothes, W.C.Fields, Century Of Progress, Original Box, 1933 ......................... 35.00
**Buttonhook,** Pan Pacific Exposition, California Bear, Folding ..................................... 32.50
**Cup,** Belfast, Maine, Ruby Flashed ............................................................................ 25.00
**Hatchet,** Glass, Indian Head, Pan American, Buffalo, 1901, 7 1/4 In. .......................... 42.00
**Plate,** Centennial, Kansas City, Missouri, 1950 ......................................................... 15.00
**Plate,** State Of Oregon, Lewis & Clark, Johnson Brothers, 11 In. ................................ 18.00
**Program,** Gone With The Wind, 1939 ......................................................................... 22.50
**Puzzle,** Jigsaw, Contest, 1933 ................................................................................... 6.00
**Spoon,** Enamel, Gibraltar ........................................................................................... 90.00
**Spoon,** Silver Plate, Century Of Progress, Chicago, 1933 .......................................... 10.00
**Spoon,** Silver Plate, Charlie McCarthy ....................................................................... 20.00
**Spoon,** Silver Plate, Columbian Exposition, Set Of 6 ................................................. 22.00
**Spoon,** Silver Plate, Dionne Quintuplets, Set Of 5 ..................................................... 90.00
**Spoon,** Silver Plate, G.A.R.Symbol, Louisville 1895 ................................................... 25.00
**Spoon,** Silver Plate, Mae Murray ................................................................................ 10.00
**Spoon,** Silver Plate, Marion Davies ............................................................................ 10.00
**Spoon,** Silver Plate, Pola Negri .................................................................................. 10.00
**Spoon,** Silver Plate, Richard Dix ................................................................................ 10.00
**Spoon,** Sterling Silver, Alaska, Gold Wash Bowl, Raised Seals On Top ...................... 40.00
**Spoon,** Sterling Silver, Amarillo, Texas, Gold Wash, Crown On Handle ...................... 20.00
**Spoon,** Sterling Silver, Antler's Hotel, Colorado Springs, Colo. .................................. 25.00
**Spoon,** Sterling Silver, Art Institute, Chicago ............................................................. 16.00
**Spoon,** Sterling Silver, Auditorium, Denver, Indian Head Handle ................................ 35.00
**Spoon,** Sterling Silver, Berlin Flats ............................................................................ 15.00
**Spoon,** Sterling Silver, Boise, Idaho, Shoshone Falls ................................................ 25.00
**Spoon,** Sterling Silver, Boston, Triennial Conclave, 1895 .......................................... 20.00

| | |
|---|---|
| Spoon, Sterling Silver, Boulder Falls, Boulder, Colorado, Wagon | 25.00 |
| Spoon, Sterling Silver, Buffalo, New York, Head Of Buffalo On Top | 50.00 |
| Spoon, Sterling Silver, Canada, Maple Leaf & Crest | 20.00 |
| Spoon, Sterling Silver, Century Of Progress Building | 12.00 |
| Spoon, Sterling Silver, Charleston, S.C., Wigwam, Canoe, State Seal | 32.00 |
| Spoon, Sterling Silver, City Hall, Pemberville, Ohio | 25.00 |
| Spoon, Sterling Silver, Colorado, Out On The Plains, Roping Steer | 35.00 |
| Spoon, Sterling Silver, Congressional Library, Gold Wash Bowl | 20.00 |
| Spoon, Sterling Silver, Court House, Mobile, Ala. | 25.00 |
| Spoon, Sterling Silver, Crocodile Handle, 1893 World's Fair | 20.00 |
| Spoon, Sterling Silver, Cutout Concord Minute Man With Rifle | 30.00 |
| Spoon, Sterling Silver, Cutout Of Washington Monument | 12.00 |
| Spoon, Sterling Silver, Death Valley, Cal., Covered Wagon, Oxen | 35.00 |
| Spoon, Sterling Silver, Denver, Colorado State Seal, Mule, Miner | 18.00 |
| Spoon, Sterling Silver, Denver, Colorado, Capital, U.S.Mint | 35.00 |
| Spoon, Sterling Silver, Duluth, Ship, Nude Handle | 29.50 |
| Spoon, Sterling Silver, Elk City | 20.00 |
| Spoon, Sterling Silver, Ellenville, Gold Wash Bowl, Demitasse | 12.00 |
| Spoon, Sterling Silver, Figural Building, Newport, R.I., Ocean Waves | 29.00 |
| Spoon, Sterling Silver, First Capitol Of Confederacy, Montgomery | 25.00 |
| Spoon, Sterling Silver, Fort Pitt, Pittsburgh, Penn., Flower Handle | 35.00 |
| Spoon, Sterling Silver, Fort Sumter, S.C., Gold Wash Bowl | 22.50 |
| Spoon, Sterling Silver, Fort Wayne, Ind. | 22.00 |
| Spoon, Sterling Silver, Havana, Cuba, Ship Maine In Bowl, Scenes | 29.00 |
| Spoon, Sterling Silver, Hawaii | 12.50 |
| Spoon, Sterling Silver, Head Of Buffalo, Buffalo, N.Y. | 38.00 |
| Spoon, Sterling Silver, Helena, Montana | 16.00 |
| Spoon, Sterling Silver, High School, Duluth | 24.00 |
| Spoon, Sterling Silver, High School, Evansville, Ind. | 25.00 |
| Spoon, Sterling Silver, Hillsdale, Michigan | 20.00 |
| Spoon, Sterling Silver, Illinois, Eagle & Wheat | 17.00 |
| Spoon, Sterling Silver, Indian Maiden, Spokane, Washington | 65.00 |
| Spoon, Sterling Silver, J.F.Kennedy, Space Capsule In Bowl | 7.00 |
| Spoon, Sterling Silver, Jackson Statue, New Orleans, La. | 25.00 |
| Spoon, Sterling Silver, Jacksonville, Florida, Art Nouveau Handle | 22.00 |
| Spoon, Sterling Silver, Knights Of Columbus | 40.00 |
| Spoon, Sterling Silver, Lewiston, Maine, Lewiston Falls | 25.00 |
| Spoon, Sterling Silver, Lulu, Christmas, 1893 | 22.00 |
| Spoon, Sterling Silver, Mackinac Island, Standing Indian | 40.00 |
| Spoon, Sterling Silver, Manitou, Colorado, State Flower Handle | 26.00 |
| Spoon, Sterling Silver, Masonic Temple, Chicago | 35.00 |
| Spoon, Sterling Silver, Mattoon, Ill., Indian | 22.00 |
| Spoon, Sterling Silver, McKinley Monument, Columbus, Ohio | 24.00 |
| Spoon, Sterling Silver, Minnesota, Name In Banner Across Handle | 25.00 |
| Spoon, Sterling Silver, Montclair, N.J., Holly Handle | 24.00 |
| Spoon, Sterling Silver, Montreal, 1920 | 60.00 |
| Spoon, Sterling Silver, Mormon Temple, Art Nouveau Handle | 28.00 |
| Spoon, Sterling Silver, Morro Castle, San Juan | 16.00 |
| Spoon, Sterling Silver, N.Hawthorne, Salem, Novels Listed On Back | 55.00 |
| Spoon, Sterling Silver, Napoleon Head, Arc De Triomphe Bowl | 95.00 |
| Spoon, Sterling Silver, New Orleans, Cabildo | 17.50 |
| Spoon, Sterling Silver, Niagara Falls, Full Figure Indian | 23.00 |
| Spoon, Sterling Silver, Ohio, 1796, Dayton In Bowl With Log Cabin | 29.00 |
| Spoon, Sterling Silver, Oklahoma City, Oklahoma, Cowboys On Bronco | 50.00 |
| Spoon, Sterling Silver, Old Kentucky Home, Log Cabin | 25.00 |
| Spoon, Sterling Silver, Old Stone Mill, Newport, R.I. | 25.00 |
| Spoon, Sterling Silver, Open Lettered Handle, Oshkosh | 14.00 |
| Spoon, Sterling Silver, Oskaloosa, Iowa | 17.50 |
| Spoon, Sterling Silver, Pan American Exposition, 1901, Indian | 24.00 |
| Spoon, Sterling Silver, Panama Canal | 16.00 |
| Spoon, Sterling Silver, Phoenix, Arizona, Figural Handle | 28.00 |
| Spoon, Sterling Silver, Plymouth, Massachusetts, Demitasse | 25.00 |
| Spoon, Sterling Silver, Poinsettias, St.Petersburg, Fla. | 10.00 |

| | |
|---|---|
| Spoon, Sterling Silver, Portland, Maine, Gold Wash Bowl, Demitasse | 27.50 |
| Spoon, Sterling Silver, Portland, Maine, Harbor & Ships | 25.00 |
| Spoon, Sterling Silver, Portland, Oregon, Mt.Hood | 28.00 To 40.00 |
| Spoon, Sterling Silver, Post Office, Pittsburgh, Pa. | 25.00 |
| Spoon, Sterling Silver, Prescott, Arizona, Jean, 1911 | 15.00 |
| Spoon, Sterling Silver, Public Square, Cleveland | 20.00 |
| Spoon, Sterling Silver, Put-In-Bay, Ohio | 20.00 |
| Spoon, Sterling Silver, Rockland, Maine | 16.00 |
| Spoon, Sterling Silver, Rocky Hill Church, Amesbury, Mass. | 12.00 |
| Spoon, Sterling Silver, Sacramento | 12.50 |
| Spoon, Sterling Silver, Saugatuck, Michigan | 20.00 |
| Spoon, Sterling Silver, Savannah Greene Monument, City Hall | 32.00 |
| Spoon, Sterling Silver, Slippery Rock State Normal, Penn. | 22.00 |
| Spoon, Sterling Silver, Soldier's Monument, Cleveland, Ohio | 24.00 |
| Spoon, Sterling Silver, South Dakota | 75.00 |
| Spoon, Sterling Silver, Springfield, Mass., Armory | 16.00 |
| Spoon, Sterling Silver, St.Augustine, Fla., Palm Tree Handle | 20.00 |
| Spoon, Sterling Silver, St.Augustine, 1890 In Gold Wash Bowl | 22.00 |
| Spoon, Sterling Silver, Statue Of Liberty | 26.00 |
| Spoon, Sterling Silver, Stewartville, Minnesota | 16.50 |
| Spoon, Sterling Silver, Tennessee, Name In Banner Across Handle | 25.00 |
| Spoon, Sterling Silver, Toledo, Ohio, Frog Playing Guitar In Bowl | 49.00 |
| Spoon, Sterling Silver, U.S.Capitol, Raised Head Of Washington | 65.00 |
| Spoon, Sterling Silver, University Of Illinois, Crest | 20.00 |
| Spoon, Sterling Silver, Utah | 55.00 |
| Spoon, Sterling Silver, Vancouver | 22.00 |
| Spoon, Sterling Silver, Washington Monument, Lincoln On Back | 25.00 |
| Spoon, Sterling Silver, West Baden, Ind., Springs Hotel | 16.00 |
| Spoon, Sterling Silver, West Baden, Ind., 1903, Gold Embossed | 20.00 |
| Spoon, Sterling Silver, 1901 Pan American Exposition, Buffalo, N.Y. | 25.00 |
| Sugar Shell, Sterling Silver, Salem Witch | 110.00 |

*Spangle glass is multicolored glass made from odds and ends of colored glass rods. It includes metallic flakes of mica covered with gold, silver, nickel, or copper. Spangle glass is usually cased with a thin layer of clear glass over the multicolored layer.*

**SPANGLE GLASS, see also Vasa Murrhina**

| | |
|---|---|
| SPANGLE GLASS, Bowl, Thorn Feet, Pink To Cranberry | 165.00 |
| Pitcher, Pink, Yellow, & Orange, Silver Mica, 5 In. | 89.00 |
| Rose Bowl, Spatter In White Opaque, Silver Flecks, 3 1/2 In. | 125.00 |

*Spanish lace is a Victorian glass pattern that seems to have white lace on a colored background. Blue, yellow, cranberry, and clear glass was made with this distinctive white pattern. It was made in England and the United States after 1885.*

| | |
|---|---|
| SPANISH LACE, Bride's Basket, Silver Plate Holder, Blue | 150.00 |
| Butter, Blue Opalescent, Covered | 125.00 To 265.00 |
| Celery, Blue | 60.00 |
| Celery, White Opalescent, 6 1/2 In. | 38.00 |
| Cruet, Flint | 50.00 |
| Cruet, Frosted Vaseline | 27.50 |
| Dish, Sweetmeat, Cranberry, Silver Plate Top & Lid | 195.00 |
| Pitcher, Blue | 160.00 |
| Pitcher, Water, Blue Opalescent, 6 Tumblers | 550.00 |
| Pitcher, Water, Green Opalescent | 450.00 |
| Rose Bowl, Blue Opalescent | 45.00 |
| Rose Bowl, Opalescent Vaseline | 40.00 |
| Rose Bowl, Ruffled, Opalescent Lace On Clear Glass, 4 1/4 In. | 40.00 |
| Sugar Shaker, Blue | 125.00 |
| Sugar, Covered, Opalescent White | 40.00 |
| Tumbler, Cranberry | 80.00 |
| Vase, Ruffled Edge, Opalescent To Clear, 6 In. | 35.00 |

*Spatter glass is a multicolored glass made from many small pieces of different colored glass. It is sometimes called End-Of-Day glass.*

| | |
|---|---:|
| **SPATTER GLASS, Alternating Vertical Bands Of Pink & Yellow,** Pinched | 60.00 |
| **Basket,** Brown & Yellow, Cased In Clear, Thorn Handle, 23 In. | 400.00 |
| **Basket,** Clear Thorn Handle, Fluted Top | 125.00 |
| **Basket,** Clear Thorn Handle, Yellow & Blue, 6 2/3 In. | 115.00 |
| **Basket,** Clear Thorn Handle, Yellow, 6 1/2 In. | 250.00 |
| **Basket,** Thorn Handle, 6 X 4 In.Diam. | 100.00 |
| **Boot,** Clear Applied Leaf, White Lining, Rigaree Top, 3 3/4 In. | 60.00 |
| **Bottle,** Perfume, Brass Topped Stopper, Handled, Label | 75.00 |
| **Box,** Hinged, Ormolu Feet, Yellow & White, 5 5/8 X 4 5/8 In. | 165.00 |
| **Box,** Ormolu Footed, Blue & White, 8 X 5 1/2 In. | 175.00 |
| **Candleholder,** Blue, Red, & Green, White Ground, 9 In., Pair | 75.00 |
| **Condiment Set,** Silver Plate Holder, Maroon & White, 4 1/4 In. | 165.00 |
| **Jar,** Covered, Crystal Leaf Finial, Mottled, 6 1/2 In. | 85.00 |
| **Jar,** Sweetmeat, Rainbow, Barrel Shaped, 7 1/2 In. | 95.00 To 110.00 |
| **Jar,** Yellow, Maroon, White, Clear Leaf Finial, 6 1/2 In. | 85.00 |
| **Lamp,** Clear Thorn Handle, Red, Yellow, & White, 3 1/2 X 5 In. | 100.00 |
| **Lamp,** Fairy, Cut Glass Pedestal Base, Dome Shade, 9 In. | 245.00 |
| **Muffineer,** Green, Wine, & Yellow, Silver Plate Cover, 6 1/2 In. | 55.00 |
| **Paperweight,** Ball, Multicolored, Round | 70.00 |
| **Pitcher Water,** Pink & White, Chartreuse & White, 6 Tumblers | 225.00 |
| **Pitcher,** Applied Handle, Green, White, & Clear, 8 In. | 40.00 |
| **Pitcher,** Pedestal, White Lining, Multicolored, 4 1/2 In. | 45.00 |
| **Pitcher,** Ruffled Top, Applied Handle, 8 1/2 In. | 125.00 |
| **Pitcher,** Ruffled, Multicolored, White Inside, 7 X 3 In.Diam. | 68.00 |
| **Pitcher,** Square Mouth, Clear Handle, White Lining, 5 3/4 In. | 65.00 |
| **Pitcher,** 3-Petal Top, Yellow Lining, Multicolored, 5 1/4 In. | 85.00 |
| **Rose Bowl,** Fluted, Gold Design, Yellow & White, 8 X 6 1/2 In. | 225.00 |
| **Salt & Pepper,** Leaf Mold Pattern, Metal Tops, 2 1/2 In. | 150.00 |
| **Shade,** Newel Post Ornament, Victorian | 35.00 |
| **Shoe,** Crystal Applied Leaf, White Lining, 5 1/4 X 2 7/8 In. | 60.00 |
| **Sugar Shaker** | 65.00 |
| **Sugar,** Blue, Chinese Celebration, 8 In. | 185.00 |
| **Sugar,** Peacock, Green Ground, 5 X 6 1/2 In.Diam. | 115.00 |
| **Toothpick,** Barrel Shape, Ribbed, Light Green | 12.00 |
| **Tumbler,** Burgundy, Emerald Green, 9 In. | 120.00 |
| **Tumbler,** Red & White | 35.00 |
| **Tumbler,** Vertical Ribbing, Pink & White Swirl | 35.00 |
| **Tumbler,** White & Blue Spatter On Green, 4 In. | 30.00 |
| **Vase,** Bulbous, Flared Ruffled Top, Purple & Yellow, 8 1/2 In. | 45.00 |
| **Vase,** Burgundy, Emerald Green, 9 In. | 120.00 |
| **Vase,** Clear Feet, 9 In. | 95.00 |
| **Vase,** Flared & Ruffled Top, Pink & Yellow, 8 In. | 46.00 |
| **Vase,** Green & Pink, White Flakes, 5 In. | 35.00 |
| **Vase,** Hat Shaped, 4 In. | 35.00 |
| **Vase,** Jack-In-The-Pulpit, Blue, White, Brown, & Maroon, 7 In. | 95.00 |
| **Vase,** Raised Pink Spatters, Crimped Edge, 4 X 5 3/4 In.Diam. | 27.00 |
| **Vase,** Ruffled Top, Pink, Green, & Amethyst, 12 1/2 In. | 185.00 |
| **Vase,** Shades Of Green & White, Flare Top | 28.00 |
| **Vase,** White Over Yellow-Green, 6 In. | 32.00 To 33.00 |
| **Vase,** White, Maroon, Yellow, White, Turquoise, Handles, 12 In. | 400.00 |

*Spatterware is a creamware or soft-paste dinnerware decorated with spatter designs. The earliest pieces were made during the late eighteenth century, but most of the wares found today were made from 1800 to 1850. The spatterware dishes were made in the Staffordshire district of England for sale on the American market.*

**SPATTERWARE, see also Spongeware**

| | |
|---|---:|
| **SPATTERWARE, Bank,** Cream & Blue, Pig, 6 In. | 50.00 |
| **Bowl,** Sugar, Open, Blue, Red Flowers, 3 3/4 In. | 335.00 |
| **Creamer,** Green & Brown On Cream | 25.00 |
| **Cup & Saucer,** Blue & White, Small | 65.00 |

| | |
|---|---|
| Cup & Saucer, Handleless, Demitasse | 100.00 |
| Cup & Saucer, Handleless, Red Transfer, Hunting Scene | 20.00 |
| Cup & Saucer, Rooster | 450.00 |
| Dish, Baby, Dutch Children, Raised Edge | 10.00 |
| Mug, Brown, 4 1/2 In., Pair | 75.00 |
| Pitcher, Blue, Green, & Red Peafowl, 7 In. | 600.00 |
| Pitcher, John Ward Cash Store, 4 1/2 In. | 29.00 |
| Plate, Castle Center, Blue Spatter Border, 9 3/4 In. | 210.00 |
| Plate, Dark Blue, 9 1/4 In. | 65.00 |
| Sugar, Covered, Blue & White, 4 In. | 60.00 |
| Tea Set, Castle Pattern, Creamer, Sugar, & Teapot, Covered | 1350.00 |

*Spelter is a synonym for a zinc alloy. Figurines, candlesticks, and other pieces were made of spelter and given a bronze or painted finish.*

| | |
|---|---|
| SPELTER, Figurine, Nude Man Wrestling Eagle, Chicks At Feet, Signed, 24 In. | 975.00 |
| Figurine, Pheasant, Marble Base, Signed Varnier, Factory Seal, 17 In. | 675.00 |

| | |
|---|---|
| SPINNING WHEEL, Flax, Dark Blue, R.T.Stewart, New England, 35 1/2 In. | 175.00 |
| Flax, Old Red Paint, Early American | 110.00 |
| Oak, Norwegian | 225.00 |
| Original Dye Trim, Swedish, Mixed Wood | 335.00 |
| Parts Complete, Walnut & Oak | 300.00 |

SPODE
Stone-China

*Spode pottery, porcelain, and bone china were made by the Stoke-on-Trent factory of England founded by Josiah Spode about 1770. The firm became Copeland and Garrett from 1833 to 1847, then W.T.Copeland or W.T.Copeland and Sons until the present time. The word Spode appears on many pieces made by the Copeland Factory. Most collectors include all the wares under the more familiar name of Spode.*

| | |
|---|---|
| SPODE COPELAND, Cup & Saucer, Blue Willow | 75.00 |
| Dish, Vegetable, Covered, Wickerdale | 75.00 |
| Dish, Vegetable, Grecian Pattern | 35.00 |
| Gravy Boat, Underplate | 45.00 |

### SPODE, see also Copeland

| | |
|---|---|
| SPODE, Bowl, Consomme, Underplate, Seasons Pattern | 24.00 |
| Bowl, Handled, Underplate, Ivory Ground, Gilt Edging, 7 1/2 In.Diam. | 45.00 |
| Cup & Plate, Handleless, 12-Sided, Blue Grapes | 58.00 |
| Cup & Saucer, Fitzhugh | 23.00 |
| Cup & Saucer, Mayflower, Demitasse | 22.00 |
| Cup & Saucer, Transfer Of View Of Potsdam, Demitasse, 4 1/2 In. | 85.00 |
| Dish, Vegetable, Blue Geisha, 10 In. | 80.00 |
| Plate, Blue Geisha, 6 In. | 25.00 |
| Plate, Blue Geisha, 10 In. | 45.00 |
| Plate, Commemorative, Imperial Plate Of Persia, 1971, Boxed | 175.00 |
| Plate, Constitution Hall, J. & E.Caldwell & Co. | 15.00 |
| Plate, Gainesborough, 10 In. | 6.00 |
| Plate, Imari Style Design, Touches Of Gold, Marked, 8 1/4 In.Diam. | 60.00 |
| Plate, Memorial Continental Hall, 4. & E.Caldwell | 15.00 |
| Platter, Well & Tree, Pashkov Palace Series, C.1790, 16 X 21 In. | 350.00 |
| Sign, Tabletop, Tent Shape, Script Letters, 1 3/4 X 3 1/4 In. | 65.00 |
| Vase, British War Relief Society, 4 1/2 In. | 15.00 |

*Spongeware is very similar to spatterware in appearance. The designs were applied to the ware by daubing the color. Many dealers do not differentiate between the two wares and use the names interchangeably.*

| | |
|---|---|
| SPONGEWARE, Bank, Piggy, Figural | 95.00 |
| Bowl, Bail, 4 Molded Feet, 5 X 10 1/4 In. | 245.00 |
| Bowl, Blue & Brown Bisque, 7 X 4 In. | 28.00 |
| Bowl, Blue & Brown On Tan, 10 In.Diam. | 60.00 |
| Bowl, Blue & Cream, Bail | 175.00 |
| Bowl, Blue & Cream, 24 In. | 66.00 |

| | |
|---|---|
| **Bowl,** Blue & Orange, Cream Ground, 3 1/2 X 6 1/2 In.Diam. | 40.00 |
| **Bowl,** Blue & Rust, Beige, 8 In. | 45.00 |
| **Bowl,** Blue, Cream, Silver Luster Top, 8 X 2 1/2 In. | 35.00 |
| **Bowl,** Blue, White, & Red, 7 In. | 60.00 |
| **Bowl,** Brown & Cream, 5 1/2 In. | 47.00 |
| **Bowl,** Brown With Blue Daubs, 10 In.Diam. | 45.00 |
| **Bowl,** Brown, 5 In.Diam. | 13.00 |
| **Bowl,** Cereal, Yellow, Trenton, N.J., 7 1/2 In.Diam. | 50.00 |
| **Bowl,** Covered | 245.00 |
| **Bowl,** Covered, Blue, 3 In.Diam. | 175.00 |
| **Bowl,** Gilded, Bedford Mold, 8 In.Diam. | 45.00 |
| **Bowl,** Green & Yellow, 3 1/2 X 7 In. | 85.00 |
| **Bowl,** Green, Yellow, Miniature | 43.00 |
| **Bowl,** Mixing, Blue & White, 5 X 10 In.Diam. | 75.00 |
| **Bowl,** Mixing, Blue Daubed On Light Brown, 12 In.Diam. | 55.00 |
| **Bowl,** Mixing, Picket Fence Band Design, Blue, 8 1/2 In.Diam. | 12.00 |
| **Bowl,** Orange & Blue, Cream Ground, 7 In.Diam. | 35.00 |
| **Bowl,** Rib Pattern On Sides, Blue & White, 3 1/2 X 9 In.Diam. | 17.50 |
| **Bowl,** Rust, Blue, Cream, 7 In. | 40.00 |
| **Bowl,** Rust, Blue, Cream, 9 1/2 In. | 49.00 |
| **Bowl,** Soup | 75.00 |
| **Bowl,** Tan & Creamy White, 17 In. | 45.00 |
| **Bowl,** Wire Bail, Blue, 10 In. | 125.00 |
| **Bowl,** 6 X 8 1/2 In.Diam. | 100.00 |
| **Butter,** Covered, Blue & White, Knob, 5 3/4 In. | 10.00 |
| **Butter,** Dragonfly | 80.00 |
| **Butter,** Lid, Blue & White | 155.00 |
| **Chamber Pot,** Blue & White | 100.00 |
| **Chamber Pot,** Blue & White, Large | 100.00 |
| **Charger,** Cut Rose, Yellow & Black Border, 11 In. | 40.00 To 42.00 |
| **Coffeepot,** Pitcher, & Sugar Bowl, Blue, Miniature | 135.00 |
| **Commode Set,** Green & White Borders, 5 Piece | 500.00 |
| **Cookie Jar,** Rust & Blue Center Band, Wooden Lid | 90.00 |
| **Cooler,** Spigot, 20 Gallon | 1800.00 |
| **Crock,** Blue Orange Daubing, 7 X 3 In. | 30.00 |
| **Crock,** Covered, Blue & White, 1/2 Gallon | 55.00 |
| **Cup & Saucer,** Handleless | 45.00 |
| **Cup,** Custard, Set Of 3 | 20.00 |
| **Cuspidor,** Blue Bands, Green & White | 175.00 |
| **Dish,** Baking, Blue & White | 125.00 |
| **Dish,** Baking, Ruffled Edge, Blue, Rust, & Yellow, 9 X 3 In. | 38.50 |
| **Holder,** Umbrella, Brown & Blue, 16 In. | 225.00 |
| **Milk Pan,** Blue & White | 75.00 |
| **Mug,** Grape | 40.00 |
| **Mush Cup,** Blue & White | 130.00 |
| **Pitcher & Bowl,** C.1830, Blue & Green | 350.00 |
| **Pitcher,** Blue & White, 2 Quart | 150.00 |
| **Pitcher,** Blue & White, 9 In. | 50.00 To 85.00 |
| **Pitcher,** Blue Daubed On Light Brown, 8 In. | 35.00 |
| **Pitcher,** Blue On Buff, 5 In. | 45.00 |
| **Pitcher,** Blue, 4 3/4 In. | 75.00 |
| **Pitcher,** Bulbous, 2 White Bands, 11 In. | 165.00 |
| **Pitcher,** Diamonds & Banding In Relief, Blue & Brown, 9 3/4 In. | 110.00 |
| **Pitcher,** Grape, Dark Blue, 9 1/2 In. | 85.00 |
| **Pitcher,** Grape, Light Blue, 9 In. | 75.00 |
| **Pitcher,** Grape, 5 In. | 65.00 |
| **Pitcher,** Green On Tan, Quart | 25.00 |
| **Pitcher,** Milk, Brown On Cream | 50.00 |
| **Pitcher,** Water, Green, 10 In. | 95.00 |
| **Pitcher,** Water, Italian Yellow, Flowers Allover, 9 In. | 178.00 |
| **Pitcher,** Water, 10 In. | 95.00 |
| **Plate,** Blue, 8 1/4 In. | 65.00 |
| **Plate,** Cobalt & White, 9 In., Pair | 500.00 |

| | |
|---|---|
| **Plate,** Kitchen, 10 In. | 90.00 |
| **Plate,** 9 In. | 42.00 |
| **Platter,** Blue, White, Deep Side, 10 In. | 145.00 |
| **Platter,** Blue, 11 In. | 70.00 |
| **Spittoon,** Blue Bands, Blue & White | 85.00 |
| **Spittoon,** Gold Band Around Middle, Green & White, 5 1/4 X 7 In. | 150.00 |
| **Sugar & Creamer,** Child's, Blue & White | 140.00 |
| **Teapot,** Blue & Rust Design, Blue Ground | 150.00 |
| **Teapot,** Brown & Green On Beige, Glazed | 39.00 |
| **Teapot,** Green, Brown, & Yellow, 6 In | 100.00 |
| **Washbowl,** 16 In.Diam. | 105.00 |

**SPOOL CABINET, see Store, Cabinet**

*Staffordshire is a district in England where pottery and porcelain have been made since the 1900s. Thousands of types of pottery and porcelain have been made in the hundreds of factories that worked in the area. Some of the most famous factories have been listed separately. See Royal Doulton, Royal Worcester, Spode, Wedgwood, and others.*

**STAFFORDSHIRE, see also Flow Blue; Mulberry**

| | |
|---|---|
| **STAFFORDSHIRE, Bank,** Cottage, Applied Flowers | 200.00 |
| **Bank,** Spaniel Head, Black & White, Gold Lock | 60.00 |
| **Basket,** Undertray, Chinoiserie & Flowers, C.1840, 9 3/4 In. | 150.00 |
| **Bowl,** Nanking Pattern | 65.00 |
| **Box,** Dog On Cushion Cover, 4 1/4 X 2 In. | 75.00 |
| **Box,** Snuff, Female Head, White Hat, Brown Hair, 2 1/2 In. | 350.00 |
| **Bust,** John Wesley, 12 In. | 350.00 |
| **Bust,** Washington, Blue Coat, 7 1/2 In. | 275.00 |
| **Butter Pat,** Flow Blue, Gold Trim | 13.50 |
| **Butter,** Covered, Rural Scenery, Lavender Transfer | 60.00 |
| **Creamer,** Royal Group, Blue & White Transfer, Bulbous | 45.00 |
| **Creamer,** View On The St.Lawrence, Indian Encampment, Blue | 175.00 |
| **Cup & Saucer,** Black American Historical Scenes, White | 80.00 |
| **Cup & Saucer,** Blue, White, Deer & Doe, Handleless | 125.00 |
| **Cup & Saucer,** Brown Transfer, W.Adams & Sons, Handleless | 28.00 |
| **Cup & Saucer,** Burslem, A Cup O' Kindness For Auld Lang Syne | 65.00 |
| **Cup & Saucer,** Candia, Floral, Purple, C.1850, Handleless | 22.00 |
| **Cup & Saucer,** Corinthia, Challinor, Blue & White, Handleless | 32.00 |
| **Cup & Saucer,** Floral Spray On White, Handleless | 25.00 |
| **Cup & Saucer,** Rosella, Basket Of Flowers At Rim, C.1891 | 46.00 |
| **Cup & Saucer,** Siam, Handleless | 45.00 |
| **Cup & Saucer,** Sowers, Adams, Pink | 35.00 |
| **Cup Plate,** American Historical Views, Cadmus, 3 5/8 In. | 195.00 |
| **Cup Plate,** British Palaces, Brown Transfer, R.Stevenson | 30.00 |
| **Desk Set,** Letter Holder, & Stamp Box, Gold Leaf Trim | 27.50 |
| **Dish,** Chicken, White, Covered, 10 X 8 In. | 225.00 |
| **Dish,** Hen On Nest Cover, White Bisque Top, 8 X 6 1/4 In. | 225.00 |
| **Dish,** Hen On Yellow Basket Weave Nest Cover, 6 1/4 In. | 150.00 |
| **Dish,** Vegetable, Open Handles, Tuscan Rose, 12 X 9 1/2 In. | 55.00 |
| **Figurine,** Babe In Cradle, Spatter Red & Green | 165.00 |
| **Figurine,** Boy With Dog, 7 1/4 In. | 48.00 |
| **Figurine,** Cat, Seated, Manganese & Green, 3 1/2 In. | 250.00 |
| **Figurine,** Cow And Calf, 10 In. | 125.00 |
| **Figurine,** Dog, Black & White, 7 In., Pair | 110.00 |
| **Figurine,** Dog, Blue Oval Platform, Gold Collar, 6 1/2 In. | 85.00 |
| **Figurine,** Dog, Gold Collar, Chain, 9 1/2 In., Pair 150.00 To | 195.00 |
| **Figurine,** Dog, Light Tan, 13 In., Pair | 250.00 |
| **Figurine,** Dog, Orange Snout, 12 In. | 95.00 |
| **Figurine,** Dog, Poodle, Small | 45.00 |
| **Figurine,** Dog, Seated, Salmon With Dark Blue Base, White | 35.00 |
| **Figurine,** Dog, White, Copper Luster, 8 1/2 In., Pair | 150.00 |
| **Figurine,** Double Figured, Inscribed Burns & Mary, 11 1/2 In. | 95.00 |
| **Figurine,** Girl Chasing Pig | 35.00 |
| **Figurine,** Girl Tambourine Player, C.1780, 9 In. | 250.00 |

Figurine, Greyhound, Standing, Hare In Mouth, 5 X 6 In. .................................................................... 65.00
Figurine, Horse, 8 In. .................................................................................................................................. 50.00
Figurine, Lady, Seated On Grass, Brown Dress, 2 1/2 In. ........................................................... 250.00
Figurine, Lamb, Vase With Stream & Tree Trunk, 6 In., Pair ..................................................... 75.00
Figurine, Lion, Lying Down, Glass Eyes, 11 X 10 1/2 In., Pair ................................................. 185.00
Figurine, Lion, Paw On Ball, Glass Eyes, Buff, 11 X 13 In.Long ........................................ 200.00
Figurine, Man & Woman In Arbor, Large Bird, 11 1/2 In. ............................................................ 95.00
Figurine, Man & Woman On Horse, Going To Market ................................................................... 65.00
Figurine, Man & Woman With Twigs On Heads, White, Gilt, 10 In. ....................................... 85.00
Figurine, Milton, With Books, Full Standing Figure, 11 In. .,................................................. 185.00
Figurine, Mongrel Dog ................................................................................................................................ 42.00
Figurine, Newsboy, 19th Century, 13 In. ........................................................................................ 220.00
Figurine, Pheasant, Female, Signed, 10 1/4 X 4 1/2 In. ........................................................ 275.00
Figurine, Rebecca At The Well, 9 In. ................................................................................................... 95.00
Figurine, Recumbent Cow, Brown, Gray & Green, 4 1/2 In. .................................................... 175.00
Figurine, Scotchman & Lady, Holding Hands, 9 In. ..................................................................... 145.00
Figurine, Shoeshine Boy, 19th Century, 13 In. ............................................................................ 220.00
Figurine, Sitting Dogs, Henna, 8 In., Pair ...................................................................................... 125.00
Figurine, Spaniel, Black & White, 4 In. ............................................................................................... 38.00
Figurine, Spaniel, Rust & White, 6 In., Pair ..................................................................................... 70.00
Figurine, Spaniel, Wistful Face, 3 1/2 In. .......................................................................................... 38.00
Figurine, Swan, Neck Touching Tail Feathers, 2 1/4 In. .............................................................. 65.00
Figurine, Victorian Sailor, 6 3/4 In. ...................................................................................................... 25.00
Figurine, Wesley, Colored & Gilded, 6 3/4 In. .............................................................................. 300.00
Figurine, Whippet, Seated, Guarding Dead Rabbit, 9 In. ......................................................... 165.00
Figurine, White Girl On Horseback, 7 In., Pair ............................................................................... 75.00
Figurine, White Seated Dog, Copper Luster Trim, 8 In., Pair ................................................... 95.00
Figurine, William Derrick As Richard III, 10 In. .............................................................................. 90.00
Figurine, Young Girl Holding Flowers In Apron, 5 1/2 In. .......................................................... 50.00
Foot Tub, Blue & White, 2-Handled, 12 1/2 X 16 X 8 In. ......................................................... 535.00
Gravy, Corella, Brown Transfer ............................................................................................................... 22.00
Holder, Toothbrush, Covered, Brown & White Transfer .............................................................. 85.00
Jug, Creamware, Enameled, C.1820, 4 1/2 In. ...................................................... *Illus* 500.00
Jug, Creamware, Enameled, C.1820, 6 1/2 In. ...................................................... *Illus* 400.00
Jug, Milk, Punch & Judy ........................................................................................................................ 295.00
Match Holder, Figural, Girl, 5 1/4 In. .................................................................................................. 35.00
Match Holder, High Boots, Pair .............................................................................................................. 45.00
Mug, Brown Bands, Florals, Gift For Charles, 2 3/4 In. ........................................................... 150.00
Mug, Child's, Man On Horse Chasing Horses ................................................................................ 55.00

Staffordshire, Jugs, Creamware, Enameled, C. 1820

| | |
|---|---|
| **Mug,** Frog, Willie Brewed A Peck Of Malt | 325.00 |
| **Mug,** Oriental Lanterns & Flowers, C.1870, Blue, 3 In. | 10.00 |
| **Mug,** Oriental Print, Pagoda, Figure, C.1850, Brown, 3 In. | 25.00 |
| **Mug,** Pastoral, Farmer & Wife, Cows, C.1840, Brown, 4 In. | 35.00 |
| **Mug,** Robin Hood, Transfer Pattern, C.1840, Green, 3 1/2 In. | 35.00 |
| **Pastille,** Cottage White | 120.00 |
| **Penholder,** Figural, Whippet Lying On Purple Cushion, 5 In. | 65.00 |
| **Pepper Pot,** Floral Design, Black Transfer, C.1840, 4 1/2 In. | 25.00 |
| **Pitcher & Bowl,** Woodbine, Lavender, J.Alcock | 225.00 |
| **Pitcher,** Milk, Abbeville, Blue & White Transfer | 75.00 |
| **Pitcher,** Overall Design Of Blue Leaves, 6 1/2 In. | 55.00 |
| **Pitcher,** Water, Columbus, Brown Transfer, Adams & Sons | 50.00 |
| **Plaque,** Comical World War I Soldier, Marked, 7 1/4 In.Diam. | 28.00 |
| **Plate,** Andalusia, Adams, Pink, 9 In. | 28.00 |
| **Plate,** Arcadia, 7 1/4 In. | 24.00 |
| **Plate,** Atlantic City, Beach Scene, C.1900 | 95.00 |
| **Plate,** Bellvue Pottery, Brown Transfer, 9 1/2 In. | 15.00 |
| **Plate,** Black American Scene, Exchange, Baltimore, 7 1/2 In. | 70.00 |
| **Plate,** Blue, Domestic Cattle, 10 In. | 65.00 |
| **Plate,** Boston Public Library, Wm.Adams & Son, 10 1/4 In. | 65.00 |
| **Plate,** Boston State House, Blue, 8 1/4 In. | 125.00 |
| **Plate,** Boston State House, Blue, 9 1/2 In. | 150.00 |
| **Plate,** Buddha, Pink & White, 8 3/4 In. | 12.00 |
| **Plate,** Caledonia, Adams, Pink Transfer, 11 1/4 In. | 28.00 |
| **Plate,** Caledonia, Pink, Adams, 8 1/2 In. | 35.00 |
| **Plate,** Canova, Brown, T.Mayer, 10 1/2 In. | 35.00 |
| **Plate,** Canova, Green Transfer, T.Mayer, 8 1/2 In. | 22.00 |
| **Plate,** Canova, Pink, 8 In. | 24.00 |
| **Plate,** Chantilly, 8 1/2 In. | 23.00 |
| **Plate,** Child's, Boy, Dog, Bird Center, Marked, 6 1/2 In. | 22.50 |
| **Plate,** Chinese Tree, Brown Transfer, 8 1/2 In. | 22.00 |
| **Plate,** Columbus, Indians Hunting, Purple, Adams, 9 1/2 In. | 56.00 |
| **Plate,** Commerce, Red Transfer, S.Alcock, 7 In. | 18.00 |
| **Plate,** Commodore MacDonnough's Victory, 7 5/8 In. | 235.00 |
| **Plate,** Corinthia, Challinor, Blue & White, 8 3/4 In. | 18.00 |
| **Plate,** Dark Blue, Batalha, Portugal, 9 3/4 In. | 30.00 |
| **Plate,** Domestic Cattle, Blue, 8 1/2 In. | 65.00 |
| **Plate,** Fountain, Pink & White, 9 1/4 In. | 28.00 |
| **Plate,** Grand Erie Canal, Legend Praising De Witt Clinton | 390.00 |
| **Plate,** Hoboken In New Jersey, Stubbs, 7 3/4 In. | 165.00 |
| **Plate,** Indian Temples, Blue, 8 In. | 85.00 |
| **Plate,** Indian Temples, Lavender Transfer, 10 1/4 In. | 22.00 |
| **Plate,** Mayer, Lavender Transfer, 10 1/2 In. | 18.00 |
| **Plate,** Mayer, Pink Transfer, 9 1/4 In. | 25.00 |
| **Plate,** Mayflower, Plymouth Harbor, 6 1/2 In.Diam. | 28.00 |
| **Plate,** Millennium, Blue Transfer | 75.00 |
| **Plate,** Millennium, Brown Transfer, C.1830, 10 1/2 In. | 45.00 |
| **Plate,** Millennium, Pink Transfer, 7 3/4 In. | 45.00 |
| **Plate,** Moulin Sur, La Marne, Blue, 9 1/2 In. | 185.00 |
| **Plate,** Palestine, Pink, 7 1/2 In., Pair | 45.00 |
| **Plate,** Palestine, Pink, 8 1/2 In. | 33.00 |
| **Plate,** Palestine, Pink, 9 1/2 In., Pair | 60.00 |
| **Plate,** Peruvian Horse Hunt, Green & Brown Transfer, 7 1/2 In. | 15.00 |
| **Plate,** Pictures Christ As Child, Raised Flowers, 6 1/8 In. | 65.00 |
| **Plate,** Rose, Adams, Pink Transfer, 9 1/3 In. | 85.00 |
| **Plate,** Rural Scenery, Lavender Transfer, 8 3/4 In. | 15.00 |
| **Plate,** Scenery, Clyde, Lavender Transfer, 8 In. | 24.00 |
| **Plate,** Scudders American Museum, Boston, 7 1/2 In.Diam. | 70.00 |
| **Plate,** Sea, Pink & White, 9 1/4 In. | 25.00 |
| **Plate,** Shannondale Springs, Va., Transfer, C.1835, Pink, 8 In. | 100.00 |
| **Plate,** Spanish Convent, Lavender Transfer, 8 1/2 In. | 15.00 |
| **Plate,** Spartan Pattern, Italian Blue, 7 In., Set Of 4 | 40.00 |
| **Plate,** Swiss, Lavender Transfer, 9 1/2 In. | 28.00 |

| | |
|---|---:|
| **Plate,** Temple Scene Center, Blue & White, 6 3/4 In. | 28.00 |
| **Plate,** Views Of Marblehead, Mass., Blue & White, 7 3/4 In. | 12.00 |
| **Plate,** Willow Design, C.1822, Impressed Stubbs, 4 In. | 50.00 |
| **Platter,** Baltimore, Blue & White, Meigh, 16 X 12 In. | 225.00 |
| **Platter,** Chinese Tree, Brown Tranfer, 10 1/2 X 8 In. | 28.00 |
| **Platter,** Dark Blue, Fruit & Bird Design, 16 1/2 In. | 385.00 |
| **Platter,** Isola Belle, Adams, 20 1/2 In. | 150.00 |
| **Platter,** Junction Of Sacandaga & Hudson Rivers, 14 In. | 1500.00 |
| **Platter,** Newburgh, Hudson River, Black, 15 1/2 In. | 295.00 |
| **Platter,** Ornithology, Green Transfer, W.Adams, 9 X 8 In. | 35.00 |
| **Platter,** Tuscan Rose, 9 1/4 X 7 1/2 In. | 35.00 |
| **Potty,** Child's, Lord Nelson, Flowers | 19.00 |
| **Ring Tree,** Figural, 2 Portraits, Flow Blue | 35.00 |
| **Soup Dish,** Bosphorus, Brown Transfer | 18.00 |
| **Soup Dish,** Caledonia, Adams, Lavender Transfer, 11 5/8 In. | 35.00 |
| **Soup Dish,** Carrara | 27.00 |
| **Soup Dish,** The Valentine, Clews, Dark Blue, 10 In. | 275.00 |
| **Stirrup Cup,** Fox, Gold Sponging On Ears | 110.00 |
| **Sugar,** Medina, Lavender Transfer | 45.00 |
| **Swan,** Neck Touching Tail Feathers, 2 1/4 In. | 65.00 |
| **Syrup,** Hinged Sheffield Lid, Butterflies, C.1870 | 85.00 |
| **Tea Set,** Child's, Pink & White, C.1890, 16 Piece | 125.00 |
| **Teapot & Tureen,** Sauce, Brian, Brown Transfer | 95.00 |
| **Teapot & Tureen,** Sauce, Melbourne, Brown Transfer | 95.00 |
| **Teapot,** Cover, Modeled As 3-Story House, C.1740, 8 1/4 In. | 700.00 |
| **Teapot,** Goat With Kid, Blue & White | 250.00 |
| **Teapot,** Nonpareil, Lavender Transfer, 6 In. | 85.00 |
| **Teapot,** Sardinia, Hall, Brown | 125.00 |
| **Tureen,** Underplate, Rhine Pattern, Gray Black Transfer, 12 In. | 45.00 |
| **Vase,** Gilt Flowers, Leaves, Cobalt Blue, Marked, 3 1/4 In. | 135.00 |
| **Watch Holder,** Tower Shape, 2 Applied Figures, 8 X 9 1/2 In. | 75.00 |

*Stangl pottery was organized in 1929, succeeding the Fulper Pottery
Company. Stangl porcelain birds are popular collectibles.*

| | |
|---|---:|
| **STANGL, Ashtray,** Game Series, Flying Duck | 25.00 |
| **Ashtray,** Spectrum, 11 In. | 6.00 |
| **Bird,** Allen Hummingbird, No.3634 | 45.00 |
| **Bird,** Bird Of Paradise, No.3408 | 60.00 To 85.00 |
| **Bird,** Black-Throated Green Warbler, No.3814 | 45.00 |
| **Bird,** Blue-Headed Vireo, No.3448 | 40.00 To 65.00 |
| **Bird,** Bluebird, No.3276, 5 In. | 40.00 To 65.00 |
| **Bird,** Bluebirds, Double, No.3276d | 45.00 To 90.00 |
| **Bird,** Bobolink, No.3595 | 70.00 |
| **Bird,** Cardinal, No.3444 | 38.00 To 80.00 |
| **Bird,** Carolina Wren, No.3590 | 35.00 To 45.00 |
| **Bird,** Cerulean Warbler, No.3456, 4 1/4 In. | 35.00 To 59.50 |
| **Bird,** Cockatoo, No.3405, Pink, 6 1/2 In. | 38.00 To 50.00 |
| **Bird,** Cockatoo, No.3405s | 46.50 |
| **Bird,** Cockatoo, No.3580, 9 In. | 35.00 To 85.50 |
| **Bird,** Cockatoo, No.3584, Signed Jacabs, 11 3/8 In. | 165.00 To 225.00 |
| **Bird,** Cockatoo, No.3584, 12 1/2 In. | 145.00 |
| **Bird,** Cockatoos, Double, No.3405d, 9 1/2 In. | 65.00 To 110.00 |
| **Bird,** Evening Grosbeak, No.3813 | 60.00 |
| **Bird,** Finch, No.3849 | 55.00 |
| **Bird,** Flying Duck, No.3443, Blue Glaze, 9 In. | 225.00 To 250.00 |
| **Bird,** Goldfinch, No.3849 | 35.00 |
| **Bird,** Gray Cardinal, No.3596 | 38.00 To 55.00 |
| **Bird,** Gray Hen, No.3446 | 55.00 |
| **Bird,** Hen, No.3286 | 30.00 |

**Bird,** Hen, No.3446, 7 In. .................................................................................. 95.00
**Bird,** Indigo Bunting, No.3589 ...................................................... 35.00 To 49.50
**Bird,** Kentucky Warbler, No.3598 ................................................ 30.00 To 70.00
**Bird,** Key West Quail Dove, No.3454 ........................................ 225.00 To 290.00
**Bird,** Kingfisher, No.3406 ............................................................ 35.00 To 68.00
**Bird,** Lovebird, No.3400 .............................................................. 35.00 To 55.00
**Bird,** Nuthatch, No.3593 ............................................................. 35.00 To 38.00
**Bird,** Oriole, No.3402 .................................................................. 32.00 To 45.00
**Bird,** Painted Bunting, No.3452 .................................................. 45.00 To 65.00
**Bird,** Pair Of Hummingbirds, No.3599d ..................................................... 175.00
**Bird,** Pair Of Kingfishers, No.3406d .......................................................... 75.00
**Bird,** Pair Of Orioles, No.3402d ................................................................. 65.00
**Bird,** Parakeet, 6 In. .................................................................................. 70.00
**Bird,** Parakeets, Double, No.3582d, Blue, 7 In. ........................................ 175.00
**Bird,** Parrot, No.3449, Seated On Limb ..................................................... 75.00
**Bird,** Parula Warbler, No.3583 ................................................... 35.00 To 40.00
**Bird,** Passenger Pigeon, No.3450, 19 X 9 In. ........................................... 135.00
**Bird,** Prothonatary Warbler, No.3447 ........................................ 45.00 To 55.00
**Bird,** Redstarts, Double, No.3490 ........................................ 150.00 To 195.00
**Bird,** Rivoli Hummingbird, No.3627 ........................................... 85.00 To 95.00
**Bird,** Rooster, No.3285 ............................................................................. 30.00
**Bird,** Rooster, No.3445 ............................................................................. 65.00
**Bird,** Rufous Hummingbird, No.3585 ......................................... 33.00 To 45.00
**Bird,** Scissor-Tail Flycatcher, No.3757 .................................................... 270.00
**Bird,** Titmouse, No.3592 .......................................................... 30.00 To 40.00
**Bird,** Western Bluebird, No.3815, Original Label ........................................ 85.00
**Bird,** Wilson Warbler, No.3597, 3 1/2 In. .................................. 30.00 To 50.00
**Bird,** Wren, No.3401 ................................................................ 35.00 To 85.00
**Bird,** Wrens, Double, No.3401d ................................................ 75.00 To 95.00
**Bowl,** Fluted Pattern, White, Oval, Marked, 9 X 5 In. .................................. 9.95
**Box,** Painted Apple Tree On Lid, 5 1/2 X 4 1/2 In. ..................................... 35.00
**Candleholder,** Lily, Pair ............................................................................ 32.00
**Console Set,** Paper Sticker, 3 Piece ......................................................... 22.00
**Cup & Saucer,** Fruit Pattern ...................................................................... 6.00
**Dinner Set,** Old Orchard Pattern, Service For 8, Extra Pieces, Signed ....................... 300.00
**Dish,** Candy, Leaf Shape, 2-Part, Metal Post, Green .................................... 4.00
**Eggcup,** Fruit Pattern, Green Band On Base .............................................. 6.50
**Pitcher,** Long-Nosed, Signed, Green ........................................................ 10.00
**Planter,** Rose Tan Interior, Blossom Shape Rim, Marked, 5 3/4 In. ............. 16.95
**Plate,** Blueberry ........................................................................................ 5.00
**Sign,** Dealer's, Ceramic ............................................................................ 50.00
**Sugar,** Handleless, Fruit Pattern, Ball Shape, 2 X 2 In. ............................... 3.50
**Toby Mug,** Sport Scene, Beige ................................................................ 20.00
**Vase,** Terra Rose, 14 In. ........................................................................... 10.00

*Star Holly is a milk glass type of glass made by the Imperial Glass
Company of Bellaire, Ohio, in 1957. The pieces were made to look like
Wedgwood jasperware. White holly leaves appear against colored borders of
blue, green, or rust. It is marked on the bottom of every piece.*

**STAR HOLLY, Sherbet,** Blue ................................................................... 85.00

*Steins have been used for over 500 years. They have been made of ivory,
porcelain, stoneware, faience, silver, pewter, wood, or glass in sizes up to nine
gallons. Although some were made by Meissen, Capo-Di-Monte, and other
famous factories, most were made in Germany. The words Geschutz or
Musterschutz on a stein are the German for patented or registered design,
not company names.*

**STEIN, Amber Body,** Rosette Bands, Pewter Lid, , Germany, C.1740, 8 1/4 In. ....................... 1100.00
  **Bavarian Maid,** 1/2 Liter, Pewter Hat ............................................... 275.00

| | |
|---|---:|
| Bavarian Man, 1/2 Liter, 8 In. | 200.00 |
| Beer, Figural, Monkey, 1/2 Liter, Pottery, 9 In. | 225.00 |
| Bicycle Club, Munich, 1904, Man On Bike, Cyclist In Relief On Lid | 250.00 |
| Bike Rider Tipping Hat, Pewter Lid | 165.00 |
| Bownfield Carnival, Pewter Lid, C.1840, Marked, 7 In. | 50.00 |
| Castles & Cathedral, Dom Zu Koln, Pewter Lid, C.1710, Germany | 45.00 |
| Character, Satan, E.C.S.412, 4 Liter | 600.00 |
| Character, Skull Figural, Bisque, 4 X 4 1/2 In. | 275.00 |
| Coachdriver, Steeple Lid, Occupational, Porcelain | 65.00 |
| Compliments Of John Kress Brewing, New York, Pottery, 1/2 Liter | 125.00 |
| Creamware, 2 Liter, Monkeys & Bears, Pewter Lid, Monkey Finial & Lid | 250.00 |
| Drinking Scene, Hinged Pewter Lid, Germany, 1/4 Liter | 22.00 |
| Dwarf, Musterschutz, 1/2 Liter | 595.00 |
| Dwarfs On Lid, 1/2 Liter, Pottery | 80.00 |
| Elk, B.P.O.E., Germany | 72.00 |
| Glass Of Casiav, 3/10 Liter | 100.00 |
| Hand-Painted Porcelain, Lithophane, Pewter Top & Bottom, 1/2 Liter | 120.00 |
| Hinged Cover, Etched, 1/5 Liter, Signed JWR, 9 In. | 190.00 |
| Human Skull Resting On Book, Anchor Mark, 5 1/4 In. | 175.00 |
| Incised Tavern Scene, Pewter Top, Merkelback & Wick, 2 Liter | 210.00 |
| Indian Chief In Headdress, Taylor Decorating Co., 1i 1/2 In. | 150.00 |
| Indian Chief, 1/2 Liter | 450.00 |
| Inlayed & Etched, Marzi Remy, 1/2 Liter | 225.00 |
| John Kress Brewing Co., N.Y., Pottery, 1/2 Liter | 125.00 |
| Jolly Monk, Figural | 40.00 |
| Laughing Radish, Musterchutz | 325.00 |
| Lithophane Man & Woman's Head, Pewter Top, Porcelain, Wiesbaden | 125.00 |
| Lowenbrau, Clear, New Ulm, Germany | 35.00 |
| Man Playing Mandolin, Native Costume, Geshultz, No.1526, 1/2 Liter | 150.00 |
| STEIN, METTLACH, see Mettlach, Stein | |
| Monk, Hinged Cover Is Monk's Head, Lithophane, 7 X 5 1/2 In. | 250.00 |
| Monk, Lithophane Bottom, 7 X 5 1/2 In. | 269.00 |
| Monk, Munchen, Gesetzlicht, Germany, 1/2 Liter | 170.00 |
| Monkeys & Skull On Lid, Germany, No.1257, 5 Liter | 250.00 |
| Munich Maid, Pottery, 1/2 Liter | 150.00 |
| Owl Shape, Pewter Thumbpiece With Lady's Head, 8 1/4 In. | 250.00 |
| Owl, Hinged Top, Pewter Thumbpiece, Blue & Gray, 8 1/2 In. | 225.00 |
| Painted Tavern Scene, Peasants, Lithophane Bottom, 9 In. | 55.00 |
| Pressed Glass, Flute Panel Design, 8 In. | 65.00 |
| Puzzle Jug, Lithophane Nude In Bottom, Porcelain | 225.00 |
| Regimental, No.1464, Germany, 1 Liter | 225.00 |
| Regimental, Prince Carl Of Bayern, 1895, Rampant Lion Handle, 11 In. | 550.00 |
| Rich Man, Gray & Blue Stoneware, 1/2 Liter | 285.00 |
| Satan, 1/2 Liter | 450.00 |
| Scenic, Figures, Lithophane, Lid, Germany, 1/2 Liter | 299.00 |
| Skull On Book, Pewter Lid, 19th Century, European, 6 In. | 175.00 |
| Skull, Pewter Thumbpiece, Bisque, 4/10 Liter, 6 In. | 225.00 |
| Stoneware, Blue, Germany, 1/2 Liter | 70.00 |
| Tavern Scene On Dark Blue Ground, Germany, 1/2 Liter | 45.00 |
| Tavern Scene, Pottery, 1/2 Liter | 125.00 |
| Twig Handle, Figural, Jolly Fat Man, 7 1/4 In. | 145.00 |
| Woman Holding Dog, Glass With Porcelain Top, German, 5 In. | 50.00 |
| Yellow & Blue Flowers, Blue Glass Lid, Lithophane Bottom, 8 1/2 In. | 110.00 |

*Stereo cards that were made for stereopticon viewers became popular after 1840. Two almost identical pictures were mounted on a stiff cardboard backing so that, when viewed through a stereoscope, a three-dimensional picture could be seen.*

| | |
|---|---:|
| STEREO, Card, Civil War, Set Of 4 | 8.00 |
| Card, Disasters, U.S., Set Of 5 | 7.00 |
| Card, European Views, Set Of 50 | 22.00 |

| | |
|---|---|
| **Card,** Galveston Disaster | 1.50 |
| **Card,** Inside Factory Scenes, Set Of 6 | 8.00 |
| **Card,** Klondike Gold Rush, Set Of 4 | 7.50 |
| **Card,** People, Set Of 25 | 10.00 |
| **Card,** U.S.Battleships, Set Of 11 | 15.00 |
| **Card,** U.S.Scenes, Set Of 55 | 25.00 |

*Stereoscopes, or stereopticons, were used for viewing the stereo cards. The hand viewer was invented by Oliver Wendell Holmes, although more complicated table models were used before his was placed in production in 1859.*

**STEREOSCOPE, Viewer,** Cards, New York, Underwood & Underwood, Set Of 170 .......... 200.00

*Steuben glass was made at the Steuben Glass Works of Corning, New York. The factory, founded by Frederick Carder and T.C.Hawkes, Sr., was purchased by the Corning Glass Company. They continued to make glass called Steuben. Many types of art glass were made at Steuben. The firm is still producing glass of exceptional quality.*

**STEUBEN, see also Aurene**

| | |
|---|---|
| **STEUBEN, Ashtray,** Man's Head On Corner, Cire Perdue, Signed, 4 1/2 In.Square | 5000.00 |
| **Banana Boat,** Clear, Signed, 16 In.Long | 115.00 |
| **Base,** Lamp, Air Trapped Bubbles, Cone Shape, Signed, 6 1/2 In. | 225.00 |
| **Basket,** Black Handle, Green Jade, 6 In.Long | 285.00 |
| **Basket,** Black Threading, Clear Handle, Berries, 4 1/2 X 7 1/2 In. | 110.00 |
| **Bonbon,** Gold Aurene, Signed Aurene, 6 In.Diam. | 295.00 |
| **Bottle,** Cologne, Crystal, Sterling Overlay, 6 1/2 In. | 225.00 |
| **Bottle,** Cologne, Gold Aurene, 5 In. | 675.00 |
| **Bottle,** Cologne, Pink Reeding & Central Flower, Clear, Signed | 150.00 |
| **Bottle,** Cologne, Sterling Overlay, Crystal, 6 1/2 In. | 225.00 |
| **Bottle,** Cologne, Verre De Soie, Green Stopper, 5 In. | 225.00 |
| **Bottle,** Perfume, Flame Stopper, Signed, 10 In. | 135.00 |
| **Bottle,** Perfume, Optic Rib, Mushroom-Shaped Stopper, Blue, 7 1/2 In. | 45.00 |
| **Bowl,** Aurene & Calcite, Gold, 10 In.Diam. | 200.00 |
| **Bowl,** Aurene On Calcite, Blue, 9 1/2 In.Diam. | 750.00 |
| **Bowl,** Aurene On Calcite, Underplate, Signed, 2 1/2 X 4 1/2 In.Diam. | 350.00 |
| **Bowl,** Aurene, Footed, Green & Gold Luster, Signed, 4 X 10 In.Diam. | 375.00 |
| **Bowl,** Aurene, Urn Shape, Curved In Top, Blue, Signed, 5 1/2 X 10 In. | 475.00 |
| **Bowl,** Calcite, Iridescent, Signed, 11 X 5 In. | 450.00 |
| **Bowl,** Centerpiece, Green Jade, Alabaster Pedestal, Signed, 12 In. | 450.00 |
| **Bowl,** Covered, Panel Cut Lid & Base, Signed, 6 X 10 In. | 420.00 |
| **Bowl,** Diamond-Quilted, Mica Flecked Handles, Signed, 10 In.Diam. | 200.00 |
| **Bowl,** Fleur-De-Lis, Apple Green Jade, Signed, 14 X 5 1/2 In. | 550.00 |
| **Bowl,** Footed, Ruffled Edge, Controlled Bubbles, Blue Threading, 9 In. | 125.00 |
| **Bowl,** Free-Form, Clear, 13 X 8 X 5 In. | 125.00 |
| **Bowl,** Fruit, Aurene, Rolled Lip, Signed, 4 1/2 X 12 In.Diam. | 450.00 |
| **Bowl,** Fruit, Footed, Bristol Yellow, Signed | 130.00 |
| **Bowl,** Ginger, Underplate, Roseline, Bowl, 4 3/4 In.Diam. | 125.00 |
| **Bowl,** Gold Aurene & Calcite, Footed, Turned-Down Rim, 7 1/4 In. | 345.00 |
| **Bowl,** Gold Aurene & Calcite, 2 X 10 In.Diam. | 275.00 |
| **Bowl,** Green Jade & Alabaster, Handled, Footed, Signed, 16 X 5 1/2 In. | 950.00 |
| **Bowl,** Green Swirl, Signed, 12 X 4 1/2 In. | 95.00 |
| **Bowl,** Grotesque Shape, Cranberry, Signed, 5 X 12 X 6 In. | 175.00 |
| **Bowl,** Grotesque Shape, Crystal, 12 1/2 X 6 1/2 In. | 55.00 |
| **Bowl,** Grotesque, Clear, 7 In. | 100.00 |
| **Bowl,** Ivorene, Iridescence, 5 1/2 X 2 1/4 In. | 100.00 |
| **Bowl,** Ivorene, Lotus Shape, Pink & Blue, 14 1/2 X 9 X 7 In. | 550.00 |
| **Bowl,** Pedestal, Cranberry Cut To Clear, 3 X 4 1/2 In.Diam. | 125.00 |
| **Bowl,** Pomona Green, Signed, 4 1/2 In.Diam. | 18.00 |
| **Bowl,** Ribbed Bristol Yellow, Pedestal, Foot In Deep Purple, Signed | 45.00 |
| **Bowl,** Ribbed, Purple, Signed, 11 1/2 In.Diam. | 105.00 |
| **Bowl,** Ruffled, Blue Aurene, Signed, 12 In. | 850.00 |

Bowl, Turned-Down Rim, Gold With Calcite, 12 In.Diam. ............................................................ 200.00
Bowl, Vertical Ribs, Emerald Green, Signed, 5 X 10 In.Diam. .................................................... 100.00
Bowl, 3 Feet, Blue Aurene, Signed, 10 In.Diam. ...................................................................... 400.00
Bowl, 4 Rolled Feet, Signed, 11 X 4 In. ................................................................................... 175.00
Brandy Snifter, Bristol, Yellow Bowl, Green Pedestal, Signed ................................................. 50.00
Candleholder, Amber Cased In Yellow, Paperweight Fruit, 10 In., Pair ................................... 179.00
Candleholder, Aurene, Twisted Stem, Signed, 8 In., Pair ........................................................ 575.00
Candleholder, Green Jade & Alabaster, Signed, 9 3/4 In., Pair ............................................... 475.00
Candleholder, Mushroom Shape, Blue Aurene, Signed, 4 In. .................................................. 675.00
Candlestick, Aurene, Iridescent Blue, Signed & Numbered, 10 In., Pr. ..................................1950.00
Candlestick, Blue Silverene, Mushroom Type, Signed, 4 1/2 X 5 In. ...................................... 125.00
Candlestick, Bristol Yellow Optic Rib Vase & Socket, Signed, 10 In. ..................................... 135.00
Candlestick, Candle Cups, Blue Aurene, Art Nouveau, 12 In., Pair .......................................2500.00
Candlestick, Cerise, Ruby Holder, Clear Body, Signed, 10 In., Pair ....................................... 300.00
Candlestick, Engraved Calcite Gold, Signed, 6 X 6 In., Pair .................................................1250.00
Candlestick, Epergne Shape, Ivory & Black, 12 In. ................................................................. 325.00
Candlestick, Green Swirl, Signed, 9 1/2 In., Pair ................................................................... 250.00
Candlestick, Holder, Mushroom Design, Signed, 4 1/2 X 5 In. ............................................... 150.00
Candlestick, Hourglass Shaped Stem, Amber, Signed, 12 In. ................................................. 85.00
Candlestick, Mushroom Design, Crystal, Signed, 4 1/2 X 5 In. .............................................. 150.00
Candlestick, Pink Reeding, Clear, Signed ............................................................................... 40.00
Candlestick, Pomona Green Ball Stem, Topaz Top, Foot, Signed, 12 In. ............................... 95.00
Candlestick, Topaz, 12 In. ...................................................................................................... 95.00
Champagne, Blue, 6 5/8 In. .................................................................................................... 45.00
Champagne, Cluthra Pattern ................................................................................................... 375.00
Champagne, Colored Bowl, Twisted Stems, Set Of 6 .............................................................. 225.00
Chandelier, Calcite & Black, Acid Cut Back Dome, 20 In. .....................................................1100.00
Cocktail, Amethyst, Signed, 3 In. ............................................................................................ 30.00
Cocktail, Teardrop In Base, C.1900, S Mark ............................................................................ 110.00
Compote, Alabaster Base, Rosaline, 5 In.Diam. ...................................................................... 195.00
Compote, Aurene, Blue, 7 X 8 In. ............................................................................................ 565.00
Compote, Aurene, Twisted Stem, Ruffled, Signed, 6 X 6 1/2 In.Diam. ................................... 750.00
Compote, Calcite & Gold Aurene, Pedestal, Inward Roll Rim, 8 1/4 In. .................................. 335.00
Compote, Green Crystal, Bubbly & Reeded, Signed, 4 1/2 In. ................................................ 110.00
Compote, Pedestal, Calcite & Gold Aurene, 2 3/4 In. .............................................................. 185.00
Compote, Rosaline, Alabaster Footed, Top, 5 In.Diam. ........................................................... 225.00
Compote, Teardrop Stem, Amethyst Cut To Clear, Signed, 7 X 7 In. ...................................... 275.00
Compote, Twisted Stem, Ruffled Edge, 6 X 6 1/2 In., Pair .....................................................1400.00
Console Set, Gold Threaded Bubble Glass, Bowl, Oval, 14 X 10 In. ....................................... 400.00
Console Set, Ruby To Clear, Leaf Design, Bowl, 6 X 12 In.Diam. ........................................... 750.00
Cordial, Flemish Blue Bands On Rim & Foot, Topaz, 5 3/4 In. ................................................ 50.00
Cordial, Funnel-Shaped Bowl, Domed Foot, 3 3/4 In., Set Of 12 ............................................ 175.00
Cordial, Opalescent Stem, Apricot Top .................................................................................... 85.00
Cup & Saucer, Demitasse, Gold Aurene, Sterling Silver Holder .............................................. 265.00
Darner, Stocking, Gold Aurene ................................................................................................ 425.00
Dish, Aurene, Iridescent Gold, Signed, 5 3/4 In.Diam. ........................................................... 225.00
Dish, Covered, Panel Design, Doughnut Handle, Signed, 6 X 10 In. ...................................... 350.00
Figurine, American Eagle, Signed, 4 3/4 X 5 1/4 In. .............................................................. 535.00
Figurine, Beaver, Sitting Up, 3 1/2 X 4 1/2 In. ...................................................................... 335.00
Figurine, Leaping Trout, Signed, 9 1/4 In. .............................................................................. 625.00
Figurine, Owl, Frosted Eyes, Crystal, Signed, 5 1/2 In. .......................................................... 225.00
Figurine, Seated Rabbit, Signed, 3 1/2 X 4 In. ....................................................................... 215.00
Finger Bowl, Cluthra ............................................................................................................... 200.00
Finger Bowl, Gold Aurene On Calcite Rib, 5 In.Diam. ............................................................. 120.00
Finger Bowl, Green Cut To Clear .............................................................................................. 30.00
Finger Bowl, Underplate, Aurene & Calcite, Iridescent ........................................................... 165.00
Finger Bowl, Underplate, Selenium Red, Signed ..................................................................... 195.00
Fixture, Ceiling, Bowl Shape, Calcite & Alabaster, 3-Bulb, 16 In. ........................................4000.00
Fixture, Ceiling, 3-Bulb, Calcite & Alabaster, Bowl, 16 In.Diam. ..........................................4000.00
Glass, Ice Tea, Pale Green, 6 1/4 In. ....................................................................................... 70.00
Glass, Pale Green, Signed, 4 3/4 In. ....................................................................................... 30.00
Goblet, Aurene, Twisted Stem, Signed, 4 1/2 In. .................................................................... 165.00
Goblet, Blue & Topaz Turned Stem, Ribbed, Signed, 8 1/2 In. ............................................... 95.00

**Goblet,** Celeste Blue Bowl, Topaz Stem & Foot, Signed, 6 1/2 In. .......... 45.00
**Goblet,** Clear Stem, Green Bowl, Signed .......... 30.00
**Goblet,** Diamond-Quilted, Green Threaded, Swirled Stem, 8 1/2 In. .......... 55.00
**Goblet,** Funnel Shaped, Trapped Bubble Stem, 6 1/2 In., Set Of 12 .......... 250.00
**Goblet,** Gold Aurene, Twisted Stem, Signed, 4 1/2 In. .......... 165.00
**Goblet,** Green Bowl, Intaglio Thistles, Leaves, Signed, 6 X 4 In.Diam. .......... 258.00
**Goblet,** Ribbed Topaz With Clear Swirled Stem, Signed, Set Of 4 .......... 155.00
**Goblet,** Selenium Red, Set Of 8 .......... 560.00
**Goblet,** Verre De Soie Underplate, Amethyst, Signed .......... 85.00
**Goblet,** Water, Amethyst, Signed, 4 3/4 In. .......... 35.00
**Goblet,** Water, Blue, 8 1/2 In. .......... 45.00
**Ice Bucket,** Amber, 2 Blue Rings At Top, Signed .......... 125.00
**Jar,** Candy, Covered, Rosaline, Alabaster Finial .......... 335.00
**Lamp,** Jade & Alabaster, Acid Cut Back, Oriental Scenes, 30 In. .......... 1500.00
**Light,** Ceiling, Bowl Shaped, Calcite & Alabaster, 16 In. .......... 4000.00
**Liqueur Set,** Gold Decanter, Dimpled Sides, 6 Matching Glasses .......... 1350.00
**Nut Dish,** Verre De Soie, Optic Swirl, 3 1/2 In. .......... 35.00
**Pitcher,** Fleur-De-Lis, 6-Sided, Amber To Green, Signed, 5 In. .......... 225.00
**Pitcher,** Green Jade, Black Handle, Signed, 9 1/2 In. .......... 350.00
**Pitcher,** Green, Applied Handle, Signed, 8 3/4 In. .......... 200.00
**Plate,** Applied Pink Threading, Signed, 8 1/2 In.Diam. .......... 25.00
**Plate,** Applied Yellow Threading, Signed, 8 1/2 In.Diam. .......... 25.00
**Plate,** Aurene, Gold Stretched Edge, Signed, 7 1/2 In.Diam. .......... 150.00
**Plate,** Chinese Pattern, Jade & Alabaster, Signed, 10 In. .......... 255.00
**Plate,** Cobalt Blue To Clear, Cased, Rim, 13 1/2 In.Diam. .......... 195.00
**Plate,** Green Jade, Cut To Alabaster, 8 1/2 In. .......... 75.00
**Plate,** Green Jade, 8 1/2 In. .......... 25.00
**Plate,** Green Swirled, Signed, 8 In. .......... 30.00
**Plate,** Ivorene, Black Rim, 8 1/2 In. .......... 125.00
**Plate,** Jade Green, Copper Wheel Engraved, Signed, Set Of 8 .......... 225.00
**Plate,** Rosaline, 5 1/2 In. .......... 20.00
**Plate,** Rosaline, 8 3/4 In.Diam. .......... 75.00
**Plate,** Salad, Topaz, Signed, 8 1/2 In. .......... 15.00
**Plate,** Selenium Red, Signed, 8 1/2 In.Diam. .......... 125.00
**Rose Bowl,** Chrysanthemum, Cut Jade To Jade, 7 1/4 X 8 1/2 In.Wide .......... 600.00
**Rose Bowl,** Fleur-De-Lis, Shaded Pink, Clear Vine Ring, 5 1/2 In. .......... 165.00
**Rose Bowl,** Green Jade, Signed, 3 1/2 X 6 In.Diam. .......... 150.00
**Rose Bowl,** Reeded Feet, Applied Red Grapes, Ruffled .......... 400.00
**Rose Bowl,** Ruffled, Vertical Ribbed Pattern, Signed, Green, 4 In. .......... 50.00
**Salt,** Gold Design, Calcite Swirls, Signed, 1 3/4 X 2 3/4 In. .......... 195.00
**Salt,** Pedestal, Verre De Soie .......... 50.00
**Salt,** Rosa Pattern, Signed .......... 95.00
**Sandwich Set,** Verre De Soie, 6 Plates, Cake Plate 11 1/2 In. .......... 250.00
**Shade,** Aurene, Calcite & Gold, Pleated Crimps, Signed .......... 30.00
**Shade,** Brown, Aurene, Gold Leaf & Vines, Signed .......... 195.00
**Shade,** Calcite, Glared Ribbed Body, C.1910, Signed, 3 7/8 In. .......... 125.00
**Shade,** Dark Green Design, Gold Lined, Signed .......... 155.00
**Shade,** Diamond-Quilted, Green Crystal Feather, Gold .......... 200.00
**Shade,** Etched Medallions & Ribbons, Calcite, Signed, Set Of 3 .......... 225.00
**Shade,** Feather On Diamond-Quilted, Green, Ruffled, Signed .......... 190.00
**Shade,** Flaring Design, White Ground, Marked, C.1910, 5 3/4 In., Pair .......... 175.00
**Shade,** Gold Aurene, Wheel Engraved, Signed, 4 1/2 In., Set Of 5 .......... 575.00
**Shade,** Gold Iridescent, Signed, Set Of 4 .......... 400.00
**Shade,** Green Drag-Loop On Calcite, Gold Border & Lining, Set Of 6 .......... 1050.00
**Shade,** Ribbed, Gold, 2 1/4 In., Pair .......... 250.00
**Shade,** 12 Vertical Ribs, Iridescent Gold, 5 1/2 In., Set Of 5 .......... 425.00
**Shades,** Green Feather, Opal, Gold Lining, Signed, 5 In., Pair .......... 250.00
**Shaker,** Cocktail, Black Base & Top, Black Threading Throughout .......... 85.00
**Sherbet,** Hand Applied Pink Reeding On Bowl, 4 X 4 In. .......... 50.00
**Sherbet,** Underplate, Alabaster Base & Stem, Blue Jade .......... 485.00
**Sherbet,** Underplate, Alabaster Stem, Blue Plate & Bowl .......... 485.00
**Sherbet,** Underplate, Calcite & Gold Aurene, Pedestal Stem .......... 170.00
**Sherbet,** Underplate, Clear Ribbed, Yellow Stem & Rim, Signed .......... 50.00

**Sherbet,** Underplate, Gold Aurene, Pedestal ............................................. 170.00
**Sherbet,** Underplate, Rosaline Pattern, Alabaster Foot, 5 In. ...................... 75.00
**Sherbet,** Underplate, Verre De Soie, Signed ........................................... 495.00
**Sugar,** Verre De Soie, 2 Cobalt Blue Handles, Large ................................ 50.00
**Toothpick,** Clear Twist Stem, Signed .................................................. 56.00
**Tumbler,** Aurene, Slightly Flared, Numbered ......................................... 175.00
**Tumbler,** Ice Tea, Pale Green, Signed, 6 1/4 In., Pair ............................. 70.00
**Tumbler,** Ribbed, Translucent Amethyst, Signed, 6 In. ........................... 95.00
**Urn,** Cigarette, 2 Strand Twist Stem, Signed ........................................ 37.00
**Urn,** Jade To Alabaster, Floral Swags, 9 In. ......................................... 750.00
**Vase,** Acid Cut Back, Jade Green, 12 In. .............................................2500.00
**Vase,** Alabaster Foot, Acid Cut Peacock & Foliage, Label, 12 In. ..............1950.00
**Vase,** Alabaster Handles, Green Jade, Ovoid, 12 In. ............................... 625.00
**Vase,** Alabaster, Applied Black Jade Band, Signed, 6 1/2 In. ................... 165.00
**Vase,** Amber Footed, Vertical Ribbed, 6 3/4 In. .................................... 50.00
**Vase,** Amber Reeding Around Ruffled Top, Signed, Clear, 4 X 6 1/2 In. ...... 75.00
**Vase,** Amber, Optic Ribbed, 11 In. ...................................................... 100.00
**Vase,** Aquamarine, 11 In. ................................................................... 425.00
**Vase,** Art Deco Shape, Random Threads At Top, Signed, 8 In. ................. 125.00
**Vase,** Aurene On Calcite, 3 5/8 In. ...................................................... 295.00
**Vase,** Aurene, Embedded Hearts, Random Threading, Signed, 9 In. ..........1750.00
**Vase,** Aurene, Flared Rim, Tapered Body, Paper Label, Blue, 10 In. .......... 225.00
**Vase,** Aurene, Flared Ruffled Top, 9 3/4 In. .......................................... 425.00
**Vase,** Blue Aurene, Signed Aurene 355, 6 1/2 In. .................................. 475.00
**Vase,** Blue Aurene, Signed, 8 In. ........................................................ 375.00
**Vase,** Bristol Yellow, Threaded, Signed, 8 In. ....................................... 100.00
**Vase,** Bubbly Bristol Yellow, Signed, 5 X 7 In. ...................................... 80.00
**Vase,** Bubbly, Reeding At Top, Spinach Green, Signed, 8 X 7 In. ............. 85.00
**Vase,** Bud, Alabaster Base, Green Jade, 10 1/2 In. ................................ 100.00
**Vase,** Bud, Aurene, Jack-In-The-Pulpit Top, Signed, 7 In. ...................... 995.00
**Vase,** Bud, Blue, Green, & Purple Iridescence, Verre De Soie, 8 In. .......... 85.00
**Vase,** Bud, Stick, Blue Aurene, Signed, 6 In. ........................................ 275.00
**Vase,** Calcite & Gold Aurene, Stretch Lavender, 5 1/4 X 5 1/4 In. ........... 325.00
**Vase,** Calcite & Gold Aurene, 5 1/4 In. ................................................ 325.00
**Vase,** Classic Cluthra, Yellow, Green, Signed, 8 In. ............................... 950.00
**Vase,** Clear Bubbly, Green Reeding, Signed, 8 In. ................................. 135.00
**Vase,** Clear Diamond-Quilted, Green Threads, 7 In. ............................... 125.00
**Vase,** Clear, Swirled, Flared Top, Signed, 7 In. ..................................... 165.00
**Vase,** Cluthra, Opalescent Shaded Greens, C.1910, 8 In. ....................... 550.00
**Vase,** Controlled Bubbles, Bands Top Third, Green, 8 In. ........................ 140.00
**Vase,** Cranberry Swirls, Marked, 7 In. ................................................. 150.00
**Vase,** Crystal Optic, Cranberry Threading, 6 3/4 X 6 1/2 In. ................... 65.00
**Vase,** Cut Back Black Jade, Matte Finish, Dragons, Clouds, 8 1/2 In. .......1250.00
**Vase,** Diagonal Swirl, Crystal, Signed, 6 1/4 In. .................................... 90.00
**Vase,** Diagonal Swirl, 4-Sided, Green Jade, Signed, 5 1/2 In. .................. 155.00
**Vase,** Diamond-Quilted, Platinum Aurene, Signed, Sticker, 4 1/2 In. ......... 400.00
**Vase,** Double Gourd, Alabaster, Signed, 6 In. ....................................... 160.00
**Vase,** Double Knobbed Pedestal, Ivory, Wafer Base, 10 1/4 In. ............... 275.00
**Vase,** Etched Floral Design, Amber Rim, 8 3/4 X 16 In.Diam. .................. 70.00
**Vase,** Fan Shape, Dark Green Threading At Top, Signed, 8 1/2 In. .......... 195.00
**Vase,** Fan Shape, Electric Blue, Signed, 6 1/2 In. .................................. 110.00
**Vase,** Fan, Amber, Ribbed, Knob Stem, Signed, 8 3/4 In. ....................... 125.00
**Vase,** Fan, Black Reeding At Top, Spanish Green, Marked, 8 1/2 In. ........ 150.00
**Vase,** Fan, Gold Aurene, Leaves & Vines, Blue Base, Signed, 8 In. ..........1750.00
**Vase,** Fan, Jade Green, Alabaster Base, Optic Rib, Signed, 9 X 10 In. ...... 165.00
**Vase,** Fan, Miniature, Electric Blue, Signed, 6 1/4 In. ............................ 110.00
**Vase,** Fan, Reeded & Bubbly, Spanish Green, Signed, 11 1/4 In. ............. 165.00
**Vase,** Fan, Rouge Flambe Design On Base, Jade Green, Signed, 8 1/2 In. . 150.00
**Vase,** Flared, 10 Vertical Ribs, Blue, C.1910, Signed, 5 1/2 In. ............... 325.00
**Vase,** Fluted Top, Iridescent Colors, Signed, 6 X 8 In. ........................... 550.00
**Vase,** Footed, 6 Blue Applied Prunts, Bands, Signed, 5 In. ..................... 75.00
**Vase,** Galleon Ship, 8 In. ................................................................... 175.00
**Vase,** Gold Aurene, Jack-In-The-Pulpit, 6 In. ........................................ 400.00

**Vase,** Gold Aurene, Trumpet Body, Round Base, Signed, 7 In. .................................................... 365.00
**Vase,** Green Jade & Alabaster, 6 Prong, Signed, 14 1/2 In. ........................................................ 850.00
**Vase,** Green Jade, Oriental, Signed, 4 1/2 X 8 In. ...................................................................... 265.00
**Vase,** Green Jade, Swirled, 10 In. ............................................................................................ 110.00
**Vase,** Green Jade, 5 In. ............................................................................................................ 125.00
**Vase,** Green Ribbed Fan, Signed, 6 1/2 In. .............................................................................. 125.00
**Vase,** Greenish Blue Tint, Polished Pontil, Signed, 5 In. ......................................................... 150.00
**Vase,** Grotesque, Pedestal Foot, Ruffled Top, Signed, 9 In. .................................................... 95.00
**Vase,** Iridescent Blue, Signed, 5 1/2 In. .................................................................................. 395.00
**Vase,** Ivorene, Signed, 10 In. .................................................................................................. 350.00
**Vase,** Ivory, Shape No.2230, 6 1/2 In. ..................................................................................... 145.00
**Vase,** Jack-In-The-Pulpit, 10 Colors, 6 In. ............................................................................... 400.00
**Vase,** Jade Green Flowers, Citrus Ground, Signed, Acid Cut, 8 In. ........................................ 1650.00
**Vase,** Jade Green, 9 1/2 In. ..................................................................................................... 600.00
**Vase,** Light Blue, Reeded & Bubbled, 6 In. .............................................................................. 60.00
**Vase,** Light Green, Bubbles, 8 X 7 1/2 X 4 In. ......................................................................... 110.00
**Vase,** Matzu Pattern, Black Jade, 12 In. .................................................................................. 550.00
**Vase,** Optic Drape, Pomona Green, 6 3/4 In. ........................................................................... 65.00
**Vase,** Optic Rib, Egyptian Urn Shape, Blue Prunts, Amber, 8 X 24 In. .................................... 195.00
**Vase,** Optic Swirl, Pomona Green, Signed, 10 X 8 In.Diam. ..................................................... 120.00
**Vase,** Oriental Poppy, Urn Shape, Transparent Green Foot, 10 In. ......................................... 450.00
**Vase,** Oriental, Poppy Design, Ribbed, 7 X 7 In. ..................................................................... 675.00
**Vase,** Pale Green, Random Bubbles, Signed, 10 X 9 In.Diam. ................................................. 125.00
**Vase,** Paneled Body, Wafer Stem, French Blue, Signed, 12 1/4 In. ......................................... 175.00
**Vase,** Pedestal, Gold Aurene, Flared, Blue, Signed, 5 1/4 In. .................................................. 365.00
**Vase,** Pedestal, Green Jade & Alabaster, Signed, 5 In. ............................................................ 145.00
**Vase,** Pomona Green Diagonal Swirl, Hexagon Shape, Signed, 8 In. ....................................... 95.00
**Vase,** Red Fluted Top, Signed, Iridescent Coloring, 8 X 6 In. .................................................. 600.00
**Vase,** Rose Cluthra, Signed, 6 1/2 In. ..................................................................................... 575.00
**Vase,** Silverene, Flared Top, 12 1/4 X 6 In.Diam. .................................................................... 395.00
**Vase,** Soft Green, Controlled Bubbles, 8 In. ............................................................................ 139.00
**Vase,** Spinach Green, Bubbly, Reeding At Top, Signed, 8 X 7 In. ............................................ 85.00
**Vase,** Stick, Blue Aurene, Sterling Silver Over Bronze Base, 14 In. ........................................ 450.00
**Vase,** Swirl Pedestal, Bristol Yellow, Signed, 12 In. ................................................................ 175.00
**Vase,** Swirl, Green, No.5017 ................................................................................................... 195.00
**Vase,** Topaz Diagonal Swirl, 6 Lobe Top, Green, Signed, 8 In. ................................................ 145.00
**Vase,** Topaz, Cobalt Trim, 9 In. .............................................................................................. 165.00
**Vase,** Topaz, 10 1/2 In. ........................................................................................................... 65.00
**Vase,** Trumpet, Gold Aurene, Blue Highlights, Signed, 14 In. .................................................. 625.00
**Vase,** Verre De Soie, 10 1/4 In. ............................................................................................... 200.00
**Vase,** Vertical Ribbed, Ruffled Top, Green, 3 1/2 In. ................................................................ 50.00
**Vase,** Vertical Ribs, Flared Top, Ivory Ground, 5 1/4 In. .......................................................... 135.00
**Vase,** Vertical Ribs, Flared Top, Jade Green, Marked, 6 5/8 In. ............................................... 127.00
**Vase,** Violet, Flared Rim, Signed, 3 In. .................................................................................... 30.00
**Vase,** White Foot, Blue Jade, 9 In. ........................................................................................... 495.00
**Vase,** 3-Pronged Tree Trunk Shape, Signed & Numbered, 6 1/2 In. ........................................ 450.00
**Vase,** 3-Pronged Tree Trunk, Blue Aurene, Signed, 10 In.Diam. .............................................. 475.00
**Vase,** 3-Pronged Tree Trunk, Gold Aurene, Signed, 6 1/2 In. .................................................. 450.00
**Water Set,** Aurene, Pitcher, 6 Glasses, Blue Rims, C.1915 ...................................................... 2100.00
**Whiskey,** Green Reeding, 2 1/2 In. ........................................................................................... 35.00
**Wine,** Blue & Topaz Turned Stem, Ribbed, Signed, 6 1/2 In. ................................................... 95.00
**Wine,** Clear, Controlled Bubbles, Amber Threading Around Bowl ............................................. 75.00
**Wine,** Controlled Bubbles In Bowl, Golden Amber Threading, 6 1/4 In. .................................... 75.00

*Stevengraphs are woven pictures made like ribbons. They were manufactured*
*by Thomas Stevens of Coventry, England, and became popular in 1862.*

**STEVENGRAPH, Are You Ready,** Matted ................................................................................ 190.00
  **Bookmark,** A Merry Christmas ............................................................................................ 100.00
  **Bookmark,** Blessing, Green & White Floral On Pink, 10 In. .................................................. 55.00
  **Bookmark,** Blessings Attend Thee, 2 X 10 1/4 In. ............................................................... 55.00
  **Bookmark,** Blue, Brown, & Red Bird, Roses, Tassel, Black Silk ............................................. 100.00
  **Bookmark,** George Washington, Centennial ........................................................................ 108.00

Bookmark, Happy New Year ..................................................................................... 48.00
Bookmark, Many Happy Returns Of The Day ......................................................... 125.00
Bookmark, May The Giver & Receiver Meet In Heaven ........................................... 50.00
Bookmark, New Year's Wish, Poem, Bird, Grapes, Tassel ..................................... 100.00
Bookmark, Norwich Celebration, 1909 ................................................................ 150.00
Bookmark, Red, Green, & Blue Flowers On White, 5 1/2 In. .................................. 65.00
Bookmark, Remember Me ................................................................................... 75.00
Bookmark, To A Dear Sister, Signed & Dated, Verse .......................................... 60.00
Bookmark, To My Darling, On Original Card ........................................................ 125.00
Bookmark, Washington Centennial ...................................................................... 85.00
Bookmark, 1876 Philadelphia Centennial, Washington, Flags ............................... 70.00
Called To The Rescue, Framed, Signed ............................................................... 150.00
English Hunt Scene, Framed ............................................................................... 55.00
Faith, Hope, & Charity ....................................................................................... 75.00
For Life Or Death, Original Frame ...................................................................... 235.00
Full Cry, Hounds, Horseman Chasing Fox, C.1880, Framed .................................. 200.00
The Finish, Original Mounts, Signed ...................................... 125.00 To 150.00
The Lady Godiva Procession, Framed .................................................................. 150.00
The Meet ............................................................................................................ 150.00
The Start, Original Mounts, Signed ..................................................................... 125.00
Ye Ladie Godiva, Framed, Signed ....................................................................... 118.00

*Stevens & Williams of Stourbridge, England, made many types of glass,*
*including layered, etched, cameo, and art glass, between the 1830s and*
*the 1930s. Some pieces are signed S and W.*

STEVENS & WILLIAMS, Biscuit Jar, Peacock, Applied Eyes, Plated Lid, Handle ................... 125.00
Bottle, Cologne, Intaglio Cut, Silver Neck, Stopper, 8 In. ..................................... 245.00
Bottle, Perfume, Amber Cut To Clear .................................................................. 425.00
Bowl, Marquetry Handles, Applied Roses, 14 X 9 In. ......................................... 1250.00
Compote, Intaglio Cut, Royal Blue On Crystal, 5 1/4 In. ...................................... 395.00
Cup & Saucer, Demitasse, Rosaline, Signed, 2 In. ............................................... 100.00
Dish, Jam, Silver Holder, Applied Lily Pads, 7 X 6 In. ........................................ 110.00
Jar, Sweetmeat, Applied Leaf, Cow Finial, 3 3/4 In. ........................................... 195.00
Plate, Intaglio Cut, Royal Blue On Crystal, 8 In. ................................................ 175.00
Rose Bowl, Applied Matsu-No-Ke Design, Signed ............................................ 1250.00
Rose Bowl, Clear Outside, Glossy Casing, Signed, 3 In. ....................................... 325.00
Rose Bowl, Du Barry, Underplate, Signed ............................................................ 350.00
Rose Bowl, Green Pull-Ups ................................................................................. 195.00
Rose Bowl, Pull-Up Pattern, Chartreuse Lining, 7 1/2 In. ..................................... 295.00
Spittoon, Woman's, Flower Bowl ........................................................................ 115.00
Spittoon, Woman's, Green Glass ........................................................................ 95.00
Sugar & Creamer, Matsu-No-Ke, Amber Rosettes ............................................... 500.00
Syrup, Cranberry, Threaded ............................................................................... 145.00
Vase, Acid Cut Back, Threading, 15 In. ............................................................. 295.00
Vase, Amberina Mother-Of-Pearl, Blue Lining, 11 1/2 In. ..................................... 795.00
Vase, Applied Clear Green Feet & Leaves, Flowers, 7 In. ..................................... 325.00
Vase, Applied Glass Flowers, 9 1/2 In., Pair ...................................................... 450.00
Vase, Applied Leaves & Acorns, 12 In. ............................................................... 135.00
Vase, Appliqued Pears, Applied Branch, Amber Base, 6 In. .................................. 495.00
Vase, Cream, Apple Green Feet, White, Blue Handle, 6 In. ................................... 240.00
Vase, Flowers, Applied Amber Leaves, Pink Lining, 10 In. .................................... 245.00
Vase, Jewel Pattern, Amber, Numbered, 5 In. ..................................................... 150.00
Vase, Reversed Amberina Swirl, 9 1/2 In. ......................................................... 1200.00
Vase, Roses, Turquoise Overlaid White, Label, 14 In., Pair .................................. 1150.00
Vase, Ruffled, Applied Rigaree Flowers, Signed, 11 In. ....................................... 275.00
Vase, Striped Jack-In-The-Pulpit, 13 5/8 In., Pair .............................................. 385.00
Vase, Turquoise Overlaid White, Rose Design, 14 In. ......................................... 3800.00
Vase, White Opaque Stripes, 6 7/8 In. ............................................................... 145.00

*Henry William Stiegel started his first factory in Pennsylvania in 1763. He remained in business until 1774. Glassware in the Stiegel style has been made by many factories. The wares are made in clear or colored glass and are decorated in various styles.*

| | |
|---|---:|
| **STIEGEL TYPE, Bowl,** 3 X 3 X 6 In.Diam. | 50.00 |
| **Flask,** Sheared Lip, Amethyst, 5 1/2 In. | 395.00 |
| **Vase,** Hand-Painted Design, Clear, 6 1/2 In. | 45.00 |

*Stoneware is a coarse glazed and fired potter's ware that is used to make crocks, jugs, etc.*

| | |
|---|---:|
| **STONEWARE, Bottle,** B.F. & C.C. Haley, 1895, California Pop Beer, 9 In. | 60.00 |
| **Bottle,** Beer, Brown | 25.00 |
| **Bottle,** Blue Lip, J.Hingle's, Blue Mark In Star, 10 1/4 In. | 35.00 |
| **Bottle,** D.W.DeFreest, Blue R For Root Beer, 10 3/4 In. | 25.00 |
| **Bottle,** Dr.Brown's Root Beer | 85.00 |
| **Bottle,** Eureka House Hotel, 10 1/4 In. | 30.00 |
| **Bottle,** Pig, Snout, Eyes, Ears, Tail Blue, 3 1/2 X 8 1/2 In. | 525.00 |
| **Bottle,** Root Beer, Dark Brown Shiny Slip, 1 Quart | 18.00 |
| **Bottle,** Tan Slip, Impressed Star, George, Reynolds, 1 Quart, 10 In. | 20.00 |
| **Bottle,** Thick Lip, D.W.Tarr & Co., 1 Quart, 9 1/4 In. | 28.00 |
| **Bowl,** Apricot, Blue & White, 9 In. | 49.00 |
| **Bowl,** Apricot, Green & Tan, 9 In. | 49.00 |
| **Bowl,** Apricot, Green & Yellow, Bail Handled, 9 1/4 X 4 1/4 In. | 48.00 |
| **Bowl,** Apricot, Green & Yellow, 8 1/4 X 4 1/4 In. | 48.00 |
| **Bowl,** Bail, 4 Molded Feet, Blue Sponge Design, 5 X 10 1/2 In.Diam. | 245.00 |
| **Bowl,** Blue, Handled, 10 In. | 19.00 |
| **Bowl,** Brown, 10 1/2 In. | 65.00 |
| **Bowl,** Dark Brown, 10 In. | 14.00 |
| **Bowl,** Dough, Blue & White | 55.00 |
| **Bowl,** F.C.Pope, 10 In.Diam. | 125.00 |
| **Bowl,** Hunting Scene With Dog, Green, 2 1/2 X 5 1/4 In.Diam. | 85.00 |
| **Bowl,** Light, Brown, 9 In. | 12.00 |
| **Bowl,** Mixing, Ribbed Base, 1 1/2 X 3 1/2 In.Diam. | 22.00 |
| **Bowl,** Raised Panels Rings Outside, Blue, 9 1/2 X 5 In. | 30.00 |
| **Bowl,** Rings Attached To Handles, 5 1/2 In.Diam. | 25.00 |
| **Bowl,** Wedding Ring, Blue & White, 8 In.Diam. | 40.00 |
| **Box,** Salt, Wooden Lid, Hanging, Blue, Round | 55.00 |
| **Bucket,** Beer, Bail Handle, Lettering, Gray & Cobalt Blue, 1 Liter | 78.00 |
| **Bucket,** Lard, Blue & White | 38.00 |
| **Bucket,** White With Blue Stripes, Bail Handle, 6 In. | 45.00 |
| **Butter Tub,** Marked Pacific, 3 Pound | 12.50 |
| **Butter,** Covered, Lambrecht's | 32.00 |
| **Butter,** Good Luck, Lid, Blue & White | 140.00 |
| **Canister,** Cinnamon, 3 Blue Rings, 4 In. | 25.00 |
| **Canister,** Tea, Snowflake Pattern, Blue & White | 80.00 |
| **Canister,** Windflower, Coffee | 80.00 |
| **Chamber Pot,** Bowtie Pattern, Blue & White | 75.00 |
| **Chamber Pot,** Open, Rose & Trellis | 75.00 |
| **Chicken Waterer,** Diamond Brand | 25.00 |
| **Chicken Waterer,** Knob Top, Blue Stripe Where Joined, 20 Ounce | 250.00 |
| **Churn,** Brown, Signed, 6 Gallon | 30.00 |
| **Churn,** Butter, Blue & Gray | 75.00 |
| **Churn,** Cobalt Blue Double Lovebirds, S.Hart, Fulton, N.Y., 4 Gallon | 800.00 |
| **Churn,** Cobalt Blue, Chicken, Haxton Bros., Ft.Edward, 6 Gallon | 385.00 |
| **Churn,** Dasher, Lid, Love & Fields Pottery, Dallas, 4 Gallon | 69.50 |
| **Churn,** F.B.Norton & Co., Worchester, Mass., Cobalt Design, 18 In. | 685.00 |
| **Churn,** Macomb Pottery Co., Macomb, Ill. | 45.00 |
| **Churn,** White's Utica, 5 Gallon | 195.00 |
| **Cookie Jar,** Sponge Band | 48.00 |
| **Creamer,** Blue Letters, York, Pa., White, 1926 | 28.00 |
| **Cream Pot,** Blue Leaf & Dots, E. & L.P.Norton, 1861-81, 1 1/2 Gallon | 130.00 |

**Cream Pot,** Parrot On Perch, Tin Lid, White's, Utica, 1865, 10 In. ........ 145.00
**Crock,** A.D.Graham & Co., Braddock, Pa., Gray & Blue, 7 In. ................. 40.00
**Crock,** Advertising Friffin's Spiced Herring, Blue & White ................... 90.00
**Crock,** Barnabas Edmands, Charlestown, Mass., C.1830, 1 Gallon ......... 95.00
**Crock,** Bird On Leaf, New York Stoneware Co., 1865-81, 4 Gallon ........ 225.00
**Crock,** Bird, Cobalt Blue, Hart, Fulton, N.Y., 2 Gallon ....................... 285.00
**Crock,** Blue Leaf Design, E. & L.P.Norton, 7 1/4 In. .......................... 65.00
**Crock,** Blue Leaves & Flowers, Wide Mouth, Signed, 2 Gallon ........... 130.00
**Crock,** Blue Letters, New Brighton, Penn., 3 Gallon ......................... 75.00
**Crock,** Blue Splashes At Top, 10 1/2 X 6 In.Diam. ............................ 95.00
**Crock,** Bluebird, Norton, Bennington, Vt., 1850-65, 1 Gallon, 11 In. ...... 125.00
**Crock,** Bluebird, Tall Stump, Riedinger & Caire, 1857-78, 9 3/4 In. ...... 200.00
**Crock,** Brush Strokes, Gray & Cobalt, 1 1/2 In. ............................... 27.50
**Crock,** Butter Stenciled, 7 In. ................................................... 77.50
**Crock,** Butter, Blue, Raised Design ............................................ 33.00
**Crock,** Butter, Butterfly ......................................................... 70.00
**Crock,** Butter, Clamp Glass Lid, 6 1/2 In. .................................... 14.00
**Crock,** Butter, Covered, Cobalt Clover Design ............................... 175.00
**Crock,** Butter, Daisy ............................................................. 55.00
**Crock,** Butter, Embossed Hunters & Moose, Blue Gray ...................... 195.00
**Crock,** Butter, Good Luck Pattern, Blue & White ............................. 135.00
**Crock,** Butter, Red Rose, Madison, Wisconsin ................................ 125.00
**Crock,** Butter, Swastika Bands Top & Bottom, Blue & Gray ................ 95.00
**Crock,** Butterfly, E. & L.P.Norton, Bennington, Vt., 2 Gallon .............. 165.00
**Crock,** Canning, John Bell ...................................................... 180.00
**Crock,** Cobalt Bird, Adam Claire, Poughkeepsie, N.Y., 4 Gallon .......... 285.00
**Crock,** Cobalt Bird, Flack & Vanarsdale, Ontario, 3 Gallon ................ 450.00
**Crock,** Cobalt Bird, S.Hart, Fulton, N.Y., 2 Gallon .......................... 285.00
**Crock,** Cobalt Iris Design, Seymour, Hartford, Conn., 3 Gallon ........... 125.00
**Crock,** Cobalt Orchid, Whites, Utica, N.Y., 5 Gallon ........................ 200.00
**Crock,** Cobalt Paddletail Bird, N.A.White & Son, 4 Gallon .................. 325.00
**Crock,** Cobalt Robin On Branch, Whites, Utica, N.Y., 3 Gallon ............ 165.00
**Crock,** Cobalt Thistle, Whites, Utica, N.Y., 5 Gallon ........................ 120.00
**Crock,** E.J.Miller & Son, Alexandria, Va., Blue Design, 1 Gallon .......... 110.00
**Crock,** Eared, Cobalt Swags, Commeraw, New York, Ovoid, 1 Gallon ..... 1400.00
**Crock,** Embossed Minnesota Stoneware, 1 Gallon ........................... 32.00
**Crock,** Fairfax, Vermont, 3 Gallon ............................................. 150.00
**Crock,** Five Leaves, Cobalt Blue, Burger, Rochester, N.Y., 2 Gallon ...... 165.00
**Crock,** Floral, Cobalt Blue, Norton, Bennington, Vt., 1 1/2 Gallon ........ 175.00
**Crock,** Flower, Blue, Ovoid, Clark & Co., Lyons, N.Y., 1 Gallon ........... 120.00
**Crock,** Flowers On Side, Western, 2 Gallon .................................. 65.00
**Crock,** Freehand Design, Sailing Vessel, MacQoid & Co., 9 1/4 In. ....... 600.00
**Crock,** Handled, Ovoid Shape, Charlestown, Mass., 4 Gallon, 14 In. ..... 200.00
**Crock,** Horse, Cobalt Blue, Lyons, 1 Gallon ................................. 1850.00
**Crock,** Impressed Cow, Gardiner Stoneware Co., 3 Gallon, 10 In. ........ 150.00
**Crock,** J. & E.Norton, Bennington, Vt., 1850-59, Cobalt, 2 Gallon ........ 245.00
**Crock,** North Star, 2 Gallon .................................................... 15.00
**Crock,** Patent 1886, Gate City Water Cooler, Flower ....................... 350.00
**Crock,** Riedinger & Caire, Poug Keepsie, Misspelled, 1857, 11 In. ........ 190.00
**Crock,** Salt, Blue & White Butterfly ........................................... 85.00
**Crock,** Salt, Lid, Apricots, Blue & White ..................................... 135.00
**Crock,** Salt, Peacock, Blue & White ........................................... 85.00
**Crock,** Sonner, Strasburg, Virginia, 1 Gallon ............................... 75.00
**Crock,** Stenciled American Eagle, Arrow, Norwich Pottery, 10 In. ....... 135.00
**Crock,** Thistle, Cobalt Blue, Whites, Utica, N.Y., 5 Gallon ................ 120.00
**Crock,** Two Eagles, Impressed, 4 Gallon ..................................... 175.00
**Crock,** 3 Impressed Swans, Flack & Vanarsdale, Ontario, 3 Gallon ...... 145.00
**Cruet,** Blue ........................................................................ 28.00
**Custard Cup,** Fish Scale, Blue & White ....................................... 58.00
**Dish,** Soap, Beaded Rose, Blue To White ..................................... 75.00
**Dish,** Soap, Blue & White ........................................................ 95.00
**Dish,** Soap, Cat Face, White, Round ........................................... 65.00
**Dish,** Soap, Rose Fish Scale, Blue To White ................................. 75.00

| | |
|---|---|
| **Dutch Oven,** Blue Chain Pattern | 58.00 |
| **Feeder,** Chicken, Blue Design Of Chickens & Chicks | 68.00 |
| **Feeder,** Chicken, Ko-Rec | 45.00 |
| **Feeder,** Chicken, Oak Leaf, Simmons | 42.00 |
| **Flask,** Tea, Gray Clay, Shiny Salt Glaze, 1/2 Pint, 5 1/8 In. | 70.00 |
| **Flowerpot,** New York Stoneware Co., Ft.Edward, N.Y., 4 Gallon | 365.00 |
| **Foot Warmer,** Advertising, Blue & White | 145.00 |
| **Foot Warmer,** Gray, 10 1/2 X 5 In. | 30.00 |
| **Foot Warmer,** Marked A Warm Friend, Signed Logan Pottery, Ohio | 85.00 |
| **Fruit,** Yellow Grapes, Apple, Lemon, Orange, & Peach, Set | 125.00 |
| **Holder,** Toothbrush, Basket Weave Rose, Blue & White | 85.00 |
| **Humidor,** Snake Finial | 250.00 |
| **Inkwell,** Orange Sides & Top, Mottled Gray, 3 Pen Holes, 6 1/2 In. | 58.00 |
| **Jar,** Apple Butter, Bail Handle | 15.00 |
| **Jar,** Beater, Blue Band, Gray | 12.00 |
| **Jar,** Butter, Brown, Self-Sealing, C.1884, Signed, 1 Gallon | 35.00 |
| **Jar,** Canning, Monmouth, Illinois, Lock Lid | 55.00 |
| **Jar,** Fruit, Denver Stone Ware Co., Brown, 1/2 Gallon | 15.00 |
| **Jar,** Horseradish, As You Like It | 25.00 |
| **Jardiniere,** Indian Head Profile, Full Headdress, Glazed Interior | 35.00 |
| **Jug,** Batter, Copper Lid, Brown | 65.00 |
| **Jug,** Blue Bands At Middle, Williams & Repperts, Penna., 2 Gallon | 125.00 |
| **Jug,** Blue Center Blossom, E. & L.P.Norton, 3 Gallon | 200.00 |
| **Jug,** Blue Scroll Design, E. & L.P.Norton, Bennington, 1 Gallon | 75.00 |
| **Jug,** Blue Star Design, Bennett & Chollar Homer, C.1840, 10 1/2 In. | 160.00 |
| **Jug,** Blue, Bird On Floral Spray, White & Son, N.Y., 5 In. | 475.00 |
| **Jug,** Bluebird Design, 5 Gallon | 300.00 |
| **Jug,** Boston, Buff Color, 19th Century, Ovoid, 2 Gallon | 140.00 |
| **Jug,** Butterfly, Julius Norton, 1838-43, Ovoid, 2 Gallon | 325.00 |
| **Jug,** Cobalt Blue Floral Sprig, Signed, F.B.Norton, 1 Gallon | 135.00 |
| **Jug,** Cobalt Blue Paddletail Bird, N.A.White & Son, 2 Gallon | 370.00 |
| **Jug,** Cobalt Blue Peacock On Stump, J. & E.Norton, Vermont, 2 Gallon | 275.00 |
| **Jug,** Cobalt Blue Peafowl, Albany, N.Y., 3 Gallon | 350.00 |
| **Jug,** Cobalt Leaf, Gray, E. & L.P.Norton, Bennington, 1 Gallon | 78.00 |
| **Jug,** Crolius, Cobalt Blue Around Name & Handle, 1794-1838 | 625.00 |
| **Jug,** Druggist's, Impressed Mortars & Pestles, J.Caire, 13 3/4 In. | 250.00 |
| **Jug,** Dutch Scene, 7 1/2 In. | 50.00 |
| **Jug,** Floral, J. & E.Norton, Bennington, Vt., Ovoid, 2 Gallon | 200.00 |
| **Jug,** G.S.Guy & Co., Fort Edward, N.Y., 1 Gallon | 45.00 |
| **Jug,** Gray Glaze, Marked Boston, Ovoid, 2 Gallon | 165.00 |
| **Jug,** Gray Glaze, Marked Charlestown, Ovoid, 1 Gallon | 87.00 |
| **Jug,** Green Mill Whiskey, Chillicothe, Ohio, Miniature | 48.00 |
| **Jug,** Handled, Stenciled Design, Alderman & Scott, Ohio, 15 3/4 In. | 200.00 |
| **Jug,** Impressed D.Goodale, 8 1/2 In. | 65.00 |
| **Jug,** Incised Leaves, Blue Lines, 18th Century, 11 1/2 In. | 435.00 |
| **Jug,** J. & E.Norton, Bennington, Vt., 11 1/2 In. | 285.00 |
| **Jug,** Liquor, Brown Dotted Glaze, Letter In Blue, 1 Gallon | 100.00 |
| **Jug,** Lyons & Co., Established 1825, 1 Gallon | 45.00 |
| **Jug,** Mottled Gray & Crown, New England, C.1820s, 1 Pint, 7 In. | 45.00 |
| **Jug,** Mottled Tan & Gray, Salt Glaze, C.1825, Ovoid, 6 5/8 In. | 35.00 |
| **Jug,** North Star, 1 Gallon | 300.00 |
| **Jug,** Norton & Fenton, Bennington, Vt., Ovoid, 13 1/2 In. | 310.00 |
| **Jug,** Ocher Slip At Top & Base, F.Carpenter, 1805-20, 16 1/4 In. | 235.00 |
| **Jug,** Ovoid, Julius Norton, Bennington, Vt., 2 Gallon | 130.00 |
| **Jug,** Ovoid, Line Design Of Bird, D.Goodale, Hartford, 16 1/4 In. | 225.00 |
| **Jug,** Ovoid, Tulip Flower, C.1830, L.Norton & Son, 17 1/2 In. | 250.00 |
| **Jug,** Ringed Neck & Base, F.Carpenter, 1805-20, Ovoid, 7 1/2 In. | 55.00 |
| **Jug,** Ringed Neck, J.Remmey, 1800-10, Ovoid, 12 In. | 450.00 |
| **Jug,** Straight Sides, Reddish Brown Glaze, 19th Century, 11 1/2 In. | 24.00 |
| **Jug,** William Radam's Microbe Killer, 1 Gallon | 65.00 |
| **Jug,** 4-Section Circles, Heart Center, Blue, C.1820, Stopper, 15 In. | 275.00 |
| **Kettle,** Apricot, Blue & White, Bail | 100.00 |
| **Match Holder,** Elves, Tree Stump | 25.00 |

**Mortar & Pestle,** Wooden Handle, Stamped U.S.1862, 7 3/8 In. ............................ 65.00
**Mug,** Brown, Impressed H In Circle ................................................................. 24.00
**Mug,** Drink Hires, It Is Pure, Pair ...................................................................... 38.00
**Mug,** Embossed Lady & Man, Monmouth, Illinois, Blue .................................... 55.00
**Mug,** Flying Bird, Blue & White ........................................................................ 125.00
**Mug,** Fraternal Order Of Eagles, Brown, Eagle, Stars, H In Circle ...................... 28.00
**Mug,** Gibson Girl & Flatiron Building Design, Blue & White ............................... 40.00
**Mug,** Grapes, Green, 5 1/4 In. ........................................................................... 27.00
**Mug,** Man Drinking, Green, 5 In. ....................................................................... 20.00
**Mug,** Nelson, 2-Handled .................................................................................. 240.00
**Mug,** Relief, Gray & Blue ................................................................................... 28.00
**Mug,** Stenciled Rose, Blue & White .................................................................. 50.00
**Mustard,** Advertising, Blue & White .................................................................. 28.00
**Mustard,** French, Blue Lettering & Logo, 3 1/2 In. ............................................ 35.00
**Pan,** Bed, White, 1903 ..................................................................................... 30.00
**Pan,** Milk, Double Dab Leaves, Penn., 4 1/2 X 12 1/4 In.Wide .......................... 95.00
**Pitcher & Bowl,** Blue & White, Large ................................................................ 165.00
**Pitcher & Bowl,** Fish Scale & Roses, Blue & White ........................................... 130.00
**Pitcher,** Albany Slip, Lid, S.Pepson, Albany, N.Y., 1866-90, 1 Gallon ................ 115.00
**Pitcher,** Apricot, Blue & White, 2 Quart ........................................................... 120.00
**Pitcher,** Apricot, Blue & White, 8 1/4 In. .......................................................... 125.00
**Pitcher,** Batter, Handled, Signed F.T.Wright, 10 In. ........................................... 125.00
**Pitcher,** Beer, Depicts Washington & Lincoln In Relief, 1 Gallon ........................ 165.00
**Pitcher,** Blue & Gray, Fish Scale & Roses, 1 Quart ........................................... 65.00
**Pitcher,** Blue & White, Cow, 8 In. ..................................................................... 60.00
**Pitcher,** Blue, White, Iris, 8 1/2 In. .................................................................... 55.00
**Pitcher,** Brown, Dog Handle ............................................................. 100.00 To 130.00
**Pitcher,** Brown, Green, & Yellow, 5 1/2 In. ........................................................ 40.00
**Pitcher,** Brown, Impressed H In Circle, 9 1/2 In. ............................................... 60.00
**Pitcher,** Castle, 4 3/4 In. .................................................................................. 100.00
**Pitcher,** Cobalt Abstract Design, 9 3/8 In. ........................................................ 120.00
**Pitcher,** Cold Water, Fish Scale Rose, Blue & White .......................................... 130.00
**Pitcher,** Cow, Blue & White, 7 1/2 In. ............................................................... 105.00
**Pitcher,** Cow, Blue & White, 8 In. ..................................................................... 155.00
**Pitcher,** Cow, Green & Yellow, 7 1/4 In. ............................................. 75.00 To 90.00
**Pitcher,** Deer & Fawn, Italian Blue, 8 1/4 In. ..................................................... 140.00
**Pitcher,** Dutch Scene, Blue & White, 7 1/2 In. .................................................. 85.00
**Pitcher,** Face Of Smiling Man, Rosy Cheeks, Blue & White, 8 In. ....................... 225.00
**Pitcher,** Grape & Treebark, Cream & Green, 8 1/4 In. ......................... 45.00 To 55.00
**Pitcher,** Grape & Treebark, Cream & Green, 9 In. ............................................. 65.00
**Pitcher,** Grapes & Leaves, Blue & Gray, Star Mark, 9 1/4 In. ............................ 75.00
**Pitcher,** Gray Bark Texture, Blue Daisies, 6 1/2 In. ........................................... 68.00
**Pitcher,** Green, Grape-Treebark Design, 8 In. ................................................... 50.00
**Pitcher,** Green, 7 1/2 In. ................................................................................... 55.00
**Pitcher,** Indian Boy & Girl, 2 In. ....................................................................... 75.00
**Pitcher,** Lattice & Roses, Blue & Beige, 6 3/4 In. .............................................. 50.00
**Pitcher,** Lincoln Head, Blue & White, 5 1/2 In. .................................................. 90.00
**Pitcher,** Marked F.T.Wright & Son, Taunton, Mass., 8 1/2 In. ............................ 75.00
**Pitcher,** Medalllions Of Grapes, Green & Beige, 8 1/2 In. .................................. 38.00
**Pitcher,** Milk, Dark Brown Glaze, 4 X 5 In.Diam. ................................................ 12.00
**Pitcher,** Milk, Dutch Boy & Girl Kissing, Blue & White ....................................... 90.00
**Pitcher,** Milk, Indian Head Both Sides, Blue & White ......................................... 220.00
**Pitcher,** Milk, Park Scene, Cream Ground, 6 In. ................................................ 25.00
**Pitcher,** Milk, Park Scene, Rust, Blue, & Green, Cream Ground, 6 In. ................. 25.00
**Pitcher,** Ocher Slip, D.Goodale, Hartford, Conn., 1825-30, 7 1/4 In. ................. 250.00
**Pitcher,** Partial Ocher Coloring, C.1805-20, 11 1/2 In. ...................................... 140.00
**Pitcher,** Squatty, Dutch Scene, Blue & White, 7 In. ........................................... 85.00
**Pitcher,** Water, Blue Fish Scale, Blue To White ................................................. 85.00
**Planter,** Tree Trunk Form, F.B.Norton & Co., 11 1/4 In. ..................................... 125.00
**Plate,** Pie, Crimped Edge, Brown Glaze, 8 3/4 In. ............................................. 80.00
**Plate,** Pie, White & Blue .................................................................................. 65.00
**Pot,** Blue Blossoms, Norton & Fenton, Semiovoid, 2 Gallon ............................. 125.00
**Pot,** Embossed Grapes, Leaves, Elf, Blue & Gray, German, 1 Gallon .................. 185.00

Stoneware, Vases, Martin Brothers

Pot, Incised Fleur-De-Lis Both Sides, 1775-1800, 11 3/4 In. ........................................... 450.00
Pot, Incised Silly Goose, Blue Lines, C.1820s, Ovoid, 13 1/2 In. ............................................. 95.00
Pot, Vertical Loop Handle, 1775-1800, Ovoid, 10 1/2 In. .......................................... 275.00
Pot, 3 Blue Blossoms, Norton & Fenton, C.1844, 10 1/2 In. ........................................ 135.00
Potlid, Knob On Top, Impressed Humiston & Warner, N.J., 3 In. .................................... 25.00
Rolling Pin, Blue Band ........................................................................................... 135.00
Rolling Pin, Wild Flower ..................................................................... 160.00 To 175.00
Rolling Pink, Blue Band ........................................................................................ 140.00
Salt & Pepper, Ships, Blue & White, Signed M.A.Malls, 5 X 3 In. ................................ 100.00
Salt, Butterfly, Blue & White ................................................................................. 60.00
Salt, Raspberry .................................................................................................... 65.00
Spittoon, Basket Weave, Green Rose ...................................................................... 35.00
Spittoon, Blue & Gray .......................................................................................... 40.00
Spittoon, Bowtie, Blue & White ............................................................................. 85.00
Spittoon, Leaf Design, Circling Bowl, Blue & White .................................................. 65.00
Spittoon, Rose Stemmed & Scroll .......................................................................... 65.00
Spittoon, Rose Waffle, Blue & White ...................................................................... 85.00
Spittoon, Sponge ................................................................................................ 145.00
Stein, Incised Design, Blue Tulip, Pewter Lid, Germany, 6 1/4 In. ................................ 50.00
Stein, Pewter Lid, Polychrome Scenes, Signed, R.Briggs, 14 In. ................................ 225.00
Teapot, Advertising McCormick's Tea ..................................................................... 28.00
Tub, Butter, Blue Stripe, White, Wooden Cover ........................................................ 45.00
Vase, Blue, Gold Trim, Slater, 6 In., Pair ................................................................ 90.00
Vase, Incised Fish, Martin Brothers, 7 In. ........................................ Illus 250.00
Vase, Incised Flowers, Martin Brothers, 7 In. .................................... Illus 200.00
Vase, Martin Brothers, 1887, 10 1/4 In. ............................................... Illus 1000.00
Vase, Roses, Florie Jones, 10 In. .......................................................................... 125.00
Vase, Slip Foliage, 9 In. ....................................................................................... 200.00
Vase, Yellow Roses, 8 1/2 In., Pair ....................................................................... 185.00
Vase, 11 1/4 In., Pair ........................................................................................... 200.00
Waterer, Chicken, Jug Shape, Closed Top, Open Trough, Brown ................................. 45.00
Wine Crock, Finger-Painted In Cobalt Blue, F.H.Cowden, 3 Gallon .............................. 200.00
        STORE, see also Card; Coffee Grinder; Scale; Tool
STORE, Ashtray, Carter Hall Tobacco, Embossed Metal ................................................ 2.00
Ashtray, Champion Spark Plug Screwed In Center, Black Porcelain ............................. 37.50
Ashtray, Chesterfield, 1930s, Porcelain ................................................................... 16.00
Ashtray, Firestone 500 ......................................................................................... 18.00
Ashtray, Goodrich Tire, Akro Insert ....................................................................... 15.00
Ashtray, Goodyear, Super Torque ............................................................................ 7.00
Ashtray, Green River Whiskey, Match Holder, Embossed, Metal ................................. 10.00
Ashtray, Guinness Beer, Pottery ............................................................................ 11.50
Ashtray, Independent Card Co. ............................................................................... 6.00
Ashtray, Iron Fireman, Figural Robot Holding Shovel, Cast Iron ................................. 16.00

**Ashtray,** Mack Truck Bulldog ............................................... 28.00
**Ashtray,** Moxie, Pictures Frank Archer ................................... 48.00
**Ashtray,** Mr.Peanut's 50th Anniversary ................................. 35.00
**Ashtray,** Phoenix Soda Fountain Co., N.Y. ............................. 15.00
**Ashtray,** Salem Cigarettes, Embossed ................................... 6.00
**Ashtray,** Tuxedo Tobacco, Giveaway .................................... 10.00
**Ashtray,** Union Oil Co., Bronze ........................................... 45.00
**Bag,** Flour, Blue Lettering, Shaker Mills, New Gloucester ...... 190.00
**Bank,** Mr.Peanut, 8 In. ...................................................... 20.00
**Bank,** Nash's Prepared Mustard, Lucky Joe, Glass .............. 8.00
**Banner,** Sideshow, King Dodo, 8 X 10 Ft. ............................ 150.00
**Barrel,** Dixie Brewing, New Orleans, Metal Bands, Wooden ... 200.00
**Barrel,** Planters Peanut, Label ............................................ 175.00
**Barrel,** Richardson Root Beer, Spigot, Wooden, 19 X 12 In.Diam. ... 150.00
**Barrel,** Royal Baking Powder, Wooden, 28 X 18 In. .............. 58.00
**Barrel,** Tobacco, Schuber & Co., Wood, Paper Label, 13 X 11 In. ... 65.00
**Baseball,** Autographed By Babe Ruth, Greensboro, N.C., 1924 ... 200.00
**Beater,** Carpet, Braided Wire ............................................. 8.00
**Beater,** Rug, Name Bat Wing On Wooden Handle ................ 11.00
**Bench,** Red Star Shoes, Oak, 5 Ft.Long ............................. 325.00
**Bill Holder,** Black Cat Stove & Shoe Polish ......................... 10.00
**Bill Holder,** Hanging, Victorian, Lady's Hand, Brass, 5 1/2 In. ... 28.00
**Bill Hook,** Ceresota Flour, Lithograph, Cardboard ................ 15.00
**Bin,** A. & P.Coffee, Floor Model, Wooden ............................ 295.00
**Bin,** Bean, 3 Compartment, Glass Front .............................. 465.00
**Bin,** Beechnut Coffee ............................... 85.00 To 95.00
**Bin,** Beechnut Tobacco, Blue ............................................ 150.00
**Bin,** Coffee, Black & Red Slant Top, Tin ............................. 150.00
**Bin,** Counter, Haring's Allspice, Rooster, Red, Tin ............... 85.00
**Bin,** Game Tobacco .......................................................... 285.00
**Bin,** Gregg's Coffee .......................................................... 165.00
**Bin,** Honest Scrap Tobacco, Metal ..................................... 900.00
**Bin,** Honest Scrap, Slant Front, Dog & Cat Pictured ............ 500.00
**Bin,** Luxury Coffee ........................................................... 200.00
**Bin,** Meldrum Coffee, Chicago, 12 X 12 X 16 In. ................. 125.00
**Bin,** Munyon's, Homeopathic Home Remedies, 1895, 14 X 12 X 15 In. ... 350.00
**Bin,** National Biscuit, Glass & Brass .................................. 98.00
**Bin,** Rosebud Match ......................................................... 140.00
**Bin,** Slant, Van Melle Toffee, Birds, Tin .............................. 135.00
**Bin,** Spice, White Squadron, Pictures U.S.S.Philadelphia ...... 65.00
**Bin,** Sugar, Grocery, Wooden ............................................ 225.00
**Bin,** Sweet Clover Tobacco, Tin ......................................... 250.00
**Bin,** Sweet Cuba Tobacco, Green, Pretty Girl, 8 X 8 X 10 In. ... 145.00
**Bin,** Tea, Slant Cover, Oriental Scenes, C.1870, 22 1/2 In., Pair ... 750.00
**Bin,** Tobacco, Polar Bear Tobacco, 18 X 14 X 12 In. ............ 350.00
**Bin,** Tobacco, Slant Front, Old English Curve Cut, 11 X 13 X 8 1/2 In. ... 105.00
**Blackboard,** Barg's Root Beer, 19 X 28 In. .......................... 15.00
    **STORE, BOTTLE, see Bottle**
**Bowl,** Cereal, Uneeda Biscuit, Boy In Raincoat .................... 12.00
**Bowl,** Planters Peanut, 4 Sided, Tin ................................... 12.00
**Box,** Allen & Ginter Imperial Tobacco ................................. 25.00
**Box,** Baker's Chocolate, Dovetailed, Lady One Side, 9 X 5 X 6 1/4 In. ... 24.50
**Box,** Baker's Chocolate, Lady On Side, Original Label, 9 X 6 X 5 In. ... 24.50
**Box,** Beechnut, Canada & Mohawk Valley Scenes, Lithograph, Tin ... 35.00
**Box,** Bixby Shoe Polish, Girl Polishing Shoes, 8 X 8 X 11 1/2 In. ... 36.00
**Box,** Bread, Oblong, U.S. Frigate Constitution ..................... 60.00
**Box,** Butter Carrying, Covered, Wire Bail, Handled, Wood, 9 1/2 In. ... 32.00
**Box,** Camel's Flat 50, Cardboard ........................................ 7.50
**Box,** Cigar, Pollack's Improved Crown Cigars, C.1859, 250 Count ... 40.00
**Box,** Cigar, Rudolph Valentino, Cardboard .......................... 35.00
**Box,** Critic Chop Cut Tobacco ............................................ 25.00
**Box,** Display, Collars & Cuffs, Oak ..................................... 25.00
**Box,** Display, Hairnet, Vogue, Wood, Labels, C.1920, 8 X 9 X 14 In. ... 60.00

Box, Dobbs, 5th Avenue, N.Y.C., View Of 5th Avenue ........................................ 12.00
Box, Ferry Seed, Oak, 11 X 7 In. ........................................................................... 35.00
Box, Gold Dust Washing Powder, Black Twins, 5-Ounce Box ............... 6.50 To 14.00
Box, Gold Shore Tobacco, Tin .............................................................................. 25.00
Box, Hat, Duryeas Satin Glass Starch, Dovetailed, Slotted Cover, 12 In. ........... 15.00
Box, Kis-Me Gum, Glass, Lid, 11 In. ................................................................... 115.00
Box, Koehler's Old Dobbin Ale, Erie, Pennsylvania, Wooden, 16 X 11 In. ........... 12.50
Box, Lyman's Seeds, Wooden ............................................................................. 100.00
Box, Match, Golden Wedding Coffee, Tin ............................................................ 10.00
Box, Melachrino Cigarettes, Cardborad ............................................................... 5.00
Box, Milk, Gateway Pure Milk, Wooden, Outside Use ......................................... 30.00
Box, Opium, 1 Pound .......................................................................................... 75.00
Box, Pocket, Bulldog Tobacco, Cardboard, Upright ............................................ 150.00
Box, Pocket, Checkers Tobacco, Upright, Cardboard .......................................... 185.00
Box, Pocket, Wagon Wheel Tobacco, Upright, Cardboard ................................... 185.00
Box, Recipe, Aunt Jemima .................................................................................. 2.50
Box, Red J Tobacco, Redbird .............................................................................. 65.00
Box, Schepp's Cake, Cream & Green, 20 In.Diam. ............................................. 100.00
Box, Security Cigars, Pineapple & Fan Pattern, Glass, Tin Lid ........................... 60.00
Box, Seed, Manderville, Oak, 19 X 14 In. ........................................................... 30.00
Box, Senate Tobacco, White-Haired Gentleman Reading Paper ......................... 40.00
Box, Sir Walter Raleigh, Christmas ..................................................................... 30.00
Box, Tea, Silver Fox Brand, Wooden ................................................................... 25.00
Box, Walter Baker Chocolate Co., Wooden, Covered, 6 X 5 X 9 !n. .................... 35.00
Box, Woolson's Golden Sun Coffee, Wooden, 30 X 22 X 18 In. .......................... 32.00
Bracelet, Charm, Mini-Cigarette Packs ............................................................... 25.00
Bracelet, Charm, Planters Peanut ....................................................................... 20.00
Bread Raiser, Handle & Pierced Lid, Patina, Tin, 15 1/2 In. ............................... 28.00
Brush, Jim Patterson Hatter, Sacramento, California ........................................... 9.50
Bucket, Miner's Puddler Tobacco ........................................................................ 45.00
Bust, Figural, Pabst, Barbershop Quartet, 11 X 9 In. .......................................... 65.00
Cabinet, Ace Comb, Revolving, Wood & Glass .................................................... 75.00
Cabinet, Angel Dainty Dyes, Brass Knobs & Hinges, 28 Bins, 18 X 15 In. .......... 150.00
Cabinet, Bronco Homeopathic Remedies, 30 Compartments, 15 X 19 In. ........... 150.00
Cabinet, Clark's, 5 Drawer, Tin ........................................................................... 35.00
Cabinet, Cleveland Twist Drill, Oak ..................................................................... 220.00
Cabinet, Diamond Dye, Children With Large Balloon .......................................... 450.00
Cabinet, Diamond Dye, Evolution Of Woman ...................................................... 375.00
Cabinet, Diamond Dye, Governess With Children ............................................... 600.00
Cabinet, Diamond Musical Strings, Tin, 19 X 21 In. ........................................... 25.00
Cabinet, Display, Waltham Clocks, Slant Glass Front .......................................... 15.00
Cabinet, Dr.A.C.Daniels Dog & Cat Remedies, Tin ............................................. 900.00
Cabinet, Dr.Daniel's Veterinarian Supplies, Sign Front, Metal ............................ 195.00
Cabinet, Dr.Lesurg, Veterinarian, Picture Of Horse ............................................ 800.00
Cabinet, Dyola Dye, Tin Front & Back, Advertising ............................................. 65.00
Cabinet, P.Lorillard Tobacco, Inlaid, Mahogany ............................................... 1700.00
Cabinet, Peerless Dye, Roll Top .......................................................................... 300.00
Cabinet, Putnam Dye, Revolving, Tin .................................................................. 25.00
Cabinet, Putnam Fadeless Dye, Tin, Wooden Inserts, Man On Horse Design ...... 100.00
Cabinet, Putnam Fadeless Dyes, Slanted Front, Tin & Wood, 15 X 11 In. ........... 69.00
Cabinet, Rit Dye, Multicolored, Tin ...................................................................... 150.00
Cabinet, Stollwerck's Chocolates, Etched Glass, 9 X 15 X 23 In. ........................ 225.00
Canister, Bagdad Tobacco, Small ....................................................................... 850.00
Canister, Bonta-Fine Confectionery, Round, Red, Gold, 10 Pound ...................... 45.00
Canister, Borden's Malted Milk, Drugstore ......................................................... 50.00
Canister, Camel Cigarette, Tin ............................................................................ 30.00
Canister, Central Union Tobacco, 4 X 6 In. ......................................................... 25.00
Canister, City Club Tobacco, Small ..................................................................... 250.00
Canister, Coffee, Battleship Coffee, Pictures Battleship ...................................... 35.00
Canister, Country Doctor Tobacco, Pictures Jean Hersholt, Flip Lid .................... 15.00
Canister, Dark Sweet Cuba, Brown & Gold, Tin ................................................. 100.00
Canister, Dill's Best, 3 1/2 X 2 1/2 X 3/4 In. ....................................................... 10.00
Canister, Droste's Cocoa, 5 1/2 In. ..................................................................... 20.00

| | |
|---|---:|
| Canister, Dupont Powder, Pictures Dogs, 4 In. | 45.00 |
| Canister, Edgeworth Tobacco, Dome Top, Concave, Tin, 6 In. | 20.00 |
| Canister, Fry's Cocoa Extract, Egyptian | 22.00 |
| Canister, George Washington Cigars, Pry Lid | 15.00 |
| Canister, Good Morning Coffee, Black On Red, 1890s, 4 X 3 1/2 In. | 65.00 |
| Canister, Graham Wafer, U-Needa Baker, Round | 25.00 |
| Canister, Heinz Peanut Butter, 10 Pound | 40.00 |
| Canister, Horlick's Malted Milk, Drugstore | 50.00 |
| Canister, Jumbo Dixie Peanuts, Black Boy, 10 Pound | 175.00 |
| Canister, Kim-Bo Cut Plug Tobacco, 1902 | 25.00 |
| Canister, Luzianne Coffee, Red, Pictures Mammy | 30.00 |
| Canister, Mara Cuba Cigars | 15.00 |
| Canister, Mayo's Coffee, Tin | 35.00 |
| Canister, Mayo's Tea, Tin | 35.00 |
| Canister, Mayo's Tobacco, Small | 60.00 |
| Canister, North Carolina Cigarettes, Tin | 115.00 |
| Canister, Old Colony Tobacco, Large | 255.00 |
| Canister, Old Colony Tobacco, Small | 225.00 |
| Canister, Peanut, Elephant, Black, White, 10 Pound, 11 In. | 60.00 |
| Canister, Ploy Boy, Bail Handle, Paper Label | 35.00 |
| Canister, Prince Albert Tobacco, Pry Lid, Small | 15.00 |
| Canister, Prince Albert, Dated 1907, Cardboard | 17.00 |
| Canister, Red Cross, Coffee, 6 In. | 30.00 |
| Canister, Red Tiger Tobacco | 95.00 |
| Canister, Rose Leaf Tobacco, Lorillard | 175.00 |
| Canister, Seal Of North Carolina Cut Plug | 115.00 |
| Canister, Sears Tea, Round, Red & White Striped | 65.00 |
| Canister, Senate Coffee, Capital | 26.00 |
| Canister, Sir Walter Raleigh Cigars | 15.00 |
| Canister, Squirrel Peanut Butter, 10 Pound | 135.00 |
| Canister, Sweet Burley Tobacco, Yellow Design, Large | 75.00 |
| Canister, Sweet Burley, Dark Red | 65.00 |
| Canister, Sweet Cuba Tobacco, Round | 85.00 |
| Canister, Sweet Mist Tobacco, Tin, Children At Fountain | 95.00 To 115.00 |
| Canister, The Nut House, Picture Nut House, 10 In. | 65.00 |
| Canister, Union Leader Tobacco, Picture Of Uncle Sam | 30.00 To 50.00 |
| Canister, White Ash Cigar | 15.00 |
| Canister, White Owl Cigars | 15.00 |
| Canister, Wright's Winner | 65.00 |
| Carrier, Star Egg, Wooden, Slide Handle, Holds 1 Dozen | 32.00 |
| Case, Blue Jar Corn Plasters, Bums Walking Tracks, 2 Drawer | 80.00 |
| Case, Cigar, Round Glass, Shelves, Oak, 27 X 26 X 49 In. | 375.00 |
| Case, Display, Collars & Cuffs, Oak | 25.00 |
| Case, Display, Kaywoodie Pipe | 20.00 |
| Case, Display, Revolving, Oak Pedestal & Trim | *Illus* 2100.00 |
| Case, Display, Rexall Pen, Oak | 30.00 |
| Case, Display, Royal Demuth Pipe | 20.00 |
| Case, Henfer Shoe Lace, Glass Front, With Laces | 35.00 |
| Case, J.C.Primley California Gum | 395.00 |
| Case, Show, Renauld, Glass & Brass, 18 In. | 40.00 |
| Cash Drawer, Under Counter, Wooden | 85.00 |
| Chain, Key, Caterpillar, 50th Year, 1954 | 8.50 |
| Change Mat, Black & White Scotty | 18.00 |
| Charm, Figural, Swift's Premium Ham, Shape Like Ham | 10.00 |
| Charm, Flako Piecrust Mix, Plastic With Paper Label | 3.00 |
| Checkerboard, Hires | 95.00 |
| Checkwriter, Todd Protectograph, Model 29 | 20.00 |
| Cheese Safe, Country Store, 1800s, Wheels, Back Opens | 750.00 |
| Cheese Safe, General Store, Original Wavy Glass | 300.00 |
| Chopper, Nut, Planters Peanut | 13.00 |
| Cigar Case, Beveled Panels & Top, Oak | 800.00 |
| Clicker, Forbes Coffee | 5.00 |
| Colgate Toothpaste, Sample, C.1927 | 5.00 |

Store, Case, Display, Revolving, Oak Pedestal & Trim

| | |
|---|---:|
| **Comb,** Mustache, Compliments Flint Wagon Works, Flint, Michigan | 14.00 |
| **Compact,** Blanke's Coffee, Christmas Souvenir | 15.00 |
| **Compact,** Lady's, Falls City High Brew, Plastic | 20.00 |
| **Compact,** Lydia Pinkham, Picture, Inside Mirror | 15.00 |
| **Cookie Jar,** Quaker Oats | 30.00 |
| **Creamer,** Kellogg's, Advertising Measure, Pink | 6.00 |
| **Creamer,** Union Leader Tobacco | 85.00 |
| **Crock,** Apple Butter, Heinz | 125.00 |
| **Crock,** Bishop's Apple Butter, Blue & White, 14 X 13 In. | 100.00 |
| **Crock,** Bishop's Peanut Butter, Lid, Blue & White, 14 X 13 In. | 100.00 |
| **Cup,** Measuring, Kellog's, Green, 3 Spouts | 9.00 |
| **Cuspidor,** Reland & Matthews Mfg.Co., Brass, Sales Sample, 2 1/2 In. | 39.00 |
| **Cutter & Match Dispenser,** Cigar, Mechanical, Patent 1909, 7 In. | 350.00 |
| **Cutter,** Cheese, Lever Dial, Iron Frame, Red & Gold Stencil, 15 1/2 In. | 265.00 |
| **Cutter,** Cigar, Brunholl Co., Embossed Ash Base, Cast Iron, 9 X 6 In. | 145.00 |
| **Cutter,** Cigar, Bulbous, Side Hinge, Silver Plate | 24.00 |
| **Cutter,** Cigar, Cudahy Hams, Pocket | 12.00 |
| **Cutter,** Cigar, East Rock Cigars, Mountain Scene On Glass Top, 1800s | 75.00 |
| **Cutter,** Cigar, Eisenlohrs Cinco 5 Cent, Clockwork Mechanism | 85.00 |
| **Cutter,** Cigar, Engraved Floral, Double Blade, Dated 1916, Gold Filled | 32.00 |
| **Cutter,** Cigar, Kelly's Havana Cigars, Pocket | 11.50 |
| **Cutter,** Cigar, New Bachelor, Brass, Pocket | 24.00 |
| **Cutter,** Cigar, Optimates 10 Cent, Cast Iron | 210.00 |
| **Cutter,** Cigar, Tortoise Trim | 27.00 |
| **Cutter,** Cigar, Wilson, Iron & Wood | 60.00 |
| **Cutter,** String, Handy Twine Knife Co. | 8.00 |
| **Cutter,** Tobacco, Arrow Plug | 30.00 |
| **Cutter,** Tobacco, Brown's Mule Plug | 40.00 |
| **Cutter,** Tobacco, Climax, Cast Iron | 30.00 |
| **Cutter,** Tobacco, Enterprise Mfg., Philadelphia, Patent 1871 | 45.00 |
| **Cutter,** Tobacco, Figural Battle-Ax | 110.00 |
| **Cutter,** Tobacco, John Finzer & Bros., Cast Iron, 20 In. | 30.00 |
| **Cutter,** Tobacco, Little Imp, Cast Iron | 125.00 |
| **Cutter,** Tobacco, R.J.R.Tobacco Co., Counter | 75.00 |
| **Cutter,** Tobacco, Spearhead Plug | 40.00 |
| **Cutter,** Tobacco, Star Plug | 25.00 To 40.00 |
| **Cutter,** Tobacco, Superb Plug | 30.00 |
| **Decanter,** I.W.Harper's Whiskey, Engraved Gold Letters | 35.00 |
| **Dish,** Cigar Bands, Under Glass, 9 In. | 20.00 |
| **Dish,** Planters Peanut, 1939 World's Fair | 12.00 |
| **Dish,** Raggedy Ann & Andy, 1941 | 23.00 |
| **Dispenser,** Adams Chewing Gum | 50.00 |
| **Dispenser,** Arctic Soda, 1863 | *Illus* 4600.00 |
| **Dispenser,** Black Buckeye | 525.00 |

Store, Dispenser, Arctic Soda, 1863 (See Page 629)

Store, Dispenser, Green
River Syrup

| | |
|---|---:|
| **Dispenser,** Carnation Malted Milk | 50.00 |
| **Dispenser,** Cherri Bon | 400.00 |
| **Dispenser,** Cherry Smash, 5 Cent, Plunger | 750.00 |
| **Dispenser,** Dixie Cup, 1 Cent, Original Glass Cup, Holder, & Key | 180.00 |
| **Dispenser,** Gold Orange, Crockware Interior, Orange Shaped Metal | 435.00 |
| **Dispenser,** Goldens 5 Orangeade, 14 X 13 In.Round | 110.00 |
| **Dispenser,** Green River Syrup ..............................................................*Illus* | 200.00 |
| **Dispenser,** Green's Muscadine Punch | 325.00 |
| **Dispenser,** Gum, Norwestern, 1920s | 250.00 |
| **Dispenser,** Heinz Vinegar, Glass Barrel | 145.00 |
| **Dispenser,** Horlick's Malted Milk, Knobbed Lid, Tin | 25.00 |
| **Dispenser,** Hoskin's 5 Cent Gum & Mints | 185.00 |
| **Dispenser,** Howel's Orange Julep, Ceramic | 500.00 |
| **Dispenser,** Lash's Orangeade, Complete | 225.00 |
| **Dispenser,** Lashe's, Lime Green, Black Deco Base | 145.00 |
| **Dispenser,** Liggett's Grape Juice, White China, Purple Grapes, Flared | 995.00 |
| **Dispenser,** Magnus Lime Rickey, Lime Shape | 675.00 |
| **Dispenser,** Malt, Wall Mount | 18.00 |
| **Dispenser,** Match, 1 Cent, Columbus Vending Co. | 175.00 |
| **Dispenser,** Mission Lime Syrup, 1930s | 45.00 |
| **Dispenser,** Mission Orange, Spigots, Glass & Metal .................... 60.00 To | 75.00 |
| **Dispenser,** O.C.B. Cigarette Paper, Wall, Tin | 15.00 |
| **Dispenser,** Ornage Julep, Plunger | 500.00 |
| **Dispenser,** Peanut, Columbus, 1 Cent, Slug Ejector, C.1920 ..............*Illus* | 200.00 |
| **Dispenser,** Pepsi-Cola, Radio Shape | 95.00 |
| **Dispenser,** Pump, Orange Crush | 195.00 |
| **Dispenser,** Rochester 5 Cent Root Beer | 450.00 |
| **Dispenser,** Safe-T Cone, On Stand, Store Slogan, Metal | 65.00 |
| **Dispenser,** Schuster's Root Beer | 325.00 |
| **Dispenser,** Soap, White King, Glass & Metal | 16.50 |
| **Dispenser,** Straw, Light Green Glass | 28.00 |
| **Dispenser,** Tape, Iron & Brass, Counter | 18.00 |
| **Dispenser,** Tex Joy Tea, Teapot Shape, Embossed Letters, Brown | 300.00 |
| **Dispenser,** Try-Me Shoe Laces | 5.00 |
| **Dispenser,** Ver-Ba | 350.00 |
| **Dispenser,** Ward's Lemon | 300.00 |
| **Dispenser,** Ward's Lemon Crush ..............................................................*Illus* | 175.00 |
| **Dispenser,** Ward's Orange Crush, Dark Orange ...................................*Illus* | 350.00 |

Store, Dispenser, Peanut,
Columbus, 1 Cent, Slug Ejector,
C.1920

**Dispenser,** Ward's Orange Crush, Light Orange ........................................................ *Illus* 285.00
**Dispenser,** Welchade, Milk Glass ........................................................................................ 100.00
**Dispenser,** Zeno Collar Button ............................................................................................ 700.00
**Display Case,** Arrow Collar, Original Collars .................................................................... 250.00
**Display Case,** Beechnut Gum, Girl With 1916 Pack, Metal, 14 In. .................................... 80.00
**Display Case,** Counter, Baby Ruth Gum ............................................................................ 75.00
**Display Case,** Curtis-Butterfinger, 3 Shelves, Glass Doors, 16 X 22 In. ........................... 30.00
**Display Case,** Dry Slitz Cigar, 2 For 5 Cents, 3 Tiers, Glass & Tin ................................... 85.00
**Display Form,** Girdle, LaMode ............................................................................................. 35.00
**Display,** Hohner Harmonica, Revolves, Wood & Metal, C.1890, 32 In. ............................ 195.00
**Door Push,** All Vick's Products, Porcelain ........................................................................ 35.00
**Door Push,** Branreth's Pills ................................................................................................. 18.00
**Door Push,** Hires Root Beer ................................................................................................ 20.00
**Door Push,** Old Gold Dancing Pack, Tin ........................................................................... 14.00

Store, Dispensers, from left to right, Ward's Lemon Crush; Ward's Orange Crush, Dark
Orange; Ward's Orange Crush, Light Orange

| | |
|---|---|
| **Door Push,** Senate Beer, 1940s, Tin | 20.00 |
| **Door Push,** Texas Punch, 1940s, Tin | 25.00 |
| **Door Push,** Three Brothers | 18.00 |
| **Figure,** Nipper, R.C.A.Dog, Papier-Mache, 12 In. | 200.00 |
| **Figure,** Nipper, R.C.A.Dog, Papier-Mache, 18 In. | 100.00 |
| **Figurine,** Cobbler, Sandler Shoes, Cobbler, Bench, Tool, 15 X 15 In. | 90.00 |
| **Figurine,** Nipper, R.C.A.Dog, Papier-Mache, 32 In. | 900.00 |
| **Figurine,** Nipper, Victor Trademark, Painted Eyes, Hard Rubber, 30 In. | 500.00 |
| **Glass,** Anheuser-Busch, Advertising, Footed | 35.00 |
| **Glass,** Coors Beer, Waterfall, Gold Rim, 7 1/4 In. | 7.00 |
| **Glass,** Lemp Brewing Co. | 23.00 |
| **Glass,** Schlitz Beer, Globe Trademark | 28.00 |
| **Grabber** | 27.00 To 35.00 |
| **Head,** Fowlers & Wells, Phrenology, Composition | 135.00 |
| **Holder,** Buggy Whip, Hanging | 50.00 |
| **Holder,** Buggy Whips, Floor Model | 250.00 |
| **Holder,** Cones, Milk-E Ice Cream, Handled, 1920s, Tin, 15 X 12 In. | 30.00 |
| **Holder,** Straw, Chrome | 45.00 |
| **Holder,** Straw, Clear Glass, Metal Lid | 49.50 |
| **Holder,** Straw, Purple Glass, Metal Lid | 85.00 |
| **Holder,** String, Black Mammy, Cast Iron | 15.00 |
| **Holder,** String, The Old Lamplighter's Lamplighter | 25.00 |
| **Holder,** String, 7-Up | 45.00 |
| **Humidor,** Crock, Blue Boar | 125.00 |
| **Humidor,** Edgeworth's, Tin, 6 X 4 1/2 In. | 20.00 |
| **Humidor,** La Palina, Glass | 30.00 |
| **Humidor,** Pocket, Lady Churchill Cigars, Tin | 12.00 |
| **Humidor,** Spaulding & Merric Sunny Bank, Chicago, Chesapeake Pottery | 75.00 |
| **Humidor,** Tobacco, House, Wood Frame, Glass Side, 20 X 17 X 16 In. | 225.00 |
| **Indianopolis Brewing Co.,** Man Drinking Near Fireplace | 125.00 |
| **Jar,** Cigar, Mercantile, Amber | 42.00 |
| **Jar,** Counter Top, Heinz Sweet Gerkins, 2 Gallon | 14.00 |
| **Jar,** Curtiss Chico's Spanish Peanuts, 5 Cents, Glass, Tin Base | 95.00 |
| **Jar,** Globe Tobacco, 1882, Glass | 50.00 |
| **Jar,** Kis-Me-Gum, Square | 65.00 |
| **Jar,** Lance Cracker, Glass | 20.00 |
| **Jar,** Lance Peanut, Lid | 28.00 |
| **Jar,** Luden's Cough Drops, Scoop | 265.00 |
| **Jar,** Milkose Malted Milk, Tin Knobbed Dome Lid | 69.00 |
| **Jar,** Num-Num Pretzels, Counter, Glass, Tin Lid | 20.00 |
| **Jar,** Peanut, Embossed Buffalo | 200.00 |
| **Jar,** Peanut, Embossed Elephant | 200.00 |
| **Jar,** Pennant Salted Peanuts, 8-Sided, Embossed, Peanut Finial | 165.00 |
| **Jar,** Planters Peanuts, Barrel Shape, Peanut Finial, Lid, 8 In.Diam. | 175.00 |
| **Jar,** Planters Peanuts, Corner Jar | 225.00 |
| **Jar,** Planters Peanuts, Embossed Peanut, 4-Sided | 225.00 |
| **Jar,** Planters Peanuts, Slanted Sides, Tin Lid | 35.00 |
| **Jar,** Planters Peanuts, Square | 69.50 |
| **Jar,** Planters Peanuts, 4-Sided, Embossed, Peanut Finial, Square | 85.00 |
| **Jar,** Planters Peanuts, 6-Sided, Peanut Finial, Covered | 60.00 To 85.00 |
| **Jar,** Planters Peanuts, 1940 Leap Year | 65.00 |
| **Jar,** Squirrel Brand Salted Peanuts, Embossed Tin Lid | 25.00 |
| **Jar,** Taffy-Tow Gum | 195.00 |
| **Jar,** Tom's Toasted Peanuts, Cover, 1 Gallon | 28.00 |
| **Jar,** Tuxedo Tobacco, Label On 2 Sides, 1910 Tax Stamp, Glass, 6 In. | 28.00 |
| **Jar,** Vasiform Pickle, Large | 60.00 |
| **Jug,** Old Continental Whiskey, Acorn, Miniature, 3 1/2 In. | 35.00 |
| **Keg,** Heinz, Stone, Gallon, Lid, Dated 1883 | 35.00 |
| **Knob,** Old Lowenbrau, Nickel Over Brass | 22.00 |
| **Knob,** Tap, Anheuser-Busch, Eagle Insert, Lucite, 6 In. | 15.00 |
| **Knob,** Tap, Bud On Tap, Colorful Insert, Lucite, 6 In. | 15.00 |
| **Knob,** Tap, Busch Bavarian Beer, Plastic, 3 In. | 10.00 |
| **Knob,** Tap, Lite Olympia On Tap, Plastic, 6 In. | 8.00 |

Armchair with rush seat marked
B 1640

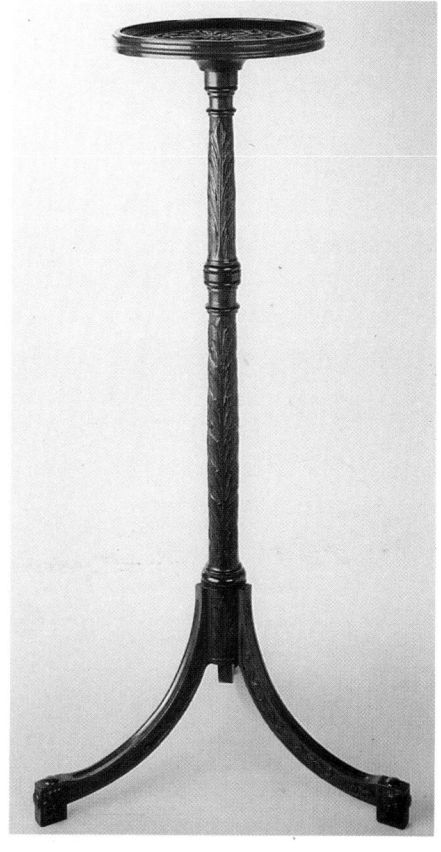

Sheraton-style mahogany
candlestand

Rococo marquetry wardrobe, Dutch, 19th century

Hepplewhite-style wardrobe, inlaid doors

Gateleg table, oak, 19th century

Papier-mâché table inlaid with mother-of-pearl, English, 19th century

Hepplewhite-style double desk

Louis XIV Boulle work bureau plat, c. 1700, Spanish rococo armchair

Netsuke, kneeling lady, ivory

Ivory netsuke, two children, signed

Pair of vases marked "Made for Tiffany by Royal Worcester,"
10 in. high

Enterprise coffee mill, c. 1900

Enterprise sausage stuffer,
c. 1880

Indian, Mille-Fleur rug, late 17th–early 18th century

Caucasian Soumak rug, late 19th century

Eastern facade, Biltmore house and gardens

South bedroom

Oak sitting room

Louis XVI bedroom

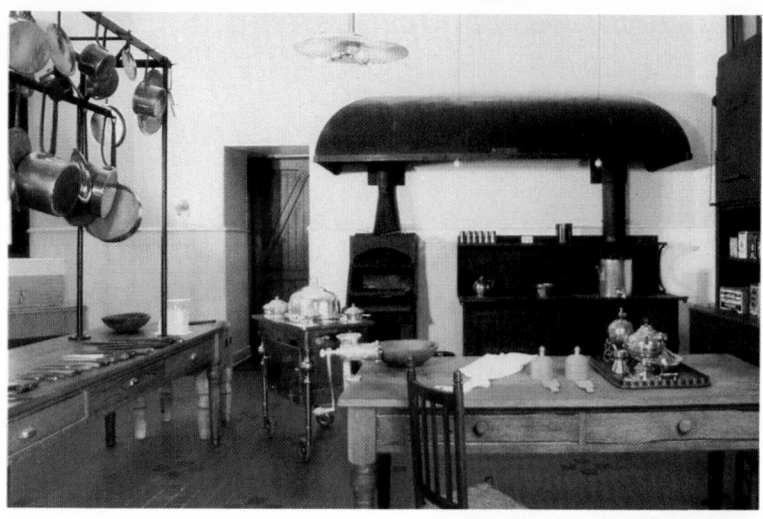

Main kitchen

One of sixty-eight Baroque-style chairs in Banquet Hall

Banquet hall

Napoleon's chess set, used at Longwood Estate, ivory, c. 1815–1821

**Knob,** Tap, Lucky Lager, Wood, 12 In. ............................................................ 12.00
**Knob,** Tap, Miller High Life, Wood, 14 In. ....................................................... 12.00
**Knob,** Tap, Miller Munchener Black Beer, Wood, 14 In. ................................. 12.00
**Label,** Apple, Hula, Topless Hula Girl Seated Beneath Palm Tree .................. 1.00
**Label,** Apple, Kentucky Cardinal, Pictures Red Apple & Blossoms .................. 10.00
**Label,** Apple, Trout, Leaping Trout, Profile Indian On Arrowhead ................... 1.00
**Label,** Apple, Wenoka Apples, Profile Of Indian On White Arrowhead ............. 3.00
**Label,** Apples, Art Nouveau Lady Sniffing Pink Roses ................................... 3.00
**Label,** Can, La Perla, Old-Fashioned Boy, California Olives ............................ .10
**Label,** Can, Rowley's, Red Tomatoes, Green Leaves ..................................... .50
**Label,** Can, Rowley's, 2-Handled Bowl Of Red Kidney Beans ........................ .50
**Label,** Can, Shaker Tomatoes ........................................................................ 35.00
**Label,** Can, Tomatoes, Winged Wheel, Big Fish, Red ................................... 5.00
**Label,** Can, Verera, 2 Squid & Sailing Ship .................................................. .10
**Label,** Cherry, Villa Bellota, Ranch & Home, Sun Over Mountains ................ .15
**Label,** Coffee, Star Fine .................................................................................. 9.00
**Label,** Grapes, C.D.Pruner, Vineyard Scene, Bunch Of Red Grapes ............ .25
**Label,** Grapes, Sunset Brand, Sunset Scene Over Mountain, 13 X 4 In. ....... .25
**Label,** Lemon, Collie, Full Figure Brown & White Collie ............................... 15.00
**Label,** Lemon, Fido, Comical Puppy, Black Spot Over One Eye ................... 10.00
**Label,** Lemon, Sea Groves, Map Of Ventura County, Stylized Waves .......... 1.00
**Label,** Orange, Bronco, Cowboy Swinging Lariat, On Galloping Horse ........ 2.00
**Label,** Orange, Cal-Flavor, Blossoms & Leaves, Woodgrain, Blue, Black ..... 1.00
**Label,** Orange, Caledonia, Thistle Spray On Plaid ...................................... 1.00
**Label,** Orange, Cupid, Golden Haired, Dimpled Cupid's Face ..................... 10.00
**Label,** Orange, Dragon, Fierce Dragon, Yellow Sun .................................... 10.00
**Label,** Orange, Golden Trout, Trout Leaping Out Of Water ......................... 10.00
**Label,** Orange, Good Year, Blossoms, Leaves, Blue .................................... 1.00
**Label,** Orange, La Reina, Spanish Senorita Holding A Black Fan ............... 1.00
**Label,** Orange, Orchard King, Orange Wearing Crown, Royal Blue ............ 1.00
**Label,** Orange, Rialto Redskin, Profile Of Indian Chief, Peace Pipe .......... 10.00
**Label,** Pear, Blue Goose, Orange Ground .................................................. .50
**Label,** Pear, Capital Pak, California Capital Buildings & Grounds ............... .50
**Label,** Pear, White Swan, Black Ground .................................................... 3.00
**Label,** Powder, DuPont, Lithograph, 1908, Set Of 6 ................................. 20.00
**Label,** Vegetable, Big B, Cute Striped Honeybee ...................................... .25
**Label,** Vegetable, Celery, Blue Goose, Narrow Label ............................... .50
**Light,** Budweiser, Revolving, Miniature 8-Horse Team ............................. 650.00
**Lighter,** Cigar, Countertop, Cherub Blowing Horn For Flame, 7 1/4 In. ...... 140.00
**Lighter,** Cigar, Kerosene, Germany, Brass .............................................. 35.00
**Lighter,** Cigar, Kerosene, Twin Lighters, Iron Base, White Ball Shade ...... 150.00
**Lighter,** Cigar, Midland Spark, Walnut Case .......................................... 395.00
**Lighter,** Cigar, Scratch Type, Fresh Havana Blended Cigars, 1903 ......... 25.00
**Lighter,** Cigarette, Genuine Rockingham Poultry, Pictures Colonel .......... 17.50
**Lighter,** Cigarette, Royal Crown Cola, Bottle Shaped .............................. 10.00
**Lighter,** Cigarettes, Lucky Strike ........................................................... 3.00
**Luggage Tag,** Planters Peanuts .......................................................... 6.00
**Lunch Box,** Allen's Rum & Butter Toffee, 1930, Masonic Design On Lid ..... 20.00
**Lunch Box,** Black Dixie Kid .................................................................. 375.00
**Lunch Box,** Central Leader Tobacco ..................................................... 30.00
**Lunch Box,** Central Union Tobacco.7 1/2 X 4 1/2 X 5 1/4 In. ................... 40.00
**Lunch Box,** Dan Patch Tobacco, Handled ............................................. 45.00
**Lunch Box,** Dixie Kid Tobacco, Black Baby ............................... 225.00 To 250.00
**Lunch Box,** Dixie Queen Tobacco, Basket Weave ..................... 15.00 To 20.00
**Lunch Box,** Dixie Queen Tobacco, Victorian Girl ..................................... 65.00
**Lunch Box,** Family Affair ....................................................................... 8.00
**Lunch Box,** Fashion Tobacco, Man, Woman In Car ................... 65.00 To 150.00
**Lunch Box,** Folding, Metal Bail, C.1900, 8 X 3 3/4 X 3 3/4 In. ................. 25.00
**Lunch Box,** Green Turtle Cigars .............................................. 125.00 To 175.00
**Lunch Box,** Green Turtle Tobacco ......................................................... 50.00
**Lunch Box,** Handbag Tobacco .............................................................. 85.00
**Lunch Box,** Joe Palooka ...................................................................... 40.00
**Lunch Box,** Just Suits Tobacco ............................................... 18.00 To 20.00

**Lunch Box,** Kandies For The Kiddies ............................................ 60.00
**Lunch Box,** Lorillard's, Blue Tiger .............................................. 25.00
**Lunch Box,** Lorillard's, Red Tiger .............................................. 25.00
**Lunch Box,** Marine Tobacco, Basket Weave ................................. 25.00
**Lunch Box,** Mayo's Tobacco, Blue ............................................. 20.00
**Lunch Box,** Miner's, 1889 ......................................................... 85.00
**Lunch Box,** Nursery Candies For The Little Folks ........................ 60.00
**Lunch Box,** Patterson Cut Plug, Basket Weave ............................ 26.50
**Lunch Box,** Patterson's Seal, Basket Weave, Yellow & Black ........ 25.00
**Lunch Box,** Pedro Cut Plug Tobacco ............................ 45.00 To 75.00
**Lunch Box,** Penny Post Tobacco ............................................... 80.00
**Lunch Box,** Peter Rabbit ........................................... 30.00 To 75.00
**Lunch Box,** Peter Rabbit, Chicks, Ducks .................................... 20.00
**Lunch Box,** Picture Of Southern Belle ........................................ 80.00
**Lunch Box,** Red Crown ............................................................ 60.00
**Lunch Box,** Red Tiger Tobacco, 8 X 6 X 6 In. ............................ 12.50
**Lunch Box,** Redicut Tobacco ................................................... 125.00
**Lunch Box,** Round Trip Tobacco .............................................. 125.00
**Lunch Box,** Sweet Cuba, Pie Shaped ........................................ 18.00
**Lunch Box,** Tiger Bright Sweet, P.Lorillard Co. .......................... 45.00
**Lunch Box,** Tiger Tobacco, 8 1/2 X 6 X 6 In. ............................ 20.00
**Lunch Box,** Union Leader Tobacco, Basket Weave ............ 16.00 To 25.00
**Lunch Box,** Warnick, Brown, Tin .............................................. 60.00
**Lunch Box,** Winner Tobacco, Race Cars ..................... 75.00 To 110.00
**Lunch Box,** Worker Cut Plug .................................................... 60.00
**Machine,** Vending, Postcard, Counter Top, Wooden .................... 150.00
**Match Holder,** Schlitz Hotel, 1914 ........................................... 90.00
**Mirror,** Carmen Complexion Powder, Picture Of Lady, Oval, 1 3/4 In. .... 38.00
**Mirror,** Carta Blanca, Oval, 12 X 16 In. ................................... 12.00
**Mirror,** Clipper Beer, 18 In. Square ......................................... 40.00
**Mirror,** Lone Star Served Here, Picture Of Alamo Girl, Oval, 18 In. .... 24.00
**Mirror,** Lone Star, Alamo Girl, 1903, Framed, 14 X 21 In. ........... 55.00
**Mirror,** Mother & Flowers, Bell Shaped, C.1880, Beaded Trim, 5 X 6 In. .... 40.00
**Mirror,** Pepsi-Cola, Girl Looking Into Mirror, 14 X 6 In. .............. 10.00
**Mirror,** Photoframe, Penny Arcade, 1945 ................................. 35.00
**Mirror,** Pocket, Aetna Life Insurance, Red & White, Round .......... 15.00
**Mirror,** Pocket, Agents For Pellets Magneto, Chicago, 1890, Oval .... 50.00
**Mirror,** Pocket, Akin, Ershine Milling Co. ................................. 20.00
**Mirror,** Pocket, Ballard's Graham Flour ................................... 35.00
**Mirror,** Pocket, Ballard's Obelisk Flour ................................... 25.00
**Mirror,** Pocket, Buy White Cat Union Suits, Kenosha, Wisc., Oval .... 18.50
**Mirror,** Pocket, Cascarets, Little Girl Sitting On Pot .................. 48.50
**Mirror,** Pocket, Ceresota Flour .............................................. 33.00
**Mirror,** Pocket, Cleveland ...................................................... 6.00
**Mirror,** Pocket, Daily Reminder, Pierre, S.D. ............................ 9.50
**Mirror,** Pocket, Dockash Stoves & Ranges, Scranton, Pa., Round .... 50.00
**Mirror,** Pocket, Dr.Pepper, 10-2-4, 2 In.Diam. .......................... 8.50
**Mirror,** Pocket, Draughon's Business College ............................ 10.00
**Mirror,** Pocket, Duffy's Pure Malt Whiskey, 2 3/4 X 1 1/4 In. ...... 24.00
**Mirror,** Pocket, Fleischmann Yeast .......................................... 7.50
**Mirror,** Pocket, Gillette Safety Razor ...................................... 45.00
**Mirror,** Pocket, Grinnell Bros., Music House, Pictures Building ...... 18.00
**Mirror,** Pocket, Hibbard Hardware .......................................... 16.00
**Mirror,** Pocket, Hood Rubbers, N.Y., Zodiac Border, Round .......... 40.00
**Mirror,** Pocket, Huyler's Candy, Pretty Girl, Celluloid ................ 22.00
**Mirror,** Pocket, I Wear Skeezix Shoes ..................................... 35.00
**Mirror,** Pocket, I.O.O.F., Dated October 1920, Matching Pinback .... 25.00
**Mirror,** Pocket, Immaculate Tailors & Cleaners ......................... 20.00
**Mirror,** Pocket, International Salt Co., Salt Sample ..................... 19.00
**Mirror,** Pocket, Kansas Expansion Flour ................................... 15.00
**Mirror,** Pocket, Kibler's Sugits, 1907 Indian Penny In Center ....... 15.00
**Mirror,** Pocket, Kingan's Hams & Bacon .................................. 36.00
**Mirror,** Pocket, Kingan's Sausage ........................................... 15.00

Mirror, Pocket, Kyanize Paints, Metamorphic Face ........................................... 15.00
Mirror, Pocket, Lucky Strike Cigarettes ........................................................ 4.50
Mirror, Pocket, M.C.Canada Dry Soda ......................................................... 6.50
Mirror, Pocket, Mascot Crushed Cut Tobacco ............................... 15.00 To 30.00
Mirror, Pocket, Meadow Gold Butter, Topeka, Kansas ................................... 12.00
Mirror, Pocket, Monitor Stoves & Ranges .................................................... 25.00
Mirror, Pocket, Morrell's Pride Meats, Man In Red Heart ............................... 7.50
Mirror, Pocket, Nature's Remedy .............................................................. 12.00
Mirror, Pocket, New King Snuff ................................................................ 38.00
Mirror, Pocket, Old Crane Whiskey ........................................................... 35.00
Mirror, Pocket, Parry Carriage Factory ....................................................... 32.00
Mirror, Pocket, Paul Vallette Swiss Watches, Beveled .................................. 15.00
Mirror, Pocket, Pittsburgh National League Champions, 1909, Picture ............. 95.00
Mirror, Pocket, Plumbing, Roman Fountain & Lady ...................................... 40.00
Mirror, Pocket, Polarine Motor Oil, 2 1/4 In.Diam. ....................................... 14.00
Mirror, Pocket, Rainbow Academy Of Beauty Culture ................................... 16.00
Mirror, Pocket, Reliable Coffee, Round ...................................................... 28.00
Mirror, Pocket, Ryer's Jewelry, Kansas City, Mo. ........................................ 10.00
Mirror, Pocket, Scony Motor Gasoline, Reg.Pat.Off., 3 1/2 In. ....................... 32.00
Mirror, Pocket, Shoe Repair, Nashville, Tenn., 1910 .................................... 10.00
Mirror, Pocket, Spencer Petroleum ........................................................... 28.00
Mirror, Pocket, Stacey's Chocolates .......................................................... 15.00
Mirror, Pocket, Star Soap ........................................................................ 18.00
Mirror, Pocket, Star Soap, Zanesville, Ohio, 2 In. ........................................ 25.00
Mirror, Pocket, State Life Insurance, With Baby .......................................... 14.00
Mirror, Pocket, Sunkist, Orange ............................................................... 4.50
Mirror, Pocket, Ted Williams With Bat, Boston ........................................... 10.00
Mirror, Pocket, The Allies, Five Flags, Oval ............................................... 20.00
Mirror, Pocket, Union Pacific, Shield, Logo, Red, White, Blue ....................... 7.00
Mirror, Pocket, Vanity, Liberty Mills Flour, Oval ......................................... 35.00
Mirror, Pocket, Walkrite Shoes, J.P.Hartray Shoe Co., Chicago ..................... 15.00
Mirror, Pocket, Welch's Grape Juice .......................................................... 37.50
Mirror, Pocket, White House Saloon .......................................................... 5.00
Mirror, Priest Of Palace, Kansas City, 1902, Cast Iron ................................. 45.00
Mirror, Royal Tailors, With Tiger, Tin, 15 3/4 X 11 3/4 In. ............................ 75.00
    STORE, MOLD, see Pewter, Mold; Tin, Mold
    STORE, MOLD, ICE CREAM, see Pewter, Mold, Ice Cream
Mug, A. & W.Root Beer ........................................................................... 5.00
Mug, Beer, Krueger, Gold Lines ............................................................... 125.00
Mug, Borden's, Elsie The Cow .................................................................. 15.00
Mug, Buckeye Root Beer, Blue & White Stripes ........................................... 23.00
Mug, Century Of Progress, Chicago, 1934, Copper ...................................... 10.00
Mug, Crystal Spring Brewing Co., Trademark .............................................. 55.00
Mug, Dad's Root Beer, Glass ................................................................... 12.00
Mug, Fred Sehring Brewery, 1868-1903 .................................................... 150.00
Mug, Hamm's Beer .................................................................................. 40.00
Mug, Lash's Root Beer, Tan, Blue Stripes, 5 1/2 In. .................................... 22.00
Mug, Miller Beer, Copper ..................................................... 10.00 To 11.00
Mug, Mortons Salt, Umbrella Girl On Front, Logo, 1956 ............................... 15.00
Mug, Old Colony Brewing Co., Boston, Mass., Blue, Tan, Pottery, 4 1/4 In. ..... 22.00
Mug, Old Heidelberg, Green Glazed ......................................................... 19.00
Mug, Ovaltine, Uncle Wiggily, 1924 ....................................... 12.00 To 30.00
Mug, Planters Peanuts, Pewterlike ............................................................ 35.00
Mug, Quaker Oats ................................................................................. 4.00
Mug, Richardson Root Beer, Embossed, Paneled, Glass, 5 1/4 In. .................. 12.00
Mug, Round Oak Stoves, Dowagiac, Michigan, 1907 .................................... 75.00
Net, Horse Fly, Leather, Handmade ........................................ 7.00 To 25.00
Nippers, Sugar, Ball Handles For Crushing, Steel ........................................ 75.00
Nut Set, Mr.Peanut, Tin, 5 Piece .............................................................. 10.00
Nut Set, Planters Peanuts, 1939 World's Fair, Emblem In Center .................... 35.00
Opener, Beer Can, Drewry's ..................................................................... 2.50
Pail, Armour Veribest Peanut Butter, Nursery Rhyme Figures, 1 Pound ............ 15.00
Pail, Aunt Jemima, Dated 1928 ................................................................ 20.00

Pail, Axheart Peanut Butter ........................................................................ 45.00
Pail, Bagley's Wild Fruit, Tin .................................................................... 65.00
Pail, Brothers Tobacco ............................................................................... 40.00
Pail, Buffalo Brand Peanut Butter ............................................................ 95.00
Pail, California Peanut Co. ......................................................................... 75.00
Pail, Central Union Tobacco ...................................................................... 28.00
Pail, Dixie Queen ....................................................................................... 18.00
Pail, Eight Brothers Tobacco, Brown ......................................................... 40.00
Pail, Eight Brothers Tobacco, Mustard Color ........................................... 40.00
Pail, F.F.Adam's Tobacco, Liberty Lady Pictured ..................................... 30.00
Pail, Fontenac Peanut Butter .................................................................... 20.00
Pail, George Washington Plug Cut ............................................................. 35.00
Pail, Just Suits Cut Plug ........................................................................... 35.00
Pail, Krespeanut Butter, Red ..................................................................... 28.00
Pail, Mammy's Coffee, Black Lady, 3 Lb. .......................... 115.00 To 125.00
Pail, Naphey's Lad, 1876 ........................................................................... 30.00
Pail, Nigger Hair, Tobacco ......................................................................... 125.00
Pail, Ojibwa, Tin ........................................................................................ 75.00
Pail, Old Partner Tobacco, Civil War Soldiers .......................................... 110.00
Pail, Old Partner Tobacco, Confederate & Civil War Soldiers .................. 110.00
Pail, Ontario Peanut Butter, 2 Pound ....................................................... 5.00
Pail, Pep Boys Motor Oil, Cartooned Cowboys, Large ............................. 25.00
Pail, Peter Rabbit, Peanut Butter .............................................................. 150.00
Pail, Pickaninny Peanut Butter .................................................................. 90.00
Pail, Planters Peanut Butter, Characters .................................................. 175.00
Pail, Plow Boy Tobacco, Paper Label, Bail ............................................... 35.00
Pail, Redicut Tobacco ................................................................................ 85.00
Pail, Shedd's Peanut Butter, 5 Pound ...................................................... 13.00
Pail, Squirrel Peanut Butter ...................................................................... 50.00
Pail, Sultana Peanut Butter, Dog Chasing Rabbits .................................. 28.00
Pail, Sunset Trail Cigars ............................................................................ 125.00
Pail, Sweet Mist, Bail ................................................................................ 95.00
Pail, Swift's Silverleaf Lard, Handles, 8 Ounce ....................................... 15.00
Pail, Swift's Silverleaf Lard, 5 Pound ...................................................... 3.00
Pail, This Little Piggy Went To Market ..................................................... 45.00
Pail, Tiger Tobacco, Red, 8 X 6 X 6 1/2 In. ...................... 35.00 To 40.00
Pail, Tip Top Tobacco ................................................................................ 40.00
Pail, Toyland Peanut Butter, Cartooned Soldiers ................ 95.00 To 125.00
Pail, Well Done Chewing Tobacco, Paper Label, Wooden, 1898 .............. 110.00
Paper Clip, Head Of Girl With Large Bonnet, Bronze Finish .................... 45.00
Pennant, Planters Peanut, 10 Pound ........................................................ 25.00
Pin, Aunt Jemima, Premium, 2 1/4 In. ..................................................... 1.00
Pin, Prohibition, No Beer, No Work, Mug Pictured ................................... 40.00
Pin, Royal Scarlet Canned Goods ............................................................. 3.00
Pinback, Kellogg's Pep ............................................................................. 7.50
Plaque, Say When, Tin, 16 In.Diam. ......................................................... 130.00
Plaque, Seal Of North Carolina Tobacco, Bisque, Seminudes ................. 60.00
Plate, Anger Baking Co., Fireside Dreams, 10 In. ................................... 62.00
Plate, C.D.Kenny Co., Chile With Doll, Premium, Tin .............................. 45.00
Plate, Lord Calvert Whiskey, Brass, 18 In.Diam. ..................................... 12.00
Plate, Souvenir, L.J.Honze Convex Glass Co., 50th Anniversary ............ 15.00
Poster, Cleveland Cycles, Pictures Indian On Bicycle, 42 X 55 In. ......... 650.00
Poster, Clyde Beatty Circus, C.1935 ........................................................ 30.00
Poster, Dr. Meyer's Foot Soap, Occupational People, 1920, 38 X 25 In. .... 95.00
Poster, Marlow Coaster Brake, Boy, Bike, 1920, 28 X 21 In. .................. 110.00
Poster, Queen Quality Shoes, Victorian Girl, 1900, 7 X 10 In. ............... 75.00
Poster, Remington Arms, Hunter, Canoe, Grizzly Bear, 1915, 17 X 26 In. ... 250.00
Poster, Ringling Barnum & Bailey, C.1945, 27 X 21 In. .......................... 25.00
Poster, Tiny Tot Toilet Powder, Baby, Powder, Tin, 1930, 36 X 22 In. .... 95.00
Poster, Western Ammo, 2 Elks In Combat, 1929, 15 X 24 In. ................. 175.00
Pouch, Laredo Cut Plug Tobacco .............................................................. 5.00
Pump, Vinegar Barrel, Wooden .................................................................. 6.00
Punchboard, Planters Peanuts, 2 Cent, 400 Punches, 8 1/2 X 13 1/2 In. ... 24.00

**Punchboard,** Prince Edward Cigars ........................................................... 12.00
**Push Plate,** Hires Root Beer, Metal ........................................................ 25.00
**Push Plate,** Nugrape, Porcelain ............................................................. 20.00
**Puzzle,** Uncle Sam Tar Soap, C.1920 ................................................... 30.00
**Rack,** Cavalier Shoe Polish, Tin ............................................................. 20.00
**Rack,** Gayla 10 Cent Hairnets, Counter Top, Tin ................................... 15.00
**Rack,** Prince Albert, For Pocket Tins, Tin .............................................. 15.00
**Roller,** Cigarette, Brown & Williamson, Tin ........................... 9.00 To 17.50
**Roller,** Cigarette, Pioneer, Chrome ........................................................ 10.00
**Ruler,** White Sewing Machine, Wooden, 12 In. ....................................... 8.00
**Salt & Pepper,** Coil Top Refrigerator, Milk Glass ................................. 30.00
**Salt & Pepper,** Gingerbread Boy & Girl ................................................. 4.50
**Salt & Pepper,** Grand Union Tea ........................................................... 17.00
**Salt & Pepper,** Jiggs & Maggie, Marked 1942 ....................................... 12.00
**Salt & Pepper,** Monk, West Germany ..................................................... 15.00
**Salt & Pepper,** Mr.Peanut, Black & Tan Plastic ..................................... 7.00
**Salt & Pepper,** Nipper, RCA, Large .................................... 10.00 To 15.00
**Salt & Pepper,** Penguin, Kool Cigarettes ............................................... 5.00
**Salt & Pepper,** Phillips 66, Pumps, Orange, Black, Plastic, Original Box ... 6.00
**Salt & Pepper,** Schlitz, Milk Glass ....................................................... 10.00
**Salt & Pepper,** Sewing Machine ............................................................. 9.00
**Scoop,** Barrington Hall Coffee, Tin ........................................................ 9.00
**Scoop,** Cranberry, Ames Plow Co., Boston, Carved Handle, 4 Ft.Long ... 75.00
**Scoop,** Pressed Horn, 12 In. ................................................................ 35.00
**Scraper,** Foam, Potosi Beer ................................................................. 15.00
**Shaker,** Ovaltine, Metal ....................................................................... 8.00
**Sharpener,** Pencil, Cast Iron, Small ..................................................... 18.00
**Sharpener,** Pencil, Gem, Crank ............................................................. 4.00
**Sharpener,** Pencil, National Cash Register ............................................. 8.00
**Shaving Brush,** Bauer ......................................................................... 5.00
**Shirt Board,** Patented 1881, Original Canvas ....................................... 45.00
**Shoe,** Wooden, Heineken's Beer, Yellow Ground, 9 In. .......................... 10.00
**Showcase,** Candy, 19th Century, Nickel Plated, 72 X 16 X 31 In. .......... 375.00
**Sign,** A.Humphry's Inn, C.1830, New York, Wooden, Iron Scrolls, 31 In. ... 750.00
**Sign,** Abbott's Ice Cream, Waitress, 1920, Tin, 30 X 22 In. .................. 195.00
**Sign,** Abc Beer, Bulldog Watching Bottle, 1905, Tin, 25 X 21 In. .......... 450.00
**Sign,** Acco Balm, 1930s, Embossed Tin, 8 X 4 In., Set Of 3 .................. 30.00
**Sign,** Ada Olive Oil, 1920s, Tin, 16 X 20 In. ........................................ 85.00
**Sign,** Allis Chalmer, Tin, 26 X 9 In. ..................................................... 15.00
**Sign,** Alt Heidelberg Brand Beer, 3-D, Bartender, 13 X 9 X 3 In. .......... 125.00
**Sign,** American Brewing, Rochester, N.Y., C.1900, Celluloid, 10 X 14 In. ... 300.00
**Sign,** American Lady Corsets, 1909, Paper, Framed, 11 X 36 In. ........... 185.00
**Sign,** American Sewer Co., Picture Old Factories, 26 X 32 In. .............. 275.00
**Sign,** Anheuser-Busch, Picture Of Stein, Paper, 14 X 18 In. ................. 60.00
**Sign,** Arm & Hammer, Bird Pictured In Color, 15 X 11 In. ...................... 12.50
**Sign,** Armour Peanut Butter, Tin, 9 1/2 X 13 1/2 In. ............................ 50.00
**Sign,** Armour Star Ham, Black Man, Tin, 38 X 13 In. ............................ 650.00
**Sign,** Armour's Glendale Oleomargarine, Boy & Sandwich, 13 X 19 In. ... 325.00
**Sign,** B-l Lemon & Lime Soda, 1940s, Tin, 3 X 14 In. ........................... 7.00
**Sign,** Bank Note, Cigars, 2 Men Smoking, Cardboard, 1930, 22 X 14 In. ... 55.00
**Sign,** Bargs Root Beer, Oval, Porcelain, 56 In. ..................................... 25.00
**Sign,** Bartels Beer, Blue & White, Convex, 18 In.Diam. ........................ 125.00
**Sign,** Bartels Beer, Tin, 18 In.Diam. ................................................... 42.00
**Sign,** Beechnut Tobacco, Porcelain, Red, White, & Blue, 22 X 11 In. ..... 150.00
**Sign,** Beef, Wine, & Iron Patent Medicine, Oiled Paper, 26 X 40 In. ...... 100.00
**Sign,** Beer, Wiedemann's, Tramp Reading Paper, Cardboard, 22 X 20 In. ... 95.00
**Sign,** Belcourt's Grocery, Black, Green, 6 X 60 In. ............................... 40.00
**Sign,** Bell System, In Blue Bell, Double Porcelain, 18 X 18 In. .............. 45.00
**Sign,** Bell System, Public Telephone One Side, Porcelain, 11 X 11 In. .... 50.00
**Sign,** Benidecto Cigar, Cardboard, Signed, Framed, 37 1/2 X 29 1/3 In. ... 395.00
**Sign,** Bickmore's Gall Cure, Cardboard, 30 X 50 In. ............................. 75.00
**Sign,** Big Boy Soda, Boy & Bottle, Self-Framed, Tin, 34 1/2 X 10 1/2 In. ... 65.00
**Sign,** Bire-Ley's, Dated 1949, Tin, 24 X 36 In. .................................... 20.00

Store, Sign, Bull Durham, Lithographed Tin, 38 X 35 1/2 In.

| | |
|---|---|
| Sign, Blacksmith's, Anvil & Horseshoes, Sheet Iron, Frame, 25 X 50 In. | 175.00 |
| Sign, Blackstone Tobacco, Raised Letters, Porcelain, 26 X 12 In. | 150.00 |
| Sign, Blatz Beer, Both Sides, Wooden, 1950s, 8 X 5 In. | 7.00 |
| Sign, Blatz Beer, Wooden, 1940s, 24 X 12 In. | 15.00 |
| Sign, Blatz, Outdoor Scene, 1913 Auto, Canvas On Wood, 28 X 20 In. | 350.00 |
| Sign, Boone Whiskey, Log Cabin, Daniel Boone, 1904, 36 X 28 In. | 475.00 |
| Sign, Bottle Cap, Hippo Beverage, Texas Size Drink, Tin, 28 In. | 44.00 |
| Sign, Brickmore's Gall Cure, Man & Horse, Cardboard, 30 X 50 In. | 75.00 |
| Sign, Buckeye Beer, 1930s, Tin, 3 X 12 In. | 15.00 |
| Sign, Budweiser Beer, Figural, Bottle, Tin, 15 In. | 95.00 |
| Sign, Budweiser, Man, Woman, Pouring Beer, 1900, Round, 16 In. | 225.00 |
| Sign, Buffalo Smoking Tobacco, Pictured Buffalo, Tin, 1920, 18 X 13 In. | 165.00 |
| Sign, Bull Durham, Lithographed Tin, 38 X 35 1/2 In. ...............*Illus* | 1600.00 |
| Sign, C.H.Pendleton, Graduate Optician, Eye In Corner, Tin, 6 X 20 In. | 45.00 |
| Sign, Camels, Tin, 18 X 12 | 12.00 |
| Sign, Campbell Vegetable Soup, Can Shape, 1900, Porcelain, 22 X 12 In. | 155.00 |
| Sign, Carling's, Nine Pints Of The Law, Keystone Cops, 20 X 13 In. | 75.00 |
| Sign, Carter's Ink Co., Carter's Kittens, Framed, 7 1/2 X 9 1/2 In. | 75.00 |
| Sign, Champagne Velvet, Comical Scene Man Fishing, Tin, 16 X 14 In. | 55.00 |
| Sign, Chesterfield Cigarettes, Joe Louis In Ring, Framed, 25 X 26 In. | 100.00 |
| Sign, Citizens National Bank, Roosevelt, 1900, Tin, 19 X 13 In. | 95.00 |
| Sign, Clabber Girl Baking Powder, 1940s, Tin, 12 X 28 In. | 25.00 |
| Sign, Clark's Rye, Man Pouring Drink, Canvas, 1900, 38 X 28 In. | 325.00 |
| Sign, Cliquot Club, Cardboard, 13 X 19 In. | 35.00 |
| Sign, Cole's Penetrating Liniment, Blue & White, Porcelain, 16 X 6 In. | 45.00 |
| Sign, Cole's Peruvian Bark & Cherry Bitters, Porcelain, 16 X 6 In. | 145.00 |
| Sign, Columbia Records, Shaped Like Record, 1920, Porcelain, 28 In. | 225.00 |
| Sign, Cook's Beer, Indians Attacking, Tin, 27 X 19 In. ............ 195.00 To | 225.00 |
| Sign, Cook's Beer, Irate Cop, Horseless Carriage, Tin, 1930, 21 X 13 In. | 85.00 |
| Sign, Coors Beer, 2-Sided, Metal, 14 X 28 In. | 15.00 |
| Sign, Cream Of Kentucky Whiskey, Shenley, Painting On Glass, 14 In. | 60.00 |
| Sign, Crosse & Blackwell, Full Color, Paper, 30 X 46 In. | 28.00 |
| Sign, Crown Ice Cream, Embossed Tin, 1920s, 28 X 19 In. | 85.00 |
| Sign, Crystal Club Soda, 10 X 28 In. | 30.00 |
| Sign, Cyclone Twister 5 Cent Cigar, Embossed, Cardboard, 9 X 11 In. | 12.00 |
| Sign, Daisy Hair Tonic, Tin, 9 X 10 In. | 20.00 |
| Sign, Dead Shot Smokeless Powder, Cloth, 11 X 13 In. | 48.50 |
| Sign, Devilish Good 5 Cent Cigar, 1910, Embossed Tin, 10 X 14 In. | 85.00 |
| Sign, Diamond Edge Tools, Tin, 28 X 10 In. | 25.00 |
| Sign, Ditto Cigar, Indian Princess, Celluloid, 8 X 12 In. | 225.00 |
| Sign, Dodge Bros., Service Station, Porcelain, 1930s, 15 X 45 In. | 90.00 |
| Sign, Dolly Madison Cigar, Embossed, 1910, Tin, 5 X 20 In. | 30.00 |
| Sign, Domino Cigarettes, Cardboard, 13 X 19 In. | 35.00 |
| Sign, Don't Forget Dexter's Mother's Bread, Porcelain, 16 X 24 In. | 20.00 |
| Sign, Down Goes Dandy Shandy, 1930s, Cardboard, 12 X 9 In. | 20.00 |
| Sign, Dr.D.Jaynes, Tonic Vermifuge, Reverse On Glass, 11 1/2 X 13 In. | 225.00 |
| Sign, Dr.Lynas Hair Grower, 1905, Cardboard, 9 X 12 In. | 10.00 |
| Sign, Dr.Pepper, Checkerboard Ground, 26 X 10 In. | 55.00 |
| Sign, Dr.Pepper, Good For Life, Porcelain, 27 X 10 In. | 75.00 |

**Sign,** Drink Orange Squeeze, C.1930, Embossed Tin, 12 X 1i In. .............................................. 40.00
**Sign,** Drink Orange Squeeze, 1940s, Tin, 18 X 24 In. ............................................................... 30.00
**Sign,** Drink Tom Tucker, Boy, Top Hat, 1920, Tin, Embossed, 12 X 18 In. ......................... 115.00
**Sign,** Dutch Masters Cigars, 6 Men Around Table, Canvas, 18 X 12 In. .............................. 125.00
**Sign,** E. & O.Pilsner Beer, Tin, 9 X 12 In. ............................................................................... 30.00
**Sign,** Edgeworth Tobacco, Embossed, 1920s, Tin, 12 X 28 In. ............................................. 35.00
**Sign,** Edison Mazda Lamps, Fold-Out Christmas Scene, 21 X 26 In. ..................................... 35.00
**Sign,** Ehlermann Brewery, Factory Scene, Workers, 1900, Tin, 26 X 18 In. ......................... 650.00
**Sign,** El Wadora Cigars, 1930s, Embossed Tin, 16 X 20 In. ................................................... 35.00
**Sign,** Eletric Work By Memphis Electric Co., Yellow, Tin, 9 X 20 In. ..................................... 10.00
**Sign,** Elgin Watches, Father Time, Dealer Name & Address, 6 X 8 In. ................................. 25.00
**Sign,** Elgin Watches, Father Time, 1900, Cardboard & Wood, 16 X 22 In. ........................... 195.00
**Sign,** English Ovals Cigarettes, Cardboard, 27 X 19 In. ......................................................... 25.00
**Sign,** Erickson's Pure Rye Whiskey, Man Firing Cannon, Tin, 34 X 24 In. ............................ 150.00
**Sign,** Falstaff Beer, Maiden Serving Sir Falstaff, Tin, 28 In. .................................................. 35.00
**Sign,** Falstaff Lamp, Falstaff, Child, Barmaid, 1912, Tin, 24 In. ........................................... 250.00
**Sign,** Fatima Cigarettes, Tin, Calendar, Harem Girl, 12 X 20 In. ........................................... 225.00
**Sign,** Fatima Cigarettes, Turkish Girl, Cardboard, 1900, 40 X 31 In. ..................................... 195.00
**Sign,** Favorite Straight Cut Cigarettes, 2-Sided Tin, 18 X 9 In. ............................................. 125.00
**Sign,** Fawn Corset, Lady, Corset, Cardboard & Wood, 1920, 12 X 17 In. .............................. 75.00
**Sign,** Fehr's Malt Tonic, Nude, Bottle, Cherubs, Tin, 1900, 28 X 22 In. ................................ 550.00
**Sign,** Ferry-Morse Seeds, Tin, 27 1/2 X 19 In. ....................................................................... 25.00
**Sign,** Firestone Tires, 2-Sided Oval, Porcelain, 21 X 16 In. .................................................. 60.00
**Sign,** Fox Old Emerald, Tin, 28 X 9 In. .................................................................................. 15.00
**Sign,** Freedom Oil, Double Sided, Bulldog, Metal, 22 X 30 In. ............................................. 75.00
**Sign,** Fremlins Ale, Man, Elephant, Wood, 51 1/2 X 48 In. .................................................... 195.00
**Sign,** Fruit-Ola, Beverage, Tin, 1930, 12 X 23 In. .................................................................. 22.00
**Sign,** Furbeck & Nellis, Druggists, C.1905, Wooden, 11 1/2 X 24 In. .................................... 145.00
**Sign,** Furniture, Undertaking, Dated 1877, Gold Leaf Frame, 10 X 12 In. ............................. 35.00
**Sign,** Garland Stoves, Cloth, 20 X 21 1/2 In. ......................................................................... 55.00
**Sign,** Gasoline, Black Letters, Both Sides, 10 X 36 In. .......................................................... 45.00
**Sign,** Gas Stores, Black, Red, & Green, Glass, 10 In.Diam. .................................................. 30.00
**Sign,** Gayoso Gin Bottle, Tin, 15 X 15 In, 1900 ...................................................................... 95.00
**Sign,** Gerhard Long, Celluloid, 7 X 14 In. .............................................................................. 70.00
**Sign,** Gets It For Corns, Tin, 10 1/2 X 6 In. ............................................................................ 20.00
**Sign,** Good-Will Soap, Black & Yellow, Embossed, Tin, 20 X 2 1/4 In. ................................. 12.50
**Sign,** Grand Cigarettes, Horse & Cigarette Pack, Cardboard, 24 X 31 In. ............................ 65.00
**Sign,** Grape Nuts, Girl, St.Bernard, Tin, Self-Framed, 20 X 31 In. ........................................ 650.00
**Sign,** Grapette Soda, Oval, Tin, 27 In. ................................................................................... 22.00
**Sign,** Green River Whiskey, Black Man & Horse, 1899, Frame, 42 X 32 In. .......................... 950.00
**Sign,** Green River Whiskey, Black Man, Mule, Paperboard, 28 X 22 In. ................................ 95.00
**Sign,** Green River Whiskey, Bowl Shape, Tin, 24 In.Diam. ..................................................... 450.00
**Sign,** Green River Whiskey, Cardboard, Pine Frame, 28 X 21 In. .......................................... 85.00
**Sign,** Haberdasher, Top Hat Shape, Red & Silver, Tin, 18 1/2 X 12 In. ................................. 650.00
**Sign,** Handley's Ale, 3-D Bulldog, Composition, 18 X 9 In. .................................................... 65.00
**Sign,** Hartford Fire Insurance, Elk, Tin, 12 X 18 In. ................................................................ 40.00
**Sign,** Harvard Rye, Harvard Man Drinking, Tin, 1900, 29 X 22 In. ........................................ 475.00
**Sign,** Hecker Jones Family, Flour, Barrel, Tin, 10 1/2 X 29 In. .............................................. 550.00
**Sign,** Heileman's Old Style Beer, Tavern Scene, Cardboard, 28 X 24 In. .............................. 45.00
**Sign,** Heinekin, Windmill, Electric, 18 X 11 In. ...................................................................... 25.00
**Sign,** Hershey's Chocolate, Picture Of 2 Boys, Cardboard, 12 X 29 In. ................................ 30.00
**Sign,** High Rollers, Cigars, 3 Girls Smoking, 1890, Tin, 10 X 14 In. ...................................... 150.00
**Sign,** Highest Octane, Crown Gold, 2-Sided, 22 3/4 X 35 1/2 In. .......................................... 15.00
**Sign,** Hires Root Beer, Tin, 16 X 24 In. .................................................................................. 8.00
**Sign,** Hires, Man & Woman At Soda Fountain, Cardboard, 35 X 24 In. ................................. 500.00
**Sign,** Home Paint, House On Paint Can, Tin, 25 X 10 In. ........................................................ 95.00
**Sign,** Home Underwriters, New York, Bronze, 14 X 9 In. ........................................................ 195.00
**Sign,** Hood's Tires, Porcelain, 2-Sided, 32 X 36 In. ............................................................... 65.00
**Sign,** Horse Blankets, Black & White, Cardboard, 27 X 6 In. ................................................. 12.00
**Sign,** Hump Hairpins, Giant Hairpin, Camel, Tin, 1910, 16 X 14 In. ...................................... 150.00
**Sign,** Hudson Essex, Porcelain, 1930s, 16 X 30 In. ............................................................... 95.00
**Sign,** Imperial Bicycles, Plate Glass, Beveled & Etched, 22 X 10 In. .................................... 125.00
**Sign,** Imperial Club 5 Cent Cigar, C.1910, Tin, 10 X 14 In. .................................................... 65.00

**Sign,** Indian Gasoline, Curved Porcelain, 12 X 18 In. ............................................. 45.00
**Sign,** Indiana Billiard Co., Nude, Peacock, Paper, 22 X 13 In. ............................. 165.00
**Sign,** Indianapolis Brewing Co., Girl, Worker, Angel, Paper, 27 X 19 In. ............. 195.00
**Sign,** Indianapolis Brewing Co., Winged Nude, 1904, Tin, 38 X 26 In. ............... 1250.00
**Sign,** International Stock Food, Man Feeding Pigs, Paper, 28 X 21 In. ................. 65.00
**Sign,** It's Cott To Be Good, Tin, 24 X 20 In. .................................................... 10.00
**Sign,** J B Williams Talc, Mother & Baby, Dated 1917, 26 X 22 In. ..................... 150.00
**Sign,** J.W.Allen Wine, Liquor & Cigars, Nude Maiden, 1908, 29 X 16 In. .......... 115.00
**Sign,** Jacob Ruppert Beer, Celluloid, 22 X 16 In. ............................................ 72.00
**Sign,** Jenkinson Fire Insurance, 1930s, Tin, 12 X 23 In. ................................... 30.00
**Sign,** Jersey Ice Cream, 1940s, Embossed Tin, 18 X 24 In. ............................. 30.00
**Sign,** Jewel Stoves & Ranges, Tin, Self-Framed, 12 1/2 X 19 1/2 In. ................ 275.00
**Sign,** Jewel Stoves & Ranges, Wooden Back, Porcelain, 20 X 21 In. ................. 295.00
**Sign,** John Gund Co., Cowboy, Rifle, Bear, 1910, 27 X 19 In. .......................... 175.00
**Sign,** Johnnie Walker Whiskey, Original White Frame, 4 X 23 In. ...................... 35.00
**Sign,** Judge Day Cigars, Cardboard, Supreme Court, Framed, 28 X 21 In. ......... 200.00
**Sign,** Kamp's Rye, Fishing Camp, Men Drinking, 1905, Tin, 24 X 21 In. ........... 650.00
**Sign,** Kato Beer, Convex Glass, Eagle, 16 In.Diam. .................. 90.00 To 125.00
**Sign,** Keen's Mustard, Shows Product, Porcelain, 30 X 15 In. ......................... 60.00
**Sign,** Kellogg's Castor Oil, Bottle & Box, Canvas, 30 X 18 In. ........................ 95.00
**Sign,** Kellogg's Corn Flakes, Baby, Basket, Metal, 1910, 13 X 19 In. .............. 75.00
**Sign,** Kessler Brewery, Helena, Montana, Embossed Tin, 1899, 17 X 23 In. ...... 800.00
**Sign,** Kopper's Coke, Porcelain, 16 X 12 In. ..................................................... 75.00
**Sign,** Korbel Sec, Champagne, Girl, Grapes, 1920, Tin, 13 X 19 In. ................. 115.00
**Sign,** Lang Ale, 6 1/2 X 13 In. ........................................................................ 65.00
**Sign,** Larkin, Chautauqua Desk, Cardboard, 4 X 7 1/2 In. .............................. 22.00
**Sign,** LaSalle Wine, Redhead On Veranda, Tin, 1930, 15 X 11 In. ................... 125.00
**Sign,** LaSalle Wine, Redhead, Red Dress, Tin, 1930, 15 X 10 In. ................... 110.00
**Sign,** Latest Styles, C.E.Hungen, Clothing & Shoes, Tin, 12 X 49 In. ............... 165.00
**Sign,** Laughlin Fountain Pen, Porcelain, 24 X 8 In. ........................................ 75.00
**Sign,** Lemon Julep, Picture Of Bottle, Metal, 10 X 28 In. ............................... 30.00
**Sign,** Lifebuoy, Cardboard, 9 X 23 In. ............................................................ 35.00
**Sign,** London Life, Cigarettes, Man In Tux, Cardboard, 34 X 18 In. ................. 225.00
**Sign,** London, Lancashire Insurance Co., Ltd, Tin, 22 1/2 X 26 1/2 In. ........... 125.00
**Sign,** Lone Star, Fireworks, Animated, 13 X 21 In. ........................................ 50.00
**Sign,** MacMillian Oil, 7 Shape, Metal, 30 X 27 In. ......................................... 25.00
**Sign,** Mail Pouch, Baby Holding Package, 1900, Metal, 19 X 16 In. ................. 425.00
**Sign,** Majestic Hams, Lady Holding Ham, Tin, Self-Framed, 36 X 28 In. .......... 595.00
**Sign,** Maumee Coal, Indian Chief, 1920, Metal, 15 X 16 In. .......................... 95.00
**Sign,** Mayo's Plug, Cock 'o The Walk, Porcelain, 6 1/2 X 13 In. .................... 125.00
**Sign,** McLean's Liver & Kidney Balm, 1905, Cardboard, 5 X 20 In. ................. 10.00
**Sign,** Mecca Cigarettes, 1920, Metal, 15 X 5 In. ........................................... 95.00
**Sign,** Michelin, Porcelain, 1920s, 18 X 60 In. ................................................ 95.00
**Sign,** Miller Beer, Metal, 20 X 24 In. ............................................................. 15.00
**Sign,** Miller Buggy Co., Indian, Lance, Horse, Paper, 1910, 16 X 19 In. .......... 75.00
**Sign,** Mission Orange, Pictures Bottle, Tin, 27 X 11 In. ................................. 25.00
**Sign,** Mitchell's & Butler's Ales & Stouts, Tin, 1910, 18 X 19 In. .................. 145.00
**Sign,** Mother's Oats, Mother's Boy, Dated 1901, 28 X 21 In. ........................ 325.00
**Sign,** Moxie, Cardboard, 1920s, 16 X 16 In. ................................................. 60.00
**Sign,** Moxie, Horse & Girl Driving Car, Tin, Framed, 27 X 16 In. ................... 275.00
**Sign,** Munsingwear, Mother & Child, Union Suits, 33 X 21 In. ...................... 350.00
**Sign,** Murrey & Lenman's Perfume, Reverse Painting, 23 X 15 In. ................. 225.00
**Sign,** Napoleon Cigar, 1910, Paper Lithograph, 10 X 30 In. .......................... 40.00
**Sign,** Nehi Sold Here, Curb Service, Embossed, Tin, 19 X 28 In. ................... 30.00
**Sign,** New Bachelor, Cigars, Bachelor, Cardboard, 31 X 39 In. ..................... 275.00
**Sign,** New England Brewery, Fishing Camp, Hunters, Tin, 33 23, 1900 .......... 585.00
**Sign,** New Yorker Ginger Ale, Porcelain, 36 X 52 In. .................................... 30.00
**Sign,** Nobel & Lacey Whiskey, Roulette Wheel, Signed, 1910, 42 X 29 In. ...... 1100.00
**Sign,** O.F.C.Whiskey, Deer Drinking, 1900, Tin, 28 X 40 In. .......................... 550.00
**Sign,** Old Boone Whiskey, Log Cabin Scene, Tin, 1904, 26 X 18 In. ............... 375.00
**Sign,** Old Continental Whiskey, Beveled Glass, 16 X 16 In. ........................... 59.00
**Sign,** Old Emerald Soda, Tin, 9 X 28 In. ........................................................ 20.00
**Sign,** Oliver Chilled Plows, Farmer Talking To Cowboy, Tin, 25 X 33 In. ......... 600.00

**Sign,** Orange Crush, Orange, Green, & White, Tin, 7 1/2 In.Diam. ............................................. 4.00
**Sign,** Orange Crush, Tin, 24 X 12 In. ....................................................................................... 8.50
**Sign,** Owensboro Wagon, Under The Apple Tree, Tin, 37 1/2 X 25 1/2 In. ...................... 1250.00
**Sign,** Pabst Beer, Two Heads, Pressed Board, 11 X 24 In. ..................................................... 10.00
**Sign,** Pabst Brewing, Factory Picture, C.1900, Self-Framed, 36 X 48 In. .......................... 375.00
**Sign,** Pabst, Cardboard Under Glass, 10 X 12 In. ................................................................... 10.00
**Sign,** Paul Jones Whiskey, Comrades For 81 Years, Tin, 22 X 28 1/2 In. .......................... 350.00
**Sign,** Paul Jones, 4 Roses, Gun, Birds, Duck, 1914, 24 X 35 1/2 In. .................................. 150.00
**Sign,** Pender & Co., Clothiers, Mother-Of-Pearl Lettering, 14 X 20 In. .............................. 90.00
**Sign,** Pendleton, Optician, Embossed, 1910, Tin, 5 X 20 In. ................................................ 40.00
**Sign,** Pepsi-Cola, Red, White, Blue, & Gray, Old Logo, Tin, 30 X 26 In. ............................ 50.00
**Sign,** Pepsi-Cola, 3-Dimensional, Bottle Cap Shape, Tin, 28 In.Diam. ................................ 35.00
**Sign,** Permit Cigars, Girl In Dress, Cardboard, 1910, 32 X 25 In. ...................................... 250.00
**Sign,** Phillip Morris, 1940s, Embossed Tin, 48 X 18 In. ....................................................... 125.00
**Sign,** Phoenix Insurance, Hartford, Conn., Porcelain, 16 X 28 1/2 In. ................................ 125.00
**Sign,** Photographer, Outdoor, Sandpaper Ground, 1-Sided, 68 X 13 1/2 In. ...................... 235.00
**Sign,** Pickwick Ale, Horses Pulling Carriage, Tin, 23 X 6 In. ................................................ 50.00
**Sign,** Piedmont Cigarettes, Canvas, 30 X 60 In. .................................................................... 30.00
**Sign,** Pilsen Root Beer, 1920s, Cardboard, 11 X 19 In. ........................................................ 25.00
**Sign,** Planters Peanuts, Cardboard, Counter, 12 In. ............................................................. 10.00
**Sign,** Planters Peanuts, Pennant, Tin, 9 1/2 X 8 1/2 In.Diam. ............................................. 38.00
**Sign,** Pony Express, Goetz Beer, Framed, 44 X 33 In. .......................................................... 60.00
**Sign,** Possum Hollow Whiskey, Picture Of Bottle, 8 X 16 In. ................................................ 80.00
**Sign,** Prince Albert Tobacco, Porcelain, 36 X 12 In. .............................................................. 32.00
**Sign,** Quaker Lace, Cloth Framed Cardboard, 13 X 18 In. ..................................................... 50.00
**Sign,** R & G Corset, Lady Moves Torso, Mechanical, 24 X 36 In. ........................................ 950.00
**Sign,** Railway Express, Porcelain, 5 X 72 In. .......................................................................... 45.00
**Sign,** Raissac, A Good Laxative, 1930s, Cardboard, 17 X 12 In. ........................................... 60.00
**Sign,** Red Cross Tobacco, Medieval Knight, Cardboard, 1870, 32 X 47 In. ......................... 650.00
**Sign,** Red Rock Cola, 1940s, Cardboard, 11 X 14 In. ............................................ 8.00 To 10.00
**Sign,** Rich's Ice Cream, Porcelain, 1930s, 28 X 20 In. ........................................................... 60.00
**Sign,** Riverside Campground, Wooden, 11 X 24 In. ................................................................ 45.00
**Sign,** Royal Tailors, Colorful Tigers, Tin, Diecut, 20 X 9 In. ................................................ 125.00
**Sign,** Santa Fe R.R., Glass Drumhead, Picture Of The Chief, 25 In.Diam. .......................... 225.00
**Sign,** Schenley Rye, Man, Lady, Glass Of Rye, C.1900, Tin, 23 X 19 In. ............................ 325.00
**Sign,** Schlitz, Porcelain, 12 In.Diam. ....................................................................................... 50.00
**Sign,** Schmidt Bros., Roosevelt, Hunters, 1900, Canvas, 33 X 24 In. .................................. 375.00
**Sign,** Sealtest Ice Cream, Red Glass Light-Up Sign, 26 X 5 1/2 In. .................................... 55.00
**Sign,** Sealtest Ice Cream, 2-Sided, Porcelain, 17 X 17 In. .................................................... 45.00
**Sign,** Sealtest Milk, Lighted, 18 X 32 In. ................................................................................ 15.00
**Sign,** Sharples Cream Separators, Tin, 10 X 14 In. ............................................................... 45.00
**Sign,** Shell Gasoline, Porcelain, 3 1/2 Ft.Diam. .................................................................... 150.00
**Sign,** Shell Motor Oil, 1920s, Porcelain, 24 X 24 In. ............................................................. 45.00
**Sign,** Sherwin Williams, Porcelain, 16 X 22 In. ...................................................................... 25.00
**Sign,** Sierra Beer, Embossed Picture, Tin, 12 X 16 In. .......................................................... 12.00
**Sign,** Silver Spring Brewery, Matted Lithograph, C.1915, 1.X 19 In. .................................... 35.00
**Sign,** Sir Walter Raleigh, Tin, 17 X 26 In. ............................................................................... 30.00
**Sign,** Skelly Oil, 15 Years, Metal, 6 1/4 X 8 1/4 In. ............................................................... 30.00
**Sign,** Skelly, Oils & Greases, 1930s, Porcelain, 36 X 60 In. ................................................. 45.00
**Sign,** Smith Piano, Victorian Lady, Man Playing, C.1890, Paper, 31 In. ............................. 275.00
**Sign,** Socony Vacuum, Oil Can With Gargoyle, Canvas, 40 X 29 In. ..................................... 25.00
**Sign,** South Bend Brewery, Woman, Tiger Skin, Tin, Round, 16 In. ..................................... 175.00
**Sign,** Sparrows Chocolate, Boy Serving Queen, Tin, 1910, 19 X 13 In. .............................. 195.00
**Sign,** Spearhead Chewing Tobacco, Porcelain, 14 X 6 In. ..................................................... 68.00
**Sign,** Square Snuff, Container Shape, 1930s, Tin, 18 X 11 In. .............................................. 40.00
**Sign,** Standard Red Crown, White Crown, Porcelain, 15 X 12 In. ......................................... 22.50
**Sign,** Star Cut Plug, Porcelain, 11 X 24 In. ............................................................................. 65.00
**Sign,** Stetson Hats, Street, Man, Hat, 1920, Canvas, 30 X 22 In. ....................................... 195.00
**Sign,** Stoechlke Diamond State, Brewery, Horse, Tin, Framed, 38 X 26 In. ........................ 650.00
**Sign,** Stroh's, Man Drinking, Tin, Wood Frame, 15 X 22 In. ............................................... 110.00
**Sign,** Sun Drop Cola, 1940s, Pictures Bottle, Tin, 48 X 18 In. ............................................. 40.00
**Sign,** Sweet Orr Overalls, Figures Having Tug-Of-War, , 23 X 10 In. .................................. 160.00
**Sign,** Sweet Orr, Porcelain, 27 X 9 1/2 In. ............................................................................. 115.00

Store, Sign, The Temptation Of St.Anthony,
19 1/2 X 13 3/4 In.

| | |
|---|---:|
| **Sign,** Sweetie Beverages, 1940s, Tin, 11 X 28 In. | 20.00 |
| **Sign,** Taffy, Black On Maroon, 4 X 20 In. | 25.00 |
| **Sign,** Tamo Shanter Ale, Porcelain On Steel, Round, 30 In. | 75.00 |
| **Sign,** Tangee Lipstick, Lady In Nightgown, Cardboard, 34 X 24 In. | 55.00 |
| **Sign,** Texaco Skychief Supreme Gasoline, Tin, 20 X 15 In. | 15.00 |
| **Sign,** Texaco Skychief Supreme, Porcelain, 12 X 8 In. | 18.00 |
| **Sign,** The Temptation Of St.Anthony, 19 1/2 X 13 3/4 In. ................*Illus* | 675.00 |
| **Sign,** Threemor, Milk Chocolate Bracer, 1930s, Tin, 9 X 19 In. | 45.00 |
| **Sign,** Tivoli Pale, Fox Hunter, Horse, Tin, Framed, 22 X 28 In. | 125.00 |
| **Sign,** Travelers Insurance, Metal, 10 X 14 In. | 16.00 |
| **Sign,** True Fruit, Tin, Table Of Fruit, Goddess, Cupids, 26 X 38 In. | 165.00 |
| **Sign,** Turkish Crosscut, Cigarettes, Victorian Girl, 1900, 40 X 12 In. | 165.00 |
| **Sign,** Tuttles Horse Elixir, Paper, 42 X 26 In. | 55.00 |
| **Sign,** Union Workman, 1950s, Tin, 16 X 20 In. | 30.00 |
| **Sign,** Van Houten Cocoa, Lady Pouring Cocoa, C.1890, Cardboard, 31 In. | 300.00 |
| **Sign,** Vess Cola, Contains No Caffeine, 1940s, Tin, 26 X 26 In. | 30.00 |
| **Sign,** Vesta Cola, Gowned Woman With Torch, Porcelain, 20 X 12 In. | 55.00 |
| **Sign,** Vicks Vapo Rub, Tin, 23 X 17 In. | 15.00 |
| **Sign,** Vigorator Hair Tonic, 1920s, Tin, 5 X 10 In. | 18.00 |
| **Sign,** Vigorite Iron Tonic, Strong Man With Package, 22 X 14 In. | 14.00 |
| **Sign,** Virginia Dare Soda, Tin, 10 X 28 In. | 25.00 |
| **Sign,** Waterman's Pen, Makes Its Mark Around The World, 20 X 10 In. | 125.00 |
| **Sign,** We Pay For Dead Stock, 1930s, Tin, 9 X 12 In. | 30.00 |
| **Sign,** We Sell Grape Tobacco, Tin, 13 In.Diam. | 50.00 |
| **Sign,** We Sell Old Dutch Cleanser, Dutch Woman, Porcelain, 14 X 20 In. | 225.00 |
| **Sign,** Weatherbird Shoes, Pictures Peter Weatherbird, Metal, 6 X 11 In. | 65.00 |
| **Sign,** Weatherbird Shoes, Rooster Shape, Tin, 23 In. | 175.00 |
| **Sign,** Whippet, Porcelain, 1930s, 24 X 36 In. | 175.00 |
| **Sign,** Whippet, Willys, Overland Co., 1930s, Tin, 10 X 24 In. | 125.00 |
| **Sign,** White Owl Cigar, Framed Glass, 21 X 32 In. | 30.00 |
| **Sign,** Wildroot, 1950, Embossed Tin, 12 X 28 In. | 30.00 |
| **Sign,** Winchester, Hunt Camp Scene, Cardboard, 26 X 20 In. | 28.00 |
| **Sign,** Yeast Foam, C.1917, Heavy Paper, 10 X 15 In. | 25.00 |
| **Spittoon,** Lady's, Yellow & White, Ceramic, 2 1/2 In. | 20.00 |
| **Spool Cabinet,** Clark's O.N.T., Desk Style, 30 X 21 In. | 450.00 |
| **Spool Cabinet,** Clark's O.N.T., Desk Style, 4 Drawer, Oak, 30 In. | 450.00 |
| **Spool Cabinet,** Clark's O.N.T., 2 Drawer, Walnut | 135.00 |
| **Spool Cabinet,** Coats & Clark, Slant Desk Style, Oak | 350.00 |
| **Spool Cabinet,** Desk Top, 6 Drawer, Oak, 33 X 23 X 17 In. | 235.00 |
| **Spool Cabinet,** J.P.Coats, Slant Top, Hinged Glass Lid, 24 X 16 In. | 45.00 |
| **Spool Cabinet,** J. P.Coats, Top Load, Swivel Base, Roll-Up Sides | 300.00 |
| **Spool Cabinet,** Star Twist Thread, Glass Front, 30 Compartments | 25.00 |
| **Spool Cabinet,** Willard's, 2 Drawer, Oak, 13 1/4 X 8 1/4 X 5 1/4 In. | 80.00 |
| **Spoon,** Mr.Peanut | 17.50 |
| **Squeezer,** Lemon, Alligator Jaws, Aluminum | 8.00 |
| **Stand,** Teaberry Gum, Vaseline Glass | 32.50 |
| **Stand,** Wrapping Paper, Counter, Iron & Wood, Original Paper | 35.00 |

| | |
|---|---|
| **Stretcher,** Sock, Wire, 14 In., Pair | 10.00 |
| **Tankard,** Budweiser, Eagle & A In Gold Medallions, Ceramic | 8.00 |
| **Teapot,** Lipton, Yellow | 25.00 |
| **Teapot,** Salada Tea | 10.00 |
| **Thermometer,** Black Boy, 1949 | 12.00 |
| **Thermometer,** Bubble-Up Record, Wooden | 22.00 |
| **Thermometer,** Camel Cigarettes, Tin | 20.00 |
| **Thermometer,** Conrad Laurel Springs, St.Louis, Wooden, 15 In. | 35.00 |
| **Thermometer,** Dad's Root Beer, Metal, 25 In. | 24.00 |
| **Thermometer,** Dr.Pepper, Tin | 18.00 |
| **Thermometer,** Dr.Wells, The Cooler Doctor, Tin, 6 X 16 In. | 6.00 |
| **Thermometer,** Dwight's Soda, Wooden | 180.00 |
| **Thermometer,** Ex-Lax, Constipation & Liver Complaints, Wooden, 15 In. | 45.00 |
| **Thermometer,** Ex-Lax, Porcelain, 9 X 36 In. | 50.00 |
| **Thermometer,** Fatima | 125.00 |
| **Thermometer,** Havoline Tower, 4 3/4 In. | 21.00 |
| **Thermometer,** Hires Bottle, 28 In. | 40.00 |
| **Thermometer,** Hires Root Beer, Diecut, 8 X 29 In. | 45.00 |
| **Thermometer,** Jamaica Loan Co., Wooden, 39 X 8 In. | 95.00 |
| **Thermometer,** Mail Pouch, Porcelain, 39 X 8 In. | 68.00 |
| **Thermometer,** Martin-Senore Paints, Orange, Porcelain, 36 In. | 110.00 |
| **Thermometer,** Marvel Cigarettes, Wooden | 30.00 |
| **Thermometer,** Mission Orange | 20.00 |
| **Thermometer,** Nesbitt Orange Drink, Dated 1936, 27 In. | 210.00 |
| **Thermometer,** Orange Crush, Blue & Orange, Wooden, 16 X 6 In. | 18.00 |
| **Thermometer,** Pabst Blue Ribbon Beer | 20.00 |
| **Thermometer,** Pepsi-Cola, Old Style Bottle, Double Hyphen After Pepsi | 75.00 |
| **Thermometer,** Pepsi, Bigger & Better, 12 Ounce Bottle | 46.00 |
| **Thermometer,** Pepsi, Say Pepsi Please, Porcelain, 27 In. | 32.50 |
| **Thermometer,** Prestolite, 27 X 8 In. | 20.00 |
| **Thermometer,** Prestone Anti-Freeze, Porcelain, Large | 45.00 |
| **Thermometer,** Prestone Anti-Freeze, Red, Blue, Gray, Tin, 36 In. | 22.00 |
| **Thermometer,** RC Cola, 25 X 10 In. | 25.00 |
| **Thermometer,** Reuter Brewery, 1880s | 125.00 |
| **Thermometer,** Salem Cigarettes, Triangular Shaped, Tin | 7.50 |
| **Thermometer,** Standard Fuel & Oil, Tin, 12 In. | 10.00 |
| **Thermometer,** Stark Tire Co., Quincy, Ill., On Wood, 6 1/2 In.Diam. | 6.50 |
| **Thermometer,** Teem, Wooden, 28 X 8 In. | 14.00 |
| **Thermometer,** Tru-Ade | 20.00 |
| **Thermometer,** Winston Cigarettes, Raised Pack, 5 X 17 In. | 25.00 |
| **Thermometer,** Wolfschmidt, 12 In.Diam. | 18.00 |
| **Thermos,** Monarch Coffee | 25.00 |
| **Tin,** Abbey, Tobacco, Pocket | 80.00 |
| **Tin,** Acme Coffee, 1 Pound | 18.00 |
| **Tin,** Airfloat Talc, Lady, Purple & Green | 12.00 |
| **Tin,** Allen & Gitner Tobacco, Genuine Perique, 3 X 1 1/2 X 2 In. | 25.00 |
| **Tin,** Angelus Marshmallow | 20.00 |
| **Tin,** Baby Educator, Baby's Blessing, 3 In. | 65.00 |
| **Tin,** Bagdad Tobacco, Man In Native Costume, Pocket | 45.00 To 65.00 |
| **Tin,** Bagley's Old Colony, Tobacco, Pocket | 40.00 |
| **Tin,** Baker's Chocolate, Label, Paper, Embossed Top | 15.00 |
| **Tin,** Bank Note Cigars | 20.00 |
| **Tin,** Beech-Nut Tobacco, U.S.Frigate Constitution | 40.00 |
| **Tin,** Beech-Nut 5 Cent Cigar | 15.00 |
| **Tin,** Belfast Cut Plug, 4 X 6 In. | 20.00 |
| **Tin,** Benson & Hedges, Virginia Rounds, Fifth Ave., N.Y., Flat Fifties | 15.00 |
| **Tin,** Big Ben Tobacco, Pocket | 10.00 |
| **Tin,** Bill's Best, 3 X 4 In. | 8.00 |
| **Tin,** Biscuit, Cracker Jack, Hinged Lid, 10 X 7 In. | 27.50 |
| **Tin,** Borden's Meadow, Malted Milk, 10 Pound | 35.00 |
| **Tin,** Box, Beechnut, Mohawk Valley Scene | 18.00 |
| **Tin,** Box, Lucky Strike Sliced Plug | 12.00 |
| **Tin,** Box, Spice, Mexican Design, Burros, 10 X 8 In. | 87.00 |

| | |
|---|---|
| **Tin,** Brewster & Crittenden's Gladiator Blend, Coffee, Floor Size | 285.00 |
| **Tin,** Buckingham Cut Plug Tobacco, Pocket, Contents | 25.00 To 35.00 |
| **Tin,** Buckingham Tobacco, Pocket | 25.00 To 50.00 |
| **Tin,** Buckingham Tobacco, Trial Size | 100.00 |
| **Tin,** Bunte Mashmallow | 285.00 |
| **Tin,** C.D.Kenny Mammy Coffee | 100.00 |
| **Tin,** Cadet Soldier, Gray, Talc | 50.00 |
| **Tin,** California Nugget, Tobacco, Pocket | 125.00 |
| **Tin,** California Perfume Talc | 12.50 |
| **Tin,** Campbell's Coffee, Yellow With Camel, 4 Pound | 35.00 |
| **Tin,** Campbell's Pictures Camels, Coffee, 4 Pound | 55.00 |
| **Tin,** Campfire Marshmallows, Scene, Round, 1 Pound | 20.00 |
| **Tin,** Campfire Marshmallows, 5 Pound | 23.00 |
| **Tin,** Central Union Tobacco, 6 X 4 X 3 In. | 14.00 |
| **Tin,** Chicago Cub, Tobacco | 125.00 |
| **Tin,** Clayton's Killflea Powder | 15.00 |
| **Tin,** Cleveland Baking Powder, 1890, Embossed | 15.00 |
| **Tin,** Coach & Four, Tobacco, Pocket | 45.00 |
| **Tin,** Coffee Pail, Grossman's, Milwaukee, 5 Pound | 9.50 |
| **Tin,** Continental Cubes Tobacco, 5 X 5 X 5 In.Square | 775.00 |
| **Tin,** Continental Tea, Trunk Shape | 15.00 |
| **Tin,** Copenhagen Snuff, Counter | 90.00 |
| **Tin,** Coronation Coach | 325.00 |
| **Tin,** Corylapsis, Talc, Oriental Lady | 22.00 |
| **Tin,** Cuticura Talcum, Baby On One Side, Lady On Other | 25.00 |
| **Tin,** Dayton Nut, Vintage Airplane, 5 Pound | 195.00 |
| **Tin,** Dill's Best, Pocket, Flat, 3 1/2 X 2 1/4 X 2 1/2 In. | 4.00 |
| **Tin,** Dill's Best, Round, 2 1/2 X 5 In.Diam. | 15.00 |
| **Tin,** Dixie Peanut, 10 Pound | 12.50 |
| **Tin,** Dr.Johnson's Educator, Cracker, 5 1/2 X 5 1/2 X 6 In. | 55.00 |
| **Tin,** Dr.Palmer's Almoeal, Lady's Face On Front & Back | 20.00 |
| **Tin,** Drostes Cocoa | 9.00 |
| **Tin,** Edgemont Crackers, White & Green | 22.00 |
| **Tin,** Edgeworth, Tobacco, Concave Hinged Cover, 4 In.Square | 15.00 |
| **Tin,** Edgeworth Tobacco, Pocket | 1.00 To 2.75 |
| **Tin,** Egyptian Rameses II Cigarettes, Paper Label, 3 X 6 In. | 7.00 |
| **Tin,** Elk Baking Powder, Paper Label | 5.00 |
| **Tin,** Ensign, Tobacco, Pocket | 100.00 |
| **Tin,** Epicure Tobacco, Pocket | 95.00 |
| **Tin,** Esso Anti-Rust, 3 In. | 7.00 |
| **Tin,** Eve Cube Cut, Pocket, Tin | 15.00 |
| **Tin,** Eve Tobacco, Pictures Nude, Pocket | 65.00 |
| **Tin,** Ex-Cel-Sis Talcum | 15.00 |
| **Tin,** Fast Mail Tobacco, Pocket | 200.00 |
| **Tin,** Forbes Coffee No.1, 1912 | 30.00 |
| **Tin,** Four Roses Tobacco, Curved Top, Pocket | 15.00 |
| **Tin,** Gail & Ax Brass, Pictures Factory, Tobacco, Sample, Pocket | 175.00 |
| **Tin,** George Washington Cut Plug, Round | 10.00 |
| **Tin,** Globe Tobacco, Pocket | 85.00 |
| **Tin,** Gold Bond, Tobacco, Pocket | 50.00 |
| **Tin,** Gold Medal, Tobacco, Square | 75.00 |
| **Tin,** Golden Cup Coffee | 10.00 |
| **Tin,** Golden Rule Pepper, Round, 1 Pound | 7.00 |
| **Tin,** Golden Rule Tea, 5 Pound | 40.00 |
| **Tin,** Granulated "54", Pocket | 47.00 |
| **Tin,** Great Blend Flake, Tobacco, Pocket | 48.00 |
| **Tin,** Half-And-Half, Barrel, 4 1/2 X 6 1/2 In. | 80.00 |
| **Tin,** Half-And-Half, Burley Bright, 5 In. | 3.00 |
| **Tin,** Half-And-Half, Tobacco, Sample, Pocket | 45.00 |
| **Tin,** Handmade Tobacco, Pocket | 55.00 |
| **Tin,** Harper's Dustless Mop, Tin With Mop Inside, C.1920 | 35.00 |
| **Tin,** Hatchet Brand Cocoa, 6 Pound Size | 25.00 |

**Tin,** Helmar Turkish Cigarettes, P.Lorillard, Flat 50s .......................................... 12.00
**Tin,** Hercules Gun Powder, Square ................................................................... 6.50
**Tin,** Honest Labor Cut Plug, Pocket .............................................. 10.00 To 25.00
**Tin,** Honeymoon Breakfast Coffee ..................................................................... 45.00
**Tin,** Honeymoon Trail, Coffee ............................................................................. 55.00
**Tin,** Hunki Dori, Pictures Trained Frog With Trainer, Tobacco ....................... 425.00
**Tin,** Huntley & Palmer, Black, Oriental Scene, Brass Trim, 8 1/2 In. ............. 45.00
**Tin,** Huntley & Palmer, Book Shape ................................................................. 115.00
**Tin,** Huntley & Palmer, Marble Column ............................................................ 45.00
**Tin,** Huntley & Palmer, Palace Of Westminster ............................................... 30.00
**Tin,** Huntley & Palmer, Two Strings To Her Bow, 7 In.Diam. ......................... 30.00
**Tin,** Huntley & Palmer, Chest ............................................................................. 65.00
**Tin,** Idle Hour Tobacco, Pictures Hourglass, Pocket ........................................ 40.00
**Tin,** Imperial Ginger, 5 X 3 X 1 In. .................................................................... 10.00
**Tin,** Ivin's Biscuits, Butter Jumble ................................................................... 15.00
**Tin,** Jersey Cream Toilet Soap ........................................................................... 12.00
**Tin,** Joe Louis Hair Pomade, C.1930, Original Contents ................................. 25.00
**Tin,** Johnson's Log Cabin Coffee ...................................................................... 850.00
**Tin,** Just Suits, Cut Plug, Slot For Bank .......................................................... 25.00
**Tin,** Justrite Tobacco, Pocket ............................................................................. 15.00
**Tin,** Kentucky Club Tobacco, Jockey On Horse, Pocket ................................... 10.00
**Tin,** Kipling, Tobacco, Pocket ............................................................................. 25.00
**Tin,** La Palina Cigars, Pictures Lady, Flat, Pocket ........................................... 20.00
**Tin,** Lady Churchill, Cigars ................................................................................. 8.50
**Tin,** LaSalle Cigarette, Canister Shape .............................................................. 18.00
**Tin,** Light Sweet Cuba Tobacco ......................................................................... 40.00
**Tin,** Lilacs & Roses, Talc .................................................................................... 10.00
**Tin,** Lily Of The Valley, Talc ............................................................................... 9.00
**Tin,** Lipton Tea, Female Tea Pickers In Fields, 2 Sides, 3 Pound ................... 45.00
**Tin,** Log Cabin Syrup, Boy In Door ................................................................... 75.00
**Tin,** London Sherbet, Tobacco, Pocket ............................................................. 65.00
**Tin,** Loose Wiles Biscuit Co., Pictures Hiawatha ............................................. 65.00
**Tin,** Loose Wiles Biscuit, Pictures Statue Of Liberty, Octagonal ..................... 20.00
**Tin,** Lowney's Cocoa .......................................................................................... 12.00
**Tin,** Lucky Strike Cigarettes, Round, 3 1/4 X 4 In. .......................................... 20.00
**Tin,** Lucky Strike Cigarettes, White .................................................................. 250.00
**Tin,** Lucky Strike Cut Plug ................................................................................. 20.00
**Tin,** Lucky Strike, Flat, Green, 50s ................................................... 4.00 To 6.00
**Tin,** Lucky Strike, Gets Smaller As Tobacco Is Used ...................................... 15.00
**Tin,** Lucky Strike, Pocket, 4 1/2 X 2 1/2 In. ..................................................... 3.00
**Tin,** Lucky Tobacco, Flat, Yellow ....................................................................... 35.00
**Tin,** Luden's Cough Drops, Pocket ..................................................................... 45.00
**Tin,** Luzianne Coffee, Mammy ............................................................................ 55.00
**Tin,** M.Melachrino & Co., Egyptian Cigarettes, Flat Fifties ............................. 9.00
**Tin,** M.Melachrino Egyptian Cigarettes, Square, 5 In. ..................................... 7.50
**Tin,** Mammy Coffee, Pictures Black Man .......................................................... 125.00
**Tin,** Mammy's Favorite Brand Coffee, Orange ................................................. 75.00
**Tin,** Maryland Club Tobacco, Pocket ................................................................ 200.00
**Tin,** McCormick Tea Banquet .............................................................................. 12.50
**Tin,** McVittie & Price, Shape Of Chest .............................................................. 135.00
**Tin,** Melachrine Egyptian Cigarettes, Flat ......................................................... 20.00
**Tin,** Monarch Peanut Butter, Round, 55 Pound, 14 1/2 In. .............................. 135.00
**Tin,** Monarch Tea, 1/2 Pound ............................................................................ 12.50
**Tin,** Monte Cristo Slabs Tobacco ....................................................................... 10.00
**Tin,** Monte Cristo Tobacco, C.1888, 8 1/2 In.Long ......................................... 35.00
**Tin,** Mother's Brand, Nut, Barsam Bros., Springfield, Mass. .......................... 35.00
**Tin,** Muriel Cigars, Round Canister, White & Red, 50 Cigar Size, Pair .......... 12.00
**Tin,** North Star, Seminude, Cherubs, Tobacco .................................................. 350.00
**Tin,** Ogburn, Hill, & Co., 2 Pound Stamp ......................................................... 75.00
**Tin,** Ojibwa Tobacco, Round .............................................................................. 70.00
**Tin,** Old Colony, Pocket ...................................................................................... 50.00
**Tin,** Old Glory Tobacco, Pocket ......................................................................... 525.00

**Tin**, Old Gold Cigarettes, Flat .................................................. 18.00
**Tin**, Old Mansion Tea, Contents, 2 1/2 X 3 In. ........................ 15.00
**Tin**, Opossum Cigar .............................................................. 25.00
**Tin**, Our Hero Coffee, Hexagon, Admiral Dewey, Other Heroes, 1 Pound ........ 75.00
**Tin**, Pat Hand Tobacco, Pocket ............................................ 35.00
**Tin**, Patterson Tuxedo, Seated Gentleman, Pocket ................ 12.50
**Tin**, Penn's Yellow, Tobacco, Square .................................. 25.00
**Tin**, Pennyroyal Pills, Diamond Brand, Jan.1, 1888, Girl On Moon ........ 15.00
**Tin**, Persian Wood, Tall, No Cap ......................................... 8.00
**Tin**, Peter Rabbit Tobacco, Pocket ...................................... 25.00
**Tin**, Philip Morris Cigarettes, Round, 50s .................... 8.00 To 18.00
**Tin**, Pickwick Peanut Butter ................................................ 30.00
**Tin**, Piper Champagne Chewing Tobacco ............................ 13.50
**Tin**, Piper Heidsieck Chewing Tobacco, Flat ....................... 15.00
**Tin**, Piper Heidsieck, Chewing Tobacco, Tin ....................... 10.00
**Tin**, Piper Heidsieck, Tobacco, Flat ..................................... 3.50
**Tin**, Planters Novola Peanut Oil, 5 Gallon .......................... 30.00
**Tin**, Planters Peanuts, 10 Pound ......................................... 15.00
**Tin**, Players Navy Cut Cigarettes, Flat 50 ........................... 7.00
**Tin**, Postmaster Tobacco, Round, 6 In. ............................... 18.00
**Tin**, Powder, Dead Shot Gun Powder, Duck Falling ............. 135.00
**Tin**, Premier Crystallized Ginger ......................................... 7.50
**Tin**, Pride Of Virginia Sliced Plug Tobacco ........................ 8.00
**Tin**, Pride Of Virginia, Pocket ............................................. 5.00
**Tin**, Prince Albert Tobacco, Round, 5 In. ............................ 35.00
**Tin**, Psylla Laxative, 5 Pound ............................................. 40.00
**Tin**, Puritan Tobacco, Pocket .............................................. 80.00
**Tin**, Red Dot Jr., Cigar ........................................................ 4.00
**Tin**, Revelation Tobacco, Pocket ......................................... 15.00
**Tin**, Roly Poly, Dutchman .................................................... 600.00
**Tin**, Roly Poly, Dutchman, Dixie Queen .................... 400.00 To 650.00
**Tin**, Roly Poly, inspector .................................................... 1050.00
**Tin**, Roly Poly, Mammy ............................................ 250.00 To 325.00
**Tin**, Roly Poly, Mammy, Mayo's Tobacco .................. 575.00 To 750.00
**Tin**, Roly Poly, Mammy, U.S.Marine ..................................... 350.00
**Tin**, Roly Poly, Satisfied Customer ..................................... 400.00
**Tin**, Roly Poly, Storekeeper, Dixie Queen ........................... 650.00
**Tin**, Roseleaf Tobacco, With Compass, Pocket .................... 65.00
**Tin**, Rosemary, Coffee ........................................................ 45.00
**Tin**, Rough Rider, Baking Powder, Pictures Man On Horse, 1909 ........ 30.00
**Tin**, Rumford Baking Powder ............................................... 6.00
**Tin**, Rumford Baking Powder, Sample Size .......................... 15.00
**Tin**, Saraka Laxative ........................................................... 6.00
**Tin**, Savoy Coffee ............................................................... 10.00
**Tin**, Sayman Salve, Picture Of Doctor Sayman ................... 5.00
**Tin**, Schepp's Coconut Cake ............................................... 165.00
**Tin**, Swee-Touch-Nee Tea, Small Trunk Shape .................... 11.00
**Tin**, Sensible Sliced Plug Tobacco ..................................... 10.00
**Tin**, Silver Sea Coffee ........................................................ 10.00
**Tin**, Sir Walter Raleigh, Christmas ...................................... 15.00
**Tin**, Sir Walter Releigh, Tobacco Canister, Round, 1926 Stamp ........ 10.00
**Tin**, Snap Shot Gun Powder, Duck Failing ........................... 85.00
**Tin**, St.Leger, Little Cigars, 4 In. ........................................ 10.00
**Tin**, Steer Brand Coffee, Pictures Bull, 3 Pound ................. 45.00
**Tin**, Sultana Peanut Butter ................................................. 25.00
**Tin**, Summer Girl Coffee ..................................................... 17.50
**Tin**, Summer Time Tobacco, Paper Label, Pocket ................ 45.00
**Tin**, Sunshine Biscuits, 16 In. ............................................. 10.00
**Tin**, Superior, Peanut, 10 Pound ......................................... 30.00
**Tin**, Surburg's Golden Sceptre, Tobacco, 5 X 5 In. ............. 25.00
**Tin**, Swansdown, Coffee ..................................................... 55.00
**Tin**, Sweet Burley, Dark, 8 1/2 X 10 3/4 In. ......................... 90.00
**Tin**, Sweet Clover Tobacco, Pocket ..................................... 225.00

| | |
|---|---|
| Tin, Sweet Cuba, Pie Shaped, Pocket | 25.00 |
| Tin, Sweet Cuba, Yellow | 100.00 |
| Tin, Sweet Pea Talc | 10.00 |
| Tin, Taite, Baby Talc, C.1890 | 15.00 |
| Tin, Target Tobacco, Pocket | 5.00 |
| Tin, Ten Strike Baking Powder, 5 Pound | 12.00 |
| Tin, Terry Window, Prophylactic, Alumium | 16.00 |
| Tin, Tetley Tea Bags, Round | 4.00 |
| Tin, Tetley Tea, Elephant, Flat, 2 X 3 In. | 35.00 |
| Tin, Tetley Tea, 5 1/2 X 3 1/2 In. | 10.00 |
| Tin, Tiger Chewing Tobacco, Red, 5 Pound | 125.00 To 135.00 |
| Tin, Tiger Tobacco, Pocket | 85.00 To 200.00 |
| Tin, Tiny Tot Talcum, Pictures Baby, Elves & Flowers | 30.00 |
| Tin, Tobacco, Buckingham, Pocket | 55.00 |
| Tin, Turf, Roulette Wheel On Lid, Cigarette | 65.00 |
| Tin, Tuxedo Tobacco, Pocket | 8.00 To 10.00 |
| Tin, Twin Oaks Tobacco, Pocket | 10.00 To 20.00 |
| Tin, Two Belles Tobacco, 4 X 5 X 1 In. | 25.00 |
| Tin, Tydol Oil Can | 8.00 |
| Tin, U-All-No, Mints | 5.00 |
| Tin, Uneeda Biscuits, Colonial Scene, 8 X 11 1/2 In. | 15.00 |
| Tin, Union Leader, Pocket | 3.00 |
| Tin, Union Leader, Uncle Sam Pictured, 1910, Pocket | 20.00 To 40.00 |
| Tin, Union Leader, 6 X 4 In. | 30.00 |
| Tin, Union Sanitary, Flask, Pint | 20.00 |
| Tin, Van Melles Toffees, Windmill | 175.00 |
| Tin, Velvet, Gold Shield, Pocket | 3.00 |
| Tin, Watkins Tooth Powder, Full | 10.00 |
| Tin, White Rose Coffee, 1 Pound | 20.00 To 25.00 |
| Tin, White Rose, Tea | 5.00 |
| Tin, Wiles Biscuit Co., W.W.II War Ship | 40.00 |
| Tin, Will Taylor Tobacco, Pocket | 15.00 |
| Tin, Willoughby Taylor, Original Contents, Pocket | 14.00 |
| Tin, Yankee Boy Tobacco, Tin, Pocket | 195.00 |
| Tin, Yellow Label Whiskey, Victorian Lady, Morris Chair, 13 X 10 In. | 175.00 |
| Tin, Yucatan Gum | 55.00 |
| Tom, Bulldog Tobacco, Pocket | 100.00 |
| Torch, Parade, Kerosene, Aluminum | 10.00 |
| Towel, Miller Beer | 3.00 |
| Tray, A Lady Of Quality, Advertising, 1904, Oval | 45.00 |
| Tray, A.Miller Wines & Liquors, Red Wind, Minn., Oval, 16 In. | 90.00 |
| Tray, Aberdeen Bottling Works, Carnation Girl, 1908 | 200.00 |
| Tray, Allen's Ice Cream, Rose O'Neill Kewpie Holding Tray, 1910 | 125.00 |
| Tray, Amsdell Albany Ale, Pre-Prohibition, Enamel | 125.00 |
| Tray, Anheuser-Busch, Factory, Train, Wagon, Pre-Prohibition, 19 In. | 395.00 |
| Tray, Anheuser-Busch, Vienna Art Plate, Seminude | 75.00 |
| Tray, Anheuser-Busch, Woman With Cherubs, 1900 | 235.00 |
| Tray, Arrow Beer, Tavern Scene With King Of Lager | 65.00 |
| Tray, B.W.O.E. Rye, Brunette, Oval, 1900 | 125.00 |
| Tray, Bartholomay Brewery, Brass | 85.00 |
| Tray, Bevo Soft Drink | 60.00 |
| Tray, Bissantz Ice Cream, Lady, Oval | 65.00 |
| Tray, Blatz, Milwaukee, Wisc., 16 In. | 10.00 |
| Tray, Blue Ribbon Beer, Gentleman Pouring Beer | 40.00 |
| Tray, Bolton Beer, Pre-Prohibition, Monks | 200.00 |
| Tray, Budweiser, Fox Hunter & Dog, Fireplace | 110.00 |
| Tray, Budweiser, King Of Beers | 13.00 |
| Tray, Budweiser, Levy Scene | 75.00 |
| Tray, Budweiser, Riverfront Scene, 1914 | 50.00 |
| Tray, Budweiser, St.Louis Levee, 1914 | 75.00 |
| Tray, Budweiser, Steamboat Scene | 60.00 |
| Tray, Buffalo Club Whiskey, C.1910, Buffalo Head | 125.00 |
| Tray, Camomile Tea, Peter Rabbit Drinking Tea, 1920 | 110.00 |

| | |
|---|---|
| Tray, Chippawa's Pride, Pictures Indian Maiden | 55.00 |
| Tray, Christian Feiganspan, Signed Asti | 38.00 |
| Tray, Claussen, 3 Tramps Drinking | 175.00 To 195.00 |
| Tray, Columbia Ice Cream, Woman & Horse, St.Bernard, 1913 | 175.00 |
| Tray, Coors Beer | 5.00 |
| Tray, Country Club Whiskey, Toothless Monk, Bottle, Barrel, 1900 | 145.00 |
| Tray, Dairy Made Ice Cream, Picture Of Small Boy | 35.00 |
| Tray, Dawe's Black Horse Ale & Porter, Porcelain | 75.00 |
| Tray, Detroit, Black Haired Girl Sipping | 145.00 |
| Tray, Diamond Wedding Rye, Girl In Red, Drinking, 1900 | 195.00 |
| Tray, Diehl Brewery, Seminude Maiden | 40.00 |
| Tray, Duquesne Pilsner, Finest Beer In Town | 17.50 |
| Tray, Eagle Brewing, Gypsy Lady | 165.00 |
| Tray, East Side Beer, Yama Yama Boy | 45.00 |
| Tray, Ecoma Ice Cream, Girl Sitting At Table, 1921 | 115.00 |
| Tray, Emil T.Raddant Brewing Co., Shawano, Wisc. | 150.00 |
| Tray, Falstaff Beer, Metal | 7.50 |
| Tray, Fatima Cigarettes, Harem Girl, Metal Oval, 22 In. | 275.00 |
| Tray, Fehr's, King Toasting Queen, Pre-Prohibition | 125.00 To 165.00 |
| Tray, Fort Dearborn, Chicago World's Fair | 8.00 |
| Tray, Gambrinus, King Holding Goblet | 155.00 |
| Tray, Genessee, Ask For Jenny, 12 In.Diam. | 20.00 |
| Tray, Gilt Edge Beer, Detroit, Patriotic Shield | 250.00 |
| Tray, Ginger Ale, 2 Blacks Serving Indian | 130.00 |
| Tray, Goodyear, Glass Top | 25.00 |
| Tray, Green River Whiskey, Black Man & Horse, 12 In.Diam. | 75.00 |
| Tray, Hampden, Handsome Waiter | 50.00 |
| Tray, Handen Beer & Ale, Willimansett, Mass. | 15.00 |
| Tray, Handley's, Providence, R.I., Old Man | 65.00 |
| Tray, Harvard Clipper Ale | 85.00 |
| Tray, Hedrick Ale & Lager, 16 In.Diam. | 15.00 |
| Tray, Heptol Splits, Cowboy On Bucking Branco, 1904 | 125.00 |
| Tray, Highlander Beer, 13 In.Diam. | 11.00 |
| Tray, Hittleman Goldenrod Brewery, C.1920, Oval | 120.00 |
| Tray, Hohenadel, Monk's Watchdog Smoking Cigar | 55.00 |
| Tray, Howel's Root Beer | 25.00 |
| Tray, Hull's Cream Ale Light Beer, New Haven, Conn. | 10.00 |
| Tray, Hull's Export Beer, Always Brewery Fresh | 12.50 |
| Tray, Imperial Ice Cream, Woman Eating Ice Cream, 1921 | 110.00 |
| Tray, Jack Daniel's Whiskey, Oval | 18.00 |
| Tray, Jax Beer, Pictures Gen.Jackson On Horse | 75.00 |
| Tray, Jersey Creme, Profile Of Pretty Girl With Bonnet, 12 In.Diam. | 250.00 |
| Tray, Kaier's, Smart Buyers Call For Kaier's | 15.00 |
| Tray, Kaier's, Star Of Excellence | 17.50 |
| Tray, Kansas City Breweries Co. | 300.00 |
| Tray, Kimballs Ice Cream, Blonde Girl Holding Tray | 110.00 |
| Tray, King's Bohemian Beer, Boston, 14 In. | 15.00 |
| Tray, Kruger Pilsner | 8.00 |
| Tray, Lawrence Welk & Alice In 1914 Dodge | 37.50 |
| Tray, Leinenkugel, Pictures Chippewa Indian, 1930 | 75.00 |
| Tray, Lemp, Sir Falstaff Holding Stein, 15 In. | 145.00 |
| Tray, Liberty Co., Seltzer Bottle | 10.00 |
| Tray, Loewers, King Holding Goblet | 110.00 |
| Tray, Mexican Beer, Spanish Writing, Girl In Bathing Suit, 16 In.Diam. | 15.00 |
| Tray, Miller High Life Beer, Lady In Quarter Moon | 36.50 To 65.00 |
| Tray, Millers Beer, 1907 | 175.00 |
| Tray, Moore Ice Cream, Boy, Girl Eating, 1915 | 125.00 |
| Tray, New Haven Ice Cream, Rose O'Neill Kewpies, Blowing Bubbles | 155.00 |
| Tray, Old Barbee Whiskey, Man, Old Cabin, 2 Ladies, 1905 | 125.00 |
| Tray, Old Grimes Whiskey, Man Drinks Toast, 1905 | 125.00 |
| Tray, Old Pepper Whiskey, Soldier Drinking, Red, White, Blue Flag | 225.00 |
| Tray, Olympia Beer, Girl On Bottle | 5.00 |
| Tray, Olympia, Cavalier Holding Bottle | 225.00 |

Tray, Olympia, Cavalier Pouring Drink ............................................. 155.00
Tray, Orange Crush Soda, Ask For A Crush, 14 In. ............................. 15.00
Tray, Orange Julep, Girl In Green Bathing Suit ................................. 150.00
Tray, Oxcart Dry Beer, 14 In.Diam. .................................................... 25.00
Tray, Pabst, Man Serving ................................................................... 55.00
Tray, Pabst, 2 Medieval Elves In Cellar, Oval, 18 1/2 In. ................. 245.00
Tray, Pacific Beer, 1912, Mountain Scene ........................................ 50.00
Tray, Paul Beer, Bremen, Pretty Girl Picture .................................... 45.00
Tray, Pepsi-Cola, Beach Scene ........................................ 15.00 To 20.00
Tray, Pepsi-Cola, Bigger & Better ..................................................... 20.00
Tray, Pepsi-Cola, Victorian Woman By Soda Bar, 1900 .................. 450.00
Tray, Pfieffers, 3 Monks Drinking ............................... 175.00 To 195.00
Tray, Phoenix Beer, Pre-Prohibition ................................................. 150.00
Tray, Pickwick Ale & Beer .................................................................. 30.00
Tray, Piel's, Pictures Elf Holding Glass ............................................ 55.00
Tray, Pin, Doe-Wah-Jack .................................................................... 15.00
Tray, Pure Milk Ice Cream, Giant Milk Bottle, 1900 ........................ 110.00
Tray, Rainier Beer, Seattle, Washington, Cowgirl On Horse ............ 295.00
Tray, Ranier Beer, Lady & Bear ......................................................... 250.00
Tray, Red Raven, Bird & Bottle .......................................................... 75.00
Tray, Red Raven, Naked Little Girl .................................................... 75.00
Tray, Red Raven, Red Bird & Bottle, 12 In.Diam. ............................. 75.00
Tray, Red Raven, Woman Hugging Raven, 1900 ................................ 125.00
Tray, Red Ribbon, Bear Inspecting Beer Case .................................. 225.00
Tray, Remember The Maine, Battleship Maine .................................. 100.00
Tray, Rheingold Extra Dry Lager Beer ............................................... 10.00
Tray, Rockford Watches, Picture Of Lady, Rectangular .................... 75.00
Tray, Ruthstaller Beer, Factory Scene, C.1910 ................................. 275.00
Tray, Schaefer Beer ............................................................................ 7.50
Tray, Schlitz Malt Liquor, 16 In.Diam. ............................................... 7.00
Tray, Schmidts Of Phila., 16 In. ........................................................ 10.00
Tray, Schuster's Root Beer, Boy, Girl, Dog, Drinking, 1920 ............. 175.00
Tray, Shafer, Red, White, & Gold, 12 In.Diam. .................................. 8.00
Tray, Sonora Brewery, Factory Truck & Cars, Mexican .................... 145.00
Tray, Star, Girl In Red Suit By Horse ................................................. 175.00
Tray, Stegmaier, Brunette, Low-Cut Dress, 1904 ............................. 145.00
Tray, Sunshine Beer, Black & Gold, 12 In.Diam. ............................... 60.00
Tray, Teacher's Highland Cream Whiskey, Engraved Copper, 12 In. . 15.00
Tray, Tip, A.B.Co., Brewers, Robin Hood Ale, Scranton, Pa. ............ 45.00
Tray, Tip, American Beauty ................................................................. 20.00
Tray, Tip, American Line ..................................................................... 125.00
Tray, Tip, American Ocean Lines, Lithographed Ocean Liner ........... 45.00
Tray, Tip, Anheuser-Busch .................................................................. 85.00
Tray, Tip, Anti-Kamnia Tablets, Wording .......................................... 30.00
Tray, Tip, Barthalomay ........................................................................ 115.00
Tray, Tip, Beck's Beer, American Eagle ............................................. 48.00
Tray, Tip, Big Jo Flour ........................................................................ 35.00
Tray, Tip, Black Angus Scotch ........................................................... 16.00
Tray, Tip, Broadway, Buffalo, N.Y. ..................................................... 90.00
Tray, Tip, Buffalo Brewing Co., California ......................................... 175.00
Tray, Tip, Centennial Beer, Seminude On Mountaintop .................... 55.00
Tray, Tip, Century Of Progress, Chicago, 1933 ................................. 15.00
Tray, Tip, Century, Trinidad, Colorado .............................................. 125.00
Tray, Tip, Champagne Velvet .............................................................. 140.00
Tray, Tip, Columbus Brewing, Picture Of Columbus ........................ 65.00
Tray, Tip, Cortez Cigars For Men Of Brains ...................................... 18.00
Tray, Tip, Cottonlene Shortening, Negroes Picking Cotton .............. 48.00
Tray, Tip, Davenport Malting Co. ....................................................... 100.00
Tray, Tip, DeLaval .............................................................................. 75.00
Tray, Tip, Diehl, Lady, 3 1/2 In.Diam. ................................................ 30.00
Tray, Tip, Dixie Queen Plug Cut, Cows In Stream, Signed ............... 20.00
Tray, Tip, Don Fino Cigar ................................................................... 24.00
Tray, Tip, Dr.Pepper .......................................................................... 50.00

Tray, Tip, El Verso Cigars, Man In Chair Smoking ........ 48.00
Tray, Tip, Elgin Hats, Brunette In Low-Cut Dress ........ 48.00
Tray, Tip, Fairy Soap, Girl Sitting On Soap ........ 25.00 To 65.00
Tray, Tip, Fairy Soap, Little Girl Holding Violets ........ 55.00
Tray, Tip, Feigenspan, Lady, Swimsuit ........ 40.00
Tray, Tip, Franklin Life Insurance ........ 12.50
Tray, Tip, Grainbelt Beer, Round ........ 35.00
Tray, Tip, Heptol Splits, Cowboy On Bucking Bronco, 1904 ........ 48.00
Tray, Tip, Hyroler Whiskey, Gentleman In Evening Dress, 4 In. ........ 45.00
Tray, Tip, Indianapolis Brewing, Gold Medal Beer Bottle, 4 In.Diam. ........ 50.00
Tray, Tip, Iroquois Beer, Indian Chief ........ 55.00
Tray, Tip, Jenney Aero Gasoline, Old Cars & Plane ........ 40.00
Tray, Tip, Kentucky Tavern ........ 10.00
Tray, Tip, King's Pure Malt ........ 30.00 To 50.00
Tray, Tip, Knickerbocker, 3 In. ........ 5.00
Tray, Tip, Lehnert's Beer, Portrait Of Gypsy Girl ........ 75.00
Tray, Tip, Lehnert's Beer, 1907 ........ 55.00
Tray, Tip, Lehnert's, Catasququa, Pa. ........ 100.00
Tray, Tip, Lewis 66 Whiskey, Man Drinking, Eating Lobster ........ 45.00
Tray, Tip, Marilyn Monroe ........ 18.00 To 45.00
Tray, Tip, Miller Beer, 1950s, Set Of 3 ........ 18.00
Tray, Tip, Miller's, Birds ........ 5.00
Tray, Tip, Monticello Whiskey ........ 35.00
Tray, Tip, Moroney Whiskey ........ 40.00
Tray, Tip, Moxie, Girl Holding Glass, 1900, 6 In. ........ 86.00
Tray, Tip, National Cigar Stands Co. ........ 80.00
Tray, Tip, Northampton Brewing ........ 125.00
Tray, Tip, Nulife, Sioux City, Iowa ........ 175.00
Tray, Tip, Oconto Brewing Co. ........ 125.00
Tray, Tip, Oertel's Brewery, Purity ........ 60.00
Tray, Tip, Old Schenly ........ 15.00
Tray, Tip, Ortlieb's Brewery ........ 75.00
Tray, Tip, Parsley Brand Salmon ........ 38.00
Tray, Tip, Pepsi-Cola, Compliments Of ........ 10.00
Tray, Tip, Pepsi, 1908 ........ 800.00
Tray, Tip, Prudential Life Insurance ........ 9.00 To 15.00
Tray, Tip, Quandt's Beer ........ 20.00
Tray, Tip, Quick Meal Ranges, Baby Chicks After Bee ........ 48.00
Tray, Tip, Rainier Beer, 1909 ........ 45.00
Tray, Tip, Red Raven Splits, 2 Birds With Bottle ........ 48.00
Tray, Tip, Robert Burns Cigars ........ 35.00
Tray, Tip, Rock Island Brewery ........ 40.00
Tray, Tip, Rockford Watches, Pretty Girl, C.1910 ........ 65.00
Tray, Tip, Round Oak, Michigan ........ 8.50
Tray, Tip, Ruhstaller, Waitress ........ 65.00
Tray, Tip, Ryan's, Syracuse ........ 75.00
Tray, Tip, Sears Roebuck Co. ........ 30.00
Tray, Tip, Sen-Sen ........ 14.00
Tray, Tip, Simon Pure ........ 15.00
Tray, Tip, Stag Tobaccos, Oval, Tin ........ 22.00
Tray, Tip, Success, Manure Spreader Machine ........ 35.00
Tray, Tip, Tam O'Shanter Ale ........ 125.00
Tray, Tip, Tom Moore Cigars, Portrait In Center ........ 35.00
Tray, Tip, Union Brewing Co., Peoria, Ill. ........ 75.00
Tray, Tip, Urbana Wine Co., Bottle & Grapes, 4 1/2 X 6 1/2 In. ........ 45.00
Tray, Tip, Wellsbach Lighting, Mother & Child In Home ........ 48.00
Tray, Tip, West End Brewing Co, Miss Liberty On Tray ........ 75.00
Tray, Tip, White Rock Table Water, Seminude On Rock ........ 48.00
Tray, Tip, Yuengling's Beer, Girl With Big Hat ........ 42.00
Tray, Tip, Zipp's Extracts ........ 100.00
Tray, Trommers Malt Beer, 16 In. ........ 25.00
Tray, Utica Club Beer ........ 16.00
Tray, Utica Club, New York, Factory ........ 40.00

Tray, Vani Kola, Girl With Horse, 1904, Oval ................................................................ 135.00 To 175.00
Tray, Weatherly Ice Cream, Lady, Fur Hat & Stole, Holly, 1925 ................................ 155.00
Tray, Webco Natural Beer ............................................................................................ 10.00
Tray, Wehle Mule Hard ................................................................................................ 35.00
Tray, Weinhard, Portland, Table Scene ...................................................................... 130.00
Tray, Westend Liberty Girl, Pre-Prohibition .............................................................. 395.00
Tray, Westside, Viking Holding Stein .......................................................................... 155.00
Tray, William Peter Palisade Beer, Oval, River Scene .............................................. 215.00
Tray, Yellowstone Whiskey, Bottle By Waterfall, 1910 ............................................ 150.00
Tray, Yosemite Beer, Cowgirl Hugging Horse, A Winner .......................................... 165.00
Tumbler, Moxie, Embossed ........................................................................................ 12.00
Whistle, Figural, Shoe, Robin Hood ............................................................................ 12.00
Whistle, Mr.Peanut ...................................................................................................... 15.00
STOVE, Alcohol, Brass, Round, Small ........................................................................ 15.00
Bridge Beach & Co., Iron ............................................................................................ 1250.00
Buddy Stove, Coal & Wood, Green Porcelain Front, 1940s ...................................... 125.00
E-Z Way, 3 Burner, 3 Warming Burners, Kerosene, 21 X 12 In. .............................. 60.00
No.18, Round, Oak ...................................................................................................... 425.00
Potbelly, Railroad, Depot ............................................................................................ 1100.00
Quick Meal, Ornate Brass, Enamel & Nickle Plated .................................................. 300.00
Riverside, Brass Top, Heating, Cast Iron, 5 Ft. ........................................................ 100.00
Round Oak, No.14, Wood-Burning, Nickel Skirt, Finial, 51 In. ................................ 750.00
Saratoga Wood Burner, 1853, Warren, Sweetland & Little, Crescent, N.Y. ............ 150.00
Treadwell & Perry, New York, Parlor, C.1845, 4 1/3 X 2 Ft. 10 1/4 In. .................. 650.00
Vanwormer McGarvey, Albany, N.Y., Parlor, Cast Iron, 4 Ft. 8 In. .......................... 250.00
     STRAWBERRY, see Soft Paste

STRETCH GLASS, Bonbon, Covered, Green ................................................................ 30.00
Bowl, Black Glass Stand, Blue Iridescent, 10 In.Diam. .............................................. 55.00
Bowl, Blue, Rolled Rim, 8 In.Diam. ............................................................................ 28.00
Bowl, Console, Clear, 12 In.Diam. .............................................................................. 8.00
Bowl, Fruit, Blue, 9 1/2 In. .......................................................................................... 20.00
Bowl, Ice Green, 10 In. ................................................................................................ 30.00
Bowl, Pink, 10 In.Diam. .............................................................................................. 35.00
Bowl, Red, 8 1/2 In. .................................................................................................... 80.00
Bowl, Vaseline, 6 1/2 In. ............................................................................................ 12.50
Candlestick, Baluster Shape, Blue, 10 In., Pair .......................................................... 45.00
Candlestick, Console Base, Amethyst, 7 In., Pair ...................................................... 50.00
Compote, Blue Opaque, 7 1/4 X 3 1/2 In. .................................................................. 20.00
Compote, Covered, Iridescent Vaseline, 9 In. ............................................................ 35.00
Compote, Open, Ribbed & Scalloped, Blue, 7 X 6 1/2 In. .......................................... 25.00
Compote, Scalloped, Lemon Yellow, 7 1/2 X 4 In. .................................................... 35.00
Dish, Candy, Covered, Purple ...................................................................................... 45.00
Goblet, Iridescent Blue, Red Interior, 8 1/2 In. .......................................................... 18.00
Jar, Candy, Covered, Northwood, Topaz, 9 In. .......................................................... 45.00
Parfait, Fluted, Aqua, 5 1/2 X 5 1/2 In. ...................................................................... 22.00
Plate, Flanged Base, 8 1/4 In., Set Of 4 .................................................................... 38.50
Plate, Pierced Border, Hand-Painted Violets, White, 8 In. ........................................ 16.00
Plate, Red, 8 In. .......................................................................................................... 49.00
Plate, Red, 10 In. ........................................................................................................ 90.00
Plate, Serving, Center Handle, Gold Trim .................................................................. 16.00
Tumble-Up, Blue, 6 3/4 In. .......................................................................................... 45.00
Tumble-Up, Iridescent Pink ........................................................................................ 25.00
Tumble-Up, White Pitcher & Tumbler, Cobalt Blue Handle ........................................ 85.00
Vase, Blue Over White, Clear Blue Cased, Handle, 8 1/4 In. .................................... 28.00
Vase, Bud, Iridescent Green, 12 In. ............................................................................ 28.00
Vase, Fan, Blue, 6 In. .................................................................................. 25.00 To 30.00
Vase, Flared Rim, Blue, 7 X 5 In. ................................................................................ 28.00

*Sunbonnet Babies were first introduced in 1902 in the Sunbonnet Babies*
*Primer. The stories were by Eulalie Osgood Grover, illustrated by*
*Bertha Corbett. The children's faces were completely hidden by the*

*sunbonnets, and had been pictured in black and white before this time. The color pictures in the book were immediately successful. The Royal Bayreuth China Company made a full line of children's dishes decorated with the Sunbonnet Babies.*

| | |
|---|---:|
| **SUNBONNET BABIES, Book,** Diane's, Rag | 35.00 |
| **Book,** In Holland, Grover, 1915 | 85.00 |
| **Bookends** | 55.00 |
| **Bowl,** Cereal, Fishing | 125.00 |
| **Box,** Dresser, Covered, 4 1/2 In. | 90.00 |
| **Candlestick,** Mending, Pair | 135.00 |
| **Card,** Set Of 4 | 12.00 |
| **Card,** Seven Days Of The Week, Set Of 7 | 20.00 |
| **Coverlet,** 28 Squares, Pink Framing, White Ruffle | 150.00 |
| **Creamer,** Wash Day, Bulbous, Royal Bayreuth, 2 1/2 In. | 135.00 |
| **Creamer,** Wash Day, 4 In. | 150.00 |
| **Cup & Saucer,** Christmas, 1910, Sunday School Name In Gold | 35.00 |
| **Dish,** Child's, Sweeping, 4 1/2 In. | 110.00 To 135.00 |
| **Hanger,** Plant, Girls Pouring From Can, Wooden, 12 In., Pair | 45.00 |
| **Hatpin Holder,** Signed Royal Bayreuth, Blue Mark, 4 3/4 In. | 300.00 |
| **Mug,** Royal Bayreuth, Blue Mark, 3 In. | 115.00 |
| **Paperweight,** Kissed By Boy, Base, 3 1/4 In. | 32.00 |
| **Pitcher,** Cleaning, 4 In. | 95.00 |
| **Pitcher,** Doing Wash, 3 3/5 In. | 150.00 |
| **Plate,** Cake, Blue Mark, 10 3/4 In. | 245.00 |
| **Plate,** Ironing, Blue Mark, 9 In. | 160.00 |
| **Plate,** Ironing, 7 1/2 In. | 110.00 To 150.00 |
| **Plate,** Sewing, 7 In. | 25.00 |
| **Plate,** Washing, Blue Mark, 7 1/2 In. | 80.00 To 100.00 |
| **Plate,** 8 In. | 110.00 |
| **Postcard,** Summer, Winter, 1907, Pair | 22.00 |
| **Print,** All Days Of The Week, 1905, Original Frame | 100.00 |
| **Print,** Wash Day, Signed, Dated | 35.00 |
| **Sugar,** Fishing, Royal Bayreuth, Blue Mark | 125.00 |
| **Toothpick,** Sewing, Gold Handle, 3 1/8 X 2 1/2 In.Diam. | 95.00 |
| **Vase,** Sweeping, Handled, 2 3/4 X 2 3/4 In. | 110.00 |

*Sunderland luster is a name given to a characteristic pink luster made by Leeds, Newcastle, and other English firms during the nineteenth century. The luster glaze is metallic and glossy and sometimes appears to have bubbles as a decoration.*

| | |
|---|---:|
| **SUNDERLAND, Cup & Saucer,** Pink Luster, Grape Leaves, C.1840 | 40.00 |
| **Cup & Saucer,** Pink Luster, Orange & Yellow Balls, C.1820 | 40.00 |
| **Mustache Cup & Saucer,** Pink Luster, Sailing Ship & Prayer | 110.00 |
| **Mustache Cup,** Saucer, Sailing Ship Front, Poem On Back, Pink | 165.00 |
| **Pitcher,** Luster Lining, 5 In. | 65.00 |
| **Pitcher,** Luster, Wearmouth Bridge, C.1825, 5 1/2 X 5 In.Diam. | 200.00 |
| **Pitcher,** Pad Feet, Pink Luster, 4 In. | 60.00 |
| **Plaque,** Copper Luster, The Farmer's Arms, Scene & Poem, 8 X 9 In. | 135.00 |
| **Plaque,** Wall, Farmer's Prayer, 19th Century, 8 X 9 In. | 125.00 |
| **Plate,** Luster, 6 3/4 In. | 35.00 |
| **Plate,** Pink Splash Luster, 5 1/4 In.Diam. | 22.00 |
| **Plate,** Pink Splash Luster, 7 1/4 In.Diam. | 28.00 |
| **Tumbler,** Luster, 2 1/2 In. | 50.00 |
| **Tureen,** Luster, Underplate, Ladle, View Of Iron Bridge, 1793 | 500.00 |

| | |
|---|---:|
| **SUPERMAN, Bank,** China | 65.00 |
| **Card Game,** Ideal | 12.00 |
| **Costume,** Child's, 1940s | 55.00 |
| **Crayon By Numbers Set,** 1954, Boxed | 65.00 |
| **Doll,** Wood Jointed, 1940s, 12 In. | 395.00 |
| **Game,** In Original Box, 1940s | 90.00 |

| | |
|---|---|
| Krypto Ray Gun | 125.00 |
| **Mug,** 1964 | 6.00 |
| **Pin,** Kellogg's Pep Premium | 15.00 |
| **Puzzle,** Jigsaw, Boxed, 1940 | 25.00 |
| **Reel,** Photograph, 5 Films, Original Box | 135.00 |
| **Valentine,** 1940 | 10.00 |

| | |
|---|---|
| **SWORD, Dress,** Trenton, N.J., 1863, Signed Emerson & Silver | 85.00 |
| **History On Handle,** Mutsu No Kami Daimichi, C.1661 | 365.00 |
| **Military,** Sheath, Chilean | 95.00 |
| **Spanish Officer's,** Brass Guard, Sharkskin Grip, 1871 | 125.00 |
| **U.S.Navy,** Boarding Cutlass | 200.00 |

*Syracuse is a trademark used by the Onondaga Pottery of Syracuse, New York. The firm was established in 1871. It is still working.*

| | |
|---|---|
| **SYRACUSE, Cake Plate,** Wayne, Blue | 30.00 |
| **Luncheon Set,** Wayne, 48 Piece | 275.00 |
|     **TAFFETA GLASS, see Carnival Glass** | |
|     **TANKARD, see Stein** | |
|     **TAPESTRY, PORCELAIN, see Rose Tapestry** | |
|     **TEA CADDY, see Furniture, Tea Caddy** | |
| **TEA LEAF IRONSTONE, Bowl,** Oblong, 9 1/2 In. | 45.00 |
| **Butter Pat,** Luster, 3 In.Diam. | 9.50 |
| **Compote,** Open, Handled, Crow's-Foot, 6 X 9 1/2 In.Diam. | 60.00 |
| **Cup & Saucer,** Handleless, Copper Luster Band, 3 3/8 In. | 22.00 |
| **Dish,** Bone, Set Of 6 | 360.00 |
| **Pitcher & Bowl,** Copper Luster Band | 250.00 |
| **Pitcher,** 7 In. | 75.00 |
| **Plate,** Copper Luster Band, C.1897, 6 3/4 In. | 13.00 |
| **Plate,** Copper Luster Band, Leaf In Well, C.1897, 8 In. | 22.00 |
| **Plate,** Luster, Copper, 8 In. | 12.00 |
| **Plate,** Mellor Taylor | 15.00 |
| **Plate,** 2-Handled, Square, 8 3/4 In. | 65.00 |
| **Plate,** 8 3/4 In. | 17.50 |
| **Platter,** Luster, 13 1/2 X 10 In. | 25.00 |
| **Platter,** Luster, 15 1/2 X 11 1/4 In. | 35.00 |
| **Platter,** Wedgwood & Co., 10 X 13 In. | 30.00 |
| **Platter,** 15 In. | 100.00 |
| **Saucer** | 12.00 |
| **Teapot,** Luster | 80.00 |

*Teco pottery is the art pottery line made by the Terra Cotta Tile Works of Terra Cotta, Illinois. The company was founded by William D.Gates in 1881. The Teco line was first made in 1902 and continued into the 1920s. It included over 500 designs, made in a variety of colors, shapes, and glazes.*

| | |
|---|---|
| **TECO, Vase,** Apple Green Matte, Urn Form Body, Buttress Handles, 15 1/2 In. | 950.00 |
| **Vase,** Blue-Green, Square Form, Pierced Stem Feet, Impressed, 13 In. | 450.00 |

| | |
|---|---|
| **TELEPHONE, Ashtray,** New York Telephone Co., Telephone On Top, Green & White | 15.00 |
| **Booth,** Embossed Tin Interiors, Oak | 650.00 |
| **Candlestick,** American Telephone & Telegraph Co.Original Cabinet | 275.00 |
| **Candlestick,** Generator & Crank, Oak Box | 75.00 |
| **Candlestick,** Kellogg, Con-Dial | 75.00 |
| **Candlestick,** Kellogg, Jax Plug, Brass | 85.00 |
| **Candlestick,** Montgomery Ward | 100.00 |
| **Candlestick,** Western Electric, Dial | 150.00 |
| **Cradle Type,** Stromberg, Carlson, Built-In Magneto, Crank, C.1930 | 50.00 |

**Crank,** Gray Mfg., Patent 1911, Coin Operated ....................................................... 700.00
**Desk,** Black, With Crank ................................................................................................ 25.00
**Dialstick,** Original Finish, Brass ................................................................................ 125.00
**Double Box,** Wall, Oak ............................................................................................... 140.00
**Earpiece,** Metal, Nickel & Hard Rubber, Pair ....................................................... 100.00
**Hand Crank,** Coin Operated, Patent 1911, Gray Mfg. ........................................... 700.00
**Kellogg,** Candlestick, Black, 1901-07 ........................................................................ 50.00
**Kellogg,** Patent 1890, Complete ............................................................................... 125.00
**Marked Rock Island Telegraph** ................................................................................ 175.00
**Pay,** Chrome, Key, 1949 ............................................................................................... 65.00
**Portable,** Forest Service, Model C ............................................................................. 35.00
**Sign,** Emergency Telephone, Black & White, 5 X 5 In. ............................................ 10.00
**Sign,** Public Telephone Bell System, 7 In.Diam. ...................................................... 15.00
**Stick,** Headset, C.1892, Black Over Brass ................................................................. 75.00
**Stick,** Oak Bell Box With Crank, 7 X 9 In. ............................................................... 110.00
**Switchboard,** C.1900, Oak ......................................................................................... 150.00
**Switchboard,** Tabletop, Cherry Case ....................................................................... 240.00
**Wall,** Monarch, Oak ................................................................................................... 250.00
**Wall,** Swedish-American & Hercules, Batteries, C.1879 ........................................ 225.00
**Wall,** Western Electric, Oak ...................................................................................... 175.00

**TELEVISION, General Electric,** Table Model, Bakelite, 1948, Screen, 10 In. ............ 75.00

 Teplitz refers to art pottery manufactured by a number of companies in the Teplitz-Turn area of Bohemia during the late nineteenth and early twentieth centuries. The Amphora Porcelain Works and the Alexandra Works were two of these companies.

**TEPLITZ, Basket,** Angels & Garland Of Rosettes, High Glaze, 15 X 11 In.Diam. ...................... 550.00
**Basket,** Cherubs On Limbs, Gold & Red Accent, 8 X 8 1/2 In.Diam. .................................... 750.00
**Basket,** Figural, Cupid ................................................................................................ 265.00
**Bowl,** Amphora, 4-Handled, Enameled Poppies, Signed, 9 X 8 In. ..................................... 265.00
**Bowl,** Green To Dusty Pink, Purple Iridized, Gold, 5 X 3 In. ............................................. 135.00
**Bowl,** Rooster Sitting In Center, Feathers Form Back, 10 In. .............................................. 395.00
**Bowl,** Rose Briar, Pheasant, Beige Ground, Marked, 7 1/2 X 3 1/2 In. .............................. 115.00
**Canister Set,** Bluebirds, Porcelain, Marked, 8 Piece ...................................................... 80.00
**Centerpiece,** Portrait Of Maiden, Amphora, 10 In. ..............................................*Illus* 1200.00
**Compote,** Double Handles, Applied Blackberries, Imperial Mark ...................................... 190.00
**Ewer,** Purple, Blue, Yellow Floral, Beige Ground, 12 1/2 In. ............................................. 95.00
**Figurine,** Amphora, Rider Kidnapping Cub, Lioness Attacking Camel ................................. 725.00
**Figurine,** Camel Rider, Arab Sitting Playing Lyre, 9 X 12 In. ............................................. 675.00
**Figurine,** Colonial Lady, Flowers At Base, 16 In., Pair ..................................................... 750.00
**Figurine,** Farm Girl Bends To Pick Up Basket, Signed, 9 In. .............................................. 325.00
**Figurine,** Hawk, Marked, 12 In. .................................................................................. 250.00
**Figurine,** Hen, Stands By Broken Egg, Round Base ........................................................ 195.00
**Figurine,** Lady At Small Fountain, Signed, 12 In. ........................................................... 295.00
**Mug,** 2 Foxes, 5 3/4 In. ................................................................................................. 75.00
**Pitcher,** Floral Design, Gold Overlay, Crown Mark, C.1900, 7 In. ....................................... 145.00
**Pitcher,** Flowers, Blue Ground, Italian Green, 9 In. ......................................................... 115.00
**Pitcher,** Milk, Amphora, Figural Leaves, White Flowers, Marked, 5 In. ................................ 40.00
**Rose Bowl,** Amphora, Pebble Surface, Enameled Poppies, 4 3/4 In. ................................... 85.00
**Vase,** Applied Blossoms, 22 In. ................................................................................... 295.00
**Vase,** Applied Roses, Gold Trim, Green Ground, 13 In. .................................................... 195.00
**Vase,** Applied Yellow Roses, Signed, Amphora, 8 In. ....................................................... 69.50
**Vase,** Art Deco, Owls, Cobalt Blue Top & Bottom, Handled, 10 In. .................................... 230.00
**Vase,** Bird Heads Around Body, Raised Deco Design, Gold Trim, 9 In. ............................... 245.00
**Vase,** Blooming Thistle Plant, Enameled, Gilding & Jewels, 6 In. ....................................... 185.00
**Vase,** Blue Glazed Jewels, Green & Beige, Imperial Mark, 9 In. ........................................ 129.00
**Vase,** Blue, Orange, Green, Black, & Brown Birds, Blue Oval Mark, 6 In. ............................ 295.00
**Vase,** Border Ducks, Gold Cattails, Signed, Oval Mark, 8 1/2 In. ...................................... 200.00
**Vase,** Classical Design, Relief Animals, Blue & Green, Signed, 12 In. ................................ 165.00
**Vase,** Cobalt Blue, Gold Trim, 11 In. ............................................................................. 135.00

**Vase,** Double Figures, Girl Feeds Sea Lion, Imperial Mark, 5 In. ............................................. 210.00
**Vase,** Drummer In Colored Enamel, Green Ground, 2-Handled, 4 3/4 In. .............................. 110.00
**Vase,** Embossed Village Scene, Girl With Ducks, 7 1/2 In.Diam. ....................................... 125.00
**Vase,** Enameled Bird, 11 In. ............................................................................................... 85.00
**Vase,** Enameled Classical Figures, Textured Ground, 10 1/2 In. ....................................... 235.00
**Vase,** Enameled Inlaid Gentleman In Knickers & Cape, 7 In. ........................................... 80.00
**Vase,** Enameled Minstrel Man, Handled, Amphora Mark ................................................... 110.00
**Vase,** Enameled Musketeer In Green Jacket, 2-Handled, 4 1/2 In. ................................... 55.00
**Vase,** Farm Woman With White Goose, 3-Handled, Signed, 10 In. ................................... 75.00
**Vase,** Gold Accented Top, 3 Bird Heads, Embossed Deco Design, 9 In. .......................... 245.00
**Vase,** Gold Ground, Jeweled Flowers, Signed, 19 1/2 In. ................................................ 395.00
**Vase,** Gold Iridescent, Applied Leaves, Jewels, 19 In. .................................................... 349.00
**Vase,** Gold Webbing, Birds In Flight, Iridescent Ground, 8 1/2 In. .................................. 210.00
**Vase,** Gold, Jeweled Bull's-Eyes, Blue Enamel, Signed, 10 In. ....................................... 249.00
**Vase,** Gourd Shape, Young Woman's Portrait, Signed, Amphora, 6 1/4 In. ...................... 595.00
**Vase,** Gray Green Flowers In Relief, Handled, Signed, 10 In. ........................................... 150.00
**Vase,** Greek Woman On Knees, Satin Blue, Huge Bird, 8 1/2 In. ..................................... 190.00
**Vase,** Hand-Painted Musician & Instrument, Glazed, 7 1/4 In. ........................................ 125.00
**Vase,** Handled, Art Deco, Stylized Duck, Brown Ground, 3 1/2 In. .................................. 145.00
**Vase,** Indian Design, Double Handled, 5 3/4 In. .............................................................. 110.00
**Vase,** Iridescent Center, Colored Ducks In Flight, 8 1/2 In. ............................................ 225.00
**Vase,** Iridescent Cobwebs, Jewels, 9 In. ........................................................................ 175.00
**Vase,** Lavender Flower Trim, Green, Yellow, & Cream, Signed, 8 In. ............................... 80.00
**Vase,** Leaf Design, 4-Handled, Crown Mark, 12 In. ......................................................... 100.00
**Vase,** Leaves, Beaded, Cream, Gold, Elephant Handles, Amphora, 11 In. ....................... 319.00
**Vase,** Molded Ribbed Bulbous Body, Blue & Green Glaze ............................................... 25.00
**Vase,** Multicolored Enameled Drummer, Double Handle, 8 In. ......................................... 110.00
**Vase,** Multicolored Enameled Drummer, 5 In. .................................................................. 110.00
**Vase,** Musician In Full Color, Handled, Amphora Mark, 7 1/2 In. ..................................... 120.00
**Vase,** Opening Drips To Clusters Of Grapes, Pearlized, Amphora, 9 In. .......................... 189.00
**Vase,** Openwork Rim, Gold Trimmed, Garlands, Signed, Turin, 15 In. ............................. 125.00
**Vase,** Pinecone Design, Gold & Mauve, Signed .............................................................. 350.00
**Vase,** Pink Flowers, High Relief, Green Ground, 10 In., Pair ............................................ 285.00
**Vase,** Portrait Of Maiden,    8 In. ..................................................................... *Illus* 950.00
**Vase,** Red Poppies, Buds, Painted Collar, Ivory Ground, 11 In. ....................................... 275.00
**Vase,** Reticulated Flowers Top Neck, Art Nouveau Handles, 11 In. .................................. 250.00

Teplitz, from left to right, Vase, Portrait Of Maiden; Centerpiece, Portrait Of Maiden, Amphora

| | |
|---|---|
| **Vase,** Rooster, Blue, 2-Handled, Amphora, 7 1/2 X 9 In. | 98.00 |
| **Vase,** Standing Lion & Shield Design, Amphora, 9 In. | 175.00 |
| **Vase,** Sunrise Scene, Purple & Gold, Signed | 225.00 |
| **Vase,** Thistle Design, Red, Green, & Gold, Relief Foliage, Large | 225.00 |
| **Vase,** 3-Figural, Boy & Girl Pulling On Doll, 13 In. | 495.00 |
| **Vase,** 4 Bottom Handles, Art Deco Birds, Imperial Mark, 7 1/2 In. | 169.00 |

| | |
|---|---|
| **TERRA-COTTA, Ashtray,** Square | 40.00 |
| **Bust,** Madame Recamier, 19th Century, Joseph Chinard, 23 In. | 500.00 |
| **Figurine,** Barefooted Black Boy & Girl, 1850 Mark, 8 In., Pair | 100.00 |
| **Pitcher,** Syrup, Egyptian Design, Pewter Lid, 8 In. | 145.00 |
| **Sphinx,** Large | 175.00 |

*Textile includes all types of table linens and household linens such as coverlets, quilts, fabrics, etc.*

| | |
|---|---|
| **TEXTILE, Bag,** Black Lace, Beaded, Olive, Pink, Blue, Turquoise, Metal Clasp | 250.00 |
| **Bag,** Stones, Beaded Overall In Floral Design | 90.00 |
| **Bathing Suit,** Man's, Wool, C.1920, Blue & White Stripes | 25.00 |
| **Bedspread,** Candlewick, Star In A Circle, 10 Ft.Square | 150.00 |
| **Bedspread,** Crocheted Medallions, Popcorn Stitch, Ecru, Double Size | 150.00 |
| **Bedspread,** Crocheted, Fringe, 76 X 110 In., Pair | 175.00 |
| **Bedspread,** Crocheted, Lord's Prayer, Twin Size | 150.00 |
| **Bedspread,** Crocheted, Popcorn Stitching, Scalloped, Double Size | 150.00 |
| **Bedspread,** Crocheted, Scalloped Edges, Star-Type Design, 96 X 96 In. | 125.00 |
| **Bedspread,** Crocheted, Star With Popcorn, C.1925, 84 X 108 In. | 150.00 |
| **Bedspread,** Crocheted, 6-Pointed Star, Full Size | 65.00 |
| **Bedspread,** Damask, Allover Cupids, French, C.1900, Twin Size, Pair | 35.00 |
| **Bedspread,** French Net & Lace, Single, Pair | 250.00 |
| **Bedspread,** Popcorn Diamonds, Crocheted, Ecru, Full Size | 90.00 |
| **Bedspread,** Popcorn Star, White, Crocheted, Double Size | 100.00 |
| **Bedspread,** Popcorn, 82 X 96 In. | 150.00 |
| **Blanket,** Homespun, Blue On Natural Wool, Twin Size, Pair | 225.00 |
| **Blanket,** Homespun, Brown, Blue, & Natural, Large | 145.00 |
| **Bodice,** Crocheted, Gigot Sleeves, Irish Lace, C.1905, Waist, 27 In. | 160.00 |
| **Bonnet,** Bashful Bonnet, Green, Silk, Collapsible, C.1790 | 85.00 |
| **Bonnet,** Lace Inserts, White | 6.00 |
| **Bookmark,** Rochester Exposition, 1909, Silk | 5.00 |
| **Bookmark,** Silk, Passaic Falls, Eagle & Flag, .R.M.G.S.C. | 75.00 |
| **Bookmark,** Woven Silk, Tassel, Birthday, British Mark | 25.00 |
| **Camisole,** Crocheted Lace | 6.00 |
| **Cap,** Boudoir, Satin & Crocheted Lace, Flapper | 8.00 |
| **Cap,** Duster, Lady's, Unused | 4.00 |
| **Cape,** Velvet, Sequined, Black, 3/4 Length | 35.00 |
| **Carpet,** Chinese, Art Deco, Camel's Hair, Flower Border, 14 X 10 Ft. | 8500.00 |
| **Carpet,** Spanish, Trellis Design, Polychrome Border, 24 X 12 Ft. | 600.00 |
| **Chair Set,** Crocheted, Pineapple Pattern, 3 Piece | 30.00 |
| **Coat,** Aquamarine Silk Damask, Lace Trimmed, 1910s | 250.00 |
| **Coat,** Christening, Victorian, Embroidered | 50.00 |
| **Coat,** Cutaway Front, Orange Wool, 1950s, Charles James | 425.00 |
| **Coat,** Evening, Periwinkle Blue, Panne Velvet, Blue Silk Lined, 1920s | 115.00 |
| **Coat,** Frock, Lt.Edwin Thomas, 13th Artillery, Civil War | 10.00 |
| **Coat,** Mandarin, C.1900 | 950.00 |
| **Coat,** Wool, Plush Trimmed, 1890 | 185.00 |
| **Cocktail Dress,** Strapless Bodice, Black Satin, 1950s, Mainbocher | 120.00 |
| **Collar & Cuffs,** Point D'angleterre Lace, 19th Century | 50.00 |
| **Combing Sacque,** Rose Silk, Band Of Gold At Neck, 1910s, London | 175.00 |
| **Costume,** Santa Claus, Jacket, Pants, Canvas Mask, Beard, 1920 | 25.00 |

*Linen or wool coverlets were made during the nineteenth century. Most of the coverlets date from 1800 to 1850. Four types were made, the double woven, jacquard, summer and winter, and overshot.*

Coverlet, Bird Pattern, Red, Blue, Green, & Brown, 76 X 72 In. .......................................... 320.00
Coverlet, Bird, Tulip Leaf & Urn Design, Red & Cream, 84 X 90 In. ........................................ 775.00
Coverlet, Brown & Beige, New England, 68 X 80 In. ................................................................ 135.00
Coverlet, Dated 1847, Red, Green & Blue ................................................................................ 475.00
Coverlet, Dated 1847, Signed J.Cunningham, Weaver, N.Hartford, N.Y. ................................. 850.00
Coverlet, Flowers & Bird In Corners, C.1850, Signed, 80 X 88 In. .......................................... 325.00
Coverlet, Frenchman's Fancy, Overshot Fringe, C.1820, 68 X 95 In. ....................................... 275.00
Coverlet, Genesee County, N.Y., Reversible, Blue & White, 1839, Double ............................... 300.00
Coverlet, Geometric Design, Blue & White, New England, 66 X 84 In. .................................... 175.00
Coverlet, Geometric Pattern, Blue, Tan, & Red, 80 X 104 In. .................................................. 275.00
Coverlet, Geometric Pattern, Overshot, Fringe, 66 X 94 In. ..................................................... 250.00
Coverlet, Geometric Pattern, Rusty Red & Natural, 72 X 99 In. .............................................. 170.00
Coverlet, Hired Man's Bed, Navy, Cedar, & White, Woven, 60 X 90 In. .................................... 85.00
Coverlet, Jacquard, Geometric Design, Signed, Dated 1839, 72 X 88 In. ............................... 550.00
Coverlet, Jacquard, John Jackson, 1841, Pennsylvania, 55 X 62 In. ....................................... 485.00
Coverlet, Jacquard, Varied Design, Red & White ................................................................... 550.00
Coverlet, Jaquard, Cupids, Flowers, Scrolls, Tassels, Wool, Double ........................................ 600.00
Coverlet, Multicolored Jacquard, 3/4 Size .............................................................................. 495.00
Coverlet, Overshot, Geometric Design, Blue & White, 66 X 90 In. .......................................... 100.00
Coverlet, Peacock In Corner, Signed 1846, Pennsylvania ....................................................... 475.00
Coverlet, Red, White Stripes, Blue Fields, White Stars, 7 1/5 Ft. ...........................................1200.00
Coverlet, Seamed Center, Nut Brown & Natural ..................................................................... 125.00
Coverlet, Snowball Pattern, Navy & White, 80 X 90 In. ........................................................... 455.00
Coverlet, Star Pattern, New England, C.1935, 96 In.Square .................................................... 275.00
Coverlet, Whig Rose Pattern, Double Woven, Reversible, 68 X 96 In. ...................................... 55.00
Coverlet, Wool & Linen, Milton Twsp., Ohio, C.1844 .............................................................. 495.00
Coverlet, Woven Churches, Schools On Edge, Signed, 1850, 86 X 68 In. ................................ 450.00
Coverlet, Yo-Yo Pattern, Pastels, Pink Trim & Lining, Double Size ........................................ 115.00
Curtains, Parlor, Lace, 4 Panels, C.1915 ................................................................................. 28.00
Dinner Suit, Black Cashmere Jacket, Satin Dress, 1950s, C.James ......................................... 200.00
Doll, Uncut, Soldiers, 1892, Arnold Print ................................................................................ 55.00
Dress, Beaded, Victorian, Long, 3 Piece, Size 3 ...................................................................... 25.00
Dress, Bergdorf-Goodman, Vionnet, Green Satin, C.1920 ............................................... *Illus* 500.00
Dress, Black Chiffon, Evening Gown, C.1911 .......................................................................... 150.00
Dress, Bride's, White Silk, Tulle Train, Beaded, C.1910, Size 10 ............................................ 95.00
Dress, Christening, Cotton ...................................................................................................... 12.00
Dress, Christening, Victorian, White ....................................................................................... 60.00
Dress, Evening, Beaded Green Chiffon, French, 1920s ...................................................*Illus* 190.00
Dress, Evening, Gold Lame, Henri Bendel, Bias Cut Dress & Cape, 1930s ............................. 150.00
Dress, Flapper, Beaded, Black ................................................................................................ 40.00

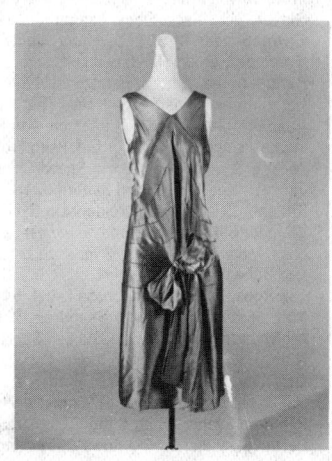

Textile, Dress, Bergdorf-Goodman,
Vionnet, Green Satin, C.1920

Textile, Dress, Evening, Beaded Green Chiffon, French, 1920s (See Page 657)

| | |
|---|---:|
| **Dress,** Flapper, Cotton Voile, Hand-Embroidered | 75.00 |
| **Dress,** Garden Party, White Organdy & Lace, 1910-15 | 65.00 |
| **Dress,** Georgette, Lace & Blue Trim, Floating Panels | 25.00 |
| **Dress,** Lace Peplum & Cuffs, Black Taffeta, Large | 25.00 |
| **Dress,** Silk Crepe, Navy Blue, Beaded, Peacock Eye Design, C.1919 | 300.00 |
| **Dress,** Silk Taffeta, Black, Wing Sleeves, Pleated Skirt, C.1890 | 85.00 |
| **Dress,** Velvet, Rust, Evening Gown, Sleeveless, Gold Beads, C.1925 | 200.00 |
| **Dress,** Victorian, Lace, Light Green, 2 Piece | 85.00 |
| **Dress,** Wedding, Veil, 3 Tier Drape, Seed Pearls, Lined, C.1915 | 125.00 |
| **Dress,** White Batiste, Tucks & Lace Inserts, Ankle Length, Size 7 | 65.00 |
| **Dress,** White Cotton, Lace Trim | 25.00 |
| **Duster,** Auto, Lady's, Linen, C.1910 | 45.00 |
| **Duster,** Lady's, Beige Linen, Small | 35.00 |
| **Duster,** Man's, Wool | 55.00 |
| **Evening Dress,** Gray Taffeta, Stand-Out Panel At Neck, C.Chapman | 70.00 |
| **Evening Dress,** Ivory Slipper Satin, Scoop Neck, C.1960, Balenciaga | 100.00 |
| **Evening Dress,** Printed Rose Chiffon, Backless, 1950s, Balmain | 200.00 |
| **Evening Dress,** Red Satin, Narrow Straps, 1950s, Lanvin Castillo | 40.00 |
| **Flag,** American, 36 Star, 16 X 10 In. | 35.00 |
| **Fruit,** Velvet, Fruits & Vegetables, 8 Piece | 250.00 |
| **Gloves,** Silk, Black, Elbow Length | 9.00 |
| **Gown,** Shades Of Pink, Lavender Hip Drape Bow, Silk & Lace, Small | 75.00 |
| **Greatcoat,** Chesterfield, Black | 40.00 |
| **Handkerchief,** Bride's, Hand-Embroidered Design, Ivory, Silk, C.1910 | 22.00 |
| **Handkerchief,** Poem, The House That Jack Built, C.1800, Framed | 165.00 |
| **Handkerchief,** Terrytoon, Character On Each, Set Of 6 | 25.00 |
| **Jacket,** Linen Stenciled In Gilt, Palm Fronds, 1940s, Fortuny | 250.00 |
| **Jacket,** Sequin, Sewn Down Shawl Collar, Piped In Bugle Beads | 225.00 |
| **Jacket,** Tape Lace, Floral Pattern, C.1910 | 325.00 |
| **Kimono,** Silk, Puffy Embroidery On Back, Bird On Shoulder, 45 In. | 135.00 |
| **Kimono,** Silk, Rayon, Crepe, Japanese | 45.00 |
| **Lace,** Madeira, 70 X 8 1/2 In. | 25.00 |
| **Lap Robe,** Carriage, Velour | 25.00 |
| **Lap Robe,** Earth Colors, Chase Label, 64 X 56 In. | 48.00 |
| **Mat,** Sarouk, Medallion & Spandrels, Blue Edge, 2 Ft. 1 In. X 3 Ft. | 200.00 |
| **Nightgown,** Long Sleeves, Tucked Back, 19th Century, White | 80.00 |
| **Nightgown,** White Cotton, Some Lace | 18.00 |
| **Obi,** Kimono, Embroidered In Gold | 125.00 |
| **Pajamas,** Embroidered, Silk, Chinese, World War II | 135.00 |
| **Peignoir,** Eyelet, White Cotton | 35.00 |
| **Petticoat,** Victorian, 30 Rows Of Tucking | 28.00 |

**Picture,** Berlin Woolwork Type, Grospoint & Petitpoint, Framed ........................... 350.00
**Picture,** Head Of Christ, Black & White Jacquard, Signed, 8 X 11 In. .................... 50.00
**Picture,** Memorial, Cemetery Scene, Chenille On Silk, 8 X 11 1/2 In. .................... 150.00
**Picture,** The Golden-Headed Vulture, A.Adams, 1797, 12 X 13 In. ........................ 1000.00
**Pillow,** Needlepoint Fronts, Flowers On Tan Ground, Pair ................................... 24.00
**Pillow,** Needlework, Scene Of Maiden On Horse, 20 X 18 In. ................................ 50.00
**Pillow,** Oilcloth, Feather Stuffed, Woman's Face On Both Sides ......................... 18.00
**Pillow,** Ribbonwork, Victorian ...................................................................... 18.00
**Quilt,** Amish Basket, Black Sateen Ground, C.1930, 62 X 84 In. ......................... 625.00
**Quilt,** Appliqued, Medallion Of Washington, 1789-1889, 19th Century .................. 2800.00
**Quilt,** Art Deco, Fan, Full Size ...................................................................... 140.00
**Quilt,** Baby, Appliqued, Mama Cat With Kittens ................................................ 55.00
**Quilt,** Baskets, Set In Red Garden Maze, 19th Century, 64 X 84 In. ...................... 450.00
**Quilt,** Bear's Claw, Red & Brown, White Ground, C.1899, 84 X 84 In. ................... 375.00
**Quilt,** Bear's Paw Pattern, Blue & White, C.1880, Double Size ........................... 350.00
**Quilt,** Berry Baskets, Plaids & Solids, C.1875, 62 X 76 In. ............................... 250.00
**Quilt,** Birds In The Air, Prints On Red & Cream, C.1850, 78 X 78 In. .................... 295.00
**Quilt,** Black-Eyed Susan, Yellow Petals, C.1830, 79 1/4 X 74 In. ........................ 225.00
**Quilt,** Bowtie Pattern, Hand-Stitched, Full Size ................................................ 135.00
**Quilt,** Bowtie Pattern, Pink & White, Double Size .............................................. 75.00
**Quilt,** Brown Stripes, Fan Quilting, Scalloped, C.1830, 72 X 82 In. ...................... 150.00
**Quilt,** Checkerboard, 9-Patch Sections, 1880-1900, 78 X 91 In. ......................... 275.00
**Quilt,** Chimney Sweep, Prints, Solids & Calicos, C.1860, 69 X 83 In. .................... 295.00
**Quilt,** Chintz, Floral Alternating Panels, 104 X 104 In. ..................................... 525.00
**Quilt,** Country Star, Flower Designs, C.1830, 100 X 100 In. ............................... 175.00
**Quilt,** Courthouse Steps Pattern ................................................................... 210.00
**Quilt,** Cover Garland, Green On Ivoried Ground, C.1850, 60 X 90 In. ................... 375.00
**Quilt,** Crazy Pattern, 72 X 90 In. ................................................................. 150.00
**Quilt,** Crazy, Silk, Cradle Size ..................................................................... 35.00
**Quilt,** Crazy, Silks & Satins, Embroidered, Dated 1886, 60 X 66 In. .................... 100.00
**Quilt,** Crazy, Various Stitches, Blue Ribbon Winner, Wichita, Kansas ................... 400.00
**Quilt,** Crazy, Wedding Bell Centered, Dated 1880, Signed, 41 X 68 In. ................. 1250.00
**Quilt,** Crib, Sunbonnet Babies ..................................................................... 20.00
**Quilt,** Crown, Blue & White Prints, Red Ground, C.1875, 74 X 74 In. ................... 195.00
**Quilt,** Double Irish Chain, Prints, Blue Backing, 81 X 91 In. .............................. 150.00
**Quilt,** Double Star, Prints & Solids, 1830-40, 82 X 76 In. .................................. 400.00
**Quilt,** Double Wedding Ring, White Ground, Handmade, 68 X 88 In. ..................... 245.00
**Quilt,** Double Wedding Ring, 20th Century, Double Size ..................................... 95.00
**Quilt,** Dresden Plate Pattern, Cotton, Full Size ................................................ 150.00
**Quilt,** Dresden Plate Pattern, Handmade, Yellow Ground, Full Size ..................... 100.00
**Quilt,** Drunkard's Path, Red & White, 76 X 65 In. .............................................. 195.00
**Quilt,** Dutch Rose Pattern, Full Size .............................................................. 85.00
**Quilt,** Eagle, Chintz & Trapunto Applique, C.1860 ............................................ 7500.00
**Quilt,** Eagle, Upper Half Turkey, C.1860, 66 X 70 In. ......................................... 850.00
**Quilt,** 8 Point Stars, Herringbone Quilting, C.1880, 82 X 84 In. .......................... 750.00
**Quilt,** Embroidery, 2 Shades Of Pink With White, 85 X 106 In. ........................... 125.00
**Quilt,** Flower Garden, Diamond Shaped Flowers, Dark Edge, 77 X 65 In. ............. 90.00
**Quilt,** Flower Garden, Hand-Stitched, Lavender Ground, Full Size ...................... 55.00
**Quilt,** Flower Garden, 1920s, 78 X 88 In. ........................................................ 175.00
**Quilt,** Friendship, White & Blue Stitching, Double, 1800s .................................. 50.00
**Quilt,** Geometric, Silk, 3 In.Lace Hem, 68 X 66 In. ............................................ 40.00
**Quilt,** Handmade, Blocks Of 8 Point Multicolored Stars, 81 X 68 In. .................... 85.00
**Quilt,** Handmade, Pyramids, Multicolored, 78 X 64 In. ....................................... 65.00
**Quilt,** Hearts & Stars, Corner Designs, 1840-60, 68 X 76 In. .............................. 625.00
**Quilt,** Hole In The Barn, Signed Frank L.Burtoph, C.1870, 83 X 83 In. .................. 265.00
**Quilt,** Irish Chain Pattern, Double Size ........................................................... 245.00
**Quilt,** Light Blue & White, Binding Wear, Full Size ............................................. 45.00
**Quilt,** Log Cabin, Silk, Blue & White, 1800 ..................................................... 155.00
**Quilt,** Lone Star, Large Size ......................................................................... 90.00
**Quilt,** Multicolored 9 Patch, Green Ground, C.1860, 72 X 72 In. ......................... 165.00
**Quilt,** Old Maid's Puzzle, Blue, White, & Rose, C.1890, 76 X 88 In. ..................... 175.00
**Quilt,** 1 Patch, Red, White, & Blue, C.1900, 76 X 84 In. .................................... 185.00
**Quilt,** Patchwork, White Ground, 19th Century, 90 In.Square ............................. 300.00

Quilt, Pennsylvania Star, Hand-Stitched, Gray, Blue & Red, Double ............................... 90.00
Quilt, Red Star, Tacked, 9 Stars, C.1900, 62 X 78 In. ................................................ 225.00
Quilt, Rising Sun Pattern, Full Size ......................................................................... 800.00
Quilt, Robbing Peter To Pay Paul, Calico Prints, Large ............................................. 185.00
Quilt, Star Pattern, Blue, Orange, & Yellow, 73 X 82 In. ............................................. 95.00
Quilt, Star, Red, Yellow, Pink, & Green, White Ground, 67 In.Square ......................... 110.00
Quilt, State Bird, Each State, Mennonite, 84 X 104 In. ............................................... 225.00
Quilt, Striped & Paisley Border, Hand-Sewn, Double Size ......................................... 140.00
Quilt, Striped Sawtooth, Solids & Prints, C.1850, 70 X 88 In. .................................... 195.00
Quilt, The Schoolhouse, Pieced & Appliqued, C.1880, 68 X 76 In. ............................ 595.00
Quilt, Tulip Pattern, C.1850, New Jersey, Full Size .................................................. 650.00
Quilt, Tulips, Pink & White, Appliqued, 66 X 86 In. .................................................. 150.00
Quilt, Turkey Trot, Red & Green, White Ground, 1850-60, 84 X 84 In. ....................... 265.00
Quilt, Variable Star On Blue, Fan Quilted, C.1890, 74 X 90 In. ................................. 325.00
Quilt, Wedding Ring, Twin Bed, C.1920 ................................................................. 125.00
Quilt, Wild Goose Chase, Blue & White, C.1880, 60 X 62 In. ................................... 150.00
Quilt, Yo-Yo, Peach, 1920, Double ........................................................................ 55.00
Quilt, Yo-Yo, 72 X 94 In. ..................................................................................... 80.00
Quilt, 8 Point Star, Black, Blue, & White, 76 X 76 In. .............................................. 60.00
Quilt, 9 Patch, Red, Pink, & Dark Brown, 76 X 76 In. .............................................. 55.00
Robe, Car, Mohair ............................................................................................... 50.00
Robe, Horse, Brown Hair, Green Wool Back ........................................................... 125.00
Robe, Lap, Buggy, C.1880 .................................................................................... 50.00
Robe, Lap, Gray & Black, Wool ............................................................................ 25.00
Robe, Oriental, Dragons ...................................................................................... 30.00
Sack, Flour, Bird Design & Advertisment, 1940s, Cotton, 25 Pound .......................... 3.50
Saddlebag, Boukara, Red, 2 Ft.3 In. X 1 Ft.7 In. .................................................... 275.00

*Samplers were made in the United States during the early 1700s. The
best examples were made from 1790 to 1840. Long narrow samplers are
usually older than the square ones. Early samplers just had stitching or
alphabets. The later examples had numerals, borders, and pictorial decorations.
Those with mottos are mid-Victorian.*

Sampler, ABC, Dated 1822, Signed Mary E.Cross, Newburyport ................................ 165.00
Sampler, ABC, Signed, 1840, 16 1/4 X 4 3/4 In. ..................................................... 125.00
Sampler, ABC, Verse, Charlotte Donald, 1827, 16 3/4 In.Square ............................... 485.00
Sampler, Alphabet, Polly & Mary Potter, C.1830, 7 1/2 X 5 1/8 In. ........................... 100.00
Sampler, Betsy Perry Fuller, Dated 8-7-1837, 17 X 13 In. ........................................ 75.00
Sampler, C.B.Dutton, 8 Years, Alphabet, Verse, 1828, 10 3/4 X 14 In. ..................... 265.00
Sampler, Dated 1817, Red, Gray, Brown, Unframed, 10 X 11 1/2 In. ......................... 70.00
Sampler, Flower Edge, Isabella Hempstock, Aged 11, 1776, 11 X 16 In. .................. 1350.00
Sampler, Sewed By Janet Brown In 1845, House, Alphabet, 12 X 17 In. .................... 310.00
Sampler, Stitched Panels, Dated Ano 1871, Spanish, 27 X 34 In. ............................. 300.00
Sampler, 3 Alphabets, Signed Lucy Lay, 1824, 10 3/8 X 7 1/4 In. .............................. 150.00
Scarf, Bureau, Cotton, Lace Edged, Cutwork Design, 13 X 38 In. .............................. 4.00
Scarf, Dresser, Crocheted Ends, 17 X 38 In. .......................................................... 24.00
Scarf, Piano, Fringe, Reversible Silk Tapestry, 56 In.Square ..................................... 40.00
Scarf, Piano, Silk & Cotton Damask, 56 In.Square .................................................. 40.00
Scarf, Silk, Yellow, Brown, & Green, Occupied Japan, 36 X 36 In. ............................. 9.00
Scarf, Table, Ecru, Embroidered, Crocheted Ends, 24 X 56 In. ................................. 18.00
Shawl, Handwoven, Stylized Designs, Cashmere, 54 X 122 In. ................................. 150.00
Shawl, Kerman, Twill Border, White Wool, 7 Ft. 2 In. X 5 1/2 Ft. ............................. 275.00
Shawl, Open Weave, Red, Wool, 104 X 104 In. ...................................................... 10.00
Shawl, Overall Woven With Silvered Metal, Egyptian ............................................... 80.00
Shawl, Piano, Cream Embroidery, 20 In.Fringe, Silk, Large ...................................... 68.00
Shawl, Piano, Orange On Black Silk ...................................................................... 175.00
Shawl, Piano, Silk Chenille & Velvet, French, C.1900, 78 X 64 In. ............................ 500.00
Shawl, Piano, White Embroidery On Black, Fringe, Silk, 7 Ft.Square ......................... 300.00
Shawl, Wool, Fringe, Black, 3 Ft.Square ................................................................ 11.00
Sheet, Wool, Homespun, Seamed ........................................................................ 20.00
Shirtwaist, Lawn, Lace Inserts, Pair ...................................................................... 35.00
Shoe, Hi-Top, Star Brand, Never Worn, Pair ........................................................... 8.20

Textile, Suit, Lady's, Dinner, Adrian, Navy Faille, C.1950

**Skirt & Jacket,** Ribbon Bands, Battenberg Lace, C.1905, Waist, 23 In. .................................. 200.00
**Skirt,** Lace Waist, Hand Crocheted, Ribbon Drawstring ......................................................... 15.00
**Skirt,** Tulip, Kelly Green Tweed, 2 Pleats 2 Zippers, Charles James ......................................... 180.00
**Spats,** 4 Button ............................................................................................................... 40.00
**Spats,** 10 Button ............................................................................................................. 6.00
**Spread,** Steamship, The Great Eastern, Double ................................................................ 150.00
**Stockings,** Openwork Diamond Pattern, Knitted, Over The Knee ............................................ 22.00
**Suit,** Lady's, Dinner, Adrian, Navy Faille, C.1950 .......................................................*Illus* 100.00
**Suit,** Lady's, Eyelet Flowers, White Linen, 1910s, Waist 30 In. ............................................. 275.00
**Suit,** Wedding, Gentleman's, Black Wool, Barbthea, Cutaway Coat ........................................ 110.00
**Tablecloth,** Appliqued Water Lilies, Linen, 52 X 68 In. ....................................................... 45.00
**Tablecloth,** Banquet, Lace Nude Ladies, 176 X 71 In. ........................................................ 700.00
**Tablecloth,** Battenburg Lace, Grape Pattern, 64 In.Diam. .................................................... 135.00
**Tablecloth,** Battenburg, 30 In.Diam ................................................................................... 50.00
**Tablecloth,** Crocheted, Fruit Design, 60 X 72 In. ................................................................ 72.00
**Tablecloth,** Crocheted, Popcorn Pattern, 63 X 63 In. .......................................................... 55.00
**Tablecloth,** Crocheted, Star Pattern, Ecru, 24 X 86 In. ........................................................ 75.00
**Tablecloth,** Deer Design, 4 Napkins, 54 X 66 In. ................................................................ 25.00
**Tablecloth,** Drawnwork, Embroidered, Linen, 66 X 52 In. .................................................... 55.00
**Tablecloth,** Embroidered With Openwork & Inset, Linen, 42 X 60 In. ..................................... 110.00
**Tablecloth,** Fringe, Woven Design, Japanese, 72 X 88 In. ..................................................... 50.00
**Tablecloth,** Hand Crocheted, Lacy Rosettes, Ecru, 60 X 120 In. ............................................ 65.00
**Tablecloth,** Irish Linen Damask, 5 Hemstitched Napkins, 63 X 90 In. ..................................... 95.00
**Tablecloth,** Italian Silk Finish, 54 X 54 In. ........................................................................ 30.00
**Tablecloth,** Lace, Battenberg, Round, 20 In. ...................................................................... 18.00
**Tablecloth,** Lace, Fringed Edge, 70 X 85 In. ....................................................................... 75.00
**Tablecloth,** Linen, Satin Damask, 72 X 86 In. ..................................................................... 25.00
**Tablecloth,** Paisley Overall, 130 X 68 In. ........................................................................... 125.00
**Tablecloth,** Paisley, 60 X 132 In. ...................................................................................... 140.00
**Tablecloth,** Pinapple Pattern, Hand-Crocheted, 90 In.Diam. ................................................. 95.00
**Tablecloth,** Pulled-Thread Openwork, 17 X 72 In. ............................................................... 50.00
**Tapestry,** Aubusson Panel, Vase, Flower Medallion, 8 1/2 X 3 1/3 Ft. .................................... 300.00
**Tapestry,** Courtyard Scene, Belgian, 20 X 38 In. ................................................................ 25.00
**Tapestry,** Crane At Riber, Farm, Verdure, 5 1/2 X 2 Ft.10 In. ............................................... 2000.00
**Tapestry,** Pictorial Scene, 56 X 19 1/2 In. ......................................................................... 75.00
**Tapestry,** Pictorial, Silk, 19th Century, 22K Gold Thread, 8 X 3 Ft. ....................................... 4000.00
**Tapestry,** Pictorial, 19th Century, 22K Gold Thread, 8 1/2 X 3 Ft. ......................................... 4000.00
**Tapestry,** Shades Of Green, 17th Century, 6 X 12 Ft. .......................................................... 4500.00
**Tapestry,** Silk, 19th Century, 22K Gold Thread, 8 X 6 Ft. ..................................................... 4000.00
**Tapestry,** Spanish Courtyard, Belgian, 60 X 18 In. .............................................................. 12.00

Tapestry, Virgin Mary, Attendants, 6 Ft. 2 In. X 3 Ft. 5 In. ........................ 1700.00
Tapestry, Wheat Harvesters, Mother & Babies, Fringed, 18 X 35 In. .......... 28.00
Tea Gown, Lavender Pleated Silk Satin, Fortuny ...................................... 1200.00
Tent Bag, Turkoman Boukara, 2 Ft.6 In. X 4 Ft.4 In. .............................. 550.00
Texas Star Pattern, Full Size ................................................................. 235.00
Throw, Crocheted, Beige With Cat Figure In Center, 55 X 32 In. ............ 35.00
Uniform, Baseball, Child's, Dizzy & Daffy Dean ..................................... 45.00
Uniform, Train Porter, Rock Island, Complete ........................................ 150.00
Veil, Mourning, Black Lace, Victorian .................................................... 6.75
Veil, Point D'Esprit, Duchess Type Lace, 29 X 89 In. ............................ 160.00
Yoke, Lingerie, Crochet ......................................................................... 9.00

THERMOMETER, Hires Bottle, 28 In. ...................................................... 40.00

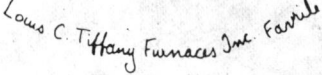

*Louis C. Tiffany*   Tiffany glass was made by Louis Comfort Tiffany, the American glass
designer who worked from about 1879 to 1933. His work included iridescent
glass, Art Nouveau styles of design, and original contemporary styles.
He was also noted for his stained glass windows, his unusual lamps, bronze
work, pottery, and silver.

TIFFANY GLASS, Bottle, Cologne, Leaf & Vine, Gold Ground, Signed, 4 1/2 In. ............. 1100.00
Bottle, Perfume, Blue Iridescent, Stopper, Signed, 3 3/4 In. ........................... 675.00
Bowl & Underplate, Gold Iridescent, Twisted Pigs' Tails ............................... 425.00
Bowl, Curved Body, Ribs, Gold Iridescent, Signed, 2 1/4 In. ........................ 250.00
Bowl, Dimpled Edge, Gold Iridescence, Signed, 6 1/4 In.Diam. .................... 595.00
Bowl, Feather Ribbing, Stretch Iridescent, Signed, 9 In.Diam. ...................... 475.00
Bowl, Flower Frog, Leaves, Vines, Gold, Signed, 12 In. Diam. ..................... 1100.00
Bowl, Gold, Iridescent, Scalloped Rim, Signed, 10 In. ................................. 895.00
Bowl, Gold, Paneled Body, Scalloped Edge, Signed, 6 In. ........................... 275.00
Bowl, Green Leaves, Blue, Signed, 12 1/2 In. ............................................. 975.00
Bowl, Green, Gold Chain Design, Gold Threads, Squat ............................... 1500.00
Bowl, Intaglio Etched Leaves Allover, Gold, 6 In.Diam. .............................. 675.00
Bowl, Iridescent Blue, Scalloped, Signed, 2 1/2 X 6 In.Diam. ..................... 495.00
Bowl, Iridescent Gold, Signed, 13 X 5 In. ................................................ 995.00
Bowl, Iridescent Peacock Blue, Gold Trim, Signed, 13 In. .......................... 1500.00
Bowl, Leaf, Ribbed, Stretched, Blue, Gold, 9 1/2 In.Diam. ........................ 485.00
Bowl, Marigold Iridescence, Melon Ribbed, Signed, 7 1/2 In. ..................... 650.00
Bowl, Nut, Blue & Gold Design, Ruffled Top, Signed, 2 3/4 In. ................... 165.00
Bowl, Orchid Pastel, Opalescent Stripes, 8 In. .......................................... 475.00
Bowl, Pedestal, Crackled Blue & Gold, Approved Sample, 13 In. ................ 950.00
Bowl, Pedestal, Fluted, Swirled & Ribbed, Signed, Blue, 7 In. .................... 740.00
Bowl, Pink, Iridescent Interior, Signed, 5 3/4 In.Diam. ............................. 295.00
Bowl, Quilted, Inverted Base, Green & Gold, Signed, 18 1/2 In. ................. 540.00
Bowl, Red & Blue Highlights, Flower Frog, Signed, 9 1/2 In. ..................... 900.00
Bowl, Ribbed, Leaf Design, Gold Luster, Signed, 9 1/2 In. ......................... 490.00
Bowl, Ruffled Edge, Gold Iridescent, Signed, 4 1/2 In.Diam. ..................... 260.00
Bowl, Ruffled Rim, Iridescent Gold, Signed, 2 1/2 X 6 1/2 In. ................... 210.00
Bowl, Ruffled, Gold Iridescent, Signed, 2 1/4 X 6 In.Diam. ....................... 300.00
Bowl, Scalloped & Ribbed, Signed, 2 1/4 X 8 1/2 In.Diam. ....................... 695.00
Bowl, Scalloped Rim, Iridescent Gold, Signed, 4 X 10 In.Diam. ................. 895.00
Bowl, Undulating Rim, Ribbed & Paneled, Marked, 8 In.Diam. ................... 400.00
Box, Open, Cypriote Texture, Dore Edge, Signed, 6 X 3 1/2 In. ................. 400.00
Brandy Snifter, Threaded, Lily Pad Design, Signed, 3 3/4 In. ..................... 350.00
Butter Pat, Ruffled, Gold Trim, Signed, 3 In.Wide .................................... 185.00
Candle Shade, Linenfold, Amber ............................................................. 300.00
Candlestick, Blue, Gold Iridescence, Signed, Numbered, 4 In. .................... 345.00
Candlestick, Damascene Design, Blue Luster, Signed, 10 In. ...................... 395.00
Candlestick, Gold Aurene, Signed, 5 1/2 In. ............................................ 325.00
Candlestick, Gold Dore, Signed & Numbered, 12 1/2 In. ........................... 500.00

**Candlestick,** Gold Iridescent, Candle Saucer, Signed, 4 In. .......................................................... 345.00
**Candlestick,** Green Patina, Signed, 7 In. ...................................................................................... 600.00
**Candlestick,** Pedestal Foot, Pink Top, Green, Signed, 7 In. ......................................................... 525.00
**Champagne,** Gold, Pink Tone, Signed & Numbered, Set Of 4 ....................................................... 850.00
**Champagne,** Hollow Stem, Signed ................................................................. 215.00 To 280.00
**Champagne,** Prinz Pattern, Gold Luster, 5 3/4 In., Set Of 12 ....................................................... 2100.00
**Champagne,** Yellow, Opal Threads, Flower, Signed, 4 1/2 In. ...................................................... 235.00
**Chandelier,** Greek Key, Green Border, Yellow Ground, 22 In. ...................................................... 5000.00
**Chandelier,** Mottled Green, Geometric, Signed, 20 In. ................................................................. 3000.00
**Compote,** Blue & Opalescent Top, Footed & Stem, 8 1/2 In. ........................................................ 550.00
**Compote,** Floral, Aqua, Opalescent, Stretch Bowl, 7 1/2 In. ....................................................... 750.00
**Compote,** Green Pastel Ribbed, Signed, 5 1/2 In. ........................................................................ 595.00
**Compote,** Intaglio Band, Gold, Signed, 3 1/2 X 4 1/2 In.Diam. ................................................... 300.00
**Compote,** Iridescent Gold, Signed, 3 X 4 1/4 In.Diam. ................................................................. 395.00
**Compote,** Low, Peacock Blue, Signed, 1 3/4 X 6 In.Diam. ........................................................... 495.00
**Compote,** Opalescent Stem & Foot, Blue, Signed, 8 1/2 In.Diam. ............................................... 475.00
**Compote,** Peacock Blue, Knobbed Stem, Iridescent, 5 In. .......................................................... 750.00
**Compote,** Peacock Blue, Signed, 6 In.Diam. ................................................................................ 495.00
**Compote,** Ribbed, Molded Design, Signed, 5 X 6 1/4 In.Diam. ................................................... 500.00
**Compote,** Ruffled Rim, Gold Iridescent, Signed, 2 3/4 X 8 In. ................................................... 450.00
**Cordial Set,** Decanter & 5 Glasses, Signed, Decanter, 10 In. ...................................................... 625.00
**Cordial,** Cameo Carved, Tulip Flower, Pedestal Foot, 4 In. ......................................................... 385.00
**Cup,** Gold, Platinum Highlights, Lily Pad Design, 3 1/4 In. .......................................................... 395.00
**Cup,** Tea, Amber, 7 Lily Pads, Platinum & Silver, 2 X 3 In. ......................................................... 375.00
**Decanter,** Bottom Facets, Engraved, Signed, 11 1/2 In. .............................................................. 2500.00
**Decanter,** 12 Shot Glasses, Gold Luster, Signed, 10 5/8 In. ....................................................... 2100.00
**Dish,** Mint, Iridescent Blue, Scalloped, Signed, 1 1/2 X 5 In. ...................................................... 350.00
**Dish,** Mint, Raised Edge, Gold Iridescent, Signed, 5 3/4 In. ....................................................... 110.00
**Dish,** Nut, Gold Iridescence, Signed, 2 X 3 In.Diam. .................................................................... 140.00
**Dish,** Nut, Gold Iridescent, Flared Top, Signed, 1 1/4 X 3 In. ..................................................... 140.00
**Finger Bowl & Underplate,** Swirled, Signed, Bowl, 2 1/4 X 4 In. ................................................. 425.00
**Flacon,** Ovoid, Blue Iridescent, Stopper, Signed, 7 3/4 In. .......................................................... 750.00
**Globe,** Hanging, Reticulated, Wire Design, Signed, 9 X 12 In. ..................................................... 5500.00
**Globe,** Paperweight, Intaglio Cut, Bronze Holder, Signed, 8 In. .................................................. 2500.00
**Goblet,** Etched, Cranberry, Signed, 8 1/2 In. .............................................................................. 325.00
**Goblet,** Twisted Stem, Signed, 6 In. ............................................................................................ 350.00
**Inkwell,** Open, Yellow Pulled Feather Design, Signed, 2 X 4 In. .................................................. 550.00
**Jardiniere,** Orange Swirl Spots, Amethyst, Signed, 4 1/4 In. ...................................................... 700.00
**Nut Cup,** Gold Ribbed, Signed, 1 X 3 1/4 In.Diam. ..................................................................... 125.00
**Pepper,** Iridescent Gold, Silver Top, Pinched, Signed, 2 3/4 In. .................................................. 150.00
**Pitcher,** Handled, Gold Threading, Signed, 4 1/2 In. ................................................................... 450.00
**Plate,** Dinner, Feather-Like Design, Yellow, Signed ..................................................................... 180.00
**Plate,** Fernery Design, Scalloped Edge, Signed, 8 In.Diam. ......................................................... 325.00
**Plate,** Gold Iridescence, Signed, 4 In.Diam. ................................................................................ 165.00
**Plate,** Pastel Pink, Signed, Original Label, 8 1/2 In.Diam. ........................................................... 295.00
**Platter,** Short Pedestal, Gold Iridescence, Signed, 8 In. ............................................................. 225.00
**Ribbed,** Scalloped, Waisted Above Base, Signed, 8 1/2 In. ........................................................ 650.00
**Salt,** Blue & Gold, Shape Of Bowl, Saucer Base, Signed ............................................................ 194.00
**Salt,** Crimped, Blue Iridescent, Signed, 4 X 3 1/2 In.Diam. ......................................................... 240.00
**Salt,** Crimped, Gold Iridescent, Signed, 1 1/8 X 2 1/2 In.Diam. .................................................. 135.00
**Salt,** Gold Iridescent, Twisted Pulls, Signed & Numbered, 2 In. .................................................. 200.00
**Salt,** Gold, 4 Feet, Paneled Body, Scalloped, Signed, 2 1/2 In. ................................................... 145.00
**Salt,** Handled, Swirled Prunt, Signed ........................................................................................... 160.00
**Salt,** Iridescent Blue, Signed ....................................................................................................... 140.00
**Salt,** Paperweight, Gold Iridescence, Scalloped, Signed, 2 In. .................................................... 200.00
**Salt,** Raised Prunts, Blue Green Inside, Signed, 2 1/4 In.Diam. ................................................... 150.00
**Salt,** Rolled Edge, Gold Aurene, Signed ...................................................................................... 195.00
**Salt,** Ruffled Edge, Gold Iridescence, Signed .............................................................................. 135.00
**Salt,** Serpentine Rim, Blue, Signed ............................................................................................. 115.00
**Salt,** Thorn Design, Blue & Gold, Signed ..................................................................................... 250.00
**Salt,** 4 Feet, Gold Iridescent, Signed ........................................................................................... 115.00
**Sherbet,** Green Opalescent, Signed LCT Favrile, 3 1/2 In. .......................................................... 275.00
**Shot Glass,** Dimpled, Signed, 1 3/4 In. ....................................................................................... 150.00

Tazza, Grecian Swag Design, 9 X 3 3/4 In. .................................................................... 750.00
Tazza, Quilted, Inverted Base, Gold Plated, Signed, Base, 6 In. ................................ 470.00
Tile, Raised Medallion, Red & Yellow Marbleized, 4 In.Square ................................ 125.00
Tile, Raised 4-Leaf Clover, Brown & Yellow Marbleized, 3 In. .................................... 55.00
Tile, 4-Lobed Molded Center Floret, Multicolored, 3 In.Square ................................ 55.00
Toothpick, Depressed Sides, Blue, Signed ................................................................ 195.00
Toothpick, Gold Dimpled, Signed, 2 In. ............................................... 100.00 To 120.00
Toothpick, 4-Sided, Dimple In Each Side, Signed, 2 In. ............................................ 175.00
Tumbler, Iridescent Gold, Threaded Midsection, Signed, 4 In. ................................ 200.00
Tumbler, Ribbed, Apple Green Pulled Feather, Signed, 5 In. .................................... 150.00
Urn, Covered, Iridescent Midnight Blue, Signed, 9 1/2 In. .................................... 1750.00
Urn, Star On Knob Finial, Covered, Pedestal, Signed, 9 1/2 In. ............................ 1250.00
Vase, Agate, Beige & Yellow Columns, Signed, 5 1/4 In. ...................................... 3450.00
Vase, Allover Raindrops, Iridescent Gold, Signed, 4 In. .......................................... 650.00
Vase, Amber & Purple Lower Half, Pistachio Upper Half, 6 In. ............................ 1000.00
Vase, Amber Ground, Purple Iridescent Swirl, Signed, 3 3/4 In. .......................... 1200.00
Vase, Ball Form, Gold & Green, C.1910, Signed, 2 1/2 In. .................................... 700.00
Vase, Balustrade Shape, Heart & Vine Design, Signed, 6 1/2 In. ............................ 595.00
Vase, Blue & Gold Iridescent, Signed, 4 3/4 In. ...................................................... 425.00
Vase, Blue Base, Yellow, Opaque, Numbered, Label, 11 3/4 In. .............................. 630.00
Vase, Blue Favrile, Blue-Purple Design, Oviform, 6 1/2 In. .................................... 525.00
Vase, Blue, Violet, Green, & Gold, Wave Life Motif, 6 In. ...................................... 770.00
Vase, Bud, Peacock Blue, Hexagon Shaped Top, Signed, 15 1/2 In. ...................... 950.00
Vase, Classic Shape, Iridescent Gold, Signed, 4 1/2 In. .......................................... 325.00
Vase, Conical Stick, Gold Luster, Signed, 14 1/2 X 5 In.Diam. .............................. 675.00
Vase, Corona, Hooked Feathers, Gold & Blue, C.1890, 4 1/4 In. ............................ 775.00
Vase, Cypriote, Gold, Lined In White, Signed, 8 1/2 In. ...................................... 2750.00
Vase, Cypriote, Iridescent, Signed, 4 3/4 In. ......................................... *Illus* 850.00
Vase, Cypriote, Pink, Blue & Green Iridescence, Signed, 8 In. ............................ 2750.00
Vase, Dimpled, Elephant Tails In Gold Luster, Signed, 2 In. .................................. 165.00
Vase, Double Gourd, Signed & Numbered, 2 1/2 In. ................................................ 425.00
Vase, Egyptian Design, Onion Shape, Gold Top, Signed, 10 In. ............................ 2090.00
Vase, Feather Border, Silver Plate Holder, Signed, 12 1/4 In. ................................ 985.00
Vase, Fishscale, Iridescent Amber, C.1900, Signed, 9 1/2 In. ................................ 150.00
Vase, Flower Form, Domed Pedestal Foot, Ribbed, Signed, 15 In. ........................ 1075.00
Vase, Flower Form, Fluted Rim, Marked, 4 1/4 X 5 1/2 In.Diam. ............................ 675.00
Vase, Flower Form, Gold Luster, Leaf & Vine, Signed, 6 1/4 In. .......................... 1250.00
Vase, Flower Form, Green Feather On White, Signed, 11 1/2 In. .......................... 1850.00

Tiffany Glass, Vase, Cypriote, Iridescent, Signed, 4 3/4 In.

**Vase,** Flower Form, Iridescent Gold, Blue, Signed, 9 7/8 In. .................................................... 1250.00
**Vase,** Flower Form, Opal & Yellow, Signed, 11 In. ................................................................. 1750.00
**Vase,** Flower Form, White Pulled Feather, Signed, 8 1/2 In. ................................................. 1500.00
**Vase,** Free-Form Butterfly, Blue Iridescent, Signed, 3 1/2 In. .............................................. 575.00
**Vase,** Gold Body, Venetian Lace Center, Label, 6 In. ............................................................ 950.00
**Vase,** Gold Flower Form, Red & Blue Iridescent, Signed, 11 In. .......................................... 1350.00
**Vase,** Gold Flower Form, Ribbed, Knob, Stem, Signed, 17 In. ............................................. 1175.00
**Vase,** Gold Ground, Green Leaf & Vine, Signed, C.1910, 2 1/2 In. ...................................... 700.00
**Vase,** Gold Ground, Green Violet, Domed Pedestal Foot, 15 In. .......................................... 995.00
**Vase,** Gold Iridescent, Fan Shaped, Signed, 5 1/2 In. ......................................................... 575.00
**Vase,** Gold Iridescent, Wide Bessel, Turned Collar, Signed .................................................. 485.00
**Vase,** Gold Iridescent, Wide Body, Signed & Numbered, 5 In. ............................................. 495.00
**Vase,** Gold Leaves, Vines, Black Iridescence, Signed, 6 In. .............................................. 3250.00
**Vase,** Gold Ribbed, Scalloped Mouth, Signed, 3 1/2 X 4 In.Diam. ...................................... 325.00
**Vase,** Gold To Platinum, Signed, 8930j, 20 In. ................................................................... 1375.00
**Vase,** Gold Trumpet, Ribbed, Signed, 11 3/4 In. ................................................................. 750.00
**Vase,** Gold With Light Gold Swirls, Translucent, Signed, 5 In. ............................................ 525.00
**Vase,** Gold With Platinum & Purple, Ribbed Sides, Signed, 2 In. ......................................... 350.00
**Vase,** Gold, Green Iridescent, Lily Shaped, Numbered, 6 1/5 In. ........................................ 495.00
**Vase,** Gold, Trumpet, Signed, 12 In. ................................................................................... 650.00
**Vase,** Intaglio Cut Design, Foil Label, 5 1/8 In. ................................................................... 1200.00
**Vase,** Iridescent Black & Blue, Signed ..................................................................*Illus* 1400.00
**Vase,** Iridescent Gold, Pink & Blue Highlights, Signed, 2 In. .............................................. 170.00
**Vase,** Iridescent Gold, Rainbow Color, Dimpled, 3 3/5 In. .................................................. 295.00
**Vase,** Jack-In-The-Pulpit, Pink & Blue, Signed, 13 In. ....................................................... 1950.00
**Vase,** Melon Ribbed & Dimples, Gold Iridescent, Signed, 6 In. .......................................... 525.00
**Vase,** Onion Shape, 2 Tiered Shoulder, C.1892, Signed, 9 1/2 In. ..................................... 950.00
**Vase,** Opal Peacock Feathers, Green, Gold Ground, Signed, 12 In. ................................... 695.00
**Vase,** Optic Swirled Body, Signed, Label, 4 3/4 In. ............................................................ 785.00
**Vase,** Paperweight, Bulbous, Engraved Design, Signed, 8 1/2 In. ...................................... 3000.00
**Vase,** Peacock Feather Design, Dark Red, Signed, 2 1/2 In. ............................................. 3000.00
**Vase,** Pearly White, Blue, Pink, Gold, Green, Signed, 8 In. ............................................... 1450.00
**Vase,** Pedestal, Opalescent Knob & Edge, Signed, 6 1/2 In. .............................................. 565.00
**Vase,** Pedestal, Ruffled Top, Rainbow Colors, Signed, 4 3/4 In. ......................................... 395.00
**Vase,** Pinched Sides, Gold Luster, Blue & Pink, Signed, 2 In. ............................................ 170.00
**Vase,** Pink Inside, Oyster White Outside, Signed, 4 3/4 In. ................................................ 595.00
**Vase,** Pink, Silver, & Gold, Turned-In Rim, Signed, 3 1/2 X 5 In. ........................................ 375.00
**Vase,** Round Center Flares To Ruffled Top, Signed, 4 3/4 In. ............................................. 395.00

Tiffany Glass, Vase, Iridescent Black & Blue, Signed

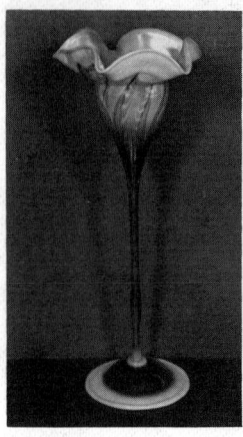

Tiffany Glass, Vase, Ruffled Flower
Form, Signed, 13 1/2 In.

**Vase,** Ruffled Flower Form, Signed, 13 1/2 In. ....................................................................*Illus* 2025.00
**Vase,** Scalloped Mouth, Gold Ribbed, Signed, 3 1/2 X 4 In. .......................................... 325.00
**Vase,** Swirl Line Design, Ribbed, Iridescent, Signed, 8 In. ........................................... 495.00
**Vase,** Trumpet Shape, Iridescent Blue, C.1910, Signed, 18 In. ................................... 225.00
**Vase,** Trumpet, Iridescent Blue, Signed & Numbered, 12 1/4 In. ............................. 1295.00
**Vase,** Trumpet, Peacock Feather, Gold Ground, Signed, 12 1/2 In. ........................... 985.00
**Vase,** Urn Shape, Blue Butterfly & Iridescent, Signed, 9 In. ...................................... 825.00
**Vase,** Vertical Ribs Pulled In To Crescents, Signed, 7 In. ........................................... 585.00
**Vase,** Violet Fold-In Top, Bronze Holder, Signed, 10 In. ............................................. 645.00
**Vase,** Waisted Neck, Scalloped, Signed, Paper Label, 3 In. ....................................... 350.00
**Vase,** Wave Life Design, Peacock Blue, Signed, 6 In. .................................................. 770.00
**Vase,** White Iridescent Top, Rainbow Bottom, Signed, 8 1/2 In. .............................. 1195.00
**Vase,** Yellow Body, Blue Throat & Base, Labeled, 11 In. ............................................. 630.00
**Vase,** Yellow, White Columns, Gold Scroll, Signed, 9 In. ......................................... 1150.00
**Vase,** 4 Pinched Openings, Blue Iridescent, Signed, 1i 1/2 In. ............................... 1500.00
**Wine,** Antique Green, Venetian Style, Phantom Luster, 4 3/4 In. ............................. 125.00
**Wine,** Cut Amber Stem, Signed L.C.T., 4 In. ................................................................ 210.00
**Wine,** Intaglio Carved, Signed, 3 3/4 In. ....................................................................... 210.00
**Wine,** Intaglio Leaves & Lappets, Signed, Set Of 8 .................................................. 1700.00
**Wine,** Intaglio Leaves, Gold Iridescent, Signed, 5 1/4 In. ........................................... 175.00
**Wine,** Iridized Stem, Foot, Green Opalescent, Signed, 4 3/4 In. ................................ 265.00
**Wine,** Stem, Gold Iridescent, Signed, 6 1/2 In. ............................................................ 295.00
**Witch Pot,** Handled, Blue, Signed & Numbered, 2 X 1 1/4 In. .................................... 380.00

**TIFFANY GOLD, Bowl,** Beaded Rim, Engraved, Christmas, 1931, 18K, 4 1/4 In. ................ 1900.00
**Dish,** Gold Iridescent, Scalloped Edge, Signed, 6 X 2 1/2 In. ...................................... 245.00
**Dish,** Nut, Blue Iridescent, Signed Favrile, 3 In. .......................................................... 210.00
**Dish,** Nut, Scalloped Rim, Signed L.C.T., 1 1/8 X 3 In. ................................................ 210.00
**Dish,** Nut, Stemmed & Footed, Signed & Numbered, 4 In. .......................................... 325.00
**Dish,** Pink Feathered Edge, White Striped, Signed, 7 3/4 In. ..................................... 400.00
**Martini,** Faceted Stem, C.1930, 18K, 4 1/4 In. ........................................................... 1200.00
**Pencil,** Collapsible, 14K Yellow Gold, Signed ............................................................. 425.00
**Vase,** Elongated Pear Form, 18K, 11 In. ..................................................................... 7500.00

**TIFFANY POTTERY, Vase,** Stylized Leaves, Cream Color, 8 1/2 In. .............................. 900.00

**TIFFANY SILVER, Beaker,** Art Nouveau Floral Design, C.1915, 13 Ounce ................ 575.00
**Bowl,** Audubon, Embossed Peacock Fills Bowl, 13 1/2 In.Diam. ............................. 1750.00
**Bowl,** Chased Design, Brass Insert, 4 X 19 In.Diam. ................................................. 2250.00

Bowl, Clover & Leaf Border, C.1900, 14 In. ............................................................................ 1800.00
Bowl, Grape Design Around Edges, Openwork, 28 Ounce ............................................ 1500.00
Bowl, Reticulated Border, Dated 1920, 1 3/4 X 6 1/2 In.Diam. ................................. 120.00
Bowl, Scalloped Rim, Openwork, Tassel Trim, Signed, 11 In. .................................. 1200.00
Box, Jewel, Gold Wash, C.1907, 4 X 3 In. ........................................................................ 300.00
Candlestick, Detachable Bobeches, 7 1/2 In., Pair ...................................................... 750.00
Candlestick, Hexagonal, 9 1/2 In., Pair .............................................................................. 500.00
Case, Cigarette, Gold Wash Inside, 3 X 5 In. .................................................................. 155.00
Castor, Scrolls & Feathering, C.1854, M Mark, 5 1/2 In. ........................................... 135.00
Compote, Pedestal, Egyptian Style, Handles, 12 1/2 In.Diam. ................................. 725.00
Dish, Pineapple Shape, Plant Top Handle, Marked, 5 1/2 In. ................................... 115.00
Dish, Swag Border Of Ribbon & Shells, C.1900, 8 3/4 X 11 In. .............................. 450.00
Dresser Set, Oakleaf Pattern, Signed, 6 Piece .............................................................. 375.00
Fork, Lettuce, Audubon, 4 Prong ......................................................................................... 225.00
Fork, Pickle, Colonial .................................................................................................................. 45.00
Fork, Salad, Audubon ................................................................................................................. 60.00
Fork, Serving, English King, 8 1/2 In. ................................................................................. 175.00
Fork, Serving, Olympian ............................................................................................................ 135.00
Frame, Picture, Repousse ........................................................................................................ 160.00
Ladle, Fluted Rim On Bowl, Marked .................................................................................... 395.00
Ladle, Punch, Gold Wash Bowl, Medallion Handle, Signed, 13 In. ........................ 350.00
Ladle, Soup, Richelieu ............................................................................................................... 435.00
Manicure Set, Fitted Leather Case, 19th Century, 7 Piece ....................................... 200.00
Money Clip, Applied Figural Heart, Marked ..................................................................... 40.00
Nut Set, 6 Individual Bowls, Ruffled Edge, Signed, Bowl, 5 In. ............................. 1295.00
Pitcher, Egyptian Revival Repousse Band, 7 In. ............................................................ 450.00
Pitcher, Griffins & Scrolls, 9 In. ....................................................................*Illus* 1700.00
Pitcher, Hinged Cover, Signed, 9 1/2 X 9 In. ................................................................. 145.00
Pitcher, Water, Cat On Pillow On Top Of Handle, 9 1/4 In. ...................................... 1500.00
Pitcher, Water, Vase Shape, C.1911, 9 1/4 In. .............................................................. 550.00
Plate, Applied Bead & Ball Edge, C.1900, 10 3/8 In. ................................................. 300.00
Server, Fish, English King, 19th Century, 11 1/4 In. ................................................... 265.00
Server, Pea, Beekman, Gold Wash Bowl ............................................................................ 195.00
Serving Set, Salad, Shell & Thread, Gold Wash Bowl ................................................. 400.00
Slice, Fish, Flemish .................................................................................................................... 225.00
Spoon, Berry, Clinton, 7 5/8 In. ............................................................................................ 85.00

Tiffany Silver, Pitcher, Griffins & Scrolls, 9 In.

**Spoon,** English King, Serving ............................................................................... 175.00
**Spoon,** Persian Pattern, Demitasse ...................................................................... 35.00
**Spoon,** Persian, Gold Wash Bowl, Patent 1872, 7 In. ........................................ 95.00
**Spoon,** Renaissance, 9 3/4 In. ............................................................................ 410.00
**Spoon,** Soup, Chrysanthemum ............................................................................ 67.00
**Sugar Tongs,** Richelieu, 4 1/2 In. ........................................................................ 52.00
**Tablespoon,** Audubon ........................................................................ 72.00 To 150.00
**Tablespoon,** Wave Edge Pattern .......................................................................... 85.00
**Tea & Coffee Set,** Octagonal, C.1925, Tray, 24 3/4 In., 7 Piece ..................... 4500.00
**Tea Ball,** Cylinder Shape, Hinged Cover, 3 X 1 1/4 In.Diam. ........................... 95.00
**Teaspoon,** Chrysanthemum ................................................................................. 43.00
**Teaspoon,** English King ....................................................................................... 30.00
**Teaspoon,** Persian, Set Of 6 ............................................................................... 275.00
**Telephone Dialer,** Sterling, 23 Grams ................................................................. 95.00
**Tray,** Gallery, Footed, Signed, 18 In. ................................................................. 3000.00
**Trowel,** Ice Cream, Empire, Bright Cut Blade, 9 1/8 In. ..................................... 200.00
**Tureen,** Soup, Foliate Banding, C.1870, 11 In. ................................................. 1300.00
**Urn,** Amphora Shape, Incised Design, C.1907, 17 In. ....................................... 1800.00
**Vase,** Trumpet Shape, Lobed Rim, Fluted Stem, Marked, 25 In. ....................... 2000.00

**TIFFANY, Ashtray & Match Holder,** Sculpture Design, Bronze, Signed, 6 1/2 In. ............... 175.00
**Ashtray,** Gold Dore Finish, Radial Design, Bronze, Signed, 4 1/2 In. ............... 125.00
**Ashtray,** Gold Dore Finish, 2-Handled, Bronze, Signed, 4 In.Diam. .................. 135.00
**Ashtray,** Gold Dore, Scalloped, Bronze, Signed, Nest Of 4 ............................... 350.00
**Ashtray,** Green Glass Insert, Bronze, Signed ..................................................... 425.00
**Blotter Corner,** Pine Needle, Bronze, 5 3/4 X 5 3/4, Set Of 4 ........................... 150.00
**Blotter Ends,** Venetian Pattern, 19 In. Pair ........................................................ 210.00
**Blotter Ends,** Zodiac, Bronze, 3 1/2 X 3 1/2 In., Set Of 4 ................................. 125.00
**Blotter,** Hand, Abalone, Iridescent Discs, Bronze, 2 3/4 X 5 3/4 In. ................. 150.00
**Blotter,** Hand, Bookmark Pattern, Bronze, Signed, 5 1/2 X 2 1/4 In. ................ 150.00
**Bookends,** Bronze, Zodiac Design, Polychrome .................................................. 320.00
**Bookends,** Venetian, 14K Gold Plate, Bronze, Signed, 6 X 4 3/4 In. ................. 495.00
**Bookends,** Zodiac, Circle & Line Design, Bronze, 5 X 6 In. ............................... 295.00
**Bowl,** Centerpiece, Ribs Form Scallop Edge, Bronze, Signed, 8 In.Diam. .......... 250.00
**Bowl,** Globular Form, Prunus & Foliage Rim, Bronze, Signed, 3 1/4 In. ............. 200.00
**Box,** Azalea Pattern, Green Slag, Bronze, Signed, 6 1/2 X 4 In. ........................ 395.00
**Box,** Covered, Venetian Pattern, Bronze, 5 1/4 X 2 3/4 In. ................................ 150.00
**Box,** Grapevine Pattern, Amber Slag, Signed, 4 1/4 X 3 1/4 In. ......................... 225.00
**Box,** Stamp, Spanish, 3 Compartment Tray, Bronze, Signed, 4 X 2 In. .............. 350.00
**Box,** Stamp, Venetian Pattern, Bronze .............................................................. 225.00
**Box,** Stamp, Zodiac Design On Hinged Cover, Bronze, 3 3/4 X 1 3/4 In. ........... 195.00
**Box,** Twine, Pine Needle Pattern, Bronze & Glass, Signed ................................ 495.00
**Brooch,** Center Black Opal, Rimmed By Design Of Lamps ............................... 4000.00
**Bust,** Shakespeare, Bronze, Signed, 9 1/2 Lbs. ................................................. 465.00
**Calendar,** Desk, Brass Frame, Green Slag Insert, Marble Ashtrays ................... 150.00
**Candelabra,** 4-Branch, Oval Base, Snuffer, Bronze, Signed, 15 In. .................. 1800.00
**Candleholder & Snuffer,** Art Glass On Candleholder, Bronze, Signed ............... 900.00
**Candlestick,** Bronzed, Sheriffs Jury, 1905-1906, Inscribed On Base ................. 250.00
**Candlestick,** Flower Form, Green Socket, Bronze, Marked, 20 1/2 In. ................ 175.00
**Candlestick,** Magnolia, Reticulated, Glass & Bronze, Signed, 15 In. ................ 1100.00
**Chamberstick,** 2 Curved Arms, Fleur-De-Lis Base, Bronze, Signed .................... 900.00
**Clip,** Paper, Graduate, Bronze, Signed ................................................................ 95.00
**Clock,** Boudoir, Key Wind, 8 Day, Silver Alarm, Marcasite Hands, 3 In. .......... 1800.00
**Clock,** Carriage, Porcelain Dial, 11-Jewel, Brass ............................................... 500.00
**Clock,** Grandfather, Colonial Works, Dated 1909 ............................................. 9000.00
**Clock,** Regulator, French Crystal, 10 3/4 X 6 3/4 In. ........................................ 525.00
**Clock,** Russian Pattern, Bronze & Enamel, Signed, Key, 4 1/2 X 6 In. .............. 975.00
**Compote,** Geometric Rim Design, Pedestal, Bronze, Signed, 6 In.Diam. ........... 150.00
**Cordial Set,** Flemish, Bronze Tray, Glass Decanter, 8 Cups, Signed ............... 2000.00
**Desk Set,** Adam's Pattern, Bronze, 6 Piece ..................................................... 1175.00
**Desk Set,** Bill File, Letter Rack, Bookends, Abalone ......................................... 600.00
**Desk Set,** Bookmark Pattern, Bronze, 10 Piece ............................................... 1250.00

**Desk Set,** Filigree Design, Bronze, 8 Piece .................................................................... 200.00
**Desk Set,** Twentieth Century Pattern, Bronze, 4 Piece ................................................. 850.00
**Desk Set,** Zodiac Pattern, Brown Patina, Bronze, Signed, 9 Piece .......................... 1295.00
**Desk Set,** Zodiac, Gilt, 1899-1920, Bronze, Signed ...................................................... 800.00
**Figurine,** Bulldog, Bronze, Signed & Numbered ........................................................... 275.00
**Frame,** Abalone Discs, Bronze, Signed, 7 1/4 X 9 1/4 In. ........................................... 650.00
**Frame,** Beading On Edge, Bronze & Green Slag, 3 1/2 X 2 1/2 In. ............................ 135.00
**Frame,** Calendar, Bookmark Pattern, Bronze, Signed, 5 1/2 X 6 1/4 In. ................... 250.00
**Frame,** Double, Azalea Pattern, Bronze, Signed, Opening, 3 X 2 In. .......................... 550.00
**Frame,** Perpetual Calendar, Spanish Pattern, Bronze, Signed ..................................... 275.00
**Frame,** Pine Needle, Amber Slag, Bronze & Glass, 10 1/4 X 12 1/4 In. ..................... 650.00
**Frog,** Gold, Iridescent, 3 1/2 X 3 1/2 In.Signed .......................................................... 100.00
**Glass,** Shot, Dimpled, Signed, 1 1/2 In. ........................................................................ 115.00
**Holder,** Matchbox, Zodiac Design, 4 1/2 In. ................................................................. 150.00
**Holder,** Note Pad, Graduate, Bronze, Signed, 7 3/4 X 4 3/4 In. ................................... 95.00
**Holder,** Note Pad, Zodiac Pattern On Hinged Cover, Bronze, Signed ......................... 125.00
**Humidor,** Bronze, Chinese Design, 8 X 5 In. ............................................................... 600.00
**Inkwell & Blotter Corners,** Grapevine Pattern, Bronze ............................................. 250.00
**Inkwell,** Abalone, Octagon Shape, Bronze, Signed, 3 1/2 X 3 1/2 In. ....................... 300.00
**Inkwell,** Adams Pattern, Dore, Oval, Insert, Bronze ..................................................... 199.50
**Inkwell,** Blown Glass In Bronze Frame, Signed, 4 1/2 In.Diam. ............................... 1500.00
**Inkwell,** Bookmark Pattern, Bronze ............................................................................... 199.00
**Inkwell,** Bronze, Double, Signed, 9 X 12 1/2 In. ........................................................ 595.00
**Inkwell,** Chinese Pattern, Octagon Shaped, Bronze, Signed, 4 In. ............................ 325.00
**Inkwell,** Graduate, Hinged Cover, Bronze, Signed, 2 1/2 In.Square ........................ 225.00
**Inkwell,** Indian Pattern, Glass Inserts, Bronze, Signed .............................................. 165.00
**Inkwell,** Pine Needle, Amber Slag, Bronze, Signed, 4 In.Square .............................. 300.00
**Inkwell,** Spanish, Hinged Lid, Bronze, 2 1/2 X 2 3/4 In.Square ............................... 450.00
**Inkwell,** Turtleback Lid, Insert, Bronze, Signed, 3 1/2 X 4 1/2 In. .......................... 1500.00
**Inkwell,** Venetian, Double, Bronze ................................................................................ 295.00
**Inkwell,** Zodiac ............................................................................................................... 120.00
**Inkwell,** Zodiac Hexagon Shape, Insert, Bronze, Signed, 6 1/2 In. .......................... 295.00
**Jar,** Jam, Clear Glass Liner & Silver Cover ................................................................... 125.00
**Lamp,** Acorn Pattern Shade, Baluster Base, Signed, 22 In. ...................................... 3100.00
**Lamp,** Acorn, Green, Yellow, White, Urn Style, Signed, 16 In. ................................. 3850.00
**Lamp,** Adjustable Double Arm, Diamond Pattern, Signed, 20 In. ............................ 1800.00
**Lamp,** American Indian, Etched Design, Tapered, Signed, 17 In. ............................. 3800.00
**Lamp,** Base, Floor, Vinson Design, Rope Twist, Signed, 60 In. ................................ 4500.00
**Lamp,** Base, Oil, Brass, Gold Dore, Lotus Leaf Design, Signed, 10 In. ................... 1475.00
**Lamp,** Bellflower, Yellow Blossoms, Footed, Signed, 23 In. .................................... 8000.00
**Lamp,** Blue Honeycomb Shade, Signed, 13 In. ........................................................ 2100.00
**Lamp,** Bridge, Curved Arms Around Shade, Signed, Shade, 12 In. ......................... 2200.00
**Lamp,** Bridge, Leaded Border, Green Slag Glass, Signed, 53 In. ............................ 3500.00
**Lamp,** Candle, Honeycomb Pattern On Shade, Cobalt, Signed ............................... 1450.00
**Lamp,** Cast As Lady In Stylized Robe, 4-Light, Signed, 15 In. ................................ 1350.00
**Lamp,** Chandelier, Turtleback, Round Globe, Hanging Rod, Signed, 32 In. ............ 3500.00
**Lamp,** Desk, Abalone, Gold Dore, Ruffled Edge, Signed, 20 In. ............................. 4000.00
**Lamp,** Desk, Bell Shaped Arms, Feather Design, Signed ........................................ 1200.00
**Lamp,** Desk, Bell Shaped Bronze Shade, Signed, 14 In. ........................................... 650.00
**Lamp,** Desk, Chinese Pattern, Green Slag Glass, Signed, 17 In. ............................ 3000.00
**Lamp,** Desk, Damascene Shade, Gold Ground, Signed, 20 In. ............................... 2800.00
**Lamp,** Desk, Dichroic Glass, Textured & Mottled, Signed, 21 In. ........................... 3500.00
**Lamp,** Desk, Green & Gold Wave Design, Signed, 7 In. .......................................... 2700.00
**Lamp,** Desk, Mottled Green Glass, Geometric, Signed, 22 In. ................................ 3200.00
**Lamp,** Desk, Sculptured Edge, Wave Design, Signed, 15 1/2 In. ........................... 2200.00
**Lamp,** Desk, Shell Shape Arms & Shade, Ribbed Platform, Signed ....................... 1200.00
**Lamp,** Desk, Zodiac Harp, Gold Aurene Shade ......................................................... 850.00
**Lamp,** Desk, Zodiac Pattern, Kapa Shell Shade, Signed ........................................ 1150.00
**Lamp,** Desk, Zodiac, Bronze Harp Base, Kapa Shell Shade, Signed ...................... 1150.00
**Lamp,** Desk, Zodiac, Turtleback, Swivels, Signed, 15 In. ....................................... 2500.00
**Lamp,** Double Arm, Tulip Form, Glass & Silver, C.1910, Signed, 22 In. .................. 475.00
**Lamp,** Etched-Out Shade, 65 Iridescent Prisms, Signed, 24 In. ............................ 5000.00
**Lamp,** Floor, Ivy Leaf, Green & White Shade, Signed, 58 In. ................................. 4250.00

**Lamp,** Font In 4 Shaped Legs, Leaded Shade, Signed, 14 1/2 In. ...........................................1150.00
**Lamp,** Green & Yellow Acorn Shade, Tripod Base, Signed, 21 In. ....................................3350.00
**Lamp,** Ivorene Flowers, Green Enamel Design, Signed, 24 In. ......................................1200.00
**Lamp,** Ivy Leaf Border, Curved Body, Signed, 21 In. ......................................................4000.00
**Lamp,** Kerosene, Pomegranate Shade, Signed, 22 In. ...................................................7500.00
**Lamp,** Lily, 3-Branch, Red Shades, Dore Finish, Signed ................................................4000.00
**Lamp,** Linenfold, Emerald Green, Signed, 19 1/2 In. ....................................................4600.00
**Lamp,** Orange Stems Form Leaves At Top, Beaded, Signed, 16 In. ..............................6500.00
**Lamp,** Piano, 2-Light, Opalescent Glass, Signed Base ..................................................1500.00
**Lamp,** Shade, Arrowroot, Yellow, White Flowers, Leaves, Signed, 20 In. .....................6000.00
**Lamp,** Shade, Maize To Burnt Orange, Striations, Label, 12 1/2 In. .............................1000.00
**Lamp,** Shade, Stalactite, Damascene Trailings, Signed, 10 1/2 In. ...............................125.00
**Lamp,** Student, 12 Panel Slag Shade, Mission Style ....................................................2400.00
**Lamp,** Table, Bellflower, Shade Fits On Arms, Signed, 23 In. .......................................8000.00
**Lamp,** Table, Chippendale, Octagon Shape Shade, Signed, 17 In. ..............................2500.00
**Lamp,** Table, Fabrique, 10 Panel, Ruffled, Signed, 20 In. .............................................4500.00
**Lamp,** Table, Fleur-De-Lis, Mottled & Striated, Signed, 21 In. ....................................6500.00
**Lamp,** Table, Greek Key, Green & Yellow, Signed, 21 In. .............................................6500.00
**Lamp,** Table, Linenfold, Amber, 10 Panels, Signed, 20 In. ..........................................4500.00
**Lamp,** Table, Linenfold, 16-Sided, Scalloped Rim, Signed, 21 In. ..............................3000.00
**Lamp,** Table, Roman, Helmet Shape Shade, Mottled, Signed, 31 In. ..........................8500.00
**Lamp,** Table, Spider & Web, Striated, Signed, 18 In. ....................................................9500.00
**Lamp,** Whirling Leaf, Orange & Yellow, Signed, 22 In. .................................................8500.00
**Lamp,** White, Yellow Leaves, Vine Border, Signed, 30 In. ...........................................5500.00
**Lamp,** Yellow Blossoms Of Mottled Glass, Signed, 16 In. ...........................................8000.00
**Lamp,** 3-Light Lily, Amber, Ribbed Shade, Signed, 13 In. ...........................................1400.00
**Lamp,** 7-Light Lily, Yellow, Purple-Gold, Lily Pad Base, 21 In. ...................................6000.00
**Letter Holder,** Blown-Glass Inserts, Bronze ................................................................550.00
**Letter Holder,** Zodiac Pattern, C.1920, Bronze, 12 X 8 1/4 In. ....................................200.00
**Letter Opener,** Bookmark Pattern, Dore Patina, Bronze ...............................................125.00
**Letter Opener,** Indian Pattern, Bronze, Signed & Numbered .........................................45.00
**Letter Opener,** Venetian Pattern, Bronze .....................................................................175.00
**Letter Rack,** Abalone, 2 Compartment, Iridescent Discs, Bronze ..................................325.00
**Letter Rack,** Bookmark Pattern, Bronze, Signed, 9 X 5 In. ..........................................300.00
**Letter Rack,** Graduate, 2 Section, Bronze, Signed, 5 1/2 X 9 1/2 In. ..........................225.00
**Letter Rack,** Spanish, 2 Compartments, Bronze, Signed, 10 In.Wide .........................650.00
**Letter Rack,** Zodiac Pattern, 2 Section, Green Patina, Bronze, Signed ........................175.00
**Lighter,** American Indian, Raised Masks, Bronze, Signed, Bottom, 3 In. ......................150.00
**Magnifying Glass,** American Indian, Bronze, Signed, 8 1/2 In.Long ...........................275.00
**Magnifying Glass,** Pine Needle, Gold Dore, Slag, Bronze, 8 In. .................................325.00
**Magnifying Glass,** Zodiac Pattern .............................................................................275.00
**Match Holder,** Bronze, Marked Tiffany Studios, 6 X 3 X 3 3/4 In. ...............................150.00
**Paper Clip,** Lady's Hand, Decorated Sleeve Cuff ..........................................................85.00
**Paperweight,** Bulldog, Bronze, Signed, 3 3/4 X 2 1/4 X 2 1/4 In. ...............................600.00
**Paperweight,** Lioness, Dark Patina, Bronze, Signed, 4 3/4 X 1 1/2 In. .......................350.00
**Paperweight,** Sphinx, Dark Patina, Bronze, Signed, 2 1/2 X 1 In. ...............................495.00
**Pen Brush,** Octagon Shape, Bronze, Original Brush, 2 1/4 X 2 1/4 In. .........................195.00
**Picture Frame,** Grapevine Design, Etched Metal & Glass, Signed .................................450.00
**Planter,** Sailboat In Relief At Front, Bronze, 4 X 8 In.Diam. ........................................225.00
**Platter,** Geometric Design On Rim, Center Well, Bronze, Signed, 9 In. ........................110.00
**Scale,** Letter, Grapevine Pattern, Amber Slag, Glass & Bronze, Signed ......................350.00
**Scissors,** Line Design, Bronze & Steel, Signed ...........................................................165.00
**Sconce,** 7-Arm, Beaded Back Plate, Lotton Shade, Bronze, 16 In. ...........................1500.00
**Seal,** Scarab, A At Base, Iridescent Gold, 2 In. ..........................................................250.00
**Service Plate,** Border Of Multicolored Flowers, Marked, 10 1/2 In. ...............................65.00
**Stamp Box,** Chinese Pattern, Dore, Insert, Bronze, Large ...........................................150.00
**Tray,** Card, Glass Center, Tab Handles In Enamel, Bronze, Signed ..............................900.00
**Tray,** Card, Raised Edge, Etched Design, Bronze, Signed, 7 In.Diam. ..........................110.00
**Tray,** Pen, Abalone, 3 Section, Center Discs, Bronze, 8 1/2 X 2 1/2 In .......................125.00
**Tray,** Pen, Bookmark Pattern, Bronze, Signed, 8 1/2 X 2 3/4 In. .................................125.00
**Tray,** Pen, Graduate, 4 Ball Feet, Bronze, Signed, 2 1/2 X 9 In. ...................................95.00
**Tray,** Pen, Jewels, Bronze, 9th Century, Signed, 9 3/4 X 3 1/2 In. ..............................225.00
**Tray,** Pen, Jigsaw Grape & Leaf Over Green Slag, Bronze, 10 X 2 In. .........................170.00

Tray, Pen, Pine Needle, Ball Feet, Bronze, 9 1/2 X 2 3/4 In. ............................................. 150.00
Tray, Pen, Zodiac Pattern At Each End, Bronze, 9 1/2 X 3 In. .......................................... 110.00
Tray, Raised Border Design, Dore Finish, Signed, 12 In.Diam. ........................................ 175.00
Tray, Raised Border, Geometric Design, Bronze, Signed, 14 In.Diam. ......................... 225.00
Tray, Serving, Raised Border, Line Design, Bronze, 12 X 15 In. ..................................... 450.00
Vase, Lamp, Cypriote, Multicolored, Signed, 12 In. ................................................. 2250.00
Vase, Prisms & Hobstar Design, Silver Rim, Signed, 9 In. ............................................. 395.00
Warmer, Brandy, Aladdin's Lamp Shape, Dragon Handle, C.1890 ............................... 450.00

*Tiffin Glass Company of Tiffin, Ohio, was a subsidiary of the United
States Glass Co.of Pittsburgh, Pennsylvania. Black satin glass, made by the
company between 1923 and 1926, is very popular among collectors. Other
types were also made.*

TIFFIN, Bowl, Green, Covered ........................................................................................ 37.50
Candleholder & Bowl, Satin, Chartreuse, 3 Piece ...................................................... 50.00
Pitcher, Shawl Dancer ..................................................................................................... 75.00
Vase, Poppies, Black Amethyst, 9 In. .............................................................................. 38.50
Vase, Silver Overlay Flowers, 6 In. ............................................................................... 129.00
Vase, Silver Overlay On Black Satin Glass, 6 1/2 In. ................................................... 196.00

TILE, see also listing by company name
TILE, Art Nouveau Goat, Wheeling, 6 X 6 In. ................................................................. 20.00
Art Nouveau, Gold Rim & Beading, Angled Corners, 5 In.Square .............................. 28.00
Art Nouveau, Portrait, French, Signed Daniellatsk, 4 1/8 In.Square ....................... 350.00
Black Bears, Mosaic, 10 1/4 X 5 3/4 In. ......................................................................... 80.00
Blue Basket Of Flowers Center, Border Design, Bavaria, 6 3/4 In. .............................. 9.50
California Faience, Sailing Ship, Blue, Brown, Tan, C.1920, Marked, 5 In. ............... 175.00
Fireplace, 6 Colored Scenics, Colored Scenes, Set Of 6 ............................................. 175.00
Indian Woman, Wrapped In Robe, C.1840, Sepia, Staffordshire, 9 X 6 In. ............... 325.00
Portrait, Terriers, Sherwin & Cotton Co., C.1890, Oak Frame, Pair .......................... 250.00
Profile Of Bearded & Helmeted Roman Soldier, Marked Robertson, 6 In. ............... 95.00
Relief Female Portrait, 10 1/2 In.Square ...................................................................... 65.00
Scrolls, Flowers, Glass, Sterling Silver Overlay, 6 In.Diam. ......................................... 45.00
Stove, Woman's Head, Brown & Gold, Beaver Falls, 2 1/4 In.Square .......................... 10.00
Tea, Dandelion Design, Austria ....................................................................................... 12.50
Tea, Horse & Rider, Stoneware ........................................................................................ 12.50
Tea, Silver Overlay On Clear Glass ................................................................................. 55.00
Tea, Tulip Design, German ............................................................................................... 20.00
Woodrow Wilson Picture, Stoke On Trent, 1910, 9 X 6 In. ........................................... 60.00

TIN, see also Store
TIN, Apple, For String, Painted ........................................................................................ 38.00
Baking Powder, Dr.Price's Phosphate, 12 Ounce .......................................................... 10.00
Baking Powder, Rough Rider, Pictures Man On Horse, 1909 ........................................ 30.00
Biscuit Jar, Figural, Organ Grinder, Crawford, English ............................................... 325.00
Biscuit, History Of Reading, Poetry, Travels, Science ................................................. 110.00
Biscuit, Poems Of Keats, Macaulay's Essays, Queen Of Hearts ................................ 110.00
Bowl, Shaving, C.1820 ..................................................................................................... 235.00
Box, Candle, Black Paint, 11 In. ...................................................................................... 200.00
Box, Candle, Hinged Cover, Tin Straps, American, 14 In. .............................................. 70.00
Box, Document, Brass Handle, Lock & Key, Black, Gold Design, 6 1/2 X 9 In. ............. 20.00
Box, Document, Hinged Lid, Handle, Hasp, Amber Finish, 4 X 7 In. ............................. 40.00
Box, Document, Red & Gold, Key, 12 X 8 X 5 1/4 In. ..................................................... 23.00
Box, Dome Lid, Wire Handle, Fruit Design, Brushstrokes, 6 1/2 X 3 In. ..................... 150.00
Box, Large Red Flowers, Original Design ....................................................................... 250.00
Box, Pencil, Charlie Chaplin Figure On Front, Red ........................................................ 28.00
Box, Tinder, Flat Top, Inside Snuffer Cover, Striker & Flint, Red Paint ..................... 295.00
Bucket, Sap, 8 3/8 X 11 1/2 In.Diam. ............................................................................... 9.50
Candle Box, Asphaltum Finish, Hanging Ring, 12 In. .................................................... 190.00
Candle Box, Hangers At Back, Pewter Gray, 15 7/8 In. ................................................ 235.00
Candle Snuffer & Tray, Stenciled Leaf Pattern, Handwrought .................................... 50.00
Candlebox, Gray Paint, 15 7/8 In. ................................................................................... 225.00
Candleholder, Saucer, Push-Up ....................................................................................... 28.00

**Canister,** Brushstrokes In Green, Red Flowers, 4 1/2 In. ..................... 125.0 0
**Canteen,** G.A.R., We Drank From The Same Canteen, 1861-95 ..................... 65.00
**Canteen,** Old Orange Paint, 6 1/4 In.Diam. ..................... 99.00
**Carrier,** Oyster ..................... 10.00
**Case,** Comb, Red Paint ..................... 35.00
**Case,** Eyeglass, C.Parker, C.1860 ..................... 15.00
**Chamberstick,** Crimped Edge, Handled ..................... 36.00
**Churn,** Butter, Bulbous, Wood Blades, 19th Century, 10 X 13 1/2 X 13 In. ..................... 195.00
**Coffeepot,** Conical Shape, Side Spout, Finial, 19th Century, 8 1/2 In. ..................... 70.00
**Coffeepot,** Domed Cover, Straight Spout, 11 1/2 In. ..................... 37.00
**Coffeepot,** Pewter Gooseneck Spout, Lid & Finial, C.1860, 12 1/2 In. ..................... 120.00
**Coffeepot,** Slant Side, Straight Spout, Lid Red, C.1860 ..................... 60.00
**Creamer,** Union Leader ..................... 150.00
**Cup & Saucer,** Little Red Riding Hood ..................... 10.00
**Cylinder,** Holding 9 Asphaltum Tin Tumblers, 3 In. ..................... 85.00
**Daisy Fly Poison,** Flat, 6 X 6 In. ..................... 10.00
**Ear Trumpet,** Black, Flared Pierced Bell ..................... 120.00
**Egg Coddler,** 2 Tiers Of 5, Double Hinged Lid, Dover Stamping Co. ..................... 125.00
**Figurine,** Dutch Boy & Girl, C.1850, Pair ..................... 175.00
**Foot Warmer,** Original Finish, Heart Punching, Wooden ..................... 120.00
**Foot Warmer,** Pierced Metal, Wood Frame, Fuel Container ..................... 88.75
**Foot Warmer,** Punched, Maple ..................... 125.00
**Foot Warmer,** Wooden Frame, Turned Post, Tin Box, Heart Design, 5 5/8 In. ..................... 120.00
**Hatbox,** Dobb's, Lithographed, Miniature ..................... 22.00
**Horn,** Fish Peddlar's ..................... 21.00
**Lamp,** Whale Oil, Oven, Original Wooden Handle ..................... 85.00
**Lantern,** Pierced, Paul Revere's Lantern, 6 X 15 In. ..................... 125.00
**Light,** Street, Dietz, 26 X 15 In. ..................... 65.00
**Log Cabin Syrup,** Large ..................... 48.00
**Lucky Strike Flat 50s,** Green ..................... 5.00
**Marshmallow,** Campfire, Round ..................... 21.00
**Match Holder,** Wall, Holds Box, Handmade, 1900 ..................... 15.00
**Match Safe,** Wall, Original Brushstroke Design ..................... 85.00
**Mold,** Candle, Arch Base, 6 Stand ..................... 165.00
**Mold,** Candle, Double Handled, 12 Hole, 19th Century, 11 In. ..................... 75.00
**Mold,** Candle, 1 Tube ..................... 45.00
**Mold,** Candle, 12 Tube, Handhold ..................... 48.00
**Mold,** Candle, 4 Tube ..................... 32.00
**Mold,** Candle, 8 Large Tubes ..................... 64.00
**Mold,** Candle, 8 Tube, Hanging Ring ..................... 38.00
**Mold,** Candle, 8 Tube, Painted Black ..................... 40.00
**Mold,** Candle, 48 Tube, 6 X 8 In. ..................... 290.00
**Mold,** Maple Sugar, Butterfly, Outspread Wings ..................... 3.00
**Mold,** Maple Sugar, Heart ..................... 3.00
**Mold,** Maple Sugar, Horseshoe ..................... 3.00
**Mold,** Maple Sugar, Swirl ..................... 3.00
**Mold,** Maple Sugar, 4 Hearts ..................... 3.00
**Mold,** Maple Sugar, 4 Stars ..................... 3.00
**Mold,** Plug Tobacco, 6 Rows Of 4 Schnapp's Logos, 12 X 12 In. ..................... 32.00
**Mold,** St.Nick, 2 Piece, 8 In. ..................... 48.00
**Peanut Roaster,** Stand, Acme, Tin ..................... 120.00
**Plaque,** Wall, Say When, 16 In. ..................... 130.00
**Rattle & Whistle,** Mother's Head In Relief, Drum Shape, 4 In. ..................... 36.00
**Reflector,** Bird Roaster For Fireplace, 6 Hooks ..................... 145.00
**Sconce,** Wall, Strap Style, 13 In. ..................... 85.00
**Sconce,** Wall, Strap, Original Green Paint, 7 1/2 In. ..................... 245.00
**Shaving Kit,** Soldier, Original Brush & Soap Dish ..................... 10.00
**Spittoon,** Figural, Turtle, Step On Head, Back Flips Open ..................... 275.00
**Spittoon,** Lady's, Asphaltum, Handled & Lidded, 3 1/4 X 4 1/4 In.Diam. ..................... 68.00
**Sugar,** Red Brushstrokes On Cover, Mustard Paint Strokes, 3 1/4 In. ..................... 125.00
**Syrup,** Covered, Red Tomato Pattern, Original, 3 3/4 In. ..................... 155.00
**Tinderbox,** Candleholder Top, Inside Snuffer, 4 3/8 In. ..................... 285.00
**Tray,** Coffin, White Band, Red & Green Brushwork ..................... 95.00

| | |
|---|---:|
| **Tray,** Flowers, Bird, Gold Scroll Border, Penna., 22 3/4 X 17 1/2 In. | 350.00 |
| **Tray,** Knife & Fork | 95.00 |
| **Tray,** New England, C.1850, Original Painted Fruit & Flowers, 22 X 17 In. | 195.00 |
| | |
| **TOBACCO JAR, Austrian Boy,** Holder For Matches, Figural, Pastels, 7 1/2 In. | 35.00 |
| **Bird Finial,** Snails & Fruit Design, Marked N. & H., 7 3/4 In. | 135.00 |
| **Black Boy** | 65.00 |
| **Black Girl** | 65.00 |
| **Black Holding Watermelon** | 110.00 |
| **Black Man,** Covered, Smoking Pipe, Bisque, 4 5/8 X 4 In.Diam. | 85.00 |
| **Black Man,** Victorian, Carlsbad, Austria | 165.00 |
| **Black Woman,** Handkerchief Tied Around Head | 85.00 |
| **Boar Finial,** Acid Finish Blue Glass, 8 1/2 X 5 3/4 In. | 91.00 |
| **Cossack Man,** Figural | 85.00 |
| **Edgeworth,** C.1920, Covered | 10.00 |
| **Figural,** Bisque, Black Boy Smoking Pipe, 5 In. | 115.00 |
| **Fisherman** | 65.00 |
| **French Legionnaire,** Figural, German | 65.00 |
| **Geisha** | 68.00 |
| **Hand-Painted Brass Lid,** Milk Glass | 65.00 |
| **Hand-Painted Cigars & Pipes,** Gold Lid, Porcelain, Signed | 195.00 |
| **Indian,** Blue Ground, Peace Pipe Top, Glazed Porcelain, 5 1/2 In. | 97.50 |
| **Lady,** Lid Is Turban, Pottery | 40.00 |
| **Marbleized Blues,** Brown, Glazed Brass Frog, English, 4 3/4 In. | 265.00 |
| **Round Feet & Finial,** 6-Sided, Cast Iron, 5 1/4 In. | 120.00 |
| **Skull** | 68.00 |
| **Stoneware,** German, Covered | 9.75 |
|      **TOBACCO, TIN, see Store, Tin** | |

*Toby jugs have been made since the seventeenth century.*
     **TOBY JUG, see also Royal Doulton, Toby Jug**

| | |
|---|---:|
| **TOBY, Jug,** Dog, 10 In. | 75.00 |
| **Long John Silver,** C.1850, Marked, 9 7/8 In. | 75.00 |
| **Standing With Snuffbox,** Colored Clothes, 8 1/4 In. | 265.00 |
| | |
| **TOLE, Box,** Deed, Stenciled, Brushwork, Azurine & Blue, Dome Top, 8 In. | 65.00 |
| **Box,** Document, Curved Top, Freehand Painting, 6 1/2 X 3 X 3 1/2 In. | 85.00 |
| **Box,** Document, Polychrome Design Of Swags, American, 13 1/2 X 7 1/2 In. | 275.00 |
| **Cache p**    Design At Top & Base, 18th Century French, 11 1/2 In.Diam. | 565.00 |
| **Can,** Tea, Printed Word, Cover, 5 1/2 X 4 In.Diam. | 6.00 |
| **Candleholder,** Push-Up, 8 1/2 In.Diam. | 55.00 |
| **Jardiniere,** Footed, D-Shape, Gilt Foliate, 11 1/4 In.     *Illus* | 950.00 |

Tole, Jardiniere, Footed, D-Shape, Gilt Foliate, 11 1/4 In.

Lantern, Candle, Hanging, English ............................................................ 75.00
Spice Cabinet, 6 Section, Beveled Mirror, 24 X 11 1/2 X 13 3/4 In. ................. 500.00
Tea Caddy, Brown, 19th Century Design .................................................... 95.00
Tray, Black, Flower Basket Center, Oval, 17 1/2 In. ..................................... 135.00
Tray, Black, Leafy Gold Border, Oval, 16 3/4 In. ......................................... 135.00
Tray, Handholds, Hunter Firing Gun, .C.1850, 19 X 26 In. .............................. 300.00
Tray, Serving, Russian, Vivid Flowers, 12 X 14 In. ....................................... 45.00
Vase, Flowers & Scene, Hand-Painted, French, C.1800 ................................. 50.00

TOM MIX, Book, Trail Of The Terrible Six .................................................. 38.00
Buckle, Belt ....................................................................................... 30.00
Card, Arcade, Set Of 17 ....................................................................... 100.00
Handkerchief ...................................................................................... 3.00
Knife, Pocket ..................................................................................... 27.50
Movie Still, Ralston Straight Shooters Series, Copyrighted .......................... 30.00
Pin, Ralston ....................................................................................... 12.50
Ring, Periscope .................................................................................. 45.00
Ring, Sliding Whistle ........................................................................... 20.00
Spinner, Good Luck ............................................................................. 22.00
Telescope, Metal ................................................................................ 45.00
Telescope, Ralston ............................................................................. 15.00
Wrapper, Bubble Gum, Adventure Stories, Panel Advertising Ring ................. 75.00

TOOL, see also Iron; Kitchen; Store; Tin; Wooden
TOOL, Adze, Cooper's ......................................................................... 22.00
Adze, Cooper's, Bowl, 7 1/4 In. .............................................................. 85.00
Adze, Hand, Strap, Connecticut ............................................................. 150.00
Alimer, Sawtooth, Stanley ..................................................................... 8.00
Anvil, Cavalry, 45 Pound ...................................................................... 65.00
Anvil, Centennial 1776, Bronze, 3 1/2 In. ................................................. 49.00
Anvil, Lap ......................................................................................... 70.00
Auger, Barrel Bung ............................................................................. 9.00
Auger, Cooper's Bung Hole, 11 1/2 In. .................................................... 28.00
Auger, Lemay, Casey, Ill., Removes Molasses From Barrel, Brass, 15 In. ......... 22.00
Auger, Long Nose, 1 1/2 X 64 In. ........................................................... 35.00
Auger, Pod, Dated 1871 ....................................................................... 17.00
Auger, Wooden Handle, C.1890, 7 In. ...................................................... 11.50
Ax, Cooper's ...................................................................................... 50.00
Ax, Goosewing .................................................................................... 150.00
Ax, Hatchet Marble Safety Ax Co., Metal Guard, Leather Cover ...................... 125.00
Back Saw, H.Disston, Blade, 8 In. ........................................................... 18.50
Baler, Copper's, Pair ........................................................................... 65.00
Baler, Wool, Handmade, Pine, Primitive ................................................... 40.00
Beam Auger, Carpenter's, Wooden Handle ............................................... 5.00
Bed Smoother, Feather Bed, Paddle Shape, Pine, 1 Piece, 30 In. .................. 40.00
Bed Smoother, Feather, Maple, Ivory Tip, 21 In. Long ................................. 100.00
Bee Smoker, Bellows Type ................................................................... 9.00
Bit Brace, Sheffield, Signed J.Bee, Brass ................................................ 115.00
Bit, Expansion, Patented 1858, Clarks ..................................................... 9.00
Blowtorch, Brass, Gasoline ................................................................... 7.00
Board, Graining, Leatherworker's ........................................................... 25.00
Box Opener, Marked Buy Only Cow Brand Soda, Cast Iron ........................... 12.75
Box, Miter, Union Hardware Co., 1902, Saw, Cast Iron & Wood, 15 1/4 In. ....... 37.50
Brace, Beechwood, Brass Plated, Sheffield .............................................. 125.00
Brace, Bit, Sheffield, Wm.Marples & Sons ................................................ 145.00
Brace, Burl Head, Signed, G.R.Goff, Brass, 10 In. ...................................... 500.00
Brace, Chairmaker's, Wooden, Beech With Spoon Bit .................................. 120.00
Brace, Corner, Stanley-Frey, No.100 ...................................................... 28.00
Brace, Stanley, No.982, Right Angle, Gears Slip One Direction ...................... 18.50
Brace, T.H.Buxton, Sheffield, Brass Plated, Beechwood ............................... 125.00
Brace, Wagon Builder's, Rosewood Head, 16 In. ........................................ 45.00
Brace, Wheelwright's ........................................................................... 28.00
Brace, Wooden, Mahogany, Brass Trim, Sheffield Style ................................ 165.00

Brace, Yankee, No.75 ..................................................................................... 16.00
Branding Iron, Bar H O, Blacksmith Made ..................................................... 30.00
Branding Iron, 20 In. ...................................................................................... 35.00
Broadax, 30 In. ............................................................................................... 25.00
Broom, Splinted Birch, 19th Century, 47 In. ................................................. 125.00
Buck Saw, Meat Market ................................................................................. 65.00
Bucket, Grease, Car & Airplane, C.1920, 6 In.Diameter .............................. 58.00
Buncher, Asparagus ...................................................................................... 45.00
Cabinet Scraper, Brass Wear Plate, Beechwood ......................................... 20.00
Cabinet Scraper, Stanley, No.82, C.1934 .................................................... 16.00
Cabinet Scraper, Stanley, No.83, 1896, Roller Type .................................... 22.50
Carpet Beater, Shaker, Bentwood, Wooden Handle .................................... 35.00
Carpet Beater, Wicker ................................................................................... 35.00
Chest, Carpenter's, Folding, 12 Wooden Tools, Pine ................................... 150.00
Chest, Inlaid Design In Top Of Inside, Dovetailed ....................................... 550.00
Chisel, Keen Kutter ....................................................................................... 8.50
Chisel, Mortise, Swan Neck Lock, Marples & Sons ..................................... 65.00
Chisel, Wood, W.Butcher, Cast Steel, 1 3/4 X 14 1/2 In. ............................ 27.50
Chisel, Wood, Winchester, 3/4 In. ................................................................ 12.00
Chopper, Fram, Blades, Wooden Handle, 28 In. .......................................... 35.00
Clamp, C, P.S. & W.Co., Patent, 1885, Throat, 5 1/2 In. ........................... 17.50
Clamp, Carpenter's, Wooden Screws, Wood, 10 In. .................................... 16.00
Clamp, Oxbow, Metal ..................................................................................... 10.00
Coachman's, C.1810, Cast Iron, Set ............................................................. 25.00
Comb, Curry, Cast Iron, Wooden Handle ...................................................... 7.50
Comb, Flax, Hexed Pennsylvania Dutch, Wood & Iron, 1700s, 11 1/2 X 6 In. ..... 95.00
Compass, Barn Maker's, Hand-Hewn, C.1820, Wooden, 22 1/2 In. ............. 50.00
Compass, Pocket, Surveying, Ainsworth Denver, Aluminum Case, Cover ... 67.00
Compass, Rabbet, Browning, Rowe, Mass, 1 1/2 In.Wide ........................... 22.00
Crimper, Hand, Pexto ..................................................................................... 18.00
Croze, Cooper's, Maple, 14 In. ...................................................................... 49.00
Cutter, Dowel, Wagon Spoke ......................................................................... 15.00
Cutter, Leather, Rosewood Handle, H.F.Osborne, Newark, N.J. ................. 12.00
Cutter, Soap, Turned Wooden Handle, C.1890 ............................................ 25.00
Cutter, Tombstone, Anvil, Swedgeblock, Forge, Vice, 1800's ................... 1100.00
Dehorner, Cattle, Wooden Handles ............................................................... 25.00
Dividers, Draftman's, Brass ........................................................................... 20.00
Dowser, Halls, 1-Rod, Witness Capsule, Instruction Sheet ......................... 125.00
Drag Saw, Ottawa, Gas Engine, 5 Horsepower, Reciprocating Saw & Parts ......... 400.00
Drawknife, Cooper's, Curved, French Pattern, Marked A.M. ........................ 30.00
Drill, Barn Beam ............................................................................................. 55.00
Drill, Hand, Bit Dispenser, Brass Ferule, Goodell Bros., 1891 .................... 16.50
Drill, Speed Breast, Original Paper & Box ................................................... 15.00
Embosser, Notary, Homestead Telephone Co. ............................................. 15.00
Engraver's, Rosewood Handles, Dated 1889, Signed, 8 Piece .................... 150.00
Fencing, Combination Hammer, Hatchet, Wire Cutter, & Grip, Handle, 10 In. ...... 26.50
Fillister, E. & T.Ring & Co., Worthington, Mass, 2 1/2 In.Wide ................... 28.00
Flax Comb, Diamond Cutout, Honey Brown, Wooden, 11 1/2 In. ................ 75.00
Funnel, Brewer's, Brass Thumblift, Copper .................................................. 42.00
Funnel, Maple Syrup, 1800s, 1 Piece ........................................................... 75.00
Gauge, Electrical, 8 In.Diam. ........................................................................ 15.00
Gauge, Gas Pump, Glass, 5 Gallon, 10 X 18 In. .......................................... 22.50
Gauge, Siding ................................................................................................. 7.50
Glue Pot, Double, Copper, 5 X 5 In.Diam. .................................................... 50.00
Goad, Elephant ............................................................................................... 25.00
Gouge, Shipwright's, Bit, 2 X 16 In. .............................................................. 23.00
Grindstone, Table Model, Hand Crank, Iron Trough ..................................... 48.00
Gutter Mold, Tinsmith's, Patent 1898 .......................................................... 45.00
Hacksaw, Adjustable Cast Iron Frame, Goddell & Pratt Co., Patent 1899 ... 47.50
Hammer, Claw, Hand Forged, Cast Iron ....................................................... 22.00
Hammer, Claw, Keen Kutter, Tubular Steel Handle ..................................... 12.50
Hammer, Claw, Stanley .................................................................................. 2.50
Hammer, Double Headed, Nailing Wooden Cigar Boxes, 4 In. .................... 5.00

| | |
|---|---|
| **Hammer,** Farrier's | 5.00 |
| **Hammer,** Riveting, Keen Kutter, Wooden Handle | 12.50 |
| **Hammer,** Snowball, Maine | 25.00 |
| **Hatchet,** Keen Kutter, Original Handle | 45.00 |
| **Hatchet,** With Nail Puller, Single Blade | 52.00 |
| **Hay Tester,** Hand Forged | 22.00 |
| **Header,** Bolt, Blacksmith | 12.00 |
| **Hog Ringer,** Mills, Plier-Type, Patent 1865, 7 In. | 11.50 |
| **Hook,** Bale, Wooden T Shape Handle, Steel Hook, 9 1/2 In. | 2.75 |
| **Hook,** Rug, Stag Horn Handle | 12.00 |
| **Hoop Driver,** Cooper's, Oak Hoop, Cast Iron | 14.00 |
| **Hoop Driver,** Iron, V-Groove In Bottom | 17.00 |
| **Husker,** Corn, Wrist, Leather | 4.00 |
| **Inshave,** Cooper's, Viet, Philadelphia | 55.00 |
| **Iron,** Branding, Letter J, 10 In. | 10.00 |
| **Iron,** Branding, Letter T, 13 In. | 10.00 |
| **Iron,** Flagging | 39.00 |
| **Iron,** For Silk, Cloisonne Handle | 55.00 |
| **Jack,** Conestoga Wagon | 250.00 |
| **Jack,** Miter, Mahogany, Signed, Dunford, 14 1/2 In. | 120.00 |
| **Jack,** Wagon, Conestoga, Orange-Red Finish, Dated 1858 | 150.00 |
| **Jigsaw,** Treadle Powered, Banjo Shape Surface, Cast Iron Legs, 1886 | 300.00 |
| **Knife,** Carpenter's, Drawing, Worth | 14.00 |
| **Knife,** Chamfer, Cooper's, Signed, D.R.Barton | 60.00 |
| **Knife,** Draw, Winsted, Wooden Handles, Folding | 14.00 |
| **Knive,** Cooper's Chamfer, Nos.5 X 5 1/2, Left-Handed | 40.00 |
| **Knocker,** Snow, Yankee | 27.00 |
| **Lawn Mower,** Keen Kutter, Wooden Handle | 42.50 |
| **Level Transit,** Seiler Instrument Co., Wooden Box, 18 1/2 In. | 127.00 |
| **Level,** Carpenter's, Brass Ends, Patent December 7, 1886, 30 In. | 28.00 |
| **Level,** Carpenter's, Brass On All Edges, Rosewood, 24 In. | 150.00 |
| **Level,** Carpenter's, Connecticut, Signed | 59.00 |
| **Level,** It Costs Less To Farm With Case, Wooden, 6 In. | 15.00 |
| **Level,** Keen Kutter, Wooden, 22 In. | 25.00 |
| **Level,** Masonry, Brass Bound | 18.00 |
| **Level,** Stanley Ruler & Level Co., Patent, 1896, Wooden | 18.00 |
| **Level,** Stanley, Cast Iron, 24 In. | 25.00 |
| **Level,** Stanley, Cherry, 18 In. | 22.50 |
| **Level,** Stanley, Dated 1895, 3 1/4 In. | 9.50 |
| **Level,** Stanley, No. 3 | 25.00 |
| **Level,** Stanley, No.10, Brass Trim, Patent 2869 | 45.00 |
| **Level,** Stanley, No.95, Brassbound | 78.00 |
| **Level,** Stanley, No.237, Aluminum, 24 In. | 24.00 |
| **Level,** Surveying, Young & Sons, 1918, Oak Box | 75.00 |
| **Level,** Winchester, Wooden | 40.00 |
| **Level,** Wood, Stanley, Patent 1896, 14 In. | 8.50 |
| **Lighter,** Tinder, Pistol, Notch Carved Handle, American, 9 In. | 500.00 |
| **Line & Reel,** Carpenter's, Chalk Line, Oriental | 55.00 |
| **Link Rod,** Chain Wire, Surveyor's | 45.00 |
| **Log Dog,** Wrought, Pivot End | 17.00 |
| **Loom,** Floor, 2 Harness, Hand-Hewn Walnut, C.1835, Missouri | 1500.00 |
| **Loom,** Tape.Flat, 18th Century, Used Between Knees | 185.00 |
| **Loom,** Tape, 18th Century, Darkened Wood Color, 26 1/4 In. | 225.00 |
| **Lumber Stick,** Wrought Hook End, 48 In. Long | 32.00 |
| **Machine,** Knitting, Tabletop Model, Patent 2867, 12 In. | 75.00 |
| **Machine,** Rope Making | 47.50 |
| **Mallet,** Burl, Wooden | 30.00 |
| **Micrometer,** Pocket, C.1930, Woolworth Stores Only, 1 1/4 X 2 1/2 In. | 27.00 |
| **Mold,** Bentwood Frame | 42.00 |
| **Mold,** Gutter, Tinsmith's, Patent Jan.2, 1898 | 45.00 |
| **Nail Header,** Double | 35.00 |
| **Nail Rake,** Hand Forged, 5 Teeth, 12 In. | 14.00 |
| **Napkin Press,** Platform Base, Crossbar Top Of Screw, American, 7 In. | 150.00 |

**Oiler,** Remington, Pocket .................................................................................................. 20.00
**Oiling Trough,** D.R.Sperry & Co., Batavia, Ill., Buggy Wheel, Iron ......................... 26.00
**Peavy,** American Logging Tool Co., Cast Iron ............................................................. 9.50
**Picker,** Blueberry, Walnut, Dated 1888 ..................................................................... 95.00
**Picker,** Cranberry, Metal ............................................................................................. 42.00
**Pincher,** Cobbler's, Patent 1887 .................................................................. 14.00 To 23.00
**Plane Set,** Pattern Makers, 6 Matched Soles, 4 Blades, Signed Smith ................. 105.00
**Plane,** Block, 9 1/2 In. .................................................................................................. 60.00
**Plane,** Cabinet Maker's, Stanley, Patent 1897, 6 1/2 In. ........................................... 27.50
**Plane,** Celotex, Nickle Plated ...................................................................................... 18.00
**Plane,** Chariot, Gunmetal, Steel Sole, Marples & Sons, 1 3/4 X 4 In. ..................... 210.00
**Plane,** Coachmaker's, Coffin Shaped, 1 1/8 In. Blade, 5 1/2 In. Long ..................... 28.00
**Plane,** Flow, Boxwood, Brass Hardware, 8 In. .......................................................... 165.00
**Plane,** Greenfield Tool Co., Greenfield, Mass., Hollow & Round, Pair .................... 30.00
**Plane,** Gutter, Horn Handle, Iron, 10 In. ...................................................................... 29.50
**Plane,** Jointer, Winchester, No.3035 ......................................................................... 135.00
**Plane,** Knuckle Joint, Low Angle, Sargent .................................................................. 16.00
**Plane,** Miter, Low Angle, Iron & Mahogany Wedge, 8 In. ........................................ 125.00
**Plane,** Oar Maker, Deep Hollow Radius, Beech, 7 In. Long ...................................... 35.00
**Plane,** Plow, Cabinet Maker's, Rabbeting, Cherry ..................................................... 45.00
**Plane,** Plow, Set Of Bits, C.1840 ................................................................................. 75.00
**Plane,** Plow, Z-Z Border, Beech Arms, Wood Thumb Screw, Brass Stop .................. 65.00
**Plane,** Rabbet, Brass Plated Sole, Dark Beech ........................................................... 20.00
**Plane,** Rabbet, Gunmetal, Ebony Wedge, 4 1/2 X 1/2 In. ........................................ 175.00
**Plane,** Rabbet, Sargent, Ebony Sole ........................................................................... 35.00
**Plane,** Shipbuilder's, Rabbet, Double Iron, 20 In. ...................................................... 60.00
**Plane,** Sill, Oak, 9 In. Long ........................................................................................... 45.00
**Plane,** Spar, E.W.Carpenter, Lancaster, Penn. ........................................................... 47.50
**Plane,** Spar, Shipbuilder's, Beech, 2 1/2 X 7 1/2 In. .................................................. 39.00
**Plane,** Squirrel Tail, Coachmaker's, Wooden, Beech, 6 1/2 In. ................................ 160.00
**Plane,** Stanley No.55, 50 Cutters In Wooden Box ..................................................... 165.00
**Plane,** Stanley, Model 45, Box Of Blades .................................................................... 52.50
**Plane,** Stanley, No.18, Knuckle Joint, Block, C.1897 .................................................. 13.50
**Plane,** Stanley, No.40, Scrub ....................................................................................... 22.00
**Plane,** Stanley, No.71 1/2, Router, One Blade ............................................................ 22.00
**Plane,** Tandem Bladed, Stanley ................................................................................... 30.00
**Plane,** Toothing, Beech, Signed Gorton, 7 In. ............................................................. 30.00
**Plane,** Winchester, No.3204, Corrugated, Rear Handle .............................................. 47.50
**Plane,** Wood, Bailey ..................................................................................................... 15.00
**Planter,** Corn, Wooden, C.1890 ................................................................................... 25.00
**Pliers,** Winchester, 9 In. ............................................................................................... 35.00
**Pliers,** Winchester, 10 1/2 In. ...................................................................................... 27.50
**Plow Plane,** Cabinet Maker's, Brass Screw, Maple ................................................... 50.00
**Plucker,** Anderson, Fraserburgh ................................................................................. 72.00
**Plumb & Level,** Disston, Fluted Sides, Arched Brass Top, 30 In. .............................. 23.00
**Plumb Bob,** Brass, Signed, 5 1/4 In. ........................................................................... 30.00
**Plumb Bob,** Removable Cap, Brass, 5 1/2 In. ............................................................. 13.50
**Press,** Book Binder's, Original Paint ............................................................................ 50.00
**Printing Press,** Hand, Galley Tray, Inking Stone & Roller, C.1850 ........................... 375.00
**Puller,** Boot, Leather Punch On End Of T Handle, Folding, Steel ............................. 75.00
**Puller,** Tack, Keen Kutter .............................................................................................. 12.00
**Pulley,** Hay ..................................................................................................................... 3.00
**Pulley,** Rope, Wooden ................................................................................................... 5.75
**Pulley,** Well, Cast-Iron Housing, Marked Meyers, Wooden, 6 In. .............................. 10.00
**Pulley,** Wood, Hudson, Cast Iron, 7 In. ....................................................................... 10.00
**Punch,** Eyelet ................................................................................................................ 45.00
**Punch,** Leather, Roger's, Patent 1903, 1/16 To 3/8 In. .............................................. 20.00
**Rabbet,** Beveled, Gouch & Demond, Springfield, Mass., 3/4 Size ........................... 15.00
**Rabbet,** Shipbuilder's, Hanover, Mass., 20 X 1 In. ..................................................... 40.00
**Raft Auger,** 5/8 In. Size, Wooden, Swivel Handled, 4 2/3 Ft. ................................... 12.00
**Reamer,** Cooper's, Cross Handled, Hand Forged, 15 1/2 In. ..................................... 34.00
**Router,** Stanley No.71, Dated 1901 ............................................................................. 32.00
**Rug Beater,** Wooden Handle ....................................................................................... 12.00

| | |
|---|---|
| **Rule,** Folding, Boxwood, 2 To 4 Ft. | 14.00 |
| **Rule,** Jordon, Germany, Spring Steel, 1/2 X 48 In. | 8.50 |
| **Rule,** Lufkin, Steel, 6 X 3/4 In. | 8.00 |
| **Rule,** Treen, Inscribed Merry Christmas, C.1873, 6 In. | 35.00 |
| **Rule,** Tunbridge, C.1860, 9 In. | 58.00 |
| **Rule,** Twofold, No.O, Ivory & Brass, 6 In. | 75.00 |
| **Saw,** Butcher, Steel Rod Frame, Wooden Handle | 6.00 |
| **Saw,** Hack, Starrett, Wooden Handle, 14 In. | 7.50 |
| **Saw,** Ice, Horse Drawn | 125.00 |
| **Saw,** Keyhole, 16 In. | 7.50 |
| **Sawing Machine,** One Man, 5 1/2 In.Crosscut, Adjustable Angle Cut | 800.00 |
| **Screwdriver,** Brass Ferrule, Winchester | 7.50 |
| **Screwdriver,** Carstairs Whiskey | 5.00 |
| **Screwdriver,** Winchester, Wood & Brass, Handled | 8.00 |
| **Screwdriver,** 1871, Rosewood Handle, 8 In. | 30.00 |
| **Scribe,** Carpenter's, Metal Turn Screw, Wooden | 4.50 |
| **Scribe,** Stanley, Rosewood & Brass | 36.00 |
| **Seed Broadcaster,** Patent 1925 | 20.00 |
| **Sextant,** Heath Bell, No.I, C.1860, Fitted Mahogany Case, Brass | 290.00 |
| **Sharpener,** Lawn Mower | 40.00 |
| **Sharpener,** Stone, Griggville | 12.00 |
| **Shave,** Spoke, Brass & Wood | 8.00 |
| **Shears,** Hand Forged, Hallmarked | 18.00 |
| **Shears,** Pruning, Looped Handle, C.1845, Hand Forged, Blade 2 In. | 27.00 |
| **Shears,** Sheep, 12 In., Pair | 6.50 |
| **Shears,** Tailor's, 1859, R.Heinisch, Newark, N.J., Brass | 60.00 |
| **Shears,** Tinner's, Bench | 26.00 |
| **Shears,** Tinner's, Bench Mount, 8 In. Blade, 36 In. Overall | 22.00 |
| **Shingle,** Roofer's, Hand Forged | 28.00 |
| **Shoelast Holder,** Shoemaker's, Lap, 2 Piece | 25.00 |
| **Shoulder Rebate,** Gunmetal, Mahogany Infill & Wedge, 1 X 7 In. | 240.00 |
| **Shovel,** Corncob, Wire | 30.00 |
| **Shovel,** Grain, Birch, 1 Piece, Open Handle, C.1800 | 185.00 |
| **Shovel,** Grain, Hand-Carved, 26 In. | 55.00 |
| **Shredder,** Tobacco, Walnut Base | 55.00 |
| **Shuttle,** Weaving, Wooden, 16 1/2 In. | 7.00 |
| **Sickle,** Barley, Curbed Blade, Signed W. Fox | 25.00 |
| **Slide Rule,** White Finish, K & E Co., 1900, Leather Case | 16.00 |
| **Slitting Gauge,** Rosewood Handle | 35.00 |
| **Smoker,** Beekeeper's, Leather & Wood Bellow | 16.00 |
| **Snuff Maker,** Brass, 6 Piece | 100.00 |
| **Solicitor's,** Binding & Sealing Legal Documents, 5 Brass, 1 Steel | 65.00 |
| **Spike,** Marlin | 8.00 |
| **Spinning Wheel,** C.1870, Oak & Pine | 290.00 |
| **Spoke Shave,** Cast Iron | 8.50 |
| **Square,** Brass, 8 In. | 12.00 |
| **Square,** Warranted Steel, L.H.Godkin, Framing | 8.00 |
| **Staking Set,** Watchmaker's, 68 Punches, Case | 80.00 |
| **Stretcher,** Barbed Wire | 25.00 |
| **Stretcher,** Carpet, Iron & Wood | 15.00 |
| **Stretcher,** Hat, Treen | 20.00 |
| **Stretcher,** Hat, Wood & Metal, Size Gauge | 42.50 |
| **Stretcher,** Rug, Wood & Iron, 2 Piece | 10.00 |
| **Swift,** For Winding Yarn, All Wooden, 22 1/2 In. | 65.00 |
| **Swift,** Whalebone, American, Mid-19th Century, 21 1/2 In. ..........*Illus* | 700.00 |
| **Swift,** Wooden, 22 In. | 60.00 |
| **T Square,** Moulson Brothers, Sheffield, English Walnut, 18 In. | 40.00 |
| **Tape Measure,** Coil Spring, Advertising | 3.50 |
| **Tape Measure,** Steel, Lufkin, Leather Case, 1950s | 9.50 |
| **Telescope,** Tripod, Brass | 210.00 |
| **Tinner's Stake,** Wooden, 32 In. Long | 65.00 |
| **Tongs,** Blacksmith's | 4.00 To 6.00 |
| **Tongs,** Eel, For Lifting Eels From Barrel | 22.00 |

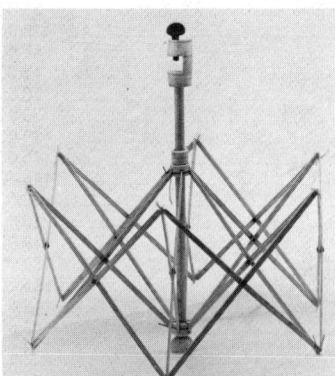

Tool, Swift, Whalebone, American,
Mid-19th Century, 21 1/2 In.

| | |
|---|---:|
| **Transit,** Keuffel & Essar & Co., Tripod, Box, Brass | 350.00 |
| **Transit,** Surveyor's, Tripod, Case, Brass | 69.50 |
| **Traveler,** Wheelwright's | 27.50 |
| **Tri-Square,** Rosewood & Brass, 3 Piece | 40.00 |
| **Trimmer,** Hoof, Bone Handle, Western Cutlery | 13.50 |
| **Trimmer,** Wallpaper, Allen's Single Keystone, Hand Crank, Dated 1892 | 65.00 |
| **Vise,** Floor, Blacksmith's, Wrought, 40 In. | 50.00 |
| **Vise,** Head, Iron | 22.00 |
| **Vise,** Jeweler's, With Anvil, Bench Clamp, Cast Iron | 12.00 |
| **Winder,** Yarn, Brass Fittings, Victorian, Glass Dome, 20 X 15 1/2 In. | 1100.00 |
| **Witchet,** Ash Handle, Iron Parts, 5 1/2 X 9 1/2 In. | 95.00 |
| **Wooden Hay Tester,** Crouch Prong, 44 In. | 4.00 |
| **Work Holder,** Blacksmith's, Wrought, Roller On Top, 25 To 33 In. | 50.00 |
| **Workbench,** Cabinet Maker's, Wood Vise | 350.00 |
| **Wrench,** Buggy, Shift Lever, Shaffer Bros., Cast Iron | 36.50 |
| **Wrench,** Center Adjustment Controls Both Ends, Model T Auto | 22.00 |
| **Wrench,** L.Coes Co., Patent July 8, 1884 | 16.00 |
| **Wrench,** Open, Marked Ford | 5.00 |
| **Wrench,** Pipe, Winchester, 6 In. | 35.00 |

*Toothpick holders are sometimes called toothpicks by collectors. The variously shaped containers made to hold the small wooden toothpicks are of glass, china, or metal. Most of the toothpicks are Victorian.*

**TOOTHPICK, see also other categories such as Bisque, Slag, etc.**

| | |
|---|---:|
| **TOOTHPICK, Alligator,** Sapphire Blue | 125.00 |
|   **Amberina** | 55.00 |
|   **Barred Hobnail** | 18.00 |
|   **Barrel Shape,** Ribbed, Green | 12.00 |
|   **Barrel,** Sapphire Blue | 40.00 |
|   **Bundled Cigars,** Milk Glass | 25.00 |
|   **Chick,** Wishbone, Cracked Egg, Best Wishes | 38.00 |
|   **Child Between 2 Cornucopia,** Bisque, 2 1/2 X 2 1/4 In. | 25.00 |
|   **Cornish Maine,** Custard, Heisey | 27.50 |
|   **Daisy & Button,** Blue | 9.00 |
|   **Daisy & Button,** Green | 18.50 |
|   **Daisy & Button,** Red Dots | 20.00 |
|   **Deer & Castle,** Ruby, Hand Cut, Bohemia | 11.00 |
|   **Delaware,** Cranberry Glass, Gold Trim | 120.00 |
|   **Delaware,** Green & Gold | 70.00 |
|   **Diamond & Fan,** Cut Glass | 18.00 |
|   **Eagle Picks Up Pick In Beak,** Cast Iron, C.1873, 4 X 3 In. | 75.00 |

| | |
|---|---:|
| **Embossed Indian Head,** Camphor Glass, Marked V In Circle | 25.00 |
| **Farm Girl Holding Gun,** Silver Plate, Square Platform | 15.00 |
| **Figural,** Porcupine, Silver Plate, Meriden | 45.00 |
| **Fleur-De-Lis** | 12.00 |
| **Fluted,** Purple, Carnival Glass, N | 50.00 |
| **Folding,** Pocket Knife Shape, Bone, 2 1/2 In. | 30.00 |
| **Frog,** Germany | 25.00 |
| **Fry Glass,** Cobalt Handles | 75.00 |
| **Girl With Bonnet Sits By Holder,** Silver Plate, Meriden | 145.00 |
| **Gypsy Kettle,** Cane Pattern | 12.00 |
| **Iris Meander,** White, Opalescent | 22.00 |
| **King's Crown** | 18.00 |
| **Lad Removes Sock,** Silver Plate, Victorian | 160.00 |
| **Lady On Horse,** Tapestry | 185.00 |
| **Lady,** C.D.Kenny | 12.00 |
| **Little Miss Muffett,** Silver Plate | 68.00 |
| **Milk Glass,** Blue, Slag Rim | 8.00 |
| **Monkeys On Tree Trunk,** Amber | 30.00 |
| **Monterey,** Zipper Slash | 22.50 |
| **Peek-A-Boo,** Holder | 24.00 |
| **Peppard Seed Co.,** K.C., Mo., Celluloid | 15.00 |
| **Pineapple & Fan,** Green | 25.00 |
| **Pointed Gothic** | 18.00 |
| **Portland,** Pressed Glass | 12.00 |
| **Rabbit Holding Egg On Back,** German, 3 1/2 In. | 20.00 |
| **Raised Diamonds & Eagles,** Green Satin Glass, Marked ABC | 15.00 |
| **Scroll,** Cane Band, Baccarat | 30.00 |
| **Shenango,** China | 10.00 |
| **Six Point,** Scalloped | 25.00 |
| **Two Mice On Side Of Egg,** White Bisque, 2 1/2 In. | 24.00 |
| **Urn Shape,** Sterling Silver | 35.00 |
| **Victoria,** Frosted, Fostoria | 75.00 |
| **Victorian Lady,** Silver Plate | 24.00 |
| **Waffle & Star Band** | 22.00 |
| **Winged Scroll,** Custard Glass, Gold | 125.00 |
| **Wishbone With Bird,** Silver Plate | 25.00 |
| **Woodpecker,** Oblong, Iron | 11.00 |
| | |
| **TORQUAY, Celery,** Red, Frosted, Silver Cover | 175.00 |

*Tortoiseshell glass was made during the 1800s and after by the Sandwich Glass Works of Massachusetts and some firms in Germany. Tortoiseshell glass has been reproduced.*

| | |
|---|---:|
| **TORTOISESHELL GLASS, Bowl,** Amber Feet, 3 5/8 X 8 In.Diam. | 88.00 |
| **Bowl,** 9 In.Diam. | 120.00 |
| **Pitcher,** Spout, Polished Pontil, 9 In. | 70.00 |
| | |
| **TORTOISESHELL, Comb,** Mustache, Gold Filled Case, Hanging Loop, C.1920, 3 In. | 65.00 |
| **Comb,** Openwork Top, 4 In.Wide | 11.50 |
| **Comb,** Pierced, A.Willard, Boston, 1830 | 45.00 |
| **Comb,** Small, Pair | 8.00 |
| **Compact,** Dragonfly Design | 28.00 |
| **Earrings,** Gypsy | 18.00 |
| **Figurine,** Violin, Green Stone, Lapis Lazuli Trim, 4 1/2 In. | 65.00 |
| **Figurine,** Violin, With Ivory, 4 1/2 In.Long | 95.00 |
| **Tea Caddy,** 8 X 6 In. | 650.00 |
| **Vase,** 7 In. | 128.00 |
| | |
| **TOY, Acrobat,** Pinocchio | 190.00 |
| **Airplane,** Army Bomber, Sun Rubber | 10.00 |
| **Airplane,** Keystone | 285.00 |
| **Airplane,** Lucky Boy, Cast Iron | 150.00 |

**Airplane,** Mechanical, 1930s, Schieble Co., 30 In. .................................................. 210.00
**Airplane,** 2 Engine, Metal, 7 X 9 In. ......................................................................... 15.00
**Al Jolson,** Dancing, Tin .................................................................................................. 75.00
**Alabama Coon Jigger,** Oh-My, Windup, 1912, Lehmann ......................................... 295.00
**Alabama Coon Jigger,** Strauss ................................................................................ 200.00
**Alligator,** Penny Toy ...................................................................................................... 95.00
**Alligator,** Wiggly, Penny, German ............................................................................... 85.00
**Alligator,** Windup, Chein ............................................................................................. 30.00
**Ally-Oop,** 1937 ............................................................................................................. 16.00
**Ambulance,** Iron Slush Cast, 3 1/2 In. ....................................................................... 25.00
**Ambulance,** Militaire, Tin, Windup, French ............................................................... 75.00
**Auto,** Coupe, C.1920, Cast Iron, 5 In. ....................................................................... 65.00
**Auto,** Ford Coupe, Arcade, Cast Iron, 5 In. .............................................................. 85.00
**Auto,** Sedan, Arcade, Cast Iron ................................................................................ 150.00
**Automatic Acrobats,** Reversible, Tin, Germany, 13 1/2 In. ..................................... 90.00
**B.O.Plenty & Sparkle,** Windup, Marx, Boxed ......................................................... 165.00
**Baby,** Crawling, Windup ............................................................................................... 10.00
**Balky Mule,** Lithographed Clowns, Clockwork, 7 1/2 In. ......................................... 90.00
**Band,** Lil Abner, Dogpatch, Windup ......................................................................... 325.00
**Band,** Merrymaker, Marx ............................................................................................ 725.00
**Banjo Player,** Mechanical, Secor .......................................................................... 4200.00
**Bareback Rider,** Original Paint, Schoenhut, 6 1/2 In. ............................................. 135.00
**Barnacle Bill The Sailor,** Walks, 1930s, Windup .................................................... 175.00
**Barney Google & Spark Plug,** Schoenhut, Pair ..................................................... 500.00
**Barney Google,** 5 1/2 In. ............................................................................................. 42.00
**Battleship,** Red Guns, Gray, 1930s, Metal, Tootsietoy, 6 In. ..................................... 6.50
**Battleship,** The Admiral, C.1890s, Lithographed Cardboard, 20 In. ...................... 200.00
**Bazooka,** Bob Burns, Original Label ........................................................................... 14.00
**Bear On Musical Base,** Tin ....................................................................................... 190.00
**Bear,** Balloon Blowing, Battery Operated .................................................................. 35.00
**Bear,** Drinking, Battery Operated ................................................................................ 20.00
**Bear,** Fur Covered, Windup ......................................................................................... 25.00
**Bear,** In Rowboat, Tin, Windup, Boxed ....................................................................... 45.00
**Bear,** Mama Feeding Baby, Battery Operated ........................................................... 40.00
**Bear,** Mohair, Shoebutton Eyes, 12 In. ...................................................................... 85.00
**Bear,** Panda, Jointed, Humpback, Straw Stuffed, Pie Shaped Eyes, 47 In. ........... 215.00
**Bear,** Playing Guitar, Windup, Boxed .......................................................................... 95.00
**Bear,** Straw Stuffed, Yellow, Jointed, 22 In. ............................................................. 195.00
**Bear,** Windup, Walks & Growls, C.1930s .................................................................. 125.00
**Bed,** Doll, Bedding & Hand-Stitched Quilt, C.1900, 11 1/2 X 7 X 9 In. .................... 50.00
**Bed,** Doll, Brass ......................................................................................................... 350.00
**Bed,** Doll, Campbell Soup Lithographed .................................................................... 85.00
**Bed,** Doll, Four-Poster, 6 X 11 In. ................................................................................. 8.50
**Bed,** Doll, Rope, 4 Low Posts, 8 X 14 In. ................................................................... 45.00
**Bed,** Doll, Slatted Bottom, Wooden, 20 X 11 In. ....................................................... 20.00
**Bell Ringer,** Dog, Doghouse, Chases Cat .............................................................. 1600.00
**Bell Ringer,** Harold Lloyd, Germany ......................................................................... 175.00
**Bell Ringer,** Monkey With Coconut .......................................................................... 375.00
**Bell Ringer,** Wild Mule Jack, 1900 .......................................................................... 475.00
      **TOY, BICYCLE, see Bicycle**
**Bimbo,** Drumming Clown, Boxed .............................................................................. 150.00
**Bird In Cage,** Tin, Windup, Japan .............................................................................. 20.00
**Bird,** Canary, Singing, Windup, Boxed ....................................................................... 20.00
**Bird,** German, Windup ................................................................................................. 10.00
**Bird,** Lithographed Paper Wings, Lehman, Tin ......................................................... 600.00
**Bird,** Pecking, 1927, Windup ....................................................................................... 20.00
**Birds,** Pull On Worm, Move On Wheels, 1900, Boxed ............................................. 325.00
**Black Minstrels,** Semimechanical, 1 Man With Accordion, Tin ............................. 2500.00
**Black Woman,** Arms Raised, Dances, Hand-Painted, 1910 .................................... 235.00
**Blimp,** Penny Toy, 4 In. .............................................................................................. 270.00
**Blocks,** Alphan, Schoenhut, Set Of 7 ........................................................................ 55.00
**Blocks,** Our Darling, Nested, McLaughlin ................................................................ 120.00

**Boat & Sailor,** Windup, Lindstrom, 7 In. ......................................................................... 22.00
**Boat,** Hydroplane, Tin, Windup ........................................................................................ 14.00
**Boat,** Lindstrom, Windup, 7 In. ........................................................................................ 22.00
**Boat,** Lionel, Cast Iron ................................................................................................... 200.00
**Boat,** Windup, Lindstrom, Tin ........................................................................................... 45.00
**Boat,** Windup, Ohio Art .................................................................................................... 15.00
**Bojangles,** Dancing, Black, Boxed .................................................................................. 60.00
**Boxes,** Nesting Alphabet, Complete Set .......................................................................... 85.00
**Boxing Dog,** Tin Face, Windup, Boxed ............................................................................. 12.50
**Boy,** With Suitcase, Windup .............................................................................................. 25.00
**Bronco Horse,** D.Sebel & Co., England, Tin, 30 X 26 In. ............................................... 150.00
**Brooklyn Bridge,** Bliss, C.1880s, Tin .............................................................................. 525.00
**Buck Rogers Rocket,** 1920s, Windup, Marx .................................................................... 175.00
**Buckboard,** 24 In. ....................................................................................... *Illus* 650.00
**Bucking Bronco,** Lehmann, Tin, Clockwork, 7 In. ........................................... *Illus* 150.00
**Buggy,** Doll, Collapsible ................................................................................................... 100.00
**Buggy,** Doll, Wicker, 35 In. ............................................................................................... 125.00
**Buggy,** Folding, 7 In. Steel Wheels, 20 X 8 In. ................................................................. 97.50
**Bugle,** Boy Scout Scenes ................................................................................................. 10.00
**Building,** Skyscraper, Marx, Tin Lithograph .................................................................... 30.00
**Bulldog,** Bulb Attachment Makes It Walk & Bark, Papier-Mache .................................. 275.00
**Bulldog,** Papier-Mache, Pull Chain Growler, French, 10 X 18 In. .................................. 325.00
**Bulldog,** U.S.Zone Germany, Tin, Windup, 8 In. ............................................................. 80.00
**Bunny,** Picnic, Battery Operated ...................................................................................... 19.00
**Bus,** Century Of Progress, Arcade .................................................................................... 75.00
**Bus,** Greyhound, Chein, Tin ............................................................................................. 28.00
**Bus,** Original Figures, Kenton, Cast Iron ......................................................................... 825.00
**Bus,** Robot, Unique Art, Tin ............................................................................................. 28.00
**Bus,** Sightseeing, 1933, Arcade, Cast Iron ...................................................................... 98.00
**Busy Bridge,** Windup, Tin, Marx ...................................................................................... 75.00
**Butcher,** On Cart, Pulled By Pig, German, 1905 ............................................................. 330.00
**Butter & Egg Man,** Windup, Boxed .................................................................................. 225.00
**Butterfly,** Wings Flap, C.1940, Tin, Friction Operated ..................................................... 7.50
**Cabin Cruiser,** Orkin, Clockwork, 33 In. .......................................................................... 785.00
**Caboose,** Lionel Standard Gauge ....................................................... 25.00 To 50.00

Toy, Buckboard, 24 In.

Toys, from left to right, Bucking Bronco, Lehmann, Tin, Clockwork; Walking Man Pushing Hand Truck, Lehmann, Lithographed Tin

(See Page 690)          (See Page 691)          (See Page 690)

Toys, from left to right, Man & Zebra Cart, Daredevil, Lehmann, Clockwork; Naughty Boy, Lehmann, Lithographed Tin, Clockwork; Man Pulling Cart, Lithographed Express, Lehmann

| | |
|---|---:|
| **Cadillac,** Sedan, Tootsietoy | 35.00 |
| **Camel,** Glass Eyes, Schoenhut | 275.00 |
| **Camel,** Walking, Windup, Strauss | 150.00 |
| **Can,** Watering, Mary, Mary Quite Contrary, Chein, Tin | 10.00 |
| **Cannon,** Capshooting, Arnold, Zone Germany | 8.00 |
| **Cannon,** Cast Iron, 9 1/2 In. | 28.00 |
| **Cannon,** On Tripod, Instructions On Can, Smith Welding Mfg., Metal | 175.00 |
| **Car,** Buick, Friction, Tin, Boxed | 37.50 |
| **Car,** Buick, 1930, Tootsietoy | 15.00 |
| **Car,** Cable, Battery Operated | 40.00 |
| **Car,** Charlie McCarthy, Windup | 125.00 |
| **Car,** Chrysler, Airflow, Arcade, Red, Cast Iron, 4 In. | 125.00 |
| **Car,** Coupe, Green, Rumble Seat, Iron, 6 In. | 50.00 |
| **Car,** Dick Tracy, Friction | 30.00 |
| **Car,** Falcon, Marx, 20 In. | 30.00 |
| **Car,** Ford Mustang, F.B.I., Tin, Friction, Bandai, Boxed | 25.00 |
| **Car,** Jag, Stunt, Battery, Boxed | 25.00 |
| **Car,** Joy Rider, Lithographed, Clockwork, Tin, Marx, 7 In. | 200.00 |
| **Car,** Leaping Lena, Key Wind, Strauss, Tin | 250.00 |
| **Car,** Lincoln Continental Ii, Plastic, Friction, Promotional, 1958 | 95.00 |
| **Car,** Mercedes Benz, Battery | 30.00 |
| **Car,** Moon Mullins, Hand, Deluxe | 325.00 |
| **Car,** Parade, Disney | 125.00 |
| **Car,** Police, 1961 Oldsmobile, Tin, Friction, 14 In. | 25.00 |
| **Car,** Racing, Mechanical, Irwin, Red, 8 In. | 4.00 |
| **Car,** Studebaker, Metal, 1949 | 65.00 |
| **Car,** Trick, Milton Berle, Boxed | 125.00 |
| **Car,** Volkswagen, K.O.Series, Tin, Friction, Boxed | 10.00 |
| **Car,** Whoopee, Various College Slogans, Marx, 7 In. | 180.00 |

Car, 007 Bond, 12 In. ......................................................................................... 35.00
Carpet Ball, Marble, 3 1/2 In. ........................................................................ 200.00
Carriage, Doll, Pink & Green, White Rubber Wheels, Wyandotte, 8 In. ......... 20.00
Carriage, Doll, Tin, 3 X 3 In. ........................................................................... 15.00
Carriage, Pull Toy, Iron, 7 In. .......................................................................... 85.00
Carrousel, Stepped Circular Base, Clockwork, Tin, German, 22 In. ........... 1700.00
Cart, Black Driver, Mule Drawn, Cast Iron .................................................... 155.00
Cart, Doll, Stenciled Hood ............................................................................. 100.00
Cash Register, Tin ............................................................................................. 7.50
Cash Register, Tom Thumb .................................................... 8.50 To 30.00
Cat, Straw Filled, Glass Eyes, Metal Wheels, Steiff, Pull Toy ...................... 195.00
Cement Mixer, Jaeger, Green, Red, Cast Iron ................................................ 85.00
Cement Mixer, Jaeger, 9 1/2 In. ................................................................... 195.00
Chair, Dollhouse, Schoenhut, Set Of 3 .......................................................... 10.00
Charlie Chaplin, Little Tramp Costume, Clockwork, German, 6 3/4 In. ......... 190.00
Charlie Chaplin, Riding Bicycle, Weighted String Toy ................................... 275.00
Charlie Weaver, Battery Operated ............................................. 25.00 To 45.00
Chicken, Fighting, Windup, Japan .................................................................... 65.00
Chicken, Roly Poly, Celluloid ............................................................................ 6.00
Chimp, Jolly, Musical ....................................................................................... 35.00
Chimp, Jolly, Musical, Battery Operated .......................................................... 40.00
Chimp, Schoenhut ......................................................................................... 200.00
Chinese Man, Pouring Tea, Battery Operated ................................................. 90.00
Chord Organ, Crank, German, Tin ................................................................. 185.00
Circus Wagon, Opens To Phonograph, 4 Records ...................................... 1500.00
Circus, Ring-A-Ling, Tin, Windup .................................................................. 200.00
City Airport, Instructions & Airplanes, Marx, Tin ........................................... 135.00
Climbing Monkey, Green Coat, Yellow Vest, Red Fez, 8 In. ............................ 65.00
Climbing Tractor, Midget, Marx, Original Tread & Box .................................... 45.00
Clown Magician, Pushes Garbage Cans, Heads Pop, German, Tin ............. 1200.00
Clown, Beats Drum, Swings Head, Mechanical, Tin, Rubber, 6 1/2 In. ........... 14.00
Clown, Blows Ball & Juggles, Battery Operated .............................................. 50.00
Clown, Clarabell, Walking, Remote Control, Boxed, Linemar ......................... 40.00
Clown, Dances, Holding Pigs, Clockwork, Tin ............................................... 595.00
Clown, Juggling, Windup, Tin ........................................................................... 35.00
Clown, Playing Drum, Battery Operated ........................................................... 25.00
Clown, Playing Piano, Battery Operated ........................................................... 30.00
Clown, Roly Poly, Schoenhut .......................................................................... 495.00
Clown, Schoenhut ............................................................................................ 40.00
Clown, Skating, Windup, Tin ............................................................................ 17.50
Clown, Unicycle, Battery Operated .................................................................. 35.00
Clown, Walking On Hands, Windup, Chein, Tin .............................................. 45.00
Coach, Cinderella, Blocks Tell Story, Bliss, Tin, 26 In. ............................... 3100.00
Coaster Wagon, Hand Brake, Signed Paris ................................................... 135.00
Cocker Spaniel, Walks, Turns Head, Wags Tail, Plush, Battery Operated ...... 30.00
Concrete Mixer, Buddy L, 1930s ................................................................... 145.00
Construction Kit, Spirit Of St.Louis, Metal, Boxed .......................................... 75.00
Cow, Pull, 21 In. ............................................................................................... 85.00
Cow, Wooden Base, Wheels, 7 X 11 In. ........................................................ 250.00
Cowboy, Twirls Lasso, On Rearing Horse, Windup, Tin ................................ 100.00
Cradle, Doll, Oak ............................................................................................. 25.00
Cradle, Doll, Wicker, Hood, Pink & White, 17 X 15 In. ................................... 35.00
Crane, Keystone ............................................................................................. 160.00
Crapshooter, Battery Operated ........................................................................ 25.00
Crawling Baby, Mechanical, Irwin, Celluloid .................................................. 20.00
Crazy Car, Charlie McCarthy, Marx, Mint ...................................................... 250.00
Crazy Car, Uncle Wiggly, Boxed .................................................................... 365.00
Crib, Doll, Wheels, Schoenhut, Green ............................................................ 75.00
Crusier, Cabin, Orkin Craft, Tin, Clockwork, 33 In.Long ............................... 785.00
Cycle, Delivery, Spinach, Cast Iron ................................................................ 75.00
Dachshund, Tin Bone In Mouth, Windup, 1930s ............................................ 25.00
Dagwood In The Airplane, Windup, Marx ...................................................... 525.00
Dan Jigger, Black Dancer, Microphone, Battery Operated, Boxed ................ 400.00

Dancing Man, Keywind, Dated 1873 .................................................................. 850.00
Dancing Man, Original Paint, Knee Pants, Rivet Joints, Tin, 11 1/2 In. ............ 225.00
Dancing Pony-Tail, Windup .................................................................................. 160.00
Dancing Sam, Lithograph, Windup, Tin ............................................................ 90.00
Daredevil, Black Man In Cart, Pulled By Zebra, Clockwork, Tin, 7 1/4 In. ...... 250.00
Daredevil, Windup, Lehmann, 1907, Tin ............................................................ 275.00
Davy Crockett Badge, Plastic, Paper, 12 Piece ................................................ 9.00
Dead Eye Dick, Tin, Windup, Marx ...................................................................... 18.52
Design-O-Scope, 8th Wonder Of The World, Scenes, Chicago Fair, 1922 ............ 20.00
Desk, Governor Winthrop, Drop Front, Wooden, Dollhouse Size ...................... 26.00
Desk, Kneehole, Miniature .................................................................................. 325.00
Dick Tracy Squad Car, 1940s, Windup, Boxed .................................................. 75.00
Dining Table & Chair, Miniature ........................................................................ 800.00
Dippy Dumper, Celluloid Driver, Clockwork, Marx, 1940s, Tin, 8 3/4 In. ........ 200.00
Dirigible, Lithographed, Buffalo Toy & Tool Works, Tin, 26 1/2 In. .................... 160.00
Dirigible, Ski Rangers, Tin .................................................................................. 55.00
Dirigible, Trans Am, Tin, Windup ........................................................................ 95.00
Dishwasher, Snow White, Tin, 12 In. .................................................................. 6.00
Doctor Set, Deco Wood, 1930, 11 Piece, Boxed .............................................. 70.00
Dog, Fuzzy Beige & Tan, Windup, Wags Tail, 4 1/4 X 5 1/2 In.Long .................. 110.00
Dog, Gray Fur, Steiff, 9 In. .................................................................................. 85.00
Dog, Stuffed, On Wheels, 8 In. ............................................................................ 100.00
Dog, Stuffed, Pull, Leather Collar, Metal Wheels, 5 1/2 X 6 1/2 In.Long ............ 65.00
Dog, Stuffed, Windup, Tin Doghouse, Japan, 4 1/2 X 4 In. .............................. 15.00
Doghouse, Musical, Fido's, Tin Lithograph, Ohio Art ........................................ 18.75
    TOY, DOLL, see Doll
Dollhouse, Antebellum, Handmade, Completely Furnished, 6 Rooms ............ 800.00
Dollhouse, Built-Rite, Cardboard, 1930s .......................................................... 12.50
Dollhouse, Cardboard, C.1930, Uncut ................................................................ 10.00
Dollhouse, Dunham's Cocoanut House .............................................................. 395.00
Dollhouse, Gabled Roof, Front Porch, 3 Bedroom ............................................ 2800.00
Dollhouse, Living Room & Furniture, Peter Pia, 1900, Folding Cardboard ........ 125.00
Dollhouse, Log Cabin, Furnished ........................................................................ 150.00
Dollhouse, Red Robin Farm & Animals, Converse .......................................... 150.00
Dollhouse, Schoenhut, Boxed, 4 Room .............................................................. 300.00
Dollhouse, Schoenhut, 13 X 10 X 9 In. .............................................................. 175.00
Dollhouse, Tudor-Style House, 1940s, Pressboard .......................................... 40.00
Dolly Sister, Black, Celluloid, Wind-Up .............................................................. 35.00
Dominoes, Ebony & Bone, Mahogany Slide-Lid Boy, Set ................................ 49.00
Donald Duck Drummer, Windup, Linemar, Tin .................................................. 150.00
Donald Duck, Windup, Chein ............................................................................ 15.00
Donkey, Glass Eyes, 1940s, Windup .................................................................. 25.00
Donkey, Laughing, Schoenhut ............................................................................ 125.00
Donkey, Voice Box & Steering Post, Wheels, Steiff, 18 X 22 In. ...................... 250.00
Dray Horse, Weeker & Crosby, Large .................................................................. 175.00
Drinking Bear, Battery Operated ........................................................................ 12.00
Drum Major, Chein, Tin, 8 3/4 In. ........................................................................ 40.00
Drum Major, Wolverine, Tin, 1o 1/2 In. .............................................................. 95.00
Drum Major, Wolverine, Tin, 13 In. .................................................................... 95.00
Drum, Chein, Tin .................................................................................................. 22.00
Drummer Boy, Windup, Marx, Tin .................................................... 65.00 To 85.00
Duck, Mother & Baby, Battery Operated ............................................................ 16.00
Duck, Mystery, Windup ........................................................................................ 25.00
Duck, Tin, Chein, Windup .................................................................................... 15.00
Duck, Tin, Windup, 5 In. ...................................................................................... 45.00
Duck, Windup, Celluloid Head, Tin .................................................................... 15.00
Dump Truck, Boycraft, 1929 .............................................................................. 90.00
Dump Truck, Friction, Red, C.1918, 14 In. ........................................................ 75.00
Dump Truck, Kilgore, Cast Iron .......................................................................... 65.00
Dump Wagon, Coal, 2-Wheel, Pulled By Donkey, Held By Black Boy, C.1898 ...... 225.00
Easter Egg Transfers, King Features, Comic Strip Characters 1936 .................. 5.00
Egg Beater & Bowl, 1933 .................................................................................... 14.00
Elephant, Circus, On Tricycle, Propeller Spins, Windup, Tin ............................ 36.00

**Elephant,** Gong Bell, Pull Toy, Cast Iron ........................................ 900.00
**Elephant,** Jumbo, Bubble Blowing, Battery, 7 1/2 X 7 1/2 In. ............. 35.00
**Elephant,** Musical, Windup, 1960s, Boxed ..................................... 7.00
**Elephant,** On Wheels, Tin, 1900, 9 In. .......................................... 190.00
**Elephant,** Schoenhut ................................................................ 175.00
**Engine,** Steam, Lionel No.2053 ................................................. 70.00
**Engine,** Tender & Passenger Car, Nickel Plated Cast Iron, 17 In. ....... 125.00
**Erector Set,** Gilbert, 1938, Instruction Book ............................... 35.00
**Erector Set,** 1913 ..................................................................... 45.00
**Erector Set,** 1934, Gilbert Co., Boxed ......................................... 115.00
**Fan,** Oscillating, German, Windup, 9 In. ....................................... 70.00
**Fast Express,** Green & Orange, C.1941, Buddy L, 19 1/2 In. ............ 50.00
**Felix The Cat,** Jointed, Wooden, Paper Label, 1922, Schoenhut, 4 In. .... 200.00
**Felix The Cat,** Leather Ears, Stand-Up, Wood, Sullivan Patent, 1925, 9 In. ..... 85.00
**Felix The Cat,** Wood, Jointed, 1925, 4 In. ................................... 95.00
**Ferdinand The Bull,** Windup, Tin ................................ 125.00 To 150.00
**Ferris Wheel,** Chein, Boxed ....................................................... 110.00
**Ferris Wheel,** Chein, 1930, Windup ............................................ 115.00
**Ferris Wheel,** Disney Characters Lithograph, Windup, 1930s, 17 In. .... 175.00
**Ferris Wheel,** Hercules, Chein, Boxed ......................................... 150.00
**Ferris Wheel,** Hercules, Tin ...................................................... 65.00
**Ferris Wheel,** Mickey Mouse, Tin ............................................... 150.00
**Fighting Chickens,** Windup, Japan .............................................. 65.00
**Fire Engine,** Horse-Drawn, Hose Reel, Kenton, 1920s, Cast Iron, 13 1/2 In. ....... 400.00
**Fire Engine,** Pedal Power ....................................................*Illus* 310.00
**Fire Engine,** Riding, Red & Yellow, Marx, Tin, 30 In. ...................... 50.00
**Fire Engine,** Wood 30 In.Aerial Ladder, Friction, Ohio Art, 20 In. ....... 200.00
**Fire Engine,** 3 Ladders, Metal, 26 X 7 In. ................................... 75.00
**Fire Pumper,** Horse-Drawn, Iron, Kenton, 18 In. .......................... 150.00
**Fire Truck,** Aerial Pumper, Keystone ......................................... 300.00
**Fire Truck,** Ladder, Arcade, Cast Iron, 6 3/4 In. ........................... 165.00
**Fireman,** Climbing, Windup, Marx, Tin ........................................ 100.00
**Fireman,** Smokey Joe, Climbs Ladder, 1930s, Boxed ..................... 265.00
**Flasho,** Sparking Grinder, Girrard, 1920s, Windup, Tin, Boxed ......... 125.00
**Flying Saucer,** Apollo, Revolving Center, Friction, Germany, 4 In.Diam. .... 25.00
**Fred Flintstone,** Riding Dino, Windup, Marx, Original Box ................ 85.00
**Furniture,** Dollhouse, Bentwood, 7 Piece ..................................... 65.00

Toy, Fire Engine, Pedal Power

Toy, Furniture, Miniature, German Silver, 5 Pieces

**Furniture,** Miniature, German Silver, 5 Piece ........................................................... *Illus* 600.00
**Furniture,** Table & Chairs, Wicker, Label ................................................................... 20.00
**G.I.Joe,** K9 Pups, Windup, Unique Art ........................................................................ 85.00
**G-Man,** Ring ......................................................................................................................... 3.50
     **TOY, GAME, see Game**
**Garage,** Folding Door, Tin, Lithograph, Marx ............................................................ 10.00
**Goat Wagon,** Beggs, Jr. ............................................................................................. *Illus* 650.00
**Goose,** Gertie The Galloping, Unique Art, C.1920s, Windup, Tin ....................... 115.00
**Goose,** Riding, Windup ..................................................................................................... 18.00
**Grasshopper,** Brass Eyes, Articulated Legs, Pull Toy, 11 In. ............................... 110.00
**Grasshopper,** Windup, Tin ............................................................................................. 10.00
**Greyhound Bus,** Tootsietoy ........................................................................................... 10.00
**Gun & Belt,** Derringer, 1958, Boxed ............................................................................ 15.00
**Gun,** Cap, Bulldog ............................................................................................................. 18.00
**Gun,** Cap, Cowboy King, Kilgore .................................................................................. 25.00
**Gun,** Cap, Frontier Smoker ............................................................................................ 10.00
**Gun,** Cap, Jr., Flintlock, Boxed ..................................................................................... 13.00

Toy, Goat Wagon, Beggs, Jr.

| | |
|---|---|
| **Gun,** Cap, Kilgore, Cast Iron | 15.00 |
| **Gun,** Cap, Lion's Head, Patent June 1890, Cast Iron | 85.00 |
| **Gun,** Cap, Revolver Style, Stevens, Cast Iron | 15.00 |
| **Gun,** Cap, Silver With Ivory Tenite Handle, 1950s, 6 Shooter | 38.00 |
| **Gun,** Cap, Stallion, Silver With Ivory Tenite Handle | 18.50 |
| **Gun,** Cap, Texas, Cast Iron | 26.00 |
| **Gun,** Cap, Trooper, Hubley, Cast Iron | 25.00 |
| **Gun,** Cap, W. & S., Nickel Plated Cast Iron | 15.00 |
| **Gun,** Disintegrator, Atomic | 45.00 |
| **Gun,** Old Mac Machine Gun, Paper Shooter | 10.00 |
| **Gun,** Red Ryder Bb | 37.00 |
| **Gun,** Ric-O-Shay, Boxed | 25.00 |
| **Gun,** Smoke, Cosmic, Green | 150.00 |
| **Ham & Sam,** Black Man Playing Piano & Dancing, Linemar | 115.00 |
| **Ham & Sam,** Windup, Ferdinand Strauss Corp, 1921, Jigs | 200.00 |
| **Hamper,** Picnic, Doll's, Woven Splintwood, C.1900 | 22.00 |
| **Hand Car,** Mickey Mouse, Track & Key, Clockwork, Lionel, 8 In. | 650.00 |
| **Hand Car,** Moon Mullins & Kayo, Deluxe | 725.00 |
| **Hand Car,** Peter Rabbit, Lionel | 625.00 |
| **Hansom Cab,** Horse-Drawn, Hubley, 1920, Cast Iron, 7 1/2 In. | 70.00 |
| **Hansom Cab,** 1890s, German, Tin | 750.00 |
| **Happy & Sad Magic Face Clown,** Battery | 45.00 |
| **Happy Holligan Walker,** Chein, Windup | 225.00 |
| **Happy Hooligan Walker,** Tin, Windup, Chein Co, , 1932 | 75.00 |
| **Happy Hooligan,** In Cart, Pulled By Horse, Iron, 1903 | 350.00 |
| **Harold Lloyd,** Walker | 275.00 |
| **Helicopter,** Military, Tin, Friction | 14.00 |
| **Helmet,** Men Into Space, Col.McCauley, 1960 | 40.00 |
| **Hen,** Laying Eggs, Battery Operated, China | 18.75 |
| **Henry On Windup Platform,** Pulling Cart, Little Brother, Celluloid | 295.00 |
| **Hercules Ferris Wheel,** Windup | 85.00 |
| **High Chair,** Pine, Doll, 30 X 10 In. | 35.00 |
| **Holster,** Cap Gun, Tooled Leather, Silver Studs, 1950s | 17.50 |
| **Honeymoon Express,** Popeye, Windup, Marx, Boxed | 550.00 |
| **Honeymoon Express,** Windup, Marx, 1927 | 140.00 |
| **Honeymoon Special,** Marx, Marked, Tin, 6 In.Diam. | 65.00 |
| **Hook & Ladder,** Kenton, 1915, Cast Iron, Cast Iron, 26 In. | 225.00 |
| **Hoppy On Horse,** Windup | 75.00 |
| **Horse & Cart,** Gibb, Cast Iron | 160.00 |
| **Horse & Cart,** Pull, Wood, 2 Ft. | 135.00 |
| **Horse & Sulky,** Pedal Power | *Illus* 200.00 |
| **Horse & Wagon,** Meadow Brook Farm, Riding, Wooden | 210.00 |
| **Horse,** Dapple, Papier-Mache, On Wheels | 65.00 |
| **Horse,** Hair Tail, Pull Toy | 36.00 |
| **Horse,** Hide Covered | 395.00 |

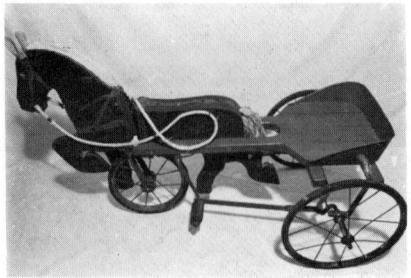

Toy, Horse & Sulky, Pedal Power

Toy, Horse, Hide Covered, Leather Bridle & Saddle, 51 In.

**Horse,** Hide Covered, Leather Bridle & Saddle, 51 In. .......................................................... *Illus* 1200.00
**Horse,** Platform With Wheels, Wool Covering, Germany, 24 X 27 In. ..................................... 360.00
**Horse,** Riding, Wooden ............................................................................................................. 350.00
**Horse,** Saddled, Lady Rider, Schoenhut .................................................................................. 125.00
**Horse,** Swing, Dappled, All Original ....................................................................................... 220.00
**Howdy Doody,** In Cart, Windup, Tin ........................................................................................ 75.00
**Hum-Burger,** Musical, 1930s ................................................................................................... 35.00
**Humpty Dumpty Circus,** Elephant, Horse, Clown, & Stool, Schoenhut, 10 Piece .................... 395.00
**Humpty Dumpty,** Fat, Sieberling, 5 In. .................................................................................... 18.00
**Humpty Dumpty,** Seiberling Rubber Co., 5 In. ......................................................................... 18.00
**Ice Skates,** C.1900, Wooden ................................................................................................... 25.00
**Ice Skates,** Iron, Heart Shaped Sole, 11 1/2 In. ..................................................................... 20.00
**Ice Skates,** Shoe Type, Winchester ..................................................................... 12.00 To 20.00
**Ice Skates,** Sonja Henie, Pictures & Endorsement On Box, White, Size 6 ............................ 40.00
**Indian,** Beating Drum, Battery Operated ............................................................. 15.00 To 35.00
**Indian,** Does War Dance, Windup, Tin, 1930s ...................................................... 20.00 To 30.00
**Ironing Board,** Wooden, 25 X 17 In. ....................................................................................... 18.00
**Jalopy,** Archie ......................................................................................................................... 35.00
**Jazzbo Jim,** Windup, Strauss, 1921, Tin ............................................................ 185.00 To 235.00
**Jeep,** Tootsietoy, Boxed .......................................................................................................... 10.00
**Jenny The Balky Mule,** Windup, Strauss ................................................................................ 150.00
**Jigger,** Dapper Dan Porter, Marx, Windup, Dated 1910 ......................................................... 295.00
**Joe Penner,** Walks, Tips Hat, Tips Cigar, Marx, Tin .............................................................. 265.00
**Jumpin' Jeep,** Marx, Boxed ............................................................................... 68.00 To 95.00
**Jupiter Robot,** Plastic, Tin, Windup, Boxed, 7 In. .................................................................. 40.00
**Kiddy Cyclist** .......................................................................................................................... 165.00
**Kitchen,** Nuremberg, 15 Piece, Tin ......................................................................................... 190.00
**Kitchen,** Water Pump, Pots & Pans, American, Tin, C.1870s ................................................ 550.00
**Knight,** Combat, Andy Gard, Battery ....................................................................................... 25.00
**Knitting Cat,** Windup, Boxed ................................................................................................... 40.00
**Laser Robot,** Mechanical, Boxed ............................................................................................. 100.00
**Leaping Lena Auto,** Tin, Windup, C.1920, 7 In. ...................................................................... 225.00
**Leopard,** Marx, Windup ............................................................................................................ 10.00
**Li'l Abner Dog Patch Band,** 1940s, Windup ..................................................... 245.00 To 285.00
**Lion,** Glass Eyes, Pull Toy ....................................................................................................... 295.00
**Lion,** Linemar, Windup ............................................................................................................. 15.00
**Little Miss Washing Machine,** 4 3/4 In. ................................................................................. 75.00
**Loader,** Sand, Automatic, Chein, Boxed .................................................................................. 55.00
**Locomotive & Tender,** Cast Iron, 18 In. ................................................................................. 225.00
**Locomotive,** Engineer & Fireman In Cab, Friction, Old Paint, 17 1/2 In. ............................... 95.00
**Locomotive,** Pressure Valve, Live Steam, 7 In. ...................................................................... 275.00
**Locomotive,** Red, Yellow, & Green, Clockwork, Painted Tin, 10 In. ...................................... 180.00

**Log House,** Old Fort Dearborn, Original Box, 1933 .................................................... 25.00
**Loom,** Weaving, Nellie Bee, Metal, Boxed ..................................................... 10.00
**Loop The Loop,** Wolverine, Windup ..................................................... 28.00
**Looping Plane,** Windup, Marx, Tin ..................................................... 50.00
**Mac The Turtle,** Battery Operated ..................................................... 38.50
**Machine Gun,** G-Man, Mini, 1930, Windup ..................................................... 29.00
**Machine Gun,** Paper Popper, Safe & Sane Mfg. ..................................................... 83.00
**Maggie & Jiggs,** Mounted On Wheels, Clockwork, 1920s, Tin, 7 In. ..................................................... 550.00
**Maggie & Jiggs,** Windup, Germany, All Original ..................................................... 1100.00
**Mama Katzenjammer,** Mechanical, Mouth Opens, 1920s, 10 In. ..................................................... 275.00
**Man & Zebra Cart,** Daredevil, Lehmann, Clockwork, 7 1/4 In. .......................... *Illus* 90.00
**Man,** Acrobat, Original Cotton Suit, Schoenhut, Wooden, 7 In. ..................................................... 65.00
**Man,** Acrobat, Top Hat, Wood ..................................................... 225.00
**Man,** Egghead, Tin, Mechanical, Boxed ..................................................... 20.00
**Man,** Pulling Cart, Lithographed Express, Lehmann, 6 1/4 In. .......................... *Illus* 120.00
**Man,** Smoking Pipe, Rocking Chair, Mechanical, Battery Operated, 7 X 4 In. ..................................................... 20.00
**Medical Kit,** Dr.Kildare ..................................................... 24.50
**Men On Hand Car,** Tin, Windup ..................................................... 68.00
**Merry-Go-Round,** Carnival, Windup ..................................................... 15.00
**Merrymakers,** Marx ..................................................... 450.00
       **TOY, MICKEY MOUSE, see Disneyana**
**Milton Berle Drives Crazy Car,** 1940s, Boxed ..................................................... 95.00 To 125.00
**Miniature,** Antique Shop ..................................................... *Illus* 1500.00
**Miniature,** Furniture, Viennese, Gilt Metal & Enamel, 5 Piece ..................................................... 1000.00
**Minstrel,** Ham & Sam ..................................................... 375.00
**Mirror,** Miniature ..................................................... 350.00
**Miss Friday,** The Typist, Battery Operated ..................................................... 25.00
**Monkey & Clown,** On High Bar, Windup ..................................................... 75.00
**Monkey & Drum,** Windup, Plays Drum, 8 In. ..................................................... 145.00
**Monkey & Elephant,** Jungle Trio, Linemar, Battery ..................................................... 400.00
**Monkey,** Bombo, Windup ..................................................... 20.00

Toy, Miniature, Antique Shop

Monkey, Bubble Blowing, Battery Operated, Boxed ........................................................ 30.00 To 40.00
Monkey, Climbing, Battery Operated, Lehmann, Boxed ........................................................ 80.00
Monkey, On Tricycle, Bell Toy, Cast Iron, C.1880 ........................................................ 300.00
Monkey, Shooting Crap, Battery Operated ........................................................ 40.00 To 45.00
Monkey, Tail Swivels Head, Organ Grinder's Costume, Jointed, 12 In. ................. 125.00
Monkey, With Cymbals, Tin Eyes, Windup, 1950s ........................................................ 25.00
Monkey, Zippo, Climbing, Tin ........................................................ 35.00
Mother Duck & Baby, Battery Operated ........................................................ 16.00
Mother Duck & Ducklings, Lehmann ........................................................ 195.00
Mother Goose, Windup, Unique Toy Co., Tin ........................................................ 45.00
Motorcycle Cop, Rider, White Rubber Tires, Champion, Cast Iron, 7 In. ................. 85.00
Motorcycle, Attached Delivery Wagon, Windup, Marx, Tin, 10 X 6 In. ................. 55.00
Motorcycle, Hubley, Cast Iron, 4 1/2 In. ........................................................ 40.00
Motorcycle, Indian, Cop Driving, Cop In Side Car, 1930s, 8 In. ................. 275.00
Motorcycle, Indian, Man In Sidecar, Red, Hubley, 9 X 4 In. ................. 225.00
Motorcycle, Indian, Tin, Friction ........................................................ 35.00
Motorcycle, Mystic, Marx, Windup ........................................................ 50.00
Motorcycle, Original Orange Paint, Cast Iron, 3 In.Long ................. 20.00
Motorcycle, Policeman, Marx, Windup ........................................................ 25.00
Motorcycle, Technofix, Tin, Windup ........................................................ 55.00
Motorcycle, Turns Left & Right, Tin, Windup, Germany, 5 1/2 In.Long ................. 46.00
Motorcycle, U.S.Air Mail Sidecar, Hubley, Iron, 9 1/2 In. ................. 500.00
Motorcycle, With Sidecar, Hubley, 8 3/4 In. ........................................................ 295.00
Mouse, Penny Toy, German ........................................................ 45.00
Mouse, Schuco, Windup ........................................................ 10.00
Mr.Baseball, Major League Teams, Battery, Boxed ........................................................ 75.00
Mr.Brain, Robot, Battery Operated, Boxed ........................................................ 125.00
Mule, Glass Eyes, Schoenhut, 8 1/2 In. ........................................................ 40.00
Music Box, Shape Of Cathedral, 1920s, Turn Crank ................. 75.00
Music Box, 3 Paper Rolls, Lithograph Of Pan Dancing, J.Chein ................. 46.00
Musician, Bubble Blowing, Battery, Boxed ........................................................ 85.00
Mutt & Jeff, Metal, Ball-Jointed, 8 In. ........................................................ 225.00
Mystery Duck, Windup ........................................................ 25.00
Naughty Boy, Lithographed Tin, Lehmann, Clockwork, 5 In. ...................*Illus* 400.00
Noma Ski Champ, Key Wind, Boxed ........................................................ 10.00
Nu Nu, Chinaman Pulls Tea Cart, Lehmann ........................................................ 395.00
Nutty Mad Indian, Tin, Windup, Marx ........................................................ 19.00 To 20.00
Nutty Nibs, Battery, Boxed ........................................................ 400.00
Oceanliner, Deck Details, Fleischmann, Tin, 11 1/2 In. ........................................................ 120.00
Old Jalopy, Marx, Windup ........................................................ 100.00
Omnibus, Penny Toy ........................................................ 400.00
Operation Airlift, Windup, Tin ........................................................ 65.00
Organ, Chein, Windup ........................................................ 30.00
Organ, Crank, Metal & Lithograph, Chein, 2 Rolls, Tin ................. 135.00
Paddy & Pig, Windup, Lehmann, 1903, Tin ........................................................ 300.00
Panda, Drummer, Windup, Tin ........................................................ 8.00
Parrot, Dome Shaped Cage, Papier-Mache Bird, Squeak, 19th Century, 5 In. ................. 225.00
Peacock, Walks, Tail Fans Out, 1930s ........................................................ 135.00
Pecking Goose, Golden, Marx, 1924, 9 1/2 In. ........................................................ 55.00
Phonograph, Portable, Windup, Brunswick ........................................................ 60.00
Piano-Organ, Schoenhut, Maple ........................................................ 65.00
Piano, Baby Grand, Schoenhut, 9 1/2 X 11 X 5 1/2 In. ........................................................ 65.00
Piano, Baby Grand, Stool, 27 Keys, 19 Flats, Schoenhut ................. 35.00
Piano, Player, Electric, 3 Rolls, Plastic, Chein, 20 X 10 X 20 In. ................. 195.00
Piano, Player, Upright, Turn Handle, It Plays, Schoenhut ................. 250.00
Piano, Upright, Dated 1900, Schoenhut ........................................................ 60.00
Piano, Upright, Schoenhut, Angels Over Keyboard, 7 1/2 X 5 X 7 In. ................. 55.00
Picnic Bunny, Battery ........................................................ 19.00
Pilot, Popeye ........................................................ 400.00
Pinocchio, The Acrobat ........................................................ 165.00 To 190.00
Pinocchio, Windup, Marx, 1939, 9 In. ........................................................ 160.00
Pipe & Bubbles, Snoopy, 1958 ........................................................ 12.00

| | |
|---|---|
| Pistol, Bigger Bang Cap | 40.00 |
| Pistol, Cork, Daisy, Tin | 16.00 |
| Pistol, Pirate, 1940s, Hubley | 125.00 |
| Pistol, Water, James Bond, 1966, Packaged | 10.00 |
| Piston Robot, Walks, Battery Operated, Tin & Plastic, 10 1/2 In. | 50.00 |
| Plane, Fighter, Spring Wheels & Wings, Hubley, Metal, 9 In. | 13.60 |
| Pluto, Mechanical, Linemar | 90.00 |
| Police, Royal Canadian Mounted, Summer Dress, C.1930s, Boxed, Set Of 8 | 92.50 |
| Poodle, French, Schoenhut, Painted Eyes, Wooden, Large | 95.00 |
| Pool Shooter, Penny, German | 75.00 |
| Pool Table & Two Men Shooting Pool, Tin, Windup | 100.00 |
| Popgun, Jones, Indians & Soldiers | 35.00 |
| Porky Pig, Windup, Leon Schlessinger, 1939, Tin | 25.00 |
| Porky Pig, With Umbrella, Windup, Marx, 1939, Tin | 125.00 |
| Postal Wagon, Penny Toy, 5 1/2 In. | 150.00 |
| Pots & Pans, Child's, 1920, Aluminum, 10 Piece | 17.50 |
| Printing Press, Swiftset Cub | 25.00 |
| Projector, Movie, Keystone, 1920s, 13 In. | 49.00 |
| Pumper, Fire Engine, Kenton, 11 In. | 165.00 |
| Pup, Perky, Battery Operated | 35.00 |
| Puppet, Hand, Dutch Boy Paints | 17.00 |
| Quick Draw McGraw, Windup, Tin | 25.00 |
| Rabbit On Egg Cart, Pulled By Rooster, Lehmann | 395.00 |
| Rabbit, In Auto, Mechanical, Tin | 35.00 |
| Racer, Hubley, Cast Iron, 7 1/2 In. | 65.00 |
| Racer, Nickel Disc Wheels & Driver, Cast Iron, Hubley, Red | 30.00 |
| Racer, Turbine, Red, Black Wheels, Buddy L, Plastic, 6 In. | 2.30 |
| Racer, Windup, Lithograph, Marx, Tin, 16 In. | 12.50 |
| Racer, 2 Drivers, Key Wind, Red, 9 In. | 45.00 |
| Railplane, Arcade | 145.00 |
| Range Rider, Windup, Marx, Tin | 40.00 |
| Range, Dolly's Favorite Iron Kitchen | 850.00 |
| Rattling Baby, Windup, Boxed | 12.50 |
| Red Devil Racer, Hood Lifts Out, Can See Motor, Hubley | 250.00 |
| Refrigerator, North Wind, Tin, Marx | 20.00 |
| Refrigerator, Snow White | 5.00 |
| Refrigerator, Tootsietoy | 15.00 |
| Rickshaw, Lehmann | 300.00 |
| Riding Goose, Windup | 18.00 |
| Rifle, The Rifleman | 10.00 |
| Roadster, Friction, Republic, Pressed Steel, 18 In. | 310.00 |
| Roadster, Rumble Set, Iron, Hubley, 11 1/2 In. | 375.00 |
| Robot, Astroid, Movable Arms, Rotating Head, Windup, Plastic, 7 In. | 10.00 |
| Robot, Attacking Martian, Gun Pops Out, Battery Operated, Tin, 9 1/2 In. | 35.00 |
| Robot, Blocky Shape, Wind Arms & He Travels, 1970s, 3 1/2 In. | 7.00 |
| Robot, Gigantor, Rotating Body, Battery Operated, Mego, 1970, 17 In. | 95.00 |
| Robot, Laser, Mechanical, Boxed | 100.00 |
| Robot, Magnor, Square Turn Action, Battery Operated, China, Plastic, 9 In. | 65.00 |
| Robot, Mister Flash, Red Body, Yellow Dome, Plastic, 8 1/2 In. | 45.00 |
| Robot, Mr.Brain, Battery, Boxed | 125.00 |
| Robot, Mr.Monster, Comical Action, Battery Operated, Plastic, 10 1/2 In. | 30.00 |
| Robot, Myrobo, Dial To Tall Or Short, Battery Operated, Plastic, 9 In. | 35.00 |
| Robot, Rotating & Walking, Torso Turns, Windup, Tin & Plastic, 4 1/2 In. | 15.00 |
| Robot, Silver Warrior, Stop 'n Go, Battery Operated, Plastic, 11 1/2 In. | 35.00 |
| Robot, Star Wars R2-D2, Radio Controlled, Kenner, Moves Up To 20 Ft. | 75.00 |
| Robot, Super Silver, Walking, Windup, Plastic & Paper, 1970s, 4 In. | 8.00 |
| Robot, Walking, Windup, Walks, Step-Over Action, Plastic, 4 In. | 12.00 |
| Robot, Walks, Shooting Sparks, Windup, Tin & Plastic, Korean, 5 1/4 In. | 15.00 |
| Robot, Windup, Shoots Sparks, Schuco | 45.00 |
| Robot, Yakkity Yob, Rolls His Eyes At You, Red Head, 1960s | 75.00 |
| Rocket, Jupiter, Retractable Nose Cone, Friction, Tin, 9 1/2 In. | 20.00 |
| Rocketship, Sparkling, V-1 | 6.00 |
| Rocking Grandpa, Battery Operated | 45.00 |

**Rocking Horse,** Leather Seat, Sponge Painted, American, 40 In. ............................................ 850.00
**Rocky Jones,** Space Pins, 24 Pins, Metal ................................................ 85.00
**Roller Coaster,** Chein, Boxed .............................................................. 110.00
**Rooster,** On Wheeled Platform, American, Tin ................................................ 140.00
**Rooster,** Papier-Mache, Moves Head, 23 In. ................................................ 225.00
**Rooster,** Penny Toy, Tin ................................................................... 210.00
**Roulette Wheel & Accessories,** 1930s, Boxed ................................................ 45.00
**Sand Mill,** Chein, Tin .................................................................... 29.00
**Sand,** Sandy Andy, Boxed ................................................................. 20.00
**Sand,** Wolverine, Boy .................................................................... 22.50
**Santa On Skies,** Windup .................................................................. 25.00
**Santa,** Long Neck, Windup ................................................................ 18.00
**Santa,** Scooter, Battery Operated ........................................................ 25.00
**Santa,** Walks, 1920s, Windup ............................................................. 125.00
**Santa,** With Sled & Reindeer, Celluloid, Occupied Japan ................................... 20.00
**Schoolbus,** Hubley, Tin, 9 1/4 In. ......................................................... 15.00
**Schoolhouse,** Figures, Crandall, Boxed .................................................... 250.00
**Scotty Dog,** Windup, Marx ................................................................ 35.00
**Screen,** Miniature ........................................................ *Illus* 300.00
**Seal,** With Ball, Windup, Lehmann ......................................................... 25.00
**Sedan,** Take Apart, Kenton, C.1938, Cast Iron, 7 In. ........................................ 900.00
**Sedan,** White Rubber Wheels, Tootsietoy ................................................... 12.00
**Sedan,** 1920s, Cast Iron, Dent, 7 1/2 In. .................................................. 800.00
**Sergeant,** U.S.Army, J.Chein, Windup ...................................................... 25.00
**Sewing Machine,** Black & Gold, Germany ................................................... 35.00
**Sewing Machine,** Box & Instructions, Little Treasure, England ............................... 30.00
**Sewing Machine,** Gateway, Metal .......................................................... 20.00
**Sewing Machine,** Hand Operated, Eldredgatee, 1920s ........................................ 55.00
**Sewing Machine,** Kayee, U.S.Zone, Germany ................................................ 15.00
**Sewing Machine,** Reliable ................................................................. 35.00
**Sewing Machine,** Singer, Cast Iron, Boxed ................................................. 60.00
**Shooting Gallery,** Wolverine, Tin .......................................................... 11.00
**Shooting Gallery,** Wyandotte, Original Box ................................................. 25.00
**Shovel,** Mickey Mouse Enterprises ......................................................... 45.00
**Shovel,** Sand, Tonka, Tin ................................................................. 20.00
**Shovel,** Steam, 1940s, Metal .............................................................. 34.00
**Sideboard,** Miniature ...................................................... *Illus* 400.00
**Singing Canary,** Windup, West Germany .................................................... 65.00
**Six Gun,** Maverick ....................................................................... 12.50
**Skates,** Ice, H. & S.Scooter, 1920, Boxed .................................................. 22.00
**Skates,** Ice, 1890s, Wooden ............................................................... 35.00
**Skates,** Racing, Brass Toes & Heels, Ankle Supports, Dated 1895 ............................ 28.00
**Skates,** Roller, Brass, Wood, Leather, Patent 1881 ......................................... 85.00
**Skates,** Roller, Winchester ............................................................... 6.00
**Skates,** Roller, Winchester, Original Key .................................................. 35.00
**Skidoodle,** 3 Clowns On Top, German, Tin ................................................. 875.00
**Sky King's Spy Detecto Writer** ........................................................... 40.00
**Skybird Flyer,** 2 Airplanes Fly Around Tower, 1930s, Boxed ................................. 125.00
**Sled,** Child's, Curved Runners, Original Stencil & Paint .................................... 135.00
**Sled,** Clipper, Hand-Painted Red, Paris Mfg.Co. ............................................ 175.00
**Sled,** Fire Fly Racer, Christmas Design .................................................... 75.00
**Sled,** Iron Runners, Hand-Painted Horse On Top ........................................... 345.00
**Sled,** Iron Runners, Wooden, Loyal Patriots Of America .................................... 78.00
**Sled,** Maple, Small ...................................................................... 65.00
**Sled,** Riding Girl, Windup, Celluloid, Occupied Japan ...................................... 25.00
**Sled,** Steel Runners, Hand-Painted, Signed, Kalamazoo, Michigan, 1902 ..................... 190.00
**Smitty On Scooter,** 1920s, Windup, Marx ................................................. 495.00
**Soldier,** Doughboy, Marching, Slope Arms, Painted, Lead, 3 In. ............................. 3.50
**Soldier,** Kneeling, Holding Shell, Lead .................................................... 6.30
**Soldier,** Lead, Brirains Grenadier Guards, Set Of 24 ....................................... 150.00
**Soldier,** Lead, Infantry & Cavalry, Spanish & Mexican, Set Of 20 ........................... 125.00
**Soldier,** Marching In Overcoat, Gray Iron ................................................. 4.60
**Soldier,** Riding Bicycle, C.1935, Silver Paint, Lead, 5 X 3 In. ............................... 12.00

| | |
|---|---|
| **Soldier,** Standing, Holding Rifle, Silver Helmet, Manoil, Lead | 6.80 |
| **Soldier,** Wooden, 4 1/2 In. | 14.00 |
| **Space Capsule,** Apollo, Astronauts At Controls, Tin & Plastic, 11 In. | 60.00 |
| **Space Guard Tank,** Fires Missiles, Boxed | 125.00 |
| **Space Patrol,** Camera & Dog, Battery Operated, Lucite, 11 1/2 X 6 1/2 In. | 65.00 |
| **Space Patrol,** No.2019, Battery Operated | 18.00 |
| **Space,** Moon Express, Magic Color, Battery Operated | 35.00 |
| **Spaceship,** Bump & Go Action, Battery Operated, Japan, 1960s, 9 In.Diam. | 40.00 |
| **Speed King,** Boy On Soapbox | 95.00 |
| **Speedboat,** Century Of Progress, Marx, Boxed | 125.00 |
| **Speedway,** Double Spiral, C.1940, J.B.Miller Co., 28 In. | 50.00 |
| **Spinner,** Poll Parrot | 6.00 |
| **Spinning Top & Holder,** Pine, Hand-Carved, 18th Century, American | 60.00 |
| **Stagecoach,** 4-Horse, Lithographed Paper On Wood, Bliss, 31 In. | 1500.00 |
| **Station,** Train, Marklin, 12 X 7 X 10 In. | 225.00 |
| **Steam Engine,** Cast Iron | 35.00 |
| **Steam Pumper,** Union Hardware, Cast Iron | 1600.00 |
| **Steam Shovel,** Keystone, Red & Black, Dated 1915, 20 In. | 68.00 |
| **Steam Shovel,** Original Paint, Buddy L | 135.00 To 225.00 |
| **Steam Shovel,** Structo, Orange, Metal | 55.00 |
| **Steamroller,** Battery Operated, Rosco, Japan | 38.50 |
| **Stool,** Piano, Swivel, Schoenhut | 125.00 |
| **Stove,** Cooking Utensils, Marked Home, Cast Iron | 125.00 |
| **Stove,** Crescent, Cast Iron, 13 X 11 In. | 52.50 |
| **Stove,** Electric, Empire, Child's, 12 X 13 1/2 In. | 30.00 |
| **Stove,** Eva, Iron | 125.00 |
| **Stove,** Gas, Royal, Cast Iron, 2 1/2 X 2 1/4 X 4 1/2 In. | 18.00 |
| **Stove,** Girart, Electric, 1937 | 30.00 |
| **Stove,** Little Orphan Annie, Blue, Metal | 20.00 |
| **Stove,** Snow White | 5.00 |
| **Stove,** Workable Doors, Flues, Grate, Cotton Plant, Abendroth Bros, 9 In. | 140.00 |
| **Street Car,** Horse-Drawn, Tin, 1890, 13 In. | 250.00 |
| **Stroller,** Doll, Rickshaw Type, Wire Spoke Wheels, Stencil Lines, 20 In. | 85.00 |
| **Stroller,** Mesh Seat & Back, Footrest, Folds | 75.00 |
| **Studebaker,** Remote Control, Boxed | 63.00 |
| **Submarine,** Diving, Clockwork Motor, Wolverine | 45.00 |
| **Submarine,** Tootsietoy, 4 In. | 8.00 |
| **Submarine,** Windup, German, Original Paint, Tin, 9 In. | 35.00 |
| **Sugar Bowl,** Lid, Amber, Tappan | 20.00 |
| **Surrey,** Horse-Drawn, 2 Passengers, Driver, 12 In. | 75.00 |
| **Surrey,** Kenton, Cast Iron | 70.00 |
| **Sweeper,** Carpet, Busy Betty | 22.50 |
| **Sweeper,** Carpet, Gong Bell | 12.00 |
| **Sweeping Mammy,** Windup, 1930s, Lindstrom, Boxed | 155.00 |
| **Swing Horse,** Victorian, All Original | 355.00 |
| **Sword & Scabbard,** Ben Hur, Marx | 20.00 |
| **Table,** Butler's, Miniature | 400.00 |
| **Table,** Tilt Top, Miniature | 350.00 |
| **Table,** Tripod, Miniature | 750.00 |
| **Tank Car,** Original Paint & Decals, No Sprinkler, Buddy L | 495.00 |
| **Tank,** Army, Cranmer No.40, Windup | 25.00 |
| **Tank,** Cap Firing, Thunderbolt, Tin | 25.00 |
| **Tank,** Domed Cannon Turret, Tin, Lithograph, Battery Driven, 8 In. | 22.70 |
| **Tank,** Mechanical, Sparkling, Marx, Boxed | 40.00 |
| **Tank,** Stars Landing, Driver In Lucite Bubble, Friction, Tin, 5 X 3 In. | 12.00 |
| **Tank,** Tin, Marx, No.3 | 35.00 |
| **Tank,** World War II, Windup, Marx | 15.00 |
| **Taxi,** Amos & Andy, Original & Complete | 500.00 |
| **Taxi,** 1930s, Arcade, Cast Iron | 625.00 |
| **Tea Drinker,** Battery Operated | 45.00 |
| **Tea Set,** Little Red Riding Hood, Tin, 7 Piece | 20.00 |
| **Tea Set,** Miniature | *Illus* 200.00 |
| **Tea Set,** Tin, Ohio Art, Circus Design, 11 Piece | 50.00 |

**Teddy Bear,** Button In Ear, Jointed, Steiff ........................................................................ 140.00
**Teddy Bear,** C.1930, 25 In. ........................................................................................... 125.00
**Teddy Bear,** Glass Eyes, Prominent Hump, Jointed, German, 24 In. ................................. 450.00
**Teddy Bear,** Gold Color, Shoebutton Eyes, Humpback, 16 In. ....................................... 95.00
**Teddy Bear,** Humpback, Straw Body, Shoebutton Eyes, 9 In. ....................................... 110.00
**Teddy Bear,** On Wheels, Steiff ...................................................................................... 195.00
**Teddy Bear,** Smoky The Bear, 14 In. .............................................................................. 12.00
**Teddy Bear,** Steiff, 12 In. ............................................................................................. 225.00
**Teddy Bear,** Steiff, 1905, Pewter Pin In Ear, 14 In. ........................................................ 250.00
**Teddy Bear,** Straw Stuffed, Smiling, 20 In. ................................................................... 150.00
**Teddy Bear,** Sun Rubber, Charcoal & White, Pink Ears, Nose, 1958, 10 In. ................... 10.00
**Teddy Bear,** Velvet Pads, Shoebutton Eyes, 14 In. ........................................................ 55.00
**Teddy,** The Artist, Battery Operated, Original Box ........................................................ 100.00
**Teeter,** Busy Mike, Runs By Sand, Tin, 7 In. ................................................................ 33.00
**Telephone,** Wall, The Gong Bell Co., Tin ...................................................................... 45.00
**Thresher,** McCormick-Deering, Arcade, Cast Iron ......................................................... 135.00
**Tiger,** Glass Eyes, Schoenhut ...................................................................................... 200.00
**Tin Lizzie,** Windup ...................................................................................................... 125.00
**Tinkling Trolley,** Battery Operated, Boxed .................................................................... 105.00
**Tip-Top,** Black Man Pushing Cart, Windup, Strauss ...................................................... 145.00
**Tobogganer,** Yellow & Red Boy Riding, Friction, Tin, 9 1/4 In. ...................................... 170.00
**Toe-Joe,** Ohio Art ........................................................................................................ 15.00
**Toilet,** Tootsietoy ........................................................................................................ 15.00
**Tom & Jerry Hand Car,** Tin & Plastic, Battery Operated ............................................... 25.00
**Tool Chest,** Complete, 3 X 5 In. ................................................................................... 25.00
**Toonerville Trolley,** Push ............................................................................................. 230.00
**Toonerville Trolley,** Windup, Boxed .......................................................... 450.00 To 675.00
**Tower,** Signal, Lionel, Cast Iron .................................................................................... 150.00
**Tower,** Wonder Woman, Collapsing .............................................................................. 6.00
**Tractor,** Arcade, Iron, 5 1/2 In. ..................................................................................... 35.00
**Tractor,** Cat, Slushmold, Rubber Treads, Tootsietoy .................................................... 15.00
**Tractor,** Fordson, Red & White Tires, Arcade, 5 1/2 In. ................................................ 110.00
**Tractor,** Fordson, Tootsietoy ........................................................................................ 45.00
**Tractor,** International F-20, C.1928, Arcade, Cast Iron, 5 In. .......................................... 95.00
**Tractor,** International, Rubber Tires, C.1935, 4 In. ......................................................... 60.00
**Tractor,** McCormick, Deering, Red & Gray, Arcade, Cast Iron, 8 In. ............................. 125.00
**Tractor,** Original Paint & Man, Ferguson ...................................................................... 125.00
**Tractor,** Red, Arcade, Iron, 5 1/2 In. ............................................................................. 47.00
**Tractor,** Seated Man, Fordson, Original Paint, Cast Iron, 6 1/2 In. ............................... 145.00
**Trailer,** Gasoline, Domaco, Toosietoy .......................................................................... 20.00
**Train Set,** Cragston Dog Shuttling, B.O., Boxed ........................................................... 65.00
**Train Set,** Freight, Marx, Model 999 ............................................................................. 40.00
**Train Station,** Marklin, 12 X 7 X 10 In. ......................................................................... 225.00
**Train,** Buddy L, Set ...................................................................................................... 700.00
**Train,** Engine & Passenger Car, Niagara, Reed, Wooden, 32 In. ................................... 160.00
**Train,** Hobo, Dog Chases Hobo On Top Of Freight Car, 1930s .................................... 250.00
**Train,** Honeymoon Express, Moves In Circle, Boxed ..................................................... 95.00
**Train,** Ice Depot, Lionel, No.352 ................................................................................... 225.00
**Train,** Lionel, No.2046, Engine & Whistling Tender ........................................................ 75.00
**Train,** Musical, Puppy Band, Battery Operated .............................................................. 25.00
**Tricky Taxi,** Friction, Marx, Tin .................................................................................... 10.00
**Trolley,** Friction, American, Painted Metal, 17 1/2 In. ......................................... *Illus* 100.00
**Trolley,** Friction, Ohio Art, 13 1/2 In. ........................................................................... 150.00
**Trolley,** Lionelville, Cast Iron, Boxed ............................................................................ 155.00
**Trolley,** Pay As You Enter, Friction, Old Paint, 22 In. .................................................... 150.00
**Trolley,** San Francisco, Friction, Boxed ........................................................................ 17.00
**Truck,** Aerial, Windup Ladder, Red, Kingsbury, 33 In. ................................................. 200.00
**Truck,** Arctic Ice Cream, 1930s, Kilgore, 6 1/2 In. ........................................................ 350.00
**Truck,** Austin, Blue, Iron, 3 5/8 In. ............................................................................... 29.00
**Truck,** Buddy L, Ride On Dump Truck, Embossed Lettering ......................................... 85.00
**Truck,** Cement, Tootsietoy ........................................................................................... 10.00
**Truck,** Cor-Cor Stake Bed, Green & Black, Riding, 23 In. ............................................. 95.00
**Truck,** Cor-Cor Van, Blue & Black, Riding, 23 In. ......................................................... 125.00

Toy, Trolley, Friction, American, Painted Metal, 17 1/2 In. (See Page 695)

| | |
|---|---:|
| **Truck,** Delivery, Coca-Cola, Buddy L, Metal | 11.00 |
| **Truck,** Delivery, H.J.Heinz Co. | 45.00 |
| **Truck,** Dump, Buddy L, Cast Iron | 200.00 |
| **Truck,** Dump, Driver, 1930s, Arcade, 10 1/2 In. | 350.00 |
| **Truck,** Dump, Hercules, Chein, Tin, 1. 1/2 In. | 195.00 |
| **Truck,** Dump, Keystone, Riding, 26 In. | 125.00 |
| **Truck,** Dump, Mack, Mechanical, Arcade, 1930s, 12 In. | 450.00 |
| **Truck,** Dump, Mack, Red & Black, Chein | 70.00 |
| **Truck,** Dump, Twin Lever, C.1927, Structo | 60.00 |
| **Truck,** Dump, Wooden Wheels, C.1940s, Buddy L, Cast Iron, 12 In. | 18.00 |
| **Truck,** Fire, Separate Ladders, Cast Iron, 3 1/2 In. | 30.00 |
| **Truck,** Gasoline, Mack, Blue, Cast Iron | 70.00 |
| **Truck,** Heinz Pickle, Metal Craft, 1930s | 75.00 |
| **Truck,** Jump, Contractor's Buddy, Cast Iron | 750.00 |
| **Truck,** Machinery Moving, Marx, Boxed, 20 In. | 35.00 |
| **Truck,** Moving, Courtland, Tin, Boxed, 8 1/2 In. | 20.00 |
| **Truck,** Oil Tank, White Rubber Tires, C.1938, Cast Iron, 5 1/2 In. | 45.00 |
| **Truck,** Panel, Arcade, Cast Iron, 4 In. | 75.00 |
| **Truck,** Penny Toy Gasoline, 1930s | 95.00 |
| **Truck,** Railway Express, Marx | 50.00 |
| **Truck,** Raising Ladders, Structo, 21 In. | 45.00 |
| **Truck,** Sand & Gravel, Buddy L | 185.00 |
| **Truck,** Semi, Marshall Field, Metal, 22 In. | 37.00 |
| **Truck,** Shell Oil, Buddy L, 13 In. | 60.00 |
| **Truck,** Stake, Chevy, 1923, Arcade, Cast Iron | 600.00 |
| **Truck,** Stake, Wyandotte, 15 In. | 20.00 |
| **Truck,** Sunshine Biscuit, White, Metalcraft, 11 1/2 In. | 175.00 |
| **Truck,** Tanker, Wyandotte | 40.00 |
| **Truck,** Telephone Repair, Poles & Trailer, 1940s, Buddy L | 100.00 |
| **Truck,** Tow, Hubley, Iron, 3 1/2 In. | 20.00 |
| **Truck,** Utility, Friction, Under Hood Motor, Structo Toyland, 31 In. | 45.00 |
| **Trucky Taxi,** Windup, Marx, 1930s, Tin, Boxed, 4 1/2 In. | 55.00 |
| **Trumpet Player,** Windup | 40.00 |
| **Trunk,** Doll, Red Metal, 19 X 10 X 10 In. | 22.00 |
| **Trunk,** Doll, Travel Stickers, Blue Metal, C.1928 | 23.00 |
| **Trunk,** Wyandotte | 30.00 |
| **Turtle,** Windup, Grass-Skirted Native Riding Back, Chein, Boxed | 125.00 |
| **Tut-Tut,** Man In Car Plays Horn, 1903, Lehmann | 575.00 |
| **Typewriter,** Berwin, Metal | 12.50 |
| **Typewriter,** Dial, Marx | 14.50 To 45.00 |
| **Typewriter,** Round Letter Wheel, Metal Carriage, Red Base, 1899 | 35.00 |
| **Typewriter,** Simplex, Boxed | 12.00 To 45.00 |
| **Typewriter,** Simplex, 1900 | 20.00 |
| **Typewriter,** Tom Thumb, Tin | 30.00 |

| | |
|---|---|
| **U-Drive-It,** Tin, Lithograph | 20.00 |
| **Uncle Wiggily,** Windup, Unused | 285.00 |
| **Van,** Market Delivery, Tootsietoy | 38.00 |
| **Van,** Moving, Keystone, Metal | 150.00 |
| **Vendor,** Peanut, Battery Operated | 145.00 |
| **Victrola,** Tootsietoy | 20.00 |
| **Village Blacksmith,** Mechanical, Sand Toy, Tin, Boxed | 22.00 |
| **Wagon,** Circus, Barnum & Bailey, Painted Wood, C.1930, 35 In. | 180.00 |
| **Wagon,** Freight, Unique Art, Tin | 28.00 |
| **Wagon,** Hay, Tin, John Deere, 10 In. | 15.00 |
| **Wagon,** Ice, Driver & 2 Horses, Rich Toys, Morrison, Ill., Wooden | 110.00 |
| **Wagon,** Junior, Signed Paris | 135.00 |
| **Wagon,** Milk, C.1795, Fallow, 12 1/2 In. | 625.00 |
| **Wagon,** Pulled By A Goat, C.1875, Cast Iron | 85.00 |
| **Wagon,** Radio Line, Tin, 4 In. | 8.00 |
| **Wagon,** Seat, Wheels Turn, Red, Tin | 35.00 |
| **Wagon,** Water Tank, European, C.1900, Tin, 26 In. | 180.00 |
| **Walking Man,** Pushing Hand Truck, Lehmann, Litho Tin, 8 In. *Illus* | 425.00 |
| **Washing Machine,** Dutch Scenes, Inside Paddle, 1930s, Tin, 12 In. | 48.50 |
| **Washing Machine,** Sunny Suzy, 1920s | 35.00 |
| **Wheelbarrow,** High-Sided, Iron, C.1910, 6 1/2 In. | 19.00 |
| **Whistle,** Chain, Purina Dog Chow, Checkerboard Button | 12.50 |
| **Whistle,** Junior G-Man | 10.00 |
| **Whistle,** Soldier On Cannon, China | 25.00 |
| **Woodpecker & Tree Stump,** Windup | 30.00 |
| **Wrecker,** Model A, 1920s, Kenton, 9 1/2 In. | 1200.00 |
| **Wrecker,** Riding, Wyandotte | 45.00 |
| **Xylophone,** Pinky Lee, Original Box | 10.00 |
| **Yellow Cab,** Arcade, Cast Iron | 95.00 |
| **Yellow Kid,** Cast Iron, 5 1/2 X 7 In. | 195.00 |
| **Yo-Yo,** Sterling, Raised Acanthus Leaf Design, Gorham | 65.00 |
| **Yo-Yo,** 1956 Chevrolet, Wooden | 10.00 |
| **Zeppelin,** Cast Iron | 30.00 To 35.00 |
| **Zeppelin,** Lehmann, 7 In. | 275.00 |
| **Zeppelin,** Sky Flier, Tin Lithograph, 4 1/2 In. | 10.00 |
| **Zeppelin,** Wheels, Cast Iron, 6 In. | 45.00 |
| **Zigzag Vehicle,** Windup, German, Tin, 7 1/2 In. | 850.00 |

*Tramp art is a form of folk art made since the Civil War. It is
usually made from chip-carved cigar boxes.*

| | |
|---|---|
| **TRAMP ART, Box,** Cigar, Deer & Trees, Carved Lid | 25.00 |
| **Box,** Jewelry | 16.00 |
| **Box,** Pedestal, Geometric Design, 9 In. | 50.00 |
| **Box,** School, Child's, Stamped Robert | 46.00 |
| **Compote,** Covered | 15.00 |
| **Desk,** Kneehole | 475.00 |
| **Frame,** Photograph | 16.50 |
| **Frame,** 10 X 12 In. | 26.00 |
| **Pincushion,** 2 Drawers, 3 1/2 X 3 X 2 1/2 In. | 35.00 |

| | |
|---|---|
| **TRAP, Bear,** Hand Forged | 95.00 |
| **Bear,** Herder, Codiak | 400.00 |
| **Bear,** Lock & Matching Strap Hinges, Wrought-Iron | 195.00 |
| **Bear,** Newhouse No.5, Teeth | 175.00 |
| **Bear,** Newhouse, 1911 | 300.00 |
| **Beaver,** Hand Forged, 6 Tally Marks | 165.00 |
| **Fox,** Easy Set Triumph Trap Co., No.1 1/2 | 7.00 |
| **Gopher,** Scissors-Type | 3.50 |
| **Mink,** S.Newhouse, No.I | 7.50 |
| **Mink,** S.Newhouse, No.1 1/2 | 9.00 |
| **Mouse,** Black Wire & Iron, C.1870 | 32.00 |
| **Mouse,** Catch 'Em Alive, C.1900, Tin & Wood | 50.00 |

| | |
|---|---|
| **Mouse,** Magill | 10.00 |
| **Mouse,** Runway Trap Co., Tinware, 4 1/4 In. | 14.00 |
| **Mouse,** Trapdoor Closes Behind, Inner Chamber, Tin | 38.00 |
| **Rat,** Automatic, Ketchall | 20.00 |
| **Rat,** Sheet Iron, 6 In. | 7.50 |
| **Tarantula,** Patent April, 1877, Brass | 60.00 |
| **Wolf,** Hand Forged | 29.50 |
| **Wolf,** Newhouse, 4 1/2 In. | 80.00 |
| **Wolf,** 18th Century, Hand Forged, Signed, 21 In. | 95.00 |

*Treen are small wooden objects such as mugs, spoons, and bowls. The term is early English but is used in the United States in many areas.*

| | |
|---|---|
| **TREEN, Dipper,** S Shaped | 85.00 |
| **Jar,** Covered, Tri-Footed, 2 1/2 In. | 45.00 |
| **Plate,** Mottled Finish, 18th Century | 195.00 |
| **Sugar,** Covered | 50.00 |

*Trivets are now used to hold hot dishes. Most of the late nineteenth and early twentieth century trivets were made to hold hot irons. Iron or brass reproductions are being made of many of the old styles.*

| | | |
|---|---|---|
| **TRIVET, Alligator,** Brass, 6 In. | | 8.00 |
| **Child's,** Open Heart Handle, Masonic Emblem, Cast Iron, 4 3/4 In. | | 65.00 |
| **Crown & Cross,** Colebrookdale Iron Co., Pottstown, Penn., Cast Iron | | 9.00 |
| **Dumb Dutch,** Cast Iron | | 35.00 |
| **Eagle,** Cast Brass, Not Polished, 10 1/4 In. | *Illus* | 65.00 |
| **Enterprise Co.,** E Center, Cast Iron | | 8.00 |
| **Grapes & Scrolls,** Brass | | 35.00 |
| **Heart Center,** Turned Feet, Brass, 9 3/8 In. | *Illus* | 45.00 |
| **Heart,** Penny Feet, Wrought-Iron, 5 X 6 In., 2 In., High | | 85.00 |
| **Hearts & W,** Handled, Cast Iron | | 17.00 |
| **Lacy Urn With Smooth Rail,** Cast Iron, 6 In. | *Illus* | 15.00 |
| **Lyre Shape,** Brass, 4 X 7 In. | | 45.00 |
| **Not Polished,** Cast Brass, 9 1/4 In. | *Illus* | 22.50 |
| **Oxford Shoe Insert,** Hand-Forged Iron | | 25.00 |
| **Penny Foot,** Heart Shaped, Handle | | 110.00 |
| **Pierced Horse Design,** Ball & Claw Feet, Brass | *Illus* | 85.00 |
| **Quatrefoil Center,** Brass, 9 1/2 In. | *Illus* | 75.00 |
| **Rectangular,** Handle, Cast Iron, 8 In. | *Illus* | 22.50 |
| **Sadiron Shape,** Footed, Wooden Handle, 11 In. | | 48.00 |
| **San Francisco Etched,** Buildings, Footed, Marked China | | 16.50 |
| **Scrolled Feet,** Turned Handle, Wrought-Iron, 11 3/4 In. | *Illus* | 57.50 |
| **Sensible,** Cast Iron | | 35.00 |
| **Serpentine Form,** 3 Drawn Legs, 18th Century, Wrought-Iron, 7 In. | | 150.00 |
| **Shoe Form Feet,** Heart Cutout, Brass, 9 In. | *Illus* | 70.00 |
| **Slides On Double Iron Rod Handle,** Fire Hook, England, 19 In. | | 75.00 |
| **Stamped G.G.,** Wrought-Iron, 10 In. | *Illus* | 25.00 |
| **Striped Center,** Brass, 11 In. | *Illus* | 30.00 |
| **Two Interlocking Hearts,** Cast Iron, 7 1/2 In. | *Illus* | 25.00 |
| **Urn With Fern,** Cast Iron, 8 1/4 In. | *Illus* | 17.50 |
| **Wilton,** Cast Iron | | 35.00 |

| | |
|---|---|
| **TRUNK, Brass Trimmed,** Large | 125.00 |
| **Doll,** Tray, Flat Top, Wooden | 40.00 |
| **Domed Lid,** Brushed Copper Interior, Black, Tin, 19 X 12 X 15 In. | 125.00 |
| **Domed Lid,** Handmade Iron Bands & Handles | 750.00 |
| **Domed Lid,** Hide Covered, 41 X 21 In. | 87.00 |
| **Domed Lid,** Original Interior Wallpaper, 1806, Paper Label | 195.00 |
| **Handmade Hardware & Lock,** Round Top, Oak | 450.00 |
| **Humpback,** Embossed Tin Of Acorns & Flowers, 1800s, Large | 350.00 |
| **Irish,** Grain Paint, J.Bligh Casterea, May 1883, Tin, Hat Box | 250.00 |
| **Leather,** Studded With Brass Tacks | 675.00 |
| **Stagecoach,** Brass Buttons, Leather, 8 X 8 X 16 In. | 75.00 |
| **Tapered,** A.Jonsdatter, 1891, 20 X 20 X 41 In. | 435.00 |

Trivet, Eagle, Cast Brass, Not Polished, 10 1/4 In.

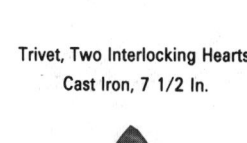

Trivet, Two Interlocking Hearts,
Cast Iron, 7 1/2 In.

Trivet, Rectangular, Handle,
Cast Iron, 8 In.

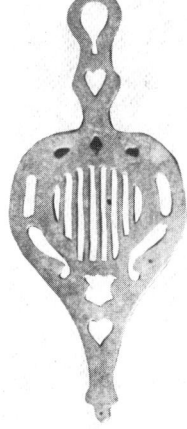

Trivet, Striped Center, Brass, 11 In.

Trivet, Heart Center, Turned
Feet, Brass, 9 3/8 In.

Trivet, Stamped G.G., Wrought-Iron, 10 In.

Trivet, Quatrefoil Center, Brass, 9 1/2 In. (See Page 698)

Trivet, Urn With Fern, Cast Iron,
8 1/4 In. (See Page 698)

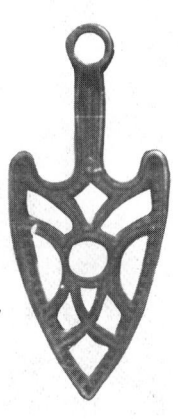

Trivet, Not Polished, Cast Brass,
9 1/4 In. (See Page 698)

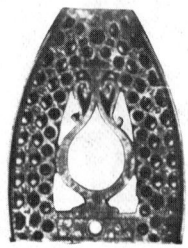

Trivet, Shoe Form Feet, Heart Cutout,
Brass, 9 In. (See Page 698)

Trivet, Lacy Urn With Smooth Rail,
Cast Iron, 6 In. (See Page 698)

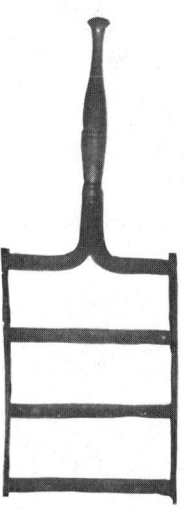

Trivet, Scrolled Feet, Turned Handle, Wrought
Iron, 11 3/4 In. (See Page 698)

Trivet, Pierced Horse Design, Ball &
Claw Feet, Brass (See Page 698)

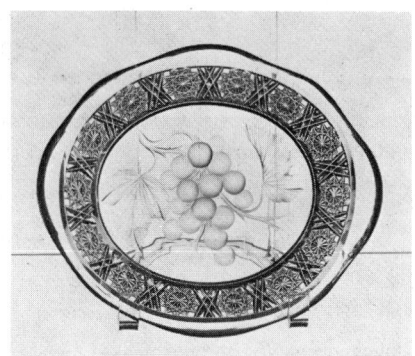

Tuthill, Dish, Cut Glass, Signed, Late 19th
Century, 8 1/2 In.

| | |
|---|---|
| **TUTHILL, Bottle,** Perfume, Wild Rose Pattern, Sterling Silver Stopper, Signed | 425.00 |
| **Bowl,** Berry, Signed, 8 In.Diam. | 345.00 |
| **Bowl,** Intaglio Flowers, Hobstar & Hobstar Base, Signed, 8 In.Diam. | 375.00 |
| **Bowl,** Poppy Pattern & Russian Cut, Signed, 3 1/2 X 8 In.Diam. | 650.00 |
| **Compote,** Bishop's Hat, Teardrop Stem, Signed, 7 1/2 X 12 In.Diam. | 600.00 |
| **Dish,** Cut Glass, Signed, Late 19th Century, 8 1/2 In. ..................*Illus* | 350.00 |
| **Dish,** Intaglio Vintage Design, 7 In. | 150.00 |
| **Dish,** Rosemere Pattern, Rectangular, Signed, 5 1/2 X 4 In. | 295.00 |
| **Jar,** Jam, Phlox Pattern, Gorham Sterling Silver Lid, Signed | 125.00 |
| **Pitcher,** Cream, Primrose, Intaglio Cut, Signed | 125.00 |
| **Plate,** Cut Central Figure, Vintage Border, Signed, 10 In.Diam. | 575.00 |
| **Sherbet,** Underplate, Copper Wheel Engraving, Signed, Plate, 6 In. | 150.00 |
| **Sugar & Creamer,** Open, Handled, Corset Shape, Signed, 4 In. | 195.00 |
| **Sugar & Creamer,** Open, Handled, Wild Rose, Signed | 450.00 |
| **Sugar,** Open, Handled, Vintage Grape, Signed | 195.00 |
| **Tray,** Ice Cream, Hobstars & Strawberry Diamond, Signed, 14 X 8 In. | 280.00 |
| **Tray,** Solid Handled, Intaglio Grape Cluster, Signed, 13 1/2 In. | 525.00 |
| **Vase,** Bud, Intaglio Cut Poppies, C.1910, Signed, 10 1/8 In. | 50.00 |
| **Vase,** Pedestal, Engraved In Leaf & Flower Design, Signed, 12 In. | 110.00 |
| | |
| **TYPEWRITER, Blickensderfer,** Original Oak Case | 95.00 |
| **Corona,** Folding, 1910 | 30.00 |
| **Hammond,** Folding, Case | 85.00 |
| **Ideal,** Oak Case | 365.00 |
| **Oliver,** No.3 | 40.00 |
| **Oliver,** No.5, Case | 47.50 |
| **Oliver,** No.9 | 55.00 |
| **Underwood,** Standard Portable, Carrying Case, 10 X 8 X 4 In. | 55.00 |
| **Underwood,** Standard, 1920s, Unusual Keyboard | 85.00 |
| **World Typewriter Co.,** Portland, Maine, Patent Papers, Case | 250.00 |
| | |
| **UMBRELLA, Child's,** Kate Greenaway Figure | 45.00 |
| **Indian Head Handle** | 30.00 |
| **Parasol,** Child's, Ruffled Edge, Curved Coral Handle, Marked P.K. | 15.00 |
| **Parasol,** Handle, Stylized Horse, 6 1/2 In. | 30.00 |

| | |
|---|---|
| **Parasol,** Pearl Chip Handle, Beige Silk | 40.00 |
| **Parasol,** Silk Embossed Roses & Vines, C.1933 | 60.00 |
| **Parasol,** Victorina, Painted Tin | 15.00 |
| **Uncle Wiggily,** Decal Of Wiggily & Pig On Handle, C.1924 | 38.00 |

UNION
PORCELAIN
WORKS
GREENPOINT
N.Y.

*Union Porcelain Works was established at Greenpoint, New York, in 1848 by Charles Cartlidge. The company went through a series of ownership changes and finally closed in the early 1900s.*

| | |
|---|---|
| **UNION PORCELAIN WORKS, Plate,** Oyster, Round, 9 1/2 In. | 125.00 |

*University City Pottery was first made in University City, Missouri, in 1907. It was made in classes taught by such famous potters as Taxile Doat, Edward Lewis, Adelaide Robineau, and Frederick Hurten Rhead. Overglaze painting on china was the largest part of the work. The experimental classes ended in 1914.*

| | |
|---|---|
| **UNIVERSITY CITY, Vase,** Crystalline Glaze, Green, 8 In. | 500.00 |

| | |
|---|---|
| **UNIVERSITY OF NORTH DAKOTA, Bowl,** Green, Prairie Rose, Signed, 5 1/2 In. | 65.00 |
| **Bowl,** Green, Sioux, Signed, 6 1/2 In. | 150.00 |
| **Tile,** Incised Grasshopper, 4 X 4 In. | 75.00 |
| **Vase,** Incised Roses, J.Mattson, 5 1/2 In. | 75.00 |

## Val St Lambert

*Val St.Lambert Cristalleries of Belgium was founded by Messieurs Kemlin and Lelievre in 1825. The company is still in operation.*

| | |
|---|---|
| **VAL ST.LAMBERT, Ashtray,** Cut & Polished, Set Of 6 | 25.00 |
| **Atomizer,** Perfume, Silk Tassel, Signed, 4 In. | 35.00 |
| **Bell,** Cut Glass | 25.00 |
| **Box,** Cameo, Frosted, Red Etched, Figures, Chariots, 4 3/4 In. | 395.00 |
| **Box,** Lilies On Stenciled Ground, Signed, 4 X 5 1/2 In. | 400.00 |
| **Candleholder,** Ruby Cut To Clear, Signed, 2 3/4 In., Pair | 125.00 |
| **Dish,** Candy, Bell Shaped Base, Finger Hold, Signed, 5 1/2 In. | 45.00 |
| **Paperweight,** Free-Form Iceberg Shape, Signed | 55.00 |
| **Plate,** Rembrandt & Reubens, 1968, Boxed | 85.00 |
| **Platter,** Art Deco, Amethyst, 16 1/2 In.Diam. | 175.00 |
| **Sugar & Creamer,** Signed | 25.00 |
| **Vase,** Cranberry, 6 In. | 75.00 |
|     **VALENTINE, see Card, Valentine** | |

## Vallerysthal

*Vallerysthal Glassworks was founded in 1836 in Lorraine, France. In 1854 the firm became Klenglin et Cie. It made table and decorative glass, opaline, cameo, and art glass. The firm is still working.*

| | |
|---|---|
| **VALLERYSTHAL, Dish,** Hen On Nest Cover, Miniature | 12.50 |
| **Dish,** Setter Dog Cover, Blue Milk Glass, Flower Base | 130.00 |
| **Dish,** Snail Cover, On Strawberry | 80.00 |
| **Dish,** Swan Cover, Gold Design, Blue, Milk Glass | 80.00 |
| **Plate,** Aqua, 7 1/2 In. | 12.00 |
| **Salt,** Hen On Nest, Cobalt | 25.00 |
| **Salt,** Hen On Nest, Individual, Set Of 4 | 75.00 |
| **Swan,** Blue | 70.00 |

Van Briggle Pottery was made by Artus Van Briggle and his wife Anna in Colorado Springs, Colorado, after 1901. Mr. Van Briggle died in 1904. The wares have modeled relief decorations with a soft dull glaze. It is still being made.

| | |
|---|---|
| **VAN BRIGGLE, Ashtray,** Hopi Maiden, Turquoise | 85.00 To 115.00 |
| **Ashtray,** Ming House, Figural | 45.00 |
| **Ashtray,** Rose, 8 1/2 In.Square | 24.00 |
| **Bookends,** Owl, Persian Rose | 80.00 |
| **Bookends,** Peacocks, Rose | 85.00 |
| **Bowl & Flower Frog,** Curled Leaf Shape, 12 1/4 X 8 1/2 In. | 45.00 |
| **Bowl,** Acorn, 6 In. | 22.50 |
| **Bowl,** Acorns & Leaves Folded Over Top, Persian Rose, 6 In. | 22.50 |
| **Bowl,** Console, Siren Of The Sea, Flower Frog | 325.00 |
| **Bowl,** Cranberry Matte Glaze, C.1903, Incised Mark, 4 1/2 In. | 150.00 |
| **Bowl,** Dragonflies, Flower Frog, Dated 1919, 8 1/4 In.Diam. | 100.00 |
| **Bowl,** Dragonfly, Persian Rose Glaze, 3 X 3 5/8 In. | 35.00 |
| **Bowl,** Duck Flower Holder, Turquoise | 70.00 |
| **Bowl,** Greenish Yellow Matte, Leaves, C.1903, Marked, 6 In. | 425.00 |
| **Bowl,** Matching Frog, Blue Over Green, 1919, 8 1/2 In. | 80.00 |
| **Bowl,** Molded Butterflies, Turquoise Blue, 3 In. | 20.00 |
| **Bowl,** Scalloped, Turquoise, Double A, 6 X 3 X 2 1/2 In. | 18.50 |
| **Bowl,** Slate Blue, Shape No.263, 1906, 10 1/2 In. | 325.00 |
| **Bowl,** Turquoise Matte, Dated 1916, 2 X 6 1/4 In.Diam. | 50.00 |
| **Candleholder,** Double, Persian Rose | 18.00 |
| **Conch Shell,** Persian, Rose Color, 12 1/2 In. | 50.00 |
| **Conch Shell,** Plum, 10 In. | 19.00 |
| **Conch Shell,** Turquoise, 17 In. | 60.00 |
| **Console Set,** Reclining Mermaid, Frog & Candlesticks, Signed | 395.00 |
| **Creamer & Sugar,** Red | 22.00 |
| **Creamer,** Rose, 3 In. | 30.00 |
| **Dish,** Candy, Maple Leaf Shape, High Gloss Jet Black, 10 In.Diam. | 11.50 |
| **Dish,** Cheese & Cracker, Sunflower, Persian Rose | 45.00 |
| **Dish,** Flat Bottom, Shades Of Blue, 14 X 10 In.Diam. | 28.00 |
| **Ewer,** Turquoise, 6 1/2 In. | 12.00 |
| **Figurine,** Elephant, Trunk Up, Turquoise, 7 1/2 In. | 55.00 |
| **Figurine,** Girl, Indian, Grinding Corn, Turquoise Blue, 6 In. | 60.00 |
| **Figurine,** Lorelei, Dark Mulberry | 200.00 |
| **Figurine,** Mule, Turquoise | 35.00 |
| **Figurine,** Owl, Perched On Stump, Turquoise Glaze, 9 1/2 In. | 45.00 |
| **Figurine,** Rabbit, Plum, 2 1/2 In. | 100.00 |
| **Figurine,** Shell Girl, Turquoise | 60.00 |
| **Jardiniere,** Head In Relief, Persian Rose, 8 In. | 325.00 |
| **Lamp,** Bedroom, Encased Butterflies & Milkweed Shade, 11 In. | 75.00 |
| **Lamp,** Damsel Of Damascus, Persian Rose | 165.00 |
| **Lamp,** Damsel Of Demascus, Blue, Shade | 225.00 |
| **Lamp,** Mulberry Moth, Original Shade | 125.00 |
| **Match Holder,** Boot Shape | 20.00 |
| **Mug,** Turquoise, High Glaze, Marked, 5 1/2 In. | 18.00 |
| **Paperweight,** Elephant, Mulberry | 45.00 |
| **Pitcher,** Turquoise, 4 In. | 20.00 |
| **Planter,** Conch Shell, Persian Rose, Signed, 12 1/2 In. | 45.00 |
| **Planter,** Dragonfly, Persian Rose Design | 65.00 |
| **Planter,** Seashell, Flower Frog, Blue, 17 In. | 45.00 |
| **Plaque,** Hanging, Indian Maiden, Little Star, 5 1/4 In. | 70.00 |
| **Plaque,** Hanging, Indian, Big Buffalo, Oval, 5 1/4 In. | 70.00 |
| **Rose Bowl,** Pinecone, Blue, Signed | 15.00 |
| **Salt & Pepper,** Penguin, Persian Rose, Ming Blue | 45.00 |
| **Shell,** Turquoise, 13 In. | 35.00 |
| **Turquoise,** Frog Insert Of Duck, 5 1/2 In. | 62.00 |
| **Vase,** Band Of Poppy Seed Pods, Green Matte, Marked, 9 1/4 In. | 2500.00 |
| **Vase,** Blue Daffodil, AA Signed, 7 In. | 35.00 |
| **Vase,** Blue Floral, AA Signed, 4 3/4 In. | 35.00 |

| | |
|---|---|
| Vase, Blue Glaze, Green Highlights, Dated, 1 3/4 X 2 3/4 In. | 70.00 |
| Vase, Blue Green, Blue Daffodil, AA Signed, 7 In. | 38.00 |
| Vase, Blue, Daffodils, 1920, 10 In. | 145.00 |
| Vase, Blue, Green, 2-Handled, 6 1/2 In. | 75.00 |
| Vase, Blue, Signed & Dated 1905, 9 In. | 265.00 |
| Vase, Brown & Green Matte, Poppy Seed Pods, Signed, 9 In. | 1050.00 |
| Vase, Bud, Triple, Volcanic Blue, 7 In. | 35.00 |
| Vase, Bud, Volcanic Brown, 6 In. | 20.00 |
| Vase, Butterfly, Light Blue With Darker Blue, 1918, 3 In. | 65.00 |
| Vase, Butterfly, Rose With Cobalt, 3 In. | 35.00 |
| Vase, Colorado Springs, Blue, 4 In. | 12.00 |
| Vase, Daffodil, Dated 1920, Blue, 9 1/2 In. | 65.00 |
| Vase, Daffodils, Blue, 1920, 10 In. | 145.00 |
| Vase, Dragonfly, Blue On Turquoise, 8 1/4 In. | 65.00 |
| Vase, Etched Wheat Design, Rose, 7 X 4 In. | 38.00 |
| Vase, Figural, Lorelei Rising From Sea, Blue, 10 1/2 In. | 100.00 |
| Vase, Figural, Lorelei Rising From Sea, White, 10 1/2 In. | 100.00 |
| Vase, Flowers, 1908-11, Green, 3 In. | 145.00 |
| Vase, Flowers, 1916, 9 In. | 125.00 |
| Vase, Frieze Of Sea Gulls At Neck, Marked, 1908-11, 4 In. | 135.00 |
| Vase, Geometric Design, 1920, Blue, 5 3/4 In. | 85.00 |
| Vase, Green Glaze, Stylized Flowers, Cranberry, 11 In. | 500.00 |
| Vase, Indian Girl Grinding Corn, 6 In. | 65.00 To 75.00 |
| Vase, Indian Heads, Mulberry, 13 1/2 In. | 155.00 |
| Vase, Indian Heads, Turquoise, 13 1/2 In. | 125.00 |
| Vase, Lorelei, Blue, 10 1/2 In. | 100.00 |
| Vase, Maroon & Blue, AA Signed, 3 1/2 In. | 20.00 |
| Vase, Molded Leaf, Aqua, 4 3/4 In. | 35.00 |
| Vase, Molded Tulips, Persian Rose, 1920s, Marked, 9 In. | 55.00 |
| Vase, Navy, Touches Of Maroon, 1917, 3 In. | 65.00 |
| Vase, Nude Lady Emerging From Top, Persian Rose, 10 In. | 145.00 |
| Vase, Overlapping Leaves, Maroon, 1918, 3 1/2 In. | 85.00 |
| Vase, Plum, Dated 1919, 5 In. | 65.00 |
| Vase, Plum, Dated 1920, 8 1/2 In. | 95.00 |
| Vase, Plum, 1921, Signed, 3 X 4 1/2 In. | 22.00 |
| Vase, Raised Floral, Maroon To Purple, Marked 9, 4 In. | 68.00 |
| Vase, Rose & Blue, 13 In. | 115.00 |
| Vase, Trumpet, Blue, 5 1/2 In. | 25.00 |
| Vase, Tulip Shape, Turquoise, 6 In.Diam. | 30.00 |
| Vase, Turquoise Glaze, Conical Form, C.1905, 4 1/2 In. | 325.00 |
| Vase, Turquoise, Blue, Tulip Leaf, 7 In. | 47.00 |
| Vase, Turquoise, Raised Flowers, Pair, 5 In. | 30.00 |
| Vase, Turquoise, 2 3/4 In. | 20.00 |
| Wall Pocket, Double, Turquoise, Dated 1926, Small | 25.00 |
| Wall Pocket, Lotus, Green With Dark Blue | 48.00 |

*Vasa Murrhina is the name of a glassware made by the Vasa Murrhina Art Glass Company of Sandwich, Massachusetts, about 1884. The glassware was transparent and was embedded with small pieces of colored glass and metallic flakes. Some of the pieces were cased. The same type of glass was made in England. Collectors often confuse Vasa Murrhina glass with aventurine, spatter, or spangle glass. There is much confusion about what actually was made by the Vasa Murrhina factory.*

### VASA MURRHINA, see also Spangle Glass

| | |
|---|---|
| VASA MURRHINA, Basket, White Lining, Pink Outside, Maroon Spatter, 6 1/2 In. | 165.00 |
| Bowl, Rose, Metallic Specks, Satin Finish | 45.00 |
| Ewer, Silver Mica, Ruffled Edge, Thorn Handle, Blue, 9 In. | 125.00 |
| Pitcher, Melon Shape, 6 In. | 47.50 |
| Rose Bowl, Multicolored, Silver Specks, 4 1/2 In. | 75.00 |
| Rose Bowl, Rose Overlay, 8 Crimp, Silver Spangles, 3 3/8 In. | 110.00 |
| Rose Bowl, Yellow, Gold Spangled, Egg Shape, 4 In. | 115.00 |
| Toothpick, Leaf Mold | 95.00 |

Toothpick, Melon Ribbed Swirl, Spangles ................................................................... 65.00
Vase, Amber With Gold Flecks, 10 1/2 X 7 In.Diam. ............................................... 135.00
Vase, Applied Shell Handles, White Lining, Pink Overlay, 7 In. ............................... 85.00
Vase, Bulbous, Ruffled Clear Rim, Rose, 5 1/2 In. .................................................. 110.00
Vase, Clear Handles, Cobalt, Gold Mica, 11 In. ....................................................... 70.00

*Vasart is the signature used on a late type of art glass made by the Streathearn Glass Company of Scotland.*

VASART, Ashtray, Mottled Blue To Pink, 4 1/2 In.Diam. ........................................ 25.00
Bowl, Aqua Swirls, Pink, Signed, 10 X 3 3/4 In. ...................................................... 68.00
Bowl, Inverted Hat Shape, Light Blue, Signed, 9 X 2 1/2 In. ................................. 28.00
Bowl, Mottled Blue, Cylindrical, Flairing Rim, 2 1/2 In. .......................................... 20.00
Bowl, Mottled Green, Scalloped Rim, 2 In. ............................................................... 25.00
Bowl, Mottled Pink To Green, Flairing Rim, 4 X 6 X 2 1/2 In. ............................... 45.00
Bowl, Pale Green, Signed, 5 X 1 1/2 In. ................................................................... 20.00
Bowl, Posey, 9 1/2 X 2 In. ........................................................................................ 35.00
Desk Set, Gold Trim, Letter Holder, Stamp Box ....................................................... 32.50
Hat, Gray Crown, Mottled Pink Brim, 2 1/4 In. ........................................................ 35.00
Vase, Cluthra, Pink & White, Turned Collar, Signed, 2 1/4 X 5 In. ....................... 125.00
Vase, Footed, Jade Green, Signed, 9 X 3 In. ........................................................... 45.00
Vase, Mottled White Base, Pink Flange, Signed, 4 1/2 X 2 In. .............................. 65.00
Vase, Pink & White, Cluthra Type, Turned Over Collar, 2 1/4 X 5 In. .................... 125.00

*Vaseline glass is a greenish yellow glassware resembling petroleum jelly. Some vaseline glass is still being made in old and new styles. Pressed glass of the 1870s was often made of vaseline-colored glass. The old glass was made with uranium, but the reproductions are being colored in a different way. See Pressed Glass for more information about patterns that were also made of vaseline-colored glass.*

VASELINE GLASS, Basket, Baby Coin Spot, Opalescent, 7 In. ............................... 20.00
Berry Bowl, Petticoat, Master .................................................................................... 38.00
Berry Master, Pressed Diamond ................................................................................ 42.00
Berry Set, Daisy & Button, 3 Cornered .................................................................... 110.00
Bottle, Clear Handled ................................................................................................. 38.00
Bottle, Ketchup, Daisy & Button ............................................................................... 90.00
Bottle, Perfume, Faceted Stopper, Square, 2 5/8 In. .............................................. 50.00
Bottle, Perfume, Purse, Sterling Collar & Cover, 3 X 1 In. ..................................... 48.00
Bottle, Perfume, Sterling Collar & Hinged Cover, 3 1/2 In. ..................................... 48.00
Bottle, Perfume, Urn Shape ....................................................................................... 60.00
Bowl, Berry, Diamond ................................................................................................. 35.00
Bowl, Diamond, 8 1/2 In., Pair .................................................................................. 45.00
Bowl, Fish, 13 X 7 In. ................................................................................................ 125.00
Bowl, Hobnail, 3 1/4 X 7 In.Diam. ............................................................................ 45.00
Bowl, Paneled Daisy, Scalloped, 9 3/4 In.Diam. ...................................................... 110.00
Compote, Daisy & Button, Loops Around Top, 9 3/4 In. .......................................... 50.00
Compote, Diamond Pattern, 8 3/4 X 6 In. ................................................................ 52.00
Compote, Open, Rose In Snow, 5 1/2 In. .................................................................. 38.00
Compote, Pedestal, Bubble Connector Ball, 14 In.Diam. ......................................... 90.00
Compote, Rose In Snow, Open, 5 1/2 In. .................................................................. 38.00
Creamer, Austrian, Miniature ..................................................................................... 78.00
Creamer, Dewey ......................................................................................................... 55.00
Creamer, Gold Band ................................................................................................... 55.00
Creamer, Oaken Bucket ............................................................... 35.00 To 45.00
Creamer, Ransom, Gold Band .................................................................................... 25.00
Creamer, 3 Panel ........................................................................................................ 35.00
Cruet, Baby Coin Spot, Opalescent, 6 1/2 In. .......................................................... 22.00
Cruet, Dewey, Original Stopper ................................................................................. 150.00
Dish, Basket Weave, Lattice Edge, 7 In.Diam. ......................................................... 12.00
Dish, Cheese, Paneled Crystal, Belltone Cover, 11 1/2 In. ...................................... 50.00
Dish, Sweetmeat, Blue Trim, Silver Plated Holder, Opalescent ............................... 135.00
Epergne, 4 Lilies, Clear Bottom, 10 In. .................................................................... 20.00
Goblet, Basket Weave ................................................................................................ 45.00

| | |
|---|---|
| Goblet, Cane Pattern | 58.00 |
| Goblet, Daisy & Button With Thumbprint | 35.00 |
| Goblet, Diamond-Quilted | 22.00 |
| Goblet, Diamond-Quilted With Star | 35.00 |
| Goblet, Etched Grapes & Vines | 85.00 |
| Goblet, Valencia Waffle | 25.00 |
| Humidor, Tobacco, Raised Red & White Design, Brass Lid | 67.50 |
| Jar, Candy, Covered, Gold Striping, 6 1/2 In. | 25.00 |
| Jar, Covered, Clear Knob Handle, 12 In. | 38.00 |
| Pitcher, Basket Weave | 32.00 |
| Pitcher, Lemonade, Blue Hobnail, Cased, 8 In. | 175.00 |
| Pitcher, Milk, Daisy & Button With Crossbars | 50.00 |
| Pitcher, Water, Cranberry & White Spatter, Leaf Mold | 325.00 |
| Pitcher, Water, Riverside, Ransom Band | 150.00 |
| Pitcher, Wild Flower | 135.00 |
| Plate, Cake, Maple Leaf | 40.00 |
| Plate, Sandwich, Fleur-De-Lis, Handled | 30.00 |
| Rose Bowl, Crimped Top, 3-Footed, Opalescent | 60.00 |
| Rose Bowl, Paneled Buttons, Northwood, 4 X 4 In. | 55.00 |
| Salt, Footed, Heart Shaped, Opalescent | 65.90 |
| Saucer, Daisy & Button With Crossbars, 4 In.Diam. | 10.00 |
| Shoe, Daisy & Button | 25.00 |
| Shoe, High Button, On Platform, Marked Bouquet Holder | 35.00 |
| Shoe, On Skates | 18.00 |
| Spooner, Basket Weave | 52.00 |
| Spooner, Fine Cut | 38.00 |
| Spooner, Gold Band | 55.00 |
| Spooner, Inverted Thumbprint | 35.00 |
| Spooner, Pressed Diamond | 40.00 |
| Spooner, Wooden Pail | 48.00 |
| Spooner, 3 Panel | 35.00 |
| Sugar Shaker, Spatter Leaf Mold | 130.00 |
| Sugar, Covered, Gold Band | 75.00 |
| Syrup, Valencia Waffle, Applied Handle | 110.00 |
| Toothpick, Button With V Ornament | 22.00 |
| Toothpick, Hand Shape | 59.00 |
| Tray, Change, Teaberry Gum | 28.00 |
| Tray, Condiment, Petticoat | 50.00 |
| Tray, Handled, Pleat & Panel, 8 1/2 X 13 In. | 60.00 |
| Tumbler, Basket Weave | 33.00 |
| Tumbler, Daisy & Button | 25.00 |
| Tumbler, Daisy & Button, Design On Bottom Half | 25.00 |
| Tumbler, Mitered Diamond | 25.00 |
| Vase, Car, Impressed Flowers & Geometric Design, Pair | 35.00 |
| Vase, Cobalt Trim, 7 1/2 In. | 37.50 |
| Vase, Hand Shape, 3 3/4 In. | 75.00 |
| Vase, Overall Raised White Floral Design, C.1870, 10 1/4 In. | 150.00 |
| Vase, Ruffled, Flared Top, Ribbed, Plated, Smoked, 3 1/2 In. | 195.00 |

*Venetian glass has been made near Venice, Italy, from the thirteenth to the twentieth century. Thin colored glass with applied decorations is favored, although many other types have been made.*

| | |
|---|---|
| VENETIAN GLASS, Bowl, Finger, Ruffled Underplate, Applied Glass Design | 35.00 |
| Cruet, Double, Swirled, Lavender | 90.00 |
| Cup & Saucer, Demitasse, Multicolored | 65.00 |
| Ewer, Figural, Dolphin, Green & Gold | 50.00 |
| Pitcher, Applied Lion Head On Handle, Gold Flecked, 9 In. | 125.00 |
| Sherbet, Blown, Pink & Green, Hollow Stem, 7 In. | 45.00 |
| Vase, Green Trails, Millefiori Flowers, C.1895, 4 3/4 In. | 100.00 |
| Vase, Hand-Painted Apple Blossoms, 14 In., Pair | 210.00 |
| Vase, Polychrome Design, Dragon Handles, Sea Green, 15 In. | 200.00 |
| Water Set, Cranberry Tint Bottom, Gold Flowers, 7 Piece | 245.00 |

*Verlys glass was made in France after 1931. Verlys was also made in the United States. The glass is either blown or molded. The American glass is signed with a diamond-point-scratched name, but the French pieces are marked with a molded signature.*

**VERLYS, Ashtray,** Frosted Swallows & Rim, Rectangular, 3 1/2 X 4 1/2 X 1 In. .................. 40.00
**Bowl,** Birds & Bumblebees, Wings Spread On Birds, Signed, 11 In.Diam. ............................ 165.00
**Bowl,** Birds & Fish, Script Signed, 14 In.Diam. ............................................................ 200.00
**Bowl,** Centerpiece, Puffed-Out Angelfish, Signed, 12 3/4 In.Diam .................................. 250.00
**Bowl,** Console, Floral & Leaf, 13 1/2 In. ...................................................................... 85.00
**Bowl,** Cupid, Arrow, & Hearts, Frosted, 6 In.Diam. ....................................................... 75.00
**Bowl,** Diamond Tassel, Frosted, Signed, 12 In. ............................................................. 76.00
**Bowl,** Flying Geese, Fish On Underside, Green, 13 1/2 In.Diam. ..................................... 80.00
**Bowl,** Irises, Frosted, Signed, 2 3/8 X 5 3/8 In. ........................................................... 75.00
**Bowl,** Large Puffed-Out Fish Center, Frosted, Signed, 12 1/2 In. .................................... 250.00
**Bowl,** Orchids, Frosted, High Relief, Signed, 14 In. ....................................................... 119.00
**Bowl,** Poppies & Buds, Frosted Underside, Signed, 13 1/2 In.Diam. ................................ 115.00
**Bowl,** Poppies & Leaves, Signed, 13 1/2 In.Diam. ........................................................ 110.00
**Bowl,** Raised Pinecones, Footed, Frosted, 6 In. ........................................................... 32.00
**Bowl,** Tassel Pattern, Amber, Signed, 11 1/2 In.Diam. ................................................. 80.00
**Bowl,** Tassel, Opalescent, Signed, 11 3/4 In. ............................................. 115.00 To 245.00
**Bowl,** Tassels, Double Signed, 11 3/4 In. .................................................................... 65.00
**Bowl,** Water Lily Pattern, Art Nouveau, Crystal, 14 In.Diam. ........................................ 180.00
**Bowl,** Wild Ducks, 13 1/2 In. .................................................................................... 75.00
**Bowl,** 3 Flowers On Bottom Form Feet, Signed, 8 1/2 In.Diam. ..................................... 59.50
**Box,** Cigarette, Ashtray, Mourning Doves .................................................................... 45.00
**Box,** Smoky Glass, Spider Chrysanthemum, Covered, Signed, 6 5/8 In. .......................... 200.00
**Candleholder,** Script, 3 X 6 In. ................................................................................... 50.00
**Charger,** Flowing Birds, Crystal ................................................................................. 110.00
**Charger,** Iris Designs ................................................................................................ 120.00
**Console Set,** Water Lily Pattern, Candleholders, Bowl, 14 In.Diam. ............................... 145.00
**Dish,** Figural Goose Perched At End, Signed, 6 X 3 3/4 In. ............................................ 58.00
**Vase,** Blue Alpine Thistle, Signed, 9 In. ...................................................................... 245.00
**Vase,** Gems, Footed, 7 X 6 3/4 In.Diam. .................................................................... 80.00
**Vase,** Lovebirds, Opalescent, Fan Shaped, Marked, 13 In. ............................................ 115.00
**Vase,** Mermaid Design, Smoky Topaz, Signed, 11 In. ................................................... 300.00
**Vase,** Pink Design, Clear, Trumpet Shaped, Square Base, Signed, 7 In. ......................... 250.00

*Verre de soie glass was first made by Frederick Carder at the Steuben Glass Works from about 1905 to 1930. It is an iridescent glass of soft white or very, very pale green. The name means glass of silk, and it does resemble silk. Other factories have made verre de soie, and some of the English examples were made of different colors. Verre de soie is an art glass and is not related to the iridescent pressed white carnival glass mistakenly called by its name.*

**VERRE DE SOIE, see also Steuben**
**VERRE DE SOIE, Bottle,** Cologne, 6 1/4 X 3 1/2 In.Diam. ............................................. 280.00
**Bowl,** Amber Edge, Etched Flowers, 10 In.Diam. ......................................................... 155.00
**Bowl,** Centerpiece, Gold Label, Pink Shading, 12 1/4 In. .............................................. 350.00
**Bowl,** Eggnog, 4-Petal Rim, Swirl Pattern, 7 1/2 X 10 1/2 In. ..................................... 175.00
**Bowl,** Signed Hawkes, 4 3/4x 8 In.Diam. ................................................................... 95.00
**Compote,** Candy, Blue Edge, 3 X 6 In.Diam. ............................................................... 50.00
**Dish,** Mint, 6 1/4 In. ................................................................................................ 65.00
**Lampshade,** Neck, 2 1/4 In., Set Of 4 ...................................................................... 145.00
**Rose Bowl,** Blue Applied Rim, Turquoise, Signed, 3 1/2 X 6 In. .................................... 135.00
**Sherbet,** Underplate .................................................................................................. 75.00
**Vase,** Applied Green Cord & Oval Discs, Signed, 8 In. .................................................. 210.00
**Vase,** Bell Shaped, Engraved Flowers, Signed Hawkes, 10 In. ...................................... 110.00
**Vase,** Copper Wheel Engraved Design, Signed Hawkes, 6 3/4 In. .................................. 135.00
**Vase,** Pinecones, Leaves, Daisies, Green, 12 In. ......................................................... 65.00
**Vase,** Stick, Engraved, 8 In. ...................................................................................... 75.00
**Vase,** 3-Prong, Iridescent ......................................................................................... 110.00
 **VIENNA, see Beehive; Royal Vienna**

*Vienna Art plates were round metal serving trays produced around the turn of the century. The designs, copied from Royal Vienna porcelain plates, usually featured a portrait of a lady encircled by a wide, ornate border. Many were used as advertising or promotional items and were produced in Coshocton, Ohio, by J.F. Meek's Tuscarora Advertising Co. and H.D. Beach's Standard Advertising Co.*

**VIENNA ART, see also Coca-Cola**

| | |
|---|---:|
| **VIENNA ART, Plate,** Anheuser-Busch, 1905 | 85.00 |
| **Plate,** Art Nouveau Woman, Draped Bosom, Dated 1905 | 50.00 |
| **Plate,** Barbee Whiskey, Mountain, Cabin, Booze Barrels | 150.00 |
| **Plate,** Budweiser Beer, On The Levee, 1914 | 145.00 |
| **Plate,** Coca-Cola, Seminude | 275.00 |
| **Plate,** Jamestown | 45.00 |
| **Plate,** Knights Of Columbus, 1905 | 28.50 |
| **Plate,** Lady, Butterflies, Cherubs, 1905, Pair | 85.00 |
| **Plate,** Long-Haired Brunette, Skullcap, Dated 1905 | 65.00 |
| **Plate,** Woman Holding Vase, Stamped Eli Spayd, Bartlesville, Okla. | 45.00 |

*Villeroy & Boch Pottery of Mettlach, Germany, was founded in 1841. The firm made many types of pottery, including the famous Mettlach steins.*

**VILLEROY & BOCH, see also Mettlach**

| | |
|---|---:|
| **VILLEROY & BOCH, Creamer,** Floral, C.1896 | 50.00 |
| **Mug,** Twig Handle, Green Figural Leaves | 50.00 |
| **Pitcher,** Blue Flowers, Cobalt & Gold Handle, 7 In. | 40.00 |
| **Plate,** Comical Hunting Scene, Black & White, 8 In. | 25.00 |
| **Plate,** Dutchman Walking His Dog, Signed, 12 In.Diam. | 40.00 |
| **Plate,** Harbor Scene With Dutch Girls, Blue & White, 10 In. | 195.00 |
| **Platter,** Blue Poppy Pattern, Oval, 19 In. | 125.00 |
| **Platter,** Cream Ground, Marked, 11 X 17 3/4 In. | 65.00 |
| **Punch Bowl,** Underplate, Russian Motif, Marked, Bowl, 14 In. | 1000.00 |
| **Sugar & Creamer,** Yellow Inside, Black Outside | 25.00 |
| **Teapot,** Figural, Terrier, Black & White | 35.00 |
| **Tile,** Dutch Scene, Blue & White | 48.00 |
| **Tobacco Jar,** Raised Portraits All Around | 35.00 |
| **Tumbler,** 5 In., Set Of 6 | 350.00 |
| **Vase,** Handled, Silver Trim, Figures In Relief, 6 3/4 In. | 50.00 |
| **Vase,** Stump, Silver Leaves Design, 5 In. | 125.00 |

**VOLKMAR**
**Corona N.Y.**    *Volkmar pottery was made by Charles Volkmar from 1879 to about 1911. He was part of several firms including the Volkmar Ceramic Company, Volkmar and Cory, and Charles Volkmar and Son.*

| | |
|---|---:|
| **VOLKMAR, Lamp Base,** Oil, Green, Signed, Incised Mark, 8 X 10 In. | 150.00 |
| **Plaque,** Blue & White, Washington Home, 1896, 11 1/4 In. | 200.00 To 385.00 |
| **Plaque,** Under The Elms, Blue, 11 1/4 In. | 200.00 |

*Volkstadt was a soft paste porcelain manufactory started in 1760 by Georg Heinrich Macheleid at Volkstadt, Thuringia. Volkstadt-Rudolstadt was a porcelain factory started at Volkstadt-Rudolstadt by Beyer and Bock in 1890.*

| | |
|---|---:|
| **VOLKSTADT, Group,** Mars & Venus, Grass Mound Base, C.1770, Marked, 6 3/4 In. | 300.00 |
| **WALLACE NUTTING, see Print, Nutting** | |
| **WALLENDORF, Coffeepot,** Cover, Pear Shape, Flowers, C.1804, Blue Mark, 9 1/2 In. | 480.00 |
| **Tea Bowl & Saucer,** Flower Sprays, C.1775, Blue Mark | 160.00 |
| **Tea Bowl & Saucer,** 2 Lovebirds, Fruit, C.1775, Blue Mark | 160.00 |
| **WALT DISNEY, see Disneyana** | |
| **WALTER, see A. Walter** | |
| **WANNOPEE, Candleholder,** Loop Handle, Metallic Glaze, 12 1/2 In. | 165.00 |

*Warwick china was made in Wheeling, West Virginia, in a pottery factory founded in 1887.*

| | |
|---|---|
| **WARWICK, Butter Pat,** Hand-Painted, Gold Rim | 6.00 |
| **Compote,** Currants, Brown Ground, Pedestaled | 85.00 |
| **Cornucopia,** Pair | 55.00 |
| **Creamer,** Flowers, 5 In. | 20.00 |
| **Dish,** Cheese, Rose & Gold Swirls, Gold Handle, Covered | 42.00 |
| **Dish,** Relish, Gold Edge, 12 In. | 18.00 |
| **Holder,** Toothbrush, Flowers | 25.00 |
| **Humidor,** Hunt Scene, Brown | 150.00 |
| **Mug,** B.P.O.E., IOGA Mark, 5 In. | 65.00 |
| **Mug,** Champion Bulldog, IOGA | 25.00 |
| **Mug,** Clergyman Smelling Flowers, IOGA, 4 1/2 In. | 50.00 |
| **Mug,** Elk, IOGA Mark | 35.00 |
| **Mug,** Hobo Wearing Top Hat, Strumming Guitar, IOGA, 4 1/2 In. | 68.00 |
| **Mug,** Indian, IOGA, 4 In. | 65.00 |
| **Mug,** Picture Of Bulldog, Rodney Stone Covering, IOGA, 4 1/4 In. | 75.00 |
| **Mug,** Portrait Of Fat Man, Holding Glass Of Ale, IOGA | 75.00 |
| **Pitcher,** Ale, Portrait Of Jovial Monk, IOGA Mark | 145.00 |
| **Pitcher,** Lemonade, Flowers | 95.00 |
| **Pitcher,** Monk, 5 Mugs | 350.00 |
| **Pitcher,** Pine Needles, Cones, Matte Finish, IOGA, 7 1/2 In. | 48.00 |
| **Plate,** Gold Panels, Flowered Insert Panels, Helmet Mark, 9 In. | 20.00 |
| **Plate,** Indian, Signed, IOGA, 9 1/2 In.Diam. | 95.00 To 120.00 |
| **Soup,** Underplate, Handled, Double | 13.00 |
| **Spittoon,** Melon Ribged Bottom, Flared Top, Flowers | 175.00 |
| **Tankard,** Fruit Painted, Apple Design, 15 In. | 150.00 |
| **Vase Bud,** Portrait, Lebrun Girl, 10 In. | 95.00 |
| **Vase,** Bonita, Pink Bleeding Hearts, 5 In. | 39.50 |
| **Vase,** Cylinder, Marvo, Green, 10 In. | 30.00 |
| **Vase,** Gypsy Lady, Twig Handles, IOGA, 10 1/2 In. | 115.00 To 145.00 |
| **Vase,** Pearl White, Parrot On Branch, 11 In. | 175.00 |
| **Vase,** Poinsettia, IOGA Mark, 12 In. | 40.00 |
| **Vase,** Roses, 9 In. | 35.00 |
| **Vase,** Tutone, Triangular, 9 In. | 27.50 |
| **Vase,** Twig Handles, Brown & Poinsettia, Marked IOGA, 10 In. | 85.00 |
| **Vase,** Verbena, Gray, IOGA, 9 In.Diam. | 150.00 |

*Watch fobs were worn on watch chains. They were popular during Victorian times and after.*

| | |
|---|---|
| **WATCH FOB, A.E.Anderson Co.,** Tailors, Chicago, Stitch In Time, 2 1/2 X 3 In. | 14.50 |
| **Abe Lincoln** | 55.00 |
| **Advanced Rumley Oil,** Pull Tractor | 85.00 |
| **Airship,** Akron | 5.00 |
| **Allis Chalmers** | 18.50 |
| **American Eagle,** Bronze | 5.00 |
| **American Legion Convention,** Omaha, 1925, Embossed Oxen | 25.00 |
| **American Legion,** 1946, Brass | 18.00 |
| **Annual Sheriff's Assoc.,** 1910, Lincoln Monument On Reverse | 35.00 |
| **Arrowhead Shape,** Indian In Relief, Brass | 7.00 |
| **Associated Western Yale Club,** Embossed Bulldog | 27.50 |
| **Atlas Insurance Co.,** Tulsa, Brass | 17.00 |
| **Avery Bulldog** | 60.00 |
| **B.P.O.E.,** Jeweled | 30.00 |
| **Baseball Mitt,** Ball Hanging From Crossed Bats, Bone, C.1800 | 85.00 |
| **Birdsell Hullers Since 1855** | 25.00 |
| **Buffalo,** Springfield Roller | 16.75 |
| **Bulldog,** Avery, Figural | 90.00 |
| **California Diamond Jubilee,** 1925, Presentation To Dr.Miller | 40.00 |
| **Canton Art Metal,** Brass | 16.00 |

| | |
|---|---:|
| Caterpillar Sixty | 38.00 |
| Caterpillar, Peoria | 12.00 |
| Chalmer's Motors, Brass | 21.00 |
| Chicago Tailoring, Beautiful Lady, Brass | 21.00 |
| Cigar Makers Union, Bronze | 50.00 |
| Colorado State Sunday School, Metal | 7.50 |
| Columbian Expo, 1893 Keystone Watch Case Co. | 35.00 |
| Commonwealth Of Kentucky, United We Stand, Divided We Fall | 30.00 |
| Cyrus McCormick & Reaper, Brass | 35.00 |
| Danciger Bros., Embossed World, Cook & Perry Holding Pole, Brass | 35.00 |
| DeLaval, Bronze | 40.00 |
| Dempsey & Gibbons Championship, July 4, 1923, Brass Mesh | 110.00 |
| Dobbins Furnace, Strap, Brass | 22.00 |
| East Buffalo Brewing Co., Embossed Buffalo, Lager Beer | 30.00 |
| Eimco Rocker, Shovel Shape, Strap | 20.00 |
| Elk's Tooth, Gold Cap & Hanger, Enameled Insignia | 49.50 |
| Embossed Lookout Mountain & Buffalo Bill Cody, Copper | 25.00 |
| Fire Department Supplies, Brass | 15.00 |
| Firestone Tires | 35.00 |
| Fish Form, Enameled On Sterling Silver | 35.00 |
| Football Player, Brass | 9.00 |
| Ford Trimotor Plane, Dated 1930, Dixon, Ill., Bronze | 9.50 |
| Gold Dust Twins, Enamel | 75.00 |
| Gold Medal Flour | 35.00 |
| Gold Ore | 12.00 |
| Gold Shield Center, C.1900, Hallmarked, English, 1 1/2 In. | 25.00 |
| Gold Twisted Wire, Abalone Heart | 23.00 |
| Golden Sun Coffee, Boy Drinking Coffee, Pewter | 45.00 |
| Green River Whiskey | 15.00 |
| Harley Davidson, 1930s | 40.00 |
| Harvard, Enameled, 10K Gold | 100.00 |
| Hawk-Eye Compound Co., Bronze | 15.00 |
| Horseshoe, Wishbone, I Bring Good Luck, Blum's, St.Louis, Celluloid | 25.00 |
| I.O.O.F. Of Michigan, Bronze | 10.00 |
| Ice Hockey, Embossed | 9.50 |
| Indianapolis Saddlery Co., Harness & Saddle | 47.50 |
| Int'l.Brotherhood Electrical Workers, Atlantic City, 1948 | 22.50 |
| International Harvester Caterpillar, Advertising, Metal | 25.00 |
| Iowa National Guard, 1914 Camp, Dodge, Iowa | 35.00 |
| J.I.Case Threshing Machines, Eagle On Globe | 36.00 |
| James E.Pepper Whiskey | 37.50 |
| John Deere Caterpillar, Deer On Blade | 25.00 |
| John Deere, Mother-Of-Pearl Shield With Deer | 90.00 |
| John Deere, Watertown, Conn., Equipment Co. | 35.00 |
| Keen Kutter, Shape Of Trademark | 57.00 |
| Key Shaped, Purina, Keeps Mules Up & Feed Bills Down | 37.50 |
| Large Cow, Dated 1883, Metal | 38.00 |
| Liberty Bell, Centennial | 15.00 |
| Lindbergh, 1927, Dollar Watch & Strap | 12.50 |
| Mardi Gras, New Orleans, 1892, Brass | 12.50 |
| Marion Shovel | 11.00 |
| Master Horseshowers 25th Annual Convention, 1918, Strap | 15.00 |
| Michelin Earthmover Tires | 8.00 |
| Michigan Clark Equipment, Tractor, Brass | 25.00 |
| Mineral Palace, Brass | 9.50 |
| Moose Head, Brass | 10.00 |
| Nation Cash Register, Chain | 18.50 |
| National Federation Of Post Office Clerks, 1921 | 7.00 |
| National Sportsman, Leather Strap, Brass | 27.50 |
| Night & Day Bank, St.Louis, Missouri State Seal | 30.00 |
| Ogden Union Stockyards, Figural Pig, Strap, Bronze | 20.00 |
| Ohio Power Shovel Co., Strap | 22.00 |
| Osgood General | 17.00 |

| | |
|---|---|
| **Pan,** Automobile, Enameled | 45.00 |
| **Poll-Parrot Shoes** | 60.00 |
| **Red Man,** Picture Of Indian On Horse, Brass | 10.00 |
| **Sears,** Roebuck, Mirror | 22.50 |
| **Shield Eagle Top,** National Fidelity & Casualty Co. | 25.00 |
| **Ship's Anchor In Circle,** Cutout | 15.00 |
| **Sir Knights Shoes,** Bronze | 10.00 |
| **Sun Life Insurance,** 1907, Sun Rays On Front | 26.00 |
| **Swift's Premium Ham,** Shaped | 5.00 |
| **Town Talk Flour Has No Equal** | 12.00 |
| **Union Horse Nail,** Brass | 75.00 |
| **W.H.Taft** | 45.00 |
| **W.J.Bryan** | 75.00 |
| **Ward's Tip-Top Bread,** Brass | 60.00 |
| **Willy-Knight,** Knight In Armor, Copper | 50.00 |
| **Witte Engine Works,** Pictured, Kansas City, Mo., Pewter | 18.00 |
| **Wolverine Portland Cement,** Brass | 12.00 |
| **World Globe,** Uncle Sam, Panama, Pacific, 1915 | 35.00 |
| **Yellow Gold Chain,** Initials E.S. | 29.00 |
| **4 Linked Medallions,** Relief Egyptian, Howard Carter Medallion | 85.00 |
| | |
| **WATCH, Advertising,** Levi Strauss Co., Original Riveted Clothing, Pocket | 15.00 |
| **Alvah Skinner,** 15K Gold, Porcelain Dial, C.1840, Pocket | 675.00 |
| **Barbie,** Original Condition, Working | 25.00 |
| **Bracelet,** Longine, White Gold Cover, 21 Diamonds, 14K Gold, 6 3/4 In. | 850.00 |
| **D.Charleston,** London, Alarm, Fusee Movement, 18th Century, Pocket, Pair | 525.00 |
| **E.Howard,** Pocket, Gold Fittings On Chain, Gold Filled | 325.00 |
| **Elgin,** Blind Man's, Ribbon Watch Fob, Gold Plated, Pocket, C.1890 | 100.00 |
| **Elgin,** Hunting Case, Coin Silver Hinged Box | 475.00 |
| **Elgin,** Interstate Chronometer, Open Face, 17-Jewel, Sterling Case | 250.00 |
| **Elgin,** Lady's, Hunting Case, Engraved Gold Filled Case, 1 3/8 In. | 230.00 |
| **Elgin,** Lady's, Hunting Case, 14K Gold, 7-Jewel | 425.00 |
| **Elgin,** Lady's, Lapel, Dueber, Hunting Case, Sailboat Scene, Floral, Gold | 140.00 |
| **Elgin,** Military, British Admiralty Dial, Government Case, 21-Jewel | 225.00 |
| **Elgin,** Pocket, Father Time, 21-Jewel, Silveroid Case | 175.00 |
| **Elgin,** Pocket, Hunting Case, Gold Filled Case | 85.00 |
| **Elgin,** Pocket, Veritas, 23-Jewel, Silveroid Case | 255.00 |
| **Elgin,** Pocket, 7-Jewel, Open Face, 20 Year Gold Filled Case | 17.00 |
| **Elgin,** Pocket, 15-Jewel, Coin Silver Case, Interchangeable Movement | 235.00 |
| **Elgin,** Pocket, 17-Jewel, Wheeler Model, Twin Engine Airline On Back | 55.00 |
| **Elgin,** Railroad, Pocket, 23-Jewel, 5 Position, 10K Gold Face & Chain | 125.00 |
| **Elgin,** 15-Jewel, Convertible Movement, 14K Gold Case | 500.00 |
| **Elgin,** 18K Gold & Gold Inlaid, Pocket, C.1879 | 425.00 |
| **Elgin,** 21-Jewel, C.1920, Watch & Band Are 12K Gold Filled | 100.00 |
| **Hamilton,** Pocket, Military, 2-Jewel, Military Case | 150.00 |
| **Hamilton,** Pocket, Military, 22-Jewel, Government Case | 195.00 |
| **Hamilton,** Pocket, Open Face, 17-Jewel, Size No.18, Model 924 | 60.00 |
| **Hamilton,** Pocket, Unusual Dial, 23-Jewel, Yellow Gold Filled | 555.00 |
| **Hamilton,** Railroad, 21-Jewel, Model 992b | 145.00 |
| **Hampden,** Lady's, Hunter Case, 14K Gold | 225.00 |
| **Hampden,** Pocket, Open Face, Coin Silver Swing-Out Case, Keywind, C.1879 | 70.00 |
| **Holder,** Cupid Stand On Footed Box, Drawers, Quadruplate, 11 In. | 175.00 |
| **Howard,** Independent KWKS, 15-Jewel, Coin Case | 800.00 |
| **Howard,** Pocket, Adjusted Temperature & 5 Positions, 23 Jewel | 245.00 |
| **Howard,** Pocket, Hunter, 17-Jewel | 305.00 |
| **Illinois,** Pocket, Bunn Special, 24-Jewel | 730.00 |
| **Ingersoll Trenton,** Pocket, Woman Golfer Fob, 15-Jewel | 100.00 |
| **Ingersoll,** Pocket, Black Radium Dail | 12.00 |
| **Iowa Watch Co.,** Gold, Pocket | 200.00 |
| **Jackie Robinson** | 200.00 |
| **Lapel,** Lady's, Waltham, 14K Gold, Open Face, C.1905 | 110.00 |
| **Lapel,** Lady's, 18K Gold Hunting Case, C.1894, Switzerland | 550.00 |
| **New Era,** Pocket, Lancaster, Penn., Coin Silver Open Face, C.1880 | 60.00 |

Pendant, Swiss, 18K Gold, Cathedral Shape Case, 2 In.Diam. ............................................ 1100.00
Piquet & Bachmann, Chronometer, 1/2 Hour Repeater, Pocket, C.1900 ....................... 3100.00
Seth Thomas, Pocket, Century, Size 18, Open Face, Silveroid Case ........................... 48.00
Seth Thomas, Pocket, Century, 7-Jewel, Silveroid ........................................................ 75.00
Seth Thomas, Pocket, 15-Jewel, Yellow Gold Filled ..................................................... 155.00
Seth Thomas, Pocket, 17-Jewel, Size 12, Gold Filled ................................................... 85.00
South Bend, 17-Jewel, Adjusted Double Roller, Fancy Dial ......................................... 110.00
Stop, Ferdinand Melly Locle, Coin Silver Case, C.1880 ............................................... 100.00
Swiss, J.Mathey Lockle, 18K Gold Case, Bar Movement, Pocket, C.1880 .................... 300.00
Travel, Concord Watch Co., Rectangular Sterling Case, Medallion ............................... 185.00
U.S.Watch Co., Pocket, Butterfly Cutout, Open Face ................................................... 225.00
Waltham, Broadway Model, Keywind, Pocket .............................................................. 35.00
Waltham, Chronograph, Aircraft, 8 Day, Air Force, 22-Jewel ....................................... 40.00
Waltham, Crescent Street, Up & Down Indicator, Gold Filled ....................................... 400.00
Waltham, Hunting Case, Pink Dial, Filigree Hands, Coin Silver .................................... 225.00
Waltham, Pocket, Hunting Case, 17-Jewel, Yellow Gold Filled, C.1907 ....................... 185.00
Waltham, Pocket, Size 18, Coin Silver ........................................................................ 175.00
Waltham, Pocket, Stem Wound, C.1910, Gold Plated ................................................. 110.00
Waltham, Pocket, Vanguard, 12-Jewel, Yellow Gold Filled .......................................... 200.00
Waltham, Pocket, 21-Jewel, Metal Case ..................................................................... 200.00
Waltham, Railroad, Riverside, Metal Case ................................................................... 125.00
Waltham, Railroad, Up & Down Indicator, 21-Jewel .................................................... 450.00
Waltham, Riverside, Shield, 14K Gold Case, Sunken Dial ........................................... 255.00
Waltham, 18K Gold Case, Riverside Movement, Pocket, C.1880 ................................. 325.00
Washington Watch Co., 17-Jewel, Adjusted Close Face .............................................. 235.00
Waterbury, Pocket, Open Face, Patent 1886 ............................................................. 35.00

*Waterford type glass resembles the famous glass made in the Waterford Glass Works in Ireland. It is a clear glass that was often cut for decoration. Modern glass is still being made in Waterford, Ireland.*

WATERFORD, Compote, Covered, Finial, Pair ............................................................. 395.00
Decanter, Wine, C.1780 ............................................................................................ 65.00
Dish, Sweetmeat, Covered, Cut In Flat Flutes, Trefoil Rim, 7 In. ............................... 265.00
Goblet, Tramore Pattern, Signed, Set Of 14 .............................................................. 224.00
Salt, Boat Shape, 18th Century, Pair ......................................................................... 225.00
Sherbet, Waffle Pattern, Crystal ............................................................................... 3.50
Vase, Noah, 1973, Carrying Case, Signed Certificate ............................................... 1500.00

*Wave Crest glass is a white glassware manufactured by the Pairpoint Manufacturing Company of New Bedford, Massachusetts, and some French factories. It was then decorated by the C.F.Monroe Company of Meriden, Connecticut. The glass was painted in pastel colors and decorated with flowers. The name Wave Crest was used after 1898.*

WAVE CREST, Biscuit Jar, Apple Blossom Pattern, 10 In. .......................................... 325.00
Biscuit Jar, Barrel Shape, Florals & Scrolls ............................................................... 375.00
Biscuit Jar, Bulging Rib Form, Flowers, Silver Plate Cover ......................................... 175.00
Biscuit Jar, Cream To Blue, Pink Daisies, Square Shape, 10 In. ................................. 295.00
Biscuit Jar, Lid Marked C F Monroe & Co. ................................................................ 295.00
Biscuit Jar, Molded Scrolls, Flowers, Silver Plate Lid, Marked .................................... 110.00
Biscuit Jar, Multicolored Flowers & Leaves, Ovoid, Signed ........................................ 125.00
Biscuit Jar, Pink & Yellow Flowers All Sides, Square ................................................. 195.00
Biscuit Jar, Soft Yellow Tall Lid ................................................................................ 325.00
Box, Baroque Shell, Red Banner Mark, Velvet Lined, 7 In.Diam. ................................ 750.00
Box, Blue & White Daisies, Gold Lining, Brass Closing, 3 In. ...................................... 125.00
Box, Brass Collar, Hand-Painted, Scrolls, Marked, 1 3/8 X 3 In. ................................ 125.00
Box, Cherub On Lid, Hinged, 2 X 3 In. ...................................................................... 125.00
Box, Cigar, Shell Lid, Medallions On Sides, Signed ................................................... 400.00
Box, Collar & Cuff, 6 1/2 X 5 1/4 In. .......................................................................... 600.00
Box, Collar & Cuff, 7 In.Square ................................................................................ 925.00
Box, Collar, Beige, 2 Cherubs, Flower Garden, Signed, 8 In. ..................................... 450.00
Box, Covered, Helmschmied Swirl, Pink Bottom, Cream Top, 3 1/4 In. ....................... 135.00

**Box,** Covered, Pink Flower, Lined, Blue, Signed, 4 1/4 X 2 3/4 In. .......................... 170.00
**Box,** Covered, Polychrome Floral Design, Puffy, 2 1/2 X 7 In.Diam. ...................... 425.00
**Box,** Covered, Shell Shape, Pink & White, Signed, 5 In.Square ........................... 215.00
**Box,** Covered, 7 1/2 In.Diam. ........................................................................ 490.00
**Box,** Cream Swirl With Enameled Flowers, Signed, 4 1/2 In.Square ..................... 295.00
**Box,** Cupid & Bird On Lid, Hinged, Signed, 3 1/4 X 3 1/4 In. ............................ 250.00
**Box,** Dresser, Swirled Body, Daisy Design, 3 In.Diam. ..................................... 85.00
**Box,** Embossed Flowers, Hinged, Pink Lining, 8 In. .......................................... 400.00
**Box,** Embossed Rococo, Hinged, Signed, Square, 3 In. ...................................... 350.00
**Box,** Floral & Jeweled, Hinged, Enamel Beads, 5 1/2 X 3 In. ............................. 395.00
**Box,** Floral Design, Hinged Cover, Signed, 3 1/4 X 2 1/2 In. ............................ 150.00
**Box,** Floral Top, Hinged, Oval, Red Banner Mark, Signed, 3 X 5 In. .................... 250.00
**Box,** Footed, Covered, 2 X 2 In. ................................................................... 65.00
**Box,** Gold Lining, Maiden Dancing, Trees, Lake, 7 In. ...................................... 425.00
**Box,** Hinged Cover, Embossed Scroll Design, Blue, Signed, 5 1/2 In. .................. 275.00
**Box,** Hinged Cover, Helmschmied Swirl, Hand-Painted, 3 1/2 In. ....................... 145.00
**Box,** Hinged Lid, Enameled Beading, Violets, Signed, 5 1/2 In. .......................... 375.00
**Box,** Hinged Lid, Jeweled, Enameled Beads, 5 1/2 X 3 In. ................................ 395.00
**Box,** Hinged, Apple Blossoms, Signed, 3 1/2 X 3 In.Square .............................. 155.00
**Box,** Hinged, Blown-Out Pansy, Yellow, Gold Trim, Marked, 4 1/2 In. ................ 325.00
**Box,** Hinged, Cobalt Enameled Flowers, Small .............................................. 200.00
**Box,** Hinged, Molded Shell, Top & Bottom, 2 3/4 X 3 1/4 In.Diam. ..................... 185.00
**Box,** Hinged, Puffy Swirl Shape, Paper Label, 3 X 3 In. ................................... 325.00
**Box,** Hinged, Shells & Pink Flowers, 3 In. ..................................................... 190.00
**Box,** Jewel, Cherub, Pale Green, 5 X 3 X 3 In. ............................................... 275.00
**Box,** Jewel, Hinged Lid, Violets, Beading, Signed, 6-Sided, 5 1/2 In. .................. 350.00
**Box,** Jewel, Open, Ormolu Handles, Luster Rim, Signed, 4 1/2 In. ..................... 165.00
**Box,** Jewel, Ormolu Hinge, Satin Lining, Signed, 4 X 3 In. ............................... 360.00
**Box,** Jewel, Pansy, Brass Rim & Handles, Red Mark, 5 In.Diam. ....................... 145.00
**Box,** Jewel, Pink Flowers, Lined, Signed, 3 1/2 In. .......................................... 335.00
**Box,** Niagara Falls On Lid, 4 In. .................................................................. 195.00
**Box,** Open, Ormolu Footed, C Scrolls, Roses, Enameled Dots ........................... 145.00
**Box,** Open, Ormolu Handles, Blue Flower, Signed, 3 1/4 In.Square ..................... 95.00
**Box,** Pin, Pink Floral, Blown Out Flowers, Marked, 2 In. ................................. 135.00
**Box,** Pink Roses, Brown Leaves, Green Ground, Footed, 7 In. ........................... 750.00
**Box,** Pink, Yellow, White, Satin Lined, Enameled, Signed ................................. 700.00
**Box,** Puffed Out All Around Top & Bottom, Signed, 4 1/2 In. ............................ 275.00
**Box,** Puffy Swirl Shape, Hinged, Paper Label, 3 X 3 In. ................................... 325.00
**Box,** Puffy, Scrolls & Flowers, Signed, 3 1/2 In.Diam. ..................................... 175.00
**Box,** Red Enameled Flowers On Top & 3 Sides, 3 1/2 X 5 1/2 In. ....................... 350.00
**Box,** Ring, Enameled, Cherubs On Lid, Signed, 2 1/4 X 1 3/4 In. ....................... 225.00
**Box,** Scene, Green, 3 1/2 In. ........................................................................ 135.00
**Box,** Shell, Baroque, Red Banner Mark, Lining, 7 1/2 In. ................................. 775.00
**Box,** Sprays Of Flower, Cream, Gold Holder, Signed, 2 1/2 X 4 In. ..................... 245.00
**Box,** Swirl, Flowers, 5 In. ............................................................................ 295.00
**Box,** Swirled & Floral Design, Signed, 4 1/2 X 3 In. ........................................ 175.00
**Box,** Trinket, Ormolu Rim & Handles, Beaded, Blue, Signed, 3 In. ..................... 125.00
**Box,** Trinket, Swirl Pattern, Enamel Blue Flowers, 3 1/4 In.Diam. ..................... 65.00
**Box,** Watch, Double Shell, Hand-Painted, Red Banner Mark, 3 In. ..................... 295.00
**Card Holder,** Brass Rim, Hand-Painted Flowers, Signed ................................... 255.00
**Card Holder,** Rose Buds, Banner Mark ......................................................... 285.00
**Casket,** Covered, Floral Design, Signed, 19 In.Diam. ...................................... 140.00
**Casket,** Floral Cover, Ormolu Legs, Apple Green, Signed, 14 In. ....................... 372.00
**Casket,** Puffed-Out Body, Floral Cover, Ormolu Feet, 12 In. ............................. 285.00
**Cigar Set,** White Ground, Pink Clover Design, Red Banner Mark ....................... 550.00
**Creamer,** Blue Forget-Me-Nots, Silver Handle & Spout ................................... 135.00
**Creamer,** Silver Plated Handle, Swirled, Flowers, 3 1/2 In. .............................. 95.00
**Creamer,** Swirled Small Flowers, Silver Plate Rim, 3 1/2 In. ............................ 95.00
**Dish,** Enameled Flowers, Brass Rim, Red Banner Mark, 3 In.Diam. .................... 65.00
**Dish,** Floral On Beige, Open, 3 In. ................................................................ 90.00
**Dish,** Flowers On Beige Ground, Signed, 3 X 3 In. .......................................... 95.00
**Dish,** Sweetmeat, Enameled, Silver Plate Cover ............................................. 275.00
**Dish,** Trinket, Ormolu Handle, Flowers, Black Mark, 4 X 3 1/4 In. ..................... 95.00

Dish, Vanity, Floral, 4 In. ........................................................................................ 65.00
Dish, Wild Rose On Mottled Green, Silver Rim, Signed, 5 1/4 In. ................................ 320.00
Ewer, Fern Design, Yellow Satin Ground, Metal Handled, 16 In. ................................ 75.00
Ferner, Ring Handled, Brass Insert, Red Banner Mark, 5 In. ...................................... 349.00
Fernery, Brass Insert, Red Banner Mark, Signed, 6 1/2 In. ........................................ 350.00
Fernery, Brass Insert, Signed, Red Banner Mark, 5 In.Square .................................. 349.00
Fernery, Dark Green, Brass Insert, White Plaque, Floral, 5 In. .................................. 350.00
Fernery, Mold Blown, Puffy Corners, Scrollwork, Signed, 6 1/2 In. ........................... 365.00
Fernery, Ormolu Feet, Purple, Octagonal, Signed, 8 1/2 In. ...................................... 345.00
Fernery, Pink Flowers, Blue, 8 X 4 1/4 In. ................................................................ 220.00
Frame, Embossed Rococo, Pink Tones, Floral Design .............................................. 575.00
Frame, Puffy Egg Crate, Ormolu Rim, Enameled Flowers ......................................... 240.00
Hatpin Holder, Hand-Painted Flowers, Marked .......................................................... 225.00
Holder, Letter, Orchids, Metal Rim, 5 1/2 X 4 1/4 In. ............................................... 210.00
Holder, Letter, Puffy, Ormolu Rim .............................................................................. 350.00
Humidor, Marked Cigars, Shell Top, Red Banner Mark, 6 In. .................................... 300.00
Jar, Sweetmeat, Covered, Barrel Shape, Silver Collar, Cover, Bail ............................ 250.00
Letter Holder, Bronze Trim, Pink Flowers ................................................................. 185.00
Letter Holder, Ormolu Border, Puffy, Signed ........................................................... 240.00
Letter Holder, Puffy, Brass Rim ................................................................................. 225.00
Match Holder, Footed, Hand-Painted Pansies, Banner Mark .................................... 225.00
Mustard, Pansies, Yellow Ground .............................................................................. 50.00
Mustard, Rococo, Enameled Flowers, Cover, 1 1/2 X 4 1/2 In.Diam. ........................ 225.00
Paperweight, Winged Ormolu Angel Playing Cymbals, 4 X 4 In. ............................... 98.00
Planter, Insert, Puffy, Flowers & Vines, 7 In.Diam. ................................................... 225.00
Planter, Puffed Blue Flowers, Ormolu Rim, 2 3/4 X 5 1/4 In. .................................... 240.00
Planter, Puffy, Flowers & Vine, Insert, 7 In.Diam. .................................................... 225.00
Pot, Glass, Floral Enamel Design, Hinged Lid, 3 In. ................................................. 260.00
Rose Bowl, Brass Wire Lid, 6 3/4 X 6 In. .................................................................. 165.00
Salt & Pepper, Swirl Pattern, Flowers ....................................................................... 87.00
Salt & Pepper, Swirled, Pair ...................................................................................... 95.00
Salt & Pepper, White Satin, Square, 4 In. ................................................................. 75.00
Shaker, Scrolls, Blue Flowers .................................................................................... 50.00
Sugar & Creamer, Cherubs, Metal Rope Type Handles, Finial .................................. 195.00
Sugar Shaker, Glossy White, Beige, Blue Floral, 2-Piece Top ................................. 70.00
Sugar Shaker, Pink Flower, White To Italian Blue, 5 In. ........................................... 210.00
Syrup, Dangling Loop Mold, Flowers, Cover, C.1872, 7 1/2 In. ................................. 130.00
Toothpick, Opera Glasses, Glossy White, Blue Flower .............................................. 55.00
Tray, Handled, Enameled Flowers, Green, Black, Signed, 6 1/2 In. ........................... 325.00
Tray, Pin, Floral, Pink, Jeweled, Brass Rim, Signed, 4 X 1 In. .................................. 110.00
Tray, Pin, Flowers, Jeweled, Brass Rim, Signed, 1 1/2 X 4 1/4 In. ............................ 110.00
Tray, Trinket, Beaded Ormolu Rim, Swirl Design, Red Mark, 6 In. ............................ 249.00
Vase, Blue-Gray Ground, Red-Cream Roses, Signed, 14 In. ..................................... 650.00
Vase, Coral Ground, Floral Reserves, Ormolu Frame, 5 In. ...................................... 345.00
Vase, Deep Coral Ground, Floral Design, Ormolu Frame, 5 In. ................................. 345.00
Vase, Footed, Handled, Ormolu Rim, Flowers, Signed, 14 1/2 In. ............................ 350.00
Vase, Little Bopeep & Sheep, Gold Embossing, Signed, 12 1/2 In. .......................... 1380.00
Vase, Metal Handles, Gold Feet, Enamel Flowers, Red Banner, 12 In. ..................... 1100.00
Vase, Orange & Yellow, Floral, Ormolu Rim, Footed Base, 6 In. ............................... 255.00
Vase, Orange & Yellow, Hip Floral Design, Footed, 6 In. .......................................... 225.00
Vase, Ormolu Footed Base & Trim, 6 1/2 In. ............................................................ 150.00
Vase, Ormolu Rim & Handles, Colored Florals, Signed, 8 1/4 In. ............................. 375.00
Vase, Ormolu Rim, Sculptured Base & Neck, Signed, 128 In. .................................. 495.00
Vase, Ormolu Top, Blue & Pink & White Floral Design .............................................. 265.00
Vase, Portrait, Lipped Top, Pansy Flowers, Cherub, Signed, 6 In. ............................ 225.00
Vase, Red & Cream Roses, Gray Ground, Signed Kelva, 14 In. ................................ 650.00
Vase, Scrolled Bottom, Enameled Flowers, Signed, 5 1/2 In., Pair .......................... 250.00
Vase, White Roses, Pink, Pair ................................................................................... 400.00

WEAPON, Bayonet, Dress, Nazi Police, Eagles' Heads, Bone Grip, Sheath .............. 130.00
Bayonet, Fits Brown Bess Musket, Revolutionary War .............................................. 150.00
Bayonet, Indian Wars ................................................................................................ 25.00
Bayonet, Mauser Rifle Style, Sheath ......................................................................... 12.75

Billy Club, Constable, Bowerston, Ohio, 1892, 14 In. ....................................................... 21.50
Box, Cartridge, Indian Wars Era ............................................................................... 35.00
Box, Cartridge, V.L. & A.Wood .................................................................................. 35.00
Cannon, Signal, Cast Iron, French ............................................................................. 16.00
Carbine, Frank Wesson, Civil War ............................................................................. 150.00
Carbine, Spencer, Civil War Issue ............................................................................. 400.00
Crossbow, Ivory Trigger, Malay .................................................................................. 125.00
Dagger, Gambler's, Ivory Twist Handle, German Silver Beading ................................ 165.00
Dagger, Gentleman's, Tortoiseshell & Silver Mounted, C.1850, 14 In. ....................... 375.00
Dagger, Military Dress, Brass, Snake & Sharkskin Sheath, Japanese ........................ 150.00
Gun Powder Horn, Wooden Plug, Brass Brads, 7 In. .................................................. 20.00
Gun, BB, Daisy, Golden Eagle, 1936 ......................................................................... 65.00
Mold, Bullet, Colonial American, Pine, Lead Insert, 4 1/4 X 2 1/4 In. ......................... 55.00
Mold, Bullet, Winchester ........................................................................................... 40.00
Musket, Civil War Import, Austrian ............................................................................. 160.00
Oil Can, Remington, For Guns .................................................................................... 22.50
Pistol, Air, Brass Barrel, Benjamin Franklin, Brass ..................................................... 35.00
Pistol, Allen & Thurber, Single Shot, 31 Caliber, Half Octagon Barrel ........................ 95.00
Pistol, Colt Derringer, Bone Handle, 41 Caliber ......................................................... 350.00
Pistol, Colt, Peacemaker, 45 Caliber, Dated 1878, Barrel, 7 1/2 In. ........................ 1000.00
Pistol, Derringer, Lady's, Allen Bird Head, Single Shot, Ivory Grips ........................... 750.00
Pistol, Dueling, 1860 Colt Army, Centennial Arms, Chicago, Pair .............................. 350.00
Pistol, Engraved, Percussion, Richard, London ......................................................... 750.00
Pistol, Hawkeye, Repeat, Boxed ................................................................................ 26.00
Pistol, Military, European Flintlock ............................................................................. 165.00
Pistol, Smith & Wesson, Vest Pocket, Single Action, 1864 ........................................ 700.00
Pistol, Williamson, Berringer, 1866, Lady's, Gold & Silver .......................................... 985.00
Revolver, Colt, Conversion, 1862, Brass Frame, Blue Grips, Case .............................. 420.00
Revolver, Colt, 1851, Navy, Scene ............................................................................ 390.00
Revolver, Moore, Teat-Fire, 1864 .............................................................................. 175.00
Revolver, Smith & Wesson, Pocket, 1874 .................................................................. 300.00
Shotgun, Ithaca, 28 Gauge ...................................................................................... 1500.00
Shotgun, J.Stevens, Single Barrel, 12 Gauge ............................................................ 35.00
Spike, Enfield, Case ................................................................................................... 5.00

WEATHER VANE, Bull, Dimensional, American, 26 X 49 In. ...................................... 2600.00
Cow, Copper, 10 X 28 In. ............................................................................... Illus 450.00
Cow, Gilded Patina, American, 20th Century, Copper, 27 In. ...................................... 250.00
Cow, Hand Forged, Cast Iron & Tin ............................................................................ 450.00
Cow, Molded Body, American, 19th Century, Copper, 27 In. ....................................... 275.00
Eagle Standing On Globe, American, Gilt Zinc, 12 In. ................................................ 50.00
Eagle, Flagpole, Wings Spread, Copper, 20 X 17 X 31 In. .......................................... 475.00
Eagle, Spread Wing .................................................................................................... 80.00
Fireman, Wooden Pedestal, Iron ................................................................................ 425.00

Weather Vane, Cow, Copper, 10 X 28 In.

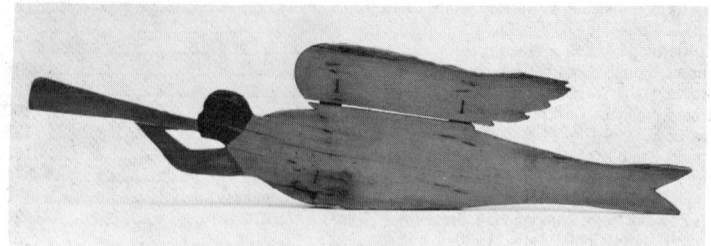

Weather Vane, Planked Angel Gabriel, Wooden, 8 1/2 X 34 In.

| | |
|---|---|
| Fish, Dated 1939, Cape Cod, Wooden, 17 In. | 65.00 |
| Fish, Molded Construction, Attached Fins, Copper, 23 In. | 250.00 |
| Fish, Salmon, 19th Century, Copper, 36 In. | 300.00 |
| Fish, Tin | 185.00 |
| Fish, Wooden, 34 In. | 325.00 |
| Game Cock, Molded Body & Head, 19th Century, Copper, 14 In. | 700.00 |
| Hackney Horse, At Trot, Copper, 33 X 7 1/2 X 27 In. | 1250.00 |
| Horse & Jockey, Carved Wood | 2050.00 |
| Horse & Sulky, Copper | 250.00 |
| Horse, Iron Arrow, Tin | 50.00 |
| Horse, Running, Massachusetts, Copper, 25 X 13 In. | 350.00 |
| Horse, Running, Sheet Iron | 875.00 |
| Horse, Zinc Head, Copper, Gilding, 1800s, No Directionals | 495.00 |
| Lumberjack With Ax, Counter Balance | 58.00 |
| Pig & Piglet On Arrow, C.1910, Sheet Iron, 8 X 20 In. | 125.00 |
| Pig & Piglet On Arrow, Iron, C.1899, 8 X 20 In. | 125.00 |
| Pig, Full Size, Large Ears & Curled Tail, Copper, 23 X 38 In. | 500.00 |
| Planked Angel Gabriel, Wooden, 8 1/2 X 34 In. ...............................Illus | 700.00 |
| Rooster, Copper, Cast Iron Directionals, Large | 350.00 |
| Rooster, Molded Body, American, C.1880, Copper, 32 X 29 In. | 850.00 |
| Rooster, Molded Copper, Brass Directionals, 25 X 25 In. | 785.00 |
| Rooster, Molded, Trace Of Gold Leaf & Verdigris, Copper, 28 In. | 1150.00 |
| Rooster, On Arrow, C.1910, Iron, 15 X 10 1/2 In. | 125.00 |
| Rooster, Painted Blue, American, Sheet Iron, 28 1/2 In. | 900.00 |
| Rooster, Profile, Trace Of White Paint, American, Pine, 17 In. | 350.00 |
| Running Horse, Cast-Iron Directionals, American, Copper, 23 In. | 400.00 |
| Running Horse, Molded Copper, Brass Directionals, 20 X 30 In. | 750.00 |
| Scotty, Copper Arrow, C.1910, Brass, 17 X 26 In. | 265.00 |
| Scroll Design, American, 19th Century, Copper & Iron, 37 In. | 300.00 |
| Stallion, Stackney, Hollow Pewter, 1840 | 900.00 |
| Trotter, Small | 68.00 |
| Trotting Horse, Tin | 60.00 |
| Whale, Raised Tail, 2-Dimensional, Copper, American, 32 In. | 300.00 |

*Webb glass was made by Thomas Webb & Sons of Stourbridge, England.
Many types of art and cameo glass were made by them during the Victorian
era. The factory is still producing glass.*

| | |
|---|---|
| WEBB BURMESE, Cup, Punch, Silver Hallmarked Band, Leaves & Berries, 2 1/2 In. | 275.00 |
| Epergne, Silver Trefoil Base, Enameled Flowers, C.1880s | 750.00 |
| Fairy Lamp, Brass Holder Attached To Mirror, Signed, 8 1/2 In. | 895.00 |
| Fairy Lamp, Clarke Green & Pink Pottery Base, 5 In. | 425.00 |
| Fairy Lamp, Matching Square Base, Signed, 5 3/4 X 6 In.Diam. | 695.00 |
| Fairy Lamp, Menu Card, Applied Yellow Leaf, Signed, 5 3/8 In. | 550.00 |
| Fairy Lamp, Moss Rose, Butterfly, Clarke Base, 5 1/8 In. | 395.00 |
| Fairy Lamp, Satin Finish, Clear Clarke Base, 3 3/4 In. | 165.00 |

**Finger Bowl,** Lavender 5 Petal Flower, Leaves, 4 5/8 In. ............................................. 375.00
**Jar,** Sweetmeat, Brass Collar, Cover & Bail, Signed, 5 In. ........................................ 675.00
**Jar,** Sweetmeat, Butterfly & Prunus Blossoms, 5 In. ............................................... 495.00
**Lamp,** Fairy, Ruffled Base, Acid Finish, Signed ..................................................... 495.00
**Match Holder,** Salmon To Yellow, Bulbous, 6 Sided Top, 2 1/2 In. ........................... 295.00
**Match Holder,** Square Top, Salmon Pink To Yellow, 2 3/4 In. ................................. 200.00
**Pitcher,** Floral Sprays, Signed, 7 In. .................................................................1200.00
**Pitcher,** Water, Signed, 7 In. ...........................................................................1200.00
**Rose Bowl,** 6-Sided Top, 2 1/8 X 2 5/8 In.Diam. ................................................... 175.00
**Rose Bowl,** 8 Crimped Top, Salmon To Pale Yellow, 2 1/4 In. ................................ 235.00
**Rose Bowl,** 8 Point Crimp, 2 X 2 1/2 In. ............................................................. 250.00
**Toothpick,** Blueberries, Brown Leaves, Square Mouth ........................................... 275.00
**Vase,** Ball Shaped, Flower Petal Top, Queen's Ware, 2 3/4 In. ................................ 245.00
**Vase,** Collared 6-Sided Top, Lavender Flowers, 3 1/8 In. ....................................... 325.00
**Vase,** Egg Shaped, Ruffled Pedestal, Crimped, 3 5/8 In. ....................................... 275.00
**Vase,** Enameled Leaves & Acorns, 5 Point Edge, Signed, 3 In. ................................ 380.00
**Vase,** Flower Petal Sahped Top, Red Flowers, Salmon Pink, 3 In. ........................... 295.00
**Vase,** Flower Petal Shaped Top, Enameled Flowers, 3 In. ...................................... 295.00
**Vase,** Fluted Scalloped Top, Dimpled Sides, Square, 3 3/4 In. ................................ 225.00
**Vase,** Green & Tan Ivy, Signed, 6 1/4 X 3 1/8 In.Diam. .......................................... 850.00
**Vase,** Ivy Design, Brown Dots At Top Edge, Signed, 6 1/4 In. ................................. 850.00
**Vase,** Ivy Design, Pink, Yellow, Brown Dots, Signed, 6 1/4 In. ............................... 850.00
**Vase,** Ivy Leaves, Brown Dots Around Top, Signed, 6 1/4 In. ................................. 875.00
**Vase,** Pinecones, Salmon To Yellow, 2 7/8 X 4 1/8 In. ........................................... 295.00
**Vase,** Ruffled, Salmon To Yellow, Oak Leaves, Acorns, 4 1/4 In. ............................ 295.00
**Vase,** Salmon Pink To Yellow, Coral Buds, 6-Sided, 3 1/4 In. ................................. 295.00
**Vase,** Striped, Fluted, Red Berries, Salmon To Yellow, 3 1/2 In. ............................. 275.00

**WEBB PEACHBLOW, Bottle,** Perfume, Enameled Butterfly, Silver Cap, 4 In. ............... 325.00
**Bowl,** Green Handles, Cream Lining, Rose Shading, 8 1/4 In. .................................. 175.00
**Bowl,** Green Handles, Gold Prunus, Cream Lining, 8 1/4 In. ................................... 750.00
**Bowl,** Pinch 5-Sided, White Lining, 3 X 5 3/4 ...................................................... 335.00
**Creamer,** Clear Applied Handles Cream Inside 3 1/2 In. ........................................ 275.00
**Creamer,** Clear Handled, 3 1/2 X 2 3/4 In.Diam. ................................................... 325.00
**Cup,** Punch .................................................................................................... 250.00
**Finger Bowl,** Underplate, Crimped Edge .............................................................. 275.00
**Pitcher,** Pink To White, Ivory Lining, Frosted Handle, 9 In. ................................... 725.00
**Rose Bowl,** Crimp Top, Cream Lining, 3 3/8 X 3 1/8 In. ........................................ 295.00
**Rose Bowl,** Crimp Top, Gold Design, 3 In.Diam. ................................................... 395.00
**Rose Bowl,** Mat-Su-Noke Design, Pinch-Pleat Top, Cream Lining ........................1150.00
**Toothpick,** Hand-Painted Flowers, 2 1/2 In. ........................................................ 365.00
**Tumbler** ........................................................................................................ 115.00
**Vase,** Bottle Shape, Gold Prunus & Butterfly, 9 In. ............................................... 495.00
**Vase,** Butter, Limbs, Blossoms, Double Handle, 5 In. ............................................ 500.00
**Vase,** Egg Shaped, Crystal Applique & Feet, Scalloped, 8 In. .................................. 695.00
**Vase,** Egg Shaped, Pedestal Ruffled Foot, Gold Berries, 4 In. ................................ 295.00
**Vase,** Gold Blossoms & Leaves, Cream Lining, 4 1/2 In. ........................................ 395.00
**Vase,** Gold Butterfly, Limbs, Flowers, Handled, Signed, 5 In. ................................. 525.00
**Vase,** Gold Prunus & Bee, 6 3/8 X 3 1/2 In.Diam. ................................................. 335.00
**Vase,** Gold Prunus Blossoms, Enameled Bug, 5 3/4 In. ......................................... 275.00
**Vase,** Mat-Su-Noke Appliqued Design, 12 Crimp, 4 3/4 In. ................................... 325.00
**Vase,** Raspberry Pink Top, Acorns & Leaves, 8 1/4 In. .......................................... 395.00
**Vase,** Urn-Shaped, Red Top, Pinky-White Bottom, 6 In. ........................................ 300.00
**Vase,** 3 Enameled Birds, Flowers, Cream Lining, 6 In. ........................................... 295.00

**WEBB, Bottle,** Perfume, Cameo, White Shell, Yellow, Green Ground, 2 In. ................ 425.00
**Bottle,** Perfume, Eagle Form, Sterling Fittings, Yellow, Marked, 7 In. ....................2000.00
**Bottle,** Perfume, Embossed Silver Top, White Flowers, Signed, 8 In. ......................2250.00
**Bottle,** Perfume, Floral & Butterfly, 2-Color, C.1900, 6 5/8 In. ............................... 400.00
**Bottle,** Perfume, Lay Down, Flowers & Branches, Sterling Cap, 3 1/4 In. ................. 475.00
**Bottle,** Perfume, Lay Down, Silver Hinged Cap, White, Green Ground, 4 In. ............. 425.00
**Bottle,** Perfume, 2-Color, Sterling Fittings, 7 In. ...............................*Illus*2000.00
**Bowl,** Cameo, Footed, Intaglio, Yellow Inside, 3 Feet, 4 X 5 3/4 In.Diam. ............... 795.00

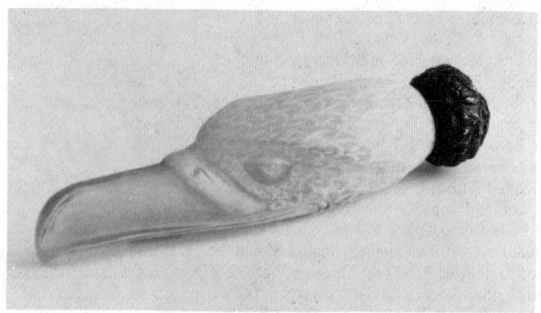

Webb, Bottle, Perfume, 2-Color, Sterling Fittings, 7 In. (See Page 717)

Webb, Bowl, White & Blue, Silver Rim, 9 1/2 In.

Bowl, Cranberry & Vaseline Ruffle, Gold Enameled Flowers, 13 In. ......................................... 185.00
Bowl, Flowers & Butterfly, Hallmarked Silver Rim, Marked, 9 1/2 X 5 In. ............................... 1350.00
Bowl, Footed, Crystal Applied Garland, Berry Prunts, Cranberry, 5 In. ..................................... 395.00
Bowl, Molded, Cut & Etched, 9 In. ........................................................................................... 190.00
Bowl, Scissor-Cut Top, Enameled Feet, Gold Trim, 4 3/4 X 5 In.Diam. ..................................... 265.00
Bowl, Turned-Over Edge, Pad-Type Base, Floral Center, 5 X 10 In.Diam. ................................. 1000.00
Bowl, White & Blue, Silver Rim, 9 1/2 In. .......................................................................*Illus* 1350.00
Bowl, White To Blue Floral & Butterfly, Silver Base, Marked, 9 1/2 In. ..................................... 1350.00
Bride's Basket, Crimped, Cream Lining, Silver Plated Holder, 10 1/2 In. .................................. 495.00
Chalice, Cameo Flowers, Diaper Pattern Around Collar, 2 1/4 In. ............................................ 635.00
Chalice, White Stylized Flowers, Brown Ground, 2 1/4 In. ...................................................... 585.00
Compote, Alexandrite, Shades Of Amber, Red, & Fuchsia, 5 1/2 In. ....................................... 750.00
Creamer, Burmese, Green Ivy Leaves, Bulbous, Round Mouth, 3 3/4 In. ................................. 675.00
Creamer, Floral Front, Butterfly Back, Carved Handle, Signed, 3 1/2 In. ............................... 1300.00
Dish, Bride's, Fiery Red To Deep Pink, Signed ...................................................................... 275.00
Finger Bowl, Pink Lining, Yellow Outside, Gold Design, 4 1/4 X 3 In. ..................................... 70.00
Finger Bowl, Pink Overlay, Crimped, Cream Inside, Butterfly, 4 1/8 In. ................................. 110.00
Flask, Head Of Duck, Yellow Bill, Signed, T.W. & Son, 8 3/4 In. ........................................... 1950.00
Jar, Jam, Crosscut Diamonds, Flutes, Signed Silver Cover ..................................................... 65.00
Lamp, Fairy, Pottery Base, Bird & Flower Design, 5 X 4 1/4 In.Diam. ..................................... 375.00
Match Striker, Filled With Controlled Bubbles, Signed ........................................................... 215.00

Webb, Vase, Cameo Cased, Green,
Yellow, & White, C.1900, 9 In.

| | |
|---|---:|
| **Pitcher,** Water, Yellow, Satin, White Lining, Signed | 275.00 |
| **Rose Bowl,** Blue Satin, Gold Enameled, Signed | 395.00 |
| **Rose Bowl,** Diamond-Quilted, 8 Crimp, Cream Lining, 2 1/2 X 2 1/4 In. | 275.00 |
| **Salt,** Figural, Swan, Crystal | 24.00 |
| **Shade,** Gas, Yellow Seaweed, Coralene, Brass Collar, 2 1/4 In. | 250.00 |
| **Toothpick,** Blue Swirl Stripe With Clambroth, Signed | 85.00 |
| **Vase,** Apple Blossom & Butterfly, 2-Color, C.1900, Marked, 3 5/8 In. | 600.00 |
| **Vase,** Applied Gold Flowers, Burgundy, Signed, 6 In. | 250.00 |
| **Vase,** Cameo Carved Flower, Buds, & Leaves, Bands At Top & Base, 5 In. | 1750.00 |
| **Vase,** Cameo Cased, Green, Yellow, & White, C.1900, 9 In. *Illus* | 3300.00 |
| **Vase,** Colored Enamel Bird In Flight, Gold Accent, 6 1/4 In., Pair | 295.00 |
| **Vase,** Coral Overlay, Gold & Silver Design, Cream Lining, 5 In. | 595.00 |
| **Vase,** Coral Overlay, Roman Gold Branches & Bird, White Lining, 6 In. | 275.00 |
| **Vase,** Cranberry, White Tulip, Vine & Butterfly Design, 7 3/4 In. | 2800.00 |
| **Vase,** Flower Shaped Top, Red Berries, 3 In. | 325.00 |
| **Vase,** Gold Florals, Brown Trim, Butterfly, 5 7/8 X 3 1/2 In.Diam. | 450.00 |
| **Vase,** Gold Prunus & Butterfly Design, Green To Yellow, 8 1/8 In. | 495.00 |
| **Vase,** Gold Prunus Blossom Design, Green Ground, 5 1/2 In. | 525.00 |
| **Vase,** Gold Prunus Flower Design, Pink Ground, 10 1/2 In. | 675.00 |
| **Vase,** Iridescent Amber, Paneled Flared Form, C.1900, Signed, 5 In. | 175.00 |
| **Vase,** Lily, Salmon To Pale Yellow, Ribbed, 6 In. | 355.00 |
| **Vase,** Minature, White, Floral, Yellow Body, Signed, 3 In. | 875.00 |
| **Vase,** Mocha Colored, Raspberry Stripe, Enameled | 375.00 |
| **Vase,** Mother-Of-Pearl, Diamond-Quilted, Blue, Signed, 5 1/4 In. | 225.00 |
| **Vase,** Opaque Floral Carving, Cranberry Ground, 5 1/2 In. | 1895.00 |
| **Vase,** Red Ground, White Cameo Ferns, Leaves, Flower Buds, 5 In. | 1375.00 |
| **Vase,** Satin Glass, Flowers & Butterflies, Brown, Gold, 5 7/8 In. | 450.00 |
| **Vase,** Satin-Quilted, Coralene Decorated, Signed, 6 In. | 595.00 |
| **Vase,** Stick, Blue Satin, Gold Enameled, 9 1/2 In. | 395.00 |
| **Vase,** White Cameo Floral, Yellow Body, Signed, 3 In. | 875.00 |
| **Vase,** Yellow & White, Apple Blossom, Butterfly, C.1900, Signed, 3 5/8 In. | 600.00 |

# WEDGWOOD

*Wedgwood pottery has been made at the famous Wedgwood factory in
England since 1759. A large variety of wares has been made, including the
well-known jasperware, basalt, creamware, and even a limited amount of
porcelain.*

**WEDGWOOD, see also Gibson Girl**

| | |
|---|---:|
| **WEDGWOOD, Ashtray,** Basalt, Classical Scene, Diamond Shape | 45.00 |
| **Ashtray,** Creamware, Advertising, Falls Rubber Co., Marked | 45.00 |
| **Ashtray,** Crimson, Bermuda Coat Of Arms In Center, 4 1/2 In. | 225.00 |
| **Ashtray,** Pegasus, Dark Blue, 3 5/8 In.Diam. | 25.00 |

**Ashtray,** Terra-Cotta Jasper, Spade Shape, 4 1/2 In. ........ 40.00
**Basket & Tray,** Pearlware, C.1820, 8 3/4 X 2 3/4 X 10 1/4 In. ........ 95.00
**Basket,** Creamware, Oval, 9 In. ........ 135.00
**Beaker,** Armorial Black Jasper & Terra-Cotta, St.John, N.B., 4 In. ........ 75.00
**Beaker,** Caneware, White Slipware Dot Design, C.1820, 4 1/2 In. ........ 250.00
**Beaker,** Hummingbirds, Orange Interior, Blue Luster, 5 1/2 In. ........ 295.00
**Biscuit Jar,** Jasperware, Blue & White, Marked, 6 X 5 1/4 In.Diam. ........ 145.00
**Biscuit Jar,** Jasperware, Blue & White, Silver Plated Bail & Cover ........ 145.00
**Biscuit Jar,** Jasperware, Cameo, Lilac, Ball Feet, Marked ........ 256.00
**Biscuit Jar,** Jasperware, Lilac ........ 325.00
**Biscuit Jar,** Jasperware, Tricolor, Gold Bands, Figures, 4 7/8 In. ........ 750.00
**Biscuit Jar,** Jasperware, Tricolor, Green Bands, Figures, 6 In. ........ 750.00
**Biscuit Jar,** Jasperware, Tricolor, Silver Plated Top, Rim, & Handle ........ 325.00
**Biscuit Jar,** Jasperware, Washington, Jefferson, & Franklin, Green ........ 345.00
**Biscuit Jar,** Jasperware, White Classical Figures, Blue, 6 1/4 In. ........ 395.00
**Biscuit Jar,** Lilac & White, 7 1/2 In. ........ 390.00
**Biscuit Jar,** White Figures, Silver Plated Bail & Handle, Green ........ 180.00
**Biscuit Jar,** White Trees & People, Blue ........ 155.00
**Bottle,** Scent, Jasperware, Silver Plated Embossed Lid, 2 1/2 In. ........ 145.00
**Bottle,** Scent, Light Green & White, Silver Mounted, 4 1/2 In. ........ 150.00
**Bowl,** Bowl, Daventry Pattern, 5 In.Diam. ........ 620.00
**Bowl,** Butterfly Luster, Mother-Of-Pearl Lining, Marked, 2 1/8 In. ........ 165.00
**Bowl,** Butterfly Luster, Orange Mottled Interior, 3 1/2 In.Diam. ........ 200.00
**Bowl,** Butterfly Luster, Orange, Blue Inside, 6 1/2 In. ........ 359.00
**Bowl,** Butterfly, Orange Luster, Blue Inside, Gold Peacock, 6 1/2 In. ........ 385.00
**Bowl,** Drabware, Blue Trim, 4 X 6 In.Diam. ........ 250.00
**Bowl,** Dragon Luster, Blue, Gilt, Aqua, Birds Inside, 8 1/4 In. ........ 490.00
**Bowl,** Dragon Luster, Gold Dragons, Marked, 3 5/8 X 2 1/8 In. ........ 165.00
**Bowl,** Dragon Luster, Inside & Out, Green & Ivory, 4 3/4 In. ........ 360.00
**Bowl,** Dragon Luster, Mother-Of-Pearl Inside, 9 3/4 In. ........ 650.00
**Bowl,** Dragon Luster, Mottled Blue Marked, 2 1/2 In. ........ 195.00
**Bowl,** Dragon Luster, Orange & Gold, 9 X 2 1/2 In. ........ 395.00
**Bowl,** Dragon Luster, 3 1/2 X 8 In.Diam. ........ 345.00
**Bowl,** Fairlyland Luster, Fruit Inside, Out, Gold Rim, 4 1/2 In.Diam. ........ 250.00
**Bowl,** Fairyland Luster, Cranes, Hummers, Set Of 2, 2 To 3 1/2 In. ........ 250.00
**Bowl,** Fairyland Luster, Dragons, Blue Ground, 4 In.Diam. ........ 175.00
**Bowl,** Fairyland Luster, Garden Of Paradise, Marked, 7 1/4 In.Diam. ........ 1695.00
**Bowl,** Fairyland Luster, Gold Butterfly & Border, 3 1/2 In.Diam. ........ 295.00
**Bowl,** Fairyland Luster, Gold Butterfly & Border, 4 In.Diam. ........ 250.00
**Bowl,** Fairyland Luster, Hummingbird On Orange Luster, 4 3/4 In. ........ 315.00
**Bowl,** Fairyland Luster, Picnic On Rock, Woodland Bridge, 8 In.Diam. ........ 2000.00
**Bowl,** Fairyland, Feather Hat Interior, 9 1/2 In.Diam. ........ 1950.00
**Bowl,** Fairyland, Magpie & Masks, Rosette Pattern, 9 In.Diam. ........ 1800.00
**Bowl,** Hummingbird Luster, Blue Mottled Outside, Bird Inside, 4 In. ........ 200.00
**Bowl,** Hummingbird Luster, Flying Geese Border, Marked, 3 1/4 In. ........ 195.00
**Bowl,** Jasperware, Widow Finial, White Raised Figures, 5 3/4 In. ........ 195.00
**Bowl,** Luster, Orange Out, Blue Inside, Gilt Figures, 2 3/4 In. ........ 118.00
**Bowl,** Terra-Cotta & Black, 4 1/4 X 10 In.Diam. ........ 500.00
**Box,** Covered, Heart Shaped, Crimson, 5 X 3 3/4 In. ........ 595.00
**Box,** Diary, Locking, 7 Cameos, Rosewood & Brass, 8 1/2 X 5 In. ........ 450.00
**Box,** Dragon Luster, Widow Finial, Mosque Design, Covered, 6 X 6 In. ........ 550.00
**Box,** Dresser, Jasperware, Art Nouveau, Jeweled, Star Mark ........ 75.00
**Box,** Jasperware, Lady Seated Near Tree, 2 Cupids, 1 1/2 In.Diam. ........ 158.00
**Box,** Match, Dark Blue Jasper, Scratcher ........ 54.00
**Box,** Powder, Jasperware, Draped Lady With Cupid On Lid, 4 In.Diam. ........ 55.00
**Box,** White Mythological Figures On Black, 4 1/4 X 2 1/4 In.Square ........ 150.00
**Bridge Set,** Terra-Cotta, Club, Spade, Diamond, & Heart ........ 160.00
**Bust,** Basalt Figural, Shakespeare, Marked, 12 1/4 In. ........ 425.00 To 590.00
**Bust,** Basalt, Robert Burns, Black, 7 1/2 X 5 1/2 In.Diam. ........ 595.00
**Bust,** Basalt, Winston Churchill, 1940, 7 In. ........ 90.00
**Bust,** G.Stephenson, Parian, Dated July 12, 1858 ........ *Illus* 275.00
**Bust,** Mercury, Basalt, C.1895, 21 In. ........ 950.00
**Bust,** Mercury, Basalt, Victorian, Marked Wedgwood, 19 In. ........ 800.00

Wedgwood, from left to right, G. Stephenson, Parian, Dated July 12, 1858;
Urn, Covered, Black & White (See Page 727)

| | |
|---|---|
| **Bust,** Mercury, Black Basalt, Marked, 17 1/2 X 10 1/2 In.Diam. | 1200.00 |
| **Bust,** Winston Churchill, 1940, 7 In. | 90.00 |
| **Butter Pat,** Seaweed & Shell | 18.00 |
| **Cake Plate,** Terra-Cotta, 6 3/4 In.Diam. | 60.00 |
| **Cake Plate,** Terra-Cotta, 9 1/2 In.Diam. | 125.00 |
| **Calendar Plate,** 1971, Queensware | 20.00 |
| **Candlestick,** Basalt, Etruria, 8 1/2 In., Pair | 490.00 |
| **Candlestick,** Black Jasperware, Classical Figures, 8 1/2 In. | 175.00 |
| **Candlestick,** Jasperware, Dark Blue, 8 In., Pair | 285.00 |
| **Candlestick,** Jasperware, White Design At Top & Foot, 8 In. | 115.00 |
| **Candlestick,** Light Blue & White, 6 In., Pair | 220.00 |
| **Candlestick,** Terra-Cotta, Low, Pair | 130.00 |
| **Chalice,** Zodiac, Green & Tan On White, 7 1/2 In. | 200.00 |
| **Chamberstick,** 3 Scenes Wreath Border, Candlesnuffer Rest, Blue | 150.00 |
| **Cheese Dish,** Covered, Acorn Finial, White Cameos, 9 X 10 In.Diam. | 425.00 |
| **Chess Piece,** Bishop, Lilac & White, 18th Century | 890.00 |
| **Chocolate Cup Set,** Covered, Jasperware, White, C.1840, 4 1/2 In. | 250.00 |
| **Clock,** Blue & White, Classical Figures, 6 In. | 350.00 |
| **Coffeepot,** Basalt, Swan Finial, Raised Shields, 1800s, Black, 6 In. | 200.00 |
| **Compote,** Footed, Embossed Grape & Vine, Ivory, 8 1/2 X 5 1/2 In. | 85.00 |
| **Compote,** Lilac, 6 X 3 1/2 In. | 125.00 |
| **Cookie Jar,** Flowers, Gold Berries, Cream Ground, Marked, 5 1/2 In. | 175.00 |
| **Creamer,** Basket Weave, Stoneware, 1840-50, 12 In. | 135.00 |
| **Creamer,** Black Basalt, Encaustic Enameling, Marked | 195.00 |
| **Creamer,** Bone, Shell Shaped, C, 1880, 9 In. | 28.00 |
| **Creamer,** Caneware, White | 110.00 |
| **Creamer,** Green, White Figures, Marked Wedgwood, English, 3 3/4 In. | 65.00 |
| **Creamer,** Jasperware, White Lady, Bust Profile, Green | 17.00 |
| **Creamer,** Raised Metal Luster Design, Ivory Ground, 6 In. | 75.00 |
| **Creamer,** White Classic Figures, Dark Blue, 4 1/2 In. | 115.00 |
| **Cup & Saucer,** Basalt, Figures, Leaves | 140.00 |
| **Cup & Saucer,** Cameos, Dark Blue & White, 5 In. | 165.00 |

Wedgwood, from left to right, top row, Flower Basket, Pierced Cover, Caneware, Blue; Teapot, Caneware, Bamboo, Bentley (See Page 726); Teapot, Caneware, Branch Handle, Primrose (See Page 726); bottom row, Teapot, Smear Glazed Caneware Marked (See Page 726); Teapot, Miniature, Smear Glazed Caneware (See Page 726); Teapot, Caneware, Oriental Figures

| | |
|---|---:|
| **Cup & Saucer,** Deep Blue & White, Figures In Relief, 5 5/8 In. | 125.00 |
| **Cup & Saucer,** Dragon Luster, Oriental Design, Demitasse | 115.00 |
| **Cup & Saucer,** Jasperware, Cobalt Blue & White | 125.00 |
| **Cup & Saucer,** Jasperware, Figures In White, Blue & White | 125.00 |
| **Cup & Saucer,** Terra-Cotta | 70.00 |
| **Cup,** Fairyland Luster, Leapfrogging Elves, Marked, 3 1/8 In. | 795.00 |
| **Decanter,** Prince Of Wales, Facing Left, Black | 35.00 |
| **Decanter,** Prince Of Wales, Facing Right, Black | 35.00 |
| **Dish,** Game, Rabbit Finial, Terra-Cotta, Liner, 12 X 8 In. | 395.00 |
| **Ewer,** Deep Blue & White, 8 In. | 275.00 |
| **Fernery,** 3-Color, Footed, 8 X 5 In. | 349.00 |
| **Figurine,** Asiatic Pheasant, Blue & White, Marked, 9 1/2 In. | 20.00 |
| **Figurine,** Bulldog, Basalt, Glass Eyes, C.1916, Black, 2 3/4 In. | 395.00 |
| **Figurine,** Raven, Basalt, C.1916, Black, 4 1/2 X 5 In.Diam. | 595.00 |
| **Flower Basket,** Pierced Cover, Caneware, Blue, 5 In. *Illus* | 250.00 |
| **Flower Basket,** Pierced Lid, Fern Leaves, White, 5 In. *Illus* | 300.00 |
| **Flower Holder,** Basalt, Hedgehog, Signed, Tray, 11 1/2 In. | 990.00 |
| **Flowerpot,** Insert, Sage Green | 125.00 |
| **Flowerpot,** Jasperware, Ladies & Cupid, 3 7/8 X 4 1/8 In.Diam. | 95.00 |
| **Game Dish,** Caneware, Rabbit Finial, 8 In.Long | 425.00 |
| **Hair Receiver,** Dark Blue Jasper, English | 135.00 |
| **Hatpin Holder,** Jasperware, Cameo Inside Gilded Frame, Marked, 5 In. | 95.00 |
| **Hatpin Holder,** Oriental Lady, Pink & Gold, Crown & Shield | 125.00 |
| **Hatpin Holder,** Shoe Shape, Jasperware, Cameo, Crown & Shield | 125.00 |
| **Hatpin Holder,** Tower Shape, White Roses, Green, Crown & Shield | 65.00 |
| **Holder,** Flower, Cobalt, Compana Shape, Potpourri Cover, 6 In. | 275.00 |
| **Holder,** Spill, Figural, Sphinx, Multicolored, 12 In. | 690.00 |
| **Humidor,** Jasperware, 4 Full-Figured Men, Green | 160.00 |
| **Inkwell,** Basalt, Engine Turned, 18th Century, 2 1/2 X 4 In.Diam. | 250.00 |

Wedgwood, Jar, Covered, Crimson Ware, 4 1/2 In.

Wedgwood, Vase, White Stoneware, Blue Florets, 7 In., Pair

(See Page 727)

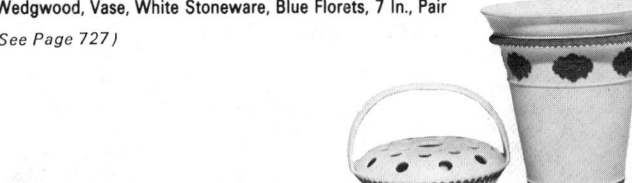

Wedgwood, Flower Basket, Pierced

Lid, Fern Leaves, White, 5 In.

Jar, Covered, Crimson Ware, 4 1/2 In. ................................................................................*Illus* 400.00
Jar, Dragon, Blue & Gold, 9 X 6 In. ................................................................................ 175.00
Jar, Jam, Blue, White Classical Figures, Lid & Spoon, 3 In. ............................................. 115.00
Jar, Sweetmeat, Jasperware, Figures, Silver Plated Rim, Top & Handle ........................... 110.00
Jardiniere, Blue & White, Lion Heads 6 X 5 In. ............................................................. 259.00
Jardiniere, Crimson, 8 1/2 In. ....................................................................................... 750.00
Jardiniere, Ladies & Garlands, Lion Heads, Marked, 5 1/2 X 6 In. ................................... 95.00
Jardiniere, White Classical Figures, Green ..................................................................... 210.00
Jasper, Lilac, Cameo Figures In White, 4 Ball Feet ........................................................ 256.00
Jasper, Pitcher, Classical Figures, Marked, 6 In. ........................................................... 100.00
Jug, Dark Blue, Etruscan, Marked, 7 1/4 In. ................................................................. 125.00
Jug, Jasperware, Figures & Acorns In White, Blue & White, 4 1/8 In. .............................. 110.00
Jug, Salt Glaze, White Stoneware, 7 1/4 In. .................................................................. 275.00
Jug, Yellow & Black, 5 1/2 In. ...................................................................................... 450.00
Matchbox & Scratcher, Jasperware, Dark Blue ............................................................... 54.00
Mirror, Hand, Jasperware, Brass Frame, Blue & White ..................................................... 30.00
Mug, Christmas 1971 .................................................................................................... 25.00
Mug, Jasperware, Washington & Franklin Medallion, Green, 5 1/4 In. ............................. 200.00
Mug, Prince Charles, Investiture, Prince Of Wales, 1969, 4 In. ........................................ 48.00
Mug, Queensware, Churchill, Speech On Base, Portrait & Lion, Blue ............................... 75.00
Mug, Queensware, Coronation Of Edward VIII, 1937, 4 3/4 In. ........................................ 75.00
Mug, White Handled, Dark Blue, 4 1/2 In. ..................................................................... 225.00
Pipe Rest, Jasperware, White Classical Figures, Blue, 3 1/2 In. ....................................... 175.00
Pitcher & Bowl, Corn Pattern, Dated 1863 .................................................................... 100.00
Pitcher & Bowl, 8-Sided Bowl, 13 In.Diam., Pitcher, 12 In. ........................................... 115.00
Pitcher, Bulbous, Hunt Scene, Blue Piping, Unicorn Mark, 5 1/2 In. ............................... 155.00
Pitcher, Classical Figures & Cupids, Green, 4 3/4 In. ..................................................... 95.00
Pitcher, Commemorative, Longfellow, Etruria, 7 X 7 X 9 In. ............................................ 110.00
Pitcher, Cream, Classical Figures, Cherubs, Animals, Marked, 4 In. ................................ 60.00
Pitcher, Creamware, Pitcher, Handle & Top Half Brown Glaze, 3 In. ................................. 20.00
Pitcher, Fox Hunt, Hound Handle, 6 In. ......................................................................... 70.00
Pitcher, Hound Handle, Scene Of Horses, Silver Luster Band, 7 In. ................................. 65.00
Pitcher, Jasper, Blue, White Cameo, Woman, Cherubs, 4 1/2 In. ..................................... 75.00
Pitcher, Jasperware, Black Relief, Yellow, C.1900, 6 1/8 In. ........................................... 440.00
Pitcher, Jasperware, Classical White Figures, C.1900, 4 1/2 In. ...................................... 125.00
Pitcher, Jasperware, Dark Blue, 7 In. ............................................................................ 175.00
Pitcher, Jasperware, Figure, Grape & Leaf Border, 1877, 5 1/4 In. .................................. 165.00
Pitcher, Jasperware, Purplish-Blue, White Figure, C.1877, 5 In. ...................................... 165.00
Pitcher, Jasperware, Relief Scene, Dark Blue, 7 In. ........................................................ 175.00
Pitcher, Light Blue, White Grape, Classical Figures, 5 In. ................................................ 155.00
Pitcher, Pearl Stoneware, Washington, Sepia, 1834-59, 12 In. ........................................ 200.00
Pitcher, Rope Handle, Grapes & Vines At Top, Dark Blue, 5 5/8 In. ................................. 150.00
Pitcher, Stoneware, White Body, Green Top, Rim, & Handle, 7 1/4 In. ............................. 295.00
Pitcher, Terra-Cotta, Rope Handle, 3 3/4 In. .................................................................. 100.00
Pitcher, Terra-Cotta, Rope Handle, 5 1/4 In. .................................................................. 125.00
Pitcher, White Flower, Green, 3 1/2 In. ......................................................................... 25.00
Planter, Footed, White Figures, Liner, Dark Green, 6 In.Diam. ........................................ 195.00
Planter, Green & White Figures, Signed, 6 In. ............................................................... 95.00
Planter, White Figures, Matching Base, Blue & White, 7 1/2 In. ...................................... 295.00

Wedgwood, Plaque, Archimedes,
Black Basalt, Brass Bezel, 3 In.

Wedgwood, Plaque, Black Basalt
On Brass Bezel, 3 In.

| | |
|---|---|
| **Planter,** 3 Legs, Liner, Green, White Classical Figures, 6 X 4 In. ............................................. *Illus* | 200.00 |
| **Plaque,** Archimedes, Black Basalt, Brass Bezel, 3 In. ............................................................. *Illus* | 375.00 |
| **Plaque,** Black Basalt On Brass Bezel, 3 In. ................................................................. *Illus* | 325.00 |
| **Plaque,** Blue & White, Oliver Wendell Holmes, Signed, 5 X 6 In. ............................................. | 65.00 |
| **Plaque,** Blue Ground, White Relief, Green Border, 5 1/2 X 10 In. ............................................. | 550.00 |
| **Plaque,** C.1875, Brown & Tan, 14 X 6 In., Pair ............................................................. | 790.00 |
| **Plaque,** Dancing Hours, Light Green & White, Frame, 11 1/2 X 7 In. ..................................... | 290.00 |
| **Plaque,** Fairyland, Elves, Sky, & Rainbow, 9 X 12 In. ................................................. | 3500.00 |
| **Plaque,** Impressed Perseus Poet, Copper Frame ...................................................... *Illus* | 625.00 |
| **Plaque,** Ladies In Different Poses, Blue, Framed, 6 X 4 In., Pair ......................................... | 595.00 |
| **Plaque,** Louis XVI, White Stoneware, C.1795, Oval, 3 1/4 In. ......................................... | 250.00 |
| **Plaque,** Trophy, Zodiac, Framed ......................................................................... *Illus* | 2250.00 |
| **Plate,** Asiatic Pheasant, Blue & White, 9 1/2 In. ...................................................... | 25.00 |
| **Plate,** Barometer, Lilac, 9 1/4 In.Diam. .............................................................. | 350.00 |
| **Plate,** Beatrice, Dated June 16, 1880 ................................................................. | 25.00 |
| **Plate,** Blue Willow, 10 In., Set Of 4 ................................................................. | 60.00 |
| **Plate,** Capture Of Vincennes, Saratoga Battle Monument, Blue ....................................... | 30.00 |
| **Plate,** Christian Temperance Union, 1908, Dark Blue ................................................. | 34.00 |
| **Plate,** Christmas, 1969 .................................................................. 200.00 To | 210.00 |
| **Plate,** Christmas, 1970 ............................................................................... | 20.00 |
| **Plate,** Christmas, 1971 ............................................................................... | 25.00 |
| **Plate,** Christmas, 1972 ............................................................................... | 30.00 |
| **Plate,** Christmas, 1973 ............................................................................... | 30.00 |
| **Plate,** Colored Shells & Seaweed, 9 In. ............................................................. | 56.00 |
| **Plate,** Commemorative, Creamware, Amherst College, C.1933, Set Of 8 ............................. | 150.00 |
| **Plate,** Creamware, C.1820, Floral, 8 In. ............................................................. | 39.00 |
| **Plate,** Dark Blue, Floral Border, White House, 9 In. ................................................. | 35.00 |
| **Plate,** Drabware, Oriental Florals, Enameled, C.1830, 8 In. ......................................... | 65.00 |
| **Plate,** Dragon Luster, 9 1/8 In.Diam. ............................................................... | 345.00 |
| **Plate,** Engraved For Newark, N.J.Art Club, 1925, 10 1/4 In. ......................................... | 25.00 |
| **Plate,** Etruria, N.Y.U., 100 Years, School Of Commerce, 10 1/4 In. ................................. | 27.50 |
| **Plate,** Fresno County Courthouse, Blue ............................................................. | 30.00 |
| **Plate,** Gunston Hall ................................................................................. | 18.00 |
| **Plate,** Harrison & Tecumseh, Blue & White, 9 1/4 In. ............................................... | 30.00 |
| **Plate,** Harvard Universtiy Memorial Hall, Blue Transfer, 10 In. ..................................... | 35.00 |
| **Plate,** Ivanhoe, Rebecca Gives Purse To Gurth, Blue & White, 9 In. ............................... | 32.00 |
| **Plate,** Ivanhoe, Rebecca Repelling The Templar ..................................................... | 55.00 |
| **Plate,** Ivanhoe, Urfried Relating Her Story .......................................................... | 45.00 |
| **Plate,** Lilac, Medallion Center, 6 3/4 In.Diam. ...................................................... | 55.00 |
| **Plate,** Longfellow House .............................................................................. | 38.00 |
| **Plate,** Mass. General Hospital, 9 1/4 In. ............................................................ | 40.00 |

Wedgwood, Plaque, Impressed
Perseus Poet, Copper Frame

Wedgwood, Plaque, Trophy,
Zodiac, Framed

| | |
|---|---|
| **Plate,** Mount Vernon | 35.00 |
| **Plate,** Old Brick Church | 40.00 |
| **Plate,** Old Man Of The Mountain, Hexagonal, C.1890 | 38.00 |
| **Plate,** Patrician Pattern, Raised Scroll Pattern Edge, 10 1/2 In. | 12.50 |
| **Plate,** President Harrison & Tecumseh, Blue & White, 9 1/4 In. | 30.00 |
| **Plate,** President Harrison, Blue & White, 10 1/2 In. | 30.00 |
| **Plate,** Public Library, Boston | 30.00 |
| **Plate,** Saratoga Battle Monument, Blue | 30.00 |
| **Plate,** Serving, Creamwear Shell, C.1800, 8 In. | 110.00 |
| **Plate,** Shell & Seaweed, Dated 1878, 9 In. | 40.00 |
| **Plate,** Sponge Center, Reticulated Edge, C.1870, 8 1/2 In. | 56.00 |
| **Plate,** Stratford Hall, Pink Transfer, 9 1/2 In.Diam | 15.00 |
| **Plate,** The Medical School & Straus, Blue & White, Signed, 10 In. | 25.00 |
| **Plate,** View Of Commonwealth, Boston, Brown | 30.00 |
| **Plate,** Vine Border, Grape Leaves Design, 12 In. | 60.00 |
| **Plate,** White, Mulberry Grape Leaf, 8 1/2 In., Set Of 4 | 50.00 |
| **Platter,** Blue, Cows, 17 In. | 95.00 |
| **Platter,** Grape Design | 25.00 |
| **Platter,** Handled, 7 3/4 X 10 1/2 In. | 210.00 |
| **Platter,** Regina, C.1862, 18 X 14 In. | 34.00 |
| **Pudding,** Corn Mold, C.1820, 7 In. | 125.00 |
| **Ring Tree,** Black Basalt | 65.00 |
| **Saucer,** Wavette Pattern | 6.00 |
| **Shaker,** Salt & Pepper, Dar Blue Jasper, Pair | 120.00 |
| **Sugar & Creamer,** Blue & White, Signed, 3 1/2 In. | 95.00 |
| **Sugar & Creamer,** Dark Blue, White Relief, Figures | 110.00 |
| **Sugar & Creamer,** Flags Of Allies Of World War I, Cream | 35.00 |
| **Sugar & Creamer,** Jasperware, Bamboo Mold, Terra-Cotta Leaves | 95.00 |
| **Sugar & Creamer,** Jasperware, Blue, White Classical Figures | 110.00 |
| **Sugar Pot,** Gray Jasper, Lilac Figural, Scroll Decorated, 5 1/2 In. | 350.00 |
| **Syrup,** Blue Jasper, Pewter Lid, Grecian Figures | 95.00 |
| **Syrup,** Jasperware, Washington & Franklin, Green & White, 5 In. | 165.00 |
| **Syrup,** Light Blue, Jasper, Pewter Lid, Grecian Figures | 95.00 |
| **Tankard,** Jasperware, White Relief Figures, Pewter Lid, 8 In. | 285.00 |
| **Tea Cup & Saucer,** Jasperware, Classical Figures, Panels, 2 1/8 In. | 125.00 |
| **Tea Set,** Blue Jasperware, Commemorative, Elizabeth Regina 1953 | 225.00 |
| **Tea Set,** Caneware, Applied Terra-Cotta Flowers, Bamboo Spout | 195.00 |
| **Tea Set,** Jasperware, Commemorative, Elizabeth Regina, 1953, 3 Piece | 225.00 |
| **Tea Set,** Lilac, Covered Teapot, Sugar & Creamer | 550.00 |
| **Teapot,** Basalt, Classical Figures, 1881 Mark | 145.00 |
| **Teapot,** Blue & White Jasper, 8 In. | 120.00 |
| **Teapot,** Blue & White, Jasperware, Classical Figures Of Ladies | 165.00 |

**Teapot,** Caneware Bamboo, Wedgwood Bentley, 7 3/4 In. ................................................. *Illus* 2000.00
**Teapot,** Caneware, Branch Handle, Primrose, 6 3/4 In. .................................................. *Illus* 100.00
**Teapot,** Cobalt Blue & White, 4 X 8 1/4 In. ..................................................................... 300.00
**Teapot,** Countryside, Blue & White ..................................................................................... 15.00
**Teapot,** Cover, Redware, Raised Design ................................................................ *Illus* 5200.00
**Teapot,** Drabware, White Rose Design ............................................................................ 285.00
**Teapot,** Flower, White High Relief .................................................................................... 285.00
**Teapot,** Green & White, Jasper, 9 In. .............................................................................. 145.00
**Teapot,** Jasperware, Blue & White, Marked, 5 1/4 In. .................................................... 165.00
**Teapot,** Jasperware, C.1900, Dark Blue ........................................................................... 125.00
**Teapot,** Jasperware, Figures, Animals, & Cherubs, 19th Century, Marked ...................... 50.00
**Teapot,** Jasperware, Terra-Cotta, Small .......................................................................... 195.00
**Teapot,** King Edward VIII, Dark Blue, Covered, Sugar & Creamer ................................... 395.00
**Teapot,** Miniature, Smear Glazed Caneware, 5 1/2 In. ................................................. *Illus* 125.00
**Teapot,** Smear Glazed Caneware, Marked, 6 3/4 In. ..................................................... *Illus* 75.00
**Teapot,** Smear Glazed, Dog Finial, C.1810, 4 In. ........................................................... 175.00
**Teapot,** Stand, Marked, 6 Cup Size, 6 In. ...................................................................... 250.00
**Tile,** Boston, 1947 ........................................................................................................... 28.00
**Tile,** Calendar, Frigate Constitution & Florida ................................................................. 45.00
**Tile,** Calendar, 1901, Bunker Hill Monument ................................................................... 50.00
**Tile,** Calendar, 1903 ....................................................................................................... 45.00
**Tile,** Calendar, 1918, Boston Light, Brown ...................................................................... 38.00
**Tile,** Cobweb, C.1880, 8 In. ............................................................................................ 80.00
**Tile,** Helena Of A Midsummer Night's Dream, Sepia, 6 In.Square ................................... 95.00
**Tile,** March, Blue, 6 In.Square ......................................................................................... 50.00
**Tile,** October, Blue & White ............................................................................................. 65.00
**Tile,** Puck Of A Midsummer Night's Dream, Blue, 9 In.Square ....................................... 110.00
**Tile,** Wall, Molded, Brown Tones, C.1870, 6 X 14 In., Pair ............................................. 890.00
**Tile,** Whimsical Man Fishing, Entitled Folly, Blue, 6 In.Square ......................................... 95.00
**Tile,** 1908, Harvard Medical ............................................................................................ 50.00
**Tobacco Jar,** Classical Scenes, Acorn Finial, Dark Blue, 6 1/2 In. ................................ 200.00
**Tobacco Jar,** Egyptian Cameos, Black & White, 6 In. ..................................................... 550.00
**Toby Jug,** Elihu Yale, Blue ............................................................................................. 150.00
**Toby Jug,** Elihu Yale, Yellow, 6 In. ................................................................................. 150.00
**Toothpick,** Holder, Jasper, Dark Blue, White Figures, 1890, 2 1/2 In. ............................ 225.00
**Toothpick,** Jasperware, Black .......................................................................................... 33.00
**Toothpick,** Jasperware, Dark Blue ................................................................................... 50.00
**Tray,** Creamware, Pagoda, Oval, 7 3/4 In. ....................................................................... 18.00
**Tray,** Creamware, Pagoda, Rectangular, 8 1/4 In. ............................................................ 22.00
**Tray,** Dresser, Jasperware, Wreath Border, Classical Scenes, 6 In. ............................... 45.00
**Tray,** Dresser, Wreath Border, 3 Classical Scenes, 6 X 3 1/4 In. .................................... 45.00
**Tray,** Jasperware, Elizabeth II, Silver Jubilee, Cameo, 4 1/4 In. ..................................... 30.00
**Tray,** Jasperware, Shell Design, White ............................................................................ 35.00
**Tray,** Jasperware, 2 Scenes, Figures & Horses, Oval, 9 1/4 In. ..................................... 175.00
**Tray,** Lilac, Round, Flat, 4 1/2 In. .................................................................................... 40.00
**Tray,** Pin, Lilac, Oval, 3 1/2 X 5 In. .................................................................................. 50.00
**Tray,** Pink, Grapevine Rim, Roses, Angel Center, Blue, 4 1/2 In. .................................... 25.00

Wedgwood, Teapot, Cover, Redware, Raised Design

Wedgwood, Vase, Black Basalt, Polychrome
Enameled Floral, 6 In.

| | |
|---|---|
| Tureen, Underplate, Ladle, Blue Pattern, Pearlware, Rope Edging | 350.00 |
| Urn, Classical Figures, Trees, Wreaths, Marked, 13 1/4 In. | 125.00 |
| Urn, Covered, Black & White, 9 In. .......... *Illus* | 225.00 |
| Urn, Covered, Garlands, Gold Handles, C.1900, 9 1/2 In. | 252.00 |
| Urn, Covered, Jasperware, Sage Green & White, C.1850, 10 1/4 In. | 325.00 |
| Urn, Zodiac, Jasperware, 19th Century, Signs In Relief, Green | 370.00 |
| Vase, Bird Of Paradise, Gold Design, Mottled Orange, C.1860, 5 In. | 200.00 |
| Vase, Black & White, 1890-1915, 5 1/4 In. | 95.00 |
| Vase, Black Basalt, Polychrome Enameled Floral, 6 In. .......... *Illus* | 110.00 |
| Vase, Blue Luster, Beaker Shaped, Footed, Hummingbirds, 7 In. | 275.00 |
| Vase, Blue, Hummingbird Luster, Flame Luster Interior, 8 1/2 In. | 395.00 |
| Vase, Caneware, Yelow, Blue Jasper Figures, Miniature | 525.00 |
| Vase, Cherubs, Laurel Draped, Blue, 7 11/16 In. | 100.00 |
| Vase, Chinese Luster, Gilded, Green Celadon Prunus Pattern, 11 In. | 550.00 |
| Vase, Cylindrical, Classical Scene, Dark Blue, 5 3/4 In. | 155.00 |
| Vase, Dragon Design, Mottled Blue, 8 1/4 In. | 315.00 |
| Vase, Dragon Luster, Blue & Gold, Portland Mark, 8 In. | 375.00 |
| Vase, Dragon Luster, Blue, Gold Design, Covered, 11 In. | 520.00 |
| Vase, Dragon Luster, Blue, Marked, 8 3/4 In. | 675.00 |
| Vase, Dragon Luster, Gold Dragon, Mottled Orange, Blue Inside, 6 In. | 225.00 |
| Vase, Dragon Luster, Mottled Blue, Portland Mark, 9 In. | 350.00 |
| Vase, Dragon Luster, Mottled, Blue Mark, 8 In. | 395.00 |
| Vase, Dragon Luster, 2 Gold Dragons, Blue, 10 In. | 280.00 |
| Vase, Fairyland Luster, Figures On Bridge, , 7 3/4 In., Pair | 3900.00 |
| Vase, Fairyland Luster, Torches, Tree Serpent Design, 12 1/2 In. | 2500.00 |
| Vase, Fairyland Luster, 14 In. .......... *Illus* | 3000.00 |
| Vase, Firbolgs, Fairyland, Ruby Luster, Marked, 8 1/2 In. | 1450.00 |
| Vase, Hummingbird Luster, Blue Exterior, Flame Interior, 8 1/2 In. | 450.00 |
| Vase, Hummingbird Luster, 5 Birds, Blue Exterior, 11 1/2 In. | 510.00 |
| Vase, Hummingbird, Luster Interior, Blue Exterior, 8 In. | 375.00 |
| Vase, Jasper Dip, White Reliefs, Classical Figures, 11 In. | 900.00 |
| Vase, Jasperware, Dark Blue, Classical Scene, 7 1/2 In. | 135.00 |
| Vase, Jasperware, Handled, Raised White Ladies, Marked, 10 1/4 In. | 650.00 |
| Vase, Jasperware, Handled, White Cameo Design, 19th Century, 8 In. | 225.00 |
| Vase, Jasperware, Raised Grecian Figures, Black & White, 10 5/8 In. | 475.00 |
| Vase, Jasperware, Tricolor, Green Bands, 4 Medallions, Marked, 5 In. | 750.00 |
| Vase, Mottled Blue, Gold Dragon, Portland Mark, 9 In. | 375.00 |
| Vase, Portland, Blue, 6 1/2 In. | 350.00 |
| Vase, Portland, Green, 4 In. .......... *Illus* | 275.00 |
| Vase, Portland, Lilac, 5 1/2 In. | 425.00 |
| Vase, Pottery, Raised Gold Leaves, Black, 7 1/4 In. | 265.00 |
| Vase, White Ground, Classical Figures, C.1860, 8 In. | 400.00 |
| Vase, White Stoneware, Blue Florets, 7 In., Pair .......... *Illus* | 250.00 |

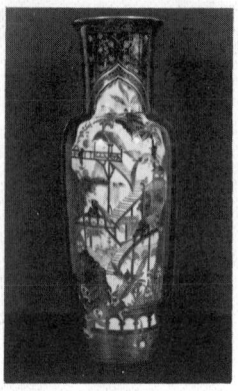

Wedgwood, Vase, Fairyland Luster,
14 In. (See Page 727)

Wedgwood, Vase, Portland, Green, 4 In.

*(See Page 727)*

| | |
|---|---:|
| **Vase,** Yellow, Relief Figures, Twisted Handles, 4 1/2 In. | 525.00 |
| **Weights,** Pearlware, Signature & Regulatory Marks, Set Of 4 | 650.00 |

**LOUWELSA**
**WELLER**

*Weller pottery was first made in 1873 in Fultonham, Ohio. The firm moved to Zanesville, Ohio, in 1882. Art wares were first made in 1893. Hundreds of lines of pottery were made including Louwelsa, Eocean, Dickens, and Sicardo before the pottery closed in 1948.*

| | |
|---|---:|
| **WELLER, Base,** Bonito, 4 In. | 55.00 |
| **Basket,** Cameo, Rust, 7 1/2 In. | 18.00 |
| **Basket,** Ivory, Scroll Handle, Blue Floral, 6 1/2 X 6 1/2 In. | 24.00 |
| **Basket,** Magnolia, Blue Ground, 7 In. | 30.00 |
| **Basket,** Souevo, Hanging | 95.00 |
| **Bowl & Frog,** Monochrome, Aqua, 9 1/2 In. | 20.00 |
| **Bowl,** Claywood, With Mice, 2 In. | 18.00 |
| **Bowl,** Console, Ardsley, 16 1/2 In. | 95.00 |
| **Bowl,** Console, Rosemont, Black, 12 In. | 30.00 |
| **Bowl,** Console, Woodcraft, Leaves, Twigs, 10 In. | 26.00 |
| **Bowl,** Coppertone, Square Handle, 8 In. | 65.00 |
| **Bowl,** Marvo, Woodcraft Glaze, 8 In. | 35.00 |
| **Bowl,** Nut, Panels Of Squirrels & Trees | 25.00 |
| **Bowl,** Panella, Yellow Flowers, Blue, 12 In. | 20.00 |
| **Bowl,** Roma, 7 1/2 In. | 25.00 |
| **Bowl,** Scandia, 9 In. | 35.00 |
| **Bowl,** Squirrel Eating A Nut, 6 X 7 In. | 45.00 |
| **Bowl,** Turada, 2 X 5 In. | 90.00 |
| **Bowl,** Wild Rose, Brown Raised Flower, 11 In. | 45.00 |
| **Bowl,** Woodcraft, Squirrels, 3 1/2 In. | 115.00 |
| **Bowl,** Woodcraft, Squirrels, 6 In. | 98.00 |
| **Bowl,** Woodcraft, With Liner, 7 X 3 In. | 15.00 |
| **Candleholder,** Cameo, Creamware, 11 In. | 90.00 |
| **Candleholder,** Coppertone, Turtle | 95.00 |
| **Candleholder,** Evergreen, Triple, Script Mark, 8 X 10 X 3 In. | 55.00 |
| **Candleholder,** Greora, 3-Legged, 3 1/2 In. | 13.00 |
| **Candlestick,** Cornish, Blue, Pair | 40.00 |
| **Cornucopia,** Blossom, Green, 8 1/2 In. | 18.50 |
| **Cornucopia,** Panella, Blue, 5 1/2 In., Pair | 25.00 |
| **Cornucopia,** Sydonia, Green, 6 1/2 In. | 32.00 |
| **Creamer,** Dickens Ware, Indian Handle, Signed | 135.00 |
| **Creamer,** Zona, Duck, 3 1/2 In. | 25.00 |

| | |
|---|---|
| **Dish,** Muskota, Squirrel | 85.00 |
| **Ewer,** Ansonia, Pink, Gray, & Yellow, 11 In. | 65.00 |
| **Ewer,** Cameo, Green, 10 In. | 25.00 |
| **Ewer,** Floral, Rust & Gold, Bulbous, Trefoil Spout, Signed, 11 1/4 In. | 225.00 |
| **Ewer,** Gloria, Green, 9 In. | 25.00 |
| **Ewer,** Oak Leaf, Brown, 8 1/2 In. | 25.00 |
| **Ewer,** Roba, Orange, Script Mark, 11 In. | 52.50 |
| **Figurine,** Hobart Girl, Ink Stamp On Base, 7 1/2 In. | 32.50 |
| **Figurine,** Muskota Girl With Doll, Marked, 8 In. | 175.00 |
| **Flower Frog,** Crab | 35.00 |
| **Flower Frog,** Glendale | 25.00 |
| **Flower Frog,** Muskota, Frog On Lily Pad | 15.00 |
| **Flower Frog,** Muskota, Toad On Toadstool, Marked | 25.00 |
| **Flower Frog,** Pedestaled Mushroom, Frog On Top | 48.00 |
| **Flower Frog,** Tree Trunk | 35.00 |
| **Flower Frog,** Tutone, Brown | 12.00 |
| **Flower Frog,** Woodcraft | 34.00 |
| **Humidor,** 3 Pipes Design, Mary Gillies | 175.00 |
| **Jardiniere & Pedestal,** Flemish, 38 In. | 450.00 |
| **Jardiniere,** Claywood, Spider Webs, 3 1/2 In. | 20.00 |
| **Jardiniere,** Dickens Ware, Golden Flowers, Blue Ground, 10 In. | 360.00 |
| **Jardiniere,** Dickens Ware, Underglazed Flowers, Blue, 9 X 8 1/2 In. | 350.00 |
| **Jardiniere,** Flemish, 7 1/2 In. | 85.00 |
| **Jardiniere,** Forest, Block Mark, 5 1/2 In. | 75.00 |
| **Jardiniere,** Forest, 4 1/2 In. | 30.00 |
| **Jardiniere,** Roma, 6-Sided, 4 1/2 In. | 12.00 |
| **Jardiniere,** Rudlor, Glaze Crackle, Blue-Green, 6 1/2 In. | 9.00 |
| **Jug,** Louwelsa, Cherry & Leaf Design, Short Spout, Handled, 6 In. | 125.00 |
| **Lamp,** Hudson, Gray To Cream, 6 1/2 In. | 120.00 |
| **Loving Cup,** Lonhuda | 235.00 |
| **Mug,** Burnt Wood, Owl On Side, Hooded Man On Reverse | 90.00 |
| **Mug,** Claywood, Owl & Jester | 60.00 |
| **Mug,** Dickens Ware, Monk In Brown Cloak, Blue Stein, 5 1/2 In. | 300.00 |
| **Mug,** Dresden, Windmill & Boat, 5 In. | 215.00 |
| **Mug,** Eocean, Red Flowers, Gray Ground | 85.00 |
| **Mug,** Ivory, Marked, 5 In. | 45.00 |
| **Mug,** Ivory, Set Of 5 | 160.00 |
| **Mug,** Suevo, 5 In. | 45.00 |
| **Mushroom,** Muskota, Bug On Top | 12.00 |
| **Pedestal,** Eocean, Iris, Pink To Gray, 24 In. | 175.00 |
| **Pitcher,** Coppertone, Fish Handled, 7 1/2 In. | 135.00 To 175.00 |
| **Pitcher,** Louwelsa, Pansy Design, Signed, 6 In. | 160.00 |
| **Pitcher,** Sabrinian, Seahorse Handle, Pastel | 95.00 |
| **Pitcher,** Zona, Kingfisher, Red, 8 In. | 48.00 |
| **Pitcher,** Zona, Peaches, 7 In. | 75.00 |
| **Planter Bookends,** Roba, Blue | 65.00 |
| **Planter,** Blue Drapery, 9 1/2 X 4 1/2 X 2 3/4 In. | 35.00 |
| **Planter,** Bonita, Handled, 6 In. | 56.00 |
| **Planter,** Evergreen, Pelican, Marked, 9 1/2 In. | 70.00 |
| **Planter,** Evergreen, Pelican, 6 1/2 In.Long | 70.00 |
| **Planter,** Roma, Cutouts, 4 In.Square | 20.00 |
| **Planter,** Woodcraft, Log, 9 X 4 In. | 35.00 |
| **Planter,** Woodcraft, 3 Foxes | 175.00 |
| **Plaque,** Abraham Lincoln, 4 1/2 In. | 75.00 |
| **Plaque,** Lincoln, Art Nouveau | 58.00 |
| **Smoking Set,** Roma, Humidor, Cigarette Holder, Ashtray, Signed | 235.00 |
| **Strawberry Pot,** Greora, Script Mark, 5 In. | 35.00 |
| **Tankard,** Dickens Ware Iii, Deer Scene, 14 In. | 750.00 |
| **Tankard,** Dickens Ware, Cobalt Blue, Signed, 17 In. | 950.00 |
| **Tea Set,** Zona, 3 Piece | 85.00 |
| **Umbrella Stand,** Bedford, Matte | 100.00 |
| **Umbrella Stand,** Ivory | 150.00 |
| **Umbrella Stand,** Louwelsa, Iris, 20 In. | 375.00 |

| | |
|---|---|
| Vase, Ardsley, Iris, Green, 9 1/2 In. | 21.00 |
| Vase, Baldin, Blue Ground, 9 X 9 In. | 95.00 |
| Vase, Baldin, Blue, 13 1/4 In. | 195.00 |
| Vase, Baldin, Earth Tones, Twig Handles, 9 3/4 X 9 1/2 In. | 150.00 |
| Vase, Baldwin, Earth Tones, 7 In. | 45.00 |
| Vase, Bonita, 7 In. | 50.00 |
| Vase, Bonita, 9 In. | 68.00 |
| Vase, Bonita, 10 1/2 In. | 100.00 |
| Vase, Bouquet, Blue, Pink, White Blossoms, Green Leaves, 8 1/2 In. | 28.00 |
| Vase, Bud, Florenzo, Double | 13.00 |
| Vase, Bud, LaSa, Signed, Paper Label, 6 1/4 In. | 395.00 |
| Vase, Bud, Roma, Triple, Marked, 8 In. | 28.00 |
| Vase, Bud, Woodcraft, Double | 30.00 To 48.00 |
| Vase, Bud, Woodcraft, 6 3/4 In. | 24.00 |
| Vase, Bud, Woodcraft, 7 In. | 20.00 |
| Vase, Burnt Wood, Flowers, 5 In. | 12.00 |
| Vase, Burnt Wood, Incised Birds & Flowers, 11 1/2 In. | 70.00 |
| Vase, Candis, White, 7 1/2 In. | 18.50 |
| Vase, Chengtu, 11 In. | 50.00 |
| Vase, Claywood, Pinecones, 6 1/2 In. | 20.00 |
| Vase, Claywood, Spider Web, 4 In. | 15.00 |
| Vase, Coppertone, Bulbous, 6 In. | 55.00 |
| Vase, Coppertone, Frogs Holding Lily, 4 In., Pair | 120.00 |
| Vase, Coppertone, 6 In. | 38.00 To 40.00 |
| Vase, Cornish, Brown, 8 1/2 In. | 18.50 |
| Vase, Darsie, Green, 6 In. | 14.00 |
| Vase, Dickens Ware, Blackbird, Indian Portrait, 1908, 7 1/2 In. | 550.00 |
| Vase, Dynasty, Blue & Green, 6 In. | 22.00 |
| Vase, Eclair, Black Ground, Marked, 8 In. | 45.00 |
| Vase, Etna, Blooming Pink Carnations, 7 In. | 95.00 |
| Vase, Etna, Red Blossoms, Blue Ground, Shaded To Ivory, Marked, 10 In. | 85.00 |
| Vase, Etna, Red Flower, 8 X 8 In. | 100.00 |
| Vase, Fleron, 7 1/2 In. | 40.00 |
| Vase, Florenzo, Footed, 7 In. | 35.00 |
| Vase, Floretta Matte, 3 Textured Flowers At Top, 13 1/2 In. | 90.00 |
| Vase, Floretta, Berries, Brown, 5 In. | 62.00 |
| Vase, Floretta, Pears, Rose Bowl Shape, 7 1/4 In. | 95.00 |
| Vase, Forest, 8 In. | 55.00 |
| Vase, Gloria, Brown, 9 1/2 In. | 20.00 To 25.00 |
| Vase, Gloria, Brown, 10 In. | 30.00 |
| Vase, Golden Glow, 10 In. | 45.00 |
| Vase, Hudson, Iridescent Design, 9 In. | 325.00 |
| Vase, Hudson, 8-Sided Floral, 7 1/2 In. | 140.00 |
| Vase, Hudson, 8-Sided, Dogwood, Gray To White, 9 1/2 In. | 35.00 |
| Vase, LaSa, Red & Gold Metallic Iridescent Landscape, Signed, 7 In. | 175.00 |
| Vase, LaSa, Signed, 7 In. | 165.00 |
| Vase, Loru, Green, 8 In. | 20.00 |
| Vase, Louwelsa, Daffodils, Artist Signed, 9 In. | 195.00 |
| Vase, Louwelsa, Flowers, 8 In. | 90.00 |
| Vase, Louwelsa, Green & Brown Glaze, Yellow Daffodil, Signed, 9 In. | 150.00 |
| Vase, Louwelsa, Indian, Full Headdress, Signed LJB, 15 In. | 1900.00 |
| Vase, Malvern, Pillow, 8 1/2 In. | 48.00 |
| Vase, Marvo, Blue-Gray, 10 In. | 50.00 |
| Vase, Marvo, Brown, 12 In. | 12.00 |
| Vase, Mi-Flo, 7 1/2 In. | 18.00 |
| Vase, Mirror Black, 6 In. | 35.00 |
| Vase, Panella, Blue, 10 In. | 25.00 |
| Vase, Panella, Tan, 10 In. | 25.00 |
| Vase, Rochelle, 6 In. | 65.00 |
| Vase, Roma, Pinecones, 7 In. | 24.00 |
| Vase, Silvertone, Signed H, 7 In. | 80.00 |
| Vase, Silvertone, Twisted Handles, 6 1/2 X 6 In. | 85.00 |
| Vase, Softone, Pink, 5 In. | 15.00 |

| | |
|---|---|
| Vase, Sydonia, Ruffled, Mottled Green, Double Hand Signed, 9 X 9 In. | 38.00 |
| Vase, Voile, 7 In. | 60.00 |
| Vase, Wall, Ivory | 28.50 |
| Vase, Warwick, 6 1/2 In. | 15.00 |
| Vase, Woodcraft, Flowers On Trellis, 7 In. | 12.00 |
| Vase, Woodcraft, Goblet Shape, Twig Supports From Base, Labels, 9 In. | 120.00 |
| Vase, Woodcraft, Owl, Tree Trunk, Limb Handle, 13 In. | 185.00 To 215.00 |
| Vase, Woodcraft, Pink Flowers, 10 In. | 28.00 |
| Vase, Woodcraft, 11 In. | 40.00 |
| Vase, Woodcraft, 1928, 10 1/2 In. | 45.00 |
| Vase, Yellow Roses, Louwelsa, Signed Madge Hurst, Bulbous, 5 In. | 120.00 |
| Wall Pocket, Luster, Black Roma-Type Design, 7 1/2 In. | 15.00 |
| Wall Pocket, Roma, 8 In. | 45.00 |
| Wall Pocket, Roma, 10 In. | 60.00 |
| Wall Pocket, Warwick, Half Bottle Mark, 11 1/2 In. | 52.00 |
| Wall Pocket, Woodcraft, Squirrel, 9 In. | 50.00 |
| | |
| WHEATLEY, Vase, 3-Handled, Drip Green Glaze, Flecked, 6 1/2 In. | 75.00 |

*Willets Manufacturing Company of Trenton, New Jersey, worked from 1879. The company made Belleek in the late 1880s and 1890s in shapes similar to those used by the Irish Belleek factory.*

| | |
|---|---|
| WILLETS, Bouillon & Underplate, Raised Gold Leaves, Water Lily Handles | 225.00 |
| Bowl & Underplate, White Blossoms, Wide Rimmed, 1 1/2 X 5 1/2 In. | 42.00 |
| Bowl, Covered, Sterling Overlay On Dragon Handles | 75.00 |
| Bowl, Heart Shaped, Crimped, Fluted Edge, Coin Gold Grapes, 6 1/2 In. | 55.00 |
| Bowl, 2-Handled, Scalloped Rim, Flowers, 5 X 7 In.Diam. | 250.00 |
| Chalice, Pinecones, Leaves, Multicolored Ground, Gold Inside, 11 In. | 275.00 |
| Chalice, Portrait Of Monk Drinking Tea, Leafy Ground, 11 In. | 395.00 |
| Chocolate Pot, 4 Cups & Saucers, Silver Deposit, Dragon Handle | 400.00 |
| Coffeepot, Molded Scrollwork Handle & Finial, 8 1/4 In. | 70.00 |
| Creamer, Pedestal, Art Deco, Angular Handle, 5 1/4 In. | 30.00 |
| Cup & Saucer, Pink Floral, Green, Serpent Mark | 46.50 |
| Hatpin Holder, Art Nouveau, Heart-Shaped Flowers, Signed, 5 In. | 75.00 |
| Hatpin Holder, Pink Roses, Mint Green Ground | 75.00 |
| Mug, Monk, Wine, Barrels, Hand-Painted, Signed, 5 1/2 In. | 140.00 |
| Pitcher, Cider, Bulbous, Yellow, Hand-Painted Flowers | 95.00 |
| Pitcher, Pastel Roses On Both Sides, Twig Handle, Jewels, 5 In. | 185.00 |
| Rose Bowl, Single, Pink Rose Design, Signed, Dated 1911 | 125.00 |
| Salt, Blue, Set Of 3 | 28.00 |
| Salt, Flowers On Cream Ground, Gold Ball Feet & Trim, Pair | 32.00 |
| Salt, Iridescent, Gold Trim, Set Of 8 | 80.00 |
| Salt, Ruffled Rim, Applied Gold Design | 25.00 |
| Sugar, Covered, Pedestal, Urn Shaped, 6 1/2 In. | 35.00 |
| Toothpick, 2-Handled, Creamy Translucent | 32.00 |
| Trivet, Art Nouveau, Silver Overlay, 7 In.Diam. | 85.00 |
| Vase, Allover Multicolored Mum Design, 16 In. | 300.00 |
| Vase, Bulbous, Purple Flowers, Signed, 10 In. | 90.00 |
| Vase, Cylinder Shape, Hollyhock Blossoms, 1928, Signed, 16 In. | 135.00 |
| Vase, Cylinder, Hand-Painted, Chrysanthemums, 16 In. | 250.00 |
| Vase, Deep Red Roses, 14 In. | 350.00 |
| Vase, Green With Red Carnations, 10 1/4 In. | 150.00 |
| Vase, Hand-Painted Flowers, Green, Yellow, & White, 11 1/2 In. | 235.00 |
| Vase, Hand-Painted Geraniums, Green Ground, 15 In. | 265.00 |
| Vase, Hand-Painted, Green, Lavender, & Purple, 1909, 13 In. | 85.00 |
| Vase, Hand-Painted, 1909, 11 1/2 In. | 235.00 |
| Vase, Oriental Junks, Night Scene, 15 1/2 In. | 145.00 |
| Vase, Painted Man & Woman Dancing, Gold Beading, Dated 1886, 23 In. | 385.00 |
| Vase, Pink Roses, Gold Rim, Cream Ground, Artist Signed, 10 In. | 125.00 |
| Vase, Roses, Hand-Painted, Artist Signed & Dated 1903, 16 In. | 270.00 |
| Vase, Silver Overlay, 12 1/2 In. | 290.00 |

**Vase,** Wisteria Design, 1909, 14 In. .................................................................................... 170.00
**Vase,** 3 Gold Handles, Hand-Painted Flowers, 3 5/8 X 3 1/4 In. ................................ 50.00
**WILLOW, see Blue Willow**
**WINDOW, Angel,** Drapery Glass, 4 1/2 X 6 Ft. .................................................... 4500.00
   **Beveled,** Set In Zinc, Diamond Shape, Arch Shaped, 77 X 24 In. ............................ 1500.00
   **Bow,** 4 Panel Stained Glass, Oak Frame, C.1904, Panel, 4 1/2 30 1/2 In. ............... 650.00
   **Geometric Design In Clear,** White, & Pressed Design, 12 X 38 In., Pair ................. 1300.00
   **Leaded Glass,** St.George Slaying The Dragon, C.1860, 42 X 67 In. ..................... 7000.00
   **Stained Glass,** Arched Top, Oak Tracery, Original Frames, 10 X 12 Ft. ................. 1500.00
   **Stained Glass,** Flowering Tree, Original Casement, 31 X 81 In., Pair ..................... 1550.00
   **Stained Glass,** Jeweled, 5 Part, C.1880, 42 X 102 In. ........................................... 2500.00
   **Stained Glass,** Medieval Rondel, 8 In.Diam. ......................................................... 300.00
   **Stained Glass,** Panel, 21 1/2 X 67 In. .................................................................. 800.00
   **Stained Glass,** Stylized Tree, Clambroth Ground, 15 1/2 X 10 In. ........................ 175.00
   **Stained Glass,** Villa By The Sea, Mural, 6 Panels, Each 20 X 30 In. ..................... 2200.00
   **Stained Glass,** 1 Large Flower, Blue, Orange, & Gold, 40 X 24 In. ..................... 775.00
   **Triple Bay,** Leaded Glass, Oak Frame & Hardware, 57 X 88 In. ......................... 750.00
   **Victorian,** Beveled, Art Glass & Jewel Center, 64 X 27 In. ................................ 1500.00
   **Victorian,** Beveled, Curved Pieces, 84 X 24 In., Pair ......................................... 3500.00

**WOOD CARVING, Angel,** 19th Century, 2 Ft., Pair ....................................... *Illus* 500.00
   **Bust,** Abe Lincoln ................................................................................................. 95.00
   **Eagle,** Polychrome, Maine, 1910 ......................................................................... 450.00
   **Figure,** Eagle, Gesso & Wood, C.1860, 29 X 48 X 42 In. ................................ 2750.00
   **Figurine,** Angel, Detachable Wings, 1830-50, Teak, 40 In. ............................... 1975.00
   **Figurine,** Black Man, 28 In. ................................................................................ 995.00
   **Figurine,** Bulldog, Head, 1/2 Life-Size ................................................................. 40.00
   **Figurine,** Thai Fertility, 18th Century, 24 In. ....................................................... 275.00
   **Mirror,** Eagle, Claws On Top, Half-Moon Shape, 12 5/8 In.Square ..................... 295.00

**WOODEN, see also Kitchen; Store; Tool**
**WOODEN, Ashtray Stand,** Bellhop ........................................................................ 50.00
   **Ashtray Stand,** Black Cat .................................................................................... 60.00
   **Ashtray Stand,** Brown Dog ................................................................................. 15.00
   **Ashtray Stand,** Moxie Man ................................................................................. 75.00
   **Ashtray Stand,** Moxie Woman ............................................................................ 60.00
   **Ashtray Stand,** Mutt, Comic Character, 28 In. .................................................... 90.00
   **Ashtray Stand,** White Horse ............................................................................... 10.00
   **Barrel,** Rose-Headed Nails, V Laps, Green Paint, 14 X 14 In. ............................. 75.00
   **Barrel,** Spigot, Curly Maple ................................................................................ 40.00
   **Bootjack,** Folding, Tiger Stripe Maple, 4 X 10 In. ............................................... 16.00
   **Bowl & Scoop,** Handholds, Butter Worker, American, Burl, 7 1/2 In. ................... 1300.00
   **Bowl,** Butter, Butternut, 19 X 10 In. ................................................................. 48.00
   **Bowl,** Chopping, Carved, 19th Century, 6 3/4 X 24 In. ............................. *Illus* 75.00
   **Bowl,** Chopping, Tab Holds, New England, 18th Century, Burl, 22 1/2 In. .......... 1300.00
   **Bowl,** Molded Rim, 19th Century, Burl, 11 3/4 In. ................................... *Illus* 550.00
   **Bowl,** Raised Base, New England, 18th Century, Burl, 7 In. ............................... 275.00
   **Bowl,** Ridged, Old Dark Green Paint Inside & Out, 8 1/2 In. .............................. 75.00
   **Bowl,** Ridged, Old Red Paint Inside & Out, 8 1/2 In. ......................................... 75.00
   **Bowl,** Ridged, Original Paint Inside & Out, 9 1/2 In. ......................................... 115.00
   **Bowl,** Ridged, 18th Century, Old Red Paint, 10 1/2 In. ..................................... 70.00
   **Bowl,** Rounded-Over Edge, Light Mustard Paint, Hand-Turned, 12 In. ................. 68.00
   **Bowl,** Turned Rim, 19th Century, Burl, 22 1/4 In. ..................................... *Illus* 900.00
   **Box,** Dome Top, Wallpapered, Figure In Uniform On Top, 9 X 6 1/2 In. ............. 120.00
   **Box,** Farm Landscape, Rose Flowers, Eliza Cass Cornville, 1824, 3 In. ............. 1900.00
   **Box,** Knife, 2 Sections, Divided By 2 Running Horses, 6 1/4 In. ......................... 525.00
   **Box,** Razor, Heart End, Mahogany, 2 X 9 1/2 In. .............................................. 35.00
   **Box,** Stamp, Hinged Lid, C.1845, 4 1/2 X 1 1/2 X 1 In. ................................... 8.50
   **Box,** Tool, Pine, 36 X 12 In. ............................................................................. 100.00
   **Bucket,** Lock-Lapped Wood Hoops, 10 1/2 X 10 In. ......................................... 35.00
   **Bucket,** Water, Split Oak .................................................................................... 78.00
   **Bucket,** Well, 3 Iron Bands ............................................................................... 125.00
   **Canteen,** Staved Sides, Ash Hoops, Old Red Paint, 18th Century ....................... 150.00
   **Carrier,** Butter, Round, Flat, Wooden Bail, 11 X 7 1/4 In. ................................. 68.00

Wood Carving, Angel, 19th Century, 2 Ft., Pair

Wooden, Bowl, Chopping, Carved, 19th Century, 6 3/4 X 24 In.

Wooden, Bowl, Molded Rim, 19th Century, Burl, 11 3/4 In.

Wooden, Bowl, Turned Rim, 19th Century, Burl, 22 1/4 In.

| | |
|---|---:|
| **Chalice,** Drinking, Waterfall Base, Maple, 5 In. | 25.00 |
| **Chest,** Carpenter's, Pine | 130.00 |
| **Chest,** Tool, Cobbler's, Handled, Metal Corners, Hasp, 19 X 12 X 19 In. | 95.00 |
| **Chest,** Tool, Union, Boy's, C.1907, Tools, 17 1/2 X 8 1/2 X 6 1/2 In. | 150.00 |
| **Chopping Block,** Butcher, Maple, 30 X 40 In. | 150.00 |
| **Curler,** Butter, Corrugated Curved Spoon Shape, 6 1/2 In. | 35.00 |
| **Fork,** Hand-Carved, Long Handle, Dark Age Color, 18 In. | 28.00 |

Fork, Hay, 3 Prong, 5 In.Overall ............................................................................... 85.00
Gavel, Burl Head, Ash Handle, 9 In. ....................................................................... 24.00
Mortar & Pestle, Double Ended, Tiger Maple, 9 3/4 In. ...................................... 60.00
Mortar & Pestle, Pewter Gray Paint, 7 1/4 In. ...................................................... 72.00
Mortar, Burl, Molded Rim & Base, 18th Century, 6 In. ........................................ 130.00
Pail, Sugar, Maple, Painesville Finial, 2 1/4 X 3 1/2 In. ...................................... 120.00
Pitcher, Maple Noggin, 1 Piece, 9 1/4 In. .............................................................. 195.00
Rack, Candle Dipping, Removable Sticks, 23 X 9 1/4 In. ..................................... 145.00
Rack, Letter, Eagle, Antelope, Walnut, 2 Tier, Carved, 8 1/2 X 17 In. ................. 130.00
Rattle, Fireman's ...................................................................................................... 75.00
Sander, Ink, 3 In. ...................................................................................................... 30.00
Sieve, Winnowing, Woven Splint Bottom, New England, 22 1/4 In.Diam. ........... 225.00
Stick, Walking, Hound Head Handle, Brass Collar, Solid Cherry .......................... 85.00
Stirrup, Pair ............................................................................................................... 12.00
Stretcher, Sock, Child's, 9 Cutout Holes, 32 In. .................................................... 18.00
Sword, Child's, Curved Blade, Bend Handle, Hand Hewn, 22 In. ......................... 23.00
Trammel, Lighting, 18th Century, Chestnut & Pine, Extended, 42 In. .................. 540.00
Tray, Knife, Blue, Dovetailed, 8 3/4 X 12 In. .......................................................... 75.00
Tray, Knife, Hand Hole Center, 1 1/2 X 6 3/4 In. ................................................... 9.00
Tray, Knife, Slanted Sides, Maple, 12 X 7 7/8 In. .................................................. 14.50
Wash Stick, Corrugated, Handled, 30 In. ............................................................... 140.00
Wash Stick, Hand-Carved, 33 In. ........................................................................... 85.00
Washboard, Hand-Carved, Corrugated, 13 X 21 In. .............................................. 35.00
Whirligig, Cowboy On Bucking Horse, C.1930s ..................................................... 75.00
Wine, Ring Carved Around Stem, Maine, 3 In. ....................................................... 22.00
Wool Carder, Pair ..................................................................................................... 10.00
Wringer, Tremont, 2 Roller ...................................................................................... 150.00

**WORCESTER, see also Royal Worcester**
WORCESTER, Creamer, Embossed Oak Leaves, Cream Satin, Marked Kerr ........... 20.00
Cup & Saucer, Imari Pattern, FBB Mark Under Crown ......................................... 65.00
Cup & Saucer, Iron Red, Cobalt & Gold, Kerr & Binns ........................................ 135.00
Ewer, Melon Shape, Mask Spout, Gold & Olive Green, C.1884, 14 In. ............... 1400.00
Inkwell, Hinged Cover, Enamel Floral, Crystal, 2 In.Square ................................ 44.00
Pitcher, Flatback, C.1870, 7 1/2 In. ........................................................................ 165.00
Saucer, Exotic Birds, Insets, Fretwork Mark, 5 1/4 In. ......................................... 295.00
Sugar & Creamer, 4 Cups & Saucers, 1783-88, Flight Period .............................. 185.00
Sweetmeat Stand, Formed As 4 Pierced Baskets, C.1765, 6 1/2 In. .................... 2800.00
Teapot, Celadon Green, Gilded Design, Ribbed Sides & Lid, 5 In. ....................... 90.00
Vase, Flowers, Butterflies, & 3 Serpents, Green Mark, 7 1/2 In. .......................... 395.00
Vase, 4 Floral Panels, Hadley, 3 1/4 In. ................................................................. 95.00

WORLD WAR I, Apron, Red Cross Nurse's ............................................................. 20.00
Belt, Ammo, Canvas ................................................................................................. 5.00
Butcher Bayonet, German ....................................................................................... 20.00
Canteen, French ....................................................................................................... 25.00
Helmet, Camouflage, German ................................................................................. 43.00
Helmet, Felt, Spike, Line Eagle .............................................................................. 200.00
Helmet, Leather Spike, Fish Scale Chin Strap, German ....................................... 175.00
Helmet, Leather Spike, Gray Bavarian Lion, German ........................................... 150.00
Helmet, Police, Leather, Germany .......................................................................... 65.00
Leggings, Leather ..................................................................................................... 25.00
Periscope, Trench, Belt & Clip, Wooden ................................................................ 15.00
Ring, German, Iron Cross In Center, Dated 1914 ................................................. 30.00
Saddlebag, Leather .................................................................................................. 16.00

WORLD WAR II, Banner, Nazi, 6 X 15 Ft. ............................................................... 75.00
Bayonet, Police, Scabbard, Nazi, Eagle's Head, Bone Grips ............................... 100.00
Belt, Cartridge ......................................................................................................... 10.00
Box, Cartridge, Japanese, Rubber .......................................................................... 30.00
Buckle, Nazi, Marked D.C.P. & Co ......................................................................... 22.00
Canteen, Japanese ........................................................................... 14.00 To 20.00
Dagger, Dress, Medical Corps. ............................................................................... 150.00

| | |
|---|---:|
| **Dagger,** Dress, Pilot's | 185.00 |
| **Dagger,** Nazi, Youth, Blut Und Ehre On Blade | 215.00 |
| **Dagger,** Scabbard, Nazi Air Force, Blade Marked K.W.C. | 85.00 |
| **Dagger,** Scabbard, SS Leader's | 195.00 |
| **Flag,** Nazi, With Swastika, 100 X 170 In. | 75.00 |
| **Flask,** German, Army Field | 10.00 |
| **Flight Suit,** Nazi, Pressed Insignia, Dated 1942 | 495.00 |
| **Hat,** Peaked, Green, Gold Cord, Nazi | 70.00 |
| **Helmet,** French Army, Steel | 9.00 |
| **Helmet,** Liner, Nazi | 85.00 |
| **Knife,** Cattaraugus | 16.00 |
| **Knife,** Youth, Hitler, Sheath | 60.00 |
| **Lantern,** Blackout, Pair | 95.00 |
| **Micrometer,** Japanese Writing On Box Top | 75.00 |
| **Sea Bag,** Guadalcanal, 1943, Stenciled Date & Unit | 15.00 |
| **Stickpin,** Nazi | 25.00 |
| **Watch Fob,** Nazi, 3 Enameled Swastikas On Sterling Silver | 85.00 |
| | |
| **WORLD'S FAIR, Ashtray,** 1933, Chrysler Giveaway, Copper | 19.00 |
| **Cane,** 1933 Chicago | 20.00 |
| **Compact,** 1933 | 20.00 |
| **Corkscrew,** 1893, Chicago | 12.50 |
| **Dustpan,** Chicago, Small | 8.00 |
| **Fan,** St.Louis | 32.50 |
| **Handkerchief,** Mother, Chicago, 1893, Silk | 10.00 |
| **Mirror,** Pocket, St.Louis, 1904 | 38.00 |
| **Mortar & Pestle,** Embossed St.Louis World's Fair 1904, Brass | 35.00 |
| **Napkin Ring,** Chicago | 35.00 |
| **Napkin Ring,** St.Louis | 22.50 |
| **Pencil Sharpener,** Trylon & Perisphere, Desk Type, 4 In. | 12.00 |
| **Pencil,** Last Nail, 1893, Metal | 12.00 |
| **Pillow,** Rose With Green Back, Skyride, 5 Buildings, 1933 | 45.00 |
| **Pinback,** American Flag Ribbon, Pan American Exposition | 8.00 |
| **Pincushion,** Beaded, Chicago | 35.00 |
| **Postcard,** 1939, Set Of 18 | 10.00 |
| **Salt & Pepper,** Trylon & Perisphere, Silver Plate | 22.50 |
| **Shot Glass,** 1893 | 22.50 |
| **Thermometer,** Chicago | 7.75 |
| | |
| **YELLOWWARE, Bank,** Figural, Pig, Green, Brown, & Yellow | 28.00 |
| **Bowl,** Brown Bands, 5 In. | 14.00 |
| **Bowl,** Green Seaweed On White Band, 5 1/4 X 11 1/4 In. | 145.00 |
| **Bowl,** Green Seaweed On Wide Cream Band, 11 3/4 X 6 In. | 135.00 |
| **Bowl,** Mixing, Pouring Spout, 5 7/8 X 14 1/4 In. | 35.00 |
| **Bowl,** Mixing, 10 1/2 In. | 27.50 |
| **Cup,** Custard, Set Of 6 | 20.00 |
| **Jug,** Hound Handled, Embossed Animals, New Jersey, 8 3/4 In. | 250.00 |
| **Mold,** Food, Grapes | 30.00 |
| **Mold,** Strawberry & Leaf, Paneled Sides | 50.00 |
| **Pan,** Milk, 12 In. | 20.00 |
| **Pie Plate** | 35.00 |
| **Pitcher,** Banded, 7 In. | 125.00 |
| **Rolling Pin** | 95.00 |
| **Wax Sealer** | 30.00 |

## ZANE WARE

Zane pottery was founded in 1921 by Adam, Reed, and McClelland in
South Zanesville, Ohio. It was sold in 1941.

**ZANE, see also Peters & Reed**

| | |
|---|---:|
| **ZANE, Vase,** Flare Top, Pulled Tan & Blue Finish, Signed, 5 1/4 In. | 32.00 |

# LA MORO

Zanesville Art Pottery was founded in 1900 by David Schmidt in Zanesville, Ohio. The firm made faience, umbrella stands, jardinieres, and pedestals. It worked until 1962.

ZANESVILLE, Jardiniere, Mottled ............................................................................................ 85.00

ZS BAVARIA, Plate, Queen Louise, Gold Rim Designs, 8 1/4 In. .............................. 30.00
    Plate, Roses, Marked, 8 In. ................................................................................................ 20.00

Zsolnay pottery was made in Hungary after 1862, and was characterized by Persian, Art Nouveau, or Hungarian motifs. A series of new Zsolnay figurines with green-gold luster finish is available in many shops today.

ZSOLNAY, Basket, 2 Sculptured Horses, Enclosed Top, Open Sides ......................... 425.00
    Bowl, Gondola Shape, Design Inside & Out, Castle Blue Mark, 12 In. ................... 195.00
    Bowl, Heart Shaped, Fish & Sea Flowers Design ..................................................... 435.00
    Bowl, Molded Out Flowers, Reticulated, Impressed, 2 In. ...................................... 335.00
    Bowl, Reticulated, Flower Design, Miniature ............................................................. 105.00
    Ewer, Shades Of Brown, Gold Design, High Glaze, Reticulated, 12 In. ................. 375.00
    Fernery, Reticulated Top, 6 X 8 In. ........................................................................... 150.00
    Figurine, Boxer, 5 In. .................................................................................................... 60.00
    Figurine, Deer, Metallic Bronze, Deer On Stomach, 2 1/2 X 3 1/4 In. .................. 35.00
    Figurine, Frog With Girl Feeding Hen, Iridescent Green ......................................... 40.00
    Figurine, Horse, Standing, Art Deco, 6 X 5 1/2 In. ................................................. 70.00
    Figurine, Nude Girl, Bending, Green & Gold, Five Castle Mark, 10 In. ................. 280.00
    Figurine, Owl ................................................................................................................ 125.00
    Figurine, Rooster, Standing, Metallic Green Luster, 5 X 8 1/4 In. ......................... 65.00
    Jug, Pink, Gold, Floral Design, Pink Handles, Signed, 7 3/4 In. ............................ 140.00
    Vase, Blue & Red Flowers, White Ground, 9 1/4 In. ............................................... 275.00
    Vase, Bud, Blue & Red Flowers, Small ....................................................................... 80.00
    Vase, Cylindrical, Stylized Flowers, Gold Luster, Marked, 10 In. ........................... 600.00
    Vase, Gold Luster, Flowers & Foliage, Salmon, 10 In. ..................... 550.00 To 600.00
    Vase, Luster Iridescent Metallic, Red Body, 8 In. .................................................... 210.00
    Vase, People, Green, Iridescent, 6 In. ......................................................................... 50.00
    Vase, Pink & Gold, Double Walled, Handles, Signed, 7 In. .................................... 395.00
    Vase, Reticulated Blue Jewels In Enamel, 3 1/2 In. ................................................. 110.00
    Vase, Rose Ground, Rose Medallions, Gold Handle, 8 In. ...................................... 310.00

# INDEX

Note: entries in capital letters refer to principal categories

A. WALTER, 1
Abacus, ivory, 278
ABC, 1; napkin ring, 368; textile sampler, 660
ABINGDON, 1-2
Accordion, 361
ADAMS, 2. See also Flow blue
Advertising. See Poster; Sign; Store; and specific makers, materials, companies, and objects
Adze, 674
African: bell, 33; bracelets, 56; elephant tusk, 278; map, 330; postcard album, 427
AGATA, 2
Airplane, toy, 680-81
AKRO AGATE, 3
ALABASTER, 3
Aladdin lamp, 302-3
Alarm, fire, 187
Alarm clock, 106-10; Mickey Mouse, 163; Roy Rogers, 516
Album: Mickey Mouse, 163; photograph, 310, 361; 417; record, see Records
Alcohol lamp, laboratory, 340
ALEXANDRITE, 3
ALHAMBRA, 4
Alice in Wonderland (Disney character), 163, 164; doll, 163, 166, 171, 172
Alimer, 674
Almanac: Ayer's, 404; Farmer's, 404; Kate Greenaway, 286
Alphabet plates, 1
ALUMINUM, 4
AMBER, 4
AMBER GLASS, 4
AMBERETTE. See Pressed glass, Klondike
AMBERINA, 4-7; cruet, 5, 131; PLATED, 423. See also Baccarat; Bluerina
Ambrotype, 417
AMERICAN ENCAUSTIC TILING CO., 7
American Legion: bottle, 46; watch fob, 709
AMETHYST GLASS, 7-8
Ammunition belt, World War 1, 734
Ammunition box, 51
AMOS & ANDY, 8; record, 365; sheet music, 366; taxi, 694
AMPHORA. See Teplitz
Amputation kit, Civil War, 104
Andirons (firedogs), 188; brass, 53, 188; iron, 188, 273
Andy Gump: Christmas card, 82; Christmas tree light bulb, 102
Anheuser-Busch: corkscrew, 125; glass, 632; match safe, 335; plate, 708; pocket knife, 296; sheet music, 367; sign, 637; tap knob, 632; tip tray, 649; tray, 647
ANIMAL TROPHY, 8
Anvil, 674
Apostle bell, 33
Apothecary: bottles, 45, 241, 251; cabinet, 8;

chest, 214, 340; cup, 356; jar, 150; scale, 569. See also Pharmacy
Apple: basket, 29; corer, 289; peeler, 293
Apple butter: crock, store, 629; jar, stoneware, 623; kettle, 291
Aquarium, 273
Arcade card set, Tom Mix, 674
Arcade machines, coin-operated, 117-20
ARCHITECTURAL, 8-9
ARITA, 10
Armchair, 207-8, 211
Army. See Military; Weapon
ART DECO, 10. See also specific makers, materials, and objects
ART GLASS, 10-11. See also specific makers, materials, and objects
ART NOUVEAU, 11. See also specific makers, materials, and objects
Art pottery. See under factory name
Ashtray. See specific makers, materials, and objects
Ashtray, wooden, 732
Asparagus: buncher, 675; fork, sterling silver, 598; plate, Limoges, 318
Atlas bottles, 47
Atomizer: Aurene, 11; Baccarat, 16; Cambridge, 68; cranberry glass, 126; D'Argental, 143; Devilbiss, 162; Hawkes, 249; Lalique, 298; Lenox, 311; Mary Gregory, 332; Pairpoint, 401; Val St. Lambert, 702
Audubon: bowl, Tiffany silver, 666; print, 487
Auger, 674; raft, 677
Aunt Jemima: banks, 18; doorstop, 42; figurine, 42; pail, 636; pin, 636; recipe box, 627; salt & pepper, 42; shaker, 42; syrup, 42
AURENE, 11. See also Steuben
Austria. See Royal Dux; Kauffmann; Porcelain
AUTO, 11-15; ashtray, Baccarat, 16; candy container, 77; hood ornament, 14, 300; lady's duster, 658; mascot, Lalique, 299; robe, 660. See also License plate, auto; Car, toy
Autry, Gene. See Gene Autry
AUTUMN LEAF, 15-16
Avon bottle, 45
AVON POTTERY, 16
Awl case, Plains Indian, 269
Ax, 674
AYNSLEY, 16. See also Chelsea Grape

B.P.O.E.: ashtray, 503; flask, 47; mug, 709; platter, 334; shaving mug, 577; stein, 614; watch fob, 709
Baby: buggy, 63; cup, silver, 581; dish, spatterware, 607; sterling silver, 598; quilt, 659; scale, 569; set, Royal Doulton, 526; spoon, sterling silver 599
BACCARAT, 16-17
Back saw, 674
Backbar, 8
BADGE, 17; Boy Scout, 52; Buck Rogers, 61; Captain Midnight, 82; Dick Tracy, 162; fireman's, 17, 187; Hopalong Cassidy, 261; Lone Ranger, 323; railroad, 493; Roy Rogers, 516
Bag, 656; beaded, 31; Coca-Cola, 114; Indian,

Bunsen burner, brass, 53
Bureau, 210. See also Chest
BURGUN & SCHVERER, 63
BURMESE, 63–64; Webb, 716–17. See also Gunderson
BUSTER BROWN, 64; bank, 18; calendar, 64, 66; plate, 1
Butcher's: case, 8; chopping block, 733; saw, 678
Butler's tray, 234
Butter: bowl, wooden, 732; box, 626; carrier, wooden, 732; churn, see Churn; crock, 289, 622; curler, wooden, 733; dish, see specific makers and materials; jar, stoneware, 623; knife, silver, 582, 583, 590; mold, 291; paddle, 293; plate, Belleek, 35; roller, 294; scale, 570; stamp, 295
Butter pat: Buffalo Pottery, 62; cut glass, 137; Delft, 150; flow blue, 192; Haviland, 248; Heisey, 252; Majolica, 328; moss rose, 357; Rose Medallion, 507; RS Tillowitz, 554; Staffordshire, 609; tea leaf ironstone, 653; Tiffany glass, 662; Warwick, 709; Wedgwood, 721
Butter tub: mocha, 353; Nippon, 375; Noritake, 384; stoneware, 621, 625
Buttermilk glass. See Custard glass
BUTTON, 64–65; carnival glass, 87; celluloid, 98; Kate Greenaway, 286; King George V and Queen Mary coronation, 125; political campaign, 424; Satsuma, 568
BUTTONHOOK, 65; Pan Pacific Exposition, 603; sterling silver, 598
BYBEE, 65

C clamp, brass, 54
Cabbage cutter, 289
Cabinet: barber, 29; card, 417–18; dental, 340; scraper, 675; store, 8, 627
Caboose: lamp, 494; toy, 683; whistle, 496
Cachepot: Daum Nancy, 144; ironstone, 276; Meissen, 341; Moorcroft, 353; tole, 673
Cake: basket, silver, 590; knife, silver, 583; mold, 275, 291, 499; pan, 243, 293; plate, see specific makers and materials; safe, Autumn Leaf, 15; salver, Duncan & Miller, 179; tray, cut glass, 137
Cake set: Dresden, 178; Nippon, 375; Noritake, 384; Old Ivory, 390; RS Germany, 542; RS Prussia, 547; Rudolstadt, 558
Cake stand: amber glass, 4; cut glass, 137; Dresden, 178; Majolica, 328; milk glass, 348; Sevres, 572
CALENDAR, 67; Buster Brown, 64, 66; Coca-Cola, 115; desk, Tiffany, 668; Dionne quintuplets, 162; frame, Tiffany, 669; King George VI and Elizabeth, 122; PAPER, 66–67; PLATE, 67, 721; railroad, 494; tile, Wedgwood, 726
Calling card: case, 278, 589, 598; tray, see Card tray
Calliope box, 361
CAMARK, 68
CAMBRIDGE, 68–75
CAMBRIDGE POTTERY, 68
Camel bell, 33
CAMEO, 75–76
Cameo glass. See specific makers and articles
Camera, 418; Buster Brown, 64; Dick Tracy, 162; Howdy Doody, 261; Mickey Mouse, 163
Camisole, 656
Campaign chest, 216
CAMPBELL KIDS, 76; doll, 166, 169; feeding dish, 62; game, 237; plate, 1
Camphene lamp, 303
CAMPHOR GLASS, 76
Can: label, 633; opener, 289. See also specific types of cans
Canary glass. See Vaseline glass
CANDELABRA, 76; bronze, 57, 76; Cambridge, 69; Duncan & Miller, 179; New Martinsville, 371; Pairpoint, 401; Roycroft, 540; Sandwich glass, 564; silver, 582, 590, 595; Tiffany, 668

Candle: box, 51, 671; dipping rack, 734; lamp, darkroom, 418; lantern, 309, 674; mold, 54, 291–92, 672; shade, Tiffany glass, 662; shield, lithophane, 320
CANDLEHOLDER, 76. See also specific makers and materials
Candlesnuffer: iron, 274, 276; Royal Worcester, 537; silver, American, 582; sterling silver, 598; & tray, tin, 671
Candlestand, 211
CANDLESTICK, 76. See also specific makers and materials
Candy: backbar, 8; bowl, RS Germany, 541; box, 51, 517; dish, see specific makers and materials; display case, 631; kettle, 291; mold, 275, 292; scale, 570; scoop, pewter, 415; showcase, 637
CANDY CONTAINER, 77–80; bank, 21; Christmas tree ornament, 103
Candy jar: Cambridge, 72; Depression glass, 154; Sandwich glass, 564; Steuben, 617; stretch glass, 651; vaseline glass, 706
CANE, 80–81; Chicago World's Fair (1933), 735; Wilson inauguration, 424. See also Walking stick
Canister: Delft, 150; stoneware, 621; store, 627–28; tin, 672
Canister set, 289; Delft, 150; Hall, 245; Teplitz, 654
Canning: crock, 622; jar, 623
Cannon: signal, 715; toy, 682
Canoe: Clambroth, 105; ruby glass, 555
Canteen: Civil War, 105; tin, 672; wooden, 732; World War I, 734; World War II, 734
Canterbury, 211
CANTON, 81
Cap, 656; Ku Klux Klan, 297; railroad, 494
Cap gun. See Gun, toy
Cape, 656
CAPO-DI-MONTE, 81
CAPTAIN MARVEL, 82; paper doll, 403; puzzle, 239
CAPTAIN MIDNIGHT, 82
Captain Video game, 238
Car, toy, 238, 681, 683–84, 685, 689, 692, 693; Captain Marvel, 82; Charlie McCarthy, 100; Disney characters, 164, 165
Carafe: cameo, 75; cut glass, 138; Fiesta ware, 186; Gouda, 242; maize, 327; Mary Gregory, 332; Rubena, 554; wine, 130
Caramel slag. See Chocolate glass
Carbine, 715; Civil War, 105
CARD, 82–83; box, cinnabar, 104; case, silver, 582, 598; Coca-Cola, 115; dish, Sinclaire, 599; Disneyana, 163; Elvis Presley, 182; holder, 517, 713; plate, Kate Greenaway, 286; Sunbonnet Babies, 652; table, 231–33; Tom Mix, 674. See also specific types (e.g., Gum cards; Playing cards)
Card game: Buck Rogers, 61; Donald Duck, 163; Superman, 652. See also Playing cards
Card tray, 62; & holder, Duncan & Miller, 180; opalescent, 396; Rookwood, 505; Royal Bayreuth, 522; Sarreguemines, 566; silver plate, 581; Tiffany, 670
CARLSBAD, 83
CARLTON WARE, 83
CARNIVAL GLASS, 83–96. See also specific makers and articles
CAROUSEL, 96
Carpenter's: bench, 209; chest, 733; tools, see Tool
Carpet, 656; beater, 626, 675; Navajo, 269; runner, Buster Brown, 64; stretcher, 678; sweeper, toy, 694
CARRIAGE, 96; clock, 107, 108; lamp, 304; toy, 684. See also specific types
Cart, Roy Rogers, 516
Carte de visite, 418
Cartridge: belt, 734; box, 51, 715, 734
CASH REGISTER, 96–97; toy, 684
Cash till, 96
Casket, Wave Crest, 713

Cider: jug or pitcher, 140, 141, 499; set, 316, 376

Cigar: band, Buster Brown, 64; band dish, 629; box, 51, 53, 60, 626, 627, 697; canister, 627, 628; case, 310, 628; clipper, 274; cutter, 424, 581, 629; display case, 631; holder, 4, 279; humidor, see Humidor; jar, 4, 246, 328, 632; label, 405; lighter, store, 633; set, Wave Crest, 713; STORE FIGURE, 104; tin, 643, 645, 646; Truman for President, 424

Cigarette: canister, 627; case, 98, 111, 597, 598, 667; jar, Cloisonne, 111; lighter, 15, 115, 495, 633; paper dispenser, 630; pipe, 341; roller, 637; tin, 644-47, 672; urn, Steuben, 618

Cigarette box, 627: agate, 2; Cambridge, 69; Depression glass, 151; Duncan & Miller, 179; Heisey, 252; Lalique, 299; Lenox, 312; Verlys, 707

Cigarette holder: & ashtray, Cambridge, 72; celluloid, 99; Cowan, 126; cut glass, 139; Hawkes, 250; ivory, 279; Meerschaum, 340; scrimshaw, 571; & tray, Quimper, 492

CINNABAR, 104

Circus: poster, 428, 636; toy, 684, 685, 689, 697

CIVIL WAR, 104-5; Beam bottles, 45; carbine, 715; carte de visite, 418; chemist laboratory bottle, 46; daguerreotype, 419; file cabinet, 210; musket, 715; pistol, 715; revolver, 715; stereo cards, 614; sword, 653; tintype, 419. See also Confederate

CLAMBROTH, 105

Clamp, 675

CLARICE CLIFF, 105

Clarinet, 363

Cleaver, 289

CLEWELL, 105

CLEWS, 105. See also Flow blue

CLIFTON, 106

CLOCK, 106-10; auto, 11; bank, 20, 23; case, KPM, 297; Coca-Cola, 106, 115; cut glass, 138; Lalique, 300; McCoy, 336; nautical, 108, 110, 370; Occupied Japan, 387; Roy Rogers, 516; Royal Bonn, 523; Tiffany, 668; Wedgwood, 721. See also Alarm clock

CLOISONNE, 110-13. See also specific makers and articles

Clothes brush: Shaker, 576; W. C. Fields, 603

Clothing. See Textile

CLUTHRA, 113. See also Steuben

Coach: lamp, 304; lantern, 309

Coal box, 189

COALPORT, 113-14. See also Indian Tree

Coaster: Cambridge, 70; cut glass, 138; Depression glass, 152; Fostoria, 201; Nippon, 376; Occupied Japan, 387; papier-mache, 406

Coat, 656; rack, 218; tree, 218

COBALT BLUE, 114. See also specific makers and articles

COCA-COLA, 114-16; clock, 106, 115; plate, 708; toy truck, 696

Cocktail: Cambridge, 70; cut glass, 138; Depression glass, 152; dress, 656; Duncan & Miller, 179; Fostoria, 201; Heisey, 253; Honesdale, 260; Libbey, 314; Masonic, 334; set, 104, 595; shaker, 250, 253, 402, 556, 617; Steuben, 616

Cocoa: canister, 627, 628; pot, Nippon, 376; tin, 644

Coffee: bin, 626; box, 51, 627; can, Derby, 162; canister, 42, 621, 627, 628; dispenser, Hall, 245; GRINDER, 15, 116-17, 150, 290; MILL, 117; pail, advertising, 636; percolator, 15, 104; scoop, 637; tin, 643-47; urn, silver plate, 581

Coffee set: Aynsley, 16; Fulper, 206; moriage, 355; Occupied Japan, 387; Old Ivory, 390; Pickard, 420; Ridgway, 500; Royal Doulton, 527; Royal Vienna, 536; Royal Worcester, 537; silver, American, 582; tea &, silver, 587, 593, 595, 596, 668

Coffeepot. See specific makers and materials

COFFIN, 117

Coin: case, silver, 595, 598; scale, 570; vendor, 117

COIN-OPERATED MACHINE, 117-20

COIN SPOT, 117

Colander, graniteware, 243

Collar: box, 98, 137, 712; & cuff box, 51, 626, 712; & cuff display case, 628; display case, 631; lace, 656; pin, Art Nouveau, 11

Collar button, 281; box, 316, 509; dish, Nippon, 377; dispenser, 631

COLLECTOR PLATE, 121. See also Bing & Grondahl; Royal Copenhagen

Cologne bottle, 46; amethyst glass, 7; Baccarat, 16; carnival glass, 84; cranberry glass, 127; cut glass, 136; Depression glass, 151; Fenton, 185; Hawkes, 249; Hobnail, 260; Lalique, 298; Limoges, 316; Mary Gregory, 332; Nippon, 374; Quezal, 490; RS Germany, 541; Rubena, 554; Sandwich glass, 564; Sinclaire, 599; Smith Brothers, 601; Steuben, 615; Stevens & Williams, 620; Tiffany glass, 662; verre de soie, 707

Coloring book, 30, 162, 405

Columbian Exposition (Chicago World's Fair, 1892-1893): bank, 26; corkscrew, 735; handkerchief, 735; jug, 531; pencil, 735; shot glass, 734; spoon, 603; sugar, 409; watch fob, 710

Column, 8

Comb: box, 210; case, tin, 672; curry, 675; display cabinet, 627; Eskimo, 183; flax, 675; mustache, 629, 680; tortoiseshell, 680

Combing sacque, 656

COMIC ART, 121-22

COMMEMORATIVE, 122. See also Coronation; World's Fair; and specific makers

Commode, 218. See also Chest

Compact, 10, 282, 581, 629, 680, 735

Compass: Boy Scout, 52; carpentry, 675; Flash Gordon, 190; nautical, 370; surveyor's, 675

Compote. See specific makers and materials

Condensed milk holder, Nippon, 377

Condiment: spoon, silver, 585; tray, vaseline glass, 706

Condiment set: amber glass, 4; Burmese, 63; milk glass, 348; Nippon, 376; Occupied Japan, 387; porcelain, 427; Rosenthal, 509; spatter glass, 606. See also Castor set

Confederate: button, 64; flag, 105; rifle, 501; spoon, 604. See also Civil War

Console: set, see specific makers and materials; table, 232

Console bowl, 68; black amethyst, 41; Cambridge, 70; Depression glass, 152; Fenton, 185; Heisey, 251, 253; Hull, 261; Roseville, 511; Van Briggle, 703; Verlys, 707; Weller, 728

Cookbook, Kewpie, 288

Cookie: board, 288; cutter, 289-90; jar, see specific makers and materials; mold, 292

Cooler: Coca-Cola, 115; spongeware, 608; wine, 143, 235

Cooper's tools. See Tool

COORS, 122, 632, 638, 648

COPELAND, 123

COPELAND SPODE, 122-23; see also Flow blue

COPPER, 123; luster, 325

CORALENE, 124; JAPANESE, 280

CORDEY, 124-25

Cordial: glass, see specific makers and materials; set, 70, 138, 144, 663, 668

CORKSCREW, 125, 289, 735

Corn: grater, 290; holder, sterling silver, 598; husker, 676; knife, 295; planter, 677; sheller, 294; stick pan, 293

Cornet, 363

Cornucopia: Heisey, 253; Hull, 262; Occupied Japan, 387; Roseville, 512; Shawnee, 578; Warwick, 709; Weller, 728

CORONATION, 125. See also Commemorative

COSMOS, 125

HAVILAND, 248–49
HAWKES, 249–51. See also Cut glass
Hay: fork, 734; pulley, 677; tester, 676, 679
Hearing aid, 340
Hearse lamps, 306
Heater: kerosene, 189; railroad boxcar, 494
HEINTZ ART, 251
HEISEY, 251–59. See also Custard glass
Helmet: fireman's, 188; World War I, 734
Hepplewhite furniture, 214, 217, 223, 229, 231
Herb basket, 30
HEREND, 259
HEUBACH, 259–60
Hibachi, Imari, 267
HIGBEE, 260. See also Pressed glass
High chair, 222
Highboy, 222–23
Hinge, door, 9
Hip flask, 47
Historic blue. See Adams; Clews; Ridgway; Staffordshire
HOBNAIL, 260. See also Francisware; and specific makers and materials
Hog ringer, 676
HOLLY AMBER, 260
Holster, toy, 516, 688
HONESDALE, 260
Honey: dish, Royal Worcester, 538; jar, slag, 600; pot, 35, 312
Hood ornament, auto, 14, 300
Hoof trimmer, 679
Hook, jamb, 54
Hooked rug, 559–60
Hoop driver, 676
HOPALONG CASSIDY, 261; bank, 22
Horn: auto, 14; fish peddler's, 672; fox hunting, brass, 54; lantern, 309
Horn of plenty. See Cornucopia
Horse: carousel, 96; toy, 688–89
Horse fly net, 635
Horseradish jar, stoneware, 623
Horseshoe, brass, 54
Hot water bottle, 48, 340
Hotel bell, 33
HOWDY DOODY, 261
Hubcap, 14
HULL, 261-63; bank, 27
Humidor: brass, 54; bronze, 60; carnival glass, 89; Clifton, 106; cut glass, 139–40; Deldare, 61; Doulton, 177; Handel, 246; Kelva, 287; Limoges, 317; Loetz, 322; moriage, 355; Moser, 356; Nakara, 368; Niloak, 373; Nippon, 377–78; Noritake, 384; Pairpoint, 402; porcelain, 427; Rookwood, 504; Royal Bayreuth, 519; Royal Doulton, 531; Sevres, 572; silver, Irish, 596; stoneware, 623; store, 632; Tiffany, 669; vaseline glass, 706; Warwick, 709; Wave Crest, 714; Wedgwood, 722; Weller, 729
HUMMEL, 263-66
Huntboard, 223–24
Hunting: horn, brass, 54; knife, 295
Hurdy gurdy, 363
Hutch, 224
HUTSCHENREUTHER, 266; bust, 407

Icart prints, 487–88
Ice: box, 290; chest, 289; pick, 115, 275; saw, 678; scale, 570; tongs, 275, 295; tub, 72, 142
Ice bucket: Cambridge, 72; cut glass, 140; Depression glass, 154; Hawkes, 250; Limoges, 317; Pairpoint, 401; Sandwich glass, 564; Steuben, 617
Ice cream: cone holder, 632; freezer, 290; mold, pewter, 413–14; scoop, 294; spoon, silver, 596, 599; tray, 142, 701; trowel, Tiffany silver, 668
Ice cream dish: custard glass, 134; Fostoria, 202; Heisey, 254; Libbey, 315
Ice cream set: carnival glass, 89; cut glass, 140; Haviland, 248; opalescent, 393; Rosenthal, 510; RS Prussia, 546
Ice skates, 689, 693

ICON, 266
IMARI, 267–68
IMPERIAL, 268
Inaugural items, 424, 425
Incense burner: brass, 54; bronze, 56, 60; iron, 274; jade, 280; Satsuma, 568
INDIAN, 269–70; bust, bronze, 56; cigar store figure, 104; pipe, 423; postcard, 428; toy, 689. See also Eskimo
Indian Head nickel button, 65
INDIAN TREE, 268–69. See also specific pieces
Ink bottle, 48; blown glass, 42
Ink sander, 734
INKSTAND, 270; Faience, 183; silver, American, 583; silver, English, 591; sterling silver, 598
INKWELL, 270–72. See also specific makers and materials
Inshave, 676
Instrument bag, medical, 340
INSULATOR, 273
Invalid feeder, 340, 399
Iron (clothes), 291, 574; for silk, 676
IRON (metal), 273–76
Ironing board, toy, 689
IRONSTONE, 276–78
IVORY, 278–79; jewelry, 280–82; netsuke, 371; painting on, 400; walrus, Eskimo, 183. See also Scrimshaw; and specific objects
Ivy ball: amethyst glass, 7; black amethyst, 41; Cambridge, 72; Duncan & Miller, 180

Jack, auto, 14
JACK ARMSTRONG, 279
JACK-IN-THE-PULPIT VASES, 279–80
Jacket, 658
JACKFIELD, 280
Jackknife, 295–96; McKinley, 424. See also Penknife; Pocket knife
JADE, 280
Jam: bowl, cranberry glass, 127; dish, 5, 128, 554, 620; pot, Belleek, 35; set, 426, 543
Jam jar: Bing & Grondahl, 40; Kauffmann, 287; Lenox, 312; Moorcroft, 354; Nippon, 378; Pickard, 420; Royal Bayreuth, 520; RS Prussia, 549; Tiffany, 669; Tuthill, 701; Webb, 718; Wedgwood, 723
Japan. See Nippon; Occupied Japan; and specific factories
JAPANESE CORALENE, 280
Japanese prints, 488
Jar. See specific makers, materials, and types
JAR OPENER, 280
Jardiniere. See specific makers and materials
JASPERWARE, 280. See also Wedgwood
Jelly: box, cut glass, 137; bucket, 289; cabinet, 210; cupboard, 219; kettle, 54, 291; opalescent, 393
Jewel Tea Company, Autumn Leaf pattern china, 15–16
Jeweler's: box, 51; desk, 221; scale, 570; vise, 679
JEWELRY, 280–84; casket, Sevres, 572. See also specific makers, materials, and types
Jewelry box: amber glass, 4; Belle Ware, 34; cobalt blue, 114; ivory, 278; Kelva, 287; Nakara, 368; Nippon, 375; opalescent, 392; papier-mache, 406; RS Germany, 542; Tiffany silver, 667; tramp art, 697
Jigsaw, 676
Jigsaw puzzle, 146, 238, 239, 603, 653
JOHN ROGERS, 284–85
JUDAICA, 285
Jug. See specific makers, materials, and types
Jugate, political campaign, 424
JUGTOWN, 285
Jukebox, 118, 363
Julep cup, silver, 582

Kabuki doll, 170
Kas, 224
Kate Greenaway. See Greenaway, Kate
KAUFFMANN, 286–87

Organ, 364; stool, 231; toy, 684, 691
Organette, 364
ORPHAN ANNIE, 398; book, 404; Christmas tree
light bulb, 102; nodder, 383; sheet music,
366, 398; stove, 694
ORREFORS, 399
OTT & BREWER, 399
Ovaltine, 82, 398
Oven: biscuit, 293; warming, 104
OVERBECK, 399
OWENS, 399
Oyster: carrier, tin, 672; fork, silver, 583;
platter, Sarreguemines, 565; set, Limoges,
318
OYSTER PLATE, 399–400; Dresden, 178; Haviland,
248; Limoges, 317–18, 399; Quimper, 492;
Union Porcelain Works, 702

PADEN CITY, 400
Padlock, 276; brass, 54; railroad, 495
Pagods. See Nodder
Pail: brass, 54; Donald Duck, 164; granite-
ware, 243; store, 636. See also Bucket
Paint set, Popeye, 426
PAINTING, 400. See also Picture; Portrait
PAIRPOINT, 401–2; silver plate items, 581
Pajamas, 658
Pan, 293; fireplace, 189; iron, 276; milk, see
Milk pan; toy, 692. See also Saucepan
Pan American Exposition, 603–5, 735
Pancake: dish, Nippon, 377; server, Nippon,
380
Panel, carved, 9
Pantry box, 51, 269, 288–89, 576
PAPER, 404–5; clip, 636, 668, 670; knife,
agate, 2. See also specific paper articles
PAPER DOLL, 403–4; Dionne quintuplets, 163,
403; Shirley Temple, 580
PAPERWEIGHT, 405–6. See also specific makers
and materials
PAPIER-MACHE, 406–7; doll, 175, 176
Paprika shaker, Aunt Jemima, 42
Parade torch, 647
Parasol, 701–2
Parfait: Heisey, 256; stretch glass, 651
PARIAN, 407
Paring knife, 296
PARIS, 407–8
Parlor set, 225
Pasta maker, 293
Pastille, Staffordshire, 611
Pastry: cutter, 290; jigger & pie crimper, 293;
server, silver, 585; set, Orphan Annie, 398;
wheel, 293
Patch: box, 51, 332, 356, 412; Boy Scout, 52;
Girl Scout, 241
PATE-DE-VERRE, 408; A. Walter, 1. See also
Galle
PATE-SUR-PATE, 408
PAUL REVERE, 409
PAULINE POTTERY, 409
PEACHBLOW, 409–10. See also Gunderson; Webb
Peanut: canister, store, 628; dispenser, 630;
jar, store, 632; roaster, tin, 672; tin, 644,
646; vending machine, 119
Peanut butter: canister, 628; crock, 629; pail,
advertising, 636; tin, 645, 646
PEARL, 280–84, 410
Peavy, 677
Pedometer: Jack Armstrong, 279; Lone Ranger,
324
Peel, 289, 293; iron, 276
Pegboard, Shaker, 576
Peignoir, 658
PEKING GLASS, 410
PELOTON, 410
PEN, 410–11; brush, Tiffany, 670; Campbell
Kid, 76; holder, silver plate, 581; Popeye,
426; tray, Tiffany, 670–71
PEN & PENCIL SET, 410
PENAUD, 416
PENCIL, 411; Campbell Kid, 76; Columbian Ex-
position (1893), 735; set, Coca-Cola, 115;
sharpener, 115, 164, 637, 735; Tiffany gold,
666; Union Pacific, 495

Pencil box, 52; Charlie Chaplin, 99; Coca-
Cola, 115; Lindbergh, 320; Popeye, 426; Roy
Rogers, 516; tin, 671
Pendant, 283–84; pate-de-verre, 408
Penholder, 1, 60, 402, 611
Penknife, 296; Hopalong Cassidy, 261; Lone
Ranger, 324. See also Jackknife; Pocket knife
Pennant, Planters Peanuts, 636
PENNSBURY, 411
Pennsylvania Dutch: bell, 33; blanket chest,
214; cupboard, 219, 220; server, 229
Penny scale, 570
Pepper pot, Staffordshire, 611
Pepper shaker, Royal Doulton, 531
Pepperette, silver, 591
Pepsi-Cola: bank, 26; bottle, 49; bottle opener,
45; button, 64; clock, 106; dispenser, 630;
radio, 493; sign, 641; thermometer, 643; tip
tray, 650; tray, 649
Perfume: atomizer, see Atomizer; bottle, see
specific makers and materials; dispenser,
coin-operated, 118; funnel, sterling silver,
598; lamp, Fulper, 206; vial, 129, 143, 557
Periscope: Buster Brown, 64; trench, World War
I, 734
Pestle: druggist's, 340. See also Mortar &
pestle
PETERS & REED, 411. See also Zane
Petticoat, 658
Pew, church, 218, 225
PEWABIC, 412
PEWTER, 412–16. See also specific makers and
objects
Pharmacy (drugstore): backbar, 8; cabinet, 8;
delivery case, 340; jug, stoneware, 623;
pestle, 340; scale, 570. See also Apothecary
PHOENIX, 416–17
PHOENIX BIRD, 416
Phonograph, 364–65; toy, 164, 684, 691, 697
Photograph: album, 310; album, musical, 361;
Civil War, 105
PHOTOGRAPHY, 417–19. See also Camera
Photoscope, 119
Piano, 365; lamp, 247, 307; scarf, 660; shawl,
660; stool, 231, 694; toy, 691
PIANO BABY, 419–20
Pianoforte, 365
PICKARD, 420–21
Pickle: bottle, 50; castor, 5, 97–98, 127, 128,
392, 401; fork, silver, 590, 667; jar, store,
632; keg, Heinz, 632
Pickle dish: Cambridge, 71; Heisey, 255; iron-
stone, 277; Libbey, 315; Old Ivory, 390;
Royal Bayreuth, 519; RS Germany, 543; Ru-
dolstadt, 558
PICTURE, 421–22; frame, see Frame; textile,
659
Pie: bird, Royal Worcester, 538; board, 288;
crimper, 289; fork, silver, 595; juicer, 293;
lifter, 291; peel, 293; rack, 293; safe,
225–26; tin, graniteware, 243; tray, cut
glass, 142
Pie plate: Bennington, 38; Hall, 246; redware,
499; Rockingham, 502; slipware, 601; stoneware, 624; yellowware, 735
PIGEON FORGE, 422
Piggy banks, 26–27. See also Bank
PILKINGTON, 422
Pill: box, 340, 596; jar, cut glass, 140
Pillow, 659; Beatles, 31; case, Elvis Presley,
182; Chicago World's Fair (1933), 735
Pin, 284; advertising, 636; box, 98, 508, 520,
713; Coolidge, 425; Dick Tracy, 162; dish,
510, 602; Masonic, 334; Orphan Annie, 398;
Superman, 653; Tom Mix, 674; tray, see spe-
cific makers and materials. See also specific
makers, materials, and types
Pinback, Pan American Exposition, 735
Pinball games, coin-operated, 119
Pincher, cobbler's, 677
Pincushion, 573, 574; Chicago World's Fair,
735; DOLL, 422; Shaker, 576; tramp art, 697
Ping-pong paddle, Coca-Cola, 115
Pinking device, 574
Pinocchio, 163, 164; acrobat, 680; bank, 27;